ALL ▪ IN ▪ ONE

CompTIA A+® Certification

EXAM GUIDE

Ninth Edition

(Exam 220-901 & 220-902)

ABOUT THE AUTHOR

Michael Meyers is the industry's leading authority on CompTIA A+ and CompTIA Network+ certifications. He is the president and founder of Total Seminars, LLC, a major provider of computer and network repair seminars for thousands of organizations throughout the world, and a member of CompTIA.

Mike has written numerous popular textbooks, including the best-selling *Mike Meyers' CompTIA A+® Guide to Managing & Troubleshooting PCs* and *Mike Meyers' CompTIA Network+® Guide to Managing and Troubleshooting Networks.*

About the Contributor

Scott Jernigan wields a mighty red pen as Editor in Chief for Total Seminars. With a Master of Arts degree in Medieval History, Scott feels as much at home in the musty archives of London as he does in the crisp IPS glow of Total Seminars' Houston HQ. After fleeing a purely academic life, he dove headfirst into IT, working as an instructor, editor, and writer.

Scott has written, edited, and contributed to dozens of books on computer literacy, hardware, operating systems, networking, and certification, including *Computer Literacy—Your Ticket to IC³ Certification*, and co-authoring with Mike Meyers the *All-in-One CompTIA Strata® IT Fundamentals Exam Guide.*

Scott has taught computer classes all over the United States, including stints at the United Nations in New York and the FBI Academy in Quantico. Practicing what he preaches, Scott is a CompTIA A+ and CompTIA Network+ certified technician, a Microsoft Certified Professional, a Microsoft Office User Specialist, and Certiport Internet and Computing Core Certified.

About the Technical Editor

Chris Crayton (CompTIA A+, CompTIA Network+, MCSE) is an author, editor, technical consultant, and trainer. Chris has worked as a computer technology and networking instructor, information security director, network administrator, network engineer, and PC specialist. Chris has authored several print and online books on PC Repair, CompTIA A+, CompTIA Security+, and Microsoft Windows. Chris has served as technical editor on numerous professional technical titles for leading publishing companies, including the *CompTIA A+ All-in-One Exam Guide*, the *CompTIA A+ Certification Study Guide*, and the *Mike Meyers' CompTIA A+ Certification Passport.*

ALL IN ONE

CompTIA A+® Certification

EXAM GUIDE

Ninth Edition

(Exam 220-901 & 220-902)

Mike Meyers

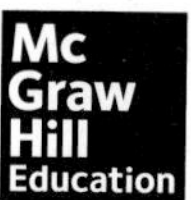

New York • Chicago • San Francisco
Athens • London • Madrid • Mexico City
Milan • New Delhi • Singapore • Sydney • Toronto

Cataloging-in-Publication Data is on file with the Library of Congress

CompTIA A+® Certification All-in-One Exam Guide, Ninth Edition (Exams 220-901 & 220-902)

3 4 5 6 7 8 9 10 LCR 20 19 18 17 16

ISBN: Book p/n 978-1-25-958869-3 and CD p/n 978-1-25-958870-9
of set 978-1-25-958951-5

MHID: Book p/n 1-25-958869-6 and CD p/n 1-25-958870-X
of set 1-25-958951-X

Sponsoring Editor
Tim Green

Editorial Supervisor
Jody McKenzie

Project Editor
Howie Severson, Fortuitous Publishing

Acquisitions Coordinator
Amy Stonebraker

Technical Editor
Christopher Crayton

Copy Editor
Bill McManus

Proofreader
Richard Camp

Indexer
Jack Lewis

Production Supervisor
James Kussow

Composition
Cenveo® Publishing Services

Illustration
Cenveo Publishing Services

Art Director, Cover
Jeff Weeks

To my grandson, Stephen Meyers Kelly.
Can't wait to dismantle our first system together!

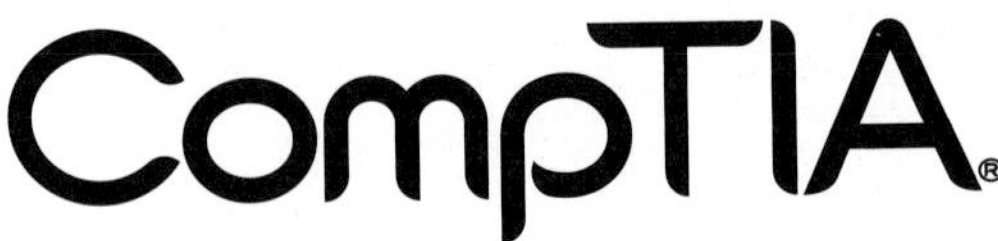

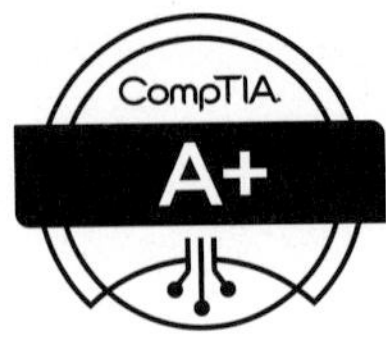

Becoming a CompTIA Certified IT Professional Is Easy

It's also the best way to reach greater professional opportunities and rewards.

Why Get CompTIA Certified?

Growing Demand

Labor estimates predict some technology fields will experience growth of more than 20% by the year 2020. (Source: CompTIA 9th Annual Information Security Trends study: 500 U.S. IT and Business Executives Responsible for Security.) CompTIA certification qualifies the skills required to join this workforce.

Higher Salaries

IT professionals with certifications on their resume command better jobs, earn higher salaries, and have more doors open to new multi-industry opportunities.

Verified Strengths

91% of hiring managers indicate CompTIA certifications are valuable in validating IT expertise, making certification the best way to demonstrate your competency and knowledge to employers. (Source: CompTIA Employer Perceptions of IT Training and Certification.)

Universal Skills

CompTIA certifications are vendor neutral—which means that certified professionals can proficiently work with an extensive variety of hardware and software found in most organizations.

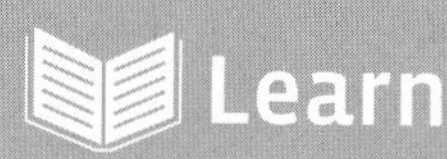

Learn more about what the exam covers by reviewing the following:

- Exam objectives for key study points.
- Sample questions for a general overview of what to expect on the exam and examples of question format.
- Visit online forums, like LinkedIn, to see what other IT professionals say about CompTIA exams.

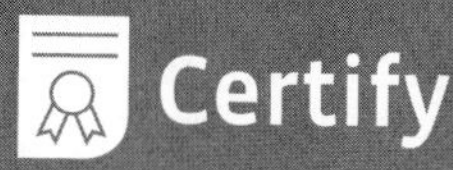

Purchase a voucher at a Pearson VUE testing center or at CompTIAstore.com.

- Register for your exam at a Pearson VUE testing center.
- Visit pearsonvue.com/CompTIA to find the closest testing center to you.
- Schedule the exam online. You will be required to enter your voucher number or provide payment information at registration.
- Take your certification exam.

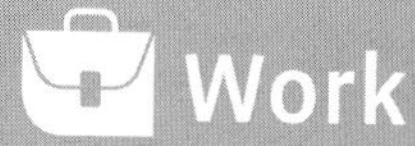

Congratulations on your CompTIA certification!

- Make sure to add your certification to your resume.
- Check out the CompTIA Certification Roadmap to plan your next career move.

Learn More: Certification.CompTIA.org/aplus

CompTIA Disclaimer

CONTENTS AT A GLANCE

CONTENTS

ACKNOWLEDGMENTS

I'd like to acknowledge the many people who contributed their talents to make this book possible:

To my in-house Editor in Chief, Scott Jernigan: I couldn't have done it without you, amigo. Truthfully, has there ever been a better combo than a wizard and a paladin?

To Christopher Crayton, technical editor: Another great project with you, Chris. Thanks for keeping my toes to the fire and for your relentless push to update, update, update! This is a much better product than it could have been without your help.

To Bill McManus, copy editor: Another amazing and excellent effort, Bill. Thank you!

To Michael Smyer, tech guru and photographer: Brilliant photos for this edition. Your technical contributions are always such a bonus. Great stuff!

To Dave Rush, technologist: Love, love, love arguing technology with you, Dave. And your research skills blow me away! Thanks for all the great work in this edition.

To Travis Everett, Internet guru and writer: Great contributions on this edition, Travis, from writing and research to copyedit and page proofing. Looking forward to many more.

To Ford Pierson, editor: Thanks for jumping in on the page proofs, Ford. And thanks for keeping it simple and diaper free.

To Dudley Lehmer, my partner at Total Seminars: As always, thanks for keeping the ship afloat while I got to play on this book!

To Amy Stonebraker, acquisitions coordinator at McGraw-Hill: Thanks for keeping us on track on so many levels. Love your quiet, but forceful voice at our weekly meetings. Looking forward to the next one!

To Jody McKenzie and Howie Severson, project editors: It was a joy to work with you both again. I couldn't have asked for a better team. In fact, I asked for the best team and got exactly what I wanted!

To Richard Camp, proofreader: Awesome work!

CHAPTER 1

The Path of the PC Tech

In this chapter, you will learn how to

- Explain the importance of CompTIA A+ certification
- Detail the CompTIA A+ certification objectives
- Describe how to become CompTIA A+ certified

The field of computing has changed dramatically over the decades since the introduction of the IBM Personal Computer (PC) in 1981, and so has the job of the people who build, maintain, and troubleshoot computers. A *PC tech* for many years serviced IBM-compatible desktop systems running a Microsoft operating system (OS), such as DOS or, later, Windows. Figure 1-1 shows a typical system from the early days, running Microsoft Windows 3.1. All a tech needed to service such a machine was a Phillips-head screwdriver and knowledge of the hardware and OS.

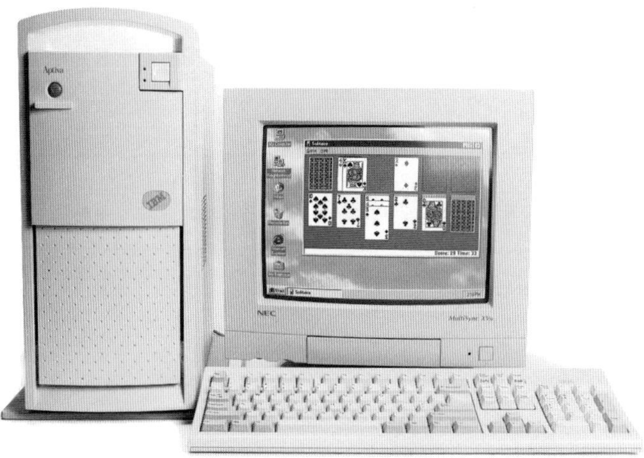

Figure 1-1 An IBM-compatible PC, circa 1996

The personal computing landscape today includes a zillion devices in all shapes, sizes, and purposes. How many computing devices do you interact with every day? Seriously, count them.

Here's my typical contact in a day. My smartphone alarm clock awakens me in the morning. I use either a Windows or Mac OS X desktop to check the morning news and my e-mail by connecting to other computers over the Internet. Or, if the family is on both systems, I'll retreat to the study with a laptop running Ubuntu Linux to do the same tasks. At the gym, my smartwatch keeps track of my exercises and my heart rate. The computer in my car handles navigation and traffic reports for my daily commute. At the office I'm literally surrounded by dozens of computing devices, because everyone has a desktop or laptop computer, a tablet, a smartphone, plus any number of wearable devices. See Figure 1-2.

Someone needs to set up, manage, maintain, and troubleshoot all of these devices. Because you're reading this book, I'm guessing that *you* are that someone. You're going to need a lot of knowledge about many systems to be a modern personal computer technician. A modern *PC tech*, therefore, works with many devices running many different systems. Almost everything interconnects as well, and a PC tech makes that connection happen.

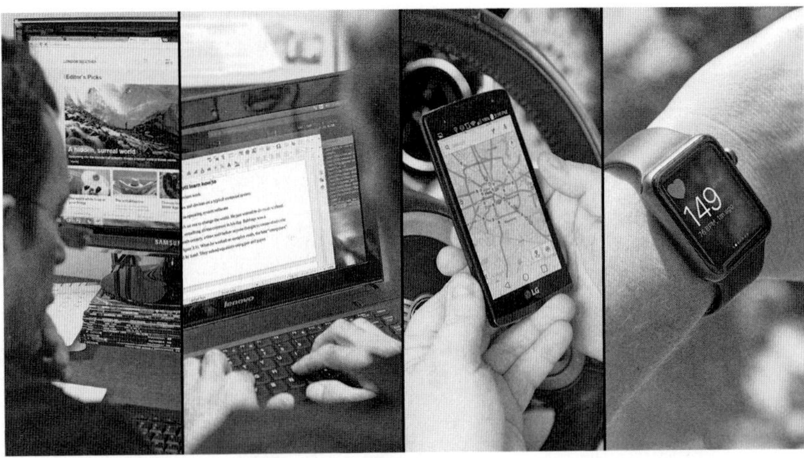

Figure 1-2 We're all PCs!

NOTE This book uses the term "personal computer" and the initials "PC" generically to refer to any kind of personal computing device. PCs here mean things that techs interact with, can set up, and repair.

This book teaches you everything you need to know to become a great tech. It might seem like a lot of information at first, but I'll show you how each system functions and interacts, so you learn the patterns they all follow. At some point in the process of reading this book and working on computers, it will all click into place. You've got this!

Along the way, you'll pick up credentials that prove your skill to employers and clients. The rest of this chapter explains those credentials and the steps you need to take to gain them.

CompTIA A+ Certification

Nearly every profession has some criteria that you must meet to show your competence and ability to perform at a certain level. Although the way this works varies widely from one profession to another, all of them will at some point make you take an exam or series of exams. Passing these exams proves that you have the necessary skills to work at a certain level in your profession, whether you're an aspiring plumber, teacher, barber, or lawyer.

If you successfully pass these exams, the organization that administers them grants you *certification*. You receive some piece of paper or pin or membership card that you can show to potential clients or employers. This certification gives those potential clients or employers a level of confidence that you can do what you say you can do. Without this certification, either you will not find suitable work in that profession or no one will trust you to do the work.

Modern PC techs attain the *CompTIA A+ certification*, the essential credential that shows competence in the modern field of *information technology (IT)*, a fancy way of saying *computing technology plus all the other stuff needed to connect and support computers.* CompTIA A+ is an industry-wide, vendor-neutral certification program developed and sponsored by the *Computing Technology Industry Association (CompTIA)*. You achieve this certification by taking two computer-based exams consisting of multiple-choice and performance-based questions. The tests cover what technicians should know after 12 months of hands-on work on personal computing devices, either from a job or as a student in the lab. CompTIA A+ certification enjoys wide recognition throughout the computer industry. To date, more than 1,000,000 technicians have become CompTIA A+ certified, making it the most popular of all IT certifications.

Who Is CompTIA?

CompTIA is a nonprofit industry trade association based in Oakbrook Terrace, Illinois. It consists of over 20,000 members in 102 countries. You'll find CompTIA offices in such diverse locales as Amsterdam, Dubai, Johannesburg, Tokyo, and São Paulo.

CompTIA provides a forum for people in these industries to network (as in meeting people), represents the interests of its members to the government, and provides certifications for many aspects of the computer industry. CompTIA sponsors CompTIA A+, CompTIA Network+, CompTIA Security+, and other certifications. CompTIA works hard to watch the IT industry and constantly looks to provide new certifications to meet the ongoing demand from its membership. Check out the CompTIA Web site at *www.comptia.org* for details on the other certifications you can obtain from CompTIA.

Virtually every company of consequence in the IT industry is a member of CompTIA. Here are a few of the biggies:

AT&T	AMD	Best Buy	Brother International
Canon	Cisco Systems	Epson	Fujitsu
Gateway	Hewlett-Packard	IBM	Intel
Kyocera	McAfee	Microsoft	NCR
Novell	Panasonic	Sharp Electronics	Siemens
Symantec	Toshiba	Total Seminars, LLC (that's my company)	Plus many thousands more

CompTIA began offering CompTIA A+ certification back in 1993. When it debuted, the IT industry largely ignored CompTIA A+ certification. Since that initial stutter, however, the CompTIA A+ certification has grown to become the de facto requirement for entrance into the PC industry. Many companies require CompTIA A+ certification for all of their PC support technicians, and the CompTIA A+ certification is widely recognized both in the United States and internationally.

The Path to Other Certifications

Most IT companies—big and small—see CompTIA A+ certification as the entry point to IT. From CompTIA A+, you have a number of certification options, depending on whether you want to focus more on hardware and operating systems or move into network administration (although these aren't mutually exclusive goals). The following three certifications are worth serious consideration:

- CompTIA Network+ certification
- Microsoft technical certifications
- Cisco certifications

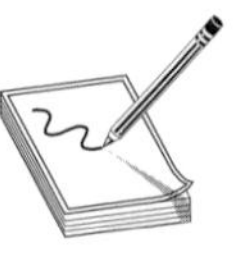

NOTE CompTIA A+ is the entry point to IT, though definitely not the only route for learning about computers and having certifications to prove that knowledge. Several certifications cover computer literacy or digital literacy, the phrase that means "what every person needs to know about computers to survive in the 21st century." The most popular computer literacy certification is Certiport's IC³ certification that tests on general computer knowledge; office productivity applications, such as Microsoft Word and PowerPoint; and Internet applications such as Web browsers and e-mail clients.

CompTIA has a pre–CompTIA A+ certification called *CompTIA IT Fundamentals* that's geared a bit more to a user preparing to become a tech. It's designed to check basic knowledge levels for people getting into IT.

CompTIA Network+ Certification

Building, maintaining, and fixing *networks*—groups of computers that enable people to share resources—represent a logical set of skills for computer technicians. Networks are so integral to modern life that you have to learn a lot about them just to get CompTIA A+ certified.

So, if you haven't already achieved CompTIA Network+ certification, make it your next certification goal after CompTIA A+ certification. Just as CompTIA A+ certification shows that you have solid competency as a PC technician, *CompTIA Network+ certification* demonstrates your skills as a network technician, including your understanding of network hardware, installation, and troubleshooting. CompTIA's Network+ certification is a natural step for continuing toward your Microsoft or Cisco certifications.

Microsoft Technical Certifications

Microsoft operating systems control a huge portion of all installed networks, and those networks need qualified support people to make them run. Pursuing Microsoft's series of certifications for networking professionals is a natural next step after completing the CompTIA certifications. They offer a whole slew of tracks and exams, ranging from specializations in Windows 8 to numerous *Microsoft Certified Solutions Expert (MCSE)* certifications and beyond. You can find more details on the Microsoft Learning Web site at

www.microsoft.com/learning/en-us/default.aspx

Cisco Certification

Cisco routers pretty much run the Internet and most intranets in the world. A *router* is a networking device that controls and directs the flow of information over networks, such as e-mail messages, Web browsing, and so on. Cisco provides multiple levels of IT certification for folks who want to show their skills at handling Cisco products, such as the *Cisco Certified Network Associate (CCNA)*, plus numerous specialty certifications. See the Cisco IT Certification Web site here for more details:

www.cisco.com/web/learning/certifications/index.html

CompTIA A+ Objectives

CompTIA splits A+ certification into two exams: *CompTIA A+ 220-901* and *CompTIA A+ 220-902*. It's common to refer to these two exams as the "2015" exams to differentiate them from older CompTIA exams.

Although you may take either of the two exams first, I recommend taking 220-901 followed by 220-902. The 220-901 exam concentrates on understanding terminology and technology, how to do fundamental tasks such as upgrading RAM, and basic network and mobile device support. The 220-902 exam builds on the first exam, concentrating on operating system support, advanced configuration, and troubleshooting scenarios.

Both of the exams are extremely practical, with little or no interest in theory, aside from troubleshooting. All questions are multiple-choice, simulation, or "click on the right part of the picture" questions. The following is an example of the type of questions you will see on the exams:

Your laser printer is printing blank pages. Which item should you check first?

A. Printer drivers

B. Toner cartridge

C. Printer settings

D. Paper feed

The correct answer is B, the toner cartridge. You can make an argument for any of the others, but common sense (and skill as a PC technician) tells you to check the simplest possibility first.

The 2015 exams use a regular test format in which you answer a set number of questions and are scored based on how many correct answers you give. CompTIA makes changes and tweaks over time, so always check the CompTIA Web site before final preparations for the exams. These exams have no more than 90–100 questions each.

Be aware that CompTIA may add new questions to the exams at any time to keep the content fresh. The subject matter covered by the exams won't change, but new questions may be added periodically at random intervals. This policy puts strong emphasis on understanding concepts and having solid PC-tech knowledge rather than on trying to memorize specific questions and answers that may have been on the tests in the past. No book or Web resource will have all the "right answers" because those answers change constantly. Luckily for you, however, this book not only teaches you what steps to follow in a particular case, but also explains how to be a knowledgeable tech who understands *why* you're doing those steps. That way, when you encounter a new problem (or test question), you can work out the answer. This will help you pass the exams and function as a master tech.

To keep up to date, we monitor the CompTIA A+ exams for new content and update the special Tech Files section of the Total Seminars Web site (www.totalsem.com) with new articles covering subjects we believe may appear on future versions of the exams.

Windows-Centric

The CompTIA A+ exams cover five different operating systems and many versions within each OS. When you review the objectives a little later in this section, though, you'll see that the majority of content focuses on the Microsoft Windows operating systems you would expect to find on a PC at a workstation or in a home. The exams cover a specific and limited scope of questions on Linux, Mac OS X, iOS, and Android.

Objectives in the exams cover the following operating systems:

- Windows Vista Home Basic, Windows Vista Home Premium, Windows Vista Business, Windows Vista Ultimate, Windows Vista Enterprise

- Windows 7 Starter, Windows 7 Home Premium, Windows 7 Professional, Windows 7 Ultimate, Windows 7 Enterprise
- Windows 8, Windows 8 Pro, Windows 8 Enterprise
- Windows 8.1, Windows 8.1 Pro, Windows 8.1 Enterprise
- Linux
- Mac OS X
- iOS
- Android

Windows 10

CompTIA has the darnedest luck when it comes to the timing of new CompTIA A+ exams compared to releases of new Windows versions. In 2006, CompTIA released an update to the CompTIA A+ exams about four months before Microsoft released Windows Vista. In 2009, CompTIA missed Windows 7 by about one month (though CompTIA released a Windows 7 update to the exams in late 2009). The 2012 objectives similarly missed the rollout of Windows 8.

It seems that CompTIA will once again run into what I'm going to call the "CompTIA Windows Curse." Microsoft released Windows 10 after CompTIA announced the objectives for the 220-901 and 220-902 exams, but before the exams went live in December 2015. Assuming CompTIA stays true to form, there's a very good chance that you'll see a Windows 10 update on the exams within a year or two of the Windows 10 rollout. Be sure to check the CompTIA Web site or contact me directly at michaelm@totalsem.com to see if any Windows 10 updates have taken place.

Try This!

Recommending an OS

Imagine this scenario. One of your first clients wants to upgrade her computing gear and doesn't know which way to go. It's up to you to make a recommendation. This is a great way to assess your knowledge at the start of your journey into CompTIA A+ certification, so Try This!

Open a Web browser on a computer or smartphone and browse to my favorite tech store, Newegg (www.newegg.com). Scan through their computer systems. What operating systems seem to be most common? What can you get from reading reviews of, say, Chrome OS vs. Windows 10? Do they sell any Apple products?

Don't get too wrapped up in this exercise. It's just a way to ease you into the standard research we techs do all the time to stay current. We'll revisit this exercise in later chapters so you can gauge your comfort and knowledge level over time.

Table 1-1 Exam 220-901 Domains and Percentages

Domain	Percentage
1.0 Hardware	34%
2.0 Networking	21%
3.0 Mobile Devices	17%
4.0 Hardware and Network Troubleshooting	28%

Exam 220-901

The questions on the CompTIA A+ 220-901 exam fit into one of four domains. The number of questions for each domain is based on the percentages shown in Table 1-1.

The 220-901 exam tests your knowledge of computer components, expecting you to be able to identify just about every common device on PCs, including variations within device types. Here's a list:

- Hard drives
- Optical drives
- Solid state drives (SSDs)
- Motherboards
- Power supplies
- CPUs
- RAM
- Monitors
- Input devices, such as keyboards, mice, and touchscreens
- Video and multimedia cards
- Network and modem cards
- Cables and connectors
- Heat sinks, fans, and liquid cooling systems
- Laptops and mobile devices
- Printers and multifunction devices
- Scanners
- Network switches, cabling, and wireless adapters
- Biometric devices

The 220-901 exam tests your ability to install, configure, and maintain all the hardware technology involved in a personal computer. You need to be able to install and set up a hard drive, for example, and configure devices in Windows Vista, Windows 7, Windows 8, and Windows 8.1. You have to understand device drivers.

The 220-901 exam tests you on mobile devices. While the smartphone and tablet market covers an impossibly wide array of hardware and software, the 220-901 exam focuses on Apple iOS and Google Android devices. You'll need to know how to interact with the hardware and software.

The 220-901 exam tests extensively on networking. You need to know how to set up a typical local area network (LAN), for example, understanding cabling standards, network protocols, and Windows configuration.

The 220-901 exam requires you to know a lot about hardware and network troubleshooting. You'll get questions, for example, on how to fix a network failure.

Table 1-2 Exam 220-902 Domains and Percentages

Domain	Percentage
1.0 Windows Operating Systems	29%
2.0 Other Operating Systems & Technologies	12%
3.0 Security	22%
4.0 Software Troubleshooting	24%
5.0 Operational Procedures	13%

Exam 220-902

The CompTIA A+ 220-902 exam covers five domains. Table 1-2 lists the domains and the percentage of questions dedicated to each domain.

The 220-902 exam covers the configuration, repair, and troubleshooting of the Windows operating system. You have to know your way around Windows and understand the tasks involved in updating, upgrading, and installing Windows Vista, Windows 7, Windows 8, and Windows 8.1. You need to know the standard diagnostic tools available in Windows so that you can fix problems and work with higher-level techs. Make sure you know Windows; 29% of the 220-902 questions are going to challenge you on this.

You need to know your way around the Linux and Mac OS X interfaces. Plus, the 220-902 exam tests you on accessing and properly using various tech tools for running maintenance, backup, and so forth. The exam goes into lots of detail on iOS and Android configuration, such as setting up e-mail and securing the devices. But it's not just mobile devices . . .

In general, security is a big topic on the 220-902 exam. You need to know quite a bit about computer security, from physical security (door locks to retinal scanners), to knowledge of security threats (malware and viruses), to the ways in which to secure an individual computer. This also includes coverage of how to recycle and dispose of computer gear properly.

You'll also be tested on methods for securing networks. You'll need to know how to access a small office/home office (SOHO) router or wireless access point and configure that device to protect your network.

Additionally, this exam puts a lot for emphasis on operational procedures, such as safety and environmental issues, communication, and professionalism. You need to understand how to avoid hazardous situations. The exam tests your ability to communicate effectively with customers and coworkers. You need to understand professional behavior and demonstrate that you have tact, discretion, and respect for others and their property.

The Path to Certification

You become CompTIA A+ certified, in the simplest sense, by taking and passing two computer-based exams. There are no prerequisites for taking the CompTIA A+ certification exams (although there's an assumption of computer literacy, whether or not you have one of the computer literacy certifications). There is no required training course and

no training materials to buy. You *do* have to pay a testing fee for each of the two exams. You pay your testing fees, go to a local testing center, and take the tests. You immediately know whether you have passed or failed. By passing both exams, you become CompTIA A+ certified.

To stay certified, every three years you'll need to either retake the exam or perform sufficient continuing education as specified by CompTIA.

Retaking the exams isn't that hard to understand, but the continuing education requirement is a bit more complex. Instead of trying to explain it all, please review CompTIA's documentation here:

https://certification.comptia.org/continuing-education

Most importantly, if you pursue the continuing education path, you'll need to earn 20 continuing education units (CEUs) each three-year period to renew your CompTIA A+ certification. How do you earn these CEUs? You can participate in industry events and seminars, complete a presentation, participate in IT training, teach a course, or earn another higher-level certification. The number of CEUs that you earn by completing each of these requirements varies, and each requires that you submit documentation to CompTIA for review.

Finding a Testing Center

Pearson VUE administers the CompTIA A+ testing at over 5000 testing centers in 165 countries. You may take the exams at any testing center. You can select the closest training center and schedule your exams right from the comfort of your favorite Web browser by going to the Pearson VUE Web site:

www.vue.com

Alternatively, in the United States and Canada, call Pearson VUE at 877-551-PLUS (7587) to schedule the exams and to locate the nearest testing center. International customers can find a list of Pearson VUE international contact numbers for various regions of the world on their Web site here:

www.pearsonvue.com/comptia/contact/

You must pay for the exam when you call to schedule. Be prepared to sit on hold for a while. Have your Social Security number (or international equivalent) and a credit card ready when you call. Pearson VUE will be glad to invoice you, but you won't be able to take the exam until they receive full payment.

Pearson VUE will accommodate any special needs, although this may limit your selection of testing locations.

Exam Costs

The cost of the exam depends on whether you work for a CompTIA member or not. At this writing, the cost for non-CompTIA members is $194 (U.S.) for each exam. International prices vary, but you can check the CompTIA Web site for international pricing.

Of course, the prices are subject to change without notice, so always check the CompTIA Web site for current pricing.

Very few people pay full price for the exam. Virtually every organization that provides CompTIA A+ training and testing also offers discount *vouchers*. You buy a discount voucher and then use the voucher number instead of a credit card when you schedule the exam. Vouchers are sold per exam, so you'll need two vouchers to take the two CompTIA A+ exams. Total Seminars is one place to get discount vouchers. You can call Total Seminars at 800-446-6004 or 281-922-4166, or get vouchers via the Web site: www.totalsem.com. No one should ever pay full price for CompTIA A+ exams.

How to Pass the CompTIA A+ Exams

CompTIA designed the A+ exams to test the knowledge of a technician with only 12 months of experience, so keep it simple! The exams aren't interested in your ability to overclock DDR4 CAS latency in CMOS or whether you can explain the differences between the Intel X99 and the AMD 990FX chipsets. Think in terms of practical knowledge and standards. Read this book, do whatever works for you to memorize the key concepts and procedures, take the practice exams on the media accompanying this book, review any topics you miss, and you should pass with no problem.

NOTE Those of you who just want more knowledge in managing and troubleshooting PCs can follow the same strategy as certification-seekers. Think in practical terms and work with the PC as you go through each chapter.

Some of you may be in or just out of school, so studying for exams is nothing novel. But if you haven't had to study for and take an exam in a while, or if you think maybe you could use some tips, you may find the next section valuable. It lays out a proven strategy for preparing to take and pass the CompTIA A+ exams. Try it. It works.

Obligate Yourself

The very first step you should take is to schedule yourself for the exams. Have you ever heard the old adage, "Heat and pressure make diamonds?" Well, if you don't give yourself a little "heat," you'll end up procrastinating and delay taking the exams, possibly forever. Do yourself a favor. Using the following information, determine how much time you'll need to study for the exams, and then call Pearson VUE or visit their Web site and schedule the exams accordingly. Knowing the exams are coming up makes it much easier to put down the game controller and crack open the book. You can schedule an exam as little as a few weeks in advance, but if you schedule an exam and can't take it at the scheduled time, you must reschedule at least a day in advance or you'll lose your money.

Set Aside the Right Amount of Study Time

After helping thousands of techs get their CompTIA A+ certification, we at Total Seminars have developed a pretty good feel for the amount of study time needed to pass the CompTIA A+ certification exams. The following table provides an estimate to help you plan how much study time you must commit to the CompTIA A+ certification exams.

Keep in mind that these are averages. If you're not a great student or if you're a little on the nervous side, add 10%; if you're a fast learner or have a good bit of computer experience, you may want to reduce the figures.

To use Table 1-3, just circle the values that are most accurate for you and add them up to get your estimated total hours of study time.

	Amount of Experience			
Tech Task	**None**	**Once or Twice**	**Every Now and Then**	**Quite a Bit**
Installing an adapter card	6	4	2	1
Installing and configuring hard drives and SSDs	12	10	8	2
Connecting a computer to the Internet	8	6	4	2
Installing printers and multifunction devices	16	8	4	2
Installing RAM	8	6	4	2
Installing CPUs	8	7	5	3
Repairing printers	6	5	4	3
Repairing boot problems	8	7	7	5
Repairing portable computers	8	6	4	2
Configuring mobile devices	4	3	2	1
Building complete systems	12	10	8	6
Using the command line	8	8	6	4
Installing and optimizing Windows	10	8	6	4
Using Windows Vista	6	6	4	2
Using Windows 7	8	6	4	2
Using Windows 8/8.1	8	6	4	2
Using Linux	8	6	6	3
Using Mac OS X	8	4	4	2
Configuring NTFS, Users, and Groups	6	4	3	2
Configuring a wireless network	6	5	3	2
Configuring a software firewall	6	4	2	1
Configuring sound	2	2	1	0
Removing malware	4	3	2	0
Using OS diagnostic tools	8	8	6	4
Using a multimeter	4	3	2	1

Table 1-3 Analyzing Skill Levels

Months of Direct, Professional Experience	Hours to Add to Your Study Time
0	50
Up to 6	30
6 to 12	10
Over 12	0

Table 1-4 Adding Up Your Study Time

To that value, add hours based on the number of months of direct, professional experience you have had supporting PCs, as shown in Table 1-4.

A total neophyte often needs roughly 240 hours of study time. An experienced tech shouldn't need more than 60 hours.

Total hours for you to study: _____________.

A Strategy for Study

Now that you have a feel for how long it's going to take to prepare for the exams, you're ready to develop a study strategy. I suggest a strategy that has worked for others who've come before you, whether they were experienced techs or total newbies.

This book accommodates the different study agendas of these two groups of students. The first group is experienced techs who already have strong PC experience but need to be sure they're ready to be tested on the specific subjects covered by the CompTIA A+ exams. The second group is those with little or no background in the computer field. These techs can benefit from a more detailed understanding of the history and concepts that underlie modern PC technology, to help them remember the specific subject matter information they must know for the exams. I'll use the shorthand terms Old Techs and New Techs for these two groups. If you're not sure which group you fall into, pick a few chapters and go through some end-of-chapter questions. If you score less than 70%, go the New Tech route.

I have broken most of the chapters into four distinct parts:

- **Historical/Conceptual** Topics that are not on the CompTIA A+ exams but will help you understand more clearly what is on the CompTIA A+ exams
- **901** Topics that clearly fit under the CompTIA A+ 220-901 exam domains
- **902** Topics that clearly fit under the CompTIA A+ 220-902 exam domains
- **Beyond A+** More advanced issues that probably will not be on the CompTIA A+ exams—yet

The beginning of each of these parts is clearly marked with a large banner that looks like this:

Historical/Conceptual

Those of you who fall into the Old Tech group may want to skip everything except the 901 and 902 parts in each chapter. After reading the sections in those parts, jump immediately to the questions at the end of the chapter. The end-of-chapter questions concentrate on information in the 901 and 902 sections. If you run into problems, review the Historical/Conceptual sections in that chapter. Note that you may need to skip back to previous chapters to get the Historical/Conceptual information you need for later chapters.

After going through every chapter as described, Old Techs can move directly to testing their knowledge by using the free practice exams on the media that accompanies the book. Once you start scoring above 90%, you're ready to take the exams. If you're a New Tech—or if you're an Old Tech who wants the full learning experience this book can offer—start by reading the book, *the whole book*, as though you were reading a novel, from page one to the end without skipping around. Because so many computer terms and concepts build on each other, skipping around greatly increases the odds that you will become confused and end up closing the book and firing up your favorite game. Not that I have anything against games, but unfortunately that skill is *not* useful for the CompTIA A+ exams!

Your goal on this first read is to understand concepts, the *whys* behind the *hows*. Having a PC nearby as you read is helpful so you can stop and inspect the PC to see a piece of hardware or how a particular concept manifests in the real world. As you read about hard drives, for example, inspect the cables. Do they look like the ones in the book? Is there a variation? Why? It is imperative that you understand why you are doing something, not just how to do it on one particular system under one specific set of conditions. Neither the exams nor real life as a PC tech will work that way.

If you're reading this book as part of a managing and troubleshooting PCs class rather than a certification-prep course, I highly recommend going the New Tech route, even if you have a decent amount of experience. The book contains a lot of details that can trip you up if you focus only on the test-specific sections of the chapters. Plus, your program might stress historical and conceptual knowledge as well as practical, hands-on skills.

The CompTIA A+ certification exams assume that you have basic user skills. The exams really try to trick you with questions on processes that you may do every day and not think much about. Here's a classic: "To move a file from the C:\DATA folder to the D:\ drive using File Explorer, what key must you hold down while dragging the file?" If you can answer that without going to your keyboard and trying a few likely keys, you're better than most techs! In the real world, you can try a few wrong answers before you hit on the right one, but for the exams, you have to *know* it. Whether Old

Tech or New Tech, make sure you are proficient at user-level Windows skills, including the following:

- Recognizing all the components of the standard Windows desktop (Start menu, notification area, etc.)
- Manipulating windows—resizing, moving, and so on
- Creating, deleting, renaming, moving, and copying files and folders within Windows
- Understanding file extensions and their relationship with program associations
- Using common keyboard shortcuts/hotkeys
- Installing, running, and closing a Windows application

When you do your initial read-through, you may be tempted to skip the Historical/Conceptual sections—don't! Understanding the history and technological developments behind today's personal computing devices helps you understand why they work—or don't work—the way they do. Basically, I'm passing on to you the kind of knowledge you might get by apprenticing yourself to an older, experienced PC tech.

After you've completed the first read-through, go through the book again, this time in textbook mode. If you're an Old Tech, start your studying here. Try to cover one chapter at a sitting. Concentrate on the 901 and 902 sections. Get a highlighter and mark the phrases and sentences that bring out major points. Be sure you understand how the pictures and illustrations relate to the concepts being discussed.

Once you feel you have a good grasp of the material in the book, you can check your knowledge by using the practice exams included on the media accompanying this book. You can take these in Practice mode or Final mode. In Practice mode, you can use the Assistance window to get a helpful hint for the current questions, use the Reference feature to find the chapter that covers the question, check your answer for the question, and see an explanation of the correct answer. In Final mode, you answer all the questions and receive an exam score at the end, just like the real thing. You can also adjust the number of questions on a Practice or Final mode exam with the Customize option.

Both modes show you an overall grade, expressed as a percentage, as well as a breakdown of how well you did on each exam domain. The Review Questions feature lets you see which questions you missed and what the correct answers are. Use these results to guide further studying. Continue reviewing the topics you miss and taking additional exams until you are consistently scoring in the 90% range. When you get there, you are ready to pass the CompTIA A+ certification exams.

Study Tactics

Perhaps it's been a while since you had to study for a test. Or perhaps it hasn't, but you've done your best since then to block the whole experience from your mind. Either way, savvy test-takers know that certain techniques make studying for tests more efficient and effective.

Here's a trick used by students in law and medical schools who have to memorize reams of information: write it down. The act of writing something down (not typing, *writing*) in and of itself helps you to remember it, even if you never look at what you wrote again. Try taking separate notes on the material and re-creating diagrams by hand to help solidify the information in your mind.

Another oldie but goodie: Make yourself flash cards with questions and answers on topics you find difficult. A third trick: Take your notes to bed and read them just before you go to sleep. Many people find they really do learn while they sleep!

Contact

If you have any problems, any questions, or if you just want to argue about something, feel free to send an e-mail to the author—michaelm@totalsem.com—or to the editor—scottj@totalsem.com.

For any other information you might need, contact CompTIA directly at their Web site: www.comptia.org.

Chapter Review

Questions

1. What is the primary CompTIA Web site?
   - **A.** www.comptia.com
   - **B.** www.comptia.edu
   - **C.** www.comptia.net
   - **D.** www.comptia.org
2. Which certification is considered a requirement for entrance into the IT industry?
   - **A.** Certified Cisco Network Associate
   - **B.** CompTIA A+ certification
   - **C.** CompTIA Network+ certification
   - **D.** Microsoft Certified Solutions Expert
3. How many exams do you need to pass to become CompTIA A+ certified?
   - **A.** One
   - **B.** Two
   - **C.** Three
   - **D.** Four

4. Which domain receives the most coverage in the 220-902 exam?
   - **A.** Windows Operating Systems
   - **B.** Security
   - **C.** Other Operating Systems and Technologies
   - **D.** Software Troubleshooting
5. Which version of Windows is *not* tested on the 2015 versions of the CompTIA A+ exams?
   - **A.** Windows 8 Pro
   - **B.** Windows 10
   - **C.** Windows 7 Ultimate
   - **D.** Windows Vista Business
6. What company administers the CompTIA A+ certification exams?
   - **A.** CompTIA
   - **B.** Microsoft
   - **C.** Pearson VUE
   - **D.** Total Seminars
7. What pass rate should you strive for on the practice questions?
   - **A.** 75%
   - **B.** 80%
   - **C.** 90%
   - **D.** 95%
8. How many study hours to pass the CompTIA A+ exams does Mike recommend to a person just starting out learning PC repair?
   - **A.** Roughly 140
   - **B.** Roughly 240
   - **C.** Roughly 340
   - **D.** Roughly 440
9. What is the very first step you should take to pass the CompTIA A+ exams?
   - **A.** Buy more practice exams.
   - **B.** Buy two vouchers.
   - **C.** Read this book like a novel.
   - **D.** Schedule the exams.

10. After becoming CompTIA A+ certified, what's the next certification you should attain?
    A. CompTIA Network+
    B. CompTIA Security+
    C. Microsoft Certified Solutions Expert
    D. Certified Cisco Network Associate

Answers

1. **D.** The primary CompTIA Web site is www.comptia.org (although the .com and .net addresses will redirect you to the main site).
2. **B.** The CompTIA A+ certification is considered a requirement for entrance into the PC industry.
3. **B.** You need to pass two exams to become CompTIA A+ certified.
4. **A.** The 220-902 exam dedicates 29% of the questions to Windows operating systems.
5. **B.** No versions of Windows 10 are on the CompTIA A+ exams.
6. **C.** Pearson VUE administers the CompTIA A+ certification exams.
7. **C.** You should not take either exam until you are consistently getting at least 90% on the practice exams.
8. **B.** Mike recommends about 240 study hours for a person new to PC repair.
9. **D.** Schedule the exams for some point in the future.
10. **A.** The typical certification path goes from CompTIA A+ to CompTIA Network+, so you have all the basics before you choose to specialize in Microsoft or Cisco products.

CHAPTER 2

Operational Procedures

In this chapter, you will learn how to

- Present yourself with a proper appearance and professional manner
- Talk to customers in a professional, productive manner
- Discuss the tools of the trade

I am a "nerd" and I consider the term a compliment. Nerds are smart and like to work with technology—these are the good aspects of nerd-dom. On the other hand, many people think of the term nerd as an insult. Nerds are rarely portrayed in a positive manner in the media, and I think I know why. Nerds generally suffer from some pretty serious social weaknesses. These weaknesses are classics: bad clothing, shyness, and poor communication skills. If you've ever seen an episode of the TV show *The Big Bang Theory*, you know what I'm talking about.

This chapter covers some basic life skills to enable you to enjoy your nerdiness and yet function out in the real world. You'll learn how to act as a professional and how to communicate effectively. After you're well on your way to the beginnings of social graces, we'll discuss some of the hazards (such as static electricity) you may run into in your job and the tools you can use to prevent problems. After all, nerds who cannot stay organized—or who break equipment or themselves—need to learn some tricks to keep everything organized and safe. The chapter finishes with a discussion about troubleshooting. You'll learn the CompTIA A+ troubleshooting theory, an excellent tool that will serve you well in your studies and career as a tech.

902

The Professional Tech

A professional tech displays professionalism, which might seem a little trite if it weren't absolutely true. The tech presents a professional appearance and follows a proper ethical code. I call the latter the Traits of a Tech. Let's take a look at these two areas in more detail.

Appearance

Americans live in a casual society. The problem with casual is that perhaps our society is becoming *too* casual. Customers often equate casual clothing with a casual attitude. You might think you're just fixing somebody's computer, but you're doing much more than that. You are saving precious family photos. You are keeping a small business in operation. This is serious stuff, and nobody wants an unclean, slovenly person doing these important jobs. Take a look at Figure 2-1. This is our resident illustrator (among other job descriptions), Ford Pierson, casually dressed to hang with his buddies.

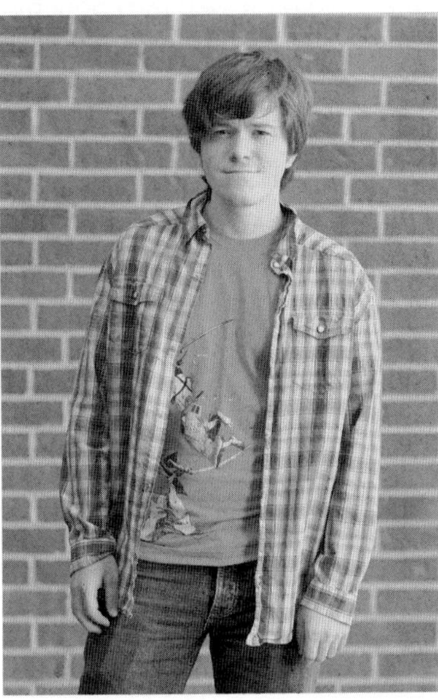

Figure 2-1
Casual Ford

I have a question for you. If you ran a small business and your primary file server died, leaving 15 employees with nothing to do, how would you feel about Ford as a tech coming into your office looking like this? I hope your answer would be "not too confident." Every company has some form of dress code for techs. Figure 2-2 shows Ford dressed in a fairly typical example, with a company polo shirt, khaki pants, and dark shoes (trust me on that score). Please also note that both his shirt and his pants are wrinkle-free. All techs either know how to iron or know the location of the nearest cleaners.

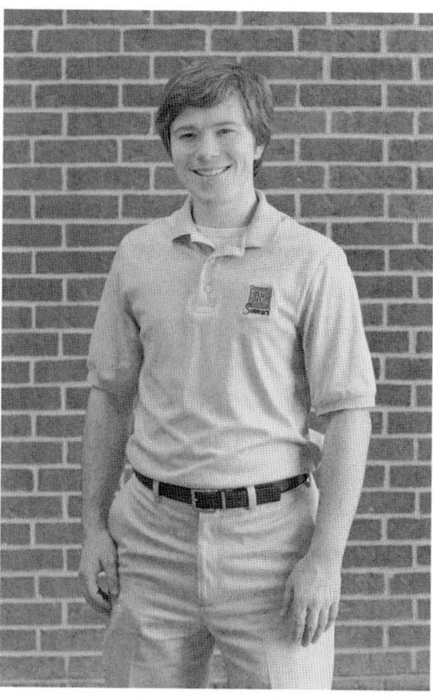

Figure 2-2 Professional Ford

While we are looking at this model of a man, do you appreciate that his hair is combed and his face is cleanly shaven? It's too bad I can't use scratch-and-sniffs, but if I could, you'd also notice that Professional Ford took a shower, used some deodorant, and brushed his teeth.

I hope that most of the people who read this smile quietly to themselves and say, "Well, of course." The sad truth tells me otherwise. Next time you look at a tech, ask yourself how many of these simple appearance and hygiene issues were missed. Then make a point not to be one of the unkempt techs.

The Traits of a Tech

When I was a Boy Scout in the United States, we learned something called the Boy Scout Law, a list of traits that define the ethics of a Boy Scout. Even though I haven't been active in Boy Scouts for a long time, I still have the Scout Law memorized: "A Scout is trustworthy, loyal, helpful, friendly, courteous, kind, obedient, cheerful, thrifty, brave, clean, and reverent."

My goal here isn't a sales pitch for scouting in any form, but rather to give you an idea of what we are trying to achieve: a list of ethics that will help you be a better technician. The list you are about to see is my own creation, but it does a great job of covering the CompTIA A+ objectives. Let's dive into the traits of a tech: honesty/integrity, dependability/responsibility, adaptability/versatility, and sensitivity.

Honesty/Integrity

Honesty and integrity are not the same thing, but for a tech, they are so closely related that it is best to think of them as one big ethic. *Honesty* means to tell the truth, and *integrity* means doing the right thing.

It's simple to say you have to be honest, but be warned that our industry often makes it difficult. IT technicians get a lot of leeway compared to most starting jobs, making dishonesty tempting. One of the biggest temptations is lying to your boss. A new tech driving around in a van all day may find it convenient to stretch the truth on how long he took for lunch or how far along he is on the next job. Being up front and honest with your boss is pretty obvious and easy to understand.

Being honest with your customers is a lot harder. Don't sell people goods and services they don't need, even if you get a cut of what you sell. Don't lie to your customers about a problem. If you can't explain the problem to them in plain English, don't create techno-babble (see note) and don't be afraid to say, "I don't know." Too many techs seem to think that not knowing exactly what a problem might be is a reflection of their skill. A skilled tech can say, "I don't know, but I know how to figure it out, and I will get you the right answer."

NOTE *Techno-babble* is the use of (often nonsensical) jargon and technical terms to intimidate and silence a challenge to a technical issue.

A computer tech must bring *integrity* to the job, just like any other service professional. You should treat anything said to you and anything you see as a personal confidence, not to be repeated to customers, coworkers, or bosses. Here's Mike's Rule of Confidentiality: "Unless it's a felony or an imminent physical danger, you didn't see nothin'." You'll learn more about dealing with prohibited content in Chapter 27.

There is an exception to this rule. Sometimes you need to separate paying customers from in-house users. A paying customer is someone who doesn't work for your company and is paying for your services. An in-house user is someone who works for the same company you work for and is not directly paying for your services. It's often your job (but not always) to police in-house IT policies. Here's a great example. If you are at a customer's site and you see a Post-it note with a password on a user's monitor, you say nothing. If you are in-house and you see the same thing, you probably need to speak to the user about the dangers of exposing passwords.

You have a lot of power when you sit in front of someone's computer. You can readily read private e-mail, discover Web sites surfed, and more. With a click of the Start button, you can know the last five programs the user ran, including Word and Solitaire, and the last few documents the user worked on. Don't do this; you really don't want to know. Plus, if you are caught violating a customer's privacy, you not only will lose credibility and respect, but you could also lose your job. *You need to deal appropriately with customers' confidential and private materials.* This includes files on the computer, items on a physical desktop, and even pages sitting in a printer tray.

Passwords are a big issue for techs. We have to reboot computers and access shares and other jobs that require passwords. The rule here is to *avoid learning other folks' passwords at all costs* (see Figure 2-3). If you know a password to access a mission-critical machine and that machine ends up compromised or with data missing, who might be blamed? You, that's who, so avoid learning passwords! If you only need a password once, let the user type it in for you. If you anticipate accessing something multiple times (the more usual situation), ask the user to change the password temporarily.

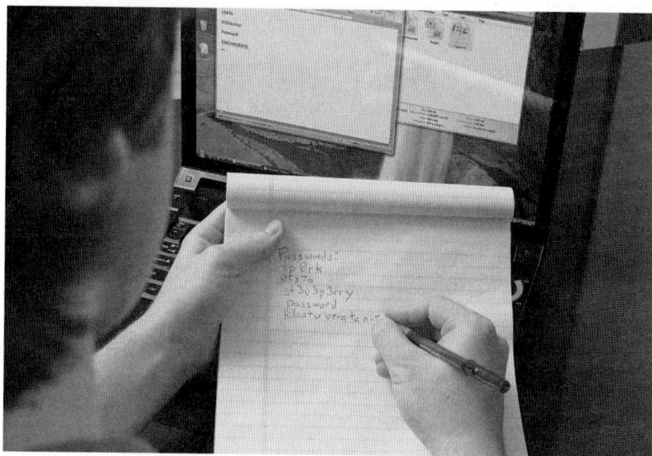

Figure 2-3 Don't do this!

It's funny, but people assume ownership of things they use at work. John in accounting doesn't call the computer he uses anything but "my PC." The phone on Susie's desk isn't the company phone, it's "Susie's phone." Regardless of the logic or illogic involved with this sense of ownership, a tech needs to respect that feeling. You'll never go wrong if you follow the *Ethic of Reciprocity*, also known as the *Golden Rule*: "Do unto others as you would have them do unto you." In a tech's life, this can translate as "treat people's things as you would have other people treat yours." Don't use or touch anything—keyboard, printer, laptop, monitor, mouse, phone, pen, paper, or cube toy—without first asking permission. Follow this rule at all times, even when the customer isn't looking.

Dependability/Responsibility

Dependability and responsibility are another pair of traits that, while they don't mean the same thing, often go together. A dependable person performs agreed-upon actions. A responsible person is answerable for her actions. Again, the freedom of the typical IT person's job makes dependability and responsibility utterly critical.

Dependable techs show up for job appointments and show up on time. Failure to show up for an appointment not only inconveniences the customer, but also can cost your customer a lot of money in lost time and productivity. So, *be on time*.

If you or your company makes an appointment for you, show up. Be there. Don't let simple problems (such as bad traffic) prevent you from showing up on time. Take some time to prepare. Figure out traffic times. Figure out if preceding appointments will cause

a problem, and check for traffic. There is a popular old saying in the United States, "Five minutes early is on time, and on time is late." Sometimes events take place that prevent you from being on time. *If late, contact the customer immediately* and give him or her your best estimate of when you will arrive. A simple apology wouldn't hurt, either.

Responsibility is a tricky subject for IT folks. Certainly you should be responsible for your actions, but the stakes are high when critical data and expensive equipment are at risk. Before you work on a computer, always ask the customer if there are up-to-date backups of the data. If there aren't, offer to make backups for the customer, even if this incurs an extra charge for the customer. If the customer chooses not to make a backup, make sure he or she understands, very clearly, the risk to the data on the system you are about to repair.

Adaptability/Versatility

Adaptability defines how someone adjusts to changes. Versatility, at least within the scope of an IT technician, is bringing a broad set of skills to the computer repair process. Every repair is to some degree a guessing game. No one knows all the possible problems a computer can have. There is no universal computing devices repair manual to which you can refer to tell you how to fix computers. Good techs must be able to adapt to any situation, both technically and in the environment. For example, good techs should be able to fix most peripherals, even if they are not experts on that particular device. As you progress through the book, you'll discover that most devices fit into one family or another and that there are certain diagnostic/repair steps that you can at least try to enact a repair.

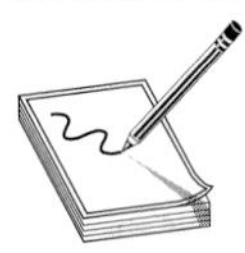

NOTE Most computer repair companies require a signed Authorization of Work or Work Authorization form to document the company name, billing information, date, scope of work, and that sort of thing. Even if you do your own repairs, these forms can save you from angst and from litigation. You can create your own or do an Internet search for examples.

Adaptability isn't required just for technical issues. Computing devices find themselves broken in the strangest places and ways. An adaptable tech doesn't have a problem if a computer sits at the top of a suspension bridge or behind a desk. An adaptable tech can work around mean dogs, broken water lines, and noisy little kids (but there are some very important rules for dealing with kids; see later in this chapter).

A technician has to be versatile. The best example of this is what I call the User Advocate. User Advocates are technicians who not only take the time to learn the processes of whatever organization they work for, but also look to create technology solutions for problems and inefficiencies. This also means a tech should be at least competent if not expert at working with all the computer applications used by the organization. When you combine your IT skills with an understanding of how the business works, you become amazingly versatile, quickly finding yourself with more responsibility and (hopefully) more money.

A big part of versatility is offering different repair options in certain situations. When there is more than one way to fix things, make sure the customer knows all the

options, but also give them your recommendation. Tell the customer why you feel your recommendation is the best course of action, but give them knowledge necessary to make their own decision.

A tech's versatility isn't limited to IT skills. Woe to the tech who doesn't understand basic electrical wiring and building codes. Skilled techs need to act in *compliance with local government regulations* on this sort of issue. I've had hundreds of repair scenarios where the fix was as simple as knowing how to turn on an electrical breaker or moving a computing device away from an electrical motor. No, these aren't IT skills, but a versatile tech knows these problems exist.

Sensitivity

Sensitivity is the ability to appreciate another's feeling and emotions. Sensitivity requires observing others closely, taking time to appreciate their feelings, and acting in such a way that makes them feel comfortable. I've rarely felt that technicians I've met were good at sensitivity. The vast majority of nerds I know, including myself, tend to be self-centered and unaware of what's going on around them. Let me give you a few tips I've learned along the way.

Understand that the customer is paying for your time and skills. Also understand that your presence invariably means something is wrong or broken, and few things make users more upset than broken computers. When you are "on the clock," you need to show possibly very upset customers that you are giving their problem your full attention. To do this, you need to avoid distractions. If you get a personal call, let it roll over to voicemail. If you get a work-related call, politely excuse yourself, walk away for privacy, and keep the call brief. Never talk to coworkers while interacting with customers. Never speak badly of a customer; you never know where you'll run into them next.

Last, *be culturally sensitive*. We live in a diverse world of races, religions, etiquettes, and traditions. If a customer's religious holiday conflicts with your work schedule, the customer wins. If the customer wants you to take off your shoes, take them off. If the customer wants you to wear a hat, wear one. *Use appropriate professional titles, when applicable.* If a customer's title is "Doctor," for example, use the title even if you don't recognize the field of medicine. When in doubt, always ask the customer for guidance.

Effective Communication

When you deal with users, managers, and owners who are frustrated and upset because a computer or network is down and they can't work, your job requires you to take on the roles of detective and psychologist. Talking with frazzled and confused people and getting answers to questions about how the personal computing device got into the state it's in takes skill. Communicating clearly and effectively is important.

This section explores techniques for effective communication. It starts with assertive communication and then looks at issues involving respect. We'll examine methods for eliciting useful answers in a timely fashion. The section finishes with a discussion about managing expectations and professional follow-up actions.

Assertive Communication

In many cases, a computer problem results from user error or neglect. As a technician, you must show users the error of their ways without creating anger or conflict. You do this by using assertive communication. *Assertive communication* isn't pushy or bossy, but it's also not the language of a pushover. Assertive communication first requires you to show the other person that you understand and appreciate the importance of his feelings. Use statements such as "I know how frustrating it feels to lose data," or "I understand how infuriating it is when the network goes out and you can't get your job done." Statements like these cool off the situation and let customers know you are on their side. Avoid using the word "you," as it can sound accusatory.

The second part of assertive communication is making sure you state the problem clearly without accusing the user directly: "Not keeping up with defragmenting your hard drive slows it down," or "Help me understand how the network cable keeps getting unplugged during your lunch hour." Last, tell the user what you need to prevent this error in the future. "Please call me whenever you hear that buzzing sound," or "Please check the company's approved software list before installing anything." Always use "I" and "me," and never make judgments. "I can't promise the keyboard will work well if it's always getting dirty" is much better than "Stop eating cookies over the keyboard, you slob!"

Respectful Communication

Generally, IT folks support the people doing a company's main business. You are there to serve their needs and, all things being equal, to do so at their convenience, not yours.

You don't do the user's job, but you should *respect* that job and person as an essential cog in the organization. Communicate with users the way you would like them to communicate with you, were the roles reversed. Again, this follows the Ethic of Reciprocity.

Don't assume the world stops the moment you walk in the door and that you may immediately interrupt a customer's work to do yours. Although most customers are thrilled and motivated to help you the moment you arrive, this may not always be the case. Ask the magic question, "May I start working on the problem now?" Give customers a chance to wrap up, shut down, or do anything else necessary to finish their business and make it safe for you to do yours.

Engage the user with the standard rules of civil conversation. *Actively listen. Don't interrupt customers* as they describe a problem; *just listen and take notes.* You might hear something that leads to resolving the problem. Rephrase and repeat the problems back to the customer to verify you understand the issue ("So the computer is locking up three times a day?"). Use an even, nonaccusatory tone, and although it's okay to try to explain a problem if the user asks, *never condescend and never argue with a customer.*

Maintain a positive attitude in the face of adversity. Don't get defensive if you can't figure something out quickly and the user starts hassling you. Remember that an angry customer isn't really angry with you—he's just frustrated—so don't take his anger personally. Instead, take it in stride; smile, *project confidence*, and assure him that computer troubleshooting sometimes takes a while.

Avoid distractions that take your focus away from the user and his or her computer problem. Things that break your concentration slow down the troubleshooting process

immensely. Plus, customers will feel insulted if you start texting or chatting on your cell phone with your significant other about a movie date later that night when you're supposed to be fixing the customer's computers! You're not being paid to socialize, so turn those cell phones to vibrate. That's why the technogods created voicemail. Avoid personal interruptions. Never take any call except one that is potentially urgent. If a call is potentially urgent, explain the urgency to the customer, step away, and deal with the call as quickly as possible.

Also, avoid accessing social media sites while on the job. Checking Facebook or tweeting while your customer waits for his computer to get fixed is rude. And definitely never post on social media anything about your interaction with your customer.

Try This!

Apply the Ethic of Reciprocity

The Ethic of Reciprocity appears in almost every religion on the planet, with versions attributed to Confucius, Jesus, Moses, and Mohammed, among others. Just for practice, try the Ethic of Reciprocity out in nontechnical situations, such as when buying something from the corner store or grocery. Consciously analyze how the clerk behind the counter would want a customer to interact with him or her. Now put yourself in the clerk's shoes. How would you want a customer to communicate with you? Act accordingly!

If you discover that the user caused the problem, either through ignorance or by accident, don't dismiss the customer's problem, but don't be judgmental or insulting about the cause. We all screw up sometimes, and these kinds of mistakes are your job security. *You get paid because people make mistakes and machines break.* Chances are you'll be back at that workstation six months or a year later, fixing something else. By becoming the user's advocate and go-to person, you create a better work environment. If a mistaken action caused the problem, explain in a positive and supportive way how to do the task correctly, and then have the user go through the process while you are there to reinforce what you said.

Eliciting Answers

Your job as a tech is to get the computer fixed, and the best way to start that process is to determine what the computer is doing or not doing. You must start by talking to the customer. Allow the customer to explain the problem fully while you record the information. Once the person has described the situation, you must then ask questions. This process is called *eliciting answers.*

Although each person is different, most users with a malfunctioning computer or peripheral will be distraught and perhaps defensive about the problem. To overcome this initial attitude, you need to ask the right questions *and* listen to the customer's answers. Then ask the proper follow-up questions.

Always avoid accusatory questions, because they won't help you in the least (see Figure 2-4). "What did you do?" generally gets a confused or defensive "Nothing" in reply, which doesn't get you closer to solving the problem. First, ask questions that help clarify the situation. Repeat what you think is the problem after you've listened all the way through the user's story.

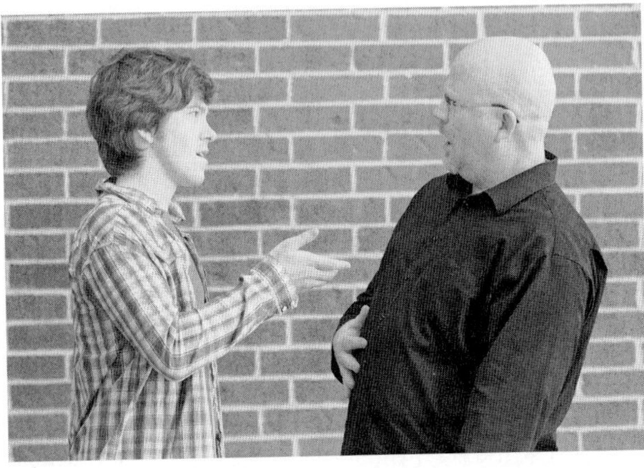

Figure 2-4 Never accuse!

Follow up with fact-seeking questions. "When did it last work?" "Has it ever worked in this way?" "Has any software changed recently?" "Has any new hardware been added?" Ask open-ended questions to narrow the scope of the problem ("Which applications are running when the computer locks up?").

By keeping your questions friendly and factual, you show users that you won't accuse them or judge their actions (see Figure 2-5). You also show them that you're there to help them. After the initial tension drops away, you'll often get more information: for instance, a recitation of something the user might have tried or changed. These clues can help lead to a quick resolution of the problem.

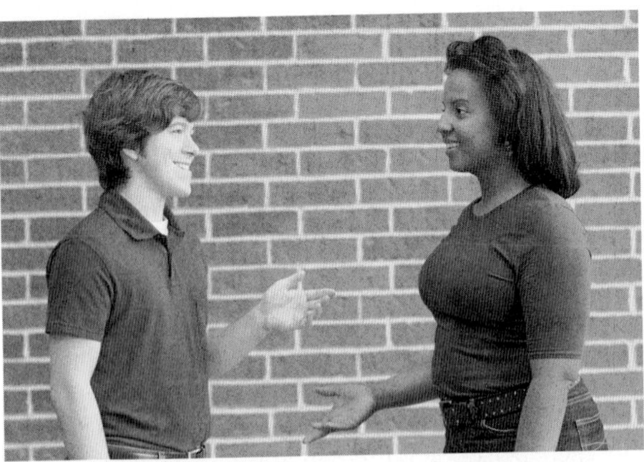

Figure 2-5 Keeping it friendly

Remember that you may know all about computer technology, but the user probably does not. This means a user will often use vague and/or incorrect terms to describe a

particular computer component or function. That's just the way it works, so don't bother to correct the user. Wherever possible, avoid using jargon, acronyms, or abbreviations specific to computers. They simply confuse the already upset user and can make you sound like you're talking down to the user. Just ask direct, factual questions in a friendly tone, using simple, non-jargon language to zero in on what the user was trying to accomplish and what happened when things went wrong. Use visual aids when possible. Point at the machine or go to a working computer to have the user show what went wrong or what she did or tried to do.

People do usually want to get a handle on what you are doing—in a simplified way. You don't want to overwhelm them, but don't be afraid to use simple analogies or concepts to give them an idea of what is happening. If you have the time (and the skills), use drawings, equipment, and other visual aids to make technical concepts more clear. If a customer is a closet tech and is really digging for answers—to the point that it's affecting your ability to do your job—compliment her initiative and then direct her to outside training opportunities. Better yet, tell her where she can get a copy of this book!

Beyond basic manners, never assume that just because you are comfortable with friendly or casual behavior, the customer will be too. Even an apparently casual user will expect you to behave with professional decorum. On the flip side, don't allow a user to put you in an awkward or even potentially dangerous or illegal situation. Never do work outside the scope of your assigned duties without the prior approval of your supervisor (when possible in such cases, try to direct users to someone who *can* help them). You are not a babysitter; never volunteer to "watch the kids" while the customer leaves the job site or tolerate a potentially unsafe situation if a customer isn't properly supervising a child. Concentrate on doing your job safely and efficiently, and maintain professional integrity.

Expectations and Follow-Up

Users are terrified when their computers and networks go down so hard that they need to call in a professional. Odds are good that they've left critical, or at least important, data on the computer. Odds are equally good they need this computer to work to do their job. When they're ready to lay down money for a professional, they're expecting you to make their system exactly the way it was before it broke. Hopefully you can do exactly that for them, but you also must deal with their expectations and let them know what to expect.

Equally, you should give your customers some follow-up after the job is finished. We've already covered data backups and Authorization of Work forms (and those are very important), but you need to keep the customer's needs in mind. You also want to keep the customer thinking about you, should they need more help in the future. Here are a few items you should consider.

Timeline

If you can give the customer a best guess as to how long the repair will take, you'll be a hero. Don't be afraid to hold off on your time frame prediction until you've diagnosed the machine. If you truly don't have a feel for the time involved, tell the customer that and then tell him or her what you'll need to know before you can make the prediction.

Stick to the timeline. If you finish more quickly, great! People love a job that goes faster than predicted. If you're moving past the predicted time frame, contact the customer and

tell him or her as soon as possible. Let him or her know what's happened, explain why you need more time, and give the customer a new time frame. The biggest secret here is to keep in communication with the customer on any change in status. People understand delays—they take place in our lives daily. People resent not knowing why a delay is occurring, especially when a precious computer is at stake.

Options

Many times with a computer issue, you can fix the problem and avoid a similar problem in the future in several ways. These options boil down to money. If applicable, offer different repair/replacement options and let the customer decide which route to take.

Route A might replace a faulty component with an upgraded component and a backup in case the new component fails in the future. Route B might replace the faulty device with an upgraded device. Route C might do an even device swap. Provide options and let the customer decide.

Documentation

At the completion of work, provide proper documentation of the services provided. Describe the problem, including the time and day you started work, the solution (again including the time and day the work ended), the number of hours you worked, and a list of all parts you replaced. If the customer owns the removed parts, offer them to the customer (this is especially true if you replace any storage media). This documentation may or may not include your charges.

Follow-Up

Follow up with a customer/user at a later date to verify satisfaction. This can be simple follow-up, usually just a phone call, to confirm that the customer is happy with your work. This gives the customer a chance to detail any special issues that may have arisen, and it also adds that final extra touch that ensures he or she will call you again when encountering a technical problem.

Tools of the Trade and Personal Safety

Effective communication with your customer enables you to *start* the troubleshooting process, getting details about the problem and clues about things that happened around the same time. To continue troubleshooting, though, you need to be adept at handling computing devices. That starts with knowing how to handle computer components safely and how to use the tools of a tech. You also need a very clear troubleshooting methodology to guide your efforts. Let's look at these issues.

Electrostatic Discharge (ESD)

If you decide to open a PC or Linux box while reading this book, as I encourage you to do, you must take proper steps to avoid a great killer of computers: *electrostatic discharge (ESD)*. ESD simply means the passage of a static electrical charge from one item to another. Have you ever rubbed a balloon against your shirt, making the balloon stick to you? That's a classic example of static electricity. When that static charge discharges, you may not notice

it happening—although on a cool, dry day, I've been shocked so hard by touching a doorknob that I could see a big, blue spark! I've never heard of a human being getting anything worse than a rather nasty shock from ESD, but I can't say the same thing about computers. ESD will destroy the sensitive parts of any computing device, so it is essential that you take steps to avoid ESD when working on a PC or other computing device.

NOTE All computing devices are well protected against ESD on the outside. Unless you take a screwdriver or pry tool and actually open up a PC or other computing device, you don't need to concern yourself with ESD.

Antistatic Tools

ESD only takes place when two objects that store different amounts (the hip electrical term to use is *potential*) of static electricity come in contact. The secret to avoiding ESD is to keep you and the parts of the computer you touch at the same electrical potential, otherwise known as grounding yourself to the computing device. You can accomplish this by connecting yourself to the computer via a handy little device called an *antistatic wrist strap*. This simple device consists of a wire that connects on one end to an alligator clip and on the other end to a small metal plate that secures to your wrist with an elastic strap. You snap the alligator clip onto any handy metal part of the computer and place the wrist strap on either wrist. Figure 2-6 shows a typical antistatic wrist strap in use.

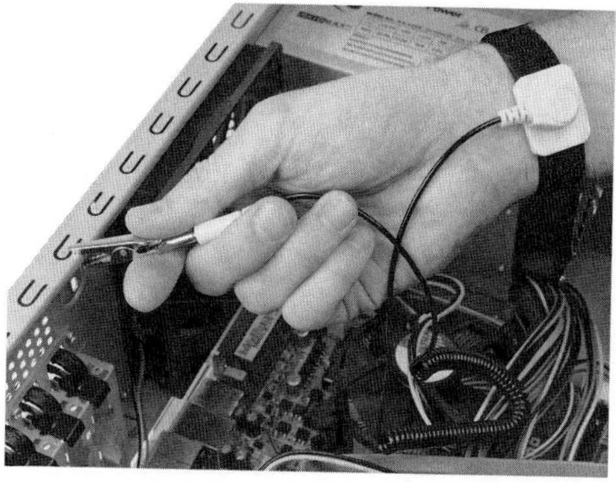

Figure 2-6 Antistatic wrist strap in use

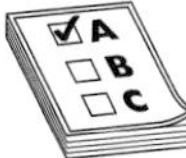

EXAM TIP Static electricity, and therefore the risk of ESD, is much more prevalent in dry, cool environments.

Antistatic wrist straps are standard equipment for anyone working on a computing device, but other tools might also come in handy. One of the big issues when working with a computer occurs if you find yourself pulling out parts from the computer and setting them aside. The moment you take a piece out of the computer, it no longer has contact with the systems and may pick up static from other sources. Techs use antistatic mats to eliminate this risk. An *antistatic mat* acts as a point of common potential; you

can purchase a combination antistatic wrist strap and mat that all connect to keep you, the computer, and any loose components at the same electrical potential (see Figure 2-7).

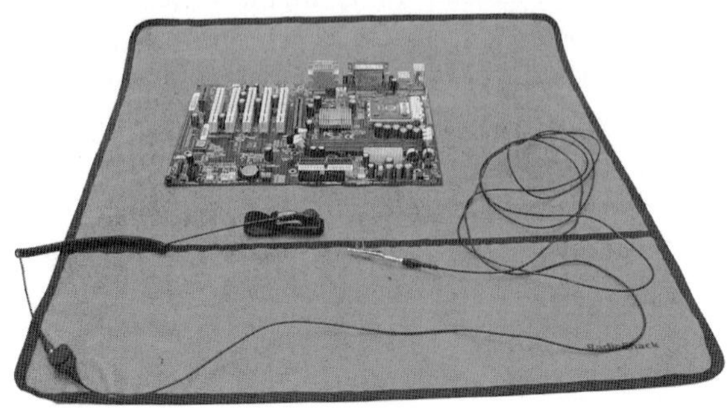

Figure 2-7 Antistatic wrist strap and mat combination

Antistatic wrist straps and mats use tiny *resistors*—devices that stop or *resist* the flow of electricity—to prevent a static charge from racing through the device. These resistors can fail over time, so it's always a good idea to read the documentation that comes with your antistatic tools to see how to test those small resistors properly.

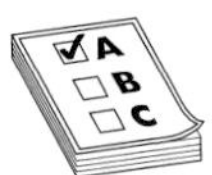

EXAM TIP Always put components *in* an antistatic bag, not on the bag.

Any electrical component not in a computer case needs to be stored in an *antistatic bag*, a specially designed bag that sheds whatever static electricity you have when you touch it, thus preventing any damage to components stored within (see Figure 2-8). Almost all components come in an antistatic bag when purchased. Experienced techs never throw these bags away, as you never know when you'll want to pull a part out and place it on a shelf for a while.

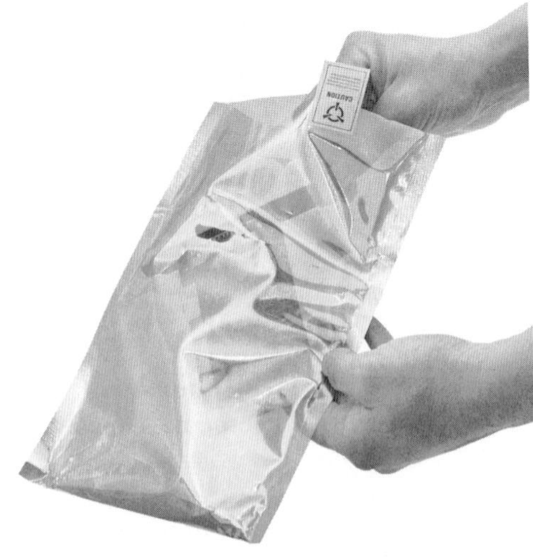

Figure 2-8 Antistatic bag

NOTE Computer gear manufacturers package their product in a variety of ways to shield against accidental damage, whether that's physical damage, ESD, EMI, or RFI. The typical pink translucent computer bag is coated with a film that prevents the bag from producing static electricity and mildly protects the contents against physical contact (and thus damage). The two types of metal bags offer shielding against EMI and RFI as well as ESD. These are the silvery bags (such as in Figure 2-8) you'll see hard drives packed in, for example, and the black and silver woven bags you'll sometimes see.

Although having an antistatic wrist strap with you at all times would be ideal, the reality is that from time to time you'll find yourself in a situation where you lack the proper antistatic tools. This shouldn't keep you from working on the computer—if you're careful! When working on a computer in such a situation, take a moment to touch the power supply before you start and then every once in a while as you work—I'll show you where it is in Chapter 3—to keep yourself at the same electrical potential as the computer. Although this isn't as good as a wrist strap, this *self-grounding* is better than nothing at all.

Try This!

Antistatic Protection Devices

In some circumstances, an antistatic wrist strap could get in the way. Manufacturers have developed some alternatives to the wrist strap, so try this:

1. Take a field trip to a local computer or electronics store.
2. Check out their selection of antistatic devices. Can you find anything other than wrist straps or mats?
3. Do a Web search for "static control products." Can you find anything other than wrist straps or mats?
4. Report what options you can find for protecting your equipment from ESD. Weigh the pros and cons and decide what you would use in various situations.

The last issue when it comes to preventing ESD is that never-ending question—should you work with the computing device plugged in or unplugged? The answer is simple: Do you really want to be physically connected to a computer that is plugged into an electrical outlet? Granted, the chances of electrocution are slim, but why take the risk?

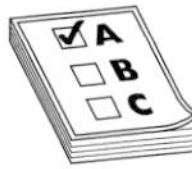

EXAM TIP Always disconnect power before repairing a personal computing device.

Removing the power applies also when working on portable computers. Disconnect both from the wall outlet and remove the battery. With mobile devices such as tablets and smartphones, this creates an issue because the battery is inside the case. Chapter 25 covers the special skills needed for working on mobile devices.

Electromagnetic Interference (EMI)

A magnetic field interfering with electronics is *electromagnetic interference (EMI)*. EMI isn't nearly as dangerous as ESD, but it can cause permanent damage to some components and erase data on some storage devices. You can prevent EMI by keeping magnets away from computer equipment. Certain components are particularly susceptible to EMI, especially storage devices like hard drives.

The biggest problem with EMI is that we often use magnets without even knowing we are doing so. Any device with an electrical motor has a magnet. Many telephones have magnets. Power bricks for laptops and speakers also have magnets. Keep them away!

Radio Frequency Interference (RFI)

Do you ever hear strange noises on your speakers even though you aren't playing any sounds? Do you ever get strange noises on your cell phone? If so, you've probably run into *radio frequency interference (RFI)*. Many devices emit radio waves:

- Cell phones
- Wireless network cards
- Cordless phones
- Baby monitors
- Microwave ovens

In general, the radio waves that these devices emit are very weak, and almost all electronic devices are shielded to prevent RFI. A few devices, speakers in particular, are susceptible to RFI. RFI will never cause any damage, but it can be incredibly irritating. The best way to prevent RFI is to keep radio-emitting devices as far away as possible from other electronics.

RFI becomes a big problem when two devices share the same frequencies. Cordless phones, baby monitors, and wireless networks share the same range of frequencies. They sometimes interfere with each other, causing poor signals or even blocking signals completely. These devices need to be tuned to avoid stomping on each other's frequencies. In Chapter 22, you'll see how to tune a wireless network to prevent RFI.

Personal Safety

IT techs live in a dangerous world. We're in constant danger of tripping, hurting our backs, and getting burned by hot components. You also need to keep in mind what you wear (in a safety sense). Let's take a moment to discuss these *personal safety* issues and what to do about them.

CAUTION When thinking about safety, keep in mind any local government regulations. You may be required to wear certain protective gear or take extra precautions while in the workplace. Make sure you also follow any environmental rules for the disposal of old parts, especially with things like CRT monitors, batteries, and toner cartridges, which may contain hazardous or toxic materials. Check with your employer or your local government's Web site for more information.

If you don't stay organized, hardware technology will take over your life. Figure 2-9 shows a corner of my office, a painful example of a cable "kludge."

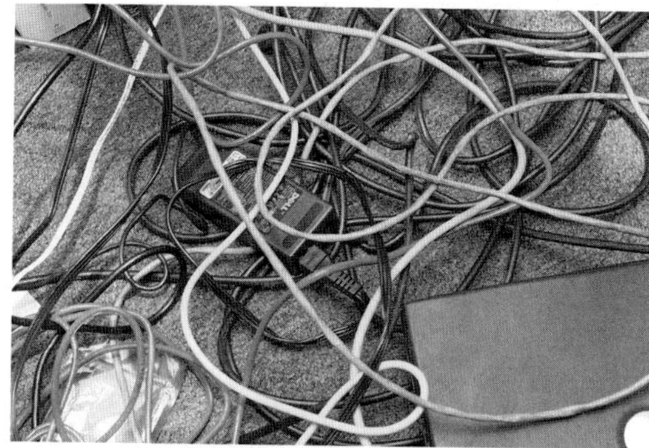

Figure 2-9 Mike's cable kludge

Cable messes such as these are dangerous tripping hazards. While I may allow a mess like this in my home office, all cables in a business environment are carefully tucked away behind computer cases, run into walls, or placed under cable runners. If you see a cable that is an obvious tripping hazard, contact the person in charge of the building to take care of it immediately. The results of ignoring such hazards can be catastrophic (see Figure 2-10). Use proper cable management to avoid these dangers.

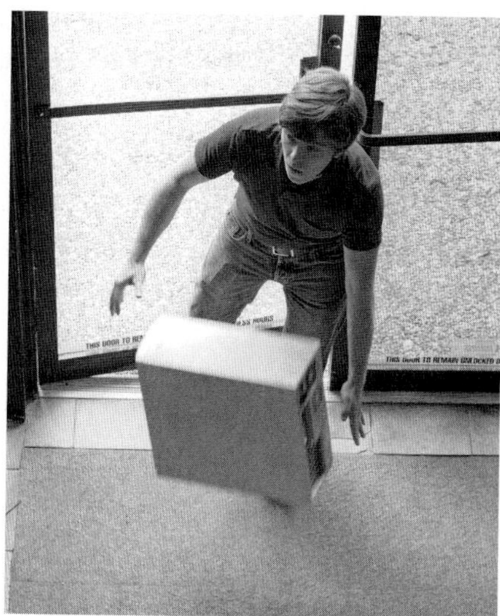

Figure 2-10 What a strange, bad trip it's been.

Another personal safety issue is heavy boxes. Computers, printers, monitors—everything we use—all seem to come to us in heavy boxes. Use proper lifting techniques. Remember never to lift with your back; lift with your legs, and always use a hand truck if available. Pay attention to weight limitations on the devices you use to move anything heavy. You are never paid enough to risk your own health.

You also need to watch out for hot components. It's hard to burn yourself unless you actually open up a computer, printer, or monitor. First, watch for anything with a cooling fin like the one shown in Figure 2-11. If you see a cooling fin, odds are good that something is hot enough to burn you. Also look for labels or stickers warning about hot components. Last, when in doubt, move your hand over components as if you were checking the heat on a stove.

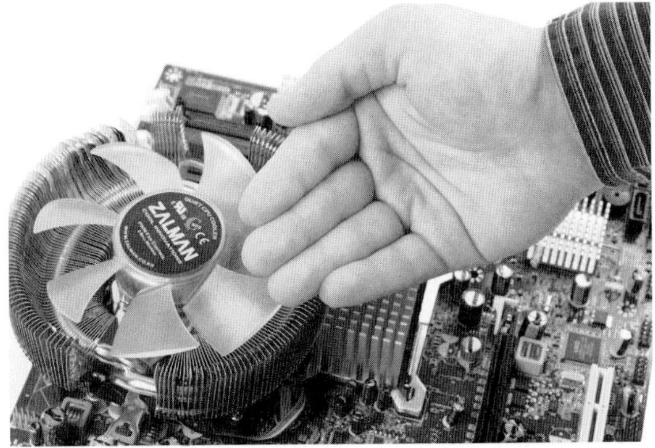

Figure 2-11 Checking for hot cooling fins

Disconnect a computer from its electrical source before you work on it, if possible. In the rare event where you need to work on a live system, take caution. Provide electrical fire safety equipment in rooms or locations that have a fire risk, such as server rooms. All those electronics and all that juice make a dangerous combination in those rare circumstances in which bad things happen. Keep properly rated (Class C) fire extinguishers handy.

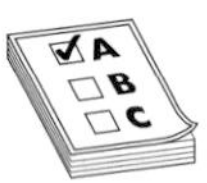

EXAM TIP When you build out a particular computer space, such as a server closet (the room that has a lot of important computers in it), use standard carpentry safety techniques. Wear an *air filter mask* when cutting drywall, for example. Wear *safety goggles* when using power tools.

Finally, remove any jewelry or loose-hanging clothing before working on a computer. If you have long hair, you might consider tying it back in a ponytail. You don't want anything getting caught in a fan or stuck on a component. This can save you and your components a lot of pain.

Physical Tools

The basic *tech toolkit* consists of a *Phillips-head screwdriver* and not much else—seriously—but a half-dozen tools round out a fully functional toolkit. Most kits have a star-headed Torx wrench, a nut driver or two, a pair of plastic tweezers, a little grabber tool (the technical term is *parts retriever*), a hemostat, an IC extractor for removing various chips, and both Phillips-head and flat-head screwdrivers (see Figure 2-12).

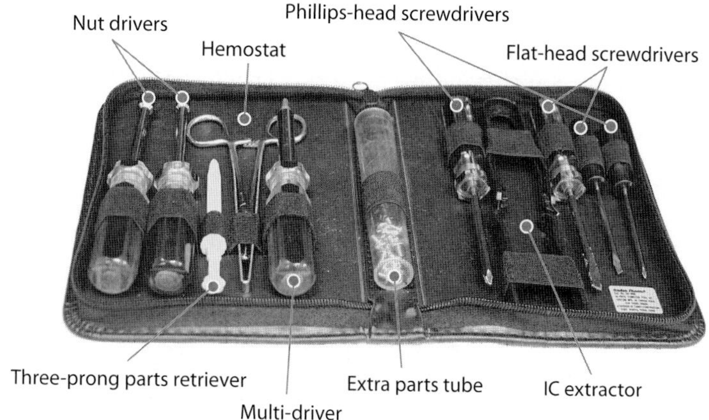

Figure 2-12 Typical technician toolkit

A lot of techs throw in an extension magnet to grab hard-to-reach bits that drop into cases (an exception to the "no magnets" rule). Many also add a magnifying glass and a flashlight for those hard-to-read numbers and text on the printed circuit boards (PCBs) that make up a large percentage of devices inside the system unit. Contrary to what you might think, techs rarely need a hammer.

Troubleshooting Theory

An effective *troubleshooting theory* follows a set of steps to diagnose and fix a computer. Troubleshooting theory includes talking to users to determine how and when the problem took place, determining a cause, testing, verification, and documentation. Techs use a number of good troubleshooting theories. Luckily for those taking the CompTIA A+ 220-902 certification exam, CompTIA clearly defines their vision of troubleshooting theory:

5.5 Given a scenario, explain the troubleshooting theory

1. Identify the problem
   - Question the user and identify user changes to computer and perform backups before making changes
2. Establish a theory of probable cause (question the obvious)
   - If necessary, conduct external or internal research based on symptoms

3. Test the theory to determine cause
   - Once theory is confirmed, determine next steps to resolve problem
   - If theory is not confirmed, re-establish new theory or escalate
4. Establish a plan of action to resolve the problem and implement the solution
5. Verify full system functionality and if applicable implement preventative measures
6. Document findings, actions and outcomes

Identify the Problem

There's a reason you're standing in front of a computer to repair it: something happened that the user of the computer has identified as "not good" and that's why you're here. First, you need to *identify the problem* by talking to the user. Get the user to show you what's not good. Is it an error code? Is something not accessible? Is a device not responding?

Then ask the user that classic tech question (remember your communication skills here!): "Has anything recently changed on the computer that might have made this problem appear?" What you're really saying is: "Have you messed with the computer? Did you install some evil program? Did you shove a USB drive in so hard that you broke the connection?" Of course, you never say these things; simply ask nicely without accusing so the user can help you troubleshoot the problem (see Figure 2-13).

Figure 2-13 Tech asking nicely

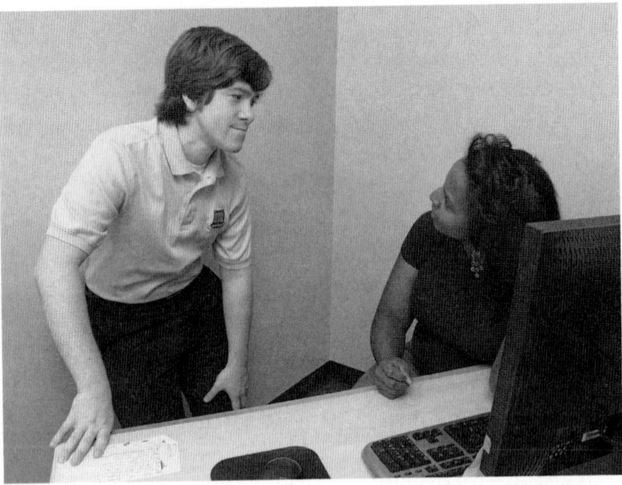

In most troubleshooting situations, it's important to back up critical files before making changes to a system. To some extent, this is a matter of proper ongoing maintenance, but if some important bit of data disappears and you don't have a backup, you know who the user will blame, don't you? We cover backup options in detail in Chapter 15.

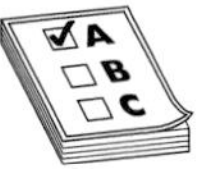

EXAM TIP The CompTIA A+ certification exams assume that all techs should back up systems *every time* before working on them, even though that's not how it works in the real world.

Establish a Theory of Probable Cause (Question the Obvious)

Now it's time to analyze the issue and come up with a theory as to what is wrong, a *theory of probable cause*. Personally, I prefer the word "guess" at this point because very few errors are so obvious that you'll know what to do. Fall back on your knowledge of the *computing process* to localize the issue based on the symptoms. Keep your guesses ... err ... theories ... simple. One of the great problems for techs is their desire to overlook the obvious problems in their desire to dig into the system (see Figure 2-14).

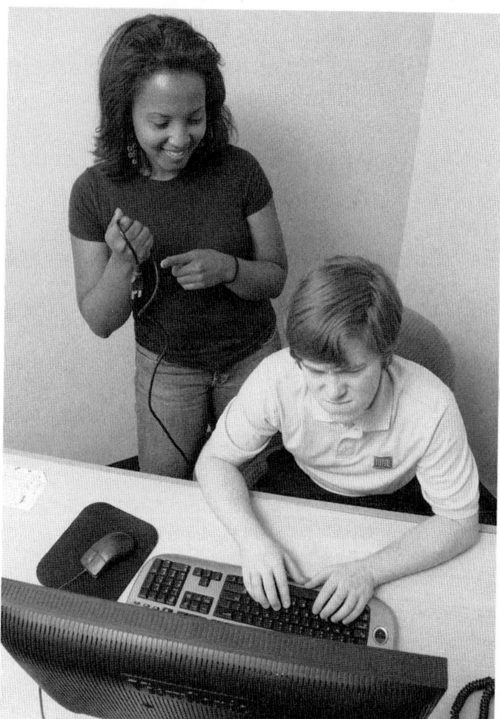

Figure 2-14 Ford the Tech misses the obvious.

Research In many situations, you'll need to access other resources to root out the most probable cause of the problem. If necessary, therefore, you should conduct external or internal research based on the symptoms.

With the Internet quite literally at the fingertips of anyone with access to a smartphone or tablet, a short search online can result in swift answers to tech problems.

Using key words and a few punctuation marks, such as – and " ", can make searches on external sites very efficient. Put the hyphen directly in front of a key term you *don't* want searched to tighten search results. If the customer's computer displays an error message, putting the whole error message into a search engine in quotes will return results on that whole string.

An internal search means asking other techs on-site for help. It means checking company records regarding a particular machine (for example, checking a problem-tracking database where previous issues have been recorded). This kind of search will reveal any known problems with the machine or with the user's actions.

Outside the Case Take a moment to look for clues before you open up the case. Most importantly, use all your senses in the process.

What do you see? Is a connector mangled or a plastic part clearly damaged? Even if that connector or part works fine, the physical abuse could provide extra information. If the user can't connect to a network, check the cable. Was something rolled over it that could have broken the thin internal wires? Is that a jelly smear near the jammed optical drive door? (No pun intended, really!) A visual examination of the external computer is important.

When you put your hand on the system unit (that's the case that houses all the computer parts), does it feel hot? Can you feel or hear the vibrations of the fans? If not, that would be a clue to an overheating or overheated computer. Modern computers can run when overly hot, but generally run very sluggishly.

If you spend a moment listening to the computer, you might get some clues to problem sources. A properly running computer doesn't make a lot of sound, just a regular hum from the spinning fans. If you hear clicking or grinding sounds, that's a very bad sign and a very important clue! We'll cover data storage devices in detail in Chapters 7 and 8—they're the usual cause of clicking and grinding sounds.

Finally, don't forget your nose. If you smell the unmistakable odor of ozone, you know that's the smell electronic components give off when they cook or are simply running much too hot.

Test the Theory to Determine Cause

Okay, so you've decided on a theory that makes sense. It's time to *test the theory* to see if it fixes the problem. A challenge to fixing a computer is that the theory and the fix pretty much prove themselves at the same time. In many cases, testing your theory does nothing more than verify that something is broken. If that's the case, then replace the broken part.

If your theory doesn't pan out, you should come up with a new theory and test it. (In CompTIA speak, if the theory is not confirmed, you need to re-establish a new theory.) If you verify and the fix lies within your skill set, excellent.

At this point, you need to check in with management to make certain you have permission to make necessary changes. Always consider corporate policies, procedures, and impacts before implementing changes. Having the boss walk in frowning while you're elbows-deep in a machine with the question "Who gave you permission?" can make for a bad day!

If you don't have the skills—or the permission—to fix the issue, you need to *escalate* the problem.

Escalation is the process your company (or sometimes just you) goes through when you—the person assigned to repair a problem—are not able to get the job done. It's okay to escalate a problem, because no one can fix every problem. All companies should have some form of escalation policy. It might mean calling your boss. It might mean filling out and sending some in-house form to another department. Escalation is sometimes a more casual process. You might want to start researching the problem online; you might want to refer to in-house documentation to see if this problem has appeared in the past. (See "Document Findings, Actions, and Outcomes," later in this chapter.) You may want to call a coworker to come check it out (see Figure 2-15).

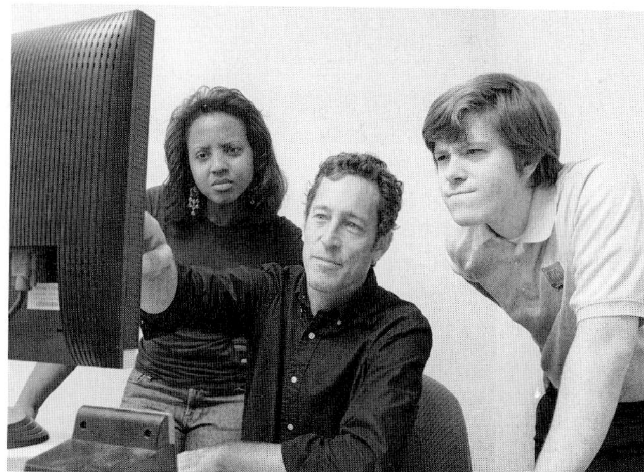

Figure 2-15 Ford the Tech asks for help from Scott.

Verify and Prevent

Fantastic! Through either your careful work or escalation, you've solved the problem, or so you think. Remember two items here. First, even though *you* think the problem is fixed, the customer/user might not think it's fixed. Second, try to do something to prevent the problem from happening again in the future, if possible.

Verify Full System Functionality You need to *verify* full system functionality to make sure the user is happy. Let's say a user can't print. You determine that the Print Spooler service is stalled due to a locked-up laser printer. You reset the printer and the jobs all start printing. Job done, right?

The best way to verify full system functionality is to have the user do whatever she needs to do on the repaired system for a few minutes while you watch. Any minor errors will quickly become apparent, and you might learn some interesting aspects of how the user does her job. Knowing what your users do is critical for good techs to help them do their jobs better (see Figure 2-16).

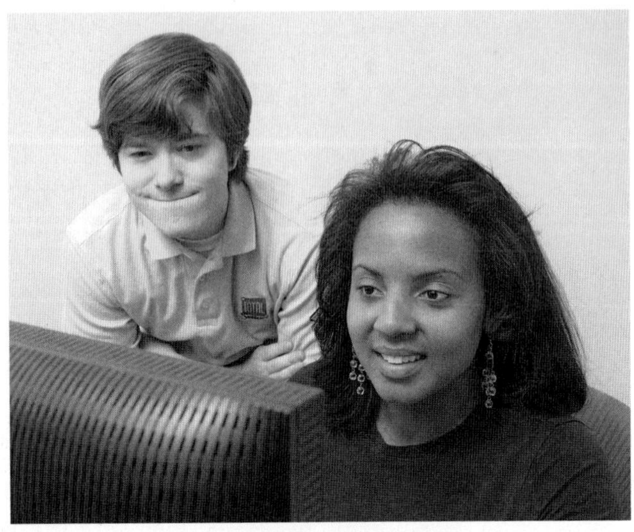

Figure 2-16 Ford the Tech sticks around and watches.

If Applicable, Implement Preventive Measures A very smart tech once told me, "A truly good support tech's work goal should be to never have to get out of his chair." That's a pretty tall order, but it makes sense to me. Do whatever you can to prevent this problem from repeating. For some problems, there are obvious actions to take, such as making sure anti-malware is installed so a computer doesn't get infected again. Sometimes there's no action to take at all: nothing can prevent a hard drive that decides to die. But you can take one more critical action in almost every case: education. Take advantage of the time with the user to informally train him about the problem. Show him the dangers of malware or tell him that sometimes hard drives just die. The more your users know, the less time you'll spend out of your chair.

Document Findings, Actions, and Outcomes

Based on his famous quote, "Those who cannot remember the past are condemned to repeat it," I think the philosopher George Santayana would have made a great technician. As a tech, the last step of every troubleshooting job should be to *document* your findings, actions, and outcomes. This documentation might be highly formalized in some organizations, or it might just be a few notes you jot down for your own use, but you must document! What was the problem? What did you do to fix it? What worked? What didn't? The best guide to use for documentation is: "What would I have liked to have known about this problem before I walked up to it?" Good documentation is the strongest sign of a good tech (see Figure 2-17).

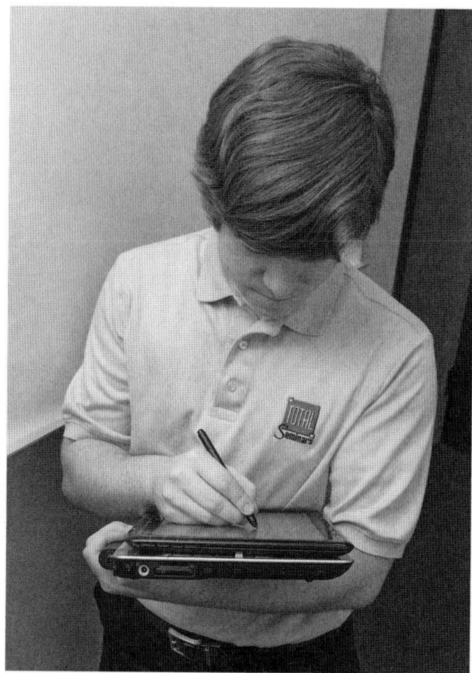

Figure 2-17 Ford documents a successful fix.

Documenting problems helps you track the troubleshooting history of a computing device over time, enabling you to make longer-term determinations about retiring it or changing out more parts. If you and fellow techs fix a specific problem with Mary's laptop several times, for example, you might decide to swap out her whole system rather than fix it a fourth time.

Documenting helps fellow techs if they have to follow up on a task you didn't finish or troubleshoot a machine you've worked on previously. The reverse is also true. If you get a call about Frank's computer, for example, and check the records to find other service calls on his computer, you might find that the fix for a particular problem is already documented. This is especially true for user-generated problems. Having documentation of what you did also means you don't have to rely on your memory when your coworker asks what you did to fix the weird problem with Jane's computer a year ago!

Documenting also comes into play when you or a user has an accident on-site. If your colleague Joe drops a monitor on his foot and breaks both the monitor and his foot, for example, you need to fill out an *incident report*, just as you would with any kind of accident: electrical, chemical, or physical. An *incident report* should detail what happened and where it happened. This helps your supervisors take the appropriate actions quickly and efficiently.

Chapter Review

Questions

1. Which of the following would be most appropriate for the workplace? (Select two.)
   A. Clean, pressed khaki trousers
   B. Clean, wrinkle-free T-shirt
   C. Clean, wrinkle-free polo shirt
   D. Clean, pressed jeans
2. While manning the help desk, you get a call from a distraught user who says she has a blank screen. What would be a useful follow-up question? (Select two.)
   A. Is the computer turned on?
   B. Is the monitor turned on?
   C. Did you reboot?
   D. What did you do?
3. At the very least, what tool should be in every technician's toolkit?
   A. Pliers
   B. Hammer
   C. Straight-slot screwdriver
   D. Phillips-head screwdriver
4. When is it appropriate to yell at a user?
   A. When he screws up the second time
   B. When he interrupts your troubleshooting
   C. When he screws up the fifth time
   D. Never
5. When troubleshooting a software problem on Phoebe's computer and listening to her describe the problem, you get a text from your boss. Which of the following is the most appropriate action for you to take?
   A. Excuse yourself, walk out of the cube, and text your boss.
   B. Pick up Phoebe's phone and dial your boss's number.
   C. Wait until Phoebe finishes her description and then ask to use her phone to call your boss.
   D. Wait until Phoebe finishes her description, run through any simple fixes, and then explain that you need to call your boss on your cell phone.

6. You are at a customer's workstation to install several software and hardware updates, a process that will take a while and will require several reboots of the computer. What should you do about the password to the user's account?

   A. Require the customer to sit with you throughout the process so she can type in her password each time.

   B. Ask the user to write down her password for you to use.

   C. Ask the user to change her password temporarily for you to use.

   D. Call your supervisor.

7. Which of the following is a good practice after completing a troubleshooting call at someone's office?

   A. Follow up with a call within a couple of days to make sure everything is going well with the fixed computer.

   B. Make copies of any passwords you used at the site for future reference.

   C. Document any particularly important people you met for future reference.

   D. Do nothing. Your work is finished there.

8. Which tool helps you avoid accidental static discharge by keeping you at the same electrical potential as the computer on which you're working?

   A. Antistatic spray

   B. Antistatic bag

   C. Antistatic wrist strap

   D. Phillips-head screwdriver

9. Once you have ascertained the computer's problem and backed up the critical data, what should you do?

   A. Establish a theory of probable cause.

   B. Start fixing the machine.

   C. Question users more to find out how they caused the problem.

   D. Document.

10. What should you do after successfully repairing a machine?

    A. Do nothing; your job is done.

    B. Admonish the user for causing so much work for the IT department.

    C. Document your findings.

    D. Lock it down so the user can't cause the same problem again.

Answers

1. **A, C.** Khaki trousers and a polo shirt trump jeans and a T-shirt every time.
2. **A, B.** Go for the simple answer first. When faced with a blank screen, check to see if the computer and the monitor are turned on.
3. **D.** Every tech's toolkit should have a Phillips-head screwdriver, at the very least.
4. **D.** Don't get angry or yell at clients.
5. **D.** Focus on the customer and don't use her things.
6. **C.** In this circumstance, asking for a temporary password is the right answer. Make sure the user changes her password back before you leave the site.
7. **A.** A simple follow-up builds good will and trust. This is a very important step to take after completing a job.
8. **C.** An antistatic wrist strap keeps you at the same electrical potential as the computer.
9. **A.** You should establish a theory of probable cause once you have ascertained the problem and backed up data.
10. **C.** At the end of a repair you should always document your findings.

CHAPTER 3

The Visible Computer

In this chapter, you will learn how to

- Describe how computing devices work
- Identify common connectors and devices on a typical computer system
- Discuss features common to operating system software

Charles Babbage didn't set out to change the world. He just wanted to do math without worrying about human error, something all too common in his day. Babbage was a mathematician in the nineteenth century, a time well before anyone thought to create electronic calculators or computers (see Figure 3-1). When he worked on complex math, the best "computers" were people who computed by hand. They solved equations using pen and paper.

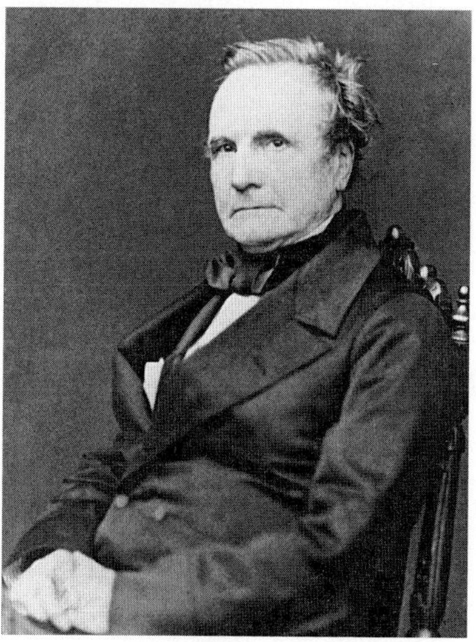

Figure 3-1 Charles Babbage, father of the computer

Babbage thought of making machines that would do calculations mechanically, so the numbers would always be right. Although his ideas were ahead of his time, inventors in the mid-twentieth century picked up the concepts and created huge calculating machines that they called *computers*.

This chapter explores how computing devices work. We'll look first at the computing process, then turn to hardware components common to all devices. The chapter finishes

with a discussion about software, exploring commonality among all operating systems and specific functions of application programming. And, there are lots of pictures.

Historical/Conceptual

The Computing Process

In modern terms, a *computer* is an electronic device that can perform calculations. The most common types use special programming languages that people, known as *computer programmers*, have written and compiled to accomplish specific tasks.

When most people hear the word "computer," they picture *general* computing devices, machines that can do all sorts of things. The typical *personal computer (PC)* runs the operating system Microsoft Windows and is used for various tasks (see Figure 3-2). You can use it to manage your money and play games, for example, without doing anything special to it, such as adding new hardware.

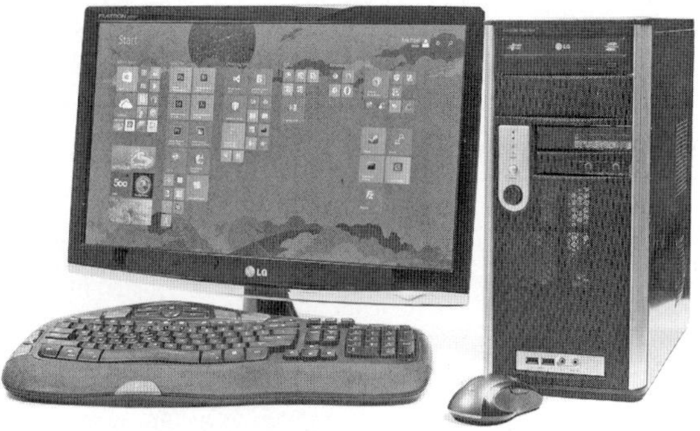

Figure 3-2
A typical PC

Here are some other general-purpose computing devices:

- Apple Mac
- Apple iPad
- Smartphone
- Portable computer (see Figure 3-3)

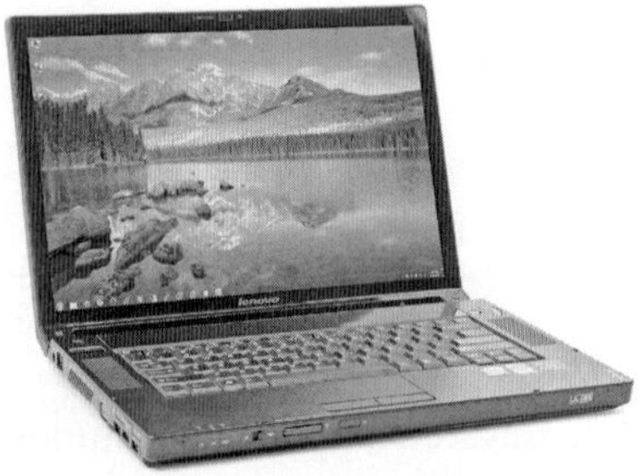

Figure 3-3
A portable computer

Plenty of other devices do *specific* computing jobs, focusing on a single task or set of similar tasks. You probably encounter them all the time. Here's a list of common specific-purpose computers:

- Apple iPod
- Pocket calculator
- Digital watch
- Digital clock
- Wi-Fi picture frame
- Basic mobile phone
- Xbox One
- PlayStation 4
- GPS (Global Positioning System, the device that helps drivers figure out how to get where they need to go)
- TiVo
- Point of sale (POS) system (see Figure 3-4)
- Digital camera
- Camcorder

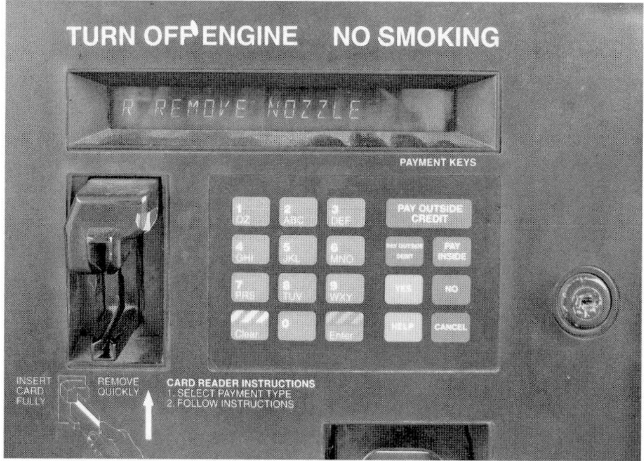

Figure 3-4
A point of sale computer in a gasoline pump

This list isn't even close to complete! Plus, there are computers *inside* a zillion other devices. Here are some:

- Modern refrigerators
- Every automobile built since 1995
- Airplanes

- Boats
- Mall lighting systems
- Zambonis
- Home security alarms

You get the idea. Computers help the modern world function.

NOTE I picked 1995 as an arbitrary date for when every new car built had a computer. Computers have been used with cars for a long time. Simple computers helped make car factories work better starting in the 1970s, for example. The earliest mass-production car I found that had a central processor chip for added performance was the BMW 3 Series. The 1985-86 BMW 325, for example, can gain a few extra horsepower just from a ~$200 chip upgrade.

Modern computer techs need to know how different types of computing devices work so they can support the many devices used by their clients. This diversity is also reflected in the CompTIA A+ exams.

If the list of devices to support seems overwhelming, relax. The secret savior for modern techs is that computing devices function similarly to each other. Once you know what a particular device should enable a user to do, you'll be able to configure and troubleshoot successfully.

The Computing Parts

A modern computer consists of three major components:

- Hardware
- Operating system
- Applications

The *hardware* is the physical stuff that you can touch or hold in your hand. With a smartphone, for example, you hold the phone. On a typical personal computer, you touch the keyboard or view images on the monitor (see Figure 3-5).

Figure 3-5 A typical computer

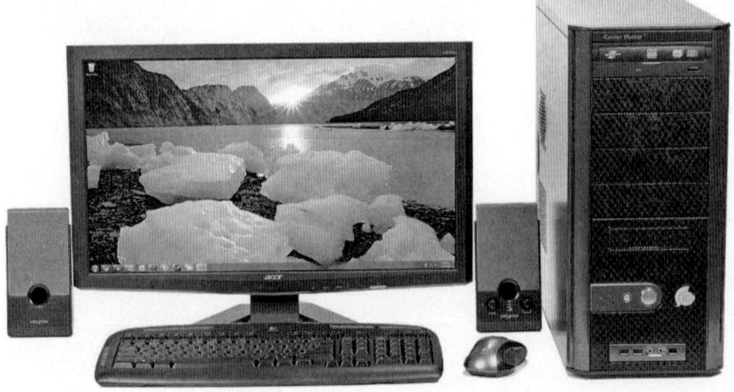

The *operating system (OS)* controls the hardware and enables you to tell the computer what to do. The operating system often appears as a collection of windows and little icons you can click or touch (see Figure 3-6). Collectively these are called the *user interface (UI),* which means the software parts with which you can interact. The UI that offers images or icons to select (as opposed to making you type commands) is called a *graphical user interface (GUI).*

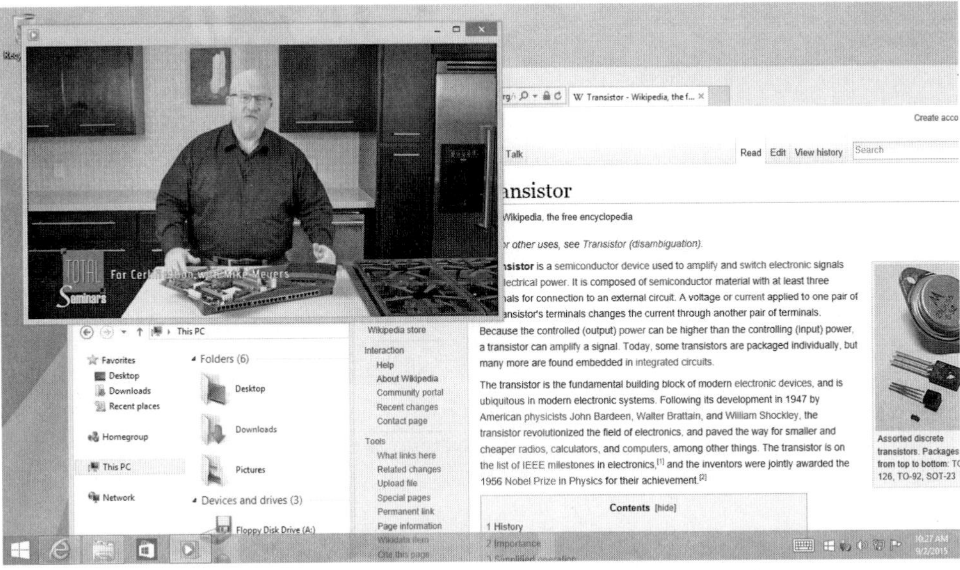

Figure 3-6 The Microsoft Windows 8.1 operating system

Applications (or programs) enable you to do specialized tasks on a computer, such as

- Type a letter
- Send a message from your computer in Houston to your friend's computer in Paris
- Wander through imaginary worlds with people all over Earth

Very simple computing devices might have an operating system with only a few features that give you choices. A digital camera, for example, has a menu system that enables you to control things like the quality of the picture taken (see Figure 3-7).

More complicated devices offer more choices. An Apple iPhone, for example, can do some cool things right out of the box, including make a phone call. But you can visit the Apple online store—the App Store—for programs and download applications (known as apps) to do all sorts of things that Apple didn't include (see Figure 3-8).

Finally, multipurpose computers like the typical Windows PC or Mac OS X computer offer applications to help you do everything from write a book on CompTIA A+ certification to talk with someone on the other side of the world, with full audio and video (see Figure 3-9).

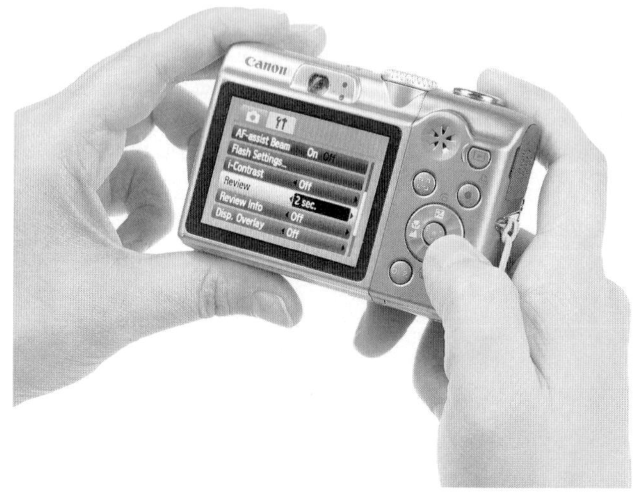

Figure 3-7 Changing settings on a digital camera

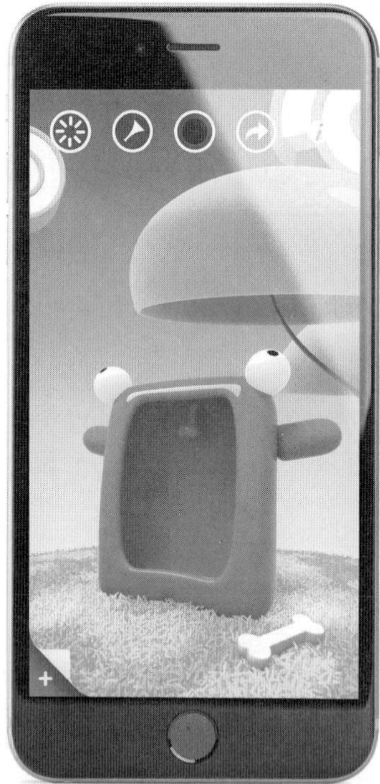

Figure 3-8 Talking Carl + talks back to you—perhaps not the most *useful* app on the planet, but amusing

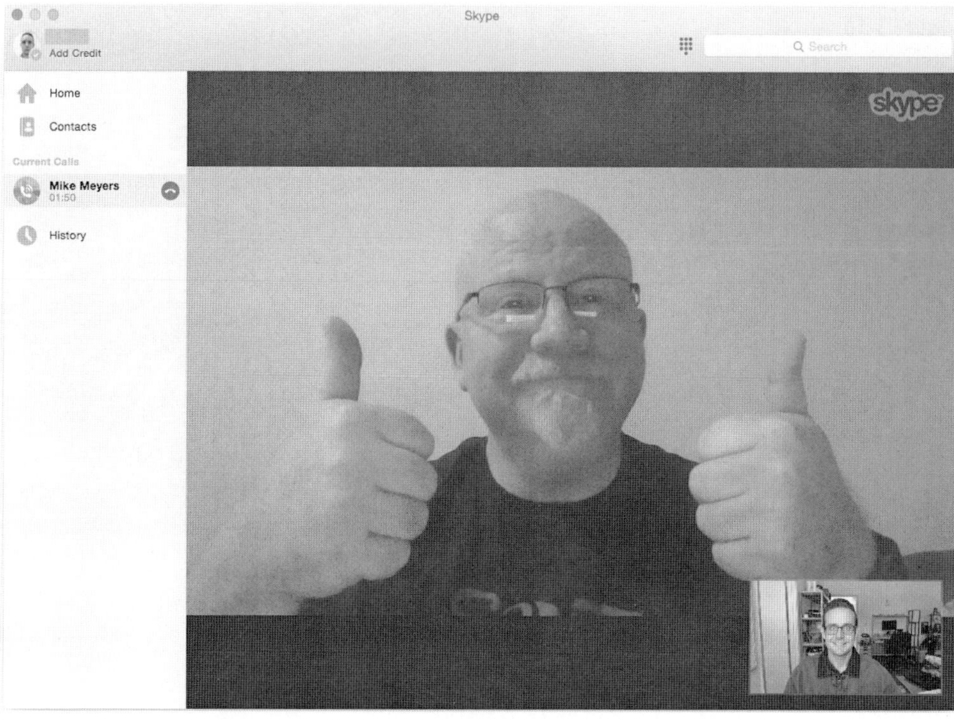

Figure 3-9 Skype communication

Stages

At the most basic level, computers work through three stages, what's called the *computing process*:

- Input
- Processing
- Output

You start the action by doing something—clicking the mouse, typing on the keyboard, or touching the touch screen. This is *input*. The parts inside the device or case take over at that point as the operating system tells the hardware to do what you've requested. This is *processing*.

In fact, at the heart of every computing device is a *central processing unit (CPU)*, usually a single, thin wafer of silicon and tiny transistors (see Figure 3-10). The CPU handles the majority of the processing tasks and is, in a way, the "brain" of the computer.

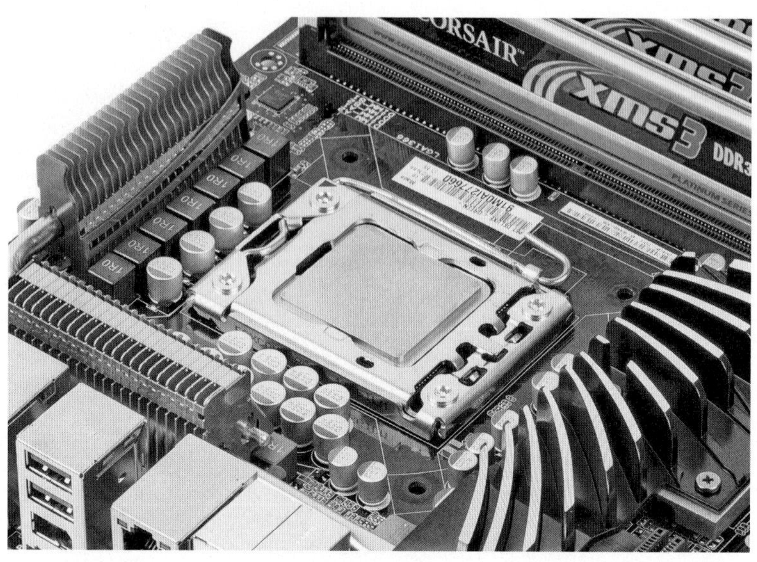

Figure 3-10 Intel Core i7 CPU on a motherboard

NOTE Chapter 4, "Microprocessors," gives a lot more information on CPUs and other processing components.

Once the computer has processed your request, it shows you the result by changing what you see on the display or playing a sound through the speakers. This is *output*. A computer wouldn't be worth much if it couldn't demonstrate that it fulfilled your commands! Figure 3-11 shows the computing process.

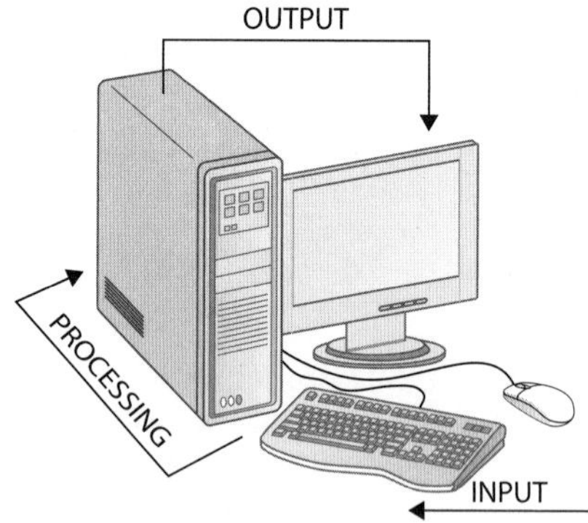

Figure 3-11 The computing process

Modern computing devices almost always have two other stages:

- Data storage
- Network connection

Data storage means saving a permanent copy of your work so that you can come back to it later. It works like this. First, you tell the computer to save something. Second, the CPU processes that command and stores the data. Third, the computer shows you something, such as a message saying that the data is stored. Any work that you *don't* save is lost when you turn the computer off or exit the application.

Most computing devices connect to other devices to access other resources. A *network connection* often describes how one computer connects to one or more other computers. And it doesn't just apply to a couple of office computers. Every smartphone, for example, can connect to the Internet and play a video from YouTube (assuming you have a signal from a cell tower and a data plan). A network connection can also mean running a cable between two devices, like connecting an iPad or iPhone to a Windows desktop machine using a Lightning-to-USB cable.

At this point, students often ask me a fundamental question: "Why should I care about the computing process?" The answer to this question defines what makes a good computer technician. Here's my response.

Why the Process Matters to Techs

Because the computing process applies to every computing device, it provides the basis for how every tech builds, upgrades, and repairs such devices. By understanding both the components involved and how they talk to each other, you can work with *any* computing device. It might take a couple minutes to figure out how to communicate with the device via input, for example, but you'll quickly master it because you know how all computing devices work.

Breaking It Down

The whole computer process from start to finish has a lot of steps and pieces that interact. The more you understand about this interaction and these pieces, the better you can troubleshoot when something goes wrong. *This is the core rule to being a great tech.*

Here are nine steps that apply to most computers and computing devices when you want to get something done:

1. Power up. Computers run on electricity.
2. Processing parts prepare for action.
3. You provide input.
4. Processing parts process your command.
5. Processing parts send output information to your output devices.
6. Output devices show you the results.
7. Repeat Steps 3–6 until you're satisfied with the outcome.
8. Save your work.
9. Power down the computer.

We'll come back to these processing steps as we tackle troubleshooting scenarios throughout the book. Keep these steps in mind to answer the essential question a tech should ask when facing a problem: What can it be? Or, in slightly longer fashion: What could cause the problem that stopped this device from functioning properly?

901

Computing Hardware

A lot of this book takes you in depth on specific computing hardware, such as CPUs and mass storage devices. CompTIA expects competent techs to know what to call every connector, socket, and slot in a variety of computing devices. Rather than describe all of those briefly here, I decided to create a photo walkthrough naming points-of-interest and the chapters that discuss them.

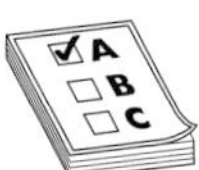

EXAM TIP Memorize the names of the components, connectors, and terms discussed and displayed in this section. You'll see them in future chapters, in the real world, and on the CompTIA A+ 901 exam.

This section serves as a visual introduction to the components and connections. Plus, it should work great as a set of study sheets for memorizing names just before taking the 901 exam. The images that follow indicate the chapters where you'll find information about a component or connection standard.

Figure 3-12 shows a typical PC. The input and output devices should be familiar to most.

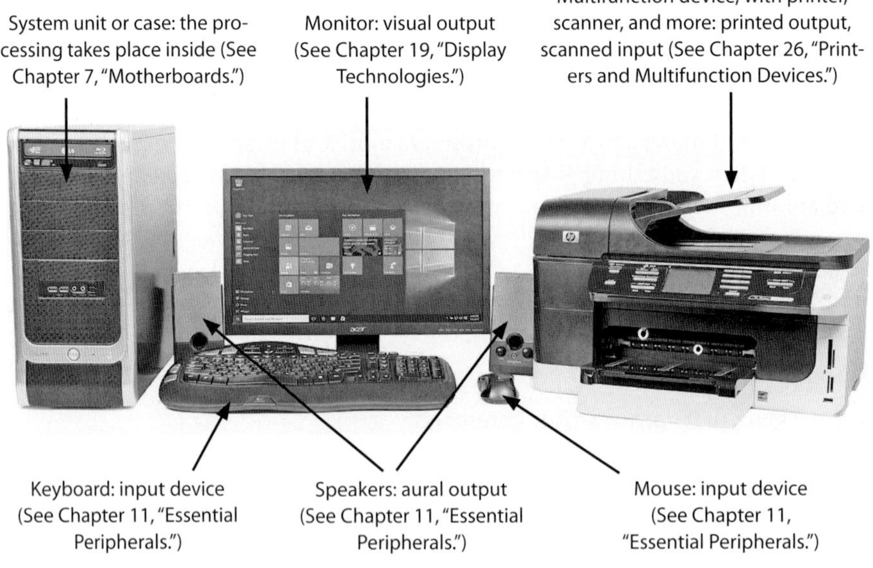

Figure 3-12 PC with common peripherals

Figure 3-13 shows the back of a PC's system unit, where you'll find the many connection points called ports. Some ports connect to output devices; a couple are exclusively used for input devices. Most (such as the universal serial bus, or USB) handle either type of device.

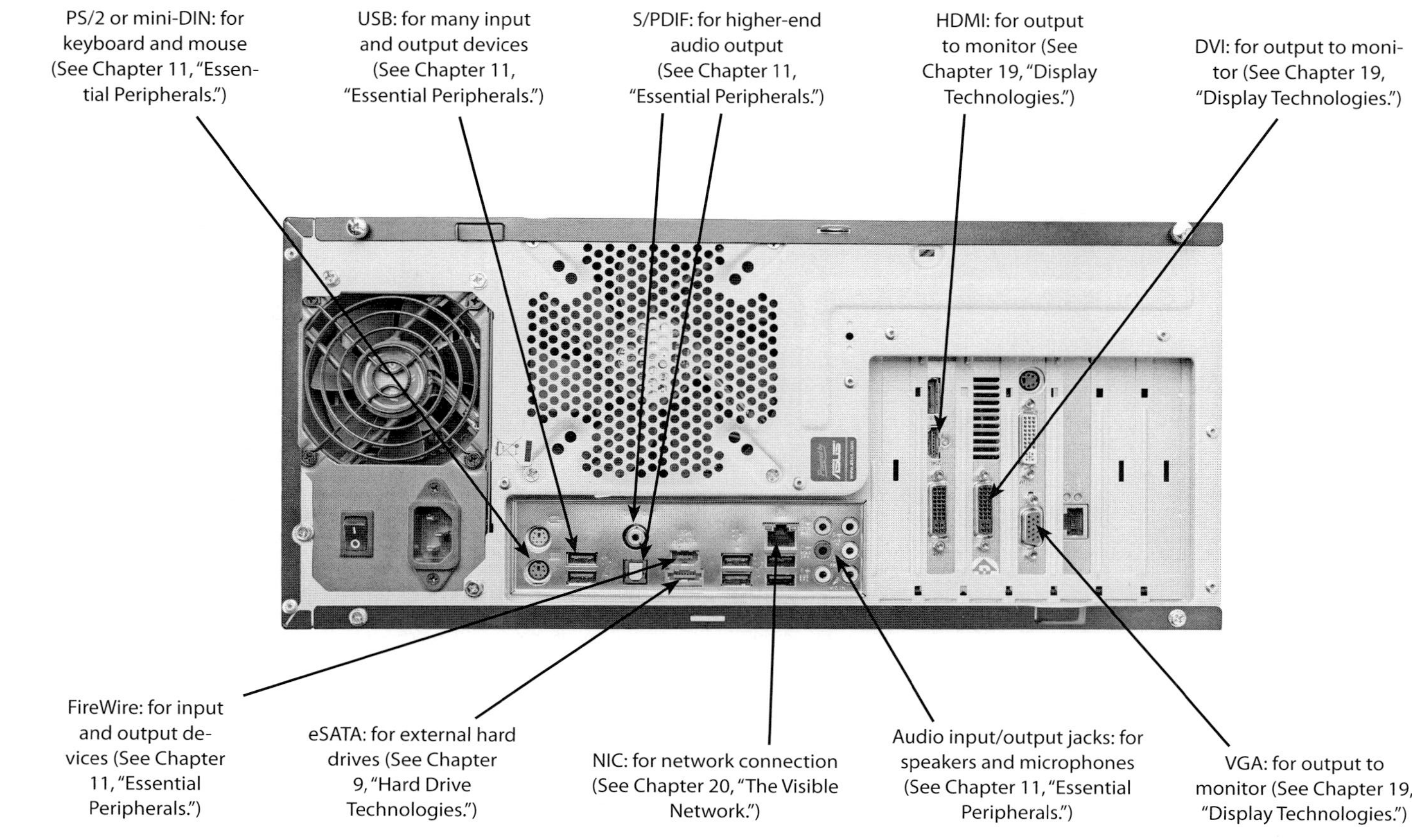
PS/2 or mini-DIN: for keyboard and mouse (See Chapter 11, "Essential Peripherals.")
USB: for many input and output devices (See Chapter 11, "Essential Peripherals.")
S/PDIF: for higher-end audio output (See Chapter 11, "Essential Peripherals.")
HDMI: for output to monitor (See Chapter 19, "Display Technologies.")
DVI: for output to monitor (See Chapter 19, "Display Technologies.")
FireWire: for input and output devices (See Chapter 11, "Essential Peripherals.")
eSATA: for external hard drives (See Chapter 9, "Hard Drive Technologies.")
NIC: for network connection (See Chapter 20, "The Visible Network.")
Audio input/output jacks: for speakers and microphones (See Chapter 11, "Essential Peripherals.")
VGA: for output to monitor (See Chapter 19, "Display Technologies.")

Figure 3-13 The business end of a PC

Figure 3-14 reveals the inside of a PC case, where you'll find the processing and storage devices. Hiding under everything is the motherboard, the component into which everything directly or indirectly connects.

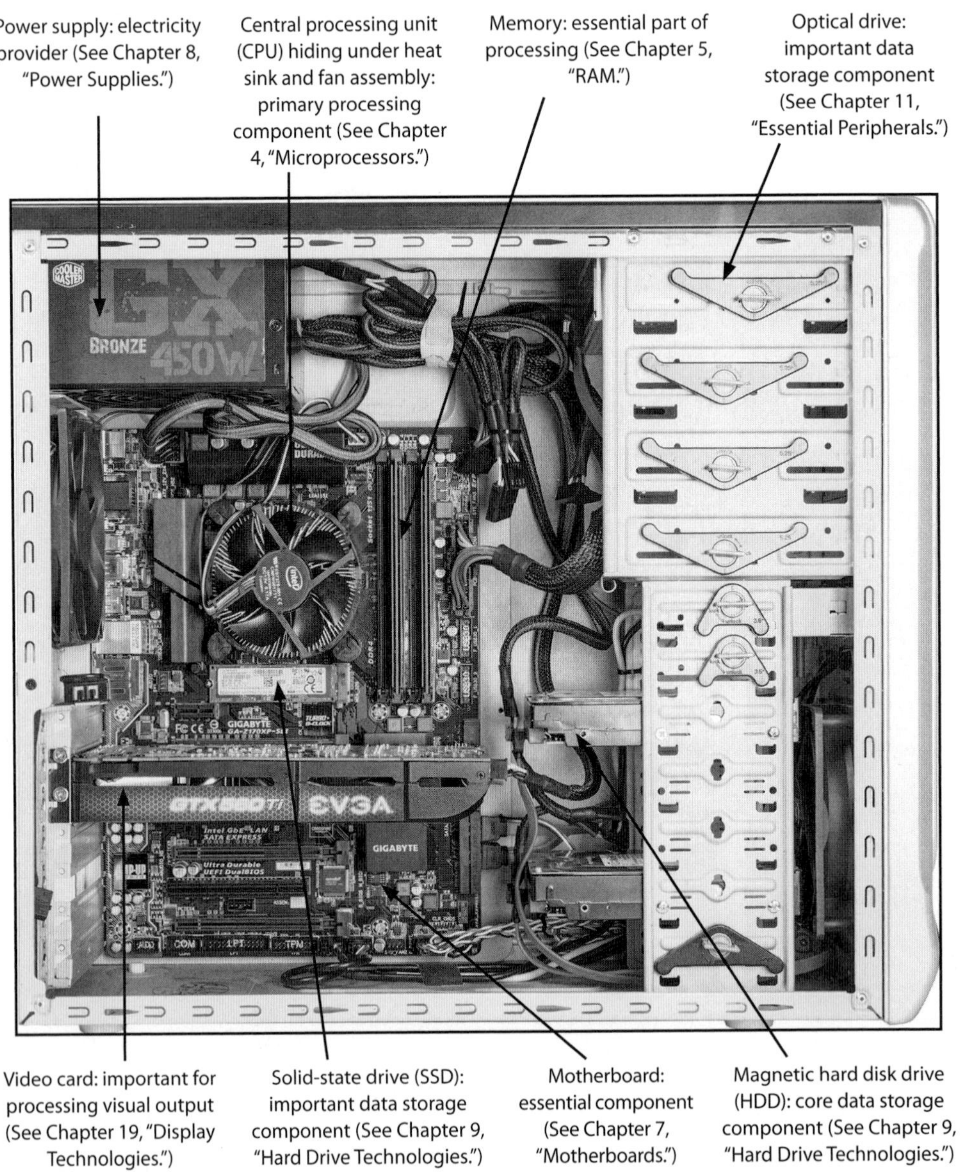

Figure 3-14 Inside the system unit

Figure 3-15 shows a clamshell-style portable computer, in this case an Apple MacBook Air. The portable nature of the device calls for input and output devices built into the case—some variation from the typical PC displayed earlier, therefore, but all the standard computing component functions apply. Chapter 24, "Portable Computing," goes into a lot of detail about each component displayed here.

Figure 3-15 Portable computer (a MacBook Air)

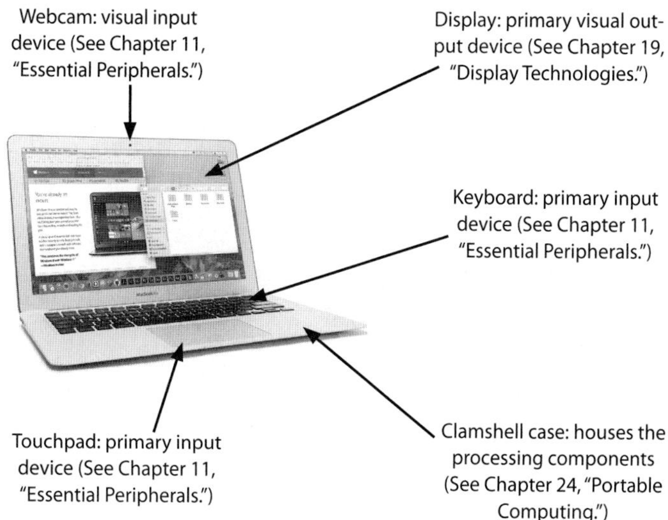

Figure 3-16 shows the side of a portable computer with three different connection types.

Figure 3-16 Ports on a portable computer

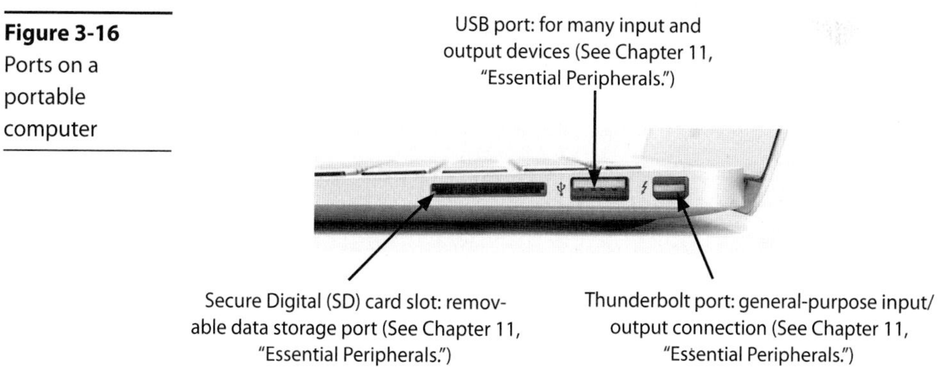

Figure 3-17 shows a tablet computer, an Apple iPad. Note that the screen has a touch interface, which makes it both an input and output device.

Figure 3-17
Tablet computer

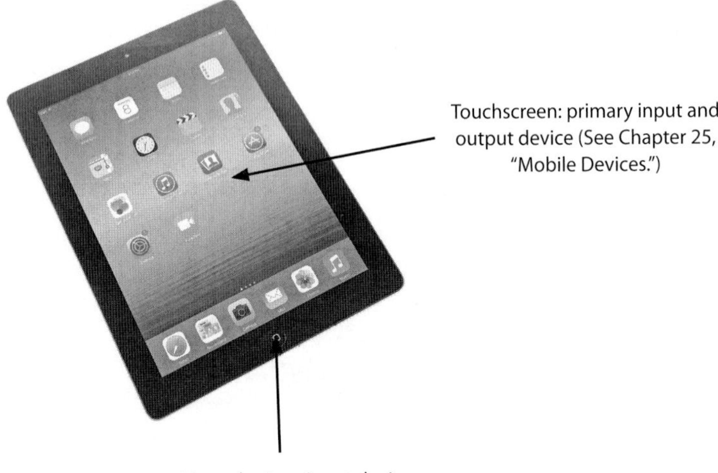

We could continue with any number of computing devices in the same picture show, but at this point the uniformity of computing component functions should be pretty clear. They all work similarly, and, as a competent tech, you should be able to support just about any customer device. Let's turn now to a visual feast of software.

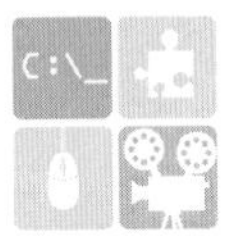

SIM Check out the excellent Chapter 3 Challenge! sim on motherboard matching at totalsem.com/90x. It's a cool sim that helps names stick in your head.

902

Computing Software

The CompTIA A+ 902 exam covers a lot of software, though mostly operating system tools rather than specific applications. Five Microsoft operating systems make up the bulk of the coverage: Windows Vista, Windows 7, Windows 8, Windows 8.1, and Windows Phone/Mobile. Windows 10 didn't make it into the objectives, but I've added it to the book because you need to know it for real-life support. Apple gets coverage of two OSs: OS X and iOS. Linux gets a generic nod (more on that in a moment), and Google Android gets some discussion.

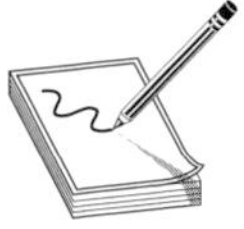

NOTE Along with the unfortunately missing Windows 10, the CompTIA A+ objectives have a few notably absent operating systems. Microsoft released Windows 10 well after CompTIA finalized the exam objectives, so it gets no coverage. Perhaps more puzzling, though, is the lack of specific Linux versions, called *distributions* or *distros*. There's a big difference in look and feel, for example, between Ubuntu and SUSE Linux. Focus here on what you can do with every OS and you'll be able to handle any distro easily. Finally, Google Chrome OS, used on Google's line of portable computers (Chromebooks), gets nary a nod.

Common Operating System Functions

All OSs are not created equal, but every OS provides certain functions. Here's a list:

- The OS communicates, or provides a method for other programs to communicate, with the hardware of the PC or device. Operating systems run on specific hardware. For example, if you have a 32-bit computer, you need to install a 32-bit version of an operating system. With a 64-bit computer, you need a 64-bit OS.
- The OS creates a *user interface (UI)*—a visual representation of the computer on the monitor that makes sense to the people using the computer.
- The OS enables users to determine the available installed programs and run, use, and shut down the programs of their choice.
- The OS enables users to add, move, and delete the installed programs and data.
- The OS provides a method to secure a system from all sorts of threats, such as data loss or improper access.

Almost every chapter in this book explores the interaction of OS and hardware. Chapter 12, "Building a PC," examines adding and removing programs. Many security features show up in multiple chapters, such as Chapter 14, "User and Groups," and Chapter 27, "Securing Computers." The rest of this chapter, therefore, focuses on the user interface and the file structures.

User Interfaces

This section tours the various operating system user interfaces. Like the hardware tours earlier, this section serves a double purpose. First, you need to know the proper names for the various UI features and have an understanding of their functions. Second, it serves as a handy quick review section before you take the 902 exam.

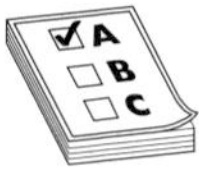

EXAM TIP Be sure you are very familiar with the operating system feature names, tools, and terms discussed and displayed in this section. Not only will you see them in future chapters, you will also encounter them in the field as well as in the CompTIA A+ 902 exam.

NOTE Chapter 25, "Mobile Devices," details the three operating systems for mobile devices—iOS, Android, and Windows Phone/Mobile.

Windows Vista/7

Figure 3-18 shows the standard interface for Windows 7, a traditional multifunction computer. Windows uses a graphical user interface primarily, so you engage with the mouse or other pointing device and click on elements. The background is called the *Desktop*. The open applications are Internet Explorer—Window's default Web browser—and a Windows Explorer window showing the Windows 7 default Libraries.

Other visible items are as follows:

- The open applications demonstrate *transparency*, where the edges of the applications show blurred background images. This feature is called *Aero*, or *Aero Glass*.
- Click on the *Start button* to get access to applications, tools, files, and folders.
- The *pinned programs* enable you to launch a program with a single left-click.
- The *taskbar* shows running programs.
- The *notification area* shows programs running in the background. Many techs also calls it the *system tray*.

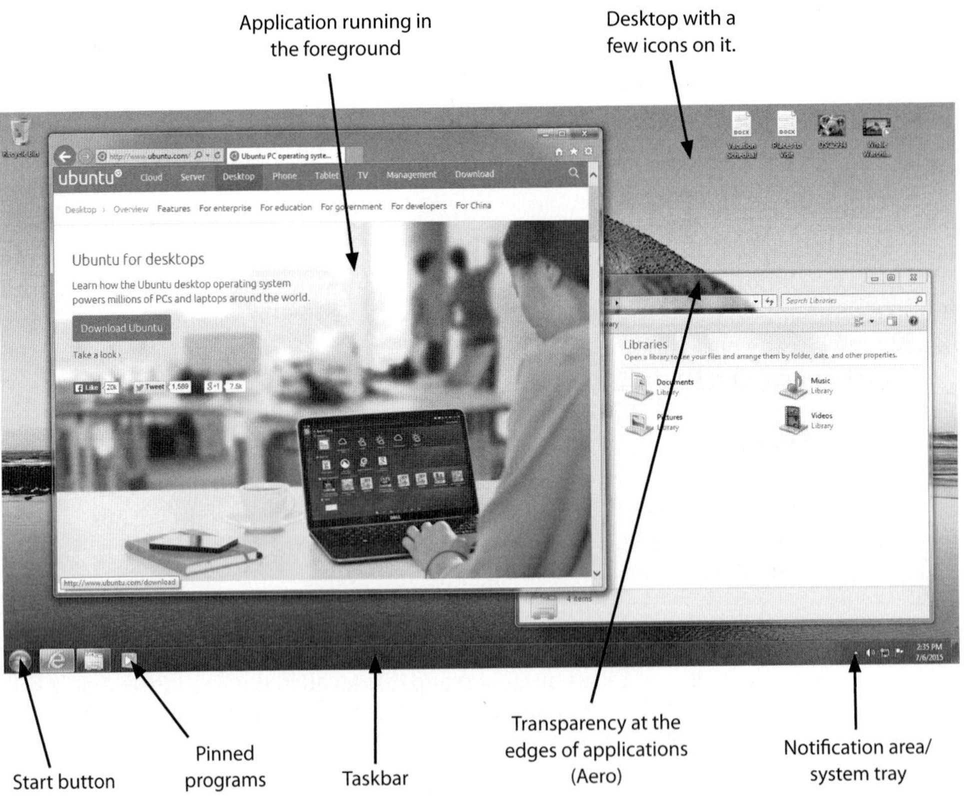

Figure 3-18 Windows 7 with applications open

Interacting with the classic Windows interface for the most part involves using a mouse or touchpad to move the cursor and either left-clicking or right-clicking on the icons. Left-clicking selects an item; double-left-clicking opens an item. Right-clicking opens a *context menu* from which you can select various options (see Figure 3-19).

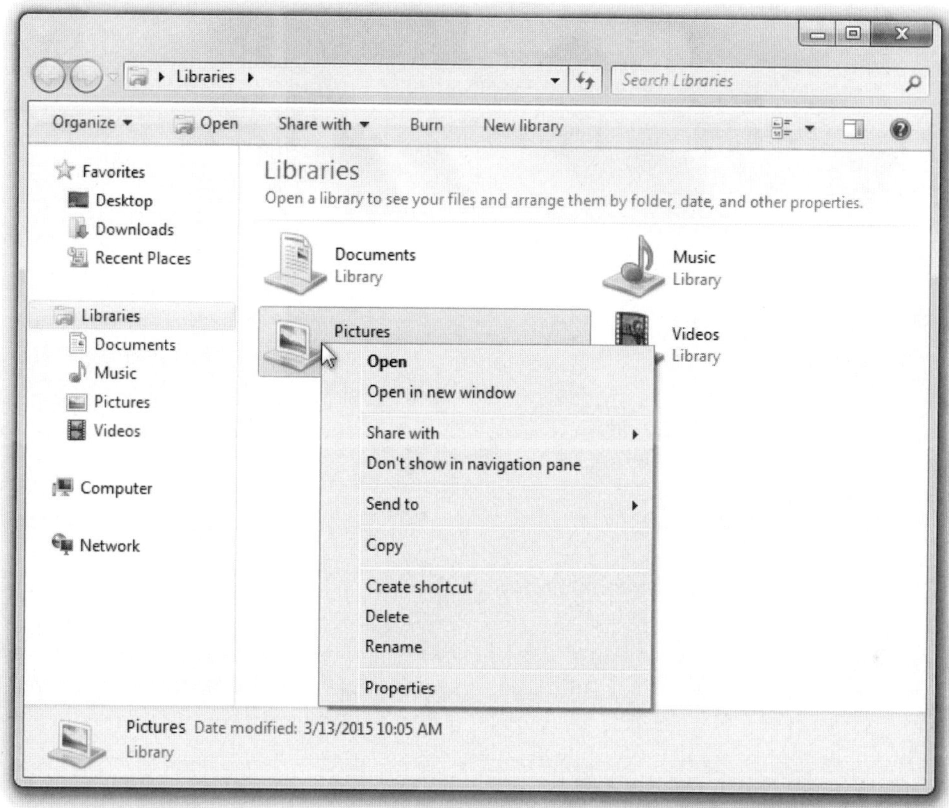

Figure 3-19 Context menu

NOTE The context menu offers options specific to the icon you right-click. Right-clicking on a file, for example, gives you a context menu that differs greatly from when you right-click an application.

Windows 7's predecessor, Windows Vista, has a similar look and feel. The most visible difference is the Vista feature called the Sidebar. Enabled by default, the *Sidebar* houses one or more *Gadgets*, such as the Clock, Calendar, and speeds you can see in Figure 3-20. Windows 7 supports Gadgets too, but doesn't have a Sidebar.

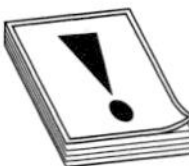

CAUTION Because of the inherent security flaws with both Sidebars and Gadgets, Microsoft recommends disabling them on Windows Vista and Windows 7 systems. Later versions of the OS do not have either.

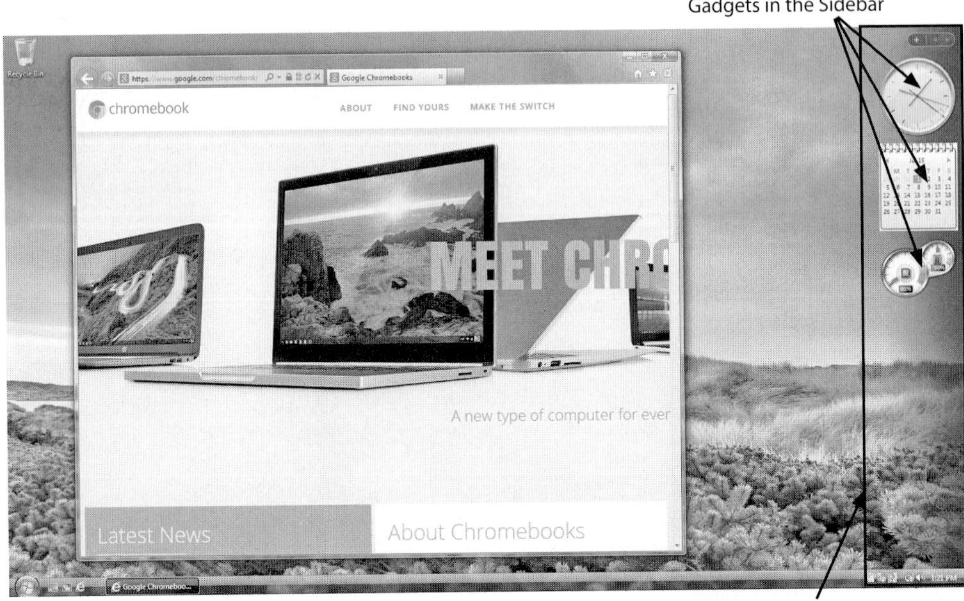

Figure 3-20 Windows Vista

Windows 8/8.1

Microsoft made significant changes to the Windows interface with the introduction of Windows 8. They borrowed from tablet operating systems, such as Windows Phone, to create a graphical set of *tiles* for full-screen programs, called *apps*. Note that the screen shows *pinned apps*—the default programs and programs selected by the user—and not all the applications installed on the computer.

The Windows 8 interface, code-named *Metro UI*, works great for touch-enabled devices. The PC becomes in essence a giant tablet. Touch an app to load, drag your finger across the screen to see other apps, and have fun. Figure 3-21 shows the default Windows 8 interface, called the *Start screen*, with various elements called out.

NOTE Microsoft dropped the "Metro UI" moniker just before releasing Windows 8 due to legal concerns, replacing it with "Modern UI." A lot of techs and IT industry pros continue to refer to the unique Windows 8/8.1 tiled interface as "Metro."

Windows 8 also features a more classic Desktop, but one with the noticeable absence of a visible Start button (see Figure 3-22). You access this screen by pressing the *Windows logo key* on a standard keyboard.

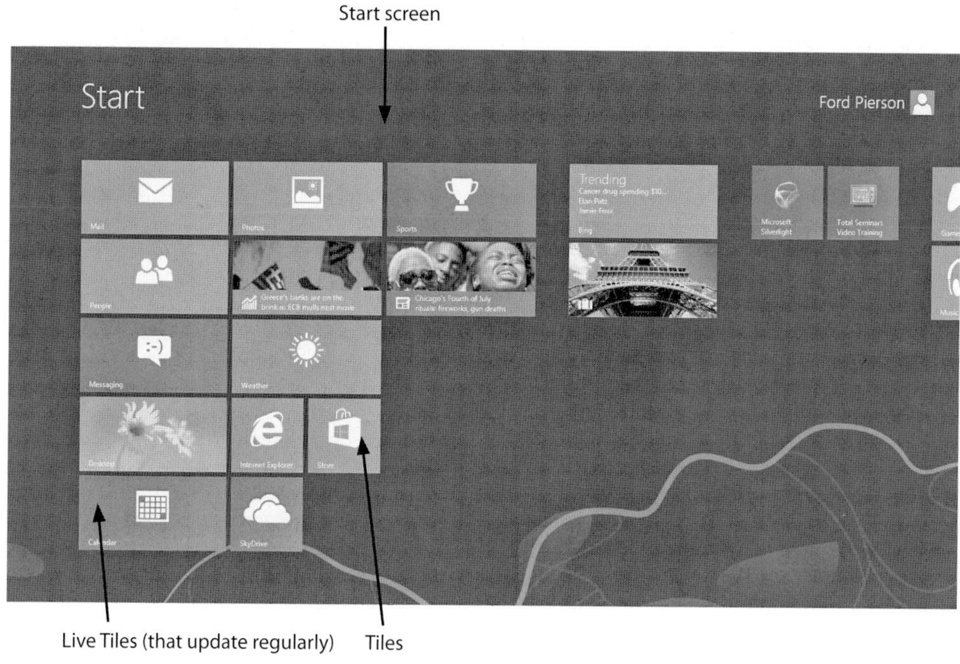

Figure 3-21 Windows 8 Start screen

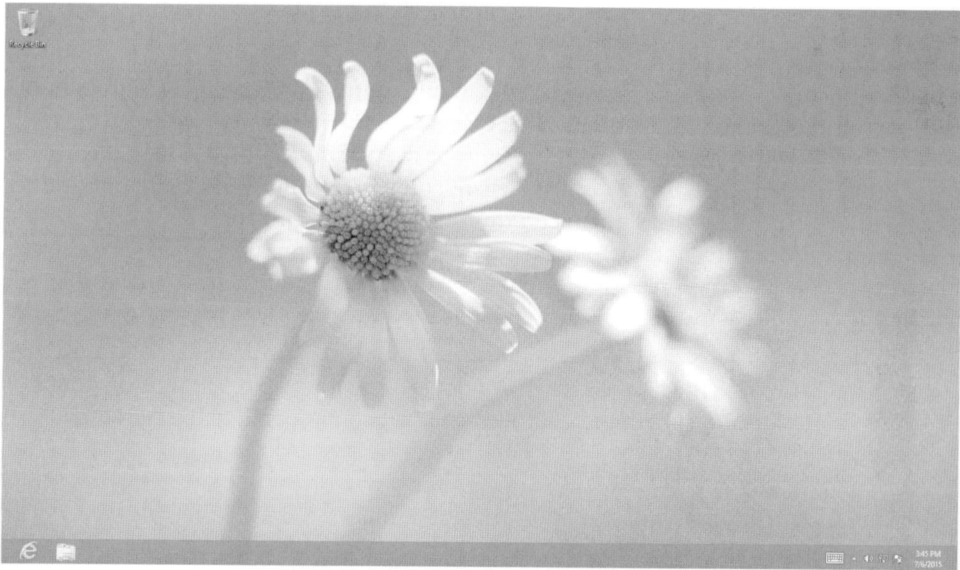

Figure 3-22 Windows 8 Desktop

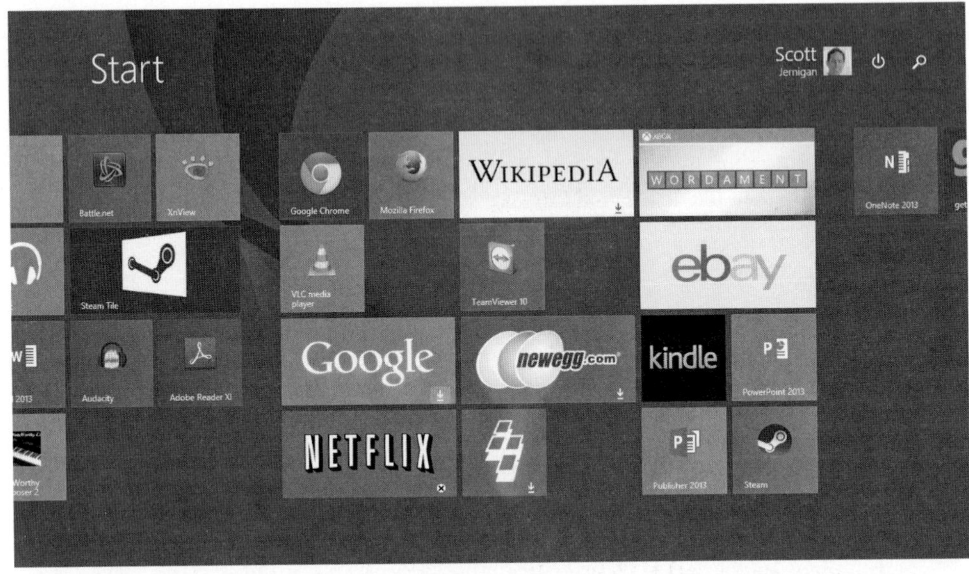

Figure 3-23 Windows 8 Start screen scrolled to the right

Using a keyboard and mouse with Windows 8 bothers a lot of users making the jump from Windows 7. Scrolling with the mouse wheel, for example, scrolls right to left rather than up and down (see Figure 3-23).

With a series of updates culminating in Windows 8.1, Microsoft brought back features such as the Start button, easy access to a Close button for apps, and the ability to boot directly to the Desktop. Figure 3-24 shows the standard interface for Windows 8.1 with the various elements called out. Note that it's very similar to Windows 7.

Windows 8.1 makes it very easy to pin apps to the Start screen. Selecting the arrow at the bottom left brings up the Apps pane where you can sort and select apps and utilities (see Figure 3-25). Right-click on an icon to pin it to the Start screen.

Windows 8/8.1 offer lots of hidden interface components that activate when you place the cursor in certain places on the screen. Dropping the cursor to the bottom left corner, for example, activates the Start button (see Figure 3-26) when in the Start screen.

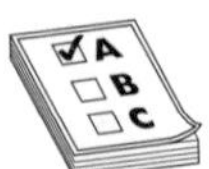

EXAM TIP The first release of Windows 8 had no visible Start button on the Desktop (except in the Charms bar). Microsoft added it to the Desktop in later patches.

Placing the cursor in the top- or bottom-right corner of the screen reveals the *Charms bar*, a location for tools called *charms*. See the right side of Figure 3-27. Charms include a robust Search tool that enables a search of the computer or even the Internet in one location. There's a Share charm for sharing photos, e-mail messages, and more. We'll revisit the charms later in this chapter when exploring how to access tech tools.

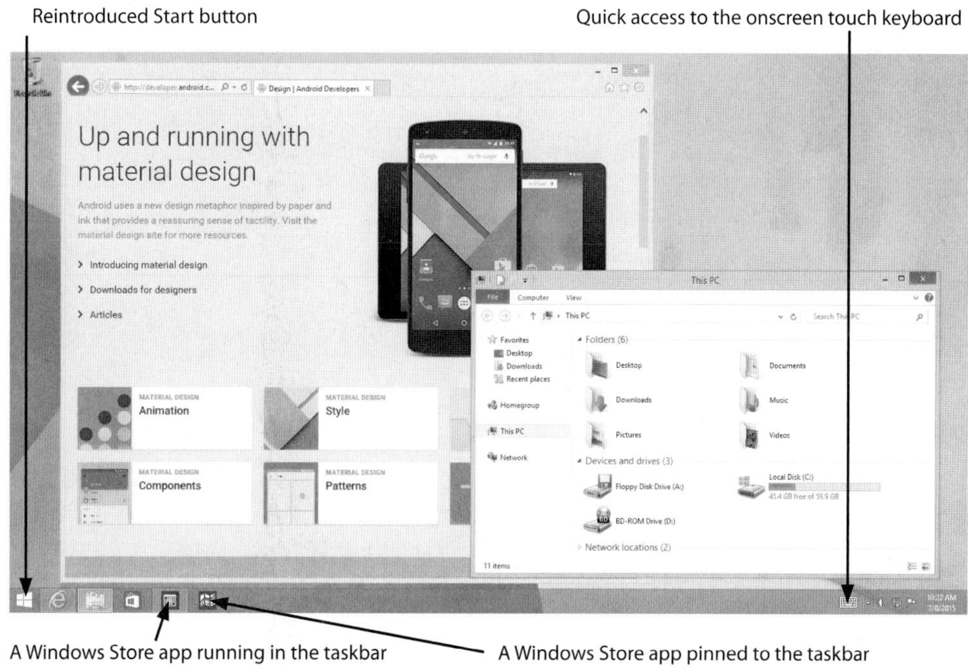

Figure 3-24 Windows 8.1

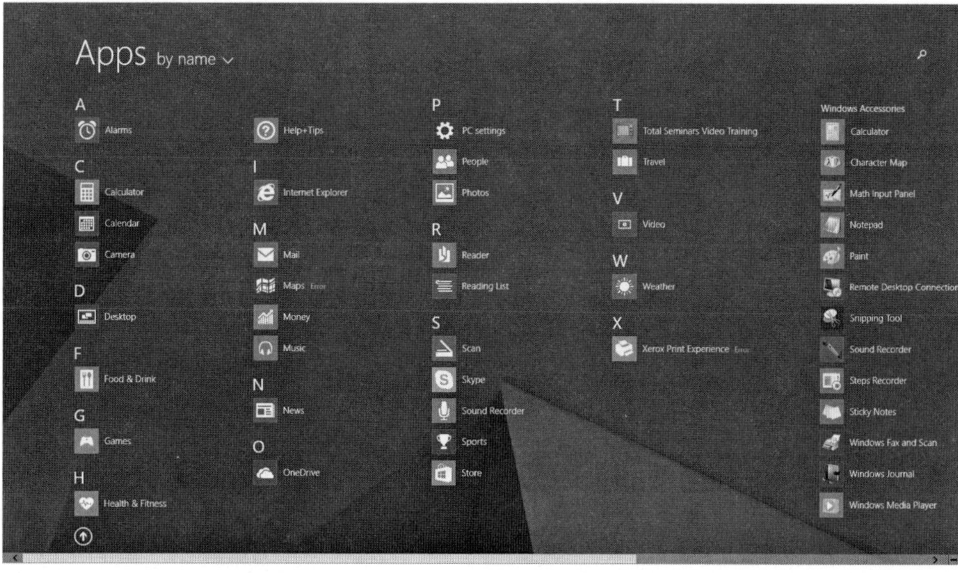

Figure 3-25 Apps sorted by name

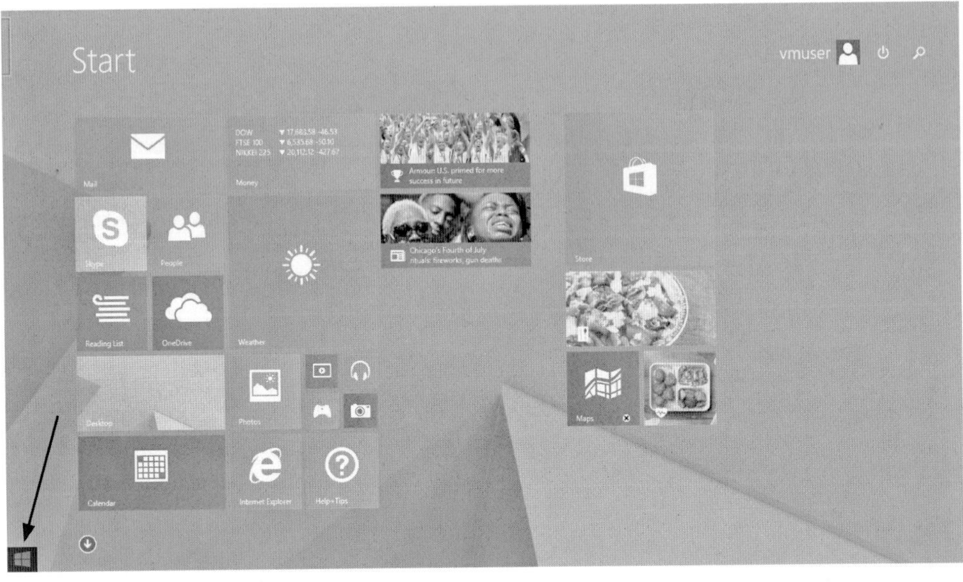

Figure 3-26 Start button magically appears

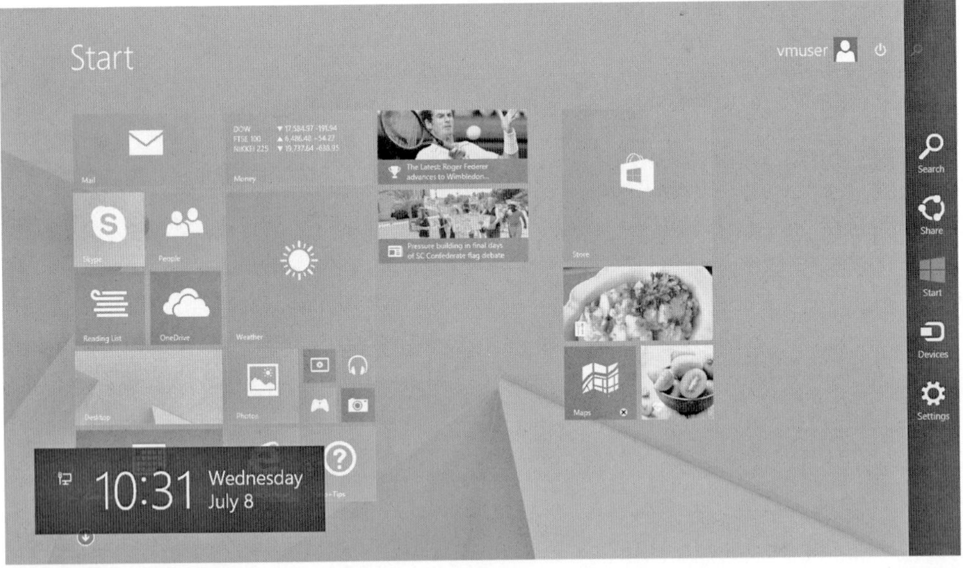

Figure 3-27 Charms accessed by cursor in upper- or lower-right corner

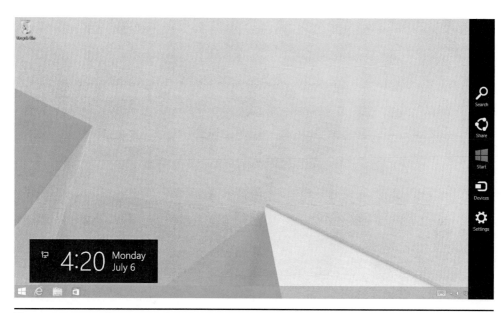

Figure 3-28 Windows 8.1 Desktop

The final version of Windows 8.1 uses the Desktop rather than the Start screen as the default interface. The Start button is visible in the bottom left (see Figure 3-28). You can still access the charms using the cursor and the upper- and lower-right corners of the screen.

Windows 10

With Windows 10, Microsoft created an OS that blends the traditional Windows 7–style Desktop experience with some of the more progressive features of the Windows 8.*x* Metro/Modern UI. In particular, Microsoft brought the Start menu back with conviction. They removed the much unloved Charms bar. Microsoft incorporated the essential tools—Search being my go-to feature—into the desktop in the lower-left corner of the taskbar. Figure 3-29 shows the Windows 10 interface with an active application in the foreground.

When you press the WINDOWS KEY on the keyboard, Windows 10 brings up the Start menu with useful tools and your most used apps on the left and pinned apps on the right (see Figure 3-30). Just like with Windows 8.1, you can click on the link helpfully named All apps (bottom left) to open a list of installed applications. Right-click to pin any app to the Start screen. Windows 10 altered the side-by-side app feature introduced in Windows 8. Use the Windows key and right or left arrow key to flip an app to one side of the screen. Do the same on another. Sweet!

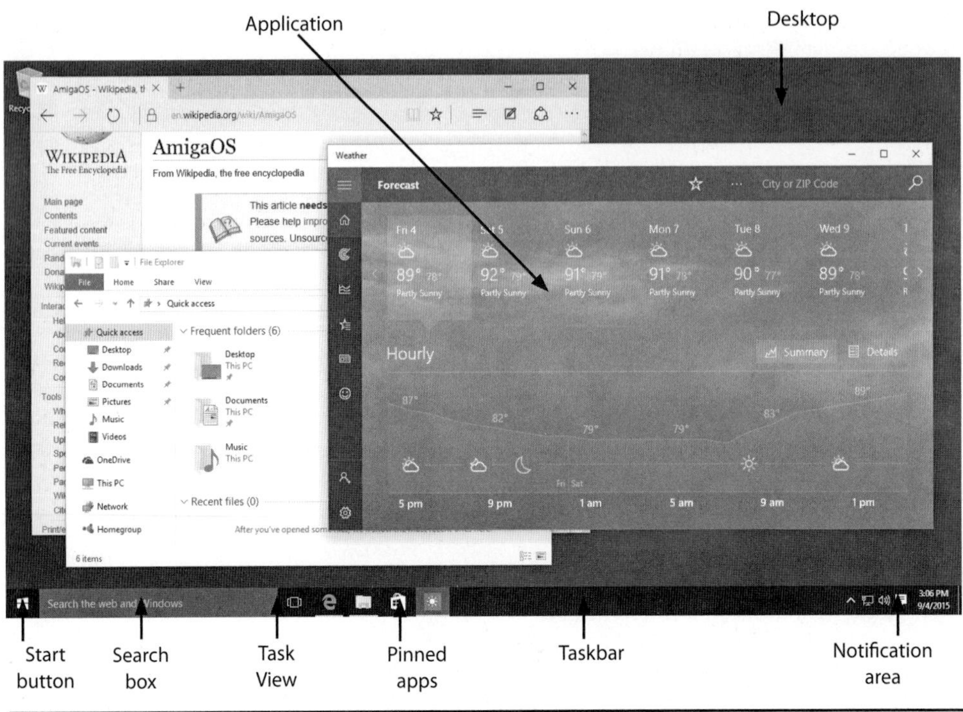

Figure 3-29 Windows 10 with a few applications open

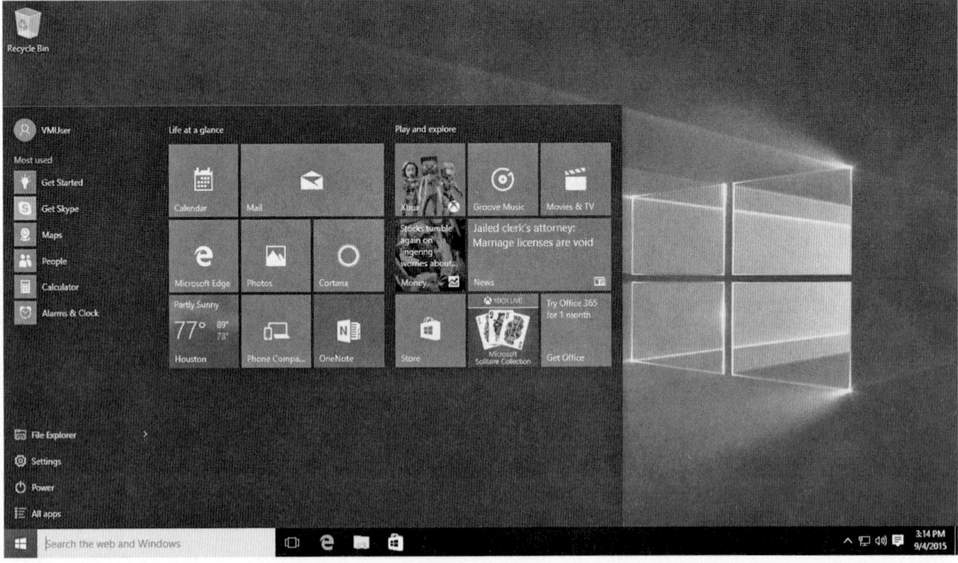

Figure 3-30 Start menu in Windows 10

Click on the Windows 10 Task View button to create and manage *multiple Desktops* for grouping your open applications. Mac OS X and Linux each have their own take on this feature, as you'll see in the following sections.

Mac OS X

The Mac OS X operating system interface offers similar functions to those found on Windows. The background of the main screen is called the *Desktop*. You can access frequently used applications by clicking on their icons on the *Dock*. Just like with the taskbar pinned apps, you can add and remove apps from the Dock with a right-click. The Dock is more than a set of apps, though. It also shows running applications (like the taskbar in Windows). Figure 3-31 shows a typical Mac OS X interface.

Pressing the Mission Control button on an Apple keyboard (see Figure 3-32) brings up a utility, called *Mission Control*, that enables you to switch between open applications, windows, and more, as shown in Figure 3-33. You can also access Mission Control by pressing and holding the control/ctrl key and pressing the up arrow key.

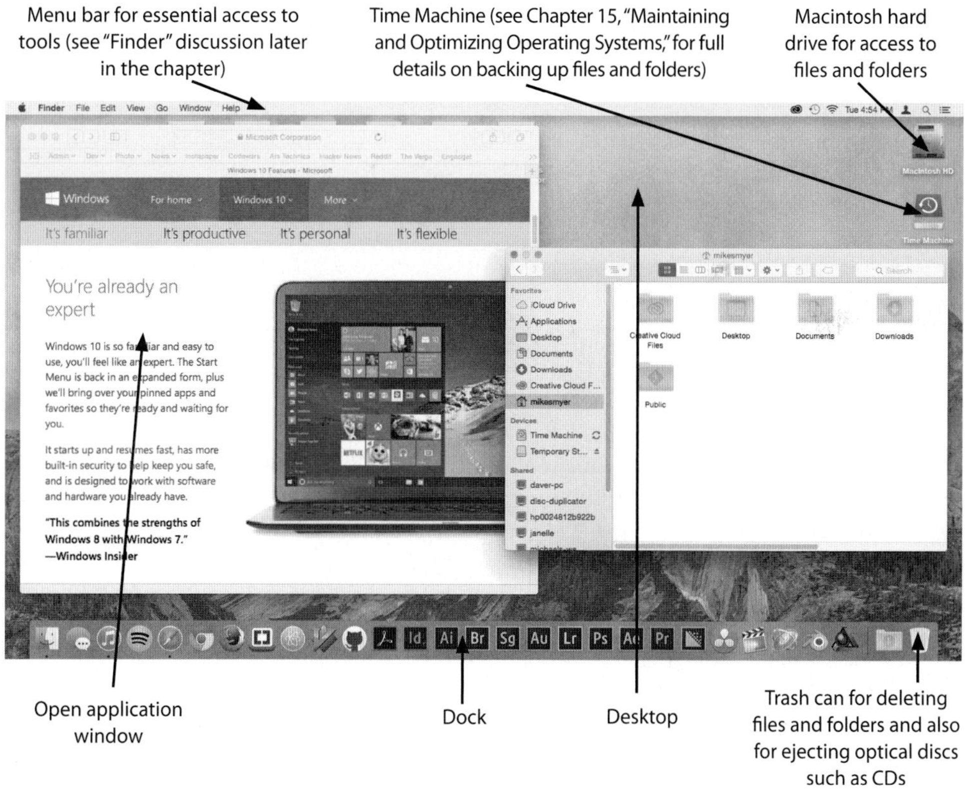

Figure 3-31 Mac OS X

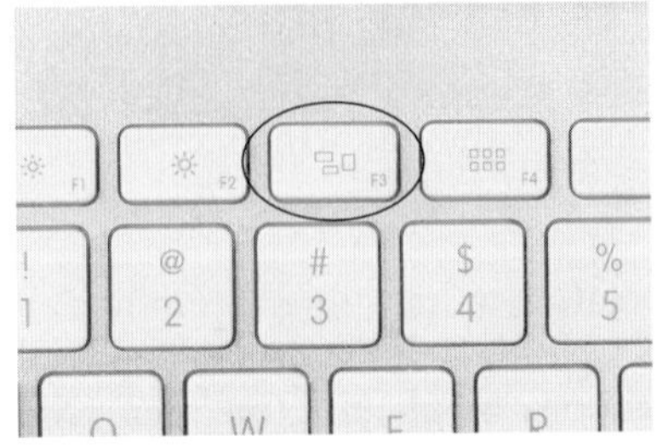

Figure 3-32 Mission Control button on keyboard

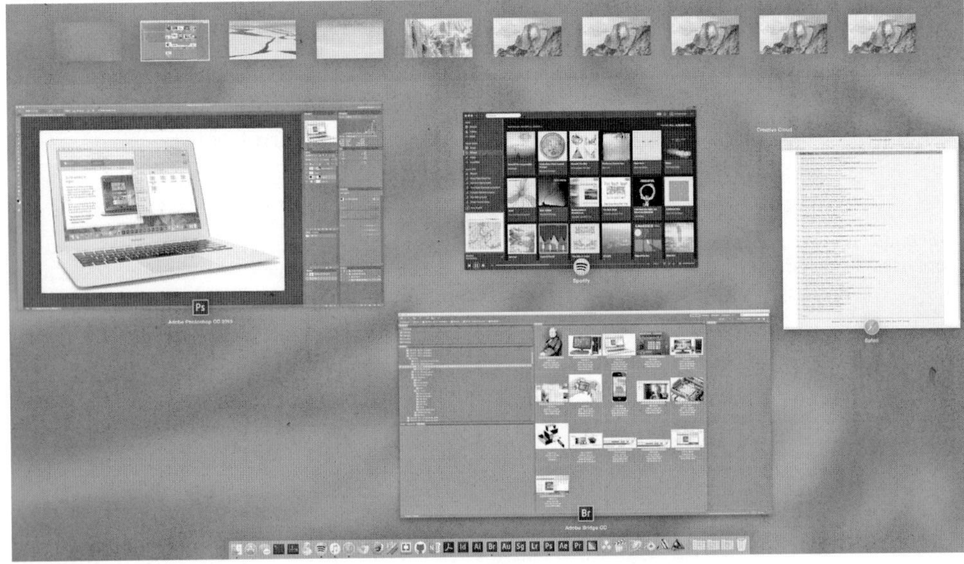

Figure 3-33 Mission Control showing four open apps and nine Desktops

Mac OS X supports *Spaces*—essentially multiple Desktops—that can have different backgrounds and programs (but keep the same Dock). You can optimize your workflow, for example, by putting your primary program full screen on Desktop 1 and putting your e-mail client on Desktop 2 (see Figure 3-34). New messages won't disturb you when working, but you can access the second Desktop easily when you want with Mission Control. On the latest versions of Mac OS X, press and hold the control key and press the right arrow and left arrow keys to scroll through Spaces.

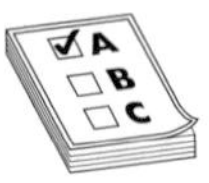

EXAM TIP Windows 10 supports multiple Desktops with Task View, but you won't find support for that feature in earlier versions of Windows.

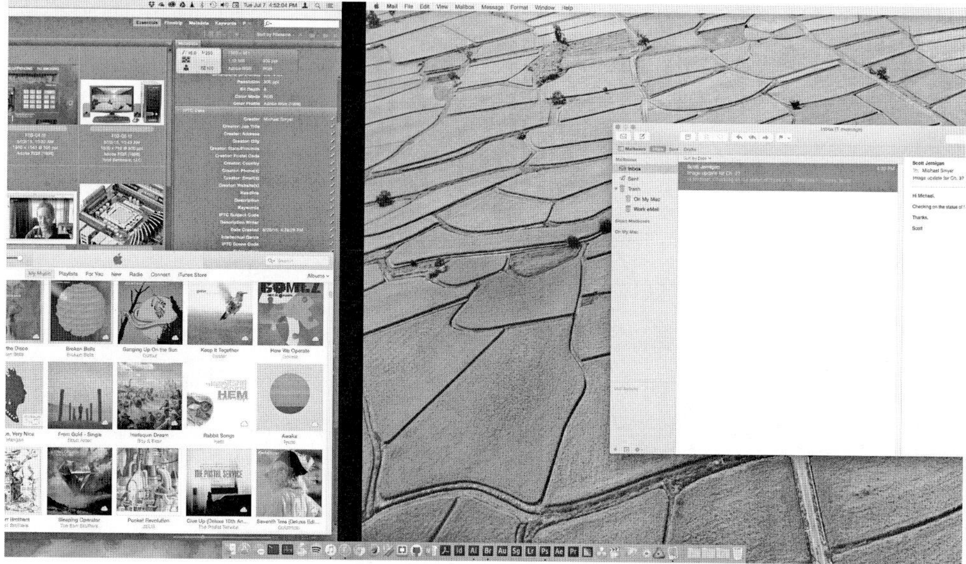

Figure 3-34 Switching between multiple Desktops

Linux

The many different distributions of Linux offer a variety of user interfaces, called *desktop environments (DEs)*, but they offer similar functions to those in Windows or Mac OS X. Figure 3-35 shows a popular Linux distro, Ubuntu Linux with the Unity DE, and notes the various features. Frequently used utilities and applications are locked on the Launcher on the left side of the screen. The top-left icon—the Ubuntu button—offers powerful system/network/Internet searching, while the next icon down enables you to access files and folders.

Try This!

Ubuntu Emulator Online

Ubuntu.com has a fairly robust emulator for Ubuntu Linux that enables you to poke around the desktop, check out settings and so forth. Try This! Open www.ubuntu.com, type **tour** in the Search option on the page, and press ENTER. In the search results, click on the first link to Take the tour. Have fun!

File Structures and Paths

Knowing where to find specific content—files and the folders in which they reside—helps techs help users do their day-to-day tasks more efficiently. Almost every operating system stores files in folders in a tree pattern. The root of the tree is the drive or disc,

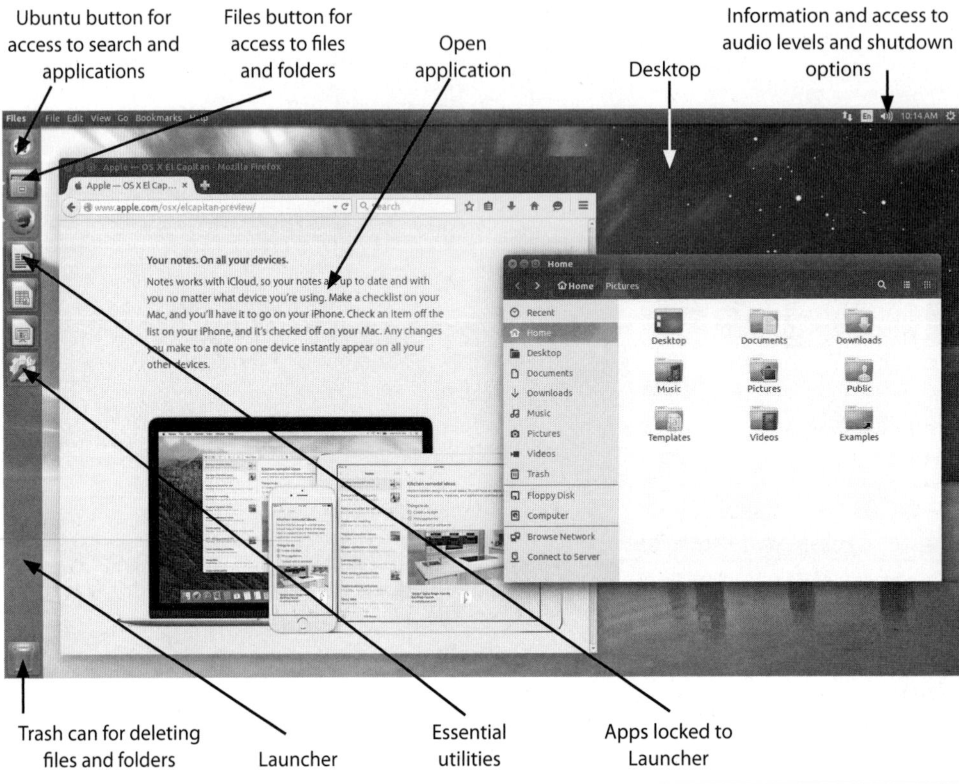

Figure 3-35 Ubuntu Linux

followed by a folder, subfolder, sub-subfolder, and so on, until you get to the desired file. The drive or disc gets some designation, most usually a *drive letter* like C:. Chapter 10, "Implementing Hard Drives," goes into gory detail on how modern operating systems implement systems for storing data. This section is more dictated by CompTIA's obsession with requiring examinees to memorize paths.

Windows

Windows has a number of important folders that help organize your programs and documents. They sit in the *root directory*—where the operating system is installed—and of course they have variations depending on the version of Windows. The following sections walk through the locations of important folders.

Most users and techs access folders and files in Windows with a tool called *Windows Explorer* in Windows Vista/7 and *File Explorer* in Windows 8/8.1/10—although you can only see that difference in name by right-clicking on the Start button or by moving your mouse over the folder icon in the taskbar (see Figure 3-36).

Figure 3-37 shows File Explorer viewing the Desktop in Windows 8. Select View to change Folder Options, such as view hidden files, hide file extensions, general options, and other view options.

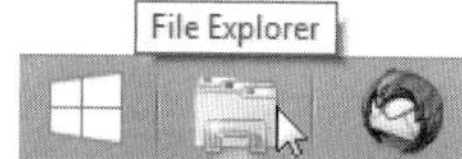

Figure 3-36 Mousing over the File Explorer icon

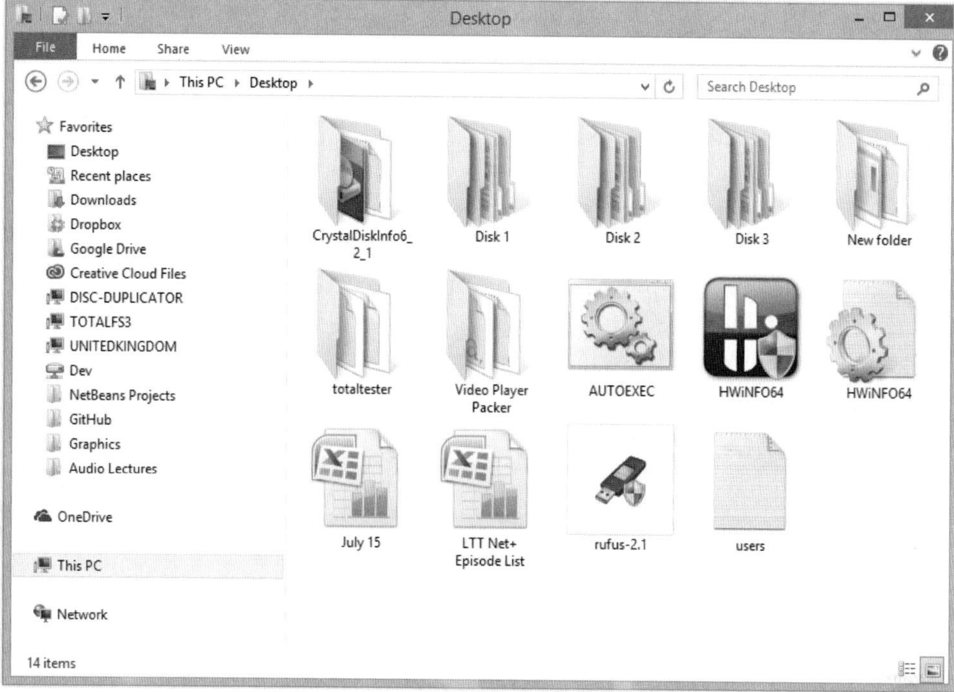

Figure 3-37 File Explorer

The folder structures that follow here use the standard formatting for describing folder structures. This is what you'll see on the 902 exam and in almost any OS. Windows hides the "\" characters at the beginning to make it prettier. File Explorer might show something like "Local Disk (C:) > Users > Mike." This translates in proper fashion as C:\Users\Mike.

C:\Program Files (All Versions) By default, most programs install some or all of their essential files into a subfolder of the Program Files folder. If you installed a program, it should have its own folder in here. Individual companies decide how to label their subfolders. Installing Photoshop made by Adobe, for example, creates the Adobe subfolder and then an Adobe Photoshop subfolder within it.

C:\Program Files (x86) The 64-bit editions of Windows create two directory structures for program files. The 64-bit applications go into the C:\Program Files folder, whereas the 32-bit applications go into the C:\Program Files (x86) folder. The separation makes it easy to find the proper version of whatever application you seek.

Personal Documents Modern versions of Windows use subfolders of the C:\Users folder to organize files for each user on a PC. Figure 3-38 shows the default folders for a user named Mike. Let's quickly survey the ones you need to know for the CompTIA A+ exams:

- **C:\Users\Mike\Desktop** This folder stores the files on the user's Desktop. If you delete this folder, you delete all the files placed on the Desktop.
- **C:\Users\Mike\Documents** This is the Documents or My Documents folder for that user. Only Windows 7 uses My Documents. The others use Documents.
- **C:\Users\Mike\Downloads** Microsoft's preferred download folder for applications to use. Most applications use this folder, but some do not.
- **C:\Users\Mike\Music** This is the default location for music you download. My guess is that more people have music in iTunes, but that's just me.

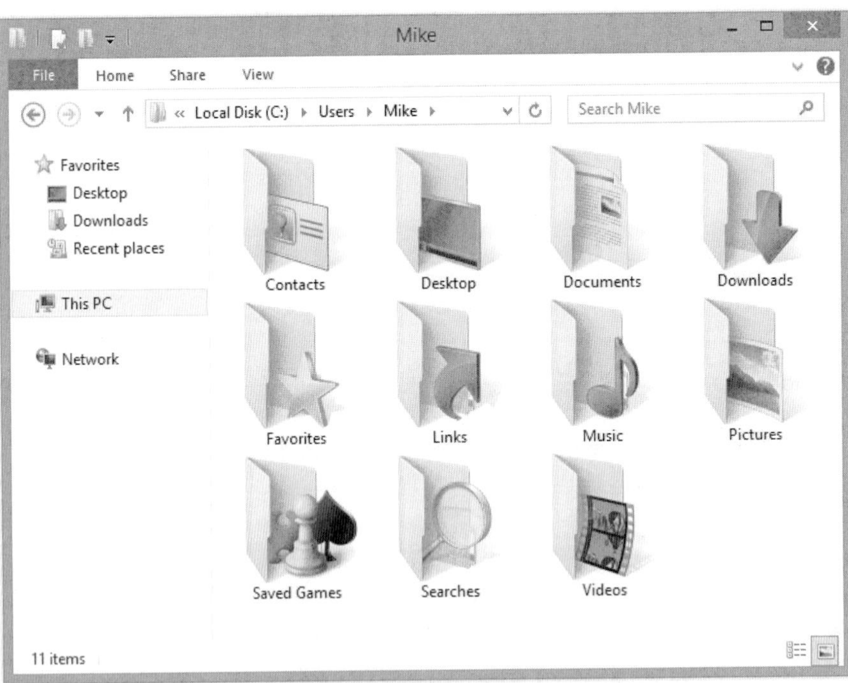

Figure 3-38 File Explorer viewing Mike's folders

- **C:\Users\Mike\Pictures** Pictures is the default location for images imported into the PC, although the Pictures library can (and does) draw from many folder locations.
- **C:\Users\Mike\Videos** Videos is the default location for movies and homebrewed videos imported into a PC.

Mac OS X

Finder holds the keys to files and folders in Mac OS X. Figure 3-39 shows Finder open to display Mike's Users folder. Note that although its style differs from the Windows screen earlier, it has functionally similar folders. These are the default locations for files on the Desktop, in Documents, Downloads, Music, Pictures, and so on. Each user account on the Mac will have a unique Users folder that is inaccessible by other users on that computer.

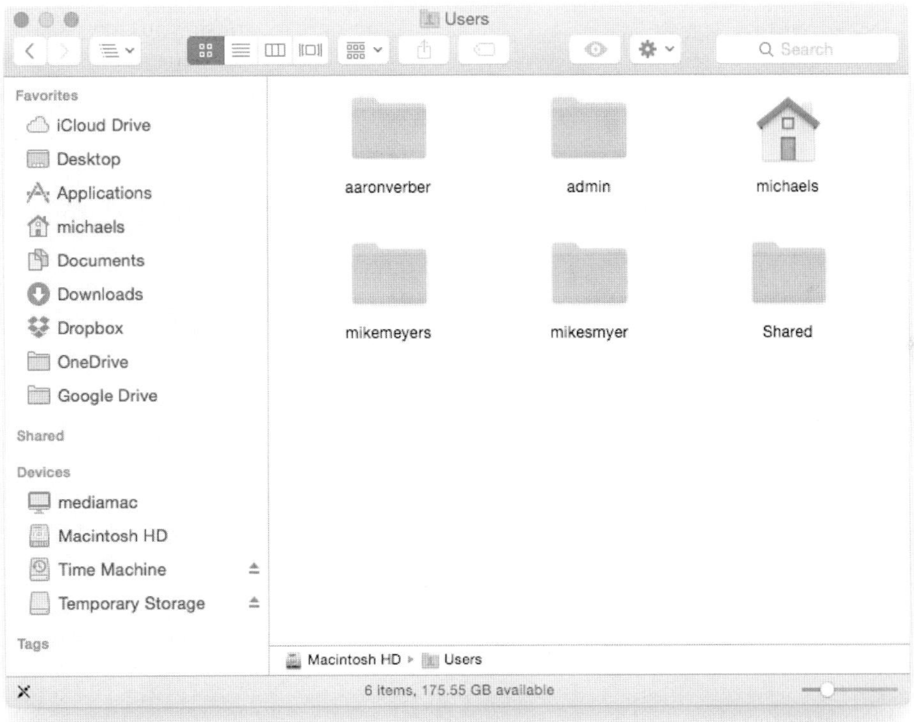

Figure 3-39 Finder

Linux

Ready to be shocked? Not surprisingly, Linux uses pretty much the same structure for user organization (see Figure 3-40). I guess once something seems logical to enough people, there's no reason to add confusion by changing the structure. The only major difference is the name: Linux uses the Home folder, rather than the Users folder.

The Tech Launch Points

Every OS has two or three areas for tech-specific utilities. This section shows you how to access those areas, primarily so that we don't have to repeat the steps to get to them when accessing them many times throughout the book. Just refer back to this section if you have difficulty remembering how to arrive at a place later on. Also, CompTIA will test your knowledge on how to access these tool locations, with specific steps. Use this section for the last-minute cram before taking the exams.

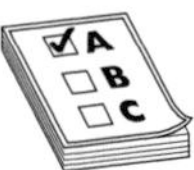

EXAM TIP The 902 exam will test you on specific paths to specific tools. You will get several of these questions as multiple-choice, scenario-based, or both types of question.

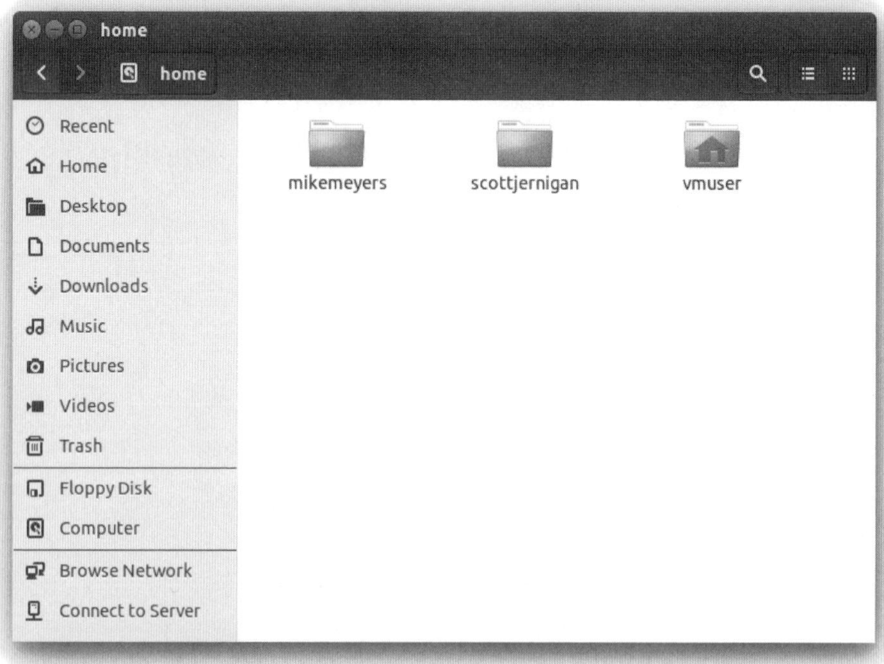

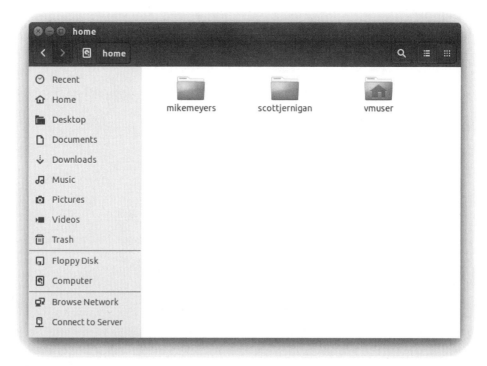

Figure 3-40 Home folder

Windows Vista/7

Windows Vista/7 have three tech launch points: the Control Panel, System Tools, and the command-line interface. You can get to each launch point in multiple ways.

Control Panel The *Control Panel* handles most of the maintenance, upgrade, and configuration aspects of Windows. As such, the Control Panel is the first set of tools for every tech to explore. You can find the Control Panel by clicking on the Start button and choosing Control Panel from the Start menu.

The Control Panel opens in the Control Panel's Category view by default, which displays the icons in groups like Hardware and Sound. See Figure 3-41. This view requires an additional click (and sometimes a guess about which category includes the applet you need), so many techs use Classic view.

The CompTIA A+ 902 exam specifically assumes Classic view with large icons, so you should do what every tech does: switch from Category view to Classic view. In Windows Vista, choose Classic View. In Windows 7, select either Large icons or Small icons from the View by drop-down list for a similar effect. Figure 3-42 shows the Windows Vista Control Panel in Classic view.

A large number of programs, called *applets*, populate the Control Panel. The names and selection of applets vary depending on the version of Windows and whether any installed programs have added applets. But all versions of Windows have applets that enable you to control specific aspects of Windows, such as the appearance, installed

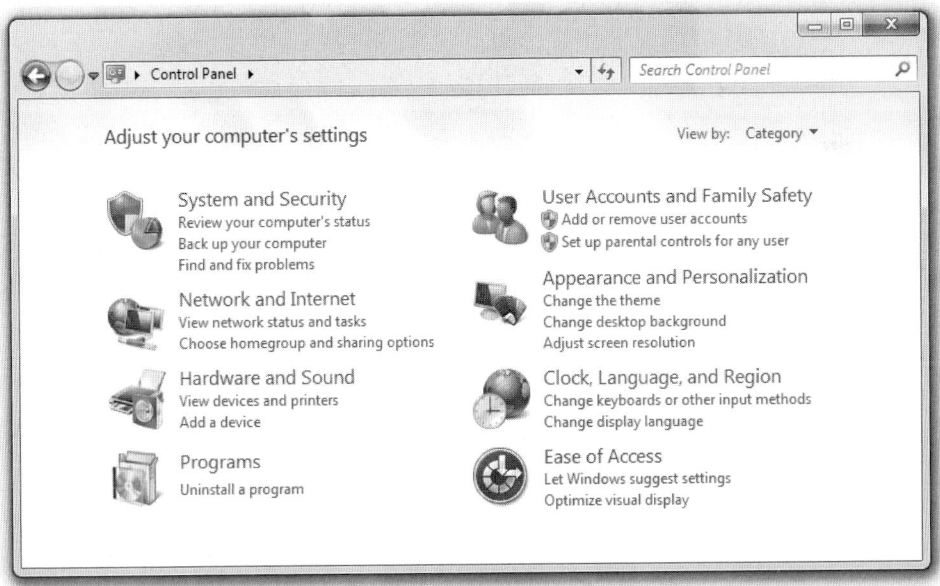

Figure 3-41 Windows 7 Control Panel (Category view)

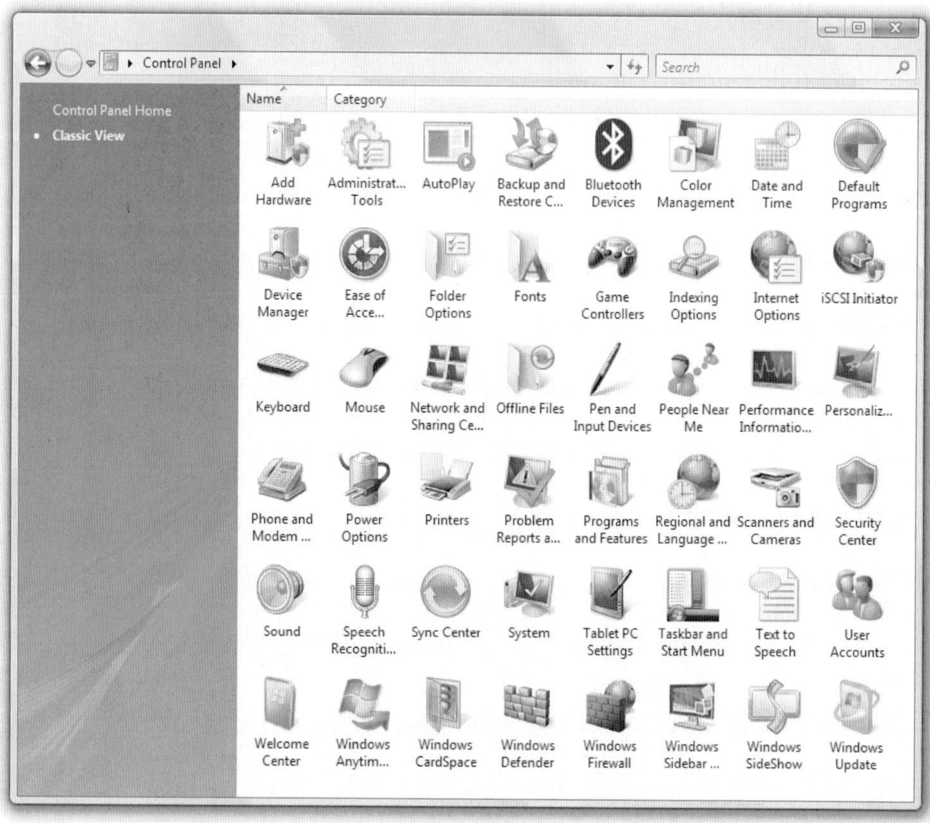

Figure 3-42 Windows Vista Control Panel (Classic view)

applications, and system settings. You will get details on each applet as we put them into use over the course of this book.

System Tools The Start menu offers a variety of tech utilities collected in one place: System Tools. In the *System Tools* menu, you'll find commonly accessed tools such as System Information and Disk Defragmenter (see Figure 3-43).

Many techs overlook memorizing how to find the appropriate Windows tool to diagnose problems, but nothing hurts your credibility with a client like fumbling around, clicking a variety of menus and applets, while mumbling, "I know it's around here somewhere." The CompTIA A+ certification 902 exam therefore tests you on a variety of paths to appropriate tools.

To access System Tools in Windows Vista/7, go to Start | All Programs | Accessories | System Tools. Each version of Windows shares many of the same tools, but each includes its own utilities as well. Rather than go through every tool here, I'll discuss each in

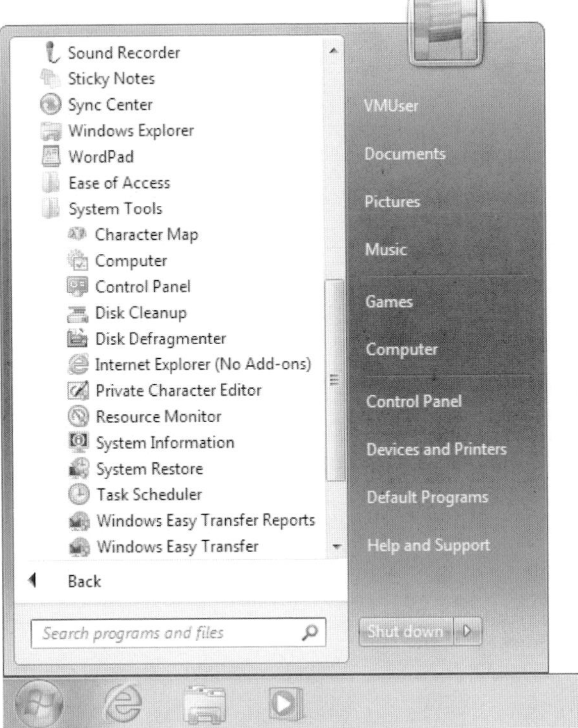

Figure 3-43 System Tools menu options

detail during the appropriate scenarios in the book. Here's one example that won't appear again, Character Map.

Ever been using a program only to discover you need to enter a strange character such as the euro character (€) but your word processor doesn't support it? That's when you need the Character Map. It enables you to copy any Unicode character into the Clipboard (see Figure 3-44) and paste into your document. Unicode has all the special symbols and alphabet characters used in languages throughout the world.

Command Line The Windows *command-line interface* is a throwback to how Microsoft operating systems worked a long, long time ago when text commands were entered at a command prompt. Figure 3-45 shows the command prompt from DOS, the first operating system commonly used in PCs.

DOS is dead, but the command-line interface is alive and well in every version of Windows. Every good tech knows how to access and use the command-line interface. It is a lifesaver when the graphical part of Windows doesn't work, and it is often faster than using a mouse if you're skilled at using it. An entire chapter (Chapter 16, "Working with the Command-Line Interface") is devoted to the command line, but let's look at one example of what the command line can do. First, you need to get there. Click on

Figure 3-44 Character Map

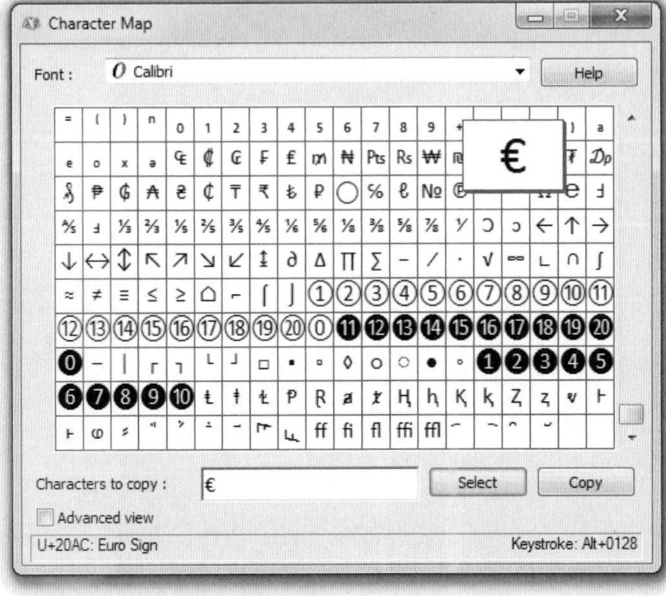

Figure 3-45 DOS command prompt

```
 Volume in drive C is SYSTEM
 Volume Serial Number is 3A95-79D2
 Directory of C:\

COMMAND  COM        54,645 05-31-94   6:22a
DOS          <DIR>         04-21-09   3:13p
WINDOWS      <DIR>         04-21-09   3:20p
WINA20   386         9,349 05-31-94   6:22a
CONFIG   OLD            71 04-21-09   3:15p
AUTOEXEC OLD            78 04-21-09   3:15p
WIN311       <DIR>         04-21-09   4:20p
CONFIG   SYS            85 04-21-09   3:32p
AUTOEXEC BAT            93 12-22-10   2:31p
GORILLA  BAS        30,702 10-21-09   4:24p
FILE0001 CHK        32,768 02-23-12   5:04p
SHMANSI      <DIR>         04-14-10   2:30p
       12 file(s)        127,791 bytes
                   2,001,423,360 bytes free

C:\>ver

MS-DOS Version 6.22


C:\>_
```

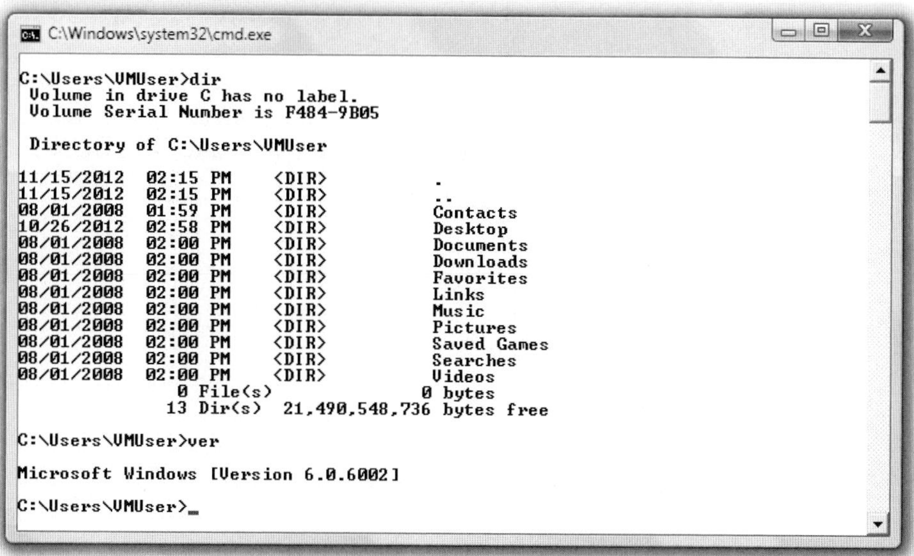

Figure 3-46 Command prompt in Windows Vista

the Start button, type **cmd** in the Search text box, and press the ENTER key. Figure 3-46 shows a command prompt in Windows Vista.

Once at a command prompt, type **dir** and press ENTER. This command displays all the files and folders in a specific directory—probably your user folder for this exercise—and gives dates, times, folder names, and other information. The dir command is just one of many useful command-line tools you'll learn about in this book.

Windows 8/8.1

Windows 8/8.1 have three tech tool starting points, but they differ a little from the big three in Windows Vista/7. The newer versions feature the Control Panel, Administrative Tools, and the command-line interface.

Control Panel The Control Panel in Windows 8/8.1 serves the same function as in previous versions of Windows—the go-to source for tech tools. You can access the Control Panel in several ways:

- Tap the down arrow on the lower right of the Start screen and scroll all the way to the right in the list of Apps. In the Windows System category, click on Control Panel (see Figure 3-47). That's the slow way, but you should know it for the exams. You can also start typing **control panel** in the Search field in the Apps list. Control Panel will quickly appear as the best option to select.
- Right-click on the Start button and select Control Panel from the menu (see Figure 3-48). You can bring up the same menu by pressing WINDOWS KEY-X.

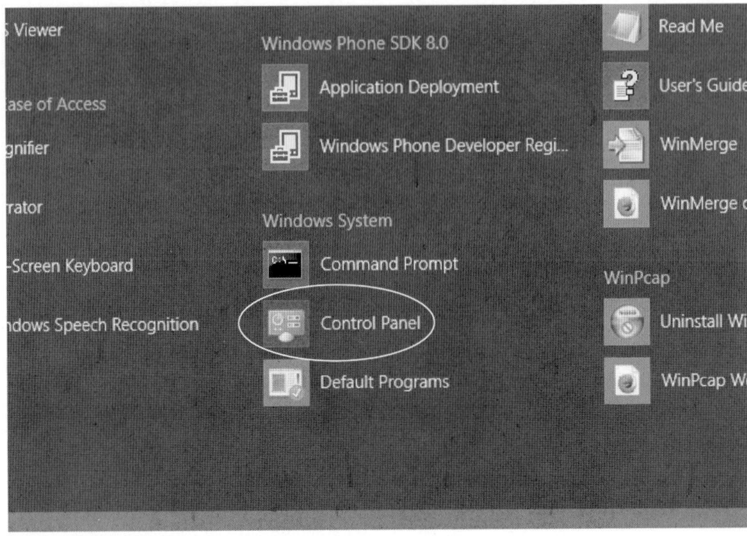

Figure 3-47 Selecting Control Panel from the list of Apps

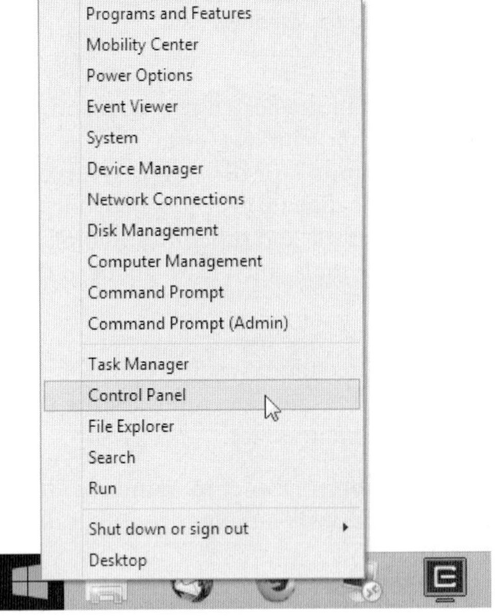

Figure 3-48 Right-clicking on the Start button

I call this menu *Tech Essentials* because it gives you very quick access not only to the Control Panel and its collection of tools but also to specific tools that every tech relies on heavily, like the Task Manager (for forcing frozen programs to close, among other things).

- In the Start screen, start typing **control panel**; the Control Panel will show up as the top option in the Search charm (see Figure 3-49). Select it to open.

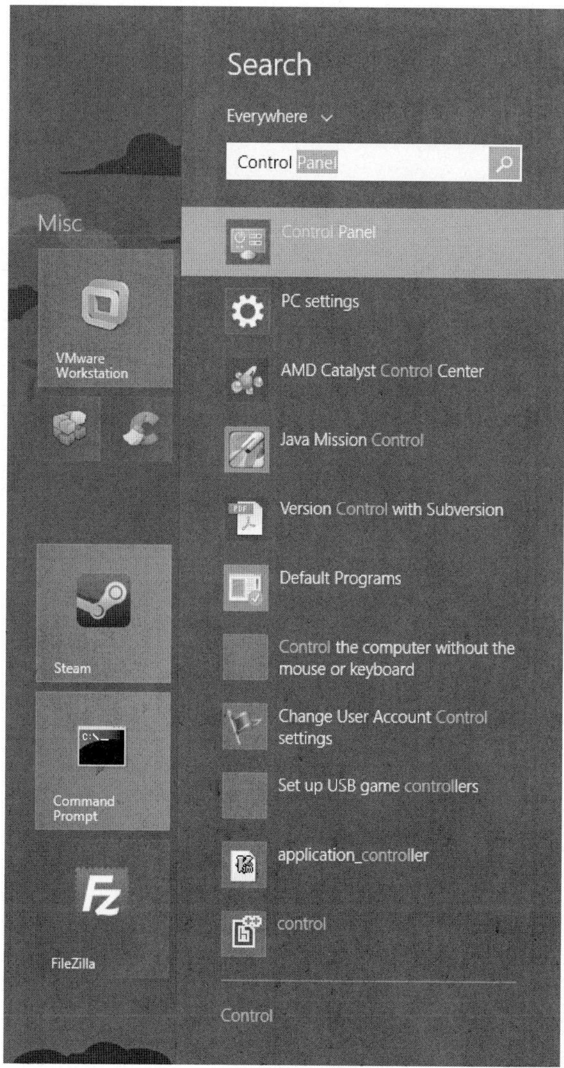

Figure 3-49 Search charm with Control Panel as top option

Administrative Tools Microsoft beefed up Administrative Tools starting in Windows 8, adding some of the tools found in the System Tools menu in previous versions of Windows. *Administrative Tools* enables you to set up hard drives, manage devices, test system performance, and much more. This is a go-to set of tools for every tech, and one that we will access many times for scenarios in this book.

As with Control Panel, you have several options for accessing Administrative Tools:

- In the Start screen, click on the down arrow to open the Apps list. Scroll a little to the right and you'll see the list of Administrative Tools (see Figure 3-50). Select the specific tool you want to open.

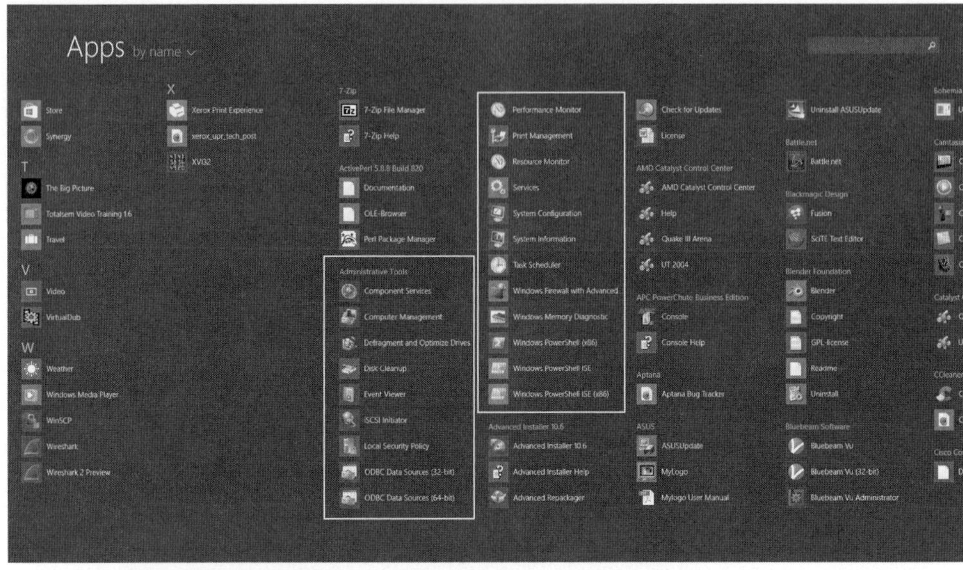

Figure 3-50 Administrative Tools in the Apps list

- Begin typing **administrative tools** in the Start screen and Administrative Tools will quickly appear as an option in the Search charm (see Figure 3-51). Select it to open.
- Right-click on the Start button (or press WINDOWS KEY-X) and select Control Panel from the context menu. In the Control Panel, select Administrative Tools to open.

Command Line The command-line interface retains its place as a go-to tool for techs. Windows 8/8.1 offers several ways to access it:

- Tap the down arrow on the lower right of the Start screen and scroll all the way to the right in the list of Apps. In the Windows System category, click on Command Prompt to open the utility. You can also start typing **command prompt** in the Search field in the Apps list. Command Prompt will quickly appear as the best option to select.
- Right-click on the Start button (or press WINDOWS KEY-X) and select Command Prompt from the context menu to open the command-line interface.
- In the Start screen, start typing **cmd** or **command prompt** and Command Prompt will appear in the Search charm. Click on it to open it.

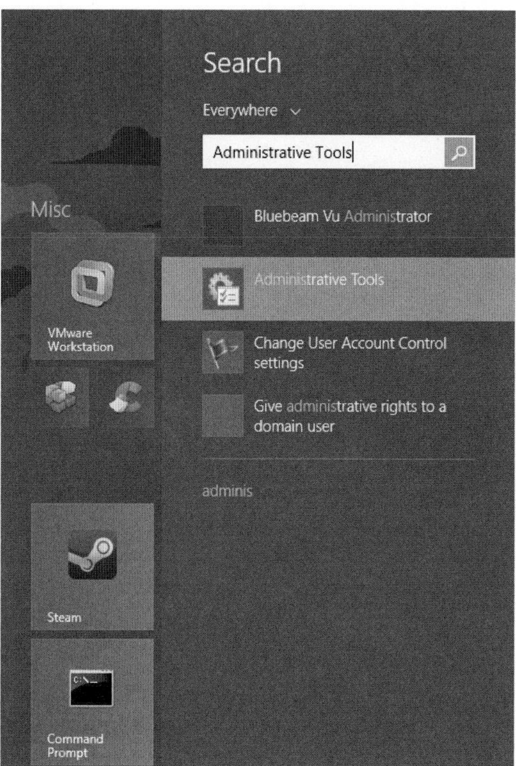

Figure 3-51 Administrative Tools option in the Search charm

Windows 10

Windows 10 keeps the Control Panel and command-line interfaces we see in earlier Windows versions, but focuses on an expanded Settings app for day-to-day administration.

Control Panel Windows 10 offers two standard ways to get to the Control Panel. Right-click on the Start button to open the Tech Essentials menu and select Control Panel. Alternatively, you can click on the Start button to open the Metro/Modern UI interface, start typing **control panel**, and select Control Panel from the Search results.

Administrative Tools is still an important part of Windows 10, a set of utilities piled together as a single Control Panel applet. You have the same options for accessing Administrative Tools in Windows 10 as listed in the prior section for Windows 8/8.1.

Settings App The Windows 10 *Settings app* combines a huge number of otherwise disparate utilities, apps, and tools traditionally spread out all over your computer into one fairly unified, handy Windows app (see Figure 3-52). Since the Settings app was introduced in Windows 8, it has taken over more and more tasks from the Control Panel. Expect it to grow as Windows 10 matures.

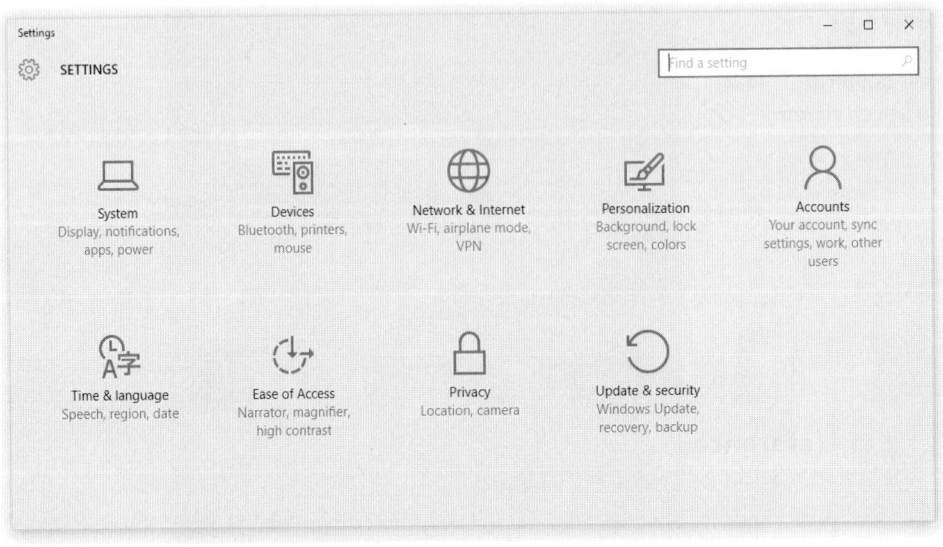

Figure 3-52 Windows Settings app

Figure 3-53 Accessing Settings in Windows 10

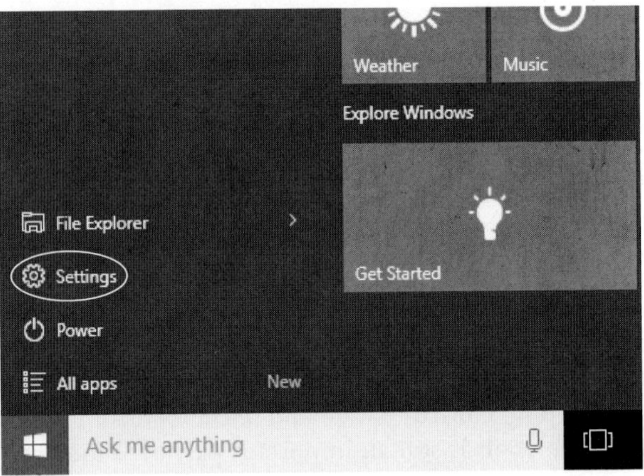

To access the Setting app, press the WINDOWS KEY to access the Start menu. Select Settings from the lower left to open the tool (see Figure 3-53).

Mac OS X

Mac OS X has two key launch points for techs: the System Preferences app and the Utilities folder. You can access both quickly.

Figure 3-54 Accessing System Preferences

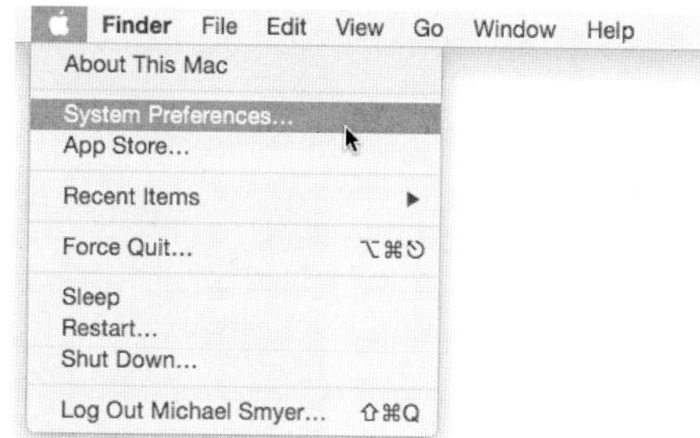

System Preferences To access *System Preferences,* click on the Apple (top-left corner of screen). Select System Preferences from the permanent Apple menu to open the app (see Figure 3-54). From System Preferences you have access to almost all settings you will need to administer a Mac OS X system.

Utilities Folder The second launch point is the *Utilities* folder, located neatly in the Applications folder. Because of its importance, Apple provides a quick shortcut to access it. With the Finder in focus, click on Go on the menu bar and select Utilities (see Figure 3-55). Alternatively, use the hot-key combination: COMMAND-SHIFT-U. This gives you access to the tools you need to perform services on a Mac beyond what's included in System Preferences, including Activity Monitor and Terminal. The latter

Figure 3-55 Accessing the Utilities folder

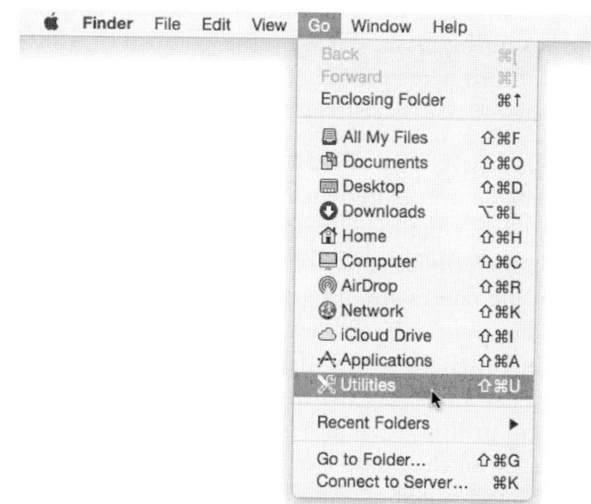

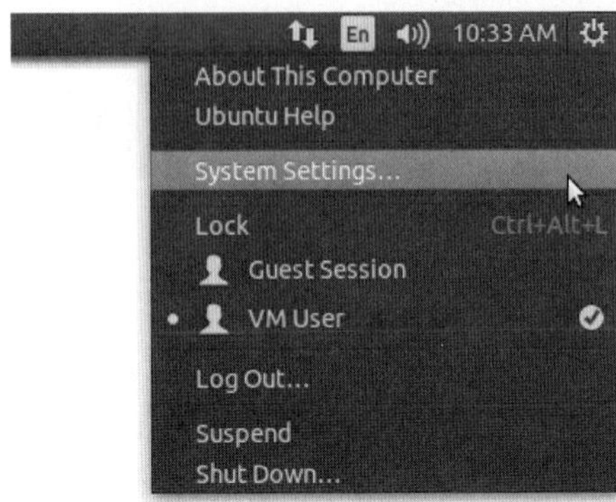

Figure 3-56 Accessing System Settings

is the command-line interface for Mac OS X, a very powerful tool for techs that we explore in detail in Chapter 16.

Linux

An essential tool in Linux for techs is the command line, called Terminal. You can get there in most distros by pressing CTRL-ALT-T. (See Chapter 16, "The Command-Line Interface," for a lot of details about essential Linux commands.)

Other launch points vary from distro to distro. Here are the locations of the launch points for the three most common desktop environments.

Unity (Default for Ubuntu Desktop) Similar to Mac OS X, Unity has a central application for managing common settings called *System Settings*. To access System Settings, click on the gear icon on the far right of the menu bar and select System Settings (see Figure 3-56).

You can find settings and utilities not in the System Settings application with the rest of the applications in the Dash. Click on the Ubuntu button at the top of the Launcher (see Figure 3-57). From here you can search or browse for handy applications such as the System Monitor or the always critical Terminal.

GNOME 3 (Default for Fedora Workstation, Red Hat Enterprise Linux) If you have any experience with Ubuntu's Unity, working with GNOME 3 should feel somewhat familiar because Unity is based on GNOME. Because of this connection, the same applications are used to administer GNOME 3–based desktops, although some of the names are different.

The first launch point is the All Settings application, which is practically the same as System Settings in Unity. To access All Settings, click on the down arrow icon on the far right of the menu bar and select the wrench and screwdriver icon (see Figure 3-58).

For other system utilities such as System Monitor or Terminal, click on the Activities button on the far left of the menu bar. From here you can search for the utility from the box at the top, or select the Show Applications grid icon from the bottom of the Dash on the left side of the screen. This will open a menu showing all installed applications, and within this list is a folder for Utilities.

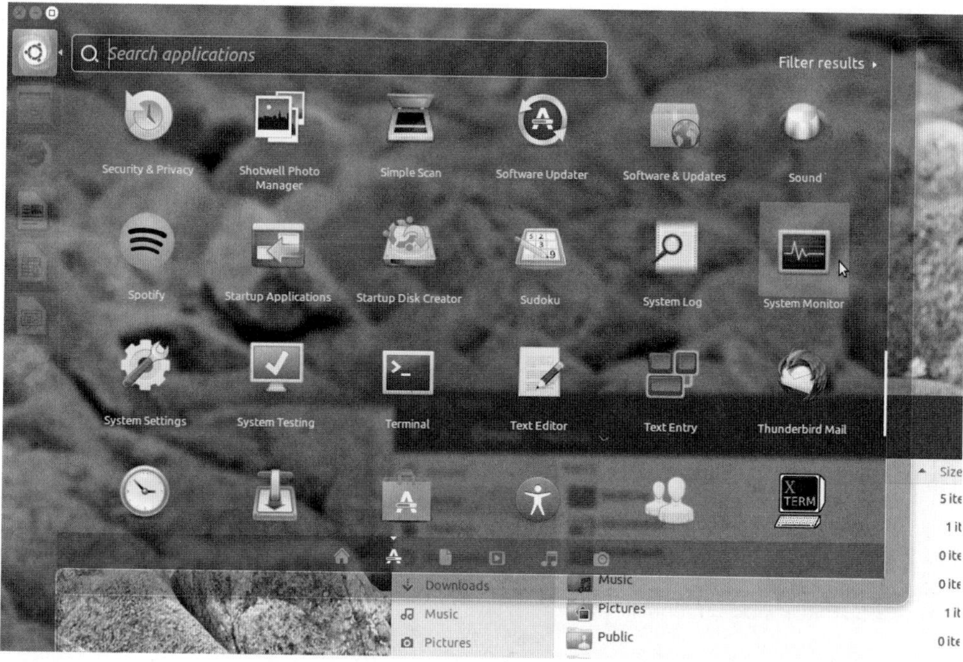

Figure 3-57 Browsing through Dash applications

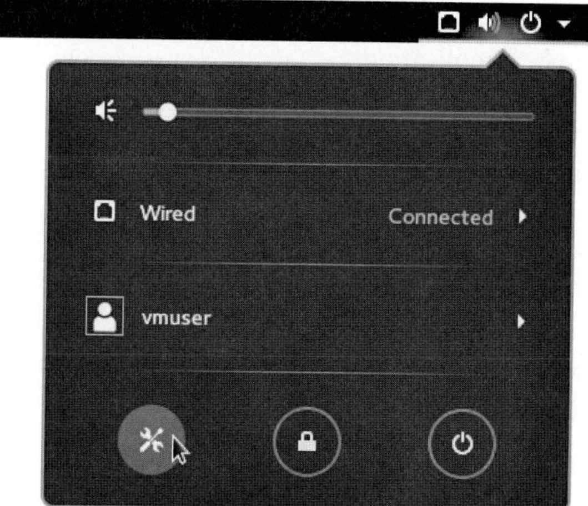

Figure 3-58 Accessing All Settings

KDE Plasma Desktop (Default for OpenSUSE, Kubuntu)

"Choice!" could be the unofficial motto of Linux, and when you are working on a KDE-based distro, you are certainly spoiled for choices. The downside to this abundance is that the configuration utilities can vary among the different KDE-based distros.

The one thing that is the same in all the KDE-based distros is that everything you need to work on the system is accessible from the *Kickoff* menu on the far left of the

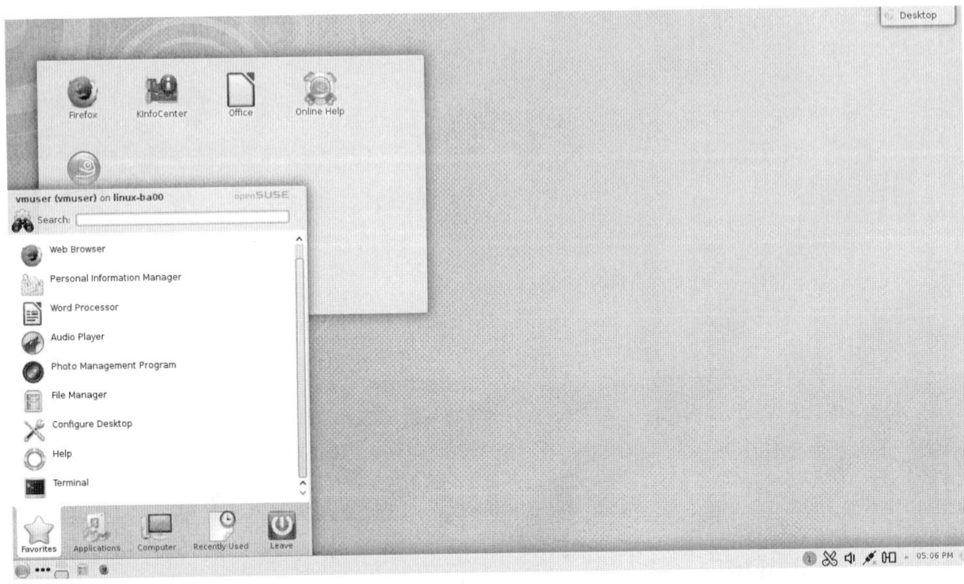

Figure 3-59 KDE Kickoff menu

Panel (see Figure 3-59). The Kickoff menu looks and works a lot like the Start menu in Windows 7, so it should be relatively easy to navigate. Once in the Kickoff menu, you can search for a needed utility or select the Applications tab at the bottom. From here, most distros have a Utilities or System menu that holds all the key system configuration and maintenance applications.

Chapter 3 Review

Questions

1. Which version of Windows introduced the Metro UI?
   - **A.** Windows 7
   - **B.** Windows 8
   - **C.** Windows 8.1
   - **D.** Windows 10
2. Which Windows 8 feature did Microsoft not include in Windows 10?
   - **A.** Metro/Modern UI
   - **B.** Start button
   - **C.** Control Panel
   - **D.** Charms bar

3. What Mac OS X feature is essentially multiple Desktops?
   A. Charms
   B. Desktop
   C. Mission Control
   D. Spaces
4. What is the default Ubuntu desktop environment?
   A. Metro UI
   B. Unity
   C. KDE
   D. GNOME 3
5. The user, Mike, has downloaded files with his Web browser. Where will they be stored by default?
   A. C:\Downloads
   B. C:\Mike\Desktop\Downloads
   C. C:\Users\Mike\Downloads
   D. C:\Users\Mike\Desktop\Downloads
6. 32-bit programs are installed into which folder by default in a 64-bit edition of Windows?
   A. C:\Program Files
   B. C:\Program Files (x32)
   C. C:\Program Files\Wins\Old
   D. C:\Program Files (x86)
7. Which Mac OS X feature is functionally equivalent to Windows File Explorer?
   A. Finder
   B. Dock
   C. Quartz
   D. File Manager
8. Which of the following paths would open Administrative Tools in Windows 8.1?
   A. Right-click the task bar and select Administrative Tools from the context menu.
   B. Right-click the Start button and select Administrative Tools from the context menu.
   C. Right-click anywhere on the desktop and select Administrative Tools from the context menu.
   D. Press the WINDOWS KEY-L combination to open Administrative Tools.

9. What feature of Mac OS X is the equivalent of the command-line interface in Windows?
   - A. Dock
   - B. Spaces
   - C. Terminal
   - D. Unity
10. What Windows app in Windows 10 combines many utilities into a unified tool?
   - A. Settings
   - B. Control
   - C. Command Center
   - D. Control Center

Answers

1. **B.** Microsoft introduced Metro UI with Windows 8.
2. **D.** Microsoft did not include the Charms bar in Windows 10. Bye!
3. **D.** *Spaces* is the term Apple uses for multiple Desktops in Mac OS X.
4. **B.** Ubuntu Linux uses the Unity DE by default.
5. **C.** The default download location in Windows is C:\Users\<user name>\Downloads.
6. **D.** By default, 32-bit applications install into the C:\Program Files (x86) folder.
7. **A.** Finder is the equivalent of File Explorer.
8. **B.** To open Administrative Tools, right-click on the Start button and select Administrative Tools. Easy!
9. **C.** Terminal is the equivalent of the Windows command-line interface.
10. **A.** The Settings app in Windows 10 offers many utilities in a unified interface.

CHAPTER 4

Microprocessors

In this chapter, you will learn how to

- Identify the core components of a CPU
- Describe the relationship of CPUs and memory
- Explain the varieties of modern CPUs
- Select and install a CPU
- Troubleshoot CPUs

The *central processing unit (CPU)* does most of the calculations that make your computer...well, a computer. The CPU, also known as a *microprocessor*, invariably hides on the motherboard below a large heat sink and often a fan assembly as well. CPU makers name their microprocessors in a fashion similar to the automobile industry: CPUs get a make and a model, such as Intel Core i7 or AMD FX-8350 Black Edition. But what's happening inside the CPU to make it able to do the amazing things asked of it every time you step up to the keyboard?

This chapter delves into microprocessors in detail. We'll first discuss how processors work and the components that enable them to interact with the rest of the computer. The second section describes how CPUs work with memory. The third section takes you on a tour of modern CPUs. The fourth section gets into practical work, selecting and installing CPUs. The final section covers troubleshooting CPUs in detail.

Historical/Conceptual

CPU Core Components

Although the computer might seem to act quite intelligently, comparing the CPU to a human brain hugely overstates its capabilities. A CPU functions more like a very powerful calculator than like a brain—but, oh, what a calculator! Today's CPUs add, subtract, multiply, divide, and move billions of numbers per second. Processing that much information so quickly makes any CPU look intelligent. It's simply the speed of the CPU, rather than actual intelligence, that enables computers to perform feats such as accessing the Internet, playing visually stunning games, or editing photos.

A good technician needs to understand some basic CPU functions to support computing devices, so let's start with an analysis of how the CPU works. If you wanted to teach someone how an automobile engine works, you would use a relatively simple example engine, right? The same principle applies here. Let's begin our study of the CPU with the granddaddy of all PC CPUs: the famous Intel 8088, invented in the late 1970s. This CPU defined the idea of the modern microprocessor and contains the same basic parts used in even the most advanced CPUs today.

The Man in the Box

Let's begin by visualizing the CPU as a man in a box (see Figure 4-1). This is one clever guy. He can perform virtually any mathematical function, manipulate data, and give answers *very quickly*.

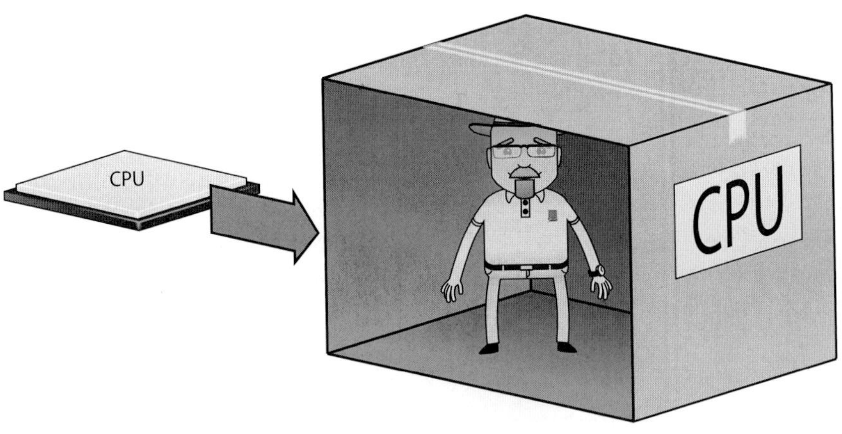

Figure 4-1 Imagine the CPU as a man in a box.

This guy is potentially very useful to us, but there's a catch—he lives closed up in a tiny box. Before he can work with us, we must come up with a way to exchange information with him (see Figure 4-2).

Imagine that we install a set of 16 light bulbs, 8 inside his box and 8 outside his box. Each of the 8 light bulbs inside the box connects to one of the 8 bulbs outside the box to form a pair. Each pair of light bulbs is always either on or off. You can control the 8 pairs of bulbs by using a set of 8 switches outside the box, and the Man in the Box can also control them by using an identical set of 8 switches inside the box. This light-bulb communication device is called the *external data bus (EDB)*.

Figure 4-3 shows a cutaway view of the external data bus. When either you or the Man in the Box flips a switch on, *both* light bulbs go on, and the switch on the other side is also flipped to the on position. If you or the Man in the Box turns a switch off, the light bulbs on both sides are turned off, along with the other switch for that pair.

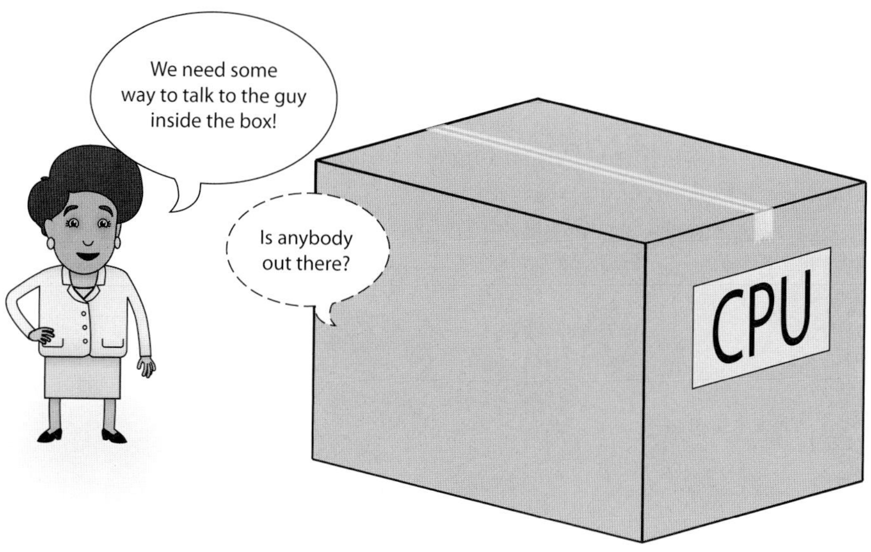

Figure 4-2 How do we talk to the Man in the Box?

Can you see how this works? By creating on/off patterns with the light bulbs that represent different pieces of data or commands, you can send that information to the Man in the Box, and he can send information back in the same way—*assuming that you agree ahead of time on what the different patterns of lights mean.* To accomplish this, you need some sort of codebook that assigns meanings to the many patterns of lights that the EDB might display. Keep this thought in mind while we push the analogy a bit more.

Before going any further, make sure you're clear on the fact that this is an analogy, not reality. There really is an EDB, but you won't see any light bulbs or switches on the CPU.

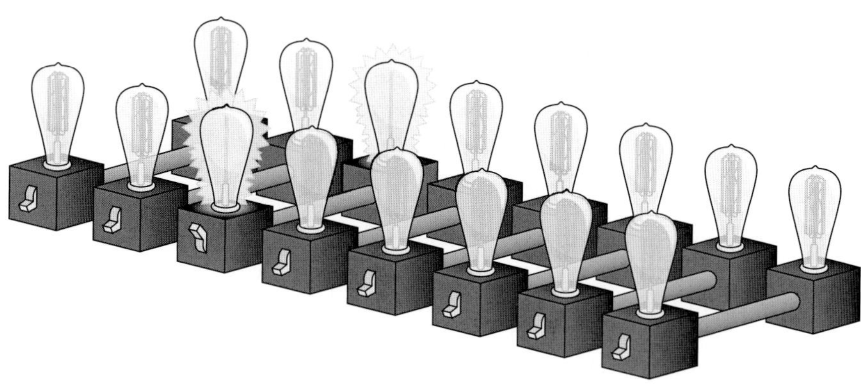

Figure 4-3 Cutaway of the external data bus—note that one light bulb pair is on.

You can, however, see little wires sticking out of many CPUs (see Figure 4-4). If you apply voltage to one of these wires, you in essence flip the switch. Get the idea? So if that wire had voltage, and if a tiny light bulb were attached to the wire, that light bulb would glow, would it not? By the same token, if the wire had no power, the light bulb would not glow. That is why the switch-and-light-bulb analogy may help you picture these little wires constantly flashing on and off.

Figure 4-4 Close-up of the underside of a CPU

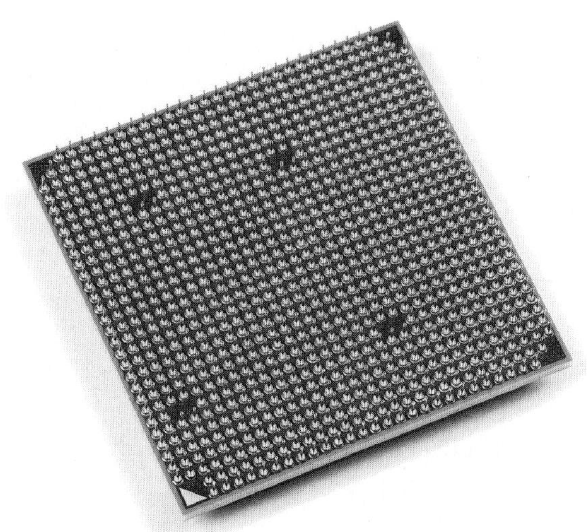

Now that the EDB enables you to communicate with the Man in the Box, you need to see how it works by placing voltages on the wires. This brings up a naming problem. It's a hassle to say something like "on-off-on-off-on-on-off-off" when talking about which wires have voltage. Rather than saying that one of the EDB wires is on or off, use the number 1 to represent on and the number 0 to represent off (see Figure 4-5). That way, instead of describing the state of the lights as "on-off-on-off-on-on-off-off," I can instead describe them by writing "10101100."

In computers, wires repeatedly turn on and off. As a result, we can use this "1 and 0," or *binary*, system to describe the state of these wires at any given moment. (See, and you just thought computer geeks spoke in binary to confuse normal people. Ha!) There's much more to binary numbering in computing, but this is a great place to start.

Registers

The Man in the Box provides good insight into the workspace inside a CPU. The EDB gives you a way to communicate with the Man in the Box so you can give him work to do. But to do this work, he needs a worktable; in fact, he needs at least four worktables. Each of these four worktables has 16 light bulbs. These light bulbs are not in pairs; they're just 16 light bulbs lined up straight across the table. Each light bulb is controlled by a single switch, operated only by the Man in the Box. By creating on/off patterns like

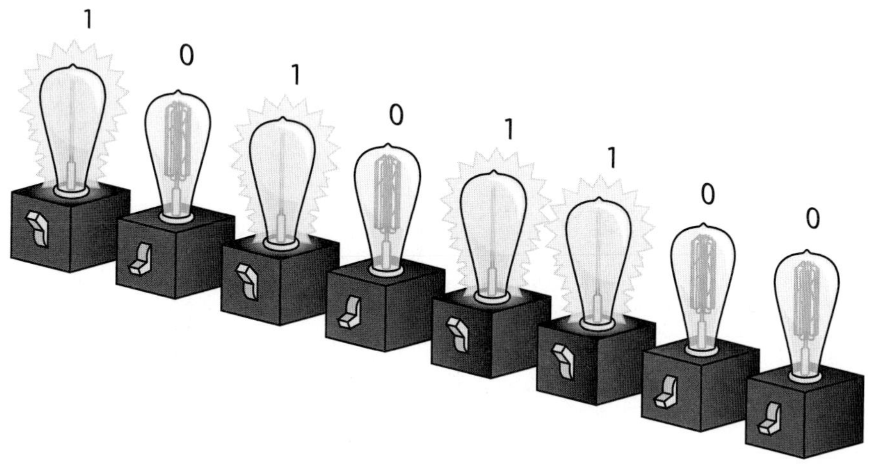

Figure 4-5 Here "1" means on, "0" means off.

the ones on the EDB, the Man in the Box can use these four sets of light bulbs to work math problems. In a real computer, these worktables are called *registers* (see Figure 4-6) and store internal commands and data.

Registers provide the Man in the Box with a workplace for the problems you give him. All CPUs contain a large number of registers, but for the moment let's concentrate on the four most common ones: the *general-purpose registers*. Intel named them AX, BX, CX, and DX.

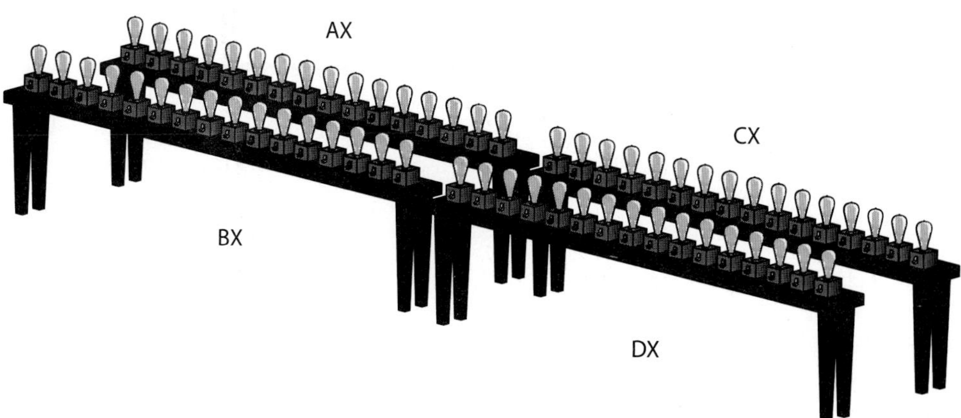

Figure 4-6 The four general-purpose registers

NOTE The 8088 was the first CPU to use the four AX–DX general-purpose registers, and they still exist in even the latest CPUs. (But they have a lot more light bulbs!) In 32-bit processors, the registers add an E for extended, so EAX, EBX, and so on. The 64-bit registers get an R for . . . I don't know, thus RAX, RBX, and so on.

Great! We're just about ready to put the Man in the Box to work, but before you close the lid on the box, you must give the Man one more tool. Remember the codebook I mentioned earlier? Let's make one to enable us to communicate with him. Figure 4-7 shows the codebook we'll use. We'll give one copy to him and make a second for us.

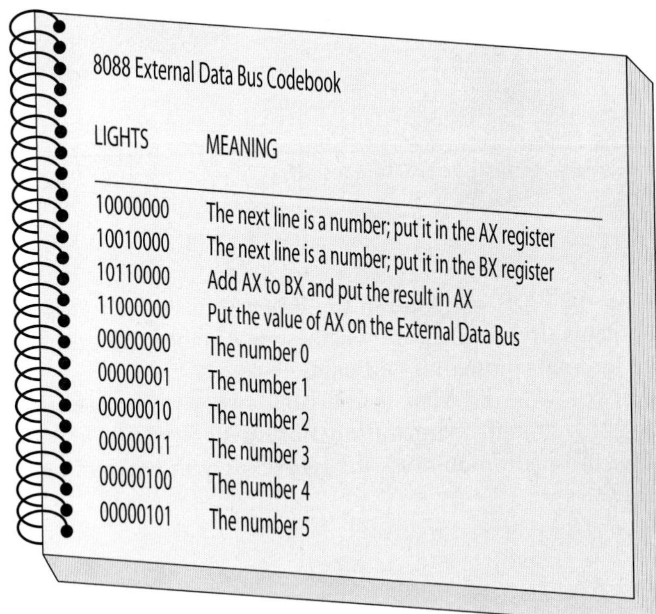
8088 External Data Bus Codebook
LIGHTS
MEANING
10000000 The next line is a number; put it in the AX register
10010000 The next line is a number; put it in the BX register
10110000 Add AX to BX and put the result in AX
11000000 Put the value of AX on the External Data Bus
00000000 The number 0
00000001 The number 1
00000010 The number 2
00000011 The number 3
00000100 The number 4
00000101 The number 5

Figure 4-7 CPU codebook

In this codebook, for example, 10000111 means *Move the number 7 into the AX register.* These commands are called the microprocessor's *machine language*. The commands listed in the figure are not actual commands; as you've probably guessed, I've simplified dramatically. The Intel 8088 CPU actually used commands very similar to these, plus a few hundred others.

Here are some examples of real machine language for the Intel 8088:

10111010	The next line of code is a number. Put that number into the DX register.
01000001	Add 1 to the number already in the CX register.
00111100	Compare the value in the AX register with the next line of code.

By placing machine language commands—called *lines of code*—onto the EDB one at a time, you can instruct the Man in the Box to do specific tasks. All of the machine language commands that the CPU understands make up the CPU's *instruction set.*

So here is the CPU so far: the Man in the Box can communicate with the outside world via the EDB; he has four registers he can use to work on the problems you give him; and he has a codebook—the instruction set—so he can understand the different patterns (machine language commands) on the EDB (see Figure 4-8).

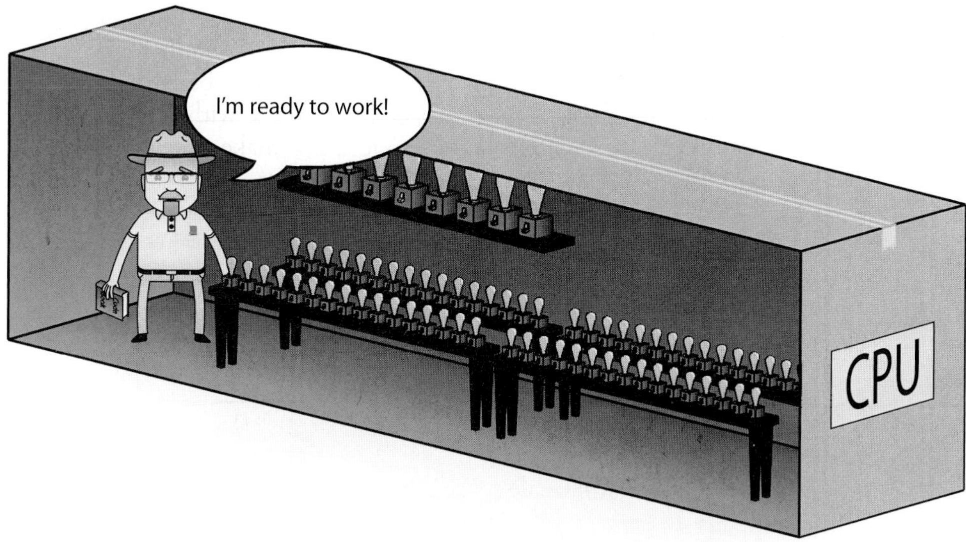

Figure 4-8 The CPU so far

Clock

Okay, so you're ready to put the Man in the Box to work. You can send the first command by lighting up wires on the EDB. How does he know when you've finished setting up the wires and it's time to act?

Have you ever seen one of those old-time manual calculators with the big crank on one side? To add two numbers, you pressed a number key, the + key, and another number key, but then to make the calculator do the calculation and give you the answer, you had to pull down the crank. That was the signal that you had finished entering data and instructions and were ready for the calculator to give you an answer.

A CPU also has a type of crank. To return to the Man in the Box, imagine there's a bell inside the box activated by a button on the outside of the box. Each time you press the button to sound the bell, the Man in the Box reads the next set of lights on the EDB. Of course, a real computer doesn't use a bell. The bell on a real CPU is a special wire called the *clock wire* (most diagrams label the clock wire CLK). A charge on the CLK wire tells the CPU that another piece of information is waiting to be processed (see Figure 4-9).

For the CPU to process a command placed on the EDB, a certain minimum voltage must be applied to the CLK wire. A single charge to the CLK wire is called a *clock cycle*. Actually, the CPU requires at least two clock cycles to act on a command, and usually

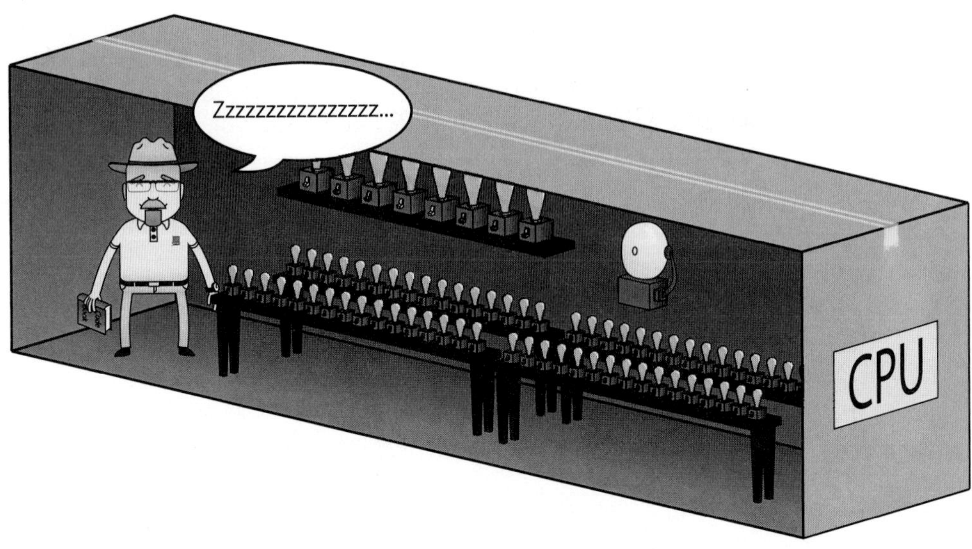

Figure 4-9 The CPU does nothing until activated by the clock.

more. Using the manual calculator analogy, you need to pull the crank at least twice before anything happens. In fact, a CPU may require hundreds of clock cycles to process some commands (see Figure 4-10).

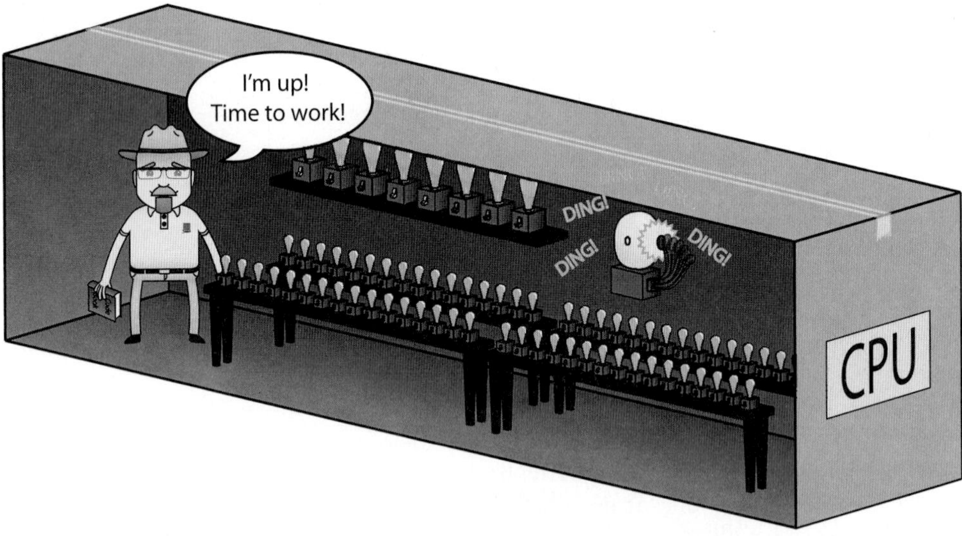

Figure 4-10 The CPU often needs more than one clock cycle to get a result.

The maximum number of clock cycles that a CPU can handle in a given period of time is referred to as its *clock speed*. The clock speed is the fastest speed at which a CPU

can operate, determined by the CPU manufacturer. The Intel 8088 processor had a clock speed of 4.77 MHz (4.77 million cycles per second), extremely slow by modern standards, but still a pretty big number compared to using a pencil and paper. CPUs today run at speeds in excess of 3 GHz (3 billion cycles per second). You'll see these "hertz" terms a lot in this chapter, so here's what they mean:

1 hertz (1 Hz) = 1 cycle per second

1 megahertz (1 MHz) = 1 million cycles per second

1 gigahertz (1 GHz) = 1 billion cycles per second

A CPU's clock speed is its *maximum* speed, not the speed at which it *must* run. A CPU can run at any speed, as long as that speed does not exceed its clock speed. Manufacturers used to print the CPU's clock speed directly onto the CPU, but for the past several years they've used cryptic codes (see Figure 4-11). As the chapter progresses, you'll see why they do this.

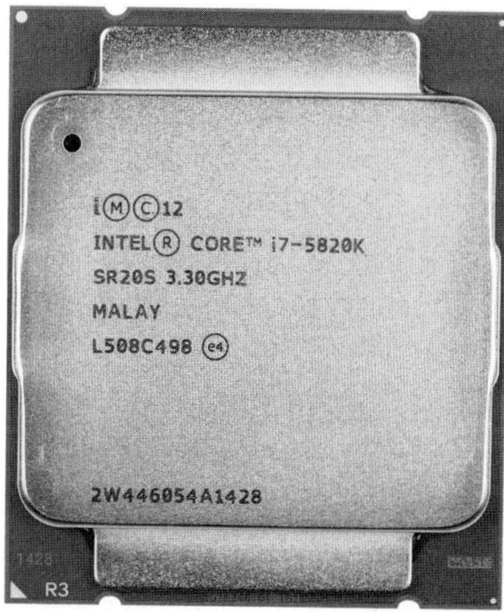

Figure 4-11 Where is the clock speed?

The *system crystal* determines the speed at which a CPU and the rest of the PC operate. The system crystal is usually a quartz oscillator, very similar to the one in a wristwatch, soldered to the motherboard (see Figure 4-12).

NOTE CPU makers sell the exact make and model of CPU at a number of different speeds. All of these CPUs come off of the same assembly lines, so why do they have different speeds? Every CPU comes with subtle differences—flaws, really—in the silicon that makes one CPU run faster than another. The speed difference comes from testing each CPU to see what speed it can handle.

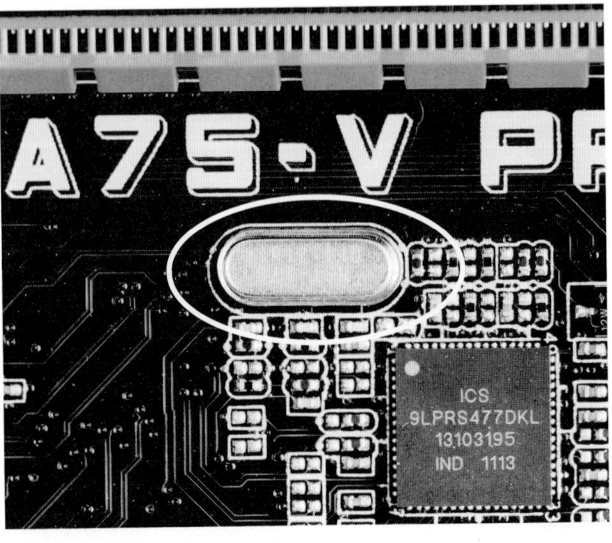

Figure 4-12 One of many types of system crystals

The quartz oscillator sends out an electric pulse at a certain speed, many millions of times per second. This signal goes first to a clock chip that adjusts the pulse, usually increasing the pulse sent by the crystal by some large multiple. (The folks who make motherboards could connect the crystal directly to the CPU's clock wire, but then if you wanted to replace your CPU with a CPU with a different clock speed, you'd need to replace the crystal too.) As long as the computer is turned on, the quartz oscillator, through the clock chip, fires a charge on the CLK wire, in essence pushing the system along.

Visualize the system crystal as a metronome for the CPU. The quartz oscillator repeatedly fires a charge on the CLK wire, setting the beat, if you will, for the CPU's activities. If the system crystal sets a beat slower than the CPU's clock speed, the CPU will work just fine, though at the slower speed of the system crystal. If the system crystal forces the CPU to run faster than its clock speed, it can overheat and stop working. Before you install a CPU into a system, you must make sure that the crystal and clock chip send out the correct clock pulse for that particular CPU. In the old days, this required very careful adjustments. With today's systems, the motherboard talks to the CPU. The CPU tells the motherboard the clock speed it needs, and the clock chip automatically adjusts for the CPU, making this process now invisible.

NOTE Aggressive users sometimes intentionally overclock CPUs by telling the clock chip to multiply the pulse faster than the CPU's designed speed. They do this to make slower (cheaper) CPUs run faster and to get more performance in demanding programs. See the "Overclocking" section, later in this chapter.

Back to the External Data Bus

One more reality check. We've been talking about tables with racks of light bulbs, but of course real CPU registers don't use light bulbs to represent on/1 and off/0. Registers are tiny storage areas on the CPU made up of microscopic semiconductor circuits that hold charges. It's just easier to imagine a light bulb lit up to represent a circuit holding a charge; when the light bulb is off, there is no charge.

Figure 4-13 is a diagram of an 8088 CPU, showing the wires that comprise the external data bus and the single clock wire. Because the registers are inside the CPU, you can't see them in this figure.

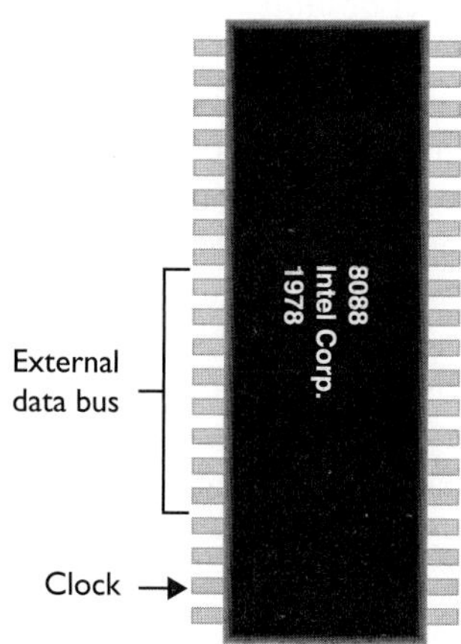

Figure 4-13 Diagram of an Intel 8088 showing the external data bus and clock wires

Now that you have learned what components are involved in the process, try the following simple exercise to see how the process works. In this example, you tell the CPU to add 2 + 3. To do this, you must send a series of commands to the CPU; the CPU will act on each command, eventually giving you an answer. Refer to the codebook in Figure 4-7 to translate the instructions you're giving the Man in the Box into binary commands.

Did you try it? Here's how it works:

1. Place 10000000 on the external data bus (EDB).
2. Place 00000010 on the EDB.
3. Place 10010000 on the EDB.
4. Place 00000011 on the EDB.
5. Place 10110000 on the EDB.
6. Place 11000000 on the EDB.

When you finish step 6, the value on the EDB will be 00000101, the decimal number 5 written in binary.

Congrats! You just added 2 + 3 by using individual commands from the codebook. This set of commands is known as a *program*, which is a series of commands sent to a

CPU in a specific order for the CPU to perform work. Each discrete setting of the EDB is a line of code. This program, therefore, has six lines of code.

Memory

Now that you've seen how the CPU executes program code, let's work backward in the process for a moment and think about how the program code gets to the external data bus. The program itself is stored on the hard drive. In theory, you could build a computer that sends data from the hard drive directly to the CPU, but there's a problem—the hard drive is too slow. Even the ancient 8088, with its clock speed of 4.77 MHz, could conceivably process several million lines of code every second. Modern CPUs crank out billions of lines every second. Hard drives simply can't give the data to the CPU at a fast enough speed.

Computers need some other device that takes copies of programs from the hard drive and then sends them, one line at a time, to the CPU quickly enough to keep up with its demands. Because each line of code is nothing more than a pattern of eight ones and zeros, any device that can store ones and zeros eight-across will do. Devices that in any way hold ones and zeros that the CPU accesses are known generically as *memory*.

Many types of devices store ones and zeros perfectly well—technically even a piece of paper counts as memory—but computers need memory that does more than just store groups of eight ones and zeros. Consider this pretend program:

1. Put 2 in the AX register.
2. Put 5 in the BX register.
3. If AX is greater than BX, run line 4; otherwise, go to line 6.
4. Add 1 to the value in AX.
5. Go back to line 1.
6. Put the value of AX on the EDB.

This program has an IF statement, also called a *branch* by CPU makers. The CPU needs a way to address each line of this memory—a way for the CPU to say to the memory, "Give me the next line of code" or "Give me line 6." Addressing memory takes care of another problem: the memory must store not only programs, but also the result of the programs. If the CPU adds 2 + 3 and gets 5, the memory needs to store that 5 in such a way that other programs may later read that 5, or possibly even store that 5 on a hard drive. By addressing each line of memory, other programs will know where to find the data.

Memory and RAM

Memory must store not only programs, but also data. The CPU needs to be able to read and write to this storage medium. Additionally, this system must enable the CPU to jump to *any* line of stored code as easily as to any other line of code. All of this must be done at or at least near the clock speed of the CPU. Fortunately, this magical device has existed for many years: *random access memory (RAM)*. Chapter 5 develops the concept of

RAM in detail, so for now let's look at RAM as an electronic spreadsheet, like one you can generate in Microsoft Excel (see Figure 4-14). Each cell in this spreadsheet can store only a one or a zero. Each cell is called a *bit*. Each row in the spreadsheet is 8 bits across to match the EDB of the 8088. Each row of 8 bits is called a *byte*. In PCs, RAM transfers and stores data to and from the CPU in byte-sized chunks. RAM is therefore arranged in byte-sized rows. Here are the terms used to talk about quantities of bits:

- Any individual 1 or 0 = a bit
- 4 bits = a nibble
- 8 bits = a byte
- 16 bits = a word
- 32 bits = a double word
- 64 bits = a paragraph or quad word

Figure 4-14 RAM as a spreadsheet

1	0	0	0	0	0	1	1
0	1	0	0	0	0	0	0
0	0	0	0	1	1	0	1
0	1	0	1	0	0	0	0
0	0	0	0	0	0	0	1
0	1	0	1	1	0	1	0
0	0	1	1	1	1	0	0
0	0	0	0	1	0	0	1
1	1	1	0	0	0	0	0
0	0	1	0	1	1	1	0
1	0	0	0	0	0	0	0
1	0	1	0	1	0	1	0

The number of bytes of RAM varies from PC to PC. In earlier PCs, from around 1980 to 1990, the typical system would have only a few hundred thousand bytes of RAM. Today's systems often have billions of bytes of RAM.

Let's stop here for a quick reality check. Electronically, RAM looks like a spreadsheet, but real RAM is made of groups of semiconductor chips soldered onto small cards that snap into your computer (see Figure 4-15). In Chapter 5, you'll see how these groups of chips actually make themselves look like a spreadsheet. For now, don't worry about real RAM and just stick with the spreadsheet idea.

Figure 4-15 Typical RAM

The CPU accesses any one row of RAM as easily and as fast as any other row, which explains the "random access" part of RAM. Not only is RAM randomly accessible, it's also fast. By storing programs on RAM, the CPU can access and run them very quickly. RAM also stores any data that the CPU actively uses.

Computers use *dynamic RAM (DRAM)* for the main system memory. DRAM needs both a constant electrical charge and a periodic refresh of the circuits; otherwise, it loses data—that's what makes it dynamic rather than static in content. The refresh can cause some delays, because the CPU has to wait for the refresh to happen, but modern CPU manufacturers have clever ways to get by this issue, as you'll see when you read about modern processor technology later in this chapter.

Don't confuse RAM with mass storage devices such as hard drives and flash drives. You use hard drives and flash drives to store programs and data permanently. Chapters 9–11 discuss permanent storage in intimate detail.

Address Bus

So far, the entire PC consists of only a CPU and RAM. But the CPU and the RAM need some connection so they can talk to each other. To do so, extend the external data bus from the CPU so it can talk to the RAM (see Figure 4-16).

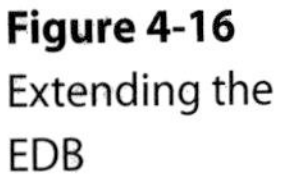

Figure 4-16 Extending the EDB

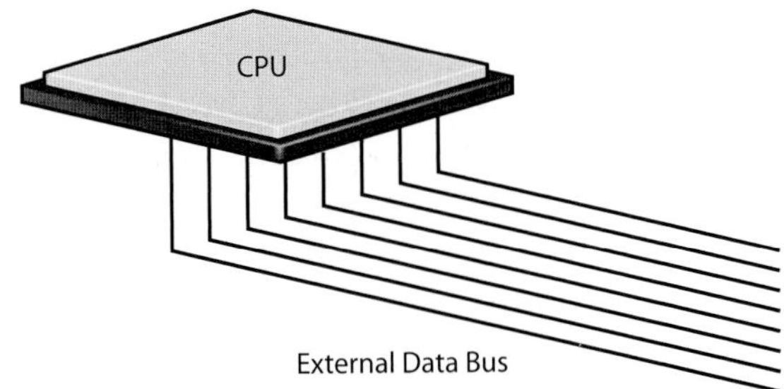

Wait a minute. This is not a matter of just plugging the RAM into the EDB wires! RAM is a spreadsheet with thousands and thousands of discrete rows, and you need to look at the contents of only one row of the spreadsheet at a time, right? So how do you connect the RAM to the EDB in such a way that the CPU can see any one given row but still give the CPU the capability to look at *any* row in RAM? We need some type of chip between the RAM and the CPU to make the connection. The CPU needs to be able to say which row of RAM it wants, and the chip should handle the mechanics of retrieving that row of data from the RAM and putting it on the EDB. Wouldn't you know I just happen to have such a chip? This chip comes with many names, but for right now just call it the *memory controller chip (MCC)*.

The MCC contains special circuitry so it can grab the contents of any single line of RAM and place that data or command on the EDB. This in turn enables the CPU to act on that code (see Figure 4-17).

Once the MCC is in place to grab any discrete byte of RAM, the CPU needs to be able to tell the MCC which line of code it needs. The CPU therefore gains a second set

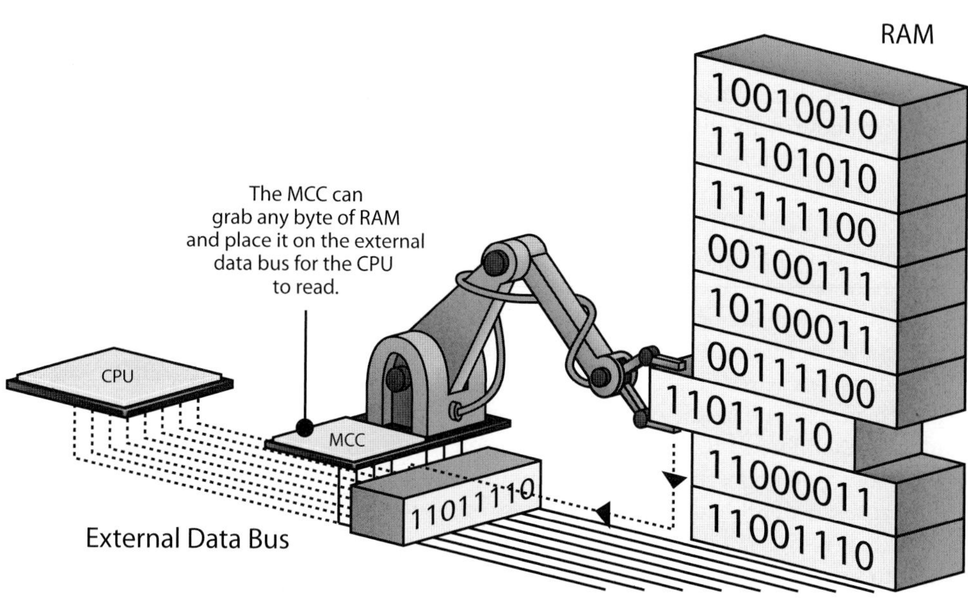

Figure 4-17 The MCC grabs a byte of RAM.

of wires, called the *address bus*, with which it can communicate with the MCC. Different CPUs have different numbers of wires (which, you will soon see, is very significant). The 8088 had 20 wires in its address bus (see Figure 4-18).

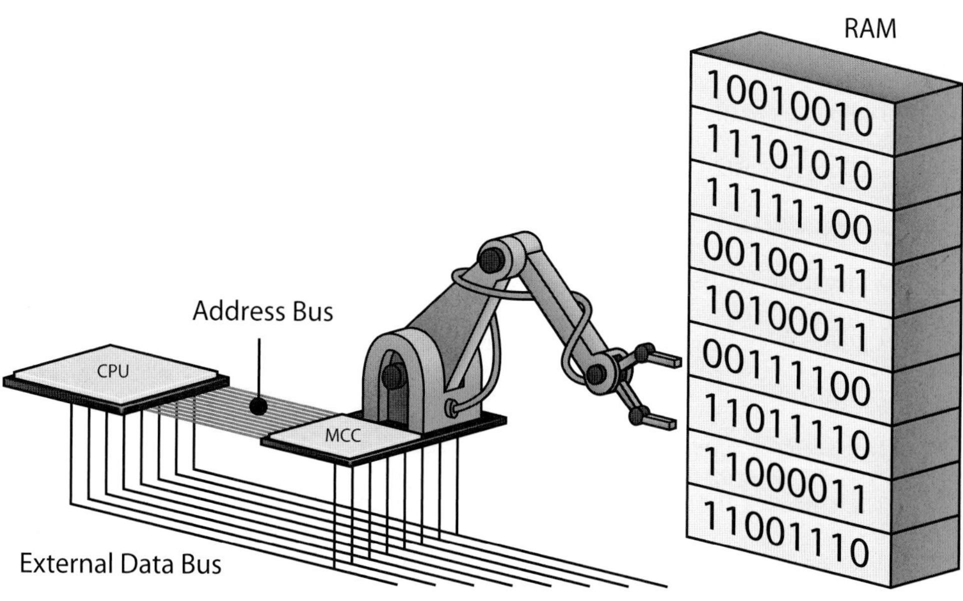

Figure 4-18 Address bus

By turning the address bus wires on and off in different patterns, the CPU tells the MCC which line of RAM it wants at any given moment. Every different pattern of ones and zeros on these 20 wires points to one byte of RAM. There are two big questions here. First, how many different patterns of on-and-off wires can exist with 20 wires? And second, which pattern goes to which row of RAM?

How Many Patterns?

Mathematics can answer the first question. Each wire in the address bus exists in only one of two states: on or off. If the address bus consisted of only one wire, that wire would at any given moment be either on or off. Mathematically, that gives you (pull out your old pre-algebra books) $2^1 = 2$ different combinations. If you have two address bus wires, the address bus wires create $2^2 = 4$ different combinations. If you have 20 wires, you would have 2^{20} (or 1,048,576) combinations. Because each pattern points to one line of code and each line of RAM is one byte, if you know the number of wires in the CPU's address bus, you know the maximum amount of RAM that a particular CPU can handle.

Because the 8088 had a 20-wire address bus, the most RAM it could handle was 2^{20}, or 1,048,576, bytes. The 8088, therefore, had an *address space* of 1,048,576 bytes. This is not to say that every computer with an 8088 CPU had 1,048,576 bytes of RAM. Far from it! The original IBM PC only had a measly 64 kilobytes—but that was considered plenty back in the Dark Ages of Computing in the early 1980s.

Okay, so you know that the 8088 had 20 address wires and a total address space of 1,048,576 bytes. Although this is accurate, no one uses such an exact term to discuss the address space of the 8088. Instead, you say that the 8088 had one *megabyte* (1 MB) of address space.

What's a "mega"? Well, let's get some terminology down. Dealing with computers means constantly dealing with the number of patterns a set of wires can handle. Certain powers of 2 have names used a lot in computing. The following list explains.

1 kilo = 2^{10} = 1024 (abbreviated as "K")

1 kilobyte = 1024 bytes (abbreviated as "KB")

1 mega = 2^{20} = 1,048,576 (abbreviated as "M")

1 megabyte = 1,048,576 bytes (abbreviated as "MB")

1 giga = 2^{30} = 1,073,741,824 (abbreviated as "G")

1 gigabyte = 1,073,741,824 bytes (abbreviated as "GB")

1 tera = 2^{40} = 1,099,511,627,776 (abbreviated as "T")

1 terabyte = 1,099,511,627,776 bytes (abbreviated as "TB")

1 peta = 2^{50} = 1,125,899,906,842,624 (abbreviated as "P")

1 petabyte = 1,125,899,906,842,624 bytes (abbreviated as "PB")

1 kilo is *not* equal to 1000 (one thousand)

1 mega is *not* equal to 1,000,000 (one million)

1 giga is *not* equal to 1,000,000,000 (one billion)

1 tera is *not* equal to 1,000,000,000,000 (one trillion)

1 peta is *not* equal to 1,000,000,000,000,000 (one quadrillion)

(But they are pretty close!)

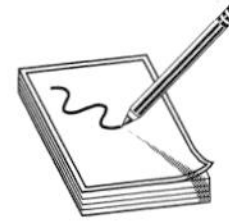

NOTE Of course, 1 kilo is equal to 1000 when you talk in terms of the metric system. It also means 1000 when you talk about the clock speed of a chip, so 1 KHz is equal to 1000 Hz. When you talk storage capacity, though, the binary numbers kick in, making 1 KB = 1024 bytes. Got it? This same bizarre dual meaning applies all the way up the food chain, so 1 MHz is 1,000,000 Hz, but 1 MB is 1,048,576 bytes; 1 GHz is 1 billion Hz, but 1 GB is 1,073,741,824 bytes; and so on.

Some techs and standards bodies use slightly different prefixes for the metric and binary numbering systems. In such a system, 1 K is a kilo, and always means 1000. So 1 kilobyte (KB) is 1000 bytes. That's the metric value. To go binary, you'd use kibibytes (KiB). 1 KiB = 1024 bytes. The industry standard is the one outlined in this chapter, however, and that's what you'll see on the CompTIA A+ exams.

Which Pattern Goes to Which Row?

The second question is a little harder: "Which pattern goes to which row of RAM?" To understand this, let's take a moment to discuss binary counting. In binary, only two numbers exist, 0 and 1, which makes binary a handy way to work with wires that turn on and off. Let's try to count in binary: 0, 1...what's next? It's not 2—you can only use zeros and ones. The next number after 1 is 10! Now let's count in binary to 1000: 0, 1, 10, 11, 100, 101, 110, 111, 1000. Try counting to 10000. Don't worry; it hardly takes any time at all.

Super; you now count in binary as well as any math professor. Let's add to the concept. Stop thinking about binary for just a moment and think about good old base 10 (regular numbers). If you have the number 365, can you put zeros in front of the 365, like this: 000365? Sure you can—it doesn't change the value at all. The same thing is true in binary. Putting zeros in front of a value doesn't change a thing! Let's count again to 1000 in binary. In this case, add enough zeros to make 20 places:

00000000000000000000

00000000000000000001

00000000000000000010

00000000000000000011

00000000000000000100

00000000000000000101

00000000000000000110

00000000000000000111

00000000000000001000

Hey, wouldn't this be a great way to represent each line of RAM on the address bus? The CPU identifies the first byte of RAM on the address bus with 00000000000000000000. The CPU identifies the last RAM row with 11111111111111111111. When the CPU turns off all of the address bus wires, it wants the first line of RAM; when it turns on all of the wires, it wants the 1,048,576th line of RAM. Obviously, the address bus also addresses all of the rows of RAM in between. So, by lighting up different patterns of ones and zeros on the address bus, the CPU can access any row of RAM it needs.

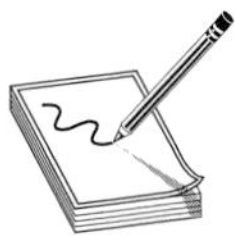

NOTE Bits and bytes are abbreviated differently. Bits get a lowercase b, whereas bytes get a capital B. So, for example, 4 Kb is four kilobits, but 4 KB is four kilobytes. The big-B little-b standard applies all the way up the food chain, so 2 Mb = 2 megabits; 2 MB = 2 megabytes; 4 Gb = 4 gigabits; 4 GB = 4 gigabytes; and so on.

901

Modern CPUs

CPU manufacturers have achieved stunning progress with microprocessors since the days of the Intel 8088, and the rate of change doesn't show any signs of slowing. At the core, though, today's CPUs function similarly to the processors of your forefathers. The arithmetic logic unit (ALU)—that's the Man in the Box—still crunches numbers many millions of times per second. CPUs rely on memory to feed them lines of programming as quickly as possible.

This section brings the CPU into the present. We'll first look at models you can buy today, and then we'll turn to essential improvements in technology you should understand.

Developers

When IBM awarded Intel the contract to provide the CPUs for its new IBM PC back in 1980, it established for Intel a virtual monopoly on all PC CPUs. The other

home-computer CPU makers of the time faded away: MOS Technology, Zilog, Motorola—no one could compete directly with Intel. Over time, other competitors have risen to challenge Intel's market-segment share dominance. In particular, a company called Advanced Micro Devices (AMD) began to make clones of Intel CPUs, creating an interesting and rather cutthroat competition with Intel that lasts to this day.

NOTE The ever-growing selection of mobile devices, such as the Apple iPhone and iPad, use a CPU architecture developed by ARM Holdings, called *ARM*. ARM-based processors use a simpler, more energy-efficient design, the reduced instruction set computing (RISC) architecture. They're not as raw powerful as the Intel and AMD complex instruction set computing (CISC) chips, but the savings in cost and battery life make ARM-based processors ideal for mobile devices.

(Note that the clear distinction between RISC and CISC processors has blurred. Each design today borrows features of the other design to increase efficiency.)

ARM Holdings designs ARM CPUs but doesn't manufacture them. Many other companies—most notably, Samsung—license the design and manufacture their own versions. Chapter 25 goes into more detail on ARM processors.

Intel

Intel Corporation thoroughly dominated the personal computer market with its CPUs and motherboard support chips. At nearly every step in the evolution of the PC, Intel has led the way with technological advances and surprising flexibility for such a huge corporation. Intel CPUs—and more specifically, their instruction sets—define the personal computer. Intel currently produces a dozen or so models of CPU for both desktop and portable computers. Most of Intel's desktop and laptop processors are sold under the Core, Pentium, and Celeron brands. Their very low-power portable/smartphone chips are branded Atom; their high-end server chips are called Xeon.

AMD

You can't really talk about CPUs without mentioning Advanced Micro Devices. AMD makes superb CPUs for the PC market and provides competition that keeps Intel on its toes. Like Intel, AMD doesn't just make CPUs, but their CPU business is certainly the part that the public notices. AMD has made CPUs that clone the function of Intel CPUs. If Intel invented the CPU used in the original IBM PC, how could AMD make clone CPUs without getting sued? Chipmakers have a habit of exchanging technologies through cross-license agreements. Way back in 1976, AMD and Intel signed just such an agreement, giving AMD the right to copy certain types of CPUs.

The trouble started with the Intel 8088. Intel needed AMD's help to supply enough CPUs to satisfy IBM's demands. But after a few years, Intel had grown tremendously and no longer wanted AMD to make CPUs. AMD said, "Too bad. See this agreement you signed?" Throughout the 1980s and into the 1990s, AMD made pin-for-pin identical

CPUs that matched the Intel lines of CPUs (see Figure 4-19). You could yank an Intel CPU out of a system and snap in an AMD CPU—no problem!

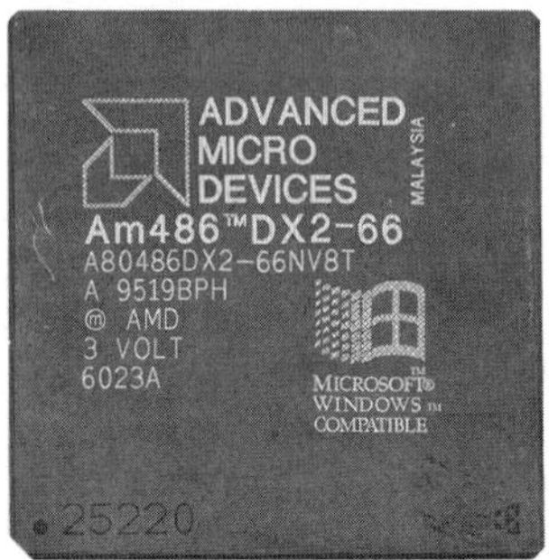

Figure 4-19 Identical Intel and AMD 486 CPUs from the early 1990s

In January 1995, after many years of legal wrangling, Intel and AMD settled and decided to end the licensing agreements. As a result of this settlement, AMD chips are no longer compatible with sockets or motherboards made for Intel CPUs—even though in some cases the chips look similar. Today, if you want to use an AMD CPU, you must purchase a motherboard designed for AMD CPUs. If you want to use an Intel CPU, you must purchase a motherboard designed for Intel CPUs. So you now have a choice: Intel or AMD.

Model Names

Intel and AMD differentiate product lines by using different product names, and these names have changed over the years. For a long time, Intel used *Pentium* for its flagship model, just adding model numbers to show successive generations—Pentium, Pentium II, Pentium III, and so on. AMD used the *Athlon* brand in a similar fashion.

Most discussions on PC CPUs focus on four end-product lines: desktop PC, budget PC, portable PC, and server computers. Table 4-1 displays many of the current product lines and names.

Market	Intel	AMD
Mainstream and enthusiast desktop	Core i7/i5/i3	A-Series, FX
Budget desktop	Pentium, Celeron	Sempron, Athlon
Portable/Mobile	Core i7/i5/i3 (mobile), Core M, Atom	A-Series
Server	Xeon	Opteron

Table 4-1 Current Intel and AMD Product Lines and Names

Both Intel and AMD reuse model names for products aimed at different markets. Yesterday's Pentium brand used to be for the highest end, for example, but now Intel uses the brand for its budget market. The same thing happened to the Athlon brand. To add a little more confusion, the budget CPUs are not the older CPUs still being sold, but low-end versions of current model lines.

Code Names

Both Intel and AMD continue to refine the CPU manufacturing process after releasing a new model, but they try to minimize the number of model names in use. This means that they release CPUs labeled as the same model, but the CPUs inside can be very different from earlier versions of that model. Both companies use *code names* to keep track of different variations within models (see Figure 4-20). As a tech, you need to know both the models and code names to be able to make proper recommendations for your clients. One example illustrates the need: the Intel Core i7.

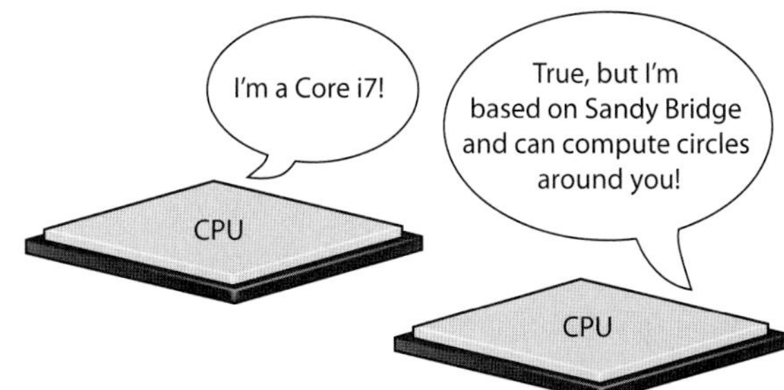

Figure 4-20 Same branding, but different capabilities

Intel released the first Core i7 in the summer of 2008. By spring of 2012, the original microarchitecture—code-named Nehalem—had gone through five variations, none of which worked on motherboards designed for one of the other variations. Plus, in 2011, Intel introduced the Sandy Bridge version of the Core i7 that eventually had two desktop versions and a mobile version, all of which used still other sockets. Just about every year since then has seen a new Core i7 based on improved architectures with different code names such as Ivy Bridge, Haswell, Broadwell, and so on. (And I'm simplifying the variations here.)

NOTE The processor number helps a lot when comparing processors once you decode the meanings. We need to cover more about modern processors before introducing processor numbers. Look for more information in the next section, "Selecting a CPU."

At this point, a lot of new techs throw their hands in the air. How do you keep up? How do you know which CPU will give your customer the best value for his or her money and provide the right computing firepower for his or her needs? Simply put, you need to research efficiently.

Your first stop should be the manufacturers' Web sites. Both companies put out a lot of information on their products.

- www.intel.com
- www.amd.com

You can also find many high-quality tech Web sites devoted to reporting on the latest CPUs. When a client needs an upgrade, surf the Web for recent articles and make comparisons. Because you'll understand the underlying technology from your CompTIA A+ studies, you'll be able to follow the conversations with confidence. Here's a list of some of the sites I use:

- www.arstechnica.com
- www.anandtech.com
- www.tomshardware.com
- www.bit-tech.net

Finally, you can find great, exhaustive articles on all things tech at Wikipedia:

- www.wikipedia.org

NOTE Wikipedia is a user-generated, self-regulated resource. I've found it to be accurate on technical issues the vast majority of the time, but you should always check other references as well. Nicely, most article authors on the site will tell you their sources through footnotes. You can often use the Wikipedia articles as jump-off points for deeper searches.

Desktop versus Mobile

Mobile devices, such as portable computers, have needs that differ from those of desktop computers, notably the need to consume as little electricity as possible. This helps in two ways: extending battery charge and creating less heat.

Both Intel and AMD have engineers devoted to making excellent mobile versions of their CPUs that sport advanced energy-saving features (see Figure 4-21). Intel's SpeedStep technology, for example, enables the CPU to run in very low power mode and scale up automatically if the user demands more power from the CPU. If you're surfing the Web at an airport terminal, the CPU doesn't draw too much power. When you switch to playing an action game, the CPU kicks into gear. Saving energy by making the CPU run more slowly when demand is light is generically called *throttling*.

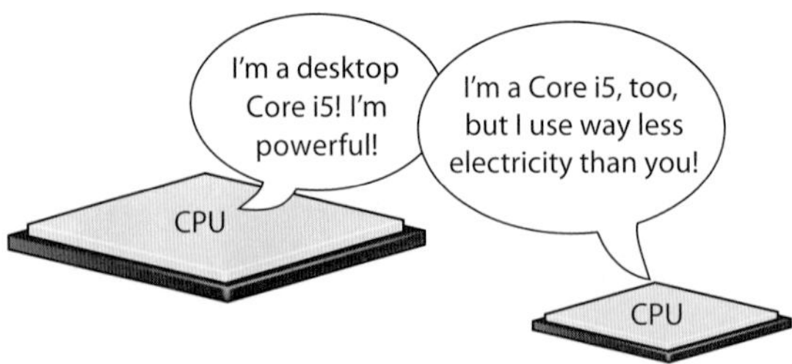

Figure 4-21 Desktop vs. mobile, fight!

Many of the technologies developed for mobile processors have migrated into their more power-hungry desktop siblings, too. That's an added bonus for the planet.

Technology

Although microprocessors today still serve the same function as the venerable 8088—crunching numbers—they do so far more efficiently. Engineers have altered, enhanced, and improved CPUs in a number of ways. This section looks at eight features:

- Clock multipliers
- 64-bit processing
- Virtualization support
- Parallel execution
- Multicore processing
- Integrated memory controller (IMC)
- Integrated graphics processing unit (GPU)
- Security

Clock Multipliers

All modern CPUs run at some multiple of the system clock speed. The system bus on my Core i7 machine, for example, runs at 100 MHz. The clock multiplier goes up to ×35 at full load to support the 3.4 GHz maximum speed. Originally, CPUs ran at the speed of the bus, but engineers early on realized the CPU was the only thing doing any work much of the time. If the engineers could speed up just the internal operations of the CPU and not anything else, they could speed up the whole computing process. Figure 4-22

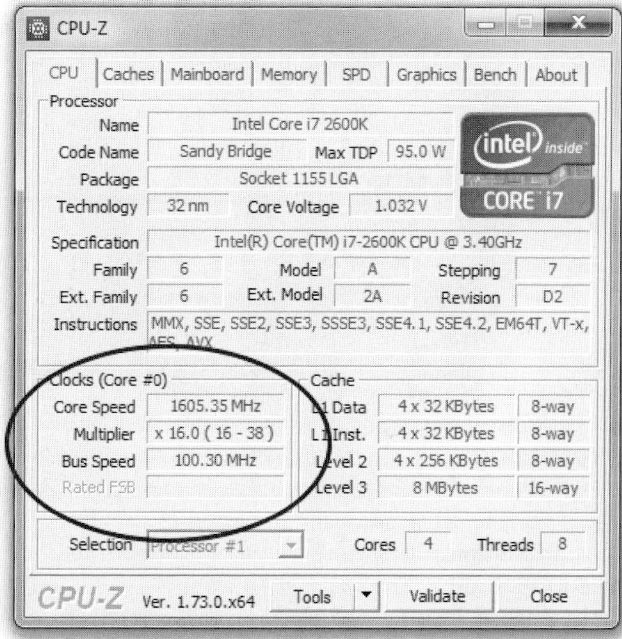

Figure 4-22 CPU-Z showing the clock speed, multiplier, and bus speed of a Core i7 processor hardly breaking a sweat

shows a nifty program called CPU-Z displaying my CPU details. Note that all I'm doing is typing at the moment, so SpeedStep has dropped the clock multiplier down to ×16 and the CPU core speed is only 1600 MHz.

> **Try This!**
>
> ### CPU-Z
>
> Imagine a scenario where you're dumped into an office full of unfamiliar PCs. There's no documentation about the systems at all, so your boss tells you to get cracking and find out as much as possible about each PC ASAP. Try This! Download a copy of the very popular and free CPU-Z utility from www.cpuid.com. CPU-Z gives you every piece of information you'll ever want to know about a CPU. Copy it to a thumb drive, then insert it into a bunch of different computers. (Ask permission, of course!) What kinds of processors do you find in your neighbors' computers? What can you tell about the different capabilities?

The clock speed and the multiplier on early clock-multiplying systems had to be manually configured via jumpers or dual in-line package (DIP) switches on the motherboard (see Figure 4-23). Today's CPUs report to the motherboard through a function called CPUID (CPU identifier), and the speed and multiplier are set automatically. (You can manually override this automatic setup on many motherboards. See "Overclocking," later in this chapter, for details.)

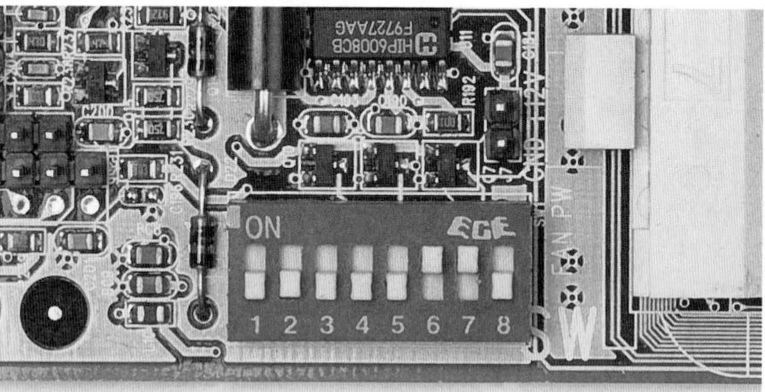

Figure 4-23 DIP switches on a motherboard

64-Bit Processing

Over successive generations of microprocessors, engineers have upgraded many physical features of CPUs. The EDB gradually increased in size, from 8- to 16- to 32- to 64-bits wide. The address bus similarly jumped, going from 20- to 24- to 32-bits wide (where it stayed for a decade).

The technological features changed as well. Engineers added new and improved registers, for example, that used fancy names like multimedia extensions (MMX) and

Streaming SIMD Extensions (SSE). A mighty shift started several years ago and continues to evolve: the move to 64-bit computing.

Most new CPUs support *64-bit processing*, meaning they can run a compatible 64-bit operating system, such as Windows 8.1, and 64-bit applications. They also support 32-bit processing for 32-bit operating systems, such as some Linux distributions, and 32-bit applications. The general-purpose registers also make the move up to 64-bit. The primary benefit to moving to 64-bit computing is that modern systems can support much more than the 4 GB of memory supported with 32-bit processing.

With a 64-bit address bus, CPUs can address 2^{64} bytes of memory, or more precisely, 18,446,744,073,709,551,616 bytes of memory—that's a lot of RAM! This number is so big that gigabytes and terabytes are no longer convenient, so we now go to an exabyte (2^{60}), abbreviated *EB*. A 64-bit address bus can address 16 EB of RAM.

In practical terms, 64-bit computing greatly enhances the performance of programs that work with large files, such as video-editing applications. You'll see a profound improvement moving from 4 GB to 8 GB or 16 GB of RAM with such programs.

x86 The terminology of CPUs can trip up new techs, so here's the scoop. CPUs from the early days can be lumped together as *x*86 CPUs, because they used an instruction set that built upon the earliest Intel CPU architecture. The Intel Core 2 Duo, for example, could run a program written for an ancient 80386 processor that was in fashion in the early 1990s.

x64 When the 64-bit CPUs went mainstream, marketing folks needed some way to mark applications, operating systems, and so on, such that consumers could quickly tell the difference between something compatible with their system or something not compatible. Since you generally cannot return software after you open it, this is a big deal. The marketing folks went with *x*64, and that created a mess.

x86-64 The earlier 32-bit stuff had been marketed as *x*86, not *x*32, so now we have *x*86 (old, 32-bit stuff) vs. *x*64 (new, 64-bit stuff). It's not pretty, but do you get the difference? To make matters even worse, however, *x*64 processors quite happily handle *x*86 code and are, by definition, *x*86 processors too! It's common to marry the two terms and describe current 64-bit CPUs as *x*86-64 processors.

Virtualization Support

Intel and AMD have built in support for running more than one operating system at a time, a process called *virtualization*. Virtualization is very cool and gets its own chapter later in the book (Chapter 18), so I'll skip the details here. The key issue from a CPU standpoint is that virtualization used to work entirely through software. Programmers had to write a ton of code to enable a CPU—which was designed to run one OS at a time—to run more than one OS at the same time. Think about the issues involved. How does the memory get allocated, for example, or how does the CPU know which OS to update when you type something or click an icon? With hardware-based virtualization support, CPUs took a lot of the burden off the programmers and made virtualization a whole lot easier.

Parallel Execution

Modern CPUs can process multiple commands and parts of commands in parallel, which is known as *parallel execution*. Early processors had to do everything in a strict,

linear fashion. The CPUs accomplish this parallelism through multiple pipelines, dedicated caches, and the capability to work with multiple threads or programs at one time. To understand the mighty leap in efficiency gained from parallel execution, you need insight into the processing stages.

Pipelining To get a command from the data bus, do the calculation, and then get the answer back out on the data bus, a CPU takes at least four steps (each of these steps is called a *stage*):

1. **Fetch** Get the data from the EDB.
2. **Decode** Figure out what type of command needs to be executed.
3. **Execute** Perform the calculation.
4. **Write** Send the data back onto the EDB.

Smart, discrete circuits inside the CPU handle each of these stages. In early CPUs, when a command was placed on the data bus, each stage did its job and the CPU handed back the answer before starting the next command, requiring at least four clock cycles to process a command. In every clock cycle, three of the four circuits sat idle. Today, the circuits are organized in a conveyer-belt fashion called a *pipeline*. With pipelining, each stage does its job with each clock-cycle pulse, creating a much more efficient process. The CPU has multiple circuits doing multiple jobs, so let's add pipelining to the Man in the Box analogy. Now, it's *Men* in the Box (see Figure 4-24)!

Pipelines keep every stage of the processor busy on every click of the clock, making a CPU run more efficiently without increasing the clock speed. Note that at this point, the CPU has four stages: fetch, decode, execute, and write—a four-stage pipeline. No CPU ever made has fewer than four stages, but advancements in caching (see "Cache," next) have increased the number of stages over the years. Current CPU pipelines contain many more stages, up to 20 in some cases.

Pipelining isn't perfect. Sometimes a stage hits a complex command that requires more than one clock cycle, forcing the pipeline to stop. Your CPU tries to avoid these stops, or *pipeline stalls*. The decode stage tends to cause the most pipeline stalls; certain commands are complex and therefore harder to decode than other commands. Current processors use multiple decode stages to reduce the chance of pipeline stalls due to complex decoding.

The inside of the CPU is composed of multiple chunks of circuitry to handle the many types of calculations your PC needs to do. For example, one part, the *arithmetic logic unit (ALU)* (or *integer unit*), handles integer math: basic math for numbers with no decimal point. A perfect example of integer math is 2 + 3 = 5. The typical CPU spends most of its work doing integer math. CPUs also have special circuitry to handle complex numbers, called the *floating point unit (FPU)*. With a single pipeline, only the ALU or the FPU worked at any execution stage. Worse yet, floating point calculation often took many, many clock cycles to execute, forcing the CPU to stall the pipeline until the FPU finished executing the complex command (see Figure 4-25). Current CPUs offer multiple pipelines to keep the processing going (see Figure 4-26).

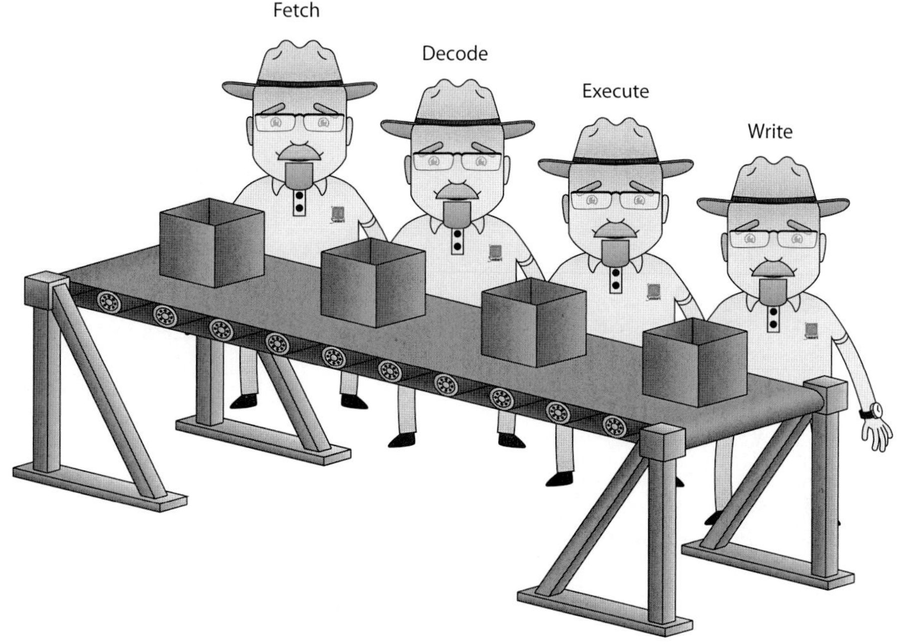

Figure 4-24 Simple pipeline

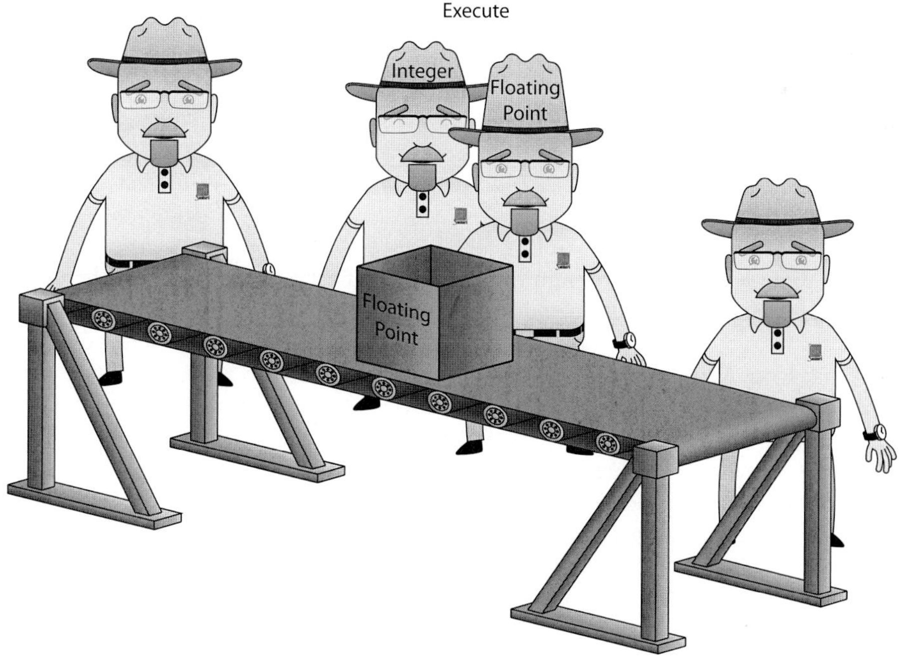

Figure 4-25 Bored integer unit

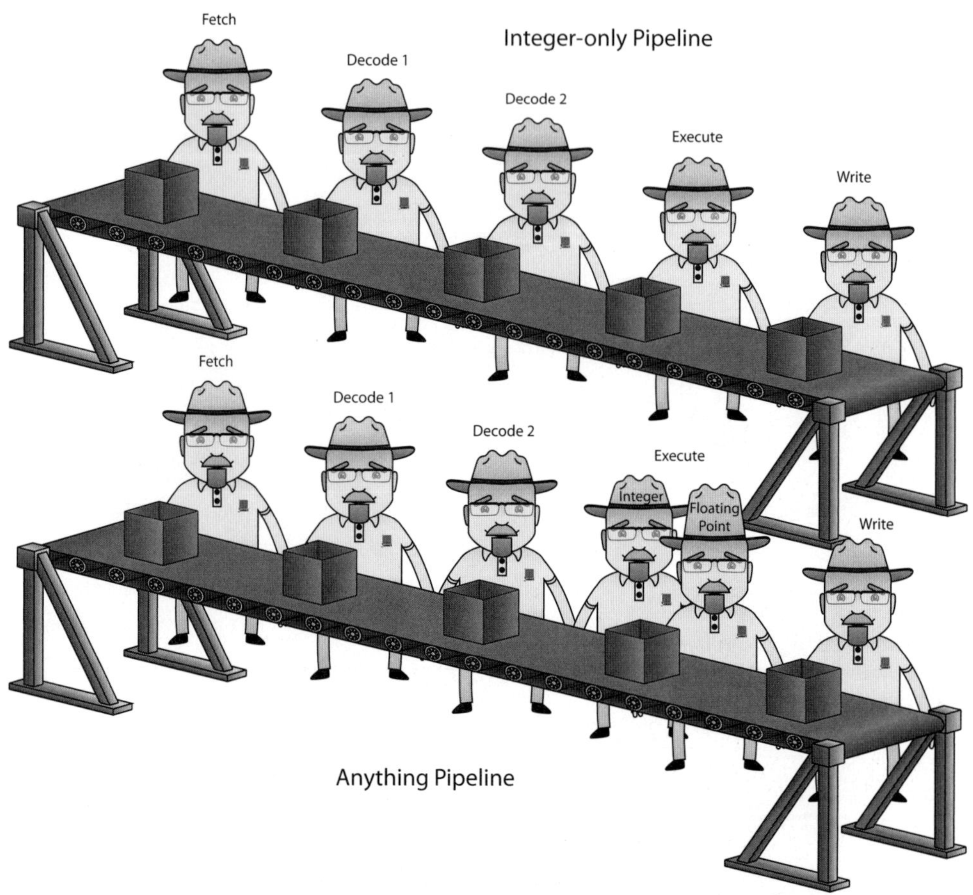

Figure 4-26 Multiple pipelines

Cache When you send a program to the CPU, you actually run lots of little programs all at the same time. Okay, let's be fair here: *you* didn't run all of these little programs—you just started your Web browser or some other program. The moment you double-clicked that icon, Windows started sending many programs to the CPU. Each of these programs breaks down into some number of little pieces, called *threads*, and data. Each thread is a series of instructions designed to do a particular job with the data.

Modern CPUs don't execute instructions sequentially—first doing step 1, then step 2, and so on—but rather process all kinds of instructions. Most applications have certain instructions and data that get reused, sometimes many times.

Pipelining CPUs work fantastically well as long as the pipelines stay filled with instructions. Because the CPU runs faster than the RAM can supply it with code, you'll always get pipeline stalls—called *wait states*—because the RAM can't keep up with the

CPU. To reduce wait states, CPUs come with built-in, very high-speed RAM called *static RAM (SRAM)*. This SRAM preloads as many instructions as possible and keeps copies of already-run instructions and data in case the CPU needs to work on them again (see Figure 4-27). SRAM used in this fashion is called a *cache*.

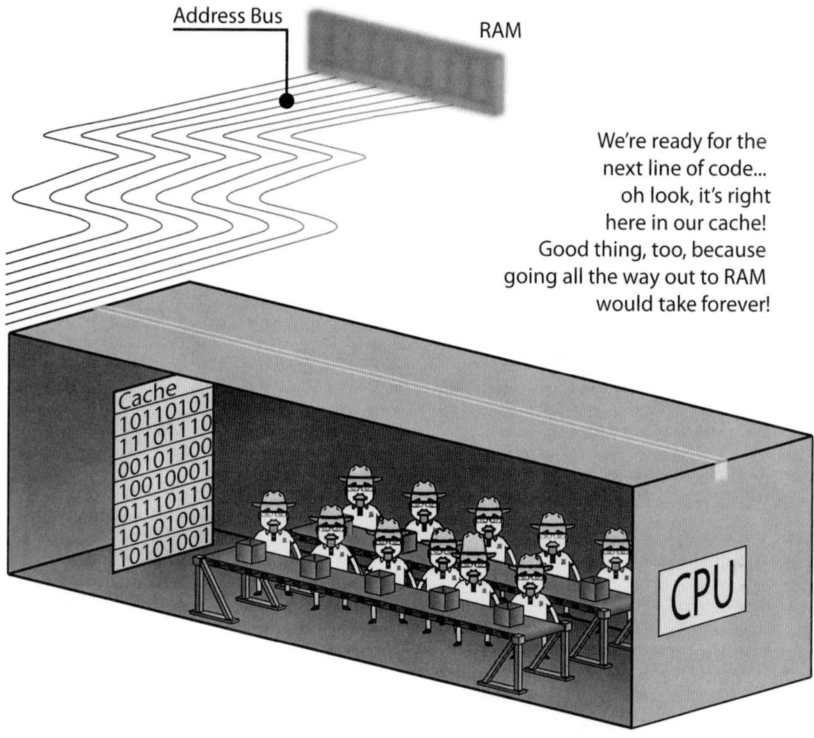

Figure 4-27 SRAM cache

The SRAM cache inside the early CPUs was tiny, only about 16 KB, but it improved performance tremendously. In fact, it helped so much that many motherboard makers began adding a cache directly to the motherboards. These caches were much larger, usually around 128 to 512 KB. When the CPU looked for a line of code, it first went to the built-in cache; if the code wasn't there, the CPU went to the cache on the motherboard. The cache on the CPU was called the *L1 cache* because it was the one the CPU first tried to use. The cache on the motherboard was called the *L2 cache*, not because it was on the motherboard, but because it was the second cache the CPU checked.

Eventually, engineers took this cache concept even further and added the L2 cache onto the CPU package. Most newer CPUs include three caches: an L1, an L2, and an L3 cache (see Figure 4-28).

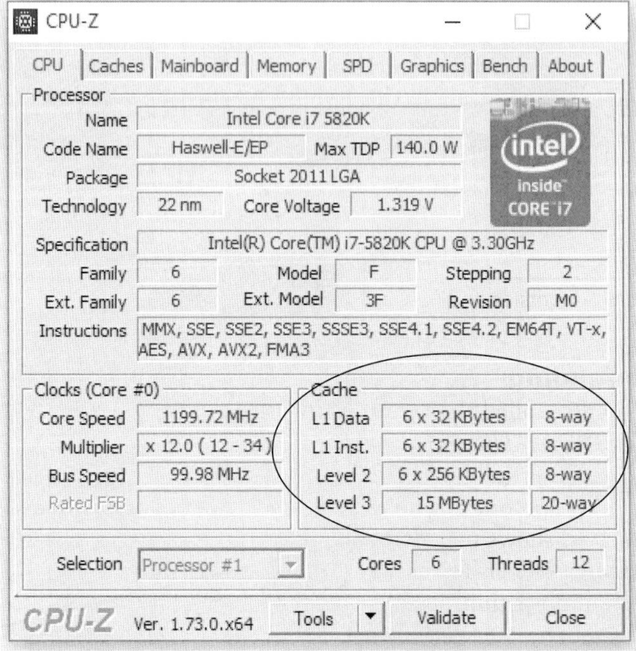

Figure 4-28 CPU-Z displaying the cache information for a Core i7 processor

The L2 cache on the early CPUs that had L2 cache included on the CPU package ran at a slower clock speed than the L1 cache. The L1 cache was in the CPU and thus ran at the speed of the CPU. The L2 cache connected to the CPU via a tiny set of wires on the CPU package. The first L2 caches ran at half the speed of the CPU.

The inclusion of the L2 cache on the chip gave rise to some new terms to describe the connections between the CPU, MCC, RAM, and L2 cache. The address bus and external data bus (connecting the CPU, MCC, and RAM) were lumped into a single term called the *frontside bus*, and the connection between the CPU and the L2 cache became known as the *backside bus* (see Figure 4-29). (These terms don't apply well to current computers, so they have fallen out of use. See the "Integrated Memory Controller" section, later in this chapter.)

NOTE To keep up with faster processors, motherboard manufacturers began to double and even quadruple the throughput of the frontside bus. Techs sometimes refer to these as *double-pumped* and *quad-pumped* frontside buses.

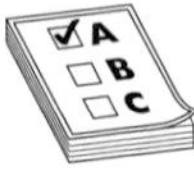

EXAM TIP Typically, the CompTIA A+ exams expect you to know that L1 cache will be the smallest and fastest cache; L2 will be bigger and slower than L1; and L3 will be the biggest and slowest cache. (This is not completely true anymore, with L1 and L2 running the same speed in many CPUs, but it is how it will appear on the exams.)

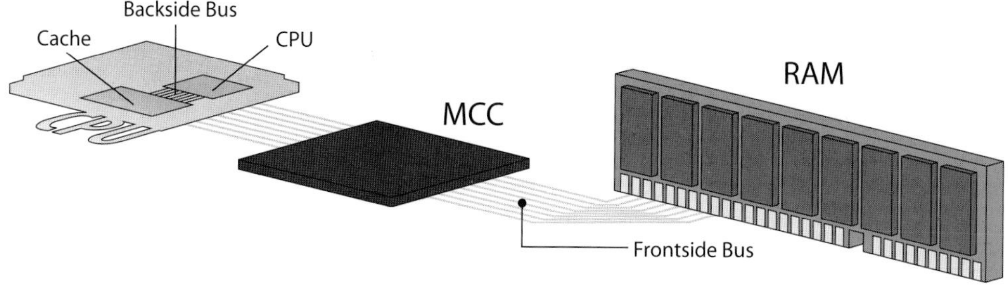

Figure 4-29 Frontside and backside buses

Multithreading At the peak of the single-CPU 32-bit computing days, Intel released a CPU called the Pentium 4 that took parallelism to the next step with Hyper-Threading. *Hyper-Threading* enabled the Pentium 4 to run multiple threads at the same time, what's generically called *simultaneous multithreading*, effectively turning the CPU into two CPUs on one chip—with a catch.

Figure 4-30 shows the Task Manager in an ancient Windows XP computer on a system running a Hyper-Threaded Pentium 4. Note how the CPU box is broken into two groups—Windows thinks this one CPU is two CPUs.

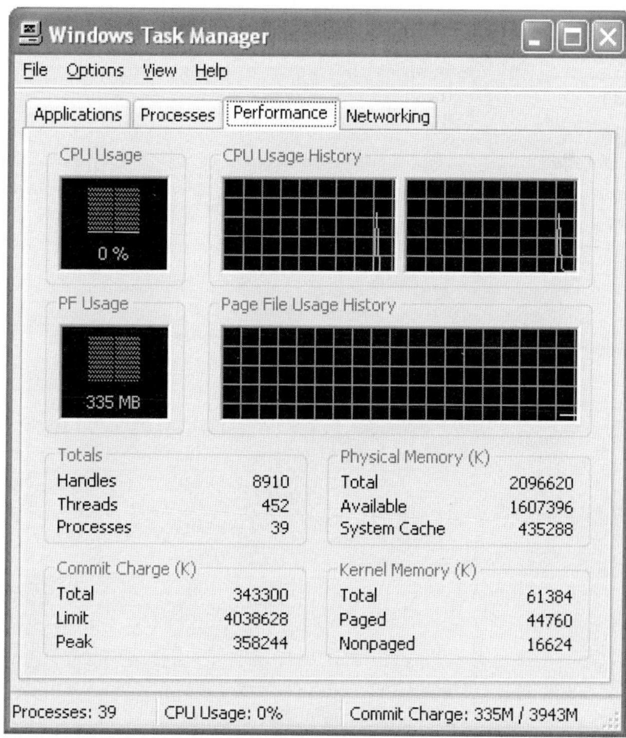

Figure 4-30 Windows Task Manager with the Performance tab displayed for a system running a Hyper-Threaded Pentium 4

Multithreading enhances a CPU's efficiency, but with a couple of limitations. First, the operating system and the application have to be designed to take advantage of the feature. Second, although the CPU simulates the actions of a second processor, it doesn't double the processing power, because the main execution resources are not duplicated.

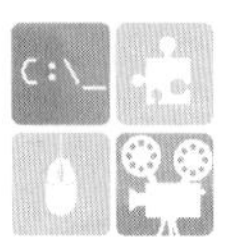

SIM This is a great time to head over to the Chapter 4 Show! and Click! sims to see how to download and use the CPU-Z utility. Head over to totalsem.com/90x and check out the "What is CPU-Z" sim.

Multicore Processing

CPU clock speeds hit a practical limit of roughly 4 GHz around 2002–2003, motivating the CPU makers to find new ways to get more processing power for CPUs. Although Intel and AMD had different opinions about 64-bit CPUs, both decided at virtually the same time to combine two CPUs (or *cores*) into a single chip, creating a *dual-core* architecture. A dual-core CPU has two execution units—two sets of pipelines—but the two sets of pipelines share caches and RAM.

Today, multicore CPUs—with four, six, or eight cores—are common. With each generation of multicore CPU, both Intel and AMD have tinkered with the mixture of how to allocate the cache among the cores. Figure 4-31 shows another screenshot of CPU-Z, this time displaying the cache breakdown of a Haswell-based Core i7.

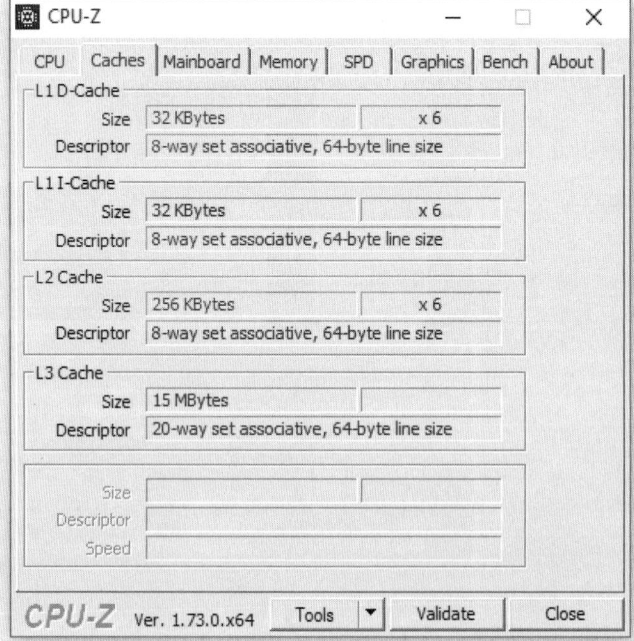

Figure 4-31 CPU-Z showing the cache details of a Haswell Core i7

Figure 4-31 reveals specific details about how this Intel CPU works with the cache. The Core i7 has L1, L2, and L3 caches of 64 KB, 256 KB, and 15 MB, respectively. (The L1 cache divides into 32 KB to handle data—the *D-Cache*—and another 32 KB for instructions—the *I-Cache*.) Each core has dedicated L1 and L2 caches. (You can tell this by the ×6 to the right of the capacity listing.) All six cores share the giant L3 cache. That pool of memory enables the cores to communicate and work together without having to access the radically slower main system RAM as much. CPU manufacturers engineered the cores in multicore CPUs to divide up work independently of the OS, known as *multicore processing*. This differs from Hyper-Threading, where the OS and applications have to be written specifically to handle the multiple threads. Note that even with multicore processors, applications have to be modified or optimized for this parallelism to have a huge impact on performance.

Integrated Memory Controller

Almost all current microprocessors have an *integrated memory controller (IMC)*, moved from the motherboard chip into the CPU to optimize the flow of information into and out from the CPU. An IMC enables faster control over things like the large L3 cache shared among multiple cores.

Just like in so many other areas of computing, manufacturers implement a variety of IMCs in their CPUs. In practice, this means that different CPUs handle different types and capacities of RAM. I'll save the details on those RAM variations for Chapter 5. For now, add "different RAM support" to your list of things to look at when making a CPU recommendation for a client.

Integrated Graphics Processing Unit

As you'll read about in much more detail in Chapter 19, the video-processing portion of the computer—made up of the parts that put a changing image on the monitor—traditionally has a discrete microprocessor that differs in both function and architecture from the CPUs designed for general-purpose computing. The generic term for the video processor is a *graphics processing unit (GPU)*. I'll spare you the details until we get to video in Chapter 19, but it turns out that graphics processors can handle certain tasks much more efficiently than the standard CPU. Integrating a GPU into the CPU enhances the overall performance of the computer while at the same time reducing energy use, size, and cost. With the proliferation of mobile devices and portable computers today, all of these benefits have obvious merit.

Both Intel and AMD produce CPUs with integrated GPUs. For many years, the quality of the GPU performance with demanding graphical programs like games made the choice between the two easy. The *Intel HD Graphics* and *Intel Iris Pro Graphics* integrated into many Core i3/i5/i7 processors pale in comparison with the AMD *accelerated processing unit* (*APU*), such as the AMD A10. AMD bought one of the two dedicated GPU manufacturers—ATI—years ago and used their technology for microprocessors with integrated CPU and GPU. (The Xbox One and PlayStation 4 gaming systems, for example, use AMD APUs.) Intel is slowly closing the gap, but isn't there as of this writing.

Security

All modern processors employ the *NX bit* technology that enables the CPU to protect certain sections of memory. This feature, coupled with implementation by the operating system, stops malicious attacks from getting to essential operating system files. Microsoft calls the feature Data Execution Prevention (DEP), turned on by default in every OS since Windows XP (see Figure 4-32).

Figure 4-32 DEP in Windows 8.1

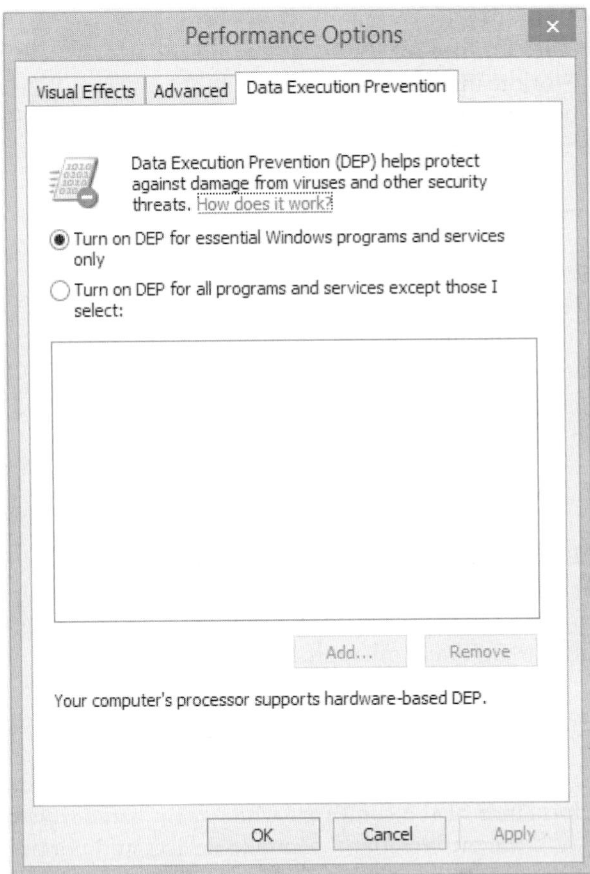

The bad news for you is that everybody calls the NX bit technology something different:

- Intel: XD bit (eXecute Disable)
- AMD: Enhanced Virus Protection
- ARM: XN (eXecute Never)
- CompTIA: Disable execute bit

Selecting and Installing CPUs

Now that you know how CPUs work, it's time to get practical. This last section discusses selecting the proper CPU, installing several types of processors, and troubleshooting the few problems techs face with CPUs.

Selecting a CPU

When selecting a CPU, you need to make certain you get one that the motherboard can accommodate. Or, if you're buying a motherboard along with the CPU, then get the right CPU for the intended purpose. Chapter 12 discusses computer roles and helps you select the proper components for each role. You need to have a lot more knowledge of all the pieces around the CPU to get the full picture, so we'll wait until then to discuss the "why" of a particular processor. Instead, this section assumes you're placing a new CPU in an already-acquired motherboard. You need to address two key points in selecting a CPU that will work. First, does the motherboard support Intel or AMD CPUs? Second, what socket does the motherboard have?

To find answers to both those questions, you have two sources: the motherboard book or manual and the manufacturer's Web site. Figure 4-33 shows a manual for an Asus motherboard open to reveal the supported processors and the socket type.

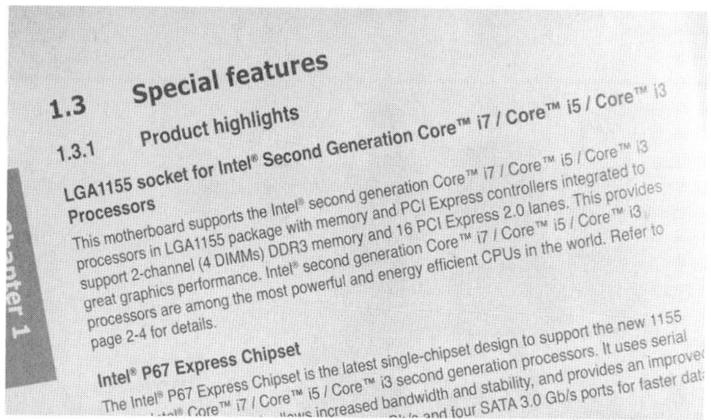
1.3 Special features

1.3.1 Product highlights

LGA1155 socket for Intel® Second Generation Core™ i7 / Core™ i5 / Core™ i3 Processors

This motherboard supports the Intel® second generation Core™ i7 / Core™ i5 / Core™ i3 processors in LGA1155 package with memory and PCI Express controllers integrated to support 2-channel (4 DIMMs) DDR3 memory and 16 PCI Express 2.0 lanes. This provides great graphics performance. Intel® second generation Core™ i7 / Core™ i5 / Core™ i3 processors are among the most powerful and energy efficient CPUs in the world. Refer to page 2-4 for details.

Intel® P67 Express Chipset

The Intel® P67 Express Chipset is the latest single-chipset design to support the new 1155 ... Core™ i7 / Core™ i5 / Core™ i3 second generation processors. It uses serial ... increased bandwidth and stability, and provides an improve... and four SATA 3.0 Gb/s ports for faster dat...

Figure 4-33 Supported processors and socket type

Just as Intel and AMD make many types of CPUs, motherboards are manufactured with various different types of sockets. The CompTIA A+ exams expect you to know which sockets go with which family of CPU. Table 4-2 charts the important Intel ones; Table 4-3 lists the AMD-based sockets. I would show you all the pictures, but, frankly, CPU sockets aren't the sexiest part of the computer.

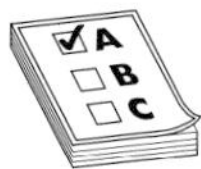

EXAM TIP I've included the number of socket pins for the AMD-based sockets because related questions have been on the CompTIA A+ certification exams in the past. You don't need to memorize the Intel numbers, because Intel names the sockets by the number of pins.

Socket	CPU
LGA 775[1]	Pentium 4, Celeron, Pentium 4 Extreme Edition, Core 2 Duo, Core 2 Quad, Xeon, and many others
LGA 1156[2]	Core i3/i5/i7, Pentium, Celeron, Xeon
LGA 1155[3]	Core i3/i5/i7, Pentium, Celeron, Xeon
LGA 1366[4]	Core i7, Xeon, Celeron
LGA 2011[5]	Core i7, Core i7 Extreme Edition, Xeon
LGA 1150[6]	Core i3/i5/i7, Pentium, Celeron, Xeon
LGA 1151[7]	Core i3/i5/i7, Pentium, Celeron, Xeon

[1] The LGA 775 socket was the only desktop or server socket used for many years by Intel and thus just about every branded Intel CPU used it at one time or another.
[2] Socket LGA 1156 CPUs are based on the pre–Sandy Bridge architecture.
[3] Socket LGA 1155 CPUs are based on Sandy Bridge or Ivy Bridge architecture.
[4] The very first Core i7 processors used LGA 1366. Socket 1366 does not support integrated graphics.
[5] Intel uses LGA 2011 for several generations of Core i7 and Core i7 Extreme Edition CPUs. Socket 2011 does not support integrated graphics. Plus, the retail version does not come with an OEM fan and heat-sink assembly. You need to buy that separately.
[6] Socket 1150 CPUs are based on Haswell or Broadwell architecture.
[7] Socket 1151 CPUs are based on Skylake architecture. Intel had just started releasing the first of these as we went to print. Skylake will not be on the 901 exam.

Table 4-2 Intel-based Sockets

Socket	Pins	CPU
AM3[1]	941	Phenom II, Athlon II, Sempron, Opteron
AM3+	942	FX
FM1	905	A-Series[2]
FM2	904	A-Series
FM2+	906	A-Series
G34	1974	Opteron
C32	1207	Opteron

[1] The names of some of the processors designed for Socket AM3 match the names of CPUs designed for earlier sockets, but they're *not* the same CPUs. They are specific to AM3 because they support different types of RAM (see Chapter 5). Just to make things even crazier, though, AM3 CPUs work just fine in earlier Socket AM2/2+ motherboards.
[2] The A-Series features integrated GPUs and other chips.

Table 4-3 AMD-based Sockets

Deciphering Processor Numbers

Intel and AMD use different processor numbering schemes that help you compare multiple CPUs with similar names, such as Core i5. Intel's system is pretty straightforward; AMD's is muddled. Here's the scoop on both.

Intel processor numbers follow a very clear pattern. An Intel Core i7 5775 C processor, for example, maps out like this:

- Intel Core = brand
- i7 = brand modifier
- 5 = generation
- 775 = SKU numbers
- C = alpha suffix (C indicates that it's a desktop processor with integrated graphics, socket LGA 1150)

Contrast the previous processor with an Intel Core i7 5950 H Q, where the numbers map like this:

- Intel Core = brand
- i7 = brand modifier
- 5 = generation
- 950 = SKU numbers
- HQ = alpha suffix (HQ indicates that it's a mobile quad-core processor with integrated graphics)

AMD started out loving techs. Here's the breakdown for an AMD FX-8350:

- AMD = brand
- FX = product line
- 8 = series and number of processing cores
- 3 = generation (higher number means it's more refined)
- 50 = model number (higher number means it's faster)

With their A-Series, though, AMD fell a little out of love. Here's the breakdown for an AMD A10-6800K:

- AMD = brand
- A10 = product line
- 6 = generation (higher number means it's more refined, usually, though not always)
- 800 = model number (higher number means it's faster)

- K = suffix (K means that the processor has an unlocked core, designed to make overclocking easier; no suffix means it's a locked desktop core; M suffix denotes mobile version)

  Note that none of the A-Series processor numbers tell you how many cores the CPU has. Most of the desktop versions have four cores. Portable and low-powered versions (E- and C-series) have one or two cores. You have to read the packaging or search online for confirmation with any given processor.

  It's a lot to take in, especially for new techs. The good news is you won't find product numbers on the CompTIA A+ exams. The other good news is that you can refer to the this section (and the Internet) to help you choose the right processor for your customer/user. The bad news is that it's complicated.

Installation Issues

When installing a CPU, you need to use caution with the tiny pins. Plus, you must make certain that the power supply can supply enough electricity for the processor to function along with all the other components on the computer. You have to provide adequate cooling. Finally, you can decide whether to leave the CPU at stock settings or overclock it.

Socket Types

When installing a CPU, you need to exercise caution not to bend any of the tiny pins. The location of the pins differs between Intel and AMD. With Intel-based motherboards, the sockets have hundreds of tiny pins that line up with contacts on the bottom of the CPU (see Figure 4-34). Intel CPUs use a *land grid array* (*LGA*) package for socketed CPUs, where the underside of the CPU has hundreds of contact points that line up with the socket pins.

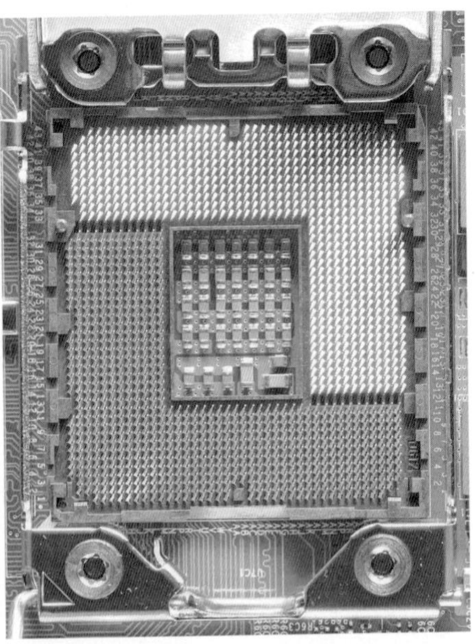

Figure 4-34 Intel-based socket with pins

AMD CPUs have the pins (see Figure 4-35); the sockets have holes. The pins on the AMD *pin grid array* (*PGA*) CPUs align with the holes in the sockets.

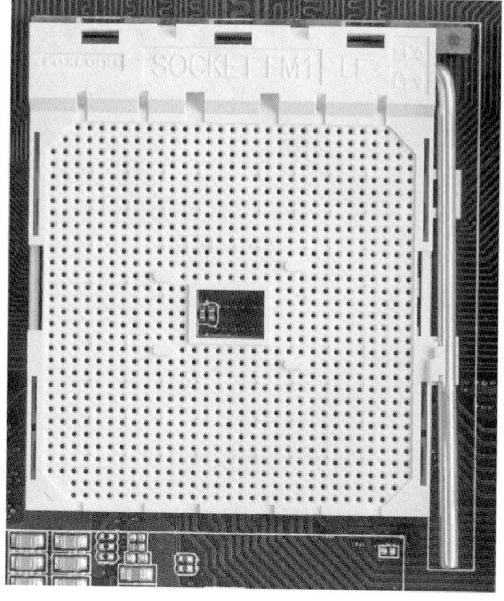

Figure 4-35 AMD-based socket without pins

All CPUs and sockets are keyed so you can't (easily) insert them incorrectly. Look at the underside of the CPU in Figure 4-36 (left). Note that the pins do not make a perfect square, because a few are missing. Now look at the top of the CPU (right). See the little mark at the corner? The socket also has tiny markings so you can line the CPU up properly with the socket.

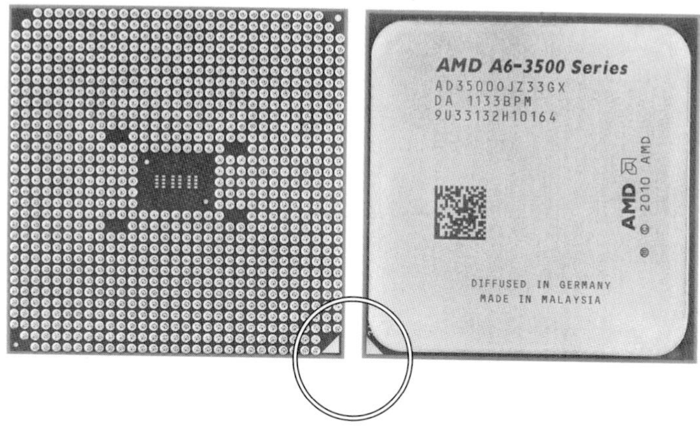

Figure 4-36 Underside and top of a CPU

In both socket styles, you release the retaining mechanism by pushing the little lever down slightly and then away from the socket (see Figure 4-37). You next raise the arm fully, and then move the retaining bracket (see Figure 4-38).

Align the processor with the socket and gently drop the processor into place. If it doesn't go in easily, check the orientation and try again. These sockets are generically called *zero insertion force (ZIF) sockets*, which means you never have to use any force at all.

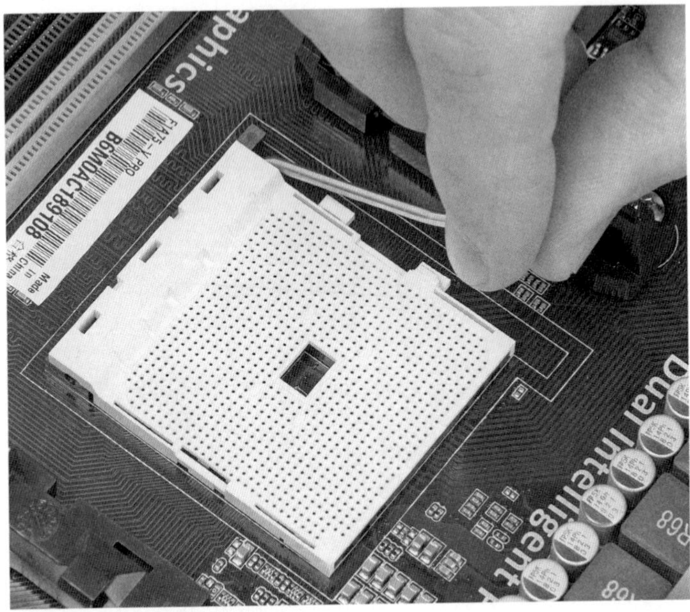

Figure 4-37 Moving the release arm

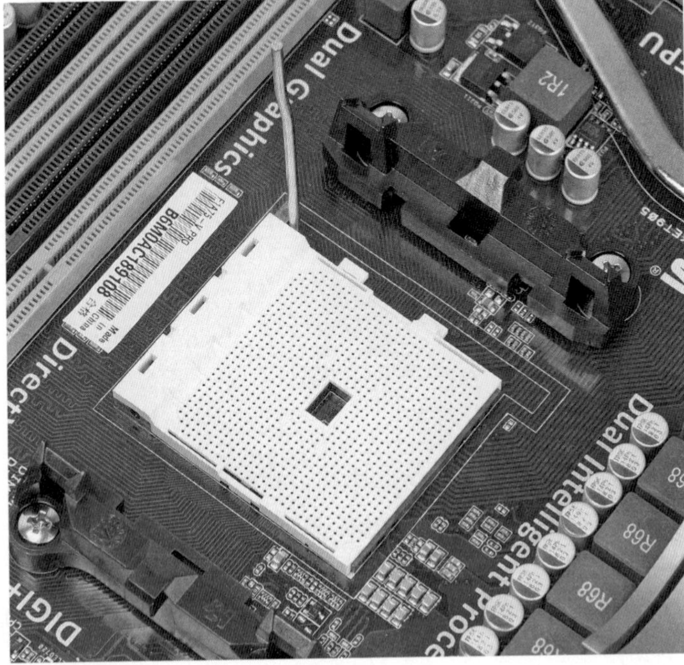

Figure 4-38 Fully opened socket

Cooling

CPUs work very hard and thus require power to function. In electrical terms, CPUs consume *wattage*, or *watts*, a unit of electrical power, just like a 100-watt light bulb consumes power whenever it's on. (See Chapter 8 for more details about electricity.) Have you ever touched a light bulb after it's been on for a while? Ouch! CPUs heat up, too.

To increase the capability of the CPUs to handle complex code, CPU manufacturers have added a lot of microscopic transistors over the years. The more transistors the CPU has, the more power they need and thus the hotter they get. CPUs don't tolerate heat well, and modern processors need active cooling solutions just to function at all. Almost every CPU uses a combination of a heat-sink and fan assembly to wick heat away from the CPU. Figure 4-39 shows the standard Intel *heat sink* and fan. Here are some cooling options:

Figure 4-39 Intel stock heat-sink and fan assembly

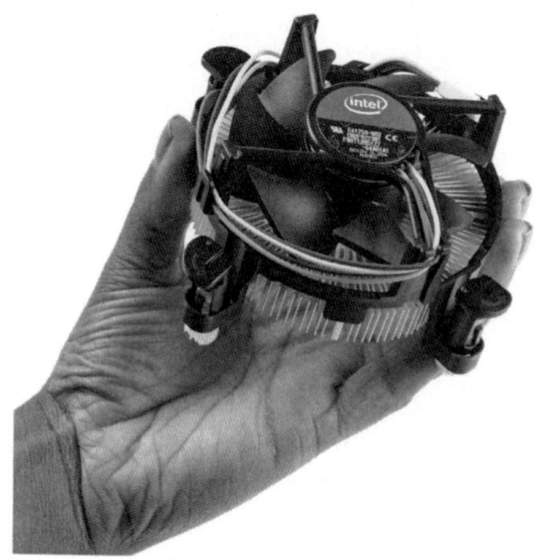

- **OEM CPU coolers** Original equipment manufacturer (OEM) heat-sink and fan assemblies are included with most Intel retail-boxed CPUs. OEM in this case means that Intel makes the heat-sink/fan assemblies. Rather confusingly, you'll see the term "OEM CPUs" used to mean CPUs you buy in bulk or not in the retail packaging. These are still made by Intel or AMD and are functionally identical to the retail versions. They don't come bundled with CPU coolers. Crazy, isn't it? OEM CPU coolers have one big advantage: you know absolutely they will work with your CPU. Intel Socket 2011 CPUs do not come with heat sinks or fans.
- **Specialized CPU coolers** Many companies sell third-party heat-sink and fan assemblies for a variety of CPUs. These usually exceed the OEM heat sinks in the amount of heat they dissipate. These CPU coolers invariably come with eye-catching designs to look really cool inside your system—some are even lighted (see Figure 4-40).

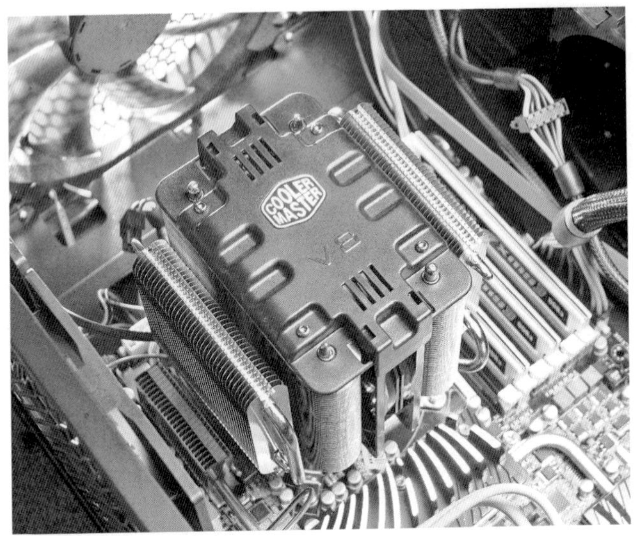

Figure 4-40 Cool retail heat sink

The last choice is the most impressive of all: liquid cooling! *Liquid cooling* works by running some liquid—usually water—through a metal block that sits on top of your CPU, absorbing heat. The liquid gets heated by the block, runs out of the block and into something that cools the liquid, and is then pumped through the block again. Any liquid-cooling system consists of three main parts:

- A hollow metal block that sits on the CPU
- A pump to move the liquid around
- Some device to cool the liquid

And of course, you need plenty of hosing to hook them all together. Figure 4-41 shows a typical liquid-cooled CPU.

A number of companies sell these liquid-based cooling systems. Although they look impressive and certainly cool your CPU, unless you're overclocking or want a quiet system, a good fan will more than suffice.

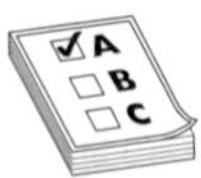

EXAM TIP In some instances, you can create a system that has no fan for the CPU, what's called *fanless* or *passive cooling*. Aside from mobile devices (like an Apple iPad) that have no fans, the term can be very misleading. The Xeon CPUs powering the servers in my office, for example, only have heat sinks with no fans. On the other hand, they have ducts directly to the case fans, which serve the same function as a an active CPU fan. So, go figure.

See also the "Beyond A+" section at the end of this chapter for interesting passive developments.

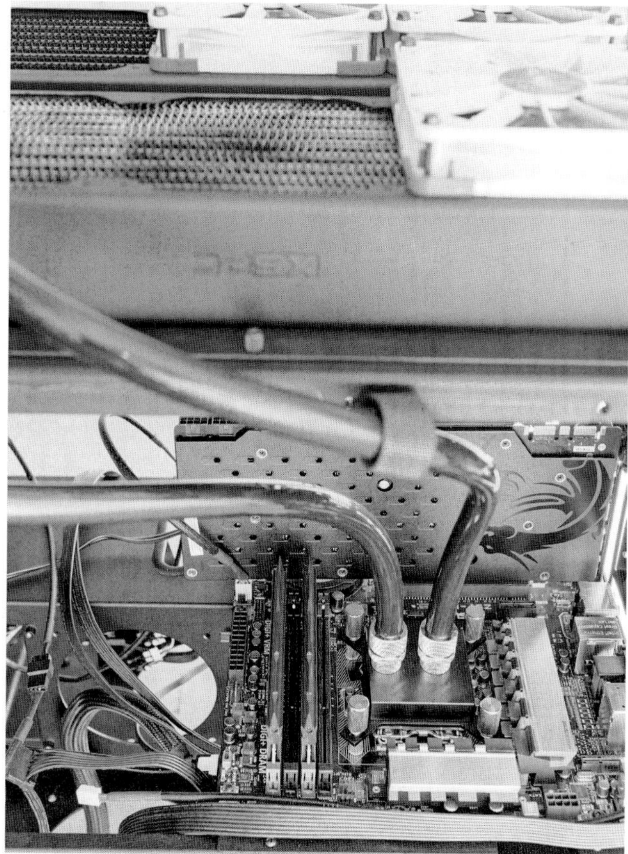

Figure 4-41 Liquid-cooled CPU

Once you've got a heat-sink and fan assembly sorted out, you need to connect them to the motherboard. To determine the orientation of the heat-sink and fan assembly, check the power cable from the fan. Make sure it can easily reach the three- or four-wire standout on the motherboard (see Figure 4-42). If it can't, rotate the heat sink until it can. (Check the motherboard manual if you have trouble locating the CPU fan power standout.)

Next, before inserting the heat sink, you need to add a small amount of *thermal paste* (also called *thermal compound*, *heat dope*, or *nasty silver goo*). Many heat sinks come with some thermal paste already on them; the thermal paste on these pre-doped heat sinks is covered by a small square of tape—take the tape off before you snap it to the CPU. If you need to put thermal paste on from a tube, know that you need to use only a tiny amount of this compound (see Figure 4-43). Spread it on as thinly, completely, and evenly as you can. Unlike so many other things in life, you *can* have too much thermal paste!

You secure heat sinks in various ways, depending on the manufacturer. Stock Intel heat sinks have four plungers that you simply push until they click into place in corresponding

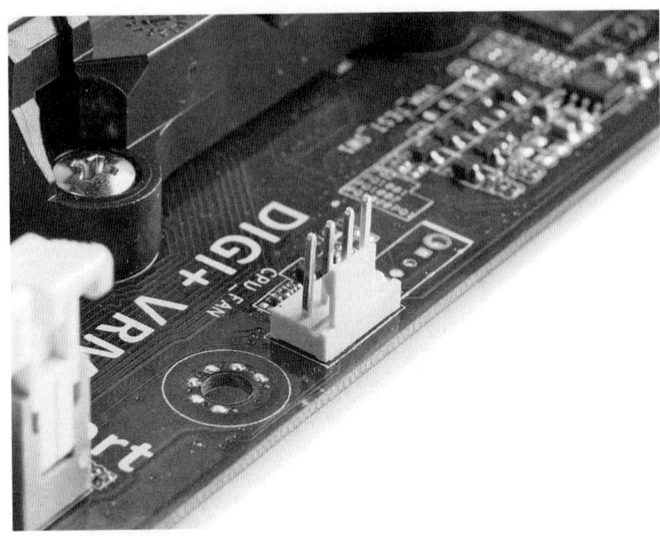

Figure 4-42 CPU fan power standout on motherboard

holes in the motherboard. AMD stock heat sinks generally have a bracket that you secure to two points on the outside of the CPU socket and a latch that you swivel to lock it down (see Figure 4-44).

Finally, you can secure many aftermarket heat-sink and fan assemblies by screwing them down from the underside of the motherboard (see Figure 4-45). You have to

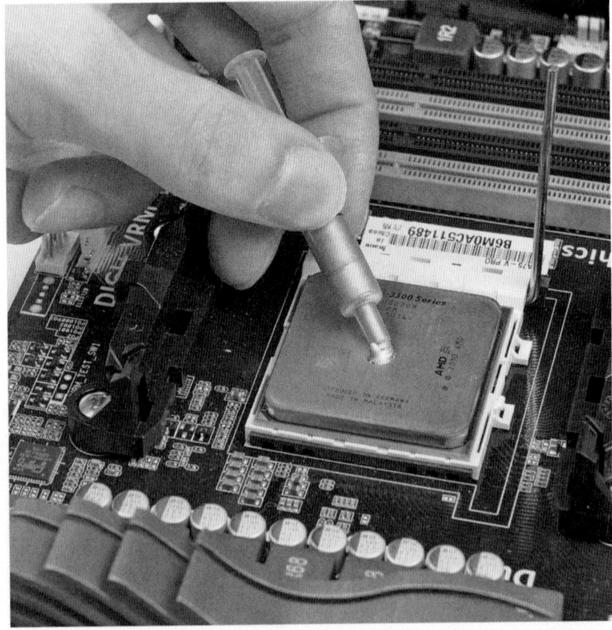

Figure 4-43 Applying thermal paste

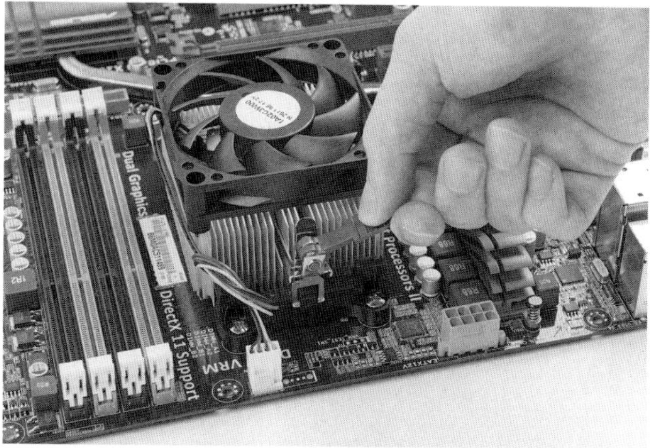

Figure 4-44
AMD stock heat-sink and fan assembly

remove the motherboard from the case or install the heat sink before you put the motherboard in the case.

For the final step, plug the fan power connector into the motherboard standout. It won't work if you don't!

Overclocking

For the CPU to work, the motherboard speed, multiplier, and voltage must be set properly. In most modern systems, the motherboard uses the CPUID functions to set these options automatically. Some motherboards enable you to adjust these settings manually by moving a jumper, changing a CMOS setting, or using software; many enthusiasts deliberately change these settings to enhance performance.

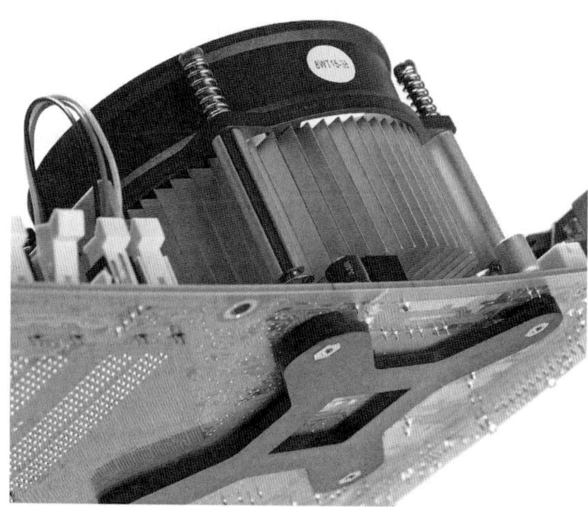

Figure 4-45
Heat-sink and fan assembly mounted to motherboard with screws

NOTE Chapter 6 goes into gory detail about the system setup utility and the area in which it stores important data (called *CMOS*), but invariably students want to experiment at this point, so I'll give you some information now. You can access the system setup utility by pressing some key as the computer starts up. This is during the text phase, well before it ever says anything about starting Windows. Most systems require you to press the DELETE key, but read the screen for details. Just be careful once you get into the system setup utility not to change anything you don't understand. And read Chapter 6!

Starting way back in the days of the Intel 80486 CPU, people intentionally ran their systems at clock speeds higher than the CPU was rated, a process called *overclocking*, and it worked. Well, *sometimes* the systems worked, and sometimes they didn't. Intel and AMD have a reason for marking a CPU at a particular clock speed—that's the highest speed they guarantee will work.

Before I say anything else, I must warn you that intentional overclocking of a CPU immediately voids most warranties. Overclocking has been known to destroy CPUs. Overclocking might make your system unstable and prone to lockups and reboots. I neither applaud nor decry the practice of overclocking. My goal here is simply to inform you of the practice. You make your own decisions.

CPU makers do not encourage overclocking. Why would you pay more for a faster processor when you can take a cheaper, slower CPU and just make it run faster? Bowing to enthusiast market pressure, both Intel and AMD make utilities that help you overclock their respective CPUs.

- **Intel Extreme Tuning Utility (Intel XTU)** Don't skip the additional Performance Tuning Protection Plan if you go this route.
- **AMD Overdrive Utility** No extra warranty is provided here; you're on your own.

Most people make a couple of adjustments to overclock successfully. First, through jumpers, CMOS settings, or software configuration, you would increase the bus speed for the system. Second, you often have to increase the voltage going into the CPU by just a little to provide stability. You do that by changing a jumper or CMOS setting (see Figure 4-46).

Overriding the defaults can completely lock up your system, to the point where even removing and reinstalling the CPU doesn't bring the motherboard back to life. (There's also a slight risk of toasting the processor, although all modern processors have circuitry that shuts them down quickly before they overheat.) Most motherboards have a jumper setting called *CMOS clear* (see Figure 4-47) that makes the CMOS go back to default settings. Before you try overclocking on a modern system, find the CMOS-clear jumper and make sure you know how to use it! Hint: Look in the motherboard manual.

To clear the CMOS, turn off the PC. Then locate one of those tiny little plastic pieces (officially called a *shunt*) and place it over the two jumper wires for a moment. Next, restart the PC and immediately go into CMOS and restore the settings you need.

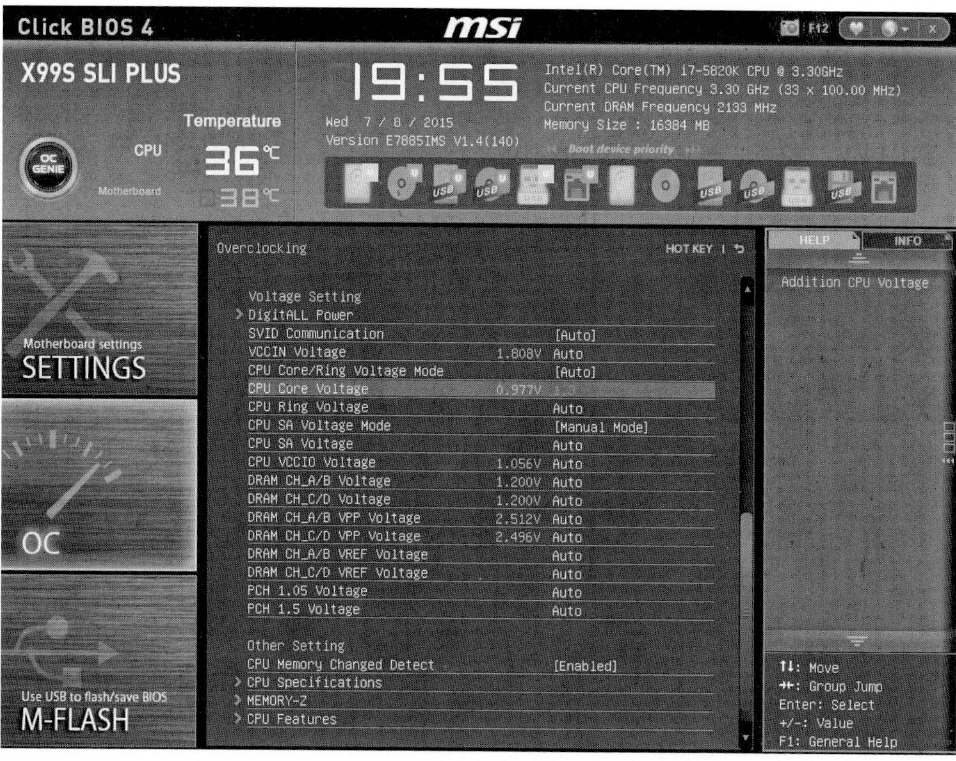

Figure 4-46 Manually overriding CPU settings in the system setup utility

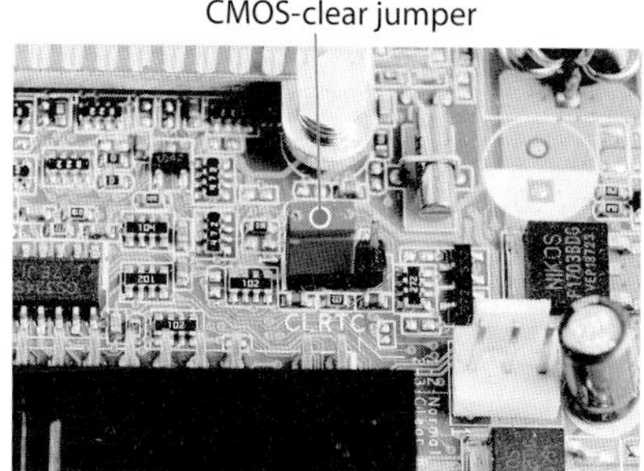

Figure 4-47 CMOS-clear jumper

Troubleshooting CPUs

Troubleshooting CPU issues falls into two categories: overheating and catastrophic failures, with overheating being far more common than the latter. Once a CPU is installed properly and functioning, it rarely causes problems. The only exception is when you ask a CPU to do too much too quickly. Then you'll get a sluggish PC. The Intel Atom pro-

cessor in my vintage netbook, for example, does a great job at surfing the Web, working on e-mail, and writing stellar chapters in your favorite textbook. But if you try to play a game more advanced than Half-Life (the original, circa 1998), the machine stutters and complains and refuses to play nice.

The vast majority of problems with CPUs come from faulty installation or environmental issues that cause overheating. Very rarely will you get a catastrophic failure, but we'll look at the signs of that, too.

Symptoms of Overheating

Failure to install a CPU properly results in either nothing—that is, you push the power button and nothing at all happens—or a system lock-up in a short period of time. Because of the nature of ZIF sockets, you're almost guaranteed that the issue isn't the CPU itself, but rather the installation of the heat-sink and fan assembly. Here's a checklist of possible problems that you need to address when faced with a CPU installation problem:

1. Too much thermal paste can impede the flow of heat from the CPU to the heat sink and cause the CPU to heat up rapidly. All modern CPUs have built-in fail-safes that tell them to shut down before getting damaged by heat.
2. Not enough thermal paste or thermal paste spread unevenly can cause the CPU to heat up and consequently shut itself down.
3. Failure to connect the fan power to the motherboard can cause the CPU to heat up and shut itself down.

The fan and heat-sink installation failures can be tricky the first few times you encounter them. You might see the text from the system setup. You might even get into an installation of Windows before the crash happens. The key is that as soon as you put the CPU under load—that is, make it work for a living—it heats up beyond where the faulty heat-sink connection can dissipate the heat and then shuts down.

With a system that's been running fine for a while, environmental factors can cause problems. An air conditioning failure in my office last summer, deep in the heart of very hot Texas, for example, caused machines throughout the office to run poorly. Some even shut down entirely. (At that point it was time to close the doors and send the staff to the beach, but that's another story.) A client called the other day to complain about his computer continuously rebooting and running slowly. When I arrived on the scene, I found a house with seven cats. Opening up his computer case revealed the hairy truth: the CPU fan was so clogged with cat hair that it barely spun at all! A quick cleaning with a computer vacuum and a can of compressed air and he was a happily computing client.

The CPU needs adequate ventilation. The CPU fan is essential, of course, but the inside of the case also needs to get hot air out through one or more exhaust fans and cool air in through the front vent. If the intake vent is clogged or the exhaust fans stop working or are blocked somehow, the inside of the case can heat up and overwhelm the CPU cooling devices. This will result in a system running slowly or spontaneously rebooting.

Catastrophic Failure

You'll know when a catastrophic error occurs. The PC will suddenly get a Blue Screen of Death (BSoD), what's technically called a Windows Stop error (see Figure 4-48). On Mac OS X, by comparison, you'll get a pin wheel on the screen that just doesn't go away or stop spinning. (CompTIA calls the BSoD and pin wheel *proprietary crash screens*. Most users just find them annoying.)

Or the entire computer will simply stop and go black, perhaps accompanied by a loud pop. The acrid smell of burnt electronics or ozone will grace your nasal passages. You might even see trails of smoke coming out of the case. You might not know immediately that the CPU has smoked, but follow your nose. Seriously. Sniff the inside of the case until you find the strongest smell. If it's the CPU, that's bad news. Whatever electrical short hit, it probably caused damage to the motherboard too, and you're looking at a long day of replacement and rebuilding.

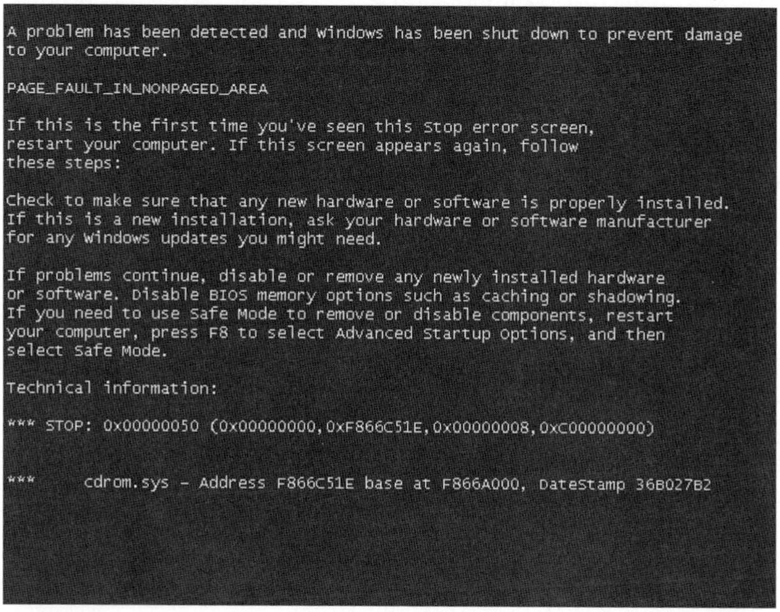

```
A problem has been detected and windows has been shut down to prevent damage
to your computer.

PAGE_FAULT_IN_NONPAGED_AREA

If this is the first time you've seen this stop error screen,
restart your computer. If this screen appears again, follow
these steps:

Check to make sure that any new hardware or software is properly installed.
If this is a new installation, ask your hardware or software manufacturer
for any windows updates you might need.

If problems continue, disable or remove any newly installed hardware
or software. Disable BIOS memory options such as caching or shadowing.
If you need to use Safe Mode to remove or disable components, restart
your computer, press F8 to select Advanced Startup Options, and then
select Safe Mode.

Technical information:

*** STOP: 0x00000050 (0x00000000,0xF866C51E,0x00000008,0xC0000000)


***     cdrom.sys - Address F866C51E base at F866A000, DateStamp 36B027B2
```

Figure 4-48 Blue Screen of Death

Beyond A+

Intel Core M

The Intel Core M runs cool and sips juice for incredibly long battery life in mobile devices. The official thermal design power (TDP) is just 4.5 watts—compared to a mobile version of a Core i7 that demands 57 watts. The trade-off Intel makes with the

Core M is in raw processing power. It falls in between the Atom and a mobile Core i3—enough to get the job done, but not enough to run a serious game or other demanding application. On the other hand, the incredibly low electricity use means manufacturers can skip the fan and make super skinny devices.

At the time of this writing, only a few portable computers run the Core M, most notably the Apple MacBook. Expect the Core M to migrate to some nonportable systems, especially Media Center PCs, where the quiet of fanless computing makes a lot of sense.

Chapter Review

Questions

1. What do registers provide for the CPU?
   - **A.** Registers determine the clock speed.
   - **B.** The CPU uses registers for temporary storage of internal commands and data.
   - **C.** Registers enable the CPU to address RAM.
   - **D.** Registers enable the CPU to control the address bus.
2. What function does the external data bus have in the PC?
   - **A.** The external data bus determines the clock speed for the CPU.
   - **B.** The CPU uses the external data bus to address RAM.
   - **C.** The external data bus provides a channel for the flow of data and commands between the CPU and RAM.
   - **D.** The CPU uses the external data bus to access registers.
3. What is the function of the address bus in the PC?
   - **A.** The address bus enables the CPU to communicate with the memory controller chip.
   - **B.** The address bus enables the memory controller chip to communicate with the RAM.
   - **C.** The address bus provides a channel for the flow of data and commands between the CPU and RAM.
   - **D.** The address bus enables the CPU to access registers.
4. Which of the following terms are measures of CPU speed?
   - **A.** Megahertz and gigahertz
   - **B.** Megabytes and gigabytes
   - **C.** Megahertz and gigabytes
   - **D.** Frontside bus, backside bus

5. Which CPU feature enables the microprocessor to support running multiple operating systems at the same time?
    A. Clock multiplying
    B. Caching
    C. Pipelining
    D. Virtualization support
6. Into which socket could you place an Intel Core i5?
    A. Socket LGA 775
    B. Socket LGA 1155
    C. Socket C
    D. Socket AM3+
7. Which feature enables a single-core CPU to function like two CPUs?
    A. Hyper-Threading
    B. SpeedStep
    C. Virtualization
    D. *x*64
8. What steps do you need to take to install a Core i3 CPU into an FM2 motherboard?
    A. Lift the ZIF socket arm; place the CPU according to the orientation markings; snap on the heat-sink and fan assembly.
    B. Lift the ZIF socket arm; place the CPU according to the orientation markings; add a dash of thermal paste; snap on the heat-sink and fan assembly.
    C. Lift the ZIF socket arm; place the CPU according to the orientation markings; snap on the heat-sink and fan assembly; plug in the fan.
    D. Take all of the steps you want to take because it's not going to work.
9. A client calls to complain that his computer starts up, but crashes when Windows starts to load. After a brief set of questions, you find out that his nephew upgraded his RAM for him over the weekend and couldn't get the computer to work right afterward. What could be the problem?
    A. Thermal paste degradation
    B. Disconnected CPU fan
    C. Bad CPU cache
    D. There's nothing wrong. It usually takes a couple of days for RAM to acclimate to the new system.

10. Darren has installed a new CPU in a client's computer, but nothing happens when he pushes the power button on the case. The LED on the motherboard is lit up, so he knows the system has power. What could the problem be?
    - **A.** He forgot to disconnect the CPU fan.
    - **B.** He forgot to apply thermal paste between the CPU and the heat-sink and fan assembly.
    - **C.** He used an AMD CPU in an Intel motherboard.
    - **D.** He used an Intel CPU in an AMD motherboard.

Answers

1. **B.** The CPU uses registers for temporary storage of internal commands and data.
2. **C.** The external data bus provides a channel for the flow of data and commands between the CPU and RAM.
3. **A.** The address bus enables the CPU to communicate with the memory controller chip.
4. **A.** The terms megahertz (MHz) and gigahertz (GHz) describe how many million or billion (respectively) cycles per second a CPU can run.
5. **D.** Intel and AMD CPUs come with virtualization support, enabling more efficient implementation of virtual machines.
6. **B.** You'll find Core i5 processors in several socket types, notably LGA 1155 and LGA 1156.
7. **A.** Intel loves its Hyper-Threading, where a single-core CPU can function like a dual-core CPU as long as it has operating system support.
8. **D.** Intel and AMD processors are not compatible at all.
9. **B.** Most likely, the nephew disconnected the CPU fan to get at the RAM slots and simply forgot to plug it back in.
10. **B.** The best answer here is that he forgot the thermal paste, though you can also make an argument for a disconnected fan.

CHAPTER 5

RAM

In this chapter, you will learn how to

- Identify the different types of DRAM packaging
- Explain the varieties of RAM
- Select and install RAM
- Perform basic RAM troubleshooting

Whenever people come up to me and start professing their computer savvy, I ask them a few questions to see how much they really know. In case you and I ever meet and you decide you want to "talk tech" with me, I'll tell you my first two questions now so you'll be ready. Both involve *random access memory* (*RAM*), the working memory for the CPU.

1. "How much RAM is in your computer?"
2. "What is RAM and why is it so important that every PC has enough?"

Can you answer either of these questions? Don't fret if you can't—you'll know how to answer both of them before you finish this chapter. Let's start by reviewing what you know about RAM thus far.

When not in use, programs and data are held in a mass storage device such as a hard disk drive (HDD), USB thumb drive, optical drive, or some other device that can hold data while the computer is off. When you load a program in Windows, your PC copies the program from the mass storage device to RAM and then runs it (see Figure 5-1).

You saw in Chapter 4 that the CPU uses *dynamic random access memory (DRAM)* as RAM for all PCs. Just like CPUs, DRAM has gone through a number of evolutionary changes over the years, resulting in improved DRAM technologies such as SDRAM, RDRAM, and DDR RAM. This chapter starts by explaining how DRAM works, and then discusses the types of DRAM used over the past several years and how they improve on the original DRAM. The third section, "Working with RAM," goes into the details of finding and installing RAM. The chapter finishes with troubleshooting RAM problems.

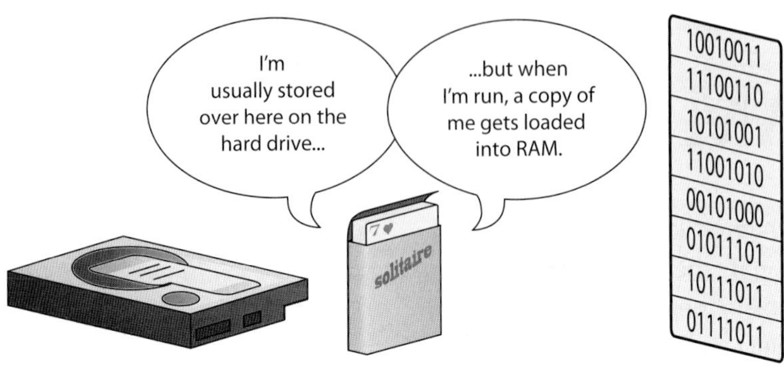

Figure 5-1 Mass storage holds programs, but programs need to run from RAM.

Historical/Conceptual

Understanding DRAM

As discussed in Chapter 4, DRAM functions like an electronic spreadsheet, with numbered rows containing cells and each cell holding a one or a zero. Now let's look at what's physically happening. Each spreadsheet cell is a special type of semiconductor that can hold a single bit—one or zero—by using microscopic capacitors and transistors. DRAM makers put these semiconductors into chips that can hold a certain number of bits. The bits inside the chips are organized in a rectangular fashion, using rows and columns.

Each chip has a limit on the number of lines of code it can contain. Think of each line of code as one of the rows on the electronic spreadsheet; one chip might be able to store a million rows of code while another chip might be able to store over a billion lines. Each chip also has a limit on the width of the lines of code it can handle. One chip might handle 8-bit-wide data while another might handle 16-bit-wide data. Techs describe chips by bits rather than bytes, so they refer to *×8* and *×16*, respectively. Just as you could describe a spreadsheet by the number of rows and columns—John's accounting spreadsheet is huge, 48 rows × 12 columns—memory makers describe RAM chips the same way. An individual DRAM chip that holds 1,048,576 rows and 8 columns, for example, would be a *1M×8* chip, with "M" as shorthand for "mega," just like in megabytes (2^{20} bytes). It is difficult if not impossible to tell the size of a DRAM chip just by looking at it—only the DRAM makers know the meaning of the tiny numbers on the chips (see Figure 5-2), although sometimes you can make a good guess.

Organizing DRAM

Because of its low cost, high speed, and capability to contain a lot of data in a relatively small package, DRAM has been the standard RAM used in all computers—not just

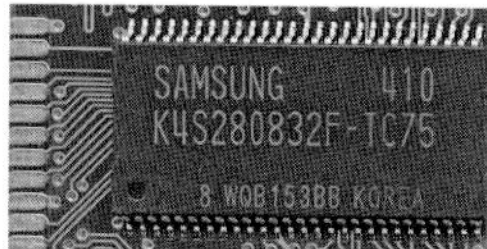

Figure 5-2 What do these numbers mean?

PCs—since the mid-1970s. DRAM can be found in just about everything, from automobiles to automatic bread makers.

The PC has very specific requirements for DRAM. The original 8088 processor had an 8-bit frontside bus. Commands given to an 8088 processor were in discrete 8-bit chunks. You needed RAM that could store data in 8-bit (1-byte) chunks, so that each time the CPU asked for a line of code, the memory controller chip (MCC) could put an 8-bit chunk on the data bus. This optimized the flow of data into (and out from) the CPU. Although today's DRAM chips may have widths greater than 1 bit, all DRAM chips back then were 1 bit wide, meaning only sizes such as 64 K × 1 or 256 K × 1 existed—always 1 bit wide. So how was 1-bit-wide DRAM turned into 8-bit-wide memory? The solution was quite simple: just take eight 1-bit-wide chips and use the MCC to organize them electronically to be eight wide (see Figure 5-3).

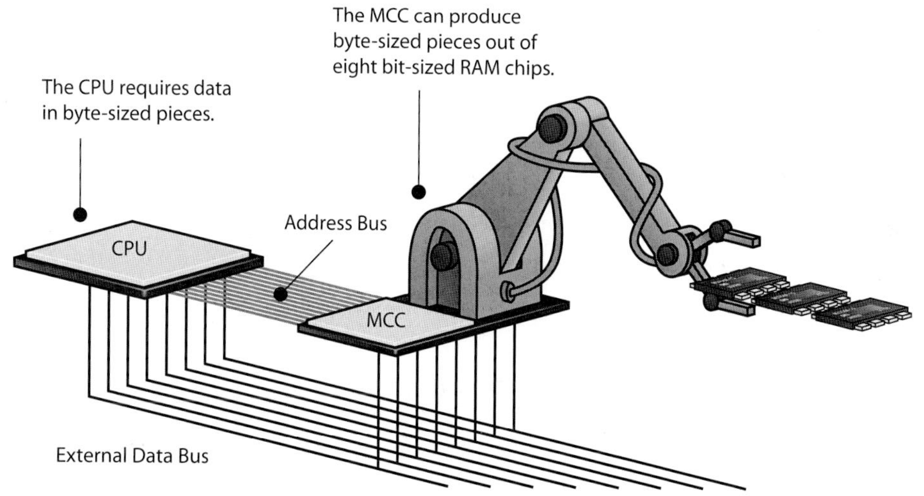

Figure 5-3 The MCC accessing data on RAM soldered onto the motherboard

Practical DRAM

Okay, before you learn more about DRAM, I need to clarify a critical point. When you first saw the 8088's machine language in Chapter 4, all the examples in the "codebook" were exactly 1-byte commands. Figure 5-4 shows the codebook again—see how all the commands are 1 byte?

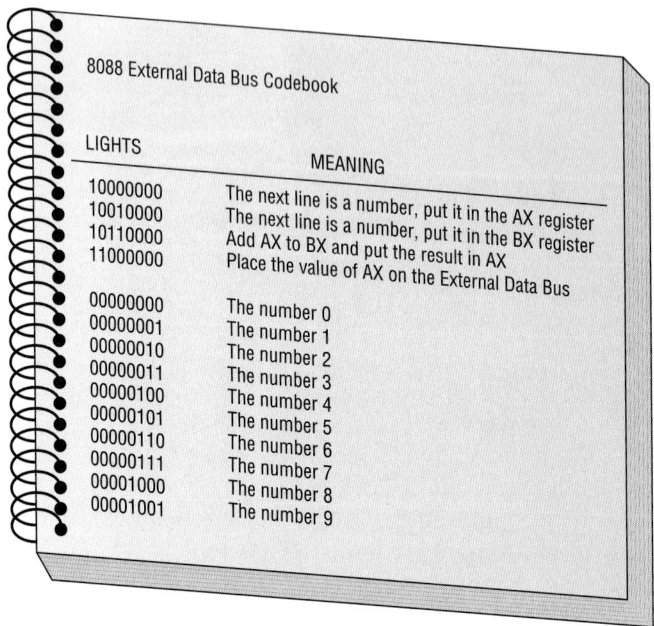

8088 External Data Bus Codebook
LIGHTS
MEANING
10000000
The next line is a number, put it in the AX register
10010000
The next line is a number, put it in the BX register
10110000
Add AX to BX and put the result in AX
11000000
Place the value of AX on the External Data Bus
00000000
The number 0
00000001
The number 1
00000010
The number 2
00000011
The number 3
00000100
The number 4
00000101
The number 5
00000110
The number 6
00000111
The number 7
00001000
The number 8
00001001
The number 9

Figure 5-4 Codebook again

Well, the reality is slightly different. Most of the 8088 machine language commands are 1 byte, but more-complex commands need 2 bytes. For example, the following command tells the CPU to move 163 bytes "up the RAM spreadsheet" and run whatever command is there. Cool, eh?

```
1110100110100011
```

The problem here is that the command is 2 bytes wide, not 1 byte. So how did the 8088 handle this? Simple—it just took the command 1 byte at a time. It took twice as long to handle the command because the MCC had to go to RAM twice, but it worked.

So if some of the commands are more than 1 byte wide, why didn't Intel make the 8088 with a 16-bit frontside bus? Wouldn't that have been better? Well, Intel did. Intel invented a CPU called the 8086. The 8086 actually predates the 8088 and was absolutely identical to the 8088 except for one small detail: it had a 16-bit frontside bus. IBM could have used the 8086 instead of the 8088 and used 2-byte-wide RAM instead of 1-byte-wide RAM. Of course, they would have needed to invent an MCC that could handle that kind of RAM (see Figure 5-5).

Why did Intel sell the 8088 to IBM instead of the 8086? There were two reasons. Nobody had invented an affordable MCC or RAM that handled 2 bytes at a time. Sure, chips had been invented, but they were *expensive* and IBM didn't think anyone would want to pay $12,000 for a personal computer. So IBM bought the Intel 8088, not the Intel 8086, and all our RAM came in bytes. But as you might imagine, it didn't stay that way for long.

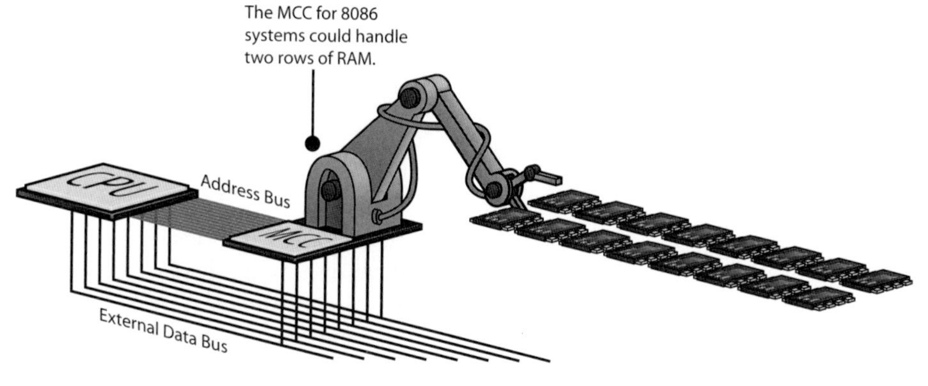

Figure 5-5 Pumped-up 8086 MCC at work

DRAM Sticks

As CPU data bus sizes increased, so too did the need for RAM wide enough to fill the bus. The Intel 80386 CPU, for example, had a 32-bit data bus and thus the need for 32-bit-wide DRAM. Imagine having to line up 32 one-bit-wide DRAM chips on a motherboard. Talk about a waste of space! Figure 5-6 shows motherboard RAM run amuck.

Figure 5-6 That's a lot of real estate used by RAM chips!

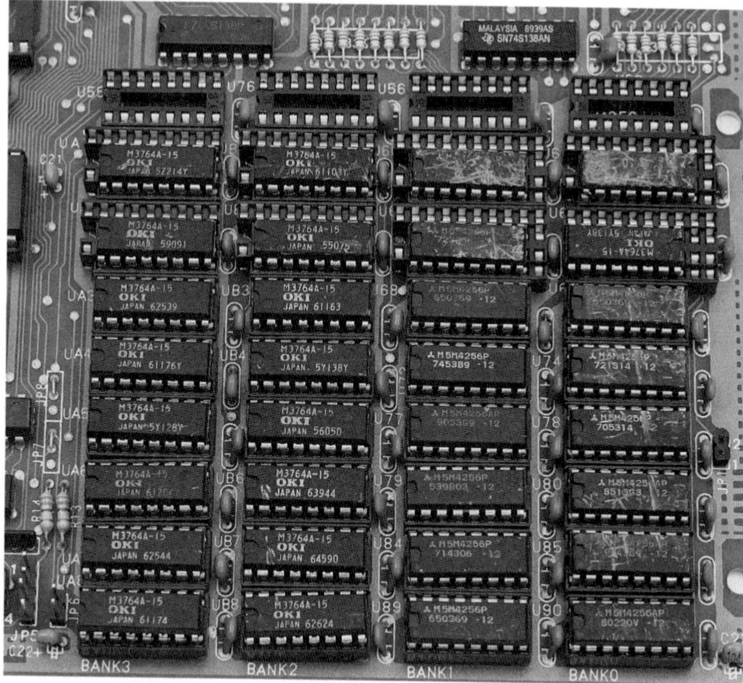

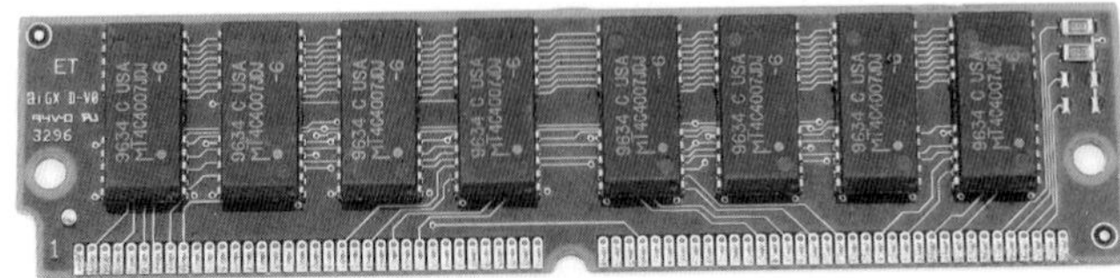

Figure 5-7 A 72-pin SIMM

DRAM manufacturers responded by creating wider DRAM chips, such as ×4, ×8, and ×16, and putting multiples of them on a small circuit board called a *stick* or *module*. Figure 5-7 shows an early stick, called a *single inline memory module (SIMM)*, with eight DRAM chips. To add RAM to a modern machine, you need to get the right stick or sticks for the particular motherboard. Your motherboard manual tells you precisely what sort of module you need and how much RAM you can install.

Modern CPUs are a lot smarter than the old Intel 8088. Their machine languages have some commands that are up to 64 bits (8 bytes) wide. They also have at least a 64-bit frontside bus that can handle more than just 8 bits. They don't want RAM to give them a puny 8 bits at a time! To optimize the flow of data into and out of the CPU, the modern MCC provides at least 64 bits of data every time the CPU requests information from RAM.

Try This!

Dealing with Old RAM

Often in the PC world, old technology and ways of doing things are reimplemented with some newer technology. A tech who knows these ancient ways will have extra opportunities. Many thousands of companies—including hospitals, auto repair places, and more—use very old proprietary applications that keep track of medical records, inventory, and so on. If you're called to work on one of these ancient systems, you need to know how to work with old parts, so try this.

Obtain an old computer. Ask your uncle, cousin, or Great Aunt Edna if they have a PC collecting dust in a closet that you can use. Failing that, go to a secondhand store or market and buy one for a few dollars.

Open up the system and check out the RAM. Remove the RAM from the motherboard and then replace it to familiarize yourself with the internals. You never know when some critical system will go down and need repair immediately—and you're the one to do it!

Modern DRAM sticks come in 32-bit- and 64-bit-wide data form factors with a varying number of chips. Many techs describe these memory modules by their width, so we call them *×32* and *×64*. Note that this number does *not* describe the width of the individual DRAM chips on the module. When you read or hear about *by whatever* memory, you need to know whether that person is talking about the DRAM width or the module

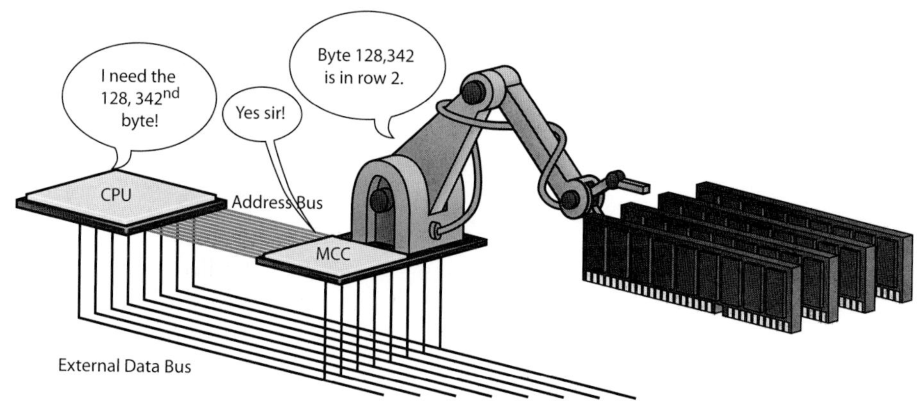

Figure 5-8 The MCC knows the real location of the DRAM.

width. When the CPU needs certain bytes of data, it requests those bytes via the address bus. The CPU does not know the physical location of the RAM that stores that data, nor the physical makeup of the RAM—such as how many DRAM chips work together to provide the 64-bit-wide memory rows. The MCC keeps track of this and just gives the CPU whichever bytes it requests (see Figure 5-8).

Consumer RAM

If modern DRAM modules come in sizes much wider than a byte, why do people still use the word "byte" to describe how much DRAM they have? Convention. Habit. Rather than using a label that describes the electronic structure of RAM, common usage describes the *total capacity of RAM on a stick in bytes*. John has a single 4-GB stick of RAM on his motherboard, for example, and Sally has two 2-GB sticks. Both systems have a total of 4 GB of system RAM. That's what your clients care about. Having enough RAM makes their systems snappy and stable; not enough RAM means their systems run poorly. As a tech, you need to know more, of course, to pick the right RAM for many different types of computers.

Types of RAM

Development of newer, wider, and faster CPUs and MCCs motivate DRAM manufacturers to invent new DRAM technologies that deliver enough data at a single pop to optimize the flow of data into and out of the CPU.

SDRAM

Most modern systems use some form of *synchronous DRAM (SDRAM)*. SDRAM is still DRAM, but it is *synchronous*—tied to the system clock, just like the CPU and MCC, so the MCC knows when data is ready to be grabbed from SDRAM. This results in little wasted time.

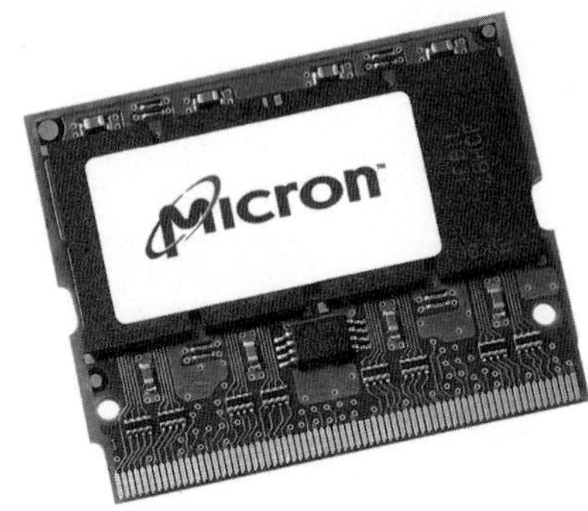

Figure 5-9 144-pin micro-DIMM (photo courtesy of Micron Technology, Inc.)

SDRAM made its debut in 1996 on a stick called a *dual inline memory module (DIMM)*. The early SDRAM DIMMs came in a wide variety of pin sizes. The most common pin sizes found on desktops were the 168-pin variety. Laptop DIMMs came in 68-pin, 144-pin (see Figure 5-9), or 172-pin *micro-DIMM* packages; and the 72-pin, 144-pin, or 200-pin *small-outline DIMM (SO-DIMM)* form factors (see Figure 5-10). With the exception of the 32-bit 72-pin SO-DIMM, all these DIMM varieties delivered 64-bit-wide data to match the 64-bit data bus of every CPU since the original Pentium.

To take advantage of SDRAM, you needed a PC designed to use SDRAM. If you had a system with slots for 168-pin DIMMs, for example, your system used SDRAM. A DIMM in any one of the DIMM slots could fill the 64-bit bus, so each slot was called a *bank*. You could install one, two, or more sticks and the system would work. Note that on laptops that used the 72-pin SO-DIMM, you needed to install two sticks of RAM to make a full bank, because each stick only provided half the bus width.

SDRAM was tied to the system clock, so its clock speed matched the frontside bus. Five clock speeds were commonly used on the early SDRAM systems: 66, 75, 83, 100, and 133 MHz. The RAM speed had to match or exceed the system speed or the computer would be unstable or wouldn't work at all. These speeds were prefixed with a "PC" in the front, based on a standard forwarded by Intel, so SDRAM speeds were PC66 through PC133. For a Pentium III computer with a 100-MHz frontside bus, you needed to buy SDRAM DIMMs rated to handle it, such as PC100 or PC133.

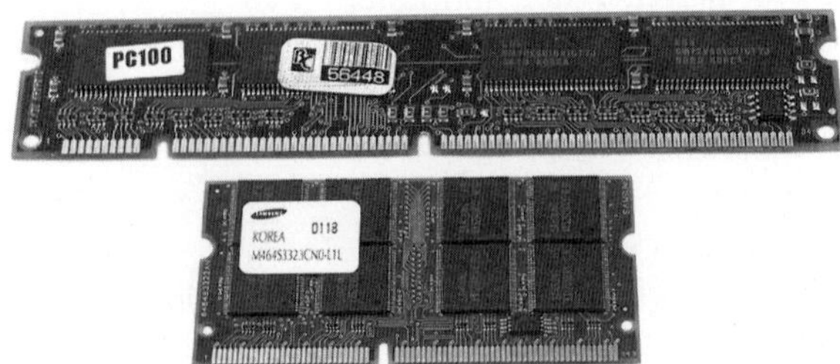

Figure 5-10 A 168-pin DIMM above a 144-pin SO-DIMM

Figure 5-11 RDRAM

RDRAM

When Intel was developing the Pentium 4, they knew that regular SDRAM just wasn't going to be fast enough to handle the quad-pumped 400-MHz frontside bus. Intel announced plans to replace SDRAM with a very fast, new type of RAM developed by Rambus, Inc., called *Rambus DRAM*, or simply *RDRAM* (see Figure 5-11). Hailed by Intel as the next great leap in DRAM technology, RDRAM could handle speeds up to 800 MHz, which gave Intel plenty of room to improve the Pentium 4.

RDRAM was greatly anticipated by the industry for years, but industry support for RDRAM proved less than enthusiastic due to significant delays in development and a price many times that of SDRAM. Despite this grudging support, almost all major PC makers sold systems that used RDRAM—for a while. From a tech's standpoint, RDRAM shared almost all of the characteristics of SDRAM. A stick of RDRAM was called a *RIMM*. In this case, however, the letters didn't actually stand for anything; they just rhymed: SIMMs, DIMMs, and RIMMs, get it?

NOTE The 400-MHz frontside bus speed wasn't achieved by making the system clock faster—it was done by making CPUs and MCCs capable of sending 64 bits of data two or four times for every clock cycle, effectively doubling or quadrupling the system bus speed.

901

DDR SDRAM

AMD and many major system and memory makers threw their support behind an alternative to RDRAM, *double data rate SDRAM (DDR SDRAM)*. DDR SDRAM basically copied Rambus, doubling the throughput of SDRAM by making two processes for every clock cycle. This synchronized (pardon the pun) nicely with the Athlon and later AMD processors' double-pumped frontside bus. DDR SDRAM could not run as fast as RDRAM—although relatively low frontside bus speeds made that a moot point—but cost only slightly more than regular SDRAM.

DDR SDRAM for desktops comes in 184-pin DIMMs. These DIMMs match 168-pin DIMMs in physical size but not in pin compatibility (see Figure 5-12). The slots for the two types of RAM appear similar as well but have different guide notches, so you

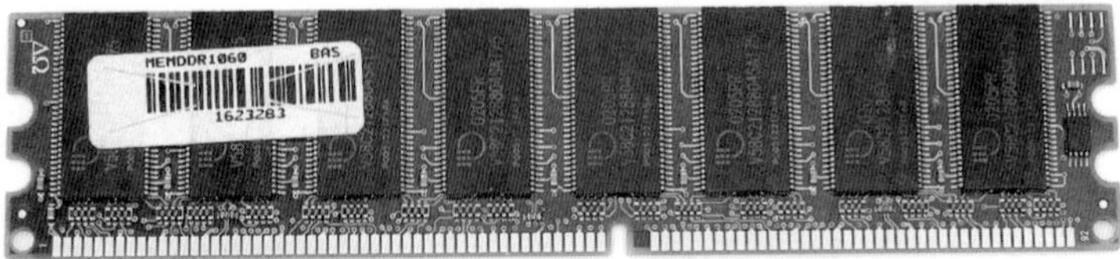

Figure 5-12 DDR SDRAM

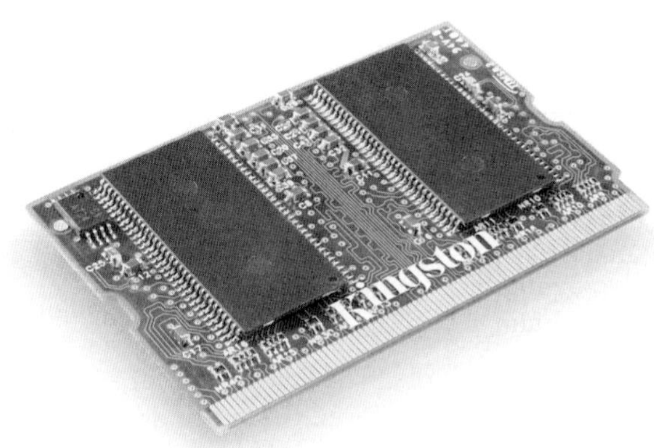

Figure 5-13 172-pin DDR SDRAM micro-DIMM (photo courtesy of Kingston/Joint Harvest)

can't insert either type of RAM into the other's slot. DDR SDRAM for laptops comes in either 200-pin SO-DIMMs or 172-pin micro-DIMMs (see Figure 5-13).

NOTE Most techs drop some or all of the SDRAM part of DDR SDRAM when engaged in normal geekspeak. You'll hear the memory referred to as DDR, DDR RAM, and the weird hybrid, DDRAM.

DDR sticks use a rather interesting naming convention based on the number of bytes per second of data throughput the RAM can handle. To determine the bytes per second, take the MHz speed and multiply by 8 bytes (the width of all DDR SDRAM sticks). So 400 MHz multiplied by 8 is 3200 megabytes per second (MBps). Put the abbreviation "PC" in the front to make the new term: PC3200. Many techs also use the naming convention used for the individual DDR chips; for example, *DDR400* refers to a 400-MHz DDR SDRAM chip running on a 200-MHz clock.

Even though the term DDR*xxx* is really just for individual DDR chips and the term PC*xxxx* is for DDR sticks, this tradition of two names for every speed of RAM is a bit of a challenge because you'll often hear both terms used interchangeably. Table 5-1 shows all the speeds for DDR—not all of these are commonly used.

Clock Speed	DDR Speed Rating	PC Speed Rating
100 MHz	DDR-200	PC-1600
133 MHz	DDR-266	PC-2100
166 MHz	DDR-333	PC-2700
200 MHz	DDR-400	PC-3200
217 MHz	DDR-433	PC-3500
233 MHz	DDR-466	PC-3700
250 MHz	DDR-500	PC-4000
275 MHz	DDR-550	PC-4400
300 MHz	DDR-600	PC-4800

Table 5-1 DDR Speeds

Following the lead of AMD and other manufacturers, the PC industry adopted DDR SDRAM as the standard system RAM. In the summer of 2003, Intel relented and stopped producing motherboards and memory controllers that required RDRAM.

One thing is certain about PC technologies: any good idea that can be copied will be copied. One of Rambus' best concepts was the *dual-channel architecture*—using two sticks of RDRAM together to increase throughput. Manufacturers have released motherboards with MCCs that support dual-channel architecture using DDR SDRAM. Dual-channel DDR motherboards use regular DDR sticks, although manufacturers often sell RAM in matched pairs, branding them as dual-channel RAM.

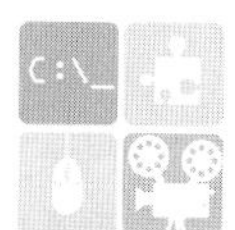

SIM I've got a great Chapter 5 Challenge! sim on calculating RAM speeds at totalsem.com/90x. Check it out right now!

Dual-channel DDR requires two identical sticks of DDR and they must snap into two paired slots. Many motherboards offer four slots (see Figure 5-14).

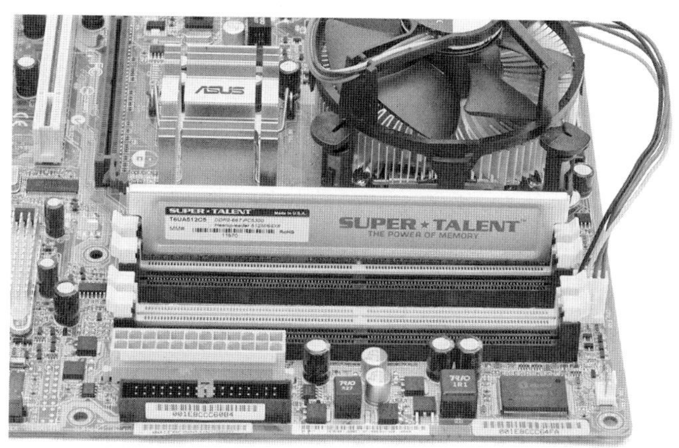

Figure 5-14 A motherboard showing four RAM slots. By populating the same-colored slots with identical RAM, you can run in dual-channel mode.

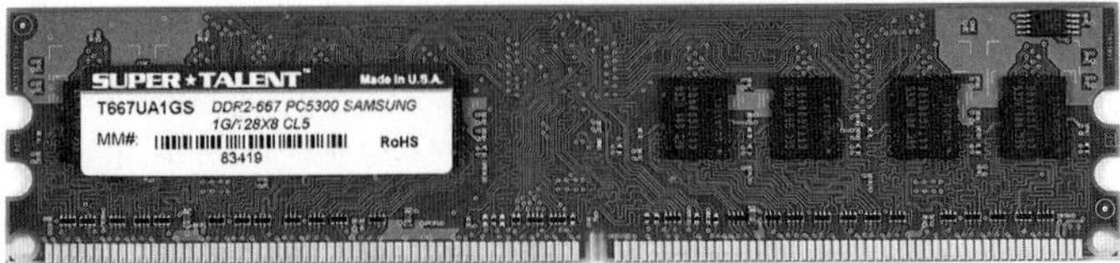

Figure 5-15 240-pin DDR2 DIMM

DDR2

DDR2 is DDR RAM with some improvements in its electrical characteristics, enabling it to run even faster than DDR while using less power. The big speed increase from DDR2 comes by clock doubling the input/output circuits on the chips. This does not speed up the core RAM—the part that holds the data—but speeding up the input/output and adding special buffers (sort of like a cache) makes DDR2 run much faster than regular DDR. DDR2 uses a 240-pin DIMM that's not compatible with DDR (see Figure 5-15). Likewise, the DDR2 200-pin SO-DIMM is incompatible with the DDR SO-DIMM. You'll find motherboards running both single-channel and dual-channel DDR2.

NOTE DDR2 RAM sticks will not fit into DDR sockets, nor are they electronically compatible.

Table 5-2 shows some of the common DDR2 speeds.

Core RAM Clock Speed	DDR I/O Speed	DDR2 Speed Rating	PC Speed Rating
100 MHz	200 MHz	DDR2-400	PC2-3200
133 MHz	266 MHz	DDR2-533	PC2-4200
166 MHz	333 MHz	DDR2-667	PC2-5300
200 MHz	400 MHz	DDR2-800	PC2-6400
266 MHz	533 MHz	DDR2-1066	PC2-8500

Table 5-2 DDR2 Speeds

DDR3

DDR3 boasts higher speeds, more efficient architecture, and around 30 percent lower power consumption than DDR2 RAM, making it a compelling choice for system builders. Just like its predecessor, DDR3 uses a 240-pin DIMM, albeit one that is slotted differently to make it difficult for users to install the wrong RAM in their system without using a hammer (see Figure 5-16). DDR3 SO-DIMMs for portable computers have 204 pins. Neither fits into a DDR2 socket.

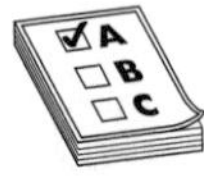

EXAM TIP The 220-901 exam will test your knowledge of the various RAM types including DDR, DDR2, and DDR3. Be sure you are familiar with their individual characteristics and differences. DDR3 DIMMs have 240 pins, for example, and DDR3 SO-DIMMs have 204 pins. They are physically and electronically incompatible with DDR2 DIMMs and SO-DIMMs.

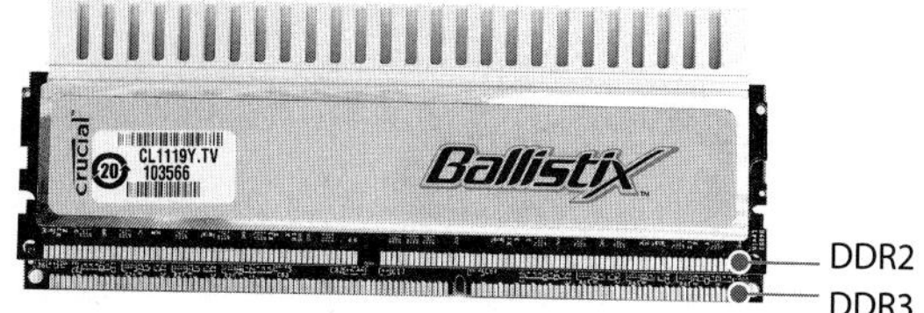

Figure 5-16 DDR2 DIMM on top of a DDR3 DIMM

NOTE Do not confuse DDR3 with GDDR3; the latter is a type of memory used solely in video cards. See Chapter 19, "Display Technologies," for the scoop on video-specific types of memory.

DDR3 doubles the buffer of DDR2 from 4 bits to 8 bits, giving it a huge boost in bandwidth over older RAM. Not only that, but some DDR3 modules also include a feature called *XMP*, or *extended memory profile*, that enables power users to overclock their RAM easily, boosting their already fast memory. DDR3 modules also use higher-density memory chips, up to 16-GB DDR3 modules.

Some motherboards that support DDR3 also support features called *triple-channel architecture* or *quad-channel architecture*, which work a lot like dual-channel, but with three or four sticks of RAM instead of two. Intel's LGA 1366 platform supports triple-channel memory; no AMD processors support a triple-channel feature. More recent Intel and AMD systems support quad-channel memory.

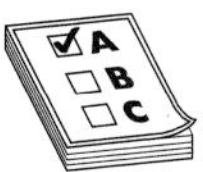

EXAM TIP Be sure you are familiar with single-, dual-, and triple-channel memory architectures.

Table 5-3 shows common DDR3 speeds. Note how DDR3 I/O speeds are quadruple the clock speeds, whereas DDR2 I/O speeds are only double the clock. This speed increase is due to the increased buffer size, which enables DDR3 to grab twice as much data every clock cycle as DDR2 can.

Core RAM Clock Speed	DDR I/O Speed	DDR3 Speed Rating	PC Speed Rating
100 MHz	400 MHz	DDR3-800	PC3-6400
133 MHz	533 MHz	DDR3-1066	PC3-8500
166 MHz	667 MHz	DDR3-1333	PC3-10667
200 MHz	800 MHz	DDR3-1600	PC3-12800
233 MHz	933 MHz	DDR3-1866	PC3-14900
266 MHz	1066 MHz	DDR3-2133	PC3-17000
300 MHz	1200 MHz	DDR3-2400	PC3-19200

Table 5-3 DDR3 Speeds

DDR3L/DDR3U

Memory manufacturers offer a low-voltage version of DDR3, most commonly labeled *DDR3L*, that provides substantial cost savings when used in massive RAM applications. (Think big data centers, like the ones that power Google.) DDR3L runs at 1.35 volts (V), compared to the 1.5 V or 1.65 V of regular DDR3, providing cost savings up to 15 percent—that adds up fast! The ultra-low-voltage version of DDR3, *DDR3U*, runs at a miserly 1.25 V.

Lower voltage means less heat generated. In a server farm or data center, that can reduce the air conditioning bill by a lot. That's a good thing.

The DIMM is slot-compatible with DDR3, although not necessarily a drama-free replacement on older motherboards. A motherboard pushing 1.5 V to the RAM slots and RAM only capable of running at 1.35 V would not result in happiness.

For best results, check the manual that came with the motherboard in question or check the manufacturer's Web site for support. Also, many RAM manufacturers produce RAM modules capable of running at 1.35 V or 1.5 V; those will work in any motherboard that supports DDR3. Some modules can handle the full gamut, from 1.25 V to 1.65 V.

DDR4

DDR4 arrived on the scene in late 2014 with much fanfare and slow adoption. DDR4 offers higher density and lower voltages than DDR3, and can handle faster data transfer rates. In theory, manufacturers could create DDR4 DIMMs up to 512 GB. As of this writing, DIMMS running DDR4 top out at 16 GB, like DDR3, but run at only 1.2 V. (There's a performance version that runs at 1.35 V and a low-voltage version at 1.05 V too.)

DDR4 uses a 288-pin DIMM, so they are not backwardly compatible with DDR3 slots. DDR4 SO-DIMMs have 260 pins that are not compatible with DDR3 204-pin SO-DIMM slots. Some motherboard manufacturers have released boards that offer support for both DDR3 and DDR4, by providing both slot types.

NOTE Intel has proposed a memory standard as of this writing that would bridge the gap between DDR3 and DDR4, called *UniDIMM*. The processor architecture released in the summer of 2015, called Skylake, can handle either type of memory. The UniDIMM memory can be either DDR3 or DDR4 and the processor can handle it.

Depending on when you're reading this note, UniDIMM might be a reality, or a blip in the past. Either way, it's not covered on the CompTIA A+ 901 exam.

With DDR4, most techs have switched from bit rate to megatransfers per second (MT/s), a way to describe the bandwidth as the number of data transfer operations happening at any given second. For DDR4, the number is pretty huge. Table 5-4 shows common DDR4 speeds and labels.

Clock Speed	Bandwidth	DDR4 Speed Rating	PC Speed Rating
200 MHz	1600 MT/s	DDR4-1600	PC4-12800
266 MHz	2133 MT/s	DDR4-2133	PC4-17000
300 MHz	2400 MT/s	DDR4-2400	PC4-19200
400 MHz	3200 MT/s	DDR4-3200	PC4-25600

Table 5-4 Standard DDR4 Varieties

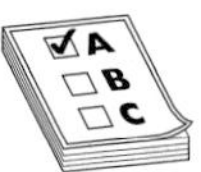

EXAM TIP The CompTIA A+ 901 exam covers only DDR, DDR2, and DDR3 sticks. You won't find DDR3L, DDR3U, or DDR4 on the exam.

RAM Variations

Within each class of RAM, you'll find variations in packaging, speed, quality, and the capability to handle data with more or fewer errors. Higher-end systems often need higher-end RAM, so knowing these variations is of crucial importance to techs.

Double-Sided DIMMs

Every type of RAM stick comes in one of two types: *single-sided RAM* and *double-sided RAM*. As their name implies, single-sided sticks have chips on only one side of the stick. Double-sided sticks have chips on both sides (see Figure 5-17). Double-sided sticks are basically two sticks of RAM soldered onto one board. There's nothing wrong with double-sided RAM sticks other than the fact that some motherboards either can't use them or can only use them in certain ways—for example, only if you use a single stick and it goes into a certain slot.

Figure 5-17 Double-sided DDR SDRAM

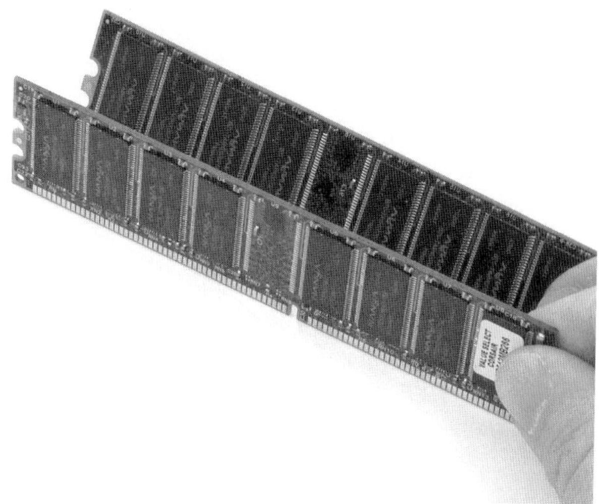

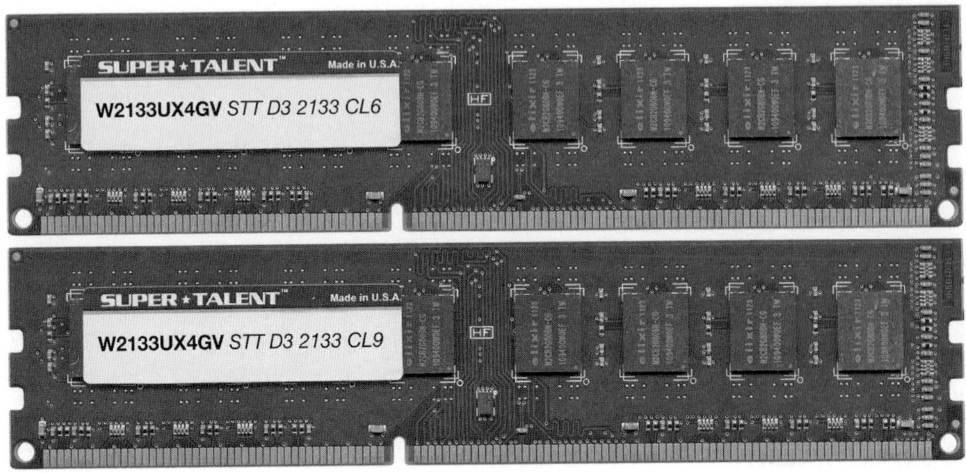

Figure 5-18 Why is one more expensive than the other?

Latency

If you've shopped for RAM lately, you may have noticed terms such as "CL6" or "low latency" as you tried to determine which RAM to purchase. You might find two otherwise identical RAM sticks with a 20 percent price difference and a salesperson pressuring you to buy the more expensive one because it's "faster" even though both sticks say DDR3-2133 (see Figure 5-18).

RAM responds to electrical signals at varying rates. When the memory controller starts to grab a line of memory, for example, a slight delay occurs; think of it as the RAM getting off the couch. After the RAM sends out the requested line of memory, there's another slight delay before the memory controller can ask for another line—the RAM sat back down. The delay in RAM's response time is called its *latency*. RAM with a lower latency—such as CL6—is faster than RAM with a higher latency—such as CL9—because it responds more quickly. The CL refers to clock cycle delays. The "6" means that the memory delays six clock cycles before delivering the requested data; the "9" means a nine-cycle delay.

The latency numbers can help you decide between two similar sticks of RAM, but can deceive you when comparing generations of memory. It's obvious that an 8-GB stick from G.SKILL with a column array strobe (CAS) latency of 11 is not as good as their "identical" and slightly more expensive stick with a CAS latency of 9. That's comparing apples to apples.

Before DDR4 debuted, however, its relatively high latency made enthusiasts question the memory companies, complaining that it would be too slow. Once released and tested, though, the added efficiency and technology improvements proved DDR4 performed equally with DDR3 at the same clock speed, even with higher latency. Plus DDR4 will eventually scale up much higher in speed that DDR3 can.

NOTE Latency numbers reflect how many ticks of the system clock it takes before the RAM responds. If you speed up the system clock—say, from 200 MHz to 266 MHz—the same stick of RAM might take an extra tick before it can respond. When you take RAM out of an older system and put it into a newer one, you might get a seemingly dead PC, even though the RAM fits in the DIMM slot. Many motherboards enable you to adjust the RAM timings manually. If yours does so, try raising the latency to give the slower RAM time to respond. See Chapter 7, "BIOS," to learn how to make these adjustments (and how to recover if you make a mistake).

From a tech's standpoint, you need to get the proper RAM for the system you're working on. If you put a high-latency stick in a motherboard set up for a low-latency stick, you'll get an unstable or completely dead PC. Check the motherboard manual or RAM manufacturer's Web site and get the quickest RAM the motherboard can handle, and you should be fine.

NOTE CAS stands for *column array strobe*, as mentioned earlier, one of the wires (along with the *row array strobe*) in the RAM that helps the memory controller find a particular bit of memory. Each of these wires requires electricity to charge up before it can do its job. This is one of the aspects of latency.

Parity and ECC

Given the high speeds and phenomenal amount of data moved by the typical DRAM chip, a RAM chip might occasionally give bad data to the memory controller. This doesn't necessarily mean that the RAM has gone bad. It could be a hiccup caused by some unknown event that makes a good DRAM chip say a bit is a zero when it's really a one. In most cases you won't even notice when such a rare event happens. In some environments, however, even these rare events are intolerable. A bank server handling thousands of online transactions per second, for example, can't risk even the smallest error. These important computers need a more robust, fault-resistant RAM.

The first type of error-detecting RAM was known as parity RAM (see Figure 5-19). *Parity RAM* stored an extra bit of data (called the parity bit) that the MCC used to verify whether the data was correct. Parity wasn't perfect. It wouldn't always detect an error, and if the MCC did find an error, it couldn't correct the error. For years, parity was the only available way to tell if the RAM made a mistake.

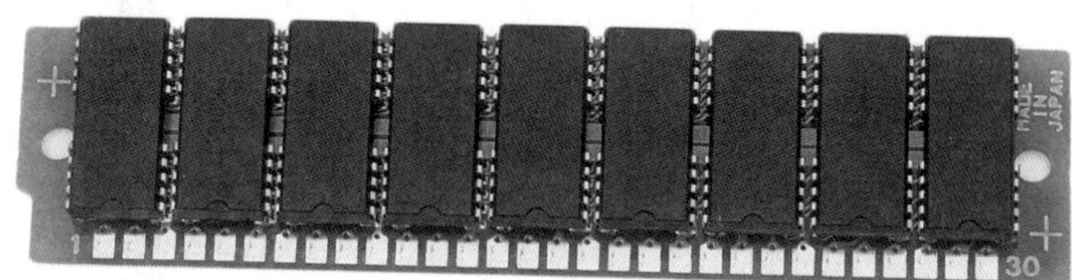

Figure 5-19 Ancient parity RAM stick

Today's PCs that need to watch for RAM errors use a special type of RAM called *error correction code RAM (ECC RAM)*. ECC is a major advance in error checking on DRAM. First, ECC detects any time a single bit is incorrect. Second, ECC fixes these errors on-the-fly. The checking and fixing come at a price, however, as ECC RAM is always slower than non-ECC RAM.

ECC DRAM comes in every DIMM package type and can lead to some odd-sounding numbers. You can find DDR2, DDR3, or DDR4 RAM sticks, for example, that come in 240-pin, *72*-bit versions. Similarly, you'll see 200-pin, 72-bit SO-DIMM format. The extra 8 bits beyond the 64-bit data stream are for the ECC.

You might be tempted to say, "Gee, maybe I want to try this ECC RAM." Well, don't! To take advantage of ECC RAM, you need a motherboard with an MCC designed to use ECC. Only expensive motherboards for high-end systems use ECC. The special-use-only nature of ECC makes it fairly rare. Plenty of techs with years of experience have never even seen ECC RAM.

NOTE Some memory manufacturers call the technology *error checking and correction* (ECC). Don't be thrown off if you see the phrase—it's the same thing, just a different marketing slant for error correction code.

Registered and Buffered Memory

When shopping for memory, especially for ECC memory, you are bound to come across the terms *registered RAM* or *buffered RAM* (CompTIA uses the latter term on the A+ 901 exam). Either term refers to a small register installed on some memory modules to act as a buffer between the DIMM and the memory controller. This little extra bit of circuitry helps compensate for electrical problems that crop up in systems with lots of memory modules, such as servers.

The key thing to remember is that a motherboard will use either buffered or *unbuffered RAM* (that's typical consumer RAM), not both. If you insert a module of the wrong type in a system you are upgrading, the worst that will happen is a blank screen and a lot of head scratching.

Working with RAM

Whenever someone comes up to me and asks what single hardware upgrade they can make to improve their system performance, I always tell them the same thing—add more RAM. Adding more RAM can improve overall system performance, processing speed, and stability—if you get it right. Botching the job can cause dramatic system instability, such as frequent, random crashes and reboots. Every tech needs to know how to install and upgrade system RAM of all types.

To get the desired results from a RAM upgrade, you must first determine if insufficient RAM is the cause of system problems. Second, you need to pick the proper RAM for the system. Finally, you must use good installation practices. Always store RAM sticks in anti-static packaging whenever they're not in use, and use strict ESD handling procedures.

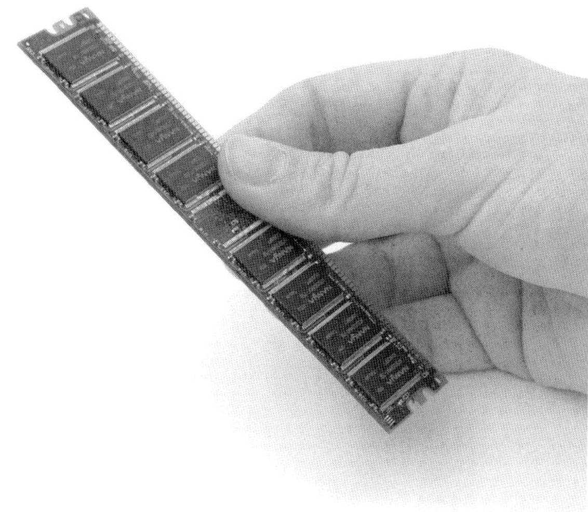

Figure 5-20 Don't do this! Grabbing the contacts is a bad idea!

Like many other pieces of the PC, RAM is *very* sensitive to ESD and other technician abuse (see Figure 5-20).

Do You Need More RAM?

Two symptoms point to the need for more RAM in a PC: general system sluggishness and excessive hard drive accessing. If programs take forever to load and running programs seem to stall and move more slowly than you would like, the problem could stem from insufficient RAM.

A friend with a Windows 7 system complained that her PC seemed snappy when she first got it but now takes a long time to do the things she wants to do with it, such as photograph retouching in Adobe Photoshop and document layout for an online magazine she produces. Her system had only 2 GB of RAM, sufficient to run Windows 7, but woefully insufficient for her tasks—she kept maxing out the RAM, and thus the system slowed to a crawl. I replaced her stick with a pair of 4-GB sticks and suddenly she had the powerhouse workstation she desired.

Excessive hard drive activity when you move between programs points to a need for more RAM. Every computer has the capability to make a portion of your hard drive work like RAM in case you run out of real RAM.

Virtual Memory

Computers use a portion of the hard drive as an extension of system RAM, through what's called virtual memory. Virtual memory is a portion of a hard drive or solid state drive set aside as what's called a *page file* or *swap file*. When a computer starts running out of real RAM because you've loaded too many programs, the system swaps programs from RAM to the page file, opening more space for programs currently active. All versions of

Windows, Mac OS X, and Linux use virtual memory. Let's use a typical Windows PC as an example of how paging works.

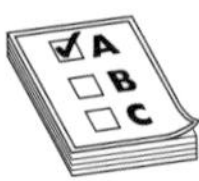

EXAM TIP The default and recommended page-file size in Windows is 1.5 times the amount of installed RAM on your computer.

Let's assume you have a PC with 4 GB of RAM. Figure 5-21 shows the system RAM as a thermometer with gradients from 0 to 4 GB. As programs load, they take up RAM, and as more and more programs are loaded (labeled A, B, and C in the figure), more RAM is used.

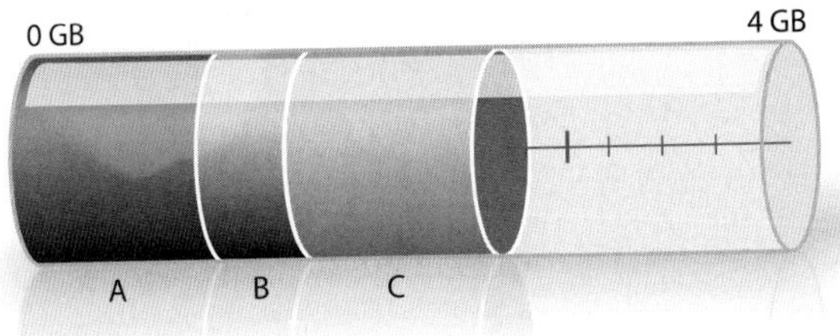

Figure 5-21 A RAM thermometer showing that more programs take more RAM

At a certain point, you won't have enough RAM to run any more programs (see Figure 5-22). Sure, you could close one or more programs to make room for yet another one, but you can't keep all of the programs running simultaneously. This is where virtual memory comes into play.

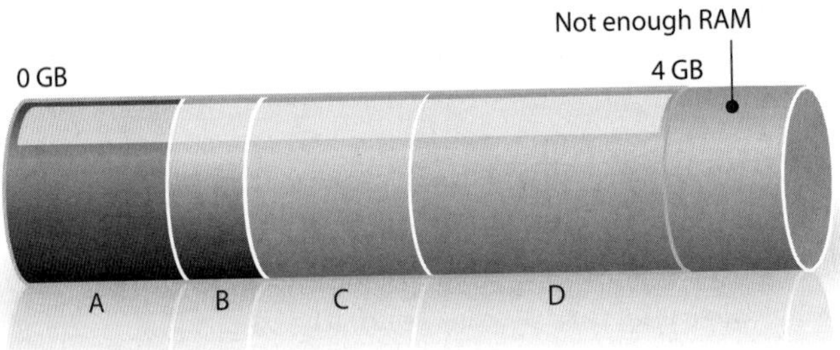

Figure 5-22 Not enough RAM to load program D

Windows' virtual memory starts by creating a page file that resides somewhere on your hard drive. The page file works like a temporary storage box. Windows removes running programs temporarily from RAM into the page file so other programs can load and run. If you have enough RAM to run all your programs, Windows does not need to use the page file—Windows brings the page file into play only when insufficient RAM is available to run all open programs.

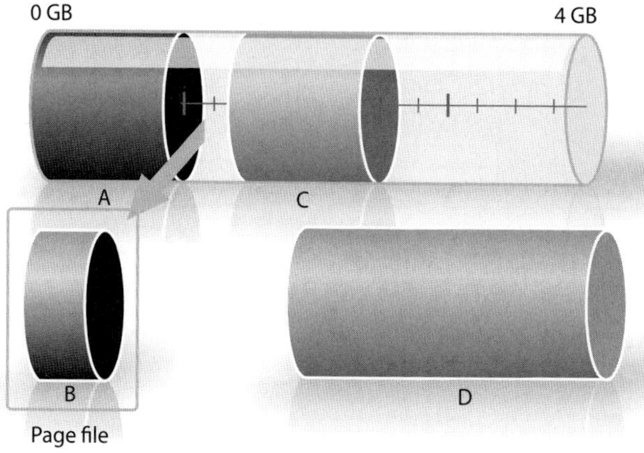

Figure 5-23 Program B being unloaded from memory

NOTE Virtual memory is a fully automated process and does not require any user intervention. This is true of virtual memory in Windows, Mac OS X, and Linux distributions ("distros").

To load, Program D needs a certain amount of free RAM. Clearly, this requires unloading some other program (or programs) from RAM without actually closing any programs. Windows looks at all running programs—in this case A, B, and C—and decides which program is the least used. That program is then cut out of or swapped from RAM and copied into the page file. In this case, Windows has chosen Program B (see Figure 5-23). Unloading Program B from RAM provides enough RAM to load Program D (see Figure 5-24).

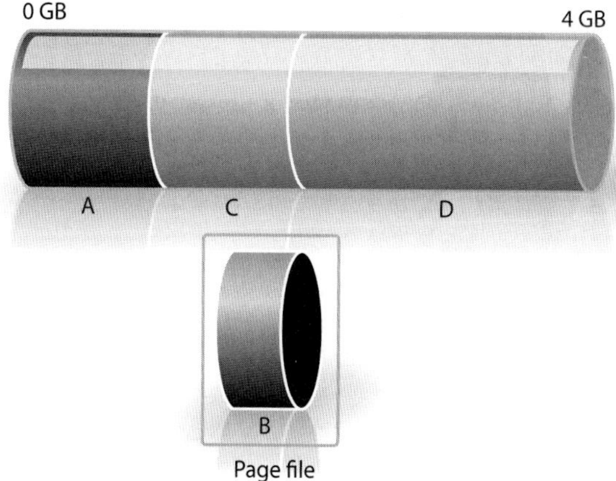

Figure 5-24 Program B stored in the page file, making room for Program D

It is important to understand that none of this activity is visible on the screen. Program B's window is still visible, along with those of all the other running programs. Nothing tells the user that Program B is no longer in RAM (see Figure 5-25).

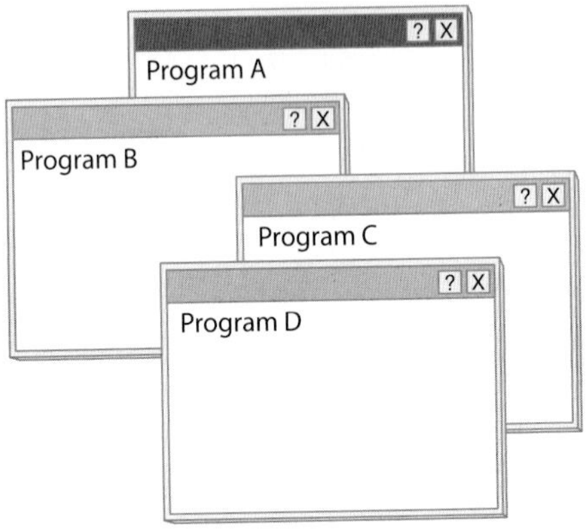

Figure 5-25 You can't tell whether a program is swapped or not.

So what happens if you click on Program B's window to bring it to the front? The program can't actually run from the page file; it must be loaded back into RAM. First, Windows decides which program must be removed from RAM, and this time Windows chooses Program C (see Figure 5-26). Then it loads Program B into RAM (see Figure 5-27).

Swapping programs to and from the page file and RAM takes time. Although no visual clues suggest that a swap is taking place, the machine slows down quite noticeably as Windows performs the swaps. Page files are a crucial aspect of Windows operation.

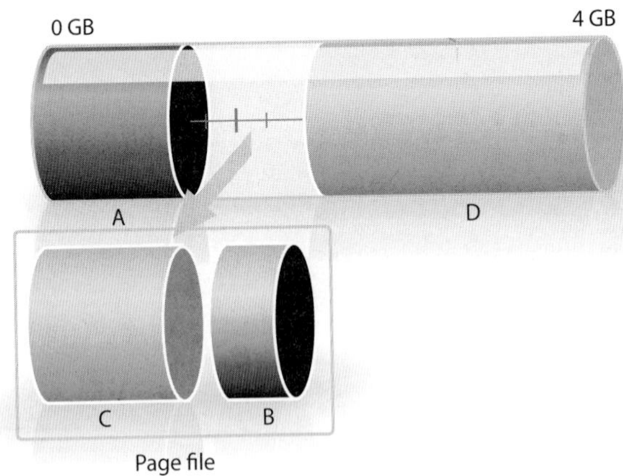

Figure 5-26 Program C is swapped to the page file.

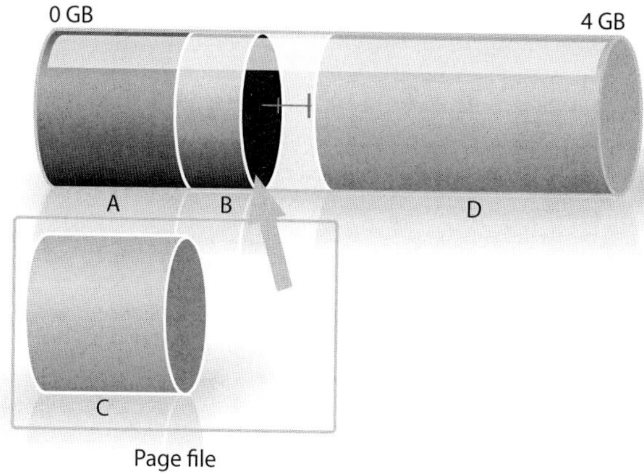

Figure 5-27 Program B is swapped back into RAM.

Windows handles page files automatically, but occasionally you'll run into problems and need to change the size of the page file or delete it and let Windows re-create it automatically. The page file is pagefile.sys. You can often find it in the root directory of the C: drive, but again, that can be changed. Wherever it is, the page file is a hidden system file, which means in practice that you'll have to play with your folder-viewing options to see it.

If Windows needs to access the page file too frequently, you will notice the hard drive access LED going crazy as Windows rushes to move programs between RAM and the page file in a process called *disk thrashing*. Windows uses the page file all the time, but excessive disk thrashing suggests that you need more RAM.

System RAM Recommendations

Microsoft sets very low minimum RAM requirements for the various Windows operating systems to get the maximum number of users to upgrade or convert, and that's fine. Old Windows machines ran well enough on 128 MB of RAM. Windows Vista raised the bar considerably, especially with the 64-bit versions of the operating system. Microsoft recommends a minimum system requirement of 1 GB of RAM for 32-bit versions of Windows and 2 GB of RAM for 64-bit versions. This applies to Windows Vista/7/8/8.1/10. I think that results in dreadfully sluggish computers. Here are my recommendations:

- **32-bit Windows** 2 GB to get by; 4 GB for best results
- **64-bit Windows** 4 GB to get by; 8 GB for a solid machine; 16+ GB for any machine doing serious, processor-intensive work

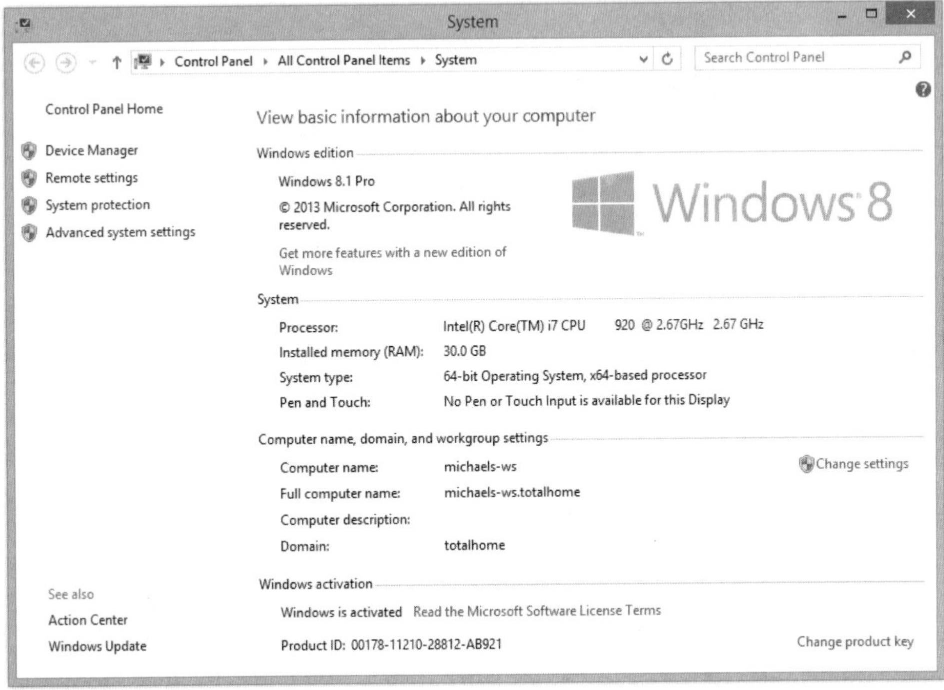

Figure 5-28 Mike has a lot of RAM!

The latest versions of Mac OS X require a minimum of 2 GB of RAM. Like Windows, however, the 64-bit-only OS does much better with a lot more RAM. I would go with 4 GB at a minimum, 8 GB for good performance, and more for peak performance.

Linux RAM requirements and recommendations depend entirely on the distro used. The mainstream ones, like Ubuntu, have requirements similar to Windows and Mac OS X. But many distros get by on very minimal system requirements.

Finally, a lot of personal computing devices have memory soldered in place and cannot be upgraded. That includes smartphones, tablets, and a host of portable computers, like the MacBook Air.

Determining Current RAM Capacity

Before you go get RAM, you obviously need to know how much RAM you currently have in your PC. Windows displays this amount in the System Control Panel applet (see Figure 5-28). You can also access the screen with the WINDOWS-PAUSE/BREAK keystroke combination.

Windows also includes the handy Performance tab in the Task Manager (as shown in Figure 5-29). The Performance tab includes a lot of information about the amount of RAM being used by your PC. Access the Task Manager by pressing CTRL-SHIFT-ESC and selecting the Performance tab.

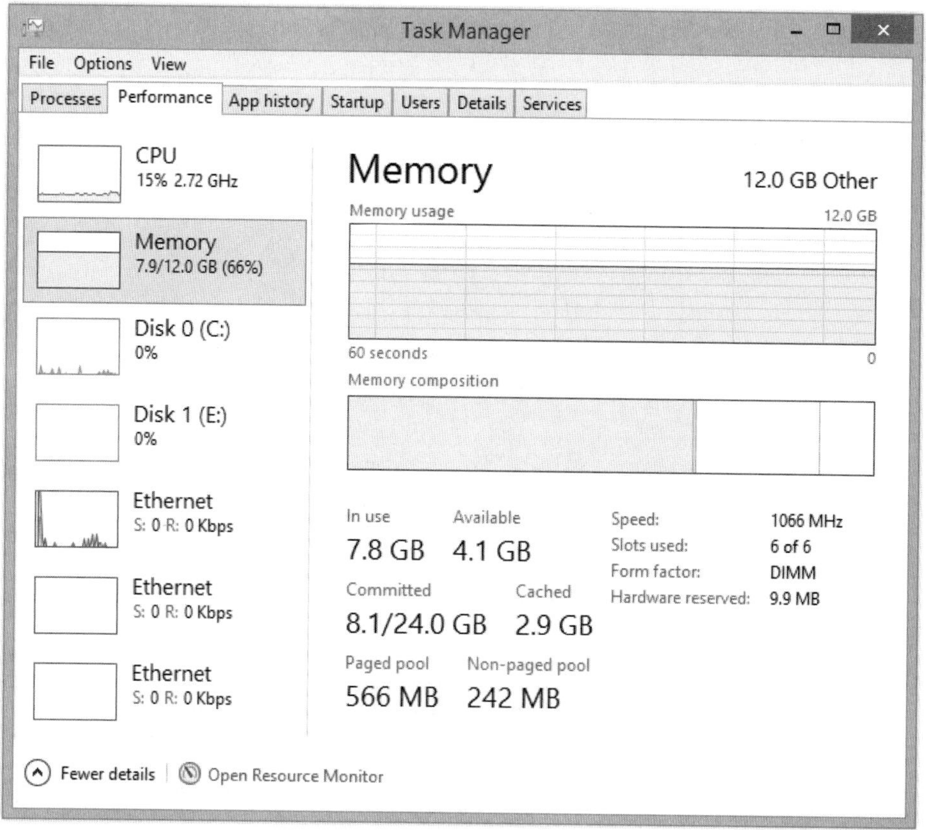

Figure 5-29 Performance tab in Windows 8.1 Task Manager

ReadyBoost

Windows Vista and later versions offer a feature called *ReadyBoost* that enables you to use flash media devices—removable USB thumb drives or memory cards—as super-fast, dedicated virtual memory. The performance gain over using only a typical hard drive for virtual memory can be significant with ReadyBoost because read/write access times on flash memory blows hard drive read/write access times away. Plus, the added ReadyBoost device or devices means Windows has multiple sources of virtual memory that it can use at the same time.

Windows 7 and later can handle up to eight flash devices, whereas Windows Vista can benefit from only one device. Devices can be between 1 and 32 GB in capacity. The flash device's file system matters in terms of how much memory Windows can use. Typically, the most you'll get out of a flash drive is 4 GB without manually changing the file system. Finally, Microsoft recommends using 1–3× the amount of system RAM for the ReadyBoost drives or devices to get optimal performance.

NOTE See Chapter 10, "Implementing Hard Drives," for an explanation of the differences between FAT, FAT32, NTFS, and exFAT.

Plug a ReadyBoost-approved device into a USB port or built-in flash memory card reader slot. Right-click the device in Computer and select Properties. Click the ReadyBoost tab and select the radio button next to either *Dedicate this device to ReadyBoost* or *Use this device* (see Figure 5-30). Click Apply to enhance your system's performance.

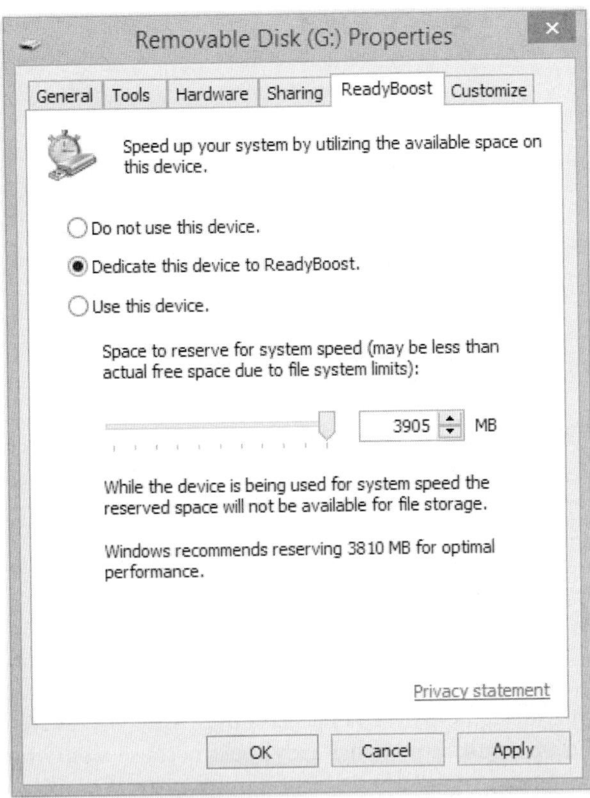

Figure 5-30 Dedicating a flash drive to ReadyBoost to enhance system performance

NOTE Adding more system memory will always give you or your clients a far better boost in performance than messing with ReadyBoost. ReadyBoost was essentially a bridge tool for Windows Vista adopters with marginal systems. RAM is relatively cheap today. Add some and blow off ReadyBoost. Just remember ReadyBoost for the exams.

Getting the Right RAM

To do the perfect RAM upgrade, determine the optimum amount of RAM to install and then get the right RAM for the motherboard. Your first two stops toward these goals are the inside of the case and your motherboard manual. Open the case to see how many sticks of RAM you have installed currently and how many free slots you have open.

Check the motherboard book or RAM manufacturer's Web site to determine the total capacity of RAM the system can handle and what specific technology works with your system.

You can't put DDR4 into a system that can only handle DDR3 SDRAM, after all, and it won't do you much good to install a pair of 4-GB DIMMs when your system tops out at 4 GB. Figure 5-31 shows the RAM limits for an ASUS Crosshair motherboard.

Crosshair specifications summary

CPU	Support AMD® Socket AM2 Athlon 64 X2 / Athlon 64 FX / Athlon 64/ Sempron AMD Cool 'n' Quiet™ Technology AMD64 architecture enables simultaneous 32-bit and 64-bit computing AMD Live!™ Ready
Chipset	NVIDIA nForce® 590 SLI™ MCP NVIDIA LinkBoost™ Technology
System bus	2000 / 1600 MT/s
Memory	Dual channel memory architecture 4 x DIMM, max. 8GB, DDR2-800/667/533, ECC and non-ECC, un-buffered memory
Expansion slots	2 x PCI Express x16 slot with NVIDIA® SLI™ technology support, at full x16, x16 speed 1 x PCI Express x4 3 x PCI 2.2
Scalable Link Interface (SLI™)	Support two identical NVIDIA SLI-Ready graphics cards (both at x16 mode) ASUS two-slot thermal design ASUS PEG Link
High Definition Audio	SupremeFX Audio Card featuring ADI 1988B 8-channel High Definition Audio CODEC Support Jack-Sensing, Enumeration, Multi-streaming and Jack-Retasking 8 channel audio ports Coaxial, Optical S/PDIF out on back I/O port * ASUS Array Mic * Noise Filter
Storage	NVIDIA nForce® 590 SLI™ MCP supports: * 1 x Ultra DMA 133 / 100 / 66 / 33 * 6 x Serial ATA 3.0Gb/s with NCQ * NVIDIA MediaShield™ RAID supports RAID 0, 1, 0+1, 5 and JBOD span cross Serial ATA drives Silicon Image® 3132 SATA controller supports: * 2 x External Serial ATA 3.0Gb/s port on back I/O (SATA On-the-Go) * Support RAID 0, 1, JBOD, RAID 0+1(10) and 5 through multiplier

(continued on the next page)

xi

Figure 5-31 The motherboard book shows how much RAM the motherboard will handle.

NOTE The freeware CPU-Z program tells you the total number of slots on your motherboard, the number of slots used, and the exact type of RAM in each slot—very handy. CPU-Z not only determines the latency of your RAM but also lists the latency at a variety of motherboard speeds. The media accompanying this book has a copy of CPU-Z, so check it out or download it from www.cpuid.com.

Mix and Match at Your Peril

All motherboards can handle different capacities of RAM. If you have three slots, you may put a 2-GB stick in one and a 4-GB stick in the other with a high chance of success. To ensure maximum stability in a system, however, shoot for as close as you can get to uniformity of RAM. Choose RAM sticks that match in technology, capacity, and speed.

Mixing Speeds

With so many different DRAM speeds available, you may often find yourself tempted to mix speeds of DRAM in the same system. Although you may get away with mixing speeds on a system, the safest, easiest rule to follow is to use the speed of DRAM specified in the motherboard book, and make sure that every piece of DRAM runs at that speed. In a worst-case scenario, mixing DRAM speeds can cause the system to lock up every few seconds or every few minutes. You might also get some data corruption. Mixing speeds sometimes works fine, but don't do your tax return on a machine with mixed DRAM speeds until the system has proven to be stable for a few days. The important thing to note here is that you won't break anything, other than possibly data, by experimenting.

Okay, I have mentioned enough disclaimers. Modern motherboards provide some flexibility regarding RAM speeds and mixing. First, you can use RAM that is faster than the motherboard specifies. For example, if the system needs PC-3200 DDR2 SDRAM, you may put in PC-4200 DDR2 SDRAM and it should work fine. Faster DRAM is not going to make the system run any faster, however, so don't look for any system improvement.

Second, you can sometimes get away with putting one speed of DRAM in one bank and another speed in another bank, as long as all the speeds are as fast as or faster than the speed specified by the motherboard. Don't bother trying to put different-speed DRAM sticks in the same bank with a motherboard that uses dual-channel DDR.

Installing DIMMs

Installing DRAM is so easy that it's one of the very few jobs I recommend to non-techie folks. First, attach an anti-static wrist strap or touch some bare metal on the power supply to ground yourself and avoid ESD. Then swing the side tabs on the RAM slots down from the upright position. Pick up a stick of RAM—don't touch those contacts—and line up the notch or notches with the raised portion(s) of the DIMM socket (see Figure 5-32). A good hard push down is usually all you need to ensure a solid connection. Make sure that the DIMM snaps into position to show it is completely seated. Also, notice that the two side tabs move in to reflect a tight connection.

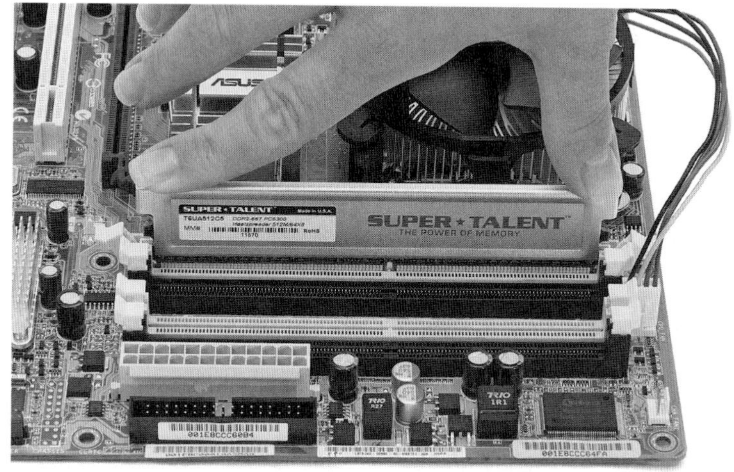

Figure 5-32 Inserting a DIMM

Serial Presence Detect (SPD)

Your motherboard should detect and automatically set up any DIMM you install, assuming you have the right RAM for the system, using a technology called *serial presence detect (SPD)*. RAM makers add a handy chip to modern sticks called the SPD chip (see Figure 5-33). The SPD chip stores all the information about your DRAM, including size, speed, ECC or non-ECC, registered or unregistered, and a number of other more technical bits of information.

When a PC boots, it queries the SPD chip so that the MCC knows how much RAM is on the stick, how fast it runs, and other information. Any program can query the SPD chip. Take a look at Figure 5-34 with the results of the popular CPU-Z program showing RAM information from the SPD chip.

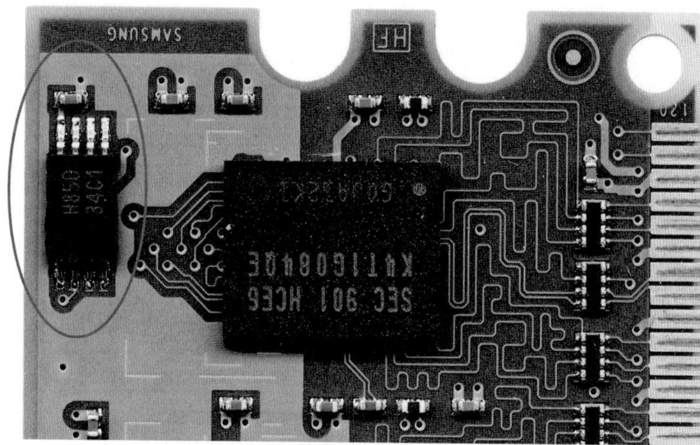

Figure 5-33 SPD chip on a stick

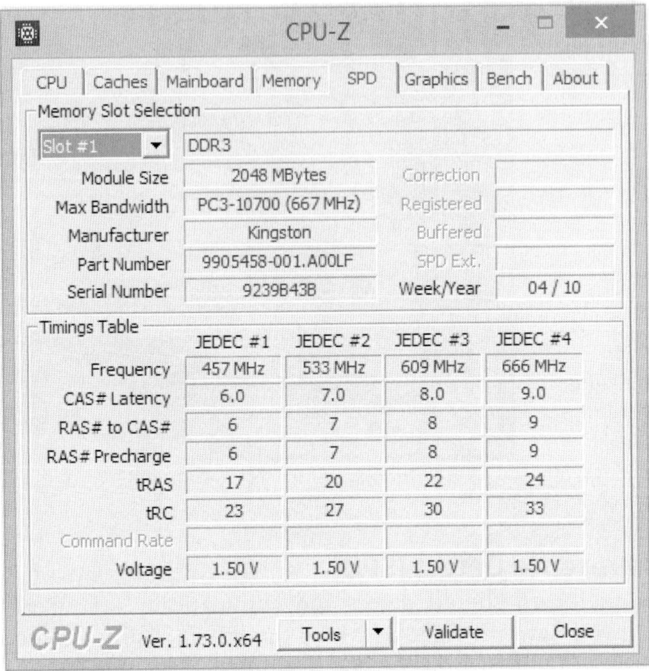

Figure 5-34 CPU-Z showing RAM information

All new systems count on SPD to set the RAM timings properly for your system when it boots. If you add a RAM stick with a bad SPD chip, you'll get a POST error message and the system will not boot. You can't fix a broken SPD chip; you just buy a new stick of RAM.

The RAM Count

Older systems display the RAM count during the initial boot sequence. After installing the new RAM, turn on the PC and watch the boot process closely. If you installed the RAM correctly, the RAM count on the PC reflects the new value (compare Figures 5.35 and 5.36). If the RAM value stays the same, you probably have installed the RAM in a slot the motherboard doesn't want you to use (for example, you may need to use a particular slot first) or have not installed the RAM properly. If the computer does not boot and you've got a blank screen, you probably have not installed all the RAM sticks correctly. Usually, a good second look is all you need to determine the problem. Reseat or reinstall the RAM stick and try again. RAM counts are confusing because RAM uses megabytes and gigabytes as opposed to millions and billions. Here are some examples of how different systems would show 256 MB of RAM:

268435456 (exactly 256 × 1 MB)
256M (some PCs try to make it easy for you)
262,144 (number of KB)

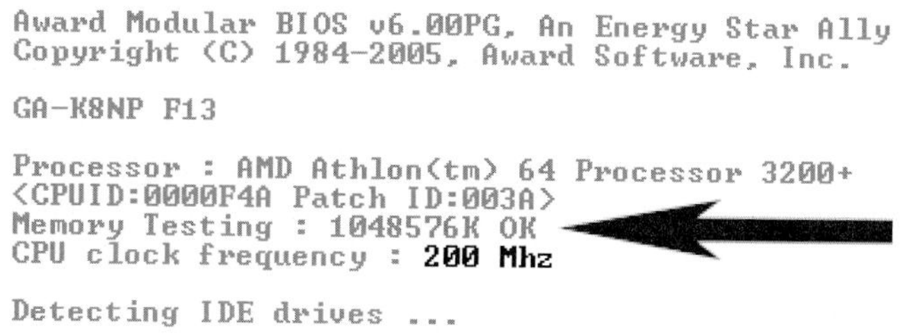

Figure 5-35
Hey, where's the rest of my RAM?!

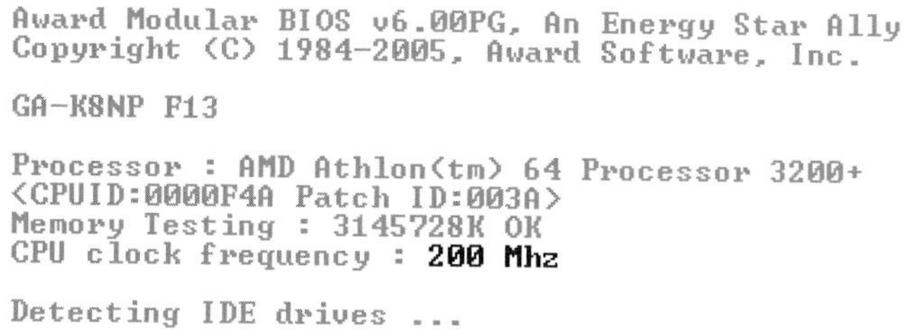

```
Award Modular BIOS v6.00PG, An Energy Star Ally
Copyright (C) 1984-2005, Award Software, Inc.

GA-K8NP F13

Processor : AMD Athlon(tm) 64 Processor 3200+
<CPUID:0000F4A Patch ID:003A>
Memory Testing : 1048576K OK
CPU clock frequency : 200 Mhz

Detecting IDE drives ...
```

Figure 5-36
RAM count after proper insertion of DIMMs

```
Award Modular BIOS v6.00PG, An Energy Star Ally
Copyright (C) 1984-2005, Award Software, Inc.

GA-K8NP F13

Processor : AMD Athlon(tm) 64 Processor 3200+
<CPUID:0000F4A Patch ID:003A>
Memory Testing : 3145728K OK
CPU clock frequency : 200 Mhz

Detecting IDE drives ...
```

You should know how much RAM you're trying to install and use some common sense. If you have 2 GB and you add another 2-GB stick, you should end up with 4 gigabytes of RAM. If you still see a RAM count of 2147483648 after you add the second stick, something went wrong!

Installing SO-DIMMs in Laptops

It wasn't that long ago that adding RAM to a laptop was either impossible or required you to send the system back to the manufacturer. For years, every laptop maker had custom-made, proprietary RAM packages that were difficult to handle and staggeringly expensive. The wide acceptance of SO-DIMMs has virtually erased these problems. Most laptops now provide relatively convenient access to their SO-DIMMs, enabling easy replacement or addition of RAM.

Access to RAM usually requires removing a panel or lifting up the keyboard—the procedure varies among laptop manufacturers. Figure 5-37 shows a typical laptop RAM access panel. You can slide the panel off to reveal the SO-DIMMs. Slide the pins into position and snap the SO-DIMM down into the retaining clips (see Figure 5-38).

Before doing any work on a laptop, turn the system off, disconnect it from the AC wall socket, and remove any removable batteries. Use an anti-static wrist strap because laptops are far more susceptible to ESD than desktop PCs.

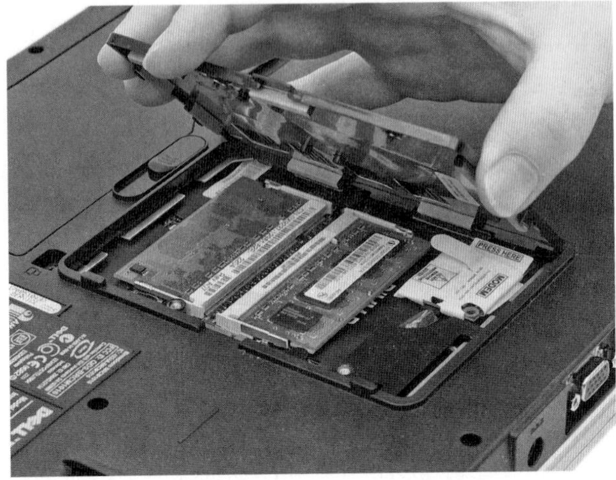

Figure 5-37 A RAM access panel on a laptop

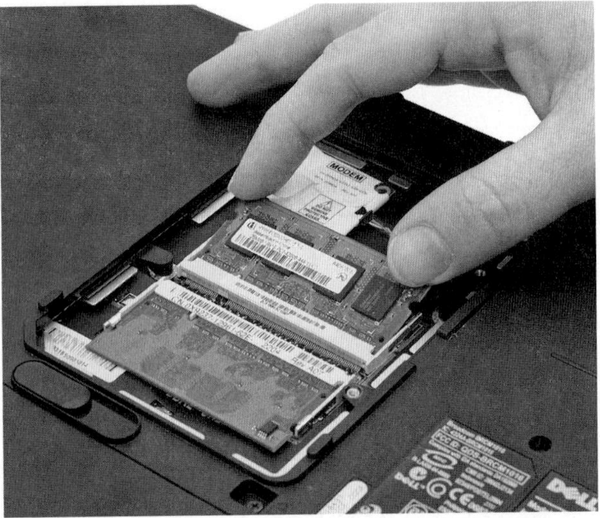

Figure 5-38 Snapping in a SO-DIMM

Troubleshooting RAM

"Memory" errors show up in a variety of ways on modern systems, including parity errors, ECC error messages, system lockups, page faults, and other error screens. These errors can indicate bad RAM but often point to something completely unrelated. This is especially true with intermittent problems. Techs need to recognize these errors and determine which part of the system caused the memory error.

You can get two radically different types of parity errors: real and phantom. *Real parity errors* are simply errors that the MCC detects from the parity or ECC chips (if you have them). The operating system then reports the problem in an error message, such as "Parity error at *xxxx:xxxxxxxx*," where *xxxx:xxxxxxxx* is a hexadecimal value (a string of

numbers and letters, such as A5F2:004EEAB9). If you get an error like this, write down the value. A real parity/ECC error shows up at the same place in memory each time and almost always indicates that you have a bad RAM stick.

Phantom parity errors show up on systems that don't have parity or ECC memory. If Windows generates parity errors with different addresses, you most likely do *not* have a problem with RAM. These phantom errors can occur for a variety of reasons, including software problems, heat or dust, solar flares, fluctuations in the Force...you get the idea.

System lockups and page faults (they often go hand in hand) in Windows can indicate a problem with RAM. A system lockup is when the computer stops functioning. A *page fault* is a milder error that can be caused by memory issues but not necessarily system RAM problems. Certainly page faults *look* like RAM issues because Windows generates frightening error messages filled with long strings of hexadecimal digits, such as "KRNL386 caused a page fault at 03F2:25A003BC." Just because the error message contains a memory address, however, does not mean that you have a problem with your RAM. Write down the address. If it repeats in later error messages, you probably have a bad RAM stick. If Windows displays different memory locations, you need to look elsewhere for the culprit.

Every once in a while, something potentially catastrophic happens within the PC, some little electron hits the big red panic button, and the operating system has to shut down certain functions before it can save data. This panic button inside the PC is called a *non-maskable interrupt (NMI)*, more simply defined as an interruption the CPU cannot ignore. An NMI manifests as a *proprietary crash screen*. In Windows Vista and Windows 7, for example, the crash screen is what techs call the *Blue Screen of Death (BSoD)*—a bright blue screen with a scary-sounding error message on it (see Figure 5-39).

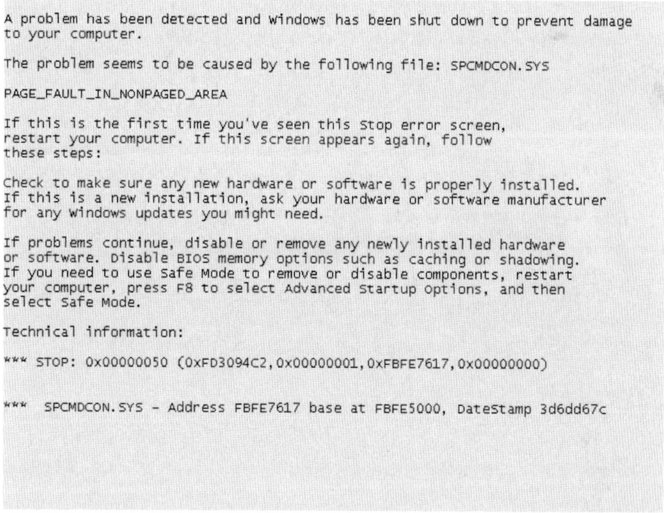

```
A problem has been detected and Windows has been shut down to prevent damage
to your computer.

The problem seems to be caused by the following file: SPCMDCON.SYS

PAGE_FAULT_IN_NONPAGED_AREA

If this is the first time you've seen this Stop error screen,
restart your computer. If this screen appears again, follow
these steps:

Check to make sure any new hardware or software is properly installed.
If this is a new installation, ask your hardware or software manufacturer
for any Windows updates you might need.

If problems continue, disable or remove any newly installed hardware
or software. Disable BIOS memory options such as caching or shadowing.
If you need to use Safe Mode to remove or disable components, restart
your computer, press F8 to select Advanced Startup Options, and then
select Safe Mode.

Technical information:

*** STOP: 0x00000050 (0xFD3094C2,0x00000001,0xFBFE7617,0x00000000)

***  SPCMDCON.SYS - Address FBFE7617 base at FBFE5000, DateStamp 3d6dd67c
```

Figure 5-39 Blue Screen of Death

Windows 8/8.1/10 display a blue screen with a sad face and the words to the effect of Windows has a problem. Restart the machine. Mac OS X will display a spinning rainbow wheel called the *pinwheel of death*. The response is the same: reboot the machine.

Bad RAM sometimes triggers an NMI, although often the culprit lies with buggy programming or clashing code. The BSoD varies according to the operating system, and it would require a much lengthier tome than this one to cover all the variations. Suffice it to say that RAM *could* be the problem when that delightful blue screen appears.

Finally, intermittent memory errors can come from a variety of sources, including a dying power supply, electrical interference, buggy applications, buggy hardware, and so on. These errors show up as lockups, general protection faults, page faults, and parity errors, but they never have the same address or happen with the same applications. I always check the power supply first.

Testing RAM

Once you discover that you may have a RAM problem, you have a couple of options. First, several companies manufacture hardware RAM-testing devices. Second, you can use the method I use—*replace and pray*. Open the system case and replace each stick, one at a time, with a known good replacement stick. (You have one of those lying around, don't you?) This method, although potentially time-consuming, certainly works. With PC prices as low as they are now, you could simply replace the whole system for less than the price of a dedicated RAM tester.

Third, you could run a software-based tester on the RAM. Because you have to load a software tester into the memory it's about to scan, there's always a small chance that simply starting the software RAM tester might cause an error. Still, you can find some pretty good free ones out there. Windows 7 and later include the *Windows Memory Diagnostic* tool, which can automatically scan your computer's RAM when you encounter a problem. If you're using another OS, my favorite tool is memtest86+ (www.memtest.org). The memtest86+ software exhaustively checks your RAM and reports bad RAM when it finds it (see Figure 5-40).

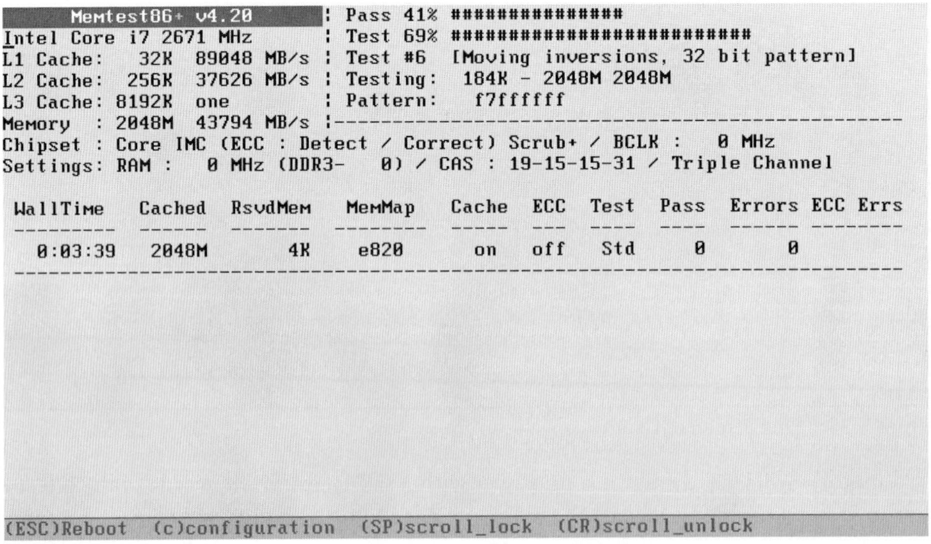

```
    Memtest86+ v4.20           : Pass 41% ###############
Intel Core i7 2671 MHz         : Test 69% ###########################
L1 Cache:    32K  89048 MB/s   : Test #6   [Moving inversions, 32 bit pattern]
L2 Cache:   256K  37626 MB/s   : Testing:   184K - 2048M 2048M
L3 Cache:  8192K  one          : Pattern:   f7ffffff
Memory  :  2048M  43794 MB/s   :-------------------------------------------
Chipset : Core IMC (ECC : Detect / Correct) Scrub+ / BCLK :   0 MHz
Settings: RAM :   0 MHz (DDR3-   0) / CAS : 19-15-15-31 / Triple Channel

 WallTime   Cached  RsvdMem   MemMap   Cache  ECC  Test  Pass  Errors ECC Errs
 ---------  ------  -------  --------  -----  ---  ----  ----  ------ --------
   0:03:39   2048M       4K    e820      on   off   Std     0       0
 -----------------------------------------------------------------------------

(ESC)Reboot  (c)configuration  (SP)scroll_lock  (CR)scroll_unlock
```

Figure 5-40 Memtest86+ in action

NOTE A *general protection fault (GPF)* is an error that can cause an application to crash. Often GPFs are caused by programs stepping on each other's toes. Chapter 17, "Troubleshooting Operating Systems," goes into more detail on GPFs and other Windows errors.

Chapter Review

Questions

1. Steve adds a second 1-GB 240-pin DIMM to his PC, which should bring the total RAM in the system up to 2 GB. The PC has an Intel Core 2 Duo 3-GHz processor and three 240-pin DIMM slots on the motherboard. When he turns on the PC, however, only 1 GB of RAM shows up during the RAM count. Which of the following is most likely to be the problem?
   - **A.** Steve failed to seat the RAM properly.
   - **B.** Steve put DDR SDRAM in a DDR 2 slot.
   - **C.** The CPU cannot handle 2 GB of RAM.
   - **D.** The motherboard can use only one RAM slot at a time.
2. Scott wants to add 512 MB of PC100 SDRAM to an aging but still useful desktop system. The system has a 100-MHz motherboard and currently has 256 MB of non-ECC SDRAM in the system. What else does he need to know before installing?
   - **A.** What speed of RAM he needs.
   - **B.** What type of RAM he needs.
   - **C.** How many pins the RAM has.
   - **D.** If the system can handle that much RAM.
3. What is the primary reason that DDR2 RAM is faster than DDR RAM?
   - **A.** The core speed of the DDR2 RAM chips is faster.
   - **B.** The input/output speed of the DDR2 RAM is faster.
   - **C.** DDR RAM is single-channel and DDR2 RAM is dual-channel.
   - **D.** DDR RAM uses 184-pin DIMMs and DDR2 uses 240-pin DIMMs.
4. What is the term for the delay in the RAM's response to a request from the MCC?
   - **A.** Variance
   - **B.** MCC gap
   - **C.** Latency
   - **D.** Fetch interval

5. How does an NMI manifest on a Mac OS X system?
   A. Blue Screen of Death.
   B. Pinwheel of death.
   C. Interrupt of death.
   D. NMIs only happen on Windows systems.
6. Silas has an AMD-based motherboard with two sticks of DDR2 RAM installed in two of the three RAM slots, for a total of 2 GB of system memory. When he runs CPU-Z to test the system, he notices that the software claims he's running single-channel memory. What could be the problem? (Select the best answer.)
   A. His motherboard only supports single-channel memory.
   B. His motherboard only supports dual-channel memory with DDR RAM, not DDR2.
   C. He needs to install a third RAM stick to enable dual-channel memory.
   D. He needs to move one of the installed sticks to a different slot to activate dual-channel memory.
7. Which of the following Control Panel applets will display the amount of RAM in your PC?
   A. System
   B. Devices and Printers
   C. Device Manager
   D. Action Center
8. What is the best way to determine the total capacity and specific type of RAM your system can handle?
   A. Check the motherboard book.
   B. Open the case and inspect the RAM.
   C. Check the Device Manager.
   D. Check the System utility in the Control Panel.
9. Gregor installed a third stick of known good RAM into his Core i7 system, bringing the total amount of RAM up to 3 GB. Within a few days, though, he started having random lockups and reboots, especially when doing memory-intensive tasks such as gaming. What is most likely the problem?
   A. Gregor installed DDR RAM into a DDR2 system.
   B. Gregor installed DDR2 RAM into a DDR3 system.
   C. Gregor installed RAM that didn't match the speed or quality of the RAM in the system.
   D. Gregor installed RAM that exceeded the speed of the RAM in the system.

10. Cindy installs a second stick of DDR3 RAM into her Core i5 system, bringing the total system memory up to 4 GB. Within a short period of time, though, she begins experiencing Blue Screens of Death. What could the problem be?
    A. She installed faulty RAM.
    B. The motherboard could only handle 2 GB of RAM.
    C. The motherboard needed dual-channel RAM.
    D. There is no problem. Windows always does this initially, but gets better after crashing a few times.

Answers

1. **A.** Steve failed to seat the RAM properly.
2. **D.** Scott needs to know if the system can handle that much RAM.
3. **B.** The input/output speed of DDR2 RAM is faster than that of DDR RAM (although the latency is higher).
4. **C.** Latency is the term for the delay in the RAM's response to a request from the MCC.
5. **B.** A non-maskable interrupt on a Mac OS X system often results in the spinning pinwheel called the pinwheel of death.
6. **D.** Motherboards can be tricky and require you to install RAM in the proper slots to enable dual-channel memory access. In this case, Silas should move one of the installed sticks to a different slot to activate dual-channel memory. (And he should check the motherboard manual for the proper slots.)
7. **A.** You can use the System applet to see how much RAM is currently in your PC.
8. **A.** The best way to determine the total capacity and specific type of RAM your system can handle is to check the motherboard book.
9. **C.** Most likely, Gregor installed RAM that didn't match the speed or quality of the RAM in the system.
10. **A.** If you have no problems with a system and then experience problems after installing something new, chances are the something new is at fault.

CHAPTER 6

BIOS

In this chapter, you will learn how to

- Explain the function of BIOS
- Distinguish among various CMOS setup utility options
- Describe option ROM and device drivers
- Troubleshoot the power-on self test (POST)
- Maintain BIOS and CMOS properly

In Chapter 4, "Microprocessors," you saw how the address bus and external data bus connect RAM to the CPU via the memory controller chip (MCC) to run programs and transfer data. Assuming you apply power in the right places, you don't need anything else to make a simple computer. The only problem with such a simple computer is that it would bore you to death—there's no way to do anything with it! A PC needs devices such as keyboards and mice to provide input, and output devices such as monitors and sound cards to communicate the current state of the running programs to you. A computer also needs permanent storage devices, such as hard drives, USB drives, and optical drives, to store programs and data when you turn off the computer.

This chapter discusses in detail the core programming and supporting hardware that enables the many different internal and external devices in a computer to function together. We'll start with a couple of sections on why and how it all works, and then we'll look at hardware and self-testing circuits. The chapter finishes with the finer points of maintaining this essential programming and hardware.

901

We Need to Talk

Simply placing a number of components into a computer is useless if the CPU can't communicate with them. Getting the CPU to communicate with a device starts with some kind of interconnection—a communication bus that enables the CPU to send commands to and from devices. To make this connection, let's promote the MCC, giving it extra firepower to act as not only the interconnection between the CPU and RAM but also the interconnection between the CPU and the other devices on the PC. The MCC

isn't just the memory controller anymore, so let's call it the *Northbridge* because it acts as the primary bridge between the CPU and the rest of the computer (see Figure 6-1).

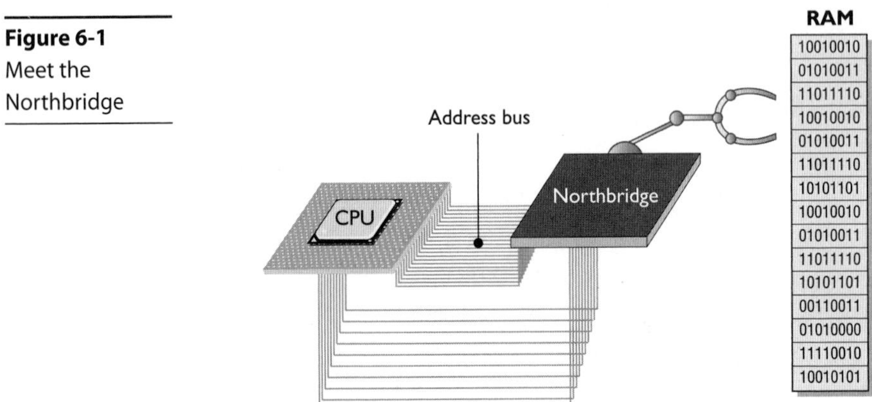

Figure 6-1 Meet the Northbridge

Your PC uses so many devices, the PC industry decided to delegate some of the interconnectivity work to a second chip called the *Southbridge*. The Northbridge deals with high-speed interfaces such as the connection to your video card and RAM. The Southbridge works mainly with lower-speed devices such as the USB controller and hard drive controllers. Chip makers design matched sets of particular models of Northbridge and Southbridge to work together. You don't buy a Northbridge from one company and a Southbridge from another—they're sold as a set. We call this set of Northbridge and Southbridge the *chipset*.

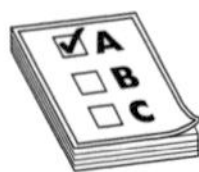

EXAM TIP Modern processors include the functions of the Northbridge directly on the CPU. The Southbridge is called the *Input/Output Controller Hub* (*ICH*) in Intel systems and the *Fusion Controller Hub* (*FCH*) in AMD systems. Current systems move the Southbridge feature to the *Platform Controller Hub* (*PCH*), connected directly to the CPU.

To help you understand their function, however, I'll still refer to the Northbridge and Southbridge as distinct elements. Also, the 901 exam refers to them as distinct chips.

The chipset extends the data bus to every device on the PC. The CPU uses the data bus to move data to and from all of the devices of the PC. Data constantly flows on the external data bus among the CPU, chipset, RAM, and other devices on the PC (see Figure 6-2).

The first use for the address bus, as you know, is for the CPU to tell the chipset to send or store data in memory and to tell the chipset which section of memory to access or use. Just as with the external data bus, the chipset extends the address bus to all of the devices (see Figure 6-3). That way, the CPU can use the address bus to send commands to devices, just as it sends commands to the chipset.

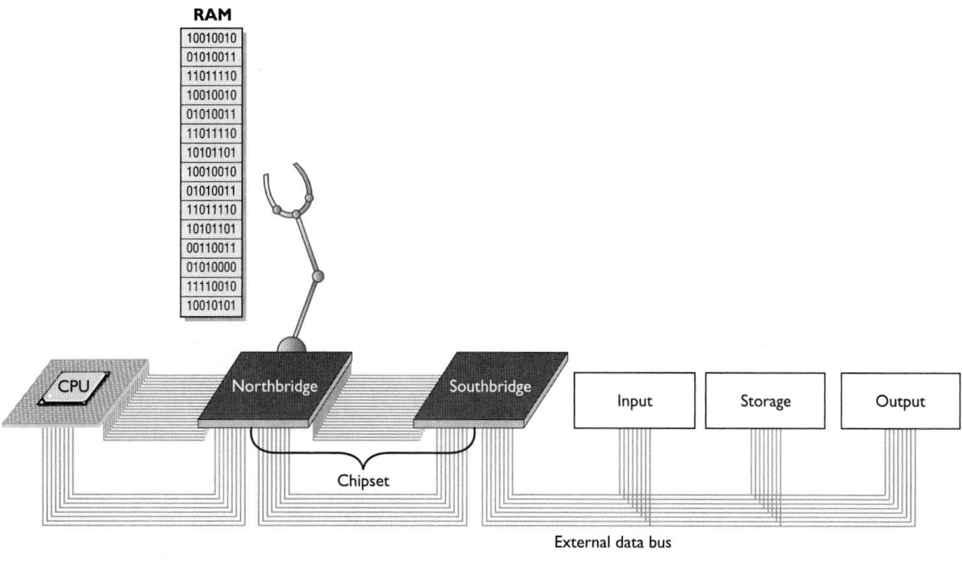

Figure 6-2 The chipset extending the data bus

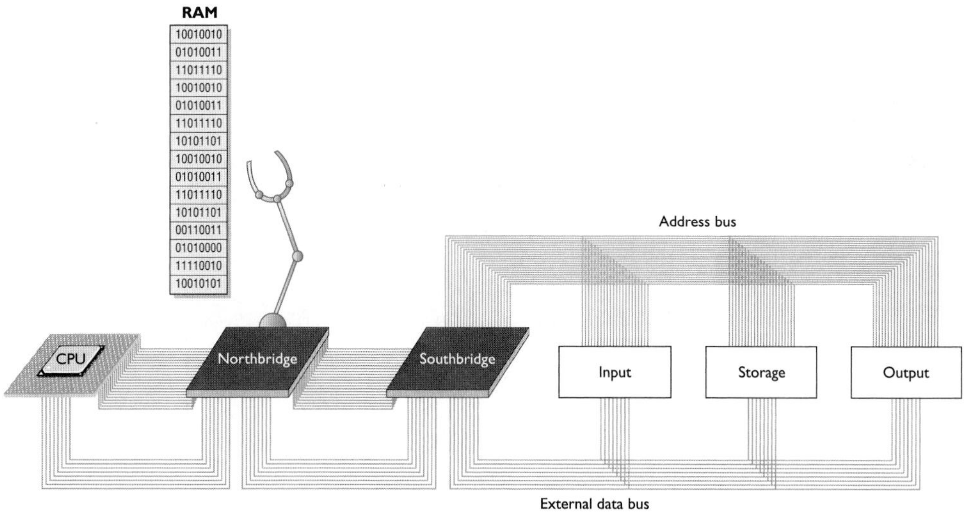

Figure 6-3 Every device in your computer connects to the address bus.

It's not too hard to swallow the concept that the CPU uses the address bus to talk to the devices, but how does it know what to *say* to them? How does it know all of the patterns of ones and zeros to place on the address bus to tell the hard drive it needs to send a file? Let's look at the interaction between the keyboard and CPU for insight into this process.

Talking to the Keyboard

The keyboard provides a great example of how the buses and support programming help the CPU get the job done. In early computers, the keyboard connected to the external data bus via a special chip known as the *keyboard controller*. Don't bother looking for this chip on your motherboard—the Southbridge now handles keyboard controller functions. The way the keyboard controller—or technically, the keyboard controller *circuitry*—works with the CPU, however, has changed only a small amount in the past 25+ years, making it a perfect tool to illustrate how the CPU talks to a device.

NOTE Techs commonly talk about various functions of the chipset as if those functions were still handled by discrete chips. So you'll hear about memory controllers, keyboard controllers, mouse controllers, USB controllers, and so on, even though they're all just circuits on the CPU, Northbridge, or Southbridge.

The keyboard controller was one of the last single-function chips to be absorbed into the chipset. For many years—in fact, well into the Pentium III/early Athlon era—most motherboards had separate keyboard controller chips. Figure 6-4 shows a typical keyboard controller from those days. Electronically, it looked like Figure 6-5.

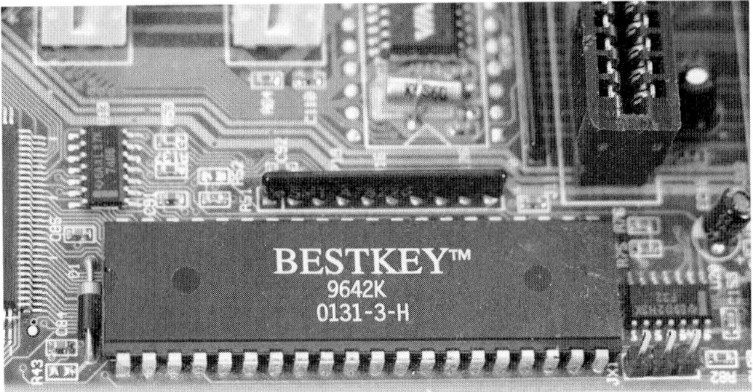

Figure 6-4 A keyboard chip on a Pentium motherboard

NOTE Even though the model numbers changed over the years, you'll still hear techs refer to the keyboard controller as the *8042*, after the original keyboard controller chip.

Every time you press a key on your keyboard, a scanning chip in the keyboard notices which key you pressed. Then the scanner sends a coded pattern of ones and zeros—called the *scan code*—to the keyboard controller. Every key on your keyboard has a unique scan code. The keyboard controller stores the scan code in its own register. Does it surprise you that the lowly keyboard controller has a register similar to a CPU? Lots of chips have registers—not just CPUs (see Figure 6-6).

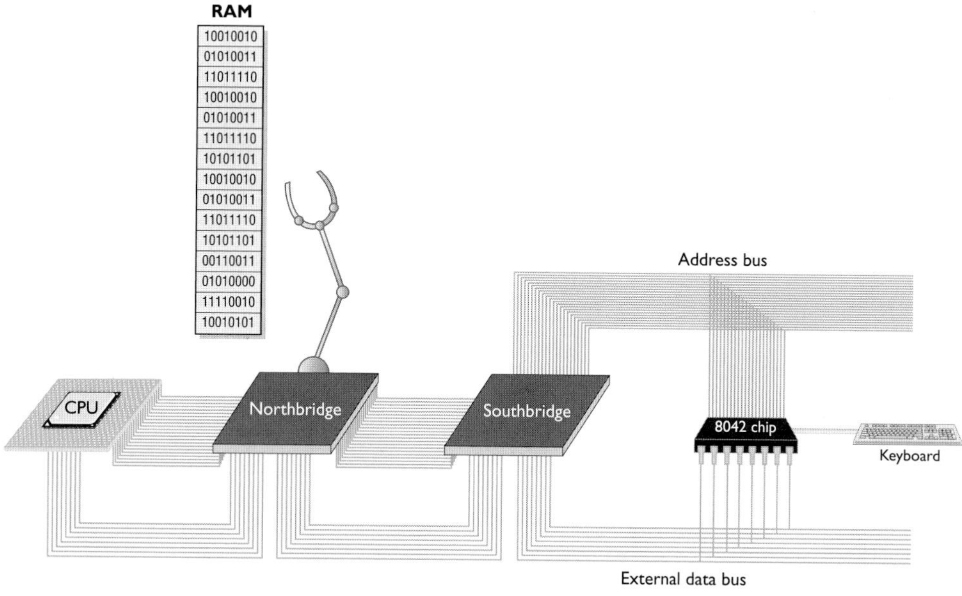

Figure 6-5 Electronic view of the keyboard controller

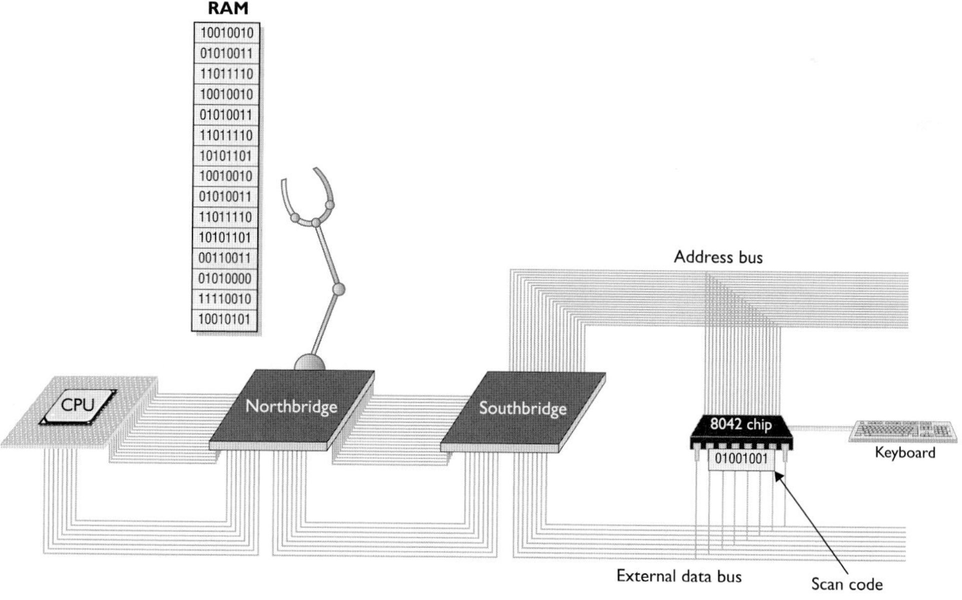

Figure 6-6 Scan code stored in keyboard controller's register

How does the CPU get the scan code out of the keyboard controller (see Figure 6-7)? While we're at it, how does the CPU tell the keyboard to change the typematic buffer rate (when you hold down a key and the letter repeats) or to turn the number lock LED on and off, to mention just a few other jobs the keyboard needs to do for the system? The point is that the keyboard controller must be able to respond to multiple commands, not just one.

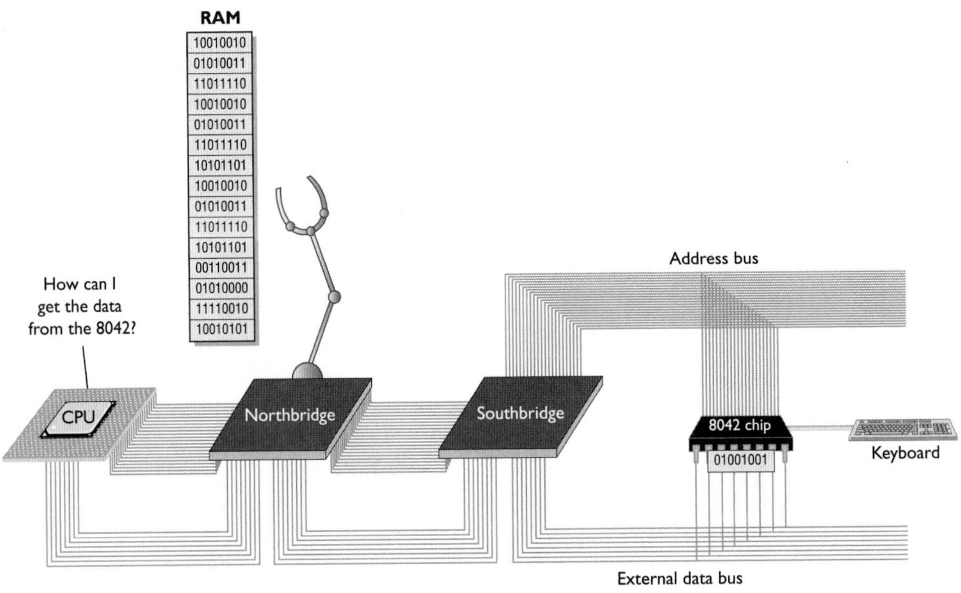

Figure 6-7 The CPU ponders the age-old dilemma of how to get the 8042 to cough up its data.

The keyboard controller accepts commands exactly as you saw the CPU accept commands in Chapter 4. Remember when you added 2 to 3 with the 8088? You had to use specific commands from the 8088's codebook to tell the CPU to do the addition and then place the answer on the external data bus. The keyboard controller has its own codebook—much simpler than any CPU's codebook, but conceptually the same. If the CPU wants to know what key was last pressed on the keyboard, the CPU needs to know the command (or series of commands) that orders the keyboard controller to put the scan code of the letter on the external data bus so the CPU can read it.

BIOS

The CPU doesn't magically or otherwise automatically know how to talk with any device; it needs some sort of support programming loaded into memory that teaches it about a particular device. This programming is called *basic input/output services (BIOS)*.

The programs dedicated to enabling the CPU to communicate with devices are called *services* (or device drivers, as you'll see later in the chapter). This goes well beyond the keyboard, by the way. In fact, *every* device on the computer needs BIOS! But let's continue with the keyboard for now.

Bringing BIOS to the PC

A talented programmer could write BIOS for a keyboard if the programmer knew the keyboard's codebook; keyboards are pretty simple devices. This begs the question: Where would this support programming be stored? Programming could be incorporated into the operating system. Storing programming to talk to the hardware of your PC in the operating system is great—all operating systems have built-in code that knows how to talk to your keyboard, your mouse, and just about every piece of hardware you may put into your PC.

That's fine once the operating system's up and running, but what about a brand new stack of parts you're about to assemble into a new PC? When a new system is being built, it has no operating system. The CPU must have access to BIOS for the most important hardware on your PC: not only the keyboard, but also the monitor, mass storage drives, optical drives, USB ports, and RAM. This code can't be stored on a hard drive or optical disc—these important devices need to be ready at any time the CPU calls them, even before installing a mass storage device or an operating system.

The perfect place to store the support programming is on the motherboard. That settles one issue, but another looms: What storage medium should the motherboard use? DRAM won't work, because all of the data would be erased every time you turned off the computer. You need some type of permanent program storage device that does not depend on other peripherals to work. And you need that storage device to sit on the motherboard.

ROM

Motherboards store the keyboard controller support programming, among other programs, on a special type of device called a *read-only memory (ROM)* chip. A ROM chip stores programs, called *services*, exactly like RAM—that is, like an 8-bit-wide spreadsheet. But ROM differs from RAM in two important ways. First, ROM chips are *nonvolatile*, meaning that the information stored on ROM isn't erased when the computer is turned off. Second, traditional ROM chips are read-only, meaning that once you store a program on one, you can't change it.

Modern motherboards use a type of ROM called *flash ROM* that differs from traditional ROM in that you can update and change the contents through a very specific process called "flashing the ROM," covered later in this chapter. Figure 6-8 shows a typical flash ROM chip on a motherboard. When the CPU wants to talk to the keyboard controller, it goes to the flash ROM chip to access the proper programming.

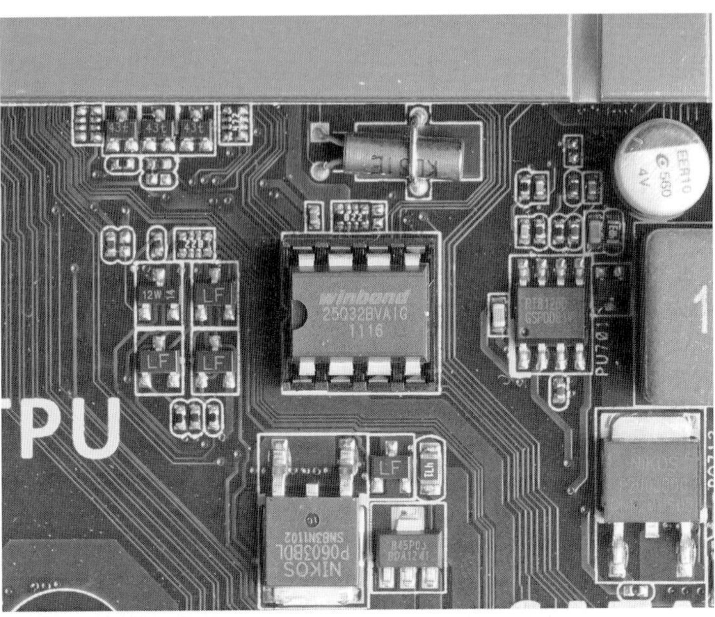
Figure 6-8 Typical flash ROM

Every motherboard has a flash ROM chip, called the *system ROM* chip because it contains code that enables your CPU to talk to the basic hardware of your PC (see Figure 6-9). As alluded to earlier, the system ROM holds BIOS for more than just the keyboard controller. It also stores programs for communicating with hard drives, optical drives, display devices, USB ports, and other basic devices on your motherboard.

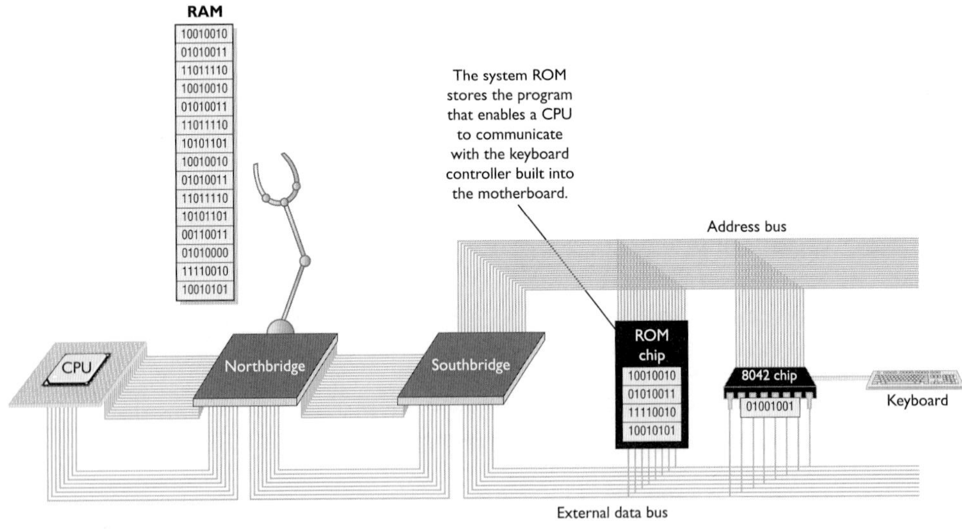

Figure 6-9 Function of the flash ROM chip

To talk to all of that hardware requires hundreds of little services (2 to 30 lines of code each). These hundreds of little programs stored on the system ROM chip on the motherboard are called, collectively, the *system BIOS* (see Figure 6-10). Techs call programs stored on ROM chips of any sort *firmware.*

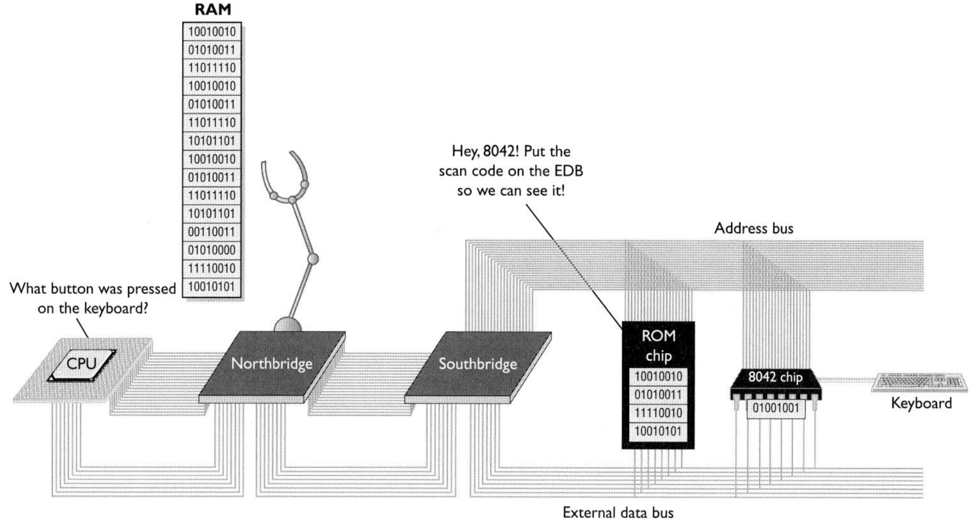

Figure 6-10 CPU running BIOS service

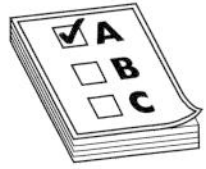

EXAM TIP Programs stored on ROM chips—flash or any other kind of ROM chip—are known collectively as *firmware*, as opposed to programs stored on dynamic media, which are collectively called *software*.

System BIOS Support

Every system BIOS has two types of hardware to support. First, the system BIOS supports all of the hardware that never changes, such as the keyboard. (You can change your keyboard, but you can't change the keyboard controller built into the Southbridge.) Another example of hardware that never changes is the PC speaker (the tiny one that beeps at you, not the ones that play music). The system ROM chip stores the BIOS for these and other devices that never change.

Second, the system BIOS supports all of the hardware that might change from time to time. This includes RAM (you can add RAM) and hard drives (you can replace your hard disk drive [HDD] with a larger drive or a solid-state drive [SSD], or add additional drives of either type). The system ROM chip stores the *BIOS* for these devices, but the system needs another place to store information about the specific *details* of a piece of hardware. This enables the system to differentiate between a Western Digital Green 2-TB HDD and a Samsung 850 EVO 500-GB SSD, and yet still support both drives right out of the box.

UEFI

For many years, PCs used 16-bit BIOS that required x86-compliant hardware. That was fine until really large hard drives (3+ terabytes) came on the market. At that point, Intel released the BIOS used in modern systems, called the *Unified Extensible Firmware Interface (UEFI)*. Here are a few advantages of UEFI over the 16-bit BIOS:

- UEFI supports file systems that enable booting to drives larger than 2.2 TB.
- UEFI supports 32-bit or 64-bit booting.
- UEFI handles all boot-loading duties.
- UEFI is not dependent on x86 firmware.

Current systems—Windows, Mac OS X, and Linux—use UEFI and also provide legacy support for BIOS services. But a zillion older systems use the older BIOS. Most techs continue to call the support software BIOS, even though technically the terms differ. There's no standardization on how to pronounce UEFI, by the way. Microsoft initializes it: "U-E-F-I." Others say "you-fee" or "you-fie." For a job interview, stick with initializing it. You can't go wrong that way.

CMOS

A separate memory chip, called the *complementary metal-oxide semiconductor (CMOS)* chip, stores the information that describes specific device parameters. CMOS does *not* store programs; it only stores data that is read by BIOS to complete the programs needed to talk to changeable hardware. CMOS also acts as a clock to keep the current date and time.

Years ago, CMOS was a separate chip on the motherboard, as shown in Figure 6-11. Today, CMOS is almost always built into the Southbridge.

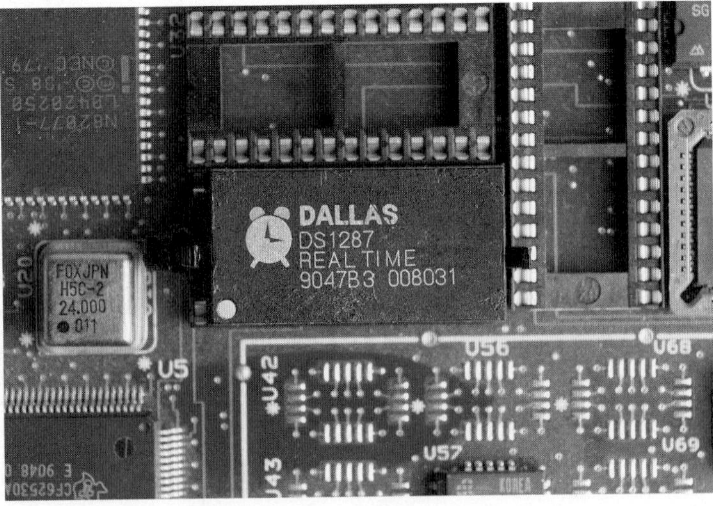

Figure 6-11 Old-style CMOS

Most CMOS chips store around 64 KB of data, but the PC usually needs only a very small amount—about 128 bytes—to store all of the necessary information on the changeable hardware. Don't let the tiny size fool you. The information stored in CMOS is absolutely necessary for the PC to function!

If the data stored on CMOS about a particular piece of hardware (or about its fancier features) is different from the specs of the actual hardware, the computer cannot access that piece of hardware (or use its fancier features). It is crucial that this information be correct. If you change any of the previously mentioned hardware, you must update CMOS to reflect those changes. You need to know, therefore, how to change the data on CMOS.

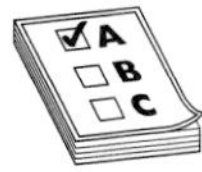

EXAM TIP All the details of BIOS and CMOS that you're going to spend many hours memorizing for the 901 exam only apply to PCs and Linux machines. Apple computers have BIOS and CMOS, but Apple designs their systems from the ground up as unified systems. Apple has done all the work for you and you simply use the Mac OS X machine. (Some older Mac Pro systems enable you to add drives; with newer systems, you'd use external drives.)

Modify CMOS: The Setup Program

Every PC ships with a program built into the system ROM called the *CMOS setup program* or the *system setup utility* that enables you to access and modify CMOS data. When you boot a computer, the first thing you likely see is the BIOS information. It might look like the example shown in Figure 6-12 or perhaps like the example shown in Figure 6-13.

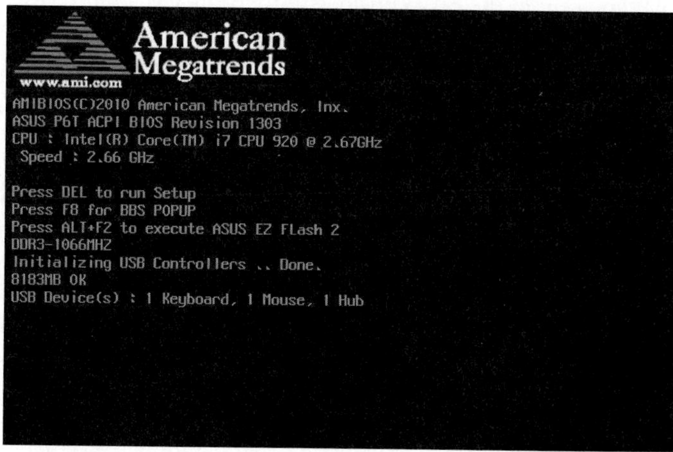

Figure 6-12 AMIBIOS information

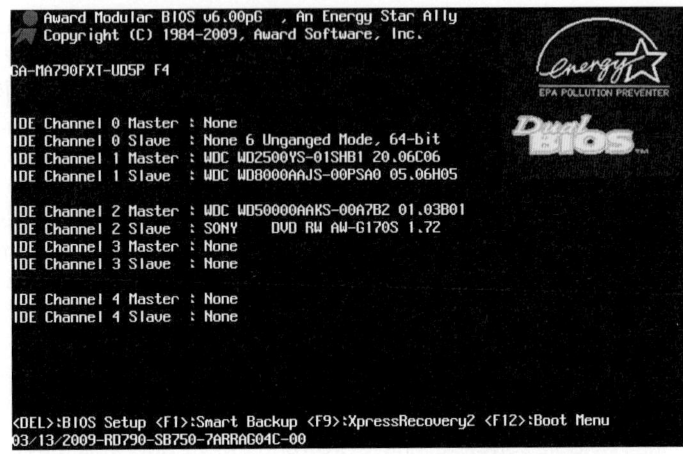

Figure 6-13 Award/Phoenix BIOS information

NOTE The terms *CMOS setup program, CMOS,* and *system setup utility* are functionally interchangeable today. You'll even hear the program referred to as the *BIOS setup utility,* UEFI/BIOS setup, or UEFI firmware settings. Most techs just call it the CMOS.

Who or what is AMIBIOS, and who or what is Phoenix Technologies? These are brand names of BIOS companies. They write BIOS programs and sell them to computer manufacturers. In today's world, motherboard makers rarely write their own BIOS. Instead, they buy their BIOS from specialized third-party BIOS makers such as Award Software and Phoenix Technologies. Although several companies write BIOS, two big companies control 99 percent of the BIOS business: American Megatrends (AMI) and Phoenix Technologies. Phoenix bought Award Software and still sells the Award brand name as a separate product line. These three are the most common brand names in the field.

Accessing CMOS Through Windows

Traditionally, you access a system's CMOS setup program at boot. In a functioning UEFI-based system running Windows 8 or 8.1, however, you can access setup from the Settings charm on the Charms bar. Here's the process in case CompTIA grills you on it for the 901 exam.

Drag your cursor to the top- or bottom-right corner of the screen to activate the Charms bar. Select Settings to open the Settings charm (see Figure 6-14). Click the option to Change PC settings.

In the PC settings app (see Figure 6-15), click the Update and recovery link (lower left) to get to the Update and recovery screen (which initially shows the Windows Update option selected). Select the Recovery link (see Figure 6-16) to see the desired options on the right (see Figure 6-17).

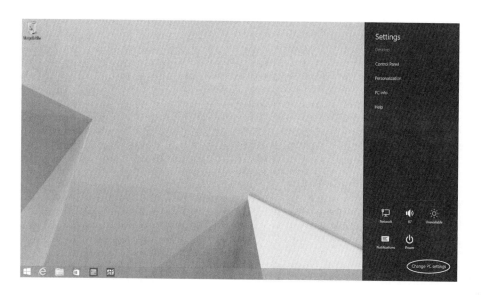

Figure 6-14 Settings charm options

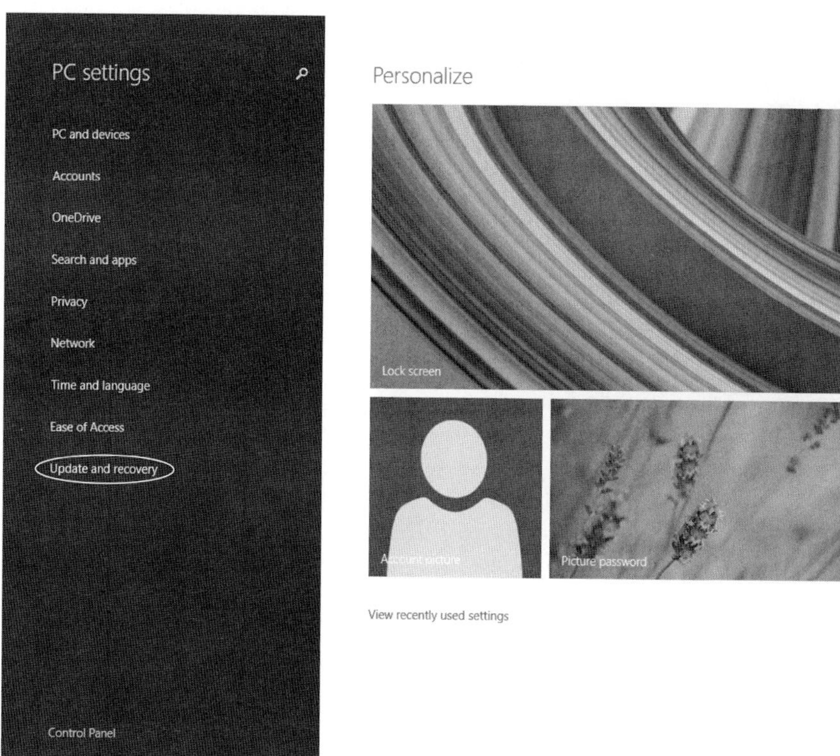

Figure 6-15 PC settings app

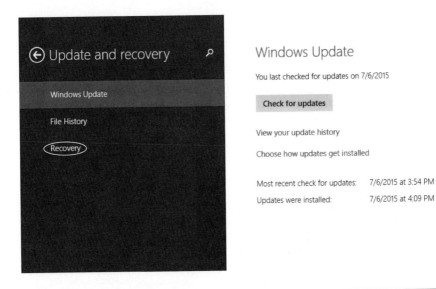

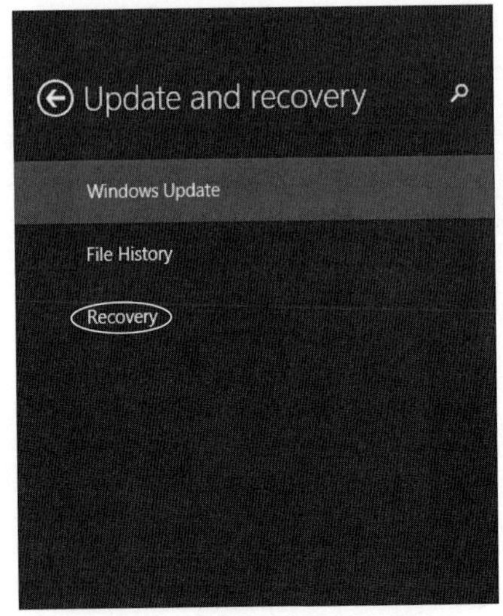

Figure 6-16 Update and recovery screen

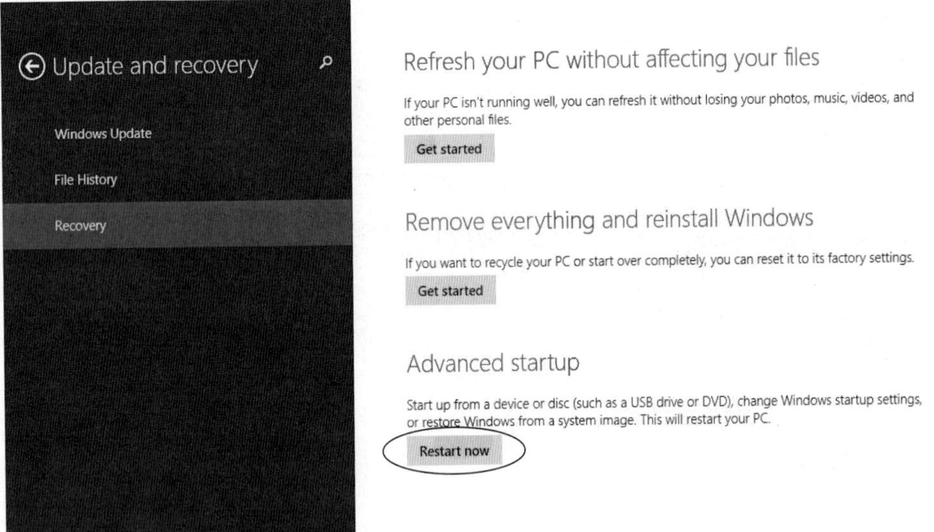

Figure 6-17 Recovery options on the Update and recovery screen

Under Advanced startup, click the Restart now button to get to the Choose an option screen, shown in Figure 6-18. Click Troubleshoot to get to the Troubleshoot screen for more options (see Figure 6-19).

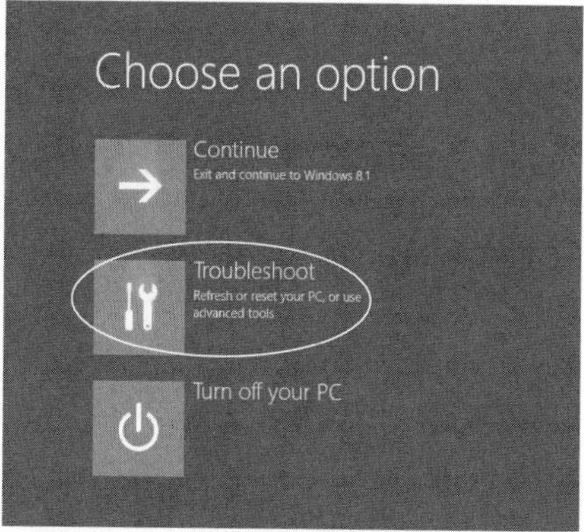

Figure 6-18 Choose an option screen

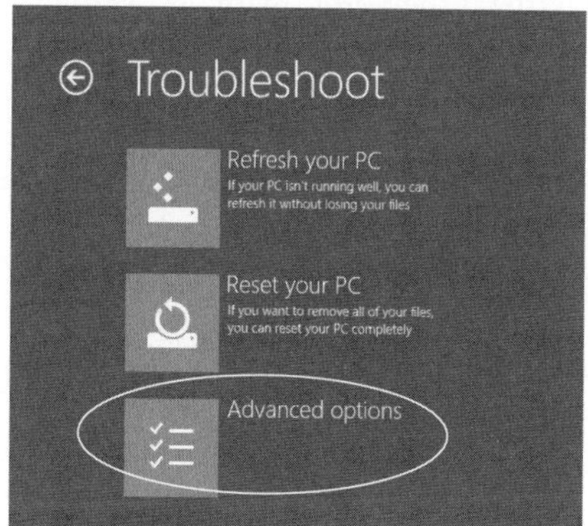

Figure 6-19 Troubleshoot options

Careful here. Windows 8.1 has three options on the Troubleshoot screen, as you can see in Figure 6-19. The first two, Refresh your PC and Reset your PC, enable you to do some *serious damage* to a working computer. Refresh will save your "files," but remove all desktop applications. Reset does a full wipe and reinstallation of Windows. Say goodbye to any data that is not backed up!

We're just trying to get to the system setup utility now, so click the third option, Advanced options. This takes you to the Advanced options screen (see Figure 6-20). From here, click the UEFI Firmware Settings option. The system will reboot and go into the system setup utility.

As you might imagine, it's a lot faster to reboot and access the CMOS setup manually. The Windows 8/8.1 process via the Charms bar is tedious at best.

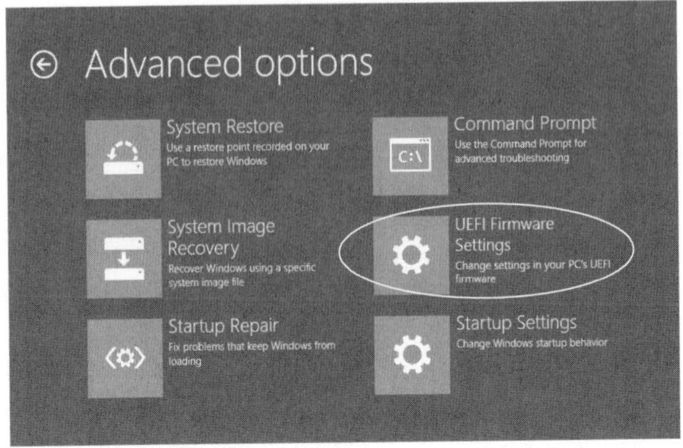

Figure 6-20 UEFI Firmware Settings option on the Advanced options screen

Accessing CMOS at Boot

So, the real question is how to access the CMOS setup at boot for your particular PC. AMI, Award, and Phoenix use different keys to access the CMOS setup program. Usually, BIOS manufacturers tell you how to access the CMOS setup right on the screen as your computer boots. For example, at the bottom of the screen in Figure 6-12 shown earlier, you can see the option to "Press DEL to run Setup." Keep in mind that this is only one possible example.

Motherboard manufacturers can change the key combinations for entering CMOS setup. You can even set up the computer so the message does not show—a smart idea if you need to keep nosy people out of your CMOS setup! If you don't see an "enter setup" message, wait until the RAM count starts and then try one of the following keys or key combinations: DELETE, ESC, F1, F2, CTRL-ALT-ESC, CTRL-ALT-INS, CTRL-ALT-ENTER, or CTRL-S. It may take a few tries, but you will eventually find the right key or key combination. If not, check the motherboard book or the manufacturer's Web site for the information.

Try This!

Accessing CMOS Setup

The key or key combination required to access CMOS setup varies, depending on your particular BIOS. When you find yourself in a setup or troubleshooting scenario that requires access to the system setup utility, it's important to know how to access it! Plus, you'll need to know how to find the BIOS information once you're in, so Try This!

1. Turn the monitor on and boot your system. Watch the information that scrolls by on the screen as your computer boots. Most BIOS makers include a line indicating what key(s) to press to access the CMOS setup program. Make a note of this useful information! You can also check your motherboard book to determine the process for accessing the CMOS setup program.
2. Reboot the system, and this time watch for information on the BIOS manufacturer. If you don't see it, and if it's okay to do so, open the system case and check the name printed on the system ROM chip. Make a note of this useful information.
3. Reboot one more time, and this time use the key or key combination you found to run the CMOS setup program. Locate and make a note of the manufacturer, date, and version number of your PC's current BIOS.
4. If you can, make a note of the exact model information for your system and visit the Web site of the company that manufactured your PC. Search their support files for the specs on your specific system and see if you can locate your BIOS information. Now take the detailed BIOS information and search the BIOS manufacturer's Web site for the same information.

Typical CMOS Setup Programs

Every BIOS maker's CMOS setup program looks a little different, but don't let that confuse you. They all contain basically the same settings; you just have to be comfortable poking around. To avoid doing something foolish, *do not save anything* unless you are sure you have it set correctly.

Several years ago, BIOS manufacturers in the consumer space migrated to graphical CMOS setup utilities that enable you to use a mouse. You'll still find plenty of examples in the field of the classic text-only CMOS setup utilities. You need to know both, so this section will show you both styles. We'll run through a graphical version first, then skim through an older text-only version.

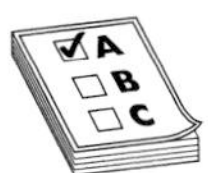

EXAM TIP UEFI does *not* specify a graphical or text-based system setup utility. The two are unrelated. I have many older motherboards with graphical system setup utilities that are 16-bit BIOS. The laptop I'm writing this chapter on has a text-based setup utility and UEFI.

Do not be surprised on the 901 exam, however, if it implies UEFI as graphical and the legacy BIOS as text mode. That's a common interpretation among some techs.

Graphical UEFI AMD-based Setup Utility

Figure 6-21 shows a typical, simple graphical setup screen. You can't do much here except view information about installed components, select one of three preset System Performance optimization options, and change the boot priority.

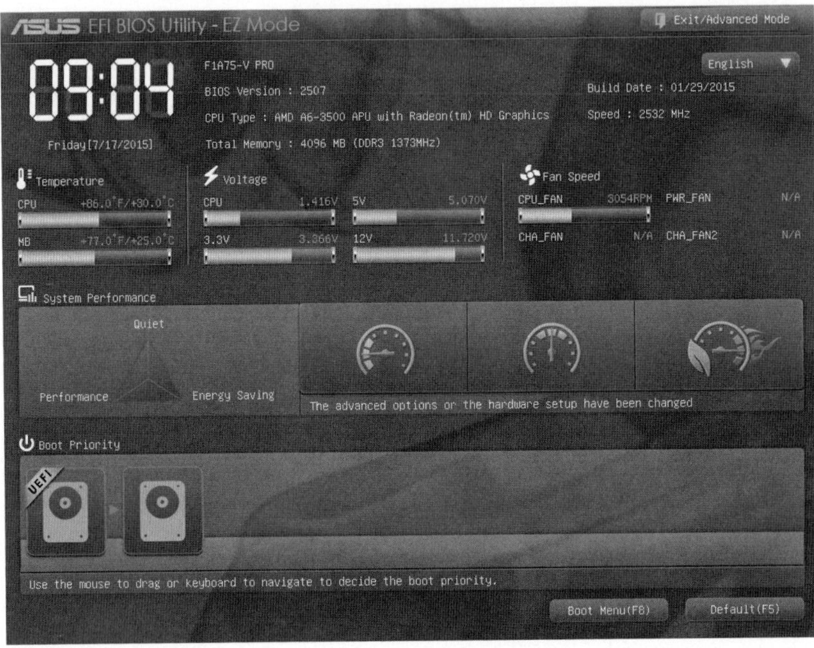

Figure 6-21 ASUS EFI BIOS Utility setup screen in EZ Mode

Click the option to go into Advanced Mode and you'll get a much more versatile utility (see Figure 6-22). The Main tab offers some *BIOS component information*, such as surface details on amount of RAM and speed of CPU, plus a couple of options to modify the language and date and time. (Some utilities will show information about installed hard drives and optical drives; this UEFI BIOS presents that information elsewhere.)

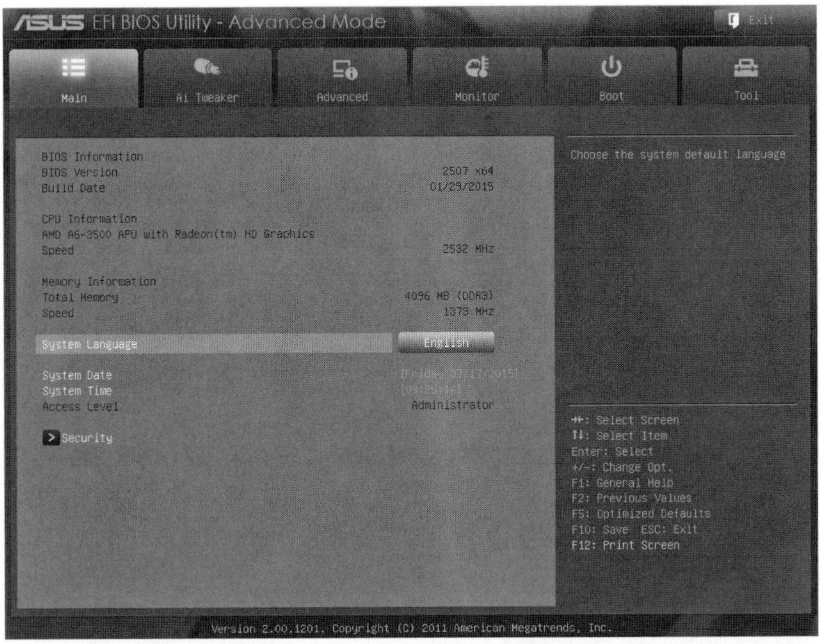

Figure 6-22 Main tab

The Main tab also enables you to configure modest *BIOS security* by setting an administrator or user password. (The default for the pictured UEFI BIOS is Access Level: Administrator. Click the Security option to change access information. UEFI setup screens differ somewhat, but you'll find similar options in all of them.)

An administrator password locks or unlocks access to the system setup utility. A user password locks or unlocks the computer booting to an operating system.

Things get far more interesting in the other tabs. Selecting the Ai Tweaker tab, for example, enables you to delve into the Dark Arts of overclocking both the CPU and RAM (see Figure 6-23). You can change the clock multiplier, clock speeds, voltages, and more here. This is a great place to go to fry a new CPU!

The Advanced tab (see Figure 6-24) gives BIOS component information about CPUs, hard drives and optical drives, and all the built-in components, such as USB ports. In this tab, as you drill down to each subcategory, you can configure drive settings, enable and disable devices, and more.

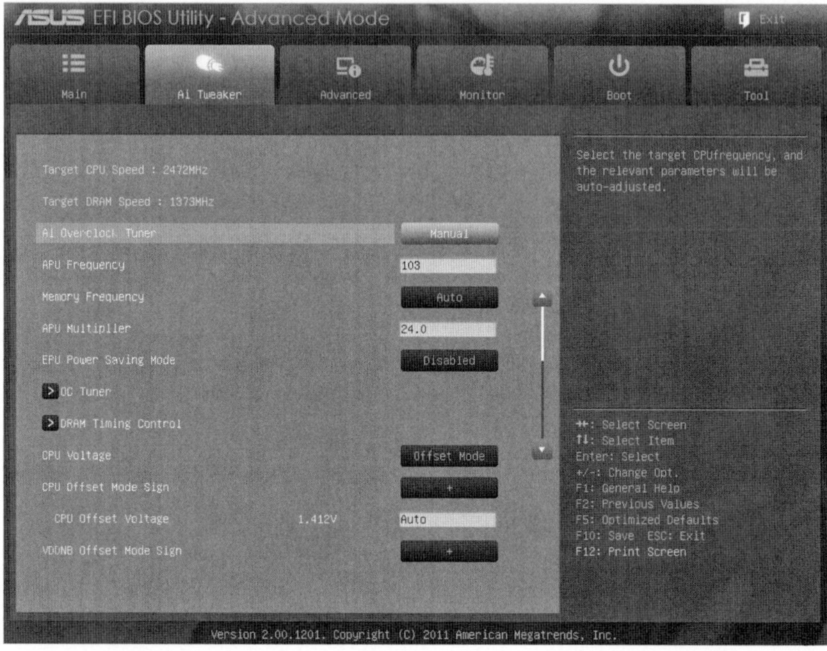

Figure 6-23 Ai Tweaker tab

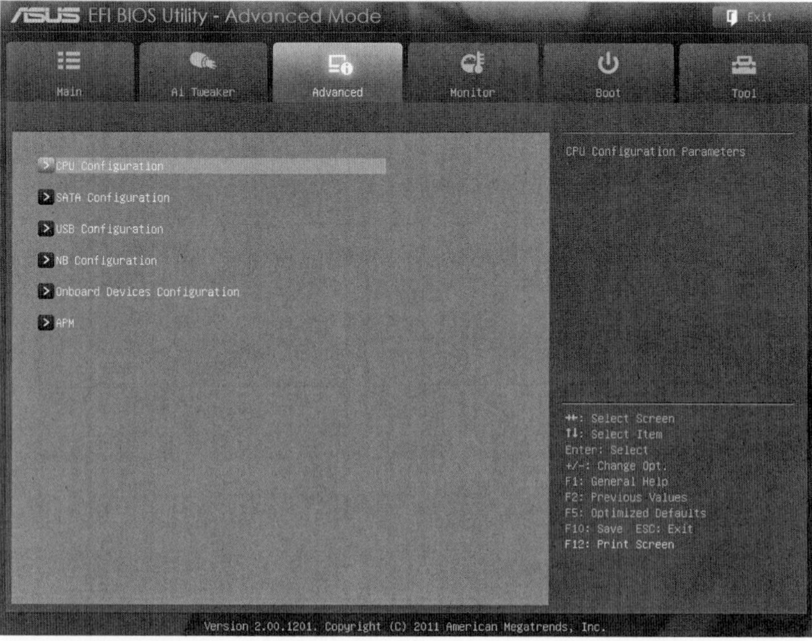

Figure 6-24 Advanced tab

The Monitor tab (see Figure 6-25) shows monitoring information for CPU and motherboard temperatures, fan speeds, and voltages. You can modify the behavior of the chassis fans here too. All of this monitoring information is considered some of the *built-in diagnostics* for both the motherboard and the full system.

The Boot tab (see Figure 6-26) enables you to adjust boot settings. You can select devices to boot by priority, setting the *boot sequence* used by the motherboard. (See "The Boot Process" later in this chapter for more information.) You can determine how the system will react/inform if booting fails, and more.

The Tool tab (see Figure 6-27) has a couple of very important features. The Flash 2 Utility enables you to update the motherboard firmware. See the "Flashing the ROM" section later in this chapter for more details.

The Tool tab also shows very detailed RAM information. That's the SPD option (for *serial presence detect*) you should recognize from Chapter 5, "RAM."

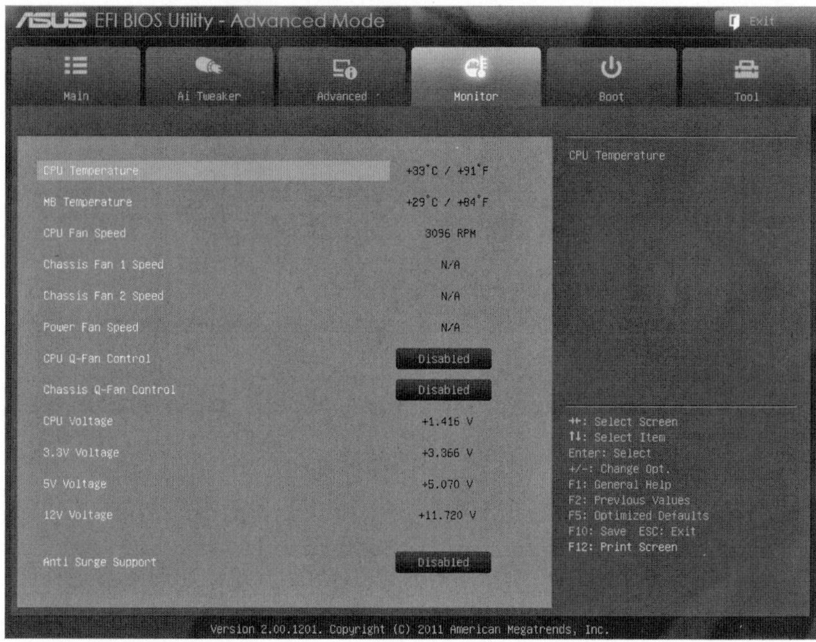

Figure 6-25 Monitor tab

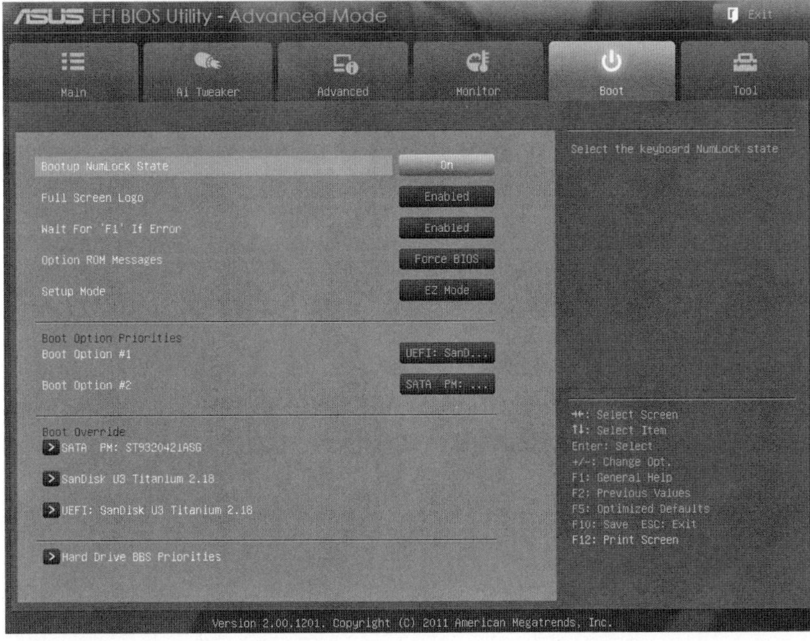

Figure 6-26 Boot tab

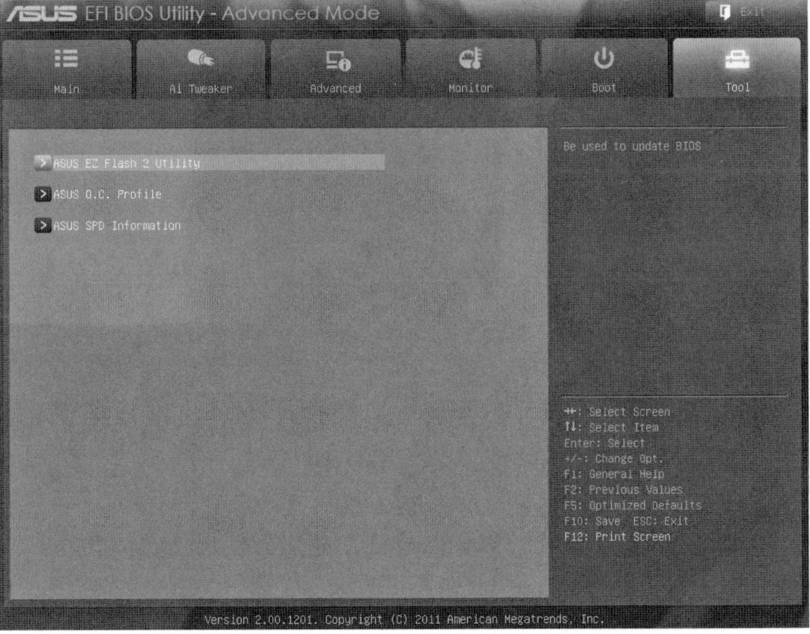

Figure 6-27 Tool tab

Text-Based UEFI Intel-Based Setup Utility

In this second walkthrough, we'll switch to a more recent UEFI motherboard, this time on an Intel-based portable computer. As we go through the screens, pay attention to the options listed on each. I'll call out features that the graphical AMD-based BIOS didn't have.

The Information tab (see Figure 6-28) offers straightforward information about the CPU and RAM amount, and cryptic information about the hard drive. Other tabs do more.

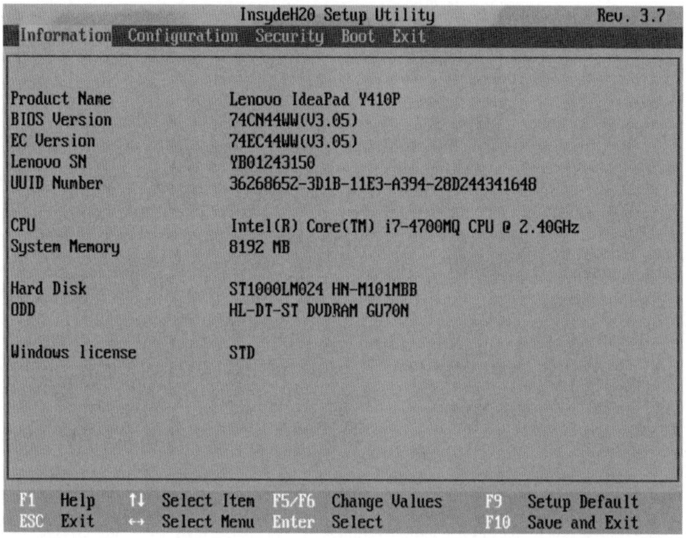

Figure 6-28
Information tab

```
InsydeH20 Setup Utility                                   Rev. 3.7
Information  Configuration  Security  Boot  Exit

Product Name          Lenovo IdeaPad Y410P
BIOS Version          74CN44WW(V3.05)
EC Version            74EC44WW(V3.05)
Lenovo SN             YB01243150
UUID Number           36268652-3D1B-11E3-A394-28D244341648

CPU                   Intel(R) Core(TM) i7-4700MQ CPU @ 2.40GHz
System Memory         8192 MB

Hard Disk             ST1000LM024 HN-M101MBB
ODD                   HL-DT-ST DVDRAM GU70N

Windows license       STD

F1   Help   ↑↓ Select Item  F5/F6 Change Values   F9  Setup Default
ESC  Exit   ↔  Select Menu  Enter Select          F10 Save and Exit
```

The Configuration tab (see Figure 6-29) shows a number of built-in devices that you configure or enable/disable here. Because this is a portable, it has an option to turn on/off wireless networking capabilities.

There are two interesting options here that are covered in detail in other chapters but warrant a brief discussion now. The Intel Virtual Technology option enables or disables *virtualization support* for virtual machines.

A *virtual machine* is a powerful type of program that enables you to run a second (or third or fourth), software-based machine inside your physical PC. It re-creates the motherboard, hard drives, RAM, network adapters, and more, and is just as powerful as a real PC. To run these virtual machines, however, you'll need a very powerful PC—you are trying to run multiple PCs at the same time, after all.

To support this, CPU manufacturers have added *hardware-assisted virtualization*. Intel calls their version Intel Virtualization Technology (Intel VT, for short), and AMD calls theirs AMD Virtualization (AMD-V) technology. This technology helps the virtual machines use your hardware more efficiently and is controlled by the BIOS. This feature is disabled by default in BIOS, so if your virtual machine requires hardware-assisted virtualization, you'll need to enable it here.

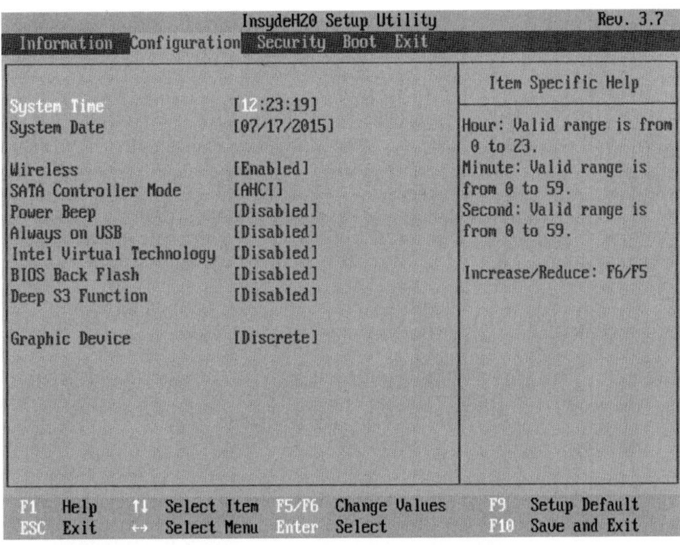

Figure 6-29 Configuration tab

NOTE Chapter 18, "Virtualization," covers virtual machines in gory detail. Stay tuned!

This particular laptop has built-in graphics courtesy of the Intel Core i7 processor, plus it has dedicated add-on video for gaming. The Graphic Device option, set here to Discrete, means to use the dedicated video card when possible. This uses more electricity than the graphics card built into the CPU, but it makes for way better gaming!

NOTE Chapter 19, "Display Technologies," goes into video options (and gaming) in modern systems.

The Security tab (see Figure 6-30) offers a lot more options for configuring BIOS security than found on the Main tab of the AMD-based system. You see the Administrator Password and User Password options, but there's also an option to set a couple of different hard drive passwords.

The *Secure Boot* feature you can see on the Security tab is a UEFI protocol that secures the boot process by requiring properly signed software. This includes boot software and software that supports specific, essential components. (See "Device Drivers" a little later in this chapter.) Secure Boot requires an Intel CPU, a UEFI BIOS, and an operating system designed for it, such as Windows 8/8.1/10.

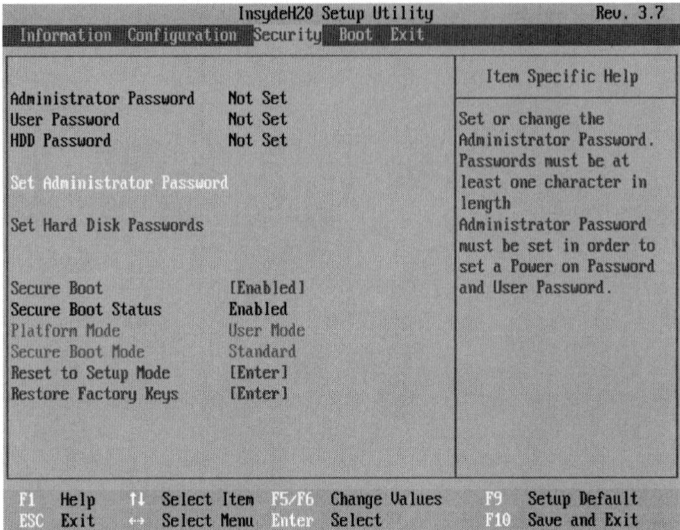

Figure 6-30 Security tab

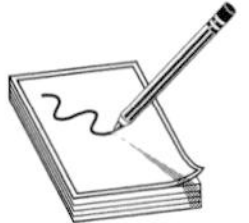

NOTE Secure Boot is an example of a tool that uses *drive encryption*. Various types of encryption—essentially scrambling the information to make it inaccessible to bad guys—secure all sorts of processes and data in modern computing. We'll hit the subject in several places later in the book. Chapter 10, "Implementing Hard Drives," discusses drive encryption specifically in more detail.

The Boot tab (see Figure 6-31) enables you to set boot options. Here is where you provide support for booting to a USB device as well. It looks a little different from the graphical example used earlier. See "The Boot Process" later in this chapter for more explanation.

Other BIOS Security Options

Motherboard manufacturers, BIOS writers, and programmers have implemented all kinds of security features over the years. This section mentions a couple you might run into on various motherboards (or on a certain exam in your near future).

Chassis Intrusion Detection/Notification Many motherboards support the *chassis intrusion detection/notification* feature provided by the computer case, or chassis. Compatible cases contain a switch that trips when someone opens the case. With motherboard support and a proper connection between the motherboard and the case, the CMOS logs whether the case has been opened and, if it has, posts a notification to the screen on the subsequent boot. How cool is that?

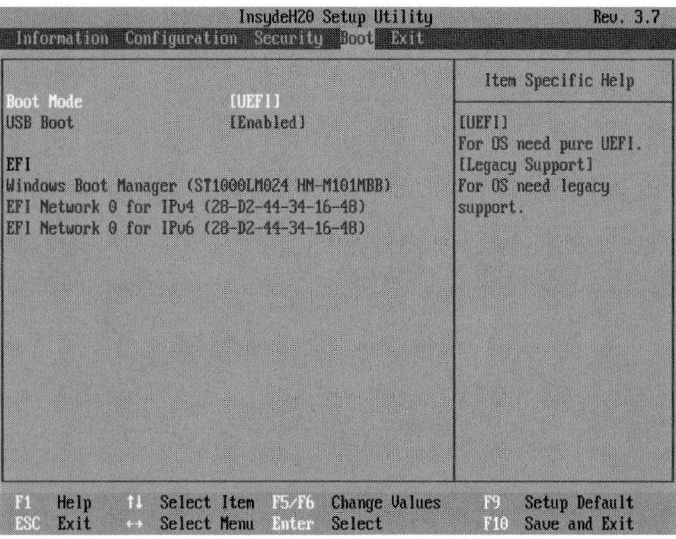

Figure 6-31 Boot tab

DriveLock On some motherboards, the CMOS setup program enables you to control the ATA Security Mode Feature Set, also commonly referred to as drive lock or *DriveLock*. ATA Security Mode is the first line of defense for protecting hard disks from unwanted access when a system is lost or stolen.

LoJack Some PC manufacturers also include *LoJack* security features in their BIOS—this way, if your PC is stolen, you can track its location, install a key logger, or even remotely shut down your computer.

Trusted Platform Module The *Trusted Platform Module (TPM)* acts as a secure cryptoprocessor, which is to say that it is a hardware platform for the acceleration of cryptographic functions and the secure storage of associated information. The specification for the TPM is published by the Trusted Computing Group, an organization whose corporate members include Intel, Microsoft, AMD, IBM, Lenovo, Dell, Hewlett-Packard, and many others.

The TPM can be a small circuit board plugged into the motherboard, or it can be built directly into the chipset. The CMOS setup program usually contains settings that can turn the TPM on or off and enable or disable it.

TPMs can be used in a wide array of cryptographic operations, but one of the most common uses of TPMs is hard disk encryption. For example, the *BitLocker Drive Encryption* feature of Microsoft Windows can be accelerated by a TPM, which is more secure because the encryption key is stored in the tamper-resistant TPM hardware rather than on an external flash drive. Other possible uses of TPMs include digital rights management (DRM), network access control, application execution control, and password protection.

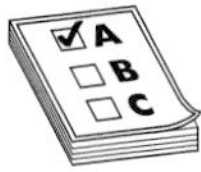

EXAM TIP BIOS security–related options can include TPM, LoJack, passwords, Secure Boot, intrusion detection/notification, and drive encryption.

Exiting and Saving Settings

Of course, all system setup utilities provide some method to Save and Exit or to Exit *Discarding* Saving (see Figure 6-32). Use these as needed for your situation. Exit Discarding Saving is particularly nice for those folks who want to poke around the CMOS setup utility but don't want to mess anything up. Use it!

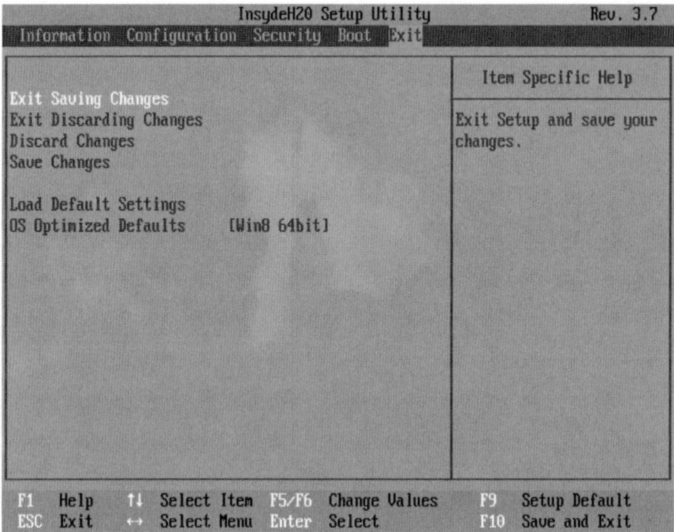

Figure 6-32 Exit options

The CMOS setup utility would meet all of the needs of a modern system for BIOS if manufacturers would just stop creating new devices. That's not going to happen, of course, so let's turn now to devices that need to have BIOS loaded from elsewhere.

Option ROM and Device Drivers

Every piece of hardware in your computer needs some kind of programming that tells the CPU how to talk to that device. When IBM invented the PC more than 30 years ago, they couldn't possibly have included all of the necessary BIOS routines for every conceivable piece of hardware on the system ROM chip. How could they? Most of the devices in use today didn't exist on the first PCs. When programmers wrote the first BIOS, for example, network cards, mice, and sound cards did not exist. Early PC designers at IBM understood that they could not anticipate every new type of hardware, so they gave us a few ways to add programming other than on the BIOS. I call this *BYOB*—Bring Your Own BIOS. You can BYOB in two ways: option ROM and device drivers. Let's look at both.

Option ROM

The first way to BYOB is to put the BIOS on the hardware device itself. Look at the card displayed in Figure 6-33. This is a serial ATA RAID hard drive controller—basically just

a card that lets you add more hard drives to a PC. The chip in the center with the wires coming out the sides is a flash ROM that stores BIOS for the card. The system BIOS does not have a clue about how to talk to this card, but that's okay, because this card brings its own BIOS on what's called an *option ROM* chip.

Figure 6-33 Option ROM

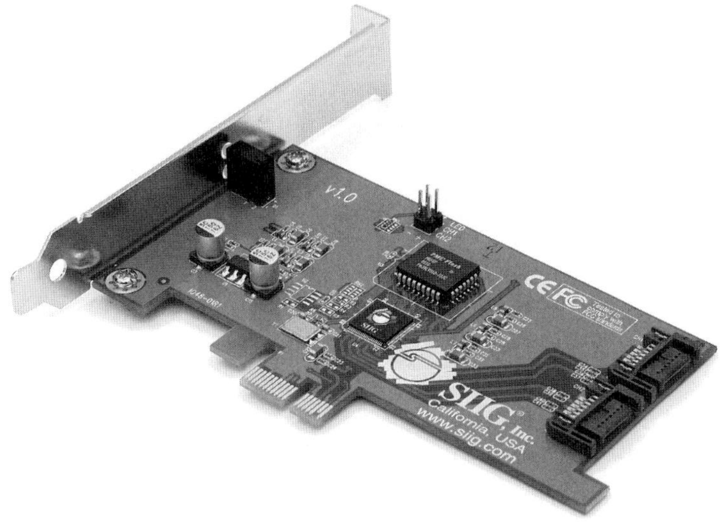

Most BIOS that come on option ROMs tell you that they exist by displaying information when you boot the system. Figure 6-34 shows a typical example of an option ROM advertising itself.

```
System Memory Size: 4.0 GB, System Memory Speed: 800 MHz, Voltage: 1.5V


Broadcom NetXtreme II Ethernet Boot Agent v5.2.7
Copyright (C) 2000-2009 Broadcom Corporation
All rights reserved.
Press Ctrl-S to Configure Device (MAC Address - 0024E867D111)


Adaptec 1225SA SATA HostRAID BIOS V6.0-0 B2328
(c) 1998-2007 Adaptec, Inc. All Rights Reserved.

◄◄◄ Press <Ctrl><A> for Adaptec RAID Configuration Utility! ►►►

Controller #00: Adaptec 1225SA at PCI Bus:03, Dev:00, Func:00
SerialNumber = 0KX0B0040013
Loading Configuration...
00:00 WDC WD20EADS-00R6B0 01.00A01     1.81 TB Healthy     3.0 Gb/s

SATA JBOD- PORT-0   WDC WD20EADS-00R     1.81 TB     Legacy

1 JBOD Device(s) Found.

_
```

Figure 6-34 Option ROM at boot

In the early days of the PC, you could find all sorts of devices with BIOS on option ROMs. Today, option ROMs have mostly been replaced by more flexible software methods (more on device driver software in the next section), with one major exception: video cards. Every video card made today contains its own BIOS. Option ROMs work well but are hard to upgrade. For this reason, most hardware relies on software for BYOB.

Device Drivers

A *device driver* is a file stored on the PC's hard drive that contains all of the commands necessary to talk to whatever device it was written to support. All operating systems employ a method of loading these device drivers into RAM every time the system boots. They know which device drivers to install by reading a file (or files) that lists which device drivers the system needs to load at boot time. All operating systems are designed to look at this list early on in the boot process and copy the listed files into RAM, thereby giving the CPU the capability to communicate with the hardware supported by the device driver.

Device drivers come with the device when you buy it. When you buy a sound card, for example, it comes with a disc that holds all of the necessary device drivers (and usually a bunch of extra goodies). The generic name for this type of CD-ROM is *installation disc*. In many cases, Windows will automatically detect and install the driver for you. If this does not work, Windows will prompt you for the installation disc (see Figure 6-35).

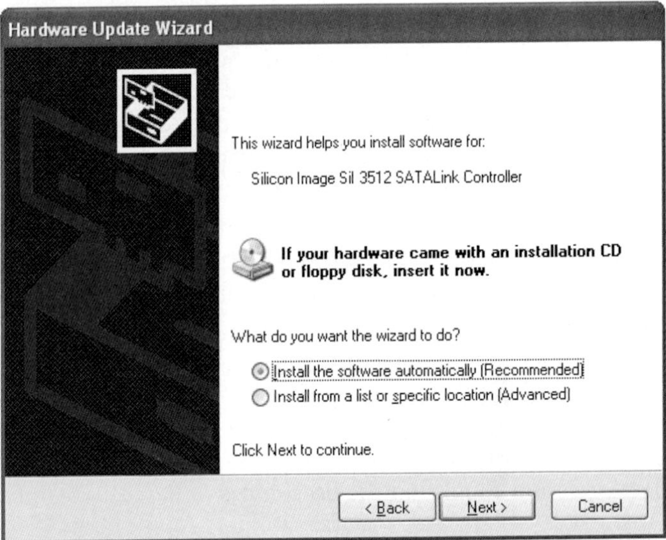

Figure 6-35 Windows XP asking for the installation disc

NOTE As you might notice, that is a Windows XP screenshot. Windows driver support has come a long way, and this dialog box, though not completely gone, is far rarer today than a decade ago.

You might want to add or remove device drivers manually at times. Windows uses a special database called the *Registry* that stores everything you want to know about your system, including the device drivers. You shouldn't access the Registry directly to access these drivers, but instead use the venerable Device Manager utility (mentioned in Chapter 3, "The Visible Computer").

BIOS, BIOS, Everywhere!

As you should now understand, every piece of hardware on a system must have an accompanying program that provides the CPU with the code necessary to communicate with that particular device. This code may reside on the system ROM on the motherboard, on ROM on a card, or in a device driver file on the hard drive loaded into RAM at boot. BIOS is everywhere on your system, and you need to deal with it occasionally.

Power-On Self Test (POST)

BIOS isn't the only program on your system ROM. When the computer is turned on or reset, it initiates a special program, also stored on the system ROM chip, called the *power-on self test (POST)*. The POST program checks out the system every time the computer boots. To perform this check, the POST sends out a command that says to all of the devices, "Check yourselves out!" All of the standard devices in the computer then run their own built-in diagnostic—the POST doesn't specify what they must check. The quality of the diagnostic is up to the people who made that particular device.

Let's consider the POST for a moment. Suppose some device—let's say it's the keyboard controller chip—runs its diagnostic and determines that it is not working properly. What can the POST do about it? Only one thing really: tell the human in front of the PC! So how does the computer tell the human? PCs convey POST information to you in two ways: beep codes and text messages.

Before and During the Video Test: The Beep Codes

The computer tests the most basic parts of the computer first, up to and including the video card. In early PCs, you'd hear a series of beeps—called *beep codes* or *POST beep codes*—if anything went wrong. By using beep codes before and during the video test, the computer could communicate with you. (If a POST error occurs before the video is available, obviously the error must manifest itself as beeps, because nothing can display on the screen.) The meaning of the beep code you'd hear varied among different BIOS manufacturers. You could find the beep codes for a specific motherboard in its motherboard manual.

Most modern PCs have only two beep codes: one for bad or missing video (one long beep followed by two or three short beeps), and one for bad or missing RAM (a single beep that repeats indefinitely).

CAUTION You'll find lots of online documentation about beep codes, but it's usually badly outdated.

You'll hear three other beep sequences on most PCs (although they're not officially beep codes). At the end of a successful POST, the PC produces one or two short beeps, simply to inform you that all is well. Most systems make a rather strange noise when the RAM is missing or very seriously damaged. Unlike traditional beep codes, this code repeats until you shut off the system. Finally, your speaker might make beeps for reasons that aren't POST or boot related. One of the more common is a series of short beeps after the system's been running for a while. That's a CPU alarm telling you the CPU is approaching its high heat limit.

Text Errors

After the video has tested okay, any POST errors display on the screen as text errors. If you get a text error, the problem is usually, but not always, self-explanatory (see Figure 6-36). Text errors are far more useful than beep codes, because you can simply read the screen to determine the bad device.

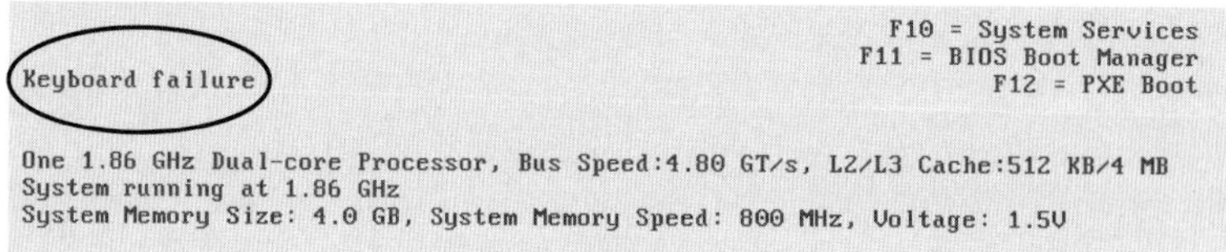

Figure 6-36 POST text error messages

POST Cards

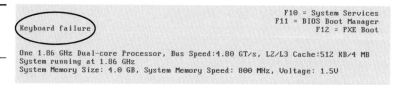

Beep codes, numeric codes, and text error codes, although helpful, can sometimes be misleading. Worse than that, an inoperative device can sometimes disrupt the POST, forcing the machine into an endless loop. This causes the PC to act dead—no beeps and nothing on the screen. In this case, you need a device, called a *POST card*, to monitor the POST and identify which piece of hardware is causing the trouble.

POST cards are simple cards that snap into expansion slots on your system. A small, two-character light-emitting diode (LED) readout on the card indicates which device the POST is currently testing (see Figure 6-37).

POST cards used to be essential tools for techs, but today I use them only when I have a "dead" PC to determine at which level it's dead. If the POST card shows no reading, I know the problem is before the POST and must be related to the power, the CPU, the RAM, or the motherboard. If the board posts, then I know to look at more issues, such as the drives and so on.

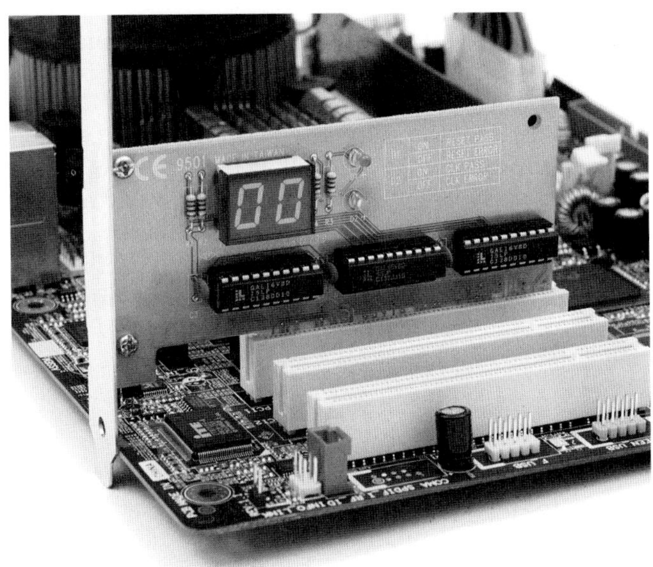

Figure 6-37 POST card in action

The Boot Process

All PCs need a process to begin their operations. Once you feed power to the PC, the tight interrelation of hardware, firmware, and software enables the PC to start itself, to "pull itself up by the bootstraps" or boot itself.

When you first power on the PC, the power supply circuitry tests for proper voltage and then sends a signal down a special wire called the *power good* wire to awaken the CPU. The moment the power good wire wakes it up, every CPU immediately sends a built-in memory address via its address bus. This special address is the same on every CPU, from the oldest 8086 to the most recent microprocessor. This address is the first line of the POST program on the system ROM! That's how the system starts the POST. After the POST has finished, there must be a way for the computer to find the programs on the hard drive to start the operating system. What happens next differs between the old BIOS way and the UEFI way.

In the older BIOS environment, the POST passes control to the last BIOS function: the bootstrap loader. The *bootstrap loader* is little more than a few dozen lines of BIOS code tacked to the end of the POST program. Its job is to find the operating system. The bootstrap loader reads CMOS information to tell it where to look first for an operating system. Your PC's CMOS setup utility has an option that you configure to tell the bootstrap loader which devices to check for an operating system and in which order—that's the *boot sequence*. (See Figure 6-38).

Figure 6-38 CMOS boot sequence

```
▶ Hard Disk Book Priority   [Press Enter]
  First Boot Device         [CDROM]
  Second Boot Device        [Hard Disk]
  Third Boot Device         [CDROM]
```

Almost all storage devices—hard disk drives, solid-state drives, CDs, DVDs, and USB thumb drives—can be configured to boot an operating system by setting aside a specific location called the *boot sector*. If the device is bootable, its boot sector contains special programming designed to tell the system where to locate the operating system. Any device with a functional operating system is called a *bootable disk* or a *system disk*. If the bootstrap loader locates a good boot sector, it passes control to the operating system and removes itself from memory. If it doesn't, it goes to the next device in the boot sequence you set in the CMOS setup utility. The boot sequence is an important tool for techs because you can set it to load in special bootable devices so you can run utilities to maintain PCs without using the primary operating system.

In UEFI systems, the POST hands control of the boot process to the boot manager, which checks the boot configuration, and then loads the operating system boot loader directly (see Figure 6-39). There's no need for scanning for a boot sector or any of that. UEFI firmware stores the boot manager and boot configuration.

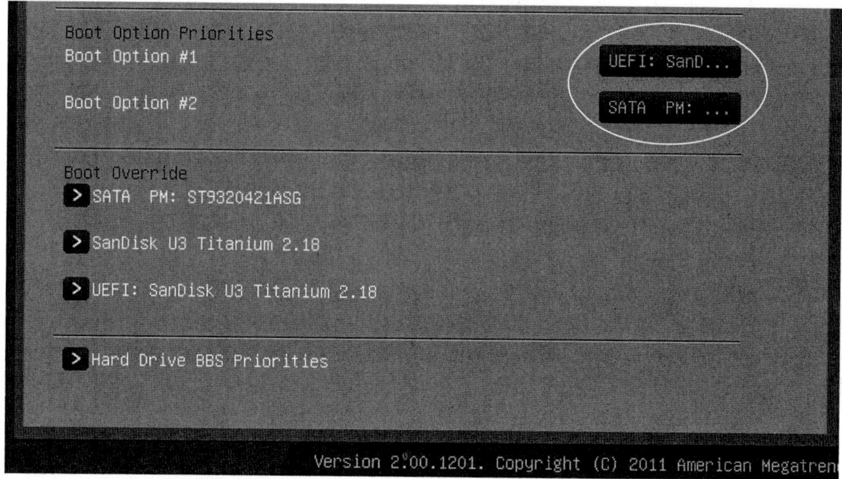

Figure 6-39 UEFI Boot Mode with Boot Manager options displayed

NOTE If you put an old-style BIOS bootable disk in a UEFI system, the system will most likely drop into BIOS compatibility mode and boot just like the old days. See Chapter 10 for more on drive structures.

Some BIOS include a feature that enables a PC to use a *preboot execution environment (PXE)*. A PXE enables you to boot a PC without any local storage by retrieving an OS from a server over a network. You'll see more on PXE when we talk about installing Windows in Chapter 12, "Building a PC."

Care and Feeding of BIOS and CMOS

BIOS and CMOS are areas in your PC that you don't go to very often. BIOS itself is invisible. The only real clue you have that it even exists is the POST. The CMOS setup utility, on the other hand, is very visible if you start it. Most CMOS setup utilities today work acceptably well without ever being touched. You're an aspiring tech, however, and all self-respecting techs start up the CMOS setup utility and make changes. That's when most CMOS setup utility problems take place.

If you mess with the CMOS setup utility, remember to make only as many changes at one time as you can remember. Document the original settings and the changes on a piece of paper or take a photo so you can put things back if necessary. Don't make changes unless you know what they mean! It's easy to screw up a computer fairly seriously by playing with CMOS settings you don't understand.

Default/Optimized Settings

Every CMOS setup utility has a couple of reset options, commonly called Load Default Settings and OS Optimized Defaults (see Figure 6-40). These options keep you from having to memorize all of those weird settings you'll never touch. Default or Fail-Safe sets everything to very simple settings—you might occasionally use this setting when very low-level problems such as freeze-ups occur and you've checked more obvious areas first. Optimized sets the CMOS to the best possible speed/stability for the system. You would use this option after you've tampered with the CMOS too much and need to put it back like it was!

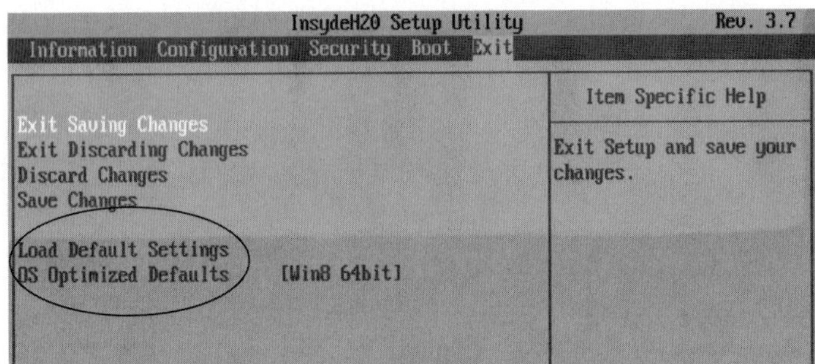

Figure 6-40 Options for resetting CMOS

Clearing CMOS

You read about the process for clearing CMOS settings back in Chapter 4, but the process is worth repeating here. When you mess up a setting (by overclocking too much or disabling something that should have remained enabled—or vice versa) that renders the computer dead, you can reset the CMOS back to factory defaults and start over.

Almost every motherboard has a dedicated set of wires called *CMOS clear* or something similar (see Figure 6-41).

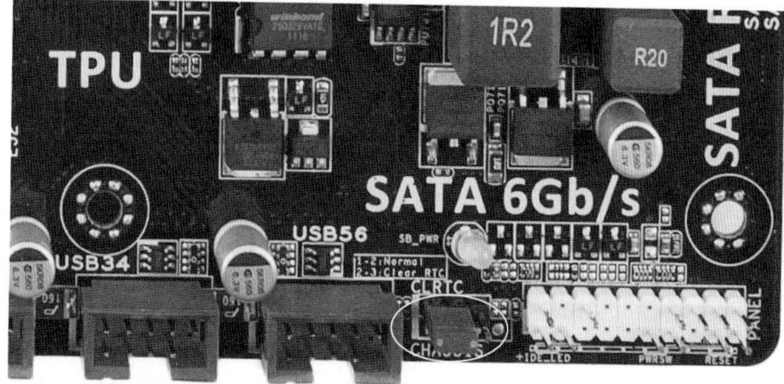

Figure 6-41 CMOS clear wires

Turn off and unplug the computer, then open the case to access the motherboard. Find the CMOS clear wires. Move the shunt (the little plastic and metal jumper thing) from wires 1 and 2 to wires 2 and 3 (see Figure 6-42). Wait for 10 seconds and then move the shunt back to the default position. Plug in and boot the system.

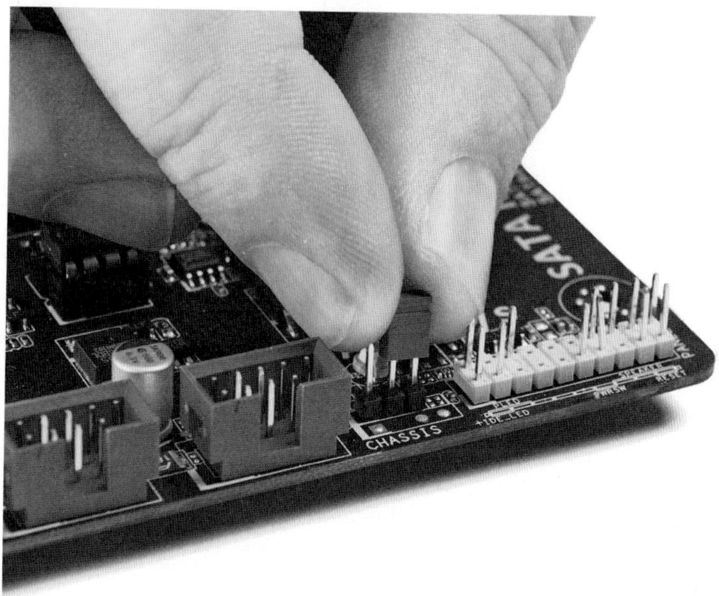

Figure 6-42 Changing shunt location to clear CMOS settings

NOTE Manufacturers of enthusiast boards designed for easy overclocking experimentation know you're going to screw up during the overclocking process. You'll find a dedicated clear CMOS button hardwired to the motherboard. Now that's service!

If that doesn't work or if you get one of the truly odd motherboards without CMOS clear jumpers, power down the system and unplug. Pry out the little coin battery (see below) and wait for several seconds. Reinstall and reboot.

Losing CMOS Settings

Your CMOS needs a continuous trickle charge to retain its data. Motherboards use some type of battery, usually a coin battery like those in wrist watches, to give the CMOS the charge it needs when the computer is turned off (see Figure 6-43). This battery also keeps track of the date and time when the PC is turned off.

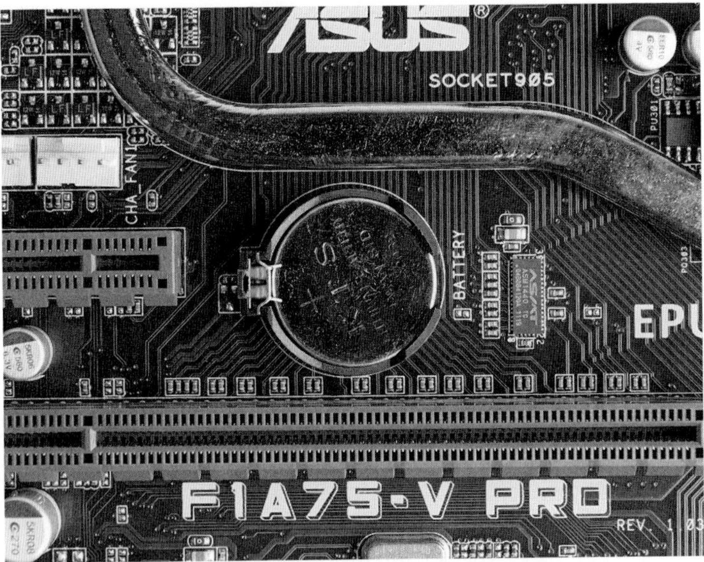

Figure 6-43 A CMOS battery

If the battery runs out of charge, you lose all of your CMOS information. If some mishap suddenly erases the information on the CMOS chip, the computer might not boot or you'll get nasty-looking errors at boot. Any PC made after 2002 will boot to factory defaults if the CMOS clears, so the chances of not booting are slim—but you'll still get errors at boot. Here are a few examples of errors that point to lost CMOS information:

- CMOS configuration mismatch
- CMOS date/time not set
- BIOS time and settings reset
- No boot device available
- CMOS battery state low

Here are some of the more common reasons for losing CMOS data:

- Pulling and inserting cards
- Touching the motherboard
- Dropping something on the motherboard
- Dirt on the motherboard
- Faulty power supplies
- Electrical surges

If you encounter any of these errors, or if the clock in Windows resets itself to January 1st every time you reboot the system, the battery on the motherboard is losing its charge and needs to be replaced. To replace the battery, use a screwdriver to pry the battery's catch gently back. The battery should pop up for easy removal. Before you install the new battery, double-check that it has the same voltage and amperage as the old battery. To retain your CMOS settings while replacing the battery, simply leave your PC plugged into an AC outlet. The 5-volt soft power on all modern motherboards provides enough electricity to keep the CMOS charged and the data secure. Of course, I know you're going to be *extremely* careful about ESD while prying up the battery from a live system!

Flashing the ROM

Flash ROM chips can be reprogrammed to update their contents. With flash ROM, when you need to update your system BIOS to add support for a new technology, you can simply run a small command-line program, combined with an update file, and voilà, you have a new, updated BIOS! This is called a *firmware upgrade*. Different BIOS makers use slightly different processes for *flashing the BIOS*, but, in general, you insert a removable disk of some sort (usually a USB thumb drive) containing an updated BIOS file and use the updating utility in CMOS setup.

Some motherboard makers provide Windows-based flash ROM update utilities that check the Internet for updates and download them for you to install (see Figure 6-44). Most of these utilities also enable you to back up your current BIOS so you can return to it if the updated version causes trouble. Without a good backup, you could end up throwing away your motherboard if a flash BIOS update goes wrong, so you should always make one.

Finally, don't update your BIOS unless you have some compelling reason to do so. As the old saying goes, "If it ain't broke, don't fix it!"

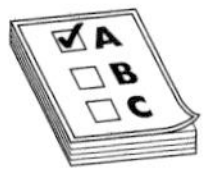

EXAM TIP While techs usually talk about "flashing the BIOS," the CompTIA A+ exams refer to this process also as "firmware upgrades" or "driver/firmware updates."

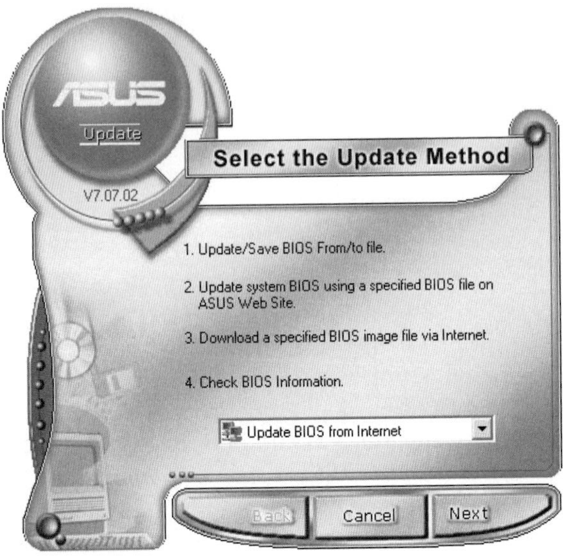

Figure 6-44 ROM-updating program for an ASUS motherboard

Chapter Review

Questions

1. What does BIOS provide for the computer? (Choose the best answer.)
   - **A.** BIOS provides the physical interface for various devices such as USB and FireWire ports.
   - **B.** BIOS provides the programming that enables the CPU to communicate with other hardware.
   - **C.** BIOS provides memory space for applications to load into from the hard drive.
   - **D.** BIOS provides memory space for applications to load into from the main system RAM.
2. What is the correct boot sequence for an older BIOS-based PC?
   - **A.** CPU, POST, power good, boot loader, operating system
   - **B.** POST, power good, CPU, boot loader, operating system
   - **C.** Power good, boot loader, CPU, POST, operating system
   - **D.** Power good, CPU, POST, boot loader, operating system

3. Jill decided to add a second hard drive to her computer. She thinks she has it physically installed correctly, but it doesn't show up in Windows. Which of the following options will most likely lead Jill where she needs to go to resolve the issue?

   A. Reboot the computer and press the F key on the keyboard twice. This signals that the computer has two hard disk drives.

   B. Reboot the computer and watch for instructions to enter the CMOS setup utility (for example, a message may say to press the DELETE key). Do what it says to go into CMOS setup.

   C. In Windows, press the DELETE key twice to enter the CMOS setup utility.

   D. In Windows, go to Start | Run and type **hard drive**. Click OK to open the Hard Drive Setup Wizard.

4. Henry bought a new card for capturing television on his computer. When he finished going through the packaging, though, he found no driver disc, only an application disc for setting up the TV capture software. After installing the card and software, it all works flawlessly. What's the most likely explanation?

   A. The device doesn't need BIOS, so there's no need for a driver disc.

   B. The device has an option ROM that loads BIOS, so there's no need for a driver disc.

   C. Windows supports TV capture cards out of the box, so there's no need for a driver disc.

   D. The manufacturer made a mistake and didn't include everything needed to set up the device.

5. Which of the following most accurately describes the relationship between BIOS and hardware?

   A. All hardware needs BIOS.

   B. All hardware that attaches to the motherboard via ribbon cables needs BIOS.

   C. All hardware built into the motherboard needs BIOS.

   D. Some hardware devices need BIOS.

6. After a sudden power outage, Samson's PC rebooted, but nothing appeared on the screen. The PC just beeps at him, over and over and over. What's most likely the problem?

   A. The power outage toasted his RAM.

   B. The power outage toasted his video card.

   C. The power outage toasted his hard drive.

   D. The power outage toasted his CPU.

7. Davos finds that a disgruntled former employee decided to sabotage her computer when she left by putting a password in CMOS that stops the computer from booting. What can Davos do to solve this problem?
   - **A.** Davos should boot the computer while holding the left SHIFT key. This will clear the CMOS information.
   - **B.** Davos should try various combinations of the former employee's name. The vast majority of people use their name or initials for CMOS passwords.
   - **C.** Davos should find the CMOS clear jumper on the motherboard. Then he can boot the computer with a shunt on the jumper to clear the CMOS information.
   - **D.** Davos should find a replacement motherboard. Unless he knows the CMOS password, there's nothing he can do.
8. Richard over in the sales department went wild in CMOS and made a bunch of changes that he thought would optimize his PC. Now most of his PC doesn't work. The computer powers up, but he can only get to CMOS, not into Windows. Which of the following tech call answers would most likely get him up and running again?
   - **A.** Reboot the computer about three times. That'll clear the CMOS and get you up and running.
   - **B.** Open up the computer and find the CMOS clear jumper. Remove a shunt from somewhere on the motherboard and put it on the CMOS clear jumper. Reboot and then put the shunt back where you got it. Reboot, and you should be up and running in no time.
   - **C.** Boot into the CMOS setup program and then find the option to load a plug-and-play operating system. Make sure it's set to On. Save and exit CMOS; boot normally into Windows. You should be up and running in no time.
   - **D.** Boot into the CMOS setup program and then find the option to load OS Optimized Defaults. Save and exit CMOS; boot normally into Windows. You should be up and running in no time.
9. Jill boots an older Pentium system that has been the cause of several user complaints at the office. The system powers up and starts to run through POST, but then stops. The screen displays a "CMOS configuration mismatch" error. Of the following list, what is the most likely cause of this error?
   - **A.** Dying CMOS battery
   - **B.** Bad CPU
   - **C.** Bad RAM
   - **D.** Corrupt system BIOS

10. Where does Windows store device drivers?
    A. Computer
    B. Hardware
    C. Registry
    D. Drivers and Settings

Answers

1. **B.** BIOS provides the programming that enables the CPU to communicate with other hardware.
2. **D.** Here's the correct boot sequence for a BIOS-based PC: power good, CPU, POST, boot loader, operating system.
3. **B.** Jill should reboot the computer and watch for instructions to enter the CMOS setup utility (for example, a message may say to press the DELETE key). She should do what it says to go into CMOS setup.
4. **B.** Most likely the device has an option ROM, because it works.
5. **A.** All hardware needs BIOS!
6. **A.** The long repeating beep and a dead PC most likely indicate a problem with RAM.
7. **C.** Davos should find the CMOS clear jumper on the motherboard and then boot the computer with a shunt on the jumper to clear the CMOS information.
8. **D.** Please don't hand Richard a screwdriver! Having him load Optimized Default settings will most likely do the trick.
9. **A.** The CMOS battery is likely dying.
10. **C.** Windows stores device drivers in the Registry.

CHAPTER 7

Motherboards

In this chapter, you will learn how to

- Explain how motherboards work
- Recognize modern expansion buses
- Upgrade and install motherboards
- Troubleshoot motherboard problems

The *motherboard* provides the foundation for the personal computer. Every piece of hardware, from the CPU to the lowliest expansion card, directly or indirectly plugs into the motherboard. The motherboard contains the wires—called *traces*—that make up the buses of the system. It holds the vast majority of the ports used by the peripherals, and it distributes the power from the power supply (see Figure 7-1). Without the motherboard, you literally have no PC.

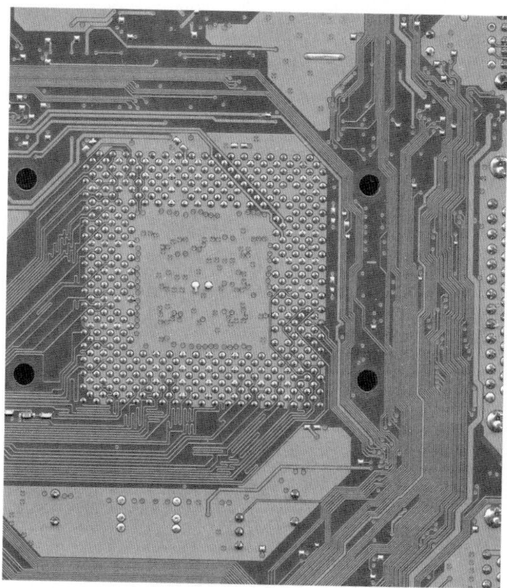

Figure 7-1 Traces visible beneath the CPU socket on a motherboard

This chapter starts with an explanation of how motherboard work, identifying various types or form factors of motherboards, including distinguishing features. The second section examines expansion capabilities on motherboards, specifically the types of expansion slots you'll run into in the wild and how to install expansion cards. The third section goes through the pragmatic steps of upgrading and installing motherboards. The chapter finishes with techniques for troubleshooting motherboard problems.

NOTE Modern motherboards are layered *printed circuit boards (PCBs)*, copper etched onto a nonconductive material and then coated with some sort of epoxy for strength. The layers mask some of their complexity. You can see some of the traces on the board, but every motherboard is four or more layers thick. The layers contain a veritable highway of wires, carrying data and commands back and forth between the CPU, RAM, and peripherals. The layered structure enables multiple wires to send data without their signals interfering with each other. The layered approach allows the manufacturer to add complexity and additional components to the board without extending the overall length and width of the board. Shorter traces also allow signals to travel faster than they would if the wires were longer, as would be necessary if motherboards did not use layers. The multiple layers also add strength to the board itself, so it doesn't bend easily.

Historical/Conceptual

How Motherboards Work

Three variable and interrelated characteristics define modern motherboards: form factor, chipset, and components. The *form factor* determines the physical size of the motherboard as well as the general location of components and ports. The *chipset* defines the type of processor and RAM the motherboard requires and determines to a degree the built-in devices the motherboard supports, including the expansion slots. Finally, the built-in components determine the core functionality of the system.

Several companies have made chipsets over the years, but all the big players of yesteryear—NVIDIA, VIA Technologies, SiS—have faded, leaving two players standing: Intel and AMD. It's fitting that the two biggest CPU manufacturers for Windows, Mac OS X, and Linux-based computers would also produce the essential supporting chipsets.

Any good tech should be able to make a recommendation to a client about a particular motherboard simply by perusing the specs. Because the motherboard determines function, expansion, and stability for the whole PC, it's essential that you know your motherboards!

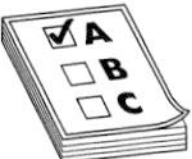

EXAM TIP CompTIA A+ 901 exam objective 1.2 focuses specifically on motherboards you find in classical Windows and Linux-based desktop PCs. This style of motherboard enables techs to do such things as update components. Thus, this chapter uses the term "PC" pretty much throughout.

Note, though, that every personal computing device has a main circuit board to which connects CPU, RAM, storage, and more. Some device makers call this PCB a *motherboard*. Others, like Apple, call it a *logic board*. Regardless of the label, the primary function is the same—it's the foundational component of the computer.

Form Factors

Form factors are industry-standardized shapes and layouts that enable motherboards to work with cases and power supplies. A single form factor applies to all three components. All motherboards come in a basic rectangular or square shape but vary in overall size and in the layout of built-in components (see Figure 7-2). You need to install a motherboard in a case designed to fit it, so the ports and slot openings on the back fit correctly.

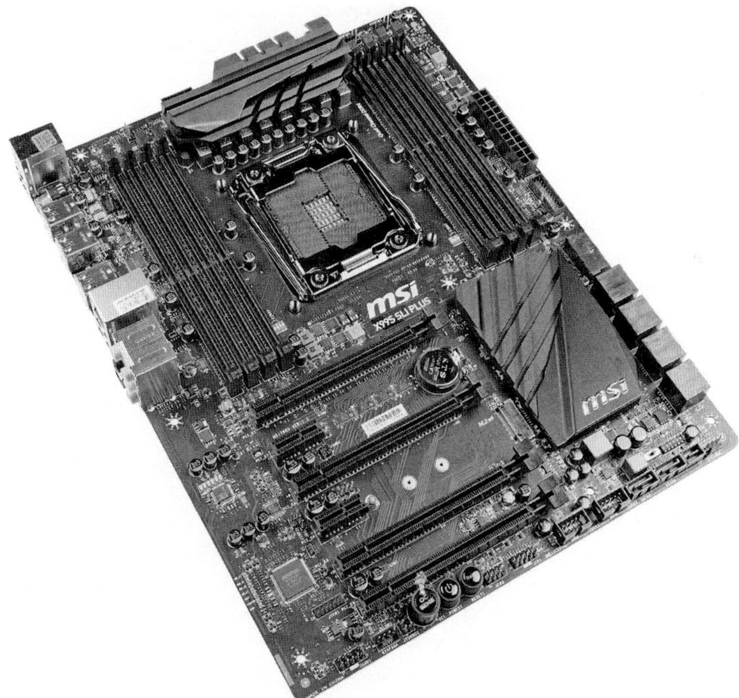

Figure 7-2 Typical motherboard

The power supply and the motherboard need matching connectors, and different form factors define different connections. Given that the term "form factor" applies to the case, motherboard, and power supply—the three parts of the PC most responsible for moving air around inside the PC—the form factor also defines how the air moves around in the case.

To perform motherboard upgrades and provide knowledgeable recommendations to clients, techs need to know their form factors. The PC industry has adopted—and dropped—a number of form factors over the years with such names as AT, ATX, and BTX. Let's start with the granddaddy of all PC form factors, AT.

AT Form Factor

The *AT* form factor (see Figure 7-3), invented by IBM in the early 1980s, was the predominant form factor for motherboards through the mid-1990s. AT is now obsolete.

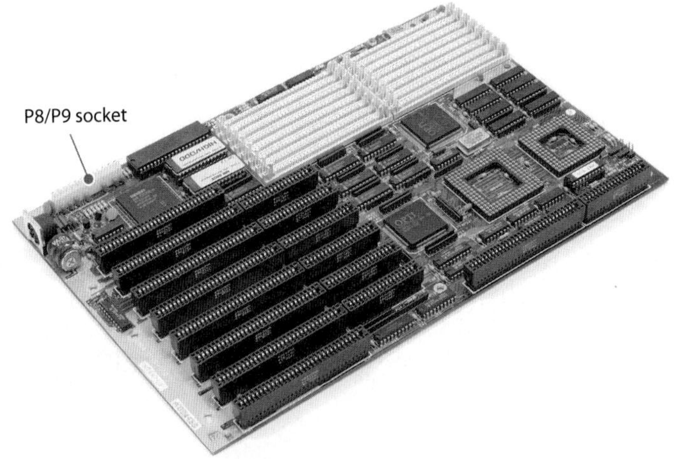

Figure 7-3 AT-style motherboard

The AT motherboard had a few size variations (see Figure 7-4), ranging from large to very large. The original AT motherboard was huge, around 12 inches wide by 13 inches deep. PC technology was new and needed lots of space for the various chips necessary to run the components of the PC.

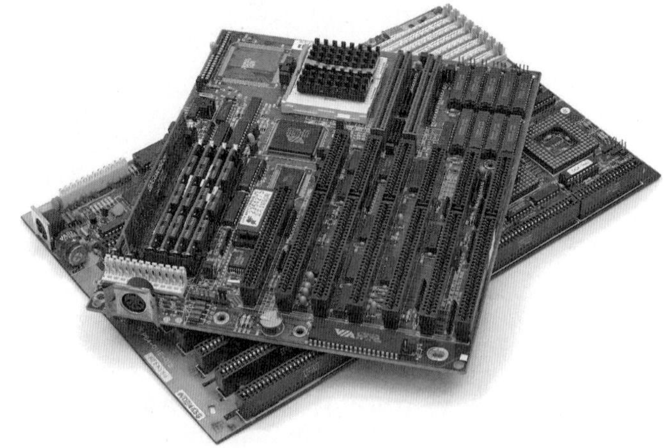

Figure 7-4 AT motherboard (bottom) and Baby AT motherboard (top)

The single greatest problem with AT motherboards was the lack of external ports. When PCs were first invented, the only devices plugged into the average PC were a monitor and a keyboard. That's what the AT was designed to handle—the only dedicated connector on an AT motherboard was the keyboard port (see Figure 7-5).

Figure 7-5 Keyboard connector on the back of an AT motherboard

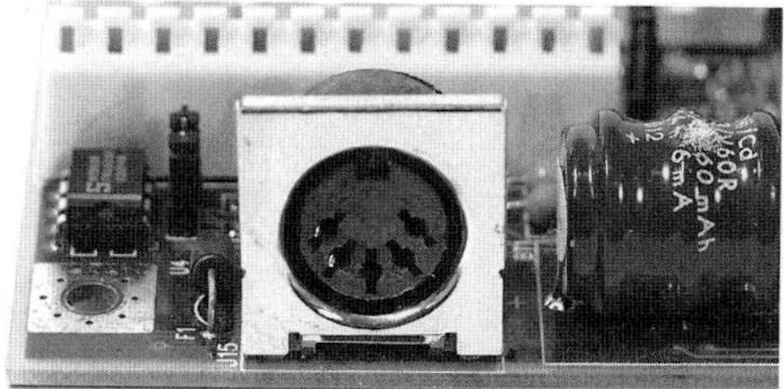

Over the years, the number of devices plugged into the back of the PC has grown tremendously. Your average PC today has a keyboard, a mouse, a printer, some speakers, a monitor, and—if your system's like mine—four to six USB devices connected to it at any given time. These added components created a demand for a new type of form factor, one with more dedicated connectors for more devices. Many attempts were made to create a new standard form factor. Invariably, these new form factors integrated dedicated connectors for at least the mouse and printer, and many even added connectors for video, sound, and phone lines.

901

ATX Form Factor

There continued to be a tremendous demand for a new form factor, one that had more standard connectors and also was flexible enough for possible changes in technology. This demand led to the creation of the ATX form factor in 1995 (see Figure 7-6). ATX got off to a slow start, but by around 1998, ATX overtook AT to become the most common form factor, a distinction it holds today.

ATX is distinct from AT in the lack of an AT keyboard port, replaced with a rear panel that has all necessary ports built in. Note the mini-DIN (PS/2) keyboard and mouse ports at the left of Figure 7-7, until recently, standard features on almost all ATX boards. You recall those from Chapter 3, right?

The ATX form factor includes many improvements over AT. The position of the power supply creates better air movement. The CPU and RAM are placed to provide easier access, and the rearrangement of components prevents long expansion cards from colliding with the CPU or Northbridge. Other improvements, such as placing the RAM closer to the Northbridge and CPU than on AT boards, offer users enhanced performance as well. The shorter the wires, the easier to shield them and make them capable of handling double or quadruple the clock speed of the motherboard. Figure 7-8 shows AT and ATX motherboards—note the radical differences in placement of internal connections.

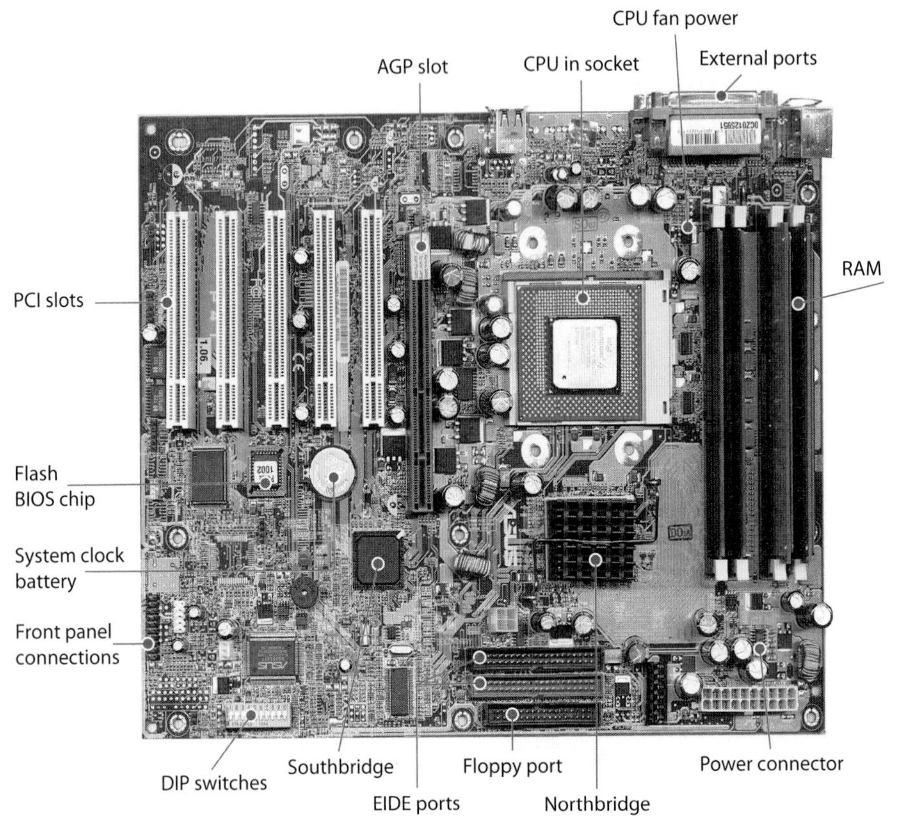

Figure 7-6 Early ATX motherboard

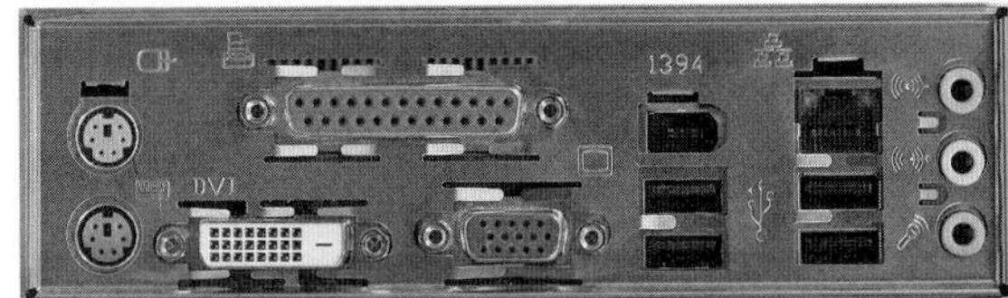

Figure 7-7 ATX ports

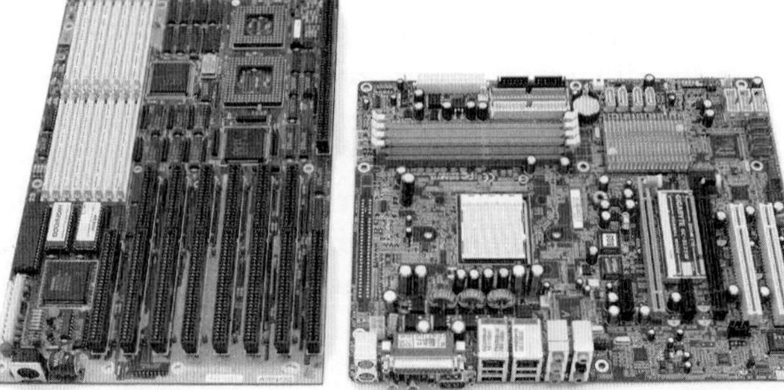

Figure 7-8 AT (left) and ATX (right) motherboards for quick visual comparison

ATX motherboards come in three variations to accommodate different types of cases. So far, you've seen the full-sized ATX form factor, which is 12 by 9.6 inches.

The *microATX* motherboard (see Figure 7-9) floats in at a svelte 9.6 by 9.6 inches (usually), or about 30 percent smaller than standard ATX, yet uses the standard ATX connections. A microATX motherboard fits into a standard ATX case or in the much smaller microATX cases. Note that not all microATX motherboards have the same physical size. You'll sometimes see microATX motherboards referred to with the Greek symbol for micro, as in µATX.

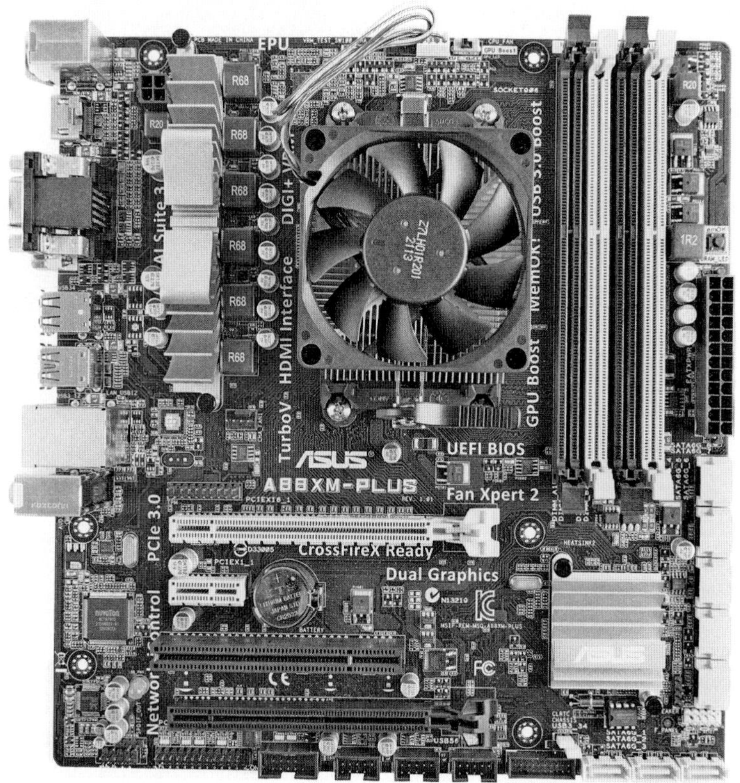

Figure 7-9 A microATX motherboard

In 1999, Intel created a variant of the microATX called the FlexATX. *FlexATX* motherboards have maximum dimensions of just 9 by 7.5 inches, which makes them the smallest motherboards in the ATX standard. FlexATX is pretty much gone now.

ITX

Not everyone wants or needs a huge desktop system. From the beginning of PCs, there's always been a demand for smaller computers. While a number of companies have made proprietary motherboards to support smaller computers, it wasn't until around 2001 that the chipset maker VIA Technologies started the process to create a small form factor

(SFF) motherboard, the *ITX*. The ITX itself wasn't a success, but VIA in turn created a number of even smaller form factors that today populate the SFF market: Mini-ITX, Nano-ITX, and Pico-ITX.

Mini-ITX is the largest and the most popular of the three ITX form factors. At a minuscule 6.7 by 6.7 inches, Mini-ITX competes head to head with the virtually identical microATX (see Figure 7-10).

Figure 7-10
Mini-ITX

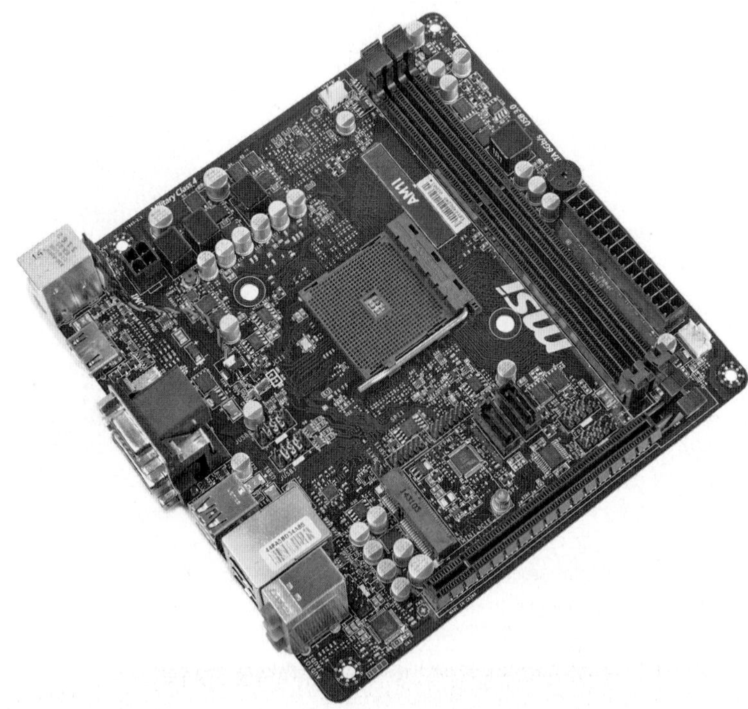

If you think that's small, *Nano-ITX* at 4.7 by 4.7 inches and *Pico-ITX* at 3.8 by 2.8 inches are even smaller (see Figure 7-11). These tiny motherboard form factors are commonly used for embedded systems and highly specialized devices such as routers.

One of the great benefits of these SFF motherboards is the tiny amount of power needed to support them. ITX power supplies are quite small compared to a typical power supply. Lower power usage produces less heat, thus enabling passive cooling on many SFF systems. The lack of fan noise makes them ideal for media center PCs.

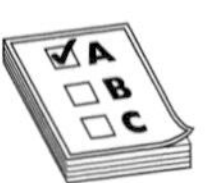

EXAM TIP You need to know the variations of the ATX standard for the CompTIA 220-901 exam, especially microATX. You should also be familiar with the low-power design of Mini-ITX boards.

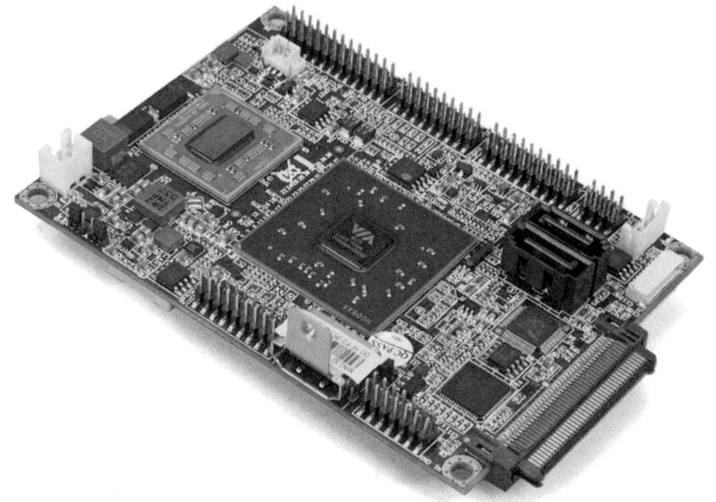

Figure 7-11 Pico-ITX (photo courtesy of VIA Technologies, Inc.)

Proprietary Form Factors

Several major PC makers make motherboards that work only with their cases. These *proprietary* motherboards enable these companies to create systems that stand out from the generic ones and, not coincidently, push you to get service and upgrades from their authorized dealers. Some of the features you'll see in proprietary systems are *riser cards*—part of a motherboard separate from the main one but connected by a cable of some sort—and unique power connections. Proprietary motherboards drive techs crazy because replacement parts tend to cost more and are not readily available.

Try This!

Motherboard Varieties

Motherboards come in a wide variety of form factors. Go to your local computer store and check out what is on display. Note the different features offered by ATX, microATX, and Mini-ITX motherboards.

1. Does the store stock Mini-ITX or proprietary motherboards?
2. Did the clerk use tech slang and call the motherboards "mobos"? (It's what most of us call them outside of formal textbooks, after all!)

Chipset

Every motherboard has a chipset, one or more discrete integrated circuit chips that support the CPU's interfacing to all the other devices on the motherboard. The chipset determines the type of processor the motherboard accepts, the type and capacity of RAM, and the sort of internal and external devices that the motherboard supports. As you learned in earlier chapters, the chips in a PC's chipset serve as electronic interfaces through which the CPU, RAM, and input/output devices interact. Chipsets vary in features, performance, and stability, so they factor hugely in the purchase or recommendation of a particular motherboard. Good techs know their chipsets!

Because the chipset facilitates communication between the CPU and other devices in the system, its component chips are relatively centrally located on the motherboard (see Figure 7-12). As you'll recall from Chapter 6, chipsets were originally composed of two primary chips: the Northbridge and the Southbridge.

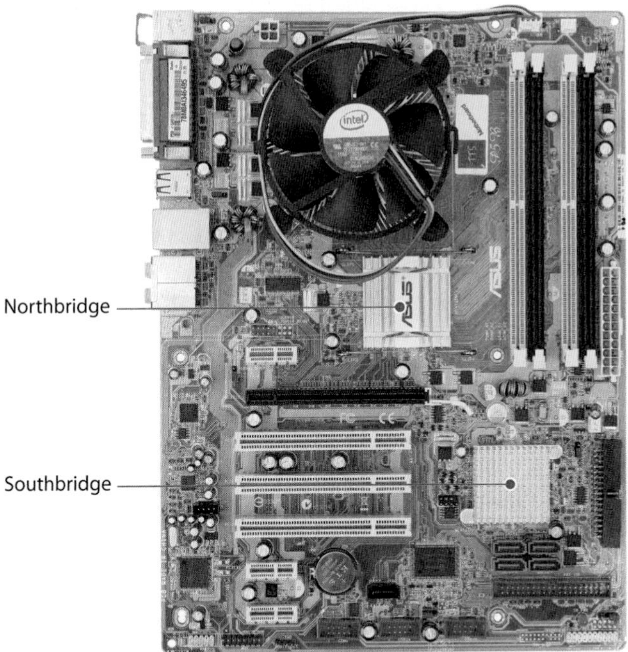

Figure 7-12 Northbridge and Southbridge

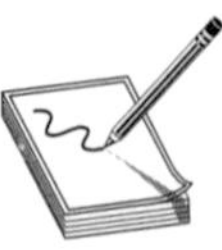

NOTE Although CompTIA continues to discuss the Northbridge and Southbridge as discrete chips, you know from Chapter 6 that their functions have been absorbed into other devices. The CPU handles all the memory controller features. The Southbridge first morphed into the Input/Output Controller Hub (ICH—Intel) or Fusion Controller Hub (FCH—AMD). Now it's just the Platform Controller Hub (PCH) that connects directly to the CPU.

The Northbridge chip handled RAM, while the Southbridge handled some expansion devices and mass storage drives, such as hard drives. Some motherboard manufacturers added (or still add) a third chip called the *super I/O chip* to handle these chores. Figure 7-13 shows a typical super I/O chip.

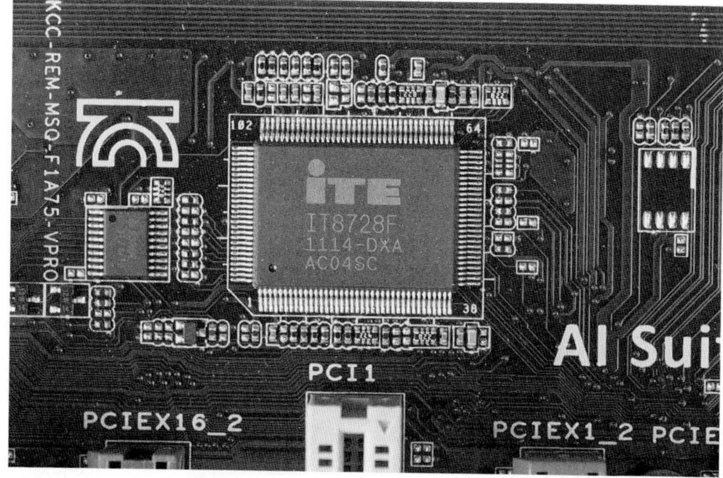

Figure 7-13 Super I/O chip on ASUS motherboard

The system ROM chip provides part of the BIOS for the chipset, but only at a barebones, generic level. The chipset still needs support for the rest of the things it can do. So how do expansion devices get BIOS? From software drivers, of course, and the same holds true for modern chipsets. You have to load the proper drivers for the specific OS to support all of the features of today's chipsets. Without software drivers, you'll never create a stable, fully functional PC. Most motherboards ship with an optical disc with drivers, support programs, and extra-special goodies such as antivirus software (see Figure 7-14).

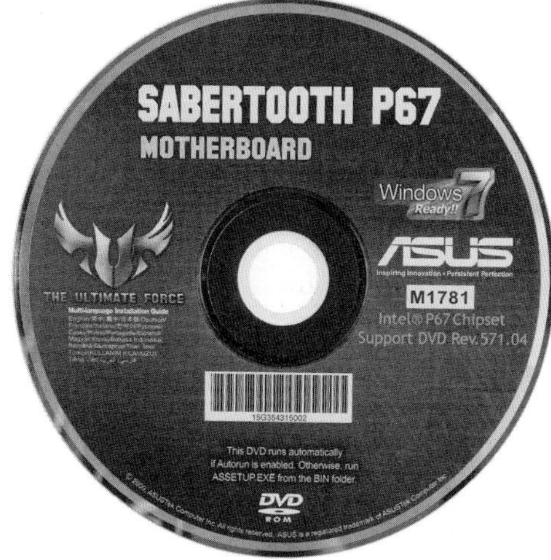

Figure 7-14 Driver disc for ASUS motherboard

Different chipsets offer support for a lot of different hardware options, including type of memory slot (DDR3 or DDR4), number and version of USB ports, various mass storage devices, and so on. Figure 7-15 shows a schematic with typical chipset chores for an Intel X99 chipset.

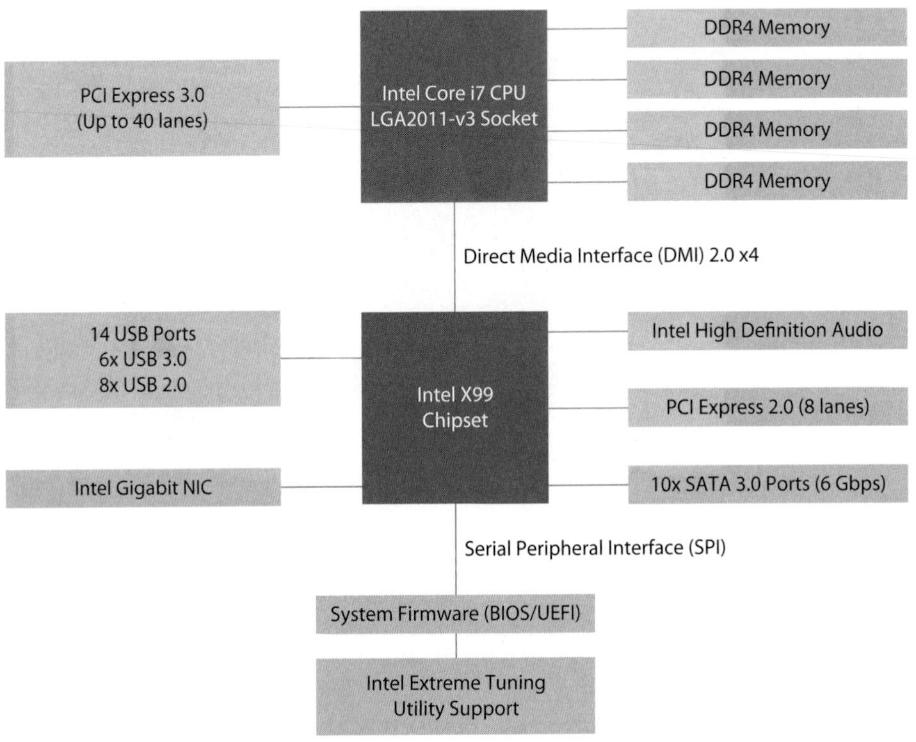

Figure 7-15 Schematic of a modern chipset

Good techs need to know the hot chipsets in detail. The chipset defines almost every motherboard feature short of the CPU itself. Techs love to discuss chipsets and expect a fellow tech to know the differences between one chipset and another. You also need to be able to recommend a motherboard that suits a client's needs. Chapter 12, "Building a PC," covers choosing components and building PCs for specific purposes, such as video editing and gaming. One of the most important choices you'll make in building a custom rig is selecting a chipset.

Motherboard Components

The connections and capabilities of a motherboard sometimes differ from those of the chipset the motherboard uses. This disparity happens for a couple of reasons. First, a particular chipset may support eight USB ports, but to keep costs down, the manufacturer might include only four ports. Second, a motherboard maker may choose to install extra features—ones not supported by the chipset—by adding additional chips. A common

example is a motherboard that supports FireWire. Other technologies you might find are built-in sound, hard drive RAID controllers, network cards, and more. Some motherboards have added convenience features, such as case fan power connectors and running lights so you can see what you're working on.

USB/FireWire

Most chipsets support USB, and many motherboards come with FireWire as well, but it seems no two motherboards offer the same port arrangement. My motherboard supports eight USB ports and two FireWire ports, for example, but if you look on the back of the motherboard, you'll only see four USB ports and one FireWire port. So, where are the other ports? Well, this motherboard has special connectors for the other ports, and the motherboard comes with the dongles you need to connect them (see Figure 7-16). These dongles typically use an extra slot on the back of the case.

Figure 7-16 USB/FireWire dongle

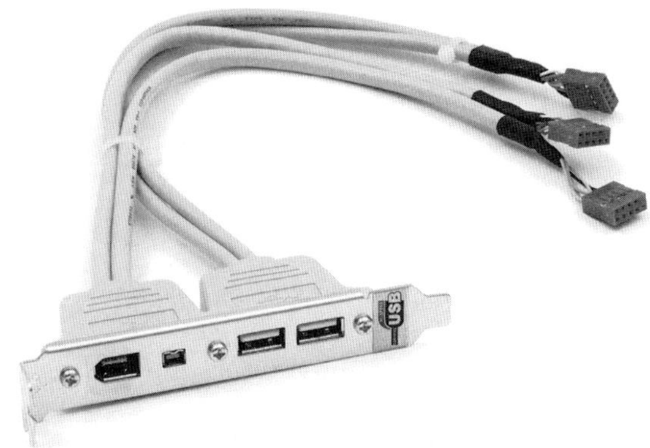

These dongle connectors are standardized, so many cases have built-in front USB/FireWire ports that have dongles attached. This is very handy for USB or FireWire devices you might want to plug and unplug frequently, such as thumb drives or digital cameras. You can also buy add-on front USB and FireWire devices that go into a 3.5-inch drive bay (see Figure 7-17).

Figure 7-17 Front USB and FireWire drive bay device

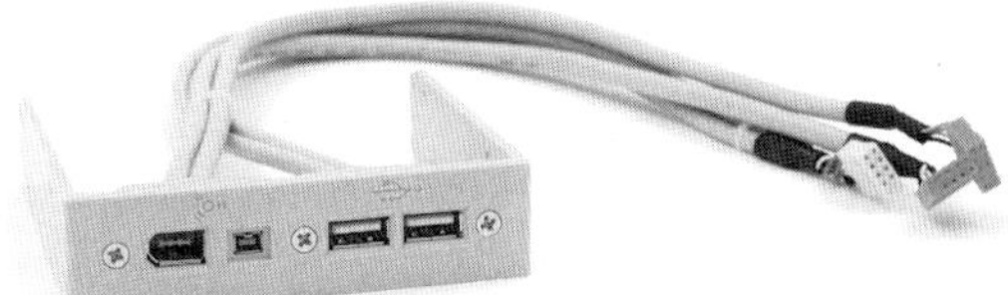

Sound

Most motherboards come with onboard sound chips. As with USB, a lot of motherboards have a port for connecting to audio jacks on the front of the case. These enable you to plug headphones or microphones into the front rather than the rear of the case, a

very convenient feature. These connectors are identical to the ones used on sound cards, so we'll save more discussion for Chapter 11, "Essential Peripherals."

RAID

RAID stands for *redundant array of independent (or inexpensive) disks* and is very common on motherboards. There are many types of RAID, such as *mirroring* (the process of using two drives to hold the same data, which is good for safety, because if one drive dies, the other still has all of the data) or *striping* (making two drives act as one drive by spreading data across them, which is good for speed). RAID is a very cool but complex topic that's discussed in detail in Chapter 9, "Hard Drive Technologies."

Case Fan Support

Every motherboard has a CPU fan power connector, as you'll recall from Chapter 4, "Microprocessors," usually a four-wire connector that supports three-wire fans too. Some motherboards offer one or more fan power connectors for case fans. These are almost always only three-wire connectors. The case fans plugged into the motherboard can be monitored and controlled in Windows, unlike case fans connected only to the power supply, so they are a nice feature.

Expansion Bus

Expansion slots have been part of the PC from the very beginning. Way back then, IBM created the PC with an eye to the future; the original IBM PC had slots built into the motherboard—called *expansion slots*—for adding expansion cards and thus new functions to the PC. The slots and accompanying wires and support chips on the first PC and on the latest and greatest PC are called the *expansion bus*.

Structure and Function of the Expansion Bus

As you've learned, every device in the computer—whether soldered to the motherboard or snapped into a socket—connects to the external data bus and the address bus. The expansion slots are no exception. They connect to the rest of the PC through the chipset. Exactly *where* on the chipset varies depending on the system. On some systems, the expansion slots connect to the Southbridge (see Figure 7-18). On other systems, the expansion slots connect to the Northbridge (see Figure 7-19). Finally, many systems have more than one type of expansion bus, with slots of one type connecting to the Northbridge and slots of another type connecting to the Southbridge (see Figure 7-20).

The chipset provides an extension of the address bus and data bus to the expansion slots, and thus to any expansion cards in those slots. If you plug a hard drive controller card into an expansion slot, it functions just as if it were built into the motherboard, albeit with one big difference: speed. As you'll recall from Chapter 4, the system crystal—the clock—pushes the CPU. The system crystal provides a critical function for the entire PC, acting like a drill sergeant calling a cadence, setting the pace of activity in the computer.

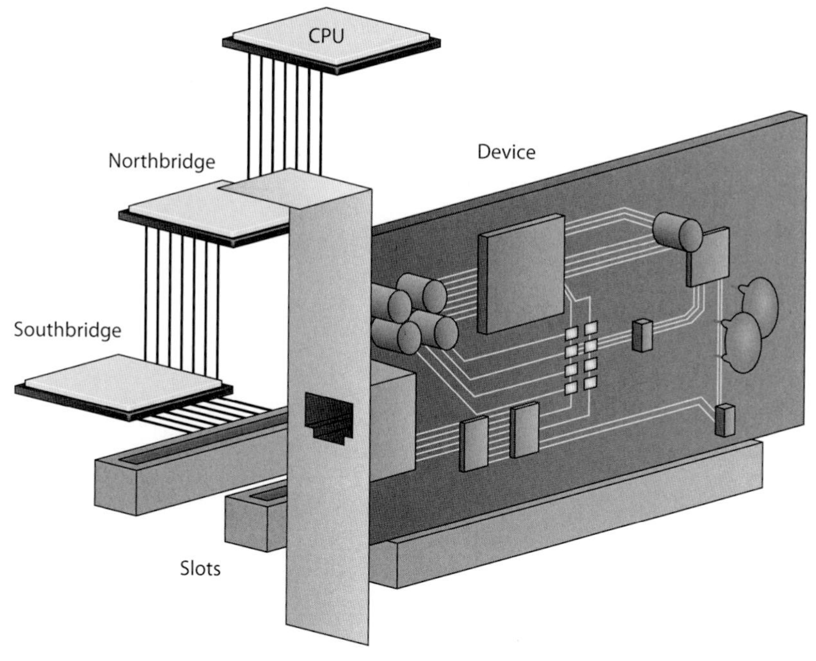

Figure 7-18 Expansion slots connecting to Southbridge

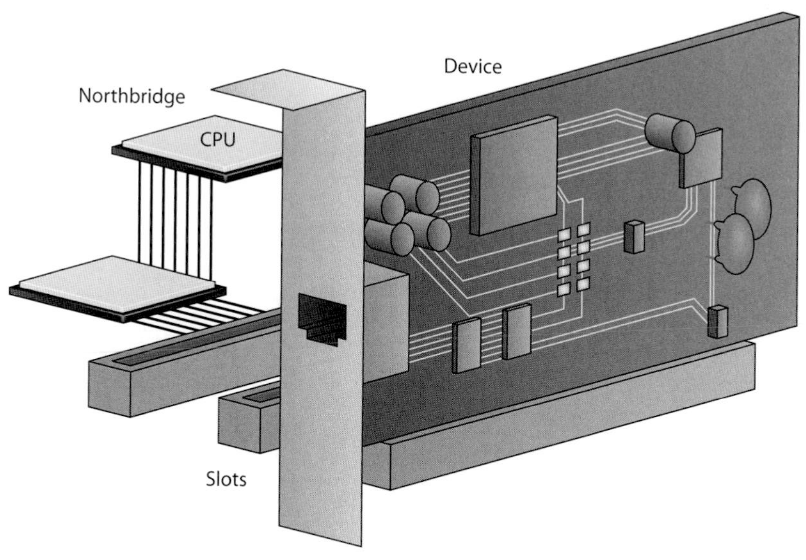

Figure 7-19 Expansion slots connecting to Northbridge

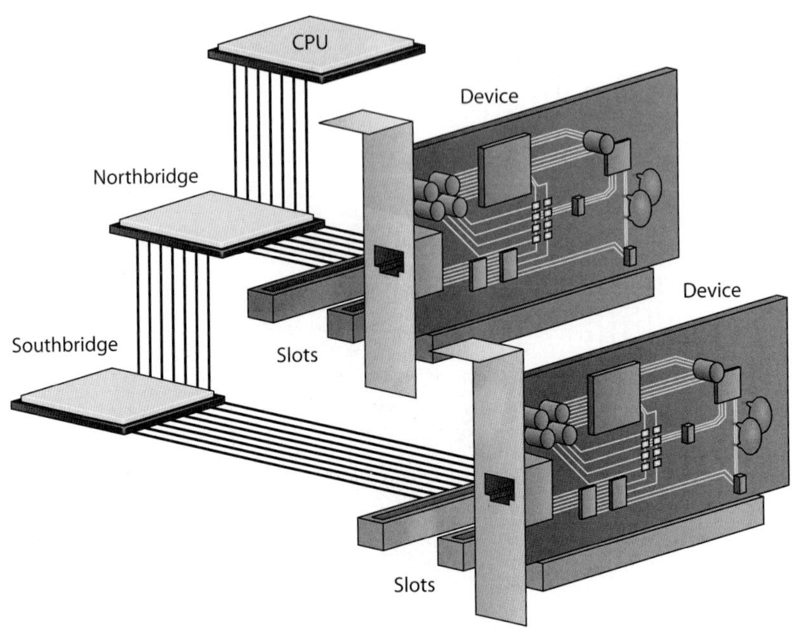

Figure 7-20 Expansion slots connecting to both Northbridge and Southbridge

Every device soldered to the motherboard is designed to run at the speed of the system crystal. A 200-MHz motherboard, for example, has its chipset chips all timed by a 200-MHz crystal (see Figure 7-21).

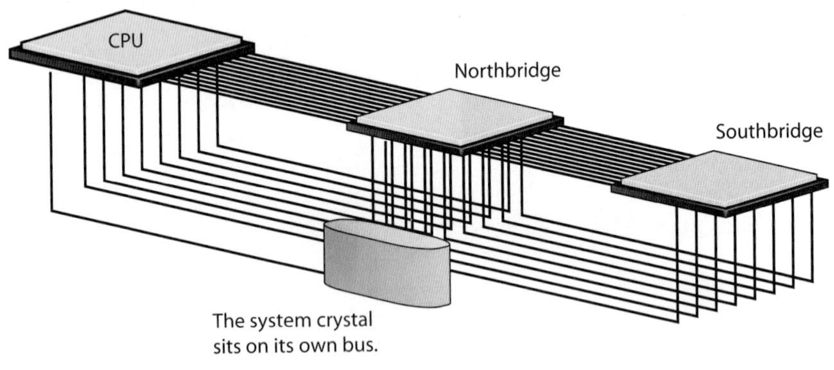

Figure 7-21 The system crystal sets the speed.

Clock crystals aren't just for CPUs and chipsets. Pretty much every chip in your computer has a CLK wire and needs to be pushed by a clock chip, including the chips on your expansion cards. Suppose you buy a device that did not come with your computer—say,

a sound card. The chips on the sound card need to be pushed by a CLK signal from a crystal. If PCs were designed to use the system crystal to push that sound card, sound card manufacturers would need to make sound cards for every possible motherboard speed. You would have to buy a 100-MHz sound card for a 100-MHz system or a 200-MHz sound card for a 200-MHz system.

That would be ridiculous, and IBM knew it when they designed the PC. They had to make an extension to the external data bus that *ran at its own standardized speed.* You would use this part of the external data bus to snap new devices into the PC. IBM achieved this goal by adding a different crystal, called the *expansion bus crystal,* which controlled the part of the external data bus connected to the expansion slots (see Figure 7-22).

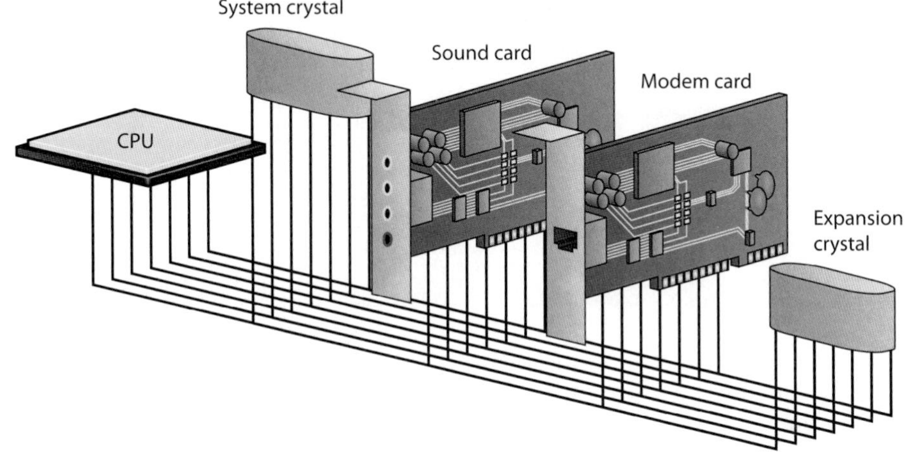

Figure 7-22 Function of system and expansion bus crystals

The expansion slots run at a much slower speed than the frontside bus. The chipset acts as the divider between the two buses, compensating for the speed difference with wait states and special buffering (storage) areas. No matter how fast the motherboard runs, the expansion slots run at a standard speed. In the original IBM PC, that speed was about 14.318 MHz ÷ 2, or about 7.16 MHz. Luckily, modern expansion buses run much faster! Let's start with the oldest of the modern expansion slots, PCI.

PCI

Intel introduced the *Peripheral Component Interconnect (PCI)* bus architecture (see Figure 7-23) in the early 1990s, and the PC expansion bus was never again the same. Intel made many smart moves with PCI, not the least of which was releasing PCI to the public domain to make PCI very attractive to manufacturers. PCI provided a wider, faster, more flexible alternative than any previous expansion bus. The exceptional technology of the new bus, combined with the lack of a price tag, made manufacturers quickly drop older buses and adopt PCI.

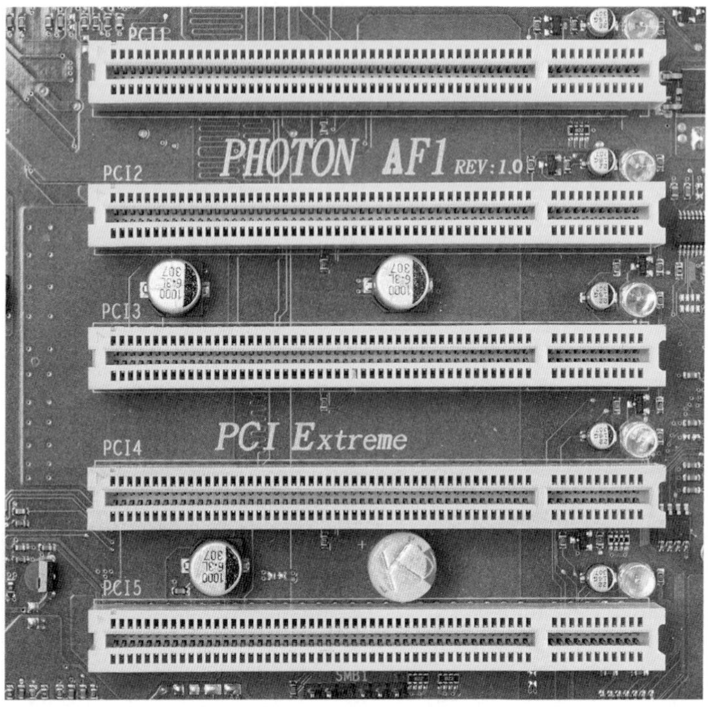

Figure 7-23 PCI expansion bus slots

PCI really shook up the PC world with its capabilities. The original PCI bus was 32 bits wide and ran at 33 MHz, which was superb, but these features were expected and not earth-shattering. The coolness of PCI came from its capability to coexist with other expansion buses. When PCI first came out, you could buy a motherboard with both PCI and older slots. This was important because users could keep their old expansion cards and slowly migrate to PCI. Equally impressive was that PCI devices were (and still are) self-configuring, a feature that led to the industry standard that became known as plug and play (PnP). Finally, PCI had a powerful burst-mode feature that enabled very efficient data transfers.

NOTE Before PCI, it was rare to see more than one type of expansion slot on a motherboard. Today this not only is common—it's expected!

The original PCI expansion bus has soldiered on in PCs for more than two decades. Replacement forms appeared over the years to dethrone the king. Although these newer PCI expansion buses were faster than the original PCI, they were only improvements to PCI, not entirely new expansion buses. The original PCI has faded to a single slot on most motherboards, but not because of the PCI improvements. Let's look at those and then turn to the serial alternatives to PCI.

AGP

When video started going graphical with the introduction of Windows, the current buses were too slow and graphics looked terrible. PCI certainly improved graphics when it came out, but Intel was thinking ahead. Shortly after Intel invented PCI, they presented a specialized, video-only version of PCI called the *Accelerated Graphics Port (AGP)*. An AGP slot was a PCI slot, but one with a direct connection to the Northbridge. AGP slots were only for video cards—you couldn't snap a sound card or modem into one. Figure 7-24 shows a typical AGP slot.

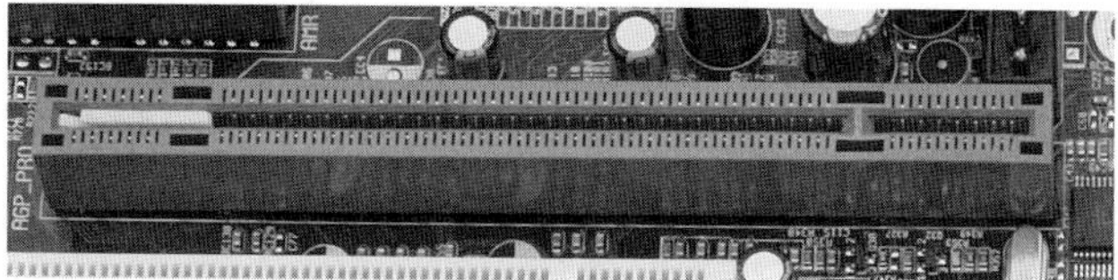

Figure 7-24
AGP slot

PCI-X

PCI Extended (PCI-X) offered a high-speed alternative to PCI (and AGP). The 64-bit AGP slots supported 32-bit PCI cards for backward compatibility and easy upgrade, and supported native 64-bit PCI-X cards (see Figure 7-25). The PCI-X 2.0 standard featured four speed grades (measured in MHz): PCI-X 66, PCI-X 133, PCI-X 266, and PCI-X 533.

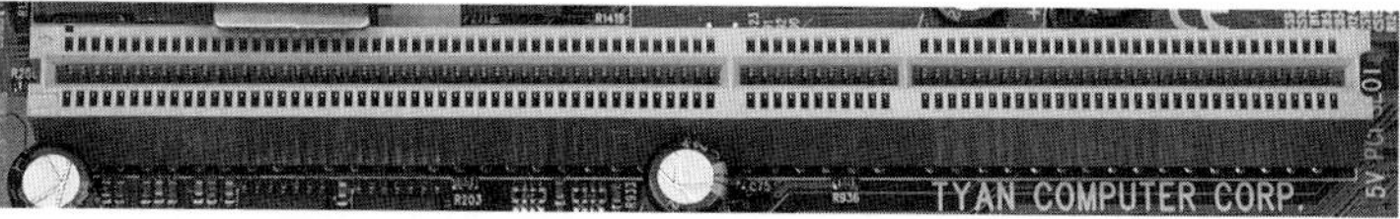

Figure 7-25
PCI-X slot

A lot of businesses rolled out PCI-X systems in advanced workstations, such as video production machines. PCI-X had a relatively short run as the dominant computer platform, replaced today by PCI Express (discussed after Mini-PCI).

Mini-PCI

PCI made it into laptops in the specialty *Mini-PCI* format (see Figure 7-26). Mini-PCI was designed to use low power and to lie flat—both good features for a laptop expansion slot. Mini-PCI returns in Chapter 24, "Portable Computing."

PCI Express

PCI Express (PCIe) is the latest, fastest, and most popular expansion bus in use today. As its name implies, PCI Express is still PCI, but it uses a point-to-point *serial* connection instead of PCI's shared *parallel* communication. Consider a single 32-bit chunk of data moving from a device to the CPU. In PCI parallel communication, 32 wires each carry

one bit of that chunk of data. In serial communication, only one wire carries those 32 bits. You'd think that 32 wires are better than one, correct?

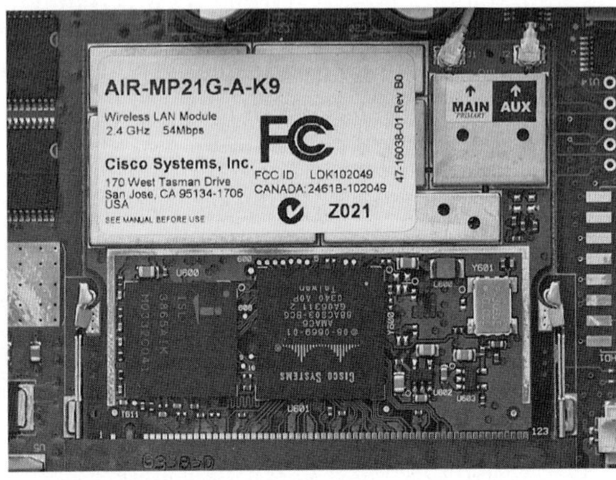

Figure 7-26 Tiny card in Mini-PCI slot. See the contacts at the bottom of the picture?

First of all, PCIe doesn't share the bus. A PCIe device has its own direct connection (a point-to-point connection) to the Northbridge, so it does not wait for other devices. Plus, when you start going really fast (think gigabits per second), getting all 32 bits of data to go from one device to another at the same time is difficult, because some bits get there slightly faster than others. That means you need some serious, high-speed checking of the data when it arrives to verify that it's all there and in good shape. Serial data doesn't have this problem, as all of the bits arrive one after the other in a single stream. When data is really going fast, a single point-to-point serial connection is faster than a shared 32-wire parallel connection.

And boy howdy, is PCIe ever fast! A PCIe connection uses one wire for sending and one for receiving. Each of these pairs of wires between a PCIe controller and a device is called a *lane*. Each direction of a lane runs at 2.5 gigatransfers per second (GTps) with PCIe 1.*x*, 5 GTps with PCIe 2.*x*, and 8 GTps with PCIe 3.*x*. Better yet, each point-to-point connection can use 1, 2, 4, 8, 12, or 16 lanes to achieve a maximum theoretical bandwidth of 128 GTps. The *transfer rate* describes the number of operations happening per second. With serial communication, you almost get a one-to-one correlation between transfer rate and binary data rate. The effective data rate drops a little bit because of the *encoding scheme*—the way the data is broken down and reassembled—but full-duplex data throughput can go up to a whopping 16 GBps on a ×16 connection.

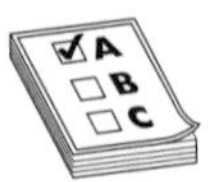

EXAM TIP You need to know the various motherboard expansion slots for the CompTIA 220-901 exam, especially PCIe. Be sure you are also familiar with PCI, PCI-X, Mini-PCI, and Mini-PCIe.

The most common PCIe slot is the 16-lane (×16) version most commonly used for video cards, as shown in Figure 7-27. The first versions of PCIe motherboards used a combination of a single PCIe ×16 slot and a number of standard PCI slots. (Remember, PCI is designed to work with other expansion slots, even other types of PCI.) There is also a popular small form factor version of PCI Express for mobile computers called PCI Express Mini Card, or Mini-PCIe, which Chapter 24, "Portable Computing," covers in detail.

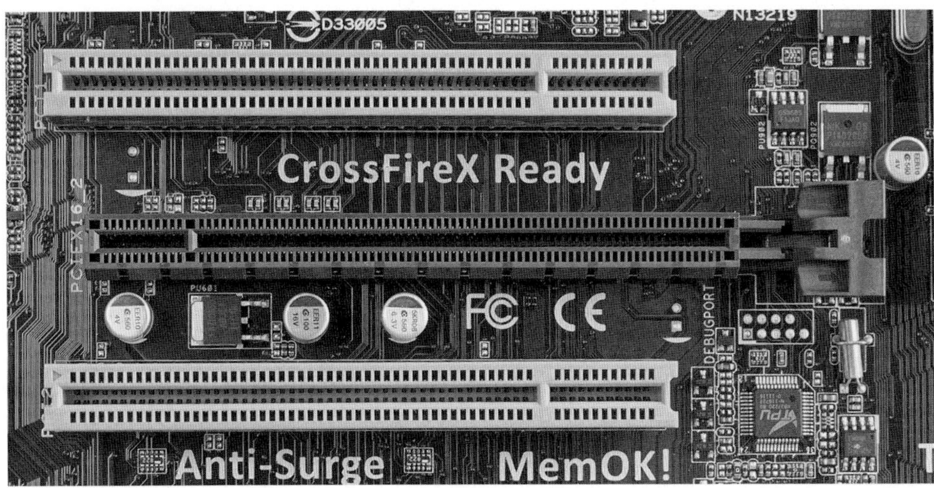

Figure 7-27 PCIe ×16 slot (center) with PCI slots (top and bottom)

The bandwidth generated by a ×16 slot is far more than anything other than a video card would need, so most PCIe motherboards also contain slots with fewer lanes. Currently ×1 is the most common general-purpose PCIe slot (see Figure 7-28).

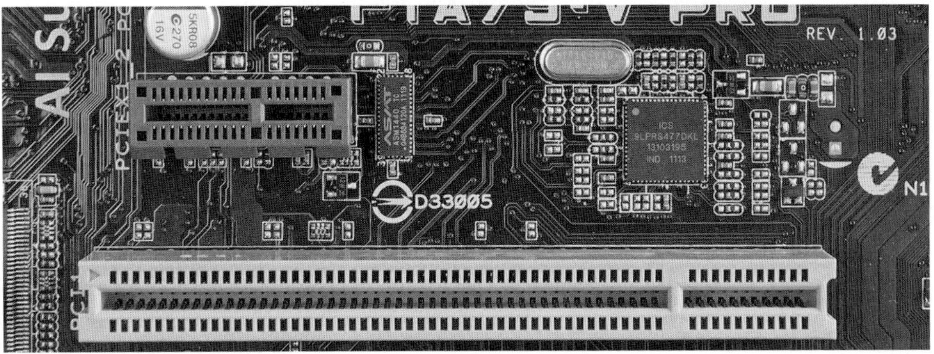

Figure 7-28 PCIe ×1 slot (top)

NOTE When you talk about the lanes, such as ×1 or ×16, use "by" rather than "ex" for the multiplication mark. So "by 1" and "by 16" is the correct pronunciation.

Try This!

Shopping Trip

So, what's the latest PCIe motherboard out there? Get online or go to your local computer store and research higher-end motherboards. What combinations of PCIe slots can you find on a single motherboard? Jot them down and compare your findings with your classmates' findings.

Installing Expansion Cards

Installing an expansion card successfully—another one of those bread-and-butter tasks for the PC tech—requires at least four steps. First, you need to know that the card works with your system and your operating system. Second, you have to insert the card in an expansion slot properly and without damaging that card or the motherboard. Third, you need to provide drivers for the operating system—*proper* drivers for the *specific* OS. Fourth, you should always verify that the card functions properly before you walk away from the PC.

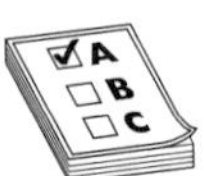

EXAM TIP The four steps involved in installing expansion cards apply to all types of expansion cards. The CompTIA A+ exams will ask you about cards ranging from common—sound, video, and networking—to other specific cards for USB, FireWire, Thunderbolt, and modem connections. They'll ask about wireless and cellular networking cards, storage cards, TV tuner cards, video capture cards, riser cards, and more, all of which we'll cover in their proper chapters in this book. You install any of them using the same four steps: knowledge, physical installation, device drivers, and verification.

Step 1: Knowledge

Learn about the device you plan to install—preferably before you purchase it! Does the device work with your system and operating system? Does it have drivers for your operating system? If you use a recent Windows operating system, the answer to these questions is almost always "yes." If you use an old, unsupported operating system such as Windows XP or a less common operating system such as Linux, these questions become important. A lot of older hardware simply won't work with new versions of Windows, especially the 64-bit versions. Check the device's documentation and check the device manufacturer's Web site to verify that you have the correct drivers. While you're checking, make sure you

have the latest version of the driver; most devices get driver updates more often than the weather changes in Texas.

For Windows systems, your best resource for this knowledge is the Microsoft Web site. The specific list of supported hardware has changed names many times. Currently Microsoft calls it the Windows Compatibility Center. Earlier operating systems called it the Hardware Compatibility List (HCL) or Windows Logo'd Product List, and you'll still hear lots of people refer to it by one of those names, especially the former.

This might list your product, but most people just look on the box of the device in question (see Figure 7-29)—all Windows-certified devices proudly display that they work with Windows.

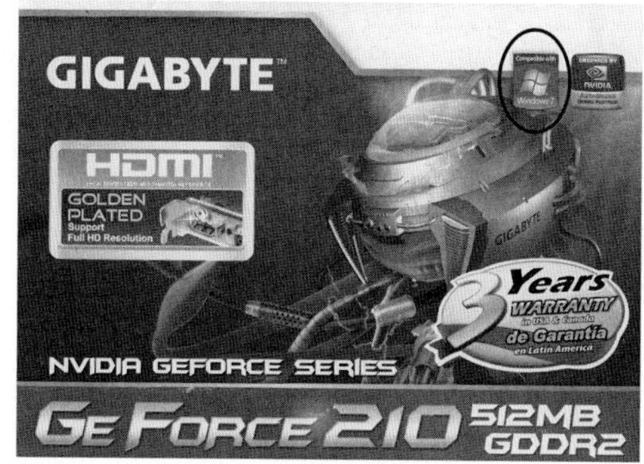

Figure 7-29 Works with Windows!

Step 2: Physical Installation

To install an expansion card successfully, you need to take steps to avoid damaging the card, the motherboard, or both. This means knowing how to handle a card and avoiding electrostatic discharge (ESD) or any other electrical issue. You also need to place the card firmly and completely into an available expansion slot.

Optimally, a card should always be in one of two places: in a computer or in an anti-static bag. When inserting or removing a card, be careful to hold the card only by its edges. Do not hold the card by the slot connectors or touch any components on the board (see Figure 7-30).

If possible, use an anti-static wrist strap properly attached to the PC, as noted in Chapter 2, "Operational Procedures." If you don't have a wrist strap, you can use the tech way of avoiding ESD by touching the power supply after you remove the expansion card from its anti-static bag. This puts you, the card, and the PC at the same electrical potential and thus minimizes the risk of ESD.

Modern systems have a trickle of voltage on the motherboard at all times when the computer is plugged into a power outlet. Chapter 8, "Power Supplies," covers power for the PC and how to deal with it in detail, but here's the short version: *Always unplug the PC before inserting an expansion card!* Failure to do so can destroy the card, the motherboard, or both. It's not worth the risk.

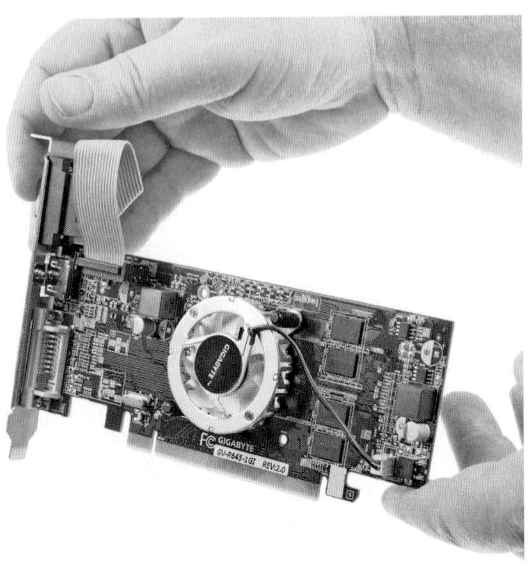

Figure 7-30 Where to handle a card

Never insert or remove a card at an extreme angle. This may damage the card. A slight angle is acceptable and even necessary when removing a card. Always secure the card to the case with a connection screw or other retaining mechanism. This keeps the card from slipping out and potentially shorting against other cards. Also, many cards use the screw connection to ground the card to the case (see Figure 7-31).

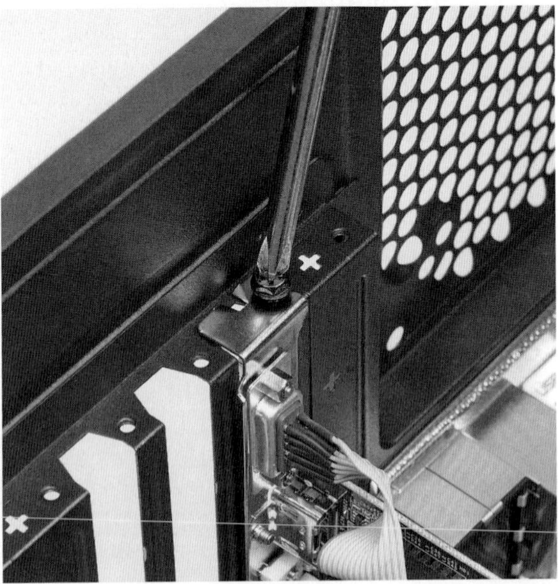

Figure 7-31 Always secure all cards properly.

Many technicians have been told to clean the slot connectors if a particular card is not working. This is almost never necessary after a card is installed and, if done improperly,

can cause damage. You should clean slot connectors only if you have a card that's been on the shelf for a while and the contacts are obviously dull.

Never use a pencil eraser for this purpose. Pencil erasers can leave behind bits of residue that wedge between the card and slot, preventing contact and causing the card to fail. Grab a can of contact cleaning solution and use it instead. Contact cleaning solution is designed exactly for this purpose, cleans contacts nicely, and doesn't leave any residue. You can find contact cleaning solution at any electronics store.

A fully inserted expansion card sits flush against the back of the PC case—assuming the motherboard is mounted properly, of course—with no gap between the mounting bracket on the card and the screw hole on the case. If the card is properly seated, no contacts are exposed above the slot. Figure 7-32 shows a properly seated (meaning fitted snugly in the slot) expansion card.

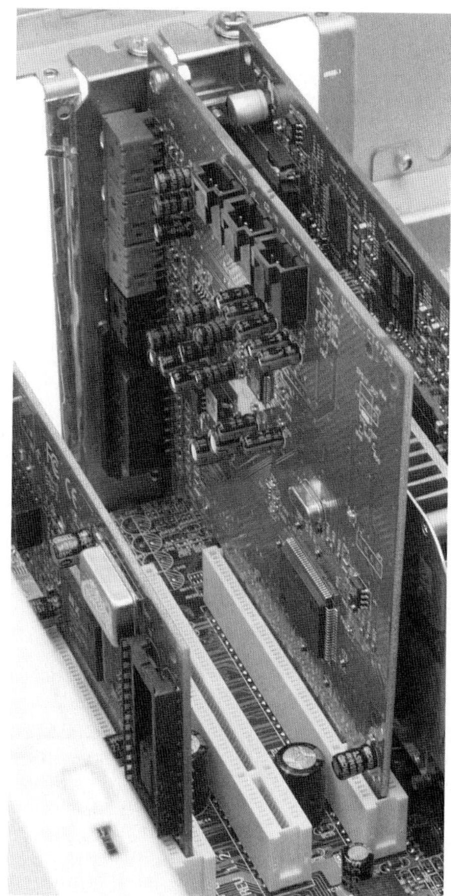

Figure 7-32 Properly seated expansion card; note the tight fit between case and mounting bracket and the evenness of the card in the slot.

Step 3: Device Drivers

You know from Chapter 6 that all devices, whether built into the motherboard or added along the way, require BIOS. For almost all expansion cards, that BIOS comes in the

form of *device drivers*—software support programs—loaded from an optical disc provided by the card manufacturer.

Installing device drivers is fairly straightforward. You should use the correct drivers—kind of obvious, but you'd be surprised how many techs mess this up—and, if you're upgrading, you might have to unload current drivers before loading new drivers. Finally, if you have a problem, you may need to uninstall the drivers you just loaded or roll back to earlier, more stable drivers.

Getting the Correct Drivers To be sure you have the best possible driver you can get for your device, you should always check the manufacturer's Web site. The drivers that come with a device may work well, but odds are good that you'll find a newer and better driver on the Web site. How do you know that the drivers on the Web site are newer? First, take the easy route: look on the disc. Often the version is printed right on the CD or DVD. If it's not printed there, you're going to have to load the disc in your optical drive and poke around. Many driver discs have an AutoRun screen that advertises the version. If nothing is on the pop-up screen, look for a Readme file (see Figure 7-33).

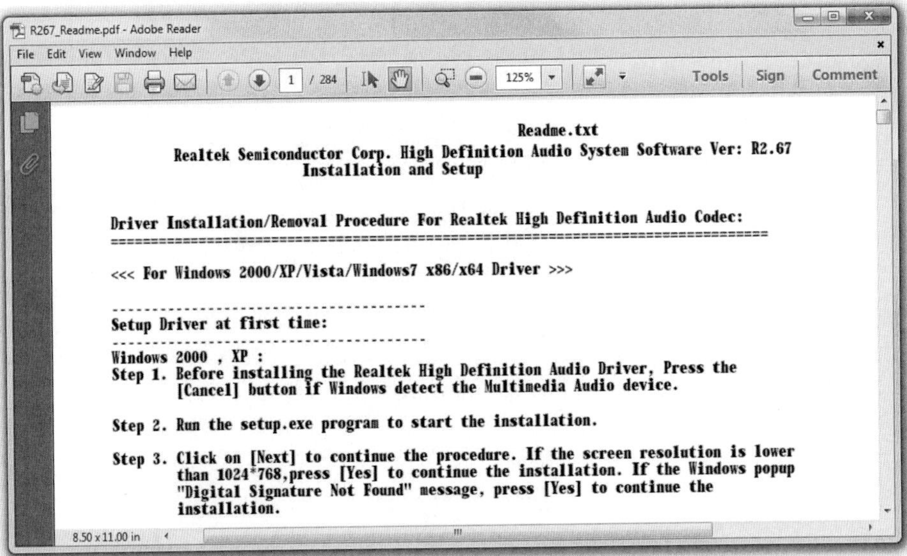

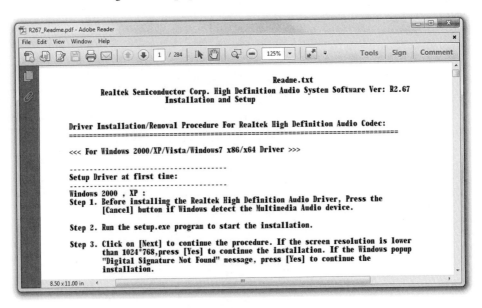

Figure 7-33 Part of a Readme file showing the driver version

Driver or Device? In almost all cases, you should install the device driver after you install the device. Without the device installed, the driver installation will not see the device and will give an error screen. The only exceptions to this rule are USB and FireWire devices—with these you should always install the driver first. (The other excellent external connection, Thunderbolt, works great however you install drivers when you're in Mac OS X. With Windows? It totally depends on the hardware manufacturer. Read the documentation.)

Removing the Old Drivers Some cards—and this is especially true with video cards—require you to remove old drivers of the same type before you install the new device. To do this, you must first locate the driver in Device Manager. Right-click the device driver you want to uninstall and select Uninstall (see Figure 7-34). Many devices, especially ones that come with a lot of applications, will have an uninstall option in the Programs and Features applet in the Control Panel (see Figure 7-35).

Figure 7-34 Uninstalling a device

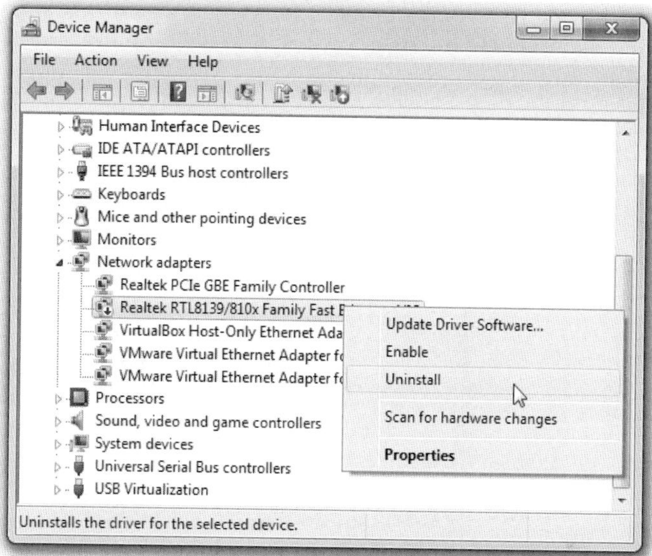

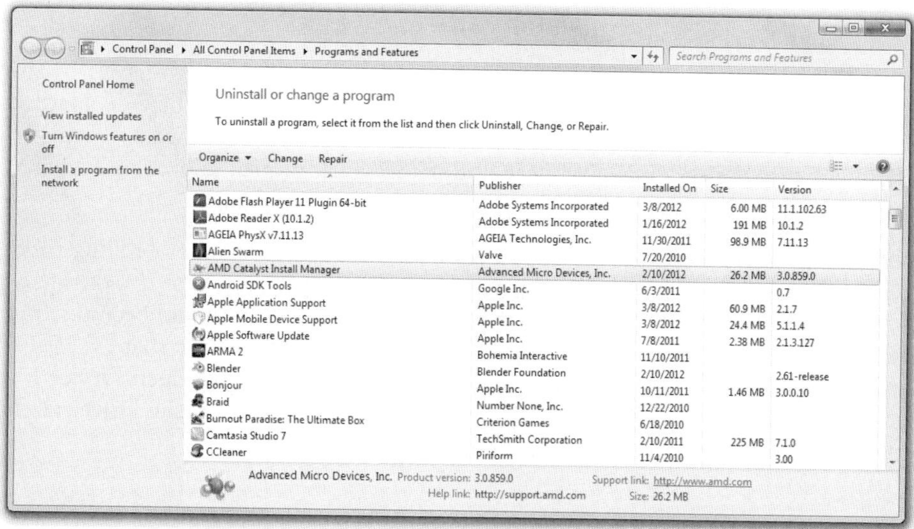

Figure 7-35 The Uninstall/Change option in Programs and Features

Unsigned Drivers Microsoft truly wants your computer to work, so they provide an excellent and rigorous testing program for hardware manufacturers called the *Windows Hardware Certification Program*. The drivers get a digital signature that says Microsoft tested them and found all was well.

The last of the 32-bit versions of Windows had support for *unsigned drivers*, essentially drivers that had not gone through the Windows Certification Program (as it was called then), so their software did not get a digital signature from Microsoft. Windows would bring up a scary-looking screen (see Figure 7-36) that warned against the driver. Although you might see unsigned drivers on the CompTIA A+ 901 exam, you won't see them on any modern Windows machine.

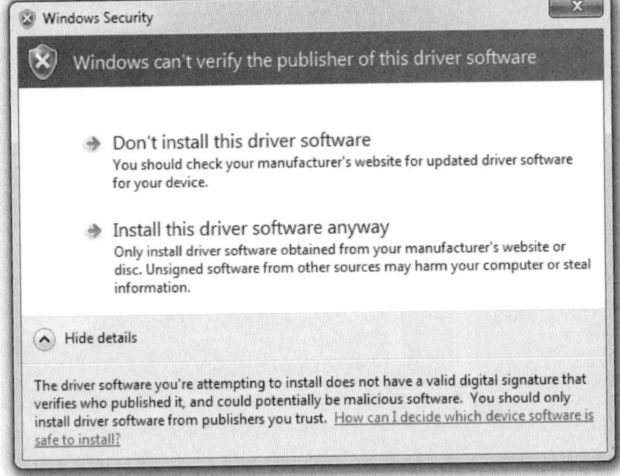

Figure 7-36 Unsigned driver warning

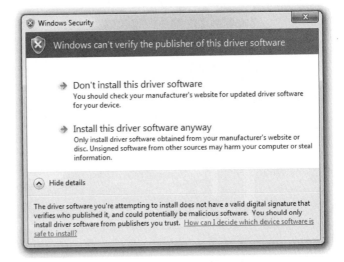

Installing the New Driver You have two ways to install a new driver: by using the installation disc directly or (in Windows Vista only) by using the Add Hardware Wizard in the Control Panel. Microsoft phased out the Add Hardware Wizard after Vista. Most installation discs give clear options so you can pick and choose what you want to install (see Figure 7-37).

Driver Rollback All versions of Windows offer the nifty feature of rolling back to previous drivers after an installation or driver upgrade. If you decide to live on the edge and install beta drivers for your video card, for example, and your system becomes frightfully unstable, you can back up to the drivers that worked before. (Not that I've ever had to use that feature, of course.) To access the rollback feature, simply open Device Manager and access the properties for the device you want to adjust. On the Driver tab (see Figure 7-38), you'll find the Roll Back Driver button.

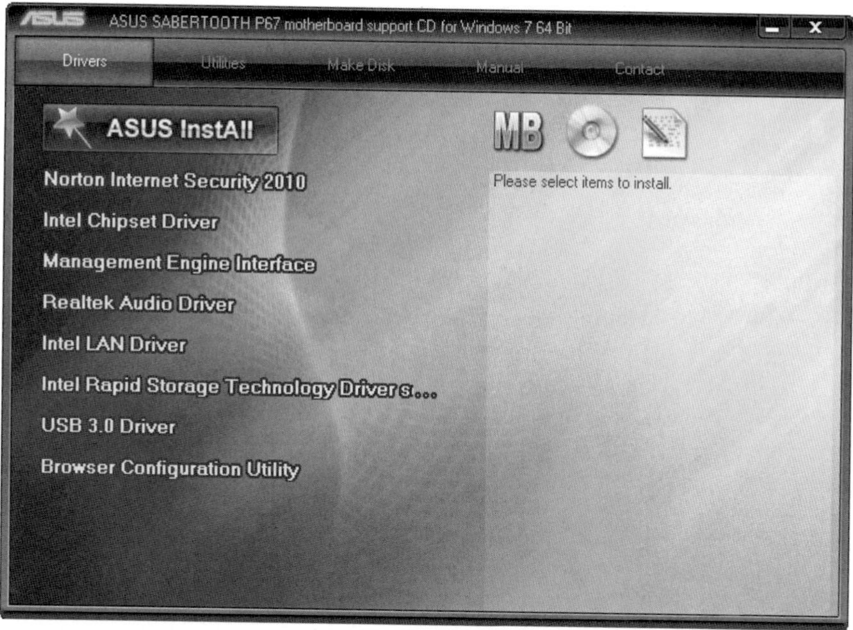

Figure 7-37 Installation menu

Figure 7-38 Driver rollback feature

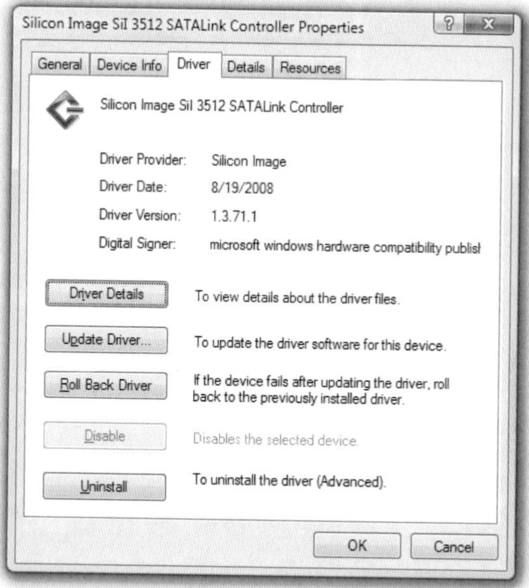

NOTE To install drivers in a Windows computer, you need to have the proper permission. I'm not talking about asking somebody if you're allowed to install the device. Permissions are granted in Windows to enable people to do certain things, such as add a printer to a local computer or install software, or to stop people from being able to do such tasks. Specifically, you need administrative permissions to install drivers.

Step 4: Verify

As a last step in the installation process, inspect the results of the installation and verify that the device works properly. Immediately after installing, you should open Device Manager and verify that Windows sees the device (see Figure 7-39). Assuming that Device Manager shows the device working properly, your next check is to put the device to work by making it do whatever it is supposed to do. If you installed a printer, print something; if you installed a scanner, scan something. If it works, you're finished!

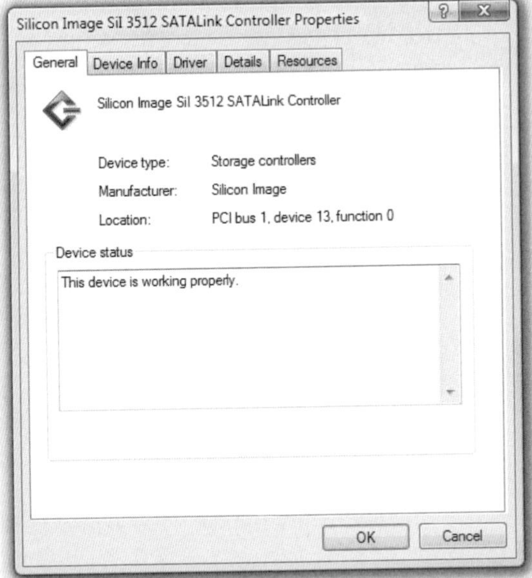

Figure 7-39 Device Manager shows the device working properly.

CAUTION Many PC enthusiasts try to squeeze every bit of performance out of their PC components, much as auto enthusiasts tinker with engine tunings to get a little extra horsepower out of their engines. Expansion card manufacturers love enthusiasts, who often act as free testers for their unpolished drivers, known as *beta drivers*. Beta drivers are fine for the most part, but they can sometimes cause amazing system instability—never a good thing! If you use beta drivers, make sure you know how to uninstall or roll back to previous drivers.

Troubleshooting Expansion Cards

A properly installed expansion card rarely makes trouble; it's the botched installations that produce headaches. Chances are high that you'll have to troubleshoot an expansion card installation at some point, usually from an installation you botched personally.

The first sign of an improperly installed card usually shows up the moment you first try to get that card to do whatever it's supposed to do and it doesn't do it. When this happens, your primary troubleshooting process is a reinstallation—after checking in with Device Manager.

Other chapters in this book cover specific hardware troubleshooting: sound cards in Chapter 11, for example, and video cards in Chapter 19, "Display Technologies." Use this section to help you decide what to look for and how to deal with the problem.

Device Manager provides the first diagnostic and troubleshooting tool in Windows. After you install a new device, Device Manager gives you many clues if something has gone wrong.

Occasionally, Device Manager may not even show the new device. If that happens, verify that you inserted the device properly and, if needed, that the device has power. Run the Add Hardware Wizard and see if Windows recognizes the device. You'll find the wizard as a Control Panel applet in Windows Vista. In Windows 7/8/8.1, you run the program by clicking Start and typing the name of the executable in the Search bar: **hdwwiz.exe**.

If Device Manager doesn't recognize the device at this point, you have one of two problems: either the device is physically damaged and you must replace it, or the device is an onboard device, not a card, and is turned off in CMOS.

Device Manager rarely completely fails to see a device. More commonly, device problems manifest themselves in Device Manager via error icons:

- A black "!" on a triangle indicates that a device is missing (see Figure 7-40), that Windows does not recognize a device, or that there's a device driver problem. A device may still work even while producing this error.
- A black downward-pointing arrow on a white field indicates a disabled device. This usually points to a device that's been manually turned off, or a damaged device. A device producing this error will not work.

The "!" symbol is the most common error symbol and usually the easiest to fix. First, double-check the device's connections. Second, try reinstalling the driver with the Update Driver button. To get to the Update Driver button, right-click the desired device in Device Manager and select Properties. In the Properties dialog box, select the Driver tab. On the Driver tab, click the Update Driver button to open the updating wizard (see Figure 7-41).

If you get a downward-pointing arrow, first check that the device isn't disabled. Right-click on the device and select Enable. If that doesn't work (it often does not), try rolling back the driver (if you updated the driver) or uninstalling (if it's a new install). Shut the system down and make triple-sure you have the card physically installed. Then redo the entire driver installation procedure, making sure you have the most current driver for that device. If none of these procedures works, return the card—it's almost certainly bad.

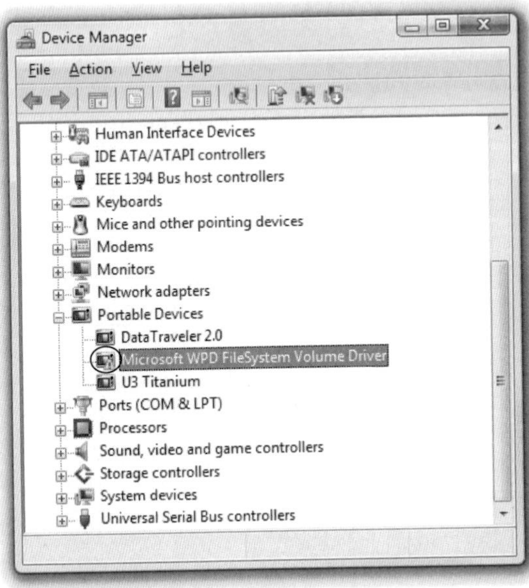

Figure 7-40 An "!" in Device Manager, indicating a problem with the selected device

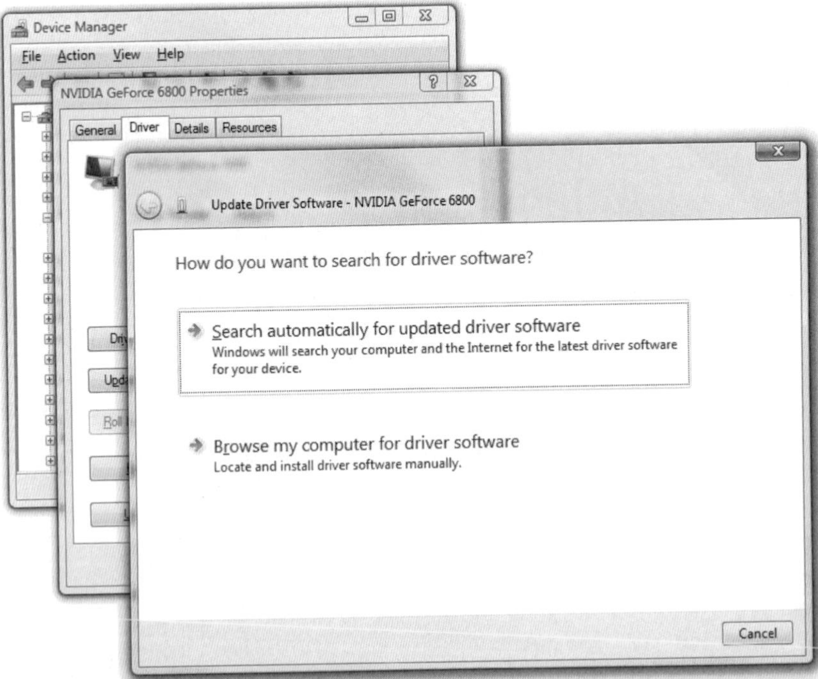

Figure 7-41 Updating the driver

Upgrading and Installing Motherboards

To most techs, the concept of adding or replacing a motherboard can be extremely intimidating. It really shouldn't be; motherboard installation is a common and necessary part of PC repair. It is inexpensive and easy, although it can sometimes be a little tedious and messy because of the large number of parts involved. This section covers the process of installation and replacement and shows you some of the tricks that make this necessary process easy to handle.

Choosing the Motherboard and Case

Choosing a motherboard and case can prove quite a challenge for any tech, whether newly minted or a seasoned veteran. You first have to figure out the type of motherboard you want, such as AMD- or Intel-based. Then you need to think about the form factor, which of course influences the type of case you'll need. Third, how rich in features is the motherboard and how tough is it to configure? You have to read the motherboard manual to find out. Finally, you need to select the case that matches your space needs, budget, and form factor. Now look at each step in a little more detail.

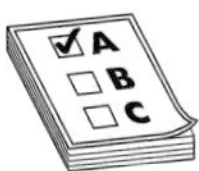

EXAM TIP Being able to select and install a motherboard appropriate for a client or customer is something every CompTIA A+ technician should know.

First, determine what motherboard you need. What CPU are you using? Will the motherboard work with that CPU? Because most of us buy the CPU and the motherboard at the same time, make the seller guarantee that the CPU will work with the motherboard. How much RAM do you intend to install? Are extra RAM sockets available for future upgrades?

NOTE Chapter 12 covers items needed for specialized PCs.

A number of excellent motherboard manufacturers currently exist. Some of the more popular brands are ASUS, BIOSTAR, GIGABYTE, Intel, and MSI. Your supplier may also have some lesser-known but perfectly acceptable brands of motherboards. As long as the supplier has an easy return policy, it's fine to try one of these.

Second, make sure you're getting a form factor that works with your case. Don't try to put a regular ATX motherboard into a microATX case!

Third, all motherboards come with a technical manual, better known as the *motherboard book* (see Figure 7-42). You must have this book! This book is your primary source for all of the critical information about the motherboard. If you set up CPU or RAM timings incorrectly in CMOS, for example, and you have a dead PC, where would you find the CMOS-clear jumper? Where do you plug in the speaker? Even if you let someone else install the motherboard, insist on the motherboard book; you will need it.

Try This!

Building a Recommendation

Family, friends, and potential clients often solicit the advice of a tech when they're thinking about upgrading their PC. This solicitation puts you on the spot to make not just any old recommendation, but one that works with the needs and budget of the potential upgrader. To handle this scenario successfully, you need to manage expectations and ask the right questions, so Try This!

What does the upgrader want to do that compels him or her to upgrade? Write it down! Some of the common motivations for upgrading are to play that hot new game or to take advantage of new technology. What's the minimum system needed to run tomorrow's action games? What do you need to make multimedia sing? Does the motherboard need to have SuperSpeed USB 3.0 or SuperSpeed+ USB 3.1 built in to accommodate digital video or some other special purpose?

How much of the current system does the upgrader want to save? Upgrading a motherboard can very quickly turn into a complete system rebuild. What form factor is the old case? If it's a microATX case, that constrains the motherboards you can use with it to microATX. If the desired motherboard is a full-sized ATX board, you'll need to get a new case. Does the new motherboard possess the same type of CPU socket as the old motherboard? If not, that's a sure sign you'll need to upgrade the CPU as well.

What about RAM? If the old motherboard was using DDR2 SDRAM, and the new motherboard requires DDR3 or DDR4 SDRAM, you'll need to replace the RAM. If you need to upgrade the memory, it is best to know how many channels the new RAM interface supports, because performance is best when all channels are populated.

Once you've gathered information on motivation and assessed the current PC of the upgrader, it's time to get down to business: field trip time! This is a great excuse to get to the computer store and check out the latest motherboards and gadgets. Don't forget to jot down notes and prices while you're there. By the end of the field trip, you should have the information to give the upgrader an honest assessment of what an upgrade will entail, at least in monetary terms. Be honest—in other words, don't just tell upgraders what you think they want to hear—and you won't get in trouble.

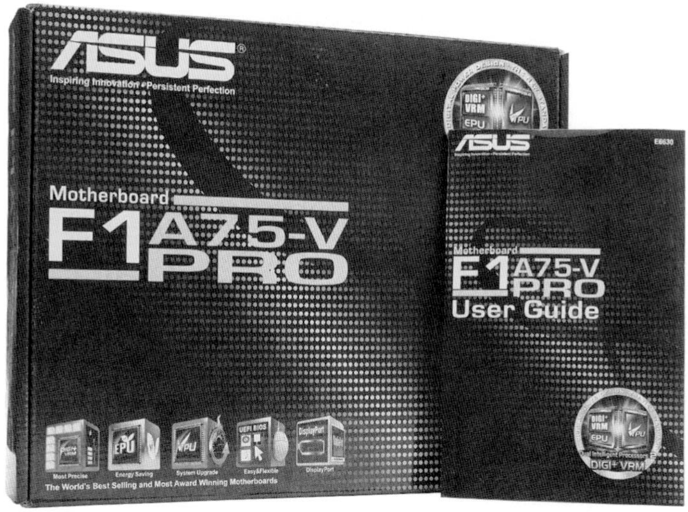

Figure 7-42 Motherboard box and book

NOTE If you have a motherboard with no manual, you can usually find a copy of the manual in Adobe Acrobat (.PDF) format online at the manufacturer's Web site. It's a good idea to grab and print a copy to keep with the motherboard. I often tape a copy (either hard copy, burned onto a disc, or copied to a USB drive) of the manual in the case where I installed the motherboard. Just don't cover any vents!

Fourth, pick your case carefully. Cases come in many sizes: slimline, desktop, mini-tower, mid-tower, tower, and cube. Plus you can get specialized cases, such as tiny cases for entertainment systems or ones that fit the same format as a stereo receiver or DVD player. The latter case is called a home theater PC (HTPC). See Figure 7-43.

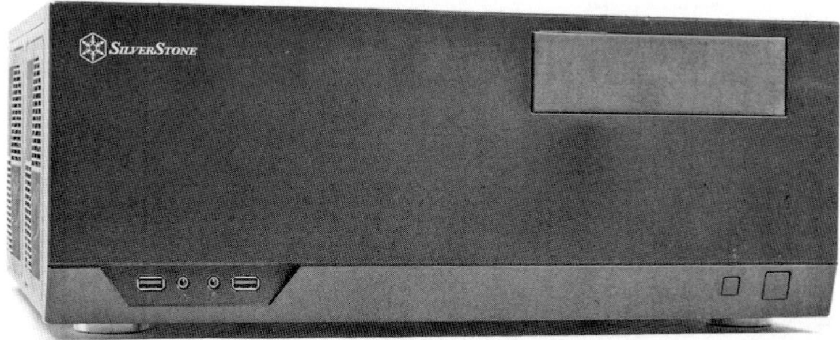

Figure 7-43 An HTPC

Slimline and desktop models generally sit on the desk, beneath the monitor. The various tower cases usually occupy a bit of floor space next to the desk. The mini-tower and mid-tower cases are the most popular choices. Make sure you get a case that fits your motherboard—most microATX cases are too small for a regular ATX motherboard.

Cube cases generally require a specific motherboard, so be prepared to buy both pieces together. A quick test-fit before you buy saves a lot of return trips to the supplier.

Better cases offer tool-free component installation, so you don't have to screw down cards or drives. They just snap into place. You'll still need a trusty screwdriver to secure the motherboard, though. No installation is completely tool-free yet.

Power supplies sometimes come with the case. Watch out for "really good deal" cases because that invariably points to a cheap or missing power supply. You also need to verify that the power supply has sufficient wattage. This issue is handled in Chapter 8.

Installing the Motherboard

If you're replacing a motherboard, first remove the old motherboard. Begin by removing all of the cards. Also remove anything else that might impede removal or installation of the motherboard, such as a hard drive. Keep track of your screws—the best idea is to return the screws to their mounting holes temporarily, at least until you can reinstall the parts. Sometimes you even have to remove the power supply temporarily to enable access to the motherboard.

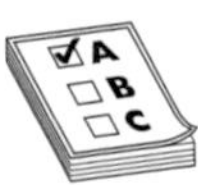

EXAM TIP The CompTIA A+ exams may test you on the basics of installing a motherboard, so you need to know this section.

Unscrew the motherboard. *It will not simply lift out.* The motherboard mounts to the case via small connectors called *standouts* that slide into keyed slots or screw into the bottom of the case (see Figure 7-44). Screws then go into the standouts to hold the motherboard in place. Be sure to place the standouts properly before installing the new motherboard.

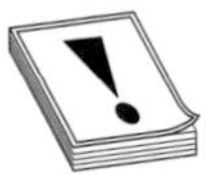

CAUTION Watch out for ESD here! Remember that it's very easy to damage or destroy a CPU and RAM with a little electrostatic discharge. It's also fairly easy to damage the motherboard with ESD. Always wear your anti-static wrist strap.

When you insert the new motherboard, do not assume that you will put the screws and standouts in the same place as they were in your old motherboard. When it comes to the placement of screws and standouts, only one rule applies: anywhere it fits. Do not be afraid to be a little tough here! Installing motherboards can be a wiggling, twisting, knuckle-scraping process.

CAUTION Pay attention to the location of the standouts if you're swapping a motherboard. If you leave a screw-type standout beneath a spot on the motherboard where you can't add a screw and then apply power to the motherboard, you run the risk of frying the motherboard.

Here are a few installation tips. A lot of techs install the CPU, CPU fan, and RAM into the motherboard before installing the motherboard into the case. This helps in sev-

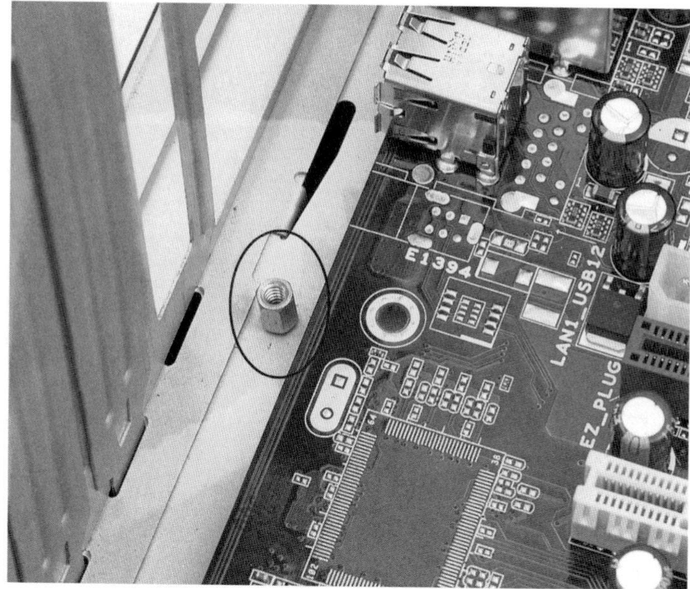

Figure 7-44 Standout in a case, ready for the motherboard

eral ways, especially with a new system. First, you want to make certain that the CPU and RAM work well with the motherboard and with each other—without that, you have no hope of setting up a stable system. Second, installing these components first prevents the phenomenon of *flexing* the motherboard. Some cases don't provide quite enough support for the motherboard, and pushing in RAM can make the board bend. Third, attaching a CPU fan can be a bear of a task, one that's considerably easier to do on a table top than within the confines of a case. A lot of third-party CPU fan and heat-sink assemblies mount on brackets on the bottom of the motherboard, requiring installation before placement in the case.

The next part of motherboard installation is connecting the LEDs, buttons, and front-mounted ports on the front of the box. This is sometimes easier to do before you install the motherboard fully in the case. You can trace the wire leads from the front of the case to the appropriate standouts on the motherboard. These usually include the following:

- Soft power button
- Reset button
- Speaker
- Hard drive activity light
- Power light
- USB
- FireWire
- Sound
- Thunderbolt

These wires have specific pin connections to the motherboard. Although you can refer to the motherboard book for their location, usually a quick inspection of the motherboard will suffice for an experienced tech (see Figure 7-45).

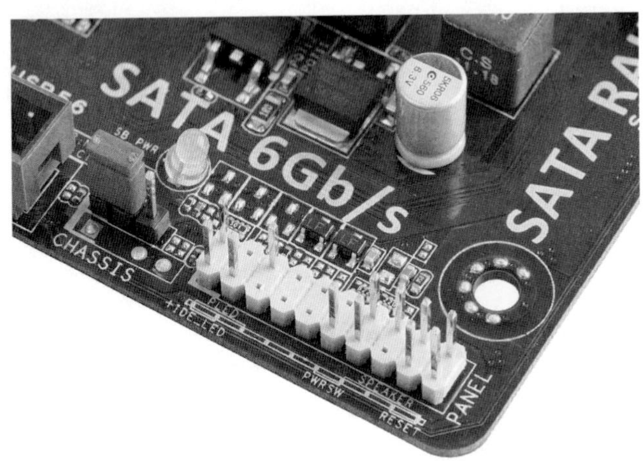

Figure 7-45 Motherboard wire connections labeled on the motherboard

You need to follow a few rules when installing these wires. First, the lights are LEDs, not light bulbs; they have a positive side and a negative side. If they don't work one way, turn the connector around and try the other. Second, when in doubt, guess. Incorrect installation only results in the device not working; it won't damage the computer. Refer to the motherboard book for the correct installation. The third and last rule is that, with the exception of the soft power switch on an ATX system, you do not need any of these wires for the computer to run.

No hard-and-fast rule exists for determining the function of each wire. Often the function of each wire is printed on the connector (see Figure 7-46). If not, track each wire to the LED or switch to determine its function.

Finally, install the motherboard into the case fully and secure it with the appropriate screws. Once you get the motherboard mounted in the case, with the CPU and RAM properly installed, it's time to insert the power connections and test it. A POST card can be helpful with the system test because you won't have to add the speaker, a video card, monitor, and keyboard to verify that the system is booting. If you have a POST card, start the system, and watch to see if the POST takes place—you should see a number of POST codes before the POST stops. If you don't have a POST card, install a keyboard, speaker, video card, and monitor. Boot the system and see if the BIOS information shows up on the screen. If it does, you're probably okay. If it doesn't, it's time to refer to the motherboard book to see where you made a mistake.

If you get no power at all, check to make sure you plugged in all the necessary power connectors. If you get power to fans but get nothing on the screen, you could have several problems. The CPU, RAM, or video card might not be connected to the motherboard properly. The only way to determine the problems is to test. Check the easy connections first (RAM and video) before removing and reseating the CPU. Also, see Chapter 8 for more on power issues.

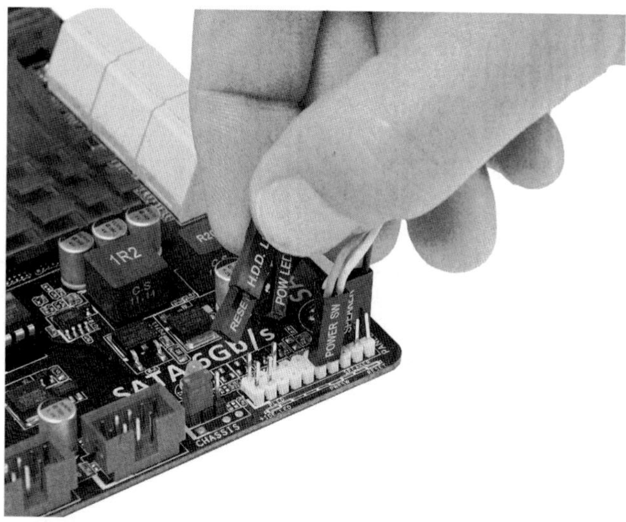

Figure 7-46 Sample of case wires

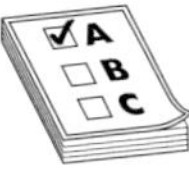

EXAM TIP Very old motherboards used to require techs to set jumpers to determine the bus speed for the motherboard. Setting these jumpers incorrectly resulted in failure-to-boot errors and overheated CPUs.

Modern motherboards autodetect CPU and RAM settings and adjust accordingly, so these errors only happen when you intentionally overclock or underclock a CPU through the CMOS setup utility.

Troubleshooting Motherboards

Motherboards fail. Not often, but motherboards and motherboard components can die from many causes: time, dust, cat hair, or simply slight manufacturing defects made worse by the millions of amps of current sluicing through the motherboard traces. Installing cards, electrostatic discharge, flexing the motherboard one time too many when swapping out RAM or drives—any of these factors can cause a motherboard to fail. The motherboard is a hard-working, often abused component of the PC. Unfortunately for the common tech, troubleshooting a motherboard problem can be difficult and time-consuming. Let's wrap up this chapter with a look at symptoms of a failing motherboard, techniques for troubleshooting, and the options you have when you discover a motherboard problem.

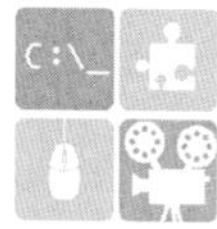

SIM There's a Chapter 7 Challenge! sim just to help you recognize motherboard components at http://totalsem.com/90x. It's a tricky sim that will really challenge you.

Symptoms

Motherboard failures commonly fall into three types: catastrophic, component, and ethereal. With a *catastrophic failure*, the PC just won't boot. Check the power and hard drive activity indicator lights on the front of the PC. Assuming they worked before, having them completely flat points to power supply failure or motherboard failure.

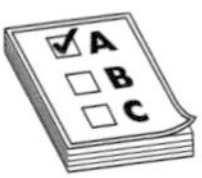

EXAM TIP For several years in the mid-2000s, suppliers of capacitors—devices that store and release energy, essentially smoothing the power on motherboards and other PCBs—released some seriously bad ones. Millions of these incorrectly formulated capacitors made it into computers and failed at high rates. The failure led to dead PCs, but the culprit was obviously the bulging capacitors, what you'll see on the 901 exam as *distended capacitors*.

This sort of problem happens to brand-new systems because of manufacturing defects—often called a *burn-in failure*—and to any system that gets a shock of ESD. Burn-in failure is uncommon and usually happens in the first 30 days of use. Swap out the motherboard for a replacement and you should be fine. If you accidentally zap your motherboard when inserting a card or moving wires around, be chagrined. Change your daring ways and wear an anti-static wrist strap!

Component failure happens rarely and appears as flaky connections between a device and motherboard, or as intermittent problems. A hard drive plugged into a faulty controller on the motherboard, for example, might show up in CMOS autodetect but be inaccessible in Windows. Another example is a serial controller that worked fine for months until a big storm took out the external modem hooked to it, and now it doesn't work, even with a replacement modem.

The most difficult of the three types of symptoms to diagnose are those I call *ethereal* symptoms. Stuff just doesn't work all of the time. The PC reboots itself. You get a Blue Screen of Death (BSoD) in the midst of heavy computing, such as right before you smack the villain and rescue the damsel. What can cause such symptoms? If you answered any of the following, you win the prize:

- Faulty component
- Buggy device driver
- Buggy application software
- Slight corruption of the operating system
- Power supply problems

Err...you get the picture.

What a nightmare scenario to troubleshoot! The Way of the Tech knows paths through such perils, though, so let's turn to troubleshooting techniques now.

Techniques

Troubleshooting a potential motherboard failure requires time, patience, and organization. Some problems will certainly be quicker to solve than others. If the hard drive doesn't work as expected, as in the previous example, check the settings on the drive. Try a different drive. Try the same drive with a different motherboard to verify that it's a good drive. Like every other troubleshooting technique, what you're trying to do with motherboard testing is to isolate the problem by eliminating potential causes.

Use a modern POST card with a good diagnostic screen. You'll find cards that plug into both PCI and PCIe slots, for example, and even USB-based POST cards that enable quick diagnostic tests on portable computers. See Figure 7-47.

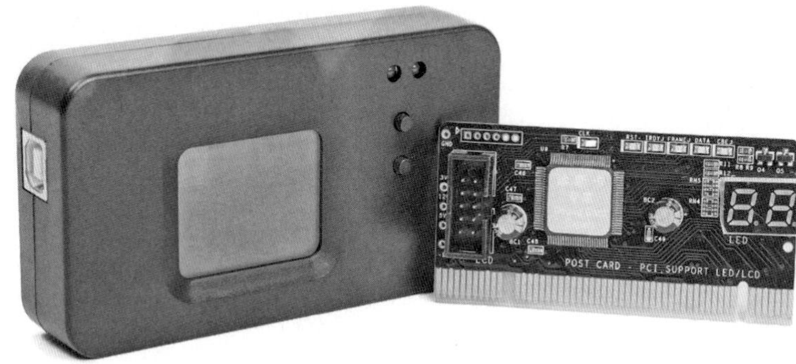

Figure 7-47 USB POST card (left) and PCI POST card (right)

This three-part system—check, replace, verify good component—works for both simple and more complicated motherboard problems. You can even apply the same technique to ethereal-type problems that might be anything, but you should add one more verb: *document*. Take notes on the individual components you test so you don't repeat efforts or waste time. Plus, taking notes can lead to the establishment of patterns. Being able to re-create a system crash by performing certain actions in a specific order can often lead you to the root of the problem. Document your actions. Motherboard testing is time-consuming enough without adding inefficiency.

Options

Once you determine that the motherboard has problems, you have several options for fixing the three types of failures. If you have a catastrophic failure, you must replace the motherboard. Even if it works somewhat, don't mess around. The motherboard should provide bedrock stability for the system. If it's even remotely buggy or problematic, get rid of it!

CAUTION If you've lost components because of ESD or a power surge, you would most likely be better off replacing the motherboard. The damage you can't see can definitely sneak up to bite you and create system instability.

If you have a component failure, you can often replace the component with an add-on card that will be as good as or better than the failed device. Adaptec, for example, makes fine cards that can replace the built-in SATA ports on the motherboard (see Figure 7-48).

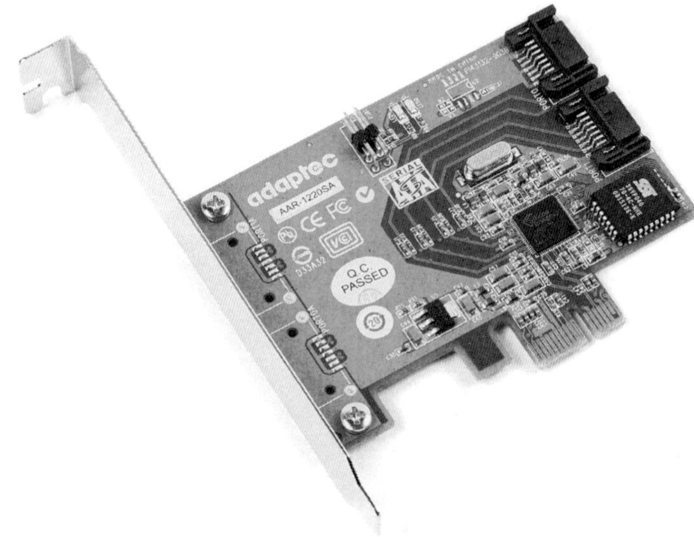

Figure 7-48 Adaptec PCIe SATA card

If your component failure is more a technology issue than physical damage, you can try upgrading the BIOS on the motherboard. As you'll recall from Chapter 6 every motherboard comes with a small set of code that enables the CPU to communicate properly with the devices built into the motherboard. You can quite readily upgrade this programming by *flashing the BIOS*: running a small command-line program to write a new BIOS in the flash ROM chip. Refer to Chapter 6 for the details on flashing.

NOTE Flashing the BIOS for a motherboard can fix a lot of system stability problems and provide better implementation of built-in technology. What it cannot do for your system is improve the hardware. If AMD comes out with a new, improved, lower-voltage A-Series CPU, for example, and your motherboard cannot scale down the voltage properly, you cannot use that CPU—even if it fits in your motherboard's Socket AM3. No amount of BIOS flashing can change the hardware built into your motherboard.

Finally, if you have an ethereal, ghost-in-the-machine type of problem that you have finally determined to be motherboard related, you have only a couple of options for fixing the problem. You can flash the BIOS in a desperate attempt to correct whatever it is, which sometimes does work and is less expensive than the other option, which is replacing the motherboard.

Chapter Review

Questions

1. Which of the following statements about the expansion bus is true?
   A. The expansion bus runs at the speed of the system clock.
   B. The expansion bus crystal sets the speed for the expansion bus.
   C. The CPU communicates with RAM via the expansion bus.
   D. The frontside bus is another name for the expansion bus.
2. What does a black down arrow next to a device in Device Manager indicate?
   A. A compatible driver has been installed that may not provide all of the functions for the device.
   B. The device is missing or Windows cannot recognize it.
   C. The system resources have been assigned manually.
   D. The device has been disabled.
3. Which variation of the PCI bus was specifically designed for laptops?
   A. PCI-X
   B. PCIe
   C. Mini-PCI
   D. AGP
4. Which of the following form factors dominates the PC industry?
   A. AT
   B. ATX
   C. ITX
   D. CTX
5. Amanda bought a new system that, right in the middle of an important presentation, gave her a Blue Screen of Death. Now her system won't boot at all, not even to CMOS. After extensive troubleshooting, she determined that the motherboard was at fault and replaced it. Now the system runs fine. What was the most likely cause of the problem?
   A. Burn-in failure
   B. Electrostatic discharge
   C. Component failure
   D. Power supply failure

6. Martin bought a new motherboard to replace his older ATX motherboard. As he left the shop, the tech on duty called after him, "Check your standouts!" What could the tech have meant?
   - **A.** Standouts are the connectors on the motherboard for the front panel buttons, such as the on/off switch and reset button.
   - **B.** Standouts are the sharp metal edges on some cases that aren't rolled.
   - **C.** Standouts are the metal connectors that attach the motherboard to the case.
   - **D.** Standouts are the dongles that enable a motherboard to support more than four USB ports.
7. Solon has a very buggy computer that keeps locking up at odd moments and rebooting spontaneously. He suspects the motherboard. How should he test it?
   - **A.** Check settings and verify good components.
   - **B.** Verify good components and document all testing.
   - **C.** Replace the motherboard first to see if the problems disappear.
   - **D.** Check settings, verify good components, replace components, and document all testing.
8. When Jane proudly displayed her new motherboard, the senior tech scratched his beard and asked, "What kind of ICH does it have?" What could he possibly be asking about?
   - **A.** The PCI slot
   - **B.** The PCIe slot
   - **C.** The Northbridge
   - **D.** The Southbridge
9. What companies dominate the chipset market? (Select two.)
   - **A.** AMD
   - **B.** Intel
   - **C.** NVIDIA
   - **D.** SiS
10. If Windows recognizes a device, where will it appear?
    - **A.** Device Manager
    - **B.** C:\Windows\System32\Devices
    - **C.** Desktop
    - **D.** Safely remove hardware applet

Answers

1. **B.** A separate expansion bus crystal enables the expansion bus to run at a different speed than the frontside bus.
2. **D.** The device has been disabled.
3. **C.** The Mini-PCI format conserves space and power, making it an ideal card type for use in laptops.
4. **B.** Almost all modern motherboards follow the ATX form factor.
5. **A.** Although all of the answers are plausible, the best answer here is that her system suffered burn-in failure.
6. **C.** Standouts are the metal connectors that attach the motherboard to the case.
7. **D.** Solon needs to check settings, verify good components, replace components, and document all testing.
8. **D.** Intel calls Southbridge chips the I/O Controller Hub (ICH) on many of their chipsets.
9. **A, B.** AMD and Intel produce the vast majority of the chipsets used in personal computers.
10. **A.** Windows displays recognized devices in Device Manager.

CHAPTER 8

Power Supplies

In this chapter, you will learn how to

- Explain the basics of electricity
- Describe the details about powering the PC
- Install and maintain power supplies
- Understand power supply troubleshooting and fire safety

Powering the PC requires a single box—the power supply—that takes electricity from the wall socket and transforms it into electricity to run the motherboard and other internal components. Figure 8-1 shows a typical power supply inside a case. All of the wires dangling out of it connect to the motherboard and peripherals.

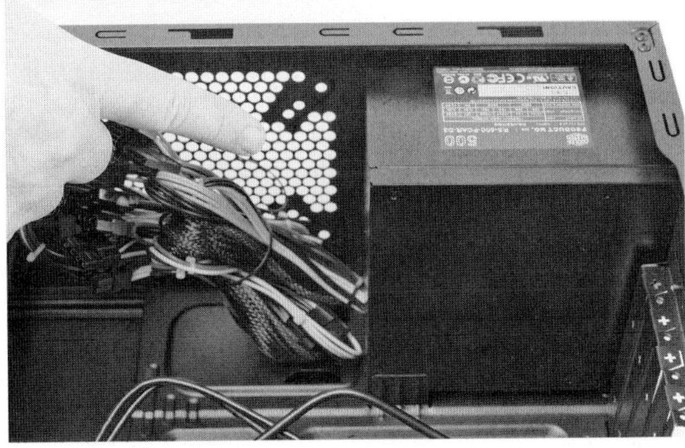

Figure 8-1 Typical power supply mounted inside the PC system unit

As simple as this appears on the surface, power supply issues are of critical importance for techs. Problems with power can create system instability, crashes, and data loss—all things most computer users would rather avoid! Good techs therefore know an awful lot about powering the PC, from understanding the basic principles of electricity to knowing the many variations of PC power supplies. Plus, you need to know how to recognize power problems and implement the proper solutions. Too many techs fall into the "just plug it in" camp and never learn how to deal with power, much to their clients' unhappiness.

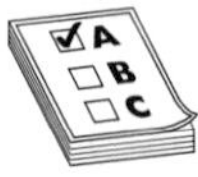

EXAM TIP Some questions on the CompTIA A+ 220-901 certification exam refer to a power supply as a *PSU*, for *power supply unit*. A power supply also falls into the category of *field replaceable unit (FRU)*, which refers to the typical parts a tech should carry, such as RAM and a hard drive.

Historical/Conceptual

Understanding Electricity

Electricity is a flow of negatively charged particles, called electrons, through matter. All matter enables the flow of electrons to some extent. This flow of electrons is very similar to the flow of water through pipes; so similar that the best way to learn about electricity is by comparing it to how water flows though pipes. So let's talk about water for a moment.

Water comes from the ground, through wells, aquifers, rivers, and so forth. In a typical city, water comes to you through pipes from the water supply company that took it from the ground. What do you pay for when you pay your water bill each month? You pay for the water you use, certainly, but built into the price of the water you use is the surety that when you turn the spigot, water will flow at a more or less constant rate. The water sits in the pipes under pressure from the water company, waiting for you to turn the spigot.

Electricity works essentially the same way as water. Electric companies gather or generate electricity and then push it to your house under pressure through wires. Just like water, the electricity sits in the wires, waiting for you to plug something into the wall socket, at which time it'll flow at a more or less constant rate. You plug a lamp into an electrical outlet and flip the switch, electricity flows, and you have light. You pay for reliability, electrical pressure, and electricity used.

The pressure of the electrons in the wire is called *voltage* and is measured in units called *volts (V)*. The amount of electrons moving past a certain point on a wire is called the *current* or *amperage*, which is measured in units called *amperes (amps* or *A)*. The amount of amps and volts needed so that a particular device will function is expressed as how much *wattage (watts* or *W)* that device needs. The correlation between the three is very simple math: V × A =. You'll learn more about wattage a little later in this chapter.

Wires of all sorts—whether copper, tin, gold, or platinum—have a slight *resistance* to the flow of electrons, just as water pipes have a slight amount of friction that resists the flow of water. Resistance to the flow of electrons is measured in *ohms (Ω)*.

- Pressure = voltage (V)
- Volume flowing = amperes (A)
- Work = wattage (W)
- Resistance = ohms (Ω)

A particular thickness of wire only handles so much current at a time. If you push too much through, the wire will overheat and break, much as an overloaded water pipe will

burst. To make sure you use the right wire for the right job, all electrical wires have an amperage rating, such as 20 amps. If you try to push 30 amps through a 20-amp wire, the wire will break and electrons will seek a way to return into the ground. Not a good thing, especially if the path back to ground is through you!

Circuit breakers and ground wires provide the basic protection from accidental overflow. A circuit breaker is a heat-sensitive or electromagnetically operated electrical switch rated for a specified amperage. If you push too much amperage through the circuit breaker, the wiring inside detects the increase in heat or current and automatically opens, stopping the flow of electricity before the wiring overheats and breaks. You reset the circuit breaker to reestablish the circuit, and electricity flows once more through the wires. A ground wire provides a path of least resistance for electrons to flow back to ground in case of an accidental overflow.

Many years ago, your home and building electrical supply used fuses instead of circuit breakers. Fuses are small devices with a tiny filament designed to break if subjected to too much current. Unfortunately, fuses had to be replaced every time they blew, making circuit breakers much more preferable. Even though you no longer see fuses in a building's electrical circuits, many electrical devices—such as a PC's power supply—often still use fuses for their own internal protection. Once blown, these fuses are not replaceable by users or technicians without special training and tools.

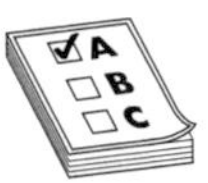

EXAM TIP An electrical outlet must have a ground wire to be suitable for PC use.

Electricity comes in two flavors: *direct current (DC)*, in which the electrons flow in one direction around a continuous circuit, and *alternating current (AC)*, in which the flow of electrons alternates direction back and forth in a circuit (see Figure 8-2). Most electronic devices use DC power, but all power companies supply AC power because AC travels long distances much more efficiently than DC.

Figure 8-2 Diagrams showing DC and AC flow of electrons

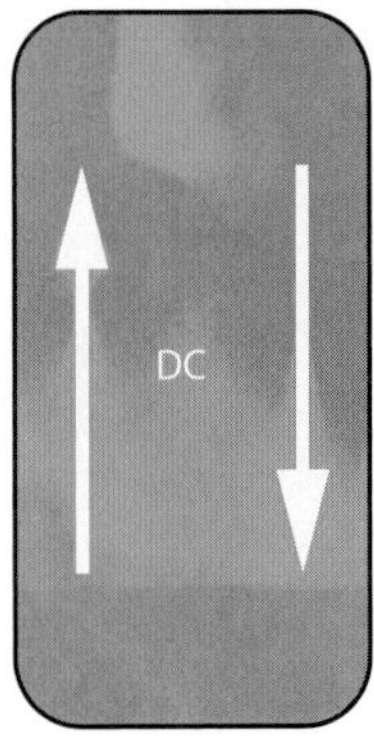

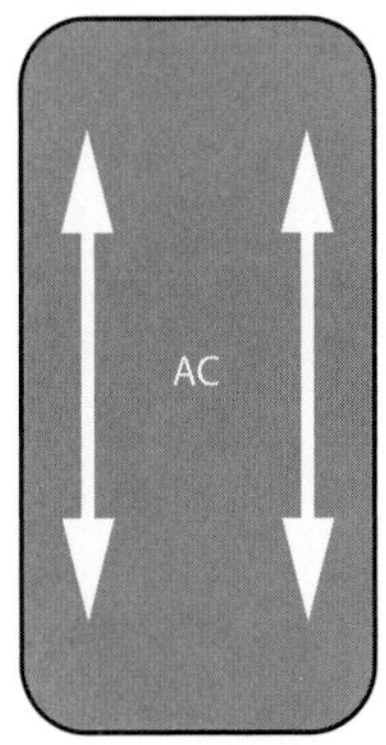

901

Powering the PC

Your PC uses DC voltage, so some conversion process must take place before the PC can use AC power from the power company. The power supply in a computer converts high-voltage AC power from the wall socket to low-voltage DC. The first step in powering the PC, therefore, is to get and maintain a good supply of AC power. Second, you need a power supply to convert AC to the proper voltage and amperage of DC power for the motherboard and peripherals. Finally, you need to control the byproduct of electricity use—namely, heat. Let's look at the specifics of powering the PC.

Supplying AC

Every PC power supply must have standard AC power from the power company, supplied steadily, rather than in fits and spurts, and protection against accidental blurps in the supply. The power supply connects to the power cord (and thus to an electrical outlet) via a standard *IEC-320* connector. In the United States, standard AC comes in somewhere between 110 and 120 V, often written as ~115 VAC (volts of alternating current). Most of the rest of the world uses 220–240 VAC, so power supplies are available with *dual-voltage options*, making them compatible with either standard. Power supplies with voltage-selection switches are referred to as fixed-input. Power supplies that you do not have to manually switch for different voltages are known as auto-switching. Figure 8-3 shows the back of a power supply. Note the three components, from top to bottom: the hard on/off switch, the 115/230 switch, and the IEC-320 connector.

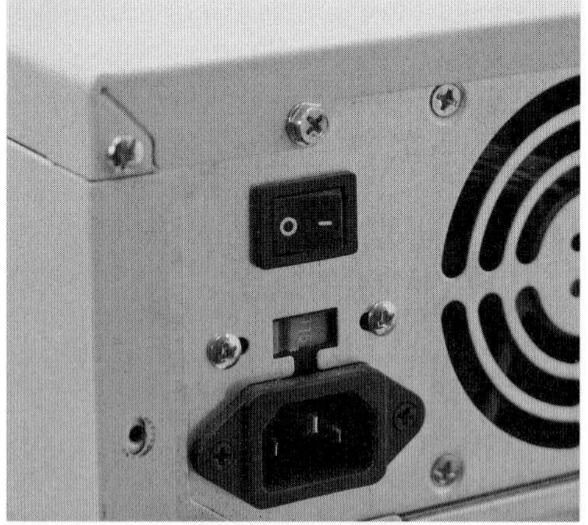

Figure 8-3 Back of fixed-input power supply, showing typical switches and power connection

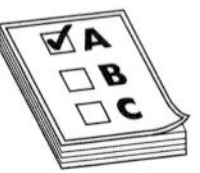

EXAM TIP The CompTIA A+ 901 exam expects you to be familiar with power supply *dual-voltage options*.

Try This!

Using a Multimeter to Test AC Outlets

Every competent technician knows how to use a multimeter, so if you haven't used one in the past, get hold of one and work through this scenario. Your boss tasks you with checking the existing electrical outlets in a new satellite location for the company. Caution: During this exercise, do *not* physically touch any of the metal parts of the probes or sockets!

First you need to set up the meter for measuring AC. Follow these steps:

1. Move the selector switch to the AC V (usually red). If multiple settings are available, put it into the first scale higher than 120 V (usually 200 V). *Auto-range* meters set their own range; they don't need any selection except AC V.
2. Place the black lead in the common (–) hole. If the black lead is permanently attached, ignore this step.
3. Place the red lead in the V-Ohm-A (+) hole. If the red lead is permanently attached, ignore this step.

Once you have the meter set up for AC, go through the process of testing the various wires on an AC socket. Just don't put your fingers on the metal parts of the leads when you stick them into the socket! Follow these steps:

1. Put either lead in hot, the other in neutral. You should read 110 to 120 V AC.
2. Put either lead in hot, the other in ground. You should read 110 to 120 V AC.
3. Put either lead in neutral, the other in ground. You should read 0 V AC.

If any of these readings is different from what is described here, it's time to call an electrician.

AC Adapters

Many computing devices use an AC adapter rather than an internal power supply. Even though it sits outside a device, an AC adapter converts AC current to DC, just like a power supply. Unlike internal power supplies, AC adapters are rarely interchangeable. Although manufacturers of different devices often use the same kind of plug on the end of the AC adapter cable, these adapters are not necessarily interchangeable. In other

words, just because you can plug an AC adapter from your friend's laptop into your laptop does not mean it's going to work.

You need to make sure that three things match before you plug an AC adapter into a device: voltage, amperage, and polarity. If either the voltage or amperage output is too low, the device won't run. If the polarity is reversed, it won't work, just like putting a battery in a flashlight backward. If either the voltage or amperage—especially the former—is too high, on the other hand, you can very quickly toast your device. Don't do it! Always check the voltage, amperage, and polarity of a replacement AC adapter before you plug it into a device.

Using Special Equipment to Test AC Voltage

A number of good AC-only testing devices are available. With these devices, you can test all voltages for an AC outlet by simply inserting them into the outlet. Be sure to test all of the outlets the computer system uses: power supply, external devices, and monitor. Although convenient, these devices aren't as accurate as a multimeter. My favorite tester is a seemingly simple tool available from a number of manufacturers (see Figure 8-7). This handy device provides three light-emitting diodes (LEDs) that describe everything that can go wrong with a plug.

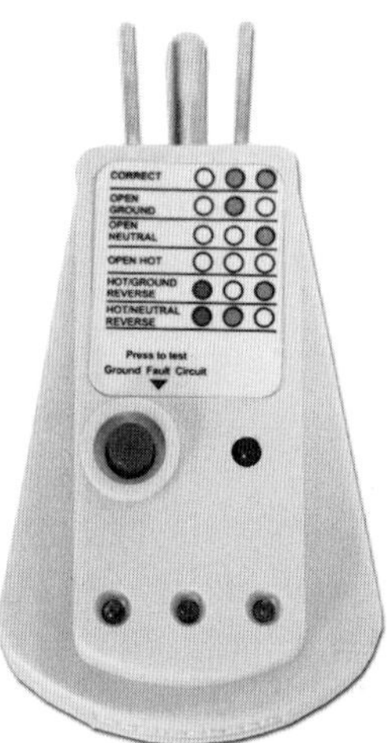

Figure 8-7 Circuit tester

902

Protecting the PC from Spikes and Sags in AC Power

If all power companies could supply electricity in smooth, continuous flows with no dips or spikes in pressure, the next two sections of this chapter would be irrelevant. Unfortunately, no matter how clean the AC supply appears to a multimeter, the truth is that voltage from the power company tends to drop well below (sag) and shoot far above (surge

or spike) the standard 115 V (in the United States). These sags and spikes usually don't affect lamps and refrigerators in such scenarios, but they can keep your PC from running or can even destroy a PC or peripheral device. Two essential devices handle spikes and sags in the supply of AC: surge suppressors and uninterruptible power supplies.

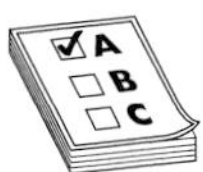

EXAM TIP Large sags in electricity are also known as *brownouts*. When the power cuts out completely, it's called a *blackout*.

Surge Suppressors Surges or spikes are far more dangerous than sags. Even a strong sag only shuts off or reboots your PC; any surge can harm your computer, and a strong surge destroys components. Given the seriousness of surges, every PC should use a *surge suppressor* device that absorbs the extra voltage from a surge to protect the PC. The power supply does a good job of surge suppression and can handle many of the smaller surges that take place fairly often. But the power supply takes a lot of damage from this and will eventually fail. To protect your power supply, a dedicated surge suppressor works between the power supply and the outlet to protect the system from power surges (see Figure 8-8).

Figure 8-8
Surge suppressor

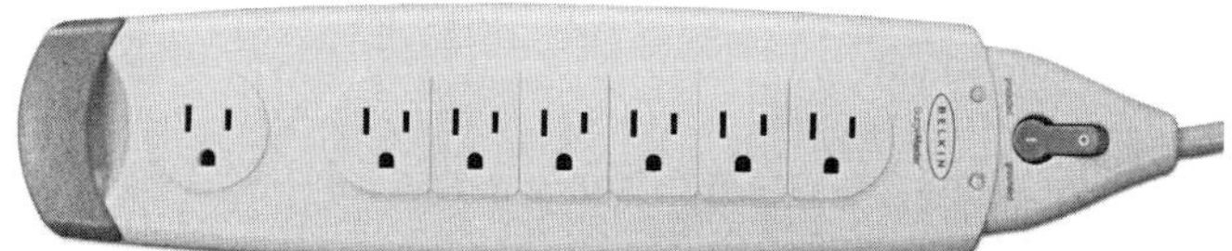

Most people tend to spend a lot of money on their PC and for some reason suddenly get cheap on the surge suppressor. Don't do that! Make sure your surge suppressor has the Underwriters Laboratories UL 1449 for 330-V rating to ensure substantial protection for your system. Underwriters Laboratories (www.ul.com) is a U.S.-based, not-for-profit, widely recognized industry testing laboratory whose testing standards are very important to the consumer electronics industry. Additionally, check the joules rating before buying a new surge suppressor. A *joule* is a unit of electrical energy. How much energy a surge suppressor can handle before it fails is described in joules. Most authorities agree that your surge suppressor should rate at a minimum of 2000 joules—and the more joules, the better the protection. My surge suppressor rates at 3500 joules.

While you're protecting your system, don't forget that surges also come from telephone and cable connections. If you use a modem, DSL, or cable modem, make sure to get a surge suppressor that includes support for these types of connections. Many manufacturers make surge suppressors with telephone line protection (see Figure 8-9).

No surge suppressor works forever. Make sure your surge suppressor has a test/reset button so you'll know when the device has—as we say in the business—turned into an extension cord. If your system takes a hit and you have a surge suppressor, call the company! Many companies provide cash guarantees against system failure due to surges, but only if you follow their guidelines.

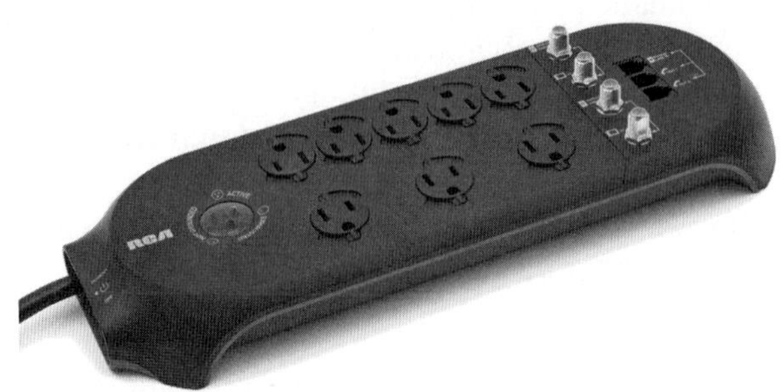

Figure 8-9 Surge suppressor with telephone line protection

CAUTION No surge suppressor in the world can handle the ultimate surge, the electrical discharge of a lightning strike. If your electrical system takes such a hit, you can kiss your PC and any other electronic devices goodbye if they were plugged in at the time. Always unplug electronics during electrical storms!

NOTE Surge suppression isn't just about joules. Surge suppressors are also rated in *clamping voltage,* in which an overvoltage condition is "clamped" to a more manageable voltage for a certain amount of time. Good consumer suppressors can clamp 600 volts down to 180 volts or less for at least 50 microseconds and can do so on either the hot line or neutral line.

If you want really great surge suppression, you need to move up to *power conditioning*. Your power lines take in all kinds of strange signals that have no business being in there, such as electromagnetic interference (EMI) and radio frequency interference (RFI). Most of the time, this line noise is so minimal it's not worth addressing, but occasionally events (such as lightning) generate enough line noise to cause weird things to happen to your PC (keyboard lockups, messed-up data). All better surge suppressors add power conditioning to filter out EMI and RFI.

UPS An *uninterruptible power supply (UPS)* protects your computer (and, more importantly, your data) in the event of a power sag or power outage. Figure 8-10 shows a typical UPS. A UPS essentially contains a big battery that provides AC power to your computer regardless of the power coming from the AC outlet.

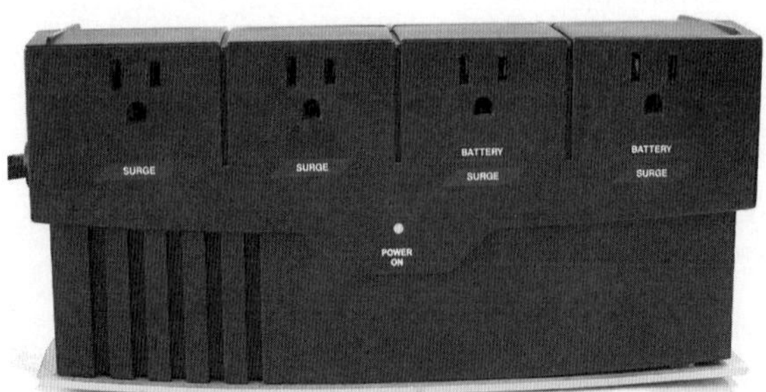

Figure 8-10 Uninterruptible power supply

All uninterruptible power supplies are measured in both watts (the true amount of power they supply in the event of a power outage) and in *volt-amps* (*VA*). Volt-amps is the amount of power the UPS could supply if the devices took power from the UPS in a perfect way. Your UPS provides perfect AC power, moving current smoothly back and forth 60 times a second (or 50 in other parts of the world). Power supplies, monitors, and other devices, however, may not take all of the power the UPS has to offer at every point as the AC power moves back and forth, resulting in inefficiencies. If your devices took all of the power the UPS offered at every point as the power moved back and forth, VA would equal watts.

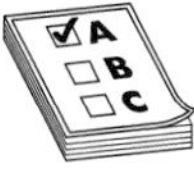

EXAM TIP You'll want to be familiar with the technology and use of surge suppressors and battery backup systems (UPS) for the CompTIA A+ 220-902 exam.

If the UPS makers knew ahead of time exactly what devices you planned to plug into their UPS, they could tell you the exact watts, but different devices have different efficiencies, forcing the UPS makers to go by what they can offer (VAs), not what your devices will take (watts). The watts value they give is a guess, and it's never as high as the VAs. The VA rating is always higher than the watt rating.

Because you have no way to calculate the exact efficiency of every device you'll plug into the UPS, go with the wattage rating. You add up the total wattage of every component in your PC and buy a UPS with a higher wattage. You'll spend a lot of time and mental energy figuring precisely how much wattage your computer, monitor, drives, and so on require to get the proper UPS for your system. But you're still not finished! Remember that the UPS is a battery with a limited amount of power, so you then need to figure out how long you want the UPS to run when you lose power.

NOTE There are two main types of UPS: *online*, where devices are constantly powered through the UPS's battery, and *standby*, where devices connected to the UPS receive battery power only when the AC sags below ~80–90 V. Another type of UPS is called *line-interactive*, which is similar to a standby UPS but has special circuitry to handle moderate AC sags and surges without the need to switch to battery power.

The quicker and far better method to use for determining the UPS you need is to go to any of the major surge suppressor/UPS makers' Web sites and use their handy power calculators. My personal favorite is on the APC by Schneider Electric (formerly known as American Power Conversion Corporation) Web site: www.apc.com (click on the Product Selectors menu item). APC makes great surge suppressors and UPSs, and the company's online calculator will show you the true wattage you need—and teach you about whatever new thing is happening in power at the same time.

Try This!

Shopping for a UPS

When it comes to getting a UPS for yourself or a client, nothing quite cuts through the hype and marketing terms like a trip to the local computer store to see for yourself. You need excuses to go to the computer store, so here's a valid one for you.

1. Go to your local computer store—or visit an online computer site if no stores are nearby—and find out what's available.
2. Answer this question: How can you tell the difference between an online and a standby UPS?

Every UPS also has surge suppression and power conditioning, so look for the joule and UL 1449 ratings. Also look for replacement battery costs—some UPS replacement batteries are very expensive. Last, look for a UPS with a USB or Ethernet (RJ-45) connection. These handy UPSs come with monitoring and maintenance software (see Figure 8-11) that tells you the status of your system and the amount of battery power available, logs power events, and provides other handy options.

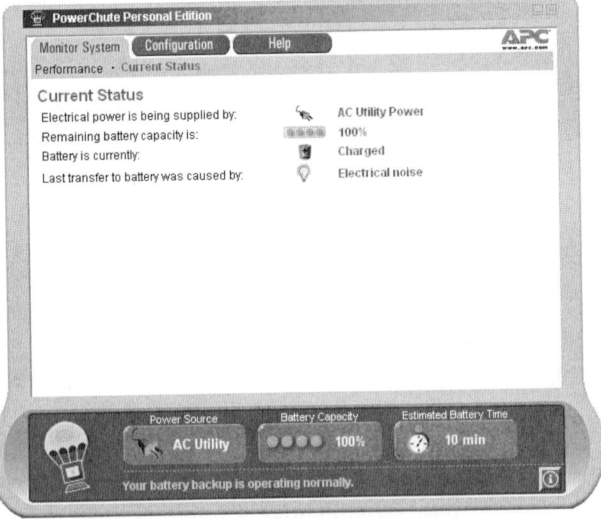

Figure 8-11 APC PowerChute software

Table 8-1 gives you a quick look at the low end and the very high end of UPS products (as of mid-2015).

Brand	Model	Outlets Protected	Backup Time	Price	Type
APC	BE350G	3 @ 120 V	3 min @ 200 W, 10 min @ 100 W	$43.99	Standby
APC	Pro 1000	4 @ 120 V	4 min @ 600 W, 64 min @ 100 W	$134.99	Standby
CyberPower	CPS1500AVR	6 @ 120 V	6 min @ 950 W, 18 min @ 475 W	$279.99	Line-interactive

Table 8-1 Typical UPS Devices

901

Supplying DC

After you've ensured the supply of good AC electricity for the PC, the power supply unit (PSU) takes over, converting high-voltage AC into several DC voltages (notably, 5.0, 12.0, and 3.3 V) usable by the delicate interior components. Power supplies come in a large number of shapes and sizes, but the most common size by far is the standard 150 mm × 140 mm × 86 mm desktop PSU shown in Figure 8-12.

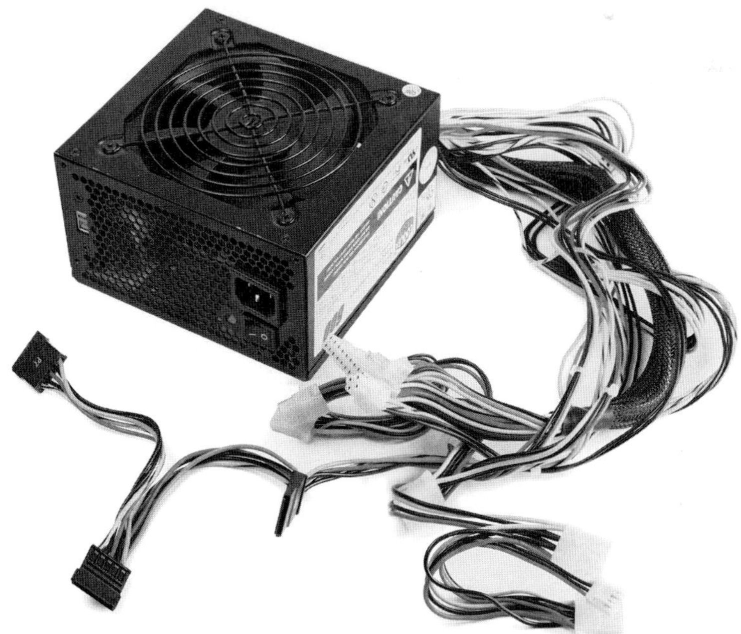

Figure 8-12 Desktop PSU

The PC uses the 12.0-V current to power motors on devices such as hard drives and optical drives, and it uses the 5.0-V and 3.3-V current for support of onboard electronics. Manufacturers may use these voltages any way they wish, however, and may deviate from these assumptions. Power supplies also come with standard connectors for the motherboard and interior devices.

Power to the Motherboard

Modern motherboards use a 20- or 24-pin *P1 power connector*. Some motherboards may require special 4-, 6-, or 8-pin connectors to supply extra power (see Figure 8-13). We'll talk about each of these connectors in the form factor standards discussion later in this chapter.

Figure 8-13 Motherboard power connectors

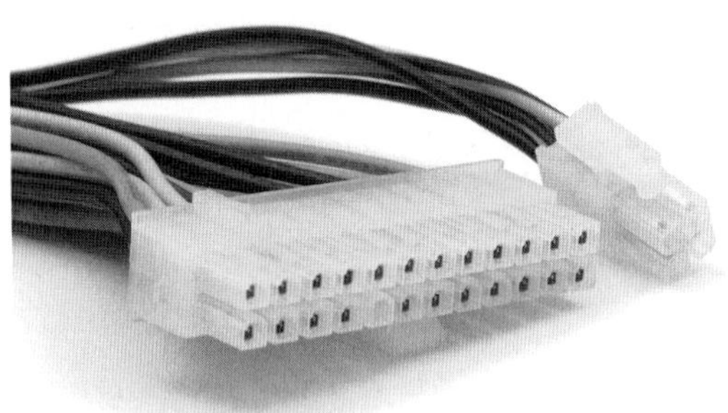

Power to Peripherals: Molex, Mini, and SATA

Many devices inside the PC require power. These include hard drives, floppy drives (back in the day), optical drives, and fans. The typical PC power supply has up to three types of connectors that plug into peripherals: Molex, mini, and SATA.

Molex Connectors The *Molex connector* supplies 5-V and 12-V current for fans and older drives (see Figure 8-14). The Molex connector has notches, called *chamfers*, that guide its installation. The tricky part is that Molex connectors require a firm push to plug in properly, and a strong person can defeat the chamfers, plugging a Molex in upside down. Not a good thing. *Always* check for proper orientation before you push it in!

Figure 8-14 Molex connector

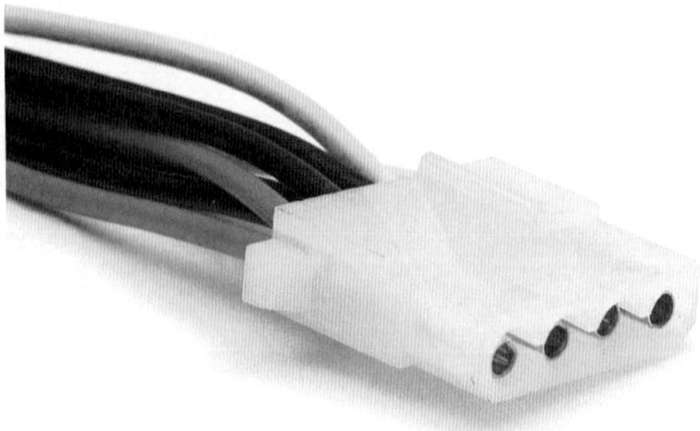

Mini Connectors All power supplies have a second type of connector, called a *mini connector* (see Figure 8-15), that supplies 5 V and 12 V to peripherals, although only the largely extinct floppy disk drives use this connector. Drive manufacturers adopted the mini as the standard connector on 3.5-inch floppy disk drives.

Figure 8-15
Mini connector

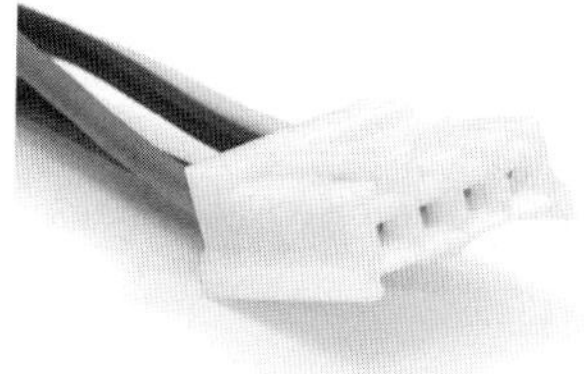

Try This!

Testing DC

A common practice for techs troubleshooting a system is to test the DC voltages coming out of the power supply. Even with good AC, a bad power supply can fail to transform AC to DC at voltages needed by the motherboard and peripherals. The best way to learn how to perform this common technique is to try it yourself, so grab your trusty multimeter and walk through the following steps on a powered-up PC with the side cover removed. Note that you must have P1 connected to the motherboard and the system must be running (you don't have to be in Windows or Linux, of course).

1. Switch your multimeter to DC, somewhere around 20 V DC if you need to make that choice. Make sure your leads are plugged into the multimeter properly: red to hot, black to ground. The key to testing DC is that which lead you touch to which wire matters. Red goes to hot wires of all colors; black *always* goes to ground.
2. Plug the red lead into the red wire socket of a free Molex connector and plug the black lead into one of the two black wire sockets. You should get a reading of ~5 V. What do you have?
3. Now move the red lead to the yellow socket. What voltage do you get?
4. Testing the P1 connector is a little more complicated. You push the red and black leads into the top of P1, sliding in alongside the wires until you bottom out. Leave the black lead in one of the black wire ground sockets. Move the red lead through all of the colored wire sockets. What voltages do you find?

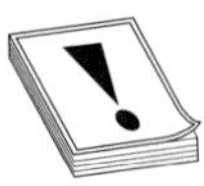

CAUTION As with any power connector, plugging a mini connector into a device the wrong way will almost certainly destroy the device. Check twice before you plug one in!

Be extra careful when plugging in a mini connector! Whereas Molex connectors are difficult to plug in backward, you can insert a mini connector incorrectly with very little effort. As with a Molex connector, doing so will almost certainly destroy the device powered by it. Figure 8-16 depicts a correctly oriented mini connection, with the small ridge on the connector away from the body of the data socket.

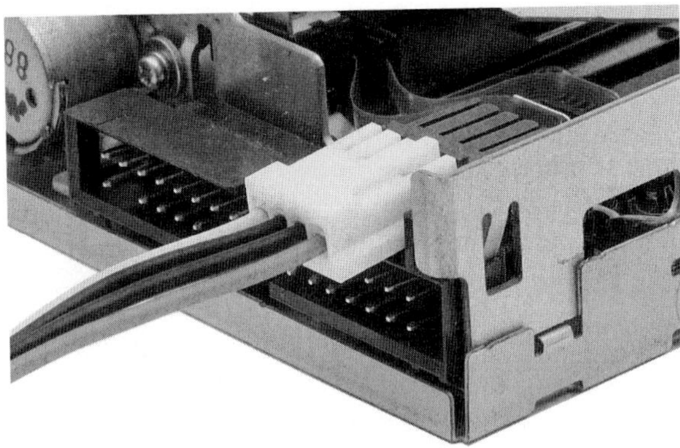

Figure 8-16 Correct orientation of a mini connector

SATA Power Connectors Serial ATA (SATA) drives need a special 15-pin *SATA power connector* (see Figure 8-17). The larger pin count supports the SATA hot-swappable feature and 3.3-, 5.0-, and 12.0-V devices. The 3.3-V pins are not used in any current iteration of SATA drives and are reserved for possible future use. All three generations of SATA use the same power connectors. SATA power connectors are L shaped, making it almost impossible to insert one incorrectly into a SATA drive. No other device on your computer uses the SATA power connector. For more information about SATA drives, see Chapter 9, "Hard Drive Technologies."

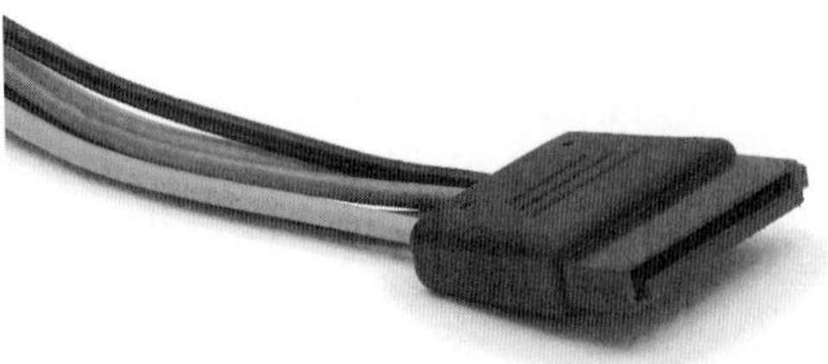

Figure 8-17 SATA power connector

Splitters and Adapters You may occasionally find yourself without enough connectors to power all of the devices inside your PC. In this case, you can purchase splitters to create more connections (see Figure 8-18). You might also run into the phenomenon of needing a SATA connector but having only a spare Molex. Because the voltages on the wires are the same, a simple adapter will take care of the problem nicely.

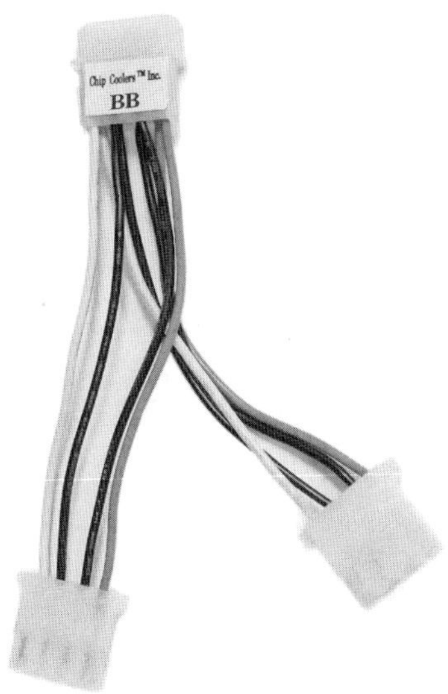

Figure 8-18
Molex splitter

ATX

The original ATX power supplies had two distinguishing physical features: the motherboard power connector and soft power. Motherboard power came from a single cable with a 20-pin P1 motherboard power connector. ATX power supplies also had at least two other cables, each populated with two or more Molex or mini connectors for peripheral power.

When plugged in, ATX systems have 5 V running to the motherboard. They're always "on," even when powered down. The power switch you press to power up the PC isn't a true power switch like the light switch on the wall in your bedroom. The power switch on an ATX system simply tells the computer whether it has been pressed. The BIOS or operating system takes over from there and handles the chore of turning the PC on or off. This is called *soft power*.

Using soft power instead of a physical switch has a number of important benefits. Soft power prevents a user from turning off a system before the operating system has been shut down. It enables the PC to use power-saving modes that put the system to sleep and then wake it up when you press a key, move a mouse, or receive an e-mail (or other network traffic). (See Chapter 24, "Portable Computing," for more details on sleep mode.)

All of the most important settings for ATX soft power reside in CMOS setup. Boot into CMOS and look for a Power Management section. Take a look at the Power On Function option in Figure 8-19. This determines the function of the on/off switch. You

may set this switch to turn off the computer, or you may set it to the more common *4-second delay*.

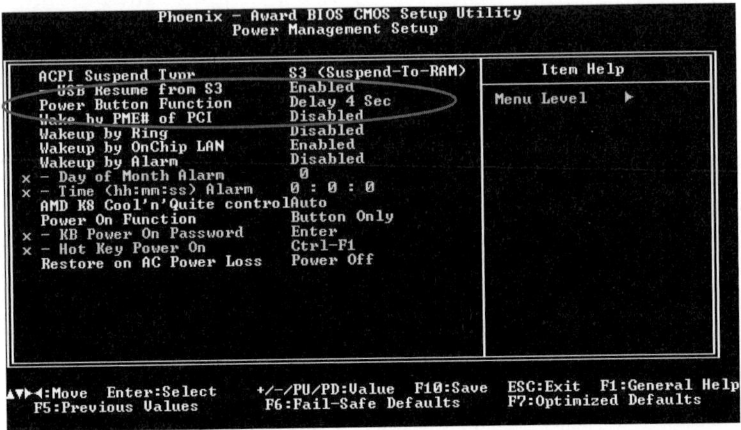

Figure 8-19 Soft power setting in CMOS

ATX did a great job supplying power for more than a decade, but over time more powerful CPUs, multiple CPUs, video cards, and other components began to need more current than the original ATX provided. This motivated the industry to introduce a number of updates to the ATX power standards: ATX12V 1.3, EPS12V, multiple rails, ATX12V 2.0, other form factors, and active PFC.

ATX12V 1.3 The first widespread update to the ATX standard, ATX12V 1.3, came out in 2003. This introduced a 4-pin motherboard power connector, unofficially but commonly called the P4, that provided more 12-V power to assist the 20-pin P1 motherboard power connector. Any power supply that provides a P4 connector is called an ATX12V power supply. The term "ATX" was dropped from the ATX power standard, so if you want to get really nerdy you can say—accurately—that there's no such thing as an ATX power supply. All power supplies—assuming they have a P4 connector—are ATX12V or one of the later standards.

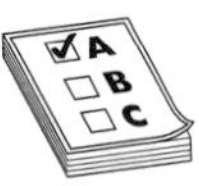

EXAM TIP SATA also supports a slimline connector that has a 6-pin power segment and a micro connector that has a 9-pin power segment.

NOTE It's normal and common to have unused power connectors inside your PC case.

The ATX12V 1.3 standard also introduced a 6-pin auxiliary connector—commonly called an *AUX* connector—to supply increased 3.3- and 5.0-V current to the motherboard

(see Figure 8-20). This connector was based on the motherboard power connector from the precursor of ATX, called *AT*.

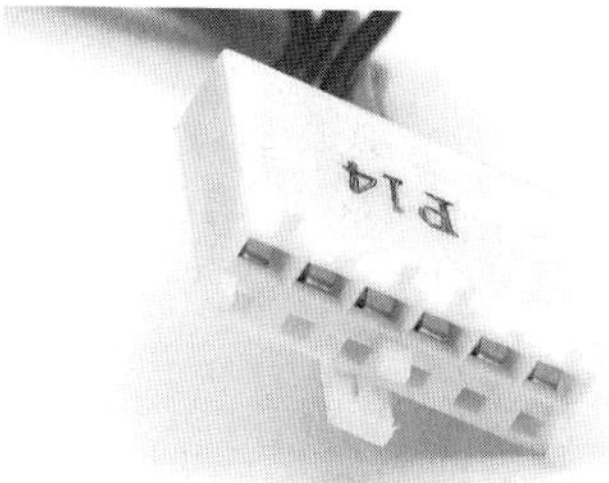

Figure 8-20 Auxiliary power connector

The introduction of these two extra power connectors caused the industry some teething problems. In particular, motherboards using AMD CPUs tended to need the AUX connector, while motherboards using Intel CPUs needed only the P4. As a result, many power supplies came with only a P4 or only an AUX connector to save money. A few motherboard makers skipped adding either connector and used a standard Molex connector so people with older power supplies wouldn't have to upgrade just because they bought a new motherboard (see Figure 8-21).

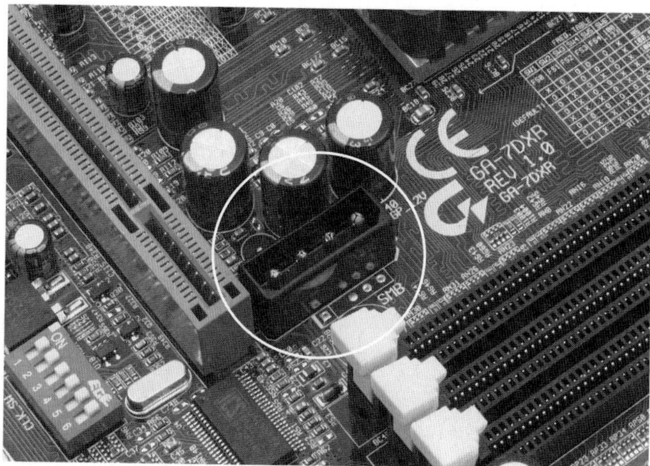

Figure 8-21 Molex power on motherboard

The biggest problem with ATX12V was its lack of teeth—it made a lot of recommendations but few requirements, giving PSU makers too much choice (such as choosing or not choosing to add AUX and P4 connectors) that weren't fixed until later versions.

EPS12V Server motherboards are thirsty for power, and sometimes ATX12V 1.3 just didn't cut it. An industry group called the Server System Infrastructure (SSI) developed a non-ATX standard motherboard and power supply called EPS12V. An EPS12V power

supply came with a 24-pin main motherboard power connector that resembled a 20-pin ATX connector, but it offered more current and thus more stability for motherboards. It also came with an AUX connector, an ATX12V P4 connector, and a unique 8-pin connector. That's a lot of connectors! EPS12V power supplies were not interchangeable with ATX12V power supplies.

EPS12V may not have seen much life beyond servers, but it introduced a number of power features, some of which eventually became part of the ATX12V standard. The most important issue was something called *rails*.

Rails Generally, all of the PC's power comes from a single transformer that takes the AC current from a wall socket and converts it into DC current that is split into three primary DC voltage rails: 12.0 V, 5.0 V, and 3.3 V. Groups of wires run from each of these voltage rails to the various connectors.

Each rail has a maximum amount of power it can supply. Normal computer use rarely approaches this ceiling, but powerful computers with advanced processors and graphics cards require more power than some rails can provide. In the past, 12-V rails only supplied about 18 amps, which wasn't enough to power all that high-end equipment.

The most popular solution was to include multiple 12-V rails in the power supply. This worked fine, but you needed to make sure that you weren't drawing all of your power from the same 12-V rail. The key circuitry that monitors the amount of amperage going through each rail, called the over-current protection (OCP), will shut down the power supply if the current goes beyond its cap. In a *single-rail* system, a single OCP monitors all the pathways. In a *multi-rail* system, each pathway gets its own OCP.

When first implemented, multi-rail (or *dual rail*, as CompTIA calls them) power supplies didn't do a great job balancing the circuitry, so enthusiasts still ran into problems with systems shutting down under heavy load. This has been fixed since 2008 or so, so any multi-rail PSU you buy today can handle whatever you throw at it.

Today's power supply manufacturers produce single- and multi-rail, high-amperage PSUs. You can find power supplies now with 12-V rails pushing 50 amps or more!

ATX12V 2.0 The ATX12V 2.0 standard incorporated many of the good ideas of EPS12V, starting with the 24-pin connector. This 24-pin motherboard power connector is backward compatible with the older 20-pin connector, so users don't have to buy a new motherboard if they use an ATX12V 2.0 power supply. ATX12V 2.0 requires two 12-V rails for any power supply rated higher than 230 W. ATX12V 2.0 dropped the AUX connector and requires SATA hard drive connectors.

In theory, a 20-pin motherboard power supply connector will work on a motherboard with a 24-pin socket, but doing this is risky because the 20-pin connector may not provide enough power to your system. Try to use the right power supply for your motherboard to avoid problems. Many ATX12V 2.0 power supplies have a convertible 24-to-20-pin converter. These are handy if you want to make a nice "clean" connection, because many 20-pin connectors have interfaces that prevent plugging in a 24-pin connector. You'll also see the occasional 24-pin connector constructed in such a way that you can slide off the extra four pins. Figure 8-22 shows 20-pin and 24-pin connectors; Figure 8-23 shows a convertible connector. Although they look similar, those extra four pins won't replace the P4 connector. They are incompatible!

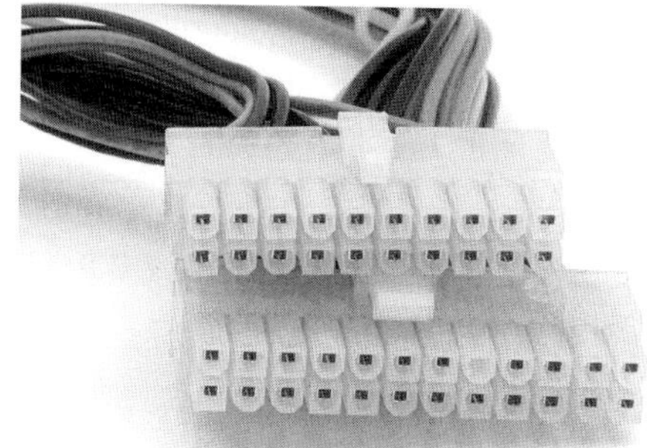

Figure 8-22
20- and 24-pin connectors

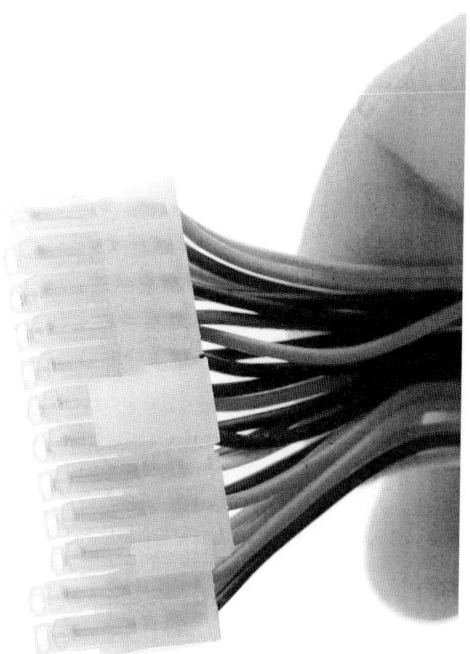

Figure 8-23
Convertible motherboard power connector

Many modern ATX motherboards feature an 8-pin CPU power connector like the one found in the EPS12V standard to help support high-end CPUs that demand a lot of power. This connector is referred to by several names, including EPS12V, EATX12V, and ATX12V 2×4. One half of this connector will be pin compatible with the P4 power connector, and the other half may be under a protective cap. Be sure to check

the motherboard installation manuals for recommendations on if and when you need to use the full 8 pins. For backward compatibility, some power supplies provide an 8-pin power connector that can split into two 4-pin sets, one of which is the P4 connector.

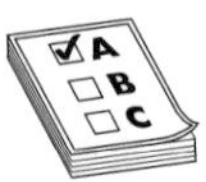

EXAM TIP The CompTIA A+ 901 exam expects you to know your pins! Be sure you are familiar with 4/8-pin 12-V, PCIe 6/8-pin, 20-pin, and 24-pin power connectors.

Another notable connector is the auxiliary PCI Express (PCIe) power connector. Figure 8-24 shows the 6-pin PCIe power connector. Some motherboards add a Molex socket for PCIe, and some cards come with a Molex socket as well. Higher-end cards have a dedicated 6-pin or 8-pin PCIe power connector, sometimes even two of them. The 8-pin PCIe connector should not be confused with the EPS12V connector, as they are not compatible. Some PCIe devices with the 8-pin connector will accept a 6-pin PCIe power connection instead, but this may put limits on their performance. Often you'll find that 8-pin PCIe power cables have two pins at the end that you can detach for easy compatibility with 6-pin devices.

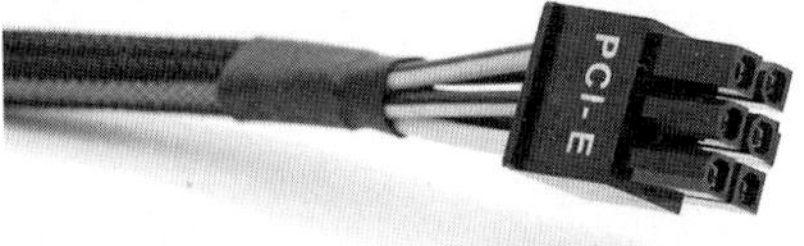

Figure 8-24 PCI Express 6-pin power connector

Niche-Market Power Supply Form Factors The demand for smaller and quieter PCs led to the development of a number of niche-market power supply form factors. All use standard ATX connectors but differ in size and shape from standard ATX power supplies.

Here are some of the more common specialty power supply types:

- **Mini-ATX** and **micro-ATX** Smaller power supply form factors designed specifically for mini-ATX and micro-ATX cases, respectively
- **TFX12V** A small power supply form factor optimized for low-profile ATX systems
- **SFX12V** A small power supply form factor optimized for systems using FlexATX motherboards (see Figure 8-25)
- **CFX12V** An L-shaped power supply optimized for microBTX systems
- **LFX12V** A small power supply form factor optimized for low-profile BTX systems

Figure 8-25 SFX power supply

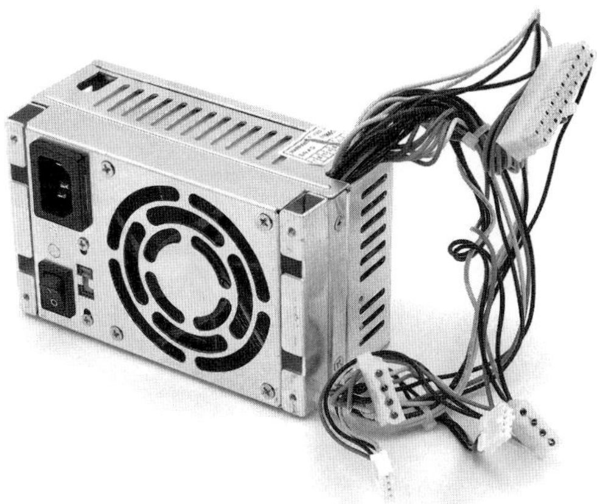

NOTE You'll commonly find niche-market power supplies bundled with computer cases (and often motherboards as well). These form factors are rarely sold alone.

Active PFC Visualize the AC current coming from the power company as water in a pipe, smoothly moving back and forth, 50 or 60 times each second. A PC's power supply, simply due to the process of changing this AC current into DC current, is like a person sucking on a straw on the end of this pipe. It takes gulps only when the current is fully pushing or pulling at the top and bottom of each cycle and creating an electrical phenomena—sort of a back pressure—that's called *harmonics* in the power industry. These harmonics create the humming sound you hear from electrical components. Over time, harmonics damage electrical equipment, causing serious problems with the power supply and other electrical devices on the circuit. Once you put a few thousand PCs with power supplies in the same local area, harmonics can even damage the electrical power supplier's equipment!

Good PC power supplies come with *active power factor correction (active PFC)*, extra circuitry that smooths out power coming from the wall before passing it to the main power supply circuits. This smoothing process eliminates any harmonics (see Figure 8-26). Never buy a power supply that does not have active PFC—all power supplies with active PFC will announce it on the box.

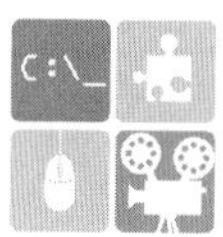

SIM There's a Chapter 8 Challenge! Sim to help you recognize power supply connections at totalsem.com/90x. Give it a try!

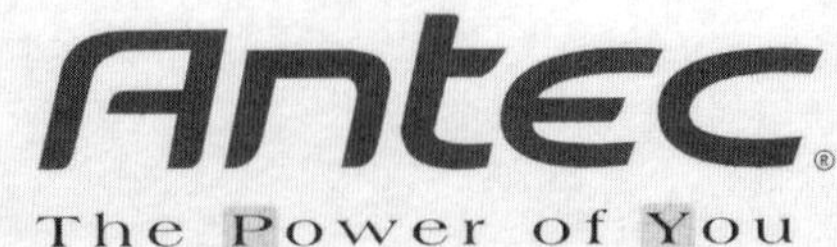

[ENGLISH] Model: Neo HE 550

- **ATX12V v2.2 and EPS12V compliant.**
- **Dual CPU and dual core ready.**
- **Advanced cable management system** improves internal airflow and reduces system clutter by allowing you to use only the cables that you need.
- **Universal Input** automatically accepts line voltages from 100V to 240V AC.
- **Active PFC** (Power Factor Correction) delivers environmentally-friendlier power.
- **Up to 85% efficiency** reduces heat generation and saves power and money.
- **Dedicated voltage outputs** to deliver more stable power.
- **Voltage feedback** and tight ±3% regulation for improved system stability.
- **Three +12V output circuits** provide maximum stable power for the CPU independently and for other peripherals.
- **Dual PCI Express** graphics card power connectors.
- **Low-speed 80mm fan** delivers whisper-quiet cooling and ensures quiet operation by varying fan speed in response to load and conditions.

Figure 8-26 Power supply advertising active PFC

Wattage Requirements

Every device in a PC requires a certain amount of wattage to function. A typical hard drive draws about 15 W of power when accessed, for example, whereas a quad-core Intel i7-4790K draws a whopping 151 W at peak usage. The total wattage of all devices combined is the minimum you need the power supply to provide.

If the power supply cannot produce the wattage a system needs, that PC won't work properly. Because most devices in the PC require maximum wattage when first starting, the most common result of insufficient wattage is a paperweight that looks like a PC. This can lead to some embarrassing moments. You might plug in a new hard drive for a client, push the power button on the case, and nothing happens—a dead PC! Eek! You can quickly determine if insufficient wattage is the problem. Unplug the drive and power up the system. If the system boots up, the power supply is a likely suspect. The only fix for this problem is to replace the power supply with one that provides more wattage (or leave the new drive out—a less-than-ideal solution).

NOTE An undersized power supply may not necessarily result in a complete paperweight. Some graphics cards that are dependent on additional rail power from a PSU may continue to operate but will do so at reduced frame rates. That means your games won't play well, but the computer will function in other capacities. See Chapter 19, "Display Technologies," for the scoop on power-hungry video cards.

No power supply can turn 100 percent of the AC power coming from the power company into DC current, so all power supplies provide less power to the system than the wattage that they draw from the wall. The difference is lost in heat generation. The amount of this differential is advertised on the box. ATX12V 2.0 standards require a power supply to be at least 70 percent efficient, but many power supplies operate with better than 80 percent efficiency.

Power supplies are typically graded for their efficiency under a voluntary standards program called *80 Plus*. Under 80 Plus, power supplies are rated from 80 percent to 94 percent efficiency for a given load and badged with "metal labels" such as Bronze (85 percent), Gold (90 percent), or Titanium (94 percent) levels. These levels are achieved within a narrow range of watts provided, while lower levels of efficiency are achieved at higher and lower power draw. Power and efficiency curves are usually provided in the power supply documentation. More efficiency can tell you how many watts the system draws to supply sufficient power to the PC in actual use. The added efficiency means the power supply wastes less power, saving you money.

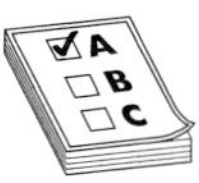

EXAM TIP The CompTIA A+ 901 exam does not require you to figure precise wattage needs for a particular system. When building a PC for a client, however, you do need to know this stuff!

One common argument these days is that people buy power supplies that provide far more wattage than a system needs and therefore waste power. This is untrue. A power supply provides only the amount of power your system needs. If you put a 1500-W power supply into a system that needs only 250 W, that big power supply will put out only 250 W to the system. So buying an efficient, higher-wattage power supply gives you two benefits. First, running a power supply at less than 100 percent load helps it live longer. Second, you'll have plenty of extra power when adding new components.

Don't cut the specifications too tightly for power supplies. All power supplies produce less wattage over time, simply because of wear and tear on the internal components. If you build a system that runs with only a few watts of extra power available from the power supply initially, that system will most likely start causing problems within a year or less. Do yourself or your clients a favor and get a power supply that has more wattage than you need.

As a general recommendation for a new system, use at least a 500-W power supply. This is a common wattage and gives you plenty of extra power for booting as well as for whatever other components you might add to the system in the future.

Installing and Maintaining Power Supplies

Although installing and maintaining power supplies takes a little less math than selecting the proper power supply for a system, they remain essential skills for any tech. Installing takes but a moment, and maintaining is almost as simple. Let's take a look.

Installing

The typical power supply connects to the PC with four standard computer screws, mounted in the back of the case (see Figure 8-27). Unscrew the four screws and the power supply lifts out easily (see Figure 8-28). Insert a new power supply that fits the case and attach it by using the same four screws.

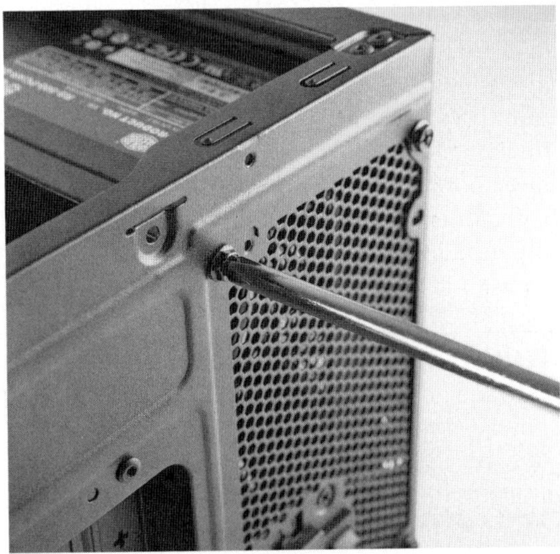

Figure 8-27 Mounting screws for power supply

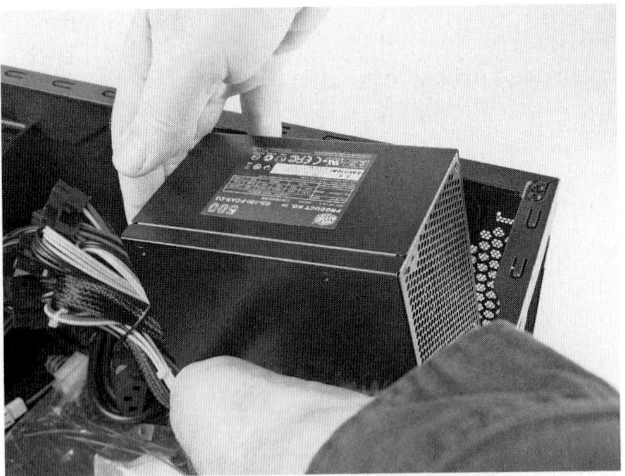

Figure 8-28 Removing power supply from system unit

Handling ATX power supplies requires special consideration. Understand that an ATX power supply *never turns off*. As long as that power supply stays connected to a power outlet, the power supply will continue to supply 5 V to the motherboard. Always unplug an ATX system before you do any work! For years, techs bickered about the

merits of leaving a PC plugged in or unplugged when servicing it. ATX settled this issue forever. Many ATX power supplies provide a real on/off switch on the back of the PSU (see Figure 8-29). If you really need the system shut down with no power to the motherboard, use this switch.

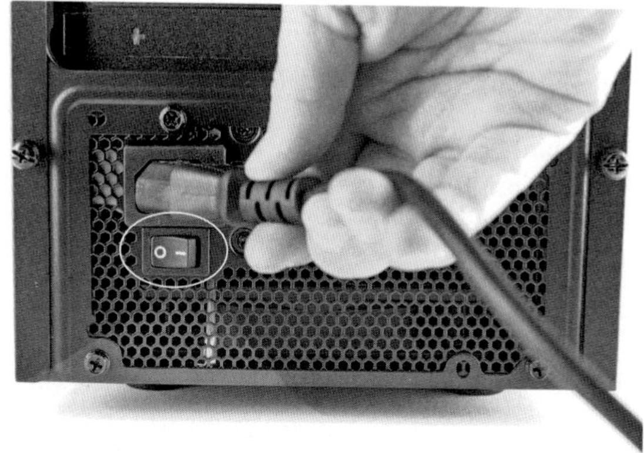

Figure 8-29
On/off switch for an ATX system

When working on an ATX system, you may find using the power button inconvenient because you're not using a case or you haven't bothered to plug the power button's leads into the motherboard. That means there is no power button. One trick when in that situation is to use a metal key or a screwdriver to contact the two wires to start and stop the system (see Figure 8-30).

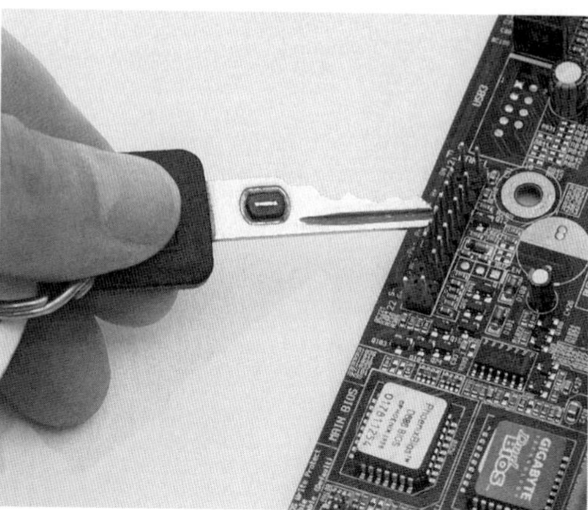

Figure 8-30
Shorting the soft on/off jumpers

Your first task after acquiring a new power supply is simply making sure it works. Insert the motherboard power connectors before starting the system. If you have video cards with power connectors, plug them in too. Other connectors such as hard drives can wait until you have one successful boot—or if you're cocky, just plug everything in!

Cooling

Heat and computers are not the best of friends. Cooling is therefore a vital consideration when building a computer. Electricity equals heat. Computers, being electrical devices, generate heat as they operate, and too much heat can seriously damage a computer's internal components.

The *power supply fan* provides the basic cooling for the PC (see Figure 8-31). It not only cools the voltage regulator circuits *within* the power supply but also provides a constant flow of outside air throughout the interior of the computer case. A dead power supply fan can rapidly cause tremendous problems, even equipment failure. If you ever turn on a computer and it boots just fine but you notice that it seems unusually quiet, check to see if the power supply fan has died. If it has, quickly turn off the PC and replace the power supply.

Figure 8-31
Power supply fan

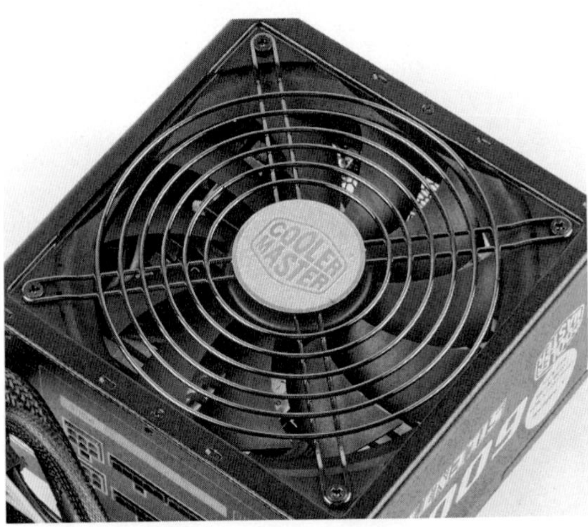

Some power supplies come with a built-in sensor to help regulate the airflow. If the system gets too hot, the power supply fan spins faster (see Figure 8-32).

Figure 8-32
3-wire fan sensor connector

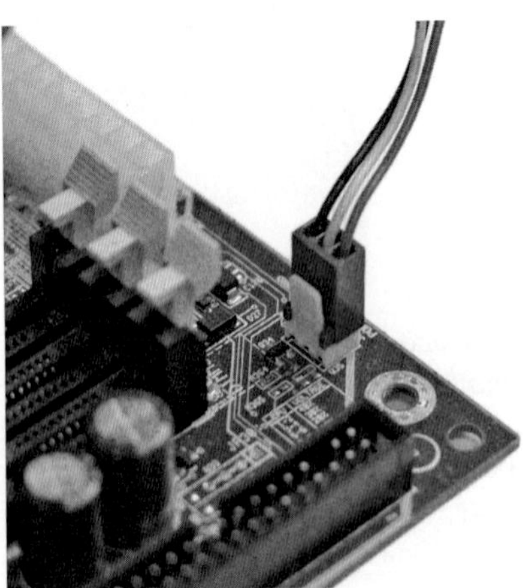

Case fans are large, square fans that snap into special brackets on the case or screw directly to the case, providing extra cooling for key components (see Figure 8-33). Most cases come with a case fan, and no modern computer should really be without one or two.

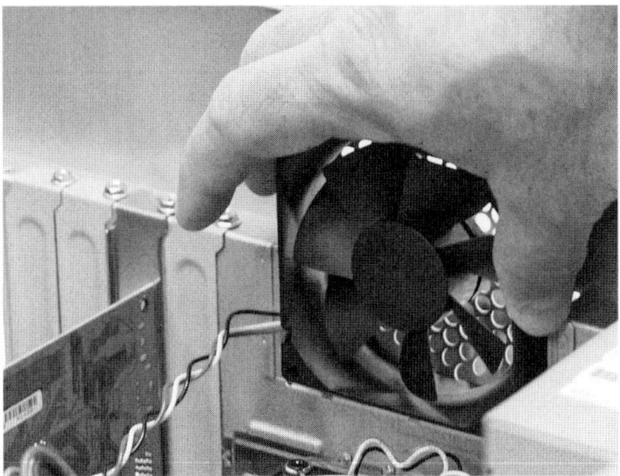

Figure 8-33 Case fan

The single biggest issue related to case fans is where to plug them in. Case fans may come with standard Molex connectors, which are easy to plug in, or they may come with special three-pronged power connectors that need to connect to the motherboard. You can get adapters to plug three-pronged connectors into Molex connectors or vice versa.

Maintaining Airflow

A computer is an enclosed system, and computer cases help the fans keep things cool: everything is inside a box. Although many tech types like to run their systems with the side panel of the case open for easy access to the components, in the end they are cheating themselves. Why? A closed case enables the fans to create airflow. This airflow substantially cools off interior components. When the side of the case is open, you ruin the airflow of the system, and you lose a lot of cooling efficiency.

An important point to remember when implementing good airflow inside your computer case is that hot air rises. Warm air always rises above cold air, and you can use this principle to your advantage in keeping your computer cool.

In the typical layout of case fans for a computer case, an intake fan is located near the bottom of the front bezel of the case. This fan draws cool air in from outside the case and blows it over the components inside the case. Near the top and rear of the case (usually near the power supply), you'll usually find an exhaust fan. This fan works the opposite of the intake fan: it takes the warm air from inside the case and sends it to the outside.

Another important part of maintaining proper airflow inside the case is ensuring that *slot covers* are covering all empty expansion bays (see Figure 8-34). To maintain good airflow inside your case, you shouldn't provide too many opportunities for air to escape. Slot covers not only assist in maintaining a steady airflow; they also help keep dust and smoke out of your case.

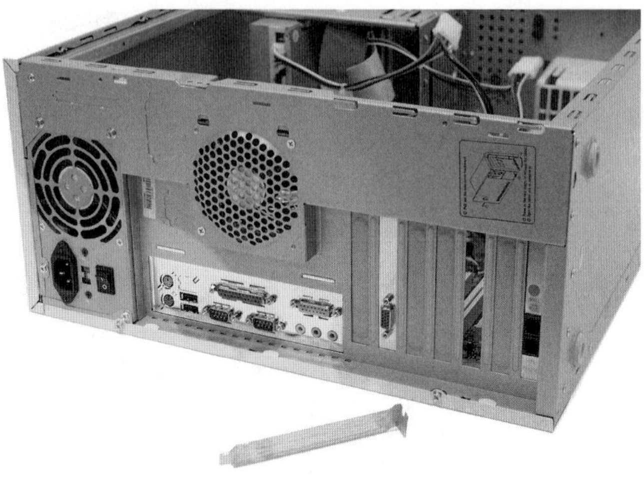

Figure 8-34 Slot covers

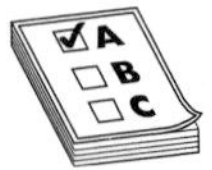

EXAM TIP Missing slot covers can cause the PC to overheat!

Reducing Fan Noise

Fans generate noise. In an effort to ensure proper cooling, many techs put several high-speed fans into a case, making the PC sound like a jet engine. You can reduce fan noise by using manually adjustable fans, larger fans, or specialty "quiet" fans. Many motherboards enable you to control fans through software.

Manually adjustable fans have a little knob you can turn to speed up or slow down the fan (see Figure 8-35). This kind of fan can reduce some of the noise, but you run the risk of slowing down the fan too much and thus letting the interior of the case heat up. A better solution is to get quieter fans.

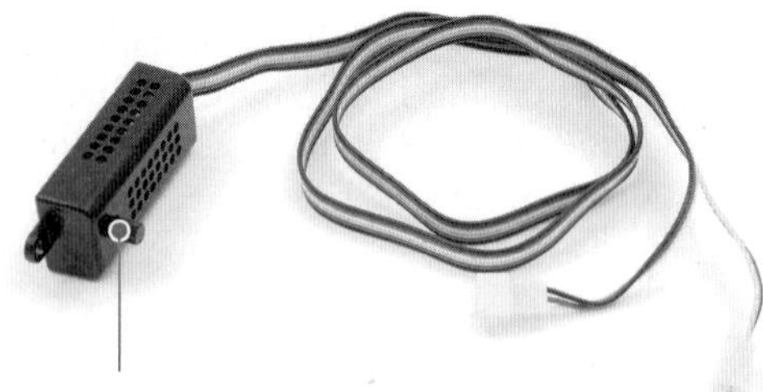

Figure 8-35 Manual fan adjustment device

Larger fans that spin more slowly are another way to reduce noise while maintaining good airflow. Fans sizes are measured in millimeters (mm) or centimeters (cm).

Traditionally, the industry used 80-mm power supply and cooling fans, but today you'll find 100-mm, 120-mm, and even larger fans in power supplies and cases.

Many companies manufacture and sell higher-end low-noise fans. The fans have better bearings than run-of-the-mill fans, so they cost a little more, but they're definitely worth it. They market these fans as "quiet" or "silencer" or other similar adjectives. If you run into a PC that sounds like a jet, try swapping out the case fans for a low-decibel fan from Cooler Master or NZXT. Just check the decibel rating to decide which one to get. Lower, of course, is better.

Because the temperature inside a PC changes depending on the load put on the PC, the best solution for noise reduction combines a good set of fans with temperature sensors to speed up or slow down the fans automatically. A PC at rest uses less than half of the power of a PC running a video-intensive computer game and therefore makes a lot less heat. Virtually all modern systems support three fans through three 3-pin fan connectors on the motherboard. The CPU fan uses one of these connectors, and the other two are for system fans or the power supply fan.

Most CMOS setup utilities provide a little control over fans plugged into the motherboard. Figure 8-36 shows typical CMOS settings for the fans. Note that you can't use CMOS settings to tell the fans when to turn on or off—only to set off an alarm if they reach a certain temperature or fall below a certain speed.

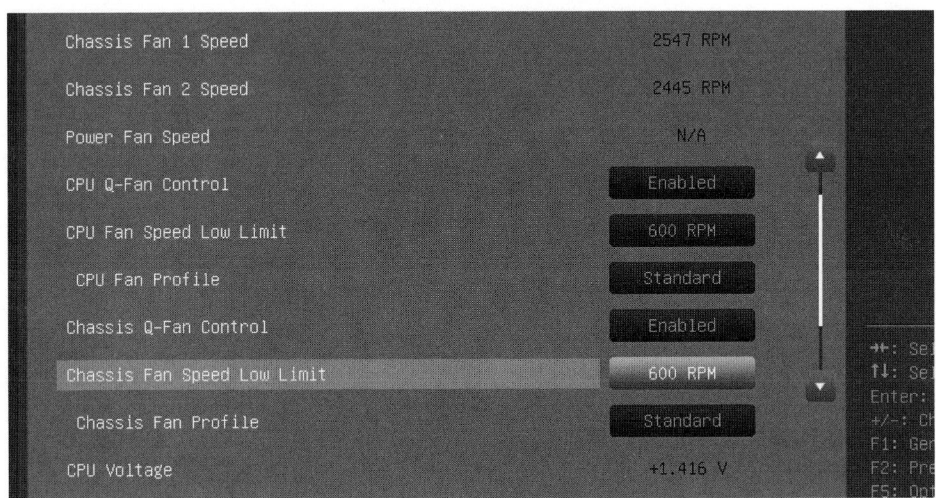

Figure 8-36 CMOS fan options

Software is the best way to control your fans. Some motherboards come with system-monitoring software that enables you to set the temperature at which you want the fans to turn on and off. If no program came with your motherboard, and the manufacturer's Web site doesn't offer one for download, try the popular freeware SpeedFan utility (see Figure 8-37). Written by Alfredo Milani Comparetti, SpeedFan monitors voltages, fan speeds, and temperatures in computers with hardware monitor chips. SpeedFan can

even access S.M.A.R.T. information (see Chapter 9) for hard disks that support this feature and show hard disk temperatures, too. You can find SpeedFan at www.almico.com/speedfan.php.

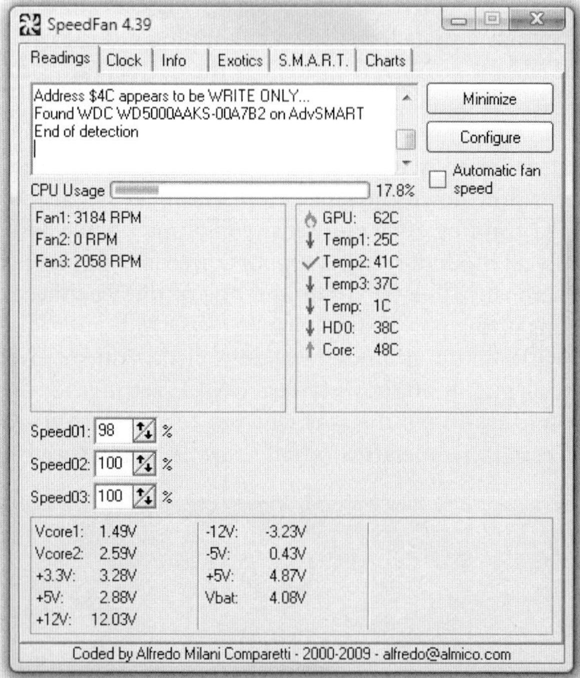

Figure 8-37 SpeedFan

NOTE When shopping for fans, remember your metric system: 80 mm = 8 cm; 120 mm = 12 cm. You'll find fans marketed both ways.

Even if you don't want to mess with your fans, always make a point to turn on your temperature alarms in CMOS. If the system gets too hot, an alarm will warn you. There's no way to know if a fan dies other than to have an alarm.

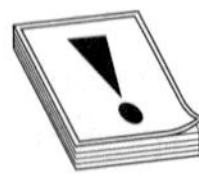

CAUTION SpeedFan is a powerful tool that does far more than work with fans. Don't tweak any settings you don't understand!

Troubleshooting Power Supplies

Power supplies fail in two ways: sudden death and slowly over time. When they die suddenly, the computer will not start and the fan in the power supply will not turn. In this case, verify that electricity is getting to the power supply before you do anything. Avoid the embarrassment of trying to repair a power supply when the only problem is a bad outlet or an extension cord that is not plugged in. Assuming that the system has electricity, the best way to verify that a power supply is working or not working is to use a multimeter to check the voltages coming out of the power supply (see Figure 8-38).

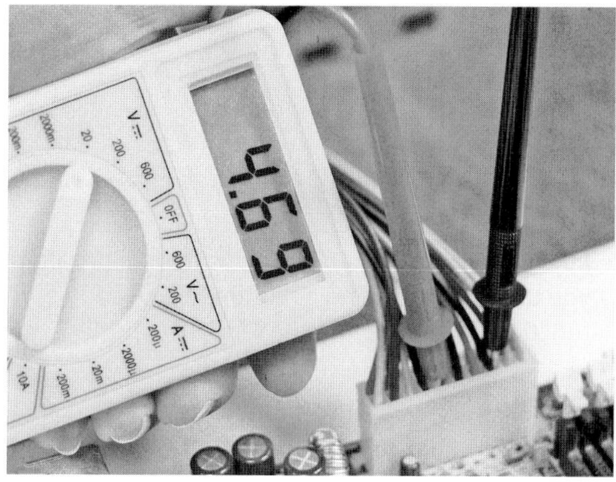

Figure 8-38 Testing one of the 5-V DC connections

Do not panic if your power supply puts out slightly more or less voltage than its nominal value. The voltages supplied by most PC power supplies can safely vary by as much as ±10 percent of their stated values. This means that the 12.0-V line can vary from roughly 10.8 to 13.2 V without exceeding the tolerance of the various systems in the PC. The 5.0- and 3.3-V lines offer similar tolerances.

Be sure to test every connection on the power supply—that means every connection on your main power as well as every Molex and mini. Because all voltages are between –20 and +20 VDC, simply set the multimeter to the 20-V DC setting for everything. If the power supply fails to provide power, throw it into the recycling bin and get a new one—even if you're a component expert and a whiz with a soldering iron. Don't waste your time or your company's time; the price of new power supplies makes replacement the obvious way to go.

No Motherboard

Power supplies will not start unless they're connected to a motherboard, so what do you do if you don't have a motherboard you trust to test? First, try an ATX tester. Many companies make these devices. Look for one that supports both 20- and 24-pin motherboard connectors as well as all of the other connectors on your power supply. Figure 8-39 shows a power supply tester.

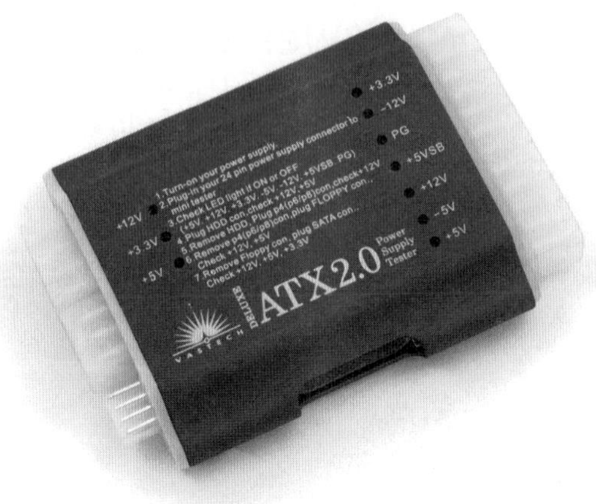

Figure 8-39 ATX power supply tester

NOTE Many CMOS utilities and software programs monitor voltage, saving you the hassle of using a multimeter. Of course, you have to have enough functionality to get into the CMOS utilities!

Switches

Broken power switches form an occasional source of problems for power supplies that fail to start. The power switch is behind the on/off button on every PC. It is usually secured to the front cover or inside front frame on your PC, making it a rather challenging part to access. To test, try shorting the soft power jumpers as described earlier. A key or screwdriver will do the trick.

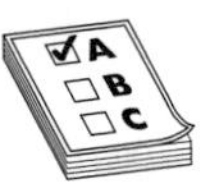

EXAM TIP Be sure you are familiar with power testing tools such as multimeters and power supply testers.

When Power Supplies Die Slowly

If all power supplies died suddenly, this would be a much shorter chapter. Unfortunately, the majority of PC problems occur when power supplies die slowly over time. This means that one of the internal electronics of the power supply has begun to fail. The failures are *always* intermittent and tend to cause some of the most difficult to diagnose problems in PC repair. The secret to discovering that a power supply is dying lies in one word: intermittent. Whenever you experience intermittent problems, your first

guess should be that the power supply is bad. Here are some other clues you may hear from users:

- "Whenever I start my computer in the morning, it starts to boot, and then locks up. If I press CTRL-ALT-DEL two or three times, it will boot up fine."
- "Sometimes when I start my PC, I get an error code. If I reboot, it goes away. Sometimes I get different errors."
- "My computer will run fine for an hour or so. Then it locks up, sometimes once or twice an hour."

Sometimes something bad happens and sometimes it does not. That's the clue for replacing the power supply. And don't bother with the multimeter; the voltages will show up within tolerances, but only *once in a while* they will spike and sag (far more quickly than your multimeter can measure) and cause these intermittent errors. When in doubt, change the power supply. Power supplies break in computers more often than any other part of the PC except components with moving parts. You might choose to keep extra power supplies on hand for swapping and testing.

Fuses and Fire

Inside every power supply resides a simple fuse. If your power supply simply pops and stops working, you might be tempted to go inside the power supply and check the fuse. This is not a good idea. First off, the capacitors in most power supplies carry high-voltage charges that can hurt a lot if you touch them. Second, fuses blow for a reason. If a power supply is malfunctioning inside, you want that fuse to blow because the alternative is much less desirable.

Failure to respect the power of electricity will eventually result in the most catastrophic of all situations: an electrical fire. Don't think it can't happen to you! Keep a fire extinguisher handy. Every PC workbench needs a fire extinguisher, but make sure you have the right one. The fire prevention industry has divided fire extinguishers into five fire classes:

- **Class A** Ordinary free-burning combustible, such as wood or paper
- **Class B** Flammable liquids, such as gasoline, solvents, or paint
- **Class C** Live electrical equipment
- **Class D** Combustible metals such as titanium or magnesium
- **Class K** Cooking oils, trans-fats, or fats

As you might expect, you should only use a Class C fire extinguisher on your PC if it catches on fire. All fire extinguishers are required to have their type labeled prominently on them. Many fire extinguishers are multiclass in that they can handle more than one type of fire. The most common fire extinguisher is type ABC—it works on all common types of fires, though it can leave residue on computing equipment.

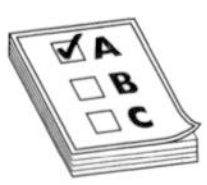

EXAM TIP If your power supply is smoking or you smell something burning inside of it, stop using it now. Replace it with a new power supply.

Beyond A+

Power supplies provide essential services for the PC, creating DC out of AC and cooling the system, but that utilitarian role does not stop the power supply from being an enthusiast's plaything. Plus, servers and high-end workstations have somewhat different needs than more typical systems, so naturally they need a boost in power. Let's take a look Beyond A+ at these issues.

It Glows!

The enthusiast community has been modifying, or *modding*, their PCs for years: cutting holes in the cases, adding fans to make overclocking feasible, and slapping in glowing strips of neon, LEDs, and cold cathode tubes. The power supply escaped the scene for a while, but it's back. A quick visit to a good computer store off- or online, such as http://directron.com, reveals power supplies that light up, sport a fancy color, or have more fans than some rock stars. Figure 8-40 shows a see-through PSU.

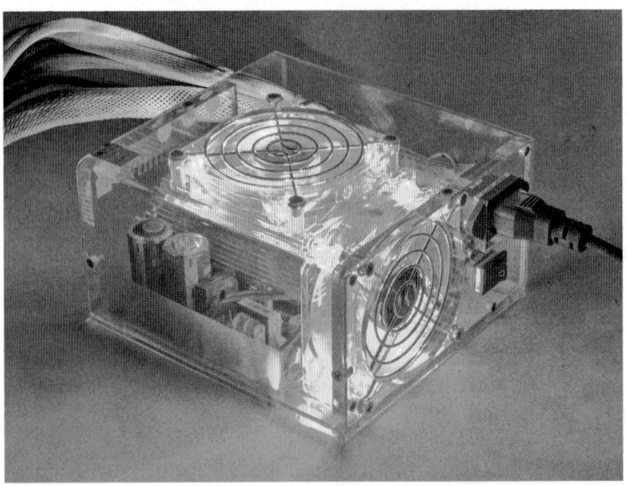

Figure 8-40 See-through power supply that glows blue

You can also find super-quiet stealth power supplies, with single or double high-end fans that react to the temperature inside your PC—speeding up when necessary but running slowly and silently when not. One of these would make a perfect power supply for a home entertainment PC because it would provide function without adding excessive noise.

Modular Power Supplies

It's getting more and more popular to make PCs look good on both the inside and the outside. Unused power cables dangling around inside PCs creates a not-so-pretty picture and can impede airflow. To help stylish people, manufacturers created power supplies with modular cables (see Figure 8-41).

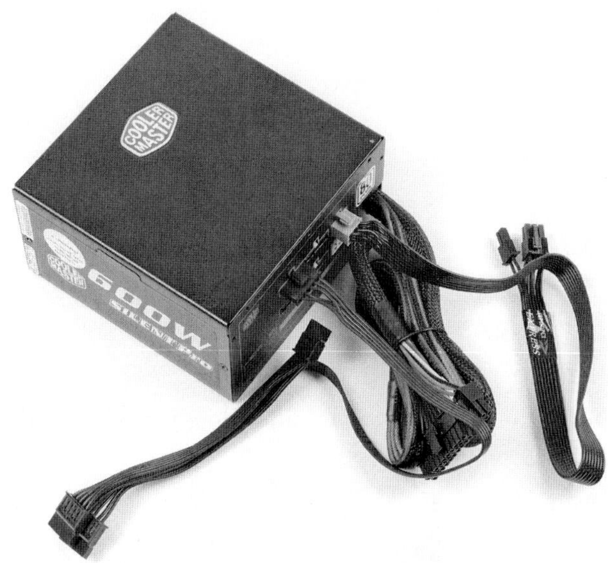

Figure 8-41 Modular-cable power supply

Modular cables are pretty cool, because you add only the lines you need for your system. On the other hand, some techs claim that modular cables hurt efficiency because the modular connectors add resistance to the lines. You make the choice: is a slight reduction in efficiency worth a clean look?

Temperature and Efficiency

Watch out for power supplies that list their operating temperature at 25° C—about room temperature. A power supply that provides 500 W at 25° C will supply substantially less in warmer temperatures, and the inside of your PC is usually 15° C warmer than the outside air. Sadly, many power supply makers—even those who make good power supplies—fudge this fact.

Chapter Review

Questions

1. What is the proper voltage for a U.S. electrical outlet?
   - A. 120 V
   - B. 60 V
   - C. 0 V
   - D. –120 V
2. What voltages does an ATX12V P1 connector provide for the motherboard?
   - A. 3.3 V, 5 V
   - B. 3.3 V, 12 V
   - C. 5 V, 12 V
   - D. 3.3 V, 5 V, 12 V
3. What sort of power connector did a floppy disk drive typically use?
   - A. Molex
   - B. Mini
   - C. Sub-mini
   - D. Micro
4. Joachim ordered a new power supply but was surprised when it arrived because it had an extra 4-wire connector. What is that connector?
   - A. P2 connector for plugging in auxiliary components
   - B. P3 connector for plugging in case fans
   - C. P4 connector for plugging into modern motherboards
   - D. Aux connector for plugging into a secondary power supply
5. What should you keep in mind when testing DC connectors?
   - A. DC has polarity. The red lead should always touch the hot wire; the black lead should touch a ground wire.
   - B. DC has polarity. The red lead should always touch the ground wire; the black lead should always touch the hot wire.
   - C. DC has no polarity, so you can touch the red lead to either hot or ground.
   - D. DC has no polarity, so you can touch the black lead to either hot or neutral but not ground.

6. What voltages should the two hot wires on a Molex connector read?
   - **A.** Red = 3.3 V; Yellow = 5 V
   - **B.** Red = 5 V; Yellow = 12 V
   - **C.** Red = 12 V; Yellow = 5 V
   - **D.** Red = 5 V; Yellow = 3.3 V
7. Why is it a good idea to ensure that the slot covers on your computer case are all covered?
   - **A.** To maintain good airflow inside your case.
   - **B.** To help keep dust and smoke out of your case.
   - **C.** Both A and B are correct reasons.
   - **D.** Trick question! Leaving a slot uncovered doesn't hurt anything.
8. A PC's power supply provides DC power in what standard configuration?
   - **A.** Two primary voltage rails, 12 volts and 5 volts, and an auxiliary 3.3-volt connector
   - **B.** Three primary voltage rails, one each for 12-volt, 5-volt, and 3.3-volt connectors
   - **C.** One primary DC voltage rail for 12-volt, 5-volt, and 3.3-volt connectors
   - **D.** One voltage rail with a 12-volt connector for the motherboard, a second voltage rail with a 12-volt connector for the CPU, and a third voltage rail for the 5-volt and 3.3-volt connectors
9. What feature of ATX systems prevents a user from turning off a system before the operating system has been shut down?
   - **A.** Motherboard power connector
   - **B.** CMOS setup
   - **C.** Sleep mode
   - **D.** Soft power
10. How many pins does a SATA power connector have?
    - **A.** 6
    - **B.** 9
    - **C.** 12
    - **D.** 15

Answers

1. **A.** U.S. outlets run at 120 V.
2. **D.** An ATX12V power supply P1 connector provides 3.3, 5, and 12 volts to the motherboard.
3. **B.** Floppy drives commonly used a mini connector.
4. **C.** The P4 connector goes into the motherboard to support more power-hungry chips.
5. **A.** DC has polarity. The red lead should always touch the hot wire; the black lead should touch a ground wire.
6. **B.** A Molex connector's red wires should be at 5 volts; the yellow wire should be at 12 volts.
7. **C.** Both A and B are correct reasons. Keeping the slots covered helps keep a good airflow in your case and keeps dust and smoke away from all those sensitive internal components.
8. **B.** The standard PC power supply configuration has three primary voltage rails, one each for 12-volt, 5-volt, and 3.3-volt connectors.
9. **D.** The soft power feature of ATX systems prevents a user from turning off a system before the operating system has been shut down.
10. **D.** SATA power connectors have 15 pins.

CHAPTER 9

Hard Drive Technologies

In this chapter, you will learn how to

- Explain how hard drives work
- Explain how solid-state drives work
- Identify and explain the PATA and SATA hard drive interfaces
- Describe how to protect data with RAID
- Install hard drives
- Configure CMOS and install drivers
- Troubleshoot hard drive installation

Of all the hardware on a PC, none gets more attention—or gives more anguish—than the hard drive. There's a good reason for this: if the hard drive breaks, you lose data. As you probably know, when data goes, you have to redo work, restore from a backup, or worse. It's good to worry about our data, because that data runs the office, maintains the payrolls, and stores the e-mail. This level of concern is so strong that even the most neophyte PC users are exposed to terms such as *IDE*, *PATA*, *SATA*, and *controller*—even if they never say these terms themselves.

This chapter focuses on how hard drives work, beginning with the internal layout and organization of hard drives. You'll look at the different types of hard drives used today (PATA, SATA, and SSD), how they interface with the PC, and how to install them properly into a system. The chapter covers how more than one drive may work with other drives to provide data safety and improve speed through a feature called RAID. Let's get started.

Historical/Conceptual

How Hard Drives Work

Hard drives come in two major types: the traditional type with moving parts: and a newer, more expensive technology that with no moving parts. Let's look at both.

NOTE Chapter 10, "Implementing Hard Drives," continues the hard drive discussion by adding in the operating systems, showing you how to prepare drives to receive data and teaching you how to maintain and upgrade drives in modern operating systems.

Magnetic Hard Drives

A traditional *hard disk drive (HDD)* is composed of individual disks, or *platters*, with read/write heads on actuator arms controlled by a servo motor—all contained in a sealed case that prevents contamination by outside air (see Figure 9-1).

Figure 9-1 Inside the magnetic hard drive

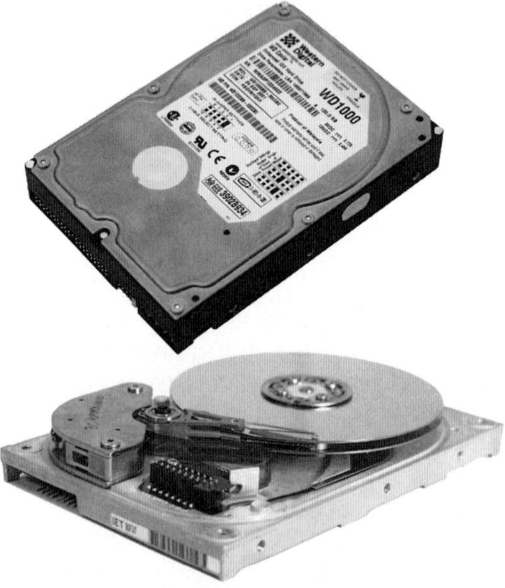

The aluminum platters are coated with a magnetic medium. Two tiny read/write heads service each platter, one to read the top of the platter and the other to read the bottom of the platter (see Figure 9-2). Many folks refer to traditional HDDs as *magnetic hard drives*, or sometimes *platter-based hard drives*.

Figure 9-2 Read/write heads on actuator arms

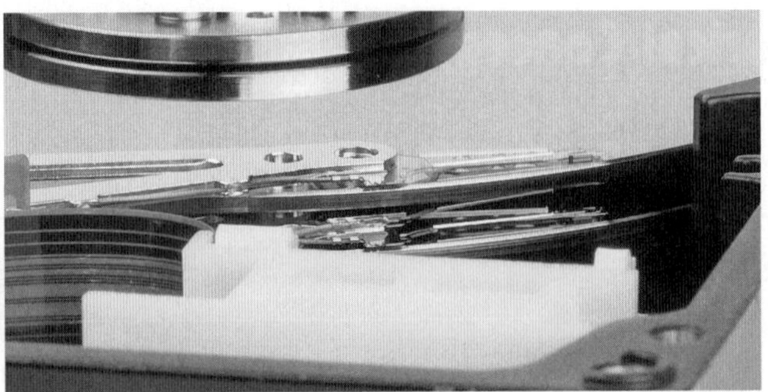

901

Spindle (or Rotational) Speed

Hard drives run at a set spindle speed, with the spinning platters measured in *revolutions per minute (RPM)*. Older drives ran at a speed of 3600 RPM, but new drives are hitting 15,000 RPM. The faster the spindle speed, the faster the controller can store and retrieve data. Here are the common speeds: 5400, 7200, 10,000, and 15,000 RPM.

Faster drives mean better system performance, but they can also cause the computer to overheat. This is especially true in tight cases, such as minitowers, and in cases containing many drives. Two 5400-RPM drives might run forever, snugly tucked together in your old case. But slap a hot new 15,000 RPM drive in that same case and watch your system start crashing right and left!

On a related note, heat can cut the life of hard drives dramatically. A rise of 5 degrees (Celsius) may reduce the life expectancy of a hard drive by as much as two years. So even if replacing an old pair of 5400-RPM drives with a shiny new pair of 15,000-RPM drives doesn't generate enough heat to crash the entire system, it may severely put your storage investment at risk of a short life cycle.

You can deal with the warmth of these very fast drives by adding drive bay fans between the drives or migrating to a more spacious case. Most enthusiasts end up doing both. Drive bay fans sit at the front of a bay and blow air across the drive. They range in price from $10 to $100 (U.S.) and can lower the temperature of your drives dramatically. Some cases come with a bay fan built in (see Figure 9-3).

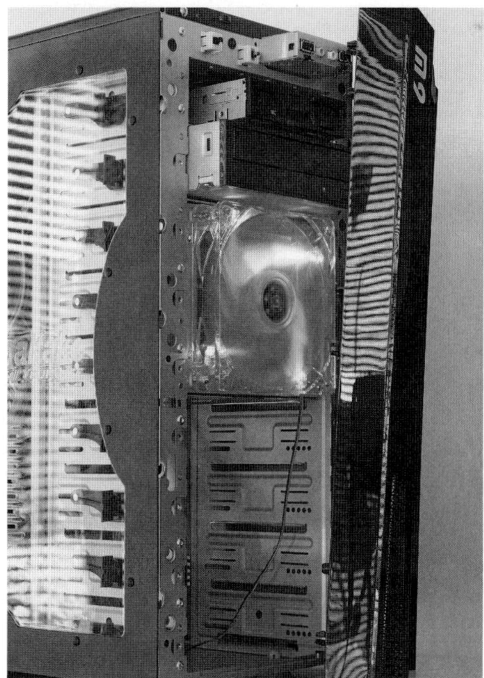

Figure 9-3 Bay fan

Airflow in a case can make or break your system stability, especially when you add new drives that increase the ambient temperature. Hot systems get flaky and lock up at odd moments. Many things can impede the airflow—jumbled-up ribbon cables (used by older storage systems, USB headers, and other attachments), drives squished together in a tiny case, fans clogged by dust or animal hair, and so on.

Technicians need to be aware of the dangers when adding a new hard drive to an older system. Get into the habit of tying off non-aerodynamic cables, adding front fans to cases when systems lock up intermittently, and making sure any fans run well. Finally, if a client wants a new drive for a system in a tiny minitower with only the power supply fan to cool it off, be gentle, but definitely steer the client to one of the slower drives!

Solid-State Drives

Booting up a computer takes time in part because a traditional hard drive needs to first spin up before the read/write heads can retrieve data off the drive and load it into RAM. All of the moving metal parts of a platter-based drive use a lot of power, create a lot of heat, take up space, wear down over time, and take a lot of nanoseconds to get things done. A *solid-state drive* (*SSD*) addresses all of these issues nicely.

In technical terms, solid-state technology and devices are based on the combination of semiconductors and transistors used to create electrical components with no moving parts. That's a mouthful! In simple terms, SSDs use memory chips to store data instead of all those pesky metal spinning parts used in platter-based hard drives (see Figure 9-4).

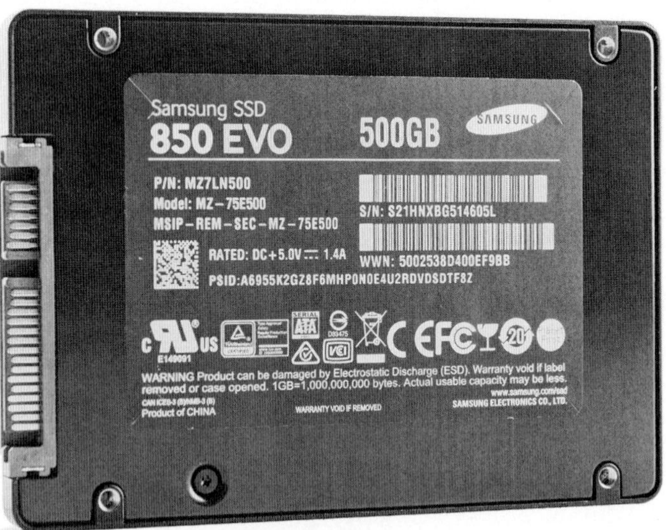

Figure 9-4 A solid-state drive

Solid-state technology is commonly used in desktop and laptop hard drives, memory cards, cameras, USB thumb drives, and other handheld devices.

SSD form factors are typically 1.8-inch, 2.5-inch, or (rarely) 3.5-inch when plugging into traditional hard drive ports. SSDs also come in exotic flavors, such as mSATA, a standardized form factor used in portable devices, and M.2 (see Figure 9-5), that have special slots on motherboards. Finally, SSDs can install as add-on PCIe cards.

Figure 9-5
M.2 SSD

SSDs can be PATA, SATA, eSATA, or USB for desktop systems. Some portable computers have mini-PCI Express versions.

Early SSDs used SDRAM cache that was volatile and lost data when powered off. Current SSDs use nonvolatile flash memory such as NAND that retains data when power is turned off or disconnected. (See Chapter 11, "Essential Peripherals," for the scoop on flash memory technology.)

SSDs are more expensive than traditional HDDs. Less expensive SSDs typically implement less reliable multi-level cell (MLC) memory technology in place of the more efficient single-level cell (SLC) technology to cut costs. The cutting-edge memory in SSDs as I write this is stacked memory, which takes NAND and adds a third dimension to it, giving it increased density and capacity.

Solid-state drives operate internally by writing data in a scattershot fashion to high-speed flash memory cells in accordance with the rules contained in the internal SSD controller. That process is hidden from the operating system by presenting an electronic façade to the OS that makes the SSD appear to be a traditional cylinder/head/sector (CHS) drive. The sheer speed of the internal read/write process far exceeds any slowdowns caused by the CHS-to–memory map translation, making SSDs operate extremely fast.

But "fast" comes at a price. In the first-generation SSDs, once data was written into a memory cell, it stayed there until the drive was full. Even if the cell contained file contents from a "deleted" file, the cell was not immediately erased or overwritten. This is because SSD memory cells have a finite number of times that they can be written to before wearing out. The first generation of protection from this was to wait until all of the cells of an SSD were filled before erasing and reusing a previously written cell.

The result of this "never reuse a memory cell until you have to" policy is kind of an electronic version of disk fragmentation. Benchmark results of this fragmentation show about a 10 percent reduction in raw read and write performance, although there is little to notice in real-world applications.

Windows and other operating systems have defragmenting utilities for magnetic HDDs, but these tools don't have much effect on SSDs. The Windows *trim* function—built into Windows 7 and later versions—is a periodic garbage collection system that seeks out SSD memory cells with deleted contents and erases them, making them available to speed up new write operations.

Hybrid Hard Drives

Windows supports hybrid hard drives (HHDs), drives that combine flash memory and spinning platters to provide fast and reliable storage. Samsung has drives with 128-MB and 256-MB flash cache, for example, that shave boot times in half and, because the platters don't have to spin all of the time, add 20–30 minutes more of battery life for portable computers.

Parallel and Serial ATA

Over the years, many interfaces have existed for hard drives, with such names as ST-506 and ESDI. Don't worry about what these abbreviations stood for; neither the CompTIA A+ certification exams nor the computer world at large have an interest in these prehistoric interfaces. Starting around 1990, an interface called *advanced technology attachment (ATA)* appeared that now virtually monopolizes the hard drive market. ATA hard drives are often referred to as *integrated drive electronics (IDE)* drives.

ATA drives come in two basic flavors. The older *parallel ATA (PATA)* drives send data in parallel, on a wide 40- or 80-wire data cable called a ribbon cable. PATA drives dominated the industry for more than a decade but have been replaced by *serial ATA (SATA)* drives that send data in serial, using only one wire for data transfers.

NOTE The term *IDE* (integrated drive electronics) refers to any hard drive with a built-in controller. All hard drives are technically IDE drives, although we only use the term IDE when discussing ATA drives.

PATA

The last PATA standard, called ATA/ATAPI-7, provides support for very large hard drives (144 petabytes [PB], a number greater than 144 million GB) at speeds up to 133 megabytes per second (MBps). All PATA drives use a standard Molex power connector (see Figure 9-6). Ancient PATA drives (33 MBps and slower) could get by with a 40-pin ribbon cable. Drives that go 66 MBps or faster required an 80-wire cable. Figure 9-7 shows both types of cables.

Figure 9-6 Molex connector and Molex socket (right) on PATA HDD

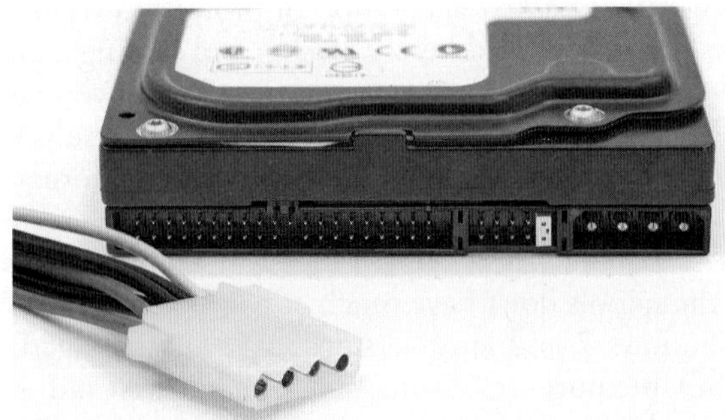

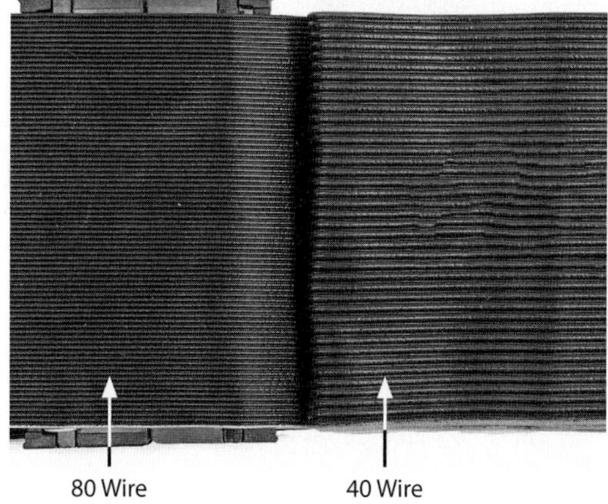

Figure 9-7 80-wire and 40-wire PATA cables

You can connect up to two PATA drives—including hard drives, optical drives, and tape drives—to a single ATA controller. You set jumpers on the drives to make one master and the other slave. (See the discussion on installation later in this chapter for the full scoop.) As a technology standard, ATA went through seven major revisions, each adding power, speed, and/or capacity to storage system capabilities. I could add 15 pages tracking the changes here, but we don't really need to know that much detail about these upgrades as A+ technicians. However, there are a few powerful features that have come from all of those upgrades that are with us today and useful for technicians to know.

ATA-3 introduced Self Monitoring And Reporting Technology (S.M.A.R.T.). Kind of what it sounds like, S.M.A.R.T. is an internal drive program that tracks errors and error conditions within the drive. This information is stored in nonvolatile memory on the drive and must be examined externally with S.M.A.R.T. reader software. There are generic S.M.A.R.T. reading programs, and every drive manufacture has software to get at the vendor-specific information being tracked. Regular usage of S.M.A.R.T. software will help you create a baseline of hard drive functionality to predict potential drive failures.

SATA

For all its longevity as the mass storage interface of choice for the PC, parallel ATA had problems. First, the flat ribbon cables impeded airflow and could be a pain to insert properly. Second, the cables had a limited length, only 18 inches. Third, you couldn't hot-swap PATA drives. You had to shut down completely before installing or replacing a drive. Finally, the technology had simply reached the limits of what it could do in terms of throughput.

Serial ATA addresses these issues. SATA creates a point-to-point connection between the SATA device—hard disk, CD-ROM, CD-RW, DVD-ROM, DVD-RW, BD-R, BD-RE, and so on—and the SATA controller, the *host bus adapter (HBA)*. At a glance, SATA devices look identical to PATA devices. Take a closer look at the cable and power connectors, however, and you'll see significant differences (see Figure 9-8).

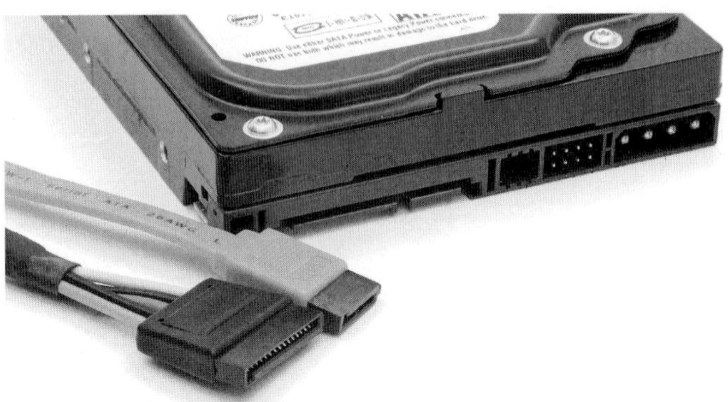

Figure 9-8 SATA hard disk power (left) and data (right) cables

Because SATA devices send data serially instead of in parallel, the SATA interface needs far fewer physical wires—seven instead of the 80 wires that was typical of PATA—resulting in much thinner cabling. Thinner cabling means better cable control and better airflow through the PC case, resulting in better cooling.

Further, the maximum SATA-device cable length is more than twice that of an IDE cable—about 40 inches (1 meter) instead of 18 inches. This facilitates drive installation in larger cases.

SATA did away with the entire master/slave concept. Each drive connects to one port. Further, there's no maximum number of drives—many motherboards today support up to eight SATA drives. Want more? Snap in a SATA HBA and load 'em up!

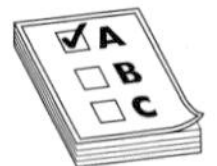

EXAM TIP Know your cable lengths:

- SATA: 1 meter
- eSATA: 2 meters
- PATA: 18 inches

Connecting many types of components to a fully functioning and powered-up computer can result in disaster. The outcome may be as simple as the component not being recognized or as dire as a destroyed component or computer. Enter the era of the hot-swap device. Hot-swapping entails two elements, the first being the capacity to plug a device into the computer without harming either. The second is that once the device is safely attached, it will be automatically recognized and become a fully functional component of the system. SATA handles hot-swapping just fine.

The biggest news about SATA is in data throughput. As the name implies, SATA devices transfer data in serial bursts instead of parallel, as PATA devices do. Typically, you might not think of serial devices as being faster than parallel, but in this case, a SATA device's single stream of data moves much faster than the multiple streams of data coming from a parallel IDE device—theoretically, up to 30 times faster. SATA drives come in three common SATA-specific varieties: *1.5 Gbps*, *3 Gbps*, and *6 Gbps*, which have a maximum throughput of 150 MBps, 300 MBps, and 600 MBps, respectively. It should be noted that if a system has an eSATA port, it will operate at the same revision and speed as the internal SATA ports.

NOTE Number-savvy readers might have noticed a discrepancy between the names and throughput of SATA drives. After all, SATA 1.0's 1.5-Gbps throughput translates to 192 MBps, a lot higher than the advertised speed of a "mere" 150 MBps. The encoding scheme used on SATA drives takes about 20 percent of the transferred bytes as overhead, leaving 80 percent for pure bandwidth.

SATA 2.0's 3-Gbps drive created all kinds of problems, because the committee working on the specifications was called the SATA II committee, and marketers picked up on the SATA II name. As a result, you'll find many hard drives labeled "SATA II" rather than 3 Gbps.

The SATA committee now goes by the name SATA-IO. In keeping with tradition, when SATA II speed doubled from 3 Gbps to 6 Gbps, two names were attached: SATA III and SATA 6 Gbps.

The latest version of SATA, *SATA Express (SATAe)* or *SATA 3.2*, ties capable drives directly into the PCI Express bus on motherboards. SATAe drops both the SATA link and transport layers, embracing the full performance of PCIe. The lack of overhead greatly enhances the speed of SATA throughput, with each lane of PCIe 3.0 capable of handling up to 8 Gbps of data throughput. A drive grabbing two lanes, therefore, could move a whopping 16 Gbps through the bus.

SATAe has unique connectors (see Figure 9-9) but provides full backward compatibility with earlier versions of SATA. Feel free to upgrade your motherboard! Oh yeah, did I forget to mention that? You'll need a motherboard with SATAe support to take advantage of these new, superfast versions of SATA drives.

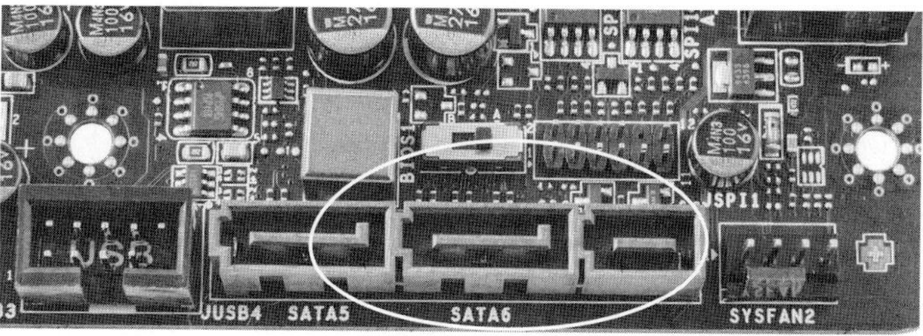

Figure 9-9 SATAe connectors

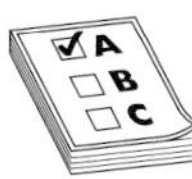

EXAM TIP Each SATA variety is named for the revision to the SATA specification that introduced it, with the exception of SATAe:

- SATA 1.0: 1.5 Gbps/150 MBps
- SATA 2.0: 3 Gbps/300 MBps
- SATA 3.0: 6 Gbps/600 MBps
- SATA 3.2: up to 16 Gbps, also known as SATAe

SATA's ease of use has made it the choice for desktop system storage. Most hard drives sold today are SATA drives.

AHCI

Current versions of Windows support the *Advanced Host Controller Interface (AHCI)*, an efficient way to work with SATA HBAs. Using AHCI unlocks some of the advanced features of SATA, such as hot-swapping and native command queuing.

When you plug in a SATA drive to a running Windows computer that does not have AHCI enabled, the drive doesn't appear automatically. In Windows Vista, you need to go to the Control Panel and run the Add New Hardware to make the drive appear, and in Windows 7 and later, you need to run **hdwwiz.exe** from the Start menu Search bar. Alternatively, you can run the Disk Management console and run Rescan Disks under the Action menu. With AHCI mode enabled, the drive should appear in Computer immediately, just what you'd expect from a hot-swappable device.

Native command queuing (NCQ) is a disk-optimization feature for SATA drives. It enables faster read and write speeds.

AHCI mode is enabled at the CMOS level (see "BIOS Support: Configuring CMOS and Installing Drivers," later in this chapter) and generally needs to be enabled before you install the operating system. Enabling it after installation will cause Windows to Blue Screen. How nice.

If you want to enable AHCI but you've already installed Windows, don't worry! Microsoft has developed a procedure (http://support.microsoft.com/kb/922976) that will have you enjoying all that AHCI fun in no time. Before you jump in, note that this procedure requires you to edit your Registry, so remember to make a backup before you start editing.

NVMe

AHCI was designed for spinning SATA drives to optimize read performance as well as to effect hot-swappability. As a configuration setting, it works for many SSDs as well, but it's not optimal. That's because in order for an SSD to work with the operating system, the SSD has to include some circuitry that the OS can see that makes the SSD appear to be a traditional spinning drive. Once a read or write operation is commenced, the virtual drive circuits pass the operation through a translator in the SSD that maps the true inner guts of the SSD. The *Non-Volatile Memory Express* (*NVMe*) specification supports a communication connection between the operating system and the SSD directly through a PCIe bus lane, reducing latency and taking full advantage of the wicked-fast speeds of high-end SSDs. NVMe SSDs come in a couple of formats, such as an add-on expansion card and a 2.5-inch drive, like the SATA drives for portables. NVMe drives are a lot more expensive currently than other SSDs, but offer much higher speeds.

eSATA and Other External Drives

External SATA (eSATA) extends the SATA bus to external devices, as the name would imply. The eSATA drives use connectors similar to internal SATA, but they're keyed differently so you can't mistake one for the other. Figure 9-10 shows eSATA connectors on the back of a motherboard.

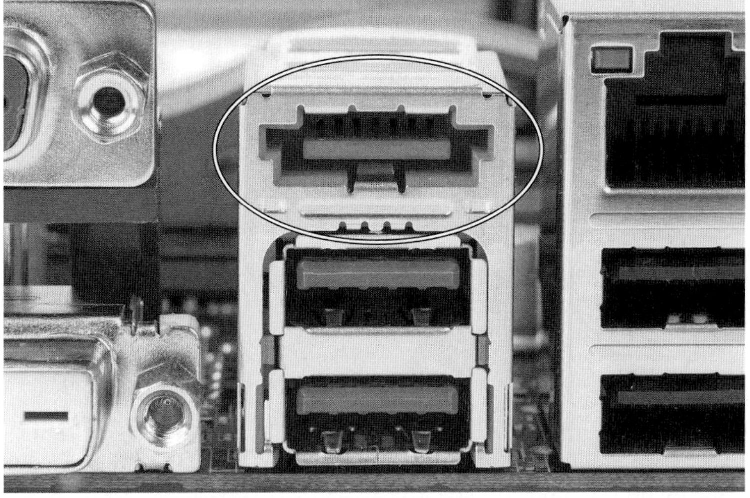

Figure 9-10 eSATA connectors

External SATA uses shielded cable in lengths up to 2 meters outside the PC and is hot-swappable. The beauty of eSATA is that it extends the SATA bus at full speed, mildly faster than the fastest USB connection. It's not that big of a speed gap, especially when you consider that neither connection type fully utilizes its bandwidth yet, but even in real-world tests, eSATA still holds its own.

If a desktop system doesn't have an eSATA external connector, or if you need more external SATA devices, you can install an eSATA HBA PCIe card or eSATA internal-to-external slot plate. You can similarly upgrade laptop systems to support external SATA devices by inserting an eSATA ExpressCard (see Figure 9-11). There are also USB-to-eSATA adapter plugs. Install eSATA PCIe, PC Card, or ExpressCard following the same rules and precautions for installing any expansion device.

NOTE For the scoop on PC Cards and ExpressCards—both technologies designed to add expansion options for portable computers—see Chapter 24, "Portable Computing."

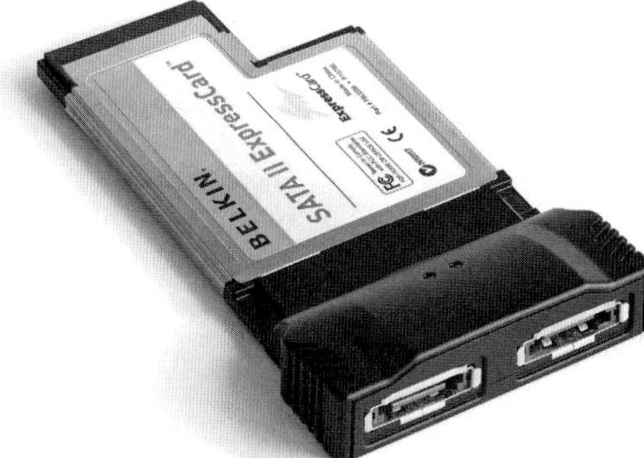

Figure 9-11 eSATA ExpressCard

A quick trip to any major computer store will reveal a thriving trade in external hard drives. External drives connect to a FireWire, USB, eSATA, or Thunderbolt port. All four interfaces offer high data transfer rates and hot-swap capability, making them ideal for transporting huge files such as digital video clips. Regardless of the external interface, however, you'll find an ordinary SATA drive inside the *external enclosure* (the name used to describe the casing of external hard drives).

Protecting Data with RAID

Ask experienced techs "What is the most expensive part of a PC?" and they'll all answer in the same way: "It's the data." You can replace any single part of your PC for a few hundred dollars at most, but if you lose critical data—well, let's just say I know of two small companies that went out of business just because they lost a hard drive full of data.

Data is king; data is your PC's *raison d'être*. Losing data is a bad thing, so you need some method to prevent data loss. Of course, you can do backups, but if a hard drive dies, you have to shut down the computer, reinstall a new hard drive, reinstall the operating system, and then restore the backup. There's nothing wrong with this as long as you can afford the time and cost of shutting down the system.

A better solution, though, would save your data if a hard drive died and enable you to continue working throughout the process. This is possible if you stop relying on a single hard drive and instead use two or more drives to store your data. Sounds good, but how do you do this? Well, first of all, you could install some fancy hard drive controller that reads and writes data to two hard drives simultaneously (see Figure 9-12). The data on each drive would always be identical. One drive would be the primary drive and the other drive, called the *mirror* drive, would not be used unless the primary drive failed. This process of reading and writing data at the same time to two drives is called *disk mirroring*.

If you really want to make data safe, you can use a separate controller for each drive. With two drives, each on a separate controller, the system will continue to operate even if the primary drive's controller stops working. This super-drive mirroring technique is called *disk duplexing* (see Figure 9-13). Disk duplexing is also faster than disk mirroring because one controller does not write each piece of data twice.

Even though duplexing is faster than mirroring, they both are slower than the classic one-drive, one-controller setup. You can use multiple drives to increase your hard drive access speed. *Disk striping* (without parity) means spreading the data among multiple (at least two) drives. Disk striping by itself provides no redundancy. If you save a small

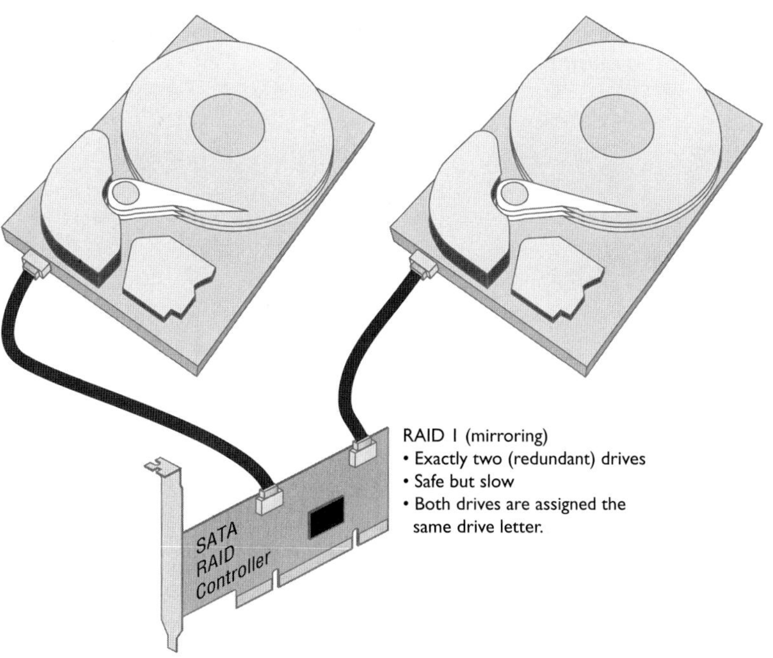

Figure 9-12 Mirrored drives

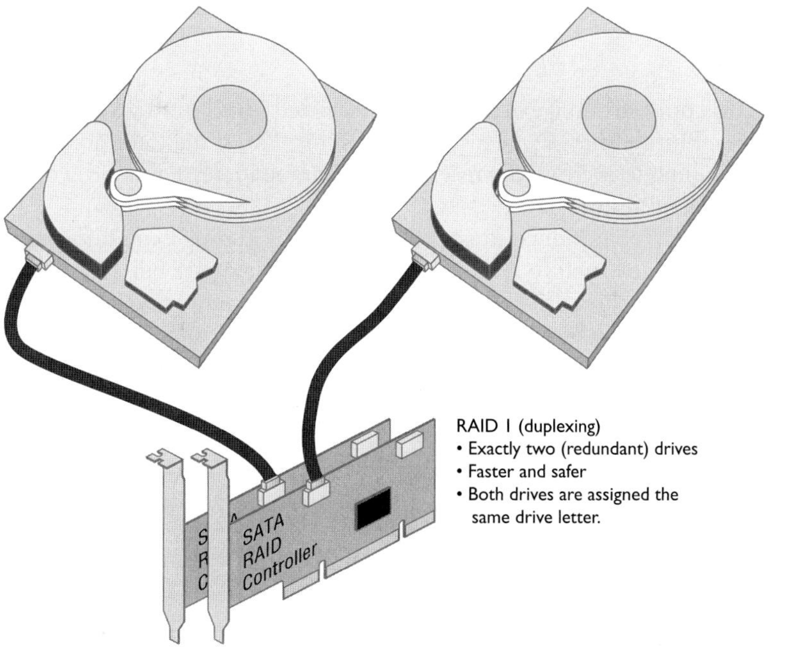

Figure 9-13 Duplexing drives

Microsoft Word file, for example, the file is split into multiple pieces; half of the pieces go on one drive and half on the other (see Figure 9-14).

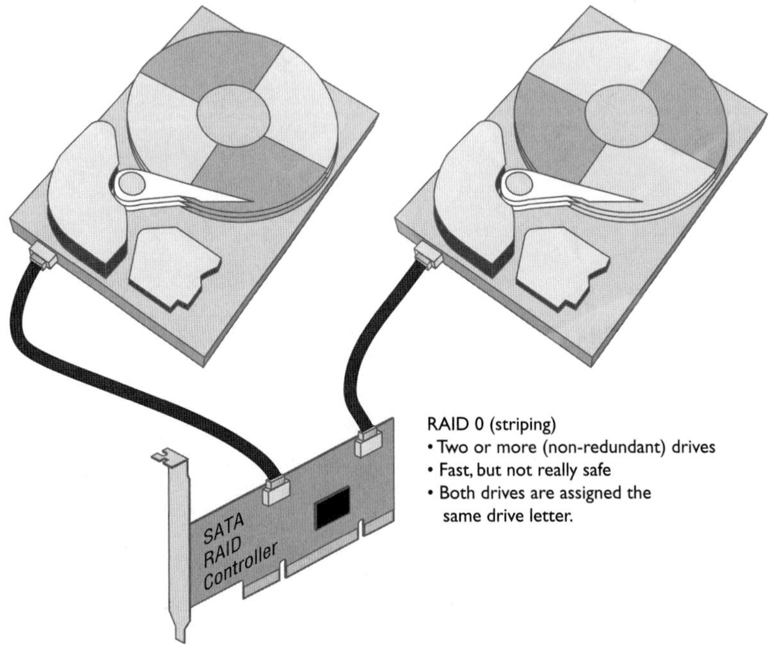
RAID 0 (striping)
• Two or more (non-redundant) drives
• Fast, but not really safe
• Both drives are assigned the same drive letter.
SATA RAID Controller

Figure 9-14 Disk striping

The one and only advantage of disk striping is speed—it is a fast way to read and write to hard drives. But if either drive fails, *all* data is lost. You should not do disk striping—unless you're willing to increase the risk of losing data to increase the speed at which your hard drives save and restore data.

Disk striping with parity, in contrast, protects data by adding extra information, called *parity data*, that can be used to rebuild data if one of the drives fails. Disk striping with parity requires at least three drives, but it is common to use more than three. Disk striping with parity combines the best of disk mirroring and plain disk striping. It protects data and is quite fast. The majority of network servers use a type of disk striping with parity.

NOTE There is actually a term for a storage system composed of multiple independent disks of various sizes, *JBOD*, which stands for *just a bunch of disks* (or *drives*). Many popular drive controllers support JBOD.

RAID

A couple of sharp guys in Berkeley back in the 1980s organized the many techniques for using multiple drives for data protection and increasing speeds as the *redundant array of*

independent (or *inexpensive*) *disks (RAID)*. An *array* describes two or more drives working as a unit. They outlined several forms or "levels" of RAID that have since been numbered 0 through 6 (plus a couple of special implementations). Only a few of these RAID types are in use today: 0, 1, 5, 6, 10, and 0+1.

- **RAID 0—Disk Striping** Disk striping requires at least two drives. It does not provide redundancy to data. If any one drive fails, all data is lost.
- **RAID 1—Disk Mirroring/Duplexing** RAID 1 arrays require at least two hard drives, although they also work with any even number of drives. RAID 1 is the ultimate in safety, but you lose storage space because the data is duplicated; you need two 2-TB drives to store 2 TB of data.
- **RAID 5—Disk Striping with Distributed Parity** Instead of dedicated data and parity drives, RAID 5 distributes data and parity information evenly across all drives. This is the fastest way to provide data redundancy. RAID 5 is by far the most common RAID implementation and requires at least three drives. RAID 5 arrays effectively use one drive's worth of space for parity. If, for example, you have three 2-TB drives, your total storage capacity is 4 TB. If you have four 2-TB drives, your total capacity is 6 TB.
- **RAID 6—Disk Striping with Extra Parity** If you lose a hard drive in a RAID 5 array, your data is at great risk until you replace the bad hard drive and rebuild the array. RAID 6 is RAID 5 with extra parity information. RAID 6 needs at least five drives, but in exchange you can lose up to two drives at the same time. RAID 6 is gaining in popularity for those willing to use larger arrays.
- **RAID 10—Nested, Striped Mirrors** RAID levels have been combined to achieve multiple benefits, including speed, capacity, and reliability, but these benefits must be purchased at a cost, and that cost is efficiency. Take for instance RAID 10, also called RAID 1+0 and sometimes a "stripe of mirrors." Requiring a minimum of four drives, a pair of drives is configured as a mirror, and then the same is done to another pair to achieve a pair of RAID 1 arrays. The arrays look like single drives to the operating system or RAID controller. So now, with two drives, we can block stripe across the two mirrored pairs (RAID 0). Cool, huh? We get the speed of striping and the reliability of mirroring at the cost of installing two bytes of storage for every byte of data saved. Need more space? Add another mirrored pair to the striped arrays!
- **RAID 0+1—Nested, Mirrored Stripes** Like RAID 10, RAID 0+1 (or a "mirror of stripes") is a nested set of arrays that works in opposite configuration from RAID 10. It takes a minimum of four drives to implement RAID 0+1. Start with two RAID 0 striped arrays, then mirror the two arrays to each other. Which is better: the RAID 10 or the RAID 0+1? Why not do a bit of research and decide for yourself?

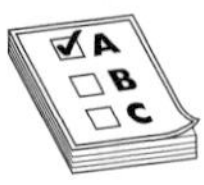

EXAM TIP In preparation for the CompTIA A+ 220-901 exam, you'll want to be familiar with common RAID levels, the minimum number of drives in a given level array, and how many failures a given array can withstand and remain functional.

RAID Level	Minimum Drives	Number of Functional Failures
RAID 0	2	0
RAID 1	2	1
RAID 5	3	1
RAID 6	5	2
RAID 10	4	Up to 2
RAID 0+1	4	Up to 2

Implementing RAID

RAID levels describe different methods of providing data redundancy or enhancing the speed of data throughput to and from groups of hard drives. They do not say *how* to implement these methods. Literally thousands of methods can be used to set up RAID. The method you use depends largely on the level of RAID you desire, the operating system you use, and the thickness of your wallet.

The obvious starting place for RAID is to connect at least two hard drives in some fashion to create a RAID array. Specialized RAID controller cards support RAID arrays of up to 15 drives—plenty to support even the most complex RAID needs.

Once you have a number of hard drives, the next question is whether to use hardware or software to control the array. Let's look at both options.

Hardware Versus Software

All RAID implementations break down into either hardware or software methods. Software is often used when price takes priority over performance. Hardware is used when you need speed along with data redundancy. Software RAID does not require special controllers; you can use the regular ATA controllers or SATA controllers to make a software RAID array. But you do need "smart" software. The most common software implementation of RAID is the built-in RAID software that comes with Windows. The Disk Management program in Windows Server versions can configure drives for RAID 0, 1, or 5, and it works with PATA or SATA (see Figure 9-15). Disk Management in Windows Vista can only do RAID 0, while Windows 7/8/8.1/10 Disk Management can do RAID 0 and 1.

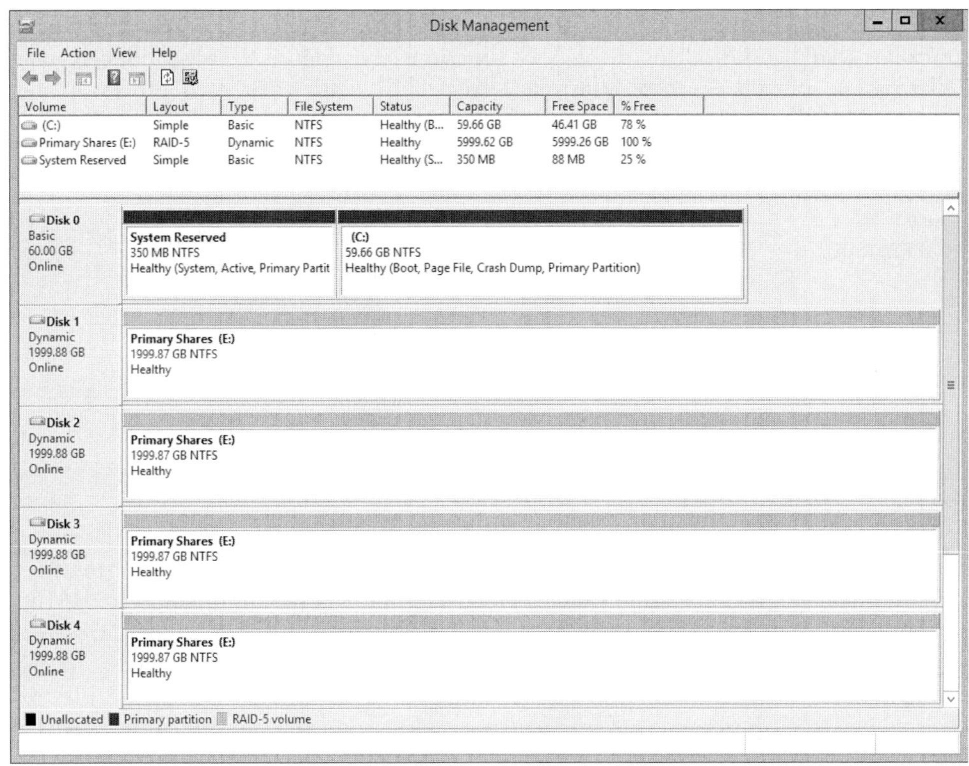

Figure 9-15 Disk Management tool of Computer Management in Windows Server

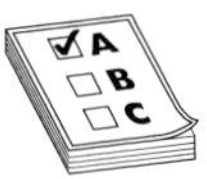

EXAM TIP Get your hands on Windows 8.1 and/or Windows 7 to play with the Disk Management utilities. Get familiar with the RAID configuration and implementation procedures, as you may see these simulated on a performance-based exam question.

Windows Disk Management is not the only software RAID game in town. A number of third-party software programs work with Windows or other operating systems.

Software RAID means the operating system is in charge of all RAID functions. It works for small RAID solutions but tends to overwork your operating system easily, creating slowdowns. When you *really* need to keep going, when you need RAID that doesn't even let the users know a problem has occurred, hardware RAID is the answer.

NOTE See Chapter 10 for a thorough discussion of *Storage Spaces*, the software RAID implementation available in Windows 8/8.1/10.

Hardware RAID centers on an *intelligent* controller—either a PATA or SATA controller that handles all of the RAID functions (see Figure 9-16). Unlike regular PATA/SATA controllers, these controllers have chips with their own processor and memory. This allows the card, instead of the operating system, to handle all of the work of implementing RAID.

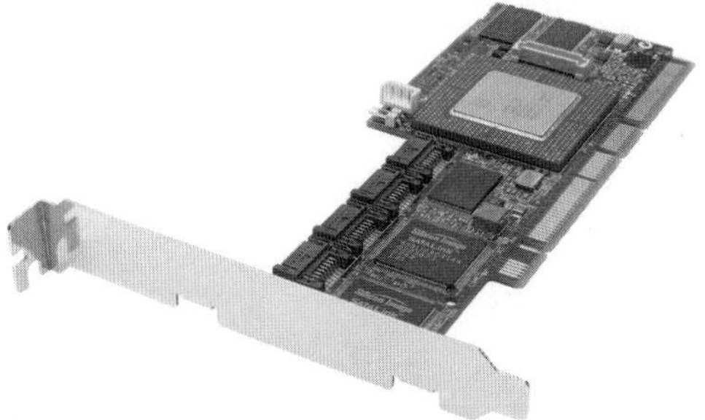

Figure 9-16 Serial ATA RAID controller

Most RAID setups in the real world are hardware-based. Almost all of the many hardware RAID solutions provide *hot-swapping*—the ability to replace a bad drive without disturbing the operating system. Hot-swapping is common in hardware RAID.

Hardware-based RAID is invisible to the operating system and is configured in several ways, depending on the specific chips involved. Most RAID systems have a special configuration utility in Flash ROM that you access after CMOS but before the OS loads. Figure 9-17 shows a typical firmware program used to configure a hardware RAID solution.

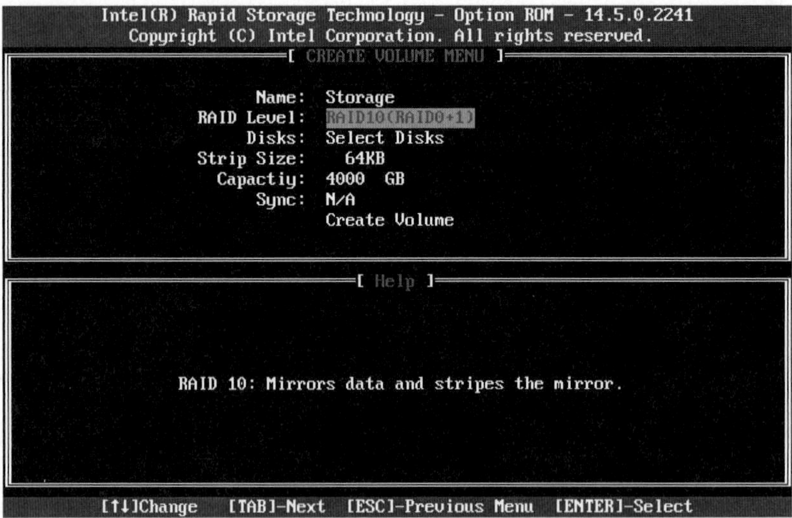

Figure 9-17 RAID configuration utility

NOTE RAID controllers aren't just for internal drives; some models can handle multiple eSATA drives configured at any of the RAID levels. If you're feeling lucky, you can create a RAID array using both internal and external SATA drives.

Installing Drives

Installing a drive is a fairly simple process if you take the time to make sure you have the right drive for your system, configure the drive properly, and do a few quick tests to see if it's running properly. Since PATA and SATA have different cabling requirements, we'll look at each separately.

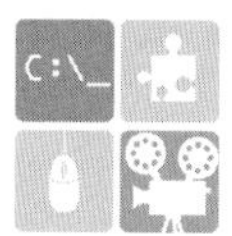

SIM Try the Chapter 9 Challenge! sim to determine the best use of capacity vs. speed considerations for a RAID array at http://totalsem.com/90x.

Choosing Your Drive

First, decide where you're going to put the drive. Look for an open ATA connection. Is it PATA or SATA? Is it a dedicated RAID controller? Many motherboards with built-in RAID controllers have a CMOS setting that enables you to turn the RAID controller on or off (see Figure 9-18).

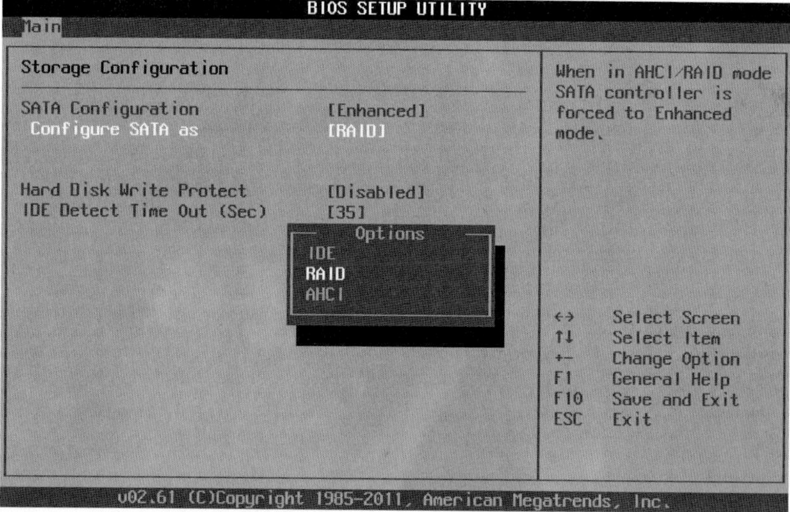

Figure 9-18 Settings for RAID in CMOS

Second, make sure you have room for the drive in the case. Where will you place it? Do you have a spare power connector? Will the data and power cables reach the drive? A quick test fit is always a good idea.

Try This!

Managing Heat with Multiple Drives

Adding three or more fast hard drives into a cramped PC case can be a recipe for disaster to the unwary tech. While the heat generated may not threaten the fabric of the time-space continuum, it is a fact that heat reduces the life expectancy of drives and computers. You have to manage the heat inside a RAID-enabled system because such systems usually have more than the typical quantity of drives found in most computers. The easiest way to do this is to add fans.

Open up your PC case and look for built-in places to mount fans. How many case fans do you have installed now? What size are they? What sizes can you use? (Most cases use 80-mm fans, but 60- and 120-mm fans are common as well.) Jot down the particulars of your system and take a trip to the local PC store to check out the fans.

Before you get all fan-happy and grab the biggest and baddest fans to throw in your case, don't forget to think about the added noise level. Try to get a compromise between keeping your case cool enough and avoiding early deafness.

Jumpers and Cabling on PATA Drives

If you have only one hard drive, set the drive's jumpers to master or standalone. If you have two drives, set one to master and the other to slave. Or set both to cable select. See Figure 9-19 for a close-up of a PATA hard drive, showing the jumpers.

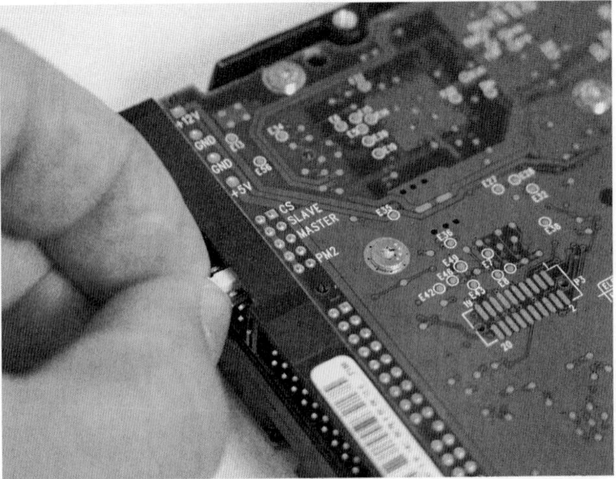

Figure 9-19 Master/slave jumpers on a hard drive

At first glance, you might notice that the jumpers aren't actually labeled *master* and *slave*. So how do you know how to set them properly? The easiest way is to read the front of the drive; most drives have a diagram on the housing that explains how to set the jumpers properly. Figure 9-20 shows the label of one of these drives, so you can see how to set the drive to master or slave.

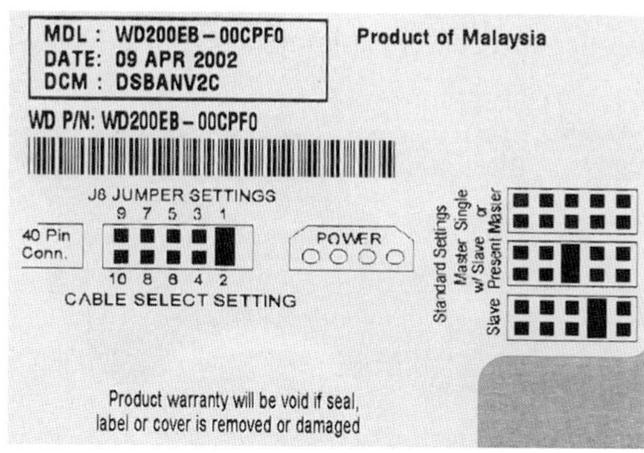

Figure 9-20 Drive label showing master/slave settings

Hard disk drives may have other jumpers that may or may not concern you during installation. One common set of jumpers is used for diagnostics at the manufacturing plant or for special settings in other kinds of devices that use hard drives. Ignore them; they have no bearing in the PC world. Second, many drives provide a third setting to be used if only one drive connects to a controller. Often, master and single drive are the same setting on the hard drive, although some hard drives require separate settings. Note that the name for the single drive setting varies among manufacturers. Some use Single; others use 1 Drive or Standalone.

Many PATA hard drives use a jumper setting called *cable select* rather than master or slave. As the name implies, the position on the cable determines which drive will be master or slave: master on the end, slave in the middle. For cable select to work properly with two drives, you must set both drives as cable select.

If you don't see a label on the drive that tells you how to set the jumpers, you have several options. First, look at the drive maker's Web site. Every drive manufacturer lists its drive jumper settings on the Web, although finding the information you want can take a while. Second, try phoning the hard drive maker directly. Unlike many other PC parts manufacturers, hard drive producers tend to stay in business for a long time and offer great technical support.

Hard drive cables have a colored stripe that corresponds to the number-one pin—called *pin 1*—on the connector. You need to make certain that pin 1 on the controller is on the same wire as pin 1 on the hard drive. Failing to plug in the drive properly will also prevent the PC from recognizing the drive. If you incorrectly set the master/slave jumpers or cable to the hard drives, you won't break anything; it just won't work.

Finally, you need to plug a Molex connector from the power supply into the drive. All modern PATA drives use a Molex connector.

Cabling SATA Drives

Installing SATA hard disk drives is much easier than installing PATA devices because there's no master, slave, or cable select configuration to mess with. In fact, there are no jumper settings to worry about at all, as SATA supports only a single device per controller channel. Simply connect the power and plug in the controller cable as shown in Figure 9-21—the OS automatically detects the drive and it's ready to go. The keying on SATA controller and power cables makes it impossible to install either incorrectly.

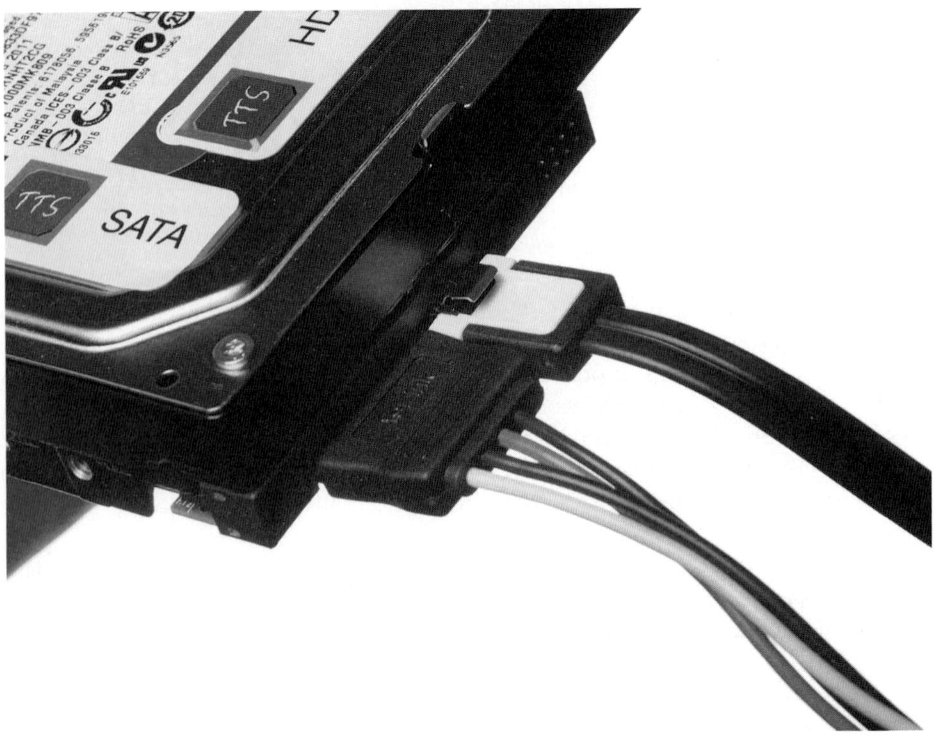

Figure 9-21 Properly connected SATA cable

Connecting Solid-State Drives

You install a solid-state drive as you would any PATA or SATA drive. They usually come in 2.5-inch laptop sizes. To install them into a desktop or tower with 3.5-inch drive bays, form-factor adapters are available to make the job easy. Just as with earlier hard drive types, you either connect SSDs correctly and they work, or you connect them incorrectly and they don't. If they fail, nine times out of ten they will need to be replaced.

M.2 and mSATA drives slip into their slot on the motherboard or add-on card, then either clip in place or secure with a tiny screw (see Figure 9-22). Both standards are keyed, so you can't install them incorrectly.

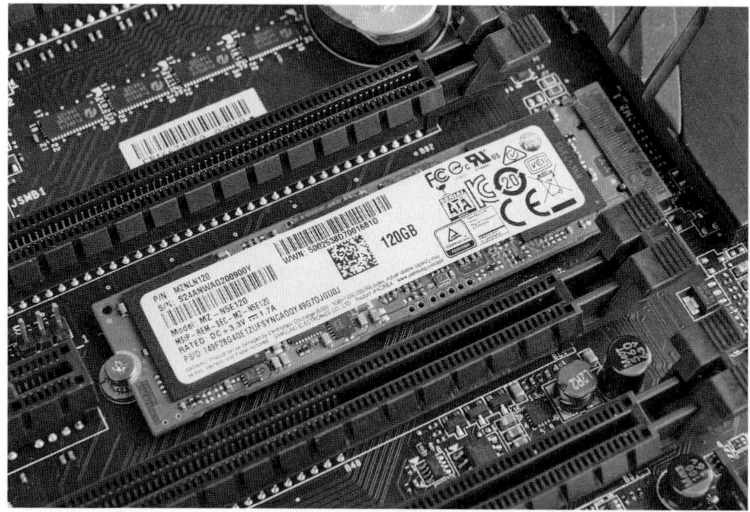

Figure 9-22 M.2 SSD secured on motherboard

Keep in mind the following considerations before installing or replacing an existing HDD with an SSD:

- Do you have the appropriate drivers and firmware for the SSD? Newer Windows versions are likely to load most currently implemented SSD drivers. As always, check the manufacturer's specifications before you do anything.
- Do you have everything important backed up? Good!

BIOS Support: Configuring CMOS and Installing Drivers

Every device in your PC needs BIOS support, whether it's traditional BIOS or UEFI BIOS. Hard drive controllers are no exception. Motherboards provide support for the ATA hard drive controllers via the system BIOS, but they require configuration in CMOS for the specific hard drives attached.

In the old days, you had to fire up CMOS and manually enter hard drive information whenever you installed a new drive. Today, this process is automated.

Configuring Controllers

As a first step in configuring controllers, make certain they're enabled. Most controllers remain active, ready to automatically detect new drives, but you can disable them. Scan through your CMOS settings to locate the controller on/off options (see Figure 9-23 for typical settings). This is also the time to check whether your onboard RAID controllers work in both RAID and non-RAID settings.

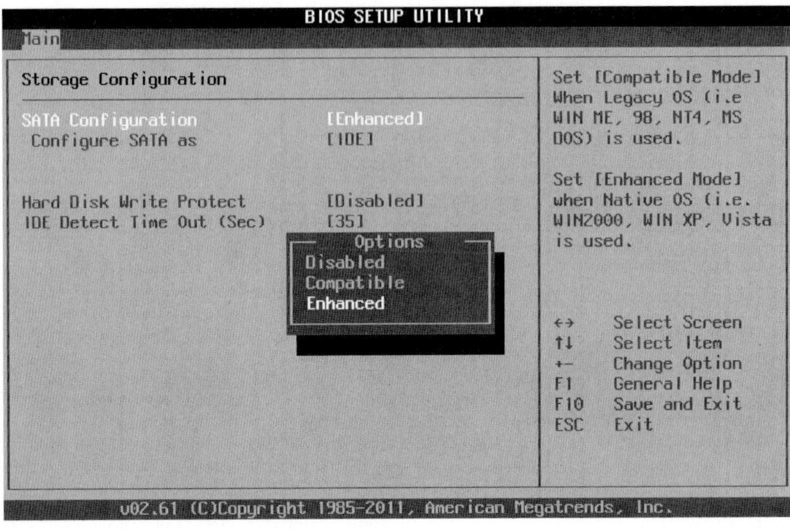

Figure 9-23 Typical controller settings in CMOS

Autodetection

If the controllers are enabled and the drive is properly connected, the drive should appear in CMOS through a process called *autodetection*. Autodetection is a powerful and handy feature that takes almost all of the work out of configuring hard drives.

PATA drives had priority according to the master/slave settings and such. You connected the drives and checked autodetect to see if you got it right and plugged/jumpered everything correctly. See Figure 9-24.

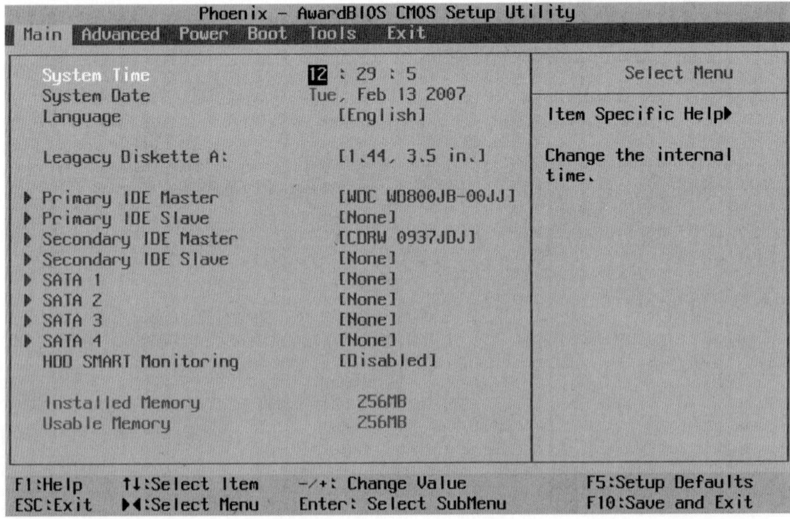

Figure 9-24 Old standard CMOS settings

SATA changed autodetection a little. Motherboards with SATA connectors use a numbering system—and every motherboard uses its own numbering system! One common numbering method uses the term *channel* for each controller. The first boot device is channel 1, the second is channel 2, and so on. So instead of names of drives, you see numbers. Take a look at Figure 9-25.

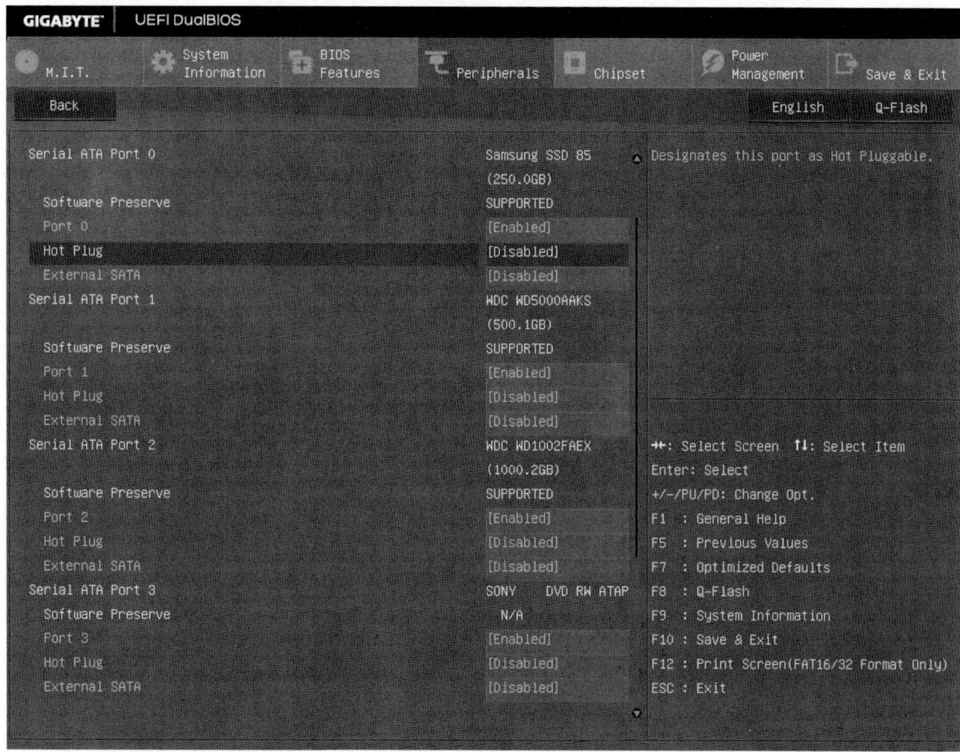

Figure 9-25 New standard CMOS features

Whew! Lots of hard drives! This motherboard supports six SATA connections. Each connection has a number, with an M.2 SSD on SATA 0, hard drives on SATA 1 and SATA 2, and the optical drive on SATA 3. Each was autodetected and configured by the BIOS without any input from me. Oh, to live in the future!

Boot Order

If you want your computer to run, it's going to need an operating system to boot. You assign *boot order* priority to drives and devices in CMOS.

Figure 9-26 shows a typical boot-order screen, with a first, second, and third boot option. Many users like to boot first from the optical drive and then from a hard drive. This enables them to put in a bootable optical disc if they're having problems with the system. Of course, you can set it to boot first from your hard drive and then go into CMOS and change it when you need to—it's your choice.

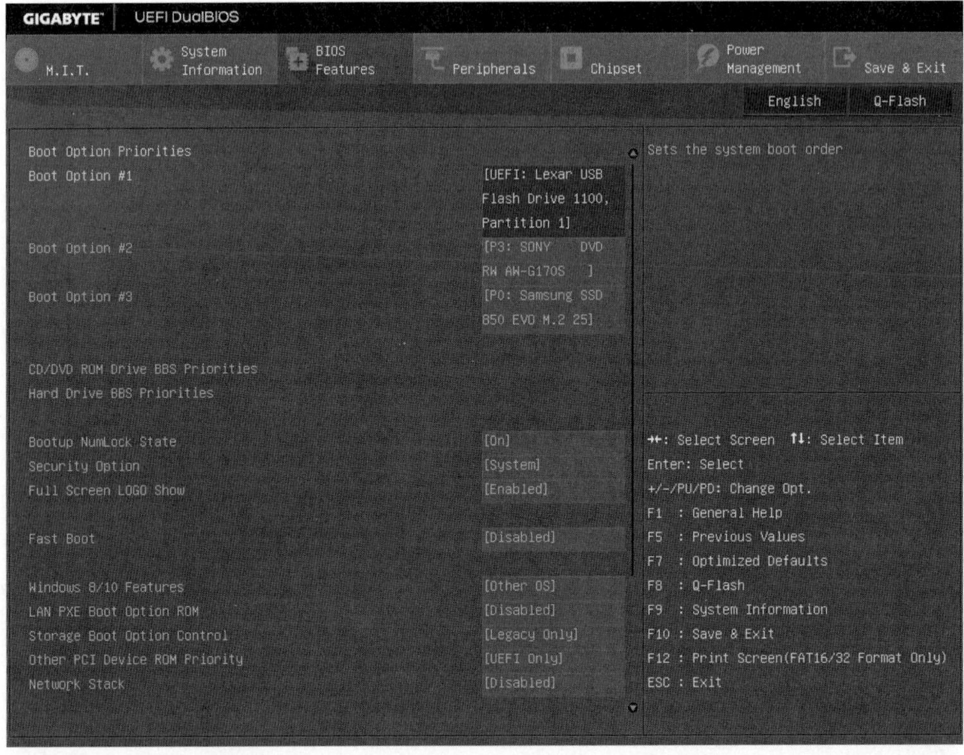

Figure 9-26 Boot order

Most modern CMOS setup utilities include a second screen for determining the boot order of your hard drives. You might want to set up a boot order that goes optical drive, followed by hard drive, and then USB thumb drive, but what if you have more than one hard drive? This screen enables you to set which hard drive goes first. If you have a different operating system on each hard drive, this can be very helpful.

Enabling AHCI

On motherboards that support AHCI, you implement it in CMOS. You'll generally have up to three options: IDE/SATA or compatibility mode, AHCI, or RAID. Use compatibility mode to install old operating systems, such as Windows XP. Going to AHCI or RAID enables the AHCI option for the HBA.

Troubleshooting Hard Drive Installation

The best friend a tech has when it comes to troubleshooting hard drive installation is the autodetection feature of the CMOS setup utility. When a drive doesn't work, the biggest question, especially during installation, is "Did I plug it in correctly? Or did

I plug both data and power in correctly?" With autodetection, the answer is simple: If the system doesn't see the drive, something is wrong with the hardware configuration. Either a device has physically failed or, more likely, you didn't give the hard drive power, plugged a cable in improperly, or messed up some other connectivity issue. To troubleshoot hard drives, simply work your way through each step to figure out what went wrong.

Make sure the BIOS recognizes your hard drive. Use the CMOS setup program to check. Check the physical connections, then run through these issues in CMOS. Is the controller enabled? Similarly, can the motherboard support the type of drive you're installing? If not, you have a couple of options. You may be able to flash the BIOS with an upgraded BIOS from the manufacturer or get a hard drive controller that goes into an expansion slot.

Chapter Review

Questions

1. Which of the following is a common spindle speed for an HDD?
   - A. 5200
   - B. 7200
   - C. 9200
   - D. Not applicable. HDDs have no moving parts.
2. Which form factor connects directly to a dedicated motherboard socket?
   - A. 2.5-inch SSD
   - B. 3.5-inch SSD
   - C. M.2 SSD
   - D. eSATA SSD
3. How many PATA hard drives can you have on a system with two PATA hard drive controllers?
   - A. 1
   - B. 2
   - C. 3
   - D. 4
4. How do you differentiate two PATA drives on the same cable?
   - A. The flat ribbon cable has a seven-wire twist that determines which is which.
   - B. You set jumpers on the individual drives to determine which is master and which is slave.
   - C. The PATA controller determines the hierarchy.
   - D. Both drives are considered equal.

5. What happens if you cable a PATA hard drive incorrectly?
   A. You can destroy that hard drive.
   B. The data will be erased, but the hard drive will be okay.
   C. The system will not be able to communicate with that hard drive.
   D. Nothing. It doesn't matter how the cable is set up; it doesn't have the seven-wire twist.
6. What is the maximum cable length of an internal SATA device?
   A. 2 meters
   B. 12 inches
   C. 18 inches
   D. 1 meter
7. What is the maximum number of SATA drives you can have on a system?
   A. One master, one slave
   B. Two, with no master/slave distinction
   C. Eight
   D. There is no maximum other than the limitations of your motherboard.
8. Which SATA version offers the least overhead (and thus best performance)?
   A. AHCI
   B. SATA 2.0
   C. PATA 3.0
   D. SATAe
9. Which standard supports magnetic SATA drives most efficiently?
   A. AHCI
   B. CMOS
   C. SATA-IO
   D. SATA 3.2
10. Which RAID standard requires at least four drives?
    A. RAID 1
    B. RAID 4
    C. RAID 5
    D. RAID 10

Answers

1. **B.** Common spindle speeds on magnetic hard drives are 5400, 7200, 10,000, and 15,000 RPM.
2. **C.** The M.2 (and mSATA) SSD has a dedicated motherboard socket.
3. **D.** Each controller supports two drives.
4. **B.** PATA drives use master/slave jumpers to differentiate between the two drives.
5. **C.** Nothing will be damaged or lost—there just won't be any communication.
6. **D.** The maximum cable length of an internal SATA device is 1 meter.
7. **D.** There is no maximum number of SATA drives you can have on a system beyond the limits imposed by the number of ports on your motherboard/host card.
8. **D.** SATA Express (SATAe) uses the PCIe bus and has none of the traditional SATA overhead.
9. **A.** The AHCI standard supports magnetic SATA drives efficiently.
10. **D.** RAID 10 requires at least four drives.

CHAPTER 10

Implementing Hard Drives

In this chapter, you will learn how to

- Explain the partitions available in Windows
- Discuss hard drive formatting options
- Partition and format hard drives
- Maintain and troubleshoot hard drives

From the standpoint of your PC, a freshly installed hard drive is nothing more than a huge pile of sectors. Sure, CMOS recognizes it as a drive—always a step in the right direction—but your operating system is clueless without more information. Your operating system must organize those sectors so you can use the drive to store data. This chapter covers that process.

NOTE This chapter uses the term "hard drive" as a generic term that covers all the drive types you learned about in Chapter 9, "Hard Drive Technologies." Once you get into Windows, the operating system doesn't particularly care if the drive is a magnetic hard disk drive (HDD), a flash-based solid-state drive (SSD), or some hybrid combination of the two. The tools and steps for preparing the drives for data are the same.

Historical/Conceptual

After you've successfully installed a hard drive, you must perform two more steps to translate a drive's geometry and circuits into something the system can use: partitioning and formatting. *Partitioning* is the process of electronically subdividing the physical hard drive into smaller units called *partitions*. A hard drive must have at least one partition, and you can create multiple partitions on a single hard drive if you wish. In Windows, each of these partitions typically is assigned a drive letter such as C: or D:. After partitioning, you must *format* the drive. Formatting installs a *file system* onto the drive that organizes each partition in such a way that the operating system can store files and folders

on the drive. Several types of file systems are used by Windows. This chapter will go through them after covering partitioning.

Partitioning and formatting a drive is one of the few areas remaining on the software side of PC assembly that requires you to perform a series of fairly complex manual steps. The CompTIA A+ 220-902 exam tests your knowledge of *what* these processes do to make the drive work, as well as the steps needed to partition and format hard drives in Windows.

This chapter continues the exploration of hard drive installation by explaining partitioning and formatting and then going through the process of partitioning and formatting hard drives. The chapter wraps with a discussion on hard drive maintenance and troubleshooting issues, the scope of which includes all the operating systems covered on the current exams.

Hard Drive Partitions

Partitions provide tremendous flexibility for hard drive organization. With partitions, you can organize a drive to suit your personal taste.

You can partition a hard drive to store more than one operating system: store one OS in one partition and create additional partitions for another OS. Granted, most people use only one OS, but if you want the option to boot to either Windows or Linux, partitions are the key.

902

Windows supports three different partitioning methods: the older master boot record (MBR) partitioning scheme, Windows' proprietary dynamic storage partitioning scheme, and the *GUID partition table (GPT)*. Microsoft calls a hard drive that uses either the MBR partitioning scheme or the GPT partitioning scheme a *basic disk* and calls a drive that uses the dynamic storage partitioning scheme a *dynamic disk*. A single Windows system with three hard drives may have one of the drives partitioned with MBR, another with GPT, and the third set up as a dynamic disk, and the system will run perfectly well. The bottom line? You get to learn about three totally different types of partitioning. I'll also cover a few other partition types, such as hidden partitions, and tell you when you can and should make your partitions.

NOTE Okay, if GPT stands for GUID Partition Table, I guess we had better see what GUID stands for, eh? GUID is the Global Unique Identifier and is a technology that we'll look at a little further on in the chapter.

Master Boot Record

The first sector of an MBR hard drive contains the *master boot record (MBR)*. To clarify, hard drives that use the MBR partitioning scheme have a tiny bit of data that is also called the "master boot record." While your computer boots up, BIOS looks at the first

sector of your hard drive for instructions. At this point, it doesn't matter which OS you use or how many partitions you have. Without this bit of code, your OS will never load.

NOTE Techs often refer to MBR-partitioned drives as "MBR drives." The same holds true for GPT-partitioned drives, which many techs refer to as "GPT drives."

The master boot record also contains the *partition table*, which describes the number and size of partitions on the disk (see Figure 10-1). MBR partition tables support up to four partitions—the partition table is large enough to store entries for only four partitions. The instructions in the master boot record use this table to determine which partition contains the active operating system.

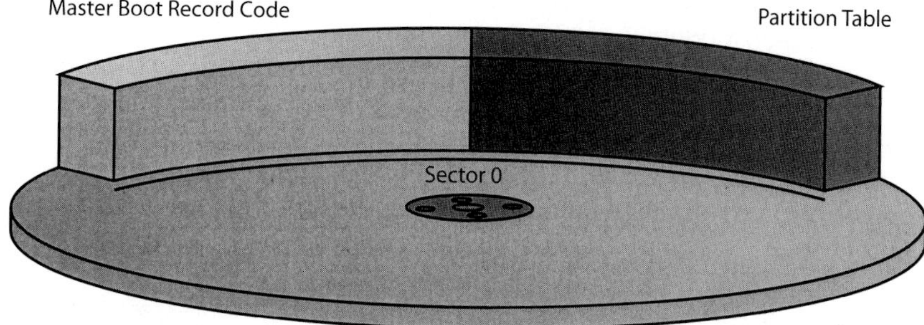

Figure 10-1 The master boot record

After the MBR locates the appropriate partition, the *partition boot sector* loads the OS on that partition. The partition boot sector stores information important to its partition, such as the location of the OS boot files (see Figure 10-2).

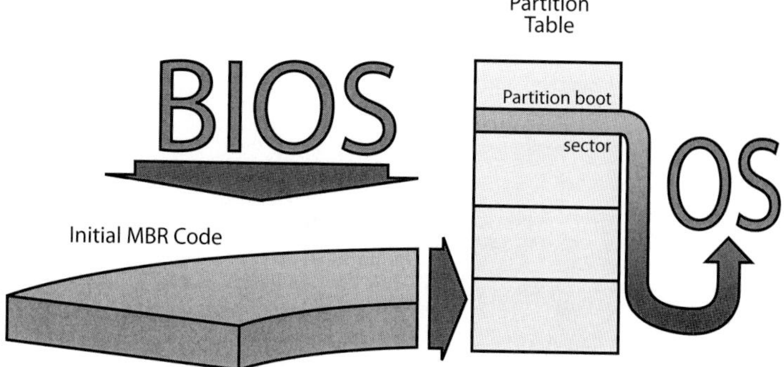

Figure 10-2 Using the master boot record to boot an OS

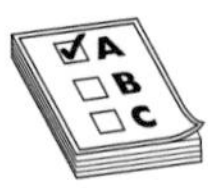

EXAM TIP Only one master boot record and one partition table within that master boot record exist per MBR disk. Each partition has a partition boot sector.

MBR partition tables support two types of partitions: primary partitions and extended partitions. *Primary partitions* are designed to support bootable operating systems. *Extended partitions* are not bootable. A single MBR disk may have up to four primary partitions or up to three primary partitions and one extended partition.

Primary Partitions and Multiple Operating Systems

Primary partitions are usually assigned drive letters and appear in Windows Explorer/File Explorer (once you format them). The first lettered primary partition in Windows is always C:. After that, you can label the partitions D: through Z:.

NOTE Partitions don't always get drive letters. Windows creates a small 100 MB primary partition named "System Reserved" for essential Windows boot files. See also the section "Mounting Partitions as Folders," later in this chapter, for details.

On a related topic, the first primary Windows partition is called "C:" because early PCs had one or two floppy drives installed and they got the "A:" and "B:" labels.

Only primary partitions can boot operating systems. On an MBR disk, you can easily install four different operating systems, each on its own primary partition, and boot to your choice each time you fire up the computer.

Every primary partition on a single drive has a special setting stored in the partition table called *active* that determines the *active partition*. During boot-up, the BIOS/POST reads the MBR to find the active partition and boots the operating system on that partition. Only one partition can be active at a time because you can run only one OS at a time (see Figure 10-3).

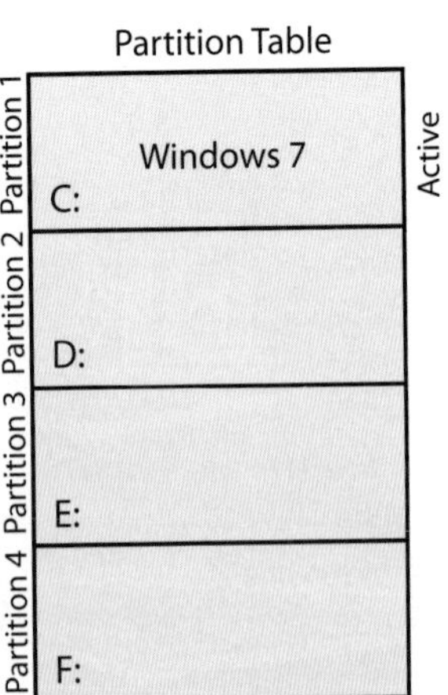

Figure 10-3 The active partition containing Windows

To control multiboot setups, many people use a free Linux-based boot manager called Grand Unified Bootloader (GRUB), shown in Figure 10-4, although some people prefer Partition Commander by Avanquest Software to set up the partitions. When the computer boots, the boot manager software yanks control from the MBR and asks which OS you want to boot. Once a partition is set as active, the partition boot sector loads the operating system.

```
GNU GRUB  version 1.99-18ubuntu1

Ubuntu, with Linux 3.2.0-20-generic-pae
Ubuntu, with Linux 3.2.0-20-generic-pae (recovery mode)
Memory test (memtest86+)
Memory test (memtest86+, serial console 115200)
Windows 7 (loader) (on /dev/sda1)

Use the ↑ and ↓ keys to select which entry is highlighted.
Press enter to boot the selected OS, 'e' to edit the commands
before booting or 'c' for a command-line.
```

Figure 10-4 GRUB in action

Extended Partitions

With a four-partition limit, an MBR disk would be limited to only four drive letters if using only primary partitions. An extended partition overcomes this limit. An extended partition can contain multiple *logical drives*, each of which can get a drive letter (see Figure 10-5).

A logical drive works like a primary partition—it usually gets a drive letter such as D: or E:—but you can't boot an OS from it. You format it just like you would a primary partition. The only difference is that each logical drive is actually in the same extended partition.

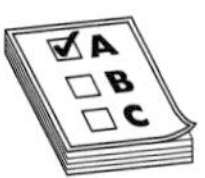

EXAM TIP Extended partitions do not receive drive letters, but the logical drives within an extended partition do.

Figure 10-5 An extended partition containing multiple logical drives

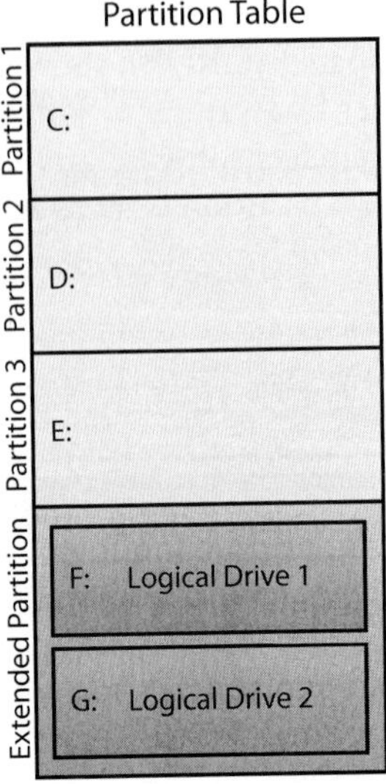

Dynamic Disks

With the introduction of Windows 2000, Microsoft defined a type of partitioning called *dynamic storage partitioning*, better known as *dynamic disks*. Microsoft calls a drive structure created with a dynamic disk a *volume*. There is no dynamic disk equivalent to primary versus extended partitions. A dynamic disk volume is still technically a partition, but it can do things a regular partition cannot do.

NOTE The terms "volume" and "partition" refer to the same thing: a defined chunk of your hard drive.

First off, when you turn a hard drive into a dynamic disk, you can create as many volumes on it as you want. You're not limited to four partitions.

Second, you can create—in software—new drive structures that you can't do with MBR drives. Specifically, you can implement RAID, span volumes over multiple drives, and extend volumes on one or more drives. Table 10-1 shows you which version of Windows supports which volume type.

Volume	Windows Vista Business/ Ultimate/Enterprise	Windows 7 Professional/ Ultimate/Enterprise	Windows 8/8.1/10	Windows Server
Simple	X	X	X	X
Spanned	X	X	X	X
Striped	X	X	X	X
Mirrored		X	X	X
RAID 5				X

Table 10-1 Dynamic Disk Compatibility

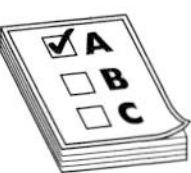

EXAM TIP Only the lower-end editions of Windows Vista and Windows 7 don't support dynamic disks. Almost every version and edition you'll run into these days supports dynamic disks.

Simple volumes work a lot like primary partitions. If you have a hard drive and you want to make half of it E: and the other half F:, for example, you create two volumes on a dynamic disk. That's it.

Spanned volumes use unallocated space on multiple drives to create a single volume. Spanned volumes are a bit risky: if any of the spanned drives fails, the entire volume is lost.

Striped volumes are RAID 0 volumes. You may take any two unallocated spaces on two separate hard drives and stripe them. But again, if either drive fails, you lose all of your data.

Mirrored volumes are RAID 1 volumes. You may take any two unallocated spaces on two separate hard drives and mirror them. If one of the two mirrored drives fails, the other keeps running.

RAID 5 volumes, as the name implies, are for RAID 5 arrays. A RAID 5 volume requires three or more dynamic disks with equal-sized unallocated spaces.

NOTE Windows 8 and later can use a software RAID system called Storage Spaces that's distinct from dynamic disks. See the appropriately named section of this chapter for the scoop.

GUID Partition Table

MBR partitioning came out a long time ago, in an age where 32-MB hard drives were thought to be larger than you would ever need. While it's lasted a long time as the partitioning standard for bootable drives, there's a newer kid in town with the power to outshine the aging partitioning scheme and assume all the functions of the older partition style.

The *globally unique identifier partition table (GPT)* partitioning scheme shares a lot with the MBR partitioning scheme, but most of the MBR scheme's limitations have been fixed. Here are the big improvements:

- While MBR drives are limited to four partitions, a GPT drive can have an almost unlimited number of primary partitions. Microsoft has limited Windows to 128 partitions.
- MBR partitions can be no larger than 2.2 TB, but GPT partitions have no such restrictions. Well, there is a maximum size limit, but it's so large, we measure it in zettabytes. A zettabyte, by the way, is a million terabytes.

On paper, a GPT drive looks a lot like an MBR drive, except it's arranged by LBA instead of sectors (see Figure 10-6). LBA 0, for instance, is the *protective MBR*. This is a

re-creation of the master boot record from MBR drives so disk utilities know it is a GPT drive and don't mistakenly overwrite any partition data.

Instead of the old master boot record and partition table, GPT drives use a GPT header and partition entry array. Both are located at the beginning and end of the drive so there is a protected backup copy. The partitions on a GPT drive go between the primary and backup headers and arrays, as shown in Figure 10-6.

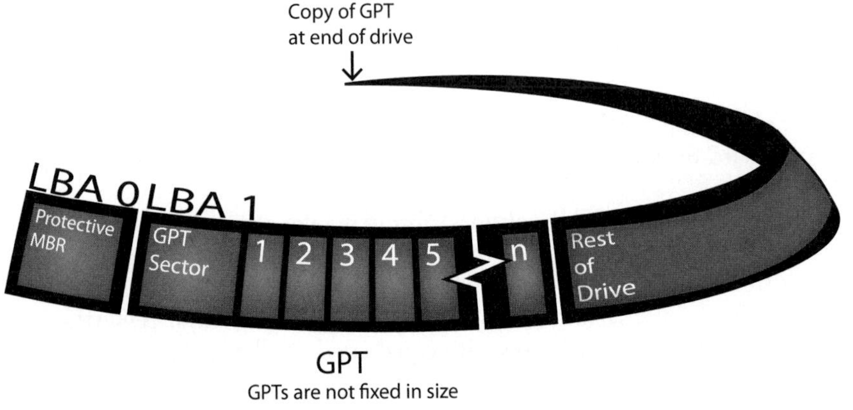

Figure 10-6 GUID partition table

You can configure the 64-bit versions of modern Windows to boot from GPT only if you use a UEFI motherboard. In other words, if you're trying to install Windows 10 on an ancient motherboard, you're stuck with MBR. The same is true of Mac OS X. Most Linux distributions can boot from GPT partitions with older BIOS or UEFI firmware.

Other Partition Types

The partition types supported by Windows are not the only partition types you may encounter; other types exist. One of the most common is called the *hidden partition*. A hidden partition is really just a primary partition that is hidden from your operating system. Only special BIOS tools may access a hidden partition. Hidden partitions are used by some PC makers to hide a backup copy of an installed OS that you can use to restore your system if you accidentally trash it—by, for example, using a partitioning program incorrectly while learning about partitions.

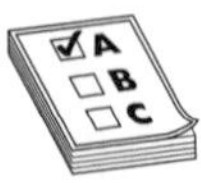

EXAM TIP CompTIA refers to a hidden partition that contains a restorable copy of an installed OS as a *factory recovery partition*.

A *swap partition* is another special type of partition, but swap partitions are found only on Linux and UNIX systems. A swap partition's only job is to act like RAM when your system needs more RAM than you have installed. Windows has a similar function with a *page file* that uses a special file instead of a partition, as you'll recall from Chapter 5, "RAM."

When to Partition

Partitioning is not a common task. The two most common situations likely to require partitioning are when you install an OS on a new system, and when you add an additional drive to an existing system. When you install a new OS, the installation program asks you how you would like to partition the drive. When you add a new hard drive to an existing system, every OS has a built-in tool to help you partition it.

Each version of Windows offers a different tool for partitioning hard drives. For more than 20 years, through the days of DOS and early Windows (up to Windows Me), we used a command-line program called *FDISK* to partition drives. Figure 10-7 shows the FDISK program. Modern versions of Windows use a graphical partitioning program called *Disk Management*, shown in Figure 10-8. You'll find it under Computer Management in Administrative Tools.

Figure 10-7 FDISK

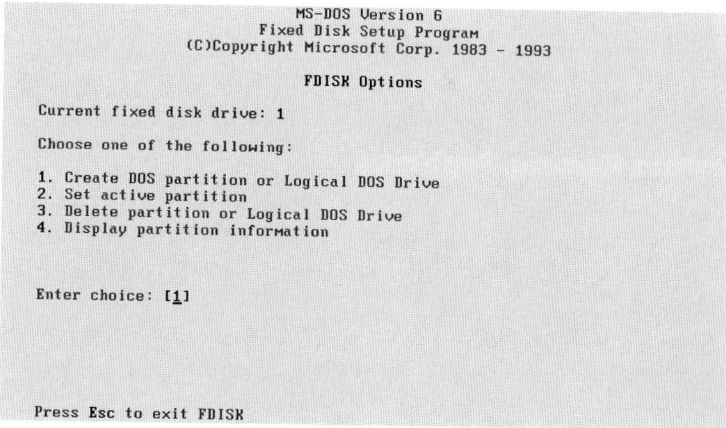

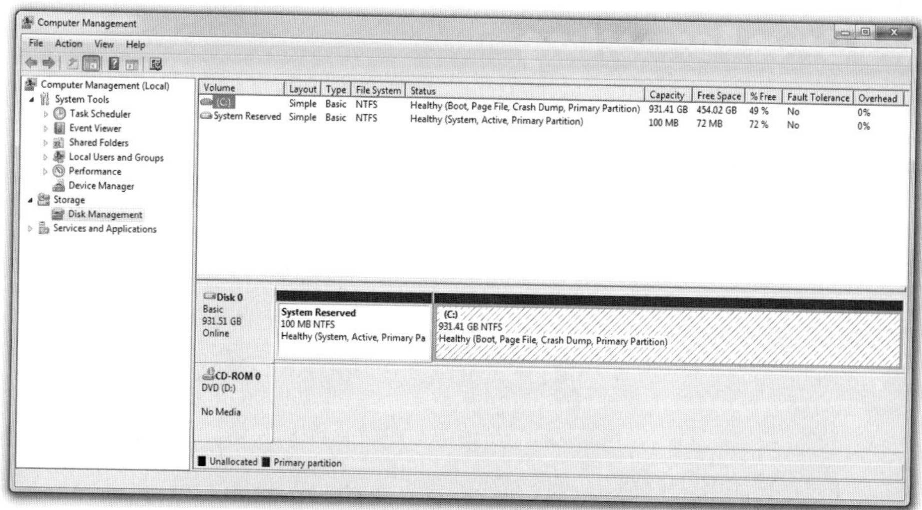

Figure 10-8 Windows 7 Disk Management tool in Computer Management

Linux uses a number of different tools for partitioning. The oldest is called FDISK—yes, the same name as the DOS/Windows version. That's where the similarities end, however, as Linux FDISK has a totally different command set. Even though every copy of Linux comes with the Linux FDISK, it's rarely used because so many better partitioning tools are available. One of the newer Linux partitioning tools is called GParted. See the "Beyond A+" section for more discussion on third-party partitioning tools.

In the early days of PCs, you couldn't change a partition's size or type (other than by erasing it) once you'd made it with any Microsoft tools. A few third-party tools, led by PartitionMagic, gave techs the understanding to resize partitions without losing the data the partitions held.

Current Microsoft tools have more. In Windows Vista and later, you can nondestructively resize partitions by shrinking or expanding existing partitions with available free space.

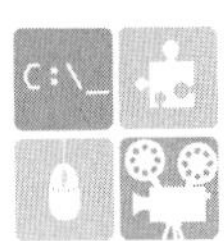

SIM Check out the excellent Chapter 10 Show! and Click! simulations "Resizing a Partition" at the Total Seminars Training Hub: http://totalsem.com/90x. These give you a quick shot at addressing probable simulation questions on the 902 exam.

Partition Naming Problems

So far, you've learned that MBR and GPT disks use partitions and dynamic disks use volumes. Unfortunately, when you create a new partition or volume in current versions of Windows, the tool (Disk Management) only shows that you're about to create a volume. See Figure 10-9.

Even though the context menu says "volumes," you create partitions on basic disks. Figure 10-10 shows Disk Management in Windows 8.1 inspecting a basic disk with four partitions. The first three (from left to right) are primary partitions. The two structures on the right are a logical drive and some blank, unpartitioned "Free space" in an extended partition. It's hard to see the extended partition; it's a color-coded border.

Hard Drive Formatting

Once you've partitioned a hard drive, you must perform one more step before your OS can use that drive: formatting. *Formatting* does two things: it creates a file system—like a library's card catalog—and makes the root directory in that file system. You must format every partition and volume you create so it can hold data that you can easily retrieve. The various versions of Windows you're likely to encounter today can use several different file systems, so we'll look at those in detail next. The *root directory* provides the foundation upon which the OS builds files and folders.

NOTE If you've ever been to a library and walked past all of the computers connected to the Internet, down the stairs into a dark basement, you might have seen a dusty old cabinet full of organized cards that have information about every book in the library. This is a "card catalog" system, invented over 2000 years ago. That concept has been carried forward and implemented electronically as the basis for file systems in many partitions and volumes. These days, you probably won't encounter this phrase anywhere outside of explanations for formatting.

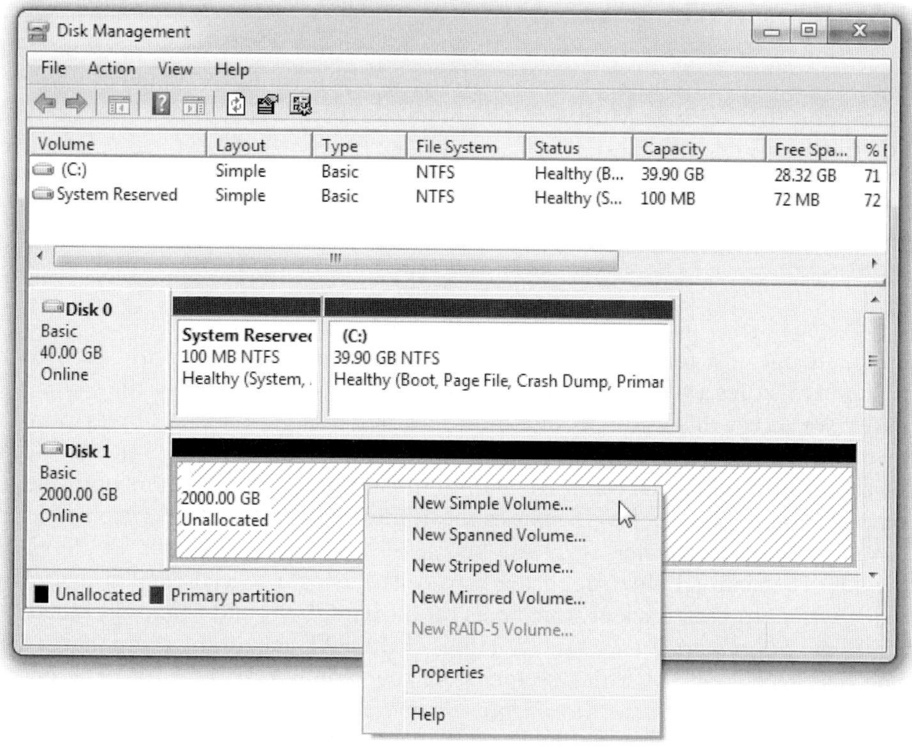

Figure 10-9 Note that the context menu only mentions volumes, not partitions.

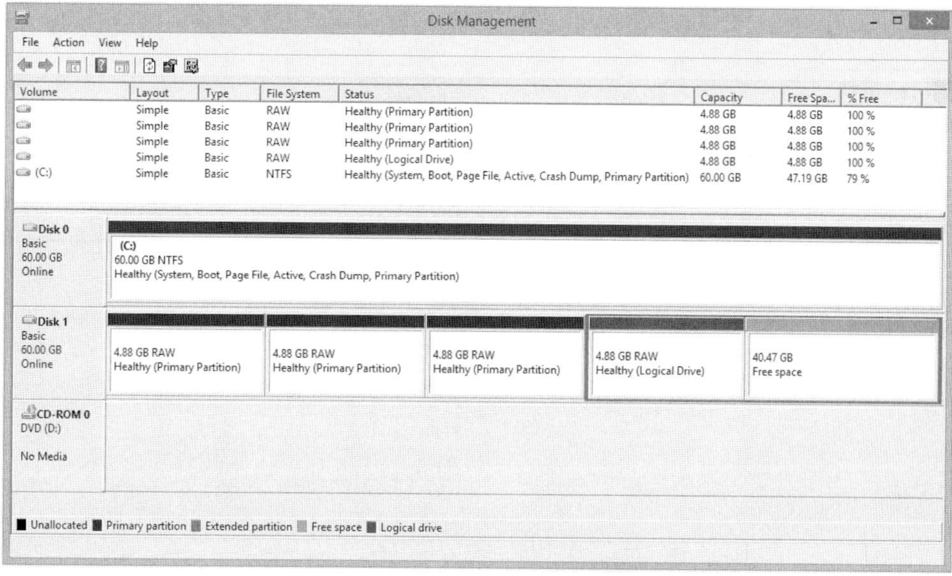

Figure 10-10 Drive with four partitions displayed in Disk Management

File Systems in Windows

Every version of Windows comes with a built-in formatting utility with which to create one or more file systems on a partition or volume. The versions of Windows currently in use support four separate Microsoft file systems: FAT16, FAT32, NTFS, and exFAT/FAT64 (for removable media).

The simplest hard drive file system, called FAT or FAT16, provides a good introduction to how file systems work. More complex file systems fix many of the problems inherent in FAT and add extra features as well.

FAT

The base storage area for hard drives is a sector; each sector stores up to 512 bytes of data. If an OS stores a file smaller than 512 bytes in a sector, the rest of the sector goes to waste. We accept this waste because most files are far larger than 512 bytes. So what happens when an OS stores a file larger than 512 bytes? The OS needs a method to fill one sector, find another that's unused, and fill it, continuing to fill sectors until the file is completely stored. Once the OS stores a file, it must remember which sectors hold the file, so it can be retrieved later.

MS-DOS version 2.1 first supported hard drives using a special data structure and indexing system to keep track of stored data on the hard drive, and Microsoft called this structure the *file allocation table (FAT)*. Think of the FAT as nothing more than a card catalog that keeps track of which sectors store the various parts of a file. The official jargon term for a FAT is *data structure*, but it is more like a two-column spreadsheet.

The left column (see Figure 10-11) gives each sector a hexadecimal number from 0000 to FFFF. Each hexadecimal character represents four binary numbers or 4 bits. Four hex characters, therefore, represent 16 bits. If you do the math (2^{16}), you'll find that there are 65,536 (64 K) sectors that can be tracked, or indexed.

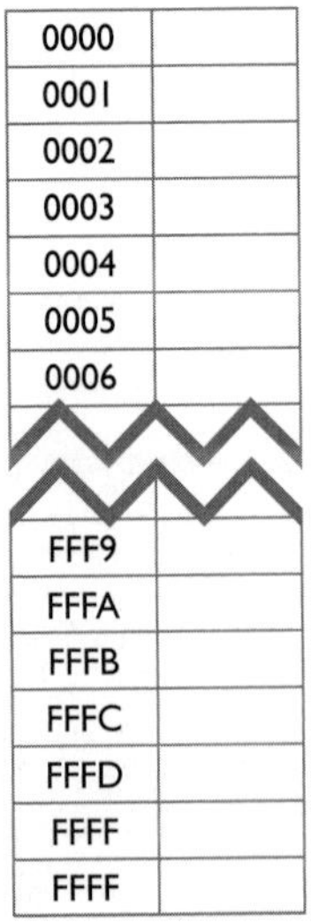

Figure 10-11 16-bit FAT

0000	
0001	
0002	
0003	
0004	
0005	
0006	
FFF9	
FFFA	
FFFB	
FFFC	
FFFD	
FFFF	
FFFF	

NOTE Hexadecimal characters cover the decimal numbers 0–15; and number 0–9, A–F; each character reflects the state of four binary characters. You add them up to make the number. So, 0000 in binary shows zero numbers and the hex number is 0. When you go up numerically in binary to 0001, this represents the number 1 in decimal and also in hex. The key to hex is when you reach the number 10. In binary, this looks like this: 1010. But because hex sticks with a single digit, it's represented as A. B translates as 11 in decimal or 1011 in binary, and so on.

We call this type of FAT a *16-bit FAT* or *FAT16*. And it's not just hard drives that have FATs. Many USB flash drives use FAT16. Floppy disks used FATs, but their FATs were only 12 bits because they stored much less data.

The right column of the FAT contains information on the status of sectors. All hard drives, even brand-new drives fresh from the factory, contain faulty sectors that cannot store data because of imperfections in the construction of the drives. The OS must locate these bad sectors, mark them as unusable, and then prevent any files from being written to them. This mapping of bad sectors is one of the functions of *high-level formatting*. After the format program creates the FAT, it marches through every sector of the entire partition, writing and attempting to read from each sector sequentially. If it finds a bad sector, it places a special status code (FFF7) in the sector's FAT location, indicating that the sector is unavailable for use. Formatting also marks the good sectors with code 0000.

NOTE There is such a thing as "low-level formatting," but that's generally done at the factory and doesn't concern techs. This is especially true if you're working with modern hard drives (post-2001). *High-level formatting*, as noted, creates the FAT and then creates a blank root directory. This process is known in Microsoft speak as a *quick format*. At your option, you can cause the format utility to test every sector to mark out the unusable ones in the FAT. This is called a *full format*.

Using the FAT to track sectors, however, creates a problem. The 16-bit FAT addresses a maximum of 64 K (2^{16}) locations. Therefore, the size of a hard drive partition should be limited to 64 K × 512 bytes per sector, or 32 MB. When Microsoft first unveiled FAT16, this 32-MB limit presented no problem because most hard drives were only 5 to 10 MB. As hard drives grew in size, you could use FDISK to break them up into multiple partitions. You could divide a 40-MB hard drive into two partitions, for example, making each partition smaller than 32 MB. But as hard drives started to become much larger, Microsoft realized that the 32-MB limit for drives was unacceptable. We needed an improvement to the 16-bit FAT, a new and improved FAT16 that would support larger drives while still maintaining backward compatibility with the old-style 16-bit FAT. This need led to the development of a dramatic improvement in FAT16, called *clustering*, that enabled us to format partitions larger than 32 MB (see Figure 10-12). This new FAT16 appeared way back in the DOS-4 days.

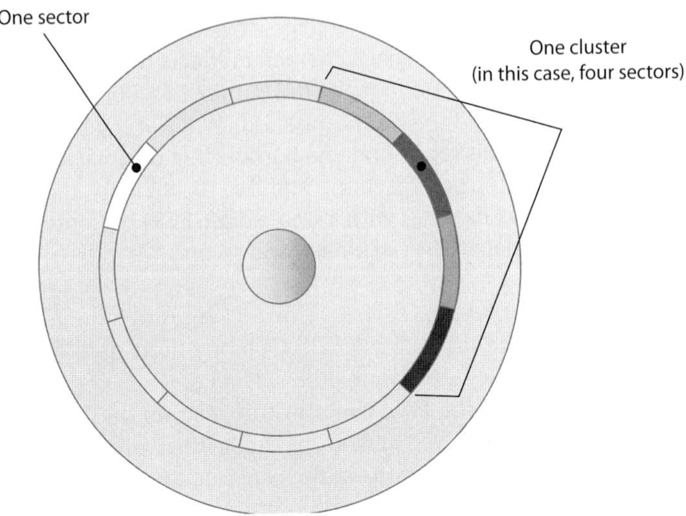

Figure 10-12 Cluster versus sector

Clustering simply refers to combining a set of contiguous sectors and treating them as a single unit in the FAT. These units are called *file allocation units* or *clusters*. Each row of the FAT then addressed a cluster instead of a sector. Unlike sectors, the size of a cluster is not fixed. Clusters improved FAT16, but it still only supported a maximum of 64 K storage units, so the formatting program set the number of sectors in each cluster according to the size of the partition. The larger the partition, the more sectors per cluster. This method kept clustering completely compatible with the 64 K locations in the old 16-bit FAT. The new FAT16 could support partitions up to 2 GB. (The old 16-bit FAT is so old it doesn't really even have a name—if someone says "FAT16," they mean the newer FAT16 that supports clustering.) Table 10-2 shows the number of sectors per cluster for FAT16.

If FDISK makes a partition this big:	You'll get this many sectors/cluster:
16 to 127.9 MB	4
128 to 255.9 MB	8
256 to 511.9 MB	16
512 to 1023.9 MB	32
1024 to 2048 MB	64

Table 10-2 FAT16 Cluster Sizes

FAT16 in Action

Assume you have a copy of Windows using FAT16. When an application such as Microsoft Word tells the OS to save a file, Windows starts at the beginning of the FAT, looking for the first space marked "open for use" (0000), and begins to write to that cluster. If the

entire file fits within that one cluster, Windows places the code *FFFF* (last cluster) into the cluster's status area in the FAT. That's called the *end-of-file marker*. Windows then goes to the folder storing the file and adds the filename and the cluster's number to the folder list. If the file requires more than one cluster, Windows searches for the next open cluster and places the number of the next cluster in the status area, filling and adding clusters until the entire file is saved. The last cluster then receives the end-of-file marker (FFFF).

Let's run through an example of this process, and start by selecting an arbitrary part of the FAT: from 3ABB to 3AC7. Suppose you want to save a file called mom.txt. Before saving the file, the FAT looks like Figure 10-13.

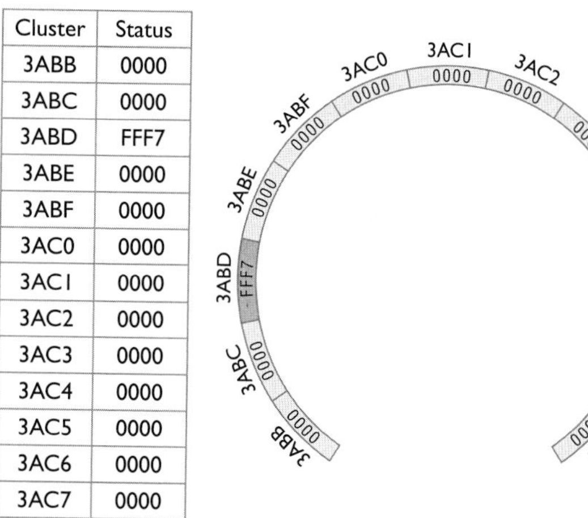

Cluster	Status
3ABB	0000
3ABC	0000
3ABD	FFF7
3ABE	0000
3ABF	0000
3AC0	0000
3AC1	0000
3AC2	0000
3AC3	0000
3AC4	0000
3AC5	0000
3AC6	0000
3AC7	0000

Figure 10-13
The initial FAT

Windows finds the first open cluster, 3ABB, and fills it. But the entire mom.txt file won't fit into that cluster. Needing more space, the OS goes through the FAT to find the next open cluster. It finds cluster 3ABC. Before filling 3ABC, the value *3ABC* is placed in 3ABB's status (see Figure 10-14).

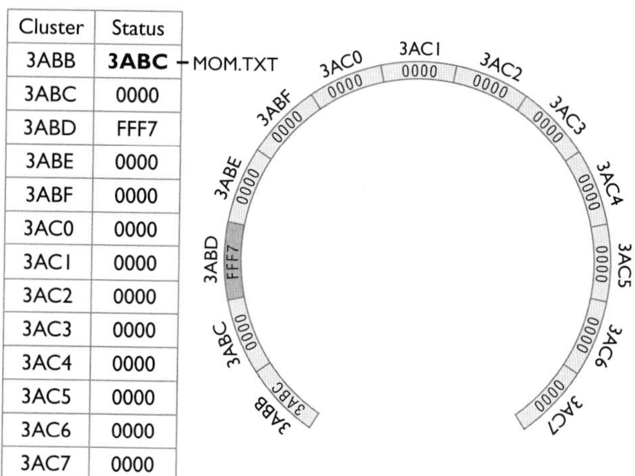

Cluster	Status
3ABB	**3ABC**
3ABC	0000
3ABD	FFF7
3ABE	0000
3ABF	0000
3AC0	0000
3AC1	0000
3AC2	0000
3AC3	0000
3AC4	0000
3AC5	0000
3AC6	0000
3AC7	0000

Figure 10-14
The first cluster used

Even after filling two clusters, more of the mom.txt file remains, so Windows must find one more cluster. The 3ABD cluster has been marked FFF7 (bad cluster or *bad-sector marker*), so Windows skips over 3ABD, finding 3ABE (see Figure 10-15).

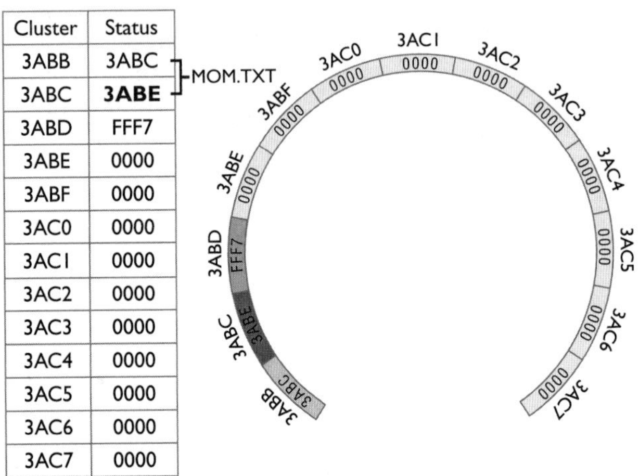

Cluster	Status
3ABB	3ABC
3ABC	**3ABE**
3ABD	FFF7
3ABE	0000
3ABF	0000
3AC0	0000
3AC1	0000
3AC2	0000
3AC3	0000
3AC4	0000
3AC5	0000
3AC6	0000
3AC7	0000

Figure 10-15 The second cluster used

Before filling 3ABE, Windows enters the value *3ABE* in 3ABC's status. Windows does not completely fill 3ABE, signifying that the entire mom.txt file has been stored. Windows enters the value *FFFF* in 3ABE's status, indicating the end of file (see Figure 10-16).

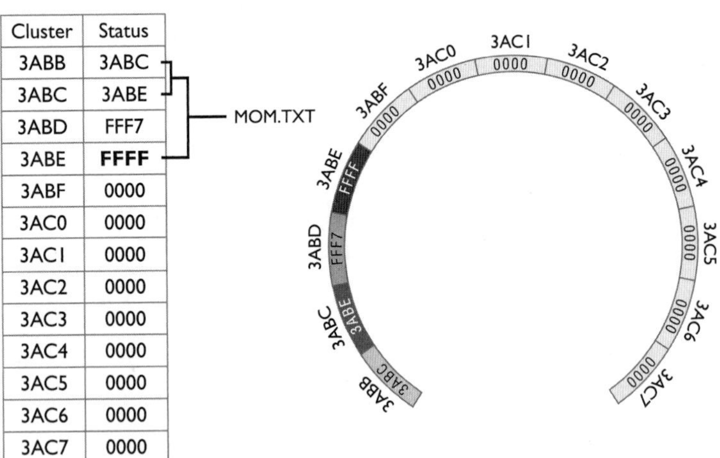

Cluster	Status
3ABB	3ABC
3ABC	3ABE
3ABD	FFF7
3ABE	**FFFF**
3ABF	0000
3AC0	0000
3AC1	0000
3AC2	0000
3AC3	0000
3AC4	0000
3AC5	0000
3AC6	0000
3AC7	0000

Figure 10-16 End of file reached

After saving all of the clusters, Windows locates the file's folder (yes, folders also are stored on clusters, but they get a different set of clusters, somewhere else on the disk) and records the filename, size, date/time, and starting cluster, like this:

mom.txt 19234 05-19-09 2:04p 3ABB

If a program requests that file, the process is reversed. Windows locates the folder containing the file to determine the starting cluster and then pulls a piece of the file from each cluster until it sees the end-of-file cluster. Windows then hands the reassembled file to the requesting application.

Clearly, without the FAT, Windows cannot locate files. FAT16 automatically makes two copies of the FAT. One FAT backs up the other to provide special utilities a way to recover a FAT that gets corrupted—a painfully common occurrence.

Even when FAT works perfectly, parts of any file can get written to separate places on the disk in a process called *fragmentation.*

Fragmentation

Continuing with the example, let's use Microsoft Word to save two more files: a letter to the IRS (irsrob.doc) and a letter to IBM (ibmhelp.doc). The irsrob.doc file takes the next three clusters—3ABF, 3AC0, and 3AC1—and ibmhelp.doc takes two clusters—3AC2 and 3AC3 (see Figure 10-17).

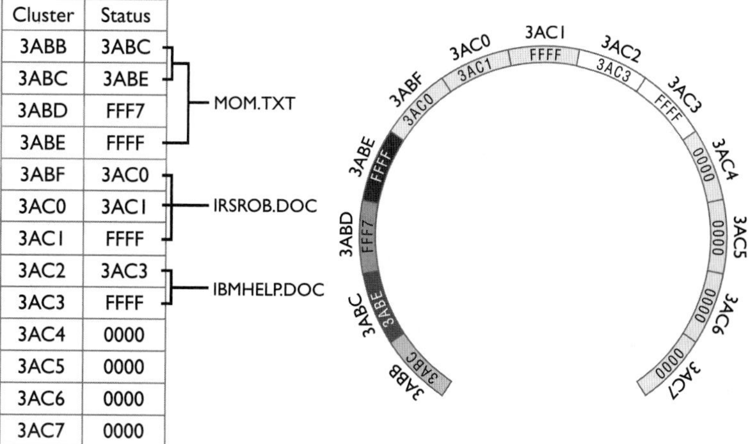

Cluster	Status
3ABB	3ABC
3ABC	3ABE
3ABD	FFF7
3ABE	FFFF
3ABF	3AC0
3AC0	3AC1
3AC1	FFFF
3AC2	3AC3
3AC3	FFFF
3AC4	0000
3AC5	0000
3AC6	0000
3AC7	0000

Figure 10-17 Three files saved

Now suppose you erase mom.txt. Windows does not delete the cluster entries for mom.txt when it erases a file. Windows only alters the information in the folder, simply changing the first letter of mom.txt to the Greek letter Σ (sigma). This causes the file to "disappear" as far as the OS knows. It won't show up, for example, in Windows Explorer, even though the data still resides on the hard drive for the moment (see Figure 10-18).

Note that under normal circumstances, Windows does not actually delete files when you press the DELETE key. Instead, Windows moves the files to a special hidden directory that you can access via the Recycle Bin. The files themselves are not actually deleted until you empty the Recycle Bin. (You can skip the Recycle Bin entirely if you wish, by highlighting a file and then holding down the SHIFT key when you press DELETE).

Because all of the data for mom.txt is intact, you could use some program to change the Σ back into another letter and thus get the document back. A number of third-party

Figure 10-18 The mom.txt file erased

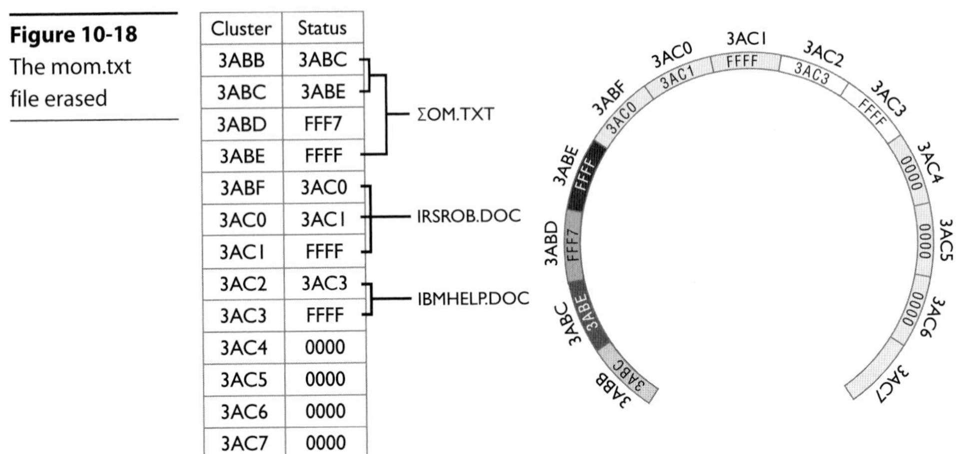

Cluster	Status
3ABB	3ABC
3ABC	3ABE
3ABD	FFF7
3ABE	FFFF
3ABF	3AC0
3AC0	3AC1
3AC1	FFFF
3AC2	3AC3
3AC3	FFFF
3AC4	0000
3AC5	0000
3AC6	0000
3AC7	0000

undelete tools are available. Figure 10-19 shows one such program at work. Just remember that if you want to use an undelete tool, you must use it quickly. The space allocated to your deleted file may soon be overwritten by a new file.

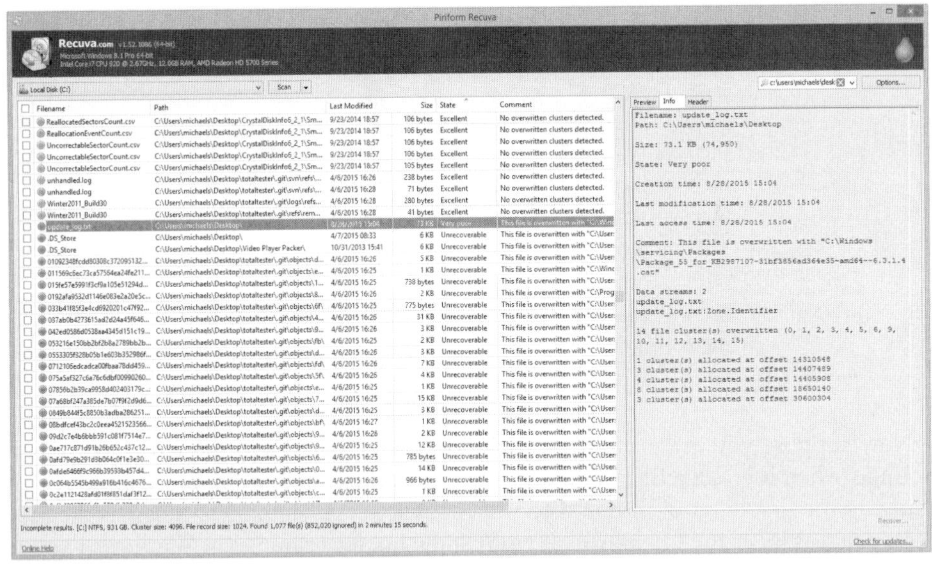

Figure 10-19 Piriform Recuva in action

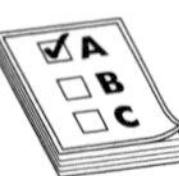

EXAM TIP CompTIA may ask you how to recover a deleted file. If the file is still in the Recycle Bin, simply browse to the Recycle Bin, right-click on the deleted file, and select Restore. If the file was deleted and bypassed the Recycle Bin or for any other reason is no longer there, Microsoft offers no utility that can recover or restore the file. You must resort to one of the third-party utilities that are available.

Let's say you just emptied your Recycle Bin. You now save one more file, taxrec.xls, a big spreadsheet that will take six clusters, into the same folder that once held mom.txt. As Windows writes the file to the drive, it overwrites the space that mom.txt used, but it needs three more clusters. The next three available clusters are 3AC4, 3AC5, and 3AC6 (see Figure 10-20).

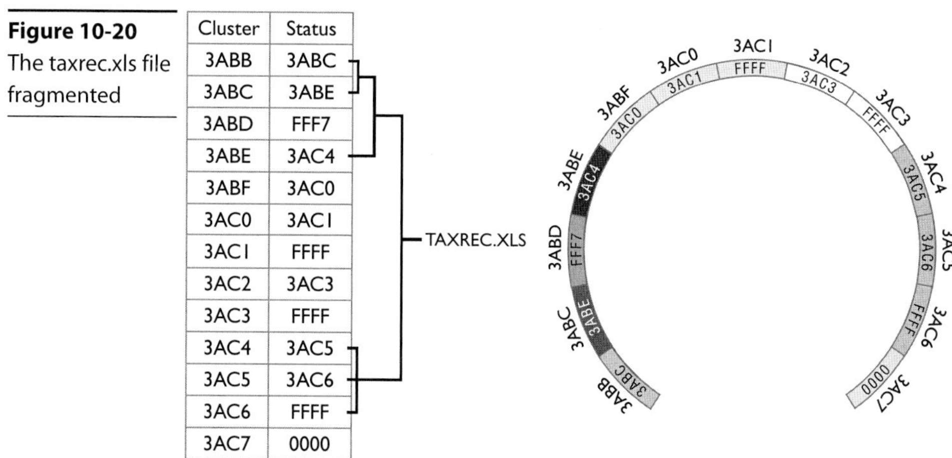

Cluster	Status
3ABB	3ABC
3ABC	3ABE
3ABD	FFF7
3ABE	3AC4
3ABF	3AC0
3AC0	3AC1
3AC1	FFFF
3AC2	3AC3
3AC3	FFFF
3AC4	3AC5
3AC5	3AC6
3AC6	FFFF
3AC7	0000

Figure 10-20 The taxrec.xls file fragmented

Notice that taxrec.xls is in two pieces, thus *fragmented*. Fragmentation takes place all of the time on FAT16 systems. Although the system easily negotiates a tiny fragmented file split into only two parts, excess fragmentation slows down the system during hard drive reads and writes. This example is fragmented into two pieces; in the real world, a file might fragment into hundreds of pieces, forcing the read/write heads to travel all over the hard drive to retrieve a single file. You can dramatically improve the speed at which the hard drive reads and writes files by eliminating this fragmentation.

Windows comes with a program called Disk Defragmenter (Windows Vista/7) and Optimize Drives (Windows 8/8.1/10) that can rearrange the files into neat contiguous chunks (see Figure 10-21). Defragmentation is crucial for ensuring the top performance of a mechanical hard drive. The "Maintaining and Troubleshooting Hard Drives" section of this chapter gives the details on working with the various Disk Defragmenters in Windows.

FAT32

When Microsoft introduced Windows 95 OSR2 (OEM Service Release 2), it also unveiled a file format called *FAT32* that brought a couple of dramatic improvements. First, FAT32 supports partitions up to 2 TB (more than 2 trillion bytes). Second, as its name implies, FAT32 uses 32 bits to describe each cluster, which means clusters can drop to more reasonable sizes. FAT32's use of so many FAT entries gives it the power to use small clusters, making the old "keep your partitions small" rule obsolete. A 2-GB partition using FAT16 would use 32-KB clusters, while the same 2-GB partition

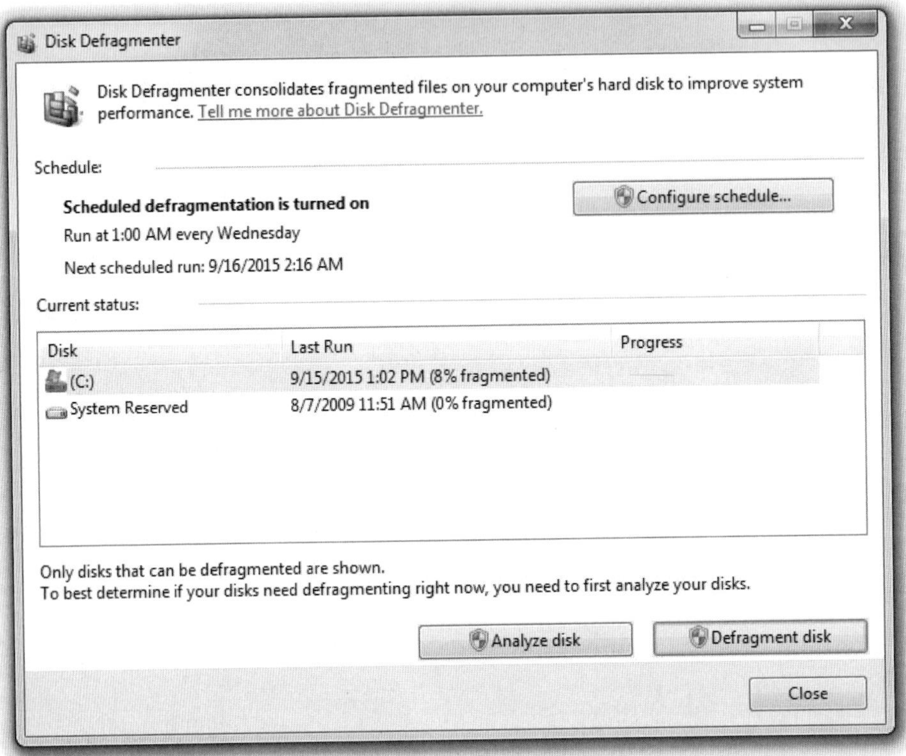

Figure 10-21 Windows 7 Disk Defragmenter

using FAT32 would use 4-KB clusters. You get far more efficient use of disk space with FAT32, without the need to make multiple small partitions. FAT32 partitions still need defragmentation, however, just as often as FAT16 partitions.

Table 10-3 shows cluster sizes for FAT32 partitions.

Table 10-3 FAT32 Cluster Sizes

Drive Size	Cluster Size
512 MB or 1023 MB	4 KB
1024 MB to 2 GB	4 KB
2 GB to 8 GB	4 KB
8 GB to 16 GB	8 KB
16 GB to 32 GB	16 KB
>32 GB	32 KB

FAT32 is still commonly used today, though not for operating system partitions. Rather, you'll see it on smaller (< 32-GB) flash-media USB drives.

NTFS

The Windows format of choice these days is the *New Technology File System (NTFS)*. NTFS came out a long time ago with the first version of Windows NT, thus the name. Over the years, NTFS has undergone a number of improvements. The version used in modern Windows is called NTFS 3.1, although you'll see it referred to as NTFS 5.0/5.1. NTFS uses clusters and file allocation tables but in a much more complex and powerful way compared to FAT or FAT32. NTFS offers six major improvements and refinements: redundancy, security, compression, encryption, disk quotas, and cluster sizing.

NOTE If you have a geeky interest in what version of NTFS you are running, open a Command Prompt as an administrator and type this command: **fsutil fsinfo ntfsinfo c:**. Then press ENTER.

NTFS Structure

NTFS utilizes an enhanced file allocation table called the *master file table (MFT)*. An NTFS partition keeps a backup copy of the most critical parts of the MFT in the middle of the disk, reducing the chance that a serious drive error can wipe out both the MFT and the MFT copy. Whenever you defragment an NTFS partition, you'll see a small, immovable chunk somewhere on the drive, often near the front; that's the MFT (see Figure 10-22).

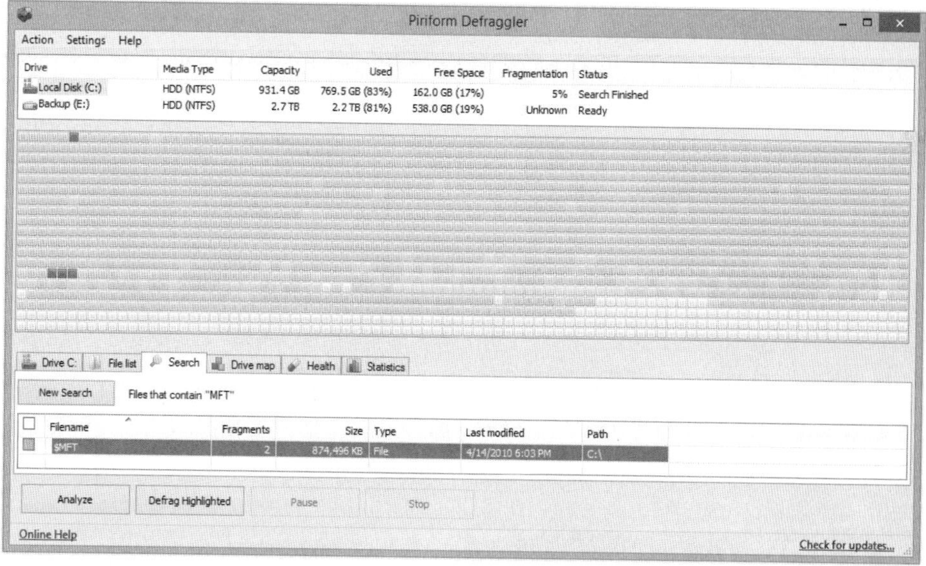

Figure 10-22 The NTFS MFT appears in a defragmenter program as the highlighted red blocks, which doesn't translate visually into black and white . . . ah, well.

Security

NTFS views individual files and folders as objects and provides security for those objects through a feature called the *Access Control List (ACL)*. Future chapters go into this in much more detail.

NOTE Microsoft has never released the exact workings of NTFS to the public.

Compression

NTFS enables you to compress individual files and folders to save space on a hard drive. Compression makes access time to the data slower because the OS has to uncompress files every time you use them, but in a space-limited environment, sometimes that's what you have to do. Windows Explorer/File Explorer displays filenames for compressed files in blue.

Encryption

One of the big draws with NTFS is file encryption, the black art of making files unreadable to anybody who doesn't have the right key. You can encrypt a single file, a folder, or a folder full of files. Microsoft calls the encryption utility in NTFS the *encrypting file system (EFS)*, but it's simply an aspect of NTFS, not a standalone file system. You'll learn more about encryption when you read Chapter 14, "Users, Groups, and Permissions."

Disk Quotas

NTFS supports *disk quotas*, enabling administrators to set limits on drive space usage for users. To set quotas, you must log on as an Administrator, right-click the hard drive name, and select Properties. In the Drive Properties dialog box, select the Quota tab and make changes. Figure 10-23 shows configured quotas for a hard drive. Although rarely used on single-user systems, setting disk quotas on multi-user systems prevents any individual user from monopolizing your hard disk space.

Cluster Sizes

Unlike FAT16 or FAT32, you can adjust the cluster sizes in NTFS, although you'll probably rarely do so. Table 10-4 shows the default cluster sizes for NTFS.

Drive Size	Cluster Size	Number of Sectors
512 MB or less	512 bytes	1
513 MB to 1024 MB (1 GB)	1024 bytes (1 KB)	2
1025 MB to 2048 MB (2 GB)	2048 bytes (2 KB)	4
2049 MB and larger	4096 bytes (4 KB)	8

Table 10-4 NTFS Cluster Sizes

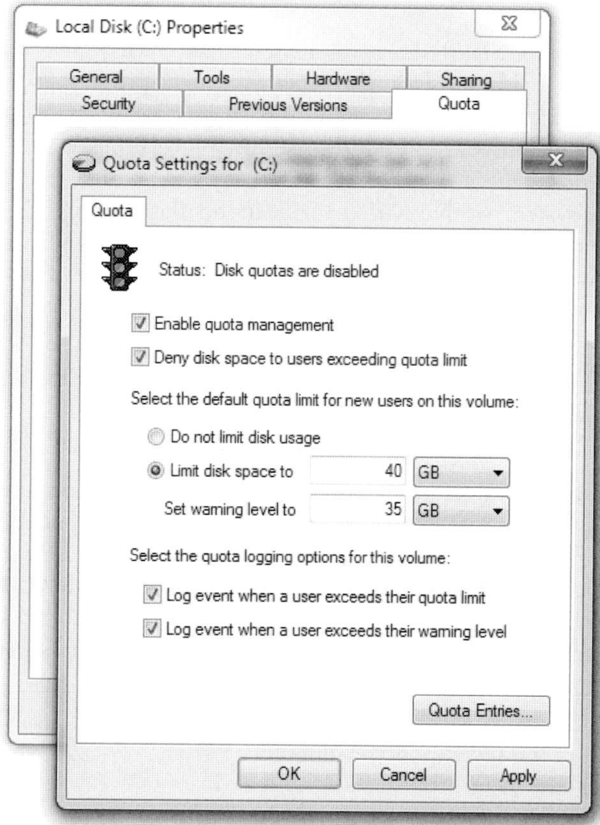

Figure 10-23 Hard drive quotas in Windows 7

By default, NTFS supports partitions up to ~16 TB on a dynamic disk (though only up to 2 TB on a basic disk). By tweaking the cluster sizes, you can get NTFS to support partitions up to 16 exabytes, or 18,446,744,073,709,551,616 bytes! That might support any and all upcoming hard drive capacities for the next 100 years or so.

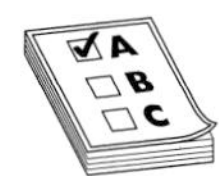

EXAM TIP NTFS supports partitions up to 16 TB by default.

With so many file systems, how do you know which one to use? In the case of internal hard drives, you should use the most feature-rich system your OS supports. For all modern versions of Windows, use NTFS. External hard drives and flash drives still often use FAT32 because NTFS features such as the ACL and encryption can make access difficult when you move the drive between systems, but with that exception, NTFS is your best choice on a Windows-based system.

FAT64

Everyone loves USB flash drives. Their ease of use and convenience make them indispensable for those of us who enjoy sharing a program, some photos, or a playlist. But people today want to share more than just a few small files, and they can do so with larger flash drives. As flash drives grow bigger in capacity, however, the file system becomes a problem.

The file system we have used for years on flash drives, FAT32, does not work on drives larger than 2 TB. Worse, FAT32 limits *file* size to 4 GB. Because there is frequent need to physically transport many files that are often larger than 4 GB, Microsoft wisely developed a replacement for FAT32.

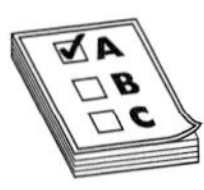

EXAM TIP FAT32 only supports drives up to 2 TB and files up to 4 GB.

The newer file system, called *exFAT* or *FAT64*, breaks the 4-GB file-size barrier, supporting files up to 16 exabytes (EB) and a theoretical partition limit of 64 zettabytes (ZB). Microsoft recommends a partition size of up to 512 TB on today's larger USB flash drives, which should be enough for a while. The exFAT file system extends FAT32 from 32-bit cluster entries to 64-bit cluster entries in the file table. Like FAT32, on the other hand, exFAT still lacks all of NTFS's extra features such as permissions, compression, and encryption.

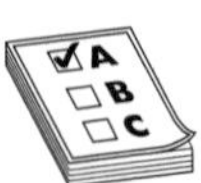

EXAM TIP Know the difference between FAT32, FAT64/exFAT, and NTFS for the exam.

Now, if you're like me, you might be thinking, "Why don't we just use NTFS?" And I would say, "Good point!" Microsoft, however, sees NTFS as too powerful for what most of us need from flash drives. For example, flash drives don't need NTFS permissions. But if for some reason you *really* want to format large USB flash drives with NTFS, Windows will gladly allow you to do so, as shown in Figure 10-24.

NOTE An exabyte is 2^{60} bytes; a zettabyte is 2^{70} bytes. For comparison, a terabyte is 2^{40} bytes. Remember from your binary practice that each superscript number doubles the overall number, so 2^{41} = 2 TB, 2^{42} = 4 TB, and so on. That means a zettabyte is really, really big!

File Systems in Mac OS X

Mac OS X uses the *Hierarchical File System Plus (HFS+)* by default, although you can read and write to several different file systems with the OS. The latest versions can read and write to FAT32 and exFAT, though only read NTFS. Surprisingly, HFS+ is not listed in the CompTIA A+ 902 exam objectives.

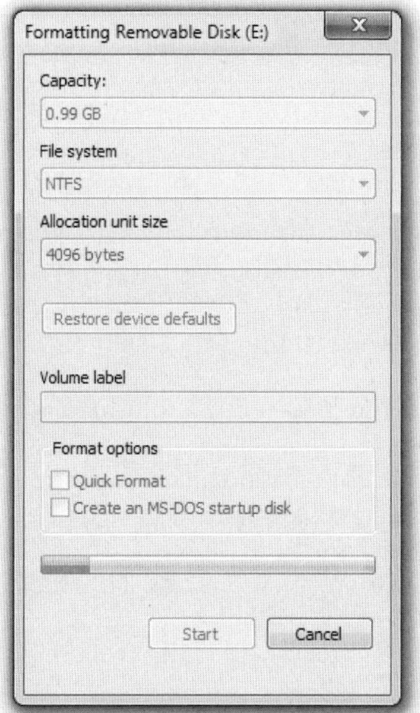

Figure 10-24 Formatting a flash drive in Windows

File Systems in Linux

Most Linux distributions use a file system known as the *Fourth Extended File System (ext4)* by default. Some older distros use one of its predecessors, such as ext2 or ext3. The ext4 file system supports volumes up to 1 exabyte (EB) with file sizes up to 16 TB and is backwardly compatible with ext2 and ext3. In other words, you can mount an ext3 volume as an ext4 volume with no problems. You don't need to know the details of ext3 or ext4, just that they are Linux file systems and that ext4 supports volumes up to 1 EB with file sizes up to 16 TB.

Linux file system capabilities exceed those of Mac OS X, being able to read and write to NTFS, FAT32, exFAT, HFS+, and ext2, ext3, and ext4. Sweet!

The Partitioning, Formatting, and Pooling Process

Now that you understand the concepts of partitioning and formatting, let's go through the process of setting up an installed hard drive by using different partitioning and formatting tools. At the end of the section, we'll look at the process of creating a storage pool by creating a virtual disk. If you have access to a system, try following along

with these descriptions. Don't make any changes to a drive you want to keep, because both partitioning and formatting are destructive processes. The pooling process is also destructive. You cannot follow the procedure in that discussion unless you have a few drives to erase.

Bootable Media

Imagine you've built a brand-new PC. The hard drive has no OS, so you need to boot up something to set up that hard drive. Any software that can boot up a system is by definition an operating system. You need an optical disc or USB flash drive with a bootable OS installed. Any removable media that has a bootable OS is generically called a *boot device* or *boot disc*. Your system boots off of the boot device, which then loads some kind of OS that enables you to partition, format, and install an OS on your new hard drive. Boot devices come from many sources. All Windows OS installation media are boot devices, as are Linux installation media. Boot devices may also be a medium that has an image of an installation disc. These images are usually stored as a file with a name that has an extension of ".iso." Image files may be on a traditional boot device, such as a disc or flash drive, but they can come from any place, such as on a network drive.

Every boot device has some kind of partitioning tool and a way to format a new partition. A hard drive has to have a partition and has to be formatted to support an OS installation.

Partitioning and Formatting with the Installation Media

When you boot up Windows installation media and the installation program detects a hard drive that is not yet partitioned, it prompts you through a sequence of steps to partition and format the hard drive. Chapter 12, "Building a PC," covers the entire installation process, but we'll jump ahead and dive into the partitioning part of the installation here to see how this is done.

The process of partitioning and formatting with the current versions of Windows is pretty straightforward. You'll go through a couple of installation screens (see Figure 10-25) where you select things such as language and get prompted for a product key and acceptance of the license agreement. Eventually you'll get to the *Where do you want to install Windows?* dialog box (see Figure 10-26).

Click Next to do the most common partitioning and formatting action: creating a single C: partition, making it active, and formatting it as NTFS. Note that Windows creates two partitions, a 100-MB System Reserved partition and the C: partition. This is normal, the way the system was designed to work. Figure 10-27 shows a typical Windows 7 installation in Disk Management.

If you want to do any custom partitioning or delete existing partitions, you click on Drive options (advanced) in the Where do you want to install Windows? dialog box. To create a new partition, click the New button. Type in an amount in gigabytes that you want to use for a new partition, then click Apply. In Windows 7, you will get a notice

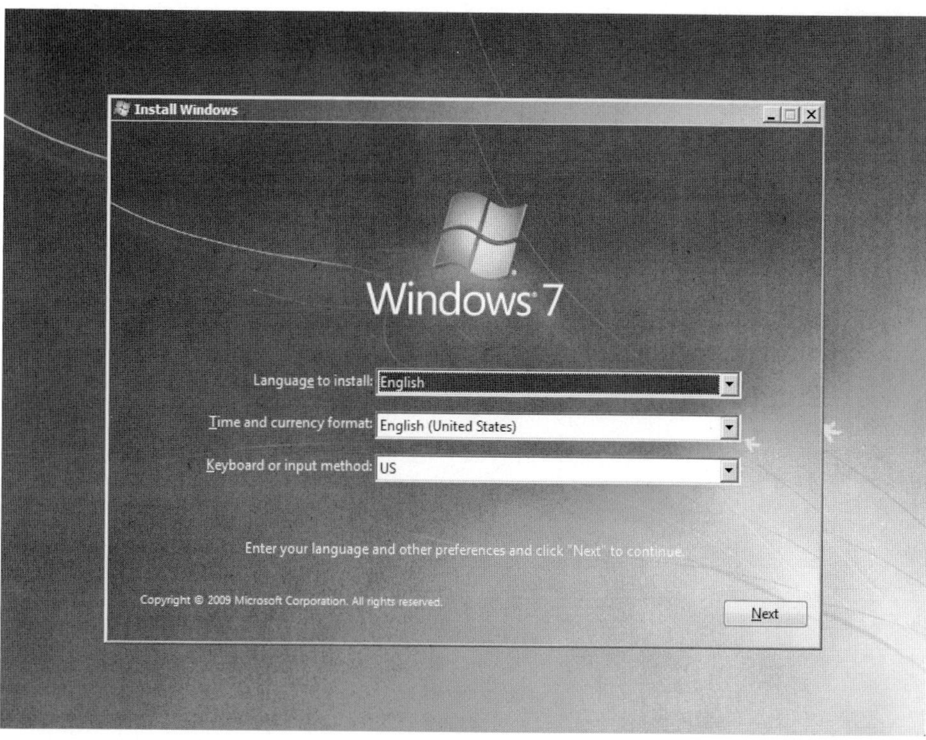

Figure 10-25 Starting the Windows 7 installation

that Windows might create additional partitions for system files. When you click OK, Windows will create the 100-MB System Reserved partition as well as the partition you specified (see Figure 10-28). Any leftover drive space will be listed as Unallocated Space.

Once you create a new partition, click the Format button. The installer won't ask you what file system to use. Newer Windows versions can read FAT and FAT32 drives, but they won't install to such a partition by default.

The example here has a 1-TB drive with a 499-GB partition and 500 GB of unallocated space. If you've gone through this process and have changed your mind, now wanting to make the partition use the full terabyte, what do you have to do? You can simply click the Extend button and then apply the rest of the unallocated space to the currently formatted partition. The Extend function enables you to tack unpartitioned space onto an already partitioned drive with a click of the mouse.

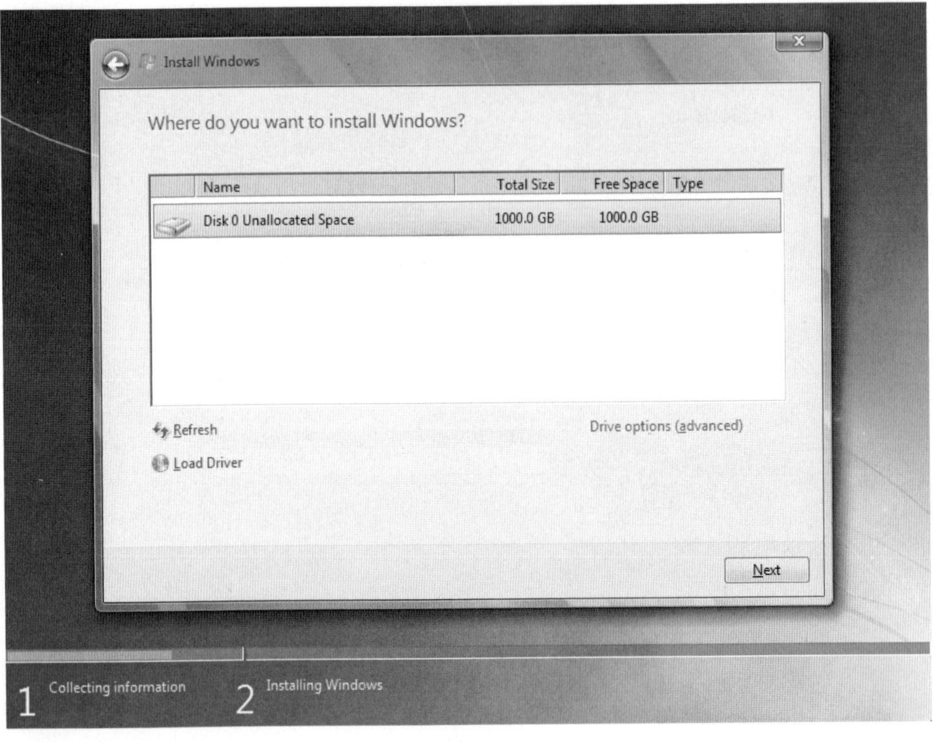

Figure 10-26 Where do you want to install Windows?

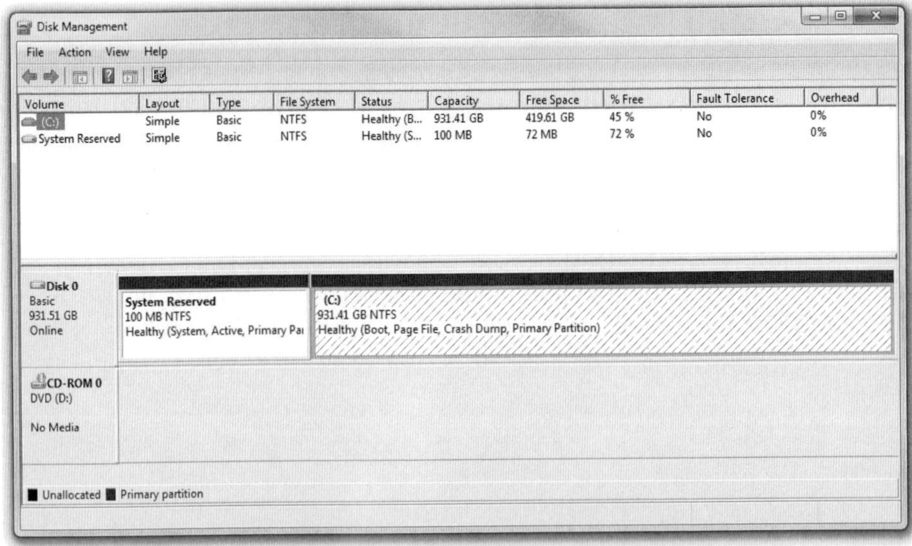

Figure 10-27 Disk Management showing the default partitions in Windows 7

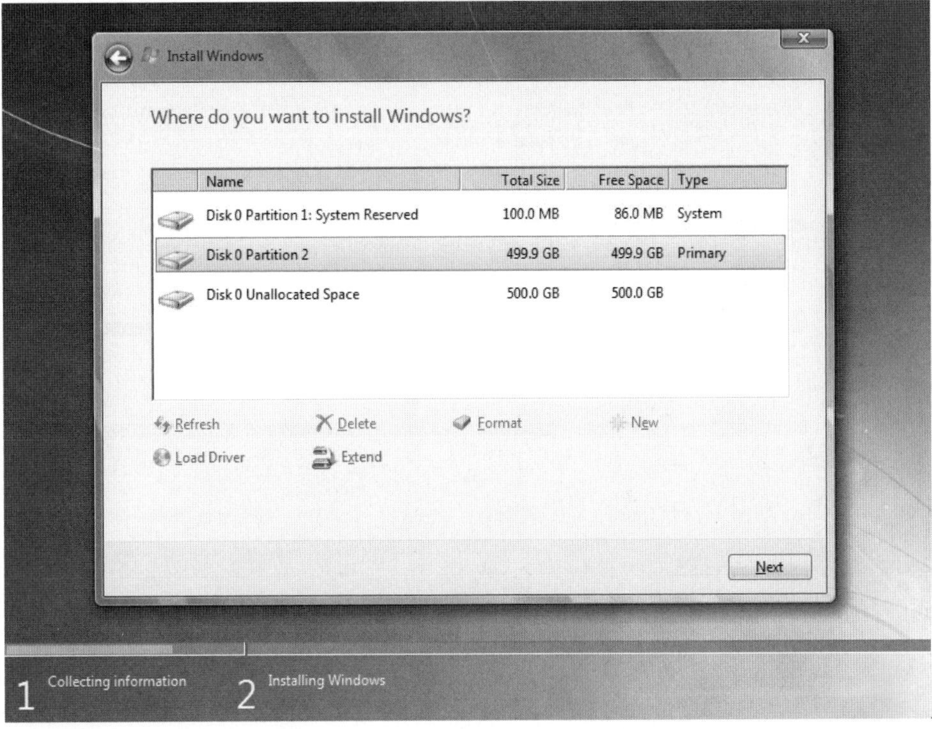

Figure 10-28 New 499-GB partition with 100-MB System Reserved partition and Unallocated Space

Disk Management

Earlier, we took a brief look at Disk Management to manipulate installed disks. It is also used to manage newly installed disks. The Disk Management utility is the primary tool for partitioning and formatting drives after installation (see Figure 10-29). You can use Disk Management to do everything you want to do to a hard drive in one handy tool.

NOTE Refer to Chapter 9, "Hard Drive Technologies," for the many ways to get to Disk Management.

Disk Initialization

Every hard drive in a Windows system has special information placed onto the drive through a process called *disk initialization*. (CompTIA refers to this as *initializing* a disk.) This initialization information includes identifiers that say "this drive belongs in this system" and other information that defines what this hard drive does in the system. If the

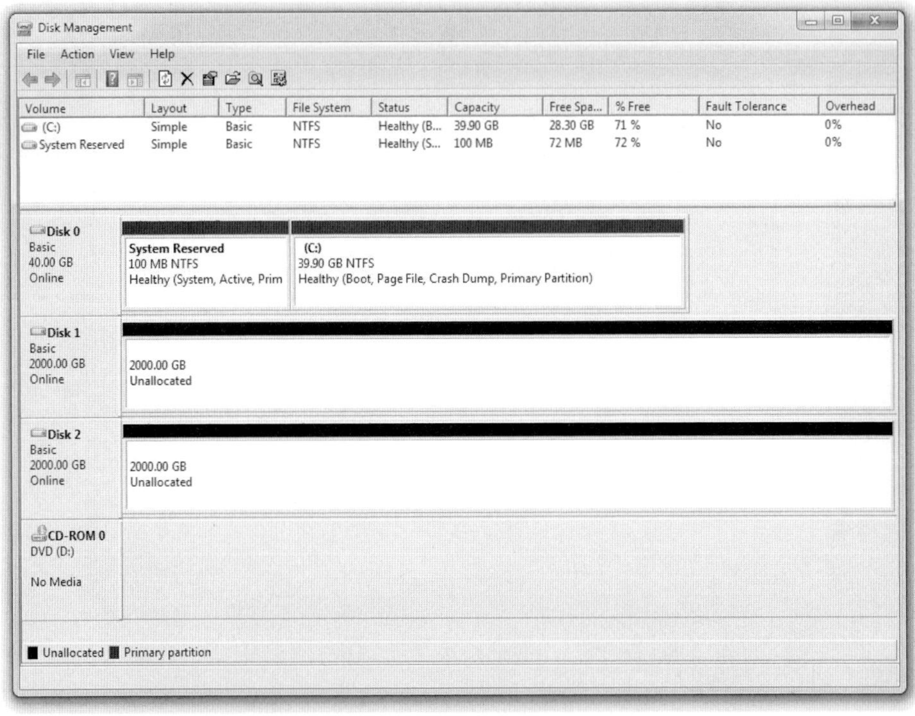

Figure 10-29 Disk Management

hard drive is part of a software RAID array, for example, its RAID information is stored in the initialization. If it's part of a spanned volume, this is also stored there.

All new drives must be initialized before you can use them. When you install an extra hard drive into a Windows system and start Disk Management, it notices the new drive and starts the Hard Drive Initialization Wizard. If you don't let the wizard run, the drive will be listed as unknown (see Figure 10-30).

To initialize a disk, right-click the disk icon and select Initialize. You will get the option to select MBR or GPT as a partition style. Once a disk is initialized, you can see the status of the drive—a handy tool for troubleshooting.

Disk Management enables you to view the *drive status* of every mass storage device in your system. Hopefully, you'll see each drive listed as Healthy, meaning that nothing is happening to it and things are going along swimmingly. You're also already familiar with the Unallocated and Active statuses, but here are a few more to be familiar with for the CompTIA A+ exams and real life as a tech:

- **Foreign drive** You see this when you move a dynamic disk from one computer to another.
- **Formatting** As you might have guessed, you see this when you're formatting a drive.

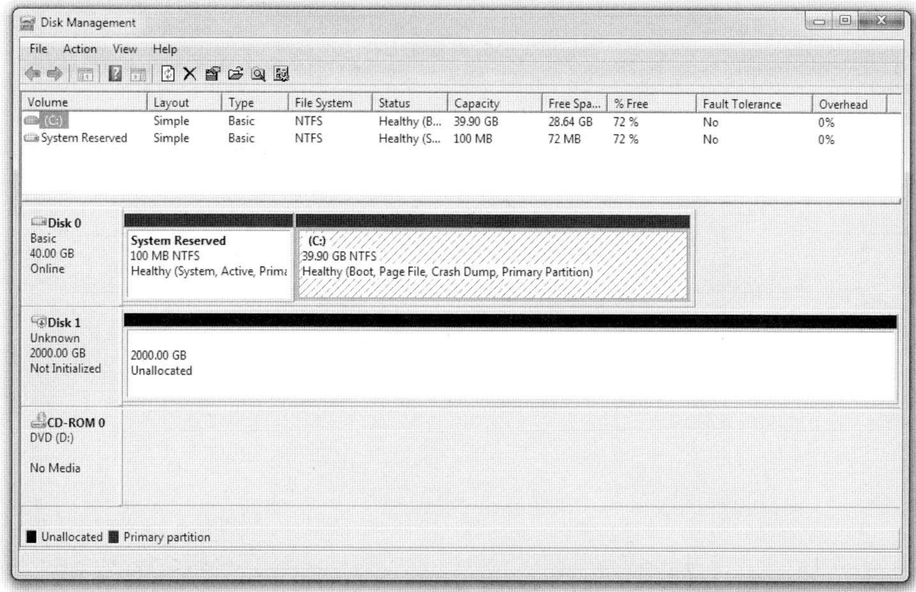

Figure 10-30 Unknown drive in Disk Management

- **Failed** Pray you never see this status, because it means that the disk is damaged or corrupt and you've probably lost some data.
- **Online** This is what you see if a disk is healthy and communicating properly with the computer.
- **Offline** The disk is either corrupted or having communication problems.

A newly installed drive is always set as a basic disk. There's nothing wrong with using basic disks, other than that you miss out on some handy features.

Creating Partitions and Volumes in Disk Management

To create partitions or volumes, right-click the unallocated part of the drive and select New Simple Volume. Disk Management runs the New Simple Volume Wizard. You'll go straight to the sizing screen (see Figure 10-31).

Specify a volume size and click Next. The wizard will ask if you want to assign a drive letter to the volume, mount it as a folder to an existing volume, or do neither (see Figure 10-32). In almost all cases, you'll want to give simple volumes a drive letter.

It's important to note here that current versions of Windows do not enable you to specify whether you want a primary or extended partition when you create a volume. The first three volumes you create will be primary partitions. Every volume thereafter will be a logical drive in an extended partition.

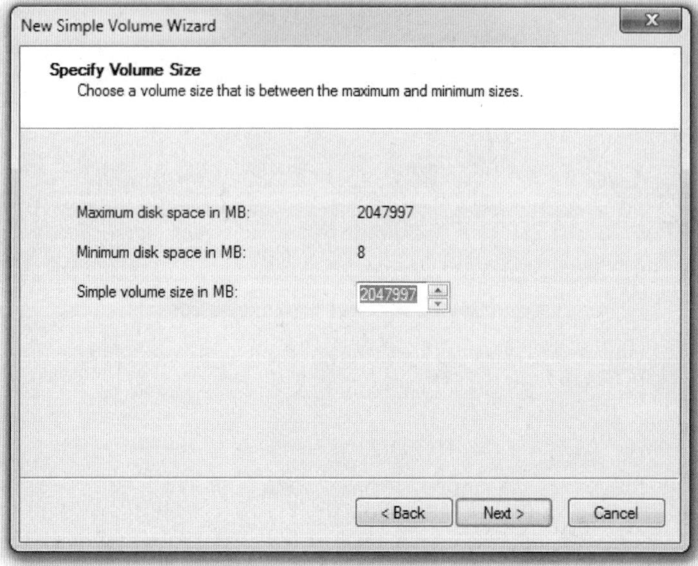

Figure 10-31 Specifying the simple volume size in the New Simple Volume Wizard

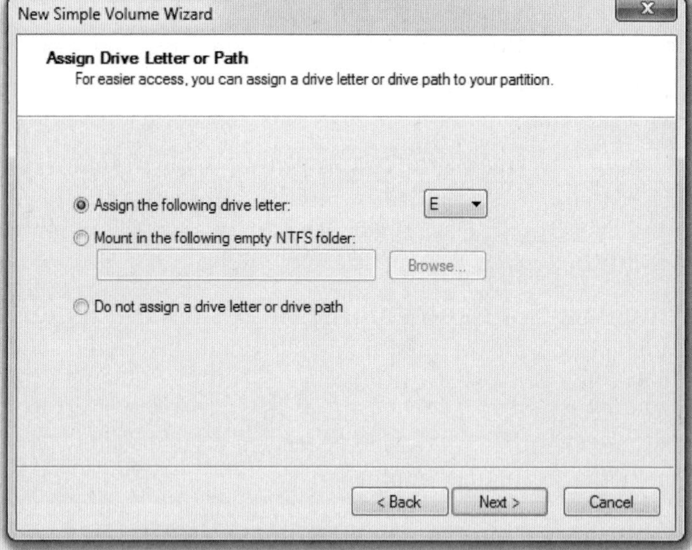

Figure 10-32 Assigning a drive letter to a volume

The last screen of the New Simple Volume Wizard asks for the type of format you want to use for this partition (see Figure 10-33). If your partition is 4 GB or less, you may format it as FAT, FAT32, or NTFS. If your partition is greater than 4 GB but less than 32 GB, you can make the drive FAT32 or NTFS. Windows requires NTFS on any partition greater than 32 GB. Although FAT32 supports partitions up to 2 TB, Microsoft wants you to use NTFS on larger partitions and creates this limit. With today's big hard drives, there's no good reason to use anything other than NTFS. In addition to the file system selection, you are offered a checkbox to perform a quick format or a full format. Remember that the quick format does not test the disk clusters as part of the format process, while the full format option does.

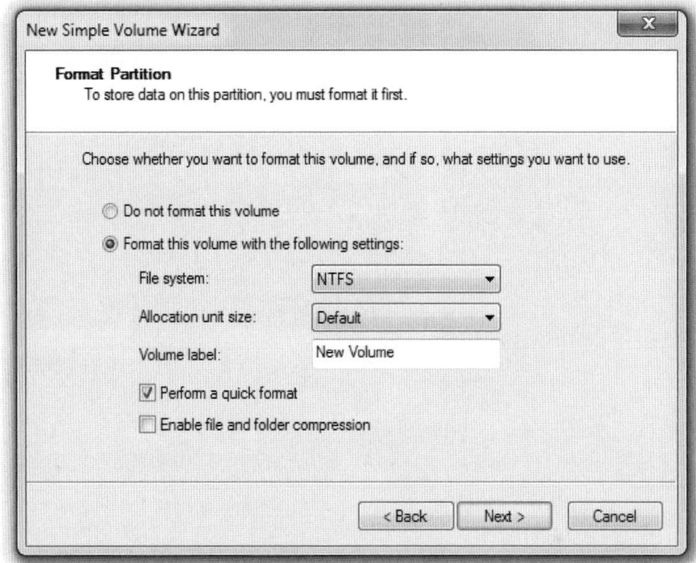

Figure 10-33 Choosing a file system type

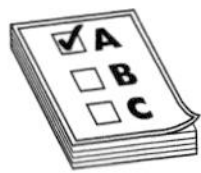

EXAM TIP Know the differences between a quick format vs. a full format for the exam.

You have a few more tasks to complete at this screen. You can add a volume label if you want. You can also choose the size of your clusters (allocation unit size). There's no reason to change the default cluster size, so leave that alone—but you can sure speed up the format if you select the Perform a quick format checkbox. This will format your drive without checking every cluster. It's fast and a bit risky, but new hard drives almost always come from the factory in perfect shape—so you must decide whether to use it or not.

Last, if you chose NTFS, you may enable file and folder compression. If you select this option, you'll be able to right-click any file or folder on this partition and compress it.

To compress a file or folder, choose the one you want to compress, right-click, and select Properties. Then click the Advanced button and turn compression on (see Figure 10-34). Compression is handy for opening up space on a hard drive that's filling up, but it also slows down disk access, so use it only when you need it.

Figure 10-34 Turning on compression

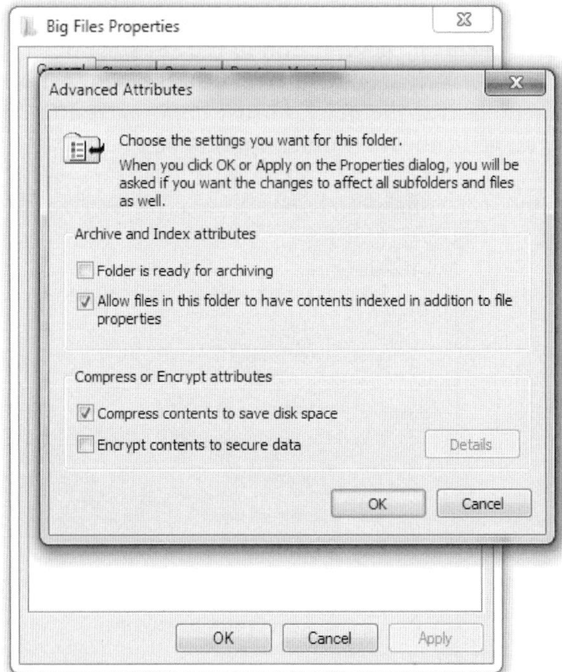

Dynamic Disks

You create dynamic disks from basic disks in Disk Management. Once you convert a drive from a basic disk to a dynamic disk, primary and extended partitions no longer exist; dynamic disks are divided into volumes instead of partitions. Because current versions of Windows call partitions *volumes*, the change to dynamic disk isn't obvious at all.

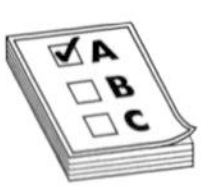

EXAM TIP When you move a dynamic disk from one computer to another, it shows up in Disk Management as a foreign drive. You can import a foreign drive into the new system by right-clicking the disk icon and selecting Import Foreign Disks.

To convert a basic disk to dynamic, just right-click the drive icon and select Convert to Dynamic Disk (see Figure 10-35). The process is very quick and safe, although the reverse is not true. The conversion from dynamic disk to basic disk first requires you to delete all volumes off of the hard drive.

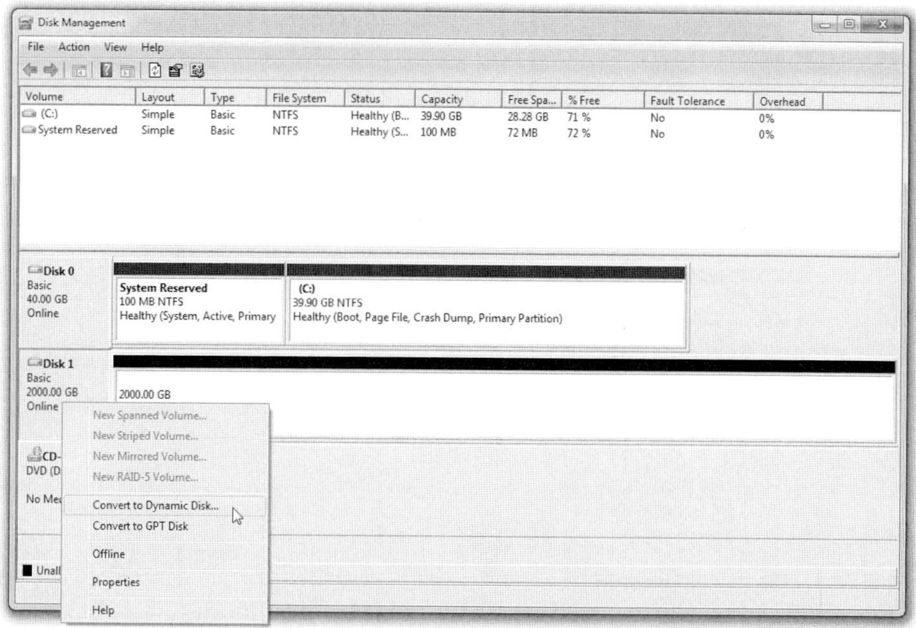

Figure 10-35 Converting to a dynamic disk

Once you've converted the disk, you can make one of the five types of volumes on a dynamic disk: simple, spanned, striped, mirrored, or RAID 5. You'll next learn how to implement the three most common volume types. The final step involves assigning a drive letter or mounting the volume as a folder.

Simple Volumes A simple volume acts just like a primary partition. If you have only one dynamic disk in a system, it can have only a simple volume. It's important to note here that a simple volume may act like a traditional primary partition, but it is very different because you cannot install an operating system on it.

In Disk Management, right-click any unallocated space on the dynamic disk and choose New Simple Volume (see Figure 10-36) to run the New Simple Volume Wizard. You'll see a series of screens that prompt you on size and file system, and then you're finished. Figure 10-37 shows Disk Management with three simple volumes.

Spanning Volumes You can extend the size of a simple volume to any unallocated space on a dynamic disk. You can also extend the volume to grab extra space on completely different dynamic disks, creating a spanned volume. To extend or span, simply right-click the volume you want to make bigger, and choose Extend Volume from the options (see Figure 10-38). This opens the Extend Volume Wizard, which prompts you for the location of free space on a dynamic disk and the increased volume size you want to assign (see Figure 10-39). If you have multiple drives, you can span the volume just as easily to one of those drives.

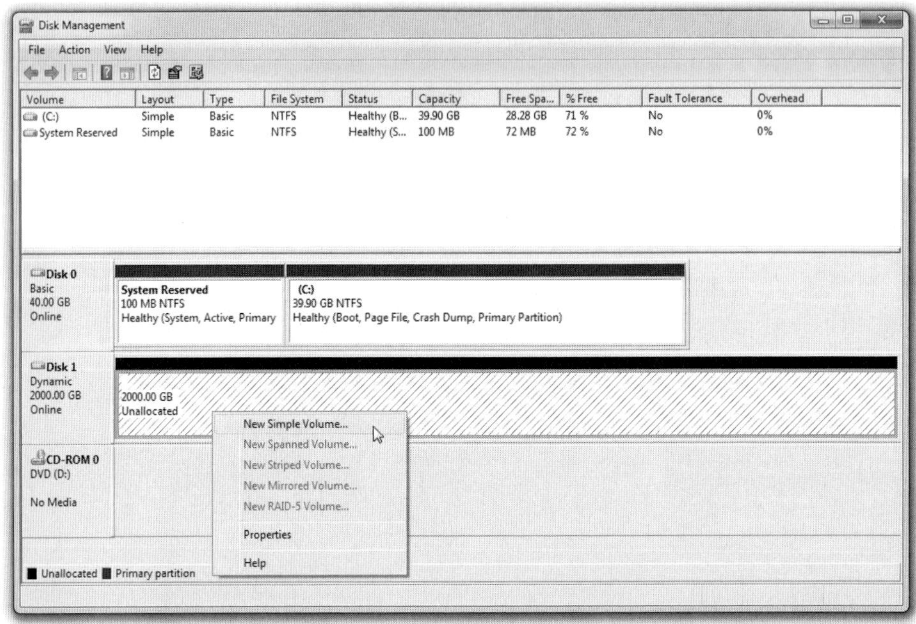

Figure 10-36 Selecting to open the New Simple Volume Wizard

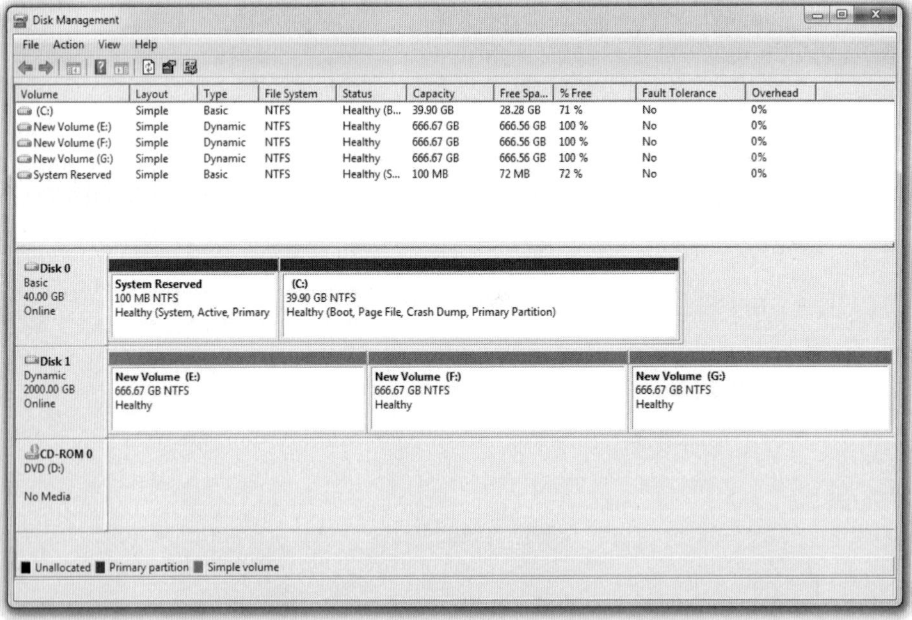

Figure 10-37 Simple volumes

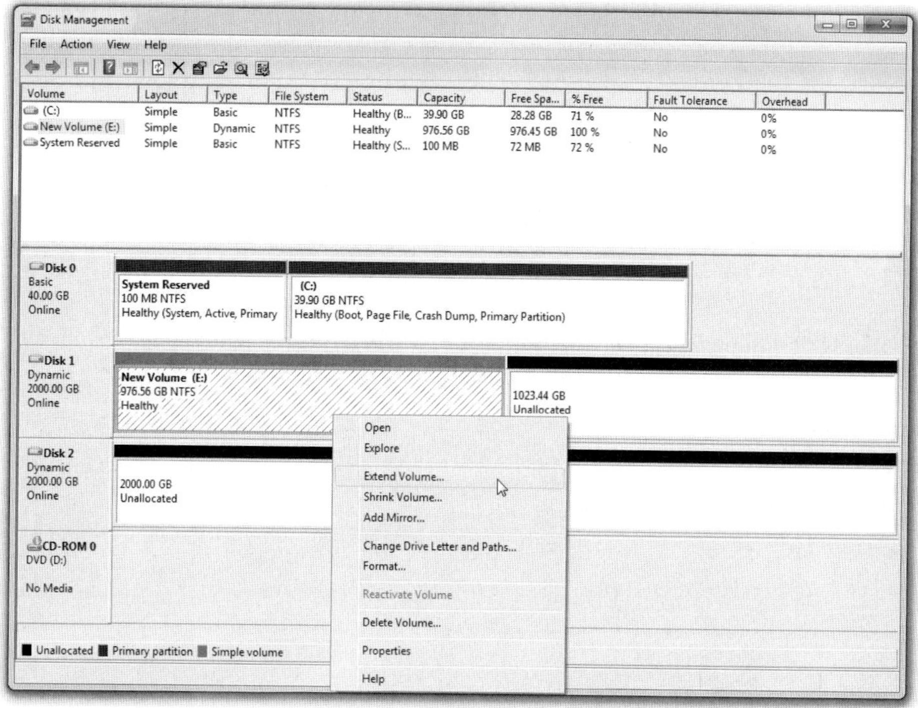

Figure 10-38 Selecting the Extend Volume option

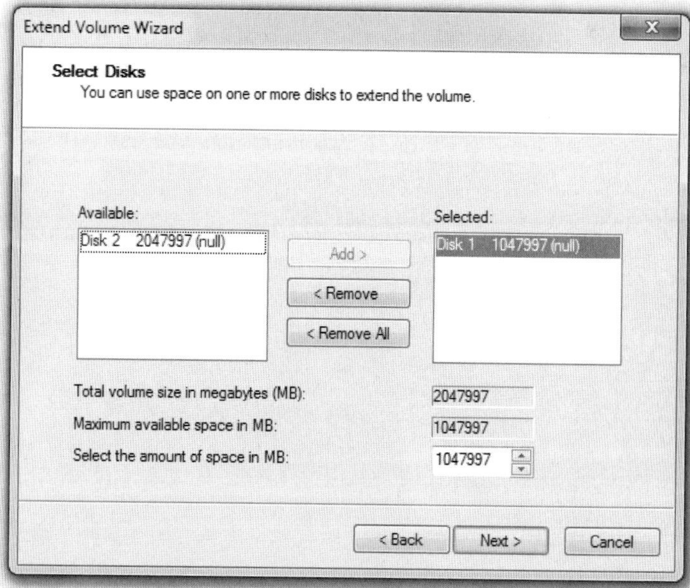

Figure 10-39 The Extend Volume Wizard

The capability to extend and span volumes makes dynamic disks worth their weight in gold. If you start running out of space on a volume, you can simply add another physical hard drive to the system and span the volume to the new drive. This keeps your drive letters consistent and unchanging so your programs don't get confused, yet enables you to expand drive space when needed.

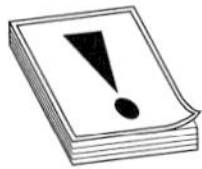

CAUTION Once you convert a drive to dynamic, you cannot revert it to a basic disk without losing all of the data on that drive. Be prepared to back up all data before you convert.

You can extend or span any simple volume on a dynamic disk, not just the "one on the end" in the Disk Management console. You simply select the volume to expand and the total volume increase you want. Figure 10-40 shows a simple 488.28-GB volume named Extended that has been enlarged an extra 1316.40 GB in a portion of the hard drive, skipping the 195.31-GB section of unallocated space contiguous to it. This created an 1804.68-GB volume. Windows has no problem skipping areas on a drive.

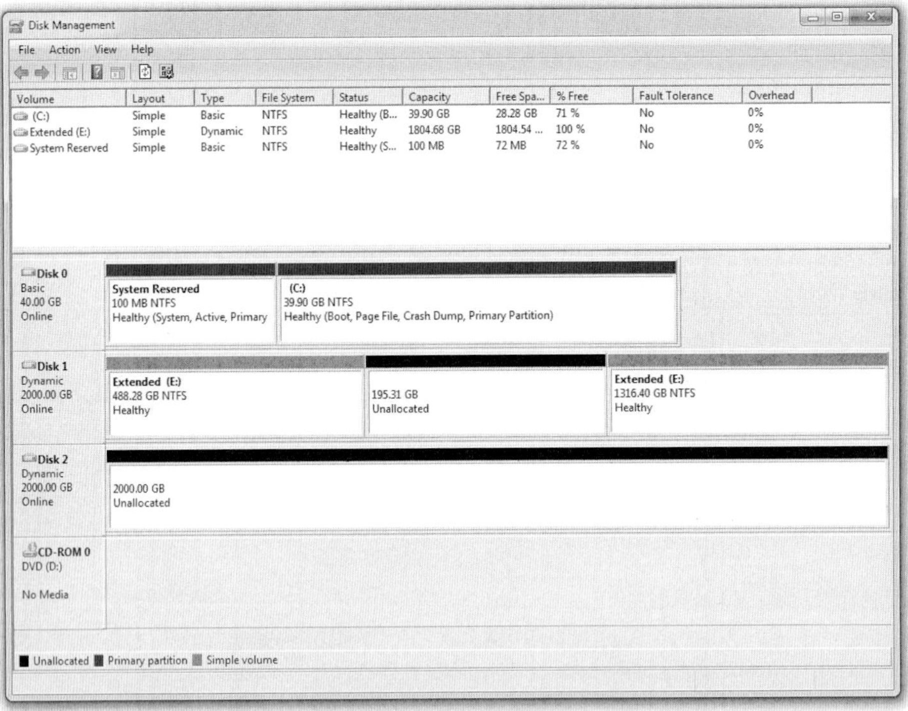

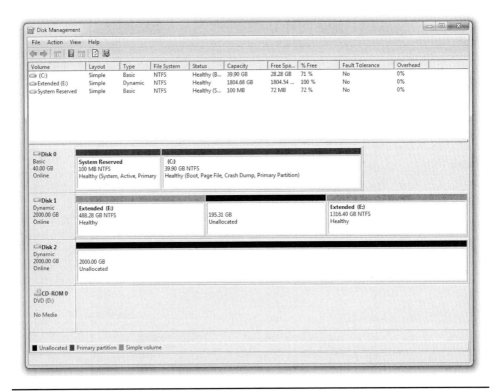

Figure 10-40 Extended volume

NOTE You can extend and shrink volumes in current versions of Windows without using dynamic disks. You can shrink any volume with available free space (though you can't shrink the volume by the whole amount of free space, based on the location of unmovable sectors such as the MBR), and you can expand volumes with unallocated space on the drive.

To shrink a volume, right-click it and select Shrink Volume. Disk Management will calculate how much you can shrink it, and then you can choose up to that amount.

Extending volumes is equally straightforward. To extend, right-click and select Extend Volume.

Note that CompTIA refers to the processes as *extending partitions* and, in an odd pairing of grammar, *shrink partitions*.

Striped Volumes If you have two or more dynamic disks in a PC, Disk Management enables you to combine them into a *striped* volume. Although Disk Management doesn't use the term, you know this as a RAID 0 array. A striped volume spreads out blocks of each file across multiple disks. Using two or more drives in a group called a *stripe set*, striping writes data first to a certain number of clusters on one drive, then to a certain number of clusters on the next drive, and so on. It speeds up data throughput because the system has to wait a much shorter time for a drive to read or write data. The drawback of striping is that if any single drive in the stripe set fails, all the data in the stripe set is lost.

To create a striped volume, right-click any unused space on a drive, choose New Volume, and then choose Striped. The wizard asks for the other drives you want to add to the stripe, and you need to select two unallocated spaces on other dynamic disks. Select the other unallocated spaces and go through the remaining screens on sizing and formatting until you've created a new striped volume (see Figure 10-41). The two stripes in Figure 10-41 appear to have different sizes, but if you look closely you'll see they are both 1000 GB. All stripes must be the same size on each drive.

Mirrored Volumes Windows 7 and later Professional, Enterprise, and Ultimate editions can create a *mirror set* with two drives for data redundancy. You know mirrors from Chapter 9 as *RAID 1*. To create a mirror, right-click on unallocated space on a drive and select New Mirrored Volume (see Figure 10-42). This runs the New Mirrored Volume Wizard. Click Next to continue. Select an available disk in the Available box and click the Add button to move it to the Selected box (see Figure 10-43). Click Next to get to the by-now-familiar Assign Drive Letter or Path dialog box and select what is appropriate for the PC.

Other Levels of RAID Disk Management enables you to create a *RAID 5 array* that uses three or more disks to create a robust solution for storage. This applies to all the Professional editions of Windows. Unfortunately for users of those operating systems, you can only make the array on a Windows Server machine that you access remotely across a network. (Starting with the Professional and Enterprise editions of Windows 8, Microsoft includes Storage Spaces, an alternative way to do software pseudo-RAID in the

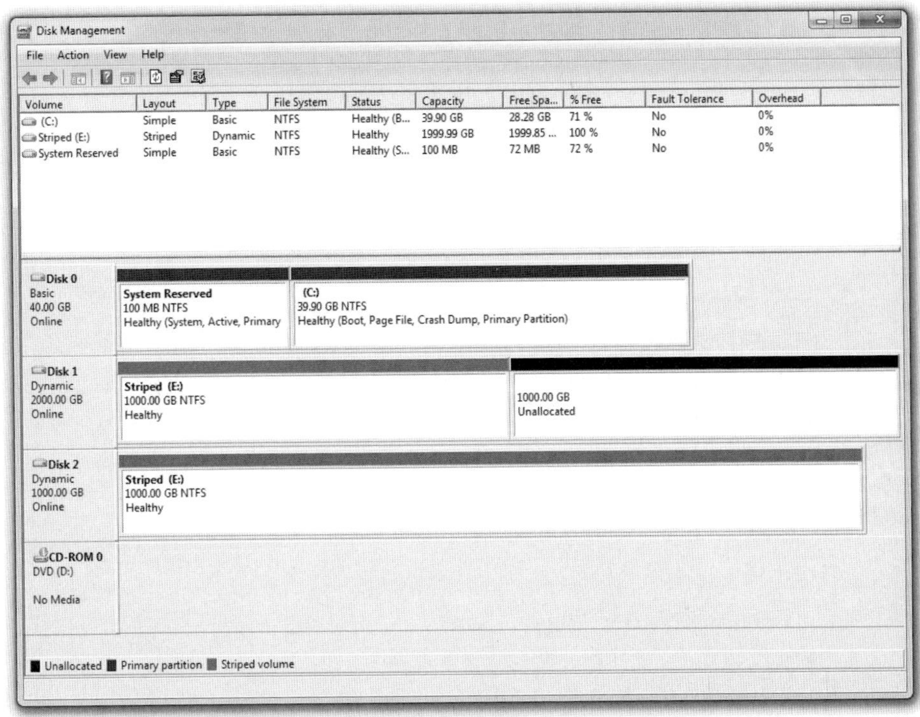

Figure 10-41 Two striped drives

form of pooling; one option closely resembles RAID 5. See the "Storage Spaces" section later in the chapter for more details.)

Disk Management cannot do any nested RAID arrays. So if you want RAID 0+1 or RAID 1+0 (RAID 10), you need to use third-party software (or go with hardware RAID).

Mounting Partitions as Folders

While partitions and volumes can be assigned a drive letter, D: through Z:, they can also be mounted as a folder on another drive, also known as a *mount point*. This enables you to use your existing folders to store more data than can fit on a single drive or partition/volume (see Figure 10-44).

Imagine you use your Documents folder on a Windows Vista machine to store your digital photos. As your collection grows, you realize your current 500-GB hard drive is running out of space. You're willing to buy another hard drive, but you have a great organizational structure in your existing Documents folder and you don't want to lose that. You don't have to move everything to the new hard drive, either.

After you install the new hard drive, you can *mount* the primary partition (or logical drive) as a folder within the existing Documents folder on your C: drive (for example,

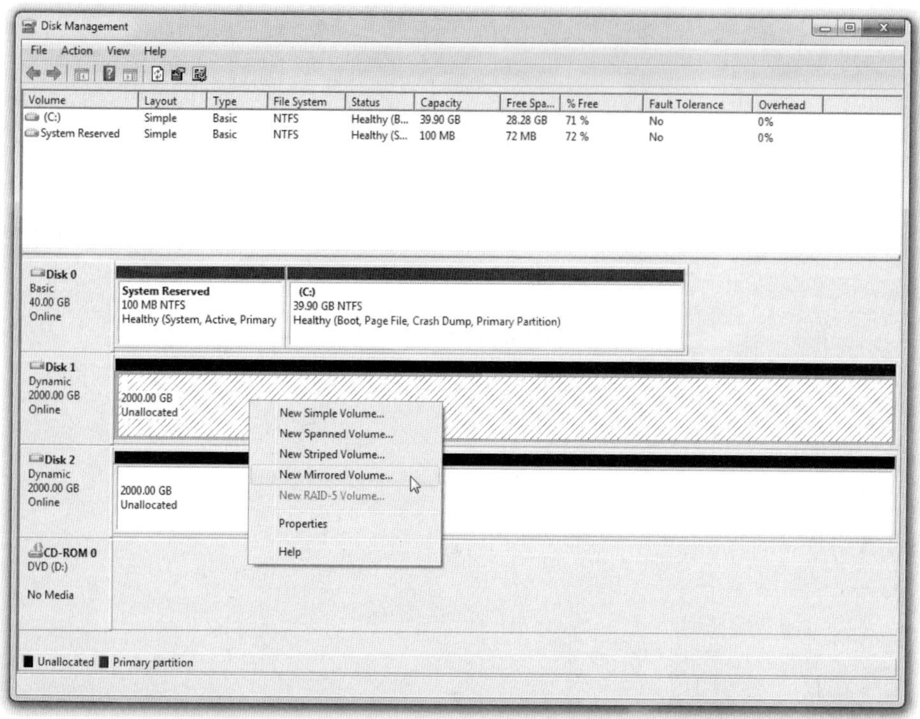

Figure 10-42 Selecting a new mirror

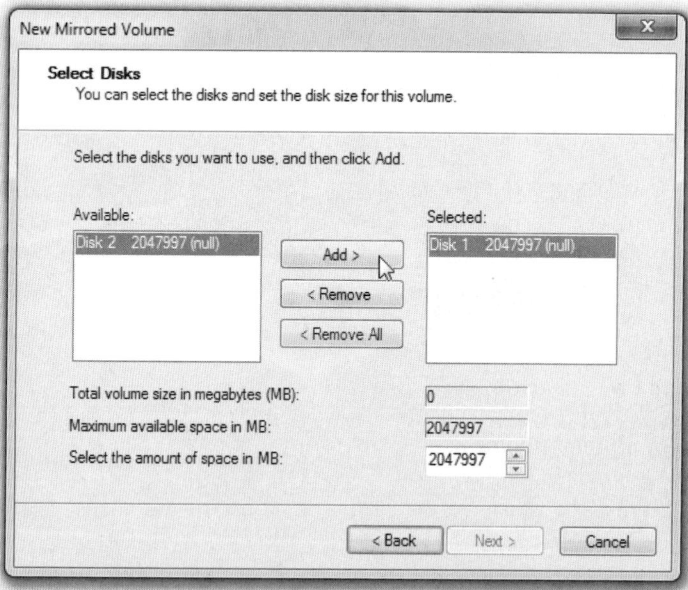

Figure 10-43 Selecting drives for the array

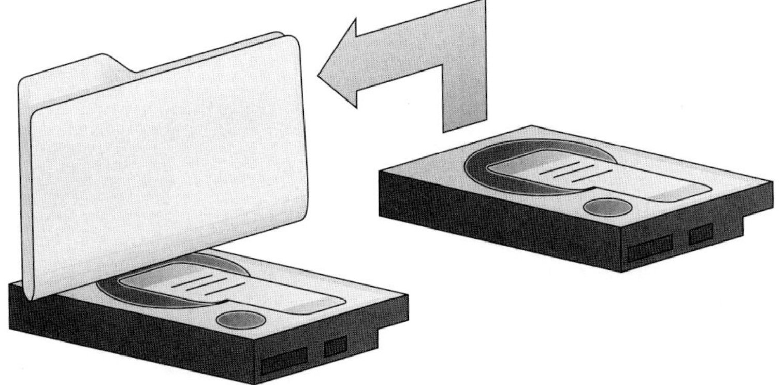

Figure 10-44 Mounting a drive as a folder

C:\Users\Mike\My Photos). At this point the drive doesn't have a letter (though you could add one later, if you wanted). To use the new drive, just drop your files into the My Photos folder. They'll be stored on the second hard drive, not the original 500-GB drive (see Figure 10-45). Amazing!

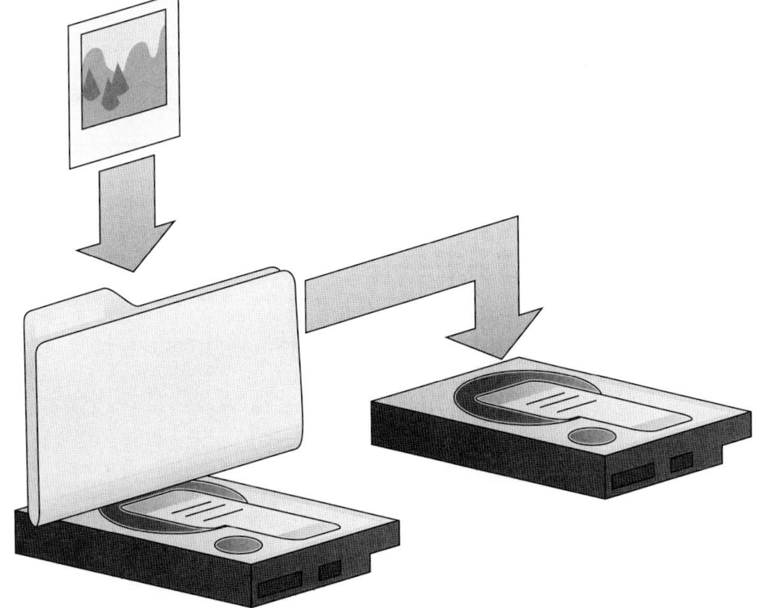

Figure 10-45 Adding photos to the mounted folder stores them on the second hard drive.

To create a mount point, right-click on an unallocated section of a disk and choose New Simple Volume. This opens the appropriately named wizard. In the second screen, you can select a mount point rather than a drive letter (see Figure 10-46). Browse to a blank folder on an NTFS-formatted drive or create a new folder and you're in business.

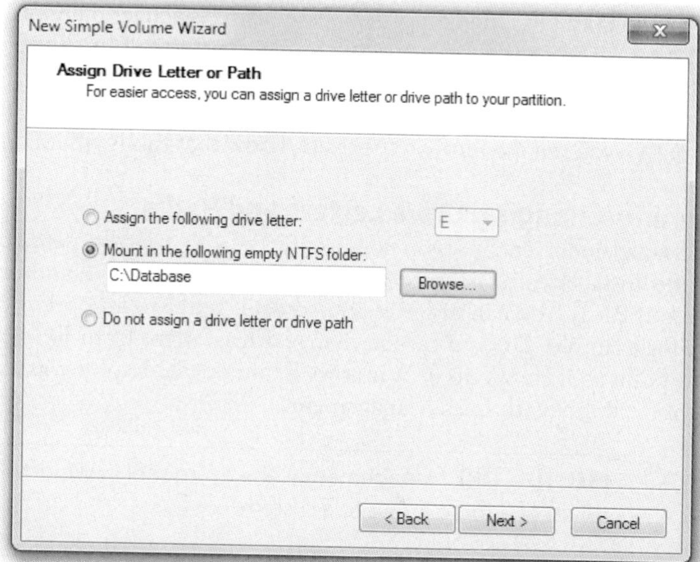

Figure 10-46 Choosing to create a mounted volume

Try This!

Working with Dynamic Drives and Mount Points

You can't begin to appreciate the ease and elegant simplicity of Disk Management until you play with it, so Try This! Get a couple of spare drives and install them into a Windows PC. Fire up the Disk Management console and try the following setups:

1. Make a mirror set.
2. Make a stripe set.
3. Make them into a single volume spanned between both drives.
4. Make a single volume that takes up a portion of one drive, and then extend that volume onto another portion of that drive. Finally, span that volume to the other hard drive as well.
5. Create a volume of some sort—you decide—and then mount that volume to a folder on the C: drive.

You'll need to format the volumes after you create them so you can see how they manifest in Windows Explorer/File Explorer. Also, you'll need to delete volumes to create a new setup. To delete a volume, simply right-click on the volume and choose Delete Volume. It's almost too easy.

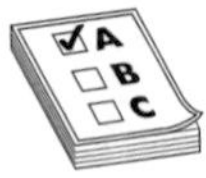

EXAM TIP The CompTIA A+ 902 exam objectives mention "splitting" partitions. To be clear, you never actually split a partition. If you want to turn one partition into two, you need to remove the existing partition and create two new ones, or shrink the existing partition and add a new one to the unallocated space. If you see the term on the exam, know that this is what CompTIA means.

Assigning/Changing Drive Letters and Paths

Disk Management enables you to modify the drive letter, path, or mount point on currently installed mass storage devices. Right-click a drive and select Change Drive Letter and Paths. You can assign a desired drive letter to an optical drive—say, from D: to Z:, for example. Or, you can or change a hard drive from D: to a non-letter named mount point so it shows up in Windows Explorer/File Explorer as a subfolder. You have a ton of flexibility with Disk Management.

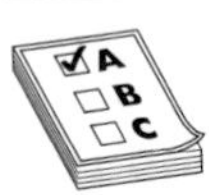

EXAM TIP Disk Management is the go-to tool in Windows when adding drives or adding arrays to a system.

Formatting a Partition

You can format any Windows partition/volume in Windows Explorer/File Explorer. Just right-click on the drive name and choose Format (see Figure 10-47). You'll see a dialog box that asks for the type of file system you want to use, the cluster size, and a volume label. You can also do a quick format or compress the volume. The Quick Format option tells Windows not to test the clusters and is a handy option when you're in a hurry—and feeling lucky. The Enable Compression option tells Windows to give users the capability to compress folders or files. It works well but slows down your hard drive.

Disk Management is today's preferred formatting tool for Windows. When you create a new partition or volume, the wizard also asks you what type of format you want to use. Always use NTFS unless you're that rare and strange person who wants to dual-boot some ancient version of Windows.

All OS installation media partition and format as part of the OS installation. Windows simply prompts you to partition and then format the drive. Read the screens and you'll do great.

Storage Spaces

With Windows 8 and later versions of the OS, you can group one or more physical drives of any size into a single *storage pool*. These drives can be internal HDD or SSD or external storage connected via USB. It's pretty sweet. *Storage Spaces* functions like a RAID management tool, except it goes well beyond the typical tool. Here's the scoop.

First off, to run the tool, get to the Start screen and type **storage spaces**. Storage Spaces will show up in the Search charm. Click on it to run the program. The opening screen gives you pretty much a single option, to *Create a new pool and storage space* (see Figure 10-48). Click that option.

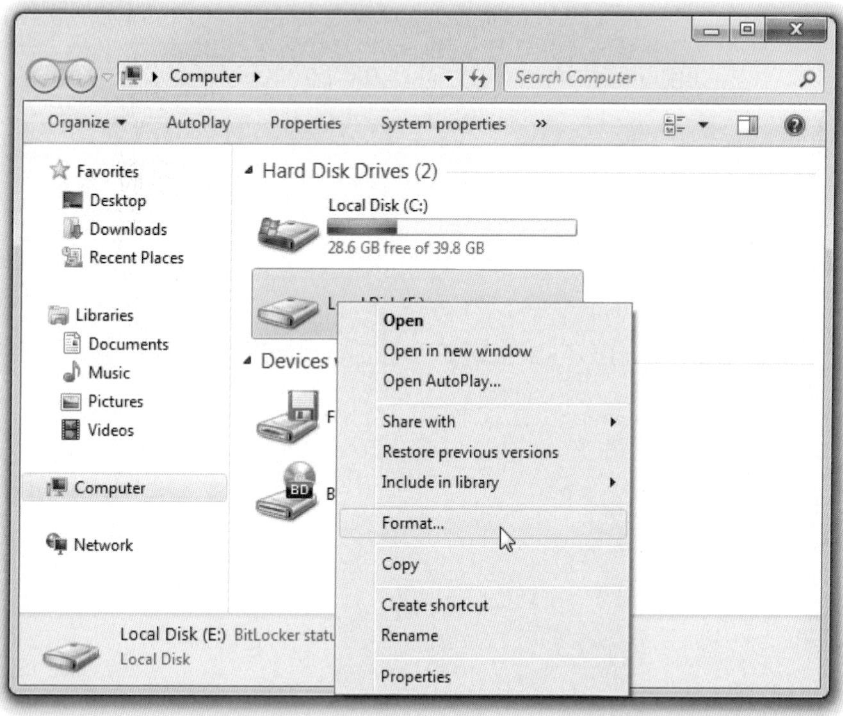

Figure 10-47 Choosing Format in Computer

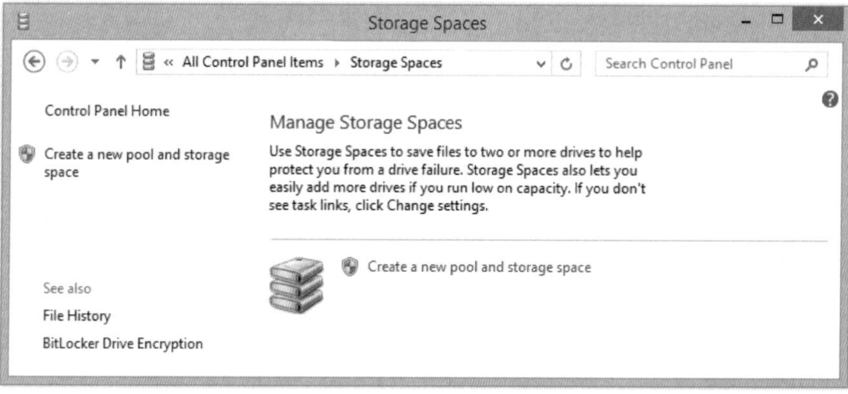

Figure 10-48 Storage Spaces opening window

Storage Spaces will show you the available installed and formatted physical drives and give you a warning that proceeding will erase the drives (see Figure 10-49). Select the drives you want to include in the pool and click the Create pool button.

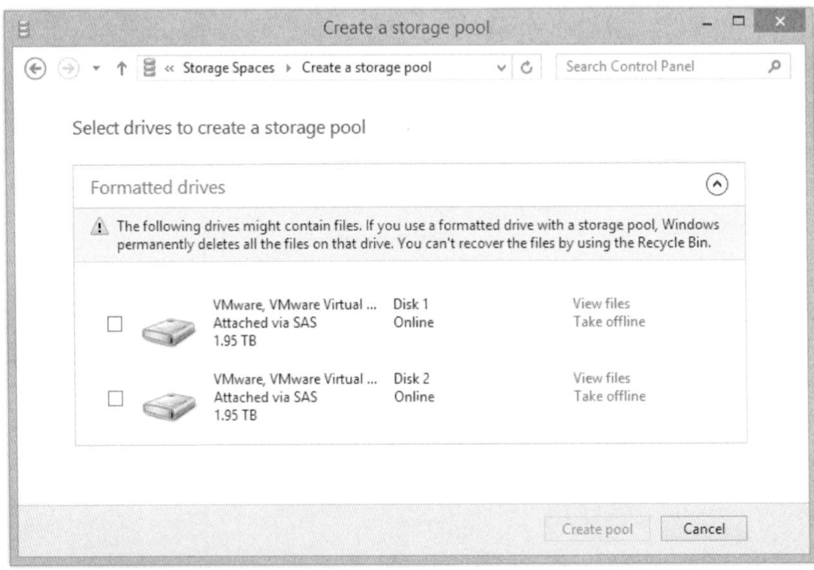

Figure 10-49 Formatted drives revealed

Once you've created a pool, you need to select what Microsoft calls the *resiliency mechanism*, which essentially means providing one or more layers of redundancy so you can lose a hard drive or two and not lose any data. Sounds a lot like RAID, doesn't it? Figure 10-50 shows the Create a storage space window with a *Two-way mirror* storage layout. Here's where Storage Spaces gets pretty much cooler than any RAID management tool.

Storage Spaces offers three different types of storage spaces:

- *Simple spaces* are just pooled storage, like JBOD, that has multiple drives of whatever capacity added together to form a single virtual drive. Simple spaces provide no resiliency, so if a drive fails, the data goes away. These are good for temporary storage, scratch files, and the like.
- *Mirror spaces* keep more than one copy of the data, like in a RAID mirror array, so you can lose one or more drives and still save your data. The number of drives in the array determines which mirror options you have. A two-way mirror requires at least two drives; a three-way mirror requires five or more. Mirror spaces work like RAID 1 or RAID 10, providing excellent redundancy and robust performance.

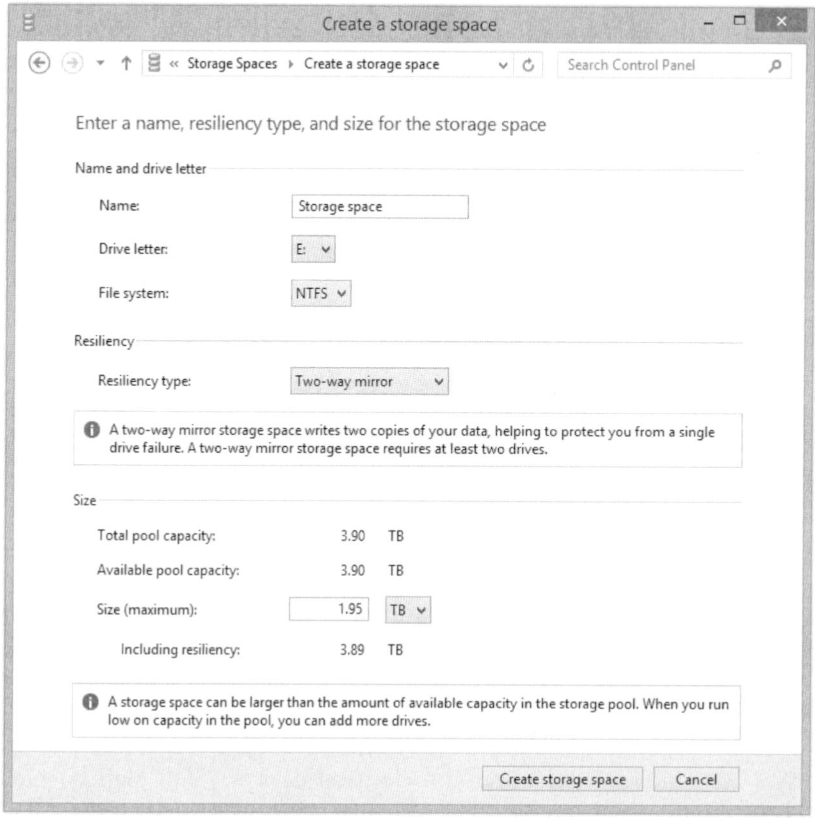

Figure 10-50 Ready to create the storage space

- *Parity spaces* add another layer of resiliency to the array, similarly to how a RAID 5 or RAID 6 provides redundancy. The added resiliency comes with both an upside and a downside. The good thing about parity spaces is that they are more space efficient than two-way mirroring. In two-way mirroring, for every 10 GB of data to be stored, 20 GB of storage must be installed. With parity spaces, for every 10 GB of stored data, only 15 GB of storage needs to be installed. The downside is that the performance overhead to manage parity spaces can have a significant impact on overall performance. Microsoft recommends using parity spaces for big files that don't change a lot, like your movie collection. You can lose one drive and recover in a three-drive parity space. It takes a seven-drive parity space (at minimum) to enable you to recover from a two-drive loss.

When a disk fails in a space, Storage Spaces sends a warning through the standard Windows Action Center messaging. You can open Storage Spaces to reveal the failed drive and replace the drive readily.

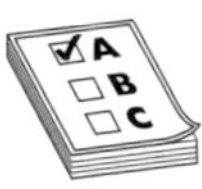

EXAM TIP A storage pool is a collection of physical drives that enables you to flexibly add and expand capacity. Storage spaces are virtual drives that are created from storage pool free space. Storage spaces have resiliency and fixed provisioning.

Storage Spaces enables you to do one more very cool action: future-proof your storage needs. The *thin provisioning* feature means you can create a space with more capacity than your current physical drives provide. You might have a storage pool composed of two 2-TB drives and one 3-TB drive, laid out as a two-way mirror. Rather than limit your new space to a 3-TB capacity, you can assign whatever capacity you want, such as 12 TB, because you know your movie collection will grow. When you start to reach the capacity of the physical drives in the pool, Storage Spaces will tell you and enable you to add more physical capacity at that time. Thin provisioning means you don't have to redo an array or space when you reach the limits of current hardware.

NOTE SSDs work great with some space types and not others. With a simple two-way or three-way mirror, go for it. You'll add some speed and lots of resiliency. With parity spaces, on the other hand, the nature of how SSDs function inside might cause premature failure. Best to use HDDs with parity spaces.

Maintaining and Troubleshooting Hard Drives

Hard drives are complex mechanical and electrical devices. With platters spinning at thousands of rotations per minute, they also generate heat and vibration. All of these factors make hard drives susceptible to failure. In this section, you will learn some basic maintenance tasks that will keep your hard drives healthy, and for those inevitable instances when a hard drive fails, you will also learn what you can do to repair them.

NOTE The "Maintaining and Troubleshooting Hard Drives" section applies primarily to HDDs, not SSDs. The few parts that apply to the latter have been salted into the discussion.

Maintenance

Hard drive maintenance can be broken down into two distinct functions: checking the disk occasionally for failed clusters, and keeping data organized on the drive so it can be accessed quickly.

Error-Checking

Individual clusters on hard drives sometimes go bad. There's nothing you can do to prevent this from happening, so it's important that you check occasionally for bad clusters on drives. The tools used to perform this checking are generically called error-checking utilities, although the terms for two older Microsoft tools—ScanDisk and *chkdsk* (pronounced "checkdisk")—are often used. ScanDisk and chkdsk are command-

line utilities. Microsoft calls the tool *Error-checking* in current versions of Windows, where it is operated as a graphical utility. Mac OS X uses the *Disk Utility*. Linux offers a command-line tool called *fsck*. Whatever the name of the utility, each does the same job: when the tool finds bad clusters, it puts the electronic equivalent of orange cones around them so the system won't try to place data in those bad clusters.

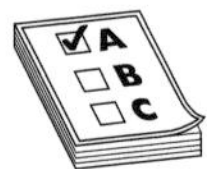

EXAM TIP CompTIA A+ uses the terms CHKDSK and check disk rather than Error-checking.

Most error-checking tools do far more than just check for bad clusters. They go through all of the drive's filenames, looking for invalid names and attempting to fix them. They look for clusters that have no filenames associated with them (we call these *lost chains*) and erase them or save them as files for your review. From time to time, the underlying links between parent and child folders are lost, so a good error-checking tool checks every parent and child folder. With a folder such as C:\Test\Data, for example, they make sure that the Data folder is properly associated with its parent folder, C:\Test, and that C:\Test is properly associated with its child folder, C:\Test\Data.

To access Error-checking on a Windows system, open Windows Explorer/File Explorer, right-click on the drive you want to check, and choose Properties to open the drive's Properties dialog box. Select the Tools tab and click the Check now button (see Figure 10-51) to display the Check Disk dialog box, which has two options

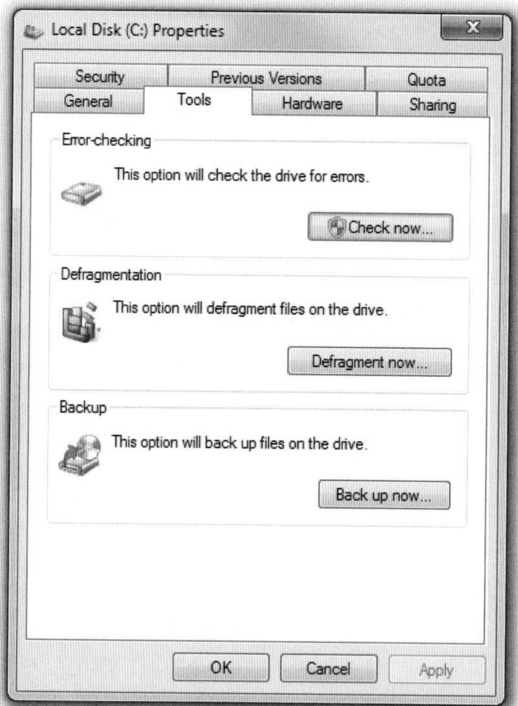

Figure 10-51 The Tools tab in the Properties dialog box

(see Figure 10-52). Check the box next to *Automatically fix file system errors*, but save the option to *Scan for and attempt recovery of bad sectors* for times when you actually suspect a problem, because it takes a while on bigger hard drives.

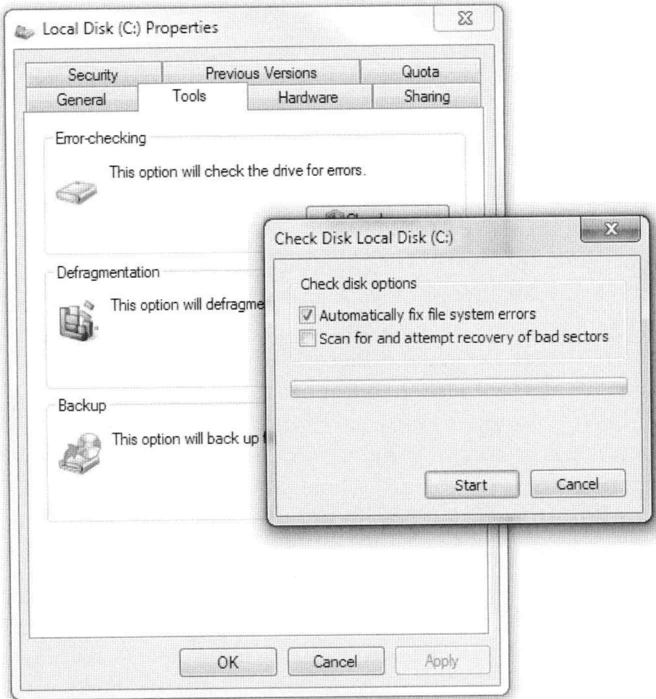

Figure 10-52 Check Disk options

In Mac OS X, you'll find Disk Utility in the Utilities folder. When open, you'll get one or two options, such as Verify Disk or both Verify Disk and Repair Disk. Figure 10-53 shows the options available for a non-startup disk. Verify Disk checks for errors; Repair Disk fixes those errors. You can verify but not fix the startup disk from within Mac OS X. If Disk Utility finds errors on the startup disk, reboot the system and press APPLE KEY-R until the Recovery partition loads. You can fix the startup disk from there.

Now that you know how to run Error-checking, your next question should be, "How often do I run it?" A reasonable maintenance plan would include running it about once a week. Error-checking is fast (unless you use the Scan for and attempt recovery option), and it's a great tool for keeping your system in top shape. The same is true for Disk Utility. Many Linux distributions run fsck periodically, automatically, so you don't have to do anything at all.

Defragmentation

Fragmentation of clusters can increase your drive access times dramatically. It's a good idea to *defragment*—or *defrag*—your drives as part of monthly maintenance. You access the defrag tool Optimize Drives the same way you access Error-checking—right-click a

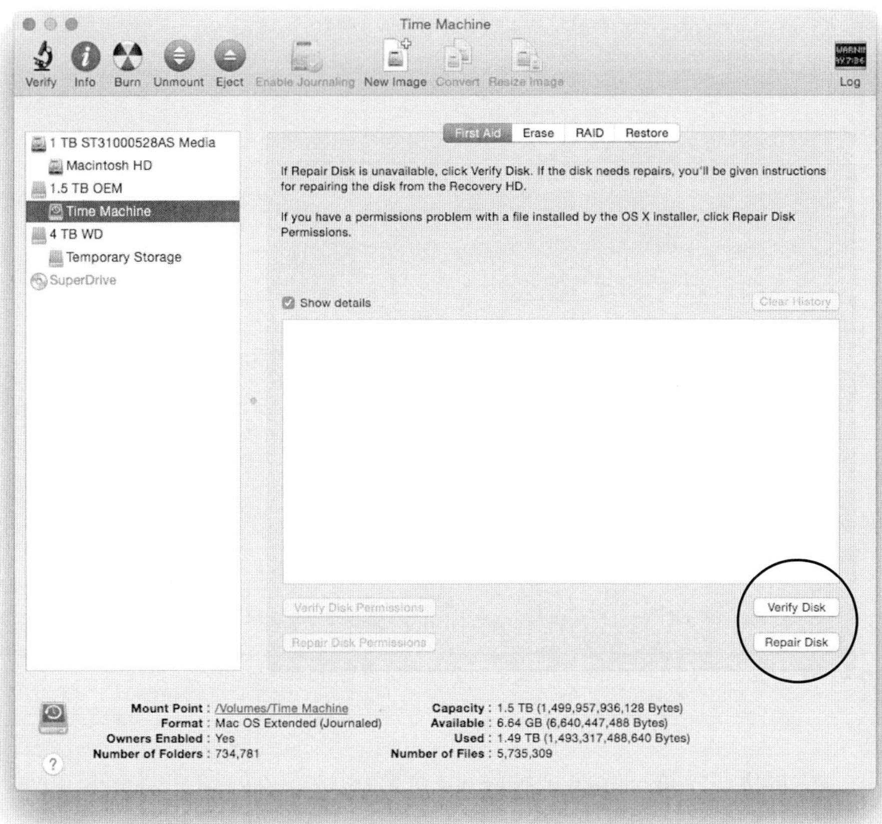

Figure 10-53 Disk Utility options

drive in Windows Explorer/File Explorer and choose Properties—except you click the Defragment now button on the Tools tab to open Optimize Drives (Figure 10-54).

Defragmentation is not interesting to watch. Schedule disk defragmentation to run late at night. You should defragment your drives about once a month, although you could run Optimize Drives every week, and if you run it every night, it takes only a few minutes. The longer you go between defrags, the longer it takes. In Windows 7 and later, Microsoft has made defragging even easier by automatically defragging disks once a week. You can adjust the schedule or even turn it off altogether, but remember that if you don't run Optimize Drives, your system will run slower. If you don't run Error-checking, you may lose data.

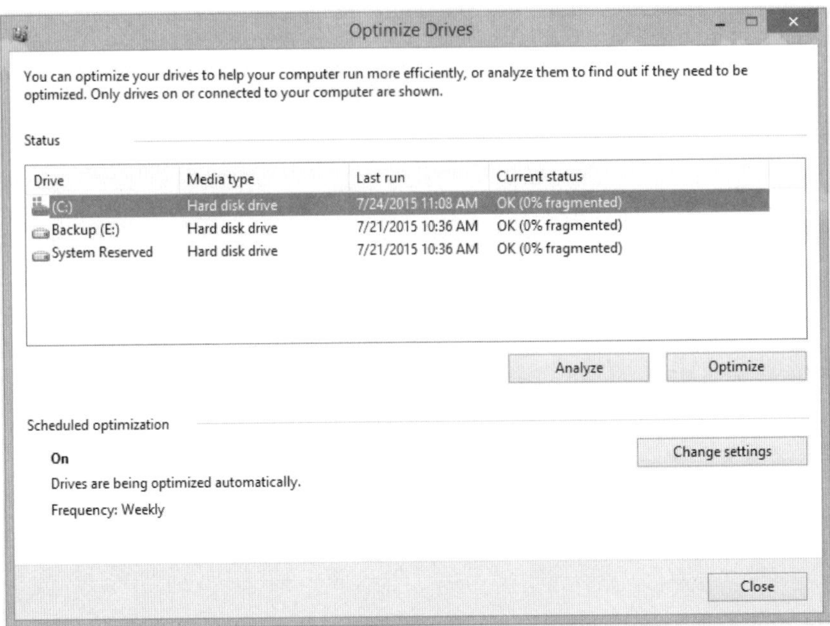

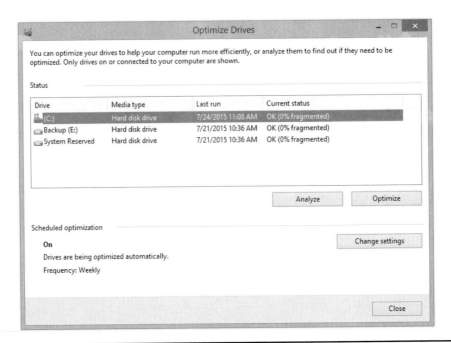

Figure 10-54 Optimize Drives, the defragmenting tool in Windows 8.1

NOTE If you happen to have one of those blazingly fast solid-state drives, you don't have to defrag your drive. In fact, you should *never* defrag an SSD, because it can shorten its lifetime. Windows will not defragment SSDs automatically.

Disk Cleanup

Did you know that the average hard drive is full of trash? Not the junk you intentionally put in your hard drive such as the 23,000 e-mail messages that you refuse to delete from your e-mail program. This kind of trash is all of the files that you never see that Windows keeps for you. Here are a few examples:

- **Files in the Recycle Bin** When you delete a file, it isn't really deleted. It's placed in the Recycle Bin in case you decide you need the file later. I just checked my Recycle Bin and found around 3 GB worth of files (see Figure 10-55). That's a lot of trash!
- **Temporary Internet files** When you go to a Web site, Windows keeps copies of the graphics and other items so the page will load more quickly the next time you access it. You can see these files by opening the Internet Options applet on

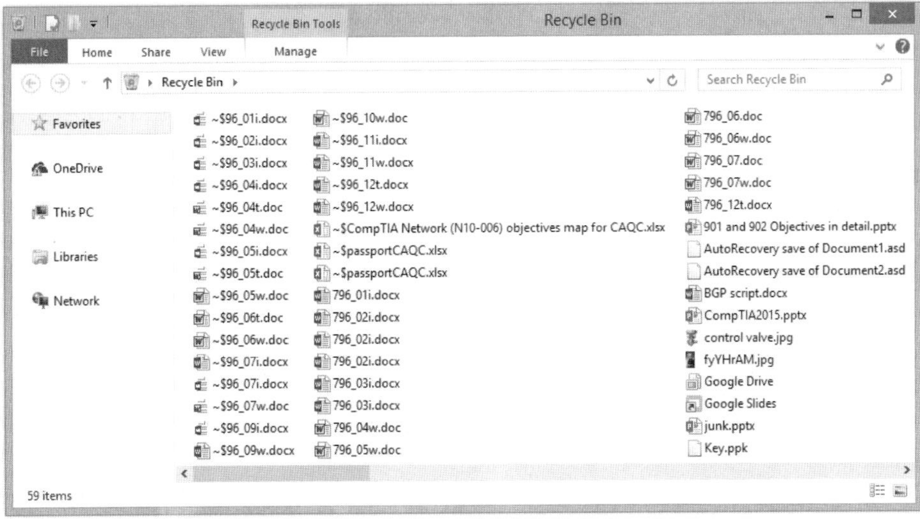

Figure 10-55 Mike's Recycle Bin

the Control Panel. Click the Settings button under the Browsing history label and then click the View files button. Figure 10-56 shows temporary Internet files from Internet Explorer.

- **Downloaded program files** Your system always keeps a copy of any Java or ActiveX applets it downloads. You can see these in the Internet Options applet by clicking the Settings button under the Browsing history label. Click the View

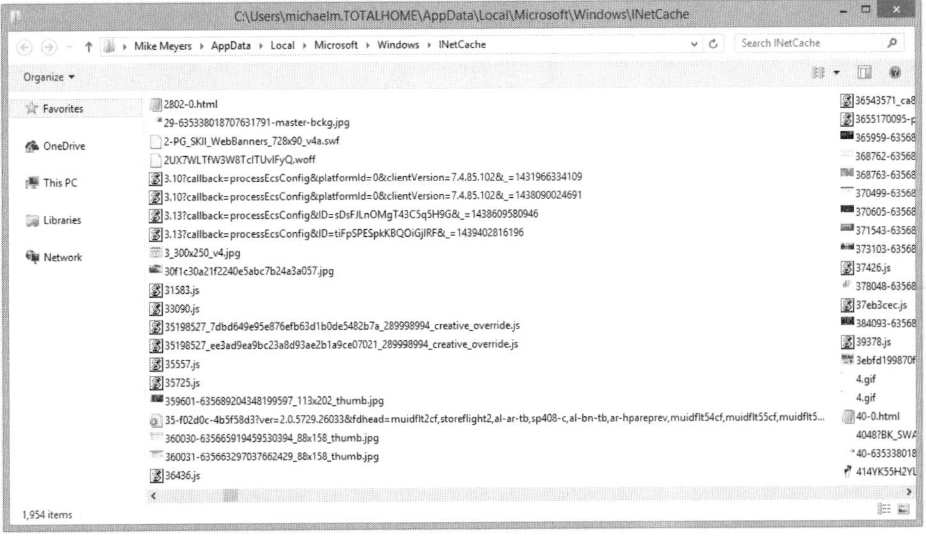

Figure 10-56 Lots of temporary Internet files

objects button on the Temporary Internet Files and History Settings dialog box. You'll generally find only a few tiny files here.

- **Temporary files** Many applications create temporary files that are supposed to be deleted when the application is closed. For one reason or another, these temporary files sometimes aren't deleted. The location of these files varies with the version of Windows, but they always reside in a folder called "Temp."

Every hard drive eventually becomes filled with lots of unnecessary trash. All versions of Windows tend to act erratically when the drives run out of unused space. Fortunately, all versions of Windows have a powerful tool called *Disk Cleanup* (see Figure 10-57). You can access Disk Cleanup in Windows Vista and Windows 7 by choosing Start | All Programs | Accessories | System Tools | Disk Cleanup. In Windows 8/8.1/10, click the Start button and type "disk cleanup." Disk Cleanup will show up in the Search charm or dialog box. Click it to run the program.

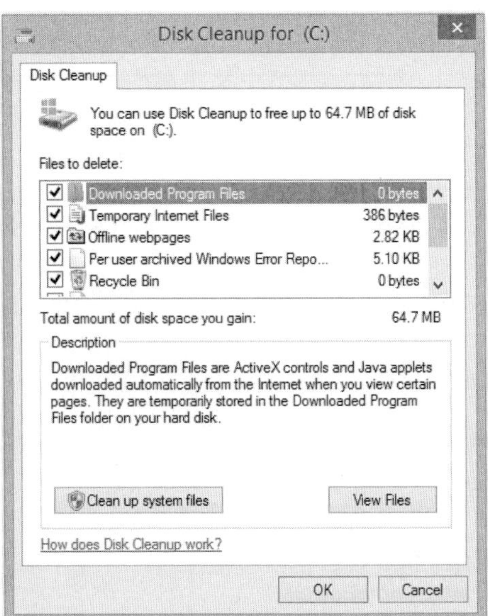

Figure 10-57 Disk Cleanup

Disk Cleanup gets rid of the four types of files just described (and a few others). Run Disk Cleanup once a month or so to keep plenty of space available on your hard drive.

NOTE Mac OS X and Linux do not have a tool equivalent to Disk Cleanup. That said, there are third-party utilities such as BleachBit for Linux that can perform similar operations as Windows Disk Cleanup.

901

Troubleshooting Hard Drive Implementation

There's no scarier computer problem than an error that points to trouble with a hard drive. This section looks at some of the more common problems that occur with hard drives and how to fix them. These issues fall into four broad categories: installation errors, data corruption, dying hard drives, and RAID issues.

Installation Errors

Installing a drive and getting to the point where it can hold data requires four distinct steps: connectivity, CMOS, partitioning, and formatting. If you make a mistake at any point on any of these steps, the drive won't work. The beauty of this is that if you make an error, you can walk back through each step and check for problems. The "Troubleshooting Hard Drive Installation" section in Chapter 9 covered physical connections and CMOS, so this section concentrates on the latter two issues.

Partitioning Partitioning errors generally fall into two groups: failing to partition at all, and making the wrong size or type of partition. You'll recognize the former type of error the first time you open Windows Explorer/File Explorer after installing a drive. If you forgot to partition it, the drive won't even show up in Windows Explorer/File Explorer, only in Disk Management. If you made the partition too small, that'll become painfully obvious when you start filling it up with files.

The fix for partitioning errors is simply to open Disk Management and do the partitioning correctly. Just right-click and select Extend Volume to correct the mistake.

Formatting Failing to format a drive makes the drive unable to hold data. Accessing the drive in Windows results in a drive "is not accessible" error, and from a C:\ prompt, you'll get the famous "Invalid media type" error. Format the drive unless you're certain that the drive has a format already. Corrupted files can create the invalid media error. Check the upcoming "Data Corruption" section for the fix.

Most of the time, formatting is a slow, boring process. But sometimes the drive makes "bad sounds" and you start seeing errors like the one shown in Figure 10-58 at the top of the screen.

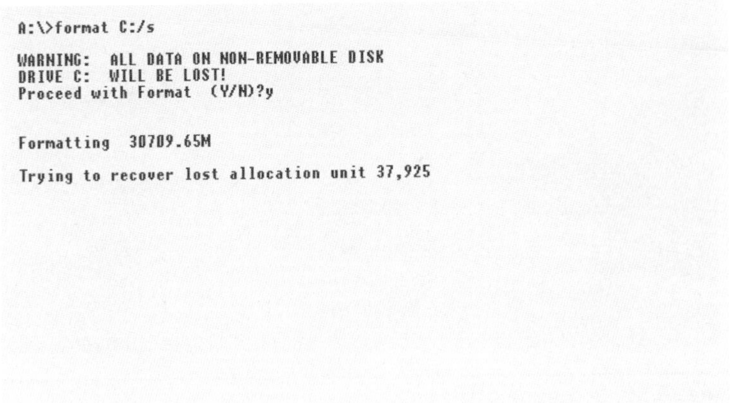

```
A:\>format C:/s

WARNING:  ALL DATA ON NON-REMOVABLE DISK
DRIVE C:  WILL BE LOST!
Proceed with Format  (Y/N)?y

Formatting  30709.65M

Trying to recover lost allocation unit 37,925
```

Figure 10-58 The "Trying to recover lost allocation unit" error

An *allocation unit* is another term for a cluster. The drive has run across a bad cluster and is trying to fix it. For years, I've told techs that seeing this error a few (610) times doesn't mean anything; every drive comes with a few bad spots. This is no longer true. Modern drives actually hide a significant number of extra sectors that they use to replace bad sectors automatically. If a new drive gets a lot of "Trying to recover lost allocation unit" errors, you can bet that the drive is dying and needs to be replaced. Get the hard drive maker's diagnostic tool to be sure. Bad clusters are reported by S.M.A.R.T. (introduced in Chapter 9), one of several S.M.A.R.T. errors possible.

Mental Reinstallation Focus on the fact that all of these errors share a common thread—you just installed a drive! Installation errors don't show up on a system that has been running correctly for three weeks; they show up the moment you try to do something with the drive you just installed. If a newly installed drive fails to work, do a "mental reinstallation." Does the drive show up in the UEFI or traditional BIOS setup screens? No? Then recheck the cables, master/slave settings on old PATA drives, and power. If it does show up, did you remember to partition and format the drive? Did it need to be set to active? These are commonsense questions that come to mind as you march through your mental reinstallation. Even if you've installed thousands of drives over the years, you'll be amazed at how often you do things such as forget to plug in power to a drive. Do the mental reinstallation—it really works!

Data Corruption

All hard drives occasionally get corrupted data in individual sectors. Power surges, accidental shutdowns, corrupted installation media, and viruses, along with hundreds of other problems, can cause this corruption. In most cases, this type of error shows up while Windows is running. Figure 10-59 shows a classic example.

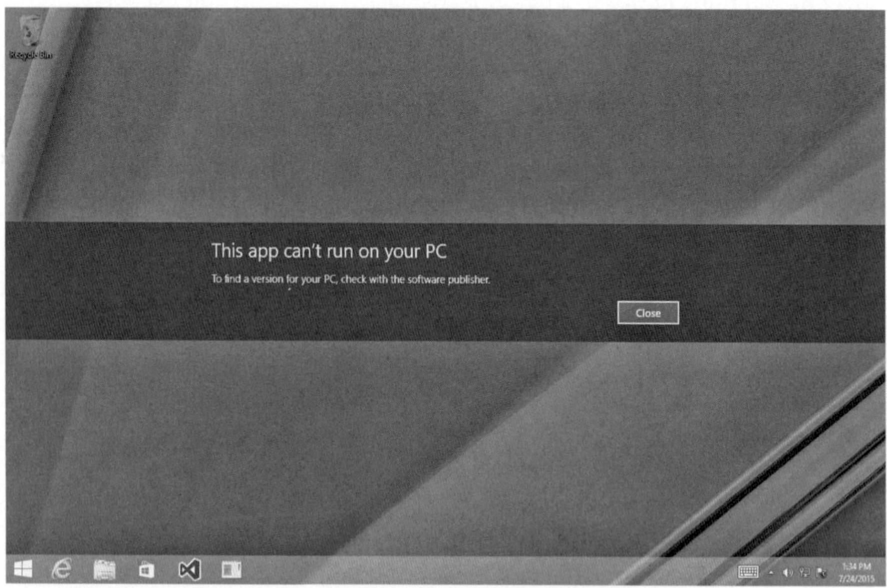

Figure 10-59 A corrupted data error

You may also see Windows error messages saying one of the following:

- "The following file is missing or corrupt"
- "The download location information is damaged"
- "Unable to load file"
- "... is not a valid Win32 application"
- "Bootmgr is missing...Press Ctrl+Alt+Del to restart"
- "Your PC ran into a problem...This problem caused your PC to restart"
- "This app can't run on your PC"

If core boot files become corrupted, you may see text errors at boot, such as the following:

- "Cannot find COMMAND.COM"
- "Error loading operating system"
- "Invalid BOOT.INI"
- "NTLDR is missing or corrupt"
- "An error occurred while attempting to read the boot configuration data"

On older programs, you may see a command prompt open with errors such as this one:

```
Sector not found reading drive C: Abort, Retry, Fail?
```

The first fix for any of these problems is to run the Error-checking utility. Error-checking will go through and mark bad clusters and, hopefully, move your data to a good cluster.

If the same errors continue to appear after you run the Error-checking utility, there's a chance that the drive has bad sectors.

Almost all drives today take advantage of built-in *error correction code (ECC)* that constantly checks the drive for bad sectors. If the ECC detects a bad sector, it marks the sector as bad in the drive's internal error map. Don't confuse this error map with a FAT. The partitioning program creates the FAT. The drive's internal error map was created at the factory on reserved drive heads and is invisible to the system. If the ECC finds a bad sector, you will get a corrupted data error as the computer attempts to read the bad sector. Disk-checking utilities fix this problem most of the time.

Many times, the ECC thinks a bad sector is good, however, and fails to update the internal error map. In this case, you need a program that goes back into the drive and marks the sectors as bad. That's where the powerful SpinRite utility from Gibson Research (www.grc.com) comes into play. SpinRite marks sectors as bad or good more accurately than ECC and does not disturb the data, enabling you to run SpinRite without fear of losing anything. And if it finds a bad sector with data in it, SpinRite has powerful

algorithms that usually recover the data on all but the most badly damaged sectors (see Figure 10-60).

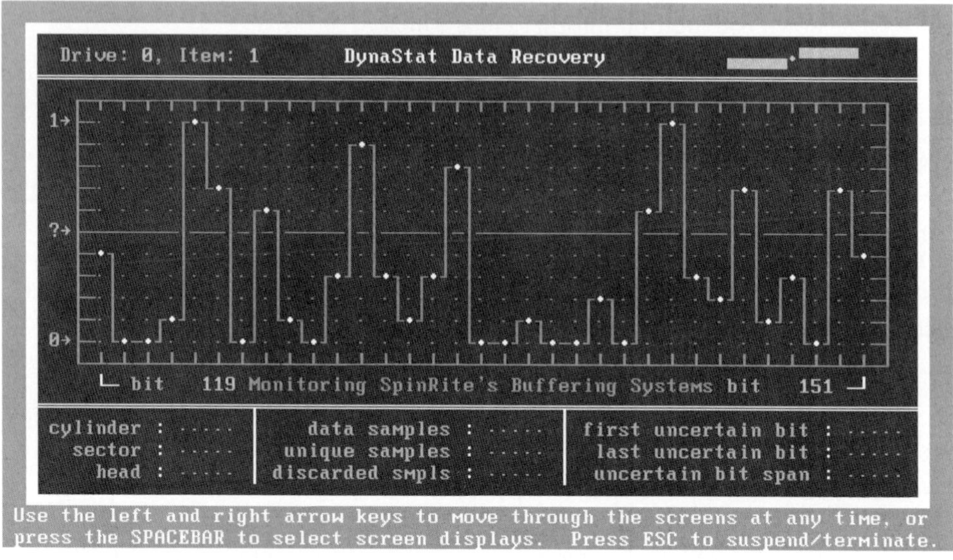

Figure 10-60 SpinRite at work

Without SpinRite, you must use a low-level format program supplied by the hard drive maker, assuming you can get one (not all are willing to distribute these). These programs work like SpinRite in that they aggressively check the hard drive's sectors and update the internal error map. Unfortunately, they wipe out all data on the drive. At least you can use the drive, even if it means repartitioning, formatting, and reinstalling everything.

Dying Hard Drive

Physical problems are rare, thankfully, but they are devastating when they happen. If a hard drive is truly damaged physically, there is nothing that you or any service technician can do to fix it. Fortunately, hard drives are designed to take a phenomenal amount of punishment without failing. Physical problems manifest themselves in several ways: you start getting read/write failures, the drive works properly but makes a lot of noise, or the drive seems to disappear. You might get a failure to boot after experiencing any of these events.

Windows will give you error messages with read/write failures. Good hard drives don't fail to read or write. Only dying ones have these problems.

All mechanical hard drives make noise—the hum as the platters spin and the occasional slight scratching noise as the read/write heads access sectors are normal. However, if your drive begins to make any of the following sounds, it is about to die:

- Continuous high-pitched squeal
- A loud clicking noise, a short pause, and then another series of clicks
- Continuous grinding or rumbling

Back up your critical data and replace the drive. Windows comes with great tools for backing up data.

You'll know when a drive simply dies. If it's the drive that contains your operating system, the system will lock up. When you try to restart the computer, you'll see this error message or something similar to it:

```
No Boot Device Present
```

If it's a second drive, it will simply stop showing up in Windows Explorer/File Explorer. The first thing to do in this case is to fire up the System Setup program and see if autodetect sees the drive. If it does, you do not have a physical problem with the drive. If autodetect fails, shut off the system and remove the data cable, but leave the power cable attached. Restart the system and listen to the drive. If the drive spins up, you know it is getting good power. This is usually a clue that the drive is probably good. In that case, you need to look for more mundane problems such as an unplugged data cord or jumpers incorrectly set. If the drive doesn't spin up, try another power connector. If it still doesn't spin up and you've triple-checked the jumpers (PATA only) and data cable, you have a problem with the onboard electronics, and the drive is dead.

If the device is a solid-state drive, the troubleshooting process is similar: either the power or motherboard controller is bad, a power or data cable has failed, or the drive electronics are dead. Start with the power cable, changing it for a known good one. Then try a known good data cable using the original motherboard connection. Next, try a different motherboard connector. Still haven't got it? It's likely a bad drive, but you should confirm so by testing it in another known good computer to see if it is detected by UEFI/BIOS and then by Windows Disk Management.

NOTE If you ever lose a hard drive that contains absolutely critical information, you can turn to a company that specializes in hard drive data recovery. The job will be expensive—prices usually start around $1000 (U.S.)—but when you have to have the data, such companies are your only hope. Do a Web search for "data recovery" or check the Yellow Pages for companies in this line of business.

Troubleshooting RAID

For the most part, drive problems in a RAID array are identical to those seen on individual drives. There are a couple of errors unique to RAID, however, that need their own separate discussion.

Drive Not Recognized If you're using hardware RAID and the configuration firmware doesn't recognize one of the drives, first check to make sure the drives are powered and that they are connected to the proper connections. This is especially true of motherboards with onboard RAID that require you to use only certain special RAID connectors.

RAID Stops Working When one of the drives in a RAID array fails, several things can happen depending on the type of array and the RAID controller. With RAID 0,

the effect is dramatic. Many enthusiasts use RAID 0 for their OS drive to make it snappier. If you're running such a rig that then loses a drive, you'll most likely get a critical stop error, a sad face or Blue Screen of Death (BSoD). On reboot, the computer will fail to boot or you'll get a message such as *OS not found*. You lose all your data because there's no redundancy on a stripe set. You may see error messages before the crash related to read/write failures. On Mac OS X machines, a failing drive or array may result in the spinning "pin wheel." If there are no other systemic problems such as low RAM or low disk space, it's time to break out RAID- or disk-diagnostic tools such as S.M.A.R.T. reader software.

All the other levels of RAID tend to do nothing extraordinary when one drive in the array fails. When you reboot the system, that's when the RAID controller (if hardware) or Windows (if you've used the built-in tools) will squeal and tell you that a drive has failed.

Often, the failure of a drive will cause access to the contents of the drive to slow to a crawl, and that *slow performance* is your clue to check Device Manager or the RAID controller firmware. Some drive failures will cause the computer to crash. Others will show no effects until you get the error messages at reboot.

Regardless of the reason a RAID stops working or the effects, the fix is simple. Replace the failed drive and let the RAID rebuild itself. Life is good. If you need to know the reason for the failure, trying running S.M.A.R.T. reader software on the failed drive. If the drive electronics have some functionality, you may get results.

RAID Not Found The CompTIA A+ 220-901 exam objectives use the term "RAID not found," which doesn't really exist as an error but instead implies a series of errors where an existing RAID array suddenly fails to appear. The problem with these errors is that they vary greatly depending on the make and model of hardware RAID or (heaven forbid) if you used software RAID.

A properly functioning hardware RAID array will always show up in the configuration utility. If an existing array stops working and you enter the configuration utility only to find the array is gone, you have big trouble. This points to either dead drives or faulty controllers. In either case they must be replaced.

If the array is gone but you can still see the drives, then the controller may have broken the array on its own. This is a rare action that some controllers do to try to save data. You should at least try to rebuild the array using whatever tools the controllers provide.

Beyond A+

Modern hard drives have many other features that are worth knowing about but that rarely impact beginning techs. A couple of the more interesting ones are spindle speed and third-party hard drive tools. If you have a burning desire to dive into hard drives in all their glory, you need not go any farther than the StorageReview.com, an excellent site dedicated solely to hard drives and other storage devices such as SANs, NAS devices, and SSDs.

Third-Party Partition Tools

Disk Management is a good tool, but it's still limited for some situations. Some really great third-party tools on the market can give you incredible flexibility and power to structure and restructure your hard drive storage to meet your changing needs. They each have interesting unique features, but in general they enable you to create, change, and delete partitions on a hard drive *without* destroying any of the programs or data stored there. Slick! These programs aren't covered on the CompTIA A+ exams, but all PC techs use at least one of them, so let's explore two of the most well-known examples: Avanquest Partition Commander Professional and the open source Linux tool GParted.

Avanquest offers a variety of related products, one of which is the very useful Partition Commander. It supports all versions of Windows and enables you to play with your partitions without destroying your data. Among its niftier features are the capability to convert a dynamic disk to a basic disk nondestructively (which you can't do with the Microsoft-supplied Windows tools), to defrag the master file table on an NTFS partition, and to move unused space from one partition to another on the same physical drive, automatically resizing the partitions based on the amount of space you tell it to move. Figure 10-61 shows the Partition Commander dialog box for moving unused space between partitions.

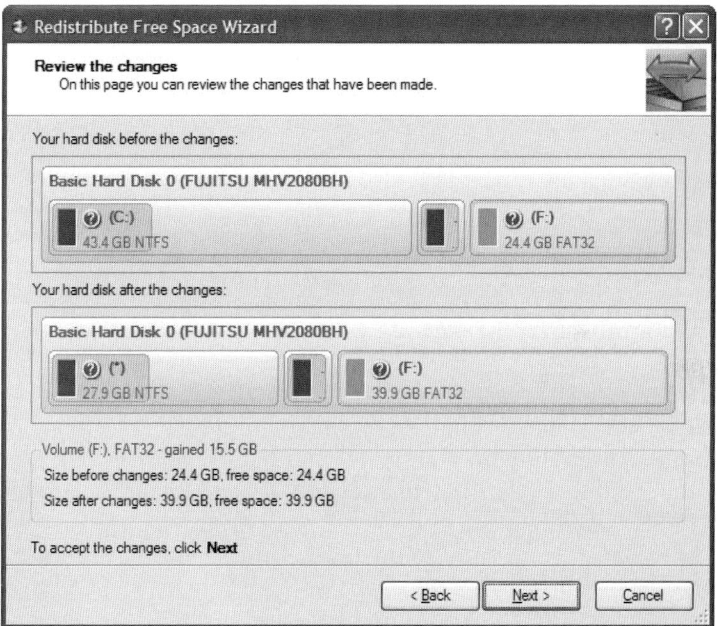

Figure 10-61 Partition Commander

The only problem with Partition Commander is that it costs money. There's nothing wrong with spending money on a good product, but if you can find something that does the job for free, why not try it? If you think like I do, check out the GNOME Partition Editor, better known as *GParted*. You can find it at http://gparted.org.

GParted is an incredibly powerful partition editor and does almost everything the for-pay partition editors do, but it's free. In fact, you might already have a copy lying around in the form of an Ubuntu desktop live CD. If you look closely at Figure 10-62, you'll notice that it uses strange names for the partitions, such as HDA1 or SDA2. These are Linux conventions and are well documented in GParted's Help screens. Take a little time and you'll love GParted too.

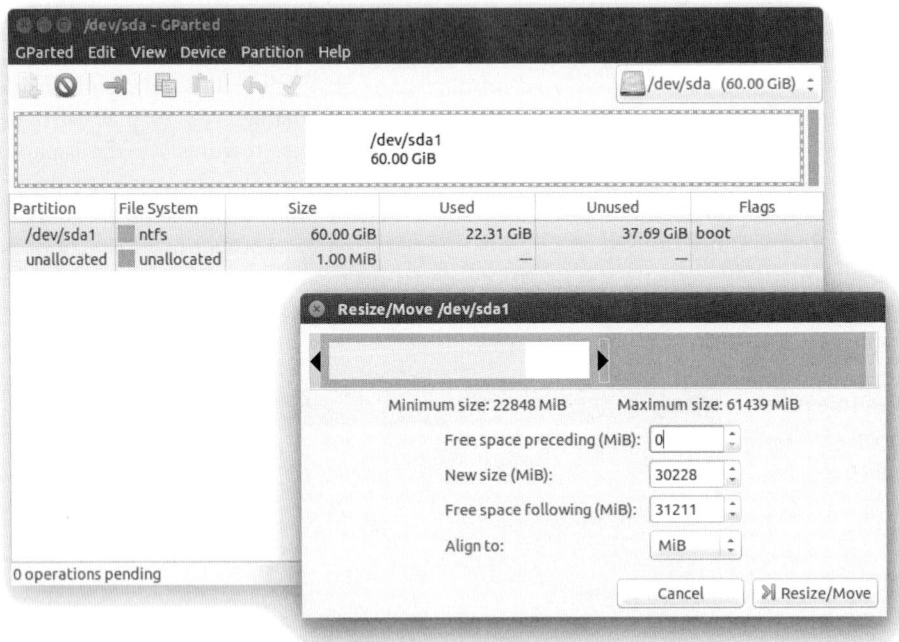

Figure 10-62 GParted in action

The one downside to GParted is that it is a Linux program—because no Windows version exists, you need Linux to run it. So how do you run Linux on a Windows system without actually installing Linux on your hard drive? The answer is easy—the folks at GParted will give you the tools to burn a live CD that boots Linux so you can run GParted!

A *live CD* is a complete OS on a CD. Understand this is not an installation CD like your Windows installation disc. The OS is already installed on the CD. You boot from the live CD and the OS loads into RAM, just like the OS on your hard drive loads into RAM at boot. As the live CD boots, it recognizes your hardware and loads the proper drivers into RAM so everything works. You get everything you'd expect from an OS with one big exception: a live CD does not touch your hard drive. Of course, you may run programs (such as GParted) that work on your hard drive, which makes live CDs popular with PC techs, because you can toss them into a cranky system and run utilities.

The truly intrepid might want to consider using The Ultimate Boot CD (UBCD), basically a huge pile of useful freeware utilities compiled by frustrated technician Ben Burrows, who couldn't find a boot disk when he needed one. His Web site is www.ultimatebootcd.com. The UBCD has more than 100 different tools, all placed on a single live CD. It has all of the low-level diagnostic tools for all of the hard drive makers, four or five different partitioning tools, S.M.A.R.T. viewers, hard drive wiping utilities, and hard drive cloning tools (nice for when you want to replace a hard drive with a larger one). Little documentation is provided, however, and many of the tools require experience way beyond the scope of the CompTIA A+ exams. I will tell you that I have a copy and I use it.

Chapter Review

Questions

1. Which is the most complete list of file systems Windows can use?
   - A. FAT16, FAT32, NTFS
   - B. FAT16, FAT32, FAT64, NTFS
   - C. FAT16, FAT32
   - D. FAT16, NTFS
2. Which of the following correctly identifies the four possible entries in a file allocation table?
   - A. Filename, date, time, size
   - B. Number of the starting cluster, number of the ending cluster, number of used clusters, number of available clusters
   - C. An end-of-file marker, a bad-sector marker, code indicating the cluster is available, the number of the cluster where the next part of the file is stored
   - D. Filename, folder location, starting cluster number, ending cluster number
3. What program does Microsoft include with Windows to partition and format a drive?
   - A. Format
   - B. Disk Management console
   - C. Disk Administrator console
   - D. System Commander

4. What does NTFS use to provide security for individual files and folders?
   A. Dynamic disks
   B. ECC
   C. Access Control List
   D. MFT
5. Jaime wishes to check her hard drive for errors. What tool should she use in Windows 8.1?
   A. FDISK
   B. Format
   C. Disk Management
   D. Error-checking
6. To make your files unreadable by others, what should you use?
   A. Clustering
   B. Compression
   C. Disk quotas
   D. Encryption
7. How can you effectively expand the capacity of an NTFS drive?
   A. Create an extended partition to extend the capacity.
   B. Install a second drive and mount it to a folder on the original smaller NTFS drive.
   C. Convert the drive to a dynamic disk and create a mirrored set.
   D. Format the drive with the Quick Format option.
8. Which configuration requires three same-sized volumes?
   A. RAID 5
   B. Mirrored set
   C. Spanned volume
   D. Striped volume
9. Which of the following partitioning schemes enables the creation of more than four partitions or volumes on a single hard drive? (Select two.)
   A. MBR
   B. GPT
   C. Dynamic disk
   D. MFT

10. Which storage option in Windows 8 or later offers the best mix of resiliency and performance with two drives?
    - **A.** Simple space
    - **B.** Two-way mirror space
    - **C.** Three-way mirror space
    - **D.** Parity space

Answers

1. **B.** Modern versions of Windows can use FAT (FAT16), FAT32, and NTFS for hard drives, and FAT64 for removable flash-media drives.
2. **C.** The four possible entries in a file allocation table are an end-of-file marker, a bad-sector marker, code indicating the cluster is available, and the number of the cluster where the next part of the file is stored.
3. **B.** Windows uses the Disk Management console to partition and format a drive.
4. **C.** Because NTFS views individual files and folders as objects, it can provide security for those objects through an Access Control List.
5. **D.** Error-checking is used to check a drive for errors.
6. **D.** To make your files unreadable by others, use encryption.
7. **B.** You can effectively expand the capacity of an NTFS drive by installing a second drive and mounting it to a folder on the original smaller NTFS drive.
8. **A.** RAID 5 requires three same-sized volumes.
9. **B, C.** Both GPT and dynamic disk partitioning schemes enable the creation of more than four partitions or volumes on a single hard drive.
10. **B.** A two-way mirror space efficiently and effectively uses two drives for resilience and performance. A simple space offers no resiliency; the other options require three or more drives.

CHAPTER 11

Essential Peripherals

In this chapter, you will learn how to

- Explain how to support multipurpose connectors
- Identify and install standard peripherals (that aren't display devices) on a PC
- Identify and install standard storage devices (that aren't SSDs or HDDs) and their media

Modern computing devices sport a variety of peripherals—stuff you plug into the system unit—that extend and enhance their capabilities. This chapter looks at common ports first, then turns to a laundry list of standard peripherals. The chapter finishes with a discussion of various mass storage devices, such as flash drives and the fading but not yet gone optical disc technologies.

901

Supporting Common Ports

Whenever you're dealing with a device that isn't playing nice, you need to remember that you're never dealing with just a device—you're dealing with a device and the port to which it is connected. Before you start troubleshooting the device, you need to take a look at the issues and technologies of some of the more common input/output (I/O) ports and see what needs to be done to keep them running well.

USB Ports

Most folks have used USB ports and USB devices. Let's go beyond the user level, now, and approach USB as techs. Here's a more in-depth look at USB and some of the issues involved with using USB devices.

Understanding USB

The *USB host controller*, an integrated circuit that is usually built into the chipset, controls every USB device that connects to it. Inside the host controller is a *USB root hub*: the part of the host controller that makes the physical connection to the USB ports.

Every USB root hub is really just a bus—similar in many ways to an expansion bus. Figure 11-1 shows a diagram of the relationship between the host controller, root hub, and USB ports.

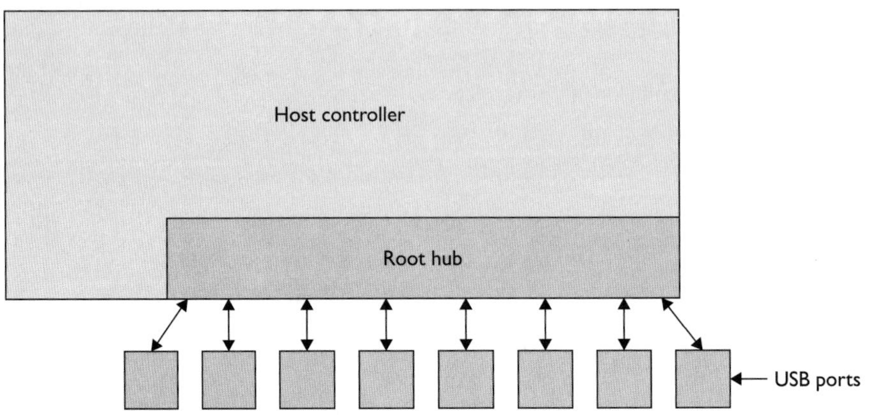

Figure 11-1 Host controller, root hub, and USB ports

A single host controller can theoretically support up to 127 devices, though real-life circumstances create sharper limits. Even if a host adapter supports a certain number of ports, there's no guarantee that the motherboard maker will supply that many ports. To give a common example, a host adapter might support eight ports while the motherboard maker only supplies four adapters.

Every USB device connected to a single host adapter/root hub *shares* that USB bus with every other device connected to it. The more devices you place on a single host adapter, the more the total USB bus slows down and the more power they use.

USB devices, like any electrical device, need power to run, but not all take care of their own power needs. A powered USB device comes with its own electrical cord that is usually connected in turn to an AC adapter. *Bus-powered* USB devices take power from the USB bus itself; they don't bring any AC or DC power with them. When too many bus-powered devices take too much power from the USB bus, bad things happen—some devices won't work; other devices will lock up. You'll also often get a simple message from Windows saying that the hub power has been exceeded, and it just won't work.

USB Standards and Compatibility

The USB standard has gone through several revisions:

- USB 1.1 was the first widely adopted standard and defined two speeds: *Low-Speed USB*, running at a maximum of 1.5 Mbps (plenty for keyboards and mice), and *Full-Speed USB*, running at up to 12 Mbps.
- The USB 2.0 standard introduced *Hi-Speed USB* running at a whopping 480 Mbps.

- USB 3.0 is capable of speeds of up to 5 Gbps—ten times faster than USB 2.0! USB 3.0 is commonly referred to as *SuperSpeed USB*. It's also referred to as *USB 3.1 Gen 1*, though *not* on the CompTIA A+ exams.
- USB 3.1 can handle speeds up to 10 Gbps. It's referred to as *SuperSpeed USB 10 Gbps* or *USB 3.1 Gen 2*.

If you think all of those names and numbers are confusing, you're right. Table 11-1 provides a quick reference to help you sort it all out.

Name	Standard	Maximum Speed
Low-Speed USB	USB 1.1	1.5 Mbps
Full-Speed USB	USB 1.1	12 Mbps
Hi-Speed USB	USB 2.0	480 Mbps
SuperSpeed USB	USB 3.0	5 Gbps
SuperSpeed USB 10 Gbps	USB 3.1 Gen 2	10 Gbps

Table 11-1 USB Standards

NOTE Each standard defines more than just the speed. Because they were incorporated into the newer standard, many Low-Speed and Full-Speed USB devices are also USB 2.0 devices.

Hi-Speed USB is fully backward compatible with USB 1.1 devices, while USB 3.0/3.1 is backward compatible with USB 2.0 devices. Those old devices won't run any faster than they used to, however. To take advantage of the fastest USB speeds, you must connect Hi-Speed USB devices to Hi-Speed USB ports by using Hi-Speed USB cables (or connect SuperSpeed USB devices to SuperSpeed USB ports with SuperSpeed USB cables). Although backward compatibility at least enables you to use the newer USB device with an older port, a quick bit of math tells you how much time you're sacrificing when you're transferring a 2-GB file at 480 Mbps instead of 10 Gbps!

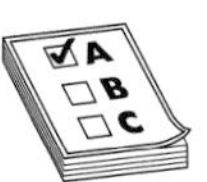

EXAM TIP The USB Implementers Forum (USB-IF) does not officially use "Low-Speed" and "Full-Speed" to describe 1.5-Mbps and 12-Mbps devices, calling both of them simply "USB 1.1." On the CompTIA A+ certification exams, though, you'll see the marketplace-standard nomenclature used here. For the 220-901 exam, focus on USB 1.1, 2.0, and 3.0.

Most people want to take advantage of these amazing speeds, but what do you do if your motherboard doesn't have built-in Hi-Speed or SuperSpeed USB ports? One option

is to add a USB 2.0 or USB 3.0 adapter card like the one shown in Figure 11-2. CompTIA refers to these cards (at any version) as *USB cards*.

Figure 11-2 USB adapter card

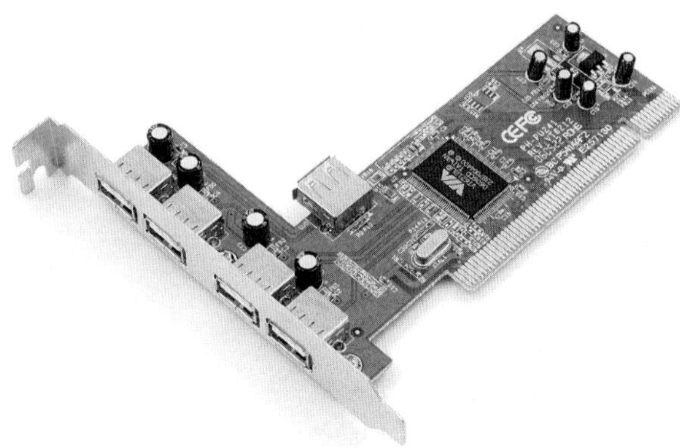

Motherboards capable of both USB 1.1 and USB 2.0 usually share the available USB ports (see Figure 11-3). For every USB port on your computer, plugging in a Low-Speed or Full-Speed device uses the USB 1.1 host controller, and plugging in a Hi-Speed device uses the USB 2.0 host controller.

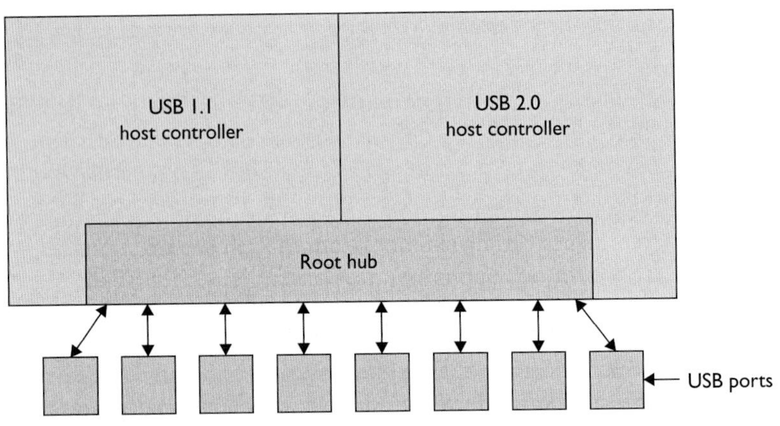

Figure 11-3 Shared USB ports

USB 3.0 and 3.1, on the other hand, are different enough from USB 2.0 that they use separate and clearly marked ports. The USB 3.0 standard suggests that these ports be colored blue to differentiate them. USB 3.1 ports are colored teal. You can still plug older USB devices into a USB 3.0 or 3.1 port, but they will run at the slower speeds. The only ports that work at 10 Gbps are the teal USB 3.1 Gen 2 ports (see Figure 11-4).

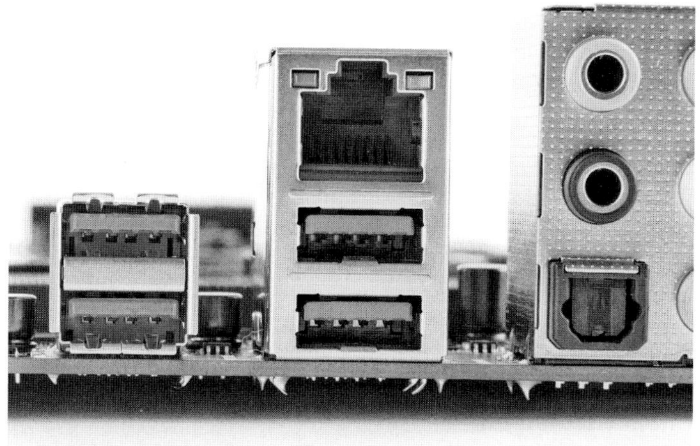

Figure 11-4 Blue USB 3.0 ports (left) and teal USB 3.1 ports (center)

USB Cables and Connectors

USB connectors and ports come in multiple sizes: A, B, mini-A, mini-B, micro-A, micro-B, and Type-C. USB A ports and connectors are for interfacing with the PC. Most peripherals use B, mini-B, or micro-B connectors and ports. Micro connections are especially popular on smartphones. Type-C connectors enable any USB device to connect. These debuted as we went to print.

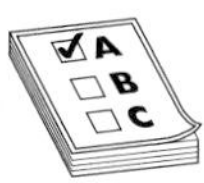

EXAM TIP On USB 1.1 and 2.0 cables, the A and B ports and connectors use four pins, while the rest use five pins. USB 3.0/3.1 A and B ports and connectors use nine pins. A larger, 11-pin USB 3.0/3.1 B connector that can supply extra power to a device also exists.

Almost any USB device can use any USB standard's cable, though you won't always get the best possible speeds. USB 1.1 and USB 2.0 cables look and work the same. Your connection speed will change primarily based on the quality of the cable.

There is one big exception to this cross-compatibility, however: to achieve SuperSpeed speeds with USB 3.0, you'll need a USB 3.0/3.1 cable (see Figure 11-5). Because the USB 3.0/3.1 B connector is larger than other B connectors, your USB 3.0/3.1 cable will only work with USB 3.0/3.1 devices.

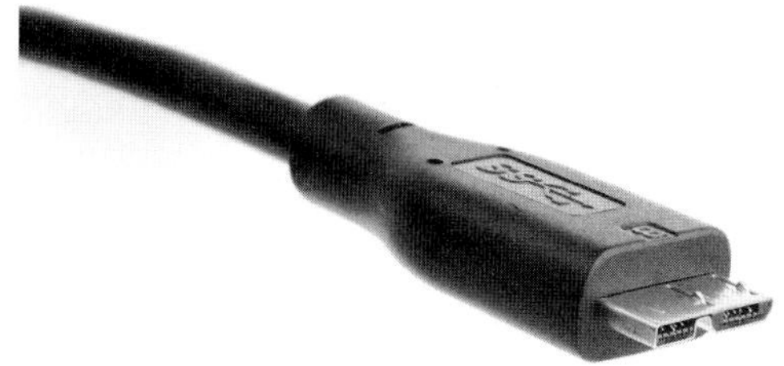

Figure 11-5 USB 3.0/3.1 cable

NOTE In general, your connection will operate at the speed of the slowest device involved. If you have a USB 2.0 device connected to a USB 3.*x* port on your PC, it will operate at USB 2.0 speeds.

Cable length is an important limitation to keep in mind with USB. USB 1.1 and USB 2.0 specifications allow for a maximum cable length of 5 meters, although you may add a powered USB hub every 5 meters to extend this distance. Although most USB devices never get near this maximum, some devices, such as digital cameras, can come with cables at or near the maximum 5-meter cable length. The USB 3.*x* standards don't define a maximum cable length, but to reach the fastest speeds possible, you shouldn't use a cable longer than 3 meters. Because USB is a two-way (bidirectional) connection, as the cable grows longer, even a standard, well-shielded, 20-gauge, twisted-pair USB cable begins to suffer from electrical interference. To avoid these problems, I stick to cables that are no more than about 2 meters long.

If you really want to play it safe, spend a few extra dollars and get a high-quality USB cable like the one shown in Figure 11-6. These cables come with extra shielding and improved electrical performance to make sure your USB data gets from the device to your computer safely.

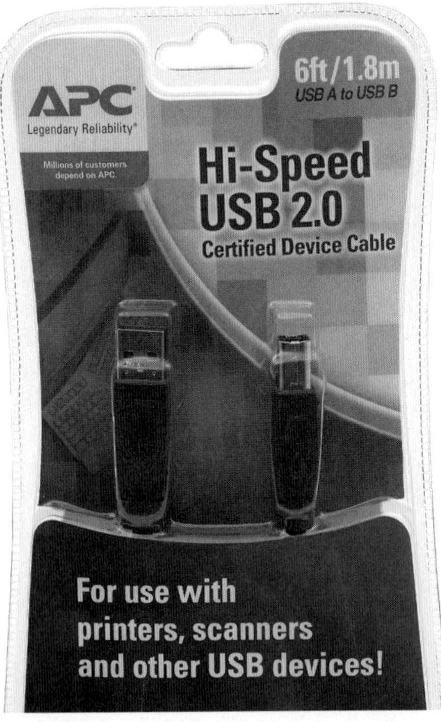

Figure 11-6 USB cable

Try This!

What Speed Is Your USB?

Here's a scenario. A client complains that a new USB device seems a little slow. You need to determine if the fault lies with the device or the USB implementation on the client's computing device—in this case, a Windows 10 PC.

Open Device Manger and locate two or three controllers under the Universal Serial Bus icon. The Standard Enhanced Host Controller is the Hi-Speed controller. The Standard OpenHCD Host Controller is the Low- and Full-Speed controller. You might also have a third controller named the Extensible Host Controller Interface (xHCI). This controller, as you might have guessed, is for USB 3.*x* SuperSpeed connections.

USB Hubs

Each USB host controller supports up to 127 USB devices, but as mentioned earlier, most motherboard makers provide only six to eight real USB ports. So what do you do when you need to add more USB devices than the motherboard provides ports? You can add more host controllers (in the form of internal cards), or you can use a USB hub. A *USB hub* is a device that extends a single USB connection to two or more USB ports, almost always directly from one of the USB ports connected to the root hub. Figure 11-7 shows a typical USB hub. USB hubs are often embedded into peripherals. The keyboard in Figure 11-8 comes with a built-in USB hub—very handy!

Figure 11-7 USB hub

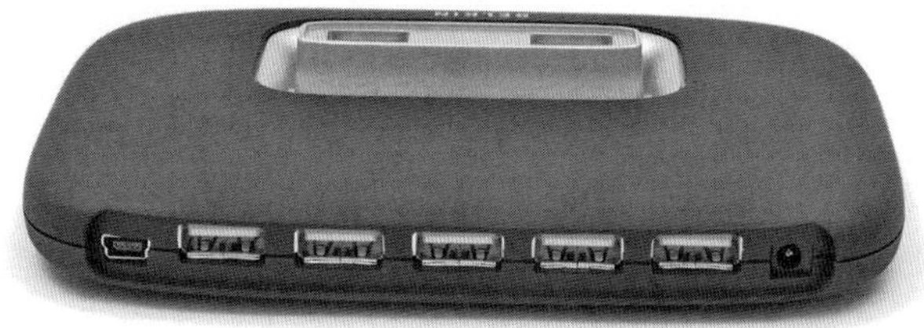

Figure 11-8 USB keyboard with built-in hub

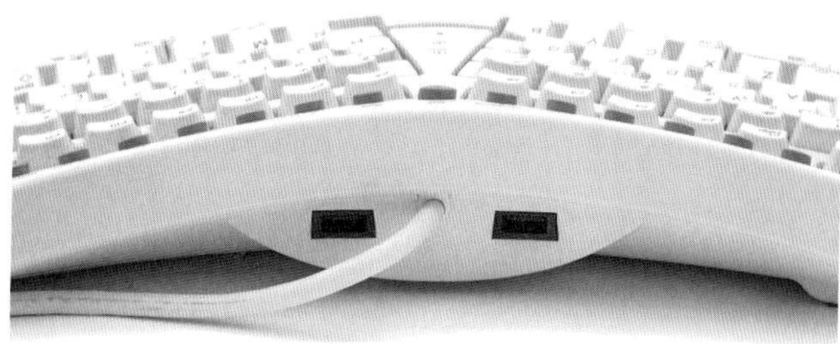

Hubs also come in powered and bus-powered versions. If you choose to use a general-purpose USB hub like the one shown in Figure 11-7, try to find a powered one, as too many devices on a single USB root hub will draw too much power and create problems.

USB Configuration

The biggest troubleshooting challenge you encounter with USB is a direct result of its widespread adoption and ease of use. Pretty much every modern PC comes with multiple USB ports, and anyone can easily pick up a cool new USB device at the local computer store. The problems arise when all of this USB installation activity gets out of control, with too many devices using the wrong types of ports or pulling too much power. But, by following a few easy steps, you can avoid or eliminate these issues.

The first rule of USB installation is this: Always install the device driver for a new USB device *before* you plug it into the USB port. Once you've installed the device driver and you know the ports are active (running properly in Device Manager), feel free to plug in the new device and hot-swap to your heart's content. USB device installation really is a breeze as long as you follow this rule!

NOTE There are exceptions to the "install the driver first" rule. USB thumb drives, for example, don't need extra drivers at all. Just plug them in and every modern OS will pick them up. (Technically speaking, though, that means the drivers came *preinstalled* with the operating system!)

Windows and Mac OS X include a large number of built-in drivers for USB devices. You can count on the OSs to recognize keyboards, mice, and other basic devices with their built-in drivers. Just be aware that if your new mouse or keyboard has some extra buttons, the default USB drivers will probably not support them. To be sure I'm not missing any added functionality, I always install the driver that comes with the device or an updated one downloaded from the manufacturer's Web site.

The last and toughest issue is power. A mismatch between available and required power for USB devices can result in nonfunctioning or malfunctioning USB devices. If you're pulling too much power, you must take devices off that root hub until the error goes away. Buy an add-in USB card if you need to use more devices than your current USB hub supports.

To check the USB power usage in Windows, open Device Manager and locate any USB hub under the Universal Serial Bus Controller icon. Right-click the hub and select Properties, and then select the Power tab. This shows you the current use for each of the devices connected to that root hub (see Figure 11-9).

Most root hubs provide 500 mA per port—more than enough for any USB device. Most power problems take place when you start adding hubs, especially bus-powered hubs, and then you add too many devices to them. Figure 11-10 shows the Power tab for a bus-powered hub; note that it provides a maximum of 100 mA per port.

There's one more problem with USB power: sometimes USB devices go to sleep and won't wake up. Actually, the system is telling them to sleep to save power. You should suspect this problem if you try to access a USB device that was working earlier but that

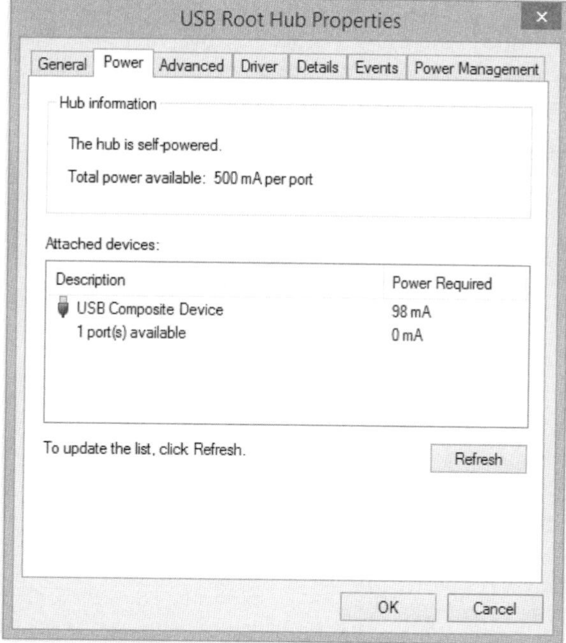

Figure 11-9 USB hub Power tab

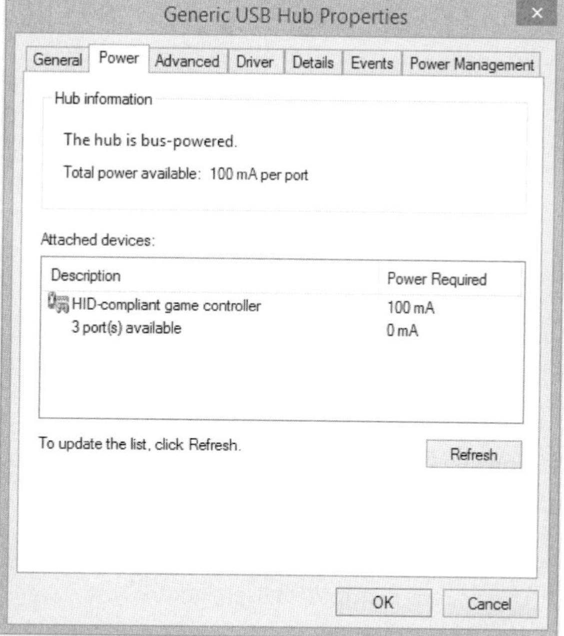

Figure 11-10 General-purpose bus-powered hub

suddenly no longer appears in Device Manager. To fix this, head back in to Device Manager to inspect the hub's Properties, but this time open the Power Management tab and uncheck the *Allow the computer to turn off this device to save power* checkbox, as shown in Figure 11-11.

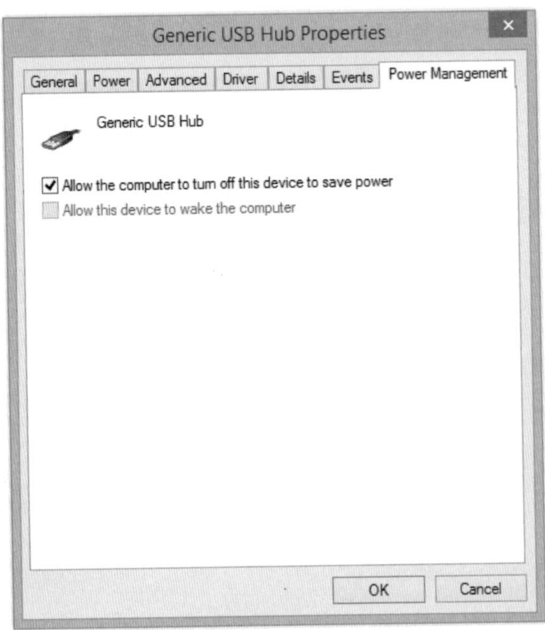

Figure 11-11 Power Management tab

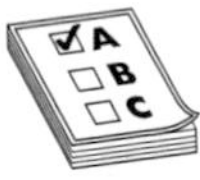

EXAM TIP *USB Type-C* connectors don't show up in the exam objectives as of this writing, but the "universal" connector for USB is rolling out quickly now. The running joke about USB is that every connector has *three* sides: Up position; Down position; and the third time you try to plug it in and it works, the Superposition. USB Type-C just plugs in either way.

FireWire Ports

At first glance, *FireWire*, also known as IEEE 1394, looks and acts much like USB. FireWire has all of the features of USB, but it uses different connectors and is actually the older of the two technologies. For years, FireWire had the upper hand when it came to moving data quickly to and from external devices. The onset of Hi-Speed and SuperSpeed USB, along with the introduction of eSATA for external hard drives, changed that, and FireWire has lost ground to USB in most areas.

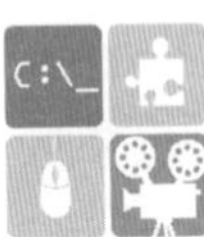

SIM Try the Chapter 11 Challenge! sim to see how well you know your USB speeds at http://totalsem.com/90x.

Understanding FireWire

FireWire has two distinct types of connectors. The first is a 6-pin *powered* connector, the type you see on some desktop computers. Like USB, a FireWire port is capable of providing power to a device, and it carries the same cautions about powering high-power devices through the port. The other type of connector is a 4-pin *bus-powered* connector, which you see on portable computers and such FireWire devices as cameras. This type of connector does not provide power to a device, so you need to find another method of powering the external device.

FireWire comes in two speeds: *IEEE 1394a*, which runs at 400 Mbps, and *IEEE 1394b*, which runs at 800 Mbps. FireWire devices can also take advantage of bus mastering, enabling two FireWire devices—such as a digital video camera and an external FireWire hard drive—to communicate directly with each other. When it comes to raw speed, FireWire 800—that would be 1394b, naturally—is faster than Hi-Speed USB but not SuperSpeed USB.

FireWire does have differences from USB other than just speed and a different-looking connector. First, a USB device must connect directly to a hub, but a FireWire device may use either a hub or daisy chaining. Figure 11-12 shows the difference between hubbed

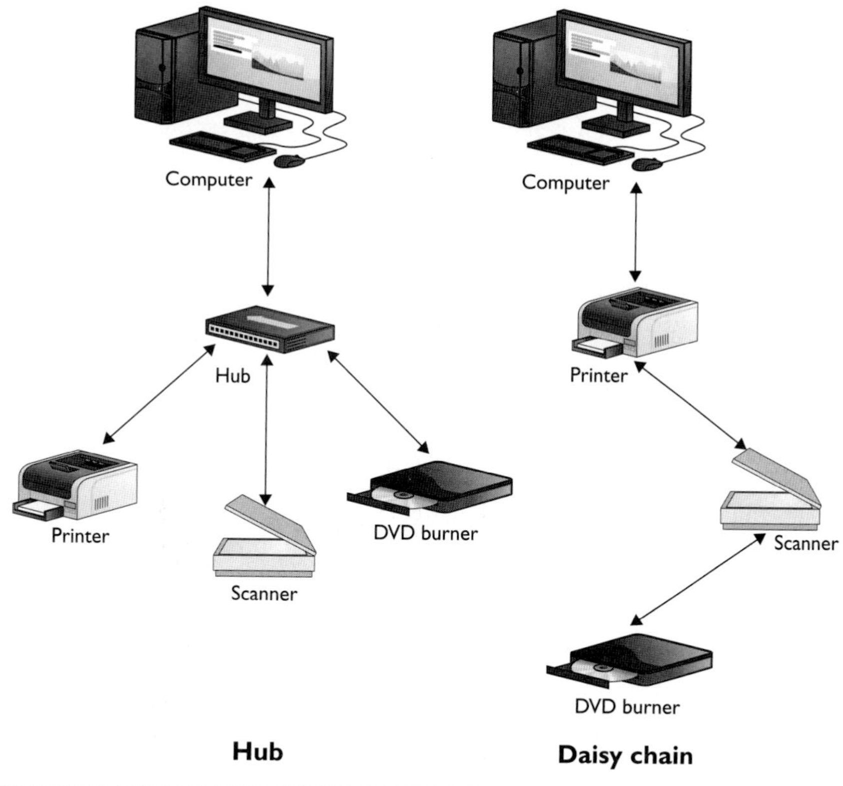

Figure 11-12 Hubbed versus daisy-chained connections

connections and daisy chaining. Second, FireWire supports a maximum of 63 devices, compared to USB's 127. Third, each cable in a FireWire daisy chain has a maximum length of 4.5 meters, as opposed to USB's 5 meters.

Configuring FireWire

In a Windows environment, FireWire is subject to many of the same issues as USB, such as the need to preinstall drivers, verify that onboard devices are active, and so on. But none of these issues are nearly as crucial with a FireWire connection. For example, as with USB, you really should install a FireWire device driver before attaching the device, but given that 95 percent of the FireWire devices used in PCs are either external hard drives or digital video connections, the preinstalled Windows drivers almost always work perfectly. FireWire devices do use much more power than USB devices, but the FireWire controllers are designed to handle higher voltages, and they'll warn you on the rare chance that your FireWire devices pull too much power.

NOTE Like USB ports (or any other ports, for that matter), you can always add more FireWire ports using a PCI or PCIe expansion card. Standard installation procedures apply.

Thunderbolt Ports

Intel developed *Thunderbolt* ports as a high-speed alternative to existing technologies such as USB, FireWire, and DisplayPort, tapping the PCI Express bus for up to six external peripherals. (See Chapter 19 for the scoop on DisplayPort.) Apple adopted Thunderbolt early, because the interface enabled the company to produce thinner portable computers. The technology has since moved to the desktop in the form of *Thunderbolt* cards. Thunderbolt supports video (up to a single 4K video monitor—see Chapter 19) and audio signals. It handles data storage devices just fine, too.

Thunderbolt 1 and Thunderbolt 2 connect computing devices with a Mini DisplayPort (MDP) connector. Thunderbolt 3 should use a USB Type-C connector.

Thunderbolt can use copper or fiber cabling. With copper, Thunderbolt chains can extend up to 3 meters. With fiber, on the other hand, a Thunderbolt chain can extend up to 60 meters.

And did I mention that Thunderbolt offers amazing bandwidth? Thunderbolt 1 runs full duplex at 10 Gbps, so it compares to the currently fastest USB, 3.1. Thunderbolt 2 aggregates (combines) internal data channels, enabling throughput at up to 20 Gbps. Intel has not released Thunderbolt 3 at the time of this writing, but the specs sheet says it will offer throughput up to 40 Gbps at half the power consumption of Thunderbolt 2. Nice!

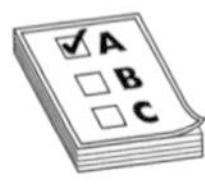

EXAM TIP Know the characteristics and purposes of USB, FireWire, and Thunderbolt connection interfaces for the exams.

General Port Issues

No matter what type of port you use, if it's not working, you should always check out a few issues. First of all, make sure you can tell a port problem from a device problem. Your best bet here is to try a second "known good" device in the same port to see if that device works. If it does *not*, you can assume the port is the problem. It's not a bad idea to reverse this and plug the device into a known good port.

NOTE A "known good" device is simply a device that you know is in good working order. All techs count heavily on the use of known good devices to check other devices. For example, if you think a PC has a bad keyboard, borrow one from the PC next door and see if that keyboard works on the broken machine.

If you're pretty sure the port's not working, you can check three things: First, make sure the port is turned on. Almost any I/O port on a motherboard can be turned off in CMOS. Reboot the system and find the device and see if the port's been turned off. You can also use Windows Device Manager to disable most ports. Figure 11-13 shows a disabled USB controller in Device Manager—you'll see a small down-pointing arrow in Windows. To turn the port back on, right-click the device's icon and choose Enable.

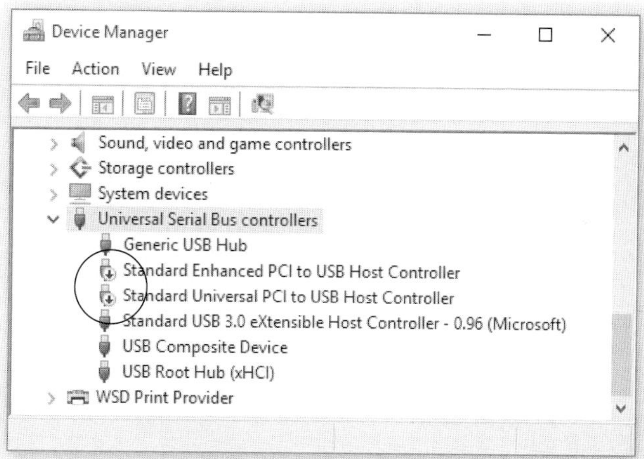

Figure 11-13 Disabled USB controller in Device Manager in Windows 10

Being able to turn off a port in Device Manager points to another not-so-obvious fact: ports need drivers just as devices need drivers. Windows has excellent built-in drivers for all common ports, so if you fail to see a port in Device Manager (and you know the port is turned on in CMOS), you can bet the port itself has a physical problem.

Common Peripherals

So what is a "common" peripheral? I'm hoping you immediately thought of the mouse and the keyboard, two of the most basic, necessary, and abused input devices on a computer.

But those aren't the only things the CompTIA A+ 220-901 exam considers as standard. Here is a list of peripherals covered in this section:

- Keyboards
- Pointing devices
    - Mouse
    - Touchpad
- Biometric devices
- Smart card readers
- Bar code readers
- Touch screens
- Motion sensors
- KVM switches
- Gamepads and joysticks
- Digitizers
- Multimedia devices
    - Digital cameras and camcorders
    - Webcams
    - Sound processors, speakers, and microphones
- Video capture
- TV tuners
- Smart TV and set-top boxes

You probably don't use all of these "common" devices every day, so I'll cover each of them in detail. (Two other common peripherals—printers and scanners—get their own chapter, Chapter 27.)

Keyboards

Keyboards are both the oldest and still the primary way you input data into a PC. All modern operating systems come with perfectly good drivers for any keyboard, although some fancier keyboards may come with specialized keys that require a special driver be installed to operate properly.

Modern keyboards connect via USB port, either wireless or wired. You can also connect an older PS/2 keyboard using a simple PS/2 to USB converter.

There's not much to do to configure a standard keyboard. The only configuration tool you might need in Windows is the Keyboard Control Panel applet. This tool enables you to change the repeat delay (the amount of time you must hold down a key before the keyboard starts repeating the character), the repeat rate (how quickly the character is

repeated after the repeat delay), and the default cursor blink rate. Figure 11-14 shows the default Windows Keyboard Properties window—some keyboard makers provide drivers that add extra tabs.

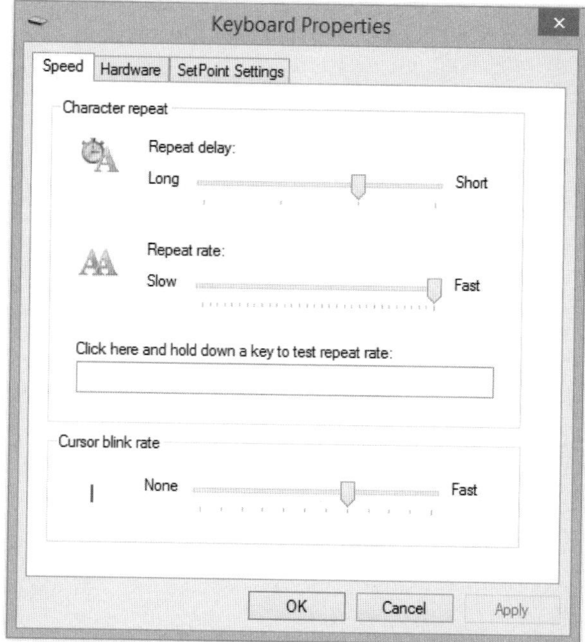

Figure 11-14 Keyboard Control Panel applet

Windows and Linux share the same standard QWERTY keyboards, including the CTRL and ALT *modifier keys* that enable you to do certain keyboard shortcuts. (Press CTRL-Z to undo an action, for example.) Windows-specific keyboards also come with the WINDOWS LOGO modifier key. Apple keyboards have three modifier keys: CONTROL, OPTION, and COMMAND. The first two correspond to CTRL and ALT; the COMMAND key is the Mac OS X special modifier key. You can use Windows keyboards with Mac OS X, but you need to go into the Keyboard preferences in System Preferences to map the modifier keys properly (see Figure 11-15).

Keyboards might be easy to install, but they do fail occasionally. Given their location—right in front of you—the three issues that cause the most keyboard problems stem from spills, physical damage, and dirt.

Spilling a soda onto your keyboard can make for a really bad day. If you're quick and unplug the keyboard from the PC before the liquid hits the electrical components, you might be able to save the keyboard. It'll take some cleaning, though. More often than not, you'll get a sticky, ill-performing keyboard that is not worth the hassle—just replace it!

Other common physical damage comes from dropping objects onto the keyboard, such as a heavy book (like the one in your hands). This can have bad results! Most keyboards are pretty resilient, though, and can bounce back from the hit.

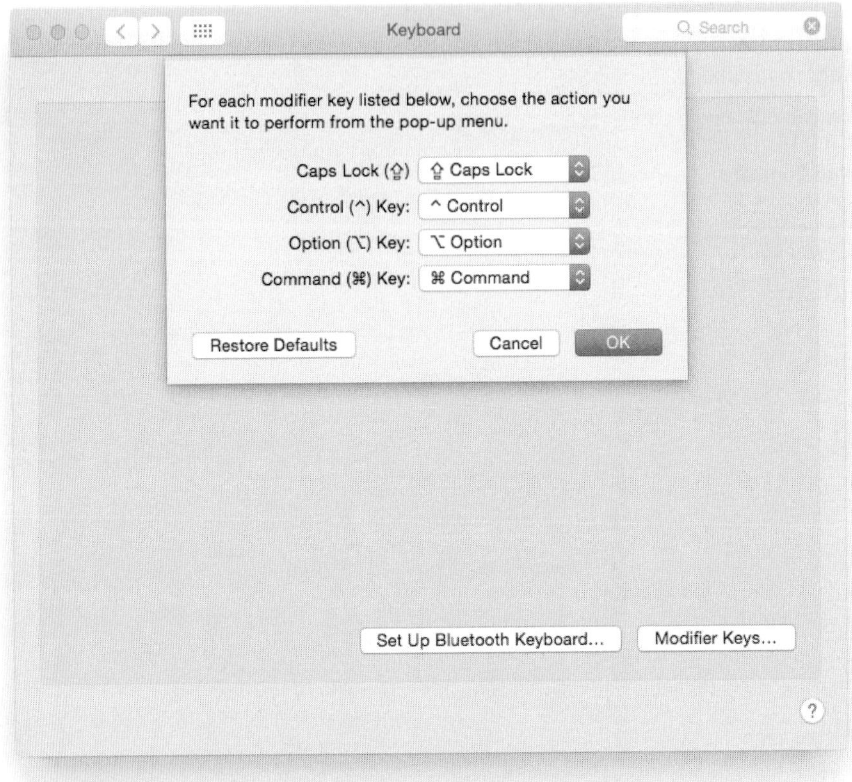

Figure 11-15 Keyboard options in Mac OS X System Preferences

Clean grime off the keys by using a cloth dampened with a little water, or if the water alone doesn't do the job, use a bit of isopropyl alcohol on a cloth (see Figure 11-16).

Figure 11-16 Cleaning keys

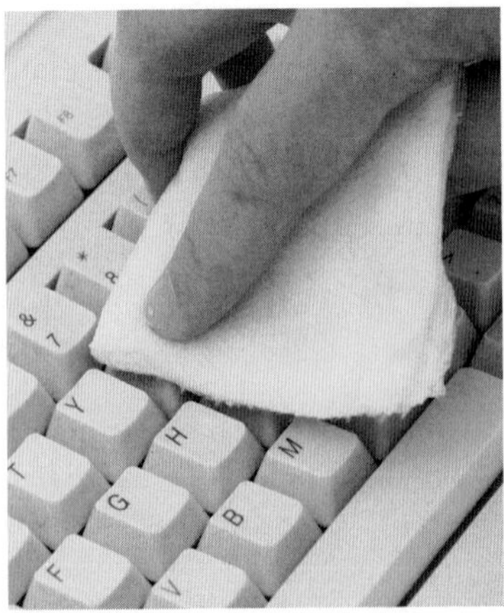

Dirty keys might be unsightly, but dirt under the keys might cause the keyboard to stop working completely. When your keys start to stick, grab a bottle of compressed air and shoot some air under the keys. Do this outside or over a trash can—you'll be amazed how much junk gets caught under the keys!

The bottom line when it comes to stuck keys is that the keyboard's probably useless with the stuck key, so you might as well try to clean it. Worst case scenario, you'll need to buy another keyboard.

Pointing Devices

Have you ever tried to use Windows or Mac OS X without a mouse or other device to move the cursor? It's not fun, but it can be done. All techs eventually learn the navigation hot keys for those times when mice fail, but all in all we do love our mice. There are two common pointing devices, mice and touchpads (CompTIA splits the term touchpad into two words, "touch pad"). A mouse moves the cursor as you move the mouse; a *touchpad* moves the cursor as you move your fingers over its surface.

Like keyboards, modern operating systems come with excellent drivers for all standard pointing devices; the exception you might encounter is the more advanced mice that come with extra buttons.

In Windows, you can adjust your mouse or touchpad settings through the Mouse Control Panel applet. Figure 11-17 shows the Windows 7 version. Mac OS X has both Mouse and Trackpad applets in System Preferences.

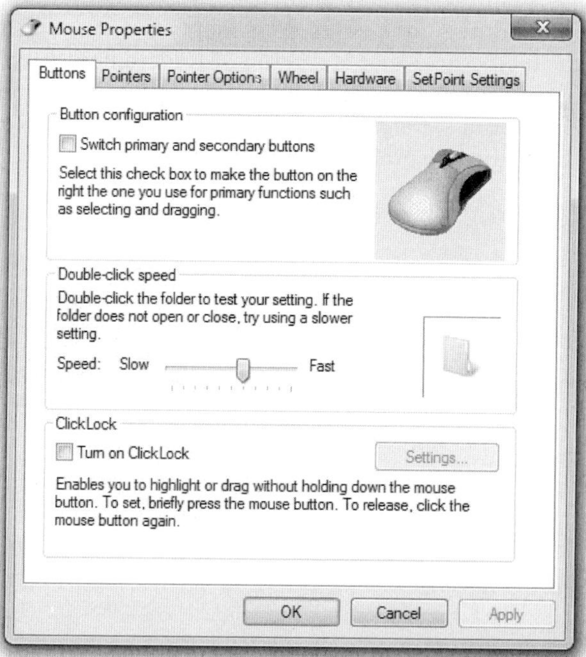

Figure 11-17 Mouse Control Panel applet

Modern pointing devices require little maintenance and almost never need cleaning, as the optics that make them work are never in contact with the grimy outside world. On the rare occasion where an optical mouse begins to act erratically, try using a cloth or damp cotton swab to clean out any bits of dirt that may be blocking the optics (see Figure 11-18).

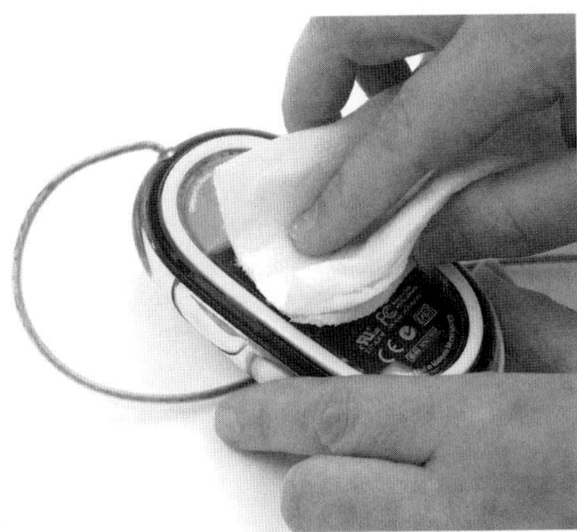

Figure 11-18 Cleaning an optical mouse

Biometric Devices

Biometric devices scan and remember unique aspects of various body parts, such as your retina, iris, head image, or fingerprint, using some form of sensing device such as a retinal scanner. This information is used as a key to prevent unauthorized people from accessing whatever the biometric device is securing. Most biometric devices currently used in personal computing devices secure only themselves. The USB thumb drive in Figure 11-19 has a tiny fingerprint scanner. You slide your finger (any finger you choose) over the drive to unlock the contents of the thumb drive.

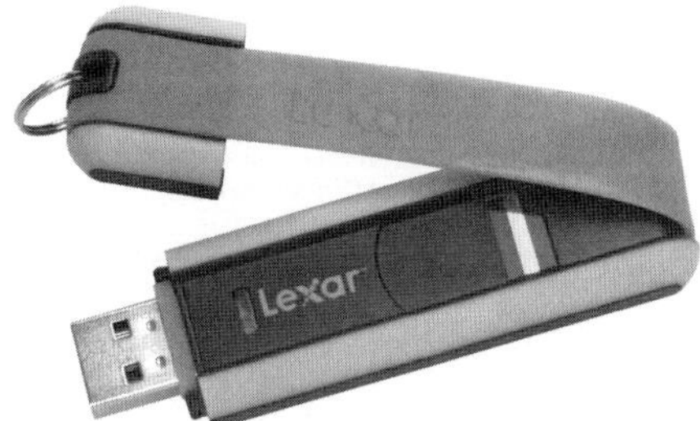

Figure 11-19 USB thumb drive with fingerprint scanner (photo courtesy of Lexar Media, Inc.)

Less common are biometric security devices that secure entire computers. The Microsoft fingerprint scanner is a USB device that replaces standard user name and password security. Figure 11-20 shows the scanner built into a keyboard. When a program or Web

site asks for a user name and password, you simply press your finger against the fingerprint scanner. It confirms your identity (assuming your fingerprint matches), and then special software that comes with the scanner supplies the program or Web site with your stored user name and password.

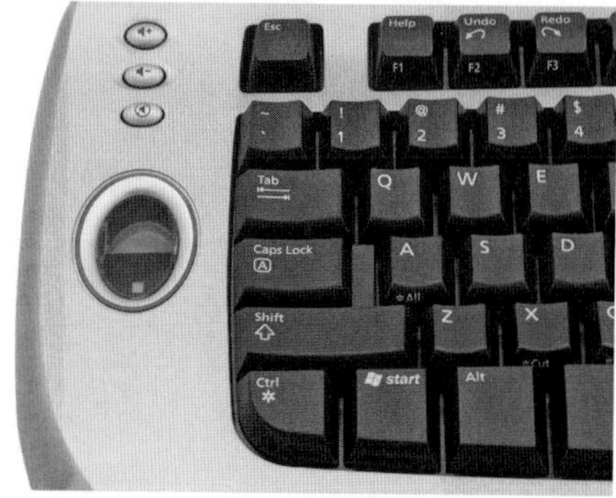

Figure 11-20 Microsoft fingerprint scanner on a keyboard

Biometric devices are also used for recognition. Recognition is different from security in that the biometric device doesn't care who you are; it just wants to know what you're doing. The best example of this is voice recognition. Voice recognition programs convert human voice input into commands or text. Apple, Microsoft, and Google use voice recognition in many forms, including the delightful Siri in iOS and the excellent Cortana in Windows 10 (both can respond to input for searching and other functions). Google uses voice recognition in its flagship office productivity app, Google Docs, so students can speak in addition to type.

No matter what biometric device you use, you use the same steps to make it work:

1. Install the device.
2. Register your identity with the device by sticking your eye, finger, or other unique body part (Why are you snickering?) into the device so it can scan you.
3. Configure its software to tell the device what to do when it recognizes your scanned identity.

Smart Card Readers

Many enterprise-level businesses use a smart-card system to enable employees to access company resources and display proper credentials so they have proper levels of access too. A *smart card reader* comes in many forms, from small devices attached to a laptop computer to a panel next to a secure door (see Figure 11-21). The smart card reader scans the chip embedded in such devices as ID badges to enhance access and security.

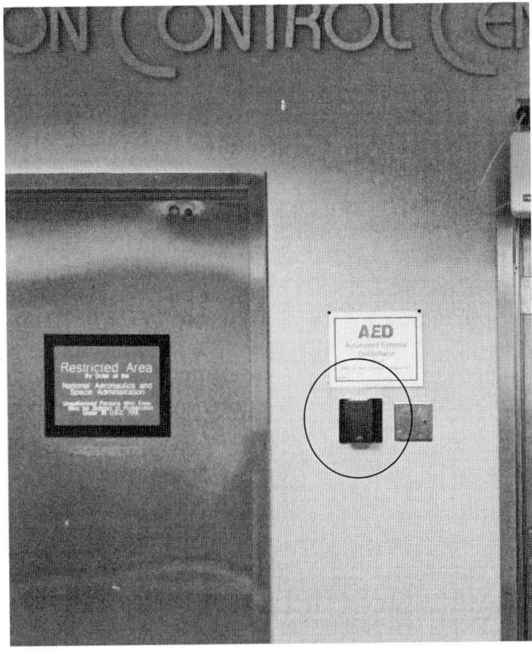

Figure 11-21 Smart card reader

Bar Code Readers

Bar code readers read standard *Universal Product Code (UPC)* bar codes (see Figure 11-22), primarily to track inventory. Bar code readers enable easy updating of inventory databases stored on computing devices.

Figure 11-22 Typical UPC code

Two types of bar code readers are commonly found with personal computers: pen scanners and hand scanners. Pen scanners look like an ink pen and must be swiped across the bar code (see Figure 11-23). Hand scanners are held in front of the UPC code while a button is pressed to scan. All bar code readers emit a tone to let you know the scan was successful.

Older bar code readers used the venerable PS/2 ports; modern ones use USB ports. No configuration is usually necessary, other than making sure that the particular bar code reader works with whatever database or point-of-sale software you use.

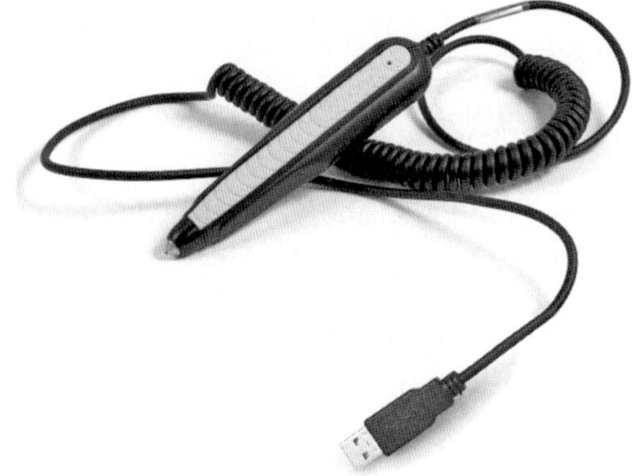

Figure 11-23 Pen scanner (photo courtesy of Wasp® Barcode Technologies)

Touch Screens

A *touch screen* is a monitor with some type of sensing device across its face that detects the location and duration of contact, usually by a finger or stylus. All touch screens then supply this contact information to the PC as though it were a click event from a mouse. Touch screens are used in situations for which conventional mouse/keyboard input is either impossible or impractical. Here are a few places you'll see touch screens at work:

- Smartphones
- Smart watches
- Fitness monitors
- Smart cameras
- Information kiosks
- Point of sale systems
- Tablets
- Phablets
- E-readers

Touch screens can be separated into two groups: built-in screens like the ones in smartphones, and standalone touch screen monitors like those used in many point of sale systems. From a technician's standpoint, you can think of a standalone touch screen as a monitor with a built-in mouse. All touch screens have a separate USB port for the "mouse" part of the device, along with drivers you install just as you would for any USB mouse.

Windows includes a Control Panel applet for configuring the touch screens on Tablet PCs. Windows Vista offers the Pen and Input Devices applet; Windows 7/8/8.1/10 have Tablet PC Settings (note that the Tablet PC Settings applet will only appear if you have a touch screen, like on a Microsoft Surface). You can use these applets to adjust how you interact with the touch screen just as you would with the Mouse or Keyboard applets. The applets enable you to configure what happens when you tap, double-tap, use gestures called "flicks," and more.

Motion Sensors

Motion sensors respond to external movement to update some function of the computing device. Cameras (think surveillance here) can have motion sensors that, when triggered, send a signal to the computer to start recording.

Microsoft sells the Kinect motion-sensing devices for its Xbox One gaming system and, increasingly, for Windows. The Kinect enables interaction and recognition to run applications, do various things in games, and a lot more. You can use your hand, for example, to select Internet Explorer; push your hand forward and then pull it back and the app will load. And you never make physical contact with anything. It's a cool technology that promises amazing things in the future.

KVM Switches

A *keyboard, video, mouse (KVM) switch* is a hardware device that most commonly enables multiple computers to be viewed and controlled by a single mouse, keyboard, and screen. Some KVMs reverse that capability, enabling a single computer to be controlled by multiple keyboards, mice, or other devices. KVMs are especially useful in data centers where multiple servers are rack mounted, space is limited, and power is a concern. An administrator can use a single KVM to control multiple server systems from a single keyboard, mouse, and monitor.

There are many brands and types of KVM switches. Some enable you to connect to only two systems, and some support hundreds. Some even come with audio output jacks to support speakers. Typical KVMs come with two or more sets of wires that are used for input devices such as PS/2 or USB mice and video output (see Figure 11-24).

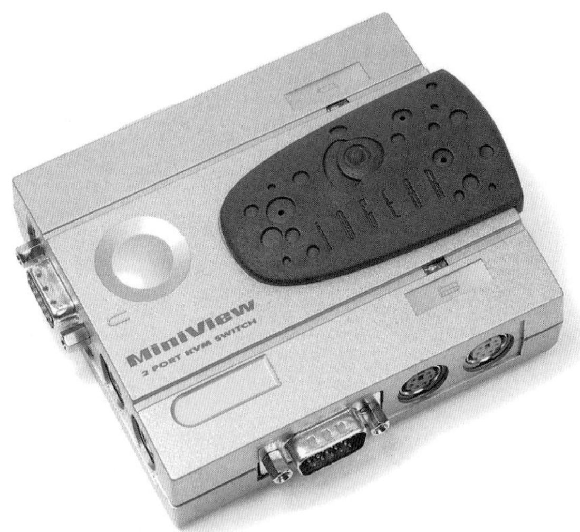

Figure 11-24 A typical KVM switch

To use a KVM, you simply connect a keyboard, mouse, and monitor to the KVM and then connect the KVM to the desired computers. Once connected and properly configured, assigned keyboard hotkeys—a combination of keys typically assigned by the KVM

manufacturer—enable you to toggle between the computers connected to the KVM. In most cases, you simply tap the SCROLL LOCK key twice to switch between sessions.

Installing a KVM is not difficult; the most important point to remember is to connect the individual sets of cables between the KVM ports and each computer one at a time, keeping track of which keyboard, mouse, and video cable go to which computers. I highly recommend labeling and using twist or zip ties.

If you get the connections wrong, the KVM won't function as desired. If you connect a mouse and keyboard wires to the correct KVM port, for example, but attach the same computer's video cable to a different port on the KVM, you won't get the correct video when you try to switch to that computer. The same holds true for the mouse and keyboard cables. Don't cross the cables!

Gamepads and Joysticks

Whether you're racing through tight turns at top speeds or flying a state-of-the-art jet fighter, having the right controller for the job is important for an enjoyable gaming experience. Two peripherals are commonly used for controlling PC games: joysticks and gamepads (CompTIA splits the term gamepad into two words, "game pad").

Over the past decade, flight simulator programs have declined in popularity, and so have *joysticks* (see Figure 11-25). Once a required component of a gamer's arsenal, you only need joysticks now if you are a *serious* flight simulator fan. Most modern games are controlled by gamepad or mouse and keyboard.

Figure 11-25
A joystick

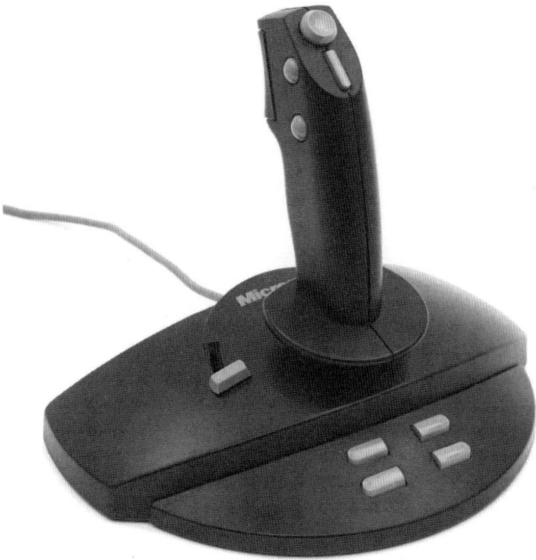

Some PC games, especially those that were designed to played on consoles like the Microsoft Xbox One or Sony PlayStation 4, are best enjoyed when using a gamepad. A

gamepad looks more like your standard video game controller, usually covered in an array of buttons and triggers (see Figure 11-26).

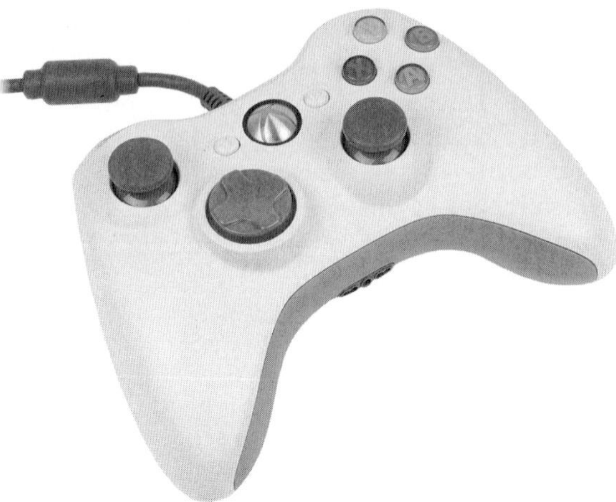

Figure 11-26
A gamepad

Joysticks and gamepads have used plenty of connectors over the years, including the eponymous joystick connector. These days, they all connect to computers via USB or wireless connections. Depending on the complexity of the controller, you may need to install drivers to get a joystick or gamepad working. Simpler controllers, however, can probably get by using the default gamepad drivers included in Windows and Mac OS X.

You'll need to configure your joystick or gamepad to make sure all the buttons and controls work properly. In Windows Vista, open the Game Controllers Control Panel applet. In Windows 7 and later, go to the Devices and Printers applet. Depending on your gamepad or joystick, you'll be able to configure the buttons, sticks, triggers, and more (see Figure 11-27). You can calibrate the analog sticks so they accurately register your movements. You can even adjust the amount of vibration used by the controller's force feedback (if available).

NOTE You might also need to configure your controller from within the game you want to play. Most games are set to use keyboard and mouse controls by default. You'll need to play around with the settings to enable your game controller.

Once you've set up your controller, you should be ready to take to the skies, or the streets, or wherever else you go to game.

Digitizers

PCs and Macs have quickly become the most powerful and flexible tools available for visual artists. Given the number of applications dedicated to producing various visual styles, including painting, sketching, animation, and more, digital art stands toe-to-toe with its more traditional counterpart. It's only reasonable that a category of hardware would appear to help users take advantage of these tools.

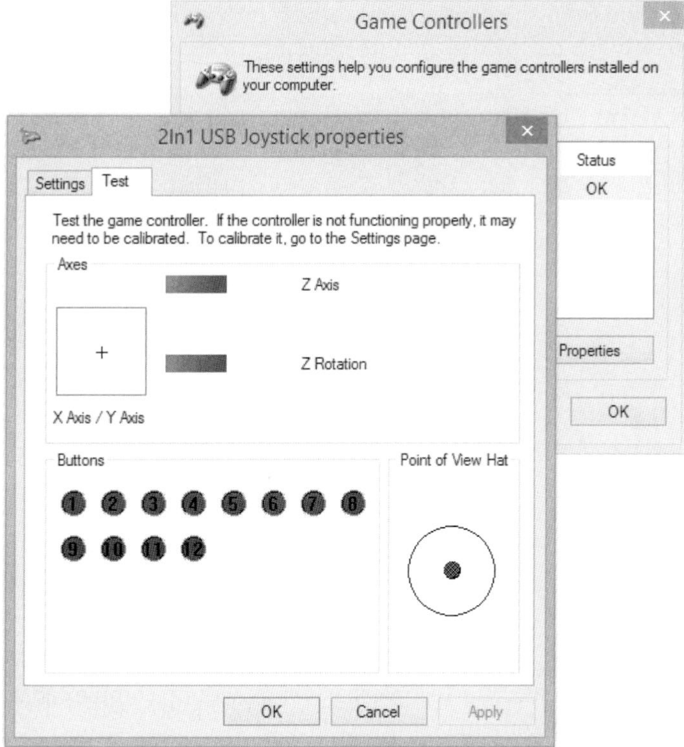

Figure 11-27 Game controller properties

A *digitizer* (otherwise known as a *pen tablet*) enables users to paint, ink, pencil, or otherwise draw on a computer (see Figure 11-28). Now, don't get carried away and start taking watercolors to your monitor. The digitizer receives input using a special surface. When a user presses against the surface, usually with a stylus, the surface transforms (or digitizes) the analog movements into digital information. The drawing application receives the

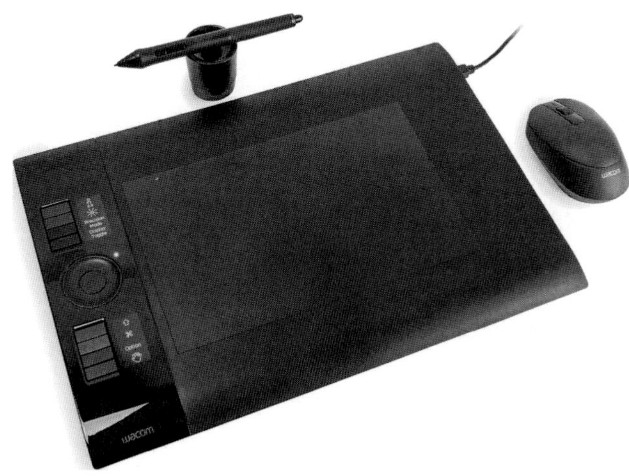

Figure 11-28 A type of digitizer known as the Wacom pen tablet

information from the digitizer and turns it into an image onscreen (see Figure 11-29). If you draw a line on the digitizer, for example, that line should appear onscreen.

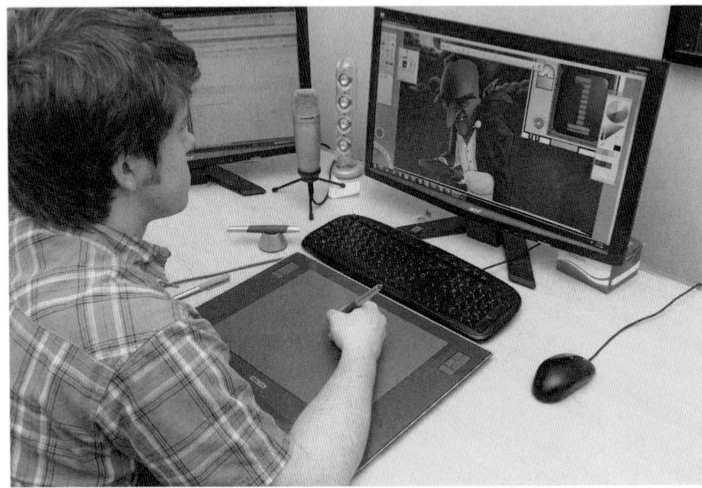

Figure 11-29 Drawing with a digitizer

NOTE Not all digitizers are designed for digital art. Some are used for handwriting, technical drawings, writing complex characters, or even as a replacement pointing device.

Most digitizers connect via a USB or wireless connection. You'll need to install drivers before you connect the device, although they should be included in the box. The digitizer should also include a configuration utility. Here you can adjust the pressure sensitivity of the stylus, configure buttons on the tablet, and set the portion of the screen to which the tablet can draw.

NOTE In addition to drivers, most digitizers require specific software to use their advanced functions. With digital art digitizers, for example, you'll need a graphic arts program like Adobe Illustrator or Autodesk SketchBook, which know how to use several brands and varieties of pen tablets.

You might also find an option to calibrate the digitizer. To ensure that where you press on the digitizer matches up with where you want it to appear on your monitor, you'll need to use the digitizer to click on a series of marks that appear on your monitor. If your digitizer is incorrectly calibrated, your inputs won't appear correctly when you are drawing.

Multimedia Devices

Popular multimedia devices like digital cameras and digital camcorders have found their way into almost every home. Their affordability and ease of use make them a no-brainer

for families looking to capture every moment of their (cats') lives. Many people also use webcams to enable video chats with friends and family around the world. Finally, almost all computing devices come with some capability to produce and record sound.

NOTE Most folks use their smartphones today for casual pictures and video, but the CompTIA A+ 901 objectives assume separate devices.

Digital Cameras and Camcorders

Digital cameras and *camcorders* electronically simulate older film and tape technology and provide a wonderful tool for capturing a moment and then sending it to friends and relatives. Because digital cameras and camcorders interface with computers, CompTIA A+ certified techs need to know the basics.

NOTE While digital cameras and digital camcorders can be considered distinct products, their features have become nearly identical. Both take pictures. Both take videos. In fact, a lot of high-end digital cameras take better video than digital camcorders. Because of this feature and function overlap, I'm presenting them here together.

Storage Media—Digital Film Digital cameras and camcorders save the pictures and videos they take onto some type of *removable storage media*. Think of it as digital film. Probably the most common removable storage media used in modern digital cameras (and probably your best choice) is the Secure Digital (SD) card (see Figure 11-30). For details about removable storage media, see the discussion in the "Storage Devices" section, later in this chapter.

NOTE Many digital camcorders include built-in hard drives for storing large amounts of high-definition (HD) video. This removes the need to constantly switch out memory cards.

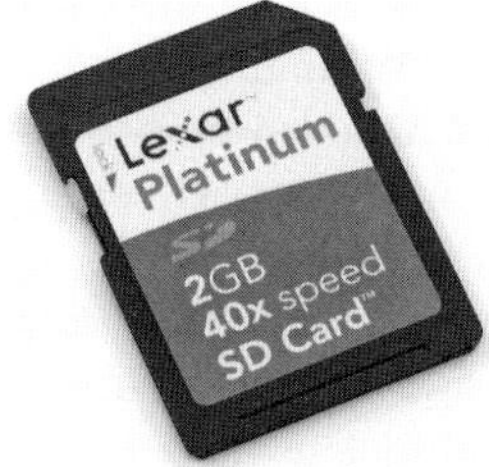

Figure 11-30 Secure Digital card

Connection These days, digital cameras plug directly into a USB port (see Figure 11-31). Another common option, though, is to connect only the camera's storage media to the computer, using one of the many digital media readers available.

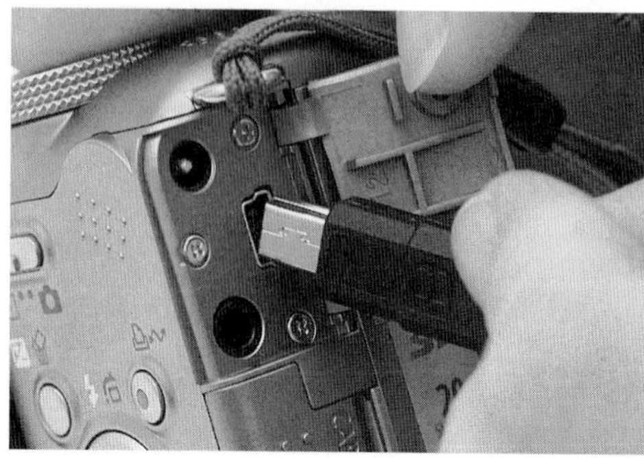

Figure 11-31 Camera connecting to USB port

You can find readers designed specifically for SD cards, as well as other types. Plenty of readers can handle multiple media formats. Many computers come with a decent built-in digital media reader (see Figure 11-32).

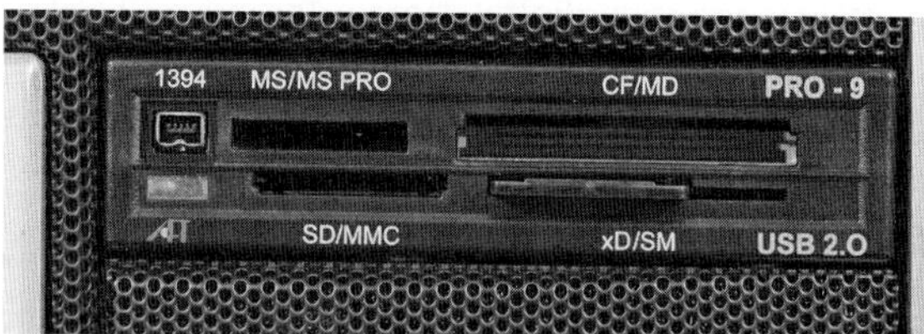

Figure 11-32 Digital media reader built into computer

Many digital camcorders use USB connections, although you'll find FireWire connections on older models (since it used to be faster than USB connections).

Quality You should consider the amount of information a particular model of camera or camcorder can capture, which in the digital world is expressed as some number of *megapixels*. Instead of light-sensitive film, digital cameras and camcorders have one CCD (charged coupled device) or CMOS (complementary metal-oxide semiconductor) sensor covered with photosensitive pixels (called *photosites*) to capture the still image or video; the more pixels on the sensor, the higher the resolution of the images it captures.

Not so long ago, a 1-megapixel digital camera was the bleeding edge of digital photographic technology, but now you can find cameras with ten times that resolution for a few hundred U.S. dollars. As a basis of reference, a 5-megapixel camera produces snapshot-sized (4 × 6 inch) pictures with print photograph quality, whereas a 10-megapixel unit can produce a high-quality 8 × 10 inch print.

Another feature of most digital cameras and camcorders is the capability to zoom in on your subject. The way you ideally want to do this is the way film cameras do it, by using the camera's optics—that's the lens. Most cameras above the basic level have some *optical zoom*—meaning the zoom is built into the lens of the camera—but almost all models include multiple levels of *digital zoom*, accomplished by some very clever software

in the camera. Choose your camera based on optical zoom: 3× at a minimum or better if you can afford it. Digital zoom is useless.

Camcorder optical zoom ranges are often much larger. You can find digital camcorders with an optical zoom of 30× or more.

Form Factor As was the case with film cameras, size matters for digital cameras and camcorders. These devices come in several form factors. They range from tiny, ultra-compact models that readily fit in a shirt pocket to monster cameras with huge lenses. Although it's not universally true, the bigger the camera/camcorder, the more features and sensors it can have. Thus bigger is usually better in terms of quality.

In shape, digital cameras come in a rectangular package, in which the lens retracts into the body, or as an SLR-type, with a lens that sticks out of the body. Figure 11-33 shows both styles.

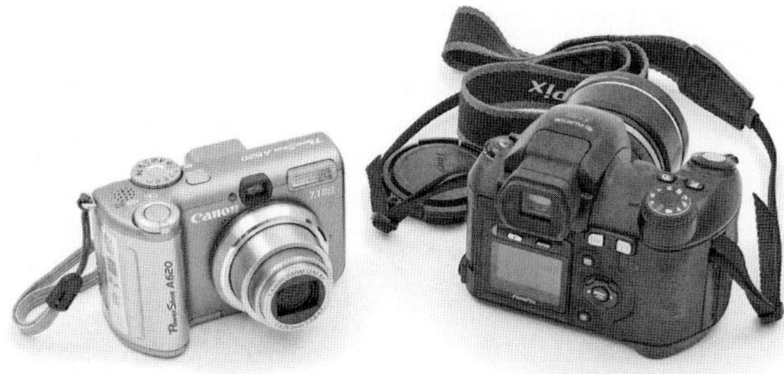

Figure 11-33 Typical digital cameras

Camcorders also come in multiple shapes (see Figure 11-34). Some are arranged vertically; others are more horizontal. Some are large enough that you need to use two hands to hold them. The latest form factors include two lenses so they can capture 3-D videos. Now your cat can fly right off the screen.

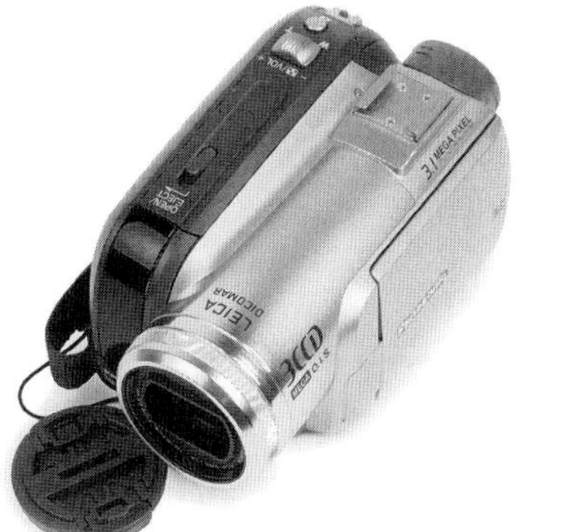
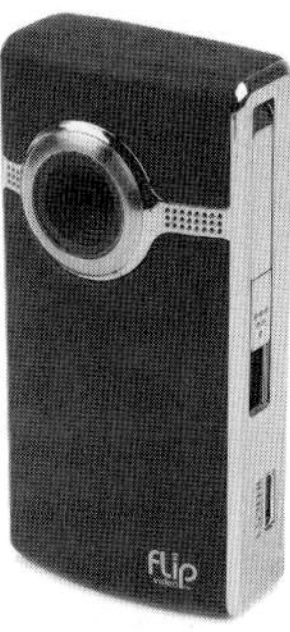

Figure 11-34 Digital camcorders

Web Cameras

Cameras in or on computer monitors, often called *webcams* because their most common use is for Internet video communication, enable people to interact over networks with both voice and video. Webcams range greatly in quality and price.

The biggest issue with webcams is the image quality. Webcams measure their resolution in pixels. You can find webcams with resolutions of as few as 100,000 pixels and webcams with millions of pixels. As broadband speeds have increased worldwide, webcam resolution has risen accordingly. The most common webcam today has 2 million pixels (2 megapixels), essentially providing a 1080p HD resolution experience.

The next issue with webcams is the frame rate, that is, the number of times the camera "takes your picture" each second. Higher frame rates make for smoother video; 30 frames per second is considered the best. A good camera with a high megapixel resolution and fast frame rate will provide you with excellent video conferencing capabilities. Figure 11-35 shows the author chatting via webcam using Skype software.

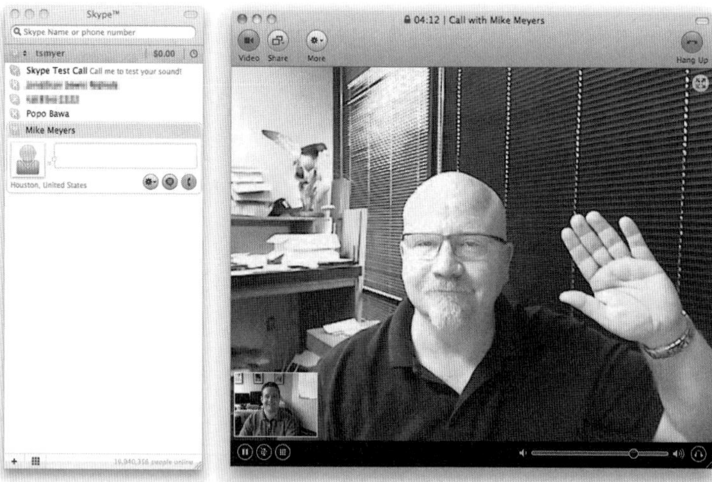

Figure 11-35 Video chatting by webcam with Skype

Most people who use online video also want a *microphone*. Many cameras come with microphones, or you can use your own. Those who do a lot of video chatting may prefer to get a camera without a microphone and then buy a good-quality headset with which to speak and listen.

Many cameras now can track you when you move, to keep your face in the picture—a handy feature for fidgety folks using video conferencing! This interesting technology recognizes a human face with little or no "training" and rotates its position to keep your face in the picture.

Almost all webcams use USB connections. Windows and Mac OS X come with limited sets of webcam drivers, so always make sure to install the drivers supplied with the camera before you plug it in. Most webcams use Hi-Speed or SuperSpeed USB, so make sure you're plugging your webcam into the proper USB port.

Once the camera is plugged in, you'll need to test it. All cameras come with some type of program, but finding the program can be a challenge. Some brands put the program in the notification area in Windows, some place it in Computer, others put it in the Control

Panel or System Preferences—and some do all of these! Figure 11-36 shows the Control Panel applet that appeared when I installed the webcam driver.

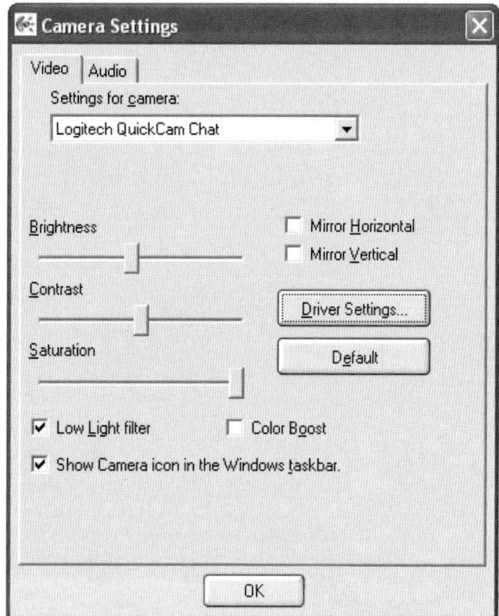

Figure 11-36 Camera Settings applet

Sound Cards

Virtually every computing device today comes with four critical components for capturing and outputting sound: a sound card or sound device built into the motherboard, speakers, microphone, and recording/playback software. Computers capture (record) sound waves in electronic format through a process called *sampling*. In its simplest sense, sampling means capturing the state or quality of a particular sound wave a set number of times each second. The sampling rate is measured in units of thousands of cycles per second, or kilohertz (KHz). The more often a sound is sampled, the better the reproduction of that sound. Most sounds in computing are recorded with a sampling rate ranging from 11 KHz (very low quality, like a telephone) to 192 KHz (ultra-high quality, better than the human ear).

NOTE Every modern motherboard comes with sound-processing capabilities built in. By default, techs refer to built-in sound as either built-in sound or as a *sound card*, even when there's no expansion card for sound. I'll do the same in this chapter.

Sounds vary according to their loudness (*amplitude*), how high or low their tone (*frequency*), and the qualities that differentiate the same note played on different instruments

(*timbre*). All the characteristics of a particular sound wave—amplitude, frequency, timbre—need to be recorded and translated into ones and zeros to reproduce that sound accurately within the computer and out to your speakers.

The number of characteristics of a particular sound captured during sampling is measured by the *bit depth* of the sample. The greater the bit depth used to capture a sample, the more characteristics of that sound can be stored and thus re-created. An 8-bit sample of a Jimi Hendrix guitar solo, for example, captures 2^8 (256) characteristics of that sound per sample. It would sound like a cheap recording of a recording, perhaps a little flat and thin. A 16-bit sample, in contrast, captures 2^{16} (65,536) different characteristics of his solo and reproduces all the fuzzy overtones and feedback that gave Hendrix his unique sound.

The last aspect of sound capture is the number of tracks of sound you capture. Most commonly, you can capture either a single track (*monaural*) or two tracks (*stereo*). More advanced captures record many more sound tracks, but that's a topic for a more advanced sound capture discussion.

The combination of sampling frequency and bit depth determines how faithfully a digital version of a sound captures what your ear would hear. A sound capture is considered *CD quality* when recorded at 44.1 KHz, with 16-bit depth and in stereo. Most recording programs let you set these values before you begin recording. Figure 11-37 shows the configuration settings for Windows Sound Recorder.

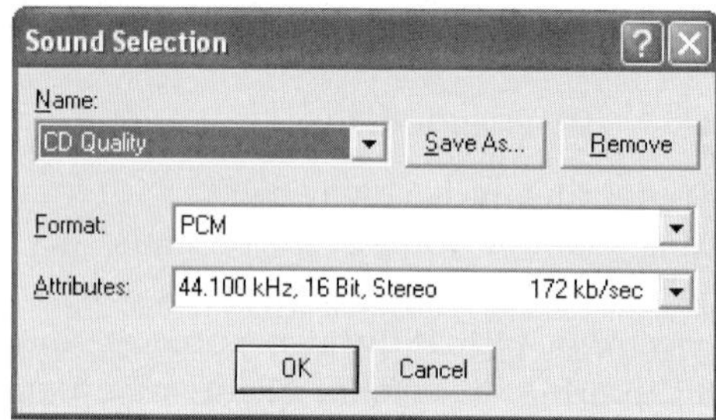

Figure 11-37 Sound Recorder settings

Hey, wait a minute! Did you notice the Format setting in Figure 11-37? What's that? You can save those sampled sounds in lots of different ways—and that's where the term *format* comes into play.

Recorded Sound Formats The granddaddy of all sound formats is *pulse code modulation (PCM)*. PCM was developed in the 1960s to carry telephone calls over the first digital lines. With just a few minor changes to allow for use in PCs, the PCM format is still alive and well, although it's better known as the *WAV* format so common in the PC world. WAV files are great for storing faithfully recorded sounds and music, but they do so at a price. WAV files can be huge, especially when sampled at high frequency and depth. A 4-minute song at 44.1 KHz and 16-bit stereo, for example, weighs in at a whopping 40-plus MB!

What's interesting about sound quality is that the human ear cannot perceive anywhere near the subtle variations of sound recorded at 44.1 KHz and 16-bit stereo. Clever

programmers have written algorithms to store full-quality WAV files as compressed files, discarding unnecessary audio qualities of that file. These algorithms—really nothing more than a series of instructions in code—are called compressor/decompressor programs or, more simply, *codecs*. The most famous of the codecs is the Fraunhoffer MPEG-1 Layer 3 codec, more often called by its file extension, *MP3*.

NOTE WAV and MP3 are only two among a large number of file formats for sound. Not all sound players can play all of these formats; however, many sound formats are nothing more than some type of compressed WAV file, so with the right codec loaded, you can play most sound formats.

Compressing WAV Files to MP3 Format Using MP3 compression, you can shrink a WAV file by a factor of 12 without losing much sound quality. When you compress a WAV file into an MP3 file, the key decision is the bit rate. The *bit rate* is the amount of information (number of bits) transferred from the compressed file to the MP3 decoder in 1 second. The higher the bit rate of an MP3 file, the higher the sound quality. The bit rate of MP3 audio files is commonly measured in thousands of bits per second, abbreviated *Kbps*. Most MP3 encoders support a range of bit rates from 24 Kbps up to 320 Kbps (or 320,000 bits per second). A CD-quality MP3 bit rate is 128 Kbps.

MIDI Every sound card can produce sounds in addition to playing prerecorded sound files. Every sound card comes with a second processor designed to interpret standardized *musical instrument digital interface* (*MIDI*) files. It's important to note that a MIDI file is not an independent music file, unlike a WAV file that sounds more or less the same on many different personal computing devices. A MIDI file is a text file that takes advantage of the sound processing hardware to enable the computing device to produce sound. Programmers use these small files to tell the sound card which notes to play; how long, how loud, and on which instruments to play them; and so forth. Think of a MIDI file as a piece of electronic sheet music, with the instruments built into your sound card.

NOTE MIDI files typically have the file extension .MID in Windows. This harkens back to the ancient three-character file extension limitation of Microsoft's first OS, DOS.

The beauty of MIDI files is that they're tiny in comparison to equivalent WAV files. The first movement of Beethoven's Fifth Symphony, for example, weighs in at a whopping 78 MB as a high-quality WAV file. The same seven-minute song as a MIDI file, in contrast, slips in at a svelte 60 KB. MIDI is hardware dependent, meaning the capabilities and quality of the individual sound card make all the difference in the world on the sound produced.

NOTE See "MIDI-enabled Devices," later in the chapter, for more on MIDI.

Playing Sounds A large number of programs can play sounds on a typical computer. First, virtually every Windows computer comes with Windows Media Player (see Figure 11-38). You can download many other players, of course, including iTunes, Apple's media program for Windows and Mac OS X. This is good, because not all sound players can play all sound formats.

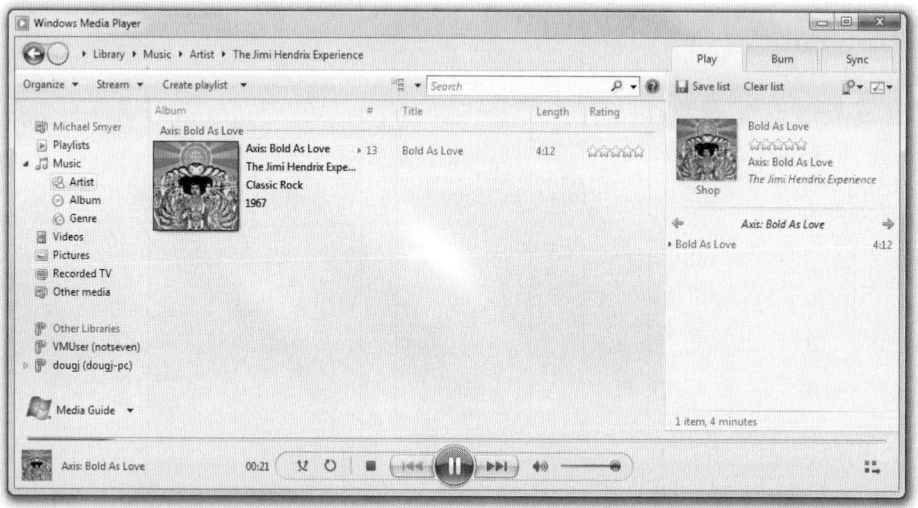

Figure 11-38 Windows Media Player

Streaming media is a broadcast of data that is played on your computer and immediately discarded. Streaming media is incredibly popular on the Internet. Streaming media has spawned an entire industry of Internet radio stations and music databases. Two popular Internet radio players include Windows Media Player and Apple's iTunes. You can use streaming services like Spotify and Pandora to pick and choose the music you want to hear.

Sound Card Standards Most sound cards follow one of two standards, AC'97 or Intel High Definition Audio, although no rule says manufacturers must follow these standards. This applies both to the sound processing hardware built into motherboards and to add-on sound cards.

The *AC'97* standard applies to lower-end audio devices, having been created when most folks listened to stereo sound at best. Both playback and recording capabilities of such sound cards offer adequate quality, certainly enough for the typical office computer. When you want to go beyond average, though, turn to a motherboard or add-on sound card that offers a newer standard.

Intel designed the *Intel High Definition Audio (HDA)* standard to support features such as true surround sound with many discrete speakers. Technically speaking, whereas AC'97 offers support for up to six channels at 48 KHz/20-bit quality, HDA cranks that

up to eight channels at 192 KHz/32-bit quality, a substantial improvement. HDA also supports sending multiple streams of audio from one computer to different output devices, so you can enjoy Internet radio in one room, for example, and listen to a CD in another room, both played on the same computer.

NOTE As they do with new microprocessor models, Intel gave the HDA standard a codename as well. Look for motherboards offering the *Azalia* sound option. That's Intel High Definition Audio.

Speaker Support Every sound card supports two speakers or a pair of headphones, but many better sound cards support five or more speakers in discrete channels. These multiple speakers provide surround sound—popular not only for games but also for those who enjoy watching movies on their personal computers. The card shown in Figure 11-39, for example, has outputs for many speakers.

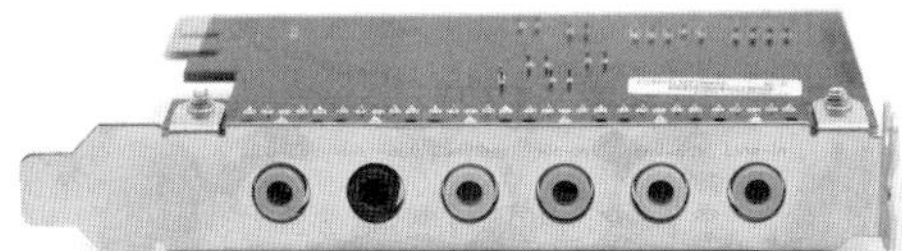

Figure 11-39 A sound card with multiple speaker connections

Another popular speaker addition is a subwoofer. A *subwoofer* provides the amazing low-frequency sounds that give an extra dimension to your movies, music, and games. Almost all modern sound cards support both surround sound and a subwoofer and advertise this with a nomenclature such as Dolby Digital or DTS. Figure 11-40 shows one type of surround speaker system. (You'll learn more about surround sound in the upcoming "Speakers" section.)

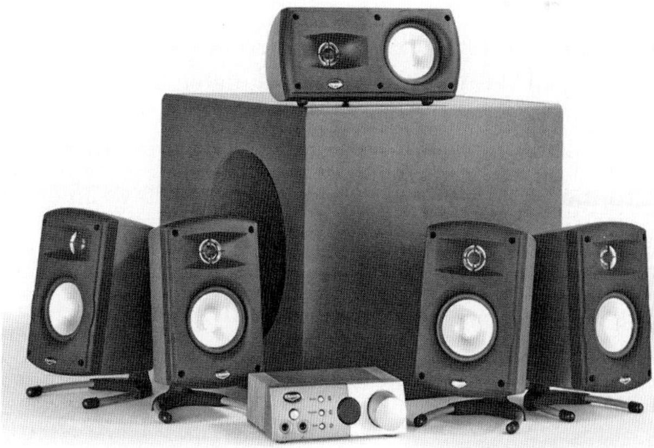

Figure 11-40 Surround speakers (photo courtesy of Klipsch Group, Inc.)

Jacks Virtually every sound card comes with at least three connections: one for a stereo speaker system, one for a microphone, and one for a secondary input called line in. If you look at the back of a motherboard with a built-in sound card, you'll invariably see these three connections. On most systems, the main stereo speaker connector is green, the line in connector is blue, and the microphone connector is pink. You'll often find plenty of other connectors as well (see Figure 11-41).

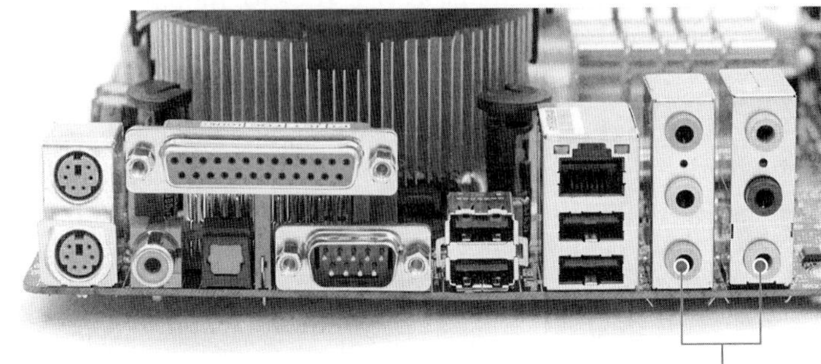

Figure 11-41 Typical audio connections on a motherboard sound card

Here's a list of some of the standard connectors:

- **Main speaker out** Just what it sounds like, the main speaker output is where you plug in the standard speaker connector.
- **Line out** Some cards will have a separate line out connector that is often used to connect to an external device such as a CD or MP3 player. This enables you to output sounds from your computer.
- **Line in** The line in port connects to an external device such as a CD or MP3 player to allow you to import sounds into your computer.
- **Rear out** The rear out connector connects to the rear speakers for surround sound audio output.
- **Analog/digital out** The multifunction analog/digital out connection acts as a special digital connection to external digital devices or digital speaker systems, and it also acts as the analog connection to center and subwoofer channels. (See the "Speakers" section, next in this chapter, for a discussion of surround sound.)
- **Microphone** The microphone port connects to an external microphone for voice input.
- **Joystick** The now-obsolete joystick port connects a joystick or a MIDI device to the sound card. The joystick port is a two-row, DB-15 female connection, but few motherboards or sound cards include the port these days.

Speakers

It always blows me away when I walk into someone's study and hear tinny music whining from a $10 pair of speakers connected to a $2000 computer. If you listen to music

or play games on your computer, a decent set of speakers can significantly improve the experience. Speakers come in a wide variety of sizes, shapes, technologies, and quality and can stump the uninformed tech who can't easily tell that the $50 set on the right sounds 100 times better than the $25 pair on the left (see Figure 11-42).

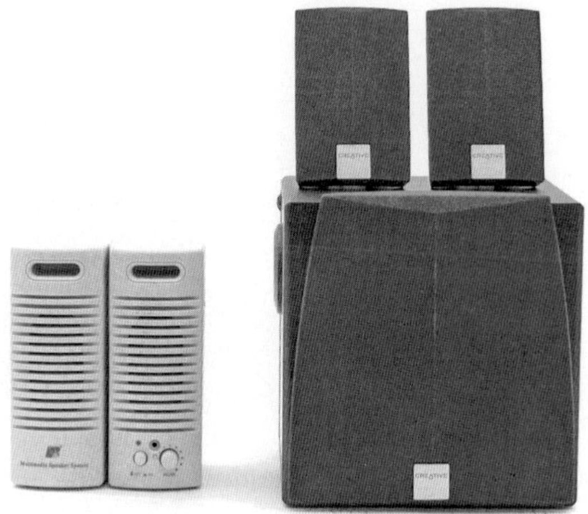

Figure 11-42 High-quality speaker set (right) versus another manufacturer's low-end speaker set (left)

The advent of surround sound in the computing world created a number of speaker standards. You should know these standards so you can choose the speakers that work best for you and your clients.

Stereo is the oldest speaker technology you'll see in typical computing devices. Stereo speakers are just what you might imagine: two speakers, a left and a right (see Figure 11-43). The two speakers share a single jack that connects to the sound card. Most cheap speakers are stereo speakers.

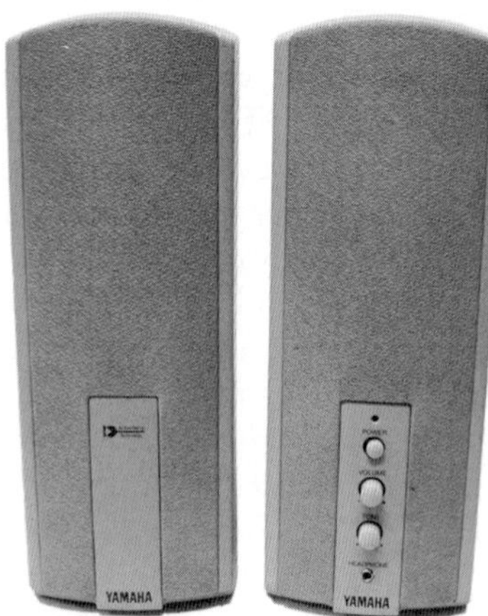

Figure 11-43 Stereo speakers

A *2.1* speaker system consists of a pair of standard stereo speakers—called *satellites*—combined with a subwoofer (see Figure 11-44). The average 2.1 speaker system has a single jack that connects to the sound card and runs into the subwoofer. Another wire runs from the subwoofer to the two stereo speakers. If you want to enjoy great music and don't need surround sound, this is your speaker standard of choice.

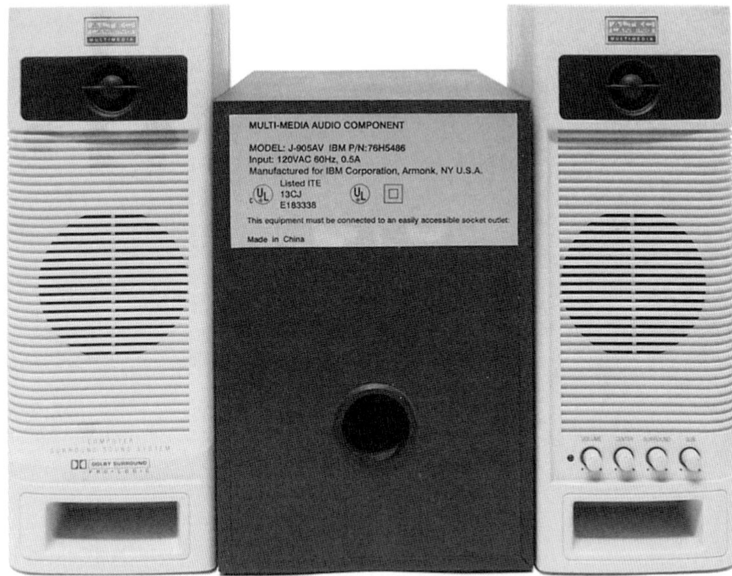

Figure 11-44 Typical 2.1 speakers

Going beyond standard two-channel (stereo) sound has been a goal in the sound world since the 1970s. However, it wasn't until the advent of Dolby Laboratory's *Dolby Digital* sound standard in the early 1990s that surround sound began to take off. The Dolby Digital sound standard is designed to support five channels of sound: front-left, front-right, front-center, rear-left, and rear-right. Dolby Digital also supports a subwoofer—thus, the term *5.1*. Another company, *Digital Theatre Systems (DTS)*, created a competing standard that also supports a 5.1 speaker system. When DVDs were introduced, they included both Dolby Digital and DTS 5.1 standards, making 5.1 speakers an overnight requirement for home theater. If you want to enjoy your movies in full surround sound, you must purchase a full 5.1 speaker system. A number of 5.1 speaker systems are available. The choice you make is usually determined by what sounds best to you.

Many sound cards also come with a special *Sony/Philips Digital Interface (S/PDIF)* connector that enables you to connect your sound card directly to a 5.1 speaker system or receiver (see Figure 11-45). Using a single S/PDIF instead of a tangle of separate wires for each speaker greatly simplifies your sound setup. S/PDIF connections come in two types, optical and coaxial. The optical variety looks like a square with a small door (at right in Figure 11-45). The coaxial is a standard RCA connector (at left), the same type used to connect a CD player to your stereo. It doesn't matter which one you use; just make sure you have an open spot on your receiver or speakers.

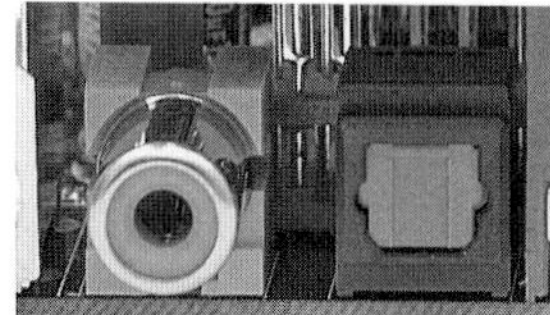

Figure 11-45 S/PDIF connectors

NOTE Only a few 5.1 PC speaker sets come with S/PDIF. In most cases, you'll have to use the regular audio outputs on the sound card. You'll find the connector more common on 6.1 and 7.1 sets.

Configure speakers and speaker settings with the Sound applet/preferences. (Go to the Control Panel in Windows; System Preferences in Mac OS X.)

Microphones

Speakers are great for listening to music, but what if you're a musician looking to record your own music? You'll need to plug a *microphone* into your sound card if you want to input audio into your computer (see Figure 11-46). A microphone records sound by detecting vibrations and turning them into an electronic signal. Microphones are most commonly used for recording voices, though you can easily record any other sounds. (Many musical instruments can be plugged into the line in port of your sound card, either directly or through a converter box.)

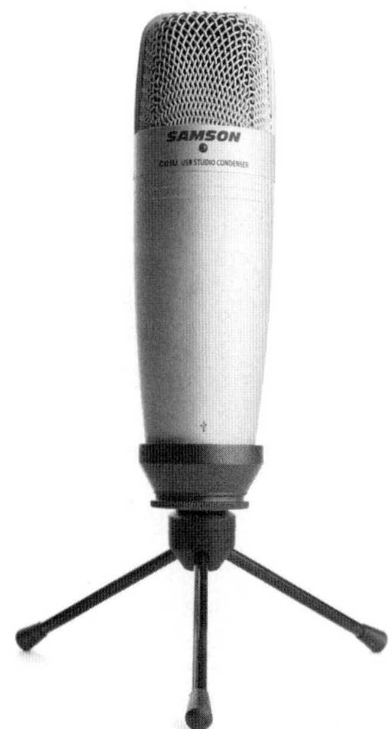

Figure 11-46 A standard microphone

NOTE You can also buy microphones that connect via USB instead of the microphone port.

Microphones can also be used with speech-to-text programs that listen to what you say and then type it out on the screen. These programs can be finicky to use, but they're still fun to play around with. If you do use speech-to-text programs, look for a headset that has a built-in microphone (see Figure 11-47). The quality will be lower, but it will keep your hands free. (These headsets are also great for voice chatting while playing games on a PC or game console.)

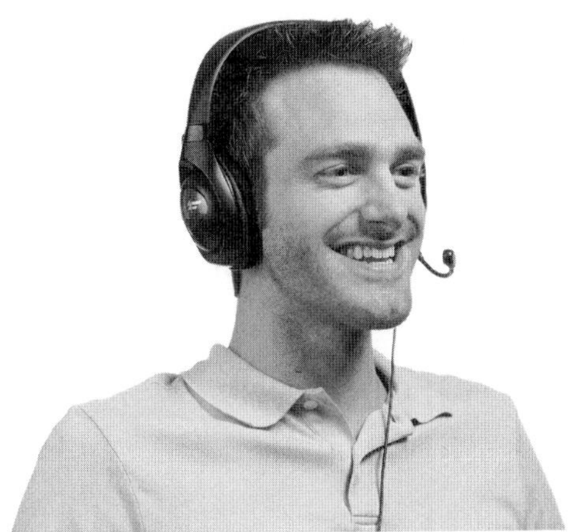

Figure 11-47 Headsets are great for gaming.

MIDI-Enabled Devices

Music composition has changed dramatically over the past few decades. What used to be a painfully analog process of writing out music on paper, recording it to tape, and hoping for the best has become almost entirely digital. Hardware and software exist that enable you to record analog sounds to digital storage, and create entirely digital sound with special audio production software. One type of software, called a *digital audio workstation*, enables you to input MIDI information using an external *MIDI-enabled device* (see Figure 11-48). *Music notation* software also exists that enables you to write out notes on sheet music either by hand or with a MIDI device.

MIDI-enabled devices, also known as *MIDI controllers*, come in several form factors, but most look and feel like standard music keyboards (see Figure 11-49). Others use a grid or row of square buttons—the best ones light up, too! Keep in mind that these devices don't play music; they are incapable of making noise on their own. Only combined with the proper software will a MIDI device be able to make music. In the past, MIDI devices used MIDI-to-serial or MIDI-to-joystick adapters, but almost all modern MIDI controllers use USB connections.

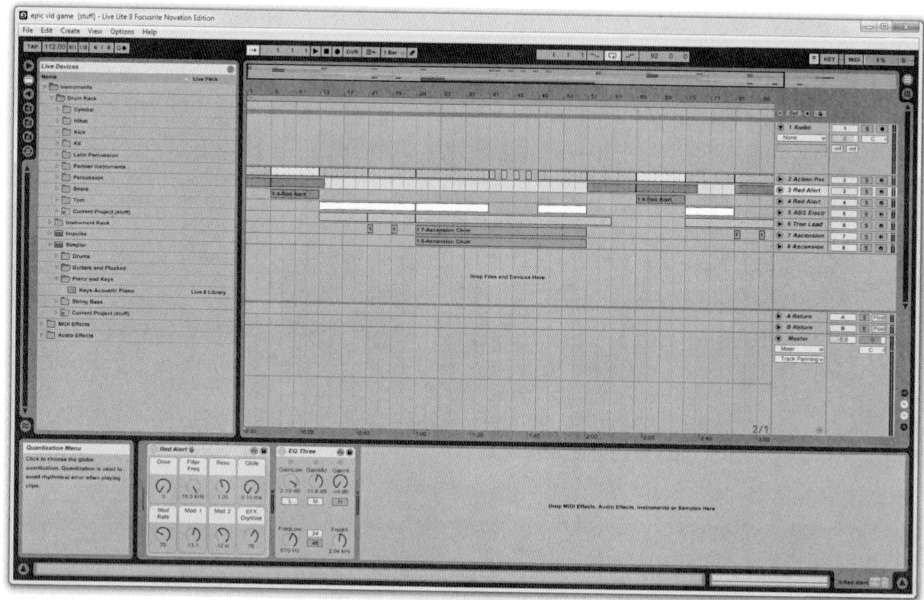

Figure 11-48 Ableton Live, a digital audio workstation

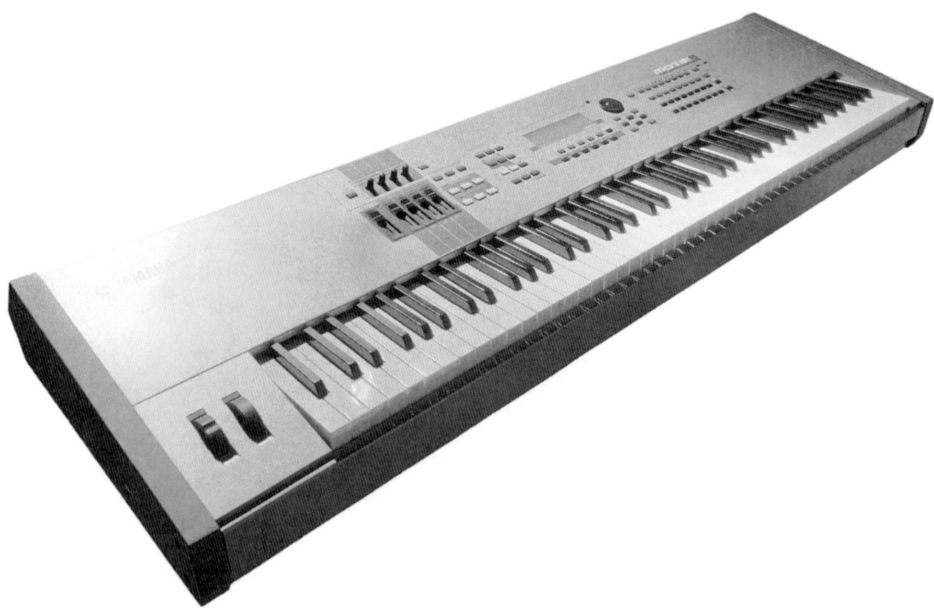

Figure 11-49 A MIDI keyboard

Video Capture

A microphone, sound card, and software enable you to capture audio, but with a camera capable of capturing full-motion video as well as sound, you can turn the PC into your very own movie studio. This is called *video capture*. If you want to capture video from another source, you to have the right hardware installed to provide an interface with the camcorder or video player and, if the source is analog, provide translation of the signal as well; plus you need a properly configured application to do the capturing. Once captured, you can use an application to edit the video file and upload it to YouTube or save it to DVD or other removable media.

Hardware

You need the proper hardware installed to capture video. From a digital signal, such as a modern camcorder that records directly to its own internal solid-state drive (SSD), you simply run a cable from the USB out port on the camcorder to the USB port on your computer. When capturing from an analog source, such as a VHS cassette player or a Hi-8 tape, you'll need some kind of connection and translation hardware.

The Pinnacle Studio MovieBox Ultimate (pictured in Figure 11-50), for example, offers two different dedicated video connections (S-Video in the middle and the yellow RCA jack next to it) and stereo RCA audio jacks. The box uses a USB connector to plug into a PC.

NOTE Some video capture devices are external, while others are internal PCI or PCIe cards. If you have an internal video capture card, install it into your PC as you would any other expansion card.

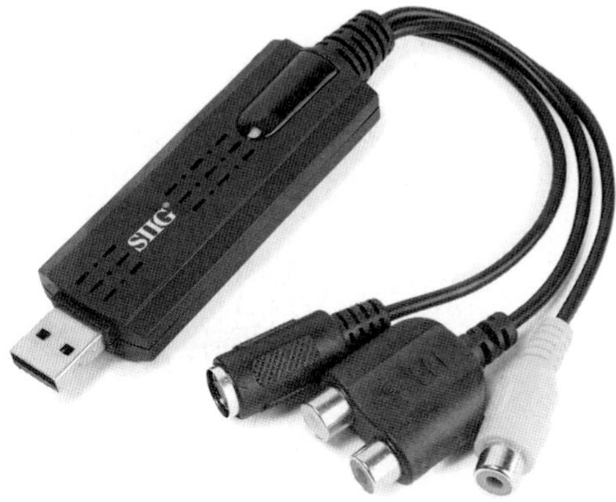

Figure 11-50 A video capture device

You need a decent-grade computer with lots of free hard drive space and a substantial amount of RAM to import the video and audio streams from an external source.

And you'll certainly need a serious processor when it comes time to edit and compile a new video from the source material. There's no simple rule for how much of any resource you'll need. Different projects have different demands on the hardware. If you're setting up a new computer for video capture, the simple rule is to get as powerful a system as possible with as much hard drive and RAM capacity as you can afford.

Once you have the hardware in place, the true heavy lifting in video capture falls on the software.

Software

With video editing applications, such as Adobe Premier Elements or Apple Final Cut, you can import video and then work with it directly. Figure 11-51 shows the former software capturing video and audio translated through the Pinnacle blueBox from a Hi-8 camcorder. Most webcams—even those built into portable computers—are analog devices rather than digital devices. Thus some software automatically creates break points in the import to make the editing process easier

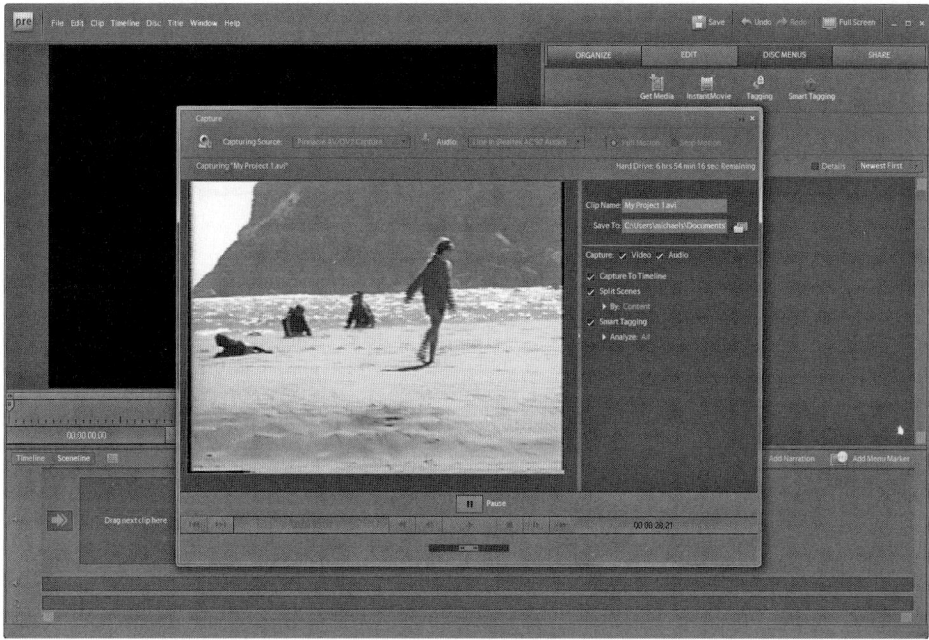

Figure 11-51 Importing video in Adobe Premier Elements

The video editing software enables you to take video and audio from one or many sources and arrange clips into a timeline. You can add and edit various transitions between

clips, shorten clips, and so on. Figure 11-52 shows the storyboard from Final Cut Pro and a how-to video my team produced in-house.

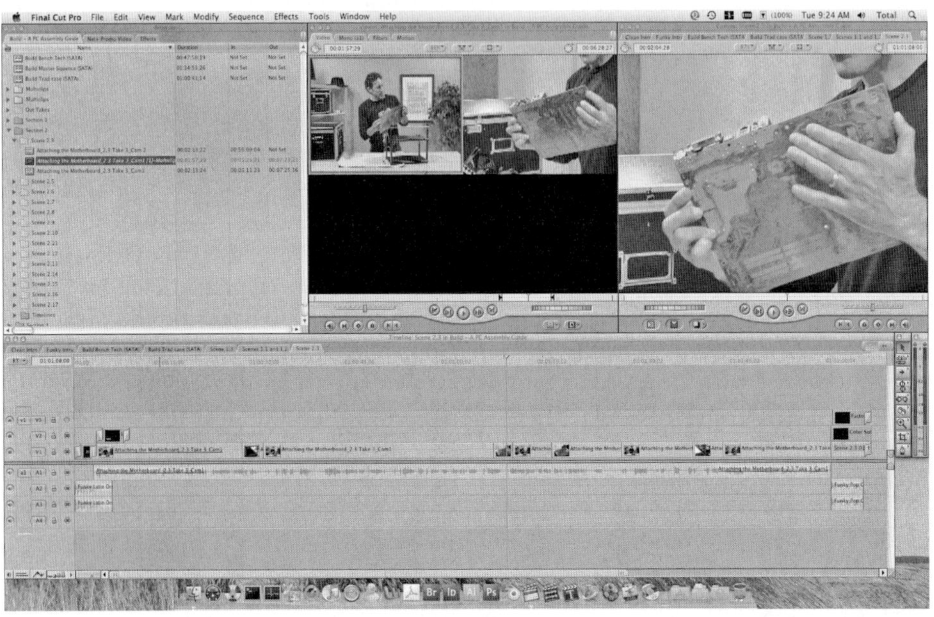

Figure 11-52 Editing in Final Cut Pro

Once you've finished the editing process, you can export to a file for archiving, sending out on optical disc/USB stick/etc., or posting to a video-sharing site. With an audio file, as discussed earlier, this is a simple process. You pick a format such as MP3 and save the file. Video is far more complicated.

A video is two or more separate tracks—moving picture and audio—that each go through a compression algorithm. Otherwise, the resulting files would be huge, even for short videos. The compressed tracks then get wrapped up into a *container file*, what's often called a *wrapper*. When you receive a file saved in a standard wrapper, such as .MOV for a QuickTime Movie file, you have no way to know for certain which codecs were used to compress the video or audio tracks inside that container file (see Figure 11-53).

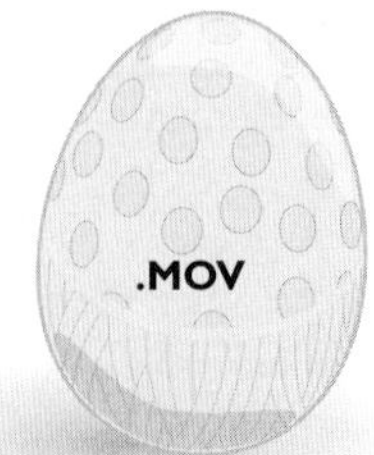

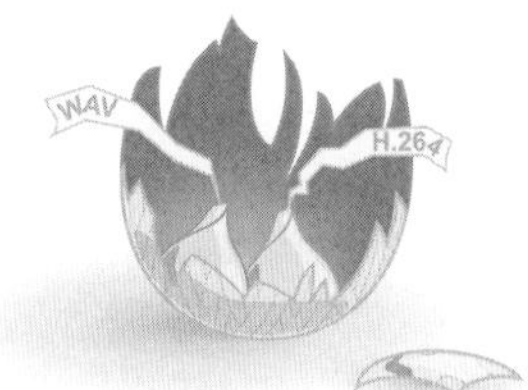

Figure 11-53 A standard container file holds multiple tracks, each encoded separately.

Codecs Video files use standard audio codecs for the audio tracks, such as WAV or MP3, but vary wildly in the type of video codecs used. Just as with audio codecs, video codecs take a video stream and compress it by using various algorithms. Here are some of the standard video codecs:

- MPEG-2 Part 2, used for DVDs
- MPEG-4 Part 2, often used for Internet broadcasts; you'll find implementations of it with other names, such as DivX
- H.264, used for high-definition movies on Blu-ray Discs, among others
- Windows Media Video (WMV), the family of Microsoft-developed codecs
- Theora, an open source codec developed to go with the Vorbis audio codec as part of the Ogg project
- TrueMotion VP6, used in Adobe Flash; and VP7, used for Skype video conferencing, among others
- VC-1, a Microsoft-designed codec that competes with H.264 and other higher-end codecs for the hearts and minds of Blu-ray Disc developers; usually wrapped in a WMV container file (see the following section)

Wrappers When both the video and audio streams of your video file are compressed, the file is placed into some sort of container file or wrapper. The key thing to note here is that the wrapper file doesn't necessarily specify how the video or audio tracks were encoded. You can look at two seemingly identical movie files—for example, both saved with the .MOV file extension—and find that one will play audio and video just fine in Windows Media Player, but the other one might play only the audio and not the video because Media Player lacks the specific codec needed to decode the video stream. Here are some of the standard video wrappers:

- ASF, a container used mainly for WMA and WMV streams; note that you can also have a WMV wrapper for a WMV-format file
- AVI, the standard container file for Windows
- FLV (Flash Video), a container file for streams encoded with various codecs, such as H.263 or VP6; it can also handle H.264 codec
- MOV, the standard container file for Apple QuickTime for both Mac OS X and Windows
- MPEG-2 Transport Stream (MPEG-TS), a container for broadcasting that can handle many streams
- Ogg, a container file made for the open source Vorbis and Theora codecs

TV Tuners

With a *TV tuner*, you can have it all in one package: a computer and the latest TV shows. Most local stations (in the United States, at least) broadcast high-definition signals, so

with the proper TV tuner, you can watch HDTV without any of the artifacting you see with both cable and satellite feeds. Plus you can make use of typical cable, fiber, or satellite feeds to watch television as you would with a regular TV. You need four components to make it all happen: a tuner device, an antenna or cable connection, a tuning application, and some sort of program guide.

Tuner Hardware

TV tuners come in just about every expansion option available for computers: expansion cards that plug into PCI or PCIe slots on the motherboard; PC Card or ExpressCard for portable computers; and Hi-Speed or SuperSpeed USB for desktop and laptop computers. Figure 11-54 shows a PCIe version of an ATI tuner card.

Figure 11-54
ATI TV tuner card

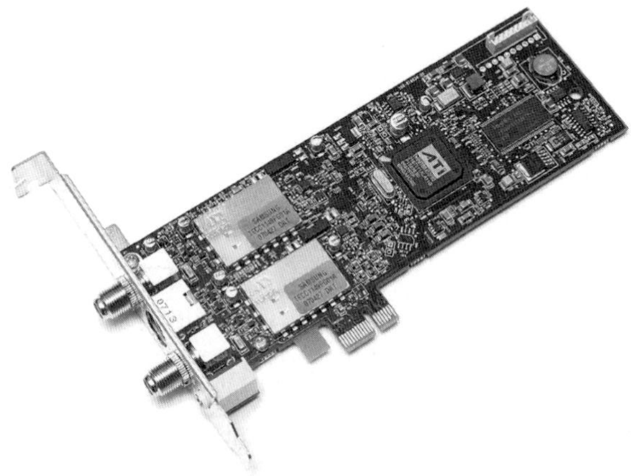

To install a TV tuner, follow standard installation procedures.

NOTE TV tuners often include components for video capture, so you can get both devices on one card or expansion device.

To pick up a signal on the TV tuner, just as with a standalone television, you need some source. Most can handle a cable TV connection, for example, or an over-the-air antenna. Figure 11-55 shows a USB Hauppauge HDTV tuner card with retractable antenna. For such a small device, it picks up HDTV signals quite well. You'll get the best results for uncompressed HD signals by using a serious, mounted-on-the-rooftop metal antenna with lots of tines.

Tuner hardware comes with a standard coaxial connection. You can plug in a cable or satellite source just as you would with any regular television.

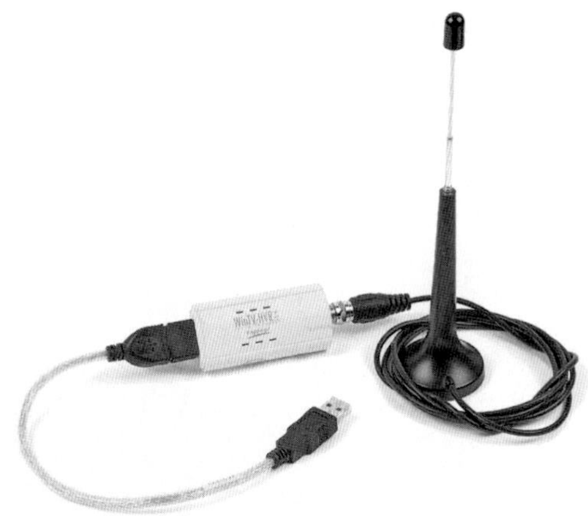

Figure 11-55 Hauppauge TV tuner with retractable antenna

Tuner Software

Once you've installed the hardware, you need to load the specific application or applications that make the tuner work as a tuner. If you have a copy of Windows Media Center, that will often be the tool of choice (until you upgrade to Windows 10). Tuner card distributors bundle third-party applications with their cards. Figure 11-56 shows the EyeTV software enabling the computer to show television shows.

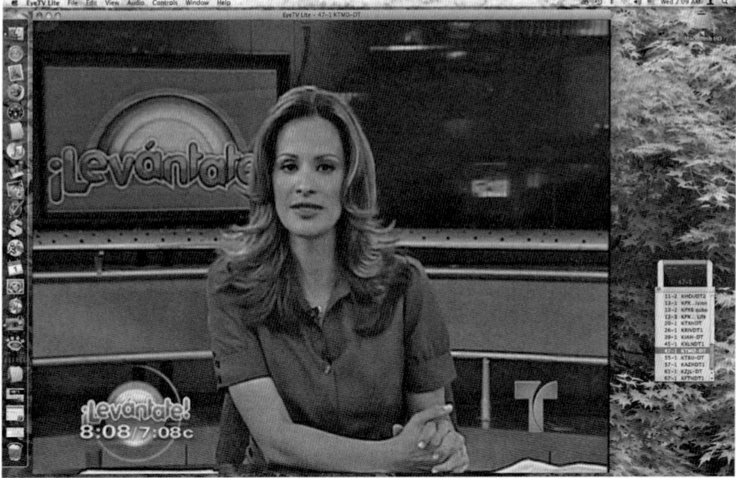

Figure 11-56 EyeTV tuner application

Online TV Channel Listings

You can find a lot of sources for local television shows. The huge name is tvguide.com, the Web site of the company that produced the absolutely essential guide book to television for decades before the Internet. The titantv.com site offers robust channel listings as well, tuned to your local time zone. And titantv has apps for various mobile devices to make finding things to watch easy.

Smart TV and Set-Top Boxes

Two types of devices function as computing devices, enabling you to watch content streamed over the Internet. A *smart TV* is a television with network capabilities—both hardware and software—so you can plug in and hit the Web. A *set-top box* is an alternative computing device that you can use if you have a dumb TV. The box, like the Roku 3 pictured in Figure 11-57, handles the Internet connectivity and interface. Streaming movies from Netflix or Amazon has never been easier. (See Chapters 20–23 for the full details about networking and networking devices.)

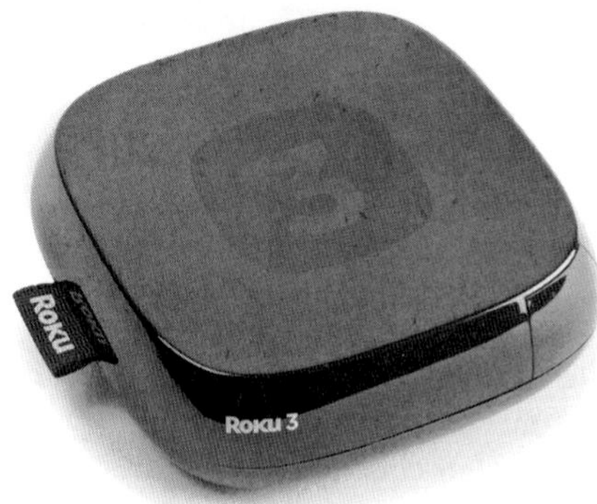

Figure 11-57
Roku 3

Storage Devices

Removable media refers to any type of mass storage device that you may use in one system and then physically remove from that system and use in another. Today's highly internetworked computers have reduced the need for removable media as a method of sharing programs and data, but removable media has so many other uses that it's still going strong. Removable media is the perfect tool for software distribution, data archiving, and system backup.

This final section of the chapter covers the most common types of removable media used today. For the sake of organization, the removable media types are broken down into these groups:

- **Flash memory** From USB thumb drives to flash memory cards
- **Optical discs** Any shiny disc technology, from CD-ROMs to DVDs and Blu-ray Discs

We can add external drives to this mix, meaning any hard drive, SSD, or optical drive that connects to a PC via an external cable. These drives manifest just like an internal drive, as you studied in Chapters 9 and 10, so there's nothing special to discuss here.

Flash Memory

Flash memory, the same flash memory that replaced CMOS technology for your system BIOS, found another home in personal computing devices in the form of removable mass storage devices. Flash memory comes in two families: USB thumb drives and memory cards. USB thumb drives are flash devices that contain a standard USB connection. "Memory card" is a generic term for a number of tiny cards that are used in cameras, smartphones, and other devices. Both of these families can manifest themselves as drives in modern OSs, but they usually perform different jobs. USB thumb drives have replaced virtually all other rewritable removable media as the way people transfer files or keep copies of important programs. My thumb drives (yes, I have two on me at all times) keep backups of my current work, important photos, and a stack of utilities I need to fix computers. Memory cards are very small and make a great way to store data on small devices and then transfer that data to your computer.

USB Thumb Drives

Moving data between computers has historically been a pain, but USB flash memory drives, also known as *USB thumb drives*, jump drives, and flash drives, make the process much easier (see Figure 11-58). For a low price, you can get a 64-GB thumb drive that holds a ton of data.

Figure 11-58 USB thumb drives

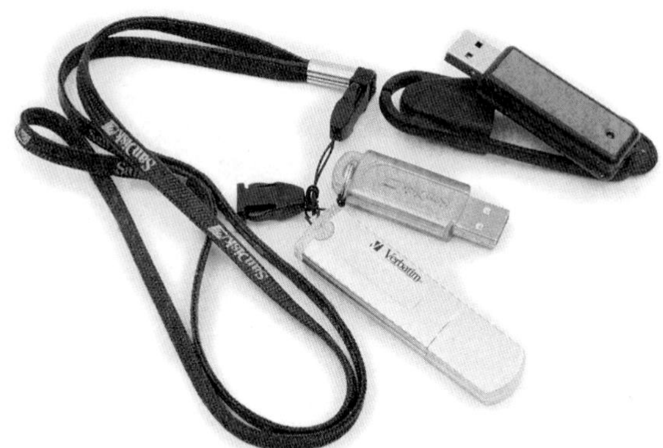

The smallest thumb drives are slightly larger than an adult thumbnail; others are larger and more rounded. The drives are hot-swappable in all modern OSs. You simply plug one into any USB port and it appears in File Explorer or on the Desktop as a removable storage device. After you plug the drive into a USB port, you can copy or move data to or from your hard drive and then unplug the unit and take it with you. You can read, write, and delete files directly from the drive. Because these are USB devices, they don't need an external power source. The nonvolatile flash memory is solid-state, so it's shock resistant and is supposed to retain data safely for a decade.

Current systems enable you to boot to a thumb drive. With a bootable thumb drive, you can replace bootable CDs and DVDs with fast flash drives. Making a thumb drive bootable is a bit of a challenge, so most of the classic bootable-utility CD makers have created USB versions that seek out your thumb drive and add an operating system with

the utilities you wish to use. Most of these are simply versions of Linux-based live CDs. If you want to try it, check out GParted Live at http://gparted.sourceforge.net and click on the Live CD/USB link.

NOTE Remember to change the boot order in CMOS when you want to boot from a USB flash drive. If you use the wrong boot order, the BIOS will skip straight to the hard drive and load an OS.

Flash Cards

Flash cards are the way people store data on small appliances. Digital cameras, smartphones, and MP3 players all come with slots for some type of memory card. Memory cards come in a number of incompatible formats, so let's start by making sure you know the more common ones.

CompactFlash *CompactFlash (CF)* is the oldest, most complex, and physically largest of all removable flash media cards (see Figure 11-59). Roughly one inch wide, CF cards use a simplified PCMCIA bus (see Chapter 24 for details) for interconnection. CF cards come in two sizes: CF I (3.3 mm thick) and CF II (5 mm thick). CF II cards are too thick to fit into CF I slots.

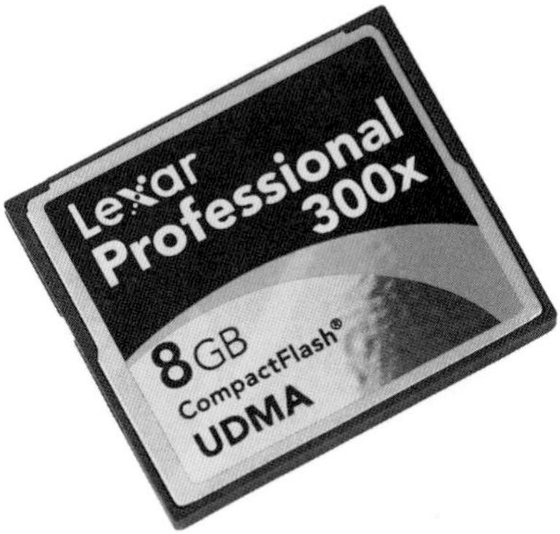

Figure 11-59
CF card

Clever manufacturers repurposed the CF form factor to create the microdrive (see Figure 11-60). *Microdrives* are true hard drives, using platters and read/write heads that

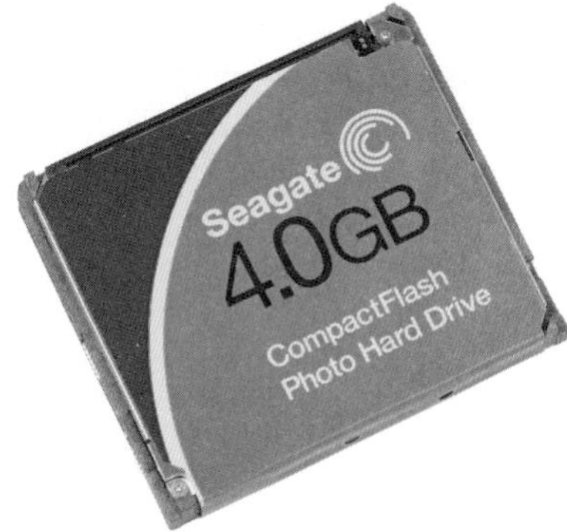

Figure 11-60
Microdrive

fit into the tiny CF form factor. Microdrives are slower and use more power than flash drives and, when they were first introduced, cost much less than an equivalent CF flash card. From the user's standpoint, CF flash cards and microdrives look and act exactly the same way, although the greater power consumption of microdrives makes them incompatible with some devices. These days, microdrives have been surpassed in size, speed, and cost by their flash cousins and have become more difficult to find.

SmartMedia SmartMedia came out as a competitor to CF cards and for a few years was quite popular in digital cameras (see Figure 11-61). The introduction of SD media reduced SmartMedia's popularity, and no new devices use this media.

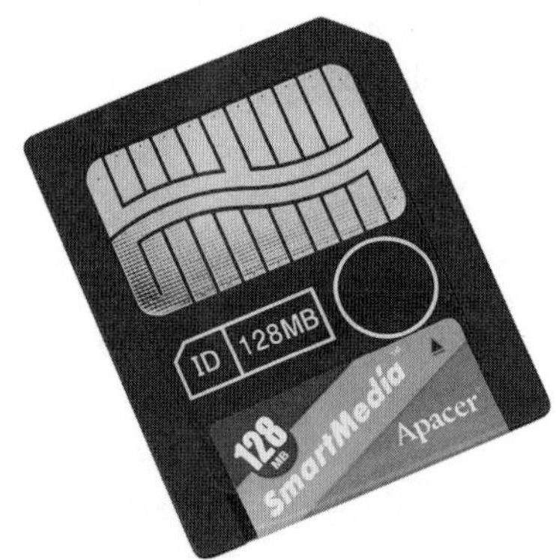

Figure 11-61 SmartMedia

Secure Digital *Secure Digital (SD)* cards are arguably the most common flash media format today. About the size of a small postage stamp, you'll see SD cards in just about any type of device that uses flash media.

SD cards come in two smaller forms called *Mini Secure Digital (MiniSD)* cards and *Micro Secure Digital (MicroSD)* cards. They're extremely popular in cellular phones that use flash memory, but they see little use in other devices. Figure 11-62 shows the three forms of SD cards.

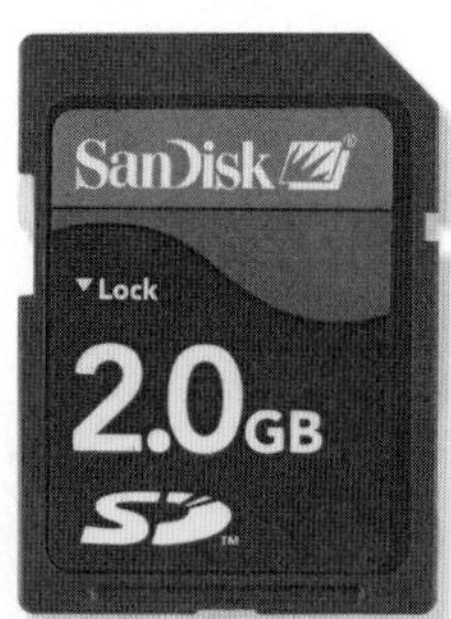

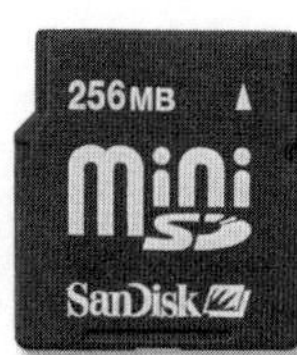

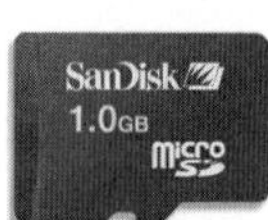

Figure 11-62 SD, MiniSD, and MicroSD cards

SD cards come in three storage capacities. *Standard SD* cards store from 4 MB to 4 GB, *Secure Digital High Capacity (SDHC)* cards store 4 GB to 32 GB, and *Secure*

Digital Extended Capacity (SDXC) cards have a storage capacity of 32 GB to 2 TB. Early SD card readers and devices cannot read the SDHC or SDXC cards, though the latter standards provide backward compatibility.

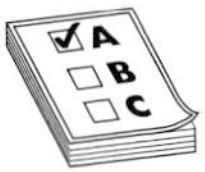

EXAM TIP SD cards developed out of an older, slower flash memory technology called *MultiMediaCard (MMC)*. If you happen to have an MMC card lying around, you can use it in almost any SD card slot. SD cards are a little thicker than MMC cards, though, so the reverse is not true.

You will see the *embedded* version of MMC cards, called *eMMC*, in very wide use, especially in mobile devices. Aside from knowing it's there, though, there's not much a tech can do aside from answering questions about it correctly on the 901 exam.

Memory Stick Sony always likes to use proprietary formats, and their *Memory Stick* flash memory is no exception. If you own something from Sony and it uses flash memory, you'll need a Memory Stick, though not all Memory Sticks are manufactured by Sony (see Figure 11-63). There are several Memory Stick formats, including Standard, Pro, Duo, Pro Duo, and Micro.

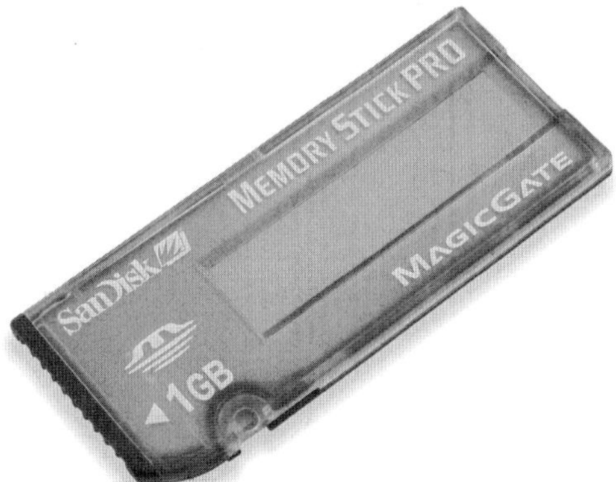

Figure 11-63 Memory Stick

xD Picture Card The proprietary *Extreme Digital (xD) Picture Cards* (see Figure 11-64) are about half the size of an SD card. They're almost exclusively used in Olympus and Fujifilm digital cameras, although Olympus (the developer of the xD technology) produces a USB housing so you can use an xD-Picture Card like any other USB flash memory drive.

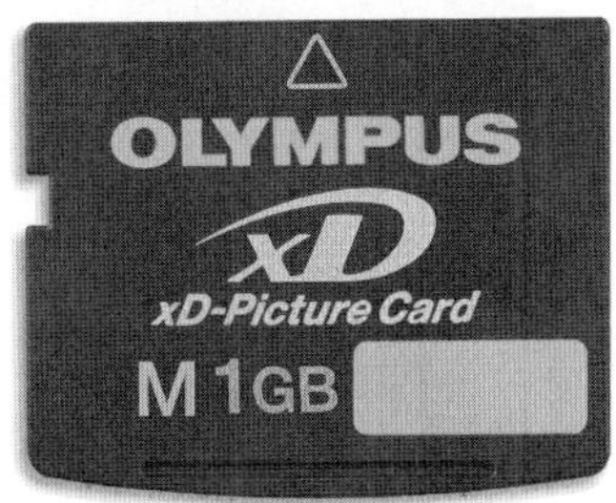

Figure 11-64 xD-Picture Card

The xD-Picture Cards come in three flavors: original, Standard (Type M), and Hi-Speed (Type H). The Standard cards are slower than the original cards but offer greater storage capacity. The Hi-Speed cards are two to three times faster than the others and enable you to capture full-motion video—assuming the camera has that capability, naturally!

Card Readers Whichever type of flash memory you use, your computer must have a *card reader* to access the data on the card directly. A number of inexpensive USB card readers are available today (see Figure 11-65), and some computers come with built-in readers—handy to have when someone pulls out an SD card and says, "Let's look at the pictures I just took!" Of course, if the person just happened to bring her camera and USB cable along, you could connect the camera to the computer and pull pictures in that way. Just make sure you have spare batteries, too! Wouldn't a card reader be a more elegant solution?

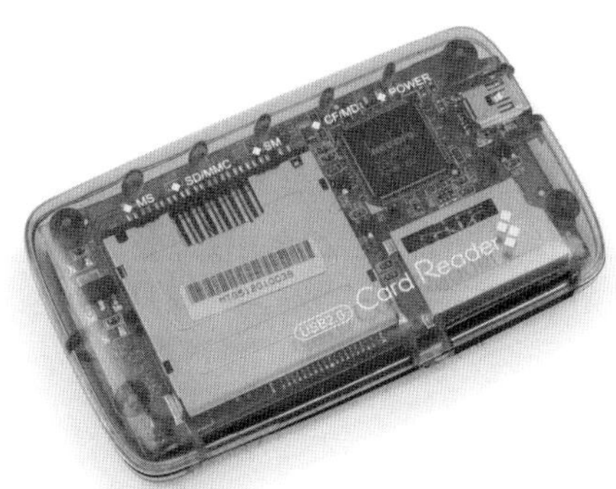

Figure 11-65
USB card reader

Whichever type of flash memory you have, understand that it acts exactly like a hard drive. If you wish, you can format a memory card or copy, paste, and rename files.

Optical Drives

CD, DVD, and Blu-ray Disc drives and discs come in a variety of flavors and formats, enabling you to back up data, record music, master home videos, and much, much more. *Optical disc* is the generic term for all those different types of shiny, 12-centimeter-wide discs that, if you're a slob like me, collect around your computer like pizza boxes. The drives that support them are called *optical drives*. This section examines optical discs, finishing with the details about installing optical drives.

CD stands for *compact disc*, a medium that was originally designed as a replacement for vinyl records. The *digital versatile disc (DVD)* first eliminated VHS cassette tapes from the commercial home movie market, and grew into a contender for backups and high-capacity storage. *Blu-ray Disc (BD)* eliminated the High-Definition DVD (HD DVD) format to become the only high-definition and high-capacity optical format.

Going beyond those big three household names, the term "optical disc" refers to technologies such as CD-ROM, CD-R, CD-RW, DVD, DVD+RW, HD DVD, BD-R, BD-RE, and so on. Each of these technologies will be discussed in detail in this chapter—for now, understand that although "optical disc" describes a variety of exciting formats, they all basically boil down to the same physical object: that little shiny disc.

CD-Media

The best way to understand optical disc technologies is to sort out the many varieties available, starting with the first: the compact disc. All you're about to read is relevant and fair game for the CompTIA A+ certification exams.

CD Formats The first CDs were designed for playing music and organized the music in a special format called *CD-Digital Audio (CDDA)*, which we usually just call CD-audio. CD-audio divides the CD's data into variable-length tracks; on music CDs, each song gets one track. CD-audio is an excellent way to store music, but it lacks any error checking, file support, or directory structure, making it a terrible way to store data. For this reason, The Powers That Be created a special method for storing data on a CD, called—are you ready—*CD-ROM*. The CD-ROM format divides the CD into fixed sectors, each holding 2353 bytes.

Most CD-ROM drives also support a number of older, less well-known formats. You may never come across these formats—CD Text, CD+G, and so forth—although you may see them listed among compatible formats on the packaging for a new drive or with a program like Nero InfoTool (see Figure 11-66). Don't let these oddball formats throw

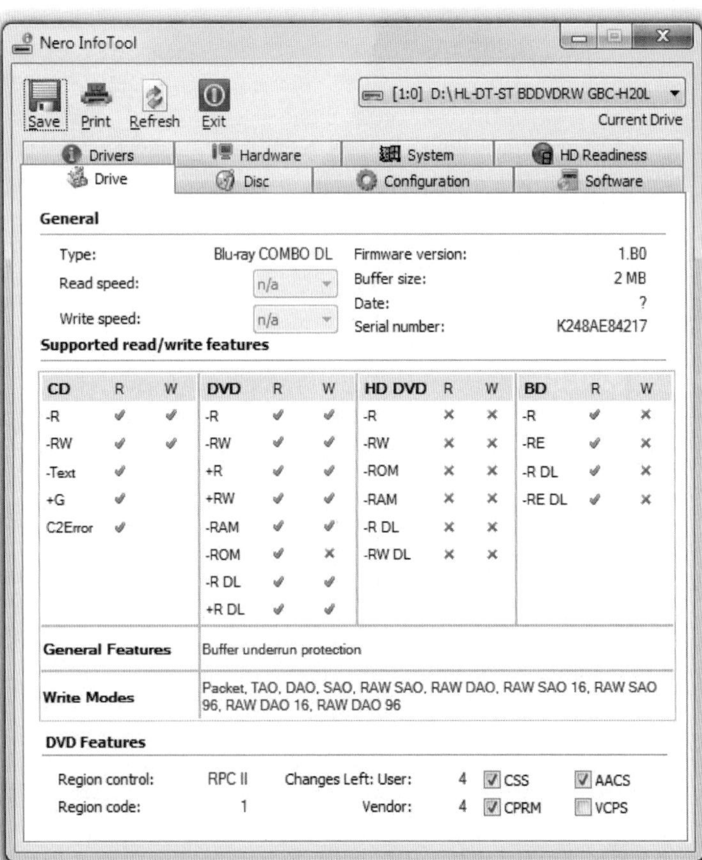

Figure 11-66 Crazy CD formats

you—with few exceptions, they've pretty much fallen by the wayside. All CD-ROM drives read all of these formats, assuming that the system is loaded with the proper software.

The CD-ROM format is something like a partition in the hard drive world. CD-ROM may define the sectors (and some other information), but it doesn't enable a CD-ROM disc to act like a hard drive, with a file structure, directories, and such. To make a CD-ROM act like a hard drive, there's another layer of formatting that defines the file system used on the drive.

At first glance you might think, "Why don't CD-ROMs just use a FAT or an NTFS format like hard drives?" Well, first of all, they could. There's no law of physics that prevented the CD-ROM world from adopting any file system. The problem is that the CD makers did not want CD-ROM to be tied to Microsoft's or Apple's or anyone else's file format. In addition, they wanted non-PC devices to read CDs, so they invented their own file system just for CD-ROMs called *ISO-9660*. This format is sometimes referred to by the more generic term, *CD File System (CDFS)*. The vast majority of data CD-ROMs today use this format.

Over the years, extensions of the ISO-9660 have addressed certain limitations, such as the characters used in file and directory names, filename length, and directory depth.

CD-ROM *Speeds* The first CD-ROM drives processed data at roughly 150,000 bytes per second (150 KBps), copying the speed from the original CD-audio format. Although this speed is excellent for listening to music, the CD-ROM industry quickly recognized that installing programs or transferring files from a CD-ROM at 150 KBps was the electronic equivalent of watching paint dry. Since the day the first CD-ROM drives for PCs hit the market, there has been a desire to speed them up to increase their data throughput. Each increase in speed is measured in multiples of the original 150-KBps drives and given an × to show speed relative to the first (1×) drives. Here's a list of the common CD-ROM speeds, including most of the early speeds that are no longer produced:

1× 150 KBps	10× 1500 KBps	40× 6000 KBps
2× 300 KBps	12× 1800 KBps	48× 7200 KBps
3× 450 KBps	16× 2400 KBps	52× 7800 KBps
4× 600 KBps	24× 3600 KBps	60× 9000 KBps
6× 900 KBps	32× 4800 KBps	72× 10800 KBps
8× 1200 KBps	36× 5400 KBps	

Keep in mind that these are maximum speeds that are rarely met in real-life operation. You can, however, count on a 32× drive to read data faster than an 8× drive. As multipliers continue to increase, so many other factors come into play that telling the difference between a 48× drive and a 52× drive, for example, becomes difficult. High-speed CD-ROM drives are so inexpensive, however, that most folks buy the fastest drive possible—at least installations go faster!

CD-R Making CD-ROMs requires specialized, expensive equipment and substantial expertise, so a relatively small number of CD-ROM production companies do it. Yet, since the day the first CD-ROMs came to market, demand was high for a way that

ordinary PC users could make their own CDs. The CD industry made a number of attempts to create a technology that would let users record, or *burn*, their own CDs.

In the mid-1990s, the CD industry introduced the *CD-recordable (CD-R)* standard, which enables affordable CD-R drives, often referred to as *CD burners*, to add data to special CD-R discs. Any CD-ROM drive can then read the data stored on the CD-R, and all CD-R drives can read regular CD-ROMs. CD-R discs come in two varieties: a 74-minute disc that holds approximately 650 MB, and an 80-minute variety that holds approximately 700 MB (see Figure 11-67). A CD-R burner must be specifically designed to support the longer, 80-minute CD-R format, but most drives you'll encounter can do this.

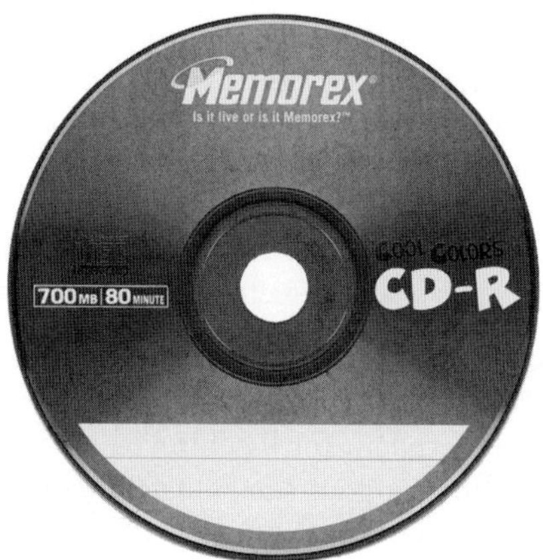

Figure 11-67 A CD-R disc, with its capacity clearly labeled

CD-R discs function similarly to regular CD-ROMs, although the chemicals used to make them produce a brightly colored recording side on almost all CD-R discs. CD-ROM discs, in contrast, have a silver recording side. CD-R technology records data by using special organic dyes embedded into the disc. This dye is what gives the CD-R its distinctive bottom color. CD-R burners have a second burn laser, roughly ten times as powerful as the read laser, that heats the organic dye. This causes a change in the reflectivity of the surface, creating the functional equivalent of a CD-ROM's pits.

NOTE Some music CD players can't handle CD-R discs.

Once the CD-R drive burns data onto a CD-R, the data cannot be erased or changed short of destroying the disc itself. Early CD-R drives required that the entire disc be burned in one burn session, wasting any unused part of the CD-R disc. These were called single-session drives. All modern CD-R drives are *multisession drives*, so you can go back and burn additional data onto the CD-R disc until the disc is full. Multisession drives also have the capability to "close" a partially filled CD-R so that no more data can be burned onto that disc.

CD-R drives have two speeds that matter: the record speed and the read speed, both expressed as multiples of the 150-KBps speed of the original CD-ROM drives. The record speed, which is listed first, is always equal to or slower than the read speed. For example, a CD-R drive with a specification of 8×24× would burn at 8× and read at 24×.

CD-RW For all their usefulness, CD-R drives have disappeared from the market. Notice that I didn't say CD-R *discs* have disappeared; more CD-R discs are burned now than ever before. Just as CD-R drives could both burn CD-R discs and read CD-ROMs, a newer type of drive called *CD-rewritable (CD-RW)* took over the burning market from CD-R drives. Although this drive has its own type of CD-RW discs, it also can burn to CD-R discs, which are much cheaper.

CD-RW technology enables you not only to burn a disc, but to *burn over* existing data on a CD-RW disc. This is not something you need for every disc. For example, I create CD-R archives of my completed books to store the text and graphics for posterity—this is data I want to access later but do not need to modify. While I'm still working on this book, however, I might make a backup copy. As I work on it, I'll update the backup. I couldn't do that with a CD-R. The CD-RW format, on the other hand, essentially takes CD-media to the functional equivalent of a 650-MB flash-media drive. Once again, CD-RW discs look exactly like CD-ROM discs with the exception of a colored bottom side. Figure 11-68 shows all three formats.

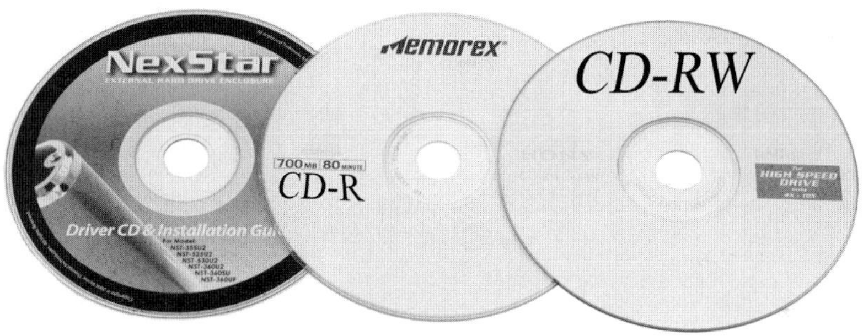

Figure 11-68 CD-ROM, CD-R, and CD-RW discs

A CD-RW drive works by using a laser to heat an amorphous (noncrystalline) substance that, when cooled, slowly becomes crystalline. The crystalline areas are reflective, whereas the amorphous areas are not. Because both CD-R and CD-RW drives require a powerful laser, making a drive that could burn CD-Rs and CD-RWs was a simple process, and plain CD-R drives disappeared almost overnight. Why buy a CD-R drive when a comparably priced CD-RW drive could burn both CD-R and CD-RW discs?

CD-RW drive specs have three multiplier values. The first shows the CD-R write speed, the second shows the CD-RW rewrite speed, and the third shows the read speed. Write, rewrite, and read speeds vary tremendously among the various brands of CD-RW drives; here are just a few representative samples: 8×4×32×, 12×10×32×, and 48×24×48×.

One of the goals with the introduction of CD-RWs was the idea of making a CD-RW act like a hard drive so you could simply drag a file onto the CD-RW (or CD-R) and just as easily drag it off again. This goal was difficult for two reasons: first, the different file formats made on-the-fly conversion risky; second, CD-RWs don't store data exactly the same way as hard drives and would quickly wear out if data were copied in the same manner.

Two developments, UDF and packet writing, enable you to treat a CD-RW just like a hard drive—with a few gotchas. The not-so-new kid in town with CD-media file formats is the *universal data format (UDF)*. UDF is a replacement for ISO-9660 and all of its various extensions, resulting in a single file format that any drive and operating system can read. UDF handles very large files and is excellent for all rewritable CD-media. *Packet-writing* is a feature built into modern operating systems that enables easy adding and deleting of files on optical media.

Windows and CD-Media Virtually all optical drives are *ATAPI-compliant*, meaning they plug into the ATA controllers on the motherboard, just like a hard drive, so you don't need to install drivers. You just plug in the drive and, assuming you didn't make any physical installation mistakes, the drive appears in Windows (see Figure 11-69).

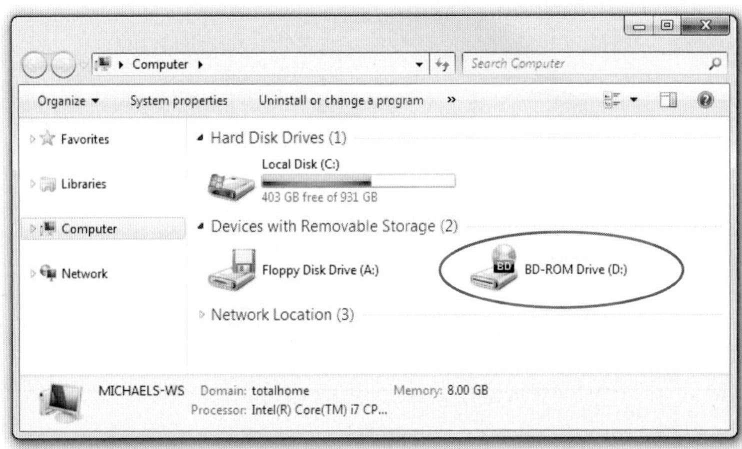

Figure 11-69 Optical drive in Windows

DVD-Media

For years, the video industry tried to create an optical-media replacement for videotape. The 12-inch diameter *laserdisc* format originally introduced by Philips gained some ground in the 1980s and 1990s. But the high cost of both the discs and the players, plus various marketing factors, meant there was never a very large laserdisc market. You may still find one of them sitting around, however, or you may know someone who invested in a small collection during the laserdisc's heyday.

The DVD was developed by a large consortium of electronics and entertainment firms during the early 1990s and released as digital *video* discs in 1995. The transformation of

DVD to a data storage medium required a name change to digital *versatile* discs. You'll still hear both terms used. The industry also uses the term *DVD-video* to distinguish the movie format from the data formats.

With the exception of the DVD logo stamped on all commercial DVDs (see Figure 11-70), DVDs look exactly like CD-media discs; but that's pretty much where the similarities end. DVD became the fastest growing media format in history and has completely overtaken VHS as the preferred media for video. Additionally, one variant of DVD called DVD-RAM has enjoyed some success as a mass storage medium.

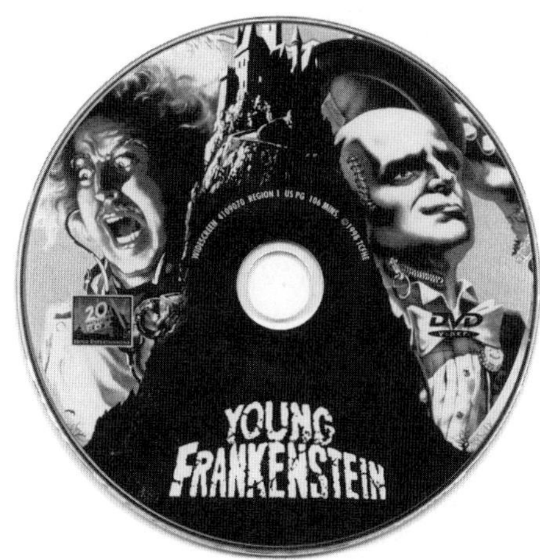

Figure 11-70 Typical DVD-video

The single best word to describe DVD is *capacity*. All previous optical discs stored a maximum of 700 MB of data or 80 minutes of video. The lowest capacity DVD holds 4.37 GB of data, or two hours of standard-definition audio. The highest capacity DVD versions store roughly 16 GB of data, or more than eight hours of video! DVD achieves these amazing capacities by using a number of technologies, but three are most important. First, DVD uses smaller pits than CD-media, and packs them much more densely. Second, DVD comes in both *single-sided (SS)* and *double-sided (DS)* formats. As the name implies, a DS disc holds twice the data of an SS disc, but it also requires you to flip the disc to read the other side. Third, DVDs come in *single-layer (SL)* and *dual-layer (DL)* formats. DL formats use two pitted layers on each side, each with a slightly different reflectivity index. Table 11-2 shows the common DVD capacities.

Table 11-2 DVD Versions/Capacities

DVD Version	Capacity
DVD-5 (12 cm, SS/SL)	4.37 GB, more than two hours of video
DVD-9 (12 cm, SS/DL)	7.95 GB, about four hours of video
DVD-10 (12 cm, DS/SL)	8.74 GB, about four and a half hours of video
DVD-18 (12 cm, DS/DL)	15.90 GB, more than eight hours of video

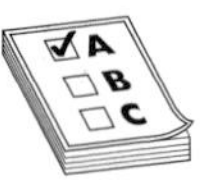

EXAM TIP The CompTIA A+ 901 exam refers to dual-layer DVDs as *DVD DL*, while a rewritable DVD—in theory—is called a *Dual Layer DVD-RW*.

DVD-Video The most beautiful trait of DVD-video is its capability to store two hours of video on one side. You drop in a DVD-video and get to watch an entire movie without flipping it over. DVD-video supports TV-style 4:3 aspect-ratio screens as well as 16:9 theater screens, but it is up to the producer to decide which to use. Many DVD-video producers used to distribute DVD movies on DS media with a 4:3 ratio on one side and 16:9 ratio on the other, though that isn't as common anymore. DVD-video relies on the *MPEG-2* standard of video and audio compression to reach the magic of two hours of video per side. *Moving Picture Experts Group (MPEG)* is a group of compression standards for both audio and video. The MPEG-2 standard offers resolutions of up to 1280 × 720 at 60 frames per second (fps), with full CD-quality audio (standard DVDs only offer 480 vertical resolution, the same as regular television).

DVD-ROM *DVD-ROM* is the DVD equivalent of the standard CD-ROM data format except that it's capable of storing up to almost 16 GB of data. Almost all DVD-ROM drives also fully support DVD-video, as well as most CD-ROM formats. Most DVD drives sold with PCs are DVD-ROM drives.

Recordable DVD The IT industry has no fewer than *five* distinct standards of recordable DVD-media: DVD-R, DVD+R, DVD+R DL, DVD-RW, and DVD+RW. Both DVD-R standard discs and DVD+R discs work like CD-Rs. You can write to them but not erase or alter what's written. DVD+R DL can be written to on two layers, doubling the capacity. DVD-RW and DVD+RW discs can be written and rewritten, just like CD-RW discs. Most DVD drives can read all formats.

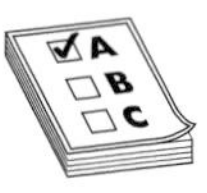

EXAM TIP The CompTIA A+ 901 objectives mention *DVD-RW DL* as a common recordable disc type. The specification has been out for several years, but the media is not around. Rewritable Blu-ray Discs have eclipsed DVD-whatever discs.

Although there is little if any difference in quality among the standards, the competition between corporations pushing their preferred standards has raged for years. Sony and Phillips, for example, pushed the + series, whereas other manufacturers pushed the – series. Worse, no recordable DVD drive manufactured before 2003 could write any format except its own. You could plop down US$250 on a brand-new DVD+RW drive and still find yourself unable to edit a disc from your friend who used the DVD-RW format! Half of the time, the drive couldn't even *read* the competing format disc.

The situation is much better today, as DVD±RW combo drives in PCs play just about anyone else's DVDs. The challenge is DVD players. If you want to make a DVD of your family picnic and then play it on the DVD player hooked to your television, take the time to read the documentation for your player to make sure it reads that particular DVD format—not all players read all formats.

Blu-ray Disc Media

Blu-ray Disc is considered the next generation in optical disc formatting and storage technology after CD and DVD. Because of its near-perfect audio and video quality; mass acceptance by industry-leading computer, electronics, game, music, retail, and motion picture companies; and huge storage capacities of up to 25 GB (single-layer disc), 50 GB (dual-layer disc), and 100 GB (BDXL), Blu-ray Disc technology might make CD- and DVD-media and devices obsolete.

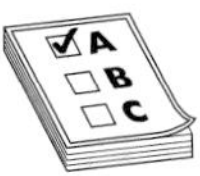

EXAM TIP Apple stopped including optical drives on both desktop and portable systems a long time ago. Because optical media enjoys some popularity, Apple gave OS X machines Remote Disc, the capability to read optical media from an optical drive in another system.

Blu-ray Discs come in two physical sizes, standard and mini. The standard size matches that of earlier optical discs, such as CD-R and DVD-RW, and is what you'll see used in computers and for movies (see Figure 11-71). The mini-size discs are a lot smaller and, naturally, offer less storage. You'll find mini Blu-ray Discs in very high-end camcorders. Table 11-3 shows the details of the two formats.

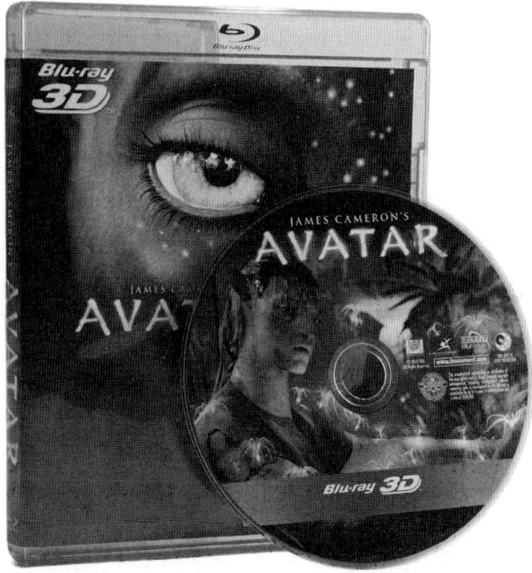

Figure 11-71 Standard Blu-ray Disc

Type	Size	Capacity (single layer)	Capacity (dual layer)
Standard disc	12 cm	25 GB	50 GB
Mini disc	8 cm	7.8 GB	15.6 GB

Table 11-3 Standard and Mini Blu-ray Disc Comparison Chart

NOTE If you own an Xbox One or PlayStation 3 or later, you already have a Blu-ray Disc player. That's the optical format the game system uses.

Blu-ray Disc technology offers several advantages over DVD aside from raw capacity. First, Blu-ray Disc uses a blue-violet laser (hence the Blu in the name) with a wavelength of 405 nanometers (nm), whereas DVD uses a red-laser technology with a wavelength of 650 nm. The 405-nm wavelength is smaller and much more precise, enabling better use of space during the creation process and ultimately resulting in a sharper image. Second, Blu-ray Disc can handle HD video in resolutions far higher than DVD. Finally, Blu-ray Disc supports many more video compression schemes, giving producers more options for putting content on discs.

BD-ROM *BD-ROM* (read only) is the Blu-ray Disc equivalent of the standard DVD-ROM data format except, as noted earlier, it can store much more data and produces superior audio and video results. Almost all BD-ROM drives are fully backward compatible and support DVD-video as well as most CD-ROM formats. If you want to display the best possible movie picture quality on your HDTV, you should get a Blu-ray Disc player and use Blu-ray Discs in place of DVDs. Most new computer systems still don't come standard with Blu-ray Disc drives installed. You can often custom-order a system with a Blu-ray Disc drive or you can simply install one yourself. Figure 11-72 shows a Blu-ray Disc drive.

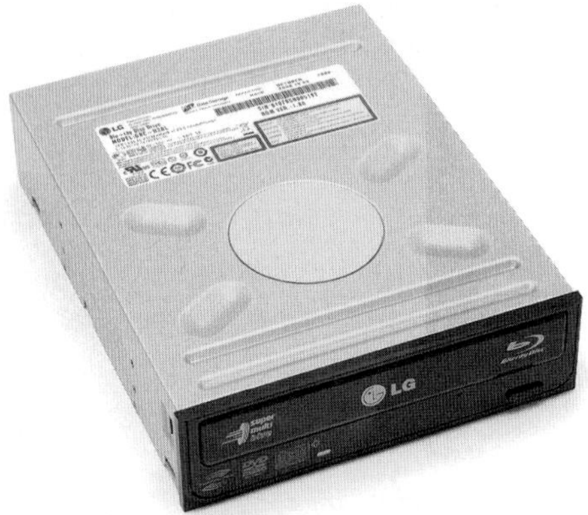

Figure 11-72 A combination CD/DVD/Blu-ray Disc drive

BD-R and BD-RE Blu-ray Discs come in two writable formats, BD-R (for recordable) and BD-RE (for rewritable). You can write to a *BD-R* disc one time. You can write to and erase a *BD-RE* disc several times. There are also BD-R and BD-RE versions of mini Blu-ray Discs.

Blu-ray Disc Burners Blu-ray Disc burners cost more than a standard optical drive and have not seen wide adoption. Blu-ray Disc burners and other Blu-ray Disc drives can be connected internally or externally to a system. It is common for them to be connected

externally via USB (3.0/3.1 usually) or eSATA, or internally through SATA. Modern Windows and Mac OS X operating systems support Blu-ray Disc burners and software. The software you use for burning is totally up to you; however, as always, you should follow the manufacturer's specifications for the best results. Most multidrive Blu-ray Disc burners offer the following support features.

- **Media support** BD-R, BD-RE, DVD-ROM, DVD-RAM, DVD-video, DVD+/-R DL, DVD+/-R, DVD+/-RW, CD-DA, CD-ROM, CD-R, and CD-RW
- **Write speed (max)** 2× BD-R, 4× DVD+/-R DL, 8× DVD+/-R(8×), and 24× CD-R
- **Rewrite speed (max)** 2× BD-RE, 8× DVD+RW, 6× DVD-RW, 5× DVD-RAM, and 16× CD-RW
- **Read speed (max)** 2× BD-ROM, 8× DVD-ROM, and 32× CD-ROM
- **Compatibility** Most Blu-ray Disc drives are backward compatible, meaning they can read and play CDs and DVDs. CD and DVD drives and players cannot read or play Blu-ray Discs.

Installing Optical Drives

From ten feet away, optical drives of all flavors look absolutely identical. Figure 11-73 shows a CD-RW drive, a DVD drive, and a BD-R drive. Can you tell them apart just by a glance? In case you were wondering, the CD-RW drive is on the bottom, the DVD drive is next, and finally the BD-R drive is on the top. If you look closely at an optical drive, you will normally see its function either stamped on the front of the case or printed on a label somewhere less obvious (see Figure 11-74).

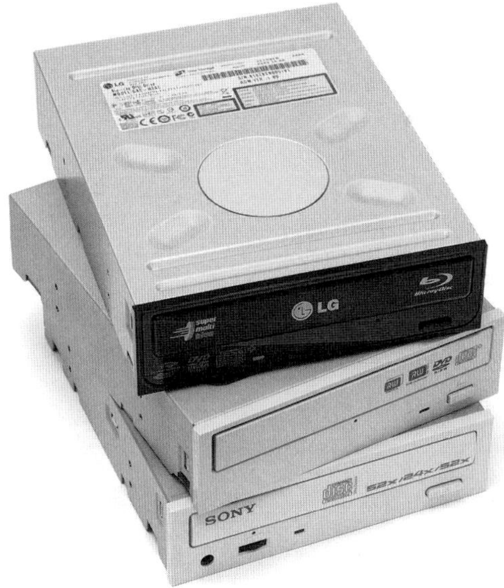

Figure 11-73 CD-RW, DVD, and BD-R drives

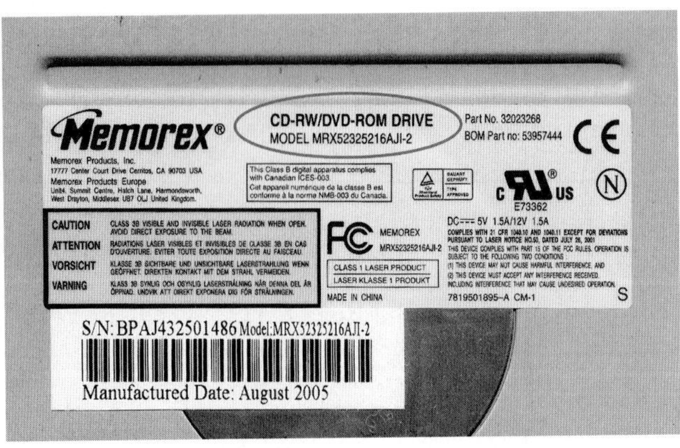

Figure 11-74 Label on optical drive indicating its type

Most internal optical drives use SATA and support the ATAPI standard. External optical drives often use USB, FireWire, eSATA, or Thunderbolt connections. Plug them in and go.

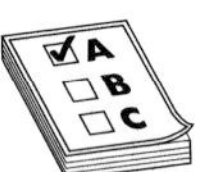

EXAM TIP You might run into magnetic tape drives as backup solutions in some businesses. The only common form factor left is called Linear Tape Open (LTO) with capacities of up to 2.5 TB per tape.

Chapter Review

Questions

1. When triggered, which of the following sends a signal to the computer to start recording?
   A. Smart card
   B. Motion sensor
   C. KVM switch
   D. Digitizer
2. What happens to bus speed and power usage when you plug multiple devices into a USB hub?
   A. The bus speed stays constant, but power usage increases.
   B. The bus speed increases because each device brings a little burst; power usage increases.
   C. The bus speed decreases because all devices share the same total bandwidth; power usage increases.
   D. The bus speed decreases because all devices share the same total bandwidth; power usage decreases.

3. Which port type offers the fastest transfer speed?
   A. IEEE 1394a
   B. SuperSpeed USB
   C. Full-Speed USB
   D. Hi-Speed USB
4. You take a tech call from a user who complains that she gets an error message, "Hub power exceeded," when she plugs her new thumb drive into her USB keyboard's external USB port. Worse, the device won't work. What's most likely the problem?
   A. Her USB port is defective.
   B. She has a defective thumb drive.
   C. She plugged a Hi-Speed device into a Full-Speed port.
   D. She plugged one too many devices into the USB hub.
5. What is the fastest speed that Hi-Speed USB 2.0 can go?
   A. 12 Mbps
   B. 120 Mbps
   C. 400 Mbps
   D. 480 Mbps
6. What is the maximum cable length for USB 2.0?
   A. 1.2 meters
   B. 1.2 yards
   C. 5 meters
   D. 5 feet
7. How many speakers are in a Dolby Digital 5.1 setup?
   A. Five speakers plus a subwoofer
   B. Six speakers plus a subwoofer
   C. Seven speakers plus a subwoofer
   D. Eight speakers plus a subwoofer
8. What type of file is a MIDI file?
   A. Audio
   B. Binary
   C. MP3
   D. Text

9. Which optical disc type offers the most capacity for writing and rewriting data files?
   - A. DVD-R
   - B. DVD+R DL
   - C. BD-RE
   - D. BD-RW
10. Jack wants to watch television through his computer. He has a cable television subscription. What else does he need?
    - A. A cable card installed in his system
    - B. TV tuner card installed in his system
    - C. Smart TV added to his system
    - D. A set-top box connected to his system

Answers

1. **B.** Motion sensors respond to external movement. When triggered, they send a signal to the computer to start recording.
2. **C.** The bus speed decreases because all devices share the same total bandwidth; power usage increases.
3. **B.** SuperSpeed USB easily spanks the competition here.
4. **D.** Just like the error message said, the thumb drive drew too much power for the hub to handle.
5. **D.** Hi-speed USB 2.0 has a theoretical maximum of 480 Mbps.
6. **C.** USB has a maximum cable length of 5 meters.
7. **A.** A Dolby Digital 5.1 setup has five speakers and one subwoofer.
8. **D.** A MIDI file is a text file.
9. **C.** BD-RE offers the highest rewritable capacity of the discs mentioned here.
10. **B.** Jack can install a TV tuner card in his computer (or attach one via USB) and then plug his cable into it.

CHAPTER 12

Building a PC

In this chapter, you will learn how to

- Research and spec out specialized PCs
- Install and upgrade Windows
- Describe Windows post-installation best practices

Techs build computers. We fix them too, of course, but very little beats the chance to show off our knowledge, research skill, and technical savvy like creating excellent custom PCs for clients.

This chapter puts together a lot of what you know about hardware from the previous 11 chapters and layers on the essential component that makes Windows PCs so excellent: Windows. Let's start with customized PCs for specialized jobs, then turn to installing and upgrading Windows. The final section covers post-installation tasks.

901

Specialized Custom PCs

Specialized computing needs require specialized PCs to get the job done well. Many techs specialize in rolling out (or deploying, in IT speak) PCs that do exactly what the customer needs.

This section looks first briefly at hardware considerations you should make, then turns to workstation PCs, such as thick clients and media workstations. The section finishes with a look at some specialized consumer PCs, such as home servers, home theaters, and gaming boxes.

Evaluating Parts

The most difficult (and most fun) part of buying a PC is picking which parts you want. Knowing which parts to buy for each type of PC is essential. Let's take a moment to consider the processes and steps you can use to discover and evaluate the right parts for specialized systems.

Read the Reviews

Every component has a review somewhere. Go to Google, type in the name and model number of a part, and add the word "review" at the end. There are two types of reviews: industry reviews written by professionals, and personal reviews written by people who purchased and use the part. Let the Google search I described show you how to the find the professional reviews. Newegg.com is one of my favorite places to read personal reviews.

Read the Fine Print

Learn everything you can about the part. Take some time to read the technical specifications. Check the return and warranty policy of both the manufacturer and retailer. Make sure you have some recourse if the part breaks or doesn't function as advertised.

Compare and Contrast

Before you buy a part, see what folks say about the competitors' parts. Are there other parts that cost less, have better reviews, or use less power?

Put It in Your Hand

If you're lucky enough to live near a big retailer like Fry's Electronics or Micro Center, go check out the part. Look for a display model. Look at the back of the box. See what extra parts are included. Talk to the salespeople about their experiences, the returns they've seen, and alternatives they like better.

Workstation PCs

In modern times, people need computers to get work done. The type of workstation a person needs depends on what types of tasks they need to perform with it and how the IT department has configured the organization's network. The CompTIA A+ 901 exam defines the standard workstation types: thick clients, thin clients, virtualization workstations, and media workstations.

Thick Clients

A standard *thick client* runs a modern operating system and general productivity applications to accomplish the vast majority of tasks needed by office and home users (see Figure 12-1). When most folks hear the term "PC," the thick client comes to mind. Thick clients are the quiet workhorses of modern computing.

The "thick" part of thick client doesn't necessarily refer (these days) to the physical thickness of the computer case or system unit that houses everything. It means more that the computer can do what the user needs to get done, be it sending e-mail, searching the Web, writing papers, or doing taxes. With thick clients, you can readily add all sorts of capabilities just by installing new software.

A trip to a computer or electronics store will reveal that most contemporary components are powerful enough to build a useful thick client. Every mainstream motherboard designed for a PC, for example, has a ton of necessary features built in, such as memory

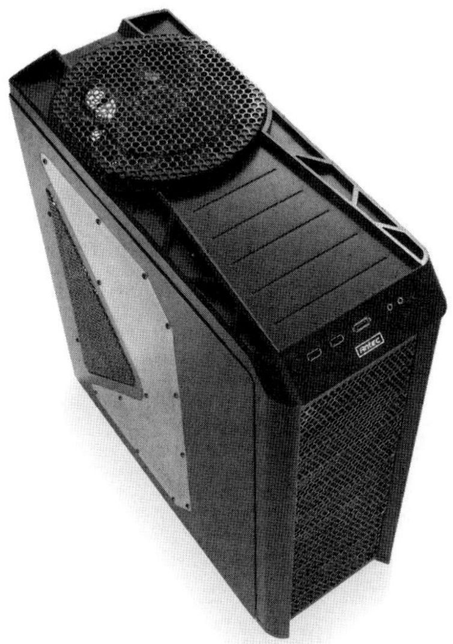

Figure 12-1 A typical thick client

slots, mass storage support, video, sound, networking, and plenty of USB ports for extensibility.

The key to a good thick client is sufficient core hardware to support the operating system and applications typical of an office or home-office environment. Table 12-1 shows the minimum hardware requirements for modern Windows (including up to Windows 10).

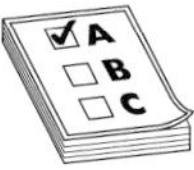

EXAM TIP A standard thick client should meet or exceed the recommended hardware specifications for Windows and offer typical desktop applications, such as office productivity and network applications (like a Web browser and an e-mail client).

Component	Hardware Requirements
CPU[1]	1 gigahertz (GHz) or faster 32-bit (x86) or 64-bit (x64)
Memory[2]	1 gigabyte (GB) RAM (32-bit) or 2 GB RAM (64-bit)
Hard drive[3]	16 GB available hard drive space (32-bit) or 20 GB (64-bit)
Graphics	DirectX 9 graphics device with WDDM driver
Network	Internet access

1. Windows Vista can get by with an 800-MHz processor.
2. Windows Vista requires a minimum 512 MB of RAM for Vista Home Basic; 1 GB for all other editions.
3. Windows Vista requires 15 GB of available hard drive space for all editions.

Table 12-1 Hardware requirements for Windows

Thin Clients

With just enough hardware and power to run the selected operating system and a few basic applications, a *thin client* is a system designed to outsource much of its work. Thin clients usually rely on resources from powerful servers, so they may not have hard drives, for example, or store any data. Thin clients often serve as single-purpose systems, like point of sale machines (cash registers). Another common example today is office workstations. A thin client might look like a thick client, but it requires fewer resources, thus making it cheaper and easier to deploy. Figure 12-2 shows a typical thin client.

Because the classic thin client relies on *network connectivity* and access to servers over those networks, we'll revisit them when we get to networking in Chapters 20–23.

Virtualization Workstations

Virtualization is a powerful technology that enables you to run more than one operating system at the same time on a single computer. With virtualized servers, you can consolidate multiple, power-hungry machines into one box, saving floor space, electricity, and a lot of running around. With *virtualization workstations*, virtualization is most often used to run a second OS within the OS installed on the computer's hard drive.

For good performance on a virtualization workstation, install lots and lots of RAM. Each virtualization workstation needs enough memory to run the native operating system, the guest operating system, and any applications running in either OS, so RAM is the most important thing in virtualization. A powerful 64-bit CPU with many cores also helps virtual machines run smoothly. Many desktop computers can run virtual machines, but if you want the best possible performance, you want lots of RAM and a good CPU.

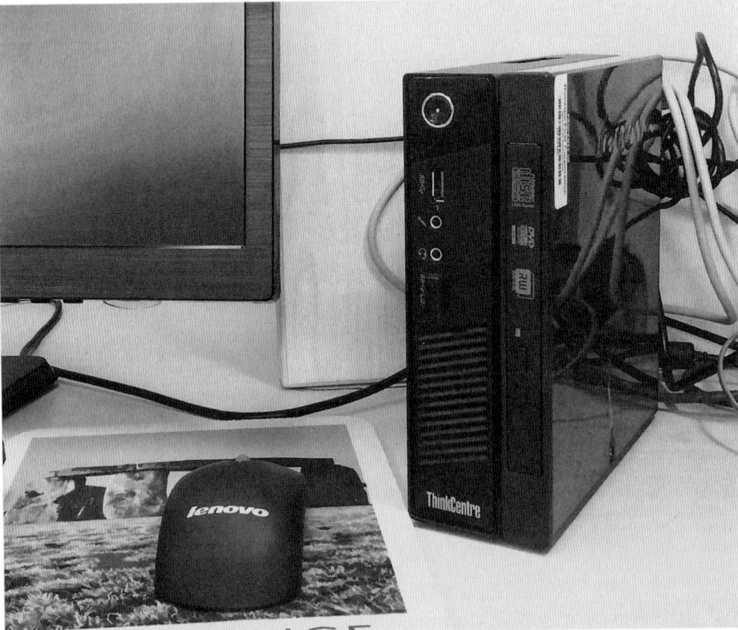

Figure 12-2 Thin client in an office

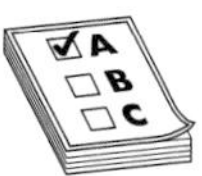

EXAM TIP You'll need lots of RAM—think *maximum RAM*—and a fast CPU with many cores to get great performance out of a virtualization workstation.

Chapter 18, "Virtualization," discusses virtual machines in great detail. We'll take the opportunity there to flesh out the discussion of virtualization workstations.

Media Workstations

When George Lucas made the first *Star Wars* movie, he used camera tricks, miniature models, and stop-motion animation to create the illusion of massive spaceships and robots battling it out in a galaxy far, far away. Twenty years later, he filmed the *Star Wars* prequels in front of massive green screens and used computer-generated imagery (CGI) to transform the bland sets into exotic planets and space stations. I won't get into an argument about which approach produced better movies, but the fact remains that the act of creating films has changed. It's not just films, either—computers have changed the way we create all types of media, including movies, television shows, photography, music, and more.

If you want to get involved in this creative revolution, you're going to need a powerful computer. Workstations for creative professionals are customized for the type of media they create. We'll start by looking at graphics workstations and then move on to audio-/video-editing workstations.

Graphics Workstations Professional photographers and graphic designers generally work with pretty hefty files, so at its core, a *graphics workstation* requires a fast, multicore CPU and maximum RAM. Because designers work visually, add to that mix the need for high-end video components. Finally, throw in specialized software to make it all work. Professional photographers use Adobe Photoshop and Adobe Lightroom. Graphics engineers have a few other options, but they fall into *computer-aided design (CAD)* and *computer-aided manufacturing (CAM)* categories.

NOTE CAD/CAM software programs enable engineers to create and build components in an industrial setting.

Graphics designers need to have the clearest view possible of their images and image-editing software. Whether you're editing photos in Adobe Photoshop or drafting mechanical components in SolidWorks, you need to make sure you can see what you're working on! Because of this, a primary need for a graphics workstation is a large, high-quality monitor. A $200 LCD panel from Best Buy won't help you here—you need to make sure that the colors you see on the screen are as accurate as possible.

Chapter 19, "Display Technologies," covers all the various high-end video components, such as IPS monitors and multi-thousand-dollar graphics workstation video cards. We'll reopen the discussion on graphics workstations in that chapter.

Audio Editing Workstations The requirements for *audio editing workstations* are very similar to those for graphics workstations—a fast, multicore CPU, gobs of RAM, and a large monitor. Plus, you need a large, fast hard drive. Add to that the need for a high-quality audio interface.

An *audio interface* is a box that you hook up to a PC with inputs that enable you to connect professional microphones and instruments (see Figure 12-3). Functionally, an audio interface is just a really high-end sound card, though they usually connect to your computer via USB or FireWire rather than plugging into the motherboard. Audio interfaces range in size from an interface you can fit in your hand to one that will take up most of your desk. A more expensive interface includes more inputs and produces higher-quality sound, though you'll also need some expensive speakers to hear the difference.

Just like with graphics workstations, audio editing workstations frequently make use of specialized input devices. These devices, referred to as *control surfaces*, mimic the look and feel of older, analog mixing consoles. They have a large number of programmable inputs that make controlling the software much faster and more accurate than with just a mouse and keyboard. These control surfaces range in size from small desktop units, all the way up to room-filling behemoths that are used in recording studios. Some of these boards also contain an audio interface.

Video Editing Workstations *Video editing workstations* combine the requirements of a graphics workstation and an audio editing workstation. Video editors often use two or more color-calibrated monitors so they can view the video stream they're working on with one monitor and see their video editor open on the other, making multiple monitors very useful. Video editing workstations require a very powerful CPU paired with as much RAM as possible, since video editing is a far more intensive process than graphics or audio editing. High-speed, high-capacity hard drives are also life-savers, since video files often take up multiple gigabytes of space. Many video editing workstations have multiple hard drives set up in a RAID array for added storage capacity and enhanced read/write speed.

Video editing workstations, like CAD/CAM workstations, benefit enormously from a professional-level graphics card. This is almost as important as the fast CPU and piles of RAM, and you'll rarely see a video editing workstation without one.

Because video editing workstations are frequently used as audio editing workstations, too, you will often find video editing workstations with the same audio interfaces and control surfaces as you'd see on an audio editing workstation. There are also video

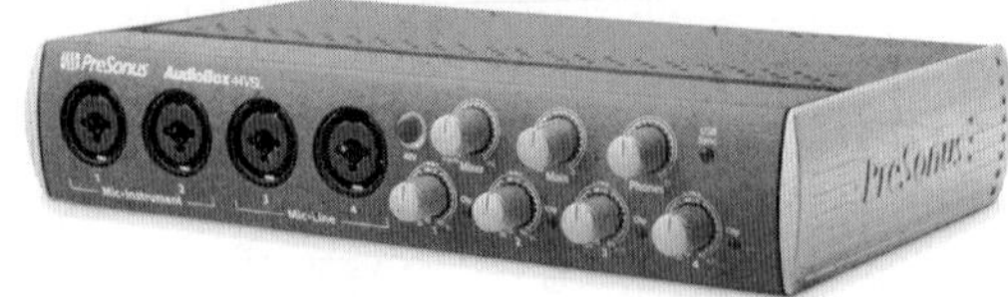

Figure 12-3 Audio interface device (photo courtesy of PreSonus)

interfaces that enable editors to connect to various cameras. Additionally, many video editors use custom keyboards that have special labels and controls for popular video editing software.

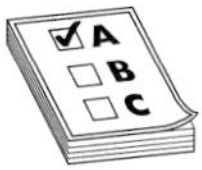

EXAM TIP The CompTIA A+ 901 objectives combine *audio and video editing workstations* into a single thing. They often do double duty, so that's cool, and keep that in mind for the exam. In practice, you'll find dedicated audio editing workstations and dedicated video editing workstations, as well as the combined units.

Specialized Consumer PCs

Once you move away from the office and into the house, computing needs change. Home is for leisure, and the workplace is for, well, work! The three common types of home systems are home servers that store everything from your music collection to last year's income tax return, home theater PCs to play music and movies, and gaming PCs to play powerful, video-intensive games.

Building a Home Server PC

How many computing devices are in your house right now? If you're like me, the answer is "a lot." Between multiple smartphones, iPods, tablets, portables, and desktop computers, you might shock yourself with the count.

As more and more computing devices move into the home environment, there's a need for a centralized storage space, a *home server PC* to dish out files and folders on demand—a place for all your media to stream to multiple devices. This home server PC has very specialized needs that take it beyond the typical thick client.

A home server PC supplies three discrete functions: media streaming, file sharing, and print sharing. Media streaming can use specialized software, but, just like file and print sharing, it works fine through the default tools in Windows and Mac OS X. The home server PC has to have a very fast network connection and gobs of storage. Plus, that storage needs to be fault tolerant. Losing your video collection because of a hard drive crash would make for a very bad day.

Software Any modern operating system enables you to share files and folders through standard sharing features. The same is true of sharing a printer. To turn a PC into a print server, open the Devices and Printers applet in the Control Panel, right-click on an installed printer, choose Printer properties, and then check the Share this printer checkbox on the Sharing tab (see Figure 12-4).

You can easily turn a Windows PC into a media streaming server by selecting that option in the Control Panel. Open the Network and Sharing Center, select the Change

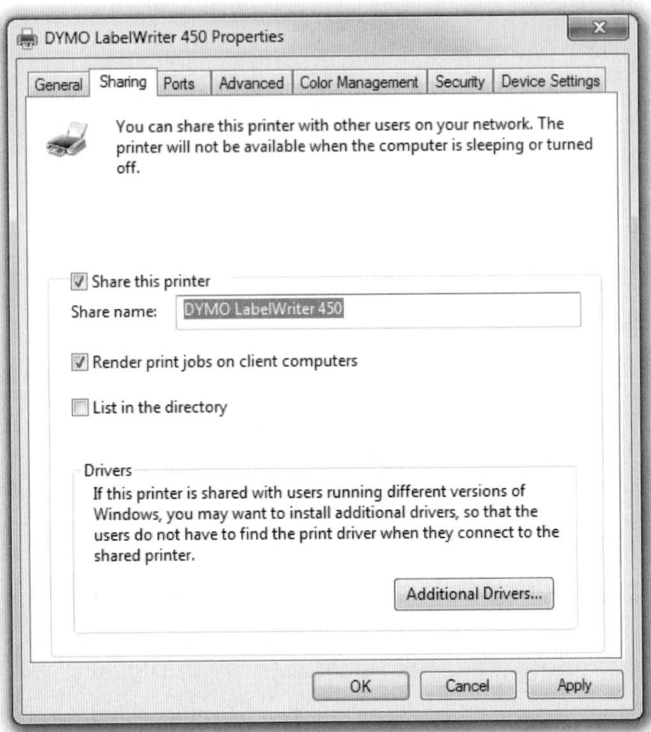
DYMO LabelWriter 450 Properties
General
Sharing
Ports
Advanced
Color Management
Security
Device Settings
You can share this printer with other users on your network. The printer will not be available when the computer is sleeping or turned off.
Share this printer
Share name:
DYMO LabelWriter 450
Render print jobs on client computers
List in the directory
Drivers
If this printer is shared with users running different versions of Windows, you may want to install additional drivers, so that the users do not have to find the print driver when they connect to the shared printer.
Additional Drivers...
OK
Cancel
Apply

Figure 12-4 Sharing a printer

advanced sharing settings link from the left Task menu, and then click the Home or Work option to get to the Advanced sharing settings screen (see Figure 12-5).

Half way down the screen you'll find a link to *Choose media streaming options*. Click it. Figure 12-6 shows the Media streaming options screen. By default, Windows wants to share everything, though you can customize what's shared in case you have young children and don't want them to have access to inappropriate content.

Finally, both Windows Media Player and iTunes have a feature to share media files on a local network. Figure 12-7 shows iTunes sharing via the Bonjour protocol.

Hardware Hardware needs on a home server PC apply primarily to the network speed and hard drive redundancy, at least according the CompTIA objectives. If you have a very active server, you should also pay attention to the amount of RAM it has and the speed of the CPU. Beefing both up above the standard thick client can help if you start getting some lag.

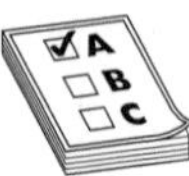

EXAM TIP You don't need to care at all about the video card in a home server PC. Anything will do because you're not going to run anything visual directly on the server.

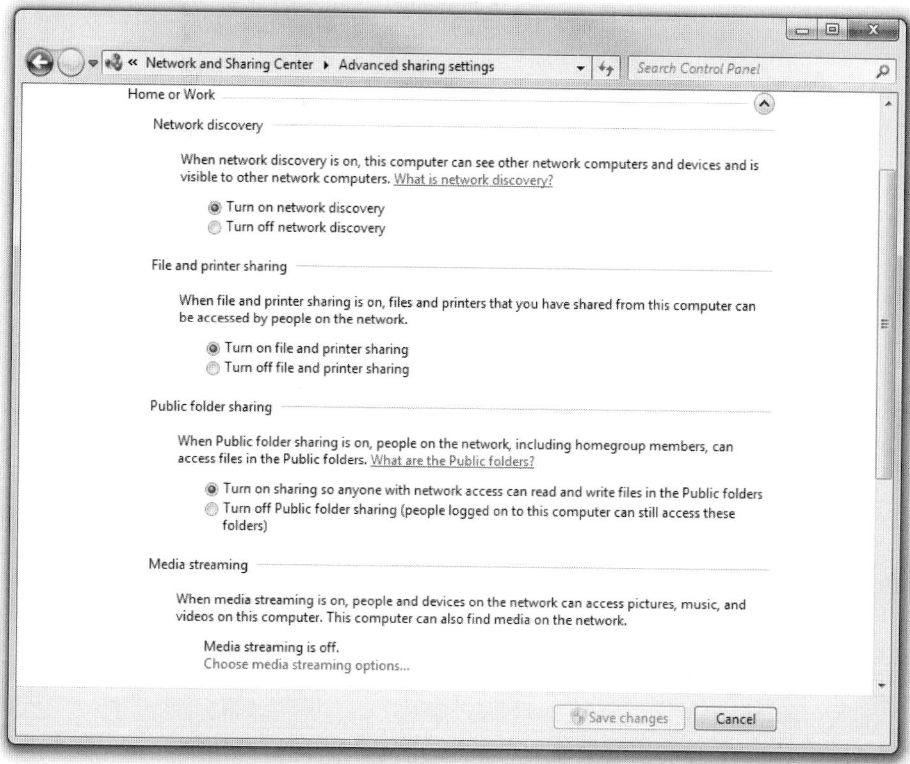

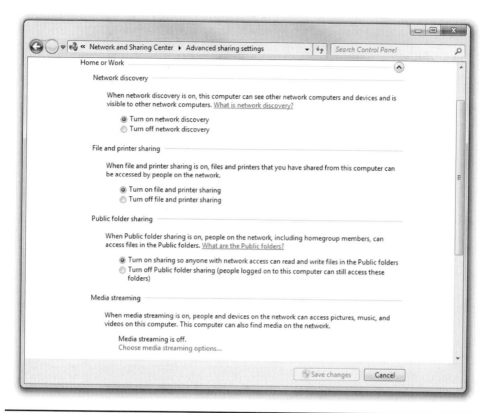

Figure 12-5 Advanced sharing settings

For the network, a wired Gigabit Ethernet NIC should be standard issue. Although it sounds cool to go wireless, you should limit the use of wireless to the single connection between the wireless access point and the client. The home server should connect via Ethernet to minimize any lag or dropped frames.

A file server's hard drives do the heavy and sustained lifting for the PC, so you should not stint on them. At a minimum, get two drives of identical size that have as much capacity as you can afford. No one *reduces* the amount of media in his or her collection over time, after all, especially if it's stored electronically. Plus, because you need fault tolerance on the data, you simply must use a RAID 1 configuration at a minimum (and thus the need to get two identical drives). If your budget can afford it and your motherboard supports it, get four identical drives and run in RAID 10.

You'll recall from Chapter 10 that Windows 8/8.1/10 offer *Storage Spaces* and storage pools where you can toss in any number of drives and create an array. If you do this sensibly, like putting three 4-TB drives into a pool and creating a single Storage Space, you're essentially creating an excellent RAID 5 array.

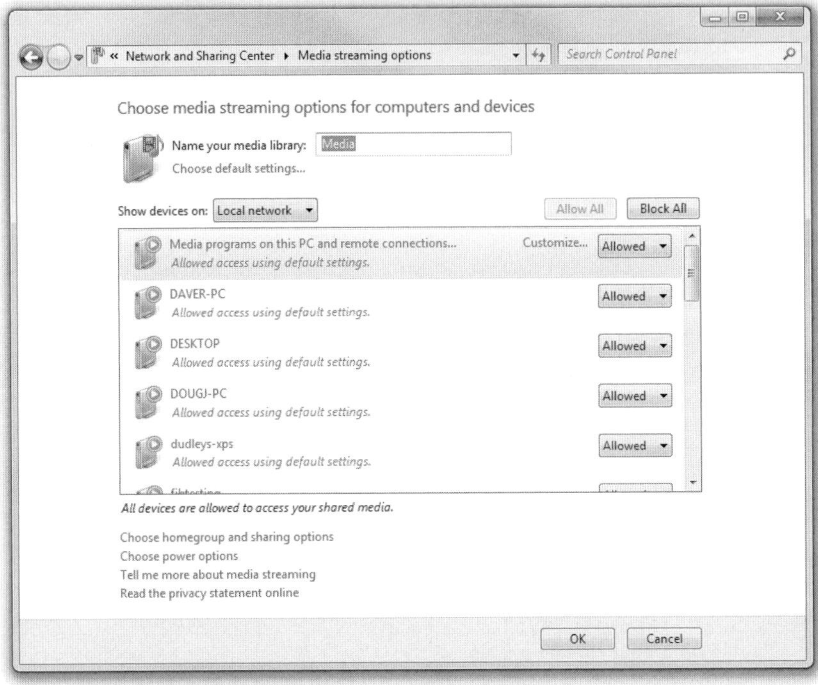

Figure 12-6 Media streaming options

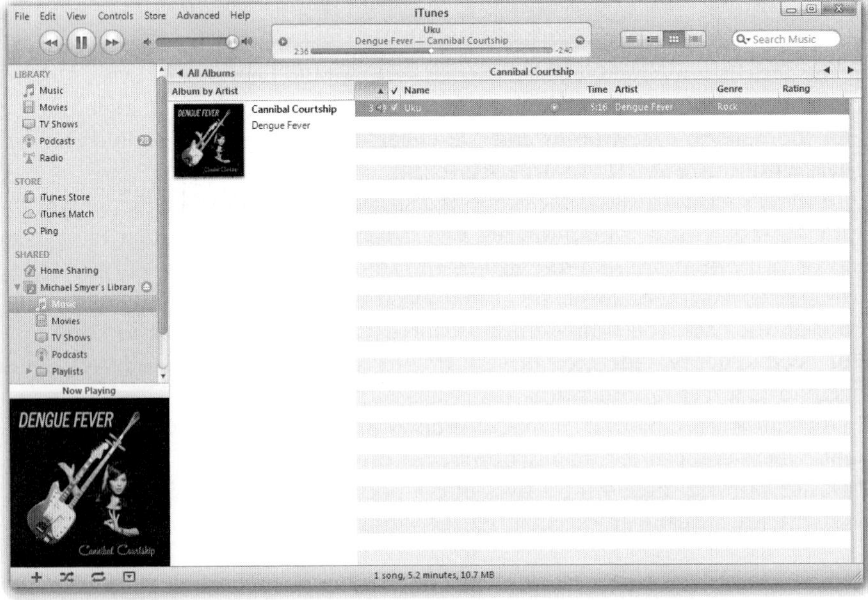

Figure 12-7 Streaming with iTunes

Setting Up a Home Theater PC

A home theater system enables you to play music and watch movies and television. If done well, the experience can rival that of watching a movie at a fine movie house. When coupled with a home theater PC, the home theater system enables the full computing experience as well.

An optimal home theater has five components:

- A monitor, television, or projector
- Surround sound speakers
- A stereo receiver
- A home theater PC
- Network connectivity (such as a cable box or Ethernet)

This section looks at the specific components and issues involved with creating a home theater PC and connecting it to other components.

Output Killer Video A home theater PC must provide support for large monitors at high resolution, a requirement that usually involves an HDMI connector on the video card (see Figure 12-8). The HDMI cable connects the home theater box to the stereo receiver, which then pushes the signal to the television. Figure 12-9 shows the basic home theater schematic.

Play It Loudly A great home theater system simply must have surround sound and a thumping subwoofer, so the home theater PC needs a sound card or built-in sound processor that supports 5.1 or 7.1 stereo. For the best output, the sound card connects to the stereo receiver via S/PDIF, through either the optical connector or coaxial connector.

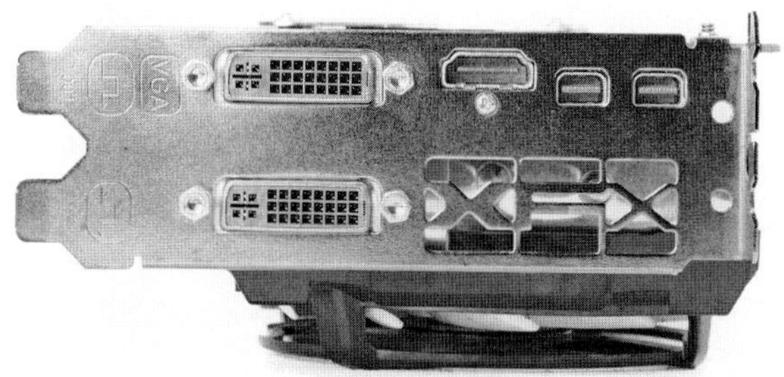

Figure 12-8 HDMI output on video card

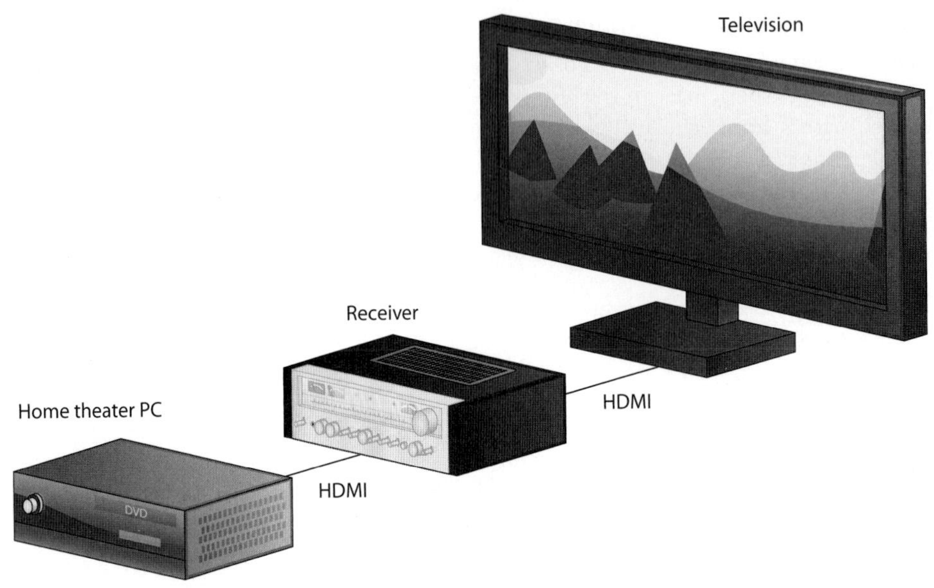

Figure 12-9 Television, receiver, home theater PC

The speakers then connect to the receiver. Figure 12-10 shows the schematic with speakers added.

HDMI carries both the video signal and the surround sound audio signal, so if you plug it into the television directly from the PC, the rig will use the television's speakers by default. If you have the surround sound speakers plugged into the computer rather

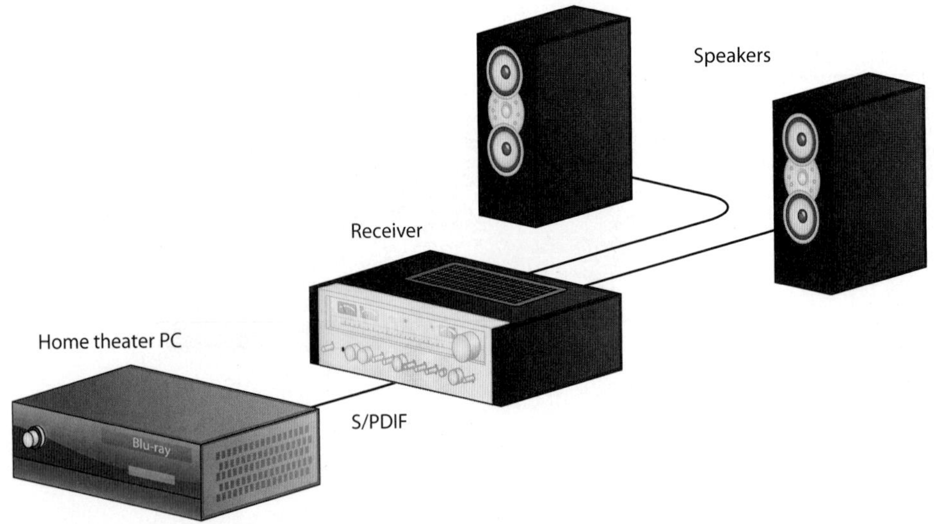

Figure 12-10 PC, receiver, speakers

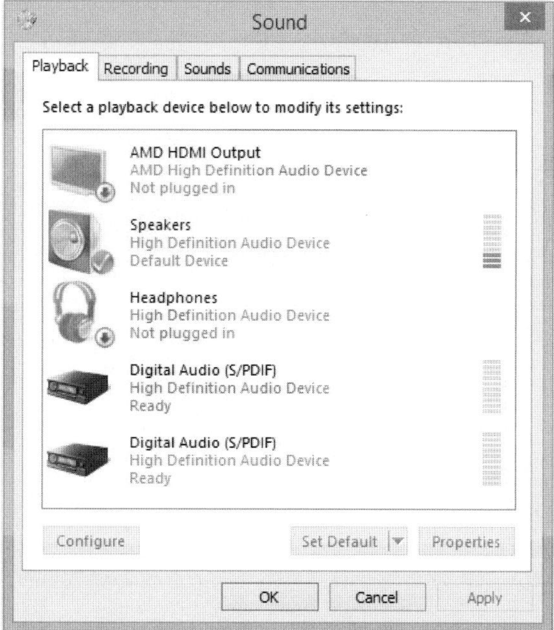

Figure 12-11 Sound applet for choosing playback device

than a receiver, you need to go into the Sound applet in the Control Panel to select the playback device you prefer (see Figure 12-11).

Look Cool in the Process Home theater components look like traditional stacking stereo components, such as a receiver, equalizer, DVD player, and so on. It simply won't do to put a beige office computer case alongside your sleek, black-clad components (see Figure 12-12).

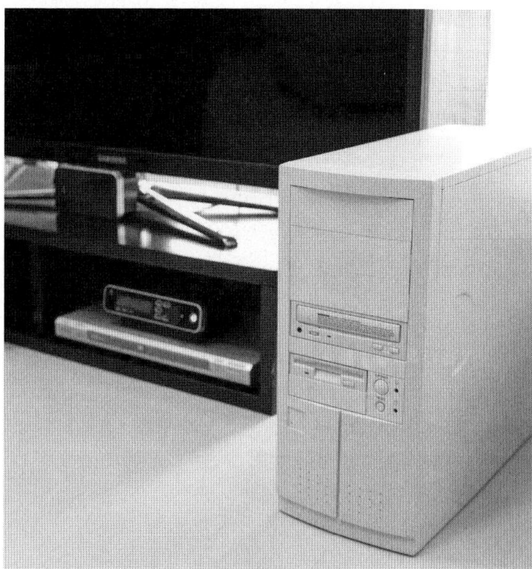

Figure 12-12 This is not right!

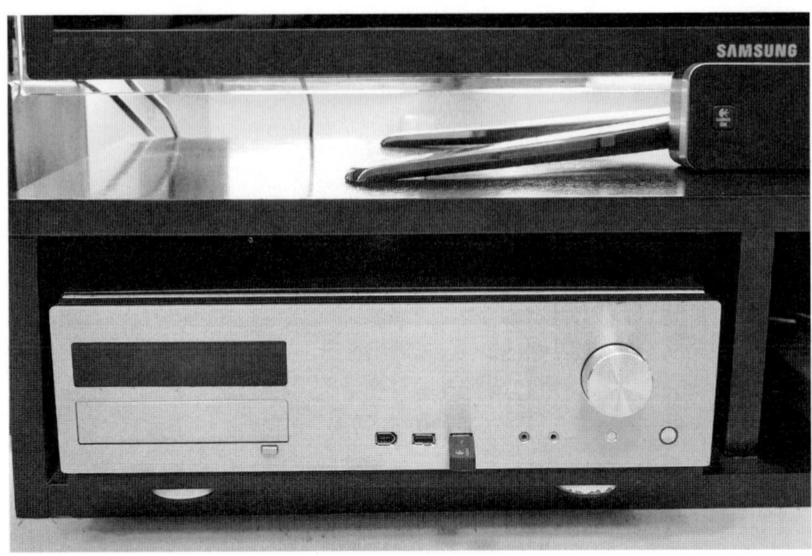

Figure 12-13 HTPC case

You can get a case for a PC that stacks nicely with other home theater components (see Figure 12-13). CompTIA calls this style of case an *HTPC*, although that's not an industry-standard form factor. The letters stand for *home theater PC*.

Access the Media—Streaming and TV The home theater PC needs access to content, usually through Gigabit Ethernet to get streaming media from the home server PC you created in the previous section of the chapter. The home theater could use Wi-Fi (802.11n or 802.11ac), though wired is best, especially for high-definition (HD) content. (See Chapter 22, "Wireless Networking," for the details on . . . wireless networks.)

The home theater PC wouldn't normally have anything to do with a signal from the cable company or from a dedicated optical disc player, like a Blu-ray Disc box. Those signals go from the applicable box to the stereo receiver directly.

The only time the home theater PC should receive a television signal directly is through broadcast over the air. For this signal, the PC needs a TV tuner, like you learned about in Chapter 11, "Essential Peripherals." You would use this to catch local news or sports programs.

Figure 12-14 shows the home theater schematic with all the media access methods included.

Software Tools for Playback Once you have the media center hardware set up properly, you need software to access streaming media. Microsoft includes Windows Media Center in some editions of Windows. If you don't have one of those editions, then you need to use a third-party tool, such as the excellent Kodi (XBMC) or Plex.

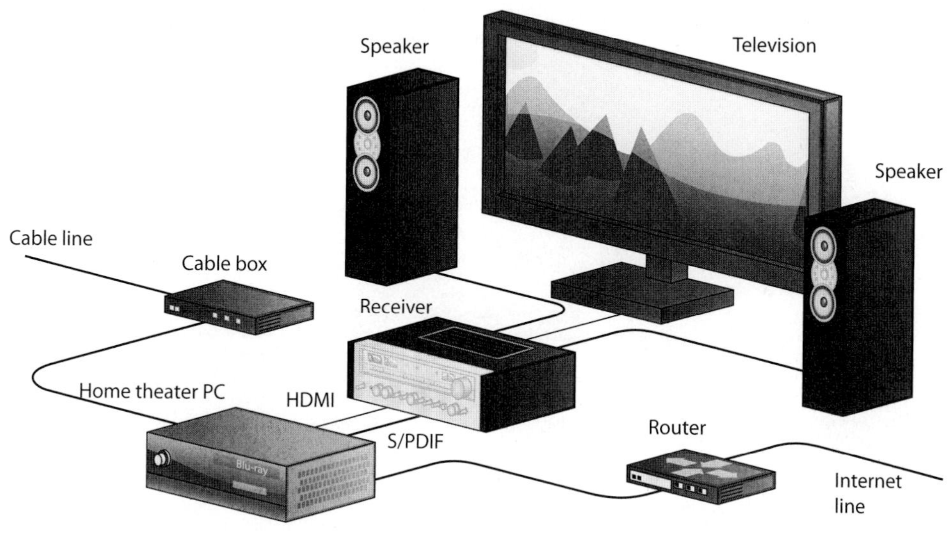

Figure 12-14 Final home theater

NOTE Microsoft dropped support for both DVD playback and Windows Media Center in Windows 10. If you want to use a Windows 10 machine for a home theater system, you'll need to use Kodi or Plex.

Kodi in particular enables you to customize the look and feel of the interface, and many people have made awesome skins available. Figure 12-15 shows the default skin for Kodi; Figure 12-16 shows the same content but displayed with a completely different skin. Plex

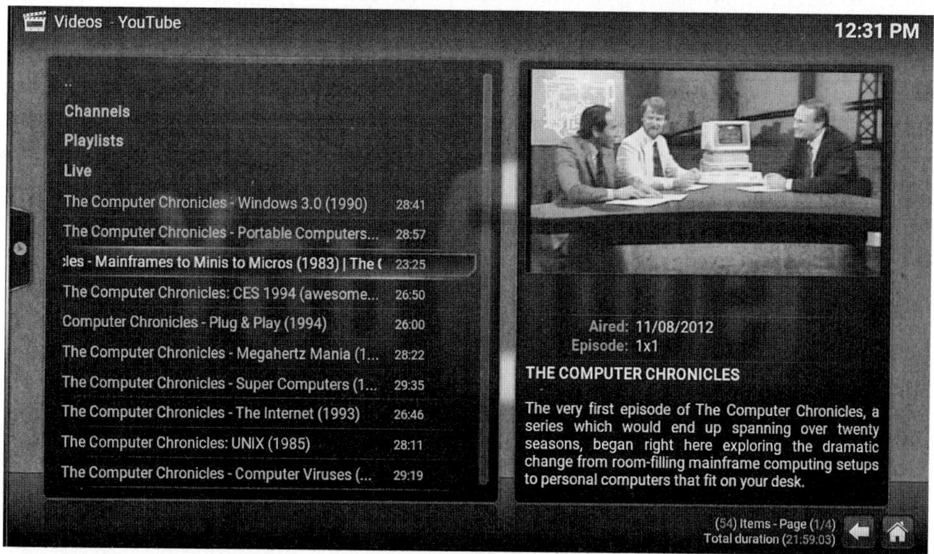

Figure 12-15 Default Kodi feeling retro on YouTube

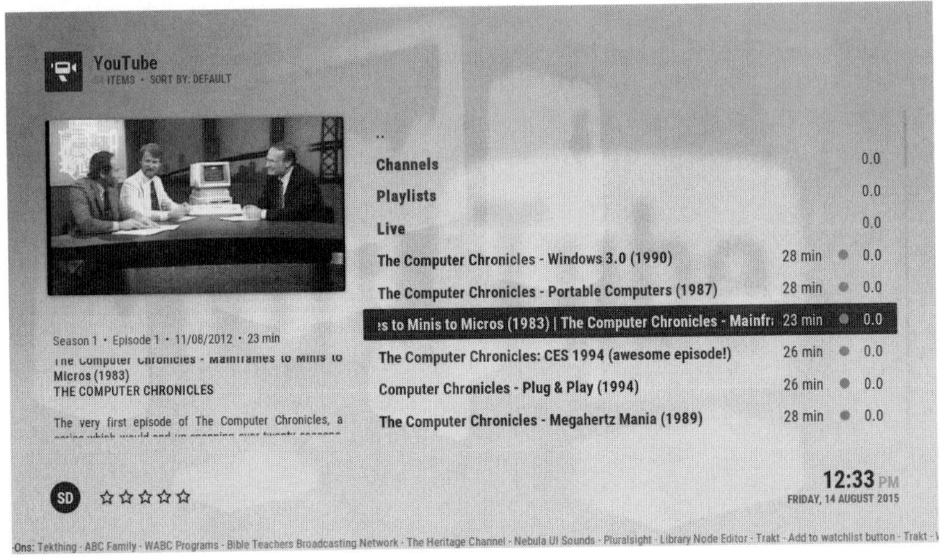

Figure 12-16 Kodi sporting the Arctic: Zephyr skin

is not flashy, but it's totally functional. There are versions of Kodi and Plex available for Windows, Mac OS X, and Linux. You can download Kodi from http://kodi.tv. Get Plex at http://plex.tv.

Gaming PC

And now for the grand finale, the PC you've been waiting for, the system you've always wanted to build. As an aspiring PC tech, you probably took your first apprehensive steps into the dark underbelly of PCs with a game: *Minecraft*, *Grand Theft Auto*, *Team Fortress 2*, *Borderlands 2*, *World of Warcraft* . . . you've played at least one of them. While casual gamers can get by with a standard desktop PC (like the thick client you read about earlier), those who take their gaming seriously want a powerful PC ready to pump out the latest graphics. A gamer goes through a game's graphics settings and sets everything to the max. And since games aren't all about how good they look, you'll also want a good sound card and headphones. Okay—you also need a good game, but one thing at a time.

So here's a list of essential features for a gaming PC:

- Fast, multicore processor
- A lot of memory, at least 8 GB, 16 GB for good measure, and 64 GB if you plan to play five games at once
- High-end video card with a specialized graphics processor unit (GPU) for gaming
- High-definition sound card to provide optimal positional audio

We haven't covered the GPUs yet, so I'll leave those until Chapter 19. The rest of the pieces should make a lot of sense at this point. Remember the high-end CPUs from Chapter 4, "Microprocessors"? Crank them up and throw on some high-end cooling, like a purpose-built *water cooling rig*, to give a gaming system the foundation for greatness.

902

Installing and Upgrading Windows

Once you have the hardware lined up for whichever specialized PC you want to build, it's time to install an operating system. For most computers, you'll want to install a version of Windows—and the appropriate edition within each version. This section looks at media selection, types of installation, then the installation and upgrade process. It completes with a discussion on troubleshooting installations.

Media Sources

At its most basic, a Windows installation has two steps. First, boot the system from the OS installation media. Second, answer the installation wizard's initial queries and let it do its thing. At the end of the 10- to 40-minute process, you'll be looking at a Welcome screen (see Figure 12-17) and be ready to begin your love affair with the PC.

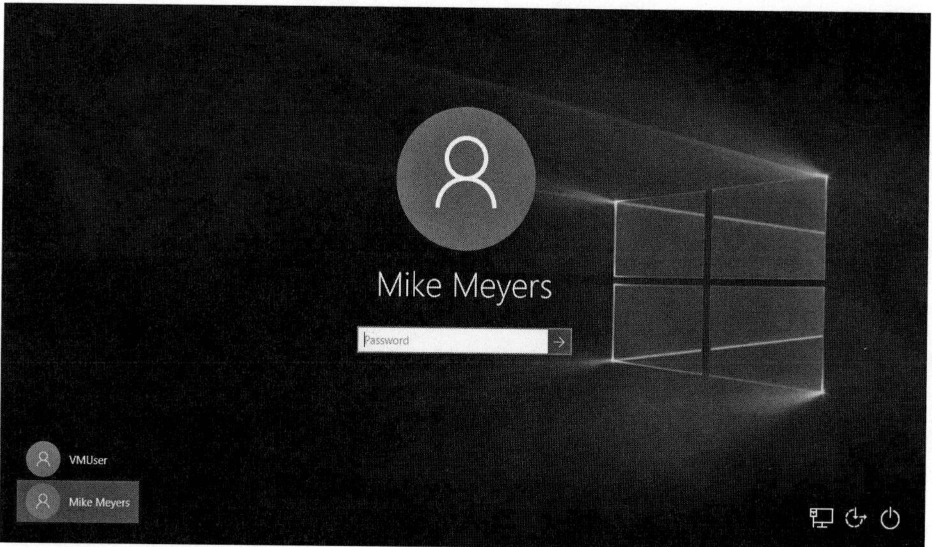

Figure 12-17 Windows 10 welcome screen

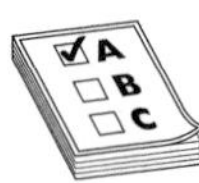

EXAM TIP Successful installation results in a properly formatted boot drive with the correct partitions/formats.

Windows offers a surprising number of *boot methods*, giving you many options to get the process started. The most common way to start—historically at least—is to insert a Windows DVD, change the boot order in the System Setup Utility (CMOS), and power up the system. Current systems make this even easier; most have a hot key you press just after the system powers on to enable you to select the preferred boot device. No need to mess with the System Setup Utility at all.

Alternatively, you can boot to any number of other removable drives that plug into USB, FireWire, eSATA, or Thunderbolt ports. That includes flash-media drives, external hard drives, or external solid-state drives. Any number of *external/hot-swappable drives* will do the job.

NOTE Microsoft has shifted with the times. The primary way to install Windows 10 is downloading an ISO image and writing that image to some bootable media. With the Windows Media Creation Tool (a quick download from Microsoft), you can easily make that bootable media a DVD or USB flash drive.

Don't have an optical drive? No problem. You can access Windows installation files over a network. See "Installing Over a Windows Network," a little later in this chapter, for details.

Finally, many system builders add a small, hidden partition to the primary hard drive containing an image of the factory-fresh version of Windows. In the event of a corrupted or very messy instance of Windows, you can reboot, access this *recovery partition*, and reinstall Windows. Chapter 17, "Troubleshooting Operating Systems," covers recovery partitions and other forms of restoration in some detail.

EXAM TIP The CompTIA A+ 220-902 exam objectives offer "internal hard drive (partition)" as a viable boot method for installing Windows. My best guess is that they mean the hidden recovery partition.

Types of Installation

You can install Windows in several ways. A *clean installation* of an OS involves installing it onto an empty hard drive or completely replacing an existing installation. An *upgrade installation* means installing an OS on top of an earlier installed version, thus inheriting all previous hardware and software settings. You can combine versions of Windows by creating a *multiboot installation*. Installing usually involves some sort of optical disc, but other methods also exist. Let's look at all the options.

Clean Installation

A clean installation means your installation ignores a previous installation of Windows, wiping out the old version as the new version of Windows installs. A clean installation

is also performed on a new system with a completely blank hard drive. The advantage of doing a clean installation is that you don't carry problems from the old OS over to the new one. The disadvantage is that you need to reinstall all your applications and reconfigure the desktop and each application to the user's preferences. You typically perform a clean installation by setting CMOS to boot from the optical drive before the hard drive. You then boot off of a Windows installation disc, and Windows gives you the opportunity to partition and format the hard drive during the installation process.

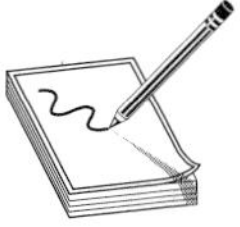

NOTE The CompTIA A+ 902 objectives mention *refresh/restore* as an appropriate method of installing Windows, and in some scenarios this is true. Both refresh and restore install some or all of an operating system as an attempt to fix an OS that's not functioning properly. We'll cover System Restore in detail in Chapter 15 and tackle Refresh your PC when we hit troubleshooting in Chapter 17.

Upgrade Installation

In an upgrade installation, the new OS installs into the same folders as the old OS, or in tech speak, the new installs *on top of* the old. The new OS replaces the old OS but retains data and applications and also inherits all of the personal settings (such as font styles, desktop themes, and so on). The best part is that you don't have to reinstall your favorite programs.

Microsoft makes a *compatibility* tool called the *Windows Upgrade Advisor* for each version of Windows that enables you to scan your current hardware to see if it can handle upgrading to a new version of Windows. (It's called the Upgrade Assistant in Windows 8/8.1. Inexplicably, CompTIA calls it the Windows upgrade OS advisor.) Do a quick search and download the tool from Microsoft if you're thinking about upgrading.

Many tech writers refer to the upgrade process as an *in-place upgrade*. Upgrades aren't always perfect, but the advantages make them worthwhile if your upgrade path allows it.

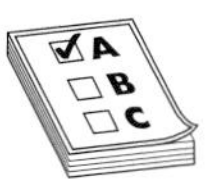

EXAM TIP Microsoft often uses the term *in-place upgrade* to define an upgrade installation, so you might see it on the CompTIA A+ 902 exam. On the other hand, Microsoft documentation also uses the term for a completely different process, called a *repair installation*, so read whatever questions you get on the exam carefully for context. For repair installations, see Chapter 17.

To begin the upgrade of Windows, you should run the appropriate program from the optical disc. This usually means inserting a Windows installation disc into your system while your old OS is running, which autostarts the installation program. The installation program will ask you whether you want to perform an upgrade or a new installation; if you select new installation, the program will remove the existing OS before installing the new one.

NOTE Before starting an OS upgrade, make sure you have shut down all other open applications!

Multiboot Installation

A third option that you need to be aware of is the dual-boot or *multiboot* installation. This means your system has more than one Windows installation and you may choose which installation to use when you boot your computer. Every time your computer boots, you'll get a menu asking you which version of Windows you wish to boot.

You'll recall from Chapter 10 that Windows enables you to shrink the C: partition, so if you want to dual boot but have only a single drive, you can make it happen even if Windows is already installed and the C: partition takes up the full drive. Use Disk Management to shrink the volume and create another partition in the newly unallocated space. Install another copy of Windows to the new partition.

Apple makes an excellent tool called Boot Camp that enables you to install Windows on an Apple machine. Once you run through the Windows installation, Boot Camp enables you to decide when you start up the computer each time whether you want to run Mac OS X or Windows. Choose Boot Camp if you have some Windows-only program that you simply must run and your only computer is an Apple.

You can also multiboot Windows and Linux. The Linux installers add this multiboot capability by default. Just note that the reverse is not true. You need to install Windows *first*, then install Linux.

NOTE When configuring a computer for multibooting, there are two basic rules: first, you must format the system partition in a file system that is common to all installed operating systems; and second, you must install the operating systems in order from oldest to newest (or from Windows to other).

Other Installation Methods

In medium to large organizations, more advanced installation methods are often employed, especially when many computers need to be configured identically. A common method is to place the source files in a shared directory on a network server. Then, whenever a tech needs to install a new OS, he or she can boot up the computer, connect to the source location on the network, and start the installation from there. This is called generically a *remote network installation*. This method alone has many variations and can be automated with special scripts that automatically select the options and components needed. The scripts can even install extra applications at the end of the OS installation, all without user intervention once the installation has been started. This type of installation is called an *unattended installation*.

Another type of installation that is very popular for re-creating standard configurations is an *image deployment*. An image is a complete copy of a hard drive volume on which an operating system and any desired application software programs have been preinstalled. Images can be stored on optical discs or USB flash drives, in which case the tech

runs special software on the computer that copies the image onto the local hard drive. Images can also be stored on special network servers, in which case the tech connects to the image server by using special software that copies the image from the server to the local hard drive. A leader in this technology for many years was Norton Ghost, which was available from Symantec. Symantec now offers Symantec Ghost Solution Suite. Other similar programs are Clonezilla and Acronis's True Image.

The Installation and Upgrade Process

At the most basic level, installing any operating system follows a fairly standard set of steps. You turn on the computer, insert an operating system disc into the optical drive or access the media some other way, and follow the installation wizard until you have everything completed. Along the way, you'll accept the *End User License Agreement (EULA)* and enter the product key that says you're not a pirate; the product key is invariably located on the installation disc's case.

Upgrade Paths

With four (or five) active Windows versions in the wild (plus the officially retired Windows XP on a zillion machines), all with multiple editions in both 32- and 64-bit, techs can spend a lot of time figuring out if a client's computer can upgrade from *X* to *Y*. The following tables outline the upgrade options from Windows Vista and 7 to Windows 8 and 8.1. (See the "Beyond A+" section at the end of this chapter for the scoop on Windows 10.) Note that you can always do a clean install as long as the system meets the hardware requirements for the new OS. Just make sure everything important is backed up first.

The first thing to note is that the bit size of the currently installed OS must match the bit size of the upgrade OS. So you can upgrade from 32-bit Windows Vista to 32-bit Windows 7, or from 64-bit Windows 7 to 64-bit Windows 8. You can't upgrade from 32-bit anything to 64-bit anything else, or vice versa. When we get into the versions and editions, it gets a little more complicated.

Table 12-2 outlines the upgrade paths from Windows Vista to Windows 7.

If you have Windows 7 and you want to upgrade to a higher edition with more features—from Windows 7 Home Premium to Windows 7 Ultimate, for example—you can use the built-in Windows Anytime Upgrade feature. You can find this option pinned to the Start menu. Don't forget your credit card!

Table 12-2 Upgrading from Windows Vista to Windows 7

From Windows Vista	Upgrade to Windows 7
Home Basic	Home Basic, Home Premium, Ultimate
Home Premium	Home Premium, Ultimate
Business	Professional, Enterprise, Ultimate
Enterprise	Enterprise
Ultimate	Ultimate

Table 12-3 Upgrading from Windows 7 to Windows 8

From Windows 7	Upgrade to Windows 8
Starter	Windows 8, Windows 8 Pro
Home Basic	Windows 8, Windows 8 Pro
Home Premium	Windows 8, Windows 8 Pro
Professional	Windows 8 Pro, Windows 8 Enterprise
Enterprise	Windows 8 Enterprise
Ultimate	Windows 8 Pro

Table 12-3 outlines the upgrade paths from Windows 7 to Windows 8.

You can upgrade from Windows 8 to Windows 8.1 pretty easily, keeping all your applications and personal files. Upgrading from previous versions? I suggest you back up your stuff and do a clean installation. Table 12-4 outlines the upgrade paths from Windows 7/8/8.1 to various Windows 8.1 editions.

The Windows Clean Installation Process

The Windows installer in Vista and all later versions of Windows has a full graphical interface, making it easy to partition drives and install an operating system. You already saw some of this process back in Chapter 10, but this chapter will go into a bit more detail.

The installation methods for Windows Vista/7/8/8.1/10 are so close to identical that it would be silly to address them as separate entries in this book. Only the splash screens and the product-key entry dialog box have changed between Windows Vista and Windows 8! Because of this trivial difference, showing the installation process for all operating systems

Table 12-4 Upgrading from Windows 7/8/8.1 to Windows 8.1

From Windows 7/8/8.1	Upgrade to Windows 8.1
Windows 7[1]	Windows 8.1
Windows 8	Windows 8.1, Windows 8.1 Pro[2]
Windows 8 Pro	Windows 8.1 Pro, Windows 8.1 Enterprise
Windows 8 Pro with Media Center	Windows 8.1 Pro, Windows 8.1 Enterprise
Windows 8 Enterprise	Windows 8.1 Pro, Windows 8.1 Enterprise
Windows 8.1	Windows 8.1 Pro
Windows 8.1 Pro	Windows 8.1 Enterprise

1. You can upgrade from Windows 7 to Windows 8.1, but you can only keep personal files, not applications.
2. You can upgrade to Windows 8.1 with one of two methods: through the Windows Store or via upgrade media, like a Windows disc. You can only change versions via upgrade media. Installing through the Windows Store locks you into the previous edition.

would waste paper. This walkthrough uses the Windows Vista screenshots just because you might never see them anywhere else.

Start by booting your computer from some sort of Windows installation media. Usually, you'll use a DVD disc, though you can also install Windows from a USB drive, over a network, or even off of several CD-ROMs that you have to specially order from Microsoft. When you've booted into the installer, the first screen you see asks you to set your language, time/currency, and keyboard settings, as shown in Figure 12-18.

The next screen enables techs to start the installation disc's repair tools (see Figure 12-19). You'll learn more about those tools in Chapter 17, but for now all you need to know is that you click where it says *Repair your computer* to use the repair tools. Because you're just installing Windows in this chapter, click *Install now*.

The next screen on Vista will prompt you to enter your product key before you do anything else, as you can see in Figure 12-20. Starting with Windows 7, this doesn't come until much, much later in the process, and there's a very interesting reason for this change.

Every Windows installation disc contains all of the available editions within a version. The product key not only verifies the legitimacy of your purchase; it also tells the installer which edition you purchased.

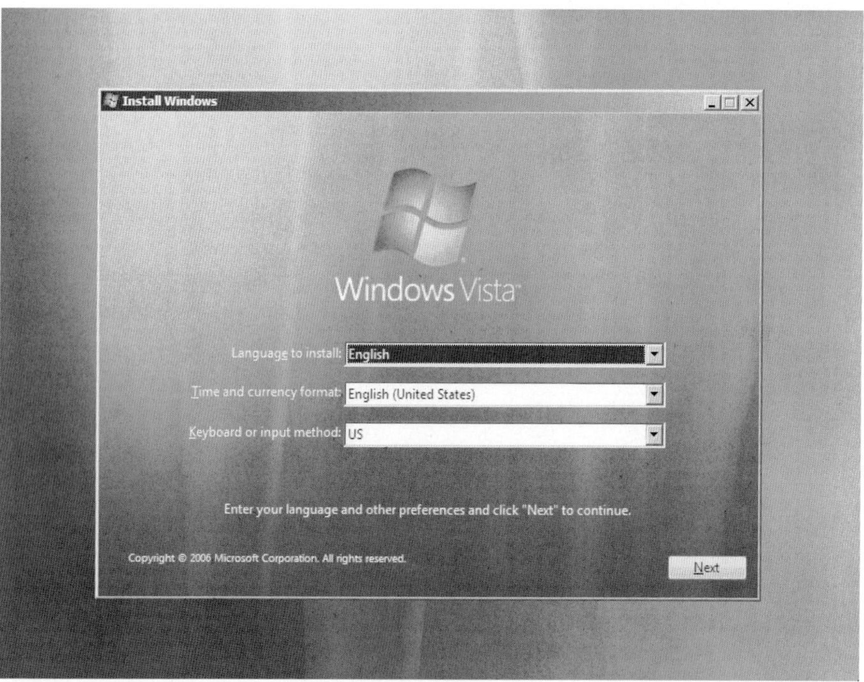

Figure 12-18 Windows Vista language settings screen

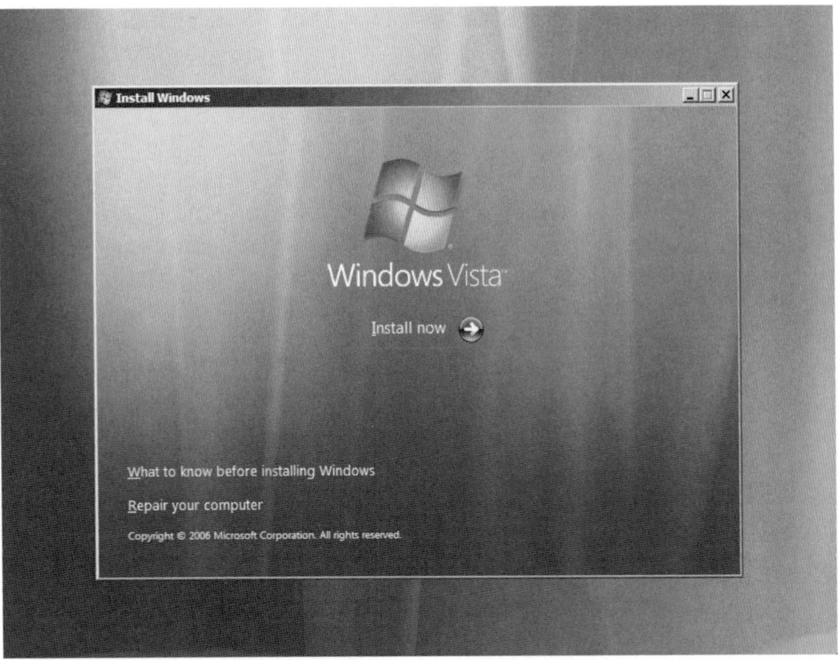

Figure 12-19 The Windows Vista setup welcome screen

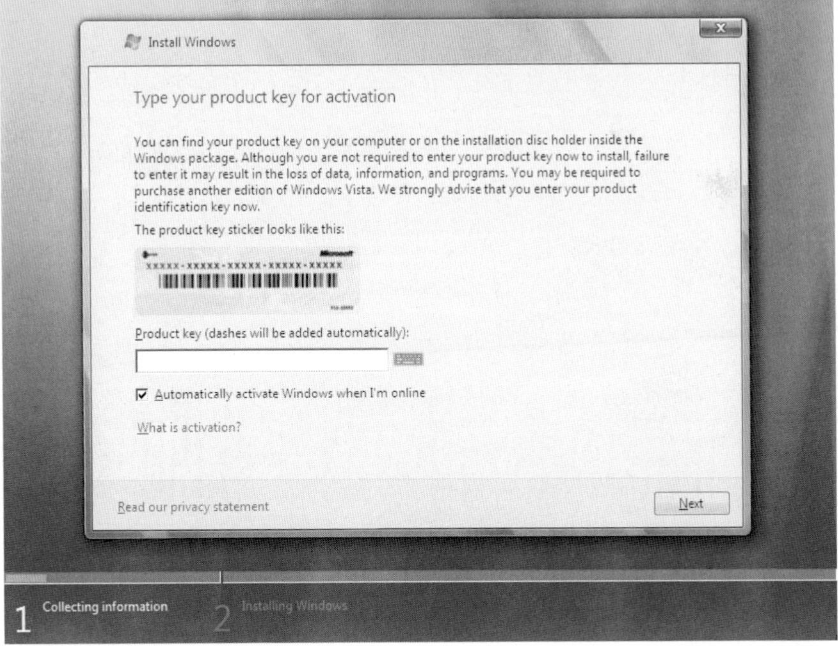

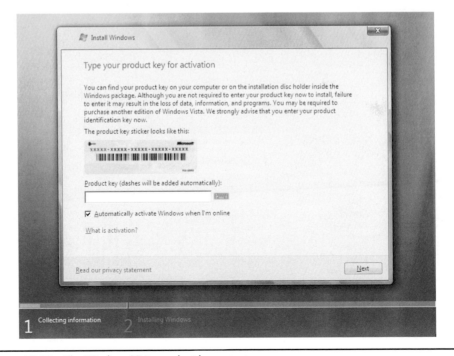

Figure 12-20 The Windows Vista product key screen

If you leave the product key blank and click the Next button, you will be taken to a screen asking you which version of Windows Vista you would like to install (see Figure 12-21). (Windows 7/8/8.1, however, disables this option—while every version is on the disc, you can only install the edition named on the box or disc label.) And lest you start to think that you've discovered a way to install Windows without paying for it, you should know that doing this simply installs a 30-day trial of the operating system (at least for Windows Vista and Windows 7–starting with Windows 8 a key is required to install). After 30 days, you will no longer be able to boot to the desktop without entering a valid product key that matches the edition of Windows you installed. Microsoft ditched the 30-day grace period in the retail copies of Windows 8, mandating that users provide a product key during setup.

After the product key screen, you'll find Microsoft's EULA, shown in Figure 12-22, which you can skip.

On the next page, you get to decide whether you'd like to do an upgrade installation or a clean installation (see Figure 12-23). As you learned earlier, you have to begin the installation process from within an older OS to use the Upgrade option, so this option will be dimmed if you've booted off of the installation disc. To do a clean installation of

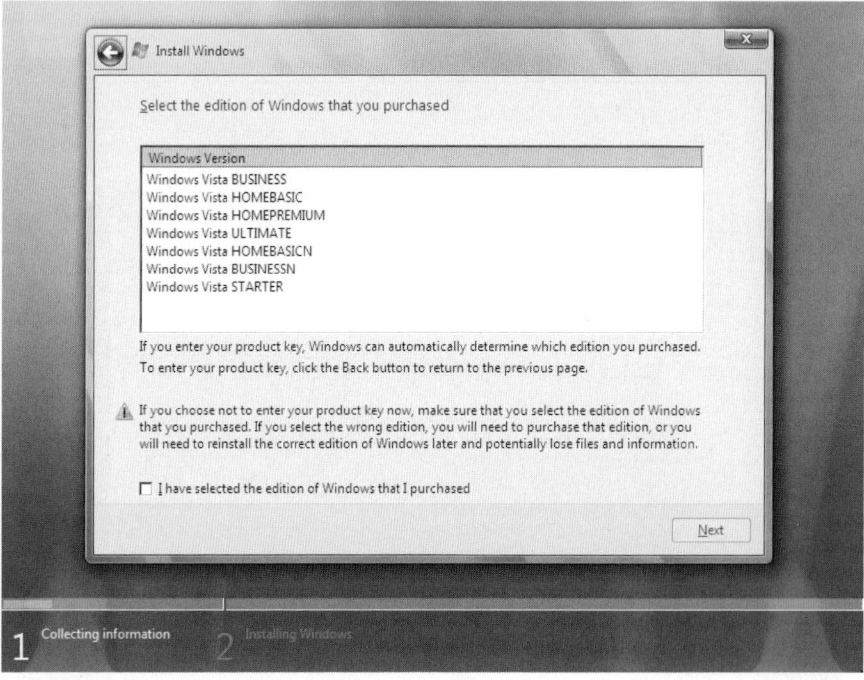

Figure 12-21 Choose the edition of Vista you want to install.

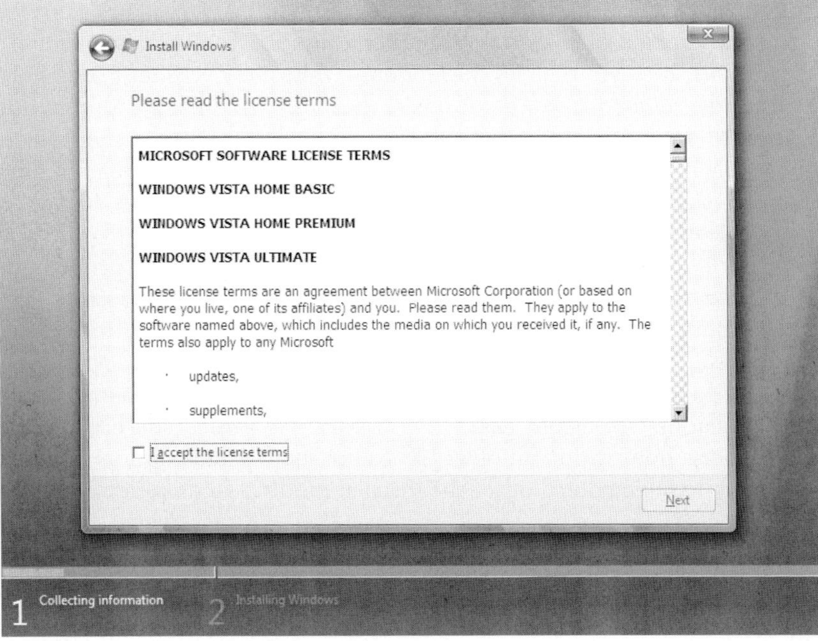

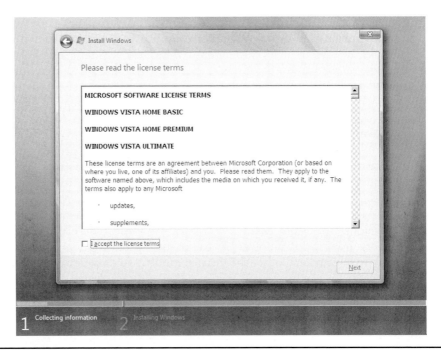

Figure 12-22 The Vista EULA

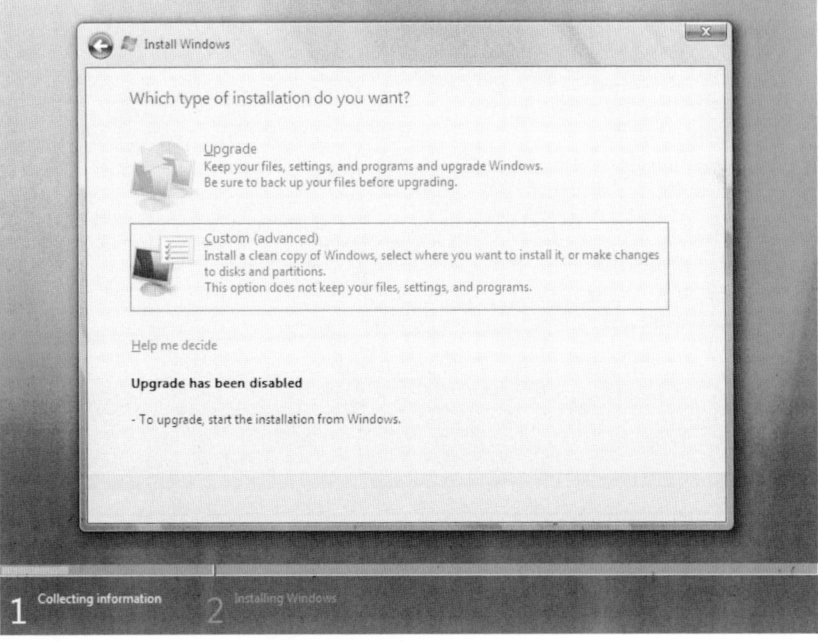

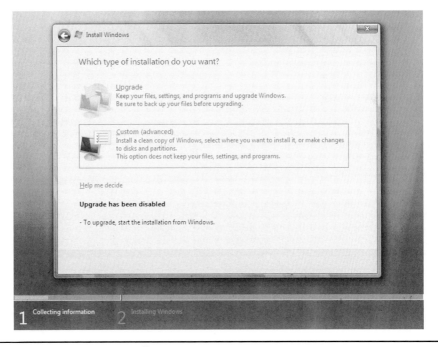

Figure 12-23 Choose your installation type.

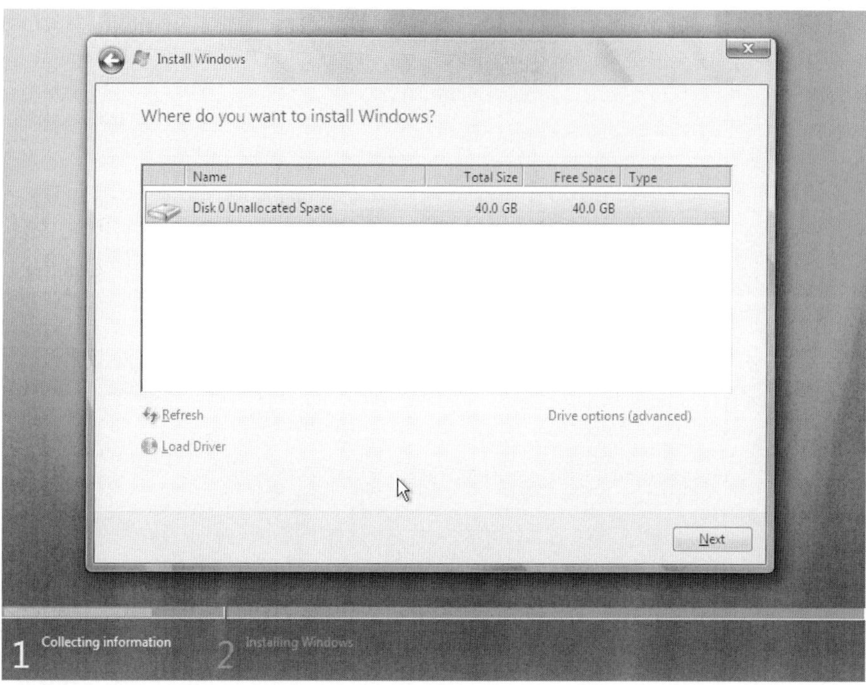

Figure 12-24 The partitioning screen

Windows, edit your partitions, and just generally install the OS like a pro, you choose the Custom (advanced) option.

You may remember the next screen, shown in Figure 12-24, from Chapter 10. This is the screen where you can partition your hard drives and choose the partition to which Windows will install. From this screen, you can click the Drive options (advanced) link to display a variety of partitioning options, and you can click the Load Driver button to load alternative, third-party drivers. The process of loading drivers is pretty straightforward: you just browse to the location of the drivers you want by using Windows' very familiar browsing window (see Figure 12-25).

Of course, you will most likely never have to load drivers for a drive, and if it is ever necessary, your drive will almost certainly come with a driver disc and documentation telling you that you'll have to load the drivers.

Once you've partitioned your drives and selected a partition on which to install Windows, the installation process takes over, copying files, expanding files, installing features, and just generally doing lots of computerish things. This can take a while, so if you need to get a snack or read *War and Peace*, do it during this part of the installation.

NOTE It doesn't take *that* long to install Windows. Each version so far is snappier than its predecessor, especially on an SSD.

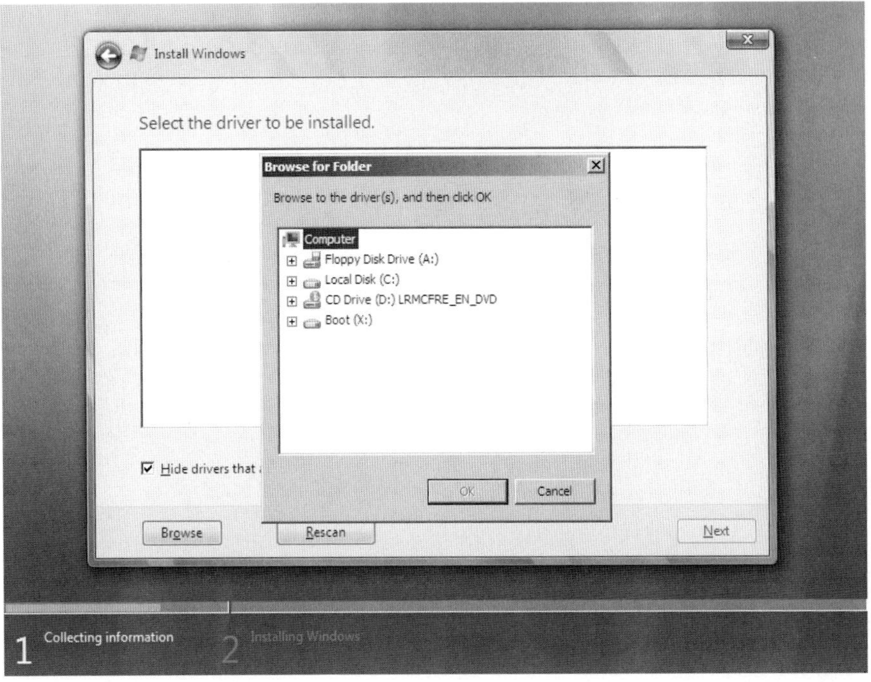

Figure 12-25 Browse for drivers.

When Windows has finished unpacking and installing itself, it asks you to choose a user name and picture (see Figure 12-26). This screen also asks you to set up a password for your main user account, which is definitely a good idea if you're going to have multiple people using the computer.

After picking your user name and password, and letting Windows know how much you like pictures of kitties, you're taken to a screen where you can type in a computer name (see Figure 12-27). By default, Windows makes your computer name the same as your user name but with "-PC" appended to it, which in most cases is fine.

This is also the screen where you can change the desktop background that Windows will start up with. You can change this easily later on, so pick whatever you like and click the Next button.

At this point, Windows 7/8/8.1 will ask for your product activation key. On Windows Vista, you did this at the beginning of the installation.

The next page asks you how you want to set up Windows Automatic Updates (see Figure 12-28). Most users want to choose the top option, Use recommended settings, as it provides the most hassle-free method for updating your computer. The middle option, Install important updates only, installs only the most critical security fixes and updates and leaves the rest of the updates up to you. This is useful when setting up computers for businesses, as many companies' IT departments like to test out any updates before

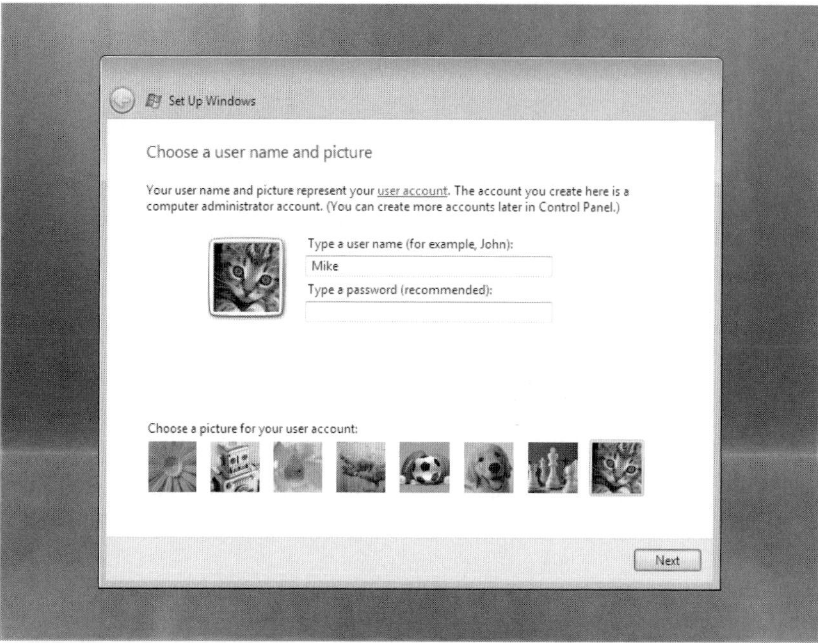

Figure 12-26 Choose a user picture.

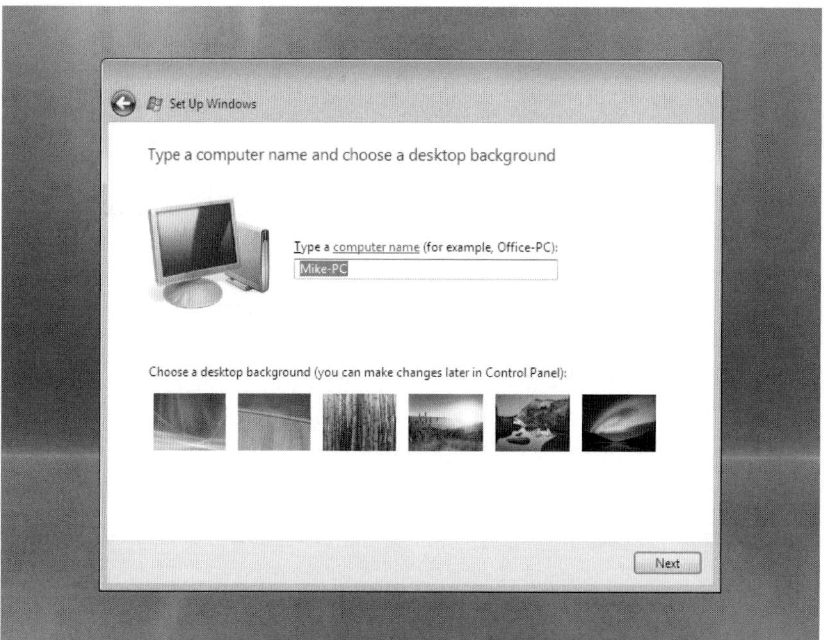

Figure 12-27 Choose your computer name.

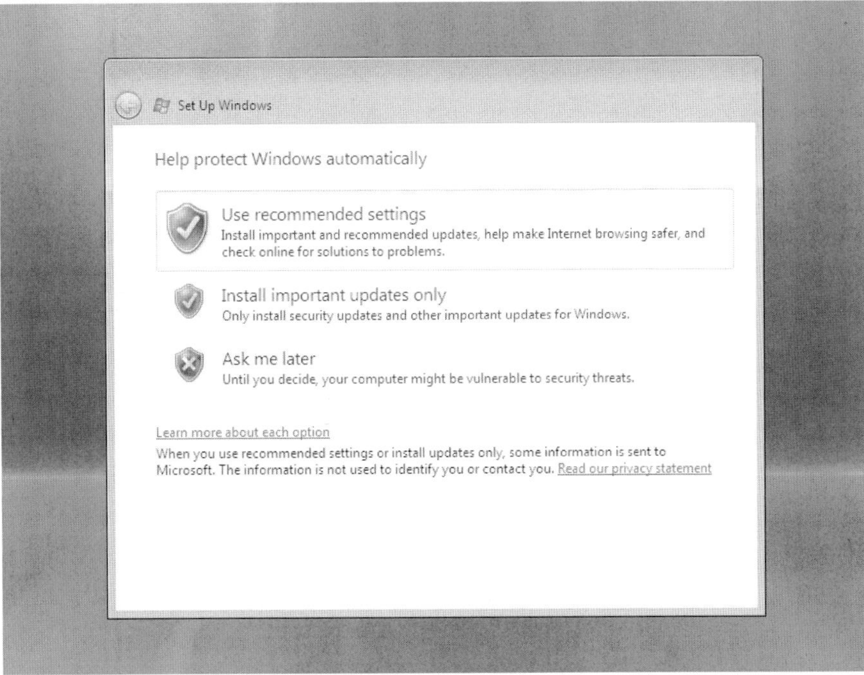

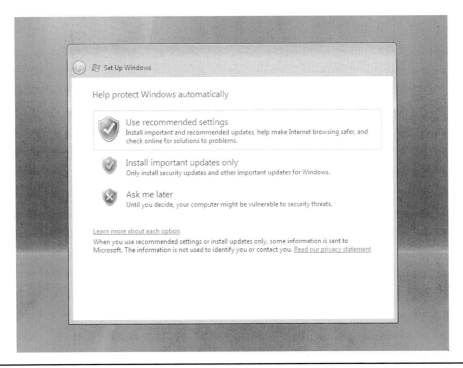

Figure 12-28 The automatic updates screen

rolling them out to the employees. You should only select the last option, Ask me later, if you can dedicate yourself to checking weekly for updates, as it will not install any automatically.

Next up is the time and date screen, where you can make sure your operating system knows what time it is, as in Figure 12-29. This screen should be pretty self-explanatory, so set the correct time zone, the correct date, and the correct time, and move to the next screen.

If you have your computer connected to a network while running the installer, the next screen will ask you about your current location (see Figure 12-30). If you're on a trusted network, such as your home or office network, make the appropriate selection and your computer will be discoverable on the network. If you're on, say, a Starbucks' network, choose Public location so the caffeine addicts around you can't see your computer and potentially do malicious things to it.

Once you're past that screen, Windows thanks you for installing it (see Figure 12-31), which is awfully polite for a piece of software, don't you think?

Lest you think you're completely through the woods, Windows Vista and 7 will run some tests on your computer to give it a performance rating, which, in theory, will tell you how well programs will run on your computer. You'll sometimes see minimum performance ratings on the sides of game boxes, but even then, you're more likely to need plain, old-fashioned minimum system requirements. This process can take anywhere

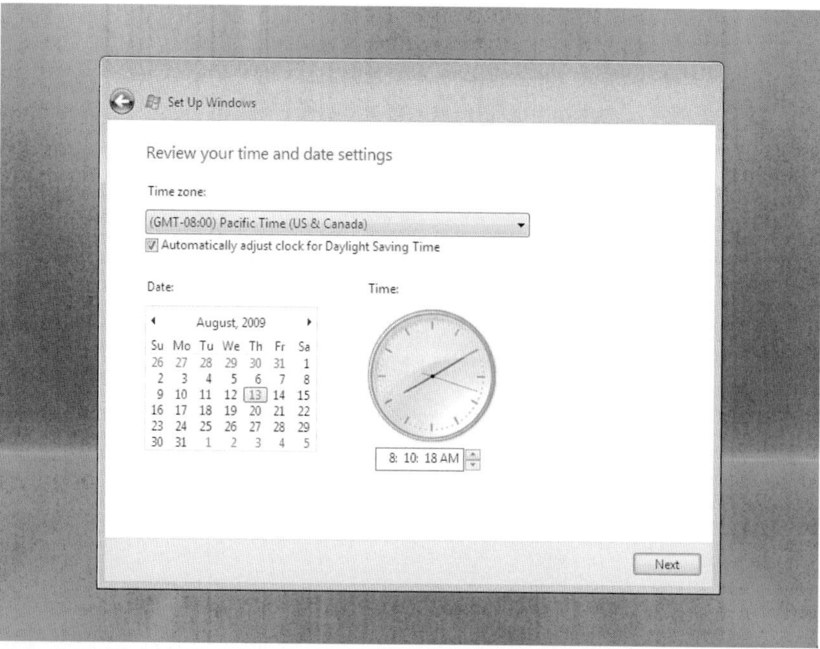

Figure 12-29 Vista pities the fool who doesn't know what time it is.

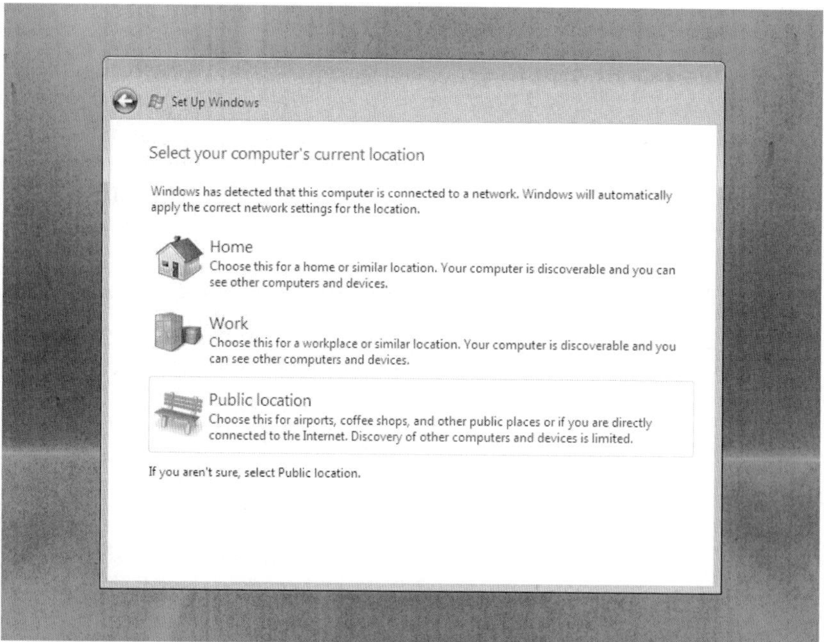

Figure 12-30 Tell Windows what kind of network you're on.

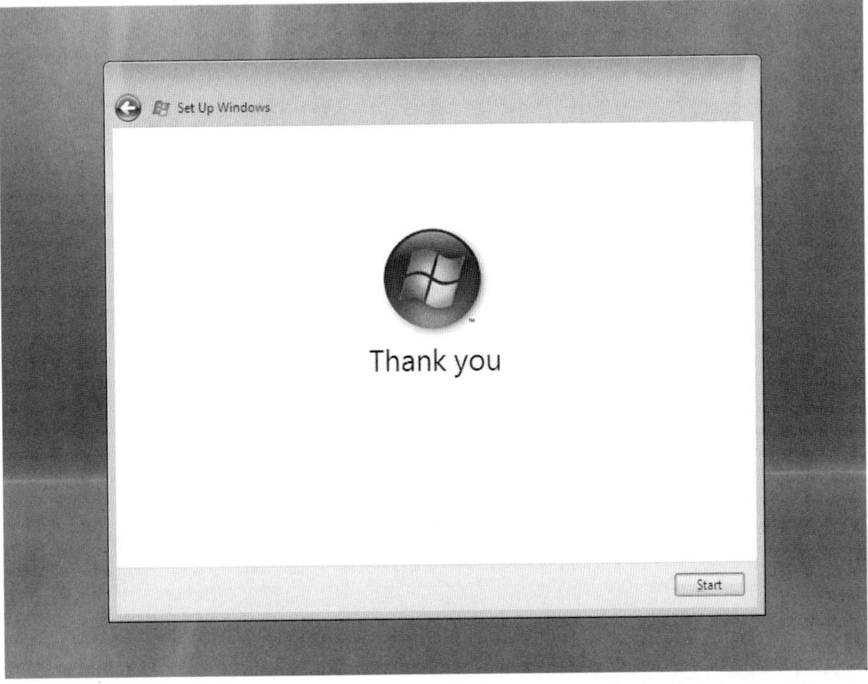

Figure 12-31 Aw, shucks, Microsoft Windows Vista. Don't mention it.

from 5 to 20 minutes, so this is another one of those coffee-break moments in the installation process.

Once the performance test finishes, Windows Vista or 7 boots up and you have 30 days to activate your new operating system if you didn't do so during installation. After 30 days, Windows will go into a non-genuine mode, which reduces the functionality of unverified Windows installations.

NOTE When it comes right down to it, you don't need a performance rating on your computer (and the option doesn't even exist beyond Windows 7). If you don't want to waste your time, use the ALT-F4 keyboard shortcut to skip this step.

Installing Windows over a Network

Techs working for big corporations can end up installing Windows a lot. When you have a hundred PCs to take care of and Microsoft launches a new version of Windows, you don't want to have to walk from cubicle to cubicle with an installation disc, running one install after the other. You already know about automated installations, but network installations take this one step further.

Imagine another scenario. You're still a tech for a large company, but your boss has decided that every new PC will use an image with a predetermined set of applications and configurations. You need to put the image on every workstation, but most of them don't have optical drives. Network installation saves the day again!

The phrase "network installation" can involve many different tools depending on which version of Windows you use. Most importantly, the machines that receive the installations (the clients) need to be connected to a server. That server might be another copy of Windows Vista, 7, 8, 8.1, or 10; or it might be a fully fledged server running Windows Server 2008, 2008 R2, 2012, and so on. The serving PC needs to host an image, which can either be the default installation of Windows or a custom image, often created by the network administrator.

All of the server-side issues should be handled by a network administrator—setting up a server to deploy Windows installations and images goes beyond what the CompTIA A+ exams cover.

Booting with PXE On the client side, you'll need to use the *Preboot Execution Environment (PXE)*. PXE uses multiple protocols such as IP, DHCP, and DNS to enable your computer to boot from a network location. That means the PC needs no installation disc or USB drive. Just plug your computer into the network and go! Okay, it's a little more complicated than that.

To enable PXE, you'll need to enter your BIOS System Setup. Find the screen that configures your NIC (which changes depending on your particular BIOS). If there is a PXE setting there, enable it. You'll also need to change the boot order so that the PC boots from a network location first.

NOTE Not every NIC supports PXE. To boot from a network location without PXE, you can create boot media that forces your PC to boot from a network location.

When you reboot the PC, you'll see the familiar first screens of the boot process. At some point, you should also see an instruction to "Press F12 for network boot." (It's almost always F12.) The PC will attempt to find a server on the network to which it can connect. When it does, you'll be asked to press F12 again to continue booting from the network, as you can see in Figure 12-32.

Depending on how many images are prepared on the server, you'll either be taken directly to the Windows installation screen or be asked to pick from multiple images. Pick the option you need, and everything else should proceed as if you were installing Windows from the local optical drive.

[cue interlude]

Installing Mac OS X over a Network

I know, I know. CompTIA 220-902 exam objective 1.2 specifically poses a scenario where you install a *Windows PC OS*, but CompTIA snuck in one tiny Mac OS X option. So let's take a very brief detour from Happy Town and look at an important Apple tool.

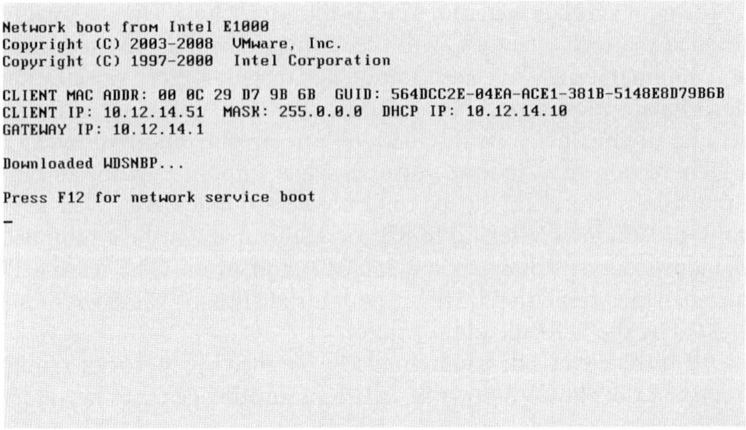

Figure 12-32 Network boot

```
Network boot from Intel E1000
Copyright (C) 2003-2008  VMware, Inc.
Copyright (C) 1997-2000  Intel Corporation

CLIENT MAC ADDR: 00 0C 29 D7 9B 6B  GUID: 564DCC2E-04EA-ACE1-381B-5148E8D79B6B
CLIENT IP: 10.12.14.51  MASK: 255.0.0.0  DHCP IP: 10.12.14.10
GATEWAY IP: 10.12.14.1

Downloaded WDSNBP...

Press F12 for network service boot

_
```

NetBoot enables you to do some amazing installation types for Mac OS X over a network. With this tool, you can boot a bunch of identical Mac OS X machines remotely—so they have the look and feel you want. Any user-generated content on them simply goes away when you reboot the machines. This is a great tool for a classroom or conference.

Secondly, you can load identical images on multiple Macs, installing OS X on the hard drives of many remote systems. This is great when you're rolling out a new corporate default build, for example, at the enterprise level.

Finally, you can use NetBoot to push specific applications to many computers at once. This is huge for product rollout throughout any organization.

Expect to see Netboot (capital *N* only) on the CompTIA A+ 902 exam, rather than capitalized all fancy like the Apple folks do it (i.e., NetBoot).

[cue end of interlude]

Troubleshooting Installation Problems

The term "installation problem" is rather deceptive. The installation process itself almost never fails. Usually, something else fails during the process that is generally interpreted as an "install failure." Let's look at some typical installation problems and how to correct them.

Media Errors

If you're going to have a problem with a Windows installation, have a media error, like a scratched DVD. It's always better to have the error right off the bat as opposed to when the installation is nearly complete.

RAID Array Not Detected If Windows fails to detect a RAID array during installation, this could be caused by Windows not having the proper driver for the hard drive or RAID controller. If the hard drives show up properly in the RAID controller setup utility, then it's almost certainly a driver issue. Get the driver disc from the manufacturer

and run setup again. Press F6 when prompted very early in the Windows installation process. Nothing happens right away when you push F6, but later in the process you'll be prompted to install drivers.

No Boot Device Present When Booting Off the Windows Installation Disc Either the startup disc is bad or the CMOS is not set to look at that optical drive first. Access the system setup utility as discussed in Chapter 6, "BIOS."

Not Ready Error on Optical Drive You probably just need to give the optical drive a moment to catch up. Press R for retry a few times. You may also have a damaged installation disc, or the optical drive may be too slow for the system.

Graphical Mode Errors

Once the graphical part of the installation begins, errors can come from a number of sources, such as hardware or driver problems.

Hardware Detection Errors Failure to detect hardware properly by any version of Windows Setup can be avoided by simply researching compatibility beforehand. Or, if you decided to skip that step, you might be lucky and only have a hardware detection error involving a noncritical hardware device. You can troubleshoot this problem at your leisure. In a sense, you are handing in your homework late, checking out compatibility and finding a proper driver after Windows is installed.

Every Windows installation depends on Windows Setup properly detecting the computer type (motherboard and BIOS stuff, in particular) and installing the correct hardware support. Microsoft designed Windows to run on several hardware platforms using a layer of software tailored specifically for the hardware, called the *hardware abstraction layer (HAL)*.

Lockups During Installation

Lockups are one of the most challenging problems that can take place during installation, because they don't give you a clue as to what's causing the problem. Here are a few things to check if you get a lockup during installation.

Unplug It Most system lockups occur when Windows Setup queries the hardware. If a system locks up once during setup, turn off the computer—literally. Unplug the system! Do *not* press CTRL-ALT-DEL. Do *not* press the Reset button. Unplug it! Then turn the system back on, boot into Setup, and rerun the Setup program. Windows will see the partial installation and restart the installation process automatically. Microsoft used to call this *Smart Recovery*, but the term has faded away over the years.

Disc, Drive, or Image Errors Bad media can mess up an installation. Bad optical discs, optical drives, or hard drives may cause lockups. Similarly, faults on a USB-based drive can stop an installation in its tracks. Finally, problems with a downloaded ISO image—also part of the media—can cause lockups. Check each media component. Check the optical disc for scratches or dirt, and clean it up or replace it. Try a known-good disc in the drive. If you get the same error, you may need to replace the drive or perhaps the ISO.

Log Files Windows generates a number of special text files called *log files* that track the progress of certain processes. Windows creates different log files for different purposes. The Windows installation process creates about 20 log files, organized by installation phase. Each phase creates a setuperr.log file to track any errors during that phase of the installation.

Windows stores these log files in the Windows directory (the location in which the OS is installed). These operating systems have powerful recovery options, so the chances of ever actually having to read a log file, understand it, and then get something fixed as a result of that understanding are pretty small. What makes log files handy is when you call Microsoft or a hardware manufacturer. They *love* to read these files, and they actually have people who understand them. Don't worry about trying to understand log files for the CompTIA A+ exams; just make sure you know the names of the log files and their location. Leave the details to the übergeeks.

Try This!

Locating Windows Setup Log Files

1. Go to the following Microsoft TechNet Web site:

   https://technet.microsoft.com/en-us/library/Hh824819.aspx

2. Identify the specific log file locations and descriptions.
3. Using Windows Explorer or Explorer on your own PC, navigate to the specific log file locations and see if you can find your setup log files.

Who knows, you may be on your way to becoming a Microsoft log file reader!

Post-Installation Tasks

You might think that's enough work for one day, but your task list has a few more things. They include updating the OS with patches and service packs, upgrading drivers, restoring user data files, and migrating and retiring systems.

Patches, Service Packs, and Updates

Someone once described an airliner as consisting of millions of parts flying in close formation. I think that's also a good description for an operating system. And we can even carry that analogy further by thinking about all of the maintenance required to keep an airliner safely flying. Like an airliner, the parts (programming code) of your OS were created by different people, and some parts may even have been contracted out. Although each component is tested as much as possible, and the assembled OS is also tested, it's

not possible to test for every possible combination of events. Sometimes a piece is simply found to be defective. The fix for such a problem is a corrective program called a *patch.*

In the past, Microsoft provided patches for individual problems. They also accumulated patches up to some sort of critical mass and then bundled them together as a *service pack*, but Windows 7 was the last version to get one.

Immediately after installing Windows, install the latest updates on the computer. The easiest way to accomplish this task it to turn on Windows Update. Chapter 15, "Managing and Optimizing Operating Systems," covers this process more thoroughly.

Upgrading Drivers

During installation, you may decide to go with the default drivers that come with Windows and then upgrade them to the latest drivers after the fact. This is a good strategy because installation is a complicated task that you can simplify by installing old but adequate drivers. Maybe those newest drivers are just a week old—waiting until after the Windows installation to install new drivers gives you a usable driver to go back to if the new driver turns out to be a lemon.

Restoring User Data Files (If Applicable)

Remember when you backed up the user data files before installation? You don't? Well, check again, because now is the time to restore that data. Your method of restoring depends on how you backed up the files in the first place. If you used a third-party backup program, you need to install it before you can restore those files, but if you used the Backup and Restore Center, you are in luck, because they are installed by default. If you did something simpler, such as copying to optical discs, USB or other external drive, or a network location, all you have to do is copy the files back to the local hard drive. Good luck!

Migrating and Retiring Systems

Seasons change and so does the state of the art in computing. At a certain point in a computer's life, you'll need to retire an old system. This means you must move the data and users to a new system or at least a new hard drive—a process called *migration*—and then safely dispose of the old system. Microsoft offers a few tools to accomplish this task, and because it's important to know about them for the CompTIA A+ exams (not to mention for your next new computer purchase), I'm going to go over them.

User State Migration Tool

If you're the sort of computer user who demands maximum functionality and power from your operating system, you'll probably want to use the *User State Migration Tool (USMT)*. The USMT's primary use is in businesses because it has to be run in a Windows Server Active Directory domain. If you need to migrate many users, the USMT is the tool. If you only need to migrate a few, Windows Easy Transfer, described next, is the way to go.

NOTE USMT is extremely handy for large-scale Windows operating system deployments. Microsoft provides a detailed overview that includes the benefits and limitations of USMT. Take a look here:
https://technet.microsoft.com/en-us/library/hh825227.aspx

Windows Easy Transfer

Windows Easy Transfer enables you to migrate user data and personalizations quickly. In Windows Vista/7, it is located in the System Tools subfolder of the Accessories folder in the Programs menu. To locate it in Windows 8/8.1, open the Start screen, type Windows Easy Transfer, and then click on Windows Easy Transfer from the results. Unfortunately, it is not available in Windows 10.

The first screen of Windows Easy Transfer simply gives you information about the process, so there's not really much to do there. When you click on Next, you're taken to a screen that asks if you want to start a new transfer or continue an old one (see Figure 12-33). If you've already set up your old computer to transfer the files, select the latter option; if you haven't, select the former.

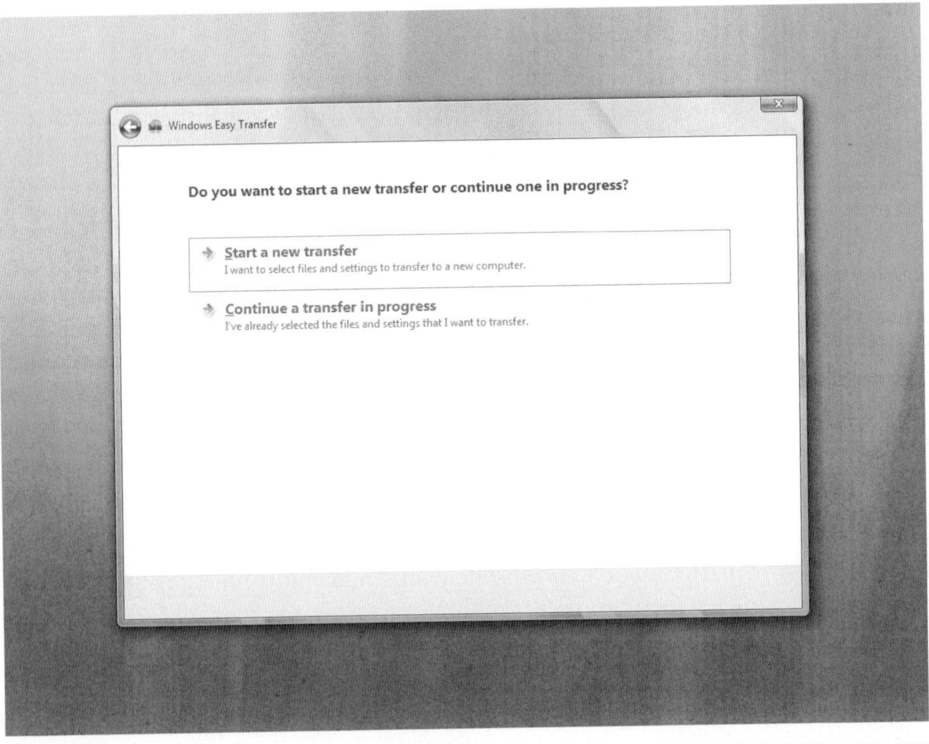

Figure 12-33 Start a new transfer or continue one?

If you choose to start a new transfer, select whether you're using your new or old computer and then follow the prompts.

Migration Practices

When talking about migration or retirement in terms of security, you need to answer one question: What do you do with the old system or drive?

All but the most vanilla new installations have sensitive data on them, even if it's simply e-mail messages or notes-to-self that would cause embarrassment if discovered. Most PCs, especially in a work environment, contain a lot of sensitive data. You can't just format C: and hand over the drive.

Follow three principles when migrating or retiring a computer. First, migrate your users and data information in a secure environment. Until you get passwords properly in place and test the security of the new system, you can't consider that system secure. Second, remove data remnants from hard drives that you store or give to charity. Third, recycle the older equipment; don't throw it in the trash. PC recyclers go through a process of deconstructing hardware, breaking system units, keyboards, printers, and even monitors into their basic plastics, metals, and glass for reuse.

The easiest way for someone to compromise or access sensitive data is to simply walk up and take it when you're not looking. This is especially true when you are in the process of copying information to a new, unprotected system. Don't set a copy to run while you go out to lunch, but rather be there to supervise and remove any remnant data that might still reside on any mass storage devices, especially hard drives.

Data Destruction

You might think that, as easy as it seems to be to lose data, you could readily get rid of data if you tried. That's definitely not the case with magnetic media such as hard drives. When you delete something in Windows, or even empty the Recycle Bin, the "deleted" data remains on your storage device (you'll see it as free space in Windows) until new data overwrites it, or replaces it. This can be a big security hole when you dispose of a drive.

Cleaning a drive completely is very difficult. You can either physically destroy the hard drive or *sanitize* it using a software utility. Physical destruction isn't complicated—you bust up the drive into tiny little bits or melt it. Tools to accomplish this include drive shredders, drills, hammers, electromagnets, and degaussing tools (which reduce or remove the magnetic fields that store data on HDDs). Incineration pretty much clears all data. Keep in mind that, as hard drives advance and pack more data into smaller spaces, you'll need to break the hard drive into smaller pieces to prevent anyone from recovering your data.

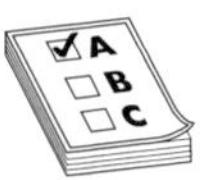

EXAM TIP Professional hard drive disposal services will guarantee they have truly, thoroughly destroyed drives by issuing a *certificate of destruction*. This certificate brings peace of mind, among other things, that precious data won't slip into unwanted hands.

Sanitizing your drive means the hard drive will still function once the data has been destroyed. There are several more or less effective ways to do this. The CompTIA A+ exams want you to know the difference between a standard format and a *low-level format*. You already learned about standard formatting back in Chapter 10, so how is low-level formatting different? With older drives (pre-1990s), low-level formatting would create the physical marks on the disk surface so that the drive knew where to store data; in the process, it erased the data from the drive. This was initially done at the factory, but utilities existed to repeat this operation later. As drives became more complex, hard drive manufacturers disabled the ability to perform low-level formats outside the factory.

Today, the term "low-level formatting" is often used to describe a *zero-fill* or *overwrite* operation. This process returns the drive to a state as close to like-new as possible by writing zeros to every location on the drive.

You can also use a *drive wiping* utility to erase any old, deleted data that hasn't been overwritten yet. Simply put, this overwrites the free space on your drive with junk data that makes the original data harder to recover. Piriform's CCleaner is a data-sanitizing utility that can erase your Web browsing history, erase your recent activity in Windows (such as what programs you ran), and even scrub your hard drive's free space to make deleted files unrecoverable (see Figure 12-34).

Recycle

An important and relatively easy way to be an environmentally conscious computer user is to follow *recycle or repurpose best practices*. Recycling products such as paper and printer cartridges not only keeps them out of overcrowded landfills but also ensures that the more toxic products are disposed of in the right way. Safely disposing of hardware containing hazardous materials, such as computer monitors, protects both people and the environment.

Anyone who's ever tried to sell a computer more than three or four years old learns a hard lesson: they're not worth much, if anything at all. It's a real temptation to take that old computer and just toss it in the garbage, but never do that!

First of all, many parts of your computer—such as your computer monitor—contain hazardous materials that pollute the environment. Luckily, thousands of companies now specialize in computer recycling and will gladly accept your old computer. If you have enough computers, they might even pick them up. If you can't find a recycler, call your local municipality's waste authority to see where to drop off your system.

An even better alternative for your old computer is donation. Many organizations actively look for old computers to refurbish and to donate to schools and other organizations. Just keep in mind that the computer can be too old—not even a school wants a computer more than five or six years old.

No Installation Is Perfect

Even when the installation seems smooth, issues may slowly surface, especially in the case of upgrades. Be prepared to reinstall applications or deal with new functions that were absent in the previous OS. If things really fall apart, you can go back to the previous OS. Or, if you have an OEM computer (one built by, for example, Dell or HP instead of by you), your computer likely came with a special recovery partition on its hard drive,

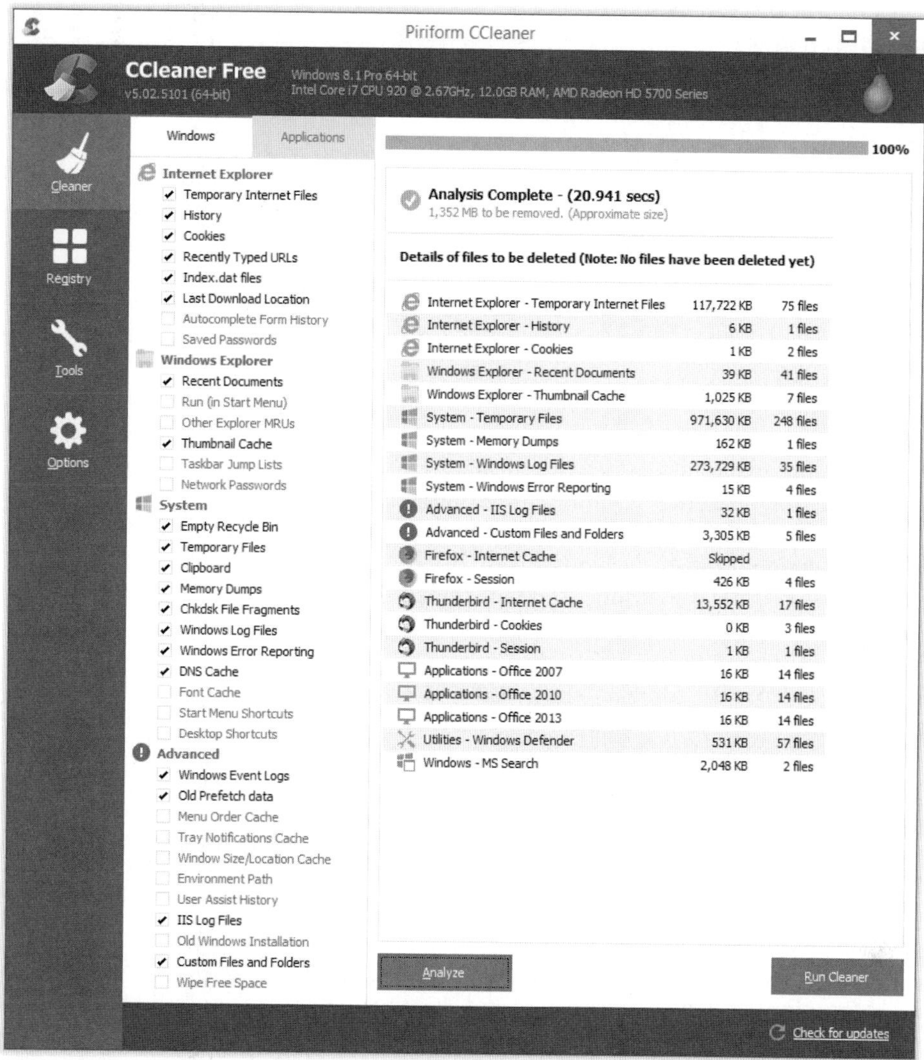

Figure 12-34 Piriform's CCleaner showing files to be removed

a recovery disc, or a recovery USB flash drive; you can use any of these to restore your operating system to its factory settings. You usually invoke a system recovery by pressing a certain key during boot-up—usually F10 or F11—and then following a set of prompts.

The procedures I've laid out in this chapter may seem like a lot of work—how bad could it be to grab an installation disc, fling a copy of Windows onto a system, and, as the saying goes, let the chips fall where they may? Plenty bad, is how bad. Not only is understanding these procedures important for the CompTIA A+ certification exams, but these procedures can also save your, ah, hide once you're a working PC tech and tasked to install the latest version of Windows on the boss's new computer!

Beyond A+

Installing Windows 10

Even though Windows 10 isn't on the CompTIA A+ 220-901/902 exams, techs need to know it. Windows 10 is slick, easy to use, and considered by many (including me) to be the best Windows version Microsoft has ever produced.

Microsoft rolled out Windows 10 in an interesting fashion, granting free upgrades to licensed users of Windows 7, 8, and 8.1—if they upgrade before July 29, 2016. For installations on new hardware (and for Enterprise users), Redmond charges a nominal fee for the OS.

To encourage users to upgrade from Windows 7 or Windows 8/8.1, Microsoft pushes a Get Windows 10 app through Windows Update. Clicking on it brings up a reservation system that, once you queue up, will download Windows 10 installation media.

The steps for installing Windows 10 from a tech's standpoint are pretty minimal. Microsoft automates the process to the point that you have to answer only a few questions at the end, but those questions are essential.

All of the positives of Windows 10 are countered by Microsoft's unprecedented and questionable use of what many consider private data. One of the most controversial questions is why Windows 10 seemingly requires you to log in using a Microsoft (Hotmail or Outlook) account. Savvy techs discovered that logging in with a Microsoft account enables Windows to grab a disturbing amount of personal information, including data such as your Wi-Fi passwords. Security-conscious users should consider creating and using an old-style local user account. Be warned that not using a Microsoft account disables the Microsoft Cortana voice command feature.

There are a number of privacy issues beyond the Microsoft account issue. Here's a list of features you should consider turning off. Most of these features may be shut down using the Privacy utility in the Settings app.

- **Let apps use my advertising ID for experiences across apps** This gives Microsoft the right to create, use, and share a unique advertising ID that will at the very least create custom advertising on Web sites.
- **Send Microsoft information about how I write to help us improve typing and writing in the future** Microsoft doesn't clearly state the purpose of this option, but suffice it to say they may capture all of your keystrokes. Scary!
- **Let websites provide locally relevant content by accessing my language list** Why does Microsoft need to access language settings given that a Web site can easily tell your default language? Unless you go between multiple languages, it's a good idea to turn this off.
- **Location** Location services enable Microsoft to track your location unless this setting is disabled.

- **Getting to know you** This happy-sounding feature tracks a large amount of information about you such as your contacts, calendar events, speech, handwriting, and more. Turn it off.
- **Wi-Fi Sense** This feature offers two settings. First is *Connect to suggested open hotspots*. If you don't turn off this setting, Windows will automatically connect you to any hotspot. Second is *Connect to networks shared by my contacts*. This feature lets any of your contacts have your Wi-Fi password, and *vice versa*.

The bottom line is this: Windows 10 is easy to use and full of features, plus the free price (for most users) is tempting. But just remember, "when software is free, you are no longer the customer, you are the product!"

Chapter Review

Questions

1. What is a thin client?
   - **A.** A computer with a 32-bit-wide address bus
   - **B.** A portable computer
   - **C.** A system designed to handle only very basic applications with the minimum hardware required by the operating system
   - **D.** A computer in a narrow, small form-factor case
2. What three functions does a home server PC provide? (Select three.)
   - **A.** Media streaming
   - **B.** File sharing
   - **C.** Web hosting
   - **D.** Print sharing
3. What does CompTIA call a PC case built for a home theater?
   - **A.** Media center case
   - **B.** XBMC
   - **C.** HTPC
   - **D.** Stereo case
4. What is the most important component for building a virtualization workstation?
   - **A.** CPU
   - **B.** Power supply
   - **C.** RAM
   - **D.** Large monitor

5. What is the most common boot method for installing Windows 8?
   A. Boot to a Windows DVD
   B. Boot to a Windows CD-ROM
   C. Boot to a PXE drive
   D. Boot to a recovery partition
6. When you install an operating system alongside an existing operating system, what do you create?
   A. A clean installation
   B. An upgrade installation
   C. A multiboot installation
   D. A network installation
7. If you do not complete the activation process for Windows 7, what will happen to your computer?
   A. Nothing. Activation is optional.
   B. The computer will work fine for 30 days and then Windows will be disabled.
   C. Microsoft will not know how to contact you to provide upgrade information.
   D. It will work if you check the "I promise to pay for Windows later" box.
8. If Windows locks up during the installation, what should you do?
   A. Press CTRL-ALT-DEL to restart the installation process.
   B. Push the Reset button to restart the installation process.
   C. Press the ESC key to cancel the installation process.
   D. Unplug the computer and restart the installation process.
9. Which term describes a combination of many updates and fixes in Windows Vista/7?
   A. Hot fix
   B. Hot pack
   C. Service pack
   D. Service release
10. You've just replaced Jane's Windows 7 PC with a new Windows 8.1 machine. What post-installation tool should you run to make the transition as painless as possible for her?
   A. Windows Activation
   B. Repair installation
   C. Windows Easy Transfer
   D. User State Migration Tool

Answers

1. **C.** Thin clients rely on servers to perform anything beyond the most basic computing tasks.
2. **A, B, D.** Home servers share files, stream media, and share printers.
3. **C.** HTPC cases enable your PC to blend in with your home theater equipment.
4. **C.** Every virtual machine you run consumes a large share of RAM, so the more RAM you have, the more VMs you can run.
5. **A.** Although in-place upgrades happen with more frequency, it's still very common to boot to the Windows 8 DVD and install from there.
6. **C.** An OS added alongside an existing OS creates a multiboot system.
7. **B.** If you do not complete the activation process for Windows 7, the computer will work fine for 30 days and then Windows will be disabled.
8. **D.** If Windows locks up during the installation, you should unplug the computer and restart the installation process.
9. **C.** A service pack is a combination of many updates and fixes in Windows Vista/7.
10. **C.** Run the Windows Easy Transfer tool to move all her Windows 7 personal files and familiar settings, like her desktop, to the new Windows 8.1 computer.

CHAPTER 13

Windows Under the Hood

In this chapter, you will learn how to

- Work with the Registry
- Understand and observe the Windows boot process in detail
- Control processes, services, and threads
- Explore Windows tools for programmers

Windows is powerful, easy to use, surprisingly idiot proof, backward compatible, and robust. A large part of Windows' power is hidden—*under the hood*—in programs and processes that Microsoft doesn't want normal users to see. For the record, I think hiding anything normal users don't need is a smart idea. Technicians, on the other hand, need to not only understand these processes and programs, but also know how to use, configure, and fix them when needed. Let's start with one of the most famous and most important items under the hood: the Registry.

902

Registry

The *Registry* is a huge database that stores everything about your PC, including information on all of the hardware, network information, user preferences, file types, and virtually anything else you might find in Windows. Almost any form of configuration you do to a Windows system involves editing the Registry. Every version of Windows stores the numerous Registry files (called *hives*) in the \%SystemRoot%\System32\config folder and each user account folder. Fortunately, you rarely have to access these massive files directly. Instead, you can use a set of relatively tech-friendly applications to edit the Registry.

The CompTIA A+ 220-902 certification exam does not expect you to memorize every aspect of the Windows Registry. You should, however, understand the basic components of the Registry, know how to edit the Registry manually, and know the best way to locate a particular setting.

Accessing the Registry

Before you look in the Registry, let's look at how you access the Registry directly by using a Registry Editor, so you can open the Registry on your machine and compare what you see to the examples in this chapter. To open the Registry Editor, enter **regedit** in the Start | Search bar.

NOTE Well before any version of Windows you'll see on the current CompTIA A+ exams, Windows came with two Registry editors: regedt32.exe and regedit.exe. You started either of these programs by going to a command prompt and typing its filename. The reason for having two different Registry editors is long and boring, and explaining it would require a dull monologue about how the Registry worked in Windows 9*x* and Windows NT (very 20th century!). While there's only one editor these days, either program name will open the Registry Editor, and you may run into seasoned techs or users calling the Registry Editor by these names.

Registry Components

The Registry is organized in a tree structure similar to the folders on the file system. Once you open the Registry Editor in Windows, you will see five main subgroups, or *root keys*:

- HKEY_CLASSES_ROOT
- HKEY_CURRENT_USER
- HKEY_USERS
- HKEY_LOCAL_MACHINE
- HKEY_CURRENT_CONFIG

Try opening one of these root keys by clicking on the plus sign to its left; note that more subkeys are listed underneath. A subkey also can have other subkeys, or *values*. Values define aspects of the subkey. Figure 13-1 shows an example of a subkey with some values. Notice that the Registry Editor shows only keys—root keys and subkeys—on the left and values on the right. Each of the root keys has a specific function, so let's take a look at them individually.

HKEY_CLASSES_ROOT

Historically, this root key defined the standard *class objects* used by Windows. A class object is a named group of functions that defines what you can do with the object it represents. Pretty much everything that has to do with files on the system is defined by a class object. For example, the Registry uses two class objects to define the popular MP3 sound file. These days, this root key combines class objects from \Software\Classes under both HKEY_CURRENT_USER and HKEY_LOCAL_MACHINE to provide backward compatibility for older applications.

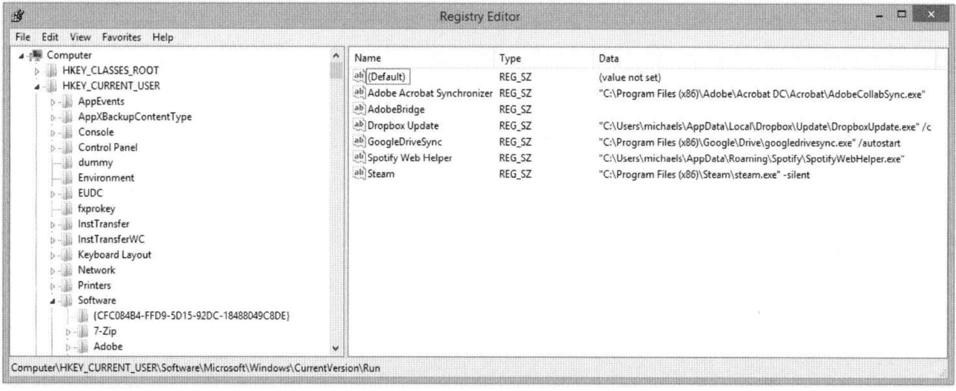

Figure 13-1 Typical Registry root keys, subkeys, and values

HKEY_CURRENT_USER and HKEY_USERS

Windows is designed to support more than one user on the same system, storing personalized information such as desktop colors, screensavers, and the contents of the desktop for every user that has an account on the system. HKEY_CURRENT_USER stores the current user settings, and HKEY_USERS stores all of the personalized information for each user. While you certainly can change items such as the screensaver here, the better way is to right-click on the desktop and select Personalize.

HKEY_LOCAL_MACHINE

This root key contains all the data for a system's non-user-specific configurations. This encompasses every device and every program in your computer.

HKEY_CURRENT_CONFIG

If the values in HKEY_LOCAL_MACHINE have more than one option, such as two different monitors, this root key defines which one is currently being used. Because most people have only one type of monitor and similar equipment, this area is almost never touched.

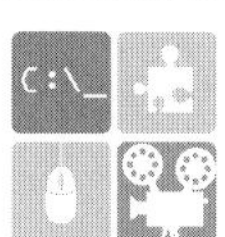

SIM Check out the excellent trio of sims on "Registry Files Location" in the Chapter 13 section of the online TotalSims here: http://totalsem.com/90x. The combination of Type!, Show!, and Click! will prepare you for any scenario-based question on the Windows Registry.

Talkin' Registry

When describing a Registry setting, we use a simple nomenclature. For example, I recently moved my copy of *World of Warcraft* from my C: drive to my D: drive and was having problems when the program started. I went online to www.blizzard.com (home of

Blizzard Entertainment, the folks who make *World of Warcraft*) and contacted the support staff, who gave me instructions to access the Registry and make this change:

> "Go to HKLM\SOFTWARE\Blizzard Technologies\World of Warcraft and change the GamePath object and the InstallPath object to reflect the new drive letter of your new WoW location."

To do so, I opened the Registry Editor. Using this nomenclature, I was able to find the location of these Registry settings. Figure 13-2 shows this location. Compare this image to the path described in the instructions from Blizzard. Note that HKEY_LOCAL_MACHINE is abbreviated as HKLM.

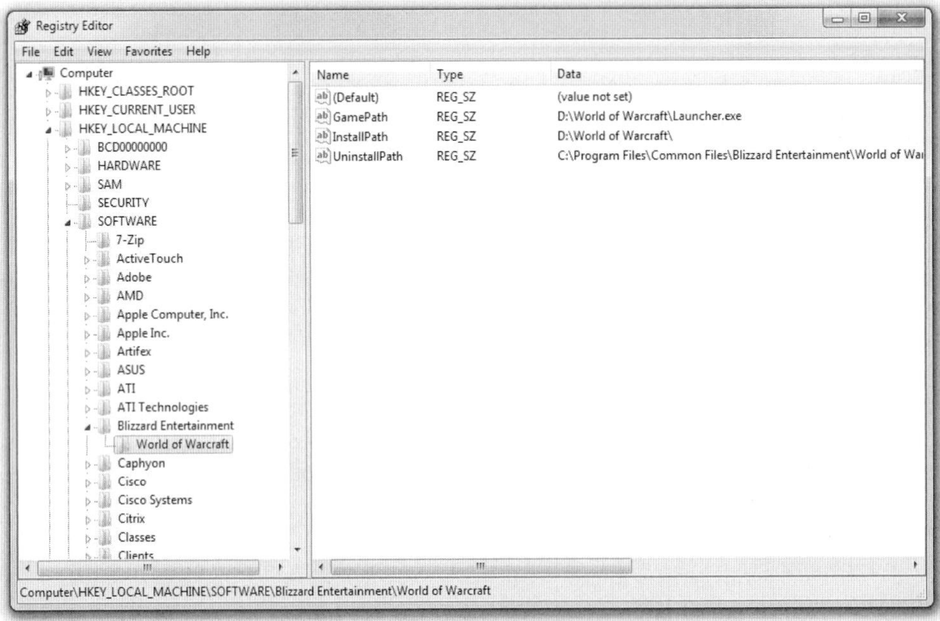

Figure 13-2 Editing the Registry to move *World of Warcraft* to a new drive

To describe the location of a specific Registry value, like where the Blizzard tech told me to go, requires a little bit of repetition. To wit, in the previous example, World of Warcraft is a subkey to Blizzard Technologies, which is in turn a subkey to the root key HKLM. The World of Warcraft subkey has four values. All keys have the (Default) value, so in this case the World of Warcraft subkey offers three functional values.

Values must have a defined type of data they store:

- **String value** These are the most flexible type of value and are very common. You can put any form of data in these.
- **Binary value** These values store nothing more than long strings of ones and zeros.

- **DWORD value** These values are like Binary values but are limited to exactly 32 bits.
- **QWORD value** These values are like Binary values but are limited to exactly 64 bits.

There are other types of values, but these four are used for most Registry entries.

Manual Registry Edits

There's little motivation for you to go into the Registry and make manual edits unless you've done some research that tells you to do so. When you do find yourself using the Registry Editor to access the Registry, you risk breaking things in Windows: applications might not start, utilities might not work, or worst of all, your computer might not boot. To prevent these problems, always make a backup of the Registry before you change anything. Once the backup is in a safe place (I like to use a thumb drive, personally), reboot the system to see if the changes you made had the desired result. If it worked, great. If not, you'll need to restore the old Registry settings using your backup. Let's watch this in action.

One of the more common manual Registry edits is to delete autostarting programs. I want to prevent three programs installed by my Logitech GamePanel keyboard and mouse from autostarting. The most common place for making this change is here:

HKLM\SOFTWARE\Microsoft\Windows\CurrentVersion\Run

Opening the Registry Editor and going to this subkey, you'll see something like Figure 13-3.

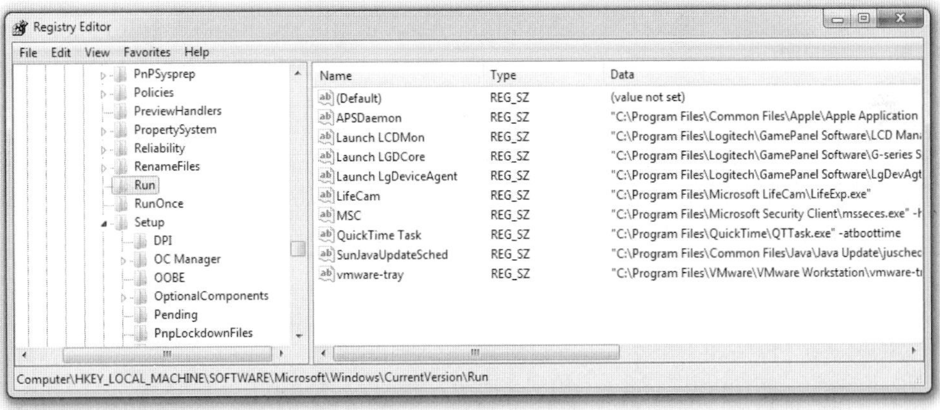

Figure 13-3 Mike's Run subkey

Before I delete these keys, I'm going to save a copy of my Registry. The Registry Editor's Export feature enables you to save either the full Registry or only a single root key or subkey (with all subkeys and values under it). Select Run from the left pane and

then click File | Export. Save the subkey as a Registration file with the extension .reg. Be sure to put that file somewhere you'll remember. Should you need to restore that key, use the File | Import command, or just right-click on the icon as shown in Figure 13-4 and click Merge.

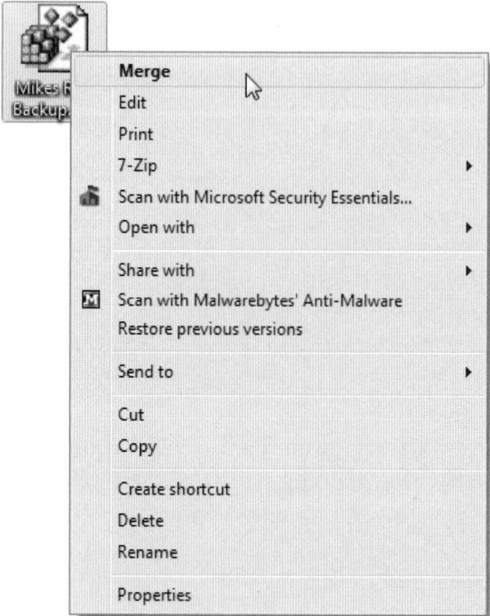

Figure 13-4 Merging keys from a backup file

Command-Line Registry Editing Tools

Windows includes a couple of command-line tools to edit the Registry (plus a lot more in PowerShell). The two that you might need on occasion are reg and regsvr32.

TIP If the command-line interface is new to you, you might want to flag this section of Chapter 13 and skip it for now, then return to it after reading about the command line and how it works in Chapter 16, "Working with the Command-Line Interface."

The *reg* command is a full Registry editing tool. You can view Registry keys and values, import and export some or all of a Registry, and even compare two different versions of a Registry. The tool is so powerful that it has multiple levels of help so you can tailor a command to accomplish very tight Registry edits. For example, typing **reg /?** brings up a list of 12 specific operations that you can search for help on, such as reg query /? and reg add /?.

The *regsvr32* command, in contrast with reg, can modify the Registry in only one way, adding (or *registering*) dynamic link library (DLL) files as command components in the Registry. By default, if you run regsvr32 in a 64-bit version of Windows, the 64-bit version runs. This can cause problems if you're trying to add a 32-bit DLL to the Registry. To accomplish the latter, run the regsvr32.exe file in the %SystemRoot%Syswow64 folder.

On the very off chance you'll ever need to run reg or regsvr32 (either version), refer to Chapter 16 for how to use the command-line interface effectively.

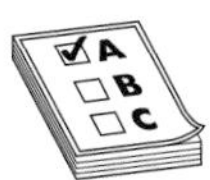

EXAM TIP Be familiar with regedit and regsvr32.

The Boot Process

The Windows installation creates a number of specific files and folders that the OS needs to run. Some of these files and folders are directly on the root of the C: drive; others can be elsewhere. The best way to remember the locations of these files and folders and to know their importance to the OS is by looking at how they interact to boot the system.

Current Windows versions support both BIOS and UEFI boot processes. The very first thing that happens when you power on a system with Windows is that either the BIOS or the UEFI starts up. The difference between BIOS and UEFI systems is in what happens next.

- In a BIOS-based system, the BIOS uses its boot order to scan a hard drive for a master boot record (MBR). The MBR holds a small bit of file system boot code that scans the partition table for the system partition and then loads its boot sector. The boot sector in turn contains code that does nothing but point the boot process toward a file called bootmgr (pronounced *Boot Manager*, or "boot mugger" if you're trying to make nerds laugh), the Windows Boot Manager. In short, the BIOS looks for the MBR, which finds the boot code to launch the OS.
- In a UEFI system, on the other hand, neither the MBR/GUID partition table (GPT) nor the file system boot code is run, and UEFI simply loads bootmgr directly.

NOTE Windows keeps bootmgr in the special 100-MB system partition you learned about in Chapter 10, "Implementing Hard Drives." If you are using a UEFI system, the helpfully named EFI system partition contains a special version of bootmgr called bootmgr.efi.

If you've ever run a dual-boot system with any Windows version from Vista on as one of the operating systems, you're probably already somewhat familiar with bootmgr; one of its jobs is displaying that "Which operating system do you want to load?" screen and then loading the appropriate operating system. When bootmgr starts, it reads data from a *Boot Configuration Data (BCD)* file that contains information about the various operating systems installed on the system as well as instructions for how to actually load (bootstrap) them. Once an operating system is selected (or immediately if only one is present), bootmgr loads a program called winload.exe, which readies your system to load the operating system kernel (called ntoskrnl.exe) itself rather like the way you clean up your house before Aunt Edna comes to visit. It does this by loading into memory the

hardware abstraction layer, the system Registry, and the drivers for any boot devices before the operating system itself takes over.

NOTE If you use Windows long enough, you may encounter an error message saying that Windows cannot boot because bootmgr is missing. This message is generated when the boot sector code is unable to locate bootmgr, which can be caused by file system corruption, a botched installation, or viruses.

Once the operating system process takes over, it loads up all of the various processes and systems that comprise Windows, the Windows logo comes up, and you're happily computing, completely oblivious to all of the complex electronic communication that just took place inside your computer.

Processes, Services, and Threads

Back in Chapter 4, "Microprocessors," you learned that CPUs run threads—bits of programs that are fed into the CPU. Let's see how all of this looks from Windows' point of view.

NOTE I'm simplifying things a little for the purposes of the CompTIA A+ 220-902 exam, but know that processes, services, and threads can get a lot more complicated.

In Windows, programs are executable files waiting on a mass storage device. When you start a program, Windows loads it into RAM as a process. Once there, the CPU reads the process and the process tells the CPU which chunks of code to run. Dealing with processes in their many forms is a big part of understanding what's happening "under the hood."

Windows is a multitasking operating system, running lots of processes simultaneously. Many of these processes appear in a window (or full screen) when you open them and end when you close that window. These processes are called applications. However, there's an entire class of processes that, due to the nature of their job, don't require a window of any form. These processes run invisibly in the background, providing a large number of necessary support roles. Collectively, these are called *services*. Let's look at applications, services, and processes and the tools we use to control them.

Task Manager

Microsoft offers the Windows *Task Manager* as the one-stop-shop for anything you need to do with applications, processes, and services (see Figure 13-5). The Microsoft development team significantly redesigned Task Manager for Windows 8. We'll look at the tool in Windows Vista/7 first, then examine Task Manager in Windows 8/8.1/10.

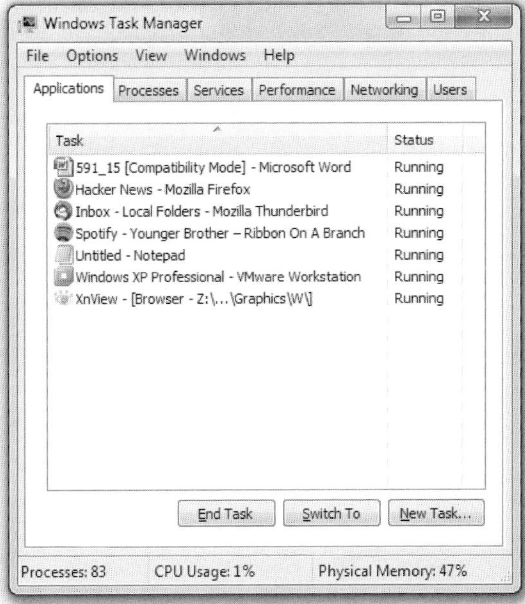

Figure 13-5 Task Manager in Windows 7

Task Manager in Windows Vista and Windows 7

The quickest way to open the Task Manager is to press CTRL-SHIFT-ESC. There are two other ways to open the Task Manager that you might see on the CompTIA A+ exams: go to Start | Search, type **taskmgr**, and press ENTER; or press CTRL-ALT-DELETE and select Task Manager.

Applications The *Applications* tab shows all the running applications on your system. If you're having trouble getting an application to close normally, this is the place to go. To force an application to shut down, select the naughty application and click End Task, or right-click on the application and select End Task from the context menu. Be careful when using this feature! There is no "Are you sure?" prompt and it's easy to accidently close the wrong application.

There are two other handy buttons on the Applications tab:

- Switch To enables you to bring any program to the front (very handy when you have a large number of applications running).
- New Task enables you to run programs if you know the executable. Click on New Task, type **cmd**, and press ENTER, for example, to open the command-line interface.

Remember that everything is a process, so every application is also listed in the Processes tab. Right-click on an application and select Go To Process to open the Processes tab and see which process is running the application.

Processes If you really want to tap the power of the Task Manager, you need to click on the *Processes* tab (see Figure 13-6). Since everything is a process, and the Processes tab shows you every running process, this is the one place that enables you to see everything running on your computer.

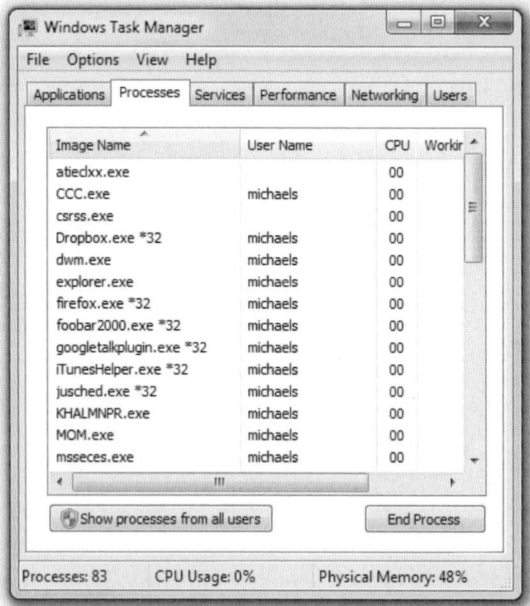

Figure 13-6 Processes tab in Windows 7

All processes have certain common features that you should recognize:

- A process is named after its executable file, which usually ends in .exe but can also end with other extensions.
- All processes have a user name to identify who started the process. A process started by Windows has the user name System.
- All processes have a Process Identifier (PID). To identify a process, you use the PID, not the process name. The Task Manager doesn't show the PID by default. Click on View | Select Columns and select the PID (Process Identifier) checkbox to see the PIDs (see Figure 13-7).

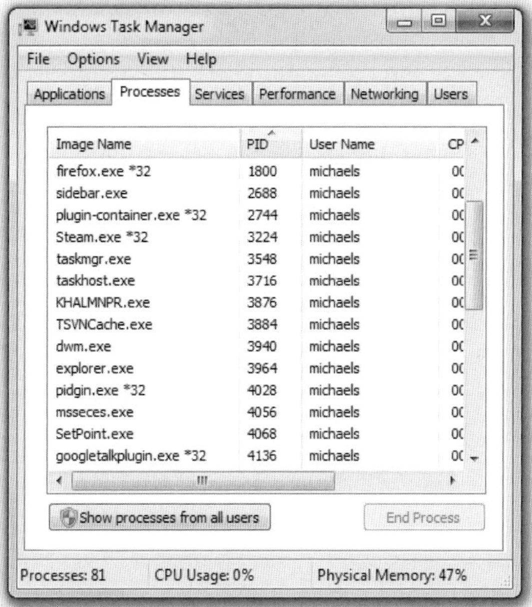

Figure 13-7 Processes tab showing the PID column in Windows 7

The Task Manager provides important information about processes. It shows the amount of CPU time (percentage) and the amount of RAM (in kilobytes) the process is using. Most processes also provide a description to help you understand what the process is doing, although you'll probably need to scroll right to see this information (see Figure 13-8).

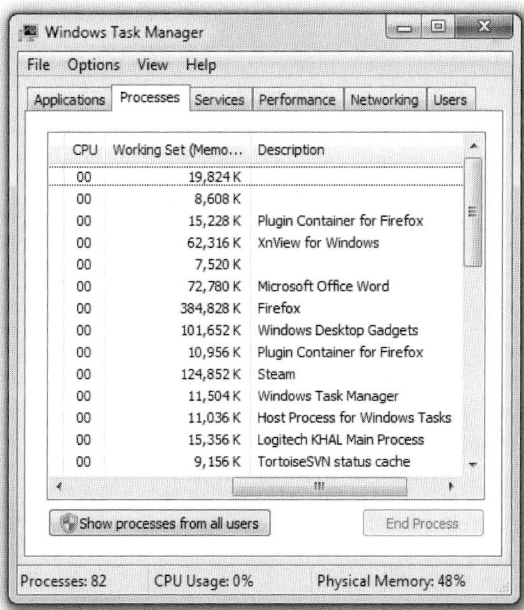

Figure 13-8 Processes details in Windows 7

You'll notice that almost all of the processes have the same user name. By default, the Task Manager shows only processes associated with the current user. Click on *Show processes from all users* to see every process on the system (see Figure 13-9). Note that some of the processes show a user name of Local Service or Network Service. As you might imagine, those are services!

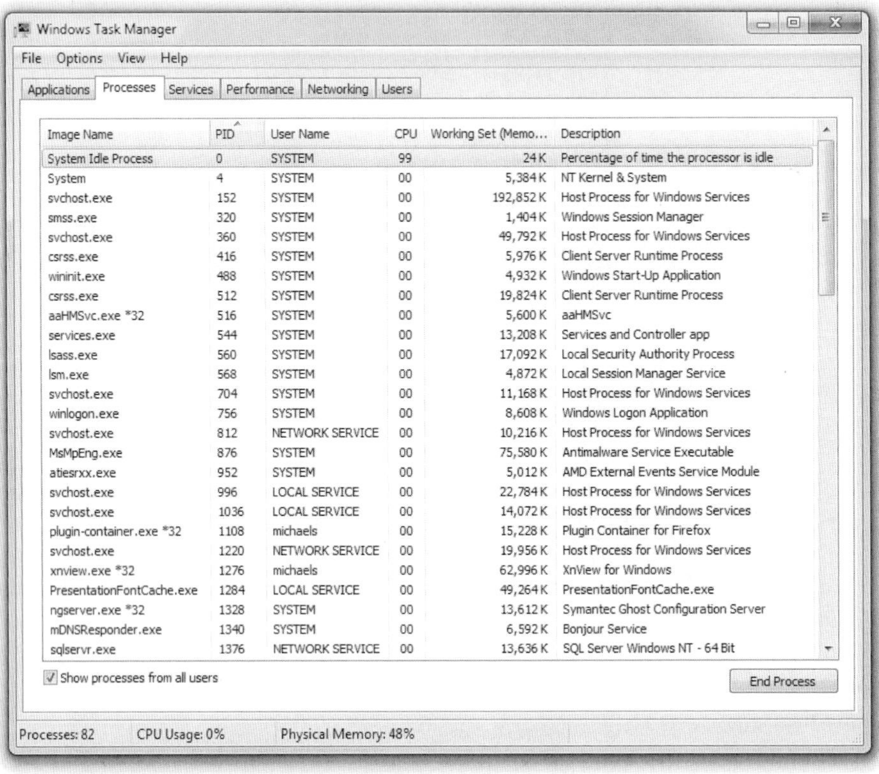

Figure 13-9 Processes from all users in Windows 7

Now that you understand the basics, let's watch the Task Manager do its magic with processes. If you select a process and click on the End Process button, you'll get a chance to confirm your intent to end it. If the process is an application, that application will close.

Try This!

Closing Applications

Start up Notepad and then start up the Task Manager. Right-click on the Notepad application and select Go To Process. It takes you to the process. Right-click and select End Process to close the application.

Closing processes is important, but to take it even further, you need to select a process and right-click on it to see a number of options. If you select a process that's an application (the name of the process is a strong clue—winword.exe is Microsoft Word), you see something like Figure 13-10.

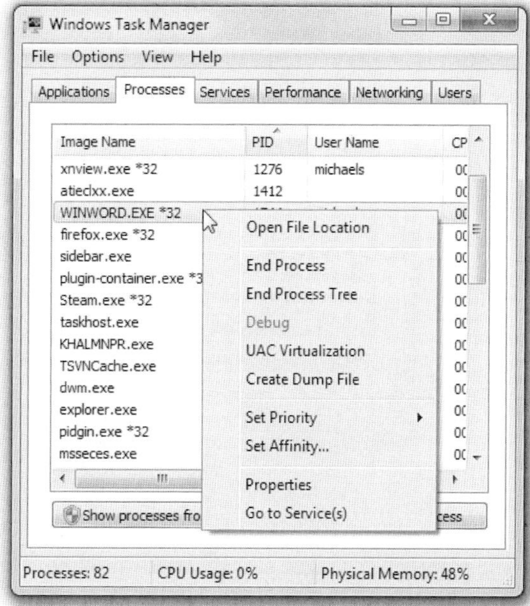

Figure 13-10 Processes detail on right-click

Open File Location takes you to wherever the file is located. This is extremely helpful when you're looking at a mysterious process and are trying to find out what it's doing on your computer.

You already know what End Process does. End Process Tree is extremely important but also complex, so let's save that for later.

Debug is grayed out, unless you're running a Windows debugger program—see the explanation of dump files below.

In Windows 7, UAC Virtualization gives older programs that weren't written to avoid accessing protected folders a way to do so by making a fake protected folder. In most cases, Windows handles this automatically, but there are rare cases where you'll need to set this manually. Again, you won't do this on your own—you'll be on the phone with the tech support for some software company and they'll tell you how to use UAC Virtualization.

Dump files show the status of the program at the moment you click Create Dump File. Developers use special debugging utilities to read dump files to analyze problems with programs. The only time you'd ever use this option is if you're having problems with a program and the support people ask you to make a dump file.

Set Priority gives you the ability to devote more or less processor time to a process (see Figure 13-11). This is very handy when you have a process that is slowing down your machine or if you have a process that is running too slowly and you want to speed it up.

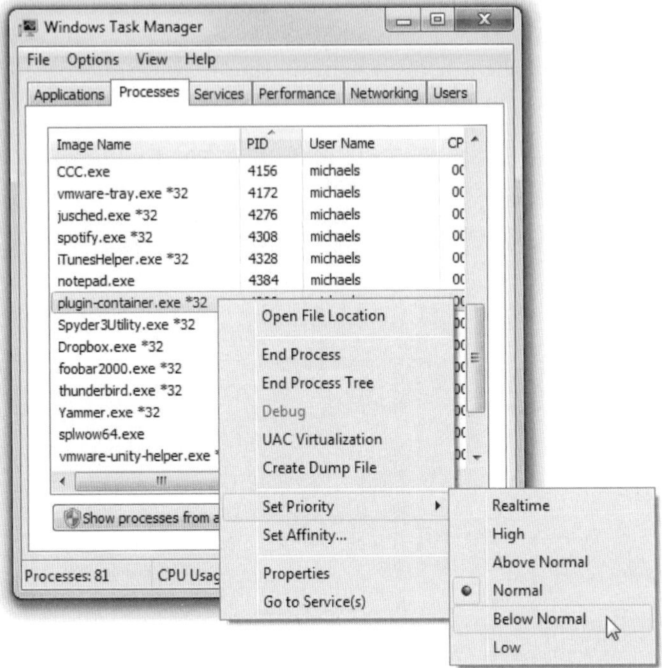

Figure 13-11 Process priority

Messing with priorities can get complicated quickly. Maybe it's best to think about priority as a bit like the VIP lines most amusement parks have these days. Having a VIP pass doesn't make the rides any faster—nor does it help you get back in line any quicker—it just changes how many people you have to wait behind to ride again. But what happens to everyone else if there are so many people in the VIP line that the non-VIP queue almost never moves?

Imagine you need to render out some video on your system, but when you start the job, you find out it'll take six hours. As soon as the job starts, your music starts skipping and jumping along. The video renders might be more important in the grand scheme of things, but you won't be able to get anything else done with your music stuttering along. The best idea here is to increase the priority of a single process you need to run normally, such as your audio player, or reduce the priority of a single process that isn't as time sensitive, such as the video renderer, without touching any other priorities. It may be better to have your system spend eight hours rendering a video while you use it for other work than to have your system rendered unusable for six.

NOTE Setting any single process to Realtime priority will often bring the entire system to a crawl as no other process gets much CPU time—avoid Realtime priority.

Set Affinity enables you to specify which CPU cores a process can run on (see Figure 13-12). You probably won't need to touch affinity; the most likely reason you would need to do so is a situation in which you have some processes (perhaps older programs that are not well designed for multicore systems) that need to be separated from others.

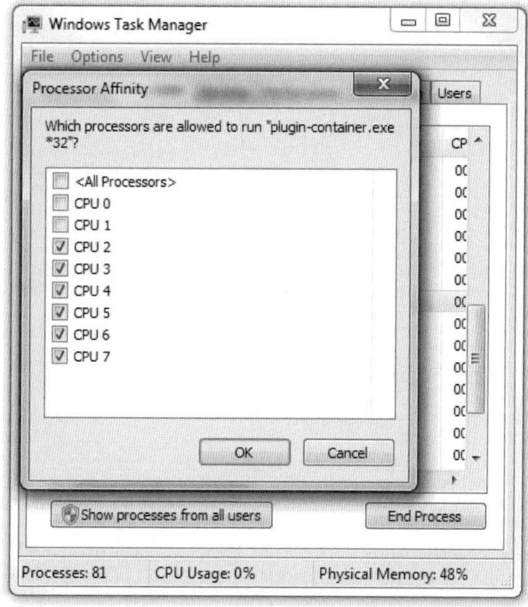

Figure 13-12 Turning off affinity to the first two cores

The Properties option isn't too exciting. It's the same as if you were to right-click on the executable file and select Properties in Windows Explorer (Windows 7). Finally, the Go to Service(s) option will move you to the Services tab of the Task Manager, showing you any and all services associated with the process. Depending on the process, it could use no services or multiple services. This is a great tool for those "Program won't start because associated services aren't running" situations. Figure 13-13 shows what happens when you use Go to Services for a process called LSASS.EXE.

Let's get back to the End Process Tree option. It's very common for a single process to be dependent on other processes (or for a process to start other processes). This creates a tree of dependencies. Sadly, the Task Manager doesn't give you any clue as to what processes depend on other processes, but it still gives you the option to End Process Tree, which ends not only the process, but any process it depends on. At first glance, this is scary since it's very common for many processes to depend on one important process. Microsoft makes this less scary, as it will not let you kill a process tree for the most important system processes.

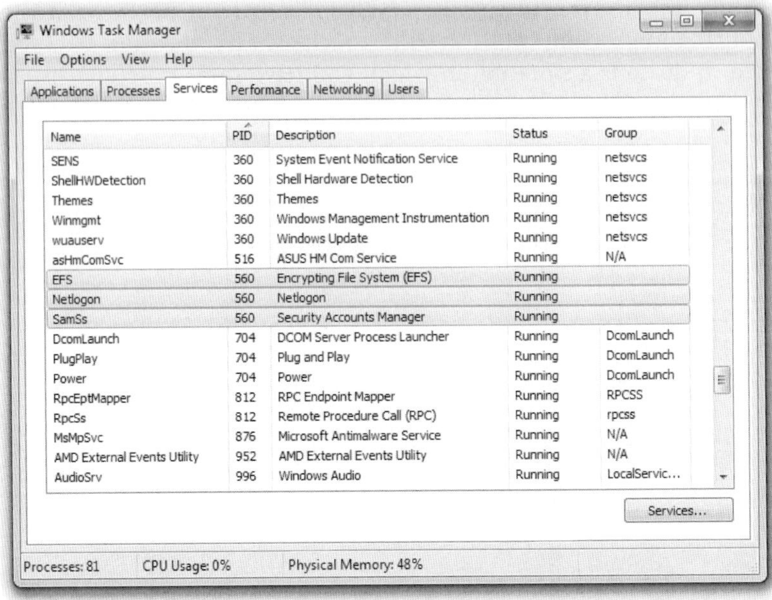

Figure 13-13 Services associated with the LSASS.EXE process

Even so, it would be nice to actually *see* what processes you're about to kill, wouldn't it? That's when the popular (and free) Process Explorer, written by Mark Russinovitch, is your go-to tool (see Figure 13-14).

Figure 13-14 Process Explorer

Think of Process Explorer as the Task Manager on steroids. It's very powerful, and a lot of techs use it instead of the Task Manager. It isn't on the CompTIA A+ exams, but it should be. Instead of just listing all of the processes, Process Explorer uses a tree structure so you can see all the dependencies.

NOTE Process Explorer does so much more than just show a tree structure. Download a copy and play with it. You'll see why it's so popular.

Services You can use the *Services* tab in the Task Manager to work with services directly (see Figure 13-15). Here, you can stop or start services, and you can go to the associated process.

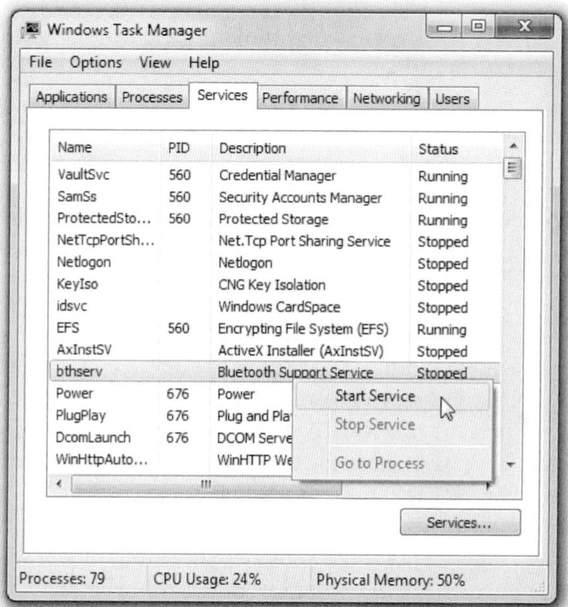

Figure 13-15 Services tab in Task Manager

The best way to see services in action is to use the Services Control Panel applet. To open it, click on the Services button at the bottom of the Services tab in the Task Manager or open Services in Administrative Tools. Figure 13-16 shows the Services applet running in Windows 7.

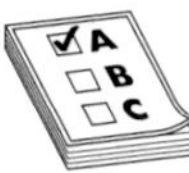

EXAM TIP You can open the Services applet from the Start | Search bar. Type **services.msc** and press ENTER. Like many other tools, you can also access Services from a Microsoft Management Console (MMC), adding it as a custom snap in. Type **mmc** and press ENTER.

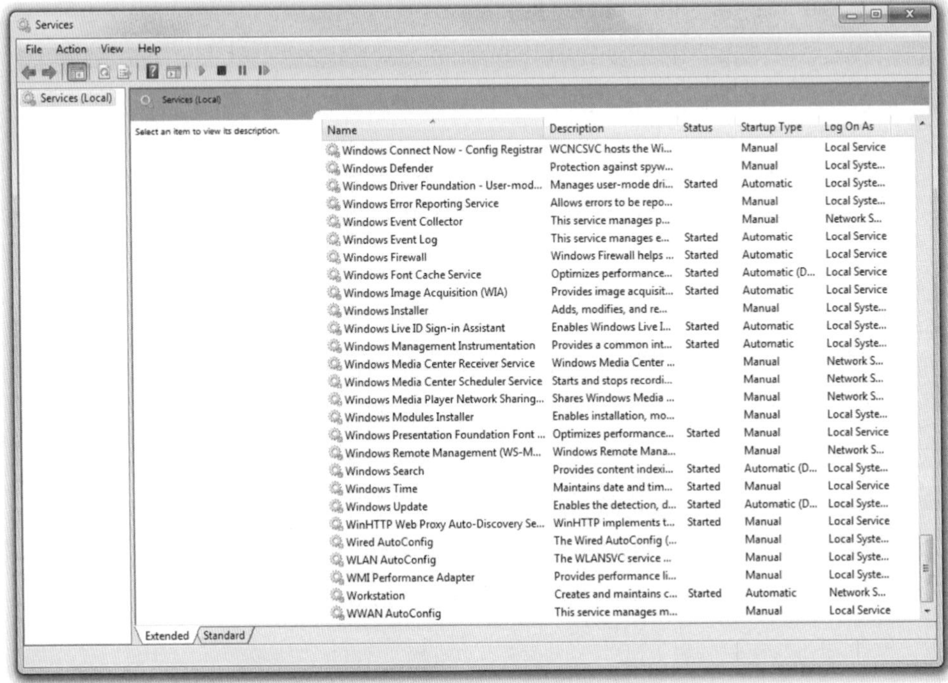

Figure 13-16 Services applet

Look closely at Figure 13-16. Each line in this applet is an individual service. Services don't have their own window, so you use the Services applet to start, stop, and configure them. You can see if a service is running by reading the Status column. To configure a service, right-click on the service name. The context menu enables you to start, stop, pause, resume, or restart any service. Click on Properties to see a dialog box similar to the one shown in Figure 13-17.

Of the four tabs you see in the Properties dialog box, General and Recovery are by far the most used. The General tab provides the name of the service, describes the service, and enables you to stop, start, pause, or resume the service. You can also define how the service starts: Manual (you go here to start it), Automatic (starts at beginning of Windows boot), Disabled (prevents the service from starting in any fashion), or Automatic (delayed start), which starts the service at boot but only after pretty much everything else has started.

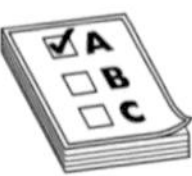

EXAM TIP You can start any service at a command prompt by typing **net start <service name>**. Likewise, you can stop a running service by typing **net stop <service name>**. You need to know the net command for the 901 exam. Just thought I'd slip a reference into this otherwise thoroughly 902 discussion.

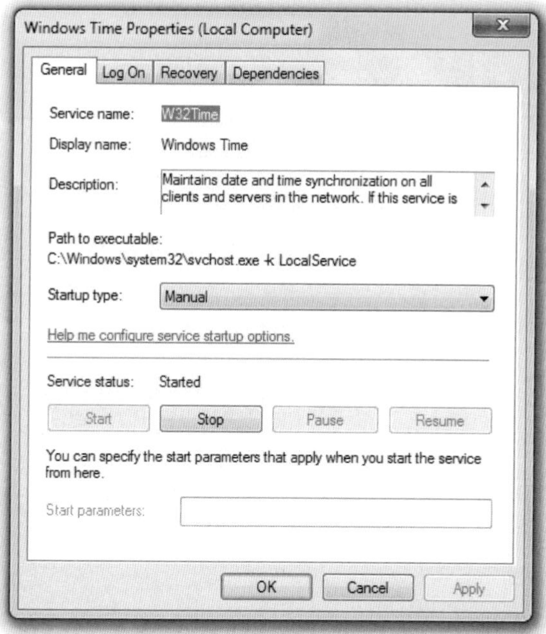

Figure 13-17 Service Properties dialog box

Performance For optimization purposes, the Task Manager is a great tool for investigating how hard your RAM and CPU are working at any given moment and why. Click the *Performance* tab to reveal a handy screen with the most commonly used information: CPU usage, available physical memory, size of the disk cache, and other details about memory and processes. Figure 13-18 shows a system with an eight-core processor, which is why you see eight graphs under CPU Usage History. A system with a single-core processor would have a single screen.

Not only does the Task Manager tell you how much CPU and RAM usage is taking place, it also tells you what program is using those resources. Let's say your system is running slowly. You open the Task Manager and see that your CPU usage is at 100 percent. You then click on the Processes tab to see all the processes running on your system. Click on the CPU column heading to sort all processes by CPU usage to see who's hogging the CPU (see Figure 13-19). If necessary, shut down the program or change its priority to fix the issue.

Networking and Users The other two tabs in the Task Manager, Networking and Users, enable you to see network use at a glance and see which users' accounts are currently logged on to the local machine. The Networking tab is a good first spot to look if you think the computer is running slowly on the network. If there's little activity displayed, then it's not traffic from your computer that's causing the slowdown, so you need to look elsewhere. Chapter 21, "Local Area Networking," covers network troubleshooting in a lot more detail, so we'll leave the Networking tab alone for now.

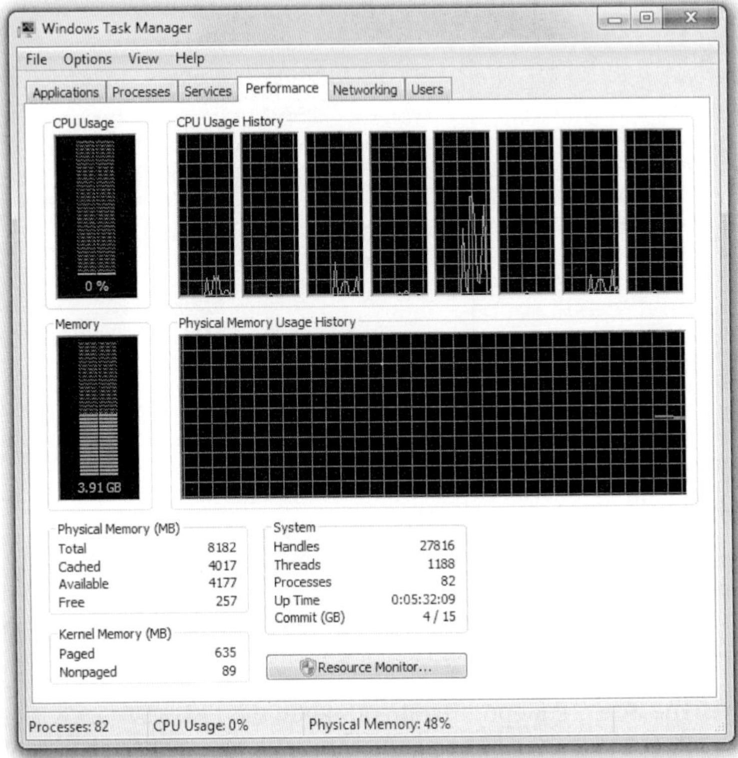

Figure 13-18 Task Manager Performance tab

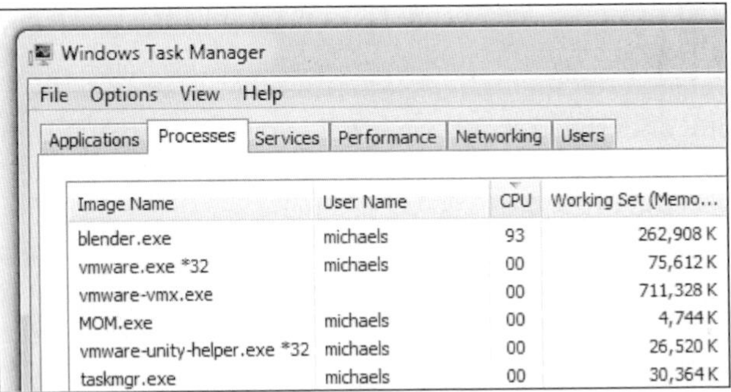

Figure 13-19 CPU usage

The Users tab enables you to log off other users if you have the proper permissions. You can also log off from here. There's not much else to say, but since the CompTIA A+ 220-902 exam may use the tab in a scenario, here's one hypothetical. Another user is still logged on and left a critical file open that you need to access. Logging the user off forces his or her applications to close and makes the file available. Of course, unsaved changes will be lost, so use caution here.

Task Manager in Windows 8/8.1/10

Now that you know a little about the Task Manager in the days before Windows 8, let's look at how the significant update it received has shuffled things around and improved its usefulness. The latest Task Manager has a new *Fewer details* view (see Figure 13-20) with a dead-simple interface for seeing and terminating running programs. For some users, this is all they'll ever need—and as a tech you need to be aware that not all users will be looking at the *More details* view by default when they open the Task Manager. Once you click More details, the Task Manager will start to look much more familiar, but don't let that trick you—a lot has changed. Let's take a moment to go over the biggest changes.

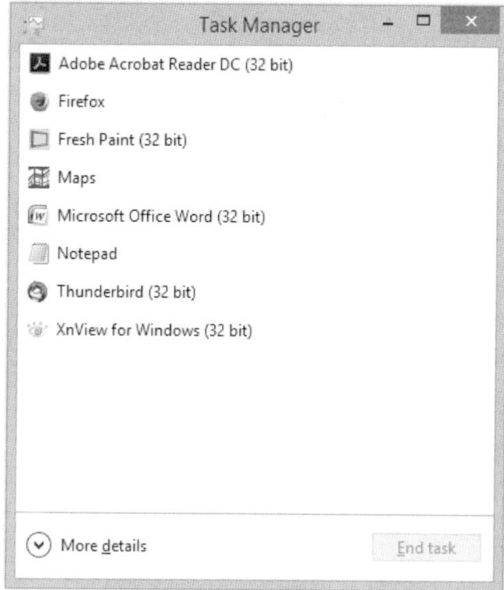

Figure 13-20 Fewer details view in Windows 8 Task Manager

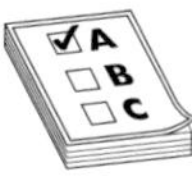

EXAM TIP While you can still open Task Manager by pressing CTRL-SHIFT-ESC, you can also right-click Start and select Task Manager from the context menu.

The new Task Manager no longer opens on the simple Applications tab; instead it opens on a much-changed Processes tab (see Figure 13-21). While the Performance, Services, and Users tabs all still exist, the Networking tab has been merged into the Performance tab (along with other new data). Finally, the Task Manager gains three new tabs: App history, Startup, and Details. There are also some huge usability improvements in this update, like the ability to simply right-click on column headers (well, on most of the tabs) to select which columns are enabled, and a Search online option any time you right-click on a process or service. Let's look at each tab.

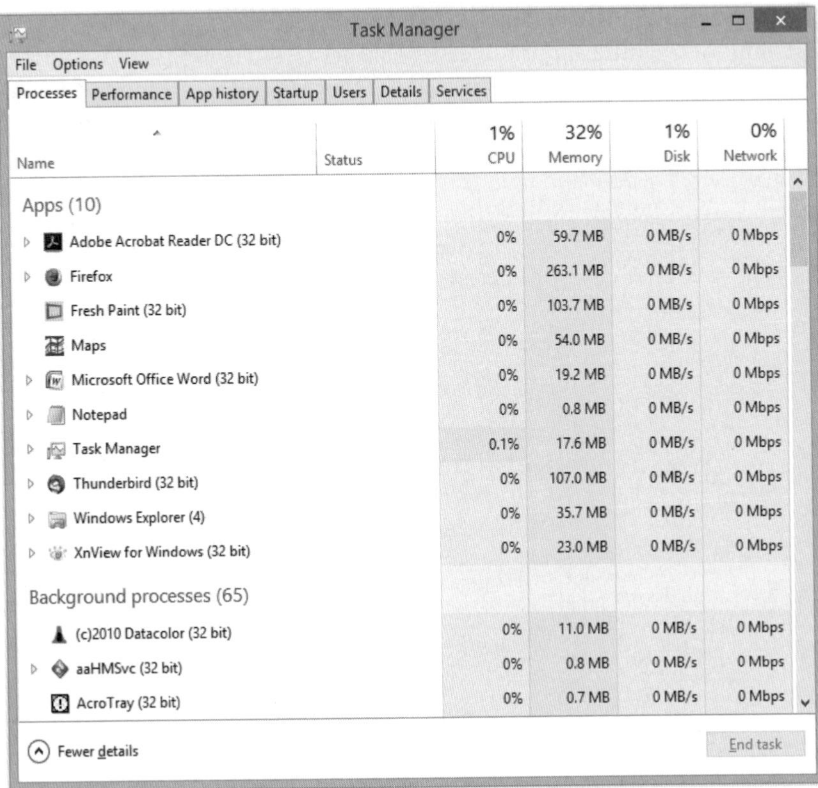

Figure 13-21 Processes tab in detailed Windows 8 Task Manager

Processes You might've noticed that the Fewer details view previously discussed looks a lot like a pared-down version of the older Task Manager Applications tab. The rest of the former Applications tab is best thought of as having been merged with Processes. In detailed mode, you might also notice that Processes is now broken down into three sections: Apps, Background processes, and Windows processes.

NOTE These three categories are only visible when the processes are sorted by name.

Beyond these changes to reorganize the Processes tab, there's also a philosophical shift in what the Processes tab is trying to communicate. Before Windows 8, the Processes tab listed the executable, user, CPU/memory use, and a description of the process (don't

worry, these values have moved to the new Details tab, which we'll discuss in a moment). Now by default the Processes tab lists a process description, its status, and its resource use, including CPU, Memory, Disk I/O, and Network I/O. These resource values are color-coded to make problems easy to spot, and you can change the enabled columns by right-clicking on a column header.

Much like the information given has changed, the context menu (see Figure 13-22) has a different focus. Most of the advanced options (End Process Tree, UAC Virtualization, Set Priority, Set Affinity, Go to Service[s]) have also moved to the context menu of the Details tab, and are replaced by some simpler options for expanding the process group, specifying whether resource use is reported as a percentage, going to the Details entry for this process, and searching for information about this process online.

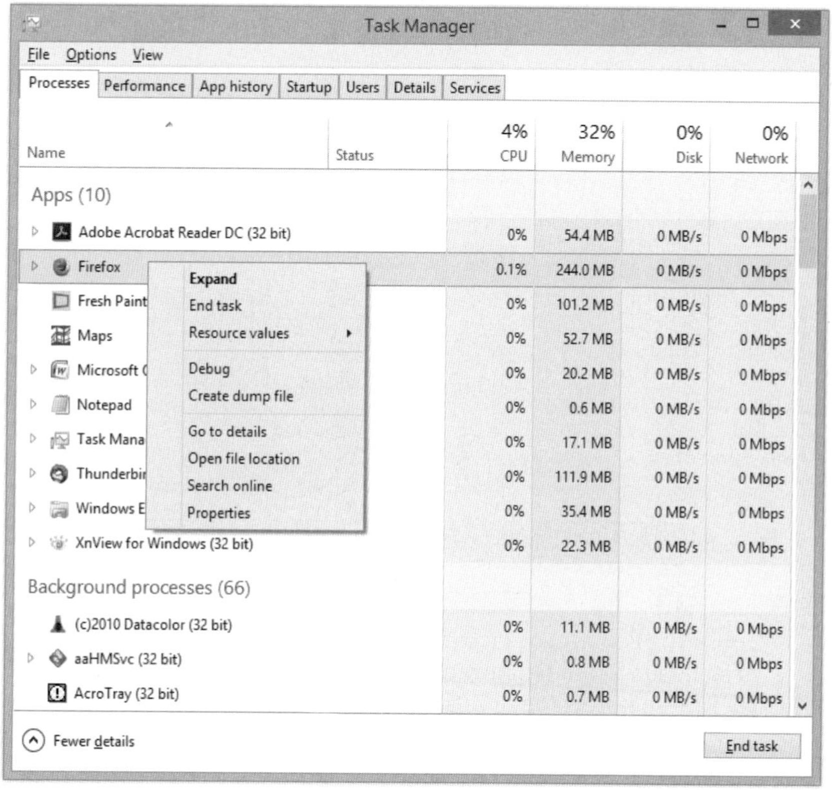

Figure 13-22 Processes tab context menu in Windows 8 Task Manager

Performance The spirit of the Performance tab (see Figure 13-23) is intact from the earlier Task Manager, and the update has made it both easier on the eyes and quite a bit better at its job. The Networking tab has been folded in with Performance, and Disk I/O

has been added as well. The result is that there's now one simple place to view all of your major performance metrics—CPU, memory, disk and network—at once.

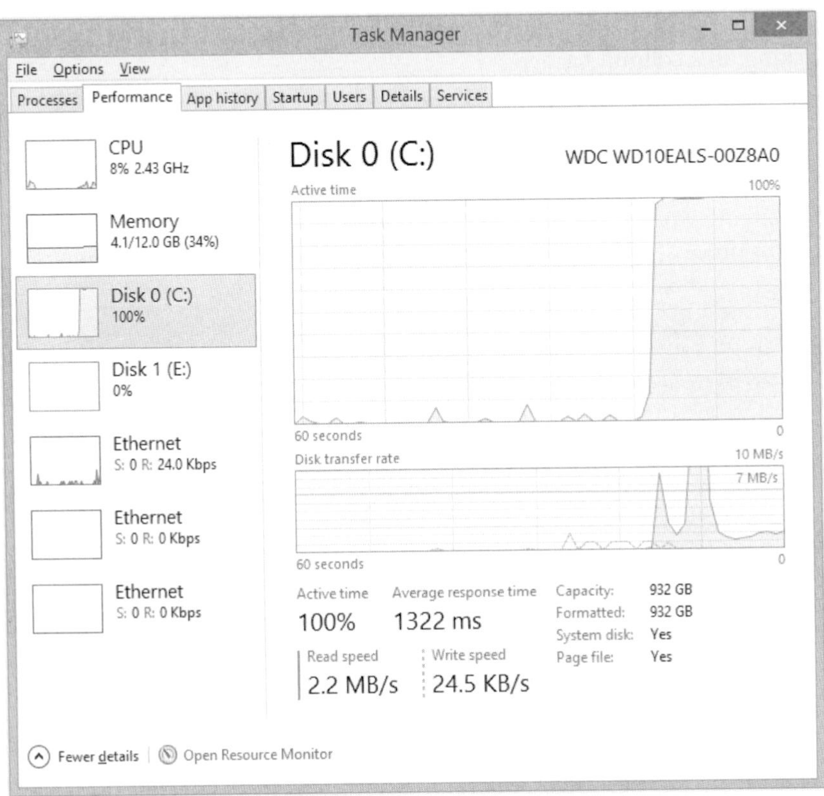

Figure 13-23 Performance tab in Windows 8 Task Manager showing a very active Disk 0

NOTE The Performance tab provides a graph of overall CPU utilization by default, but you can right-click on the graph and choose Change graph to | Logical processors to see each processor's graph.

App history When it comes to identifying resource-hungry programs, the resource consumption of a program right this second is often less important than its usage over time. The new Task Manager has an App history tab (see Figure 13-24) that collects recent statistics on CPU time and network usage. If you look at the list when you first

click on this tab, you'll notice it's not showing history for all processes; you can click Options and select *Show history for all processes* to see a more comprehensive list. Above the list is a sentence stating when the current data begins, and a chance to clear the current data by clicking Delete usage history.

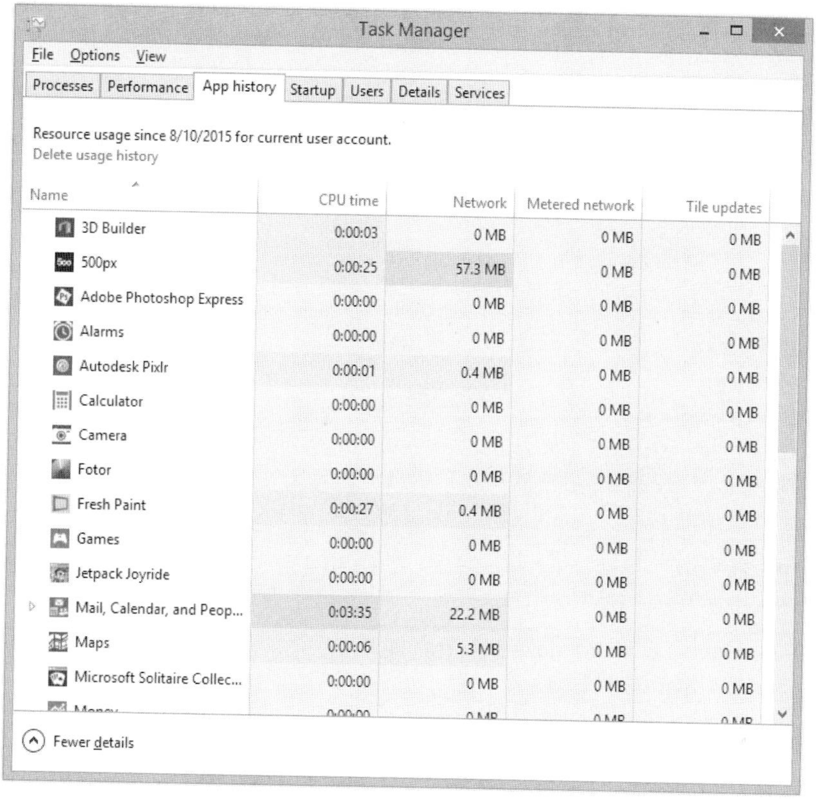

Task Manager

File Options View

Processes | Performance | App history | Startup | Users | Details | Services

Resource usage since 8/10/2015 for current user account.
Delete usage history

Name	CPU time	Network	Metered network	Tile updates
3D Builder	0:00:03	0 MB	0 MB	0 MB
500px	0:00:25	57.3 MB	0 MB	0 MB
Adobe Photoshop Express	0:00:00	0 MB	0 MB	0 MB
Alarms	0:00:00	0 MB	0 MB	0 MB
Autodesk Pixlr	0:00:01	0.4 MB	0 MB	0 MB
Calculator	0:00:00	0 MB	0 MB	0 MB
Camera	0:00:00	0 MB	0 MB	0 MB
Fotor	0:00:00	0 MB	0 MB	0 MB
Fresh Paint	0:00:27	0.4 MB	0 MB	0 MB
Games	0:00:00	0 MB	0 MB	0 MB
Jetpack Joyride	0:00:00	0 MB	0 MB	0 MB
Mail, Calendar, and Peop...	0:03:35	22.2 MB	0 MB	0 MB
Maps	0:00:06	5.3 MB	0 MB	0 MB
Microsoft Solitaire Collec...	0:00:00	0 MB	0 MB	0 MB

Fewer details

Figure 13-24 App history tab in Windows 8 Task Manager

Startup If you've used Windows for very long, you've almost inevitably had an undesired program open every time you load Windows. You might've been content to just close it every time, or uninstall the application altogether, but you also could've used the Startup tab in a utility called *msconfig* to specify programs you didn't want to load with Windows. In Windows 8 the Startup tab (see Figure 13-25) has finally been moved to its rightful place in the Task Manager, enabling you to both identify and disable rogue startup programs in the same place. It even has a Startup impact column that will help you identify which programs slow down your boot the most!

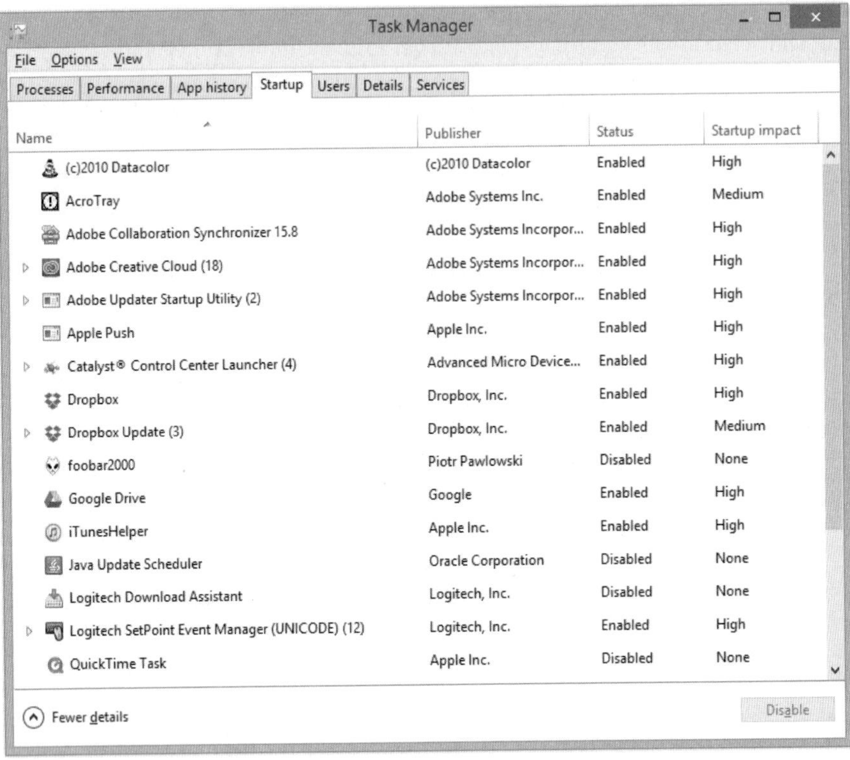

Figure 13-25 Startup tab in Windows 8 Task Manager

Users The Users tab (see Figure 13-26) allows most of the same basic functionality it used to—a place to see, disconnect, or log off connected users—but it also shows the programs running under a user's account and clearly indicates the associated resource use. This makes it easier to diagnose a system that is sluggish due to resources tied up by other logged-in users.

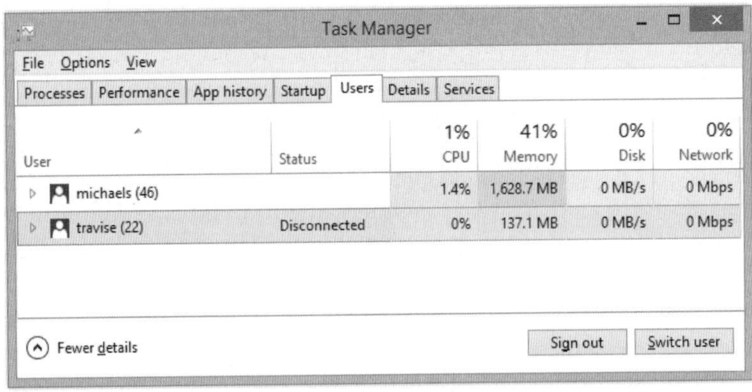

Figure 13-26 Users tab in Windows 8 Task Manager

Details As previously noted, the Details tab (see Figure 13-27) inherits most of the functionality removed from the old Processes tab. It lists your processes by executable name, and includes their PID, status, the user running them, CPU/memory use, and a description. If you right-click on any column header and choose Select columns, you can enable or disable a dizzying array of columns containing information about each running process. The context menu also introduces a debugging option called *Analyze wait chain* for identifying the cause of a frozen program.

Task Manager

File Options View

Processes | Performance | App history | Startup | Users | Details | Services

Name	PID	Status	User name	CPU	Memory (p...	Description
aaHMSvc.exe	1628	Running	SYSTEM	00	876 K	aaHMSvc
AcroRd32.exe	35796	Running	michaels	00	4,280 K	Adobe Acroba...
AcroRd32.exe	23276	Running	michaels	00	55,804 K	Adobe Acroba...
acrotray.exe	12752	Running	michaels	00	740 K	AcroTray
Adobe CEF Helper.exe	5820	Running	michaels	00	19,940 K	Adobe CEF He...
Adobe CEF Helper.exe	13420	Running	michaels	00	8,888 K	Adobe CEF He...
Adobe Desktop Servi...	32428	Running	michaels	00	16,876 K	Creative Cloud
AdobeIPCBroker.exe	14004	Running	michaels	00	1,960 K	Adobe IPC Br...
AdobeUpdateService...	1504	Running	SYSTEM	00	432 K	Adobe Update...
AppleMobileDeviceS...	1572	Running	SYSTEM	00	1,304 K	MobileDevice...
armsvc.exe	1472	Running	SYSTEM	00	344 K	Adobe Acroba...
atieclxx.exe	36584	Running	SYSTEM	00	984 K	AMD External ...
atiesrxx.exe	840	Running	SYSTEM	00	548 K	AMD External ...
audiodg.exe	30692	Running	LOCAL SE...	00	3,336 K	Windows Aud...
CCC.exe	37536	Running	michaels	00	15,496 K	Catalyst Contr...
CoreSync.exe	36984	Running	michaels	00	5,240 K	Core Sync
Creative Cloud.exe	27400	Running	michaels	00	23,260 K	Adobe Creativ...
csrss.exe	436	Running	SYSTEM	00	1,968 K	Client Server R...
csrss.exe	35724	Running	SYSTEM	00	1,796 K	Client Server R...
dasHost.exe	1908	Running	LOCAL SE...	00	1,908 K	Device Associ...
dbserv.exe	3516	Running	SYSTEM	00	360 K	Symantec Gh...
Dropbox.exe	23192	Running	michaels	00	129,504 K	Dropbox

Fewer details | End task

Figure 13-27 Details tab in Windows 8 Task Manager

Services The Services tab (see Figure 13-28) itself is virtually unchanged, aside from the cosmetic update; the same columns appear in the same order. Still, if you right-click on a service, there are a few nice usability tweaks, including the *Search online* option for investigating unknown services, and an option to restart a service with a single click (instead of only stopping it, and then starting it).

The tasklist and taskkill Commands

The two command-line utilities *tasklist* and *taskkill* enable you to work with tasks, similarly to what you can do with the Task Manager. Here is a scenario I ran into recently: I was looking at the log files from a server that was having some security problems, and

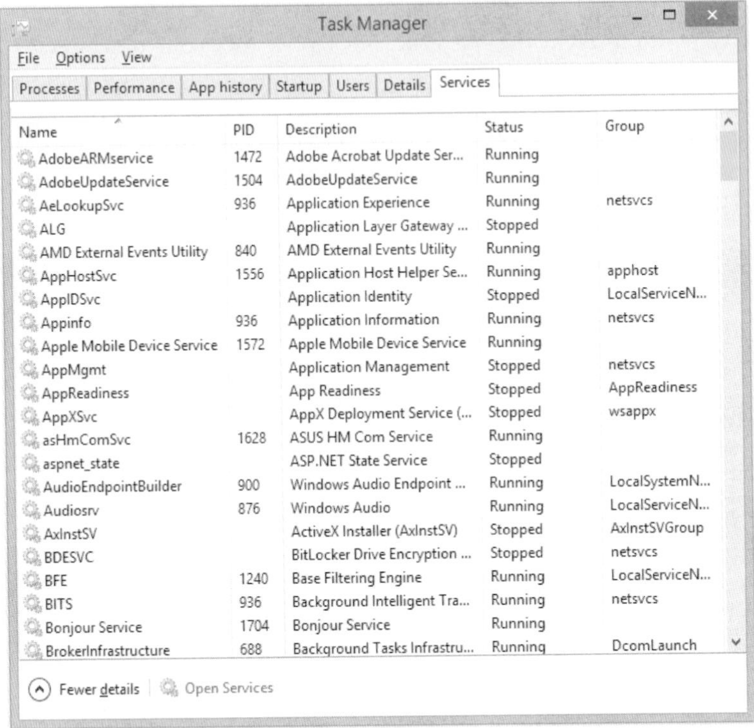

Figure 13-28 Services tab in Windows 8 Task Manager

I attempted to open one of the logs in Notepad. What I failed to notice was the size of the file, 300 MB! A bit bigger than Notepad was designed to handle, and this caused Notepad to promptly freeze. Because I was already in the command line, I decided to take advantage of a couple of useful commands to quickly kill my frozen Notepad.

The first command I used was tasklist, which enables you to view running processes on a local or remote system. Open up a command prompt and type **tasklist**. The following is a partial example of the output:

```
C:\Users\mike>tasklist

Image Name                     PID Session Name        Session#    Mem Usage
========================= ======== ================ =========== ============
System Idle Process              0 Services                   0         24 K
System                           4 Services                   0        940 K
smss.exe                       268 Services                   0        340 K
csrss.exe                      372 Services                   0      2,388 K
wininit.exe                    444 Services                   0        968 K
csrss.exe                      452 Console                    1      9,788 K
winlogon.exe                   500 Console                    1      2,420 K
services.exe                   544 Services                   0      4,536 K
svchost.exe                    756 Services                   0      4,320 K
atiesrxx.exe                   904 Services                   0        824 K
notepad.exe                   3932 Console                    1    584,868 K
```

Once I found Notepad's PID, I was ready to kill it with the taskkill command. See the memory-hungry notepad.exe in the preceding tasklist output? You can kill the process using either the name or the PID. I'm using Notepad's PID in this example along with the force flag (/f) to make sure Windows actually closes Notepad, instead of just asking it nicely. This is necessary when dealing with frozen apps like my log-jammed Notepad.

```
C:\>taskkill /f /pid 3932
SUCCESS: The process "notepad.exe" with PID 3932 has been terminated.
```

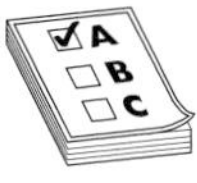

EXAM TIP You can use the *kill* command in the Windows PowerShell command-line environment to stop a running process. Kill is actually an alias for the Stop-Process cmdlet, although you don't need to know that for the exam. See Chapter 16 for a more in-depth discussion of working with the command line and PowerShell.

Performance Tools

The Task Manager is good for identifying current problems, but what about problems that happen when you're not around? What if your system is always running at a CPU utilization of 20 percent—is that good or bad? Windows comes with tools to log resource usage so you can track metrics such as CPU and RAM usage over time. In Windows Vista this was called *Reliability and Performance Monitor*, but starting with Windows 7 Microsoft pulled out the Reliability tool to make the remaining *Performance Monitor* tool smaller and tighter.

You can find Reliability and Performance Monitor/Performance Monitor in the Administrative Tools applet in Control Panel. You can also open the tool by going to Start | Search, typing **perfmon.msc**, and pressing ENTER.

Reliability and Performance Monitor in Windows Vista opens to a Resource Overview screen (see Figure 13-29). Think of the Resource Overview as an advanced Task Manager, giving details on CPU, hard drive, network, and memory usage.

When you click on one of the four bars, you get details on exactly which processes are using those resources—a powerful tool when you suspect a program might be hogging something! Figure 13-30 shows the Network bar opened to reveal the processes using the network and how much data each is sending.

NOTE The Reliability Monitor tool gives you an overview of how a system has behaved over time, showing important events such as application or OS crashes. You can find the tool in Windows 7 and later as part of the Action Center Control Panel applet.

Performance Monitor opens to a more modest screen that displays some text about Performance Monitor and a System Summary (see Figure 13-31). You can get to the Overview screen by clicking the Open Resource Monitor link on the main screen. Aside from orienting the graphical screens on the right rather than on the top, the tool is the same as the Resource Overview in Windows Vista (see Figure 13-32).

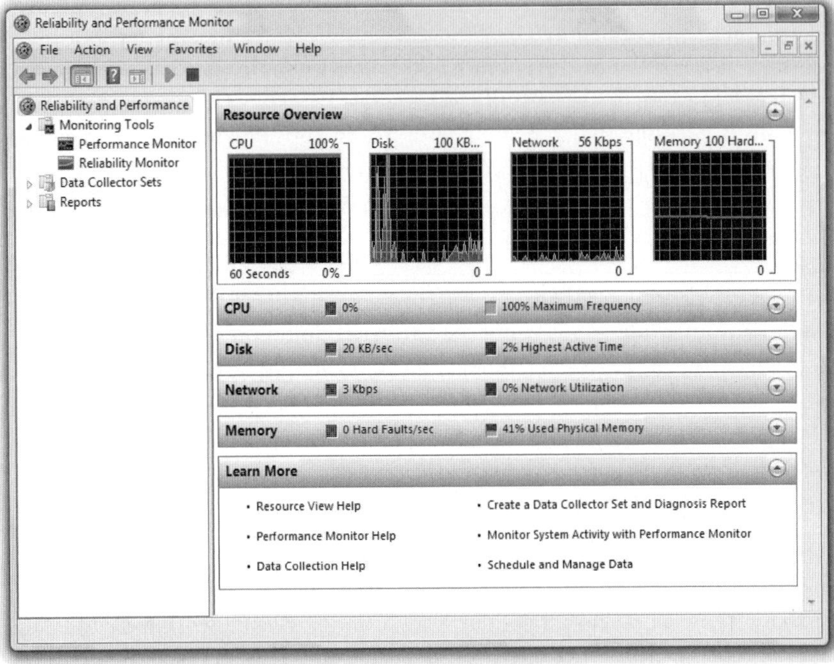

Figure 13-29 Resource Overview in Windows Vista

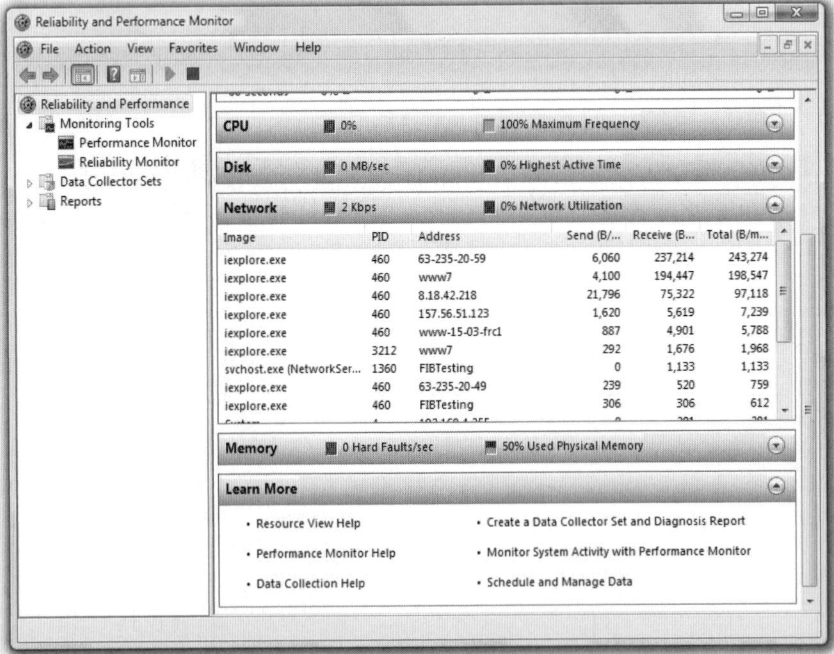

Figure 13-30 Network bar in Resource Overview

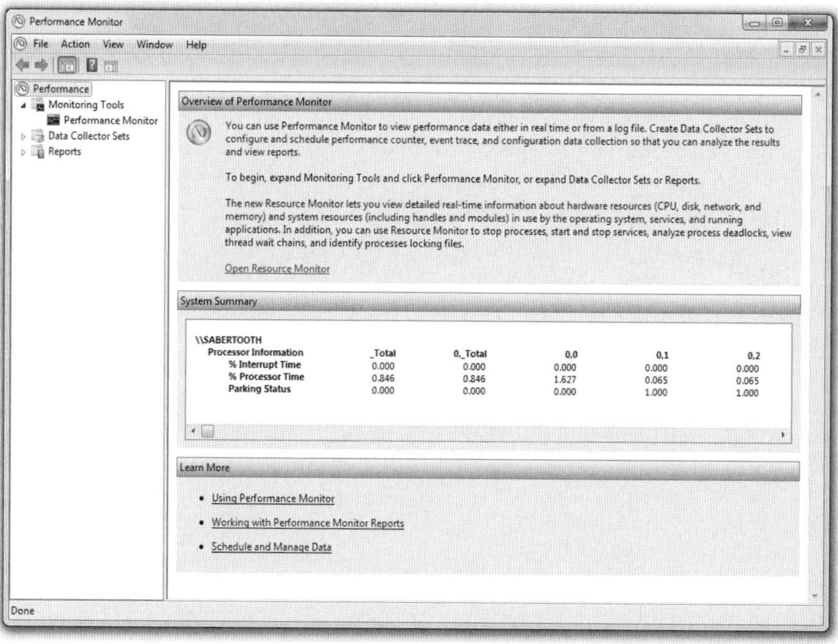

Figure 13-31 Initial Performance Monitor screen in Windows 7

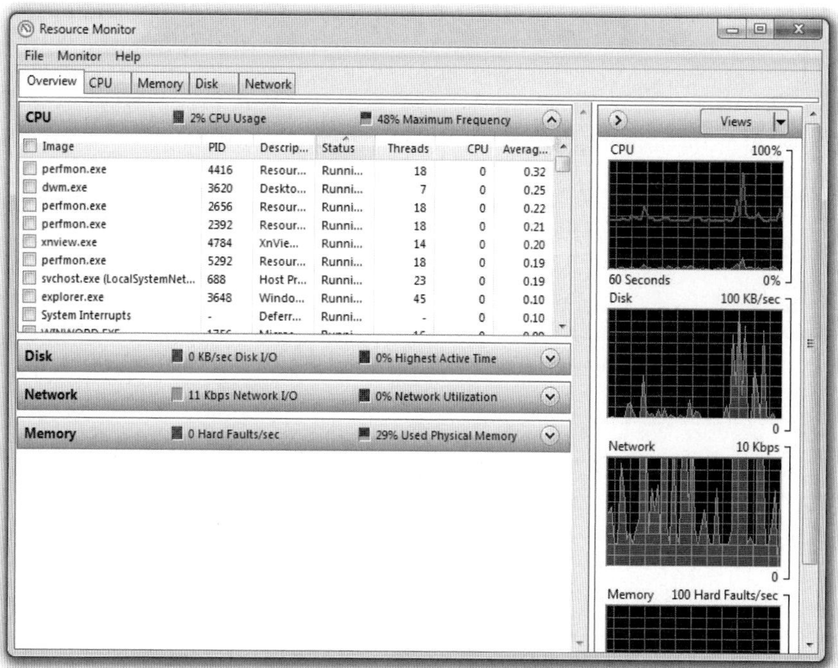

Figure 13-32 Resource Monitor displaying CPU usage

Objects and Counters

Before working with Performance Monitor, you need to understand two terms: object and counter. An *object* is a system component that is given a set of characteristics and can be managed by the operating system as a single entity. A *counter* tracks specific information about an object. For example, the Processor object has a counter, %Processor Time, that tracks the percentage of elapsed time the processor uses to execute a non-idle thread. Many counters can be associated with an object.

Working with the Tools

Performance Monitor gathers real-time data on objects such as memory, physical disk, processor, and network, and displays this data as a graph (line graph), histogram (bar graph), or simple report. When you first open it, Performance Monitor shows data in graph form. The data displayed is from the set of counters listed below the chart. If you want to add counters, click the Add button (the one that looks like a plus sign) or press CTRL-I to open the Add Counters dialog box. Click the Performance object drop-down list and select one of the many different objects you can monitor. The Add Counters dialog box includes a helpful feature: you can select a counter and click on the Explain button to learn about the counter, as shown in Figure 13-33. Try that now.

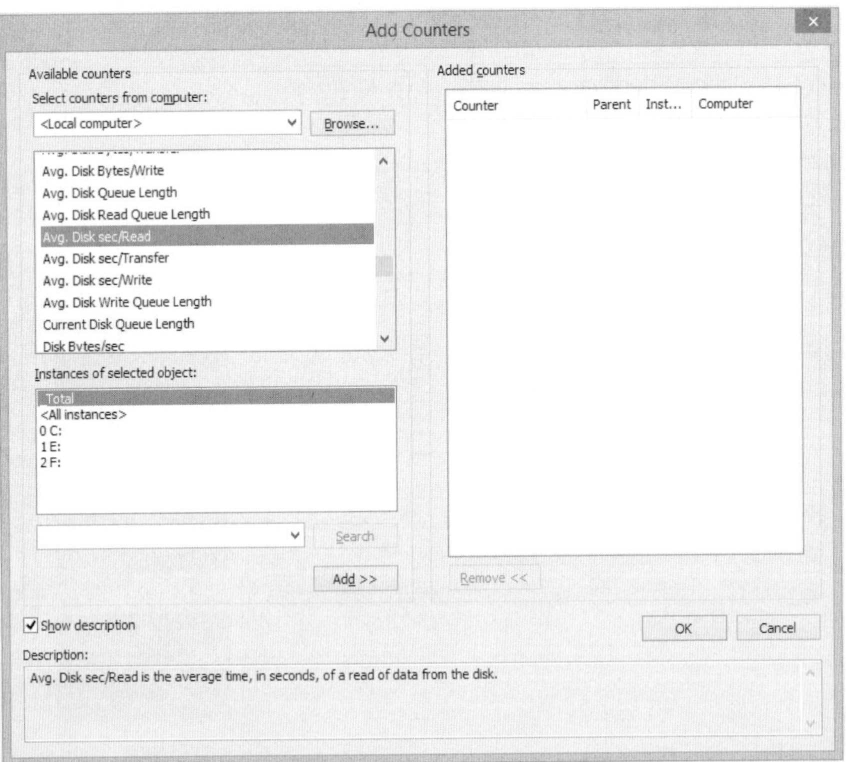

Figure 13-33 Add Counters dialog box

Even with just three counters selected, the graph can get a little busy. That's where one of my favorite Performance Monitor features shines. If you want the line of charted data from just one counter to stand out, select the counter in the list below the graph and then press CTRL-H. See how this trick makes the Bytes Received/sec line stand out in Figure 13-34? Imagine how useful that is when you are monitoring a dozen counters.

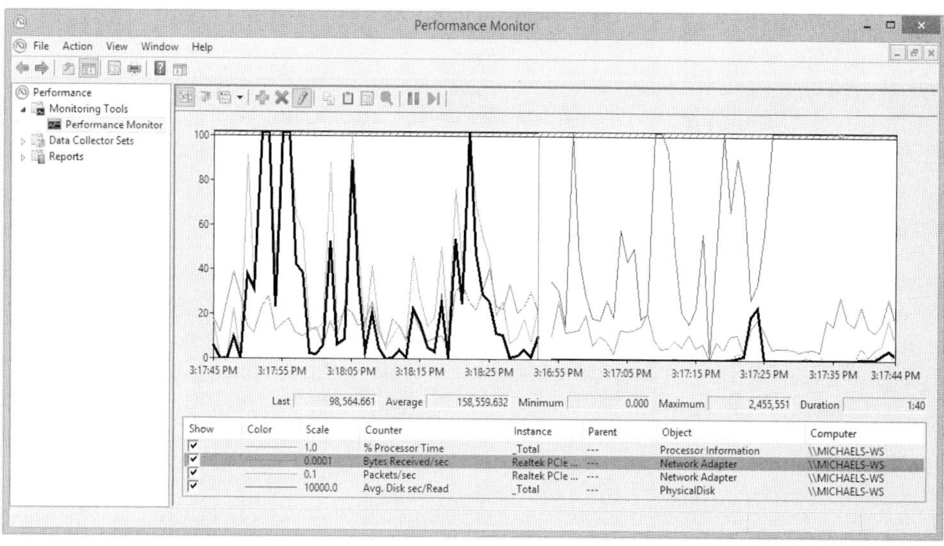

Figure 13-34 Pressing CTRL-H makes one set of data stand out.

Data Collector Sets

Microsoft included Data Collector Sets in Reliability and Performance Monitor and Performance Monitor, groupings of counters you can use to make reports. You can make your own Data Collector Sets (User Defined), or you can just grab one of the predefined system sets. Once you start a Data Collector Set, you can use the Reports option to see the results (see Figure 13-35). Data Collector Sets not only enable you to choose counter objects to track, but also enable you to schedule when you want them to run.

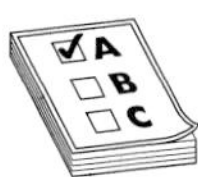

EXAM TIP The CompTIA A+ 902 exam won't ask too many detailed questions on either Performance Monitor or Reliability and Performance Monitor. That doesn't mean you can ignore these amazing tools! Make sure you understand that these tools give you the power to inspect anything happening on your system to help you diagnose problems.

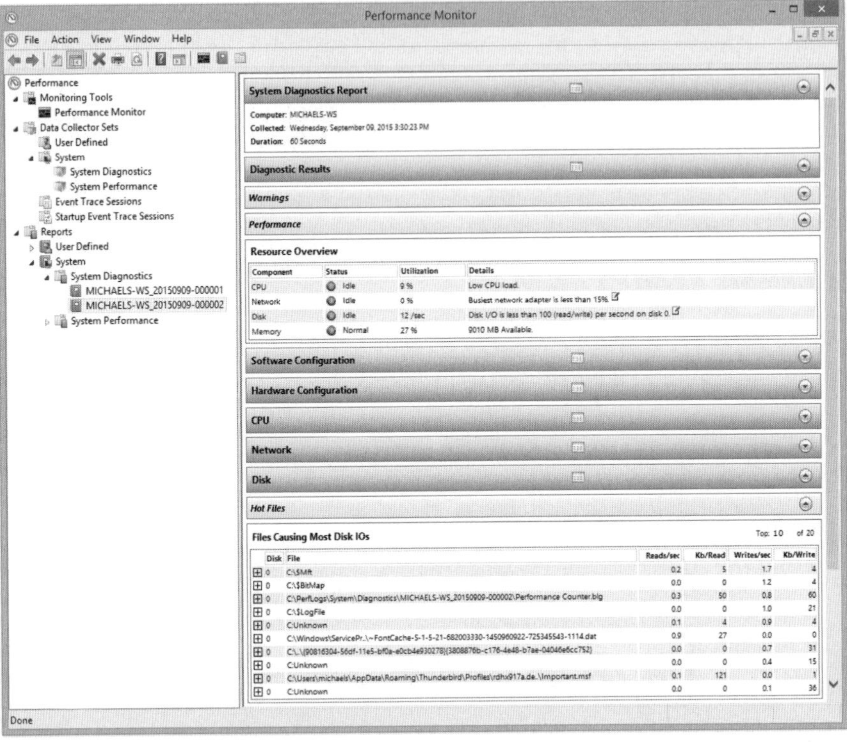

Figure 13-35 Sample report

Tools for Programmers

Microsoft provides an assortment of tools in Windows that go well beyond what techs typically need. Specifically, the CompTIA A+ 902 exam includes two such programmer-specific tools dealing with some low-level functionality in Windows that affects how a lot of applications are programmed. Read on to find out more about the Component Services and ODBC Data Sources applets, both found in Administrative Tools.

Component Services

To understand all that *Component Services* can do would require a huge amount of information—far greater than the scope of CompTIA's A+ exams. Simply put, as long as Windows has existed, Microsoft has come up with many tools (with names like COM, DCOM, and COM+) to enable programmers to share data objects (an element of programs) between applications on a single computer. Over time, this sharing was extended so that you could share objects between computers on a network.

In almost all cases, this object sharing doesn't require you to do anything more than install an application that uses these features. Component Services is there for those very rare times when something's either wrong or a programmer needs you to make manual changes (see Figure 13-36). If you have a company that creates in-house or buys custom applications, there's a better than good chance that you'll be firing up Component Services and working with programmers, manually installing programs, and tweaking those programs to get them to work the way you wish. Professional, third-party applications (the kind you buy in stores) should automatically configure any of these programs during the installation process, making it extremely rare that you'll need to go into Component Services.

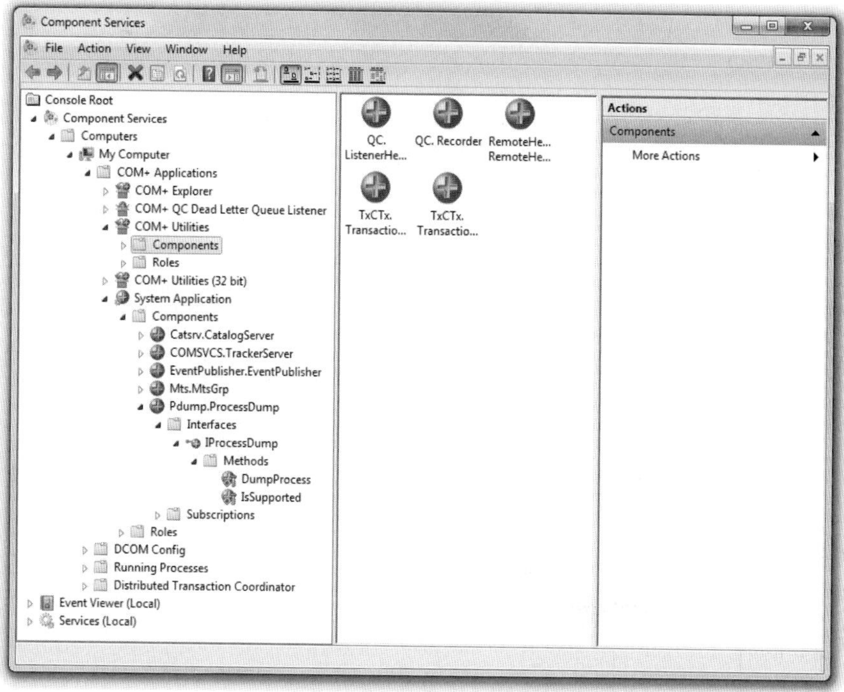

Figure 13-36 Component Services in Windows 7

Data Sources

One of the oldest and most common motivations to make networks is the idea of a number of computers accessing one or more shared databases. These computers might not all be running the same operating system, nor will they always use the same application to access those databases. That's where Open Database Connectivity (ODBC) really shines. ODBC is a coding standard that enables programmers to write databases and the applications that use them in a way that they can query ODBC on how to locate and access a database without any concern about what application or operating system is used.

Microsoft's tool to configure ODBC is called *ODBC Data Source Administrator* (see Figure 13-37). ODBC Data Source Administrator enables you to create and manage entries called Data Source Names (DSNs) that point OBDC to a database. DSNs are used by ODBC-aware applications to query ODBC to find their databases. Keep in mind that you'll rarely go into Data Source Administrator unless you're making your own shared databases.

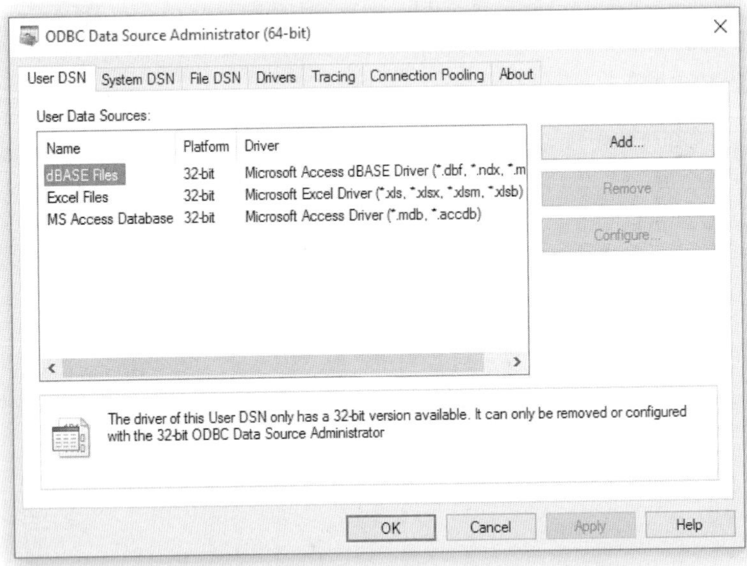

Figure 13-37 ODBC Data Source Administrator in Windows 8.1

The 64-bit versions of Windows offer both a 64-bit and a 32-bit version of the ODBC tool. The 64-bit tool is used on 64-bit databases and the 32-bit tool is used on 32-bit databases.

We'll talk a lot more about sharing resources over networks when we get to networking in depth in Chapter 21, "Local Area Networking."

Chapter Review

Questions

1. What is the name of the program that boots Windows?
   - **A.** regsvr32
   - **B.** msconfig
   - **C.** bootmgr
   - **D.** Registry

2. What is the name of the command-line version of the Task Manager?
   A. taskman
   B. tasklist
   C. taskkill
   D. tasks
3. Tim needs to register an important .DLL file as a command component in the Registry. What command-line tool should he use?
   A. regedt64
   B. regedt32
   C. regsvr32
   D. regmgr64
4. When using Performance Monitor, which settings are defined to track resource usage? (Select two.)
   A. Processes
   B. Objects
   C. Counters
   D. Values
5. Which of the following are organized inside the Registry's root keys? (Select two.)
   A. Subkeys
   B. Subfolders
   C. Values
   D. Objects
6. Which of the following root keys contains the data for a system's non-user-specific configurations?
   A. HKEY_LOCAL_MACHINE
   B. HKEY_USERS
   C. HKEY_CURRENT_USER
   D. HKEY_CLASSES_ROOT
7. Which of the following tools enables programmers to share objects between applications and computers?
   A. Task Manager
   B. Performance console
   C. bootmgr
   D. Component Services

8. Which of the following statements about booting Windows is true?
   - **A.** BIOS does not use bootmgr.
   - **B.** UEFI looks for the MBR, which finds the boot code that launches bootmgr.
   - **C.** BIOS looks for the MBR, which finds the boot code that launches bootmgr.
   - **D.** UEFI does not use bootmgr.
9. How do you open the Registry Editor from the command prompt? (Select two.)
   - **A.** regedit
   - **B.** regedt32
   - **C.** regeditor
   - **D.** rgstry
10. Sven calls the Help Desk to complain that a certain program (I won't name names here) has locked up. In such a scenario, which tool should Sven use to force the program to quit and how should he open the program?
    - **A.** Task Manager; press CTRL-SHIFT-ESC to open
    - **B.** Task Manager; press CTRL-T-M to open
    - **C.** Performance Monitor; open in Administrative Tools
    - **D.** Performance Monitor; press CTRL-P-M to open

Answers

1. **C.** On Windows machines, bootmgr is used to boot the operating system.
2. **B.** The tasklist command opens the command-line version of the Task Manager.
3. **C.** The regsvr32 command is used to register dynamic link library (DLL) files as command components in the Registry.
4. **B, C.** To track resource usage in Performance Monitor, you need to configure objects and counters.
5. **A, C.** The Registry's root keys are further organized into subkeys and values.
6. **A.** The system's non-user-specific configurations are stored in the HKEY_LOCAL_MACHINE root key of the Registry.
7. **D.** Component Services enables programmers to share objects between applications and computers.
8. **C.** When booting Windows, the BIOS looks for the MBR, which finds the boot code to launch the OS.
9. **A, B.** From the command prompt, you can use either regedit or regedt32 to open the Registry Editor.
10. **A.** Task Manager is the tool you need to force a program closed in Windows. The easiest way to access the tool is to press CTRL-SHIFT-ESC simultaneously.

CHAPTER 14

Users, Groups, and Permissions

In this chapter, you will learn how to

- Create and administer Windows users and groups
- Define and use NTFS permissions for authorization
- Share a Windows computer securely
- Secure PCs with User Account Control

Through the combination of user accounts, groups, and NTFS permissions, Windows provides incredibly powerful file and folder security. This user/group/NTFS combination scales from a single computer up to a network of computers spanning the world.

When learning about users, groups, and NTFS permissions, it's helpful to think about a single PC. To that end, this chapter focuses on Windows security from the point of view of a single, or *standalone*, machine. Chapter 21, "Local Area Networking," takes over where this chapter stops and will revisit these topics in more detail and show you how the same tools scale up to help you protect a computer in a networked environment.

This chapter begins by examining user accounts, passwords, and groups, then turns to the high level of granular security afforded by NTFS. The third section describes methods for sharing and accessing shared content. The chapter wraps with a look under the hood at User Account Control.

902

Authentication with Users and Groups

Security begins with a *user account*, a unique combination of a user name and an associated password, stored in some database on your computer, that grants the user access to the system. Although we normally assign a user account to a human user, user accounts are also assigned to everything that runs programs on your computer. For example, every Windows system has a SYSTEM account that Windows uses when it runs programs. Two mechanisms enable user account security: authentication and authorization.

Authentication is the process of identifying and granting access to some user, usually a person, who is trying to access a system. In Windows, authentication is most commonly handled by a password-protected user account. The process of logging into a system is where the user types in an active user name and password.

NOTE Authentication is the process of giving a user access to a system. Authorization is how we determine what an authenticated user can do to a system.

Once a user authenticates, he or she needs *authorization*: the process that defines what resources an authenticated user may access and what he or she may do with those resources. Authorization for Windows' files and folders is controlled by the NTFS file system, which assigns permissions to users and groups. These permissions define exactly what users may do to a resource on the system. Let's start with authentication.

User Accounts

Every user account has a user name and a password (although that password may be blank). A user name is a text string that identifies the user account assigned to a system. Three examples of possible user names are "Mike1" or "john.smith" or "some.person@somedomain.com." Associated with every user name is a password: a unique key known only by the system and the person using that user name. This user name and password are encrypted on the system—and only those with a user name and password are allowed access to the system via the login process.

Every Windows system stores the user accounts as an encrypted database of user names and passwords. Windows calls each record in this database a *local user account*. If you don't have a local user account created on a particular Windows system, you won't be able to log on to that computer (see Figure 14-1).

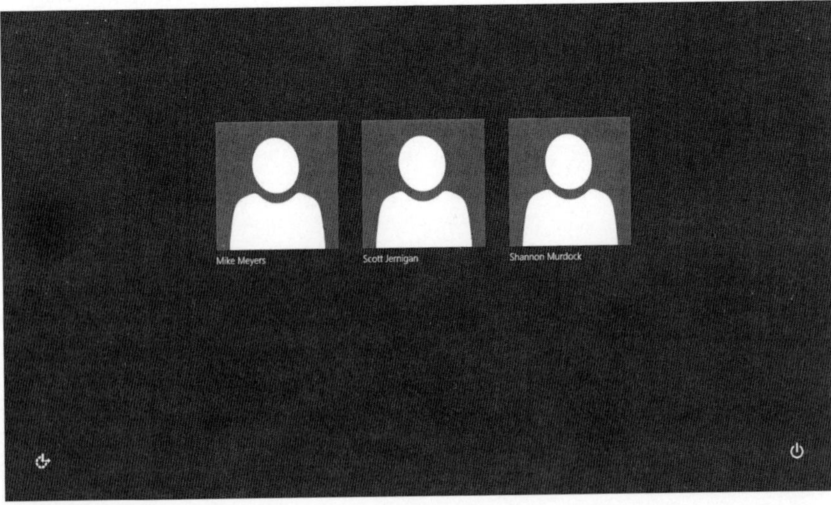

Figure 14-1 Windows logon screen

Creating a user account generates a number of folders on a computer. In Windows, for example, each user account gets unique personal folders, such as Documents, Desktop, Pictures, Music, and more. By default, only a person logged in as a specific user can access the personal folders for that user account. So the next step is to secure that user account.

Passwords

Passwords help secure user accounts. If someone learns your user name and password, he or she can log on to your computer. Even if the user account has only limited permissions—perhaps it can only read files, not edit them—you still have a security breach.

Make your users choose good passwords. I once attended a security seminar, and the speaker had everyone stand up. She then began to ask questions about our passwords—if we responded yes to the question, we were to sit down. She began to ask questions such as

"Do you use the name of your spouse as a password?"

and

"Do you use your pet's name?"

By the time she had asked about 15 questions, only 6 people out of some 300 were still standing. The reality is that most of us choose passwords that are amazingly easy to hack. Make sure users have a *strong password*: at least eight characters in length, including letters, numbers, and punctuation symbols.

Using non-alphanumeric characters makes any password much more difficult to crack, for two reasons. First, adding non-alphanumeric characters forces the hacker to consider many more possible characters than just letters and numbers. Second, most password crackers use a combination of common words and numbers to hack passwords.

Because non-alphanumeric characters don't fit into common words or numbers, a character such as an exclamation point defeats these common-word hacks. Not all systems allow you to use characters such as @, $, %, or \, however, so you need to experiment.

CompTIA also recommends that you should have users change passwords at regular intervals; this can be enforced with a *password expiration* policy that forces users to select a new password periodically. Although this concept sounds good on paper, it is a hard policy to maintain in the real world. For starters, users tend to forget passwords when they change a lot. This can lead to an even bigger security problem because users start writing passwords down.

If your organization forces you to change passwords often, one way to remember the password is to use a numbering system. I worked at a company that required me to change my password at the beginning of each month, so I did something very simple. I took a root password—let's say it was "m3y3rs5"—and simply added a number to the end representing the current month. So when June rolled around, for example, I would change my password to "m3y3rs56." It worked pretty well.

NOTE Every secure organization sets up various security policies and procedures to ensure that security is maintained. Windows has various mechanisms to implement such things as requiring a strong password, for example. Chapter 28, "Securing Computers," goes into detail about setting up Local Policies and Group Policy.

Windows enables you to create a password hint for your accounts. This clue appears after your first logon attempt fails (see Figure 14-2).

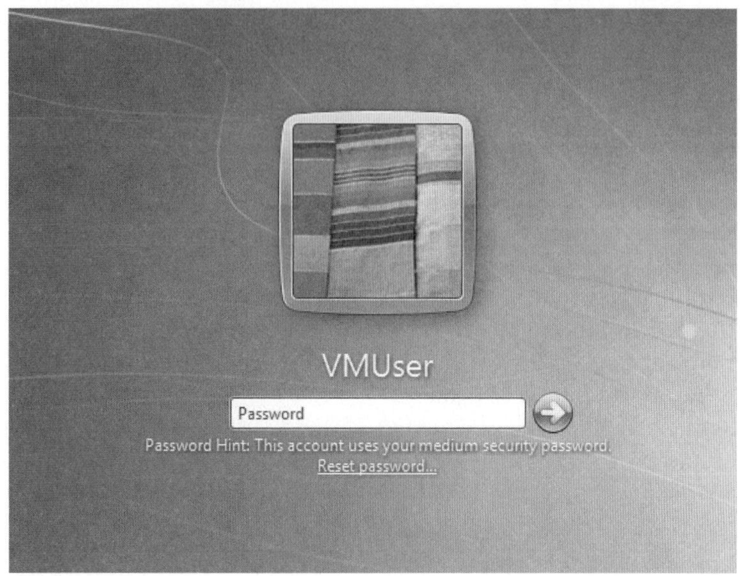

Figure 14-2 Password hint on the Windows 7 logon screen

CAUTION Blank passwords or passwords that are easily visible on a sticky note provide no security. Always insist on non-blank passwords, and do not let anyone leave a password sitting out in the open.

Groups

A *group* is a container that holds user accounts and defines the capabilities of its members. A single account can be a member of multiple groups. Groups are an efficient way of managing multiple users, especially when you are dealing with a whole network of accounts. Standalone computers rely on groups too, though Windows obscures this a little, especially with home users.

Groups make Windows administration much easier in two ways. First, you can assign a certain level of access for a file or folder to a group instead of to just a single user account. You can make a group called Accounting, for example, and put all user accounts for the accounting department in that group. If a person quits, you don't need to worry about assigning all of the proper access levels when you create a new account for his or her replacement. After you make an account for the new person, just add her account to the appropriate access group! Second, Windows provides numerous built-in groups with various access levels already predetermined.

While all versions of Windows come with a large number of these built-in groups, Windows editions aimed at home users handle these very differently than more advanced versions. For starters, make sure you are aware of the following groups for the exam:

- **Administrators** Any account that is a member of the *Administrators group* has complete administrator privileges. Administrator privileges grant complete control over a machine. It is common for the primary user of a Windows system to have her account in the Administrators group.

  When you create the Jane user account, in other words, and make Jane an administrator, you actually place the Jane account in the Administrators group. Because the Administrators group has all power over a system, Jane has all power over the system.
- **Power Users** Members of the *Power Users group* are almost as powerful as members of the Administrators group, but they cannot install new devices or access other users' files or folders unless the files or folders specifically provide them access.
- **Users** Members of the *Users group* cannot edit the Registry or access critical system files. They can create groups but can manage only those they create. Members of the Users group are called *standard users*.

  If you change the Jane account from administrator to standard user, you specifically take the Jane account out of the Administrators group and place it into the Users group. Nothing happens with her personal files or folders, but what the Jane account can do on the computer changes rather dramatically.
- **Guests** The *Guests group* enables someone who does not have an account on the system to log on by using a guest account. You might use this feature at a party, for example, to provide casual Internet access to guests, or at a library terminal. Most often, the guest account remains disabled.

Configuring Users and Groups

Configuring local user accounts and local groups requires tools in Windows for creating and managing users and groups. Every version of Windows includes either one or two users and group management tools. Most editions of Windows include a Control Panel applet called *User Accounts* (see Figure 14-3).

The more advanced Windows editions include a second, more advanced utility called Local Users and Groups (see Figure 14-4). You'll find Local Users and Groups in the Computer Management console in Administrative Tools. (Remember from Chapter 3 how to access Administrative Tools?)

NOTE To create and manage users, you must have administrator privileges.

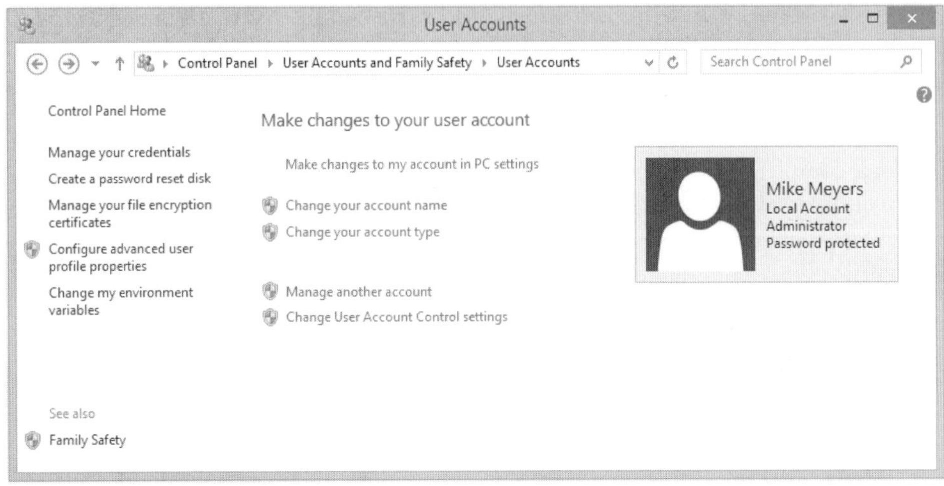

Figure 14-3 User Accounts

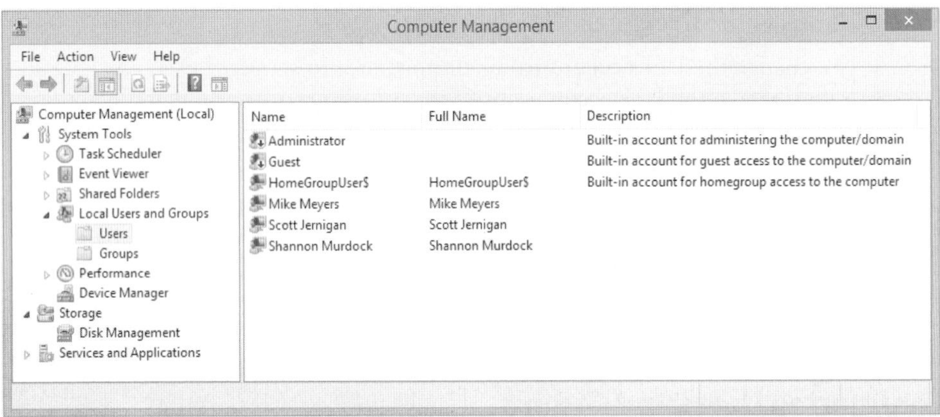

Figure 14-4 Local Users and Groups

Managing Users in Windows Vista

You create three accounts when you set up a computer: guest, administrator, and a local account that's a member of the Administrators group.

To add or modify a user account, you have numerous options depending on which Control Panel view you select and which edition and update of Vista you have installed. If your machine is on a workgroup, you'll see the User Accounts and Family Safety applet (see Figure 14-5). If you connect to a domain (discussed in Chapter 21), the default Control Panel Home view offers the User Accounts applet (see Figure 14-6). The options in each applet differ as well, as you can see in the screenshots.

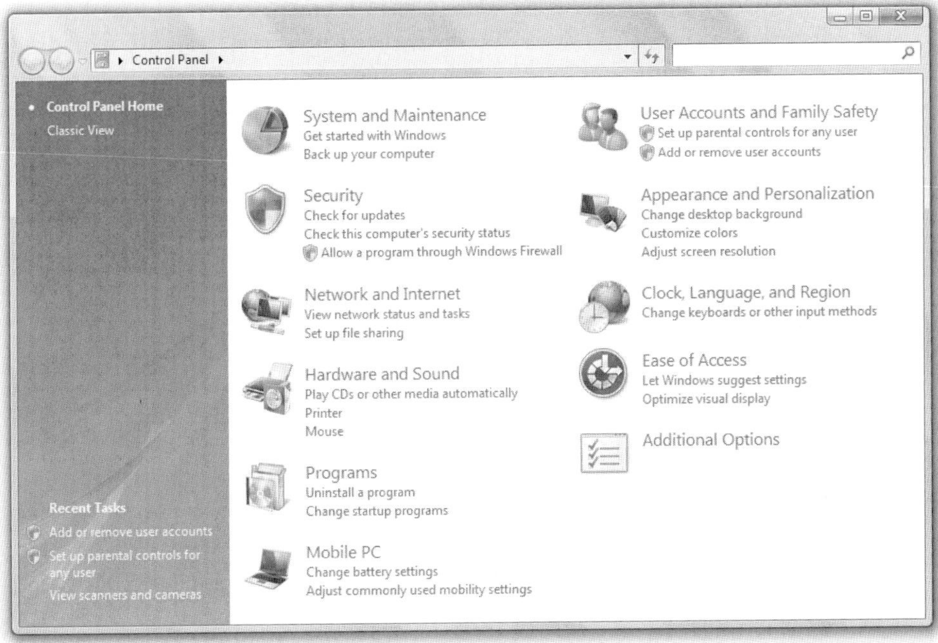

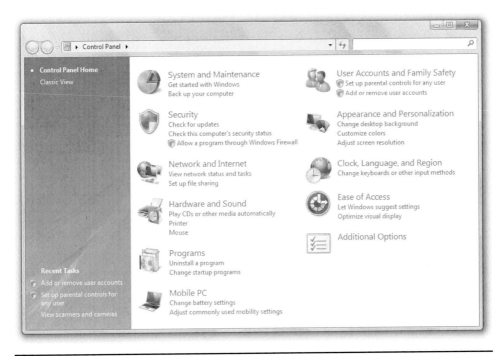

Figure 14-5 User Accounts and Family Safety applet in the Control Panel Home in Windows Vista Home Premium

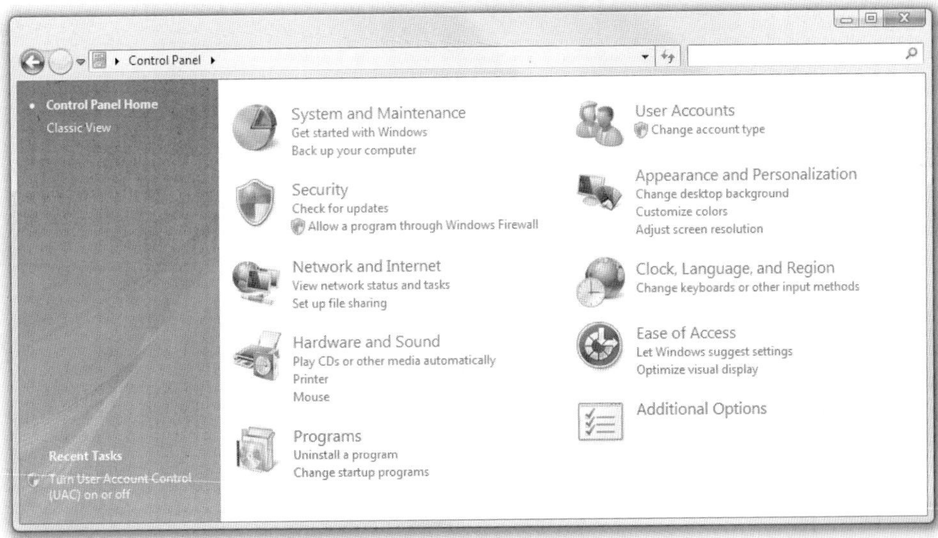

Figure 14-6 User Accounts applet in the Control Panel Home in Windows Vista Ultimate

Most techs almost immediately change the Control Panel view to Classic, but even there the different versions of Windows—and whether you're logged on to a workgroup or a domain—give you different versions of the User Accounts applet. Figure 14-7 shows the User Accounts applet in Windows Vista Business in a domain environment. Figure 14-8 shows the applet in Windows Vista Home Premium.

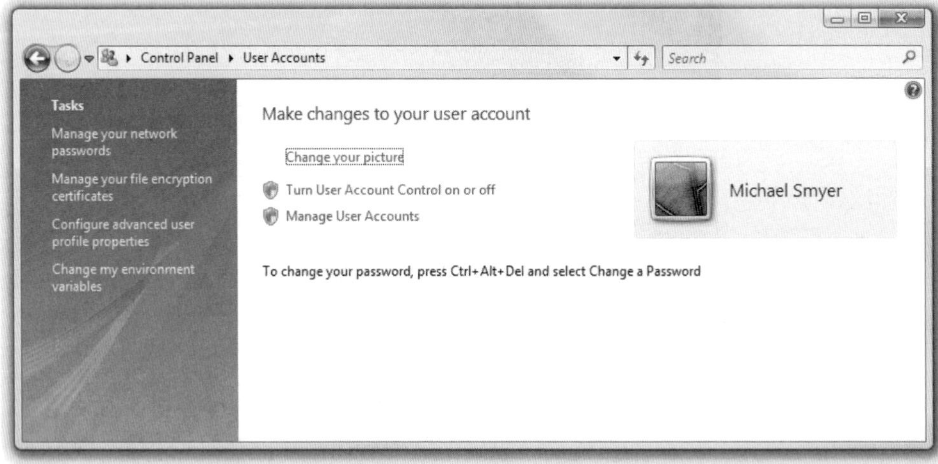

Figure 14-7 User Accounts applet in Windows Vista Business

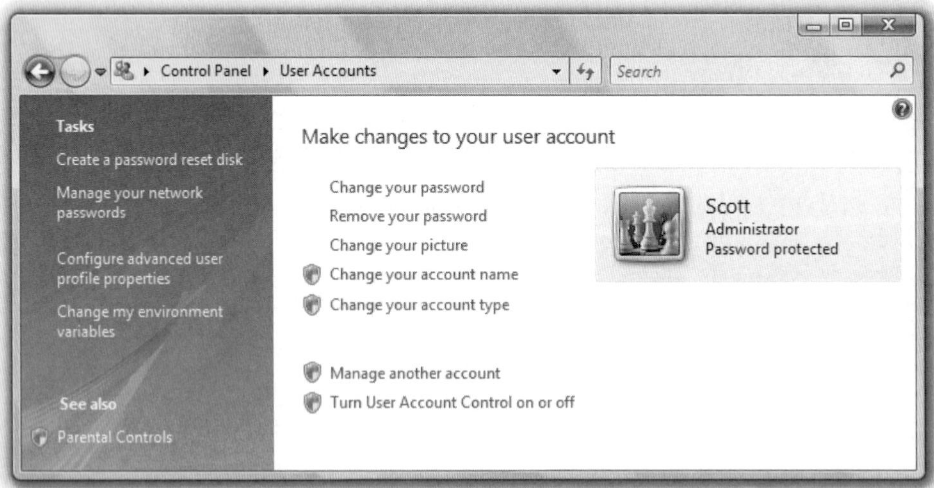

Figure 14-8 User Accounts applet in Windows Vista Home Premium

The Tasks links on the left are similar between editions of Windows (with the addition of Parental Controls in the Home Premium edition), but the main options differ a lot. This chapter focuses on standalone machines, so we'll look more closely at the options included with Vista Home Premium.

Windows Vista Home Premium uses Vista's version of the Welcome screen for logging on, so each user account has a picture associated with it. You can change the picture from the User Accounts applet. You can also change the name of the user account here and alter the account type, demoting an account from administrator to standard user, for example.

To add a user in Windows Vista, open the User Accounts applet. You may need to open User Accounts and Family Safety first. Click *Manage another account* and select *Create a new account*. Give the account a user name and select a user account type. Then click Create Account.

NOTE At least one account must be an administrator account. If you try to demote the sole administrator account, you'll find the option dimmed.

User Account Control Windows makes it too easy to make your primary account on a computer an administrator account. Because limited users can't do common tasks, such as running certain programs, installing applications, updating applications, updating Windows, and so on, most users simply create an administrator-level account and log on. Such accounts have full control over the computer, so any malware or any simple user mistake that slips in through the account can do a lot of harm.

Microsoft addressed this problem with *User Account Control (UAC)*, a feature that enables standard users to do common tasks and provides a permissions dialog box when standard users *and* administrators do certain things that could potentially harm the computer (such as attempt to install a program). We'll discuss UAC in detail at the end of this chapter.

Parental Controls With *Parental Controls*, an administrator account can monitor and limit the activities of any standard user in Windows, a feature that gives parents and managers an excellent level of control over the content their children and employees can access (see Figure 14-9). Activity Reporting logs a user's successful and blocked attempts to run an application, visit a Web site, download a file, and more. You can block various Web sites by type or specific URL, or you can allow only certain Web sites, a far more powerful option.

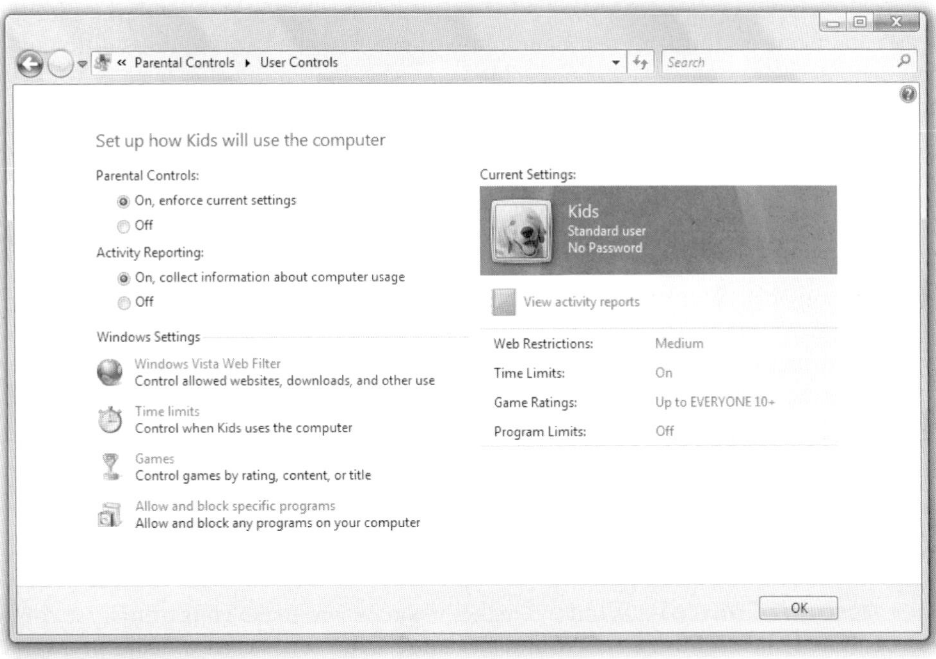

Figure 14-9 Parental Controls

Parental Controls also enable you to limit the time that standard users can spend logged on. You can specify acceptable and unacceptable times of day when standard users can log on. You can restrict access both to types of games and to specific applications. If you like playing rather gruesome games filled with monsters and blood that you don't want your kids to play, for example, you can simply block any games with certain ESRB (Entertainment Software Rating Board) ratings, such as E for Everyone, T for Teen, or M for Mature.

Managing Users in Windows 7

Windows 7 handles user creation in a manner very similar to Windows Vista, continuing the use of the User Accounts Control Panel applet. The User Accounts applet is virtually identical to the one used in Windows Vista. To create a user account, open the User Accounts applet and select *Manage another account* to see something like Figure 14-10.

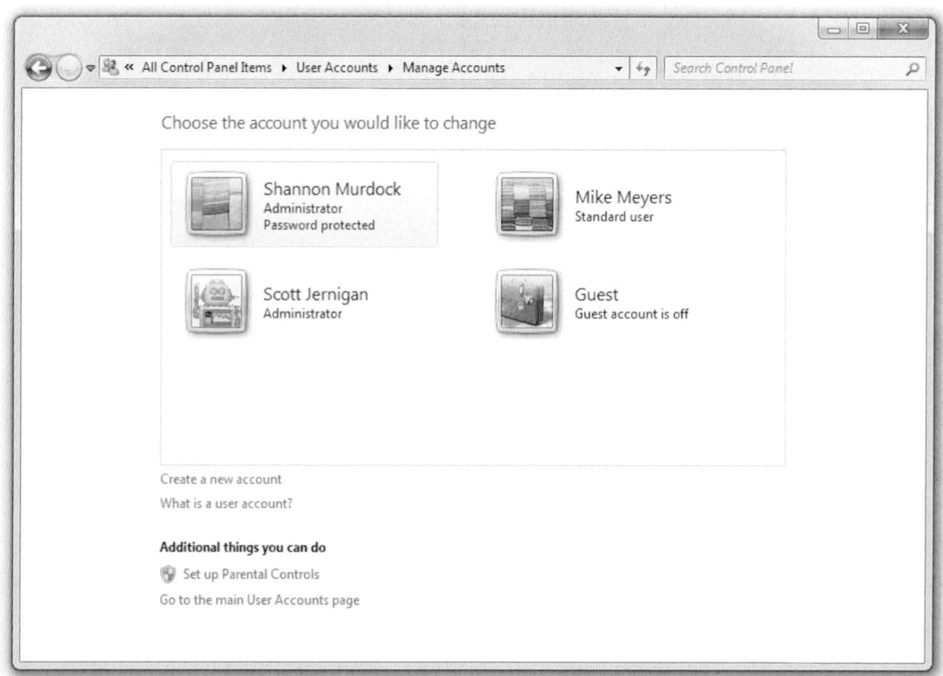

Figure 14-10 Manage Accounts

Click on *Create a new account* to see your options for making a new account (see Figure 14-11). Note that this applet only enables you to make administrator accounts (in the Administrators group) or standard users (in the Users group).

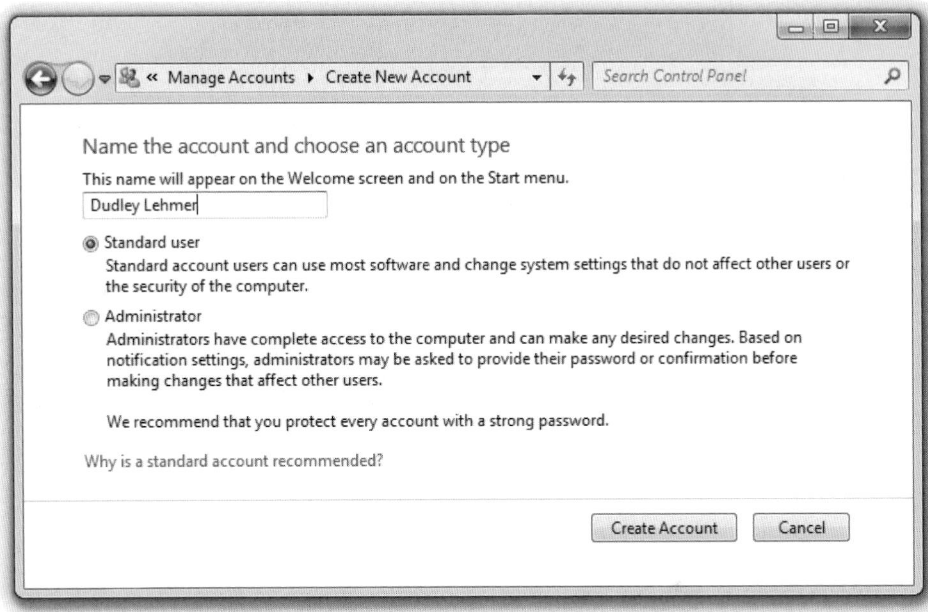

Figure 14-11 Adding a new user

Managing Users in Windows 8/8.1/10

Starting with Windows 8, Microsoft shifted the focus of user accounts from local accounts to Internet-wide Microsoft accounts. Windows 8 debuted the Settings charm (see Figure 14-12). Select *Change PC settings* from the initial charm screen to open PC settings (see Figure 14-13) and get access to the Accounts option. Note that the User Accounts applet in Control Panel enables you to make changes to current accounts (local or global), and gives you access to the Settings charm (or app in Windows 10) when you opt to add a new account.

Figure 14-12 Settings charm

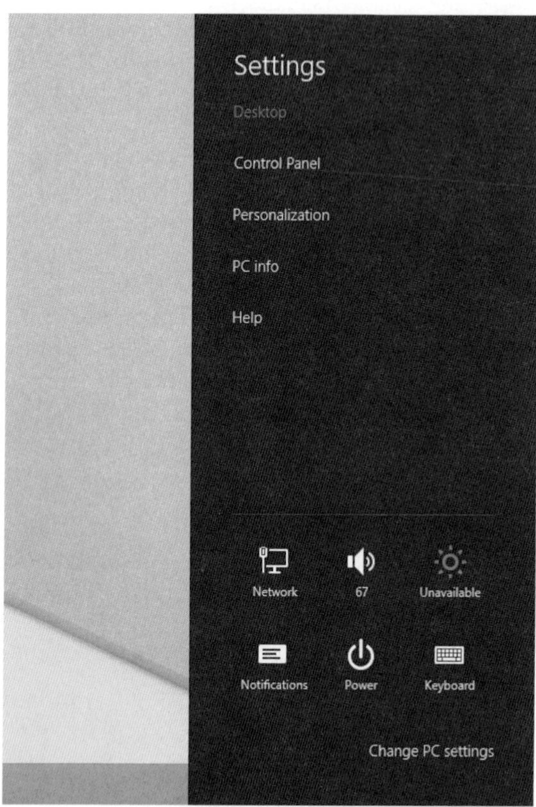

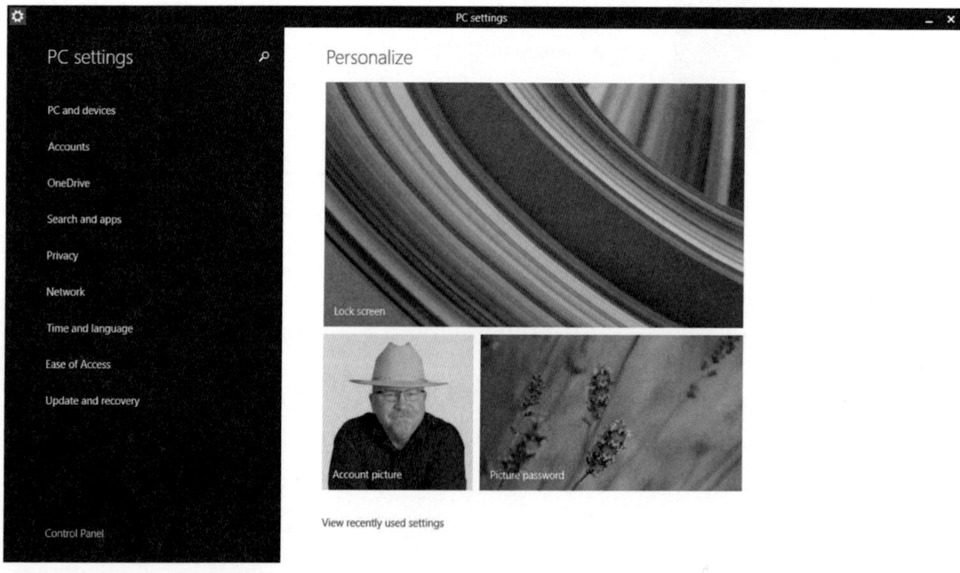

Figure 14-13 PC settings

When you first set up a Windows 8/8.1/10 PC, you're prompted either to sign in to your Microsoft global account or create one at that time. Although the language of the sign-up option for the new account suggests a Microsoft-sponsored e-mail address (like user@hotmail.com), any valid e-mail address can serve as a Microsoft account. You can opt to create a local user account instead and that will function like any local account on previous versions. But if you opt for a global Microsoft account, you'll synchronize photos, files, and Desktop settings (like the background picture and colors).

Note that creating an account—global or not—creates a local user account. If you create an account tied to your global account, the local account gets created and then Windows applies the settings from your global profile.

Once you have a valid user account set up and have a functioning system, the Accounts area of the Settings app enables you to sign out, sign in, modify your profile picture, and so on. Figure 14-14 shows a typical Accounts default screen.

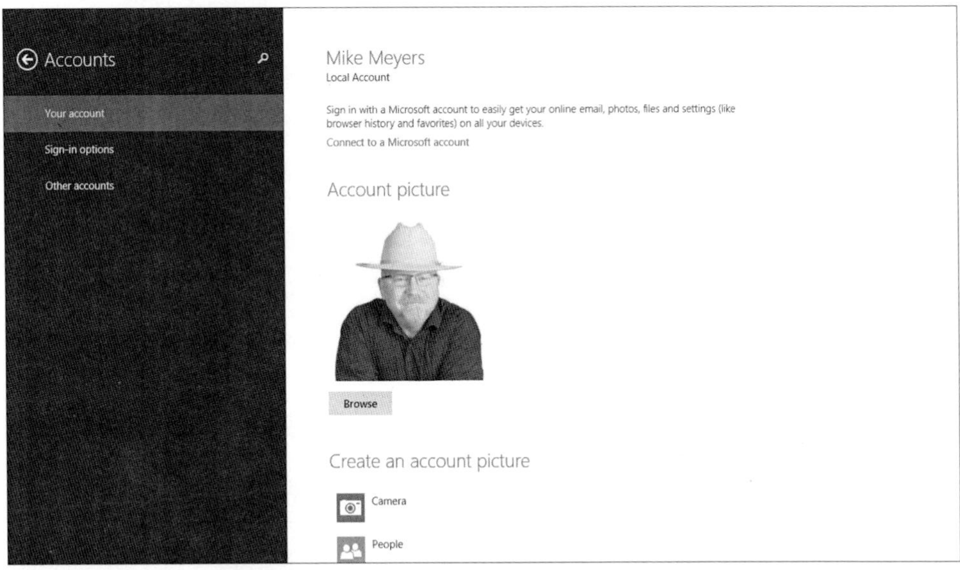

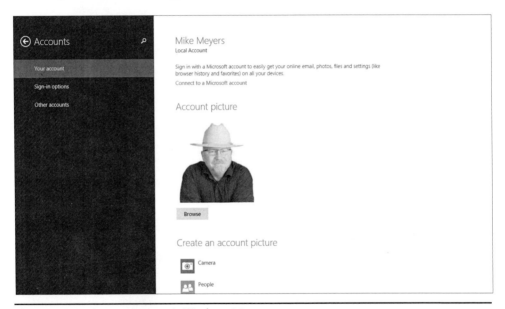

Figure 14-14 Accounts screen in Windows 8.1

To create a new account, click on the Other accounts option. This opens the Manage other accounts page (see Figure 14-15). From this page you can modify the status or group of any current local user account. Click the + symbol next to Add an account to get started.

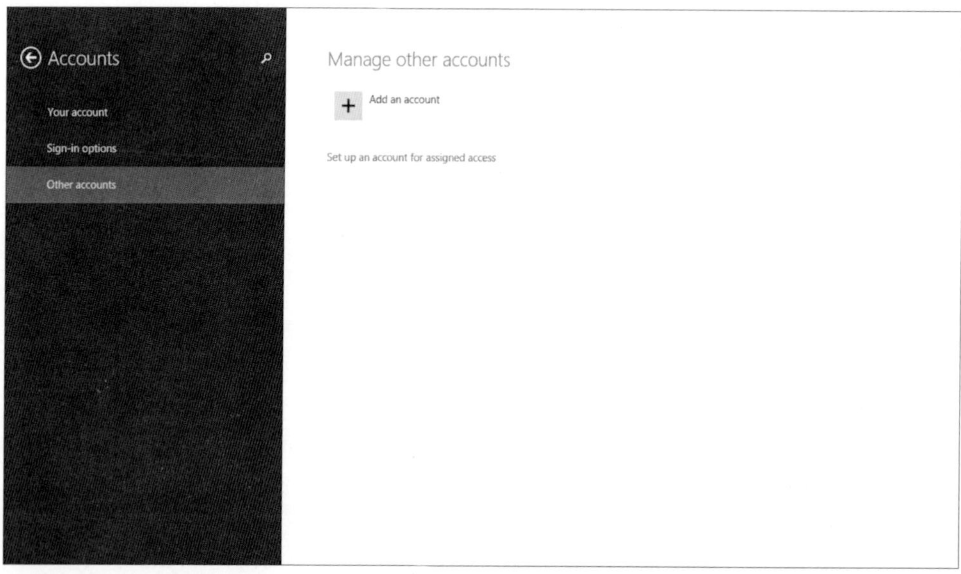

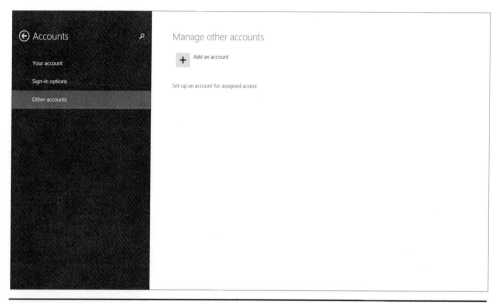

Figure 14-15 Manage other accounts

On the How will this person sign in? screen (see Figure 14-16), you'll see options to use a valid Microsoft account, get a Microsoft account, add a child's account, or create a local account only. The Add a child's account option creates an account with parental controls enabled, as you probably suspected.

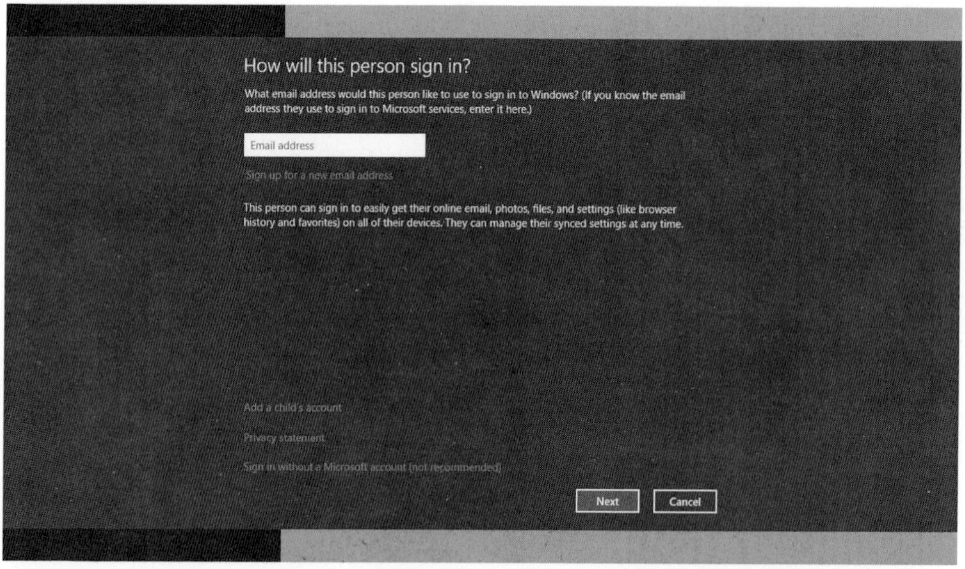

Figure 14-16 Options for a new account

Once you've opted to do either a global or local account, Windows creates that account on the local machine. This process takes a while; Windows creates all the folder structures and updates the local profile. Eventually, you'll have a new account ready to roll (see Figure 14-17).

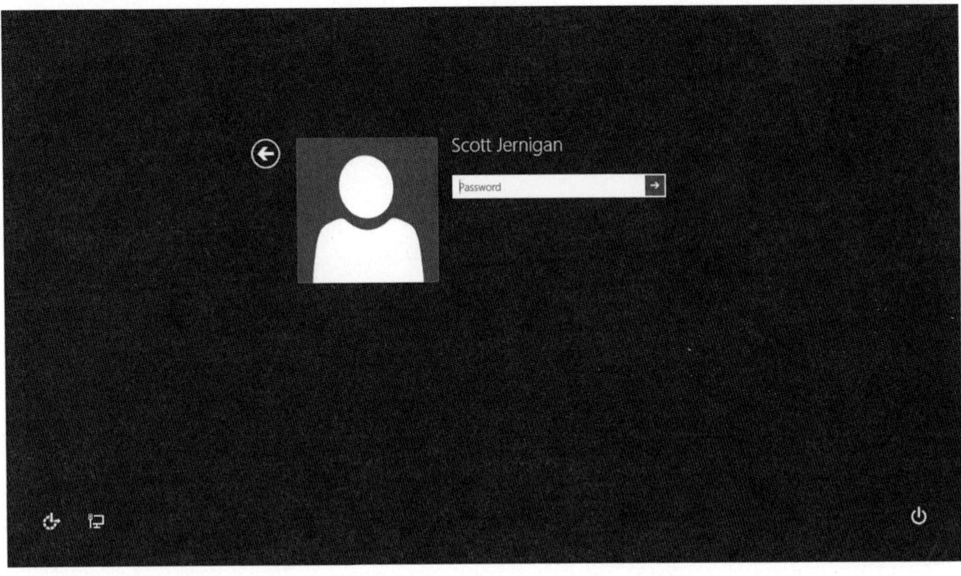

Figure 14-17 Shiny new account

Local Users and Groups

The professional editions of Windows include the *Local Users and Groups* tool, a more powerful tool for working with user accounts. You can create, modify, and remove users and groups. Keep in mind, however, that this advanced tool will not hold your hand like the Control Panel applets. Think of the Local Users and Groups tool as a bike without the training wheels of the User Accounts applet. Figure 14-18 shows the Local Users and Groups tool in Windows 8.1 with Groups selected.

To add a group, simply right-click on a blank spot in the Groups folder and select New Group. This opens the New Group dialog box, where you can type in a group name and description in their respective fields (see Figure 14-19).

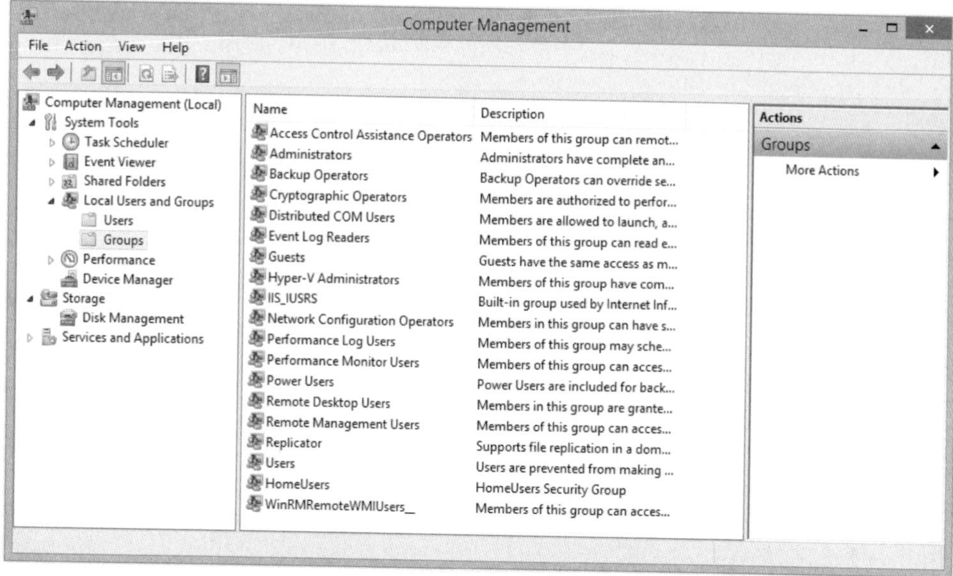

Figure 14-18 Local Users and Groups in Windows 8.1 Pro

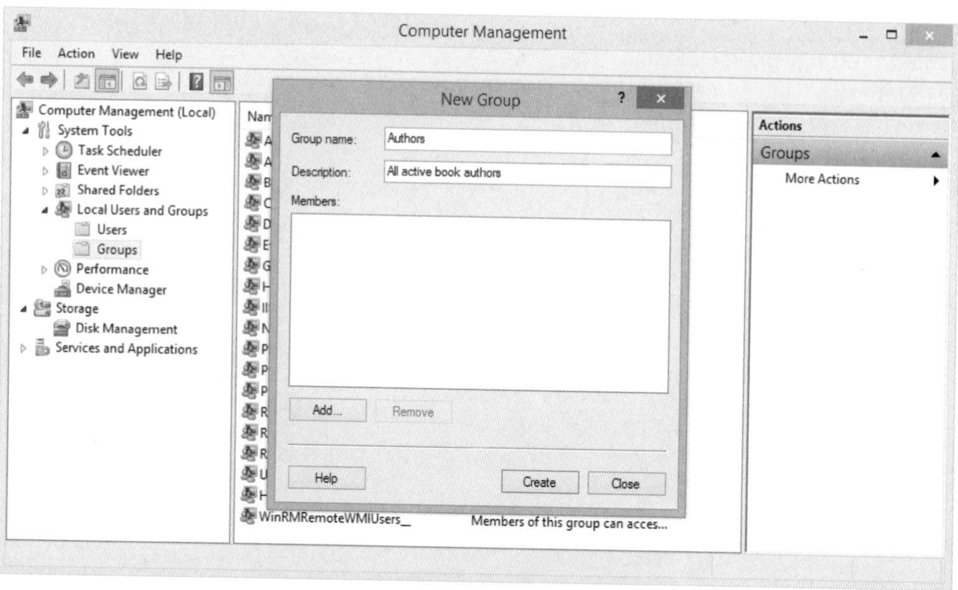

Figure 14-19 New Group dialog box in Windows 8.1 Pro

To add users to this group, click the Add button. The dialog box that opens varies a little in name among the three operating systems, though they all contain the same functionality (see Figure 14-20).

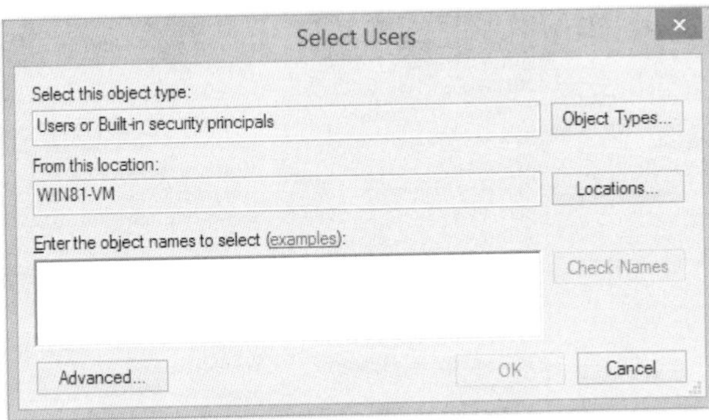

Figure 14-20 Select Users dialog box in Windows 8.1 Pro

You can add more than just users to a group. Windows uses multiple *object* types to define what you can add. Object types include user accounts, groups, and computers. Each object type can be added to a group and assigned permissions. The short version of how to add a user account is: click the Advanced button to expand the dialog box and then click the Find Now button (see Figure 14-21).

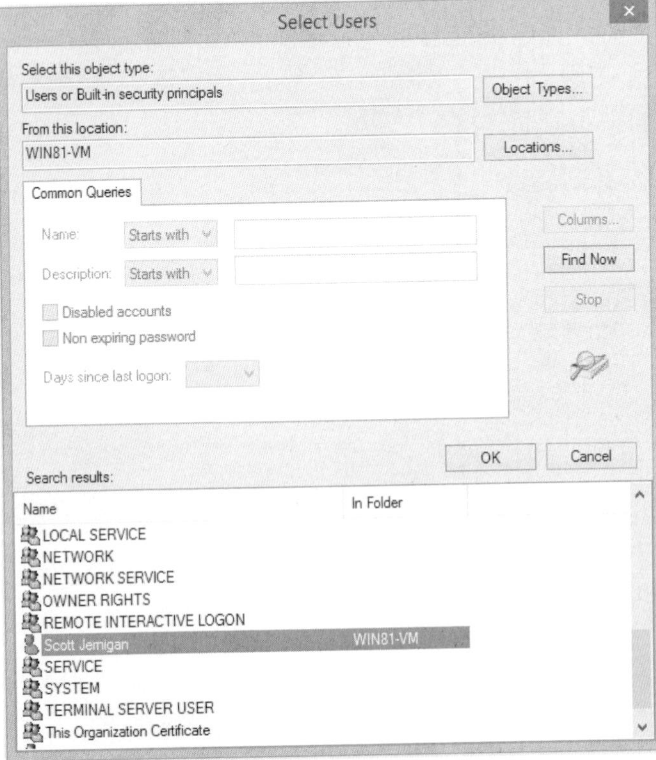

Figure 14-21 Select Users dialog box in Windows 8.1 Pro with advanced options expanded to show user accounts

You can either add group membership to a user's properties or add a user to a group's properties.

- To add group membership to a user account, select the Users folder, right-click a user account you want to change, and select Properties from the context menu. Then select the Member Of tab on the user account's Properties dialog box (see Figure 14-22). Click Add to add group membership.
- To add users via the group's properties, select the Groups folder. Right-click on a group and select Properties. Beneath the Members list, click the Add button to search for and add user accounts to the group.

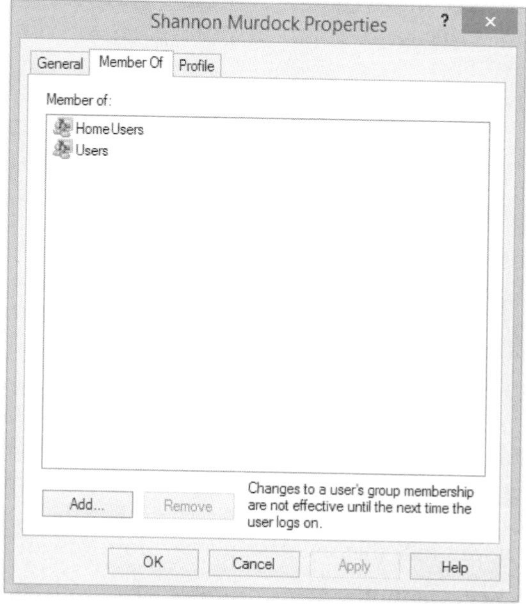

Figure 14-22 Properties dialog box of a user account, where you can change group memberships for that account

You can also use either method to remove users. This level of flexibility makes the Local Users and Groups tool much more powerful and useful than the User Accounts Control Panel applets.

NOTE Home editions of Windows do not have the Local Users and Groups utility. You must use the User Accounts applet or the Settings charm.

Authorization Through NTFS

User accounts and passwords provide the foundation for securing a Windows computer, enabling users to authenticate with a PC. After you've created a user account, you need to determine what the user can do with the available resources (files, folders, applications,

and so on). We call this process *authorization*. Windows uses the powerful NT File System (NTFS) as the primary tool for providing authorization. Let's delve into NTFS to see how this powerful file system protects folders and files.

NTFS Permissions

In Windows, every folder and file on an NTFS partition has a list that contains two sets of data. First, the list details every user and group with access to that file or folder. Second, the list specifies the level of access each user or group has to that file or folder. The level of access is defined by a set of restrictions called NTFS permissions. *NTFS permissions* define exactly what any particular account can or cannot do to the file or folder and are thus quite detailed and powerful. You can, for example, set up NTFS permissions allowing a user account to edit a file but not delete it. You could also configure NTFS permissions to enable any member of a user group to create a subfolder for a particular folder.

NTFS file and folder permissions are so complicated that entire books have been written on them! Fortunately, the CompTIA A+ 220-902 exam tests your understanding of only a few basic concepts of NTFS permissions: Ownership, Take Ownership permission, Change permission, folder permissions, and file permissions.

- **Ownership** When you create a new file or folder on an NTFS partition, you become the *owner* of that file or folder. Owners can do anything they want to the files or folders they own, including changing the permissions to prevent anybody, even administrators, from accessing them.
- **Take Ownership permission** With the *Take Ownership* permission, anyone with the permission can seize control of a file or folder. Administrator accounts have Take Ownership permission for everything. Note the difference here between owning a file and accessing a file. If you own a file, you can prevent anyone from accessing that file. An administrator whom you have blocked, however, can take that ownership away from you and *then* access that file!
- **Change permission** Another important permission for all NTFS files and folders is the Change permission. An account with this permission can give or take away permissions for other accounts.
- **Folder permissions** Folder permissions define what a user may do to a folder. One example might be "List folder contents," which gives the permission to see what's in the folder.
- **File permissions** File permissions define what a user may do to an individual file. One example might be "Read and Execute," which gives a user account the permission to run an executable program.

The primary way to set NTFS permissions is through the Security tab under the folder or files Properties (see Figure 14-23). The Security tab contains two main areas. The top area shows the list of accounts that have permissions for that resource. The lower area shows exactly what permissions have been assigned to the selected account.

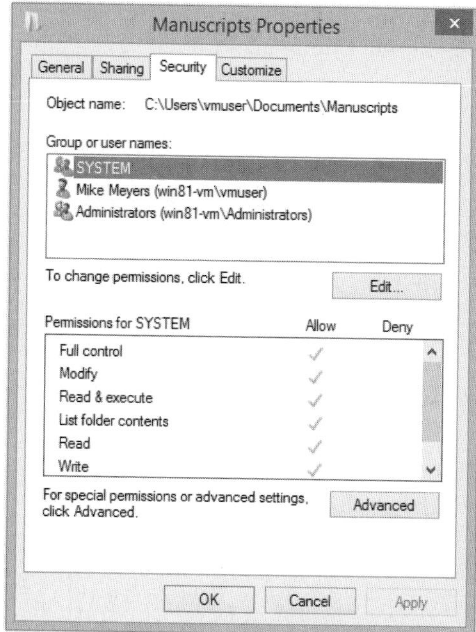

Figure 14-23 The Security tab lets you set permissions.

You add or remove NTFS permissions by first selecting the user or group you wish to change and then clicking Edit to open a Permissions dialog box. To add an NTFS permission, select the Allow checkbox next to the NTFS permission you want to add. You remove an NTFS permission by deselecting the Allow checkbox next to the NTFS permission you want to remove. The Deny checkbox is not used very often and has a very different job—see the next section, "Inheritance." For now, let's see what all the NTFS permissions are for folders and files.

Here are the standard NTFS permissions for a folder:

- **Full Control** Enables you to do anything you want
- **Modify** Enables you to read, write, and delete both files and subfolders
- **Read & Execute** Enables you to see the contents of the folder and any subfolders as well as run any executable programs or associations in that folder
- **List Folder Contents** Enables you to see the contents of the folder and any subfolders
- **Read** Enables you to view a folder's contents and open any file in the folder
- **Write** Enables you to write to files and create new files and folders

File permissions are quite similar to folder permissions, with the main difference being the Special Permissions option, which I'll talk about a bit later in the chapter.

- **Full Control** Enables you to do anything you want
- **Modify** Enables you to read, write, and delete the file
- **Read & Execute** Enables you to open and run the file
- **Read** Enables you to open the file
- **Write** Enables you to open and write to the file

Here are a few important points about NTFS permissions:

- You may see the NTFS permissions on a folder or file by accessing the Properties dialog box for that file or folder and opening the Security tab.
- NTFS permissions are assigned both to user accounts and groups, although it's considered a best practice to assign permissions to groups and then add user accounts to groups instead of adding permissions directly to individual user accounts.
- Permissions are cumulative. If you have Full Control on a folder and only Read permission on a file in the folder, you get Full Control permission on the file.
- Whoever creates a folder or a file has complete control over that folder or file. This is called *ownership*.
- Administrators do not automatically have complete control over every folder and file. If an administrator wants to access a folder or file they do not have permission to access, they may go through a process called Take Control.

Take some time to think about these permissions. Why would Microsoft create them? Think of situations where you might want to give a group Modify permission. Also, you can assign more than one permission. In many situations, we like to give users both the Read and Write permissions.

NOTE Windows editions for home use have only a limited set of permissions you can assign. As far as folder permissions go, you can assign only one: Make This Folder Private. To see this in action, right-click on a file or folder and select Sharing and Security from the options. Note that you can't just select Properties and see a Security tab as you can in the professional-oriented editions of Windows. Windows Home editions do not have file-level permissions.

Inheritance

Inheritance is the process of determining the default NTFS permissions any newly introduced files or subfolders contained in a folder receive. Inheritance is a huge issue as we tend to make lots of folder and file changes on a system. We need to let NTFS know what we want it to do when new files and folders suddenly appear (see Figure 14-24).

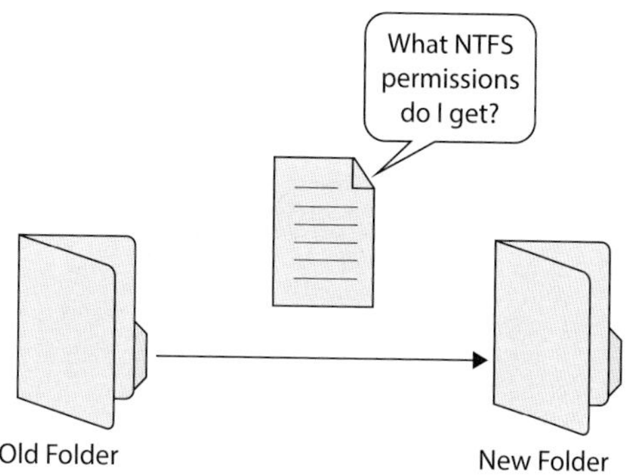

Figure 14-24 What permissions do I get?

The base rule of Windows inheritance is that any new files or folders placed into a folder automatically get all the NTFS permissions of the parent folder. So if, for example, you have Read and Execute access to a folder and someone else copies a file to that folder, you will automatically get Read and Execute permissions (see Figure 14-25).

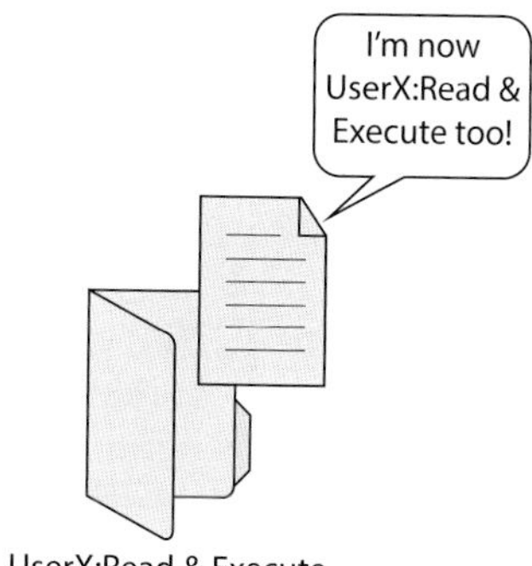

Figure 14-25 Here are your permissions!

All versions of Windows have inheritance turned on by default, which most of the time is a good idea. If you access a folder's Properties dialog box, click on the Security tab, and then click the Advanced button, you'll see a little checkbox that says *Include inheritable permissions from this object's parent*. If you wanted to turn off

inheritance, you would just uncheck this box. Don't do that. Inheritance is good. Inheritance is expected.

If you look closely at Figure 14-26, you'll see that there are a number of grayed-out NTFS Allow permissions! That's how Windows tells you that the permissions here are inherited. Grayed-out checkboxes can't be changed, so what do you do if you need to make a change here?

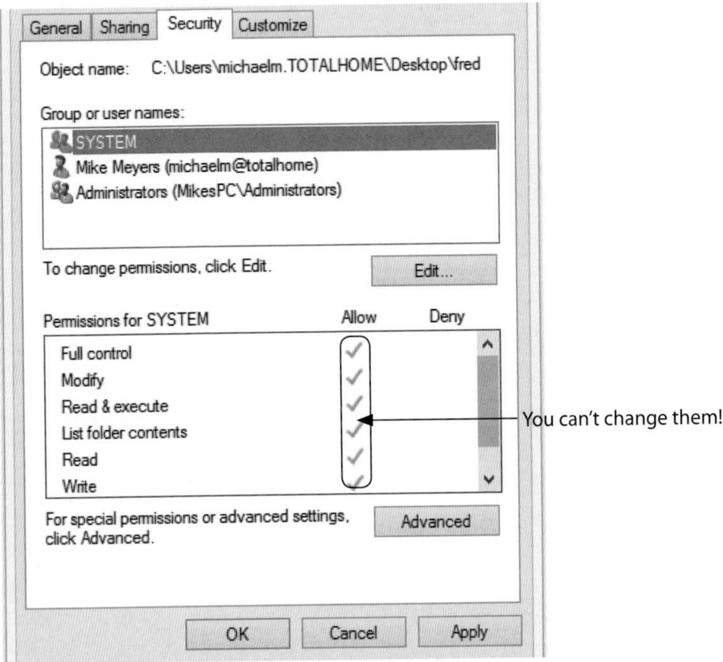

Figure 14-26 Inherited permissions

In rare situations you may want to turn off inheritance for a specific folder or file. Instead of shutting down inheritance completely, use the Deny checkbox. Clicking the Deny checkbox for a particular NTFS permission (see Figure 14-27) tells Windows to overrule inheritance and stop that particular NTFS permission.

NOTE The Deny checkbox always overrides the NTFS inheritance.

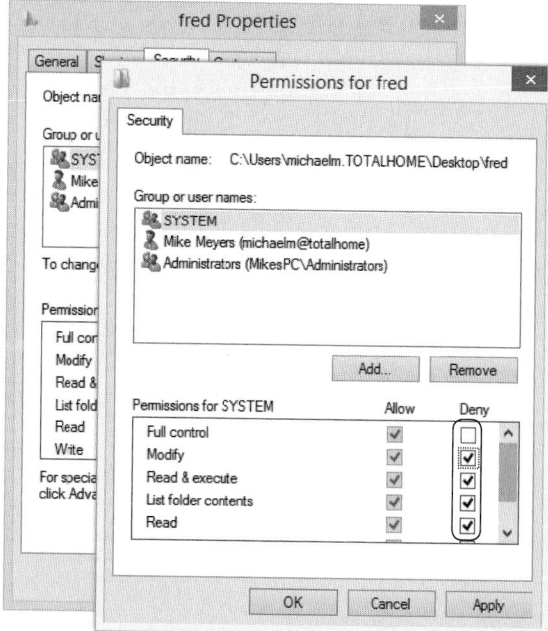

Figure 14-27 Special permissions

Permission Propagation

Permission propagation is the process of determining what NTFS permissions are applied to files that are moved or copied into a new folder. Be careful here! You might be tempted to think, given you've just learned about inheritance, that any new files/folders copied or moved into a folder would just inherit the folder's NTFS permissions. This is not always true, and CompTIA wants to make sure you know it. It really depends on two issues: whether the data is being copied or moved, and whether the data is coming from the same volume or a different one. So we need to consider four situations:

- Copying data within one NTFS-based volume
- Moving data within one NTFS-based volume
- Copying data between two NTFS-based volumes
- Moving data between two NTFS-based partitions

Let's look at our list of four things techs need to know to see what happens when you copy or move an object, such as a file or folder.

1. Copying within a volume creates two copies of the object. The copy of the object in the new location *inherits* the permissions from that new location. The new copy can have different permissions than the original.

2. Moving within a volume creates one copy of the object. That object *retains* its permissions, unchanged.
3. Copying from one NTFS volume to another creates two copies of the object. The copy of the object in the new location *inherits* the permissions from that new location. The new copy can have different permissions than the original.
4. Moving from one NTFS volume to another creates one copy of the object. The object in the new location *inherits* the permissions from that new location. The newly moved file can have different permissions than the original.

Table 14-1 Permission Propagation

	Same Volume	Different Volume
Move	Keeps original permissions	Inherits new permissions
Copy	Inherits new permissions	Inherits new permissions

From a tech's standpoint, you need to be aware of how permissions can change when you move or copy files, and if you're in doubt about a sensitive file, check it before you sign off to a client (Table 14-1).

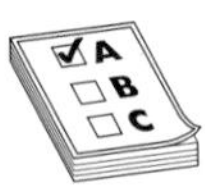

EXAM TIP Current versions of Windows refer to groupings of cylinders or transistors on an HDD or SSD as volumes, as you'll recall from Chapter 10. Earlier versions—and many techs and exams in your near future—refer to such groupings as partitions. Be prepared for either term.

Techs and Permissions

You need local administrative privileges to change almost anything on a Windows machine, such as install updates, change drivers, and install applications; most administrators hate giving out administrative permissions (for obvious reasons). If an administrator does give you administrative permission for a PC and something goes wrong with that system while you're working on it, you immediately become the primary suspect!

If you're working on a Windows system administered by someone else, make sure she understands what you are doing and how long you think it will take. Have the administrator create a new account for you that's a member of the Administrators group. Never ask for the password to a permanent administrator account! That way, you won't be blamed if anything goes wrong on that system: "Well, I told Janet the password when she installed the new hard drive…maybe she did it!" When you have fixed the system, *make sure the administrator deletes the account you used.*

This "protect yourself from passwords" attitude applies to areas other than just doing tech support on Windows. PC support folks get lots of passwords, scan cards, keys, and ID tags. New techs tend to get an "I can go anywhere and access anything" attitude, and this is dangerous. I've seen many jobs lost and friendships ruined when a backup suddenly disappears or a critical file gets erased. Everybody points to the support tech in these situations. In physical security situations, make other people unlock doors for you.

In some cases, I've literally asked the administrator or system owner to sit behind me, read a magazine, and be ready to punch in passwords as needed. What you don't have access to can't hurt you.

Permissions in Linux and Mac OS X

While the CompTIA A+ 902 exam concentrates hard on Windows users, groups, and permissions, this is a good time to consider that Linux and Mac OS X also have their own concepts pertaining to users, groups, and permissions. Let's take a short jaunt into Linux/Mac OS X users, groups, and permissions. In particular, we'll take a look at the chmod and chown commands because they are listed as objectives for the CompTIA A+ 902 exam.

NOTE Understanding this section requires some understanding of the Linux command line. You may need to refer to Chapter 16, "Working with the Command-Line Interface," to practice some of the commands shown here.

Just as in Windows, every file and folder on a Linux/Mac OS X system has permissions. You can easily see this if you go to a Linux terminal and type this command: ls –l. This shows a detailed list of all the files and folders in a particular location. Chapter 16 discusses the ls command in a lot more detail, but this is enough for our present discussion.

```
drwxrwxr-x 2 mikemyers mi6    4096 Oct  2 18:35 agent_bios
-rw-rw-r-- 1 mikemyers mi6   34405 Oct  2 18:39 datafile
-rwxrwxrwx 1 mikemyers mi6    7624 Oct  2 18:39 honeypot
-rw-rw-r-- 1 mikemyers users   299 Oct  2 18:36 launch_codes
-rw-rw-r-- 1 mikemyers mi6     905 Oct  2 18:36 passwords.txt
```

Let's zero in on one line of this output:

```
-rwxrwxrwx 1 mikemyers mi6    7624 Oct  2 18:39 honeypot
```

In particular, note the string -rwxrwxrwx—each of those letters represents a permission for this file. Ignore the dash at the beginning. That is used to tell us if this listing is a file, directory, or shortcut. What we have left are three groups of rwx. The three groups, in order, stand for:

- **Owner** Permissions for the owner of this file or folder
- **Group** Permissions for members of the group for this file or folder
- **Everyone** Permissions for anyone for this file or folder

The letters r, w, and x represent the following permissions:

- **r** Read the contents of a file
- **w** Write or modify a file or folder
- **x** Execute a file or list the folder contents

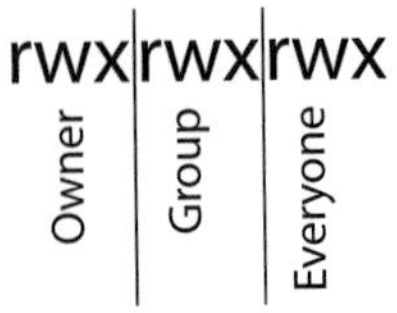

Figure 14-28 Linux file permissions

Figure 14-28 shows the relationships.

Let's look at another example:

```
-rw-rw-r-- 1 mikemyers users   299 Oct  2 18:36 launch_codes
```

- This file is called launch codes. The owner of this file is me. This file is in the users group.
- The owner, mikemyers, has read and write privileges (rw-).
- The group users has read and write privileges (rw-).
- Everyone can read the launch codes (r--). We should probably fix that.

chown Command

The *chown* command enables us to change the owner and the group with which a file or folder is associated. The chown command uses the following syntax:

```
chown <new owner> filename
```

To change the group, use the following syntax:

```
chown <owner>:<group> filename
```

So to change the owner of launch_codes to m, type

```
chown m launch_codes
```

To change the group to mi6, type

```
chown m:mi6 launch_codes
```

If you retype the ls –l command, you would see the following output:

```
-rw-rw-r-- 1   mi6     299 Oct  2 18:36 launch_codes
```

Be aware that the chown command needs superuser privileges (sudo or su). Refer to Chapter 16 for details.

chmod Command

The *chmod* command is used to change permissions. Sadly, it uses a somewhat nonintuitive numbering system that works as follows:

```
r: 4
w: 2
x: 1
```

For example, we can interpret the permissions on

```
-rw-rw-r-- 1   mi6     299 Oct  2 18:36 launch_codes
```

as follows:

- Owner's permissions are 6: 4+2 (rw-)
- Group's permissions are 6: 4+2 (rw-)
- Everyone's permissions are 4: 4 (r--)

The chmod command uses the following syntax to make permission changes:

```
chmod <permissions> <filename>
```

Using this nomenclature, we can make any permission change we want using only three numbers. The current permissions can be represented by 664. If we want to keep the launch codes out of the wrong hands, we just change the 4 to a 0: 660. To make the change, we use the chmod command as follows:

```
chmod 660 launch_codes
```

Sharing Resources Securely

Windows uses NTFS to make the folders and files in a specific user's personal folders (Documents, Music, Pictures, and so on) private. In other words, only the user who created those documents can access those documents. Members of the Administrators group can override this behavior, but members of the Users group (standard users) cannot. On a shared Windows machine, you'll need to take extra steps and actively share resources to make them available to multiple users.

Here's a scenario. The Snyder family has a computer in the media room that acts as a media server. It has accounts for each family member. The family could be smart and run something that makes sharing music easy, like iTunes, but they stuck with Windows Media Player. Each user needs access to the shared collection of MP3 files.

Windows Vista and 7 make sharing with everyone very simple through the Public libraries for Documents, Music, Pictures, and Videos. Open Windows Explorer and click the down arrow next to one of the Libraries folders; for example, click the down arrow next to Music to see My Music and Public Music (see Figure 14-29). Every user can access anything saved in the Public Music folder.

Windows 8/8.1 versions have the same Libraries as Windows Vista/7, but they are not visible by default. Right-click on some white space in File Explorer and select Show libraries (see Figure 14-30). The Libraries folders show up just fine.

Windows 10 does not work this way, and, in fact, all modern versions of Windows give you much more granular options for securely sharing specific folders with specific users.

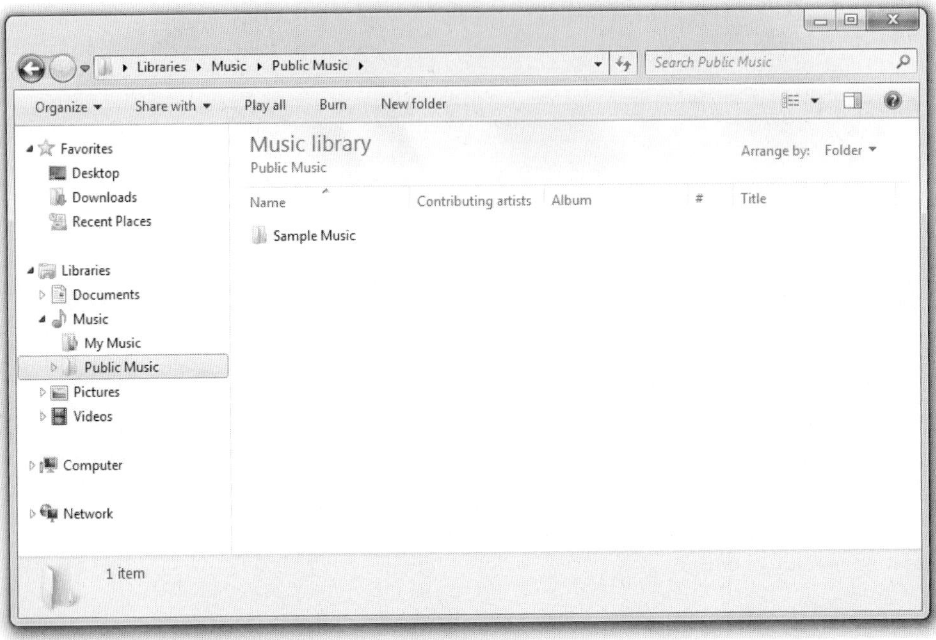

Figure 14-29 Public Libraries

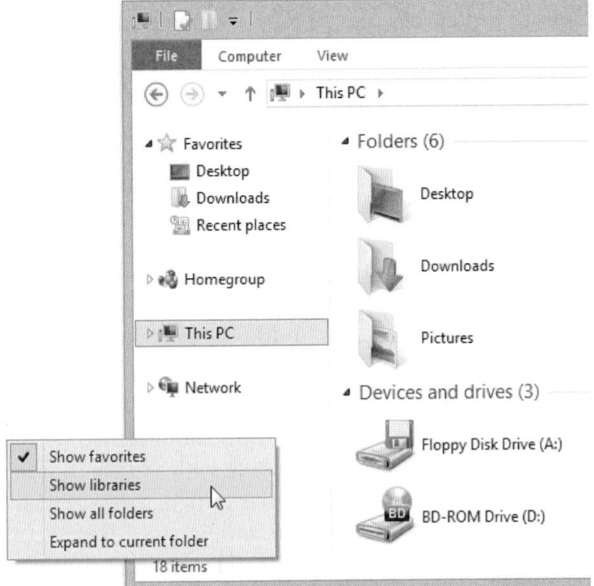

Figure 14-30 Showing libraries in File Explorer on Windows 8.1

NOTE Sharing gets more interesting and complicated when you put a computer into a network setting. We'll cover network sharing and accessing of shared resources in depth in Chapter 21.

So the next obvious question follows: How do you share non-library folders with one or more users on a single computer? The next sections walk through the details.

Sharing a Folder

Probably the easiest part of the whole securely sharing process is the sharing itself. There's more than one way to do this, so let's first look at the most tedious way. Select the folder you wish to share, right-click on it, and select Properties | Sharing tab. From here, select Advanced Sharing. Click on the Share this folder checkbox and give the folder a network share name (see Figure 14-31).

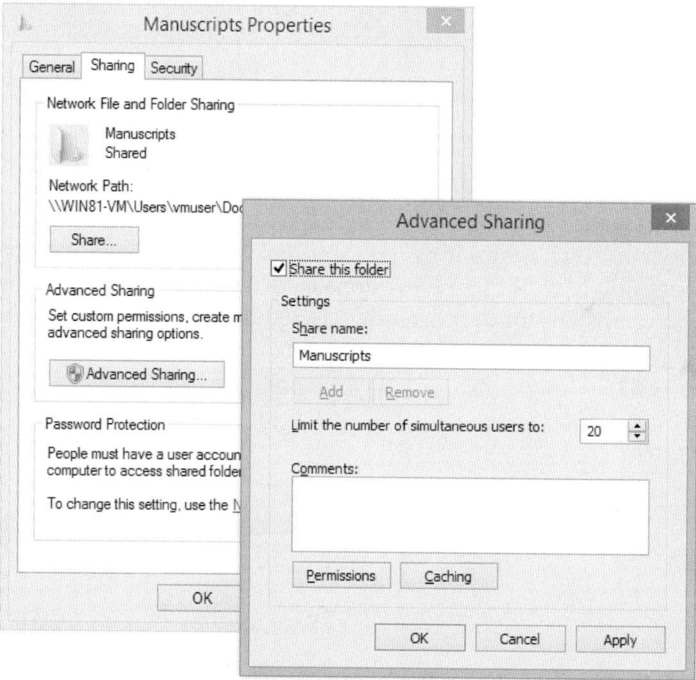

Figure 14-31 Advanced Sharing dialog box

Next, click on the Permissions button. By default, all new Windows shares only have Read permission. Here is where you set your share to Full Control, as shown in Figure 14-32. Note that the Change checkbox automatically gets checked. Click OK twice to get back to the Properties folder, and let's go to step two.

Figure 14-32 Setting the share to Full Control

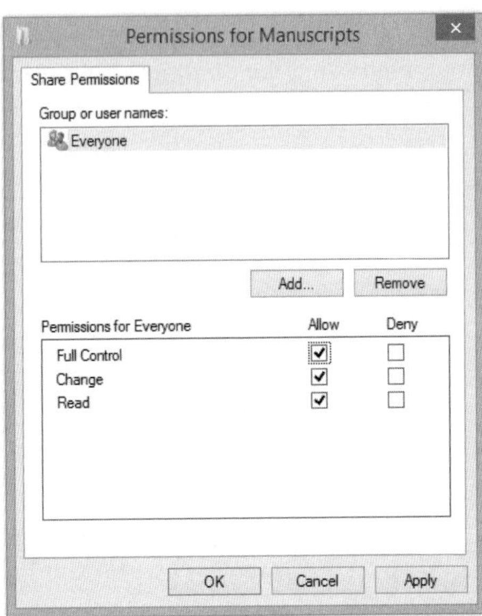

Add/Edit Users and/or Groups

It's now time to add users and groups and set their NTFS permissions. Head over to the Security tab. You'll notice it has two sections: the top section is a list of users and groups that currently have NTFS permissions to that folder, and the bottom section is a list of NTFS permissions for the currently selected users and groups (see Figure 14-33).

Figure 14-33 Folder Security tab

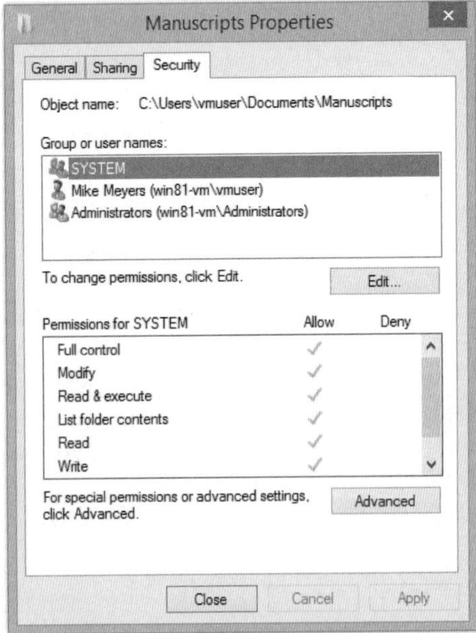

To add a new user or group, click the Edit button. In the Permissions dialog box that opens, you can not only add new users and groups but also remove them and edit existing NTFS permissions (see Figure 14-34).

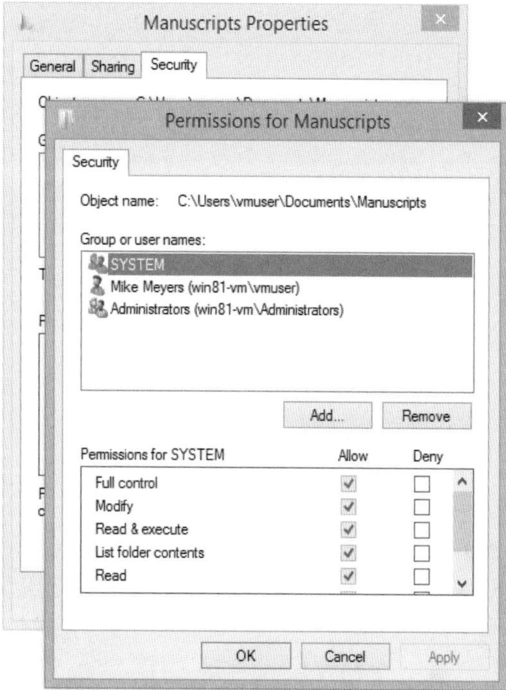

Figure 14-34 Permissions dialog box

While the method just shown works for all versions of Windows, it's a tad old fashioned. Windows provides yet another method for sharing that's less powerful but easier to use. To use this method, pick anything you want to share (even a single file) in Windows Explorer/File Explorer. Then simply right-click on it and select Share (or Share with) | Specific people. This opens the File Sharing dialog box, shown in Figure 14-35, where you can select specific user accounts from a drop-down list.

Once you select a user account, you can then choose what permission level to give to that user. You have two choices: Read and Read/Write (see Figure 14-36). *Read* simply means the user has read-only permissions. *Read/Write* gives the user read and write permissions and the permission to delete any file the user contributed to the folder.

NOTE If the computer in question is on a Windows domain, the File Sharing dialog box differs such that you can search the network for user accounts in the domain. This makes it easy to share throughout the network. See Chapter 21 for the details.

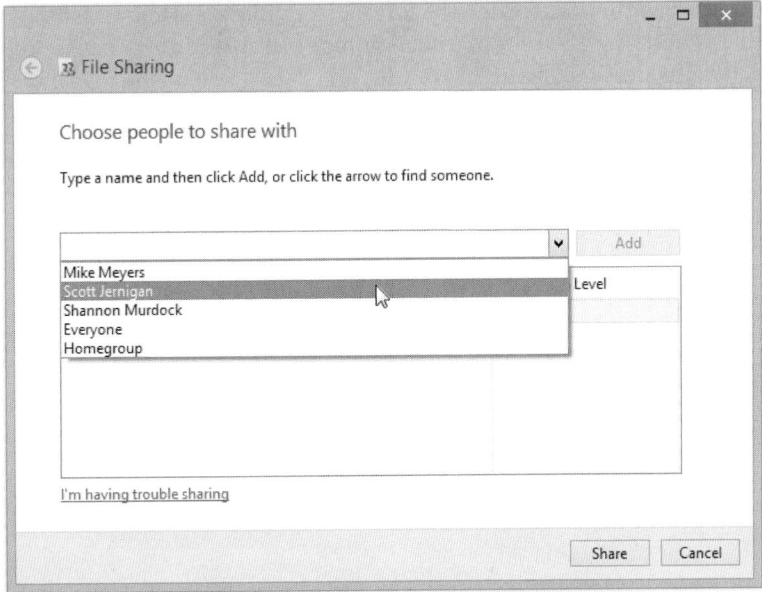

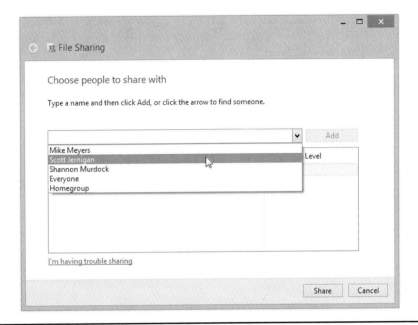

Figure 14-35 File Sharing dialog box

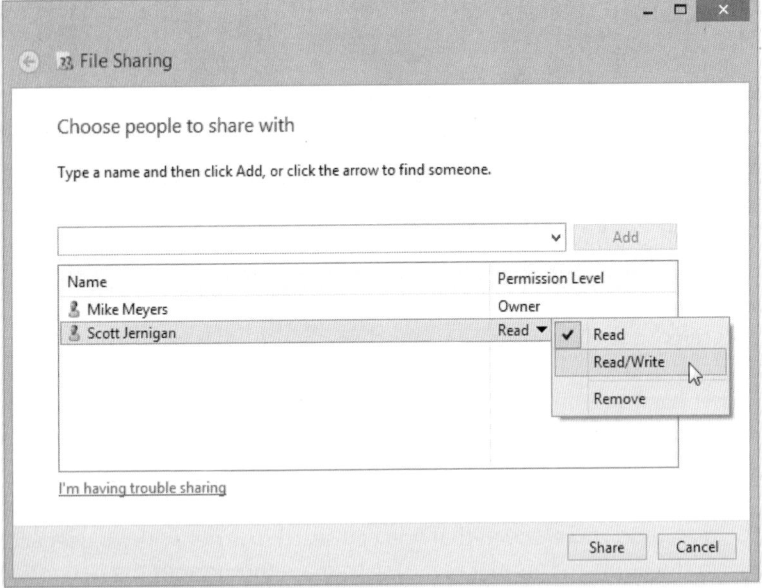

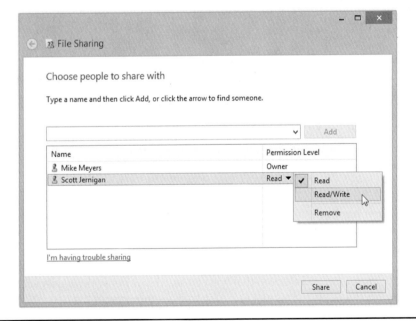

Figure 14-36 Permissions options

Locating Shared Folders

Before you walk away from a computer, you should check for any unnecessary or unknown (to you) shared folders on the hard drives. This enables you to make the computer as secure as possible for the user. When you look in Windows Explorer/File Explorer, shared folders don't just jump out at you, especially if they're buried deep within the file system. A shared C: drive is obvious, but a shared folder all the way down in D:\temp\backup\Simon\secret share would not be obvious, especially if none of the parent folders were shared.

Windows comes with a handy tool for locating all of the shared folders on a computer, regardless of where they reside on the drives. The Computer Management console in the Administrative Tools has a Shared Folders option under System Tools. Under Shared Folders are three options: Shares, Sessions, and Open Files. Select Shares to reveal all of the shared folders (see Figure 14-37).

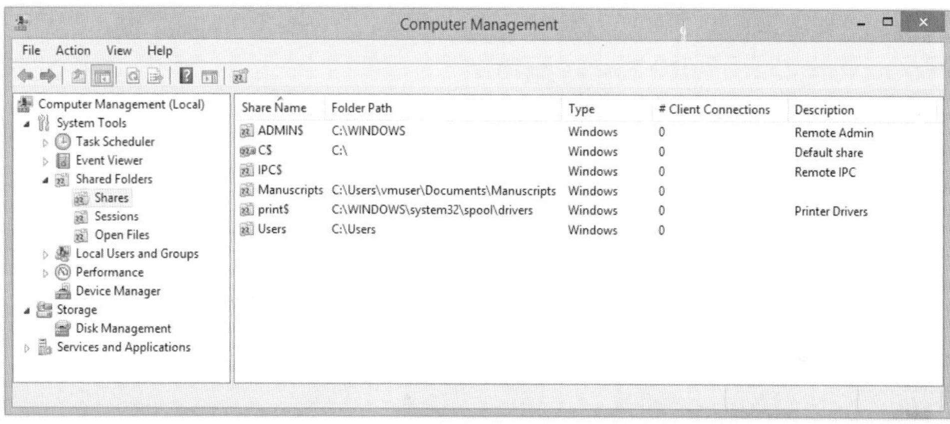

Figure 14-37 Shared Folders tool in Computer Management

You can double-click on any share to open the Properties dialog box for that folder. At that point, you can make changes to the share—such as users and permissions—just as you would from any other sharing dialog box.

Administrative Shares

A close look at the screenshot in Figure 14-37 might have left some of you with raised eyebrows and quizzical looks. What kind of share is ADMIN$ or C$?

Every version of Windows since Windows NT comes with several default shares, notably all hard drives—not optical drives or removable devices, such as thumb drives—plus the %systemroot% folder (usually C:\Windows) and a couple of others, depending on the system. These *administrative shares* give local administrators administrative access to these resources, whether they log on locally or remotely. (In contrast, shares added manually are called *local shares*.)

Administrative shares are odd ducks. You cannot change the default permissions on them. You can delete them, but Windows will re-create them automatically every time you reboot. They're hidden, so they don't appear when you browse a machine over the network, though you can map them by name. Keep the administrator password safe, and these default shares won't affect the overall security of the computer.

NOTE Administrative shares have been exploited by malware programs, especially because many users who set up their computers never give the administrator account a password. Starting with Windows XP Home, Microsoft changed the remote access permissions for such machines. If you log on to a computer remotely as administrator with no password, you get guest access rather than administrator access. That neatly nips potential exploits in the bud.

Protecting Data with Encryption

The scrambling of data through *encryption* techniques provides the only true way to secure your data from access by any other user. Administrators can use the Take Ownership permission to seize any file or folder on a computer, even those you don't actively share. Thus, you need to implement other security measures for that data that needs to be ultra secure. Depending on the version of Windows, you have between zero and three encryptions tools: Windows Home editions have basically no security features. Advanced editions of Windows add a system that can encrypt files and folders called Encrypting File System. Finally, the most advanced editions feature drive encryption through BitLocker.

Encrypting File System

The professional editions of Windows offer a feature called the *Encrypting File System (EFS)*, an encryption scheme that any user can use to encrypt individual files or folders on a computer.

You can encrypt a file or folder in seconds. Just right-click on the file or folder you want to encrypt and select Properties. In the Properties dialog box for that object, select the General tab and click the Advanced button (see Figure 14-38) to open the Advanced Attributes dialog box. Click the checkbox next to *Encrypt contents to secure data* (see Figure 14-39). Click OK to close the Advanced Attributes dialog box and then click OK again on the Properties dialog box, and you've locked that file or folder from any user account aside from your own.

NOTE Encryption is just one possible *attribute* of a file. You can also make files hidden, read-only, and more, all from a file or folder's Properties dialog box. You'll learn more about attributes in Chapter 16.

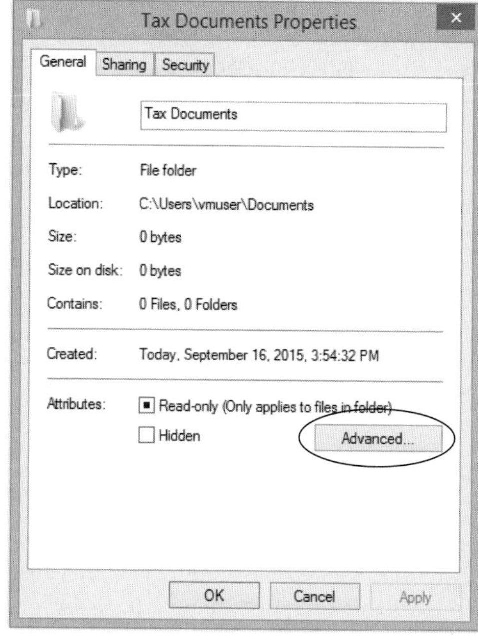

Figure 14-38 Click the Advanced button on the General tab

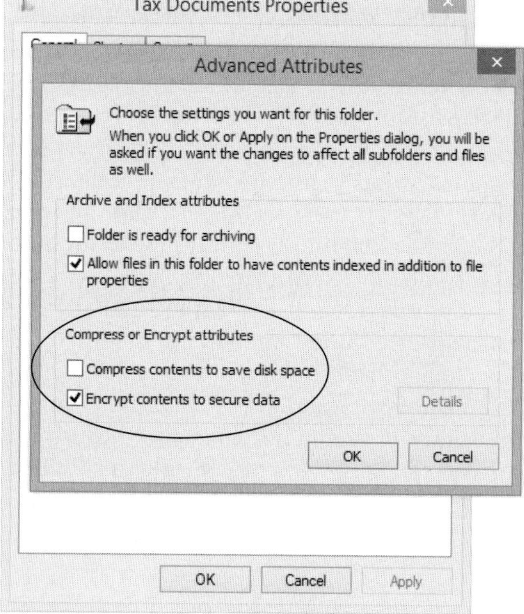

Figure 14-39 Selecting encryption

As long as you maintain the integrity of your password, any data you encrypt by using EFS is secure from prying eyes. That security comes at a potential price, though, and your password is the key. The Windows security database stores the password (securely, not plain text, so no worries there), but that means access to your encrypted files is based on that specific installation of Windows. If you lose your password or an administrator resets your password, you're locked out of your encrypted files permanently. There's no recovery. Also, if the computer dies and you try to retrieve your data by installing the hard drive in another system, you're likewise out of luck. Even if you have an identical user name on the new system, the security ID that defines the user account will differ from what you had on the old system.

NOTE If you use EFS, you simply must have a valid password reset disk in the event of some horrible catastrophe.

And one last caveat. If you copy an encrypted file to a drive formatted as anything but NTFS, you'll get a prompt saying that the copied file will not be encrypted. If you copy to a drive with NTFS, the encryption stays. The encrypted file—even if on a removable disk—will only be readable on your system with your login.

BitLocker Drive Encryption

Windows Ultimate and Enterprise editions, and Windows 8/8.1 Pro, offer full drive encryption through *BitLocker Drive Encryption*. BitLocker encrypts the whole drive, including every user's files, so it's not dependent on any one account. The beauty of BitLocker is that if your hard drive is stolen, such as in the case of a stolen portable computer, all of the data on the hard drive is safe. The thief can't get access, even if you have a user on that system who failed to secure his or her data through EFS.

BitLocker requires a special Trusted Platform Module (TPM) chip on the motherboard to function. The TPM chip validates on boot that the computer has not changed—that you still have the same operating system installed, for example, and that the computer wasn't hacked by some malevolent program. The TPM also works in cases where you move the BitLocker drive from one system to another.

If you have a legitimate BitLocker failure (rather than a theft) because of tampering or moving the drive to another system, you need to have a properly created and accessible recovery key or recovery password. The key or password is generally created at the time you enable BitLocker and should be kept somewhere secure, such as a printed copy in a safe or a file on a network server accessible only to administrators.

To enable BitLocker, double-click the BitLocker Drive Encryption icon in the Classic Control Panel, or select Security in Control Panel Home view and then click Turn on BitLocker (see Figure 14-40).

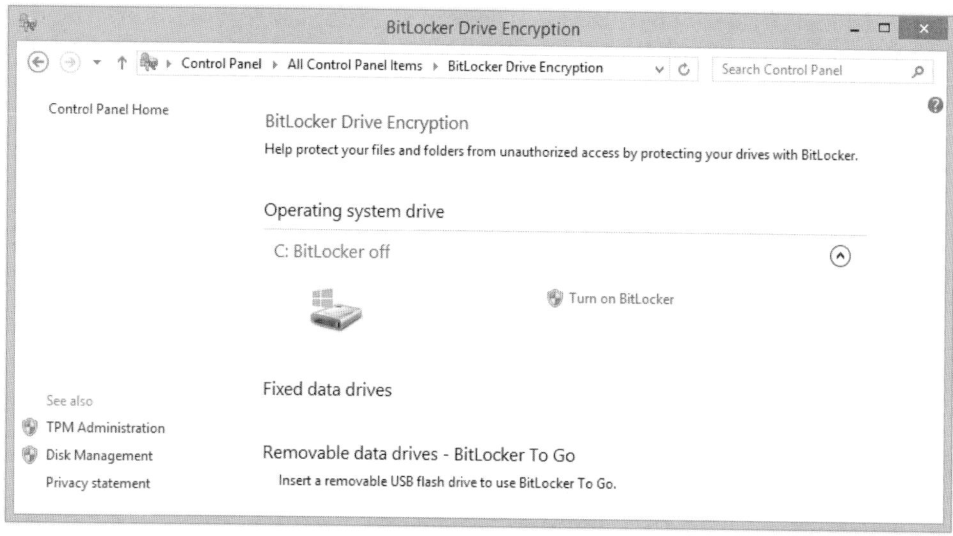

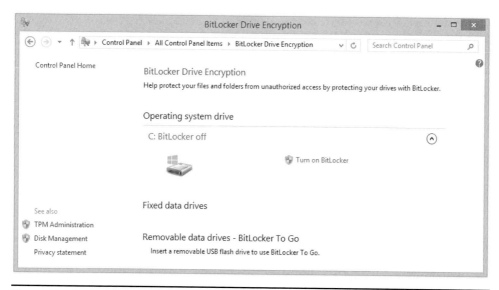

Figure 14-40 Enabling BitLocker Drive Encryption

BitLocker to Go enables you to apply BitLocker encryption to removable drives, like USB-based flash drives. Although it shares a name, BitLocker to Go applies encryption and password protection, but doesn't require a TPM chip. Still, every little bit counts when it comes to securing data.

Beyond Sharing Users and Groups

As you've just seen, users and groups are powerful tools for authenticating users to systems as well as authorizing NTFS permissions, but that's not where their power ends. There are two more areas where we use users and groups to go beyond logging on to a system or sharing folders and files: security policies and User Account Control. Let's discuss security policies first and then cover User Account Control.

Security Policies

Security policies are just rules we apply to users and groups to do, well, just about everything *but* NTFS permissions. Would you like to configure your system so that the Accounting group can only log on between 9 A.M. and 5 P.M.? There's a security policy for that. How about forcing anyone who logs on to your system to use a password that's at least eight characters long? There's a security policy for that as well. Windows provides thousands of preset security policies that you may use simply by turning them on in a utility called Local Security Policy.

All versions of Windows have the Local Security Policy utility. You may access this tool through Control Panel | Administrative Tools | Local Security Policy, but all of us cool kids just open a command line and run **secpol.msc**. However you choose to access this tool, it will look something like Figure 14-41.

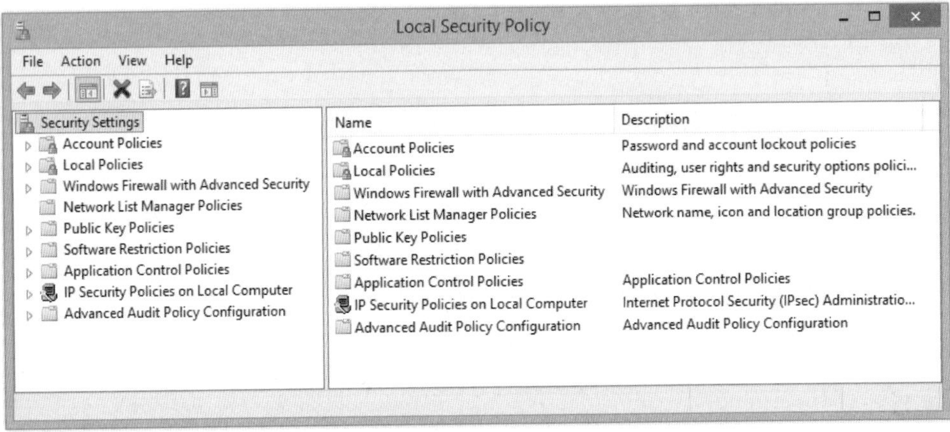

Figure 14-41 Local Security Policy utility

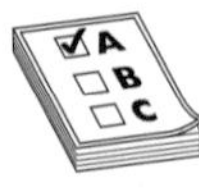

EXAM TIP Local security policies are incredibly powerful—so powerful that one could make a career out of understanding all they can do. We're covering just enough on the Local Security Policy editor to cover a few basic questions on the CompTIA A+ 220-902 exam.

Local Security Policy has a number of containers that help organize the many types of polices on a typical system. Under each container are subcontainers or preset policies. As an example, let's set a local security policy that causes user passwords to expire every 30 days—better known as account password expiration or password age. To do this, open up the Account Policies container and then open the Password Policy subcontainer.

Look at the Maximum password age setting. On almost all versions of Windows your local user accounts passwords expire after 42 days. You can easily change this to 30 days just by double-clicking on Maximum password age and adjusting the setting in the Properties dialog box, as shown in Figure 14-42. You can also set the value to 0 and the password will never expire.

NOTE This setting only works for your local user accounts.

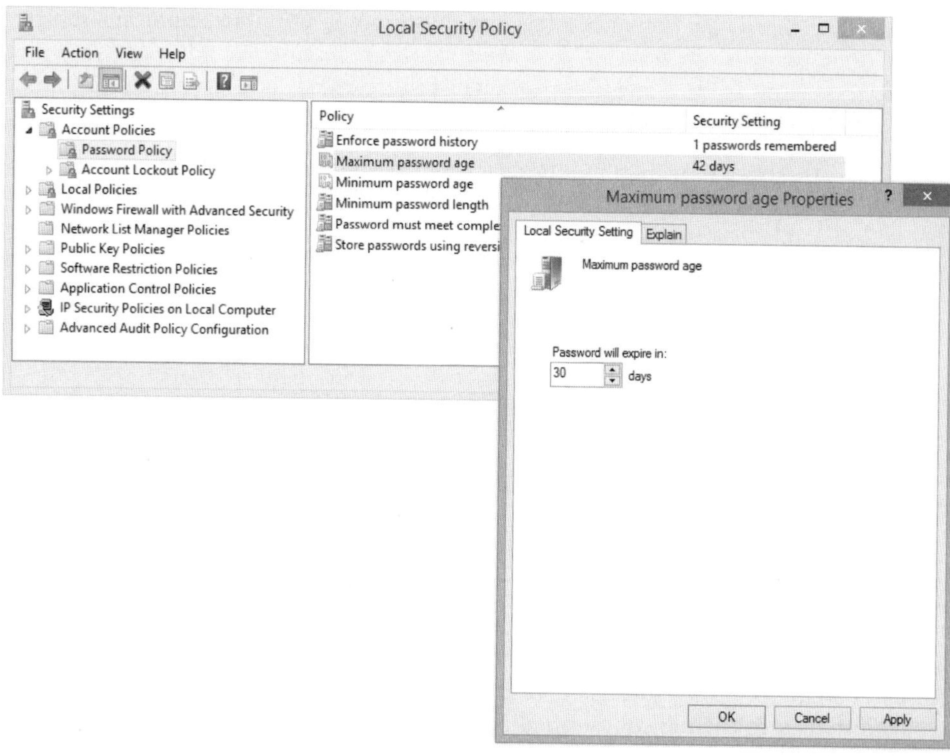

Figure 14-42 Local Security Policy editor

User Account Control

When picking the poster child for the "327 Reasons We Hated Vista" list, I'll bet most folks put Vista's *User Account Control (UAC)* at the very top. Vista's UAC manifested as a pop-up dialog box that seemed to appear every time you tried to do *anything* on a Windows Vista system (see Figure 14-43).

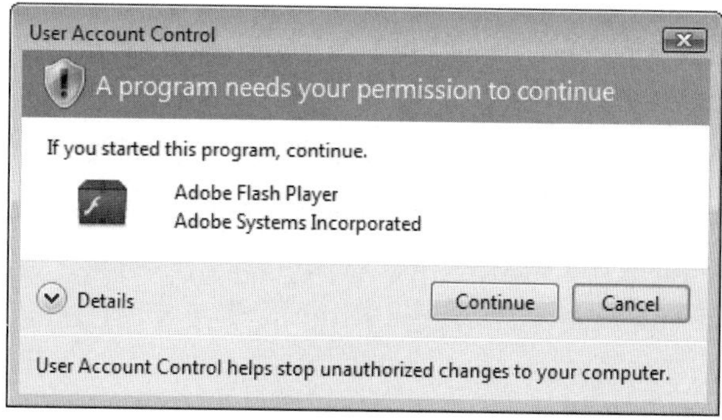

Figure 14-43 UAC in action. Arrgh!

It's too bad that UAC got such a bad rap. Not only is UAC an important security update for all versions of Windows, it is also a common feature in both Mac OS X and Linux/Unix. Figure 14-44 shows the equivalent feature on a Mac.

Figure 14-44 UAC equivalent on a Mac

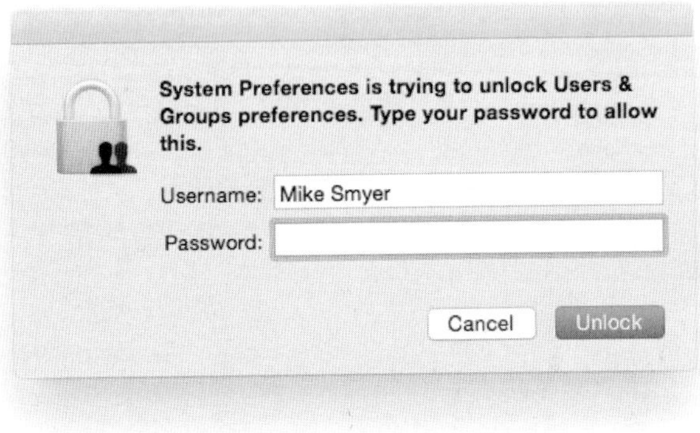

If every other major operating system uses something like UAC, why was Microsoft slammed so hard when they unveiled UAC in Windows Vista? The reason was simple: Windows users are spoiled rotten, and until UAC came along, the vast majority of users had no idea how risky their computing behavior was.

The problem started years ago when Microsoft created NTFS. NTFS uses robust user accounts and enables fine control over how users access files and folders—but at a cost: NTFS in its pure form is somewhat complicated.

User accounts have always been a bit of a challenge. The only account that can truly do *anything* on a Windows system is the administrator. Sure, you can configure a system with groups and assign NTFS permissions to those groups—and this is commonly done on large networks with a full-time IT staff—but what about small offices and home networks? These users almost never have the skill sets to deal with the complexities of users and groups, which often results in systems where the user accounts are all assigned administrator privileges by default—and that's when it gets dangerous (see Figure 14-45).

User Account Control enables users to know when they are about to do something that has serious consequences. Here are some examples of common actions that require administrator privileges:

- Installing and uninstalling applications
- Installing a driver for a device (e.g., a digital camera driver)
- Installing Windows Updates
- Adjusting Windows Firewall settings
- Changing a user's account type
- Browsing to another user's directory

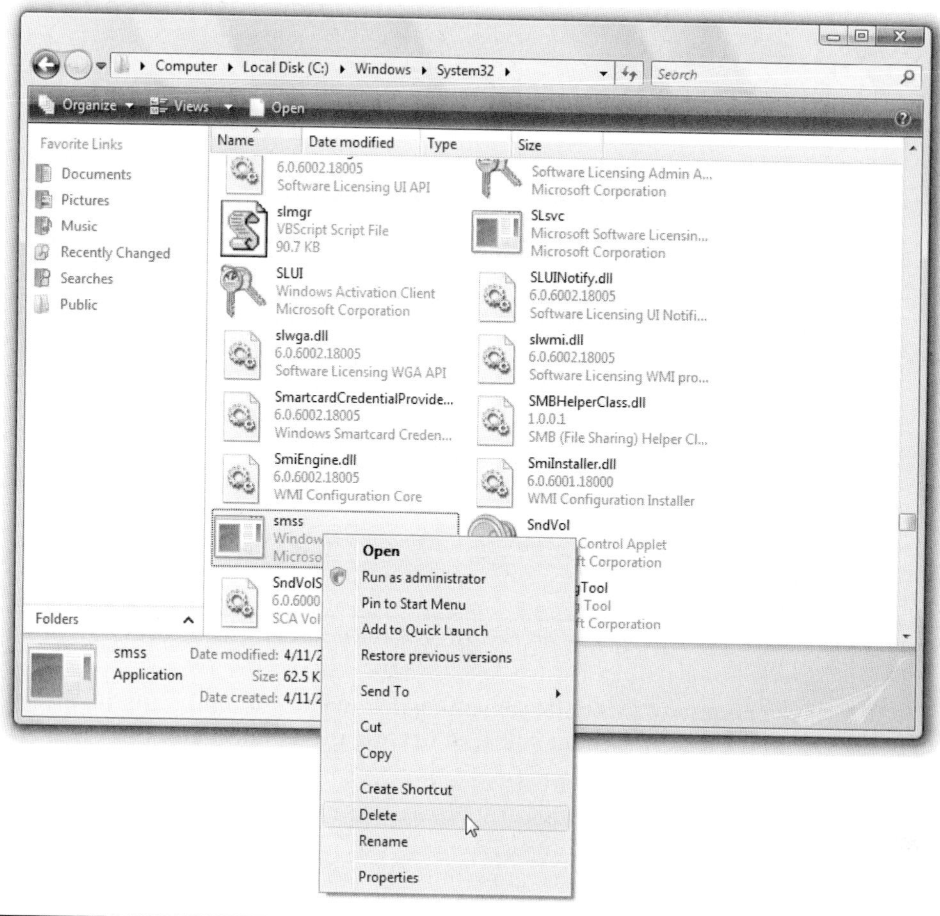

Figure 14-45 The danger of administrator privileges in the wrong hands!

Before Vista, Microsoft invented the idea of the Power Users group to give users almost all of the power of an administrator account (to handle most of the situations just described) without actually giving users the full power of the account. Assigning a user to the Power Users group still required someone who knew how to do this, however, so most folks at the small office/home level simply ignored the Power Users group (see Figure 14-46).

Clearly, Microsoft needed a better method to prevent people from running programs that they should not run. If users have the correct privileges, however—or the ability to "escalate" their privileges to that of an administrator—then they should be able to do what they need to do as simply as possible. Microsoft needed to make the following changes:

- The idea of using an administrator account for daily use needed to go away.
- Any level of account should be able to do anything as easily as possible.

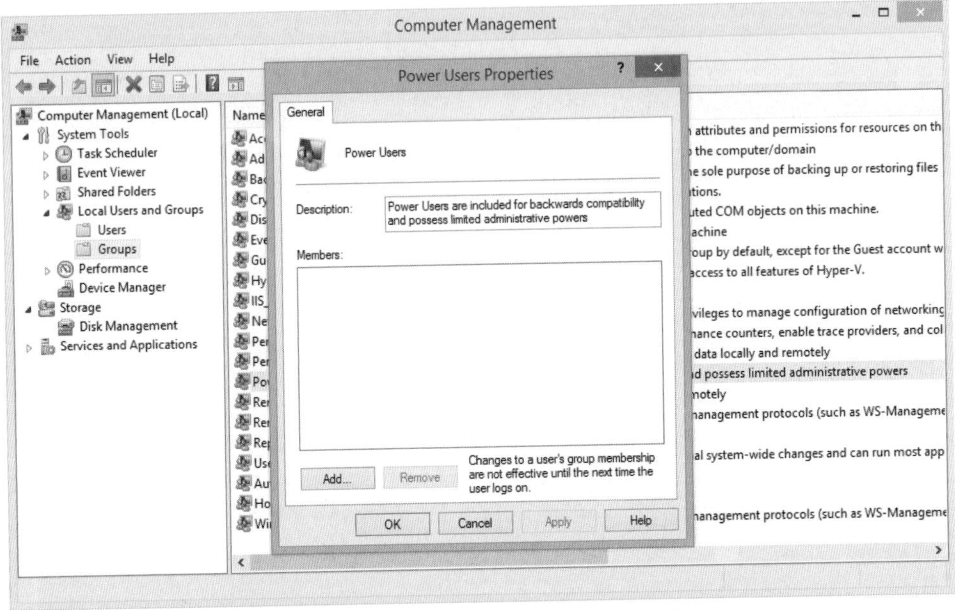

Figure 14-46 Power Users group—almost never used at the small office/home level

- If a regular account wants to do something that requires administrator privileges, the user of the regular account will need to enter the administrator password.
- If a user with administrator privileges wants to run something that requires administrator privileges, the user will not have to reenter his or her password, but the user will have to respond to an "Are you sure?"-type dialog box so he or she appreciates the gravity of the action—thus, the infamous UAC dialog box.

NOTE Both Linux and Mac OS X have been using a UAC function for a long time—it's called sudo. Check it out in Chapter 16.

How UAC Works

Sorry, but if you want to talk about UAC, you have to see how it all started with Vista. Since Vista was the first Windows OS with UAC, it has some of the classic "version 1.0" problems. Forgive me for the Vista references, but you need to see the Vista way of UAC to appreciate why it works the way it does in the most modern versions of Windows.

UAC works for both standard user accounts and administrator accounts. If a standard user attempts to do something that requires administrator privileges, he or she sees a UAC dialog box that prompts for the administrator password (see Figure 14-47).

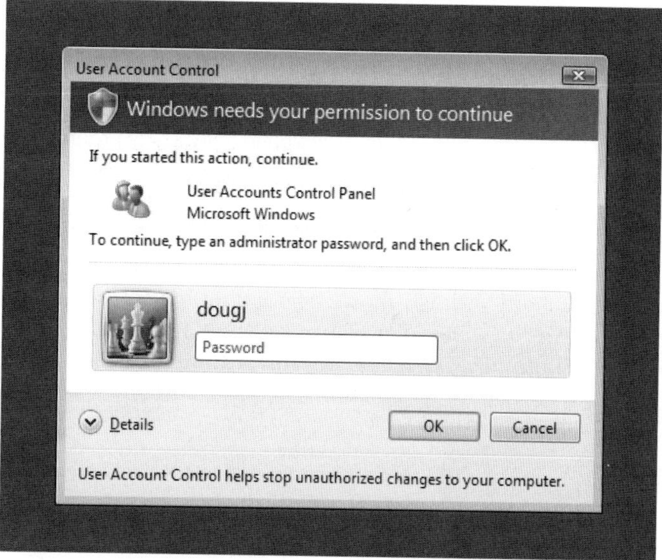

Figure 14-47 Prompting for an administrator password in Vista

If a user with administrator privileges attempts to do something that requires administrator privileges, a simpler UAC dialog box appears, like the one shown in Figure 14-48.

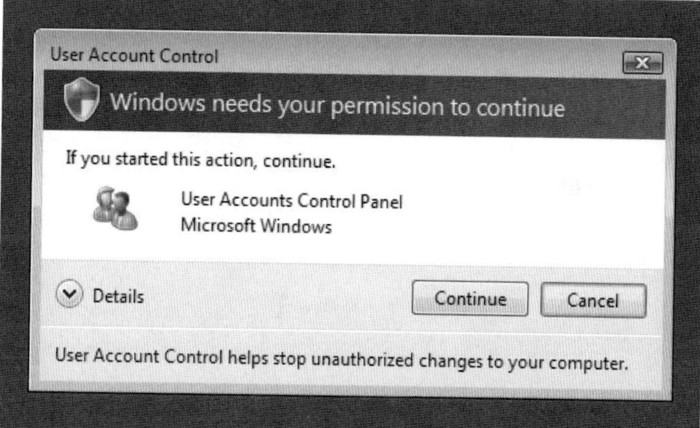

Figure 14-48 Classic UAC prompt

NOTE The official name for the UAC dialog box is the "UAC consent prompt." When the UAC consent prompt appears in Vista, the rest of the desktop darkens and you cannot take any other action until you respond to the consent prompt.

Interestingly, Vista has not one but four different UAC prompts, depending on the program/feature you wish to run, as outlined in Table 14-2.

UAC Classification	Type of Program
Blocked program	A program that has been blocked by a security policy
Unverified	An unknown third-party program
Verified	A digitally signed, third-party program or non-core OS program
Published by Vista	A program that is a core part of the operating system

Table 14-2 UAC Prompts in Windows Vista

In all versions of windows, blocked programs generate a scary-looking, red-bannered dialog box like the one shown in Figure 14-49. Note you can click OK in Windows Vista (or Close in Windows 7/8/8.1/10) or look at more details (if available).

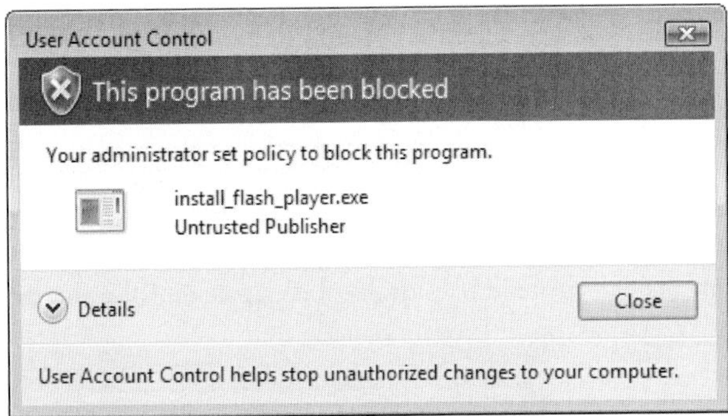

Figure 14-49 Blocked program

Unverified programs lack any form of certificate to validate. In this case, you get a yellow-bannered dialog box warning you the application is unsigned and giving you two options: allow the program to run (Yes) or not (No). See Figure 14-50 for an example of this.

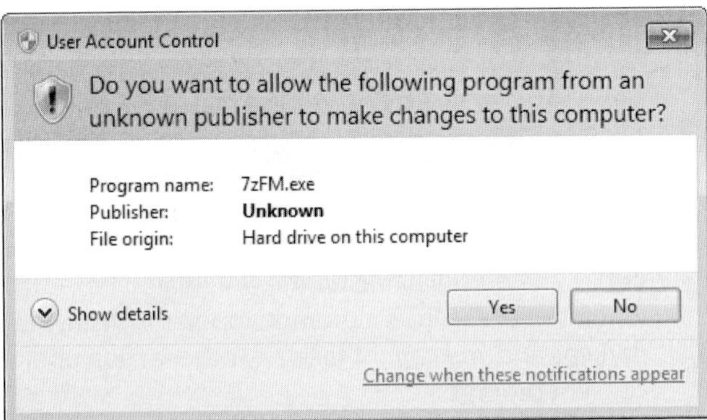

Figure 14-50 Unverified program

Verified programs aren't part of the core of Vista and are usually written by third parties. These programs do have valid, verified certificates. You can identify the dialog box by its gray-blue banner (see Figure 14-51).

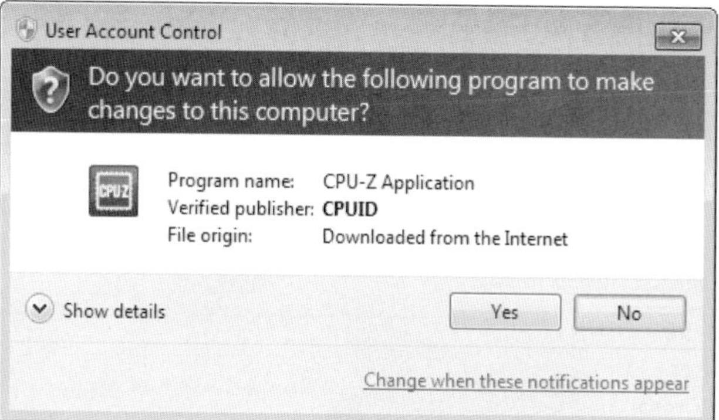

Figure 14-51
Verified program

Published by Vista programs are written as part of the core of Vista and show up with a teal-bannered dialog box (see Figure 14-52).

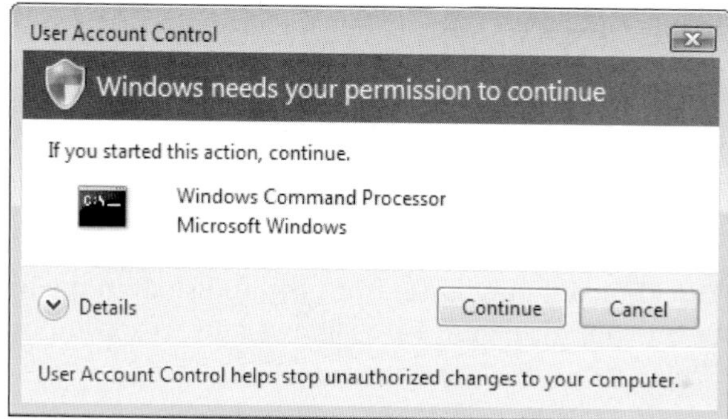

Figure 14-52
Published by Vista

UAC uses small shield icons to warn you ahead of time that it will prompt you before certain tasks, as shown in Figure 14-53. Microsoft updated this somewhat redundant feature in subsequent versions of Windows, as you'll soon see.

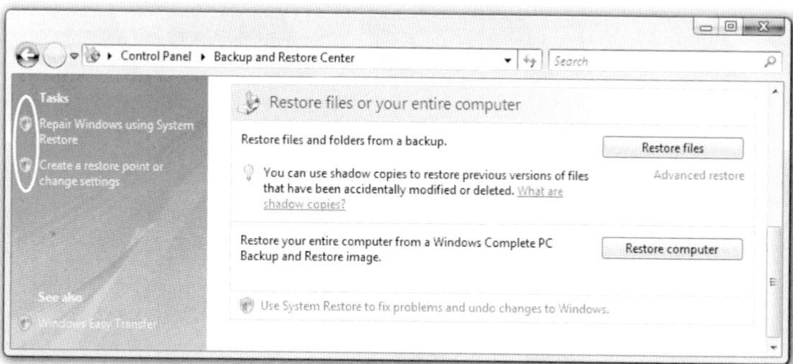

Figure 14-53
Shield icons in the Control Panel

UAC gives users running a program an opportunity to consider their actions before they move forward. It's a good thing, but spoiled Windows users aren't accustomed to something that makes them consider their actions. As a result, one of the first things everyone learned how to do when Vista came out was to turn off UAC.

How to Turn Off UAC

You can turn off UAC in a number of ways in Windows. Here are the two most common ways:

1. In the User Accounts Control Panel applet, you'll see an option to *Turn User Account Control on or off* (see Figure 14-54). Select this option and uncheck the checkbox to turn UAC off. Check the checkbox to turn it on again.

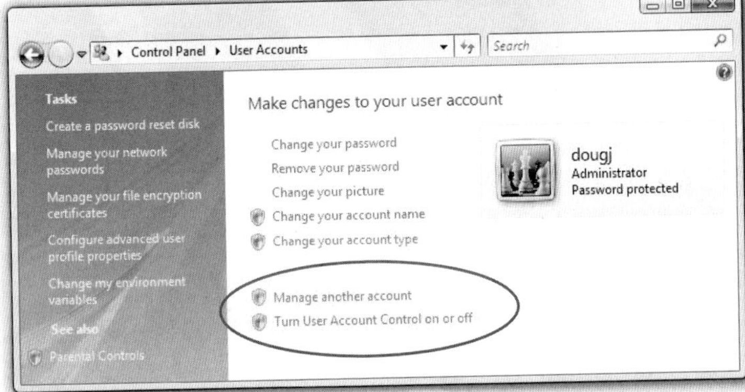

Figure 14-54 Turning User Account Control on or off

2. You can also configure UAC from the Tools tab in the System Configuration utility (msconfig); Figure 14-55 shows how to accomplish this in Windows Vista.

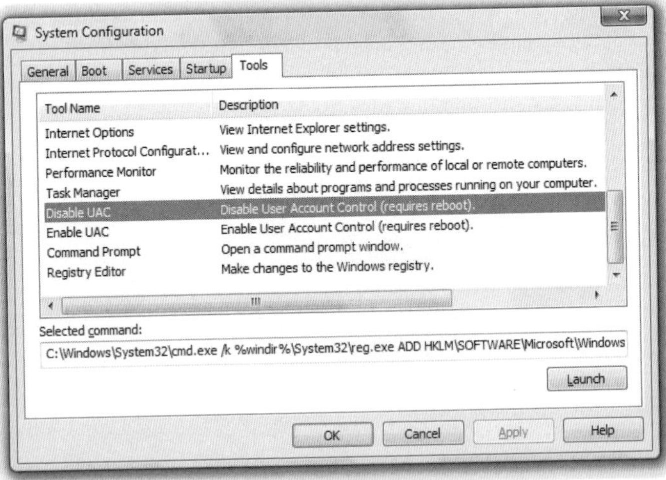

Figure 14-55 Disabling UAC in the System Configuration utility

UAC in Windows Vista worked well, but it startled users. Suddenly, users had to deal with UAC, and they didn't like that. Most users simply turned UAC off and added it to the reasons to not like Windows Vista.

UAC in Modern Windows

Microsoft may be a huge company, but it still knows how to react when its customers speak out about features they don't like. Windows 7 unveiled a more refined, less "in-your-face" UAC that makes the feature much easier to use. This is the version of UAC used in all later versions of Windows as well.

A More Granular UAC

Microsoft did some research on why UAC drove users nuts, concluding that the problem wasn't UAC itself but the "I'm constantly in your face or you can turn me off and you get no help at all" aspect. To make UAC less aggressive, Microsoft introduced four UAC levels. To see these levels, go to the User Accounts applet and select Change User Account Control settings, as shown in Figure 14-56. When you select this option, you see the dialog box in Figure 14-57.

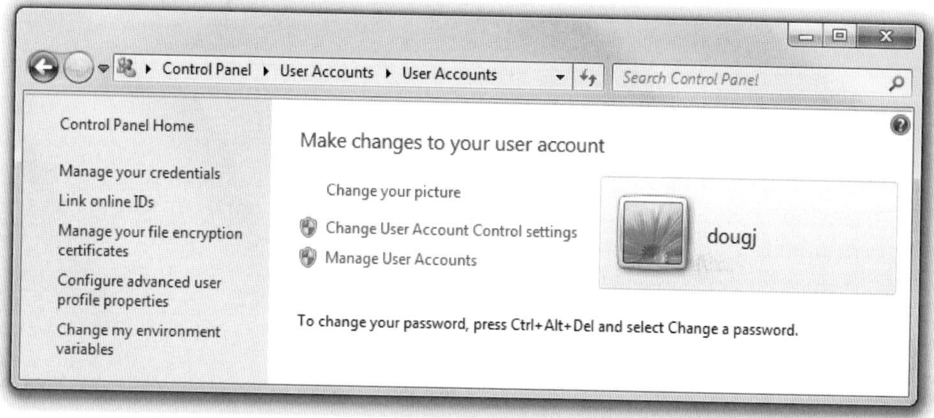

Figure 14-56 Change User Account Control settings option

In Figure 14-57, you can see a slider with four levels. The top level (Always notify) means you want UAC to work exactly as it does in Vista, displaying the aggressive consent form every time you do anything that typically requires administrator access. The bottom option (Never notify) turns off UAC. The two levels in the middle are new and are very similar. Both of them do the following:

- Don't notify me when I make changes.
- Notify me only when programs try to makes changes.

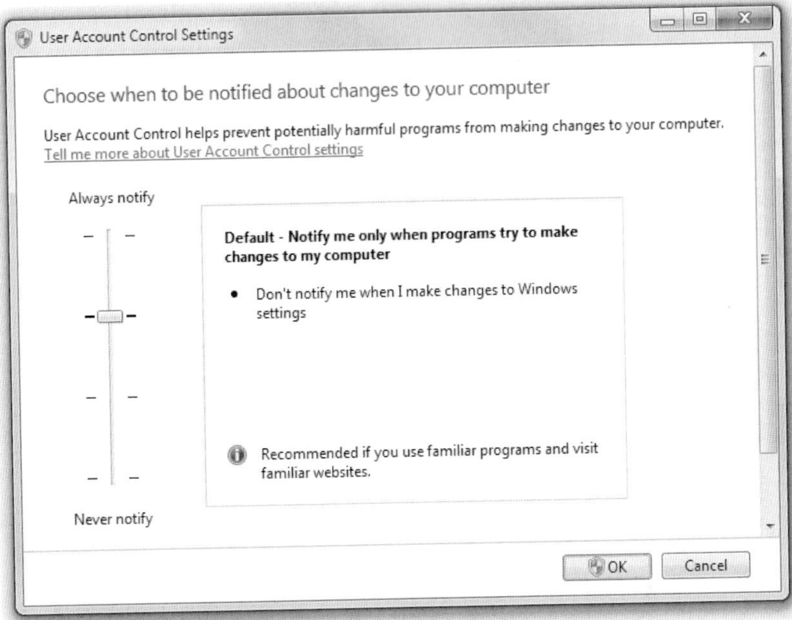

Figure 14-57 Four levels of UAC

The only difference is in *how* they show the change. The second-from-top level will display the typical consent form, but only when programs try to make changes. The third-from-top level displays a consent form, but where the normal consent form dims your desktop and doesn't allow you to do anything but address the form, this consent form just pops up like a normal dialog box.

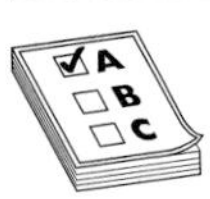

EXAM TIP Make sure you know what each of the four UAC levels does.

Program Changes Versus Changes I Make

So what's the difference between a program making a change and you making a change? Take a look at Figure 14-58. In this case, Windows 7 is set to the second-from-top option. A program (the very safe and, judging by the color of the banner, verified) Adobe Download Manager is attempting to install a feature into Internet Explorer. Because this is a program trying to make changes, the UAC consent form appears and darkens the desktop.

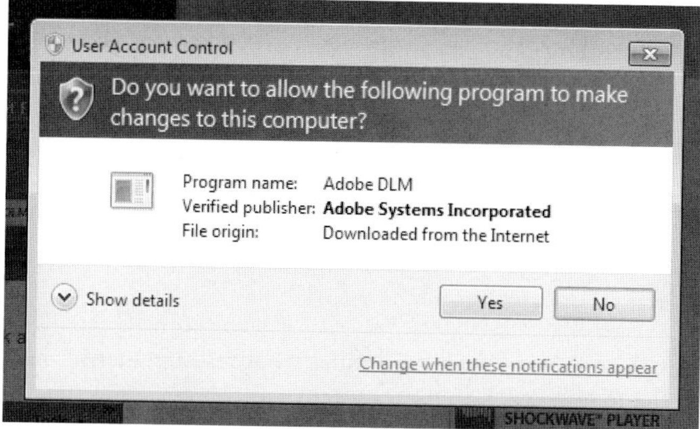

Figure 14-58 Darkened UAC

If you lower the UAC to the third-from-top option, you still see a consent form, but now it acts like a typical dialog box, as shown in Figure 14-59.

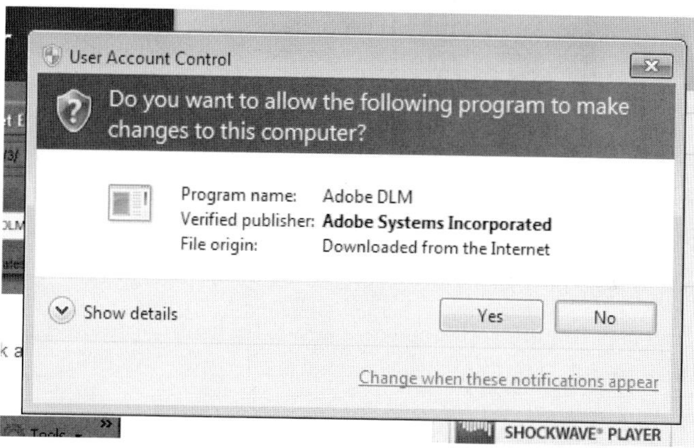

Figure 14-59 Non-darkened UAC

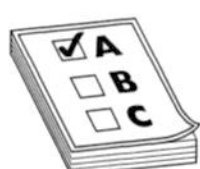

EXAM TIP The default behavior for UAC in Windows 7 is the second-from-top option, which results in a screen similar to Figure 14-58.

A program such as the Adobe program described earlier is very different from a feature *you* want to change. Notice the shields, as shown in earlier figures.

Each of these options isn't a program—each is merely a feature built into Windows. Those shields tell you that clicking the feature next to a shield will require administrator privileges. If you were to pick the Vista-strength UAC option, you'd get a UAC consent prompt when you click one of those features. If you set UAC to any of the three lower settings, however, you'd go straight to that feature without *any* form of UAC consent prompt. Of course, this isn't true if you don't have administrator privileges. If you're a standard user, you'll still be prompted for a password, just as in Vista.

Overall, the improvements to UAC in Windows 7 show that it has a place on everyone's computer. UAC might cause an occasional surprise or irritation, but that one more "Are you sure?" could mean the difference between safe and unsafe computing. So go ahead, turn UAC back on in Windows! It's well worth the small inconvenience.

Chapter Review

Questions

1. Which tool or mechanism defines what resources a user may access and what he or she may do with those resources?
   A. Authentication through user accounts and passwords
   B. Authorization through user accounts and passwords
   C. Authentication through NTFS
   D. Authorization through NTFS
2. Which is the best password for the user Joy, who has a pet named Fido and a birth date of January 8, 1982?
   A. joy1982
   B. joylovesfido
   C. 1982cutie
   D. oddvr88*
3. How can you encrypt an entire drive, including files and folders belonging to other users?
   A. EFS
   B. User Account Control
   C. Administrative Shares
   D. BitLocker
4. What feature in Windows 7 opens a consent prompt for standard users to enter administrator credentials to accomplish various tasks reserved for the latter group?
   A. User Access Command
   B. User Access Control
   C. User Account Command
   D. User Account Control

5. Which permission enables an administrator to change the ownership of a file without knowing the user account password for that file?
   A. Change permission
   B. Change Ownership permission
   C. Ownership permission
   D. Take Ownership permission
6. You copy a file from a folder on a hard drive formatted as NTFS, with permissions set to Read for everyone, to a USB thumb drive formatted as FAT32. What effective permissions does the copy of the file have?
   A. Read-only for everyone
   B. Full Control for everyone
   C. None
   D. You can't copy a file from an NTFS drive to a FAT32 drive.
7. Which of the following commands is used to change file permissions in Linux?
   A. chmod
   B. chown
   C. users
   D. pwn
8. Which tool in Windows 8.1 enables you to create a new user account based on a global Microsoft account?
   A. User Accounts in Control Panel
   B. Users and Groups in Control Panel
   C. Settings charm
   D. Users charm
9. Which option enables you to share files easily among multiple users on a single Windows 8 system?
   A. Place the files in the Public Libraries.
   B. Place the files in the Public Shares.
   C. Place the files in the EFS folders.
   D. You cannot. Windows locks down sharing on a single system.
10. Which of the following file systems enables you to encrypt files, thus making them unviewable by any account but your own?
   A. EFS
   B. FAT
   C. FAT32
   D. OSR

Answers

1. **D.** Authorization through NTFS defines resources a user may access and what he or she can do with those resources.
2. **D.** Of the choices listed, oddvr88* would be the best password; it has a non-alphanumeric character, which makes it more difficult for a hacker to crack.
3. **D.** BitLocker Drive Encryption enables you to encrypt an entire drive, including files and folders belonging to other users.
4. **D.** The User Account Control feature in Windows 7 provides a consent prompt for standard users to enter administrator credentials to accomplish various tasks normally reserved for the Administrators group.
5. **D.** The Take Ownership permission enables an administrator to change the ownership of a file without knowing the user account password for that file.
6. **C.** The key here is that you are copying from an NTFS hard drive to a FAT32 USB drive. Copying from an NTFS-based partition to a FAT- or FAT32-based partition creates two copies of the object; the copy of the object in the new location has no effective permissions at all.
7. **A.** The chmod command enables you to change file permissions in Linux.
8. **C.** The Settings charm in Windows 8.1 enables you to create a new user account based on a global Microsoft account.
9. **A.** The Public Libraries make it easy to share files among multiple users of a single system.
10. **A.** The Encrypting File System (EFS) enables you to encrypt files, making them unviewable by any account but your own.

CHAPTER 15

Maintaining and Optimizing Operating Systems

In this chapter, you will learn how to

- Perform operating system maintenance tasks
- Optimize operating systems
- Prepare for problems

Every computer running a modern operating system (OS) requires both occasional optimization to keep the system running snappily and ongoing maintenance to make sure nothing goes wrong. Microsoft, Apple, and the many Linux developers use decades of experience with operating systems to search for ways to make the tasks of maintaining and optimizing surprisingly easy and very automatic, but there's still plenty to do to keep things humming along.

The chapter covers maintenance and optimization, so let's make sure you know what these two terms mean. *Maintenance* means jobs you do from time to time to keep the OS running well, such as running hard drive utilities. CompTIA sees *optimization* as changes you make to a system to make it better—a good example is adding RAM. This chapter covers the standard maintenance and optimization activities performed on Windows, Mac OS X, and Linux, and the tools techs use to perform them.

NOTE This chapter covers maintenance and optimization techniques for all the operating systems currently on the CompTIA A+ exams. But, like the exams and the reality of market share, Windows features a lot more than Mac OS X or Linux.

Even the best maintained, most perfectly optimized computer is going to run into trouble. Hard drives crash, naïve coworkers delete files, and those super great new video card drivers sometimes fail. The secret isn't to try to avoid trouble, because trouble will find you, but rather to make sure you're ready to deal with problems when they arise. This is one area that very few users do well, and it's our jobs as techs to make recovery from trouble as painless as possible. OS developers give us plenty of tools to prepare for problems—we just need to make sure we use them.

902

Maintaining Operating Systems

Maintaining modern operating systems can be compared to maintaining a new automobile. Of course, a new automobile comes with a warranty, so most of us just take it to the dealer to get work done. In this case, however, *you* are the mechanic, so you need to think as an auto mechanic would think. First, an auto mechanic needs to apply recalls when the automaker finds a serious problem. For a PC tech, that means installing the latest system patches released by Microsoft. You also need to maintain the parts that wear down over time. On a car, that might mean changing the oil or rotating the tires. In a Windows system, that includes keeping the hard drive and Registry organized and uncluttered. Mac OS X and Linux require a little less maintenance, but I'll cover those needs as well.

Windows Patch Management

There's no such thing as a perfect operating system, and Windows is no exception. From the moment Microsoft releases a new version of Windows, malware attacks, code errors, new hardware, new features, and many other issues compel Microsoft to provide updates, known more generically as *patches* in the computing world, to the operating system. The process of keeping software updated in a safe and timely fashion is known as *patch management*. Microsoft's primary distribution tool for handling patch management is a Control Panel applet called *Windows Update*. (This applies to Windows versions covered on the 901 exam, but not to Windows 10. Just FYI.)

Windows Update separates the different type of fixes into distinct types: updates and service packs. *Updates* in Windows Vista and 7 are individual fixes that come out fairly often, on the order of once a week or so. Individual updates are usually fairly small, rarely more than a few megabytes. A *service pack* is a large bundle of updates plus anything else Microsoft might choose to add. Service packs are invariably large (hundreds of megabytes) and are often packaged with Windows, as shown in Figure 15-1.

NOTE Windows Vista has two service packs: SP1 and SP2. Window 7 has one service pack: SP1. In Window 8, 8.1, and 10, *updates* have replaced the use of service packs.

With Windows 8 and later, Microsoft ditched the service pack terminology and uses only updates to indicate changes. Big updates get a revision number, like Windows 8 to Windows 8.1.

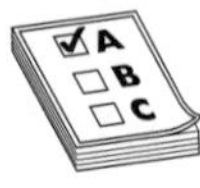

EXAM TIP You might be asked about installing service packs and updates on the CompTIA A+ exams. Pay attention to the steps listed here.

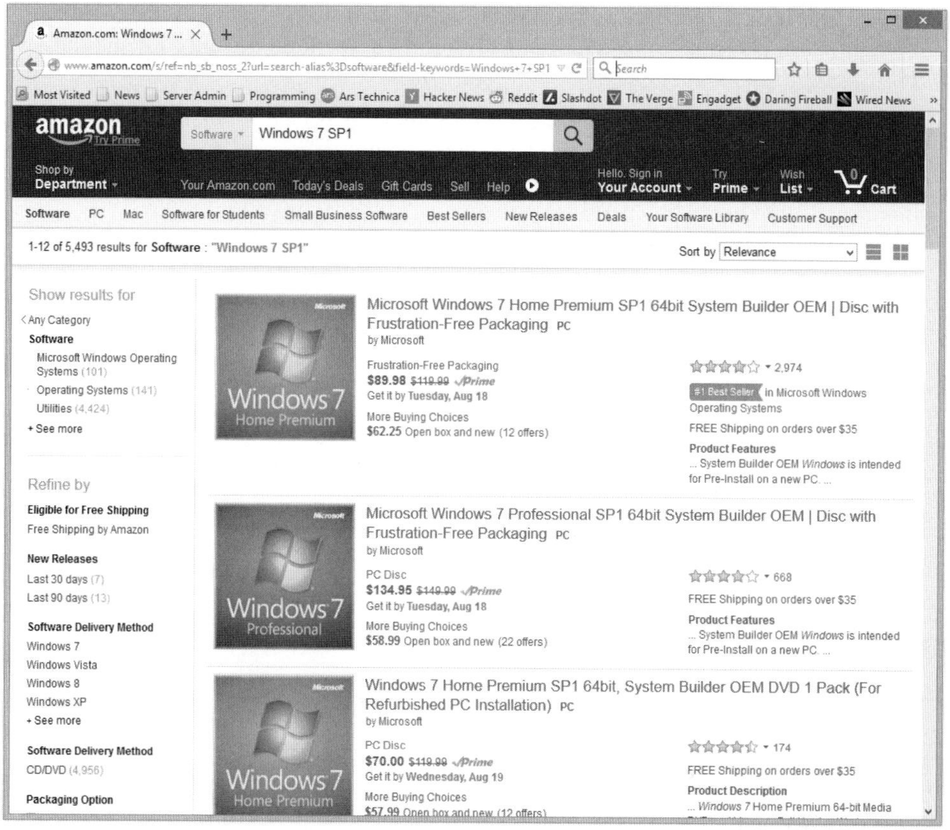

Figure 15-1 Windows 7 with Service Pack 1

Windows Update checks your system, grabs the updates, and patches your system automatically. Even if you don't want to allow Windows Update to run automatically, it'll nag you about updates until you patch your system. Microsoft provides Windows Update for all versions of Windows.

NOTE Windows 8/8.1 offers two interfaces for Windows Update: one in Control Panel and one in the PC Settings app. In Windows 10, the Control Panel Windows Update app is gone and you will find the only Windows Update interface in the Settings app under Update and Security.

Windows Update can run automatically, so you'll probably see new updates to install every time you open the applet. There are three common types of updates:

- **Important** These updates address critical security or stability issues and are the most critical. You can configure Windows Update to install these updates automatically.

- **Recommended** A recommended update is an added feature or enhancement that is not critical. You can configure Windows Update to install these updates automatically.
- **Optional** These include device drivers, language packs, and other nonessential updates. You must install these updates manually.

Figure 15-2 shows you what Windows Update looks like in Windows 7. Note that the Important update is Windows 7 Service Pack 1.

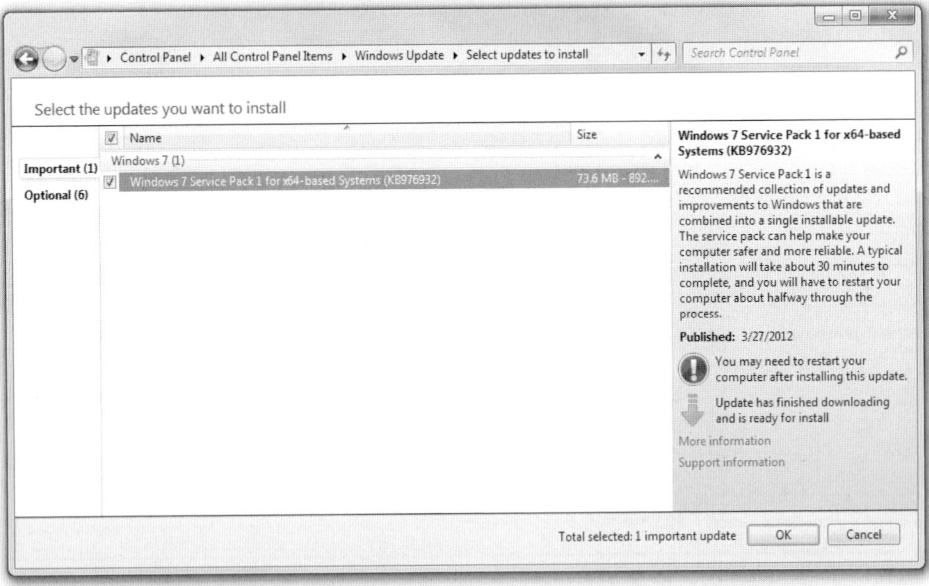

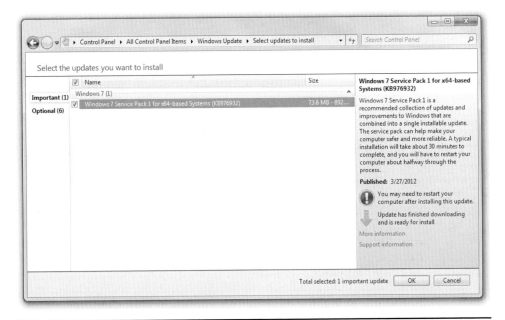

Figure 15-2 Windows Update in Windows 7

NOTE All Windows 10 updates download and install automatically by default and you cannot selectively choose individual updates to download.

Installing an update is as easy as selecting the updates you want to install and clicking OK. If you don't want to install a specific update, and don't want to look at it every time you open Windows Update, you can hide it. To hide an update, right-click on the update you wish to hide and select Hide update (see Figure 15-3).

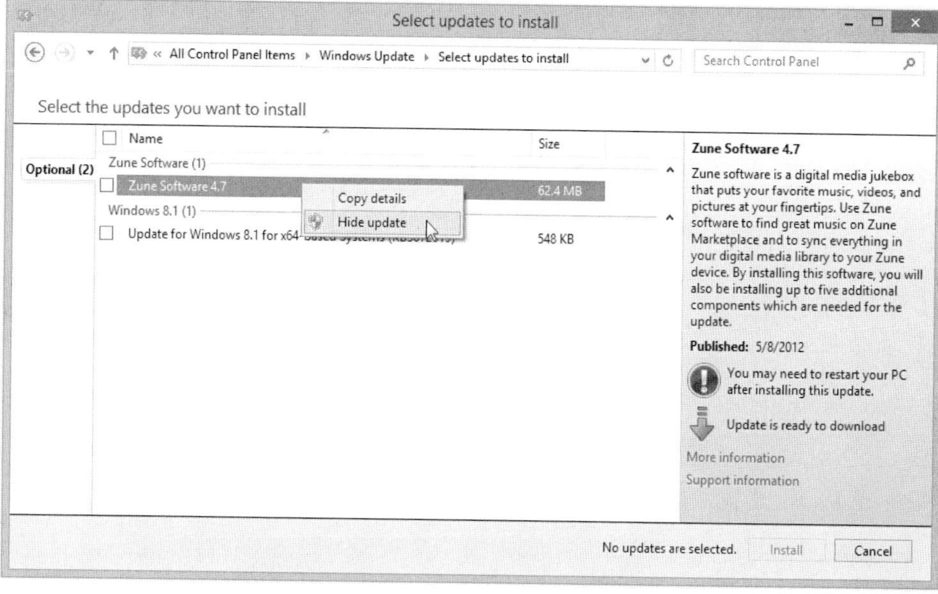

Figure 15-3 Hiding an update

Patch Management in Mac OS X and Linux

Both Mac OS X and Linux automatically alert you when software needs updating. With Mac OS X, you access updates through the *App Store* pane in System Preferences (see Figure 15-4). Most Linux distros have an updating tool like the Software Updater in Ubuntu (see Figure 15-5).

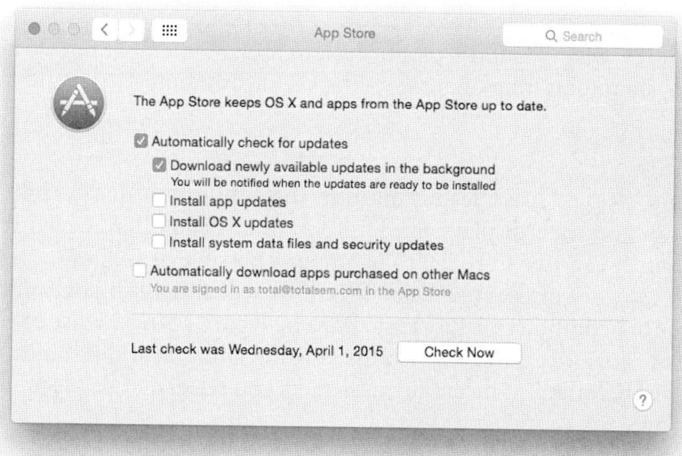

Figure 15-4 App Store update options

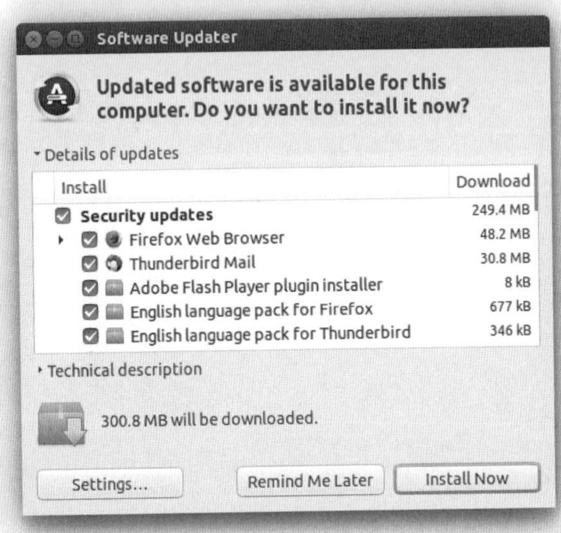

Figure 15-5 Software Updater in Ubuntu Linux

Managing Temporary Files in Windows

You should run the *Disk Cleanup* utility regularly to make sure you've cleared out the junk files that accumulate from daily use. All that late-night Web surfing doesn't just use up time; it also uses up disk space, leaving behind hundreds of temporary Internet files. Those, and other bits and pieces (such as those "deleted" files still hanging around in your Recycle Bin), can add up to a lot of wasted drive space if you don't periodically clean them out.

NOTE Disk Cleanup is part of System Tools. Remember how to access System Tools from Chapter 3, "The Visible Computer"?

When you click the Disk Cleanup button, the application first calculates the space you can free up and then displays the Disk Cleanup dialog box, which tells you how much disk space it can free up—the total amount possible as well as the amount you'll get from each category of files it checks. Windows will also ask if you want to clean up all the files on the computer or just your files. In Figure 15-6, the list of files to delete has a couple of categories checked; also listed is the amount of disk space to be gained by allowing Disk Cleanup to delete these files. As you select and deselect choices, watch this value change.

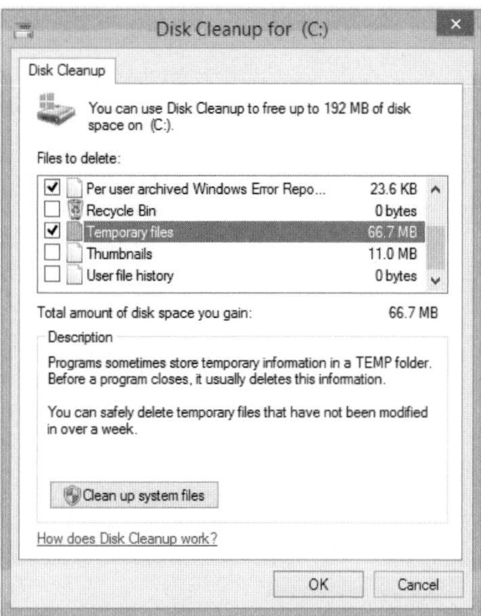

Figure 15-6 Disk Cleanup dialog box

If you scroll down through the list, you will see a choice to compress old files. What do you know—Disk Cleanup does more than just delete files! In fact, this file compression trick is where Disk Cleanup really, uh, cleans up. This is one of the few choices where you will gain the most space. The other big heavyweight category is Temporary Internet Files, which Disk Cleanup will delete. Try Disk Cleanup on a computer that gets hours of Internet use every day and you'll be pleased with the results.

Registry Maintenance

The Registry is a huge database that Windows updates every time you add a new application or hardware or make changes to existing applications or hardware. As a result, the Registry tends to be clogged with entries that are no longer valid. These usually don't cause any problems directly, but they can slow down your system. Interestingly, Microsoft does not provide a utility to clean up the Registry. To clean your Registry, you need to turn to a third-party utility. Quite a few Registry cleaner programs are out there, but my favorite is the freeware CCleaner by Piriform (see Figure 15-7). You can download the latest copy at www.piriform.com/ccleaner/.

Before you start cleaning your Registry with wild abandon, keep in mind that all Registry cleaners are risky in that they may delete something you want in the Registry. Because Microsoft makes changes to the Registry for every version of Windows, make sure your utility supports the Windows version you're running. This is especially true for any 64-bit version of Windows! I've used CCleaner for a while and it has worked well for me—your experience may differ.

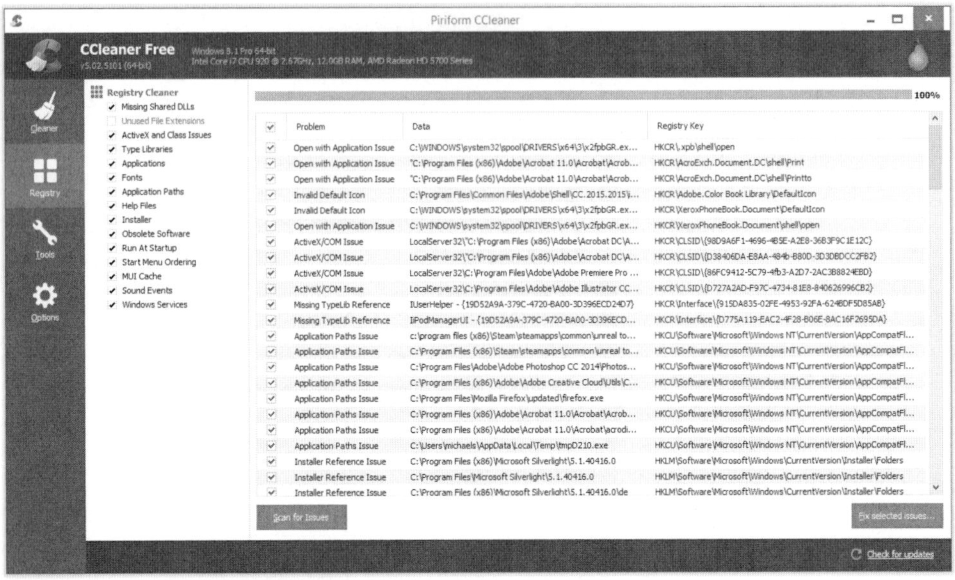

Figure 15-7 CCleaner Registry Cleaner

NOTE CCleaner also helps clean all of the most common Web browsers and a number of popular applications.

Disk Maintenance Utilities

Every modern OS has one or more utilities designed to maintain hard disk drives (HDDs) and solid-state drives (SSDs), though Windows requires a little more manual action than Mac OS X or Linux. Let's look at all three.

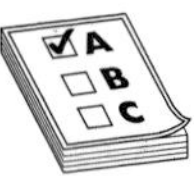

EXAM TIP Performance-based exam questions will likely test your knowledge of the various OS-related tools listed in the CompTIA objectives and in this chapter. Given a scenario, be sure you know what tool to use, where to find it, and how to achieve the desired result.

Error-Checking and Disk Defragmentation in Windows

Keeping drives healthy and happy is a key task for every tech. Error-checking and Disk Defragmenter, discussed way back in Chapter 10, "Implementing Hard Drives," are the key Windows maintenance tools used to accomplish this task.

When you can't find a software reason (and there are many possible ones) for a problem such as a system freezing on shutdown, the problem might be the actual physical

hard drive. The tool to investigate that is Error-checking. You can run Error-checking by using the chkdsk command from an elevated command prompt. You can also access the tool through the GUI by opening Computer, Explorer, or File Explorer (depending on the OS), right-clicking on the drive you want to check, selecting Properties, and then clicking the Tools tab. Click Check now, or Check in Windows 8 forward, to have Error-checking scan the drive for bad sectors, lost clusters, and similar problems, and repair them if possible.

Disk Defragmenter (see Figure 15-8) should run on a regular basis to keep your system from slowing down due to files being scattered in pieces on your hard drive. Every current version of Windows runs Disk Defragmenter automatically by default on HDDs; SSDs do not require defragmenting.

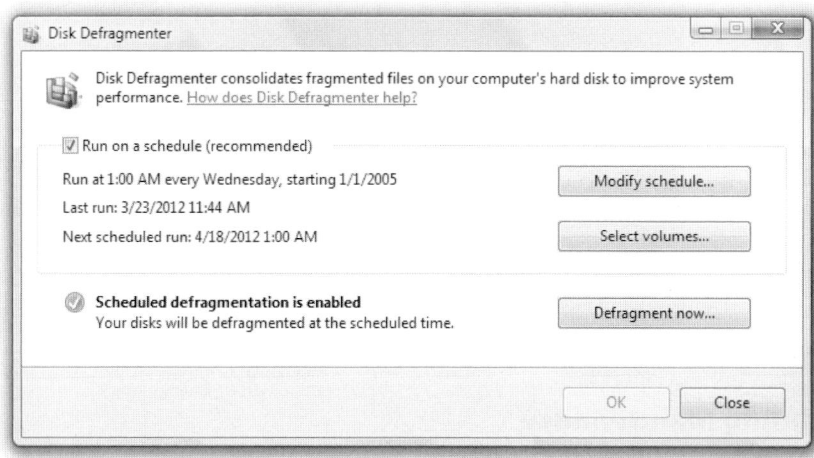

Figure 15-8 Vista Disk Defragmenter

Error-checking and Disk Defragmenter are such critical maintenance features that you really should have them run automatically. Let's glance at Mac OS X and Linux tools, then look at scheduling.

Disk Utility in Mac OS X

Mac OS X handles most chores automatically these days. Apple still includes the *Disk Utility* in Mac OS X, a disk maintenance utility/tool that used to be important for techs to run regularly. You'll encounter veteran Apple folks who still run it to verify and repair file structures. The current version of the tool also enables you to partition and format drives, a useful feature with used external drives. (Wipe them and start fresh.)

Linux Options

Just about every distro offers one or more disk maintenance utilities, plus you can download a ton of really good applications for free. The best option for most techs is to use the disk diagnostic tool on the installation DVD. Reboot with the installation media in

the drive. In some installation discs, you'll see a little keyboard icon that, when you press ENTER, shows you options to try, install, check disk for defects, test memory, and more (see Figure 15-9). Another option is to download the everything-but-the-kitchen-sink utility package, Ultimate Boot CD. Get it here: www.ultimatebootcd.com.

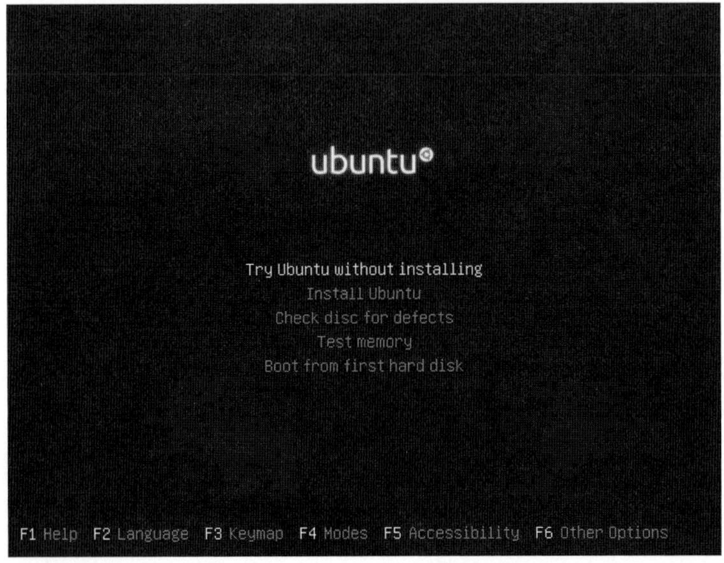

Figure 15-9 Ubuntu installation options, including one for disk diagnosis

Scheduling Maintenance

Maintenance only works properly when you do it at regular intervals. Depending on the version of Windows installed, for example, you can schedule maintenance jobs to run automatically. The CompTIA A+ 220-902 exam objectives define two areas for you to consider for scheduled maintenance: backups and disk maintenance.

Windows: Task Scheduler

Current versions of Windows use a single Administrative Tool, *Task Scheduler*, to schedule maintenance. You can choose an executable program and define when you want that program to run. The key to running scheduled maintenance is to know the names of the executable programs and any special switches you may need to enter.

Task Scheduler divides tasks into triggers, actions, and conditions. *Triggers* are actions or schedules that start a program. *Actions* are steps that define both the program to run and how it is to run. *Conditions* are extra criteria that must be met for the program to run. (Is the system idle? Is it connected to the Internet?) Figure 15-10 shows the Conditions tab for a sample task. To create a basic task, all you need to do is name it, set how often it should run, and decide what it should do.

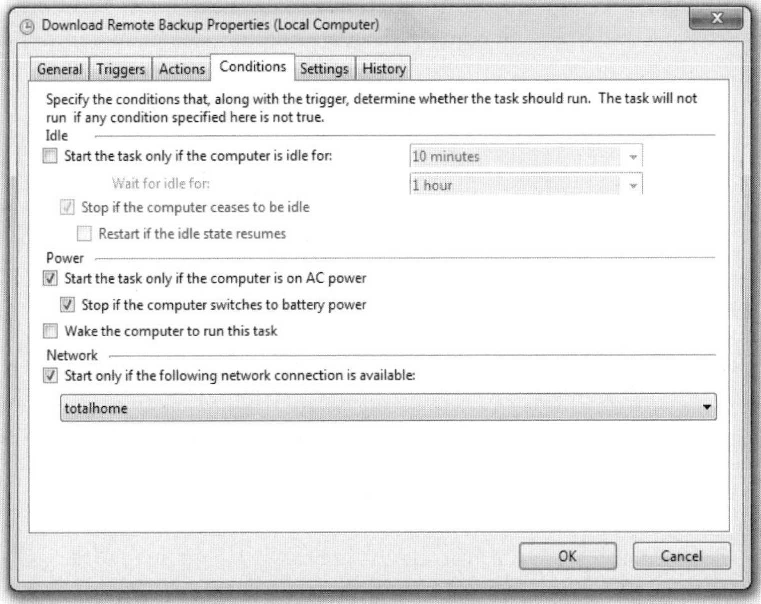

Figure 15-10 Conditions tab in Windows 7 Task Scheduler

Many Windows utilities include built-in scheduling options. Here's the twist, though: they're still using Task Scheduler. If you want to modify the automated defragmentation from within Disk Defragmenter, for example, you can open up Task Scheduler and see it listed as a scheduled task. Neat!

Mac OS X and Linux: launchd and cron

Mac OS X and most Linux distributions use one of two scripting tools to run all sorts of tasks automatically in the background. Apple developed *launchd* for automation; most Linux distros use the more universal and older *cron*. Although you can create custom launchd and cron jobs, the details on making custom scripts go way beyond CompTIA A+, so I'll leave them out here. Just remember the names of the tools for the exam.

Scheduling Backups in Windows

The backup utility varies depending on your version of Windows: in Windows Vista, it's called the Backup and Restore Center; in Windows 7, it's called Backup and Restore; Windows 8/8.1/10 use a tool called File History (although Windows 10 has a Backup and Restore tool as well). You'll learn more about each of these tools later in the chapter, but right now, let's talk about scheduling regular backups of your data, something necessary in Windows Vista and Windows 7.

Windows Vista/7's Backup and Restore Center/Backup and Restore applet includes a scheduler, too. Near the end of the Set up backup Wizard, after you've selected which folders to back up, you can click on Change schedule to set when and how often you want Windows to create the backup. It's that easy.

How often should you back up your files on the older versions of Windows? If you're creating new documents, downloading music, and taking lots of digital photos, you'll want to back up your files weekly. If you're a casual, Internet-browsing, Solitaire-playing PC user, you're probably safe making a new backup once a month.

NOTE You don't need to schedule anything, really, on Mac OS X. Once you've set up Time Machine, you're golden (see "Time Machine in Mac OS X," later in the chapter).

Scheduling Error-Checking (Check Disk)

The tool you know and love as Error-checking appears on the CompTIA A+ 220-902 exam objectives as CHKDSK (the command-line version of the tool, though it's more properly written all lowercase, chkdsk, as we'll refer to it). Regardless of what you call Error-checking, setting up Task Scheduler to run it automatically is a good thing according to CompTIA.

In a typical scenario today, only run chkdsk when you suspect a problem. Windows 8/8.1/10 don't ever need the tool to run, automatically or manually. They do periodic tests of hard drives and will notify the user if errors are detected.

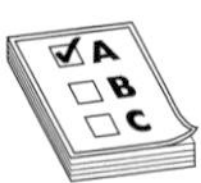

EXAM TIP You do *not* have to run any kind of scheduled drive maintenance on Mac OS X. In fact, Disk Utility doesn't provide that option at all. The OS runs scans late at night regularly and either fixes any problems or makes you aware of them when you next access the Mac.

Controlling Autostarting Software

A lot of software loads when you boot up any computing device, such as small programs that provide support for the various functions of the operating system. These small programs are called *processes* and *services*. As you add applications and peripherals to a system, software loads automatically at startup. Most of the time these autostarting programs are welcome—you want that latest peripheral to work, right? Sometimes, though, autostarting programs cause problems and need to be stopped, either temporarily or from loading at all.

Every OS gives you the capability to stop autostarting applications, processes, and services. Windows has two tools, System Configuration and Task Manager. Apple discourages startup programs, but each user account will have certain login items that load. To manage those, use the Users & Groups pane in System Preferences. In Linux, check the Startup Applications folder for automatic programs.

System Configuration

Techs use the *System Configuration* utility (also known by its executable name, *msconfig*) in Windows Vista/7 to edit and troubleshoot operating system and program startup processes and services. From Windows 8 on, you can make these changes from Task Manager.

To start the System Configuration utility, go the Start | Search bar, enter **msconfig**, and click OK or press ENTER (see Figure 15-11). The program runs after you provide the necessary credentials, depending on the User Account Control (UAC) setup.

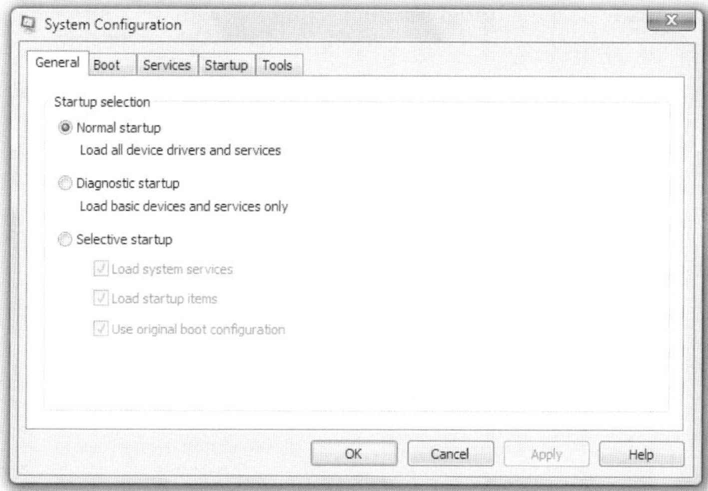

Figure 15-11 Windows Vista System Configuration utility

The System Configuration utility offers a number of handy features, distributed across the following tabs:

- **General** Select the type of startup you would like to use for the next boot. You can perform a normal startup with all programs and services launching normally, a diagnostic startup with only basic devices and services, or a custom boot.
- **Boot** This tab contains advanced boot features. Here you can see every copy of Windows you have installed, set a default OS, or delete an OS from the boot menu. You can set up a safe boot, or adjust advanced options like the number of cores or amount of memory to use. Selecting Safe boot, by the way, will force Windows to start in Safe mode on every reboot until you deselect it. *Safe mode* loads minimal, generic, trusted drivers and is used for troubleshooting purposes. It's better to use the F5 key to get into Safe mode, but see Chapter 17, "Troubleshooting Operating Systems," for troubleshooting issues.
- **Services** This tab is similar to the Services tab in the Task Manager. You can enable or disable any or all services running on your PC.
- **Startup** This tab enables you to enable or disable any startup programs (programs that load when you launch Windows). This is perhaps the most useful tab, especially if Windows is slow to load on your PC.
- **Tools** This tab lists many of the tools and utilities available in Windows, including Event Viewer, Performance Monitor, Command Prompt, and so on. There's nothing here that you can't find elsewhere in Windows, but it's a handy list all the same.

Task Manager

Microsoft placed the Startup applications and services in Task Manager (press CTRL-SHIFT-ESC) in Windows 8/8.1/10. You can readily see the status (enabled or disabled) of each application and a handy guide to the Startup impact that program has (see Figure 15-12). As you might imagine, programs that require syncing of a lot of files across the Internet will have a higher impact than applications that just load local files.

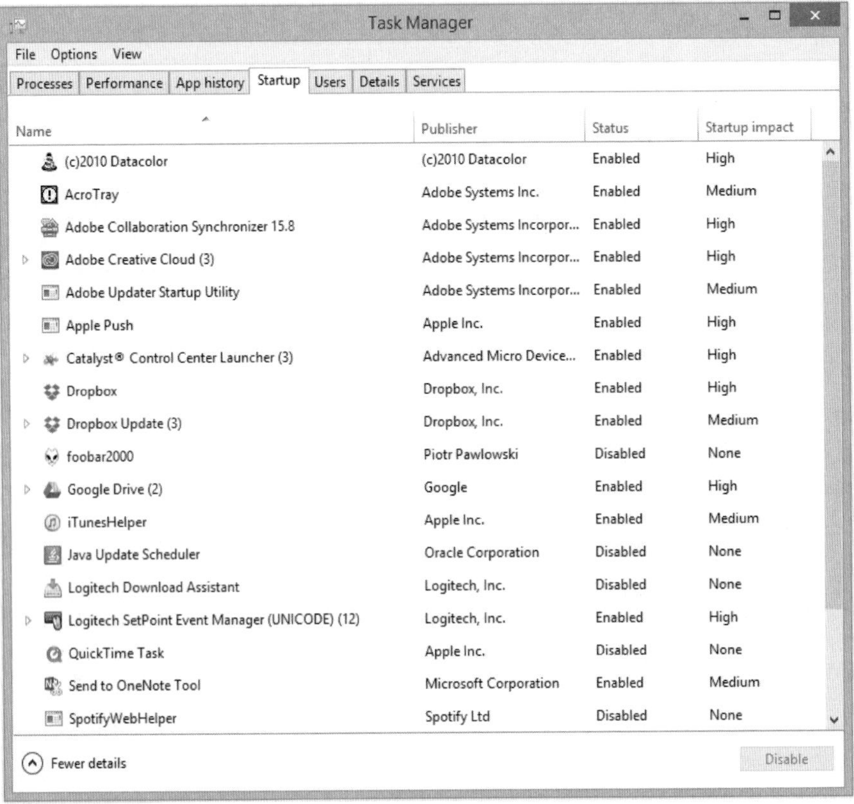

Figure 15-12 Startup tab in Task Manager

To enable or disable an application, right-click and select one of those options. When you reboot the system next, the behavior of the application will be changed according to your previous action.

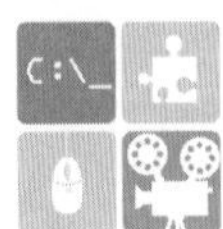

SIM Nervous about using Task Manager? Then try the Chapter 15 Click! sim to try your hand at killing a task without fear http://totalsem.com/90x.

Users & Groups in Mac OS X

In the Users & Groups pane of System Preferences, you can readily select or deselect any application that might load with specific user accounts (see Figure 15-13). There's not a lot more to say about the process, so I'll throw in some filler words for fun. Mac OS X is easy to use and maintain because Apple exercises extreme control over the platform.

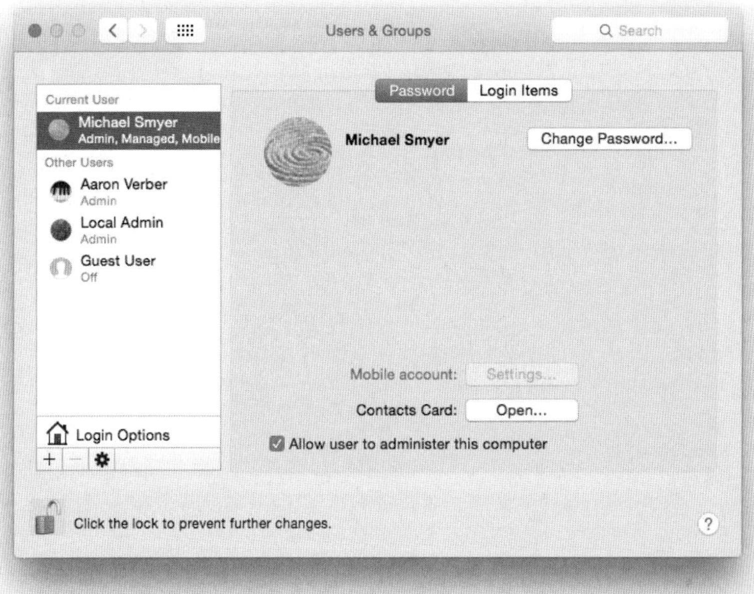

Figure 15-13 Options in Users & Groups pane

NOTE You know the importance of users and groups in Windows from Chapter 14.

Startup Applications

With Ubuntu Linux, you can access the Startup Applications preferences by searching. Click the Search button (top left of screen, on the Unity bar) and start typing **Startup**. When the Startup Applications preferences appears, click it. From there, you deselect

the check box next to a program you don't want to start at boot and you're done (see Figure 15-14).

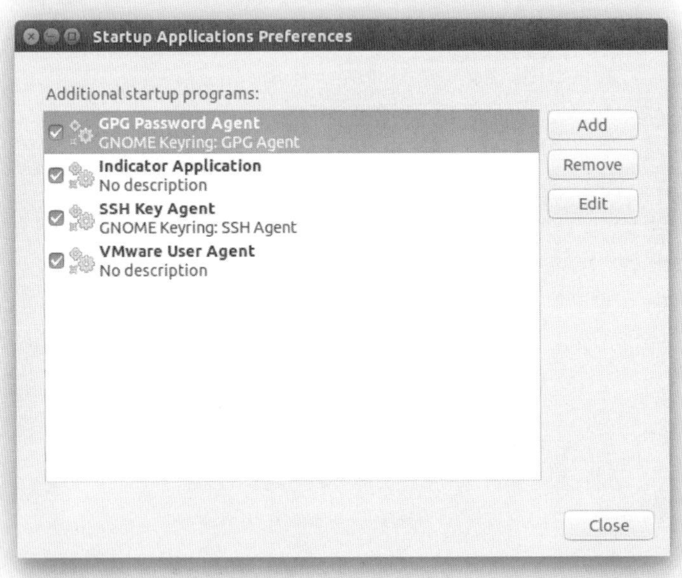

Figure 15-14 Disabling an autostarting program in Startup Applications

System Information

Windows comes with a handy built-in utility known as the *System Information tool* (see Figure 15-15) that collects information about hardware resources, components, and the software environment. When it finishes doing that, it provides a nice and tidy little report, enabling you to troubleshoot and diagnose any issues and conflicts. As with many other tools, you can access this tool from the Start | Search bar; simply enter **msinfo32**. The CompTIA A+ exams also refer to System Information by its executable, *msinfo32*.

It is also important to note that you can use System Information to gather information about remote computers by selecting View | Remote Computer and then entering the remote computer's network machine name. Under Tools, you even get quick access to System Restore and the DirectX Diagnostic Tool, a tool for checking your video card that Chapter 19, "Display Technologies," discusses.

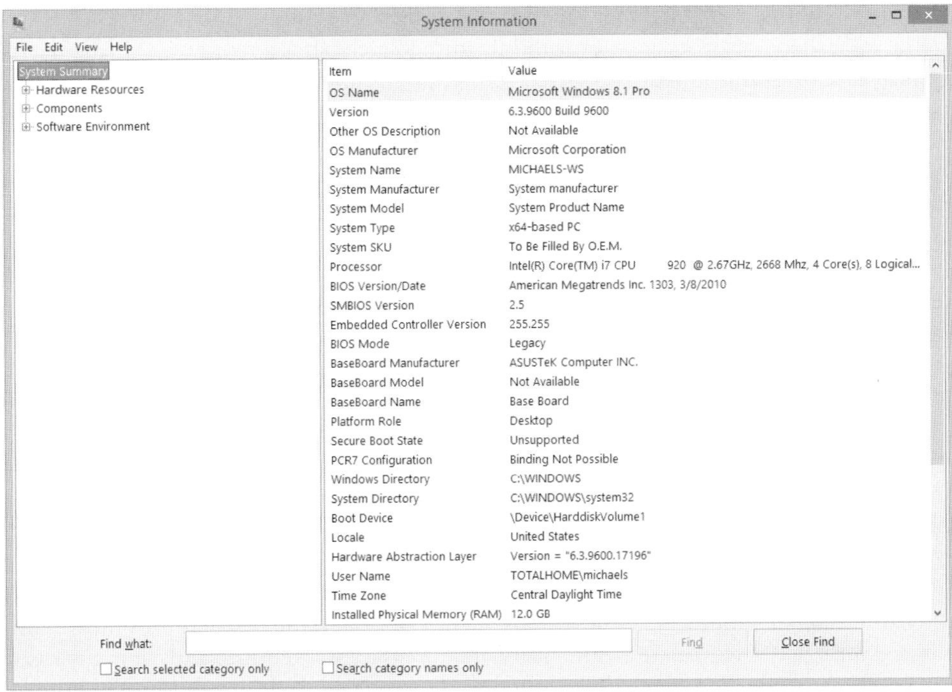

Figure 15-15 System Information

Optimizing Operating Systems

Maintenance means keeping the performance of an OS from degrading with time and use. Of course, you don't just want to keep trouble at bay—you want to make your systems better, stronger, faster! Anything you do that makes Windows better than it was before, such as adding a piece of software or hardware to make something run better, is an *optimization*.

Installing and Removing Software

Optimizing by installing and removing software is part of the normal life of any computing device. Each time you add or remove software, you make changes and decisions that can affect the system beyond whatever the program does, so it pays to know how to do it right.

Installing Software

If you can't download or access an application over the Internet, it'll probably arrive on an optical disc. Windows supports *Autorun*, known as AutoPlay in modern Windows

operating systems, a feature that enables the operating system to look for and read a special file called—wait for it—autorun.inf. Immediately after a removable media device (optical disc or thumb drive) is inserted into your computer, whatever program is listed in autorun.inf runs automatically. Most application programs distributed on removable media have an autorun file that calls up the installation program.

To start an installation manually, double-click on the disc icon in Explorer, File Explorer, Finder, or the desktop. All OSs will scan the disc or other removable media for an executable file and run it.

The UAC in Windows complicates the installation process a bit. You will most likely be prompted by UAC when installing an application, giving you time to review what is happening to your system in case you did not intend to install the program. If you are using an administrator account, you can simply click Continue and finish the installation. Should you be logged in with a less privileged account, you will need to enter a user name and password of an account with administrative privileges. Some installers have trouble letting UAC know that they need more privileges and simply fail no matter what account you are logged in with. In those cases, it is best to right-click the installer icon and select Run as administrator to give the installer the access it expects from the start.

Assuming all is well, you typically must accept the terms of a software license before you can install an application. These steps are not optional; the installation simply won't proceed until you accept all terms the software manufacturer requires and, in many cases, enter a correct code. You may also be asked to make several decisions during the installation process. For example, you may be asked where you would like to install the program and if you would like certain optional components installed. Generally speaking, it is best to accept the suggested settings unless you have a very specific reason for changing the defaults.

Installing Software in Mac OS X

You have a couple of options for installing software in Mac OS X. The most common method involves the Mac App Store; the link is in System Preferences. Installing via the App Store is pretty much just like installing an app on a cell phone. You click the Install button, add some credentials, and the app installs.

Alternatively, you can download installation programs, often .dmg files, that you drag to the Applications folder. Mac OS X will prompt you to accomplish this goal.

Installing Software in Linux

Linux distros differ in the process of installing applications. A common way is to download an installation file, double-click it, and select Install from the options. Applications generally install into the Applications folder.

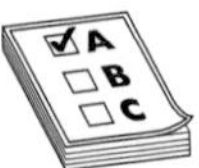

EXAM TIP Mac OS X and Linux require you to type in root credentials every time you install anything. Many times, you'll get prompted a few more times for credentials before the installation completes.

Removing Software

Each installed application program takes up space on your computer's hard drive, and programs that you no longer need waste space that could be used for other purposes. Removing unnecessary programs can be an important piece of optimization.

You remove a program from a Windows PC in much the same manner as you install it. That is, you use the application's own uninstall program, when possible. You normally find the uninstall program listed in the application's folder in the All Programs section of the Start menu, as shown in Figure 15-16.

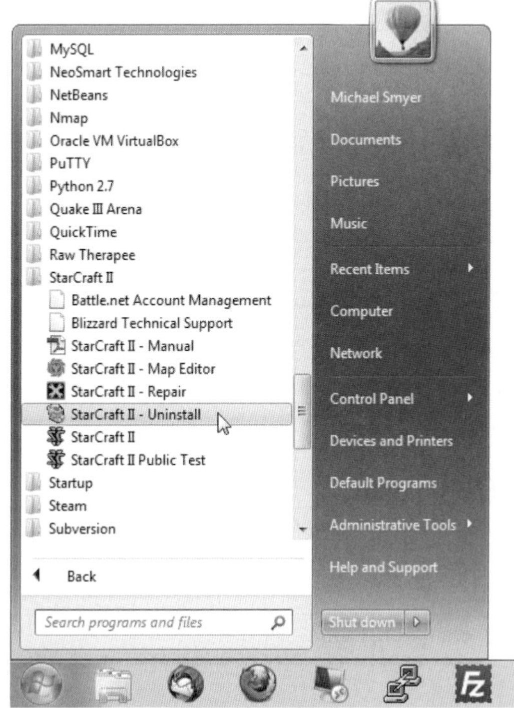

Figure 15-16 Uninstall me!

If an uninstall program is not available, use the Programs and Features applet to remove the software (see Figure 15-17). You select the program you want to remove and click the Uninstall/Change button or Change/Remove button. Windows displays a message warning you that the program will be permanently removed from your PC. If you're certain you want to continue, click Yes.

NOTE The Uninstall/Change and Change/Remove buttons change depending on the program. Not all programs can be changed.

You may then see a message telling you that a shared file that appears to no longer be in use is about to be deleted, and asking your approval. Generally speaking, it's safe to delete such files. If you do not delete them, they will likely be orphaned and remain unused on

your hard disk forever. In some cases, clicking the Uninstall/Change or Change/Remove button starts the application's install program (the one you couldn't find before) so you can modify the installed features. This is a function of the program you're attempting to remove. The end result should be the removal of the application and all of its pieces and parts, including files and Registry entries.

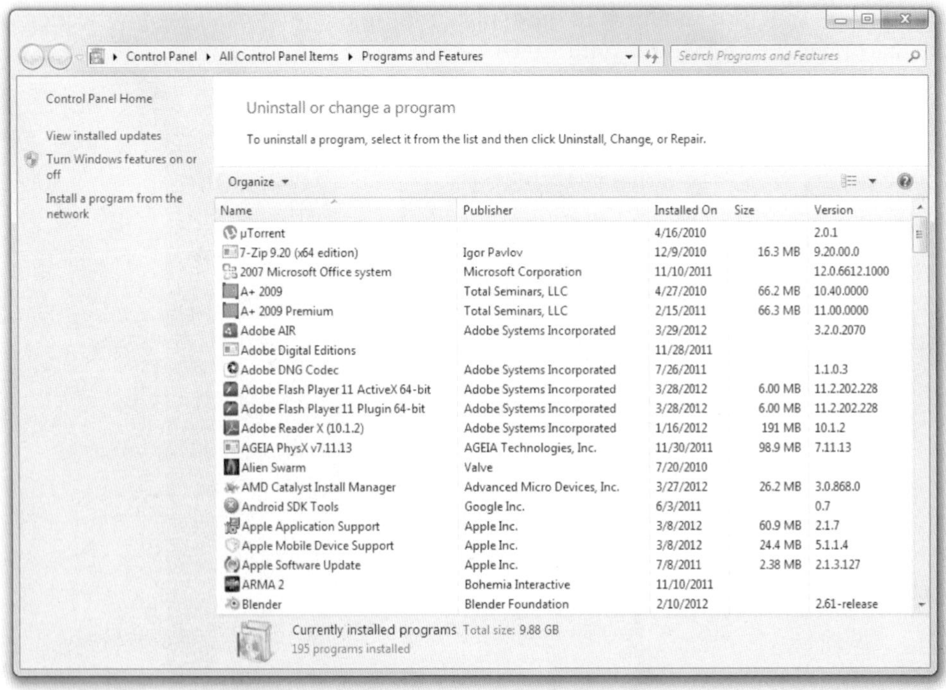

Figure 15-17 Programs and Features applet

Uninstalling applications in Mac OS X varies based on how they were installed. Mac Store apps are removed very similarly to apps on a cell phone. First, open the Launchpad app from the Dock or Applications folder (it looks like a rocket ship), then click and hold on any app icon until all the icons start to wiggle. An × in a circle will appear on the upper left of any app that can be removed (see Figure 15-18). Click the × to remove the app. If you accidentally remove an app you wanted, you can re-download it from the Mac App Store.

For all other Mac OS X apps, removing them comes down to two options. Drag the app to the Trash or run the uninstaller if the app came with one. Of the two, the first option of just deleting the app is the most common, with a dedicated uninstaller only being available for some of the larger (and often cross-platform) apps like Photoshop. Be aware that deleting an app can leave behind various files on the system, most often a few user preference files and other customizations in the user's Library folder.

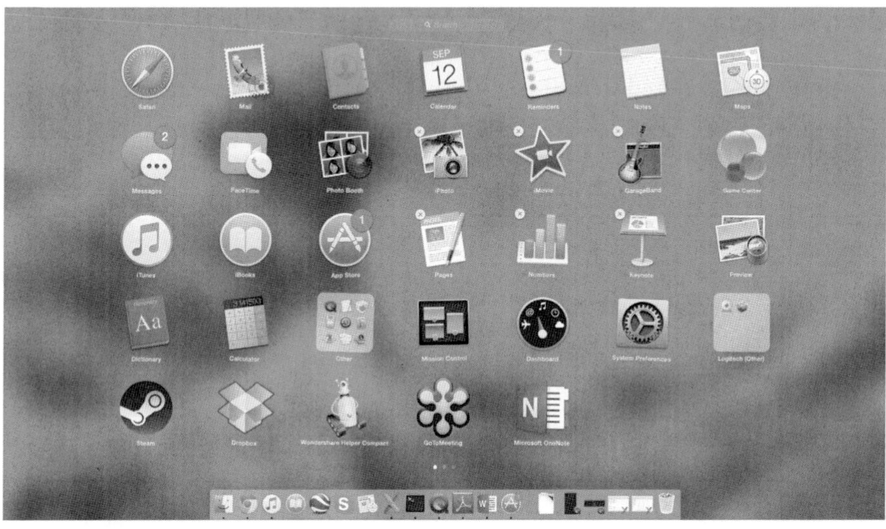

Figure 15-18 Uninstalling App Store–purchased applications using the Launchpad app

Removing software in mainstream Linux distros is just as easy as installing it. Open the software manager, find the app, and then click Remove (see Figure 15-19). The underlying package manager, which we'll work with directly in Chapter 16, "Working with the Command-line Interface," will handle all the deleting and cleanup for you.

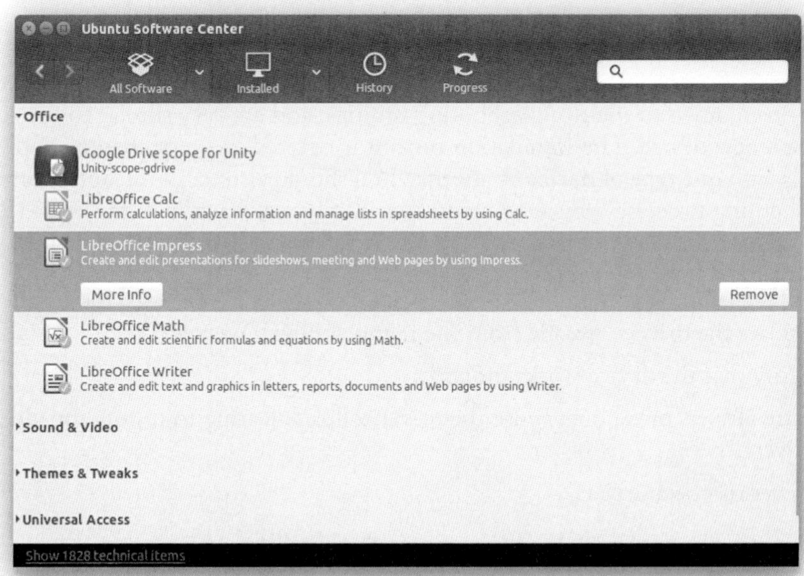

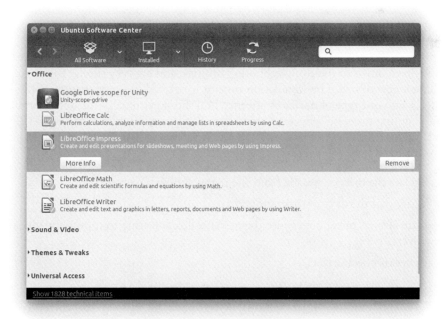

Figure 15-19 Removing an application in Ubuntu Linux

Adding or Removing Windows Components/Features

When you installed Windows, it included certain features by default. It installed Notepad, network support, and games on your computer. You can remove these Windows components from your system if you like, and add other components as well.

Open the Programs and Features applet in the Control Panel, and then click the *Turn Windows features on or off* option on the Tasks list. Click Continue if prompted by UAC and you will be presented with the Windows Features dialog box (see Figure 15-20). To toggle a feature on or off, simply click its checkbox.

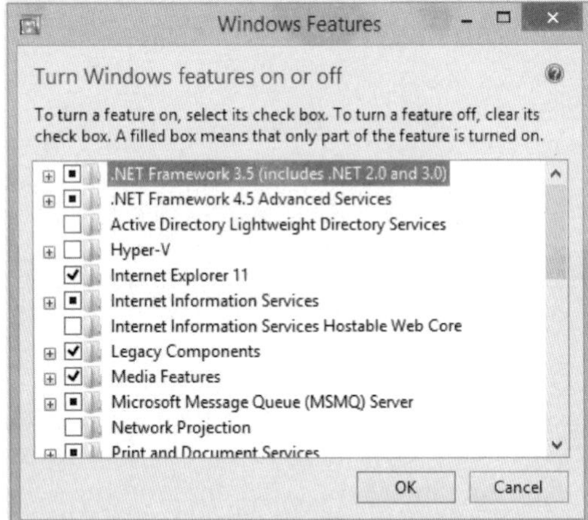

Figure 15-20 Windows Features dialog box

Installing/Optimizing a Device

The processes for optimizing hardware in Windows are absolutely identical between the versions, even down to the troubleshooting utilities, and are very similar to the steps for installing a new device. The installation process is covered in every chapter of this book that deals with one type of device or another. You should also recall the optimization and troubleshooting processes you read about specifically way back in Chapter 7. (Refer to that chapter to refresh your memory if any of the following steps don't seem crystal clear.) So, these are the important steps/action items:

- Update the drivers, usually from the manufacturer's Web site.
- Verify that the device works properly.
- If the drivers prove buggy, use the driver rollback feature to restore the older drivers.
- Never run beta drivers.

The textbook version of this book has a classroom feature called a "Cross Check" where students examine older sections of the book in light of the current section.

This completely applies right now in this book too! Check Chapter 7, "Motherboards," and make sure you can answer these questions: What's the update process? Does Windows provide any assistance? Where can you verify a working device? What do you need to select to roll back a driver? Enquiring minds want to know!

Updating Drivers in Mac OS X

Mac OS X will notify you about available *system updates* that contain driver updates for built-in components. Make a quick trip to the App Store to get updates installed (see Figure 15-21). If the system has third-party devices, like a Wacom tablet, you will need to manually check and update any drivers for those devices.

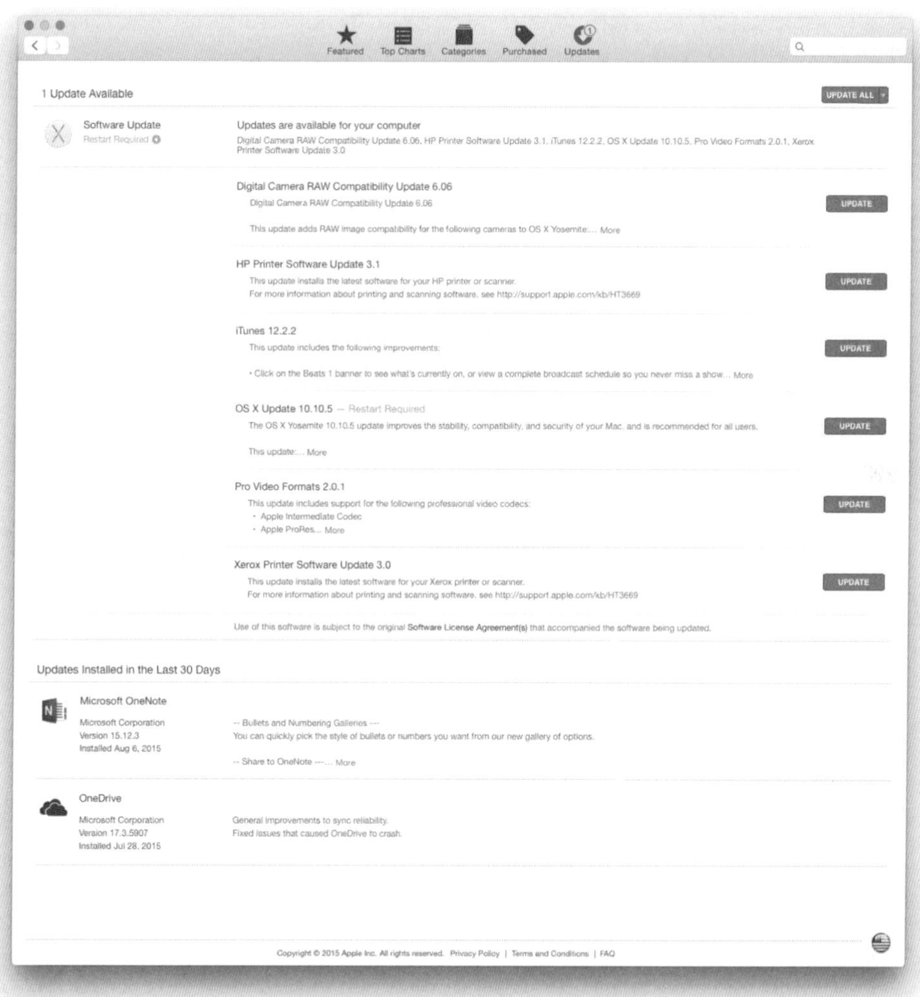

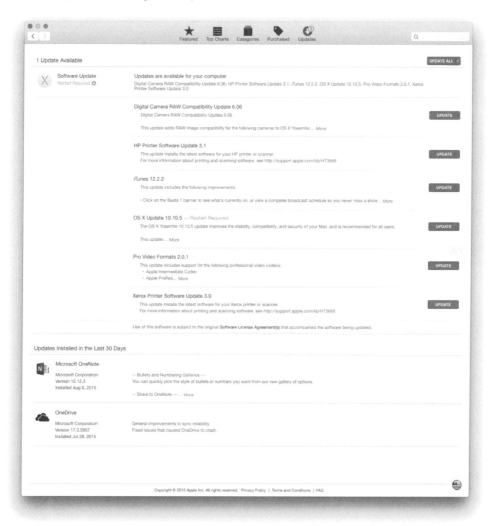

Figure 15-21 App Store showing an available update

Updating Drivers in Linux

Most Linux distros regularly check for updates and will signal any new updates. Download and install the updates using the Software Updater.

Device Manager

You've worked with *Device Manager* in other chapters when installing and troubleshooting devices; it's also the tool to use when optimizing device drivers. Right-click on a device in Device Manager to display the context menu. From here you can update or uninstall the driver, disable the device, scan for hardware changes, or display the Properties dialog box. When you open the Properties dialog box, you'll see several tabs that vary according to the specific device. Most have General, Driver, Details, and Resources. The tab that matters most for optimization is the Driver tab.

The Driver tab has buttons labeled Driver Details, Update Driver, Roll Back Driver, Uninstall, and Disable. Most of these you'll recall from Chapter 7. Driver Details lists the driver files and their locations on disk.

Adding a New Device

Windows should automatically detect any new device you install in your system. If Windows does not detect a newly connected device, use Windows Vista's Add Hardware wizard, which you can find in the Add Hardware applet, or the *Add a device* option in the Devices and Printers applet in Windows 7/8/8.1/10 to get the device recognized and drivers installed (see Figure 15-22).

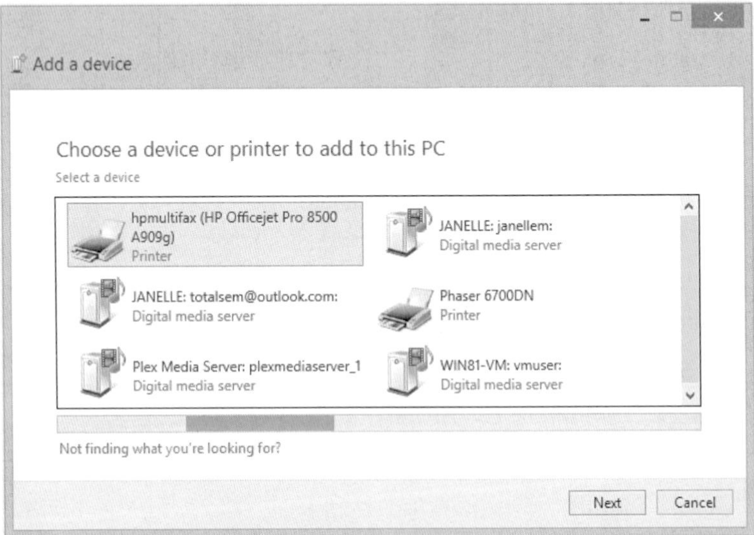

Figure 15-22 Adding a device in Windows 8.1

Windows almost completely automates the Add Hardware/Add a device wizards. The wizards present you with a list of detected hardware.

Performance Options

One optimization you can perform on all Windows versions is setting Performance Options. *Performance Options* are used to configure CPU, RAM, and virtual memory (page file) settings. To access these options right-click Computer or This PC and select Properties, and then click the Advanced system settings link in the Tasks list. On the Advanced tab, click the Settings button in the Performance section.

The Performance Options dialog box has three tabs: Visual Effects, Advanced, and Data Execution Prevention (see Figure 15-23). The Visual Effects tab enables you to adjust visual effects that impact performance, such as animations, thumbnails, and transparencies. Try clicking the top three choices in turn and watch the list of settings. Notice the tiny difference between the first two choices (*Let Windows choose what's best for my computer* and *Adjust for best appearance*). The third choice, *Adjust for best performance*, turns off all visual effects, and the fourth option is an invitation to make your own adjustments.

If you're on a computer that barely supports Windows, turning off visual effects can make a huge difference in the responsiveness of the computer. For the most part, though, just leave these settings alone.

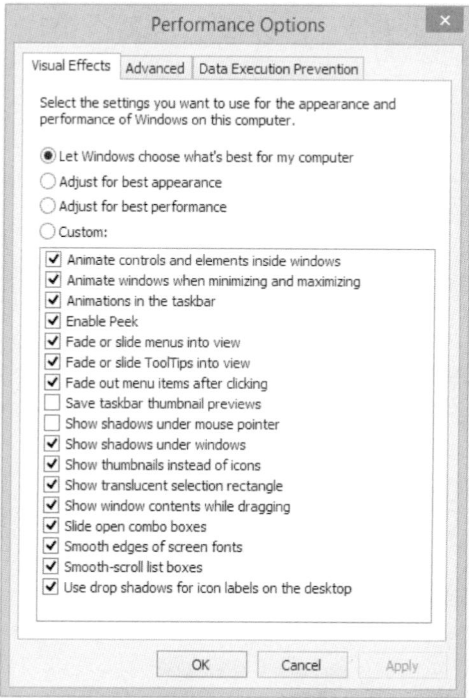

Figure 15-23 Windows 8.1 Performance Options dialog box

The Advanced tab, shown in Figure 15-24, has two sections: Processor scheduling and Virtual memory. Under the Processor scheduling section, you can choose to adjust for best performance of either Programs or Background services. The Virtual memory section of this tab enables you to modify the size and location of the page file.

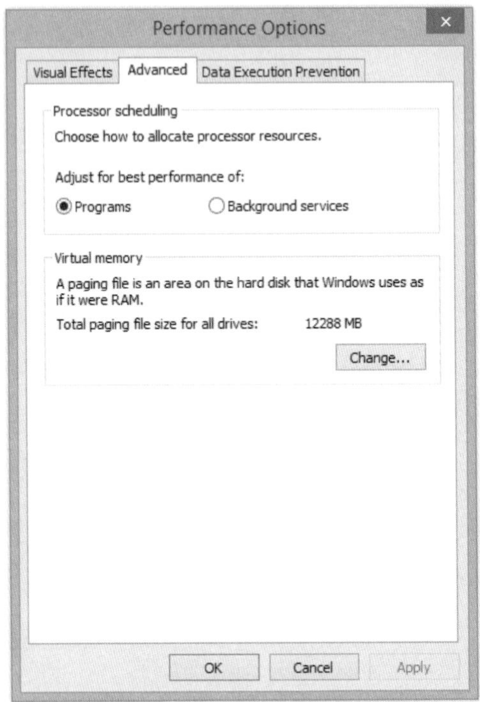

Figure 15-24 Advanced tab of Performance Options dialog box

Data Execution Prevention (DEP) works in the background to stop viruses and other malware from taking over programs loaded in system memory. It doesn't prevent viruses from being installed on your computer, but makes them less effective. By default, DEP is only enabled for critical operating system files in RAM, but the Data Execution Prevention tab enables you to have DEP turned on for all running programs. It works, but you might take a performance hit or find that some applications crash with it enabled for all programs. Like other options in Performance Options, leaving the default DEP settings is the best option most of the time.

Preparing for Problems

Techs need to prepare for problems. You must have critical system files and data backed up and tools in place for the inevitable glitches. Every modern operating system has options for backing up data and, as you might imagine, they all offer different features. Windows offers System Restore to recover from problems, too. Let's take a look.

Backing Up Personal Data

The most important data on your computer is the personal data: your documents, e-mail messages and contacts, Web favorites, photographs, and other files. To handle backing up

personal data, every version of Windows comes with some form of backup utility. Mac OS X and Linux of course have backup tools as well.

Backup and Restore Center for Windows Vista/7

Microsoft includes the automated and simple *Backup and Restore Center* (Windows Vista) and *Backup and Restore* (Windows 7) Control Panel applets. In Windows Vista, you can either back up files or back up your computer (see Figure 15-25). Both choices will first ask you where you want to store the backup (see Figure 15-26).

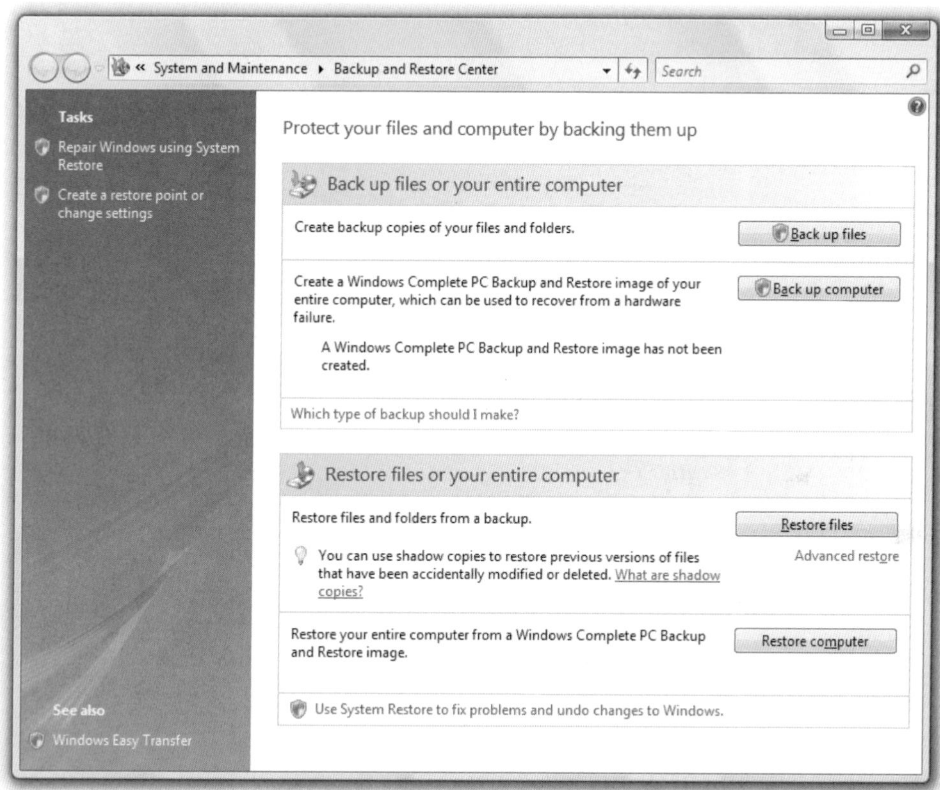

Figure 15-25 Backup options in Vista

As the name implies, the Back up computer option backs up your entire computer to a system image. All you need to do is pick a destination for the image (optical drive, hard drive, or network location) and Windows takes care of the rest. Choosing the Back up files option is another matter entirely. Clicking this button reveals the screen shown in Figure 15-27.

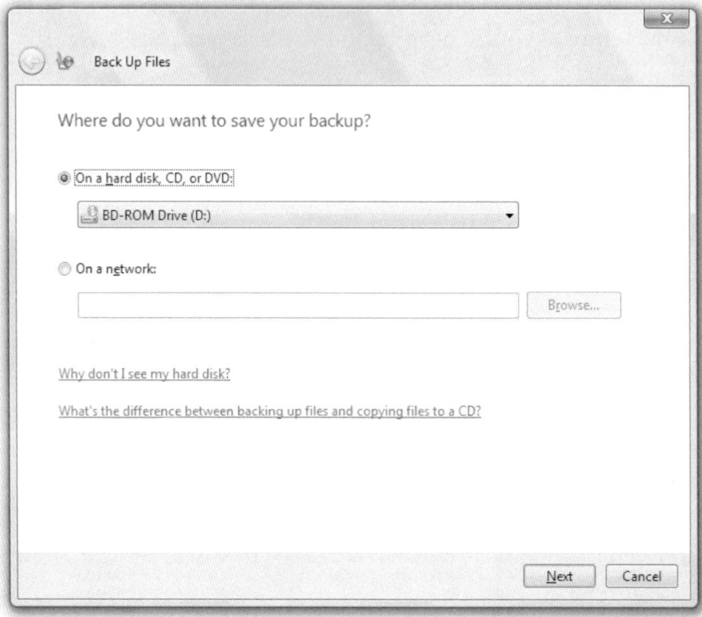

Figure 15-26 Backup location in Vista

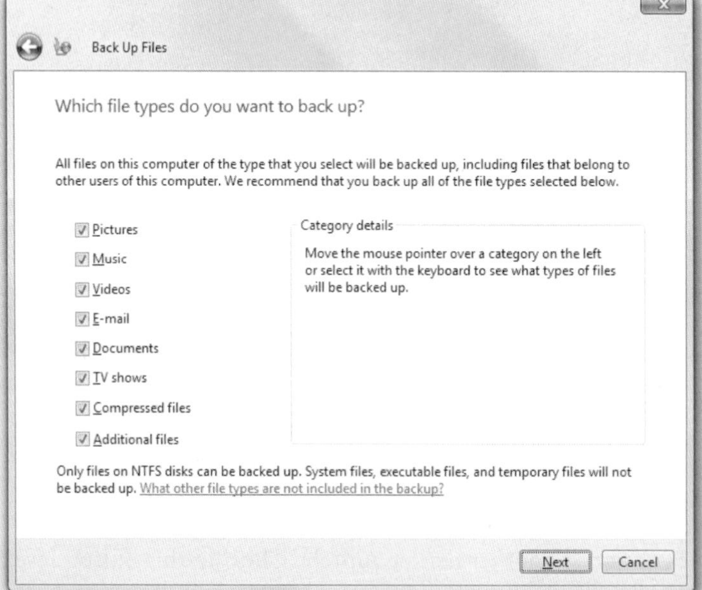

Figure 15-27 Types of files to back up

The Back up files option in Vista only enables you to back up personal information for all users. If you want to back up any installed applications, or even Windows itself, don't bother using the Back up files option that comes with Vista.

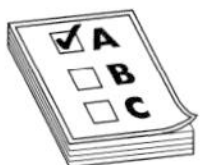

EXAM TIP Windows will not back up content stored on non-NTFS volumes.

Windows 7's Backup and Restore utility includes a number of noteworthy improvements over Windows Vista's. First of all, Microsoft changed the look of the main screen (see Figure 15-28).

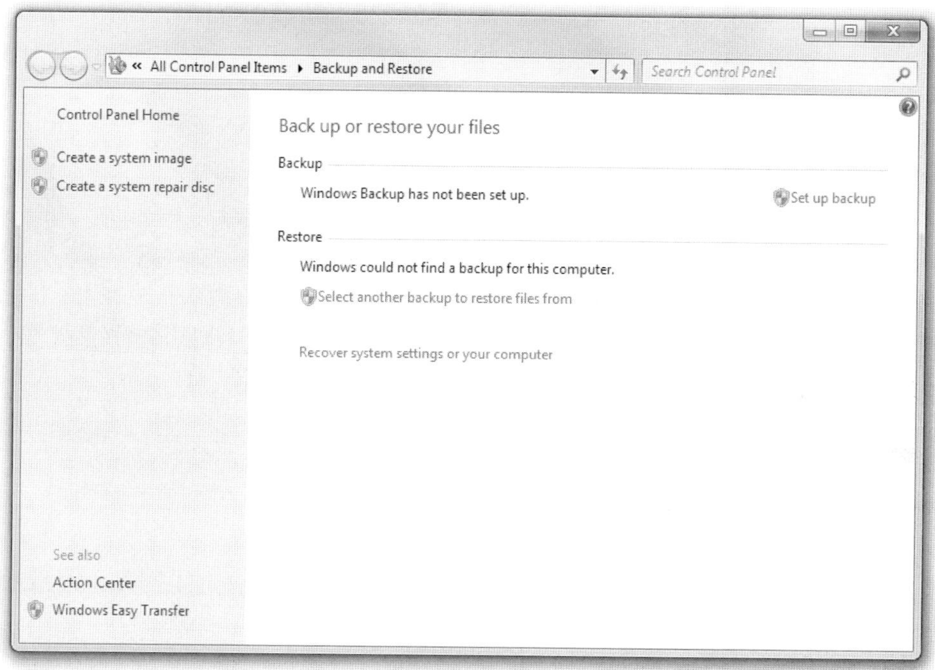

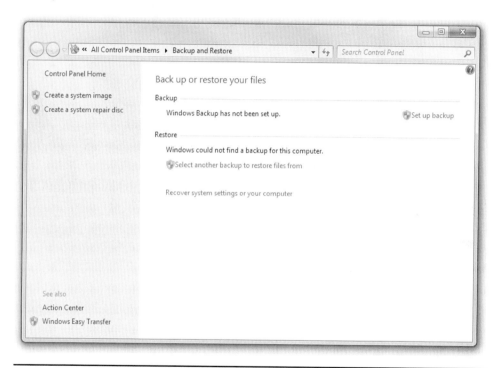

Figure 15-28 Windows 7 Backup and Restore

Clicking the Set up backup link in Windows 7 opens a dialog box asking you to choose your backup location—very similar to Vista's backup. After selecting your backup location and clicking Next, you then see the screen shown in Figure 15-29.

If you select Let Windows choose (recommended), you'll get a backup similar to the Vista backup, but with one very important difference. You'll back up each user's personal data, but Windows 7 doesn't stop there. Assuming you have enough space in your backup location, Windows 7 will automatically add a system image that includes the entire Windows operating system, every installed program, all device drivers, and even the Registry.

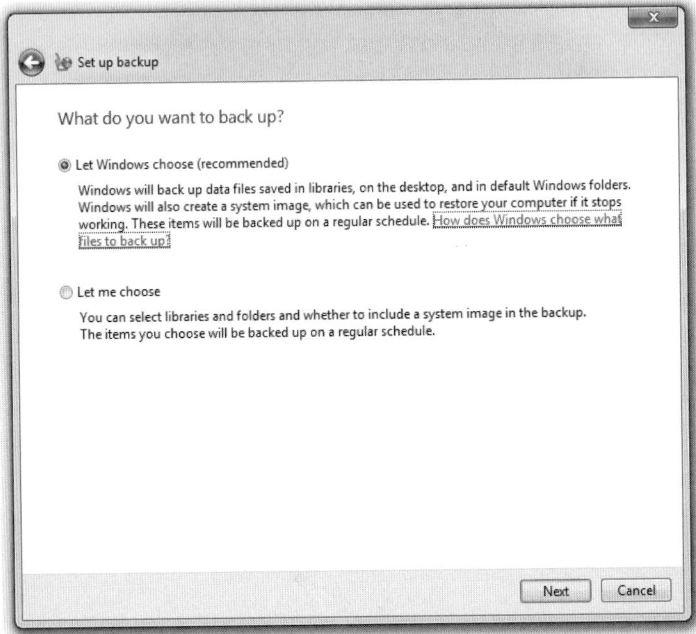

Figure 15-29 What do you want to back up?

Selecting Let me choose is equally interesting. Unlike Vista's selection, Windows 7 enables you to pick individual users' files to back up (see Figure 15-30).

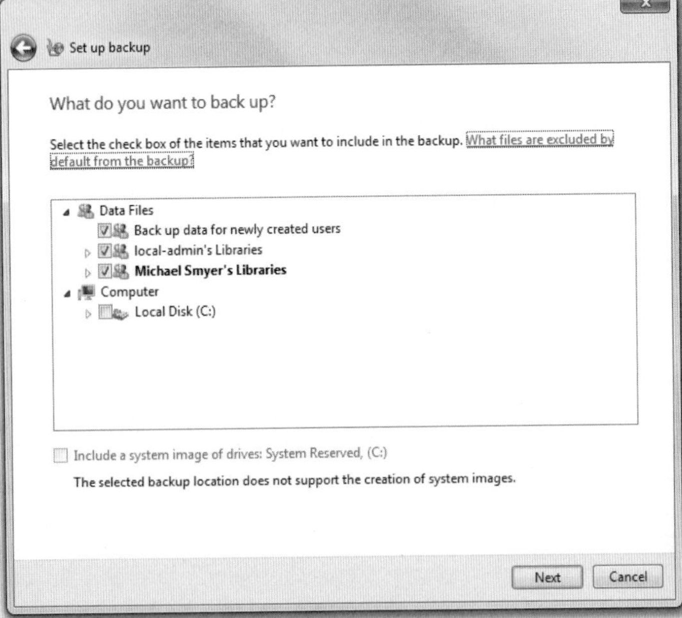

Figure 15-30 Backup showing a list of users

By selecting a user, you can choose libraries or the user's personal folders to back up, as shown in Figure 15-31. Also note the checkbox that gives you the option to make a system image, just as if you selected the Let Windows choose (recommended) option.

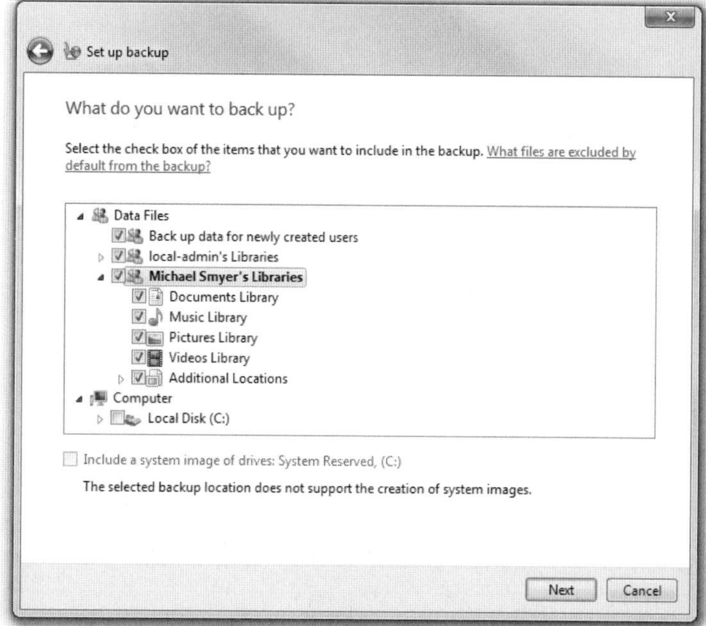

Figure 15-31 Single user, showing some of the user's libraries/folders

Once you complete the wizard, Windows starts backing up your files. While the backup runs, you can monitor its status with an exciting and handy progress bar (see Figure 15-32). If you can't handle that much excitement, you can close the backup window while the OS backs up files. The process can take a long time, many hours with a modern system with a large hard drive.

NOTE You can also choose to create just a system image in Windows 7. From the Backup and Restore applet, select Create a system image. It works like the system image function in Windows Vista.

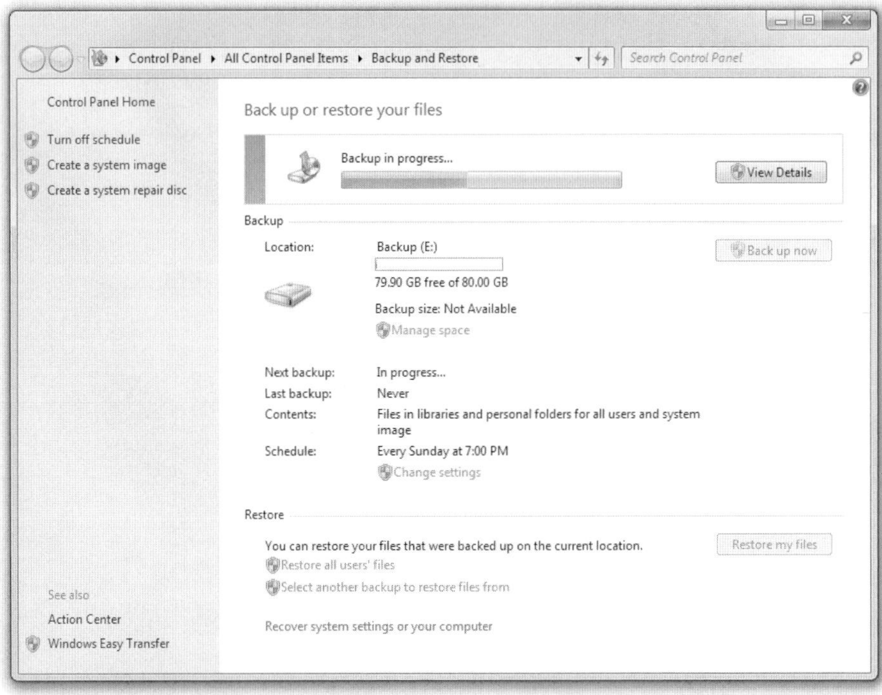

Figure 15-32 Backup in progress...

File History in Windows 8/8.1/10

Microsoft introduced the robust *File History* Control Panel applet in Windows 8 that enables aggressive backup of personal files and folders (see Figure 15-33). File History requires a second drive and is not enabled by default. You can use any type of HDD or SSD as the second drive, internal or external. (You could choose to back up to a second partition on the same drive, I suppose, but what would be the point?) Enable File History and start backing up your Libraries, Desktop, Contacts, and Favorites right now.

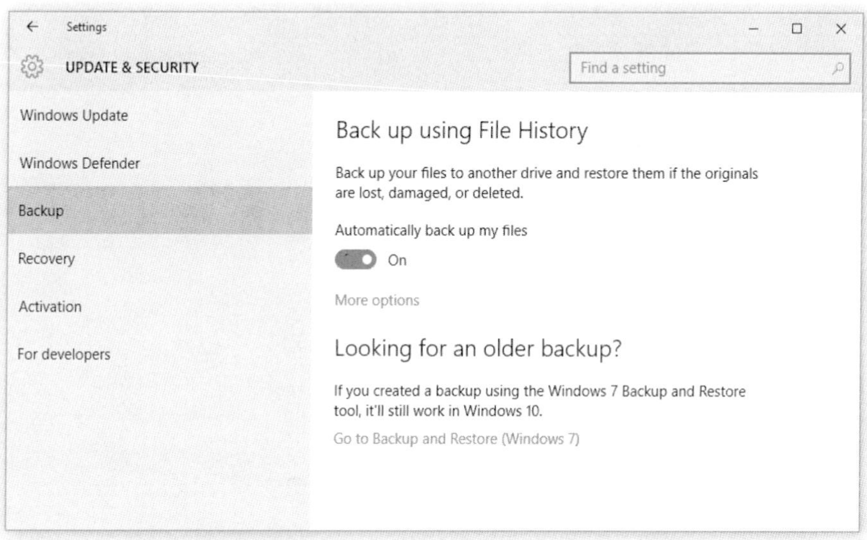

Figure 15-33 Windows 10 File History

Note that File History won't back up all your personal files unless you either add them to the default Libraries or create custom Libraries. Also, File History does not replace full system backups at all. To back up your system, select the System Image Backup option (lower left option in File History) to open the Windows 7–era Backup and Restore tool. Create a full backup to another (larger) drive.

Time Machine in Mac OS X

Mac OS X provides the excellent Time Machine to create full system backups (see Figure 15-34). These backups are called *local snapshots*. Time Machine enables you to recover some or all files in the event of a crash; it also enables you to *restore* deleted files and recover previous versions of files. Time Machine requires an external HDD or SSD, or you can use a shared network drive. Find Time Machine in System Preferences.

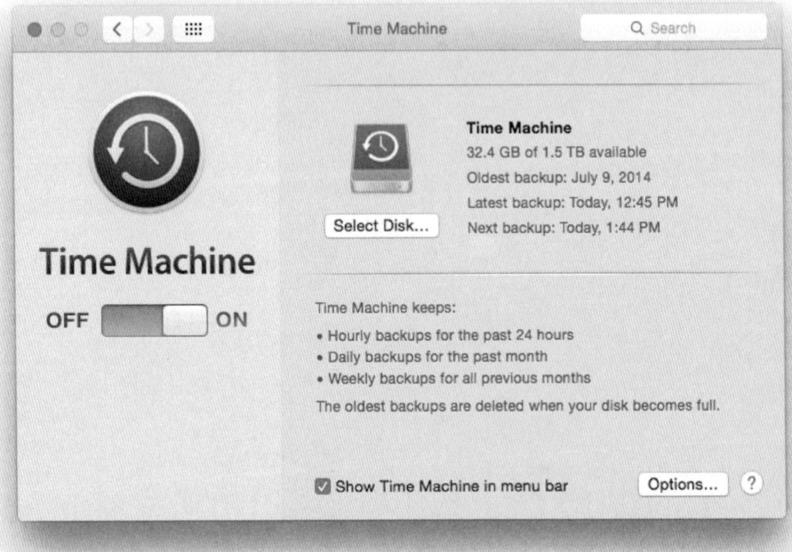

Figure 15-34 Time Machine

Backups in Linux

Different Linux distros offer different tools for backing up files, folders, and drives. Ubuntu Linux uses Déjà Dup, although it goes by the name Backups in System Settings (see Figure 15-35). Déjà Dup will happily back up your files to wherever you tell it, such as an external drive, network share, or even a folder on your main hard drive (not recommended if you care about your files!). Déjà Dup backs up a user's Home folder by default; that's where most users store all personal documents. Déjà Dup will store files and versions of files permanently, as long as the storage location has sufficient space.

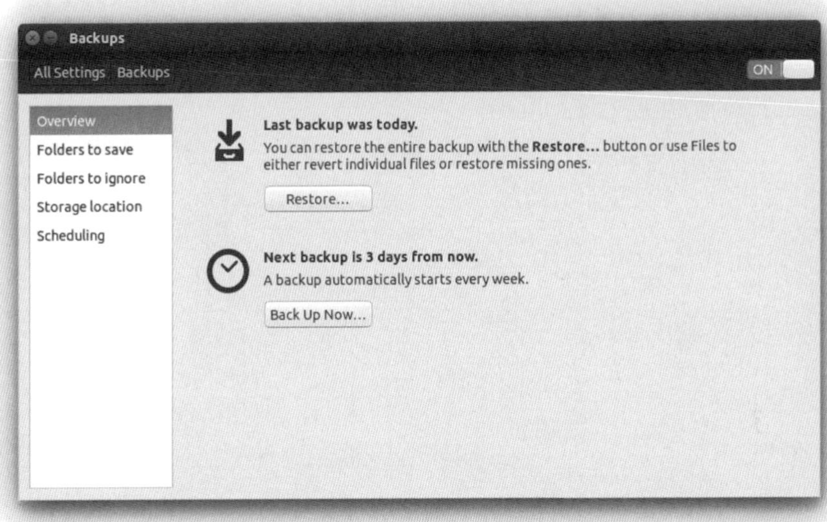

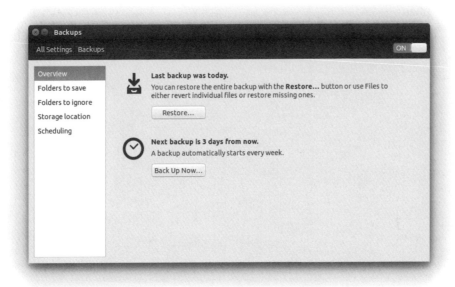

Figure 15-35 Backups under System Settings in Ubuntu

System Restore in Windows

Every technician has war stories about the user who likes to add the latest gadget and cool software to his computer. Then he's amazed when things go very, very wrong: the system locks up, refuses to boot, or simply acts weird. This guy also can't remember what he added or when. All he knows is that you should be able to fix it—fast.

The *System Restore* tool enables you to create a *restore point*, a *snapshot* of your computer's configuration at a specific point in time. If you later crash or have a corrupted OS, you can restore the system to its previous state.

System Restore makes a number of restore points automatically. To make your own restore point, right-click Computer or This PC and select Properties, and then click the System protection link in the Tasks list. On the System Protection tab, click the Create button to open the dialog box shown in Figure 15-36. Name your restore point appropriately and then click Create.

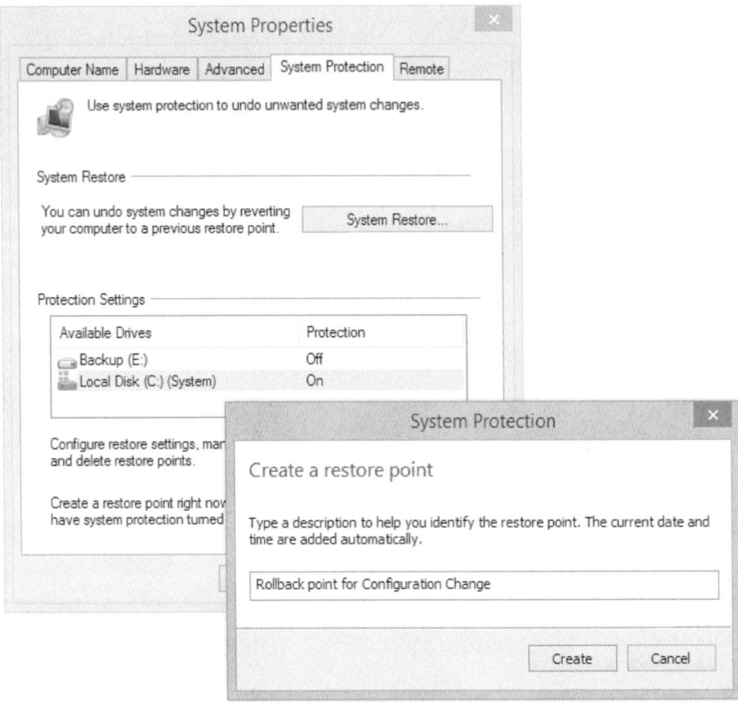

Figure 15-36 Creating a manual restore point in Windows

If you click the System Restore button on the System Protection tab, you might be surprised at how many system restore points have already been made for you automatically (see Figure 15-37).

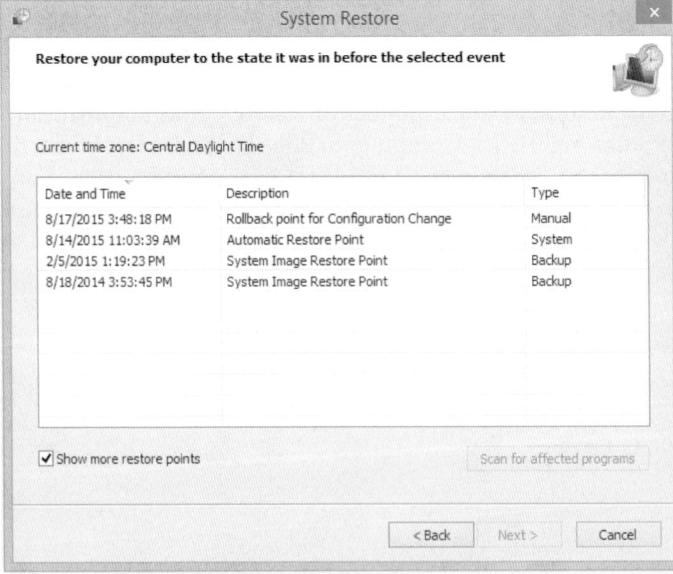

Figure 15-37 Restore points in Windows

The System Restore tool creates some of the restore points automatically, including every time you install new software. Thus, if installation of a program causes your computer to malfunction, simply restore the system to a time point prior to that installation, and the computer should work again.

During the restore process, only settings and programs are changed. No data is lost. Your computer includes all programs and settings as of the restore date. This feature is absolutely invaluable for overworked techs. A simple restore fixes many user-generated problems.

To restore to a previous time point, start the System Restore Wizard in System Tools.

You don't have to count on the automatic creation of restore points. You can open System Restore at any time and simply select Create a restore point. Consider doing this before making changes that might not trigger an automatic restore point, such as directly editing the Registry.

System Restore is turned on by default and uses some of your disk space to save information on restore points. To turn System Restore off or change the disk space usage, right-click Computer or This PC and select Properties, and then click the System protection link in the Tasks list. On the System Protection tab, click the Configure button to change System Restore configuration settings (see Figure 15-38).

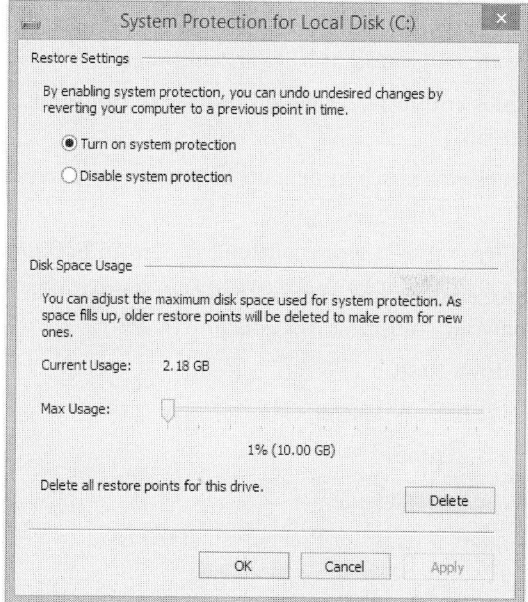

Figure 15-38 System Restore settings and Disk Space Usage options

Chapter Review

Questions

1. What tool enables you to modify which programs start when Windows 7 starts?
   - **A.** msstartup
   - **B.** msinfo32
   - **C.** msconfig
   - **D.** ipconfig
2. What tool enables you to modify which programs start when Windows 8.1 starts?
   - **A.** msstartup
   - **B.** msinfo32
   - **C.** msconfig
   - **D.** Task Manager
3. What does System Information do?
   - **A.** Provides you with a report about the hardware resources, components, and software environment in your computer
   - **B.** Enables you to select which programs and services start when Windows boots up
   - **C.** Enables you to schedule hard drive defragmentation, chkdsk scans, and other computer tasks
   - **D.** Enables you to perform automatic custom backups of your files and settings
4. What tool enables you to correct a corrupted Windows operating system by reverting your computer to a previous state?
   - **A.** Windows Restore
   - **B.** Restore State Manager
   - **C.** Time Machine
   - **D.** System Restore
5. What is Data Execution Prevention (DEP)?
   - **A.** A technology that prevents viruses from taking over programs loaded in system memory
   - **B.** A technology that enables you to set permissions for different users on your computer
   - **C.** A technology that prevents programs from being installed on your computer
   - **D.** A technology that prevents files from being written to your hard drive

6. If you install a driver on your system and it causes problems, which tool can you use to roll back to a previous driver?
   - A. Driver Manager
   - B. msconfig
   - C. Device Manager
   - D. System Info
7. When performing automatic updates, Windows 7 uses which feature to download additional updates for other Microsoft products?
   - A. Software notifications
   - B. msinfo32
   - C. Microsoft Update
   - D. Registry
8. Joan recently bought a new gamepad and used the Add a Device wizard to install it, but it still won't work. What should she do next? (Select two.)
   - A. Check the manufacturer's Web site for updated drivers
   - B. Run the Automated System Recovery tool to return the PC to a functioning state
   - C. Use a restore point in System Restore to return the PC to a functioning state
   - D. Run Windows Update to search for new drivers
9. What tool is used in Mac OS X to perform full system backups?
   - A. AppleBack
   - B. Users and Groups
   - C. Time Machine
   - D. System Preferences Backup
10. What feature included in Windows 8, 8.1, and 10 allows you to regularly back up your important files and folders?
    - A. System Configuration
    - B. Backup and Restore
    - C. AutoPlay
    - D. File History

Answers

1. **C.** msconfig enables you to select the programs and services that start with Windows Vista or Windows 7.
2. **D.** Task Manager enables you to modify the applications and services that start with Windows 8 and later.

3. **A.** System Information gives you a wide variety of information about your system.
4. **D.** Using System Restore, you can restore your computer to a previous restore point.
5. **A.** Data Execution Prevention prevents viruses from taking control of programs loaded into memory.
6. **C.** The Roll Back Driver option in Device Manager is a great tool for fixing driver problems.
7. **C.** Windows uses the Microsoft Update feature to download additional updates for other Microsoft products, such as Microsoft Office.
8. **A, D.** Joan should check both the manufacturer's Web site and Windows Update for the latest drivers.
9. **C.** Mac OS X uses Time Machine to perform full system backups.
10. **D.** File History is an awesome backup tool included with Windows 8, 8.1, and 10. It enables you to perform backups of important files and folders regularly.

CHAPTER 16

Working with the Command-Line Interface

In this chapter, you will learn how to

- Explain the operation of the command-line interface in Windows, Mac OS X, and Linux
- Manipulate files from the command line
- Execute fundamental commands from the Windows command line
- Execute fundamental commands from the Mac OS X and Linux Terminal

Whenever I teach a class of new techs and we get to the section on working with the command line, I'm invariably met with a chorus of moans and a barrage of questions and statements like "Why do we need to learn this old stuff?" and "Is this ritualistic hazing appropriate in an IT class?"

For techs who master the interface, the command line provides a powerful, quick, and flexible tool for working on a computer. Learning that interface and understanding how to make it work is not only useful, but also necessary for all techs who want to go beyond baby-tech status. You simply cannot work on modern computers without knowing the command line! I'm not the only one who thinks this way. The CompTIA A+ 220-902 certification exam tests you on a variety of command-line commands, both in Windows and Linux, for doing everything from renaming a file to rebuilding a system file.

If you're interested in moving beyond Windows and into other operating systems such as Linux, you'll find that pretty much all of the serious work is done at a command prompt. Even Mac OS X supports a command prompt.

The command prompt is popular for three reasons. First, if you know what you're doing, you can do most jobs more quickly by typing a text command than by clicking through a graphical user interface (GUI). Second, a command-line interface (CLI) doesn't take much operating system firepower, so it's the natural choice for jobs where you don't need or don't want a full-blown GUI for an OS. Third, text commands take very little bandwidth when sent across the network to another system.

So, are you sold on the idea of the command prompt? Good! This chapter gives you a tour of the Windows and Linux command-line interfaces, explaining how they work and what's happening behind the scenes. You'll learn the concepts and master essential commands, and then you'll work with files and folders. A good tactic for absorbing the material in this chapter is to try out each command or bit of information as it's presented. If you have some experience working with a command prompt, many of these commands should be familiar to you. If the command line is completely new to you, please take the red pill and join me as we step into the matrix.

NOTE If you're using a Windows system, this is a great opportunity to jump ahead to Chapter 18, "Virtualization," and try some virtualization. Consider loading up a virtual machine and installing Linux so you can practice. Check out and install my favorite virtualization tool, Oracle VirtualBox, at www.virtualbox.org, and then download an ISO file from www.ubuntu.com.

902

Deciphering the Command-Line Interface

So how does a command-line interface work? It's a little like having a Facebook Messenger conversation with your computer. The computer tells you it's ready to receive commands by displaying a specific set of characters called a *prompt*. Here's an example of a generic prompt:

```
>: Want to play a game?
>: _
```

You type a command and press ENTER to send it:

```
>: Want to play a game?
>: What kind of game?
>: _
```

The PC goes off and executes the command, and when it's finished, it displays a new prompt, often along with some information about what it did:

```
>: Want to play a game?
>: What kind of game?
>: A very fun game...
>: _
```

Once you get a new prompt, it means the computer is ready for your next instruction. Running commands from the command line is similar to clicking icons in the operating system's GUI. The results are basically the same: you tell the computer to do something and it responds.

Try This!

Opening Windows GUI Programs from the Command Prompt

Keep in mind as you go through this chapter that the command line is just another tool for communicating with the operating system. Windows responds whether you click or type and sometimes does both, so try this! At a command prompt, type **notepad** and press ENTER. What happens? The graphical program Notepad opens up, just as if you'd double-clicked its icon. Here's another: type **explorer** and press ENTER. Voilà! Windows Explorer or File Explorer loads. Windows just responds.

Shells

The command prompt, like a GUI, is just another way to interface with a computer. The command line interprets input and sends it to the OS in a form the OS understands, and then shows the results. The tool that interprets input is called the *command-line interpreter*, also known as the *shell*. The default Windows shell is cmd.exe. On Mac OS X and on most Linux distros, the default shell is called *bash*. While most operating systems have only one GUI, that's not the case with the shell. Every operating system has the ability to interface with different types of shells. On Mac OS X and Linux, it's easy to replace bash with popular shells with names like Z shell (zsh), Korn shell (ksh), and C shell (csh). In Windows you can replace cmd.exe with PowerShell. It's a standard right of nerd passage to start experimenting with these alternative shells.

NOTE When you open a command prompt, you start a shell. The shell acts as the command-line interpreter. Different shells make different command prompts. This chapter stays with common shells used in standard ways, but understand that shells are interchangeable and very customizable.

Accessing the Command-Line Interface in Windows

You access the command-line interface in Windows by starting the shell program cmd.exe. We touched on accessing the CLI in Chapter 3, "The Visible Computer," but let's develop this procedure in a bit more detail here.

A common way to access the command-line interface is through the Start menu (Windows Vista and 7) or the Start screen's Search bar (Windows 8/8.1). In Windows Vista/7, from the Start menu type **cmd** (see Figure 16-1) and press ENTER to start the command prompt.

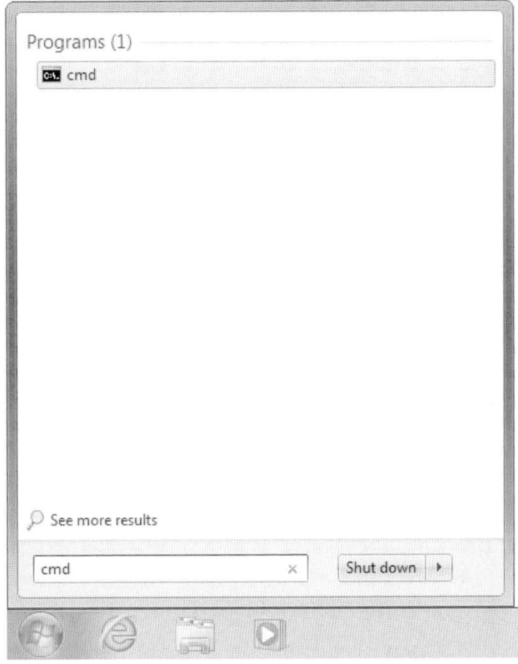

Figure 16-1 Starting the command prompt in Windows 7

In Windows 8/8.1, the search is a bit more hidden, but just start typing **cmd** from the Start screen. The Search charm will appear with the full command (see Figure 16-2). Press ENTER.

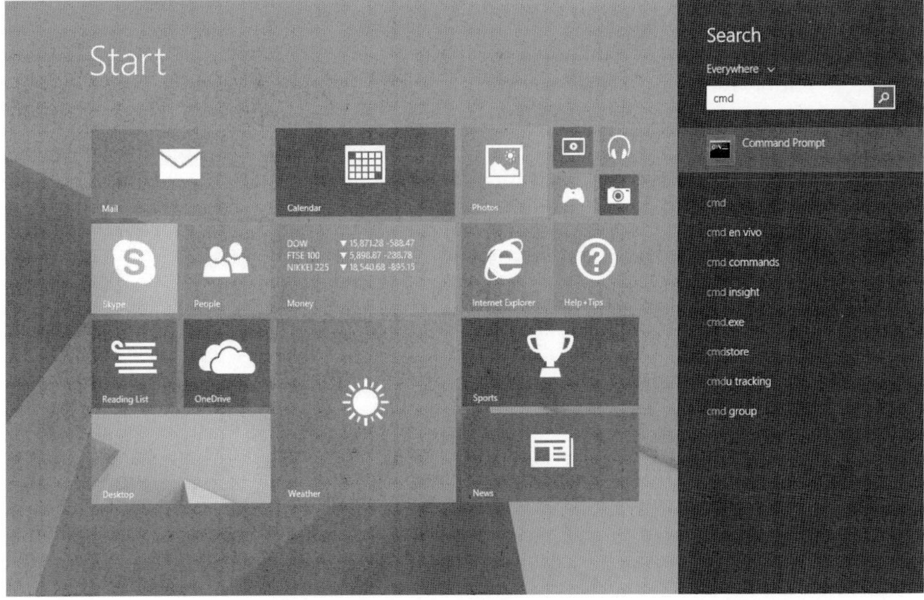

Figure 16-2 Starting the command prompt in Windows 8.1

A Command Prompt window pops up on your screen with a black background and white text—welcome to the Windows command-line interface (see Figure 16-3). To close the CLI, you can either click the Close box in the upper-right corner, as on any other window, or simply type **exit** and press ENTER.

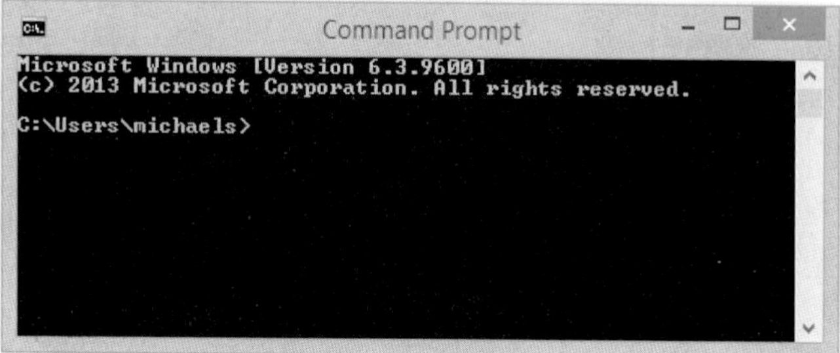
Command Prompt
Microsoft Windows [Version 6.3.9600]
(c) 2013 Microsoft Corporation. All rights reserved.
C:\Users\michaels>

Figure 16-3 The Windows 8.1 command-line interface

If you attempt to enter a command that requires elevated or administrative privileges at the Windows command prompt, you'll receive a UAC "Windows needs your permission to continue" dialog box. (You learned about UAC in Chapter 14, "Users, Groups, and Permissions.") You can also manually run a command with elevated privileges by right-clicking a command-prompt shortcut and then selecting *Run as administrator*. If you are prompted for the administrator password or credentials, enter whatever is needed.

NOTE You can create an Administrator shortcut to the Windows command prompt by right-clicking on the desktop and selecting New | Shortcut. For the location of the item, type **cmd** and click Next. Type **cmd** to name the shortcut, and click Finish. The shortcut appears on the Desktop. Next, right-click the shortcut and select the Advanced button. In the Advanced Properties dialog box, check the *Run as administrator* box and click OK. You have now created a Windows command-prompt shortcut that will always run with administrative privileges.

Accessing the Command-Line Interface in Mac OS X and Linux

The command line in Mac OS X and Linux functions virtually identically. This isn't too surprising given that they both are based on UNIX. The terminal emulator in OS X has a specific name, *Terminal*. The many distros of Linux use different emulators, such as konsole and gnome-terminal. To make things easy, we'll use the command-line interface in Ubuntu Linux, conveniently also called *Terminal*.

To open Terminal in Mac OS X, either launch the Terminal app from the Utilities folder (located in the Applications folder) or activate Spotlight (COMMAND-SPACEBAR), type **terminal**, and press ENTER to bring up the Mac OS X Terminal (see Figure 16-4).

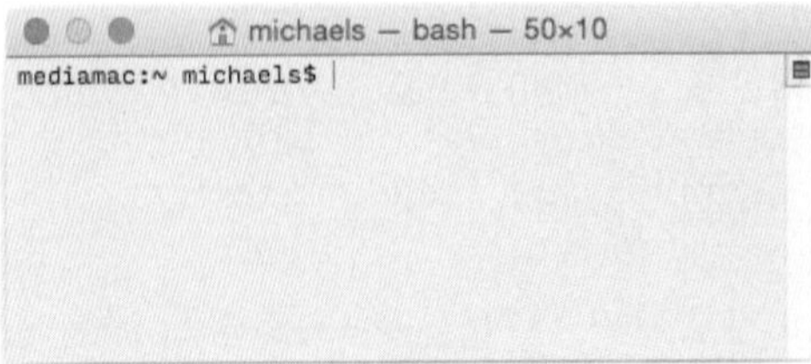

Figure 16-4 Mac OS X Terminal

The way to open a terminal emulator in Linux varies depending on the Linux distribution (distro) you use. Generally, every desktop-focused Linux distro has some form of finder or search function on the desktop that works similarly to the search tools in Mac OS X and Windows. Find this tool and then type in **terminal** to start the program. This brings up the terminal window as shown in Figure 16-5.

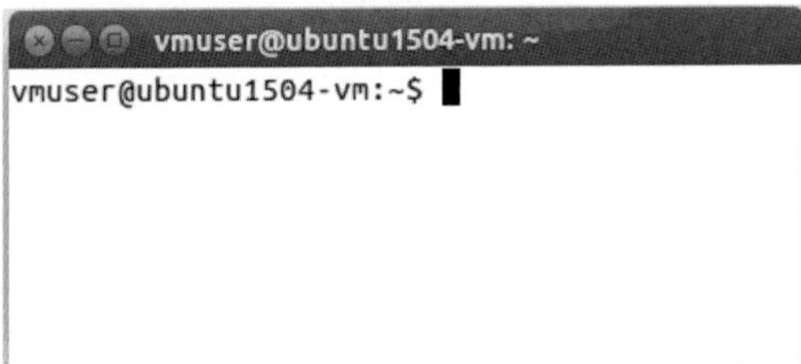

Figure 16-5 Linux Terminal

Both Mac OS X and Linux give you the ability to run the command line with advanced privileges, called *super user* or *root privileges*. Even though Mac OS X and Linux advanced privileges function is equivalent to the elevated privileges in Windows, they handle this elevation quite differently. First, open Terminal. Whenever you need to run a command as root, type **sudo** followed by the desired command. The system will prompt for a password and then run the command.

If the system doesn't have sudo, it should have its older cousin *su*. With su, you typically type **su** at the prompt and press ENTER; you will then be prompted for the root password. Once you have successfully entered the password, the prompt will change (usually changing the character at the end from a $ to a #) and every command you enter from then on will be executed as root. When you finish working as root, type **exit** and press ENTER. Terminal won't close like before, but you will return to a normal prompt. You can see how the prompt changes in the following example.

```
mike@server:~$ su
Password:_
root@server:/home/mike# exit
mike@server:~$
```

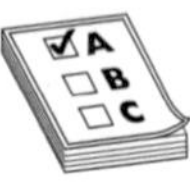

EXAM TIP Many Linux systems disable the root account for safety, rendering the su command inoperable. The sudo command enables users to do root things without having the root password.

The Command Prompt

Regardless of what shell you use, the command prompt always *focuses* on a specific folder, the *working directory*, usually indicated by the prompt. The OS executes commands in the specified folder unless otherwise directed. Here's an example of focus. In Windows, if you see a prompt that looks like the following line, you know that the focus is on the root directory of the C: drive:

```
C:\>
```

In Mac OS X and Linux the prompt is subtly different, but functionally the same. First of all, Mac OS X and Linux systems don't use the Windows drive lettering concept; all forms of storage are simply mounted as folders. Second, Linux prompts show the currently logged-on user and system as well as the current directory. Third, Mac OS X and Linux use a forward slash (/) instead of a backslash (\). This prompt shows user mike is on the "server" system and is in the home directory:

```
mike@server:/home$
```

In Windows, if you see a prompt that looks like Figure 16-6, you know that the focus is on the \Diploma\APLUS\ folder of the C: drive. The trick to using a command line is first to focus the prompt on the drive and folder where you want to work.

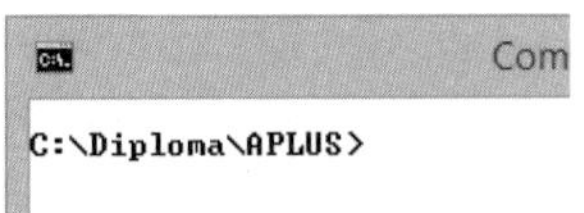

Figure 16-6 Command prompt indicating focus on the C:\Diploma\APLUS\ folder

Closing the Terminal

Closing a command prompt is easy and is done the exact same way in both Windows and OS X and Linux. At the prompt just type **exit**. The terminal window will disappear.

```
mike@server:/home$ exit
```

Filenames and File Formats

All operating systems manifest each program and piece of data as an individual file. Each file has a name, which is stored with the file on the drive. Names are broken down into two parts: the filename and the *extension*. In the early days of PCs, Microsoft used a file system that dictated the filename could be no longer than eight characters. The extension, which was optional, could be up to three characters long. The filename and extension are separated by a period, or *dot*. Here's an example of an old-style filename:

```
thisfile.txt
```

The "8.3" format does not apply to modern operating systems. Here are some examples of acceptable filenames:

fred.exe	Myfirstattempt.aes	file1.doc
driver3.h	Janet likes long file names.doc	Noextension

Whether you're running Windows, Mac OS X, or Linux, the extension is very important as it's the filename's extension that tells the operating system what type of program uses this data. This is called the file's *association*. For example, Microsoft Word is associated with any file that has the extension .docx or .doc. PowerPoint uses .pptx or .ppt. Graphics file extensions, in contrast, often reflect the graphics standard used to render the image, such as .gif for CompuServe's Graphics Interchange Format or .jpg for the JPEG (Joint Photographic Experts Group) format.

NOTE Every operating system has some method to change file associations. If you want to open Microsoft Office .docx files in LibreOffice instead of Word, there is always a way to do this.

Changing the extension of a data file does not affect its contents, but without the proper extension, your operating system won't know which program uses it. Figure 16-7 shows a folder with two identical image files. The one on the right shows a thumbnail because Windows recognizes this as a JPEG image; the one on the left shows a generic icon because I deleted the extension. Windows' GUI doesn't show file extensions by default, but Mac OS X and most Linux distros do.

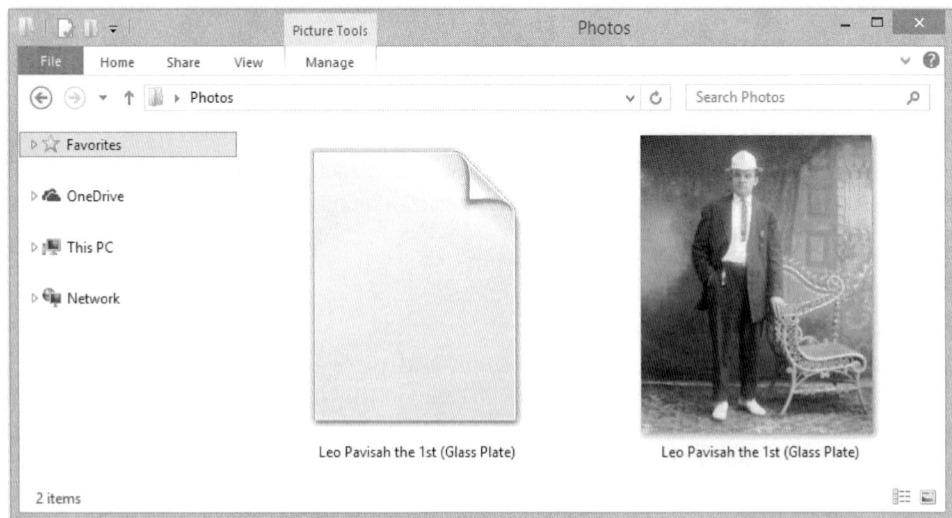

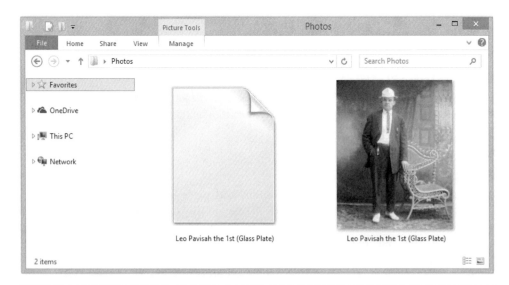

Figure 16-7 What kind of file is the one on the left?

Drives and Folders

When working from the command line, you need to be able to focus the prompt at the specific drive and folder that contains the files or programs with which you want to work. This can be a little more complicated than it seems.

Before we get too deep here, let's review what we know from Chapter 10, "Implementing Hard Drives." Windows assigns drive letters to each hard drive partition (except the system partition) and to every recognized form of mass storage. Hard drive partitions usually start with the letter C:. Optical drives by default get the next available drive letter after the last hard drive partition. On top of that, you can mount a hard drive as a volume in another drive.

Mac OS X and Linux don't use the idea of drive letters. Instead, the boot partition is defined as the root drive, shown as just a slash: /. All other storage—partitions, optical discs, thumb drives, and so on—must go through a process called *mounting* to enable the OS to just treat them as folders. These folders are most often mounted to a single folder off the root drive called /mount or /media in Linux and /Volumes in Mac OS X.

Whatever the names of the drives, all operating systems use a hierarchical directory tree to organize the contents of these drives. All files are put into groups called *folders*, although you'll often hear techs use the term *directory* rather than *folder*. Any file not in a folder *within* the tree—that is, any file in the folder at the root of the directory tree—is said to be in the *root directory*. A folder inside another folder is called a *subfolder*. Any folder can have multiple subfolders. Two or more files with the same name can exist in different folders on a PC, but two files in the same folder cannot have the same name. In the same way, no two subfolders under the same folder can have the same name, but two subfolders under different folders can have the same name.

NOTE It helps to visualize a directory tree as upside down, because in geekspeak, the trunk, or root directory, is described as "above" the folders that divide it, and those subfolders "below" root are spoken of as being "above" the other subfolders inside them. For example, "The file is in the Adobe folder under Program Files."

When describing a drive in Windows, you use its letter and a colon. For example, the hard drive would be represented by C:. To describe the root directory, put a backslash (\) after the C:, as in C:\. To describe a particular directory, add the name of the directory. For example, if a PC has a directory in the root directory called Test, it is C:\Test. Subdirectories in a directory are displayed by adding backslashes and names. If the Test directory has a subdirectory called System, it is shown like this: C:\Test\System. This naming convention provides for a complete description of the location and name of any file. If the C:\Test \System directory includes a file called test2.txt, it is C:\Test\System\test2.txt.

The exact location of a file is called its *path*. The path for the test2.txt file is C:\Test \System. Here are some examples of possible Windows paths:

```
C:\Program Files
C:\Users\mike\Desktop
F:\FRUSCH3\CLEAR
D:\
```

Mac OS X and Linux also use paths. However, folder names are separated by a forward slash (/) instead of the backslash as used by Windows. Also, Windows and Mac OS X are not case sensitive, while Linux is. For example, in Linux it's perfectly acceptable to have two folders called "Mike" and "mike" inside the same folder. Windows does not allow this. Here are some examples of Mac OS X and Linux paths:

```
/usr/local/bin
/Applications/Utilities
/home/mike/Desktop
```

Mac OS X and Linux prompts show your folder location a bit differently than Windows. Generally, your default prompt is pointing at the /home/<username>/ folder. However, by default Mac OS X and Linux do not show that path. They only show a tilde, ~, as follows:

```
mike@server:~$
```

The ~ is really just a shorthand for your users folder; in this case it means you are in /home/mike. Yes, a little confusing, but welcome to UNIX! Mac OS X and Linux provide a handy utility, *pwd*, that tells you exactly where you are if you're unsure:

```
mike@server:~$ pwd
/home/mike
```

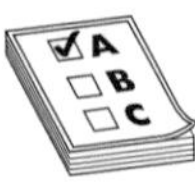

EXAM TIP The CompTIA A+ objectives want you to know the pwd and passwd commands. You've seen the pwd command; later in this chapter we'll cover passwd.

Here are a few items to remember about folder names and filenames:

- Folders and files may have spaces in their names.
- The only disallowed characters in Windows are the following eleven: * " / \ [ ] : ; | = ,
- In Mac OS X and Linux the only disallowed character is a forward slash: /
- Files aren't required to have extensions, but in most cases the OS won't know the file association type without an extension.

Mastering Fundamental Commands

It's time to try using the command line, but before you begin, a note of warning is in order: the command-line interface is picky and unforgiving. It will do what you *say*, not what you *mean*, so it always pays to double-check that those are one and the same before you press ENTER and commit the command. One careless keystroke can result in the loss of crucial data, with no warning and no going back. In this section, you'll explore the structure of commands and then play with basic commands to navigate and manipulate your OS's folder structure.

Structure: Syntax and Switches

All commands in every command-line interface use a similar structure and execute in the same way. You type the name of the command, followed by the target of that command and any modifications of that command that you want to apply. You can call up a modification by using an extra letter or number, called a *switch* or *option*, which may follow either the command or the target, depending on the command. The proper way to write a command is called its *syntax*. The key with commands is that you can't spell anything incorrectly or use a \ when the syntax calls for a /. The command line is almost completely inflexible, so you have to learn the correct syntax for each command.

```
[command] [target (if any)] [switches]
```

or

```
[command] [switches] [target (if any)]
```

How do you know what switches are allowed? How do you know whether the switches come before or after the target? If you want to find out the syntax and switches used by a particular command, in Windows type the command followed by **/?** to get help:

```
[command name] /?
```

In Mac OS X or Linux, type the command **man** (manual) followed by the command you're interested in:

```
man [command name]
```

When you are done reading the manual, press the Q key to quit back to the prompt.

Viewing Directory Contents: dir and ls

The Windows *dir command* and the Mac OS X and Linux *ls command* show you the contents of the directory where the prompt is focused. If you're like most techs, you'll use dir or ls more often than any other command at the command prompt. When you open a command-line window in Windows, it opens focused on your user folder. You will know this because the prompt looks like `C:\Users\`*`User name`*`>`. By typing **dir** and then pressing the ENTER key (remember that you must always press ENTER to execute a command from the command line), you will see something like this:

```
C:\Users>dir
 Volume in drive C has no label.
 Volume Serial Number is 98F4-E484

 Directory of C:\Users

07/16/2016  10:52 AM    <DIR>          .
07/16/2015  10:52 AM    <DIR>          ..
12/20/2016  06:59 PM    <DIR>          DefaultAppPool
08/14/2015  10:42 AM    <DIR>          Mike
07/16/2017  02:07 AM    <DIR>          Public
                0 File(s)            0 bytes
                5 Dir(s)  295,888,113,664 bytes free
C:\Users>
```

The default prompts in Linux don't show the full path, but on my Ubuntu Linux system, typing ls shows the following in the mike user's Home folder:

```
mike@server:~$ ls
Desktop      Downloads  Public      Videos
Documents    photo.jpg  timmy.doc
mike@server:~$
```

If you are following along on a PC, remember that different computers contain different files and programs, so you will absolutely see something different from what's shown in the previous example. If a lot of text scrolls quickly down the screen in Windows, try typing **dir /p** (pause). Don't forget to press ENTER. The dir /p command is a lifesaver when you're looking for something in a large directory. Just press SPACEBAR to display the next screen.

In Mac OS X and Linux, you can get the same result as dir /p by typing **ls | more**. The | symbol is called a *pipe*. You are telling the OS to take the output of ls and, instead of sending it directly to the screen, "pipe" it through a second command called more. The pipe command works in all three operating systems and is incredibly powerful. You'll see lots more of the pipe command later in this chapter.

Some commands give you the same result whether you include spaces or not. Typing **dir/p** and **dir /p**, for example, provides the same output. Some commands, however, *require* spaces between the command and switches. In general, get into the habit of putting spaces between your command and switches and you won't run into problems.

NOTE Extra text typed after a command to modify its operation, such as /w or /p after dir, is called a *switch*. Almost all switches can be used simultaneously to modify a command. For example, try typing **ls –a –l –h** in Mac OS X or Linux.

dir Command

When you type a simple **dir** command, you will see that some of the entries look like this:

```
09/04/2016   05:51 PM          63,664 photo.jpg
```

All of these entries are files. The dir command lists the creation date, creation time, file size in bytes, filename, and extension.

Any entries that look like this are folders:

```
12/31/2016  10:18 AM    <DIR>          Windows
```

The dir command lists the creation date, creation time, <*DIR*> to tell you it is a folder, and the folder name.

Now type the **dir /w** command. Note that the dir /w command shows only the filenames, but they are arranged in five columns across your screen. Finally, type **dir /?** to see the screen shown in Figure 16-8, which lists all possible switches for the command.

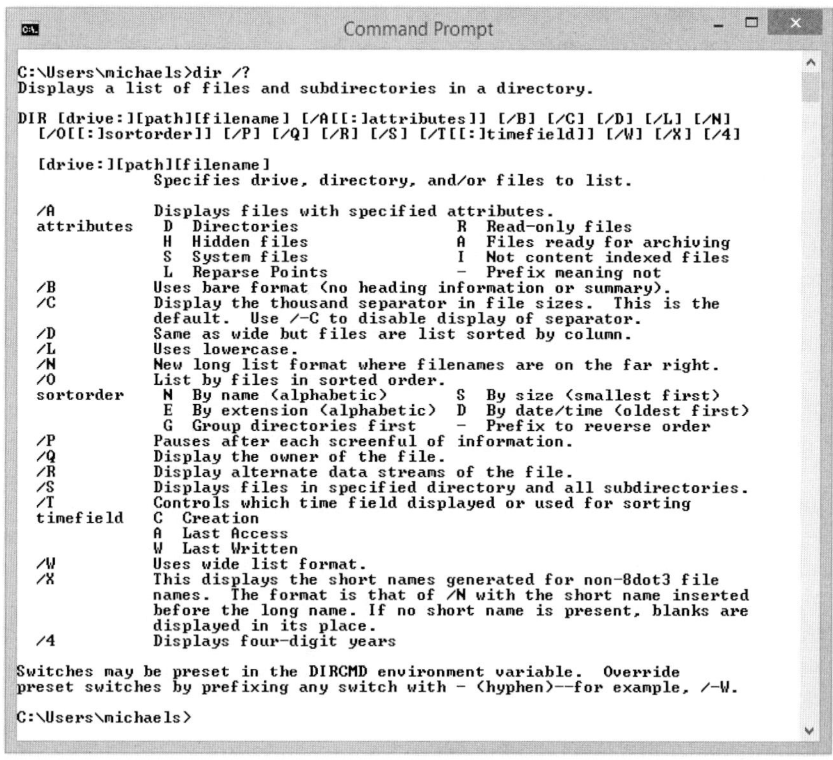

Command Prompt
C:\Users\michaels>dir /?
Displays a list of files and subdirectories in a directory.
DIR [drive:][path][filename] [/A[[:]attributes]] [/B] [/C] [/D] [/L] [/N]
[/O[[:]sortorder]] [/P] [/Q] [/R] [/S] [/T[[:]timefield]] [/W] [/X] [/4]
[drive:][path][filename]
Specifies drive, directory, and/or files to list.
/A Displays files with specified attributes.
attributes D Directories R Read-only files
H Hidden files A Files ready for archiving
S System files I Not content indexed files
L Reparse Points - Prefix meaning not
/B Uses bare format (no heading information or summary).
/C Display the thousand separator in file sizes. This is the
default. Use /-C to disable display of separator.
/D Same as wide but files are list sorted by column.
/L Uses lowercase.
/N New long list format where filenames are on the far right.
/O List by files in sorted order.
sortorder N By name (alphabetic) S By size (smallest first)
E By extension (alphabetic) D By date/time (oldest first)
G Group directories first - Prefix to reverse order
/P Pauses after each screenful of information.
/Q Display the owner of the file.
/R Display alternate data streams of the file.
/S Displays files in specified directory and all subdirectories.
/T Controls which time field displayed or used for sorting
timefield C Creation
A Last Access
W Last Written
/W Uses wide list format.
/X This displays the short names generated for non-8dot3 file
names. The format is that of /N with the short name inserted
before the long name. If no short name is present, blanks are
displayed in its place.
/4 Displays four-digit years
Switches may be preset in the DIRCMD environment variable. Override
preset switches by prefixing any switch with - (hyphen)--for example, /-W.
C:\Users\michaels>

Figure 16-8 Typing **dir /?** in Windows lists all possible switches for the dir command.

ls Command

The ls command, like most UNIX commands, is very powerful and contains over 50 different switches. For now let's just cover one of the more important ones: –l.

Using **ls** with the **–l** switch, which stands for long listing, gives detailed information about all the files:

```
$ ls -l
-rw-rw-r-- 0 mike 2313443 Jun 13 15:27 photo.jpg
```

We'll discuss this output in more detail as we continue through the chapter.

Windows help screens sometimes seem a little cryptic and Mac OS X and Linux help screens are often impossibly hard to read. Still, they're useful when you're not too familiar with a command or you can't figure out how to get a command to do what you need. Even though I have many commands memorized, I still refer to these help screens; you should use them as well. If you're really lost, type **help** at the command prompt for a list of commands you may type.

Changing Directory Focus: The cd Command

The *cd command* works in every operating system, although there are differences between Windows and Mac OS X and Linux. You can use the cd command to change the focus of the command prompt to a different directory. To use the cd command, type **cd** followed by the name of the directory on which you want the prompt to focus. For example, in Windows, to go to the Obiwan directory in the root directory, you type **cd \obiwan** and then press ENTER. If the system has an Obiwan directory there, the prompt changes focus to that directory and appears as `C:\Obiwan>`. If no Obiwan directory exists or if you accidentally type something like **obiwam**, you get the error "The system cannot find the path specified." If only I had a dollar for every time I've seen those errors! I usually get them because I've typed too fast. If you get this error, check what you typed and try again.

To return to the root directory, type **cd ** and press ENTER. You can use the cd command to point the prompt to any directory. For example, you could type **cd obiwan\my \hope** from a C:\ prompt, and the prompt would change to `C:\Obiwan\my\hope>`— assuming, of course, that your system *has* a directory called C:\Obiwan\my\hope.

Once the prompt has changed, type **dir** again. You should see a different list of files and directories. Every directory holds different files and subdirectories, so when you point the prompt to different directories, the dir command shows you different contents.

Changing directory focus in Mac OS X/Linux is similar to doing so in Windows but you use a / instead of a \. Using the same example just shown for Windows, from the root directory you type **cd /Obiwan**. To go to the /obiwan/my/hope directory you type **cd /obiwan/my/hope**.

NOTE On a Linux system it is considered bad manners to create files and folders in the root (/) directory. In fact, you need "root" permissions to even do such a thing. This is because of Linux's history as a multi-user system; it was important to include restrictions so that users couldn't break the underlying OS that everyone depended on.

In the previous examples we have been using what are known as *absolute paths*, meaning we have been typing out the entire path of a directory we are changing to. This might work OK for an ancient DOS system from the '80s, but it's way too much work to move around in today's deeply nested directory trees.

That's where relative paths come in handy; instead of starting the path with a \, you can just type the name of the directory. For example, you could go to the C:\Obiwan directory from the root directory simply by typing **cd obiwan** at the C:\> prompt. You can then move one level at a time, like this:

```
C:\>cd Obiwan
C:\Obiwan>cd my
C:\Obiwan\my>cd hope
```

Or, you can jump multiple directory levels in one step, like this:

```
C:\>cd Obiwan\my\hope
C:\Obiwan\my\hope>
```

These tricks also work for Mac OS X and Linux, but of course you always use a forward slash instead of a backslash as needed:

```
mike@server:~$ cd Obiwan
mike@server:~/Obiwan$
```

A final trick: if you want to go *up* a single directory level, you can type cd followed immediately by two periods. So, for example, if you're in the C:\Obiwan\my directory and you want to move up to the C:\Obiwan directory, you can simply type **cd ..** and you'll be there:

```
C:\Obiwan\my>cd ..
C:\Obiwan>
```

Take some time to move the prompt focus around the directories of your PC, using the cd and dir commands. Use dir to find a directory, and then use cd to move the focus to that directory. Remember, cd \ (or cd / in Mac OS X and Linux) always gets you back to the root directory.

Moving Between Drives

Windows and Mac OS X and Linux have very different techniques for moving between drives, given that Windows uses drive letters while Mac OS X and Linux do not. Let's start with Windows and then we'll take a look at Mac OS X and Linux.

Moving Between Drives in Windows

The cd command is *not* used to move between Windows' drive letters. To get the prompt to point to another drive ("point" is command-line geekspeak for "switch its focus"), just type the drive letter and a colon. If the prompt points at the C:\Users\mike directory and you want to see what is on the USB thumb drive (E:), just type **e:** and the prompt will point to the USB drive. You'll see the following on the screen:

```
C:\Users\mike>e:
E:\>
```

To return to the C: drive, just type **c:** and you'll see the following:

```
E:\>c:
C:\Users\mike>
```

Note that you return to the same directory you left. Just for fun, try typing in a drive letter that you know doesn't exist. For example, I know that my system doesn't have a W: drive. If I type in a nonexistent drive on a Windows system, I get the following error:

```
The system cannot find the drive specified.
```

Try inserting an optical disc or a thumb drive and using the **cd** command to point to its drive. Type **dir** to see the contents of the optical disc. Type **cd** to move the focus to any folders on the optical disc. Now return focus to the C: drive.

Using the dir, cd, and the drive letter commands, you can access any folder on any storage device on your system. Make sure you can use these commands comfortably to navigate inside your computer.

Moving Between Drives in Mac OS X and Linux

So if Mac OS X and Linux don't use drive letters, how do you access your other drive partitions, optical media, thumb drives, and so on? Well, all media is mounted as a folder, but the location of those folders is going to vary by the OS. In Mac OS X, you need to look in the /Volumes folder. In Ubuntu Linux, you need to look in the /mnt folder for drives and the /media/<user name> folder for removable media. In other Linux distributions, well, you're going to have to explore—good thing you know how to use the cd and ls commands, eh? The following commands show my optical drive and a thumb drive in a Ubuntu Linux system:

```
mike@server:/media/mike$ ls -l
drwx------ 3 mike mike 4096 Dec 31  1969 THUMBDRIVE
dr-xr-xr-x 6 mike mike 2048 May 13 10:15 Age of Empires
mike@server:/media/mike$
```

Making Directories: The md/mkdir Command

Now that you have learned how to navigate in a command-prompt world, it's time to start making stuff, beginning with a new directory.

To make a directory, use the *md command* in Windows. Alternatively, you can use the *mkdir command*, which works in all operating systems and is identical to md. In Windows, to create a directory called practice under your user's folder, for example, open a new command prompt window or **cd** to your users folder at \Users\<your username>. You should see the prompt

```
C:Users\mike>_
```

Now that the prompt points to the C:\Users\mike directory, type **md practice** to create the directory:

```
C:\Users\mike>md practice
```

Once you press ENTER, Windows executes the command, but it won't volunteer any information about what it did. You must use the **dir** command to see that you have, in fact, created a new directory. Note that the practice directory in this example is not listed last, as you might expect.

```
C:\>dir
 Volume in Drive C is
 Volume Serial Number is 1734-3234
Directory of C:\Users\mike
```

```
08/21/2016  03:58 PM    <DIR>          .
08/21/2016  03:58 PM    <DIR>          ..
08/21/2016  09:55 AM    <DIR>          Desktop
07/15/2016  08:25 AM    <DIR>          Documents
08/20/2016  09:16 AM    <DIR>          Downloads
07/15/2016  08:25 AM    <DIR>          Favorites
07/15/2016  08:25 AM    <DIR>          Music
07/15/2016  08:25 AM    <DIR>          Pictures
08/21/2016  03:58 PM    <DIR>          practice
07/15/2016  08:25 AM    <DIR>          Videos
               1 File(s)            240 bytes
              10 Dir(s)  216,876,089,344 bytes free
```

What about distinguishing between uppercase and lowercase? Windows displays both in file and folder names but rarely makes any distinction with commands—which is a nice way to say that Windows doesn't support case. For clarity, try using the **md** command to make a folder called Practice (note the uppercase) and see what happens. This also happens in the graphical Windows. Go to your desktop and try to make two folders, one called files and the other called FILES, and see what Windows tells you.

To create a files subdirectory in the practice directory, first use the **cd** command to point the prompt to the practice directory:

```
C:Users\mike>cd practice
C:Users\mike\practice>_
```

Then run the **md** command to make the files directory:

```
md files
```

NOTE Make sure that the prompt points to the directory in which you want to make the new subdirectory before you execute the md command.

When you're finished, type **dir** to see the new Files subdirectory. Just for fun, try the process again and add a games directory under the practice directory. Type **dir** to verify success.

Creating folders in Mac OS X and Linux is again identical, but you must use the mkdir command. Here is the same example just given but done on my Ubuntu system:

```
mike@server:~$ mkdir practice
```

You can see the results by running the **ls** command:

```
mike@server:~$ls
practice
```

Don't forget that Linux and Mac OS X are case sensitive. Check out the results of these three different folders, all different capitalizations of "files":

```
mike@server:~/practice$ ls
files  Files  FILES
mike@server:~/practice$
```

Removing Directories: The rd Command

Removing subdirectories works exactly like making them. First, get to the directory that contains the subdirectory you want to delete, and then execute either the *rmdir* or *rd* command. Both of these commands are functionally identical, but where they work is important. The rmdir command works equally well in both Windows and Mac OS X and Linux, but the rd command only works in Windows.

So, with that in mind, let's get rid of some folders. It's actually quite simple. In this example, let's use Linux as an example to delete the Files subdirectory in our ~/practice directory (remember ~ means your home directory). First, get to where the files directory is located—~/practice—by typing **cd practice** (make sure you're in your home directory first). Then type **rmdir files**. If you received no response, you probably did it right! Type **ls** to check that the Files subdirectory is gone. Windows works exactly the same, although we tend to use the rd command more often, simply because it's faster to type.

The rmdir/rd command alone will not delete a directory if the directory contains files or subdirectories. If you want to delete a directory that contains files or subdirectories, you must first empty that directory. However, Windows folks can use the rd command followed by the /s switch to delete a directory as well as all files and subdirectories. The rd command followed by the /s switch is handy but dangerous, because it's easy to delete more than you want. There is no Recycle Bin when deleting from the command line, so when deleting, always follow the maxim "Check twice and delete once."

Let's delete the practice and games directories with rd followed by the /s switch. Because the practice directory is in your home directory, point to it with **cd \Users\<your username>**. Now execute the command **rd practice /s**. In a rare display of mercy, Windows responds with the following:

```
C:\Users\mike>rd practice /s
practice, Are you sure (Y/N)?
```

Press the Y key and both C:\Users\mike\practice and C:\Users\mike\practice\games are eliminated.

Want to remove a folder and all of its contents in Linux? No problem, but we don't use rmdir. Instead we turn to the very handy rm command. With the same scenario just presented, type the **rm** command with the **–r** switch as shown:

```
mike@server:~$ rm -r practice
```

Try This!

Working with Directories

PC techs should be comfortable creating and deleting directories. To get some practice, Try This!

1. Create a new directory in your home directory by using the make directory command (md). At the command prompt from your home directory, make a directory called Jedi:

   ```
   C:\Users\padawan>md Jedi
   ```

2. As usual, the prompt tells you nothing; it just presents a fresh prompt. Do a dir (that is, type the **dir** command) to see your new directory. Windows creates the new directory wherever it is pointing when you issue the command, whether or not that's where you meant to put it. To demonstrate, point the prompt to your new directory by using the **cd** command:

   ```
   C:\Users\padawan>cd jedi
   ```

3. Now use the make directory command again to create a directory called Yoda:

   ```
   C:\Users\padawan\Jedi>md Yoda
   ```

   Do a **dir** again, and you should see that your Jedi directory now contains a Yoda directory.

4. Type **cd ..** to go up one level and return to your home directory so you can delete your new directories by using the remove directory command (**rd**):

   ```
   C:Users\padawan>rd /s jedi
   ```

   In another rare display of mercy, Windows responds with the following:

   ```
   jedi, Are you sure <Y/N>?
   ```

5. Press Y to eliminate both Jedi and Jedi\Yoda.
6. Using a Mac OS X or Linux system, repeat this entire process using the mkdir, cd, and rm commands.

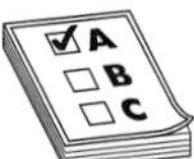

EXAM TIP Make sure you know how to use md, mkdir, rd, rmdir, rm, and cd for the CompTIA A+ 220-902 exam.

Running a Program in Windows

To run a program from the Windows command line, simply change the prompt focus to the folder where the program is located, type the name of the program, and then press ENTER. Try this safe example. Go to the C:\Windows\System32 folder—the exact name of this folder is pretty standard on all Windows systems, but your mileage may vary. Type **dir /p** to see the files one page at a time. You should see a file called mmc.exe (see Figure 16-9).

```
Command Prompt - dir /p
10/28/2014  08:28 PM            17,920 Microsoft.Management.Infrastructure.Nativ
e.Unmanaged.dll
07/25/2012  08:12 PM            29,128 microsoft.windows.softwarelogo.showdeskto
p.exe
10/28/2014  08:24 PM           160,256 MicrosoftAccountTokenProvider.dll
10/28/2014  09:42 PM            23,552 midimap.dll
10/28/2014  09:32 PM           303,616 migflt.dll
02/22/2014  05:47 AM           127,488 migisol.dll
07/14/2015  12:26 PM    <DIR>          migration
10/28/2014  09:45 PM           183,296 miguiresource.dll
12/23/2014  11:09 AM    <DIR>          migwiz
08/22/2013  01:53 AM             1,170 migwiz.lnk
10/28/2014  09:07 PM            40,448 mimefilt.dll
10/28/2014  08:26 PM           159,744 mimofcodec.dll
10/28/2014  08:26 PM            37,888 MirrorDrvCompat.dll
10/28/2014  08:09 PM         1,335,296 mispace.dll
10/28/2014  08:20 PM           234,496 miutils.dll
06/18/2013  09:48 AM           673,088 mlang.dat
10/28/2014  08:16 PM           238,592 mlang.dll
10/28/2014  09:17 PM         2,003,456 mmc.exe
10/28/2014  09:29 PM           350,208 mmcbase.dll
10/28/2014  09:27 PM            73,216 mmci.dll
10/28/2014  09:41 PM            14,336 mmcico.dll
10/28/2014  08:57 PM         2,924,032 mmcndmgr.dll
Press any key to continue . . .
```

Figure 16-9 The mmc.exe program listed in the System32 folder

As mentioned earlier, all files with extensions .exe and .com are programs, so mmc.exe is a program. To run the mmc.exe program, just type the filename, in this case **mmc**, and press ENTER (see Figure 16-10). Note that you do not have to type the .exe extension, although you can. Congratulations! You have just run another application from the command line.

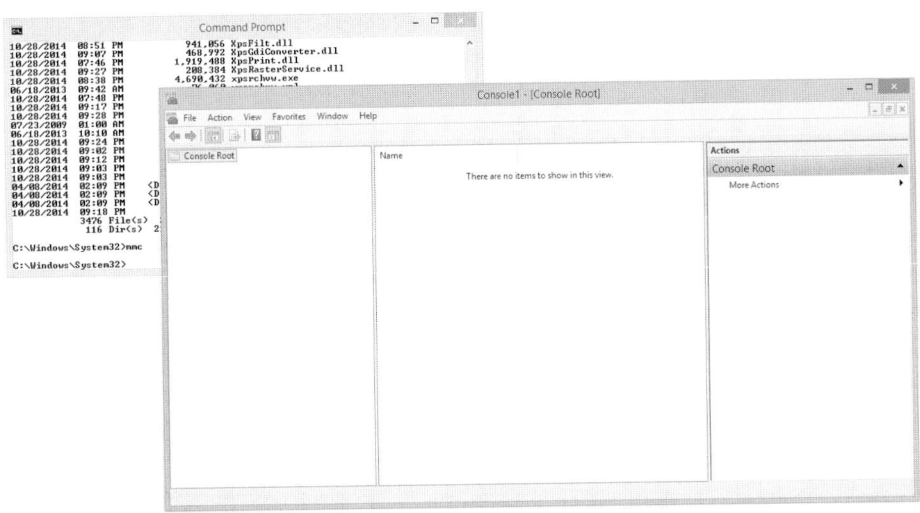

Figure 16-10 Running mmc in Windows

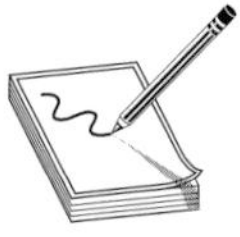

NOTE Windows includes a lot of command-line tools for specific jobs such as starting and stopping services, viewing computers on a network, converting hard drive file systems, and more. This book discusses these task-specific tools in the chapters that reflect their task. Chapter 21, "Local Area Networking," goes into detail on the versatile and powerful net command, for example.

Running a Program in Mac OS X and Linux

As much as I like to tell folks how similar Mac OS X, Linux, and Windows command lines are, they are very different in some areas, one of which is how you run executable programs from the command line. For starters, Mac OS X and Linux executable programs don't rely on any kind of extension such as .exe in Windows. Instead, any file, whether it's compiled code or a text file, can be given the property of executable, as shown in Figure 16-11.

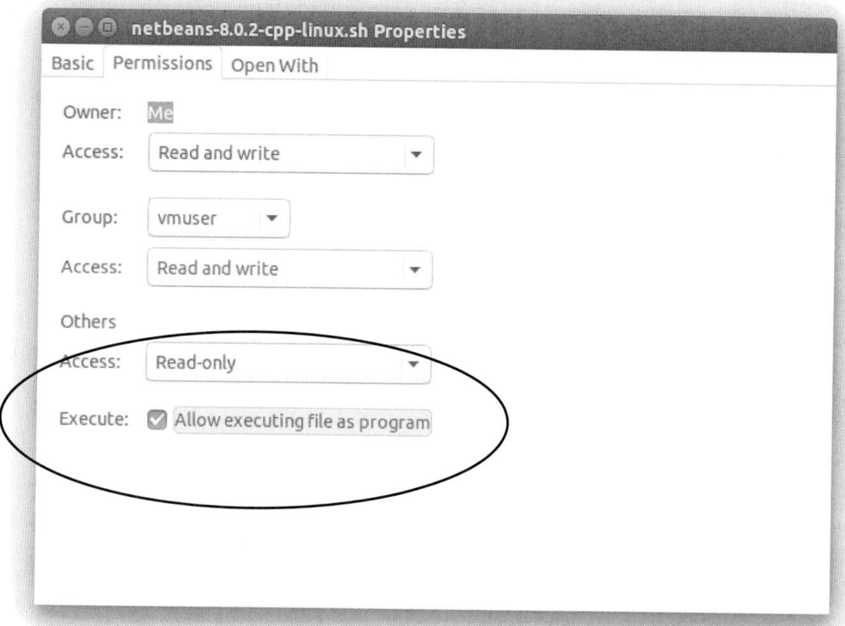

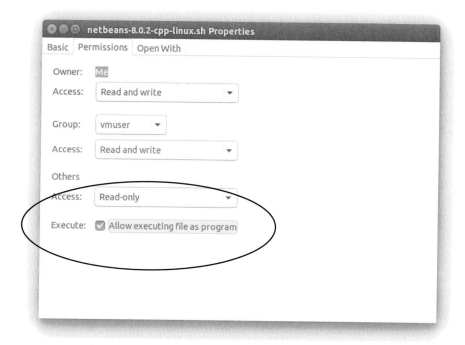

Figure 16-11 Showing file properties in Ubuntu

So it's really up to the person using the program to verify they are even using a program. One does not just start programs haphazardly in Mac OS X or Linux. You make a point to know your executable before you run it.

Mac OS X and Linux help you in the command line when it comes to executables. First of all, Mac OS X and almost all versions of Linux come with color-coded command

lines, as shown in Figure 16-12 (although you can't really tell because the book is in black and white). In this particular version the executable files are colored green.

```
vmuser@ubuntu1504-vm: /usr/bin
vmuser@ubuntu1504-vm:/usr/bin$ ls -lh gnome-*
-rwxr-xr-x 1 root root 666K Apr  7 09:42 gnome-calculator
lrwxrwxrwx 1 root root    9 Apr 23 09:10 gnome-character-map -> gucharmap
-rwxr-xr-x 1 root root 522K Sep 30  2014 gnome-contacts
-rwxr-xr-x 1 root root  40K Jan 26  2015 gnome-disk-image-mounter
-rwxr-xr-x 1 root root 622K Jan 26  2015 gnome-disks
-rwxr-xr-x 1 root root  23K Sep 27  2012 gnome-file-share-properties
-rwxr-xr-x 1 root root  61K Apr 10 13:13 gnome-font-viewer
lrwxrwxrwx 1 root root    4 Apr 23 09:10 gnome-help -> yelp
lrwxrwxrwx 1 root root   15 Apr 23 09:10 gnome-keyring -> gnome-keyring-3
-rwxr-xr-x 1 root root  15K Apr  8 10:34 gnome-keyring-3
-rwxr-xr-x 1 root root 935K Apr  8 10:34 gnome-keyring-daemon
-rwxr-xr-x 1 root root 1.5K Apr 10 09:56 gnome-language-selector
-rwxr-xr-x 1 root root  68K Oct 30  2014 gnome-power-statistics
-rwxr-xr-x 1 root root 134K Jan 26  2015 gnome-screensaver
-rwxr-xr-x 1 root root  15K Jan 26  2015 gnome-screensaver-command
-rwxr-xr-x 1 root root  82K Dec  3  2014 gnome-screenshot
-rwxr-xr-x 1 root root 206K Mar 20 01:43 gnome-session
-rwxr-xr-x 1 root root  11K Mar 20 01:43 gnome-session-inhibit
-rwxr-xr-x 1 root root  65K Mar 20 01:43 gnome-session-properties
-rwxr-xr-x 1 root root  11K Mar 20 01:43 gnome-session-quit
-rwxr-xr-x 1 root root 119K Apr 26  2014 gnome-system-log
-rwxr-xr-x 1 root root  255 Apr 12  2013 gnome-system-log-pkexec
-rwxr-xr-x 1 root root 340K Mar 16 05:14 gnome-system-monitor
-rwxr-xr-x 1 root root 3.5K Apr  8 11:34 gnome-terminal
-rwxr-xr-x 1 root root  80K Apr  8 11:34 gnome-terminal.real
-rwxr-xr-x 1 root root 1.4K Apr  8 10:18 gnome-terminal.wrapper
lrwxrwxrwx 1 root root   35 Apr 23 09:10 gnome-text-editor -> /etc/alternatives/gnome-text-editor
-rwxr-xr-x 1 root root  23K Apr 10 13:13 gnome-thumbnail-font
lrwxrwxrwx 1 root root   35 Apr 23 09:10 gnome-www-browser -> /etc/alternatives/gnome-www-browser
vmuser@ubuntu1504-vm:/usr/bin$
```

Figure 16-12 Color-coded files in Ubuntu, helpfully displayed in black and white

Mac OS X and Linux have two very different types of executable file types: built-in and executables. Built-in programs are like the ones you see in Figure 16-12: commands you've just learned such as ls, mkdir, and rm are all individual executable programs. To run a built-in program you just type it in as you have already done many times in this chapter.

Executable programs are programs that are, well, not built in. If you download a program from somewhere (and Linux people do this a lot), you first unzip the program and then run the program. But there's one problem. If you try to run it, Linux can't find it, even though it is in the exact folder you are running it from! Interestingly, this is by design. When you run a program from a Linux command line, Linux first looks through a series of folders called the *path* (not to be confused with the other type of path discussed earlier). You can see the path by typing the command **echo $PATH**:

```
mike@server:~/$ echo $PATH
/usr/local/sbin:/usr/local/bin:/usr/sbin:/usr/bin:/sbin:/bin:/usr/games:/usr/local/games
```

In order to make Linux run the executable, you need to add a period and a slash (**./**, commonly called "dot-slash") in front of the executable to make it run:

```
mike@server:~/$ ./runme
```

NOTE Downloading and running command-line programs is not a Mac OS X thing.

Working with Files

This section deals with basic file manipulation. You will learn how to look at, copy, move, rename, and delete files. The examples in this section are based on a C: root directory with the following files and directories:

```
C:\>dir
 Volume in drive C has no label.
 Volume Serial Number is 4C62-1572

 Directory of C:\

05/29/2016  05:33 PM             5,776 aoedoppl.txt
05/29/2016  05:33 PM             2,238 aoeWVlog.txt
07/12/2016  10:38 AM    <DIR>          books
07/15/2016  02:45 PM             1,708 CtDrvStp.log
06/04/2016  10:22 PM    <DIR>          Impressions Games
09/11/2017  11:32 AM    <DIR>          NVIDIA
01/03/2016  01:12 PM    <DIR>          pers-drv
09/14/2017  11:11 AM    <DIR>          Program Files
09/12/2016  08:32 PM                21 statusclient.log
07/31/2016  10:40 PM               153 systemscandata.txt
03/13/2016  09:54 AM         1,111,040 t3h0
04/21/2016  04:19 PM    <DIR>          temp
01/10/2017  07:07 PM    <DIR>          WebCam
12/31/2017  10:18 AM    <DIR>          WINDOWS
01/03/2017  09:06 AM    <DIR>          WUTemp
               6 File(s)      1,120,936 bytes
               9 Dir(s)  94,630,002,688 bytes free
```

Because you probably don't have a PC with these files and directories, follow the examples but use what's on your drive. In other words, create your own folders and copy files to them from various folders currently on your system.

Using Wildcards to Locate Files

Visualize having 273 files in one directory. A few of these files have the extension .docx, but most do not. You are looking only for files with the .docx extension. Wouldn't it be nice to be able to type the dir command in such a way that only the .docx files come up? You can do this by using wildcards.

A *wildcard* is one of two special characters—asterisk (*) and question mark (?)—that you can use in place of all or part of a filename, often so that a command-line command will act on more than one file at a time. Wildcards work with all command-line commands that take filenames. A great example is the dir command. When you execute a plain dir command, it finds and displays all of the files and folders in the

specified directory; however, you can also narrow its search by adding a filename. For example, if you type the command **dir ailog.txt** while in your root (C:\) directory, you get the following result:

```
C:\>dir ailog.txt
 Volume in drive C has no label.
 Volume Serial Number is 4C62-1572
 Directory of C:\
05/26/2016  11:37 PM                 0 AILog.txt
               1 File(s)             0 bytes
               0 Dir(s)  94,630,195,200 bytes free
```

If you just want to confirm the presence of a particular file in a particular place, this is very convenient. But suppose you want to see all files with the extension .txt. In that case, you use the * wildcard, like this: **dir *.txt**. A good way to think of the * wildcard is "I don't care." Replace the part of the filename that you don't care about with an asterisk (*). The result of dir *.txt would look like this:

```
 Volume in drive C has no label.
 Volume Serial Number is 4C62-1572

 Directory of C:\

05/26/2016  11:37 PM                 0 AILog.txt
05/29/2016  05:33 PM             5,776 aoedoppl.txt
05/29/2016  05:33 PM             2,238 aoeWVlog.txt
07/31/2016  10:40 PM               153 systemscandata.txt
               4 File(s)          8,167 bytes
               0 Dir(s)  94,630,002,688 bytes free
```

Wildcards also substitute for parts of filenames. This dir command will find every file that starts with the letter *a*:

```
C:\>dir a*.*
 Volume in drive C has no label.
 Volume Serial Number is 4C62-1572

 Directory of C:\

05/26/2016  11:37 PM                 0 AILog.txt
05/29/2016  05:33 PM             5,776 aoedoppl.txt
05/29/2016  05:33 PM             2,238 aoeWVlog.txt
               3 File(s)          8,014 bytes
               0 Dir(s)  94,629,675,008 bytes free
```

Wildcards in Mac OS X and Linux work basically the same as in Windows. Head over to the /bin directory on a typical Linux system (it's so full of files) and try using a wildcard with the ls command. Let's find everything that starts with the letter *s* by using the command **ls s* -l**:

```
mike@server:/bin$ ls s* -l
-rwxr-xr-x 1 root root 73352 Feb 13  2014 sed
-rwxr-xr-x 1 root root 36232 May 23  2013 setfacl
-rwxr-xr-x 1 root root 39896 Feb 18  2013 setfont
-rwxr-xr-x 1 root root 12052 Jan 29  2014 setupcon
lrwxrwxrwx 1 root root     4 Jun 29 13:06 sh -> dash
```

```
lrwxrwxrwx 1 root root     4 Jun 29 13:06 sh.distrib -> dash
-rwxr-xr-x 1 root root 31296 Jan 13  2015 sleep
-rwxr-xr-x 1 root root 76624 Feb 17  2014 ss
lrwxrwxrwx 1 root root     7 Jun 29 13:06 static-sh -> busybox
-rwxr-xr-x 1 root root 68256 Jan 13  2015 stty
-rwsr-xr-x 1 root root 36936 Feb 16  2014 su
-rwxr-xr-x 1 root root 27200 Jan 13  2015 sync
```

We've used wildcards only with the dir and ls commands in the previous examples, but virtually every command that deals with files and folders will take wildcards. Let's examine some more commands and see how they use wildcards.

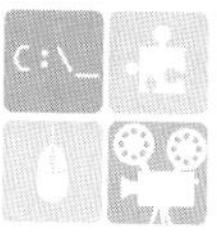

SIM Check out the four "Wildcard" sims in the Chapter 16 section of http://totalsem.com/90x. The two Type! sims plus the Show! and the Click! will prepare you for any number of performance-based questions CompTIA throws at you in the 902 exam.

Deleting Files

To delete files, you use the *del* (or *erase*) *command* in Windows and the *rm command* in Mac OS X and Linux. Deleting files is simple—maybe too simple. As I said before, deleting a file in your GUI gives you the luxury of retrieving deleted files from the Recycle Bin on those "Oops, I didn't mean to delete that" occasions everyone encounters at one time or another. The command line, however, shows no such mercy to the careless user. It has no function equivalent to the Recycle Bin or Trash. Once you have erased a file, you can recover it only by using special recovery utilities (maybe…but don't bet on it). Again, the rule here is to *check twice and delete once.*

To delete a single file in Windows, type the **del** command followed by the name of the file to delete. To delete the file reportdraft1.docx, for example, type this:

```
del reportdraft1.docx
```

In Mac OS X and Linux, do the same thing but type **rm** in place of del, like this:

```
rm reportdraft1.docx
```

Although nothing appears on the screen to confirm it, the file is now gone. To confirm that the reportdraft1.docx file is no longer listed, use the **dir** or **ls** command.

You can use wildcards with the del and rm commands to delete multiple files. For example, to delete all files with the extension .txt in a folder, you can type this in Mac OS X/Linux:

```
rm *.txt
```

You can place the wildcard anywhere in the name. For example, to delete all files with the filename "config" in a Windows directory, type **del config.***. To delete all of the files in a directory, you can use this dangerous but useful *.* wildcard (often pronounced "star-dot-star"):

```
del *.*
```

This is one of the few command-line commands that elicits a response—but only in Windows. Upon receiving the del *.* command, Windows responds with "Are you sure? (Y/N)," to which you respond with a *Y* or *N*. Pressing Y erases every file in the directory, so again, use *.* with care!

With Windows, we only use del to delete files; it will not remove directories. Use rd to delete directories. In Mac OS X and Linux, you can use the rm command to delete both files and folders. Here's an example of the rm command using the –r switch to delete the folder Jedi as well as all of its contents:

```
rm -r Jedi
```

The Windows rd command comes with a switch, /s, which makes it act identically to the rm –r command:

```
rd /s Jedi
```

Clearly it can be very dangerous to use the rm and rd commands with these switches. Use them carefully.

NOTE If you spend any time reading about Mac OS X or Linux Terminal commands online, you might see jokes involving the sudo rm –rf / command. It tells the system to delete every file and folder on the computer's hard drive! The sudo portion means run this as root, rm means to delete,–r means to go into every folder, f means to use force (in other words, delete it no matter what), and finally the / points it at the root of the drive!

Copying and Moving Files

Being able to copy and move files in a command line is crucial to all technicians. Because of its finicky nature and many options, the copy command is also rather painful to learn, especially if you're used to dragging icons in Windows, Mac OS X, or Linux. The following tried-and-true, five-step process makes it easier, but the real secret is to get in front of a prompt and just copy and move files around until you're comfortable. Keep in mind that the only difference between copying and moving is whether the original is left behind (*copy*) or not (*move*). Once you've learned the copy command, you've also learned the move command! In Mac OS X and Linux, the copy command is *cp* and the move command is *mv*. Otherwise, use the same syntax.

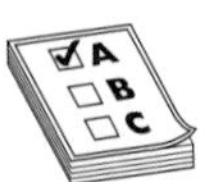

EXAM TIP As of press time, the CompTIA A+ 220-902 objectives listed *mw* rather than *mv* as the move command. I'm guessing CompTIA will fix that typo before you take the exam, but pay attention just in case.

Mike's Five-Step copy/move Process

I've been teaching folks how to copy and move files for years by using this handy process. Keep in mind that hundreds of variations on this process exist. As you become more

confident with these commands, try doing a copy /? or move /? in Windows and man cp or man mv in Mac OS X and Linux at any handy prompt to see the real power of the commands. But first, follow this process step by step:

1. Point the command prompt to the directory containing the file(s) you want to copy or move.
2. Type **copy** or **move** (Windows) or **cp** or **mv** (Mac OS X and Linux) and a space.
3. Type the *name(s)* of the file(s) to be copied/moved (with or without wildcards) and a space.
4. Type the *path* of the new location for the file(s).
5. Press ENTER.

Let's try an example using Windows. The directory Jedi (in my \users folder) contains the file notes.txt. Copy this file to a USB thumb drive (E:).

1. Type **cd Jedi** to point the command prompt to the Jedi directory.

   ```
   C:\Users\mike>cd Jedi
   ```

2. Type **copy** and a space.

   ```
   C:\Users\mike\Jedi>copy
   ```

3. Type **notes.txt** and a space.

   ```
   C:\Users\mike\Jedi>copy notes.txt
   ```

4. Type **e:**.

   ```
   C:\Users\mike\Jedi>copy notes.txt e:\
   ```

5. Press ENTER.

The entire command and response would look like this:

```
C:\Users\mike\Jedi>copy notes.txt e:\
1 file(s) copied
```

If you point the command prompt to the E: drive and type **dir**, the notes.txt file will be visible. Let's try another example, this time in Mac OS X and Linux. Suppose 100 files are in the ~/Jedi directory, 30 of which have the .odf extension, and suppose you want to move those files to ~/Screenplays/sw2018. Follow these steps:

1. Type **cd Screenplays/sw2018** to get the command prompt to the correct folder.

   ```
   mike@server:~$ cd Screenplays/sw2018
   ```

2. Type **mv** and a space.

   ```
   mike@server:~/Screenplays/sw2018$ mv_
   ```

3. Type ***.odf** and a space.

   ```
   mike@server:~/Screenplays/sw2018$ mv_*.odf_
   ```

4. Type **~/Jedi**.

```
mike@server:~/Screenplays/sw2018$ mv_*.odf_~/Jedi
```

5. Press ENTER.

```
mike@server:~/Screenplays/sw2018$
```

Mac OS X and Linux don't give you any feedback at all unless you use special switches. You can check to see if they all made it with **ls**.

Pruning and Grafting Folder Trees

There's a number of situations where you find yourself wanting to grab a folder, complete with all of the subfolders and any files that might be anywhere in any of the folders, and copy or move the whole "pile" in one command. We call this process *pruning and grafting* and it's one of the places where the command line really shines in comparison to GUI file manipulation. Done properly, command-line pruning and grafting is faster and gives you much finer control of the process.

In Windows, the standard copy and move commands can work only in one directory at a time, making them a poor choice for copying or moving files in multiple directories. To help with these multi-directory jobs, Microsoft added the *xcopy command*. (Note that there is no xmove, only xcopy.) We'll also look at robocopy, cp, and mv.

xcopy

The xcopy command works similarly to copy, but xcopy has extra switches that give it the power to work with multiple directories. Here's how it works. Let's say I have a directory called Logs in the root of my C: drive. The Logs directory has three subdirectories: Jan, Feb, and Mar. All of these directories, including the Logs directory, contain about 50 files. If I wanted to copy all of these files to my E: drive in one command, I would use xcopy in the following manner:

```
xcopy c:\Logs e:\Logs /s
```

Because xcopy works on directories, you don't have to use filenames as you would in copy, although xcopy certainly accepts filenames and wildcards. The /s switch, the most commonly used of all of the many switches that come with xcopy, tells xcopy to copy all subdirectories except for empty ones. The /e switch tells xcopy to copy empty subdirectories. When you have a lot of copying to do over many directories, xcopy is the tool to use.

robocopy

Microsoft introduced the *robocopy command*—short for Robust File Copy—many years ago as an add-on tool for Windows Server to enable techs to manage files and folders more quickly and efficiently than with xcopy or copy. The robocopy command is powerful indeed, enabling you to, for example, copy the files and folders from one computer to another across a network, fully replicating the structure on the destination system *and* deleting anything on that system that wasn't part of the copy. It can do this with a simple command.

The robocopy syntax does not resemble xcopy, so if you're going to use the tool, you need to unlearn a few things. Here's the basic syntax:

```
robocopy [source] [destination] [options]
```

Here's an example of the command in action. The following command would copy all files and subfolders from a local machine's D:\testserver\website folder to a shared folder on the remote server \\liveserver\website.

```
robocopy d:\testserver\website \\liveserver\website /mir
```

The /mir switch, for mirror, tells robocopy to copy everything from the source and make the destination mirror it. That means robocopy will also delete anything in the destination that doesn't match the source folders and files.

If that were it, robocopy would be powerful, but that's not even the tip of the iceberg. The robocopy command can copy encrypted files. It enables an administrator to copy files even if the administrator account is expressly denied access to those files. It will also resume copying after an interruption, and do so at the spot it stopped. For the full syntax, type the following:

```
robocopy /?
```

Their power and utility make the del, copy/move, xcopy, and robocopy commands indispensable for a PC technician, but that same power and utility can cause disaster. Only a trained Jedi, with The Force as his ally...well, wrong book, but the principle remains: Beware of the quick and easy keystroke, for it may spell your doom. Think twice and execute the command once. The data you save may be yours!

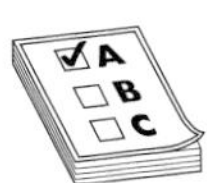

EXAM TIP Know xcopy and robocopy for the CompTIA A+ 220-902 exam.

cp and mv (again!)

If you really want to see some powerful commands, let's head over to Linux. Unlike Windows, you can both move and copy folders and their contents, using the same cp and mv commands we saw earlier for regular copying and moving. Let's say we have a folder called /home/mike/Backups. The Backups folder has ten subfolders and hundreds of files. I want to save a copy of these files to a folder called /mnt/storage. To do this I only need to run cp with the –R (recursive) switch (note that the ~ in my prompt shows that I'm in the home folder):

```
mike@server:~$ cp -R Backups /mnt/storage
```

If I want to move all of that to storage instead of copy, I use the mv command. Interestingly, the mv command doesn't even need a special switch—just run the program, pointing at the folder of interest and giving it a destination:

```
mike@server:~$ mv Desktop/Backups /mnt/storage
```

Assorted Windows Commands

As a proficient IT technician in the field, you need to be familiar with a whole slew of command-line tools and other important utilities. The CompTIA A+ 220-902 exam focuses in on several of them, and although many have been discussed in detail in previous chapters, it is extremely important that you understand and practice with chkdsk, format, hostname, gpupdate, gpresult, sfc, and shutdown.

chkdsk (/f /r)

The *chkdsk* (*checkdisk*) *command* scans, detects, and repairs file system issues and errors. You can run the chkdsk utility from a command prompt with the switches /f and /r. The /f switch attempts to fix file system–related errors, while the /r switch attempts to locate and repair bad sectors. To run successfully, chkdsk needs direct access to a drive. In other words, the drive needs to be "unlocked." For example, if you run chkdsk /f /r and chkdsk does not consider your drive unlocked, you will receive a "cannot lock current drive" message, meaning that another process has the drive locked and is preventing chkdsk from locking the drive itself. After this, chkdsk presents you with the option to run it the next time the system restarts (see Figure 16-13).

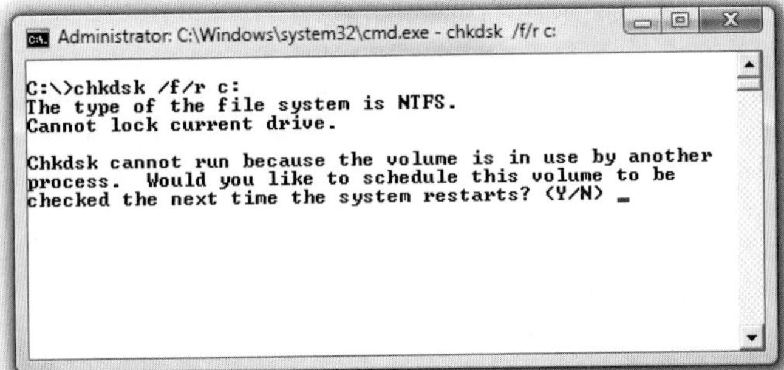

Administrator: C:\Windows\system32\cmd.exe - chkdsk /f/r c:
C:\>chkdsk /f/r c:
The type of the file system is NTFS.
Cannot lock current drive.
Chkdsk cannot run because the volume is in use by another
process. Would you like to schedule this volume to be
checked the next time the system restarts? (Y/N)

Figure 16-13 The chkdsk /f /r utility and switches on a locked drive

format

After the previous chapters, you should have an expert-level knowledge of (or, at the very least, a passing familiarity with) formatting and partitioning hard drives. Formatting, you may remember, is the process of writing a new file system to a volume (or partition, if you are old school) so it can hold an operating system or data. We have already discussed the various built-in Windows utilities available to provide the formatting of drives, and you no doubt know that many third-party formatting tools are out there. In this chapter, you just need to become familiar with the format command and its switches.

The *format command*, you may have guessed, enables you to format volumes from the command line. The very best way to familiarize yourself with the format command and its available switches is simply to enter **format /?** from the command prompt. Your results should be similar to those displayed in Figure 16-14.

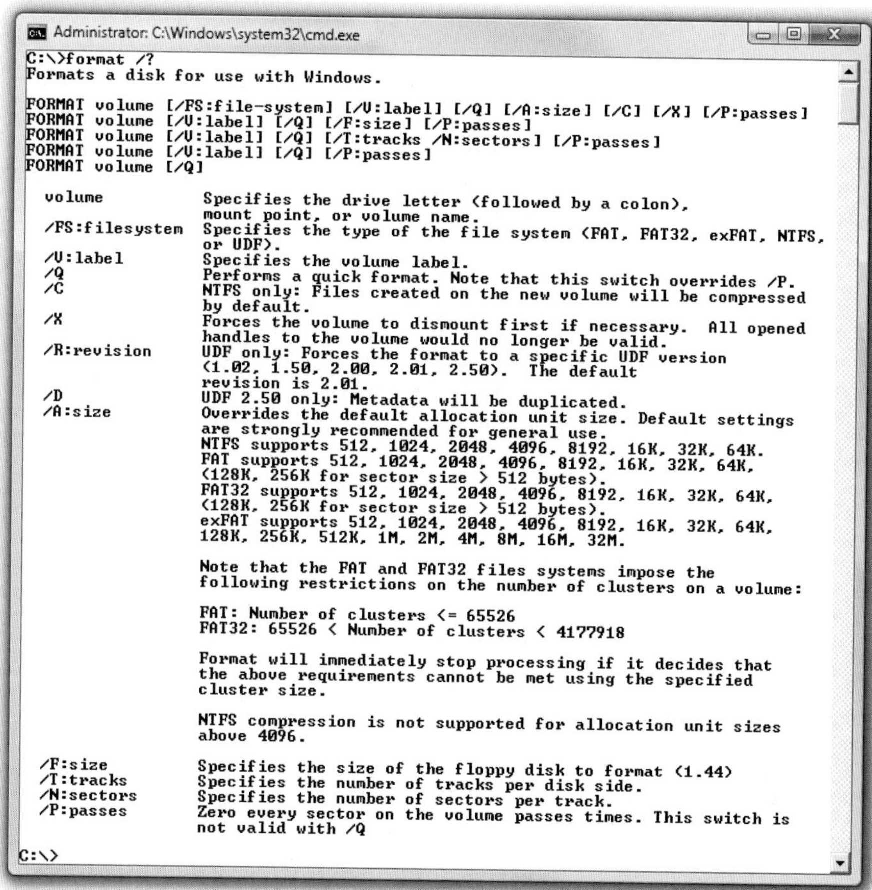

Figure 16-14 Using format /? at the command prompt

The CompTIA A+ 220-902 exam focuses on both GUI and command-line operating system formatting utilities and options, so you should familiarize yourself with the format command and its switches by practicing them on a test system you are literally not afraid to wipe out. Besides, you never know what skeletons CompTIA may pull out of the closet.

hostname

The *hostname command* is the most straightforward of all command-line commands. If you type **hostname** at the command prompt, it will display the name of your computer, also known as the hostname. When I type **hostname**, for example, it displays "MikesPC."

gpupdate

Group policies are the cornerstone of security settings for Windows systems. There are thousands of group policies. Group policies define important issues such as password complexity, logon attempts, even whether a user can install software. On an individual system it's easy to set up a group policy using GUI tools, but when you make changes on a local machine, it can take up to 16 hours before the new policy actually starts to work. If you want your newly set polices to work immediately, you use the *gpupdate* command-line utility.

gpresult

If you need a quick overview of all security policies applied to a single user or computer, the *gpresult* tool is for you. You can run gpresult for any user or computer on your network (assuming you have a valid username and password) and you can ask for detailed or summary information. This command shows the summary results for user michaelm on the local computer:

```
C:\>gpresult /USER michaelm /R

Microsoft (R) Windows (R) Operating System Group Policy Result tool v2.0
c 2013 Microsoft Corporation. All rights reserved.
Created on 8/20/2016 at 1:54:20 PM
RSOP data for TOTALBOGUS\michaelm on MIKEPC : Logging Mode
-----------------------------------------------------------
OS Configuration:            Member Workstation
OS Version:                  6.3.9600
Site Name:                   N/A
Roaming Profile:             N/A
Local Profile:               C:\Users\michaelm
Connected over a slow link?: No

USER SETTINGS
-------------
    CN=michaelm,CN=Users,DC=totalbogus
    Last time Group Policy was applied: 8/20/2016 at 1:39:10 PM
    Group Policy was applied from:      dc1.totalbogus
    Group Policy slow link threshold:   500 kbps
    Domain Name:                        TOTALBOGUS
    Domain Type:                        Windows 2008 or later

    Applied Group Policy Objects
    -----------------------------
        Default Domain Policy
    The following GPOs were not applied because they were filtered out
    -------------------------------------------------------------------
        Local Group Policy
         Filtering:  Not Applied (Empty)
    The user is a part of the following security groups
    ---------------------------------------------------
        Domain Users
        Everyone
```

sfc

The Windows *sfc (System File Checker) command*, or simply sfc.exe, scans, detects, and restores important Windows system files, folders, and paths. Techs often turn to sfc when

Windows isn't quite working correctly and use it to find and fix critical Windows system files that have become corrupt. If you run sfc and it finds issues, it attempts to replace corrupted or missing files from cached DLLs (backups of those system files) located in the Windows\System32\Dllcache\ directory. Without getting very deep into the mad science involved, just know that you can use sfc to correct corruption. To run sfc from a command prompt, enter **sfc /scannow**. To familiarize yourself with sfc's switches, enter **sfc /?** (see Figure 16-15).

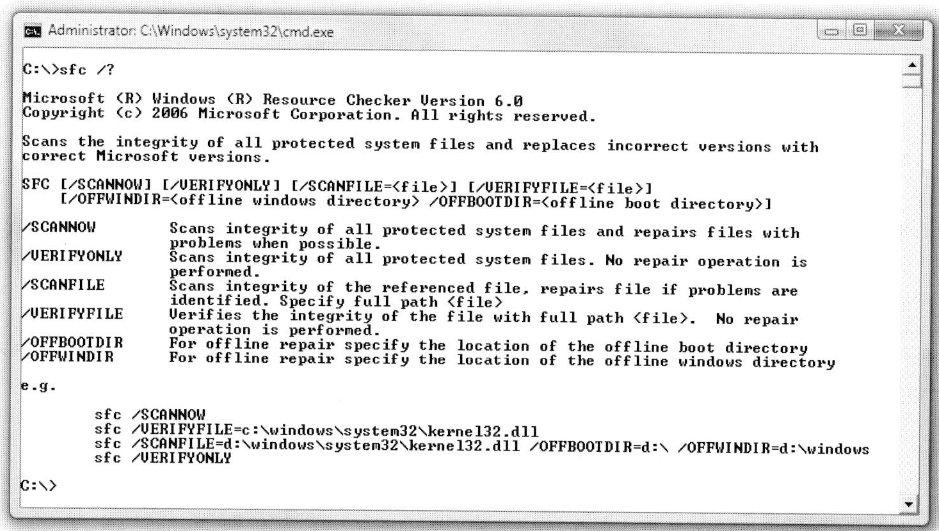

Figure 16-15 Checking sfc options with sfc /? at a command prompt

shutdown

The *shutdown command* enables you to do exactly that to a local or remote computer—namely, shut it down (or reboot it if that's your thing). The cool part of the tool is that you can use a number of switches to control and report the shutdown. A network administrator could use this tool to restart a computer remotely, for example, like this:

```
shutdown /r /m \\devserver
```

The /r switch tells shutdown to have the computer reboot rather than just shut down. If you want to see the full syntax for shutdown, type the following:

```
shutdown /?
```

Using Special Keys in Windows

You might find yourself repeatedly typing the same commands, or at least very similar commands, when working at a prompt. Microsoft has provided a number of ways to

access previously typed commands. Type the **dir** command at a command prompt. When you get back to a prompt, press F1, and the letter *d* appears. Press F1 again. Now the letter *i* appears after the *d*. Do you see what is happening? The F1 key brings back the previous command one letter at a time. Pressing F3 brings back the entire command at once. Now try running these three commands:

```
dir /w
hostname
md Skywalker
```

Now press the UP ARROW key. Keep pressing it till you see your original dir command—it's a history of all your old commands. Now use the RIGHT ARROW key to add /p to the end of your dir command. Windows command history is very handy.

Using Special Keys in Mac OS X and Linux

Mac OS X and Linux shells come with their own sets of special keys, many of which match those in Windows. Actually, Windows copied many of the handier keys, like the history feature, from the UNIX world. Mac OS X and Linux take the command history one step further and remember it even if you close the terminal or reboot the machine—useful if you accidently closed the terminal. Mac OS X and Linux shells don't use the function keys as Windows does but have many hotkeys that use the CTRL key. For example, you can search your history with the CTRL-R keystroke. This can pay for itself if you have been working with a long, complex command one day and need to use it again two weeks from now!

Beyond A+

The compact and cipher Commands

Windows offers two cool commands at the command-line interface: compact and cipher. The compact command displays or alters the compression of files on NTFS partitions. The cipher command displays or alters the encryption of folders and files on NTFS partitions. If you type just the command with no added parameters, **compact** and **cipher** display the compression state and the encryption state, respectively, of the current directory and any files it contains. You may specify multiple directory names, and you may use wildcards, as you learned earlier in the chapter. You must add parameters to make the commands change things. For example, you add /c to compress and /u to uncompress directories and/or files with the compact command, and you add /e to encrypt and /d to decrypt directories and/or files with the cipher command. When you do these operations, you also mark the directories involved so that any files you add to them in the future will take on their encryption or compression characteristics. In other words, if you encrypt a directory and all its files, any files you add later will also be encrypted. Same thing if you compress a directory. I'll run through a quick example of each.

compact

First let's try the compact command. Figure 16-16 shows the result of entering the compact command with no switches. It displays the compression status of the contents of

a directory called Tie Fighter on my desktop. Notice that after the file listing, compact helpfully tells you that zero files are compressed and six files (all of them) are not compressed, with a total compression ratio of 1.0 to 1.

```
Command Prompt

C:\Users\mike\Desktop\Tie Fighter>compact

 Listing C:\Users\mike\Desktop\Tie Fighter\
 New files added to this directory will not be compressed.

  2418317 :    2418317 = 1.0 to 1    Concept Art 1.jpg
  1267906 :    1267906 = 1.0 to 1    Concept Art 2.jpg
    40273 :      40273 = 1.0 to 1    Description.docx
   596851 :     596851 = 1.0 to 1    Diagrams.pdf
    67004 :      67004 = 1.0 to 1    Overview of New Features.pptx
  3189185 :    3189185 = 1.0 to 1    Sketchbook Sketch.png

Of 6 files within 1 directories
0 are compressed and 6 are not compressed.
7,579,536 total bytes of data are stored in 7,579,536 bytes.
The compression ratio is 1.0 to 1.

C:\Users\mike\Desktop\Tie Fighter>
```

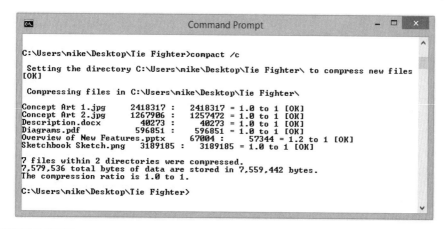

Figure 16-16 The compact command with no switches

If you enter the compact command with the /c switch, it compresses all of the files in the directory, as shown in Figure 16-17. Look closely at the listing. Notice that it includes the original and compressed file sizes and calculates the compression ratio for you. Notice also that the JPG and PNG files (both compressed graphics files) didn't compress at all, while the PowerPoint file compressed down to around a 80 percent of its original sizes. Also, can you spot what's different in the text at the bottom of the screen? The compact command claims to have compressed *seven* files in *two* directories! How can this be? The secret is that when it compresses all of the files in a directory, it must also compress the directory file itself, which is "in" my Desktop directory above it. Thus it correctly reports that it compressed seven files: six in the compact directory, and one in the Desktop directory.

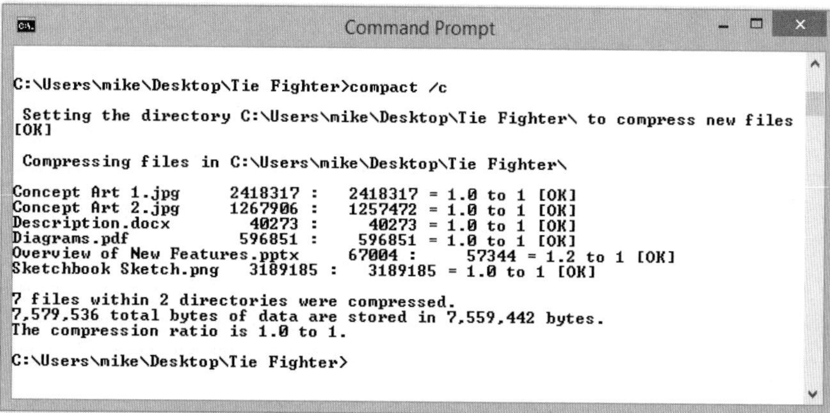

Figure 16-17 Typing **compact /c** compresses the contents of the directory.

Typing **compact** again shows you the directory listing, and now there's a *C* next to each filename, indicating that the file is compressed (see Figure 16-18).

```
Command Prompt

C:\Users\mike\Desktop\Tie Fighter>compact

 Listing C:\Users\mike\Desktop\Tie Fighter\
 New files added to this directory will be compressed.

  2418317 :    2418317 = 1.0 to 1 C Concept Art 1.jpg
  1267906 :    1257472 = 1.0 to 1 C Concept Art 2.jpg
    40273 :      40273 = 1.0 to 1 C Description.docx
   596851 :     596851 = 1.0 to 1 C Diagrams.pdf
    67004 :      57344 = 1.2 to 1 C Overview of New Features.pptx
  3189185 :    3189185 = 1.0 to 1 C Sketchbook Sketch.png

Of 6 files within 1 directories
6 are compressed and 0 are not compressed.
7,579,536 total bytes of data are stored in 7,559,442 bytes.
The compression ratio is 1.0 to 1.

C:\Users\mike\Desktop\Tie Fighter>
```

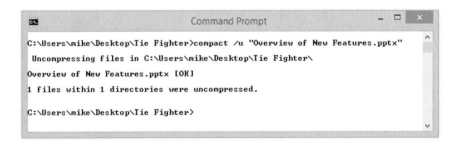

Figure 16-18 The contents of C:\Compact have been compressed.

Okay, now suppose you want to uncompress a file—say, a PowerPoint file, Session 1.ppt. To do this, you must specify the decompression operation, using the /u switch and the name of the file you want decompressed, as shown in Figure 16-19. Note that compact reports the successful decompression of one file only: Overview of New Features.pptx. You could do the same thing in reverse, using the /c switch and a filename to compress an individual file.

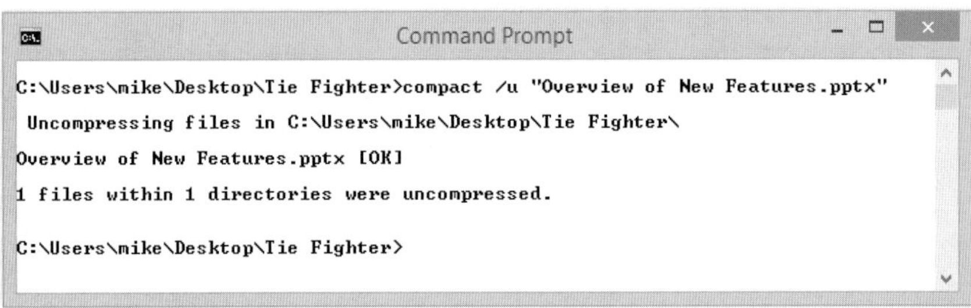

Figure 16-19 Typing **compact /u "Overview of New Features.pptx"** decompresses only that file.

cipher

The cipher command is a bit complex, but in its most basic implementation, it's pretty straightforward. Figure 16-20 shows two steps in the process. Like the compact command, the cipher command simply displays the current state of affairs when entered with no switches. In this case, it displays the encryption state of the files in

the C:\Users\mike\Pictures\Armor Pictures directory. Notice the letter *U* to the left of the filenames, which tells you they are unencrypted. The second command you can see on the screen in Figure 16-20 is this:

```
C:\Users\mike\Pictures\Armor Pictures>cipher /e
```

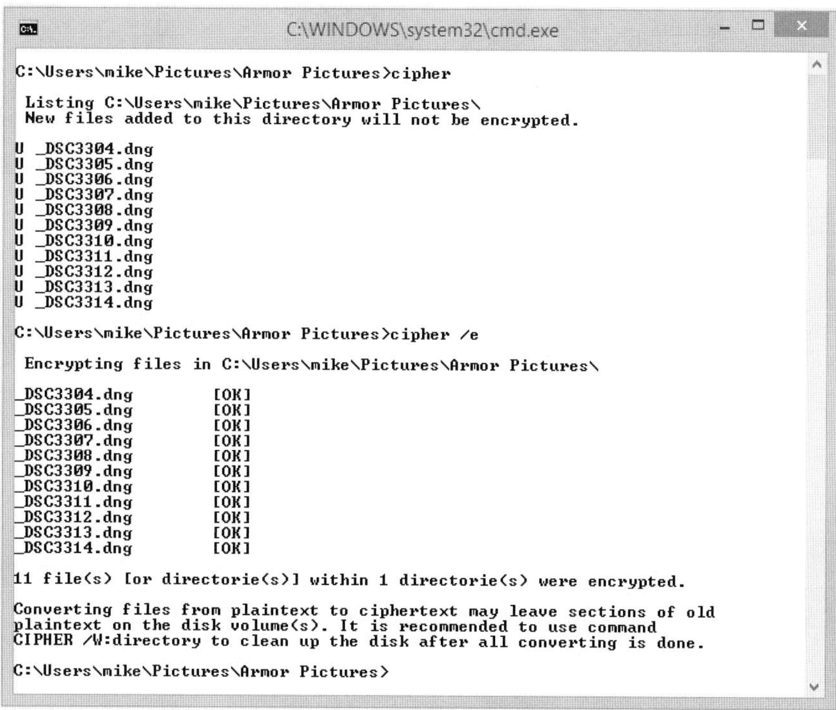

Figure 16-20 The cipher command showing the unencrypted files followed by results of running **cipher /e**

This time the cipher command carries one switch: /e specifies the encryption operation. As you can see, the command-line interface is actually pretty chatty in this case. It reports that it's doing the encryption and then tells you what it's done, and it even warns you that you should clean up any stray unencrypted bits that may have been left in the directory.

To confirm the results of the cipher operation, enter the **cipher** command again, as shown in Figure 16-21. Note that the *U* to the left of each filename has been replaced with an *E*, indicating an encrypted file. The other indication that this directory has been encrypted is the statement above the file listing:

```
New files added to this directory will not be encrypted.
```

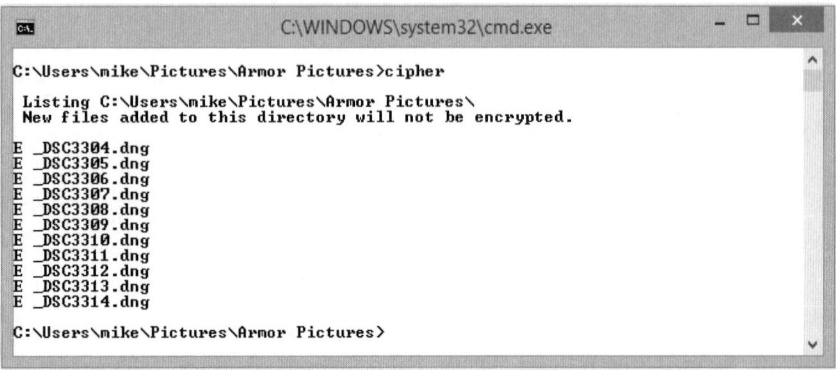
```
C:\Users\mike\Pictures\Armor Pictures>cipher

 Listing C:\Users\mike\Pictures\Armor Pictures\
 New files added to this directory will not be encrypted.

E _DSC3304.dng
E _DSC3305.dng
E _DSC3306.dng
E _DSC3307.dng
E _DSC3308.dng
E _DSC3309.dng
E _DSC3310.dng
E _DSC3311.dng
E _DSC3312.dng
E _DSC3313.dng
E _DSC3314.dng

C:\Users\mike\Pictures\Armor Pictures>
```

Figure 16-21 The cipher command confirms that the files were encrypted.

Remember that the cipher command works on directories first and foremost, and it works on individual files only when you specifically tell it to do so.

That's great, but suppose you want to decrypt just *one* of the files in the Armor Pictures directory. Can you guess how you need to alter the command? Simply add the filename of the file you want to decrypt after the command and the relevant switches. Figure 16-22 shows the cipher command being used to decipher _DSC3304.dng, a single file.

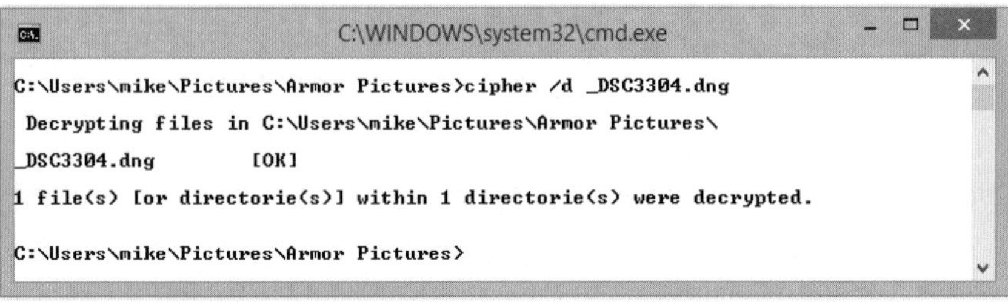
```
C:\Users\mike\Pictures\Armor Pictures>cipher /d _DSC3304.dng

 Decrypting files in C:\Users\mike\Pictures\Armor Pictures\

_DSC3304.dng         [OK]

1 file(s) [or directorie(s)] within 1 directorie(s) were decrypted.

C:\Users\mike\Pictures\Armor Pictures>
```

Figure 16-22 Typing cipher /d _DSC3304.dng decrypts only that file.

902

PowerShell

Microsoft's PowerShell is a more powerful replacement for the traditional Windows command-line interface. PowerShell enables you to do all the typical command-line activities, such as dir, cd, md, and so on, but brings a series of vastly more powerful tools called *cmdlets* that enable you to accomplish some amazing tasks. Figure 16-23 shows two commands that do the same thing by default, show the contents of a directory: dir and Get-ChildItem.

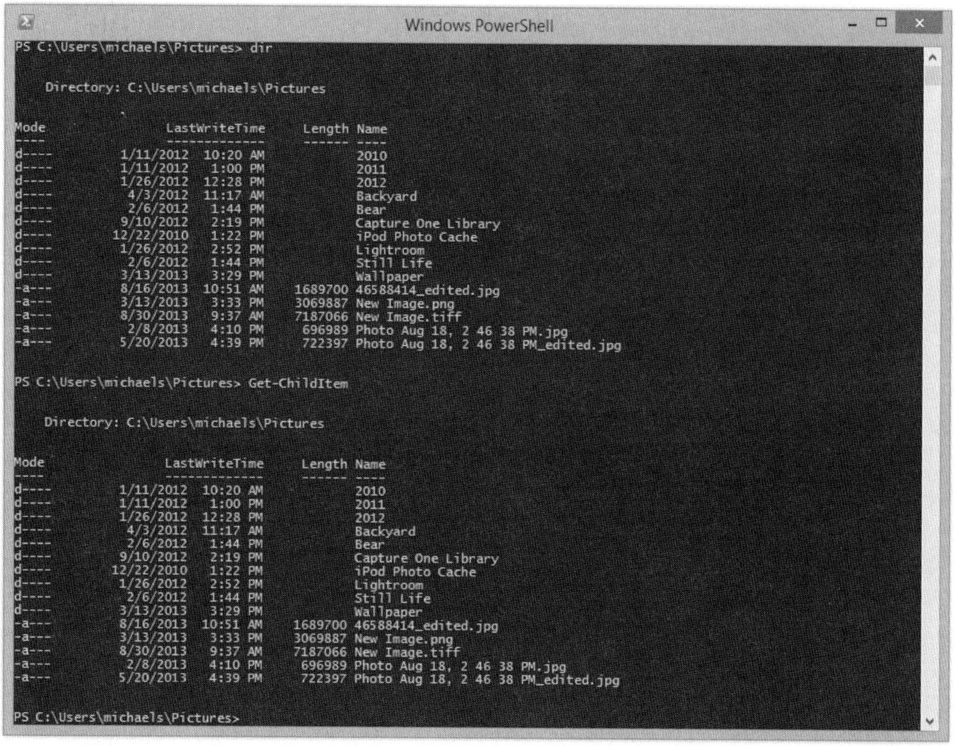

Figure 16-23 Simple commands in PowerShell

With dir, you know you can search for items in a directory, such as "find all the JPEG files in a folder" with this command:

```
dir *.jpg
```

PowerShell lets you dial it all the way to 11, though, with a few more characters on a search string. The following command will find all the JPEG files in the current directory, plus all the mentions of .jpg files in any document format, such as Word, PowerPoint, and Acrobat:

```
Get-ChildItem . -Include *.jpg -Recurse -Force
```

Just in case you want to know what each piece of that string in the cmdlet means, here's the scoop: Get-ChildItem is the main command. The dot . indicates the current directory, while –include tells the command to fetch the file type indicated next, in this case *.jpg. –Recurse means go into every subdirectory and –Force retrieves hidden and system files too. It's like dir on steroids!

This is just scratching the surface with what you can do with PowerShell. If you want to give it a try yourself, simply type **powershell** in the Search bar and press ENTER. Good luck!

NOTE PowerShell is installed by default with Windows 7 and newer. If you would like to use PowerShell on Vista, it is available for download from Microsoft.

Assorted Mac OS X and Linux Commands

Mac OS X and Linux have a massive number of built-in command-line utilities and probably hundreds of thousands of easily accessed and installed third-party tools that work amazingly well. In fact, one of the most interesting challenges to Terminal is that for almost any job, there is more than one tool for the job (see the vi command later). What you are going to see here are the commands listed by the CompTIA A+ objectives—you could spend the rest of your life learning all of the Terminal commands!

NOTE The first and second commands below are ifconfig and iwconfig, very network-specific Terminal commands. If you don't have a good grasp on networking yet, skip it until after you read Chapters 20–23. Then come back to them.

ifconfig

The *ifconfig command* enables you to view and change the settings for your network connections. Running **ifconfig** shows the following output (yours will certainly be different):

```
mike@server:~$ ifconfig
eth0      Link encap:Ethernet  HWaddr 08:00:27:c1:1f:5a
          inet addr:10.0.2.15  Bcast:10.0.2.255  Mask:255.255.255.0
          inet6 addr: fe80::a00:27ff:fec1:1f5a/64 Scope:Link
          UP BROADCAST RUNNING MULTICAST  MTU:1500  Metric:1
          RX packets:27 errors:0 dropped:0 overruns:0 frame:0
          TX packets:96 errors:0 dropped:0 overruns:0 carrier:0
          collisions:0 txqueuelen:1000
          RX bytes:3604 (3.6 KB)  TX bytes:12254 (12.2 KB)

lo        Link encap:Local Loopback
          inet addr:127.0.0.1  Mask:255.0.0.0
          inet6 addr: ::1/128 Scope:Host
          UP LOOPBACK RUNNING  MTU:65536  Metric:1
          RX packets:166 errors:0 dropped:0 overruns:0 frame:0
          TX packets:166 errors:0 dropped:0 overruns:0 carrier:0
          collisions:0 txqueuelen:0
          RX bytes:11849 (11.8 KB)  TX bytes:11849 (11.8 KB)
```

Mac OS X and Linux use special terms to define your network connections:

- eth0, eth1, en0, en1, and so on: wired Ethernet NICs
- wlan0, wlan1, and so on: wireless 802.11 NICs
- lo: loopback

You can disable a NIC using the following:

```
mike@server:~$ ifconfig eth0 down
```

You can also temporarily change any IP setting with ifconfig. This command will set the IP address of a wireless NIC to 192.168.4.15 until the computer is rebooted:

```
mike@server:~$ sudo ifconfig wlan0 192.168.4.15
```

NOTE While CompTIA wants you to be familiar with ifconfig, it is considered to be deprecated for Linux (it's still the only game in town on Mac OS X). Its replacement is called simply *ip*, and it can do everything ifconfig does and more. If you want to learn more, try reading its manual page by typing **man ip** in your terminal.

iwconfig

The ifconfig command is a powerful tool, but when you need to know about (and to change) your wireless settings, you need iwconfig. Typing **iwconfig** by itself gives you all the wireless details about your wireless NICs:

```
mike@server:~$ iwconfig
 eth0     no wireless extensions

 wlan0    IEEE 802.11abg  ESSID:"TOTALHQ"
          Mode:Managed  Frequency:2.427 GHz  Access Point: 00:0A:13:93:2F:07
          Bit Rate=48 Mb/s   Tx-Power=20 dBm   Sensitivity=8/0
          Retry limit:7   RTS thr:off   Fragment thr:off
          Link Quality=91/100  Signal level=-39 dBm  Noise level=-87 dBm
          Rx invalid nwid:0  Rx invalid crypt:860  Rx invalid frag:0
          Tx excessive retries:0  Invalid misc:39   Missed beacon:8

lo        no wireless extensions.
```

To change the SSID for wlan0 to AnotherSSID, you would type

```
mike@server:~$ sudo iwconfig wlan0 essid "AnotherSSID"
```

Note that you don't use iwconfig to view base IP information. That's ifconfig's job.

ps

If you want to see the processes running on your system, you need the *ps command*. This very old command is designed to provide detailed and customizable information about the processes running on your system. This deep history shows up even on the most basic use of ps, as it has two totally different types of switch sets! Anyway, let's look at one of the most common examples of ps, the ps aux command. The aux command is

actually three switches: a = processes for all users, u = show process owner, x = process not attached to a terminal.

```
mike@server:~$ ps aux
USER       PID %CPU %MEM    VSZ   RSS TTY      STAT START   TIME COMMand
root         1  0.0  0.2  33968  4416 ?        Ss   11:08   0:00 /sbin/init
```

Note that I'm skipping a lot of lines right here between the beginning and the end of the displayed results of the ps aux command.

```
root      2188  0.0  0.0      0     0 ?        S    11:08   0:04 [kworker/0:2]
mike      2195  0.0  0.6 385292 13836 ?        Sl   11:08   0:00 zeitgeist-datah
mike      2200  0.0  0.3 283340  7352 ?        Sl   11:08   0:00 /usr/bin/zeitge
mike      2207  0.0  0.8 325764 16832 ?        Sl   11:08   0:00 /usr/lib/x86_64
mike      2215  0.0  0.0  11416   836 ?        S    11:08   0:00 /bin/cat
mike      2218  0.0  1.5 574732 30908 ?        Sl   11:08   0:03 gnome-terminal
mike      2225  0.0  0.0  14828  1916 ?        S    11:09   0:00 gnome-pty-helpe
mike      2226  0.0  0.2  26820  5244 pts/10   Ss   11:09   0:00 bash
mike      2267  0.0  1.0 571544 20856 ?        Sl   11:09   0:00 update-notifier
mike      2290  0.0  0.3 459824  7216 ?        Sl   11:10   0:00 /usr/lib/x86_64
mike      2524  0.0  0.2 145804  5652 ?        Sl   14:12   0:00 /usr/lib/libreo
mike      2543  0.0  5.5 1140216 114080 ?      Sl   14:12   0:00 /usr/lib/libreo
root      2570  0.0  0.0      0     0 ?        S    14:19   0:00 [kworker/u2:1]
root      2577  0.0  0.0      0     0 ?        S    14:29   0:00 [kworker/u2:0]
root      2578  0.0  0.0      0     0 ?        S    14:34   0:00 [kworker/u2:2]
mike      2579  0.0  0.1  22648  2568 pts/10   R+   14:34   0:00 ps aux
mike@server:~$
```

One of the big problems with ps aux is the enormous output. There's a number of ways to make dealing with this output easier. One way is to use ps | less. The less tool makes it easy to scroll up and down through the output. Remember the | more tool we used earlier in this chapter? Well, "less" is "more." Humor! Get it? I'll see myself out… But seriously, less and more will both work for this task, the difference between the two are details for power users and programmers.

Let's discuss the output of the ps aux command:

- USER: Who is running this process
- PID: The process ID number assigned to the process
- %CPU: What percentage of CPU power this process is using
- %MEM: What percentage of memory this process is using
- VSZ: Total paged memory in kilobytes
- RSS: Total physical memory in kilobytes
- TTY: The terminal that is taking the processes output
- STAT: S = waiting, R = running, l = multithreaded, + = foreground process
- START: When the process was started
- TIME: Length of time process has been running
- COMMand: Name of the executable that created this process

One of the many reasons we run ps is to determine the PID for a process we want to kill. To kill a particular process, we use the kill command (functionally identical to Windows taskkill). The following command will stop the process with the PID 2218:

```
mike@server:~$ kill 2218
```

There's more fun to be had with the ps command output, but we will save that for the grep command next.

grep

The *grep command* is one of the handiest of all Linux commands. At its most basic level, we use grep to search through text files or command output to find specific information or to filter out unneeded information. Let's look at just two of the countless potential ways we use the powerful grep.

Finding a specific process is easy using grep with the ps command. Let's say I have a LibreOffice document that I need to kill. I have no idea what the PID is, but I can use grep with ps to find it. I know the command uses the word "libre," so I type

```
mike@server:~$ ps aux | grep libre
mike       2524  0.0  0.2 145804  5652 ?       Sl   14:12   0:00 /usr/lib/
libreoffice/program/oosplash --writer
mike       2543  0.0  5.5 1140216 114080 ?     Sl   14:12   0:01 /usr/lib/
libreoffice/program/soffice.bin --writer --splash-pipe=5
```

So I see there are two processes from LibreOffice: 2524 and 2543. Cool! The grep command can find any string of text and show you the line it was in. Let's do it again, this time using ifconfig. Let's say you want to know if any of your NICs is using 192.168.4.15. You can use **ifconfig** and **grep** together:

```
mike@server:~$ ifconfig | grep 192.168.4.15
inet addr:192.168.4.15  Bcast:10.0.2.255  Mask:255.255.255.0
collisions:0 txqueuelen:1000
```

Note that grep shows us a line from the ifconfig output indicating that something is using that IP address.

Again, this is only a light overview of grep; it is one of the most powerful tools in Linux. If you need to look in anything to find a string of text, grep is the go-to tool.

apt-get

The first ten years of Linux was interesting from the standpoint of installing programs on your computer. Linux was always a nerdy operating system used primarily by programmers and server administrators; most of the big commercial software companies didn't write applications for Linux. If you needed an application, you dug around the Internet looking for a program, downloaded the code, and tried to compile it on your system, only to find that it depended on yet more bits of code that you had to find, manually set up configuration files...Ugh! It wasn't a pretty process, especially compared to the relative ease of installing Windows or Mac programs.

Over the years many improvements have been made to the availability, acquisition, and installation of Linux programs, culminating in a number of different tools called *package managers* that give you the ability to download and fully install and update software from a single command.

Different Linux distributions use different package management systems. For Debian Linux–based distributions (like Ubuntu and Mint), we use APT, the advanced packaging tool. For Red Hat–based systems, we use RPM Package Manager (RPM). There are other package management systems available, of course, but APT and RPM are currently dominant. However, the CompTIA A+ objectives only list *apt-get*, the command-line tool for APT. This fact tells us a lot about where CompTIA is looking when it comes to what Linux distro they want you to know: Ubuntu!

Apt-get is wonderfully simple to use, assuming you know the name of the program you wish to install. For example, many Linux users aren't big fans of the old-fashioned vi text editor and prefer to use the substantially better vim. To download and install this program, you start by typing

```
mike@server:~$ sudo apt-get update
```

The first bit of business to get out of the way is to have APT go and update its package index. The package index is the list of all the available packages (software). You can technically skip this step, but you might end up installing an old version or, if the package is new enough, not finding it. Once APT's index has been updated, we're ready to install by typing

```
mike@server:~$ sudo apt-get install vim
```

That's it! Vim will now be installed and ready to use. Got vim already installed but want the newest version? No problem! Just use **apt-get** again:

```
mike@server:~$ sudo apt-get upgrade vim
```

The only downside to apt-get is that you need to know the name of the package you wish to install. While there are command-line tools that help (apt-cache), many people prefer to use whatever graphical search tool their Linux distro provides, such as the Ubuntu Software Center.

As useful as APT is for fetching and installing single applications, that's not where its real power lies. These package managers are used to manage *all* the software (minus the stuff you compiled yourself) on the system and are the tool that you use to keep the whole system up to date, just as Windows Update handles much of the software on Windows. All that it takes to upgrade all the packages on your system is to type

```
mike@server:~$ sudo apt-get update
mike@server:~$ sudo apt-get upgrade
```

If apt-get finds any out-of-date packages, it will let you know which ones and ask you to confirm the upgrade, then away it goes to download and update your system. Keeping your system up to date in this way is critical to close any security vulnerabilities that might be lurking on your system.

vi

You will sometimes need to edit raw text files in Mac OS X and Linux, and *vi* is the default text editor, built-in to Mac OS X and most distros of Linux. Figuring out how to edit a file (or even just exit) with vi in some ways is a rite of passage. Only after your have mastered vi's non-intuitive and perhaps even downright weird interface can you truly start to think of yourself as a UNIX Terminal Jedi master. Well, maybe not a Jedi master, but the fact that vi is almost always available will make you want to know how to use it. Let's get started with vi by creating a new text file called "fred":

```
mike@server:~$ vi fred
```

You'll now be in the vi text editor, staring at a blank file as shown in Figure 16-24.

Figure 16-24 vi open

The vi editor uses a non-intuitive "mode" concept where the editor is always in either *insert mode* or *command mode*. Insert mode allows you to insert and edit text. Command mode allows you to give commands such as cut, paste, delete line or characters, and save the file. By default you are in command mode, so press the I key to go into insert mode. Enter a few lines of text, such as shown in Figure 16-25, press ENTER at the end of each line, and use the BACKSPACE key if you make an error. None of the other keys you're used to working with in any other text editor (such as Windows Notepad) work here! Press the ESC key to leave insert mode and return to command mode.

To save your new file and quit vi, type **ZZ** (note the uppercase) and press ENTER. To edit an existing file, just type **vi** followed by the name of the file you wish to edit. If you wanted to edit the Fred file, for example, you would type

```
mike@server:~$ vi fred
```

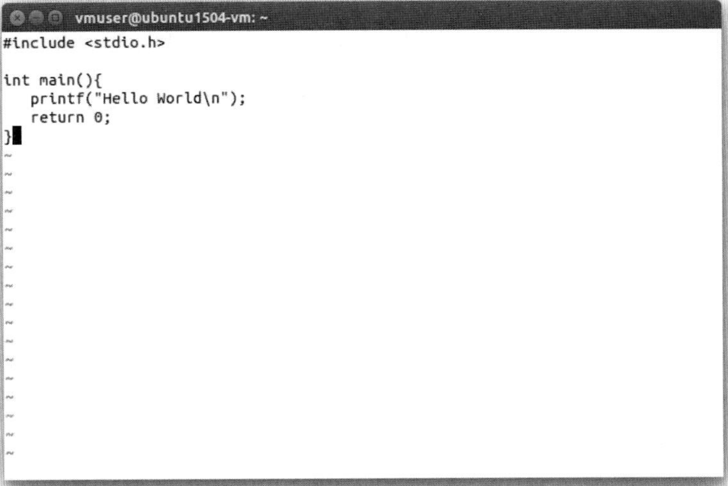
vmuser@ubuntu1504-vm: ~
#include <stdio.h>
int main(){
printf("Hello World\n");
return 0;
}

Figure 16-25 vi with text

The biggest trick to vi is making sure you know which mode you are in and how to swap between the two modes. Press ESC to get into command mode, and press I to get into insert mode. Be ready to make lots of mistakes the first few times you use vi!

The vi command set is archaic, but it is powerful if you take the time to learn it. Here is a list of a few command mode keys that you'll find helpful:

Key	Function
h	Move cursor one character to left
j	Move cursor one line down
k	Move cursor one line up
l	Move cursor one character to right
w	Move cursor one word to right
b	Move cursor one word to left
0	Move cursor to beginning of line
$	Move cursor to end of line
i	Insert to left of current cursor position
r	Change current character
dd	Delete current line
D	Delete portion of current line to right of the cursor
x	Delete current character
:w	Save file
:q!	Quit vi, do not save
ZZ	Save file and quit vi

Granted, it's important to know how to use vi, but most Linux people quickly find themselves going to one of the hundreds of alternatives. Check out one of the terminal-based editors such as vim, joe, or emacs or one of the graphical editors such as gedit or gVim.

dd

The *dd command* is primarily used to create an exact, bit-by-bit image of any form of block storage, meaning mass storage devices such as hard drive volumes, thumb drives, and optical media. In its most simple form, the dd command is just

```
$ dd if=<source block device> if=<destination image file location>
```

There's no way to show you all the possible uses for dd, so I'll just show three of the typical places I use it. Let's start with something simple: copying a hard drive.

Be careful here! The dd command name is sometimes said jokingly to stand for "Disk Destroyer." This powerful tool will wreak havoc on your data if not used correctly. There are a number of issues that I'm not covering here that could greatly affect the success of running the dd command. While all of the following commands are valid, simply running them on your systems without understanding these subtleties can wipe drives. You have been warned!

Copying a Hard Drive

Let's say you have a hard drive (sda) you want to copy onto another hard drive (sdb). In this case we will say they are exactly the same size. The following command will copy the entire sda drive, partition table, file systems…everything to the sdb drive:

```
dd if=/dev/sda of=/dev/sdb
```

Backing Up a Thumb Drive

Let's say you have thumb drive full of important files you really want to back up. Using dd as follows, you can copy the entire USB drive and make an image file (I chose to call it thumbBackup.bak) and place that image file on your Desktop:

```
dd if=/dev/sdc of=/home/mike/Desktop/thumbBackup.bak
```

Wiping a Disk

I have a drive (sdb) that I want to totally wipe. The dd command can take input from anywhere, but in this case I'll use Linux's random number generator, /dev/urandom, to write a stream of random bits completely over the entire drive. It's not a perfect wipe, but it will stop all but the most sophisticated tools.

```
dd if=/dev/urandom of=/dev/sdb
```

shutdown

Same as in Windows, you can shut down or restart the system from a terminal using the *shutdown command*. You run the command as follows:

```
shutdown <options> <time>
```

By far the most common time is now. To shut the system down immediately, type

```
shutdown now
```

To restart the system, run **shutdown** with the **–r** option:

```
shutdown -r now
```

passwd

The *passwd command* allows you to change your password or, if logged in as a root (the super user), any user's password. To change your own password, type the following:

```
mike@server:~$ passwd
changing password for mike
(current) UNIX password:
Enter new UNIX password:
Retype new UNIX password
Passwd: password updated successfully
```

Chapter Review

Questions

1. Which of the following is an illegal character in a Linux filename?
   A. * (asterisk)
   B. . (dot)
   C. / (forward slash)
   D. _ (underscore)
2. Which command pauses after displaying a screen's worth of directory contents? (Choose two.)
   A. dir p
   B. ls | more
   C. ls -p
   D. dir /p
3. Which of the following commands will delete all of the files in a directory in Linux?
   A. del *.*
   B. del all
   C. rm *
   D. rm all

4. Which command do you use to determine your exact folder location (path) in Linux?
   A. dir
   B. path
   C. pwd
   D. prompt
5. Which Windows command is functionally equivalent to the Linux ls command?
   A. dir
   B. command
   C. copy
   D. dd
6. What do you type before a Linux command to access help for that command?
   A. help
   B. ?
   C. man
   D. /?
7. Which of the following Linux commands will show detailed information about the contents of a folder?
   A. ls –l
   B. ls –e
   C. ls –h
   D. ls –k
8. What command, identical in both Windows and Linux, will tell you the name of the computer?
   A. hosts | grep
   B. whoami
   C. hostname
   D. net name
9. Of the following, which best describes the function of the Windows gpresult command?
   A. Lists all recently updated group policies
   B. Lists the group policies applied to a user
   C. Lists all changes to a user's group policies since the last refresh
   D. Lists any and all conflicting group policies

10. How do you run a command at the Windows command prompt with administrative privileges?
    A. Enter an elevated username and password at the command prompt.
    B. Right-click a command-prompt shortcut and then select Run as PowerUser.
    C. Right-click a command-prompt shortcut and then select Run as administrator.
    D. The cmd command only runs with administrator privileges.

Answers

1. **C.** Any of these characters are acceptable in a Linux filename except the forward slash (/), which is used exclusively as a path separator.
2. **B, D.** The ls | more and dir /p commands in Linux and Windows, respectively, pause a long listing at the end of the page.
3. **C.** Type **rm** * and press ENTER to delete all files in a directory in Linux.
4. **C.** The pwd command enables you to determine the current folder location in Linux.
5. **A.** The Windows dir command accomplishes a similar function to the Linux ls command.
6. **C.** Access the help for a Linux command by typing **man [command name]**.
7. **A.** Type **ls –l** and press ENTER to see detailed information about the contents of a folder in Linux.
8. **C.** Type **hostname** and press ENTER to discover the hostname for just about any computer.
9. **B.** The gpresult command in Windows lists group policies applied to a user.
10. **C.** To run a command at the Windows command prompt with administrative privileges, you would right-click a command-prompt shortcut and then select Run as administrator.

CHAPTER 17

Troubleshooting Operating Systems

In this chapter, you will learn how to

- Troubleshoot boot problems
- Troubleshoot GUI problems
- Troubleshoot application problems

This chapter looks at operating system problems from the ground up. It starts with catastrophic failure—a personal computer that won't boot—and then discusses ways to get past that problem. The next section covers the causes and workarounds when the GUI fails to load. Once you can access the GUI, the many diagnostic and troubleshooting tools that you've spent so much time learning about come to your fingertips. The chapter finishes with a discussion on application problems.

The CompTIA A+ 902 exam focuses primarily on troubleshooting in Windows, so the basic structure of this chapter follows that example. We'll look first at various issues through the prism of a PC tech working on modern Windows versions, then, when applicable, discuss the symptom, tools, and techniques in Mac OS X and Linux.

Mac OS X and Linux systems have the same problems you'll find in Windows, such as hardware failure, system and driver flaws, and buggy applications. The differences among the three OS families when troubleshooting are stark.

A ton of companies manufacture hardware and write software for Windows. The resulting *heterogeneous ecosystem* (that is, a lot of variety) of Windows greatly expands on the number of possibilities for what could be causing problems in any system.

Because Apple has always sharply controlled the hardware and drivers used with Mac OS X, hardware flaws are easier to diagnose. The same can be said with OS X and application problems. Mac OS X has a more *homogeneous ecosystem* (that is, not a lot of variety) than Windows. Aside from upgrading RAM, most Mac OS X machines get few hardware updates and thus dodge problems that dog Windows machines. Likewise, Apple provides a lot of excellent productivity software with the basic OS X system, so most users have little incentive to add much additional software. This avoids problems too.

Linux production machines—generally servers—often lack the excess complexity of Windows or Mac OS X systems and just work solidly. When you switch to the enthusiast or dabbler systems that most of us use, on the other hand, they have all kinds of problems. That's because the most common of those systems use random spare parts from old Windows machines. You get what you pay for, I suppose.

Let's dive into troubleshooting now.

902

Failure to Boot

When a computer fails to boot, you need to determine whether the problem relates to hardware or software. You'll recall from Chapter 10, "Implementing Hard Drives," that a hard drive needs proper connectivity and power, and that CMOS must be configured correctly. If not, you'll get an error like the one in Figure 17-1. We'll look more closely at these sorts of scenarios in the first part of this section as a refresher.

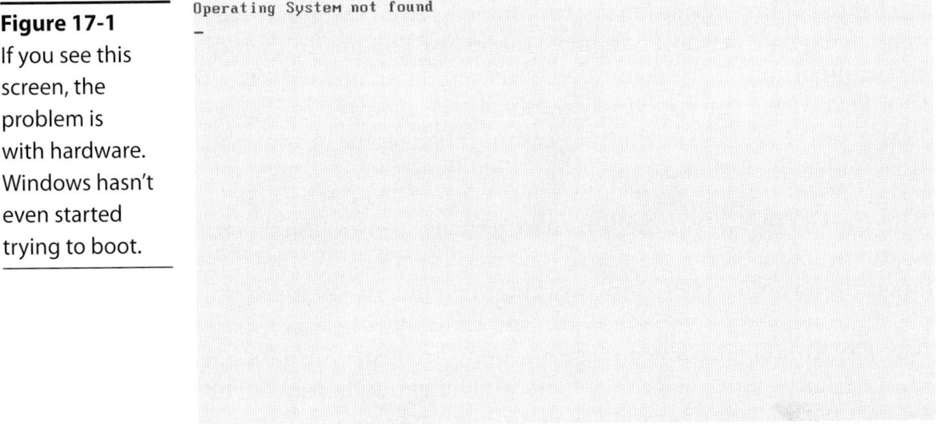
Operating System not found

Figure 17-1 If you see this screen, the problem is with hardware. Windows hasn't even started trying to boot.

But after the drive powers on and the POST completes successfully, the computer tries to boot to an OS. Failure at *this* point gives you an entirely different set of errors, such as *BOOTMGR is missing* (see Figure 17-2). You need a totally different set of tools from the ones used to troubleshoot hardware or CMOS issues.

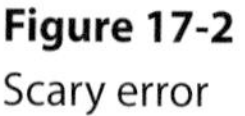

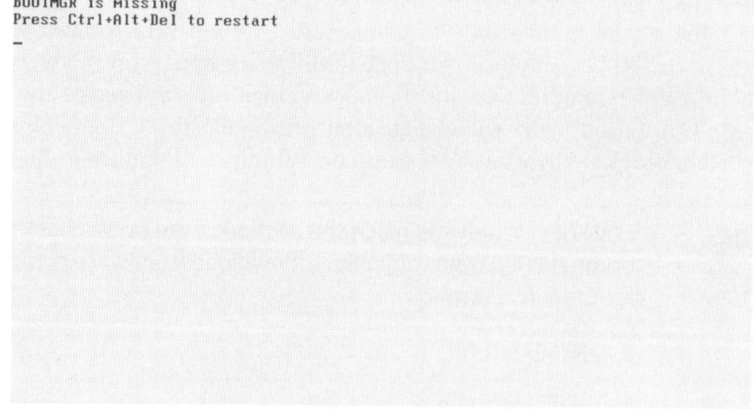

BOOTMGR is missing
Press Ctrl+Alt+Del to restart

Figure 17-2 Scary error

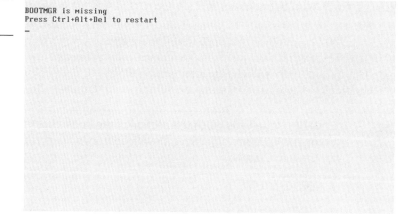

Failure to Boot: Hardware or Configuration

Most failed-boot scenarios require you to determine where the fault occurred: with the hardware and configuration, or in Windows. This is a pretty straightforward problem. Imagine that a user calls and says "My PC won't boot" or "My computer is dead." At this point, your best tools are knowledge of the boot process and asking lots of questions. Here are some I use regularly:

"What displays on the screen—if anything—after you press the power button on the case?"

"What do you hear—if anything—after you press the power button on the case?"

"Is the PC plugged in?"

"Do you smell anything weird?"

Hardware problems can give you a blank screen on boot-up, so you follow the tried-and-true troubleshooting methodology for hardware. Make sure everything is plugged in and turned on. If the PC is new, as in less than 30 days old, you know it might have suffered a burn-in failure. If the customer smells something, one of the components might have fried. Try replacing with known good devices: RAM, power supply, CPU, hard drive, motherboard.

If the user says that the screen says "No boot device detected" and the system worked fine before, it *could* mean something as simple as the computer has attempted to boot to an incorrect device, such as to something other than the primary hard drive. This scenario happens all the time. Someone plugs a thumb drive into a USB port and the CMOS is configured to boot to removable media before hard drives—boom! "No boot device detected" error. The first few times it happened to me, I nearly took my machine apart before experiencing that head-slapping moment. I removed the thumb drive and then watched Windows boot normally.

Failure to Boot: Windows XP (A CompTIA Retro Moment)

For some reason known only to CompTIA, they left very specific Windows XP references in the 902 exam objectives, specifically about boot error messages and tools for fixing those errors. Rather than just having you memorize a string of exam questions—that CompTIA undoubtedly will change after getting pushback from companies, customers, and technologies—here's a short scoop on Windows XP failure-to-boot moments.

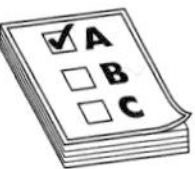

EXAM TIP When you reach this section of the book, check the latest CompTIA 902 exam objectives (download from www.comptia.org). Search for these five terms:

- Missing NTLDR
- Missing Boot.ini
- Recovery console
- Automated system recovery
- Emergency repair disk (this one refers only to Windows NT/2000 computers from last century)

If the terms are thankfully missing, then just skip this section and go on about your business prepping for the exam.

[Imagine yourself in a different age, a different time, in a simpler world . . .]

Windows XP boot errors take place in those short moments between the time POST ends and the *Loading Windows* screen begins. For Windows XP to start loading the main operating system, the critical system files ntldr, ntdetect.com, and boot.ini must reside in the root directory of the C: drive, and boot.ini must point to the Windows boot files. In a scenario where any of these requirements isn't in place, the system won't get past this step. Here are some of the common error messages you see at this point:

No Boot Device Present

NTLDR Bad or Missing

Invalid BOOT.INI

These text errors take place very early in the startup process. That's your big clue that you have a boot issue. If you get to the Windows splash screen and then the computer locks up, that's a whole different game, so know the difference.

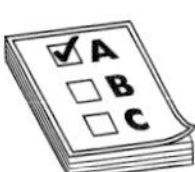

EXAM TIP The CompTIA A+ 902 exam objectives describe these error messages as "Missing NTLDR" and "Missing Boot.ini." The intent is the same, so don't be surprised by the slight difference in wording.

If you are in a failure-to-boot scenario where you get one of the catastrophic error messages with a Windows XP system, you have a three-level process to get back up and running. You first should attempt to repair. If that fails, attempt to restore from a backup copy of Windows. If restore either is not available or fails, your only recourse is to rebuild. You will lose data at the restore and rebuild phases, so you definitely want to spend a lot of energy on the repair effort first! Follow this process when faced with a corrupted system files or a missing operating system.

Attempt to Repair by Using the Recovery Console

To begin troubleshooting one of these errors, boot from the installation CD-ROM. You have three options from the initial screen: set up Windows XP, repair using the Recovery Console, and quit Setup (see Figure 17-3). The *Recovery Console* provides a command-line interface for working with Windows before the GUI starts. Press R to start the Recovery Console.

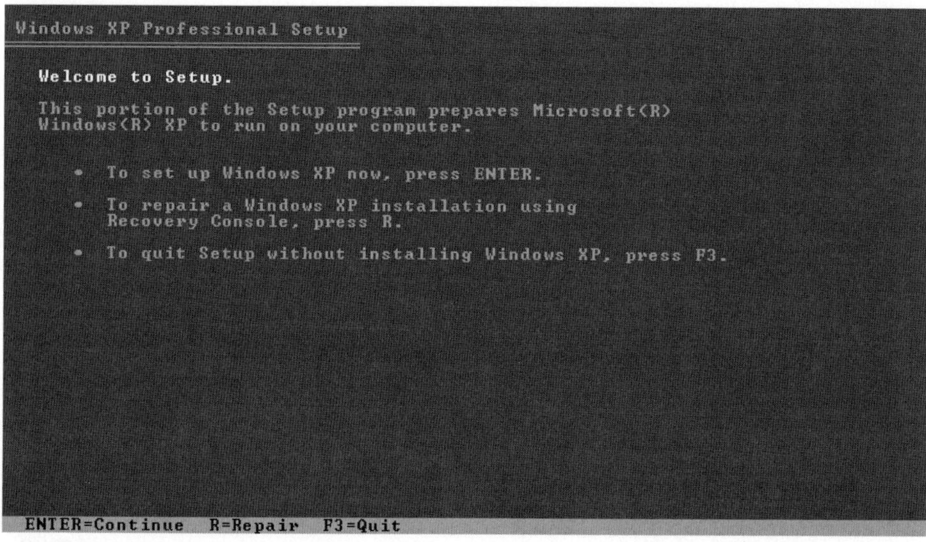

Windows XP Professional Setup
Welcome to Setup.
This portion of the Setup program prepares Microsoft(R)
Windows(R) XP to run on your computer.
• To set up Windows XP now, press ENTER.
• To repair a Windows XP installation using
Recovery Console, press R.
• To quit Setup without installing Windows XP, press F3.
ENTER=Continue R=Repair F3=Quit

Figure 17-3 Initial Windows XP Setup screen

When you select the Recovery Console, you will see a message about ntdetect, another message that the Recovery Console is starting up, and then you are greeted with the following message and command prompt:

```
Microsoft Windows XP<TM> Recovery Console.
The Recovery Console provides system repair and recovery functionality.
Type Exit to quit the Recovery Console and restart the computer.

1: C:\WINDOWS
Which Windows XP installation would you like to log onto
<To cancel, press ENTER>?
```

The cursor is a small, white rectangle sitting to the right of the question mark on the last line. If you are not accustomed to working at the command prompt, this may be disorienting. If there is only one installation of Windows XP on your computer, type the number **1** at the prompt and press the ENTER key. If you press ENTER before typing in a valid selection, the Recovery Console will cancel and the computer will reboot. The only choice you can make in this example is 1. Having made that choice, the screen displays a new line, followed by the cursor:

```
Type the Administrator password:
```

Enter the Administrator password for that computer and press ENTER. The password does not display on the screen; you see asterisks in place of the password. The screen still shows everything that has happened so far, unless something has happened to cause an error message. It now looks like this:

```
Microsoft Windows XP<TM> Recovery Console.
The Recovery Console provides system repair and recovery functionality.
Type Exit to quit the Recovery Console and restart the computer.

1: C:\WINDOWS
Which Windows XP installation would you like to log onto
<To cancel, press ENTER>? 1
Type the Administrator password: ********
C:\Windows>
```

By now, you've caught on and know that there is a rectangular prompt immediately after the last line. Now what do you do? Use the Recovery Console commands, of course. The Recovery Console uses many of the commands that work in the Windows command-line interface that you explored in Chapter 16, "Working with the Command-Line Interface," as well as some commands uniquely its own. Table 17-1 lists common Recovery Console commands.

The Recovery Console shines in the business of manually restoring Registries, stopping problem services, rebuilding partitions (other than the system partition), and using the expand program to extract copies of corrupted files from an optical disc or floppy disk.

Using the Recovery Console, you can reconfigure a service so that it starts with different settings, format partitions on the hard drive, read and write on local FAT or NTFS partitions, and copy replacement files from a floppy disk or optical disc. The Recovery Console enables you to access the file system and is still constrained by the file and folder security of NTFS, which makes it a more secure tool to use than some third-party solutions.

The Recovery Console also works great for fixing three items: repairing the MBR, reinstalling the boot files, and rebuilding boot.ini. Let's look at each of these.

A bad boot sector usually shows up as a No Boot Device error. If it turns out that this isn't the problem, using the Recovery Console command to fix it won't hurt anything. At the Recovery Console prompt, just type

```
fixmbr
```

This fixes the master boot record.

Command	Description
attrib	Changes attributes of selected file or folder
cd (or chdir)	Displays current directory or changes directories
chkdsk	Runs CheckDisk utility
cls	Clears screen
copy	Copies from removable media to system folders on hard disk. No wildcards
del (or delete)	Deletes service or folder
dir	Lists contents of selected directory on system partition only
disable	Disables service or driver
diskpart	Creates/deletes partitions
enable	Enables service or driver
expand	Extracts a single file or group of files from a compressed file
extract	Extracts components from .cab files
fixboot	Writes new partition boot sector on system partition
fixmbr	Writes new master boot record (MBR) for partition boot sector
format	Formats selected disk
listsvc	Lists all services on system
logon	Enables you to choose which Windows installation to log on to if you have more than one
map	Displays current drive letter mappings
md (or mkdir)	Creates a directory
more (or type)	Displays contents of a text file
rd (or rmdir)	Removes a directory
ren (or rename)	Renames a single file
systemroot	Change current working directory to the system root of drive
type	Displays contents of a text file

Table 17-1 Common Recovery Console commands

Missing system files are usually indicated by the error *NTLDR bad or missing*. Odds are good that if ntdlr is missing, so are the rest of the system files. To fix this, get to the root directory (cd\—remember that from Chapter 16?) and type the following line (substituting the drive letter of the optical drive for *d:* in the example):

```
copy d:\i386\ntldr
```

Then type this line:

```
copy d:\i386\ntdetect.com
```

This takes care of two of the big three and leads us to the last issue, rebuilding boot.ini. If the boot.ini file is gone or corrupted, run this command from the Recovery Console:

```
bootcfg /rebuild
```

The Recovery Console will try to locate all installed copies of Windows and ask you if you want to add them to the new boot.ini file it's about to create. Say yes to the ones you want.

If all goes well with the Recovery Console, do a thorough backup as soon as possible (just in case something else goes wrong). If the Recovery Console does not do the trick, the next step is to restore Windows XP.

Attempt to Restore

If you've been diligent about backing up, you can attempt to restore to an earlier, working copy of Windows. Assuming you made an Automated System Recovery (ASR) backup, this will restore your system to a previously installed state, but you should use it as a last resort. You lose everything on the system that was installed or added after you created the ASR disk. If that's the best option, though, follow the steps in the ASR wizard.

NOTE To use the Windows XP System Restore, you need to be able to get into Windows. In this context, "restore" means it gives you a way to get into Windows.

Rebuild

If faced with a full system rebuild, you have several options, depending on the particular system. You could simply reboot to the Windows CD-ROM and install right on top of the existing system, but that's usually not the optimal solution. To avoid losing anything important, you'd be better off swapping the C: drive for a blank hard drive and installing a clean version of Windows.

Most OEM systems come with a misleadingly named *Recovery CD* or *recovery partition*. The Recovery CD is a CD-ROM that you boot to and run. The recovery partition is a hidden partition on the hard drive that you activate at boot by holding down a key combination specific to the manufacturer of that system. (See the motherboard manual or users' guide for the key combination and other details.) Both "recovery" options do the same thing—restore your computer to the factory-installed state. If you run one of these tools, *you will wipe everything off your system*—all personal files, folders, and programs will go away! Before running either tool, make sure all important files and folders are backed up on an optical disc or spare hard drive.

[Let us return now to the present. Cue Modern Windows on camera 2.]

Failure to Boot: Modern Windows

Two critical boot files risk corruption in Windows, bootmgr and bcd, both of which you can fix with one tool, bcdedit. You can use this tool in the Windows Recovery Environment.

WinPE

With Windows Vista, Microsoft upgraded the installation environment from the 16-bit text mode environment used in every previous version of Windows to 32- and 64-bit. This upgrade enabled the Windows installation process to go graphical and support features such as a mouse pointer and clickable elements, rather than relying on command-line tools. Microsoft calls the installation environment the *Windows Preinstallation Environment* (*WinPE* or *Windows PE*).

With Windows PE, you boot directly to the Windows DVD. This loads a limited-function graphical operating system that contains both troubleshooting and diagnostic tools, along with installation options. The Windows installation media is called a *Live DVD* because WinPE loads directly from disc into memory and doesn't access or modify the hard drive.

NOTE Although here I discuss only how WinPE helps boot repair, know that WinPE goes much further. WinPE can assist unattended installations, network installations, and even booting diskless workstations on a network.

When you access Windows PE and opt for the troubleshooting and repair features, you open a special set of tools called the *Windows Recovery Environment* (*WinRE* or *Windows RE*). The terms can get a little confusing because of the similarity of letters, so mark this: Windows RE is the repair tools that run within Windows PE. WinPE powers WinRE. Got it? Let's tackle WinRE.

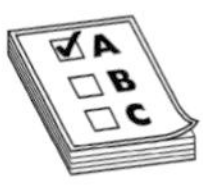

EXAM TIP Microsoft also refers to the Windows Recovery Environment as the *System Recovery Options menu*.

Enter Windows RE

It would be unfair to say that the Windows Recovery Environment only replaces the Recovery Console. WinRE includes an impressive, powerful set of both automated and manual utilities that collectively diagnose and fix all but the most serious of Windows boot problems. Although WinRE does all the hard work for you, you still need to know how to access and use it. When faced with a failure-to-boot scenario in modern versions of Windows, WinRE is one of your primary tools.

Getting to Windows RE

In Windows 7, you can access WinRE in three ways (See next Exam Tip for Windows Vista options). First, you can boot from the Windows installation media and select Repair. Second, you can use the Repair Your Computer option on the Advanced Boot Options (F8) menu (see Figure 17-4). Third, you can create a system repair disc or system image before you have problems. Go to Control Panel | System and Security | Backup and Restore and select *Create a system repair disc* or select *Create a system image.*

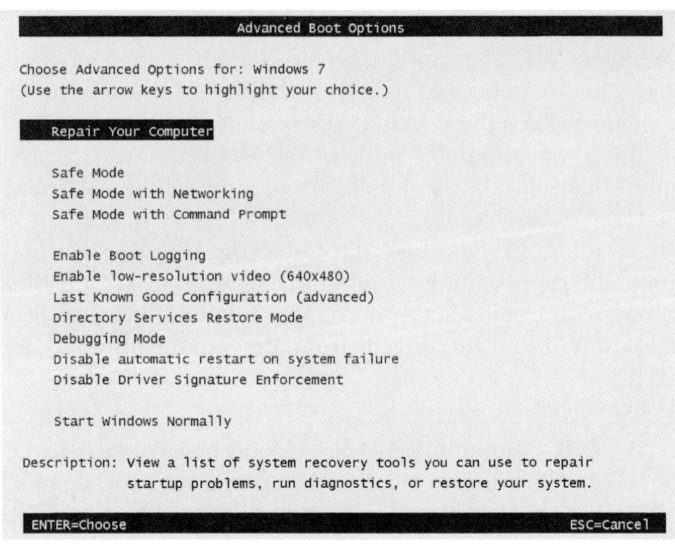

Figure 17-4 Selecting Repair Your Computer in the Advanced Boot Options menu

Windows 8/8.1 do not have the F8 Advanced Boot Options by default, nor a Backup and Restore applet. Instead, you create a recovery drive on a 16 GB+ USB flash drive by accessing the Recovery applet in Control Panel (see Figure 17-5). Advanced Boot Options is still there, mind you, but Microsoft removed the easy access via the F8 key. Boot to the recovery drive to access WinRE. (You can get to WinRE in several ways once you have access to the Windows Desktop, but this section assumes you can't get there yet.)

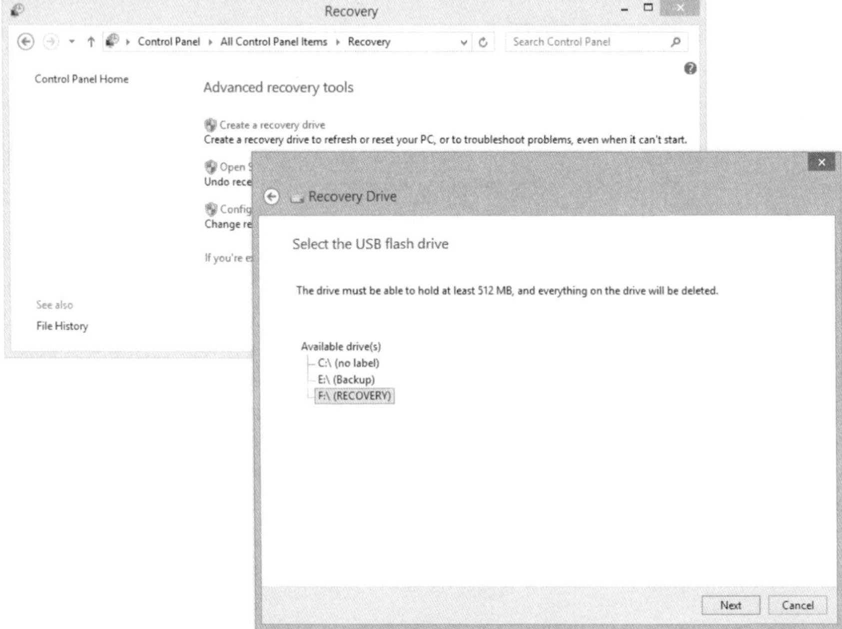

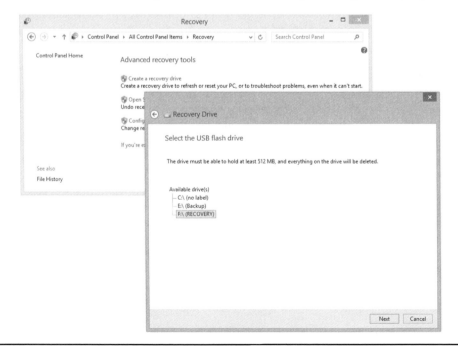

Figure 17-5 Making a recovery drive in Windows 8.1

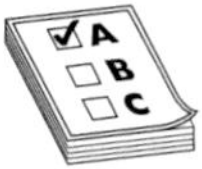

EXAM TIP Windows Vista does not have the Repair Your Computer option on the Advanced Boot Options menu. You can either use Windows installation media or, if you have SP1 or later, make a bootable system repair disc.

Although any of these methods works fine, I recommend that you access WinRE from the Windows installation media or the dedicated recovery drive for three reasons:

- The hard drive can be so messed up that you won't make it to the Advanced Boot Options menu.
- Accessing WinRE using the Repair Your Computer option in the Advanced Boot Options menu requires a local administrator password.
- Using a bootable disc/USB flash drive enables you to avoid any malware that might be on the system.

Using Windows RE

The look and feel of Windows RE differs a lot between Windows Vista/7 and Windows 8/8.1/10, although you'll find similar options in both. Windows Vista/7 WinRE has a simple interface (see Figure 17-6) with five options:

- Startup Repair
- System Restore
- System Image Recovery (Windows 7) or Windows Complete PC Restore (Vista)
- Windows Memory Diagnostic or Windows Memory Diagnostic Tool (Vista)
- Command Prompt

The name of the third option differs between Windows 7 and Windows Vista, though the intent—rebuilding from a backup—is the same. I'll talk about how these options differ a little later in the chapter.

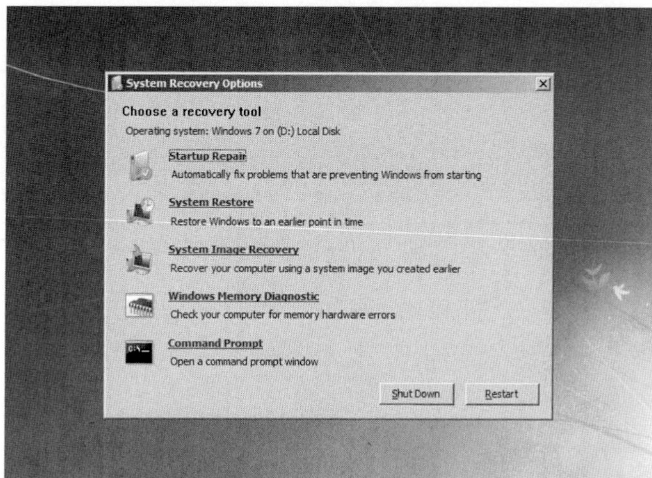

Figure 17-6 Recovery Environment main screen in Windows 7

Windows 8/8.1/10 WinRE offers fewer choices initially. The first screen requires you to choose a language, and then you get to the main menu (see Figure 17-7) with two options:

- Troubleshoot
- Turn off your PC

Click on the Troubleshoot option to see three more options (see Figure 17-8):

- Refresh your PC
- Reset your PC
- Advanced options

Understanding Refresh and Reset is critically important for troubleshooting and rebuilding a Windows 8/8.1/10 PC. We'll discuss these options in a moment.

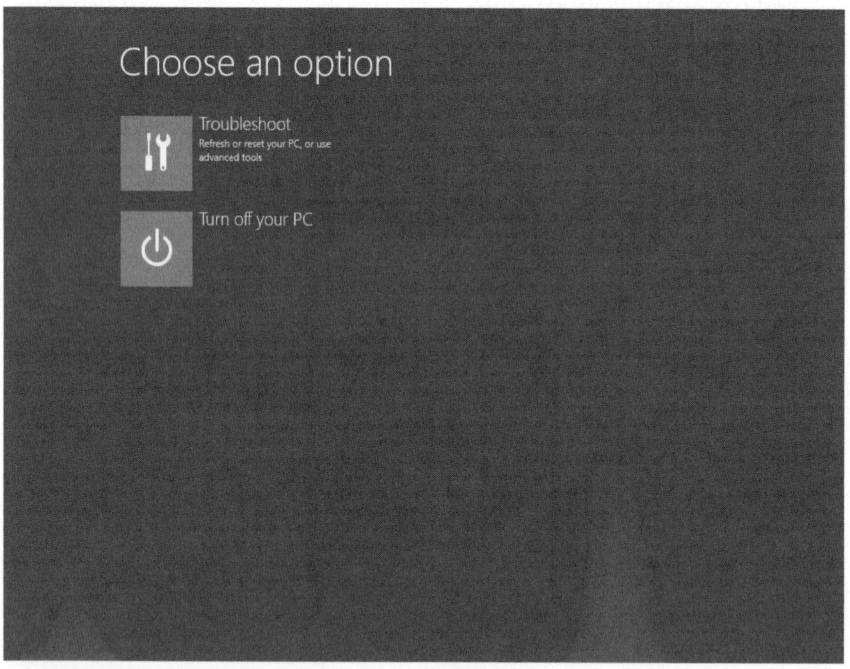

Figure 17-7 Recovery Environment main screen in Windows 8.1

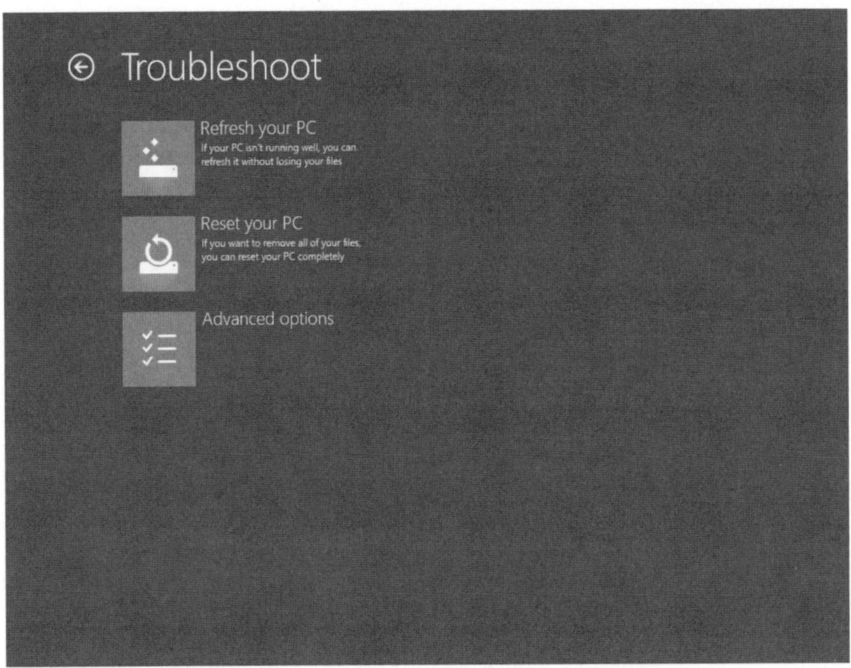

Figure 17-8 WinRE Troubleshoot screen in Windows 8.1

Clicking on Advanced options reveals another menu (see Figure 17-9) that shows a lot of the same options you see in Windows Vista/7:

- System Restore
- System Image Recovery
- Startup Repair
- Command Prompt
- UEFI Firmware Settings (available if your motherboard uses UEFI rather than classic BIOS)

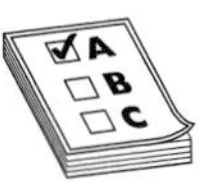

EXAM TIP Make sure you know how to access the Windows Recovery Environment and what each of the available tools does.

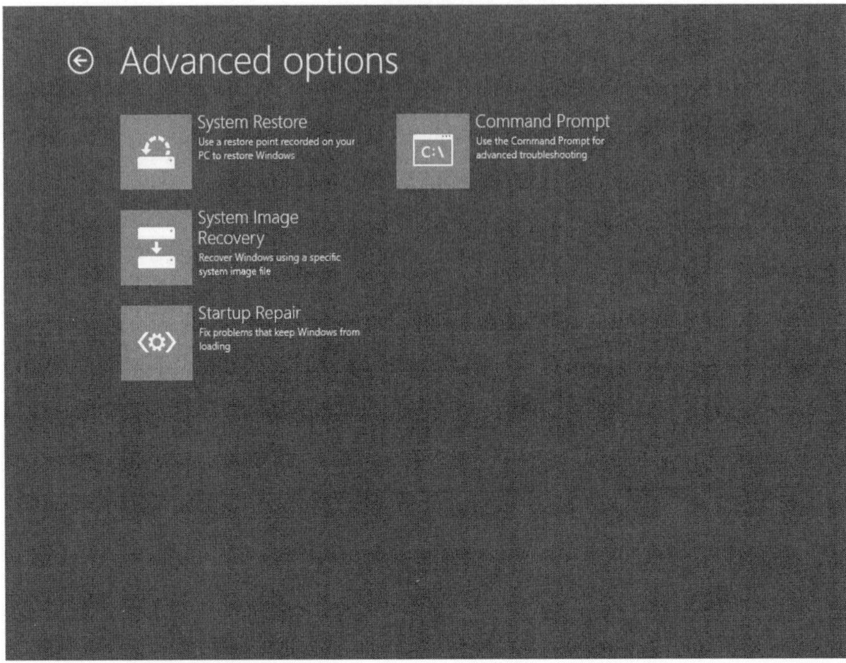

Figure 17-9 WinRE Advanced options screen in Windows 8.1

Startup Repair The *Startup Repair* utility serves as a one-stop, do-it-all option (see Figure 17-10). When run, it performs a number of repairs, including:

- Repairs a corrupted Registry by accessing the backup copy on your hard drive
- Restores critical boot files
- Restores critical system and driver files
- Rolls back any non-working drivers
- Uninstalls any incompatible service packs and patches
- Runs chkdsk
- Runs a memory test to check your RAM

Startup Repair fixes almost any Windows boot problem. In fact, if you have a system with one hard drive containing a single partition with Windows Vista or Windows 7 installed, you'd have trouble finding something Startup Repair *couldn't* fix. Upon completion, Startup Repair shows the screen shown in Figure 17-11.

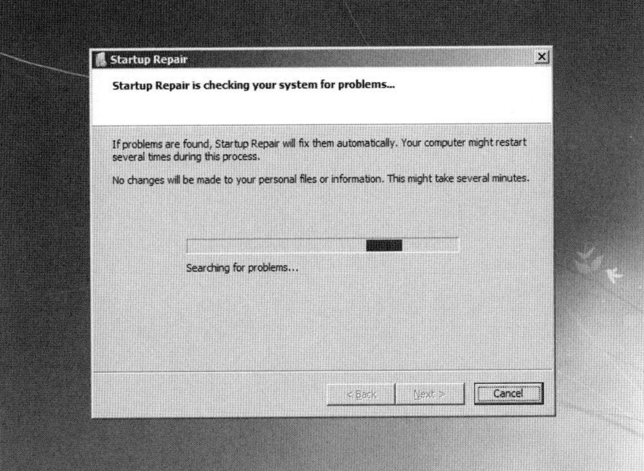

Figure 17-10 Startup Repair in action

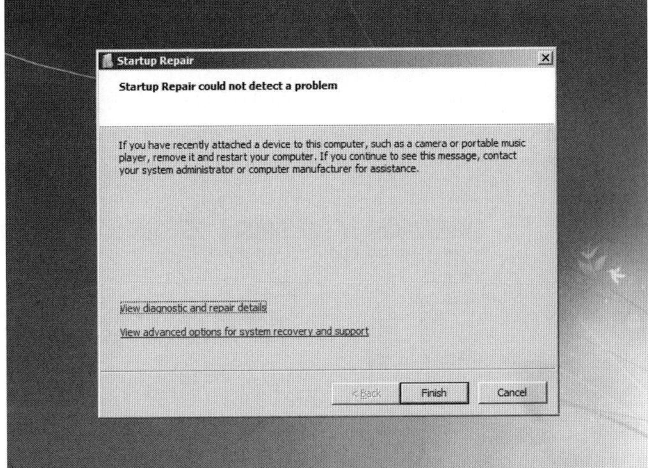

Figure 17-11 Startup Repair complete; no problems found

Note the link in Figure 17-11 that says *View diagnostic and repair details*. This opens a text file called srttrail.txt that lists exactly what the program found, what it fixed, and what it failed to do. It may look cryptic, but you can type anything you find into Google for more information. I've reproduced the beginning of the (very long) srttrail.txt file here:

```
Startup Repair diagnosis and repair log
---------------------------
Last successful boot time: 9/14/2016 2:37:43 AM (GMT)
Number of repair attempts: 6
```

```
Session details
---------------------------
System Disk = \Device\Harddisk0
Windows directory = C:\Windows
AutoChk Run = 0
Number of root causes = 1

Test Performed:
---------------------------
Name: Check for updates
Result: Completed successfully. Error code =  0x0
Time taken = 32 ms

Test Performed:
---------------------------
Name: System disk test
Result: Completed successfully. Error code =  0x0
Time taken = 0 ms
```

NOTE The *View advanced options for system recovery and support* link simply returns you to the main screen.

In Windows 7 and later, Startup Repair starts automatically if your system detects a boot problem. If you power up a Windows system and see the screen shown in Figure 17-12, Windows has detected a problem in the startup process.

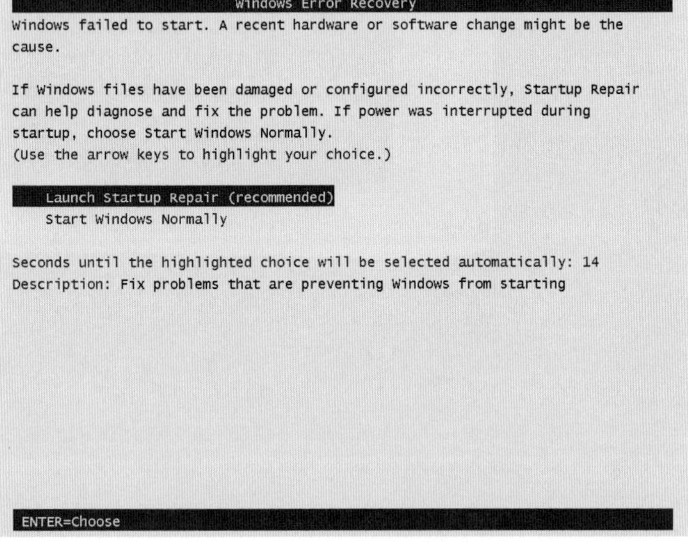

Figure 17-12 Windows Error Recovery

Personally, I think this menu pops up way too often. If you fail to shut down your computer properly, for example, this menu appears. In this case, you can save time by booting normally. When in doubt, however, go ahead and run Startup Repair. It can't hurt anything.

A powerful tool like Startup Repair still doesn't cover everything. You may have specific needs that require more finesse than a single, do-it-all approach. In many cases, you've already discovered the problem and simply want to make a single fix. You might want to perform a system restoration or check the memory. For this, we'll need to explore the other four options available in WinRE.

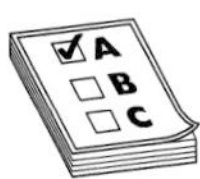

EXAM TIP If you have trouble booting your computer, you should try Startup Repair first.

System Restore *System Restore* does the same job here it has done since Microsoft first introduced it in Windows Me, enabling you to go back to a time when your computer worked properly. Placing this option in Windows RE gives those of us who make many *restore points*—snapshots of a system at a given point of time—a quick and handy way to return our systems to a previous state (see Figure 17-13).

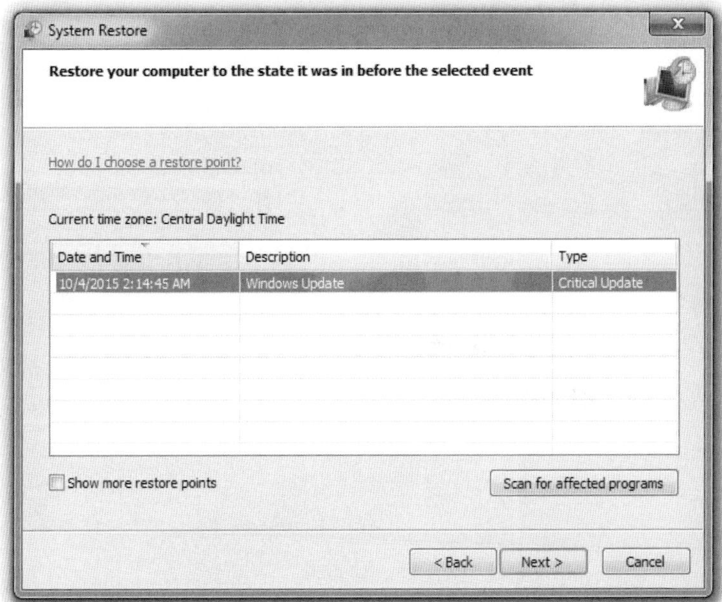

Figure 17-13 System Restore point

System Image Recovery/Windows Complete PC Restore Windows 7 and later backup tools differ from tools in Windows Vista. Note Figure 17-14, which shows the Windows Vista Recovery Environment menu on the left next to the Windows 7 Recovery Environment menu on the right. The third WinRE option differs. Windows Vista uses the Windows Complete PC Restore utility, whereas Windows 7 and later include the System Image Recovery tool.

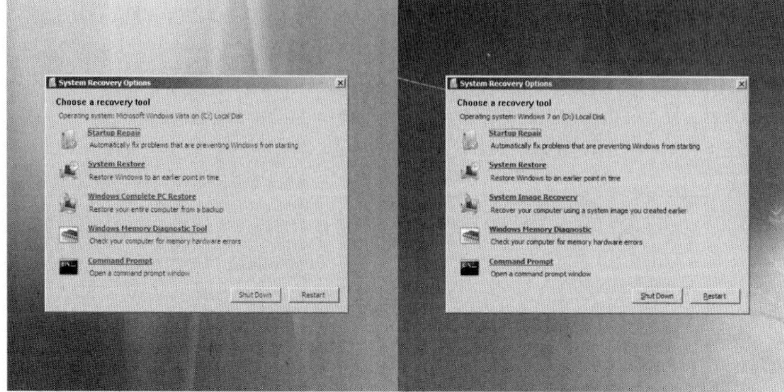

Figure 17-14 The WinRE options in Windows Vista (left) and Windows 7 (right)

With an image in hand, you can use the Windows Complete PC Restore/System Image Recovery tool to restore your system after a catastrophe.

If you have the drive containing the system image plugged in when you first run the wizard, it should detect your latest backup and present you with the dialog box shown in Figure 17-15. If it doesn't list a system image or it lists the wrong one, you can select an image from another date on the same disk or even a remote network share.

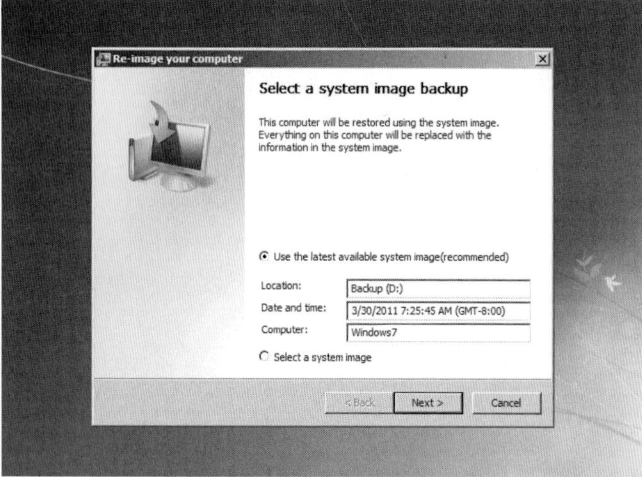

Figure 17-15 Selecting a system image

After you select the image you want to restore, the utility presents you with a few more options, as shown in Figure 17-16. Most importantly, you can choose to format and repartition disks. With this option selected, the utility wipes out the existing partitions and data on all disks so the restored system will get the same partitions that the backed-up system had.

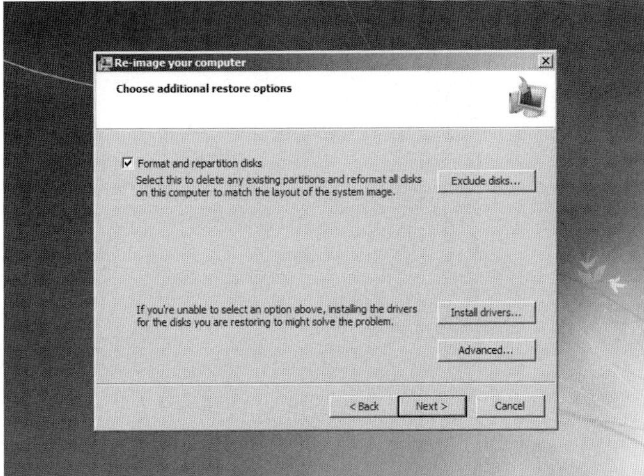

Figure 17-16 Additional restore options

After you click Finish on the confirmation screen (see Figure 17-17), which also contains a final warning, the restore process begins (see Figure 17-18). The utility removes the old system data and then copies the backed-up system image to the hard drive(s). Once the process completes, your system reboots and should start up again with all of your data and programs just where you left them when you last backed up.

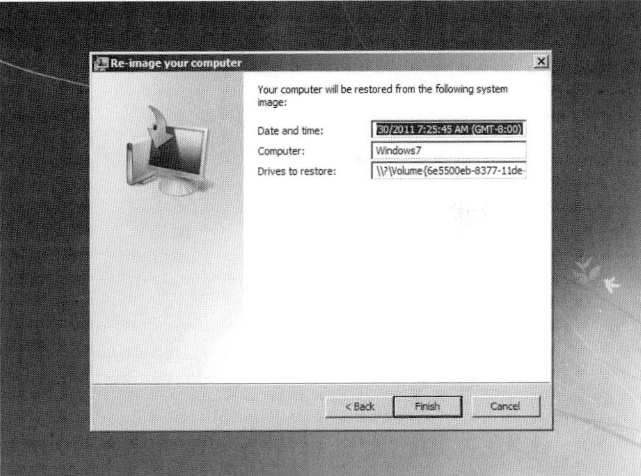

Figure 17-17 Confirming your settings

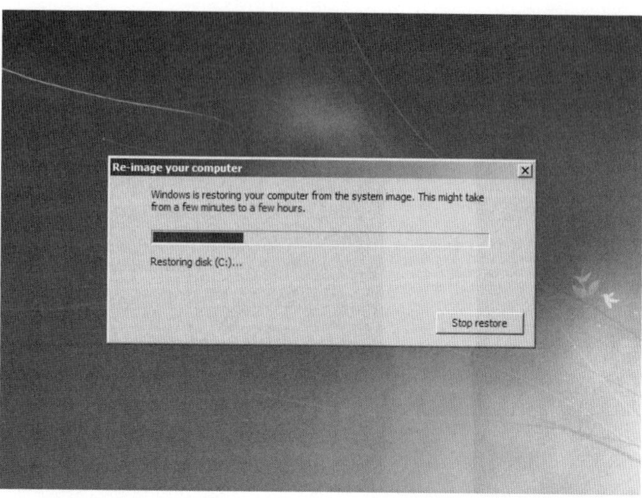

Figure 17-18 Restoring your computer

Windows Memory Diagnostic (Tool) Bad RAM causes huge problems for any operating system, creating scenarios where computers get Blue Screens of Death (BSoDs), system lockups, and continuous reboots. Starting with Windows Vista, Microsoft added a memory tester to the Windows Recovery Environment. When you click the Windows Memory Diagnostic (Tool) link from the main WinRE screen, it prompts you to *Restart now and check for problems (recommended)* or *Check for problems the next time I start my computer* (see Figure 17-19). It doesn't really matter which option you choose, but if you think you need to test the system's RAM, that probably means you should do it now.

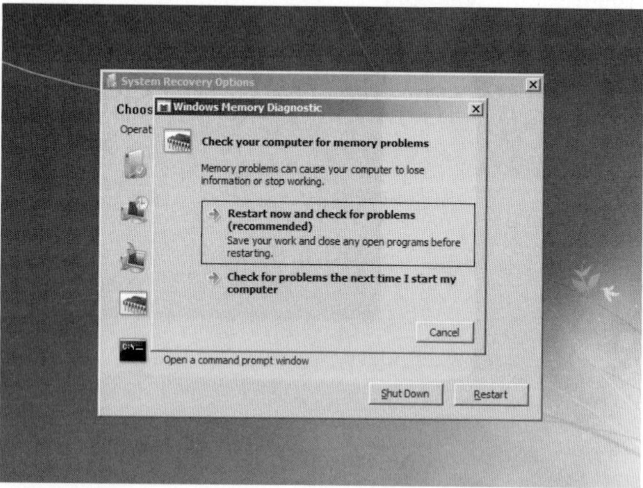

Figure 17-19 Windows Memory Diagnostic screen

Once you restart, your system immediately starts running the Windows Memory Diagnostic Tool, as shown in Figure 17-20. While the program runs, you can press F1 to see the Memory Tester options (see Figure 17-21).

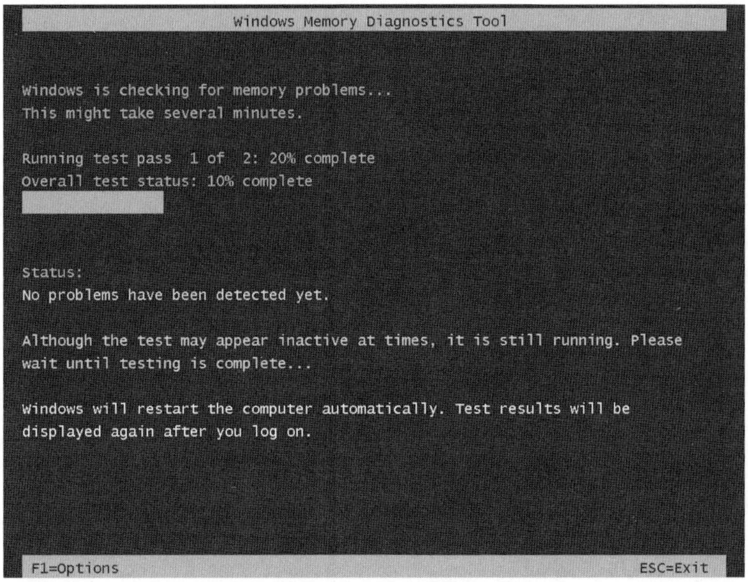

```
Windows Memory Diagnostics Tool

Windows is checking for memory problems...
This might take several minutes.

Running test pass  1 of  2: 20% complete
Overall test status: 10% complete

Status:
No problems have been detected yet.

Although the test may appear inactive at times, it is still running. Please
wait until testing is complete...

Windows will restart the computer automatically. Test results will be
displayed again after you log on.

F1=Options                                                          ESC=Exit
```

Figure 17-20 Windows Memory Diagnostic Tool running

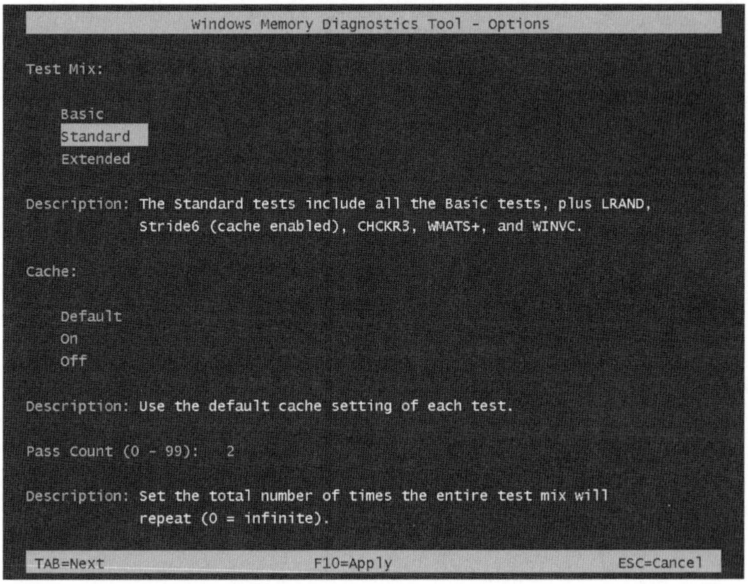

```
Windows Memory Diagnostics Tool - Options

Test Mix:

    Basic
    Standard
    Extended

Description: The Standard tests include all the Basic tests, plus LRAND,
             Stride6 (cache enabled), CHCKR3, WMATS+, and WINVC.

Cache:

    Default
    On
    Off

Description: Use the default cache setting of each test.

Pass Count (0 - 99):  2

Description: Set the total number of times the entire test mix will
             repeat (0 = infinite).

TAB=Next                     F10=Apply                            ESC=Cancel
```

Figure 17-21 Windows Memory Diagnostic Tool options

The tool lists three important Test Mix options at the top of the screen: Basic, Standard, and Extended. *Basic* runs quickly (about one minute) but performs only light testing. *Standard*, the default choice, takes a few minutes and tests more aggressively. *Extended* takes hours (you should let it run overnight), but it will very aggressively test your RAM.

NOTE You can also find the Windows Memory Diagnostic Tool in the Control Panel under System and Security | Administrative Tools, or start it from an administrative command prompt using the **mdsched** command.

This tool includes two other options: Cache and Pass Count. The *Cache* option enables you to set whether the tests use the CPU's built-in cache as well as override the default cache settings for each test type. Simply leave Cache set at Default and never touch it. *Pass Count* sets the number of times each set of tests will run. This option defaults to 2.

After the tool runs, your computer reboots normally. You can open Event Viewer to see the results (see Figure 17-22).

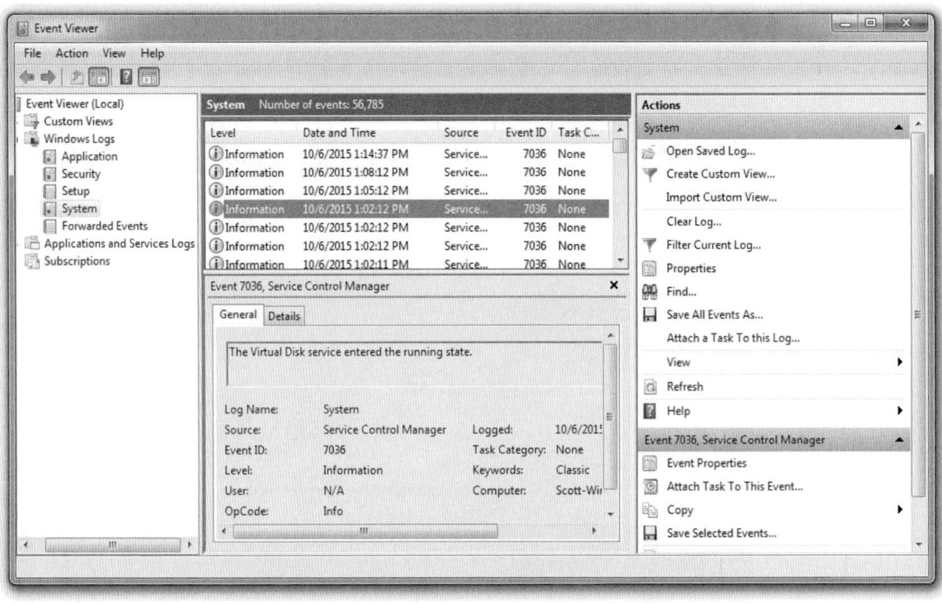

Figure 17-22 Event Viewer results

Sadly, I've had rather poor results with the Windows Memory Diagnostic Tool. We keep lots of bad RAM around the labs here at Total Seminars, and, when put to the test, we were unable to get this tool do anything other than give us a BSoD or lock up the system. We still turn to tried-and-tested tools such as the free Memtest86+ when we're worried about bad RAM.

NOTE You can find out more about Memtest86+ at www.memtest.org.

Command Prompt and bootrec The last, most interesting, and easily nerdiest option in the WinRE menu is Command Prompt. The WinRE command prompt

is a true 32- or 64-bit prompt that functions similarly to the regular cmd.exe shell in Windows. WinRE's command prompt, however, includes an important utility (bootrec) that you can't find in the regular command prompt. The WinRE command prompt also lacks a large number of the command-prompt tools you'd have in a regular Windows command prompt (though all the important ones remain). Let's begin by looking at the bootrec command. After that, we'll look at some other utilities that the WinRE command prompt offers.

NOTE The Startup Repair tool runs many of these command-prompt utilities automatically. You need to use the WinRE command prompt only for unique situations where the Startup Repair tool fails.

It's important for you to understand that the CompTIA A+ exams do not expect you to know everything about all these command-prompt utilities. The CompTIA A+ exams expect that you do know these things, however:

- Which utilities are available and their names
- How to access these utilities (WinRE in particular)
- What these utilities basically do
- Some of the basic switches used for these utilities
- With higher-level support, that you can fix computers using these tools (being led by a specialist tech over the phone, for example)

With that attitude in mind, let's take a look at probably the most important command to use in WinRE's command prompt, bootrec.

The *bootrec* command is a Windows Recovery Environment troubleshooting and repair tool that repairs the master boot record, boot sector, or BCD store. It replaced the old fixboot and fixmbr Recovery Console commands and adds two more repair features:

- **bootrec /fixboot** Rebuilds the boot sector for the active system partition
- **bootrec /fixmbr** Rebuilds the master boot record for the system partition
- **bootrec /scanos** Looks for Windows installations not currently in the BCD store and shows you the results without doing anything
- **bootrec /rebuildmbr** Looks for Windows installations not currently in the BCD store and gives you the choice to add them to the BCD store

NOTE Boot configuration data (BCD) files contain information about operating systems installed on a computer. In Microsoft speak, that information is called a *store* or *BCD store.*

You use a tool called *bcdedit* to see how Windows boots. Running bcdedit by itself (without switches) shows the boot options. The following boot information comes from a

system with a single copy of Windows installed. Note there are two sections: the *Windows Boot Manager* section describes the location of bootmgr, and the *Windows Boot Loader* section describes the location of the winload.exe file.

```
Windows Boot Manager
--------------------
identifier              {bootmgr}
device                  partition=\Device\HarddiskVolume1
description             Windows Boot Manager
locale                  en-US
inherit                 {globalsettings}
default                 {current}
resumeobject            {d4539c9b-481a-11df-a981-a17cb98be35c}
displayorder            {current}
toolsdisplayorder       {memdiag}
timeout                 30

Windows Boot Loader
-------------------
identifier              {current}
device                  partition=C:
path                    \Windows\system32\winload.exe
description             Windows 7
locale                  en-US
inherit                 {bootloadersettings}
recoverysequence        {d4539c9d-481a-11df-a981-a17cb98be35c}
recoveryenabled         Yes
osdevice                partition=C:
systemroot              \Windows
resumeobject            {d4539c9b-481a-11df-a981-a17cb98be35c}
nx                      OptIn
```

To make changes to the BCD store, you need to use switches:

- **bcdedit /export <filename>** exports a copy of the BCD store to a file. This is a very good idea whenever you use bcdedit!
- **bcdedit /import <filename>** imports a copy of the BCD store back into the store.

If you look carefully at the previous bcdedit output, you'll notice that each section has an identifier such as {bootmgr} or {current}. You can use these identifiers to make changes to the BCD store using the /set switch. Here's an example:

```
BCDEDIT /SET {current} path \BackupWindows\system32\winload.exe
```

This changes the path of the {current} identifier to point to an alternative winload.exe.

The bcdedit command supports multiple OSs. Notice how this BCD store has three identifiers: {bootmgr}, {current}, and {ntldr}—a fairly common dual-boot scenario.

```
Windows Boot Manager
--------------------
identifier              {bootmgr}
device                  partition=D:
description             Windows Boot Manager
locale                  en-US
inherit                 {globalsettings}
default                 {current}
```

```
resumeobject            {60b80a52-8267-11e0-ad8a-bdb414c1bf84}
displayorder            {ntldr}
                        {current}
toolsdisplayorder       {memdiag}
timeout                 30

Windows Legacy OS Loader
------------------------
identifier              {ntldr}
device                  partition=D:
path                    \ntldr
description             Earlier Version of Windows

Windows Boot Loader
-------------------
identifier              {current}
device                  partition=C:
path                    \Windows\system32\winload.exe
description             Windows 7
locale                  en-US
inherit                 {bootloadersettings}
recoverysequence        {60b80a54-8267-11e0-ad8a-bdb414c1bf84}
recoveryenabled         Yes
osdevice                partition=C:
systemroot              \Windows
resumeobject            {60b80a52-8267-11e0-ad8a-bdb414c1bf84}
nx                      OptIn
```

A BCD store like this will cause the menu shown in Figure 17-23 to pop up at boot.

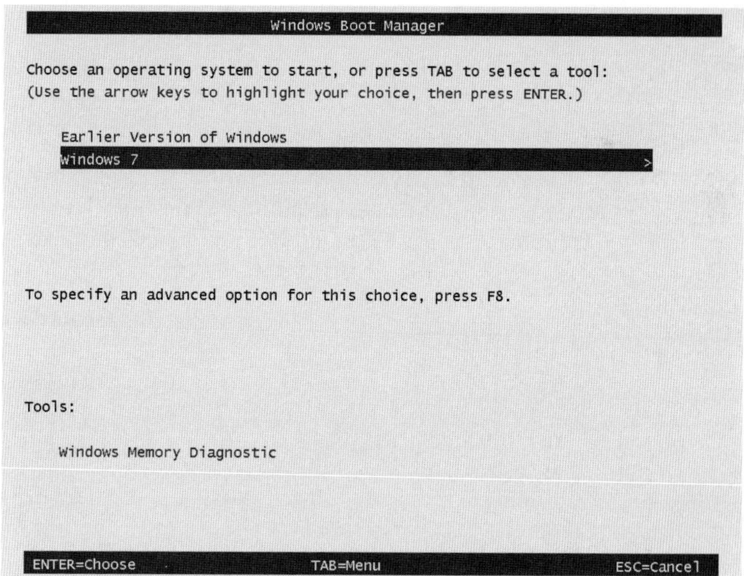

Figure 17-23 bootmgr showing available versions of Windows

The command prompt also includes *diskpart*, a fully featured partitioning tool. This tool lacks many of the safety features built into Disk Management, so proceed with

caution. You can, for example, delete any partition of any type at any time. Starting diskpart opens a special command prompt as shown here:

```
C:\Windows\system32>diskpart
Microsoft DiskPart version 6.3.9600
Copyright (C) 1999-2013 Microsoft Corporation.
On computer: MIKESPC
DISKPART>
```

You can list volumes (or partitions on Basic disks):

```
DISKPART> list volume
  Volume ###  Ltr  Label        Fs     Type        Size     Status     Info
  ----------  ---  -----------  -----  ----------  -------  ---------  --------
  Volume 0     D                       DVD-ROM         0 B  No Media
  Volume 1     C   New Volume   NTFS   Partition   1397 GB  Healthy    System

DISKPART>
```

Select a volume to manipulate (you may also select an entire drive):

```
DISKPART> select volume 1
Volume 1 is the selected volume.
DISKPART>
```

You can run commands at the diskpart prompt to add, change, or delete volumes and partitions on drives, mount or dismount volumes, and even manipulate software-level RAID arrays.

Refresh Your PC The Windows RE option to Refresh your PC in Windows 8 and later rebuilds Windows, but preserves all user files and settings and any applications purchased from the Windows Store. Note well: Refresh deletes every other application on your system.

Reset Your PC The Reset your PC option nukes your system—all apps, programs, user files, user settings—and presents a fresh installation of Windows. Use Reset as the last resort when troubleshooting a PC. And back up your data first.

Failure to Boot: OS X

Mac OS X offers a power recovery tool called *OS X Recovery* that enables you rebuild a Mac with a reboot and key combination. Hold down command + R at boot to access the Recovery environment. This enables a full Reset, but also gives options for other tools for troubleshooting. Note that CompTIA refers to the feature as *Image recovery*.

Failure to Boot: Linux

Linux offers two common boot managers: GRUB and LILO. Everyone uses GRUB these days; LILO is older, simpler, and doesn't support UEFI BIOS systems.

If GRUB gets corrupted or deleted, Linux won't start and you'll get a "Missing GRUB" error message at boot. Similarly, on older systems you'd get a "Missing LILO" error message.

You have a couple of options to fix this problem. For GRUB2-based systems, boot to the OS media disc (the Live DVD) and let it "install" into memory. In other words, don't install it to the hard drive. From there, you can access the Terminal and run the **sudo grub-install** command (along with the location of the boot drive) to repair.

Failure to Start Normally

Assuming that Windows gets past the boot part of the startup, it continues to load the graphical Windows OS. You will see the Windows startup image on the screen, hiding everything until Windows gets to the Login screen (see Figure 17-24). Once you log in, you'll get the Windows Desktop or the Start screen, depending on which version of Windows you have.

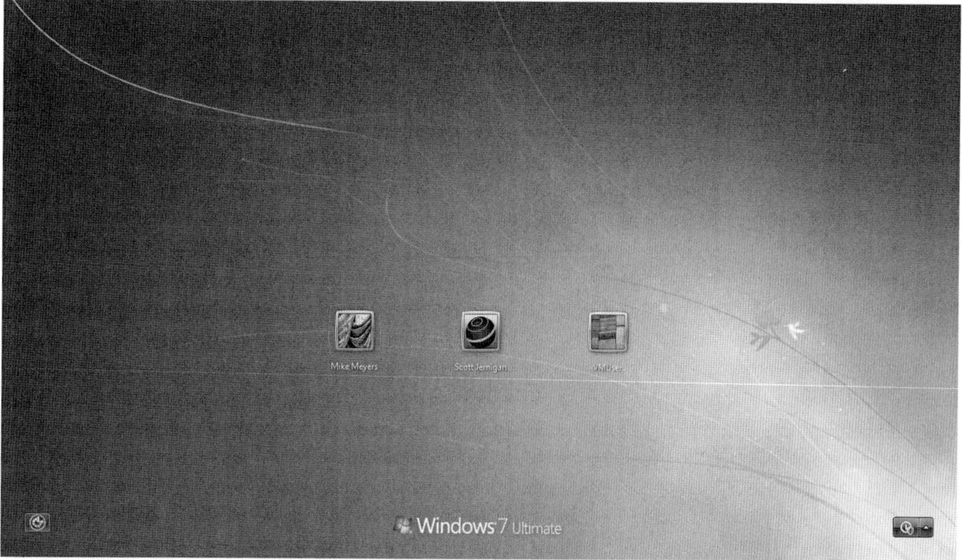

Figure 17-24 Login screen

Several issues can create a scenario where Windows fails to start normally. Windows can hang because of buggy device drivers or Registry problems. Even autoloading programs can cause Windows to hang on load. The first step in troubleshooting these sorts of scenarios is to use one of the Advanced Startup options (covered later in the chapter) to try to get past the hang spot and into Windows.

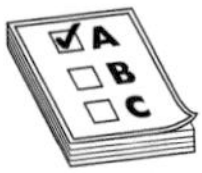

EXAM TIP If faced with a scenario where the GUI files have become corrupted, what CompTIA calls a "Missing Graphical Interface" problem, your only choices are to restore from backup or rebuild from the installation media or a recovery drive.

Device Drivers

Device driver problems that stop Windows from loading look pretty sad. Figure 17-25 shows a Windows *Stop error*, better known as the *Blue Screen of Death (BSoD)*. The BSoD only appears when something causes an error from which Windows cannot recover. The BSoD is not limited to device driver problems, but device drivers are one of the reasons you'll see the BSoD.

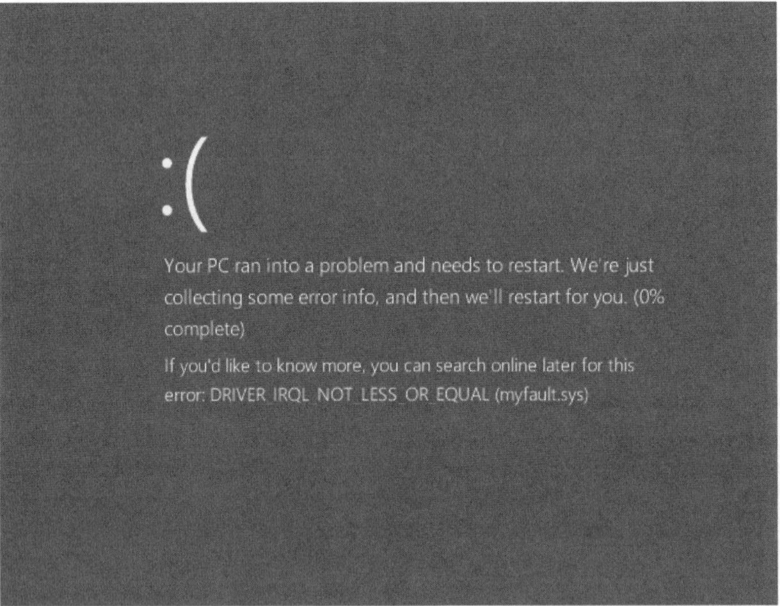

Figure 17-25 BSoD in Windows 8.1

Whenever faced with a scenario where you get a BSoD, read what it says. Windows BSoDs tell you the name of the file that caused the problem and usually suggests a course of action. Once in a while these are helpful.

BSoD problems due to device drivers almost always take place immediately after you've installed a new device and rebooted. Take out the device and reboot. If Windows loads properly, head over to the manufacturer's Web site. A new device producing this type of problem is a serious issue that should have been caught before the device was released. In many cases, the manufacturer will have updated drivers available for download or will recommend a replacement device.

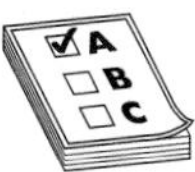

EXAM TIP Viruses can cause Windows to fail to start normally or make it appear to be missing. A nasty one running around recently, for example, caused what appeared to be a BSoD warning of imminent hard drive controller failure. Even after getting rid of the virus, Windows appeared devoid of any graphical elements at all: no Start button, icons, or files even in Computer. That's because the virus had changed the attributes of every file and folder on the hard drive to hidden! See Chapter 28, "Securing Computers," for recovery techniques for virus-attacked computers.

The second indication of a device problem that manifests during the final part of startup is a freeze-up: the Windows startup screen just stays there and you never get a chance to log on. If this happens, try one of the Advanced Startup Options, covered following the Registry.

Device drivers can trip up Linux systems too, causing their own form of BSoD, called a *kernel panic*. The fix follows along the same lines as for Windows—go to the manufacturer's Web site and find updated drivers or *kernel modules* (code that gets inserted directly into the kernel).

Note that failing hardware can create kernel panic in Mac OS X and Linux and bring the system down. Kernel panic in Mac OS X is demonstrated by a black or gray screen of death and is, I assure you, a terrifying moment to experience.

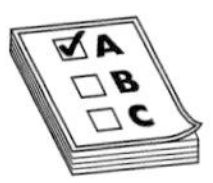

EXAM TIP The spinning pinwheel of death that you see on Mac OS X systems indicates an unresponsive system. These often get lumped into the same discussion as BSoDs and kernel panic, but the pinwheel is not nearly as bad.

Registry

The Registry files load every time the computer boots. Windows does a pretty good job of protecting your Registry files from corruption, but from time to time something may slip by Windows and it will attempt to load a bad Registry. These errors may show up as BSoDs that say "Registry File Failure" or text errors that say "Windows could not start." Whatever the case, when you run into these sorts of scenarios, you need to restore a good Registry copy. Depending on your Windows version, the best way to do this is the Last Known Good Configuration boot option (see the upcoming section). If that fails, you can restore an earlier version of the Registry through Windows RE.

Replacing the Registry

Windows keeps a regular backup of the Registry handy in case you need to overwrite a corrupted Registry. By default, the task runs every 10 days, so that's as far back as you would lose if you replaced the current Registry with the automatically backed-up files. Of course, it would be better if you kept regular backups too, but at least the damage would be limited. You can find the backed-up Registry files in \Windows\System32\config\RegBack (see Figure 17-26).

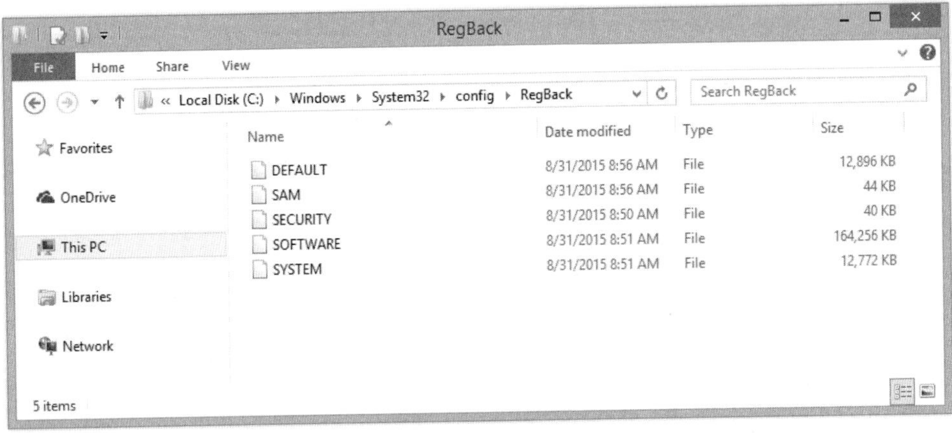

Figure 17-26 The backed-up Registry files located in the RegBack folder

To replace the Registry, boot to the Windows installation media to access Windows RE and get to the Command Prompt shell. Run the **reg** command to get to a reg prompt. From there, you have numerous commands to deal with the Registry. The simplest is probably the *copy* command. You know the location of the backed-up Registry files. Just copy the files to the location of the main Registry files—up one level in the tree under the \config folder.

Advanced Startup Options

If Windows fails to start up normally, press F5 at boot-up to boot directly to Safe Mode. Or, in Windows Vista or Windows 7, you can use the Windows *Advanced Startup Options* menu to discover the cause. To get to this menu, restart the computer and press F8 after the POST messages but before the Windows logo screen appears.

NOTE Windows 8/8.1/10 have the Advanced Startup Options, but to get there requires weird steps that will never happen in normal computing. For all intents and purposes, therefore, ignore Advanced Startup Options in Windows versions beyond Windows 7. Work with other tools.

Safe Mode (All Versions)

Safe Mode starts up Windows but loads only very basic, non-vendor-specific drivers for mouse, 800 × 600 (Vista/7) or 1024 × 768 (8/8.1) resolution monitor, keyboard, mass storage, and system services (see Figure 17-27).

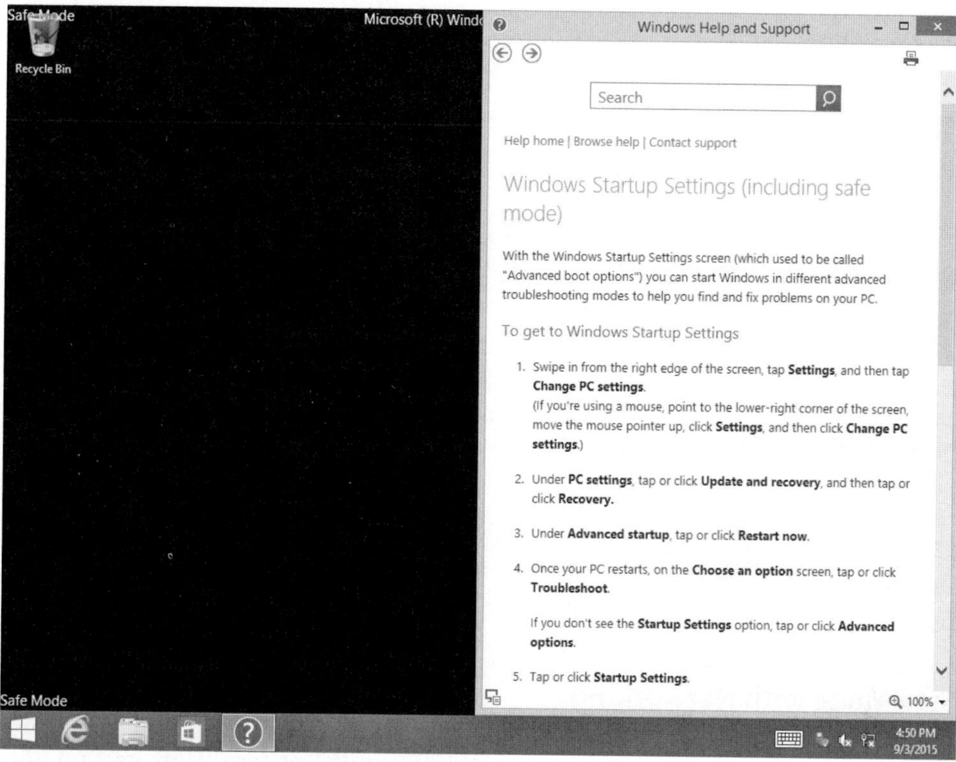

Figure 17-27 Safe Mode

Once in Safe Mode, you can use tools such as Device Manager to locate and correct the source of the problem. When you use Device Manager in Safe Mode, you can access the properties for all the devices, even those that are not working in Safe Mode. The status displayed for the device is the status for a normal startup. Even the network card will show as enabled. You can disable any suspect device or perform other tasks, such as removing or updating drivers. If a problem with a device driver is preventing the operating system from starting normally, check Device Manager for warning icons that indicate an unknown device.

There is no safety or repair feature in any version of Windows that makes the OS boot to Safe Mode automatically. In most cases, Windows automatically booting to Safe Mode indicates that someone has set the System Configuration utility to force Windows to do so. Type **msconfig** at the Start | Search or Start | Run option and press ENTER to open the System Configuration utility, and then deselect the Safe boot or Boot to Safe Mode check box (see Figure 17-28).

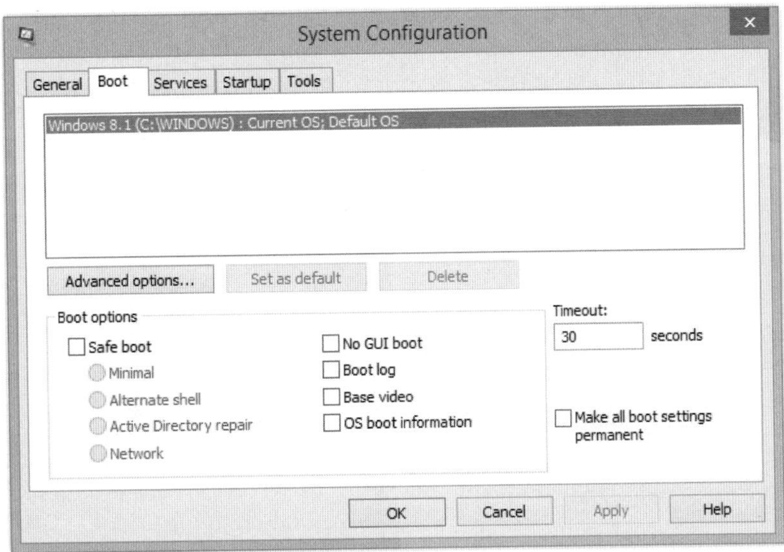

Figure 17-28 Uncheck Safe boot

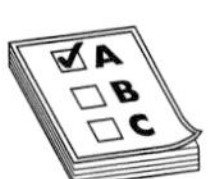

EXAM TIP The CompTIA A+ 902 exam objectives mention a scenario where Windows boots directly to Safe Mode. This can only happen if a tech specifically makes a change to the System Configuration utility.

Safe Mode with Networking

This mode is identical to plain Safe Mode except that you get network support. I use this mode to test for a problem with network drivers. If Windows won't start up normally but does start up in Safe Mode, I reboot into Safe Mode with Networking. If it fails to start up with Networking, the problem is a network driver. I reboot back to Safe Mode, open Device Manager, and start disabling network components, beginning with the network adapter.

Safe Mode with Command Prompt

When you start Windows in this mode, rather than loading the GUI desktop, it loads the command prompt (cmd.exe) as the shell to the operating system after you log on. From here you can run any of the commands you learned about in Chapter 16, plus a lot of utilities as well. Error-checking runs fine as chkdsk, for example. Disk Defragmenter probably runs even faster when you type **defrag** followed by a drive letter at the command prompt than it does from the graphical version of the tool.

Safe Mode with Command Prompt is a handy option to remember if the desktop does not display at all, which, after you have eliminated video drivers, can be caused by corruption of the explorer.exe program. From the command prompt, you can delete

the corrupted version of explorer.exe and copy in an undamaged version. This requires knowing the command-line commands for navigating the directory structure, as well as knowing the location of the file you are replacing. Although Explorer is not loaded, you can load other GUI tools that don't depend on Explorer. All you have to do is enter the correct command. For instance, to load Event Viewer, type **eventvwr.msc** at the command line and press ENTER.

Enable Boot Logging

This option starts Windows normally and creates a log file of the drivers as they load into memory. The file is named Ntbtlog.txt and is saved in the %SystemRoot% folder. If the startup failed because of a bad driver, the last entry in this file may be the driver the OS was initializing when it failed.

Reboot and go into the WinRE. Use the tools there to read the boot log and disable or enable problematic devices or services.

Enable Low-Resolution Mode

Enable Low-resolution Mode starts Windows normally, but only loads a default VGA driver. If this mode works, it may mean you have a bad driver, or it may mean you are using the correct video driver but it is configured incorrectly (perhaps with the wrong refresh rate and/or resolution). Whereas Safe Mode loads a generic VGA driver, this mode loads the driver Windows is configured to use but starts it up in standard VGA mode rather than using the settings for which it is configured. After successfully starting in this mode, open the Display applet and change the settings.

Last Known Good Configuration

When Windows' startup fails immediately after installing a new driver but before you have logged on again, try the *Last Known Good Configuration* option. This option applies specifically to new device drivers that cause failures on reboot.

Directory Services Restore Mode

The title says it all here; this option only applies to Active Directory domain controllers, and only Windows Server versions can be domain controllers. I have no idea why Microsoft includes this option. If you choose it, you simply boot into Safe Mode.

Debugging Mode (All Versions)

If you select this choice, Windows starts in kernel debug mode. It's a super-techie thing to do, and I doubt that even über techs do debug mode anymore. To do this, you have to connect the computer you are debugging to another computer via a serial connection, and as Windows starts up, a debug of the kernel is sent to the second computer, which must also be running a debugger program.

Disable Automatic Restart on System Failure

Sometimes a BSoD will appear at startup, causing your computer to spontaneously reboot. That's all well and good, but if it happens too quickly, you might not be able

to read the BSoD to see what caused the problem. Selecting *Disable automatic restart on system failure* from the Advanced Startup Options menu stops the computer from rebooting on Stop errors. This gives you the opportunity to write down the error and hopefully find a fix.

Disable Driver Signature Enforcement

Windows requires that all very low-level drivers (kernel drivers) must have a Microsoft driver signature. If you are using an older driver to connect to your hard drive controller or some other low-level feature, you must use this option to get Windows to load the driver. Hopefully you will always check your motherboard and hard drives for Windows compatibility and never have to use this option.

Start Windows Normally

This choice will simply start Windows normally, without rebooting. You already rebooted to get to this menu. Select this if you changed your mind about using any of the other exotic choices.

Reboot (All Versions)

This choice will actually do a soft reboot of the computer.

Return to OS Choices Menu

On computers with multiple operating systems, you get an OS Choices menu to select which OS to load. If you load Windows and press F8 to get the Advanced Startup Options menu, you'll see this option. Choosing it returns you to the OS Choices menu, from which you can select the operating system to load.

Troubleshooting Tools

Once you're able to load into Windows, whether through Safe Mode or one of the other options, the whole gamut of Windows tools is available for you. In the previous scenario where a bad device driver caused the startup problems, for example, you can open Device Manager and begin troubleshooting just as you've learned in previous chapters. If you suspect some service or Registry issue caused the problem, head on over to Event Viewer and see what sort of logon events have happened recently. Let's go there first.

Event Viewer

When you get to the Desktop, one of the first tools you should use is Event Viewer to see what's causing the problems on your computer. *Event Viewer* is Windows' default tattletale program, spilling the beans about a number of interesting happenings on the system. With a little tweaking, Event Viewer turns into a virtual recording of anything you might ever want to know about on your system.

Keep in mind that Event Viewer is a powerful tool for more than just troubleshooting Windows—it's a powerful tool for security as well, as you'll see in Chapter 28. But for now let's examine Event Viewer to see what we can do with this amazing utility.

Opening Event Viewer (System and Security | Administrative Tools | Event Viewer) shows you the default interface (see Figure 17-29).

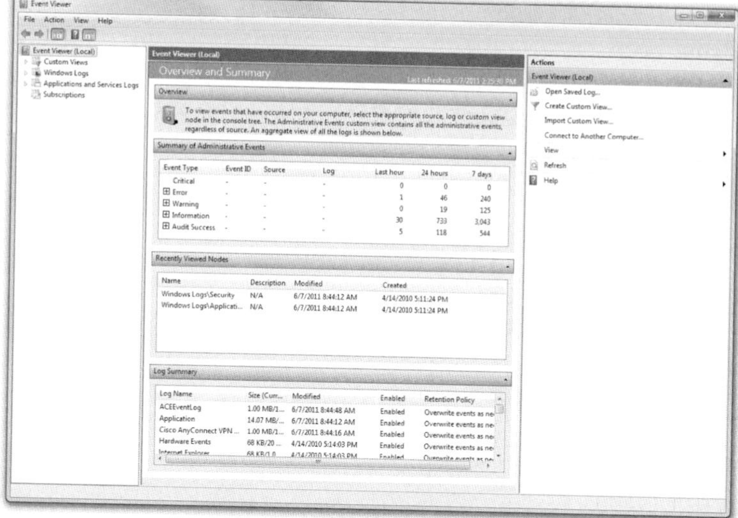

Figure 17-29
Windows 7 Event Viewer default screen

Note the four main bars in the center pane: Overview, Summary of Administrative Events, Recently Viewed Nodes, and Log Summary. Pay special attention to the Summary of Administrative Events. It breaks down the events into different levels: Critical, Error, Warning, Information, Audit Success, and Audit Failure. Figure 17-30 shows a typical Summary with the Warning Events opened. You can then click any event to see a dialog box describing the event in detail. Microsoft refers to these as *Views*.

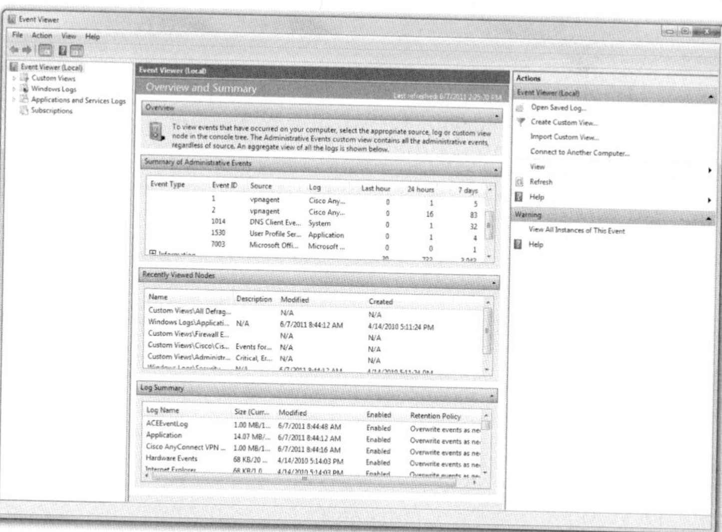

Figure 17-30
Warning Events open

Windows Event Viewer still includes the classic logs (Application, Security, and System) but leans heavily on Views to show you the contents of the logs. Views filter existing log files, making them great for custom reports using beginning/end times, levels of errors, and more. You can use the built-in Views or easily create custom Views, as shown in Figure 17-31.

NOTE By default, Event Viewer stores logs as .evtx files in the C:\Windows\System32\winevt\Logs folder.

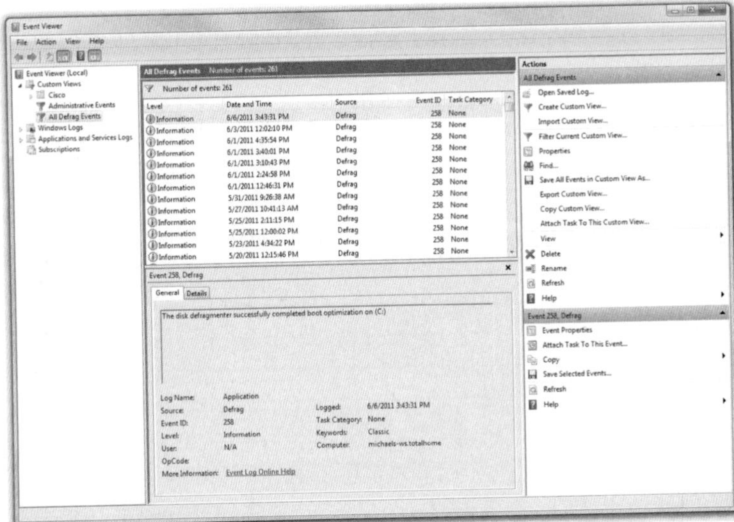

Figure 17-31 Created custom Views

You record all data to logs. Logs in Windows have limitations, such as a maximum size, a location, and a behavior for when they get too big (such as overwrite the log or make an error). Figure 17-32 shows a typical Log Properties dialog box in Windows 7. Note that only users with Administrator privileges can make changes to log files in Event Viewer.

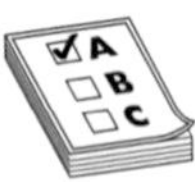

EXAM TIP If you run into a scenario where a device has failed and this created problems with Windows' startup, you would turn to the primary Windows tool for hardware issues: Device Manager. We've covered Device Manager in chapters specific to hardware, so there's no need to go into it yet again here.

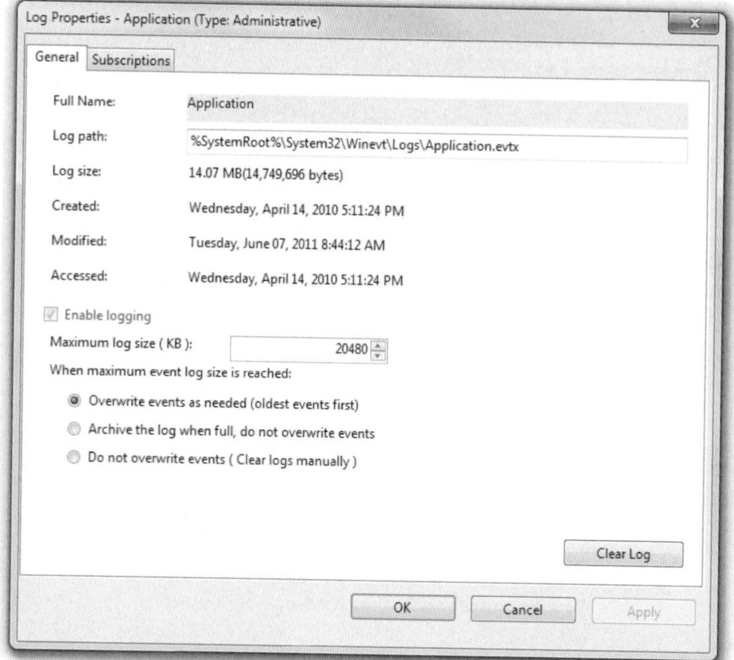

Figure 17-32 Log Properties dialog box in Windows 7

Autoloading Programs

Windows loves to autoload programs so they start at boot. Most of the time this is an incredibly handy option, used by every Windows PC in existence. The problem with autoloading programs is that when one of them starts behaving badly, you need to shut off that program! Use the System Configuration utility (Windows Vista/7) or Task Manager (8/8.1/10) to temporarily stop programs from autoloading. If you want to make the program stop forever, go into the program and find a load on startup option (see Figure 17-33).

NOTE If you can't find a load on startup option in your application, run the Registry Editor and go to where most applications autoload:

HKEY_LOCAL_MACHINE\SOFTWARE\Microsoft\Windows\CurrentVersion\Run

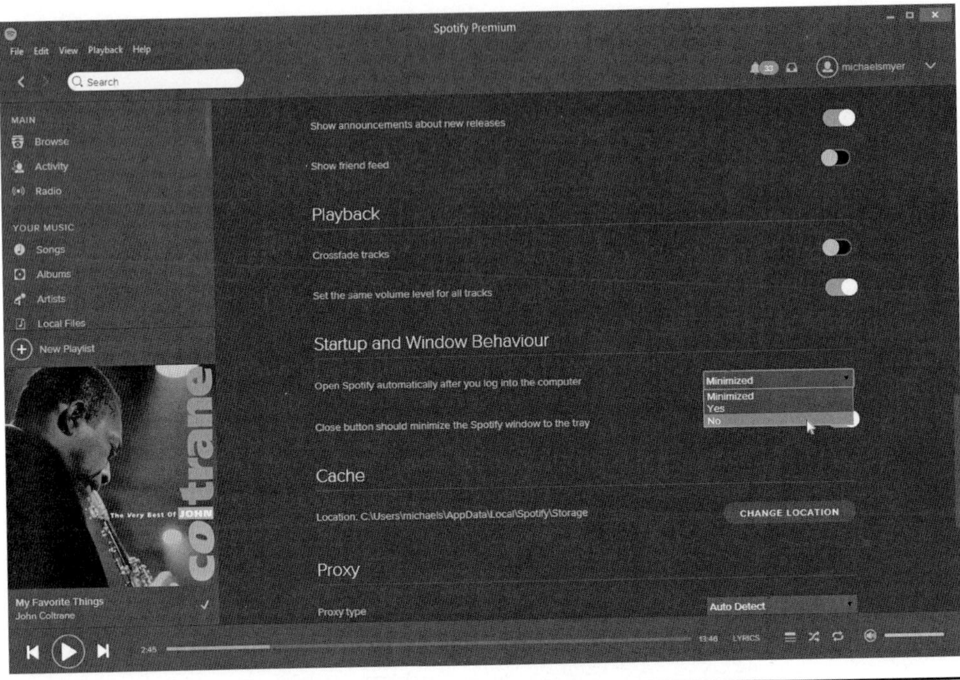

Figure 17-33 Typical load on startup option

Services

Windows loads a number of services as it starts. In a scenario where any critical service fails to load, Windows tells you at this point with an error message. The important word here is *critical*. Windows will not report *all* service failures at this point. If a service that is less than critical to Windows doesn't start, the OS usually waits until you try to use a program that needs that service before it prompts you with an error message (see Figure 17-34).

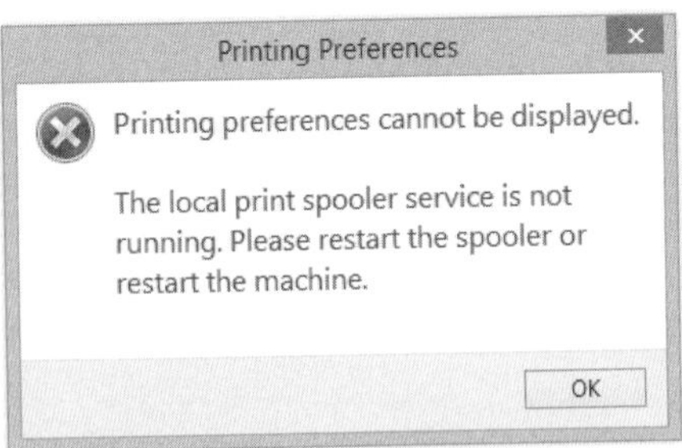

Figure 17-34 Service error

To work with your system's services, go to the Control Panel | Administrative Tools | Services and verify that the service you need is running. If not, turn it on. Also notice that each service has a Startup Type—Automatic, Manual, or Disabled—that defines when it starts. It's very common to find that a service has been set to Manual when it needs to be set to Automatic so that it starts when Windows boots (see Figure 17-35).

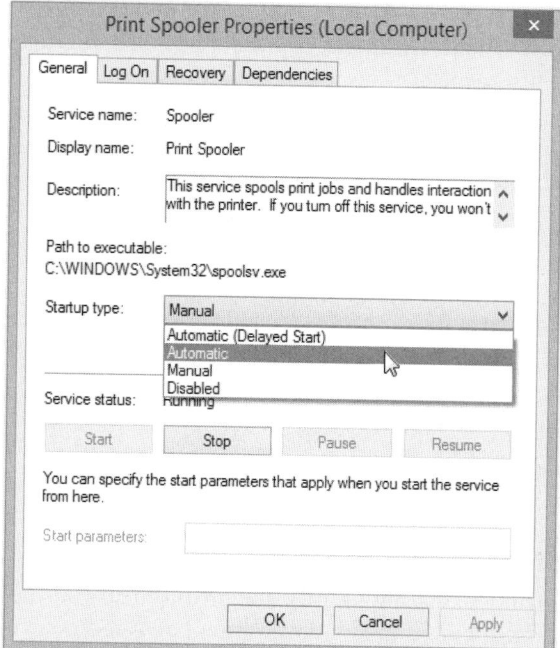

Figure 17-35 Autostarting a service

Task Manager and Command-Line Options

Task Manager is a great place to go to shut down errant processes that won't otherwise close properly. You can quickly close a program that is hogging CPU resources, for example, by right-clicking on the program under the Processes tab and selecting End Process. Task Manager enables you to see all applications or programs currently running or to close an application that has stopped working. You remember how to get to it, right? Press CTRL-SHIFT-ESC to open it directly or CTRL-ALT-DELETE to get to a list of action items, one of which opens Task Manager.

If you're unable to get to Task Manager or are comfortable with the command line, you can get to a command prompt (like in the Windows Recovery Environment) and type the command **tasklist** to find the names and process IDs of all the running processes. You can then run **taskkill** to end any process either by filename or by process ID. If you're in the Windows PowerShell, the commands are **tasklist** and **kill**.

System Files

Windows lives on dynamic link library (DLL) files. Almost every program used by Windows—and certainly all of the important ones—call to DLL files to do most of the heavy lifting that makes Windows work.

Windows protects all of the critical DLL files very carefully, but once in a while you may get an error saying Windows can't load a particular DLL. Although rare, the core system files that make up Windows itself may become corrupted, preventing Windows from starting properly. You usually see something like "Error loading XXXX.DLL," or sometimes a program you need simply won't start when you double-click its icon.

In these cases, the tool you need is the *System File Checker* that you learned about in Chapter 16. Use it to check and replace a number of critical files, including the ever-important DLL cache.

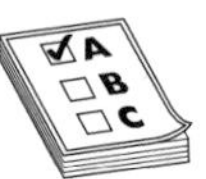

EXAM TIP Mac OS X offers a surprisingly powerful tool for application problems called Force Quit. Press the option + command + esc keyboard combination to access the Force Quit menu. It'll show you every running application.

System Restore

System Restore is the final step in recovering from a major Windows meltdown. Earlier in the chapter, you learned that you can use System Restore from the Windows Recovery Environment, but don't forget that you can also use restore points from within Windows. Follow the process explained in Chapter 15, "Maintaining and Optimizing Operating Systems."

More Control Panel Tools

Windows includes amazing utilities designed to help you support your system. Many of these tools first appeared in Windows Vista, but Windows 7 either refined them or made them easily accessible. Windows 8 and 8.1 support most of these tools as well. These Control Panel tools perform a number of different jobs, from telling you what's happening on the system to showing you how well a system's performance stacks up to other computers.

Problem Reports and Solutions (Windows Vista) and Action Center (Windows 7/8/8.1/10) centralize a lot of useful information about the status of your computer. The Performance and Information Tools applet tells you just how powerful your computer really is. Let's take a look at this crazy mixture of utilities in alphabetical order and explore the scenarios appropriate for their use.

Problem Reports and Solutions

If a computer is having a problem, wouldn't it be great to tell the people who are in charge of the program you're having that problem so they can fix it? That's the idea behind *Windows Error Reporting*. There's a good chance that, like many users, you've run into errors that look something like Figure 17-36.

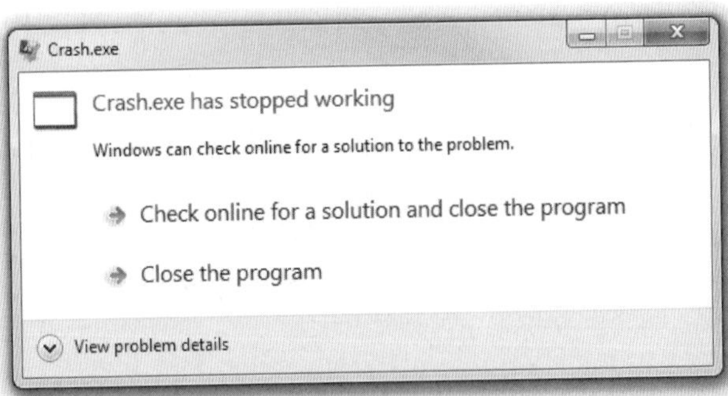

Figure 17-36 Crash.exe has stopped working.

The problem with these errors is that, while they might help Microsoft, they traditionally do little to help us fix the computer. Windows Error Reporting was a one-way tool, until Microsoft upgraded it with Vista to a much more powerful, two-way tool that gives developers a way to give you ways to fix computers.

The *Problem Reports* (called Problem Reports and Solutions in Vista) Control Panel applet in Windows lists all Windows Error Reporting issues (plus a few easy-to-check items like firewall and antimalware status), as shown in Figure 17-37. You click on the solution and, in many cases, the problem is fixed.

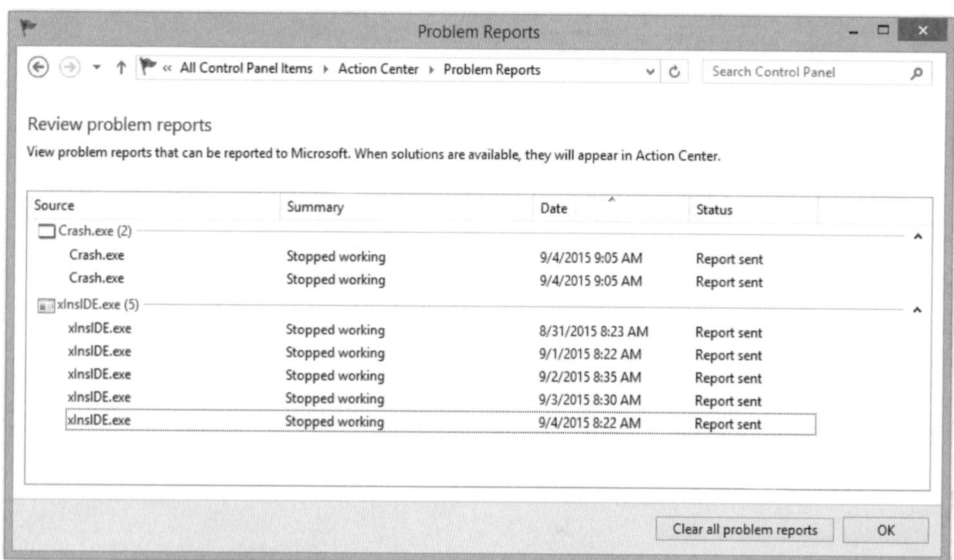

Figure 17-37 Problem Reports

Action Center

Problem Reports and Solutions is a good tool with some rough edges. For example, once you fix a problem, you have to delete the problem from the list manually. Also, there are a number of issues that don't have anything to do with Windows Error Reporting that just make sense to combine, such as Microsoft Troubleshooter and System Restore. Microsoft realized that they could organize the solutions to make it easier for you to choose what you wanted to do. *Action Center* in Windows 7/8/8.1 provides a one-page aggregation of event messages, warnings, and maintenance messages that, for many techs, might quickly replace Event Viewer as the first place to look for problems. Unlike Event Viewer, Action Center separates issues into two sections, Security and Maintenance, making it easier to review a system's issues quickly (see Figure 17-38).

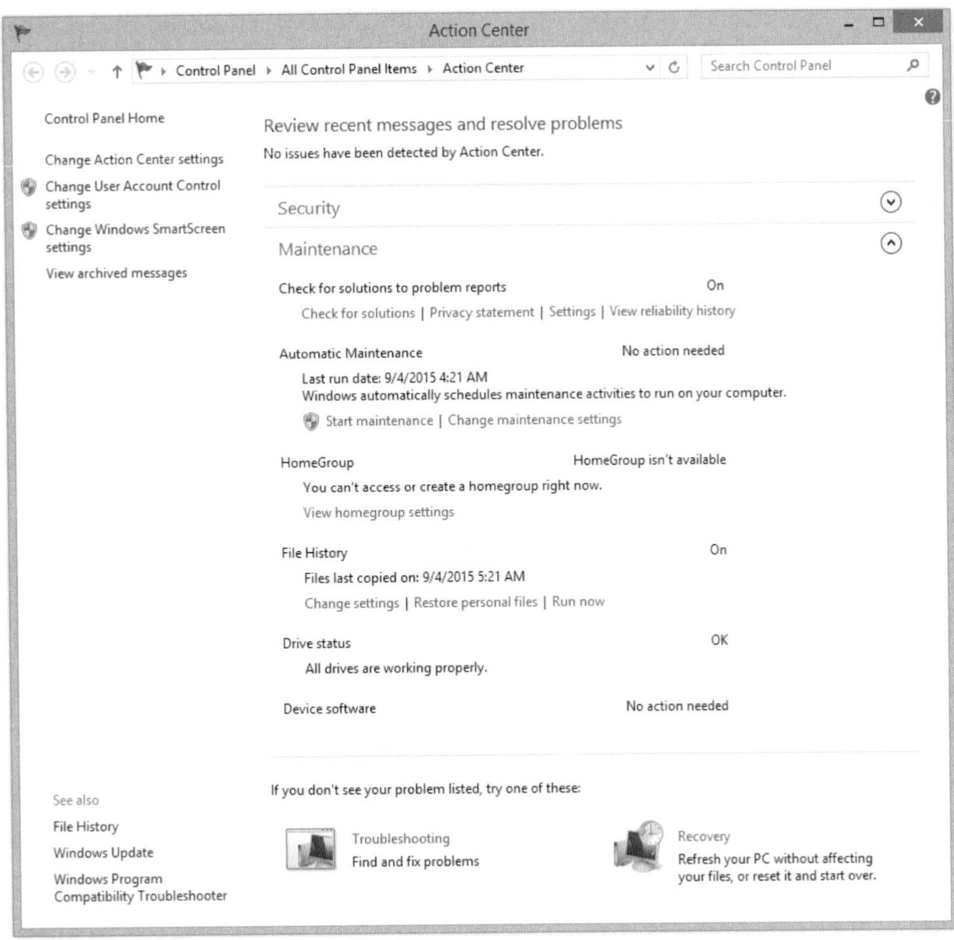

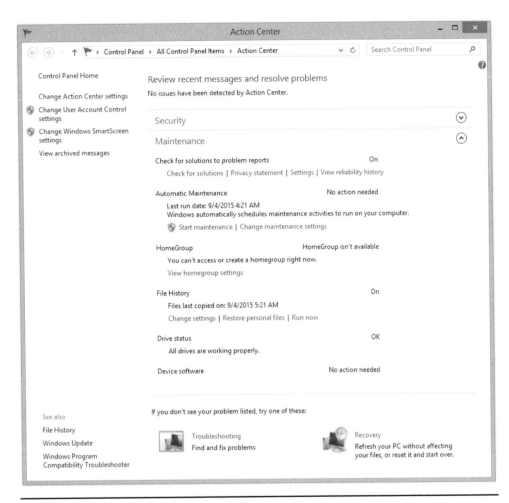

Figure 17-38 Action Center

Action Center only compiles the information, taking data from well-known utilities such as Event Viewer, Windows Update, Windows Firewall, and UAC and placing it into an easy-to-read format. If you wish, you can tell Action Center where to look for information by selecting Change Action Center settings (see Figure 17-39).

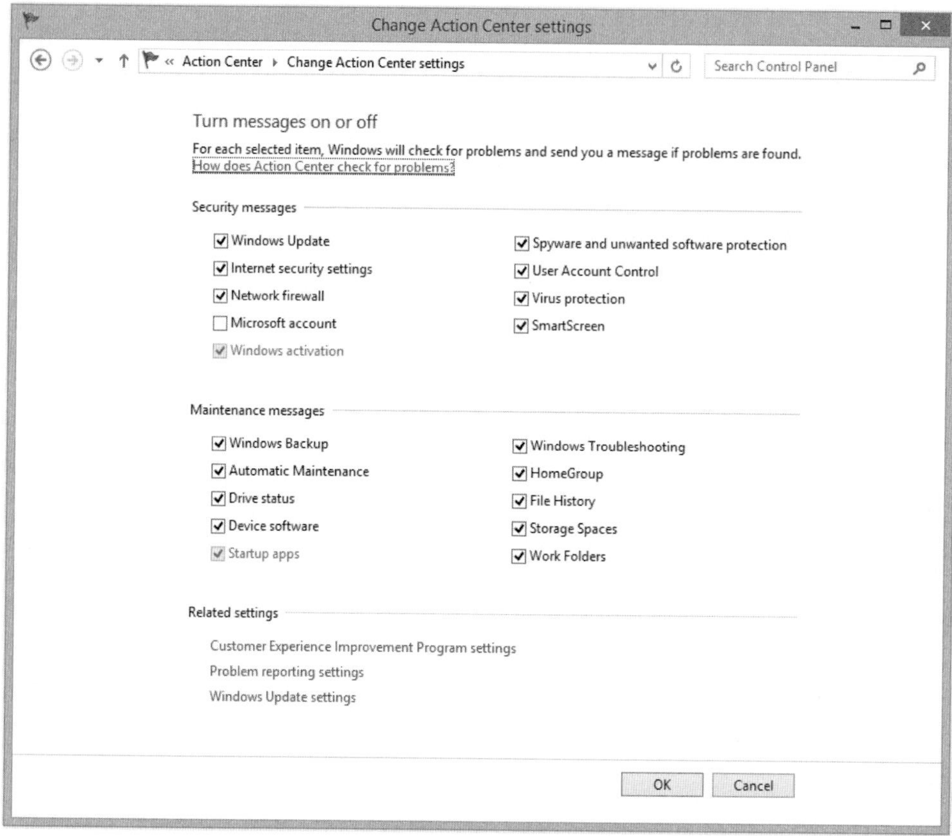

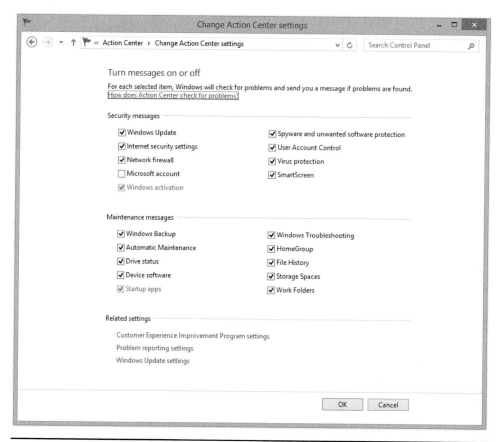

Figure 17-39 Change Action Center settings

If you see a problem, Action Center includes plenty of links to get you to the utility you need. From the Action Center applet, you get direct links to some or all of the following tools:

- UAC settings
- Performance Information and Tools
- Backup and Restore
- Windows Update
- Troubleshooting Wizard
- System Restore
- Recovery

Although Action Center does little more than reproduce information from other utilities, it makes finding problems quick and easy. Combined with quick links to most of the utilities you'll need, Action Center should become your base of operations when something goes wrong on your Windows 7/8/8.1/10 PC.

Performance Information and Tools

Techs must often answer difficult questions like "Why is my machine running so slowly?" Before Windows Vista, we could only use Performance Monitor baselines or third-party tools. Neither of these options worked very well. Baselines required you to choose the right counters—choosing the wrong counters made useless and sometimes even distracting logs. Third-party tools often measured one aspect of a system (like video quality) very well but didn't help much when you wanted an overview of your system.

This changed with Microsoft's introduction of the Performance Information and Tools Control Panel applet (see Figure 17-40).

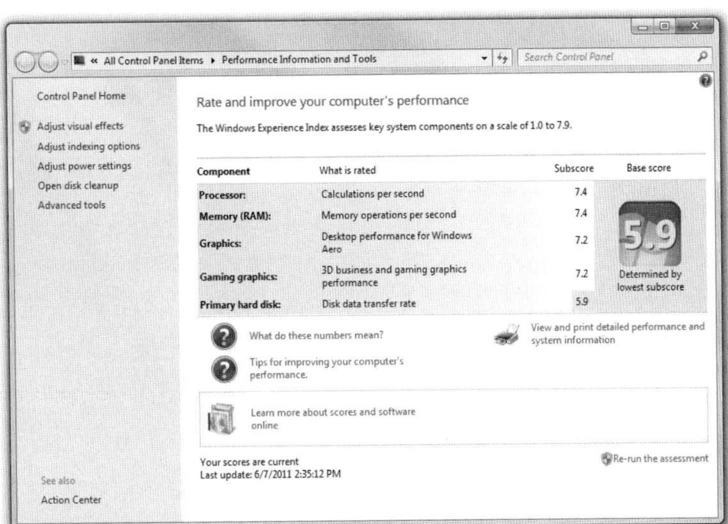

Figure 17-40 Performance Information and Tools

The *Performance Information and Tools* applet doesn't fix anything. It just provides a relative feel for how your computer stacks up against other systems using the Windows Experience Index. Windows bases this on five components:

- **Processor** Calculations per second
- **Memory (RAM)** Memory operations per second
- **Graphics** Desktop performance for Windows Aero
- **Gaming graphics** 3-D business and gaming graphics performance
- **Primary hard disk** Disk data transfer rate

Each component generates a subscore. These values range from 1 to 5.9 for Windows Vista and 1 to 7.9 for Windows 7/8. Microsoft determines the calculations that generate these numbers, so I don't know exactly what it takes to give, for example, a CPU a score of 6.1. Your system's Base score is based on the lowest subscore. Microsoft removed the Windows Experience Index and its Control Panel applet with the release of Windows 8.1.

The Performance Information and Tools applet won't fix anything, but it does tell you which component is the weakest link in overall performance.

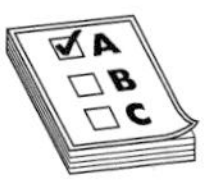

EXAM TIP You can't change a subscore in the Windows Experience Index without making some kind of hardware change.

Application Problems

Programmers want to write applications that work well, enable you to accomplish a specific task, and are good enough to earn your money. But PCs are complicated and programmers can't get it right every time for every combination of hardware and software.

Application problems show up in several ways. The typical scenario has the application failing to install or uninstall. Operating system version issues can cause compatibility problems. Another typical scenario is where an application tries to access a file and that file is either missing or won't open. The least common problems come from sloppy or poorly written code that causes the application or the operating system to crash. Finally, corrupted applications can corrupt data too, but Windows has tools for recovering previous versions of files and folders.

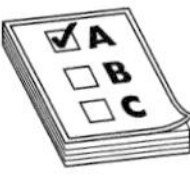

EXAM TIP Every once in a while you'll get an application that reports an error if the clock settings in Windows don't match. This can cause the application not to run. Likewise, if a computer has a failing battery and is offline for a while, the BIOS time and settings will be off. You'll get a brief "error" noting the change when you connect that computer to a network timeserver. This is both a hardware issue (failing battery) and an application issue. When the Windows clock resets, so do the BIOS time and settings.

Application Installation Problems

Almost all Windows programs come with some form of handy installer. When you insert the disc or USB drive, Windows knows to look for a text file called autorun.inf that tells it which file to run off the disc or USB drive, usually setup.exe. If you download the application, you'll need to double-click it to start the installation. Either way, you run the installer and the program runs. It almost couldn't be simpler.

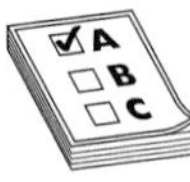

EXAM TIP The fact that Windows looks for the autorun.inf file by default when you insert a disc or USB drive creates a security issue. Someone could put a malicious program on some form of media and write an autorun.inf file to point to the virus. Insert the media and boom! There goes your clean PC. Of course, if someone has access to your computer and is fully logged on with administrator privileges, then you've already lost everything, with or without a media-born program, so this "big" security issue is pretty much not an issue at all. Nevertheless, you should know that to turn off this behavior in Windows requires opening the Registry Editor and changing up to six different settings.

A well-behaved program should always make itself easy to uninstall as well. In most cases, you should see an uninstallation option in the program's Start menu area; and in all cases (unless you have an application with a badly configured installer), the application should appear in either the Add/Remove Programs applet or the Programs and Features applet (see Figure 17-41) in the Control Panel.

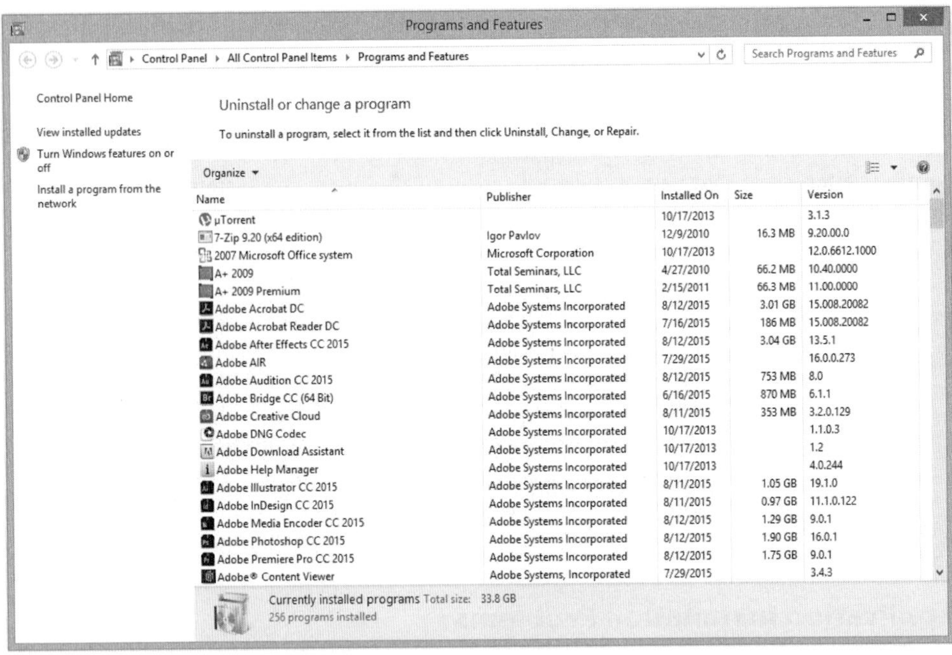

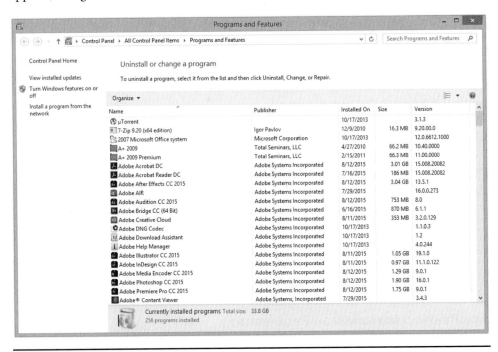

Figure 17-41 Programs and Features Control Panel applet

NOTE Remember that you need local administrator privileges to install applications in all versions of Windows.

Programs that fail to install usually aren't to blame in and of themselves. In most cases, a problem with Windows prevents them from installing, most notably the lack of some other program that the application needs so it can operate. One of the best examples of this is the popular Microsoft .NET Framework. .NET is an extension to the Windows operating system that includes support for a number of features, particularly powerful interface tools and flexible database access. If a program is written to take advantage of .NET, .NET must itself be installed. In most cases, if .NET is missing, the application should try to install it at the same time it is installed, but you can't count on this. If .NET is missing or if the version of .NET you are using is too old (there have been a number of .NET versions since it came out in 2002), you can get some of the most indecipherable errors in the history of Windows applications.

Figure 17-42 shows one such example in Windows 7 where the VMware vSphere client fails due to the wrong .NET version. Too bad the error doesn't give you any clues!

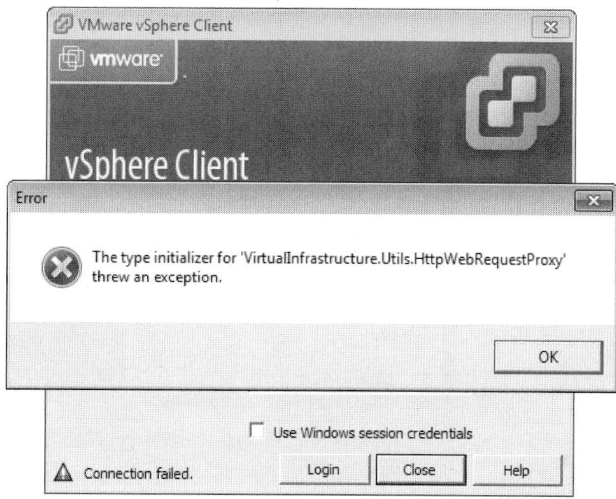

Figure 17-42 .NET error

These types of errors invariably require you to go online and do Web searches, using the application name and the error. No matter how bad the error, someone else has already suffered from the same problem. The trick is to find out what they did to get around it.

Problems with Uninstalling

The single biggest problem with uninstalling is that people try to uninstall without administrator privileges. If you try to uninstall and get an error, log back on as an administrator and you should be fine. Don't forget you can right-click on most uninstallation menu options on the Programs menu and select *Run as administrator* to switch to administrator privileges (see Figure 17-43).

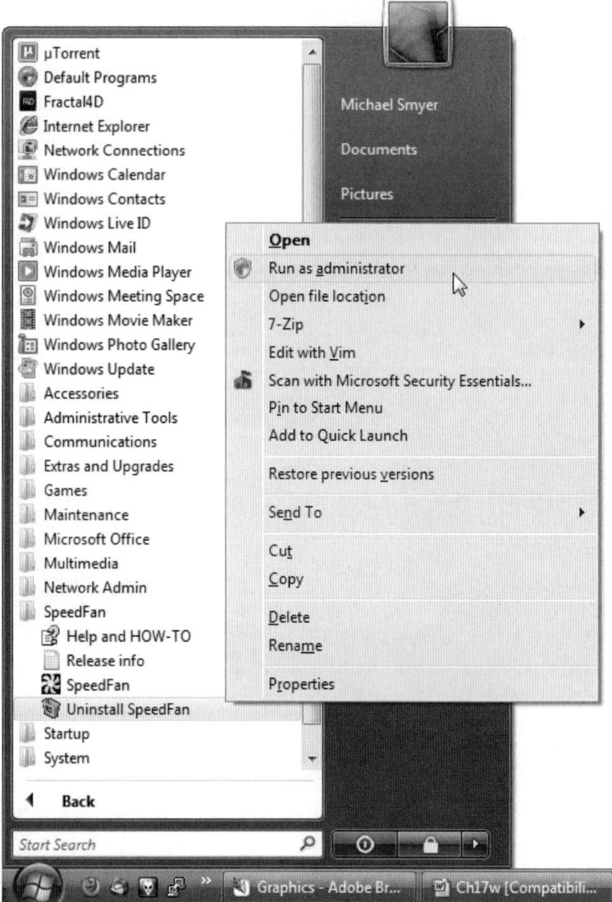

Figure 17-43 Selecting Run as administrator from the context menu

Compatibility

Most applications are written with the most recent version of Windows in mind, but as Windows versions change over time, older programs have difficulty running in more recent Windows versions. In some cases, such as the jump from Windows 7 to Windows 8, the changes are generally minor enough to cause few if any compatibility problems. In other cases, say a program written back when Windows XP reigned supreme, the underpinnings of the OS differ enough that you have to perform certain steps to ensure that the older programs run. Windows provides various different forms of *compatibility modes* to support older applications.

Windows handles compatibility using the aptly named Compatibility tab (see Figure 17-44) in every executable program's Properties dialog box (right-click on the executable file and click Properties). Select the version of Windows you want Windows to emulate and click OK; in many cases that is all you need to do to make that older program work (see Figure 17-45).

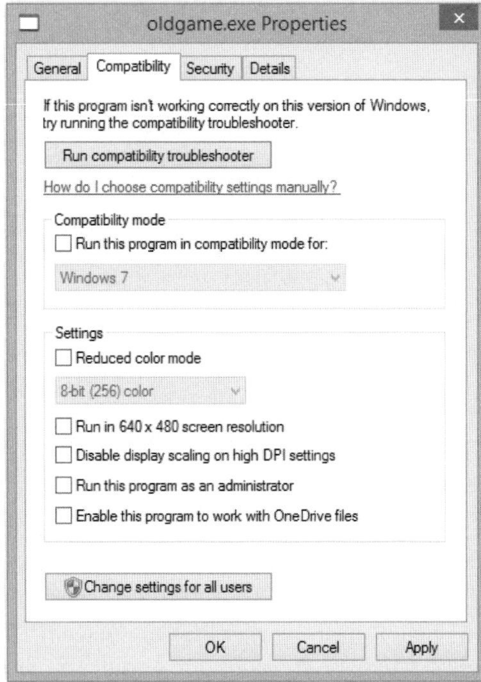

Figure 17-44 Windows 8.1 Compatibility tab

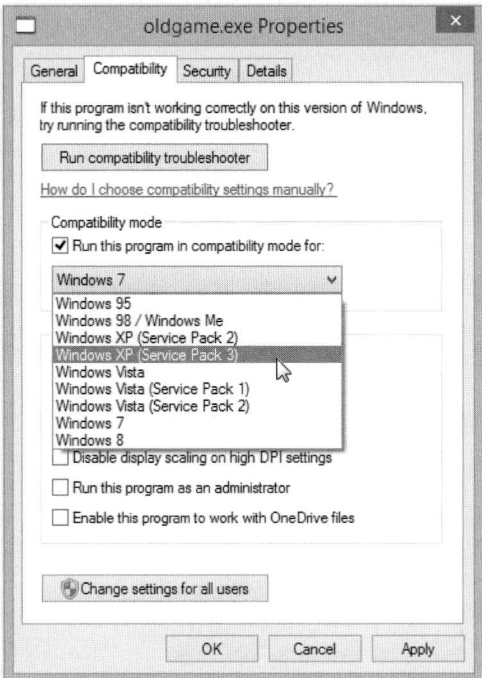

Figure 17-45 Compatibility mode options in Windows 8.1

You can also set other settings on the Compatibility tab, such as the following located under Display settings in the various versions of Windows:

- **Reduced color mode** Many old Windows programs were designed to run in 256 colors. Later versions of Windows that support more colors can confuse these older programs.
- **Run in 640 × 480 screen resolution** A few (badly written) older programs assume the screen to be at 640 × 480 resolution. This setting enables them to work.
- **Disable desktop composition (Windows Vista/7)** Disables all display features such as Aero. More advanced Windows display features often bog down older programs.
- **Disable display scaling on high DPI settings** Turns off automatic resizing of a program's windows if you're using any high DPI (dots per inch) font. This was added because many programs with large fonts would look bizarre if resized.
- **Run this program as an administrator** As stated, enables you to run the program as an administrator. If this option isn't available, log on as an administrator to see it.
- **Enable this program to work with OneDrive files (Windows 8/8.1/10)** This option provides networking support for older applications that might not understand the cloud aspects of file storage.
- **Change settings for all users** Clicking this button applies compatibility changes made to a program to every user account on the machine. Otherwise, the settings are only for the current user.

If you need to make things 100 percent compatible with Windows XP and you have Windows 7 (Pro, Ultimate, or Enterprise) on your system, you can download Windows XP Mode. *Windows XP Mode* is nothing more than a premade Windows XP SP3 virtual machine that runs under Microsoft's popular (and free) virtualization program, Windows Virtual PC (see Figure 17-46).

NOTE In April 2014 Microsoft stopped providing technical support for Windows XP, including the Windows XP Mode VM. This means that Windows XP Mode no longer gets security patches; use with caution!

The secret to using compatibility mode isn't much of a secret at all: if the program doesn't run, try a compatibly mode. If you want to be really careful, do a Web search on your application before you try to run it. Compatibility mode is a handy tool to get older applications running.

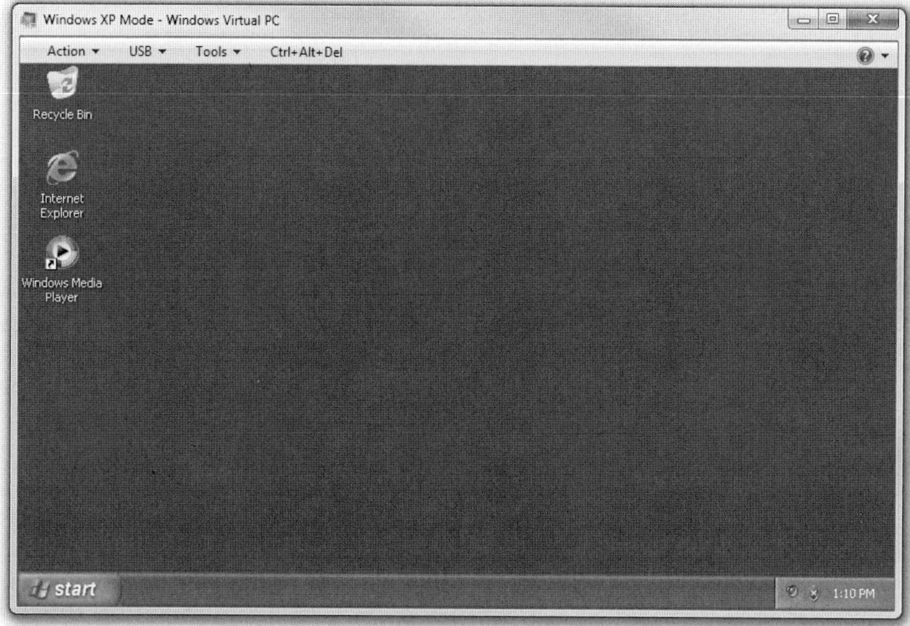

Figure 17-46 Windows XP Mode

Missing File or Incorrect File Version

An application may rely on other files—DLL files in particular—so sometimes the application's installer will replace common DLLs with its own version. Later applications might look for the earlier version of the DLL and fail when it's not found.

You'll experience this sort of scenario with error messages such as "missing DLL" or "cannot open file *xyz*." The easiest fix is to first try to reinstall the program, and check for any special instructions about versions of support files. Barring that, the usual second step for either issue is to perform an Internet search for the missing DLL or file that fails to open, along with the name of the program you're trying to use.

Crashing Programs

Occasionally, a program gets released that isn't ready for prime time and the error-prone code causes the application to crash or even causes the operating system to crash. I've seen this most often with games rushed to market near the winter holidays. The results of this rushed code can be pretty spectacular. You're right in the middle of a thrilling fight with the bad guy and then what happens? A crash to desktop (CTD).

Poorly written or buggy programs can have awful effects on you and your clients. Some of the scenarios caused by such programs are the computer locking up or unexpectedly shutting down. The system might spontaneously shut down and restart. That kind of improper shutdown can cause problems, especially to open files and folders.

The problem here is that all this crashing can be caused by hardware and driver problems, not just application problems. You've got to keep in mind all of these things as you approach troubleshooting a crash.

Here's a typical scenario where you need to troubleshoot broadly first. If you're playing a graphically intensive game that happens to be huge and takes up a lot of RAM, what could the problem be if the screen locks up and Windows locks up too? It could be that the program ran a routine that clashed with some other application or used a Windows feature improperly. It could be that the video card was marginal and failed when taxed too much. It could be that the system accessed a section of RAM that had gone bad.

In that same scenario, though, where the game runs but degrades the overall performance of Windows, what could cause that problem? That points more squarely at the application side of things rather than the hardware or drivers, especially if the computer successfully runs other programs. The bottom line with crash issues is to keep an open mind and not rule out anything without testing it first.

Volume Shadow Copy Service and System Protection

One of the big headaches with an application failure isn't so much the failure itself, but any data it may have corrupted. Sure, a good backup or a restore point might save you, but these can be a hassle. Unless the data was specifically saved (in the backup), there's a chance you don't have a backup in the first place. Microsoft came to your rescue in Windows Vista (Business, Ultimate, and Enterprise only) and Windows 7/8/8.1/10 (all editions) with a feature called System Protection.

This amazing feature is powered by Volume Shadow Copy Service (VSS). VSS enables the operating system to make backups of any file, even one that is in use. Windows uses VSS for its *System Protection* feature, enabling you to access previous versions of any data file or folder. Try right-clicking on any data file and selecting Restore previous versions, which opens the file's Properties dialog box with the Previous Versions tab displayed, as shown in Figure 17-47.

NOTE For some unknown reason, Microsoft removed the Previous Versions tab for local volumes in Windows 8/8.1 then added it back for Windows 10. If you need to restore a single file in Windows 8/8.1, you can set up and use the File History applet in Control Panel that you read about in Chapter 15. Just make sure you set it up before you need it!

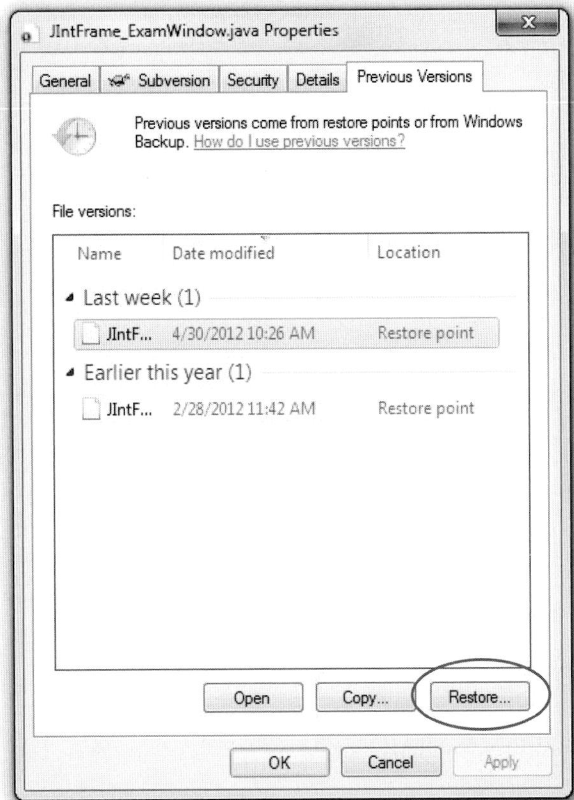

Figure 17-47 Previous Versions tab

If any of the following criteria are met, you will have at least one previous version in the list:

- The file or folder was backed up using the backup program.
- You created a restore point.
- The file or folder was changed.

You must make sure System Protection is enabled as well. Go to the System Protection tab in the System Properties dialog box (see Figure 17-48) to see if the feature is enabled (it should be running by default).

NOTE Keep in mind that System Protection doesn't have to be only for recovery of corrupted data files caused by bad applications. It's also a great tool to recover previous versions of files that users accidently overwrite.

The System Protection tab also enables you to load a restore point and to create restore points manually, very handy features.

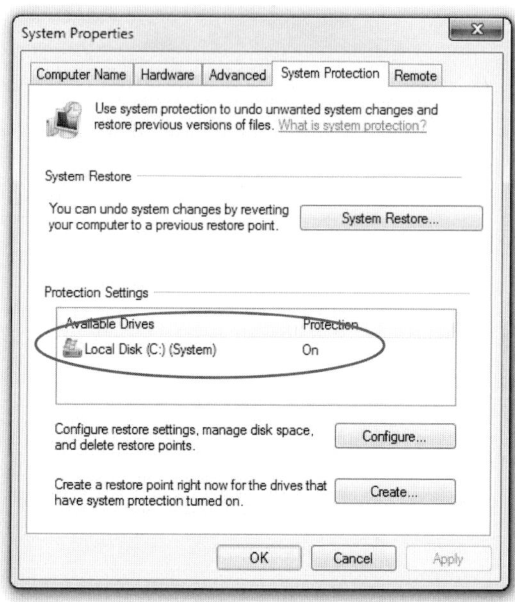

Figure 17-48 System Protection tab

System Protection falls in the category generically called *file recovery software*, and does an outstanding job. You can also get many third-party utilities that accomplish general file recovery. I've used Recuva from Piriform many times, for example, to get "deleted" data off a hard drive or RAID array.

Chapter Review

Questions

1. Which utility is useful in identifying a program that is hogging the processor?
   - A. Task Manager
   - B. Device Manager
   - C. Action Center
   - D. System Information
2. Which Windows utility uses points in time that enable you to return your system to a previous date and state?
   - A. System Configuration utility
   - B. Snapshot Manager
   - C. System Restore
   - D. GRUB or LILO

3. Scott's Windows 8.1 computer isn't performing as well as it once did. What option can he use to reset his system without deleting any personal files or changing any settings?
   - **A.** Reset your PC
   - **B.** Refresh your PC
   - **C.** Restore your computer
   - **D.** System Refresh
4. What can device drivers and failing hardware in Mac OS X and Linux cause?
   - **A.** Spinning windmill
   - **B.** Blue Screen of Death (BSoD)
   - **C.** Kernel panic
   - **D.** Terminal emulation
5. Which of the following points to a hardware or CMOS problem rather than an OS problem with a PC that won't boot.
   - **A.** A black screen with the error message "invalid boot disk"
   - **B.** A black screen with the error message "NTLDR Bad or Missing"
   - **C.** A black screen with the error message "Missing BOOT.INI"
   - **D.** A black screen with the error message "Invalid BCD"
6. John's computer has an error that says bootmgr is corrupted. What tool can he use to fix this problem?
   - **A.** bcdedit
   - **B.** chkdsk
   - **C.** diskpart
   - **D.** regedit
7. What does Microsoft call the 32- or 64-bit installation environment in Windows 7?
   - **A.** WinEE
   - **B.** WinPE
   - **C.** WinRE
   - **D.** WinVM
8. Ralph suspects a bad RAM stick is causing Windows to fail to boot. What default Windows tool can he use to check the RAM?
   - **A.** MEMMAKER
   - **B.** Memtest86+
   - **C.** Windows RAM Diagnostic Tool
   - **D.** Windows Memory Diagnostic Tool

9. Which of the following commands will repair a damaged master boot record in a Windows 8 PC?
   A. bootrec /fixboot
   B. bootrec /fixmbr
   C. fixboot
   D. fixmbr
10. Which feature in Windows 7 enables you to right-click a file or folder and restore previous versions of that file or folder?
   A. System Recovery Options
   B. System Protection
   C. File History
   D. Undelete

Review Answers

1. **A.** Task Manager will very quickly identify a program that is hogging the processor.
2. **C.** System Restore uses *restore points*—snapshots of a system at a given point of time—a quick and handy way to return your system to a previous state.
3. **B.** Refresh your PC in Windows 8 and later will rebuild Windows but preserve all user files and settings. Reset your PC removes all apps, programs, user files, user settings—and presents a fresh installation of Windows.
4. **C.** Device drivers and failing hardware can trip up Mac OS X and Linux and create kernel panic, which can bring the system down.
5. **A.** A black screen with an "invalid boot disk" error message points to a hardware or CMOS problem with a PC that won't boot.
6. **A.** The bcdedit program can fix a corrupted bootmgr.
7. **B.** Microsoft calls the 32- or 64-bit installation environment in Windows 7 the Windows Preinstallation Environment, or WinPE.
8. **D.** Ralph should use the Windows Memory Diagnostic Tool to scan his RAM.
9. **B.** Run bootrec /fixmbr in the Windows RE to repair a damaged master boot record in a Windows 8 PC.
10. **B.** The System Protection feature in Windows 7 enables you to right-click a file or folder and restore previous versions of that file or folder.

CHAPTER 18

Virtualization

In this chapter, you will learn how to

- Describe the concepts of virtualization
- Explain why virtualization is so highly adopted
- Create and use a virtual machine
- Describe how networks use virtualization
- Describe the service layers and architectures that make up cloud computing

For those of us used to the idea that a single computer system consists of one operating system running on its own hardware, virtualization challenges our understanding. In the simplest terms, *virtualization* is the process of using powerful, special software running on a computer to create a complete environment that imitates (virtualizes) all of the hardware you'd see on a real computer. We can install and run an operating system in this virtual environment exactly as if it were installed on its own physical computer. That *guest* environment is called a *virtual machine (VM)*. Figure 18-1 shows one such example: a Windows system using a program called Hyper-V to host two guest virtual machines, one running Ubuntu Linux and another running Windows 10.

This chapter begins by explaining the ideas behind virtualization. The chapter then explores the motivating factors behind the widespread adoption of virtualization throughout the IT industry. The third section outlines steps for setting up a virtual machine. The next section explores the use of virtual machines in networks, which is a little beyond where you need to go for the CompTIA A+ 220-902 exam, but where you'll run into virtualization in modern computing. With this knowledge as a foundation, the chapter finishes with an examination of important concepts in cloud computing (including the role virtualization plays).

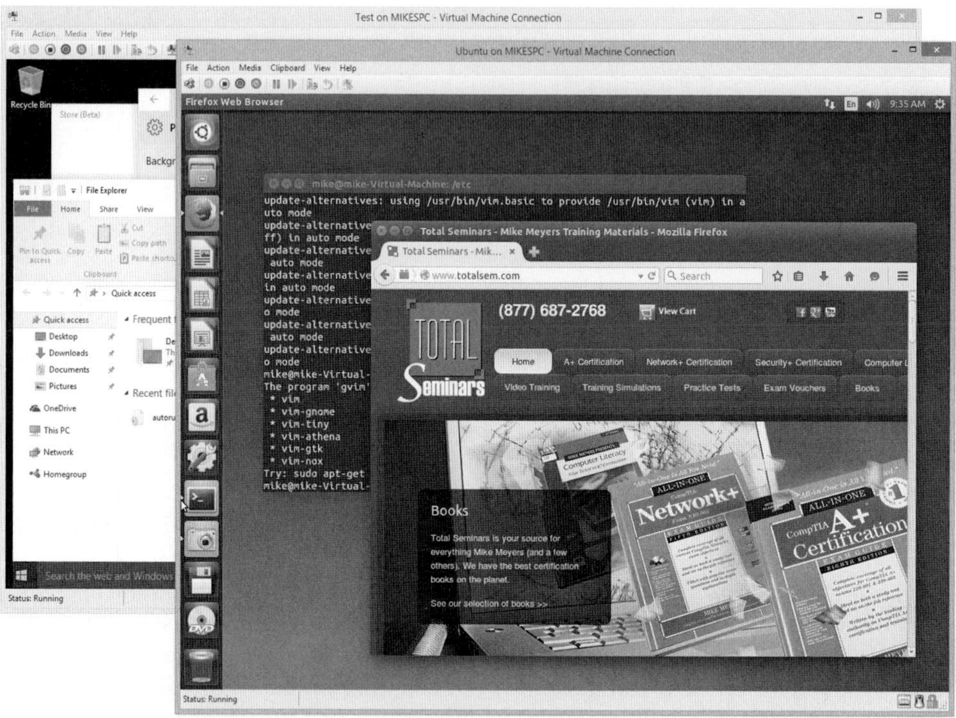

Figure 18-1 Hyper-V running Linux and Windows 10

Historical/Conceptual

What Is Virtualization?

Ask 100 people what the term *virtual* means and you'll get a lot of different answers. Most people define *virtual* with words like "fake" or "pretend," but these terms only begin to describe it. Let's try to zero in on virtualization using a term that hopefully you've heard: *virtual reality*. For most of us, the idea of virtual reality starts with someone wearing headgear and some kind of glove or handheld input device, as shown in Figure 18-2.

The headgear and the gloves work together to create a simulation of a world or environment that appears to be real, even though the person wearing them is located in a room that doesn't resemble the simulated space. Inside this virtual reality you can see the world by turning your head, just as you do in the real world. Software works with the headset's inputs to emulate a physical world. At the same time, the gloves/hand controllers enable you to touch and move objects in the virtual world.

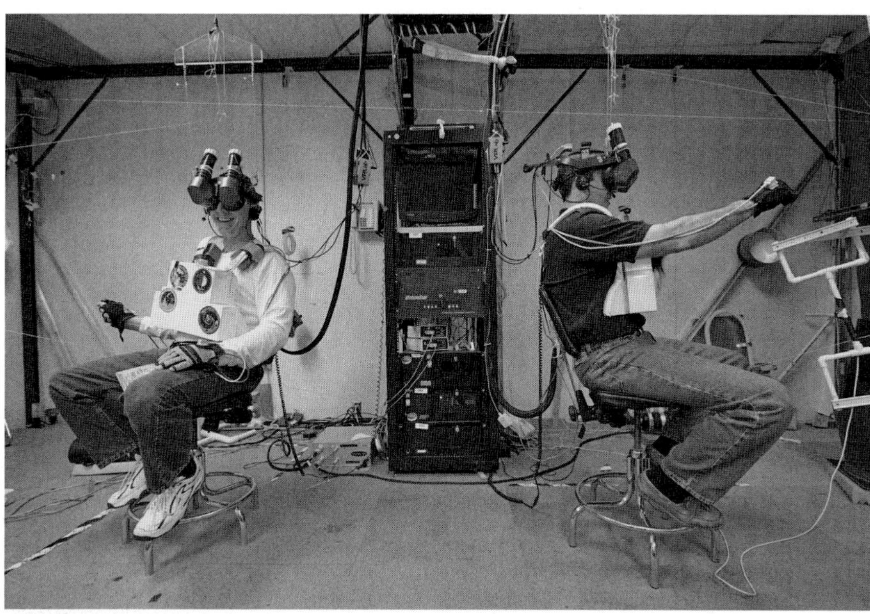

Figure 18-2 Virtual reality training (photo courtesy of NASA)

To make virtual reality effective, the hardware and software need to work together to create an environment convincing enough for a human to work within it. Virtual reality doesn't have to be perfect—it has limitations—but it's pretty cool for teaching someone how to fly a plane or do a spacewalk without having to start with the real thing (Figure 18-3).

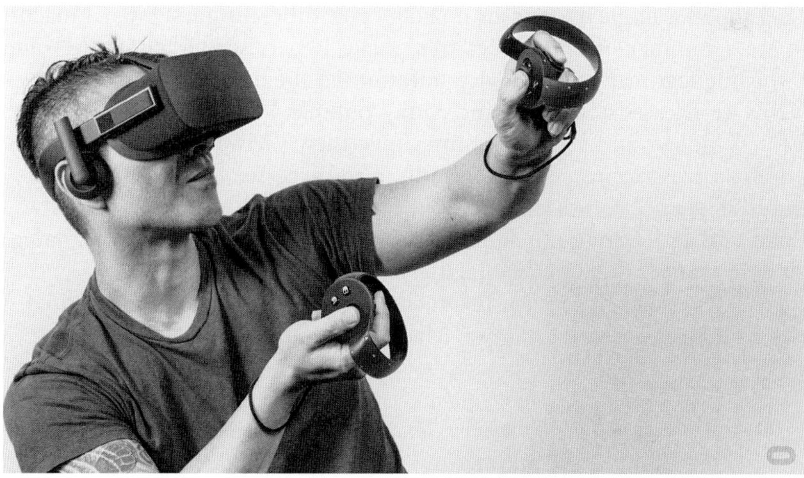

Figure 18-3 Using virtual reality with Oculus Rift (photo courtesy of Oculus VR)

Virtualization on a computer is virtually (sorry, can't pass up the pun) the same as virtual reality for humans. Just as virtual reality creates an environment that convinces humans they're in a real environment, virtualization convinces a guest operating system it is running on its own hardware by using a very cool piece of software called a hypervisor

Meet the Hypervisor

A normal operating system uses programming called a *supervisor* to handle very low-level interaction among hardware and software, such as task scheduling, allotment of time and resources, and so on. Figure 18-4 shows how the supervisor works between the OS and the hardware.

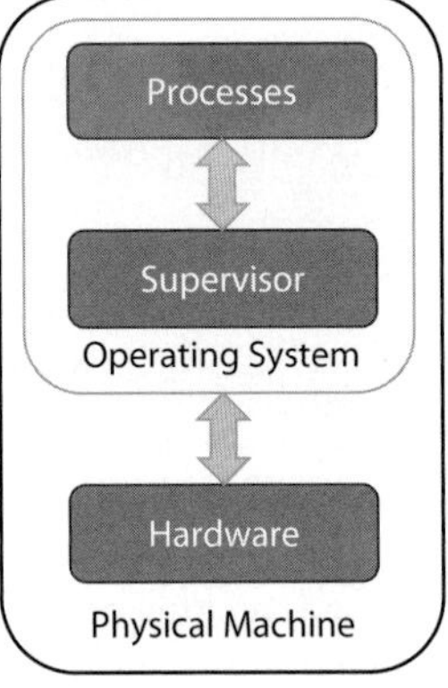

Figure 18-4 Supervisor on a generic single system

Because virtualization enables one machine—called the *host*—to run multiple guest operating systems simultaneously, full virtualization requires an extra layer of sophisticated programming called a *hypervisor* to manage the vastly more complex interactions. Figure 18-5 shows a single hypervisor hosting three different guest virtual machines.

There are a number of companies that make hypervisors. One of the oldest, and arguably the one that really put PC virtualization on the map, is VMware (www.vmware.com). VMware released their now incredibly popular VMware Workstation way back in 1999 for Windows and Linux systems. Since then VMware has grown dramatically, offering a broad cross-section of virtualization products (see Figure 18-6).

Microsoft's Hyper-V comes with Windows Server as well as desktop Windows starting with Windows 8 Pro. While not as popular as VMware products, it has a large base of users that's growing all the time (see Figure 18-7).

Another very popular hypervisor is Oracle VM VirtualBox (see Figure 18-8). VirtualBox is powerful and runs on Windows, Mac OS X, and Linux.

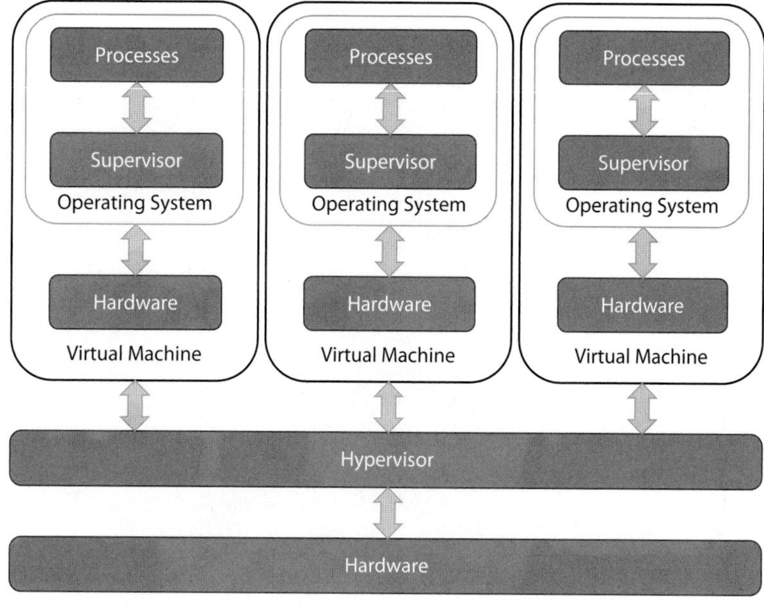

Figure 18-5 Hypervisor on a generic single system hosting three virtual machines

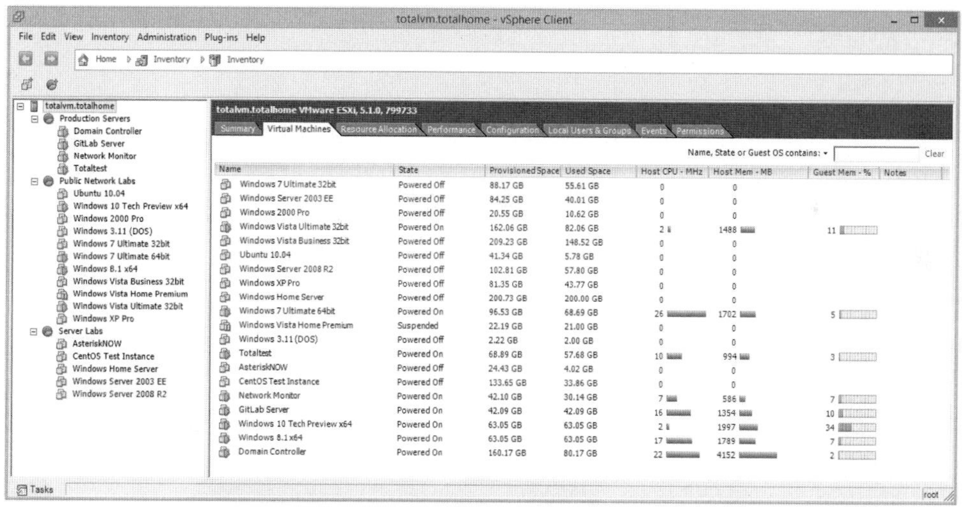

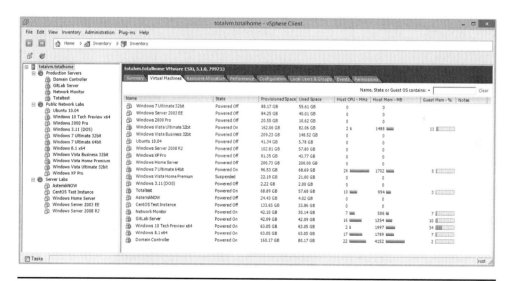

Figure 18-6 Author's busy VMware server

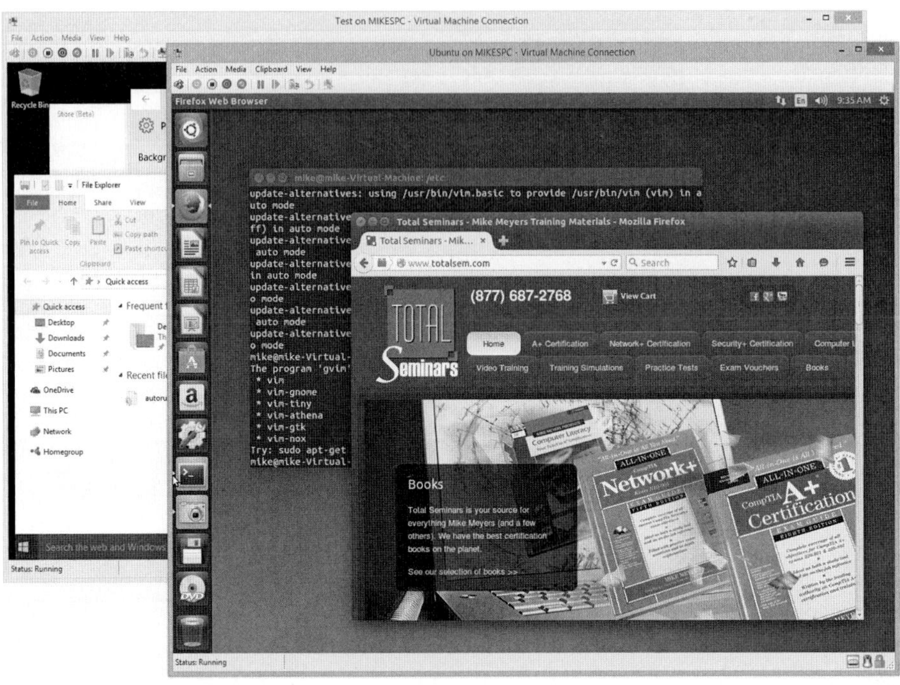

Figure 18-7 Hyper-V on a Windows 8.1 system

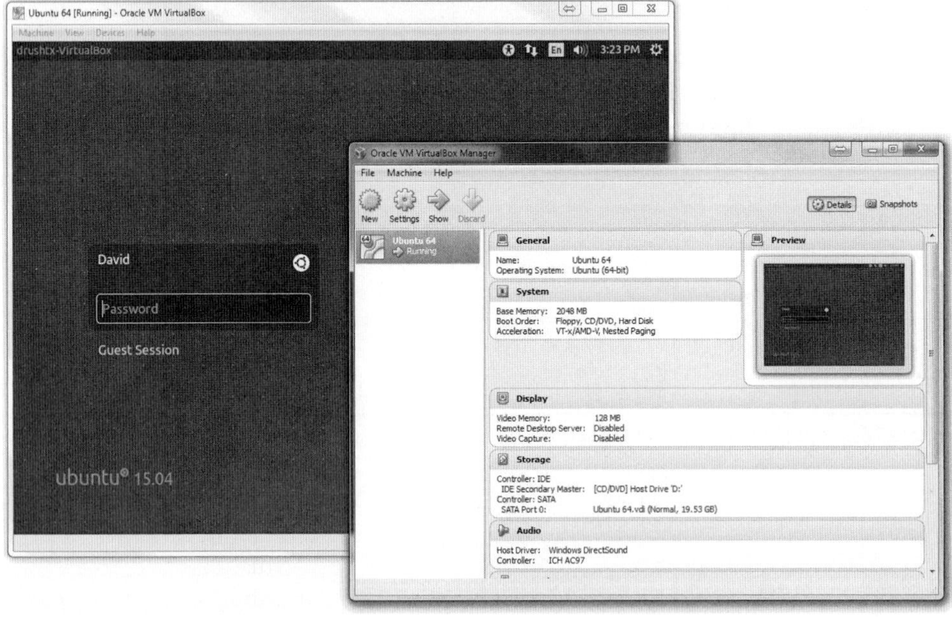

Figure 18-8 Oracle VirtualBox

If you run Mac OS X, the most popular hypervisor choices are VMware Fusion and Parallels Desktop (see Figure 18-9). Both of these Mac OS X hypervisors are quite powerful, but unlike Hyper-V or VirtualBox, they cost money.

Figure 18-9 Parallels Desktop

This is in no way a complete list of all the hypervisors available out there. Many Linux users swear by KVM, for example, but the hypervisors introduced in this section are the ones you're most likely to see on desktop systems. Make sure you are aware of at least Microsoft's Hyper-V for the exam!

NOTE VMware makes a number of amazing virtualization products, but they can be pricey. Microsoft's Hyper-V, Linux's KVM, and Oracle's VirtualBox are all free.

Emulation Versus Virtualization

Virtualization takes the hardware of the host system and allocates some portion of its power to individual virtual machines. If you have an Intel system, a hypervisor creates a virtual machine that acts exactly like the host Intel system. It cannot act like any other type of computer. For example, you cannot make a virtual machine on an Intel system that acts like a Nintendo 3DS. Hypervisors simply pass the code from the virtual machine to the actual CPU.

Emulation is very different from virtualization. An *emulator* is software or hardware that converts the commands to and from the host machine into an entirely different platform. Figure 18-10 shows a Super Nintendo Entertainment System emulator, Snes9X, running a game called *Donkey Kong Country* on a Windows system.

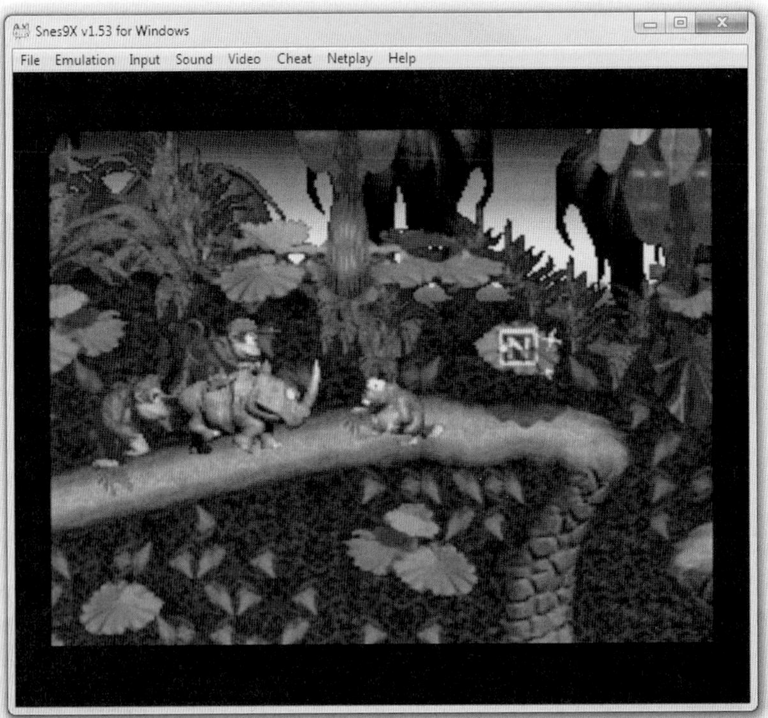

Figure 18-10 Super Nintendo emulator running on Windows

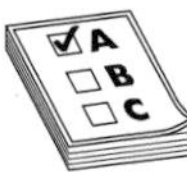

EXAM TIP While the CompTIA A+ 220-902 exam objectives include emulator requirements as a part of virtualization, the concepts are not the same. For the sake of completeness, however, know that emulating another platform (using a PC to run Sony PlayStation 3 games, for example) requires hardware several times more powerful than the platform being emulated.

Client-Side Virtualization

This chapter will show you a few of the ways you can use virtualization, but before I go any further, let's take the basic pieces you've learned about virtualization and put them together in one of its simplest forms, *client-side virtualization*.

The basic process for creating virtual machines is as follows:

1. Verify and set up your system's hardware to support virtual machines.
2. Install a hypervisor on your system.
3. Create a new virtual machine that has the proper virtualized hardware requirements for the guest OS.
4. Start the new virtual machine and install the new guest OS exactly as you'd install it on a new physical machine.

Hardware Support

While any computer running Linux, Windows, or Mac OS X will support a hypervisor, there are a few hardware requirements we need to address. First, every hypervisor will run better if you enable hardware virtualization support.

Every Intel-based CPU since the late 1980s is designed to support a supervisor for multitasking, but it's hard work for that same CPU to support multiple supervisors on multiple VMs. Around 2005, both AMD and Intel added extra features to their CPUs just to support hypervisors: Intel's *VT-x* and AMD's *AMD-V.* This is *hardware virtualization support.*

If your CPU and BIOS support hardware virtualization, you can turn it on or off inside the system setup utility. Figure 18-11 shows the virtualization setting in a typical system setup utility.

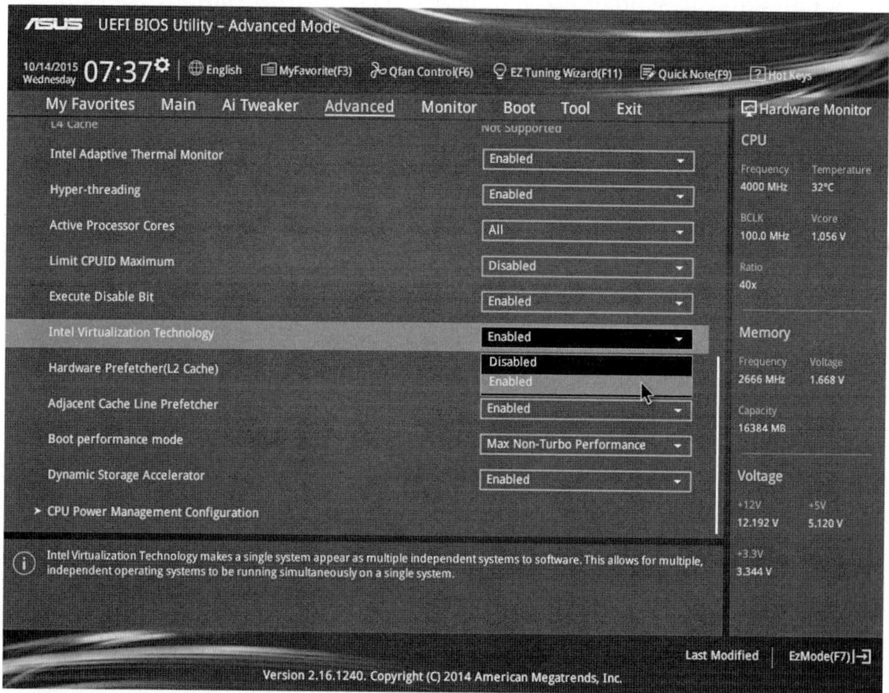

Figure 18-11 BIOS setting for CPU virtualization support

Apart from hardware virtualization support, the second most important concern is RAM. Each virtual machine needs just as much RAM as a physical one, so it's common practice to absolutely stuff your host machine with large amounts of RAM. The more virtual machines you run, the more RAM you need. Generally, there are two issues to keep in mind:

- Leave enough RAM for the hypervisor to run adequately
- Add enough RAM so that every VM you run at the same time will run adequately

It will take some research to figure out how much RAM you need. I have a VirtualBox hypervisor running on a Windows 8.1 (64-bit) host system. There are three VMs running at all times: Windows XP running a test bank simulation tool, Ubuntu Linux (64-bit) running a Web server, and Windows 10 (64-bit) being used as a remote desktop server. All of these VMs are quite busy. I determined the following requirements by looking around the Internet (and guessing a little):

- 4 GB for the host OS and VirtualBox
- 1 GB for Windows XP
- 512 MB for Ubuntu
- 2.5 GB for Windows 10

Not wanting to run short, I just dumped 32 GB of RAM into my system. So far it runs pretty well! Be careful here. It is difficult to get perfect answers for these situations. If you research this you may get a different answer.

Disk Space

Disk space can also be a problem. VM files can be huge because they include everything installed on the VM; depending on the OS and how the VM is used, the VM file could range from megabytes to hundreds of gigabytes. On top of that, every snapshot you take (snapshots are described later in this chapter) requires space. Figure 18-12 shows a newly minted Windows 10 VM taking over 11 GB of disk space. Make sure you have plenty of disk space for your VMs.

In addition, your VM files are precious. Protect them with good RAID arrays and the occasional backup as well to make sure they are available when you need them.

Emulation

Okay, I know what I said earlier, but there are some situations where hypervisors will do some simple emulation. This emulation only supports certain types of hardware. The best examples are network interface cards (NICs). Instead of writing drivers so that every imaginable guest OS can use the hypervisor's virtual NIC, the hypervisor will likely emulate a popular, widely supported hardware NIC. A great example is Microsoft's Hyper-V. If you want to set up a Linux VM on your Hyper-V system, Linux won't understand how to talk to Microsoft's default virtual NIC unless you change it to Legacy Network Adapter (see Figure 18-13).

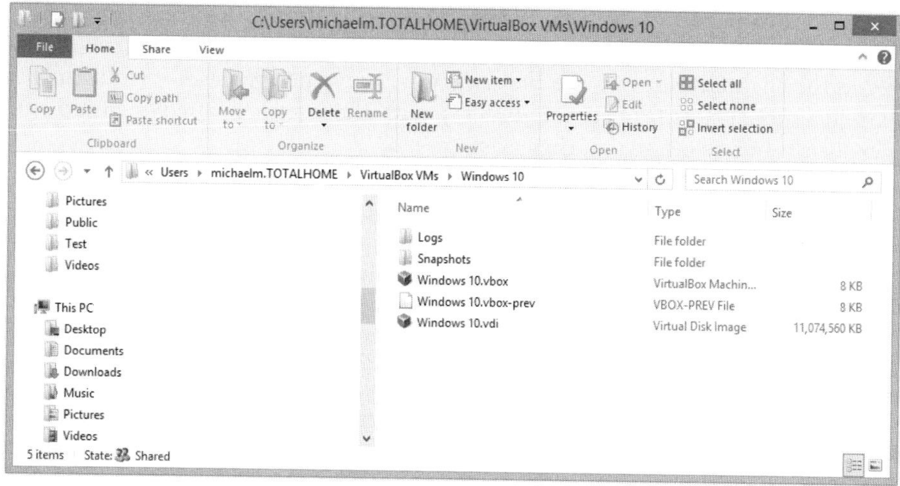

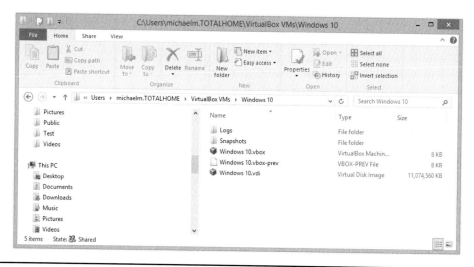

Figure 18-12 Single VM file taking 11 GB

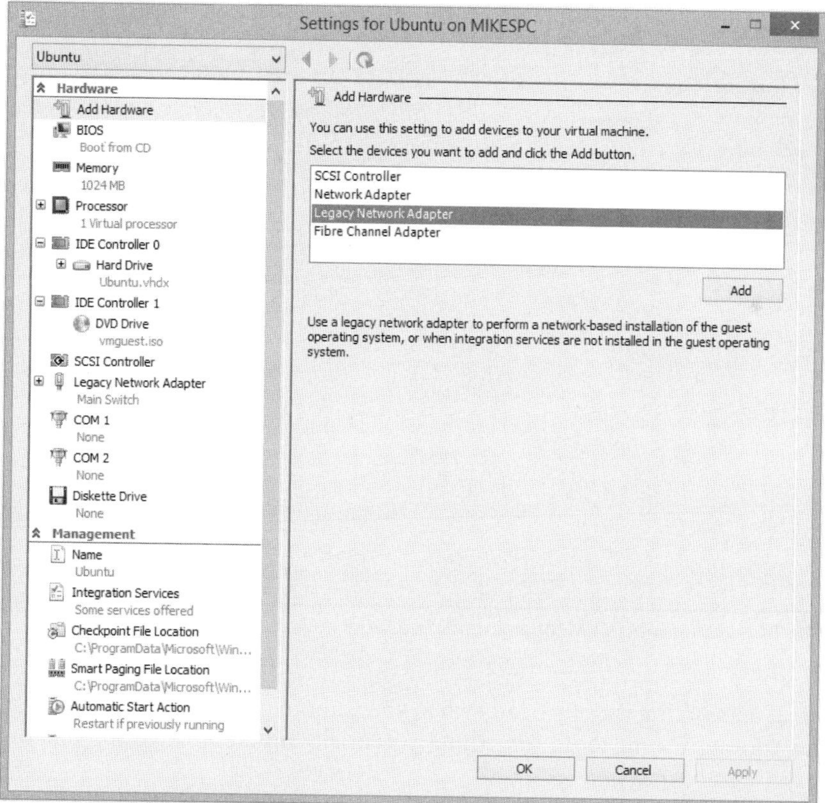

Figure 18-13 Enabling NIC emulation on Hyper-V

Basically all you are doing is turning off a few "Microsofty" features that work great when your guest VM is a Windows system. So is this really emulation as we described earlier in the chapter? Not in quite the same way; the hypervisor is not emulating a full system, just some pieces for compatibility reasons. These settings rarely mention emulation explicitly, but be aware that they exist.

Network Support

Probably one of the coolest features of VMs is the many different ways you can "virtually" network them. Don't just limit yourself to thinking, "Oh, can I get a VM to connect to the Internet?" Well, sure you can, but hypervisors do so much more. Every hypervisor has the capability to connect each of its virtual machines to a network in a number of different ways depending on your needs.

Internal Networking Let's say you have a scenario where you have four VMs and you want them to see each other, but nothing else. No Internet connection: just four VMs that think they are the only computers in existence. Go into the settings for all four VMs and set their respective virtual NICs to an *internal network* (see Figure 18-14). In this case, every VM running on that one hypervisor will act as though it is connected to its own switch and nothing else.

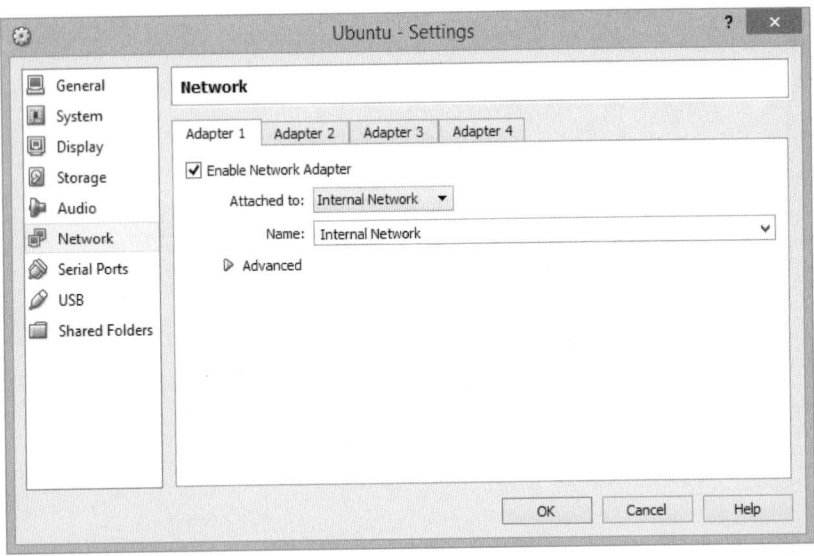

Figure 18-14 Configuring a VM for an internal network in VirtualBox

Internal networking is really handy when you want to play with some cool networking tool, but you don't want to do something potentially unsafe to anything but your little

virtual test network. I often find fun utilities that do all kinds of things that you would *never* want to do on a real network (malware utilities, network scanners, and so on). By making a few VMs and connecting them via an internal network, I can play all I wish without fear of messing up a real network.

Bridged Networking When most people think of networking a new VM, it's safe to say they are really thinking, "How do I get my new VM on the Internet?" You first connect to the Internet by connecting to a real network. There are plenty of scenarios where you might want a VM that connects to your real network, exactly as your host machine connects to the network. To do this, the VM's virtual NIC needs to piggyback (the proper word is *bridge*) the real NIC to get out to the network. A VM with a bridged network connection accesses the same network as the host system. It's a lot like the virtual machine has its own cable to connect it to the network. Bridged networking is a simple way to get a VM connected to the Internet (assuming the host machine has an Internet connection, of course).

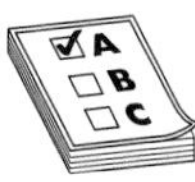

EXAM TIP A VM connected using bridged networking is subject to all the same security risks as a real computer on the Internet.

Here's a scenario where bridged networking is important. Let's say someone is trying to access my online videos, but is having trouble. I can make a VM that replicates a customer's OS and browser. In this case, I would set up the VM's NIC as a bridged network. This tells the real NIC to allow the virtual NIC to act as though it is a physical NIC on the same network. It can take Dynamic Host Configuration Protocol (DHCP) information just like a real NIC.

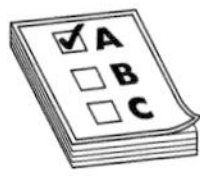

EXAM TIP On almost every hypervisor, when you create a new VM, it will by default use bridged networking unless you specifically reconfigure the VM's NIC to do otherwise.

Virtual Switches Think about this for a moment: If you are going to make an internal network of four virtual machines, aren't they going to need to somehow connect together? In a real network, we connect computers together with a switch. The answer is actually kind of cool: hypervisors make virtual switches! Every hypervisor has its own way to set up these virtual switches. Some hypervisors, like VirtualBox, just do this automatically and you don't see anything. Other hypervisors, Microsoft's Hyper-V is the best example, require you to make a virtual switch to set up networking. Figure 18-15 shows the Hyper-V Virtual Switch Manager setting up a virtual switch.

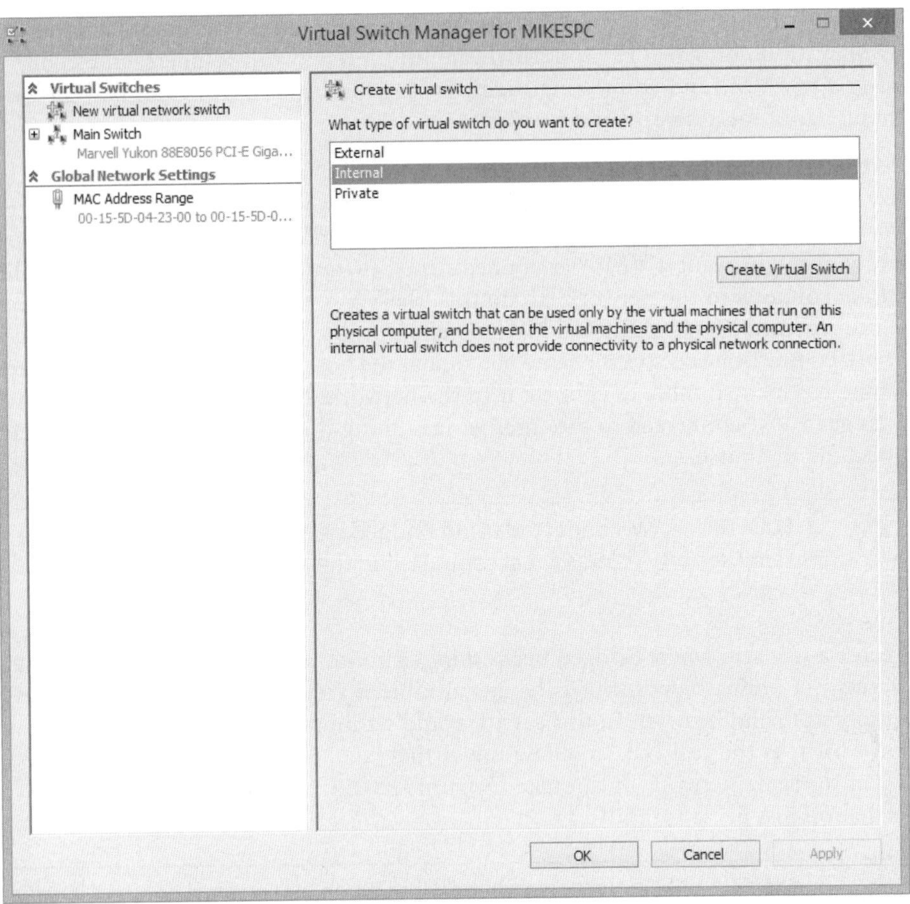

Figure 18-15 Hyper-V's Virtual Switch Manager

No Networking The last and probably least network option is no network at all. Just because you make a VM doesn't mean you need any kind of network. I have a number of VMs that I keep around just to see what my test bank software does on various standalone systems. I don't need networking at all. I just plug in a thumb drive with whatever I'm installing and test.

Installing a Virtual Machine

The actual process of installing a hypervisor is usually no more complicated than installing any other type of software. Let's use Hyper-V as an example. If you have a Windows 8/8.1/10 system, you can enable Microsoft's Hyper-V by going to the Programs and Features Control Panel applet and selecting *Turn Windows features on or off*, which opens the Windows Features dialog box, as shown in Figure 18-16.

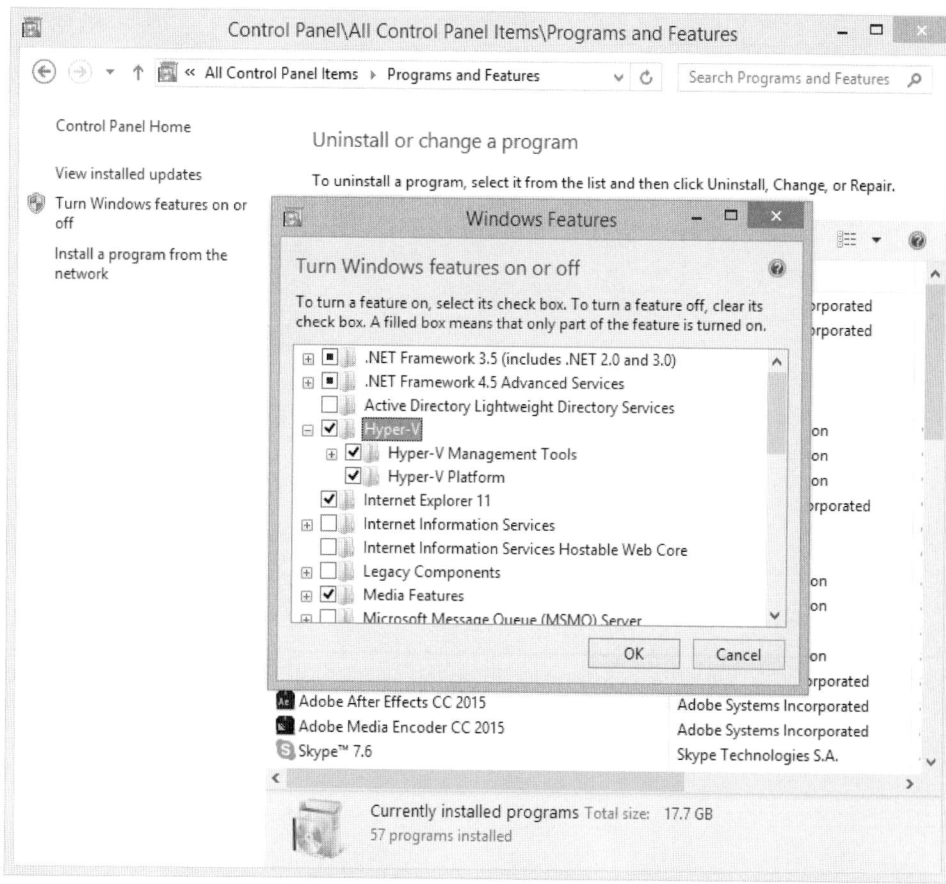

Figure 18-16 Installing Hyper-V in Windows

Once you've installed the hypervisor feature, you'll have a virtual machine manager that acts as the primary place to create, start, stop, save, and delete guest virtual machines. Figure 18-17 shows the manager for Oracle's VirtualBox.

Creating a Virtual Machine

So it's time to build a virtual machine. On pretty much any manager this is simply a matter of clicking New | Virtual Machine, which starts some kind of wizard to ensure you're creating the right virtual machine for your guest OS. Most hypervisors will have presets for a number of crucial settings to ensure your guest OS has the virtual hardware it needs to run well. Figure 18-18 shows the VirtualBox wizard asking what OS I intend to install. By selecting the correct preset, I'll make sure my guest OS has all the virtual RAM, hard drive space, and so forth, that it needs.

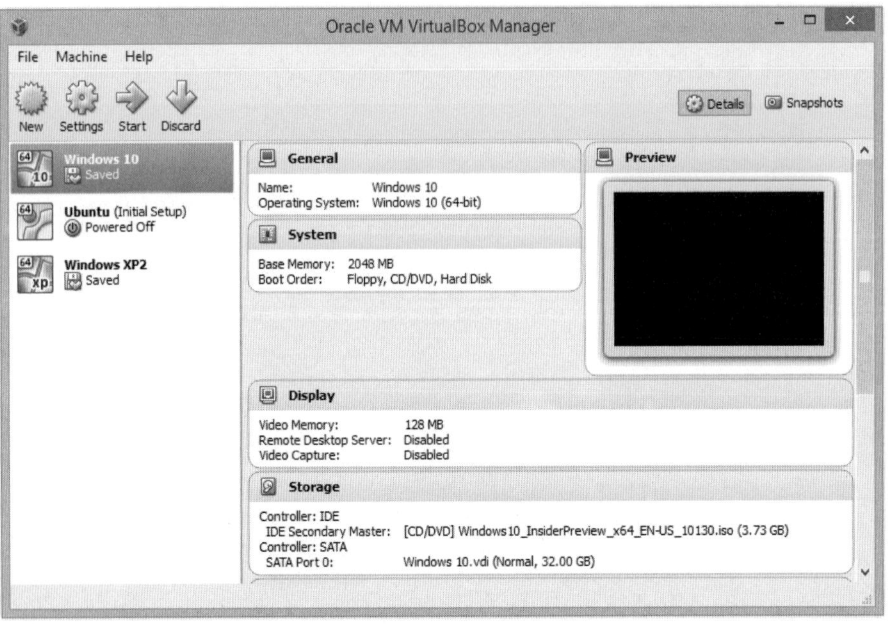

Figure 18-17 Oracle VM VirtualBox Manager (three VMs installed)

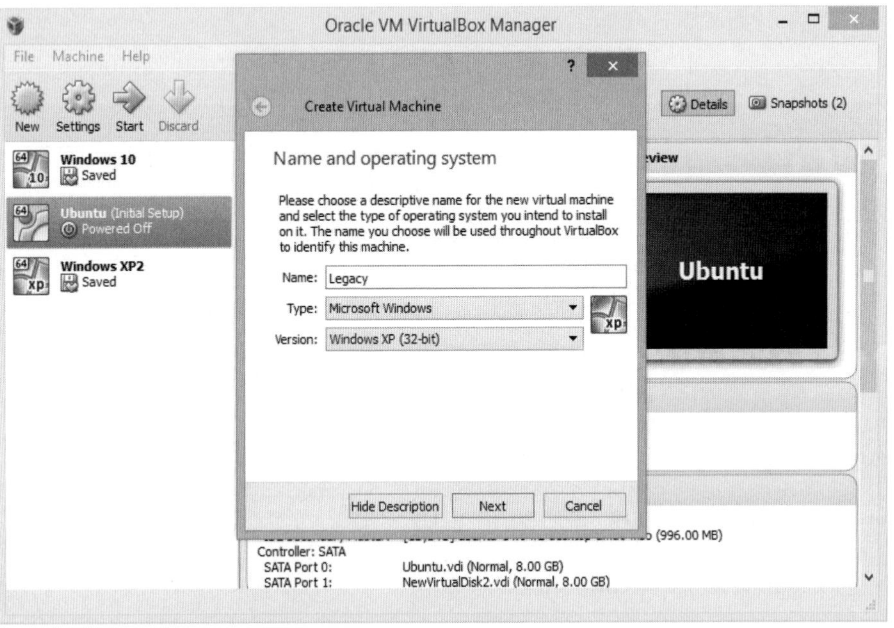

Figure 18-18 Creating a new VM in Oracle's VirtualBox

Installing the Operating System

Once you've created the new guest VM, it's time to install a guest operating system. Just because you're creating a virtual machine, don't think the operating system and applications aren't real. You need to install an operating system on that virtual machine. You can do this using some form of optical media, just as you would on a machine without virtualization. Would you like to use Microsoft Windows in your virtual machine? No problem, but know that every virtual machine on which you create and install Windows requires a separate, legal copy of Windows; this also goes for any licensed software installed in the VM.

Because virtual machines are so flexible on hardware, all good virtual machine managers enable you to use the host machine's optical drive, a USB thumb drive, or an ISO file. One of the most popular ways is to tell the new virtual machine to treat an ISO file as its own optical drive. In Figure 18-19, I'm installing Ubuntu on a VMware virtual machine. I downloaded an ISO image from the Ubuntu Web site (www.ubuntu.com), and as the figure shows, I've pointed the dialog box to that image.

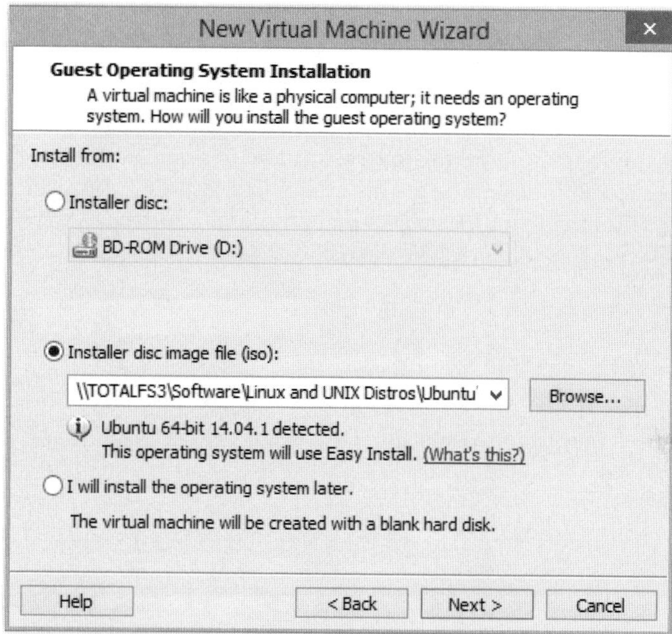

Figure 18-19 Selecting the installation media

If you look closely at Figure 18-19, you'll see that VMware reads the installation media and detects the operating system. Because VMware knows this operating system, it configures all of the virtual hardware settings automatically: amount of RAM, virtual hard drive size, and so on. You can change any of these settings, either before or after the virtual machine is created.

Next, you need to accept the size of the virtual drive, as shown in Figure 18-20.

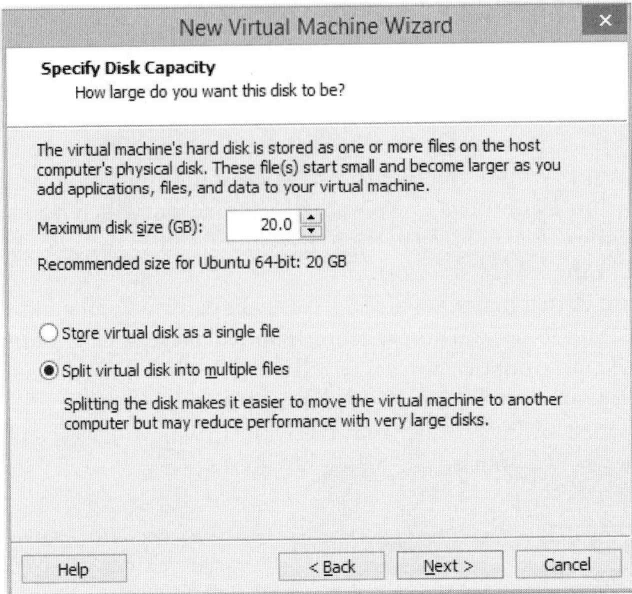

Figure 18-20 Setting the virtual drive size

You also need to give the virtual machine a name. By default, VMware Workstation uses a simple name. For this overview, accept the default name: Ubuntu (plus some version-specific information). This dialog box also lets you decide where you want to store the files that comprise the virtual machine. Note that VMware uses a folder in the user's Documents folder called Virtual Machines (see Figure 18-21).

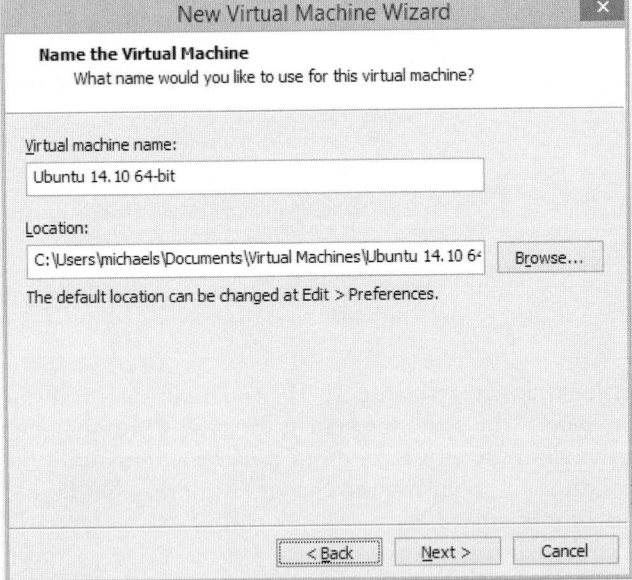

Figure 18-21 Entering VM name and location

NOTE Use descriptive names for virtual machines. This will save you a lot of confusion when you have multiple VMs on a single host.

After you've gone through all the configuration screens, you can start using your virtual machine. You can start, stop, pause, add, or remove virtual hardware.

After the virtual machine installs, you then treat the VM exactly as though it were a real machine. The only big difference is that VMware Workstation replaces CTRL-ALT-DELETE with CTRL-ALT-INSERT by default. Figure 18-22 shows VMware Workstation with the single VM installed but not running.

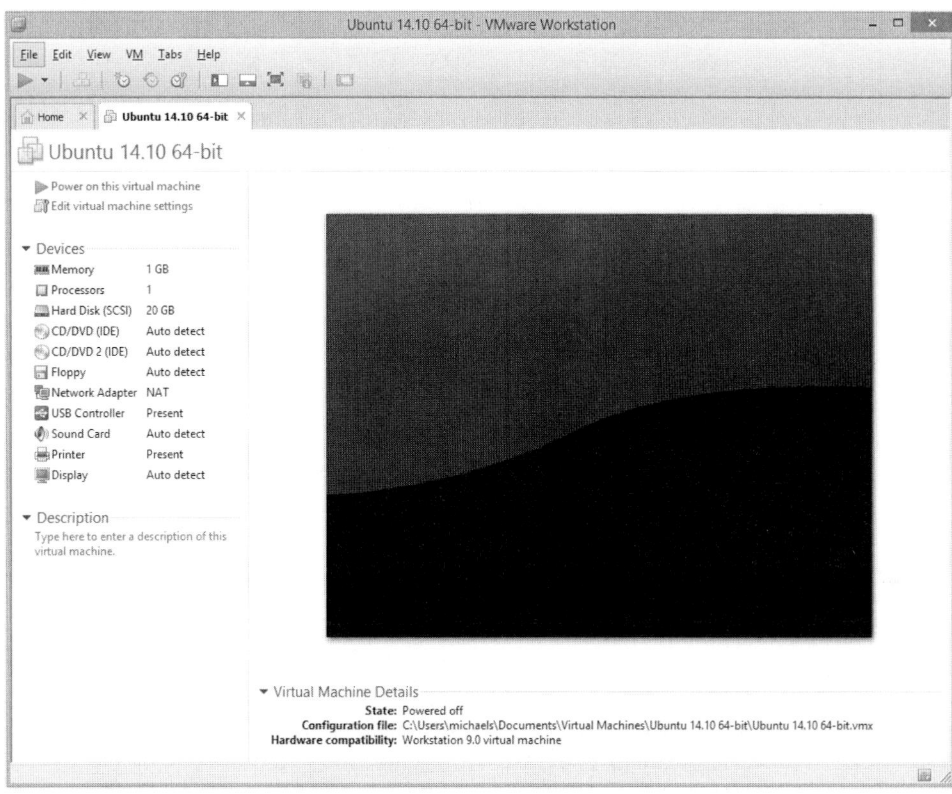

Figure 18-22 VMware Workstation with a single VM

Congratulations! You've just installed a *virtual desktop*. Like with a real system, you can add or remove hardware, but it won't take a trip to the electronics store or a box from Newegg. The real power of a hypervisor is in the flexibility of the virtual hardware. A hypervisor has to handle every input and output that the operating system would request of normal hardware. With a good hypervisor, you can easily add and remove virtual hard

drives, virtual network cards, virtual RAM, and so on, helping you adapt your virtual desktop to meet changing needs. Figure 18-23 shows the Hardware Configuration screen from VMware Workstation.

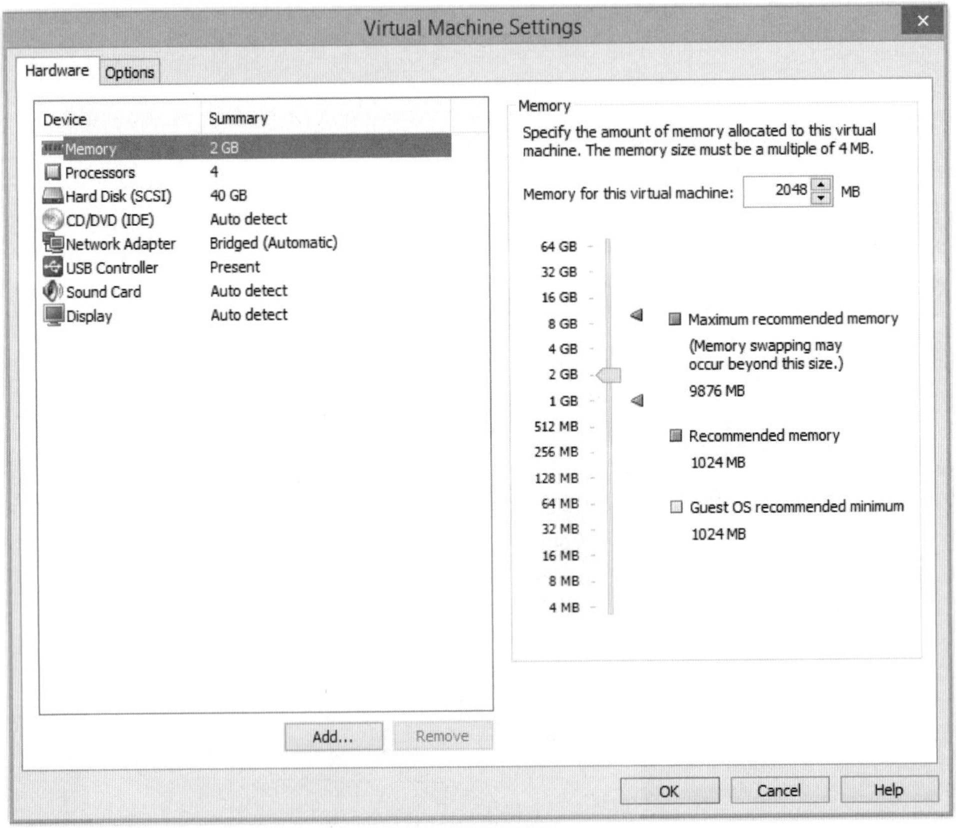

Figure 18-23 Configuring virtual hardware in VMware Workstation

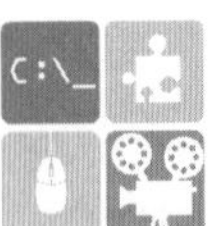

SIM Check out the excellent Chapter 18 Show! and Click! sims on "Virtual Hardware" over at http://totalsem.com/90x. These help reinforce terminology and typical steps for setting up a virtual machine.

Virtual desktops were the first type of popular virtual machines seen in the PC world, championed by VMware and quickly copied by other virtualization programs. However, there's a lot more to virtualization than just virtual desktops. Before I dive in too far, let's step back a moment and understand a very important question: Why do we virtualize?

902

Why Do We Virtualize?

Virtualization has taken IT by storm, but for those who have never seen virtualization, the big question has got to be: Why? Let's talk about the benefits of virtualization. While you read this section, keep in mind two important things:

- A single hypervisor on a single system will happily run as many virtual machines as its RAM, CPU, and drive space allow. (RAM is almost always the limiting factor.)
- A virtual machine that's shut down is no more than a file or folder sitting on a hard drive.

While you're reading about the benefits of virtualization, don't forget about the requirements. To run one or more virtual machines, you'll need a powerful machine—fast processor, loads of RAM, and a good amount of hard drive space. If you want the virtual PC to connect to a network, your physical PC needs a NIC.

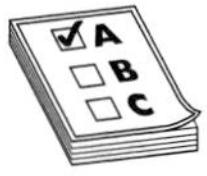

EXAM TIP Virtualized operating systems use the same security features as real operating systems. For each virtual machine user account, you'll need to keep track of user names, passwords, permissions, and so on, just like on a normal PC.

Power Saving

Before virtualization, each OS needed to be on a unique physical system. With virtualization, you can place multiple virtual servers or clients on a single physical system, reducing electrical power use substantially. Rather than one machine running a Windows file server, another Windows system acting as a DNS server, and a third machine running Linux for a DHCP server, why not take one physical computer to handle all three servers simultaneously as virtual machines (see Figure 18-24)?

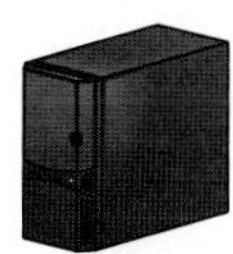
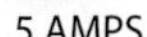

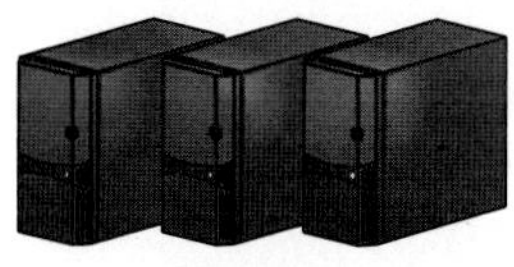

Figure 18-24 Virtualization saves power.

Hardware Consolidation

Much in the way you can save power by consolidating multiple servers or clients into a single powerful server or client, you can also avoid purchasing expensive hardware that

is rarely if ever run at full capacity during its useful lifetime. Complex desktop PCs can be replaced with simple but durable *thin clients*, which may not need hard drives, fans, or optical drives, because they only need enough power to access the remote desktop. For that matter, why buy multiple high-end servers, complete with multiple processors, RAID arrays, redundant power supplies, and so on, and only run each server using a fraction of its resources? With virtualization, you can easily build a single physical server machine and run a number of servers or clients on that one box.

System Management and Security

The most popular reason for virtualizing is probably the benefits we reap from easy-to-manage systems. We can take advantage of the fact that VMs are simply files: like any other files, they can be copied. New employees can be quickly set up with a department-specific virtual machine with all of the software they need already installed.

Let's say you have set up a new employee with a traditional physical system. If that system goes down—due to hacking, malware, or so on—you need to restore the system from a backup, which may or may not be easily at hand. With virtualization, you merely need to shut down the virtual machine and reload an alternate copy of it.

Most virtual machines let us take a *snapshot* or *checkpoint*, which saves the virtual machine's state at that moment, allowing us to quickly return to this state later. Snapshots are great for doing risky (or even not-so-risky) maintenance with a safety net. These aren't, however, a long-term backup strategy—each snapshot may reduce performance and should be removed as soon as the danger has passed. Figure 18-25 shows VMware Workstation saving a snapshot.

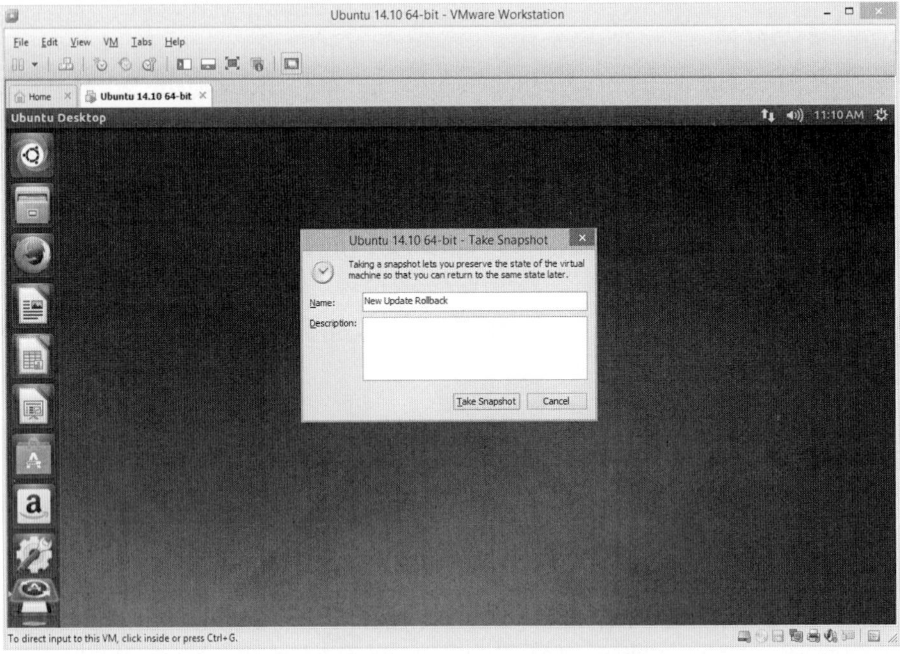

Figure 18-25 Saving a snapshot

Research

Here's a great example that happens in my own company. I sell my popular Total Tester test banks: practice questions for you to test your skills on a broad number of certification topics. As with any distributed program, I tend to get a few support calls. Running a problem through the same OS helps my team solve it. In the pre-virtualization days, I usually had seven to ten multi-boot PCs laying around my office just to keep active copies of specific Windows versions. Today, a single hypervisor enables us to support a huge number of Windows versions with one machine.

Now that we've discussed how virtualization is useful, let's look at how virtualization is implemented in networks.

Real-World Virtualization

When it comes to servers, virtualization has pretty much taken over everywhere. Many of the servers we access, particularly Web and e-mail servers, are now virtualized. Like any popular technology, there are a lot of people continually working to make virtualization better. The VMware Workstation example shown earlier in this chapter is a very powerful desktop application, but it still needs to run on top of a single system that is already running an operating system—the host operating system.

What if you could improve performance by removing the host operating system altogether and install nothing but a hypervisor? Well, you can! This is done all the time with another type of powerful hypervisor/OS combination called a *bare-metal* hypervisor. We call it bare metal because there's no other software between it and the hardware—just bare metal. The industry also refers to this class of hypervisors as *Type-1*, and applications such as VMware Workstation as *Type-2* (see Figure 18-26).

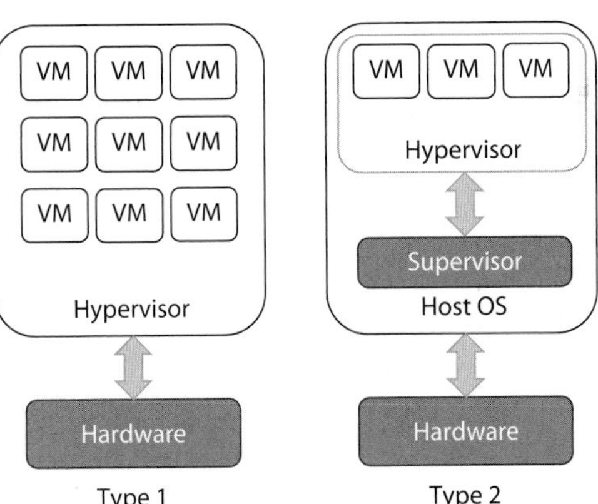

Figure 18-26 Type 1 vs. Type 2 hypervisors

In 2001 VMware introduced a bare-metal hypervisor, originally called ESX, that shed the unnecessary overhead of an operating system. ESX has since been supplanted by ESXi in VMware's product lineup. ESXi is a free hypervisor that's powerful enough to replace the host operating system on a physical box, turning the physical machine into a

system that does nothing but support virtual ones. ESXi, by itself, isn't much to look at; it's a tiny operating system/hypervisor that's often installed on something other than a hard drive. In fact, you won't manage a single VM at the ESXi server itself, as pretty much everything is done through a Web interface (see Figure 18-27).

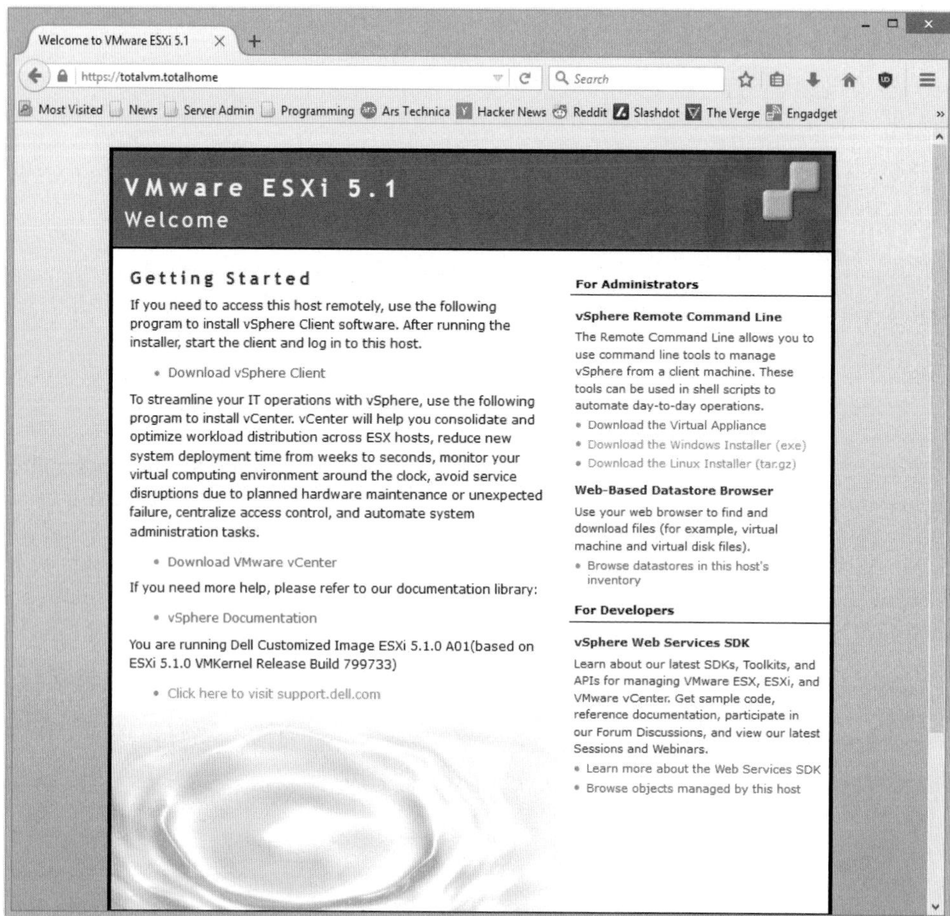

Figure 18-27 Web interface for ESXi

A host running its hypervisor from flash memory can dedicate all of its available disk space to VM storage, or even cut out the disks altogether and keep its VMs on a storage area network (SAN). Figure 18-28 shows how I loaded my copy of ESXi: via a small USB thumb drive. The server loads ESXi off the thumb drive when I power it up, and in short order a very rudimentary interface appears where I can input essential information, such as a master password and a static IP address.

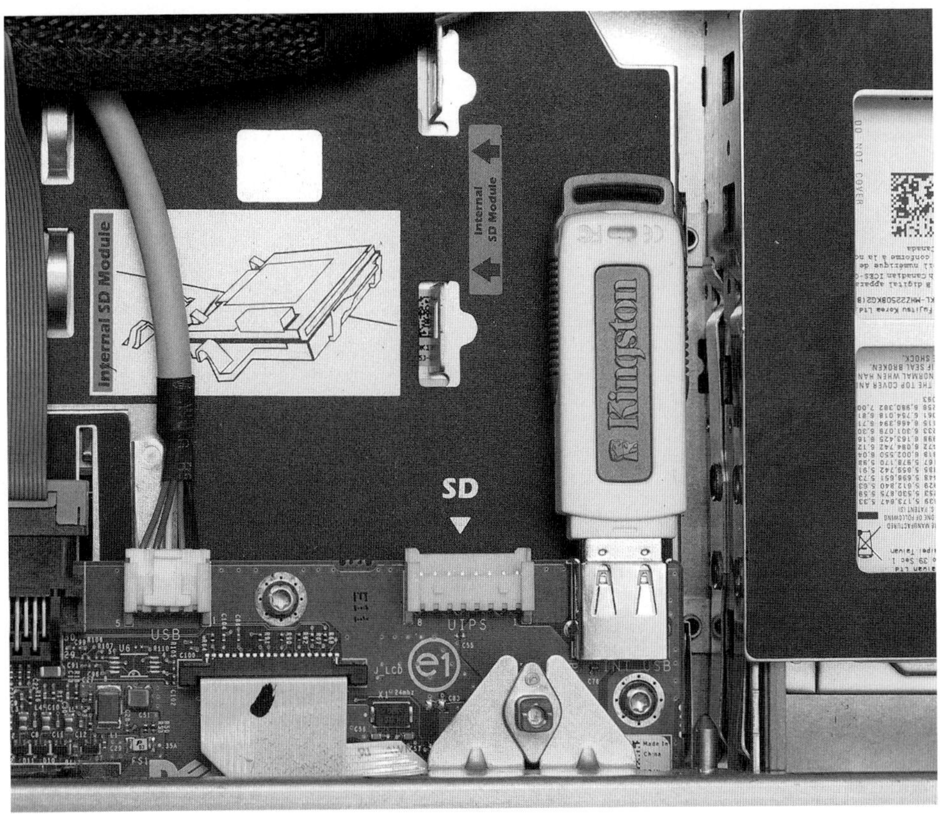

Figure 18-28 USB drive on server system

Don't let ESXi's small size fool you. It's small because it only has one job: to host virtual machines. ESXi is an extremely powerful bare-metal hypervisor.

To understand the importance of virtualization fully, you need to get a handle on how it increases flexibility as the scale of an operation increases. Let's take a step back and talk about money. One of the really great things money does is give us common, easily divisible units we can exchange for the goods and services we need. When we don't have money, we have to trade goods and services to get it, and before we had money at all we had to trade goods and services for other goods and services.

Let's say I'm starving and all I have is a hammer, and you just so happen to have a chicken. I offer to build you something with my hammer, but all you really want is a hammer of your own. This might sound like a match made in heaven, but what if my hammer is actually worth at least five chickens, and you just have one? I can't give you a fifth of a hammer, and once I trade the hammer for your chicken, I can't use it to build anything else. I have to choose between going without food and wasting most of my hammer's value. If only my hammer was money.

In the same vein, suppose Mario has only two physical servers; he basically has two really expensive hammers. If he uses one server to host an important site on his intranet,

its full potential might go almost unused (especially since his intranet site will never land on the front page of reddit). But if Mario installs a hypervisor on each of these machines, he has taken a big step toward using his servers in a new, more productive way.

In this new model, Mario's servers become less like hammers and more like money. I still can't trade a fifth of my hammer for a chicken, but Mario can easily use a virtual machine to serve his intranet site and only allocate a fifth—or any other fraction—of the host's physical resources to this VM. As he adds hosts, he can treat them more and more like a pool of common, easily divisible units used to solve problems. Each new host adds resources to the pool, and as Mario adds more and more VMs that need different amounts of resources, he increases his options for distributing them across his hosts to minimize unused resources (see Figure 18-29).

Figure 18-29
No vacancy on these hosts

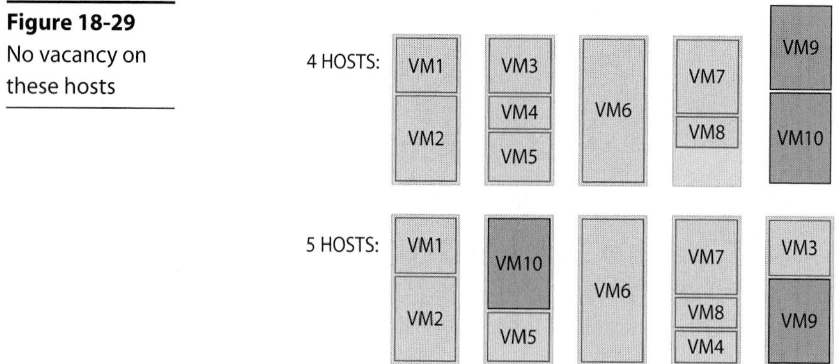

To the Cloud

While simple virtualization enabled Mario to optimize and reallocate his computing resources in response to his evolving needs (as described in the previous section), he can't exceed the capabilities of his local hardware. Luckily, he's no longer stuck with just the hardware he owns. Because his virtual machines are just files running on a hypervisor, he can run them in *the cloud* on networks of servers worldwide.

Consider a simple Web server. In the not-so-long-ago days, if you wanted a Web site, you needed to build a system, install a Web server, get a commercial-grade Internet link, obtain and properly configure the box with a public IP address, set up firewalls, and provide real-time administration to that system. The cost for even a single system would be thousands of dollars upfront for installation and hundreds of dollars a month for upkeep (and heaven forbid your system ever went down).

As time passed we began to see hosting services that took most of the work of setting up a server infrastructure away from you. You merely "hosted" some space on a single server and that server was also hosting other Web sites. This saved you from having to set up infrastructure, but it was still relatively expensive.

Around 2005/2006, a number of companies, Amazon being the best example, started offering a new kind of hosting service. Instead of individual physical computers or directories on a shared host, Amazon discovered it could use large groups of virtualized servers

combined with a powerful front end to enable customers to simply click and start the server they wanted. Cloud computing was born.

When we talk about the "cloud," we're talking not just about friendly file-storage services like Dropbox or Google Drive, but also about simple interfaces to a vast array of on-demand computing resources sold by Amazon (see Figure 18-30), Microsoft, and many other companies over the open Internet. The technology at the heart of these innovative services is virtualization.

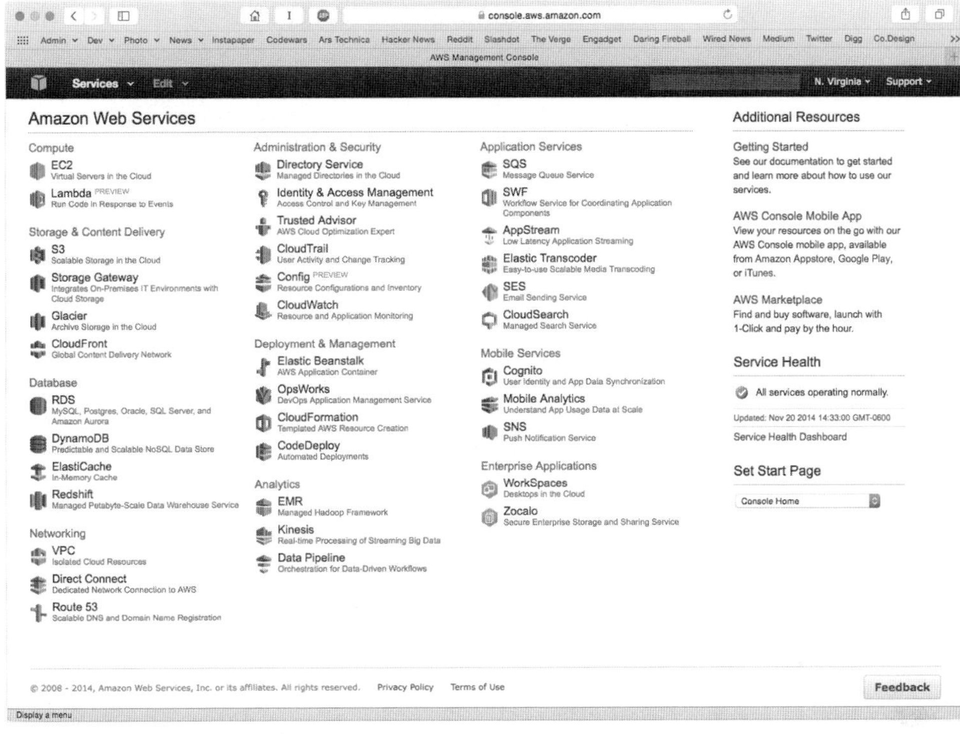

Figure 18-30 Amazon Web Services Management Console

The Service-Layer Cake

Service is the key to understanding the cloud. At the hardware level, we'd have trouble telling the difference between the cloud and the servers and networks that comprise the Internet as a whole. We use the servers and networks of the cloud through layers of software that add great value to the underlying hardware by making it simple to perform complex tasks or manage powerful hardware. As end users we generally interact with just the sweet software icing of the service-layer cake—Web applications like Dropbox, Gmail, and Facebook, which have been built atop it. The rest of the cake exists largely to support Web applications like these and their developers. Let's slice it open (see Figure 18-31) and start at the bottom.

Figure 18-31 A tasty three-layer cake

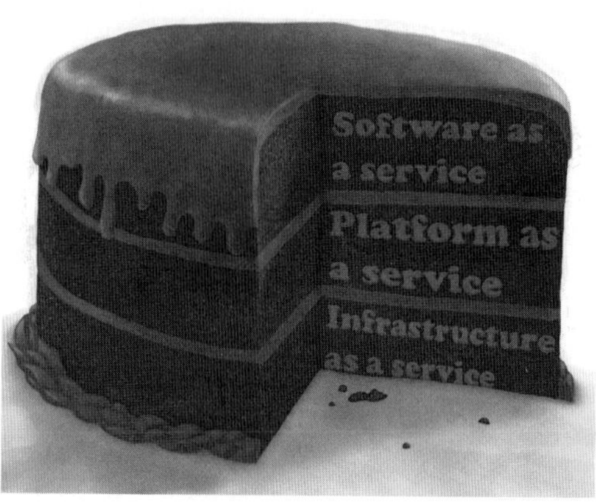

Infrastructure as a Service

Building on the ways virtualization allowed Mario to make the most efficient use of hardware in his local network, large-scale global *Infrastructure as a Service (IaaS)* providers use virtualization to minimize idle hardware, protect against data loss and downtime, and respond to spikes in demand. Mario can use big IaaS providers like Amazon Web Services (AWS) to launch new virtual servers using an operating system of his choice on demand (see Figure 18-32) for pennies an hour. The beauty of IaaS is that you no longer need to purchase expensive, heavy hardware. You are using Amazon's powerful infrastructure as a service.

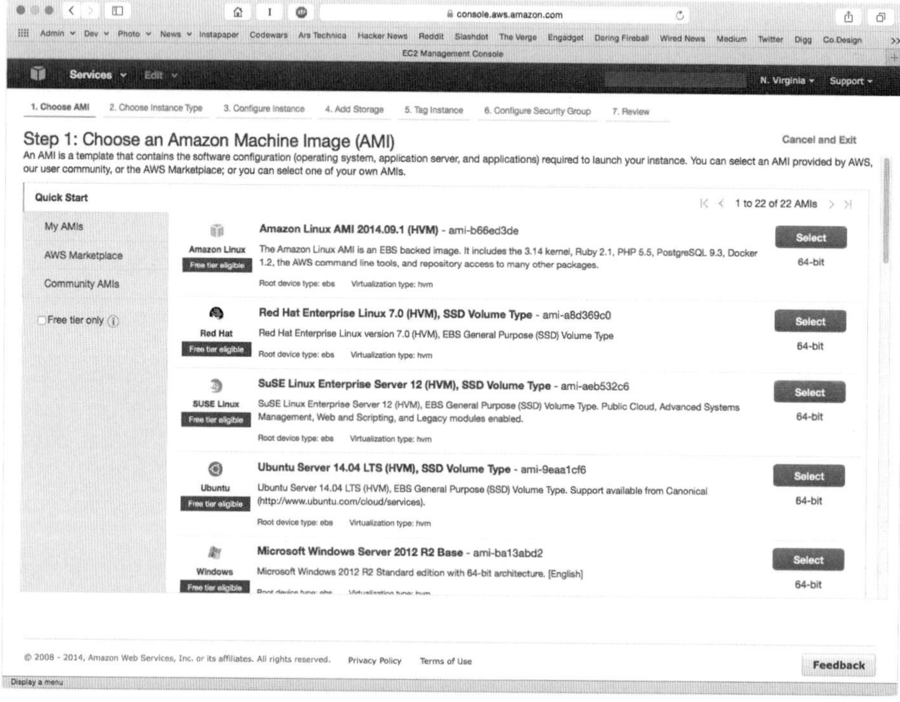

Figure 18-32 Creating an instance on AWS

A huge number of Web sites are really more easily understood if you use the term *Web applications*. If you want to access Mike Meyers' videos, you go to http://hub.totalsem.com. This Web site is really an application that you use to watch videos, practice simulation questions, and so forth. This Web application is a great tool, but as more people access the application we often need to add more capacity so you won't yell at us for a slow server. Luckily, our application is designed to run distributed across multiple servers. If we need more servers, we just add as many more virtual servers as we need. But even this is just scratching the surface. AWS provides many of the services needed to drive popular, complex Web applications—unlimited data storage (see Figure 18-33), database servers, caching, media hosting, and more—all billed by usage.

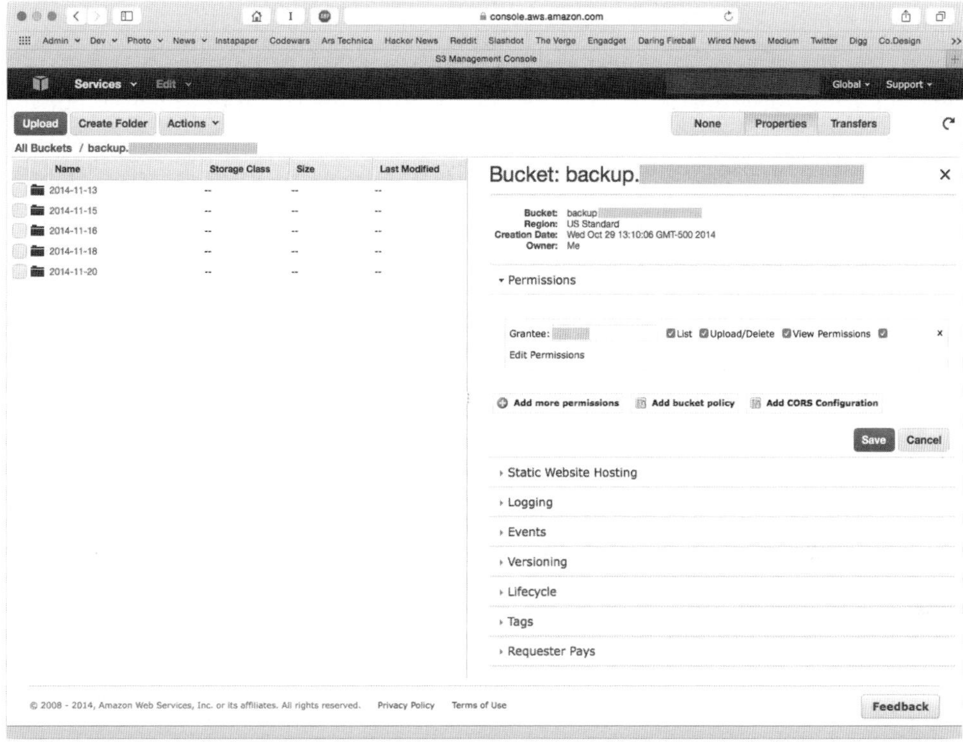

Figure 18-33 Amazon Simple Storage Service (S3)

The hitch is that, while we're no longer responsible for the hardware, we are still responsible for configuring and maintaining the operating system and software of any virtual machines we create. This can mean we have a lot of flexibility to tune it for our needs, but it also requires knowledge of the underlying OS and time to manage it. If you want someone to handle the infrastructure, the operating system, and everything else (except your application), you need to move up to Platform as a Service (PaaS).

Platform as a Service

Web applications are built by programmers. Programmers do one thing really well: they program. The problem for programmers is that a Web application needs a lot more than just a programmer. Developing a Web application requires people to manage the infrastructure: system administrators, database administrators, general network support, and so on. A Web application also needs more than just hardware and an operating system. It needs development tools, monitoring tools, database tools, and potentially hundreds of other tools and services. Getting a Web application up and running is a big job.

A *Platform as a Service (PaaS)* provider gives programmers all the tools they need to deploy, administer, and maintain a Web application. The PaaS provider starts with some form of infrastructure, which could be provided by an IaaS provider, and on top of that infrastructure the provider builds a platform: a complete deployment and management system to handle every aspect of a Web application.

The important point of PaaS is that the infrastructure underneath the PaaS is largely invisible to the developer. The PaaS provider is aware of their infrastructure, but the developer cannot control it directly, and doesn't need to think about its complexity. As far as the programmer is concerned, the PaaS is just a place to deploy and run his or her application.

Heroku, one of the earliest PaaS providers, creates a simple interface on top of the IaaS offerings of AWS, further reducing the complexity of developing and scaling Web applications. Heroku's management console (see Figure 18-34) enables developers to increase or decrease the capacity of an application with a single slider, or easily set up add-ons that add a database, monitor logs, track performance, and more. It could take days for a tech or developer unfamiliar with the software and services to install, configure, and integrate a set of these services with a running application; PaaS providers help cut this down to minutes or hours.

Software as a Service

Software as a Service (SaaS) sits at the top layer of the cake. SaaS shows up in a number of ways, but the best examples are the Web applications we just discussed. Some Web applications, such as Total Seminars Training Hub, charge for access. Other Web applications, like Google Maps, are offered for free. Users of these Web applications don't own this software; you don't get an installation DVD, nor is it something you can download once and keep using. If you want to use a Web application, you must get on the Internet and access the site. While this may seem like a disadvantage at first, the SaaS model provides access to necessary applications wherever you have an Internet connection, often without having to carry data with you or regularly update software. At the enterprise level, the subscription model of many SaaS providers makes it easier to budget and keep hundreds or thousands of computers up to date (see Figure 18-35).

The challenge to perfectly defining SaaS is an argument that almost anything you access on the Internet could be called SaaS. A decade ago we would've called the Google search engine a Web site, but it provides a service (search) that you do not own and that you must access on the Internet. If you're on the Internet, you're arguably always using SaaS.

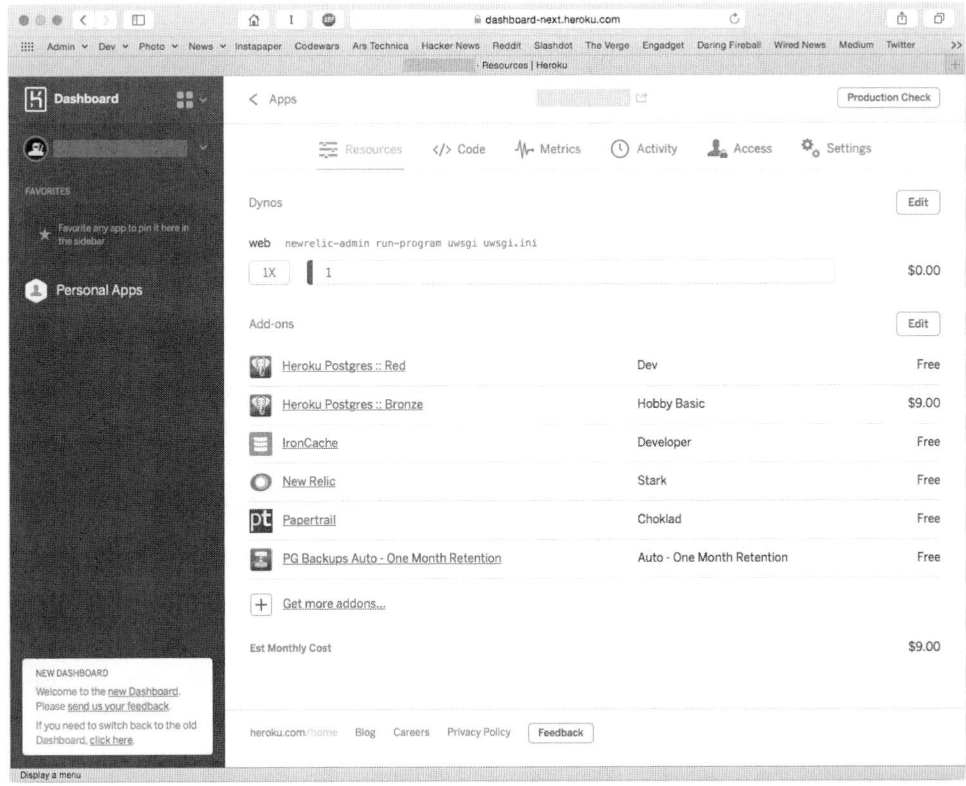

Figure 18-34 Heroku's management console

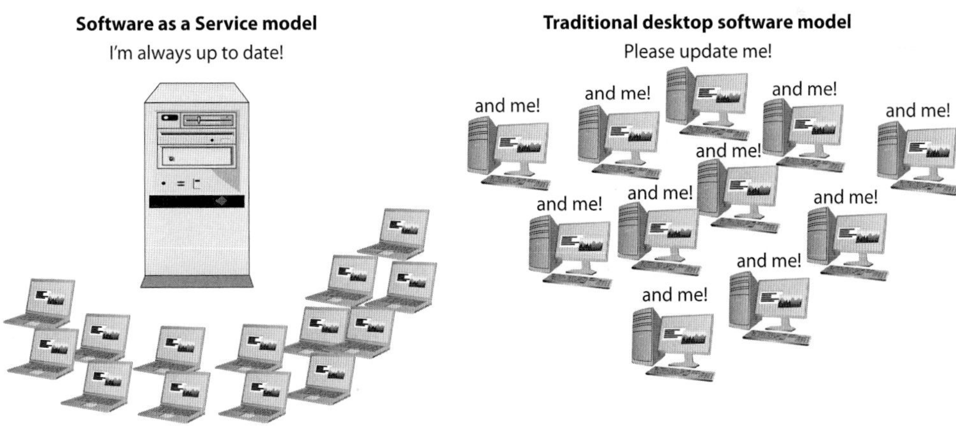

Figure 18-35 SaaS vs. every desktop for themselves

It isn't all icing, though. In exchange for the flexibility of using public, third-party SaaS, you often have to trade strict control of your data. Security might not be crucial when someone uses Google Drive to draft a blog post, but many companies are concerned about sensitive intellectual property or business secrets traveling through untrusted networks and being stored on servers they don't control.

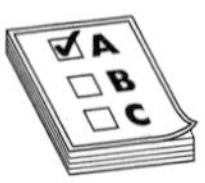

EXAM TIP Know the differences between basic cloud concepts such as SaaS, IaaS, and PaaS.

Ownership and Access

Security concerns like those just discussed don't mean organizations have to forfeit all of the advantages of cloud computing, but they do make their management think hard about the trade-offs between cost, control, customization, and privacy. Some organizations also have unique capacity, performance, or other needs no existing cloud provider can meet. Each organization makes its own decisions about these trade-offs, but the result is usually a cloud network that can be described as public, private, community, or hybrid.

Public Cloud

Most folks usually just interact with a *public cloud*, a term used to describe software, platforms, and infrastructure delivered through networks that the general public can use. When we talk about *the* cloud, this is what we mean. Out on the open, public Internet, cloud services and applications can collaborate in ways that make it easier to think of them collectively as *the cloud* than as many public clouds. The public doesn't *own* this cloud—the hardware is often owned by companies like Amazon, Google, and Microsoft—but there's nothing to stop a company like Netflix from building its Web application atop the IaaS offerings of all three of these companies at once.

The public cloud sees examples of all the *x*aaS varieties, which give specific names to these *cloud concepts*:

- Public IaaS
- Public PaaS
- Public SaaS

Private Cloud

If a business wants some of the flexibility of the cloud, needs complete ownership of its data, and can afford both, it can build an internal cloud the business actually owns—a *private cloud*. A security-minded company with enough resources could build an internal IaaS network in an onsite data center. Departments within the company could create and destroy virtual machines as needed, and develop SaaS to meet collaboration, planning, or task and time management needs all without sending the data over the open Internet. A

company with these needs but without the space or knowledge to build and maintain a private cloud can also contract a third party to maintain or host it.

Again, there are private versions of each of the cloud concepts:

- Private IaaS
- Private PaaS
- Private SaaS

Community Cloud

While a community center is usually a public gathering place for those in the community it serves, a *community cloud* is more like a private cloud paid for and used by more than one organization. Community clouds aren't run by a city or state for citizens' use; the community in this case is a group of organizations with similar goals or needs. If you're a military contractor working on classified projects, wouldn't it be nice to share the burden of defending your cloud against sophisticated attackers sponsored by foreign states with other military and intelligence contractors?

Just like with the public and private cloud, there are community cloud versions of all the *x*aaS varieties:

- Community IaaS
- Community PaaS
- Community SaaS

Hybrid Cloud

Sometimes we *can* have our cake and eat it too. Not all data is crucial, and not every document is a secret. Needs that an organization can only meet in-house might be less important than keeping an application running when demand exceeds what it can handle onsite. We can build a *hybrid cloud* by connecting some combination of public, private, and community clouds, allowing communication between them. Using a hybrid cloud model can mean not having to maintain a private cloud powerful enough to meet peak demand—an application can grow into a public cloud instead of grind to a halt, a technique called *cloud bursting*. But a hybrid cloud isn't just about letting one Web application span two types of cloud—it's also about integrating services across them. Let's take a look at how Mario could use a hybrid cloud to expand his business.

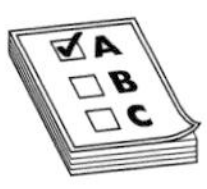

EXAM TIP Know the differences between public, private, community, and hybrid cloud models.

Mario runs a national chain of sandwich shops and is looking into drone-delivered lunch. He'll need a new application in his private cloud to calculate routes and track drones, and that application will have to integrate with the existing order-tracking application in his private cloud. But then he'll also need to integrate it with a third-party

weather application in the public cloud to avoid sending drones out in a blizzard, and a flight-plan application running in a community cloud to avoid other drones, helicopters, and aircraft (and vice versa). The sum of these integrated services and applications *is* the hybrid cloud that will power Mario's drone-delivered lunch. Like the other three clouds, the hybrid cloud sees examples of all the *x*aaS varieties, which give specific names to these cloud concepts:

- Hybrid IaaS
- Hybrid PaaS
- Hybrid SaaS

Why We Cloud

Cloud computing is the way things are done today. But let's take a moment to discuss some of the reasons we use the cloud instead of the old-style hammer of individual servers.

Virtualization

The cloud relies on virtualization. All of the power of virtualization discussed throughout this chapter applies to the cloud. Without virtualization's savings of power, resources, recovery, and security, the cloud simply could not happen.

Rapid Elasticity

Let's say you start a new Web application. If you use an IaaS provider such as Amazon, you can start with a single server and get your new Web application out there. But what happens if your application gets really, really popular? No problem! Using AWS features, you can easily expand the number of servers, even spread them out geographically, with just a click of the switch. We call this ability *rapid elasticity*.

On-Demand

So what if you have a Web application that has wild swings in demand? A local university wants to sell football tickets online. When there isn't a game coming up, their bandwidth demands are very low. But when a game is announced, the Web site is pounded with ticket requests. With cloud computing, it's easy to set up your application to add or reduce capacity based on demand with *on-demand*. The application adjusts according to the current demands.

Resource Pooling

Any time you can consolidate systems' physical and time resources, you are *resource pooling*. While a single server can pool the resources of a few physical servers, imagine the power of a company like Amazon. AWS server farms are massive, pooling resources that would normally take up millions of diverse physical servers spread all over the world!

Measured Service

Ah, the one downside to using the public cloud: you have to write a check to whoever is doing the work for you—and boy can these cloud providers get creative about how to charge you! In some cases you are charged based on the traffic that goes in and out of your Web application, and in other cases you pay for the time that every single one of your virtualized servers is running. Regardless of how costs are measured, this is called *measured service* because of how it differs from more traditional hosting with a fixed monthly or yearly fee.

Chapter Review

Questions

1. Upgrading which component of a host machine would most likely enable you to run more virtual machines simultaneously?
   - **A.** CPU
   - **B.** Hard drive
   - **C.** RAM
   - **D.** Windows
2. What is the difference between a virtual machine (VM) and an emulator?
   - **A.** A VM converts commands to and from a host machine to an entirely different platform, whereas an emulator creates an environment based on the host machine and does no converting.
   - **B.** An emulator converts commands to and from a host machine to an entirely different platform, whereas a VM creates an environment based on the host machine and does no converting.
   - **C.** An emulator requires a host OS, whereas a VM runs on bare-metal servers without an OS.
   - **D.** A VM requires a host OS, whereas an emulator runs on bare-metal servers without an OS.
3. What feature lets you save a VM's state so you can quickly restore to that point? (Choose two.)
   - **A.** Checkpoint
   - **B.** Save
   - **C.** Snapshot
   - **D.** Zip

4. What do you need to install a legal copy of Windows 8.1 into a virtual machine using VMware Workstation?
   A. A valid VM key
   B. Valid Windows 8.1 installation media
   C. A valid ESXi key
   D. A second NIC
5. Which of the following is an advantage of a virtual machine over a physical machine?
   A. Increased performance
   B. Hardware consolidation
   C. No backups needed
   D. Operating systems included
6. Janelle wants to start a new photo-sharing service for real pictures of Bigfoot, but doesn't own any servers. How can she quickly create a new server to run her service?
   A. Public cloud
   B. Private cloud
   C. Community cloud
   D. Hybrid cloud
7. After the unforeseen failure of her Bigfoot-picture-sharing service, bgFootr—which got hacked when she failed to stay on top of her security updates—Janelle has a great new idea for a new service to report Loch Ness Monster sightings. What service would help keep her from having to play system administrator?
   A. Software as a Service
   B. Infrastructure as a Service
   C. Platform as a Service
   D. Network as a Service
8. Powerful hypervisors like ESXi are often booted from ____________________.
   A. Floppy diskettes
   B. USB thumb drives
   C. Firmware
   D. Windows

9. When a virtual machine is not running, how is it stored?
    A. Firmware
    B. RAM drive
    C. Optical disc
    D. Files
10. BigTracks is a successful Bigfoot-tracking company using an internal service to manage all of its automated Bigfoot monitoring stations. A Bigfoot migration has caused a massive increase in the amount of audio and video sent back from their stations. In order to add short-term capacity, they can create new servers in the public cloud. What model of cloud computing does this describe?
    A. Public cloud
    B. Private cloud
    C. Community cloud
    D. Hybrid cloud

Answers

1. **C.** Adding more RAM will enable you to run more simultaneous VMs. Upgrading a hard drive could help, but it's not the best answer here.
2. **B.** An emulator converts from one platform to another, whereas a virtual machine mirrors the host machine.
3. **A, C.** The saved state of a VM is called a snapshot or checkpoint. Not to be confused with a true backup.
4. **B.** You need a copy of the Windows installation media to install Windows.
5. **B.** A big benefit of virtualization is hardware consolidation.
6. **A.** Using the public cloud will enable Janelle to quickly create the servers she needs.
7. **C.** By switching to a PaaS, Janelle can concentrate on creating her service and leave the lower-level administration up to the PaaS provider.
8. **B.** A good hypervisor can be tiny, loading from something as small as a USB thumb drive.
9. **D.** VMs are just files, usually stored on a hard drive.
10. **D.** BigTracks is creating a hybrid cloud by connecting its internal private cloud to a public cloud to quickly expand capacity.

CHAPTER 19

Display Technologies

In this chapter, you will learn how to

- Explain how video displays work
- Select the proper video card
- Install and configure video
- Troubleshoot basic video problems

The term *video* encompasses a complex interaction among numerous parts of personal computing devices, all designed to put a picture on the screen. The *monitor* or *video display* shows you what's going on with your programs and operating system. It's the primary output device for most computing devices. The video card or *display adapter* handles all of the communication between the CPU and the monitor or display (see Figure 19-1). The operating system needs to know how to handle communication between the CPU and the display adapter, which requires drivers specific for each card and proper setup within the operating system. Finally, each application needs to be able to interact with the rest of the video system. The components specific to video fall into the category of *display technologies*.

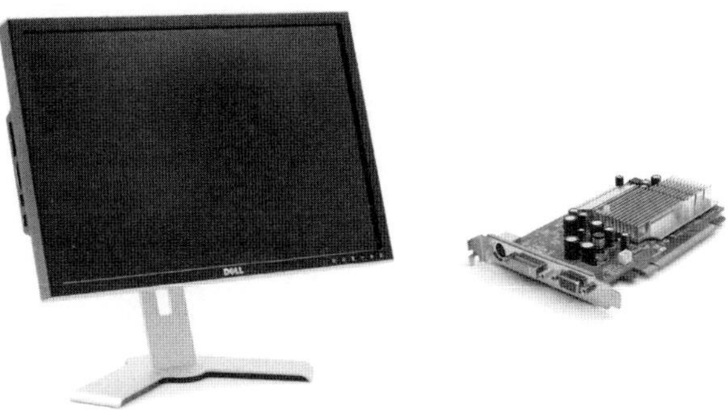

Figure 19-1 Typical monitor and video card

Let's look at monitors and display adapters individually. I'll bring them back together as a team later in the chapter so you can understand the many nuances that make video so challenging. Let's begin with the video display and then move to the display adapter.

Video Displays

To understand displays, you need a good grasp of each component and how they work together to make a beautiful (or not so beautiful) picture on the screen. Different types of displays use different methods and technologies to accomplish this task. Video displays for computing devices come in two varieties: LCD and projector. Every modern personal computer uses an LCD; you'll find projectors in boardrooms and classrooms, splashing a picture onto a screen.

PCs and Macs (well before OS X) originally used a display called a CRT, which is where the Historical/Conceptual section of this chapter starts. A lot of the terminology used with modern displays has roots in how CRTs work—understanding just a few key concepts about CRTs will help make sense of that terminology.

NOTE There's one other type of display used in computing devices, called OLED. The high cost of OLED displays means you're most likely to see them on a smartphone or tablet, so I've saved discussion of OLED for Chapter 25, which covers mobile devices. But costs are falling—so it's worth being aware that OLED has started to turn up in some high-end televisions and will inevitably make the leap to monitors when the price is right.

Historical/Conceptual

CRT Monitors

Cathode ray tube (CRT) monitors were the original computer monitors—heavy, boxy monitors that took up half the desk. As the name implies, this type of display contained a large cathode ray tube, a type of airtight vacuum tube. One end of this tube was a slender cylinder that contained three electron guns. The other end of the tube, which was fatter and wider, was the display screen.

The inside of the display screen had a phosphor coating. When power was applied to one or more of the electron guns, a stream of electrons shot toward the display end of the CRT (see Figure 19-2). Along the way, this stream was subjected to magnetic fields generated by a ring of electromagnets called a *yoke* that controlled the electron beam's point of impact. When the electron beams struck the phosphor coating, the coating released its energy as visible light.

When struck by a stream of electrons, phosphors quickly released bursts of energy. This happened far too quickly for the human eye and brain connection to register. Fortunately, the phosphors on the display screen had a quality called *persistence*, which meant the phosphors continued to glow after being struck by the electron beam. Too much persistence and the image was smeary; too little and the image appeared to flicker. The perfect combination of beam and persistence created the illusion of a solid picture.

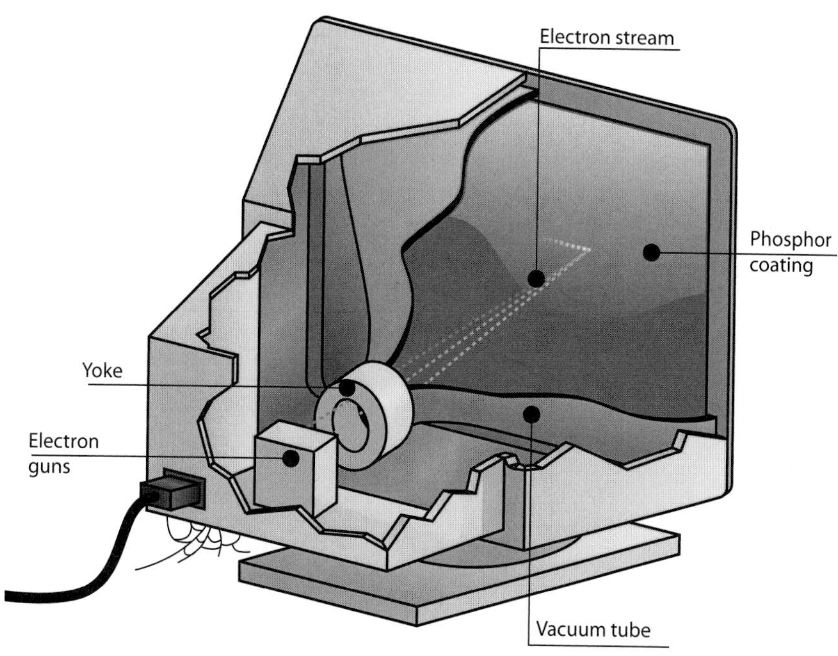

Figure 19-2 Electron stream in the CRT

Refresh Rate

The monitor displayed video data as the electron guns made a series of horizontal sweeps across the screen, energizing the appropriate areas of the phosphorous coating. The sweeps started at the upper-left corner of the monitor and moved across and down to the lower-right corner. The screen was "painted" only in one direction; then the electron guns turned and retraced their path across the screen, to be ready for the next sweep (see Figure 19-3).

Figure 19-3 Electron guns sweep from left to right.

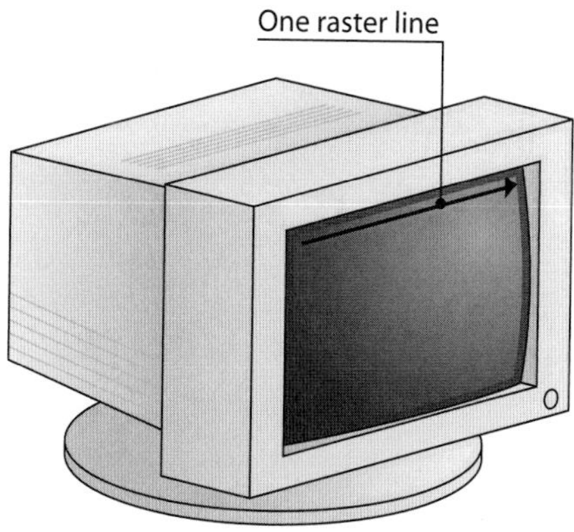

The speed at which the electron beam moved across the screen was known as the *horizontal refresh rate (HRR)*, as shown in Figure 19-4. The monitor drew a number of lines across the screen, eventually covering the screen with glowing phosphors. The number of lines was not fixed. After the guns reached the lower-right corner of the screen, they turned off and pointed back to the upper-left corner. The amount of time it took to draw the entire screen and get the electron guns back to the upper-left corner was called the *vertical refresh rate (VRR)*, shown in Figure 19-5.

Figure 19-4 Horizontal refresh rate

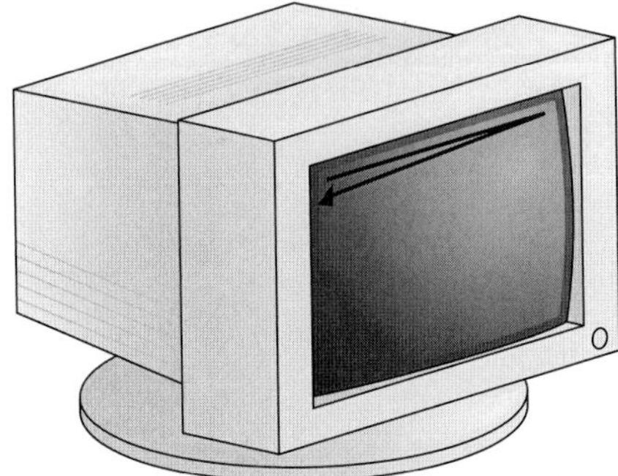

The time it takes to draw one line across the screen and be ready for the next is called the horizontal refresh rate (HRR). This is measured in KHz (thousands of lines per second).

Figure 19-5 Vertical refresh rate

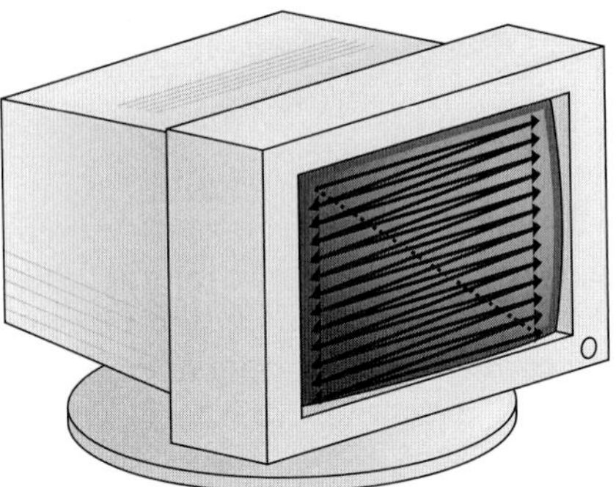

The number of times per second the electron guns can draw the entire screen and then return to the uppper left-corner is called the vertical refresh rate (VRR). This is measured in Hz (screens per second).

Today, monitor developers and technologists only refer to the *refresh rate*, meaning the time it takes for a monitor to redraw a whole screen (just like the CRT's VRR). You'll see this term again in a little while.

Phosphors and Shadow Mask

All CRT monitors had dots of phosphorous or some other light-sensitive compound that glowed *red*, *green*, or *blue* (*RGB*) when an electron gun swept over it. These *phosphors* were evenly distributed across the front of the monitor (see Figure 19-6).

Figure 19-6 A CRT monitor is a grid of red, green, and blue phosphors.

A normal CRT had three electron guns: one for the red phosphors, one for the blue phosphors, and one for the green phosphors. Directly behind the phosphors in a CRT was the *shadow mask*, a screen that allowed only the proper electron gun to light the proper phosphors (see Figure 19-7). This prevented, for example, the red electron beam from "bleeding over" and lighting neighboring blue and green dots.

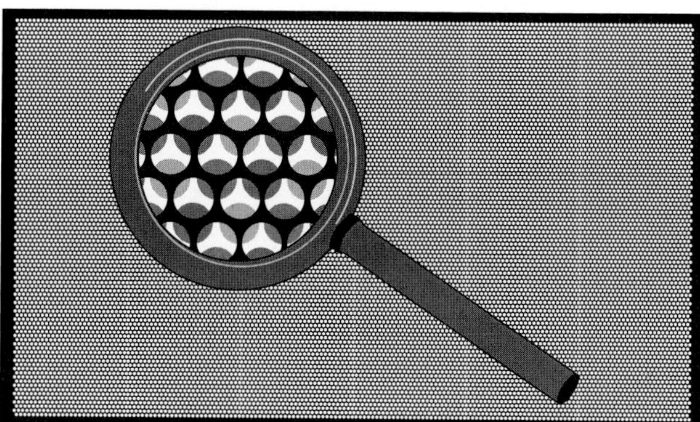

Figure 19-7 Shadow mask

The electron guns swept across the phosphors as a group, turning rapidly on and off as they moved across the screen. When the group reached the end of the screen, it moved to the next line. Turning the guns on and off, combined with moving the guns to new lines, created a mosaic that was the image you saw on the screen. The number of times the guns turned on and off, combined with the number of lines drawn on the screen, determined the number of mosaic pieces used to create the image. These individual pieces were—and are—called *pixels*, from the term *picture elements*.

901

Resolution

Monitor *resolution* is always shown as the number of horizontal pixels times the number of vertical pixels. A resolution of 640 × 480, therefore, indicates a horizontal resolution of 640 pixels and a vertical resolution of 480 pixels. If you multiply the values together,

you can see how many pixels are on each screen: 640 × 480 = 307,200 pixels per screen. An example of resolution affecting the pixel size is shown in Figure 19-8.

Figure 19-8 Resolution versus pixel size

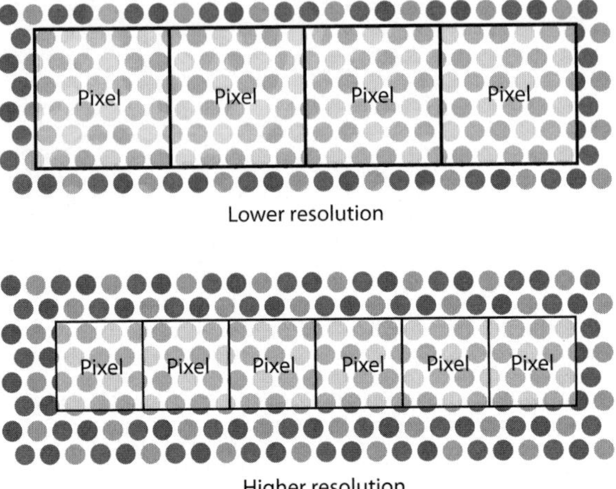

Some common resolutions for early monitors were 640 × 480, 800 × 600, and 1024 × 768. Notice that most of these resolutions match a 4:3 ratio. This is called the *aspect ratio*. You'll find some 4:3 monitors today, but the vast majority have a 16:9 or 16:10 aspect ratio. These are generically called *wide-screen monitors*. Three of the common resolutions you'll see with these monitors are 1366 × 768, 1600 × 900, and 1920 × 1080.

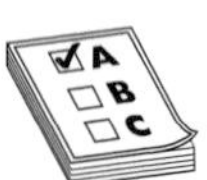

EXAM TIP Be familiar with 4:3, 16:9, and 16:10 aspect ratios for the CompTIA A+ 220-901 exam.

Now that you have the basics of CRT monitors, let's turn to LCD monitors. Although the technology differs dramatically between the monitor types, most of the terms used for CRTs also apply to LCD functions.

LCD Monitors

Almost every computing device today uses a *liquid crystal display (LCD)* as the primary visual output component. LCDs work very differently in some respects than CRTs; other aspects are similar. There's a lot of variation among LCDs, as you might imagine, considering the amazing variety of computing devices out there. Let's start with the technology and then examine variations.

How LCDs Work

The secret to understanding the most common type of LCD panels is to understand the concept of the polarity of light. Anyone who played with a prism in sixth grade or has looked at a rainbow knows that light travels in waves (no quantum mechanics here, please!), and the wavelength of the light determines the color. What you might not appreciate is the fact that light waves emanate from a light source in three dimensions.

It's impossible to draw a clear diagram of three-dimensional waves, so instead, let's use an analogy. To visualize this, think of light emanating from a flashlight. Now think of the light emanating from that flashlight as though someone was shaking a jump rope. This is not a rhythmic shaking, back and forth or up and down; it's more as if a person went crazy and was shaking the jump rope all over the place—up, down, left, right—constantly changing the speed.

That's how light really acts. Well, I guess we could take the analogy one step further by saying the person has an infinite number of arms, each holding a jump rope shooting out in every direction to show the three-dimensionality of light waves, but (a) I can't draw that and (b) one jump rope will suffice to explain the typical LCD panels. The varying speeds create wavelengths, from very short to very long. When light comes into your eyes at many different wavelengths, you see white light. If the light came in only one wavelength, you would see only that color. Light flowing through a polarized filter (like sunglasses) is like putting a picket fence between you and the people shaking the ropes. You see all of the wavelengths, but only the waves of similar orientation. You would still see all of the colors, just fewer of them because you only see the waves of the same orientation, making the image darker. That's why many sunglasses use polarizing filters.

Now, what would happen if you added another picket fence but put the slats in a horizontal direction? This would effectively cancel out all of the waves. This is what happens when two polarizing filters are combined at a 90-degree angle—no light passes through.

Now, what would happen if you added a third fence between the two fences with the slats at a 45-degree angle? Well, it would sort of "twist" some of the shakes in the rope so that the waves could then get through. The same thing is true with the polarizing filters. The third filter twists some of the light so that it gets through. If you're really feeling scientific, go to any educational supply store and pick up three polarizing filters for about US$3 each and try it. It works.

Liquid crystals take advantage of the property of polarization. Liquid crystals are composed of a specially formulated liquid full of long, thin crystals that always want to orient themselves in the same direction, as shown in Figure 19-9. This substance acts exactly like a liquid polarized filter. If you poured a thin film of this stuff between two sheets of glass, you'd get a darn good pair of sunglasses.

Figure 19-9 Waves of similar orientation

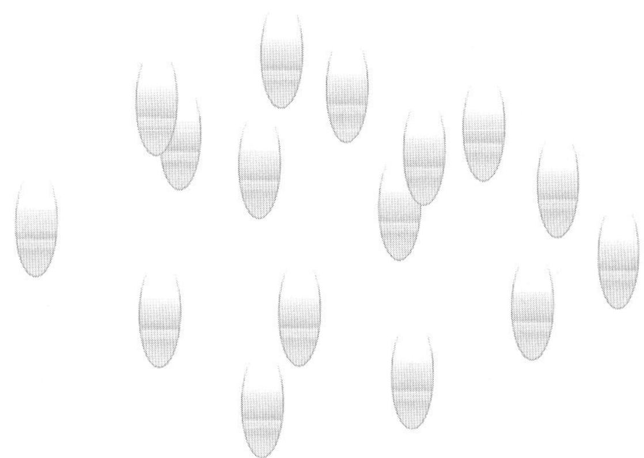

Imagine cutting extremely fine grooves on one side of one of those sheets of glass. When you place this liquid in contact with a finely grooved surface, the molecules naturally line up with the grooves in the surface (see Figure 19-10).

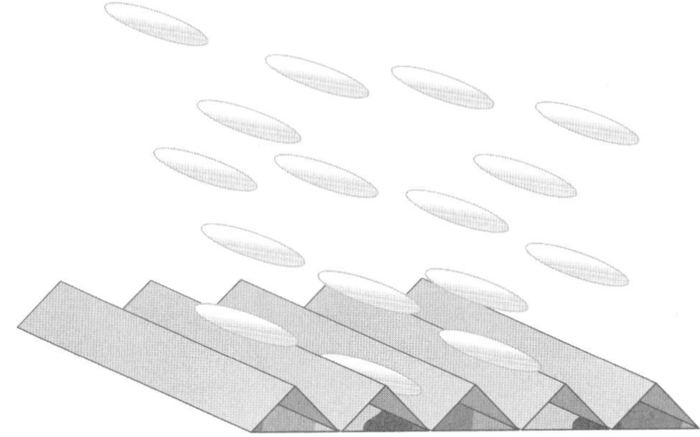

Figure 19-10 Liquid crystal molecules tend to line up together.

If you place another finely grooved surface, with the grooves at a 90-degree orientation to the other surface, opposite of the first one, the molecules in contact with that side will attempt to line up with it. The molecules in between, in trying to line up with both sides, will immediately line up in a nice twist (see Figure 19-11). If two perpendicular polarizing filters are then placed on either side of the liquid crystal, the liquid crystal will twist the light and enable it to pass (see Figure 19-12).

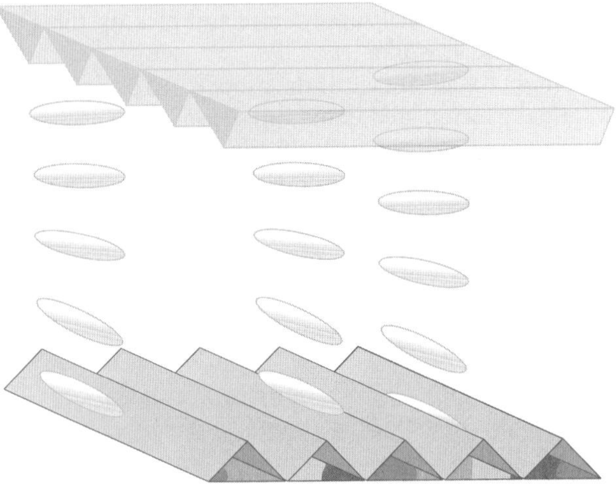

Figure 19-11 Liquid crystal molecules twisting

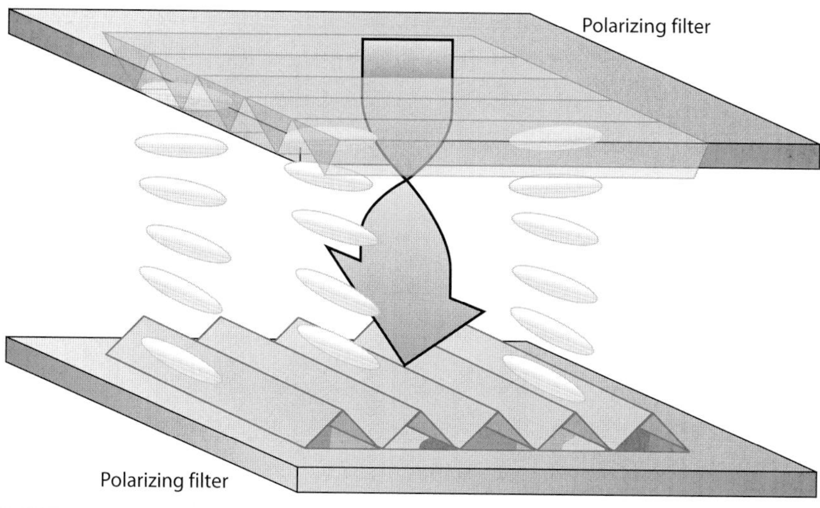

Figure 19-12 No charge, enabling light to pass

If you expose the liquid crystal to an electrical potential, however, the crystals will change their orientation to match the direction of the electrical field. The twist goes away and no light passes through (see Figure 19-13).

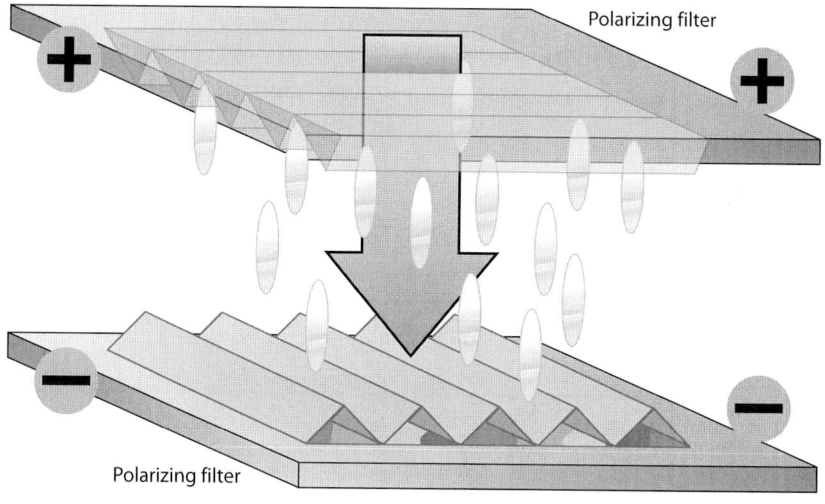

Figure 19-13 Electrical charge, no light is able to pass

A color LCD screen is composed of a large number of tiny liquid crystal molecules (called *sub-pixels*) arranged in rows and columns between polarizing filters. A translucent sheet above the sub-pixels is colored red, green, or blue. Each tiny distinct group of three sub-pixels—one red, one green, and one blue—forms a physical pixel, as shown in Figure 19-14.

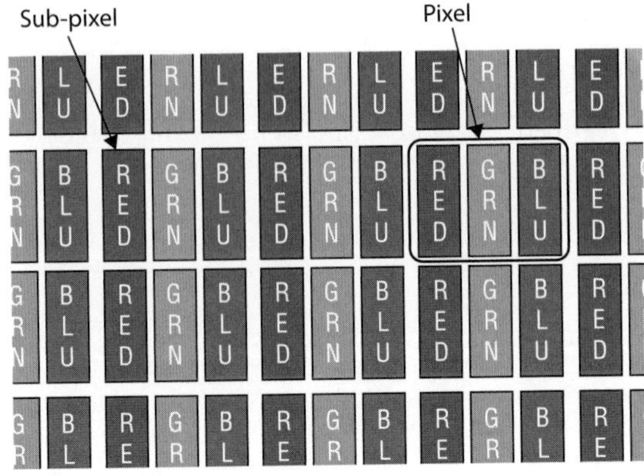

Figure 19-14 LCD pixels

NOTE LCD pixels are very different from the pixels in a CRT. A CRT pixel's size changed depending on the resolution. The pixels in an LCD panel are fixed and cannot be changed. See the section "LCD Resolution" later in the chapter for the scoop.

Once all of the pixels are laid out, how do you charge the right spots to make an image? Early LCDs didn't use rectangular pixels. Instead, images were composed of different-shaped elements, each electrically separate from the others. To create an image, each area was charged at the same time. Figure 19-15 shows the number zero, a display made possible by charging six areas to make an ellipse of sorts. This process, called *static charging*, is still quite popular in more basic numeric displays such as calculators.

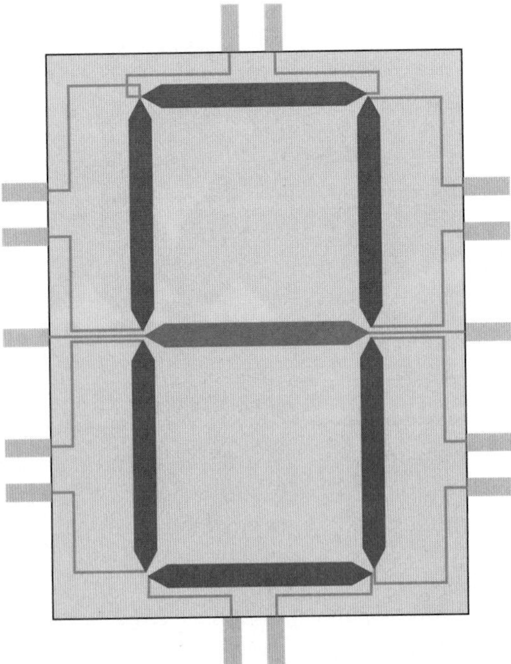

Figure 19-15 Single character for static LCD numeric display

The static method would not work in PCs due to its inherent inflexibility. Instead, early LCD screens used a matrix of wires (see Figure 19-16). The vertical wires, the Y wires, ran to every sub-pixel in the column. The horizontal wires, the X wires, ran along an entire row of sub-pixels. There had to be a charge on both the X wires and the Y wires to make enough voltage to light a single sub-pixel.

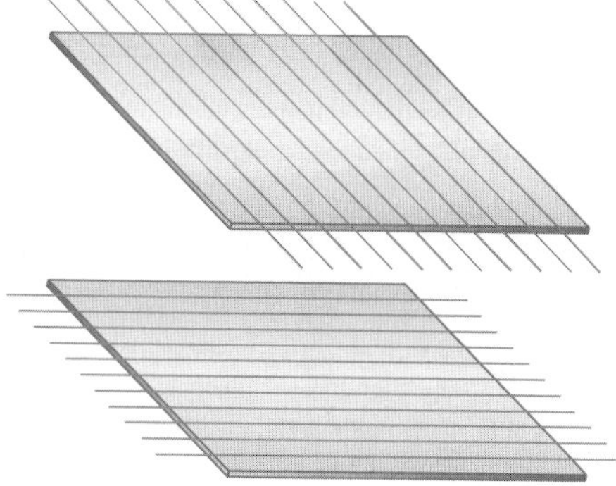

Figure 19-16 An LCD matrix of wires

If you wanted color, you had to have three matrices. The three matrices intersected very close together. Above the intersections, the glass was covered with tiny red, green, and blue dots. Varying the amount of voltage on the wires made different levels of red, green, and blue, creating colors (see Figure 19-17).

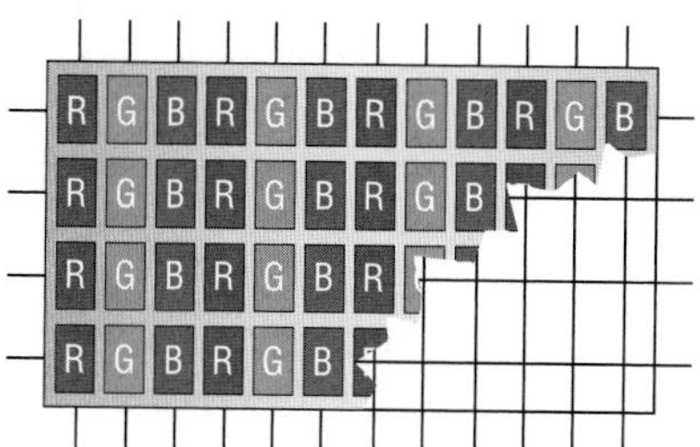

Figure 19-17 Passive matrix display

We call this usage of LCD technology *passive matrix*. All LCD displays on PCs used only passive matrix for many years. Unfortunately, passive matrix is slow and tends to create a little overlap between individual pixels. This gives a slightly blurred effect to the image displayed. Manufacturers eventually came up with a speedier method of display, called *dual-scan passive matrix*, in which the screen refreshed two lines at a time.

Thin Film Transistor

Current LCD monitors use some form of *thin film transistor (TFT)* or *active matrix* technology (see Figure 19-18). Instead of using X and Y wires, one or more tiny transistors control each color dot, providing faster picture display, crisp definition, and much tighter color control than passive or dual-scan technologies could provide.

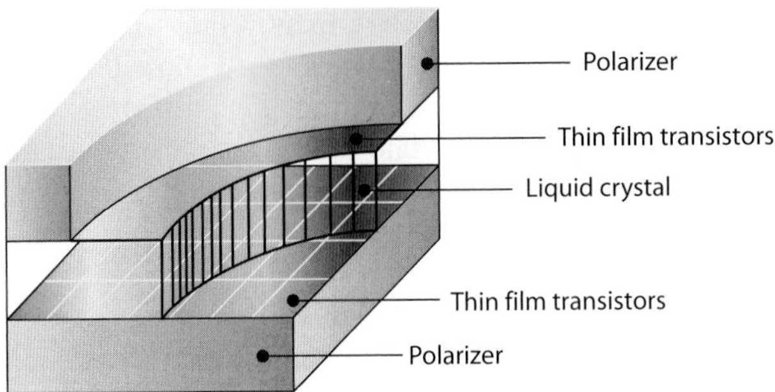

Figure 19-18 Active matrix display

The most common TFT displays use a technology called *twisted nematic (TN)*, which produces a decent display for a modest price. Most TN displays use only 6 bits for each color—red, green, and blue—and that 18-bit display will not reproduce the full 24-bit true color that video cards can send to it. This means the panel fudges a little bit when asked to do something it can't do, and this can produce noticeable problems with reproduction.

Better TFT displays use a technology called *In-Plane Switching (IPS)* to create a wider viewing angle and far better color re-creation than TN panels can provide. Graphics professionals use IPS monitors, for example, because they can display how something might print more faithfully than TN screens. Manufacturers use many types of IPS technology to find the right mix of price-to-performance.

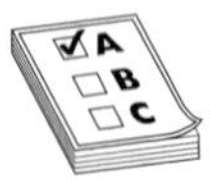

EXAM TIP You need to know the differences between TN and IPS display technologies for the CompTIA A+ 901 exam.

LCD Components

The typical LCD monitor is composed of three main components: the LCD panel, the backlight(s), and the inverters. The LCD panel creates the image, the *backlights* illuminate the image so you can see it, and the *inverters* send power to the backlights. Figure 19-19 shows a typical layout for the internal components of an LCD monitor.

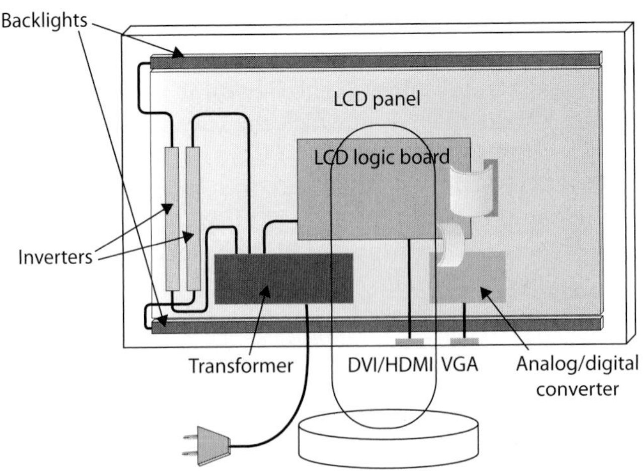

Figure 19-19 LCD internals

LCD Monitors with CCFL Backlights One of the great challenges to LCD power stems from the fact that the backlights need AC power while the electronics need DC power. Figure 19-19 shows one of the many ways that LCD monitor makers handle this issue. The AC power from your wall socket goes into an AC/DC transformer that changes the power to DC. The LCD panel uses this DC power.

Note in Figure 19-19 that this monitor has two backlights: one at the top and one at the bottom. Most LCDs have two backlights, although some have only one. Most LCD backlights use *cold cathode fluorescent lamp (CCFL)* technology, popular for its low power use, even brightness, and long life. Figure 19-20 shows a CCFL from an LCD panel.

Figure 19-20
CCFL backlight

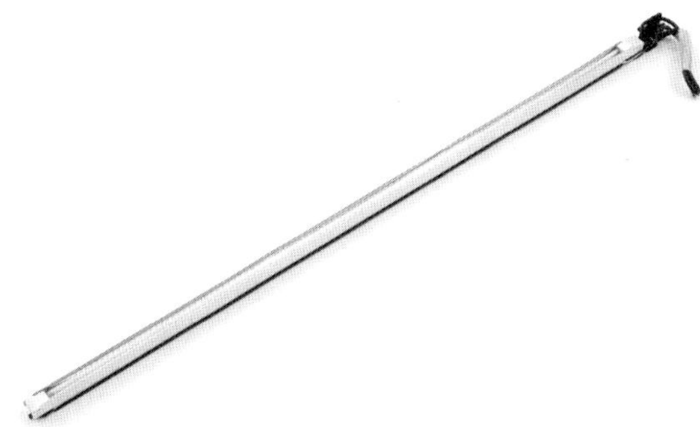

CCFLs need AC power to operate, but given that the transformer converts the incoming AC power to DC, each CCFL backlight needs a device called an inverter to convert the DC power back into AC. Figure 19-21 shows a typical inverter used in an LCD.

Figure 19-21
Inverter

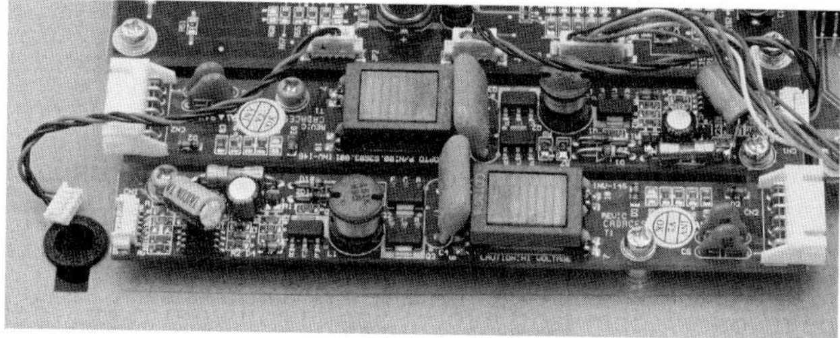

Looking once again at Figure 19-19, note the two input connectors, DVI/HDMI and VGA. DVI and HDMI are digital signals, so they connect directly to the LCD's logic circuitry. The VGA goes to an analog-to-digital converter before reaching the LCD logic board.

Keep in mind that Figure 19-19 is a generic illustration. The actual location and interconnections of the components are as variable as the number of LCD panels available today!

LED Monitors Manufacturers also use several types of *light-emitting diode (LED)* light for backlighting, either directly illuminating pixels from behind or flooding the panel from the edges of the bezel. The former produces outstanding contrast and color, but costs

a lot more than the edge types. The edge types function similarly to a CCFL-style display, so they produce similar contrast and colors to the older technology. Manufacturers have rebranded LCD monitors that use LEDs for backlighting as *LED monitors*.

NOTE Many manufacturers refer to LEDs as a display type, but such displays don't exist aside from marketing terms. LEDs manifest only as one form of backlighting for LCD monitors. Even so-called *LED monitors* and *LED televisions* are simply LCDs with LED backlights. The terms are merely marketing speak.

Using LEDs for backlighting reduces the thickness of the panels and reduces the overall electricity usage. LEDs don't need AC power, so there's no inverter to get involved in lighting the panel. Many smaller devices, such as smartphones and tablets, use LED backlights to save battery use. The better panels are also in high demand from graphics professionals.

Try This!

Test the Viewing Angle of LCDs

Take a trip to your local computer store to look at LCD and LED displays. Don't get sidetracked looking at all of the latest graphics cards, sound cards, CPUs, motherboards, and RAM—well, actually, it's okay to look at those things. Just don't forget to look at monitors!

Stand about two feet in front of an LCD display. Look directly at the image on the screen and consider the image quality, screen brightness, and color. Take a small step to your right. Compare the image you see now to the image you saw previously. Continue taking small steps to the right until you are no longer able to discern the image on the display. You've reached the edge of the viewing angle for that LCD.

Do this test with a few different monitors. Do smaller LCDs, such as 17-inch displays, have smaller viewing angles? Do larger displays have better viewing angles? How different are the LCDs with CCFL backlights from the LED monitors? You might also want to test the vertical viewing angles of some monitors. Try to find a monitor that is on your eye level; then look at it from above and below—does it have a large viewing range vertically?

LCD Resolution

All LCD monitors have a *native resolution*, such as 1920 × 1080, that enables them to display the sharpest picture possible. As mentioned earlier, the pixels are fixed. You simply cannot run an LCD monitor at a resolution higher than the native one. Worse, because LCDs have no equivalent to a shadow mask, they can't run at a *lower* than

native resolution without severely degrading image quality. The LCD has to use an edge-blurring technique called *anti-aliasing* to soften the jagged corners of the pixels when running at lower than native resolution, which simply does not look as good. The bottom line? Always set the LCD at native resolution!

NOTE Two LCD panels that have the same physical size may have different native resolutions.

The hard-wired nature of LCD resolution creates a problem for techs and consumers when dealing with bigger, better-quality monitors. A small 17-inch LCD usually has 1366 × 768 or higher resolution, for example, and the larger 20+-inch LCDs can go up to 1920 × 1080 or more. These high resolutions make the menus and fonts on a monitor super tiny, a problem for people with less-than-stellar vision. Many folks throw in the towel and run these high-end LCDs at lower resolution and just live with the lower-quality picture, but that's not the best way to resolve this problem.

Modern operating systems enable incredible interface customization. You can change the font size, shape, and color. You can resize the icons, toolbars, and more. You can even change the number of dots per inch (DPI) for the full screen, making everything bigger or smaller!

For basic customization of Windows, for example, start at the Display applet or Personalization applet in the Control Panel. To change the DPI for the display in Vista, click on the Adjust font size (DPI) option in the Tasks list. In Windows 7 and later, select one of the preset font sizes or a custom size. Your clients will thank you!

Brightness

The strength of an LCD monitor's backlights determines the brightness of the monitor. The brightness is measured in *nits*. LCD panels vary from 100 nits on the low end to over 1000 nits or more on the high end. Average LCD panels are around 300 nits, which most monitor authorities consider excellent brightness.

NOTE One nit equals one candela/m^2. One candela is roughly equal to the amount of light created by a candle.

Response Rate

An LCD panel's *response rate* is the amount of time it takes for all of the sub-pixels on the panel to go from pure black to pure white and back again. This is roughly the same concept as the CRT refresh rate, but with one important difference. Once the electron gun on a CRT lights a phosphor, that phosphor begins to fade until it is lit again. An individual LCD sub-pixel holds its intensity until the LCD circuitry changes that sub-pixel, making flicker less of an issue on LCDs.

Manufacturers measure LCD response rates in milliseconds, with lower being better. A typical lower-end or older LCD has a response rate of 20–25 ms. The screens look fine, but you'll get some ghosting if you try to watch a movie or play a fast-paced video game. In recent years, manufacturers have figured out how to overcome this issue, and you can find many LCD monitors with a response rate of 2–4 ms.

Refresh Rate

The refresh rate for an LCD monitor is described using numbers similar to those used to describe the refresh rate for a CRT monitor, such as 60 Hz, but the terms mean slightly different things between the two technologies. With CRTs, as you'll recall, the phosphors on the screen start to lose their glow and need to be hit again by the electron guns many times per second to achieve an unwavering or flicker-free image. Each dot on an active matrix LCD, in contrast, has its own transistor to light it up. There's no need to freshen up the dot; it's on or off. Regardless of the refresh rate for the LCD, therefore, there's never any flicker at all caused by refresh rate.

The refresh rate for an LCD monitor refers to how often a screen can change or update completely. Think of the refresh rate as a metronome or timer and you'll be closer to how it works in an LCD. For most computing issues, 60 Hz is fine and that's been the standard for the industry. Humans see things that change as infrequently as 24 times per second—the standard for motion pictures at the cinema, for example, and the best high-definition (HD) signal—as a full motion video. To be able to change almost three times faster is perfectly acceptable, even in higher-end applications such as fast-moving games.

Monitor manufacturers have released 120-Hz LCD monitors in a response to the convergence of LCDs, televisions, and computers to enable you to see HD movies or standard-definition (SD) content without any problems or visual artifacts on an LCD monitor. The easiest number that provides a whole-number division for both 24 frames per second and 30 frames per second was 120 Hz. The latter is the standard for SD content.

NOTE A video card needs to be able to support Dual-Link DVI to run a 120-Hz monitor or television. See the discussion on DVI later in this chapter for details.

Contrast Ratio

CRT monitors lingered in a couple of professions for a long time, because LCDs cannot produce the color saturation or richness of contrast of a CRT. It was not unusual, even a few years ago, to walk into a visual design studio and see a few working CRTs.

LCD technology continues to improve every year, and manufacturers today can produce panels that rival the old CRT technology. A good contrast ratio—the difference between the darkest and lightest spots that the monitor can display—is 450:1, although a quick trip to a computer store will reveal LCDs with lower levels (250:1) and higher levels (1000:1).

LCD monitor manufacturers market a *dynamic contrast ratio* number for their monitors, which measures the difference between a full-on, all-white screen, and a full-off,

or all-black screen. This yields a much higher number than the standard contrast ratio. My Samsung panels have a 1000:1 contrast ratio, for example, but a 20,000:1 dynamic contrast ratio. Sounds awesome, right? In general, the dynamic contrast ratio doesn't affect viewing on computer monitors. Focus on the standard contrast ratio when making decisions on LCD screens.

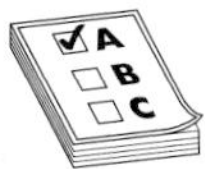

EXAM TIP The CompTIA A+ 901 exam expects you to understand the refresh rate, resolution, and native resolution of a monitor.

Comparing LCDs

At this point, you have a lot of information to sort when comparing LCDs to purchase for yourself or a client. Size and native resolution, of course, should take top consideration. The panel technology—TN vs. IPS—and backlight—CCFL vs. LED—can impact the overall quality of the display as well as the price. (Note that the CompTIA A+ 901 objectives say "fluorescent vs. LED.") Because the monitor is both the primary visual interactive component on a computer and the component most likely to stick with you the longest, these decisions matter.

For the exam, also keep in mind the brightness, response rate, and contrast ratio. Most modern monitors have acceptable specifications on those items.

Projectors

Projectors enable you to display computer images to an audience. There are two ways to project an image on a screen: rearview and front-view. As the name would suggest, a *rearview projector* (see Figure 19-22) shoots an image onto a screen from the rear. Rearview projectors are self-enclosed and were once very popular for televisions, but are virtually unheard of in the PC world.

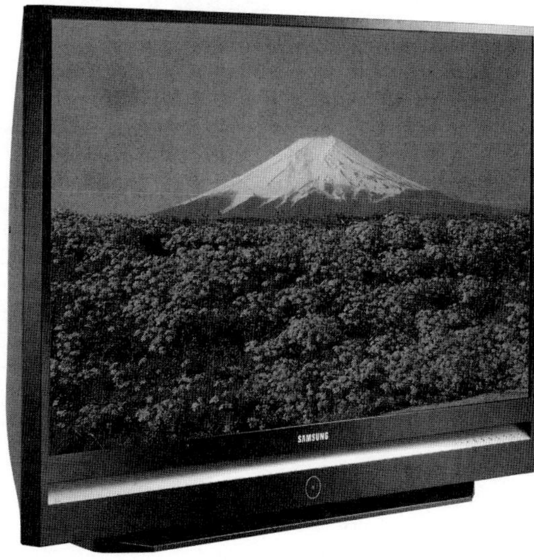

Figure 19-22 Rearview projector (photo courtesy of Samsung)

A *front-view projector* shoots the image out the front and counts on you to put a screen in front at the proper distance. Front-view projectors connected to PCs running Microsoft PowerPoint have been the cornerstone of every meeting almost everywhere since the Clinton administration (see Figure 19-23). This section deals exclusively with front-view projectors that connect to PCs.

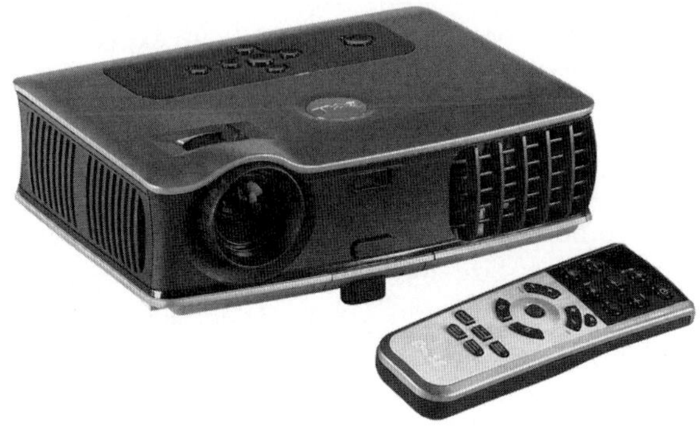

Figure 19-23 Front-view projector (photo courtesy of Dell Inc.)

Projector Technologies

Projectors that connect to PCs have been in existence for almost as long as PCs themselves. Given all that time, a number of technologies have been used in projectors. The first generation of projectors used CRTs. Each color used a separate CRT that projected the image onto a screen (see Figure 19-24). CRT projectors create beautiful images but are expensive, large, and very heavy, and have for the most part been abandoned for more recent technologies.

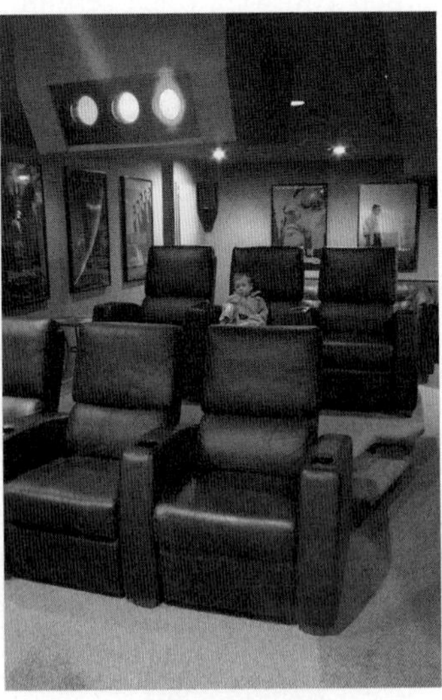

Figure 19-24 CRT projector

Given that light shines through an LCD panel, LCD projectors are a natural fit for front projection. LCD projectors are light and very inexpensive compared to CRTs but lack the image quality. LCD projectors are so light that almost all portable projectors use LCD (see Figure 19-25).

Figure 19-25 LCD projector (photo courtesy of ViewSonic)

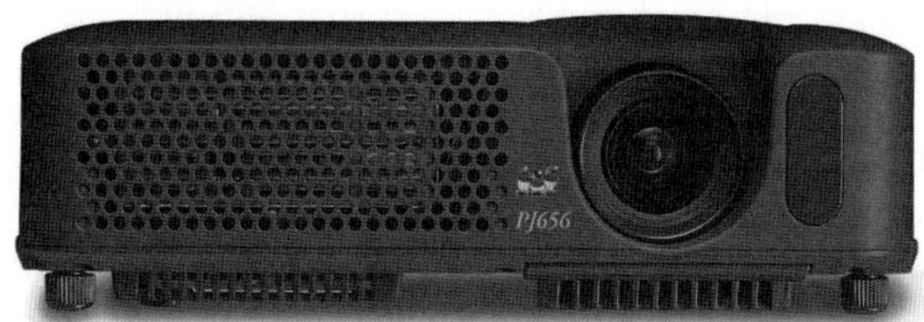

All projectors share the same issues as their equivalent-technology monitors. LCD projectors have a specific native resolution, for example. In addition, you need to understand three concepts specific to projectors: lumens, throw, and lamps.

Lumens

The brightness of a projector is measured in lumens. A *lumen* is the amount of light given off by a light source from a certain angle that is perceived by the human eye. The greater the lumen rating of a projector, the brighter the projector will be. The best lumen rating depends on the size of the room and the amount of light in the room. There's no single answer for "the right lumen rating" for a projector, but use this as a rough guide: If you use a projector in a small, darkened room, 1000 to 1500 lumens will work well. If you use a projector in a mid-sized room with typical lighting, you'll need at least 2000 lumens. Projectors for large rooms have ratings over 10,000 lumens and are very expensive.

Throw

A projector's *throw* is the size of the image at a certain distance from the screen. All projectors have a recommended minimum and maximum throw distance that you need to take into consideration. A typical throw would be expressed as follows. A projector with a 16:9 image aspect ratio needs to be 11 to 12 feet away from the projection surface to create a 100-inch diagonal screen. A *long throw lens* has about a 1:2 ratio of screen size to distance, so to display a 4-foot screen, you'd have to put the projector 8 feet away. Some *short throw lenses* drop that ratio down as low as 1:1!

Lamps

The bane of every projector is the lamp. Lamps work hard in your projector, as they must generate a tremendous amount of light. As a result, they generate quite a bit of heat, and all projectors come with a fan to keep the lamp from overheating. When you turn off a projector, the fan continues to run until the lamp is fully cooled. Lamps are also expensive, usually in the range of a few hundred dollars (U.S.), which comes as a nasty shock to someone who's not prepared for that price when the lamp dies!

Plasma Displays

Plasma display panels (PDPs) are a popular technology for displaying movies, competing directly with LCD screens for the flat-panel space. They offer a wider viewing angle and richer picture than the typical LCD and cost less. They weigh a lot more and consume much more electricity, though, compared to LCDs.

Unfortunately, plasma TVs have two issues that make them a bad choice for PC use. First is *burn-in*—the tendency for a screen to leave a "ghost" image even after the image is off the screen. Plasma TV makers have virtually eliminated burn-in, but even the latest plasma displays are subject to burn-in when used as PC displays.

The second issue is *overscan*, a problem that can affect LCD-based TVs as well. Overscan is when the TV blows up the image, cropping off the edges of the picture. TVs do this for historical reasons, but the side effect is that when used with a PC, things like your taskbar get cut off. Some manufacturers have a setting to disable this feature, but not all do. Because plasma displays can be connected to a computer, CompTIA included the plasma display device in the 220-901 exam objectives. I would advise against using a plasma screen as a monitor.

Common Features

All monitors share a number of characteristics that you need to know for purchase, installation, maintenance, and troubleshooting.

Connections

Many monitors for Windows PCs use a 15-pin, three-row, D-type connector (see Figure 19-26) and a power plug. The connector has a lot of names, such as *D-shell* or *D-subminiature* connector, DB-15, DE15, or simply *VGA connector*. CompTIA has adopted the latest name for the connector, calling it an *HD15*, for *high density*, to distinguish it from its truly ancient nine-pin forbearer.

Figure 19-26
A VGA connector

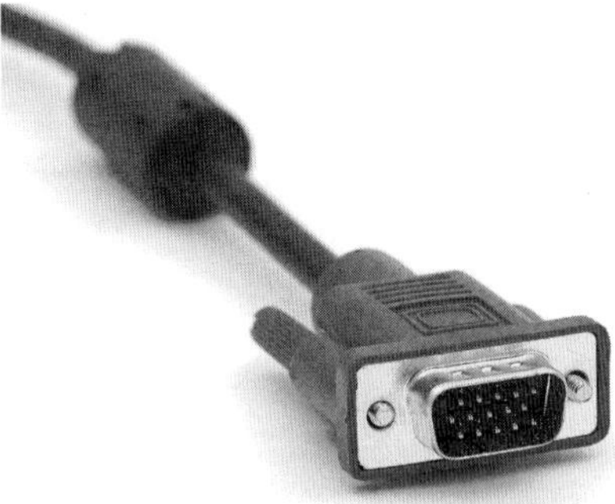

We need to step back in time a little to understand *analog versus digital signals*. Surprisingly, many modern video cards support CRT monitors just fine, so let's plug one in and talk signals.

Controlling a CRT requires an *analog signal* from the video card, meaning a signal that rises and falls in waves like a series of *S*s on their side. LCDs and computers, on the other hand, use digital signals, on or off, one or zero.

The video information stored on a video card's RAM is clearly digital. Video cards include a special chip (or function embedded into a chip that does several other jobs) called the *random access memory digital-to-analog converter (RAMDAC)*. As the name implies, the RAMDAC takes the digital signal from the video card and turns it into an analog signal for the analog CRT (see Figure 19-27).

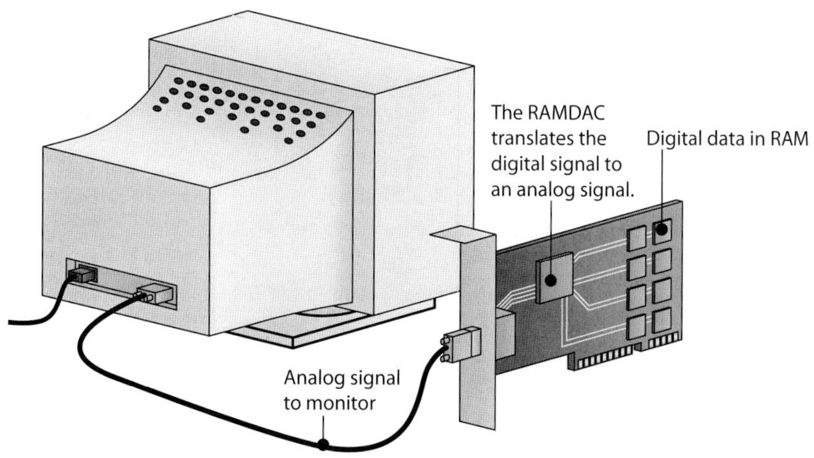

Figure 19-27 An analog signal sent to a CRT monitor

RAMDACs make sense for analog CRT monitors. If you want to plug an LCD monitor into a regular video card, however, you need circuitry on the LCD monitor to convert the signal from analog to digital (see Figure 19-28).

Many LCD monitors use exactly this process. These are called *analog LCD monitors*. The monitor really isn't analog; it's digital, but it takes a standard VGA input.

Why convert the signal from digital to analog and then back to digital? Originally, using a VGA connector with an LCD promoted adoption of the then new technology. A customer only had to swap a CRT for an LCD—no new video card required. Why many LCDs today have VGA connectors is anybody's guess.

New LCDs (and video cards) sport fully digital connections, the most common of which is the *digital visual interface (DVI)* standard. DVI is actually three different connectors that look very much alike: DVI-D is for digital, DVI-A is for analog (for backward compatibility if the monitor maker so desires), and the DVI-A/D or DVI-I (interchangeable) accepts either a DVI-D or DVI-A. DVI-D and DVI-A are keyed so that they will not connect.

DVI-D and DVI-I connectors come in two varieties, single-link and dual-link. *Single-link DVI* has a maximum bandwidth of 165 MHz, which, translated into practical terms, limits the maximum resolution of a monitor to 1920 × 1080 at 60 Hz or 1280 × 1024 at 85 Hz. *Dual-link DVI* uses more pins to double throughput and thus grant higher

resolutions (see Figure 19-29). With dual-link DVI, you can have displays up to 2048 × 1536 at 60 Hz.

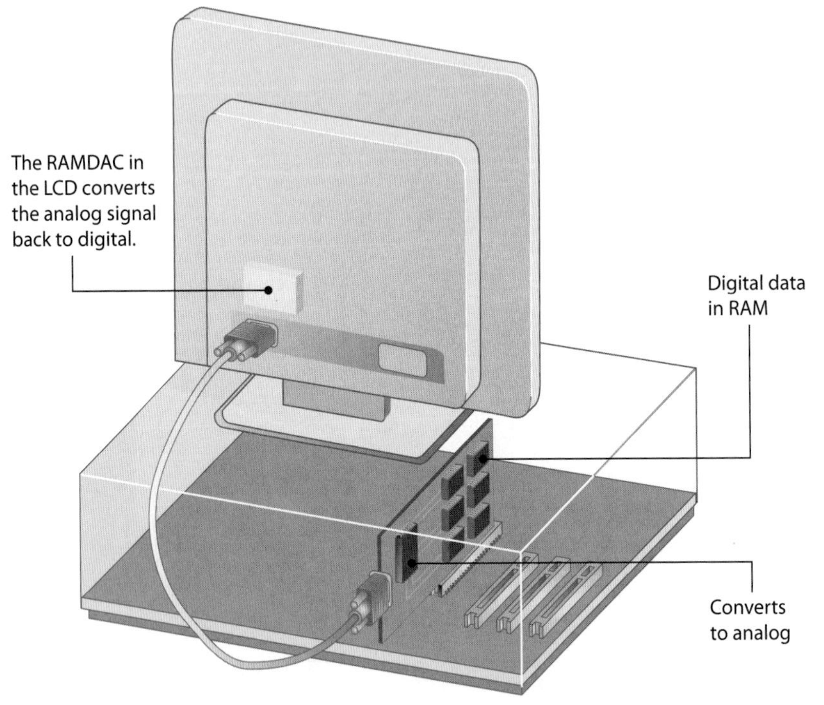

Figure 19-28 Converting analog back to digital on the LCD

Figure 19-29 Dual-link DVI-I connector

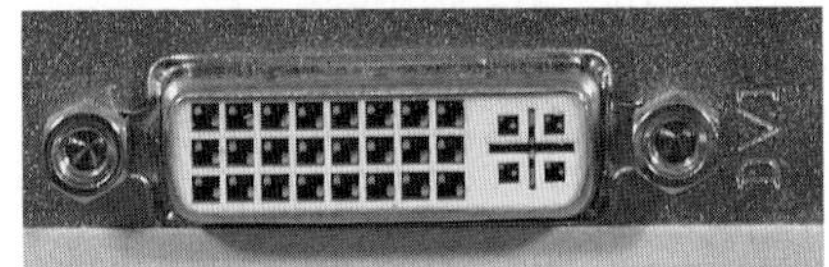

NOTE You can plug a single-link DVI monitor into a dual-link DVI connector and it'll work just fine.

The video card people have it easy. They either include both a VGA and a DVI-D connector or they use a DVI-I connector. The advantage to DVI-I is that you can add a cheap DVI-I-to-VGA adapter (one usually comes with the video card) like the one shown in Figure 19-30 and connect an analog monitor just fine.

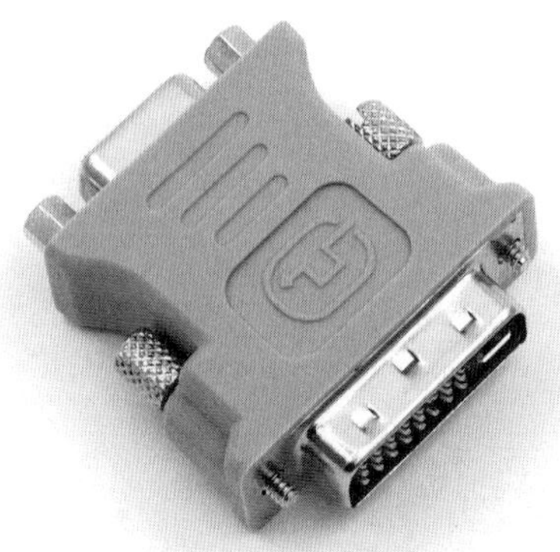

Figure 19-30 DVI-to-VGA adapter

NOTE A lot of monitors today use connector types you first read about way back in Chapter 3: HDMI, DisplayPort, and others. We'll revisit them in the discussion of display adapters later in the chapter.

Adjustments

Most adjustments to the monitor take place at installation, but for now, let's just make sure you know what they are and where they are located. Clearly, all monitors have an On/Off button or switch. Also, see if you can locate the Brightness and Contrast buttons. Beyond that, most monitors (at least the only ones you should buy) have an onboard menu system, enabling a number of adjustments. Every monitor maker provides a different way to access these menus, but they all provide two main functions: physical screen adjustment (bigger, smaller, move to the left, right, up, down, and others) and color adjustment. The color adjustment lets you adjust the red, green, and blue levels to give you the best color tones. All of these settings are a matter of personal taste. Make sure the person who will use the computer understands how to adjust these settings (see Figure 19-31).

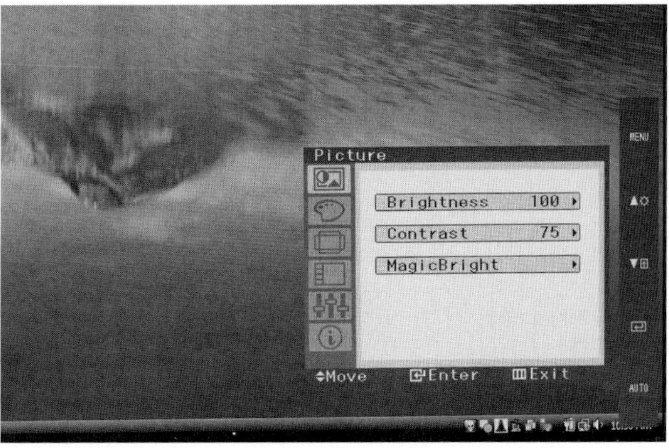

Figure 19-31 Typical menu controls

Display Adapters

The display adapter, or video card, handles the video chores within computing devices, processing information from the CPU and sending it to the display. The display adapter is a complex set of devices. A graphics processor crunches data from the CPU and outputs commands to the display. The graphics processor, like any other, needs RAM—but it also needs a fast connection with the CPU and system RAM. The display adapter must have a connection compatible with the monitor.

Traditionally, and still quite commonly in Windows PCs, the display adapter was an expansion card that plugged into the motherboard (see Figure 19-32). Although many new systems have the display adapter circuitry built into the motherboard, most techs still call it the video card, so we'll start there. This section looks at six aspects that define a video card: display modes, motherboard slot, graphics processor circuitry, video memory, integrated GPUs, and connections.

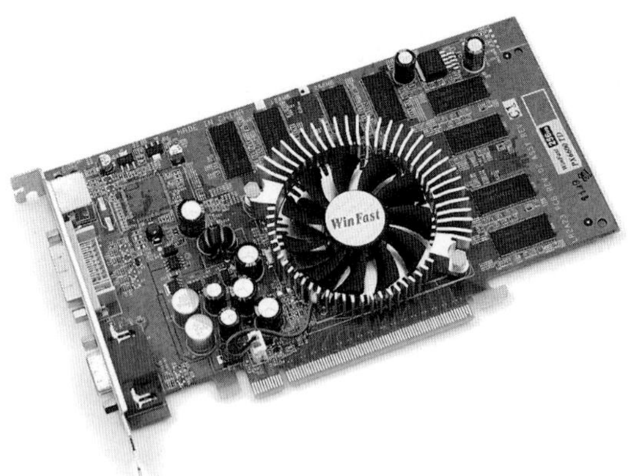

Figure 19-32 Typical video card

Historical/Conceptual

Modes

Video output to computers was around long before PCs were created. At the time PCs became popular, video was almost exclusively text-based, meaning the screen was divided into a grid of valid positions, and the video card was limited to drawing one of the 256 ASCII characters in each. These characters were made up of patterns of pixels that were stored in the system BIOS. When a program wanted to make a character, it talked to DOS or to the BIOS, which stored the image of that character in the video memory. The character then appeared on the screen.

The beauty of text video cards was that they were simple to use and cheap to make. The simplicity was based on the fact that only 256 characters existed, and no color choices were available—just monochrome text.

You could, however, choose to make the character bright, dim, normal, underlined, or blinking. Positioning the characters was easy, as space on the screen allowed for only 80 characters per row and 24 rows of characters.

Long ago, RAM was very expensive, so video card makers were interested in using the absolute least amount of RAM possible. Making a monochrome text video card was a great way to keep down RAM costs. Let's consider this for a minute. First, the video RAM is where the contents of the screen are located. You need enough video RAM to hold all of the necessary information for a completely full screen. Each ASCII character needs 8 bits (by definition), so a monitor with 80 characters/row and 24 rows will need

80 characters × 24 rows = 1920 characters = 15,360 bits or 1920 bytes

The video card would need less than 2000 bytes of memory, which isn't much, not even in 1981 when the PC first came out. Now, be warned that I'm glossing over a few things—where you store the information about underlines, blinking, and so on. The bottom line is that the tiny amount of necessary RAM kept monochrome text video cards cheap.

Very early on in the life of PCs, a new type of video, called a *graphics video card*, was invented. It was quite similar to a text card. The text card, however, was limited to the 256 ASCII characters, whereas a graphics video card enabled programs to turn any pixel on the screen on or off. It was still monochrome, but programs could access any individual pixel, enabling much more creative control of the screen. Of course, it took more video RAM. The first graphics cards ran at 320 × 200 pixels. One bit was needed for each pixel (on or off), so

320 × 200 = 64,000 bits or 8000 bytes

That's a lot more RAM than was needed for text, but it was still a pretty low amount of RAM—even in the old days. As resolutions increased, however, the amount of video RAM needed to store this information also increased.

After monochrome video was invented, moving into color for both text and graphics video cards was a relatively easy step. The only question was how to store color information for each character (text cards) or pixel (graphics cards). This was easy—just set aside a few more bits for each pixel or character. So now the question becomes, "How many bits do you set aside?" Well, that depends on how many colors you want. Basically, the number of colors determines the number of bits. For example, if you want four colors, you need 2 bits (2 bits per pixel). Then, you could do something like this:

00 = black	01 = cyan (blue)
10 = magenta (reddish pink)	11 = white

So if you set aside 2 bits, you could get 4 colors. If you want 16 colors, set aside 4 bits, which would make 16 different combinations. Nobody ever invented a text mode that used more than 16 colors, so let's start thinking in terms of only graphics mode and bits per pixels. To get 256 colors, each pixel would have to be represented with 8 bits. In PCs, the number of colors—called the *color depth*—is always a power of 2: 4, 16, 256, 64 K, and so on. Note that as more colors are added, more video RAM is needed to store the

information. Here are the most common color depths and the number of bits necessary to store the color information per pixel:

2 colors = 1 bit (mono)
4 colors = 2 bits
16 colors = 4 bits
256 colors = 8 bits
64 K colors = 16 bits
16.7 million colors = 24 bits

Most technicians won't say, for example, "I set my video card to show over 16 million colors." Instead, they'll say, "I set my color depth to 24 bits." Talk in terms of bits, not colors. It is assumed that you know the number of colors for any color depth.

A video card and monitor are capable of showing Windows or many Linux distros in a fixed number of different resolutions and color depths. The choices depend on the resolutions and color depths the video card can push to the monitor and the amount of bandwidth your monitor can support. Any single combination of resolution and color depth you set for your system is called a *mode*. For standardization, the Video Electronics Standards Association (VESA) defines a certain number of resolutions, all derived from the granddaddy of video modes: VGA.

VGA

With the introduction of the IBM Personal System/2 (PS/2), IBM introduced the *video graphics array (VGA)* standard. This standard offered 16 colors at a resolution of 640 × 480 pixels. VGA supported such an amazing variety of colors by using an analog video signal instead of a digital one, as was the case prior to the VGA standard. A digital signal is either all on or all off. By using an analog signal, the VGA standard can provide 64 distinct levels for the three colors (RGB)—that is, 64^3 or 262,144 possible colors—although only 16 or 256 can be seen at a time. For most purposes, 640 × 480 and 16 colors defines VGA mode. This is typically the display resolution and color depth referred to on many software packages as a minimum display requirement.

Beyond VGA

The 1980s were a strange time for video. Until the very late 1980s, VGA was the highest mode defined by VESA, but demand grew for modes that went beyond VGA. This motivated VESA to introduce (over time) a number of new modes with names such as SVGA, XGA, and many others. Even today, new modes are being released! Table 19-1 shows the more common modes.

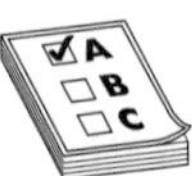

EXAM TIP You do not need to memorize all the video modes for the CompTIA A+ 901 exam. Focus on XGA, SXGA, UXGA, and WUXGA. The rest are included here so you will know what they mean when you compare various monitors and in case you get asked about them by a customer.

You also need to know the common aspect ratios on today's displays, such as 16:9, 16:10, and 4:3.

Video Mode	Resolution	Aspect Ratio	Typical Device
SVGA	800 × 600	4:3	Small monitors
HDTV 720p	1280 × 720	16:9	Lowest resolution that can be called HDTV
SXGA	1280 × 1024	5:4	Native resolution for many desktop LCD monitors
WXGA	1366 × 768	16:9	Widescreen laptops
WSXGA	1440 × 900	16:10	Widescreen laptops
SXGA+	1400 × 1050	4:3	Laptop monitors and high-end projectors
UXGA	1600 × 1200	4:3	Larger CRT monitors
HDTV 1080p	1920 × 1080	16:9	Full HDTV resolution
WUXGA	1920 × 1200	16:10	For 24"+ widescreen monitors
QWXGA	2048 × 1152	16:9	For smaller, fine monitors
WQXGA	2560 × 1600	16:10	For 27"+ widescreen monitors
WQUXGA	3840 × 2400	16:10	For smaller, fine monitors

Table 19-1 Typical Display Modes

Two other modes that have gained traction—though more on televisions than monitors—are *4K Ultra HD* and *5K Ultra HD*. The 4K means a resolution that's twice the width and twice the height of HD in one panel. 5K has even more pixel density. Both have a 16:9 aspect ratio. Here are the numbers:

4K: 3840 × 2160
5K: 5120 × 2880

It's worth noting, (again, not for the exam,) that beyond-HD standards differ depending on the standards body. For computer monitors, the Ultra HD resolution mentioned here applies as 4K. When you head to Hollywood, on the other hand, the Digital Cinema Initiatives (DCI) defines 4K as 4096 × 2160. How this discrepancy plays out is anyone's guess. What does Wikipedia say at the time you read these words?

901

Motherboard Slot

Techs will encounter four ways that display adapters connect to a motherboard. The oldest connector type, PCI, is used today only for an additional card to support extra monitors on older systems. Slightly newer, but still quite old in computer terms, is AGP. Every current discrete video card plugs into the PCIe slot on a motherboard. Finally, many motherboards have the display adapter built-in. I'll discuss integrated graphics after talking about graphics processors and memory types, at which point the topic will make more sense. For now, let's look at PCI, AGP, and PCIe.

PCI

Using more color depth slows down video functions. Data moving from the video card to the display has to go through the video card's memory chips and the expansion bus, and this can happen only so quickly. The standard PCI slots used in almost all systems for many years are limited to 32-bit transfers at roughly 33 MHz, yielding a maximum bandwidth of 132 MBps. This sounds like a lot until you start using higher resolutions, high color depths, and higher refresh rates. (The refresh rates mattered because we only had CRTs when video cards used the PCI bus.)

For example, take a typical display at 800 × 600 with a fairly low refresh rate of 70 Hz. The 70 Hz means the display screen is being redrawn 70 times per second. If you use a low color depth of 256 colors, which is 8 bits ($2^8 = 256$), you can multiply all of the values together to see how much data per second has to be sent to the display:

$$800 \times 600 \times 1 \text{ byte} \times 70 = 33.6 \text{ MBps}$$

If you use the same example at 16 million (24-bit) colors, the figure jumps to 100.8 MBps. You might say, "Well, if PCI runs at 132 MBps, it can handle that!" That statement would be true if the PCI bus had nothing else to do but tend to the video card, but almost every system has more than one PCI device, each requiring part of that throughput. The PCI bus simply cannot handle the video needs of any current systems.

AGP

Intel answered the desire for more video bandwidth than PCI provided with the *Accelerated Graphics Port (AGP)*. AGP is a single, special port, similar to a PCI slot, that is dedicated to video. You will never see a motherboard with two AGP slots; in fact, no current motherboard even has an AGP slot, so you'll only encounter these on ancient systems. Figure 19-33 shows an early-generation AGP. AGP is derived from the 66-MHz, 32-bit PCI 2.1 specification.

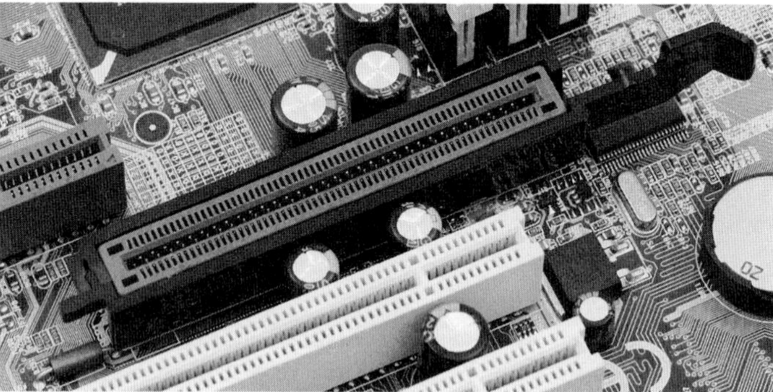

Figure 19-33
AGP

PCIe

The *PCI Express (PCIe)* interface was developed to replace PCI and, in the process, replace AGP. PCIe was a natural fit for video because it is incredibly fast. All PCIe video

cards use the PCIe ×16 connector (see Figure 19-34). PCIe replaced AGP as the primary video interface almost overnight.

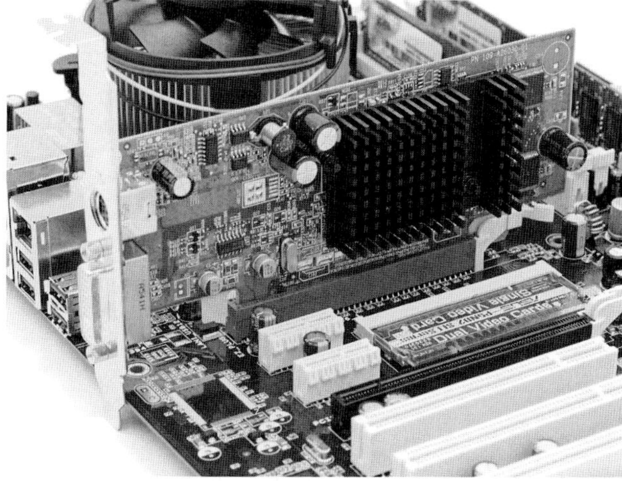

Figure 19-34 PCIe video card connected in PCIe slot

NOTE You first encountered PCIe way back in Chapter 7, but let me refresh your memory on the significant differences between the versions available. PCIe 1.0 devices transferred up to 2.5 GTps on each lane; PCIe 2.0 doubled that rate, to 5 GTps per lane, and PCIe 3.0 threw the gauntlet down at 8 GTps per lane. The motherboard, of course, needs to support the higher version to see the speed gains.

Graphics Processor

The graphics processor handles the heavy lifting of taking commands from the CPU and translating them into coordinates and color information that the monitor understands and displays. Most techs today refer to the device that processes video as a *graphics processing unit (GPU)*.

Video card discussion, at least among techs, almost always revolves around the graphics processor the video card uses and the amount of RAM onboard. A typical video card might be called an XFX Radeon HD7970 3-GB 384-bit GDDR5 PCI Express 3.0, so let's break that down. XFX is the manufacturer of the video card; Radeon HD7970 is the graphics processor; 3-GB 384-bit GDDR5 describes the dedicated video RAM and the connection between the video RAM and the graphics processor; and PCI Express 3.0 describes the motherboard expansion slot the card requires.

Many companies make the hundreds of different video cards on the market, but only three companies produce the vast majority of graphics processors found on video cards: NVIDIA, AMD, and Intel. NVIDIA and AMD make and sell graphics processors to third-party manufacturers who then design, build, and sell video cards under their own

branding. Intel made its own line of cards, but now concentrates on graphics processors built into motherboards. Figure 19-35 shows an NVIDIA GeForce GTX 570 on a board made by EVGA.

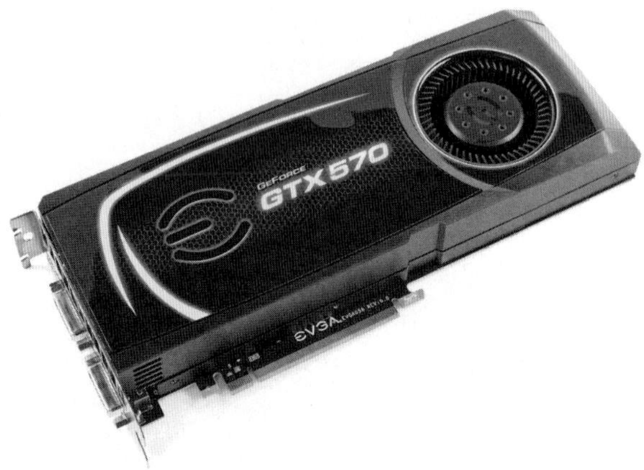

Figure 19-35 NVIDIA GeForce GTX 570

Your choice of graphics processor is your single most important decision in buying a video card. Low-end graphics processors usually work fine for the run-of-the-mill user who wants to write letters or run a Web browser. High-end graphics processors are designed to support the beautiful 3-D games that are so popular today, and they provide excellent video playback for high-definition video. We'll look at 3-D issues a little later in this chapter.

Video Memory

Video memory is crucial to the operation of a PC. It is probably the hardest-working set of electronics on the PC. Video RAM constantly updates to reflect every change that takes place on the screen. When you're working with heavy-duty applications (such as games), video memory can prove to be a serious bottleneck in three ways: data throughput speed, access speed, and simple capacity.

Manufacturers have overcome these bottlenecks by upping the width of the bus between the video RAM and video processor; using specialized, super-fast RAM; and adding more and more total RAM.

First, manufacturers reorganized the video display memory on cards to use a wider bus, giving them more memory bandwidth. Because the system bus is limited to 32 or 64 bits, this would not be of much benefit if video display cards weren't really coprocessor boards. Most of the graphics rendering and processing is handled on the card by the video processor chip rather than by the CPU. The main system simply provides the input data to the processor on the video card. Because the memory bus on the video card can be many times wider than the standard 64-bit pathway, data can be manipulated and then sent to the monitor much more quickly (see Figure 19-36).

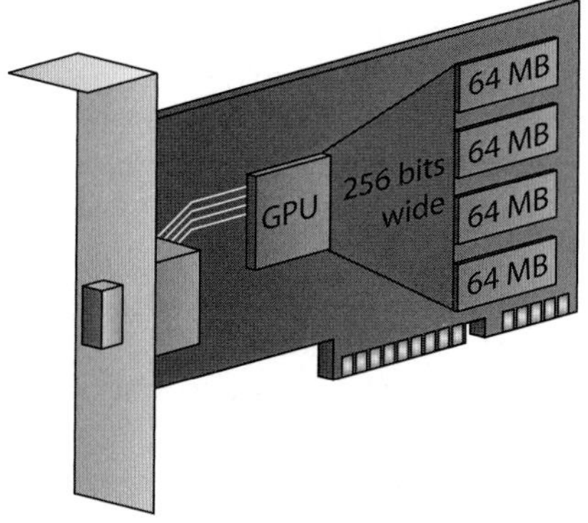

Figure 19-36 Wide path between video processor and video RAM

Specialized types of video RAM have been developed for graphics cards, and many offer substantial improvements in video speeds. The single most important feature that separates DRAM from video RAM is that video RAM can read and write data at the same time. Table 19-2 shows a list of common video memory technologies used today—make sure you know these for the exams!

Acronym	Name	Purpose
DDR SDRAM	Double Data Rate Synchronous DRAM	Used on budget graphics cards and very common on laptop video cards
DDR2 SDRAM	Double Data Rate version 2, Synchronous DRAM	Popular on video cards until GDDR3; lower voltage than DDR memory
GDDR3 SDRAM	Graphics Double Data Rate, version 3	Similar to DDR2 but runs at faster speeds; different cooling requirements
GDDR4 SDRAM	Graphics Double Data Rate, version 4	Upgrade of GDDR3; faster clock
GDDR5 SDRAM	Graphics Double Data Rate, version 5	Successor to GDDR4; double the input/output rate of GDDR4

Table 19-2 Video RAM Technologies

The majority of video cards, especially once you get into gaming-oriented cards, sport GDDR5. DDR3 RAM is the most popular memory on low-end, non-gaming cards.

Finally, many advanced 3-D video cards come with huge amounts of video RAM. It's very common to see cards with 1, 2, 3, or 4 GB of RAM! (As this book goes to press, you can drop a lot of money and get a card with 12 GB of video RAM.) Why so much? Even with PCI Express, accessing data in system RAM always takes a lot longer than accessing data stored in local RAM on the video card. The huge amount of video RAM enables game developers to optimize their games and store more essential data on the local video RAM.

Integrated GPUs

A lot of current motherboards have integrated GPUs or are ready for a CPU with an integrated GPU. The motherboard GPU can be a separate chip attached to the motherboard or can be built into the Northbridge chip. You might run into AMD Radeon chips or NVIDIA nForce chips powering the GPU. Intel has long integrated the Intel Graphics Media Accelerator (GMA) into its chipsets.

AMD, Intel, and NVIDIA make CPUs with integrated GPUs that vary a lot in graphical performance. Some of AMD's Fusion processors, for example, have a CPU/GPU combination that rivals any CPU/discrete graphics card combination, though only at a level seen in portable computers. They're good enough for casual gaming and even some medium-duty games. Intel's graphics support is geared to desktop performance, not gaming at all. NVIDIA's Tegra line is focused on gaming, but for mobile devices such as tablets and smartphones (see Chapter 25 for the details).

With an integrated GPU, the CPU circuitry is getting pretty crowded. A single AMD Accelerated Processing Unit (APU) chip, for example, integrates two to four CPU cores, a memory controller that supports DDR3 for system memory, cache memory, and a GPU that can handle advanced 3-D graphics. Wow! One of the best parts of all this integration is that the chip requires far less electricity than comparable discrete components.

Connector Types and Associated Cables

You can find many different types of connector types on video cards, plus variations within those types. CompTIA also makes a distinction between the names of the ports on the cards and the cables associated with them, though most techs will refer to the connectors and cables by multiple names interchangeably. Here's the scoop.

Standard monitors connect through one of six connectors:

- VGA
- DVI
- DB-15
- DisplayPort
- Thunderbolt
- HDMI (including Mini- and Micro- variants)

Video cards offer other connector types for connecting to things like television sets, camcorders, and other multimedia devices:

- RCA
- BNC
- Mini-DIN

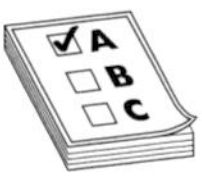

EXAM TIP The CompTIA A+ exam objectives mention *RJ-45* as a video connector type and Ethernet as a video cable type. The only place you'll find both used in video is with SP Controls' *CatLinc* system. CatLinc uses adapters to connect your VGA, DVI, HDMI, and component devices to a CAT5 cable (commonly associated with Ethernet networks). CAT5 cables enable the video signal to be transmitted across greater distances more clearly at a lower cost. Here's an example: http://spcontrols.com/prodcat.php?hierId=20.

The video card shown in Figure 19-37 has three connectors: HD15 (VGA), DVI-I, and S-video. Other connectors enable the video card to connect to composite, component, and even high-definition devices.

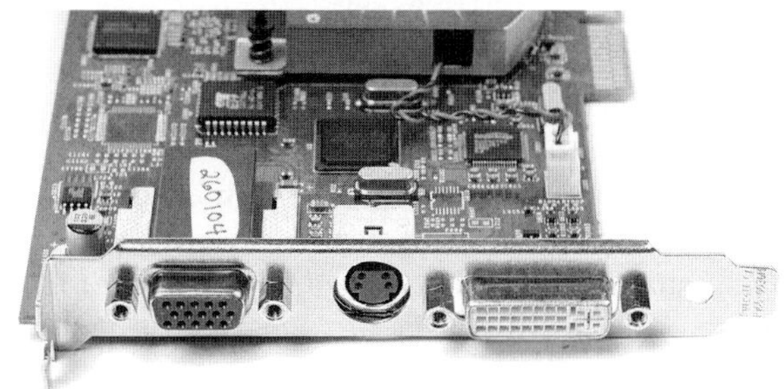

Figure 19-37 Video card connectors: VGA, S-video, and DVI-I

For Standard Monitors

You know about the standard monitor connectors, the HD15 that most people call VGA and DVI, from the monitor discussion earlier. The only thing to add is that most DVI connections on video cards these days natively support analog signals. You can use a simple DVI-to-VGA adapter, for example, for connecting a VGA cable to a video card.

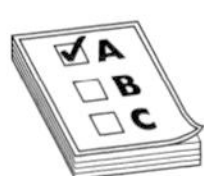

EXAM TIP The CompTIA A+ 901 exam might make a distinction between the VGA cable and the HD15 connector into which it plugs.

Many Apple Mac desktop models use a *DisplayPort* connection for connecting to a monitor. Dell offers support for DisplayPort as well at the time of this writing. Figure 19-38 shows a DisplayPort jack on a Dell portable.

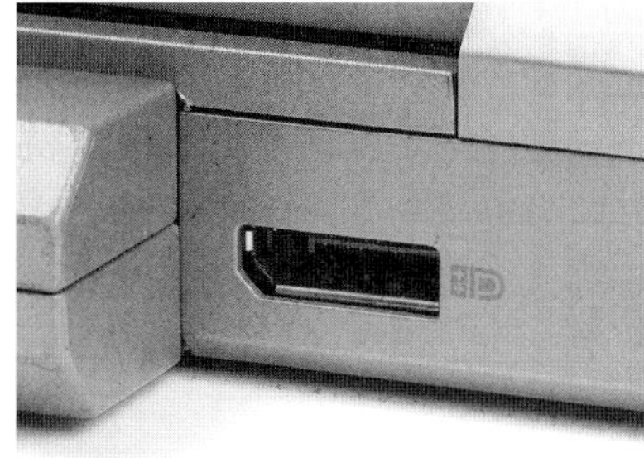

Figure 19-38 DisplayPort jack

More recent Apple offerings, such as the Mac Pro, MacBook Pro, and MacBook Air, use a Thunderbolt connector for monitors. Thunderbolt offers astounding versatility, especially with a multi-monitor setup. Figure 19-39 shows a Thunderbolt port.

Figure 19-39 Thunderbolt port

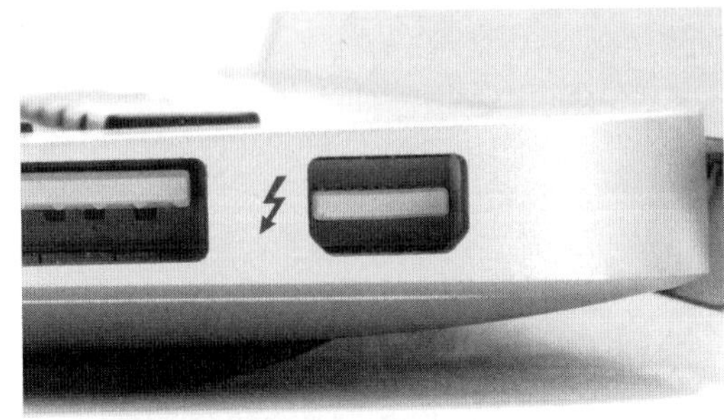

For Multimedia Devices

Video cards can have one or more standard connections plus non-standard connections for hooking the PC to a multimedia device, such as a television, DVD or Blue-ray Disc player, or video camera. The earliest type of connector commonly found is the mini-DIN for attaching an S-video cable. This provides decent-quality video output or, in some cases, input. You'll sometimes find a proprietary round connector that supports S-video and a proprietary dongle that adds support for video through either component connection or composite connections. Figure 19-40 shows the similar round ports.

Figure 19-40 S-video and proprietary round connectors

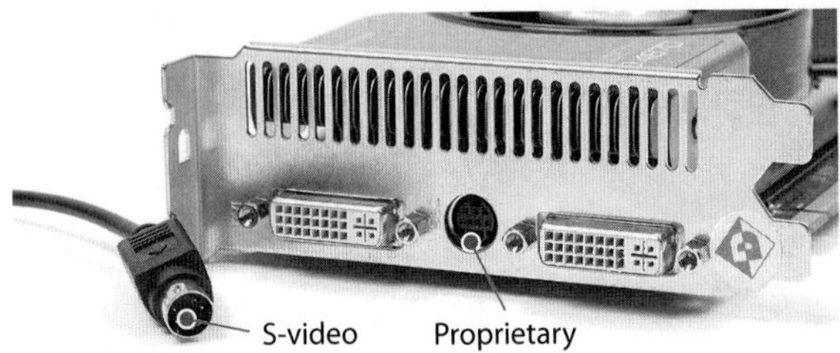

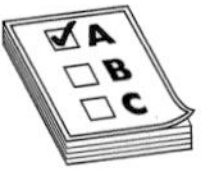

EXAM TIP CompTIA has pulled out all the stops on adding extra acronyms to your plate with connector types. The 220-901 exam objectives refer to the mini-DIN used with S-video as a *miniDIN6*. Most techs refer to the port as an *S-video port*.

A composite connector provides a video signal through a single cable that plugs into a standard *RCA* jack, whereas a component adapter provides a split signal, red, green,

and blue (RGB). Figure 19-41 shows the two connector dongles. Note that all are RCA connectors.

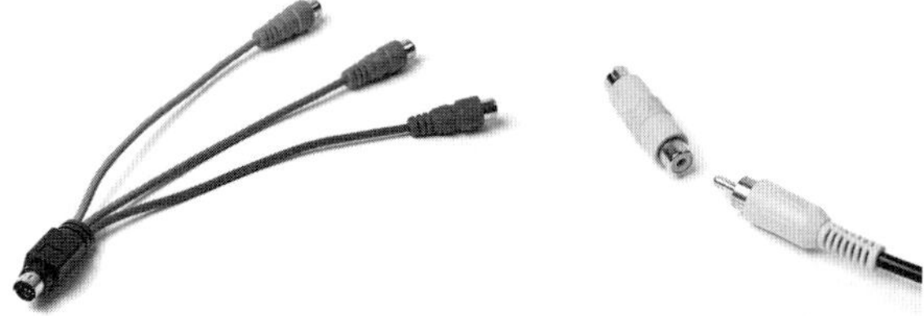

Figure 19-41 Composite and component connection options

The best connections for outputting to television are the *High Definition Multimedia Interface (HDMI)* connectors. Some devices offer HDMI output directly (such as the portable pictured in Figure 19-42), while other video cards support HDMI through a special cable that connects to a dual-link DVI port. Figure 19-43 shows an example of such a cable.

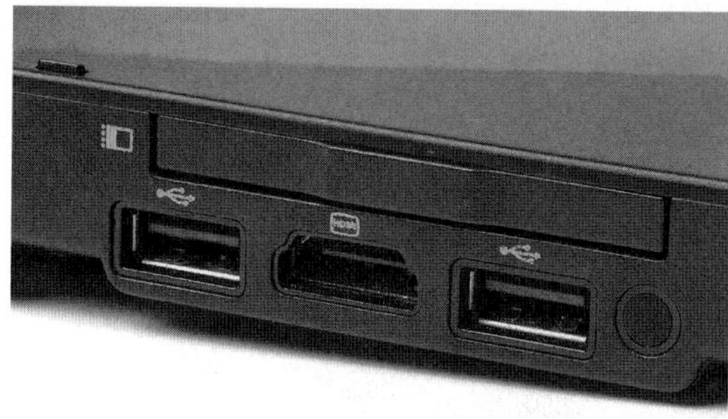

Figure 19-42 HDMI port between two USB ports on Lenovo laptop

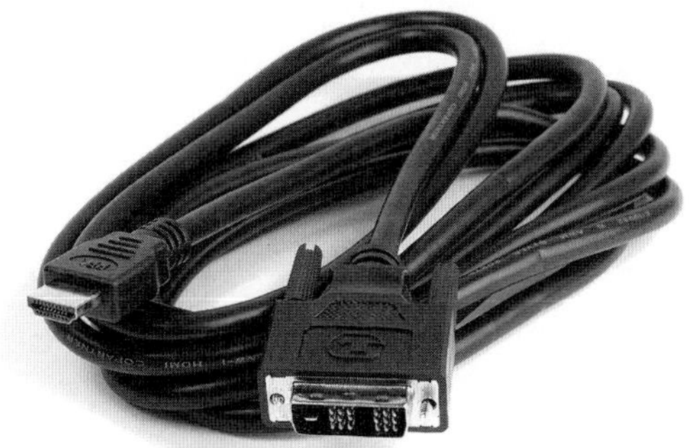

Figure 19-43 DVI-to-HDMI cable

HDMI comes in three standard sizes, Standard, Mini, and Micro. Plus there's the Type E connector used exclusively for automobile video systems—and don't we all need video while driving? Standard HDMI is what you'll find on video cards and televisions and some portable devices. Most contemporary tablet devices with an HDMI port use Mini-HDMI (see Figure 19-44). See Chapter 25 for the discussion on tablets and other mobile devices.

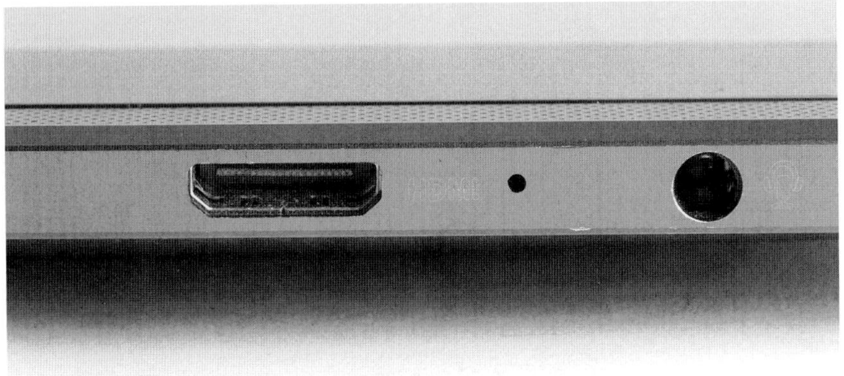

Figure 19-44 Mini-HDMI port

Adapters and Converters

What do you do if you have one video connector type on a monitor and a different video connector type on a computing device? You saw the answer earlier with the DVI-to-VGA and VGA-to-DVI converters. Not surprisingly, manufacturers provide just about any adapter and converter you need to get connected. A quick trip to a big box or online store like Newegg.com reveals a lot:

- DVI to HDMI
- Thunderbolt to DVI
- HDMI to VGA
- DisplayPort to DVI
- DisplayPort to HDMI

Plus, you can find cables that do the converting too. One of my three DVI monitors, for example, connects to the HDMI port on my video card by using a cable with DVI on one end and HDMI on the other. Sweet!

Installing and Configuring Video

Once you've decided on the features and price for your new video card and monitor, you need to install them into your system. As long as you have the right connection to your video card, installing a monitor is straightforward. The challenge comes when installing the video card.

NOTE The installation steps in this section apply to Windows PCs and Linux computers. Apple doesn't make any Mac OS X systems with an upgradable display adapter, but you can still configure it.

During the physical installation of a video card, watch out for three possible issues: long cards, the proximity of the nearest expansion card, and the presence of power connectors. Some high-end video cards simply won't fit in certain cases or will block access to needed motherboard connectors such as the SATA sockets. There's no clean fix for such a problem—you simply have to change at least one of the components (video card, motherboard, or case). Because high-end video cards run very hot, you don't want them sitting right next to another card; make sure the fan on the video card has plenty of ventilation space. A good practice is to leave the slot next to the video card empty to allow better airflow (see Figure 19-45). Many high-end video cards come as double-wide cards with built-in air vents, so you don't have any choice but to take up double the space. Mid-range to high-end video cards typically require at least one additional PCI power connector because they use more power than the PCIe slot can provide. Make sure that your power supply either supports these natively, or that you have a PCI-to-molex converter, and that your power supply can provide adequate power.

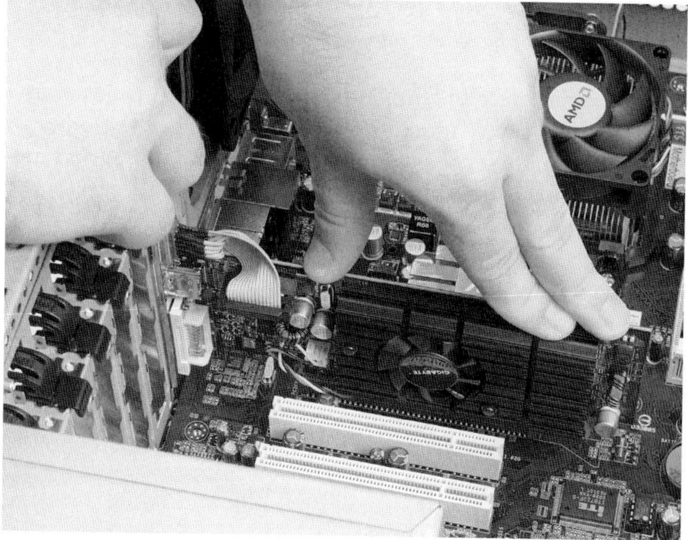

Figure 19-45 Installing a video card

Try This!

Install a Video Card

You know how to install an expansion card from your reading in earlier chapters. Installing a video card is pretty much the same, so try this:

1. Refer to Chapter 7 for the steps on installing a new card.
2. Plug the monitor cable into the video card port on the back of the PC and power up the system. If your PC seems dead after you install a video card, or if the screen is blank but you hear fans whirring and the internal speaker sounding off *long-short-short-short*, your video card likely did not get properly seated. Unplug the PC and try again.

Once you've properly installed the video card and connected it to the monitor, you've fought half the battle for making the video process work properly. You're ready to tackle the drivers and tweak the operating system, so let's go!

Software

Configuring your video software is usually a two-step process. First you need to load drivers for the video card. Then you need to open the Control Panel and go to the Display applet (Windows 7/8/8.1/10) or Personalization applet (Windows Vista) to make your adjustments. Let's explore how to make the video card and monitor work in Windows, then look briefly at display options in OS X and Linux.

Drivers

Just like any other piece of hardware, your video card needs a driver to function. Video card drivers install pretty much the same way as all of the other drivers we've discussed thus far: either the driver is already built into Windows or you must use the installation media that comes with the video card.

Video card makers are constantly updating their drivers. Odds are good that any video card more than a few months old has at least one driver update. If possible, check the manufacturer's Web site and use the driver located there if there is one. If the Web site doesn't offer a driver, it's usually best to use the installation media. Always avoid using the built-in Windows driver as it tends to be the most dated.

We'll explore driver issues in more detail after we discuss the Display and Personalization applets. Like so many things about video, you can't fully understand one topic without understanding at least one other!

902

Using the Display and Personalization Applets

With the driver installed, you're ready to configure your display settings. The *Display applet* and *Personalization applet* provide convenient, central locations for all of your display settings, including resolution, refresh rate, driver information, and color depth.

This discussion can get a little confusing for a couple of reasons. First, Microsoft titled the primary display-modifying Control Panel applet in Windows Vista "Personalization." Microsoft rebranded it "Display" in Windows 7 and later, but also included a Personalization applet. Second, Microsoft tweaked both Display and Personalization between every version of Windows, meaning you will sometimes have to hunt for the location of specific interface options.

Here's the bottom line. What you need to know as a tech is that the Control Panel applets enable you to make changes that affect many of aspects of visual output for your customers. The Personalization-branded components handle user preferences, such as background picture, colors of various interface elements, and that sort of thing. The display settings option—however you get to it or whatever Microsoft calls it in the OS you use—enables you to make tech-oriented changes to settings such as resolution, orientation, and so on.

Rather than go through four different OSs to show variations on a theme, this section focuses on Windows 8.1. Figure 19-46 shows the default Display applet.

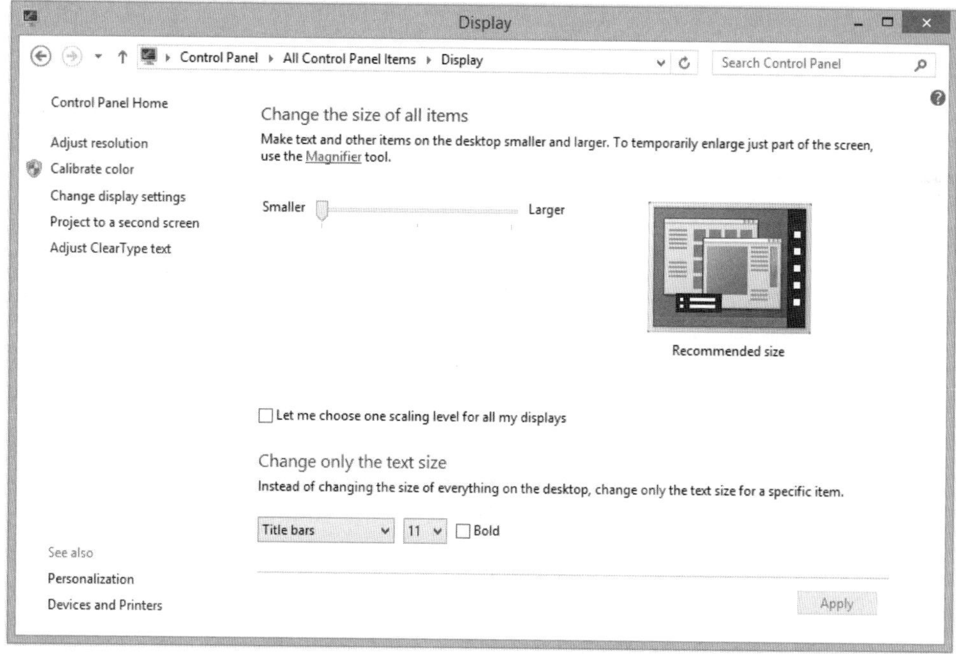

Figure 19-46 Display applet in Windows 8.1

Microsoft gives you a quick and excellent set of options for dealing with the only real issue with large, high-resolution LCD panels. You get sliders for changing the size of all interface items and just changing the text size. On the left are the Display options:

- **Adjust resolution** Change from native resolution to lower if needed
- **Adjust brightness** Available if supported by your monitor, such as a laptop
- **Calibrate color** Make the colors on your screen more closely match what you print
- **Change display settings** Another place for changing resolution; also for adding another monitor (see "Multiple Monitors," a bit later in the chapter)
- **Project to a second screen** Available if you have a second monitor connector on the video card
- **Adjust ClearType text** Enables you to tweak the font rendering used for the Windows interface, which some folks like to do

Below these options on the left are pointers to the two other possibly relevant Control Panel applets, Personalization and Devices and Printers. Figure 19-47 shows the Personalization applet default screen.

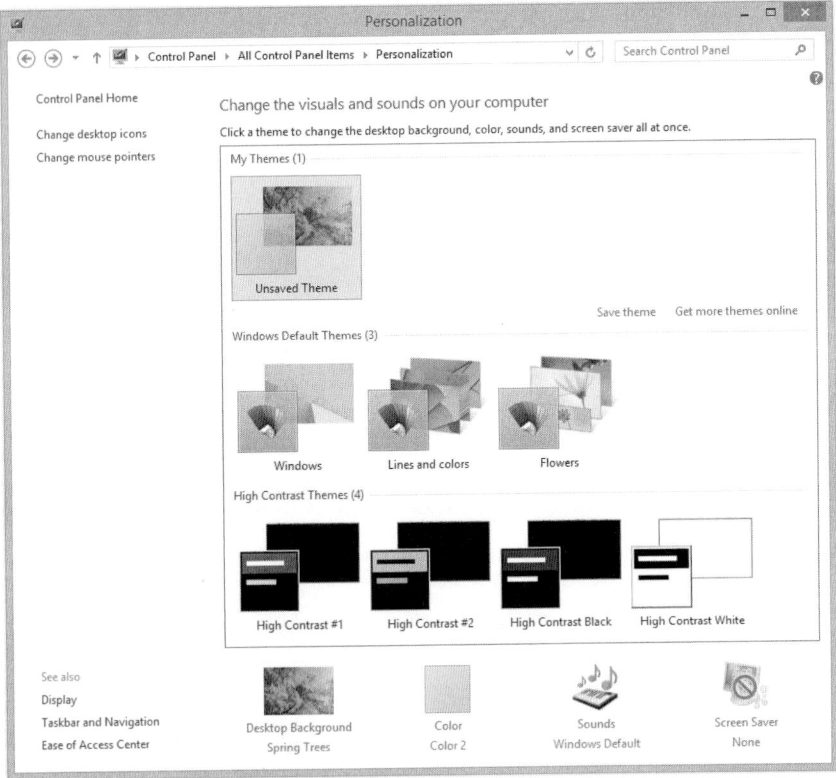

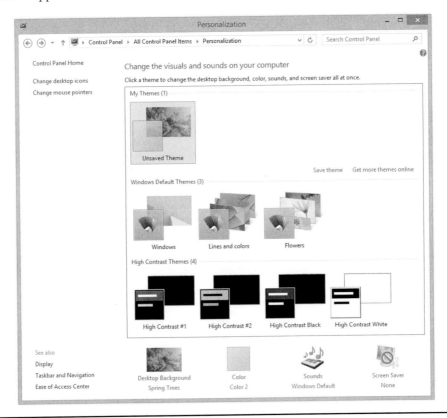

Figure 19-47 Personalization applet in Windows 8.1

Here you can change the overall theme of the Desktop, or make changes to the look and feel for individual users. The only tech-oriented items here are the Screen Saver option in the lower-right corner and the last theme option, High Contrast Themes.

Some users need to change the color palette to one of the High Contrast options for simple usability. Figure 19-48 shows how radically different you can make Windows look.

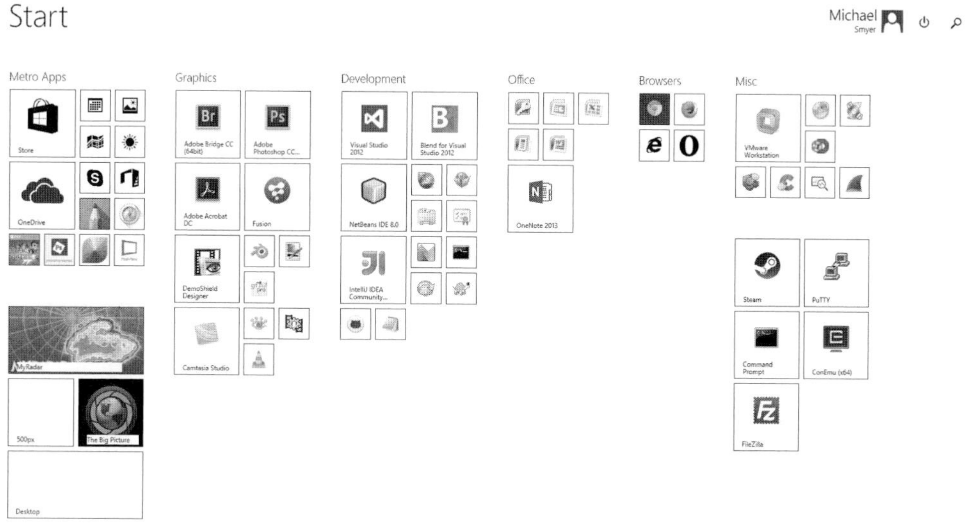

Figure 19-48 The Start screen in High Contrast White

At first glance it might not be obvious that the Screen Saver option controls more than the Windows screensaver (see Figure 19-49), but another option on the Screen Saver tab gets you to one of the most important settings of your system: power management. Click on the Power button or Change power settings option to get to the Power Options Properties dialog box or Power Options applet (see Figure 19-50).

The tabs and options define all of the power management of the system. Power management is a fairly involved process, so we'll save the big discussion for where we need to save power the most: Chapter 24, "Portable Computing."

Multiple Monitors

Adding extra monitors to a system can radically alter a user's workflow, usually for the better. As a writer and editor, for example, the ability to put text on one screen, images on another, and distracting social media feeds on a third...okay, skip the last one...makes writing and editing much easier.

Figure 19-49 Screen Saver Settings in Windows 8.1

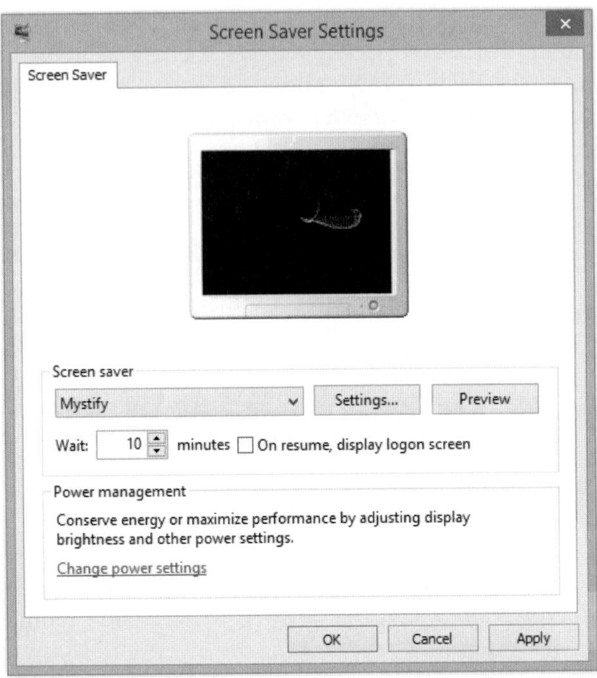

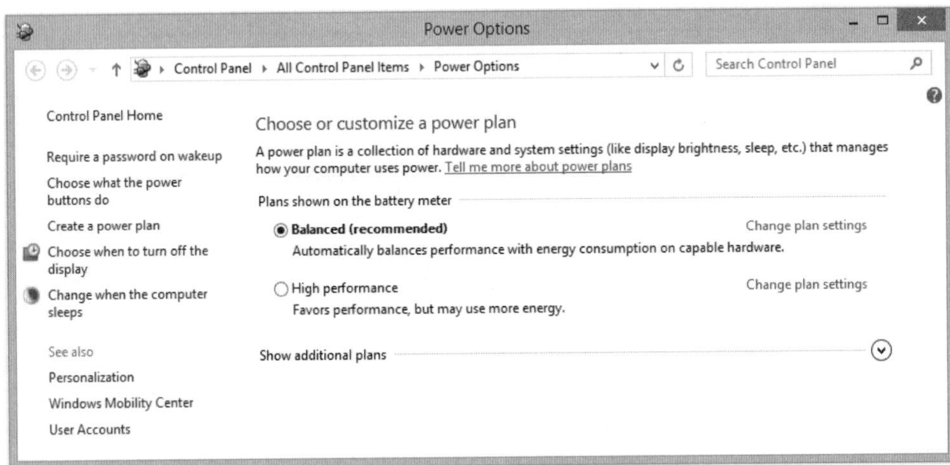

Figure 19-50 Power Options applet in Windows 8.1

The Display applet enables you to modify how multiple monitors function. Click the Change display settings link in the Display applet. Monitors may work together like two halves of one large screen, or the second monitor might simply show a duplicate of what's happening on the first monitor. Multiple monitors are handy if you need lots of screen space but don't want to buy a really large, expensive monitor (see Figure 19-51).

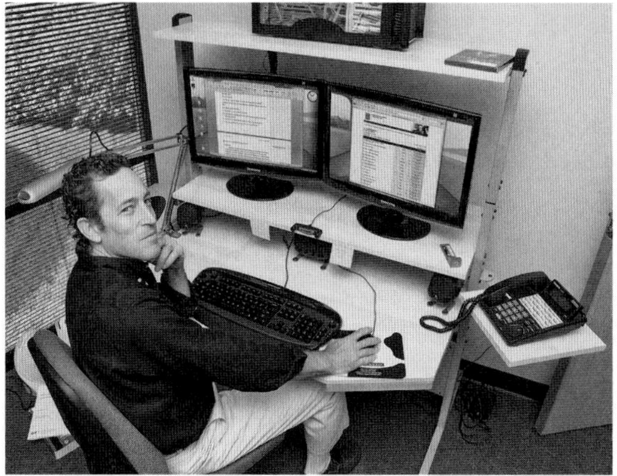

Figure 19-51 My editor hard at work with dual monitors

There are two ways to set up multiple monitors: plug in two or more video cards, or use a single video card that supports multiple monitors. Both methods are quite common and work well. Multiple monitors are easy to configure: just plug in the monitors and Windows should detect them. Windows will show the monitors in the applet, as shown in Figure 19-52 for Windows 7. By default, the second monitor is not enabled. To use the second monitor, just select *Extend the desktop onto this monitor* in Windows Vista, or use the Multiple displays dropdown box and select *Extend these displays* in Windows 7/8/8.1/10.

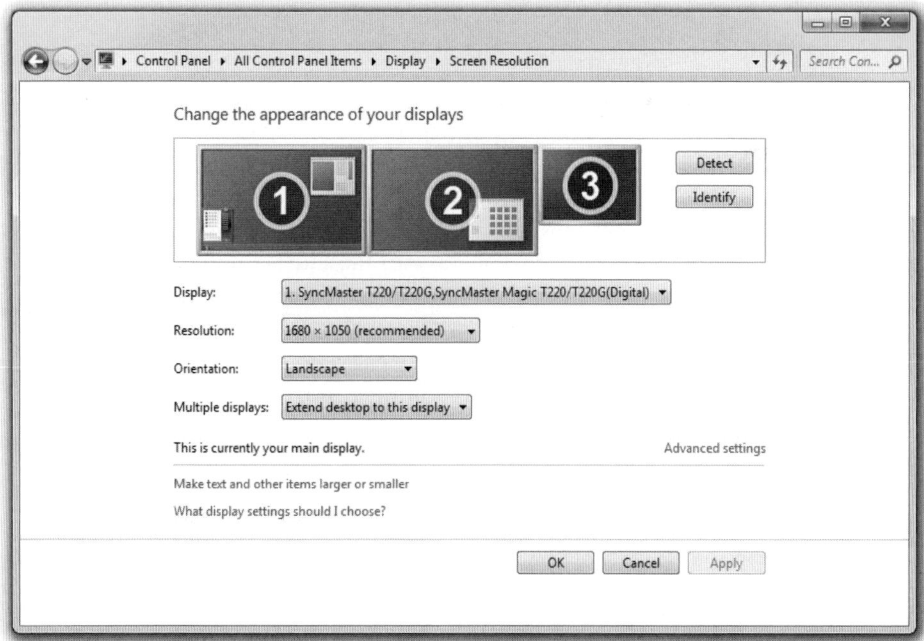

Figure 19-52 Enabling multiple monitors

If you need to see more advanced settings, click on…that's right, the Advanced or Advanced Settings button, or on the Advanced settings link in the Screen Resolution dialog box in Windows 7. The title of the dialog box that opens reflects the monitor and video card. As you can see in Figure 19-53, this particular computer uses a pair of Samsung SyncMaster T220 monitors running off of an ATI Radeon 5750 video card.

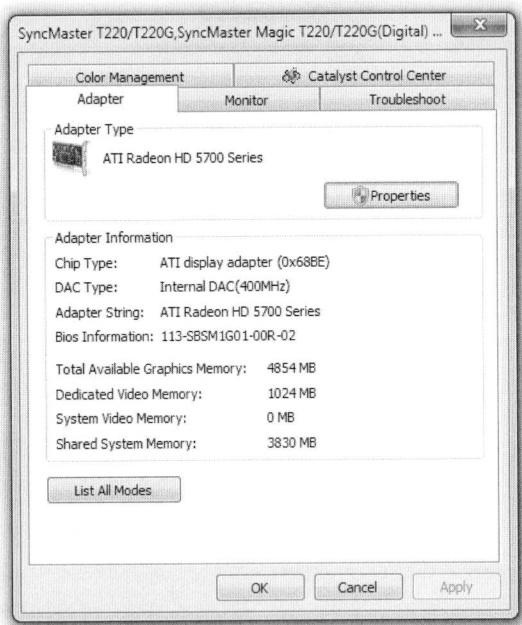

Figure 19-53 Advanced video settings, Adapter tab

The tab you're most likely to use is the Adapter tab. The Adapter tab gives detailed information about the video card, including the amount of video memory, the graphics processor, and the BIOS information (yup, your video card has a BIOS, too!). You can also click on the List All Modes button to change the current mode of the video card, although any mode you set here can also be set with the sliders on the main screen.

Most video cards add their own tab to the Advanced dialog box. In the case of the tab shown in Figure 19-54, you'd need to click on the Catalyst Control Center button to see more settings for the video card. What you see here varies by card model and driver version, but here's a list of some of the more interesting settings you might see.

Color Correction Sometimes the colors on your monitor are not close enough for your tastes to the actual color you're trying to create. In this case you use color correction to fine-tune the colors on the screen to get the look you want.

Rotation All monitors are by default wider than they are tall. This is called *landscape mode*. Some LCD monitors can be physically rotated to facilitate users who like to see their desktops taller than they are wide (*portrait mode*). Figure 19-55 shows the author's LCD monitor rotated in portrait mode. If you want to rotate your screen, you must tell the system you're rotating it.

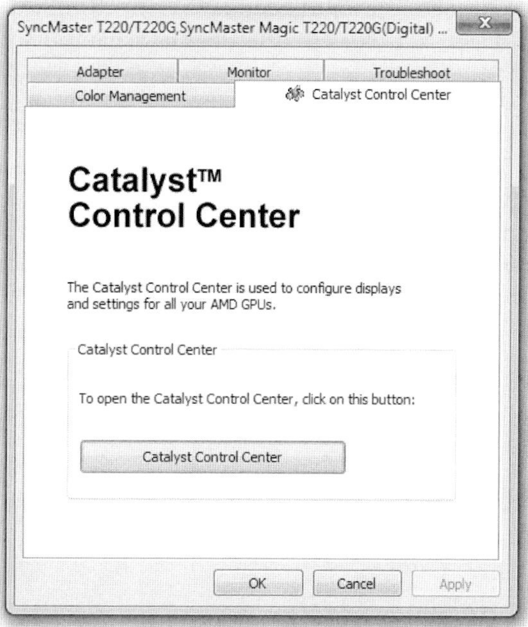

Figure 19-54 Third-party video tab

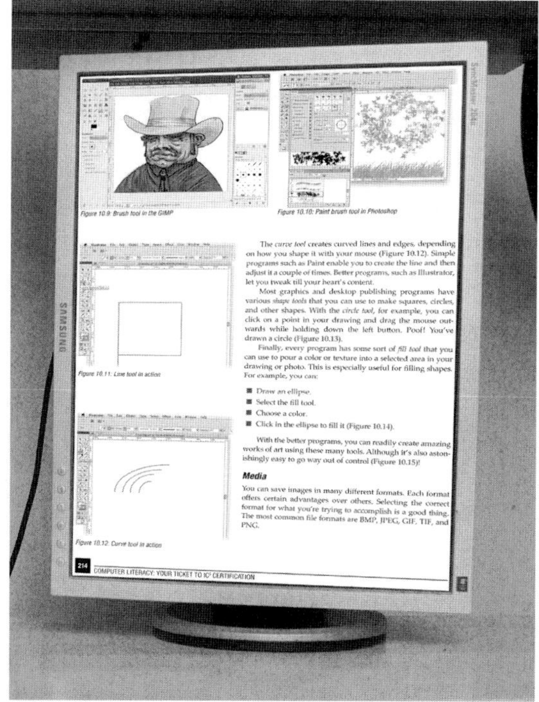

Figure 19-55 Portrait mode

Modes Most video cards add very advanced settings to enable you to finely tweak your monitor. These very dangerous settings have names such as "sync polarity" or "front porch" and are outside the scope of both CompTIA A+ certification and the needs of all but the most geeky techs. These settings are mostly used to display a non-standard resolution. Stay out of those settings!

Display Options in Mac OS X and Linux

Mac OS X and most modern Linux distros offer pretty clear options for changing display settings. To no one's surprise, you'll find the options in Mac OS X in the System Preferences (see Figure 19-56). General enables you to change color schemes. You can change the Desktop background in Desktop & Screen Saver.

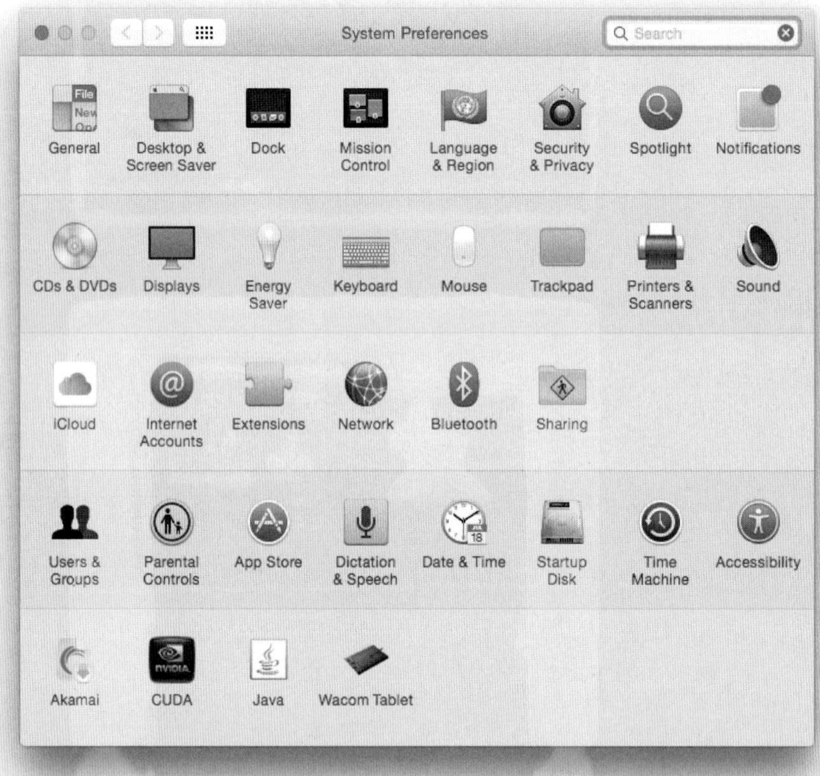

Figure 19-56 System Preferences in Mac OS X

Click the Dock option to access settings that can be used to change the user experience a lot (see Figure 19-57). The Dock resides by default along the bottom of the screen. You can make the icons tiny and less distracting. You can move it to the right or left. You can change the default animation behavior for mouseovers.

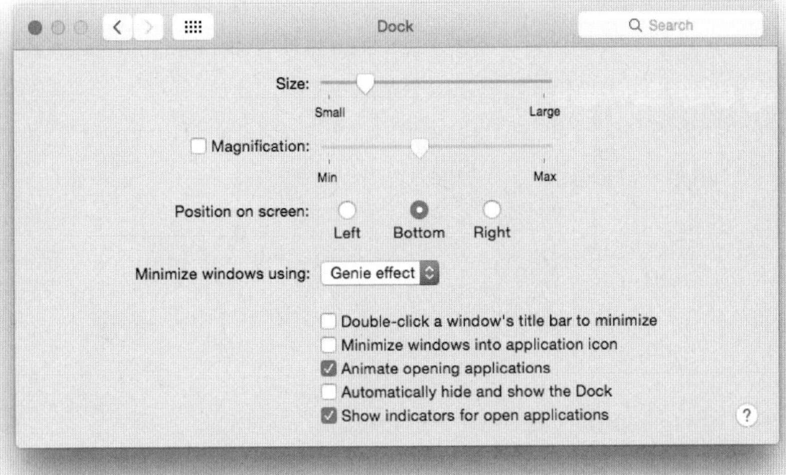

Figure 19-57 Dock options

Different Linux distros put the display options in various places, but you'll commonly find one or more utilities in the System Settings. Figure 19-58 shows the Appearance applet in Ubuntu, for example, where you can alter the background, theme, and Launcher icon size.

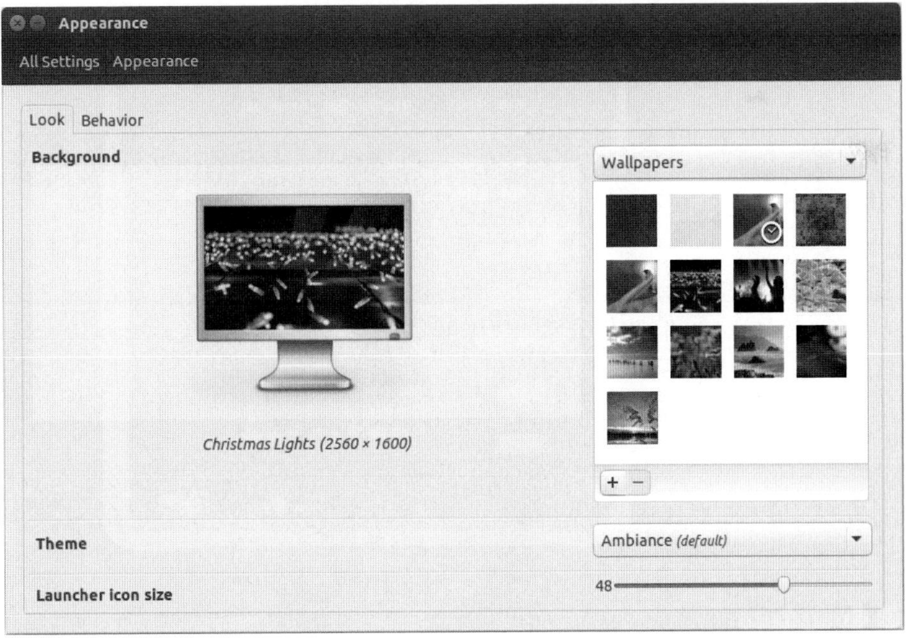

Figure 19-58 Appearance applet in System Settings

Trust that anything you can modify in Windows can be modified in Linux—you just might have to do a little hunting for it.

Working with Drivers

Now that you know the locations of the primary video tools within the operating system, it's time to learn about fine-tuning your video. You need to know how to work with video drivers from within the Display and Personalization applets, including how to update them, roll back updates, and uninstall them.

When you update the drivers for a card, you have a choice of uninstalling the outdated drivers and then installing new drivers—which makes the process the same as for installing a new card—or you can let Windows flex some digital muscle and install the new ones right over the older drivers.

To update your drivers, go to the Control Panel and double-click on the Display applet or click on the Personalization applet and click Display Settings (Windows Vista). In Windows Vista's Display Settings dialog box, select the Monitor tab and click the Advanced Settings button. In the Display applet for Windows 7/8/8.1/10, click Change display settings in the left pane and then click the Advanced settings link. In the dialog box that appears (all versions), click the Adapter tab and then click the Properties button. In the Properties dialog box for your adapter (see Figure 19-59), select the Driver tab and then click the Update Driver button to run the Hardware Update wizard.

Figure 19-59 Adapter Properties dialog box

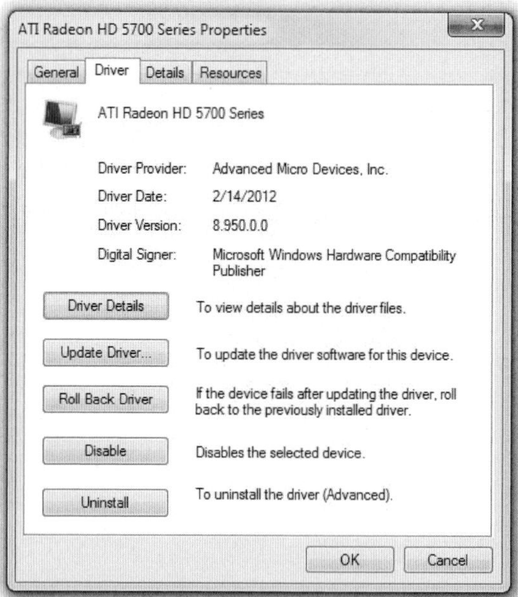

3-D Graphics

No other area of the PC world reflects the amazing acceleration of technological improvements more than *3-D graphics*—in particular, 3-D gaming—which attempts to create

images with the same depth and texture as objects seen in the real world. We are spectators to an amazing new world where software and hardware race to produce new levels of realism and complexity displayed on the computer screen. Powered by the wallets of tens of millions of PC gamers always demanding more and better, the video card industry constantly introduces new video cards and new software titles that make today's games so incredibly realistic and fun. Although the gaming world certainly leads the PC industry in 3-D technologies, many other PC applications—such as *Computer Aided Design (CAD)* programs—quickly snatch up these technologies, making 3-D useful for much more than games. In this section, we'll add to the many bits and pieces of 3-D video encountered over previous chapters in the book and build an understanding of the function and configuration of 3-D graphics.

Before the early 1990s, PCs did not mix well with 3-D graphics. Certainly, many 3-D applications existed, primarily 3-D design programs such as AutoCAD and Intergraph, but these applications would often run only on expensive, specialized hardware—not so great for casual users.

The big change took place in 1992 when a small company called id Software created a new game called *Wolfenstein 3D* (see Figure 19-60). They launched an entirely new genre of games, now called *first-person shooters (FPSs)*, in which the player looks out into a 3-D world, interacting with walls, doors, and other items, and shoots whatever bad guys the game provides.

Figure 19-60
Wolfenstein 3D

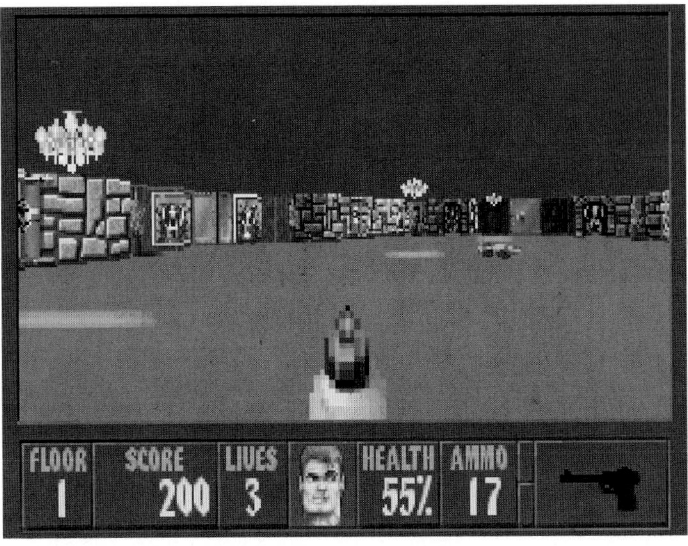

Wolfenstein 3D shook the PC gaming world to its foundations. That this innovative format came from an upstart little company made *Wolfenstein 3D* and id Software into overnight sensations. Even though their game was demanding on hardware, they gambled that enough people could run it to make it a success. The gamble paid off for John Carmack and John Romero, the creators of id Software, making them the fathers of 3-D gaming.

Early 3-D games used fixed 2-D images called *sprites* to create the 3-D world. A sprite is nothing more than a bitmapped graphic. These early first-person shooters would calculate the position of an object from the player's perspective and place a sprite to represent the object. Any single object had only a fixed number of sprites—if you walked around an object, you noticed an obvious jerk as the game replaced the current sprite with a new one to represent the new position. Figure 19-61 shows different sprites for the same bad guy in *Wolfenstein 3D*. Sprites weren't pretty, but they worked without seriously taxing the 486s and early Pentiums of the time.

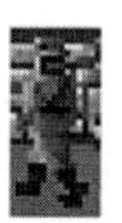
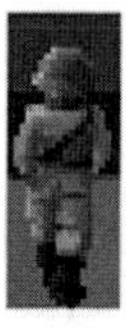
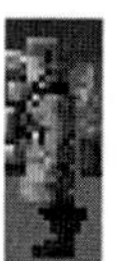

Figure 19-61 Each figure had a limited number of sprites.

The second generation of 3-D games began to replace sprites with true 3-D objects, which are drastically more complex than sprites. A true 3-D object is composed of a group of points called *vertices*. Each vertex has a defined X, Y, and Z position in a 3-D world. Figure 19-62 shows the vertices for a video game character in a 3-D world.

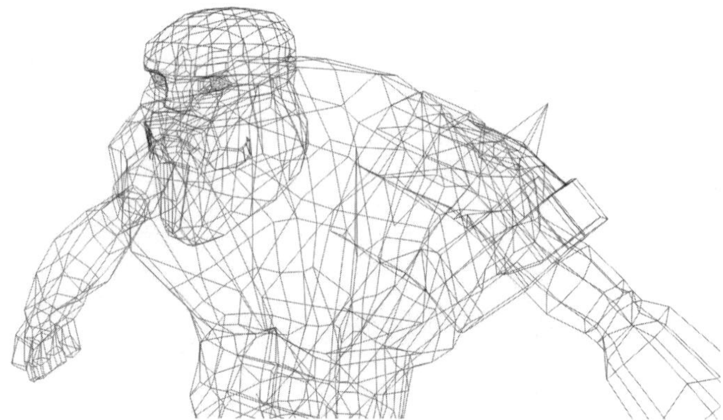

Figure 19-62 Vertices for a video game warrior

The computer must track all of the vertices of all of the objects in the 3-D world, including the ones you cannot currently see. Keep in mind that objects may be motionless in the 3-D world (a wall, for example), may have animation (such as a door opening and closing), or may be moving (like bad monsters trying to spray you with evil alien goo). This calculation process is called *transformation* and, as you might imagine, is extremely taxing to most CPUs. Intel and AMD's SIMD (SSE, etc.) processor extensions help to calculate these transformations faster.

Once the CPU has determined the positions of all vertices, the system begins to fill in the 3-D object. The process begins by drawing lines (the 3-D term is *edges*) between vertices to construct the 3-D object from many triangles. Why triangles? Well, mainly by consensus of game developers. Any shape works, but triangles make the most sense from a mathematical standpoint. I could go into more depth here, but that would

require talking about trigonometry, and I'm gambling you'd rather not read such a detailed description! All 3-D games use triangles to connect vertices. The 3-D process then groups triangles into various shapes called *polygons*. Figure 19-63 shows the same model as Figure 19-62, now displaying all of the connected vertices to create a large number of polygons.

Figure 19-63 Connected vertices forming polygons on a 3-D character

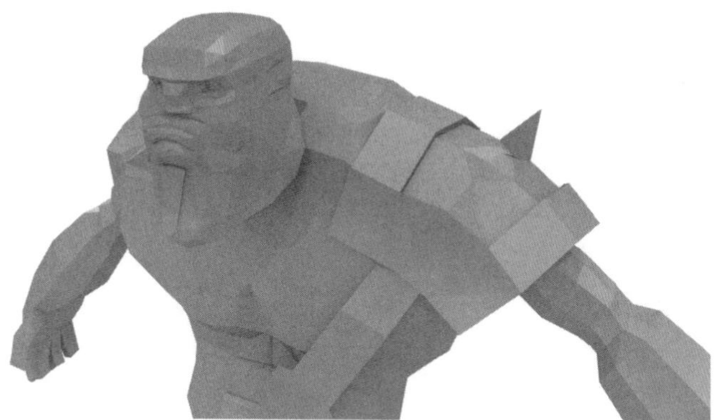

Originally, the CPU handled these calculations to create triangles. With the introduction of the GeForce 256 in 1999, this transform process was moved from the CPU to the video card, greatly accelerating 3-D performance.

The last step in second-generation games was texturing. Every 3-D game stores a number of image files called *textures*. The program wraps textures around an object to give it a surface. Textures work well to provide dramatic detail without using a lot of triangles. A single object may take one texture or many textures, applied to single triangles or groups of triangles (polygons). Figure 19-64 shows the finished character.

Figure 19-64 Video game warrior with textures added

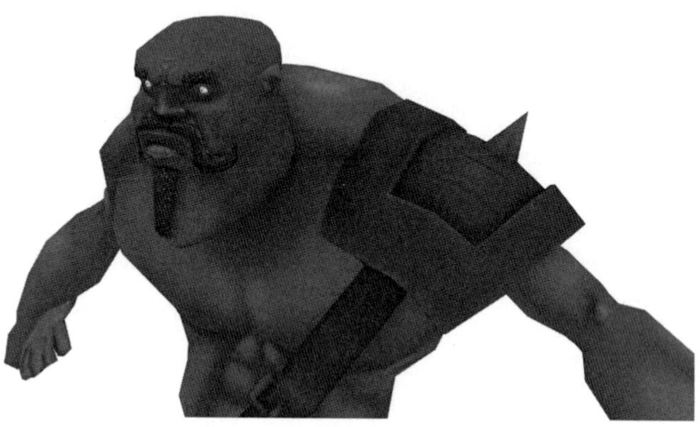

True 3-D objects immediately created the need for massively powerful video cards and much wider data buses. Intel's primary motivation for creating AGP was to provide a big enough pipe for massive data pumping between the video card and the CPU. Intel gave AGP the ability to read system RAM to support textures. If it weren't for 3-D games, AGP (and probably even PCIe) would almost certainly not exist.

3-D Video Cards

No CPU of the mid-1990s could ever hope to handle the massive processes required to render 3-D worlds. Keep in mind that to create realistic movement, the 3-D world must refresh at least 24 times per second. That means that this entire process, from transformation to texturing, must repeat once every 1/24th of a second! Furthermore, although the game re-creates each screen, it must also keep score, track the positions of all of the objects in the game, provide some type of intelligence to the bad guys, and so on. Something had to happen to take the workload off the CPU. The answer came from video cards.

Video cards were developed with smart onboard GPUs. The GPU helped the CPU by taking over some, and eventually all, of the 3-D rendering duties. These video cards not only have GPUs but also have massive amounts of RAM to store textures.

But a problem exists with this setup: How do we talk to these cards? This is done by means of a device driver, of course, but wouldn't it be great if we could create standard commands to speed up the process? The best thing to do would be to create a standardized set of instructions that any 3-D program could send to a video card to do all of the basic work, such as "make a cone" or "lay texture 237 on the cone you just made."

The video card instructions standards manifested themselves into a series of *application programming interfaces (APIs)*. In essence, an API is a library of commands that people who make 3-D games must use in their programs. The program currently using the video card sends API commands directly to the device driver. Device drivers must know how to understand the API commands. If you were to picture the graphics system of your computer as a layer cake, the top layer would be the program making a call to the video card driver that then directs the graphics hardware.

Several APIs have been developed over the years, with two clear winners among all of them: OpenGL and DirectX. The *OpenGL* standard was developed for UNIX systems but has since been *ported*, or made compatible with, a wide variety of computer systems, including Windows and Apple computers. As the demand for 3-D video grew increasingly strong, Microsoft decided to throw its hat into the 3-D graphics ring with its own API, called DirectX. We look at DirectX in depth in the next section.

Although they might accomplish the same task (for instance, translating instructions and passing them on to the video driver), every API handles things just a little bit differently. In some 3-D games, the OpenGL standard might produce more precise images with less CPU overhead than the DirectX standard. In general, however, you won't notice a large difference between the images produced by OpenGL and those produced by DirectX.

DirectX and Video Cards

In the old days, many applications communicated directly with much of the PC hardware and, as a result, could crash your computer if not written well enough. Microsoft tried to fix this problem by placing all hardware under the control of Windows, but

programmers balked because Windows added too much work for the video process and slowed everything down. For the most demanding programs, such as games, only direct access to hardware would work.

This need to "get around Windows" motivated Microsoft to unveil a new set of protocols called *DirectX*. Programmers use DirectX to take control of certain pieces of hardware and to talk directly to that hardware; it provides the speed necessary to play the advanced games so popular today. The primary impetus for DirectX was to build a series of products to enable Windows to run 3-D games. That's not to say that you couldn't run 3-D games in Windows *before* DirectX; rather, it's just that Microsoft wasn't involved in the API rat race at the time and wanted to be. Microsoft's goal in developing DirectX was to create a 100-percent stable environment, with direct hardware access, for running 3-D applications and games within Windows.

DirectX is not only for video; it also supports sound, network connections, input devices, and other parts of your PC. Each of these subsets of DirectX has a name, such as DirectDraw, Direct3D, or DirectSound.

- **DirectDraw** Supports direct access to the hardware for 2-D graphics
- **Direct3D** Supports direct access to the hardware for 3-D graphics—the most important part of DirectX
- **DirectInput** Supports direct access to the hardware for joysticks and other game controllers
- **DirectSound** Supports direct access to the hardware for waveforms
- **DirectMusic** Supports direct access to the hardware for MIDI devices
- **DirectPlay** Supports direct access to network devices for multiplayer games
- **DirectShow** Supports direct access to video and presentation devices

Microsoft constantly adds to and tweaks this list. As almost all games need DirectX and all video cards have drivers to support DirectX, you need to verify that DirectX is installed and working properly on your system. To do this, use the *DirectX Diagnostic Tool (dxdiag)* (see Figure 19-65). Go to Start and type **dxdiag** in the Search bar. Press ENTER to run the program.

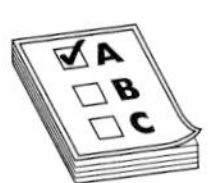

EXAM TIP The CompTIA A+ 902 exam refers to the DirectX Diagnostic Tool only by its Run command, *dxdiag*.

The System tab gives the version of DirectX. The system pictured in Figure 19-65 runs DirectX 11.

So, what does DirectX do for video cards? Back in the dark days before DirectX became popular with the game makers, many GPU makers created their own chip-specific APIs. 3dfx had Glide, for example, and S3 had ViRGE. This made buying 3-D games a mess. There would often be multiple versions of the same game for each card. Even worse, many games never used 3-D acceleration because it was just too much work to support all of the different cards.

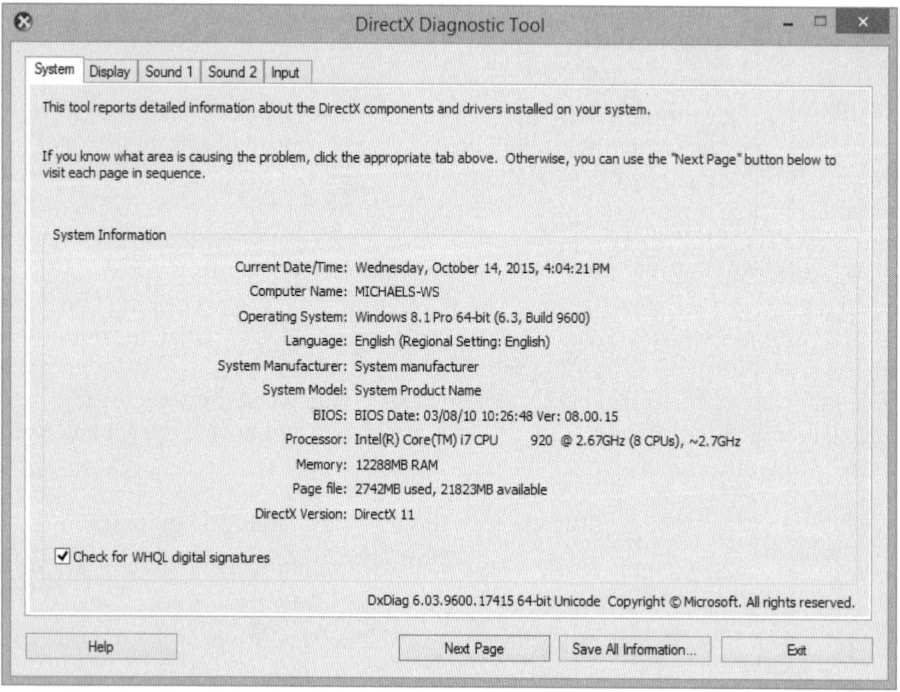

Figure 19-65 The DirectX Diagnostic Tool

That all changed when Microsoft beefed up DirectX and got more GPU makers to support it. That in turn enabled the game companies to write games by using DirectX and have them run on any card out there. The bottom line: When Microsoft comes out with a new version of DirectX, all of the GPU companies hurry to support it so they won't be left behind.

Trying to decide what video card to buy gives me the shakes—too many options! One good way to narrow down your buying decision is to see what GPU is hot at the moment. I make a point to check out these Web sites whenever I'm getting ready to buy, so I can see what everyone says is best.

- www.arstechnica.com
- www.hardocp.com
- www.tomshardware.com
- www.anandtech.com

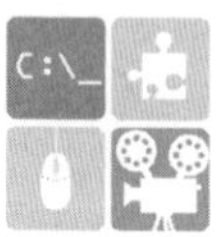

SIM Check out the excellent "DXDIAG" Show! and Click! sims in the Chapter 19 section at http://totalsem.com/90x. These will get you prepared for any performance-based questions CompTIA might throw at you.

Troubleshooting Video

People tend to notice when their monitors stop showing the Windows desktop, making video problems an urgent issue for technicians. Users might temporarily ignore a bad sound card or other device, but will holler like crazy when the screen doesn't look the way they expect. To fix video problems quickly, the best place to start is to divide your video problems into two groups: video cards/drivers, and monitors.

Troubleshooting Video Cards/Drivers

Video cards rarely go bad, so the vast majority of video card/driver problems are bad or incompatible drivers or incorrect settings. Always make sure you have the correct driver installed. If you're using an incompatible driver, you might get a Blue Screen of Death (BSoD) as soon as Windows starts to load. A system with a suddenly corrupted driver usually doesn't act up until the next reboot. If you reboot a system with a corrupted driver, Windows will do one of the following: go into SVGA mode, blank the monitor, lock up, or display a garbled screen with weird color patterns or a distorted image. You might get oversized images and icons. You might even see a 3-D image with amazingly distorted geometry.

Whatever the output, reboot into Safe mode and roll back or delete the driver. Keep in mind that more advanced video cards tend to show their drivers as installed programs under Programs and Features, so always check there first before you try deleting a driver by using Device Manager. Download the latest driver and reinstall.

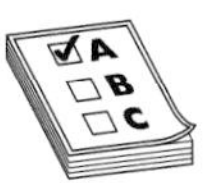

EXAM TIP The CompTIA A+ 902 objectives mention that buggy drivers can cause Windows to go into VGA mode; that's 640 × 480. This was certainly true in earlier versions of the OS, but the current versions will go 800 × 600. Be prepared for "VGA mode" to be the only correct-ish answer on an exam question.

Video cards are pretty durable but they have two components that do go bad: the fan and the RAM. Lucky for you, if either of these goes out, it tends to show the same error—bizarre screen outputs followed shortly by a screen lockup. Usually Windows keeps running; you may see your mouse pointer moving around and windows refreshing, but the screen turns into a huge mess (see Figure 19-66).

Bad drivers sometimes also make this error, so always first try going into Safe mode to see if the problem suddenly clears up. If it does, you do not have a problem with the video card!

Excessive heat inside the case, even with the video card fan running at full blast, can create some interesting effects. The computer could simply shut down due to overheating. You'll recognize this possible cause because the computer will come back up in a minute or two, but then shut down again as you use it hard and it heats up again. Sometimes the screen will get bizarre artifacts or start distorting. Check your case fans and make sure nothing is too close to the video card. You might need to blow out (outdoors!) the dust from filters, vents, and fans.

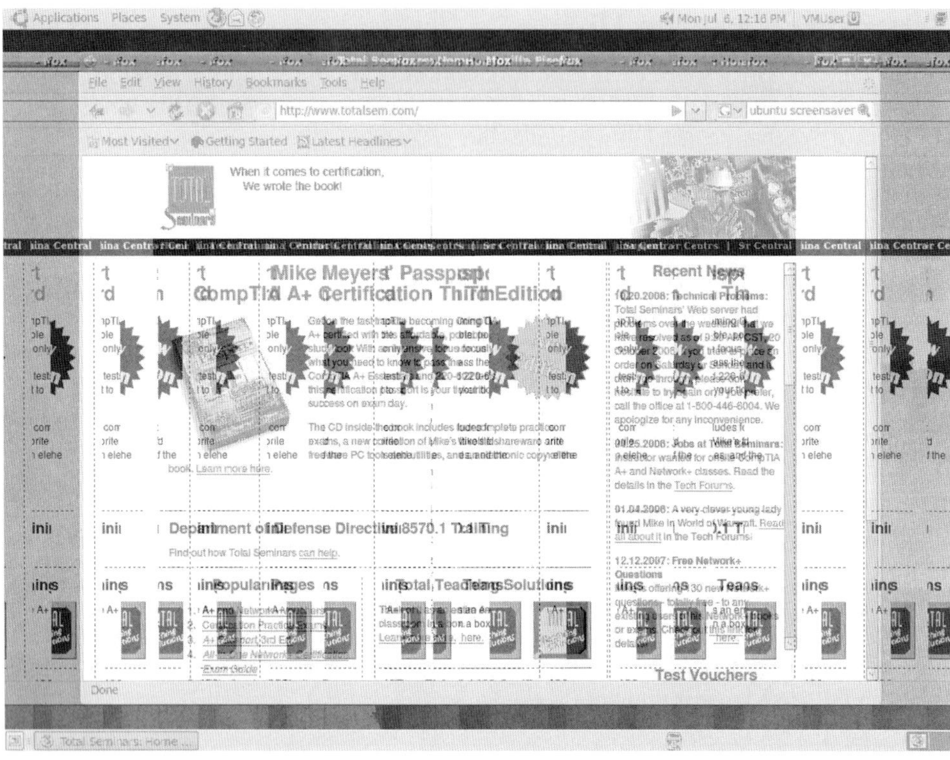

Figure 19-66 Serious video problem

Troubleshooting Monitors

Because of the inherent dangers of the high-frequency and high-voltage power required by monitors, and because proper adjustment requires specialized training, this section concentrates on giving a support person the information necessary to decide whether a trouble ticket is warranted. Virtually no monitor manufacturers make schematics of their monitors available to the public, because of liability issues regarding possible electrocution. To simplify troubleshooting, look at the process as three separate parts: common monitor problems, external adjustments, and internal adjustments.

Common Monitor Problems

Although I'm not super comfortable diving into the guts of a monitor, you can fix a substantial percentage of monitor problems yourself. The following list describes the most common monitor problems and tells you what to do—even when that means sending it to someone else.

- For problems with ghosting, streaking, and/or fuzzy vertical edges, check the cable connections and the cable itself. These problems rarely apply to monitors; more commonly, they point to the video card.

- If one color is missing, check cables for breaks or bent pins. Check the front controls for that color. If the color adjustment is already maxed out, the monitor will require internal service.
- As monitors age, they lose brightness. If the brightness control is turned all of the way up and the picture seems dim, the monitor will require internal adjustment. This is a good argument for power-management functions. Use the power switch or the power-management options in Windows to turn off the monitor after a certain amount of time.
- An LCD monitor may have bad pixels. A bad pixel is any single pixel that does not react the way it should. A pixel that never lights up is a *dead pixel*, a pixel that is stuck on pure white is a *lit pixel*, and a pixel on a certain color is a *stuck pixel*. If you discover a bad pixel on a monitor under warranty, the best course of action is to contact the manufacturer. If the monitor isn't under warranty, you can try to revive the pixel using techniques discussed online, learn to live with the bad pixels, or replace the monitor. All LCD panel makers allow a certain number of bad pixels, even on a brand-new LCD monitor! You need to check the warranty for your monitor and see how many they allow before you may return the monitor.
- If your LCD monitor cracks, it is not repairable and must be replaced.
- A flickering image with an LCD usually points to either a very inexpensive panel with too much light bleed from the backlight or a dying CCFL backlight. LEDs don't flicker, so you won't see this issue with those types of LCDs. Replace the backlight if necessary.
- A dim image, especially on only the top or bottom half of the screen, points to a dead or dying backlight in a multibacklight system. Replace as necessary.
- If the LCD goes dark but you can still barely see the image under bright lights, you lost either the backlight or the inverter. In many cases, especially with super-thin panels, you'll replace the entire panel and backlight as a unit. On the other hand, an inverter can be on a separate circuit board that you can replace, such as the one pictured in Figure 19-67.
- If your LCD makes a distinct hissing noise, an inverter is about to fail. Again, you can replace the inverter if needed.

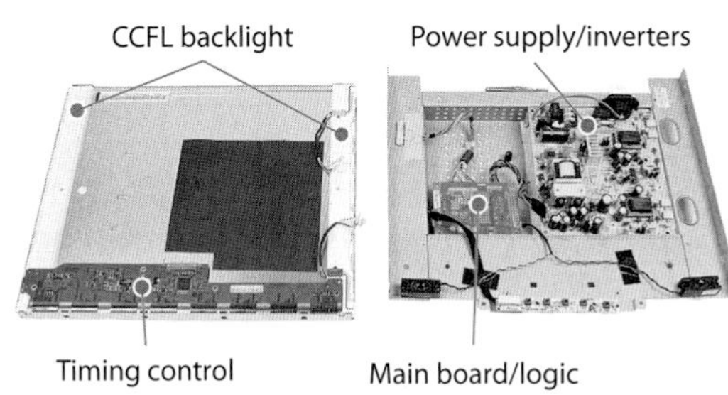

Figure 19-67 LCD components labeled

Be careful if you open an LCD to work on the inside. The inverter can bite you in several ways. First, it's powered by a high-voltage electrical circuit that can give you a nasty shock. Worse, the inverter will retain a charge for a few minutes after you unplug it, so unplug and wait for a bit. Second, inverters get very hot and present a very real danger of burning you at a touch. Again, wait for a while after you unplug it to try to replace it. Finally, if you shock an inverter, you might irreparably damage it. So use proper ESD-avoidance techniques.

Bottom line on fixing LCD monitors? You can find companies that sell replacement parts for LCDs, but repairing an LCD is difficult, and there are folks who will do it for you faster and cheaper than you can. Search for a specialty LCD repair company. Hundreds of these companies exist all over the world.

Cleaning Monitors

Cleaning monitors is easy. Always use antistatic monitor wipes or at least a general antistatic cloth. Some LCD monitors may require special cleaning equipment. Never use window cleaners that contain ammonia or any liquid because getting liquid into the monitor may create a shocking experience! Many commercial cleaning solutions will also melt older LCD screens, which is never a good thing.

Problems with Multiple Monitors

Adding a second or third monitor to your setup can create problems. The added viewing area can increase the potential for glare or reflection from other objects, making optimal monitor placement difficult. Mismatched monitors can create misalignment or odd orientation, especially with different default resolutions. The extra visual real estate and viewing angles also make it easy for even casual passersby to see what you're doing or browsing or whatever.

Monitor peripheral vendors address these problems with *privacy screens*. The screens fit over and slightly around the LCD panels. They stop wide-angle viewing of the screen and also drop the glare caused by external object reflection.

Beyond A+

Changing Technologies

For all its length, this chapter has barely scratched the surface of display technologies (don't actually scratch the surface of a display, by the way). The field changes very rapidly, with manufacturers debuting new video features on a seemingly daily basis. Some of these will stay; others will fade quickly. It's very hard to predict. As we go to print in late 2015, for example, two trends have made some headway: curved LCD panels and 3-D headsets.

Curved panels, according to the manufacturers, make the viewing experience far more 3-D like and more immersive. The panels cut down on glare and increase the viewing angle.

In practice, curved panels work only when really huge, like 60+ inches, and actually increase the glare and reflection from other objects. They're more expensive than comparably sized flat screens and don't hang on the wall well.

3-D headsets that put the "monitor" in immersive wraparound gear promise essentially virtual reality. If you imagine walking into the holodeck on the USS *Voyager* from *Star Trek*, you've got the premise of the technology. Although the technology has improved dramatically over the past couple of years, it's still not prime time as of this writing. Headaches, nausea, and disorientation are common side-effects of immersion in virtual reality.

Chapter Review

Questions

1. What do we call the time it takes for all of the sub-pixels on the panel to go from pure black to pure white and back again?
   A. Refresh rate
   B. Redraw rate
   C. Response rate
   D. Vertical refresh rate
2. What provides the illumination for LCD monitors?
   A. Backlights
   B. Inverter
   C. Lamp
   D. LCD panel
3. Dudley wants to connect his new MacBook Pro to an LCD monitor that has a Digital Visual Interface. What type of adapter should he use?
   A. BNC to DVI
   B. DisplayPort to HDMI
   C. Mini-HDMI to DB-15
   D. Thunderbolt to DVI
4. How do you measure brightness of a projector?
   A. Lumens
   B. Pixels
   C. LEDs
   D. CCFLs

5. What is 1080p resolution?
   A. 1024 × 768
   B. 1280 × 1024
   C. 1680 × 1050
   D. 1920 × 1080
6. What is the processor on a video card called?
   A. CPU
   B. GPU
   C. GDDR
   D. MPU
7. What Microsoft API supports 3-D graphics?
   A. Active Desktop
   B. DirectX
   C. Glide
   D. OpenGL
8. Which two technologies are used for backlights in LCD monitors?
   A. CCFL and LED
   B. CCFL and LCD
   C. CCFL and AC
   D. HDMI and DisplayPort
9. A customer calls complaining that his TV looks awful when he connects it to his laptop. What could cause this problem?
   A. The second monitor (the TV) connects via DisplayPort.
   B. The second monitor (the TV) connects via DVI.
   C. The second monitor (the TV) is an LCD.
   D. The second monitor (the TV) is a PDP.
10. A client calls complaining that his new LCD monitor is flickering. What is most likely the problem?
   A. The refresh rate is set too high.
   B. The refresh rate is set too low.
   C. The CCFL backlight is failing.
   D. The LED backlight is failing.

Answers

1. **C.** The amount of time it takes for all of the sub-pixels on the panel to go from pure black to pure white and back again is called the response rate.
2. **A.** The backlights provide the illumination for the LCD panel.
3. **D.** Dudley should use a Thunderbolt-to-DVI adapter to connect his new MacBook Pro to the LCD monitor.
4. **A.** The brightness of a projector is measured in lumens.
5. **D.** 1080p resolution is 1920 × 1080.
6. **B.** You'll typically see video card processors referred to as GPUs.
7. **B.** Microsoft makes the DirectX API to support 3-D programs.
8. **A.** Current LCD monitors use one of two competing backlight technologies, CCFL and LED.
9. **D.** Plasma display panels (PDPs) offer a good alternative to LCDs for television, but not as computer displays.
10. **C.** LCD monitors have a fixed refresh rate, so the most likely cause here is that the CCFL backlight is failing. LED backlights don't flicker.

CHAPTER 20

Essentials of Networking

In this chapter, you will learn how to

- Describe the basic roles of various networked computers
- Discuss network technologies and Ethernet
- Describe the differences between a LAN and a WAN and the importance of TCP/IP

It's hard to find a computer that's not connected to a network. Whether you're talking about a workstation that's part of a large enterprise network or discussing that smartphone in your pocket, every computer has some form of network connection. CompTIA has added quite a bit of networking coverage to the CompTIA A+ exams.

This chapter dives into networks in detail, especially the underlying hardware and technologies that make up the bulk of networks in today's homes and businesses. The discussion starts by examining the roles computers play in networking, helping you associate specific names with devices and services you've undoubtedly used many times already. The second portion, and the heart of the chapter, focuses on the now-standard network technology used in most networks, regardless of operating system. The final section examines how this network technology looks in a normal workplace.

902

Roles Hosts Play in Networks

Take a moment to think about what you do on a network. Most of us, when asked, would say, "surf the Internet," or "watch YouTube videos," or maybe "print to the printer downstairs." These are all good reasons to use a network, but what ties them together? In each of these situations, you use your computer (the *local host*) to access "stuff" stored

on a *remote host* (not your local computer). A *host* is any computing device connected to a network. So what do remote computers have that you might want (see Figure 20-1)?

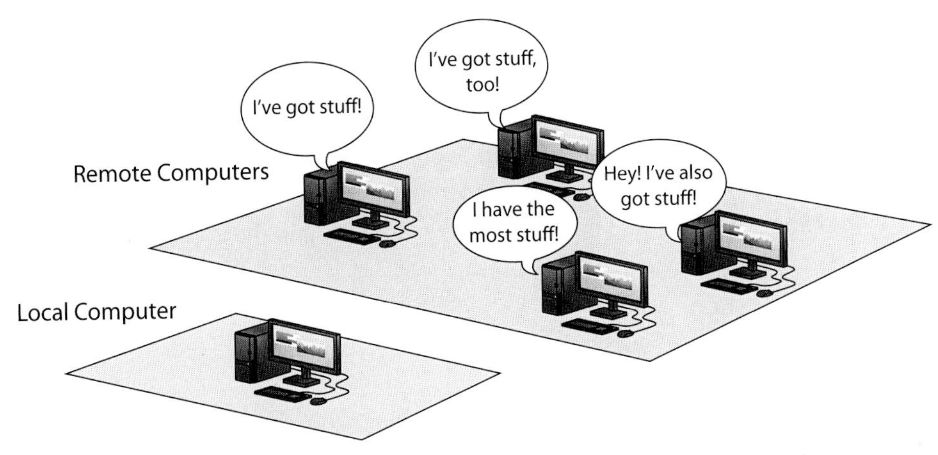

Figure 20-1 Accessing remote computers

NOTE Terminology shifts as soon as computing devices network together. Because a computing device can take many forms, not just a PC or workstation, we need a term to define networked devices. A *host* is any computing device connected to a network. A *local host*, therefore, refers to what's in front of you, like your Mac OS X workstation. A *remote host* refers to some other computing device on the network or reachable beyond the network (more on those later).

Each networked host fulfills a certain *role*. A remote computer called a *Web server* stores the files that make up a Web site. The Web server uses server programs to store and share the data. So the role of the Web server is to provide access to Web sites. Two popular Web server programs are Apache HTTP Server and Internet Information Services (IIS). When you access a Web site, your *Web browser* (likely Internet Explorer, Mozilla Firefox, Google Chrome, or Microsoft Edge) asks the Web server to share the Web page files and then displays them (see Figure 20-2). Because your computer asks for the Web page, we call it the *client*. That's the role of the local host in this example. The remote computer that serves the Web site is a *server*.

NOTE Add to this list the many legacy and embedded systems still floating about, performing specific, non-modern tasks.

Figure 20-2 Accessing a Web page

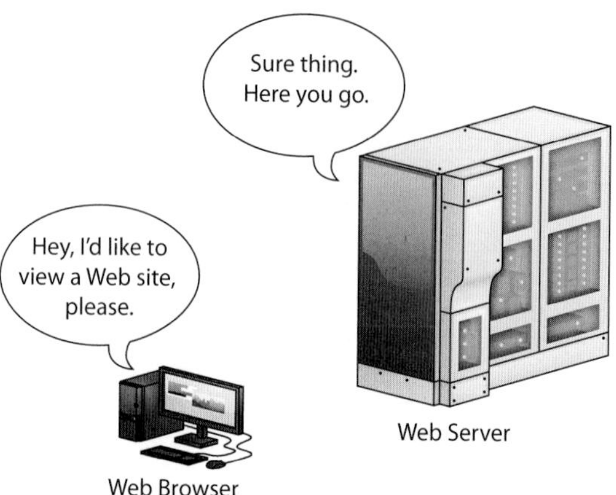

NOTE Any computer that's running a sharing program is by definition a server.

But what about YouTube? YouTube also uses Web servers, but these Web servers connect to massive video databases. Like a normal Web server, these remote computers share the videos with your client device, but they use special software capable of sending video fast enough that you can watch it without waiting (see Figure 20-3).

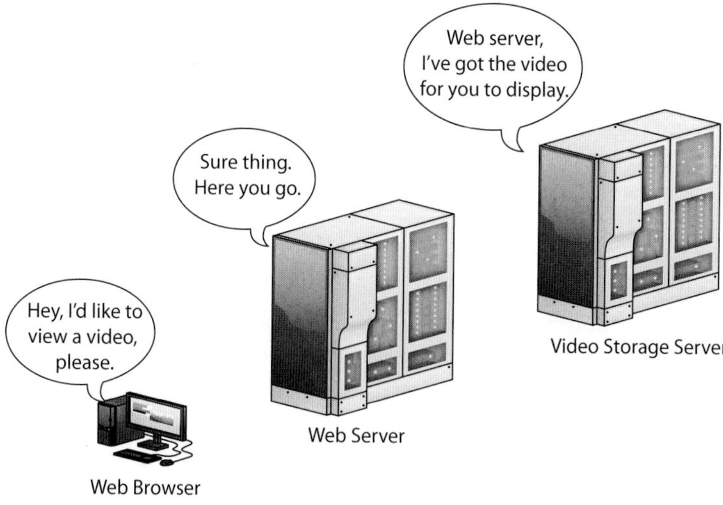

Figure 20-3 Accessing a YouTube page

But we don't need the Internet to share stuff. Figure 20-4 shows a small home network with each computer running Windows. One of the computers on the network has a printer connected via a USB port. This computer has enabled a printer-sharing program built into Windows so that the other computers on the network can use the printer. That computer, therefore, takes on the role of a *print server*.

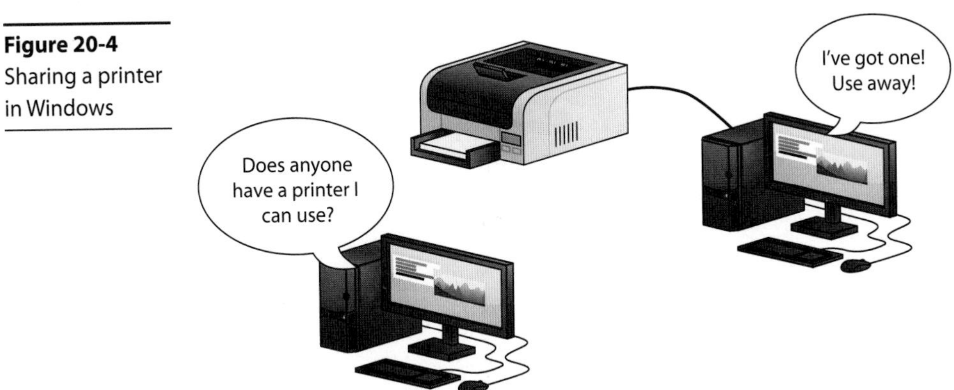

Figure 20-4 Sharing a printer in Windows

No matter how big the network, we use networks to share and access stuff. This stuff might be Web pages, videos, printers, folders, e-mail messages, music . . . what you can share and access is limited only by your ability to find a server program capable of sharing it and a client program that can access it.

Each type of server gets a label that defines its role. A networked host that enables you to access a bunch of files and folders is called a *file server*. The networked host you use to access e-mail messages? It's called a *mail server*. Truth in advertising!

Network people call anything that one computer might share with another a *resource*. The goal of networking, therefore, is to connect computers so that they can share resources or access other shared resources.

To share and access resources, a network must have the following:

1. Something that defines and standardizes the design and operation of cabling, network cards, and the interconnection of multiple computers
2. An addressing method that enables clients to find servers and enables servers to send data to clients, no matter the size of the network
3. Some method of sharing resources and accessing those shared resources

Let's look now at the first of these network needs and discuss current industry standards.

Historical/Conceptual

Networking Technologies

When the first network designers sat down at a café to figure out how to get two or more computers to share data and peripherals, they had to write a lot of notes on little white napkins to answer even the most basic questions. The first question was: *How*? It's easy to say, "Well, just run a wire between them!" But that doesn't tell us how the wire works or how the computers connect to the wire. Here are some more big-picture questions:

- How will each computer be identified?
- If two or more computers want to talk at the same time, how do you ensure that all conversations are understood?
- What kind of wire? What gauge? How many wires in the cable? Which wires do what? How long can the cable be? What type of connectors?

Clearly, making a modern network entails a lot more than just stringing up some cable! As you saw a bit earlier, most networks have one or more client machines, devices that request information or services, and a server, the machine that hosts and shares the data. Both clients and servers need *network interface controllers (NICs)* that define or label the machine on the network. A NIC also breaks files into smaller data units to send across the network and reassembles the units it receives into whole files. You also need some medium for delivering the data units between two or more devices—most often this is a wire that can carry electrical pulses; sometimes it's radio waves or other wireless methods. Finally, a computer's operating system has to be able to communicate with its own networking hardware and with other machines on the network. Figure 20-5 shows a typical network layout.

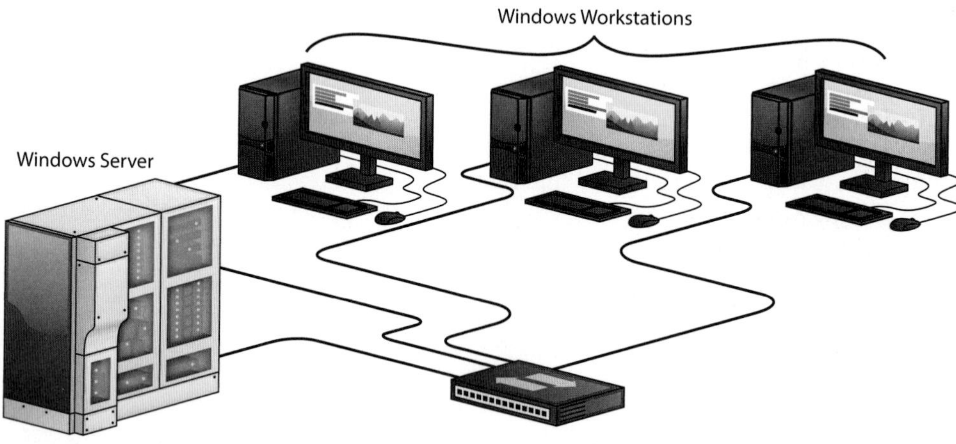

Figure 20-5 A typical network

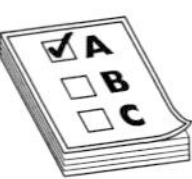

EXAM TIP Not too many years ago, every NIC came on an expansion card that you added to a motherboard. Most techs called that card a *network interface card* or *NIC*. Now that just about every motherboard has the networking feature built in, the acronym has shifted to network interface *controller*. You're likely to see only the term *NIC* on the exams, though I call them *network cards*, too.

901

Frames and NICs

Data is moved from one device to another in discrete chunks called *frames*. NICs create and process frames.

NOTE You'll sometimes hear the word *packet* used instead of frames—this is incorrect. Packets are a part of the frame. You'll find more information about packets in Chapter 21, "Local Area Networking."

Every NIC in the world has a built-in identifier, an address unique to that network card, called a *media access control (MAC) address*. A MAC address is a *binary number*, meaning it's a string of 1s and 0s. Each 1 or 0 is called a *bit*.

The MAC address is 48 bits long, providing more than 281 *trillion* MAC addresses, so there are plenty of MAC addresses to go around. Because people have trouble keeping track of that many 1s and 0s, we need another way to display the addresses. *Hexadecimal* is shorthand for representing strings of 1s and 0s. One hex character is used to represent four binary characters. Here's the key:

0000 = 0
0001 = 1
0010 = 2
0011 = 3
0100 = 4
0101 = 5
0110 = 6
0111 = 7
1000 = 8
1001 = 9
1010 = A
1011 = B
1100 = C
1101 = D
1110 = E
1111 = F

So, MAC addresses may be binary, but we represent them by using 12 hexadecimal characters. These MAC addresses are burned into every NIC, and some NIC makers print the MAC address on the card. Figure 20-6 shows the System Information utility description of a NIC, with the MAC address highlighted.

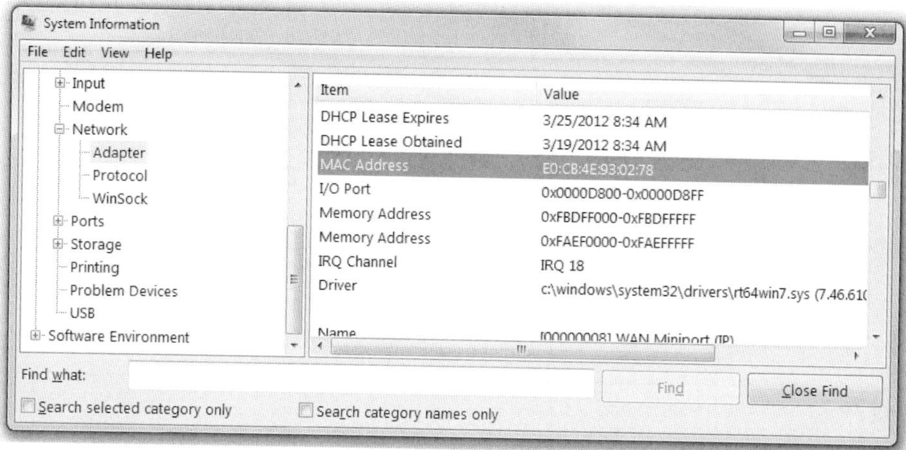

Figure 20-6 MAC address

NOTE Even though MAC addresses are embedded into the NIC, some NICs allow you to change the MAC address on the NIC. This is rarely done.

Hey! I thought we were talking about frames! Well, we are, but you needed to understand MAC addresses to understand frames.

The many varieties of frames share common features (see Figure 20-7). First, frames contain the MAC address of the network card to which the data is being sent. Second, they have the MAC address of the network card that sent the data. Third is the data itself (at this point, we have no idea what the data is—certain software handles that question), which can vary in size depending on the type of frame. Finally, the frame must contain some type of data check to verify that the data was received in good order. Most frames use a clever mathematical algorithm called a *cyclic redundancy check (CRC)*.

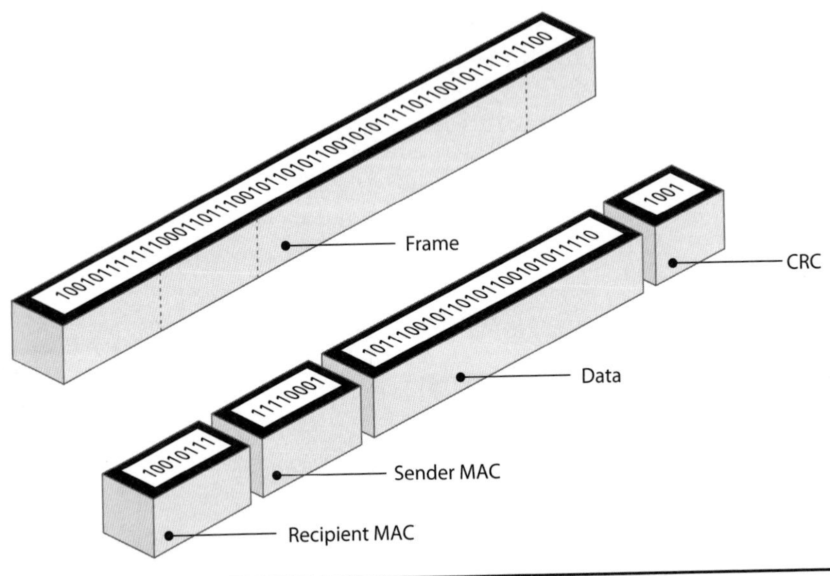

Figure 20-7 Generic frame

> **Try This!**
>
> **MAC Address Search**
>
> Every personal computing device has a MAC address assigned to each network connection type it offers. Any number of troubleshooting scenarios will have you scrambling to find a device's MAC address, so try this!
>
> You have many ways to discover the MAC address(es) in Windows, Mac OS X, and Linux. The simplest is through the command-line interface. Here's a method in Windows. At the prompt, type **ipconfig /all** and press ENTER. You'll find the MAC address listed as the "Physical Address" under the Ethernet adapter Local Area Connection category.
>
> Which command do you think would work at the Terminal in Mac OS X and Linux? How do you figure out which switch to use? (Refresh your memory of commands in Chapter 16, "Working with the Command-Line Interface.")

This discussion of frames raises a question: How big is a frame? Or more specifically, how much data do you put into each frame? How do you ensure that the receiving system understands the *way* the data was broken down by the sending machine and can

thus put the pieces back together? The hard part of answering these questions is that they encompass so many items. When the first networks were created, *everything* from the frames to the connectors to the type of cable had to be invented from scratch.

To make a successful network, you need the sending and receiving devices to use the same network technology. Over the years, many hardware protocols came and went, but today only one hardware protocol dominates the modern computing landscape: *Ethernet.* Ethernet was developed for wired networking, but even wireless networks use Ethernet as the basis for their signals. If you want to understanding networking, you need to understand Ethernet.

Ethernet

A consortium of companies centered on Digital Equipment Corporation, Intel, and Xerox invented the first network in the mid-1970s. More than just create a network, they wrote a series of standards that defined everything necessary to get data from one computer to another. This series of standards was called *Ethernet.* Over the years, Ethernet has gone through hundreds of distinct improvements in areas such as speed, signaling, and cabling. We call these improvements *Ethernet flavors.*

Through all the improvements in Ethernet, the Ethernet frame hasn't changed in over 25 years. This is very important: you can have any combination of hardware devices and cabling using different Ethernet flavors on a single Ethernet network and, in most cases, the hosts will be able to communicate just fine.

Most modern Ethernet networks employ one of three speeds: *10BaseT*, *100BaseT*, or *1000BaseT*. As the numbers in the names suggest, 10BaseT networks run at 10 Mbps, 100BaseT networks run at 100 Mbps, and 1000BaseT networks—called Gigabit Ethernet—run at 1000 Mbps, or 1 Gbps. All three technologies—sometimes referred to collectively as *10/100/1000BaseT* or just plain Ethernet—use a *star bus* topology and connect via a type of cable called unshielded twisted pair (UTP).

NOTE Ethernet developers continue to refine the technology. 1000BaseT might be the most common desktop standard now, but 10-Gigabit Ethernet is common on server-to-server connections. 40/100-Gigabit Ethernet is slowly encroaching as well.

The Ethernet Star Bus

With all Ethernet networks (with the exception of some very old flavors), every individual host connects to a central box. You attach each system to this box via cables to special ports. The box takes care of all of the tedious details required by the network to get frames sent to the correct systems. This layout, which looks something like a star, is called a *star bus* topology (see Figure 20-8). (The *bus* refers to the internal wiring in the box. The *star* refers to the wires leading from the box to the hosts.)

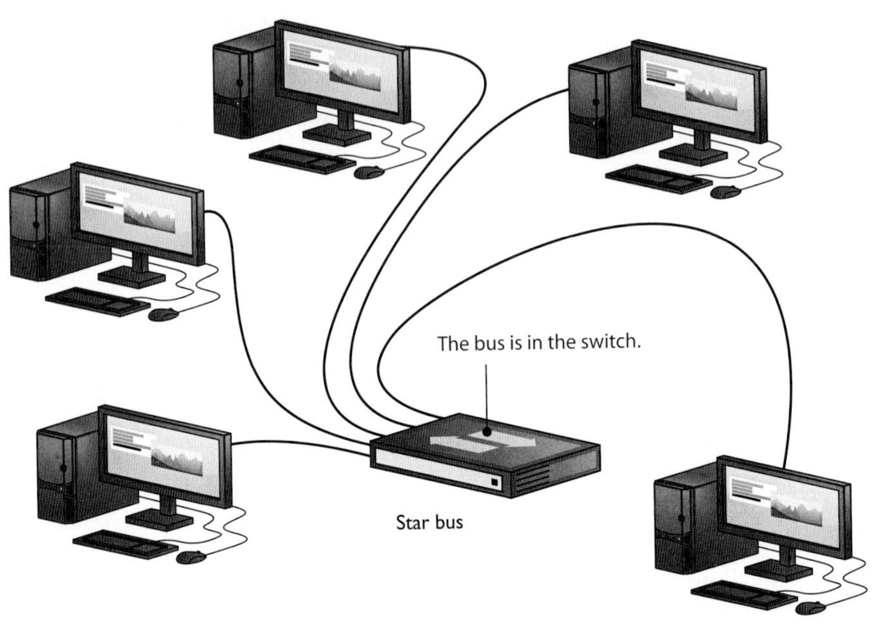

Figure 20-8 Ethernet star bus

The central box—the *switch*—provides a common point of connection for network devices. Switches can have a wide variety of ports. Most consumer-level switches have 4 or 8 ports, but business-level switches can have 32 or more ports.

Early Ethernet networks used a *hub*. A switch is a far superior and far more common version of a hub. Figure 20-9 shows a typical consumer-level switch.

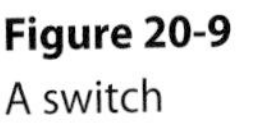

Figure 20-9
A switch

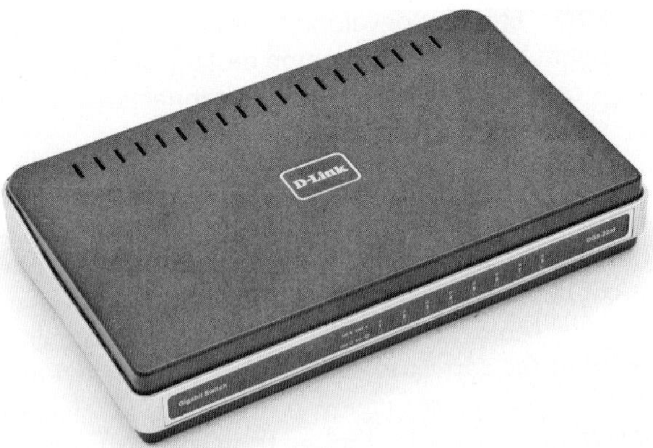

Hubs and switches look pretty much identical and they perform the same basic job: taking the signal from one host and then repeating the signal out to other hosts. Even

though they look the same and do functionally the same job, they do the job differently. Basically, hubs are stupid *repeaters*: anything sent in one port automatically goes out all the other connected ports. Switches are smart repeaters: they memorize the MAC addresses of all the connected devices and only send out repeated signals to the correct host. This makes switched networks much faster than hubbed networks.

A simple example demonstrates the difference between hubs and switches. Let's say you have a network of 32 machines, all using 100-Mbps NICs attached to a 100-Mbps hub or switch. We would say the network's *bandwidth* is 100 Mbps. If you put the 32 systems on a 32-port 100-Mbps hub, you have 32 computers *sharing* the 100 Mbps of bandwidth. A switch addresses this problem by making each port its own separate network. Each system gets to use the full bandwidth. The bottom line? Once switches became affordable, hubs went away.

The connection between a computer and a switch is called a *segment*. With most cable types, Ethernet segments are limited to 100 meters or less. You cannot use a splitter to split a single segment into two or more connections with an Ethernet network that uses this star bus topology. Doing so prevents the switch from recognizing which host is sending or receiving a signal and no hosts connected to a split segment will be able to communicate. Splitters negatively effect signal quality.

Cheap and centralized, Ethernet's star bus topology does not go down if a single cable breaks. True, the network would go down if the switch failed, but that is rare.

Unshielded Twisted Pair

Unshielded twisted pair (UTP) cabling is the specified cabling for 10/100/1000BaseT and is the predominant cabling system used today. Many types of twisted pair cabling are available, and the type used depends on the needs of the network. Twisted pair cabling consists of AWG 22–26 gauge wire twisted together into color-coded pairs. Each wire is individually insulated and encased as a group in a common jacket.

CAT Levels UTP cables come in categories that define the maximum speed at which data can be transferred (also called *bandwidth*). The major categories (CATs) are outlined in Table 20-1.

CAT 1	Standard telephone line.
CAT 3	Designed for 10-Mbps networks; a variant that used all four pairs of wires supported 100-Mbps speeds.
CAT 5	Designed for 100-Mbps networks.
CAT 5e	Enhanced to handle 1000-Mbps networks.
CAT 6	Supports 1000-Mbps networks at 100-meter segments; 10-Gbps networks up to 55-meter segments.
CAT 6a	Supports 10-Gbps networks at 100-meter segments.
CAT 6e	A nonstandard term used by a few manufacturers for CAT 6 or CAT 6a.
CAT 7	Supports 10-Gbps networks at 100-meter segments; shielding for individual wire pairs reduces crosstalk and noise problems. CAT 7 is *not* a TIA/EIA standard.

Table 20-1 CAT Levels

The CAT level should be clearly marked on the cable, as Figure 20-10 shows.

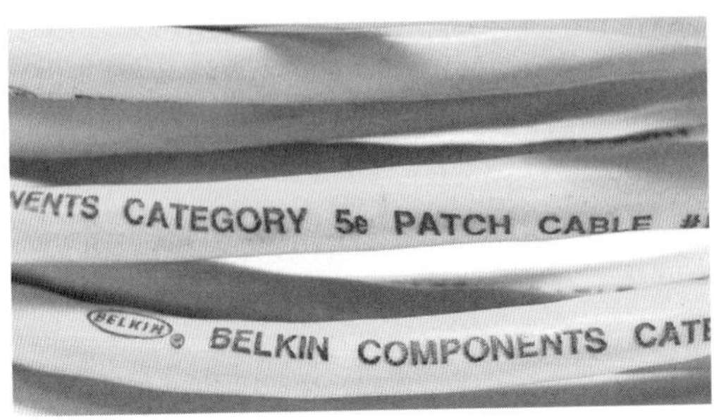

Figure 20-10 Cable markings for CAT level

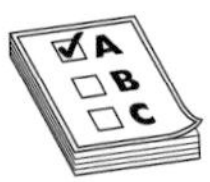

EXAM TIP Although these days you'll only find CAT 3 installed for telephones and in very old network installations, CompTIA traditionally enjoys tripping up techs who don't know it could handle 100-Mbps networks.

The *Telecommunication Industry Association/Electronics Industries Alliance (TIA/EIA)* establishes the UTP categories, which fall under the TIA/EIA 568 specification. Currently, most installers use CAT 5e, CAT 6, or CAT 6a cable.

Shielded Twisted Pair

Shielded twisted pair (STP), as its name implies, consists of twisted pairs of wires surrounded by shielding to protect them from EMI, or electromagnetic interference. STP is pretty rare, primarily because there's so little need for STP's shielding; it only really matters in locations with excessive electronic noise, such as a shop floor area with lots of lights, electric motors, or other machinery that could cause problems for other cables.

Ethernet with Twisted Pair

The 10BaseT and 100BaseT standards require two pairs of wires: a pair for sending and a pair for receiving. 10BaseT ran on an ancient CAT version called CAT 3, but typically used at least CAT 5 cable. 100BaseT requires at least CAT 5 to run. 1000BaseT needs all four pairs of wires in CAT 5e and higher cables. These cables use a connector called an *RJ-45* connector. The *RJ (registered jack)* designation was invented by Ma Bell (the phone company, for you youngsters) years ago and is still used today.

NOTE There are CAT levels for connectors as well as cables. Don't even try to use a CAT 5e RJ-45 connector with a CAT 6 cable.

Currently only two types of RJ connectors are used for networking: RJ-11 and RJ-45 (see Figure 20-11). *RJ-11* connects your telephone to the telephone jack in the wall of

your house. It supports up to two pairs of wires, though most phone lines use only one pair. The other pair is used to support a second phone line. RJ-11 connectors are primarily used for telephone-based Internet connections (see Chapter 23, "The Internet"). RJ-45 is the standard for UTP connectors. RJ-45 has connections for up to four pairs and is visibly much wider than RJ-11. Figure 20-12 shows the position of the #1 and #8 pins on an RJ-45 jack.

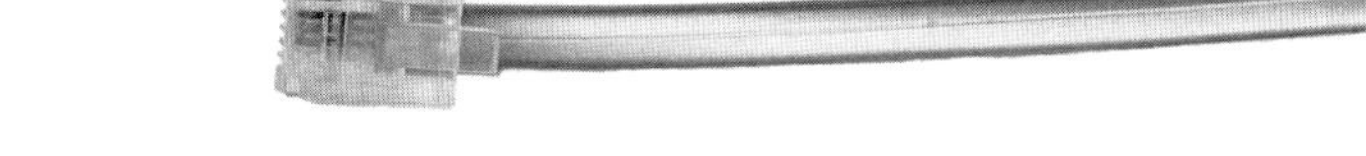

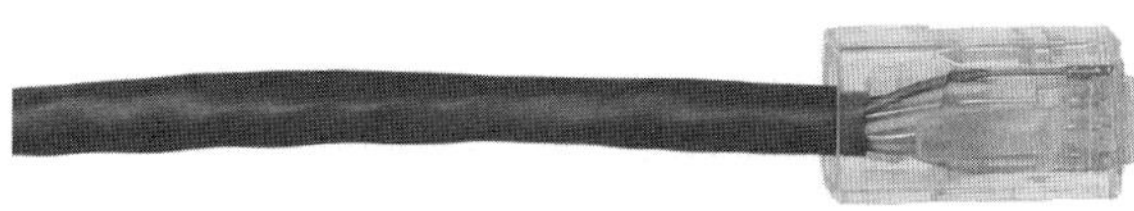

Figure 20-11 RJ-11 and RJ-45

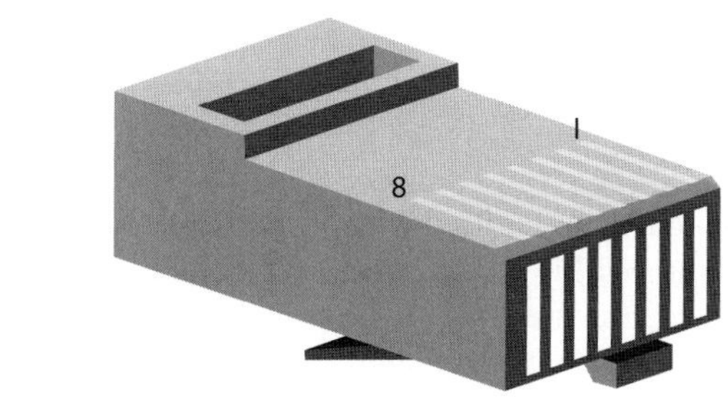

Figure 20-12 RJ-45 pin numbers

The TIA/EIA has two standards for connecting the RJ-45 connector to the UTP cable: the TIA/EIA 568A (*T568A*) and the TIA/EIA 568B (*T568B*). Both are acceptable. You do not have to follow any standard as long as you use the same pairings on each end of the cable; however, you will make your life simpler if you choose a standard. Make sure that all of your cabling uses the same standard and you will save a great deal of work in the end. Most importantly, *keep records*!

Like all wires, the wires in UTP are numbered. A number does not appear on each wire, but rather each wire has a standardized color. Table 20-2 shows the official TIA/EIA Standard Color Chart for UTP.

Pin	T568A	T568B	Pin	T568A	T568B
1	White/Green	White/Orange	5	White/Blue	White/Blue
2	Green	Orange	6	Orange	Green
3	White/Orange	White/Green	7	White/Brown	White/Brown
4	Blue	Blue	8	Brown	Brown

Table 20-2 UTP Cabling Color Chart

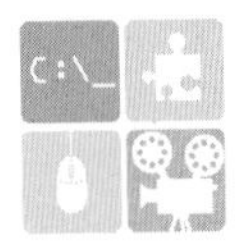

SIMS Check out the "568B" simulation at the Total Seminars Training Hub for practice on a simulation you might see on the CompTIA A+ 901 exam: http://hub.totalsem.com. You'll find it in *TotalSims for A+*, Chapter 20.

Plenum Versus PVC Cabling

Most workplace installations of network cable go up above the ceiling and then drop down through the walls to present a nice port in the wall. The space in the ceiling, under the floors, and in the walls through which cable runs is called the *plenum* space. The potential problem with this cabling running through the plenum space is that the protective sheathing for networking cables, called the *jacket*, is made from plastic, and if you get any plastic hot enough, it creates smoke and noxious fumes.

Standard network cables usually use PVC (polyvinyl chloride) for the jacket, but PVC produces noxious fumes when burned. Fumes from cables burning in the plenum space can quickly spread throughout the building, so you want to use a more fire-retardant cable in the plenum space. Plenum-grade cable is simply network cabling with a fire-retardant jacket required for cables that go in the plenum space. Plenum-grade cable costs about three to five times more than PVC, but you should use it whenever you install cable in a plenum space.

Crossover Cables

You can hook two computers directly together using a special UTP cable called a *crossover cable*. A crossover cable is a standard UTP cable with one RJ-45 connector using the T568A standard and the other using the T568B standard. This reverses the signal between sending and receiving wires and thus does the job of a hub or switch. Crossover cables work great as a quick way to connect two computers directly for a quick and dirty network. You can purchase a crossover cable at any computer store.

Ethernet with Alternative Connections

UTP is very popular, but Ethernet, as well as other types of networks, can use alternative cabling that you need to be able to identify. Every CompTIA A+ certified tech needs to know about fiber optic cable and coaxial cable, so let's start there.

Fiber Optic

Fiber optic cable is a very attractive way to transmit Ethernet network frames. First, because it uses light instead of electricity, fiber optic cable is immune to electrical problems such as lightning, short circuits, and static. Second, fiber optic signals travel much farther, 2000 meters or more (compared with 100 meters on UTP). Most fiber Ethernet networks use *62.5/125 multimode* fiber optic cable. All fiber Ethernet networks that use this type of cabling require two cables. Figure 20-13 shows three of the more common connectors used in fiber optic networks. The round connector on the left is called an *ST* connector. The square-shaped middle connecter is called an *SC* connector, and on the far right is an *LC* connector.

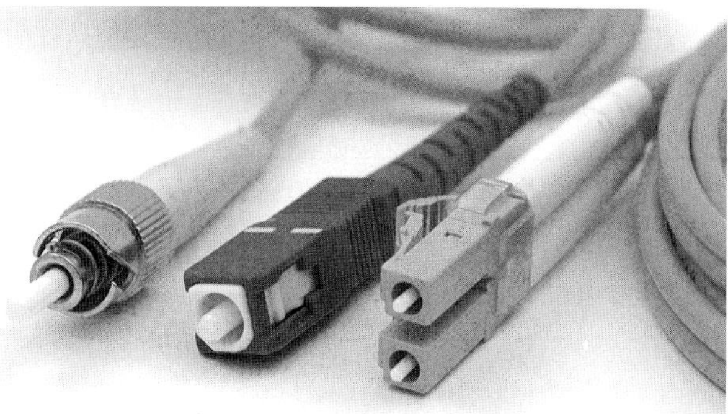

Figure 20-13 Typical fiber optic cables with ST, SC, and LC connectors

Fiber optics are half-duplex, meaning data flows only one way—hence the need for two cables in a fiber installation. With the older ST and SC connectors, you needed two connectors on every fiber connection. Newer connectors like LC are designed to support two fiber cables in one connecter, a real space saver.

Multimode and Single-Mode Light can be sent down a fiber optic cable as regular light or as laser light. Each type of light requires totally different fiber optic cables. Most network technologies that use fiber optics use light-emitting diodes (LEDs) to send light signals. These use *multimode* fiber optic cabling. Multimode fiber transmits multiple light signals at the same time, each using a different reflection angle within the core of the cable. The multiple reflection angles tend to disperse over long distances, so multimode fiber optic cables are used for relatively short distances.

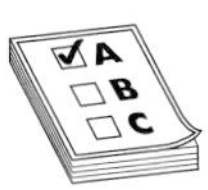

EXAM TIP Know fiber connector types and the difference between multimode and single-mode fiber.

Network technologies that use laser light use *single-mode* fiber optic cabling. Using laser light and single-mode fiber optic cables allows for phenomenally high transfer rates over long distances. Except for long-distance links, single-mode is currently quite rare; if you see fiber optic cabling, you can be relatively sure it is multimode.

There are close to 100 different Ethernet fiber optic cabling standards, with names like 1000BaseSX and 10GBaseSR. The major difference is the speed of the network (there are also some important differences in the way systems interconnect, and so on). If you want to use fiber optic cabling, you need a fiber optic switch and fiber optic network cards.

Fiber networks follow the speed and distance limitations of their networking standard, so it's hard to pin down precise numbers on true limitations. Multimode overall is slower and has a shorter range than single-mode. A typical multimode network runs at 10, 100, or 1000 Mbps, though some can go to 10,000 Mbps. Distances for multimode runs

generally top out at ~600 meters. With single-mode, speed and distance—depending on the standard—can blow multimode away. The record transmission speed way back in 2011, for example, was 100 *terabits* per second, and that was over 100 *miles*!

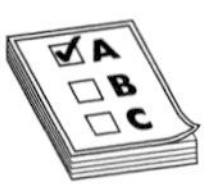

EXAM TIP There are a number of Ethernet standards that use fiber optic cable instead of UTP.

Early versions of Ethernet ran on *coaxial cable* instead of UTP. While the Ethernet standards using coax are long gone, coax lives on in the networking world, primarily for cable modems and satellite connections. Coax cable consists of a center cable (core) surrounded by insulation. This in turn is covered with a *shield* of braided cable (see Figure 20-14). The center core actually carries the signal. The shield effectively eliminates outside interference. The entire cable is then surrounded by a protective insulating cover.

Figure 20-14
Typical coax

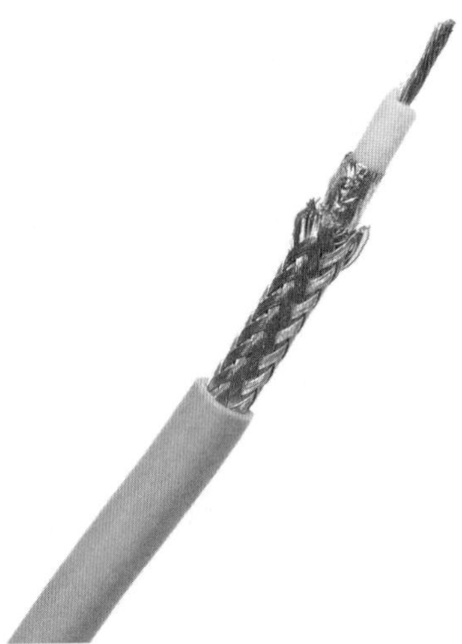

Coax cables are rated using an RG name. There are hundreds of RG ratings for coax, but the only two you need to know for the CompTIA A+ exam are RG-59 and RG-6. Both standards are rated by impedance, which is measured in ohms. (*Impedance* is the effective resistance to the flow of an alternating current electrical signal through a cable.) Both RG-6 and RG-59 have a 75-ohm impedance. Both of these coax cables are used by your cable television, but RG-59 is thinner and doesn't carry data quite as far as RG-6. The RG rating is clearly marked on the cable.

Coax most commonly uses two different types of connectors. A BNC (Bayonet Neill-Concelman or British Naval) connector (see Figure 20-15) uses a quarter twist connector, and an F-type connector uses a screw connector. BNC is uncommon, but F-type is on the back of all cable modems and most televisions (see Figure 20-16).

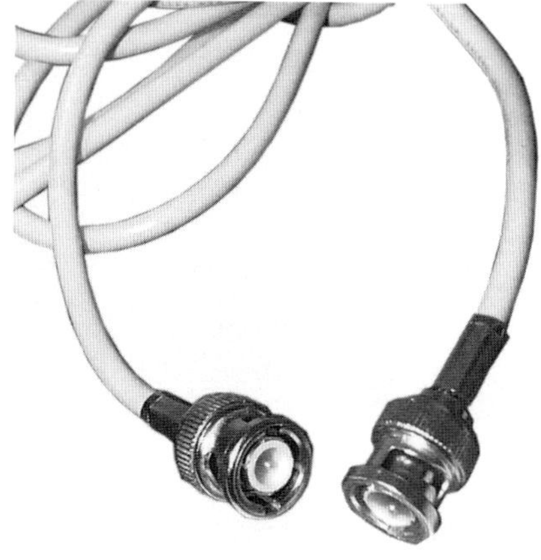

Figure 20-15
BNC connector

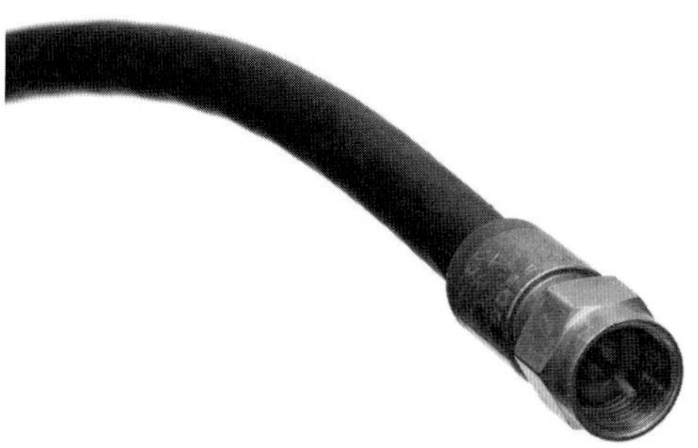

Figure 20-16
F-type connector

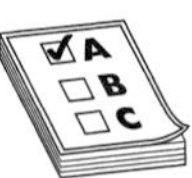

EXAM TIP Coaxial cable implementations offer amazing speeds, topping 100 Mbps in some cases. Using splitters negatively effects signal quality, lowering speeds.

Implementing Ethernet

Regardless of the cabling choice—UTP or fiber—Ethernet networks roll out into a star bus topology. The illustration of a star used earlier in the chapter doesn't quite translate into real life, so let's turn briefly to look at common implementations of Ethernet.

The Typical LAN

A *local area network (LAN)* is a group of computers located physically close to each other—no more than a few hundred meters apart at most. A LAN might be in a single room, on a single floor, or in a single building. But I'm going to add that a LAN is almost always a group of computers that are able to "hear" each other when one of them sends a broadcast. A group of computers connected by one or more switches is a *broadcast domain* (see Figure 20-17), which means that all nodes receive broadcast frames from every other node.

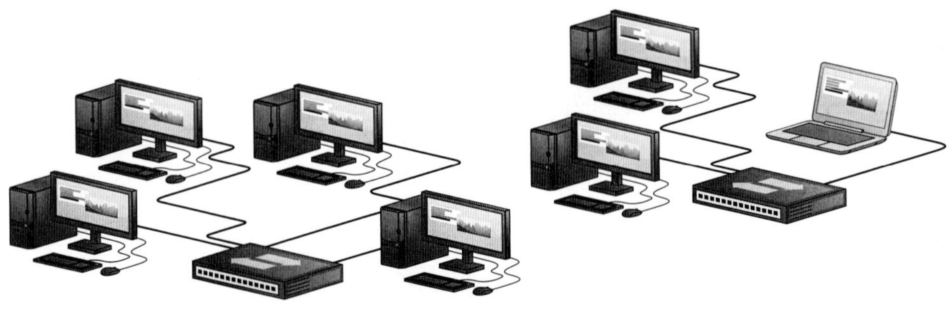

Figure 20-17 Two broadcast domains—two separate LANs

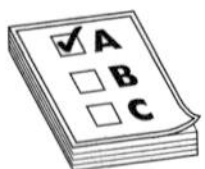

EXAM TIP For the CompTIA A+ exams, remember that a LAN is a group of networked computers that are close to each other. Also, remember that a LAN is almost always a broadcast domain.

You can set up a LAN in a small office/home office (SOHO) environment in several ways. The most common way—using wireless technology called *Wi-Fi*—dispenses with wires altogether. We'll get there in detail in Chapter 22, "Wireless Networking."

Another option uses the existing electrical network in the building for connectivity. This option, called *Ethernet over Power*, requires specialized bridges that connect to power outlets. Figure 20-18 shows a typical Ethernet over Power bridge.

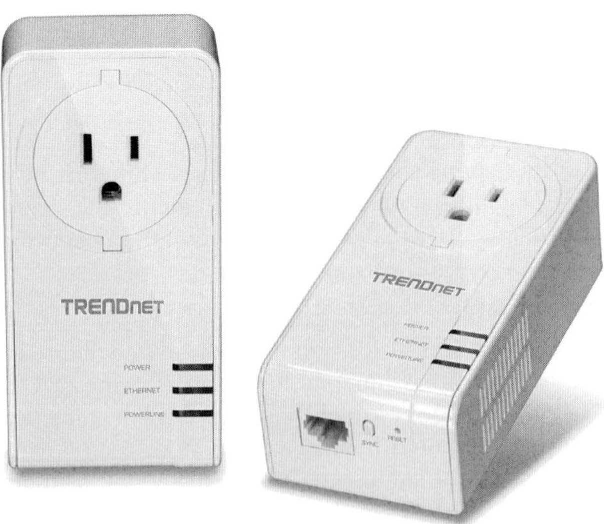

Figure 20-18 Ethernet over Power Bridge

A *bridge* is a device that connects dissimilar network technologies that transmit the same signal. In this case the bridge connects UTP to power lines. There are many other places we see bridges: there are bridge devices to connect wireless to UTP, coax to UTP, and so forth.

Ethernet over Power has its place in the right situations, but there are many challenges. First, several incompatible standards compete in the marketplace, which usually means you need to buy from the same manufacturer. Second, the fastest versions run at 100 Mbps at best, which may not be enough bandwidth for heavy use. But if you have a computer in a weird place where wireless won't work and traditional cables can't reach, try Ethernet over Power.

Structured Cabling

If you want a functioning, dependable, real-world network, you need a solid understanding of a set of standards collectively called *structured cabling*. These standards, defined by the TIA/EIA—yes, the same folks who tell you how to crimp an RJ-45 onto the end of a UTP cable—give professional cable installers detailed standards on every aspect of a cabled network, from the type of cabling to use to standards on running cable in walls, even the position of wall outlets.

The CompTIA A+ exams require you to understand the basic concepts involved in installing network cabling and to recognize the components used in a network. The CompTIA A+ exams do not, however, expect you to be as knowledgeable as a professional network designer or cable installer. Your goal should be to understand enough about real-world cabling systems to communicate knowledgeably with cable installers and to perform basic troubleshooting. Granted, by the end of this section, you'll know enough to try running your own cable (I certainly run my own cable), but consider that knowledge extra credit.

The idea of structured cabling is to create a safe, reliable cabling infrastructure for all of the devices that may need interconnection. Certainly this applies to computer networks, but also to telephone, video—anything that might need low-power, distributed cabling.

NOTE A structured cabling system is useful for more than just computer networks. You'll find structured cabling defining telephone networks and video conferencing setups, for example.

You should understand three issues with structured cabling. We'll start with the basics of how cables connect switches and computers. You'll then look at the components of a network, such as how the cable runs through the walls and where it ends up. This section wraps up with an assessment of connections leading outside your network.

Cable Basics—A Star Is Born

Earlier in this chapter we developed the idea of an Ethernet LAN in its most basic configuration: a switch, some UTP cable, and a few computers—in other words, a typical physical star network (see Figure 20-19).

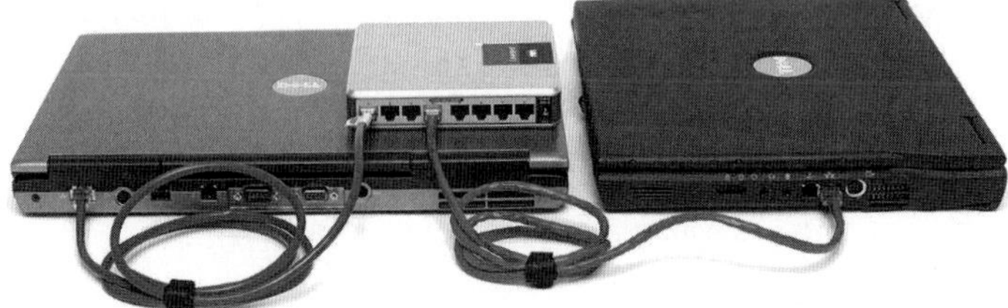

Figure 20-19 A switch connected by UTP cable to two computers

No law of physics prevents you from placing a switch in the middle of your office and running cables on the floor to all the computers in your network. This setup works, but it falls apart spectacularly when applied to a real-world environment. Three problems present themselves to the network tech. First, the exposed cables running along the floor are just waiting for someone to trip over them, giving that person a wonderful lawsuit opportunity. Simply moving and stepping on the cabling will, over time, cause a cable to fail due to wires breaking or RJ-45 connectors ripping off cable ends. Second, the presence of other electrical devices close to the cable can create interference that confuses the signals going through the wire. Third, this type of setup limits your ability to make any changes to the network. Before you can change anything, you have to figure out which cables in the huge rat's nest of cables connected to the switch go to which machines. Imagine *that* troubleshooting nightmare!

"Gosh," you're thinking (okay, I'm thinking it, but you should be, too), "there must be a better way to install a physical network." A better installation would provide safety, protecting the star from vacuum cleaners, clumsy coworkers, and electrical interference. It would have extra hardware to organize and protect the cabling. Finally, the new and improved star network installation would feature a cabling standard with the flexibility to enable the network to grow according to its needs and then to upgrade when the next great network technology comes along. That is the definition of structured cabling.

Structured Cable Network Components

Successful implementation of a basic structured cabling network requires three essential ingredients: a telecommunications room, horizontal cabling, and a work area. Let's zero in on one floor of a typical office. All the cabling runs from individual workstations to a central location, the *telecommunications room* (see Figure 20-20). What equipment goes in there—a switch or a telephone system—is not the important thing. What matters is that all the cables concentrate in this one area.

All cables run horizontally (for the most part) from the telecommunications room to the workstations. This cabling is called, appropriately, *horizontal cabling*. A single piece of installed horizontal cabling is called a *run*. At the opposite end of the horizontal cabling from the telecommunications room is the work area. The *work area* is often simply an office or cubicle that potentially contains a workstation and a telephone. Figure 20-21 shows both the horizontal cabling and work areas.

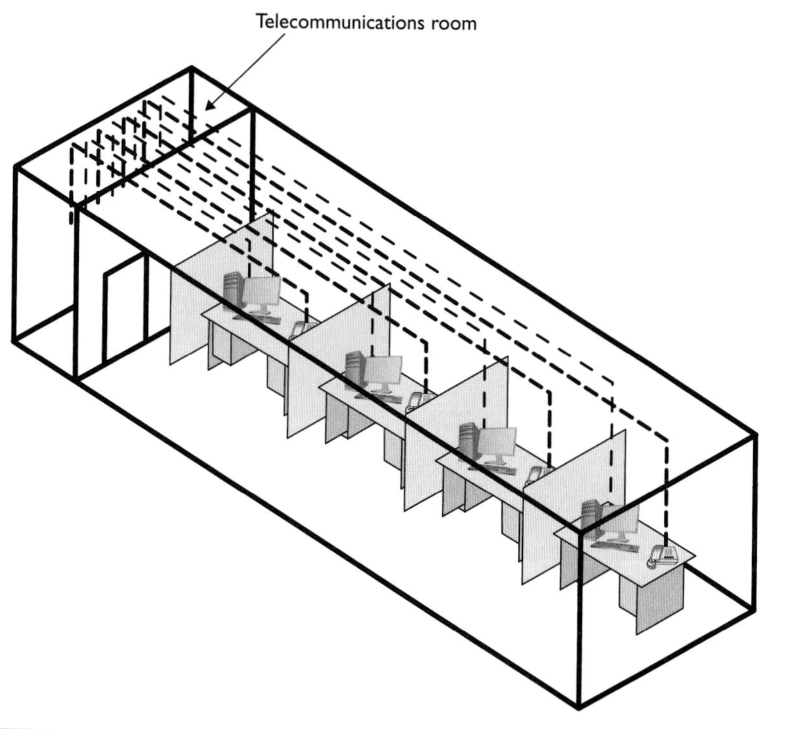

Figure 20-20 Telecommunications room

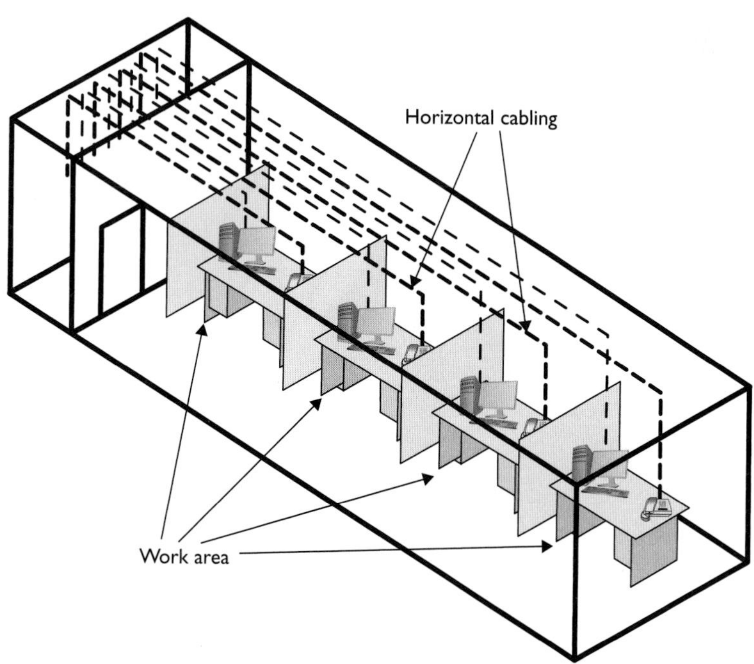

Figure 20-21 Horizontal cabling and work areas

Each of the three parts of a basic star network—the telecommunications room, the horizontal cabling, and the work area(s)—must follow a series of strict standards designed to ensure that the cabling system is reliable and easy to manage. The cabling standards set by TIA/EIA enable techs to make sensible decisions on equipment installed in the telecommunications room, so let's tackle horizontal cabling first, and then return to the telecommunications room. We'll finish up with the work area.

Horizontal Cabling A horizontal cabling run is the cabling that goes more or less horizontally from a work area to the telecommunications room. In most networks, this cable is a CAT 5e or better UTP, but when you move into structured cabling, the TIA/EIA standards define a number of other aspects of the cable, such as the type of wires, number of pairs of wires, and fire ratings.

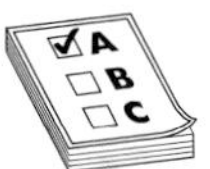

EXAM TIP A single piece of cable that runs from a work area to a telecommunications room is called a *run*. In most networks, this cable is CAT 5e or better UTP.

Solid Core Versus Stranded Core All UTP cables come in one of two types: solid core or stranded core. Each wire in *solid core* UTP uses a single solid wire. With *stranded core*, each wire is actually a bundle of tiny wire strands. Each of these cable types has its benefits and downsides. Solid core is a better conductor, but it is stiff and will break if handled too often or too roughly. Stranded core is not quite as good a conductor, but it will stand up to substantial handling without breaking. Figure 20-22 shows a close-up of solid and stranded core UTP.

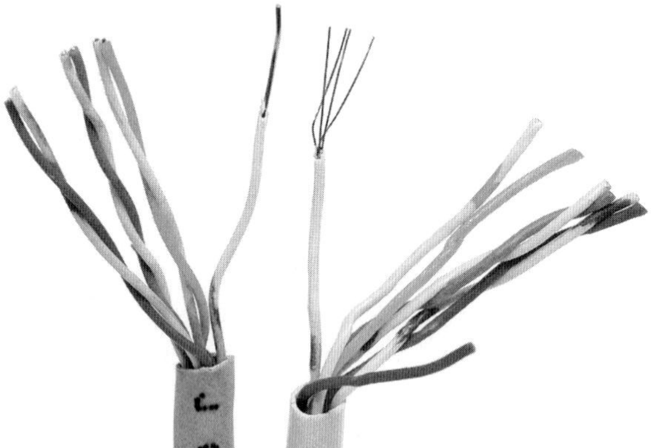

Figure 20-22 Solid and stranded core UTP

TIA/EIA specifies that horizontal cabling should always be solid core. Remember, this cabling is going into your walls and ceilings, safe from the harmful effects of shoes

and vacuum cleaners. The ceilings and walls enable you to take advantage of the better conductivity of solid core without the risk of cable damage. Stranded cable also has an important function in a structured cabling network, but I need to discuss a few more parts of the network before I talk about where to use stranded UTP cable.

The Telecommunications Room

The telecommunications room is the heart of the basic star. This room is where all the horizontal runs from all the work areas come together. The concentration of all this gear in one place makes the telecommunications room potentially one of the messiest parts of the basic star. Even if you do a nice, neat job of organizing the cables when they are first installed, networks change over time. People move computers, new work areas are added, network topologies are added or improved, and so on. Unless you impose some type of organization, this conglomeration of equipment and cables decays into a nightmarish mess.

Fortunately, the TIA/EIA structured cabling standards define the use of specialized components in the telecommunications room that make organizing a snap. In fact, it might be fair to say that there are too many options! To keep it simple, we're going to stay with the most common telecommunications room setup and then take a short peek at some other fairly common options.

Equipment Racks The central component of every telecommunications room is one or more equipment racks. An *equipment rack* provides a safe, stable platform for all the different hardware components. All equipment racks are 19 inches wide, but they vary in height from two- to three-foot-high models that bolt onto a wall (see Figure 20-23) to the more popular floor-to-ceiling models (see Figure 20-24).

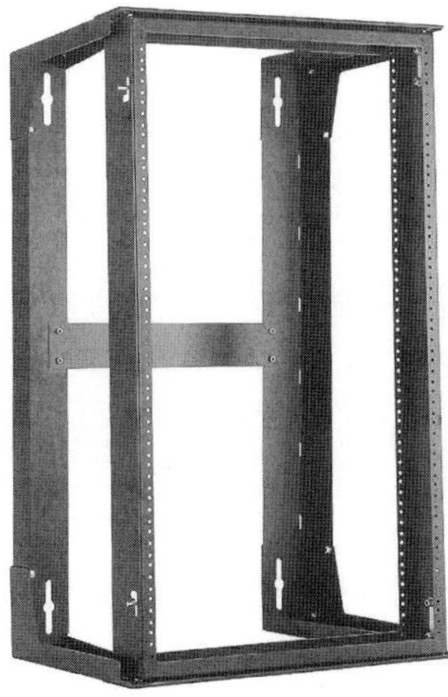

Figure 20-23 A short equipment rack

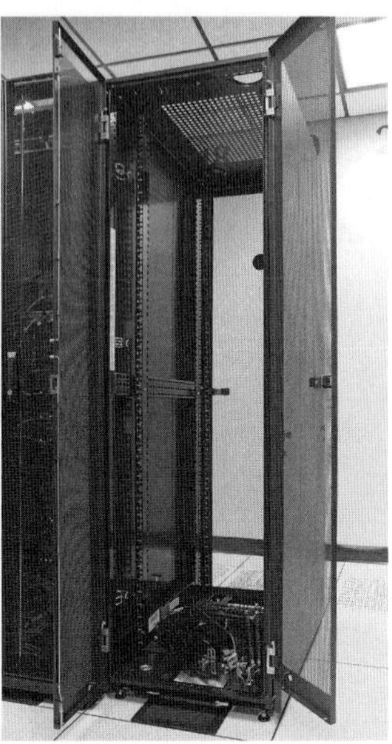

Figure 20-24 A floor-to-ceiling rack

NOTE Equipment racks evolved out of the railroad signaling racks from the 19th century. The components in a rack today obviously differ a lot from railroad signaling, but the 19-inch width has remained the standard for well over 100 years.

You can mount almost any network hardware component into a rack. All manufacturers make rack-mounted switches that mount into a rack with a few screws. These switches are available with a wide assortment of ports and capabilities. There are even rack-mounted servers, complete with slide-out keyboards, and rack-mounted uninterruptible power supplies (UPSs) to power the equipment (see Figure 20-25).

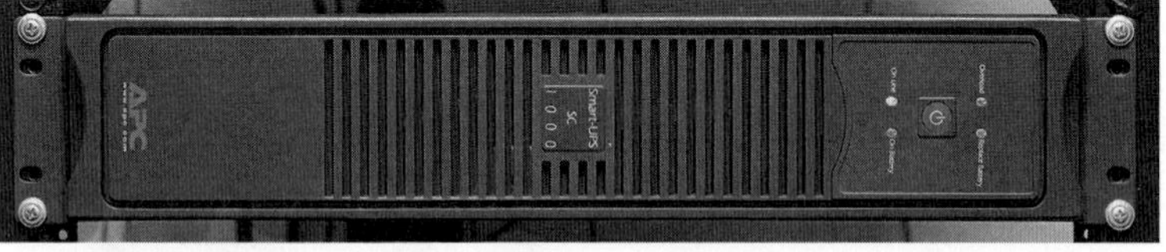

Figure 20-25 A rack-mounted UPS

All rack-mounted equipment uses a height measurement known simply as a *U*. A U is 1.75 inches. A device that fits in a 1.75-inch space is called a 1U; a device designed for a 3.5-inch space is a 2U; and a device that goes into a 7-inch space is called a 4U. Most rack-mounted devices are 1U, 2U, or 4U.

Patch Panels and Cables Ideally, once you install horizontal cabling, you should never move it. As you know, UTP horizontal cabling has a solid core, making it pretty stiff. Solid core cables can handle some rearranging, but if you insert a wad of solid core cables directly into your switches, every time you move a cable to a different port on the switch, or move the switch itself, you will jostle the cable. You don't have to move a solid core cable many times before one of the solid copper wires breaks, and there goes a network connection!

Luckily for you, you can easily avoid this problem by using a patch panel. A *patch panel* is simply a box with a row of female connectors (ports) in the front and permanent connections in the back, to which you connect the horizontal cables (see Figure 20-26).

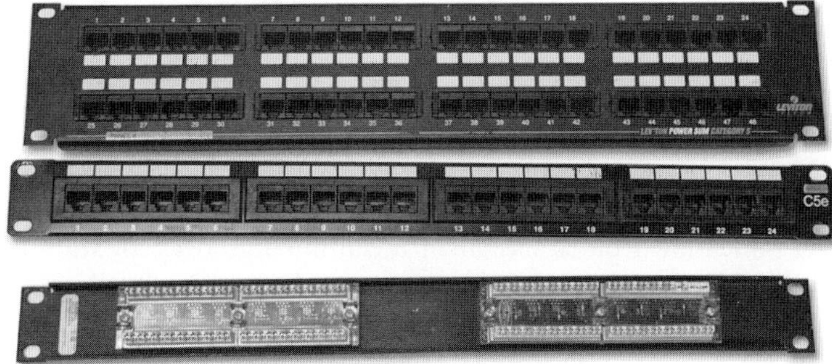

Figure 20-26 Typical patch panels

The most common type of patch panel today uses a special type of connecter called a *110 block*, or sometimes a *110-punchdown block*. UTP cables connect to a 110 block using a *punchdown tool*. Figure 20-27 shows a typical punchdown tool, and Figure 20-28 shows the punchdown tool punching down individual strands.

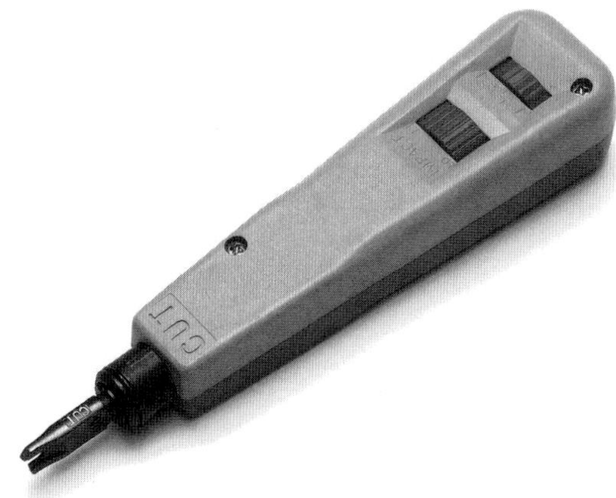

Figure 20-27 Punchdown tool

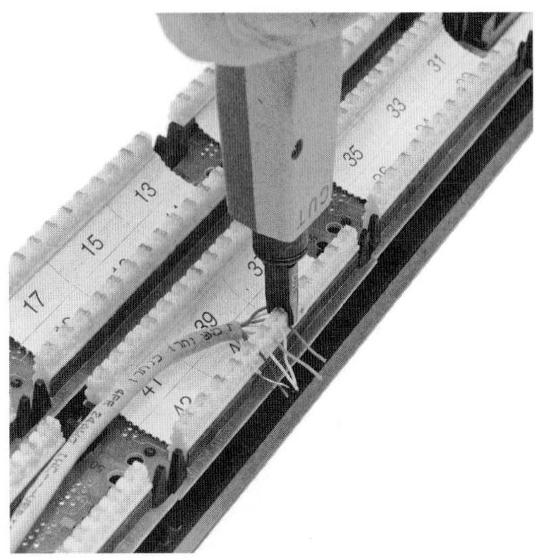

Figure 20-28 Punching down a 110 block

The punchdown block has small metal-lined grooves for the individual wires. The punchdown tool has a blunt end that forces the wire into the groove. The metal in the groove slices the cladding enough to make contact.

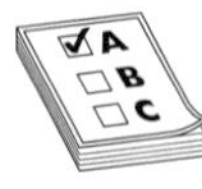

EXAM TIP The CompTIA A+ exams expect you to know that a punchdown tool is used for securing UTP connections to a punchdown block. It's not until you go for CompTIA Network+ certification that you'll be expected to know how to use these tools.

Not only do patch panels prevent the horizontal cabling from being moved, but they are also your first line of defense in organizing the cables. All patch panels have space in the front for labels, and these labels are the network tech's best friend! Simply place a tiny label on the patch panel to identify each cable, and you will never have to experience that sinking feeling of standing in the telecommunications room of your nonfunctioning network, wondering which cable is which. If you want to be a purist, there is an official, and rather confusing, TIA/EIA labeling methodology called TIA/EIA 606, but a number of real-world network techs simply use their own internal codes (see Figure 20-29).

Patch panels are available in a wide variety of configurations that include different types of ports and numbers of ports. You can get UTP, STP, or fiber ports, and some manufacturers combine several different types on the same patch panel. Panels are available with 8, 12, 24, 48, or even more ports.

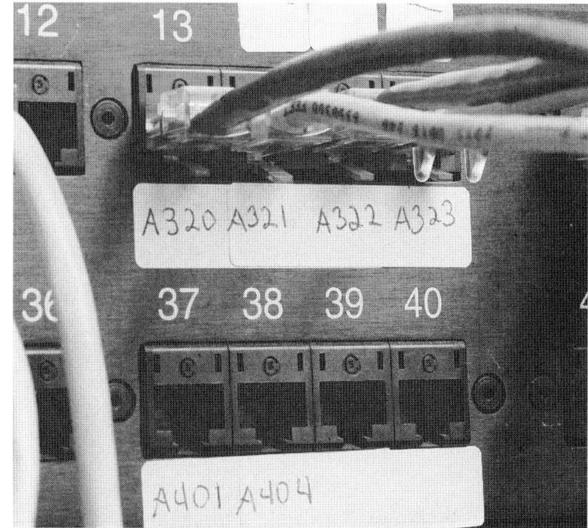

Figure 20-29 Typical patch panels with labels

UTP patch panels, like UTP cables, come with CAT ratings, which you should be sure to check. Don't blow a good CAT 6 cable installation by buying a cheap patch panel—get a CAT 6 patch panel! A higher-rated panel supports earlier standards, so you can use a CAT 6 or even CAT 6a rack with CAT 5e cabling. Most manufacturers proudly display the CAT level right on the patch panel (see Figure 20-30).

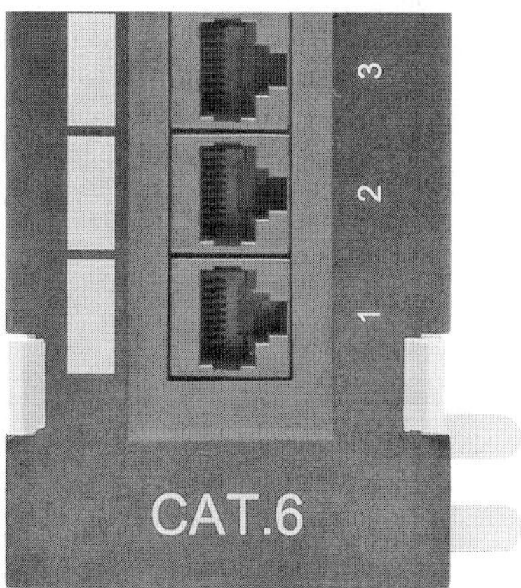

Figure 20-30 CAT level on patch panel

Once you have installed the patch panel, you need to connect the ports to the switch through *patch cables*. Patch cables are short (typically two- to five-foot) UTP cables. Patch cables use stranded rather than solid cable, so they can tolerate much more handling. Even though you can make your own patch cables, most people buy premade ones. Buying patch cables enables you to use different-colored cables to facilitate organization (yellow for accounting, blue for sales, or whatever scheme works for you). Most prefabricated patch cables also come with a reinforced (booted) connector specially designed to handle multiple insertions and removals (see Figure 20-31).

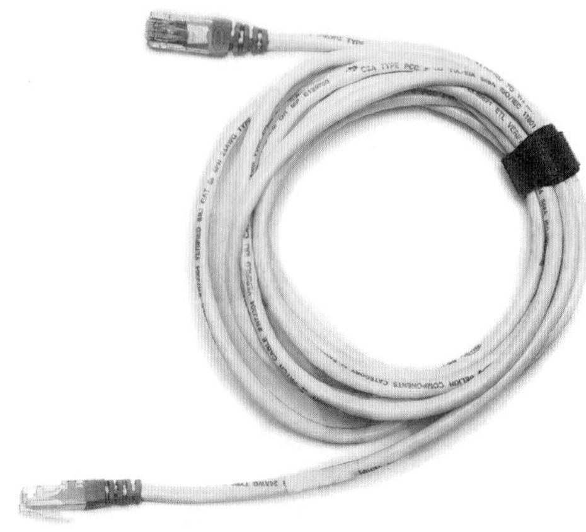

Figure 20-31 Typical patch cable

Rolling Your Own Patch Cables Although most people prefer simply to purchase premade patch cables, making your own is fairly easy. To make your own, use stranded UTP cable that matches the CAT level of your horizontal cabling. Stranded cable also requires specific crimps, so don't use crimps designed for solid cable. Crimping is simple enough, although getting it right takes some practice.

Figure 20-32 shows the two main tools of the crimping trade: an RJ-45 crimper with built-in wire stripper and a pair of wire snips. Professional cable installers naturally have a wide variety of other tools as well.

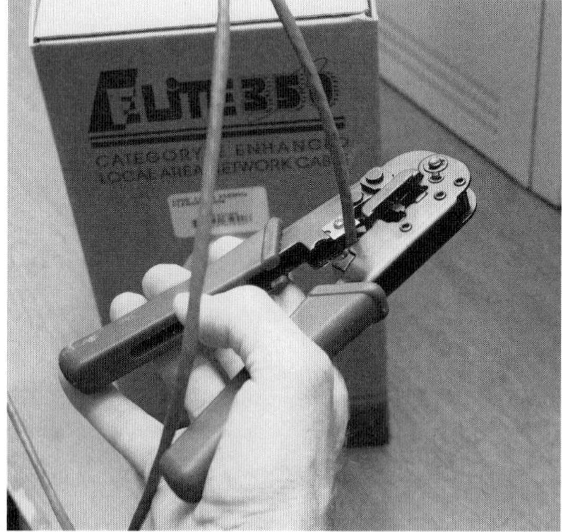

Figure 20-32 Crimper and snips

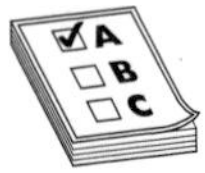

EXAM TIP The CompTIA A+ exams expect you to know that a cable tech uses a crimper or crimping tool to attach an RJ-45 to the end of a UTP cable.

Here are the steps for properly crimping an RJ-45 onto a UTP cable. If you have some crimps, cable, and a crimping tool handy, follow along!

1. Cut the cable square using RJ-45 crimpers or scissors.
2. Strip off one-half inch of plastic jacket from the end of the cable (see Figure 20-33).

Figure 20-33 Properly stripped cable

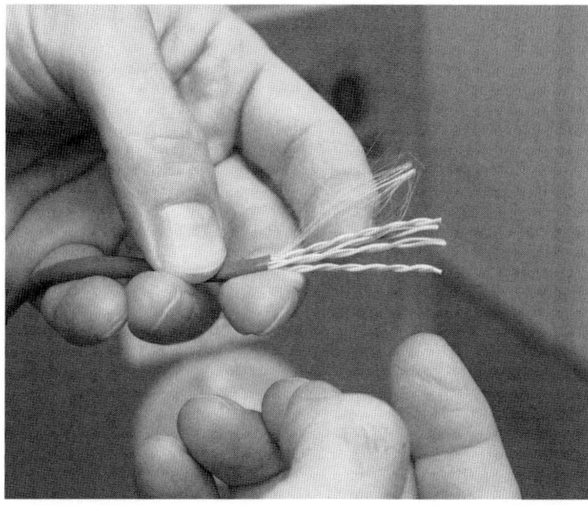

3. Slowly and carefully insert each individual wire into the correct location according to either TIA/EIA 568A or B (see Figure 20-34). Unravel as little as possible.

Figure 20-34 Inserting the individual strands

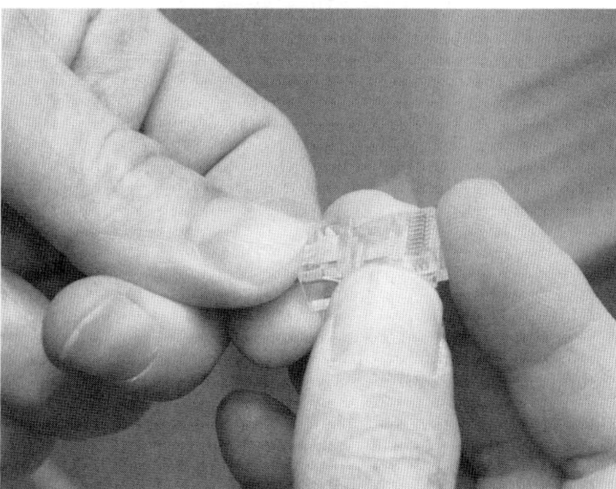

4. Insert the crimp into the crimper and press (see Figure 20-35). Don't worry about pressing too hard; the crimper has a stop to prevent you from using too much pressure.

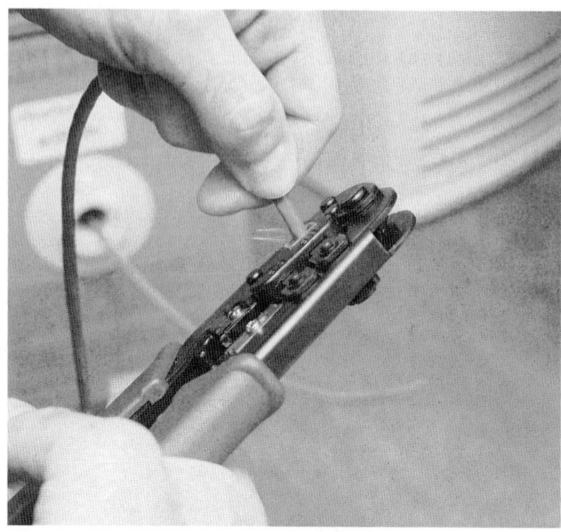

Figure 20-35 Crimping the cable

Figure 20-36 shows a nicely crimped cable. Note how the plastic jacket goes into the crimp.

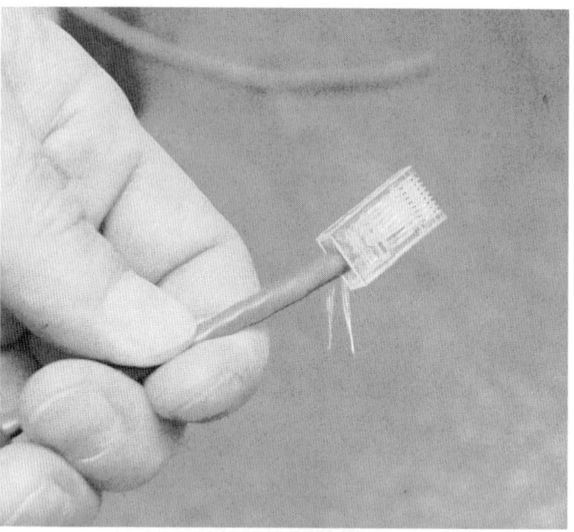

Figure 20-36 Properly crimped cable

A good patch cable should include a boot. Figure 20-37 shows a boot being slid onto a newly crimped cable. Don't forget to slide each boot onto the patch cable *before* you crimp both ends!

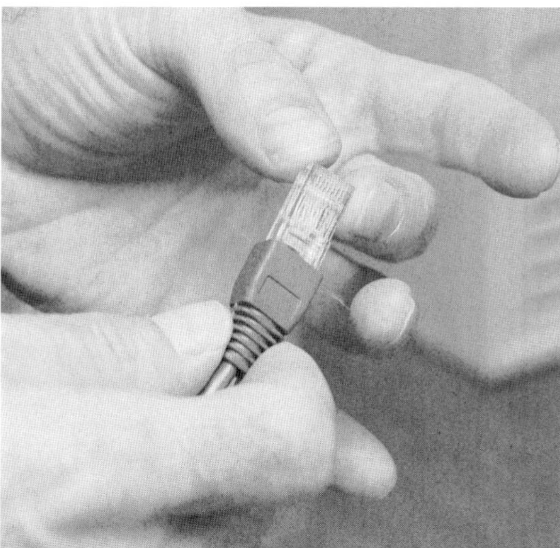

Figure 20-37
Adding a boot

After making a cable, you need to test it to make sure it's properly crimped. We use a handy cable tester, available in any good electronics store, to verify all the individual wires are properly connected and in the correct location (see Figure 20-38).

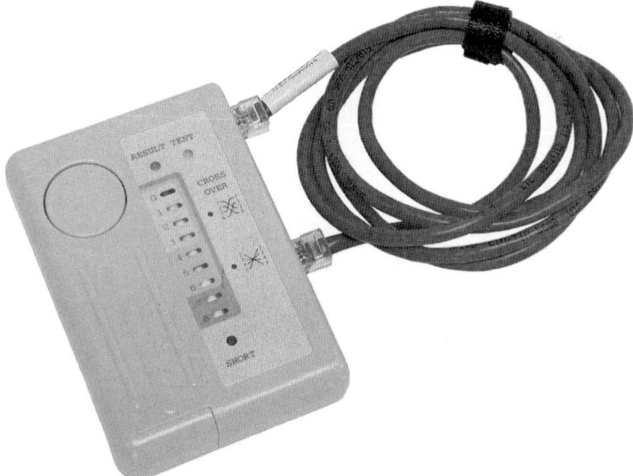

Figure 20-38
Typical tester

The Work Area

From a cabling standpoint, a work area is nothing more than a wall outlet that serves as the termination point for horizontal network cables: a convenient insertion point for a workstation and a telephone. (In practice, of course, the term "work area" includes the

office or cubicle.) A wall outlet itself consists of one or two female jacks to accept the cable, a mounting bracket, and a faceplate. You connect the workstation to the wall outlet with a patch cable (see Figure 20-39).

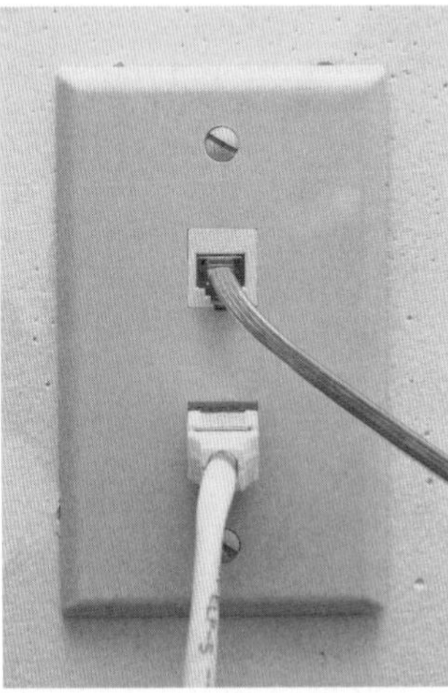

Figure 20-39 Typical work area outlet

The female RJ-45 jacks in these wall outlets also have CAT ratings. You must buy CAT-rated jacks for wall outlets to go along with the CAT rating of the cabling in your network. In fact, many network connector manufacturers use the same connectors, often 110 punchdowns, in the wall outlets that they use on the patch panels (see Figure 20-40). These modular outlets significantly increase the ease of installation.

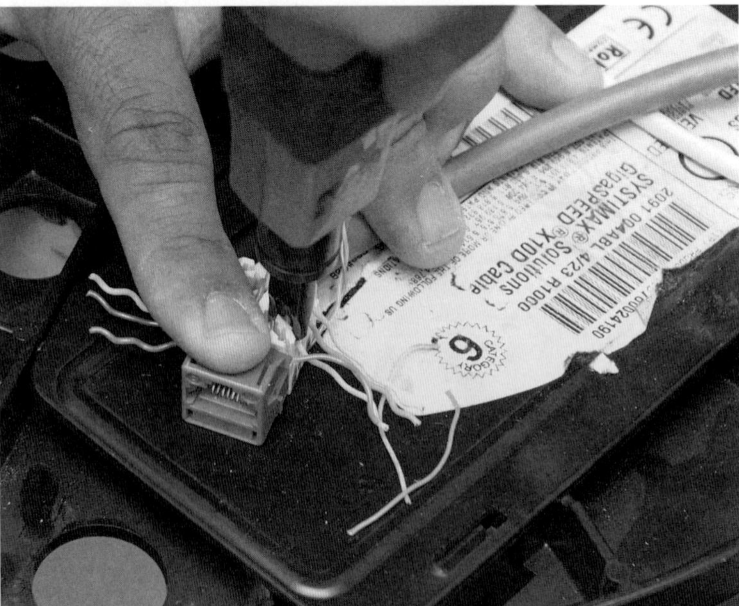

Figure 20-40 Punching down a modular jack

The last step is connecting the workstation to the wall outlet. Here again, most folks use a patch cable. Its stranded cabling stands up to the abuse caused by moving equipment, not to mention the occasional kick.

The work area may be the simplest part of the structured cabling system, but it is also the source of most network failures. When a user can't access the network and you suspect a broken cable, the first place to look is the work area.

Going Wide

A *wide area network (WAN)* is a widespread group of computers connected using long-distance technologies. You connect LANs into a WAN with a magical box called a *router* (see Figure 20-41). The best example of a WAN is the Internet.

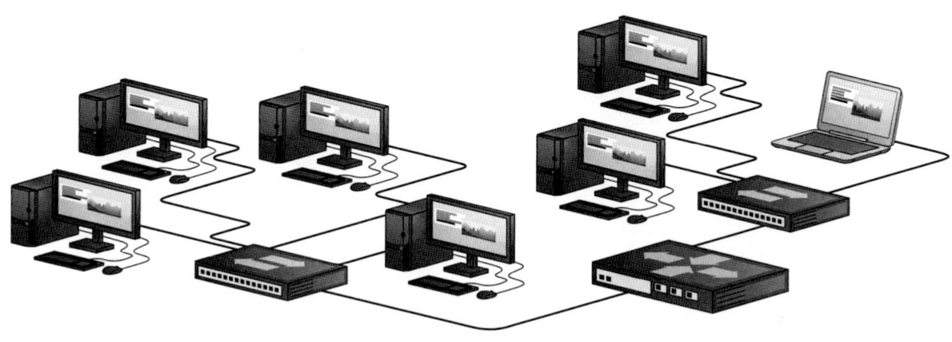

Figure 20-41 Two broadcast domains connected by a router—a WAN

You can connect multiple smaller networks into a bigger network, turning a group of LANs into one big WAN, but this raises a couple of issues with network traffic. A computer needs some form of powerful, flexible addressing to address a frame so that it goes to a computer within its own LAN or to a computer on another LAN on the same WAN. Broadcasting is also unacceptable, at least between LANs. If every computer saw every frame, the network traffic would quickly spin out of control! Plus, the addressing scheme needs to work so that routers can sort the frames and send them along to the proper LAN. This process, called *routing*, requires routers and a routing-capable protocol to function correctly.

Routers destroy any incoming broadcast frames, by design. No broadcast frame can ever go through a router. This makes broadcasting still quite common within a single broadcast domain, but never anywhere else.

To go beyond a LAN requires a network protocol—a way machines agree to communicate—that can handle routing. That protocol, for the vast majority of networks, is called TCP/IP, and Chapter 21 begins with the details. For now, review the end-of-chapter material and take some practice exams. See you in Chapter 21!

Chapter Review

Questions

1. How many bits are in a MAC address?
   A. 24
   B. 36
   C. 48
   D. 64
2. What is the minimum CAT level cable required for a 100BaseT network?
   A. CAT 1
   B. CAT 5
   C. CAT 5e
   D. CAT 6
3. Which of the following is an example of a hybrid topology?
   A. Bus
   B. Ring
   C. Star
   D. Star bus
4. A typical CAT 6 cable uses which connector?
   A. RJ-11
   B. RJ-45
   C. Plenum
   D. PVC
5. Why would you use STP over UTP cabling?
   A. Cheaper.
   B. Easier to install.
   C. Better to avoid interference.
   D. They're interchangeable terms.
6. What kind of frame gets received by all NICs in a LAN?
   A. CAT 7
   B. Broadcast
   C. WAN
   D. SC, ST, or LC

7. Microsoft Internet Explorer, Mozilla Firefox, Google Chrome, and Microsoft Edge are all examples of what?
   A. Web servers
   B. Print servers
   C. Web browsers
   D. Proxy servers
8. John's boss asks for a recommendation for connecting the company network to a small satellite building about 1 km from the main campus. The company owns the verdant land in between. Given such a scenario, what network technology implementation should John suggest?
   A. Ethernet over UTP
   B. Ethernet over STP
   C. Ethernet over multimode fiber
   D. Ethernet over single-mode fiber
9. Erin is stuck. She needs data from a friend's laptop to work on her desktop, but neither of them brought a thumb drive. She has any number of Ethernet cables at her disposal, but the last port on the switch is taken. What's her best option, given such a scenario?
   A. Connect the two computers directly using a patch cable.
   B. Connect the two computers directly using a crossover cable.
   C. Connect the two computers directly using an STP cable.
   D. Run to the store, buy a thumb drive, get back to the lab, and physically move the data.
10. Eddard hands Will a cable. Will hands it back and says, meaningfully, "That's a nice F connector you've got there." What kind of cable does Eddard have?
    A. Coaxial
    B. Fiber optic
    C. STP
    D. UTP

Answers

1. **C.** MAC addresses are 48-bit.
2. **B.** 100BaseT networks need CAT 5 or better UTP.
3. **D.** A star bus topology, like the one used with Ethernet networks, is a hybrid topology.
4. **B.** CAT 6 cables use an RJ-45 connector.

5. **C.** Shielded twisted pair cabling handles interference from other electronics much better than unshielded twisted pair.
6. **B.** All NICs in a LAN will receive broadcast frames.
7. **C.** All these programs are Web browsers.
8. **D.** John should suggest the only network technology implementation (listed here) that can cover those distances, Ethernet over single-mode fiber.
9. **B.** Erin should connect the computers directly using a crossover cable.
10. **A.** Eddard has a mighty fine coaxial cable in his hands.

CHAPTER 21

Local Area Networking

In this chapter, you will learn how to

- Explain the basics of TCP/IP
- Install and configure wired networks
- Troubleshoot wired networks

Networks dominate the modern computing environment. A vast percentage of businesses have PCs connected in a small local area network (LAN), and big businesses simply can't survive without connecting their many offices into a single wide area network (WAN).

NOTE This chapter only covers local area networks, such as a group of computers in a single office. We'll save connecting to the Internet for Chapter 23, "The Internet." But be ready! You need to understand everything in this chapter before you can take the next step and connect to the Internet.

Because networks are so common today, every good tech needs to know the basics of networking technology, operating systems, implementation, and troubleshooting. Accordingly, this chapter teaches you how to build and troubleshoot a basic network.

The first part of this chapter gets down and dirty into TCP/IP and how Windows uses it in a typical network. I'll break down the TCP/IP protocol so you can appreciate how it works.

Next, we'll go through the process of setting up a small network from start to finish. This includes details on planning a network, installing and configuring NICs, setting up switches, configuring TCP/IP—everything you need so that Windows will enable you to share folders, printers, libraries, and so on.

The chapter closes with a popular topic: troubleshooting a network. Modern operating systems come with plenty of powerful tools to help you when the network stops functioning. I'll show you the tools and combine that with a troubleshooting process that helps you get a network up and running again.

901/902

TCP/IP

The *Ethernet* hardware protocol does a fine job of moving data from one machine to another, as you learned in Chapter 20, "Networking Essentials." But Ethernet alone isn't enough to make a complete network; many other functions need to be handled. For example, an Ethernet frame holds a maximum of 1500 bytes. What if the data being moved is larger than 1500 bytes? Something has to chop up the data into chunks on one end of a connection and something else needs to reassemble those chunks on the other end so the data can be put to use.

Another issue arises if one of the machines on the network has its network card replaced. Up to this point, the only way to distinguish one machine from another was by the MAC address on the network card. To solve this, each machine must have a unique name, an identifier for the network, which is "above" the MAC address. Something needs to keep track of the MAC addresses on the network and the names of the machines so that frames and names can be correlated. If you replace a PC's network card, the network will, after some special queries, update the list to associate the name of the PC with the new network card's MAC address.

Network protocol software takes the incoming data received by the network card, keeps it organized, sends it to the application that needs it, and then takes outgoing data from the application and hands it to the NIC to be sent out over the network. All networks use some network protocol. Over the years there have been many network protocols, most combining multiple simple protocols into groups, called *protocol stacks*. This lead to some crazily named network protocols, such as TCP/IP.

The *Transmission Control Protocol/Internet Protocol (TCP/IP)* is the primary protocol of most modern networks, including the Internet. For a computing device to access the Internet, it must have TCP/IP loaded and configured properly. Let's look at some aspects of the TCP/IP protocol suite.

Network Addressing with IPv4

Any network address must provide two pieces of information: it must uniquely identify the machine and it must locate that machine within the larger network. In a TCP/IP network, the *IP address* identifies the node and the network on which it resides. If you look at an IP address, it's not apparent which part of the address identifies the network and which part is the unique identifier of the computer.

IP Addresses

The IP address is the unique identification number for your system on the network. Most systems today rely on the *Internet Protocol version 4 (IPv4)* addressing scheme. IPv4 addresses consist of four sets of eight binary numbers (octets), each set separated

by a period. This is called *dotted-decimal notation*. So, instead of a computer being called SERVER1, it gets an address like so:

202.34.16.11

Written in binary form, the address would look like this:

11001010.00100010.00010000.00001011

To make the addresses more comprehensible to users, the TCP/IP folks decided to write the decimal equivalents:

00000000 = 0
00000001 = 1
00000010 = 2
...
11111111 = 255

Subnet Mask

Part of every IP address identifies the network (the network ID), and another part identifies the local computer (the host ID, or host) on the network. A NIC uses a value called the *subnet mask* to distinguish which part of the IP address identifies the network ID and which part of the address identifies the host. The subnet mask blocks out (or masks) the network portion of an IP address.

Let's look at a typical subnet mask: 255.255.255.0. When you compare the subnet mask to the IP address, any part that's all 255s is the network ID. Any part that's all zeros is the host ID. Look at the following example:

IP address: 192.168.4.33
Subnet mask: 255.255.255.0

Because the first thee octets are 255, the network ID is 192.168.4 and the host ID is 33.

Every computer on a single LAN must have the same network ID and a unique host ID. That means every computer on the preceding network must have an IP address that starts with 192.168.4. Every computer on the network must have a unique IP address. If two computers have the same IP address, they won't be able to talk to each other, and other computers won't know where to send data. This is called an *IP conflict*.

You can never have an IP address that ends with a 0 or a 255, so for the preceding example, we can have addresses starting at 192.168.4.1 and ending at 192.168.4.254: a total of 254 addresses.

Originally, subnets fell into "classes," such as A, B, or C, determined by the corresponding octet in the subnet mask. A Class C address, like the one just discussed, had a subnet mask of 255.255.255.0. A Class B address, in contrast, had a subnet mask of 255.255.0.0. The latter class left two full octets (16 bits) just for host numbers. That meant a single Class B network ID could have $2^{16} - 2$ unique host IDs = 65,534 addresses.

Although it's still common to see subnet masks as one to three groups of "255," the class system is long gone. Because the subnet mask numbers are binary, you can make a subnet with any number of ones in the subnet mask.

The current system is called *Classless Inter-Domain Routing (CIDR)* and it works easily in binary, but a little less prettily when you show the numbers in the octets. A quick example should suffice to illustrate this point.

A subnet mask of 255.255.255.0 translates into binary as such:

11111111.11111111.11111111.00000000

With CIDR, network techs refer to the subnet mask by the number of ones it contains. The preceding subnet mask, for example, has 24 ones. Jill the tech would call this subnet a /24 (*whack twenty-four*). As you've seen already, a /24 network ID offers up to 254 host IDs.

If you want a network ID that enables more host IDs, buy one that has a subnet mask with fewer ones, like this one:

11111111.11111111.11110000.00000000

Count the ones. (There are 20.) The ones mask the network ID. That leaves 12 digits for the host IDs. Do the binary math: $2^{12} - 2 = 4094$ unique addresses in a single /20 network ID.

When you change the binary number—the string of ones—to an octet, you get the following:

255.255.240.0

It might look a little odd to a new tech, but that's a perfectly acceptable subnet mask. The binary makes sense.

From a practical standpoint, all you have to know as a tech is how to set up a computer to accept an IP address and subnet mask combination that your network administrator tells you to use.

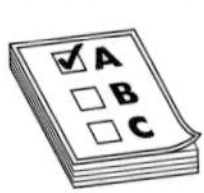

EXAM TIP Understand the basic differences between subnet masking and CIDR notation principles.

Interconnecting Networks with Routers

Sometimes you'll want to talk to computers that are outside your network. In that case, you'll need to connect to a router. A *router* is a device that has at least two IP addresses: one that connects to your LAN's switch and one that connects to the "next network." That next network could be your Internet service provider (ISP) or another router at your company—who knows (and more importantly, who cares, as long as it gets there)?

Default Gateway The port on your router that connects to your LAN is given an IP address that's part of your network ID. In most cases, this is the first address shown in Figure 21-1.

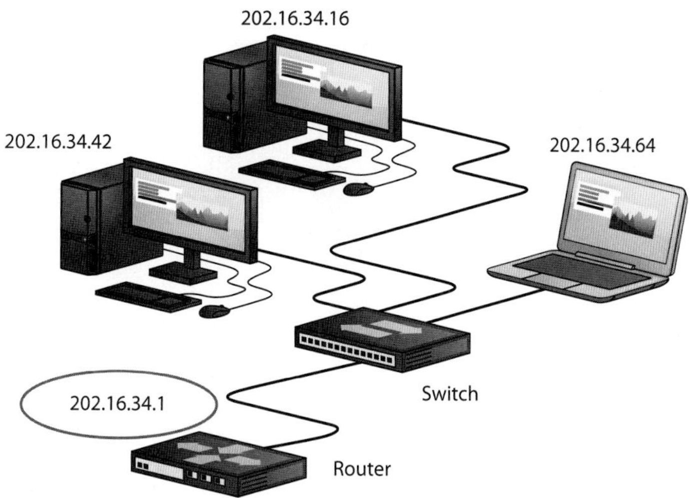

Figure 21-1 Default gateway

The IP address of the "LAN" side of your router (the port connected to your LAN) is the address your computer uses to send data to anything outside your network ID. This is called the *default gateway*.

Domain Name Service (DNS) Knowing that users could not remember lots of IP addresses, early Internet pioneers came up with a way to correlate those numbers with more human-friendly designations. Special computers, called *domain name service (DNS)* servers, keep databases of IP addresses and their corresponding names. For example, let's say a machine with the IP address 209.34.420.163 hosts a Web site and we want it to be known as www.totalsem.com. When we set up the Web site, we would pay for a DNS server to register the DNS name www.totalsem.com to the IP address 209.34.420.163. So instead of typing "http://209.34.420.163" to access the Web page, you can type "www.totalsem.com." Your system will then query the DNS server to get www.totalsem.com's IP address and use that to find the right machine. Unless you want to type in IP addresses all the time, you'll need to use DNS servers (see Figure 21-2).

NOTE Today, most Web servers host multiple Web sites using the same IP address. Accessing a single site via IP rather than name is increasingly difficult to do. For example, the address used in the previous example does not map to our Web site. Back off, hackers!

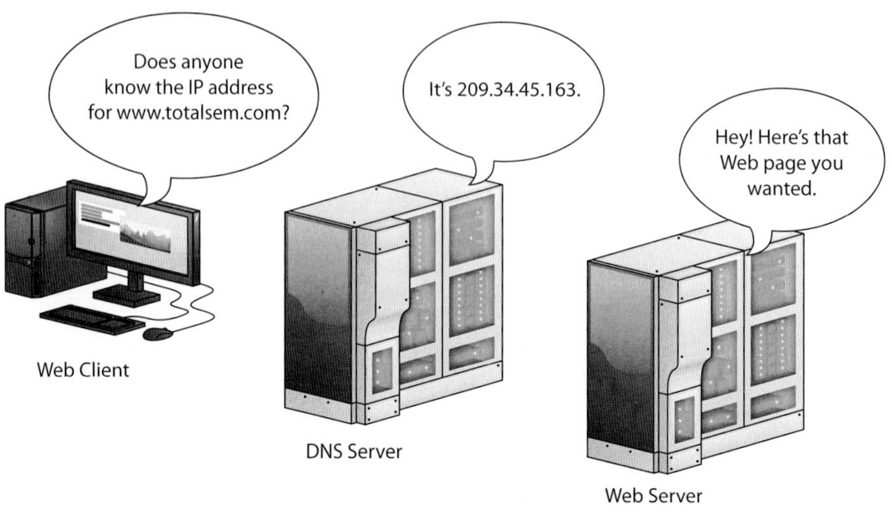

Figure 21-2 Domain name service

The Internet has regulated domain names. If you want a domain name that others can access on the Internet, you must register your domain name and pay a small yearly fee. Originally, DNS names all ended with one of the following seven domain name qualifiers, called *top-level domains (TLDs)*:

.com	General business	**.org**	Nonprofit organizations
.edu	Educational organizations	**.gov**	Government organizations
.mil	Military organizations	**.net**	Internet organizations
.int	International		

As more and more countries joined the Internet, a new level of domains was added to the original seven to indicate a DNS name from a particular country, such as .uk for the United Kingdom. It's common to see DNS names such as www.bbc.co.uk or www.louvre.fr. The *Internet Corporation for Assigned Names and Numbers (ICANN)* has added many more domains, including .name, .biz, .info, .tv, and others.

Entering the IP Information When you're configuring a computer to connect to a network, you must enter the IP address, the subnet mask, the default gateway, and at least one DNS server. Let's review:

- **IP address** Your computer's unique address on the network
- **Subnet mask** Identifies your network ID
- **Default gateway** IP address for the LAN side of your router
- **DNS server** Tracks easy-to-remember DNS names for IP addresses

Configuring the IP address differs between each version of Windows. Figure 21-3 shows the IP settings on a Windows 7 system.

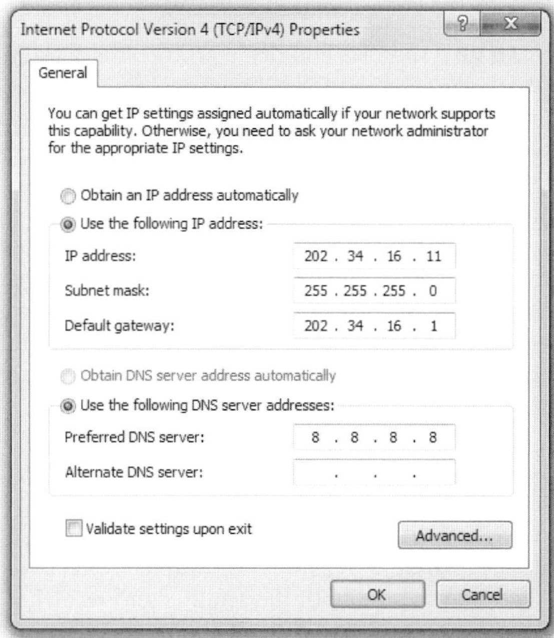

Figure 21-3 IP settings on a Windows 7 system

As you look at Figure 21-3, note the radio button for Obtain an IP address automatically. This is a common setting for which you don't need to enter any information. You can use this setting if your network uses *Dynamic Host Control Protocol (DHCP)*. If you have DHCP (most networks do) and your computer is configured to obtain an IP address automatically, your computer boots up and will broadcast a DHCP request. The DHCP server provides your computer with all the IP information it needs to get on the network (see Figure 21-4).

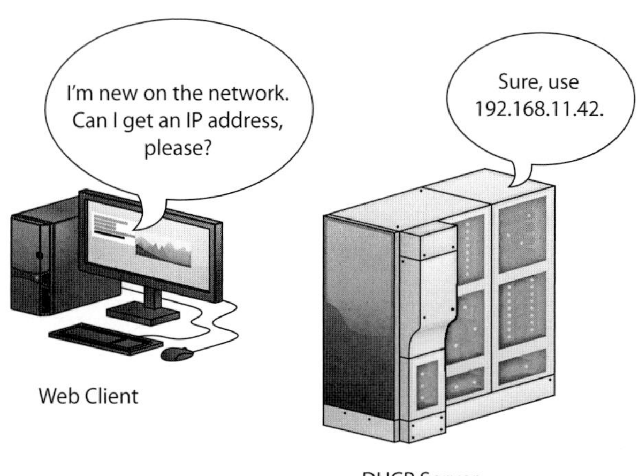

Figure 21-4 A DHCP server handing out an IP address

You can also manually input an IP address, by the way, creating a static IP address. Static means it doesn't change until you or some other tech changes it manually. We'll cover static IP addresses a little later in this chapter.

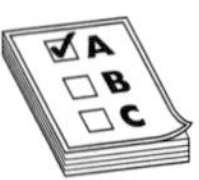

EXAM TIP The DNS and DHCP protocols and settings on a local machine—that access DNS and DHCP servers—are called client-side DNS and client-side DHCP. The client-side part tells you they're local rather than remote.

TCP/UDP

When moving data from one system to another, the TCP/IP protocol suite needs to know if the communication is connection-oriented or connectionless. When you want to be positive that the data moving between two systems gets there in good order, use a connection-oriented application. If it's not a big deal for data to miss a bit or two, then connectionless is the way to go. The connection-oriented protocol used with TCP/IP is called the *Transmission Control Protocol (TCP)*. The connectionless one is called the *User Datagram Protocol (UDP)*.

Let me be clear: you don't *choose* TCP or UDP. The people who developed the applications decide which protocol to use. When you fire up your Web browser, for example, you're using TCP because Web browsers use a protocol called HTTP. HTTP is built on TCP.

Over 95 percent of all TCP/IP applications use TCP. TCP gets an application's data from one machine to another reliably and completely. As a result, TCP comes with communication rules that require both the sending and receiving machines to acknowledge the other's presence and readiness to send and receive data.

UDP is the "fire and forget" missile of the TCP/IP protocol suite. UDP doesn't possess any of the extras you see in TCP to make sure the data is received intact. UDP works best when you have a lot of data to send that doesn't need to be perfect or when the systems are so close to each other that the chances of a problem occurring are too small to bother worrying about. A few dropped frames on a Voice over IP call, for example, won't make much difference in the communication between two people. So there's a good reason to use UDP: it's smoking fast compared to TCP.

NOTE The CompTIA A+ exams expect you to know about other TCP/IP protocols for accomplishing other goals. They're all covered in Chapter 23.

TCP/IP Services

TCP/IP is a different type of protocol. Although it supports File and Printer Sharing, it adds a number of unique sharing functions, lumped together under the umbrella term *TCP/IP services*. Most folks know the *Hypertext Transfer Protocol (HTTP)*, the language of the World Wide Web. If you want to surf the Web, you must have TCP/IP. But TCP /IP supplies many other services beyond just HTTP. By using a service called SSH, for example, you can access a remote system's terminal as though you were actually in front of that machine.

The goal of TCP/IP is to link any two hosts whether the two computers are on the same LAN or on some other network within the WAN. The LANs within the WAN are linked together with a variety of connections, ranging from basic dial-ups to dedicated high-speed (and expensive) data lines (see Figure 21-5). To move traffic between networks, you use routers (see Figure 21-6). Each host sends traffic to the router only when that data is destined for a remote network, cutting down on traffic across the more expensive WAN links. The host makes these decisions based on the destination IP address of each packet.

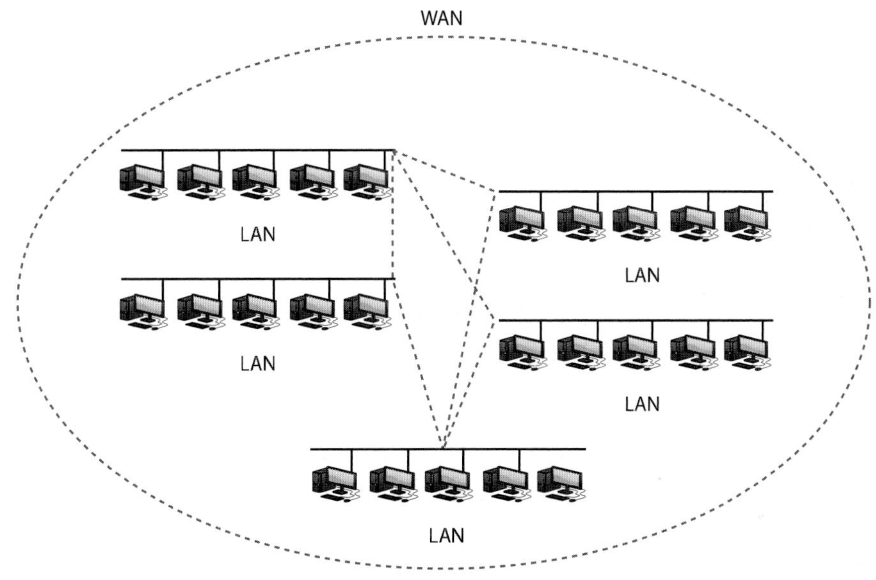

Figure 21-5 WAN concept

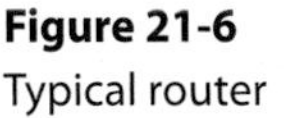

Figure 21-6 Typical router

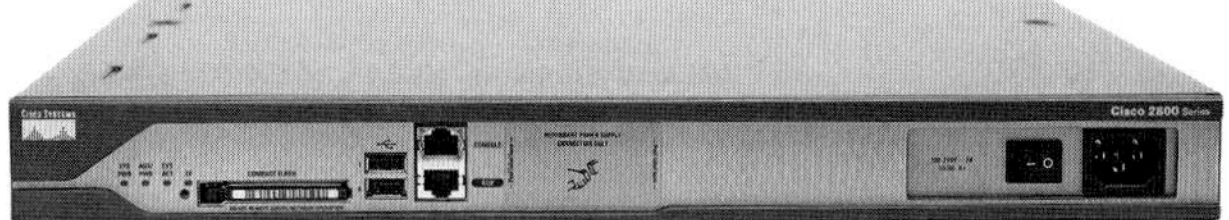

TCP/IP Settings

TCP/IP has a number of unique settings that you must configure correctly to ensure proper network functionality. Unfortunately, these settings can be quite confusing, and there are several of them. Not all settings are used for every type of TCP/IP network, and it's not always obvious where you go to set them.

In Windows, you can configure network settings from the appropriate networking applet. Right-click on Network and select Properties, or open the Control Panel and select Network and Sharing Center.

The CompTIA A+ certification exams assume that someone else, such as a tech support person or some network guru, will tell you the correct TCP/IP settings for the network. You need to understand roughly what those settings do and to know where to enter them so the system works.

TCP/IP Tools

All modern operating systems come with handy tools to test and configure TCP/IP. Those you're most likely to use in the field are ping, ipconfig, ifconfig, nslookup, tracert, and traceroute. All of these programs are command-line utilities. Open a command prompt to run them.

ping The *ping* command provides a really great way to see if you can talk to another system. Here's how it works. Get to a command prompt or terminal and type **ping** followed by an IP address or by a DNS name, such as **ping www.chivalry.com**. Press the ENTER key on your keyboard and away it goes! Figure 21-7 shows the common syntax for ping.

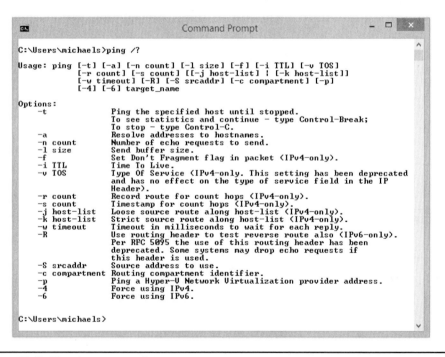

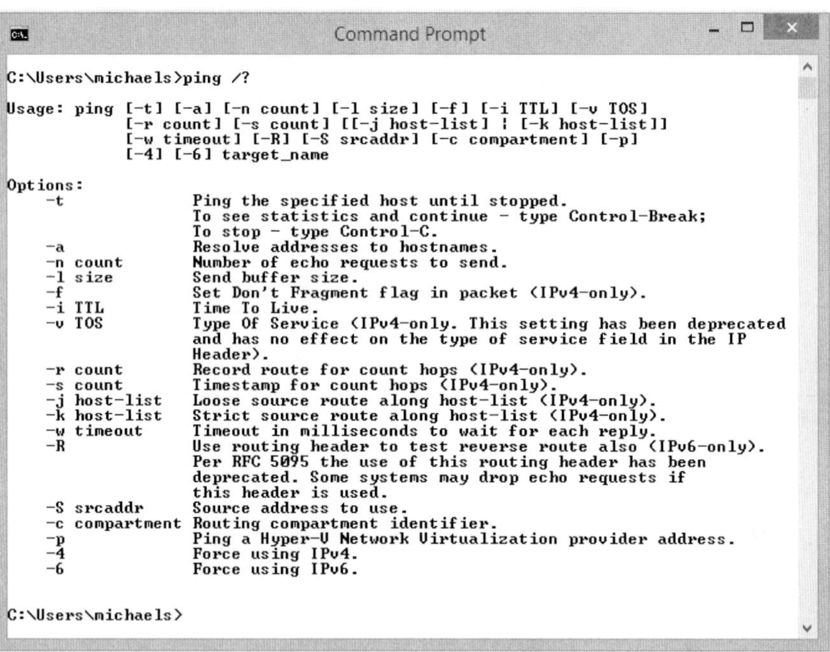

Command Prompt
C:\Users\michaels>ping /?
Usage: ping [-t] [-a] [-n count] [-l size] [-f] [-i TTL] [-v TOS]
[-r count] [-s count] [[-j host-list] | [-k host-list]]
[-w timeout] [-R] [-S srcaddr] [-c compartment] [-p]
[-4] [-6] target_name
Options:
-t Ping the specified host until stopped.
To see statistics and continue - type Control-Break;
To stop - type Control-C.
-a Resolve addresses to hostnames.
-n count Number of echo requests to send.
-l size Send buffer size.
-f Set Don't Fragment flag in packet (IPv4-only).
-i TTL Time To Live.
-v TOS Type Of Service (IPv4-only. This setting has been deprecated
and has no effect on the type of service field in the IP
Header).
-r count Record route for count hops (IPv4-only).
-s count Timestamp for count hops (IPv4-only).
-j host-list Loose source route along host-list (IPv4-only).
-k host-list Strict source route along host-list (IPv4-only).
-w timeout Timeout in milliseconds to wait for each reply.
-R Use routing header to test reverse route also (IPv6-only).
Per RFC 5095 the use of this routing header has been
deprecated. Some systems may drop echo requests if
this header is used.
-S srcaddr Source address to use.
-c compartment Routing compartment identifier.
-p Ping a Hyper-V Network Virtualization provider address.
-4 Force using IPv4.
-6 Force using IPv6.
C:\Users\michaels>

Figure 21-7 The ping command's syntax

The ping command has a few useful options beyond the basics. The first option to try in Windows is the –t switch. If you use the –t switch, ping continuously sends ping packets until you stop it with the break command (CTRL-C). That's the default behavior for ping in Mac OS X and Linux; you press the break command to make it stop. The second option in Windows is the –l switch, which enables you to specify how big a ping

packet to send. This helps in diagnosing specific problems with the routers between your computer and the computer you ping.

ipconfig/ifconfig Windows offers the command-line tool *ipconfig* for a quick glance at your network settings. From a command prompt, type **ipconfig/ all** to see all of your TCP/IP settings (see Figure 21-8). The ifconfig command in Mac OS X and Linux provides the same level of detail with no switches applied.

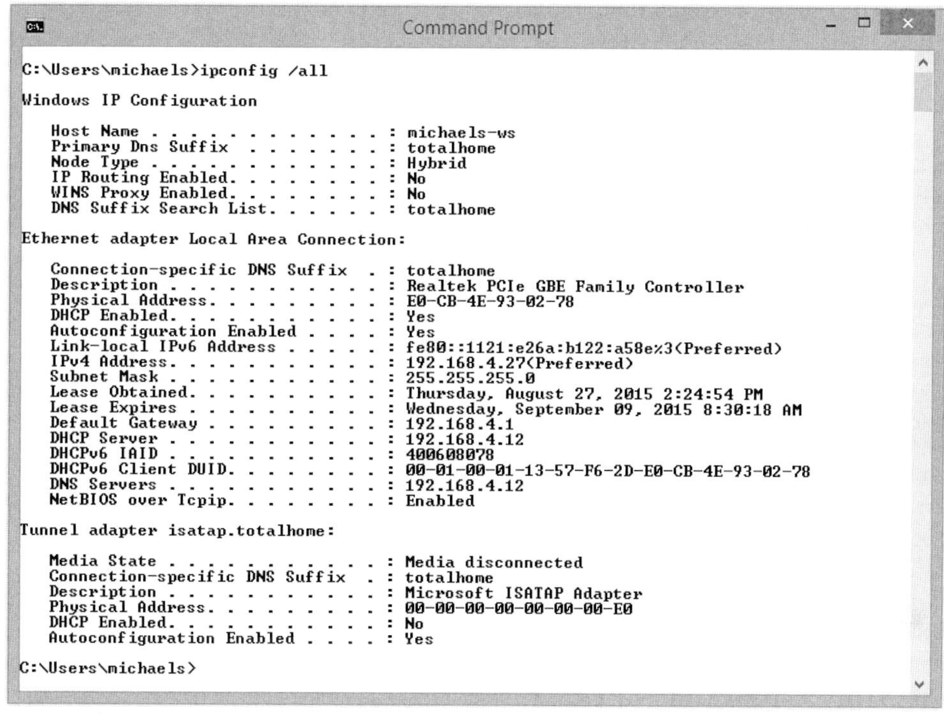

```
C:\Users\michaels>ipconfig /all

Windows IP Configuration

   Host Name . . . . . . . . . . . . : michaels-ws
   Primary Dns Suffix  . . . . . . . : totalhome
   Node Type . . . . . . . . . . . . : Hybrid
   IP Routing Enabled. . . . . . . . : No
   WINS Proxy Enabled. . . . . . . . : No
   DNS Suffix Search List. . . . . . : totalhome

Ethernet adapter Local Area Connection:

   Connection-specific DNS Suffix  . : totalhome
   Description . . . . . . . . . . . : Realtek PCIe GBE Family Controller
   Physical Address. . . . . . . . . : E0-CB-4E-93-02-78
   DHCP Enabled. . . . . . . . . . . : Yes
   Autoconfiguration Enabled . . . . : Yes
   Link-local IPv6 Address . . . . . : fe80::1121:e26a:b122:a58e%3(Preferred)
   IPv4 Address. . . . . . . . . . . : 192.168.4.27(Preferred)
   Subnet Mask . . . . . . . . . . . : 255.255.255.0
   Lease Obtained. . . . . . . . . . : Thursday, August 27, 2015 2:24:54 PM
   Lease Expires . . . . . . . . . . : Wednesday, September 09, 2015 8:30:18 AM
   Default Gateway . . . . . . . . . : 192.168.4.1
   DHCP Server . . . . . . . . . . . : 192.168.4.12
   DHCPv6 IAID . . . . . . . . . . . : 400608078
   DHCPv6 Client DUID. . . . . . . . : 00-01-00-01-13-57-F6-2D-E0-CB-4E-93-02-78
   DNS Servers . . . . . . . . . . . : 192.168.4.12
   NetBIOS over Tcpip. . . . . . . . : Enabled

Tunnel adapter isatap.totalhome:

   Media State . . . . . . . . . . . : Media disconnected
   Connection-specific DNS Suffix  . : totalhome
   Description . . . . . . . . . . . : Microsoft ISATAP Adapter
   Physical Address. . . . . . . . . : 00-00-00-00-00-00-00-E0
   DHCP Enabled. . . . . . . . . . . : No
   Autoconfiguration Enabled . . . . : Yes

C:\Users\michaels>
```

Figure 21-8 An ipconfig/ all command on Windows 8.1

When you have a static IP address, ipconfig does little beyond reporting your current IP settings, including your IP address, subnet mask, default gateway, DNS servers, and WINS servers. When using DHCP, however, ipconfig is also the primary tool for releasing and renewing your IP address. Just type **ipconfig /renew** to get a new IP address or **ipconfig /release** to give up the IP address you currently have.

nslookup The *nslookup* command is a powerful command-line program that enables you to determine exactly what information the DNS server is giving you about a specific host name. Every modern OS makes nslookup available when you install TCP/IP. To run the program, type **nslookup** from the command prompt and press the ENTER key (see Figure 21-9). Note that this gives you a little information and that the prompt has

changed. That's because you're running the application. Type **exit** and press the ENTER key to return to the command prompt.

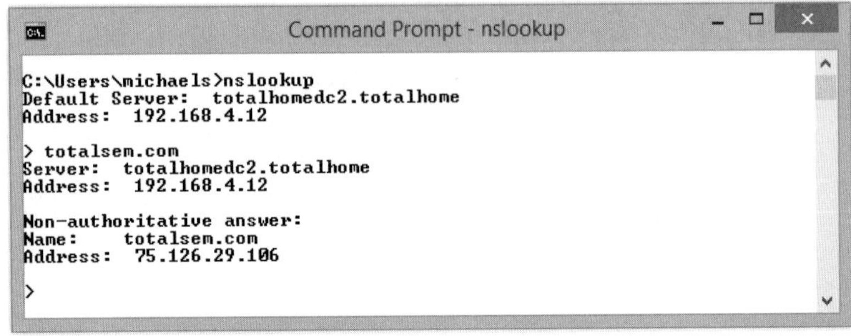

```
Command Prompt - nslookup

C:\Users\michaels>nslookup
Default Server:  totalhomedc2.totalhome
Address:  192.168.4.12

> totalsem.com
Server:  totalhomedc2.totalhome
Address:  192.168.4.12

Non-authoritative answer:
Name:    totalsem.com
Address:  75.126.29.106

>
```

Figure 21-9 The nslookup command in action

NOTE You can do some cool stuff with nslookup, and consequently some techs absolutely love the tool. Type **help** at the nslookup prompt and press ENTER to see a list of common commands and syntax.

tracert/traceroute The *tracert* (Windows) and *traceroute* (Mac OS X, Linux) utilities show the route that a packet takes to get to its destination. From a command line, type **tracert** or **traceroute** followed by a space and an IP address or URL. The output describes the route from your machine to the destination machine, including all devices the packet passes through and how long each hop between devices takes (see Figure 21-10). The tracert/traceroute command can come in handy when you have to troubleshoot bottlenecks. When users complain of difficulty reaching a particular destination by using TCP/IP, you can run this utility to determine whether the problem exists on a machine or connection over which you have control, or if it is a problem on another machine or router. Similarly, if a destination is completely unreachable, tracert/traceroute can again determine whether the problem is on a machine or router over which you have control.

```
Command Prompt

C:\Users\michaels>tracert chivalry.com

Tracing route to chivalry.com [103.224.212.239]
over a maximum of 30 hops:

  1    <1 ms    <1 ms    <1 ms  Router.totalhome [192.168.4.1]
  2    11 ms     9 ms    10 ms  96.120.17.193
  3    15 ms     9 ms    10 ms  xe-5-2-0-0-sur01.airport.tx.houston.comcast.net [68.85.251.25]
  4     9 ms    11 ms    11 ms  ae-3-0-sur02.airport.tx.houston.comcast.net [68.85.87.114]
  5    12 ms    11 ms    15 ms  ae-4-0-ar01.bearcreek.tx.houston.comcast.net [68.85.87.145]
  6    23 ms    16 ms    14 ms  4.68.71.109
  7    47 ms    47 ms    47 ms  vl-6.car1.SanDiego1.Level3.net [4.69.146.70]
  8    50 ms    49 ms    49 ms  CASTLE-ACCE.car1.SanDiego1.Level3.net [4.53.121.70]
  9    75 ms    50 ms    75 ms  sw02-ae0-san.trellian.com [103.224.213.238]
 10    53 ms    53 ms    52 ms  lb-212-239.above.com [103.224.212.239]

Trace complete.

C:\Users\michaels>
```

Figure 21-10 The tracert command in action

Try This!

Running tracert/traceroute

Ever wonder why your e-mail takes *years* to get to some people but arrives instantly for others? Or why some Web sites are slower to load than others? Part of the blame could lie with how many hops away your connection is from the target server. You can use tracert/traceroute to run a quick check of how many hops it takes to get to somewhere on a network, so Try This!

1. Run tracert or traceroute on some known source, such as www.microsoft.com or www.totalsem.com. How many hops did it take? Did your tracert/traceroute time out or make it all of the way to the server?
2. Try a tracert/traceroute to a local address. If you're in a university town, run a tracert or traceroute on the campus Web site, such as www.rice.edu for folks in Houston, or www.ucla.edu for those of you in Los Angeles. Did you get fewer hops with a local site?

Configuring TCP/IP

By default, TCP/IP is configured to receive an IP address automatically from a DHCP server on the network (and automatically assign a corresponding subnet mask). As far as the CompTIA A+ certification exams are concerned, Network+ techs and administrators give you the IP address, subnet mask, and default gateway information and you plug them into the PC. That's about it, so here's how to do it manually:

1. In Windows, open the Control Panel and go to the Network and Sharing Center applet. In Windows Vista, click the Manage network connections link, and in Windows 7/8/8.1/10, click Change adapter settings. After that, double-click the Local Area Network icon.
2. Click the Properties button, highlight Internet Protocol Version 4 (TCP/IPv4), and click the Properties button
3. In the Properties dialog box (see Figure 21-11), click the radio button next to Use the following IP address.
4. Enter the IP address in the appropriate fields.
5. Press the TAB key to skip down to the Subnet mask field. Note that the subnet mask is entered automatically, although you can type over this if you want to enter a different subnet mask.

Figure 21-11 Setting up IP

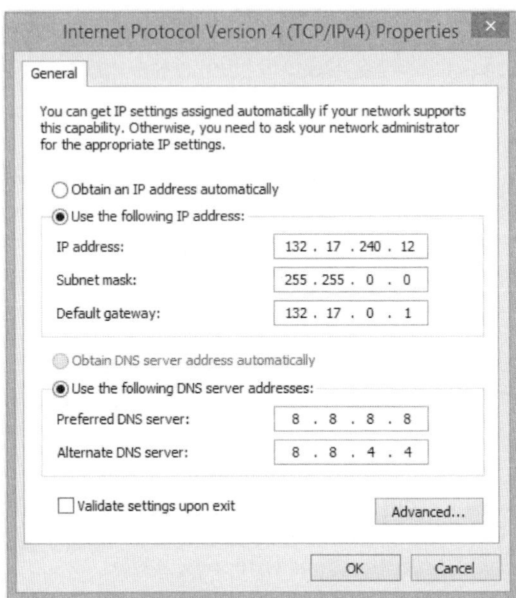

6. Optionally, enter the IP address for a default gateway.
7. Optionally, enter the IP addresses of a Preferred DNS server and an Alternate DNS server. (The configuration in Figure 21-11 uses the Google DNS servers.)
8. Click the OK button to close the Properties dialog box.
9. Click the Close button to exit the Local Area Connection Status dialog box.

Automatic Private IP Addressing

Modern operating systems support a feature called Automatic Private IP Addressing (APIPA) that automatically assigns an IP address to the system when the client cannot obtain an IP address automatically. The Internet Assigned Numbers Authority (IANA), the nonprofit corporation responsible for assigning IP addresses and managing root servers, has set aside the range of addresses from 169.254.0.1 to 169.254.255.254 for this purpose.

If the computer system cannot contact a DHCP server, the computer randomly chooses an address in the form of 169.254.*x.y* (where *x.y* is the computer's identifier) and a 16-bit subnet mask (255.255.0.0) and broadcasts it on the network segment (subnet). If no other computer responds to the address, the system assigns this address to itself. When using APIPA, the system can communicate only with other computers on the same subnet that also use the 169.254.*x.y* range with a 16-bit mask. APIPA is enabled by default if your system is configured to obtain an IP address automatically.

NOTE A computer system on a network with an active DHCP server that has an IP address in this range usually indicates a problem connecting to the DHCP server.

Network Addressing with IPv6

When the early developers of the Internet set out to create an addressing or naming scheme for devices on the Internet, they faced several issues. Of course they needed to determine how the numbers or names worked, and for that they developed the Internet Protocol and IP addresses. But beyond that, they had to determine how many computers might exist in the future, and then make the IP address space even bigger to give Internet naming longevity. But how many computers would exist in the future?

The 32-bit IPv4 standard offers only 4 billion addresses. That was plenty in the beginning, but seemed insufficient once the Internet went global.

The Internet Engineering Task Force (IETF) developed an IP addressing scheme called *Internet Protocol version 6 (IPv6)* that is slowly replacing IPv4. IPv6 extends the 32-bit IP address space to 128 bits, allowing up to 2^{128} addresses! That should hold us for the foreseeable future! This number—close to 3.4×10^{38} addresses—is something like all the grains of sand on Earth or 1/8 of all the molecules in the atmosphere.

NOTE If you really want to know how many IP addresses IPv6 provides, here's your number: 340,282,366,920,938,463,463,374,607,431,768,211,456. Say that three times fast!

Although they achieve the same function—enabling computers on IP networks to send packets to each other—IPv6 and IPv4 differ a lot when it comes to implementation. This section provides you with a quick overview to get you up to speed with IPv6 and show you how it differs from IPv4.

IPv6 Address Notation

The familiar 32-bit IPv4 addresses are written as 197.169.94.82, using four octets. The 128-bit IPv6 addresses are written like this:

2001:0000:0000:3210:0800:200C:00CF:1234

IPv6 uses a colon as a separator, instead of the period used in IPv4's dotted-decimal format. Each "group" is a hexadecimal number between 0000 and FFFF called, unofficially, a *field* or *hextet*.

NOTE For those who don't play with hex regularly, one hexadecimal character (for example, *F*) represents 4 bits, so four hexadecimal characters make a 16-bit group. For some reason, the IPv6 developers didn't provide a name for the "group of four hexadecimal characters," so many techs and writers have taken to calling them fields or "hextets" to distinguish them from IPv4 "octets."

A complete IPv6 address always has eight groups of four hexadecimal characters. If this sounds like you're going to type in really long IP addresses, don't worry, IPv6 offers a number of ways to shorten the address in written form.

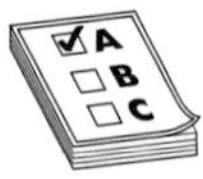

EXAM TIP IPv4 addresses use 32 bits, and IPv6 addresses use 128 bits. Be sure you can identify their address length differences and address conventions.

First, leading zeros can be dropped from any group, so 00CF becomes CF and 0000 becomes 0. Let's rewrite the previous IPv6 address using this shortening method:

2001:0:0:3210:800:200C:CF:1234

Second, you can remove one or more consecutive groups of all zeros, leaving the two colons together. For example, using the :: rule, you can write the IPv6 address

2001:0:0:3210:800:200C:CF:1234

as

2001::3210:800:200C:CF:1234

You can remove any number of consecutive groups of zeros to leave a double colon, but you can only use this trick *once* in an IPv6 address.

Take a look at this IPv6 address:

FEDC:0000:0000:0000:00CF:0000:BA98:1234

Using the double-colon rule, you can reduce four groups of zeros; three of them follow the FEDC and the fourth comes after 00CF. Because of the "only use once" stipulation, the best and shortest option is to convert the address to

FEDC::CF:0:BA98:1234

You may not use a second :: to represent the fourth groups of zeros—only one :: is allowed per address! This rule exists for a good reason. If more than one :: was used, how could you tell how many groups of zeros were in each group? Answer: you couldn't.

Here's an example of a very special IPv6 address that takes full advantage of the double-colon rule, the IPv6 loopback address:

::1

Without using the double-colon nomenclature, this IPv6 address would look like this:

0000:0000:0000:0000:0000:0000:0000:0001

NOTE The unspecified address (all zeros) can never be used, and neither can an address that contains all ones (in binary) or all *F*s (in hex notation).

IPv6 still uses subnets, but you won't find a place to type in 255s anywhere. IPv6 uses the "/x" CIDR nomenclature, where the /x refers to the number of bits in the subnet mask, just like in IPv4. Here's how to write an IP address and subnet for a typical IPv6 host:

FEDC::CF:0:BA98:1234/64

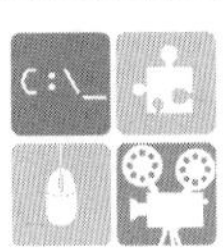

SIM Check out the excellent "IPv6 Address" Type! simulation in the Chapter 21 section of http://totalsem.com/90x. It's a good sim for reinforcing your knowledge of IPv6 and getting practice with performance-based questions.

Where Do IPv6 Addresses Come From?

With IPv4, IP addresses come from one of two places: either you type in the IP address yourself (*static IP addressing*) or you use DHCP (also called *dynamic IP addressing*). With IPv6, addressing works very differently. Instead of one IP address, you can have multiple (usually three) IP addresses on a single network card.

When a computer running IPv6 first boots up, it gives itself a *link-local address*, IPv6's equivalent to IPv4's APIPA address. Although an APIPA address can indicate a loss of network connectivity or a problem with the DHCP server, computers running IPv6 always have a link-local address. The first 64 bits of a link-local address are always FE80::. That means every address always begins with FE80:0000:0000:0000. If your operating system supports IPv6 and IPv6 is enabled, you can see this address. Figure 21-12 shows the link-local address for a typical system running the ipconfig utility.

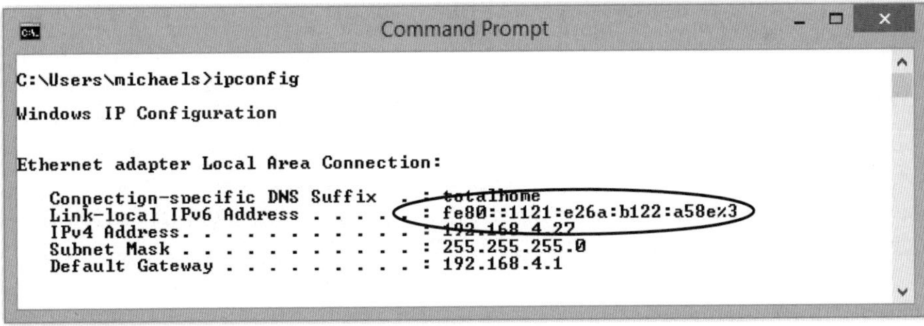
Command Prompt
C:\Users\michaels>ipconfig
Windows IP Configuration
Ethernet adapter Local Area Connection:
Connection-specific DNS Suffix . : totalhome
Link-local IPv6 Address . . . . : fe80::1121:e26a:b122:a58e%3
IPv4 Address. . . . . : 192.168.4.27
Subnet Mask . . . . : 255.255.255.0
Default Gateway . . . . : 192.168.4.1

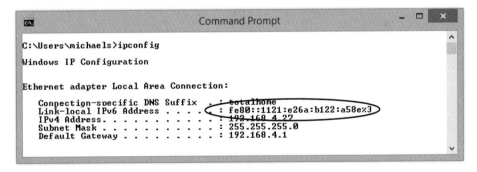

Figure 21-12 Link-local address in ipconfig

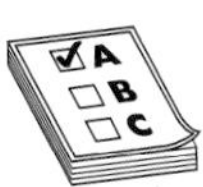

EXAM TIP Every computer running IPv6 will always have at least a link-local address.

The folks who designed IPv6 gave operating system makers a choice on how to make the last 64 bits of an IPv6 address. The first method uses a random value—and this is

the way Windows does it. When you activate a NIC, Windows simply makes a random value for the last 64 bits of the IPv6 address. Once created, this unique 64-bit value will never change.

Linux and Mac OS X use the other method to create IPv6 addresses: building them from the MAC address of the network card (called the *Extended Unique Identifier, 64-bit*, or *EUI-64*). Be warned! The CompTIA A+ exams are Windows-centric, and Windows does not use this second method by default. Even though Windows does not currently use this method by default, understanding this is critical to understanding IPv6.

NOTE If you want to force Windows to use the MAC address, just go to a command prompt and type this:

```
netsh interface ipv6 set global randomizeidentifiers=disabled
```

IPv6 Subnet Masks

IPv6 subnets function the same as IPv4 subnets, but you need to know two new rules:

- The last 64 bits of an IPv6 address are generated randomly or using the MAC address, leaving a maximum of 64 bits for the network ID. Therefore, no subnet is ever longer than /64.
- The IANA passes out /32 subnets to big ISPs and end users who need large allotments. ISPs and others may pass out /48 and /64 subnets to end users.

Therefore, the vast majority of IPv6 subnets are between /48 and /64.

Subnet masks are just as important in IPv6 networks as they are in IPv4 networks. Unlike with IPv4 networks, however, all IPv6 networks with computers have a /64 subnet mask, so you'll rarely if ever need to make any changes manually.

Global Addresses

To get on the Internet, a system needs a second IPv6 address called a *global address*. The most common way to get a global address is to request it from the default gateway router, which must be configured to pass out global IPv6 addresses. When you plug a computer into a network, it sends out a very special packet called a *router solicitation (RS)* message, looking for a router (see Figure 21-13). The router hears this message and responds with a *router advertisement (RA)*. This RA tells the computer its network ID and subnet (together called the *prefix*) and DNS server (if configured).

NOTE A router solicitation message uses the address FF02::2. This address is read only by other computers running IPv6 in the network. This type of address is different from a broadcast address and is called a *multicast address*. In IPv6, there is no broadcast, only multicast!

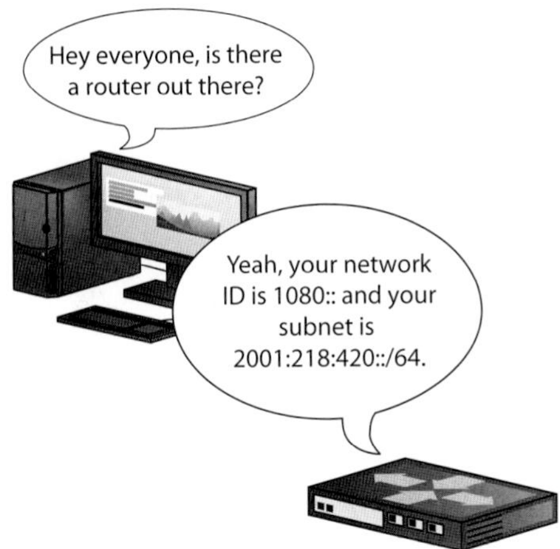

Figure 21-13 Getting a global address

Once the computer gets a prefix, it generates the rest of the address just like with the link-local address. The computer ends up with a legitimate, 128-bit public IPv6 address as well as a link-local address. Figure 21-14 shows the IPv6 information in Windows 8.1.

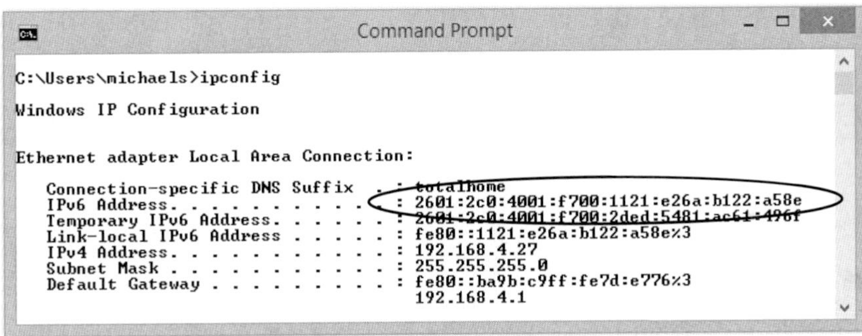

Figure 21-14 Windows system with a global IPv6 address

NOTE Most Windows machines have three IPv6 addresses: one link-local address and two global addresses. One global address stays the same, while the second is a temporary address used to make it harder for your system to be tracked by IP address.

Let's look at this process in detail with an example:

1. An IPv6-capable computer boots up. As it boots, it sends out a router solicitation message (FF02::2).
2. An IPv6-configured router hears the request and then sends to the computer a router advertisement containing the prefix and DNS. In this example, let's say it is 2001:470:ABCD:1/64.

3. The computer takes the prefix and adds the EUI-64 or a random value to the end of the prefix. If the MAC address is 00-0C-29-53-45-CA, then the address is 20C:29FF:FE53:45CA.
4. Putting the prefix with the last half of the address, you get the following global address: 2001:470:ABCD:1:20C:29FF:FE53:45CA.

NOTE At the moment, IANA only passes out global addresses that begin with the number 2 (for example, 2001::, 2002::, and so on). As demand increases, this will certainly change, but for now, knowing a global address when you see one is easy.

A global address is a true Internet address. If another computer is running IPv6 and also has a global address, it can access your system unless you have some form of firewall.

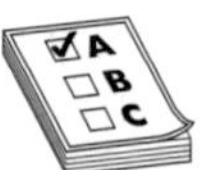

EXAM TIP Computers using IPv6 need a *global* address to access the Internet.

The addition of IPv6 makes programs such as ipconfig fairly complex. Take a look at Figure 21-15.

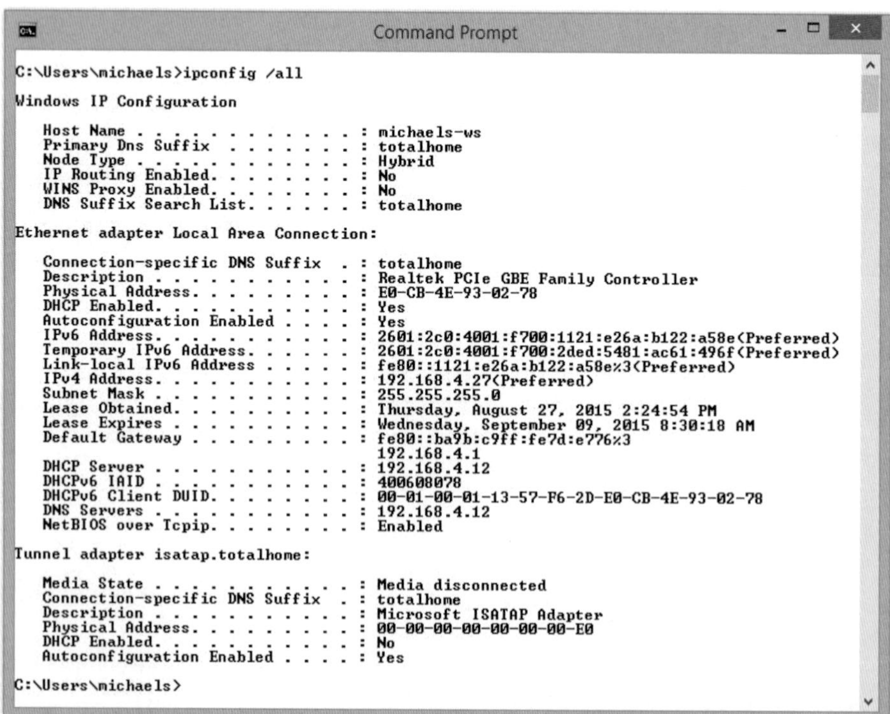

Command Prompt
C:\Users\michaels>ipconfig /all
Windows IP Configuration
Host Name . . . . : michaels-ws
Primary Dns Suffix . . . . : totalhome
Node Type . . . . : Hybrid
IP Routing Enabled. . . . . : No
WINS Proxy Enabled. . . . . : No
DNS Suffix Search List. . . . . . : totalhome
Ethernet adapter Local Area Connection:
Connection-specific DNS Suffix . : totalhome
Description . . . . : Realtek PCIe GBE Family Controller
Physical Address. . . . . : E0-CB-4E-93-02-78
DHCP Enabled. . . . . : Yes
Autoconfiguration Enabled . . . . : Yes
IPv6 Address. . . . . : 2601:2c0:4001:f700:1121:e26a:b122:a58e(Preferred)
Temporary IPv6 Address. . . . . . : 2601:2c0:4001:f700:2ded:5481:ac61:496f(Preferred)
Link-local IPv6 Address . . . . . : fe80::1121:e26a:b122:a58e%3(Preferred)
IPv4 Address. . . . . : 192.168.4.27(Preferred)
Subnet Mask . . . . : 255.255.255.0
Lease Obtained. . . . . : Thursday, August 27, 2015 2:24:54 PM
Lease Expires . . . . : Wednesday, September 09, 2015 8:30:18 AM
Default Gateway . . . . : fe80::ba9b:c9ff:fe7d:e776%3
192.168.4.1
DHCP Server . . . . : 192.168.4.12
DHCPv6 IAID . . . . : 400608078
DHCPv6 Client DUID. . . . . : 00-01-00-01-13-57-F6-2D-E0-CB-4E-93-02-78
DNS Servers . . . . : 192.168.4.12
NetBIOS over Tcpip. . . . . : Enabled
Tunnel adapter isatap.totalhome:
Media State . . . . : Media disconnected
Connection-specific DNS Suffix . : totalhome
Description . . . . : Microsoft ISATAP Adapter
Physical Address. . . . . : 00-00-00-00-00-00-00-E0
DHCP Enabled. . . . . : No
Autoconfiguration Enabled . . . . : Yes
C:\Users\michaels>

Figure 21-15 The ipconfig command with IPv6 and IPv4

Installing and Configuring a Wired Network

To have network connectivity, you need to have three things in place:

- **Connected NIC** The physical hardware that connects the computer system to the network media.
- **Properly configured TCP/IP** Your device needs correct TCP/IP setting for your network.
- **Network client** The interface that allows the computer system to speak to the protocol.

If you want to share resources on your PC with other network users, you also need to enable Microsoft's File and Printer Sharing. Plus, of course, you need to connect the PC to the network switch via some sort of cable (preferably CAT 6 with Gigabit Ethernet cranking through the wires, but that's just me!). When you install a NIC, by default Windows installs upon setup the TCP/IP protocol, the Client for Microsoft Networks, and File and Printer Sharing for Microsoft Networks. Mac OS X computers come fully set up for networking. Different Linux distros offer setup options similar to the Windows options.

Installing a NIC

The NIC is your computer system's link to the network, and installing one is the first step required to connect to a network. NICs are manufactured to operate on specific media and network types, such as 1000BaseT Ethernet. Follow the manufacturer's instructions for installation. If your system is of recent vintage, your motherboard almost certainly has a built-in NIC that you can disable in the BIOS. Assuming your OS has drivers for the new NIC, it will be detected, installed, and configured automatically. Your OS may have trouble installing drivers for a cutting-edge NIC without a functioning network connection; in that case, you'll need removable media containing drivers from the manufacturer or downloaded from their Web site.

If, for some reason, Windows doesn't automatically detect a new NIC after you turn the PC back on, go to Start | Control Panel | Add Hardware in Windows Vista or Start | Devices and Printers and click on *Add a device* in later versions of Windows to install it.

Full-Duplex and Half-Duplex

All modern NICs can run in *full-duplex* mode, meaning they can send and receive data at the same time. The vast majority of NICs and switches use a feature called *autosensing* to accommodate very old devices that might attach to the network and need to run in half-duplex mode. *Half-duplex* means that the device can send and receive, but not at the same time. An obvious example of a half-duplex device is the walkie-talkies you played with as a kid that required you to press and hold the orange button to transmit—at which time you couldn't hear anything.

Link Lights

NICs made today have some type of light-emitting diode (LED) *status indicator* that gives information about the state of the NIC's link to whatever is on the other end of the connection. Even though you know the lights are actually LEDs, get used to calling them *link lights*, because that's the term all network techs use. NICs can have between one and four different link lights, and the LEDs can be any color. These lights give you clues about what's happening with the link and are one of the first items to check whenever you think a system is disconnected from the network (see Figure 21-16).

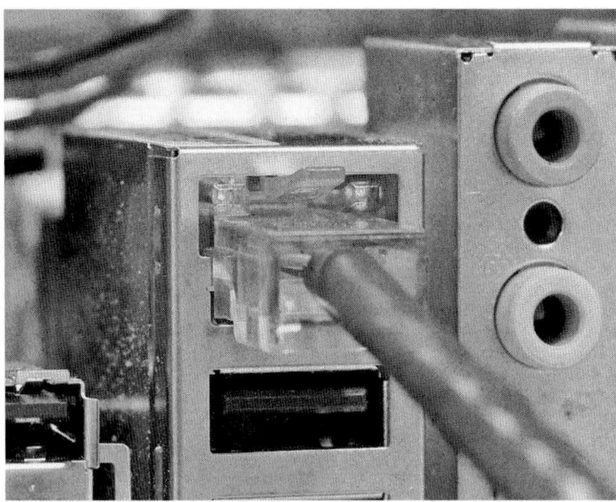

Figure 21-16 Mmmm, pretty lights!

Switches also have link lights, enabling you to check the connectivity at both ends of the cable. If a PC can't access a network, always check the link lights first. Multispeed devices usually have a link light that tells you the speed of the connection. In Figure 21-17, the light for port 2 on the top photo is orange, for example, signifying that the other end of the cable is plugged into either a 10BaseT or 100BaseT NIC. The same port connected to a Gigabit NIC—that's the lower picture—displays a green LED.

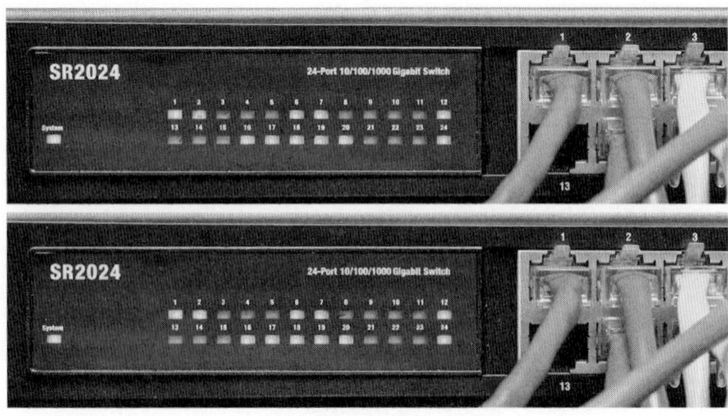

Figure 21-17 Multispeed lights

A properly functioning link light is steady on when the NIC is connected to another device. No flickering, no on and off, just on. A link light that is off or flickering shows a connection problem.

Another light is the *activity light*. This little guy turns on when the card detects network traffic, so it makes an intermittent flickering when operating properly. The activity light is a lifesaver for detecting problems, because in the real world, the connection light sometimes lies to you. If the connection light says the connection is good, the next step is to try to copy a file or do something else to create network traffic. If the activity light does not flicker, you have a problem.

No standard governs how NIC manufacturers use their lights; as a result, LEDs in NICs come in an amazing array of colors and layouts. When you encounter a NIC with a number of LEDs, take a moment to try to figure out what each one means. Although different NICs have different ways of arranging and using their LEDs, the functions are always the same: link, activity, and speed.

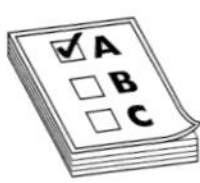

EXAM TIP Though no real standard exists for NIC LEDs, the CompTIA A+ exams will test you on some more-or-less *de facto* LED meanings. You should know that a solid green light means connectivity, a flashing green light means intermittent connectivity, no green light means no connectivity, and a flashing amber light means there are collisions on the network (which is sometimes okay). Also, know that the first things you should check when having connectivity issues are the NIC's LEDs.

Wake-on-LAN

A popular feature of most NICs is the ability to turn on or wake up a powered-down or sleeping PC. You'll learn more about power management in Chapter 24, "Portable Computing," but for now, know that *Wake-on-LAN* is handy when you want to wake up one or multiple computers that you aren't physically near. To wake up a PC with Wake-on-LAN, you'll need to use a second PC to send either a special pattern or a *magic packet* (a broadcast packet that essentially repeats the destination MAC address many times).

A powered-down or sleeping PC knows to look for this special pattern or packet, at least after configured to do so. Go to the Control Panel and open Network and Sharing Center. Click *Manage network connections* or *Change adapter settings* on the left. For all versions of Windows, right-click on the adapter and select Properties. Click the Configure button in the Properties dialog box and then select the Power Management tab (see Figure 21-18). To enable Wake-on-LAN, make sure the checkbox next to *Allow this device to wake the computer* is checked. Optionally, you can select *Only allow a magic packet to wake the computer*, which will instruct the NIC to ignore everything but magic packets.

Figure 21-18 Wake-on-LAN settings on the Power Management tab

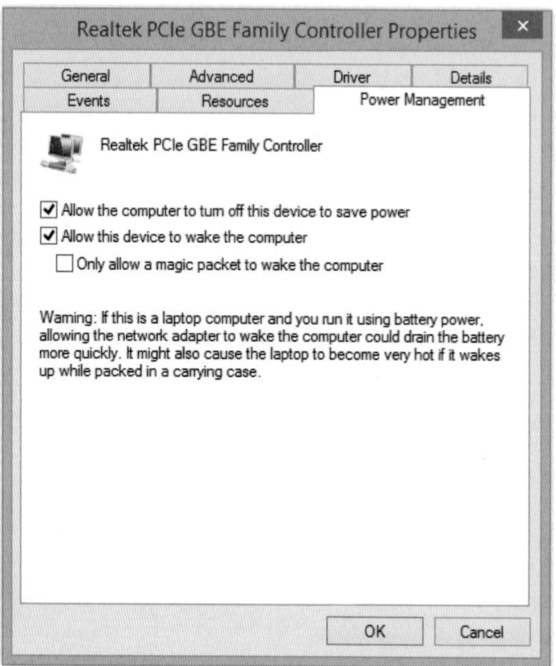
Realtek PCIe GBE Family Controller Properties
General
Advanced
Driver
Details
Events
Resources
Power Management
Realtek PCIe GBE Family Controller
Allow the computer to turn off this device to save power
Allow this device to wake the computer
Only allow a magic packet to wake the computer
Warning: If this is a laptop computer and you run it using battery power, allowing the network adapter to wake the computer could drain the battery more quickly. It might also cause the laptop to become very hot if it wakes up while packed in a carrying case.
OK
Cancel

NOTE Your BIOS might also have settings for controlling Wake-on-LAN functions. Check your CMOS System Configuration tool to find out.

Wake-on-LAN is very convenient, but it has one nasty downside. As noted in the Properties dialog box, Wake-on-LAN can wake up or turn on laptops using wireless connections, even when they aren't plugged in or are inside a carrying case. Don't let your laptop overheat or drain its battery—unless you know that you'll need it, turn off Wake-on-LAN on your laptop.

QoS

Quality of service (QoS) enables busy networks to prioritize traffic. While we'll look at QoS from the router's perspective in Chapter 23, "The Internet," individual systems play an important role in the QoS process by tagging their frames, enabling networking hardware to treat them according to rules defined by network administrators. Support for QoS tagging (or priority) should be enabled by default on most network adapters—but if you need to modify this setting you can find the Priority & VLAN option on the Advanced tab of your NIC's Properties dialog box (see Figure 21.19).

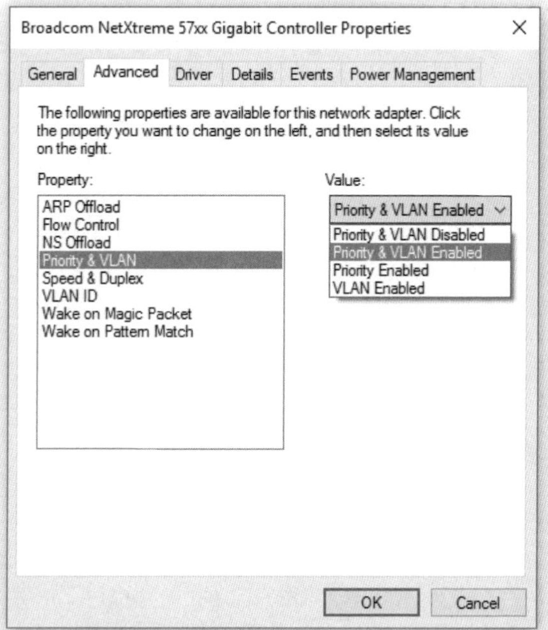

Figure 21-19 Network adapter Priority & VLAN setting

Configuring a Network Client

To establish network connectivity, you need a network client installed and configured properly. Let's look at Microsoft's client.

Installed as part of the OS installation, the Client for Microsoft Networks rarely needs configuration, and, in fact, few configuration options are available. To start it in Windows Vista, click Start, right-click Network, and select Properties. In Windows 7 and later, open the Control Panel and select Network and Sharing Center. Then click Manage network connections (Vista) or Change adapter settings (7/8/8.1/10) on the left.

In all versions of Windows, the next step is to right-click the Local Area Connection icon, click the Properties button, and highlight Client for Microsoft Networks. In Windows Vista, click the Properties button. Windows 7 and later disable this option. Note, however, that there's not much to do here. Unless told to do something by a network administrator, just leave this alone.

Sharing and Security

Windows systems can share all kinds of *resources* across your network: files, folders, entire drives, printers, faxes, Internet connections, and much more. Conveniently for you, the scope of the CompTIA A+ certification exams is limited to sharing a system's folders, printers, multifunction devices, and Internet connections. You'll see how to share folders and printers now; multifunction devices are discussed in Chapter 26, "Printers and Multifunction Devices"; and Internet connection sharing is discussed in Chapter 23.

Network Shares

When you share over a network, every OS uses specific network sharing permissions to allow or restrict access to shared resources. These permissions do not have anything to do with file- or folder-level permissions like you find in Windows with NTFS (covered in Chapter 14, "Users, Groups, and Permissions"). But file- and folder-level permissions definitely affect share permissions. Here's the scoop.

On a non-NTFS volume like an optical media disc or a flash-media USB drive, you only have three levels of permission: Read, Read/Write, and Owner, which are discussed later in this chapter. That's because Microsoft uses NTFS for authorization with both local users and network users. So that means you use the network share to actually share the resource, but use NTFS to say what folks can do with that resource.

If you share a folder on an NTFS drive, as you normally do these days, you must set *both* the network permissions and the NTFS permissions to let others access your shared resources. Some good news: This is actually no big deal! Just set the network permissions to give everyone Full Control, and then use the NTFS permissions to exercise more precise control over *who* accesses the shared resources and *how* they access them. Open the Security tab to set the NTFS permissions.

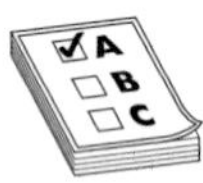

EXAM TIP You need to understand the difference between share permissions and NTFS permissions. Share permissions only apply to network sharing. NTFS permissions affect both network and local access to shared resources.

Network Organization

Once a network is created using appropriate network technology like Ethernet, users need to be able to share resources in some organized fashion. Resources such as folders and printers need a way to determine who can and cannot use them and how they can be used. Microsoft designed Windows networks to work in one of three categories: workgroups, domains, or homegroups. (These are the Microsoft terms, but the concepts have been adopted by the entire computer industry and apply to Mac OS X and other operating systems.) These three organizations differ in control, number of machines needed, compatibility, and security.

Let's start with the oldest and most common network organization: workgroups.

Workgroups

Workgroups are the most basic and simplistic of the three network organizations. They are also the default for almost every fresh installation of Windows.

By default, all computers on the network are assigned to a workgroup called WORKGROUP. You can see your workgroup name by opening the System applet, as shown in Figure 21-20.

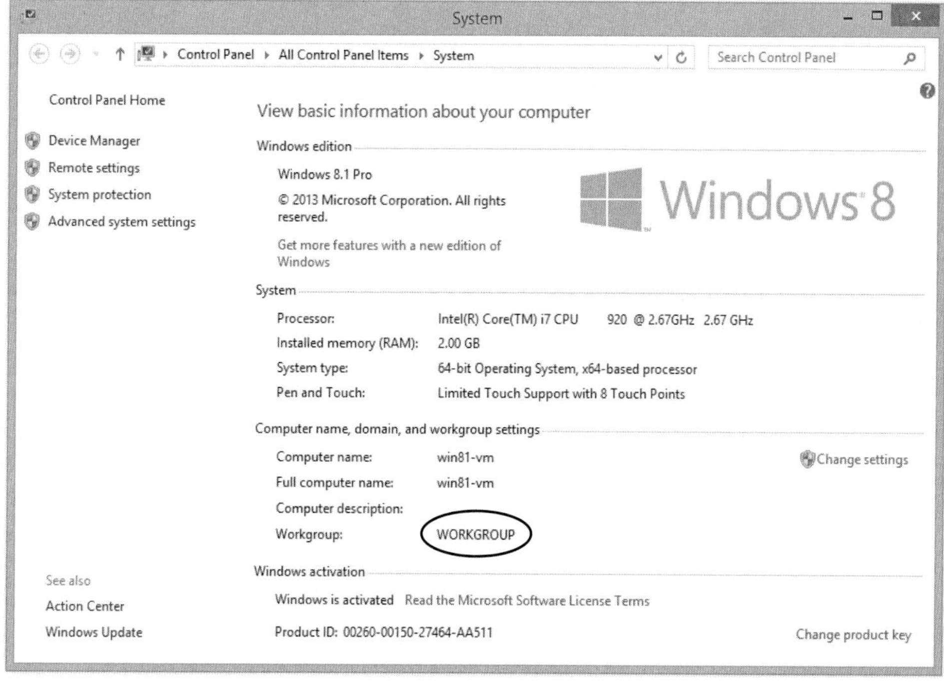

Figure 21-20 Default workgroup

There's nothing special about the name WORKGROUP, except that every computer on the network needs the same workgroup name to be able to share resources. If you want to change your workgroup name, you need to use the System applet. Click the Change settings link to open the System Properties dialog box. Then click the Change button to change your workgroup name (see Figure 21-21).

NOTE Most workgroup-based Windows networks keep the default name of WORKGROUP.

Workgroups lack centralized control over the network; all systems connected to the network are equals. This works well for smaller networks because there are fewer users, connections, and security concerns to think about. But what do you do when your network encompasses dozens or hundreds of users and systems? How can you control all of that?

User Names and Passwords As you'll recall from Chapter 14, when you log on to a Windows computer, you need to enter a user name and password. Windows makes this easy by giving you a pretty logon interface, as shown in Figure 21-22.

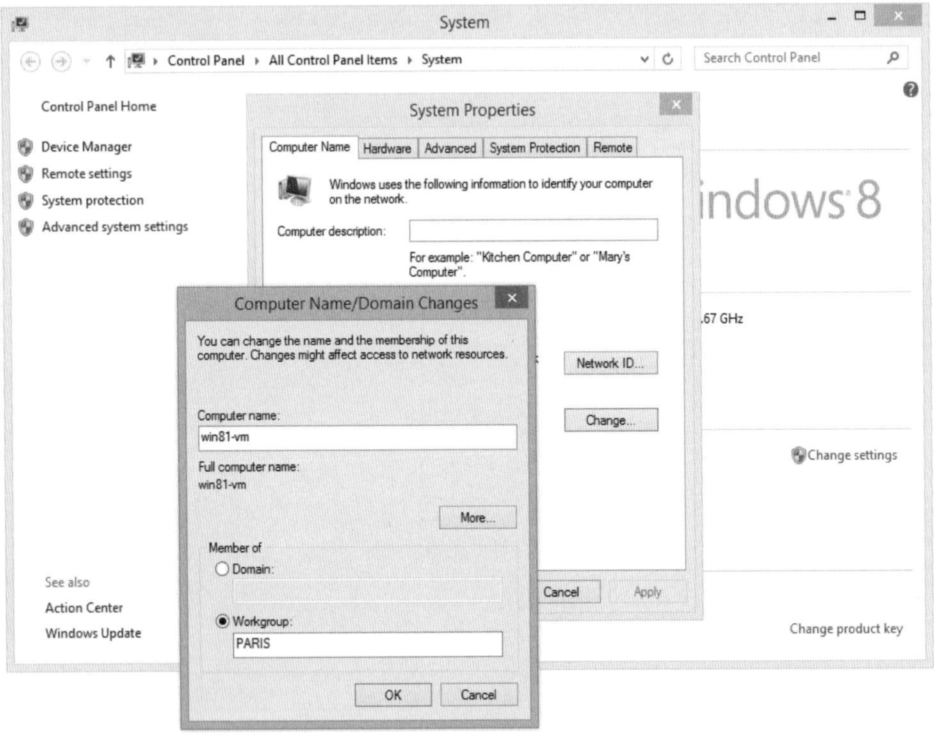

Figure 21-21 Changing the workgroup name in advanced settings

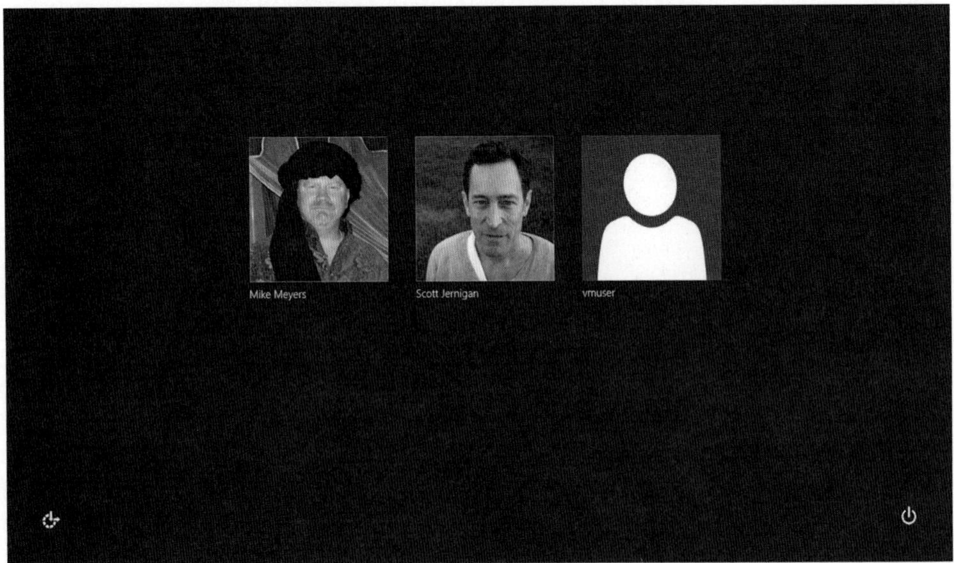

Figure 21-22 Windows logon screen

The user names and their passwords are stored in an encrypted format on your computer. User names have a number of jobs on your computer, but at this point the job most interesting to us is to give a user access to the computer. User names work well when you access your own computer, but these same user names and passwords are used to access shared resources on other computers in the network—and that's where we run into trouble. To appreciate this problem, let's watch a typical folder share take place on a network of Windows 7 systems.

Sharing a Folder All personal computers can share folders and printers out of the box. Sharing a folder in Windows is easy, for example. Just right-click on the folder and select Share with | Specific people to get to the File Sharing dialog box (see Figure 21-23). On Windows 7 systems, you'll see options called Homegroup in the context menu—ignore these for now as all will be explained in the next section.

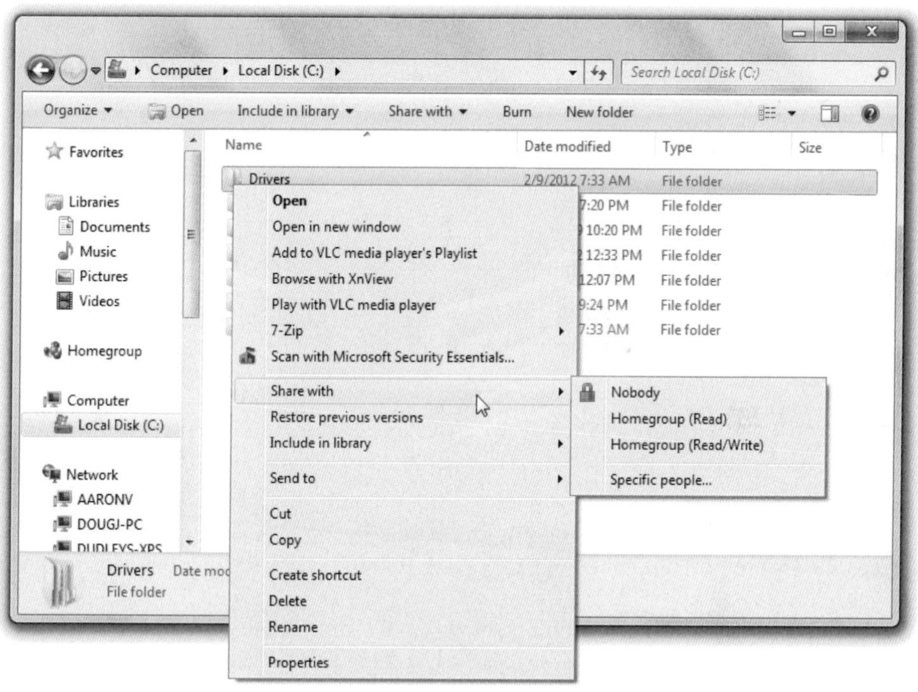

Figure 21-23 Folder Sharing with context menu

By default, you'll see every user account that's currently on this system. You may give an account Read or Read/Write permission, while the person who created the folder is assigned as Owner. The following list describes these permissions:

- **Read** You can see what's in the folder. You may open files in the folder, but you can't save anything back into the folder.

- **Read/Write** Same as Read but you can save files into the folder.
- **Owner** Same as Read/Write plus you can set the permissions for other users on the folder.

NOTE You'll recall from Chapter 14 that all versions of Windows come with a far more powerful and much more complex form of permissions based on the NTFS file system.

So all this sharing seems to work quite nicely, except for one big issue: When you log on to your computer, you are accessing a user name and database on that computer. The accounts you are giving access to are stored on your computer, so how do you give someone from another computer access to that shared folder? You have to give that other person a valid user name and password. We use the nomenclature <computer name>\<user name> to track our logons. If you log on to Computer A as Mike, we say you are logged on to ComputerA\Mike. This nomenclature comes in very handy when networked computers become part of the process.

Figure 21-24 shows Computers A and B. Assume there is a shared folder called Timmy on Computer A and the Mike account has Read/Write permission.

Figure 21-24 Computers A and B

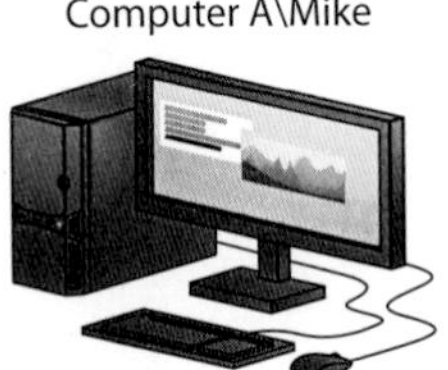

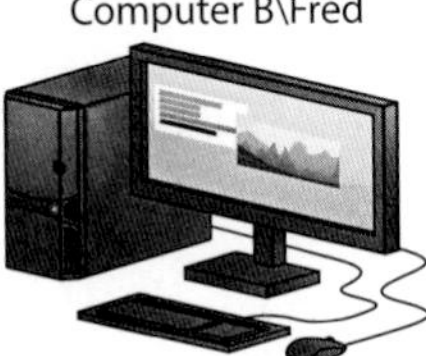

A person fires up Computer B, logging in as Fred. He opens his Network menu option and sees Computer A, but when he clicks on it he sees a network password prompt (see Figure 21-25).

The reason is that the person is logged on as ComputerB\Fred and he needs to be logged on as ComputerA\Mike to successfully access this folder. So the user needs to know the password for ComputerA\Mike. This isn't a very pretty way to protect user names and passwords. So what can you do? You have three choices:

1. You can make people log on to shares as just shown.
2. You can create the same accounts (same user name and same password) on all the computers and give sharing permissions to all the users for all the shares.
3. You can use one account on all computers. Everyone logs on with the same account, and then all shares are by default assigned to the same account.

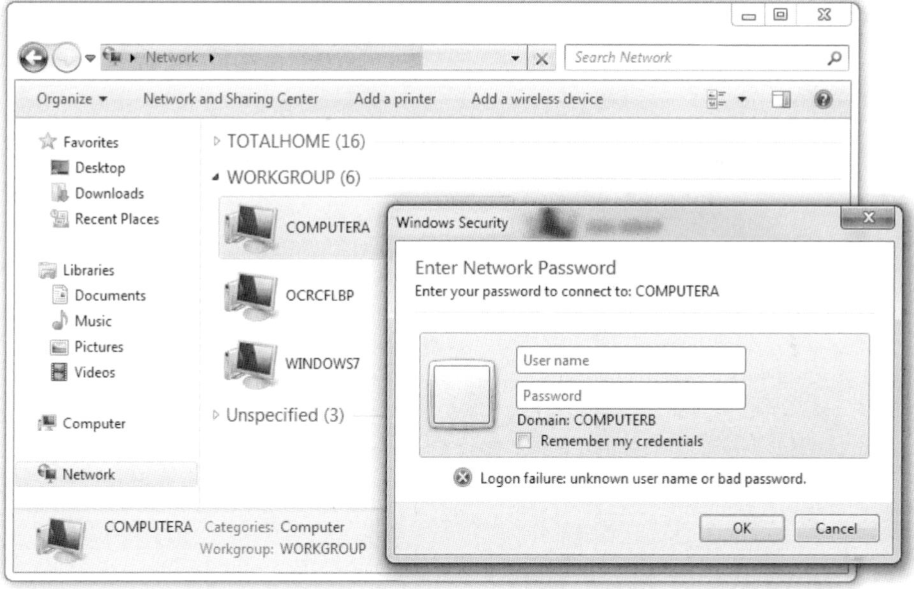

Figure 21-25 Prompt for entering user name and password

Domains

Larger networks that need more control use *domains*. Opposite the decentralized nature of workgroups, domains require a specific server to control access to the network's resources. This means tracking each user, each resource, and what each user can do to each resource.

To use a domain on a network of Windows machines, for example, you must have a computer running a version of Windows Server (see Figure 21-26). Windows Server is a completely different, much more powerful, and much more expensive version of Windows.

An administrator creates a domain on the Windows Server system, which makes that system the *domain controller (DC)*. The administrator also creates new user accounts on the domain controller. These accounts are called *domain accounts*. Once a network is set up as a domain, each PC on the network needs to join the domain (which kicks you off the workgroup). When you log on to a computer that's a member of a domain, Windows will prompt you for a user name instead of showing you icons for all the users on the network (see Figure 21-27).

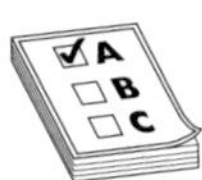

EXAM TIP You can manage a domain from the command line with the netdom command.

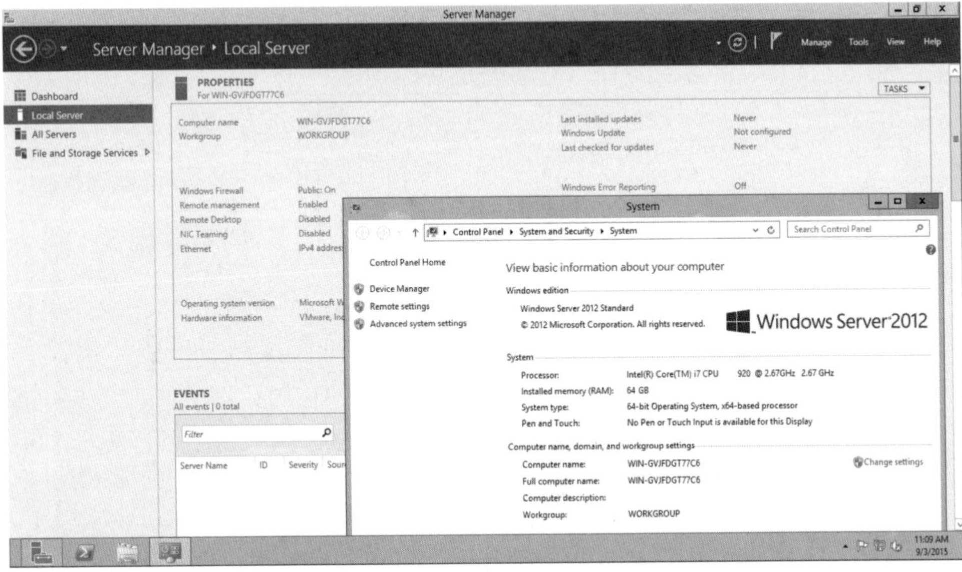

Figure 21-26 Windows Server

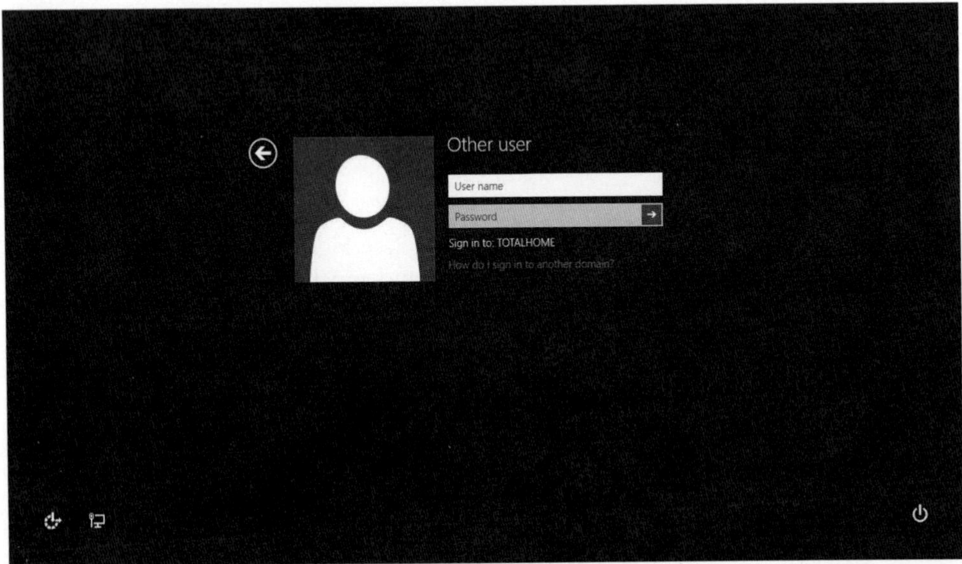

Figure 21-27 Domain logon screen

When using a domain, you don't log on to your computer. Instead, you log on directly to the domain. All user accounts are stored on the domain controller, as shown in Figure 21-28. A lot of domains have names that look like Web addresses, like totalhome .com, totalhome.local, or even just totalhome. Using the previous nomenclature, you can log on to a domain using <domain>\<domain user name>. If the domain totalhome. local has a user account called Mike, for example, you would use totalhome.local\Mike to log on.

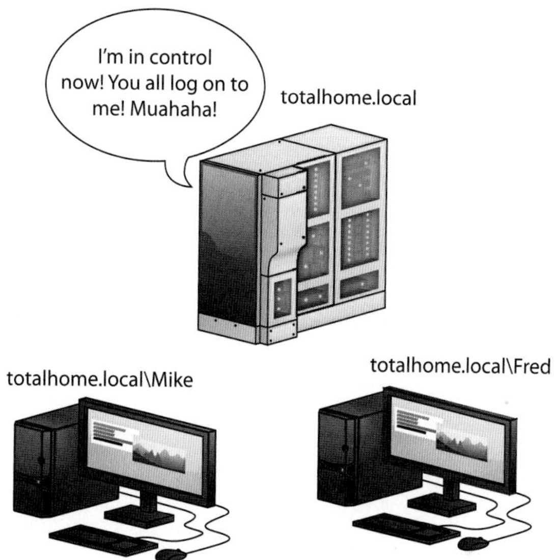

Figure 21-28 Domain network

One of the best features of domains is that you can log on to any computer on the domain using the same domain account. You don't have to set up local accounts on each computer. We call this feature *single sign-on*, and for most users, this is the biggest benefit to using a Windows domain.

NOTE There is much more to a Windows domain than single sign-on. For the CompTIA A+ certification, however, that's the big selling point. If you want to delve deeper into Windows domains, consider pursuing the CompTIA Network+ certification or one of the Microsoft certifications.

Homegroups

The problem with workgroups is that they provide almost no security and require lots of signing on to access resources. Domains provide single sign-on and lots of security, but require special servers and lots of administration. To address this, Microsoft introduced a new feature in Windows 7 called *HomeGroup*.

NOTE Homegroups are not available in Windows Vista, Mac OS X, or any Linux distro.

HomeGroup uses the idea that people want to share data, not folders. Most people just want to share their music, not their My Music or Music folder. So homegroups skip folders completely and share your Windows libraries. A homegroup connects a group of computers using a common password—no special user names required. Each computer can be a member of only one homegroup at a time. Let's make a homegroup and see how this works.

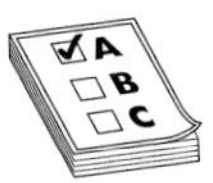

EXAM TIP Homegroups require the IPv6 protocol. Luckily, IPv6 is enabled by default.

To make a homegroup, open the HomeGroup Control Panel applet. Assuming you currently connect to a workgroup and haven't already created a homegroup, you'll see a dialog box like the one shown in Figure 21-29.

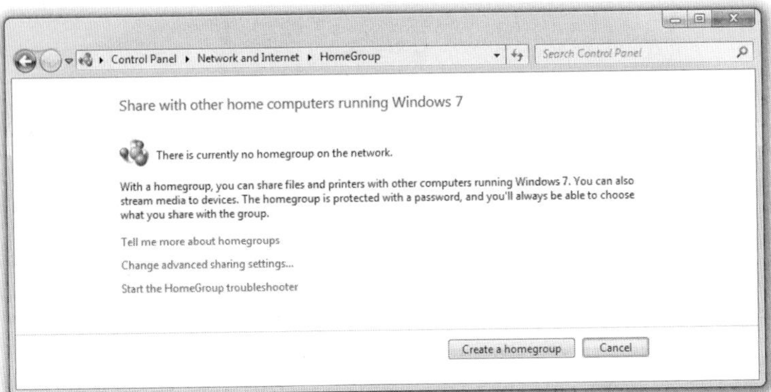

Figure 21-29 Default HomeGroup dialog box

Click the Create a homegroup button to create a homegroup. You'll then see the Create a Homegroup dialog box shown in Figure 21-30.

Notice the five options: Pictures, Music, Videos, Documents, and Printers. The Documents checkbox is probably not checked, but go ahead and check it to share all five things. Click Next to see the homegroup's password (see Figure 21-31).

NOTE Interestingly, all homegroup data is encrypted between systems.

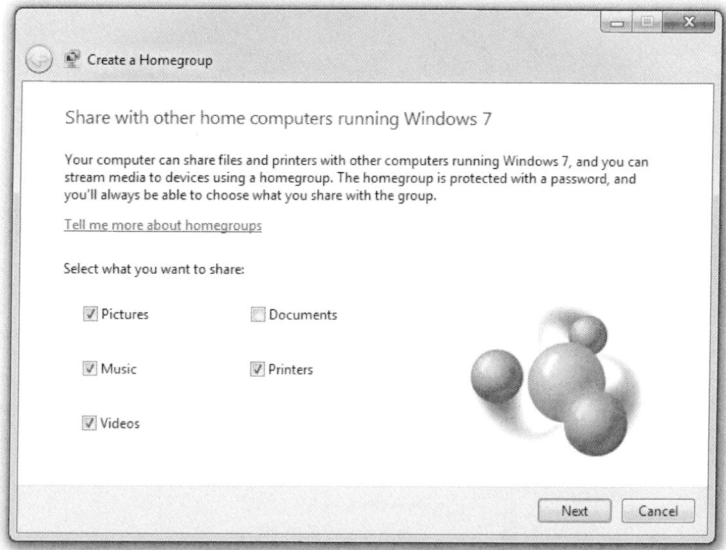

Figure 21-30 Create a Homegroup dialog box

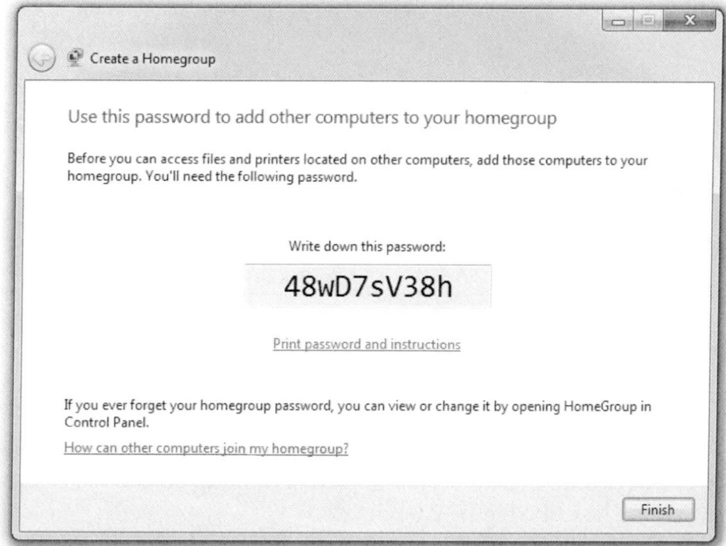

Figure 21-31 The homegroup's password

Perhaps you've heard that you shouldn't write down passwords? Well, this password is so long that you might *need* to write it down. The dialog box even gives you a way to print it out! Click Next one more time to see the dialog box shown in Figure 21-32. This is the dialog box you will now see every time you click the HomeGroup applet in the Control Panel.

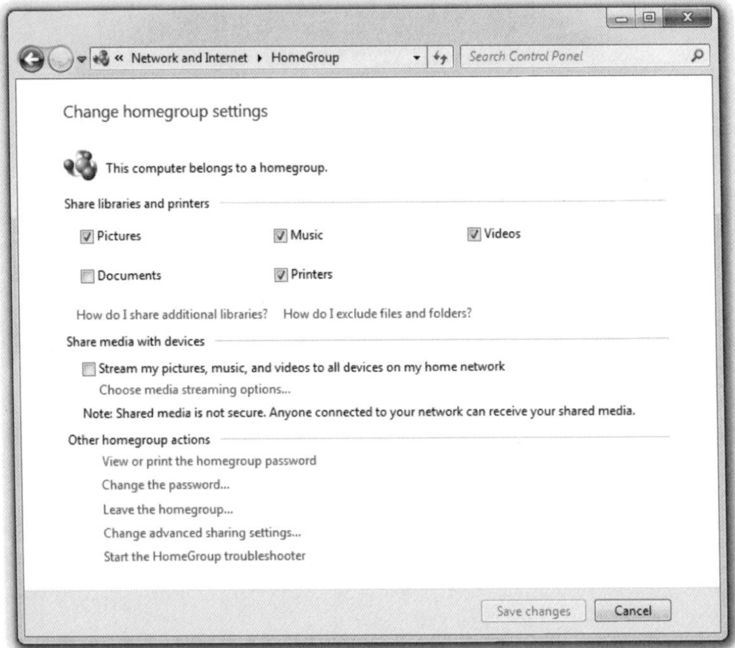

Figure 21-32 Homegroup configured

Let's look at this carefully. Notice where it says *Share libraries and printers* and, a bit lower, *How do I share additional libraries?* By default, homegroups share libraries, not individual folders. The Music, Pictures, Videos, and Documents libraries are shared by default. Although printers get their own checkbox, this setting remains the same as a normal printer share. It's just a handy place to add printer sharing, as even the most basic users like to share printers.

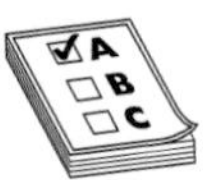

EXAM TIP Remember that homegroups share libraries, not folders, by default.

Once you've created a homegroup, go to another computer on the network and open the HomeGroup Control Panel applet. Assuming all the factors stated earlier, you will see a dialog box like Figure 21-33.

Click the Join now button, enter the password, choose which libraries you want to share with everyone else, and the new computer is in the homegroup!

Access the files shared through a homegroup by opening Windows Explorer or File Explorer, as shown in Figure 21-34. To see what others are sharing, select the corresponding computer name. You can then open those libraries to see the shared folders.

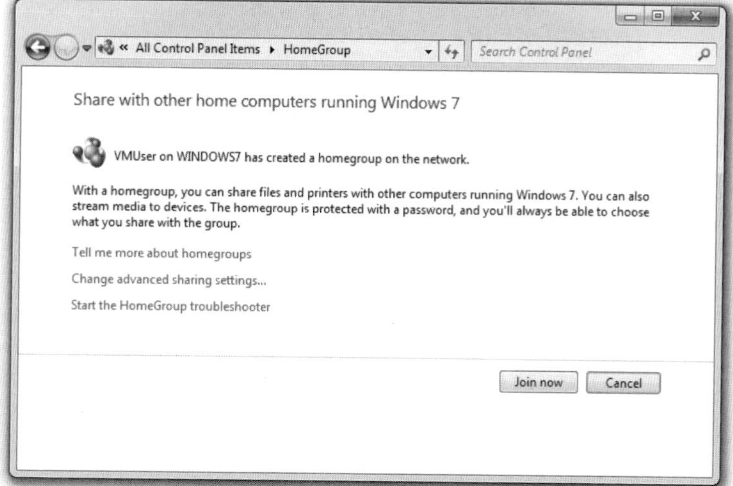

Figure 21-33 HomeGroup showing an existing homegroup

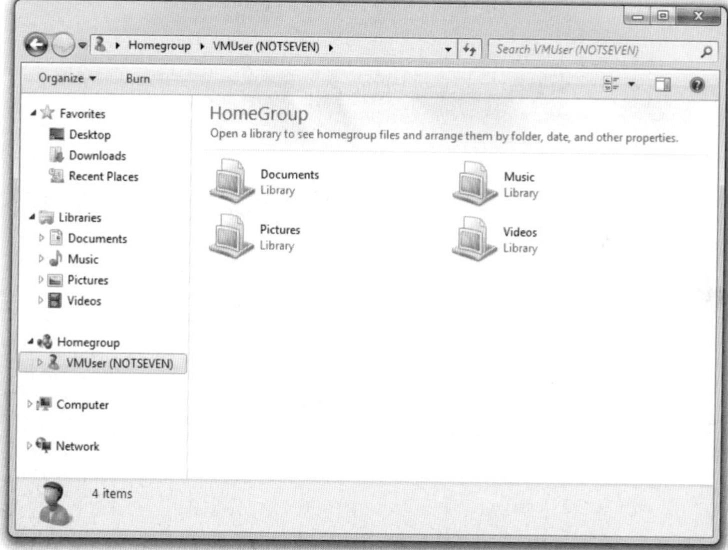

Figure 21-34 Using homegroups

NOTE Once you create a homegroup, you can access it from Windows Explorer/File Explorer.

Sharing more libraries is easy, and, if you'd like, you can even share individual folders. Just right-click on the library or folder and select Share with, as shown in Figure 21-35.

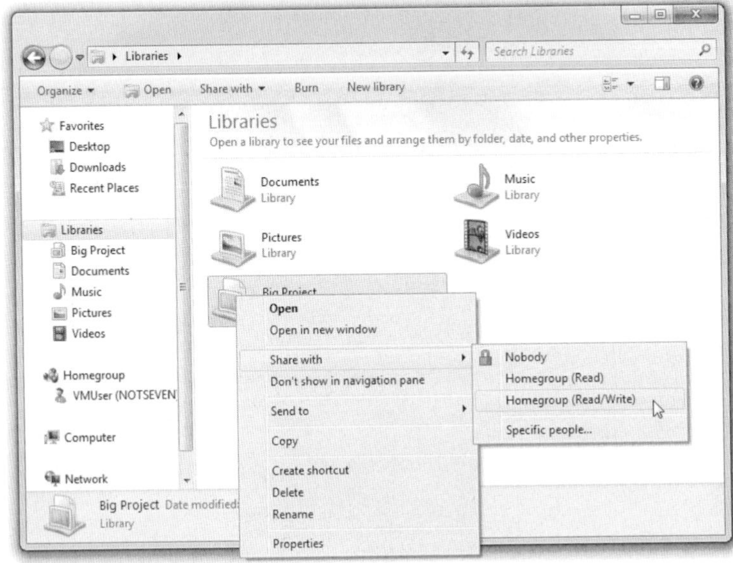

Figure 21-35 The Share with menu

Notice you have four options: Nobody, Homegroup (Read), Homegroup (Read/Write), and Specific people. The Nobody option means the item is not shared.

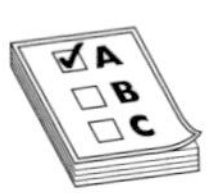

EXAM TIP Windows Explorer also adds a *Share with* toolbar button that works exactly like the menu shown in Figure 21-35.

By sharing libraries with homegroups, Microsoft hides folders for most users, helping users share their stuff (documents, pictures, music, and videos) instead of folders. Homegroups fit a very specific world—smaller, non-domain home networks—but within that realm, they work wonderfully.

Sharing Printers

Sharing printers in Windows follows the same process as sharing drives and folders. Assuming that the system has printer sharing services loaded, in Windows Vista go to the Printers folder in the Control Panel or Start menu and right-click the printer you wish to share. Select Sharing, and then click *Share this printer* and give it a name. In Windows 7/8/8.1/10, open Devices and Printers in the Control Panel, right-click on the printer you wish to share, select Printer properties, and then select the Sharing tab (see Figure 21-36). From here it's just like Vista—click *Share this printer* and you're done.

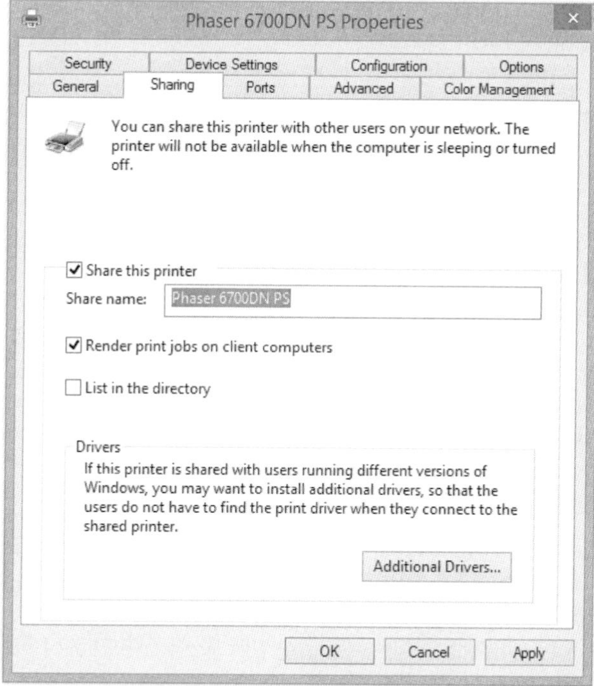
Phaser 6700DN PS Properties
Security
Device Settings
Configuration
Options
General
Sharing
Ports
Advanced
Color Management
You can share this printer with other users on your network. The printer will not be available when the computer is sleeping or turned off.
Share this printer
Share name:
Phaser 6700DN PS
Render print jobs on client computers
List in the directory
Drivers
If this printer is shared with users running different versions of Windows, you may want to install additional drivers, so that the users do not have to find the print driver when they connect to the shared printer.
Additional Drivers...
OK
Cancel
Apply

Figure 21-36 Giving a name to a shared printer on Windows 8.1

NOTE To learn about accessing shared printers in Windows, check out Chapter 26 for more information.

One of the most pleasant aspects of configuring a system for networking under all versions of Microsoft Windows is the amazing amount of the process that is automated. For example, if Windows detects a NIC in a system, it automatically installs the NIC driver, a network protocol (TCP/IP), and Client for Microsoft Networks. So if you want to share a resource, everything you need is automatically installed. Note that although File and Printer Sharing is also automatically installed, you still must activate it by clicking the appropriate checkbox in the Local Area Connection Properties dialog box.

Troubleshooting Networks

Once you go beyond a single PC and enter the realm of networked computers, your troubleshooting skills need to take a giant leap up in quality. The secret to finding the right answer to networking problems on the CompTIA A+ exams is to remember that the exams only ask about the skills to get a single computer back on the network. Granted, this might mean you'll need to check a switch or verify another system's connectivity, but

in general, always focus your network troubleshooting answers on getting a single system up and running.

NOTE The troubleshooting issues discussed here apply only to a LAN, and do not cover issues related to troubleshooting Internet access. We'll cover Internet troubleshooting in Chapter 23, using the knowledge you've gained in this chapter and adding even more tools.

CompTIA likes to ask questions that deal with "no connectivity" or "intermittent connectivity." There are two ways to look at connectivity issues, and CompTIA A+ exam objectives don't specify which type is covered on the exams. The first type of connectivity issue (and probably the one CompTIA means) is when your computer loses physical connectivity. The second type is when you're on the network and can't access a particular resource (you can access other resources, just not the one you want right now). Let's consider both.

Repairing Physical Cabling

"The network's down!" is one of the most terrifying phrases a network tech will ever hear. Networks fail for many reasons, and the first thing to know is that good-quality, professionally installed cabling rarely goes bad, but you need to know what to do when it does. Let's take a moment now to discuss what to do when you think you've got a problem with your physical network.

Symptoms

Physical connectivity interruptions stand out in Windows. Windows displays a red X over the network icon in the notification area to show you're not connected (see Figure 21-37).

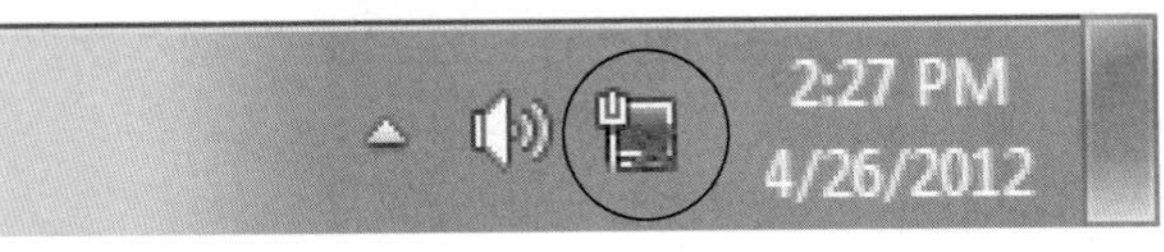

Figure 21-37 Windows 7 red X error notification icon

If you encounter this problem, first check the obvious: Is the cable unplugged at your system? At the wall outlet? Then go for the less obvious: Is the NIC disabled in Device Manager? If these checks don't solve the problem, take a peek on the other side of the cable. If you're not connected to a running switch, you're going to get the disconnect errors.

Intermittent connectivity is often the same issue but typically is harder to figure out. Either way, read the next section to see how to get serious about testing for these pesky connectivity problems.

Diagnosing Physical Problems

Look for errors that point to physical disconnection. A key clue that the computer may have a physical problem is that a user gets a "No server is found" error, or tries to use the operating system's network explorer utility (like Network in Windows) and doesn't see any systems besides his or her own.

Multiple systems failing to access the network often points to hardware problems. This is where knowledge of your network cabling helps. If all the systems connected to one switch suddenly no longer see the network, but all the other systems in your network still function, you not only have a probable hardware problem, but also have a suspect—the switch.

Check the Lights

If you suspect a hardware problem, first check the link lights on the NIC and switch. If they're not lit, you know the cable isn't connected somewhere. If you're not physically at the system in question (if you're on a tech call, for example), you can have the user check his or her connection status through the link lights or through software.

If the problem system clearly cannot connect, eliminate the possibility of a failed switch or other larger problem by checking to make sure other people can access the network, and that other systems can access the shared resource (server) that the problem system can't see. Inspect the cable running from the back of the computer to the outlet. Finally, if you can, plug the system into a known-good outlet and see if it works. A veteran network tech keeps a long patch cable for just this purpose. If you get connectivity with the second outlet, you should begin to suspect the structured cable running from the first outlet to the switch. Assuming the cable is installed properly and has been working correctly before this event, a simple continuity test will confirm your suspicion in most cases.

Check the NIC

Be warned that a bad NIC can also generate a "can't see the network" problem. Use the utility provided by the OS to verify that the NIC works. If you've got a NIC with diagnostic software, run it—this software will check the NIC's circuitry. The NIC's female connector is a common failure point, so NICs that come with diagnostic software often include a special test called a *loopback test*. A loopback test sends data out of the NIC and checks to see if it comes back. Some NICs perform only an internal loopback, which tests the circuitry that sends and receives, but not the actual connecting pins. A true external loopback requires a *loopback plug* inserted into the NIC's port (see Figure 21-38). If a NIC is bad, replace it.

Figure 21-38 Loopback plug

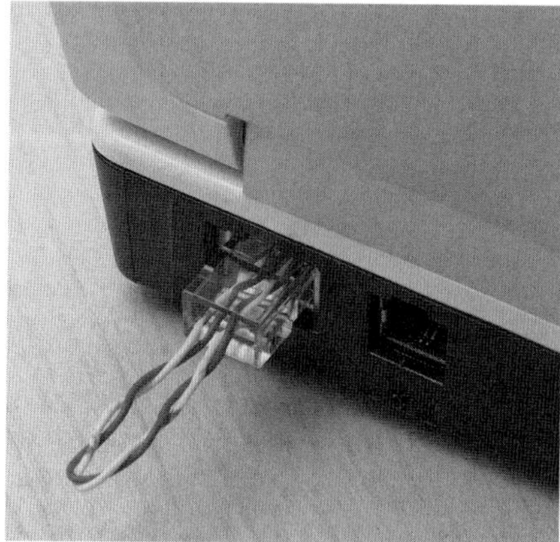

NOTE Onboard NICs on laptops are especially notorious for breaking due to frequent plugging and unplugging. On some laptops, the NICs are easy to replace; others require a motherboard replacement.

Cable Testing

The vast majority of network disconnection problems occur at the work area. If you've tested those connections, though, and the work area seems fine, it's time to consider deeper issues.

With the right equipment, diagnosing a bad horizontal cabling run is easy. Anyone with a network should own a midrange time-domain reflectometer (TDR) tester such as the Fluke MicroScanner. A TDR measures impedance in network cabling. If the tester measures any impedance, something is wrong with the cable. With a little practice, you can easily determine not only whether a cable is disconnected but also where the disconnection takes place. Sometimes patience is required, especially if you've failed to label your cable runs, but you will find the problem.

When you're testing a cable run, always include the patch cables as you test. This means unplugging the patch cable from the PC, attaching a tester, and then going to the telecommunications room. Here you'll want to unplug the patch cable from the switch and plug the tester into that patch cable, making a complete test, as shown in Figure 21-39.

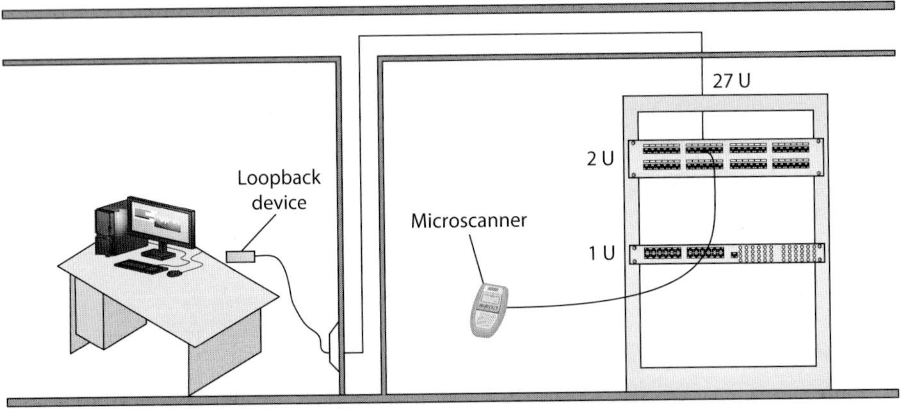

Figure 21-39 Cable tester in action

Testing in this manner gives you a complete test from the switch to the system. In general, a broken cable must be replaced. A bad patch cable is an easy fix, but what happens if the horizontal cable is to blame? In these cases, I get on the phone and call my local installer. If a cable is bad in one spot, the risk of it being bad in another is simply too great to try anything other than total replacement.

Toners

It would be nice to say that all cable installations are perfect and that over the years they won't tend to grow into horrific piles of spaghetti-like, unlabeled cables. In the real world, though, you might eventually find yourself having to locate or *trace* cables. Even in the best-planned networks, labels fall off ports and outlets, mystery cables appear behind walls, new cable runs are added, and mistakes are made counting rows and columns on patch panels. Sooner or later, most network techs will have to be able to pick out one particular cable or port from a stack.

When the time comes to trace cables, network techs turn to a device called a toner for help. *Toner* is the generic term for two separate devices that are used together: a tone generator and a tone probe. The *tone generator* connects to the cable using alligator clips, tiny hooks, or a network jack, and it sends an electrical signal along the wire at a certain frequency. The *tone probe* emits a sound when it is placed near a cable connected to the tone generator. These two devices are often referred to by the brand-name Fox and Hound, a popular model of toner made by the Triplett Corporation (see Figure 21-40).

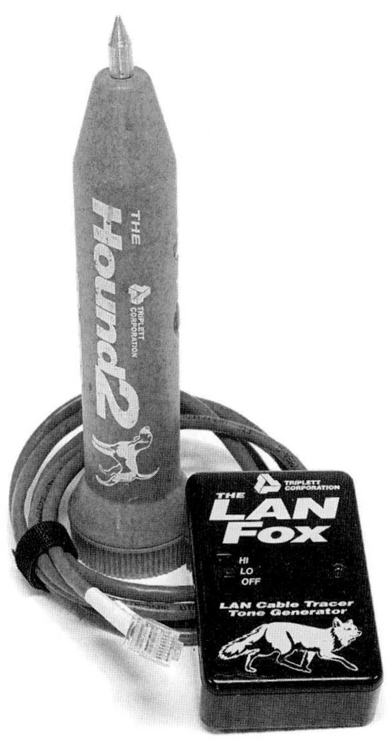

Figure 21-40 Fox and Hound

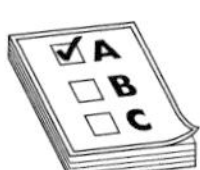

EXAM TIP You'll see a tone probe referred to on the CompTIA A+ exam as a *toner probe.*

To trace a cable, connect the tone generator to the known end of the cable in question, and then position the tone probe next to the other end of each of the cables that might be the right one. The tone probe makes a sound when it's placed next to the right cable. Some toners have one tone probe that works with multiple tone generators. Each generator emits a separate frequency, and the probe sounds a different tone for each one. Even good toners are relatively inexpensive ($75 or so); although inexpensive toners can cost less than $25, they don't tend to work well, so spending a little more is worthwhile. Just keep in mind that if you have to support a network, you'd do best to own a decent toner.

Fixing Common Problems

Let's go back and look at the second possible meaning for a loss in connectivity. It's very common to try to connect to a shared resource and either fail or find that a shared resource you've used time and again has suddenly disappeared.

Failing to Connect to a New Resource

When you can't connect to a resource on the first try, it often points to a configuration issue. In most cases, a quick double-check of the sharing system will reveal one of the following problems (and call for the associated solution):

- You don't have the right share name? Go check at the serving system.
- You don't have the required user name/password? Ask someone who might have this knowledge, or double-check that your account has access.
- You don't have permission to use/access/connect to the shared resource? Make sure you have the correct permissions.
- You're not on the right homegroup/domain/workgroup? Check your system and the sharing system to verify which workgroup/domain name to use. On a homegroup, make sure you've used the proper password.
- The folder or printer isn't shared? Share it!
- The folder or printer doesn't exist? Make sure the serving system still hosts the folder you want. Install the network printer if you haven't yet.

Failing to Connect to a Previously Used Resource

If you suddenly can't connect to a resource that you've used many times before, go with the easy answers first:

- Check that you can see the resource using Network.
- Check that the serving system is on.
- Check that the computer is physically connected to the serving system.

The net Command

Windows enables you to view a network quickly from the command line through the *net command*. This works great when you plug into a network for the first time and, naturally, don't know the names of the other computers on that network. To see the many options that net offers, type **net** at a command prompt and press ENTER. The view and use options offer excellent network tools.

You can think of net view as the command-line version of Network. When run, net view returns a list of Windows computers on the network:

```
C:\Users\Mike>net view
Server Name            Remark
--------------------------------------------------
\\SABERTOOTH
\\UBERBOX
\\SERVER1
The command completed successfully.
C:\Users\Mike>
```

Once you know the names of the computers, you type **net view** followed by the computer name. The net view command will show any shares on that machine and whether they are mapped drives:

```
C:\>net view server1
Shared resources at SERVER1
Share name  Type  Used as  Comment
-------------------------------------------------------------
FREDC       Disk
Research    Disk  W:
The command completed successfully.
```

The net use command is a command-line method for mapping network shares. For example, if you wanted to map the Research share shown in the previous example to the X: drive, you simply type

```
C:\>net use x: \\server1\research
```

This will map drive X: to the Research share on the SERVER1 computer.

The nbtstat Command

The nbtstat command is an old command-line utility that predates Windows. It stands for NetBIOS over TCP/IP Statistics. Many versions ago, Windows used NetBIOS for many aspects of LAN file sharing, and even though NetBIOS is long gone, bits of NetBIOS hang on as a way for Windows to resolve host names on the network when a DNS server is not available.

While not as useful as it once was, nbtstat can still provide insight when troubleshooting naming issues in small workgroups. Here are a couple of usage examples. To see what your computer's NetBIOS name is, use the nbtstat –n command.

```
C:\Users\mmeyers>nbtstat -n

Local Area Connection:
```

```
Node IpAddress: [192.168.4.43] Scope Id: []

                NetBIOS Local Name Table

       Name               Type         Status
    ---------------------------------------------
    mmyers-ws      <00>  UNIQUE      Registered
    WORKGROUP      <00>  GROUP       Registered
    mmyers-ws      <20>  UNIQUE      Registered

C:\Users\mmeyers>
```

You can also query a remote machine by IP to find out its NetBIOS name with nbtstat –A (note the upper case "A", use a lowercase "a" if you know the machines NetBIOS name already).

```
C:\Users\mmeyers>nbtstat -A 192.168.4.52

Local Area Connection:
Node IpAddress: [192.168.4.43] Scope Id: []

           NetBIOS Remote Machine Name Table

       Name               Type         Status
    ---------------------------------------------
    UNITEDKINGDOM  <00>  UNIQUE      Registered
    UNITEDKINGDOM  <03>  UNIQUE      Registered
    UNITEDKINGDOM  <20>  UNIQUE      Registered
    ..__MSBROWSE__.<01>  GROUP       Registered
    TOTALHOME      <00>  GROUP       Registered
    TOTALHOME      <1D>  UNIQUE      Registered
    TOTALHOME      <1E>  GROUP       Registered

    MAC Address = 00-00-00-00-00-00
```

Finally, you can see all the names that NetBIOS has in its local cache with nbtstat –c.

```
C:\Users\mmeyers>nbtstat -c

Local Area Connection:
Node IpAddress: [192.168.4.43] Scope Id: []

                NetBIOS Remote Cache Name Table

       Name               Type       Host Address    Life [sec]
    ------------------------------------------------------------
    CLASS-SERVER   <00>  UNIQUE          192.168.4.50        447
    CLASS-SERVER   <20>  UNIQUE          192.168.4.50        447
    TOTALHOME      <1B>  UNIQUE          192.168.4.12        450
    UNITEDKINGDOM  <20>  UNIQUE          192.168.4.52        417
    UNITEDKINGDOM  <00>  UNIQUE          192.168.4.52        417
    WIN7-64        <20>  UNIQUE          192.168.4.220       450
```

Because the cache is temporary, you may find that it is empty if you haven't browsed your LAN or interacted with another machine recently.

Chapter Review

Questions

1. Steven's Windows system can't connect to the Internet, and he comes to you, his PC tech, for help. You figure out that it's a DHCP problem. What program should you run to troubleshoot his DHCP problem from the client side?
   - **A.** ipconfig
   - **B.** ifconfig
   - **C.** config
   - **D.** dhcp /review
2. What command would you use to view the path taken by an Ethernet packet?
   - **A.** ping
   - **B.** ipconfig
   - **C.** tracert
   - **D.** nslookup
3. Which of the following is the correct net syntax for discovering which network shares on a particular server are mapped on your computer?
   - **A.** net view \\fileserver
   - **B.** net \\fileserver
   - **C.** net map \\fileserver
   - **D.** net share \\fileserver
4. What small device enables you to test a NIC's circuitry?
   - **A.** Loopback plug
   - **B.** Port tester
   - **C.** Multimeter
   - **D.** Integrated network and logic probe
5. Which command can be used to display the cached NetBIOS names for a Windows system?
   - **A.** nslookup
   - **B.** dig --cache
   - **C.** nbtstat -c
   - **D.** nbtstat -a

6. You are down under your desk organizing some wires when you notice that the activity light on your NIC is blinking erratically. Is there a problem?
   - **A.** Yes, the activity light should be on steadily when the computer is running.
   - **B.** Yes, the activity light should be blinking steadily, not randomly.
   - **C.** No, the light blinks when there is network traffic.
   - **D.** No, the light blinks to show bus activity.
7. What is a common symptom of a bad network cable?
   - **A.** Rapidly blinking link lights
   - **B.** No link lights
   - **C.** Solid on link lights
   - **D.** Steady blinking link lights
8. What command-line utility would you run to show a list of network computers?
   - **A.** net send
   - **B.** show net_servers
   - **C.** net use
   - **D.** net view
9. What benefit does full-duplex offer?
   - **A.** It enables NICs to send and receive signals at the same time.
   - **B.** It enables NICs to send data twice as fast.
   - **C.** It enables NICs to receive data twice as fast.
   - **D.** It enables a switch to connect to both coaxial and fiber optic cables.
10. What do most techs call a toner or tone generator?
    - **A.** TDR
    - **B.** UTP
    - **C.** UDP
    - **D.** Fox and Hound

Answers

1. **A.** You should run ipconfig, or more specifically ipconfig /release and then ipconfig /renew to get a new IP address if a DHCP server is available for Steven's Windows system. This typically resolves most DHCP client-side problems. ifconfig is the program used by Mac OS X and Linux systems for this task. Neither config nor dhcp is valid.
2. **C.** The tracert command in Windows traces the path a data packet takes to get to its destination. Mac OS X and Linux use the traceroute utility for similar purposes.

3. **A.** To see the network shares mapped on your computer, use net view \\fileserver.
4. **A.** A loopback plug will test the NIC's Ethernet port and circuitry.
5. **C.** Nslookup and dig only work with DNS, not NetBIOS. Nbtstat -a is for querying a remote system's name, but nbtstat -c displays the cached names.
6. **C.** The lights should be blinking to show activity—this is normal.
7. **B.** If there are no link lights, you probably have a bad network cable.
8. **D.** Use the net view command to show a list of computers on the network.
9. **A.** Full-duplex technology enables NICs to send and receive signals at the same time.
10. **D.** Most techs refer to a toner or tone generator as a Fox and Hound, the name of a popular brand of tone generator.

CHAPTER 22

Wireless Networking

In this chapter, you will learn how to

- Discuss wireless networking components
- Analyze and explain wireless networking standards
- Install and configure wireless networks
- Troubleshoot wireless networks

Wireless networks have been popular for many years now, but unlike wired networks, so much of how wireless works continues to elude people. Part of the problem might be that a simple wireless network is so inexpensive and easy to configure that most users and techs never really get into the *hows* of wireless. The chance to get away from all the cables and mess and just *connect* has a phenomenal appeal. Let's change all that and dive deeply into wireless networking.

Historical/Conceptual

Wireless Networking Components

Instead of a physical set of wires running between network nodes, wireless networks use either radio waves or beams of infrared light to communicate with each other. Various kinds of wireless networking solutions have come and gone in the past. The wireless radio wave networks you'll find yourself supporting these days are based on the *IEEE 802.11* wireless Ethernet standard—marketed as Wi-Fi—and on Bluetooth technology. Wireless networks using infrared light are limited to those that use the Infrared Data Association (IrDA) protocol. Finally, the cell phone companies have gotten into the mix and offer access to the Internet through cellular networks.

Wireless networking capabilities of one form or another are built into many modern computing devices. Infrared *transceiver* ports have been standard issue on portable computers and high-end printers for years, although they're absent from most of the latest PCs and portable computers. Figure 22-1 shows the infrared transceiver ports on an older laptop and personal digital assistant (PDA)—a precursor to the smartphone. Back in the day, these infrared capabilities were used to transfer data between nearby devices. Today an infrared interface on a device such as a smartphone is present primarily so the device can be used as a wireless remote control. In place of infrared as a data transfer mechanism, Wi-Fi and Bluetooth capabilities are now common as integrated components and you can easily add them when they aren't. Figure 22-2 shows a PCIe Wi-Fi adapter. Built-in cellular networking is less common, but it is similarly easy to add. You can also add wireless network capabilities by using external USB wireless network adapters, as shown in Figure 22-3.

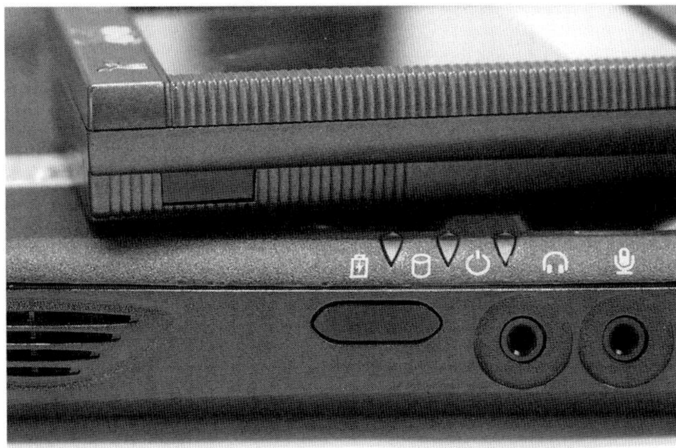

Figure 22-1 Infrared transceiver ports on a laptop and PDA

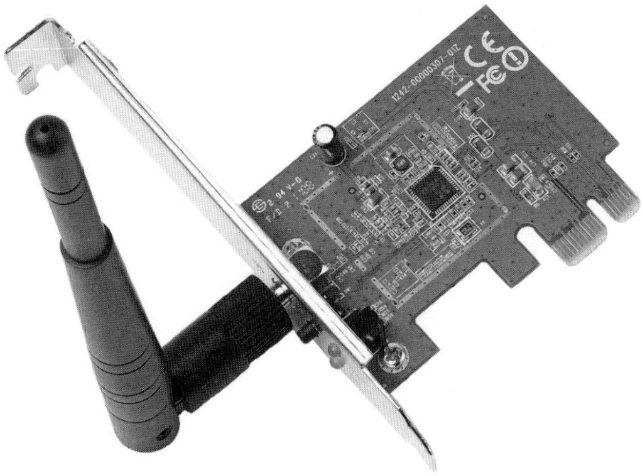

Figure 22-2 Wireless PCIe add-on card

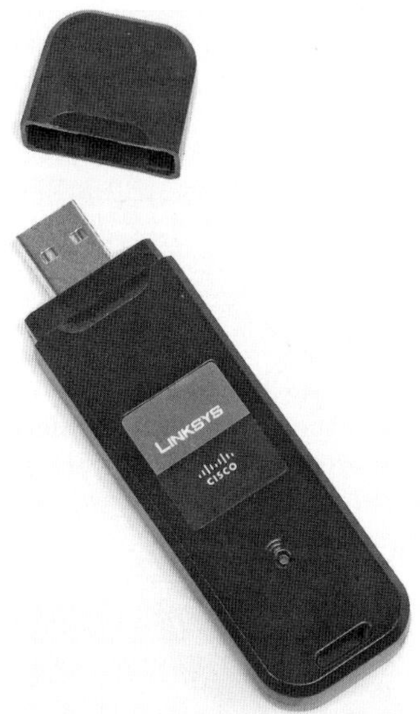

Figure 22-3 External USB wireless NIC

Wireless networking is not limited to PCs. Most smartphones and tablets have wireless capabilities built-in or available as add-on options. Figure 22-4 shows a smartphone accessing the Internet over a Wi-Fi connection.

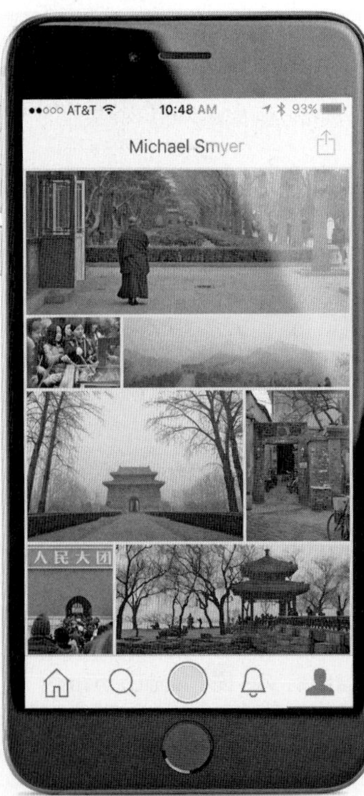

Figure 22-4 Smartphone with wireless capability

NOTE See Chapter 25 for the scoop on mobile devices like smartphones and tablets.

901

To extend the capabilities of a wireless Ethernet network, such as connecting to a wired network or sharing a high-speed Internet connection, you need a *wireless access point (WAP)*. A WAP centrally connects wireless network nodes in the same way that a hub connects wired Ethernet PCs. Many WAPs also act as switches and Internet routers, such as the Linksys device shown in Figure 22-5.

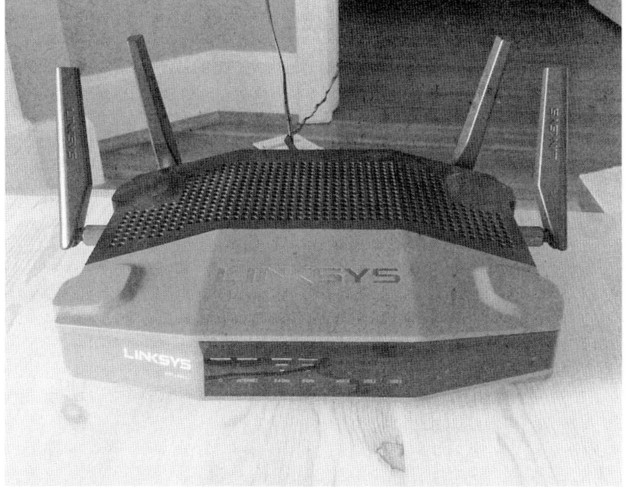

Figure 22-5 Linksys device that acts as wireless access point, switch, and router

Like any other electronic devices, most WAPs draw their power from a wall outlet. More advanced WAPs, especially those used in corporate settings, can also use a feature called *Power over Ethernet (PoE)*. Using PoE, you only need to plug a single Ethernet cable into the WAP to provide both power and a network connection.

NOTE Other devices can use PoE, even in places where there's no power. A Power over Ethernet injector, for example, can extend a PoE connection 100 meters. This is great for security cameras.

Wireless communication via Bluetooth comes as a built-in option on newer PCs and peripheral devices, or you can add it to an older PC via an external USB Bluetooth adapter. Figure 22-6 shows a Bluetooth adapter with a Bluetooth-enabled mouse and keyboard.

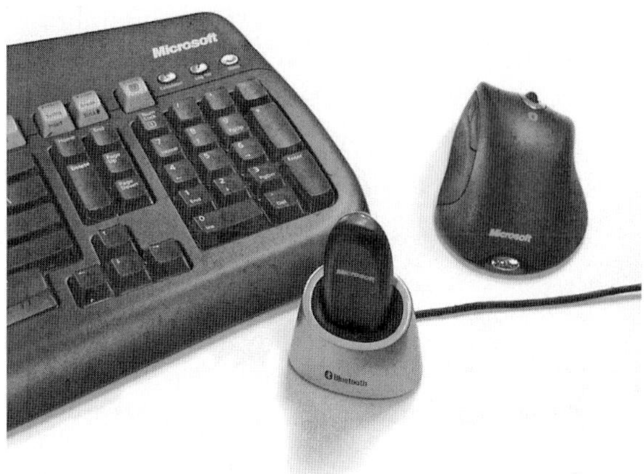

Figure 22-6 External USB Bluetooth adapter, keyboard, and mouse

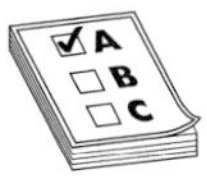

EXAM TIP Wireless access points are commonly known as WAPs, APs, or access points.

Wireless Networking Software

Wireless devices use the same networking protocols and client that their wired counterparts use, and they operate by using the *carrier sense multiple access/collision avoidance (CSMA/CA)* networking scheme. The *collision avoidance* aspect differs slightly from the *collision detection* standard used in wired Ethernet. A wireless node listens in on the wireless medium to see if another node is currently broadcasting data. If so, it waits a random amount of time before retrying. So far, this method is exactly the same as the method used by wired Ethernet networks. Because wireless nodes have a more difficult time detecting data collisions, however, they offer the option of using the *Request to Send/Clear to Send (RTS/CTS)* protocol. With this protocol enabled, a transmitting node sends an RTS frame to the receiving node after it determines the wireless medium is clear to use. The receiving node responds with a CTS frame, telling the sending node that it's okay to transmit. Then, once the data is sent, the transmitting node waits for an acknowledgment (ACK) from the receiving node before sending the next data packet. This option is very elegant, but keep in mind that using RTS/CTS introduces significant overhead to the process and can impede performance.

In terms of configuring wireless networking software, you need to do very little. Wireless network adapters are plug and play, so any modern version of Windows immediately recognizes one when it is installed, prompting you to load any needed hardware drivers. You will, however, need a utility to set parameters such as the network name.

Current versions of Windows include built-in tools for configuring these settings, but some wireless adapters also come with configuration tools provided by the wireless

network adapter vendor (see Figure 22-7). Using this utility, you can determine your link state and signal strength, configure your wireless networking *mode* (discussed next), and set options for security encryption, power saving, and so on.

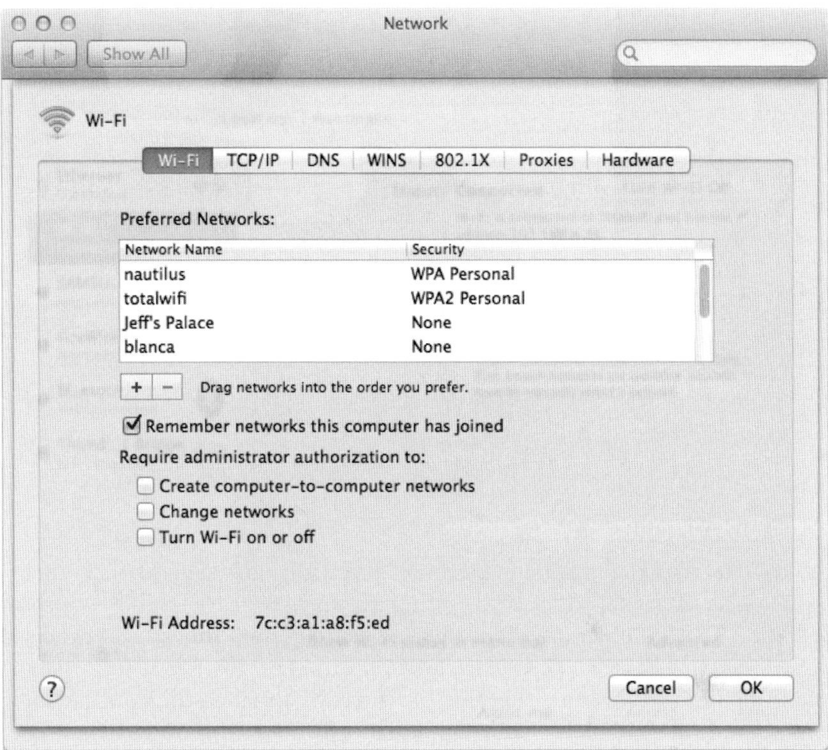

Figure 22-7 Wireless configuration utility

Wireless Network Modes

The simplest wireless network consists of two or more PCs communicating directly with each other without cabling or any other intermediary hardware. More complicated wireless networks use a WAP to centralize wireless communication and bridge wireless network segments to wired network segments. These two methods are called ad hoc mode and infrastructure mode.

Ad Hoc Mode

Ad hoc mode is sometimes called *peer-to-peer mode*, with each wireless node in direct contact with every other node in a decentralized free-for-all, as shown in Figure 22-8. Two or more wireless nodes communicating in ad hoc mode form what's called an *Independent Basic Service Set (IBSS)*. Ad hoc mode networks are suited for small groups

of computers (less than a dozen or so) that need to transfer files or share printers. Ad hoc mode networks are also good for temporary networks such as study groups or business meetings.

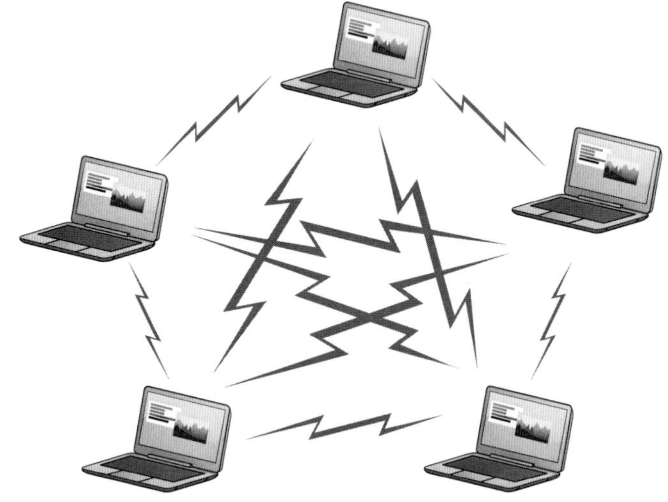

Figure 22-8 Wireless ad hoc mode network

Infrastructure Mode

Wireless networks running in *infrastructure mode* use one or more WAPs to connect the wireless network nodes to a wired network segment, as shown in Figure 22-9. A single WAP servicing a given area is called a *Basic Service Set (BSS)*. This service area can be extended by adding more WAPs. This is called, appropriately, an *Extended Basic Service Set (EBSS)*.

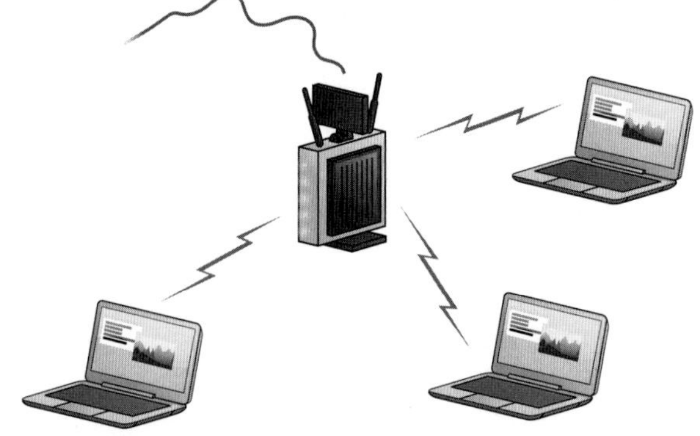

Figure 22-9 Wireless infrastructure mode network

Wireless networks running in infrastructure mode require more planning and are more complicated to configure than ad hoc mode networks, but they also give you fine control over how the network operates. Infrastructure mode is better suited to networks that need to share dedicated resources such as Internet connections and centralized

databases. Infrastructure networks are created to support small office/home office (SOHO) networks and the access points in these environments are known as SOHO WAPs and SOHO routers.

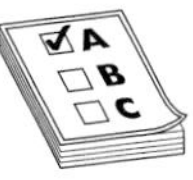

EXAM TIP The CompTIA A+ 220-901 exam will most likely ask you about the appropriate scenario for implementing an infrastructure vs. adhoc (*sic*) Wi-Fi network. Infrastructure is the default, but ad hoc makes sense for limited impromptu networks.

902

Wireless Networking Security

One of the major complaints against wireless networking is that it offers weak security, but the industry has made progress on this front in recent years. After all, data packets are floating through the air instead of safely wrapped up inside network cabling—what's to stop an unscrupulous person with the right equipment from grabbing those packets out of the air and reading that data? In the past, you could access a wireless network by walking into a WAP's coverage area, turning on a wireless device, and connecting. These days, it has grown hard to find accidentally open networks as hardware makers have trended toward using some type of security by default. Still, issues with these well-intentioned defaults are common, so it's still important to take a critical look at the settings on new equipment.

Wireless networks use three methods to secure access to the network itself and secure the data being transferred: MAC address filtering, authentication, and data encryption. But before anyone encounters our on-network security, there are some measures we can take to reduce the likelihood our network will be targeted in the first place. Let's take a look at these practices first, followed by the methods for securing the network itself.

SSID

The *service set identifier (SSID)* parameter—also called the *network name*—defines the wireless network. Wireless devices *want* to be heard, and WAPs are usually configured to announce their presence by broadcasting the SSID to their maximum range. This is very handy when you have a number of wireless networks in the same area, but a default SSID also gives away important clues about the manufacturer (and maybe even model) of your access point.

Always change the default SSID to something unique, and change the password right away. Configuring a unique SSID name and password is the very least that you should do to secure a wireless network. Older default SSID names and passwords are well known and widely available online. While newer models may come with unique SSIDs and passwords, the SSID may still leak information about your hardware—and the generated password may use rules that make it easy to break.

These defaults are intended to make setting up a wireless network as easy as possible but can cause problems in places with a lot of overlapping wireless networks. Keep in mind that each wireless network node and access point needs to be configured with the same unique SSID name. This SSID name is then included in the header of every data packet broadcast in the wireless network's coverage area. Data packets that lack the correct SSID name in the header are rejected. When it comes to picking a new unique SSID, it's still good to think about whether the name will make your network a more interesting target, or give away details that could help an attacker gain physical or remote access.

Another trick often seen in wireless networks is to tell the WAP not to broadcast the SSID. People not authorized to access the network will have a harder time knowing it's there, as it won't show up in the list of nearby networks on most devices.

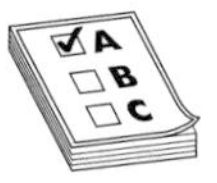

EXAM TIP CompTIA lists changing the default SSID and disabling SSID broadcast on the WAP as steps for securing a new wireless network. These practices for managing your SSID don't secure your network, but they can keep you from catching the attention of someone targeting known vulnerabilities with specific hardware and default settings.

Access Point Placement and Radio Power

When setting up a wireless network, keep the space in mind; you can limit risk by hiding the network from outsiders. When using an omni-directional antenna that sends and receives signals in all directions, for example, keep it near the center of the home or office. The closer you place it to a wall, the further away someone outside the home or office can be and still detect the wireless network.

Many wireless access points enable you to adjust the radio power levels of the antenna. Decrease the radio power until you can get reception at the furthest point *inside* the target network space, but not outside. This will take some trial and error.

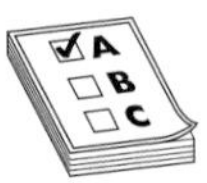

EXAM TIP Don't forget to secure the WAP. Most WAPs have physical Ethernet ports in addition to their wireless capabilities. These ports are not password-protected or encrypted. Keep the WAP in a location where unscrupulous folks can't get to it.

MAC Address Filtering

Most WAPs also support *MAC address filtering*, a method that enables you to limit access to your wireless network based on the physical, hard-wired address of the units' wireless NIC. MAC address filtering is a handy way of creating a type of "accepted users" list to limit access to your wireless network, but it works best when you have a small number of users. A table stored in the WAP lists the MAC addresses that are permitted to participate in the wireless network. Any data packets that don't contain the MAC address of a node listed in the table are rejected.

NOTE Many techs shorten the term "MAC address filtering" to simply "MAC filtering." Either way works.

WEP

Early on, Wi-Fi developers introduced the *Wired Equivalent Privacy (WEP)* protocol to attempt to ensure that data is secured while in transit over the airwaves. WEP encryption uses a standard 40-bit encryption to scramble data packets. Many vendors also support 104-bit encryption. Note that some vendors advertise 128-bit encryption, but they actually use a 104-bit encryption key. Unfortunately, WEP encryption includes a flaw that makes it extremely vulnerable to attack. Although WEP is better than no encryption at all, keep in mind that WEP will not protect you from knowledgeable intruders.

It's worth knowing that all WEP traffic is encrypted with the same key, so one user's traffic isn't protected from other members of the network. For improved encryption which uses a different key for each client, see WPA or WPA2, both discussed next.

WPA

The *Wi-Fi Protected Access (WPA)* protocol addresses the weaknesses of WEP and acts as a security protocol upgrade to WEP. WPA uses the *Temporal Key Integrity Protocol (TKIP)*, which provides a new encryption key for every sent packet. This protects WPA from many of the attacks that make WEP vulnerable, though TKIP has since been deprecated, as it has flaws of its own. WPA also offers security enhancements over WEP such as an encryption key integrity-checking feature and user authentication through the industry-standard *Extensible Authentication Protocol (EAP)*. EAP provides a huge security improvement over WEP encryption. Even with these enhancements, WPA was intended only as an interim security solution until the IEEE 802.11i (wireless security standards committee) finalized and implemented the next generation of wireless security: WPA2.

WPA2

Today, Linux, Mac OS X, and Windows support the full IEEE 802.11i standard, more commonly known as *Wi-Fi Protected Access 2 (WPA2)*, to lock down wireless networks. WPA2 uses the *Advanced Encryption Standard (AES)*, among other improvements, to provide a secure wireless environment. If you haven't upgraded to WPA2, you should. All current WAPs and wireless clients support WPA2 and most routers have a "backward compatible" mode for the handful of client devices that still use first-generation WPA. This is necessary when using older network cards or WAPs—think early implementations of 802.11b wireless networking—because the old hardware in these products cannot support WPA2. Later iterations of these devices have upgrades to support AES and WPA2.

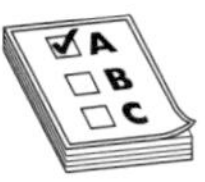

EXAM TIP Be sure you are familiar with WEP, WPA, WPA2, TKIP, and AES wireless encryption types.

WPS

While most techs can configure wireless networks blindfolded, the thought of passwords and encryption might intimidate the average user. Most people just plug in their wireless router and go on their merry way. Because everyone should secure their wireless network, the developers of Wi-Fi created *Wi-Fi Protected Setup (WPS)*, a standard included on most WAPs and clients to make secure connections easier to configure.

WPS works in one of two ways. Some devices use a push button, such as the one shown in Figure 22-10, and others use a password or code.

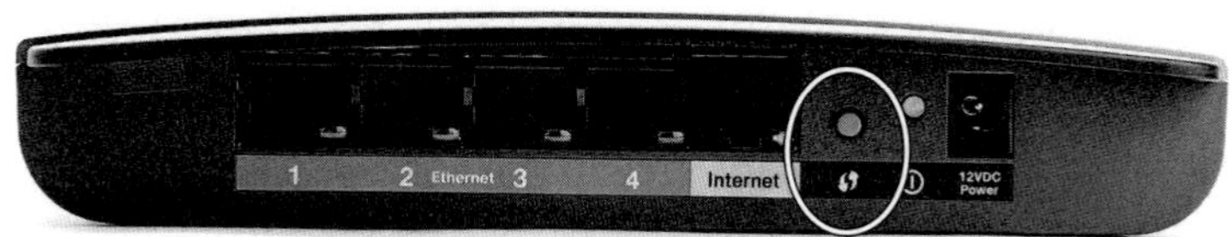

Figure 22-10 WPS button on an e2500 Router

Let's say you want to connect a WPS-capable wireless printer to a WPS-capable WAP. First, you would press the button on the printer for a short moment (usually two seconds). You then have a set time (usually two minutes) to press the button on the WAP. This should automatically configure a secure connection.

Some devices enable you to use a code. A WPS-capable WAP will have an eight-digit numeric code printed on the device. To access the WAP, just enter the code in Windows as you would a WPA/WPA2 password. Now you're on the network.

Sadly, WPS has a security flaw. A hacker can use a program to repeatedly guess the eight-digit code. Because of how the code is set up, it's very easy to guess. As long you have WPS enabled on your WAP, you are vulnerable. The only way to stop this hack is to shut down WPS. Check the WAP manufacturer's Web site for instructions on turning off WPS.

901

Speed and Range Issues

Wireless networking data throughput speeds depend on several factors. Foremost is the standard that the wireless devices use. Depending on the standard used, wireless throughput speeds range from a measly 2 Mbps to a snappy 1+ Gbps. One of the other factors affecting speed is the distance between wireless nodes (or between wireless nodes and centralized access points). Wireless devices dynamically negotiate the top speed at which they can communicate without dropping too many data packets. Speed decreases

as distance increases, so the maximum throughput speed is achieved only at extremely close range (less than 25 feet or so). At the outer reaches of a device's effective range, speed may decrease to around 1 Mbps before it drops out altogether.

Interference caused by solid objects and other wireless devices operating in the same frequency range—such as cordless phones or baby monitors—can reduce both speed and range. So-called *dead spots* occur when something capable of blocking the radio signal comes between the wireless network nodes. Large electrical appliances such as refrigerators block wireless network signals *very* effectively. Other culprits include electrical fuse boxes, metal plumbing, air conditioning units, and similar objects.

NOTE You can see the speed and signal strength on your wireless network by looking at the wireless NIC's properties. In current versions of Windows, open the Network and Sharing Center, select Change Adapter Settings, then right-click your wireless NIC and select Status.

Wireless networking range is difficult to define, and you'll see most descriptions listed with qualifiers, such as "*around* 150 feet" and "*about* 300 feet." This is simply because, like throughput speed, range is greatly affected by outside factors. Interference from other wireless devices affects range, as does interference from solid objects. The maximum ranges listed in the next section are those presented by wireless manufacturers as the theoretical maximum ranges. In the real world, you'll experience these ranges only under the most ideal circumstances. True effective range is probably about half what you see listed.

You can increase range in a couple of ways. You can install multiple WAPs to permit "roaming" between one WAP's coverage area and another's—an EBSS, described earlier in this chapter. Or, you can install a replacement WAP with greater signal strength and range. If that is still not enough, signal boosters that can give you even more power are available, as are *wireless repeaters/extenders* which can receive and re-broadcast your Wi-Fi signal.

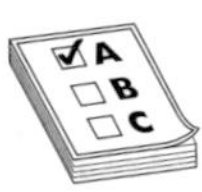

EXAM TIP Look for basic troubleshooting questions on the CompTIA A+ certification exams dealing with factors that affect wireless connectivity, range, and speed.

Wireless Networking Standards

Today's wireless world is dominated by *radio frequency (RF)* technologies, in particular the 802.11 (Wi-Fi) standards. Other standards, such as infrared, Bluetooth, and cellular, hold a strong place in today's market, as well. To help you gain a better understanding of wireless network technologies, this section provides a brief look at the standards they use.

IEEE 802.11-Based Wireless Networking

The IEEE 802.11 wireless Ethernet standard, more commonly known as *Wi-Fi*, defines methods devices may use to communicate via *spread-spectrum* radio waves. Spread-spectrum

broadcasts data in small, discrete chunks over the frequencies available within a certain frequency range.

NOTE In the early days of wireless networking, many techs and marketing people assumed Wi-Fi stood for *Wireless Fidelity*, a sort of play on the common sound signal of high fidelity. It might have at one time, but the Wi-Fi Alliance, the governing standards body for 802.11-based networking, just uses the term Wi-Fi today.

The 802.11-based wireless technologies broadcast and receive on one of two radio bands: 2.4 GHz and 5 GHz. A band is a contiguous range of frequencies that is usually divided up into discrete slices called *channels*. Over the years, the original 802.11 standard has been extended to 802.11a, 802.11b, 802.11g, 802.11n, and 802.11ac variations used in Wi-Fi wireless networks. Each of these versions of 802.11 uses one of the two bands, with the exception of 802.11n, which uses one but may use both. Don't worry; I'll break this down for you in a moment.

NOTE Wi-Fi is by far the most widely adopted wireless local networking type today, while cellular is the big dog in wide area roaming networks. Not only do millions of private businesses and homes have wireless networks, but many public places such as coffee shops and libraries also offer Internet access through wireless networks.

Newer wireless devices typically provide backward compatibility with older wireless devices. If you are using an 802.11n WAP, all of your 802.11g devices can use it. An 802.11ac WAP is backward compatible with 802.11b, g, and n. The exception to this is 802.11a, which requires a 5 GHz radio, meaning only 802.11ac and dual-band 802.11n WAPs are backwards compatible with 802.11a devices. The following paragraphs describe the important specifications of each of the popular 802.11-based wireless networking standards.

802.11a Despite the "a" designation for this extension to the 802.11 standard, *802.11a* was actually on the market *after* 802.11b. The 802.11a standard differs from the other 802.11-based standards in significant ways. Foremost is that it operates in the 5-GHz frequency range. This means devices using this standard are less prone to interference from other devices that use the same frequency range. 802.11a also offers considerably greater throughput than 802.11 and 802.11b at speeds up to 54 Mbps, though its actual throughput is no more than 25 Mbps in normal traffic conditions. Although its theoretical range tops out at about 150 feet, its maximum range will be lower in a typical office environment. Despite the superior speed of 802.11a, it isn't as widely adopted in the PC world as some of the following 802.11 versions.

802.11b *802.11b* was the first standard to take off and become ubiquitous in wireless networking. The 802.11b standard supports data throughput of up to 11 Mbps (with actual throughput averaging 4 to 6 Mbps)—on par with older wired 10BaseT

networks—and a maximum range of 300 feet under ideal conditions. In a typical office environment, its maximum range is lower. The main downside to using 802.11b is that it uses a very popular frequency. The 2.4-GHz ISM band is already crowded with baby monitors, garage door openers, microwaves, and wireless phones, so you're likely to run into interference from other wireless devices.

802.11g *802.11g* came out in 2003, taking the best of 802.11a and b and rolling them into a single standard. 802.11g offers data transfer speeds equivalent to 802.11a, up to 54 Mbps, with the wider 300-foot range of 802.11b. More important, 802.11g runs in the 2.4-GHz ISM band, so it is backward compatible with 802.11b, meaning that the same 802.11g WAP can service both 802.11b and 802.11g wireless nodes.

802.11n The *802.11n* standard brought several improvements to Wi-Fi networking, including faster speeds and new antenna technology implementations.

The 802.11n specification requires all but hand-held devices to use multiple antennas to implement a feature called *multiple in/multiple out (MIMO)*, which enables the devices to make multiple simultaneous connections. With up to four antennas, 802.11n devices can achieve amazing speeds. The official standard supports throughput of up to 600 Mbps, although practical implementation drops that down substantially.

NOTE Because cellular telephones typically support both cellular networks and 802.11x Wi-Fi networks, many can be used to bridge the gap. Using internal utilities or apps, you can set up your phone as a Wi-Fi WAP that can pass signals to and from the Internet via the cellular connection. Turning your phone into a WAP is known as *creating a hotspot*; using it to bridge to the cellular network is called *tethering*. Check out Chapters 23, 24, and 25 for the scoop on these techniques.

Many 802.11n WAPs employ *transmit beamforming*, a multiple-antenna technology that helps get rid of dead spots—or at least make them not so bad. The antennas adjust the signal once the WAP discovers a client to optimize the radio signal.

Like 802.11g, 802.11n WAPs can run in the 2.4-GHz ISM band, supporting earlier, slower 802.11b/g devices. 802.11n also supports the more powerful, so-called *dual-band* operation. To use dual-band, you need a more advanced (and more expensive) WAP that runs at both 5 GHz and 2.4 GHz simultaneously; some support 802.11a devices as well as 802.11b/g devices.

802.11ac 802.11ac is a natural expansion of the 802.11n standard, incorporating even more streams, wider bandwidth, and higher speed. To avoid *device density* issues in the 2.4-GHz band, 802.11ac only uses the 5-GHz band. The latest versions of 802.11ac include a new version of MIMO called *Multiuser MIMO (MU-MIMO)*. MU-MIMO gives a WAP the ability to broadcast to multiple users simultaneously. Like 802.11n, 802.11ac supports dual-band operation.

Table 22-1 compares the important differences among the versions of 802.11*x*.

Standard	802.11a	802.11b	802.11g	802.11n	802.11ac
Max. throughput	54 Mbps	11 Mbps	54 Mbps	100+ Mbps	1+ Gbps
Max. range	150 feet	300 feet	300 feet	300+ feet	300+ feet
Frequency	5 GHz	2.4 GHz	2.4 GHz	2.4 and 5 GHz	5 GHz
Security	SSID, MAC filtering, industry-standard WEP, WPA, WPA2	SSID, MAC filtering, industry-standard WEP, WPA, WPA2 (later hardware)	SSID, MAC filtering, industry-standard WEP, WPA, WPA2	SSID, MAC filtering, industry-standard WEP, WPA, WPA2	SSID, MAC filtering, industry-standard WEP, WPA, WPA2
Compatibility	802.11a	802.11b	802.11b, 802.11g	802.11b, 802.11g, 802.11n, (802.11a in some cases)	802.11a, 802.11b, 802.11g, 802.11n
Communication mode	Ad hoc or infrastructure	Ad hoc or infrastructure	Ad hoc or infrastructure	Ad hoc or infrastructure	Ad hoc or infrastructure
Description	Eight available channels. Less prone to interference than 802.11b and 802.11g.	Fourteen channels available in the 2.4-GHz band (only eleven of which can be used in the U.S. due to FCC regulations). Three non-overlapping channels.	Improved security enhancements. Fourteen channels available in the 2.4-GHz band (only eleven of which can be used in the U.S. due to FCC regulations). Three non-overlapping channels.	Same as 802.11g but adds the 5-GHz band that 802.11a uses. 802.11n can also make use of multiple antennas (MIMO) to increase its range and speed.	Expands on 802.11n by adding streams, bandwidth, and higher speed in the 5-GHz band. Uses MU-MIMO and beamforming antenna technology to optimize wireless connections.

Table 22-1 Comparison of 802.11 Standards

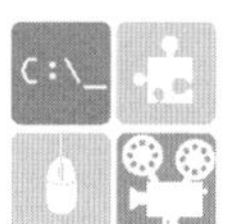

SIM Check out the "Wireless Technologies" Challenge! sim in the Chapter 22 section of http://totalsem.com/90x to reinforce the differences among 802.11a, 802.11b, 802.11g, 802.11n, and 802.11ac. This will help you with any performance-based questions CompTIA might throw your way.

Other Wireless Standards

While Wi-Fi dominates the wireless networking market, it isn't the only standard. A lot of smaller networks (we're talking two computers small) use infrared or Bluetooth to connect devices. Mobile devices, such as smartphones, wearables, and tablets, connect wirelessly via cellular networks. They often use other standards to connect with each other or to other technologies such as car stereos, GPS devices, smart televisions, flying drones, and an endless litany of wireless-enabled products.

Infrared Wireless Networking

Wireless networking using infrared technology is largely overlooked these days, probably because of the explosion of interest in newer, faster wireless and cellular standards. But it is still a viable method to transfer files on some older devices.

Communication through infrared devices is implemented via the *Infrared Data Association (IrDA)* protocol. The IrDA protocol stack is a widely supported industry standard and has been included in all versions of Windows since Windows 95.

NOTE Apple and Linux computers also support IrDA.

In speed and range, infrared isn't very impressive. Infrared devices are capable of transferring data up to 4 Mbps—not too shabby, but hardly stellar. The maximum distance between infrared devices is 1 meter. Infrared links are direct line-of-sight and are susceptible to interference. Anything that breaks the beam of light can disrupt an infrared link: a badly placed can of Mountain Dew, a coworker passing between desks, or even bright sunlight hitting the infrared transceiver can cause interference.

Infrared is designed to make a point-to-point connection between two devices only in ad hoc mode. No infrastructure mode is available. You can, however, use an infrared access point device to enable Ethernet network communication using IrDA. Infrared devices operate at half-duplex, meaning that while one is talking, the other is listening—they can't talk and listen at the same time. IrDA has a mode that emulates full-duplex communication, but it's really half-duplex. The IrDA protocol offers exactly nothing in the way of encryption or authentication. Infrared's main security feature is the fact that you have to be literally within arm's reach to establish a link. Clearly, infrared is not the best solution for a dedicated network connection, but for a quick file transfer or print job without getting your hands dirty, it'll do in a pinch.

Max. throughput	Up to 4 Mbps
Max. range	1 meter (39 inches)
Security	None
Compatibility	IrDA
Communication mode	Point-to-point ad hoc

NOTE You may find some older laptops with a little infrared window, but don't let that fool you into thinking the laptop has IrDA networking. These IR receivers are for use with remotes so you can use the laptop just like a TV or DVD player.

Bluetooth

Bluetooth wireless technology (named for tenth-century Danish king Harald Bluetooth) is designed to create small wireless networks preconfigured to do very specific jobs. Some great examples are wearable technology, audio devices such as headsets or automotive entertainment systems that connect to your smartphone, *personal area networks (PANs)* that link two PCs for a quick-and-dirty wireless network, and input devices such as keyboards and mice. Bluetooth is *not* designed to be a full-function networking solution, nor is it meant to compete with Wi-Fi.

Bluetooth, like any technology, has been upgraded over the years to make it faster and more secure. The first generation (versions 1.1 and 1.2) supports speeds around 1 Mbps. The second generation (2.0 and 2.1) is backward compatible with its first-generation cousins and adds support for more speed by introducing Enhanced Data Rate (EDR), which pushes top speeds to around 3 Mbps. The third generation (3.0 + HS) tops out at 24 Mbps, but this is accomplished over an 802.11 connection after Bluetooth negotiation. The High Speed (+ HS) feature is optional. Instead of continuing to increase top speed, the fourth generation (4.0, 4.1, and 4.2), also called Bluetooth Smart, is largely focused on improving Bluetooth's suitability for use in networked "smart" devices/appliances by reducing cost and power consumption, improving speed and security, and introducing IP connectivity.

The IEEE organization has made first-generation Bluetooth the basis for its 802.15 standard for wireless PANs. Bluetooth uses a broadcasting method that switches between any of the 79 frequencies available in the 2.45-GHz range. Bluetooth hops frequencies some 1600 times per second, making it highly resistant to interference.

Generally, the faster and further a device sends data, the more power it needs to do so, and the Bluetooth designers understood a long time ago that some devices (such as a Bluetooth headset) could save power by not sending data as quickly or as far as other Bluetooth devices may need. To address this, all Bluetooth devices are configured for one of three classes that define maximum power usage in milliwatts (mW) and maximum distance:

Class 1	100 mW	100 meters
Class 2	2.5 mW	10 meters
Class 3	1 mW	1 meter

Bluetooth personal networks are made to replace the snake's nest of cables that currently connects most PCs to their various peripheral devices—keyboard, mouse, printer, speakers, scanner, and the like—but you probably won't be swapping out your 802.11-based networking devices with Bluetooth-based replacements anytime soon. Despite this, Bluetooth's recent introduction of IP connectivity may bring more and more Bluetooth-related traffic to 802.11 devices in the future.

Having said that, Bluetooth-enabled wireless networking is comparable to other wireless technologies in a few ways:

- Like infrared, Bluetooth is acceptable for quick file transfers where a wired connection (or a faster wireless connection) is unavailable.
- Bluetooth's speed and range make it a good match for wireless print server solutions.

Bluetooth hardware comes either built into most newer portable electronic gadgets such as smartphones or as an adapter added to an internal or external expansion bus. Bluetooth networking is enabled through ad hoc device-to-device connections, or in an infrastructure-like mode through Bluetooth access points. Bluetooth access points are very similar to 802.11-based access points, bridging wireless Bluetooth PAN segments to wired LAN segments.

Cellular

A *cellular wireless network* enables you to connect to the Internet through a network-aware smartphone, tablet, or other mobile device. To learn more about cellular data networks, check out Chapter 23.

902

Installing and Configuring Wireless Networking

The mechanics of setting up a wireless network don't differ much from a wired network. Physically installing a wireless network adapter is the same as installing a wired NIC, whether it's an internal card, a laptop add-on wireless card, or an external USB device. Simply install the device and let plug and play handle the rest. Install the device's supplied driver when prompted and you're practically finished.

The trick is in configuring the wireless network so that only specific wireless nodes are able to use it, and securing the data that's being sent through the air.

Wi-Fi Configuration

Wi-Fi networks support ad hoc and infrastructure operation modes. Which mode you choose depends on the number of wireless nodes you need to support, the type of data sharing they'll perform, and your management requirements.

Ad Hoc Mode

Ad hoc mode wireless networks don't need a WAP. The only requirements in an ad hoc mode wireless network are that each wireless node be configured with the same network name (SSID) and that no two nodes use the same IP address. Figure 22-11 shows a wireless network configuration utility with ad hoc mode selected.

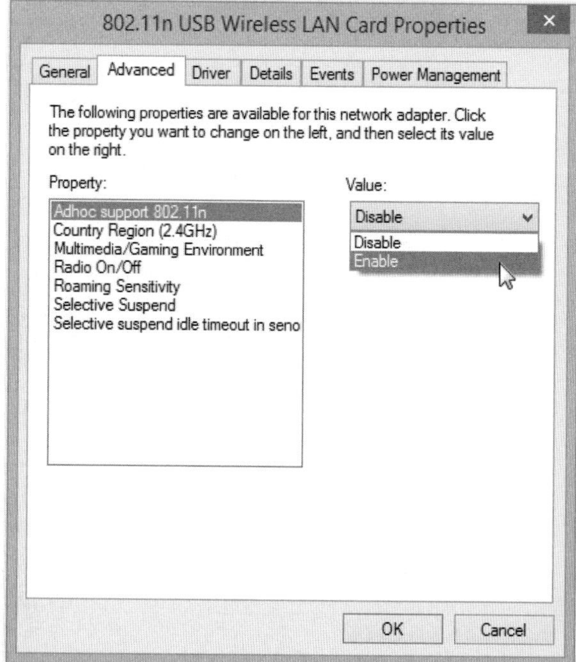

Figure 22-11 Selecting ad hoc mode in a wireless configuration utility

The only other configuration steps to take are to make sure no two nodes are using the same IP address (this step is usually unnecessary if all nodes are using DHCP) and ensuring that the File and Printer Sharing service is running on all nodes.

Infrastructure Mode

Typically, infrastructure mode wireless networks employ one or more WAPs connected to a wired network segment, such as a corporate intranet, the Internet, or both. As with ad hoc mode wireless networks, infrastructure mode networks require that the same SSID be configured on all nodes and WAPs. Figure 22-12 shows Ubuntu's Wi-Fi configuration screen set to infrastructure mode.

WAPs have an integrated Web server and are configured through a browser-based setup utility. Typically, you open a Web browser on a networked computer and enter the WAP's default IP address, such as 192.168.1.1, to bring up the configuration page. You will need to supply an administrative password, included with your WAP's documentation, to log in (see Figure 22-13). Setup screens vary from vendor to vendor and from model to model. Figure 22-14 shows the initial setup screen for a popular Linksys WAP/router.

To make life easier, current WAPs come with a Web-based utility that autodetects the WAP and guides the user through setting up all of its features.

When you purchase a new WAP, there is a pretty good chance the vendor already has updated firmware for it. This is even more true if you've had your WAP for a while. Before configuring your WAP for your users to access it, you should check for updates. Refer to the section "Software Troubleshooting," later in the chapter, for more on updating WAP firmware.

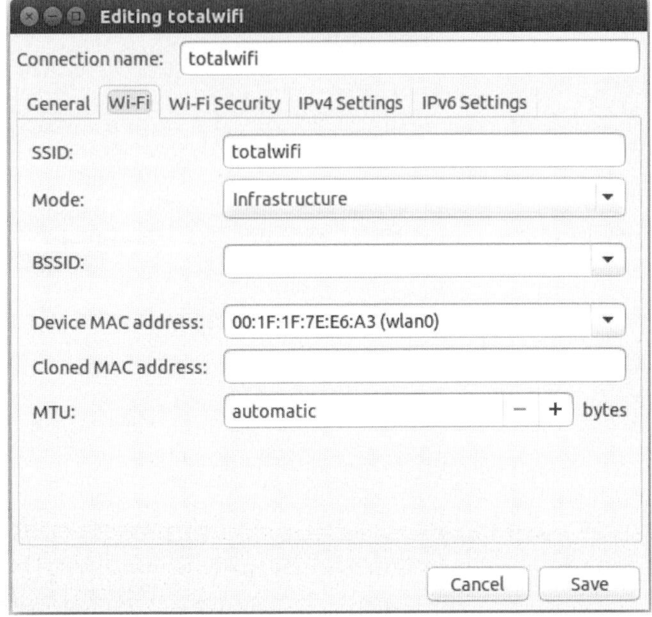

Figure 22-12 Infrastructure mode is set in a wireless configuration utility.

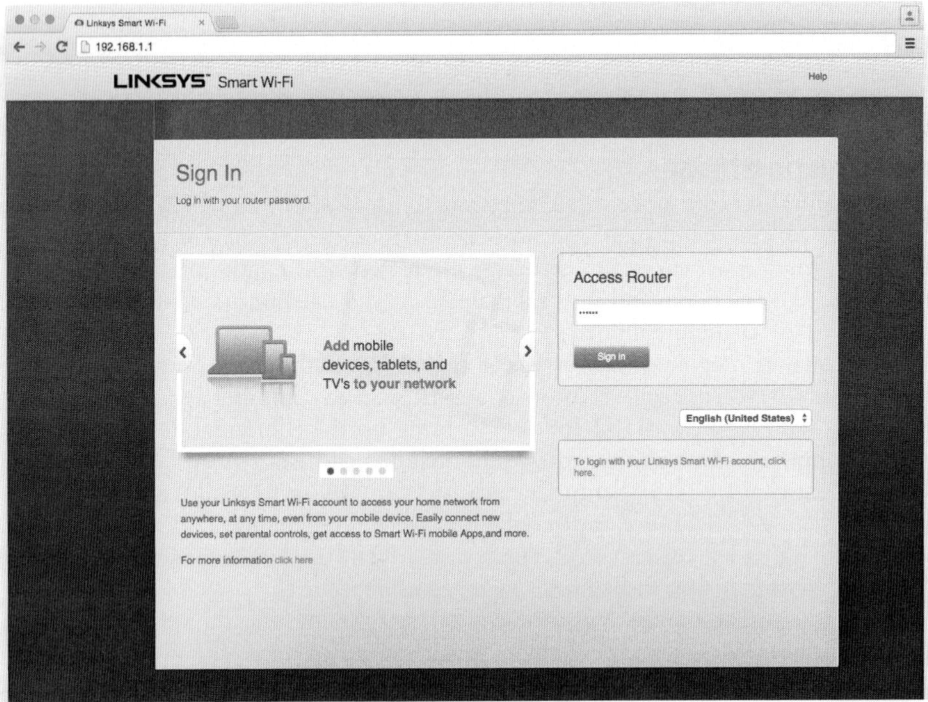

Figure 22-13 Security login for Linksys WAP

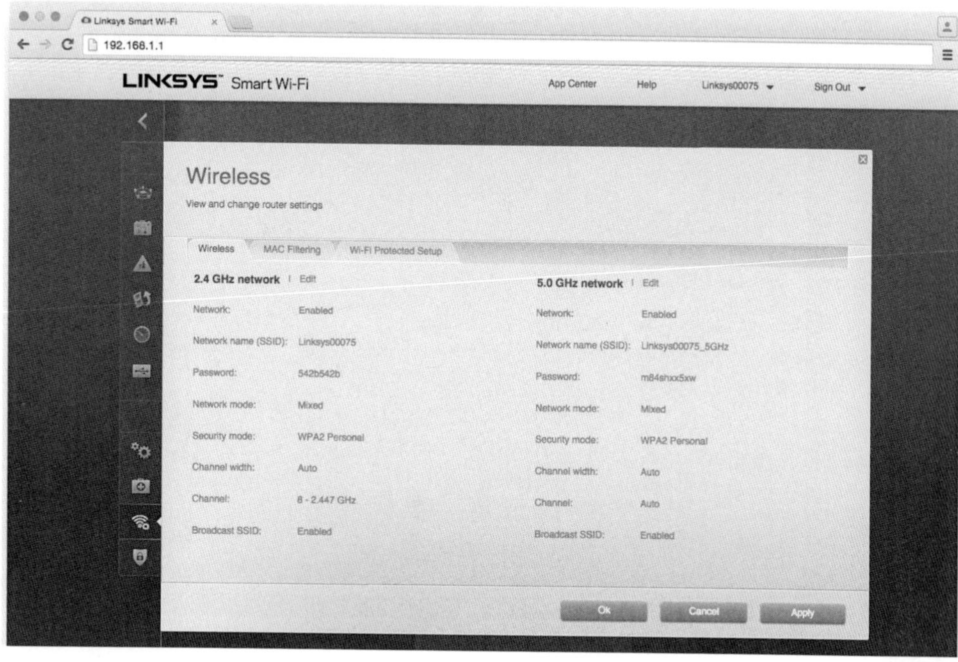

Figure 22-14 Linksys WAP setup screen

Configure the SSID option where indicated. Remember that it's always more secure to configure a unique SSID than it is to accept the well-known default one. You should also make sure that the option to allow broadcasting of the SSID is disabled. This ensures that only wireless nodes specifically configured with the correct SSID can join the wireless network.

Channel selection is usually automatic, but you can reconfigure this option if you have particular needs in your organization (for example, if you have multiple wireless networks operating in the same area). Use a wireless analyzer to find the "quietest" channel where you intend to install the WAP and select that channel in the appropriate WAP setup/configuration screen. This provides the lowest chance of interference from other WAPs. Clients automatically search through all frequencies and channels when searching for broadcasted SSIDs.

To increase security even more, use MAC filtering. Figure 22-15 shows the MAC filtering configuration screen for a Linksys WAP. Simply click the Add MAC Address button and enter the MAC address of a wireless node that you wish to allow (or deny) access to your wireless network. Set up encryption by setting the security mode on the WAP and then generating a unique security key or password. Then configure all connected wireless nodes on the network with the same credentials. Figure 22-16 shows a basic WAP properties panel configured for WPA2 Personal wireless security.

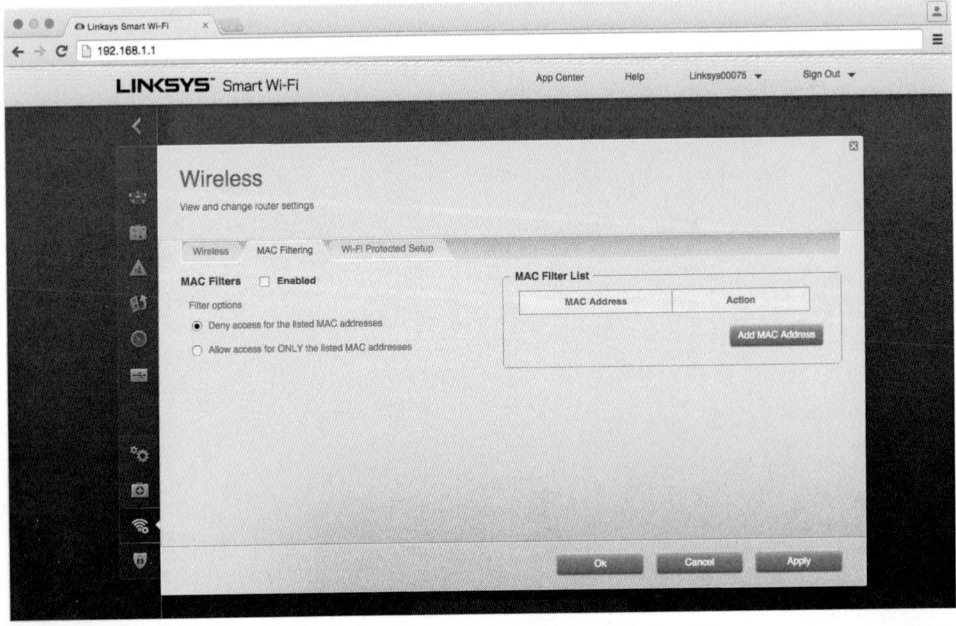

Figure 22-15 MAC filtering configuration screen for a Linksys WAP

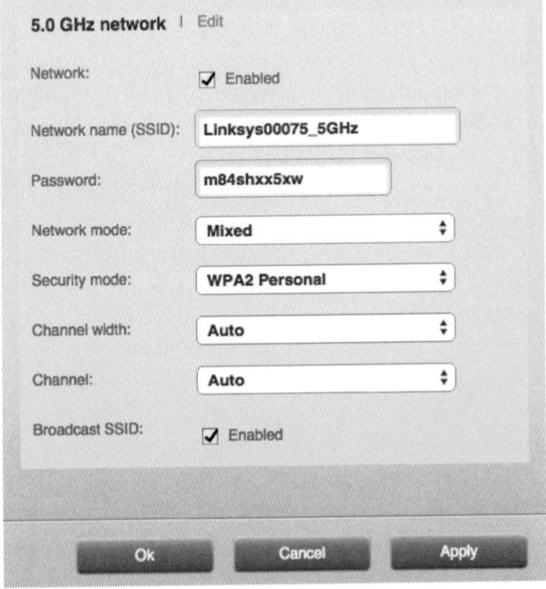

Figure 22-16 Basic properties panel for a Linksys WAP

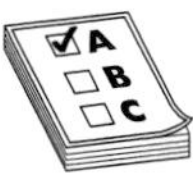

EXAM TIP As noted earlier in the chapter, the WEP protocol provides security, but it's easily cracked. Use WPA2 or, if you have older equipment, settle for WPA until you can upgrade.

If you're dealing with older equipment and find yourself performing the unseemly task of setting up WEP, you should have the option of automatically generating a set of encryption keys or doing it manually; save yourself a headache and use the automatic method. Select an encryption level—the usual choices are either 64-bit or 128-bit—and then enter a unique *passphrase* and click the **Generate** button (or whatever the equivalent button is called on your WAP). Then select a default key and save the settings. The encryption level, key, and passphrase must match on the wireless client node or communication will fail. Many WAPs have the capability to export the WEP encryption key data onto a media storage device so you can easily import it on a client workstation, or you can manually configure encryption by using the Windows wireless configuration utility.

WPA and WPA2 encryption are configured in much the same way. While it may seem that there are many configuration options, there are effectively two ways to set up WPA/WPA2: Personal/Pre-shared Key (PSK) or Enterprise. WPA/WPA2 Personal is the most common for small and home networks (see Figure 22-17). Enterprise is much more complex, requires extra equipment, and is only used in the most serious and secure wireless networks. After selecting the Personal option, there may be "subselections" such as Mixed mode, which allows a WPA2-encrypted WAP to also support WPA. You may see the term PSK, Pre-Shared Key, or just Personal in the configuration options.

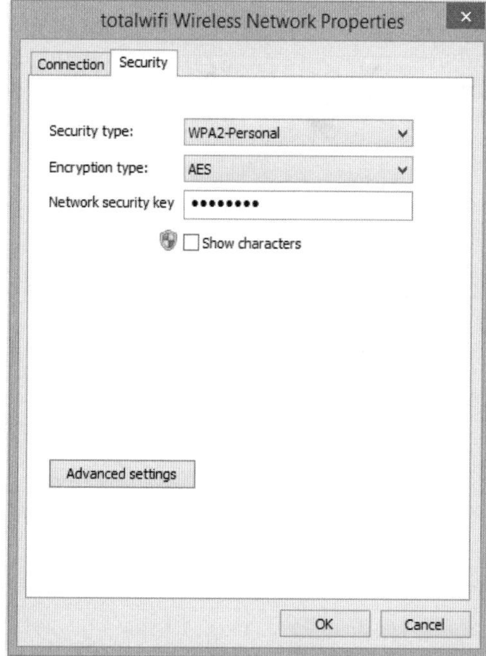

Figure 22-17 Encryption screen on client wireless network adapter configuration utility

If you have the option, choose WPA2 encryption for the WAP as well as the NICs in your network. Note that the settings such as WPA2 for the Enterprise assume you'll enable authentication by using a RADIUS server (see Figure 22-18). This way, businesses can allow only people with the proper credentials to connect to their Wi-Fi networks. For home use, select the Personal version of WPA/WPA2. Use the best encryption you can. If you have WPA2, use it. If not, use WPA. While WEP is configured in much the same way as WPA and WPA2, it is always a terrible choice.

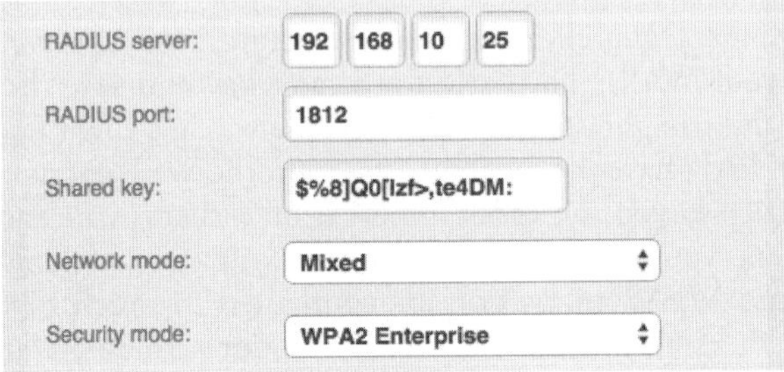

Figure 22-18 Encryption screen with RADIUS option

NOTE Always try WPA2-Personal first. If you then have wireless computers that can't connect to your WAP, fall back to WPA-Personal. Use Mixed mode so the newer clients can still take advantage of the extra security provided by WPA2 while older clients can use WPA-Personal.

With most home networks, you can simply leave the channel and frequency of the WAP at the factory defaults, but in an environment with overlapping Wi-Fi signals, you'll want to adjust one or both features. To adjust the channel, find the option in the WAP configuration screens and simply change it. Figure 22-19 shows the channel option in a Linksys WAP.

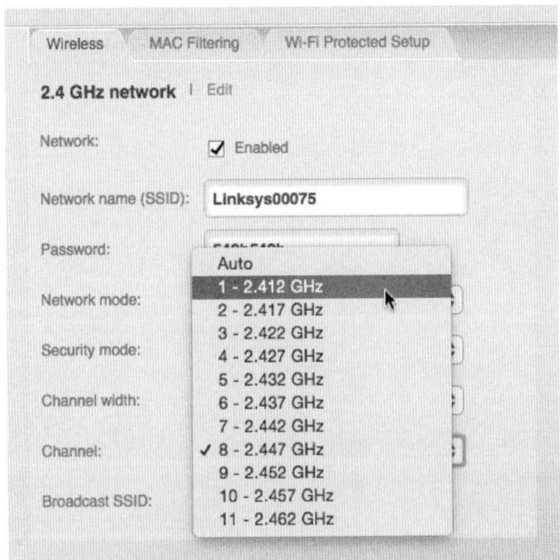

Figure 22-19 Changing the channel

With dual-band 802.11n and 802.11ac WAPs, you can choose which band to put traffic on: either 2.4 GHz or 5 GHz. In an area with overlapping signals, most of the traffic (at least as of this writing) will be on the 2.4-GHz frequency. In addition to other wireless devices (such as cordless phones), microwaves also use the 2.4-GHz frequency and can cause a great deal of interference. 802.11ac devices can avoid conflicts like these by using the 5-GHz frequency instead. Figure 22-20 shows the configuration screen for a dual-band 802.11ac WAP.

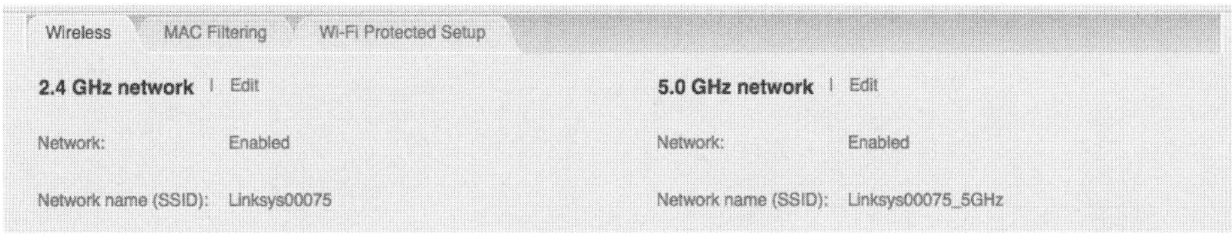

Figure 22-20 Linksys router sporting dual bands

Placing the Access Point(s)

The optimal location for an access point depends on the area you want to cover, whether you care if the signal bleeds out beyond the borders, and what interference exists from other wireless sources. You start by doing a site survey. A site survey can be as trivial as firing up a wireless-capable laptop and looking for existing SSIDs. Or it can be a complex job where you hire people with specialized equipment to come in and make lots of careful plans defining the best place to put WAPs and which wireless channels to use. To make sure the wireless signal goes where you want it to go and not where you don't, you need to use the right antenna. Let's see what types of antennas are available.

Omni-directional and Centered For a typical network, you want blanket coverage and would place a WAP with an omni-directional antenna in the center of the area (see Figure 22-21). With an omni-directional antenna, the radio wave flows outward from the WAP. This has the advantage of ease of use—anything within the signal radius can potentially access the network. Most wireless networks use this combination, especially in the consumer space. The standard straight-wire antennas that provide most omni-directional function are called *dipole antennas*. Dipole antennas look like a stick, but inside they have two antenna arms or poles aligned on the antenna's axis; hence the term "dipole."

Gaining Gain An antenna strengthens and focuses the radio frequency (RF) output from a WAP. The ratio of increase—what's called *gain*—is measured in decibels (dB). The gain from a typical WAP is 2 dB, enough to cover a reasonable area but not a very large room. Luckily, the signal power can be increased with a bigger antenna. Many WAPs have removable antennas that you can replace. To increase the signal in an omni-directional and centered setup, simply replace the factory antennas with one or more bigger antennas (see Figure 22-22). Get a big enough antenna and you can crank it all the way up to 11 dB!

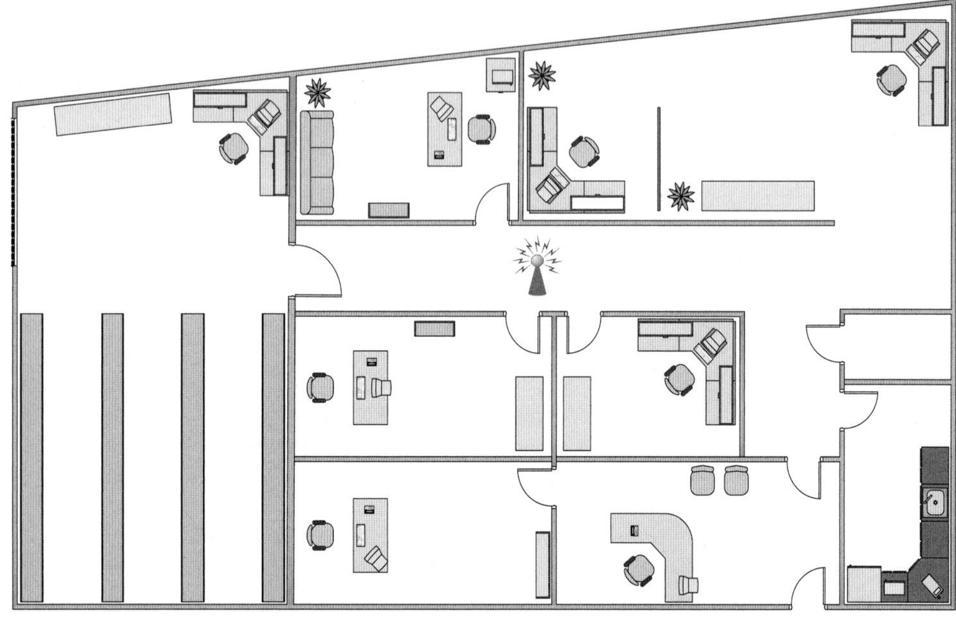

Figure 22-21 Room layout with WAP in the center

Figure 22-22 Replacement antenna on a WAP

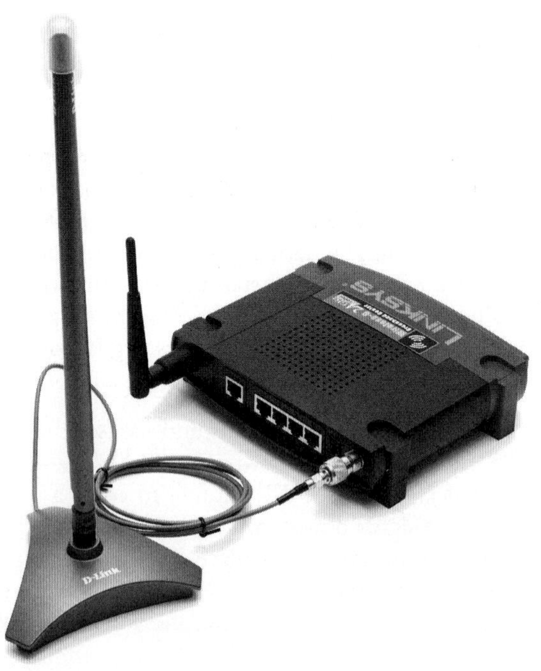

Gain antennas cause the antenna to pick up weaker signals and have an amplifying effect on transmitted signals. They come in several common flavors. Increasing the size of a dipole will increase its gain evenly in all directions. Parabolic dish-type antennas and multi-element *Yagi* antennas increase gain in a specific direction and reduce gain in all the other directions. You'll know a Yagi antenna when you see one; it looks like the old television antennas that we used to use to receive over-the-air television signals, only much smaller. In general, the more elements that a Yagi has, the higher the directional gain.

It's a Polarizing Issue Antennas and the signals that they transmit have an electromagnetic property called *polarization*. Without getting too deep into the weeds, think of polarization as the signal having the same alignment as the antenna. If the antenna on your WAP or computer is aligned up and down, your transmitted signal will have vertical alignment. Likewise, if you tilt your antenna over on its side, the signal will have horizontal polarization. Of course, you can also align your antenna somewhere between vertical and horizontal. You may have not thought about it before, but your laptop or notebook usually has vertical polarization because the antenna goes up the side of the lid, next to the screen. When the screen is open, it's generally open to a near vertical position.

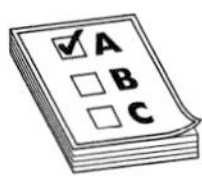

EXAM TIP To achieve a good compromise in supporting connections to clients with different antenna polarization, orient the WAP antennas on a 45-degree angle.

For the best connection between a client and a WAP, the wireless signals should have the same polarization. The worst connection strength between WAPs and clients happens when one has vertical antennas and the other has horizontal. While it is pretty easy to make sure the antenna on a desktop computer is optimally aligned, it is more challenging to dictate antenna orientation in laptops, notebooks, smartphones, and tablets. If your WAP has more than one antenna, consider orienting them differently to accommodate different client configurations. What is the right orientation? The best way to determine that is with testing; try one vertical and another horizontal and then sample the clients throughout the coverage area to check connection strength. Then try some other orientations until you achieve the strongest coverage.

NOTE If you want to know whether your local café, bookstore, airport, or other public place has a Wi-Fi access point (a hotspot), you can use a *Wi-Fi* or *wireless locator*. The locator is usually the size of your car remote and lights up or otherwise signals you whenever you are in range of a Wi-Fi access point. Wi-Fi locators, also called Wi-Fi analyzers, can also be installed as an app on a Wi-Fi smartphone.

Bluetooth Configuration

As with other wireless networking solutions, Bluetooth devices are completely plug and play. Just connect the adapter and follow the prompts to install the appropriate drivers if

your OS needs them. Once installed, you'll need to start the *pairing* process to enable the devices to create a secure connection—you wouldn't want every Bluetooth client in range to automatically connect with your smartphone! Figure 22-23 shows an iPhone receiving a pairing request from an iMac called "mediamac."

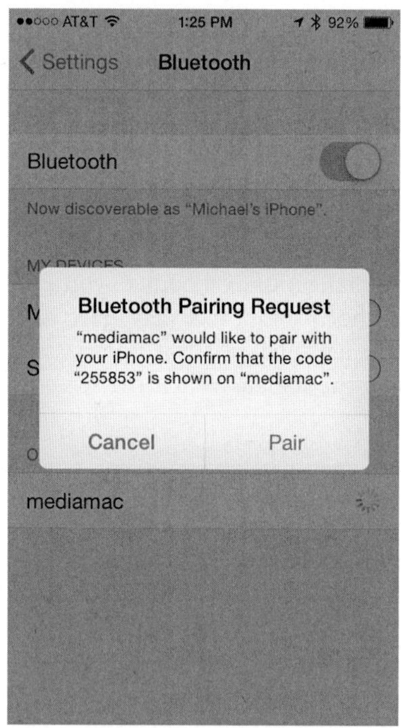

Figure 22-23 iPhone receiving a pairing request from "mediamac"

Pairing takes a few steps. The first step, of course, is to enable Bluetooth. Some devices, such as Bluetooth headsets, always have Bluetooth enabled because, it's their sole communication method. Others, like a Bluetooth adapter in your computer, may be enabled or disabled in the Network and Sharing Center.

Once enabled, the two devices must be placed into pairing mode. Some devices, like the stereo in my car, continuously listen for a pairing request, while others must be set to pairing (or discovery) mode. The devices in pairing mode will discover each other and agree on a compatible Bluetooth version, speed, and set of features.

The final step of the pairing process, the security component, requires you to confirm your intent to pair the devices. Depending on Bluetooth version and device capabilities, there are a number of different ways this could go; these range from the devices confirming the connection without user input to requiring the user to input a short code on one or both devices. If used, these codes are most often 4 or 6 digits, but older devices may differ. Refer to your device's documentation for specific details on its pairing process.

Done, right? Well, almost. There remains the final step: make sure everything works. Are you getting sound into your Bluetooth headset or speakers? Does the Bluetooth microphone work when making phone calls or recording notes on your smartphone

app? Can you stream music from your smartphone to your car stereo? You get the idea. If something isn't working, it's time to check for two common problems: unsuccessful /incomplete pairing, and configuration issues.

The pairing process is quick and easy to repeat. You may have to delete the pairing from one of the devices first. After re-pairing, test again. If the pairing process never gets started, you have no Bluetooth connectivity. Make sure both devices are on, have Bluetooth enabled, and are in pairing mode. Check battery power in wireless devices and check configuration settings.

If the pairing appears successful but the connection test is not, look for configuration issues. Check microphone input settings and audio output settings. Use any vendor-provided testing and troubleshooting utilities. Keep at it until it works or until you confirm that one or both devices are bad or incompatible.

You'll need to do a little more than just pair devices to connect to a Bluetooth PAN. This connection is handled by your OS in most cases. Figure 22-24 shows the Mac OS X network configuration for a Bluetooth PAN with the iPhone selected and ready to connect.

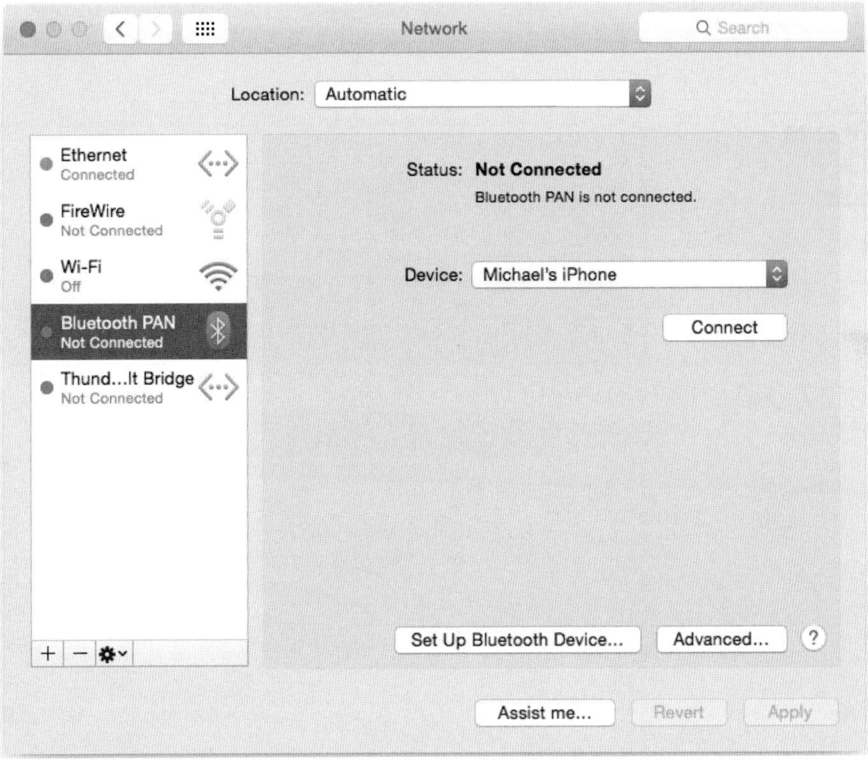

Figure 22-24 Mac OS X Bluetooth PAN ready to connect using "Michael's iPhone"

NOTE A Bluetooth Internet connection is a rare sight out in the real world. Today, mobile devices use Wi-Fi or a cellular connection to access network and Internet resources.

Cellular Configuration

There is no single standard for configuring a cellular network card because the cards and software change based on your service provider. Fortunately, those same cell phone companies have made installing their cards very simple. In most cases you just need to plug in the card and install the software.

With most cellular cards, you simply plug the card into your computer, usually via USB, and the setup program automatically launches. These cards almost always have all the required software and drivers built into the cards themselves, so there are no optical discs or other installation media to worry about. Once you've installed the necessary software, launch the connection application. Follow the instructions that came with the software; in Figure 22-25, for example, double-click on the VZAccess network listed in the window. This initiates the connection to Verizon's network. You can also go to the Options menu and select Statistics to see the specifics of your connection, as shown in Figure 22-26.

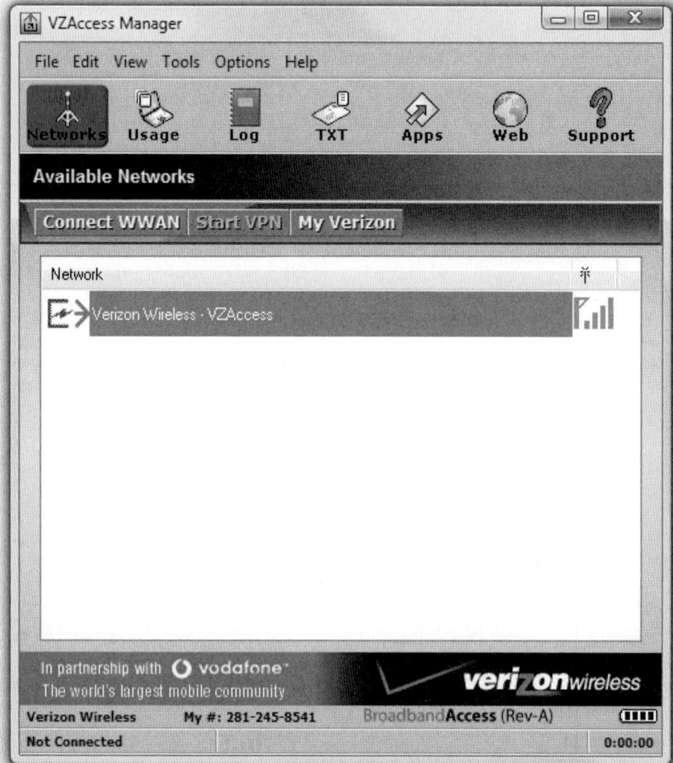

Figure 22-25 VZAccess Manager

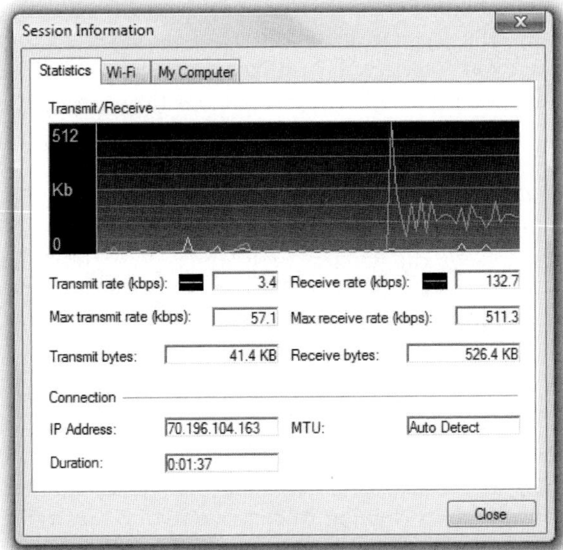

Figure 22-26 Session statistics for VZAccess Manager

The key thing to remember about cellular Internet access is that it is almost completely configured and controlled by the provider. A tech has very little to do except to make sure the cellular card is plugged in, recognized by the computer, and properly installed.

Troubleshooting Wi-Fi

Wireless networks are a real boon when they work right, but they can also be one of the most vexing things to troubleshoot when they don't. Let's turn to some practical advice on how to detect and correct wireless hardware, software, and configuration problems.

As with any troubleshooting scenario, your first step in troubleshooting a wireless network is to break down your tasks into logical steps. Your first step should be to figure out the scope of your wireless networking problem. Ask yourself *who*, *what*, and *when*:

- Who is affected by the problem?
- What is the nature of their network problem?
- When did the problem start?

In the formal process of troubleshooting, answering these questions is step one, known as gathering information. The answers to these questions dictate at least the initial direction of your troubleshooting.

So, who's affected? If all machines on your network—wired and wireless—have lost connectivity, you have bigger problems than a few wireless machines that cannot access the network. Troubleshoot this situation the way you'd troubleshoot any network failure. Once you determine which wireless nodes are affected, it's easier to pinpoint whether the problem lies in one or more wireless clients or in one or more access points.

After you narrow down the number of affected machines, your next task is to figure out specifically what type of error the users are experiencing. If they can access some, but not all, network services, it's unlikely that the problem is limited to their wireless equipment. For example, if they can browse the Internet but can't access any shared resources on a server, they're probably experiencing a permissions-related issue rather than a wireless one.

The last bit of gathering information for this issue is to determine when the problem started. What has changed that might explain your loss of connectivity? Did you or somebody else change the wireless network configuration? For example, if the network worked fine two minutes ago, and then you changed the encryption key or level on the access point, and now nobody can see the network, you have your solution—or at least your culprit! Did your office experience a power outage, power sag, or power surge? Any of these might cause a WAP to fail. And that leads us to the next step of the formal troubleshooting process, establishing a theory, which was discussed back in Chapter 2. For now, let's focus on the specifics of troubleshooting Wi-Fi issues.

Once you figure out the who, what, and when, you can start troubleshooting in earnest. Typically, your problem is going to center on your hardware, software, connectivity, or configuration.

Hardware Troubleshooting

Wireless networking hardware components are subject to the same kind of abuse and faulty installation as any other hardware component. Troubleshooting a suspected hardware problem should bring out the technician in you.

Open Windows Device Manager and look for an error or conflict with the wireless adapter. If you see a big exclamation point next to the device, you have a driver error. A downward-facing arrow next to the device indicates that it has been disabled. Enable it if possible or reinstall the device driver as needed.

If you don't see the device listed at all, perhaps it is not seated properly or plugged all the way in. These problems are easy to fix. Just remove them and reinstall the device.

NOTE As with all things computing, don't forget to do the standard PC troubleshooting thing and reboot the computer before you make any configuration or hardware changes!

Software Troubleshooting

Because you've already checked to confirm your hardware is using the correct drivers, what kind of software-related problems are left? Two things come immediately to mind: the wireless adapter configuration utility and the WAP's firmware version.

As I mentioned earlier, some wireless devices won't work correctly unless you install the vendor-provided drivers and configuration utility before plugging in the device. This is particularly true of wireless USB devices. If you didn't do this already, go into Device Manager and uninstall the device, then start again from scratch.

By the time you unpack your new WAP, there's a good chance its firmware is already out of date. Out-of-date firmware could manifest in many ways. Your WAP may enable clients to connect, but only at such slow speeds that they experience frequent timeout errors; you may find that, after a week, your clients can connect but have no Internet access until you reboot the WAP; Apple devices may have trouble connecting or running at advertised speeds. The important thing here is to be on the lookout for strange or erratic behavior.

Manufacturers regularly release firmware updates to fix issues just like these—and many more—so it's good to update the access point's firmware. For older WAPs, go to the manufacturer's Web site and follow the support links until you find the latest firmware version. You'll need your device's exact model number and hardware version, as well as the current firmware version—this is important, because installing the wrong firmware version on your device is a guaranteed way to render it useless! Modern WAPs have built-in administration pages to upload the newly downloaded firmware. Some can even check for firmware updates and install them. Because there are too many WAP variations to cover here, always look up and follow the manufacturer's instructions for updating the firmware to the letter.

NOTE When updating the firmware of any device, including your WAP, there's always a chance something could go wrong and render it unusable—and you may hear techs say such a device has been "bricked." Why? It's no more useful than a brick!

Connectivity Troubleshooting

Properly configured wireless clients should automatically and quickly connect to the desired SSID, assuming both the client and WAP support the correct bands. If this isn't taking place, it's time for some troubleshooting. Most wireless connectivity problems come down to either an incorrect configuration (such as an incorrect password) or low signal strength. Without a strong signal, even a properly configured wireless client isn't going to work. Wireless clients use a multi-bar graph (usually five bars) to give an idea of signal strength: zero bars indicates no wireless connectivity and five bars indicates maximum signal. Weak signals can result in slow overall data transfer and intermittent wireless connections.

Whether configuration or signal strength, the process to diagnose and repair uses the same methods you use for a wired network. First, if your wireless NIC has link lights, check to see whether it's passing data packets to and from the network. Second, check the wireless NIC's configuration utility. Figure 22-27 shows Windows 8.1 Pro displaying the link state and signal strength.

The link state defines the wireless NIC's connection status to a wireless network: connected or disconnected. If your link state indicates that your computer is currently disconnected, you may have a problem with your WAP. If your signal is too weak to receive a signal (referred to on the CompTIA A+ exams as a "low RF signal"), you may be out of range of your access point, or there may be a device causing interference.

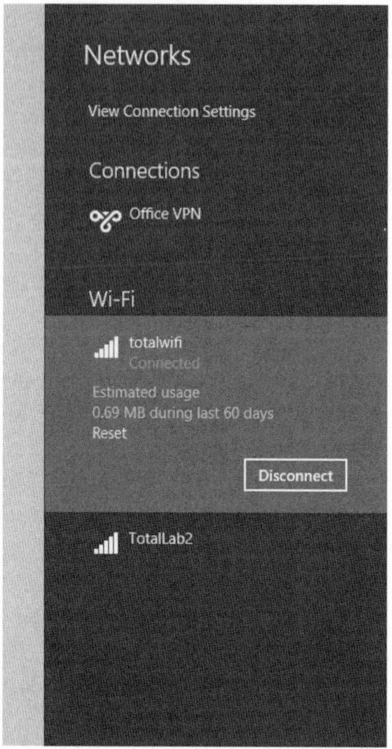

Figure 22-27 Windows 8.1 Pro's wireless configuration utility

You can fix these problems in a number of ways. Because Wi-Fi signals bounce off of objects, you can try small adjustments to your antennas to see if the signal improves. You can swap out the standard antenna for one or more higher-gain antennas. You can relocate the PC or access point, or locate and move the device causing interference.

Other wireless devices that operate in the same frequency range as your wireless nodes can cause interference as well. Look for wireless telephones, intercoms, and so on as possible culprits. One fix for interference caused by other wireless devices is to change the channel your network uses. Another is to change the channel the offending device uses, if possible. If you can't change channels, try moving the interfering device to another area or replacing it with a different device.

Configuration Troubleshooting

With all due respect to the fine network techs in the field, the most common type of wireless networking problem is misconfigured hardware or software. That's right—the dreaded *user error*! Given the complexities of wireless networking, this isn't so surprising. All it takes is one slip of the typing finger to throw off your configuration completely. The things you're most likely to get wrong are the SSID and security configuration, though dual-band routers have introduced some additional complexity.

Verify SSID configuration (for any bands in use) on your access point first, and then check on the affected wireless nodes. With most wireless devices, you can use any

characters in the SSID, including blank spaces. Be careful not to add blank characters where they don't belong, such as trailing blank spaces behind any other characters typed into the name field.

In some situations, clients that have always connected to a WAP with a particular SSID may no longer be able to connect. The client may or may not give an error message indicating "SSID not found." There are a couple possible explanations for this and they are easy to troubleshoot and fix. The simplest culprit is that the WAP is down—easy to find and easy to fix. On the opposite end of the spectrum is a change to the WAP. Changing the SSID of a WAP or disabling SSID broadcast will prevent the client from connecting. The fix can be as simple as changing the SSID back or updating the client configuration. A client may not connect to a new WAP, even if it has the same SSID and connection configuration as the previous one. Simply delete the old connection profile from the client and create a new one.

If you're using MAC address filtering, make sure the MAC address of the client that's attempting to access the wireless network is on the list of accepted users. This is particularly important if you swap out NICs on a PC, or if you introduce a new PC to your wireless network.

Check the security configuration to make sure that all wireless nodes and access points match. Mistyping an encryption key prevents the affected node from talking to the wireless network, even if your signal strength is 100 percent! Remember that many access points have the capability to export encryption keys onto a thumb drive or other removable media. It's then a simple matter to import the encryption key onto the PC by using the wireless NIC's configuration utility. Remember that the encryption level must match on access points and wireless nodes. If your WAP is configured for WPA2, all nodes must also use WPA2.

Chapter Review

Questions

1. Which of the following 802.11 standards functions only on the 5-GHz band?
   A. 802.11g
   B. 802.11n
   C. 802.11ac
   D. 802.11i
2. Which encryption protocol offers the best security?
   A. Hi-Encrypt
   B. WEP
   C. WPA
   D. WPA2

3. Which device enables you to extend the capabilities of a wireless network?
   A. WAP
   B. WEP
   C. WPA
   D. WPA2
4. In which mode do all the wireless devices connect directly to each other?
   A. Ad hoc mode
   B. Circular mode
   C. Infrastructure mode
   D. Mesh mode
5. What determines the name of a wireless network?
   A. EAP
   B. MAC address
   C. SSID
   D. WAP
6. What technology enables 802.11n networks to make multiple simultaneous connections and thus improve speed over previous Wi-Fi standards?
   A. Use of the 2.4-GHz frequency
   B. Use of the 5-GHz frequency
   C. MIMO
   D. WPA2
7. What's the top speed for data transfers using IrDA technology?
   A. 2 Mbps
   B. 4 Mbps
   C. 11 Mbps
   D. 54 Mbps
8. Bluetooth technology enables computers to link into what sort of network?
   A. Bluetooth area network (BAN)
   B. Personal area network (PAN)
   C. Local area network (LAN)
   D. Wide area network (WAN)

9. What is the name for the common omni-directional antennas found on wireless access points?
   A. Bipole antennas
   B. Dipole antennas
   C. Omni antennas
   D. RF antennas
10. Ralph has installed a wireless network in his house, placing the wireless access point in the kitchen, a centralized location. The Wi-Fi works fine in the living room and dining room but goes out almost completely in the bedroom. What's most likely the problem?
    A. Interference with some metal object
    B. Improper antenna set up
    C. Use of the default SSID
    D. The SSID overlapping with a neighbor's SSID

Answers

1. **C.** The 802.11ac standard functions exclusively on the 5-GHz band, while 802.11g functions on 2.4 GHz, 802.11n functions on both, and 802.11i is a security standard called WPA2.
2. **D.** WPA2 is the best of the encryption technologies listed.
3. **A.** A wireless access point (WAP) enables you to extend the capabilities of a wireless network.
4. **A.** In ad hoc mode networks, all the nodes connect directly to each other.
5. **C.** The SSID determines the name of a wireless network.
6. **C.** The multiple in/multiple out (MIMO) technology implementing multiple antennas enables 802.11n networks to run at much faster speeds than previous Wi-Fi networks.
7. **B.** Data transfers using the IrDA protocol top out at 4 Mbps.
8. **B.** Bluetooth creates personal area networks.
9. **B.** Standard omni-directional antennas are called dipole antennas.
10. **A.** Watch out for microwave ovens, refrigerators, and pipes in the walls. They can interfere with a Wi-Fi signal and create dead spots.

CHAPTER 23

The Internet

In this chapter, you will learn how to

- Explain how the Internet works
- Connect to the Internet
- Use Internet application protocols
- Troubleshoot an Internet connection

Imagine coming home from a long day at work building and fixing computers, sitting down in front of your shiny new computer, double-clicking the single icon that sits dead center on your monitor…and suddenly you're enveloped in an otherworldly scene, where 200-foot trees slope smoothly into snow-white beaches and rich blue ocean. Overhead, pterodactyls soar through the air while you talk to a small chap with pointy ears and a long robe about heading up the mountain in search of a giant monster…. A TV show from the Syfy channel? Spielberg's latest film offering? How about an interactive game played by millions of people all over the planet on a daily basis by connecting to the Internet? If you guessed the last one, you're right.

This chapter covers the skills you need as a tech to help people connect to the Internet. It starts with a brief section on how the Internet works, along with the concepts of connectivity, and then it goes into the specifics of hardware, protocols, and software that you use to make the Internet work for you (or for your client). Finally, you'll learn how to troubleshoot a bad Internet connection. Let's get started!

Historical/Conceptual

How the Internet Works

Thanks to the Internet, people can communicate with one another over vast distances, often in the blink of an eye. As a tech, you need to know how computers communicate with the larger world for two reasons. First, knowing the process and pieces involved in the communication enables you to troubleshoot effectively when that communication goes away. Second, you need to be able to communicate knowledgeably with a network technician who comes in to solve a more complex issue.

Internet Tiers

You probably know that the Internet is millions and millions of computers all joined together to form the largest network on earth, but not many folks know much about how these computers are organized. To keep everything running smoothly, the Internet is broken down into groups called *tiers*. The main tier, called *Tier 1*, consists of a small number of companies called *Tier 1 providers*. The Tier 1 providers own long-distance, high-speed fiber-optic networks called *backbones*. These backbones span the major cities of the earth (not all Tier 1 backbones go to all cities) and interconnect at special locations called *network access points (NAPs)*. Anyone wishing to connect to any of the Tier 1 providers must pay large sums of money. The Tier 1 providers do not charge each other to connect.

Tier 2 providers own smaller, regional networks and must pay the Tier 1 providers. Most of the famous companies that provide Internet access to the general public are Tier 2 providers. *Tier 3 providers* are even more regional and connect to Tier 2 providers.

The piece of equipment that makes this tiered Internet concept work is called a backbone router. *Backbone routers* connect to more than one other backbone router, creating a big, interwoven framework for communication. Figure 23-1 illustrates the decentralized and interwoven nature of the Internet. The key reason for interweaving the backbones of the Internet was to provide alternative pathways for data if one or more of the routers went down. If Jane in Houston sends a message to her friend Polly in New York City, for example, the shortest path between Jane and Polly in this hypothetical situation might be: Jane's message originates at Rice University in Houston, bounces to Emory University in Atlanta, flits through Virginia Commonwealth University in Richmond, and then zips into SUNY in New York City (see Figure 23-2). Polly happily reads the message and life is great. The Internet functions as planned.

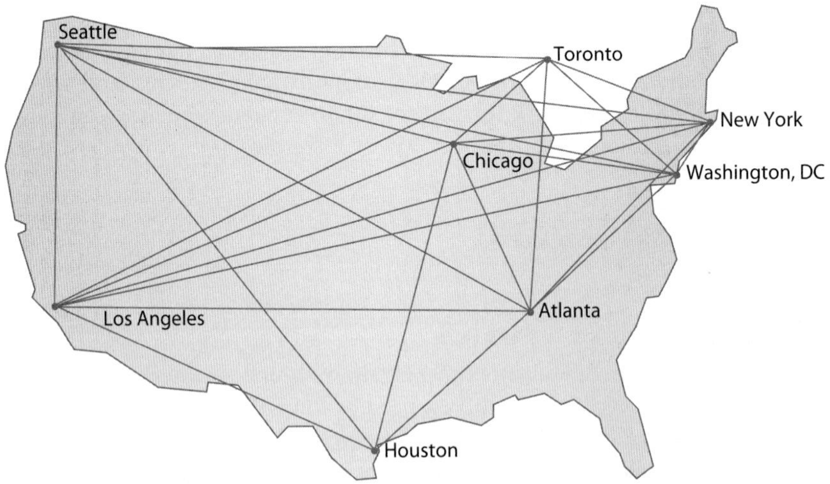

Figure 23-1 Internet Tier 1 connections

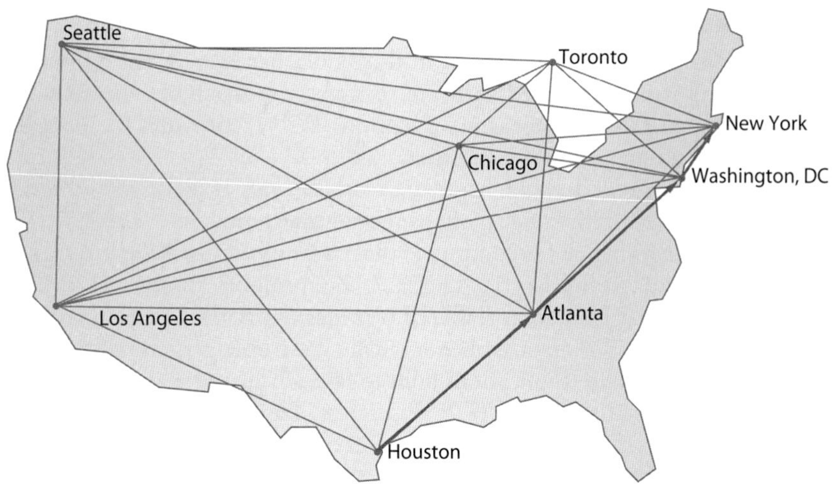

Figure 23-2 Message traveling from Houston to NYC

But what would happen if the entire southeastern United States were to experience a huge power outage and Internet backbones in every state from Virginia to Florida were to go down? Jane's message would fail to go through, so the Rice computers would resend Jane's message. Meanwhile, the routers would update their list of good routes and then attempt to reroute the message to functioning nodes—say, Rice to University of Chicago, to University of Toronto, and then to SUNY (see Figure 23-3). It's all in a day's work for the highly redundant and adaptable Internet. At this point in the game, the Internet simply cannot go down fully—barring, of course, a catastrophe of Biblical proportions.

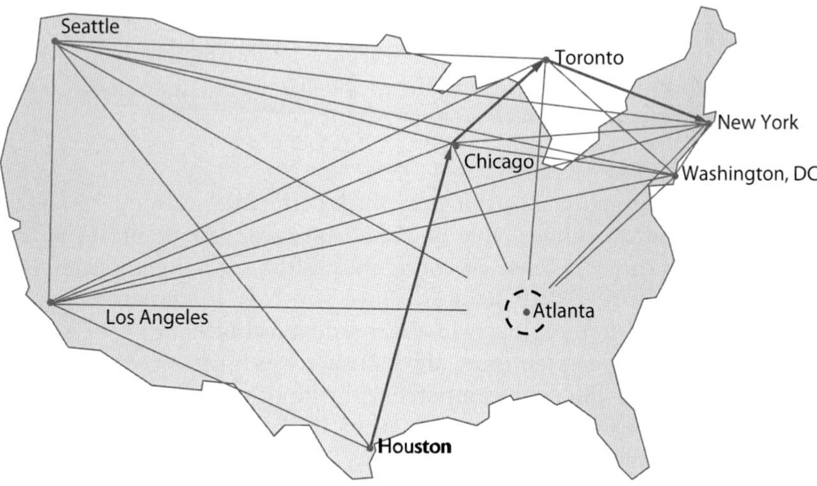

Figure 23-3 Rerouted message from Houston to NYC

TCP/IP—The Common Language of the Internet

As you know from all the earlier chapters in this book, hardware alone doesn't cut it in the world of computing. You need software to make the machines run and create an interface for humans. The Internet is no exception. TCP/IP provides the basic software structure for communication on the Internet.

Because you spent a good deal of Chapter 21 working with TCP/IP, you should have an appreciation for its adaptability and, perhaps more importantly, its extensibility. TCP/IP provides the addressing scheme for computers that communicate on the Internet through IP addresses, such as 192.168.4.1 or 16.45.123.7. As a protocol, though, TCP/IP is much more than just an addressing system. TCP/IP provides the framework and common language for the Internet. And it offers a phenomenally wide-open structure for creative purposes. Programmers can write applications built to take advantage of the TCP/IP structure and features, creating what are called TCP/IP services. The cool thing about TCP/IP services is that they're limited only by the imagination of the programmers.

At this point, you have an enormous functioning network. All the backbone routers connect redundant, high-speed backbone lines, and TCP/IP enables communication and services for building applications that enable humans and machines to interface across vast distances. What's left? Oh, of course: How do you tap into this great network and partake of its goodness?

Internet Service Providers

Every Tier 1 and Tier 2 provider leases connections to the Internet to companies called *Internet service providers (ISPs)*. ISPs essentially sit along the edges of the Tier 1 and Tier 2 Internet and tap into the flow. In turn, you can lease connections from an ISP to get on the Internet.

ISPs come in all sizes. Comcast, the cable television provider, has multiple, huge-capacity connections into the Internet, enabling its millions of customers to connect from their local machines and surf the Web. Contrast Comcast with Electric Power Board (EPB) of Chattanooga, an ISP in Chattanooga, Tennessee (see Figure 23-4), which bills itself as "...the fastest Internet available. Period." Unfortunately, EPB only offers its blazingly fast gigabit fiber connections to the lucky citizens of Chattanooga.

Connection Concepts

Connecting to an ISP requires two things to work perfectly: hardware for connectivity, such as a modem and a working cable line; and software, such as protocols to govern the connections and the data flow (all configured in the OS) and applications to take advantage of the various TCP/IP services. Once you have a contract with an ISP to grant you access to the Internet, they will either send a technician to your house or mail you a package containing any hardware and software you might need. With most ISPs, a DHCP server will provide your computer with the proper TCP/IP information. As you know, the router to which you connect at the ISP is often referred to as the *default gateway*. Once your computer is configured, you can connect to the ISP and get to the greater Internet. Figure 23-5 shows a standard computer-to-ISP-to-Internet connection. Note that various protocols and other software manage the connectivity between your computer and the default gateway.

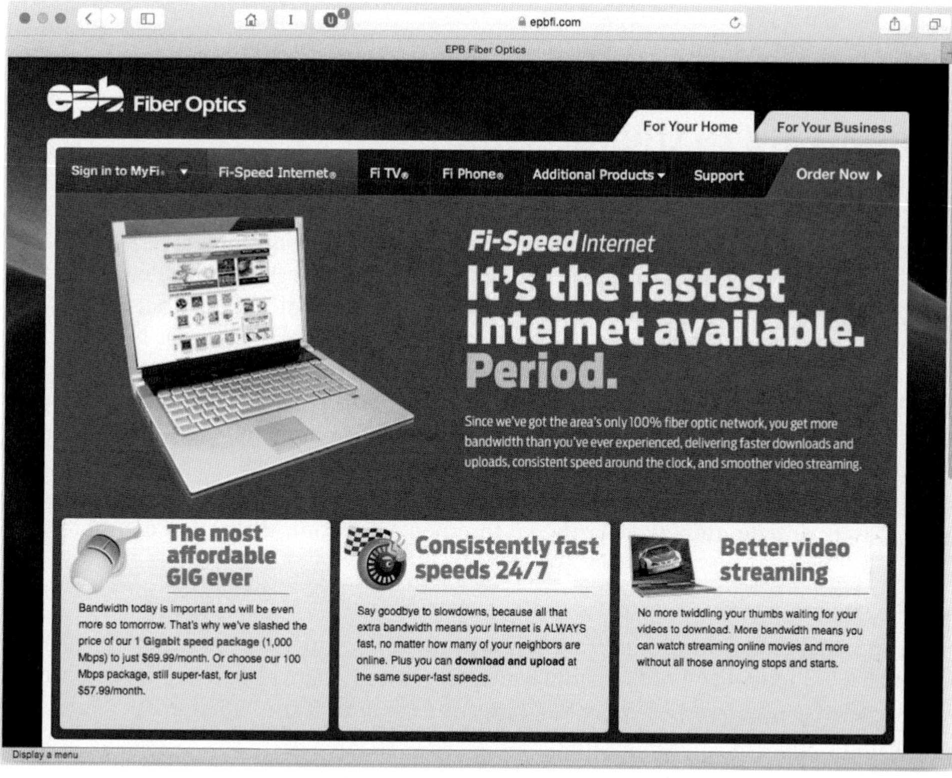

Figure 23-4 Electric Power Board (EPB) of Chattanooga home page

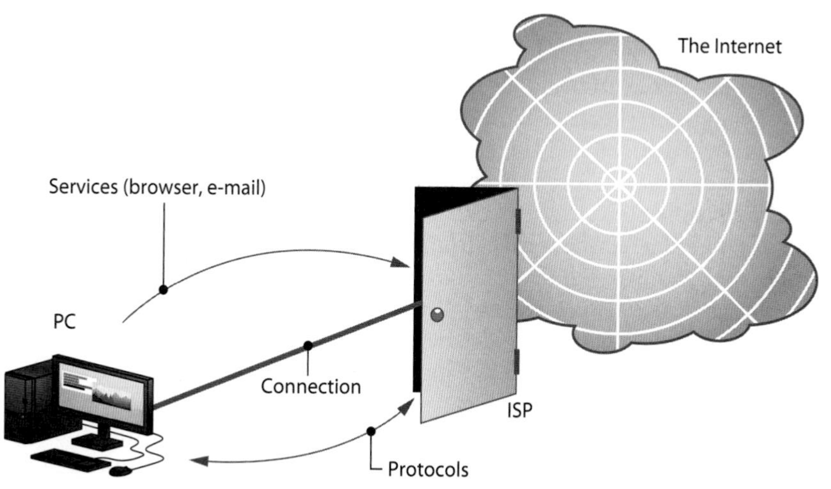

Figure 23-5 Simplified Internet connectivity

901

Connecting to the Internet

Computers commonly connect to an ISP by using one of eight technologies that fit into four categories: dial-up, both analog and ISDN; dedicated, such as DSL, cable, and fiber; wireless, including Wi-Fi and cellular; and satellite. Analog dial-up is the slowest of the bunch and requires a telephone line and a special networking device called a modem. ISDN uses digital dial-up and has much greater speed. Dedicated connections (DSL, cable, and fiber) most often use a box that connects to a regular Ethernet NIC like you played with in Chapter 21. Wireless connections are a mixed bag, depending on the device and service you have. Some are built-in, while others use a box you attach to your LAN. Satellite is the odd one out here; it may use either a modem or a NIC, depending on the particular configuration you have, although most folks will use a NIC. Let's take a look at all these various connection options, and then finish this section by discussing basic router configuration and sharing an Internet connection with other computers.

Dial-Up

A dial-up connection to the Internet requires two pieces to work: hardware to dial the ISP, such as a modem or ISDN terminal adapter; and software to govern the connection, such as Microsoft's *Dial-up Networking (DUN)*. Let's look at the hardware first, and then we'll explore software configuration.

Modems

At some point in the early days of computing, some bright guy or gal noticed a colleague talking on a telephone, glanced down at a computer, and then put two and two together: Why not use telephone lines for data communication? The basic problem with this idea is that traditional telephone lines use analog signals, while computers use digital signals (see Figure 23-6). Creating a dial-up network required equipment that could turn digital data into an analog signal to send it over the telephone line, and then turn it back into digital data when it reached the other end of the connection. A device called a modem solved this dilemma.

Modems enable computers to talk to each other via standard commercial telephone lines by converting analog signals to digital signals, and vice versa. The term *modem* is short for modulator/demodulator, a description of transforming the signals. Telephone wires transfer data via analog signals that continuously change voltages on a wire. Computers hate analog signals. Instead, they need digital signals, voltages that are either on or off, meaning the wire has voltage present or it does not. Computers, being binary by nature, use only two states of voltage: zero volts and positive volts. Modems take analog signals from telephone lines and turn them into digital signals that the computer can understand (see Figure 23-7). Modems also take digital signals from the computer and convert them into analog signals for the outgoing telephone line.

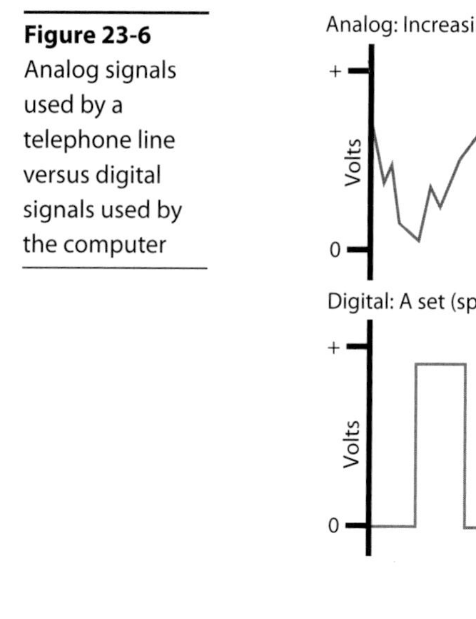
Analog: Increasing and decreasing waves of electricity
+
Volts
0
Digital: A set (specific) increase and decrease in electrical current
+
Volts
0

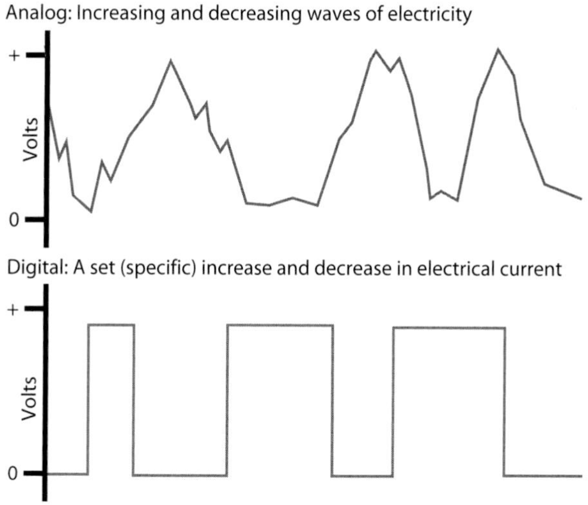

Figure 23-6 Analog signals used by a telephone line versus digital signals used by the computer

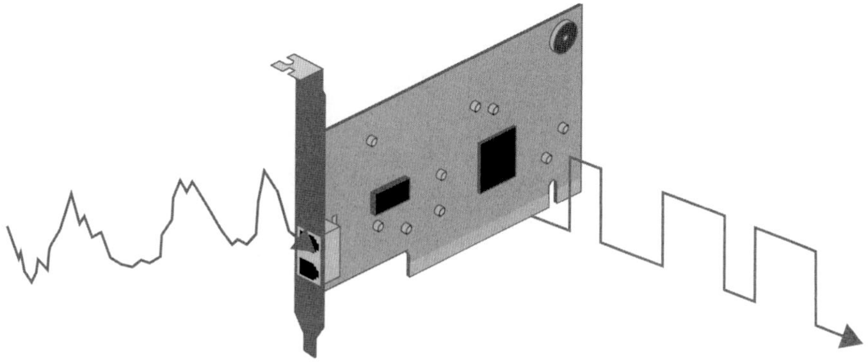

Figure 23-7 Modem converting analog signal to digital signal

Phone lines have a speed based on a unit called a *baud*, which is one cycle per second. The fastest rate a phone line can achieve is 2400 baud. Modems can pack multiple bits of data into each baud; a 33.6 kilobits per second (Kbps) modem, for example, packs 14 bits into every baud: 2400 × 14 = 33.6 Kbps.

Modem Connections Internal modems connect to the computer very differently from how external modems connect. Almost all internal modems connect to a PCI or PCI Express (PCIe) expansion bus slot inside the computer (see Figure 23-8).

Contemporary external modems connect to the computer through an available USB port (see Figure 23-9). USB offers simple plug and play and easy portability between machines, plus such modems require no external electrical source, getting all the power they need from the USB connection.

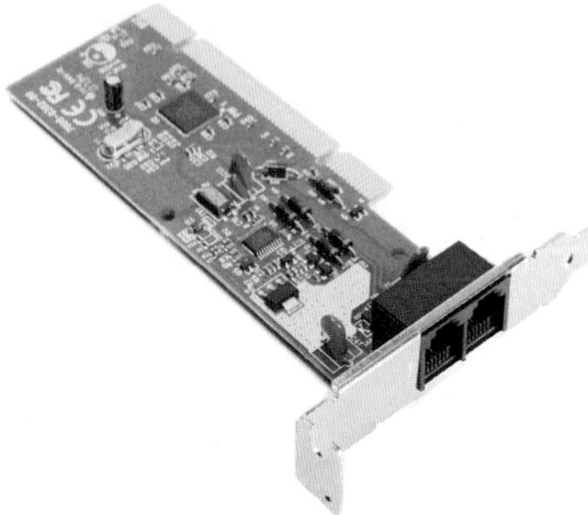

Figure 23-8 An internal modem

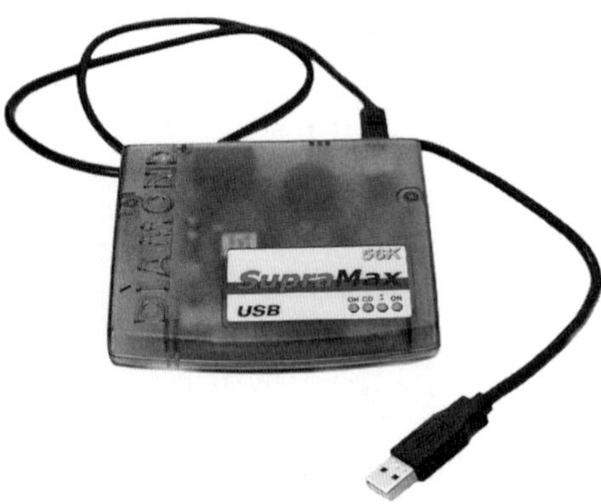

Figure 23-9 A USB modem

Dial-Up Networking

The software side of dial-up networks requires configuration within the OS to include information provided by your ISP. The ISP provides a dial-up telephone number or numbers, as well as your user name and initial password. In addition, the ISP will tell you about any special configuration options you need to specify in the software setup. The full configuration of dial-up networking is beyond the scope of this book, but you should at least know where to go to follow instructions from your ISP. Let's take a look at the Network and Sharing Center applet in Windows 7.

Configuring Dial-Up To start configuring a dial-up connection, open the Network and Sharing Center applet and click on *Set up a new connection or network* (see Figure 23-10).

Select Connect to the Internet and enter your dial-up information, as shown in Figure 23-11.

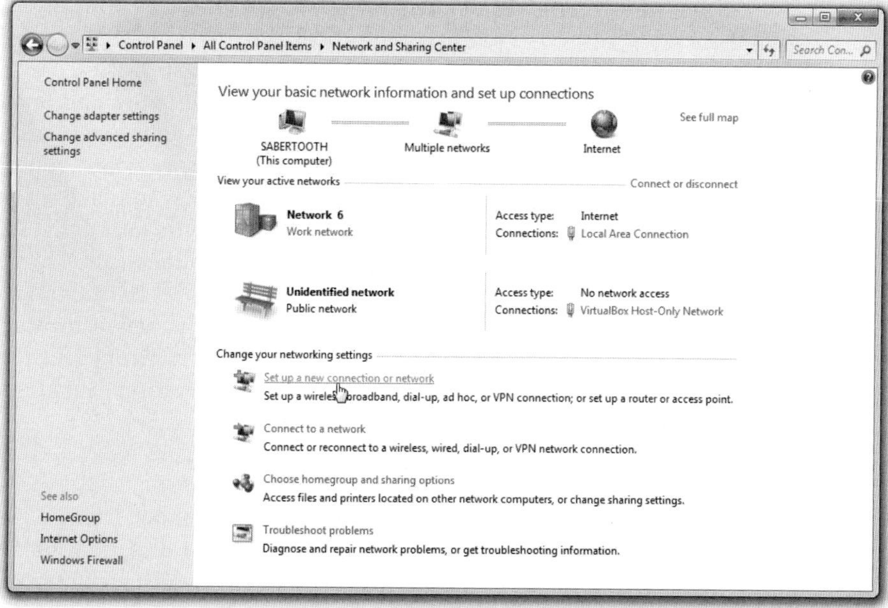

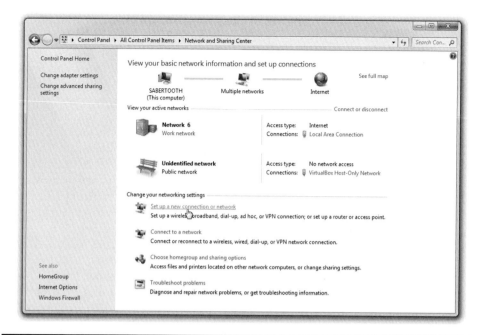

Figure 23-10 Setting up a new connection or network in Windows 7

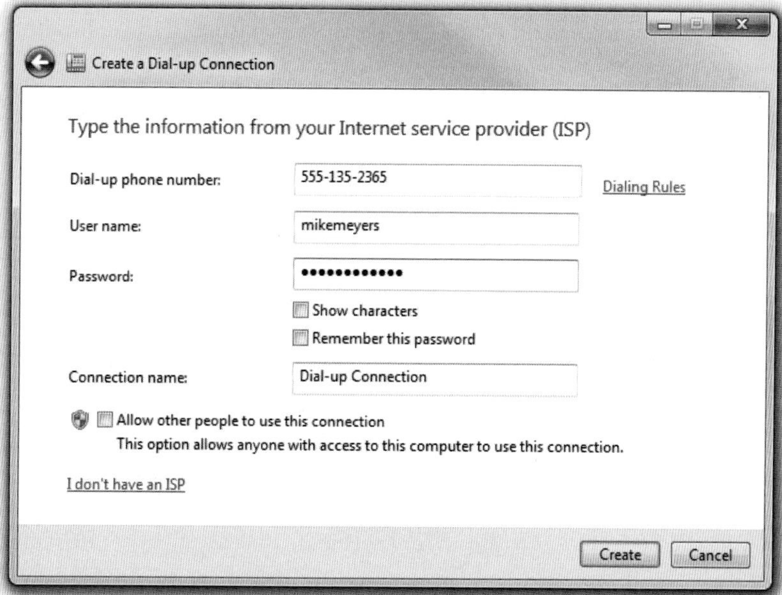

Figure 23-11 Creating a dial-up connection in Windows 7

PPP Dial-up links to the Internet have their own special hardware protocol called *Point-to-Point Protocol (PPP)*. PPP is a streaming protocol developed especially for dial-up Internet access. To Windows, a modem is nothing more than a special type of network adapter. You can configure a new dial-up connection in the Network and Sharing Center in current versions of Windows.

Most dial-up "I can't connect to the Internet"–type problems are user errors. Your first area of investigation is the modem itself. Use the modem's properties to make sure the volume is turned up. Have the user listen to the connection. Does she hear a dial tone? If she doesn't, make sure the modem's line is plugged into a good phone jack. Does she hear the modem dial and then hear someone saying, "Hello? Hello?" If so, she probably dialed the wrong number! Wrong password error messages are fairly straightforward—remember that the password may be correct but the user name may be wrong. If she still fails to connect, it's time to call the network folks to see what is not properly configured in your dial-up modem's Properties dialog box.

ISDN

A standard telephone connection comprises many pieces. First, the phone line runs from your phone out to a network interface box (the little box on the side of your house) and into a central switch belonging to the telephone company. (In some cases, intermediary steps are present.) Standard metropolitan areas have a large number of central offices, each with a central switch. Houston, Texas, for example, has nearly 100 offices in the general metro area. These central switches connect to each other through high-capacity *trunk lines*. Before 1970, the entire phone system was analog; over time, however, phone companies began to upgrade their trunk lines to digital systems. Today, the entire telephone system, with the exception of the line from your phone to the central office (and sometimes even that) is digital.

During this upgrade period, customers continued to demand higher throughput from their phone lines. The old telephone line was not expected to produce more than 28.8 Kbps (56-Kbps modems, which were a *big* surprise to the phone companies, didn't appear until 1995). Needless to say, the phone companies were very motivated to come up with a way to generate higher capacities. Their answer was actually fairly straightforward: make the entire phone system digital. By adding special equipment at the central office and the user's location, phone companies can now achieve a throughput of up to 64 Kbps per line over the same copper wires already used by telephone lines. This process of sending telephone transmission across fully digital lines end-to-end is called *integrated services digital network (ISDN)* service.

ISDN service consists of two types of channels: Bearer (B) channels and Delta (D) channels. B channels carry data and voice information at 64 Kbps. D channels carry setup and configuration information and data at 16 Kbps. Most ISDN providers allow the user to choose either one or two B channels. The more common setup is two B/one D, usually called a *basic rate interface (BRI)* setup. A BRI setup uses only one physical line, but each B channel sends 64 Kbps, doubling the throughput total to 128 Kbps. ISDN also connects much faster than modems, eliminating that long, annoying mating call you get with phone modems. The monthly cost per B channel is slightly more than

a regular phone line, and usually a fairly steep initial fee is levied for the installation and equipment. The big limitation is that you usually need to be within about 18,000 feet of a central office to use ISDN.

The physical connections for ISDN bear some similarity to analog modems. An ISDN wall socket usually looks something like a standard RJ-45 network jack. The most common interface for your computer is a device called a *terminal adapter (TA)*. TAs look much like regular modems, and like modems, they come in external and internal variants. You can even get TAs that connect directly to your LAN.

NOTE Another type of ISDN, called a primary rate interface (PRI), is composed of twenty-three 64-Kbps B channels and one 64-Kbps D channel, giving it a total throughput of 1.544 megabits per second (Mbps). PRI ISDN lines are also known as T1 lines.

DSL

Digital subscriber line (DSL) connections to ISPs use a standard telephone line with special equipment on each end to create always-on Internet connections at speeds much greater than dial-up.

NOTE The two most common forms of DSL you'll find are *asynchronous (ADSL)* and *synchronous (SDSL)*. ADSL lines differ between slow upload speed (such as 384 Kbps, 768 Kbps, and 1 Mbps) and faster download speed (usually 3–15 Mbps). SDSL has the same upload and download speeds, but telecom companies charge a lot more for the privilege. DSL encompasses many such variations, so you'll often see it referred to as *x*DSL.

Service levels for DSL can vary widely. At the low end of the spectrum, speeds are generally in the single digits—less than 1 Mbps upload and around 3 Mbps download. Where available, more recent *x*DSL technologies can offer competitive broadband speeds measured in tens or hundreds of megabits per second.

DSL requires little setup from a user standpoint. A tech comes to the house to install the DSL receiver, often called a DSL modem (see Figure 23-12), and possibly hook up a wireless router. Even if you skip the tech and have the installation equipment mailed to you, all you have to do is plug a couple cords in and call your ISP. The receiver connects to the telephone line and the computer (see Figure 23-13). The tech (or the user, if knowledgeable) then configures the DSL modem and router (if there is one) with the settings provided by the ISP, and that's about it! Within moments, you're surfing the Web. You don't need a second telephone line. You don't need to wear a special propeller hat or anything. The only kicker is that your house has to be within a fairly short distance from a main phone service switching center (central office). This distance can depend on the DSL variant and can range from several hundred feet to around 18,000 feet.

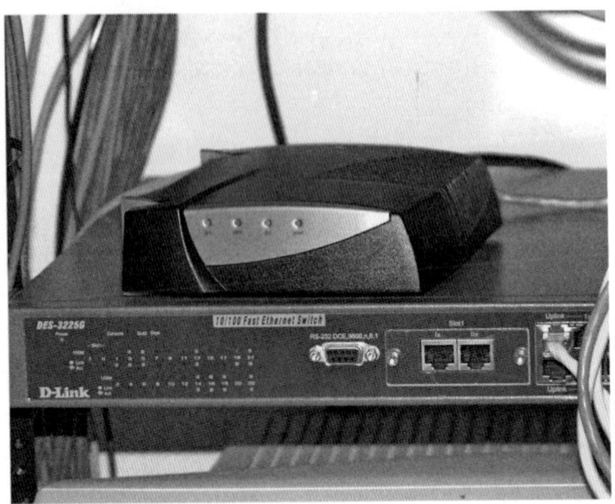

Figure 23-12 A DSL receiver

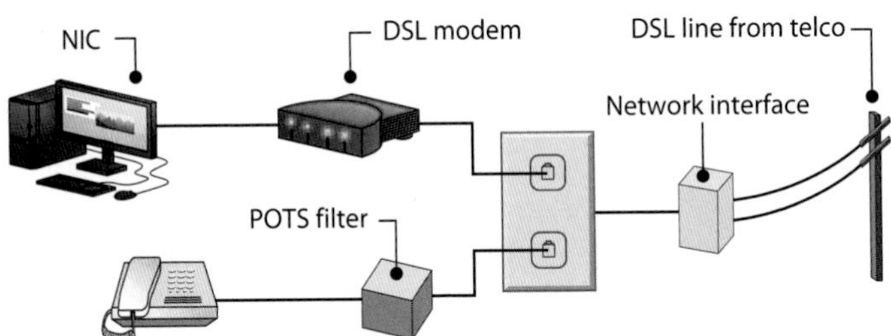

Figure 23-13 DSL connections

Cable

Cable offers a different approach to high-speed Internet access, using regular cable TV cables to serve up lightning-fast speeds. It offers faster service than most DSL connections, with upload speeds from 1 to 20 Mbps and download speeds ranging anywhere from 6 to 100+ Mbps, with gigabit speeds on the horizon. Cable Internet connections are theoretically available anywhere you can get cable TV.

Cable Internet connections start with an RG-6 or RG-59 cable coming into your house. The cable connects to a cable modem that then connects to a small home router or your network interface card (NIC) via Ethernet. Figure 23-14 shows a typical cable setup using a router.

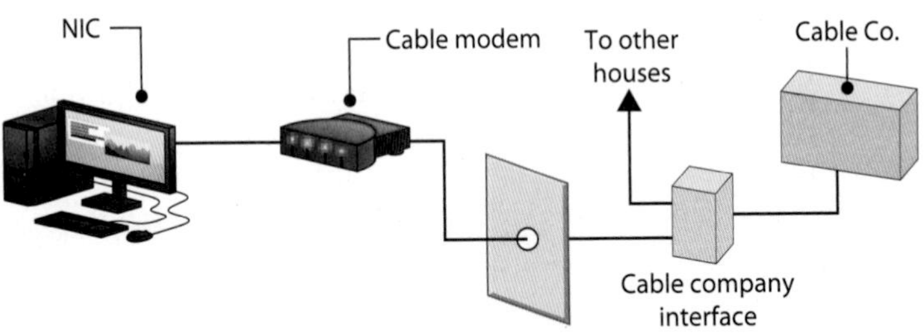

Figure 23-14 Cable connections

NOTE The term *modem* has been warped and changed beyond recognition in modern networking. Both DSL and cable—fully digital Internet connections—use the term *modem* to describe the box that takes the incoming signal from the Internet and translates it into something the computer can understand.

Fiber

In the past, high costs meant that only those with money to burn could enjoy the super-fast speeds of a fiber connection. Subsequently, DSL providers developed very popular fiber-to-the-node (FTTN) and fiber-to-the-premises (FTTP) services that provide Internet (and more), making them head-to-head competitors with the cable companies. More recently, entrants like Google Fiber and local municipalities have added momentum to the fiber rollout.

With FTTN, the fiber connection runs from the provider to a box somewhere in your neighborhood. This box is connected to your home or office using normal coaxial or Ethernet cabling. FTTP runs from the provider straight to a home or office, using fiber the whole way. Once inside the home or office, you can use any standard cabling (or wireless) to connect your computers to the Internet.

One popular FTTN service is AT&T's U-verse, which generally offers download speeds from 1 to 75 Mbps and upload speeds from 384 Kbps to 8 Mbps (see Figure 23-15). In a few locations, AT&T has deployed its GigaPower service, which gives you 1 Gbps for download and upload! Verizon's FiOS service is the most popular and widely available FTTP service in the United States, providing upload and download speeds ranging from 25 Mbps to 500 Mbps (if you can afford it, of course). Google Fiber, for its part, offers a 1 Gbps upload/download service. While these high numbers sound great, availability of service at this end of the scale is still pretty limited. (Google, please, please, please choose Houston next.)

Figure 23-15
U-verse gateway

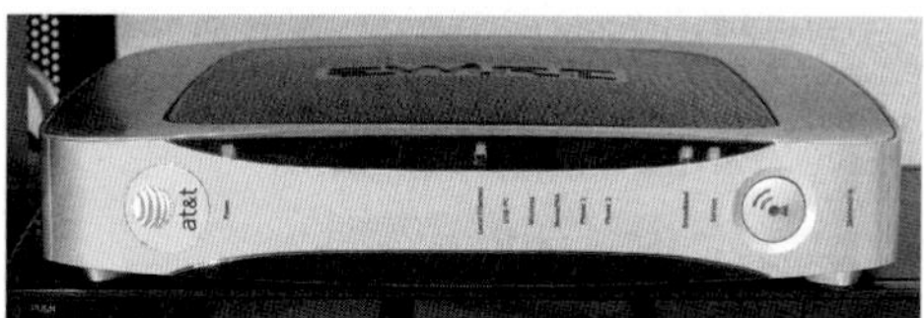

Wi-Fi

Wi-Fi (or 802.11 wireless) is so prevalent that it's the way many of us get to the Internet. Wireless access points (WAPs) designed to serve the public abound in coffee shops, airports, fast-food chains, and bars. Even some cities provide partial to full Wi-Fi coverage.

We covered 802.11 in detail in Chapter 22, "Wireless Networking," so there's no reason to repeat the process of connecting to a hotspot. Do remember that most open hotspots do not provide any level of encryption, meaning it's easy for a bad guy to monitor your connection and read everything you send or receive.

CAUTION Secure your public hotspot Web browsing using HTTPS-secured sites. It's surprisingly easy to do. Instead of typing www.facebook.com, for example, type in https://www.facebook.com or use a browser extension like the Electronic Frontier Foundation's HTTPS Everywhere.

Wi-Fi works well as an Internet access option for densely populated areas, but Wi-Fi's short range makes it impractical in areas where it's not easy to place new access points. In certain circumstances, you can address the range issue by using high-powered, directional antennas and Ethernet bridge devices. These can give you a *line-of-site wireless Internet connection* up to eight miles or more. These work great in places such as ski resorts, where you want to connect the restaurant halfway up the mountain to the main lodge, or lake cottages, where you want to connect a boat house to the main house.

NOTE An 802.11 network that covers a single city is an excellent example of a metropolitan area network (MAN).

Cellular

Who needs computers when you can get online with any number of mobile devices? Okay, there are plenty of things a smartphone or tablet can't do, but with the latest advances in cellular data services, your mobile Internet experience will feel a lot more like your home Internet experience than it ever has before.

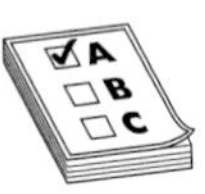

EXAM TIP You can share your smartphone's or tablet's connection to a cellular network using a process called *tethering*. You'll need to turn on the service on your device, and then connect your phone to your computer, either wirelessly as a *mobile hotspot* or directly using a USB connection. Most carriers charge extra to enable tethering on your smartphone or tablet. Check with your carrier to see if your service plan supports tethering.

Cellular data services have gone through a number of names over the years, so many that trying to keep track of them and place them in any order is extremely challenging. In an attempt to make organization somewhat clearer, the cellular industry developed a string of marketing terms using the idea of generations: first-generation devices are called 1G, second-generation are 2G, followed by 3G and 4G. On top of that, many technologies use G-names such as 2.5G to show they're not 2G but not quite 3G. You'll see these terms all over the place, especially on your phones (see Figure 23-16). Marketing folks tend to bend and flex the definition of these terms in advertisements, so you should always read more about the device and not just its generation.

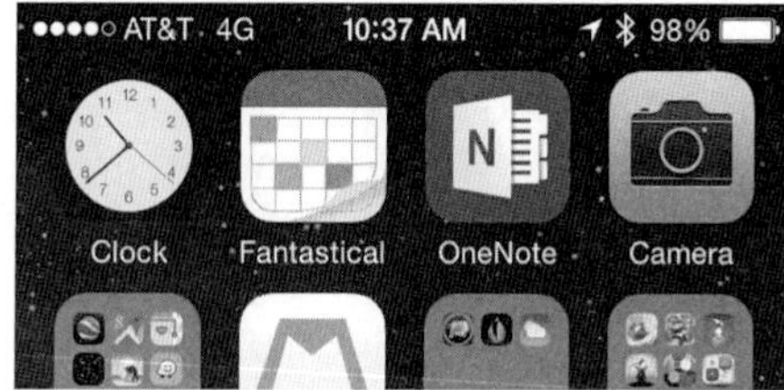

Figure 23-16 iPhone connecting over 4G

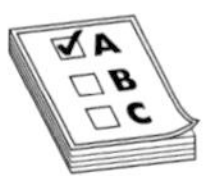

EXAM TIP The CompTIA A+ exams will not ask you to define a G-level for a particular cellular technology.

The first generation (1G) of cell phone data services was analog and not at all designed to carry packetized data. It wasn't until the early 1990s that two fully digital technologies called the Global System for Mobile Communications (GSM) and code division multiple access (CDMA) came into wide acceptance. GSM evolved into GPRS and EDGE, while CDMA introduced EV-DO. GPRS and EDGE were 2.5G technologies, while EV-DO was true 3G. Standards, with names like UTMS, HSPA+, and HSDPA, have brought GSM-based networks into the world of 3G and 3.5G. These mobile data services provide modest real-world download speeds of a few Mbps (generally under 10, usually 3 or 4).

We're now well into the fourth generation. Devices and networks using *Long Term Evolution (LTE)* technology rolled out worldwide in the early 2010s and now dominate wireless services. As early as 2013, for example, LTE already had ~20 percent market share in the United States, and even higher in parts of Asia. The numbers have only grown since then. Marketed as and now generally accepted as a true *4G* technology, LTE networks feature speeds of (in theory) up to 300 Mbps download and 75 Mbps upload (see Figure 23-17).

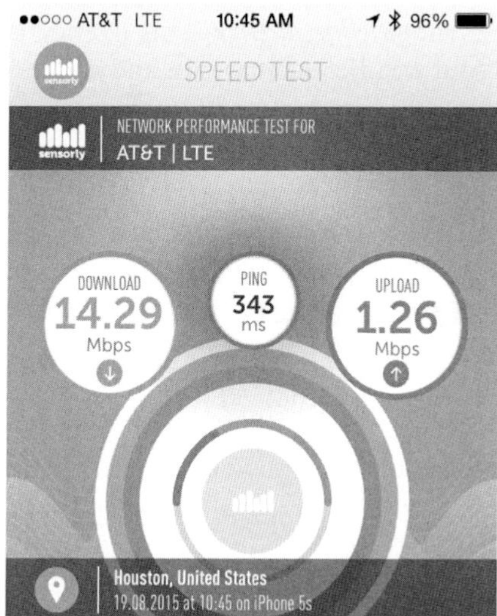

Figure 23-17 Real-world LTE speed test

NOTE LTE has become synonymous with 4G these days. You'll often see the mashed-up term *4G LTE*, which I guess is an attempt by marketing folks to make sure they get all the buzzwords out there.

With excellent speed and broad coverage of cell towers, LTE can readily replace wired network technology. In rural areas, for example, you can connect a computer to the Internet without a physical connection such as DSL, cable, or fiber, to an ISP. You can instead connect to a wireless *hotspot*—a device that connects via cellular and enables other devices to access the Internet—and be on your merry way. Hotspots can be dedicated devices, or simply one feature of a modern smartphone.

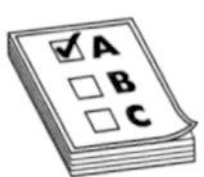

EXAM TIP Just like LANs and WANs, we also have WLANs and WWANs. A wireless wide area network (WWAN) works similarly to a wireless LAN (WLAN), but connects multiple networks similarly to a WAN.

Satellite

Satellite connections to the Internet get the data beamed to a satellite dish on your house or office; a receiver handles the flow of data, eventually sending it through an Ethernet cable to the NIC in your computer. I can already sense people's eyebrows raising. The early days of satellite required you to connect via a modem. You would upload at the slow 26- to 48-Kbps modem speed, but then get speedier downloads from the dish. It worked, so why complain? You really can move to that shack on the side of the Himalayas to write the great Tibetan novel and still have DSL-speed Internet connectivity. Sweet!

Satellite might be the most intriguing of all the technologies used to connect to the Internet today. As with satellite television, though, you need to make sure the satellite dish points toward the satellites (toward the south if you live in the United States). The only significant issue with satellite is that the distance the signal must travel creates a small delay called the *satellite latency*. This latency is usually unnoticeable unless the signal degrades in foul weather such as rain and snow.

Satellite setup requires a dish, professionally installed with line-of-sight to the satellite. A coax cable runs from the dish to your satellite modem. The satellite modem has an RJ-45 connection, which you may then connect directly to your computer or to a router.

Connection to the Internet

So you went out and signed up for an Internet connection. Now it's time to get connected. You basically have two choices:

1. Connect a single computer to your Internet connection
2. Connect a network of computers to your Internet connection

Connecting a single computer to the Internet is easy. If you're using wireless, you connect to the wireless box using the provided information, although a good tech will always go through the proper steps described in Chapter 22 to protect the wireless network. If you choose to go wired, you run a cable from whatever type of box is provided to the computer.

If you want to connect a number of computers using wired connections, you'll need to grab a router. Several manufacturers offer robust, easy-to-configure routers that enable multiple computers to connect to a single Internet connection. These boxes require very little configuration and provide firewall protection between the primary computer and the Internet, which you'll learn more about in Chapter 27. All it takes to install one of these routers is simply to plug your computer into any of the LAN ports on the back, and then to plug the cable from your Internet connection into the port labeled Internet or WAN.

There are hundreds of perfectly fine choices for SOHO (small office/home office) routers (see Figure 23-18 for an example). Most have four Ethernet ports for wired connections, and one or more Wi-Fi radios for any wireless computers you may have. All home routers use a technology called *Network Address Translation (NAT)* to perform a little network subterfuge: It presents an entire LAN of computers to the Internet as a single machine. It effectively hides all of your computers and makes them appear invisible to other computers on the Internet. All anyone on the Internet sees is your *public* IP address. This is the address your ISP gives you, while all the computers in your LAN use private addresses that are invisible to the world. NAT therefore acts as a firewall, protecting your internal network from probing or malicious users on the outside.

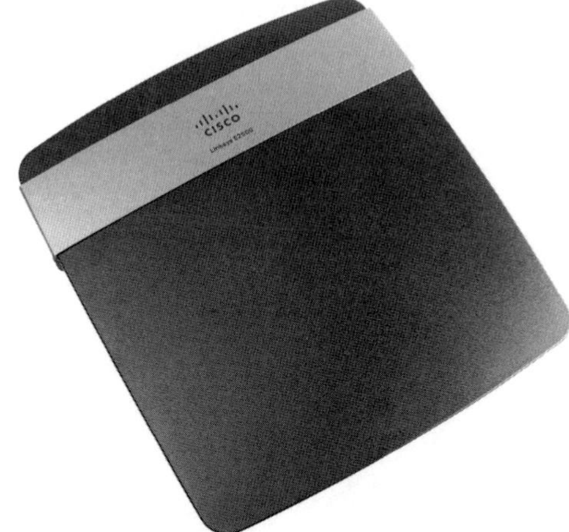

Figure 23-18 Common home router with Wi-Fi

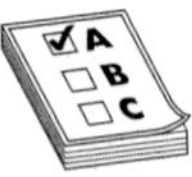

EXAM TIP Many computers can share a smaller pool of routable IP addresses with dynamic NAT (DNAT). A NAT might have 10 routable IP addresses, for example, to serve 40 computers on the LAN. LAN traffic uses the internal, private IP addresses. When a computer requests information beyond the network, the NAT doles out a routable IP address from its pool for that communication. Dynamic NAT is also called Pooled NAT.

This works well enough—unless you're the unlucky 11th person to try to access the Internet from behind the company NAT—but has the obvious limitation of still needing many true, expensive, routable IP addresses.

Basic Router Configuration

SOHO routers require very little in the way of configuration and in many cases will work perfectly (if unsafely) right out of the box. In some cases, though, you may have to deal with a more complex network that requires changing the router's settings. The vast majority of these routers have built-in configuration Web pages that you access by typing the router's IP address into a browser. The address varies by manufacturer, so check the router's documentation. If you typed in the correct address, you should then receive a prompt for a user name and password, as in Figure 23-19. As with the IP address, the default user name and password vary depending on the model/manufacturer. Once you enter the correct credentials, you will be greeted by the router's configuration pages (see Figure 23-20). From these pages, you can change any of the router's settings.

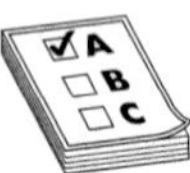

EXAM TIP A lot of networking devices designed for the residential space use a feature called *universal plug and play (UPnP)* to seek out and connect to other UPnP devices. This feature enables seamless interconnectivity at the cost of somewhat lowered security.

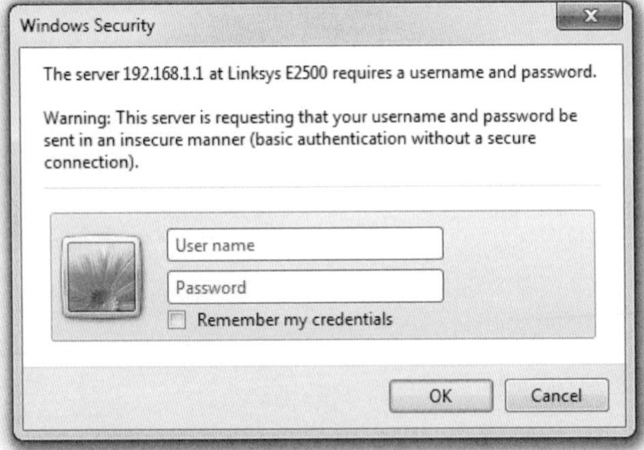

Figure 23-19 Router asking for user name and password

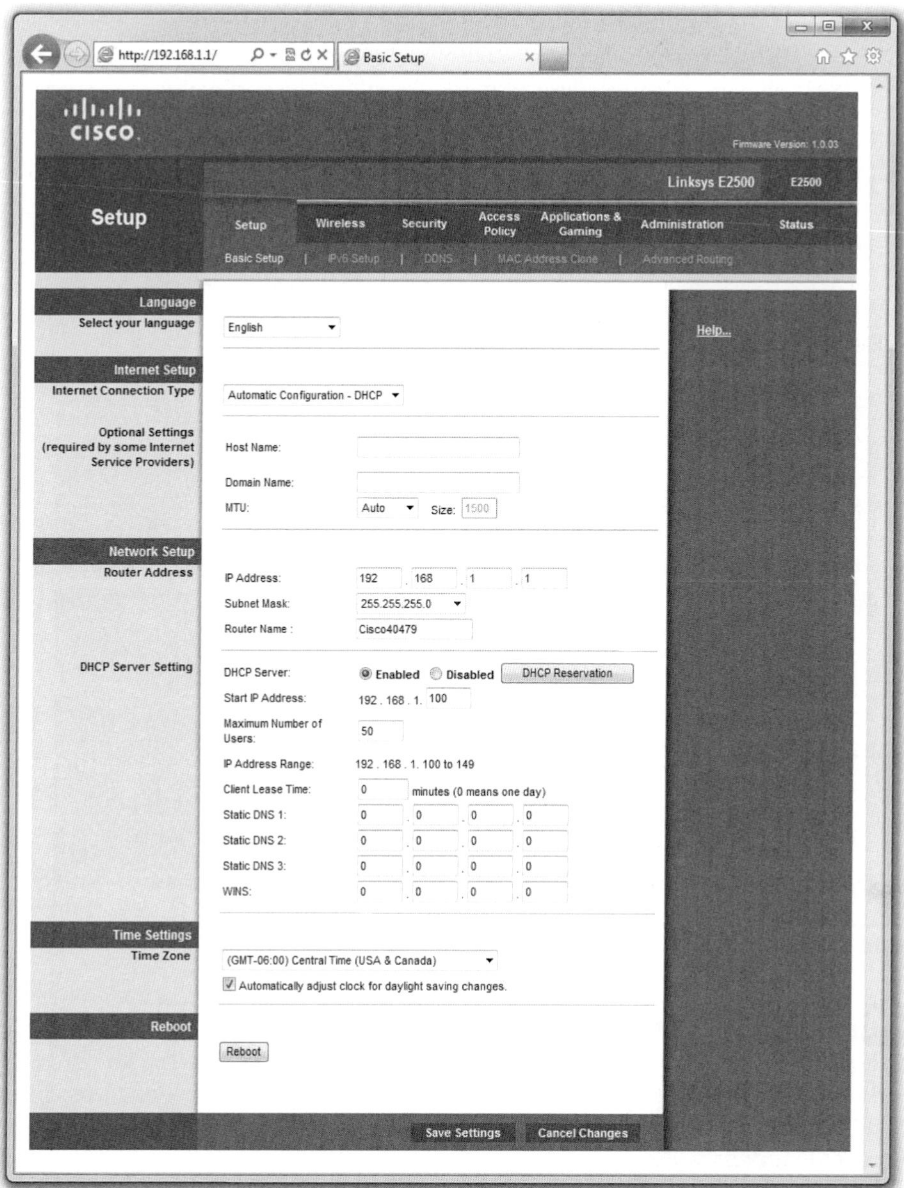

Figure 23-20 Configuration home page

Now we'll take a look at a few of the basic settings that CompTIA wants you to be familiar with. Later on in Chapter 28, "Securing Computers," we'll discuss a number of more advanced settings that help keep your network and the computers on it secure while they use services available over the Internet.

Changing User Name and Password All routers have a user name and password that gives you access to the configuration screen. One of the first changes you should make to your router after you have it working is to change the user name and password to something other than the default. This is especially important if you have open wireless turned on, which you'll recall from Chapter 22. If you leave the default user name and password, anyone who has access to your LAN can easily gain access to the router and change its settings. Fortunately, router manufacturers make it easy to change a router's login credentials, as shown in Figure 23-21.

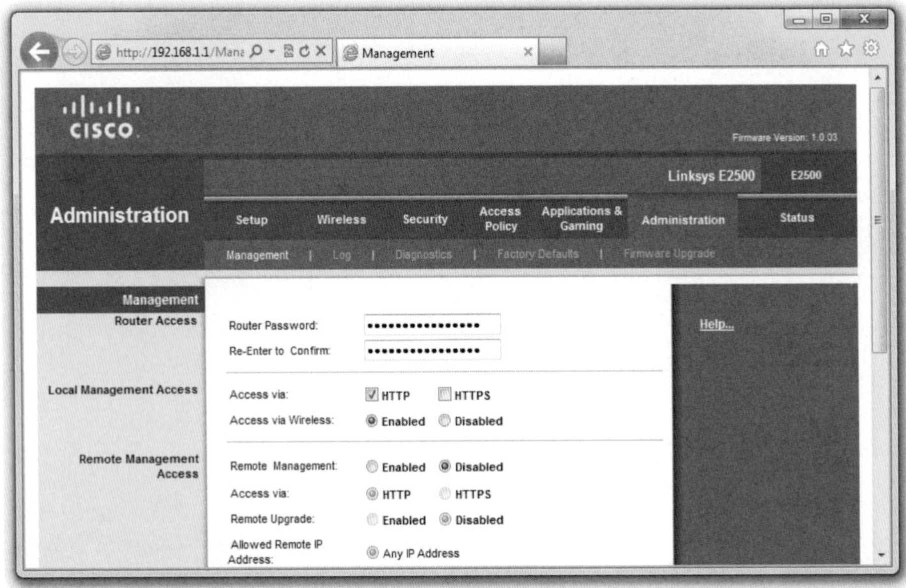

Figure 23-21 Changing the password

Setting Static IP Addresses With the user name and password taken care of, let's look at setting up the router to use a static IP address for the Internet or WAN connection. In most cases, when you plug in the router's Internet connection, it receives an IP address using DHCP just like any other computer. Of course, this means that your Internet IP address will change from time to time, which can be a bit of a downside. This does not affect most people, but for some home users and businesses, it can present a problem. To solve this problem, most ISPs enable you to order a static IP (for an extra monthly charge). Once your ISP has allocated you a static IP address, you must manually enter it into your router. You do this the same way as the previous change you've just looked at. My router has an Internet Setup configuration section where I can enter all the settings that my ISP has provided to me (see Figure 23-22). Remember,

you must change your connection type from Automatic/DHCP to Static IP to enter the new addresses.

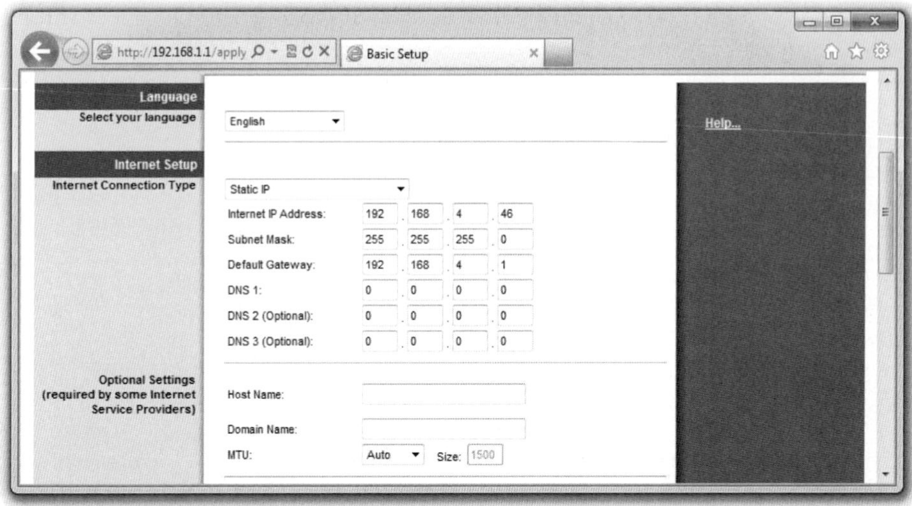

Figure 23-22 Entering a static IP address

Updating Firmware

Routers are just like any other computer in that they run software—and software has bugs, vulnerabilities, and other issues that sometimes require updating. The router manufacturers call these "firmware updates" and make them available either through the router's administration interface or on their Web sites for easy download.

NOTE While these methods are generally true of routers available commercially, routers provided by your ISP may update automatically.

If the firmware update is available directly through your router's administration interface, a firmware update may be a few clicks away. If not, download the latest firmware from the manufacturer's Web site to your computer. Then enter the router's configuration Web page and find the firmware update screen. On my router, it looks like Figure 23-23. From here, just follow the directions and click Upgrade (or your router's equivalent). A quick word of caution: Unlike a Windows update, a firmware update gone bad can *brick* your router. In other words, it can render the hardware inoperable and make it as useful as a brick sitting on your desk. This rarely happens, but you should keep it in mind when doing a firmware update.

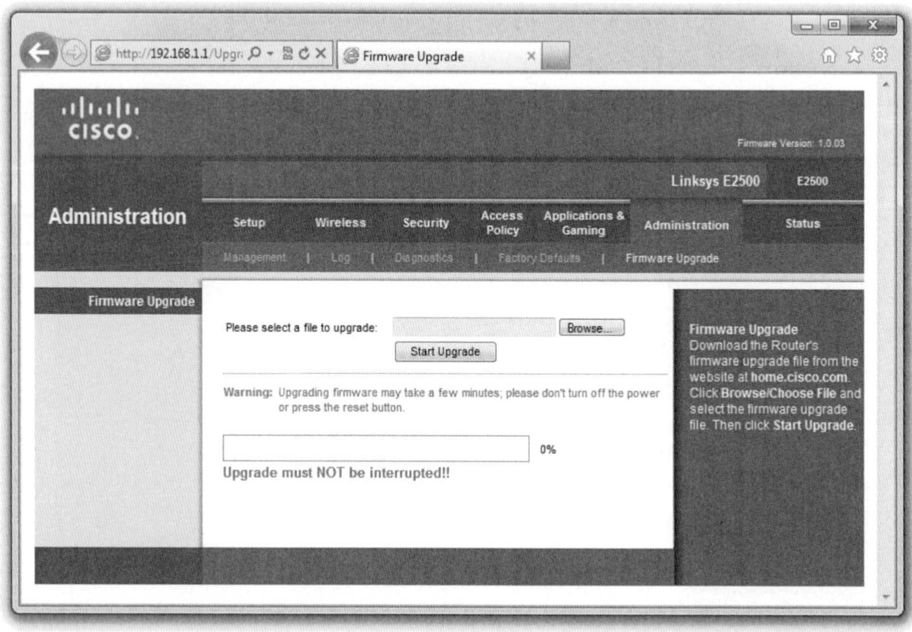

Figure 23-23 Firmware update page

Internet Application Protocols

Once you've established a connection to the Internet, you need applications to get anything done. If you want to surf the Web, you need an application called a *Web browser*, such as Mozilla Firefox, Google Chrome, or Microsoft Edge. If you want to make a VoIP phone call, you need an application like Skype or Google Voice. These applications in turn use very clearly designed application protocols. All Web browsers use the *Hypertext Transfer Protocol (HTTP)*. All e-mail clients use Post Office Protocol 3 (POP3) or Internet Message Access Protocol (IMAP) to receive e-mail. All e-mail applications use Simple Mail Transfer Protocol (SMTP) to send their e-mails. Every Internet protocol has its own rules and its own port numbers. Though there are tens of thousands of application protocols in existence, lucky for you, CompTIA only wants you to understand the following commonly used application protocols (except SFTP and VoIP, which CompTIA doesn't list but I've added for completeness):

- World Wide Web (HTTP and HTTPS)
- E-mail (POP3, IMAP, and SMTP)
- Telnet
- SSH

- FTP/SFTP
- Remote Desktop Protocol (RDP)
- VoIP (SIP)

In addition to the application protocols we see and use daily, there are hundreds, maybe thousands, of application protocols that run behind the scenes, taking care of important jobs to ensure that the application protocols we do see run well. You've encountered a number of these hidden application protocols back in Chapter 21. Take DNS. Without DNS, you couldn't type www.google.com in your Web browser and end up at the right address. DHCP is another great example. You don't see DHCP do its job, but without it, any computers relying on DHCP won't receive IP addresses.

Here's another one: People don't like to send credit card information, home phone numbers, or other personal information over the Web for fear this information might be intercepted by hackers. Fortunately, there are methods for encrypting this information, the most common being *Hypertext Transfer Protocol Secure (HTTPS)*. Although HTTPS looks a lot like HTTP from the point of view of a Web browser, HTTPS uses port 443. It's easy to tell if a Web site is using HTTPS because the Web address starts with *https*, as shown in Figure 23-24, instead of just *http*. But you don't deal with HTTPS directly; it just works in your browser automatically.

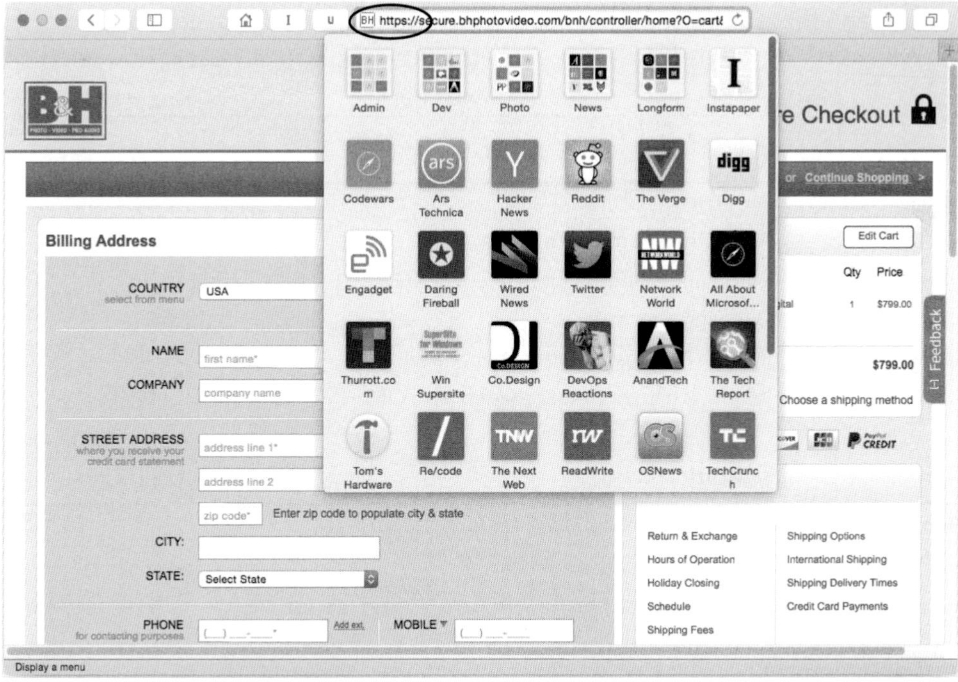

Figure 23-24 A secure Web page

In order to differentiate the application protocols you see from the application protocols you don't see, I'm going to coin the term "utility protocol" to define any of the hidden application protocols. So, using your author's definition, HTTP is an application protocol and DNS is a utility protocol. All TCP/IP protocols use defined ports, require an application to run, and have special settings unique to that application. You'll look at several of these services and learn how to configure them. As a quick reference, Table 23-1 lists the names, functions, and port numbers of the application protocols CompTIA would like you to know. Table 23-2 does the same for utility protocols.

Table 23-1 Application Protocol Port Numbers

Application Protocol	Function	Port Number
HTTP	Web pages	80
HTTPS	Secure Web pages	443
FTP	File transfer	20, 21
SFTP	Secure file transfer	22
IMAP	Incoming e-mail	143
POP3	Incoming e-mail	110
SMTP	Outgoing e-mail	25
Telnet	Terminal emulation	23
SSH	Encrypted terminal emulation	22
RDP	Remote Desktop	3389
SIP	Voice over IP	5060

Utility Protocol	Function		Port Number
DNS	Allows the use of DNS naming	UDP	53
DHCP	Automatic IP addressing	UDP	67, 68
LDAP	Querying directories	TCP	389
SNMP	Remote management of network devices	UDP	161
SMB	Windows naming/folder sharing; also CIFS	TCP	445
		UDP	137, 138, 139
AFP	Mac OS X file services	TCP	548, 427

Table 23-2 Utility Protocol Port Numbers

After you've read about these protocols, you'll learn about Virtual Private Networks and the protocols they use. I'll also tell you about a few more Internet support utilities that don't quite fit anywhere else.

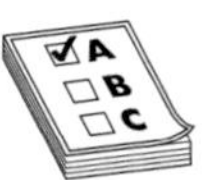

EXAM TIP Know all of the protocols and ports listed in Tables 1 and 2 for the 901 exam.

902

The World Wide Web

The Web provides a graphical face for the Internet. *Web servers* (servers running specialized software) provide Web sites that you access by using the HTTP protocol on port 80 and thus get more-or-less useful information. Using a Web browser, such as Internet Explorer, Microsoft Edge, Google Chrome, or Mozilla Firefox, you can click a link on a Web page and be instantly transported—not just to some Web server in your home town—to anywhere in the world. Figure 23-25 shows Firefox at the home page of my company's Web site, www.totalsem.com. Where is the server located? Does it matter? It could be in a closet in my office or in a huge data center in Houston. The great part about the Web is that you can get from here to there and access the information you need with few clicks or taps.

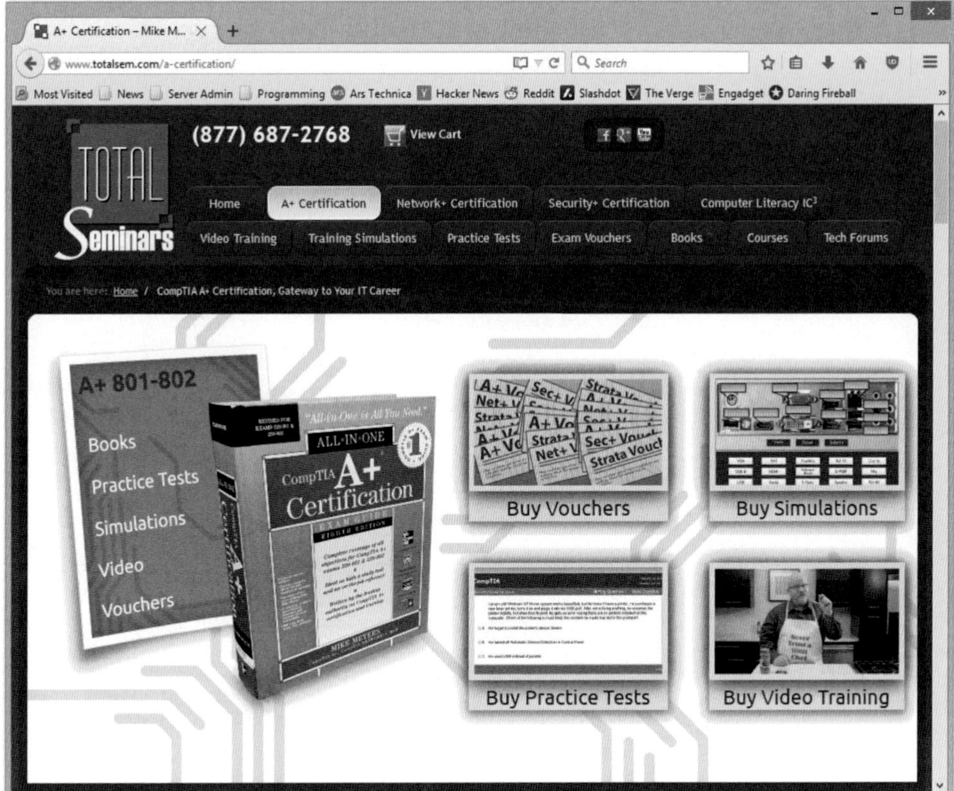

Figure 23-25 Mozilla Firefox showing a Web page

Setting up a Web browser takes almost no effort. As long as the Internet connection is working, Web browsers work automatically. This is not to say you can't make plenty of custom settings, but the default browser settings work almost every time. If you type in a Web address, such as that of the best search engine on the planet—www.google.com—and it doesn't work, check the line and your network settings and you'll figure out where the problem is.

Configuring Internet Explorer

Web browsers are highly configurable. On most Web browsers, you can set the default font size, choose whether to display graphics, and adjust several other settings. Although all Web browsers support these settings, where you go to make these changes varies dramatically. If you are using the popular Internet Explorer (IE) that comes with Windows versions up to 8.1, you will find configuration tools in the Internet Options Control Panel applet or under the Tools menu in Internet Explorer (see Figure 23-26). The applet is called Internet Options, but the window it launches is labeled Internet Properties.

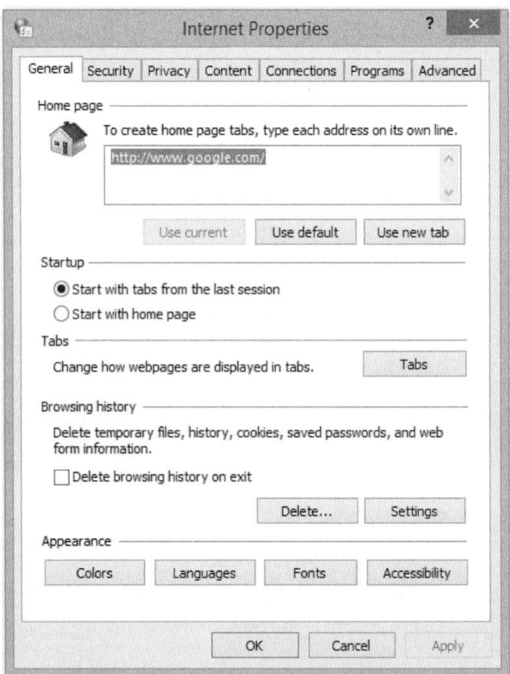

Figure 23-26 Internet Options applet

NOTE For more than a decade, Internet Explorer earned much ill will among Web developers because of its tendency to ignore the standards that make modern Web sites work. The need to support older IE versions became notorious for holding back progress on the Web, and the end result of this reputation was Microsoft's announcement that the current version, IE11, would be the last. Microsoft Edge takes over as the Microsoft browser of choice on Windows versions beyond 8.1, but the Internet Options Control Panel applet is only for Internet Explorer. Because Internet Options has no effect on any other browser—including Edge, Firefox, Chrome, and so on—its days are probably numbered.

I find it bizarre that CompTIA specifically lists Internet Options as an objective on the CompTIA A+ 220-902 exam. It's just so…Microsofty. There are obviously more browsers than just Internet Explorer, so I'll begin by explaining the options available to you in Internet Explorer, and then show you some of the common options found in other browsers, too.

When you open the Internet Options applet, you'll see seven tabs along the top. The first tab is the General tab. These settings control the most basic features of Internet Explorer: the home page, tab management, your browsing history, searching, and other appearance controls. If you want to delete or change how Internet Explorer stores the Web sites you've visited, use this tab.

The Security tab enables you set how severely Internet Explorer safeguards your Web browsing (see Figure 23-27). Each setting can be adjusted for a particular zone, such as the Internet, your local intranet, trusted sites, and restricted sites. You can configure which Web sites fall into which zones. Once you've picked a zone to control, you can set Internet Explorer's security level. The High security level blocks more Web sites and disables some plug-ins, while Medium-high and Medium allow less-secure Web sites and features to display and operate.

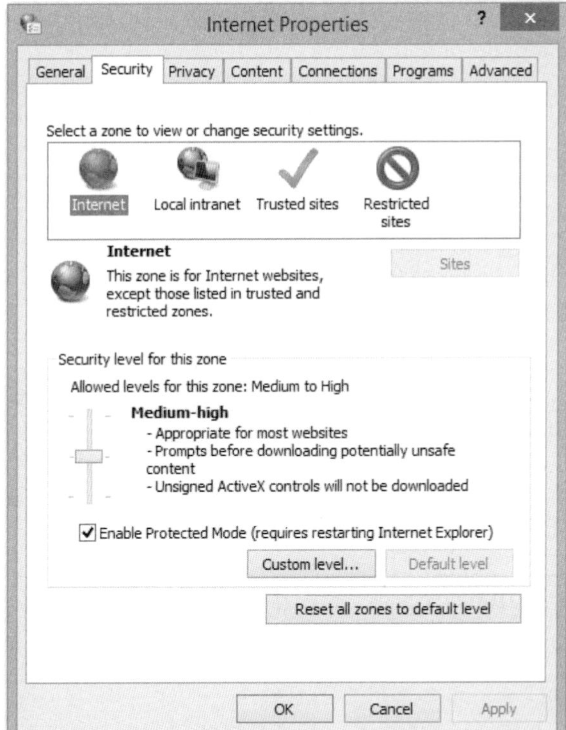

Figure 23-27 The Security tab in Internet Options

The Privacy tab works a lot like the Security tab, except it controls privacy matters, such as cookies, location tracking, pop-ups, and whether browser extensions will run in private browsing mode. There is a slider that enables you to control what is blocked—everything is blocked on the highest setting; nothing is blocked on the lowest. Go here if you don't like the idea of Web sites tracking your browsing history (though cookies do other things, too, like authenticate users).

The Content tab controls what your browser will and will not display. This time, however, it enables you to gate access to insecure or objectionable sites—a practice called *content filtering*—using certificates and a *parental-control* tool called Family Safety, which lets system administrators restrict Web, game, and app usage (by rating system and exception lists) and even control when an account can log in. The Content tab also enables you to adjust the AutoComplete feature that fills in Web addresses for you, as well as control settings for RSS feeds and Web Slices (both methods for subscribing to a Web page's content updates).

The Connections tab enables you to do a lot of things. You can set up your connection to the Internet, via broadband or dial-up, connect to a VPN, or adjust some LAN settings, which you probably won't need to deal with except perhaps to configure a proxy server connection. Because proxy servers are a little complicated and CompTIA wants you to know about them, let's quickly talk about what they are used for.

Many corporations use a proxy server to filter employee Internet access, and when you're on their corporate network, you need to set your proxy settings within the Web browser (and any other Internet software you want to use). A *proxy server* is software that enables multiple connections to the Internet to go through one protected computer. Applications that want to access Internet resources send requests to the proxy server instead of trying to access the Internet directly, which both protects the client computers and enables the network administrator to monitor and restrict Internet access. Each application must therefore be configured to use the proxy server.

Moving on, the Programs tab in Internet Options contains settings for your default Web browser, any add-ons you use (like Java), and how other programs deal with HTML files and e-mail messages.

The Advanced tab does exactly what it sounds like: lists a bunch of advanced options that you can turn on and off with the check of a box (see Figure 23-28). The available options include accessibility, browsing, international, and, most importantly, security settings. From here, you can control how Internet Explorer checks Web site certificates, among many other settings. It also hosts a settings-reset button in case you need a fresh start.

EXAM TIP Given a specific scenario, be sure you know how to use the various Internet Options.

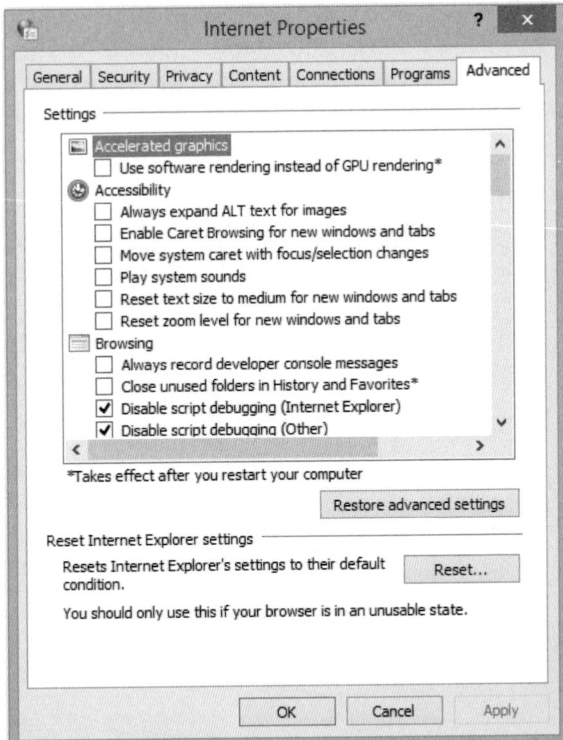

Figure 23-28 The Advanced tab in Internet Options

Configuring Other Web Browsers

I want to stomp all over Internet Explorer and tell you how bad it is—but the truth of the matter is that, after a big push to get IE back on track in recent versions, Microsoft has done the right thing to help the Web move beyond IE by focusing on its replacement, Microsoft Edge. Still, Edge is just for versions of Windows beyond 8.1, so you'll probably want to download one of several other Web browsers that run faster and support more Web standards than IE11. Two of the big browser heavyweights that fit this description are Mozilla Firefox and Google Chrome.

You control their settings much like you do in Internet Explorer, though you won't find an applet tucked away in Control Panel. In Google Chrome, you can click on the three-line icon in the upper-right corner of the browser and select Settings. In Mozilla Firefox, the icon looks like a stack of horizontal lines, but it's also in the upper-right corner, and you're looking for the Options button.

In these menus, you'll find a lot of settings very similar to the ones you find in Internet Options. In fact, Firefox's controls are laid out almost exactly the same, though you won't

find everything in the same place (see Figure 23-29). Google Chrome's settings look more like a Web page, but they still control the same features: home page, security, font size, cookies, and all your old favorites (see Figure 23-30). Take some time to use these browsers and explore their settings. You'll be surprised how well your knowledge of one browser helps you set up another.

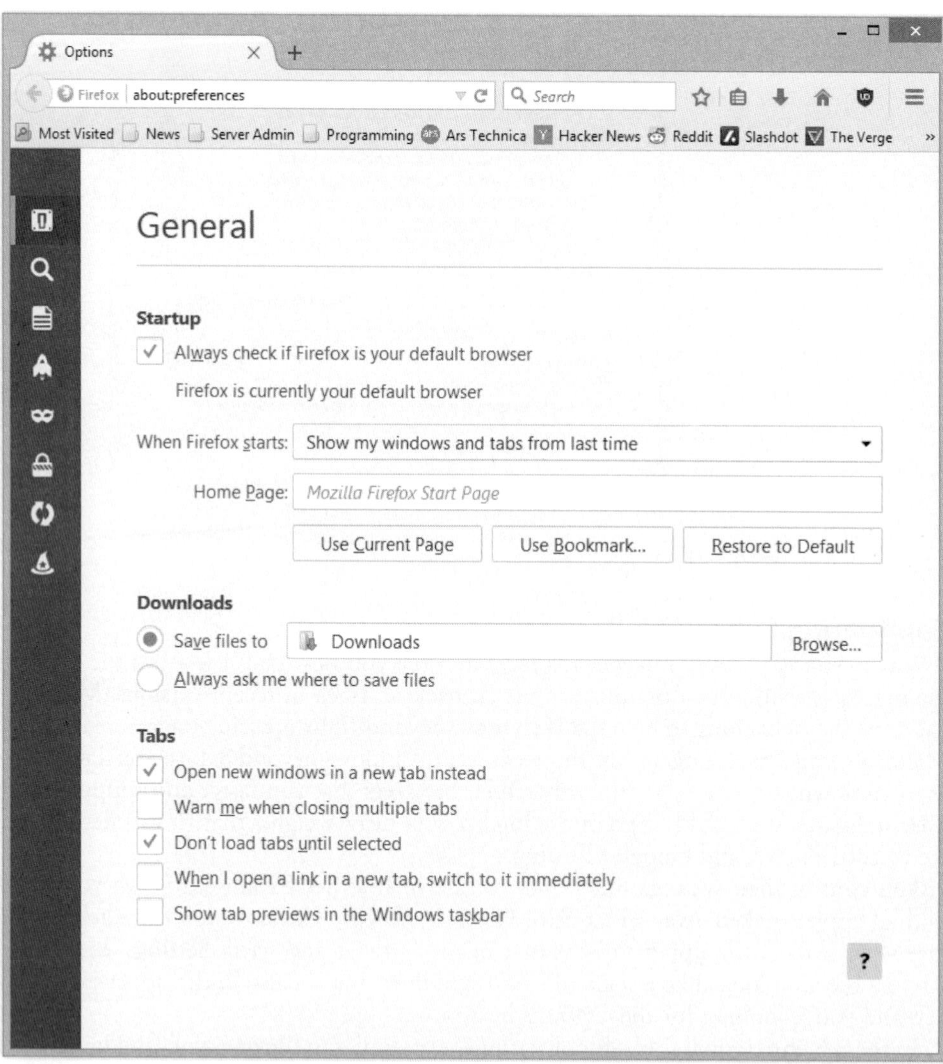

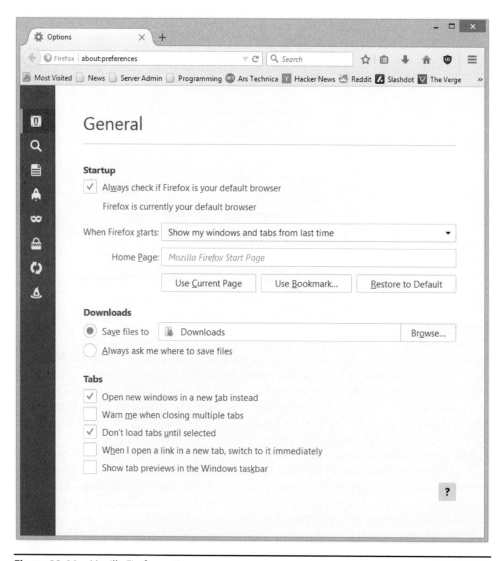

Figure 23-29 Mozilla Firefox options

assumes you'll use iCloud for all that sending and receiving stuff and thus you have no other configuration to do. All the IMAP, POP, SMTP, S/MIME, and so on settings happen behind the scenes. CompTIA calls this sort of lack of configuration *integrated commercial provider email configuration*. That's pretty accurate, if a little bland. You will see more of this in the mobile devices chapters.

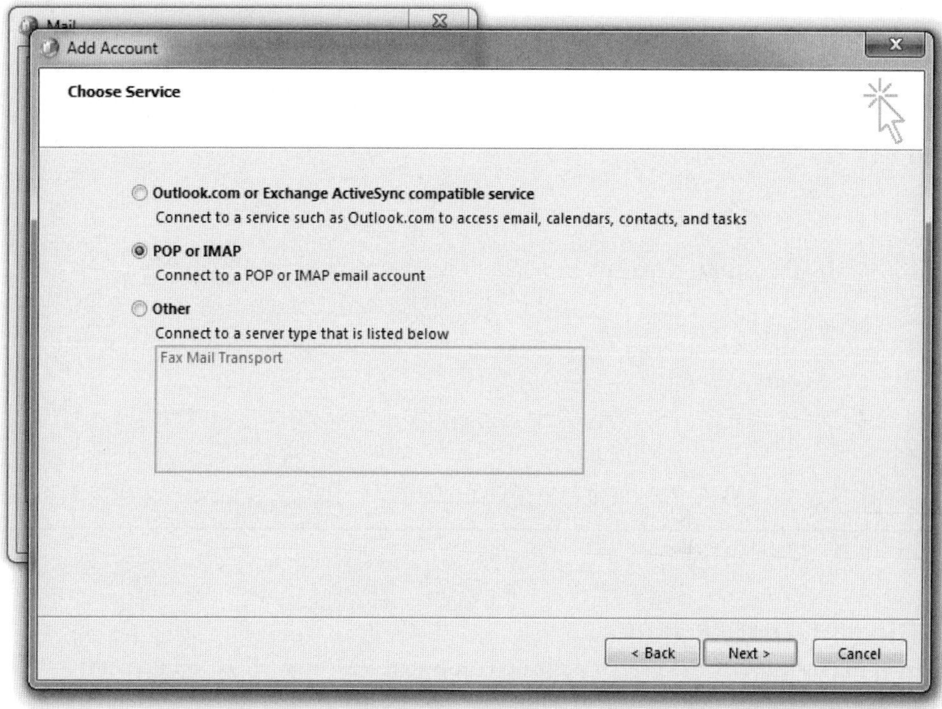

Figure 23-37 Manual setup in Outlook 2016

Web Mail

Most people use Web-based e-mail, such as Yahoo! Mail, Gmail from Google, or Outlook.com from Microsoft, to handle all of their e-mail needs (see Figure 23-38). Web-based mail offers the convenience of having access to your e-mail from any Internet-connected computer, smartphone, tablet, or other Internet-connected device. While desktop clients may offer more control over your messages and their content, Web-based e-mail has caught up in most respects. For example, Web services can provide superior spam-filtering experience by relying on feedback from a large user base to detect unwanted or dangerous messages.

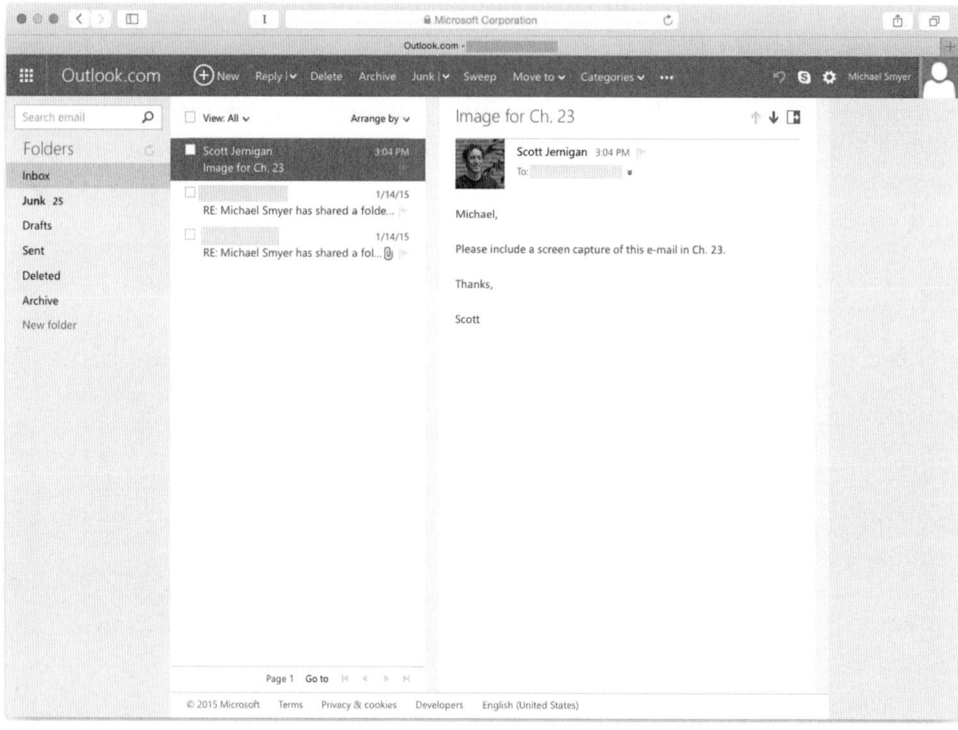

Figure 23-38 Web-based e-mail

Unified Internet Accounts

When I log into my Windows 10 desktop computer, I use my Microsoft account, a fully functional e-mail account hosted by Hotmail. Doing so defines the default e-mail experience on that machine. When I access the Mail client, for example, it immediately accesses my Hotmail account (see Figure 23-39). There's no configuration from a user's or tech's perspective. The same is true when you log in to any Apple device, whether it's a mobile device or smartphone, or a Mac OS X desktop machine.

Microsoft calls this feature Live sign in. That's what CompTIA calls it too.

File Transfer Protocol (FTP)

File transfer protocol (FTP), using ports 20 and 21, is a great way to share files between systems. FTP server software exists for most operating systems, so you can use FTP to transfer data between any two systems regardless of the OS. To access an FTP site, you must use an FTP client such as FileZilla, although most Web browsers provide at least download support for FTP. Just type in the name of the FTP site. Figure 23-40 shows Firefox accessing ftp.kernel.org.

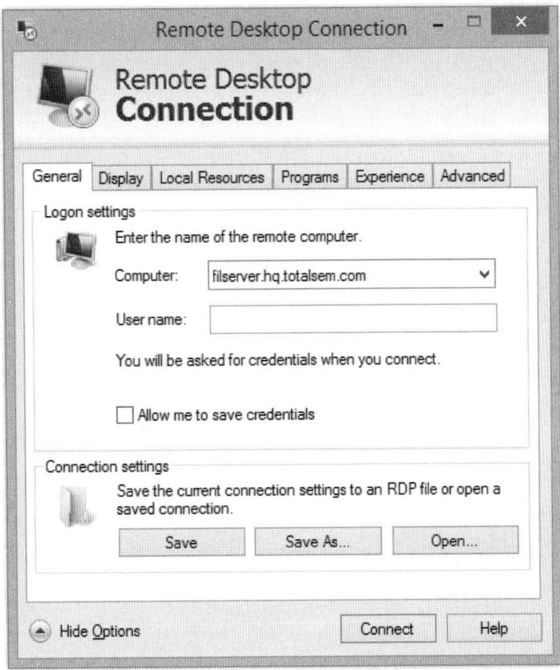

Figure 23-45 Windows Remote Desktop Connection dialog box

NOTE The name of the Remote Desktop Connection executable file is mstsc .exe. You can also open Remote Desktop Connection from a command-line interface or the search bar by typing **mstsc** and pressing ENTER.

Wouldn't it be cool if, when called about a technical support issue, you could simply see what the client sees? When the client says that something doesn't work, it would be great if you could transfer yourself from your desk to your client's desk to see precisely what the client sees. This would dramatically cut down on the miscommunication that can make a tech's life so tedious. Windows Remote Assistance does just that. *Remote Assistance* enables you to give anyone control of your desktop or take control of anyone else's desktop. If a user has a problem, that user can request support directly from you. Upon receiving the support-request e-mail, you can then log on to the user's system and, with permission, take the driver's seat. Figure 23-46 shows Remote Assistance in action.

With Remote Assistance, you can do anything you would do from the actual computer. You can troubleshoot some hardware configuration or driver problem. You can install drivers, roll back drivers, download new ones, and so forth. You're in command of the remote machine as long as the client allows you to be. The client sees everything you do, by the way, and can stop you cold if you get out of line or do something that makes the client nervous! Remote Assistance can help you teach someone how to use a particu-

NOTE Because "remote desktop" is a generic term, you may find some programs with confusingly similar names. Microsoft and Apple both at one point made a program called *Remote Desktop* (the latter is a paid offering), though Microsoft's version is called *Remote Desktop Connection* in current versions of Windows. Then there's Microsoft's *Remote Desktop Connection for Mac*, which is just for enabling Mac OS X machines to connect to a Windows remote desktop.

While some operating systems include a remote desktop client, many third-party remote desktop applications are also available. Most of these make use of either the *Remote Desktop Protocol (RDP)* or *Virtual Network Computing (VNC)*. TightVNC, for example, is totally cross-platform, enabling you to run and control a Windows system remotely from your Mac or vice versa, for example. Figure 23-44 shows TightVNC in action.

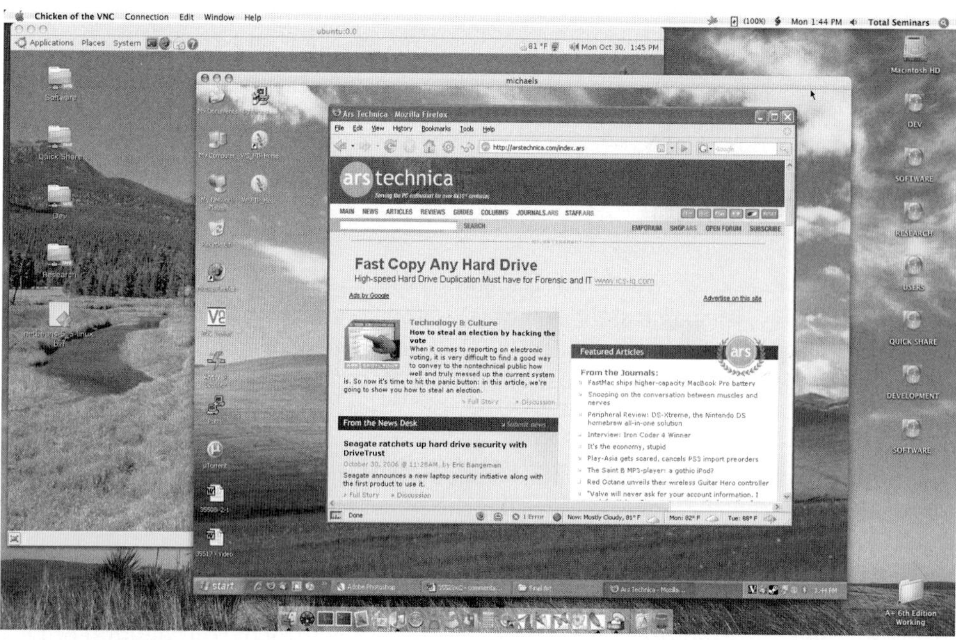

Figure 23-44 TightVNC in action

NOTE All terminal emulation programs require separate server and client programs.

Windows offers an alternative to VNC: Remote Desktop Connection. *Remote Desktop Connection* provides control over a remote server with a fully graphical interface. Your desktop *becomes* the server desktop (see Figure 23-45).

VoIP isn't confined to your computer, either. It can completely replace your old copper phone line. Two popular ways to set up a VoIP system are to either use dedicated *VoIP phones*, like the ones that Cisco makes, or use a small VoIP phone adapter (see Figure 23-43) that can interface with your existing analog phones.

Figure 23-43 Vonage Box VoIP phone adapter

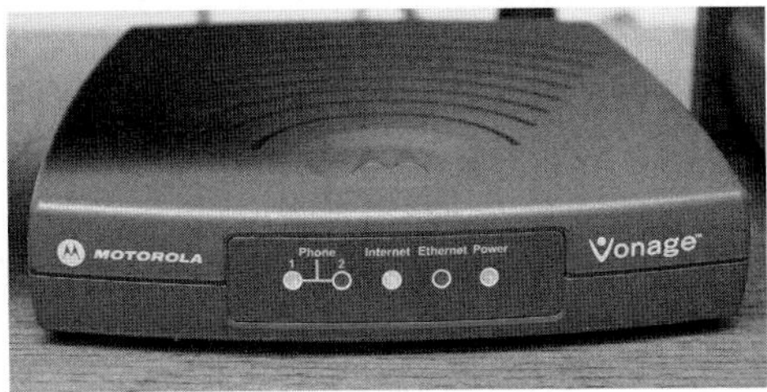

True VoIP phones have RJ-45 connections that plug directly into the network and offer advanced features such as HD-quality audio and video calling. Unfortunately, these phones require a complex and expensive network to function, which puts them out of reach of most home users.

For home users, it's much more common to use a VoIP phone adaptor to connect your old-school analog phones. These little boxes are very simple to set up: just connect it to your network, plug in a phone, and then check for a dial tone. With the VoIP service provided by cable companies, the adapter is often built right into the cable modem itself, making setup a breeze.

Try This!

Checking Latency with ping

Latency is the bane of any VoIP call because of all the problems it causes if it is too high. A quick way to check your current latency is to use the ever-handy ping, so Try This!

1. Run ping on some known source, such as www.microsoft.com or www.totalsem.com.
2. When the ping finishes, take note of the average round-trip time at the bottom of the screen. This is your current latency to that site.

Remote Desktop

While folders and printers might be the primary things shared over a network, sometimes it would be convenient to be "transported" to another computer—to feel as if your hands were actually on its keyboard. There are plenty of programs that do exactly this, generically called remote desktops.

popular. To the user, SSH works just like Telnet. Behind the scenes, SSH uses port 22, and the entire connection is encrypted, preventing any eavesdroppers from reading your data. SSH has one other trick up its sleeve: it can move files or any type of TCP/IP network traffic through its secure connection. In networking parlance, this is called *tunneling*, and it is the core of most secure versions of Internet technologies such as SFTP (discussed next) and VPN, which I will discuss in more depth later in the chapter.

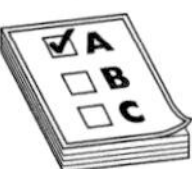

EXAM TIP The CompTIA A+ 902 exam tests your knowledge of a few networking tools, such as Telnet, but only enough to let you support a Network+ tech or network administrator. If you need to run Telnet or SSH, you will get the details from a network administrator. Implementation of Telnet and SSH falls well beyond CompTIA A+.

SFTP

Secure FTP is nothing more than FTP running through an SSH tunnel. This can be done in a number of ways. You can, for example, start an SSH session between two computers. Then, through a moderately painful process, start an FTP server on one machine and an FTP client on the other and redirect the input and output of the FTP data to go through the tunnel. You can also get a dedicated SFTP server and client. Figure 23-42 shows OpenSSH, a popular SSH server with a built-in SFTP feature as well.

Figure 23-42 OpenSSH

```
vmuser@ubuntu1504-vm: ~
vmuser@ubuntu1504-vm:~$ ssh -V
OpenSSH_6.7p1 Ubuntu-5ubuntu1.3, OpenSSL 1.0.1f 6 Jan 2014
vmuser@ubuntu1504-vm:~$
```

Voice over IP

You can use *Voice over IP (VoIP)* to make voice calls over your computer network. Why have two sets of wires, one for voice and one for data, going to every desk? Why not just use the extra capacity on the data network for your phone calls? That's exactly what VoIP does for you. VoIP works with every type of high-speed Internet connection, from DSL to cable to satellite.

VoIP doesn't refer to a single protocol but rather to a collection of protocols that make phone calls over the data network possible. The most common VoIP application protocol is Session Initiation Protocol (SIP), but some popular VoIP applications such as Skype are completely proprietary.

Vendors such as Skype, Cisco, Vonage, and Comcast offer popular VoIP solutions, and many corporations use VoIP for their internal phone networks. A key to remember when installing and troubleshooting VoIP is that low network latency is more important than high network speed. *Latency* is the amount of time a packet takes to get to its destination and is measured in milliseconds. The higher the latency, the more problems, such as noticeable delays during your VoIP call.

Although you can use a Web browser, all FTP sites require you to log on. Your Web browser will assume that you want to log on as "anonymous." If you want to log on as a specific user, you have to add your user name to the URL. (Instead of typing **ftp://ftp.example.com**, you would type **ftp://mikem@ftp.example.com**.) An anonymous logon works fine for most public FTP sites. Many techs prefer to use third-party programs such as FileZilla or Cyberduck on Mac OS X (see Figure 23-41) for FTP access because these third-party applications can store user name and password settings. This enables you to access the FTP site more easily later. Keep in mind that FTP was developed during a more trusting time, and that whatever user name and password you send over the network is sent in clear text. Don't use the same password for an FTP site that you use for your domain logon at the office!

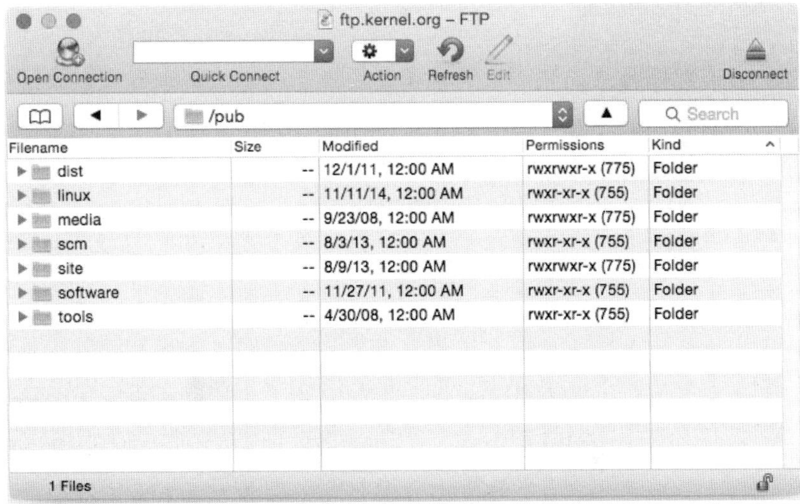

Figure 23-41 The Cyberduck FTP program

Telnet and SSH

Telnet is a terminal emulation program for TCP/IP networks that uses port 23 and enables you to connect to a server or fancy router and run commands on that machine as if you were sitting in front of it. This way, you can remotely administer a server and communicate with other servers on your network. As you can imagine, this is rather risky. If *you* can remotely control a computer, what's to stop others from doing the same? Of course, Telnet does not allow just *anyone* to log on and wreak havoc with your network. You must enter a special user name and password to run Telnet. Unfortunately, Telnet shares FTP's bad habit of sending passwords and user names as clear text, so you should generally use it only within your own LAN.

If you need a remote terminal that works securely across the Internet, you need *Secure Shell (SSH)*. In fact, today SSH has replaced Telnet in almost all places Telnet used to be

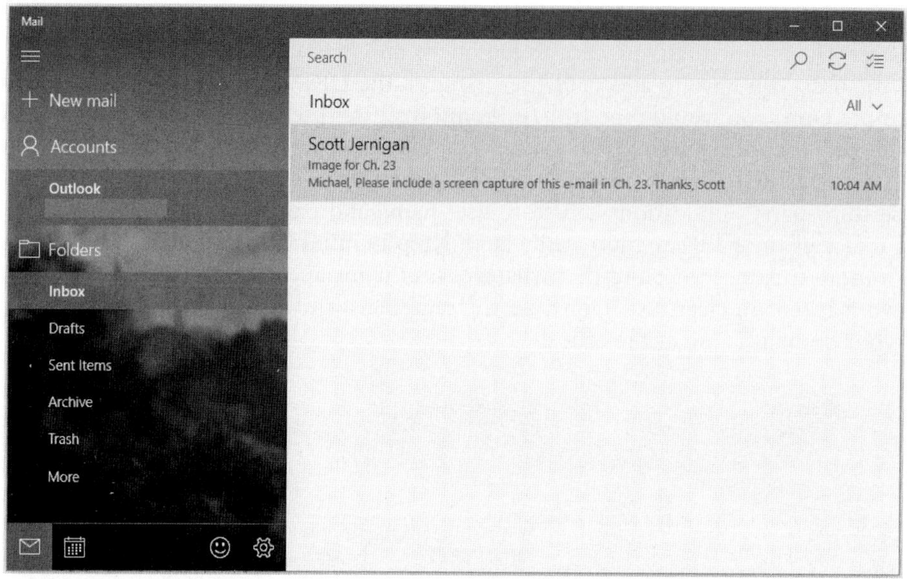

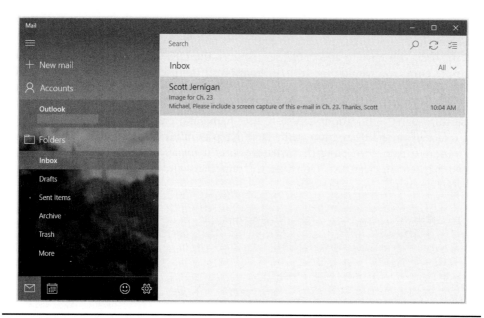

Figure 23-39 Windows 10 Mail

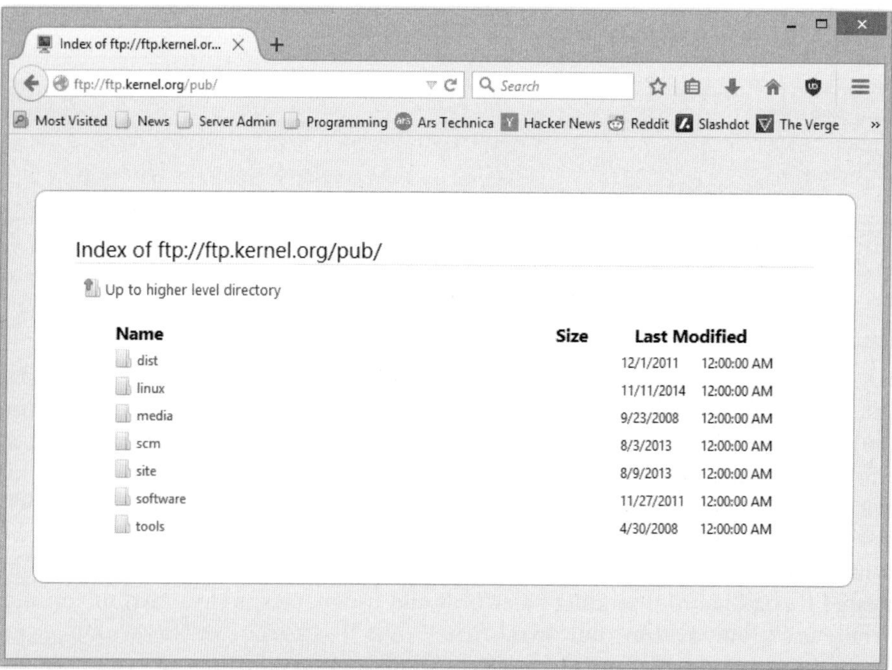

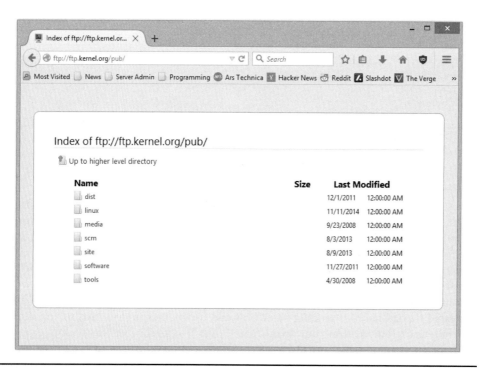

Figure 23-40 Accessing an FTP site in Firefox

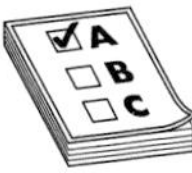

EXAM TIP Most e-mail servers have traditionally used Secure Sockets Layer (SSL) encryption for extra security, though Transport Layer Security (TLS) is becoming more and more popular due to its increased security. Every major e-mail client will have a setting called Connection security, or Security, or something like that. If your e-mail server uses encryption, change this setting to SSL and check the port setting.

Later versions of Windows and Outlook assume you're using a Microsoft or Exchange account. When you type in a user name, for example, Windows will seek out the valid sending and receiving servers automatically (see Figure 23-36). You can always instead click the *Manual setup or additional server types* option on the initial page to get access to SMTP and POP or IMAP server setup (see Figure 23-37).

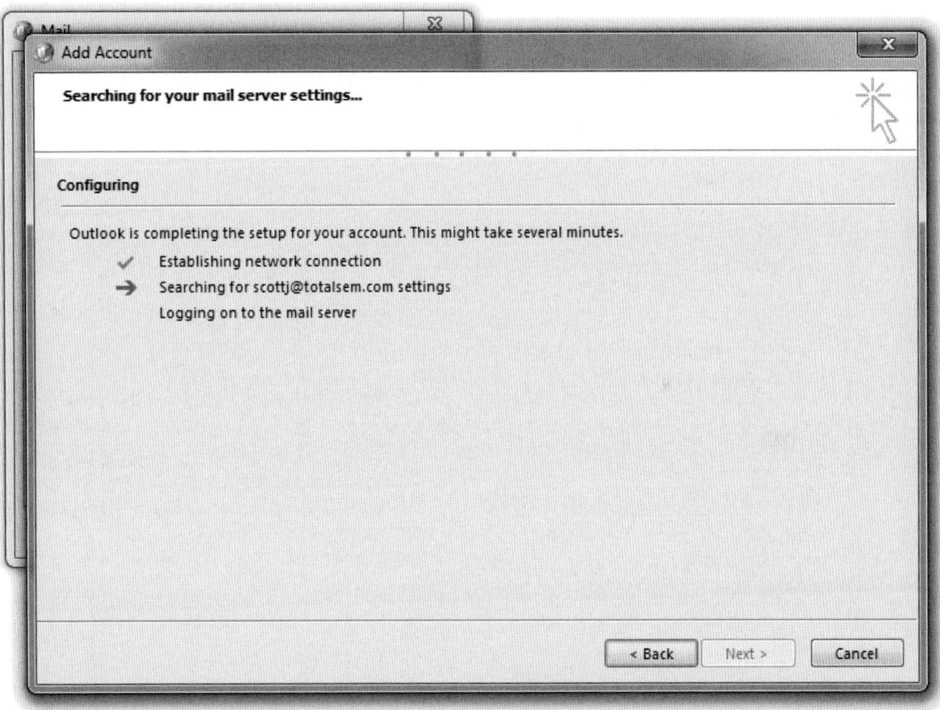

Figure 23-36 Searching for information in Outlook 2016

Integrated Solutions

All mobile devices have an integrated e-mail client, fully configured to work within the mobile ecosystem. Apple devices, such as the iPad, enable you to create and use an iCloud account that syncs across all your Apple devices. The iCloud e-mail setup process

When I'm given the name of a POP3 or SMTP server, I use ping to determine the IP address for the device, as shown in Figure 23-34. I make a point to write this down. If I ever have a problem getting mail, I'll go into my SMTP or POP3 settings and type in the IP address (see Figure 23-35). If my mail starts to work, I know the DNS server is not working.

```
C:\Windows\system32\cmd.exe

C:\>ping pop-server.totalsem.com

Pinging pop-server.totalsem.com [69.94.71.175] with 32 bytes of data:
Reply from 69.94.71.175: bytes=32 time=96ms TTL=47
Reply from 69.94.71.175: bytes=32 time=122ms TTL=47
Reply from 69.94.71.175: bytes=32 time=166ms TTL=47
Reply from 69.94.71.175: bytes=32 time=153ms TTL=47

Ping statistics for 69.94.71.175:
    Packets: Sent = 4, Received = 4, Lost = 0 (0% loss),
Approximate round trip times in milli-seconds:
    Minimum = 96ms, Maximum = 166ms, Average = 134ms

C:\>
```

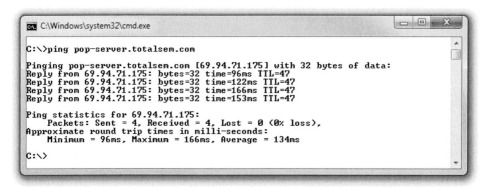

Figure 23-34 Using ping to determine the IP address

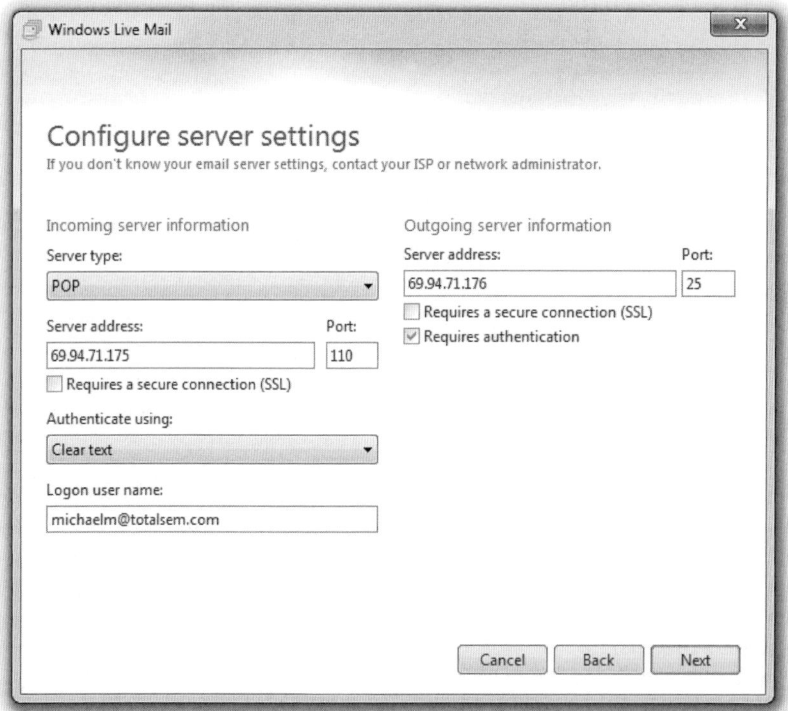

Figure 23-35 Entering IP addresses into POP3 and SMTP settings

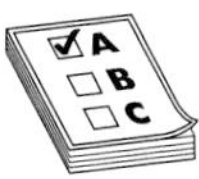

EXAM TIP You might also encounter *Secure/Multipurpose Internet Mail Extensions (S/MIME)* in place of SMTP. S/MIME offers encryption and digital signatures.

These two systems may often have the same name, or close to the same name, as shown in Figure 23-33. Your ISP should provide you with all these settings. If not, you should be comfortable knowing what to ask for. If one of these names is incorrect, you will either not get your e-mail or not be able to send e-mail. If an e-mail setup that has been working well for a while suddenly gives you errors, it is likely that either the POP3 or SMTP server is down or that the DNS server has quit working.

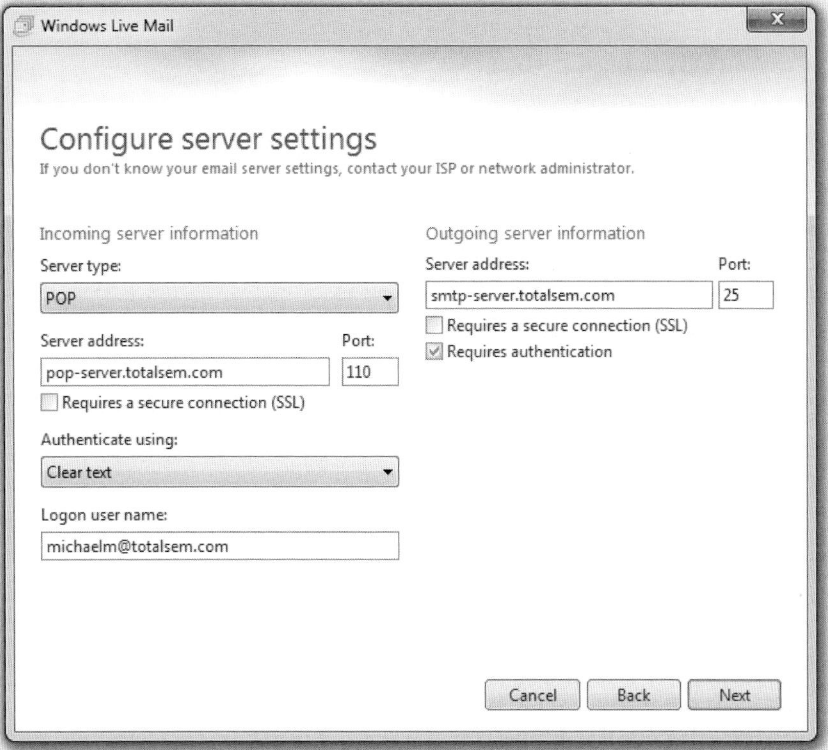

Figure 23-33 Adding POP3 and SMTP information in Windows Live Mail

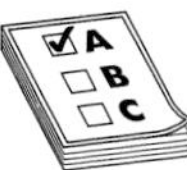

EXAM TIP Microsoft provides a special type of e-mail server called an Exchange server. This is used mainly in large businesses so that employees can access their e-mail, calendars, and instant messages from a variety of locations. To set up an Exchange e-mail client, go to the Control Panel and run the Mail applet, which is available if you have Microsoft Outlook installed. Then click E-mail Accounts and then New. After that, click Next and fill in your e-mail address and password.

address information entered into the Windows Live Mail account setup. To enter a password, the user would click Next.

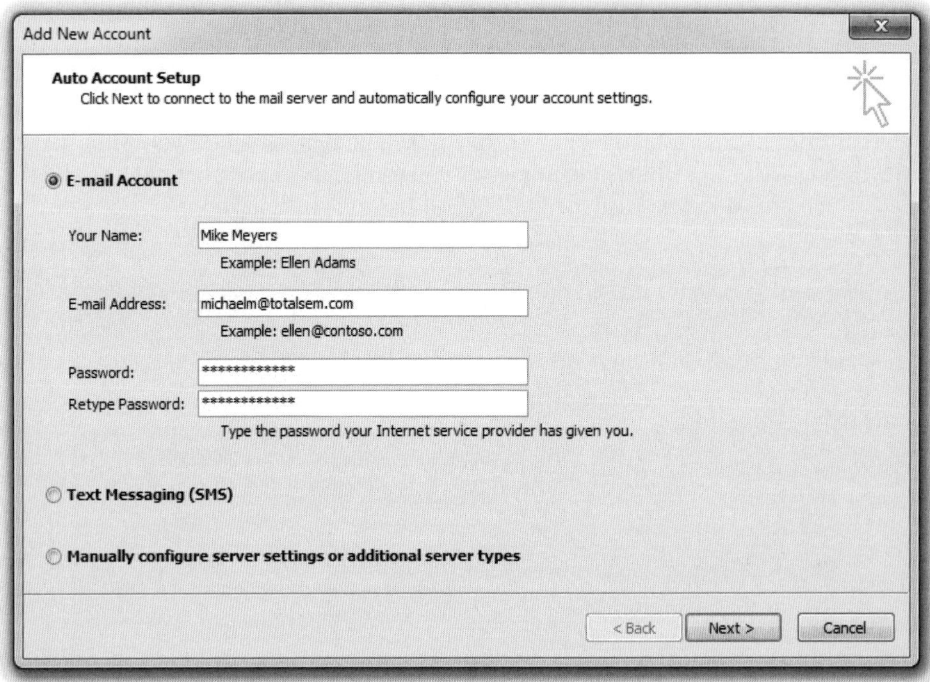

Figure 23-32 Adding an e-mail account to Windows Live Mail

At this point, things differ pretty dramatically among the different versions of Windows. Here's what happens traditionally and in third-party e-mail clients. (I'll get to the integrated stuff thereafter.)

Next you must add the names of the *Post Office Protocol version 3 (POP3)* or *Internet Message Access Protocol version 4 (IMAP4)* server and the *Simple Mail Transfer Protocol (SMTP)* server. The POP3 or IMAP server is the computer that handles incoming (to you) e-mail. POP3 is by far the most widely used standard, although the latest version of IMAP, *IMAP4*, supports some features POP3 doesn't. For example, IMAP4 enables you to search through messages on the mail server to find specific keywords and select the messages you want to download onto your machine.

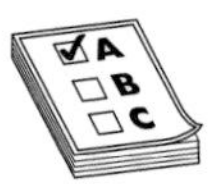

EXAM TIP Make sure you know your port numbers for these e-mail protocols! POP3 uses port 110, IMAP uses port 143, and SMTP uses port 25.

The SMTP server handles your outgoing e-mail.

E-mail

To set up and access e-mail, you have a lot of choices today. You can use the traditional corporate or ISP method that requires a dedicated e-mail application. Increasingly though, people use e-mail clients built into their devices. Finally, you can use a Web-based e-mail client accessible from any device. The difficulty with this section is that all of this is blending somewhat with the advent of account-based access to devices, such as using your Hotmail account to log into your Windows PC.

Corporate/ISP Solutions

Corporate and ISP e-mail configuration means setting up your client software to match the settings of the e-mail server software. The most popular client by far is Microsoft Outlook.

Open the e-mail client and access setup or preferences (the option varies among the many applications). In Outlook, for example, go to the Control Panel and click the Mail applet. Click Add to start adding a new mail account (see Figure 23-31).

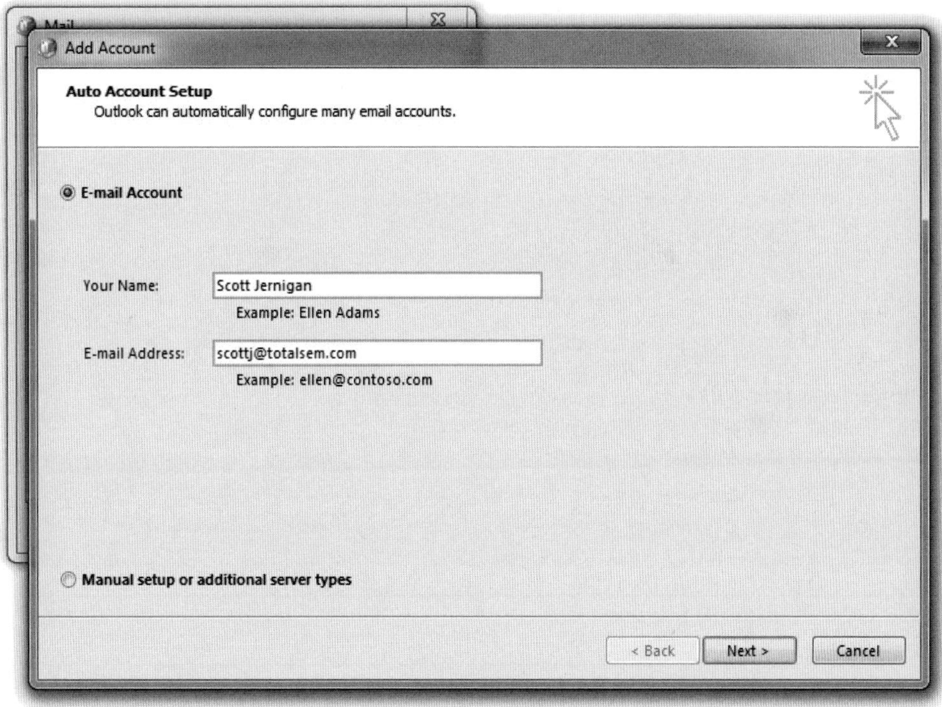

Figure 23-31 Adding an account with the Mail applet in Control Panel

Add a new account, then provide your name, e-mail address, and password. All e-mail addresses come in the *accountname@Internet domain* format. Figure 23-32 shows e-mail

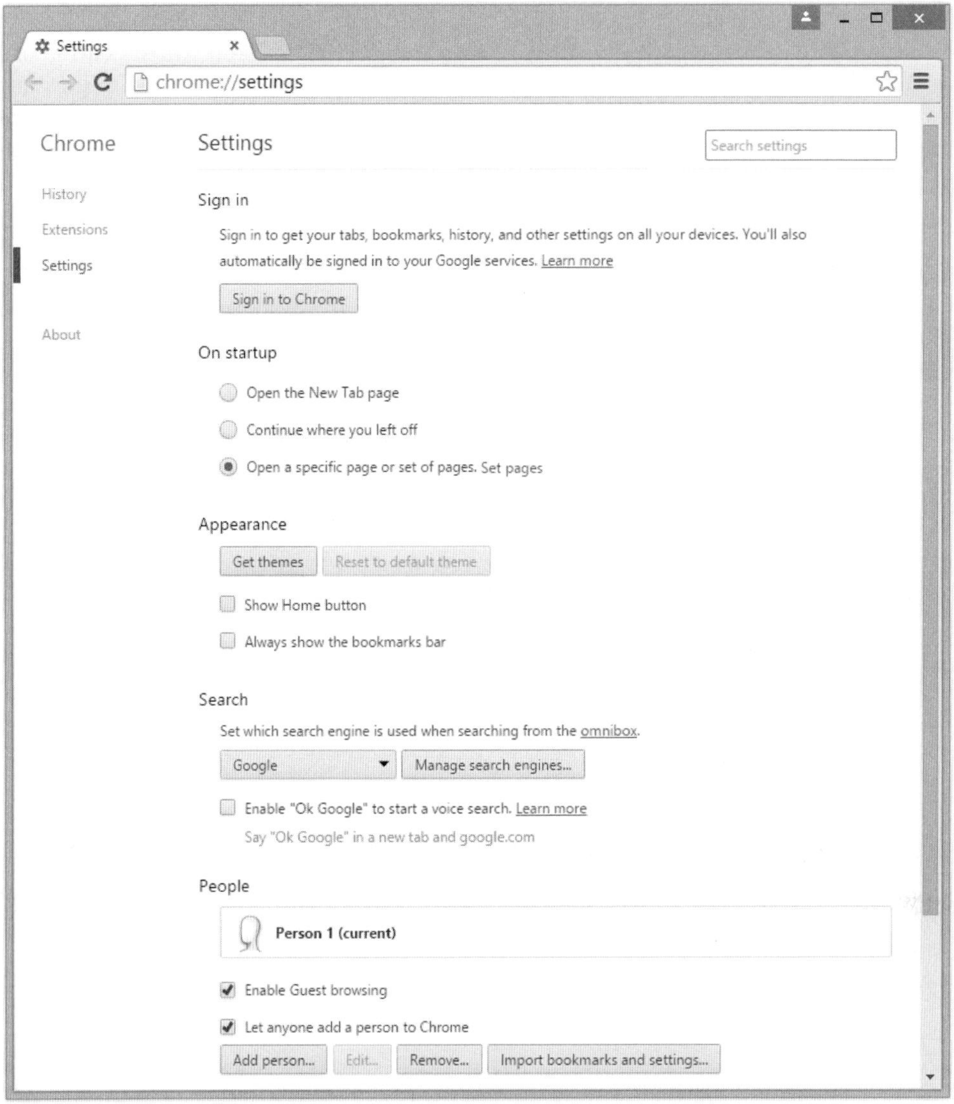

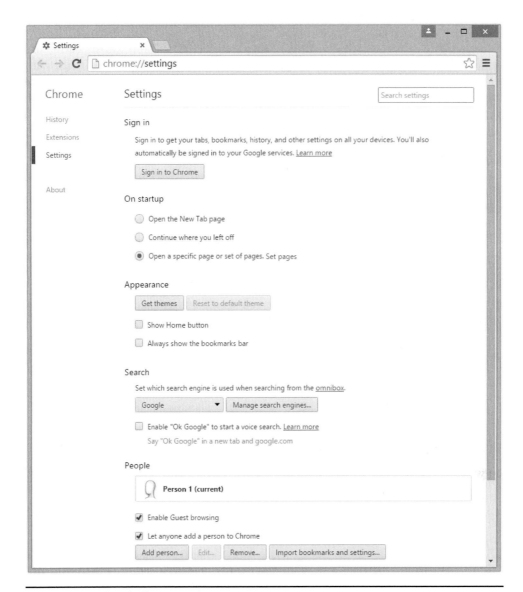

Figure 23-30 Google Chrome settings

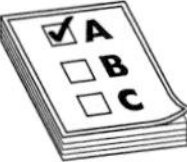

EXAM TIP The term *Internet appliance* enjoyed some popularity in the 1990s to describe the first wave of consumer devices accessible via TCP/IP, such as refrigerators and stoves. However, today, it is largely used to indicate a single-purpose network tool often installed on a server rack. These appliances frequently serve a security function, with names like *Unified Threat Management (UTM)*, *Intrusion Detection System (IDS)*, or *Intrusion Prevention System (IPS)*. We'll talk a little more about Internet appliances in Chapter 28, "Securing Computers."

lar application. You can log on to a user's computer and fire up Outlook, for example, and then walk through the steps to configure it while the user watches. The user can then take over the machine and walk through the steps while you watch, chatting with one another the whole time. Sweet!

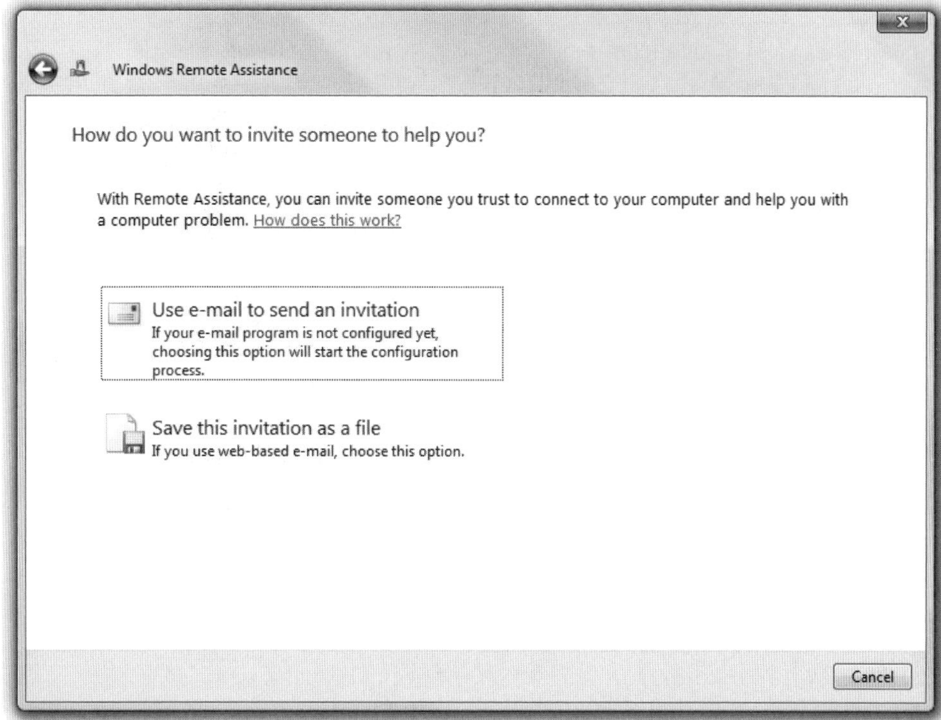

Figure 23-46 Remote Assistance in action

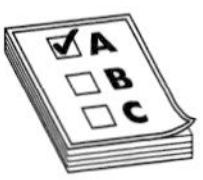

EXAM TIP While Apple sells a Remote Desktop product marketed to business customers that includes remote assistance features, Mac OS X also has more modest *screen sharing* built in to the operating system. This built-in functionality, which can be enabled in System Preferences, should suffice for general remote access, collaboration, and light remote troubleshooting.

Remote desktop applications provide everything you need to access one system from another. They are common, especially considering that Microsoft provides Remote Desktop for free. Whichever application you use, remember that you will always need both a server and a client program. The server goes on the system you want to access and the client goes on the system you use to access the server. With many solutions, the server and client software are integrated into a single product.

In Windows, you can turn Remote Assistance and Remote Desktop on and off and configure other settings. Go to the System applet in Control Panel and then select the Remote settings link on the left. Under the Remote tab in System Properties you will see checkboxes for both Remote Assistance and Remote Desktop, along with buttons to configure more detailed settings.

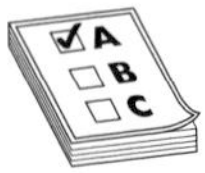

EXAM TIP Windows is also capable of running specific applications hosted on another machine. Think of it as Remote Desktop without the desktop—a single application run on one machine (a server) and appearing on another desktop (a client). You can set up your connection using the RemoteApp and Desktop Connections applet in Control Panel.

Virtual Private Networks

Remote connections have been around for a long time, long before the Internet existed. The biggest drawback about remote connections was the cost to connect. If you were on one side of the continent and had to connect to your LAN on the other side of the continent, the only connection option was a telephone. Or, if you needed to connect two LANs across the continent, you ended up paying outrageous monthly charges for a private connection. The introduction of the Internet gave people wishing to connect to their home networks a very cheap connection option, but with one problem: the whole Internet is open to the public. People wanted to stop using dial-up and expensive private connections and use the Internet instead, but they wanted to do it securely.

Those clever network engineers worked long and hard and came up with several solutions to this problem. Standards have been created that use encrypted tunnels between a computer (or a remote network) to create a private network through the Internet (see Figure 23-47), resulting in what is called a *Virtual Private Network (VPN)*.

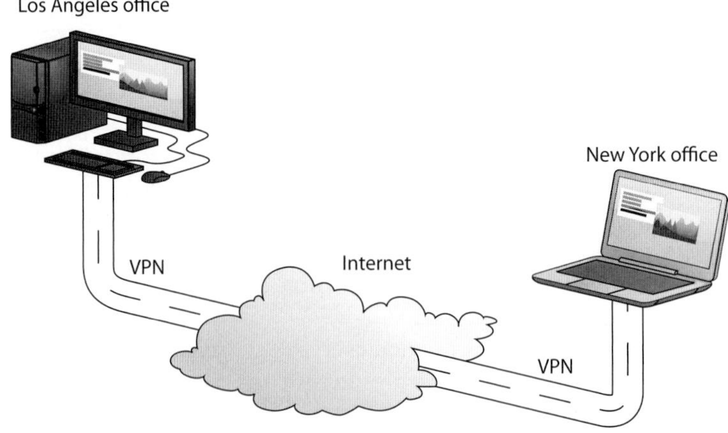

Figure 23-47 VPN connecting computers across the United States

An encrypted tunnel requires endpoints—the ends of the tunnel where the data is encrypted and decrypted. In the SSH tunnel you've seen thus far, the client for the application sits on one end and the server sits on the other. VPNs do the same thing. Either some software running on a computer or, in some cases, a dedicated box must act as an endpoint for a VPN (see Figure 23-48).

Figure 23-48 Typical tunnel

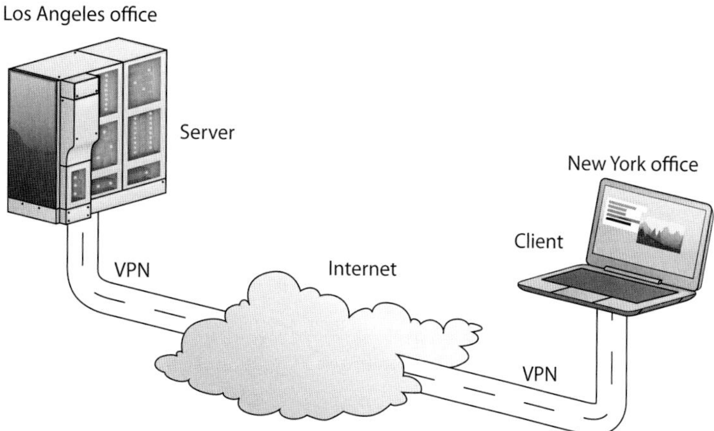

VPNs require a protocol that itself uses one of the many tunneling protocols available and adds the capability to ask for an IP address from a local DHCP server to give the tunnel an IP address that matches the subnet of the local LAN. The connection keeps the IP address to connect to the Internet, but the tunnel endpoints must act like NICs (see Figure 23-49). Let's look at one of the protocols, PPTP.

Figure 23-49 Endpoints must have their own IP addresses.

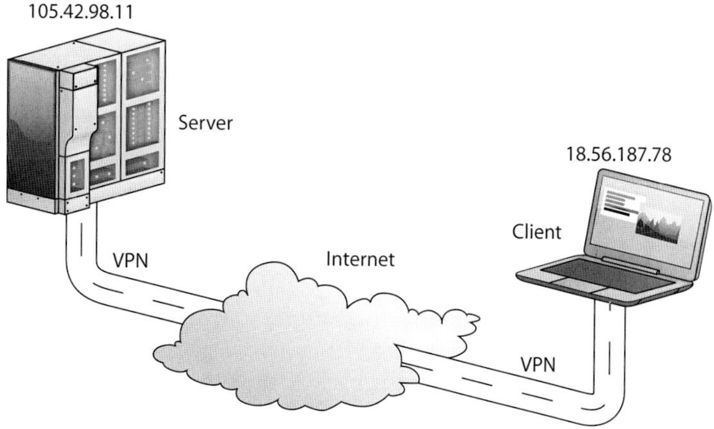

PPTP VPNs

So how do we make IP addresses appear out of thin air? Microsoft got the ball rolling with the *Point-to-Point Tunneling Protocol (PPTP)*, an advanced version of PPP (used for dial-up Internet, as discussed earlier) that handles all of this right out of the box. The only trick is the endpoints. In Microsoft's view, a VPN is intended for individual clients (think employees on the road) to connect back to the office network, so Microsoft places the PPTP endpoints on the client and a special remote access server program called Routing and Remote Access Service (RRAS), available on Server versions of Windows (see Figure 23-50).

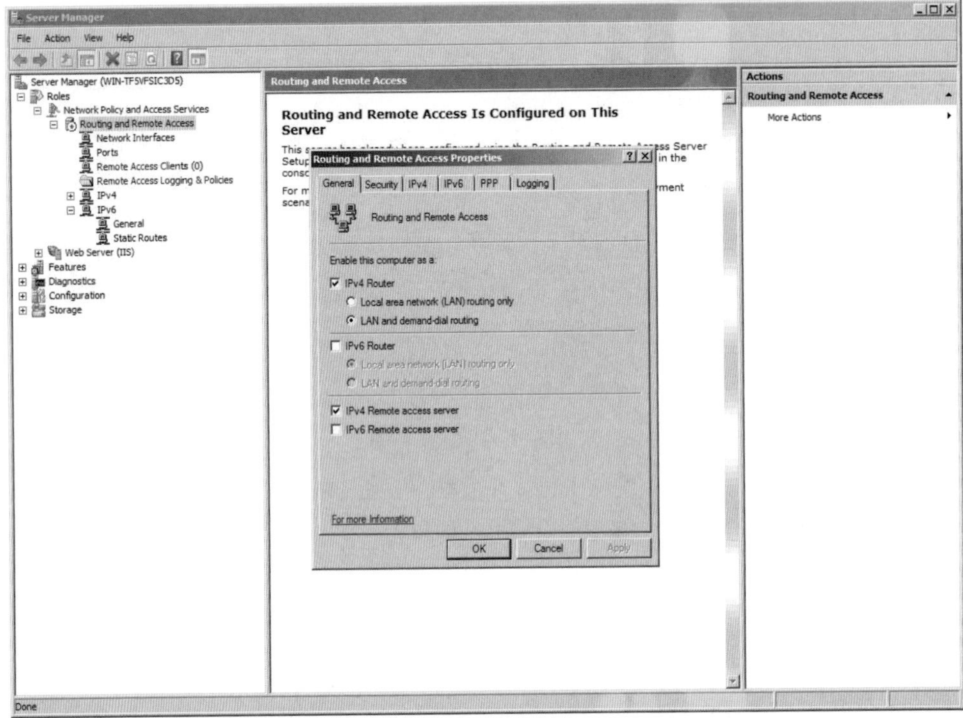

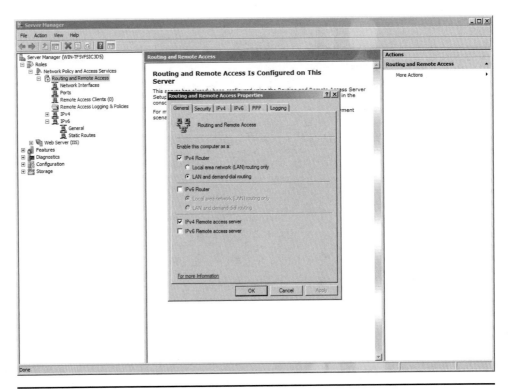

Figure 23-50 RRAS in action

On the Windows client side, type **VPN** into the Start Search bar (Windows Vista and 7) and press ENTER. In Windows 8 and 8.1, type **VPN** at the Start screen and select *Manage virtual private networks (VPN)*. This presents you with a dialog box where you can enter all your VPN server information. Your network administrator will most likely provide this to you. The result is a virtual network card that, like any other NIC, gets an IP address from the DHCP server back at the office (see Figure 23-51).

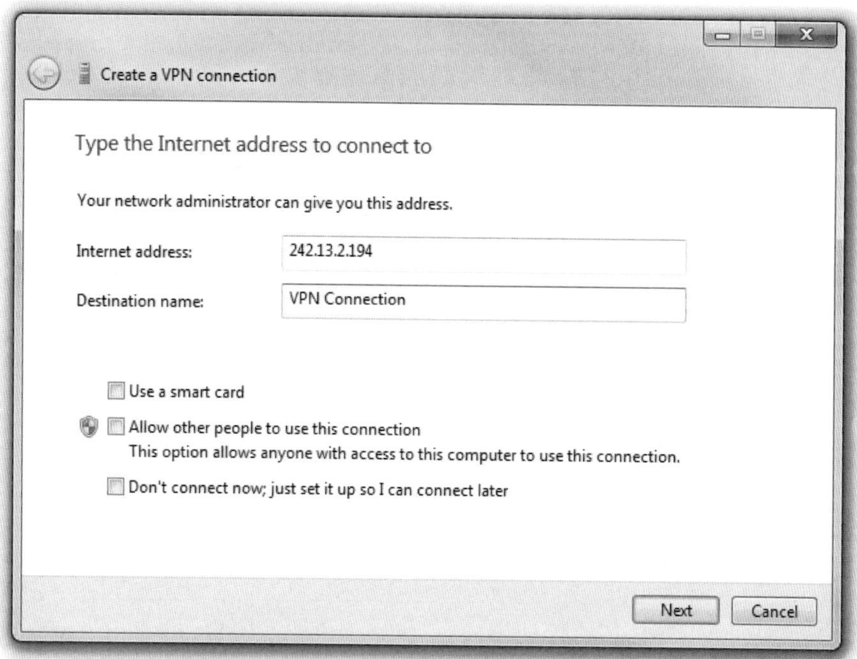

Figure 23-51 VPN connection in Windows

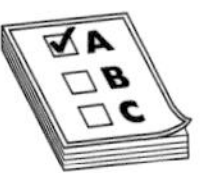

EXAM TIP A system connected to a VPN looks as though it's on the local network but often performs much slower than if the system were connected directly back at the office.

When your computer connects to the RRAS server on the private network, PPTP creates a secure tunnel through the Internet back to the private LAN. Your client takes on an IP address of that network, as if your computer were plugged into the LAN back at the office. Even your Internet traffic will go through your office first. If you open your Web browser, your client will go across the Internet to the office LAN and then use the LAN's Internet connection! Because of this, Web browsing is very slow over a VPN.

Support Applications (Internet Utilities)

The CompTIA A+ 220-902 objectives list four rather unique protocols. Personally, I doubt you'll ever deal directly with two of them, LDAP and SNMP. The third, SMB, is more common to LANs, not the Internet. And the fourth, AFP is specific to Mac OS X. You should know a little bit about all four anyway.

LDAP

The *Lightweight Directory Access Protocol (LDAP)* enables operating systems and applications to access directories. If you've got a Windows Server system running Active

Directory, for example, Windows uses LDAP to do anything with Active Directory. If you're sitting at a computer and add it to an Active Directory domain, Windows uses LDAP commands to update the Active Directory with the computer's information. You don't see LDAP, but it works hard to keep networks running smoothly.

SNMP

The *Simple Network Management Protocol (SNMP)* enables remote query and remote configuration of just about anything on a network. Assuming all your computers, switches, routers, and so on, are SNMP-capable, you can use programs to query the network for an unimaginable amount of data. SNMP is a popular protocol for checking up on your network, but it's the sort of thing you probably won't need to use unless you're a Network+ tech.

SMB

The *Server Message Block (SMB)* protocol is Windows' network file and print sharing protocol. UNIX and Linux systems used a competing protocol, Network File System (NFS), but that use has declined. Today, every major OS uses SMB: Windows, Mac OS X, and Linux (using SAMBA). SMB is the protocol of choice for LAN file servers.

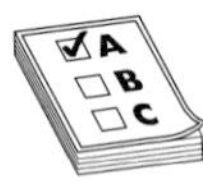

EXAM TIP Over the years, Microsoft has introduced several versions (what Microsoft calls dialects) of SMB, and one of the more widespread dialects is *Common Internet File System (CIFS)*. CIFS is currently deprecated but still widely supported, making knowledge of it important for passing the CompTIA A+ 902 exam.

AFP

Like Microsoft and SMB, Apple developed the *Apple Filing Protocol (AFP)* in late 1980s to support file sharing between Macintosh computers on early LANs. Just like SMB, AFP survives to this day as a way for Mac OS X machines to share files with Macs new and old. AFP is also the protocol used by Mac OS X Time Machine for backing up OS X over the network due to its support for HFS+ file system particularities. Support for AFP beyond OS X is solid on Linux, but Windows lacks out-of-box support for the protocol.

901

Internet Troubleshooting

There isn't a person who's spent more than a few hours on a computer connected to the Internet who hasn't run into some form of connectivity problem. I love it when I get a call from someone saying "The Internet is down!" as I always respond the same way:

"No, the Internet is fine. It's the way you're trying to get to it that's down." Okay, so I don't make a lot of friends with that remark, but it's actually a really good reminder of why we run into problems on the Internet. Let's review the common symptoms CompTIA lists on their objectives for the CompTIA A+ 220-901 exam and see what we can do to fix these all-too-common problems.

The dominant Internet setup for a SOHO environment consists of some box from your ISP: a cable or fiber modem, a DSL modem, etc. that connects via Ethernet cable to a home router. This router is usually 802.11 capable and includes four Ethernet ports. Some computers in the network connect through a wire and some connect wirelessly (see Figure 23-52). It's a pretty safe assumption that CompTIA has a setup like this in mind when talking about Internet troubleshooting, and we'll refer to this setup here as well.

Figure 23-52 Typical SOHO setup

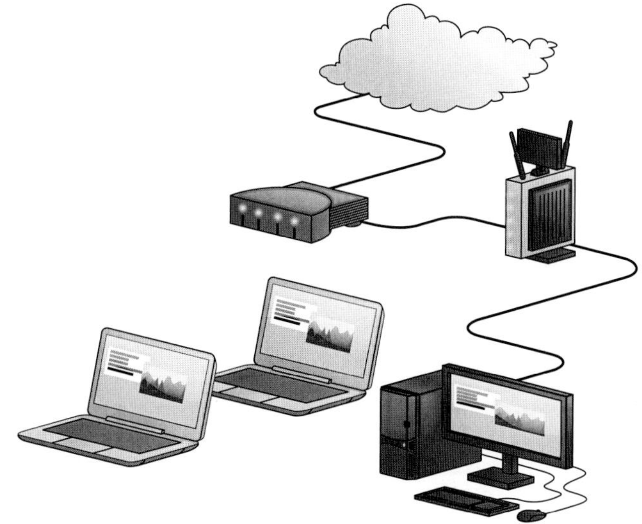

One quick note before we dive in: Most Internet connection problems are actually network connection problems. In other words, everything you learned in Chapter 21 still applies here. We're not going to rehash those repair problems in this chapter. The following issues are Internet-only problems, so don't let a bad cable fool you into thinking a bigger problem is taking place.

No Connectivity

As you'll remember from Chapter 21, "no connectivity" has two meanings: a disconnected NIC or an inability to connect to a resource. Since Chapter 21 already covers wired connectivity issues and Chapter 22 covers wireless issues, let's look at lack of connectivity from a "you're on the Internet but you can't get to a Web site" point of view:

1. Can you get to other Web sites? If not, go back and triple-check your local connectivity.

2. Can you ping the site? Go to a command prompt and try pinging the URL as follows:

```
C:\>ping www.cheetos1.com
Ping request could not find host www.cheetos1.com. Please check the name and try
 again.
C:\>
```

The ping is a failure, but we learn a lot from it. The ping shows that your computer can't get an IP address for that Web site. This points to a DNS failure, a very common problem. To fix a failing DNS:

1. In Windows, go to a command prompt and type **ipconfig /flushdns**:

```
C:\>ipconfig /flushdns
Windows IP Configuration
Successfully flushed the DNS Resolver Cache.
C:\>
```

NOTE While the commands are similar, ifconfig and iwconfig aren't suitable for flushing the DNS cache, if it exists, in Mac OS X or Linux.

2. In Windows, go to the Network and Sharing Center and click *Change adapter settings*. Right-click on your network connection and select Diagnose to run the troubleshooter (see Figure 23-53).

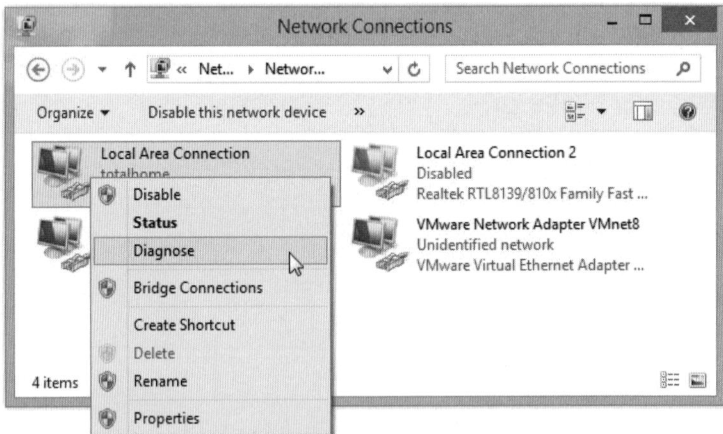

Figure 23-53 Diagnosing a network problem in Windows 8.1

3. Try using another DNS server. There are lots of DNS servers out there that are open to the public. Try Google's famous 8.8.8.8 and 8.8.4.4.

If DNS is OK, make sure you're using the right URL. This is especially true when you're entering DNS names into applications such as e-mail clients.

Limited Connectivity

Limited connectivity points to a DHCP problem, assuming you're connected to a DHCP server. Run **ipconfig** and see if you have an APIPA address:

```
C:\>ipconfig
Windows IP Configuration
Ethernet adapter Local Area Connection:
        Connection-specific DNS Suffix  . :
        IP Address. . . . . . . . . . . . : 169.254.0.16
        Subnet Mask . . . . . . . . . . . : 255.255.0.0
        Default Gateway . . . . . . . . . :
C:\>
```

Uh-oh! No DHCP server! If your router is your DHCP server, try restarting the router. If you know the Network ID for your network and the IP address for your default gateway (something you should know—it's your network!), try setting up your NIC statically.

Local Connectivity

Local connectivity means you can access network resources but not the Internet. First, this is a classic symptom of a downed DHCP server since all the systems in the local network will have APIPA/link local addresses. However, you might also have a problem with your router. You need to ping the default gateway; if that's successful, ping the other port (the WAN port) on your router. The only way to determine the IP address of the other port on your router is to access the router's configuration Web page and find it (see Figure 23-54). Every router is different—good luck!

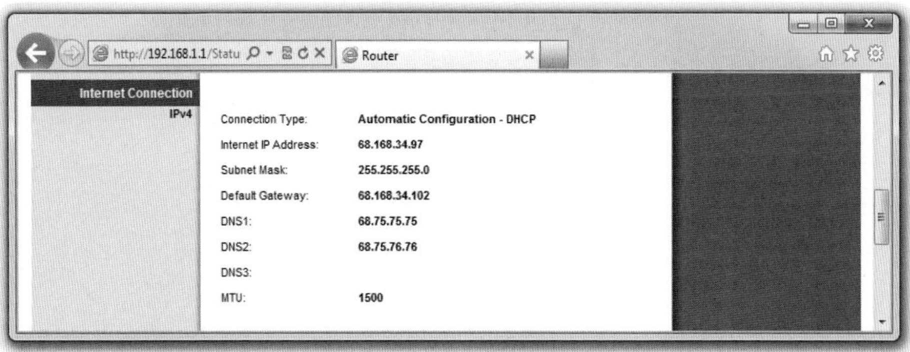

Figure 23-54 Router's WAN IP address

You can learn a lot by looking at your WAN IP address. Take a look at Figure 23-55. At first glance, it looks the same as Figure 23-54, but notice that there is no IP address.

Most ISPs don't provide static IP addresses—they simply give you the physical connection, and your router's WAN network card uses DHCP, just like most internal networks. If you're lucky, you can renew your DHCP address using some button on the router's configuration. If not, try resetting the cable/fiber/DSL modem. If that doesn't work, it's time to call your ISP.

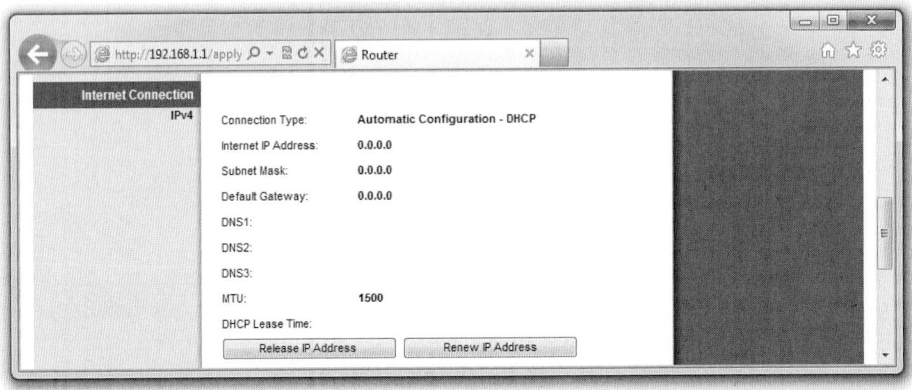

Figure 23-55 No WAN connection

Slow Transfer Speeds

No matter how fast the connection is, we all want our Internet to go faster. People tolerate a certain amount of waiting for a large program to download or an HD video to buffer, but your connection can sometimes slow down to unacceptable speeds.

Remember that your Internet connection has a maximum speed at which it can transfer. If you divide that connection between multiple programs trying to use the Internet, all of your programs will connect very slowly. To see what's happening on your network, open a command prompt and type **netstat**, which shows all the connections between your computer and any other computer. Here's a very simplified example of netstat output:

```
C:\>netstat
Active Connections
  Proto  Local Address          Foreign Address          State
  TCP    10.12.14.47:57788      totalfs3:microsoft-ds    ESTABLISHED
  TCP    192.168.15.102:139     Sabertooth:20508         ESTABLISHED
  TCP    192.168.15.102:50283   Theater:netbios-ssn      ESTABLISHED
  TCP    192.168.15.102:60222   dts1.google.com:https    ESTABLISHED
  TCP    192.168.15.102:60456   www.serve2.le.com:http    ESTABLISHED
  TCP    192.168.15.102:60482   64.145.92.65:http        ESTABLISHED
  TCP    192.168.15.102:60483   12.162.15.1:57080        TIME_WAIT
C:\>
```

If you look at the Foreign Address column, you'll see that most of the connections are Web pages (HTTP and HTTPS) or shared folders (microsoft-ds, netbios-ssn), but what is the connection to 12.162.15.1:57080? Not knowing every connection by heart,

I looked it up on Google and found out that there was a background torrent program running on my machine. I found the program and shut it down.

When everyone on the network is getting slow Internet connectivity, it's time to check out the router. In all probability, you have too many people that need too much bandwidth—go buy more bandwidth!

When additional bandwidth isn't an acceptable solution, you'll need to make the most of what you have. Your router can use a feature called *Quality of Service (QoS)* to prioritize access to network resources. QoS enables you to ensure certain users, applications, or services are prioritized when there isn't enough bandwidth to go around by limiting the bandwidth for certain types of data based on application protocol, the IP address of a computer, and all sorts of other features. Figure 23-56 is a typical router's QoS page.

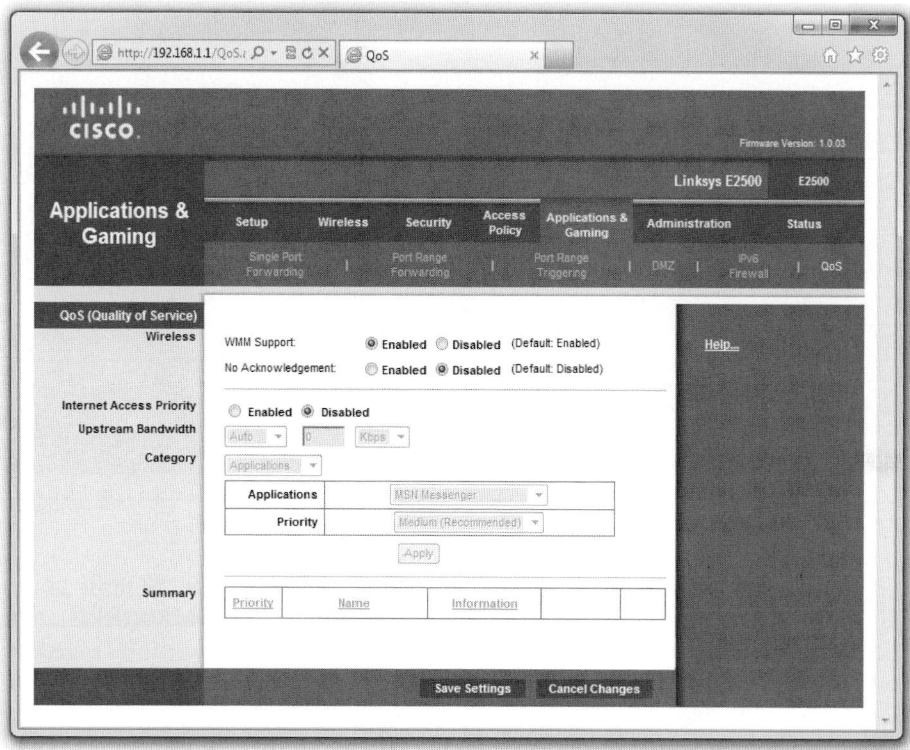

Figure 23-56 QoS

Beyond A+

The areas covered by the CompTIA A+ certification exams do a great job on the more common issues of dealing with the Internet, but a few hot topics (although beyond the scope of the CompTIA A+ exams) are so common and important that you need to know them: online gaming, chatting, and file sharing.

Online Gaming

One of the more exciting and certainly more fun aspects of the Internet is online gaming. Competing online against one or more real people makes for some pleasant gaming. Enjoying classics such as Hearts and Backgammon with another human can be challenging and fun. Another popular genre of online gaming is the "first-person shooter." These games place you in a small world with up to 64 other players. A great example is Valve Software's *Counter-Strike: Global Offensive* (see Figure 23-57).

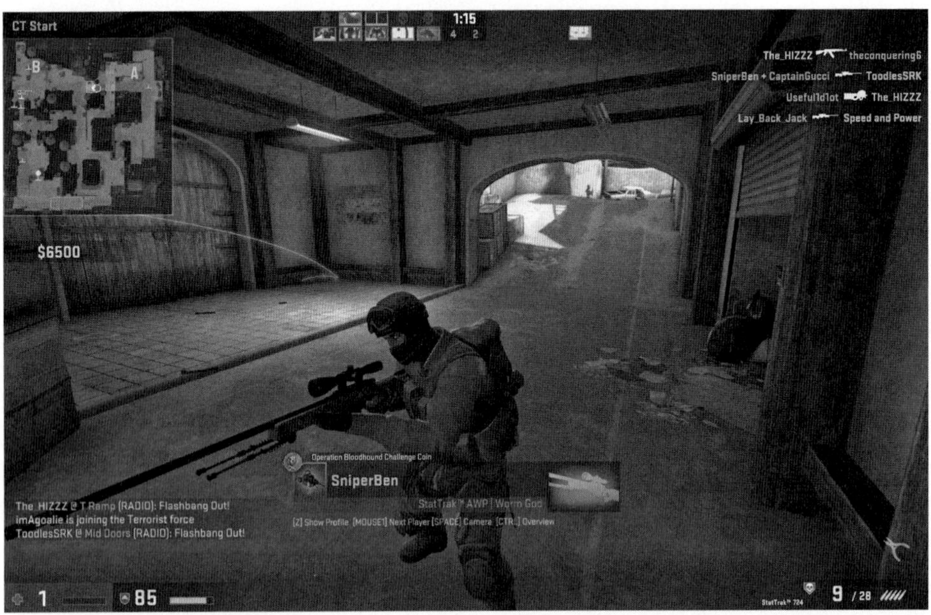

Figure 23-57 Counter-Strike: GO

No discussion of online gaming is complete without talking about the most amazing game type of all: the massively multiplayer online role-playing game (MMORPG). Imagine being an elfin wizard, joined by a band of friends, all going on adventures together in a world so large that it would take a real 24-hour day to journey across it! Imagine that in this same world, 2000 to 3000 other players, as well as thousands of game-controlled characters, are participating! Plenty of MMORPGs are out there, but the most popular today is still, surprisingly, *World of Warcraft* (see Figure 23-58).

Each of these games employs good old TCP/IP to send information, using ports reserved by the game.

Chat

If there's one thing we human beings love to do, it's chat. The Internet provides a multitude of ways to do so, whether by typing or actual talking. Keep in mind that chatting occurs in real time. As fast as you can type or talk, whoever is at the other end hears or

sees what you have to say. To chat, however, you need some form of chat software. The oldest family of chat programs is based on the Internet Relay Chat (IRC) protocol; a very common IRC chat program is mIRC. IRC protocols allow for a number of other little extras as well, such as being able to share files.

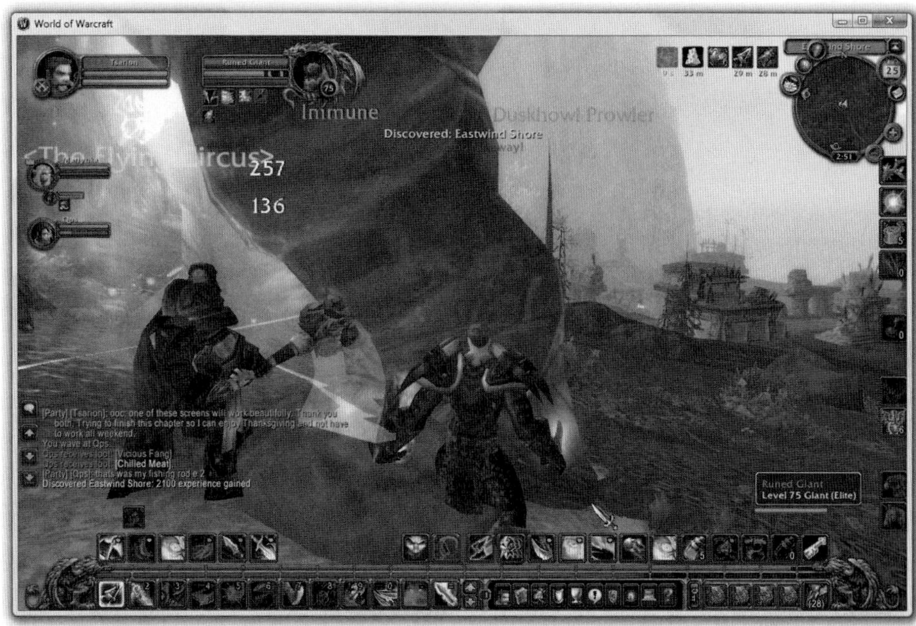

Figure 23-58 My editor playing World of Warcraft

Today, companies such as Google, AOL, Yahoo!, Microsoft, Facebook, Skype, WhatsApp, and Steam (plus many more) have made their own chat programs (otherwise known as instant messengers, or IMs) that not only provide text chat but sometimes add features such as voice and video, turning your computer or device into a VoIP phone! Figure 23-59 shows Google Hangouts being used from an iOS device.

File Sharing

The last extra Internet function to discuss is also probably the most controversial: file sharing. Modern file sharing started in the late 1990s and consisted of a whole bunch of computers running the same program, such as Napster or Kazaa. The file-sharing program enables each of the computers running that program to offer files to share, such as music and movies. Once all of the file-sharing programs are connected to the Internet, any of them can download any file offered by any other in the group.

File sharing through such *distributed* sharing software feels almost anonymous and free—and that's the problem. You can share *anything*, even copyright-protected music, movies, and more. The music industry (and later the film industry) came out swinging

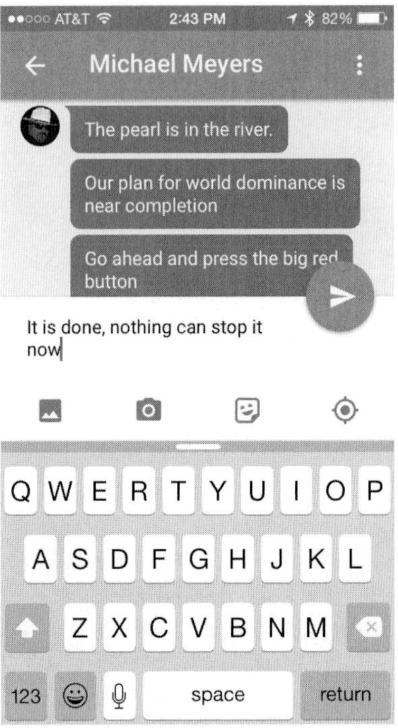

Figure 23-59 Google Hangouts in action

to try to stop file-sharing practices. The result has been a series of legal campaigns against sites and companies that facilitate file sharing, and to shut down individuals who share lots of files.

Software developers and file sharers didn't back down, responding to the pressure by creating Internet protocols such as BitTorrent that can share files faster and more efficiently. Figure 23-60 shows one of the more popular BitTorrent protocol programs, called Transmission. BitTorrent has many legitimate uses as well—it is extremely efficient for the distribution of large files and has become the method of choice for distributing Linux distributions and is even used to distribute Blizzard games (and patches for those games) like *World of Warcraft* and *Starcraft II*! Still, BitTorrent users need the ability to discover valid trackers for the files they want to obtain, and sites listing these trackers have been a big target of continual legal action.

For all of the legal maneuvering, the last several years suggest the evolving business models of content-creation companies have helped defuse the situation by providing consumers with better access to digital content. Before, the options for obtaining digital copies of most content online were almost always illegal. In the past few years, industry-sanctioned streaming services by Netflix, HBO, and Spotify (see Figure 23-61), among others, have provided legal avenues for consumers to get the content they want, when they want it, without buying physical media (or even dealing with the very real risk of downloading malware instead of a legitimate file).

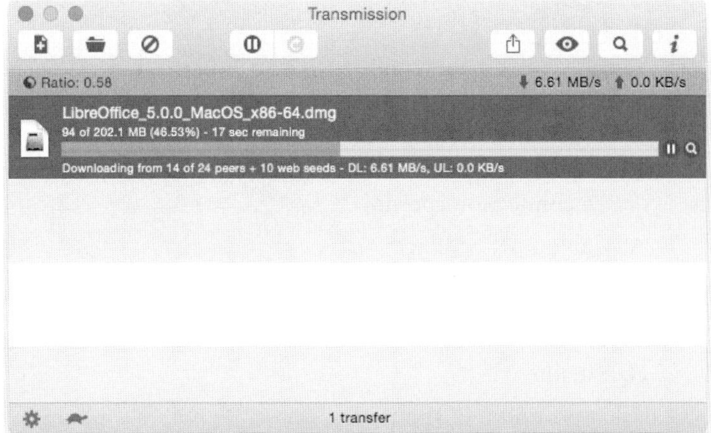

Figure 23-60 Transmission

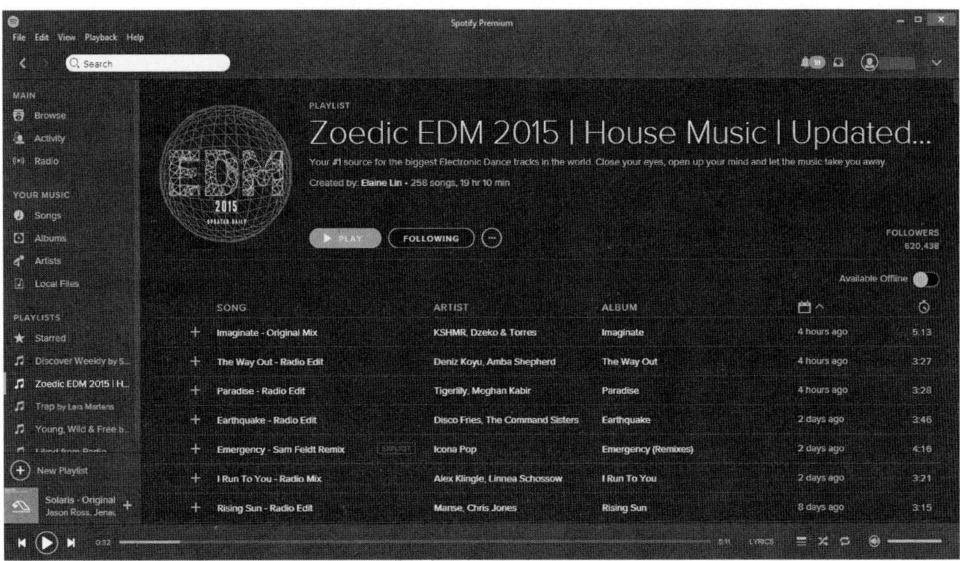

Figure 23-61 A great EDM playlist on Spotify

These example programs just scratch the surface of the many applications that use the Internet. One of the more amazing aspects of TCP/IP is that its basic design is around 40 years old. We use TCP/IP in ways completely outside the original concept of its designers, yet TCP/IP continues to show its power and flexibility. Pretty amazing!

Chapter Review

Questions

1. Of the following four Internet connection options, which typically offers the *slowest* connection speed?
   A. Cable
   B. Dial-up
   C. DSL
   D. Satellite
2. What port does POP3 use?
   A. 22
   B. 110
   C. 42
   D. 256
3. What advantage does dial-up have over DSL?
   A. Dial-up is faster than DSL.
   B. You can be farther than 18,000 feet from a main phone service switching center.
   C. You can get a second phone line to use just for dial-up.
   D. None. Dial-up has no advantages over DSL.
4. Which protocol can you use to send e-mail?
   A. IMAP
   B. POP3
   C. PPP
   D. SMTP
5. Which protocols can you use to receive e-mail? (Select two.)
   A. IMAP
   B. POP3
   C. PPP
   D. SMTP
6. What advantage does satellite have over cable for connecting to the Internet?
   A. Satellite is faster than cable.
   B. Cable degrades in stormy weather; satellite does not.

C. Satellite requires you to be within 18,000 feet of a central switch.

D. Cable is limited to areas with cable installed; satellite is not.

7. Which of the following represent invalid port to protocol matchups? (Select two.)

A. 137, 138, 139, 445 = SMB

B. 3398 = RDP

C. 80 = HTTPS

D. 22 = SSH

8. What command often enables you to diagnose TCP/IP errors such as connection problems?

A. FTP

B. ping

C. QoS

D. APIPA

9. Which of the following cellular data technologies is often considered 4G?

A. EDGE

B. UMTS

C. LTE

D. CDMA

10. Which of the following programs enable you to access and work on a remote computer from your local computer? (Select two.)

A. FTP

B. DNAT

C. Remote Desktop Connection

D. Telnet

Answers

1. **B.** Dial-up connections are robust but much slower than the other connection types.
2. **B.** Post Office Protocol 3 (POP3) uses port 110.
3. **B.** DSL has a fairly short limit of 18,000 feet from a main switch, leaving people in rural areas (in the United States, at least) out of luck. Dial-up just requires a phone line.
4. **D.** You can use Simple Mail Transfer Protocol (SMTP) to send e-mail messages.
5. **A, B.** You can use either Internet Message Access Protocol (IMAP) or POP3 to receive e-mail messages.

6. **D.** Clearly, satellite cuts you loose from the wires!
7. **B, C.** Remote Desktop Protocol (RDP) uses port 3389. Hypertext Transfer Protocol Secure (HTTPS) uses port 443; HTTP uses port 80.
8. **B.** You can often use the ping command to diagnose TCP/IP problems.
9. **C.** Long Term Evolution (LTE) is usually considered a 4G cellular data technology.
10. **C, D.** Both Remote Desktop Connection and Telnet enable you to access and work on a remote computer. The former is just prettier and more secure!

CHAPTER 24

Portable Computing

In this chapter, you will learn how to

- Describe the many types of portable computing devices available
- Explain ways to expand portable computers
- Manage and maintain portable computers
- Upgrade and repair portable computers
- Troubleshoot portable computers

There are times when the walls close in, when you need a change of scenery to get that elusive spark that inspires greatness…or sometimes you just need to get away from your coworkers for a few hours because they're driving you nuts! For many occupations, that's difficult to do. You need access to your documents and spreadsheets; you can't function without e-mail or the Internet. In short, you need a computer to get your job done.

Portable computing devices combine mobility with accessibility to bring you the best of both worlds; portables enable you to take some or even all of your computing capabilities with you when you go. Featuring all the bells and whistles of a desktop system, many portables offer a seamless transition from desk to café table.

This chapter looks at the classic portable computer, essentially a desktop transformed into a mobile format. While classic portables usually run Windows, Mac OS X, or some flavor of Linux, operating systems based on Linux—like Chrome OS—can also be found on portable computers.

Other portable devices, such as smartphones and tablets, run mobile operating systems—such as Apple iOS on the iPad and iPhone—designed to take advantage of small form factors and touchscreens. In practice (and on the CompTIA A+ exams), such mobile devices differ a lot from classic portable computers. While these devices get their own chapters later in the book, it is worth being aware that mobility has encouraged a lot of innovation in recent years and some of the resulting products do a really good job of blurring the line between these categories.

Historical/Conceptual

Portable Computing Devices

All portable devices share certain features. For output, they use LCD screens, although these vary from 20-inch behemoths to diminutive 10-inch displays. Portable computing devices employ sound of varying quality, from bland mono playback to fairly nice faux-surround reproductions. All of them run on DC electricity stored in batteries when not plugged into an AC outlet.

When asked about portable computing devices, most folks describe the traditional clamshell *notebook* computer, such as the one in Figure 24-1, with built-in LCD monitor, keyboard, and input device (a *touchpad*, in this case). The notebook is also called a portable or a *laptop*. All the terms are synonymous. A typical laptop functions as a fully standalone computer, potentially even replacing the desktop. The one in Figure 24-1, for example, has all of the features you expect a modern computer to have, such as a fast CPU, lots of RAM, a high-capacity hard drive, an optical drive, and an adequate sound system. Attach it to a network and you can browse the Internet and send e-mail.

Figure 24-1 A notebook computer

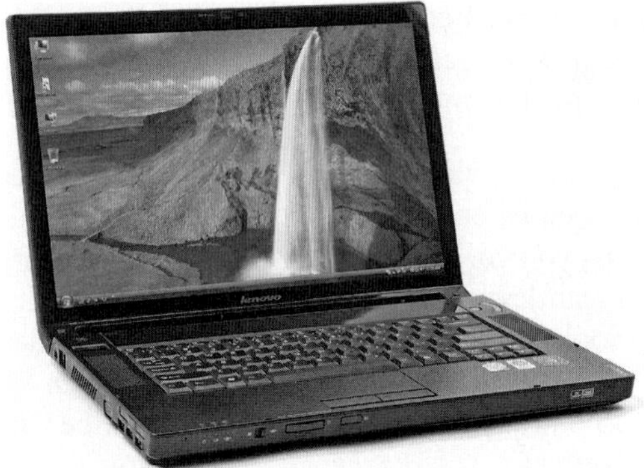

Taxonomy

The rampant experimentation and innovation within the mobile and portable device categories in recent years (driven in part by the evolution of Windows as a combined desktop/mobile device OS) has introduced new device categories, made others obsolete, and continued blurring the lines between them. Let's take a look at some of the terms used to describe these devices and put them in context. Keep in mind that, because these categories can be slippery, you shouldn't think of them as mutually exclusive. Sometimes more than one of these terms can be applied to a single device.

Desktop Replacements

A *desktop replacement* features a massive screen, a full-size keyboard, an optical drive (or maybe two), and plenty of hard drive space (see the portable on the left in Figure 24-2). Considering that it weighs almost as much as a mini-tower (or at least it feels like it does when I'm lugging it through the airport!), such a portable can be considered a *desktop replacement* because it does everything most people want to do with a desktop and doesn't compromise on performance just to make the laptop a few pounds lighter or the battery last an extra hour. Think power first, portability second.

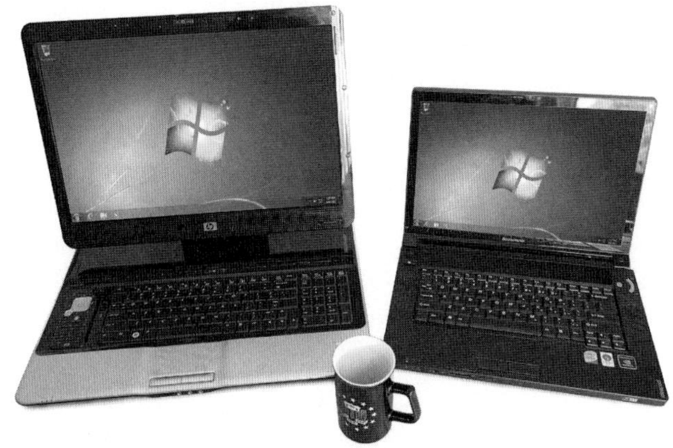

Figure 24-2 Desktop replacement (left) next to a standard portable computer (right)

The current sweet spot for desktop replacements is a 15- to 17-inch monitor with 16+ GB of memory and either dual 1- to 2-TB HDDs or a single 512-GB to 1-TB SSD. Dedicated graphics are a must. Desktop replacements run the latest Intel high-end mobile processors and, of course, Windows 10 Pro. Such perfection in computing in a sub-8-pound format doesn't come cheap, so the question that immediately arises is, why buy a desktop replacement?

Desktop replacements appeal to a diverse group of users. Most obviously, dedicated road warriors need to do everything on the plane, on the train, and in the hotel room. Second, having a computer that can work well on the road and in the office is convenient. Finally, some folks just prefer the compactness of a laptop. You can, after all, put it out of sight when you're finished with it and not have to dedicate space to an equally powerful desktop computer.

Gaming Laptops There's a lot of overlap between the broad category of desktop replacements and a popular subcategory: gaming laptops. *Gaming laptops* are an expensive compromise between the high requirements of the latest computer games and the ability to set up shop away from home. While they tend to have flashy designs that distinguish them from more reserved desktop replacements, it helps to look past the stylistics and realize that gaming laptops are purpose-built to replace desktop gaming rigs. They'll typically come loaded with the latest top-end processors, graphics cards, RAM, SSDs, and large, high-quality displays. They also tend to come with thoughtful touches like high-quality keyboards that are extensively customizable.

Subnotebooks

Unsurprisingly, the term *subnotebook* describes a portable computer that is smaller and lighter than a regular notebook or laptop. This distinction is becoming increasingly moot as more and more of the portable computer sales consist of devices that are technically subnotebooks.

Netbooks For a time, *netbooks* offered a lightweight computing platform with low cost and long battery life. These machines usually had displays in the 10-inch range, small hard drives, and CPUs geared more for minimal power usage than raw speed. While you may find some netbooks still in use, the category is basically dead. It's worth realizing that even though the term *netbook* has fallen out of vogue, the need it met for highly portable computing is bigger than ever. The netbook lives on in a few of the newer portable device categories we're about to discuss.

A prime example of the netbook is the ASUS Eee PC, shown in Figure 24-3 sitting on a full-sized laptop. This netbook has a 9-inch screen, a 1.6-GHz Intel Atom CPU, a small solid-state drive, and runs a customized Linux distribution. One distinguishing feature of these netbooks is the use of Intel's Atom processor. The Atom CPU is very useful for keeping power usage down but has much less computing power than its more power-hungry siblings. Therefore, most netbooks run lightweight operating systems better suited for their limited resources.

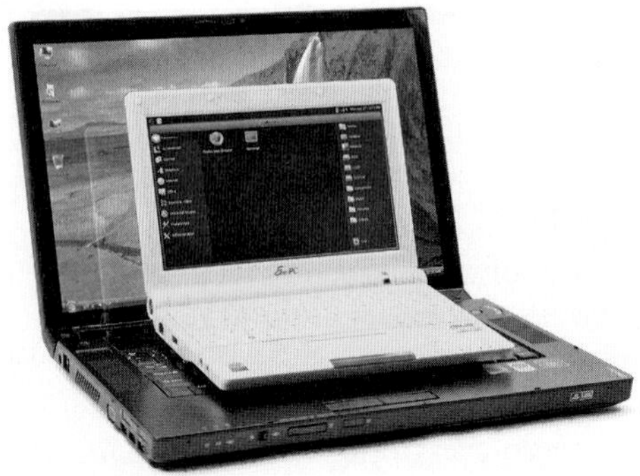

Figure 24-3 ASUS Eee PC sitting on a normal laptop

Chromebooks The most direct successor to the netbook is the *Chromebook*. Technically a Chromebook is just a portable computer running Google's Linux-based Chrome OS, but the majority of Chromebooks are light, inexpensive, relatively modest in computing power and storage, and on the small end of the laptop spectrum. Where netbooks had to make a lot of sacrifices to deliver an ultra-portable with an emphasis on e-mail and Web browsing, Chromebooks offer an experience focused on Web applications by making use of virtually unlimited data storage in the cloud and software as a service (SaaS) applications available over the Web. The rapid adoption of Chromebooks, especially in schools, is in many ways a story about just how far Web applications have come in the last several years.

Ultrabooks Thin, light, and powerful, *Ultrabooks* are as much about power and portability as they are about looks. Ultrabooks are for people who can't give up the

power of high-end computers but can afford to pay more for a smaller package. Intel set up the Ultrabook specifications in 2011, defining the form factor to use power-sipping Intel processors with integrated graphics. According to the most recent 2013 update, Ultrabooks have maximum dimensions (20 to 23 mm thick, depending on the size of the screen) and a minimum battery life (6 hours of HD video playback). You won't find optical drives on these, and most use solid-state drives for storage.

Ultrabooks reveal how the near-ubiquity of portable computers and the demanding expectations of consumers are driving the industry to marry form and function in lightweight, attractive, powerful portable computers that aren't a chore to carry, use, or keep charged. As such, most major laptop makers have at least a few Ultrabook models. Though many copy the thin-slice aesthetic of the MacBook Air (see Figure 24-4 for an example), some Ultrabooks come equipped with touchscreens and can also be used as tablets. We'll discuss these so-called *convertibles* later in this chapter.

Figure 24-4
MacBook Air

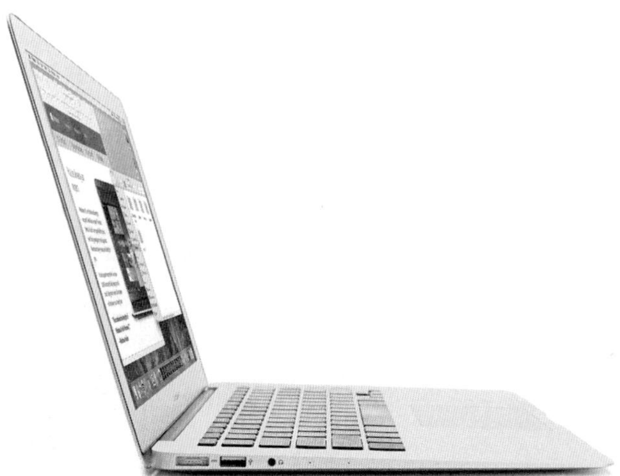

2-in-1s

Today, devices marketed or sold as a *2-in-1* can be roughly understood as a touchscreen computer somewhere along the spectrum from laptop-and-tablet to tablet-and-laptop. Because this is a pretty large spectrum covering several form factors, there are a number of more specific terms floating around, each with its own slippery definition, much overlap among them, and plenty of misuse to keep everything clear as mud. First we'll take a look at the Microsoft Tablet PCs that pioneered the category, and then we'll take a look at two terms used to describe these devices today: hybrid, and convertible.

NOTE You may run into a recent term, *laplet,* which describes a hybrid device with a full desktop OS and laptop-level specs—all in a tablet form factor.

Tablet PCs Microsoft started the *Tablet PC* initiative way back in 2001, defining the devices as fully featured portables running a tablet-aware version of Windows and using a stylus to interact directly with the screen. Many Tablet PCs have come to market since then, fulfilling the needs of specific professions, notably medicine.

NOTE *Tablet PC* is a Microsoft term (though you'll rarely catch Microsoft using the term itself anymore) and is *not* the equivalent of a tablet such as the Apple iPad or Samsung Galaxy Tab. The latter devices derive from the mobile phone market. Chapters 25 and 26 cover mobile devices in detail.

Instead of (or in addition to) a keyboard and mouse, Tablet PCs provide a screen that doubles as an input device. With a special pen, called a *stylus*, you can actually write on the screen (see Figure 24-5). Unlike some touchscreens, most Tablet PC screens are not pressure sensitive—you have to use the stylus to write on the screen. There are two main Tablet PC form factors: *convertibles*, which include a keyboard that you can fold out of the way, and *slates*, which do away with the keyboard entirely. The convertible Tablet PC in Figure 24-5, for example, looks and functions just like the typical clamshell laptop shown back in Figure 24-1. But here it's shown with the screen rotated 180 degrees and snapped flat so it functions as a slate.

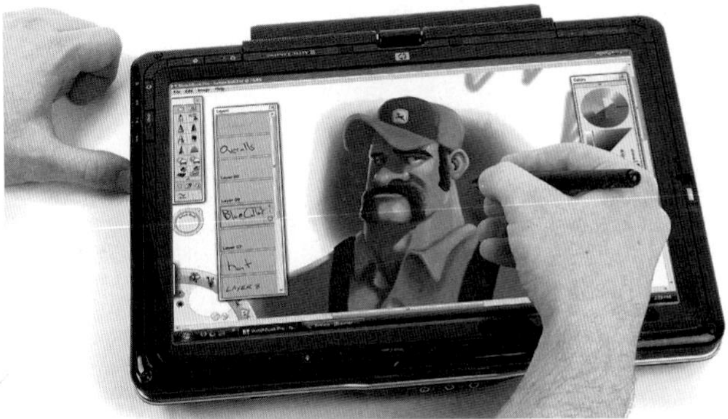

Figure 24-5
A Tablet PC

Tablet PCs worked well when you had limited space or had to walk around and use a laptop. Anyone who has ever tried to type with one hand while walking around holding a laptop with the other will immediately appreciate the beauty of a Tablet PC. In this scenario, Tablet PCs were most effective when combined with applications designed to be used with a stylus instead of a keyboard. An inventory control program, for example, might present drop-down lists and radio buttons to the user, making a stylus the perfect input tool.

Convertible Most of the time, the term *convertible* is used (much like it was in the preceding "Tablet PCs" section) to describe a laptop that uses one of several mechanisms to "convert" into something you can use like a tablet. More specifically, you can find convertibles with completely removable screens that become standalone tablets (leaving

behind any functionality or power that depends on hardware built into the keyboard portion of the device), and others that use one of a few hinge-based mechanisms:

- The laptop's hinges allow the screen to open all the way until it's flush with the bottom of the laptop, leaving the keyboard exposed on the underside of the tablet.
- The laptop's hinge has a vertical or horizontal swivel mechanism so you can rotate the screen and leave it exposed when you close the lid.
- The laptop has novel hinges that pop the screen up from a default tablet position and angle it toward the user, exposing a keyboard (usually a narrow one) underneath.

Hybrid A *hybrid* laptop/tablet is most often a device with a tablet form factor that is designed to integrate with a detachable keyboard (which may or may not come bundled with the device). Some of these keyboards may double as soft/pliable covers for the tablet (see Figure 24-6), while others are built more like a traditional keyboard in miniature. The line between a hybrid tablet that can attach to a separate hardware keyboard and a convertible laptop with a removable tablet screen can be hard to draw—but focus on whether any functionality or power is lost when the tablet portion is used alone. If all you lose is a keyboard, it's a hybrid.

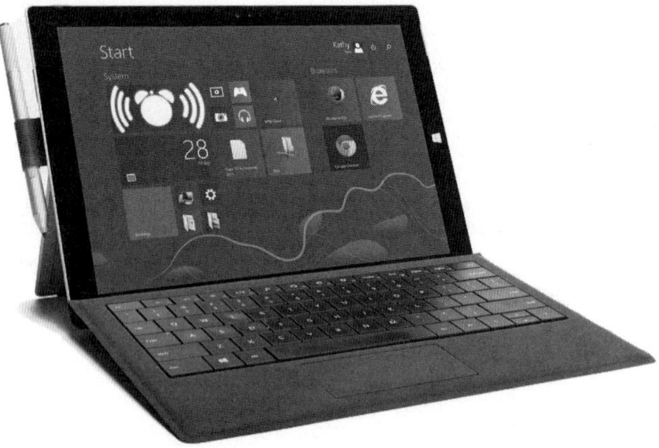

Figure 24-6 Microsoft Surface Pro 3 with its keyboard cover

NOTE Innovative portable form factors like those in the hybrid and convertible categories are often designed to be handled, rotated, flipped, and passed around. As a result, Windows now supports the automatic screen-rotation tricks we've seen on smartphones and tablets for years. Anyone who has used a device like this for long knows that occasionally you'll run into problems with the automatic screen-orientation sensor; see the troubleshooting section later in the chapter for fixes.

901

Input Devices

Portable computers come with a variety of input devices. Most have a fully functional keyboard and a device to control the mouse pointer.

Keyboard Quirks

Laptop keyboards differ somewhat from those of desktop computers, primarily because manufacturers have to cram all the keys onto a smaller form factor. They use the QWERTY format, but manufacturers make choices with key size and placement of the non-alphabet characters. Almost every portable keyboard uses a *Function (FN) key* to enable some keys to perform an extra duty. Figure 24-7 compares a standard desktop keyboard with a large portable keyboard. You'll note that the latter has no separate number pad on the right. To use the number pad, you press the FN key (lower left in this case) to transform the (7, 8, 9), (U, I, O), (J, K, L), and (M) keys into the (7, 8, 9), (4, 5, 6), (1, 2, 3), and (0) keys.

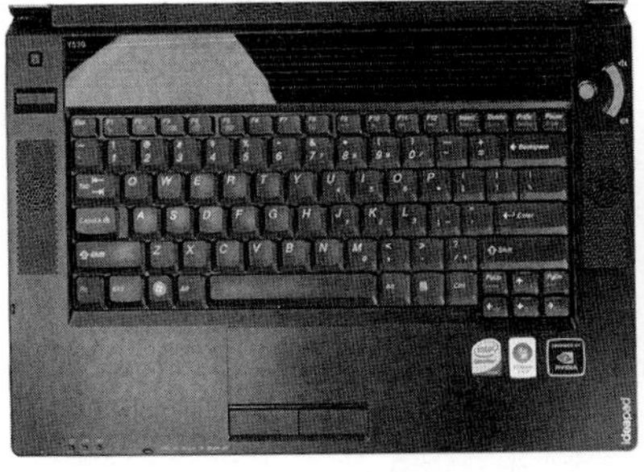
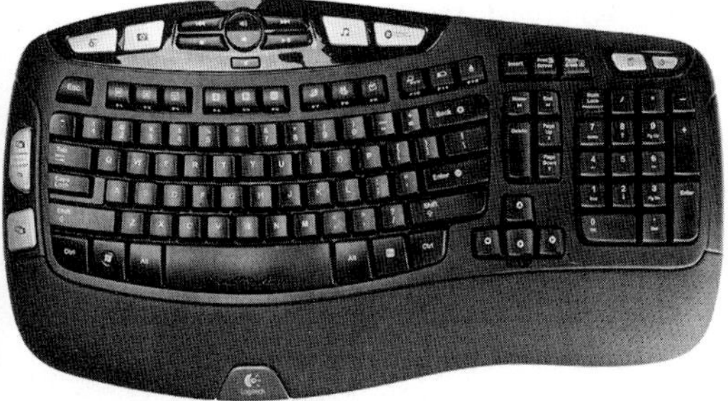

Figure 24-7 Keyboard comparison

NOTE The FN key also enables you to toggle other features specific to a portable, such as GPS tracking or the keyboard backlight to save battery life.

Pointing Devices

Portables need a way to control your mouse pointer, but their smaller size requires manufacturers to come up with clever solutions. Beyond the built-in solutions, portables usually have USB ports and can use every type of pointing device you'd see on a desktop. Early portables used *trackballs*, often plugged in like a mouse and clipped to the side of the case. Other models with trackballs placed them in front of the keyboard at the edge of the case nearest the user, or behind the keyboard at the edge nearest the screen.

The next wave to hit the laptop market was IBM's *TrackPoint* device, a joystick the size of a pencil eraser, situated in the center of the keyboard (see Figure 24-8). With the TrackPoint, you can move the pointer around without taking your fingers away from the "home" typing position. You use a forefinger to push the joystick around, and then click or right-click, using two buttons below the spacebar. This type of pointing device has since been licensed for use by other manufacturers, and it continues to appear on laptops today.

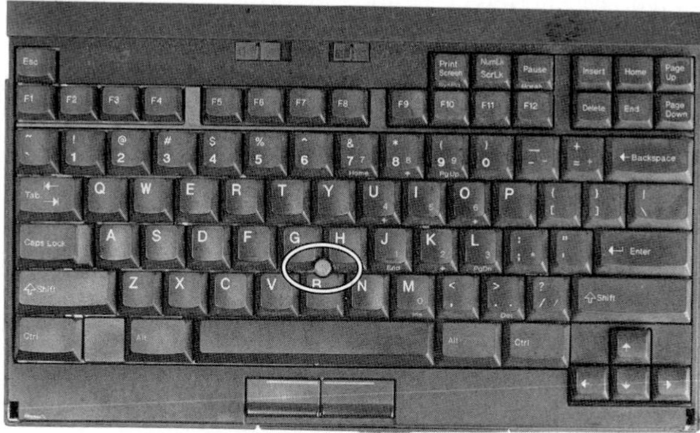

Figure 24-8
IBM TrackPoint

By far the most common laptop pointing device found today is the *touchpad* (see Figure 24-9)—a flat, touch-sensitive pad just in front of the keyboard. To operate a touchpad, you simply glide your finger across its surface to move the pointer, and tap the surface once or twice to single- or double-click. You can also click by using buttons just below the pad. Most people get the hang of this technique after just a few minutes of practice. The main advantage of the touchpad over previous laptop pointing devices is that it uses no moving parts—a fact that can really extend the life of a hard-working laptop.

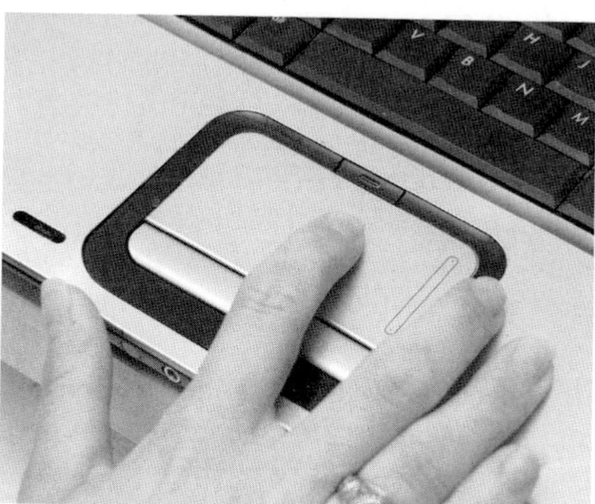

Figure 24-9
Touchpad on a laptop

Some manufacturers today include a *multitouch* touchpad that enables you to perform *gestures*, or actions with multiple fingers, such as scrolling up and down or swiping to

another screen or desktop. The *Multi-Touch trackpad* on Apple's laptops pioneered such great improvements to the laptop-pointing-device experience that the lack of a mouse is no longer a handicap on many laptops.

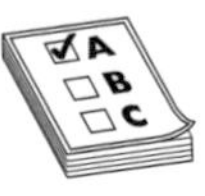

EXAM TIP In the past it was common to accidentally "use" a touchpad with your palm while typing, so you may find some devices with a hardware switch or FN key combination for disabling the touchpad. More recent touchpads are usually capable of detecting and ignoring accidental input like this on their own.

Continuing the trend of mobile's influence on more traditional portables, a growing number of laptops now come equipped with a *touchscreen* like you would find on a smartphone or tablet, again relying heavily on gestures to enable users to fluidly perform complex actions. In some cases these are otherwise very traditional laptops that happen to include a touchscreen, but in other cases they are devices that are intended to be used as both a tablet *and* a laptop.

Webcams and Microphones

The ability to communicate with others through real-time video is such a common expectation of mobile and portable devices these days that most of these devices (including laptops) come equipped with some sort of front-facing video camera—a *webcam* in the case of laptops—and one or more built-in microphones. A single *microphone* may be suitable for picking up the user's voice, and additional microphones can help noise-cancellation routines improve the audio quality.

Even though most of us may just use the microphone in conjunction with the webcam, a growing number of programs support voice commands. Take Google, for example, which has ported its popular "Ok Google" functionality from its Google Now Android app to its full Chrome browser. Any Chrome user on a system with a microphone, as long as they can live with letting Chrome listen in on them, can perform voice searches and other actions from anywhere within earshot (mic-shot?) of their device.

The downside of these input devices becoming ubiquitous is the security risk they pose. It might be bad enough if a nefarious hacker or government agency (from any country…) managed to get malware into my computer to see everything I click or type, but the risks are amplified if they can also hear and see anything going on near the device. It's common enough for webcams to include a light that indicates when they're recording, but built-in microphones don't do the same. In some cases, vulnerabilities allow the recording indicator to be disabled anyway.

NOTE If you pay careful attention when you're visiting offices or in a place people with laptops congregate, you may see tape over someone's built-in webcam; risks like these are why.

Display Types

Laptops come in a variety of sizes and at varying costs. One major contributor to the overall cost of a laptop is the size of the LCD screen. Most laptops offer a range between

10.1-inch to 17.3-inch screens (measured diagonally), while a few offer just over 20-inch screens.

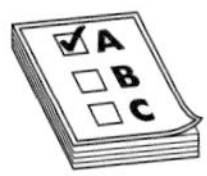

EXAM TIP Laptop LCDs are the same in almost every way as desktop LCDs with a TFT screen, an inverter (if using a CCFL backlight), and a backlight (CCFL or LED). You know all about these screens from Chapter 19, "Display Technologies." Expect questions about laptop displays, but know that they're pretty much the same as desktop displays. The only major difference is that the LCD frame contains an antenna, and may contain a camera and microphone, but we'll discuss this later in the chapter.

In the past, 4:3 aspect ratio screens were common, but these days it's hard to find one on anything but special-purpose or ruggedized laptops; almost all regular laptops come in one of two widescreen format ratios. *Aspect ratio* is the comparison of the screen width to the screen height, as you'll recall from Chapter 19. While widescreens can have varying aspect ratios, almost all of the screens you find in present-day laptops will be 16:9 or 16:10.

Laptop LCD screens come in a variety of supported resolutions, described with acronyms such as XGA, WXGA, WSXGA, and more. The *W* in front of the letters indicates widescreen. Though the number of aspect ratios on new laptops has fallen quickly, you'll still find a few resolutions for each ratio, and you may find more resolutions in use on older systems.

Laptop screens typically come with one of two types of finish: *matte* or *high-gloss*. The matte finish was the industry standard for many years and offered a good trade-off between richness of colors and the reduction of glare. The better screens have a wide viewing angle and decent response time. The major drawback for matte-finished laptop screens is that they wash out a lot in bright light. Using such a laptop at an outdoor café, for example, is almost hopeless during daylight.

Manufacturers released high-gloss laptop screens in 2006, and they rapidly took over many store shelves. The high-gloss finish offers sharper contrast, richer colors, and wider viewing angles when compared to the matte screens. The drawback to the high-gloss screens is that, contrary to what the manufacturers' claim, they pick up lots of reflection from nearby objects, including the user! So although they're usable outside during the day, you'll need to contend with increased reflection as well.

With the advent of LED backlighting for LCD panels, many manufacturers have switched back to an anti-glare screen, though they're not quite the matte screens of old. When the LED brightness is up high, these are lovely screens. (See the "Troubleshooting Portable Computers" section, later in this chapter, for issues specific to LED-backlit portables.)

As with other LCD technologies that you'll recall from Chapter 19, most LCD/LED screens use *twisted nematic (TN)* technology. Some laptop screens use *In-Plane Switching (IPS)* panels for the greater viewing angle and better color quality. You'll mostly find IPS panels on higher-grade portables.

What you will *not* find on portables are two other display technologies, plasma and organic light-emitting diode (OLED). Plasma displays demand a lot more electricity than LCDs demand and are completely inappropriate for portable devices. OLED screens sip energy when compared to LCDs, but they're still so expensive that you'll only find them on smartphones and tablets today. Chapter 25, "Mobile Devices," discusses OLED screen technology.

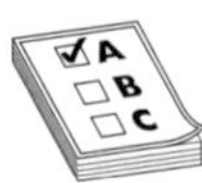

EXAM TIP The CompTIA A+ 901 exam objectives refer to OLED displays for laptops, but these don't exist. You'll find OLED displays on a few smartphones, but not on portable PCs, at least not at the time of this writing.

Extending Portable Computers

In the dark ages of mobile computing, you had to shell out top dollar for any device that would operate unplugged, and what you purchased was what you got. Upgrade a laptop? Connect to external devices? You had few if any options, so you simply paid for a device that would be way behind the technology curve within a year and functionally obsolete within two.

Portable computers today offer a few ways to enhance their capabilities. Most feature external ports that enable you to add completely new functions, such as attaching a scanner, mobile printer, or both. You can take advantage of the latest wireless technology breakthrough simply by slipping a card into the appropriate slot on the laptop.

I'll first describe single-function ports, and then turn to networking options. Next, I'll cover card slots, and then finish with a discussion of general-purpose ports.

Single-Function Ports

All portable computers come with one or more single-function ports. You'd have a hard time finding a portable computing device that doesn't have an audio port, for example. Laptops often provide a video port for hooking up an external monitor, though wireless screen sharing and screencasting are gaining popularity as an alternative.

Ports work the same way on portable computers as they do on desktop models. You plug in a device to a particular port and, as long as the operating system has the proper drivers, you will have a functioning device when you boot.

Audio

Portable computers have a standard 3.5-mm audio-out port and some have a similarly sized microphone-in port (see Figure 24-10), though built-in microphones are increasingly common. You can plug in headphones, regular PC speakers, or even a nice surround sound set to enable the laptop to play music just as well as a desktop computer can.

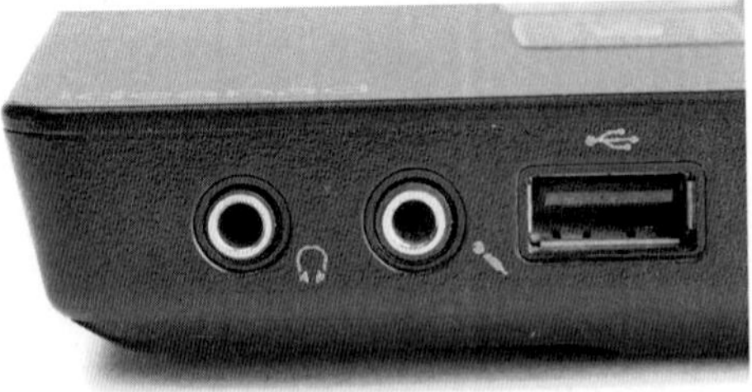

Figure 24-10 Standard audio ports

You can control the sound (both out and in) through either the appropriate Control Panel applet in Windows, System Preferences in Mac OS X, or some kind of switches on

the laptop. The portable in Figure 24-11, for example, enables you to mute the speakers by pressing a special mute button above the keyboard. Other portables use a combination of the fn key and another key to toggle mute on and off, as well as to play, pause, fast-forward, and rewind audio (or any other media options). Most portables will have volume up/down controls in the same location.

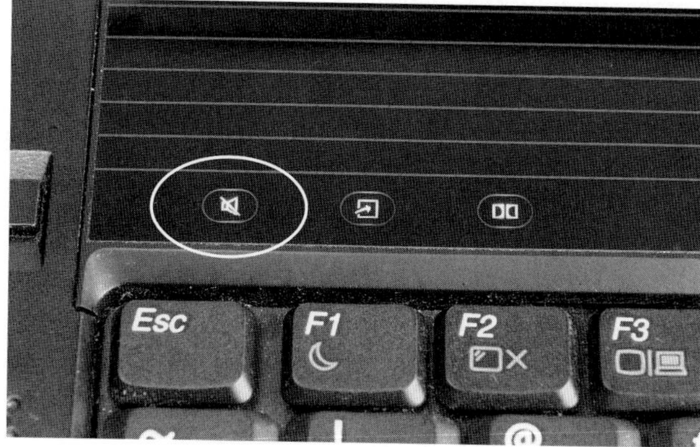

Figure 24-11 The mute button on a laptop

Display

Most laptops support a second monitor via a digital port of some sort. There are many of these—you may find HDMI (including Mini-HDMI and Micro-HDMI), DisplayPort (including USB Type-C and Thunderbolt), and DVI; on ancient or special-purpose portables, there's even a chance you may still find an analog VGA. With a second monitor attached, you can duplicate your screen to the new monitor, or extend your desktop across both displays, letting you move windows between them. Not all portables can do all variations, but they're more common than not.

Most portables use the FN key plus another key on the keyboard to cycle through display options. Figure 24-12 shows a close-up of a typical keyboard with the FN key; note the other options you can access with the FN key, such as indicated on the F2 key. To engage the second monitor or to cycle through the modes, hold the FN key and press F2.

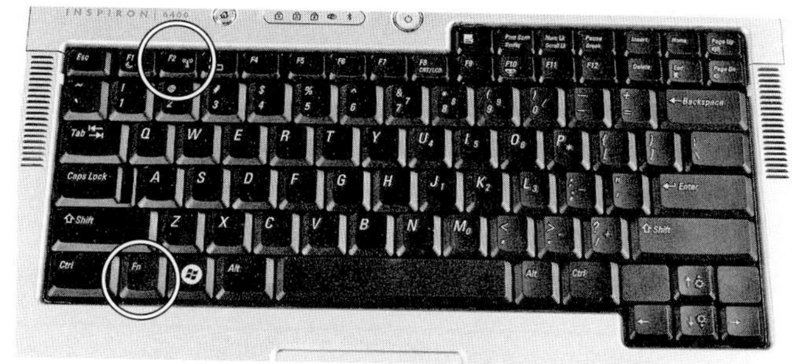

Figure 24-12 Laptop keyboard showing Function (FN) key that enables you to access additional key options, as on the F2 key

NOTE Although many laptops use the Function key method to cycle the monitor selections, that's not always the case. You might have to pop into the Display applet or System Preferences to click a checkbox. Just be assured that if the laptop has a video output port, you can cycle through monitor choices!

You can control how the external monitor displays through the Display applet in the Control Panel in Windows. (Other OSs have similar options.) Open Display and click on *Change display settings* (see Figure 24-13). On the Screen Resolution panel, click the drop-down arrow next to Multiple displays (see Figure 24-14). You'll see several options. *Extend these displays* makes your desktop encompass both the laptop and the external monitor. *Duplicate these displays* places the same thing on both displays. You'd use that for a presentation, for example, rather than for a work space. The other two options shown in Figure 24-14 temporarily blank one or the other display.

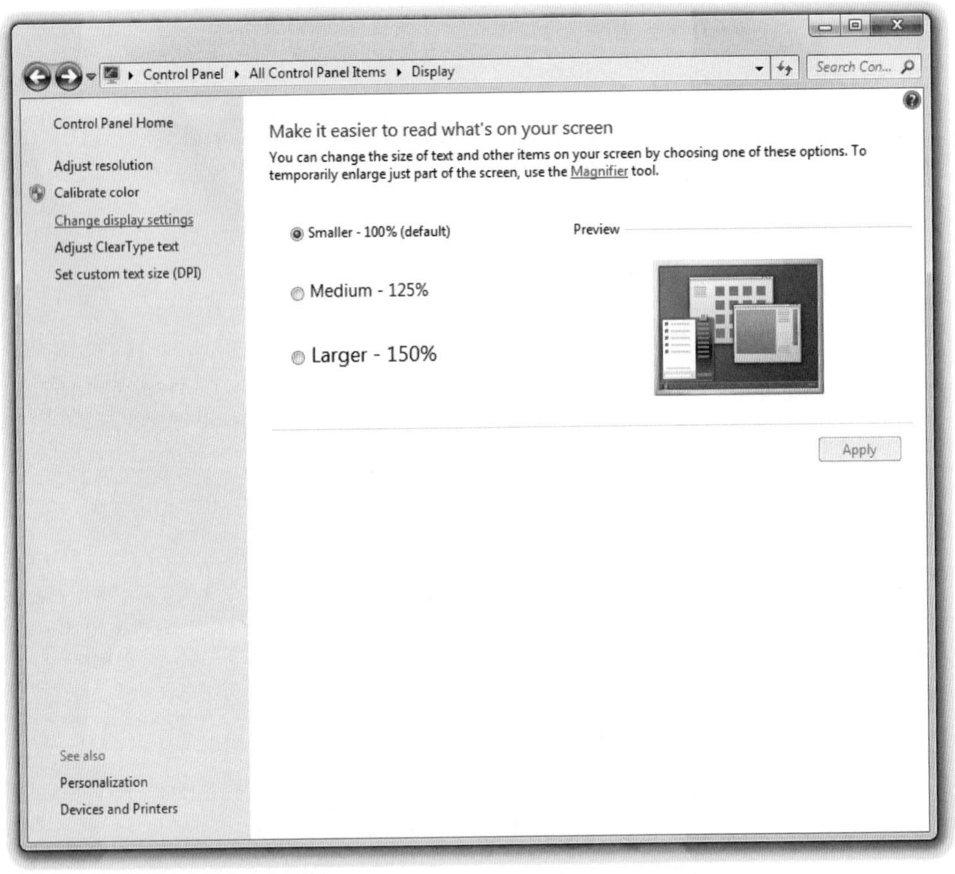

Figure 24-13 Display applet in Windows 7

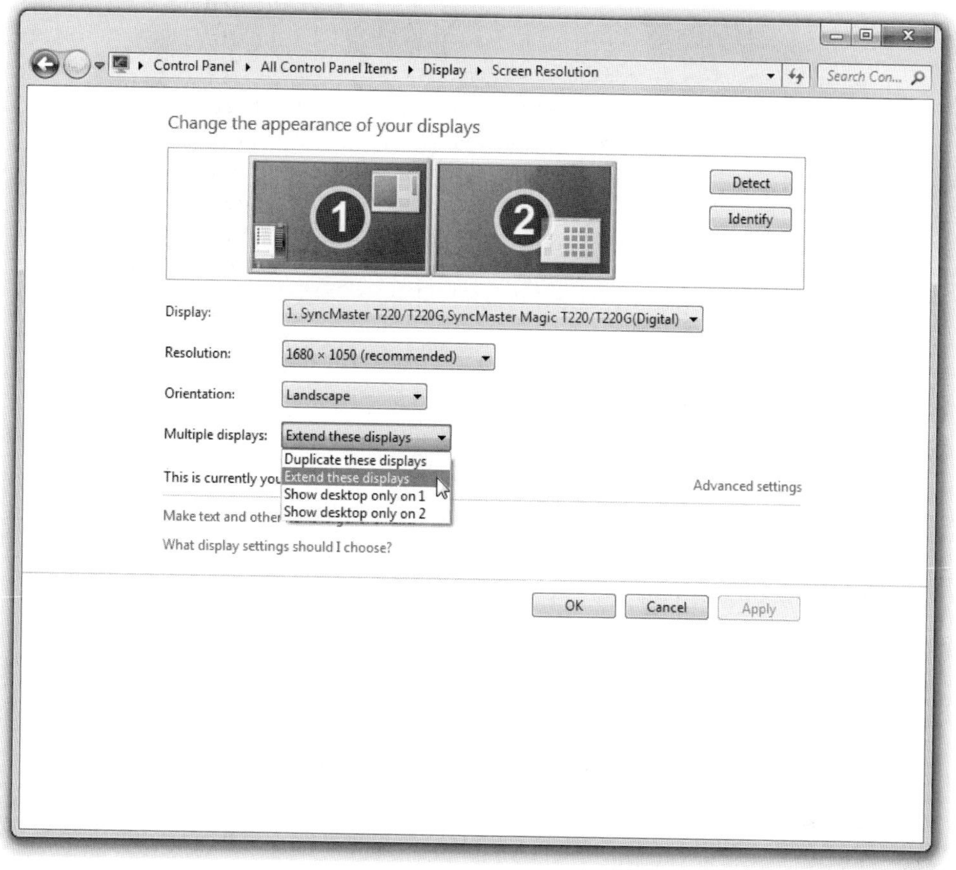

Figure 24-14 Multiple-display options menu in Windows 7

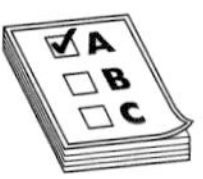

EXAM TIP The CompTIA A+ 901 exam objectives refer to multiple monitors as *dual displays*, though they can be in several modes

Smart Card Reader

It isn't really a port, but you'll find some portable computers—especially ones designed for and marketed to business users—with a very thin slot the width of a credit card on one side or the other. No, it isn't an expansion or memory card slot—it's a *smart card reader*. If you've seen a credit or debit card with a little metallic chip (see Figure 24-15), you've seen a smart card. While smart cards have tons of uses, what matters here is that you can log in to a portable device (if it has a built-in or USB smart card reader) using *your* smart card and a PIN number.

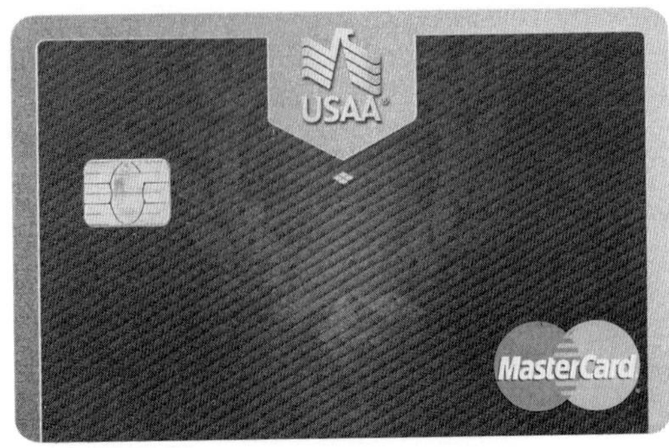

Figure 24-15
Smart card

Networking Options

It's a rare item to find a portable computer without at least one network connection option. Today's portables come with some combination 802.11, Bluetooth, or wired Ethernet connections. Generally they work exactly as you've seen in previous chapters, but you may stumble into a few issues that are unique to portables.

802.11 Wireless

Most portables today have Wi-Fi built directly into the chipset for connecting the device to a wireless access point (WAP) and from there to a bigger network, such as the Internet. The 802.11b and 802.11g standards are common on older laptops; newer portable computers use 802.11n or 802.11ac.

NOTE While the newest portables are shipping with 802.11ac, be aware that, especially as portables are getting powerful enough to live longer useful lives, you may see a few previous standards built into devices in the wild.

Bluetooth

While not quite as ubiquitous as 802.11, most portables use Bluetooth as well. Bluetooth is really handy on a laptop because it gives you the ability to add wireless peripherals such as mice, keyboards, and headsets, as well as communicate with smartphones, speakers, and other Bluetooth devices.

Hardware Switches

Portable computers that come with wireless technologies such as 802.11, mobile broadband, GPS, or Bluetooth have some form of on/off switch to toggle the antenna off or on so that you may use the laptop in areas where emissions aren't allowed (like a commercial aircraft). The switch may be hard wired, like the one shown in Figure 24-16, or it may be a toggle of the FN key plus another key on the keyboard. Also, if you're not using Wi-Fi or Bluetooth, turn them off to save electricity and lengthen the portable's battery life.

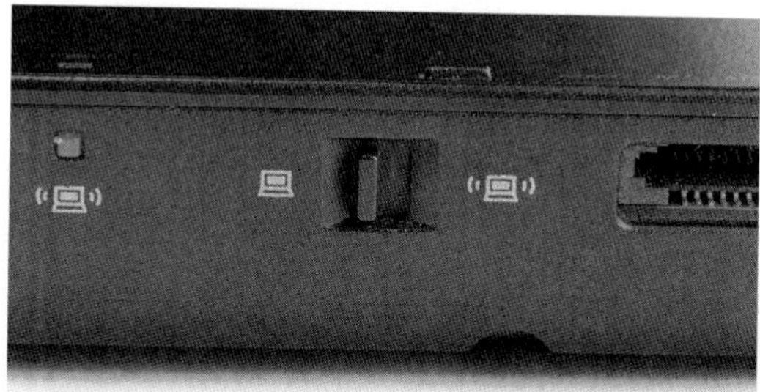

Figure 24-16 Wireless switch

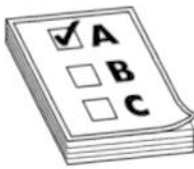

EXAM TIP Hardware switches or special Function key toggles enable you to switch features on and off, such as wireless networking, cellular networking, and Bluetooth. Toggle them off when in a scenario where battery life takes priority over networking.

Wired Ethernet

Most full-size laptops have an RJ-45 wired Ethernet connection like the one shown in Figure 24-17. These work exactly like any other Ethernet jack—they have link lights and connect via UTP cable. Be aware, however, that wired Ethernet is one of the things hybrids, Ultrabooks, and other smaller portables usually leave out.

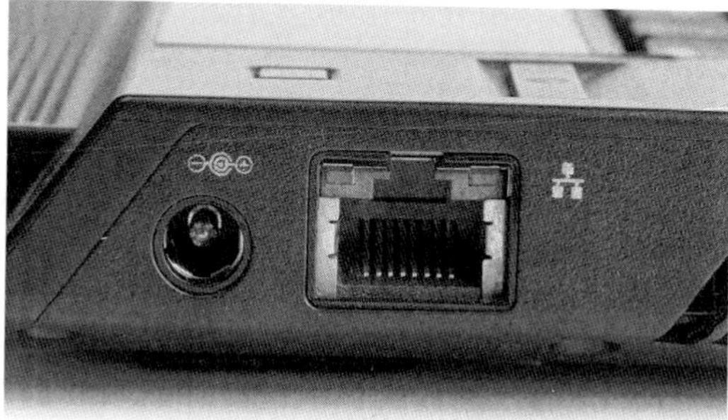

Figure 24-17 Ethernet port on laptop

There are two issues with RJ-45s on laptops. First, they do not have an on/off switch like the 802.11 and Bluetooth connections. You can turn them off just like you would turn off the NIC on a desktop: disable the NIC in Device Manager or turn the NIC off in BIOS. The other issue is the relative weakness of the physical connection. If you ever plug a laptop into a wired network and the OS doesn't see a connection, check the RJ-45 port.

Portable-Specific Expansion Slots

The makers of portable computers have developed methods for you to add features to a portable via specialized connections known generically as *expansion slots*. For many years,

the *Personal Computer Memory Card International Association (PCMCIA)* established standards involving portable computers, especially when it came to expansion cards and slots. Once a common feature on laptops, these specialized expansion slots are almost impossible to find due to the dominance of USB. The last standard was called ExpressCard.

ExpressCard

ExpressCard comes in two widths: 34 mm and 54 mm, called *ExpressCard/34* and *ExpressCard/54*. Figure 24-18 shows both ExpressCard varieties. Both cards are 75 mm long and 5 mm thick.

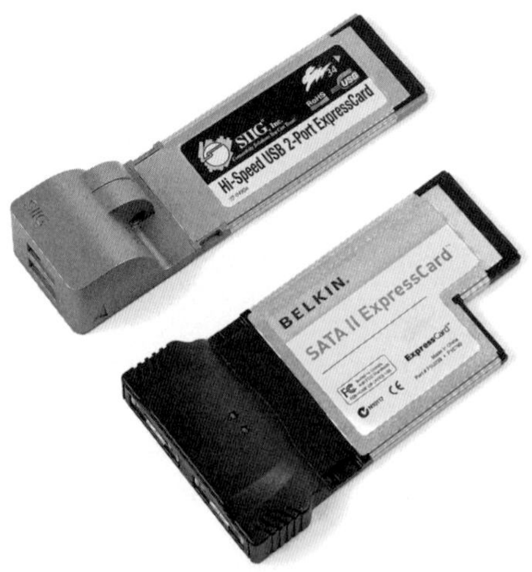

Figure 24-18 34-mm and 54-mm ExpressCards

ExpressCards connect to either the USB 2.0 bus or the PCI Express bus. These differ phenomenally in speed. The amazingly slow-in-comparison USB version has a maximum throughput of 480 Mbps. The PCIe version, in contrast, roars in at 2.5 Gbps in unidirectional communication.

Table 24-1 shows the throughput and variations for the parallel and serial PC Cards currently on the market.

Standard	Maximum Theoretical Throughput
ExpressCard using USB 2.0 bus	480 Mbps
ExpressCard using PCIe bus	2.5 Gbps

Table 24-1 ExpressCard Speeds

PCMCIA announced ExpressCard 2.0 in 2009 with speeds up to 5 Gbps and support for SuperSpeed USB 3.0, and we expected to see devices roll out in 2010, but that's not what happened. PCMCIA instead dissolved and shut its offices. The USB Implementer's Forum manages all ExpressCard standards, and there has been no further development.

NOTE You may find ExpressCards that supposedly support USB 3.0. While technically these cards have USB 3.0 ports, they connect to the PCIe bus and therefore aren't capable of true USB 3.0 speeds of up to 5 Gbps.

Storage Card Slots

Many portable computers offer one or more flash-memory card slots to enable you to add storage to the portable. These slots also enable the fast transfer of data from the card to the portable, and vice versa. They come in the standard varieties that you already know from Chapter 11, "Essential Peripherals," such as SD or Micro-SD.

General-Purpose Ports

Portable computers rarely come with all of the hardware you want. Today's laptops usually include at least USB ports to give you the option to add more hardware. Some special-purpose laptops may still provide legacy general-purpose expansion ports (PS/2, RS-232 serial ports, and so on) for installing peripheral hardware, while other portables focus on more modern ports like Thunderbolt, eSATA, and FireWire. If you're lucky, you will have a docking station so you don't have to plug in all of your peripheral devices one at a time.

USB, Thunderbolt, FireWire, and eSATA

Universal serial bus (USB), Thunderbolt, FireWire (or more properly, IEEE 1394), and eSATA enable users to connect a device while the PC is running—you won't have to reboot the system to install a new peripheral. With USB, FireWire, and eSATA, just plug the device in and go! Because portable PCs don't have a desktop's multiple internal expansion capabilities, USB, Thunderbolt, FireWire, and eSATA are some of the more popular methods for attaching peripherals to laptops (see Figure 24-19).

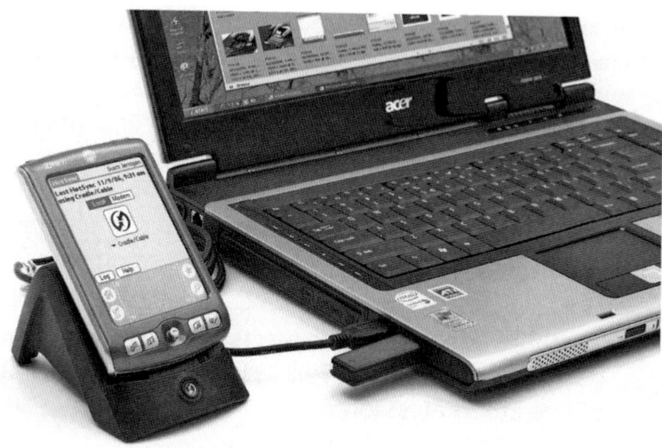

Figure 24-19 Devices attached to USB on a portable PC (Whooooa, retro PDA, dude!)

NOTE The small device resting in a stand in Figure 24-19, a *personal digital assistant (PDA)*, was a precursor to modern smartphones and tablets. You could view pictures, take notes, check a calendar, listen to music, and more on these devices.

Docking Stations

Docking stations offer legacy and modern single- and multi-function ports (see Figure 24-20). The typical docking station uses a proprietary connection but has extra features built in, such as an optica drive or ExpressCard slot for extra enhancements. You can find docking stations for many older small laptops. A docking station makes an excellent companion to such portables.

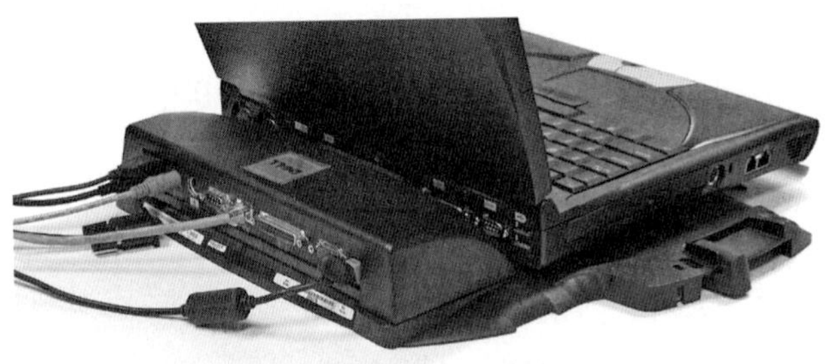

Figure 24-20 Docking station

USB Adapters

When you don't need access to a number of ports at once, you can often find a USB adapter for whatever you need to connect. There are tons of these things, but CompTIA wants you to know about a few in particular. When it comes to drives or connectors that you need only occasionally, these adapters can enable you to use a much more portable device.

Two great examples of this are wired Ethernet and optical drives. I don't know about you, but I haven't spun up an optical disc in months, nor am I sure when I last opened my laptop within a few feet of a wired Ethernet connection. A USB to RJ-45 dongle and a USB optical drive can provide these features when and where I need them, leaving me a much smaller laptop to carry the rest of the time.

Another good use for USB adapters is updating connectivity support for older devices. A USB to Wi-Fi dongle or a USB Bluetooth adapter can let me update an old laptop to 802.11ac, or add Bluetooth to a laptop that didn't come with it built in.

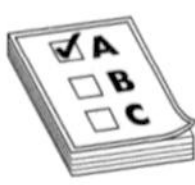

EXAM TIP The 901 exam expects you to be familiar with USB to RJ-45 and USB to Wi-Fi dongles as well as USB to Bluetooth, USB to optical drive, and USB to Ethernet adapters.

Managing and Maintaining Portable Computers

Most portables come from the factory fully assembled and configured. From a tech's standpoint, your most common work on managing and maintaining portables involves taking care of the batteries and extending the battery life through proper power management, keeping the machine clean, and avoiding excessive heat.

Everything you normally do to maintain a computer applies to portable computers. You need to keep current on OS updates and use stable, recent drivers. Use appropriate tools to monitor the health of your storage drives and clean up unwanted files. That said, let's look at issues specifically involving portables.

Batteries

Manufacturers over the years have used a few types of batteries for portable computers: Nickel-Cadmium (Ni-Cd), Nickel–Metal Hydride (Ni-MH), and *Lithium-Ion (Li-Ion)*. Today, only Li-Ion is used because that battery chemistry provides the highest energy density for the weight and has few problems with external factors.

Lithium-Ion

Li-Ion batteries are powerful, and last much longer than the Ni-MH and Ni-Cd ones we used in the 1990s. If Li-Ion batteries have a downside, it's that they will explode if overcharged or punctured, so all Li-Ion batteries have built-in circuitry to prevent accidental overcharging. Lithium batteries can only be used on systems designed to use them. They can't be used as replacement batteries to keep that retro laptop from 1998 going. Figure 24-21 shows a typical Li-Ion battery.

Figure 24-21
Li-Ion battery

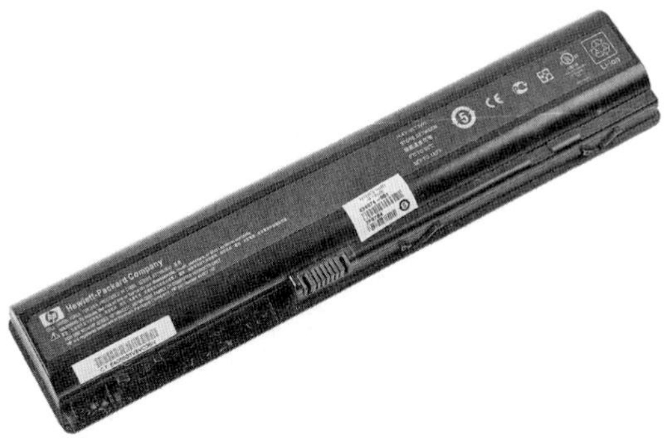

NOTE *Lithium polymer (LiPO)* batteries are a variation of Li-Ion that places the heart of the battery—the electrolyte—into a solid polymer shape rather than an organic solvent. This enables the batteries to take on unusual forms beyond the simple cylinder or rectangle shapes. LiPO batteries haven't replaced Li-Ion in most portables (with the Apple MacBook an exception), but they are used a lot in smaller electronics such as tablets, smartphones, and portable media players.

The Care and Feeding of Batteries

In general, keep in mind the following basics. First, always store batteries in a cool place. Although a freezer might seem like an excellent storage place, the moisture, extreme freezing cold, metal racks, and food make it a bad idea. Second, keep the battery charged, at least to 70–80 percent. Third, never drain a battery all the way down unless required to do so as part of a *battery calibration* (where you, in essence, reset the battery according to steps provided by the manufacturer). Rechargeable batteries have only a limited number of charge-discharge cycles before overall battery performance is reduced. Fourth, *never* handle a battery that has ruptured or broken; battery chemicals are very dangerous and flammable (check YouTube for videos of what happens when you puncture a Li-Ion or LiPO battery). Finally, always recycle old batteries.

Try This!

Recycling Old Portable PC Batteries

Got an old portable PC battery lying around? Well, you need to get rid of it, and there are some pretty nasty chemicals in that battery, so you can't just throw it in the trash. Sooner or later, you'll probably need to deal with such a battery, so Try This!

1. Do an online search to find the battery recycling center nearest to you. Electronics retailers are getting much better about accepting a wide array of e-waste, including batteries, though they often place quantity limits.
2. Sometimes, you can take old laptop batteries to an auto parts store that disposes of old car batteries—I know it sounds odd, but it's true! See if you can find one in your area that will do this.
3. Many cities offer a hazardous materials disposal or recycling service. Check to see if and how your local government will help you dispose of your old batteries.

Power Management

Many different parts are included in the typical laptop, and each part uses power. The problem with early laptops was that every one of these parts used power continuously, whether or not the system needed the device at that time. For example, the hard drive continued to spin even when it was not being accessed, the CPU ran at full speed even when the system was doing light work, and the LCD panel continued to display even when the user walked away from the machine.

The optimal situation would be a system where the computer shuts down unused devices selectively, preferably by defining a maximum period of inactivity that, when reached, would trigger the system to shut down the inactive device. Longer periods of inactivity

would eventually enable the entire system to shut itself down, leaving critical information loaded in RAM, ready to restart if a wake-up event (such as moving the mouse or pressing a key) told the system to resume. The system would have to be sensitive to potential hazards, such as shutting down in the middle of writing to a drive, and so on. Also, this feature could not add significantly to the cost of the computer. Clearly, a machine that could perform these functions would need specialized hardware and a specialized BIOS and operating system to operate properly. This process of cooperation among the hardware, the BIOS, and the OS to reduce power use is known generically as *power management.*

System Management Mode

Intel began the process of power management with a series of new features built into the 386SX CPU. These new features enabled the CPU to slow down or stop its clock without erasing the register information, as well as enabling power saving in peripherals. These features were collectively called *System Management Mode (SMM)*. All modern CPUs have SMM. Although a power-saving CPU was okay, power management was relegated to special "sleep" or "doze" buttons that would stop the CPU and all of the peripherals on the laptop. To take real advantage of SMM, the system needed a specialized BIOS and OS to go with the SMM CPU. To this end, Intel put forward the *Advanced Power Management (APM)* specification in 1992 and the *Advanced Configuration and Power Interface (ACPI)* standard in 1996.

Requirements for APM/ACPI

To function fully, APM and ACPI require a number of items. First, they require an SMM-capable CPU. As virtually all CPUs are SMM-capable, this is easy. Second, they need an APM-compliant BIOS that enables the CPU to shut off the peripherals when desired. The third requirement is devices that will accept being shut off. These devices are usually called Energy Star devices, which signals their compliance with the EPA's Energy Star standard. To be an Energy Star device, a peripheral must be able to shut down without actually turning off and show that it uses much less power than the non–Energy Star equivalent. Last, the system's OS must know how to request that a particular device be shut down, and the CPU's clock must be slowed down or stopped.

ACPI goes beyond the APM standard by supplying support for hot-swappable devices—always a huge problem with APM. This feature aside, it is a challenge to tell the difference between an APM system and an ACPI system at first glance.

NOTE Don't limit your perception of APM, ACPI, and Energy Star just to laptops. Virtually all desktop systems and many appliances also use the power management functions.

APM/ACPI Levels

APM defined four power-usage operating levels for a system. These levels are intentionally fuzzy to give manufacturers considerable leeway in their use; the only real difference

among them is the amount of time each takes to return to normal usage. These levels are as follows:

- **Full On** Everything in the system is running at full power. There is no power management.
- **APM Enabled** CPU and RAM are running at full power. Power management is enabled. An unused device may or may not be shut down.
- **APM Standby** CPU is stopped. RAM still stores all programs. All peripherals are shut down, although configuration options are still stored. In other words, you won't have to reinitialize the devices to get back to APM Enabled.
- **APM Suspend** Everything in the system is shut down or at its lowest power-consumption setting. Many systems use a special type of Suspend called *hibernation*, where critical configuration information is written to the hard drive. Upon a wake-up event, the system is reinitialized, and the data is read from the drive to return the system to the APM Enabled mode. Clearly, the recovery time between Suspend and Enabled will be much longer than the time between Standby and Enabled.

ACPI, the successor to APM, handles all these levels plus a few more, such as "soft power on/off," which enables you to define the function of the power button. You should familiarize yourself with the following ACPI global (G) and sleeping (S) system power state specifications for both the CompTIA A+ exams and your own practical application:

- **G0 (S0)** Working state
- **G1** Sleeping state mode. Further subdivided into four *S* states.
  - **S1** CPU stops processing. Power to CPU and memory (RAM) is maintained.
  - **S2** CPU is powered down.
  - **S3** Sleep or Standby mode. Power to RAM still on.
  - **S4** Hibernation mode. Information in RAM is stored to nonvolatile memory or drive and powered off.
- **G2 (S5)** Soft power off mode. Certain devices used to wake a system—such as keyboard, LAN, USB, and other devices—remain on, while most other components are powered to a mechanical off state (G3).
- **G3** Mechanical off mode. The system and all components, with the exception of the real-time clock (RTC), are completely powered down.

Configuration of APM/ACPI

You configure APM/ACPI via CMOS settings or through your operating system. OS settings override CMOS settings. Although the APM/ACPI standards permit a great deal of flexibility, which can create some confusion among different implementations, certain

settings apply generally to CMOS configuration. First is the ability to initialize power management; this enables the system to enter the APM Enabled mode. Often CMOS then presents time frames for entering Standby and Suspend modes, as well as settings to determine which events take place in each of these modes.

Many CMOS versions present settings to determine wake-up events, such as directing the system to monitor a modem or a NIC (see Figure 24-22). You'll see this feature as *Wake on LAN*, or something similar. A true ACPI-compliant CMOS provides an ACPI setup option. Figure 24-23 shows a typical modern BIOS that provides this setting.

```
Phoenix - AwardBIOS CMOS Utility
Power
APM Configuration                                    Select Menu
Restore on AC Power Loss        [Power-Off]          Item Specific Help▸▸
PWR Button < 4 secs             [Instant-Off]
Power Up On PCI/PCIE Devices    [Disabled]           Set the Data, Time
USB Resume from S5              [Disabled]           resume by Alarm.
Power On By RTC Alarm           [Enabled]
Date(of Month) Alarm            [ 5]
Alarm Time(hh:mm)                 2 : 9 : 5
Power Up By PS/2 Mouse          [Disabled]
Power Up By PS/2 Keyboard       [Disabled]
F1:Help    ↑↓:Select Item    -/+: Change Value          F5:Setup Defaults
ESC:Exit   ▸◂:Select Menu    Enter: Select SubMenu      F10:Save and Exit
```

Figure 24-22 Setting a wake-up event in CMOS

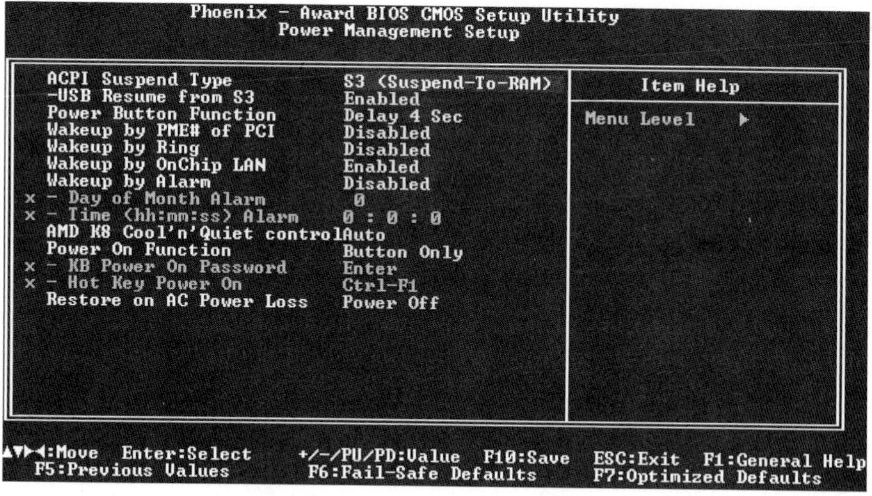

Figure 24-23 CMOS with ACPI setup option

In Windows, APM/ACPI settings can be found in the Control Panel applet Power Options. Windows offers *power plans* that enable better control over power use by customizing a Balanced, High performance, or Power saver power plan (see Figure 24-24). You can customize a power plan for your laptop, for example, and configure it to turn off the display at a certain time interval while on battery or plugged in and configure it to put the computer to sleep as desired (see Figure 24-25).

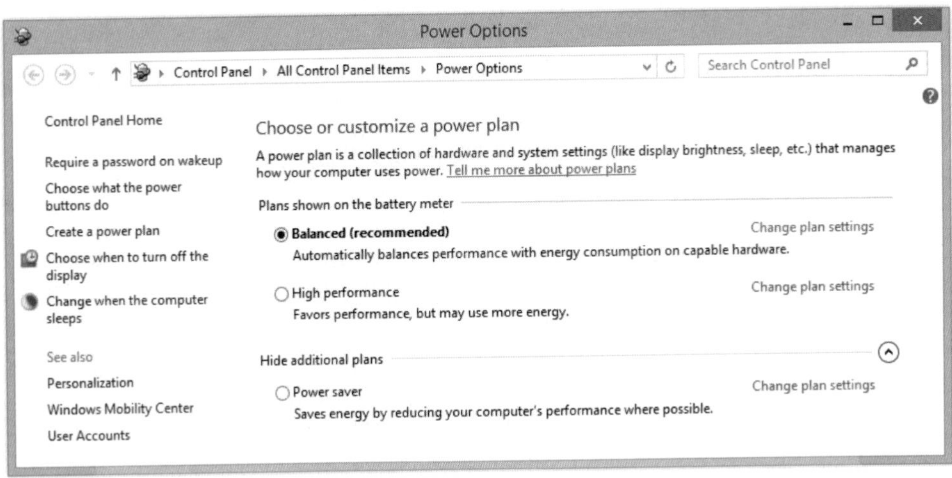

Figure 24-24 Windows Balanced, High performance, and Power saver power plan options

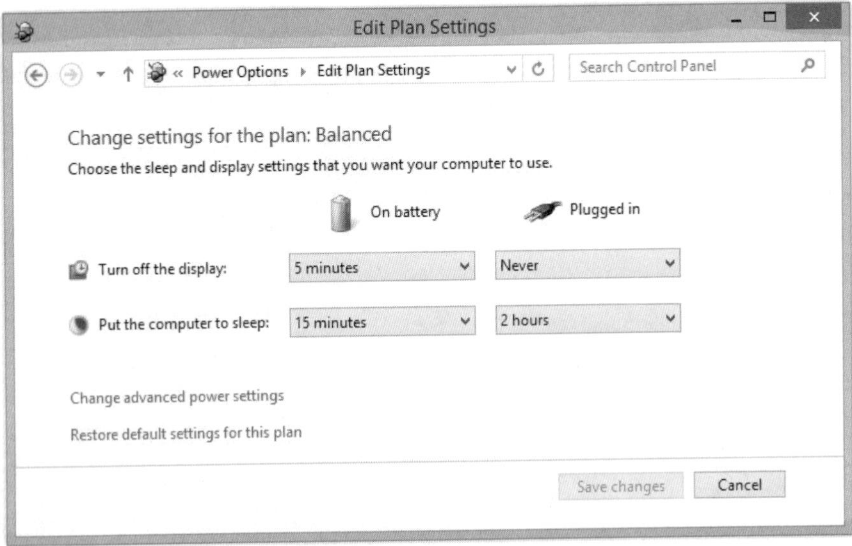

Figure 24-25 Customizing a laptop power plan in Windows

NOTE You can also access your power options by clicking on the Power icon in the notification area if it is present.

Another feature, Hibernate mode, takes everything in active memory and stores it on the hard drive just before the system powers down. When the system comes out of hibernation, Windows reloads all the files and applications into RAM. Figure 24-26 shows the hibernation options in Windows.

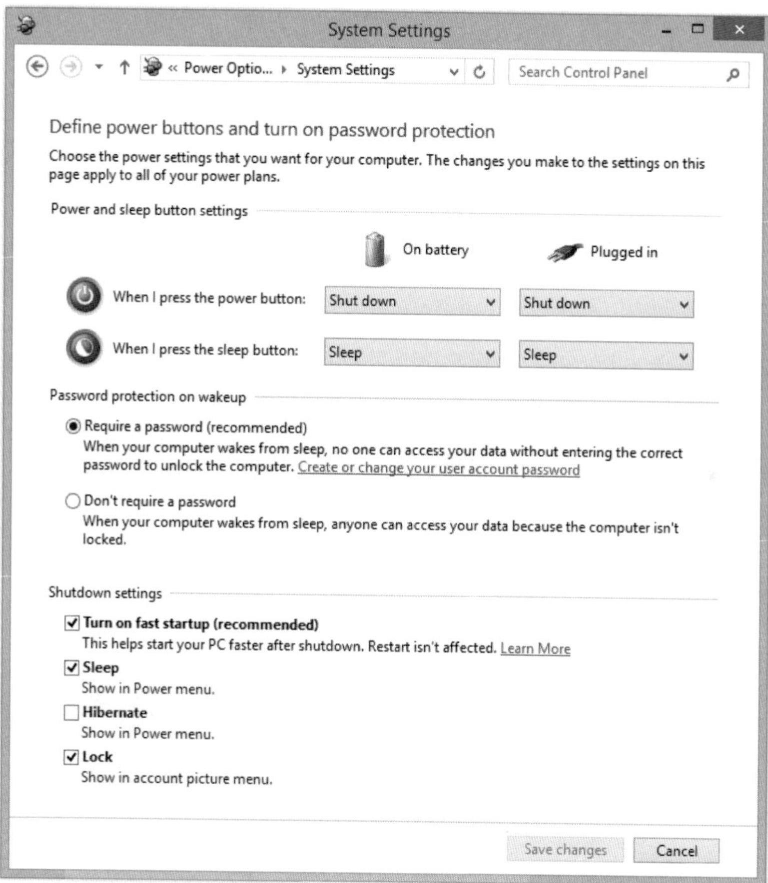

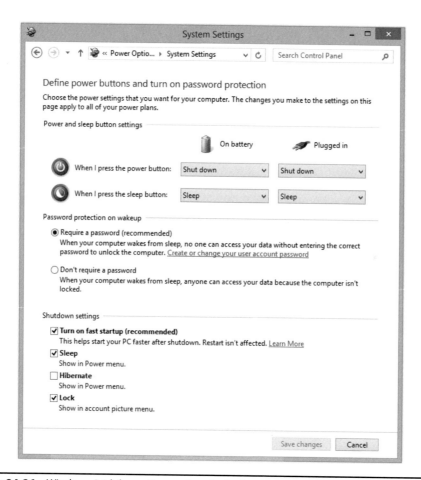

Figure 24-26 Windows 8.1 hibernation settings in the Power Options applet

Try This!

Adjusting Your System's Power Management

Go into the Power Options applet on a Windows computer and take a look at the various settings. What is the current power plan for the computer? Check to see if it is running a Balanced or High performance power plan. If it is, change the power plan to Power saver and click *Change plan settings*. Familiarize yourself with some of the advanced power settings (click on the *Change advanced power settings* link).

Try changing the individual settings for each power scheme. For instance, set a new value for the *Turn off the display* setting—try making your display turn off after five minutes. Don't worry; you aren't going to hurt anything if you fiddle with these settings.

Manual Control over Power Use

Most portables give you several manual options for reducing battery use in certain circumstances. We've already discussed using the on/off switch or keyboard combination for disabling the Wi-Fi antenna, for example, and shutting off Bluetooth, but many newer portables (not to mention Windows 8 and later) also borrow a feature from smartphones and tablets for disabling most or all of their wireless components at once: *airplane mode*. Beyond its intended use, airplane mode is also a great way to disable a number of power-sucking components quickly.

Laptops with backlit keyboards will have some way you can disable this feature when it's not needed, usually with a keyboard combination. You can also reduce the output of the LCD backlight using a combination of FN and another key to eke out a few more precious minutes of computing time before you have to shut down. Figure 24-27 shows a close-up of the FN-activated keys for adjusting screen brightness.

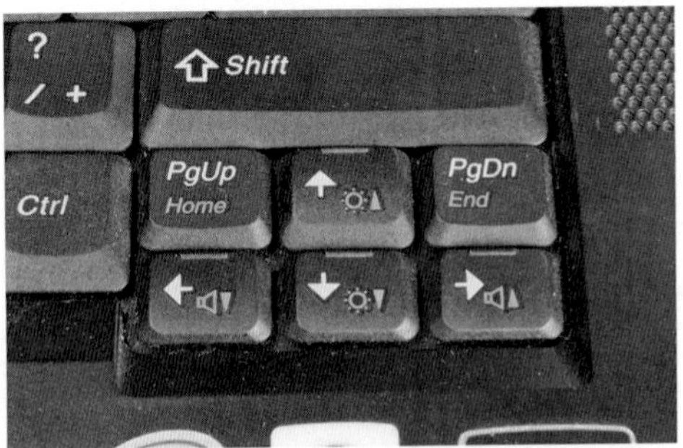

Figure 24-27 Keys for adjusting screen brightness

One of the best ways to conserve battery use is to plan ahead for times when you'll be unplugged. This can mean a lot of different things in practice, but they all boil down to thinking of ways to minimize the number of programs and hardware devices/radios you'll need to use while your laptop is running on battery power. When I travel, for example, and know that I'm going to need a certain set of files stored on my file server at the office, I put those files on my laptop before I leave, while it's still plugged into the AC. It's tempting to throw the files on a thumb drive so I don't have to break out my laptop at the office, or to let Dropbox do my syncing for me when I get to a Wi-Fi hotspot, but both USB and Wi-Fi use electricity.

Better than that, Windows enables me to designate the files and folders I need as *offline files*, storing a local, duplicate copy of the files and folders on my hard drive. When I connect my laptop into my office network, those offline files are automatically synced with the files and folders on the file server. Anything I changed on the laptop gets written to the server. Anything anyone changed in those folders on the server gets written to my laptop. (If changes were made on both sides, a sync conflict pops up automatically, enabling me to resolve problems without fear of overwriting anything important.)

To designate a folder and its contents as offline files, right-click on the folder you want and select *Always available offline* from the menu (see Figure 24-28). The sync will occur and you're done. When you want to open the files offline, go to the Control Panel and open the Sync Center applet (see Figure 24-29). Click the *Manage offline files* link in the Tasks list to open the Offline Files dialog box (see Figure 24-30). Click the *View your offline files* button and you're in.

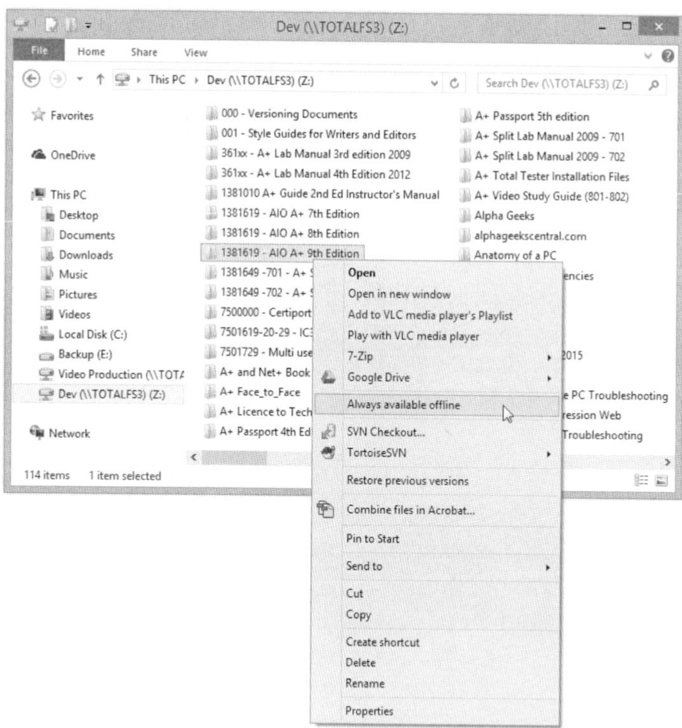

Figure 24-28 Setting up offline files

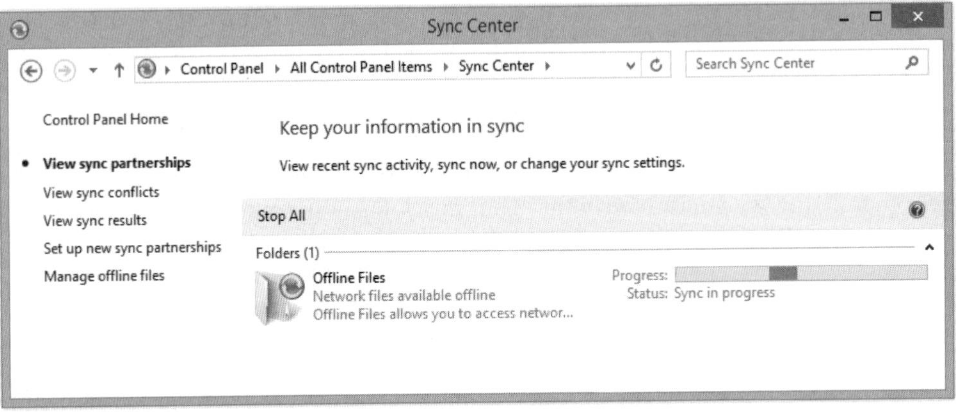

Figure 24-29 Sync Center applet

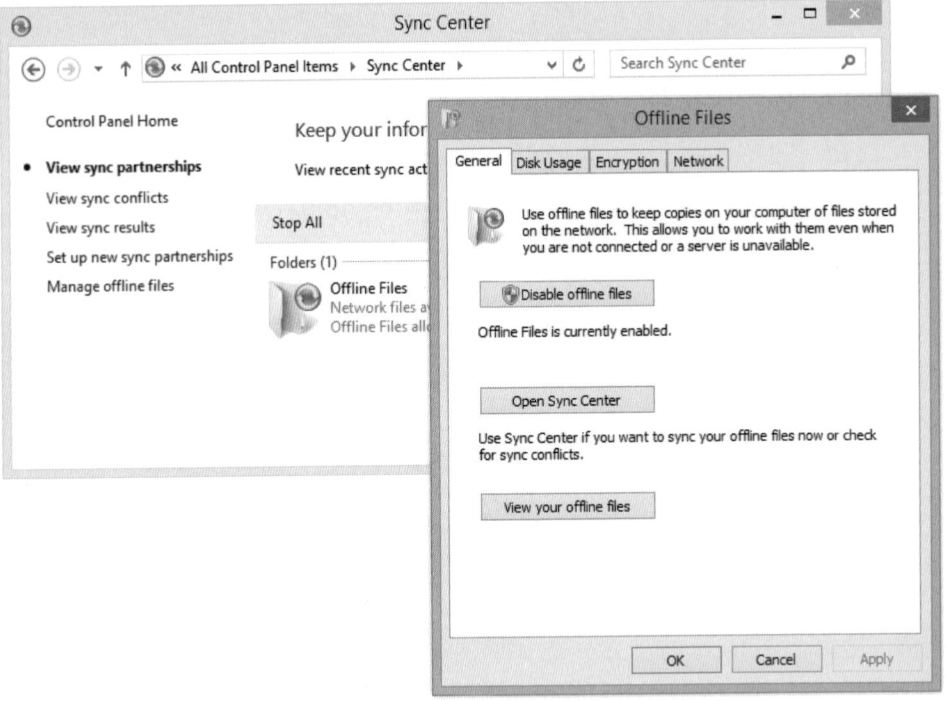

Figure 24-30 Offline Files dialog box

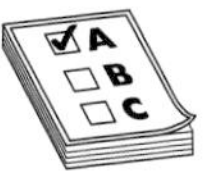

EXAM TIP Another option for extending battery life is to just bring a spare battery. Some smaller portable devices have range-extending external rechargers that can also help.

Cleaning

Most portable computers take substantially more abuse than a corresponding desktop model. Constant handling, travel, airport food on the run, and so on, can radically shorten the life of a portable if you don't take action. One of the most important things you should do is clean the laptop regularly. Use an appropriate screen cleaner (not a glass cleaner!) to remove fingerprints and dust from the fragile LCD panel. (Refer to Chapter 19 for specifics.)

If you've had the laptop in a smoky or dusty environment where the air quality alone causes problems, try cleaning it with compressed air. Compressed air works great for blowing out dust and crumbs from the keyboard and for keeping any ports, slots, and sockets clear. Don't use water on your keyboard! Even a little moisture inside the portable can toast a component.

Heat

To manage and maintain a healthy portable computer, you need to deal with heat issues. Every portable has a stack of electronic components crammed into a very small space. Unlike their desktop brethren, portables don't have lots of freely moving air space that enables fans to cool everything down. Even with lots of low-power-consumption devices inside, portable computers crank out a good deal of heat. Excessive heat can cause system lockups and hardware failures, so you should handle the issue wisely. Try this as a starter guide:

- Use power management, even if you're plugged into the AC outlet. This is especially important if you're working in a warm (more than 80 degrees Fahrenheit) room.
- Keep air space between the bottom of the laptop and the surface on which it rests. Putting a laptop on a soft surface, such as a pillow on your lap, creates a great heat-retention system—not a good thing! Always use a hard, flat surface.
- Don't use a keyboard protector for extended amounts of time.
- Listen to your fan, assuming the laptop has one. If it's often running very fast—you can tell by the whirring sound—examine your power management settings, environment, and running programs so you can change whatever is causing heat retention.
- Speaking of fans, be alert to a fan that suddenly goes silent. Fans do fail on laptops, causing overheating and failure.

Protecting the Machine

Although prices continue to drop for basic laptops, a fully loaded system is still pricey. To protect your investment, you'll want to adhere to certain best practices. You've already read tips in this chapter to deal with cleaning and heat, so let's look at the "portable" part of portable computers.

Tripping

Pay attention to where you run the power cord when you plug in a laptop. One of the primary causes of laptop destruction is people tripping over the power cord and knocking the laptop off of a desk. This is especially true if you plug in at a public place such as a café or airport. Remember, the life you save could be your portable's!

Storage

If you aren't going to use your portable for a while, storing it safely will go a long way toward keeping it operable when you do power it up again. Investing in a quality case is worth the extra few dollars—preferably one with ample padding. Not only will this protect your system on a daily basis when transporting it from home to office, but it will keep dust and pet hair away as well. Also, protect from battery leakage, at least on devices with removable batteries, by removing the battery if you plan to store the device for an extended time. Regardless of whether the battery is removable or built in, it's a good idea to store the battery partially charged and top it up occasionally to keep it from fully discharging.

Travel

If you travel with a laptop, guard against theft. If possible, use a case that doesn't look like a computer case. A well-padded backpack makes a great travel bag for a laptop and appears less tempting to would-be thieves, though some brands and styles of these are still quite obvious. Smaller portables like Ultrabooks can often hide in less obvious bags. Don't forget to pack any accessories you might need, like modular devices, spare batteries, and AC adapters. Make sure to remove any optical disks from their drives. Most importantly—back up any important data before you leave!

Make sure to have at least a little battery power available. Heightened security at airports means you might have to power on your system to prove it's really a computer and not a transport case for questionable materials. And never let your laptop out of your sight. If going through an x-ray machine, request a manual search. The x-ray won't harm your computer like a metal detector would, but if the laptop gets through the line at security before you do, someone else might walk away with it. If flying, stow your laptop under the seat in front of you where you can keep an eye on it.

If you travel to a foreign country, be very careful about the electricity. North America uses ~115-V power outlets, but most of the world uses ~230-V outlets. Many portable computers have *auto-switching power supplies*, meaning they detect the voltage at the outlet and adjust accordingly. For these portables, a simple plug converter will do the trick. Other portable computers, however, have *fixed-input power supplies*, which means they

run only on ~115-V or on ~230-V power. For these portables, you need a full-blown electricity converting device, either a step-down or step-up *transformer*. You should be able to find converters and transformers at electronics retailers, travel stores, and most other stores with a large electronics department.

Shipping

Much of the storage and travel advice can be applied to shipping. If possible, remove batteries and optical discs from their drives. Pack the portable well and disguise the container as best you can. Back up any data and verify the warranty coverage. Ship with a reputable carrier and always request a tracking number and, if possible, delivery signature. It's also worth the extra couple of bucks to pay for the shipping insurance. And when the clerk asks what's in the box, it's safer to say "electronics" rather than "a new 20-inch laptop computer."

Security

The fact is, if someone really wants to steal your laptop, they'll find a way. There are, however, some things you can do to make yourself, and your equipment, less desirable targets. As you've already learned, disguise is a good idea.

Another physical deterrent is a laptop lock. Similar to a steel bicycle cable, there is a loop on one end and a lock on the other. The idea is to loop the cable around a solid object, such as a bed frame, and secure the lock to the small security hole on the side of the laptop (see Figure 24-31). Again, if someone really wants to steal your computer, they'll find a way. They'll dismantle the bed frame if they're desperate. The best protection is to be vigilant and not let the computer out of your sight.

Figure 24-31
Cable lock

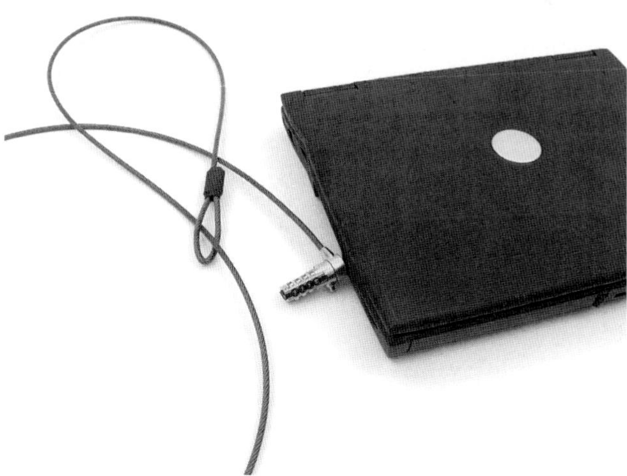

An alternative to securing a laptop with a physical lock is to use a software tracking system that makes use of GPS. It won't keep your device from being taken, but tracking

software can use the many sensors and networking capabilities of modern devices to help recover them. While functionality differs by application, common features include seeing the location of the stolen computer, capturing images or audio with its sensors, and wiping sensitive files from the device.

Upgrading and Repairing Laptop Computers

A competent tech can upgrade and repair portable computers to a degree, though true laptop techs are specialists. Upgrading the basics usually means breaking out the trusty screwdriver and avoiding electrostatic discharge (ESD). *Repairing* portables successfully, on the other hand, requires research, patience, organization, special tools, and documentation. Plus you need a ridiculously steady hand. This section provides an overview of the upgrade and repair process. Keep in mind that the growing number of form factors and the shrinking size of portable devices mean there are many exceptions, especially for very compact portables; these devices may be trickier to take apart, and components may be soldered on or use less-common interfaces.

Disassembly Process

Disassembling a portable PC is usually pretty easy, if it was designed to be upgraded or serviced by casual users. Putting it back together in working condition is the hard part! You need to follow a four-step process to succeed in disassembly/reassembly.

First, *document and label every cable and screw location*. Laptops don't use standard connectors or screws. Often you'll run into many tiny screws of varying threads. If you try to put a screw into the wrong hole, you could end up stripping the screw, stripping the hole, or getting the screw wedged into the wrong place.

Second, *organize any parts you extract from the laptop*. Seriously, put a big white piece of construction paper on your work surface, lay each extracted piece out in logical fashion, and clearly mark where each component connects and what it connects to as well. You may even want to use a smartphone camera to take pictures or a webcam to record your workspace in case something goes missing.

Third, *refer to the manufacturer's resources*. I can't stress this point enough. Unlike desktops, portables have no standardization of internal structure. Everything in the portable is designed according to the manufacturer's best engineering efforts. Two portables from the same manufacturer might have a similar layout inside, but it's far more likely that every model differs a lot.

Finally, you need to *use the appropriate hand tools*. A portable, especially on the inside, will have a remarkable variety of tiny screws that you can't remove/reinsert without tiny-headed Phillips or Torx drivers. You'll need tiny pry bars—metal and plastic—to open components. Figure 24-32 shows an entry-level toolkit for a laptop tech that you can order from iFixit.com (more on this site in a moment). Their professional version of the toolkit has 70 tools, plus there's an expansion kit! Like I said at the beginning of the section portable techs are specialists.

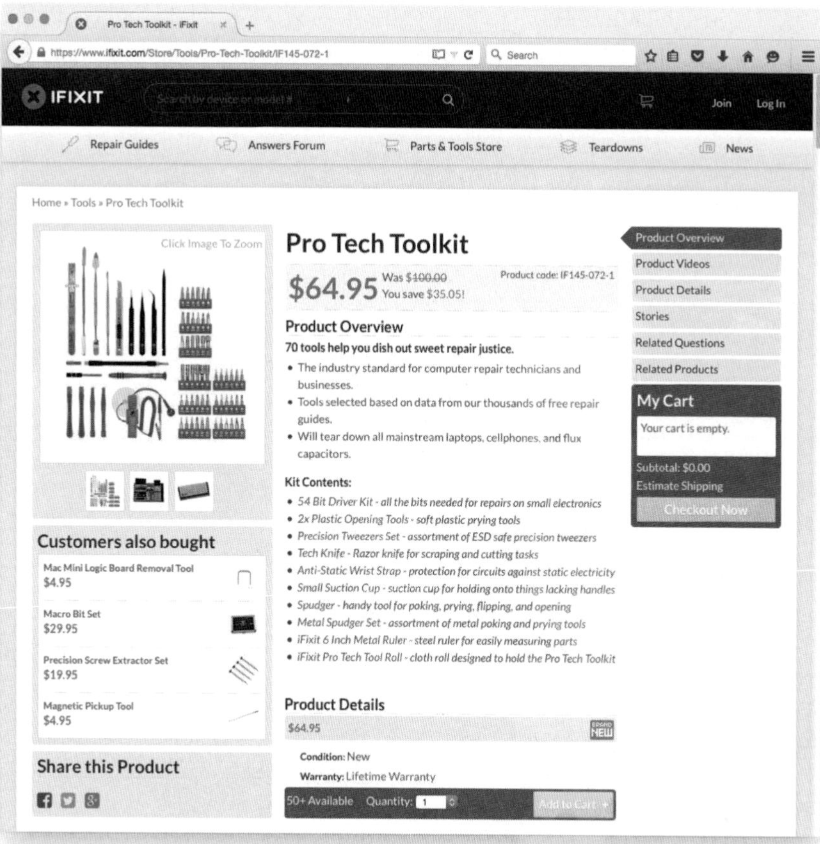

Figure 24-32 Bare-minimum laptop repair tools

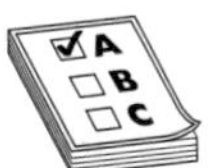

EXAM TIP Know the four-step disassembly process for the CompTIA A+ 220-901 exam:

- Document and label cable and screw locations.
- Organize parts.
- Refer to the manufacturer's resources.
- Use appropriate hand tools.

Now that you have the official line on the disassembly process, let's get one thing clear: A lot of manufacturers don't provide access to their resources to just any tech, but only to authorized repair centers. So what do you do when faced with an unfamiliar laptop that a client brought in for repair?

You have essentially two options. First, you can find a dedicated laptop tech and refer your client to that person. If the problem is exceptionally complicated and the portable in question is mission critical, that's often the best option. If you want to tackle the

problem or it looks like something you should be able to do, then you go to third-party sources: YouTube and iFixit.com.

Every portable computer has a specific make and model. Open up a Web browser and go to YouTube. Type in precisely what you want to do, such as "replace the keyboard on a Lenovo y530," and see what pops up (see Figure 24-33). You'll most likely get results back, especially if the laptop in question is a couple of years old. People all over the world have to deal with broken devices, so you're not alone.

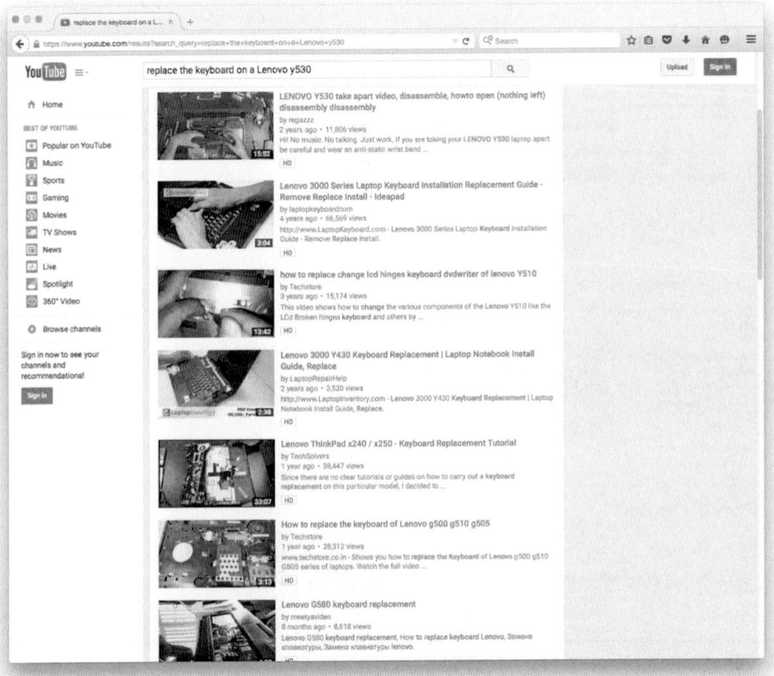

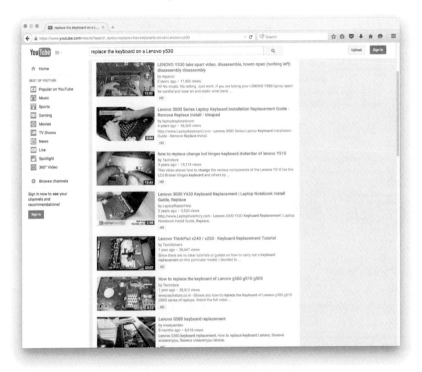

Figure 24-33 YouTube search result

Once you've found the appropriate video or something that's close enough to enable the repair attempt, watch it. If it's too difficult for your skill level or requires a set of expensive tools, then fall back to step one and go find a dedicated tech. Otherwise, figure out what tools and parts you need. Parts specific to a laptop (as in that Lenovo keyboard in preceding the example) will need to be purchased from the manufacturer. More generic parts, like hard drives, CPUs, and so on, can be purchased from Newegg (my favorite tech store) or some other online retailer.

For general tools, parts, and a lot of very detailed step-by-step instructions, I highly recommend iFixit.com. Billed as a "free repair manual you can edit," iFixit is built by techs like you and me who conquer a problem, document the steps, and post the details (see Figure 24-34). This means the next tech along who runs into the same problem doesn't have to reinvent the wheel. Just go to iFixit.com. The proceeds from parts and tools they sell, by the way, go toward supporting the site.

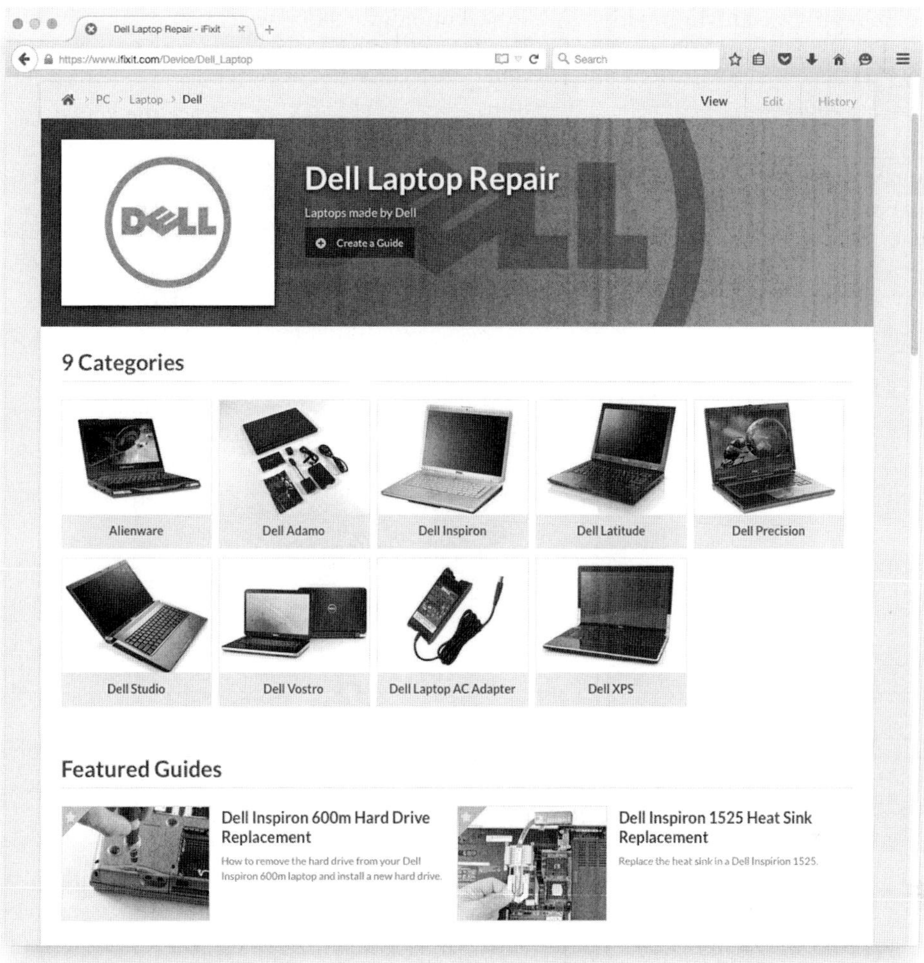

Figure 24-34 Some of the Dell laptop repair walkthroughs at iFixit.com

Standard Upgrades

Every CompTIA A+ tech should know how to perform the two standard upgrades to portable computers: adding RAM and replacing a hard drive. Let's go through the steps.

Upgrading RAM

Stock factory portable computers almost always come with a minimal amount of RAM, so one of the first laptop upgrades you'll be called on to do is to add more RAM. Economy laptops running Windows 8.1 routinely sit on store shelves and go home to consumers with as little as 2 GB of RAM, an amount guaranteed to limit the use and performance of the laptop. Luckily, most laptops have upgradeable RAM slots. Ancient laptops may

use 144-pin SO-DIMMs with SDRAM technology. Older systems use 200-pin DDR and DDR2 SO-DIMMs (see Figure 24-35), and current systems use 204-pin DDR3 SO-DIMMs.

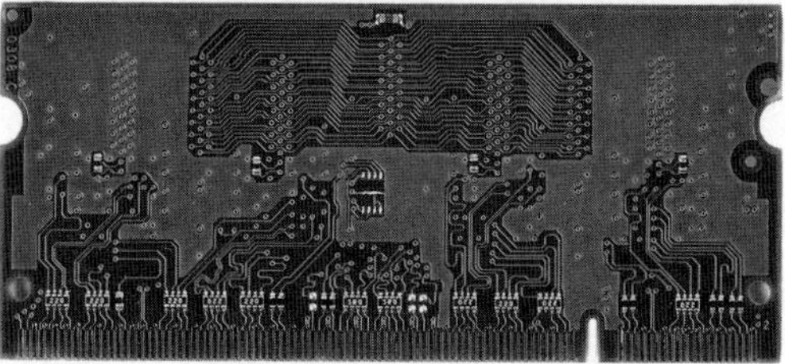

Figure 24-35 200-pin SO-DIMM stick (front and back)

NOTE The amount of RAM needed to run a computer—portable or otherwise—smoothly and stably depends on both the type of applications that it will run and the needs of the OS. When making a recommendation to a client about upgrading a laptop's memory, you should ask the basic questions, such as what the client plans to do on the laptop.

If the laptop will be used for e-mail, word processing, and Web surfing, a medium level of RAM, such as 2–4 GB, might be adequate. If the user travels, uses a high-res digital camera, and wants to use Photoshop to edit huge images, you'll need to augment the RAM accordingly. Then add the needs of the OS to give a good recommendation.

How to Add or Replace RAM Upgrading the RAM in a portable PC requires a couple of steps. First, you need to get the correct RAM. Refer to the manufacturer's Web site or to the manual (if any) that came with the portable for the specific RAM needed. Once you know the type, you need to make sure you know the configuration of any existing RAM in the system. If you are planning to upgrade from 4 GB to 8 GB, you need to know if your portable already has one module at 4 GB, or two modules at 2 GB.

Second, every portable offers a unique challenge to the tech who wants to upgrade the RAM, because there's no standard location for RAM placement in portables. The RAM slots may not even be in the same spot. More often than not, you need to unscrew or pop open a panel on the underside of the portable (see Figure 24-36). Then you press out on

the restraining clips and the RAM stick pops up (see Figure 24-37). Gently remove the old stick of RAM and insert the new one by reversing the steps.

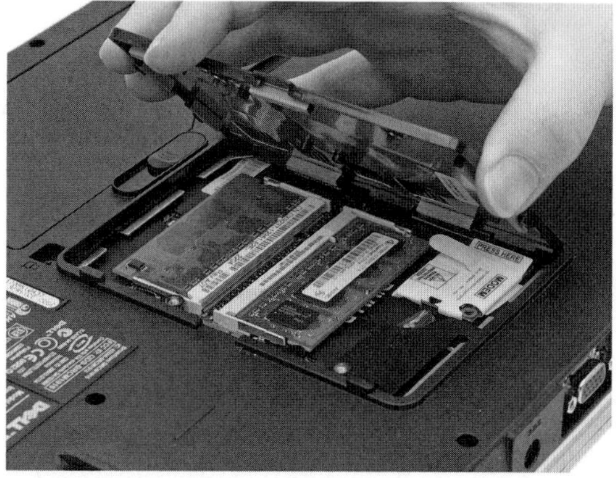

Figure 24-36 Removing a RAM panel

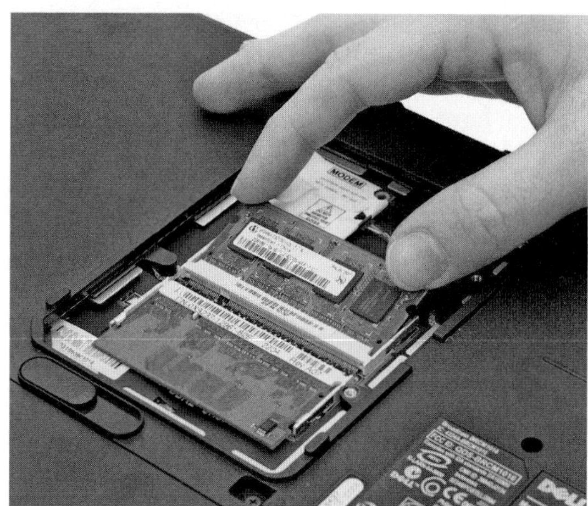

Figure 24-37 Releasing the RAM

Always remove all electrical power from the laptop before removing or inserting memory. Disconnect the AC cord from the wall outlet. Take out any removable batteries! Failure to disconnect from power can result in a fried laptop. In the case of systems with built-in batteries, consult the manufacturer's resources to evaluate the safety of working on the system and any additional steps or precautions you should take.

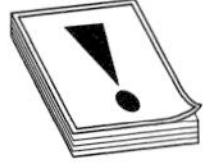

CAUTION Some portables may have both built-in and removable batteries.

Shared Memory Some laptops (and desktops) support *shared memory*. Shared memory reduces the cost of video cards by reducing the amount of memory on the video card itself. The video card uses regular system RAM to make up for the loss.

The obvious benefit of shared memory is a less expensive video card (and a less expensive laptop!) with performance comparable to its mega-memory alternative. The downside is that your overall system performance will suffer because a portion of the system RAM is no longer available to programs. (The term *shared* is a bit misleading because the video card takes control of a portion of RAM. The video portion of system RAM is *not* shared back and forth between the video card processor and the CPU.)

Some systems give you control over the amount of shared memory, while others simply allow you to turn shared memory on or off. The settings are found in CMOS setup on systems that support shared memory.

Adding more system RAM to a laptop with shared memory will improve laptop performance. Although it might appear to improve video performance, that doesn't tell the true story. It'll improve overall performance because the OS and CPU get more usable RAM. On some laptops, you can improve video performance as well, but that depends on the CMOS setup. If the shared memory is not set to maximum by default, increasing the overall memory and upping the portion reserved for video will improve video performance specifically.

Upgrading Mass Storage

You can replace a hard disk drive (HDD), solid-state drive (SSD), or solid-state hybrid drive (SSHD) in a portable PC fairly easily, especially if the laptop is only a few years old. SATA drives in the 2.5-inch drive format now rule in all laptops. Although much smaller than regular 3.5-inch hard drives, they use all the same features and configurations. These smaller hard drives have suffered, however, from diminished storage capacity as compared to their 3.5-inch brothers. Currently, large 2.5-inch hard drives hold up to 2 TB, while 3.5-inch hard drives top out at more than 8 TB of data!

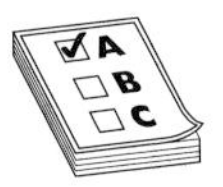

EXAM TIP 1.8-inch drives exist, though they have fallen out of favor as flash memory usurps their role in portable music players and other small portables. These days, they are quite rare. If you find one, it almost certainly will be in an older portable on the small end of the scale.

If you have an ancient laptop, it might have a PATA drive, which means you need to pay more attention to cabling and jumpers. Some PATA drive manufacturers may require you to set the drive to use a cable-select setting as opposed to master or slave, so check with the laptop maker for any special issues. Otherwise, no difference exists between 2.5-inch drives and their larger 3.5-inch brethren (see Figure 24-38).

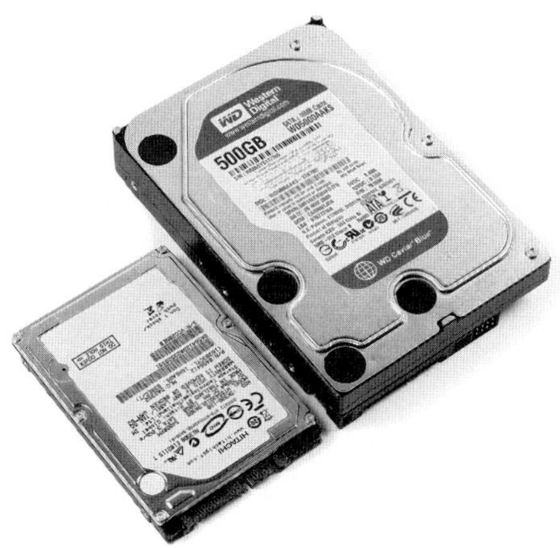

Figure 24-38 The 2.5-inch and 3.5-inch drives are mostly the same.

One of the best upgrades you can make on a laptop is to go from an HDD to an SSD. Obviously, you'll get a lot less storage capacity for the money, but the trade-offs can be worth it. First, the SSD will use a lot less electricity than an HDD, thus extending battery life. Second, any SSD is rip-roaringly faster than an HDD and performance across the board will be boosted. For a time, SSHDs, or hybrid drives, were a good compromise between the speed of an SSD and the size of a traditional HDD. These days, the inroads SSDs have made on price and capacity have made SSHDs look more and more like a lukewarm choice. 2-TB SSDs are already available, matching the top end of available HDDs (though admittedly for the price of a decent laptop), while 500-GB SSDs are under $200.

Try This!

Comparing HDD with SSD Today

As I write this chapter, you can get roughly eight times the storage capacity on an HDD for the same cost as an SSD. In other words, $100 spent on an SSD could give you ~250 GB of storage, whereas you could purchase a 2-TB, 2.5-inch HDD for the same $100. So do some comparison shopping. What's the price point now? Are the trade-offs worth it for you or for your clients to make the switch from HDD to SSD?

The process of replacing a hard drive mirrors that of replacing RAM. You find the hard drive hatch—either along one edge or in a compartment on the underside of the computer—and release the screws (see Figure 24-39). Remove the old drive and then slide the new drive into its place (see Figure 24-40). Reattach the hatch or cover and boot the computer. Grab a Windows DVD or bootable USB flash drive and prepare to reinstall.

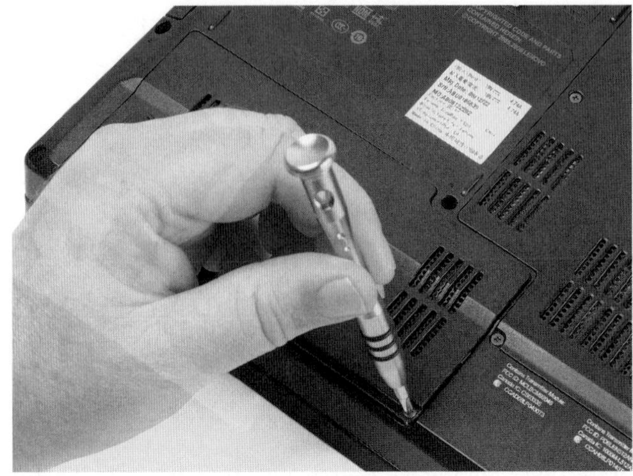

Figure 24-39 Removing the drive compartment cover

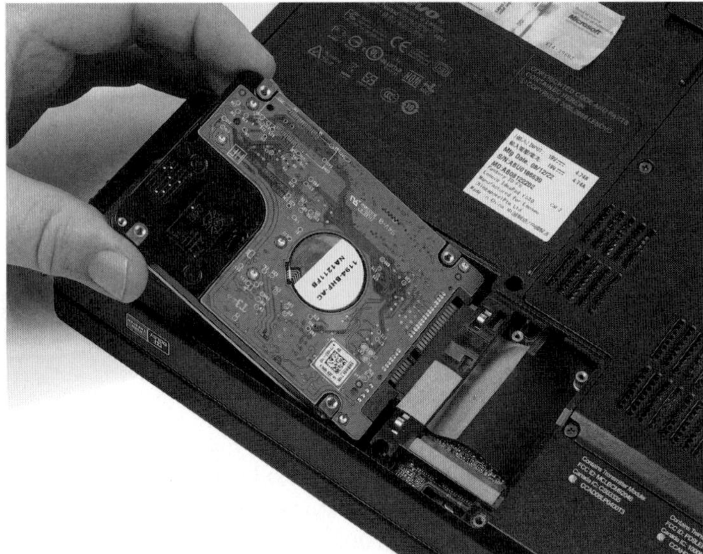

Figure 24-40 Inserting a replacement drive

Hardware Replacement

Once you get beyond upgrading RAM and replacing a hard drive on a portable, you take the plunge into the laptop-repair specialty. You can replace some components by lifting them out, detaching a ribbon cable, and then reversing the steps with the replacement part. Other parts require a full teardown of the laptop to the bare bones, which presents a much greater magnitude of difficulty. Because every portable differs, this section provides guidance, but not concrete steps, for replacement. Be aware,

as mentioned earlier, that some systems are trending toward more integrated parts; make sure the part you're replacing is actually replaceable in the specific system you're working on.

Components

Replaceable components require more work than the RAM or drive upgrades, but replacing them generally falls into the category of "doable." What I call *components* are the battery, keyboard, optical drive, internal speaker(s), and plastic parts.

Battery If a battery's performance falls below an acceptable level, you can replace it with a battery from the manufacturer or from an aftermarket vendor. Although this should be a simple swap replacement (and usually is, at least if the battery isn't built in), you might encounter a situation where the real problem wasn't the battery *per se*, but an inadequate or malfunctioning charging system. The new battery might not give you any better performance than the old one. Try it.

Keyboard Getting a keyboard off a laptop computer often requires little pry bars, but also look for screws, clips, and so on. Keyboards connect via a tiny, short, and very delicate cable, often held down by tape. Replacing one is tricky, but doable.

Optical Drive Replacing an optical drive can present a challenge. If the drive is part of a modular system, just pop out the old drive and pop in a new one. If the drive is part of the internal chassis of the portable, on the other hand, you're looking at a full dissection. (See the upcoming "Integral Parts" section for tips on dismantling the portable.)

Speaker Replacing the internal speaker or speakers on a laptop can be simple or a total pain, depending on where the speakers connect. Some laptops have speakers mounted on the outside of the chassis. You pry off the covers, pull out the little speakers, disconnect the cable, and then reverse the process for replacement speakers. If the speakers are inside the chassis, on the other hand, you need to dismantle the portable to get to them. (See the "Integral Parts" section.)

Frame All of the sophisticated electrified components that make our portables work are held together by a variety of plastic, metal, and rubber parts. Generally these are pretty durable, but over time—or in an accident—these components can warp, bend, crack, split, dent, and chip. These too can be replaced, provided you can locate a suitable replacement part.

You'll need to know the device model to get started, and you may also need to hunt down the part number using manufacturer or third-party resources. Many device parts appear similar, and some parts will appear in many other portables. You may also find that the part you need is only available as a piece of a larger assembly or group of parts, in which case you may end up paying a silly sum to get the part you need.

Expansion Cards Not to be confused with ExpressCards, many portables have one or more true expansion slots for add-on cards. The more modular varieties will have a hatch on the bottom of the case that opens like the RAM hatch that gives you access to

the slot(s). This enables you to change out an 802.11n wireless card, for example, for an 802.11ac card, thus greatly enhancing the Wi-Fi experience on this device. Figure 24-41 shows a wide-open laptop with the expansion slot exposed.

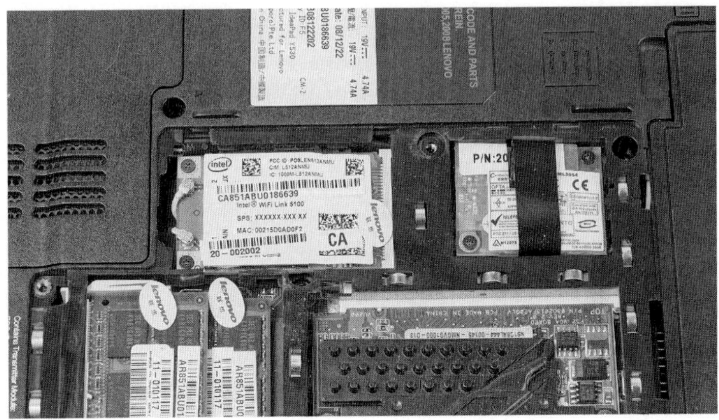

Figure 24-41 Mini-PCIe expansion slot on laptop

Just like when installing RAM in a portable, you must avoid ESD and remove all electricity before you take out or put in an expansion card. Failure to remove the battery and the AC adapter (or follow any extra steps and precautions in the manufacturer's resources if the battery is built in) can and probably will result in a shorted-out laptop motherboard, and that just makes for a bad day.

The only other consideration with expansion cards applies specifically to wireless. Not only will you need to connect the card to the slot properly, but you must reattach the antenna connection and often a separate power cable. Pay attention when you remove the card as to the placement of these vital connections.

You'll find one of two types of expansion slot in a portable: Mini-PCIe and M.2 (formerly Next Generation Form Factor [NGFF]). The older ones (think 2013 and earlier) use *Mini-PCIe*, while newer devices are quickly adopting M.2.

CPU Replacing a CPU on a modern portable takes a lot more work than replacing RAM or a Mini-PCIe expansion card, but follows the same general steps. Many CPUs mount facing the bottom of the portable, so that the venting goes away from your hands. When sitting properly on a flat surface, the heated air also goes to the back of the laptop and not toward the user. You access the CPU in this sort of system from the bottom of the portable.

As you can see in Figure 24-42, the CPU has an elaborate heat-sink and fan assembly that includes both the CPU and the chipset. Each of the pieces screws down in multiple places, plus the fan has a power connection. Aside from the tiny screws, there's no difference here in process between replacing a mobile CPU and a desktop CPU that you learned way back in Chapter 4, "Microprocessors."

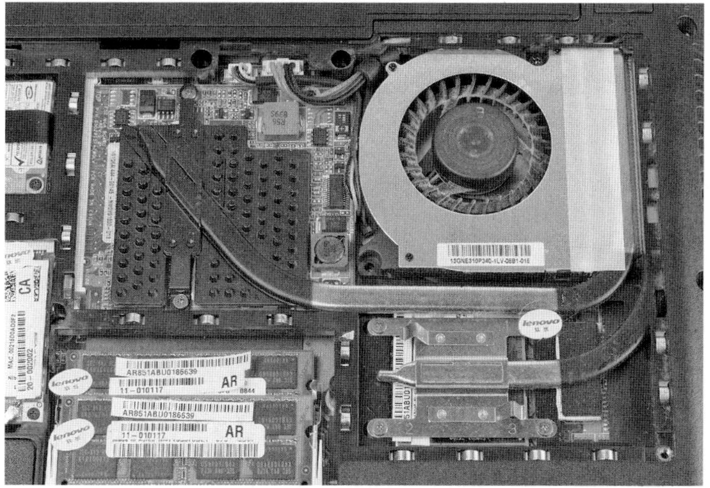

Figure 24-42 CPU heat-sink and fan assembly exposed

First, remove all power from the laptop, including the battery if possible; consult manufacturer or third-party resources for any extra steps or precautions for systems with built-in batteries. Remove the hatch to expose the CPU. Remove the heat-sink and fan assembly and lift out the CPU. Replace it with another CPU, apply thermal paste, and reattach the heat-sink and fan assembly. Reconnect the fan power connector and you're good to go.

Some laptops use passive cooling and may have the CPU pointed up rather than down. They have a heat sink beneath the keyboard that cools everything down. With that style laptop, you remove the keyboard and heat sink to expose the CPU.

Integral Parts

Some hardware replacements require you to get serious with the laptop, opening it fully to the outside, removing many delicate parts, and even stripping it down to the bare chassis. I leave these repairs to the professional laptop repair folks, simply because they have the specific tools and expertise to do the job efficiently. CompTIA expects you to understand the process, though, so I've outlined it here. This pertains to four components: screen, DC jack, touchpad, and system board.

Portables open in two different ways, depending on the manufacturer. You either peel away layers from the top down, through the keyboard, or from the bottom up, through the base. Either direction requires careful attention to detail, part connectivity, and locations. You'll need a system to keep track of the dozens of tiny screws.

Every one of the replacements here requires you to detach the screen from the main chassis of the portable. Aside from finding the connection points and removing the proper screws, you need to pay attention to the connection points for the data stream to the monitor and the antenna that's in the frame of the display.

Once you have the portable stripped down, you replace whichever component you're in there to replace and then begin the process of building it back up into a coherent unit. Pay incredibly careful attention to getting data cables connected properly as you rebuild.

I can't imagine a worse tech experience than replacing a touchpad and rebuilding a laptop only to have missed a connection and having to do it all over again.

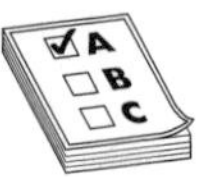

EXAM TIP The DC jack requires extra-special love when you need to replace one. The part is soldered to the main board, so replacing it means you'll need to not only strip the laptop to the bare metal, but also unsolder the old part and solder the new part. Then you'll rebuild the laptop and hope you got everything right. CompTIA cannot expect a CompTIA A+ technician to know how to do this stuff. Expect a question that explores whether it *can* be done. Rest assured, specialized techs can replace *any* component on a laptop, even the DC jack.

Troubleshooting Portable Computers

Many of the troubleshooting techniques you learned about for desktop systems can be applied to laptops. For example, take the proper precautions before and during disassembly. Use the proper hand tools, and document, label, and organize each plastic part and screw location for reassembly. Additionally, here are some laptop-specific procedures to try.

Power and Performance

Laptop Won't Power On

- Verify AC power by plugging another electronic device into the wall outlet. If the other device receives power, the outlet is good.
- If the outlet is good, connect the laptop to the wall outlet and try to power on. If no LEDs light up, you may have a bad AC adapter. Swap it out with a known-good power adapter.
- A faulty peripheral device might keep the laptop from powering up. Remove any peripherals such as USB, FireWire, or Thunderbolt devices.

Poor Performance

- The most common reason for slow performance is running applications and processes consuming high resources. All operating systems have a way to check this—such as the Task Manager in Windows or Activity Monitor in Mac OS X—and look into problems with any you find. They may need to be closed or stopped, you may need to reboot, or the application may need an update.
- Extreme performance issues may lead to a frozen system. If they don't resolve on their own and you can't interact with the device, you may need to perform a hard reboot (which may result in the loss of any unsaved work). Usually, holding down the power button for 10 seconds is sufficient, though you may need to check the manufacturer's resources for the proper procedure. If the battery is removable, you may be able to reboot the device by pulling the battery out and replacing it.

NOTE Be aware, especially when working with hybrid devices, that you might find official or third-party resources discussing hard and soft resets. These are *not* the same as hard and soft reboots, so you should pay careful attention to the instructions and make sure you're performing the correct procedure. See Chapter 26, "Care and Feeding of Mobile Devices," for more on hard and soft resets.

Battery Issues

- A swollen battery will probably go unnoticed at first, and the symptoms it creates may be hard to identify if you aren't aware it can happen. The cause is usually overcharging, perhaps due to a failure in the circuits that should prevent it, but the early symptoms might be a laptop that doesn't quite sit right on flat surfaces, a screen that doesn't fit flush when closed, problems with input devices like the touchpad or keyboard, and trouble removing or inserting a removable battery. Eventually, the device's case may be obviously deformed. While battery packs are designed to handle a little swelling, it increases the risk they'll puncture—and a punctured battery can be dangerous. Don't ignore these symptoms; open the case carefully to check the battery, and very carefully deliver it to an e-waste recycling or disposal site.
- If you have a laptop with a battery that won't charge up, it could be one of two things: the battery might be cooked or the AC adapter isn't doing its job. To troubleshoot, replace the battery with a known-good battery. If the new battery works, you've found the problem. Just replace the battery. Alternatively, remove the battery and run the laptop on AC only. If that works, you know the AC adapter is good. If it doesn't, replace the AC adapter.
- The reasons for very short battery life in a battery that charges properly are fairly benign. The battery has usually outlived its useful life and needs to be replaced, or some programs or hardware are drawing much more power than usual. Check wireless devices you usually keep disabled to make sure they aren't on. Follow recommendations in the preceding "Poor Performance" section to address problem programs.

Overheating

- Because overheating can be both a symptom and a cause of a variety issues, you should be alert to any device that is hot to the touch, or is running hotter than usual. Note which parts of the device are hot—this can give you important clues. If the device feels dangerously hot, err on the side of protecting the device from heat damage instead of trying to diagnose the cause. Power the device down and remove the battery if possible. Set it on a cool, hard surface, out of direct sunlight, with the hottest part of the device exposed to air if possible.
- Likewise, look for possible signs a device is overheating—like inconsistent reboots, graphical glitches, system beeps—and rule out heat issues.

- Listen for fans. While some portables don't have any, complete silence may indicate a failed fan, and unusual noise may signal one on its way out.
- Know when to expect a hot device. Busy or charging devices create a lot of heat; follow the steps mentioned in the preceding "Poor Performance" and "Battery Issues" sections for identifying components that shouldn't be on, especially if they are hot to the touch, and finding runaway programs. If the device is charging, unplug it and see if the device cools. If you find nothing unexpected and the device is unusually hot, it may have an airflow problem. Check any fan vents for blockages, and open the device if necessary to check any fans and heat sinks for issues.
- If the entire device is hot, it was most likely left in direct sunlight or a hot environment. Cool the device down and see if the trouble goes away.

Components

Various hardware components can use help too. Such devices include the display, wireless networking, audio, and input devices.

Display Problems

- If the laptop is booting (you hear the beeps and the drives) but the screen doesn't come on properly, first make sure the display is turned on. Press the FN key and the key to activate the screen a number of times until the laptop display comes on. If that doesn't work, check the LCD cutoff switch—on many laptops, this is the small nub somewhere near the screen hinge that shuts the monitor off when you close the laptop—and make sure it isn't stuck in the down position. If the device is a convertible with a removable screen, make sure it is properly attached and that it is receiving power.
- If the laptop display is very dim, you may have lost an inverter. The clue here is that inverters never go quietly. They can make a nasty hum as they are about to die and an equally nasty popping noise when they actually fail. Failure often occurs when you plug in the laptop's AC adapter, as the inverters take power directly from the AC adapter. It's also possible that the backlights in the LCD panel have died, though this is much less common than a bad inverter.
- If the screen won't come on or is cracked, most laptops have a port for plugging in an external monitor, which you can use to log in to your laptop.
- If you plug a laptop into an external monitor and that monitor does not display, remember that you have both a hardware and an OS component to making dual displays successful. There's usually a combination of FN and another key to toggle among only portable, only external, and both displays. Plus you have the Display applet in the Control Panel or the System Preferences to mirror or extend the desktop to a second monitor.

- Many manufacturers have switched to LED displays on laptops, which has led to a phenomenon many techs thought long behind us: *flickering displays*. The LED backlights don't work quite the same as CCFL backlights, especially when you lower the brightness. This doesn't affect desktop LED displays, because they're usually so bright it doesn't matter. But portables need to be able to dim to save battery life. One technique for dimming LEDs is to have them turn on and off rapidly enough to keep the pixels lit, but slowly enough that there's a reduction in visible light and electricity use. With some of these panels, that flickering is not only noticeable, but headache and eyestrain inducing.
- There are two things you can do with a flickering LED display: crank up the brightness so that it goes away (and thus live with reduced battery life) or replace the laptop.
- If the screen orientation on a Windows portable doesn't change when the device is rotated, auto-rotation may be disabled. Likewise, if the orientation changes at the wrong time, you can lock rotation via the Screen option in the Settings charm, or via the Display applet in the Control Panel. If the rotation needs to remain locked, the orientation can still be changed via the Display applet, or possibly with FN key combinations.

Wireless Devices (Bluetooth, Wi-Fi, Mobile Broadband, NFC, or GPS) Don't Work or Work Intermittently

- If the wireless doesn't work at all, check along the front, rear, or side edges of the laptop for a physical switch that toggles the internal wireless adapter, Bluetooth adapter, or airplane mode on and off. Also check your notification area for an airplane icon.
- If a tech has recently replaced a component that required removal of the laptop display, dead wireless could mean simply a disconnected antenna. Most portables have the antenna built into the display panel, so check that connection.
- Try the special key combination for your laptop to toggle the wireless or Bluetooth adapter, or one for toggling airplane mode. You usually press the FN key in combination with another key.
- You might simply be out of range or, if the wireless works intermittently, right at the edge of the range. Physically walk the laptop over to the wireless router or access point to ensure there are no out-of-range issues.
- With Bluetooth specifically, remember that the pairing process takes action or configuration on both devices to succeed. Turn on the Bluetooth device, actively seek it, and try again.

- If only the GPS is not functioning, privacy options may be preventing applications from accessing your GPS location information. Check the Location Settings applet in the Control Panel or the Privacy section of the Settings app to see if the GPS device is enabled, and whether location services are enabled both system wide and for the appropriate applications. Check System Preferences in Mac OS X or a similar location in Linux for the same options.
- If only near field communication (NFC) is not functioning, you may need to enable a setting to allow communication with nearby devices. In Windows, open the Proximity applet in the Control Panel and make sure Proximity support is enabled.

Audio Problems

- If audio isn't working when it should be, check for a hardware mute or volume button or switch and verify through the notification area Volume icon that the audio output isn't muted. Verify proper output device configuration through the operating system, and verify the application is using the right output device.
- If the device has had repairs or upgrades lately, make sure the speakers are properly connected.
- If no sound is coming from the device speakers, try plugging in a pair of headphones or some external speakers. If these work fine, there's a chance the built-in speakers have been damaged. Depending on their location, it can be easy to get them wet.
- If headphones work fine with the device, the speakers may need replacing. First, make sure the device has been rebooted, double-check the audio output device settings, try changing and resetting the default output device, and try disabling and re-enabling the appropriate device.

Input Problems

- Before assuming an input problem is hardware related, confirm that the system is otherwise running smoothly. Input devices may appear not to work or work erratically if the system is freezing up. Refer to the previous "Power and Performance" section for troubleshooting a frozen system.
- If none of the keys work on your laptop, there's a good chance you've unseated the keypad connector. These connectors are quite fragile and are prone to unseating from any physical stress on the laptop. Check the manufacturer's disassembly procedures to locate and reseat the keypad.
- If you're getting numbers when you're expecting to get letters, the number lock (NUMLOCK) function key is turned on. Turn it off.
- Laptop keyboards take far more abuse than the typical desktop keyboard, because of all those lunch meetings and café brainstorm sessions. Eating and drinking

while over or around a keyboard just begs for problems. If you have a portable with sticking keys, look for the obvious debris in the keys. Used compressed air to clean them out. If you have serious goo and need to use a cleaning solution, disconnect the keyboard from the portable first. Make sure it's fully dried out before you reconnect it or you'll short it out.

- A laptop keyboard key that doesn't register presses or feels sticky may also have had its switch knocked out of place, especially if the key appears slightly raised or tilted. These switches can be delicate, so be careful if you want to avoid ordering replacements. Research what kind of switch your device's keyboard uses, and be aware that a single keyboard may use a few different kinds. Look up steps for detaching and reattaching keys on that specific device if possible, and otherwise find generic instructions for the clip type before proceeding.
- If the touchpad is having problems, a shot of compressed air does wonders for cleaning pet hair out of the touchpad sensors. You might get a cleaner shot if you remove the keyboard before using the compressed air. Remember to be gentle when lifting off the keyboard and make sure to follow the manufacturer's instructions.
- The touchpad driver might need to be reconfigured. Try the various options in the Control Panel | Mouse applet, or the equivalent location in System Preferences.
- If the touchscreen is unresponsive or erratic, a good first step is checking the screen for dirt, grease, or liquids, which can make the sensors go haywire; wipe it down with a dry microfiber cloth.
- Some touchscreens may appear to work improperly if they are registering an unintentional touch. Depending on the design of the device, it may be tempting to hold it in a way that leaves some part of your hand or arm too close to the edge of the screen; some devices will register this as a touch.
- Your device may have touchscreen diagnostics available through hardware troubleshooting menus accessible through the BIOS. Refer to the manufacturer's resources for how to access these diagnostics. If available, they are a quick way to identify whether you're looking at a hardware or software/configuration issue. The Tablet PC Settings applet in the Control Panel enables you to calibrate or reset your touch support. Attempt to reset and recalibrate the display.

EXAM TIP The troubleshooting issue known as a *ghost cursor* can mean one of two things. First, the display shows a trail of ghost cursors behind your real cursor as you move it. This might point to an aging display or an improperly configured refresh rate. Second, the cursor moves erratically or drifts slowly in a steady direction (also known as *pointer drift*), whether you are touching the touchpad or not. This probably means the touchpad has been damaged in some way and needs to be replaced.

Chapter 24 Review

Questions

1. Which of the following are good ideas when it comes to batteries? (Select two.)
   - A. Keep the contacts clean by using alcohol and a soft cloth.
   - B. Store them in the freezer if they will not be used for a long period of time.
   - C. Toss them in the garbage when they wear out.
   - D. Store them in a cool, dry place.
2. Tablet PCs come in which of the following form factors? (Select two.)
   - A. Convertible
   - B. Desktop
   - C. Secure Digital
   - D. Slate
3. ExpressCards connect to which buses? (Select two.)
   - A. ACPI
   - B. PCI
   - C. PCIe
   - D. USB
4. Clara's laptop has a DVI connector to which she has connected a projector. As she prepares to make her presentation, however, nothing comes on the projector screen. The laptop shows the presentation, and the projector appears to be functional, with a bright white bulb making a blank image on the screen. What's most likely the problem?
   - A. She needs to plug in the projector.
   - B. She's running the laptop on batteries. She needs to plug in the laptop to use the DVI connector.
   - C. She needs to update her ExpressCard services to support projectors.
   - D. She needs to press the Function key combination on her keyboard to cycle through monitor modes.
5. What is the primary benefit to adding more RAM to a laptop that uses shared memory? (Select the best answer.)
   - A. Improved battery life.
   - B. Improved system performance.
   - C. Improved video performance.
   - D. None. Adding more RAM is pointless with systems that use shared memory.

6. Which of the following display types will you commonly find on a portable PC today? (Select two.)
   - A. LCD
   - B. LED
   - C. OLED
   - D. Plasma
7. Steve complains that his aging Windows 7 laptop still isn't snappy enough after upgrading the RAM. What might improve system performance?
   - A. Add more RAM.
   - B. Replace the power supply.
   - C. Replace the battery.
   - D. Replace the HDD with an SSD.
8. Jim likes his laptop but complains that his wireless seems slow compared to all the new laptops. On further inspection, you determine his laptop runs 802.11n. What can be done to improve his network connection speed?
   - A. Add more RAM.
   - B. Replace the display with one with a better antenna.
   - C. Replace the Mini-PCIe 802.11n card with an 802.11ac card.
   - D. Get a new laptop, because this one can't be upgraded.
9. Edgar successfully replaced the display on a laptop (a toddler had taken a ballpoint pen to it), but the customer called back almost immediately complaining that his wireless didn't work. What could the problem be?
   - A. The problems are unrelated, so it could be anything.
   - B. Edgar inadvertently disconnected the antenna from the Mini-PCIe 802.11 card.
   - C. Edgar replaced the display with one without an internal antenna.
   - D. Edgar failed to reconnect the antenna in the new display.
10. Rafael gets a tech call from a user with a brand new laptop complaining that working on it was causing headaches. What could the problem be?
    - A. The laptop uses a plasma display.
    - B. The laptop uses a CRT display.
    - C. The laptop uses an LED display in power saving mode.
    - D. The laptop uses an LED display in full power mode.

Answers

1. **A, D.** Keeping a battery in the freezer is a good idea in theory, but not in practice. All batteries contain toxic chemicals and should *never* be treated like regular trash.
2. **A, D.** Tablet PCs come in convertible and slate form factors.
3. **C, D.** ExpressCards connect to either the PCI Express bus or the USB bus.
4. **D.** Clara needs to press the Function key combination on her keyboard to cycle through monitor modes.
5. **B.** Improved overall system performance is the primary benefit to adding more RAM to a laptop that uses shared memory.
6. **A, B.** You'll only see LCD and LED displays on portables today.
7. **D.** Replacing the HDD with an SSD will speed up the system.
8. **C.** He can have the 802.11n NIC replaced with an 802.11ac NIC.
9. **D.** A disconnected antenna makes Wi-Fi unhappy.
10. **C.** Flicker is a side effect of dimming on some lower-end LED monitors.

CHAPTER 25

Understanding Mobile Devices

In this chapter, you will learn how to

- Explain the features and capabilities of mobile devices
- Describe the three major mobile OSs
- Describe how to configure mobile devices

It's almost hard to imagine that mobile devices—in particular the popular iPhone and Android devices—didn't even exist ten years ago. Mobile devices revolutionized the way we work and play. Devices such as smartphones, tablets, and even smart watches enable people to access unique tools and features from just about anywhere and accomplish essential tasks on the go.

As amazing as mobile devices are, it's not easy to find a definition of *mobile device* that everyone agrees on. If you ask folks who are comfortable with these devices, you'll get lots of descriptions of functions and capabilities as opposed to what they are. In essence, the following aspects make a device mobile (and even these will sometimes create debate):

- Lightweight, usually less than two pounds
- Small, designed to move with you in your hand or in your pocket
- Touch or stylus interface; no keyboard or mice
- Sealed unit lacking any field replaceable units (FRUs)
- Non-desktop OS; mobile devices use special mobile operating systems

The last one is important as it's the one way to differentiate easily classic laptops from mobile devices. Your typical laptop runs a desktop OS like Windows, Mac OS X, or some Linux distribution such as Ubuntu. A true mobile device will run Apple iOS, Google Android, or Microsoft Windows Phone.

This chapter is all about mobile devices and explores mobile devices in detail. We'll first look at the features and capabilities of devices that are common in the mobile market. The chapter then jumps into the details of configuring the devices for personal use, doing such things as setting up e-mail and adding productivity devices. The CompTIA

A+ certification exams are serious about mobile devices and we have a lot of ground to cover, so let's get started. (We'll conclude the mobile device discussion in Chapter 26.)

901

Types of Mobile Devices

Modern mobile devices fall into various categories, including smartphones, tablets, wearable technology, and other mobile device types, which all have similar features and capabilities. The CompTIA A+ 901 exam has a pretty long list of devices, so let's go through them one at a time to understand what they do, starting with easily the most popular, smartphones.

Smartphones

One of the earliest type of mobile devices was known as the *personal digital assistant (PDA)*, such as the Compaq iPaq from the late 1990s. PDAs had all the basic features of today's mobile devices but didn't have cellular connectivity, so you couldn't make a phone call. Many people, your author included, spent close to ten years carrying a mobile phone and a PDA, wondering when somebody would combine these two things. Starting around 2003–2005, companies began marketing PDAs that included cellular telephones (although cool features like using the PDA to access Internet data wasn't well developed). Figure 25-1 shows an early PDA-with-a-phone, the once very popular RIM Blackberry.

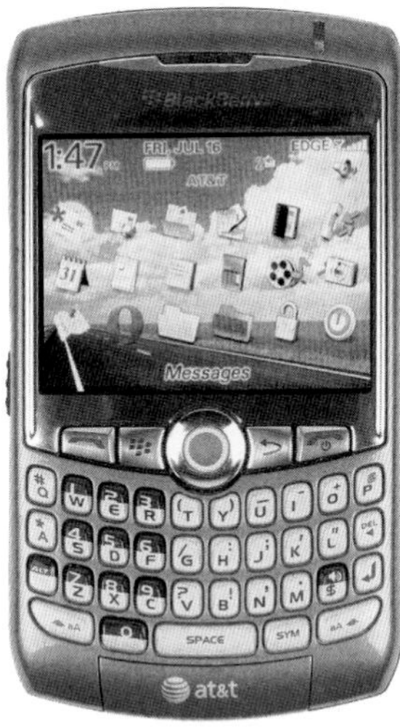

Figure 25-1
RIM Blackberry

While these tools were powerful for their time, it wasn't until Apple introduced the iPhone (see Figure 25-2) in 2007 that we saw the elements that define a modern *smartphone*:

- A multi-touch interface as the primary input method for using the smartphone
- Tight consolidation of cellular data to the device, enabling any application (Web browsers, e-mail clients, games, and so on) to access the Internet to exchange data through a seamless application programming interface (API)
- A well-standardized application API to enable developers to create new apps to work on the system
- Synchronization and distribution tools to enable users to install new apps and synchronize and back up data

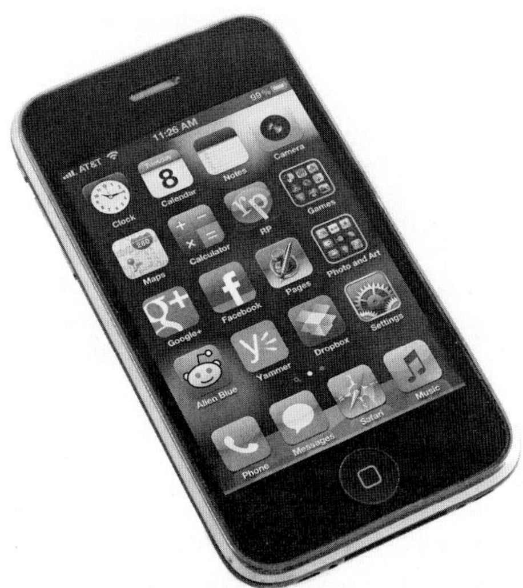

Figure 25-2 Early Apple iPhone

Since then, smartphones have developed many more tools, applications, and features. They have become part of the ubiquitous computing trend we've seen in the past few years, meaning that we expect a constant data connection and accessibility to all of our data and content on every device we own and use. Because smartphones do so much more than simply make and receive phone calls—we surf the Web with them, stream music and video, send and receive e-mail, and even perform business functions with them—the technologies and infrastructure that connect smartphones and data together has to be fast, robust, and secure.

Most smartphones run one of the big three operating systems: Apple iOS, Google Android, or Microsoft Windows Phone/10 Mobile (see Figure 25-3). Only the iPhone runs iOS, as Apple designs and builds the hardware and OS together. Phones running Android or Windows come from a multitude of manufacturers. Smartphones typically have no user-replaceable or field-replaceable components, and have to be brought into specialized (and in some cases, authorized) service centers for repair.

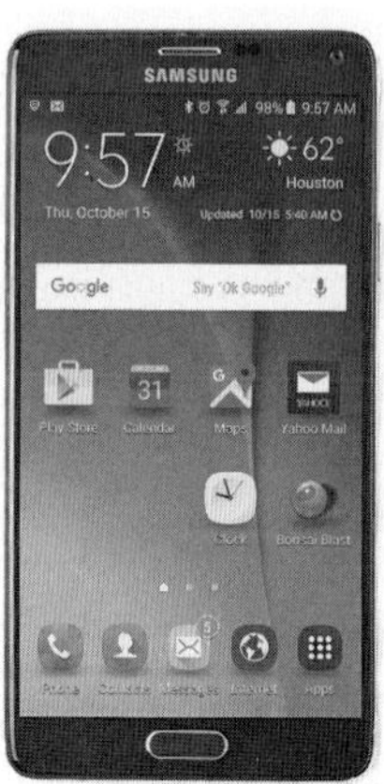
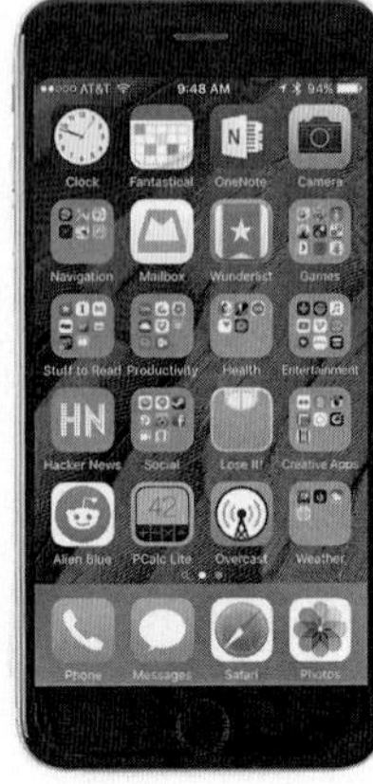
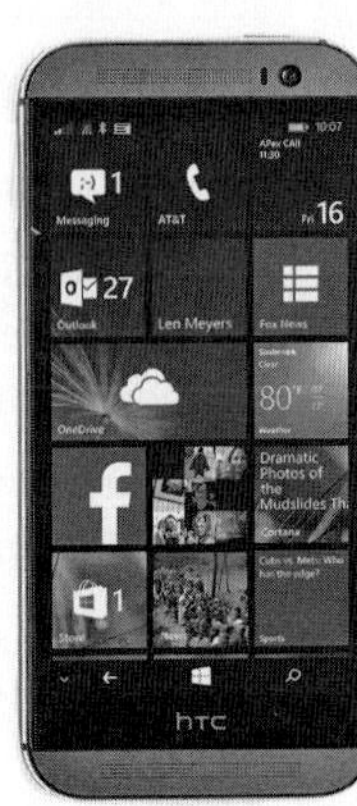

Figure 25-3 Examples of the big three smartphone OSs: Android (left), iOS (center), and Windows Phone (right)

Tablets

Tablet computers are very similar to smartphones; they run the same OSs, run the same apps, and use the same multi-touch screens. From a tech's perspective, they are large smartphones, without the phone. While a typical smartphone screen is around 5 inches, tablets run around 8 to 10 inches (see Figure 25-4).

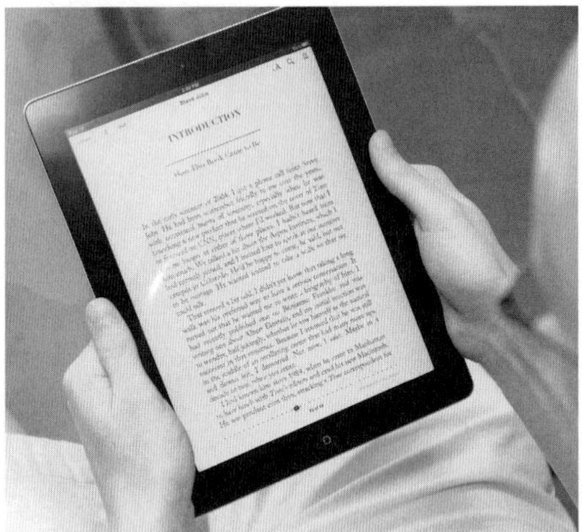

Figure 25-4 Typical tablet

Unlike smartphones, tablets generally lack a cellular data connection, instead counting on 802.11 Wi-Fi to provide Internet connectivity (there are a few exceptions). Like smartphones, you will find tablets running any of the big three operating systems. There are low-end tablets, usually running some variation of Android with limited hardware, and then there are the higher-end tablets, such as the ubiquitous Apple iPad and Microsoft Surface Pro (see Figure 25-5). The differences between the low end and the high end of the spectrum are hardware quality, capabilities, features, and cost.

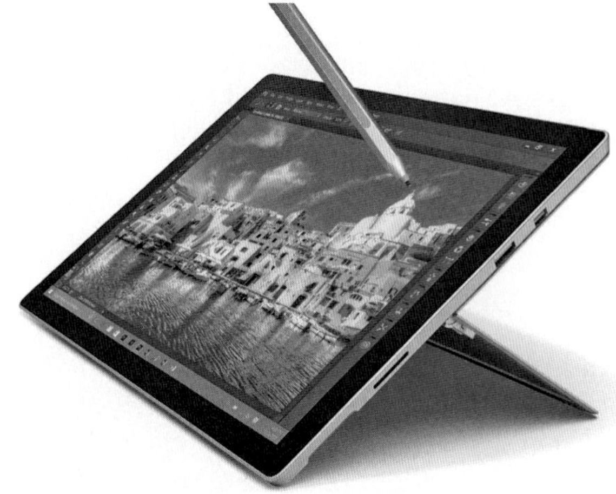

Figure 25-5 Microsoft Surface Pro 4 (photo courtesy of Microsoft)

Phablets

So, let's say you're the kind of person who absolutely must have a smartphone and tablet with you at all times. Carrying a phone and a tablet around is a bit cumbersome, so what's a geek to do? *Phablets* offer a solution. Phablets straddle the line between tablets and smartphones, providing all the features of a smartphone with the expansive vistas of a huge screen.

Today, most manufactures have a line of phablets with screen sizes ranging from 5.5 to 6.5 inches; Samsung's Galaxy Note series is a great example. Apple has gotten into the phablet game with its 5.5-inch iPhone Plus. Figure 25-6 shows two examples of phablets: a Samsung Note 4 and iPhone 6 Plus.

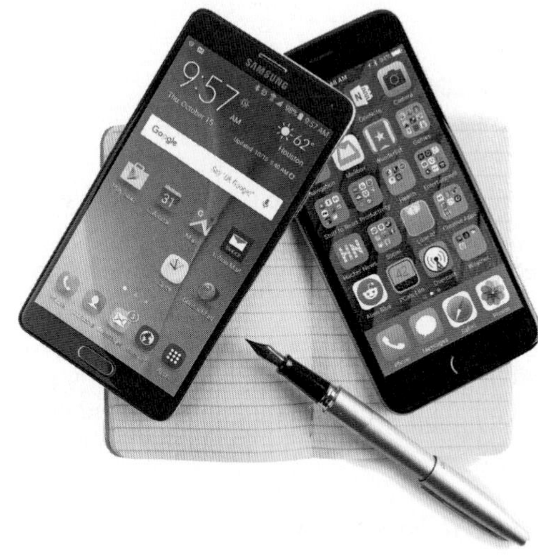

Figure 25-6 Two popular phablets: the Samsung Note 4 (left) and the iPhone 6 Plus (right)

E-Readers

E-readers enable you to access and read electronic books (e-books). Although many e-reader offerings have gotten more tablet-like over the years, some, such as the ePaper-based Amazon Kindle, offer only a black-and-white screen and the ability to turn pages in a book (see Figure 25-7).

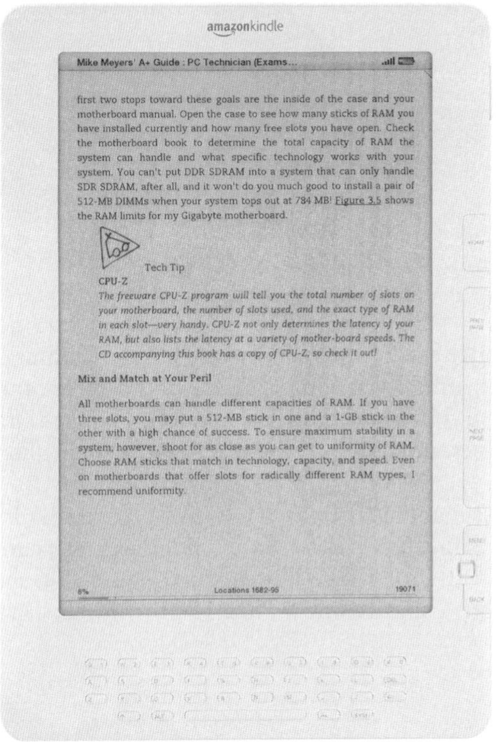

Figure 25-7 Kindle Paperwhite e-Reader

Barnes and Noble's Nook device also started out as simply a black-and-white e-reader; current models are fully fledged tablets. The Amazon Kindle has advanced in recent years, becoming a fully fledged tablet as well. Amazon still sells basic e-readers, as does Barnes and Noble, and has separated those product lines from their tablets. The real advantage to using an e-reader over a tablet is that e-readers often have displays specifically built to handle reading in adverse conditions, such as bright or variable light conditions, often adjusting for light dynamically. Other than that, most folks likely will want a fully fledged tablet that offers the e-reader capabilities through apps. Both Kindle and Nook have e-reader apps available for other platforms. Like standalone e-readers, these apps can connect to online bookstores, download e-books, and maintain a library of books for the user.

Wearable Technology Devices

The one downside to mobile devices is that if they're not in your hand, they're basically useless. Our demand for data creates a motivation to bring the data closer to us via

wearable technology devices. Wearable tech has been around for a few years, but with the recent advent of smart watches, such as the Apple Watch and Android-based watches, it's evident that the major players in the mobile tech world have embraced wearable devices.

Wearable devices have a number of features that separate them from other mobile devices:

- Very small; almost always well under a pound, usually a few ounces
- Small interfaces; screens less than 2 inches, often much less
- Light OSs used to perform a small subset of function of a typical mobile device OS
- Limited hardware, although accelerometers are very common (for step counting)
- Pairing to a host device (often a smartphone)

The CompTIA A+ 220-901 exam specifically lists three type of wearable devices: smart watches, fitness monitors, and glasses/headsets. Let's see what these are all about.

NOTE Wearable devices aren't designed to replace a smartphone, only handle some of the simpler functions. Many functions should never be done on a wearable device.

Smart Watches

A *smart watch's* main job is to take away many of the interruptions that using a smartphone involve. Some great examples are checking e-mail, playing music, reading texts, and receiving notifications of all sorts. Figure 25-8 shows a typical smart watch, the Apple Watch.

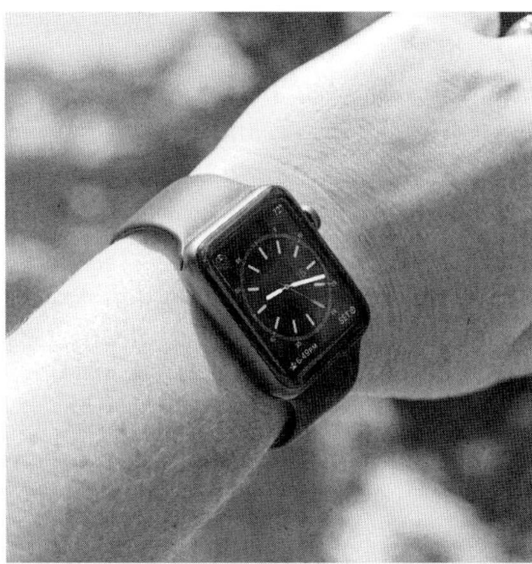

Figure 25-8
Apple Watch

Fitness Monitors

A growing number of fitness monitors or trackers hope to help you meet your fitness goals. Some of the most common fitness tracker features are counting your steps using accelerometers, registering your heart rate through sensors, using the Global Positioning System (GPS) network to track your exercise, and vibration tools to remind you to get moving. Fitness trackers fit into one of two types: fobs that clip to your body, and more sophisticated fitness wristbands. Fobs usually do little more than count steps. Wristbands, like your author's well-worn Fitbit Surge (see Figure 25-9) provide a wealth of features including GPS and heart-rate monitoring.

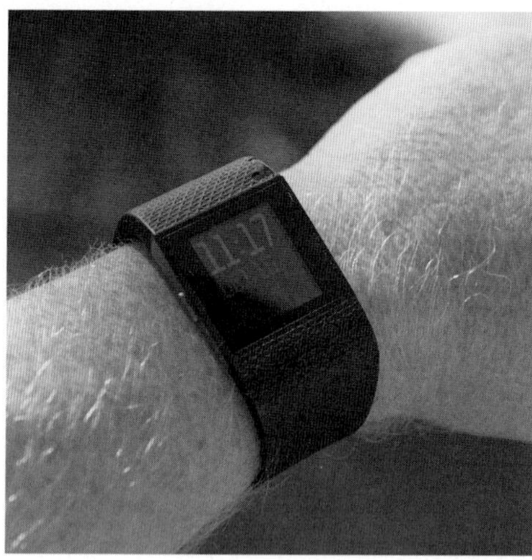

Figure 25-9 Mike's battered Fitbit Surge

Glasses/Headsets

Wearable glasses and headsets haven't made it to the mainstream yet, although there's been one close call. *Google Glass* had a built-in camera and Bluetooth connectivity, enabling an individual to take video and photos from a first-person view. It also enabled you to connect to your smartphone via Bluetooth, so you could answer calls and see information from your phone in the lens of the glass.

One of the big issues with Google Glass, as people later discovered, was privacy. Since it was quite simple for someone wearing Google Glass to film or photograph his or her surroundings, often without the knowledge of others, it created an uncomfortable invasion of personal space. In fact, some business establishments, such as restaurants, bars, and other public places, actually banned the use of Google Glass on their premises. As of this writing, Google has pulled Glass from distribution, although you shouldn't be surprised if it makes another appearance sometime in the near future, since this round was supposedly a type of beta-testing period.

Another example we can offer here is the Microsoft HoloLens. These rather futuristic-looking glasses project images in front of the user, such as videos, apps, and, yes, of course, games. HoloLens is essentially a compact Windows 10 computer with sensors,

3-D display, great sound, and an optimized user interface, all compacted into a single set of glasses. Although it's only in its preproduction stages as of this writing, HoloLens promises to help revolutionize the wearable technology arena.

In any event, wearable tech is only going to get more attention and spread much more from here on out. We'll have to deal with issues such as privacy, as well as how wearable tech integrates into our devices and clothes. Additionally, policies and procedures in organizations that have sensitive areas will have to deal with how wearable tech is used in these areas. It's one thing to ask people to place their phones in a box outside of a secure area, but often people will forget about their watch or their glasses.

Further, video cameras and voice recorders are often found in innocuous devices that we may keep on our person, such as ink pens and key fobs, which also present security issues. From a technician's perspective, there are typically no user replaceable or field replaceable units with wearable tech; these devices typically have to go to an authorized service center to be repaired or replaced.

Mobile Hardware Features

Mobile devices include many hardware features. This section explores screen technologies, cameras, microphones, digitizers, and GPS connectivity.

Screen Technologies

Mobile devices use a variety of screen types. Most tablets use some type of LCD panel, just like portable PCs and desktop monitors. The less expensive ones use twisted nematic (TN); the better ones, like the Apple iPad, use an In-Plane Switching (IPS) panel for richer colors and better viewing angles.

Some smaller devices, like the better smartphones, use a related but different technology called *organic light-emitting diode (OLED)* screens that provides the light for the screen via an organic compound. Applying an electric current causes the organic layer to glow in the precise spots desired. Displaying a checkerboard pattern of black and white, in other words, only lights up the white squares. OLEDs don't use backlights at all, which means they can display true black, they're lighter, and they use less electricity than LCDs of any sort. Screens larger than half a dozen inches, as of this writing, are too expensive to make for mainstream consumer devices.

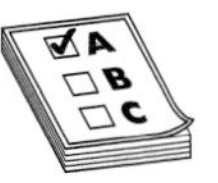

EXAM TIP OLED screens use an organic compound exposed to electrical current for lighting; they don't have a traditional backlight.

Cameras

Many mobile devices have two distinct cameras, a front-facing camera and a rear-facing camera. These cameras enable chatting with Grandma over Skype, tearful YouTube confessionals, and Instagram selfies! The cameras can transmit video over networks, including cellular and IP-based networks, such as the Internet.

The most recent round of camera upgrades on mobile devices, particularly on smartphones, rival and sometimes beat dedicated point-and-shoot cameras (see Figure 25-10).

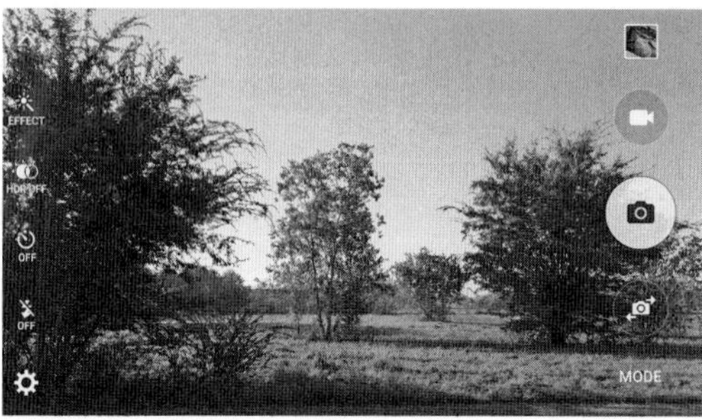

Figure 25-10 Author's camera app on his Galaxy S6

Modern smartphone camera features include high dynamic range (HDR), light compensation, and other functions that enable the user to finely tune a photo or video. Additionally, these cameras offer a variety of options when taking photos and video; some cameras allow you to take "bursts" of shots (like ten in a single second) to make sure you capture faster-moving objects or action shots, as well as slow-motion video. When coupled with the multitude of apps available for mobile devices, such as filter and editing apps, you can edit photos and videos on-the-fly, adding light-filter effects, cleaning up shots, and even adding special effects.

Finally, if you want to go completely to the edges of photography, several companies sell add-on *smart cameras* that connect physically to smartphones to enhance their photographic capabilities. Smart camera add-on devices leverage the sophisticated computing power of smartphones to create some pretty spectacular images. Alternatively, some smart cameras hook up wirelessly to smartphones, enabling them to use the cell network to post pictures immediately.

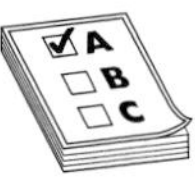

EXAM TIP The CompTIA A+ 901 objectives list *smart camera* as a type of mobile device, but it's unclear which device they mean. The sophistication and quality of front- and rear-facing cameras in smartphones certainly qualify those devices as smart cameras. The smart camera add-on devices just discussed are branded as smart cameras. Finally, many dedicated cameras run with Linux or Android for their OS. Doesn't that make them smart cameras too?

Microphones

Almost all mobile devices incorporate a microphone. Smartphones certainly wouldn't be of much value without microphones and you wouldn't be very effective communicating over Skype or FaceTime without them. Additionally, many people use mobile devices to dictate speech or record other sounds so microphones serve many purposes on mobile devices.

Digitizers

When electrical engineers talk about a digitizer, they are referring to a component that transforms analog signals into digital ones; that is to say, it digitizes them. That's not what we techs talk about when discussing digitizers on mobile devices. A *digitizer* refers to the component that provides the "touch" part of a touch screen. When your finger contacts a touch screen, the digitizer's fine grid of sensors under the glass detects your finger and signals the OS its location on the grid.

GPS

One major feature of mobile devices is the ability to track the device's location through GPS, cellular, or Wi-Fi connections. Users rely on location services to conveniently find things near them, such as stores and restaurants, or to determine how far out that Uber is.

A great example of GPS on smartphones is the traffic and navigation app *Waze* (see Figure 25-11). Waze not only navigates, but its crowd-sourced data collection provides you with amazing real-time knowledge of the road ahead.

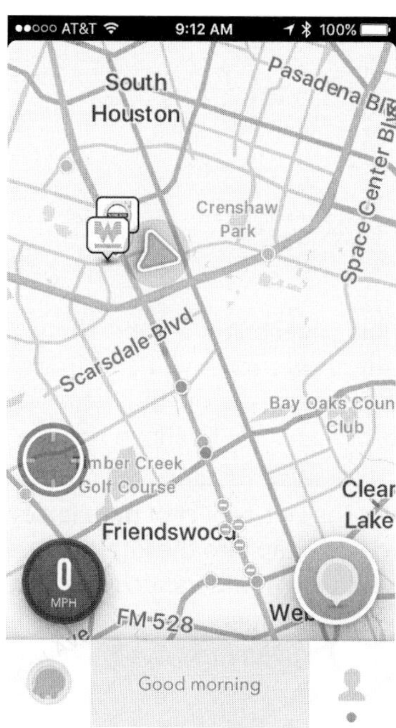

Figure 25-11
Waze in action

Another cool use of GPS is finding your phone when it's missing. The iPhone offers the Find My iPhone app (see Figure 25-12), for example. This feature is part of the iCloud service that comes free with any iOS device.

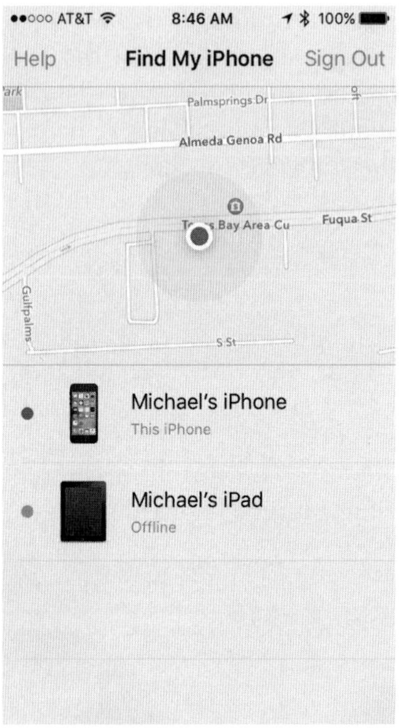

Figure 25-12 Find My iPhone app

902

Tracking your location is generally a good thing…when you want to be tracked. All mobile OSs by default always track you and in many cases record your location for an extended amount of time. This is called *geotracking*. So, for those of us who don't like this feature, turn it off. Figure 25-13 shows turning off Location on an Android phone.

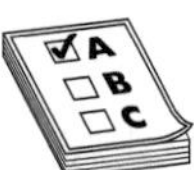

EXAM TIP The GPS aspect of mobile devices goes both ways. Because mobile devices tap into the Internet or cellular phone networks, the devices have identifying numbers such as a MAC address. The cell phone companies and government agencies can use the ID or MAC address to pinpoint where you are at any given time. *Geotracking* clearly has a lot of room for abuse of power.

Meet the Big Three Mobile OSs

Two OSs run the vast majority of mobile devices, Apple iOS and Google Android. This section discusses their development and implementation models, as well as some of their major features, including how their app stores work. Microsoft Windows Phone is in the mix as well, though with substantially smaller market share than iOS or Android.

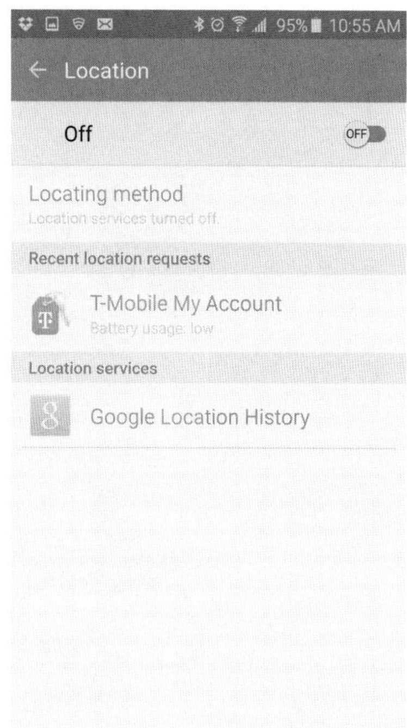

Figure 25-13 Turning off Location

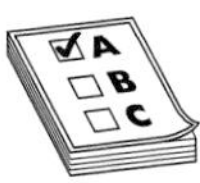

EXAM TIP The 902 exam wants you to compare features among the three mobile OS competitors, *Android vs. iOS vs. Windows*. The next sections explore those variations, though not in that order.

Apple iOS

Apple's mobile operating system, *iOS*, runs on the iPhone, iPad, and iPod Touch (see Figure 25-14). The Apple model of development is very monolithic: Apple tightly controls the development of the hardware, OS, developer tools, and app deployment. Apple has very strict development policies and controls for developers, and this contributes to the high level of security in iOS. iOS apps are almost exclusively purchased, installed, and updated through Apple's *App Store*. An exception is providers of line-of-business apps specific to a particular organization. These internal development groups reside within an organization and can develop iOS apps, but deploy only to devices that are under the organization's control, skipping the public App Store. They still have to undergo a type of Apple partnering and enterprise licensing approval process.

Google Android

In many different ways, Android devices can be considered almost the opposite of Apple. Android is an open source platform, based on yet another open platform, Linux, and is owned by Google (see Figure 25-15). Open source means device manufacturers can alter or customize Android as they see fit, so there are differences among the implementations from

various vendors. While Google writes the core Android code, vendors customize it to provide unique hardware features or a branded look and feel. Apps are available to purchase and download through various apps stores, such as Google Play and the Amazon Appstore.

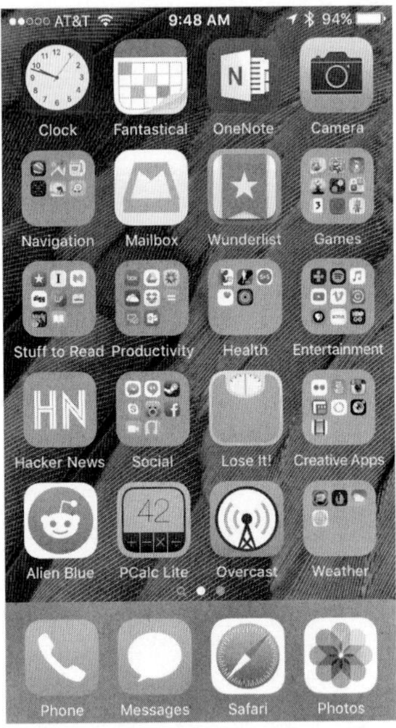

Figure 25-14 iOS 9

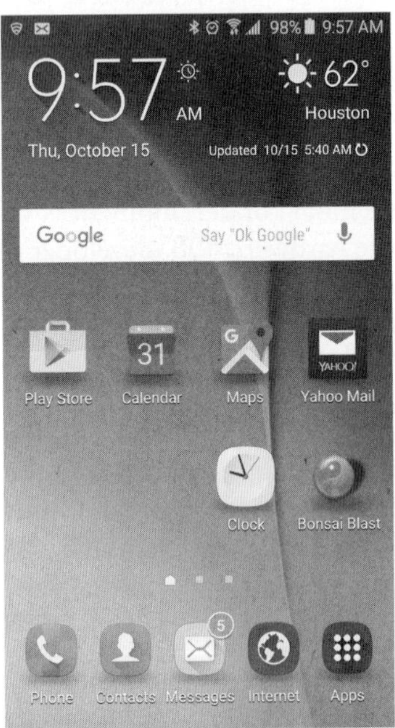

Figure 25-15 Android 5

Microsoft Windows Phone

Microsoft has a long history of developing software for mobile devices. In the pre-iPhone era, Microsoft's Windows Mobile OS powered millions of PDAs, tablets, and smartphones for both the consumer and enterprise markets. After the introduction of the iPhone, however, Microsoft failed to adopt the multi-touch UI, allowing iOS and Android to eclipse Windows Mobile in the market. Google's giving away Android didn't help Microsoft either.

Microsoft finally delivered a modern multi-touch OS with Windows Phone 7 in 2010, and its unique interface became the foundation of the tile-based interface introduced in Windows 8. Microsoft's vision of one OS and one experience, regardless of device, has signaled a turnaround for Microsoft in the mobile device space (see Figure 25-16). Microsoft maintains its own app store, but there are also third-party app providers. Microsoft primarily controls the OS portion of its platform, but naturally has developer requirements as well, although these are not as restrictive as Apple's.

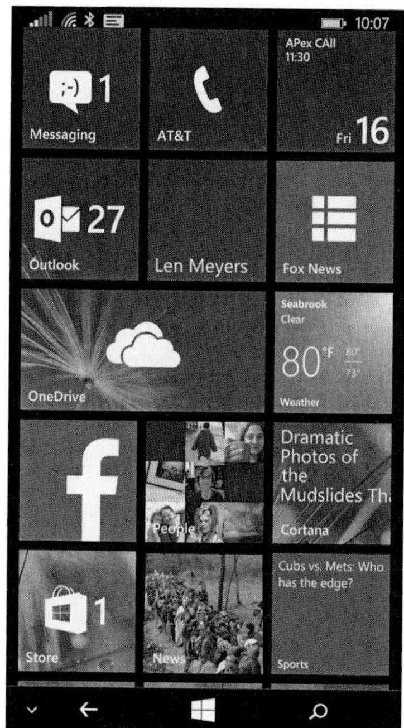

Figure 25-16 Windows Phone 8.1

Mobile OS Features

Mobile operating systems come in a variety of flavors and sometimes have different features as well as different interfaces. But they also have a great deal in common, because consumers expect them to perform some of the same functions that they are used to seeing in other mobile devices, regardless of operating system. For instance, regardless of whether you are using an iPhone or an Android phone, you still expect to be able to

check your e-mail and make video calls. So the differences in operating systems really boil down to more refined features, hardware and app support, as well as how they look and feel. We'll take a quick look at some of the features common to all mobile operating systems and point out differences along the way.

User Interfaces

All mobile OSes use a purely *graphical user interface (GUI)*, meaning you interact with them by accessing icons on the screen. Current models do not offer any command-line interface.

Each OS usually has either a major button or a row of icons that enables the user to navigate to the most prominent features of the device. They also all use touch features, such as swiping, to navigate between screens. Most have some type of menu system that enables the user to find different apps and data.

iOS offers some customization of the user interface. You can group apps together into folders, for example, and reposition most apps for your convenience. The iOS look and feel, however, will remain consistent.

Android offers a very different GUI experience by employing *launchers*, software that enables users to customize their Android device extensively. Many companies make launchers and different manufacturers of devices ship with launchers they prefer. Samsung devices use the TouchWiz launcher, for example. I use the Nova launcher on my Android phablet. The launcher enables you to change nearly every aspect of the GUI, such as putting only the apps you want on the home screen and changing the grid to add or remove apps.

NOTE Windows Phone accommodates different launchers. Microsoft is changing things a lot with Windows Phone as I'm putting this chapter together, so I can't give definitive details at this time.

Most mobile devices include an accelerometer and a gyroscope, one to measure movement in space and the other to maintain proper orientation of up and down. The mobile OSes use these hardware features to change the *screen orientation* in many apps. You can flip an iPhone from vertical to horizontal, for example, to enhance watching videos on YouTube. (See also "Adding Apps" later in this chapter for more uses of these technologies.)

Wi-Fi Calling

While every mobile device that calls itself a phone must have support for cellular wireless, another feature that many mobile devices include is *Wi-Fi calling*, the capability to make both audio and video calls over Wi-Fi networks. Smartphones have cellular networks enabled on them, but some tablets don't. That doesn't keep the latter devices from making calls using Wi-Fi networks. Applications such as Skype (see Figure 25-17), for example, can be used on a tablet that does not have cellular capability, as long as it can make a good Wi-Fi connection.

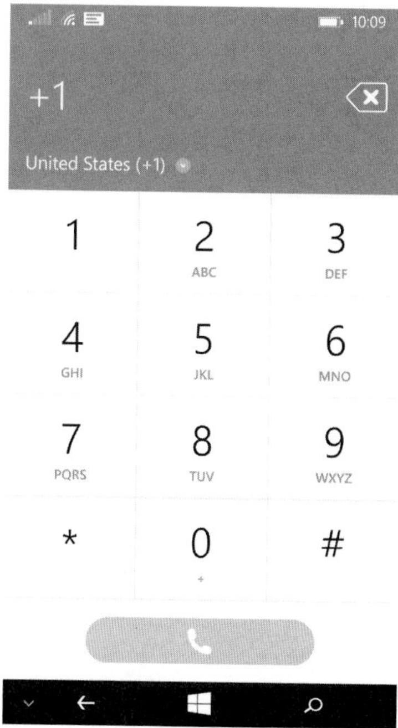

Figure 25-17 Skype app on Windows Phone

Virtual Assistants

"Hey, Siri!"

"Yes, Mike?"

"What's the weather like today?"

"Always sunny where you are, Mike."

Okay, maybe they're not quite that cool, but the *virtual assistants* on the latest smartphones and tablets enable quick, vocal interaction to accomplish common goals. For example, one only has to ask Siri (Apple's virtual assistant) how to find the nearest restaurant or tourist attraction, and she (Siri's voice is female by default) will respond with the information sought. Virtual assistants can also be useful in performing Internet searches and, in some cases, even activating and using certain apps on the mobile device. This helps people who may have certain disabilities that may prevent them from tapping or typing on the device, by enabling them to use voice commands.

A virtual assistant is also useful (although not recommended, for safety reasons) when you have to use your smartphone while driving. You can speak to the smartphone's virtual assistant to place a call or get directions while driving, particularly if you're using the smartphone paired with the car's Bluetooth system. The Windows 10 equivalent to Siri is called Cortana, and essentially serves the same functions and provides the same services and features. Google's virtual assistant found on many Android devices is called Google Now, and is available not only for Android smart devices, but also for iOS and PCs. In addition to the big three's virtual assistants, there are also apps you can download that provide other virtual assistant services, depending upon your platform.

Software Development Kits

Most mobile operating systems come with some sort of *software development kit (SDK)* or application development kit that you can use to create custom apps or add features to existing apps on the device. Figure 25-18 shows Xcode, the development environment for the iOS SDK, testing an app.

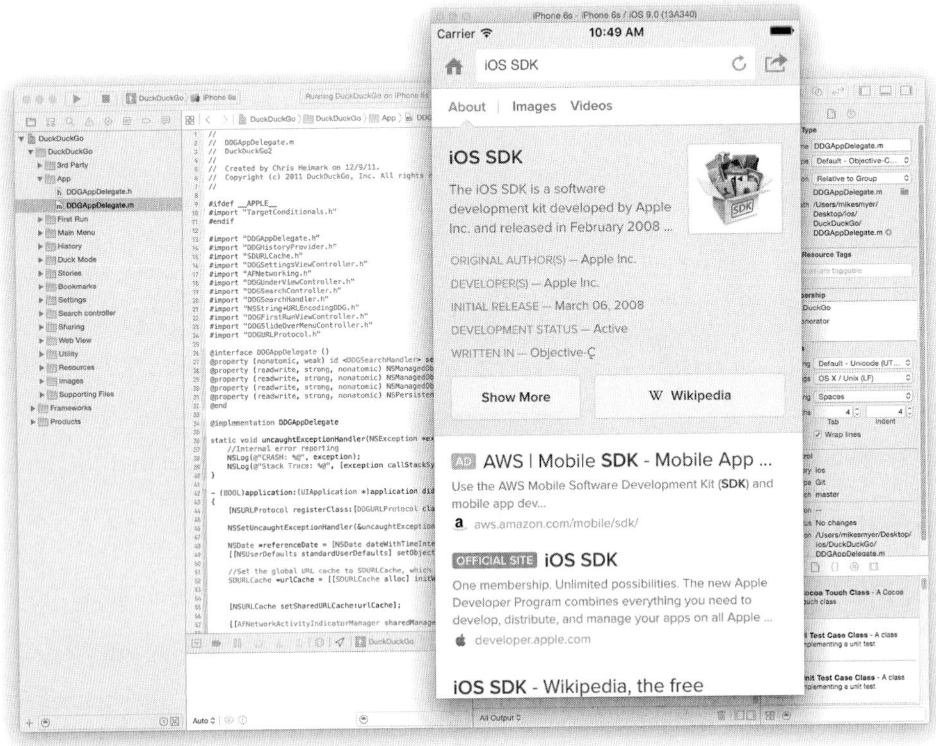

Figure 25-18 Xcode running an app written with the iOS SDK

Each mobile OS offers different challenges for app developers. Apple's rigid development model makes it such that your app must pass a rigorous testing program before it is allowed into the App Store. Microsoft's development model, while not typically as rigid, is similar in nature. Google, on the other hand, allows anyone to create Android apps and distribute them to the masses without much interference. The *Android application package (APK)* is the installation software developed after compiling an app's code, which can be written in a variety of languages.

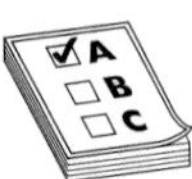

EXAM TIP A software development kit (SDK) is used to write apps. With Android, the Android application package (APK) generates the installation for apps.

Capabilities

One feature almost all currently marketed smartphones have built in is the *emergency notification* feature that enables them to receive broadcasts from national emergency broadcast systems, such as the Emergency Alert System (EAS) in the United States. This can be a very useful feature during severe weather, enabling you to receive warning text messages, or in the event of a report of a missing child in your immediate area, enabling you to get AMBER Alerts. Many of these emergency broadcast system alerts also force your phone to omit a very loud sound, even if the volume is turned all the way down, in order to get your attention.

Most smartphones also have the capability to place 911 calls, the lack of which capability was a significant issue prior to the 21st century. The older 911 system relied on the Public Switched Telephone Network (PSTN) to trace a call and determine its location, allowing emergency responders to get to the correct address quickly. This was problematic with mobile devices, so legislation was passed (the Wireless Communications and Public Safety Act of 1999) requiring carriers to be able to pinpoint the location of a mobile device, such as a smartphone. The system uses GPS and cellular networks to triangulate the location of a phone by its distance from cell towers, its transmission delay time, and other factors. The current system is called *E911* (for Enhanced 911 system).

Mobile Payment Service

As smartphones and other mobile devices have become so much more commonplace in our daily lives, we've become very reliant on them to store our personal and sensitive information. Often people store financial information, such as credit card information, in their phones as well. Over time, smartphone manufacturers, as well as merchants, realized that the next logical step was to enable your smartphone to be able to pay for goods and services simply by scanning the smartphone or by using an app to pay. Your app would be connected to your bank information, and would automatically transfer the funds from your bank to the merchant. This feature is called *mobile payment service*.

In some cases, you don't even have to use an app, and many Near Field Communication (NFC) applications have been implemented by merchants in order to simply receive payment approval from the phone by placing the phone onto or near the special pad at the register. (See "NFC" later in this chapter for the scoop on these tiny networks.)

Additionally, smartphone manufacturers have also started to produce their own payment systems. Apple, for example, has recently come out with a payment system, called *Apple Pay*. Apple Pay was first implemented with the iPhone 6, and support has even been integrated into the Apple Watch. Apple Pay supports major credit card payment terminals and point-of-sale systems, including those fielded by Visa, MasterCard, and American Express, as these card vendors were included by (and teamed up with) Apple in the development process. Apple Pay can use contactless payment terminals with NFC, and supports in-app payments for online purchases. While Apple's efforts aren't the first attempt at mobile payment systems, Apple Pay seems to be the first that is mature enough to be accepted and workable by both merchants and consumers. Other mobile device and operating system providers will no doubt introduce their own payment systems in the future.

Airplane Mode

Airplane mode is simply a switch (either an actual hardware switch located on the mobile device or a software switch that can be located in the device's configuration settings) that turns off all cellular and wireless services, including Bluetooth, from the device (see Figure 25-19). It ensures that no signal can be transmitted or received. Airplane mode, because of its name, is most commonly used on aircraft when passengers are directed to turn off their mobile devices.

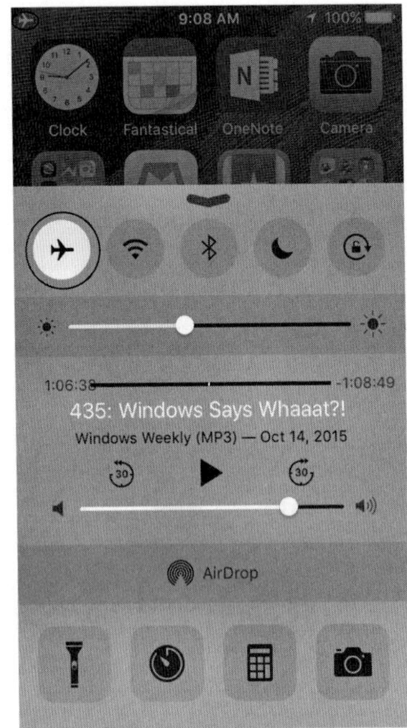

Figure 25-19 Airplane mode enabled on iOS 9

Web Browsing and E-mail

Every multifunctional mobile device—think smartphone and tablet here—enables you to do standard Internet-computing tasks. You can surf the Web using Wi-Fi connections or cellular, for example, and access just about any type of e-mail, including corporate-style e-mail and Web-based e-mail. The Web access differs according to the device you use. iOS devices, for example, all feature the Safari Web browser. Android devices bring the Chrome browser, as you might suspect (because Google makes both). Can you guess what browser Windows Phone uses by default? (If you guessed Edge, you win a prize!)

Radio Firmware

Mobile devices use a wide variety of radio technologies to access the Internet, e-mail, and corporate infrastructures. Generally, mobile devices have two types of radios: 802.11 and Bluetooth. If the device can make calls, it also has some form of cellular radio.

PRL, PRI, and Baseband Updates As mobile devices travel, they frequently have to pass through areas that don't have strong signals, or into areas that the carrier does not service. When a mobile device connects to different carriers' networks, this is called *roaming*, and in some cases can incur service charges, depending upon the carriers in question. The *Preferred Roaming List (PRL)* is occasionally and automatically updated to your phone's firmware by the carrier so that your phone will be configured with particular carriers' networks and frequencies, in a priority order, that it should search for when it can't locate its home carrier network.

Updates to this list are sent via your phone's cellular connection (called baseband updates, or over-the-air updates) or, in some cases, through firmware updates during normal operating system and firmware upgrades via synchronization. *PRI updates* are intended to control the data rates between the mobile device and the cell tower, and are sent to ensure that the mobile device can send data at the rate the carrier network can receive it.

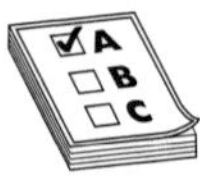

EXAM TIP PRL and PRI updates are handled automatically during firmware/OS updates. They are only for CDMA networks. No one but the nerdiest of nerds will ever see these updates.

IMEI, ICCID, and IMSI There are three particular identifiers you will need to understand both for the exam and for real-life management of mobile devices. The *International Mobile Equipment Identity (IMEI)* number is a 15-digit number used to uniquely identify a mobile device, typically a smartphone or other device that connects to a cellular network. IMEI numbers are unique to the *Global System for Mobile Communications (GSM)* family of devices, including current devices that descended from GSM technologies (including current-day 4G LTE and LTE-Advanced). You can typically find this number printed inside the battery compartment of the mobile device, but you may not necessarily need to take the device apart, as some operating systems enables you to find it inside the device configuration settings (see Figure 25-20).

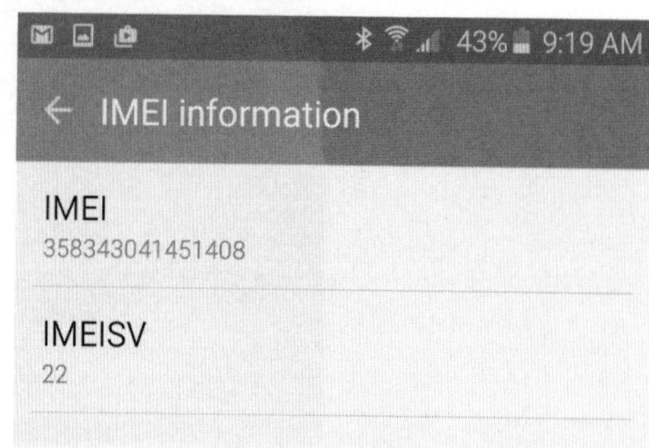

Figure 25-20 IMEI settings on an Android phone

The IMEI number can be used to identify a specific device and even to block that device from accessing the carrier's network. So, if the device is lost or stolen, the user can notify her carrier, and the carrier can make sure that the device can't be used on the network.

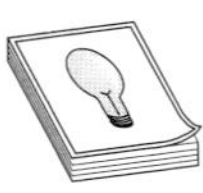

TIP Always write down your IMEI number when you get a new phone, as it can prove you are the actual owner if it ever is stolen or lost.

The ICCID number, which stands for Integrated Circuit Card Identifier, uniquely identifies a subscriber identity module (SIM). The SIM contains information unique to the subscriber (the owner of the phone), and is used to authenticate the subscriber to the network. SIMs can be moved from phone to phone, usually with no problems.

The third number is the *International Mobile Subscriber Identity (IMSI)* number. It is also included on the SIM, but represents the actual user associated with the SIM. This number is not normally accessible from the phone, but is usually available from the carrier, to ensure that stolen phones are not misused. The IMSI number can be used to unlock a phone as well. There may be some cases where you might want to record these numbers for each managed device in the enterprise, for inventory purposes or so that you have them handy when you work with your mobile device management (MDM) software. Typically, during the device provisioning process, those identifiers, as well as other information particular to the device, such as telephone number and MAC address, are collected by the server and stored in the mobile device inventory for you. Figure 25-21 shows how IMEI and ICCID numbers are listed for a newer Android device in the device settings.

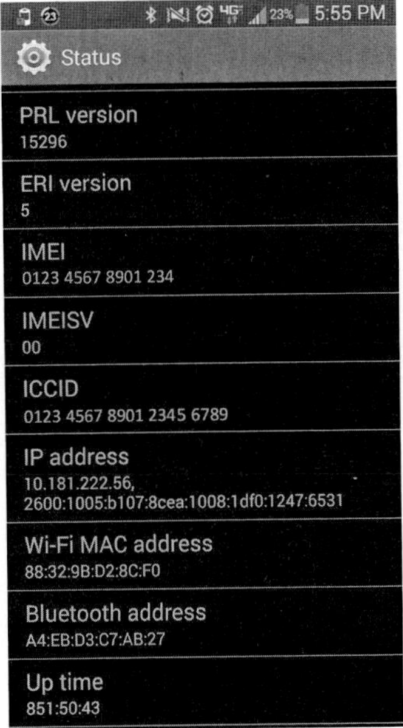

Figure 25-21 IMEI and ICCID numbers

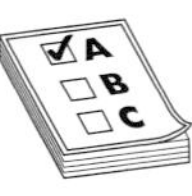

EXAM TIP Remember the differences between the IMEI and IMSI numbers for the CompTIA A+ 902 exam. The IMEI number represents the device. The IMSI number is tied to the user's account with the carrier, and is included with the SIM.

VPN

As you'll recall from earlier chapters, VPNs establish secure connections between a remote client and the corporate infrastructure, or between two different sites, such as a branch office and the corporate office. VPNs are typically implemented using tunneling methods through an unsecure network, such as the Internet. In a client VPN setup, the host has client VPN software specially configured to match the corporate VPN server or concentrator configuration. This would include encryption method and strength, as well as authentication methods, such as a user name and password combination and a digital certificate. A site-to-site VPN scenario uses VPN devices on both ends of the connection, configured to communicate only with each other, while the hosts on both ends use their respective VPN concentrators as a gateway. This arrangement is usually transparent to the users at both sites; hosts at the other site appear as if they are directly connected to the user's network.

VPNs can be created using a variety of technologies and protocols. The most popular ways to create a VPN is to use either a combination of the Layer 2 Tunneling Protocol (L2TP) and IPsec (see Figure 25-22), or Secure Sockets Layer. When using the L2TP /IPsec method, UDP port 1701 is used and must be opened on packet-filtering devices. In this form of VPN, users connect to the corporate network and can use all of their typical applications, such as their e-mail client, and can map shares and drives as they would if they were actually connected onsite to the corporate infrastructure. An SSL-based VPN, on the other hand, uses the standard SSL port, TCP 443, and is typically used through a client's Web browser. It doesn't normally require any special software or configuration on the client itself. However, SSL-based VPNs can be somewhat limited in functionality, and present the corporate resources through the client browser in the form of an access portal.

Figure 25-22 Configuring a VPN

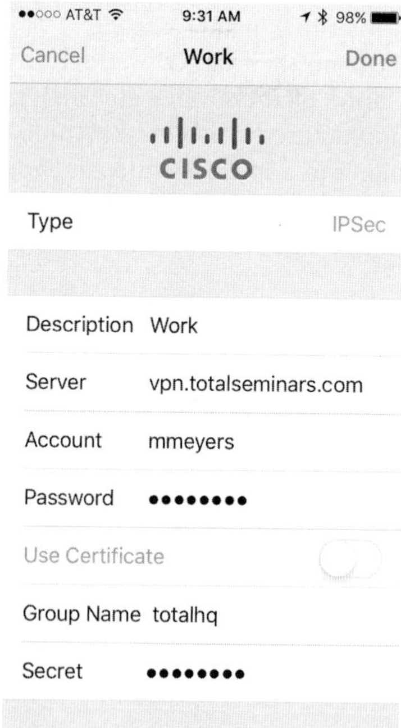

Configuring a Mobile Device

Mobile devices require some setup and configuration to function seamlessly in your online life. Initial setup requires *screen calibration*, where you touch various corners of the screen to set how your fingers interact with the device. Such calibration can recur after a major update as well.

You can add capabilities by enhancing hardware and installing productivity apps. You also need to set up network connectivity, add Bluetooth devices, configure e-mail account(s), and enable the devices to synchronize with a PC. Plus you have a lot of add-on options. Let's look at these options.

Enhancing Hardware

A mobile device is a computer, just like your desktop PC or laptop, with the same basic components doing the same basic things. The construction centers on a primary circuit board, the *motherboard*, onto which every other component is attached. The biggest of these components is often the *system on a chip (SoC)*. This wonder of miniaturization combines a CPU, GPU, and sundry other support logic onto a single silicon die, saving a lot of space and power in the process. An interesting aside about the CPUs used in these devices is that they are rarely Intel x86 based; instead, you are much more likely to run across an ARM architecture chip when perusing the spec sheets of your new tablet. The iPad uses an Apple-designed ARM A-series chip, for example, and the ASUS Transformer features an NVIDIA-designed Tegra ARM SoC.

Mobile devices use storage, though not usually a traditional magnetic hard disk drive (HDD) with spinning platters. More commonly, mobile devices use a *solid state drive (SSD)* because SSDs are smaller, use less power, and are much, much faster than spinning HDDs. Plus they're cooler in general.

Mobile devices vary from their larger brethren in two very significant areas of importance to techs. First, none of them offer any FRUs. If something breaks, you send the device back to the manufacturer, visit a local manufacturer-supported retail outlet such as the Apple Store, or take it to a specialized repair shop. Second, you can't upgrade mobile devices at all. Even a laptop enables you to upgrade RAM or a hard drive, for example, but the mobile device you buy is exactly what you get. You want something better? Buy a new one.

That said, every mobile device enables you to attach some kind of peripheral or external storage device. But every device offers different expansion capabilities, so it's hard to generalize about them.

The one exception to the rule that you can't generalize about mobile devices relates to sound. Every mobile device has a single 3.5-mm audio jack for plugging in earbuds or speakers (see Figure 25-23). This applies to smartphones and tablets from all vendors.

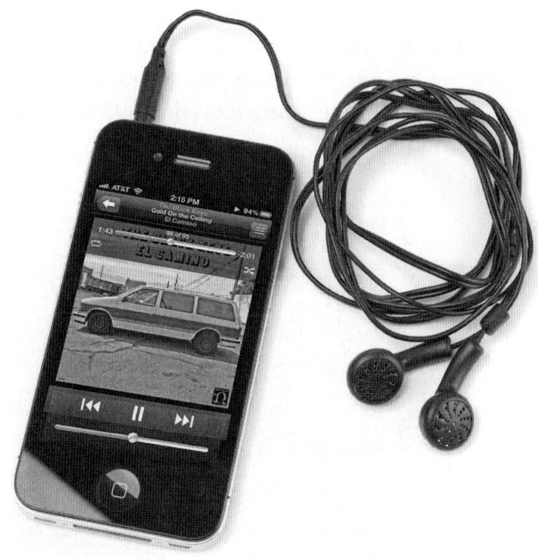

Figure 25-23 Earbuds plugged into a smartphone

Apple Expansion Options

Apple devices offer the least expansion capability of all the mobile devices, so even though they dominate the marketplace, there's not much to say about them. Most of the expansion on Apple devices is limited to proprietary cables and devices. The iPhone and iPad use a single proprietary port for recharging the device and connecting to the few external devices available. Figure 25-24 shows the typical use for the port, a dongle that connects to a USB AC adapter for recharge. We'll cover other types of connectors later in the chapter.

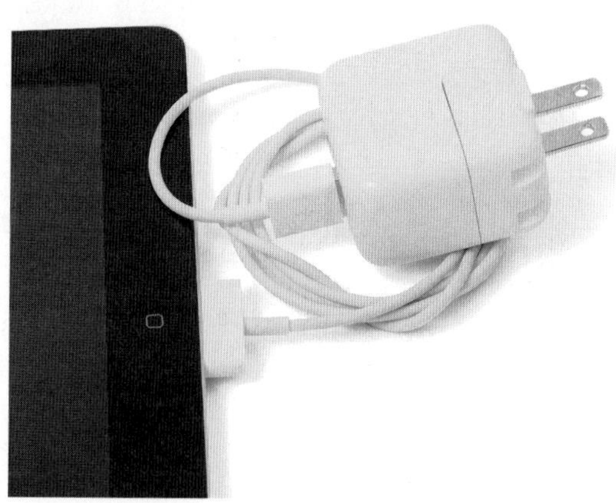

Figure 25-24 Recharger dongle

Early iPhones and iPads had limited multimedia capabilities, but current devices enable you to mirror the screen to a multimedia device such as a projector. This enables seamless presentations, for example, through the excellent Apple Keynote program (see Figure 25-25). The multimedia connection requires another dongle adapter (see Figure 25-26).

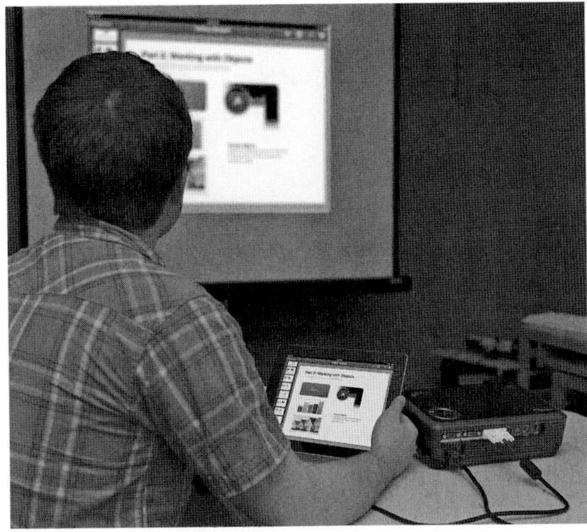

Figure 25-25 Apple Keynote on an iPad and a projector

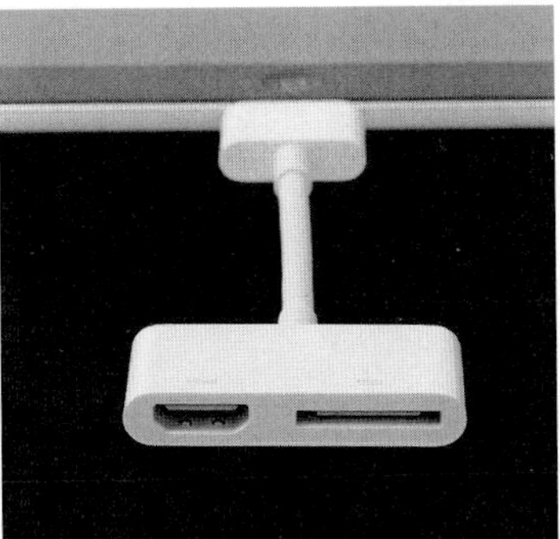

Figure 25-26 Apple Digital AV Adapter

Android Expansion Options

Devices that use Google Android come with a variety of connections and expansion capabilities. Many offer MicroSD slots for adding storage in the form of the tiny flash memory cards (see Figure 25-27). Some offer bigger slots, and a few feature micro-USB or even full-sized USB ports.

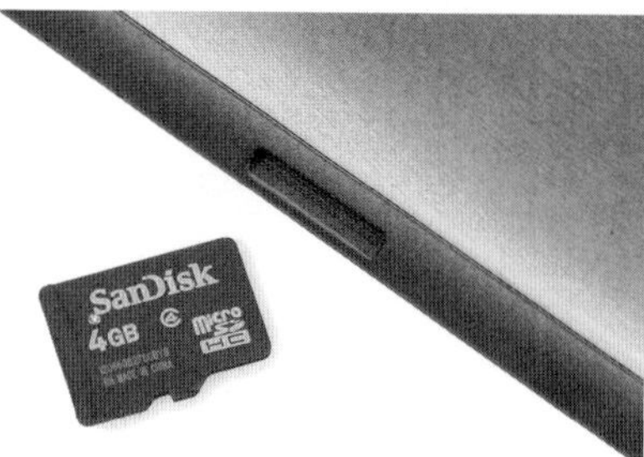

Figure 25-27 MicroSD card and slot

Many Android devices offer a proprietary socket that mimics the functions of Apple's dongle port, providing a way to recharge the tablet or smartphone and get data from a PC to the tablet and vice versa. Figure 25-28 shows a proprietary connector for power.

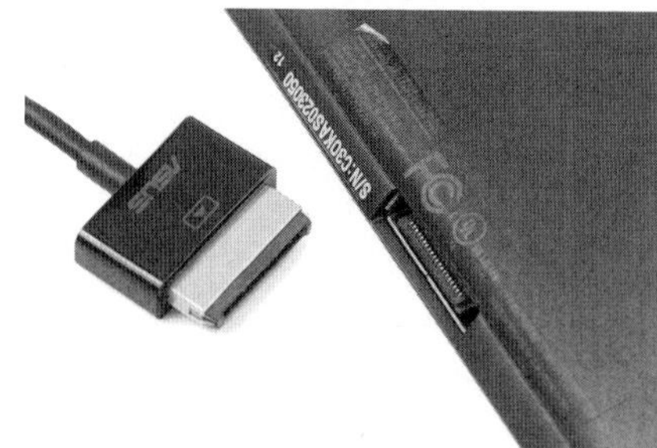

Figure 25-28 ASUS proprietary power connector

Finally, many tablets sport a connector for attaching the device to an external monitor, such as a big screen or projector. (Smartphones don't generally have this connector.) Figure 25-29 shows a Micro-HDMI port and connector.

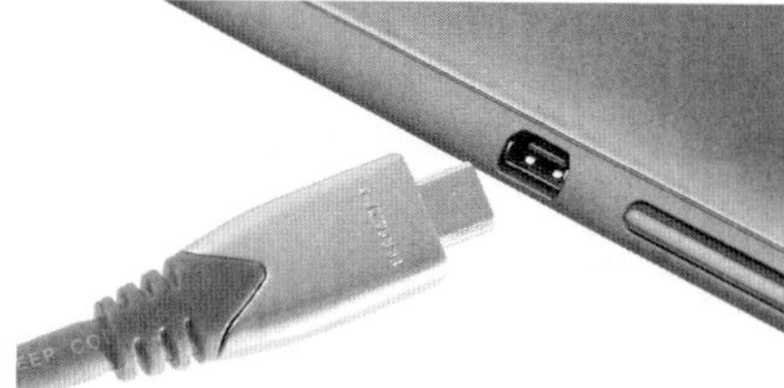

Figure 25-29 Micro-HDMI port and connector

Bluetooth

The last way that mobile devices expand their physical capabilities is wirelessly, most often using the Bluetooth standard for adding a keyboard (all) or mouse (not with Apple products). In theory, you could attach all sorts of Bluetooth devices to the mobile device,

but the reality seems limited to keyboards. Figure 25-30 shows a diminutive Apple keyboard for the iPad and the iPad resting in a stand to make typing this chapter a little easier than using the virtual keyboard.

Figure 25-30 Keyboard associated with iPad

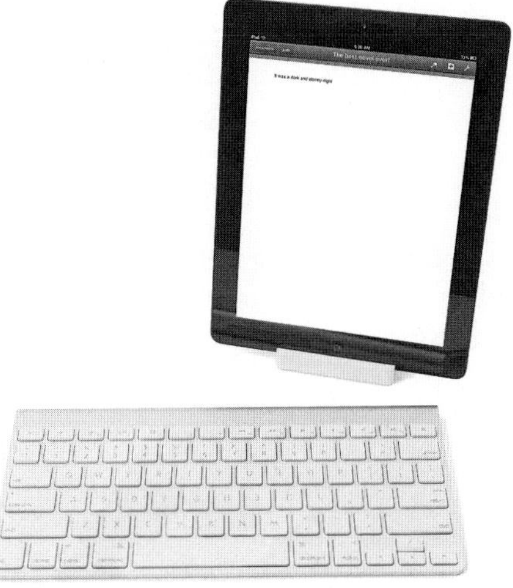

NOTE See the "Bluetooth" section toward the end of this chapter for the steps to set up a tablet with a Bluetooth keyboard.

Adding Apps

Mobile devices come from the manufacturer with a certain number of vital apps installed for accessing e-mail, surfing the Web, taking notes, making entries in a calendar, and so on. Almost all mobile devices offer multimedia apps to enable you to listen to music, take pictures, watch YouTube videos, and view photos. You'll find instant messaging tools and, in the case of smartphones, telephone capabilities.

Apple and Closed Source

Apple makes the most popular mobile devices in the iPhone and the iPad. Both devices use the iOS operating system. Unlike every other manufacturer, Apple tightly controls the user experience, insisting that all developers of apps for iOS follow the same guidelines.

Apple maintains strict control over what apps can be installed onto iOS devices, meaning that if you want to get an app for your iPhone or iPad, you can only get it from the Apple App Store (see Figure 25-31). Apple must approve any app before it goes into the App Store, and Apple reserves the right to refuse to list on the App Store any app that fails to measure up. This controlled environment is called a *closed source* or *vendor specific* system. Apple is the source for all iOS goodness.

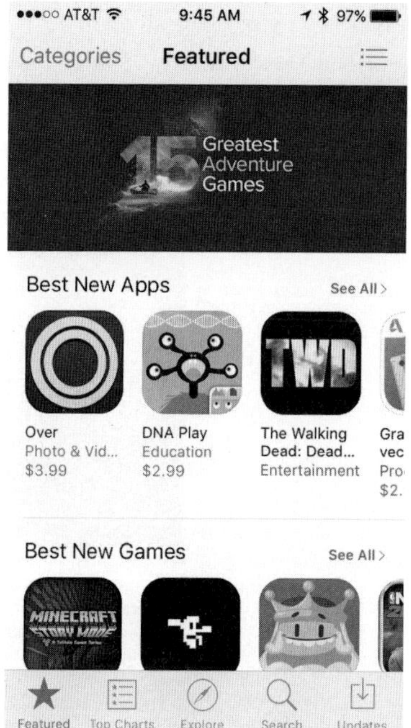

Figure 25-31 App Store

NOTE CompTIA's use of the term "closed source" to describe the distribution of apps with Apple products differs from the more common meaning of the term. *Closed source* typically means that a company that develops software doesn't release the underlying programming to other developers. Oppose this term with *open source*, like Linux distributions where anyone can download and modify the underlying source code.

To add an app, select the App Store icon from the home screen. You can select from featured apps or view by category. You can check out the top 25 paid or free apps or simply search for what you want (see Figure 25-32).

The first time you try to purchase an app through the App Store, you'll be prompted to set up an account. You can use an account that you created previously through the Apple iTunes music and video store or create a new account using the Apple iCloud service. Creating a new iCloud account takes a few steps and a lot of typing in of passwords and such (see Figure 25-33), but eventually you'll get the account figured out. You'll need a valid credit card to set up the account.

The iCloud Key Chain builds on the Key Chain feature in OS X to synchronize user information, passwords, and other credentials with all your Apple devices. (See "Syncronization" a little later in the chapter.) Key Chain can seamlessly store many non-Apple credentials as well, such as from Facebook, Amazon, and other providers.

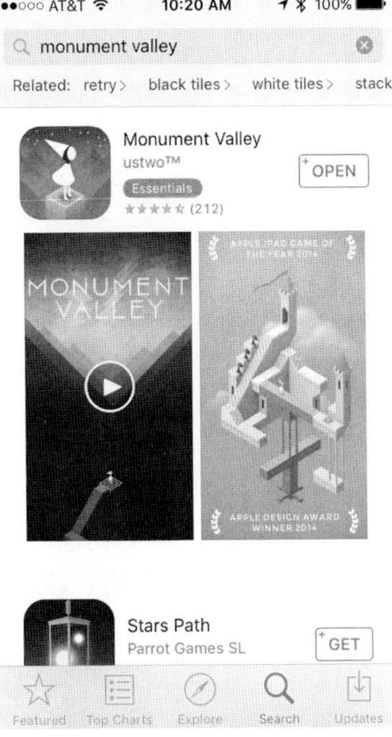

Figure 25-32 Searching for Monument Valley

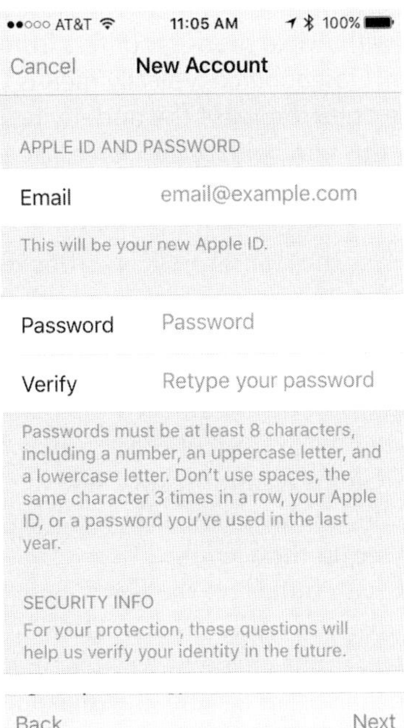

Figure 25-33 Creating an Apple ID for iCloud and App Store purchases

Android Applications

Google Android powers many smartphones and a solid percentage of tablets, but Android differs greatly from Apple iOS in that Google gives the OS away and developers create versions suited to their devices. That means in practice that when you have a smartphone or tablet that uses Google Android for an OS, you have to amend that description to include the manufacturer as well. A Samsung tablet, in other words, uses a version of Android that differs somewhat from the Android an ASUS tablet uses. HTC, for example, uses a custom interface for its Android devices called HTC Sense that changes the look and feel of Android. When you want to get an app for an Android device, you have alternative sources for that app.

Many vendors offer a store with apps developed or customized to work with their devices. These *vendor-specific* stores enable you to get apps that should work well with your Android smartphone or tablet.

You can also go to a third-party app store or market for apps developed "for Android" that probably will work with your device, but there's not a guarantee that they'll work on all Android devices. Google Play (Android's default app store), for example, offers well over 1 million apps. This Wild West approach to apps makes the Android experience vastly different from the iOS experience when it comes to smartphones and tablets.

NOTE Microsoft has a substantial presence in the mobile devices market with Windows Phone 7, 8, and 8.1 and Windows 10 Mobile. Expect the market share to increase over the coming years. Microsoft embraces an app marketplace somewhere in between that of Apple and Google, with both Microsoft-created apps and those created by other developers available through the Windows Phone Marketplace and other venues.

Windows Applications

Windows apps closely mirror Apple apps in terms of Microsoft's close development and control of apps. While anyone can write an app for Windows Phone, it must be accepted by the Windows Phone Store if the developer wants to distribute it publicly (see Figure 25-34).

Network Connectivity

Mobile devices connect to the outside world through the cellular networks or through various 802.11 Wi-Fi standards. You learned specifics about the standards in Chapter 22, "Wireless Networking," so I won't rehash them here. This section looks at standard configuration issues from the perspective of a mobile device.

When you want to connect to a Wi-Fi network, you need to turn on Wi-Fi on your device and then actively connect to a network. If the network is properly configured with WPA or WPA2 encryption, then you also need to have the logon information to access the network. The most common way to connect is through the Settings app (see Figure 25-35).

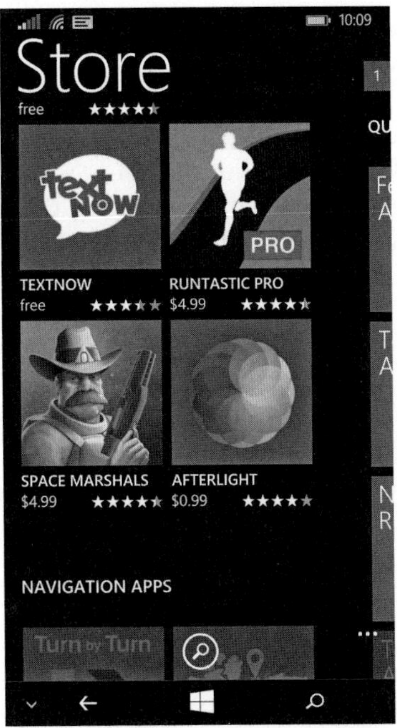

Figure 25-34 Windows Phone Store

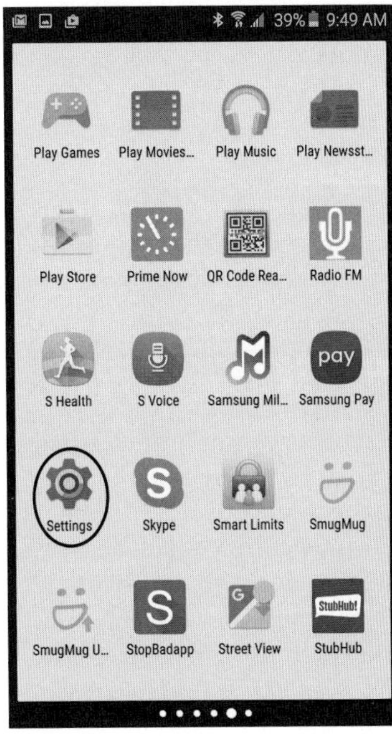

Figure 25-35 Selecting the Settings icon

Settings enables you to do the vast majority of configuration necessary to a mobile device. To join a network, for example, tap the Wi-Fi (or Networks) option to see available networks (see Figure 25-36). Simply select the network you want to join and type in the passphrase or passcode. Give the mobile device a moment to get IP and DNS information from the DHCP server, and you're on the network.

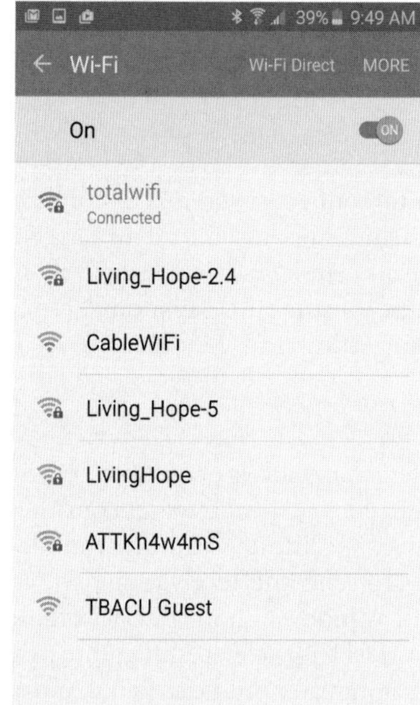

Figure 25-36 Browsing available networks

After you connect to a network successfully, all mobile devices store that network access information automatically, creating a *profile* of that network based on the SSID (the name of the network). This works just like with any other device that connects to a Wi-Fi network. If the SSID of a network changes after you've connected to that network, your mobile device will fail to connect to the rechristened network. You need to delete the profile and reconnect. You do this through the Settings app by selecting the Wi-Fi network and selecting *Forget this network*.

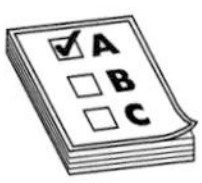

EXAM TIP You can use the Settings app to turn off Wi-Fi or to go into Airplane Mode to stop the device from sending any signals out.

Data

Many mobile devices can use the cellular data services discussed in Chapter 22 to access the Internet. This way you can use your smartphone, tablet, or other mobile devices to get e-mail or browse the Web pretty much anywhere.

By default, mobile devices that use cellular networks for Internet connectivity use *data roaming*, meaning they'll jump from cell tower to cell tower and from your provider to another provider without obvious notice. This is no big deal when you travel within your own country where competing providers have inexpensive roaming agreements.

Watch out for data roaming outside your country! If you travel outside of your country, your mobile device will also happily and seamlessly connect via some other available cell provider. This can lead to some shockingly huge bills from your cell phone company when you get back from that cruise or out-of-country trip. If you're going outside your cell provider's coverage area, get a plan that specifies that you're traveling. It'll still be more expensive than your regular plan, but not nearly as crazy as an accidental roaming charge.

If you don't need to connect when out of country, turn data roaming off. You'll find the feature in the Settings app, as you might expect. You can also turn off cellular data entirely or only turn off cellular services selectively if your device can do more than one type. (You would want to turn off cellular data, for example, if you don't have an unlimited data plan and are getting near your limits.)

E-mail

Setting up e-mail offers many levels of complexity with mobile devices, primarily because of the many different types of e-mail servers out there. Every mobile device comes with an e-mail service set up specifically from the mobile OS developer as a starter. Plus you can configure devices to send and receive standard e-mail as well.

iOS, Android, and Windows Phone devices offer e-mail services from Apple, Google, and Microsoft, respectively. iOS devices integrate perfectly with iCloud, Apple's one-stop shop for e-mail, messaging, and online storage. Android devices assume a Gmail account, so have a Google/Inbox option front and center (see below). Windows devices integrate Outlook.com e-mail options. The 902 exam describes these options with a whale of a phrase: *integrated commercial provider email [sic] configuration*. Yeah.

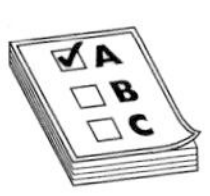

EXAM TIP The 902 exam adds Yahoo! e-mail to the list of integrated commercial providers on mobile devices. Yahoo! does great e-mail, granted, but hasn't been a default option on mobile devices since the Blackberry (a device that died at the hands of the smartphones). Just be aware that the exam might throw Yahoo! into the mix (and not include the exclamation point).

Aside from the integrated e-mail options, mobile devices enable you to set up standard corporate and ISP e-mail configurations as well. The process is similar to that of setting up e-mail accounts that you learned about in Chapter 23. Apple devices go through the Settings app, then the Mail, Contacts, Calendars option (see Figure 25-37). Tap the Add Account option to bring up the default e-mail options (see Figure 25-38). If you want to connect to a Microsoft Exchange Server–based e-mail account, tap the appropriate option here and type in your e-mail address, domain, user name, password, and description.

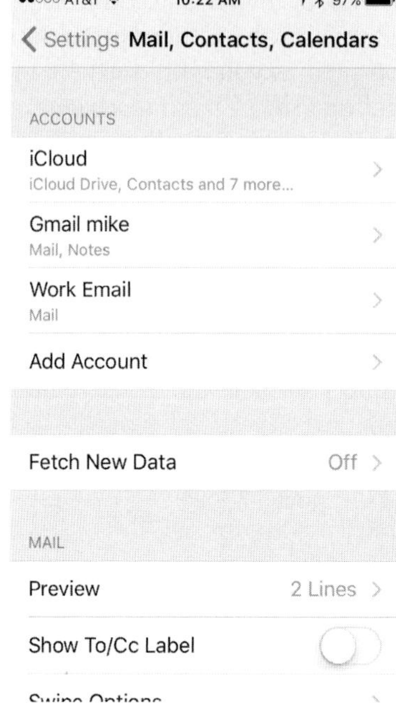

Figure 25-37 Mail, Contacts, Calendars screen on iPhone

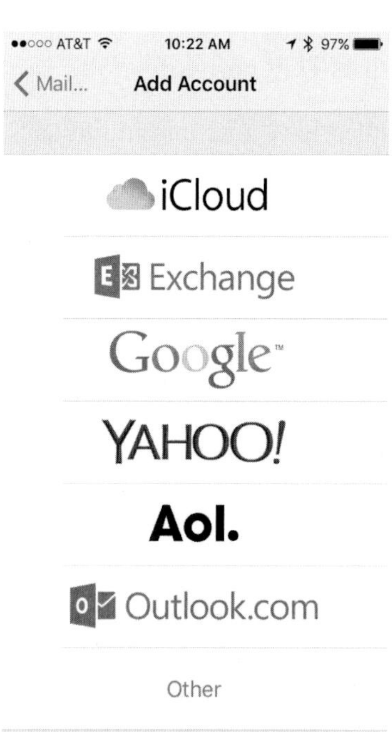

Figure 25-38 Default e-mail types on iPhone

If you want a POP3 or IMAP4 account set up, that's not one of Apple's default options, so you need to click the Other option on the initial Add Account screen. Eventually you'll get prompted as you would expect to choose POP3 or IMAP and type in addresses for the sending (SMTP) and receiving servers.

Android-based devices assume you'll have a Gmail account as your primary account, so that option is offered as a distinctive icon on the home screen (see Figure 25-39). You'll also have an e-mail icon for setting up Exchange, POP3, or IMAP4 accounts. You configure them the same way as you would a desktop e-mail application, including putting in the port number and security type, such as SSL or TLS (see Figure 25-40).

The 902 exam will hit you pretty hard on e-mail settings, specifically on TCP port numbers for the various e-mail protocols. We've covered these in earlier chapters, but here's a quick cheat sheet and a few alternative numbers for real-world applications.

- POP3 uses TCP port 110
- IMAP4 uses TCP port 123
- SMTP uses TCP port 25

Many servers block these default ports; plus, when you move to more secure versions of the protocols, you need to use other port numbers. No clue whether CompTIA will quiz on the secure ports for POP3, IMAP4, and SMTP, but here they are.

- Secure POP3 uses TCP port 995
- Secure IMAP4 uses TCP port 993
- Secure SMTP uses TCP port 465 or 587

Finally, you may also have to configure other settings, such as *Secure/Multipurpose Internet Mail Extensions (S/MIME)*, which are used to configure digital signature settings for e-mail, and contacts from the corporate address book, depending on how the corporate e-mail server is set up.

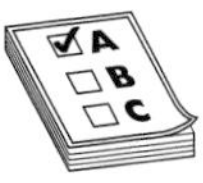

EXAM TIP Be familiar with integrated commercial provider e-mail configuration settings for Google's Inbox (Inbox by Gmail), Yahoo!, Outlook.com, and iCloud. Know the corporate and ISP e-mail configuration settings for POP3, IMAP4, port and SSL settings, Exchange, and S/MIME.

Synchronization

From the first day mobile devices came into existence there was a problem: their data. People don't want their contacts on their mobile devices to be different than the contacts on their desktop—or online contacts. People don't want to edit e-mail on their mobile device and then have to go online to make the same changes. People only want one calendar. If you have a mobile device, you're going to want a method for all these different sets of data to synchronize so you only have one set of contacts, one e-mail inbox, one calendar, and so forth.

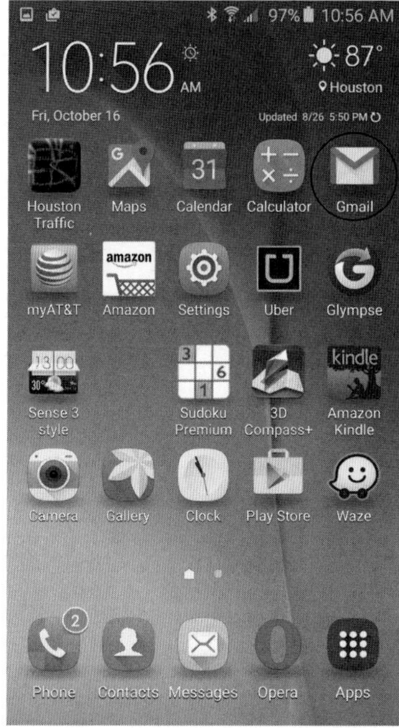

Figure 25-39 Gmail app

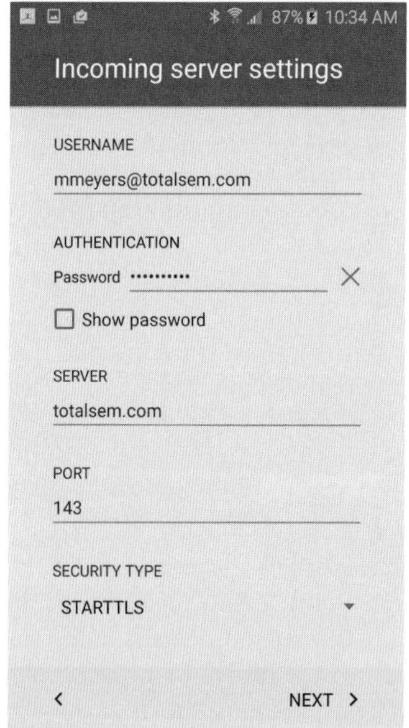

Figure 25-40 Setting up a secure IMAP account

Smartphones and tablets can *synchronize*, or *sync*, with local machines or over the Internet with cloud-based servers to keep files and data up-to-date. These files and data include personal documents, Internet bookmarks, calendar appointments, social media data, eBooks, and even location data. Older devices, such as BlackBerrys and Palm Pilots, had a specialized sync program that installed onto your PC that you could use to sync contacts, calendars, and so on. Today's devices either use a dedicated program or sync through the cloud.

Various mobile devices sync differently, depending upon the device vendor and software required. iOS devices use Apple iTunes software to play media and purchase from the iTunes Store, and also to sync iPhones, iPads, and iPods. Android and Windows devices also have an app store, similar to the iTunes Store, that can sync certain configuration settings, apps, software upgrades, and so on. In some cases, these other mobile devices—Android devices, for example—don't necessarily require any particular app to synchronize with, and may use individual apps to synchronize their parts of the device. For example, an e-mail app may be perfectly capable of synchronizing its data to include e-mail and contacts. Like the later versions of iOS, most of these other devices are capable of syncing over the air using Wi-Fi or cellular technologies.

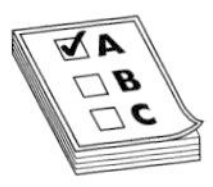

EXAM TIP Synchronization enables mobile devices to keep up-to-date with a lot of essential information. You should know the types of data typically synced, including contacts, programs (apps), e-mail, pictures, music, videos, calendar information, bookmarks, documents, location data, social media data, and e-books. It's a lot. You can do this!

Exchange ActiveSync

Exchange ActiveSync (EAS) is a Microsoft protocol used to synchronize Microsoft Exchange e-mail, contacts, and calendars that has become widely used across a range of mobile OS platforms and hardware vendors, including Apple and Android devices. It was originally developed as a synchronization protocol for Microsoft Exchange corporate users, but has evolved over time to include more device control and management features. EAS not only has the capability to set up and configure network connectivity and secure e-mail options for clients that connect to Microsoft Exchange corporate servers, but also has the capability to control the much wider range of functions. Some of these functions include the capability to set password policies, remotely wipe or lock a mobile device, and control some device settings.

Synchronization Methods

In the old days, mobile devices were synchronized to a desktop, using a specific type of synchronization software provided with the device. Also, the type of data to be synced was typically limited to contact information. Now, there are various ways you can sync a device, enabling you to sync contacts, media files, and even apps. You can also get updates and patches from the device manufacturer by syncing your device. You are now also no longer tied to just syncing to the desktop; with faster cellular and Wi-Fi networking technologies, you can sync even large amounts of data to the cloud. Each phone

vendor has its own version of cloud technologies that you can tie to your user account and use to store your personal data from your mobile device. Apple has iCloud, Microsoft has OneDrive, and Google has its own user cloud services, as do some of the individual manufacturers that make Android devices. There are also independent cloud providers that enable you to store your personal data, and even share it with others. Dropbox is a prime example of this type of provider, although there are many others. Most cloud storage services require you to set up security measures to protect your data, such as requiring a user name or password as authentication. Some cloud providers also allow you to encrypt data stored in their cloud.

Synchronizing your data to a personal computer (or laptop) has both advantages and disadvantages. The advantages of syncing to a personal computer are that you can be in full control of storing and protecting your own data, encrypted anyway you choose, and can also move it to portable storage in case you need a backup of it later. Disadvantages would be that you must be connected to that computer or within wireless range of it, if you sync wirelessly. That means that you couldn't be on vacation and simply sync your device, unless you are also lugging your big desktop with you.

Syncing to the cloud also has its advantages and disadvantages. If you have a good cellular or wireless signal, you can sync from anywhere. You do have to be careful of syncing over unsecure public wireless networks, however, since there is a possibility that your data could be intercepted and read over these unsecure networks. Another disadvantage of syncing to the cloud is that once your data is in the cloud, you no longer fully control it. You are at the mercy of the security mechanisms and privacy policies of your provider. You have to accept whatever security mechanisms, such as encryption strength (or lack thereof) they use, and you have to abide by their privacy policies, which may allow them to turn your data over to third parties, such as other companies for marketing, or even law enforcement. Additionally, some cloud providers may limit the type and amount of data you are allowed to store in their cloud. There may be particular types of media files, for example, with certain size limits that you may not be allowed to store, or certain types of software. These restrictions are typically in place to prevent software and media (for example, video and music) piracy.

These are all considerations you'll have to think carefully about when choosing whether to sync to the desktop, the cloud, or both.

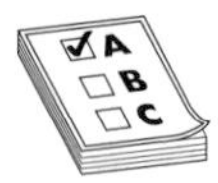

EXAM TIP The 902 objectives add a curious phrase in the discussion of synchronization, "mutual authentication for multiple services." This means a little or a lot and it's hard to tell precisely what CompTIA wants here. Certainly, when you log into your iOS device, you effectively authenticate with iCloud, iTunes, and iApple (kidding on that one). That's a lot of services. And, by using an Apple device with a specific hardware ID, the Apple services know precisely your device and user ID as well. That's mutual authentication of a sort.

In a completely different way, though, mutual authentication can deal with mobile payment information, authenticating a device with specific credit card data. This doesn't seem relevant to synchronization, but we don't know the direction CompTIA is taking this specific phrase. Be aware of both concepts for the 902 exam.

Synchronization Issues

The most common synchronization issue is incomplete sync of data due to connectivity issues, device issues, or even remote infrastructure issues. Sometimes synchronization issues can cause an incomplete downloading of e-mail or even duplicate e-mail—for example, as the device may retry the synchronization process over and over if it can't get a good connection, continually downloading the same e-mail messages. A device may attempt to sync to download an OS patch or update and may fail. The most likely culprit is connectivity issues with Wi-Fi or cellular connections, and the problem can usually be resolved by moving the device to an area with a stronger signal. This doesn't prevent upstream connectivity issues, which may also have to be examined.

In some cases, there may be other issues that prevent synchronization. These can be any of a wide range of problems, including authentication issues, OS version issues, or incorrect configuration settings. If a device won't sync even after getting it to a stronger, more stable connection, these are some of the things you should examine. Another problem may be the remote end of the connection. This may be the enterprise e-mail server, or even the entry point into the enterprise network. Failure to properly authenticate or meet the requirements of the entry device may prevent a device from synchronizing.

One other issue you may want to examine when you have synchronization issues is that in some cases synchronization can occur from multiple sources. A device can synchronize from an enterprise app store, for example, as well as the vendor app store; personal e-mail services, such as Gmail and Yahoo! Mail; and even from third-party providers of "whatever-as-a-service" and cloud storage. So in troubleshooting synchronization issues, you may have to take into account that different providers may have different configuration settings (to include encryption network settings), and in turn these configuration settings could conflict. In the enterprise environment, it's probably incumbent upon the mobile device management team to put together a management and technical strategy that will ensure minimal conflict between different synchronization sources.

iTunes and iCloud

Apple iPhones and iPads sync through Apple iTunes installed on a Mac or a PC. Everything, such as music, videos, contacts, pictures, e-mail, programs, and so on, can be stored locally. You can choose to back up all the apps on your iPhone or iPad to iTunes as well. This single source for backup makes it easy to recover from something catastrophic happening to your Apple device. If you replace an Apple device, for example, you can simply sync that new device and all your files, contact information, and apps copy to the new device.

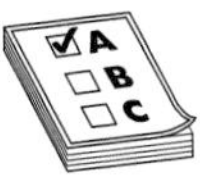

EXAM TIP Apple iTunes will run on just about any Mac OS X or Windows machine. To install the latest iTunes for Windows (64-bit), Apple specifies a Windows 7 (64-bit) or later PC with a 1-GHz Intel or AMD CPU with support for SSE2 and 512-MB RAM. You can play music with a 1-GHz CPU and a 16-bit sound card, for example, but to scale up to play more complex media, such as HD video, you need a 2.4-GHz CPU with two or more cores. For a Mac, the basic software requirements are OS X version 10.7.5 or later. For more information, visit

www.apple.com/support/itunes/getstarted/

With iCloud, you can have all your iPhone or iPad data backed up online and thus accessible from anywhere. This includes any media purchased through iTunes and calendars, contacts, reminders, and so forth.

Android and Gmail

Android-based mobile devices don't have a central desktop application similar to iTunes for Apple devices. Rather, they sync over the Internet—but only some data. Contacts, calendars, and e-mail (through Gmail) are all that sync by default. For every other type of data or media, you treat the Android device like a fat thumb drive—you drag and drop files into the appropriate folder on the smartphone or tablet.

Mobile Device Communication and Ports

Mobile devices are, well, mobile and need as many possible ways to interconnect with the outside world as possible. This section looks at the many technologies and connections mobile device use to get the data flowing to the Internet and other devices.

NFC

Near Field Communication (NFC) uses chips embedded in mobile devices that create electromagnetic fields when these devices are close to each other. The typical range for NFC communications is anywhere from a very few centimeters to only a few inches. The devices must be very close to or touching each other, and can be used for data exchange for information such as contact information, small files, and even payment transactions through stored credit cards using systems like Apple Pay and Android Pay. This technology is seeing widespread adoption in newer mobile devices, as well as the infrastructures and applications that support them.

Micro-USB/Mini-USB

Unless your devices are manufactured by Apple, it's very likely they use either a micro- or mini-USB port to charge, connect to laptops and PCs, and sync between those devices. *Micro-USB* and *mini-USB* connectors, as well as much faster USB 3.0 connectors, are standard on most Android devices, as well as Windows devices. That's not to say that each of these doesn't have their own proprietary connectors as well, since Google and Microsoft provide the OS to multiple device manufacturers, some manufacturers do maintain a proprietary connector that you can only get from them. However, we're seeing less and less of this trend, as most device manufacturers are jumping on the micro- and mini-USB bandwagon. This makes it easier to find cables and connectors that will fit almost any mobile device.

Lightning Connector

With the iPhone 5, Apple introduced its current proprietary connector, known as the *Lightning* connector. It replaced the older 30-pin connectors that Apple used on previous iPhones and iPads. The Lightning connector is an 8-pin connector (see Figure 25-41), and can be inserted without regard to proper orientation; in other words, it's not "keyed" to insert a specific way (such as right-side up or upside down, as traditional USB connectors are)

into the device. The proprietary nature of the Lightning cable means it's more expensive than a normal USB cable. It is licensed on a limited basis to other manufacturers, but to prevent widespread production of fake Lightning connectors by non-licensed manufactures, it contains a small chip that identifies it as a true Lightning connector, and cables without that chip typically won't work or will only have limited use.

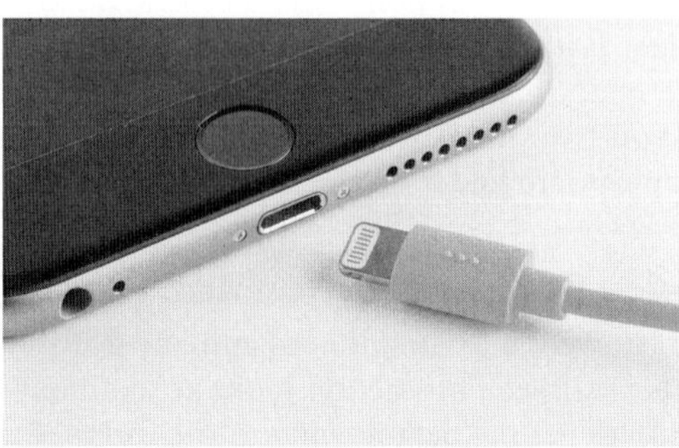

Figure 25-41 Lightning connector

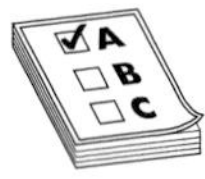

EXAM TIP The Apple Lightning standard is the poster child for *proprietary vendor-specific ports and connectors*. Only iOS devices use Lightning for communication and power. Android and Windows Phone devices use industry-standard, vendor-neutral ports and connectors.

USB Type-C

USB Type-C (see Figure 25-42) is the newest iteration of USB connectors, and is not yet commonly found on too many mobile devices, but you can expect to see it more frequently in the near future. In fact, Apple has hinted strongly that they are going to use this type of connector in the future to replace the Lightning connector as the technology matures. Like the Lightning connector, the USB Type-C connector is not keyed, allowing it to be inserted right-side up or upside down. It supports USB 3.1 technology up to 10 Gbps, making it very fast for data transfers. With any luck, this will be the standardized connector for all future mobile devices, making it easier to buy cables to fit any device, without the worry of proprietary standards.

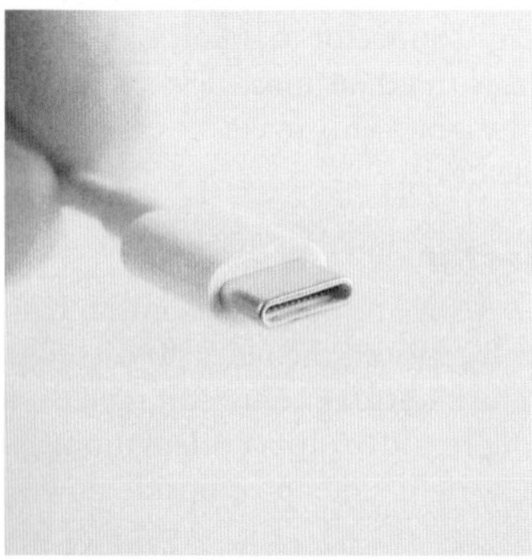

Figure 25-42 USB Type-C connector

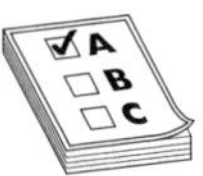

EXAM TIP You will likely see micro- and mini-USB, USB Type-C, and Lightning mobile device connection types on the exams. Know their characteristics and differences.

Bluetooth

Pairing a Bluetooth device with a mobile device follows a similar, simple pattern through the Settings icon. You turn on Bluetooth on the smartphone or tablet, then power on the Bluetooth device. Return to the mobile device to select to pair with the Bluetooth device, and then enter the appropriate personal identification number (PIN) code. For a keyboard, for example, the smartphone or tablet will display a set of characters for you to type on the keyboard (see Figure 25-43). Once you type in the PIN code, the devices connect.

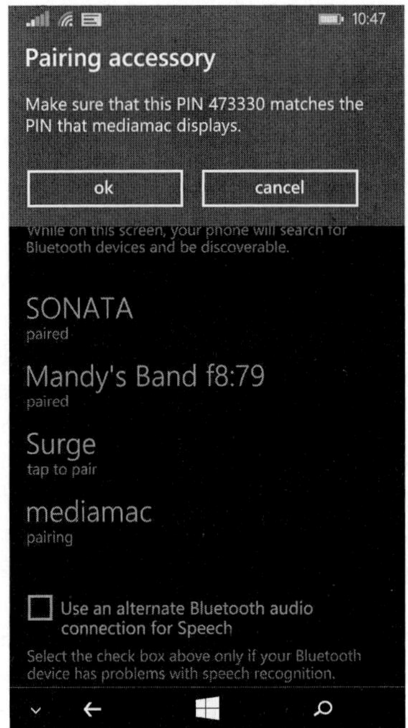

Figure 25-43 Prompting for PIN

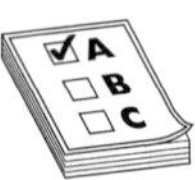

EXAM TIP Not all Bluetooth pairings require a PIN code, but there's always some kind of pairing action to do on both devices to make a pairing.

Always test the connectivity between a mobile device and a newly added Bluetooth accessory. If you've added a keyboard, for example, open up a note-taking app and start typing to make sure it works.

NOTE Most mobile devices have Bluetooth discovery disabled by default to conserve battery life. Actively seeking pairing uses electricity, as does completed pairing, so use Bluetooth only when you need to use it and be prepared for the battery hit.

Infrared

Now largely replaced by other, faster technologies, such as Bluetooth and 802.11 wireless, infrared (IR) was previously used between mobile devices, such as laptops and some older PDAs, to transfer data between them. Infrared was used to create the first real personal area networks (PANs). Infrared uses the wireless Infrared Data Association (IrDA) standard, and at one time was widely used to connect devices such as wireless remotes, printers, wireless mice, digitizers, and other serial devices. Infrared requires *line of sight*, meaning that devices have to be directly facing each other, requires very short distances (sometimes inches) between devices, and has very slow data rates.

Hotspots and Tethering

A *mobile hotspot* is typically a small device that has access to cellular technologies such as 3G, 4G, and 4G LTE, and provides access to these networks for Wi-Fi devices. Most of these devices can be purchased from wireless providers such as Verizon, Sprint, AT&T, T-Mobile, or other carriers, and are usually specific to their type of broadband network. These devices can provide wireless access for up to five to ten devices at a time. They're basically wireless routers that route traffic between Wi-Fi devices and broadband technologies. Many of these devices can be purchased as dedicated hotspots. Depending upon the carrier, many cellular phones, as well as tablets, can act as portable hotspots. When used in this manner, it's called *tethering* to the cell phone.

The popular term used for these portable hotspots, as well as devices like cellular phones that also provide hotspot service, is *MiFi*, which stands for My Wi-Fi. Novatel Wireless actually owns the trademark to this name in the United States, but it has become common to refer to most of these devices as MiFi-capable. While some devices configured as hotspots can use your existing data plan with your carrier, some carriers separate out and limit the amount of data that can be used for tethering.

To configure a device as a hotspot, you typically enable its Wi-Fi connection as sort of a router, between the cellular network and a traditional 802.11-based wireless network. Then any devices that you wish to tether to the hotspot simply see the device as a wireless router. You can also configure a password so that not just anyone can connect to the hotspot. Any device that needs to connect to the hotspot must have the password manually entered into it when configuring its Wi-Fi connection to the device providing the hotspot connectivity. Figure 25-44 shows a screenshot of an Android phone acting as a portable hotspot.

Accessories

Mobile device accessories come in a wide variety of types, packing a huge range of features. Some of the most common accessories that people want for their mobile device, particularly smartphones and tablets, include devices that wirelessly connect to them,

typically using Bluetooth technologies. It's not unusual to find Bluetooth *headsets* and high-quality *external speakers* for users to listen to music and chat with friends. *Gamepads*, including controllers and other accessories that plug into tablets via a USB port or connect via Bluetooth, are also common, effectively turning tablets into full-scale gaming platforms. Additionally, there are also specialized tablets that are outfitted with gaming controllers built in and used specifically as gaming platforms. The NVIDIA SHIELD is one such example of a specialized Android device used as a gaming platform, and it can perform the same functions as other Android tablets. One feature that Android and some Microsoft mobile devices offer is the ability to use removable external storage, such as *mini-* or *micro-USB memory cards*, effectively upgrading the storage capabilities of the device. This is something that Apple hasn't quite embraced yet with its devices.

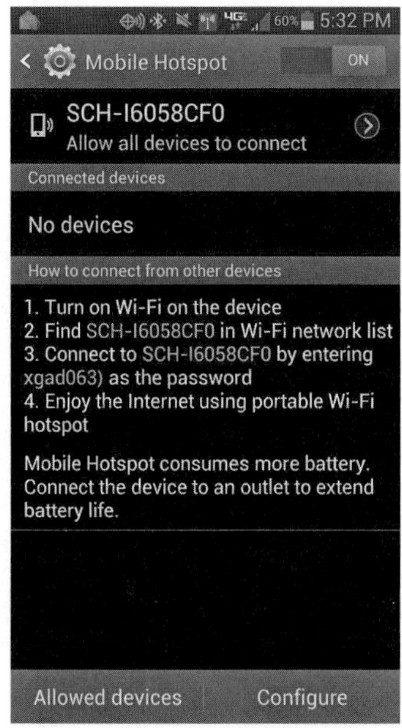

Figure 25-44 An Android phone acting as a portable hotspot

In addition to the accessories previously mentioned, there are also accessories that no mobile device user should be without, including *extra battery packs* (if your mobile device supports battery removal and replacement, which many mobile devices don't) or a *battery charger*. To recharge mobile devices, battery chargers either plug into a wall outlet and the mobile device, or plug into a computer and the mobile device. Some battery chargers don't require connection to the device at all; they simply require you to lay the device on top of a special pad, from which power is transferred to the device without the need for cables.

Depending upon the type of mobile device in use, there are also specialized accessories, including *docking stations* (typically for tablets) produced by the device manufacturer, and even *credit card readers*, allowing small businesses to take credit card payments from their mobile device. It's not unusual to see a business have a portable credit card reader plugged into the headphone port on an iPhone, for example.

One other important accessory to have for the mobile device user is a cover for the device. These include designer covers with any imaginable designer picture on them that you could think of, as well as hardened covers designed to withstand the impact of dropping a mobile device on the floor, keeping it from breaking into a million pieces. There also screen protectors that range from flimsy plastic all the way to hardened glass that can protect a mobile device screen from scratches and impact. Some of these cases are made of plastic, others of leather or rubber. Some of these cases are even waterproof, allowing the more adventurous folks to take their phones with them while they are diving in oceans or swimming pools.

We've covered only a few of the hundreds of accessories that are available out there for mobile devices. Many accessories also come with apps that help control them or get the most out of the accessory.

Chapter Review

Questions

1. Which of the following is used in mobile devices to convert analog video and sound to digital video and sound?
   - **A.** Calibrator
   - **B.** SDK
   - **C.** Virtual assistant
   - **D.** Digitizer
2. Which type of display responds to the difference in electrical potential between you and the screen?
   - **A.** Capacitive
   - **B.** LCD
   - **C.** IPS
   - **D.** Resistive
3. Which mobile device screen technology uses no backlight?
   - **A.** BYOD
   - **B.** LCD
   - **C.** LED
   - **D.** OLED
4. What can a government use to determine your location at a specific time as long as you're using your mobile device?
   - **A.** Multifactor authentication
   - **B.** Geotracking

C. Google Earth
D. Authenticator applications

5. What are the steps involved in pairing a Bluetooth keyboard with a tablet?
   A. Enable Bluetooth on the tablet; turn on the Bluetooth device; find the device with the tablet; enter a PIN code or other pairing sequence.
   B. Turn on the Bluetooth device; find the device with the tablet; enter a PIN code or other pairing sequence.
   C. Search for a Bluetooth device from the tablet; select **pair** from the options to enable the device.
   D. Enable Bluetooth on the tablet; turn on the Bluetooth device; find the device with the tablet; select **pair** from the options to enable the device.
6. Which of the following is a 15-digit number used to uniquely identify a mobile device that connects to a cellular network?
   A. IMEI
   B. GSM
   C. ICCID
   D. IMSI
7. A client calls and is upset that he's misplaced his iPad. The mobile device has literally thousands of client records, including business addresses, e-mail addresses, phone numbers, and, in some cases, credit card information. What should he do first?
   A. There's nothing he can do.
   B. He should call his ISP and have them track his iPad.
   C. He should access his iCloud account and remotely wipe his iPad to erase all personal data.
   D. He should purchase another iPad and sync with his iTunes account. This automatically erases the information on the old tablet.
8. Leonard just purchased a very expensive comic book and paid for it using the stored credit card information on his smartphone. What technology did he use to make the transaction?
   A. Swipe lock
   B. Wi-Fi calling
   C. NFC
   D. BitLocker To Go

9. What information do you need to connect an Android-based tablet to an IMAP account?
   A. POP3 server DNS name
   B. User name and password
   C. User name, password, sending and receiving server addresses
   D. Exchange server name, user name, and password
10. Which mobile OS enables developers to customize the user experience without restrictions?
   A. Android
   B. Blackberry
   C. iOS
   D. Windows Phone

Answers

1. **D.** Digitizers are used in mobile devices to convert analog video and sound to digital video and sound, or to interpret analog signals associated with touch movement on a screen into digital equivalents.
2. **A.** A capacitive touchscreen display responds to the difference in electrical potential between you and the screen.
3. **D.** OLED technology does not use a backlight.
4. **B.** Geotracking can locate you and your GPS-equipped mobile device.
5. **A.** To pair a Bluetooth keyboard with a tablet, enable Bluetooth on the tablet, turn on the Bluetooth device, find the Bluetooth device in the tablet's settings screen, then enter a PIN code or finalize the pairing.
6. **A.** The International Mobile Equipment Identity (IMEI) number is a 15-digit number used to uniquely identify a mobile device, typically a smartphone or other device that connects to a cellular network.
7. **C.** To protect his data, the client should log in to his iCloud account and remotely wipe the iPad and erase all personal data.
8. **C.** Leonard likely purchased his comic book using Near Field Communication (NFC) technology, which can be used for payment transactions through stored credit card information in mobile applications.
9. **C.** To connect an Android-based tablet to an IMAP account, you'll need a user name and password and the sending and receiving server addresses.
10. **A.** Google Android is open source, enabling developers to create custom versions for their devices.

CHAPTER 26

Care and Feeding of Mobile Devices

In this chapter, you will learn how to

- Troubleshoot common mobile device issues
- Explain basic mobile device security
- Describe typical mobile security troubleshooting issues
- Describe typical mobile application troubleshooting issues

By their very nature, mobile devices require troubleshooting and security practices that differ a lot from desktop computers and somewhat from other portable devices. This chapter explores general troubleshooting first, then covers security features and capabilities of devices common in the mobile market. The chapter finishes by jumping into the details of two different troubleshooting aspects: security troubleshooting and application troubleshooting. CompTIA loves those scenario questions, so get ready for some real-world issues when it comes to security and application troubleshooting.

901/902

Troubleshooting Mobile Device Issues

The CompTIA A+ exam objectives divide mobile device problems into two groups: hardware and OS issues, and security and application issues. In this section we're going to cover the hardware and OS issues. These common problems happen across all varieties, types, and manufacturers of mobile devices. There are also issues that may affect network connectivity.

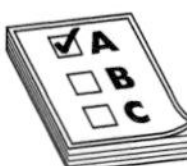

EXAM TIP Traditionally, there are rarely any field technician–serviceable components on most mobile devices, so typically, in the event of a hardware problem, the device should be taken to a service center for repair. Companies like iFixit (www.ifixit.com) are making some components field replaceable, but usually only for skilled techs.

Touchscreen Is Nonresponsive

A nonresponsive touchscreen can be caused by several things. The first and simplest issue to resolve is a dirty screen. Sometimes simply wiping the touchscreen down and getting rid of fingerprints, dust, dirt, and other foreign objects may fix a responsiveness problem (see Figure 26-1).

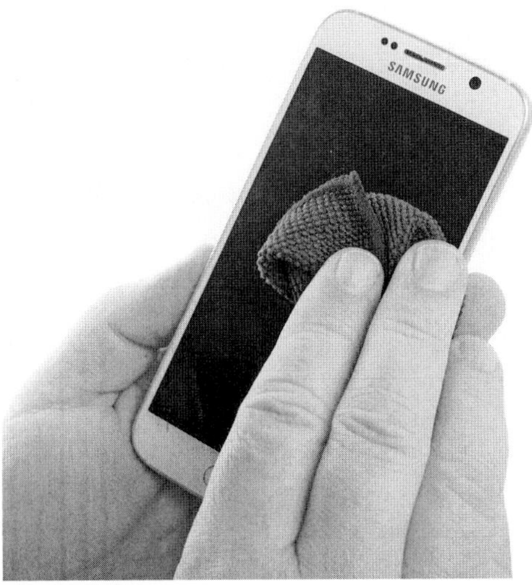

Figure 26-1 Cleaning a smartphone

Dropping or getting a mobile device wet can cause issues with the touchscreen. Even if the glass doesn't break, dropping a device can break internal connections. Moisture can cause internal shorts. Avoid both problem areas if possible.

There's also the possibility that touchscreen responsiveness could be affected by apps or the device's configuration settings. These might manifest in odd ways. You might touch a control or option, for example, and something completely unexpected occurs. The 902 exam calls these events "inaccurate touch screen responses," but the rest of us call them, "really?" These issues are typically easy to fix, because they may involve reconfiguring an app, removing it and reinstalling it, or reconfiguring the display settings on the device itself.

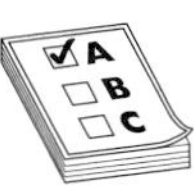

EXAM TIP App not working or experiencing battery draining *high resource utilization*? Try the *uninstall/reinstall apps* process. App developers love you, they really do, and they want you to love their programs. Sometimes the best option with an app that doesn't function the way you think it should is to ditch it and reinstall a more recent version. The Apple Store does a good job notifying you about new versions. When you go Android or Windows Phone, the app landscape is a bit more fluid.

App Not Loading

A mobile device app may not load properly or install correctly for several reasons. First, the app may not be intended for the mobile device, including the operating system version or flavor currently running. With Android devices, for example, there is a possibility that the version of the Android OS on the device itself is not compatible with the app. This is because different manufacturers can tweak the OS to suit their own needs, which may cause compatibility issues with other vendors' apps.

Another reason an app may not load is that the device may not meet the hardware requirements of the app, such as amount of available RAM, storage space, and processor type. It's always a good idea to review an app's requirements before installing it.

Slow Performance

Mobile devices can suffer from performance issues just as regular desktop computers and laptops can, and often for the same reasons. Performance issues can be caused by storage space being almost filled up on a mobile device, making it unable to save data or install apps efficiently. Additionally, mobile devices can suffer from having too many apps running at the same time, eating up RAM. Usually, the mobile device's OS has configuration settings that enable you to stop apps or view their resource usage, including memory and storage space. If storage space is an issue, you may have to uninstall some apps, or reinstall them so that they are stored on removable storage devices, such as micro- or mini-USB memory cards.

One of the first troubleshooting steps you can take in resolving slow-performance issues is to perform a hard reboot of the device, which clears RAM of all running apps, and maybe even apps that could be hanging up and not running properly. As far as troubleshooting tools go, there are plenty of apps that measure the device's performance, telling you how much RAM, storage space, CPU time, and so forth, are being used. Sometimes those apps can help point the way to what's causing the performance problems. If, in the end, you determine that a hardware issue is causing performance problems, you should take the device to an authorized repair facility.

E-mail Issues

Basically, we live in a world where e-mail is easily divided into two different types: Web-based e-mail like Google Gmail and Yahoo! Mail that uses a Web browser to access your mail, and traditional e-mail where you use a dedicated client like Microsoft Outlook or Mozilla Thunderbird to get your e-mail. In either case, issues may arise. Thankfully, we can deal with most e-mail issues by looking in just a few places.

The Best App

With mobile e-mail, almost all Web mail providers have a specialized app just for their e-mail. If you want to access Gmail, download the Gmail app. If you want to connect to a Microsoft Exchange server, you download a copy of Outlook for your mobile device. Make sure you have the correct app for your e-mail.

User Name/Password

Whatever e-mail app your mobile device uses, there will be a place to enter your e-mail account's user name and password. On personal accounts, a common scenario after getting a new phone is to enter your password at the e-mail app's prompting, only to discover you've forgotten the password! This typically requires going through the process of resetting your password.

Server Settings

If you're configuring a traditional SMTP/IMAP/POP3 client, at some point you're going to need to enter the name for your SMTP server and your IMAP/POP3 server. Figure 26-2 shows the e-mail server settings for Apple's iOS e-mail app.

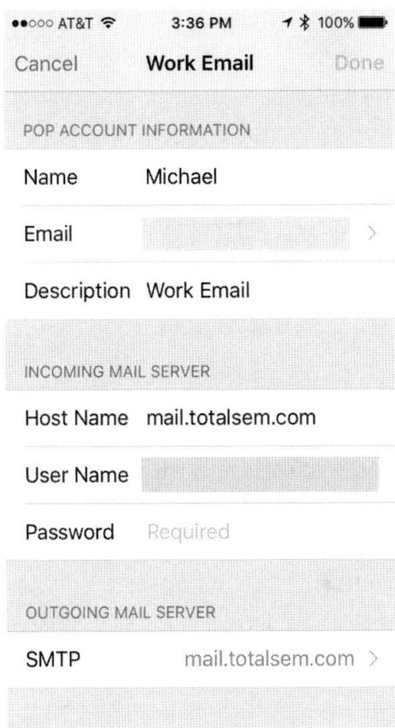

Figure 26-2 E-mail server settings

Encryption Problems

Using methods to secure e-mail messages from anyone but the intended recipient generally fall well outside the accepted parameters of the CompTIA A+ certification. The 902 exam has one line on troubleshooting mobile devices that reads, "unable to decrypt e-mail." To go into any detail on these methods would take a lot of pages and provide you with a ton of information on a topic you won't truly see until you take the CompTIA Security+ exam. So here's the issue in a very tight nutshell.

For an e-mail message to be secure, it must be *encrypted*—scrambled according to some kind of standard like Pretty Good Privacy (PGP). For the recipient to read the e-mail message, he or she needs to have software that can unscramble or *decrypt* the message. To ensure the sender and recipient only can access the contents of the e-mail message, both people need specific keys that enable encryption and decryption.

In practice, if you receive a message and you are unable to decrypt the e-mail, you need to contact the sender to set up your mail client and exchange keys.

If you find the idea of securing e-mail on your computers interesting, the PGP Corporation has a great intro Web site here: http://www.pgpi.org/doc/pgpintro/

Battery Life

Mobile devices run on batteries and batteries eventually run out of power. These two simple facts don't adequately address the issues that battery life can cause, and the issues that can cause problems with battery life itself. Mobile devices are rated differently in terms of how long the battery should power a device during normal use, how long the device can go between battery charges, and the levels of power that both the battery provides and requires in order to charge.

Most modern mobile devices use Lithium-Ion (Li-Ion) batteries. Over the years, as device features have increased, displays have gotten bigger, mobile CPUs have gotten faster, and apps have become more graphics intensive, battery power has become a premium for mobile devices. Batteries have not necessarily kept pace with the other rapidly evolving hardware and features on mobile devices, however. While marketing ads proclaim extended battery life as a feature of the latest and greatest models, newer, faster hardware and features in proportion seem to neutralize any benefits of that extended battery life.

Several factors can affect battery life. One of the main factors is network usage. Any time the device is connected to a network, such as a wireless network or even the cellular one, the device is constantly transmitting and receiving data, sometimes in the form of simple management messages that are sent back and forth to the network entry point device. Even when there is no real data being transmitted or received over the network, these management messages require power from the device, and they can, over time, significantly reduce the battery charge. Often, when traveling, a device such as a smartphone or tablet will constantly roam or try to pick up the strongest cellular or wireless signal it can find, and this constant search for stronger signals can significantly drain battery power. This unintended power drain can be controlled with most smart devices, however, through configuration changes that limit device roaming or searching for new wireless networks.

Another significant cause of battery charge reduction is the constant use of GPS or location services. When location services are turned on, the device is constantly receiving GPS data in order to fix its location. This could be for apps that require location data in the background, or for active apps, such as mapping software, that use the GPS receiver. In any event, the user will notice significant reduction in battery charge, and over the life of the device this will reduce the life of the battery as well. The simple solution to this is to be judicious with networking location services. When they are not required, they should be turned off. Another tip is to review configuration settings for apps that use location services and disable the ones that don't need to have immediate location data. In the event that you may actually use an app that requires location data, you can always turn the setting back on and let the app get a location fix. Some examples of apps

that require location data include those used to find restaurants and movie theaters, for example, as well as specialized apps, such as geocaching, mapping, and navigation apps.

Another factor that affects battery life is screen display and brightness. A screen that is configured to constantly show the brightest level will significantly reduce the battery life. Users often mistakenly adjust the screen brightness to be constantly at the highest level, thinking that they will see it better in bright sunlight or in darkened indoor areas, when often this isn't the case. The display controls on a mobile device should typically be configured to automatically adjust the screen brightness based upon factors such as device sleep or suspension, app usage, or even smartphone call use. Figure 26-3 displays the battery usage for an Android smartphone. Notice how much of the battery is being drained from the screen configuration alone!

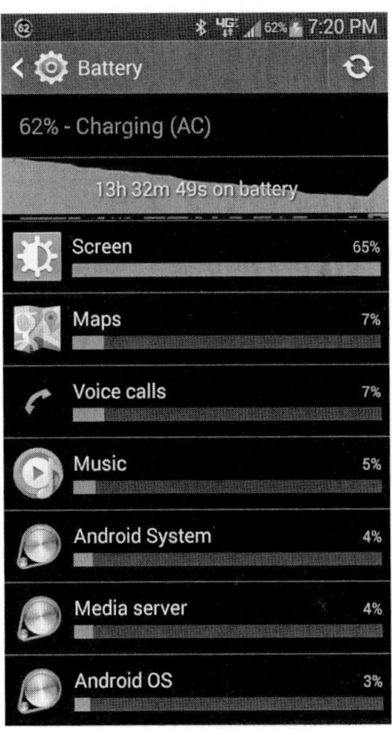

Figure 26-3 Battery usage for a smartphone

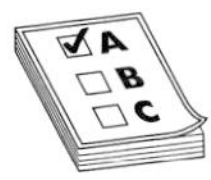

EXAM TIP Be familiar with the factors that can reduce battery power and battery life.

Swollen Battery

Batteries on mobile devices can experience a phenomenon known as swelling. When this happens, the battery casing actually swells; it heats up, often cracks, and can cause leakage of the material inside. There a few reasons why this might happen. First, overcharging the battery by leaving it on the charger for long periods of time can cause swelling. Li-Ion batteries have been known to swell due to overcharging. The device should be removed

from the charger when it's fully charged. Second, using a non-OEM charger may cause swelling, if you are using a charger that is not rated for the correct voltage and wattage the computer requires. An overheated computer or battery can also cause swelling. Finally, in rare cases, you may occasionally get a battery that is simply bad from the manufacturer.

When you encounter a swollen battery, there really is no recourse except to replace it with a known good battery, preferably an OEM battery that came from the original device vendor.

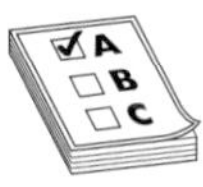

EXAM TIP You should never try to repair a battery under any circumstances, let alone when it's swollen, as it can cause bodily harm and damage to equipment.

Overheating

A mobile device that overheats is never a good thing. An obvious reason for overheating would be leaving it in contact with direct sunlight for long periods of time. That can damage the screen and other components. Our concern here primarily, however, is a device that overheats on its own. This is almost always caused by some sort of hardware issue, possibly a defective battery or other power circuit within the device. There's really not much you can do for this issue, except take it to a service center. The dangers of not addressing an overheating mobile device are, at least, an eventual device failure, resulting in lost data, and, at worst, a device that overheats so much it becomes a safety issue for the user by becoming so hot that it burns to the touch, electrically shocks the user, or causes the battery to leak or explode.

Frozen System

A mobile device that locks up or freezes can be a huge annoyance. There are several possible causes for this issue. First, an app that's not written properly, or is incompatible with the device, may cause the device to freeze because it is using too many resources, or using them incorrectly. An example of this would be an app that uses too much RAM, improperly accesses particular memory addresses, or consumes too much CPU time. A second cause could be a network connectivity issue. A device will often seem to freeze when it's desperately trying to find or maintain a network connection, and this will consume a lot of resources until it finally gives up. Finally, faulty hardware can cause a device to freeze. This can manifest itself as a frozen touchscreen, hanging apps, and generally poor performance.

The solution to a frozen system is often to reboot it, clearing its RAM and restarting it. If the device frequently freezes, especially when using a particular app, then the solution is probably to reinstall that app or find a replacement for it. Sometimes operating system issues can cause device freezes, so look for OS patches that may correct those types of issues. If the device randomly (and with increased frequency) freezes up, whenever using any type of app, then it's likely a hardware issue and the device may need to be serviced.

Cannot Broadcast to an External Monitor

Back in Chapter 25, "Understanding Mobile Devices," we saw that the vast majority of mobile devices have some form of video output that enables you to broadcast the display onto an external monitor or projector. When done correctly this is usually an almost automatic process: plug some adapter into your mobile device then plug that adapter into your external monitor's VGA or HDMI port and it just all works.

Well, that's the theory. In reality, broadcasting your mobile device's screen to an external monitor is fraught with problems. While these vary by type of device, here are a few tried and true issues to look at when your device *cannot broadcast to an external monitor*:

- Is your source correct on the external monitor? All monitors, TVs, projectors, whatever have lots of inputs. Is the external monitor pointing at the right source?
- Do you have the right adapter for your device? Apple alone has come out with five different types of videos adapters in the last few years—and don't even get me started on the many dongles for Android! Make sure you have an adapter that is known to work for your device!
- Does your dongle need its own power source? Many do not. Many do.
- For HDMI: Did the HDMI recognize your device and your external monitor? Depending on the make and model, it's common to have to reset one or both devices to give the HDMI time to see who its plugging into and set itself up.

No Sound from Speakers

Sound issues are also common in mobile devices. The most obvious, and probably most common, issue is that the volume is turned down through software configuration or an app, or the speakers are muted. This is easy to fix, but sometimes you have to go through many configuration settings for both the device and apps to figure out which one is controlling the volume at the moment or which one may actually be muting the speakers. Many mobile devices have hardware volume controls on them, so check them. If that doesn't work, then start going into the configuration settings for the device and apps. If none of these steps works, then you may have a hardware issue, in that the speakers simply may no longer be connected properly inside the device, or they may be damaged. As with all other hardware issues, you'll likely have to take the device into a service center to be fixed.

GPS and Location Services Problems

Aside from some of the issues with devices, hardware, and the operating system itself, there are occasionally issues with location services on mobile devices. Most mobile devices today are made with some type of built-in technology designed to ascertain the device's location. Some devices use built-in GPS capabilities, while others use 3G and 4G cellular technologies and Wi-Fi in place of GPS (or to supplement it) to get location data for the device. Location data is used for some of the obvious things, such as map apps, GPS coordinates, and so forth, but it's also used for some things that are not so obvious to the user.

Most apps use location data for a variety of reasons. In some cases, it's used to assist the user with whatever functions the app performs, such as locating a restaurant or a bank, for example, near the user. In other cases, location data may be used to provide services such as weather or local traffic conditions. And, for better or for worse, some apps use location data rather covertly for the purposes of marketing and reporting user data back to their respective vendors for various reasons. For the most part, this particular use is usually unknown by and undetected by the user. In any case, there are many different uses for location data, so it's considered an important feature of most modern mobile devices.

Symptoms of location issues include a map app not being able to identify the exact location of the device, or error or other messages from the device, OS, or various apps that rely on location data (see Figure 26-4).

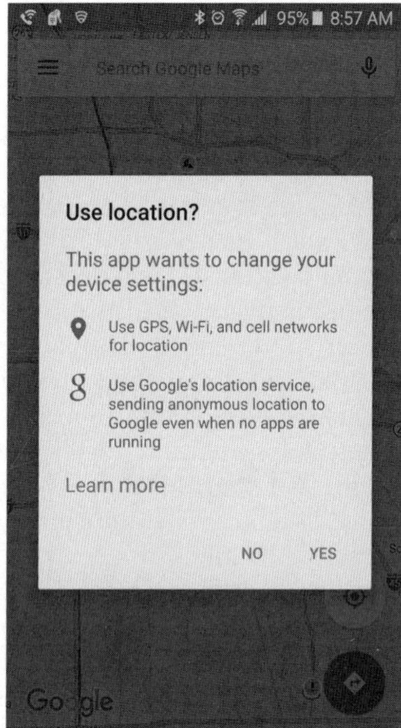

Figure 26-4
GPS prompt

Troubleshooting location problems begins with simple actions such as making sure that your GPS, cellular data, and Wi-Fi are turned on and functioning properly, as sometimes these services can be inadvertently turned off by the user or by an app, and have to be periodically reactivated. Typically, a warning message would indicate whether or not GPS or data services are turned off, so this would be an easy problem to identify and fix. Other issues may only affect specific apps because they may have been configured such that they are not allowed to access or use location services. This is usually a matter of going into the app configuration or location services settings and allowing the app to make use of those services.

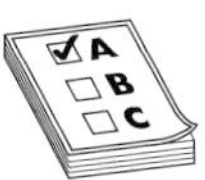

EXAM TIP If you run into GPS error questions on the exam, remember that all apps will tell you if GPS is turned off and usually ask you if want to turn on GPS. Otherwise, before digging deeper, first consider simple issues such as whether you are in a place where you can get a good GPS signal.

There also other problems that may cause location issues that are related to the operating system and the hardware in the device. Along with the OS issues discussed previously, there could be OS configuration settings that are configured incorrectly for GPS, cellular, and Wi-Fi services that may prevent location services from functioning properly. These configuration items should be checked when location service symptoms are being seen with more than one app. Hardware problems may lie in the actual GPS or network hardware with the device, and should be treated as described in the previous sections on hardware. Although laptops and other mobile devices may have removable network or GPS modules in them, most of these components are not user serviceable and have to be replaced or repaired by authorized service technicians.

System Lockout

System lockouts can occur for a couple of reasons. The first, and most common, reason is that the user forgets her PIN. With some mobile devices, the user may only get a certain amount of tries before the device locks and doesn't allow her to continue to attempt to unlock it. An additional issue would be that some devices are configured to completely erase themselves after a certain number of failed unlock attempts. This can be configured on the device itself, or centrally through the organization's *mobile device management (MDM)* software. Either way, you should probably advise the user to not exceed the maximum number of retries for unlocking the device. If it is a company-owned device, the company should probably securely store PINs for all the mobile devices it owns, in case just such an issue occurs, as well as maintain current backups of all its mobile devices. With devices owned by individual users, you have to hope that they have backed up their data as well.

If the device can be unlocked through finger swipe patterns or fingerprint authentication, then a failure of either of these two methods to unlock the device probably means that the device has lost its configuration and the user needs to be reenrolled with the authentication configuration on the device to use those methods. Typically, when these methods are used, the backup method to unlock the device is by using a PIN.

In any event, if the device is controlled through centrally managed MDM software, the organization has the ability to remotely unlock the device. If it's not centrally controlled, then the user may have to plug the device in to a computer and use an application provided by the manufacturer to access the device with a passcode. In the end, if the user can't unlock the device, the only solution may be to restore the device from a backup, if available, or completely reinstall the OS and apps from scratch. This may cause the user to lose data on the device.

Troubleshooting Steps and Tools

Because mobile devices typically aren't user or field technician serviceable, there aren't many things that can be done to fix them out in the field. The few things that can be done are fairly common to all mobile devices, and typically follow a kind of common-sense pattern of steps, much like troubleshooting steps for desktop computers. If these initial troubleshooting steps do not work, then the end solution is to take the device to an authorized service center. Some of these steps may involve data loss, if active apps and data are in memory when the steps are taken, and some steps may involve data loss simply because the device may have to be reinstalled from scratch.

In order of precedence from least damage to data and apps to the worst-case scenarios, the most common troubleshooting steps for mobile devices include the following:

1. Close running apps.
2. Force an app to stop running.
3. Adjust configurations/settings.
4. Uninstall/reinstall apps.
5. Soft reset.
6. Hard reset.
7. Restore the device from a complete backup.
8. Reset the device to factory defaults.

This is simply notional order of troubleshooting steps; the order that you take may be dictated by your organization or your repair facility. You can also use the different troubleshooting methodologies discussed elsewhere in this book. The steps you take depend upon the nature the problem in the first place, and affect which steps you may take and in which order. Additionally, different devices have different ways to perform some of these steps. For example, Android devices enable you to *force stop* an app in its configuration settings. There are also different ways to perform soft and hard resets on the different mobile devices, depending upon the manufacturer. You'll have to research these particular steps based upon the type of device you are working on. Many of them, including forcing apps to stop, reinstalling apps, and any kind of resets, will probably cause you to lose some data, which may require restoration from a backup, if a backup exists for that device.

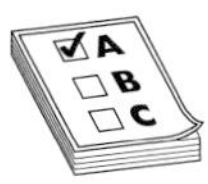

EXAM TIP What's the last resort when you have a poorly functioning or misfiring mobile device? Do a factory reset/clean install on it. Every mobile device has that doomsday option. This is also a must-do option when you move on to the next device and donate your older mobile to your charity of choice.

Securing Mobile Devices

Mobile devices require security. This applies to company-owned devices and personal ones. All need to handle damage, malware, data loss, and theft.

BYOD Versus Corporate-Owned Devices

The *Bring Your Own Device (BYOD)* war was one that was briefly fought and lost by organizations hoping to continue the long-held tradition that IT assets belonged to (and were strictly controlled by) the company, not the individual. As more and more mobile devices were brought into the infrastructure, however, IT folks realized that the genie was out of the bottle and they would never completely be able to control these new technologies. In some cases, companies may be able to enforce a policy that prohibits the use of personal devices to access corporate data and resources, particularly those in high-security environments. At the other end of the spectrum, some companies allow (and even encourage) personal devices, as it saves corporate IT dollars and can contribute to a much happier employee. Most organizations, however, probably fall into the middle of the spectrum and have a mixed environment of both corporate-owned and personally owned mobile devices. In some cases the organization may institute a cost-sharing program, subsidizing an employee's personally owned device by offering a monthly phone stipend or through discount agreements with mobile device and telecommunications vendors. Regardless of the degree of BYOD in the organization, there are challenges that must be dealt with.

One challenge is device control and how much control the corporation has versus the individual. If corporate data is processed or stored on the device, then, rightfully so, the organization should have some degree of control over the device. On the other hand, if the device also belongs to the employee, then the employee should have some control over it. Another challenge is who pays for the device and its use. If the organization allows the user to use her own device for company work, does the organization help pay for the monthly bill or compensate the user for its use? Again, this issue is probably better solved by defined formal policy and procedures. Yet another and equally important challenge in a BYOD environment is employee privacy. If policy allows the organization some degree of control over the device, what degree of privacy does the user maintain on her own device? Can the organization see private data or have the ability to remotely access or control a user's personal device and its use?

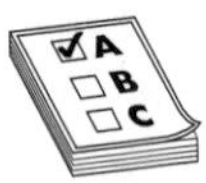

EXAM TIP The two critical issues with BYOD are personal data privacy versus protection of corporate data, and level of organizational control versus individual control.

Profile Security Requirements

A profile is a collection of configuration and security settings that an administrator has created in order to apply them to particular categories of users or devices. A profile can be created in several different ways, including through the MDM software, or in a program

such as the Apple configurator, for example. Profiles are typically text-based files, usually in an eXtensible Markup Language (XML) format, and are pushed out to the different devices that require them. Profiles should be developed based upon the needs of the organization. You can develop a profile that is device-specific, and applies to only certain platforms or operating systems, so that a particular type of device will get certain settings.

You can also develop profiles that are specific to different user categories or management groupings. For example, if you have a group of mobile sales users, you might create a profile that would contain certain settings for security, apps, network connections, and so forth. Your senior organizational executives may have a specific profile that is applied to them based upon their unique requirements. Frequently, senior managers or executives may be allowed to do more with a corporate device, in terms of what's acceptable to the organization. There also may be unique apps or connection requirements for these executives. Likewise, middle managers may require unique profiles that have configuration settings applicable to what functions they need to perform on the network using a mobile device. These managers also may have specific apps such as human resources or payroll-related apps installed on devices.

There are also group-specific profiles that may apply to external users, such as consultants or business partners, for example. These users may require limited access to organizational resources using their own mobile device, their organization's mobile devices, or even mobile devices issued from your organization. A group-specific profile applied to these external users may give them particular network configuration and security settings so that they can access a business extranet, for example, or use specific VPN settings. They may also require access to particular enterprise or business-to-business (B2B) apps hosted on your organization's servers. In any case, both device- and user-specific profiles can be very helpful in managing larger groups of users, delivering uniform security and configuration settings to their devices based upon different mission or business requirements.

Depending upon your organizational needs, you could conceivably apply several different profiles to a device at once, based upon platform, user group, and so forth. It's possible that some profile settings will conflict with those in a different profile. For example, some restrictive settings for a device profile may not be consistent with some less-restrictive ones in a group or user profile. When both are applied to the device, the different configuration settings may conflict and overwrite each other so you may want to pay special attention to profile precedence when applying them to the device. You may decide to configure settings precedence in the MDM server to resolve conflicts based upon a number of criteria, including user group membership, or security requirements, for instance.

As far as devices go, in addition to vendor- or OS platform–specific profiles, you should also develop profiles that may apply to corporate-owned versus personally owned devices. A profile applied to a device in a BYOD environment may be considerably different than one applied to an organizationally owned device. This would be based upon policy settings affecting privacy, acceptable use of the device, and so on. Figure 26-5 shows how you can conceptually apply different profiles to different device and user groups.

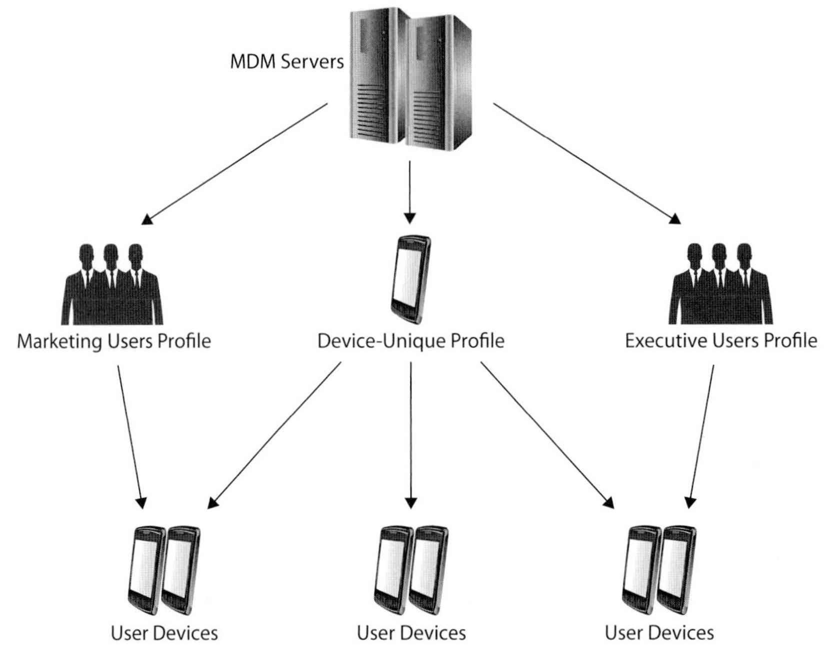

Figure 26-5 Applying profiles to different device and user groups

Preventing Physical Damage

Mobile devices cost a fair amount of money and thus aren't disposable media for most people. That means you need to take steps to prevent damage. The first step you must take is to get a *protective cover* or sleeve for the mobile device. It doesn't help the HD camcorder in your new iPad if you get a scratch across the lens! You'll get a scratched, blurry movie even though the camcorder is capable of much, much more. Apple makes very nice covers for iPhones and iPads, plus you can get many third-party covers and sleeves (see Figure 26-6).

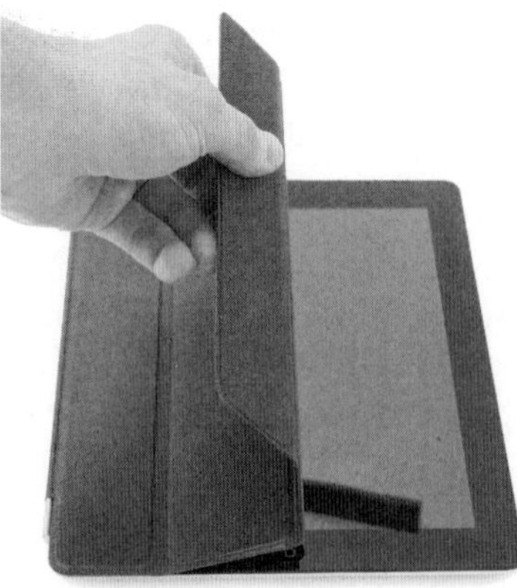

Figure 26-6 Putting an Apple Smart cover on an iPad

Depending on the amount of money you're willing to spend, you can get a cover that helps protect your screen from scratches, impacts, and small amounts of water. Like to scuba with your Android device? There are waterproof cases that enable you to check your Facebook account from 40 feet underwater. (These are specialty cases and not very typical.)

Do the obvious to protect your devices. Don't get them anywhere near liquids. Don't run your smartphone through the wash in your trousers. Don't even think about placing heavy objects on that ~$600 tablet! Use common sense.

Combating Malware

Malware on mobile devices is an interesting issue. Tight controls on the OS and apps make traditional malware infections almost impossible on iOS and Windows Phone devices. When malware strikes, the OS maker supplies periodic *patching/OS updates*, automatic updates and operating system patches. Android lacks a few of the controls that we see in iOS and Windows Phone. To plug the gap, there are third-party antivirus and anti-malware single-user (user-level) and enterprise-level solutions available. Figure 26-7 shows an example of user-level antivirus software for an Android device.

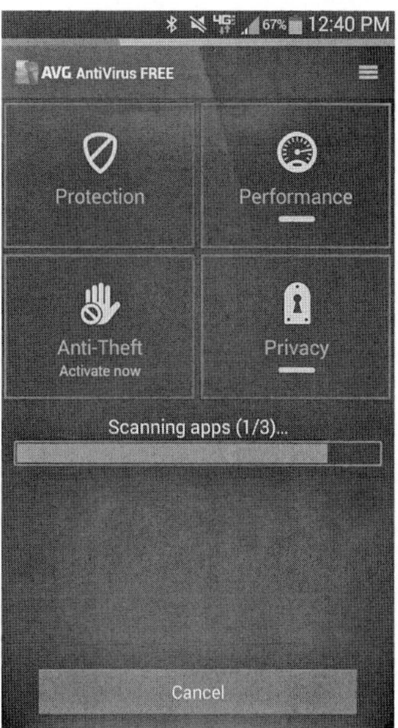

Figure 26-7 Antivirus app for Android

Any anti-malware solutions used on mobile devices should cover the widest possible range of malware threats, and should, to the best degree possible, cover the widest range of mobile devices used in the corporate network. In a heterogeneous infrastructure, because there may be different varieties of mobile devices using different operating systems and coming from different vendors, a one-size-fits-all anti-malware solution may not work. Different solutions may be necessary for the different devices present on a network, or, in

some cases, different modules that cover specific types of devices may be available from the vendor to integrate into an enterprise-level anti-malware solution.

In any case, the important part of an enterprise-level anti-malware solution is to deliver timely updates to the devices on a routine basis. Network access control solutions can ensure that when a device attempts to connect to the network, it is checked for the latest anti-malware signatures and updated as necessary before being allowed to connect to the network. In the case of user-managed solutions, when necessary, policy, network access control, and other technical solutions may be needed to ensure users are updating their own devices in a timely manner.

Dealing with Loss

Losing a mobile device creates a series of issues that you need to address. First, protect your data from access by putting a good *passcode lock* or *screen lock* on the device, which requires you to type in a series of letters and/or numbers, or perhaps use motion patterns, fingerprints, or even facial recognition, to unlock the mobile device each time you press the power button or touch the screen. Don't assume that you'll never set the phone down in the lavatory at an airport and forget about it or lose it to a thief. Most mobile devices enable you to set a passcode lock or screen lock from Settings (see Figure 26-8). Do it right now! Modern versions of iOS and Android encrypt the contents of the built-in storage, so even if a "finder" dismantles the device to access the drive, he or she will not get your documents.

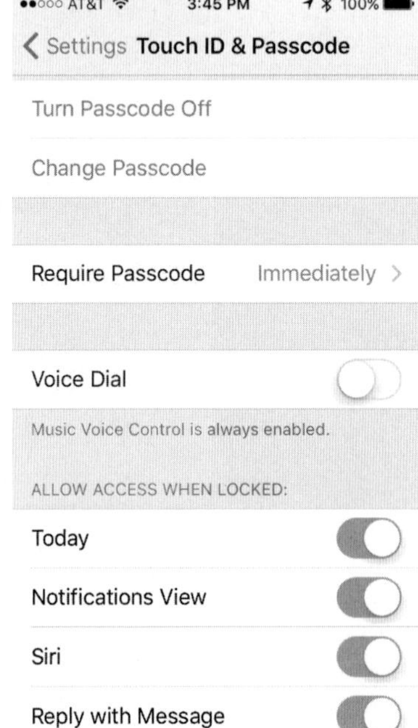

Figure 26-8 Passcode option in Settings

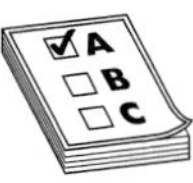

EXAM TIP Fingerprint lock, face lock, swipe lock, and passcode lock are various screen lock methods used for securing mobile devices.

Mobile devices may also have a preset restriction on the number of failed login attempts that, when exceeded, locks up the mobile device. This system lockout slows down someone trying to hack into a found mobile device while you use locator services or applications to try to recover it or remotely wipe it.

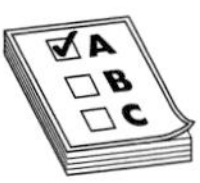

EXAM TIP You can set up many mobile devices to lockout or even automatically wipe after a certain number of failed login attempts.

Apple, Microsoft, and Google offer locator services for discovering the whereabouts of a misplaced mobile device. Using Apple's iCloud as an example, log in to your iCloud account and click the Find My iPhone button. (This works for both iPhones and iPads.) As soon as the device in question accesses the Internet (and thus receives an IP address and posts its MAC address), iCloud will pinpoint the location within a few yards (see Figure 26-9). Very slick!

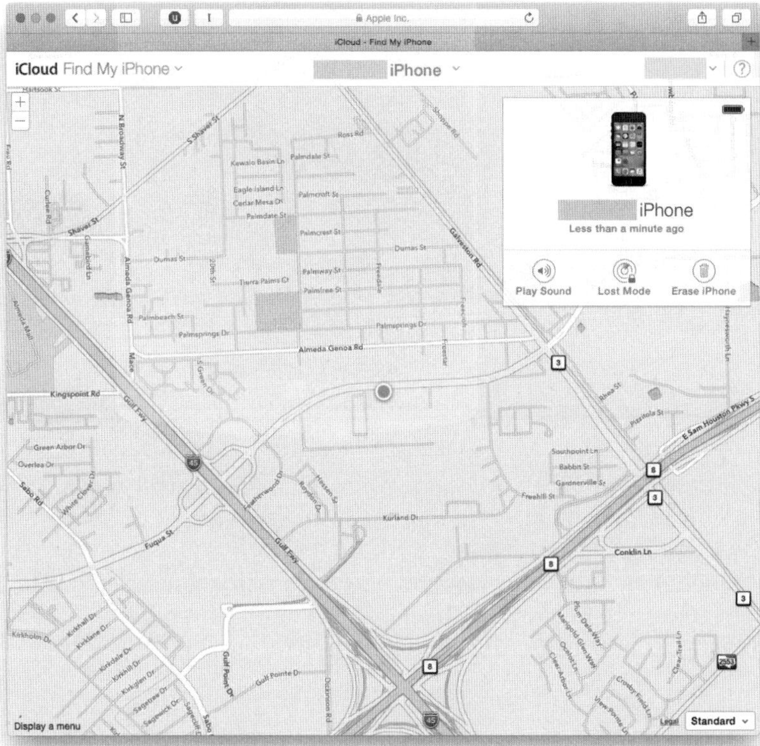

Figure 26-9 Locating a device in iCloud

Recovering from Theft

If your mobile device gets stolen and contains sensitive information, then you have a couple of options for dealing with it. Certainly the locator services help, but if you have credit card information or other very damaging information on your mobile device, you need to act quickly.

First, make sure you have your data backed up. You should have everything synced to a local machine and, if possible, backed up to one of the remote backup applications—like Microsoft's One Drive cloud service—to put your data beyond the reach of even a disaster that takes out your house. With Windows Phone 8.1, for example, go into Settings and select Backup. This screen lets you select what items on your phone get backed up (see Figure 26-10).

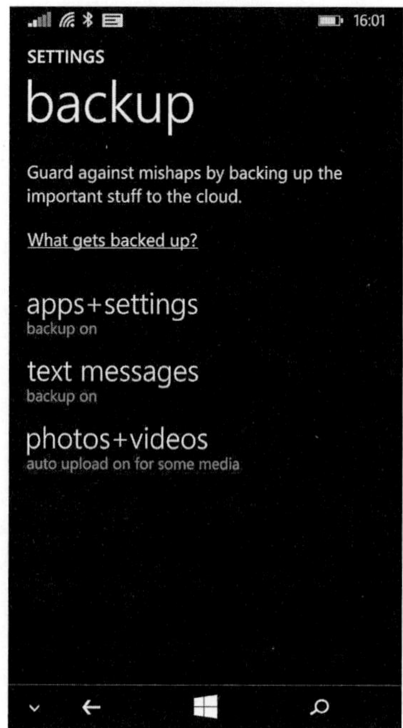

Figure 26-10 Selecting items to get backed up

For Apple devices, you back up to one of several services, such as iTunes or iCloud, and use the Apple Configurator to restore. Android devices use the Google Sync feature to backup and restore.

Second, you can remotely wipe your mobile device. Microsoft makes it supremely easy through your Microsoft account. Log in, locate, and nuke your device (see Figure 26-11). You may never get the device back, but at least the bad guys won't have your data.

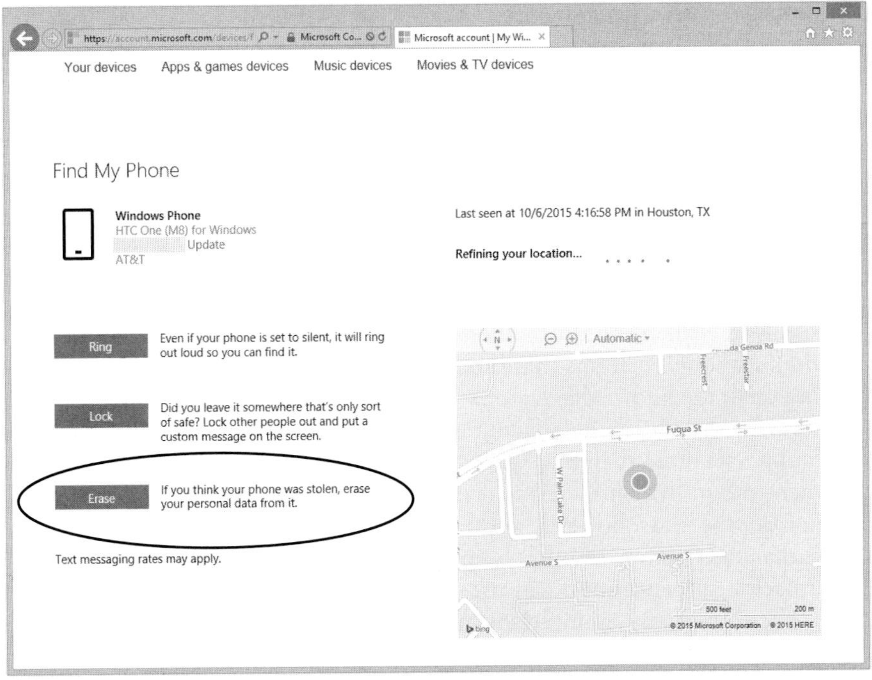

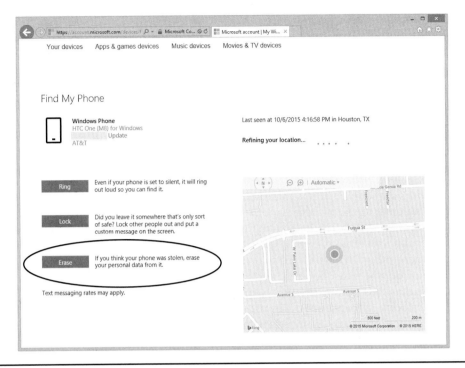

Figure 26-11 Remote wipe

Securing Your Data

Every security scenario we've discussed so far (remote wipe excepted) was designed to secure the device itself. Let's now get into what we can do to protect our actual data.

Multifactor Authentication

Before we discuss multifactor authentication, it's worth explaining single-factor authentication, as well as the different factors that exist. In order to understand single-factor authentication, it helps to understand what the authentication factors actually are. First, there is the *knowledge* factor. This is attributed to something the user knows, such as a user name and password. The second factor is the *ownership* or *possession* factor. This is something the user has in her possession, such as a smartcard or token. A third factor is the *inherence* factor. This is something the user either is or something they do. An example of an inherence factor is a biometric identifier, such as a fingerprint or retinal pattern. You commonly hear these three factors referred to as something the user knows, something the user has, and something the user is.

There are other authentication factors as well that are not as commonly considered in security authentication, but exist nonetheless. For example, something you do (an inherence factor) could be used in an authentication scheme whereby the user draws a certain pattern on the screen of a mobile device. Another authentication factor is the

location factor, or somewhere you are. This can be used if the individual's location can be pinpointed via GPS or some other method. The individual may be required to be at a certain location in order to log in to the system, for example. Yet another factor is the *temporal* factor. This factor is time based, and may require logon at a certain time of day, for example, within a narrowly defined time period, or even within so many seconds or minutes of another event. Token methods of authentication also use time factors, as the PIN displayed on a token is only good for a finite amount of time.

Now that you know what the various authentication factors are, let's get back to the simplest form of authentication, single-factor authentication. In single-factor authentication, the user has to use only one of the factors in order to authenticate. You most commonly see this in authentication methods that require only a user name and password combination. Although it seems that these are two different elements, it is still only one factor being used, the knowledge factor.

It makes sense that since single-factor authentication uses only one factor, multifactor authentication uses more than one factor. In the past, the trend was to refer to it as *two-factor* authentication, which meant that the authentication scheme required more than one factor. Over the years, however, authentication methods have developed that require even more than two factors, so it has become more correct to say *multifactor* authentication. Multifactor authentication can use a variety of methods, as long as it uses more than one. There are many examples of multifactor authentication that you may see in your everyday life. For example, when you use a bank's ATM, you're using multifactor authentication because of something you possess (the ATM card) and something you know (the correct PIN). To access data and systems, multifactor authentication can use that method as well.

EXAM TIP Don't confuse the user name and password combination with multifactor authentication. Only one factor is being used here, the knowledge factor. This makes the user name and password combination a form of single-factor authentication.

Biometric Authentication

Combined with other authentication factors, biometric elements can provide a very secure multifactor authentication mechanism. An example of biometric authentication might be presenting a smartcard to a proximity badge reader and then having your fingerprint scanned on a fingerprint reader before being granted access to a secure area.

Mobile devices are now using biometrics as well to authenticate to them. Laptops have included fingerprint readers for a few years now, and we are now seeing other mobile devices, such as smartphones, that are able to use these readers as well. A prime example of this is Apple's Touch ID; starting with the iPhone 5s, the iPhone can unlock with a fingerprint. To enable Touch ID, use the Settings app to enroll a finger, or five! (see Figure 26-12).

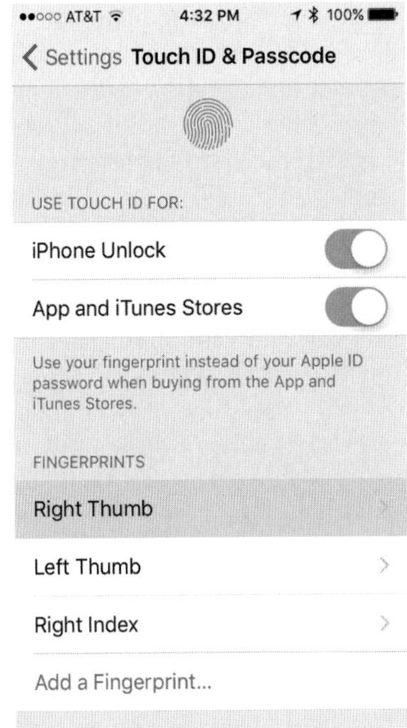

Figure 26-12 Touch ID options

Authenticator Applications

Access into third-party or corporate networks often requires strong authentication methods. Most often, authenticating to a network or service requires some type of app to facilitate the authentication process. To access a corporate VPN, for example, may require a specific app, approved and published by the organization, configured with the correct security settings. There are also generic applications that can be used for a variety of authentication needs, and may offer the ability to use multiple sets of credentials to access different Web sites, networks, or network-based services (for example, corporate e-mail, VPN access, and so forth). There are also several apps that can handle multifactor authentication and act as tokens or issue temporary session PINs.

They key consideration about any of these apps is configuration. This means that you must have the right network configuration, to include IP address, subnet mask, DNS servers, and using the correct port and secure protocol. Configuring any of these items incorrectly will likely result in no connection to the service or network you're trying to connect to. Additionally, however, from the security perspective, you also need the correct authentication and encryption settings (if encryption is required during authentication, which, hopefully, should be). These settings might include the correct authentication method, the right encryption algorithm, and the right settings for both. If anything is configured incorrectly, the mobile device won't be able to authenticate to the network.

Trusted Sources Versus Untrusted Sources

For the most part, getting software from legitimate app stores run by the major vendors, such as Apple, Google, Microsoft, and Amazon, is not only easy, but usually secure.

Different vendors have different requirements for developers to get an app into the app store, and these include security requirements as well. Some of this stems from the development and support model used by the vendor. Apple is very monolithic in their device and application structure, strictly controlling all aspects of both the device and the apps that run on it. Apple is extremely strict, for example, in terms of how developers must create an application that is sold in iTunes. Android, on the other hand, is based upon a multitier model, where the devices are developed separately from the apps, and even the operating systems that run on them. There are variations in the Android devices' operating system flavors that require developers to develop differently for each variation. What may run on devices sold by one vendor isn't necessarily guaranteed to run on another vendor's device, although they all use variations of the Android operating system. A prime example of this is Amazon's line of Kindle devices, which can only get apps from the Amazon Appstore. Additionally, Android apps aren't always subject to the same strict developer guidelines that Apple apps are. That doesn't necessarily mean they are less secure, but this can cause issues for secure development.

The security weakness that exists with third-party app stores is essentially getting apps from unapproved or unofficial sources. There are definitely legitimate app sources outside of Google Play, for example, such as device manufacturers, communications carriers, and in-house corporate development sources. Some sources, however, are not so legitimate, and are usually unapproved by the vendors, manufactureres, and corporate customers for use. In some cases, you can get just the app, but getting it to run on the device may be problematic, as some of these apps require root-level access to the device. This is typically not allowed on most consumer devices unless the device is rooted or hacked. See "Unauthorized Root Access" later in the chapter for more details.

When getting apps from questionable sources, problems include apps that contain malware, apps that steal personal data and transmit it to a third party, and even apps that can be used as hacking tools. Additionally, some apps require replacing the operating system with one that's not approved by the vendor, which not only invalidates the warranty on most devices, but also could cause the device to be unstable and not operate properly.

Firewalls

Software firewalls are typically installed on individual hosts, and as such, are normally used to protect the host itself from network-based threats. A software firewall is typically installed into an existing operating system. Apple and Windows systems have built-in firewalling features that are part of the mobile OS. Android systems require third-party firewalls. There is a surprising number of software firewalls for Android devices. One example of a software firewall for Android is shown in Figure 26-13.

Android software firewall packages include basic rule elements that can be used to construct rules to filter specific traffic coming into the host. Many of these packages also include anti-malware solutions and basic intrusion detection solutions. Some of these software firewall solutions are standalone and have to be configured and managed

by the user, whereas some are enterprise-level solutions and can be centrally configured, updated, and managed by the systems administrator. Keep in mind that the software firewall packages work at the very basic level and can't possibly keep out every single network threat that the host is exposed to. But they serve as a second line of defense for the host, and are part of any good layered defense-in-depth security design.

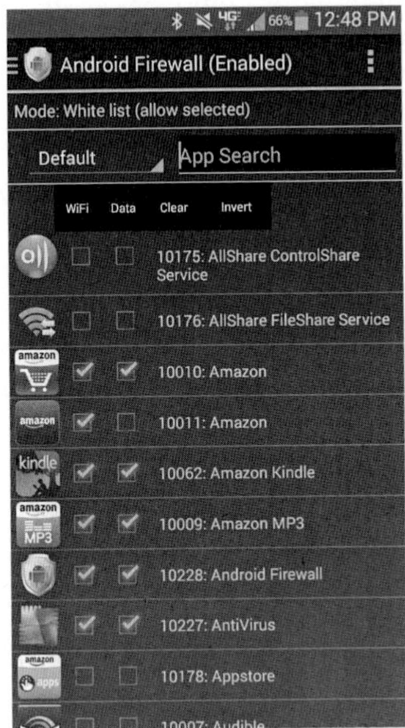

Figure 26-13 An Android firewall app

Mobile OS and Application Security Issues

We've already discussed mobile device security at various points in the chapter in different contexts, but it's worth mentioning some other security issues here that could affect mobile device usage. These are things that the user and the organization need to be aware of, and take steps to prevent. This set of issues that mobile devices can encounter includes network connectivity and security issues, issues that are frequently outside of the control of the user or even the technician. Some, however, have to do with device configuration. We'll look at each of these factors in the upcoming sections. We'll also talk about security issues that could occur with mobile devices that may involve data loss or unauthorized access.

Connectivity and Data Usage Issues

Network connectivity issues in general that affect all devices have been covered elsewhere within the book. For mobile devices in particular, there are some additional network connectivity issues you should be aware of that you will likely encounter at some point.

Some of these have to do with the cellular signal from the mobile device, and others have to do with Wi-Fi and Bluetooth network connections.

One of the most prominent issues plaguing mobile devices is weak signals or signal drops in signals, typically from cellular networks. This issue usually occurs when traveling between carrier coverage areas, or in rural areas where there aren't enough cell towers. There isn't much you can do to troubleshoot this, except monitor it. There are cellular signal boosters you can purchase, but these are of dubious value in some situations. Usually these are effective when the user stays in a location that's far from the cell tower, and typically aren't very effective while the user is actively traveling.

Another issue that typically comes from cellular networks is slow data speeds. If the device is between geographic cells, or farther away from cell towers, data speeds may get slower. Also, roaming between carriers may cause slow data speeds, as some carriers may limit data rates for nonsubscribers.

In addition to cellular issues that can cause slow data speeds, there also performance issues on the device itself that may cause an appearance of slow data connectivity. Most of these have been discussed already, but include high resource utilization, such as CPU and RAM usage, and a device's struggle to maintain a solid network connection.

Yet another issue that users may encounter doesn't necessarily affect connectivity, but it may affect their ability to use cellular data services. This may happen when a user exceeds their data usage limits set by the carrier. CompTIA calls this *data transmission overlimit*. Typically a user will be notified, via e-mail or text message, before this happens, but they may not notice it. Some carriers may restrict or stop cellular data usage beyond the preset limits. The biggest problem with exceeding the data transmission limits set by the carrier, however, is that any additional data usage beyond those limits is charged to the user at a much higher cost. This will cause the user's bill to go up significantly, and if it is a company-owned device, will cause the company's expenses to go up. In this case, the user or the company may consider raising the data limits, albeit at a modest increase in cost. Another solution is to disable cellular data usage in the configuration settings of the device (see Figure 26-14).

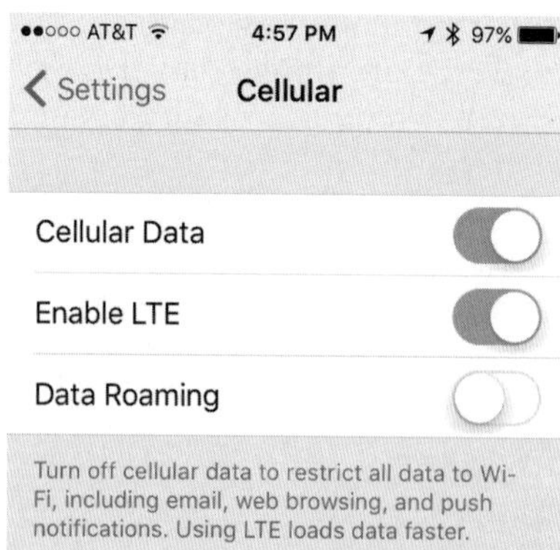

Figure 26-14 Option to disable cellular data in iOS

Unauthorized Connections

A major security issue is unintended network connections, such as those that would apply to cellular, Wi-Fi, and Bluetooth networks. Unintended cellular network connections aren't common, since these are preprogrammed into the phone by the carrier, and periodically updated, but there is a technique called *tower spoofing* that we should discuss here. Tower spoofing involves setting up equipment that can spoof a carrier's tower and infrastructure and cause a cellular device to use it instead of the normal tower equipment. It requires overpowering the nearest legitimate cell signal, causing the cellular device to lock onto it instead. Equipment used in tower spoofing can also be used to eavesdrop on any conversation, even if it is encrypted. In some cases, the equipment can be used to fool the device into turning off encryption completely.

Just as hackers have been using this technique for a few years, law enforcement officials have been reportedly using it as well. Since 2010, there have been numerous court cases highlighted in the media questioning the admissibility of evidence obtained from cell signal interception. A device called a "Stingray" has been reported by the media as used by various federal, state, and local law enforcement agencies to intercept a suspect's cell traffic using tower spoofing equipment and techniques.

Wi-Fi and Bluetooth connections are typically controlled in the configuration settings for the device. *Unintended Wi-Fi and Bluetooth connections* can lead to unauthorized access to the device over those connections, allowing data access, theft, and modification by malicious persons. To prevent connections to unauthorized Wi-Fi networks, or pairing with unauthorized Bluetooth devices, you typically only have to configure these options in the configuration settings. This includes settings that tell your mobile device to not automatically connect to unknown Wi-Fi networks, and settings that turn Bluetooth pairing off by default. This will require you to manually connect to a known and trusted Wi-Fi network, and manually pair to a Bluetooth device. The same settings can also be enforced through MDM software to the device through profile settings, if the device is centrally managed.

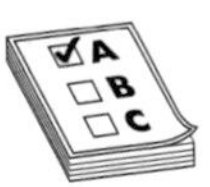

EXAM TIP The 902 exam suggests a couple of options for dealing with rogue connections, namely through apps called *cell tower analyzers* and *WiFi analyzers*. Although you can install such apps on a mobile device, they don't do much to help you in the exceedingly rare circumstance of encountering a rogue connection.

Unauthorized Data Access

Data access can be an issue with mobile devices, simply because they can be lost or stolen. Typically, device locks and remote wipe can prevent unauthorized users from accessing data on a mobile device. Data can also be leaked through other means, however, such as removable memory storage cards, as well as configuration settings on the device or in different applications. Removable memory cards should be encrypted if they contain sensitive data, so that if they are removed from the device, data can't be accessed by an unauthorized person. Configuration settings on the device can be set to protect personal data

by setting privacy and security settings, and the same settings can be configured in different apps that are allowed to access personal data.

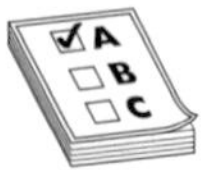

EXAM TIP Portable and mobile devices present amazing opportunities for your personal information to become much less personal and a lot more public. The 902 exam notes this potential as "leaked personal files/data," but it could just as easily be translated as "your phone password wasn't good and you left the phone in a kiosk at the ski resort." (Not that this has ever happened to me.)

Unauthorized Account Access

Unauthorized account access is not only a big deal for the mobile device itself, but also the organizational network it may connect to. If account credentials are disclosed, or someone is able to access the mobile device, then they have an entry point into an organizational network. VPNs and e-mail connections should be secured on the device, meaning that user names and passwords should not be stored by default, allowing the device to automatically connect to the service in question. This way, if the device is lost or stolen, the services can't be automatically accessed, since they still require authentication. Unauthorized account access can lead to a malicious person stealing or accessing data not only on the device, but also on the larger network.

Unauthorized Root Access

All mobile operating systems have an all-powerful root account that is normally locked so that no one but the manufacturer of the device may access it. Locking the root account is critical for mobile device security. In order to gain true root access to a mobile device, a user has to either *jailbreak* (iOS) or *root* (Android/Windows) the device.

Jailbreaking means that the user installs a program on the device that changes settings on the device that are not normally intended by the manufacturer to be changed. Jailbreaking allows a user to install software not normally allowed, such as apps that don't come from the manufacturer's legitimate app store or apps that don't meet legal or quality requirements of the device manufacturer. Jailbreaking also allows a user to unlock functionality on the device. For example, some iPhones that use AT&T as a service provider can't be used to tether (which means to allow another device to use their Internet connection). Jailbreaking an iPhone can unlock that functionality and allow other devices to use the iPhone's connection to the Internet.

Jailbreaking is normally not supported by the manufacturer at all; in fact, jailbreaking typically voids the warranty on a device. Additionally, the manufacturer or service provider, if they detect that jailbreaking has taken place on the device, can prevent the device from connecting to their services. In some cases, the jailbreaking process fails, and the device is rendered non-operational. Usually this can be fixed by restoring the device completely using a backup; however, this also removes the jailbreaking software. Rendering a device non-operational due to jailbreaking is popularly called "bricking" the device. In rare occasions, bricking a device can be permanent and can't be fixed by restoring from a clean backup.

Rooting an Android or Windows device means that the user now has full administrative access to the lower-level functionality of the device. This is useful in that it allows the user to perform functions on the device that they would not normally be able to, and access functions that may be prohibited by the device manufacturer. Again, as in the case of jailbreaking, this is done to install software that could not otherwise be used on the device, or to unlock functionality from a device. Although none of the popular device vendors condone rooting, in most cases, since the device belongs to the user, the vendors really have no recourse against this practice, except to void the warranty.

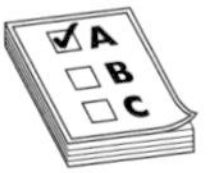

EXAM TIP Although you may hear or read the terms used interchangeably, technically, "jailbreaking" applies to an Apple iOS device, and "rooting" applies to an Android or Windows device.

Unauthorized Location Tracking

We discussed the benefits of GPS and location tracking earlier, but there are also issues that go with this. The primary one is unauthorized location tracking. Configuration settings on the device and apps may allow a user's location to be sent to third parties, sometimes without their consent or knowledge. When not in use, the best way to prevent this is to turn off the GPS function, which also saves battery power. Another way is to configure the device and apps that use geotracking in such a way as to prevent unauthorized tracking, if the device allows it. Some apps simply won't allow geotracking to be turned off, and others simply won't work without geotracking. Keep in mind that the GPS functionality in a mobile device is not the only way to track its location; cellular networks and Wi-Fi are also used to track locations of devices, although they are not as precise as GPS.

An organization could conceivably geotrack its employees, a process called *geofencing*, and this might not sit too well with users. Employees might consider this a form of workplace surveillance, and in some cases may rebel somewhat against the organization's use of geofencing. In the most benign cases, employees may simply leave the device somewhere on a desk and leave the building anyway, or, in the most serious instances, they may seek legal advice and consider bringing litigation against the organization for invasion of privacy. Depending upon how geofencing is used to track employee movement within the bounds of the employer's property, there may be legal ramifications to using it to track workers. It's a good idea to research the legal issues of using geofencing to track employees, as well as intelligently discuss the merits and pitfalls from an employee satisfaction perspective so that you can get a realistic view of what benefit your organization may or may not actually accrue from this practice.

Unauthorized Camera and Microphone Activation

There are ways that malicious individuals can remotely activate different features on a mobile device. This may be through app features, or even malware on the device. It can also be accomplished through unauthorized network connections to the device. Two of the features that can be activated remotely that are of serious concern are the built-in camera and microphone. This would allow a malicious person to effectively spy on the

mobile device user, through video or by eavesdropping on conversations (or both). The ways to prevent these sorts of actions are by restricting camera and microphone permissions in apps or operating systems (when they allow it), by taking the steps previously described to prevent unauthorized network connections, and by using anti-malware solutions on the device.

Troubleshooting Steps and Tools

Which tools you should use to troubleshoot network, security, app, and device issues vary between the different types of devices, depending upon the operating system being used and the manufacturer of the device. Examples of these tools are the iTunes/iCloud /Apple Configurator, the Windows Phone app for a desktop PC, and different third-party apps that may help you with Android and Microsoft devices. Additionally, some of these providers may also have cloud-based apps that can remotely analyze and help troubleshoot problems with your mobile devices. You can also send diagnostics information files from the devices to the different manufacturers, simply by running diagnostics commands or software apps on the devices.

There are also generic tools that will help you, regardless of the type of device you are working on. These include anti-malware apps and application scanners. Anti-malware apps can scan for, detect, and remove malware from the device. App scanners typically run before an app is installed or updated, and can give you information such as what network connectivity the app requires, what permissions it needs, and what access the app has to certain hardware and functions on your device. App scanners can also tell you what type of data access the app has to your personal information, such as contacts and media files (see Figure 26-15).

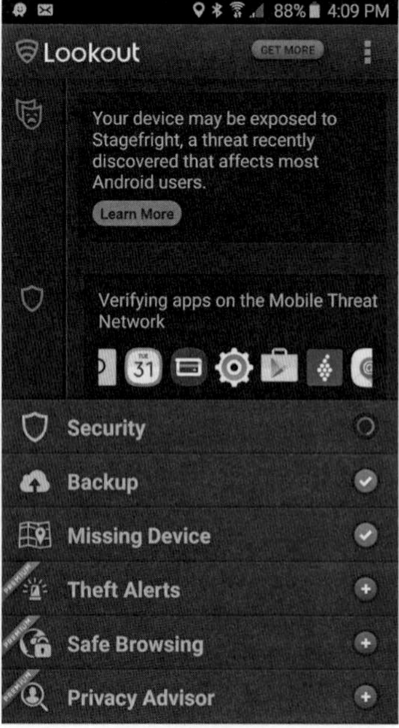

Figure 26-15 Combined anti-malware and app scanner

Always maintaining a current backup of your device is one measure you need to take in case all else fails. Different tools used to perform backups and restore data include iTunes and the various synchronization tools for Android and Microsoft devices; another option is to back up the data to the manufacturer's user cloud storage, such as Microsoft OneDrive or Apple iCloud.

Chapter Review

Questions

1. Which of the following would be a legitimate reason a mobile device is running slowly?
   - **A.** Incorrect calibration
   - **B.** RAM too slow
   - **C.** Lack of storage space
   - **D.** Incorrect version of application
2. Patty has both Gmail and a traditional (SMTP/POP3) e-mail account. She wants to consolidate the traditional account into her Gmail account. Where does she do this? (Select two.)
   - **A.** In the Gmail app
   - **B.** In the mobile device's connection settings
   - **C.** In the traditional e-mail server's settings
   - **D.** This happens automatically on all mobile devices
3. Pamela decides to add a traditional e-mail app to get her e-mail. Which of the following will she most probably need to configure the app? (Select two).
   - **A.** Name of her DNS server
   - **B.** Name of her IMAP server
   - **C.** Name of her DHCP server
   - **D.** Name of her SMTP server
4. Joyce notices her GPS map app gives the error "GPS coordinates not available." What should she try first?
   - **A.** Try running another GPS app
   - **B.** Stop and start GPS on the mobile device
   - **C.** Move to a place where she can get a good GPS signal
   - **D.** Update the mobile device's firmware

5. You've lost your iPhone. What would you use to try to find it?
   A. iTunes
   B. iFind
   C. Location Services
   D. iCloud
6. Fred wants to play *World of Warcraft* on his desktop system. He logs in and then the game asks for a code that is generated by an authenticator app on his Android phone. This is an example of:
   A. Multifactor authentication
   B. Factor authorization
   C. Multifactor authorization
   D. Factor authentication
7. Jailbreaking an iPhone gives access to:
   A. The administrator account
   B. The root account
   C. The /bin folder
   D. The system BIOS
8. A great way to protect data on a removable media card is to
   A. Encrypt it
   B. Lock it
   C. Remove it when unneeded
   D. Format it
9. Which mobile operating system requires a third-party software firewall?
   A. Android
   B. Mac OS X
   C. Windows Mobile
   D. iOS
10. Users bringing personally owned mobile devices into an enterprise environment is called:
   A. Importing
   B. CYMK
   C. Providing
   D. BYOD

Answers

1. **C.** Lack of storage space would be a legitimate reason a mobile device is running slowly.
2. **A, C.** She can add an account to her Gmail app and forward the e-mail in the traditional e-mail server's settings to Gmail.
3. **B, D.** A traditional e-mail app would need the name of the SMTP server and the name of either the IMAP or POP3 e-mail server.
4. **C.** Joyce needs to move to a place where she can get a good GPS signal.
5. **D.** Apple's iPhone uses the Find My iPhone feature of iCloud.
6. **A.** Using both a password and a security code is an example of multifactor authentication.
7. **B.** Jailbreaking is unique to iOS to provide access to the root account.
8. **A.** A great way to protect data on a removable media card is to encrypt it.
9. **A.** Only Android requires a third-party software firewall.
10. **D.** Users bringing personally owned mobile device into an enterprise environment is known as Bring Your Own Device (BYOD).

CHAPTER 27

Printers and Multifunction Devices

In this chapter, you will learn how to

- Describe current printer and multifunction device technologies
- Explain the laser printing process
- Install and configure a printer or multifunction device
- Recognize and fix basic printer and multifunction device problems

Despite all of the talk about the "paperless office," paper documents continue to be a vital part of the typical office. Some computers are even used exclusively for the purpose of producing paper documents. Many people simply still prefer dealing with a hard copy, even as portable devices have proliferated. Developers cater to this preference by using metaphors such as *page*, *workbook*, and *binder* in their applications.

In the past, your average office had an array of electronic and mechanical devices dedicated to performing a single task with paper documents. Think printers, copiers, scanners, and fax machines. Back in the 1990s, the *multifunction device (MFD)*, also known as the multifunction printer (MFP), tried to consolidate multiple functions (often printing and scanning) into a single device. At first these devices weren't terribly great at any of their functions, but today's mature multifunction devices are more common than their single-function counterparts.

The CompTIA A+ certification strongly stresses the area of printing and expects a high degree of technical knowledge of the function, components, maintenance, and repair of all types of printers and multifunction devices.

This chapter examines the common varieties of printers and scanners, then looks at specifics of how a laser printer works. The chapter continues with the steps for installing a multifunction device in a typical personal computer, and concludes with troubleshooting issues.

901

Printer and Multifunction Device Components and Technologies

The multifunction devices your average person encounters in daily life probably sit on a desk, shelf, or countertop, and they tend to be fairly similar in appearance. Because of this, when most of us think about multifunction devices, we tend to picture small desktop *all-in-one* devices (which can usually be used as a printer, scanner, copier, and fax machine) connected to a nearby computer (see Figure 27-1 for an example).

Figure 27-1 All-in-one printer/scanner/fax machine/copier/iPod dock

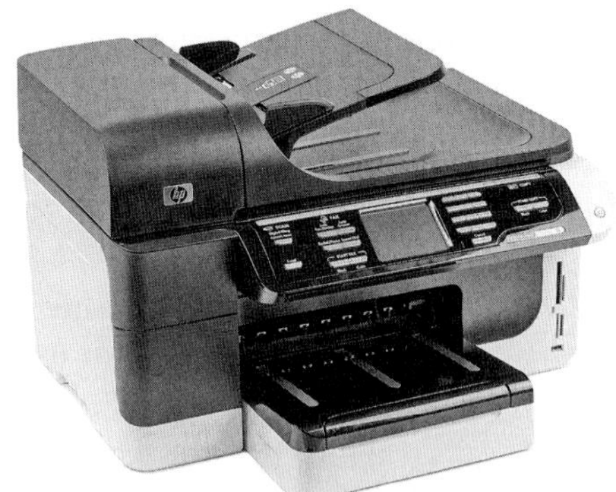

The reality is that these desktop devices, descendants of the desktop printer and scanner, are just the low end of the market. As you head upmarket, multifunction printers look more like the descendants of copy machines and even small printing presses. Despite how different these high-end devices may look, they still share a core set of components—a printer and scanner of some sort—with the all-in-ones you're probably familiar with. As you go upmarket, the greatest improvements tend to be in speed/capacity, durability, and document handling/finishing features such as sorting, stapling, binding, and so on.

Because multifunction devices are so varied, we'll take a look at some of the individual components and technologies you may find inside them separately—be prepared to encounter these components as both standalone devices and included with other components in a multifunction device.

Printers

No other piece of your computer system is available in a wider range of styles, configurations, and feature sets than a printer, or at such a wide price variation. What a printer can and can't do is largely determined by the type of printer technology it uses—that is, how

it gets the image onto the paper. Modern printers can be categorized into several broad types: impact, inkjet, dye-sublimation, thermal, laser, and solid ink.

Impact Printers

Printers that create an image on paper by physically striking an ink ribbon against the paper's surface are known as *impact printers*. Although *daisy-wheel* printers (essentially an electric typewriter attached to the computer instead of directly to a keyboard) have largely disappeared, their cousins, *dot-matrix printers*, still soldier on in many offices. Although dot-matrix printers don't deliver what most home users want—high quality and flexibility at a low cost—they're still widely found in businesses for two reasons: dot-matrix printers have a large installed base in businesses, and they can be used for multipart forms because they actually strike the paper. Impact printers tend to be relatively slow and noisy, but when speed, flexibility, and print quality are not critical, they provide acceptable results. Computers that print multipart forms, such as *point of sale (POS)* machines, use special *impact paper* that can print receipts in duplicate, triplicate, or more. These POS machines represent the major market for new impact printers, although many older dot-matrix printers remain in use.

Dot-matrix printers use a grid, or matrix, of tiny pins, also known as *printwires*, to strike an inked printer ribbon and produce images on paper (see Figure 27-2). The case that holds the printwires is called a *printhead*. Using either 9 or 24 pins, dot-matrix printers treat each page as a picture broken up into a dot-based raster image. The 9-pin dot-matrix printers are generically called *draft quality*, while the 24-pin printers are known as *letter quality* or *near-letter quality (NLQ)*. The BIOS for the printer (either built into the printer or a printer driver) interprets the raster image in the same way a monitor does, "painting" the image as individual dots. Naturally, the more pins, the higher the resolution. Figure 27-3 illustrates the components common to dot-matrix printers. Many dot-matrix printers use continuous-feed paper with holes on its sides that are engaged by metal sprockets to pull the paper through—this is known as *tractor-feed paper* because the sprockets are reminiscent of the wheels on a tractor.

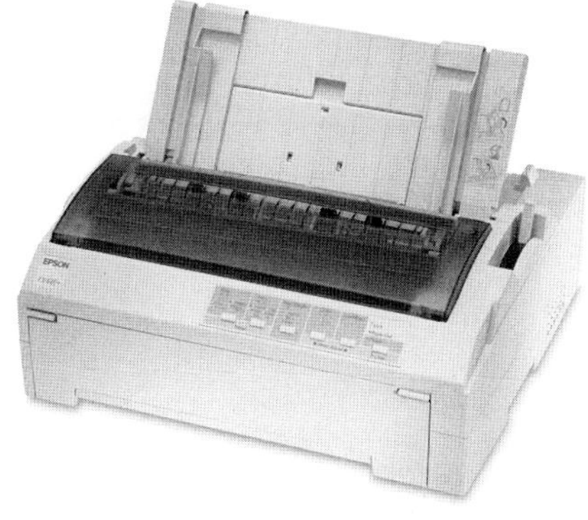

Figure 27-2 An Epson FX-880+ dot-matrix printer (photo courtesy of Epson America, Inc.)

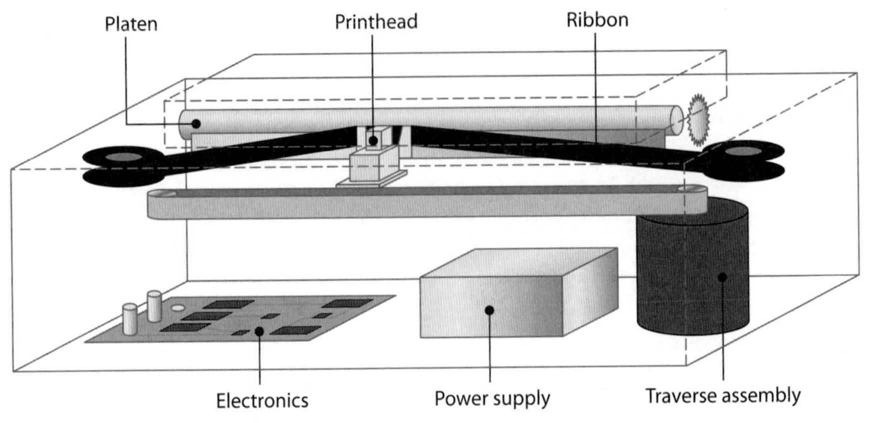

Figure 27-3 Inside a dot-matrix printer

Inkjet Printers

Inkjet printers (also called *ink-dispersion printers*) like the one in Figure 27-4 are relatively simple devices. An inkjet printer uses a *printhead* connected to a *carriage* that contains the ink. A belt and motor move the carriage back and forth so the ink can cover the whole page. A *roller* grabs paper from a paper tray (usually under or inside the printer) or feeder (usually on the back of the printer) and advances it through the printer (see Figure 27-5).

Figure 27-4 Typical inkjet printer

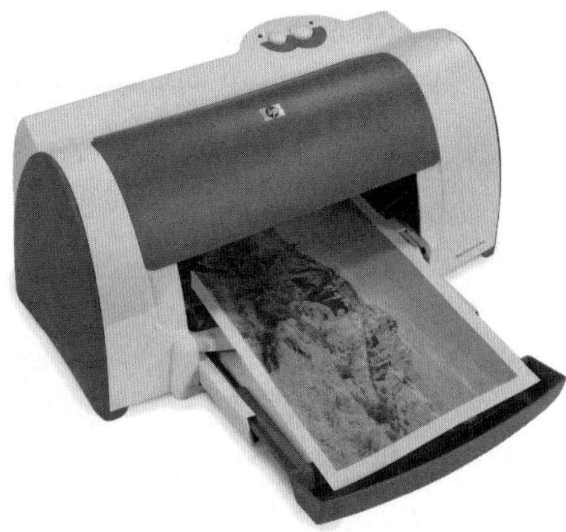

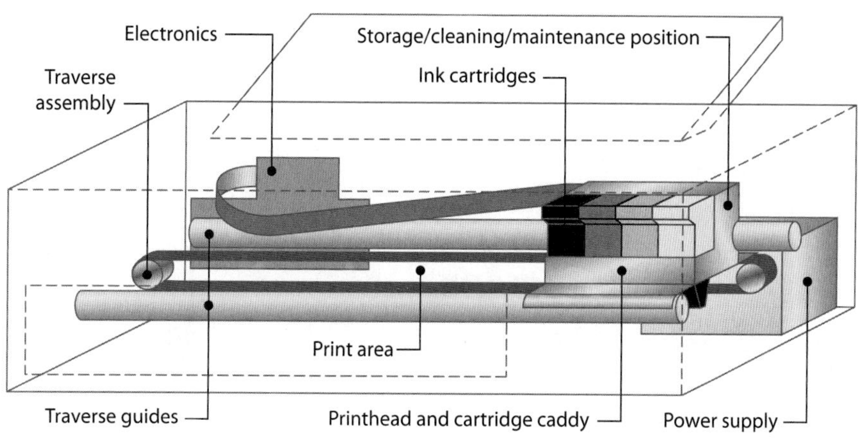

Figure 27-5 Inside an inkjet printer

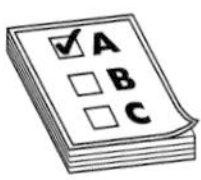

EXAM TIP Printers can also use *duplex assemblies*, which enable the printer to automatically print on both sides of the paper. Some printers include this feature built in, while others require a piece of additional hardware that flips the paper for the printer.

The ink is ejected through tiny tubes. Most inkjet printers use heat to move the ink, while a few use a mechanical method. The heat-method printers use tiny resistors or electroconductive plates at the end of each tube that literally boil the ink; this creates a tiny air bubble that ejects a droplet of ink onto the paper, thus creating a portion of the image (see Figure 27-6).

The ink is stored in special small containers called *ink cartridges*. Older inkjet printers had two cartridges: one for black ink and another for colored ink. The color cartridge had separate compartments for cyan (blue), magenta (red), and yellow ink, to print colors by using a method known as CMYK (you'll read more about CMYK later in this chapter). If your color cartridge ran out of one of the colors, you had to purchase a whole new color cartridge or deal with a messy refill kit.

Printer manufacturers began to separate the ink colors into three separate cartridges so that printers came with four cartridges: one for each color and a fourth for black (see Figure 27-7). This not only was more cost-effective for the user, but it also resulted in higher quality printouts. Today you can find color inkjet printers with six, eight, or more color cartridges. In addition to the basic CMYK inks, the additional cartridges provide for green, blue, gray, light cyan, dark cyan, and more. Typically, printers using more ink cartridges produce higher quality printed images—and cost more.

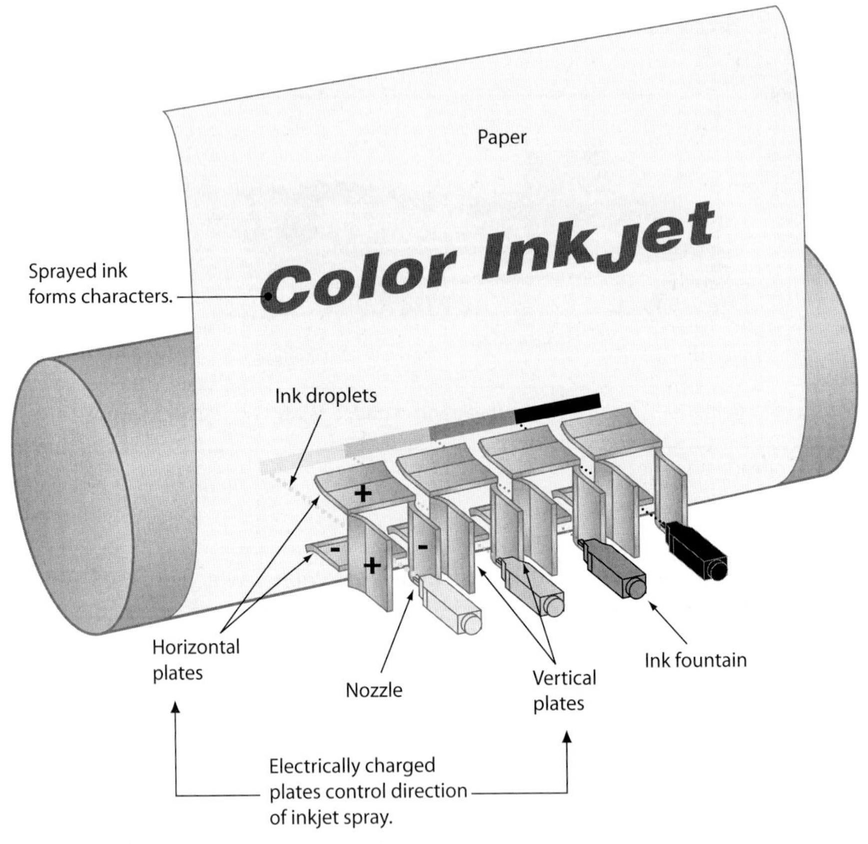

Figure 27-6 Detail of the inkjet printhead

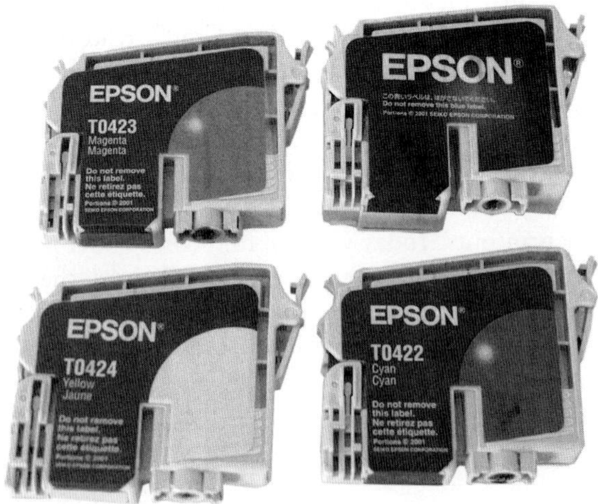

Figure 27-7 Inkjet ink cartridges

The two key features of an inkjet printer are the *print resolution*—how densely the printer lays down ink on the page—and the print speed. Resolution is measured in *dots per inch (dpi)*; higher numbers mean that the ink dots on the page are closer together, so your printed documents will look better. Resolution is most important when you're printing complex images such as full-color photos, or when you're printing for duplication and you care that your printouts look good. Print speed is measured in *pages per minute (ppm)*, and this specification is normally indicated right on the printer's box. Most printers have one (faster) speed for monochrome printing—that is, using only black ink—and another for full-color printing.

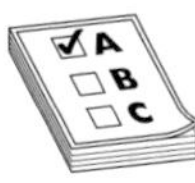

EXAM TIP Print resolution is measured in dots per inch (dpi) and print speed is measured in pages per minute (ppm).

Another feature of inkjet printers is that they can support a staggering array of print media. Using an inkjet printer, you can print on a variety of matte or glossy photo papers, iron-on transfers, and other specialty media; some printers can print directly onto specially coated optical discs, or even fabric. Imagine running a T-shirt through your printer with your own custom slogan (how about "I'm CompTIA A+ Certified!"). The inks have improved over the years, too, now delivering better quality and longevity than ever. Where older inks would smudge if the paper got wet or start to fade after a short time, modern inks are smudge proof and of archival quality—for example, some inks by Epson are projected to last up to 200 years.

Try This!

Pages per Minute Versus Price

Printer speed is a key determinant of a printer's price, and this is an easy assertion to prove, so Try This!

1. Fire up your browser and head over to the Web site for Hewlett-Packard (www.hp.com), Canon (www.canon.com), Epson (www.epson.com), Brother (www.brother.com), or Samsung (www.samsung.com). These five companies make most of the printers on the market today.
2. Pick a particular printer technology and check the price, from the cheapest to the most expensive. Then look for printers that have the same resolution but different ppm rates.
3. Check the prices and see how the ppm rate affects the price of two otherwise identical printers.

Dye-Sublimation Printers

The term *sublimation* means to cause something to change from a solid form into a vapor and then back into a solid. This is exactly the process behind *dye-sublimation printing*, sometimes called *thermal dye transfer* printing. *Dye-sublimation printers* are used mainly for photo printing, high-end desktop publishing, medical and scientific imaging, and other applications for which fine detail and rich color are more important than cost and speed. Smaller, specialized printers called *snapshot* printers use dye-sublimation specifically for printing photos at a reduced cost compared to their full-sized counterparts.

The dye-sublimation printing technique is an example of the so-called CMYK (**c**yan, **m**agenta, **y**ellow, blac**k**) method of color printing. It uses a roll of heat-sensitive plastic film embedded with page-sized sections of cyan (blue), magenta (red), and yellow dye; many also have a section of black dye. A printhead containing thousands of heating elements, capable of precise temperature control, moves across the film, vaporizing the dyes and causing them to soak into specially coated paper underneath before cooling and reverting to a solid form. This process requires one pass per page for each color. Some printers also use a final finishing pass that applies a protective laminate coating to the page. Figure 27-8 shows how a dye-sublimation printer works.

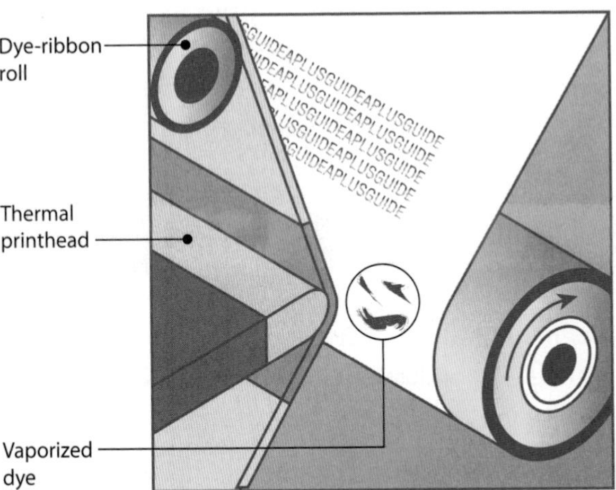

Figure 27-8 The dye-sublimation printing process

Documents printed through the dye-sublimation process display *continuous-tone* images, meaning that the printed image is not constructed of pixel dots but a continuous blend of overlaid differing dye colors. This is in contrast to other print technologies' *dithered* images, which use closely packed, single-color dots to simulate blended colors. Dye-sublimation printers produce high-quality color output that rivals professional photo-lab processing.

Thermal Printers

Thermal printers use a heated printhead to create a high-quality image on special or plain paper. You'll see two kinds of thermal printers in use. The first is the *direct thermal*

printer, and the other is the *thermal wax transfer* printer. Direct thermal printers use a heating element to burn dots into the surface of special heat-sensitive paper. If you remember the first generation of fax machines, you're already familiar with this type of printer. Many retail businesses still use it as a receipt printer, using large rolls of thermal paper housed in a *feed assembly* that automatically draws the paper past the heating element; some receipt printers can even cut the paper off the roll for you.

Thermal wax printers work similarly to dye-sublimation printers, except that instead of using rolls of dye-embedded film, the film is coated with colored wax. The thermal printhead passes over the ribbon and melts the wax onto the paper. Thermal wax printers don't require special papers like dye-sublimation printers do, so they're more flexible and somewhat cheaper to use, but their output isn't quite as good because they use color dithering.

Laser Printers

Using a process called *electro-photographic imaging*, *laser printers* produce high-quality and high-speed output of both text and graphics. Figure 27-9 shows a typical laser printer. Laser printers rely on the photoconductive properties of certain organic compounds. *Photoconductive* means that particles of these compounds, when exposed to light (that's the "photo" part), will *conduct* electricity. Laser printers usually use lasers as a light source because of their precision. Some lower-cost printers use LED arrays instead.

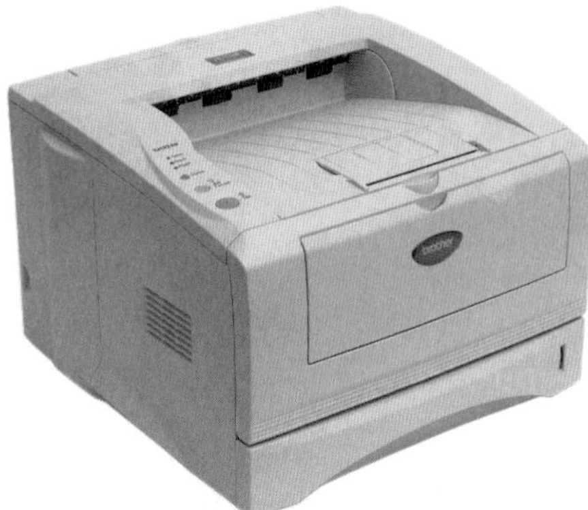

Figure 27-9 Typical laser printer

The first laser printers created only monochrome images; you can also buy a color laser printer, but most laser printers produced today are still monochrome. Although a color laser printer can produce complex full-color images such as photographs, they really shine for printing what's known as *spot color*—for example, eye-catching headings, lines, charts, or other graphical elements that dress up an otherwise plain printed presentation.

NOTE Some printers use consumables—such as ink—at a much faster rate than others, prompting the industry to rank printers in terms of their cost per page. Using an inexpensive printer (laser or inkjet) costs around 4 cents per page, while an expensive printer can cost more than 20 cents per page—a huge difference if you do any volume of printing. This hidden cost is particularly pernicious in the sub-$100 inkjet printers on the market. Their low prices often entice buyers, who then discover that the cost of consumables is outrageous—these days, a *single* set of color and black inkjet cartridges can cost as much as the printer itself, if not more!

The CompTIA A+ certification exams take a keen interest in the particulars of the laser printing process—or specifically, the *imaging process*—so it pays to know your way around a laser printer (see Figure 27-10). Let's take a look at the many components of laser printers and their functions.

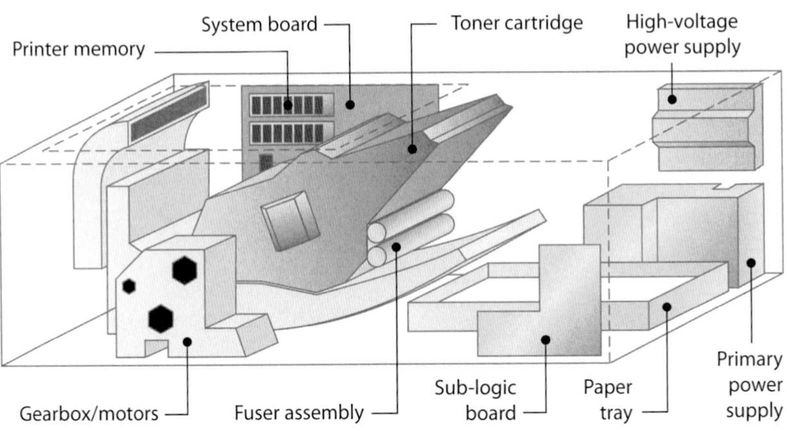

Figure 27-10 Components inside a laser printer

Toner Cartridge The *toner cartridge* in a laser printer is so named because of its most obvious activity: supplying the toner that creates the image on the page (see Figure 27-11). To reduce maintenance costs, however, many other laser printer parts, especially those that suffer the most wear and tear, have been incorporated into the toner cartridge. Although this makes replacement of individual parts nearly impossible, it greatly reduces the need for replacement; those parts that are most likely to break are replaced every time you replace the toner cartridge.

NOTE Color laser printers have four toner cartridges: black, cyan, magenta, and yellow.

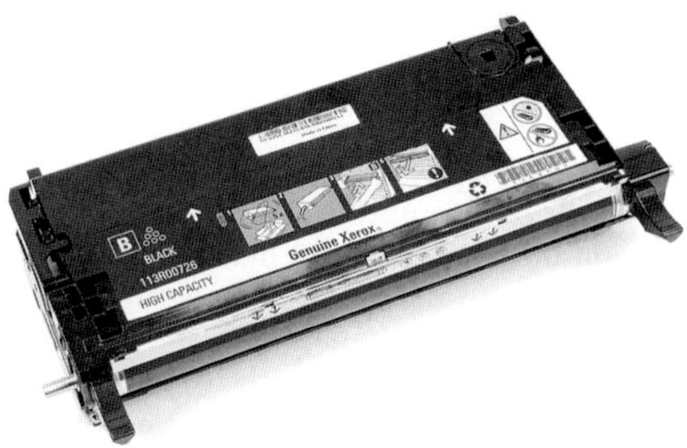

Figure 27-11 Laser printer's toner cartridge

Imaging Drum The *imaging drum* (also called the *photosensitive drum*) is an aluminum cylinder coated with particles of photosensitive compounds. The drum itself is grounded to the power supply, but the coating is not. When light hits these particles, whatever electrical charge they may have "drains" out through the grounded cylinder.

Erase Lamp The *erase lamp* exposes the entire surface of the photosensitive drum to light, making the photosensitive coating conductive. Any electrical charge present in the particles bleeds away into the grounded drum, leaving the surface particles electrically neutral.

Primary Corona/Charge Roller The *primary corona* wire (or *primary charge roller*, in newer laser printers), located close to the photosensitive drum, never touches the drum. When the primary corona or primary charge roller is charged with an extremely high voltage, an electric field (or corona) forms, enabling voltage to pass to the drum and charge the photosensitive particles on its surface. The *primary grid* regulates the transfer of voltage, ensuring that the surface of the drum receives a uniform negative voltage of between –600 and –1000 volts.

Laser The *laser* acts as the writing mechanism of the printer. Any particle on the drum struck by the laser becomes conductive and its charge is drained away into the grounded core of the drum. The entire surface of the drum has a uniform negative charge of between –600 and –1000 volts following its charging by the primary corona wire or charge roller. When particles are struck by the laser, they are discharged and left with a –100-volt negative charge. Using the laser, we can "write" an image onto the drum. Note that the laser writes a positive image to the drum.

Toner The *toner* in a laser printer is a fine powder made up of plastic particles bonded to pigment particles. The *toner cylinder* charges the toner with a negative charge of between –200 and –500 volts. Because that charge falls between the original uniform negative charge of the photosensitive drum (–600 to –1000 volts) and the charge of the particles on the drum's surface hit by the laser (–100 volts), particles of toner are attracted to the areas of the photosensitive drum that have been hit by the laser (that is, areas that have a *relatively* more positive charge than the toner particles).

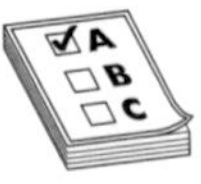

EXAM TIP The black toner used in laser printers is typically carbon melt mixed with a polyester resin, while color toner trades carbon for other pigments.

Transfer Corona/Transfer Roller To transfer the image from the photosensitive drum to the paper, the paper must be given a charge that will attract the toner particles off of the drum and onto the paper. In older printers, the *transfer corona*, a thin wire, applied a positive charge to the paper, drawing the negatively charged toner particles to the paper. Newer printers accomplish the same feat using a *transfer roller* that draws the toner onto the paper. The paper, with its positive charge, is also attracted to the negatively charged drum. To prevent the paper from wrapping around the drum, a *static charge eliminator* removes the charge from the paper.

In most laser printers, the transfer corona/roller is outside the toner cartridge, especially in large, commercial-grade machines. The transfer corona/roller is prone to a build-up of dirt, toner, and debris through electrostatic attraction, and it must be cleaned. It is also quite fragile—usually finer than a human hair. Most printers with an exposed transfer corona/roller provide a special tool to clean it, but you can also—very delicately—use a cotton swab soaked in 90 percent denatured alcohol (don't use rubbing alcohol, because it contains emollients). As always, never service any printer without first turning it off and unplugging it from its power source.

Fuser Assembly The *fuser assembly* is almost always separate from the toner cartridge. It is usually quite easy to locate, as it is close to the bottom of the toner cartridge and usually has two rollers to fuse the toner. Sometimes the fuser is somewhat enclosed and difficult to recognize because the rollers are hidden from view. To help you determine the location of the fuser, think about the path of the paper and the fact that fusing is the final step of printing.

The toner is merely resting on top of the paper after the static charge eliminator has removed the paper's static charge. The toner must be melted to the paper to make the image permanent. Two rollers, a pressure roller and a heated roller, are used to fuse the toner to the paper. The pressure roller presses against the bottom of the page, and the heated roller presses down on the top of the page, melting the toner into the paper. The heated roller has a nonstick coating such as Teflon to prevent the toner from sticking to it.

Power Supplies All of the devices described in this chapter have power supplies, but when dealing with laser printers, techs should take extra caution. The corona in a laser printer requires extremely high voltage from the power supply, making a laser printer power supply one of the most dangerous devices in computing! Turn off and unplug the printer as a safety precaution before performing any maintenance.

Turning Gears A laser printer has many mechanical functions. First, the paper must be grabbed by the *pickup roller* and passed over the *separation pad*, which uses friction to separate a single sheet from any others that were picked up. Next, the photosensitive roller must be turned and the laser, or a mirror, must be moved back and forth. The toner must be evenly distributed, and the fuser assembly must squish the toner into the paper. Finally, the paper must be kicked out of the printer and the assembly must be cleaned to prepare for the next page.

More sophisticated laser printers enable duplex printing, meaning they can print on both sides of the paper. This is another mechanical function with a dedicated *duplexing assembly* for reversing the paper.

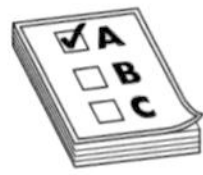

EXAM TIP Be sure you are familiar with laser printer components, including the imaging drum, fuser assembly, transfer roller, pickup rollers, separation pads, and duplexing assembly. The CompTIA A+ 901 exam objectives refer to the *separate pad*; don't get tripped up if you see it worded this way.

All of these functions are served by complex gear systems. In most laser printers, these gear systems are packed together in discrete units generically called *gear packs* or *gearboxes*. Most laser printers have two or three gearboxes that you can remove relatively easily in the rare case one of them fails. Most gearboxes also have their own motor or solenoid to move the gears.

All of these mechanical features can wear out or break and require service or replacement. See the "Troubleshooting Printers" section later in this chapter for more details.

System Board Every laser printer contains at least one electronic board. On this board is the main processor, the printer's ROM, and the RAM used to store the image before it is printed. Many printers divide these functions among two or three boards dispersed around the printer (also known as sub-logic boards, as seen in Figure 27-10). An older printer may also have an extra ROM chip and/or a special slot where you can install an extra ROM chip, usually for special functions such as PostScript.

On some printer models, you can upgrade the contents of these ROM chips (the *firmware*) by performing a process called *flashing* the ROM. Flashing is a lot like upgrading the system BIOS, which you learned about in Chapter 6, "BIOS." Upgrading the firmware can help fix bugs, add new features, or update the fonts in the printer.

Of particular importance is the printer's RAM. When the printer doesn't have enough RAM to store the image before it prints, you get a memory overflow problem. Also, some printers store other information in the RAM, including fonts or special commands. Adding RAM is usually a simple job—just snapping in a SIMM or DIMM stick or two—but getting the *right* RAM is important. Call or check the printer manufacturer's Web site to see what type of RAM you need. Although most printer companies will happily sell you their expensive RAM, most printers can use generic DRAM like the kind you use in a computer.

Ozone Filter The coronas inside laser printers generate ozone (O_3). Although not harmful to humans in small amounts, even tiny concentrations of ozone will cause damage to printer components. To counter this problem, most laser printers have a special ozone filter that needs to be vacuumed or replaced periodically.

Sensors and Switches Every laser printer has a large number of sensors and switches spread throughout the machine. The sensors are used to detect a broad range of conditions such as paper jams, empty paper trays, or low toner levels. Many of these sensors are really tiny switches that detect open doors and so on. Most of the time these

sensors/switches work reliably, yet occasionally they become dirty or broken, sending a false signal to the printer. Simple inspection is usually sufficient to determine if a problem is real or just the result of a faulty sensor/switch.

Solid Ink Printers

Solid ink printers use just what you'd expect—solid inks. The technology was originally developed by Tektronix, whose printer division was acquired by Xerox. Solid ink printers use solid sticks of nontoxic "ink" that produce more vibrant color than other print methods. The solid ink is melted and absorbed into the paper fibers; it then solidifies, producing a continuous-tone output. Unlike dye-sublimation printers, all colors are applied to the media in a single pass, reducing the chances of misalignment. Solid ink sticks do not rely on containers (as does ink for inkjet printers) and can be "topped off" midway through a print job by inserting additional color sticks without taking the printer offline.

These printers are fast, too! A full-color print job outputs the first page in about six seconds. Of course, all that speed and quality comes at a price. Xerox's base model starts at about twice the cost of a laser printer, with the expensive model selling for about six times the cost! Solid ink printers become a bit more affordable when you factor in the cost of consumables. A single stick of ink costs about as much as an inkjet cartridge, for example, but with a print capacity of 1000 pages, that completely beats the cost of inkjet cartridges over time.

Virtual Printers

The most quizzical printer of all, the *virtual printer*, doesn't look like much, but it's actually still pretty similar to physical or "real" printing. When you print to a virtual printer, your system goes through all the steps to prepare a document for printing, and sends it off to a virtual printer—a program which converts the output from your computer into a specific format and saves the result to a portable file that looks like the printed page would have. You can print this file later if you like, or maybe send it to someone else to print, but you can also just keep it in digital format. Virtual printers provide a nice way to save anything you can print, and they're particularly good for saving reference copies of information found on the Web. CompTIA wants you to know specifically about a few of these options, so we'll discuss them in a little more depth.

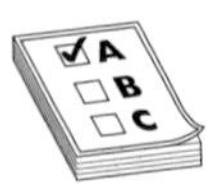

EXAM TIP The CompTIA A+ 901 exam objectives include *Print to file*, which produces a file that can be later printed without access to the program that created it, but you usually won't want to use it as a virtual printer. Print to file is a legacy option you'll often see as a checkbox on your print screen, but it may not work well with USB printers (and even if it works, the resulting file will be difficult to work with). Be aware that this option exists, but use one of the other options described here instead.

Print to PDF One of the most popular virtual printing options is the ability to *print to PDF*, a feature many operating systems support out of the box these days. Windows doesn't join the party until Windows 10, however, so be aware that you'll need to install

a virtual PDF printer on older versions of Windows. You can get these through official Adobe software, but there are also some third-party options.

Print to XPS We'll talk a little about what exactly XPS is in the next section, but Windows versions since Vista include the Microsoft XPS Document Writer as a printer, which you can use to create a .xps file that can be opened by the included XPS Viewer program. Support in other operating systems varies, but most of them have third-party software available for working with XPS files.

Print to Image This option lets you save a regular image file, such as BMP, GIF, JPG, PNG, TIFF, and more. Image formats tend to have some problems when being used for documents—text won't scale as well and can't be easily searched/selected/copied, for example—but they are very portable, and can often be viewed with software included in any operating system and on many types of devices. You will generally need to find and install third-party virtual printer software in order to print to the image format you desire on a given operating system.

Cloud and Remote Printing Blurring the line between traditional and virtual printing, a variety of applications, such as Google Cloud Print, will install a virtual printer on your system that wraps up your document and sends it out over the Internet or other network to a cloud server, which eventually ends up routing it to a real printer for printing—all without needing to have a driver installed for it.

Printer Languages

Now that you've learned about the different types of print devices and techniques, it's time to take a look at how they communicate with the computer. How do you tell a printer to make a letter *A* or to print a picture of your pet iguana? Printers are designed to accept predefined printer languages that handle both characters and graphics. Your software must use the proper language when communicating with your printer, in order to output paper documents. Following are the more common printer languages.

ASCII You might think of the *American Standard Code for Information Interchange (ASCII)* language as nothing more than a standard set of characters, the basic alphabet in upper- and lowercase with a few strange symbols thrown in. ASCII actually contains a variety of control codes for transferring data, some of which can be used to control printers. For example, ASCII code 10 (or 0A in hex) means "Line Feed," and ASCII code 12 (0C) means "Form Feed." These commands have been standard since before the creation of IBM computers, and all printers respond to them. If they did not, the PRT SCR (print screen) key would not work with every printer. Being highly standardized has advantages, but the control codes are extremely limited. Printing high-end graphics and a wide variety of fonts requires more advanced languages.

PostScript Adobe Systems developed the *PostScript* page description language in the early 1980s as a device-independent printer language capable of high-resolution graphics and scalable fonts. PostScript interpreters are embedded in the printing device. Because PostScript is understood by printers at a hardware level, the majority of the image

processing is done by the printer and not the computer's CPU, so PostScript printers print faster. PostScript defines the page as a single raster image; this makes PostScript files extremely portable—they can be created on one machine or platform and reliably printed out on another machine or platform (including, for example, high-end typesetters).

Hewlett-Packard Printer Control Language (PCL) Hewlett-Packard developed its *printer control language (PCL)* as a more advanced printer language to supersede simple ASCII codes. PCL features a set of printer commands greatly expanded from ASCII. Hewlett-Packard designed PCL with text-based output in mind; it does not support advanced graphical functions. The most recent version of PCL, PCL6, features scalable fonts and additional line drawing commands. Unlike PostScript, however, PCL is not a true page description language; it uses a series of commands to define the characters on the page. Those commands must be supported by each individual printer model, making PCL files less portable than PostScript files.

Windows GDI and XPS Windows uses the *graphical device interface (GDI)* component of the operating system to handle print functions. Although you *can* use an external printer language such as PostScript, most users simply install printer drivers and let Windows do all the work. The GDI uses the CPU rather than the printer to process a print job and then sends the completed job to the printer. When you print a letter with a TrueType font in Windows, for example, the GDI processes the print job and then sends bitmapped images of each page to the printer. The printer sees a page of TrueType text, therefore, as a picture, not as text. As long as the printer has a capable enough raster image processor (explained later in this chapter) and plenty of RAM, you don't need to worry about the printer language in most situations. We'll revisit printing in Windows in more detail later in this chapter.

Windows Vista also introduced a new printing subsystem called the *XML Paper Specification (XPS) print path*. XPS provides several improvements over GDI, including enhanced color management (which works with Windows Color System) and better print layout fidelity. The XPS print path requires a driver that supports XPS. Additionally, some printers natively support XPS, eliminating the requirement that the output be converted to a device-specific printer control language before printing.

Scanners

You can use a scanner to make digital copies of existing paper photos, documents, drawings, and more. Better scanners give you the option of copying directly from a photographic negative or slide, providing images of stunning visual quality—assuming the original photo was halfway decent, of course! In this section, you'll look at how scanners work and then turn to what you need to know to select the correct scanner for you or your clients.

How Scanners Work

All *flatbed scanners*, the most common variety of scanner, work the same way. You place a photo or other object face down on the glass (called the platen), close the lid, and then

use software to initiate the scan. The scanner runs a bright light along the length of the platen once or more to capture the image. Figure 27-12 shows an open scanner.

NOTE Many serious scanners and multifunction devices will have an automatic document feeder (ADF), a tray which holds a multi-page document and feeds it into the scanner one page at a time, which can remove most of the manual labor from this process.

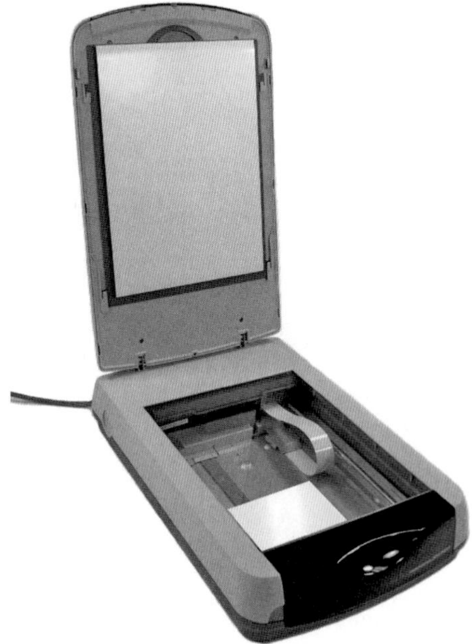

Figure 27-12 Scanner open with photograph face down

The scanning software that controls the hardware can manifest in a variety of ways. Nearly every manufacturer has some sort of drivers and other software to create an interface between your computer and the scanner. When you push the front button on the Epson Perfection scanner in Figure 27-13, for example, the Epson software opens ready to start scanning.

You can also open your favorite image-editing software first and choose to acquire a file from a scanner. Figure 27-14 shows the process of acquiring an image from a scanner in the popular free image-editing software GNU Image Manipulation Program (otherwise known as GIMP). As in most such software, you choose File | Create and then select Scanner. In this case, the scanner uses the traditional TWAIN drivers. *TWAIN* stands for *Technology Without an Interesting Name*—I'm not making this up!—and has been the default driver type for scanners for a long time.

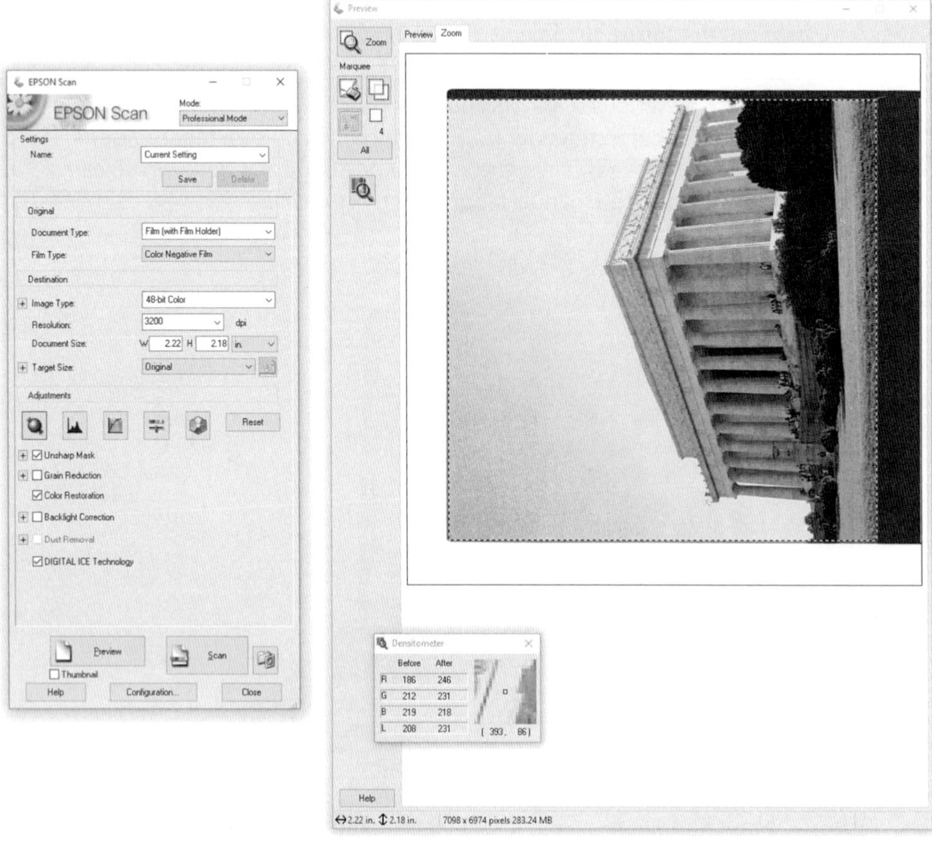

Figure 27-13 Epson software

At this point, the drivers and other software controlling the scanner pop up, providing an interface with the scanner (as shown in Figure 27-13). Here you can set the resolution of the image as well as many other options.

How to Choose a Scanner

You must consider four primary variables when choosing a scanner: resolution, color depth, grayscale depth, and scan speed. You can and will adjust the first three during the scanning process, although probably only down from their maximum. The scan speed relates to all four of the other variables, and the maximum speed is hard-coded into the scanner.

Configurable Variables Scanners convert the scanned image into a grid of pixels (often referred to as dots). The maximum number of pixels determines how well you can capture an image and how the image will look when scaled up in size. Most folks use the term *resolution* to define the grid size. As you might imagine, the higher resolution images capture more fine detail.

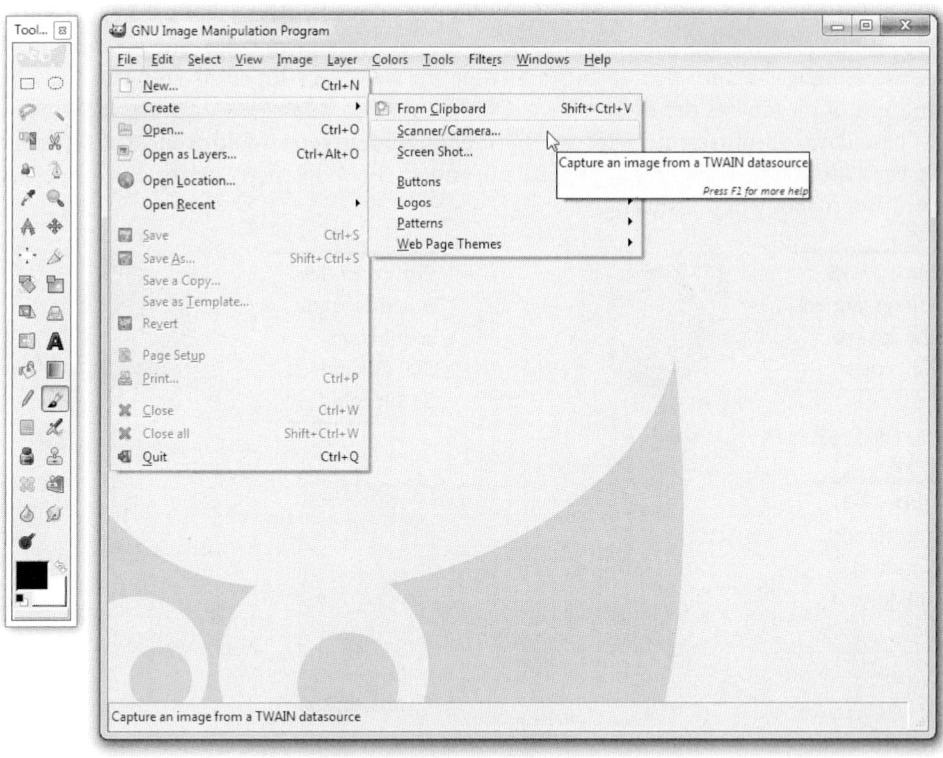

Figure 27-14 Acquiring an image in GNU Image Manipulation Program

Older scanners can create images of only 600 × 600 dots per inch (dpi), while newer models commonly achieve four times that density, and high-end machines do much more. Manufacturers cite *two* sets of numbers for a scanner's resolution: the resolution it achieves mechanically—called the *optical resolution*—and the enhanced resolution it can achieve with assistance from some onboard software.

The enhanced resolution numbers are useless. I recommend at least 2400 × 2400 dpi optical resolution or better, although you can get by with a lower resolution for purely Web-destined images.

The *color depth* of a scan defines the number of bits of information the scanner can use to describe each individual pixel. This number determines color, shade, hue, and so forth, so color depth makes a dramatic difference in how easily you can adjust the color and tone in your photo editor. With binary numbers, each extra bit of information *doubles* the color detail in the scan. The most common color depth options you will run across in scanners today are 24-bit and 48-bit. A 24-bit scan, for example, can save up to 256 shades for each of the red, green, and blue subpixels that make up an individual pixel. This gives you a total of 16,777,216 color variations in the scanned image, which explains why some scanners refer to this as "millions of colors" in their settings. A 48-bit

scan, in contrast, can save up to 65,536 shades per subpixel, giving you a scan that holds a massive 281,474,976,710,656 color variations. All this extra color does come with a downside: images scanned at 48 bits are twice the size of 24-bit scans and can easily be hundreds of megabytes per file!

These days, 48-bit scanners are common enough that you shouldn't have to settle for less, even on a budget. Figures 27-15, 27-16, and 27-17 show pretty clearly the difference resolution makes when scanning.

Figure 27-15 Earring scanned at 72 dpi and 24-bit color

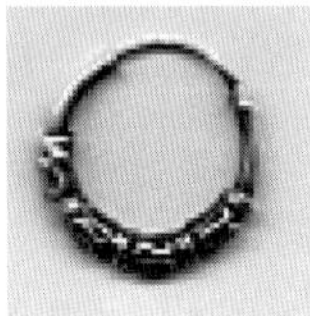

Figure 27-16 Same earring, scanned at 300 dpi and 24-bit color

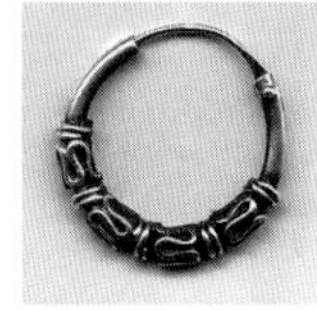

Figure 27-17 Same earring, scanned at 1200 dpi and 24-bit color

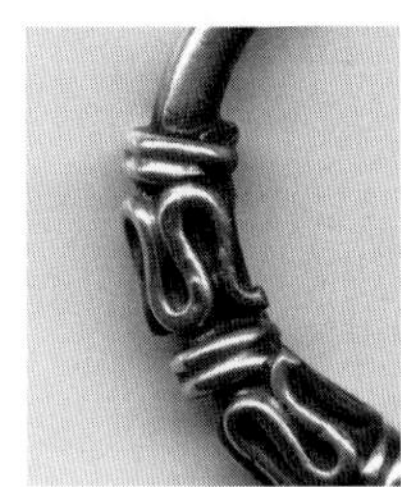

Scanners differ a lot in *grayscale depth*, a number that defines how many shades of gray the scanner can save per pixel. This matters if you work with black-and-white images in any significant way, because grayscale depth may be advertised with a much lower number than color depth. Current consumer-level scanners come in 8-bit, 12-bit, and 16-bit grayscale varieties. You might recognize these three numbers from the previous color depth discussion, because grayscale images only need a third the information it takes to represent the red, green, and blue values that make up a color image. I recommend 16-bit.

Scanning Speed Scanners have a maximum scanning speed defined by the manufacturer. The time required to complete a scan is also affected by the parameters you set; the time increases as you increase the amount of detail captured. A typical low-end scanner, for example, takes upward of 30 seconds to scan a 4 × 6 photo at 300 dpi. A faster scanner, in contrast, can crank out the same scan in 10 seconds.

Raise the resolution of the scan to 600 dpi at 48-bit resolution, and that faster scanner can take a full minute to complete the scan. Adjust your scanning settings to optimize for your project. Don't always go for the highest possible scan if you don't need the resolution and color depth.

Scanning Tips

As a general rule, you should obtain the highest quality scan you can manage, and then play with the size and image quality when it's time to print it or share it over the Web.

The amount of RAM in your system—and to a lesser extent, the processor speed—dictates how big a file you can handle.

If you travel a lot, you'll want to make sure to use the locking mechanism for the scanner light assembly. Just be sure to unlock before you try to use it or you'll get a light that's stuck in one position. That won't make for very good scans!

Copy and Fax Components

The scanning and printing capabilities of a multifunction device enable manufacturers to add copy-machine features easily. To copy a document or photo, you essentially scan a document or photo and then print it, but all with a single press of the Copy button.

Faxing generally requires separate functions in the machine, such as a document feed and a connection to a traditional, analog phone line. Assuming you have those and an account with the local telecom company, the process of faxing is pretty simple. You put a document in the feeder, plug in the fax number, and press the Send button (or whatever the manufacturer labels it).

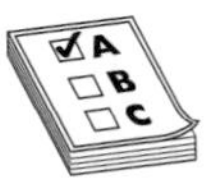

EXAM TIP Although CompTIA added multifunction devices to the 901 objectives, you're likely only to get questions on various printer technologies.

Connectivity

Most printers, scanners, and multifunction devices connect to a computer via a USB port, but Wi-Fi or Ethernet network connections are also very popular. You'll need to know how to support networked connections as well as the plug-and-play USB ones.

USB Connections

New printers and multifunction devices use USB connections that you can plug into any USB port on your computer. USB printers may not come with a USB cable, so you need to purchase one when you purchase a printer. (It's quite a disappointment to come home with your new printer only to find you can't connect it because it didn't come with a USB cable.) Most printers use the standard USB type A connector on one end and the smaller USB type B connector on the other end, although some use two type A connectors. Whichever configuration your USB printer has, just plug in the USB cable—it's that easy!

Network Connections

Connecting a printer or multifunction device to a network isn't just for offices anymore. More and more homes and home offices are enjoying the benefits of network printing. It used to be that you would physically connect the printer to a single computer and then share the printer on the network. The downside to this was that the computer connected to the printer had to be left on for others to use the printer.

Today, the typical *network printer* comes with its own built-in Wi-Fi adapter to enable wireless printing over infrastructure or ad hoc network connections, though you should

avoid ad hoc (CompTIA uses *adhoc*, all one word) connection for security reasons when possible (see Chapter 22, "Wireless Networking," for more on setting up an ad hoc wireless network).

Other printers include an onboard network adapter that uses a standard RJ-45 Ethernet cable to connect the printer directly to the network by way of a router. The printer can typically be assigned a static IP address, or it can acquire one dynamically from a DHCP server. (Don't know what a router, IP address, or DHCP server is? Take a look back at Chapters 20 and 21.) Once connected to the network, the printer acts independently of any single computer. Alternatively, some printers offer a Bluetooth interface for networking.

NOTE Since printers tend to have longer lives than most other computing devices, be aware that printers with a built-in wireless print connection may be using older Wi-Fi or Bluetooth standards than you're used to encountering.

Even if a printer does not come with built-in Ethernet, Wi-Fi, or Bluetooth, you can purchase a standalone network device known as a *print server* to connect your printer to the network—but beware that you may not be able to use all features of a multifunction device connected to a print server. These print servers, which can be Ethernet or Wi-Fi, enable one or several printers to attach via USB cable (or even parallel port, if you still have a printer that old). You may not need to go to the store to find a print server, though—check your router, first, to see if it has an *integrated print server*. If it does, you may be able to plug your printer into a USB port on the router. So take that ancient ImageWriter dot-matrix printer and network it—I dare you!

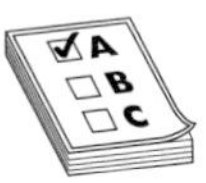

EXAM TIP You'll find print servers outside network devices. In fact, your Windows system is capable of operating as a print server. Anytime you plug a printer into a computer and share the printer over the network, the sharing system can be referred to as a print server.

Other Connections

Plenty of other connection types are available for printers. We've focused mainly on USB and networked connections. Be aware that you may run into old printers using a parallel port, a serial port, or SCSI. Although this is unlikely, know that it's a possibility. You might also see standalone scanners using Thunderbolt.

The Laser Printing Process

The *imaging process* with a laser printer breaks down into seven steps, and the CompTIA A+ 901 exam expects you to know them all. As a tech, you should be familiar with these phases, as this can help you troubleshoot printing problems. If an odd line is printed down the middle of every page, for example, you know there's a problem with the photosensitive drum or cleaning mechanism and the toner cartridge needs to be replaced.

The seven steps to the laser printing process may be performed in a different order, depending on the printer, but it usually goes like this:

1. Processing
2. Charging
3. Exposing
4. Developing
5. Transferring
6. Fusing
7. Cleaning

Processing

When you click the Print button in an application, several things happen. First, the CPU processes your request and sends a print job to an area of memory called the print spooler. The *print spooler* enables you to queue up multiple print jobs that the printer will handle sequentially. Next, Windows sends the first print job to the printer. That's your first potential bottleneck—if it's a big job, the OS has to dole out a piece at a time and you'll see the little printer icon in the notification area at the bottom right of your screen. Once the printer icon goes away, you know the print queue is empty—all jobs have gone to the printer.

Once the printer receives some or all of a print job, the hardware of the printer takes over and processes the image. That's your second potential bottleneck, and it has multiple components.

Raster Images

Impact printers transfer data to the printer one character or one line at a time, whereas laser printers transfer entire pages at a time to the printer. A laser printer generates a *raster image* (a pattern of dots) of the page, representing what the final product should look like. It uses a device (the laser imaging unit) to "paint" a raster image on the photosensitive drum. Because a laser printer has to paint the entire surface of the photosensitive drum before it can begin to transfer the image to paper, it processes the image one page at a time.

A laser printer uses a chip called the *raster image processor (RIP)* to translate the raster image into commands to the laser. The RIP takes the digital information about fonts and graphics and converts it to a rasterized image made up of dots that can then be printed. An inkjet printer also has a RIP, but it's part of the software driver instead of onboard hardware circuitry. The RIP needs memory (RAM) to store the data that it must process.

A laser printer must have enough memory to process an entire page. Some images that require high resolutions require more memory. Insufficient memory to process the image will usually be indicated by a memory overflow ("MEM OVERFLOW") error. If you get a memory overflow error, try reducing the resolution, printing smaller graphics, or

turning off RET (see the following section for the last option). Of course, the best solution to a memory overflow error is simply to add more RAM to the laser printer.

Do not assume that every error with the word *memory* in it can be fixed simply by adding more RAM to the printer. Just as adding more RAM chips will not solve every conventional computer memory problem, adding more RAM will not solve every laser printer memory problem. The message "21 ERROR" on an HP LaserJet, for example, indicates that "the printer is unable to process very complex data fast enough for the print engine." This means that the data is simply too complex for the RIP to handle. Adding more memory would *not* solve this problem; it would only make your wallet lighter. The only answer in this case is to reduce the complexity of the page image (that is, fewer fonts, less formatting, reduced graphics resolution, and so on).

Resolution

Laser printers can print at different resolutions, just as monitors can display different resolutions. The maximum resolution a laser printer can handle is determined by its physical characteristics. Laser printer resolution is expressed in dots per inch (dpi). Common resolutions are 600 × 600 dpi or 1200 × 1200 dpi. The first number, the horizontal resolution, is determined by how fine a focus can be achieved by the laser. The second number is determined by the smallest increment by which the drum can be turned. Higher resolutions produce higher-quality output, but keep in mind that higher resolutions also require more memory. In some instances, complex images can be printed only at lower resolutions because of their high memory demands. Even printing at 300 dpi, laser printers produce far better quality than dot-matrix printers because of *resolution enhancement technology (RET).*

RET enables the printer to insert smaller dots among the characters, smoothing out the jagged curves that are typical of printers that do not use RET (see Figure 27-18). Using RET enables laser printers to output high-quality print jobs, but it also requires a portion of the printer's RAM. If you get a MEM OVERFLOW error, sometimes disabling RET will free up enough memory to complete the print job.

Figure 27-18 RET fills in gaps with smaller dots to smooth out jagged characters.

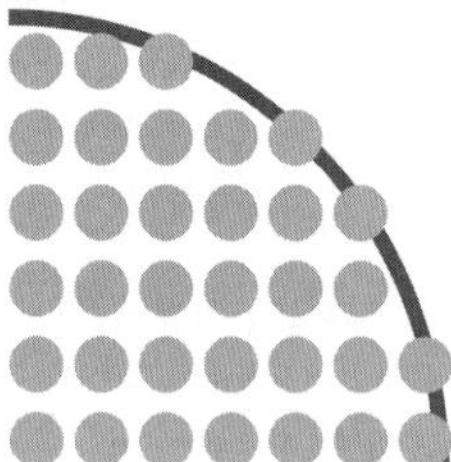

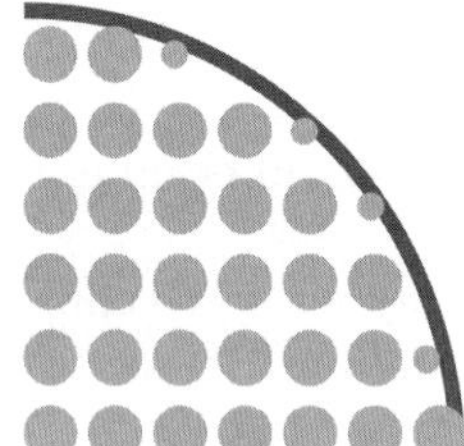

Charging

Now we turn to the physical side of the printing process. To make the drum receptive to new images, it must be charged (see Figure 27-19). Using the primary corona wire or primary charge roller, a uniform negative charge is applied to the entire surface of the drum (usually between -600 and -1000 volts).

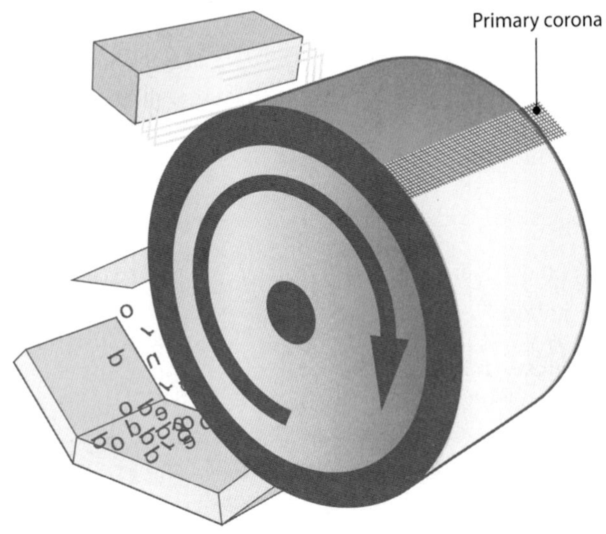

Figure 27-19 Charging the drum with a uniform negative charge

Exposing

A laser is used to create a positive image on the surface of the drum. Every particle on the drum hit by the laser releases most of its negative charge into the drum.

Developing

Those particles with a lesser negative charge are positively charged relative to the toner particles and attract them, creating a developed image (see Figure 27-20).

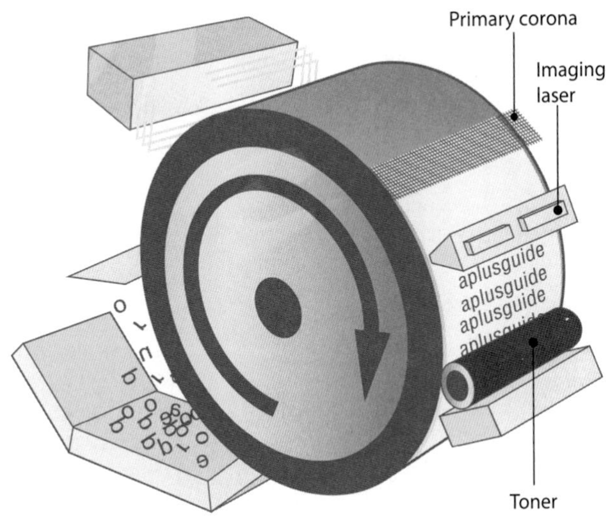

Figure 27-20 Writing the image and applying the toner

Transferring

The printer must transfer the image from the drum onto the paper. The transfer corona or transfer roller gives the paper a positive charge; then the negatively charged toner particles leap from the drum to the paper. At this point, the particles are merely resting on the paper and must still be permanently fused to the paper.

Fusing

The particles have been attracted to the paper because of the paper's positive charge, but if the process stopped here, the toner particles would fall off the page as soon as you lift it. Because the toner particles are mostly composed of plastic, they can be melted to the page. Two rollers—a heated roller coated in a nonstick material and a pressure roller—melt the toner to the paper, permanently affixing it. Finally, a static charge eliminator removes the paper's positive charge (see Figure 27-21). Once the page is complete, the printer ejects the printed copy and the process begins again with the physical and electrical cleaning of the printer.

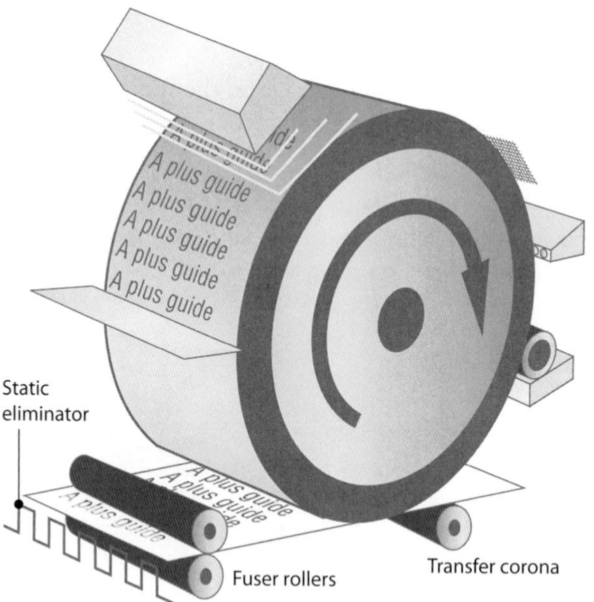

Figure 27-21 Transferring the image to the paper and fusing the final image

Cleaning

The printing process ends with the physical and electrical cleaning of the photosensitive drum (see Figure 27-22). Before printing another new page, the drum must be returned to a clean, fresh condition. All residual toner left over from printing the previous page must be removed, usually by scraping the surface of the drum with a rubber cleaning blade. If residual particles remain on the drum, they will appear as random black spots

and streaks on the next page. The physical cleaning mechanism either deposits the residual toner in a debris cavity or recycles it by returning it to the toner supply in the toner cartridge. The physical cleaning must be done carefully—a damaged drum will cause a mark to be printed on every page until it is replaced.

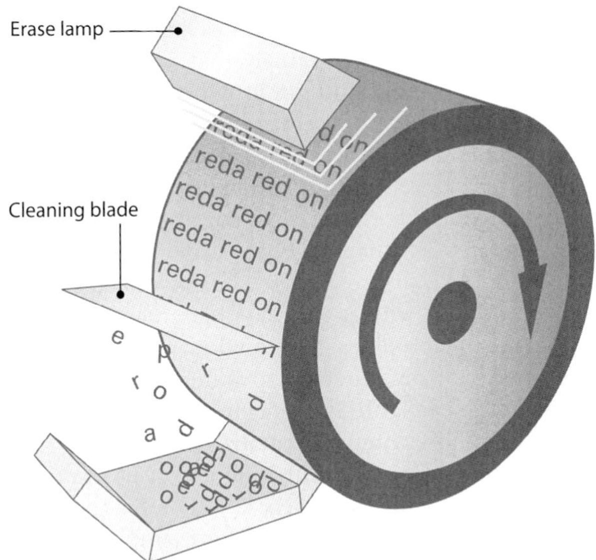

Figure 27-22 Cleaning and erasing the drum

The printer must also be electrically cleaned. One or more erase lamps bombard the surface of the drum with the appropriate wavelengths of light, causing the surface particles to discharge into the grounded drum. After the cleaning process, the drum should be completely free of toner and have a neutral charge.

NOTE Color laser printers use four different colors of toner (cyan, magenta, yellow, and black) to create their printouts. Most models send each page through four different passes, adding one color at each pass to create the needed results, while others place all the colors onto a special *transfer belt* and then transfer them to the page in one pass. In some cases, the printer uses four separate toner cartridges and four lasers for the four toner colors, and in others the printer simply lays down one color after the other on the same drum, cleaning after each of four passes per page.

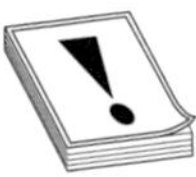

CAUTION The heated roller produces enough heat to melt some types of plastic media, particularly overhead transparency materials. This could damage your laser printer (and void your warranty), so make sure you print on transparencies designed for laser printers!

Installing a Multifunction Device

Installing a multifunction device differs a lot from installing single-function devices. In the consumer space, the process is messy because of the complexity of the devices. Here's the scoop.

First, most multifunction devices today connect via USB and wirelessly, so you need to consider connectivity. Second, you need to install drivers for each of the various functions of the multifunction device. Initially, that seems fine, because you can use the driver disc that came with the device and can install everything for the OS you choose.

That default process can rapidly turn into a mess, though, because of several factors. The drivers are often outdated. Updating specific drivers takes time and clicking. Worse, manufacturers often add absurdly bad applications to "support" specific functions of multifunction devices, such as special photo organization tools that bog down the system and function far worse than readily available tools like Picasa from Google (free) or Lightroom from Adobe (not free, but reasonably priced).

Third, you're dealing with a very complex machine that can break in interesting ways. Maintenance and troubleshooting take on new dimensions by the sheer number of options to consider, from ink levels to scanner mechanics to dogged-out phone lines. Although none of these fall into the category of installation, you can minimize the problems by practicing a more compartmentalized installation.

Rather than focus on the multifunction aspect of multifunction machines, you will fare better for you and your customers if you think about each function as a separate action. Pull the machine apart in essence, for example, and install a printer, a scanner, a copy machine, and a fax machine. Share these individual parts as needed on a network. Update drivers for each component separately. Conceptualize each function as a separate device to simplify troubleshooting. This way, if your print output goes south, for example, think about the printer aspects of the multifunction device. You don't have to worry about the scanner, copy, or fax aspects of the machine.

The next sections cover installation of single-function devices, though the bulk of information is on printers. That's both what the CompTIA A+ exams cover and what you'll have to deal with as a tech for the most part.

Setting Up Printers in Windows

You need to take a moment to understand how Windows handles printing, and then you'll see how to install, configure, and troubleshoot printers.

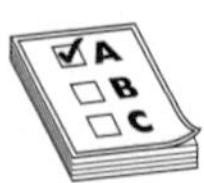

EXAM TIP The CompTIA A+ exams test you on installing and troubleshooting printers, so read these sections carefully!

To Windows, a printer is not a physical device; it is a *program* that controls one or more physical printers. The *physical* printer is called a print device by Windows (although I continue to use the term "printer" for most purposes, just like almost every tech on the

planet). Printer drivers and a spooler are still present, but in Windows, they are integrated into the printer itself (see Figure 27-23). This arrangement gives Windows amazing flexibility. For example, one printer can support multiple print devices, enabling a system to act as a print server. If one print device goes down, the printer automatically redirects the output to a working print device.

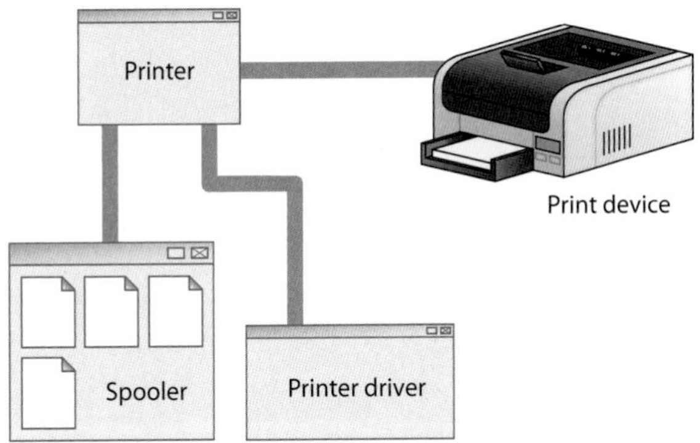

Figure 27-23 Printer driver and spooler in Windows

The general installation, configuration, and troubleshooting issues are basically identical in all modern versions of Windows. Here's a review of a typical Windows printer installation. I'll mention the trivial differences among Windows Vista, 7, and 8/8.1 as I go along. Setting up a printer is so easy it's almost scary. Most printers are plug-and-play, so installing a printer is reduced to simply plugging it in and loading the driver if needed. With USB printers, Windows won't even wait for you to do anything—Windows immediately detects and installs a printer once you connect it. If the system does not detect the printer in Vista, you need to open the Control Panel and find the Printer menu item—it is either by itself or, in the categorized view, under Hardware. With Windows 7 and newer, the applet has been renamed Devices and Printers. As you might guess, you install a new printer by clicking the Add a Printer icon/button (somehow Microsoft has managed to leave the name of this option unchanged through all Windows versions since 95!). This starts the Add Printer Wizard.

The Add Printer Wizard enables you to install a local printer or a network printer. This distinction is actually a little misleading. Windows divides printer installation into two scenarios: a printer connected directly to a computer (your local system or another one on a network), or a standalone printer directly connected to a switch or router. While you might expect the local and network installation options to divide these scenarios nicely, they don't. Let's take a quick look at both local and network installations so you know when to use each.

Installing a Local Printer

At first glance, you might think the local printer installation option is used to install your standard USB printer, but don't forget that Windows will automatically detect and install USB printers (or any other plug-and-play printer). So what do you use it for? This option is most commonly used to install standalone network printers using an IP address. Using

current versions of Windows and a modern printer, you shouldn't need to use the IP address to install a standalone network printer, but it can be a helpful alternative if Windows refuses to detect it any other way.

If you need to install a standalone network printer, use its IP address or hostname. In Windows Vista and Windows 7, click *Add a local printer*. In the *Create a new port* drop-down box, select Standard TCP/IP Port. Click Next. Type the IP address here. Windows 8/8.1/10 is even simpler: If Windows doesn't automatically detect your new printer, click *The printer that I want isn't listed* and select *Add a printer using TCP/IP address or hostname*.

Whether you use a USB port or a TCP/IP port, you'll need to manually select the proper driver (see Figure 27-24). Windows includes a lot of printer drivers, but you can also use the handy Have Disk option to use the disc that came with the printer. If you use the driver included on the disc, Windows will require administrator privileges to proceed; otherwise, you won't be able to finish the installation. The Windows Update button enables you to grab the latest printer drivers via the Internet.

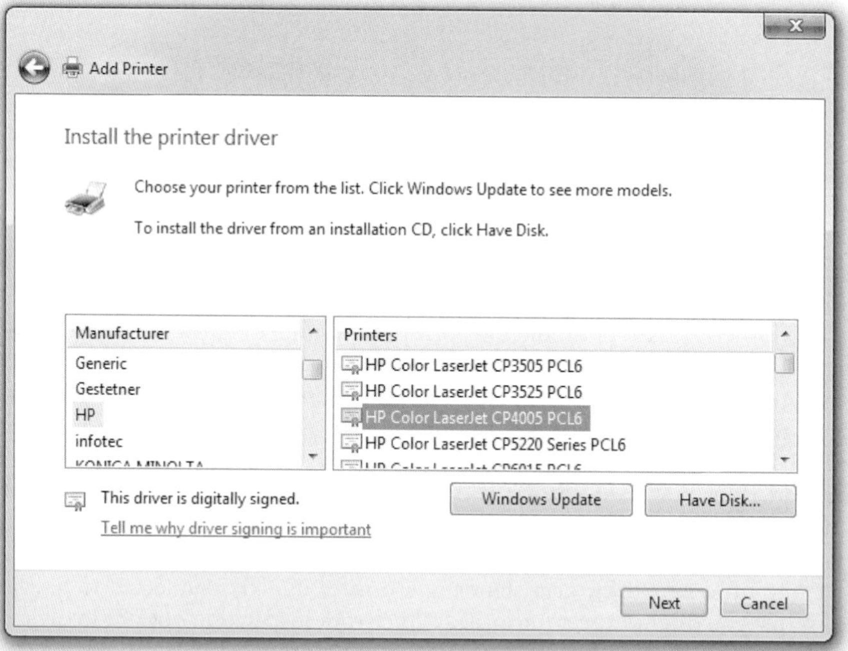

Figure 27-24 Selecting drivers

After clicking the Next button, you'll be asked if the new local printer should be the default printer and whether you want to share it with other computers on the network. And before you ask, yes, you can share a standalone network printer connected to your computer via a TCP/IP port using File and Printer Sharing, though the printer would be

disabled for other users any time you turned off your computer. You'll be asked to print a test page to make sure everything works. Then you're done!

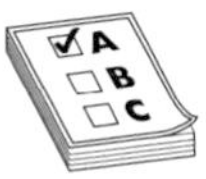

EXAM TIP Windows-based printer sharing isn't the only game in town. Apple's *AirPrint* functionality can be used in conjunction with its *Bonjour Print Service* (installed separately, or along with iTunes) to share a printer connected to a Windows system with AirPrint-compatible Mac OS X and Apple iOS devices.

Installing a Network Printer

Surprisingly, setting up network printers doesn't require much more effort than setting up local printers. When you try to install a network printer the Add Printer Wizard will scan for any available printers on your local network. More often than not, the printer you are looking for will pop up in a list (see Figure 27-25). When you select that printer and click Next, Windows will search for drivers. If you need to, you can pick from a list of available drivers or use the disc that came with the printer. Either way, you're already done.

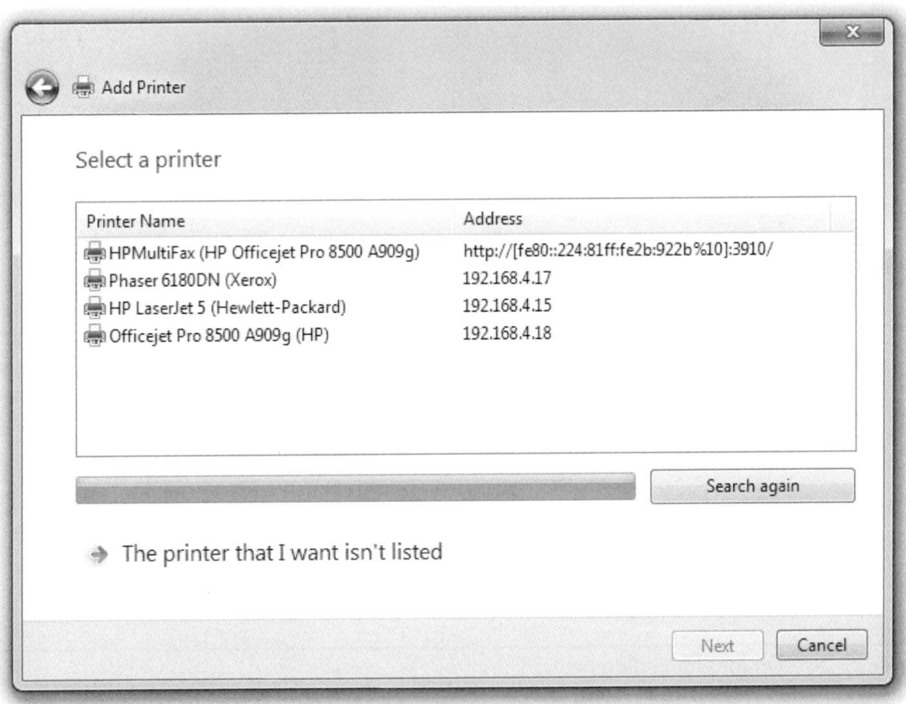

Figure 27-25 List of available shared printers on a network

NOTE Remember printer sharing from Chapter 21, "Local Area Networking"? Here's the other side of the operation. Keep in mind that after you install a shared printer onto your computer, you can actually share it with others. Windows considers it *your* printer, so you can do what you want with it, including sharing it again.

If Windows fails to find your printer, you'll need to configure the network printer manually. Every version of Windows includes multiple methods of doing this. These methods change depending on whether you are connected to a domain or a workgroup.

If you are on a workgroup, you can browse for a printer on your network, connect to a specific printer (using its name or URL), or use a TCP/IP address or hostname, as you see in Figure 27-26. In a domain, most of these options remain the same, except that instead of browsing the workgroup, you can search and browse the domain using several search parameters, including printer features, printer location, and more. Once you've found your printer, you might be prompted for drivers. Provide them using the usual methods described earlier and then you are finished!

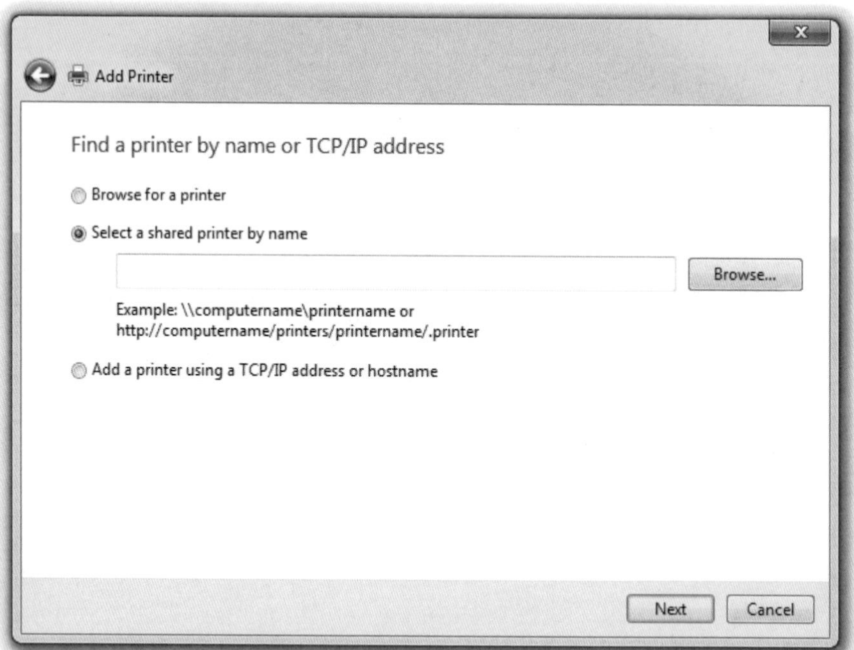

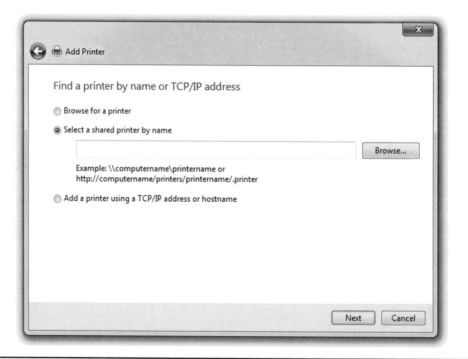

Figure 27-26 Options for finding network printers

NOTE If you are a member of a Windows homegroup and printer sharing is enabled, all printers connected to the homegroup are shared with you automatically.

Remember that Windows doesn't always see your network's printers exactly how they are physically arranged. Imagine you have a network with three computers. Andy's computer has a printer connected via USB, whereas Beth's computer and Carol's computer have no printers. There is, however, a second printer connected directly to their router via Ethernet. Beth has configured her system to connect directly to the network printer using an IP address. As such, she can actually share that printer with the rest of her network, even though it's not attached to her computer—Windows doesn't care where it is. The process for sharing a local printer and a network printer is identical because Windows considers both printers to be installed on your computer and under your control. So now Andy and Beth both share printers. When Carol goes looking for shared printers to use, the network printer attached to the router will look like Beth's printer, as if it were directly connected to Beth's machine.

NOTE Depending upon how your network shares printers, you can end up seeing the same printer shared multiple ways. Everyone who has a shared printer installed can share the same printer again as their own printer. This can lead to some confusing printer usage, especially once people start turning off their computers and breaking the connections to the shared printer. Avoid this web of print sharing.

Figure 27-27 shows a typical Windows Devices and Printers screen on a system with one printer installed. Note the small checkmark on the icon; this shows that the device is the default printer. If you have multiple printers, you can change the default printer by right-clicking the printer's icon and selecting Set as default printer.

In addition to the regular driver installation outlined previously, some installations use printer emulation. *Printer emulation* simply means using a substitute printer driver for a printer, as opposed to using one made exclusively for that printer. You'll run into printer emulation in two circumstances. First, some new printers do not come with their own drivers. They instead emulate a well-known printer (such as an HP LaserJet 4) and run perfectly well on that printer driver. Second, you may see emulation in the "I don't have the right driver!" scenario. I keep about three different HP LaserJet and Epson inkjet printers installed on my computer because I know that with these printer drivers I can print to almost any printer. Some printers may require you to set them into an *emulation mode* to handle a driver other than their native one.

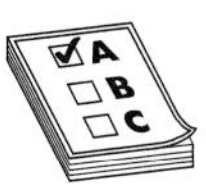

EXAM TIP In addition to the Devices and Printers applet, Windows 7 and newer (excluding the Home Premium edition) also include the Print Management console. This tool enables you to view and modify all the printers and drivers on your system or connected to your network. You can also manage any Windows print servers connected to the network. Many of Print Management's advanced features go beyond the scope of the CompTIA A+ exams, but know that it centralizes (and in a few cases, enhances) the standard printer controls in Windows. You can find Print Management in Control Panel | Administrative Tools | Print Management.

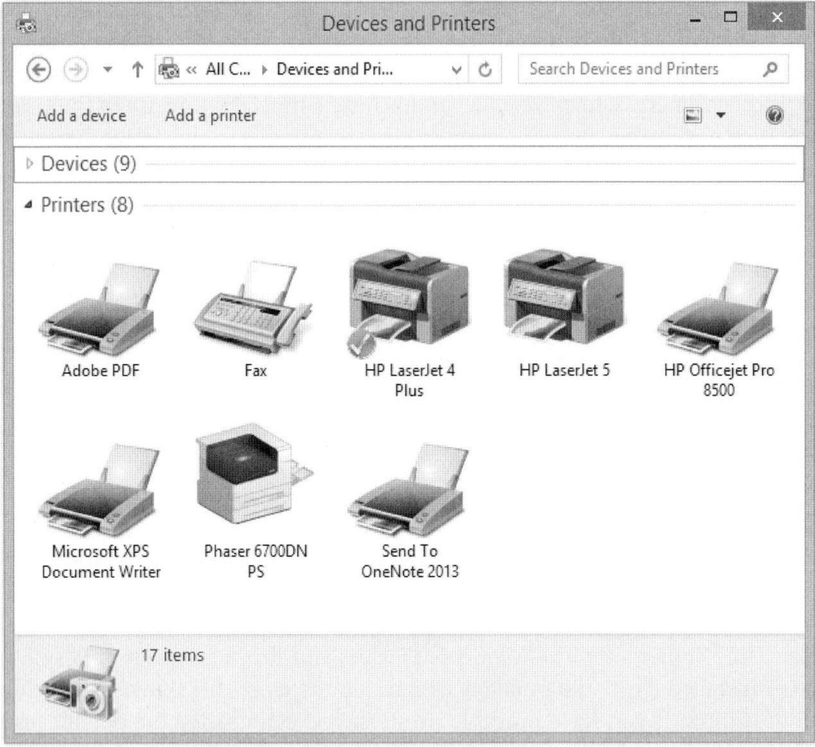

Figure 27-27 Installed default printer in the Devices and Printers applet

Configuring Print Settings

Once your printer is installed, a good first stop is the Printing preferences menu, accessible by right-clicking on the desired printer in the Devices and Printers applet in the Control Panel. This is where you'll be able to control how your printer will print your documents. Be aware that these settings can vary depending on features available on your printer or multifunction device, but let's take a look at some of the ones you're most likely to find.

Layout

The settings you're most likely to change from time to time are probably the layout settings, which control how the printer determines what to print where.

- The *duplex* setting lets you specify whether and how to use each side of a printed page. Simple duplexing will just use the front and back of each sheet sequentially, but you may find more advanced options for laying out booklets.
- The *orientation* setting lets you specify whether to print in *landscape* or *portrait* mode.
- The *multiple page* setting will let you print multiple document pages on each physical page.

- The *scaling* setting, not to be confused with the multiple page setting, is usually for fitting a large document to a single page, or scaling a small document up to the size of a full page.
- *Reverse* or *invert* options let you print the mirror image of your document, which is useful for printing on transfer paper and other special-use cases.

Paper

Many of the settings you'll find are for telling your printer what kind of paper it will be using, and (especially if the printer has multiple paper trays) where to find it.

- Set the *paper size* to one of several common paper sizes, or define a custom one.
- Specify the *paper type*, which may involve setting thickness, coating, and special formats such as envelopes and labels.
- A *paper source* setting will let you select any available paper trays, and possibly *manual feed*, in which case the printer will wait for you to feed it each sheet individually. This is useful if you need to feed in one-off items or paper that won't fit in the tray.

Quality

There are usually a number of different settings that have bearing on quality, but be aware that the name or description of some settings that affect quality may discuss ink or toner use (and may as such be located with other ink/toner-related settings).

- The most obvious of these, *resolution*, specifies what DPI the document should be printed at.
- Some printers may let you choose some mode or quality presets that optimize printing for graphics or text, or choose to manually configure your own advanced settings.
- Some printers may have settings that reduce ink or toner used, for economic and environmental reasons.

Other Common Settings

Some print devices offer options useful in specific, but limited, occasions.

- The *apply a watermark* setting will let you choose from presets or define your own. A watermark is a lightly printed mark across every page. Use a watermark to designate a draft copy of a document, for example, rather than a final copy.
- *Header/footer* settings can be used to add information about when a document was printed and who printed it.
- A *collate* option lets you specify the order in which multiple copies of a multi-page document are printed. If the option is unchecked and you print ten copies, each page will be printed ten times before the printer moves on. If the option is checked, the printer will print the full document before starting over.

Optimizing Print Performance

Although a quality printer is the first step toward quality output, your output relies on factors other than the printer itself. What you see on the screen may not match what comes out of the printer, so calibration is important. Using the wrong type of paper can result in less-than-acceptable printed documents. Configuring the printer driver and spool settings can also affect your print jobs.

Calibration

If you've ever tweaked a photograph so it looks perfect on your screen, only to discover the final printout was darker than you had hoped, consider calibrating your monitor. *Calibration* uses hardware to generate an International Color Consortium (ICC) color profile, a file that defines the color characteristics of a hardware device. The operating system then uses this profile to correct any color shifts in your monitor. With a calibrated monitor, you know any color shifts in your photograph are really in the photo, not an artifact of your monitor.

Where these ICC color profiles really start to get interesting is that they can be created for printers as well. Just like with a monitor, they let the computer know the unique color quirks of a specific printer. When your printer and monitor have been properly calibrated and the profiles installed, your prints and monitor display should match. Color profiles are sometimes included on the installation media with a printer, but you can create or purchase custom profiles as well. Windows includes *Windows Color System (WCS)* to help build color profiles for use across devices. WCS is based on a newer standard Microsoft calls *color infrastructure and translation engine (CITE)*.

Managing Shared/Public/Networked Devices

While we've looked at a few of the ways you can share a printer or multifunction device over a network, there's more to know about sharing these devices than just how to set them up. A few big issues are network security and data privacy.

Network Security

The ease of access that makes wired or wireless network printers and multifunction devices so useful is also a big risk; at best it means they're vulnerable to attacks over the LAN, and at worst it means they may be open to attack from the entire Internet. While hardening a network printer or multifunction device is beyond the scope of this book, it's important to be aware of the risks these devices present. There are the obvious immediate risks to the data and documents flowing through the device, but because security is often overlooked on these devices, they are also common starting points for an attack on the broader network.

Data Privacy

If you think about it, a lot of sensitive information can pass through a printer or multifunction device in most organizations, especially in places like schools and hospitals where privacy is strictly regulated. When all of this information passes through the printer, it's important to make sure it isn't leaking out. Unfortunately, it's common for

modern devices to contain a hard drive or other storage media used to cache copies of documents the device prints, scans, copies, or faxes. Depending on the device, you may be able to disable this feature, schedule regular deletion of the cache, or manually clear the cache regularly to limit the amount of damage a compromise could cause. It's also important to clear this information before disposing of the device.

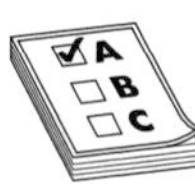

EXAM TIP The CompTIA A+ 901 objectives refer to this as *hard drive caching*, so be prepared to see this phrasing on the exam.

Disabling features like this wouldn't be much good if anyone who could use the device could also change the settings, so enterprise models often allow for *user authentication* on the device. This can address a number of the risks these devices present by limiting use to authenticated users, and restricting the features each user can access to only what they need.

Just because the data on your device is secure doesn't mean documents rolling off of it are free from prying eyes. User authentication can also help out by letting users send documents to the printer, but waiting to print them until the user authenticates at the device. It can also minimize some of the risk to unsupervised documents by restricting the ability of less-trusted users to scan/copy/e-mail a document from the device, limiting the ease with which they could steal a copy of an unattended document and leave the original.

Troubleshooting Printers

Once set up, printers tend to run with few issues, assuming that you install the proper drivers and keep the printer well maintained. But printer errors do occasionally develop. Take a look at the most common print problems, as well as problems that crop up with specific printer types.

NOTE Every printer is different. Read the documentation included with your printer to learn how you can perform the tasks listed in this section.

Troubleshooting General Issues

Printers of all stripes share some common problems, such as print jobs that don't print, strangely sized prints, and misalignment. Other issues include disposing of consumables, sharing multiple printers, and crashing on power-up. Let's take a look at these general troubleshooting issues, but start with a recap of the tools of the trade.

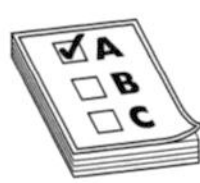

EXAM TIP Don't forget to check the obvious. Many printers include tiny displays that can clue you in to what's wrong. Most brands use a series of *error codes* that indicate the problem. Use the manual or the manufacturer's Web site to translate the error code into meaningful information.

Tools of the Trade

Before you jump in and start to work on a printer that's giving you fits, you'll need some tools. You can use the standard computer tech tools in your toolkit, plus a couple of printer-specific devices. Here are some that will come in handy:

- A multimeter for troubleshooting electrical problems such as faulty wall outlets
- Various cleaning solutions, such as denatured alcohol
- An extension magnet for grabbing loose screws in tight spaces and cleaning up iron-based toner
- An optical disc or USB thumb drive with test patterns for checking print quality
- Your trusty screwdriver—both a Phillips-head and flat-head, because if you bring just one kind, it's a sure bet that you'll need the other

Print Job Never Prints

If you click Print but nothing comes out of the printer, first check all the obvious things. Is the printer on? Is it connected? Is it online? Does it have paper? Is your computer online?

If you can't connect to the printer, check all cables, ports, and power involved. If everything is plugged in and ready to go, check the appropriate printer applet for your version of Windows. If you don't see the printer you are looking for, you'll need to reinstall it using the Add Printer Wizard.

If you attempt to use a printer shared by another computer but Windows pops up with an "Access Denied" error, you might not have permission to use the printer. Go to the host system and check the Security tab of the Printer Properties dialog box. Make sure your user account is allowed to use the printer.

Assuming the printer is in good order, it's time to look at the spooler. You can see the spooler status either by double-clicking the printer's icon in the appropriate printer Control Panel applet or by double-clicking the tiny printer icon in the notification area if it's present. If you're having a problem, the printer icon will almost always be there. Figure 27-28 shows the print spooler open.

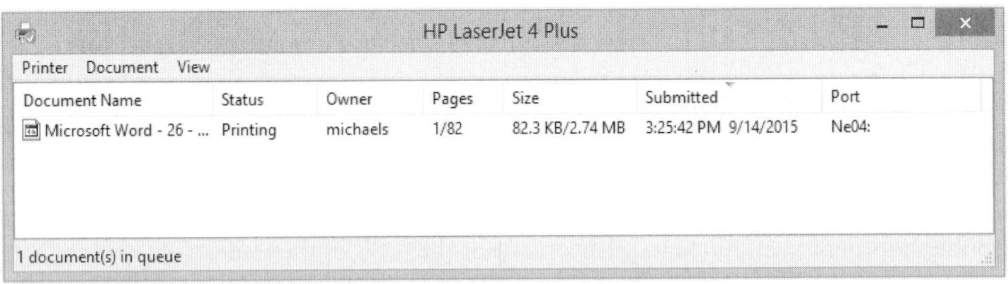

Figure 27-28 Print spooler

Print spoolers can easily overflow or become corrupt due to a lack of disk space, too many print jobs, or one of a thousand other factors. The status window shows all of the

pending print jobs and enables you to delete, start, or pause jobs. I usually just delete the affected print job(s) and try again.

Print spoolers are handy. If the printer goes down, you can just leave the print jobs in the spooler until the printer comes back online. If you have a printer that isn't coming on anytime soon, you can simply delete the print job in the spooler window and try another printer.

If you have problems with the print spooler, you can get around them by changing your print spool settings. Go into the Printers/Devices and Printers applet, right-click the icon of the printer in question, and choose Printer properties. In the resulting Properties dialog box (see Figure 27-29), choose the *Print directly to the printer* radio button on the Advanced tab and click OK; then try sending your print job again. Note that this window also offers you the choice of printing immediately—that is, starting to print pages as soon as the spooler has enough information to feed to the printer—or holding off on printing until the entire job is spooled.

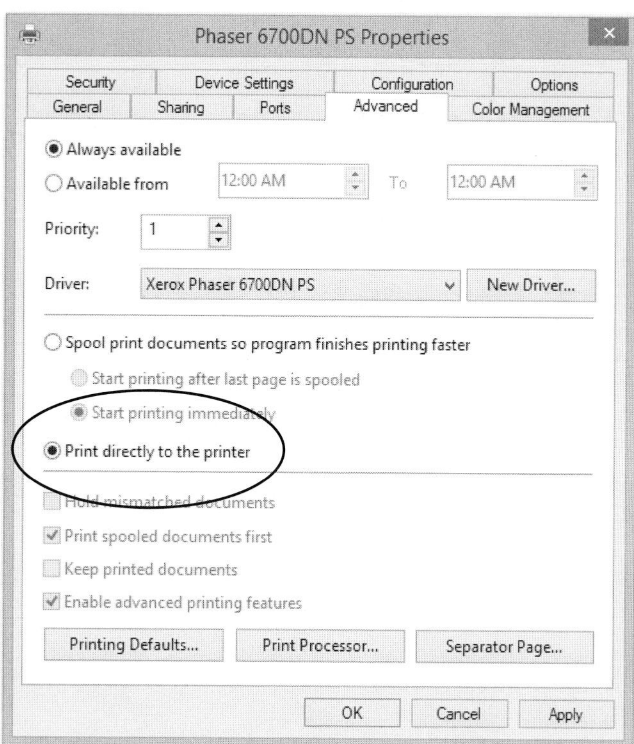

Figure 27-29
Print spool settings

If that isn't enough, try restarting the print spooler service. Open the Start menu and right-click on Computer. Select Manage—you'll need administrator privileges to continue. In the column on the left, double-click on Services and Applications, and then click on Services. The Services console should appear in the center of the Computer Management window. Scroll down and find the service named Print Spooler. Right-click on the service and simply click Restart, if available; otherwise, select Stop, wait for it to stop, right-click on the service again, and select Start. You should be able to print using the print spooler again.

Another possible cause for a stalled print job is that the printer is simply waiting for the correct paper! Laser printers in particular have settings that tell them what size paper is in their standard paper tray or trays. If the application sending a print job specifies a different paper size—for example, it wants to print a standard No. 10 envelope, or perhaps a legal sheet, but the standard paper tray holds only 8.5 × 11 letter paper—the printer usually pauses and holds up the queue until someone switches out the tray or manually feeds the type of paper that this print job requires. You can usually override this pause, even without having the specified paper, by pressing the OK or GO button on the printer.

The printer's default paper tray and paper size options will differ greatly depending on the printer type and model. To find these settings, go into the printer's Properties dialog box from the Printers/Devices and Printers applet, and then select the Device Settings tab. This list of settings includes Form To Tray Assignment, where you can specify which tray (in the case of a printer with multiple paper trays) holds which size paper.

Strange Sizes

A print job that comes out an unexpected size usually points to a user mistake in setting up the print job. All applications have a Print command and a Page Setup interface. The Page Setup interface enables you to define a number of print options, which vary from application to application. Figure 27-30 shows the Page Setup options for Microsoft Word. Make sure the page is set up properly before you blame the printer for a problem.

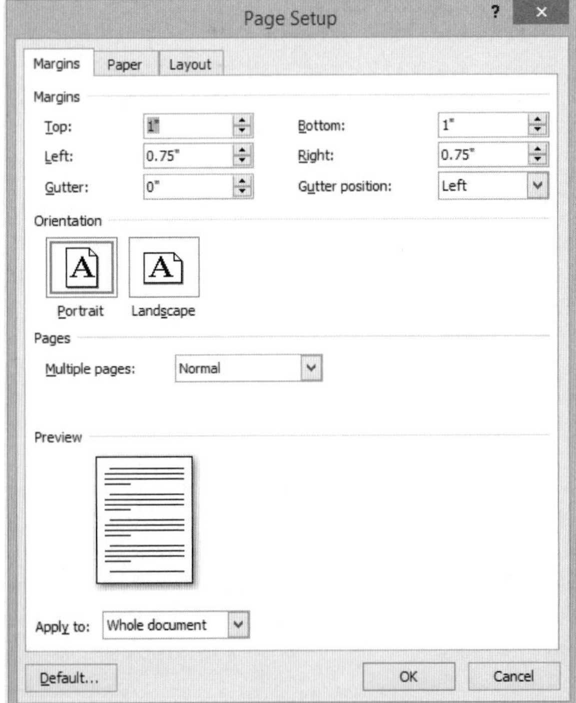

Figure 27-30 Page Setup options for Microsoft Word

If you know the page is set up correctly, recheck the printer drivers. If necessary, uninstall and reinstall the printer drivers. If the problem persists, you may have a serious problem with the printer's print engine, but that comes up as a likely answer only when you continually get the same strangely sized printouts using a variety of applications.

Misaligned or Garbage Prints

Misaligned or garbage printouts invariably point to a corrupted or incorrect driver. Make sure you're using the right driver (it's hard to mess this up, but not impossible) and then uninstall and reinstall the printer driver. If the problem persists, you may be asking the printer to do something it cannot do. For example, you may be printing to a PostScript printer with a PCL driver. Check the printer type to verify that you haven't installed the wrong type of driver for that printer!

Dealing with Consumables

All printers tend to generate a lot of trash in the form of *consumables*. Impact printers use paper and ribbons, inkjet printers use paper and ink cartridges, and laser printers use paper and toner cartridges. In today's environmentally sensitive world, many laws regulate the proper disposal of most printer components. Be sure to check with the local sanitation department or disposal services company before throwing away any component. Of course, you should never throw away toner cartridges—certain companies will *pay* for used cartridges!

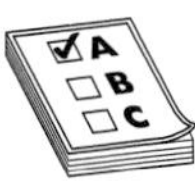

EXAM TIP *Material safety data sheets (MSDSs)* contain important information regarding hazardous materials such as safe use procedures and emergency response instructions. An MSDS is typically posted anywhere a hazardous chemical is used.

Crashes on Power-Up

Both laser printers and computers require more power during their initial power-up (the POST on a computer and the warm-up on a laser printer) than once they are running. Hewlett-Packard recommends a *reverse power-up*. Turn on the laser printer first and allow it to finish its warm-up before turning on the computer. This avoids having two devices drawing their peak loads simultaneously.

Display Screen Malfunction

The small menu display screens included on many modern printers and multifunction devices can, like any other display screen, have a number of issues such as freezing, not coming on at all, displaying a single color, or artifacts such as lines showing on the display. Unfortunately, there's not a lot you can do about these problems. Turning the device off and back on is a good start, and some manufacturers recommend completely unplugging it for a few minutes. If the screen is still misbehaving but the device is otherwise functional and the problem didn't appear immediately after a firmware update, it's time to take the device to a service center.

Troubleshooting Impact Printers

Impact printers require regular maintenance but will run forever as long as you're diligent. Keep the platen (the roller or plate on which the pins impact) and the printhead clean with denatured alcohol. Be sure to lubricate gears and pulleys according to the manufacturer's specifications. Never lubricate the printhead, however, because the lubricant will smear and stain the paper. Don't forget to replace the ink ribbon every so often.

Bad-Looking Text

White bars going through the text point to a dirty or damaged printhead. Try cleaning the printhead with a little denatured alcohol. If the problem persists, replace the printhead. Printheads for most printers are readily available from the manufacturer or from companies that rebuild them. If the characters look chopped off at the top or bottom, the printhead probably needs to be adjusted. Refer to the manufacturer's instructions for proper adjustment.

Bad-Looking Page

If the page is covered with dots and small smudges—the "pepper look"—the platen is dirty. Clean the platen with denatured alcohol. If the image is faded, and you know the ribbon is good, try adjusting the printhead closer to the platen. If the image is okay on one side of the paper but fades as you move to the other, the platen is out of adjustment. Platens are generally difficult to adjust, so your best plan is to take it to the manufacturer's local warranty/repair center.

Troubleshooting Thermal Printers

Compared to other printer styles, thermal printers are simple to troubleshoot and maintain. With direct thermal printers, you only need to worry about three things: the heating element, the rollers, and the paper. With thermal wax printers, you also need to care for the wax ribbon.

To clean the heating element, turn off the thermal printer and open it according to the manufacturer's instructions. Use denatured alcohol and a lint-free cloth to wipe off the heating element. You might need to use a little pressure to get it completely clean. Clean the rollers with a cloth or compressed air. You want to keep them free of debris so they can properly grip the paper. Replacing the paper is as easy as sliding off the old roll and replacing it with a new one. Remember to feed the paper through the heating element, because otherwise you won't print anything. Replacing the ribbon is similar to replacing the roll of paper; make sure to feed it past the heating element, or the printer won't work properly. Your printer's manufacturer should include any special instructions for installing a new ribbon.

Troubleshooting Inkjet Printers

Inkjet printers are reliable devices that require little maintenance as long as they are used within their design parameters (high-use machines will require more intensive maintenance). Because of the low price of these printers, manufacturers know that people don't

want to spend a lot of money keeping them running. If you perform even the most basic maintenance tasks, they will soldier on for years without a whimper. Inkjets generally have built-in maintenance programs that you should run from time to time to keep your inkjet in good operating order.

Inkjet Printer Maintenance

Inkjet printers don't get nearly as dirty as laser printers, and most manufacturers do not recommend periodic cleaning. Unless your manufacturer explicitly tells you to do so, don't vacuum an inkjet. Inkjets generally do not have maintenance kits, but most inkjet printers come with extensive maintenance software (see Figure 27-31). Usually, the hardest part of using this software is finding it in the first place. Look for an option in Printing Preferences, a selection on the Start menu, or an option on the printer's management Web page. Don't worry—it's there!

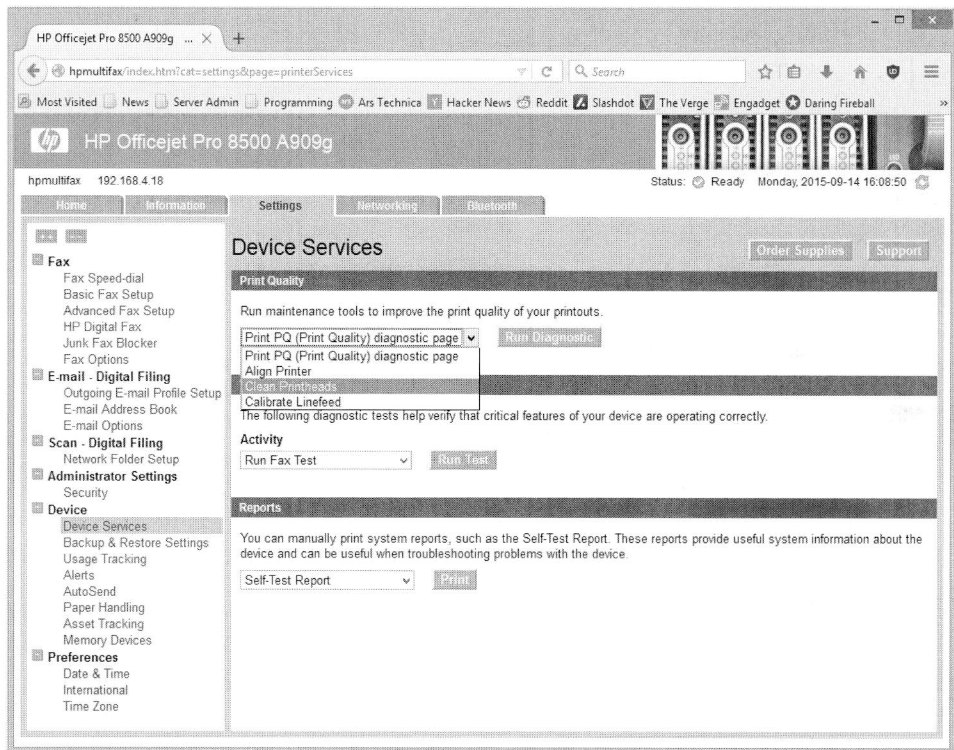

Figure 27-31 Inkjet printer maintenance screen

When you first set up an inkjet printer, it normally instructs you to perform a routine (sometimes referred to as *calibration*) to align the printheads properly, wherein you print out a page and select from sets of numbered lines. If this isn't done, the print quality will

show it, but the good news is that you can perform this procedure at any time. If a printer is moved or dropped or it's just been working away untended for a while, it's often worth running the alignment routine.

Inkjet Problems

Did I say that you never should clean an inkjet? Well, that may be true for the printer itself, but there is one part of your printer that will benefit from an occasional cleaning: the inkjet's printer head nozzles. The nozzles are the tiny pipes that squirt the ink onto the paper. A common problem with inkjet printers is the tendency for the ink inside the nozzles to dry out when not used even for a relatively short time, blocking any ink from exiting. If your printer is telling Windows that it's printing and feeding paper through, but either nothing is coming out (usually the case if you're just printing black text) or only certain colors are printing, the culprit is almost certainly dried ink clogging the nozzles.

NOTE All inkjet inks are water-based, and water works better than denatured alcohol to clean them up.

Every inkjet printer has a different procedure for cleaning the printhead nozzles. On older inkjets, you usually have to press buttons on the printer to start a maintenance program. On more modern inkjets, you can access the head-cleaning maintenance program from Windows.

NOTE Cleaning the heads on an inkjet printer is sometimes necessary, but I don't recommend that you do it on a regular basis as preventive maintenance. The head-cleaning process uses up a lot of that very expensive inkjet ink—so do this only when a printing problem seems to indicate clogged or dirty printheads!

Another problem that sometimes arises is the dreaded multi-sheet paper grab. This is often not actually your printer's fault—humidity can cause sheets of paper to cling to each other—but sometimes the culprit is an overheated printer, so if you've been cranking out a lot of documents without stopping, try giving the printer a bit of a coffee break. Also, fan the sheets of the paper stack before inserting it into the paper tray.

Finally, check to see if excess ink overflow is a problem. In the area where the printheads park, look for a small tank or tray that catches excess ink from the cleaning process. If the printer has one, check to see how full it is. If this tray overflows onto the main board or even the power supply, it will kill your printer. If you discover that the tray is about to overflow, you can remove excess ink by inserting a twisted paper towel into the tank to soak up some of the ink. It is advisable to wear latex or vinyl gloves while doing this. Clean up any spilled ink with a paper towel dampened with distilled water.

Troubleshooting Laser Printers

Quite a few problems can arise with laser printers, but before getting into those details, you need to review some recommended procedures for *avoiding* those problems.

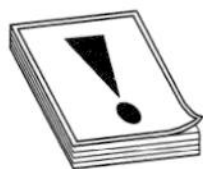

CAUTION Before you service a laser printer, always, *always* turn it off and unplug it! Don't expose yourself to the very dangerous high voltages found inside these machines.

Laser Printer Maintenance

Unlike computer maintenance, laser printer maintenance follows a fairly well-established procedure. Of course, you'll need to replace the toner cartridge every so often, but keeping your laser printer healthy requires following these maintenance steps.

Keep It Clean Laser printers are quite robust as a rule. A good cleaning every time you replace the toner cartridge will help that printer last for many years. I know of many examples of original HP LaserJet I printers continuing to run perfectly after a dozen or more years of operation. The secret is that they were kept immaculately clean.

Your laser printer gets dirty in two ways: Excess toner, over time, will slowly coat the entire printer. Paper dust, sometimes called *paper dander*, tends to build up where the paper is bent around rollers or where pickup rollers grab paper. Unlike (black) toner, paper dust is easy to see and is usually a good indicator that a printer needs to be cleaned. Usually, a thorough cleaning using a can of compressed air to blow out the printer is the best cleaning you can do. It's best to do this outdoors, or you may end up looking like one of those chimney sweeps from *Mary Poppins*! If you must clean a printer indoors, use a special low-static vacuum designed especially for electronic components (see Figure 27-32).

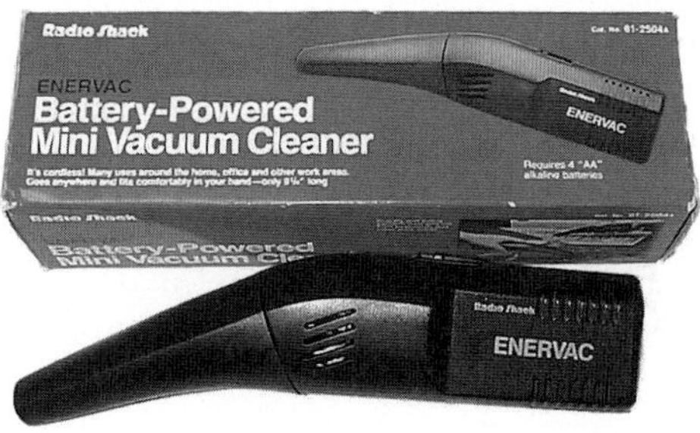

Figure 27-32 Low-static vacuum

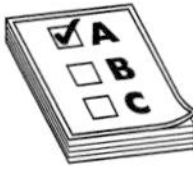

EXAM TIP The CompTIA A+ 220-901 exam refers to a "toner vacuum," which is the same as a low-static vacuum.

Every laser printer has its own unique cleaning method, but the cleaning instructions tend to skip one little area. Every laser printer has a number of rubber guide rollers through which the paper is run during the print process. These little rollers tend to

pick up dirt and paper dust over time, making them slip and jam paper. They are easily cleaned with a small amount of 90 percent or better alcohol on a fibrous cleaning towel. The alcohol will remove the debris and any dead rubber. If the paper won't feed, you can give the rollers and separator pads a textured surface that will restore their feeding properties by rubbing them with a little denatured alcohol on a nonmetallic scouring pad.

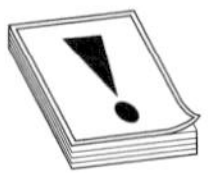

CAUTION The photosensitive drum, usually contained in the toner cartridge, can be wiped clean if it becomes dirty, but be very careful if you do so! If the drum becomes scratched, the scratch will appear on every page printed from that point on. The only repair in the event of a scratch is to replace the toner cartridge.

If you're ready to get specific, get the printer's service manual. They are a key source for information on how to keep a printer clean and running. Sadly, not all printer manufacturers provide these, but most do. While you're at it, see if the manufacturer has a Quick Reference Guide; these can be very handy for most printer problems!

Periodic Maintenance Although keeping the printer clean is critical to its health and well being, every laser printer has certain components that you need to replace periodically. Your ultimate source for determining the parts that need to be replaced (and when to replace them) is the printer manufacturer. Following the manufacturer's maintenance guidelines will help to ensure years of trouble-free, dependable printing from your laser printer.

Many manufacturers provide kits that contain components that you should replace on a regular schedule. These *maintenance kits* include sets of replacement parts, such as a fuser, as well as one or more rollers or pads. Typically, you need to reset the page counter after installing a maintenance kit so the printer can remind you to perform maintenance again after a certain number of pages have been printed.

Some ozone filters can be cleaned with a vacuum and some can only be replaced—follow the manufacturer's recommendation. You can clean the fuser assembly with 90 percent or better denatured alcohol. Check the heat roller (the Teflon-coated one with the light bulb inside) for pits and scratches. If you see surface damage on the rollers, replace the fuser unit.

Most printers will give you an error code when the fuser is damaged or overheating and needs to be replaced; others will produce the error code at a preset copy count as a preventive maintenance measure. Again, follow the manufacturer's recommendations.

NOTE Failure of the thermal fuse (used to keep the fuser from overheating) can necessitate replacing the fuser assembly. Some machines contain more than one thermal fuse. As always, follow the manufacturer's recommendations. Many manufacturers have kits that alert you with an alarm code to replace the fuser unit and key rollers and guides at predetermined page counts.

The transfer corona can be cleaned with a 90 percent denatured alcohol solution on a cotton swab. If the wire is broken, you can replace it; many just snap in or are held in by a couple of screws. Paper guides can also be cleaned with alcohol on a fibrous towel.

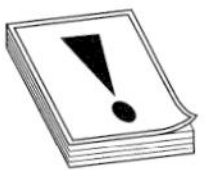

CAUTION The fuser assembly operates at 200 to 300 degrees Fahrenheit, so always allow time for this component to cool down before you attempt to clean it.

Laser Printer Problems

Laser printer problems usually result in poor output. One of the most important tests you can do on any printer, not just a laser printer, is called a *diagnostic print page* or an *engine test page*. You do this either by holding down the On Line button as the printer is started or by using the printer's maintenance software.

Blank Pages If a printer is spitting out blank pages, that usually means the printer is out of toner. If the printer does have toner and nothing prints, print a diagnostic print page. If that is also blank, remove the toner cartridge and look at the imaging drum inside. If the image is still there, you know the transfer corona or the high-voltage power supply has failed. Check the printer's maintenance guide to see how to focus on the bad part and replace it.

Dirty or Smudged Printouts If the fusing mechanism in a laser printer gets dirty, it will leave a light dusting of toner all over the paper, particularly on the back of the page. When you see toner speckles on your printouts, you should get the printer cleaned.

If the printout looks smudged, the fuser isn't properly fusing the toner to the paper. Depending on the paper used, the fuser needs to reach a certain temperature to fuse the toner. If the toner won't fuse to the paper, try using a lighter-weight paper. You might also need to replace the fuser.

Ghosting Ghost images sometimes appear at regular intervals on the printed page. This happens when the imaging drum has not fully discharged and is picking up toner from a previous image or when a previous image has used up so much toner that either the supply of charged toner is insufficient or the toner has not been adequately charged. Sometimes it can also be caused by a worn-out cleaning blade that isn't removing the toner from the drum.

Light Ghosting Versus Dark Ghosting A variety of problems can cause both light and dark ghosting, but the most common source of light ghosting is "developer starvation." If you ask a laser printer to print an extremely dark or complex image, it can use up so much toner that the toner cartridge will not be able to charge enough toner to print the next image. The proper solution is to use less toner. You can fix ghosting problems in the following ways:

- Lower the resolution of the page (print at 300 dpi instead of 600 dpi).
- Use a different pattern.

- Avoid 50 percent grayscale and "dot-on/dot-off patterns."
- Change the layout so that grayscale patterns do not follow black areas.
- Make dark patterns lighter and light patterns darker.
- Print in landscape orientation.
- Adjust print density and RET settings.
- Print a completely blank page immediately prior to the page with the ghosting image, as part of the same print job.

In addition to these possibilities, low temperature and low humidity can aggravate ghosting problems. Check your user's manual for environmental recommendations. Dark ghosting can sometimes be caused by a damaged drum. It may be fixed by replacing the toner cartridge. Light ghosting would *not* be solved in this way. Switching other components will not usually affect ghosting problems because they are a side effect of the entire printing process.

Vertical White Lines Vertical white lines usually happen when the toner is clogged, preventing the proper dispersion of toner on the drum. Try shaking the toner cartridge to dislodge the clog. If that doesn't work, replace the toner cartridge.

Blotchy Print Blotches are commonly a result of uneven dispersion of toner, especially if the toner is low. Shake the toner from side to side and then try to print. Also be sure that the printer is sitting level. Finally, make sure the paper is not wet in spots. If the blotches are in a regular order, check the fusing rollers and the photosensitive drum for any foreign objects.

Spotty Print If the spots appear at regular intervals, the drum may be damaged or some toner may be stuck to the fuser rollers. Try wiping off the fuser rollers. Check the drum for damage. If the drum is damaged, get a new toner cartridge.

Embossed Effect If your prints are getting an embossed effect (like putting a penny under a piece of paper and rubbing it with a lead pencil), there is almost certainly a foreign object on a roller. Use 90 percent denatured alcohol or regular water with a soft cloth to try to remove it. If the foreign object is on the photosensitive drum, you're going to have to use a new toner cartridge. An embossed effect can also be caused by the contrast control being set too high. The contrast control is actually a knob on the inside of the unit (sometimes accessible from the outside, on older models). Check your manual for the specific location.

Incomplete Characters You can sometimes correct incompletely printed characters on laser-printed transparencies by adjusting the print density. Be extremely careful to use only materials approved for use in laser printers.

Creased Pages Laser printers have up to four rollers. In addition to the heat and pressure rollers of the fuser assembly, other rollers move the paper from the source tray to the output tray. These rollers crease the paper to avoid curling that would cause paper

jams in the printer. If the creases are noticeable, try using a different paper type. Cotton bond paper is usually more susceptible to noticeable creasing than other bonds. You might also try sending the output to the face-up tray, which avoids one roller. There is no hardware solution to this problem; it is simply a side effect of the process.

Paper Jams Every printer jams now and then. If you get a jam, always refer first to the manufacturer's jam removal procedure. It is simply too easy to damage a printer by pulling on the jammed paper! If the printer reports a jam but there's no paper inside, you've almost certainly got a problem with one of the many jam sensors or paper feed sensors inside the printer, and you'll need to take it to a repair center.

Pulling Multiple Sheets If the printer grabs multiple sheets at a time, first try opening a new ream of paper and loading that in the printer. If that works, you have a humidity problem. If the new paper doesn't work, check the separation pad on the printer. The separation pad is a small piece of cork or rubber that separates the sheets as they are pulled from the paper feed tray. A worn separation pad looks shiny and, well, *worn*! Most separation pads are easy to replace. Check out www.printerworks.com to see if you can replace yours.

Warped, Overprinted, or Poorly Formed Characters Poorly formed characters can indicate either a problem with the paper (or other media) or a problem with the hardware.

Incorrect media cause a number of these types of problems. Avoid paper that is too rough or too smooth. Paper that is too rough interferes with the fusing of characters and their initial definition. If the paper is too smooth (like some coated papers, for example), it may feed improperly, causing distorted or overwritten characters. Even though you can purchase laser printer–specific paper, all laser printers print acceptably on standard photocopy paper. Try to keep the paper from becoming too wet. Don't open a ream of paper until it is time to load it into the printer. Always fan the paper before loading it into the printer, especially if the paper has been left out of the package for more than just a few days.

The durability of a well-maintained laser printer makes hardware a much rarer source of character printing problems, but you should be aware of the possibility. Fortunately, it is fairly easy to check the hardware. Most laser printers have a self-test function—often combined with a diagnostic printout, but sometimes as a separate process. This self-test shows whether the laser printer can properly develop an image without actually having to send print commands from the computer. The self-test is quite handy to verify the question "Is it the printer or is it the computer?" Run the self-test to check for connectivity and configuration problems.

Possible solutions include replacing the toner cartridge, especially if you hear popping noises; checking the cabling; and replacing the data cable, especially if it has bends or crimps or if objects are resting on the cable. If you have a front menu panel, turn off advanced functions and high-speed settings to determine whether the advanced functions are either not working properly or not supported by your current software configuration (check your manuals for configuration information). If these solutions do not work, the problem may not be user serviceable. Contact an authorized service center.

Chapter Review

Questions

1. What mechanism is used by most inkjet printers to push ink onto the paper?
   - A. Electrostatic discharge
   - B. Gravity
   - C. Air pressure
   - D. Electroconductive plates
2. With a laser printer, what creates the image on the photosensitive drum?
   - A. Primary corona
   - B. Laser imaging unit
   - C. Transfer corona
   - D. Toner
3. What is the proper order of the laser printing process?
   - A. Process, clean, charge, expose, develop, transfer, and fuse
   - B. Process, charge, expose, develop, transfer, fuse, and clean
   - C. Clean, expose, develop, transfer, process, fuse, and charge
   - D. Clean, charge, expose, process, develop, fuse, and transfer
4. On a dot-matrix printer, what physically strikes the ribbon to form an image?
   - A. Electromagnets
   - B. Printwires
   - C. Character wheel
   - D. Print hammers
5. Which of these items are considered to be dot-matrix printer consumables? (Select all that apply.)
   - A. Drive motor
   - B. Paper
   - C. Flywheel
   - D. Ribbon

CHAPTER 28

Securing Computers

In this chapter, you will learn how to

- Explain the threats to your computers and data
- Describe key security concepts and technologies
- Explain how to protect computers from network threats

Your PC is under siege. Through your PC, a malicious person can gain valuable information about you and your habits. He can steal your files. He can run programs that log your keystrokes and thus gain account names and passwords, credit card information, and more. He can run software that takes over much of your computer processing time and use it to send spam or steal from others. The threat is real and immediate. Worse, he's doing one or more of these things to your clients as I write these words. You need to secure your computer and your users' computers from these attacks.

But what does computer security mean? Is it an antimalware program? Is it big, complex passwords? Sure, it's both of these things, but what about the fact that your laptop can be stolen easily or that improper ventilation can cause hard drives and other components to die?

To secure computers, you need both a sound strategy and proper tactics. For strategic reasons, you need to understand the threat from unauthorized access to local machines as well as the big threats posed to networked computers. Part of the big picture is knowing what policies, software, and hardware to put in place to stop those threats. From a tactical, in-the-trenches perspective, you need to master the details to know how to implement and maintain the proper tools. Not only do you need to install antimalware programs in your users' computers, for example, but you also need to update those programs regularly to keep up with the constant barrage of new malware.

902

Analyzing Threats

Threats to your data and PC come from two directions: accidents and malicious people. All sorts of things can go wrong with your computer, from users getting access to folders they shouldn't see to a virus striking and deleting folders. Files can be deleted, renamed,

or simply lost. Hard drives can die, and optical discs get scratched and rendered unreadable. Accidents happen, and even well-meaning people can make mistakes.

Unfortunately, a lot of people out there intend to do you harm. Combine that intent with a talent for computers, and you have a dangerous combination. Let's look at the following issues:

- Unauthorized access
- Data destruction, whether accidental or deliberate
- Administrative access
- Catastrophic hardware failures
- Malware
- Environmental threats

Unauthorized Access

Unauthorized access occurs when a person accesses resources without permission. "Resources" in this case means data, applications, and hardware. A user can alter or delete data; access sensitive information, such as financial data, personnel files, or e-mail messages; or use a computer for purposes the owner did not intend.

Not all unauthorized access is malicious—often this problem arises when users who are poking around in a computer out of curiosity or boredom discover they can access resources in a fashion the primary user did not have in mind. Unauthorized access becomes malicious when people knowingly and intentionally take advantage of weaknesses in your security to gain information, use resources, or destroy data!

One way to gain unauthorized access is intrusion. You might imagine someone kicking in a door and hacking into a computer, but more often than not it's someone sitting at a home computer, trying various passwords over the Internet. Not quite as glamorous, but it'll do.

Dumpster diving is the generic term for searching refuse for information. This is also a form of intrusion. The amount of sensitive information that makes it into any organization's trash bin boggles the mind! Years ago, I worked with an IT security guru who gave me and a few other IT people a tour of our office's trash. In one 20-minute tour of the personal wastebaskets of one office area, we had enough information to access the network easily, as well as to seriously embarrass more than a few people. When it comes to getting information, the trash is the place to look!

Shoulder surfing is another technique for gaining unauthorized access. Shoulder surfing is simply observing someone's screen or keyboard to get information, often passwords. As the name implies, it usually requires the bad guy looking over your shoulder to see what you are doing.

Social Engineering

Although you're more likely to lose data through accidents, the acts of malicious users get the headlines. Most of these attacks come under the heading of *social engineering*—the process of using or manipulating people inside the organization to gain access to its

network or facilities—which covers the many ways humans can use other humans to gain unauthorized information. This information may be a network login, a credit card number, company customer data—almost anything you might imagine that one person or organization may not want outsiders to access.

Social engineering attacks aren't hacking—at least in the classic sense of the word—but the goals are the same. Let's look at a few of the more classic types of social engineering attacks.

NOTE Social engineering attacks are often used together, so if you discover one of them being used against your organization, it's a good idea to look for others.

Infiltration

Hackers can physically enter your building under the guise of someone who might have a legitimate reason for being there, such as cleaning personnel, repair technicians, or messengers. They then snoop around desks, looking for whatever they can find. They might talk with people inside the organization, gathering names, office numbers, department names—little things in and of themselves but powerful tools when combined later with other social engineering attacks.

Dressing the part of a legitimate user—with fake badge and everything—enables malicious people to gain access to locations and thus potentially your data. Following someone through the door, for example, as if you belong, is called *tailgating*. Tailgating is a common form of infiltration.

To combat tailgating, facilities often install a *mantrap* at the entrance to sensitive areas, or sometimes at the entrance to the whole building. A mantrap is a small room with a set of two doors, one to the outside, unsecured area and one to the inner, secure area. When walking through the mantrap, the outer door must be closed before the inner door can be opened. In addition to the double doors, the user must present some form of authentication. For additional security, a mantrap is often controlled by a security guard who keeps an *entry control roster*. This document keeps a record of all comings and goings from the building.

Telephone Scams

Telephone scams are probably the most common social engineering attack. In this case, the attacker makes a phone call to someone in the organization to gain information. The attacker attempts to come across as someone inside the organization and uses this to get the desired information. Probably the most famous of these scams is the "I forgot my user name and password" scam. In this gambit, the attacker first learns the account name of a legitimate person in the organization, usually using the infiltration method. The attacker then calls someone in the organization, usually the help desk, in an attempt to gather information, in this case a password.

> **Hacker:** "Hi, this is John Anderson in accounting. I forgot my password. Can you reset it, please?"

Help Desk: "Sure, what's your user name?"
Hacker: "j_w_Anderson"
Help Desk: "OK, I reset it to e34rd3."

Telephone scams certainly aren't limited to attempts to get network access. There are documented telephone scams against organizations aimed at getting cash, blackmail material, or other valuables.

Phishing

Phishing is the act of trying to get people to give their user names, passwords, or other security information by pretending to be someone else electronically. A classic example is when a bad guy sends you an e-mail that's supposed to be from your local credit card company asking you to send them your user name and password. Phishing is by far the most common form of social engineering done today.

Phishing refers to a fairly random act of badness. The attacker targets anyone silly enough to take the bait. *Spear phishing* is the term used for targeted attacks, like when a bad guy goes after a specific celebrity. The dangerous thing about spear phishing is that the bait can be carefully tailored using details from the target's life.

Data Destruction

Often an extension of unauthorized access, data destruction means more than just intentionally or accidentally erasing or corrupting data. It's easy to imagine some evil hacker accessing your network and deleting all your important files, but authorized users may also access certain data and then use that data beyond what they are authorized to do. A good example is the person who legitimately accesses a Microsoft Access product database to modify the product descriptions, only to discover that she can change the prices of the products, too.

This type of threat is particularly dangerous when users are not clearly informed about the extent to which they are authorized to make changes. A fellow tech once told me about a user who managed to mangle an important database when someone gave him incorrect access. When confronted, the user said: "If I wasn't allowed to change it, the system wouldn't let me do it!" Many users believe that systems are configured in a paternalistic way that wouldn't allow them to do anything inappropriate. As a result, users often assume they're authorized to make any changes they believe are necessary when working on a piece of data they know they're authorized to access.

Administrative Access

Every operating system enables you to create user accounts and grant those accounts a certain level of access to files and folders in that computer. As an administrator, supervisor, or root user, you have full control over just about every aspect of the computer. This increased control means these accounts can do vastly more damage when compromised, amplifying the danger of several other threats. The idea is to minimize both the number of accounts with full control and the time they spend logged in.

Even if a user absolutely needs this access, uses strong passwords, and practices good physical security, Malware installed by a convincing spear phishing attack could leverage that control to access files, install software, and change settings a typical account couldn't touch.

System Crash/Hardware Failure

As with any technology, computers can and will fail—usually when you can least afford for it to happen. Hard drives crash, the power fails…it's all part of the joy of working in the computing business. You need to create redundancy in areas prone to failure (such as installing backup power in case of electrical failure) and perform those all-important data backups. Chapter 15, "Maintaining and Optimizing Operating Systems," goes into detail about using backups and other issues involved in creating a stable and reliable system.

Physical Theft

A fellow network geek once challenged me to try to bring down his newly installed network. He had just installed a powerful and expensive firewall router and was convinced that I couldn't get to a test server he added to his network just for me to try to access. After a few attempts to hack in over the Internet, I saw that I wasn't going to get anywhere that way.

So I jumped in my car and drove to his office, having first outfitted myself in a techy-looking jumpsuit and an ancient ID badge I just happened to have in my sock drawer. I smiled sweetly at the receptionist and walked right by my friend's office (I noticed he was smugly monitoring incoming IP traffic by using some neato packet-sniffing program) to his new server.

I quickly pulled the wires out of the back of his precious server, picked it up, and walked out the door. The receptionist was too busy trying to figure out why her e-mail wasn't working to notice me as I whisked by her carrying the 65-pound server box. I stopped in the hall and called him from my cell phone.

Me (cheerily): "Dude, I got all your data!"
Him (not cheerily): "You rebooted my server! How did you do it?"
Me (smiling): "I didn't reboot it—go over and look at it!"
Him (really mad now): "YOU <EXPLETIVE> THIEF! YOU STOLE MY SERVER!"
Me (cordially): "Why, yes. Yes, I did. Give me two days to hack your password in the comfort of my home, and I'll see everything! Bye!"

I immediately walked back in and handed him the test server. It was fun. The moral here is simple: Never forget that the best network software security measures can be rendered useless if you fail to protect your systems physically!

NOTE Physical security for your systems extends beyond the confines of the office as well. The very thing that makes laptops portable also makes them tempting targets for thieves. One of the simplest ways to protect your laptop is to use a simple *cable lock*. The idea is to loop the cable around a solid object, such as a bed frame, and secure the lock to the small security hole on the side of the laptop.

Malware

Networks are without a doubt the fastest and most efficient vehicles for transferring computer viruses among systems. News reports focus attention on the many malicious software attacks from the Internet, but a huge number of such attacks still come from users who bring in programs on optical discs and USB drives. The "Network Security" section of this chapter describes the various methods of virus infection and other malware and what you need to do to prevent such attacks from damaging your networked systems.

Environmental Threats

Your computer is surrounded by a host of dangers all just waiting to wreak havoc: bad electricity from the power company, a host of chemicals stored near your computer, dust, heat, cold, wet…it's a jungle out there!

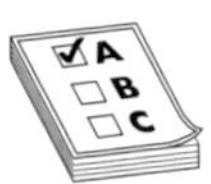

EXAM TIP Expect questions on environmental threats on the CompTIA A+ 220-902 exam.

Power

We've covered power issues extensively back in Chapter 8, "Power Supplies." Don't ever fail to appreciate the importance of surge suppressors and uninterruptible power supplies (UPSs) to protect your electronics from surges, brownouts, and blackouts. Also remember that network devices need power protection as well. Figure 28-1 shows a typical UPS protecting a network rack.

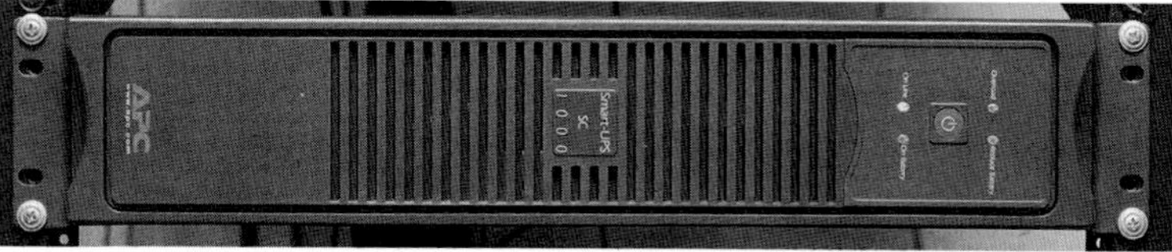

Figure 28-1 UPS on rack

How's the Air in There?

Proper environmental controls help secure servers and workstations from the environmental impact of excessive heat, dust, and humidity. Such *environmental controls* include air conditioning, proper ventilation, air filtration, and monitors for temperature and humidity. A CompTIA A+ technician maintains an awareness of temperature, humidity level, and ventilation, so that he or she can tell very quickly when levels or settings are out of whack.

A computer works best in an environment where the air is clean, dry, and room temperature. CompTIA doesn't expect you to become an environmental engineer, but it does expect you to explain and deal with how dirty or humid or hot air can affect a computer. We've covered all of these topics to some extent throughout the book, so let's just do a quick overview with security in mind.

Dirty Air Dust and debris aren't good for any electronic components. Your typical office air conditioning does a pretty good job of eliminating the worst offenders, but not all computers are in nice offices. No matter where the computers reside, you need to monitor your systems for dirt. The best way to do this is observation as part of your regular work. Dust and debris will show up all over the systems, but the best place to look are the fans. Fans will collect dust and dirt quickly (see Figure 28-2).

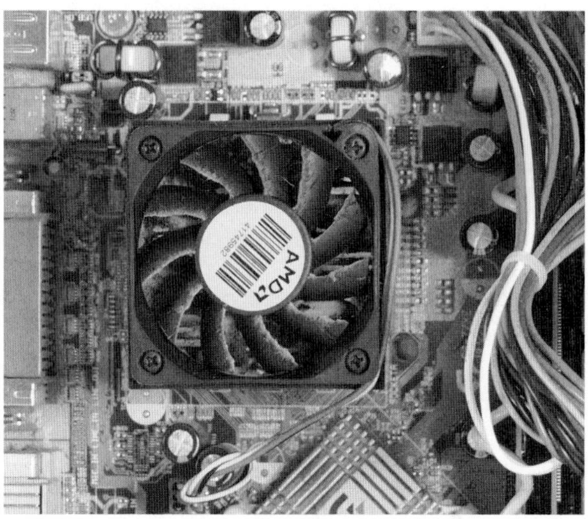

Figure 28-2 Dirty fan

All electronic components get dirty over time. To clean them, you need to use either compressed air or a nonstatic vacuum. So which one do you use? The rule is simple: If you don't mind dust blowing all over the place, use compressed air. If you don't want dust blowing all over the place, use a vacuum.

Equipment closets filled with racks of servers need proper airflow to keep things cool and to control dusty air. Make sure that the room is ventilated and air-conditioned (see Figure 28-3) and that the air filters are changed regularly.

Figure 28-3 Air-conditioning vent in a small server closet

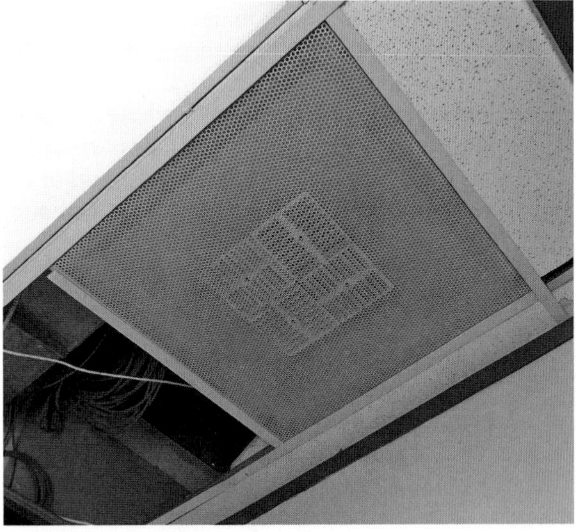

If things are really bad, you can enclose a system in a dust shield. Dust shields come complete with their own filters to keep a computer clean and happy even in the worst of environments.

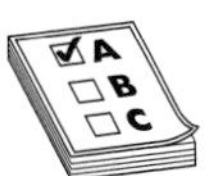

EXAM TIP Always use proper ventilation, air filters, and enclosures. To protect against airborne particles, consider wearing a protective mask.

Temperature and Humidity Most computers are designed to operate at room temperature, which is somewhere in the area of 22°C (72°F) with the relative humidity in the 30–40 percent range. Colder and dryer is better for computers (but not for people), so the real challenge is when the temperature and the humidity go higher.

A modern office will usually have good air conditioning and heating, so your job as a tech is to make sure that things don't happen to prevent your air conditioning from doing its job. That means you're pretty much always on ventilation patrol. Watch for the following to make sure air is flowing:

- Make sure ducts are always clear of obstructions.
- Make sure ducts are adjusted (not too hot or too cold).
- Don't let equipment get closed off from proper ventilation.

Toxic Materials

Every office is filled with chemicals, compounds that invariably get stored, spilled, or dumped. If something you aren't familiar with spills, refer to the Material Safety Data Sheet (MSDS) for proper documentation on handling and disposal. Always comply with local government regulations when dealing with chemicals, including batteries and the metals on circuit boards.

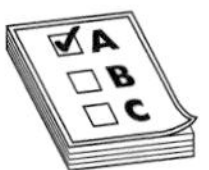

EXAM TIP Most U.S. cities have one or more environmental services centers that you can use to recycle electronic components. For your city, try a Google (or other search engine) search on the term "environmental services" and you'll almost certainly find a convenient place for e-waste disposal.

Security Concepts and Technologies

Once you've assessed the threats to your computers and networks, you need to take steps to protect those valuable resources. Depending on the complexity of your organization, this can be a small job encompassing some basic security concepts and procedures, or it can be exceedingly complex. The security needs for a three-person desktop publishing firm, for example, would differ wildly from those of a defense contractor supplying top-secret toys to the Pentagon.

From a CompTIA A+ certified technician's perspective, you need to understand the big picture (that's the strategic side), knowing the concepts and available technologies for security. At the implementation level (that's the tactical side), you're expected to know where to find such things as security policies in Windows. A CompTIA Network+ or CompTIA Security+ tech will give you the specific options to implement. (The exception to this level of knowledge comes in dealing with malicious software such as viruses, but we'll tackle that subject in the second half of the chapter.) So let's look at three concept and technology areas: access control, data classification and compliance, and reporting.

NOTE Part of establishing local control over resources involves setting up the computer properly in the first place, a topic covered in depth in Chapter 14, "Users, Groups, and Permissions." Turn to that chapter to refresh your memory on steps to control a computer's resources and NTFS.

Access Control

Access is the key. If you can control access to the data, programs, and other computing resources, you've secured your systems. *Access control* is composed of four interlinked areas that a good security-minded tech should think about: physical security, authentication, users and groups, and security policies. Much of this you know from previous chapters, but this section should help tie it all together as a security topic.

Secure Physical Area and Lock Down Systems

The first order of security is to keep people who shouldn't have access away from the physical hardware. This isn't rocket science. Lock the door to your workspace. Don't leave

a PC unattended when logged in. In fact, don't ever leave a system logged in, even as a Standard or Guest user. God help you if you walk away from a server still logged in as an administrator. You're tempting fate.

Employee *ID badges* are so common that even relatively small organizations use them. Badges are a great way not only to control building access but also to store authentication tools such as *radio frequency identification (RFID)* or smart cards (see "Authentication," later in this chapter). Figure 28-4 shows a typical badge.

Figure 28-4 Typical employee badge/smart card

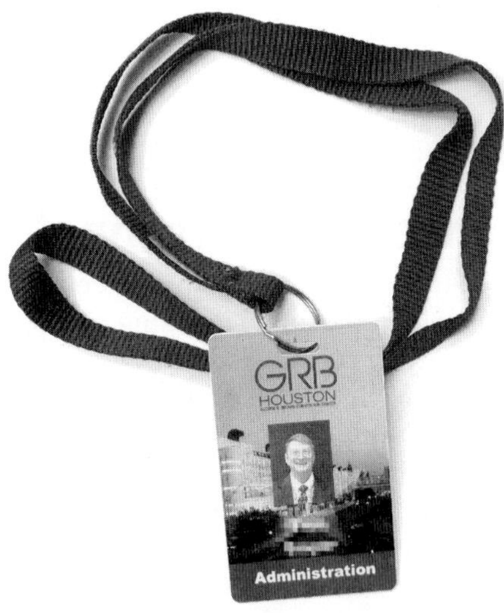

Be aware of the risk of shoulder surfing. One handy tool to prevent this is a privacy filter. A privacy filter is little more than a framed sheet or film that you apply to the front of your monitor. Privacy filters reduce the viewing angle, making it impossible to see the contents on the screen for anyone except those directly in front of the screen (see Figure 28-5).

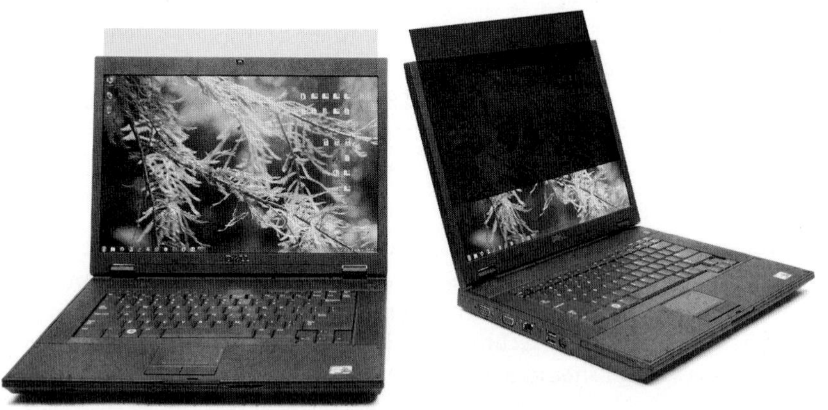

Figure 28-5 Privacy filter

Security is more of an issue when users walk away from their computers, even for a moment. When you see a user's computer logged in and unattended, do the user and your company a huge favor and lock the computer. Just walk up and press WINDOWS-L on the keyboard to lock the system. It works in all versions of Windows. Better yet, make a point to make users aware of this issue so they understand the risk and can take the precaution themselves. You should also instruct them how to password-protect their screensaver. When the password feature is enabled, a user won't be able to return to the desktop until they've entered the proper password. It's a little like locking the computer, and good for those who like using screensavers.

While you're at a user's monitor, look around his or her desk. Is the user writing down passwords and putting them in plain sight? If so, tell the user to get rid of them! Teach users to create easy-to-remember passwords, following the guidelines set forth in Chapter 14. Are critical, personal, or sensitive documents also lying about in plain sight? The user should put them in a closed, secure place. Documents no longer needed should be shredded immediately.

Authentication

Security requires properly implemented *authentication*, which means in essence how the computer determines who can or should access it and, once accessed, what that user can do. A computer can authenticate users through software or hardware, or a combination of both.

You can categorize ways to authenticate into three broad areas: knowledge factors, ownership factors, and inherent factors. You read about *multifactor authentication* in detail in Chapter 26 when talking about mobile device security. It works the same way when securing a desktop computer, a laptop, a server, or a building. There's no reason to rehash it here. The only thing to add is that many organizations use *two-factor authentication*. An example is a key fob that generates a numeric key. A user authenticates by entering his or her user name and password (something the user knows) and enters the key (something the user has) when prompted.

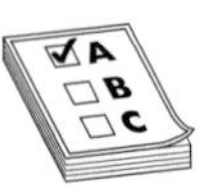

EXAM TIP The 902 exam will quiz you on multifactor and two-factor authentication. This applies to all computing devices.

Software Authentication: Proper Passwords It's still rather shocking to me to power up a friend's computer and go straight to his or her desktop, or with my married-with-kids friends, to click one of the parents' user account icons and not be prompted for a password. This is just wrong! I'm always tempted to assign passwords right then and there—and not tell them the passwords, of course—so they'll see the error of their ways when they try to log on next. I don't do it but always try to explain gently the importance of good passwords.

You know about passwords from Chapter 14, so I won't belabor the point here. Suffice it to say that you must require that your users have proper passwords, and ensure they are set to expire on a regular basis. Don't let them write passwords down or tape them to the underside of their mouse pads either!

It's not just access to Windows that you need to think about. There's always the temptation for people to do other mean things, such as change CMOS settings, open up the case, and even steal hard drives. Any of these actions renders the computer inoperable to the casual user until a tech can undo the damage or replace components. All modern CMOS setup utilities come with a number of tools to protect your computer, such as drive lock, intrusion detection, and of course system access BIOS/UEFI passwords such as the one shown in Figure 28-6. Refer to Chapter 6 to refresh yourself on what you can do at a BIOS level to protect your computer.

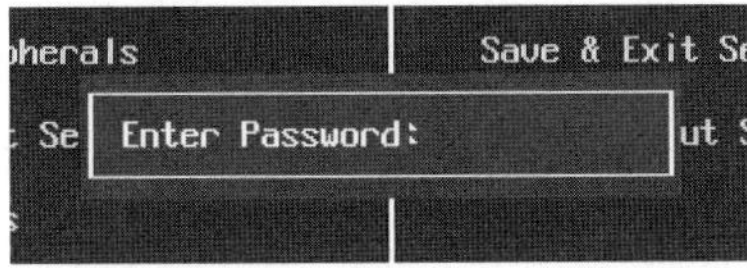

Figure 28-6 BIOS/UEFI access password request

Hardware Authentication Smart cards and biometric devices enable modern systems to authenticate users with more authority than mere passwords. *Smart cards* are credit card–sized cards with circuitry that can identify the bearer of the card. Smart cards are relatively common for tasks such as authenticating users for mass transit systems but are fairly uncommon in computers. Figure 28-7 shows a smart card and keyboard combination.

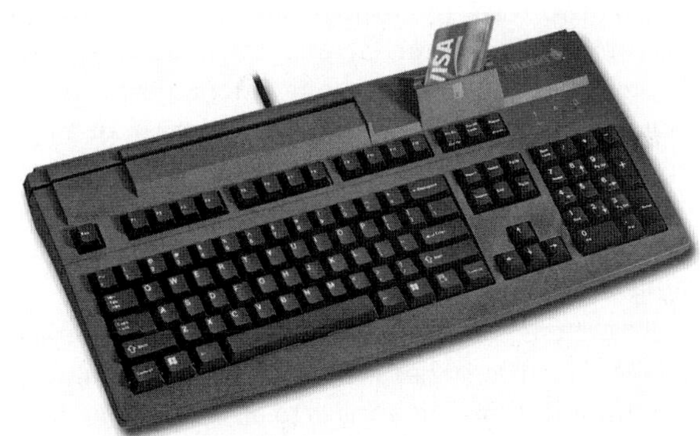

Figure 28-7 Keyboard-mounted smart card reader being used for a commercial application (photo courtesy of Cherry Corp.)

Security tokens are devices that store some unique information that the user carries on their person. They may be digital certificates, passwords, or biometric data. They may also store an RSA token. *RSA tokens* are random-number generators that are used with user names and passwords to ensure extra security. Most security tokens come in the form of key fobs, as shown in Figure 28-8.

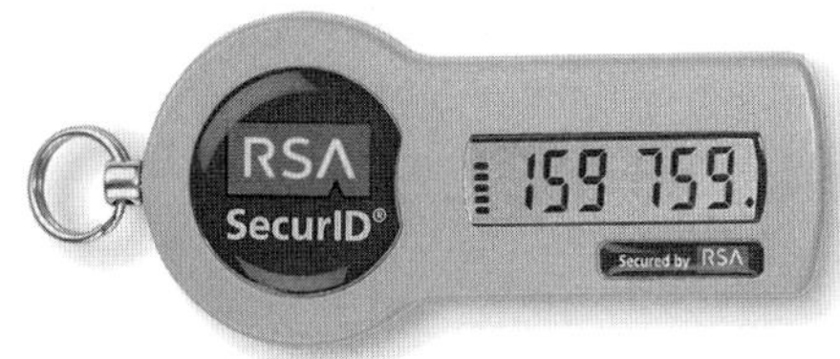

Figure 28-8 RSA key fob (photo courtesy of EMC Corp.)

You can also get many types of security tokens as software. Anyone who plays *World of Warcraft* knows that there's an entire illegal industry known as "gold farmers" who like to hack accounts and steal all the hard-earned loot your character collects. It's a terrible feeling to log in to the game only to find your character cleaned out (see Figure 28-9).

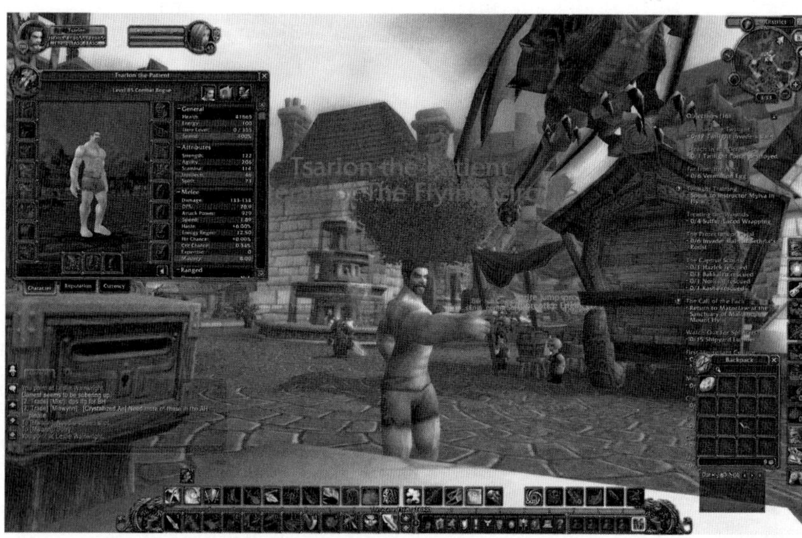

Figure 28-9 I've been robbed! My fine armor is gone, my bags are empty, and my bank account only has a few copper pieces!

To counter this problem, Blizzard Entertainment, the folks who own *World of Warcraft*, provide free security tokens. Most folks think "hardware" in the form of key fobs when they hear the words "security tokens," but you can also download a security token as software—Blizzard offers an app for your smartphone, as shown in Figure 28-10.

People can guess or discover passwords, but it's a lot harder to forge someone's fingerprints. The keyboard in Figure 28-11 authenticates users on a local machine by using a fingerprint lock. Other devices that will do the trick are key fobs and retinal scanners. Devices that require some sort of physical, flesh-and-blood authentication are called *biometric devices.*

NOTE How's this for full disclosure? Microsoft does not claim that the keyboard in Figure 28-11 offers any security at all. In fact, the documentation specifically claims that the fingerprint reader is an accessibility tool, not a security device. Because it enables a person to log on to a local machine, though, I think it falls into the category of authentication devices.

Figure 28-10 Blizzard Entertainment software security token for iPhone

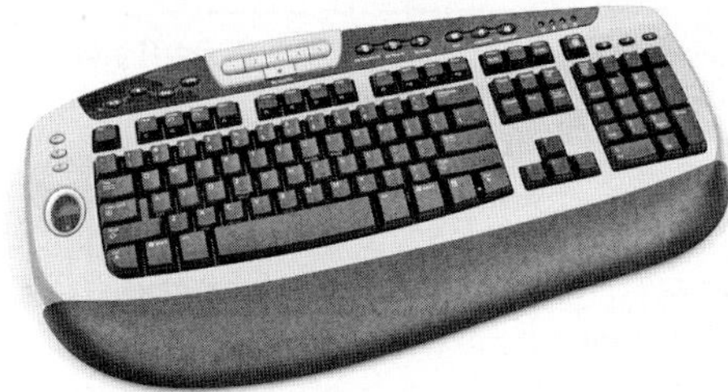

Figure 28-11 Microsoft keyboard with fingerprint accessibility

Clever manufacturers have developed key fobs and smart cards that use RFID to transmit authentication information so users don't have to insert something into a computer or card reader. The Privaris plusID combines, for example, a biometric fingerprint fob with an RFID tag that makes security as easy as opening a garage door remotely! Figure 28-12 shows a plusID device.

Retinal scanners loom large in media as a form of biometric security, where you place your eye up to a scanning device. While retinal scanners do exist, I have been in hundreds of high-security facilities and have only seen one retinal scanner in operation in almost 30 years as a tech. Figure 28-13 shows about the only image of a retinal scanner in operation you'll ever encounter.

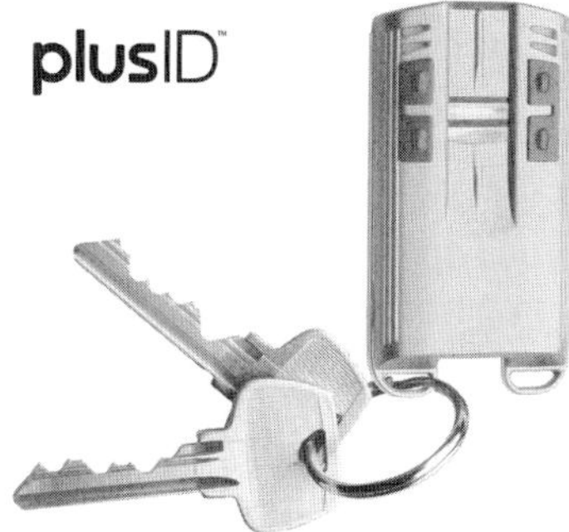

Figure 28-12 plusID (photo courtesy of Privaris, Inc.)

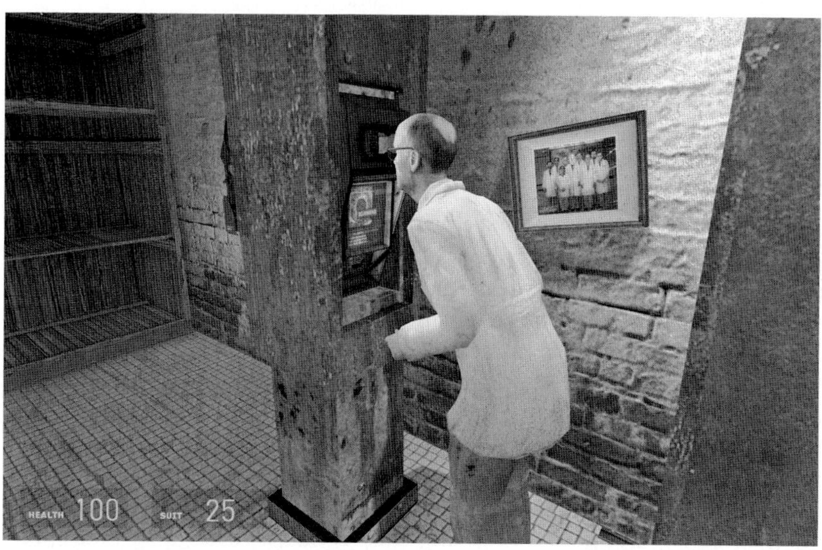

Figure 28-13 Retinal scanner in *Half-Life 2*

Users and Groups

Windows uses user accounts and groups as the bedrock of access control. A user account is assigned to a group, such as Users, Power Users, or Administrators, and by association gets certain permissions on the computer. Using NTFS enables the highest level of control over data resources.

Assigning users to groups is a great first step in controlling a local machine, but this feature really shines in a networked environment. Let's take a look.

NOTE The file system on a hard drive matters a lot when it comes to security. On modern systems, the file system on the boot drive has support for rich users and groups permissions/ACLs. But this security only extends to drives/cards formatted with modern files systems such as NTFS, HFS+, and ext3/4. If you copy a file to a drive/card formatted with the older FAT32, such as many cameras and USB flash drives use, the OS will strip all permissions and the file will be available for anyone to read!

Access to user accounts should be restricted to the assigned individuals, and those who configure the permissions to those accounts must follow the *Principle of Least Privilege*: Accounts should have permission to access only the resources they need and no more. Tight control of user accounts is critical to preventing unauthorized access. Disabling unused accounts is an important part of this strategy, but good user account management goes far deeper than that.

Groups are a great way to achieve increased complexity without increasing the administrative burden on network administrators, because all operating systems combine permissions. When a user is a member of more than one group, which permissions does that user have with respect to any particular resource? In all operating systems, the permissions of the groups are *combined*, and the result is what you call the *effective permissions* the user has to access the resource. As an example, if Rita is a member of the Sales group, which has List Folder Contents permission to a folder, and she is also a member of the Managers group, which has Read and Execute permissions to the same folder, Rita will have both List Folder Contents *and* Read and Execute permissions to that folder.

Watch out for *default* user accounts and groups—they can become secret backdoors to your network! All network operating systems have a default Everyone group that can be used to sneak into shared resources easily. This Everyone group, as its name implies, literally includes anyone who connects to that resource. Windows gives full control to the Everyone group by default, for example, so make sure you know to lock this down! The other scary one is the Guest account. The Guest account is the only way to access a system without a user name and password. Unless you have a compelling reason to provide guest access, you should always make sure the Guest account is disabled.

All of the default groups—Everyone, Guest, Users—define broad groups of users. Never use them unless you intend to permit all of those folks access to a resource. If you use one of the default groups, remember to configure them with the proper permissions to prevent users from doing things you don't want them to do with a shared resource!

Security Policies

Although permissions control how users access shared resources, there are other functions you should control that are outside the scope of resources. For example, do you want users to be able to access a command prompt on their Windows system? Do you want users to be able to install software? Would you like to control what systems a user

can log on to or at what time of day a user can log on? All network operating systems provide you with some capability to control these and literally hundreds of other security parameters, under what Windows calls *policies*. I like to think of policies as permissions for activities, as opposed to true permissions, which control access to resources.

A policy is usually applied to a user account, a computer, or a group. Let's use the example of a network composed of Windows systems with a Windows Server. Every Windows client has its own local policies program, which enables policies to be placed on that system only. Figure 28-14 shows the tool you use to set local policies on an individual system, called *Local Security Policy*, being used to deny the Guest account the capability to log on locally.

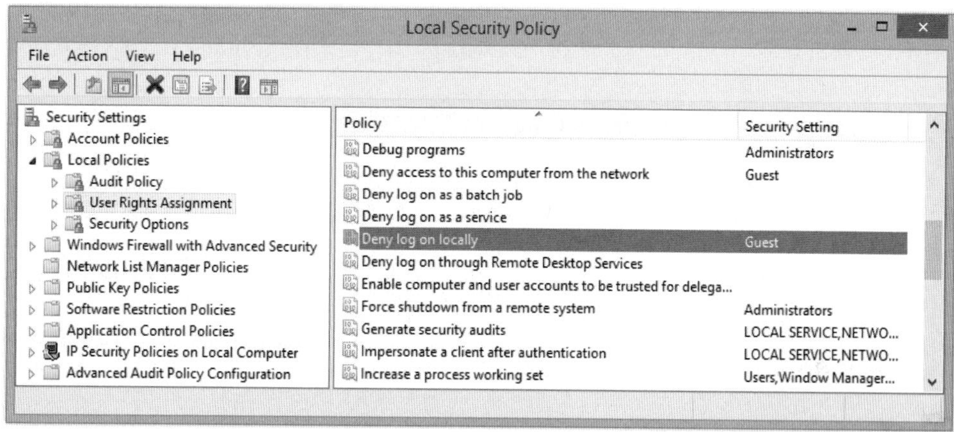

Figure 28-14 Local Security Policy

Local policies work great for individual systems, but they can be a pain to configure if you want to apply the same settings to more than one PC on your network. If you want to apply policy settings *en masse*, you need to step up to Windows Active Directory domain-based *Group Policy*. By using Group Policy, you can exercise deity-like—Microsoft prefers the term *granular*—control over your network clients.

Want to set default wallpaper for every PC in your domain? Group Policy can do that. Want to make certain tools inaccessible to everyone but authorized users? Group Policy can do that, too. Want to control access to the Internet, redirect home folders, run scripts, deploy software, or just remind folks that unauthorized access to the network will get them nowhere fast? Group Policy is the answer. Figure 28-15 shows Group Policy; I'm about to change the default title on every instance of Internet Explorer on every computer in my domain!

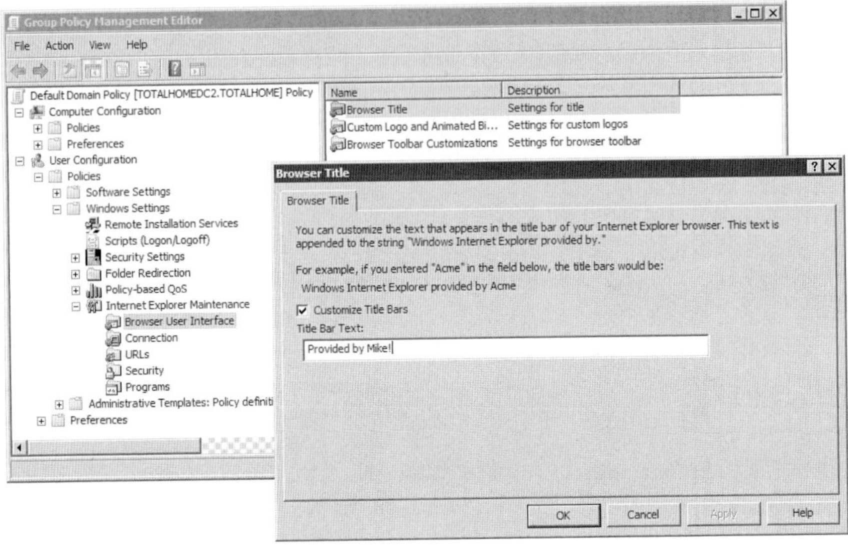

Figure 28-15 Using Group Policy to make IE title say "Provided by Mike!"

That's just one simple example of the settings you can configure by using Group Policy. You can apply literally hundreds of tweaks through Group Policy, from the great to the small, but don't worry too much about familiarizing yourself with each and every one. Group Policy settings are a big topic on most of the Microsoft certification tracks, but for the purposes of the CompTIA A+ exams, you simply have to be comfortable with the concept behind Group Policy.

Although I could never list every possible policy you can enable on a Windows system, here's a list of some commonly used ones:

- **Prevent Registry Edits** If you try to edit the Registry, you get a failure message.
- **Prevent Access to the Command Prompt** Keeps users from getting to the command prompt by turning off the Run command and the Command Prompt shortcut.
- **Log on Locally** Defines who may log on to the system locally.
- **Shut Down System** Defines who may shut down the system.
- **Minimum Password Length** Forces a minimum password length.
- **Account Lockout Threshold** Sets the maximum number of logon attempts a person can make before being locked out of the account.
- **Disable Windows Installer** Prevents users from installing software.
- **Printer Browsing** Enables users to browse for printers on the network, as opposed to using only assigned printers.

Although the CompTIA A+ exams don't expect you to know how to implement policies on any type of network, you are expected to understand that policies exist, especially on Windows networks, and that they can do amazing things to control what users can do on their systems. If you ever try to get to a command prompt on a Windows system only to discover the Run command is dimmed, blame it on a policy, not the computer!

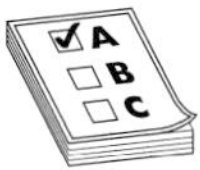

EXAM TIP Account management security policy best practices dictate that you should implement restrictive user permissions, login time restrictions, account lockout based on failed attempts, and disable the operating system's built-in AutoRun or AutoPlay features. Finally, you should always change default system user names and passwords where possible.

Data Classification and Compliance

Larger organizations, such as government entities, benefit greatly from organizing their data according to its sensitivity—what's called *data classification*—and making certain that computer hardware and software stay as uniform as possible. In addition, many government and internal regulations apply fairly rigorously to these organizations.

Data classification systems vary by the organization, but a common scheme classifies documents as public, internal use only, highly confidential, top secret, and so on. Using a classification scheme enables employees such as techs to know very quickly what to do with documents, the drives containing documents, and more. Your strategy for recycling a computer system left from a migrated user, for example, will differ a lot if the data on the drive was classified as internal use only or top secret.

Compliance means, in a nutshell, that members of an organization or company must abide by or comply with all of the rules that apply to the organization or company. Statutes with funny names such as Sarbanes-Oxley impose certain behaviors or prohibitions on what people can and cannot do in the workplace.

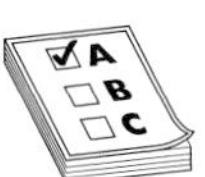

EXAM TIP The CompTIA A+ 902 objectives use specific language for compliance. People must *follow corporate end-user policies and security best practices*. Follow the rules, in other words.

From a technician's point of view, the most common compliance issue revolves around software, such as what sort of software users can be allowed to install on their computers or, conversely, why you have to tell a user that he can't install the latest application that may help him do the job more effectively because that software isn't on the approved list. This can lead to some uncomfortable confrontations, but it's part of a tech's job.

Unapproved or non-compliant software added by users can be a serious vulnerability. These non-compliant systems are clearly violations of security best practices and should be fixed.

The concepts behind compliance in IT are not, as some might imagine at first blush, to stop you from being able to work effectively. Rather, they're designed to stop users with insufficient technical skill or knowledge from installing malicious programs or

applications that will destabilize their systems. This keeps technical support calls down and enables techs to focus on more serious problems.

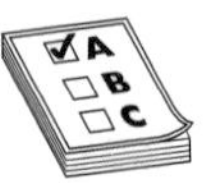

EXAM TIP *Personally identifiable information (PII)* is any data that can lead back to a specific individual. The CompTIA A+ 902 exam tests you on special classifications that apply when working with data. Be sure to consult your superiors on what your organization's policy is when working with personally identifiable information.

Licensing

Software licensing has many twists that can easily lead a user or a tech out of compliance. Like other creative acts, programmers are granted copyright to the software they create. The copyright owner then decides how he or she or it (the corporation) will license that software for others to use. The licensing can be commercial or non-commercial, personal or enterprise. The software can be closed source or open source. Each of these options has variations as well, so this gets complex. Let's start at the top and work through the variations.

Commercial Licensing

When software is released under a commercial license, you have a legal obligation to pay money for access to it—but a lot of variations apply. Traditionally, you bought a copy of a program and could use it forever, sell it to someone else, or give it away. You bought copies for each user with a personal license, or multiple users with an enterprise license.

Today, the picture is muddier. You can buy the use of Microsoft Office, for example, as long as you pay a monthly or yearly fee. The personal license enables you to share the software with several other people or accounts and use it on several of your personal machines.

The *End User License Agreement (EULA)* you agree to abide by when you open or install new software obligates you to abide by the use and sharing guidelines stipulated by the software copyright holder. You agree to the EULA for Microsoft Office, in other words, and you don't try to make illegal copies or share beyond what Microsoft says is okay.

Various forms of *digital rights management (DRM)* enforce how you use commercial software. Many programs require activation over the Internet, for example, or a special account with the copyright holder. To use Adobe software, such as Photoshop, you need an account with Adobe.com.

Non-Commercial Licensing

For moral or philosophical reasons, some developers want their software to be free for some or all purposes. When Linus Torvalds created the Linux operating system, for example, he made it freely available for people. Google Picasa image editing and cataloging software likewise is available to download and use for free.

Non-commercial licensing has variations. Many non-commercial programs are only "free" for personal use. If you want to use the excellent TeamViewer remote access program at your office, for example, you need to buy a commercial license. But if you want to log in to your home machine from your personal laptop, you can use TeamViewer for free.

Open Source Versus Closed Source

Another huge variation in software use and licensing is what you can do with the source code of an application. *Open source software* licenses generally allow you to take the original code and modify it. Some open source licenses require you to make the modified code available for free download; others don't require that at all. *Closed source software* licenses stipulate that you can't modify the source code or make it part of some other software suite.

Although CompTIA A+ 902 exam objective 5.3 lists "open source vs. commercial license," that distinction does not exist in the real world. There are plenty of open source programs with licensing fees, like server versions of Linux. Many "free" programs are likewise closed source.

The key for a tech is to know the specific licenses paid for by her company and ensure that the company abides by those licenses. Using pirated software or exceeding the use limits set by a EULA, or using private-license programs in a commercial enterprise, is *theft*, no matter how easy it is to do in practice.

Reporting

As a final weapon in your security arsenal, you need to report any security issues so a network administrator or technician can take steps resolve them. You can set up auditing within Windows so that the OS reports problems to you. *Event Viewer* enables you to read the logs created by auditing. You can then do your work and report those problems. Let's take a look.

Auditing

The Security section of Event Viewer doesn't show much by default. To unlock the full potential of Event Viewer, you need to set up auditing. *Auditing* in the security sense means to tell Windows to create an entry in the Security Log when certain events happen, such as when a user logs on—called *event auditing*—or tries to access a certain file or folder—called *object access auditing*. Figure 28-16 shows Event Viewer tracking logon and logoff events.

The CompTIA A+ certification exams don't test you on creating a brilliant auditing policy for your office—that's what network administrators do. You simply need to know what auditing does and how to turn it on or off so you can provide support for the network administrators in the field. To turn on auditing at a local level, go to Local Security Policy in Administrative Tools. Select Local Policies and then click Audit Policy. Double-click one of the policy options and select one or both of the checkboxes in the Properties dialog box that opens. Figure 28-17 shows the Audit object access Properties dialog box.

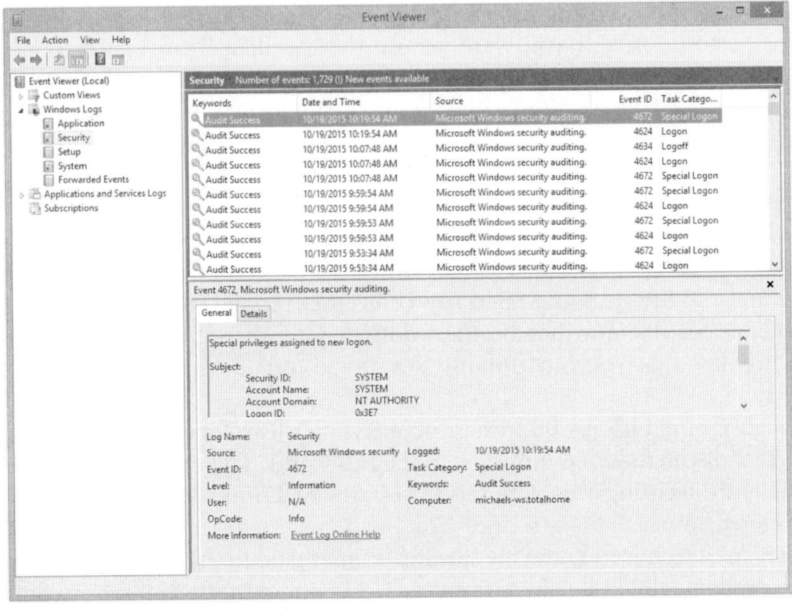

Figure 28-16 Event Viewer displaying security alerts

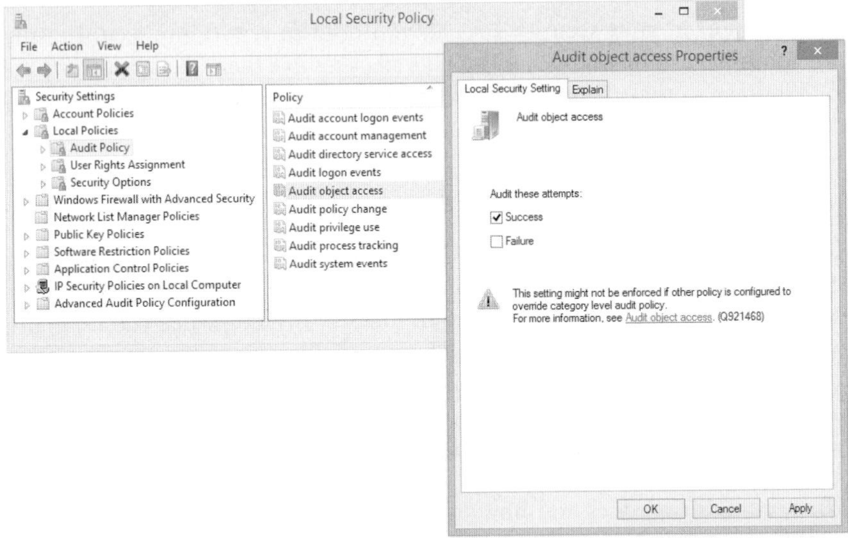

Figure 28-17 Audit object access Properties dialog box, with Local Security Policy open in the background

NOTE Event Viewer stores log files in %SystemRoot%\System32\Config.

Incident Reporting

Once you've gathered data about a particular system or you've dealt with a computer or network problem, you need to complete the mission by telling your supervisor. This is called *incident reporting*. Many companies have pre-made forms that you simply fill out and submit. Other places are less formal. Regardless, you need to do this!

Incident reporting does a couple of things for you. First, it provides a record of work you've accomplished. Second, it provides a piece of information that, when combined with other information you might or might not know, reveals a pattern or bigger problem to someone higher up the chain. A seemingly innocuous security audit report, for example, might match other such events in numerous places in the building at the same time and thus show the cause was conscious, coordinated action rather than a glitch.

Evidence Handling

As a tech, you'll need to deal with people who use company computers in prohibited ways. In most cases, you're not paid to be the police and should not get involved. There are times, however, where something bad—really bad—takes place on one of the systems you support, and if you're the first tech person there, everyone is going to turn to you for action.

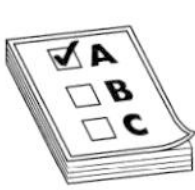

EXAM TIP Look for evidence handling questions on the CompTIA A+ 220-902 exam.

A technician should ignore personal information in and around a person's computer. As mentioned back in Chapter 2, you should treat anything said to you and anything you see as a personal confidence, not to be repeated to customers, coworkers, or bosses. Here's Mike's Rule of Confidentiality: "Unless it's a felony or an imminent physical danger, you didn't see nothin'." This includes any confidential customer materials. Try not to look at anything that isn't directly related to your job. Sometimes that's impossible, but limit your exposure. If you're waiting on a printout at a printer and suddenly there's a bunch of printed pages coming out of the printer with employee payroll information, set it to the side and pretend you never saw it.

But what about the scary stuff? Obvious espionage? Pornography? People passing out personal information? Hacking? In these cases, you've just become the first line of defense and you need to act accordingly. Let's address the objectives as listed by CompTIA for the 220-902 exam.

Identify the Action or Content as Prohibited Use common sense, but keep in mind that most organizations have an *Acceptable Use Policy (AUP)* that employees must sign. The Acceptable Use Policy defines what actions employees may or may not

perform on company equipment. Remember that these polices aren't just for obvious issues such as using a computer for personal use. These policies cover computers, phones, printers, and even the network itself. This policy will define the handling of passwords, e-mail, and many other issues.

NOTE The SANS Institute provides an excellent boilerplate Acceptable Use Policy on their Web site: www.sans.org/security-resources/policies/Acceptable_Use_Policy.pdf.

Report Through Proper Channels In most cases, you'll report any prohibited actions or content directly to your supervisor. There's also a chance your company will have a security officer or *incident response leader* who you'll contact instead. Do *not* speak to the person making the infraction unless your supervisor approves that contact.

Data/Device Preservation You might end up in a situation serious enough that a computer or other device becomes evidence. In these cases, the location of the system and who has touched it may come into question, so you need to establish a *chain of custody*: a documented history of who has been in possession of the system. You should have a legal expert to guide you, but the following are fairly common rules:

1. Isolate the system. Shut down the system and store it in a place where no one else can access it.
2. Document when you took control of the system and the actions you took: shutting it down, unplugging it, moving it, and so on. Don't worry about too much detail, but you must track its location.
3. If another person takes control of the system, document the transfer of custody.

Network Security

Networks are under threat from the outside as well, so this section looks at issues involving Internet-borne attacks, firewalls, and wireless networking. This content is the security bread and butter for a CompTIA A+ technician, so you need to understand the concepts and procedures and be able to implement them properly.

Malicious Software

The beauty of the Internet is the ease of accessing resources just about anywhere on the globe, all from the comfort of your favorite chair. This connection, however, runs both ways, and people from all over the world can potentially access your computer from the comfort of their evil lairs. The Internet is awash with malicious software that is, even at this moment, trying to infect your systems.

The term *malware* defines any program or code that's designed to do something on a system or network that you don't want done. Malware comes in quite a variety of guises,

such as viruses, worms, ransomware, spyware, Trojan horses, and rootkits. Let's examine all these forms of malware, look at what they do to infected systems, and then examine how these nasties get onto your machines in the first place.

Forms of Malware

Malware has been pestering PC users since the 1980s and has evolved into many forms over the years. From the classic boot sector viruses of the '90s to the modern threats of CryptoLocker and drive-by downloads, malware is an ever-changing threat to your users and data. To better understand these threats, you need to understand the different forms that malware can take.

Virus A *virus* is a program that has two jobs: to replicate and to activate. *Replication* means it makes copies of itself, by injecting itself as extra code added to the end of executable programs, or by hiding out in a drive's boot sector. *Activation* is when a virus does something like corrupting data or stealing private information. A virus only replicates to other drives, such as thumb drives or optical media. It does not self-replicate across networks. A virus needs human action to spread.

Worm A *worm* functions similarly to a virus, except it does not need to attach itself to other programs to replicate. It can replicate on its own through networks, or even hardware like Thunderbolt accessories. If the infected computer is on a network, a worm will start scanning the network for other vulnerable systems to infect.

Trojan Horse A *Trojan horse* is a piece of malware that appears or pretends to do one thing while, at the same time, it does something evil. A Trojan horse may be a game, like poker, or ironically, a fake security program. The sky is the limit. Once installed, a Trojan horse can have a hold on the system as tenacious as any virus or worm; a key difference is that installed Trojan horses do not replicate.

Rootkit For malware to succeed, it often needs to come up with some method to hide itself. As awareness of malware has grown, anti-malware programs make it harder to find new locations on a computer to hide malware. A *rootkit* is a program that takes advantage of very low-level operating system functions to hide itself from all but the most aggressive of anti-malware tools. Worse, a rootkit, by definition, gains privileged access to the computer. Rootkits can strike operating systems, hypervisors, and even firmware (including hard drives and accessories…yikes!).

The most infamous rootkit appeared a while back as an antipiracy attempt by Sony on its music CDs. Unfortunately for the media giant, the rootkit software installed when you played a music CD and opened a backdoor that could be used maliciously.

Behavior

Knowing what form the malware takes is all well and good, but what really matters is how "mal" the malware will be when it's running rampant on a system. To get things started, let's dive into an old favorite: spyware.

Spyware Classic spyware often sneaks onto systems by being bundled with legitimate software—software that functions correctly and provides some form of benefit to the user.

What kind of benefit? Way back in 2005, Movieland (otherwise known as Movieland.com and Popcorn.net) released a "handy" movie download service. They didn't tell users, of course, that everyone who installed the software was "automatically enrolled" in a three-day trial. If you didn't cancel the "trial," a pop-up window filled your screen demanding you pay them for the service that you never signed up for. The best part, however, was that you couldn't uninstall the application completely. The uninstaller redirected users to a Web page demanding money again. (Movieland was shut down in 2007.)

For another classic example, look at Figure 28-18: the dialog box asks the user if she trusts the Gator Corporation (a well-known spyware producer from several years ago). Because everyone eventually knew not to trust Gator, they would click No, and the company faded away several years ago.

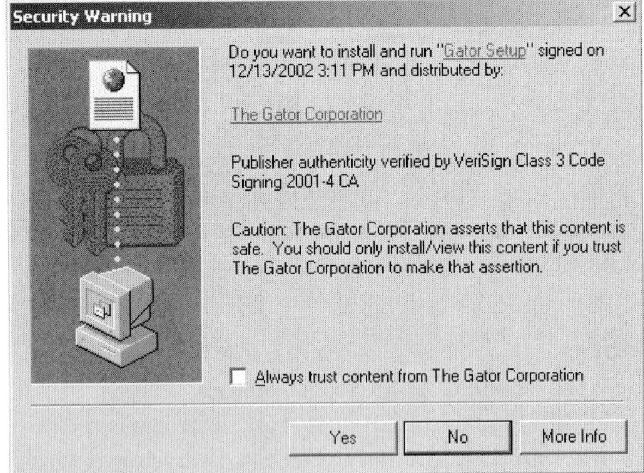

Figure 28-18 Gator Corporation's acknowledgment warning

If Movieland was a problem back in 2005, what are the big spyware applications today? Unfortunately, I can't tell you—not because it's a secret, but because we don't know about them yet.

Ransomware As bad as spyware can be, at least you still have access to your data. *Ransomware*, on the other hand, encrypts all the data it can gain access to on a system. To top it off, many versions of ransomware can even encrypt data on mapped network drives!

Once it has locked up all your data, the ransomware application pops up a message asking for money (often bitcoins) to decrypt your data. Also, to encourage a faster payment, this ransom is presented with a timer that, when it reaches 0, triggers deletion of the encryption keys, leaving you with a drive full of scrambled data.

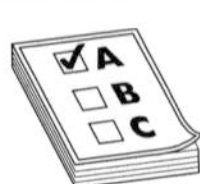

EXAM TIP Know the various types of malware, including viruses, worms, Trojan horses, rootkits, spyware, and ransomware.

A Bot on the Net Full of Zombies Another type of malware I want to talk about is the botnet ("bot" as in *robot*, get it!). A *botnet*, as "net" in its name implies, isn't a single type of malware, but a network of infected computers (*zombies*) under the control of a single person or group, with sizes easily growing into the millions of zombies for the largest networks.

With that many machines under their control, botnet operators have command of massive computing and network resources. One of the most common uses of botnets is sending spam. If you've ever wondered how spammers pay for all that bandwidth, they don't! They use the bandwidth of millions of zombie machines spread all around the world, from grandma's e-mail machine to hacked Web servers.

Spam is but one use of a botnet. The criminals who run these networks also use all that collective power to attack companies and governments and demand a ransom to call off the attack. This might be the only sign to a novice user that a computer is infected and is in fact a zombie.

Attack Methods and Sources

As bad as all this malware is, it doesn't seep onto a computer via osmosis; it needs what security people call an *attack vector*—the route the malware takes to get into and infect the system. As a good CompTIA A+ tech, you need to know where the vulnerabilities lie so you can make sure your computers are protected.

As with everything else in computing, there are multiple ways to try and get malware into a system, everything from the first floppy boot sector virus all the way up to modern Internet worms and drive-by downloads.

Zero-Day Attacks A *zero-day attack* is an attack on a vulnerability that wasn't already known to the software developers. It gets the name because the developer of the flawed software has had zero days to fix the vulnerability. Microsoft, Apple, and other software developers regularly post patches to fix flaws as they're discovered.

Spoofing *Spoofing* is the process of pretending to be someone or something you are not by placing false information into your packets. Any data sent on a network can be spoofed. Here are a few quick examples of commonly spoofed data:

- Source MAC address and IP address, to make you think a packet came from somewhere else
- E-mail address, to make you think an e-mail came from somewhere else
- Web address, to make you think you are on a Web page you are not on
- User name, to make you think a certain user is contacting you when in reality it's someone completely different

Generally, spoofing isn't so much a threat as it is a tool to make threats. If you spoof my e-mail address, for example, that by itself isn't a threat. If you use my e-mail address to pretend to be me, however, and to ask my employees to send in their user names and passwords for network login? That's clearly a threat. (And also a waste of time; my employees would *never* trust me with their user names and passwords.)

Man-in-the-Middle In a *man-in-the-middle* attack, an attacker taps into communications between two systems, covertly intercepting traffic thought to be only between those systems, reading or in some cases even changing the data and then sending the data on. A classic man-in-the-middle attack would be a person using special software on a wireless network to make all the clients think his laptop is a wireless access point. He could then listen in on that wireless network, gathering up all the conversations and gaining access to passwords, shared keys, or other sensitive information.

Session Hijacking Somewhat similarly to man-in-the-middle attacks, *session hijacking* tries to intercept a valid computer session to get authentication information. Unlike man-in-the-middle attacks, session hijacking only tries to grab authentication information, not necessarily listening in like a man-in-the-middle attack.

Brute Force CompTIA describes *brute force* as a threat, but it's more of a method that threat agents use. Brute force is a method where a threat agent guesses many or all possible values for some data. Most of the time the term *brute force* refers to an attempt to crack a password, but the term applies to other attacks. You can brute force a search for open ports, network IDs, user names, and so on. Pretty much any attempt to guess the contents of some kind of data field that isn't obvious (or is hidden) is considered a brute force attack.

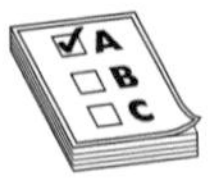

EXAM TIP A *dictionary attack* is a form of brute-force attack which essentially guesses every word in a dictionary. Don't just think of Webster's dictionary—a dictionary used to attack passwords might contain every password ever leaked online.

Pop-Ups and Drive-By Downloads *Pop-ups* are those surprise browser windows that appear automatically when you visit a Web site, proving themselves irritating and unwanted. Getting rid of pop-ups is actually rather tricky. You've probably noticed that most of these pop-up browser windows don't look like browser windows at all. They have no menu bar, button bar, or address window, yet they are separate browser windows. HTML coding permits Web site and advertising designers to remove the usual navigation aids from a browser window so all you're left with is the content. In fact, as I'll describe in a minute, some pop-up browser windows are deliberately designed to mimic similar pop-up alerts from the Windows OS. They might even have buttons similar to Windows' own exit buttons, but you might find that when you click them, you wind up with more pop-up windows instead! What to do?

The first thing you need to know when dealing with pop-ups is how to close them without actually having to risk clicking them. As I said, most pop-ups have removed all navigation aids, and many are also configured to appear on your monitor screen in a position that places the browser window's exit button—the little × button in the upper-right corner—outside of your visible screen area. Some even pop up behind the active browser window and wait there in the background. Most annoying! To remedy this, use alternate means to close the pop-up browser window. For instance, you can right-click

the browser window's taskbar icon to generate a pop-up menu of your own. Select Close, and the window should go away. You can also press ALT-TAB to bring the browser window in question to the forefront and then press ALT-F4 to close it.

Most Web browsers have features to prevent pop-up ads in the first place, but I've found that these features often miss the types of annoyances and threats that greet modern Web users. To combat these new problems, extensions such as uBlock Origin and Ghostery control a variety of Internet annoyances, including pop-up windows, cookies, and trackers, and are more configurable—you can specify what you want to allow on any particular domain address—but that much control is too confusing for most novice-level users.

Another popular spyware method is to use pop-up browser windows crudely disguised as Windows' own system warnings (see Figure 28-19). When clicked, these may trigger a flood of other browser windows, or may even start a file download. Those unwanted, unknown, or unplanned file downloads are called *drive-by downloads.*

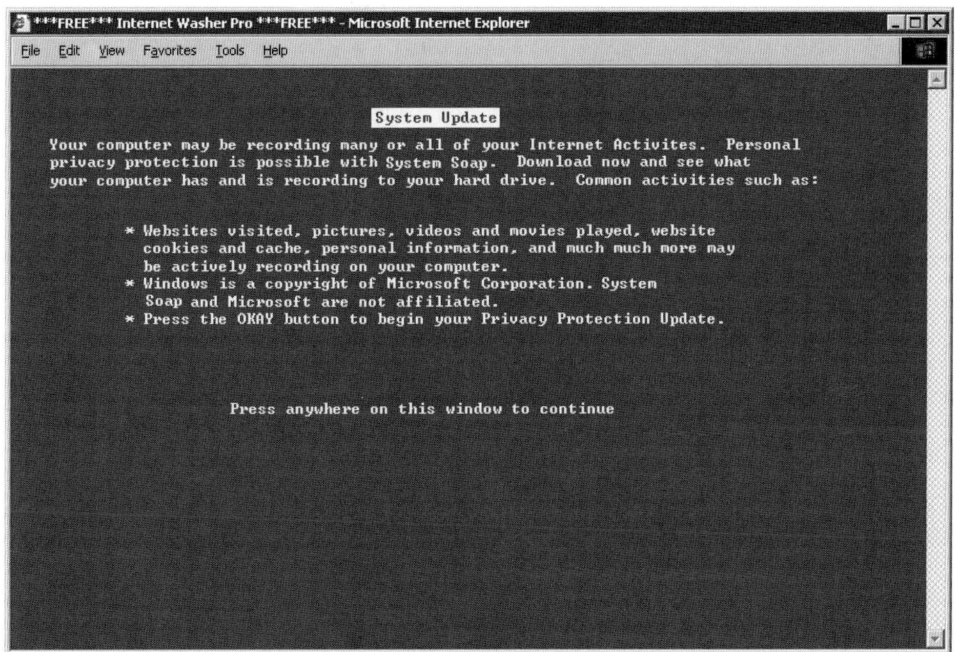

Figure 28-19 A spyware pop-up browser window, disguised as a Windows alert

The lesson here is simple: *Don't click*, at least not without researching the suspicious-looking program first. If you visit a Web site that prompts you to install a third-party application or plug-in that you've never heard of, *don't install it.* Well-known and reputable plug-ins, such as Adobe's Shockwave or Flash, are safe, but be suspicious of any others. Don't click *anywhere* inside of a pop-up browser window, even if it looks just like a Windows alert window or DOS command-line prompt—as I just mentioned, it's probably fake and the Close button is likely a hyperlink. Instead, use other means to close

the window, such as pressing ALT-F4 or right-clicking the browser window's icon on the taskbar and selecting Close.

You can also install spyware detection and removal software on your system and run it regularly. Let's look at how to do that.

Some spyware makers are reputable enough to include a routine for uninstalling their software. Gator, for instance, made it fairly easy to get rid of their programs; you just used the Windows Add/Remove Programs or Programs and Features applet in the Control Panel. Others, however, aren't quite so cooperative. In fact, because spyware is so . . . well, *sneaky*, it's entirely possible that your system already has some installed that you don't even know about.

Windows comes with Windows Defender, a fine tool for catching most spyware (Figure 28-20), but it's not perfect. You can also supplement Windows Defender with a second spyware removal program. There are several on the market, such Lavasoft's Ad-Aware and Safer-Networking's Spybot. My personal favorite is Malwarebytes.

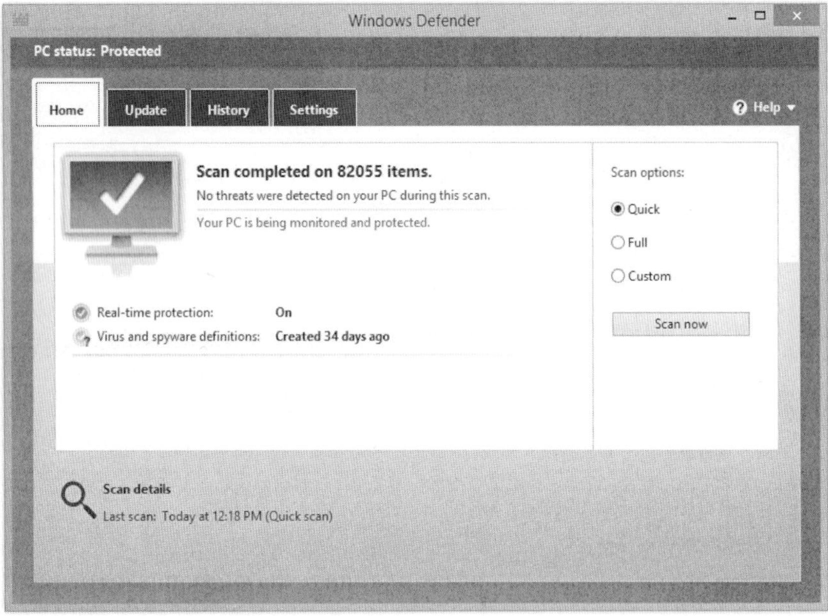

Figure 28-20 Windows Defender

These applications work exactly as advertised. They detect and delete spyware of all sorts—hidden files and folders, cookies, Registry keys and values, you name it. Malwarebytes and Ad-Aware are free for personal use, while Spybot is shareware. Figure 28-21 shows Malwarebytes in action.

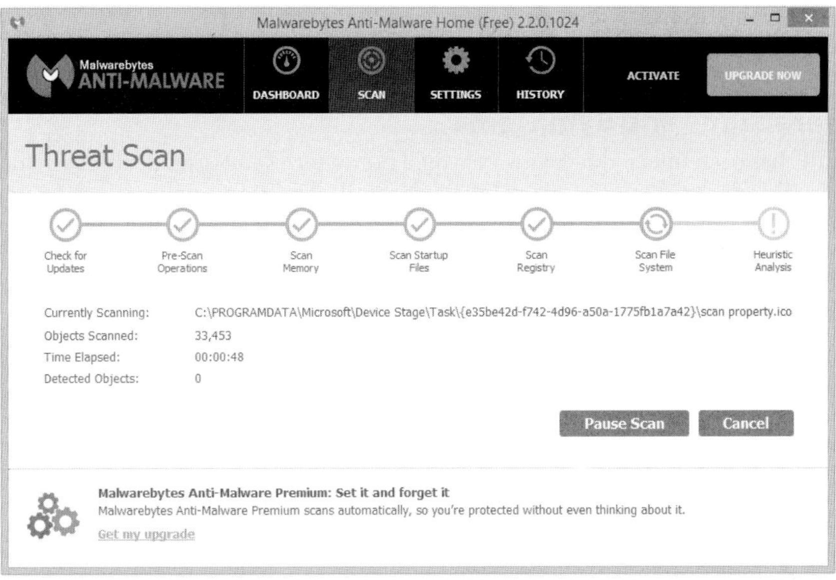

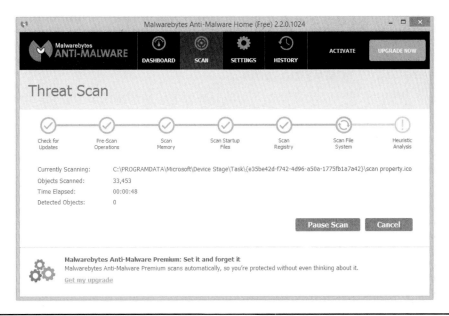

Figure 28-21 Malwarebytes

Spam E-mail that arrives in your Inbox from a source that's not a friend, family member, or colleague, and that you didn't ask for, can create huge problems for you and your computer. This unsolicited e-mail, called *spam*, accounts for a huge percentage of traffic on the Internet. Spam comes in many flavors, from legitimate businesses trying to sell you real products to scammers who just want to take your money. Hoaxes, pornography, and get-rich-quick schemes pour into the Inboxes of most e-mail users. They waste your time and can easily offend.

You can use several options to cope with the flood of spam. The first option is defense. Never post your e-mail address on the Internet. Spammers crawl the Web looking for e-mail addresses posted out in the open.

Filters and e-mail filtering software can block spam at your mail server and at your computer. Google Gmail has powerful blocking schemes, for example, that drop the average spam received by its subscribers by a large percentage, usually more than 90 percent. You can set most e-mail programs to block e-mail from specific people—good to use if someone is harassing you—or to specific people. You can block by subject line or keywords.

A lot of spam contains malware or points to dangerous Web sites. Never click on any link or open an e-mail from someone you don't know! You might just save your computer.

Spam is also notorious for phishing scams. As discussed earlier in the chapter, phishing works by sending you an e-mail message that looks legitimate, like a bill or account information, hoping you will enter important personal information. If you receive an

e-mail from Amazon.com, eBay.com, or some other site (like your bank), don't click on it! Like Admiral Ackbar said in *Star Wars*, "It's a trap!"

Malware Signs and Symptoms

If your PC has been infected by malware, you'll bump into some strange things before you can even run an anti-malware scan. Like a medical condition, malware causes unusual symptoms that should stand out from your everyday computer use. You need to become a PC physician and understand what each of these symptoms means.

Malware's biggest strength is its flexibility: it can look like anything. In fact, a lot of malware attacks can feel like normal PC "wonkiness"—momentary slowdowns, random one-time crashes, and so on. Knowing when a weird application crash is actually a malware attack is half the battle.

A slow PC can mean you're running too many applications at once, or that you've been hit with malware. Applications can crash at random, even if you don't have too many loaded. How do you tell the difference? In this case, it's the frequency. If it's happening a lot, even when all of your applications are closed, you've got a problem. This goes for frequent lockups, too. If Windows starts misbehaving (more than usual), run your anti-malware application right away.

Malware, however, doesn't always jump out at you with big system crashes. Some malware tries to rename system files, change file permissions, or hide files completely. You might start getting e-mail messages from colleagues or friends questioning a message "you" sent to them that seemed spammy. (CompTIA terms this *responses from users regarding email.*) You might get *automated replies from unknown sent e-mail* that you know you didn't send. Most of these issues are easily caught by a regular anti-malware scan, so as long as you remain vigilant, you'll be okay.

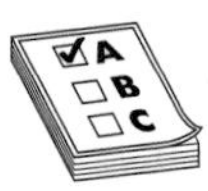

EXAM TIP While it's not necessarily a malware attack, watch out for hijacked e-mail accounts belonging either to you or to someone you know. Hackers can hit both e-mail clients and Webmail users. If you start receiving some fishy (or phishy) e-mail messages, change your Webmail user name and password and scan your PC for malware.

Some malware even fights back, defending itself from your many attempts to remove it. If your Windows Update feature stops working, preventing you from patching your PC, you've got malware. If other tools and utilities throw up an "Access Denied" road block, you've got malware. If you lose all Internet connectivity, either the malware is stopping you or the process of removing the malware broke your connection. In this case, you might need to reconfigure your Internet connection: reinstall your NIC and its drivers, reboot your router, and so on.

Even your browser and anti-malware applications can turn against you. If you type in one Web address and end up at a different site than you anticipated, a malware infection might have overwritten your HOSTS file. The HOSTS file overrules any DNS settings and can redirect your browser to whatever site the malware adds to the file. Most

browser redirections point you to phishing scams or Web sites full of free downloads (that are, of course, covered in even more malware). In fact, some free anti-malware applications are actually malware—what techs call *rogue anti-malware* programs. You can avoid these rogue applications by sticking to the recommended lists of anti-malware software found online.

Watch for security alerts in Windows, either from Windows' built-in security tools or from your third-party anti-malware program. Windows Vista includes the Security Center, a Control Panel applet that monitors your software firewall, automatic updates, malware protection, and more. Windows 7 morphed the Security Center into the Action Center, which you learned about back in Chapter 17 (see Figure 28-22). You don't actually configure much using these applets; they just tell you whether or not you are protected. Both of these tools place an icon and pop up a notification in the notification area whenever Windows detects a problem. Vista uses a red shield with a white × to notify you, while Windows 7 through 8.1 use a white flag with a red ×.

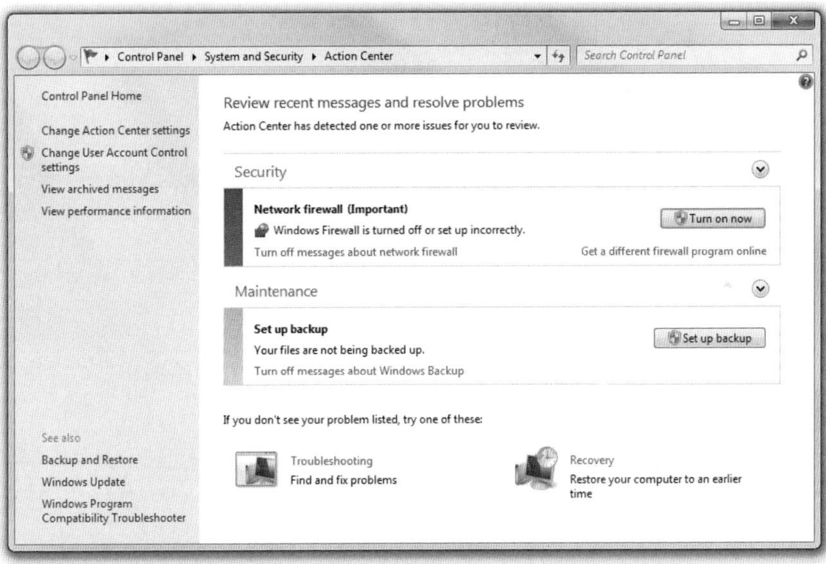

Figure 28-22 Windows 7 Action Center

Malware Prevention and Recovery

The only way to permanently protect your PC from malware is to disconnect it from the Internet and never permit any potentially infected software to touch your precious computer. Because neither scenario is likely these days, you need to use specialized anti-malware programs to help stave off the inevitable assaults. Even with the best anti-malware tools, there are times when malware still manages to strike your computer. When you discover infected systems, you need to know how to stop the spread of the

malware to other computers, how to fix infected computers, and how to remediate (restore) the system as close to its original state as possible.

Dealing with Malware

You can deal with malware in several ways: anti-malware programs, training and awareness, patch/update management, and remediation.

At the very least, every computer should run an anti-malware program. If possible, add an appliance that runs anti-malware programs against incoming data from your network. Also remember that an anti-malware program is only as good as its updates—keep everyone's definition file (explained a bit later) up to date with, literally, nightly updates! Users must be trained to look for suspicious ads, programs, and pop-ups, and understand that they must not click these things. The more you teach users about malware, the more aware they'll be of potential threats. Your organization should have policies and procedures in place so everyone knows what to do if they encounter malware. Finally, a good tech maintains proper incident response records to see if any pattern to attacks emerges. He or she can then adjust policies and procedures to mitigate these attacks.

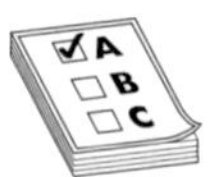

EXAM TIP One of the most important malware mitigation procedures is to keep systems under your control patched and up to date through proper *patch management*. Microsoft, Apple, and the Linux maintainers do a very good job of putting out bug fixes and patches as soon as problems occur. If your systems aren't set up to update automatically, then perform manual updates regularly.

Anti-Malware Programs

An *anti-malware program* such as a classic *antivirus* program protects your PC in two ways. It can be both sword and shield, working in an active seek-and-destroy mode and in a passive sentry mode. When ordered to seek and destroy, the program scans the computer's boot sector and files for viruses and, if it finds any, presents you with the available options for removing or disabling them. Antivirus programs can also operate as *virus shields* that passively monitor a computer's activity, checking for viruses only when certain events occur, such as a program execution or file download.

NOTE The term *antivirus* (and antispyware, or anti-anything) is becoming obsolete. Viruses are only a small component of the many types of malware. Many people continue to use the term as a synonym for anti-malware.

Antivirus programs use different techniques to combat different types of viruses. They detect boot sector viruses simply by comparing the drive's boot sector to a standard boot sector. This works because most boot sectors are basically the same. Some antivirus programs make a backup copy of the boot sector. If they detect a virus, the programs use that backup copy to replace the infected boot sector. Executable viruses are a little

more difficult to find because they can be on any file in the drive. To detect executable viruses, the antivirus program uses a library of signatures. A *signature* is the code pattern of a known virus. The antivirus program compares an executable file to its library of signatures. There have been instances where a perfectly clean program coincidentally held a virus signature. Usually the antivirus program's creator provides a patch to prevent further alarms.

Now that you understand the types of viruses and how antivirus programs try to protect against them, let's review a few terms that are often used when to describe virus traits.

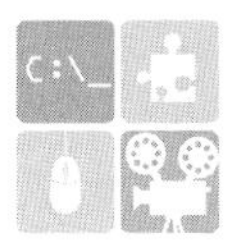

SIM Check out the excellent Challenge! sim, "Fixing Viruses," in the Chapter 28 sims over at http://totalsem.com/90x.

Polymorphic/Polymorphs A *polymorph virus* attempts to change its signature to prevent detection by antivirus programs, usually by continually scrambling a bit of useless code. Fortunately, the scrambling code itself can be identified and used as the signature—once the antivirus makers become aware of the virus. One technique used to combat unknown polymorphs is to have the antivirus program create a checksum on every file in the drive. A *checksum* in this context is a number generated by the software based on the contents of the file rather than the name, date, or size of that file. The algorithms for creating these checksums vary among different antivirus programs (they are also usually kept secret to help prevent virus makers from coming up with ways to beat them). Every time a program is run, the antivirus program calculates a new checksum and compares it with the earlier calculation. If the checksums are different, it is a sure sign of a virus.

Stealth The term "stealth" is more of a concept than an actual virus function. Most *stealth virus* programs are boot sector viruses that use various methods to hide from antivirus software. The AntiEXE stealth virus hooks on to a little-known but often-used software interrupt, for example, running only when that interrupt runs. Others make copies of innocent-looking files.

User Education

A powerful tool to prevent malware attacks and to reduce the impact of malware attacks when they happen is to educate your users. Teach users to be cautious of incoming e-mail they don't clearly recognize and to never click on an attachment or URL in an e-mail unless they are 100 percent certain of the source.

Explain the dangers of going to questionable Web sites to your users and teach them how to react when they see questionable actions take place. All Web browsers have built-in attack site warnings like the one shown in Figure 28-23.

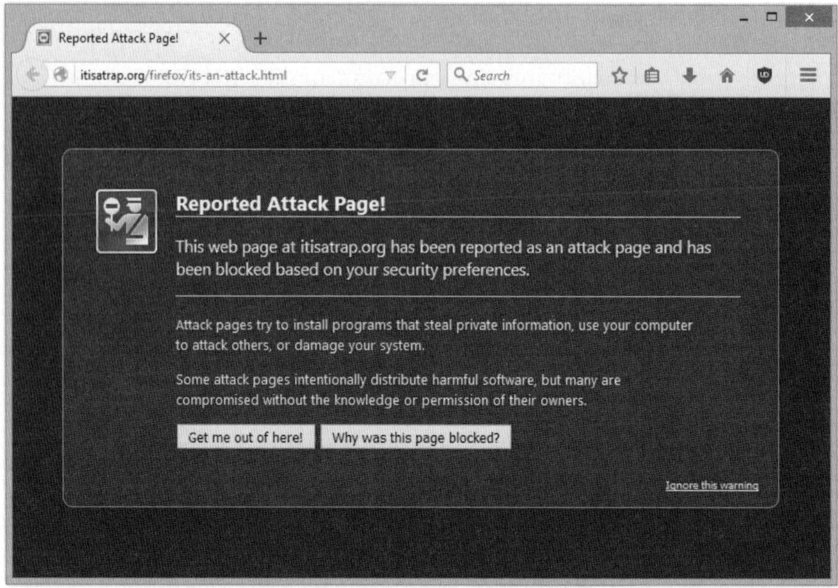

Figure 28-23 Attack site warning

Nobody wants their systems infected with malware. Users are motivated and happy when you give them the skills necessary to protect themselves. The bottom line is that educated and aware users will make your life a lot easier.

Malware Prevention Tips

The secret to preventing damage from a malicious software attack is to keep from getting malware on your system in the first place. As discussed earlier, for example, all good antivirus programs include a virus shield that scans e-mail, downloads, running programs, and so on automatically (see Figure 28-24).

Use your antivirus shield. It is also a good idea to scan PCs daily for possible virus attacks. All antivirus programs include terminate-and-stay-resident programs (TSRs) that run every time the PC is booted. Last but not least, know the source of any software before you load it. Only install apps from trusted sources, such as the manufacturer's Web site, or well-known app stores like Valve's Steam service. Avoid untrusted software sources, like free registry cleaners from some .support domain, at all costs.

Keep your antivirus and anti-malware programs updated. New viruses and other malware appear daily, and your programs need to know about them. The list of virus signatures your antivirus program can recognize, for example, is called the *definition file*, and you must keep that definition file up to date so your antivirus software has the latest signatures. Fortunately, most antivirus programs update themselves automatically. Further, you should periodically update the core anti-malware software programming—called the *engine*—to employ the latest refinements the developers have included.

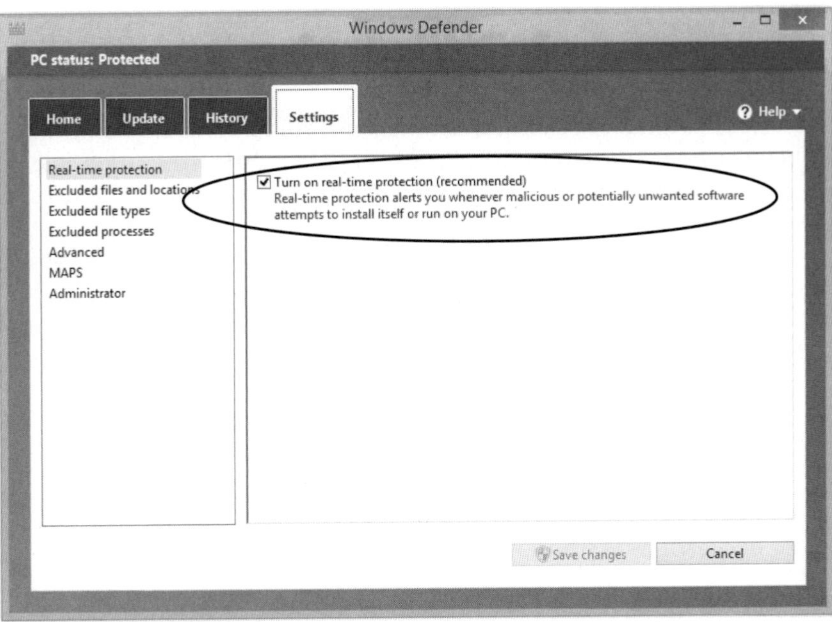

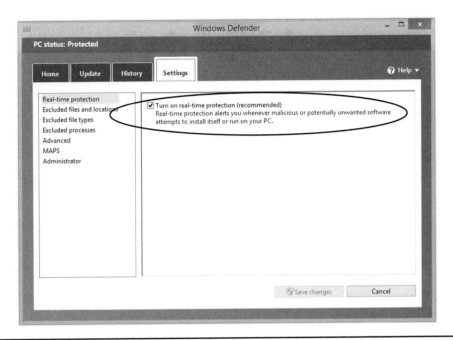

Figure 28-24 A virus shield in action

Try This!

Scoring Excellent Anti-Malware Programs

You can download many excellent anti-malware programs for free, either for extended trial periods or for indefinite use. Since you need these programs to keep your systems happy, Try This! Download one or more anti-malware programs, such as the following:

- **Malwarebytes Anti-Malware (www.malwarebytes.org)** Malwarebytes' Anti-Malware program rocks the house in terms of dealing with malicious software. They offer both a free version that scans your computer for malware and quarantines it and a Premium version that "Crushes online threats instantly, automatically." Anti-Malware is my first choice in dealing with malware on a client's computer.

Try This! (*Continued*)

- **Lavasoft Ad-Aware (www.lavasoft.com)** Ad-Aware is an excellent anti-malware program. Ad-Aware 11 offers free antivirus and spyware protection and will root out all sorts of files and programs that can cause your computer to run slowly (or worse). Ad-Aware Pro Security is available at a cost and offers advanced protection with a two-way firewall, threat blocking algorithms, and phishing protection.
- **Spybot (www.safer-networking.org)** Spybot from Safer Networking Ltd. is another superb anti-malware/antispyware program. Many folks use both Ad-Aware and Spybot—though sometimes the two programs detect each other as spyware! You can also purchase Spybot Home or Spybot Pro, both of which offer additional protection and features.

Boot Media Anti-Malware Tools

If you run anti-malware software and your computer still gets infected, especially after a reboot, you need a more serious anti-malware tool. Many anti-malware companies provide bootable CDs or USB flash drives (or show you how to make one) that enable you to boot from a known-clean OS and run the same anti-malware software, but this time not corrupted by the malware on your system.

Malware Recovery Tips

When the inevitable happens and either your computer or one of your user's computers gets infected by malware such as a computer virus, you need to follow certain steps to stop the problem from spreading and get the computer back up safely into service. The 902 exam outlines the following multi-step process as the *best practice procedure for malware removal*:

1. Identify malware symptoms
2. Quarantine infected system
3. Disable System Restore (in Windows)
4. Remediate infected systems
    a. Update anti-malware software
    b. Use scan and removal techniques (Windows Safe Mode, Preinstallation Environment)
5. Schedule scans and run updates
6. Enable System Restore and create restore point (in Windows)
7. Educate end user

Recognize and Quarantine The first step is to identify and recognize that a potential malware outbreak has occurred. If you're monitoring network traffic and one computer starts spewing e-mail, that's a good indicator of malware. Or users might complain that a computer that was running snappily the day before seems very sluggish.

Many networks employ software such as the open source PacketFence that automatically monitors network traffic and can cut a machine off the network if that machine starts sending suspicious packets. You can also quarantine a computer manually by disconnecting the network cable. Once you're sure the machine isn't capable of infecting others, you're ready to find the virus or other malware and get rid of it.

At this point, you should disable System Restore. If you make any changes going forward, you don't want the virus to be included in any saved restore points. To turn off System Restore in Windows, open the Control Panel and then the System applet. Click on the System protection link. In the Protection Settings section, select a drive and click on Configure. In the System Protection dialog box that opens, select Turn off system protection. Repeat the procedure for each hard drive on the system.

Search and Destroy Once you've isolated the infected computer (or computers), you need to get to a safe boot environment and run anti-malware software. You can try Windows Safe Mode in Windows Vista/7, or the Windows Recovery Environment in Windows 8/8.1/10 first, because they don't require anything but a reboot. If that doesn't work, or you suspect a boot sector virus, you need to turn to an external bootable source, such as a bootable CD or USB flash drive.

Get into the habit of keeping around a bootable anti-malware flash drive or optical media. If you suspect a virus or other malware, use the boot media, even if your anti-malware program claims to have eliminated the problem. Turn off the PC and reboot it from the anti-malware disc or drive (you might have to change CMOS settings to boot to optical or USB media). This will put you in a clean boot environment that you know is free from any boot sector viruses. If you only support fairly recent computers, you will likely be booting to a USB flash drive, so you can put a boot environment on a thumb drive for even faster start-up speeds.

You have several options for creating the bootable optical disc or flash drive. First, some antivirus software comes in a bootable version, such as the avast! Virus Cleaner Tool (see Figure 28-25).

Second, you can download a copy of Linux that offers a live CD or DVD option such as Ubuntu. With a live disc, you boot to the disc and install a complete working copy of the operating system into RAM, never touching or accessing the hard drive, to give you full Internet-ready access so you can reach the many online anti-malware sites you'll need for access to anti-malware tools. Kaspersky Labs provides a nice option at www.kaspersky.com.

Finally, you can download and burn a copy of the Ultimate Boot CD. It comes stocked with several antivirus and anti-malware programs, so you won't need any other tool. Find it at www.ultimatebootcd.com. The only downside is that the anti-malware engines will quickly be out of date, as will their malware libraries.

Once you get to a boot environment, update your anti-malware software and then run its most comprehensive scan. Then check all removable media that were exposed to the system, and any other machine that might have received data from the system or that is networked to the cleaned machine. A virus or other malicious program can often lie dormant for months before anyone knows of its presence.

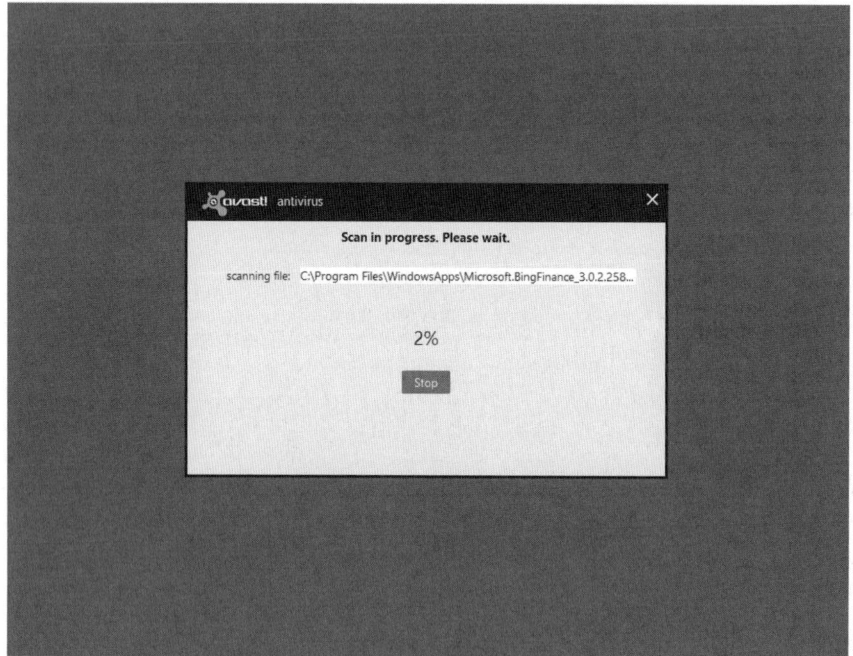

Figure 28-25 avast! Virus Cleaner Tool

E-mail is still a common source of viruses, and opening infected e-mails is a common way to get infected. Viewing an e-mail in a preview window opens the e-mail message and exposes your computer to some viruses. Download files only from sites you know to be safe and avoid the less reputable corners of the Internet, the most likely places to pick up computer infections.

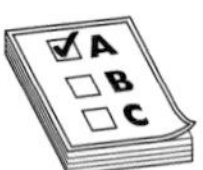

EXAM TIP CompTIA considers the process of removing a virus part of the remediation step. Since you can't remediate a PC until after a virus is gone, I've laid out the steps as you see here.

Remediate Malware infections can do a lot of damage to a system, especially to sensitive files needed to load Windows, so you might need to remediate formerly infected systems after cleaning off the drive or drives. *Remediation* simply means that you fix things the virus or other malware harmed. This can mean replacing corrupted Windows Registry files or even startup files.

If you can't start Windows after the malware scan is finished, you need to boot to the Windows Preinstallation Environment and use the Windows Recovery Environment/System Recovery Options.

With the Windows Recovery Environment, you have access to more repair tools, such as Startup Repair, System Restore, Windows Complete PC Restore (System Image Recovery in Windows 7 and later), Refresh, and the command prompt (see Figure 28-26). Run the appropriate option for the situation and you should have the machine properly remediated in a jiffy.

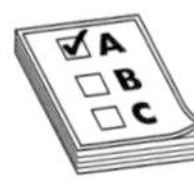

EXAM TIP Remember to re-enable System Restore and create a new restore point once the system has been repaired.

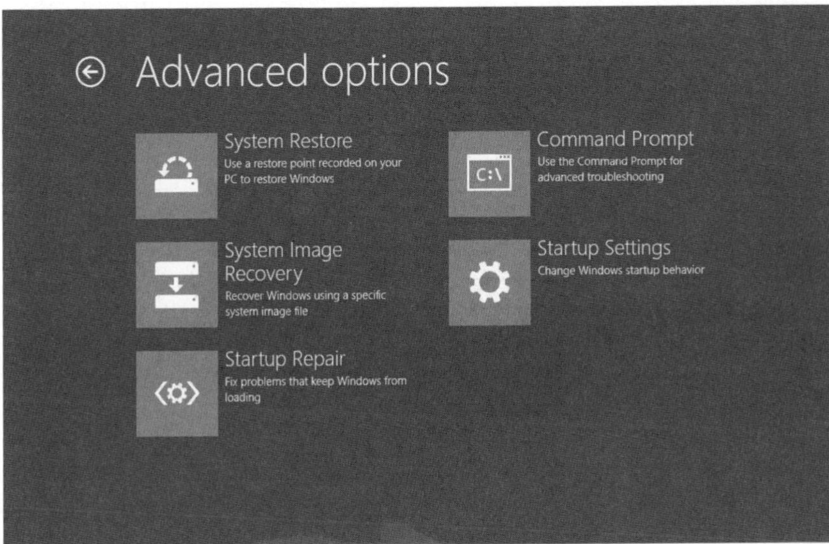

Figure 28-26 System Recovery Options in Windows Vista

Educate The best way to keep from having to deal with malware is education. It's your job as the IT person to talk to users, especially the ones whose systems you've just spent an hour ridding of nasties, about how to avoid these programs. Show them samples of dangerous e-mails they should not open, Web sites to avoid, and the types of programs they should not install and use on the network. Any user who understands the risks of questionable actions on their computers will usually do the right thing and stay away from malware.

Finally, have your users run antivirus and antispyware programs regularly. Schedule them while interfacing with the user so you know it will happen.

Firewalls

Firewalls are an essential tool in the fight against malicious programs on the Internet. *Firewalls* are devices or software that protect an internal network from unauthorized access to and from the Internet at large. Firewalls use a number of methods to protect networks, such as hiding IP addresses and blocking TCP/IP ports.

A typical network uses one of two types of firewalls: *hardware firewalls*, often built into routers, and *software firewalls* that run on your computers. Both types of firewall protect your computer and your network. You also run them at the same time. Let's look at both a typical SOHO router's firewall features and your computer's software firewall to see how they protect your network and your computers.

Hardware Firewall Settings

Most SOHO networks use a hardware firewall, often as a feature built into a router like the Linksys model shown in Figure 28-27. A hardware firewall protects a LAN from outside threats by filtering the packets before they reach your internal machines, which you learned about back in Chapter 23, "The Internet." Routers, however, have a few other tricks up their sleeves. From the router's browser-based settings screen, you can configure a hardware firewall (see Figure 28-28). Let's walk through a few of the available settings.

A hardware firewall watches for and stops many common threats—all you have to do is turn it on (see Figure 28-29). Hardware firewalls use *Stateful Packet Inspection (SPI)* to inspect each incoming packet individually. SPI also blocks any incoming traffic that isn't in response to your outgoing traffic. You can even disable ports entirely, blocking all traffic in or out. But what if you want to allow outside users access to a Web server on the LAN? Because Network Address Translation (NAT) hides the true IP address of that system (as described in Chapter 23), you'll need a way to allow incoming traffic past the router/firewall and a way to redirect that traffic to the right PC.

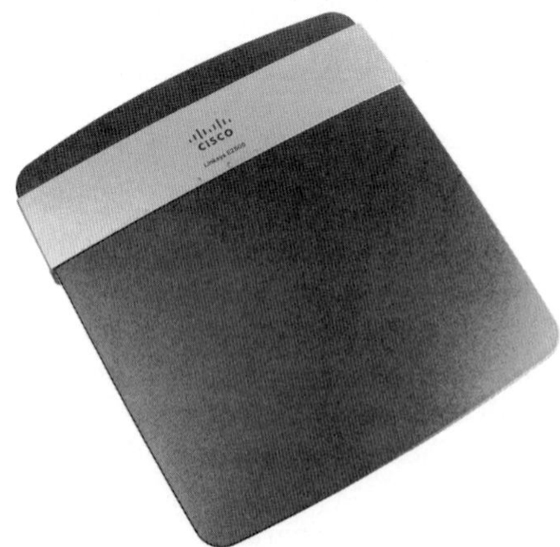

Figure 28-27 Linksys router as a firewall

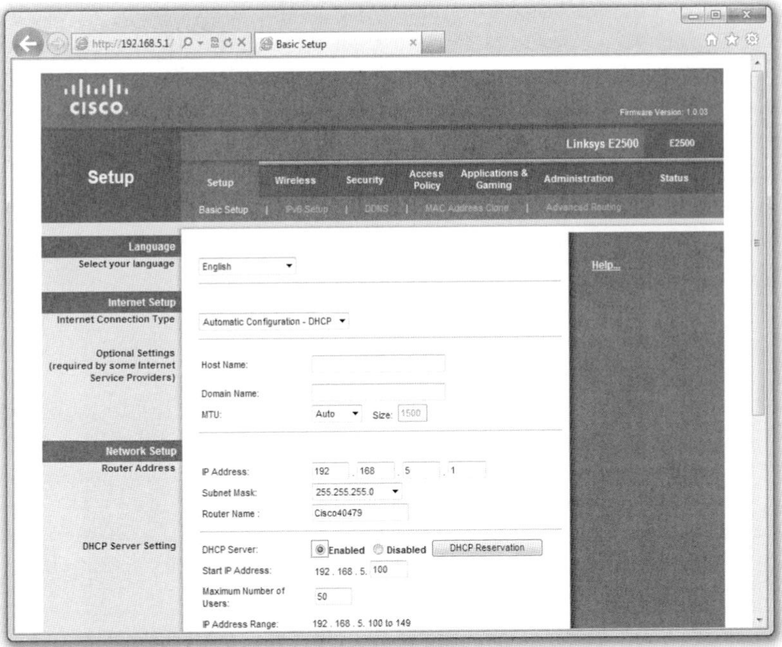

Figure 28-28 Default Web interface

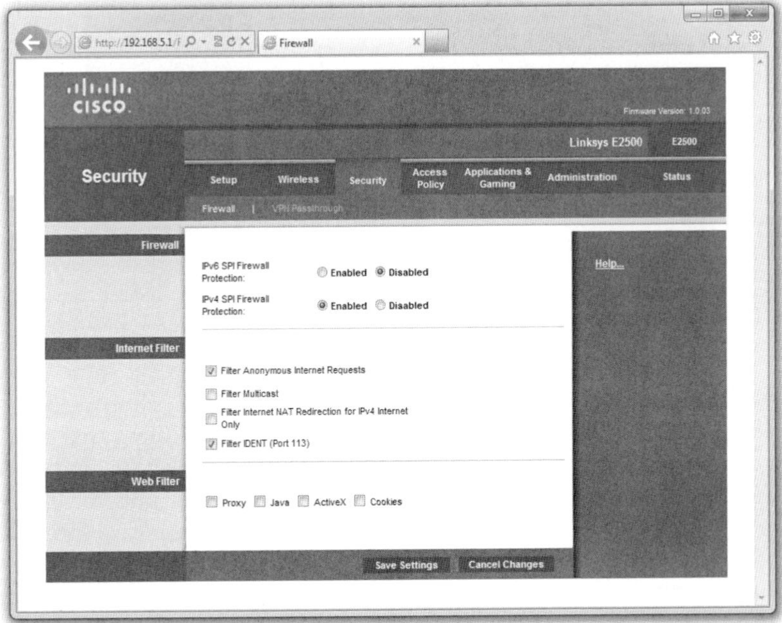

Figure 28-29 SPI firewall settings

Port forwarding enables you to open a port in the firewall and direct incoming traffic on that port to a specific IP address on your LAN. In the case of the Web server referenced in the previous paragraph, you would open port 80 (for HTTP packets) and instruct the router to send all incoming traffic to the server machine. Figure 28-30 shows port forwarding configured to send all HTTP packets to an internal Web server.

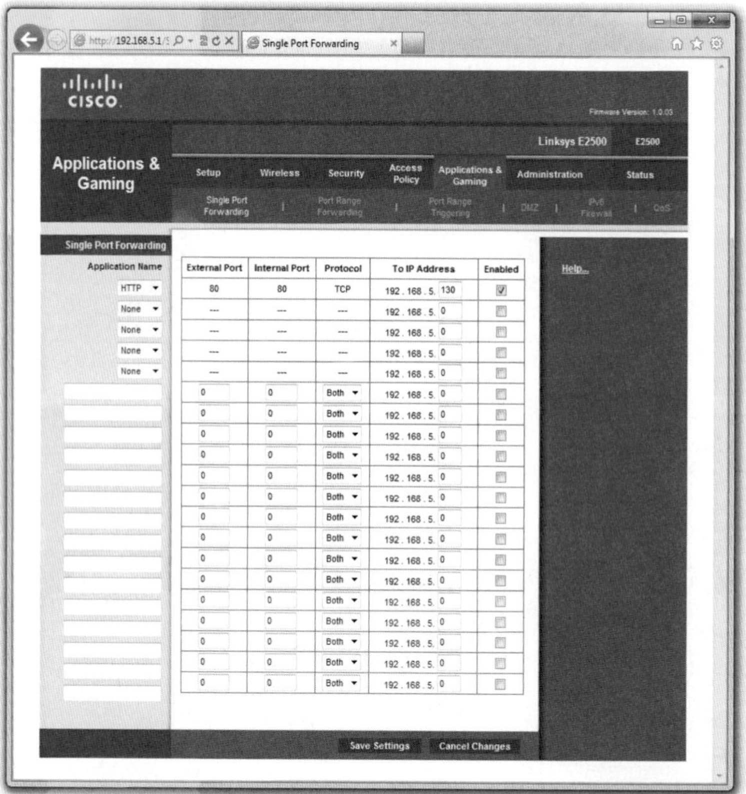

Figure 28-30 Port forwarding

Port forwarding isn't the only way to open ports on a firewall. *Port triggering* enables you to open an incoming connection to one computer automatically based on a specific outgoing connection. The *trigger port* defines the outgoing connection, and the *destination port* defines the incoming connection. If you set the trigger port to 3434 and the destination port to 1234, for example, any outgoing traffic on port 3434 will trigger the router to open port 1234 and send any received data back to the system that sent the original outgoing traffic. Figure 28-31 shows a router set up with port triggering for an Internet Relay Chat (IRC) server.

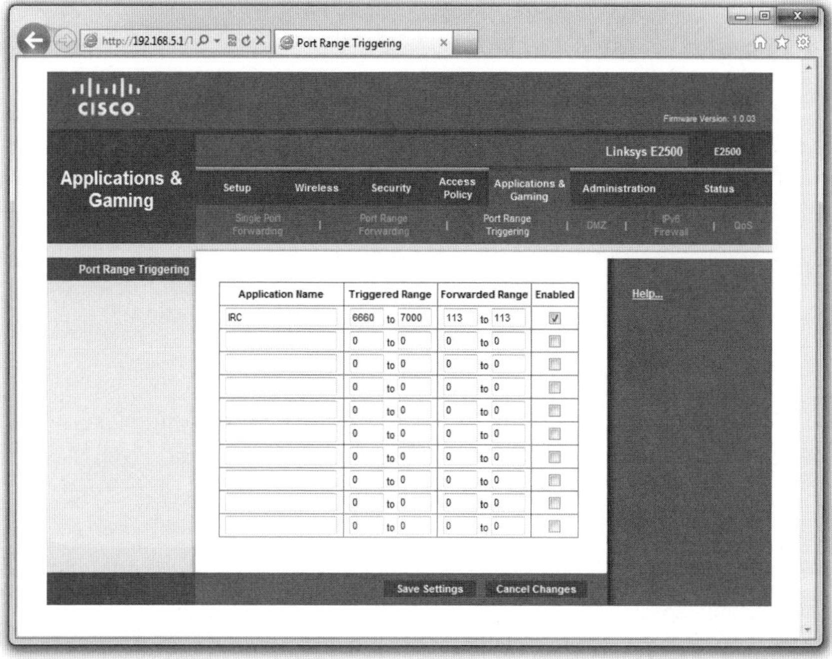

Figure 28-31 Port triggering

If you want to go beyond port forwarding and port triggering and open every port on a machine, you need a demilitarized zone (DMZ). A DMZ puts systems with the specified IP addresses outside the protection of the firewall, opening all ports and enabling all incoming traffic (see Figure 28-32). If you think this sounds incredibly dangerous, you are right! Any PC inside the DMZ will be completely exposed to outside attacks. Don't use it!

Software Firewalls

While a hardware firewall does a lot to protect you from outside intruders, you should also use a software firewall, such as the firewalls built into each version of Windows, called (appropriately) Windows Firewall or Windows Firewall with Advanced Security. Windows Firewall (see Figure 28-33) handles the heavy lifting of port blocking, security logging, and more.

You can access Windows Firewall by opening the Windows Firewall applet in the Control Panel. Configuring Windows Firewall involves turning it on or off, and choosing which programs and services can pass through the firewall, known as *exceptions*. If you wanted to run a *Minecraft* server (a game that requires an Internet connection), for example, it would need to be on the list of exceptions for your firewall—most programs you install add themselves to this list automatically, otherwise Windows Firewall prompts you the first time you run it and asks if you want to add the program as an exception.

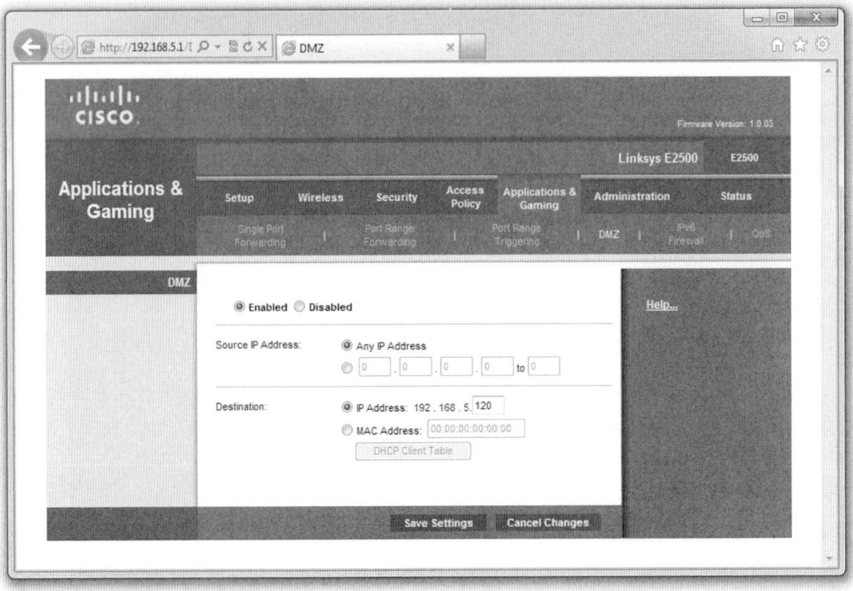

Figure 28-32 DMZ set up on a SOHO router

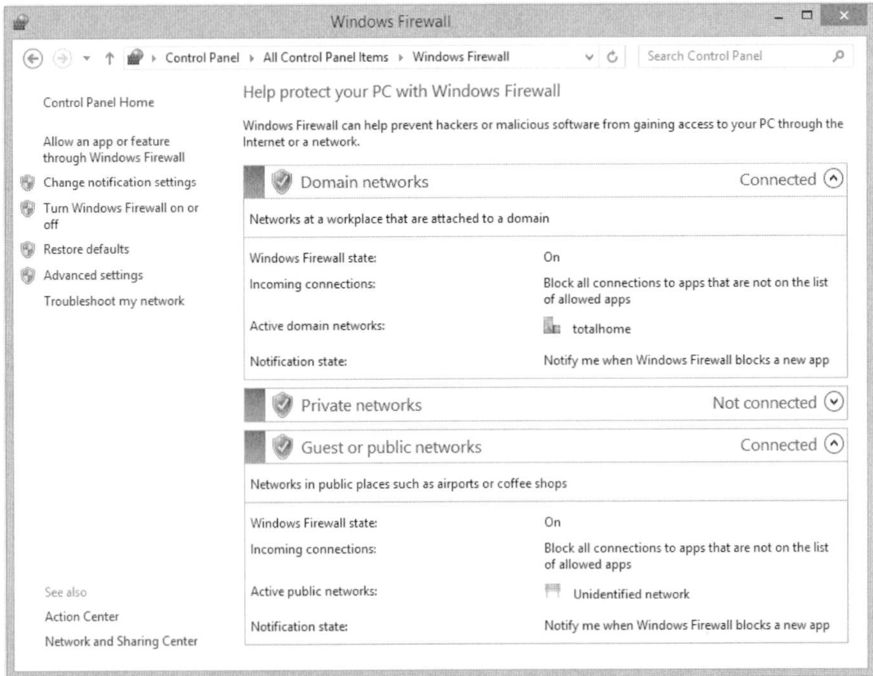

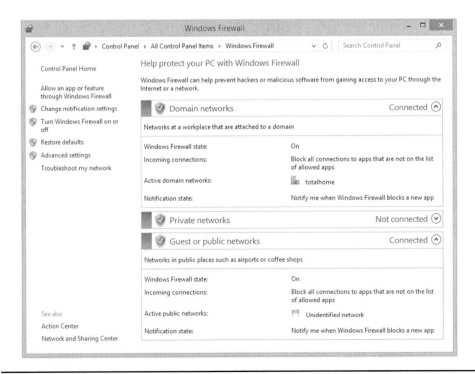

Figure 28-33 Windows 7 Firewall applet

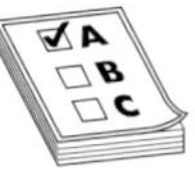

EXAM TIP To turn Windows Firewall off (which I don't recommend doing), open the Windows Firewall applet. In Windows Vista, click on *Turn Windows Firewall on or off*, then select *Off (not recommended)*. In Windows 7 and later, select *Turn Windows Firewall on or off*, then select *Turn off Windows Firewall (not recommended)* for each network type you use.

When Microsoft first introduced Windows Firewall, way back with Windows XP, its biggest shortcoming was that it failed to consider that a single PC, especially a portable, might connect to multiple networks. You don't necessarily want the same firewall settings used for both public and private networks. Microsoft needed to develop a way for you to separate trustworthy networks (like the one in your house or at the office) from non-trustworthy networks (like a public Wi-Fi Internet connection at the airport). Microsoft fixed this shortcoming in Vista (and later) by including three network types: Domain, Private, and Guest or Public.

- A *Domain* network is a Windows network controlled by a Windows domain controller that runs Active Directory Domain Services. In this case, the domain controller itself tells your machine what it can and cannot share. You don't need to do anything when your computer joins a domain.
- A *Private* network enables you to share resources, discover other devices, and allow other devices to discover your computer safely.
- A *Guest or Public* network prevents your computer from sharing and disables all discovery protocols.

When your computer connects to a network for the first time, Windows will prompt you to choose the network type: Home, Work, or Guest or Public location (see Figure 28-34).

First, notice that Domain is not an option. There's a good reason for this: If your computer is on a domain, you won't see the dialog box in Figure 28-34. When your computer joins a domain, Windows automatically sets your network location to Domain (unless your domain controller chooses something different, which is unlikely).

So what exactly does Windows do when you select Home, Work, or Guest or Public location? Windows configures Windows Firewall to block or unblock discovery and sharing services. When running on a Private (Home or Work) network, Windows enables Network Discovery and File and Printer Sharing as exceptions. When running on a Guest or Public network, Windows disables these exceptions.

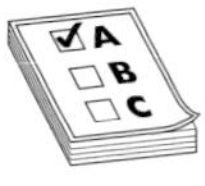

EXAM TIP The Network Discovery setting dictates whether a computer can find other computers or devices on a network, and vice versa. Even with Network Discovery activated, several firewall settings can overrule certain connections.

In Windows Vista, Microsoft cleverly used Windows Firewall and the network type to turn services on and off, but Microsoft made one mistake: the firewall configuration

and network type remain the same for every connection. If your Windows machine never changes networks, you won't have a problem. But what about machines (mainly laptops) that hop from one network to another (see Figure 28-35)? In that case, you need different firewall settings for each network the system might encounter.

Figure 28-34 Set Network Location in Windows 8.1

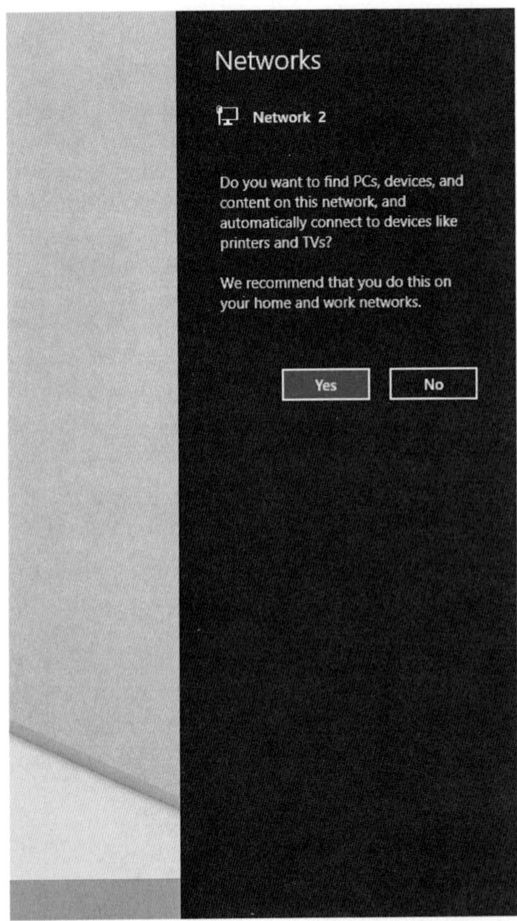
Networks
Network 2
Do you want to find PCs, devices, and content on this network, and automatically connect to devices like printers and TVs?
We recommend that you do this on your home and work networks.
Yes
No

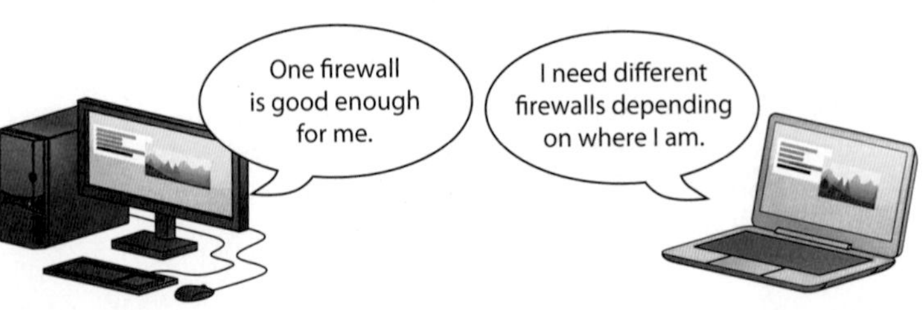
One firewall is good enough for me.
I need different firewalls depending on where I am.

Figure 28-35 Many machines need more than one network setting.

In this regard, Windows 7 and later make a big departure from Windows Vista. In the later versions of Windows, the Set Network Location dialog box appears every time you connect to a new network. Windows even includes three different firewall settings: one for Domains, one for Private networks (Home or Work), and one for Guest or Public networks.

Once you've picked a network type, you might want to customize the firewall settings further. If you click the Advanced Settings option in the Windows Firewall applet, you'll discover a much deeper level of firewall configuration (see Figure 28-36). In fact, it's an entirely different tool (actually an MMC snap-in) called Windows Firewall with Advanced Security.

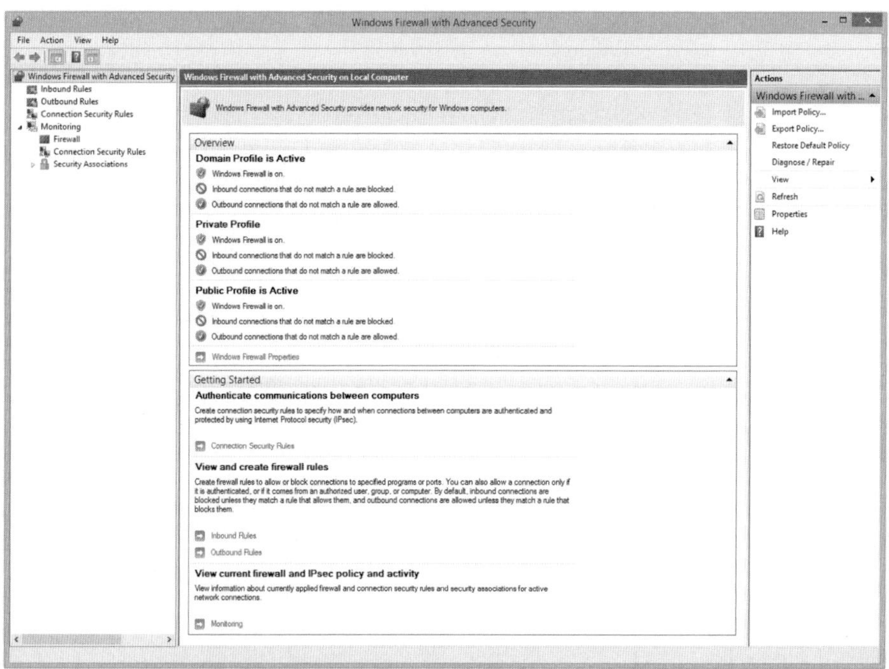

Figure 28-36 Windows Firewall with Advanced Security

From the Windows Firewall with Advanced Security snap-in, you have much more control over how Windows treats exceptions. In the standard Windows Firewall applet, you can only choose a program and make it an exception, giving it permission to pass through the firewall. But programs both send and receive network data, and the basic applet doesn't give you much control over the "inbound" and "outbound" aspect of firewalls. The Windows Firewall with Advanced Security snap-in takes the exceptions concept and expands it to include custom rules for both inbound and outbound data. Figure 28-37 shows the outbound rules for a typical Windows system.

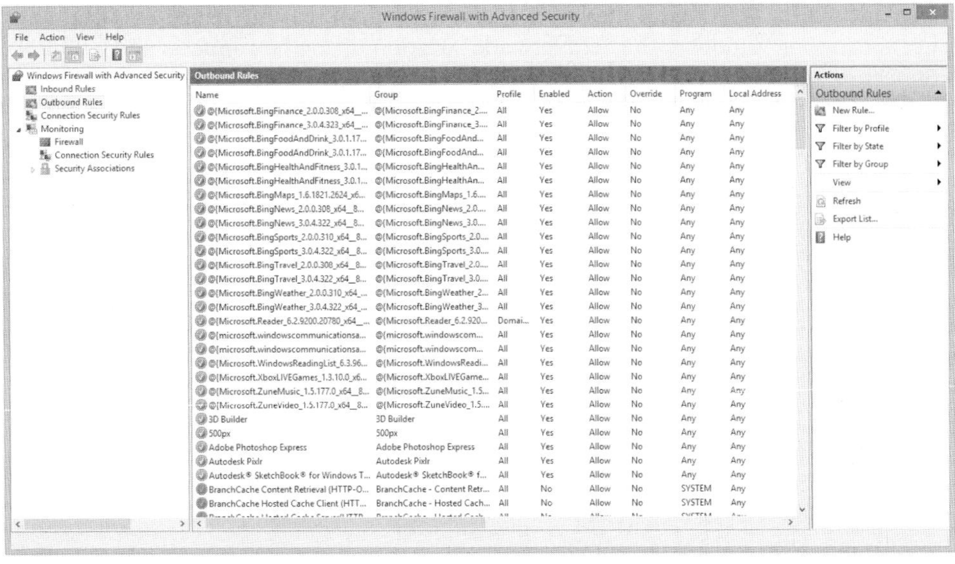

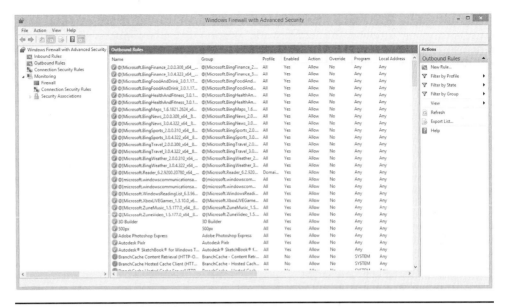

Figure 28-37 Outbound Rules list

A rule always includes at least the following:

- The name of the program
- Group: an organizational group that helps sort all the rules
- The associated profile (All, Domain, Public, Private)
- Enabled/disabled status
- Remote and local address
- Remote and local port number

You can add, remove, and customize any rule to your liking. It quickly gets complicated, so unless you need to set a lot of custom rules, stick to the standard Windows Firewall applet.

Internet Appliances

The discussion of firewalls barely scratches the surface of tools used to secure a large network. While enterprise networking is generally beyond the scope of an A+ tech's duties, the CompTIA 902 objectives cover two devices critical to modern network security—IDS and IPS—plus the concept of unified threat management. Let's take a look.

An *intrusion detection system (IDS)* is an internet application that inspects packets, looking for active intrusions. An IDS functions inside the network watching for threats that a firewall might miss, such as viruses, illegal logon attempts, and other well-known attacks. Plus, because it inspects traffic inside the network, the IDS can discover internal threats, like the activity of a vulnerability scanner smuggled in on a flash drive by a disgruntled worker planning an attack on an internal database server.

An IDS always has some way to let the network administrators know if an attack is taking place: at the very least the attack is logged, but some IDSes offer a pop-up message, an e-mail, or even a text message to an administrator's phone. An IDS can also respond to detected intrusions with action. The IDS can't stop the attack directly, but can request assistance from other devices—like a firewall—that can.

An *intrusion prevention system (IPS)* is very similar to an IDS, but an IPS sits directly in the flow of network traffic. This active monitoring has a trio of consequences. First, an IPS can stop an attack while it is happening. No need to request help from any other devices. Second, the network bandwidth and latency take a hit. Third, if the IPS goes down, the network link might go down too. Depending on the IPS, it can block incoming packets on-the-fly based on IP address, port number, or application type. An IPS might go even further, literally fixing certain packets on-the-fly.

All these network Internet appliances, no matter how advanced and aware they become, are still singular tools in the box used to protect networks. That is why modern dedicated firewall/Internet appliances are built around providing *unified threat management (UTM)*. UTM takes the traditional firewall and packages it with many other security services such as IPS, VPN, load balancing, antivirus, and many other features depending on the make and model. The UTM approach to building network gear helps build robust security deep into the network, protecting what really matters: our data.

Authentication and Encryption

You know that the first step in securing data is authentication, through a user name and password. But when you throw in networking, you're suddenly not just a single user sitting in front of a computer and typing. You're accessing a remote resource and sending login information over the Internet. What's to stop someone from intercepting your user name and password?

Firewalls do a great job of controlling traffic coming into a network from the Internet and going out of a network to the Internet, but they do nothing to stop interceptor hackers who monitor traffic on the public Internet looking for vulnerabilities. Worse, once a packet is on the Internet itself, anyone with the right equipment can intercept and inspect it. Inspected packets are a cornucopia of passwords, account names, and other tidbits that hackers can use to intrude into your network. Because we can't stop hackers from inspecting these packets, we must turn to *encryption* to make them unreadable.

Network encryption occurs at many levels and is in no way limited to Internet-based activities. Not only are there many levels of network encryption, but each encryption level also provides multiple standards and options, making encryption one of the most complicated of all networking issues. You need to understand where encryption comes into play, what options are available, and what you can use to protect your network.

Network Authentication

Have you ever considered the process that takes place each time a person types in a user name and password to access a network, rather than just a local machine? What happens when this *network* authentication is requested? If you're thinking that information is sent to a server of some sort to be authenticated, you're right—but do you

know how the user name and password get to the serving system? That's where encryption becomes important in authentication.

In a local network, authentication and encryption are usually handled by the OS. In today's increasingly interconnected and diverse networking environment, there is a motivation to enable different operating systems to authenticate any client system from any other OS. Modern operating systems such as Windows and Mac OS X use standard authentication encryptions such as MIT's *Kerberos*, enabling multiple brands of servers to authenticate multiple brands of clients. These LAN authentication methods are usually transparent and work quite nicely, even in mixed networks.

Data Encryption

Encryption methods don't stop at the authentication level. There are a number of ways to encrypt network *data* as well. The encryption method is dictated to a large degree by what method the communicating systems will connect with. Many networks consist of multiple networks linked together by some sort of private connection, usually some kind of WAN connection such as old T1s or Metro Ethernet. Microsoft's encryption method of choice for this type of network is called *IPsec* (derived from *IP security*). IPsec provides transparent encryption between the server and the client. IPsec also works in VPNs, but other encryption methods are more commonly used in those situations.

Application Encryption

When it comes to encryption, even TCP/IP applications can get into the swing of things. The most famous of all application encryptions is the *Secure Sockets Layer (SSL)* security protocol, which was used to secure Web sites. Microsoft incorporates Transport Layer Security (TLS) into its more far-reaching *HTTPS* (HTTP over TLS) protocol these days. These protocols make it possible to secure the Web sites people use to make purchases over the Internet. You can identify HTTPS Web sites by the *https://* (rather than http://) included in the URL (see Figure 28-38).

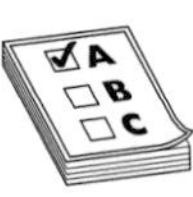

EXAM TIP Many security appliances include a context-based set of rules called Data Loss Prevention (DLP) to help companies avoid accidental leakage of data. DLP works by scanning packets flowing out of the network, stopping the flow when something triggers.

To make a secure connection, your Web browser and the Web server must encrypt their data. That means there must be a way for both the Web server and your browser to encrypt and decrypt each other's data. To do this, the server sends a public key to your Web browser so the browser knows how to decrypt the incoming data. These public keys are sent in the form of a *digital certificate*. This certificate is signed by a trusted certificate authority (CA) that guarantees that the public key you are about to get is actually from the Web server and not from some evil person trying to pretend to be the Web server. A number of companies issue digital certificates, such as Symantec (formally VeriSign), Comodo, and many others.

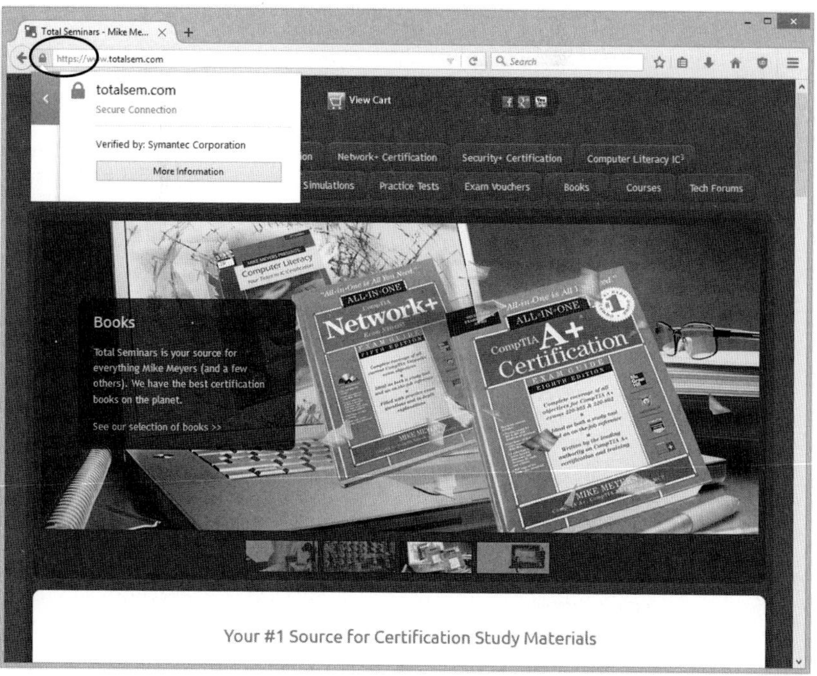

Figure 28-38 A secure Web site

Your Web browser has a built-in list of trusted authorities, referred to as *trusted root CAs*. If a certificate comes in from a Web site that uses one of these highly respected companies, you won't see anything happen in your browser; you'll just go to the secure Web page, where a small lock will appear in the corner of your browser. Figure 28-39 shows the list of trusted authorities built into the Firefox Web browser.

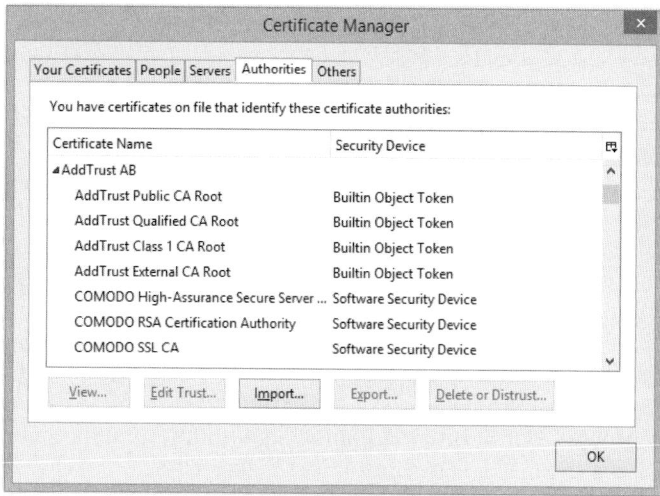

Figure 28-39 Trusted authorities

If you receive a certificate that your browser thinks is fishy, such as one that is expired or one for which the browser does not have a trusted root CA, the browser will warn you and ask you if you wish to accept the certificate, as shown in Figure 28-40.

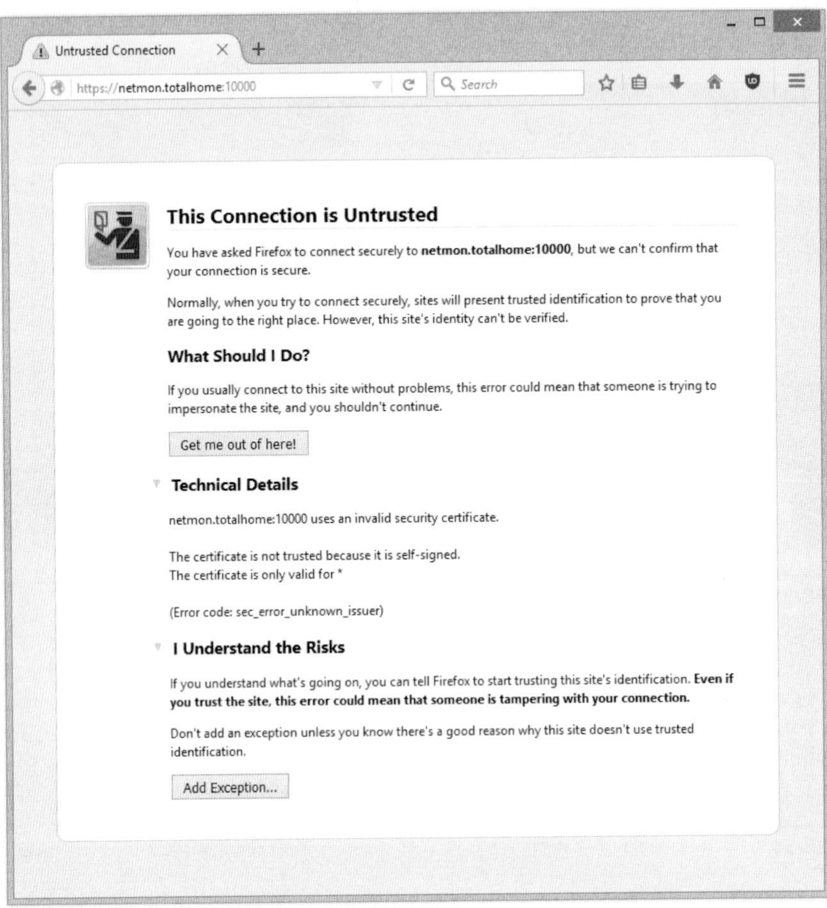

Figure 28-40 Incoming certificate

What you do here is up to you. Do you wish to trust this certificate? In most cases, you simply say yes, and this certificate is added to your SSL cache of certificates. An accepted certificate may become invalid, however, usually because of something boring; for instance, it may go out of date or the public key may change. This very rarely happens with the "big name" sites—you'll see this more often when a certificate is used, for example, in-house on a company intranet and the administrator forgets to update the certificates. If a certificate goes bad, your browser issues a warning the next time you visit that site. To clear invalid certificates, you need to clear the SSL cache. The process varies in every browser, but in Internet Explorer, go to the Content tab under Internet Options and click the Clear SSL state button (see Figure 28-41).

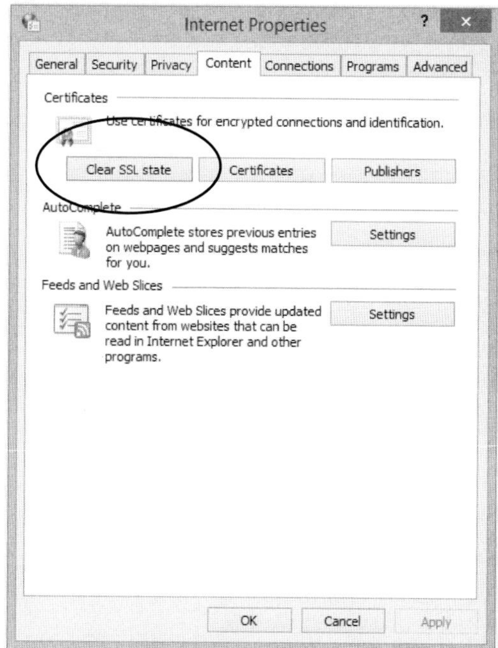

Figure 28-41 Internet Options Content tab in Internet Explorer

Wireless Issues

Wireless networks add a whole level of additional security headaches for techs to face, as you know from Chapter 22. Here are a few points to consider:

- Set up wireless encryption, at least WPA but preferably the more secure WPA2, and configure clients to use it.
- Disable DHCP and require your wireless clients to use a static IP address.
- If you need to use DHCP, only allot enough DHCP addresses to meet the needs of your network, to avoid unused wireless connections.
- Change the WAP's SSID from default.
- Filter by MAC address to allow only known clients on the network.
- Change the default user name and password. Even if the defaults are generated and look secure, knowledge of how they were generated might make them easier to guess.
- Update the firmware as needed.
- If available, make sure the WAP's firewall settings are turned on.
- Configure SOHO router NAT/DNAT settings.
- Use SOHO router content filtering/parental controls.
- Consider physical security of SOHO router.

Chapter 28 Review

Questions

1. What is the process for using or manipulating people to gain access to network resources?
   A. Cracking
   B. Hacking
   C. Network engineering
   D. Social engineering
2. Which of the following might offer good hardware authentication?
   A. Strong passwords
   B. Encrypted passwords
   C. NTFS
   D. Smart cards
3. Which of the following tools would enable you to stop a user from logging on to a local machine but still enable him to log on to the domain?
   A. AD Policy Filter
   B. Group Policy Auditing
   C. Local Security Policy
   D. User Settings
4. Which hardware firewall feature enables incoming traffic on a specific port to reach an IP address on the LAN?
   A. Port forwarding
   B. NAT
   C. DMZ
   D. Multifactor authentication
5. Zander downloaded a game off the Internet and installed it, but as soon as he started to play, he got a Blue Screen of Death. Upon rebooting, he discovered that his Documents folder had been erased. What happened?
   A. He installed spyware.
   B. He installed a Trojan horse.
   C. He broke the Group Policy.
   D. He broke the Local Security Policy.

6. Which of the following should Mary set up on her Wi-Fi router to make it the most secure?
   - **A.** NTFS
   - **B.** WEP
   - **C.** WPA
   - **D.** WPA2
7. What tool would you use to enable auditing on a local level?
   - **A.** AD Policy
   - **B.** Group Policy
   - **C.** Local Security Policy
   - **D.** User Settings
8. John dressed up in a fake security guard uniform matching the ones used by a company and then walked into the company's headquarters with some legitimate employees in an attempt to gain access to company resources. What kind of attack is this?
   - **A.** Administrative access
   - **B.** Data destruction
   - **C.** Spoofing
   - **D.** Tailgating
9. The first day on the job, Jill received a spreadsheet that listed approved software for users and clear instructions not to allow any unapproved software. What kind of policy must she follow?
   - **A.** Classification
   - **B.** Compliance
   - **C.** Group
   - **D.** Security
10. Edna wants to put a policy in place at her company to prevent or at least limit viruses. What policies would offer the best solution?
    - **A.** Install antivirus software on every computer. Teach users how to run it.
    - **B.** Install antivirus software on every computer. Set the software up to scan regularly.
    - **C.** Install antivirus software on every computer. Set the software up to update the definitions and engine automatically. Set the software up to scan regularly.
    - **D.** Install antivirus software on every computer. Set the software up to update the definitions and engine automatically. Set the software up to scan regularly. Educate the users about sites and downloads to avoid.

Answers

1. **D.** Social engineering is the process of using or manipulating people to gain access to network resources.
2. **D.** Smart cards are an example of hardware authentication devices.
3. **C.** You can use Local Security Policy to stop someone from logging on to a local machine.
4. **A.** To open a port on your hardware firewall and send incoming traffic to a specific PC, use port forwarding.
5. **B.** Zander clearly installed a Trojan horse, a virus masquerading as a game.
6. **D.** Mary should set up WPA2 on her Wi-Fi router.
7. **C.** You can enable local auditing through Local Security Policy.
8. **D.** John just practiced tailgating on the unsuspecting company.
9. **B.** Jill needs to enforce compliance to help keep the tech support calls at a minimum and the uptime for users at a maximum.
10. **D.** The best policy includes updating the software engine and definitions, scanning PCs regularly, and educating users.

Mapping to the CompTIA A+ Objectives

220-901 Exam Objectives

Competency	Chapter(s)
1.0 Hardware	
1.1 Given a scenario, configure settings and use BIOS/UEFI tools on a PC.	
• Firmware upgrades – flash BIOS	6
• BIOS component information	6
• RAM	6
• Hard drive	6
• Optical drive	6
• CPU	6
• BIOS configurations	6
• Boot sequence	6
• Enabling and disabling devices	6
• Date/time	6
• Clock speeds	6
• Virtualization support	6
• BIOS security (passwords, drive encryption: TPM, lo-jack, secure boot)	6
• Built-in diagnostics	6
• Monitoring	6
• Temperature monitoring	6
• Fan speeds	6
• Intrusion detection/notification	6
• Voltage	6
• Clock	6
• Bus speed	6

Competency	Chapter(s)
1.2 Explain the importance of motherboard components, their purpose, and properties.	
• Sizes	7
• ATX	7
• Micro-ATX	7
• Mini-ITX	7
• ITX	7
• Expansion slots	7
• PCI	7
• PCI-X	7
• PCIe	7
• miniPCI	7
• RAM slots	4
• CPU sockets	5
• Chipsets	7
• North Bridge	7
• South Bridge	7
• CMOS battery	6
• Power connections and types	8
• Fan connectors	7
• Front/Top panel connectors	7
• USB	7
• Audio	7
• Power button	7
• Power light	7
• Drive activity lights	7
• Reset button	7
• Bus speeds	7
1.3 Compare and contrast various RAM types and their features.	
• Types	5
• DDR	5
• DDR2	5
• DDR3	5
• SODIMM	5
• DIMM	5
• Parity vs. non-parity	5

Competency	Chapter(s)
• ECC vs. non-ECC	5
• RAM configurations	5
• Single channel vs. dual channel vs. triple channel	5
• Single sided vs. double sided	5
• Buffered vs. unbuffered	5
• RAM compatibility	5
1.4 Install and configure PC expansion cards.	
• Sound cards	11
• Video cards	19
• Network cards	20
• USB cards	11
• Firewire cards	11
• Thunderbolt cards	11
• Storage cards	11
• Modem cards	23
• Wireless/cellular cards	22
• TV tuner cards	11
• Video capture cards	11
• Riser cards	7
1.5 Install and configure storage devices and use appropriate media.	
• Optical drives	11
• CD-ROM / CD-RW	11
• DVD-ROM / DVD-RW / DVD-RW DL	11
• Blu-Ray	11
• BD-R	11
• BD-RE	11
• Magnetic hard disk drives	9
• 5400 rpm	9
• 7200 rpm	9
• 10,000 rpm	9
• Hot swappable drives	9
• Solid state/flash drives	9, 11
• Compact flash	11
• SD	11
• Micro-SD	11
• Mini-SD	11

Competency	Chapter(s)
• xD	11
• SSD	9
• Hybrid	9
• eMMC	11
• RAID types	9
• 0	9
• 1	9
• 5	9
• 10	9
• Tape drive	11
• Media capacity	11
• CD	11
• CD-RW	11
• DVD-RW	11
• DVD	11
• Blu-Ray	11
• Tape	11
• DVD DL	11
1.6 Install various types of CPUs and apply the appropriate cooling methods.	
• Socket types	4
• Intel: 775, 1155, 1156, 1366, 1150, 2011	4
• AMD: AM3, AM3+, FM1, FM2, FM2+	4
• Characteristics	4
• Speeds	4
• Cores	4
• Cache size/type	4
• Hyperthreading	4
• Virtualization support	4
• Architecture (32-bit vs. 64-bit)	4
• Integrated GPU	4
• Disable execute bit	4
• Cooling	4
• Heat sink	4
• Fans	4
• Thermal paste	4

Competency	Chapter(s)
• Liquid-based	4
• Fanless/passive	4
1.7 Compare and contrast various PC connection interfaces, their characteristics and purpose.	
• Physical connections	9, 11, 19, 20, 23
• USB 1.1 vs. 2.0 vs. 3.0	11
• Connector types: A, B, mini, micro	11
• Firewire 400 vs. Firewire 800	11
• SATA1 vs. SATA2 vs. SATA3, eSATA	9
• Other connector types	11, 19, 20, 23
• VGA	19
• HDMI	19
• DVI	19
• Audio	11
• Analog	11
• Digital (Optical connector)	11
• RJ-45	20
• RJ-11	23
• Thunderbolt	11
• Wireless connections	22, 25
• Bluetooth	22
• RF	22
• IR	22
• NFC	25
• Characteristics	11, 19, 20, 21, 22, 23, 28
• Analog	11, 19, 23
• Digital	11, 19, 20
• Distance limitations	11, 20, 21, 22, 23
• Data transfer speeds	9, 11, 22, 23
• Quality	11
• DRM	28
• Frequencies	11, 19, 20, 23
1.8 Install a power supply based on given specifications.	
• Connector types and their voltages	8
• SATA	8
• Molex	8

Competency	Chapter(s)
• 4/8-pin 12v	8
• PCIe 6/8-pin	8
• 20-pin	8
• 24-pin	8
• Specifications	8
• Wattage	8
• Dual rail	8
• Size	8
• Number of connectors	8
• ATX	8
• Micro-ATX	8
• Dual voltage options	8
1.9 Given a scenario, select the appropriate components for a custom PC configuration, to meet customer specifications or needs.	
• Graphic / CAD / CAM design workstation	12
• Multicore processor	12
• High-end video	12
• Maximum RAM	12
• Audio/Video editing workstation	12
• Specialized audio and video card	12
• Large fast hard drive	12
• Dual monitors	12
• Virtualization workstation	12
• Maximum RAM and CPU cores	12
• Gaming PC	12
• Multicore processor	12
• High-end video/specialized GPU	12
• High definition sound card	12
• High-end cooling	12
• Home Theater PC	12
• Surround sound audio	12
• HDMI output	12
• HTPC compact form factor	12
• TV tuner	12

Competency	Chapter(s)
• Standard thick client	12
• Desktop applications	12
• Meets recommended requirements for selected OS	12
• Thin client	12
• Basic applications	12
• Meets minimum requirements for selected OS	12
• Network connectivity	12
• Home Server PC	12
• Media streaming	12
• File sharing o	12
• Print sharing o	12
• Gigabit NIC o	12
• RAID array	12
1.10 Compare and contrast types of display devices and their features.	
• Types	19, 25
• LCD	19
• TN vs. IPS	19
• Flourescent vs. LED backlighting	19
• Plasma	19
• Projector	19
• OLED	25
• Refresh / frame rates	19
• Resolution	19
• Native resolution	19
• Brightness/lumens	19
• Analog vs. digital	19
• Privacy/antiglare filters	19
• Multiple displays	19
• Aspect ratios	19
• 16:09	19
• 16:10	19
• 4:03	19

Competency	Chapter(s)
1.11 Identify common PC connector types and associated cables.	
• Display connector types	19
• DVI-D	19
• DVI-I	19
• DVI-A	19
• DisplayPort	19
• RCA	19
• HD15 (i.e. DE15 or DB15)	19
• BNC	19
• miniHDMI	19
• miniDin-6	19
• Display cable types	11, 19
• HDMI	19
• DVI	19
• VGA	19
• Component o	19
• Composite o	19
• Coaxial	11
• Device cables and connectors	9, 11
• SATA	9
• eSATA	9
• USB	11
• Firewire (IEEE1394)	11
• PS/2	11
• Audio	11
• Adapters and convertors	11, 19, 24
• DVI to HDMI	19
• USB A to USB B	11
• USB to Ethernet	24
• DVI to VGA	19
• Thunderbolt to DVI	19
• PS/2 to USB	11
• HDMI to VGA	19

Competency	Chapter(s)
1.12 Install and configure common peripheral devices.	
• Input devices	11, 20, 27
• Mouse	11
• Keyboard	11
• Scanner	27
• Barcode reader	11
• Biometric devices	11
• Game pads	11
• Joysticks	11
• Digitizer	11
• Motion sensor	11
• Touch pads	11
• Smart card readers	11
• Digital cameras	11
• Microphone	11
• Webcam	11
• Camcorder	11
• MIDI enabled devices	20
• Output devices	11, 19, 27
• Printers	27
• Speakers	11
• Display devices	19
• Input & Output devices	11
• Touch screen	11
• KVM	11
• Smart TV	11
• Set-Top Box	11
1.13 Install SOHO multifunction device / printers and configure appropriate settings.	
• Use appropriate drivers for a given operating system	27
• Configuration settings	27
• Duplex	27
• Collate	27
• Orientation	27
• Quality	27

Competency	Chapter(s)
• Device sharing	27
• Wired	27
• USB	27
• Serial	27
• Ethernet	27
• Wireless	27
• Bluetooth	27
• 802.11(a,b,g,n,ac)	27
• Infrastructure vs. adhoc	27
• Integrated print server (hardware)	27
• Cloud printing/remote printing	27
• Public/shared devices	27
• Sharing local/networked device via Operating System settings	27
• TCP/Bonjour/AirPrint	27
• Data privacy	27
• User authentication on the device	27
• Hard drive caching	27
1.14 Compare and contrast differences between the various print technologies and the associated imaging process.	
• Laser	27
• Imaging drum, fuser assembly, transfer belt, transfer roller, pickup rollers, separate pads, duplexing assembly	27
• Imaging process: processing, charging, exposing, developing, transferring, fusing and cleaning	27
• Inkjet	27
• Ink cartridge, print head, roller, feeder, duplexing assembly, carriage and belt	27
• Calibration	27
• Thermal	27
• Feed assembly, heating element	27
• Special thermal paper	27
• Impact	27
• Print head, ribbon, tractor feed	27
• Impact paper	27
• Virtual	27
• Print to file	27
• Print to PDF	27

Competency	Chapter(s)
• Print to XPS	27
• Print to image	27
1.15 Given a scenario, perform appropriate printer maintenance.	
• Laser	27
• Replacing toner, applying maintenance kit, calibration, cleaning	27
• Thermal	27
• Replace paper, clean heating element, remove debris	27
• Impact	27
• Replace ribbon, replace print head, replace paper	27
• Inkjet	27
• Clean heads, replace cartridges, calibration, clear jams	27
2.0 Networking	
2.1 Identify the various types of network cables and connectors.	
• Fiber	20
• Connectors: SC, ST and LC	20
• Twisted Pair	20
• Connectors: RJ-11, RJ-45	20
• Wiring standards: T568A, T568B	20
• Coaxial	20
• Connectors: BNC, F-connector	20
2.2 Compare and contrast the characteristics of connectors and cabling.	
• Fiber	20
• Types (single-mode vs. multi-mode)	20
• Speed and transmission limitations	20
• Twisted pair	20
• Types: STP, UTP, CAT3, CAT5, CAT5e, CAT6, CAT6e, CAT7, plenum, PVC	20
• Speed and transmission limitations	20
• Splitters and effects on signal quality	20
• Coaxial	20
• Types: RG-6, RG-59	20
• Speed and transmission limitations	20
• Splitters and effects on signal quality	20
2.3 Explain the properties and characteristics of TCP/IP.	
• IPv4 vs. IPv6	21
• Public vs. private vs. APIPA/link local	21
• Static vs. dynamic	21

Competency	Chapter(s)
• Client-side DNS settings	21
• Client-side DHCP	21
• Subnet mask vs. CIDR	21
• Gateway	21
2.4 Explain common TCP and UDP ports, protocols, and their purpose.	
• Ports	23
• 21 – FTP	23
• 22 – SSH	23
• 23 – TELNET	23
• 25 – SMTP	23
• 53 – DNS o	23
• 80 – HTTP o	23
• 110 – POP3	23
• 143 – IMAP	23
• 443 – HTTPS o	23
• 3389 – RDP	23
• 137-139, 445 - SMB	23
• 548 or 427 - AFP	23
• Protocols	23
• DHCP	23
• DNS	23
• LDAP	23
• SNMP	23
• SMB	23
• CIFS	23
• SSH	23
• AFP	23
• TCP vs. UDP	21
2.5 Compare and contrast various WiFi networking standards and encryption types.	
• Standards	22
• 802.11 a/b/g/n/ac	22
• Speeds, distances and frequencies	22
• Encryption types	22
• WEP, WPA, WPA2, TKIP, AES	22

Competency	Chapter(s)
2.6 Given a scenario, install and configure SOHO wireless/wired router and apply appropriate settings.	
• Channels	22
• Port forwarding, port triggering	28
• DHCP (on/off)	21, 23, 28
• DMZ	28
• NAT / DNAT	28
• Basic QoS	23
• Firmware	23
• UPnP	23
2.7 Compare and contrast Internet connection types, network types, and their features.	
• Internet Connection Types	23
• Cable	23
• DSL	23
• Dial-up	23
• Fiber	23
• Satellite	23
• ISDN	23
• Cellular	23
• Tethering	23
• Mobile hotspot	23
• Line of sight wireless internet service	23
• Network Types	20, 21, 22, 23
• LAN	20
• WAN	20, 21
• PAN	22
• MAN	23
2.8 Compare and contrast network architecture devices, their functions, and features.	
• Hub	20
• Switch	20
• Router	20
• Access point	22
• Bridge	20
• Modem	23

Competency	Chapter(s)
• Firewall	28
• Patch panel	20
• Repeaters/extenders	20
• Ethernet over Power	20
• Power over Ethernet injector	22
2.9 Given a scenario, use appropriate networking tools.	
• Crimper	20
• Cable stripper	20
• Multimeter	20
• Tone generator & probe	20
• Cable tester	20
• Loopback plug	20
• Punchdown tool	20
• WiFi analyzer	22
3.0 Mobile Devices	
3.1 Install and configure laptop hardware and components.	
• Expansion options	5, 24
• Express card /34	24
• Express card /54	24
• SODIMM	5
• Flash	24
• Ports/Adapters	24
• Thunderbolt	24
• DisplayPort	24
• USB to RJ-45 dongle	24
• USB to WiFi dongle	24
• USB to Bluetooth	24
• USB Optical Drive	24
• Hardware/device replacement	24
• Keyboard	24
• Hard Drive	24
• SSD vs. Hybrid vs. Magnetic disk	24
• 1.8in vs. 2.5in	24
• Memory	24

Competency	Chapter(s)
• Smart card reader	24
• Optical drive	24
• Wireless card	24
• Mini-PCIe	24
• Screen	24
• DC jack	24
• Battery	24
• Touchpad	24
• Plastics/frames	24
• Speaker	24
• System board	24
• CPU	24
3.2 Explain the function of components within the display of a laptop.	
• Types	15, 19, 24, 25
• LCD	24
• TTL vs. IPS	19, 25
• Fluorescent vs. LED backlighting	19, 24
• OLED	25
• Wi-Fi antenna connector/placement	24
• Webcam	24, 25
• Microphone	24, 25
• Inverter	24
• Digitizer	25
3.3 Given a scenario, use appropriate laptop features.	
• Special function keys	24
• Dual displays	24
• Wireless (on/off)	24
• Cellular (on/off)	24
• Volume settings	24
• Screen brightness	24
• Bluetooth (on/off)	24
• Keyboard backlight	24
• Touch pad (on/off)	24
• Screen orientation	24
• Media options (fast forward/rewind)	24

Competency	Chapter(s)
• GPS (on/off)	24
• Airplane mode	24
• Docking station	24
• Physical laptop lock and cable lock	24
• Rotating / removable screens	24
3.4 Explain the characteristics of various types of other mobile devices.	
• Tablets	25
• Smart phones	25
• Wearable technology devices	25
• Smart watches	25
• Fitness monitors	25
• Glasses and headsets	25
• Phablets	25
• e-Readers	25
• Smart camera	25
• GPS	25
3.5 Compare and contrast accessories & ports of other mobile devices.	
• Connection types	25
• NFC	25
• Proprietary vendor specific ports (communication/power)	25
• microUSB/miniUSB	25
• Lightning	25
• Bluetooth	25
• IR	25
• Hotspot / tethering	25
• Accessories	25
• Headsets	25
• Speakers	25
• Game pads	25
• Docking stations	25
• Extra battery packs/battery chargers	25
• Protective covers / water proofing	25
• Credit card readers	25
• Memory/MicroSD	25

Competency	Chapter(s)
4.0 Hardware and Network Troubleshooting	
4.1 Given a scenario, troubleshoot common problems related to motherboards, RAM, CPU and power with appropriate tools.	
• Common symptoms	4, 6, 7, 8, 17, 18
• Unexpected shutdowns	4
• System lockups	4
• POST code beeps	6
• Blank screen on bootup	17
• BIOS time and settings resets	17
• Attempts to boot to incorrect device	17
• Continuous reboots	17
• No power	7
• Overheating	4, 8, 24
• Loud noise	18
• Intermittent device failure	7, 8
• Fans spin – no power to other devices	7
• Indicator lights	7
• Smoke	4, 8
• Burning smell	4, 8
• Proprietary crash screens (BSOD/pin wheel)	4
• Distended capacitors	7
• Tools	7, 8, 21
• Multimeter	8
• Power supply tester	8
• Loopback plugs	21
• POST card / USB	7
4.2 Given a scenario, troubleshoot hard drives and RAID arrays with appropriate tools.	
• Common symptoms	10
• Read/write failure	10
• Slow performance	10
• Loud clicking noise	10
• Failure to boot	10
• Drive not recognized	10
• OS not found	10

Competency	Chapter(s)
• RAID not found	10
• RAID stops working	10
• Proprietary crash screens (BSOD/pin wheel)	10
• S.M.A.R.T. errors	10
• Tools	2, 9, 10, 15, 16, 17
• Screwdriver	2
• External enclosures	9
• CHKDSK	10, 16
• FORMAT	16
• File recovery software	17
• Bootrec	17
• Diskpart	17
• Defragmentation tool	10, 15
4.3 Given a scenario, troubleshoot common video, projector and display issues.	
• Common symptoms	19
• VGA mode	19
• No image on screen	19
• Overheat shutdown	19
• Dead pixels	19
• Artifacts	19
• Color patterns incorrect	19
• Dim image	19
• Flickering image	19
• Distorted image	19
• Distorted geometry	19
• Burn-in	19
• Oversized images and icons	19
4.4 Given a scenario, troubleshoot wired and wireless networks with appropriate tools.	
• Common symptoms	21, 22, 23
• No connectivity	21, 22
• APIPA/link local address	21
• Limited connectivity	23
• Local connectivity	23

Competency	Chapter(s)
• Intermittent connectivity	21
• IP conflict	21
• Slow transfer speeds	23
• Low RF signal	22
• SSID not found	22
• Hardware tools	20, 21, 22
• Cable tester	21
• Loopback plug	21
• Punch down tools	20
• Tone generator and probe	21
• Wire strippers	20
• Crimper	20
• Wireless locator	22
• Command line tools	21, 23
• PING	21
• IPCONFIG/IFCONFIG	21
• TRACERT	21
• NETSTAT	23
• NBTSTAT	21
• NET	21
• NETDOM	21
• NSLOOKUP	21
4.5 Given a scenario, troubleshoot and repair common mobile device issues while adhering to the appropriate procedures.	
• Common symptoms	24
• No display	24
• Dim display	24
• Flickering display	24
• Sticking keys	24
• Intermittent wireless	24
• Battery not charging	24
• Ghost cursor/pointer drift	24
• No power	24
• Num lock indicator lights	24
• No wireless connectivity	24

Competency	Chapter(s)
• No Bluetooth connectivity	24
• Cannot display to external monitor	24
• Touchscreen non-responsive	24, 26
• Apps not loading	26
• Slow performance	26
• Unable to decrypt email	26
• Extremely short battery life	26
• Overheating	26
• Frozen system	26
• No sound from speakers	26
• GPS not functioning	26
• Swollen battery	26
• Disassembling processes for proper re-assembly	24
• Document and label cable and screw locations	24
• Organize parts	24
• Refer to manufacturer resources	24
• Use appropriate hand tools	24
4.6 Given a scenario, troubleshoot printers with appropriate tools.	
• Common symptoms	27
• Streaks	27
• Faded prints	27
• Ghost images	27
• Toner not fused to the paper	27
• Creased paper	27
• Paper not feeding	27
• Paper jam	27
• No connectivity	27
• Garbled characters on paper	27
• Vertical lines on page	27
• Backed up print queue	27
• Low memory errors	27
• Access denied	27
• Printer will not print	27
• Color prints in wrong print color	27

Competency	Chapter(s)
• Unable to install printer	27
• Error codes	27
• Printing blank pages	27
• No image on printer display	27
• Tools	27
• Maintenance kit	27
• Toner vacuum	27
• Compressed air	27
• Printer spooler	27

220-902 Exam Objectives

Competency	Chapter(s)
1.0 Windows Operating Systems	
1.1 Compare and contrast various features and requirements of Microsoft Operating Systems (Windows Vista, Windows 7, Windows 8, Windows 8.1).	
• Features:	
• 32-bit vs. 64-bit	3, 4
• Aero, gadgets, user account control, bit-locker, shadow copy, system restore, ready boost, sidebar, compatibility mode, virtual XP mode, easy transfer, administrative tools, defender, Windows firewall, security center, event viewer, file structure and paths, category view vs. classic view, previous versions.	3, 4, 6, 9, 12, 14, 17, 28
• Side by side apps, Metro UI, Pinning, One Drive, Windows store, Multimonitor task bars, Charms, Start Screen, Power Shell, Live sign in, Action Center.	3, 16, 17, 19, 25
• Upgrade paths – differences between in place upgrades, compatibility tools, Windows upgrade OS advisor	12
1.2 Given a scenario, install Windows PC operating systems using appropriate methods.	
• Boot methods	12
• USB	12
• CD-ROM	12
• DVD	12
• PXE	12
• Solid state/flash drives	12

Competency	Chapter(s)
• Netboot	12
• External/hot swappable drive	12
• Internal hard drive (partition)	12
• Type of installations	12
• Unattended installation	12
• Upgrade	12
• Clean install	12
• Repair installation	17
• Multiboot	12
• Remote network installation	12
• Image deployment	12
• Recovery partition	12
• Refresh/restore	12
• Partitioning	10
• Dynamic	10
• Basic	10
• Primary	10
• Extended	10
• Logical	10
• GPT	10
• File system types/formatting	10, 11, 23
• ExFAT	10
• FAT32	10
• NTFS	10
• CDFS	11
• NFS	23
• ext3, ext4	10
• Quick format vs. full format	10
• Load alternate third party drivers when necessary	12
• Workgroup vs. Domain setup	21
• Time/date/region/language settings	12
• Driver installation, software and windows updates	15
• Factory recovery partition	10
• Properly formatted boot drive with the correct partitions/format	12

Competency	Chapter(s)
1.3 Given a scenario, apply appropriate Microsoft command line tools.	
• TASKKILL	17
• BOOTREC	17
• SHUTDOWN	16
• TASKLIST	17
• MD	16
• RD	16
• CD	16
• DEL	16
• FORMAT	17
• COPY	16
• XCOPY	16
• ROBOCOPY	16
• DISKPART	17
• SFC	16
• CHKDSK	16
• GPUPDATE	16
• GPRESULT	16
• DIR	16
• EXIT	16
• HELP	16
• EXTRACT	17
• [command name] /?	16
• Commands available with standard privileges vs. administrative privileges.	16
1.4 Given a scenario, use appropriate Microsoft operating system features and tools.	
• Administrative	3, 13, 14, 15, 17, 27, 28
• Computer management	14
• Device manager	3, 15
• Users and groups	14
• Local security policy	28
• Performance monitor	13
• Services	13
• System configuration	15
• Task scheduler	15

Competency	Chapter(s)
• Component services	13
• Data sources	13
• Print management	27
• Windows memory diagnostics	17
• Windows firewall	28
• Advanced security	28
• MSCONFIG	15
• General	15
• Boot	15
• Services	15
• Startup	15
• Tools	15
• Task Manager	13
• Applications	13
• Processes	13
• Performance	13
• Networking	13
• Users	13
• Disk management	10
• Drive status	10
• Mounting	10
• Initializing	10
• Extending partitions	10
• Splitting partitions	10
• Shrink partitions	10
• Assigning/changing drive letters	10
• Adding drives	10
• Adding arrays	10
• Storage spaces	10
• Other	12
• User State Migration tool (USMT)	12
• Windows Easy Transfer	12
• Windows Upgrade Advisor	12

Competency	Chapter(s)
• System utilities	10, 12, 13, 15, 16, 17, 19, 23
• REGEDIT	13
• COMMAND	16
• SERVICES.MSC	13
• MMC	13
• MSTSC	23
• NOTEPAD	16
• EXPLORER	16
• MSINFO32	15
• DXDIAG	19
• DEFRAG	10
• System restore	17
• Windows Update	12, 15
1.5 Given a scenario, use Windows Control Panel utilities.	
• Internet options	23
• Connections	23
• Security	23
• General	23
• Privacy	23
• Programs	23
• Advanced	23
• Display/Display Settings	19
• Resolution	19
• Color depth	19
• Refresh rate	19
• User accounts	14
• Folder options	3
• View hidden files	3
• Hide extensions	3
• General options	3
• View options	3
• System	3, 5, 7, 11, 15, 17, 21, 22, 24, 27, 28
• Performance (virtual memory)	5
• Remote settings	22
• System protection	28

Competency	Chapter(s)
• Windows firewall	28
• Power options	24
• Hibernate	24
• Power plans	24
• Sleep/suspend	24
• Standby	24
• Programs and features	7
• HomeGroup	21
• Devices and Printers	15, 27
• Sound	11
• Troubleshooting	17
• Network and Sharing Center	21
• Device Manager	3, 15
1.6 Given a scenario, install and configure Windows networking on a client/desktop.	
• HomeGroup vs. WorkGroup	21
• Domain setup	21
• Network shares/administrative shares/mapping drives	21
• Printer sharing vs. network printer mapping	27
• Establish networking connections	20, 21, 22
• VPN	23
• Dialups	23
• Wireless	22
• Wired	21
• WWAN (Cellular)	23
• Proxy settings	23
• Remote Desktop Connection	23
• Remote Assistance	23
• Home vs. Work vs. Public network settings	28
• Firewall settings	28
• Exceptions	28
• Configuration	28
• Enabling/disabling Windows firewall	28

Competency	Chapter(s)
• Configuring an alternative IP address in Windows	21
• IP addressing	21
• Subnet mask	21
• DNS	21
• Gateway	21
• Network card properties	21
• Half duplex/full duplex/auto	21
• Speed	21
• Wake-on-LAN	21
• QoS	21
• BIOS (on-board NIC)	21
1.7 Perform common preventive maintenance procedures using the appropriate Windows OS tools.	
• Best practices	15, 28
• Scheduled backups	15
• Scheduled disk maintenance	15
• Windows updates	15
• Patch management	15
• Driver/firmware updates	15
• Antivirus/ Antimalware updates	28
• Tools	15, 17
• Backup	15
• System restore	15
• Recovery image	17
• Disk maintenance utilities	15
2.0 Other Operating Systems and Technologies	
2.1 Identify common features and functionality of the Mac OS and Linux operating systems.	
• Best practices	15
• Scheduled backups	15
• Scheduled disk maintenance	15
• System updates/App store	15
• Patch management	15
• Driver/firmware updates	15
• Antivirus/ Antimalware updates	28

Competency	Chapter(s)
• Tools	15, 16, 17, 23
• Backup/Time Machine	15
• Restore/snapshot	15
• Image recovery	17
• Disk maintenance utilities	15
• Shell/Terminal	16
• Screen sharing	23
• Force Quit	17
• Features	3, 11, 12, 15, 16, 23, 24, 25, 26
• Multiple desktops/Mission Controls	3
• Key Chain	25
• Spot Light	16
• iCloud	23, 25, 26
• Gestures	24
• Finder	3, 15
• Remote Disk	11
• Dock	3
• Boot Camp	12
• Basic Linux commands	16
• ls	16
• grep	16
• cd	16
• shutdown	16
• pwd vs. passwd	16
• mv	16
• cp	16
• rm	16
• chmod	16
• chown	16
• iwconfig/ifconfig	16
• ps	16
• q	16
• su/sudo	16
• apt-get	16
• vi	16
• dd	16

Competency	Chapter(s)
2.2 Given a scenario, setup and use client-side virtualization.	
• Purpose of virtual machines	18
• Resource requirements	18
• Emulator requirements	18
• Security requirements	18
• Network requirements	18
• Hypervisor	18
2.3 Identify basic cloud concepts.	
• SaaS	18
• IaaS	18
• PaaS	18
• Public vs. Private vs. Hybrid vs. Community	18
• Rapid Elasticity	18
• On-demand	18
• Resource pooling	18
• Measured service	18
2.4 Summarize the properties and purpose of services provided by networked hosts.	
• Server roles	20
• Web server	20
• File server	20
• Print server	20
• DHCP server	20
• DNS server	20
• Proxy server	20
• Mail server	20
• Authentication server	20
• Internet appliance	20, 28
• UTM	28
• IDS	28
• IPS	28
• Legacy / embedded systems	20
2.5 Identify basic features of mobile operating systems.	
• Android vs. iOS vs. Windows	25
• Open source vs. closed source/vendor specific	25
• App source (play store, app store and store)	25

Competency	Chapter(s)
• Screen orientation (accelerometer/gyroscope)	25
• Screen calibration	25
• GPS and geotracking	25
• WiFi calling	25
• Launcher/GUI	25
• Virtual assistant	25
• SDK/APK	25
• Emergency notification	25
• Mobile payment service	25
2.6 Install and configure basic mobile device network connectivity and email.	
• Wireless / cellular data network (enable/disable)	25
• Hotspot	25
• Tethering	25
• Airplane mode	25
• Bluetooth	25
• Enable Bluetooth	25
• Enable pairing	25
• Find device for pairing	25
• Enter appropriate pin code	25
• Test connectivity	25
• Corporate and ISP email configuration	25
• POP3	25
• IMAP	25
• Port and SSL settings	25
• Exchange, S/MIME	25
• Integrated commercial provider email configuration	25
• Google/Inbox	25
• Yahoo	25
• Outlook.com	25
• iCloud	25
• PRI updates/PRL updates/Baseband updates	25
• Radio firmware	25
• IMEI vs. IMSI	25
• VPN	25

Competency	Chapter(s)
2.7 Summarize methods and data related to mobile device synchronization.	
• Types of data to synchronize	25
• Contacts	25
• Programs	25
• Email	25
• Pictures	25
• Music	25
• Videos	25
• Calendar	25
• Bookmarks	25
• Documents	25
• Location data	25
• Social media data	25
• eBooks	25
• Synchronization methods	25
• Synchronize to the Cloud	25
• Synchronize to the Desktop	25
• Mutual authentication for multiple services	25
• Software requirements to install the application on the PC	25
• Connection types to enable synchronization	25
3.0 Security	
3.1 Identify common security threats and vulnerabilities.	
• Malware	28
• Spyware	28
• Viruses	28
• Worms	28
• Trojans	28
• Rootkits	28
• Ransomware	28
• Phishing	28
• Spear phishing	28
• Spoofing	28
• Social engineering	28
• Shoulder surfing	28

Competency	Chapter(s)
• Zero day attack	28
• Zombie/botnet	28
• Brute forcing	28
• Dictionary attacks	28
• Non-compliant systems	28
• Violations of security best practices	28
• Tailgating	28
• Man-in-the-middle	28
3.2 Compare and contrast common prevention methods.	
• Physical security	28
• Lock doors	28
• Mantrap	28
• Cable locks	28
• Securing physical documents/passwords/shredding	28
• Biometrics	28
• ID badges	28
• Key fobs	28
• RFID badge	28
• Smart card	28
• Tokens	28
• Privacy filters	28
• Entry control roster	28
• Digital security	28
• Antivirus/Antimalware	28
• Firewalls	28
• User authentication/strong passwords	28
• Multifactor authentication	28
• Directory permissions	28
• VPN	28
• DLP	28
• Disabling ports	28
• Access control lists	28
• Smart card	28
• Email filtering	28
• Trusted/untrusted software sources	28

Competency	Chapter(s)
• User education/AUP	28
• Principle of least privilege	28
3.3 Compare and contrast differences of basic Windows OS security settings.	
• User and groups	14
• Administrator	14
• Power user	14
• Guest	14
• Standard user	14
• NTFS vs. Share permissions	14
• Allow vs. deny	14
• Moving vs. copying folders and files	14
• File attributes	14
• Shared files and folders	14
• Administrative shares vs. local shares	14
• Permission propagation	14
• Inheritance	14
• System files and folders	14
• User authentication	14
• Single sign-on	14
• Run as administrator vs. standard user	14
• Bitlocker	14
• Bitlocker-To-Go	14
• EFS	14
3.4 Given a scenario, deploy and enforce security best practices to secure a workstation.	
• Password best practices	6, 14, 28
• Setting strong passwords	14
• Password expiration	14
• Changing default user names/passwords	28
• Screensaver required password	28
• BIOS/UEFI passwords	6
• Requiring passwords	28
• Account management	28
• Restricting user permissions	28
• Login time restrictions	28

Competency	Chapter(s)
• Disabling guest account	28
• Failed attempts lockout	28
• Timeout/screen lock	28
• Disable autorun	28
• Data encryption	28
• Patch/update management	28
3.5 Compare and contrast various methods for securing mobile devices.	
• Screen locks	26
• Fingerprint lock	26
• Face lock	26
• Swipe lock	26
• Passcode lock	26
• Remote wipes	26
• Locator applications	26
• Remote backup applications	26
• Failed login attempts restrictions	26
• Antivirus/Antimalware	26
• Patching/OS updates	26
• Biometric authentication	26
• Full device encryption	26
• Multifactor authentication	26
• Authenticator applications	26
• Trusted sources vs. untrusted sources	26
• Firewalls	26
• Policies and procedures	26
• BYOD vs. corporate owned	26
• Profile security requirements	26
3.6 Given a scenario, use appropriate data destruction and disposal methods.	
• Physical destruction	12
• Shredder	12
• Drill / Hammer	12
• Electromagnetic (Degaussing)	12
• Incineration	12
• Certificate of destruction	12

Competency	Chapter(s)
• Recycling or repurposing best practices	12
• Low level format vs. standard format	12
• Overwrite	12
• Drive wipe	12
3.7 Given a scenario, secure SOHO wireless and wired networks.	
• Wireless specific	22
• Changing default SSID	22
• Setting encryption	22
• Disabling SSID broadcast	22
• Antenna and access point placement	22
• Radio power levels	22
• WPS	22
• Change default user-names and passwords	22, 23
• Enable MAC filtering	22
• Assign static IP addresses	22, 23
• Firewall settings	28
• Port forwarding/mapping	28
• Disabling ports	28
• Content filtering / parental controls	28
• Update firmware	28
• Physical security	28
4.0 Software Troubleshooting	
4.1 Given a scenario, troubleshoot PC operating system problems with appropriate tools.	
• Common symptoms	17, 19
• Proprietary crash screens (BSOD/pin wheel)	17
• Failure to boot	17
• Improper shutdown	17
• Spontaneous shutdown/restart	17
• Device fails to start/detected	17
• Missing dll message	17
• Services fails to start	17
• Compatibility error	17
• Slow system performance	17
• Boots to safe mode	17

Competency	Chapter(s)
• File fails to open	17
• Missing NTLDR	17
• Missing Boot.ini	17
• Missing operating system	17
• Missing Graphical Interface	17
• Missing GRUB/LILO	17
• Kernel panic	17
• Graphical Interface fails to load	17
• Multiple monitor misalignment/orientation	19
• Tools	6, 17
• BIOS/UEFI	6
• SFC	17
• Logs	17
• Recovery console	17
• Repair disks	17
• Pre-installation environments	17
• MSCONFIG	17
• DEFRAG	17
• REGSRV32	17
• REGEDIT	17
• Event viewer	17
• Safe mode	17
• Command prompt	17
• Emergency repair disk	17
• Automated system recovery	17
• Uninstall/reinstall/repair	17
4.2 Given a scenario, troubleshoot common PC security issues with appropriate tools and best practices.	
• Common symptoms	28
• Pop-ups	28
• Browser redirection	28
• Security alerts	28
• Slow performance	28
• Internet connectivity issues	28

Competency	Chapter(s)
• PC/OS lock up	28
• Application crash	28
• OS updates failures	28
• Rogue antivirus	28
• Spam	28
• Renamed system files	28
• Files disappearing	28
• File permission changes	28
• Hijacked email	28
• Responses from users regarding email	28
• Automated replies from unknown sent email	28
• Access denied	28
• Invalid certificate (trusted root CA)	28
• Tools	16, 17, 28
• Antivirus software	28
• Antimalware software	28
• Recovery console	28
• Terminal	16
• System restore/Snapshot	28
• Pre-installation environments	17
• Event viewer	28
• Refresh/restore	17
• MSCONFIG/Safe boot	17
• Best practice procedure for malware removal	28
1. Identify malware symptoms	28
2. Quarantine infected system	28
3. Disable system restore (in Windows)	28
4. Remediate infected systems	28
a. Update antimalware software	28
b. Scan and removal techniques (safe mode, pre-installation environment)	28
5. Schedule scans and run updates	28
6. Enable system restore and create restore point (in Windows)	28
7. Educate end user	28

Competency	Chapter(s)
4.3 Given a scenario, troubleshoot common mobile OS and application issues with appropriate tools.	
• Common symptoms	24, 26
• Dim display	24
• Intermittent wireless	24
• No wireless connectivity	24
• No bluetooth connectivity	24
• Cannot broadcast to external monitor	26
• Touchscreen non-responsive	24, 26
• Apps not loading	26
• Slow performance	26
• Unable to decrypt email	26
• Extremely short battery life	26
• Overheating	26
• Frozen system	26
• No sound from speakers	26
• Inaccurate touch screen response	26
• System lockout	26
• Tools	26
• Hard reset	26
• Soft reset	26
• Close running applications	26
• Reset to factory default	26
• Adjust configurations/settings	26
• Uninstall/reinstall apps	26
• Force stop	26
4.4 Given a scenario, troubleshoot common mobile OS and application security issues with appropriate tools.	
• Common symptoms	26
• Signal drop/weak signal	26
• Power drain	26
• Slow data speeds	26
• Unintended WiFi connection	26
• Unintended Bluetooth pairing	26
• Leaked personal files/data	26

Competency	Chapter(s)
• Data transmission overlimit	26
• Unauthorized account access	26
• Unauthorized root access	26
• Unauthorized location tracking	26
• Unauthorized camera/microphone activation	26
• High resource utilization	26
• Tools	26
• Antimalware	26
• App scanner	26
• Factory reset/Clean install	26
• Uninstall/reinstall apps	26
• WiFi analyzer	26
• Force stop	26
• Cell tower analyzer	26
• Backup/restore	26
• iTunes/iCloud/Apple Configurator	26
• Google sync	26
• One Drive	26
5.0 Operational Procedures	
5.1 Given a scenario, use appropriate safety procedures.	
• Equipment grounding	2
• Proper component handling and storage	2
• Antistatic bags	2
• ESD straps	2
• ESD mats	2
• Self-grounding	2
• Toxic waste handling	19, 24, 27
• Batteries	24
• Toner	27
• CRT	19
• Personal safety	2, 8
• Disconnect power before repairing PC	2
• Remove jewelry	2
• Lifting techniques	2
• Weight limitations	2

Competency	Chapter(s)
• Electrical fire safety	8
• Cable management	2
• Safety goggles	2
• Air filter mask	2
• Compliance with local government regulations	2
5.2 Given a scenario with potential environmental impacts, apply the appropriate controls.	
• MSDS documentation for handling and disposal	27, 28
• Temperature, humidity level awareness and proper ventilation	28
• Power surges, brownouts, blackouts	8
• Battery backup	8
• Surge suppressor	8
• Protection from airborne particles	28
• Enclosures	28
• Air filters/Mask	28
• Dust and debris	28
• Compressed air	28
• Vacuums	28
• Compliance to local government regulations	28
5.3 Summarize the process of addressing prohibited content/activity, and explain privacy, licensing, and policy concepts.	
• Incident Response	28
• First response	28
• Identify	28
• Report through proper channels	28
• Data/device preservation	28
• Use of documentation/documentation changes	28
• Chain of custody	28
• Tracking of evidence/documenting process	28
• Licensing / DRM / EULA	28
• Open source vs. commercial license	28
• Personal license vs. enterprise licenses	28
• Personally Identifiable Information	28
• Follow corporate end-user policies and security best practices	28

Competency	Chapter(s)
5.4 Demonstrate proper communication techniques and professionalism.	
• Use proper language – avoid jargon, acronyms, slang when applicable	2
• Maintain a positive attitude / Project confidence	2
• Actively listen (taking notes) and avoid interrupting the customer	2
• Be culturally sensitive	2
• Use appropriate professional titles, when applicable	2
• Be on time (if late contact the customer)	2
• Avoid distractions	2
• Personal calls	2
• Texting / Social media sites	2
• Talking to co-workers while interacting with customers	2
• Personal interruptions	2
• Dealing with difficult customer or situation	2
• Do not argue with customers and/or be defensive	2
• Avoid dismissing customer problems	2
• Avoid being judgmental	2
• Clarify customer statements (ask open ended questions to narrow the scope of the problem, restate the issue or question to verify understanding)	2
• Do not disclose experiences via social media outlets	2
• Set and meet expectations/timeline and communicate status with the customer	2
• Offer different repair/replacement options if applicable	2
• Provide proper documentation on the services provided	2
• Follow up with customer/user at a later date to verify satisfaction	2
• Deal appropriately with customers confidential and private materials	2
• Located on a computer, desktop, printer, etc	2
5.5 Given a scenario, explain the troubleshooting theory.	
• Always consider corporate policies, procedures and impacts before implementing changes.	2
1. Identify the problem	2
• Question the user and identify user changes to computer and perform backups before making changes	2
2. Establish a theory of probable cause (question the obvious)	2
• If necessary, conduct external or internal research based on symptoms	2

Competency	Chapter(s)
3. Test the theory to determine cause	2
• Once theory is confirmed determine next steps to resolve problem	2
• If theory is not confirmed re-establish new theory or escalate	2
4. Establish a plan of action to resolve the problem and implement the solution	2
5. Verify full system functionality and if applicable implement preventive measures	2
6. Document findings, actions and outcomes	2

About the CD-ROM

The CD-ROM included with this book includes the following:

- A video from author Mike Meyers introducing the CompTIA A+ certification exam
- A link to the Total Tester practice exam software, which includes practice exam questions for both exam 220-901 and exam 220-902
- A link to more than 25 sample TotalSim interactive simulations from Total Seminars
- A link to more than an hour of video training episodes from Mike Meyers' CompTIA A+ Certification Video Training series
- A link to a collection of Mike's favorite tools and utilities for PC troubleshooting
- An electronic copy of the book in secure PDF format

Playing the Mike Meyers Introduction Video

If your computer's optical drive is configured to auto-run, the menu will automatically start upon inserting the CD-ROM. If the auto-run feature does not launch the CD-ROM, browse to the disc and double-click the Launch.exe icon.

From the opening screen you can launch the video message from Mike by clicking the Mike Meyers Introduction Video button. This launches the video file using your system's default video player.

System Requirements

The software requires Windows XP or higher, in addition to a current or prior major release of Chrome, Firefox, or Internet Explorer. To run, the screen resolution must be set to 1024 × 768 or higher. The PDF files require Adobe Acrobat, Adobe Reader, or Adobe Digital Editions to view.

Total Tester Exam Software

Total Tester provides you with a simulation of the CompTIA A+ exams. You may select practice exams for CompTIA A+ exam 901 or CompTIA A+ exam 902. The exams can be taken in either Practice mode or Exam mode. Practice mode provides an assistance window with hints, references to the book, explanations of the correct and incorrect

answers, and the option to check your answers as you take the test. Exam mode provides a simulation of the actual exam. Both Practice mode and Exam mode provide an overall grade and a grade broken down by certification objectives.

The link on the CD takes you to a Web download page. On the main page of the CD, click the **Software and Videos** link, then select **Total Tester A+ Practice Exams Online**. Click the download and follow the prompts to install the software. To take a test, launch the program and select A+ Demo from the Installed Question Packs list. Select either exam 220-901 or 220-902. You can then select Practice Mode, Exam mode, or Custom Mode. In Custom mode, you can select the number of questions and the duration of the exam. After making your selection, click Start Exam to begin.

Pre-assessment Test

In addition to the sample CompTIA A+ exam questions, the Total Tester also includes an A+ Pre-assessment test option to help you assess your understanding of the topics before reading the book. To launch the Assessment tests, click A+ Assessment from the Installed Question Packs list. Select either exam 220-901 or 220-902. The A+ Assessment tests include 50 questions and run in Exam mode. When you complete the test, you can review the questions with answers and detailed explanation by clicking See Detailed Results.

TotalSims for CompTIA A+

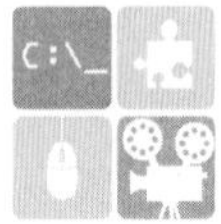

The CD contains a link that takes you to Total Seminars Training Hub. On the main page of the CD, click the **Software and Videos** link and then select TotalSims for A+ Online. The simulations are organized by chapter, and there are more than 20 free simulations available for reviewing topics referenced in the book, with an option to purchase access to the full TotalSims for A+ 220-901 and 220-902 with more than 250 simulations.

Mike's Video Training

The CD comes with links to training videos, starring Mike Meyers, for the first four chapters of the book. On the main page of the CD, click the Software And Videos link and then select Mike Meyers Video Training Online. Along with access to the videos from the first four chapters of the book, you'll find an option to purchase Mike's complete video training series.

Mike's Cool Tools

Mike loves freeware/open source troubleshooting tools! Most of the utilities mentioned in the text can be found via the CD. On the main page of the CD, click the Software And Videos link and then select Mike's Cool Tools Online. This will take you to the Total Seminars Web site, where you can download Mike's favorite tools.

PDF Copy of the Book

The entire contents of the book are provided as a PDF file on the CD-ROM. This file is viewable on your computer and many portable devices. Adobe Acrobat, Adobe Reader, or Adobe Digital Editions is required to view the file on your computer. The CD-ROM includes a link to Adobe's Web site, where you can download and install Adobe Reader.

NOTE For more information on Adobe Reader and to check for the most recent version of the software, visit Adobe's Web site at www.adobe.com and search for the free Adobe Reader or look for Adobe Reader on the product page. Adobe Digital Editions can also be downloaded from the Adobe Web site.

To view the PDF copy of the book on a portable device, copy the PDF file to your computer from the CD-ROM, and then copy the file to your portable device using a USB or other connection. Adobe offers a mobile version of Adobe Reader, the Adobe Reader mobile app, which currently supports iOS and Android. For customers using Adobe Digital Editions and an iPad, you may have to download and install a separate reader program on your device. The Adobe Web site has a list of recommended applications, and McGraw-Hill Education recommends the Bluefire Reader.

Technical Support

Technical support information is provided in the following sections by feature.

Total Seminars Technical Support

For questions regarding the Total Tester software, the operation of the CD-ROM, the Mike Meyers videos, TotalSims simulations, or Mike's Cool Tools, visit www.totalsem.com or e-mail support@totalsem.com.

McGraw-Hill Education Content Support

For questions regarding the PDF copy of the book, e-mail techsolutions@mhedu.com or visit http://mhp.softwareassist.com.

For questions regarding book content, e-mail customer.service@mheducation.com. For customers outside the United States, e-mail international_cs@mheducation.com.

%SystemRoot% The path where the operating system is installed.

4G Most popularly implemented as Long Term Evolution (LTE), a wireless data standard with theoretical download speeds of 300 Mbps and upload speeds of 75 Mbps.

10BaseT Ethernet LAN designed to run on twisted pair cabling. 10BaseT runs at 10 Mbps. The maximum length for the cabling between the NIC and the switch (or hub, repeater, etc.) is 100 meters. It uses baseband signaling. No industry-standard naming convention exists, so sometimes it's written 10BASE-T or 10Base-T.

100BaseT Ethernet cabling system designed to run at 100 Mbps on twisted pair cabling. It uses baseband signaling. No industry-standard naming convention exists, so sometimes it's written 100BASE-T or 100Base-T.

1000BaseT Gigabit Ethernet on UTP.

10 Gigabit Ethernet (10GbE) Ethernet standard that supports speeds of up to 10 Gbps. Requires CAT 6 or better twisted pair or fiber optic cabling.

110 block The most common connection used with structured cabling, connecting horizontal cable runs with patch panels.

16-bit (PC Card) Type of PC Card that can have up to two distinct functions or devices, such as a modem/network card combination.

2.1 speaker system Speaker setup consisting of two stereo speakers combined with a subwoofer.

3.5-inch floppy drive Size of all modern floppy disk drives; the format was introduced in 1986 and is one of the longest surviving pieces of computer hardware.

34-pin ribbon cable Type of cable used by floppy disk drives.

3-D graphics Video technology that attempts to create images with the same depth and texture as objects seen in the real world.

40-pin ribbon cable PATA cable used to attach EIDE devices (such as hard drives) or ATAPI devices (such as optical drives) to a system. (*See* PATA.)

5.1 speaker system Speaker setup consisting of four satellite speakers plus a center speaker and a subwoofer.

7.1 speaker system Speaker setup consisting of six satellite speakers (two front, two side, two rear) plus a center speaker and a subwoofer.

64-bit processing A type of processing that can run a compatible 64-bit operating system, such as Windows 7, 8, 8.1, or 10, and 64-bit applications. 64-bit PCs have a 64-bit-wide address bus, enabling them to use more than 4 GB of RAM.

8.3 naming system File-naming convention that specified a maximum of eight characters for a filename, followed by a three-character file extension. Has been replaced by LFN (long filename) support.

80-wire ribbon cable PATA cable used to attach fast EIDE devices (such as ATA/100 hard drives) or ATAPI devices (such as optical drives) to a system. (*See* PATA.)

802.11a Wireless networking standard that operates in the 5-GHz band with a theoretical maximum throughput of 54 Mbps.

802.11ac Wireless networking standard that operates in the 5-GHz band and uses multiple in/multiple out (MIMO) and multi-user MIMO (MU-MIMO) to achieve a theoretical maximum throughput of 1 Gbps.

802.11b Wireless networking standard that operates in the 2.4-GHz band with a theoretical maximum throughput of 11 Mbps.

802.11g Wireless networking standard that operates in the 2.4-GHz band with a theoretical maximum throughput of 54 Mbps and is backward compatible with 802.11b.

802.11n Wireless networking standard that can operate in both the 2.4-GHz and 5-GHz bands and uses multiple in/multiple out (MIMO) to achieve a theoretical maximum throughput of 100+ Mbps.

A/V sync Process of synchronizing audio and video.

AC (alternating current) Type of electricity in which the flow of electrons alternates direction, back and forth, in a circuit.

AC'97 Sound card standard for lower-end audio devices; created when most folks listened to stereo sound at best.

accelerometer Feature in smartphones and tablets that rotates the screen when the device is physically rotated.

access control Security concept using physical security, authentication, users and groups, and security policies.

access control list (ACL) A clearly defined list of permissions that specifies what actions an authenticated user may perform on a shared resource.

ACPI (Advanced Configuration and Power Interface) Power management specification that far surpasses its predecessor, APM, by providing support for hot-swappable devices and better control of power modes.

Action Center A one-page aggregation of event messages, warnings, and maintenance messages in Windows 7.

activation Process of confirming that an installed copy of a Microsoft product (most commonly Windows or a Microsoft Office application) is legitimate. Usually done at the end of software installation.

active matrix Type of liquid crystal display (LCD) that replaced the passive matrix technology used in most portable computer displays. Also called TFT (thin film transistor).

active partition On a hard drive, primary partition that contains an operating system.

active PFC (power factor correction) Circuitry built into PC power supplies to reduce harmonics.

actively listen Part of respectful communication involving listening and taking notes without interrupting.

activity light An LED on a NIC, hub, or switch that blinks rapidly to show data transfers over the network.

ad hoc mode Decentralized wireless network mode, otherwise known as peer-to-peer mode, where each wireless node is in meshed contact with every other node.

Add or Remove Programs Applet allowing users to add or remove a program manually to or from a Windows system.

address bus Set of wires leading from the CPU to the memory controller chip (traditionally the Northbridge) that enables the CPU to address RAM. Also used by the CPU for I/O addressing. On current CPUs with built-in memory controllers, the address bus refers to the internal electronic channel from the microprocessor to RAM, along which the addresses of memory storage locations are transmitted. Like a post office box, each memory location has a distinct number or address; the address bus provides the means by which the microprocessor can access every location in memory.

address space Total amount of memory addresses that an address bus can contain.

administrative shares Administrator tool to give local admins access to hard drives and system root folders.

Administrative Tools Group of Control Panel applets, including Computer Management, Event Viewer, and Reliability and Performance Monitor.

administrator account User account, created when the OS is first installed, that is allowed complete, unfettered access to the system without restriction.

Administrators group List of members with complete administrator privileges.

ADSL (asymmetric digital subscriber line) Fully digital, dedicated connection to the telephone system that provides average download speeds of 3–15 Mbps and upload speeds of 384 Kbps to 15 Mbps. *Asymmetric* identifies that upload and download speeds are different, with download usually being significantly faster than upload.

Advanced Encryption Standard (AES) A block cipher created in the late 1990s that uses a 128-bit block size and a 128-, 192-, or 256-bit key size. Practically uncrackable.

Advanced Host Controller Interface (AHCI) An efficient way for motherboards to work with SATA host bus adapters. Using AHCI unlocks some of the advanced features of SATA, such as hot-swapping and native command queuing.

Advanced Startup Options menu Menu that can be reached during the boot process that offers advanced OS startup options, such as to boot to Safe Mode or boot into Last Known Good Configuration.

adware Type of malicious program that downloads ads to a user's computer, generating undesirable network traffic.

Aero The Windows Vista/7 desktop environment. Aero adds some interesting aesthetic effects such as window transparency and Flip 3D.

AGP (Accelerated Graphics Port) An older 32/64-bit expansion slot designed by Intel specifically for video that ran at 66 MHz and yielded a throughput of at least 254 Mbps. Later versions (2×, 4×, 8×) gave substantially higher throughput.

air filter mask A mask designed to keep users from inhaling particulate matter, as when cutting drywall.

airplane mode Mode for mobile devices that disables all wireless and cellular communication for use on airplanes.

algorithm Set of rules for solving a problem in a given number of steps.

ALU (arithmetic logic unit) CPU logic circuits that perform basic arithmetic (add, subtract, multiply, and divide).

AMD (Advanced Micro Devices) CPU and chipset manufacturer that competes with Intel. Produces FX, A-Series, Phenom II, Athlon, Sempron, and Opteron CPUs and APUs. Also produces video card processors under its ATI brand.

AMI (American Megatrends, Inc.) Major producer of BIOS and UEFI software for motherboards, as well as many other computer-related components and software.

amperes (amps or A) Unit of measure for amperage, or electrical current.

amplitude Loudness of a sound card.

analog Device that uses a physical quantity, such as length or voltage, to represent the value of a number. By contrast, digital storage relies on a coding system of numeric units.

AnandTech (anandtech.com) Computer, technology, and Internet news and information site.

Android Smartphone and tablet OS created by Google.

Android application package (APK) Installation software for Android apps.

anti-aliasing In computer imaging, blending effect that smoothes sharp contrasts between two regions—e.g., jagged lines or different colors. Reduces jagged edges of text or objects. In voice signal processing, process of removing or smoothing out spurious frequencies from waveforms produced by converting digital signals back to analog.

antistatic bag Bag made of antistatic plastic into which electronics are placed for temporary or long-term storage. Used to protect components from electrostatic discharge.

antistatic mat Special surface on which to lay electronics. These mats come with a grounding connection designed to equalize electrical potential between a workbench and one or more electronic devices. Used to prevent electrostatic discharge.

antistatic wrist strap Special device worn around the wrist with a grounding connection designed to equalize electrical potential between a technician and an electronic device. Used to prevent electrostatic discharge.

antivirus program Software designed to combat viruses by either seeking out and destroying them or passively guarding against them.

AOL You've got mail!

API (application programming interface) Software definition that describes operating system calls for application software; conventions defining how a service is invoked.

APIPA (Automatic Private IP Addressing) Feature of Windows that automatically assigns an IP address to the system when the client cannot obtain an IP address automatically.

APM (Advanced Power Management) BIOS routines (developed by Intel in 1992 and upgraded over time) that enable the CPU to turn on and off selected peripherals. In 1996, APM was supplanted by Advanced Configuration and Power Interface (ACPI).

app A program for a tablet or smartphone. Also, a program written for the Windows 8 Metro interface.

applet Generic term for a program in the Windows Control Panel.

Applications Name of the tab in Task Manager that lists running applications.

App Store Apple's mobile software storefront, where you can purchase apps for your smartphone, tablet, or other Apple products.

apt-get Linux command for installing or updating a program using the advanced packaging tool.

archive To copy programs and data onto a relatively inexpensive storage medium (drive, tape, etc.) for long-term retention.

archive attribute Attribute of a file that shows whether the file has been backed up since the last change. Each time a file is opened, changed, or saved, the archive bit is turned on. Some types of backups turn off this archive bit to indicate that a good backup of the file exists on tape.

ARM Energy-efficient processor design frequently used in mobile devices.

ARP (Address Resolution Protocol) Protocol in the TCP/IP suite used with the command-line utility of the same name (arp) to determine the MAC address that corresponds to a particular IP address.

Ars Technica (arstechnica.com) Internet technology news site.

ASCII (American Standard Code for Information Interchange) Industry-standard 8-bit characters used to define text characters, consisting of 96 upper- and lowercase letters, plus 32 nonprinting control characters, each of which is numbered. These numbers were designed to achieve uniformity among computer devices for printing and the exchange of simple text documents.

aspect ratio Ratio of width to height of an object. Standard television has a 4:3 aspect ratio. High-definition television is 16:9. Desktop computer monitors tend to be either 16:9 or 16:10.

ASR (Automated System Recovery) Windows XP tool designed to recover a badly corrupted Windows system; similar to the ERD in Windows 2000.

assertive communication Means of communication that is not pushy or bossy but is also not soft. Useful in dealing with upset customers as it both defuses their anger and gives them confidence that you know what you're doing.

AT (Advanced Technology) Model name of the second-generation, 80286-based IBM computer. Many aspects of the AT, such as the BIOS, CMOS, and expansion bus, have become de facto standards in the PC industry. The physical organization of the components on the motherboard is called the AT form factor.

ATA (AT Attachment) Type of hard drive and controller designed to replace the earlier ST506 and ESDI drives without requiring replacement of the AT BIOS—hence, AT attachment. These drives are more popularly known as IDE drives. (*See* IDE.) The ATA/33 standard has drive transfer speeds up to 33 MBps; the ATA/66 up to 66 MBps; the ATA/100 up to 100 MBps; and the ATA/133 up to 133 MBps. (*See* Ultra DMA.)

ATA/ATAPI-6 Also known as ATA-6 or "Big Drive." Replaced the INT13 extensions and allowed for hard drives as large as 144 petabytes (144 million GB).

ATAPI (ATA Packet Interface) Series of standards that enables mass storage devices other than hard drives to use the IDE/ATA controllers. Popular with optical drives. (*See* EIDE.)

ATAPI-compliant Devices that utilize the ATAPI standard. (*See* ATAPI.)

Athlon Name used for a series of CPUs manufactured by AMD.

ATM (Asynchronous Transfer Mode) A network technology that runs at speeds between 25 and 622 Mbps using fiber-optic cabling or CAT 5 or better UTP.

attrib.exe Command used to view the specific properties of a file; can also be used to modify or remove file properties, such as read-only, system, or archive.

attributes Values in a file that determine the hidden, read-only, system, and archive status of the file.

ATX (Advanced Technology Extended) Popular motherboard form factor that generally replaced the AT form factor.

audio interface High-end external sound device used by audio engineers and recording artists.

AUP (Acceptable Use Policy) Defines what actions employees may or may not perform on company equipment, including computers, phones, printers, and even the network itself. This policy defines the handling of passwords, e-mail, and many other issues.

authentication Any method a computer uses to determine who can access it.

authorization Any method a computer uses to determine what an authenticated user can do.

autodetection Process through which new disks are automatically recognized by the BIOS.

Automatic Updates Feature allowing updates to Windows to be retrieved automatically over the Internet.

AutoPlay Windows setting, along with autorun.inf, enabling Windows to detect media files automatically and begin using them. (*See* autorun.inf.)

autorun.inf File included on some media that automatically launches a program or installation routine when the media is inserted/attached to a system.

autosensing Used by better-quality sound cards to detect a device plugged into a port and to adapt the features of that port.

auto-switching power supply Type of power supply able to detect the voltage of a particular outlet and adjust accordingly.

Award Software Major brand of BIOS and UEFI software for motherboards. Merged with Phoenix Technologies.

backlight One of three main components used in LCDs to illuminate an image.

backside bus Set of wires that connects the CPU to Level 2 cache. First appearing in the Pentium Pro, all modern CPUs have a backside bus. Some buses run at the full speed of the CPU, whereas others run at a fraction. Earlier Pentium IIs, for example, had backside buses running at half the speed of the processor. (*See also* frontside bus *and* external data bus.)

Backup and Restore Center Windows Vista/7's backup utility (Windows 7 drops "Center" from the name). It offers two options: create a backup or restore from a backup.

Backup or Restore Wizard Older Windows utility that enables users to create system backups and set system restore points.

bandwidth Piece of the spectrum occupied by some form of signal, such as television, voice, or fax data. Signals require a certain size and location of bandwidth to be transmitted. The higher the bandwidth, the faster the signal transmission, allowing for a more complex signal such as audio or video. Because bandwidth is a limited space, when one user is occupying it, others must wait their turn. Bandwidth is also the capacity of a network to transmit a given amount of data during a given period.

bank Total number of DIMMs that can be accessed simultaneously by the chipset. The "width" of the external data bus divided by the "width" of the DIMM sticks. Specific DIMM slots must be populated to activate dual-, triple-, or quad-channel memory.

bar code reader Tool to read Universal Product Code (UPC) bar codes.

basic disk Hard drive partitioned in the "classic" way with a master boot record (MBR) and partition table. (*See also* dynamic disks.)

baud One analog cycle on a telephone line. In the early days of telephone data transmission, the baud rate was often analogous to bits per second. Due to advanced modulation of baud cycles as well as data compression, this is no longer true.

bcdedit A command-line tool that enables you to view the BCD store, which lists the Windows boot options.

BD-R (Blu-ray Disc-Recordable) Blu-ray Disc format that enables writing data to blank discs.

BD-RE (Blu-ray Disc-REwritable) Blu-ray Disc equivalent of the rewritable DVD, allows writing and rewriting several times on the same BD. (*See* Blu-ray Disc.)

BD-ROM (Blu-ray Disc-Read Only Media) Blu-ray Disc equivalent of a DVD-ROM or CD-ROM. (*See* Blu-ray Disc.)

beep codes Series of audible tones produced by a motherboard during the POST. These tones identify whether the POST has completed successfully or whether some piece of system hardware is not working properly. Consult the manual for your particular motherboard for a specific list of beep codes.

binary numbers Number system with a base of 2, unlike the number systems most of us use that have bases of 10 (decimal numbers), 12 (measurement in feet and inches), and 60 (time). Binary numbers are preferred for computers for precision and economy. An electronic circuit that can detect the difference between two states (on–off, 0–1) is easier and more inexpensive to build than one that could detect the differences among ten states (0–9).

biometric device Hardware device used to support authentication; works by scanning and remembering a unique aspect of a user's various body parts (e.g., retina, iris, face, or fingerprint) by using some form of sensing device such as a retinal scanner.

BIOS (basic input/output services) (basic input/output system) Classically, software routines burned onto the system ROM of a PC. More commonly seen as any software that directly controls a particular piece of hardware. A set of programs encoded in read-only memory (ROM) on computers. These programs handle startup operations and low-level control of hardware such as disk drives, the keyboard, and monitor.

bit Single binary digit. Also, any device that can be in an on or off state.

bit depth Number of colors a video card is capable of producing. Common bit depths are 16-bit and 32-bit, representing 65,536 colors and 16.7 million colors (plus an 8-bit alpha channel for transparency levels), respectively.

BitLocker Drive Encryption Drive encryption software offered in high-end versions of Windows. BitLocker requires a special chip to validate hardware status and to ensure that the computer hasn't been hacked.

Bluetooth Wireless technology designed to create small wireless networks preconfigured to do specific jobs, but not meant to replace full-function networks or Wi-Fi.

Blu-ray Disc (BD) Optical disc format that stores 25 or 50 GB of data, designed to be the replacement media for DVD. Competed with HD DVD.

boot To initiate an automatic routine that clears the memory, loads the operating system, and prepares the computer for use. Term is derived from "pull yourself up by your bootstraps." Computers must do that because RAM doesn't retain program instructions when power is turned off. A cold boot occurs when the PC is physically switched on. A warm boot loads a fresh OS without turning off the computer, lessening the strain on the electronic circuitry. To do a warm boot, press the CTRL-ALT-DELETE keys twice in rapid succession (the three-fingered salute).

Boot Camp Apple tool used to install and boot to versions of Windows on a Mac OS X computer.

Boot Configuration Data (BCD) file File that contains information about the various operating systems installed on the system as well as instructions for how to actually load (bootstrap) them.

boot sector First sector on a PC hard drive or floppy disk, track 0. The boot-up software in ROM tells the computer to load whatever program is found there. If a system disk is read, the program in the boot record directs the computer to the root directory to load the operating system.

boot sequence List containing information telling the bootstrap loader in which order to check the available storage devices for an OS. Configurable in CMOS setup.

boot.ini Text file used during the boot process that provides a list of all OSs currently installed and available for ntldr (NT Loader). Also tells where each OS is located on the system. Used in Windows XP and earlier Microsoft operating systems.

bootable disk Disk that contains a functional operating system; can also be a floppy disk, USB thumb drive, or optical disc.

bootmgr Windows Boot Manager for Vista and later versions.

bootrec A Windows Recovery Environment troubleshooting and repair tool that repairs the master boot record, boot sector, or BCD store. It replaces the fixboot and fixmbr Recovery Console commands used in Windows XP and earlier operating systems.

bootstrap loader Segment of code in a system's BIOS that scans for an operating system, looks specifically for a valid boot sector, and, when one is found, hands control over to the boot sector; then the bootstrap loader removes itself from memory.

bps (bits per second) Measurement of how fast data is moved from one place to another. A 56K modem can move ~56,000 bits per second.

bridge A device that connects two networks and passes traffic between them based only on the node address, so that traffic between nodes on one network does not appear on the other network. For example, an Ethernet bridge only looks at the MAC address. Bridges filter and forward packets based on MAC addresses and operate at Level 2 (Data Link layer) of the OSI seven-layer model.

broadband Commonly understood as a reference to high-speed, always-on communication links that can move large files much more quickly than a regular phone line.

broadcast A network transmission addressed for every node on the network.

browser Program specifically designed to retrieve, interpret, and display Web pages.

BSoD (Blue Screen of Death) Infamous error screen that appears when Windows encounters an unrecoverable error.

BTX (Balanced Technology eXtended) Motherboard form factor designed as an improvement over ATX.

buffered/registered DRAM Usually seen in motherboards supporting more than four sticks of RAM, required to address interference issues caused by the additional sticks.

bug Programming error that causes a program or a computer system to perform erratically, produce incorrect results, or crash. The term was coined when a real bug was found in one of the circuits of one of the first ENIAC computers.

burn Process of writing data to a writable optical disc, such as a DVD-R.

burn-in failure Critical failure usually associated with manufacturing defects.

bus Series of wires connecting two or more separate electronic devices, enabling those devices to communicate. Also, a network topology where computers all connect to a main line called a bus cable.

bus mastering Circuitry allowing devices to avoid conflicts on the external data bus.

bus topology Network configuration wherein all computers connect to the network via a central bus cable.

BYOD (bring your own device) An arrangement in some companies' IT departments where employees are permitted to use their own phones or other mobile devices instead of company-issued ones. Also, a feature of some wireless carriers where you can buy an unsubsidized device and use it to get cheaper wireless rates.

byte Unit of 8 bits; fundamental data unit of personal computers. Storing the equivalent of one character, the byte is also the basic unit of measurement for computer storage.

CAB files Short for cabinet files. These files are compressed and most commonly used during OS installation to store many smaller files, such as device drivers.

cache (disk) Special area of RAM that stores the data most frequently accessed from the hard drive. Cache memory can optimize the use of your systems.

cache (L1, L2, L3, etc.) Special section of fast memory, usually built into the CPU, used by the onboard logic to store information most frequently accessed by the CPU.

calibration Process of matching the print output of a printer to the visual output of a monitor.

capacitive touchscreen Type of touchscreen that uses electrical current in your body to determine movement of your fingers across the screen.

CAPTCHA (Completely Automated Public Turing Test to tell Computers and Humans Apart) Authentication challenge using images, videos, sounds, or other media to be identified by a user. Computers have a much more difficult time discerning the content of these tests than humans, making the challenge useful in determining if a human or a computer is attempting access.

card reader Device with which you can read data from one of several types of flash memory.

CardBus 32-bit PC cards that can support up to eight devices on each card. Electrically incompatible with earlier PC cards (3.3 V versus 5 V).

CAT 5 Category 5 wire; a TIA/EIA standard for UTP wiring that can operate at up to 100 Mbps.

CAT 5e Category 5e wire; TIA/EIA standard for UTP wiring that can operate at up to 1 Gbps.

CAT 6 Category 6 wire; TIA/EIA standard for UTP wiring that can operate at up to 10 Gbps.

CAT 6a Category 6a wire; augmented CAT 6 UTP wiring that supports 10GbE networks at the full 100-meter distance between a node and a switch.

CAT 7 Supports 10-Gbps networks at 100-meter segments; shielding for individual wire pairs reduces crosstalk and noise problems. CAT 7 is not a TIA/EIA standard.

catastrophic failure Describes a failure in which a component or whole system will not boot; usually related to a manufacturing defect of a component. Could also be caused by overheating and physical damage to computer components.

CCFL (cold cathode fluorescent lamp) Light technology used in LCDs and flatbed scanners. CCFLs use relatively little power for the amount of light they provide.

cd (chdir) Shorthand for "change directory." Enables you to change the focus of the command prompt from one directory to another.

CD (compact disc) Originally designed as the replacement for vinyl records, has become the primary method of long-term storage of music and data.

CD quality Audio quality that has a sample rate of 44.4 KHz and a bit rate of 128 bits.

CDDA (CD-Digital Audio) Special format used for early CD-ROMs and all audio CDs; divides data into variable-length tracks. A good format to use for audio tracks but terrible for data because of lack of error checking.

CDFS (compact disc file system) File structure, rules, and conventions used when organizing and storing files and data on a CD.

CD-R (CD-recordable) CD technology that accepts a single "burn" but cannot be erased after that one burn.

CD-ROM (compact disc/read-only memory) Read-only compact storage disc for audio or video data. CD-ROMs are read by using CD-ROM drives and optical drives with backward compatibility, such as DVD and Blu-ray Disc drives.

CD-RW (CD-rewritable) CD technology that accepts multiple reads/writes like a hard drive.

Celeron Lower-cost brand of Intel CPUs.

cellular wireless networks Networks that enable cell phones, smartphones, and other mobile devices to connect to the Internet.

certification License that demonstrates competency in some specialized skill.

Certified Cisco Network Associate (CCNA) One of the certifications demonstrating a knowledge of Cisco networking products.

CFS (Central File System) Method to unify all storage devices within a network or organization to facilitate a single management point and to provide user access to any file or data within the organization.

CFS (Command File System) Along with CFS (**Common** File System), this term is found in the Acronym List of the CompTIA A+ learning objectives, and nowhere else. After diligent research, your intrepid author has not found a satisfactory reference to this alleged technology and believes that your ability to recognize that CFS can stand for Command File System will be sufficient knowledge to pass any exam questions about this topic on the corresponding test. —Mike Meyers

CFS (Common File System) Along with CFS (**Command** File System), this term is found in the Acronym List of the CompTIA A+ learning objectives, and nowhere else. After diligent research, your intrepid author has not found a satisfactory reference to this alleged technology and believes that your ability to recognize that CFS can stand for Common File System will be sufficient knowledge to pass any exam questions about this topic on the corresponding test. —Mike Meyers

chain of custody A documented history of who has been in possession of a system.

CHAP (Challenge Handshake Authentication Protocol) Common remote access protocol; the serving system challenges the remote client, usually by means of asking for a password.

charms In Windows 8 and 8.1, tools located in the hidden Charms bar, such as a search function, a sharing tool, a settings tool, and more.

Charms bar The location in Windows 8 and 8.1 of the charms tools. Accessed by moving the cursor to the upper-right corner of the screen.

chassis intrusion detection Feature offered in some chassis that trips a switch when the chassis is opened.

chipset Electronic chips, specially designed to work together, that handle all of the low-level functions of a PC. In the original PC, the chipset consisted of close to 30 different chips; today, chipsets usually consist of one, two, or three separate chips embedded into a motherboard.

chkdsk (CheckDisk) Hard drive error detection and, to a certain extent, correction utility in Windows, launched from the command-line interface. Originally a DOS command (chkdsk.exe); also the executable for the graphical Error-checking tool.

chmod Linux command used to change permissions.

chown Linux command used to change the owner and the group to which a file or folder is associated.

CIFS (Common Internet File System) The protocol that NetBIOS uses to share folders and printers. Still very common, even on UNIX/Linux systems.

clean installation Installing an operating system on a fresh drive, following a reformat of that drive. Often it's the only way to correct a problem with a system when many of the crucial operating system files have become corrupted.

client Computer program that uses the services of another computer program. Also, software that extracts information from a server; your auto-dial phone is a client, and the phone company is its server. Also, a machine that accesses shared resources on a server.

client/server Relationship in which client software obtains services from a server on behalf of a person.

client/server network Network that has dedicated server machines and client machines.

clock cycle Single charge to the clock wire of a CPU.

clock-multiplying CPU CPU that takes the incoming clock signal and multiples it inside the CPU to let the internal circuitry of the CPU run faster.

clock speed Speed at which a CPU executes instructions, measured in MHz or GHz. In modern CPUs, the internal speed is a multiple of the external speed. (*See also* clock-multiplying CPU.)

clock (CLK) wire A special wire that, when charged, tells the CPU that another piece of information is waiting to be processed.

closed source Software that is solely controlled by its creator or distributor.

Cloud computing A model for enabling and accessing computing storage and other shared (or not shared) resources on-demand. The "cloud" is based on servicing models that include IaaS, PaaS, and SaaS, or hybrid mixtures of these services.

cluster Basic unit of storage on a floppy or hard disk. Multiple sectors are contained in a cluster. When Windows stores a file on a disk, it writes those files into dozens or even hundreds of contiguous clusters. If there aren't enough contiguous open clusters available, the operating system finds the next open cluster and writes there, continuing this process until the entire file is saved. The FAT or MFT tracks how the files are distributed among the clusters on the disk.

CMOS (complementary metal-oxide semiconductor) Originally, the type of nonvolatile RAM that held information about the most basic parts of your PC, such as hard drives, floppies, and amount of DRAM. Today, actual CMOS chips have been

replaced by flash-type nonvolatile RAM. The information is the same, however, and is still called CMOS—even though it is now almost always stored on Flash RAM.

CMOS clear A jumper on the motherboard that, when set, will revert CMOS settings to the factory defaults.

CMOS setup program Program enabling you to access and update CMOS data. Also referred to as the System Setup Utility or BIOS setup.

CNR (communications and networking riser) Proprietary slot used on some motherboards to provide a sound interference–free connection for modems, sound cards, and NICs.

coaxial cable Cabling in which an internal conductor is surrounded by another, outer conductor, thus sharing the same axis.

code Set of symbols representing characters (e.g., ASCII code) or instructions in a computer program (a programmer writes source code, which must be translated into executable or machine code for the computer to use).

code names Names that keep track of different variations within CPU models.

codec (compressor/decompressor) Software that compresses or decompresses media streams.

color depth Term to define a scanner's ability to produce color, hue, and shade.

COM port(s) Serial communications ports available on a computer. COM*x* is used to designate a uniquely numbered COM port such as COM1, COM2, etc.

command A request, typed from a terminal or embedded in a file, to perform an operation or to execute a particular program.

command-line interface User interface for an OS devoid of all graphical trappings.

command prompt Text prompt for entering commands.

CompactFlash (CF) One of the older but still popular flash media formats. Its interface uses a simplified PC Card bus, so it also supports I/O devices.

compatibility modes Feature of Windows to enable software written for previous versions of Windows to operate in newer operating systems.

compliance Concept that members of an organization must abide by the rules of that organization. For a technician, this often revolves around what software can or cannot be installed on an organization's computer.

component failure Occurs when a system device fails due to a manufacturing or some other type of defect.

Component Services Programming tools in Windows for the sharing of data objects between programs.

compression Process of squeezing data to eliminate redundancies, allowing files to use less space when stored or transmitted.

CompTIA A+ 220-901 The first half of the CompTIA A+ certification for computer technicians. The 901 exam focuses primarily on understanding terminology and technology, how to do fundamental tasks such as upgrading RAM, and basic network and mobile device support.

CompTIA A+ 220-902 The second half of the CompTIA A+ certification for computer technicians. The 902 exam focuses primarily on software, security, and troubleshooting.

CompTIA A+ certification Industry-wide, vendor-neutral computer certification program that demonstrates competency as a computer technician.

CompTIA Network+ certification Industry-wide, vendor-neutral certification for network technicians, covering network hardware, installation, and troubleshooting.

Computer Default interface in Windows Vista and Windows 7 for Windows Explorer; displays hard drives and devices with removable storage.

Computer Management Applet in Windows' Administrative Tools that contains several useful snap-ins, such as Device Manager and Disk Management.

computing process Four parts of a computer's operation: input, processing, output, and storage.

Computing Technology Industry Association (CompTIA) Nonprofit IT trade association that administers the CompTIA A+ and CompTIA Network+ exams, and many other vendor-neutral IT certification exams.

connectors Small receptacles used to attach cables to a system. Common types of connectors include USB, PS/2, DB-25, RJ-45, HDMI, DVI, HD15, DisplayPort, and Thunderbolt.

consumables Materials used up by printers, including paper, ink, ribbons, and toner cartridges.

container file File containing two or more separate, compressed tracks, typically an audio track and a moving-picture track. Also known as a *wrapper*.

context menu Small menu brought up by right-clicking on objects in Windows.

Control Panel Collection of Windows applets, or small programs, that can be used to configure various pieces of hardware and software in a system.

controller card Card adapter that connects devices, such as a drive, to the main computer bus/motherboard.

convergence Measure of how sharply a single pixel appears on a CRT; a monitor with poor convergence produces images that are not sharply defined.

copy backup Type of backup similar to a normal or full backup, in that all selected files on a system are backed up. This type of backup does not change the archive bit of the files being backed up.

copy command Command in the command-line interface for making a copy of a file and pasting it in another location.

Core Name used for the family of Intel CPUs that succeeded the Pentium 4, such as the Core i3, Core i5, and Core i7.

counter Used to track data about a particular object when using the Performance Monitor.

cp Copy command in Linux.

CPU (central processing unit) "Brain" of the computer. Microprocessor that handles primary calculations for the computer. CPUs are known by names such as Core i5 and Phenom II.

CRC (cyclic redundancy check) Very accurate mathematical method used to check for errors in long streams of transmitted data. Before data is sent, the main computer uses the data to calculate a CRC value from the data's contents. If the receiver calculates from the received data a different CRC value, the data was corrupted during transmission and is re-sent. Ethernet packets use the CRC algorithm in the FCS portion of the frame.

credit card reader Device that can be attached to mobile phones and tablets to take credit card payments.

crimper A specialized tool for connecting twisted pair wires to an RJ-45 connector. Also called a *crimping tool.*

CrossFire Technology that combines the power of multiple AMD graphics cards in a system.

crossover cable A standard UTP cable with one RJ-45 connector using the T568A standard and the other using the T568B standard. This reverses the signal between sending and receiving wires and thus simulates the connection to a switch.

CRT (cathode ray tube) Tube of a monitor in which rays of electrons are beamed onto a phosphorescent screen to produce images. Also, a shorthand way to describe a monitor that uses CRT rather than LCD technology.

CSMA/CA (carrier sense multiple access/collision avoidance) Networking scheme used by wireless devices to transmit data while avoiding data collisions, which wireless nodes have difficulty detecting.

CSMA/CD (carrier sense multiple access/collision detection) Networking scheme used by Ethernet devices to transmit data and resend data after detection of data collisions.

cylinder Single concentric track passing through all the platters in a hard disk drive. Imagine a hard disk drive as a series of metal cans, nested one inside another; a single can would represent a cylinder.

DAC (Discretionary Access Control) Authorization method based on the idea that there is an owner of a resource who may at his or her discretion assign access to that resource. DAC is considered much more flexible than mandatory access control (MAC).

daily backup Backup of all files that have been changed on that day without changing the archive bits of those files. Also called *daily copy backup*.

daisy-chaining Method of connecting several devices along a bus and managing the signals for each device.

data classification System of organizing data according to its sensitivity. Common classifications include public, highly confidential, and top secret.

data roaming A feature of cellular data systems that enables the signal to jump from cell tower to cell tower and from your provider to another provider without obvious notice.

data storage Saving a permanent copy of your work so that you can come back to it later.

data structure Scheme that directs how an OS stores and retrieves data on and off a drive. Used interchangeably with the term file system. (*See also* file system.)

DB connectors D-shaped connectors used for a variety of connections in the PC and networking world. Can be male (with prongs) or female (with holes) and have a varying number of pins or sockets. Also called D-sub, D-subminiature, or D-shell connectors.

DB-9 A two-row DB connector (male) used to connect the computer's serial port to a serial-communication device such as a modem or a console port on a managed switch.

DB-15 connector A two- or three-row D-sub connector (female) used for 10Base5 networks, MIDI/joysticks, and analog video.

DB-25 connector D-sub connector (female), commonly referred to as a parallel port connector.

DC (direct current) Type of electricity in which the flow of electrons is in a complete circle in one direction.

dd Linux command for copying entire block volumes.

DDOS (distributed denial of service) An attack on a computer or network device in which multiple computers send data and requests to the device in an attempt to overwhelm it so that it cannot perform normal operations.

DDR SDRAM (double data rate SDRAM) Type of DRAM that makes two processes for every clock cycle. (*See also* DRAM.)

DDR2 SDRAM Type of SDRAM that sends 4 bits of data in every clock cycle. (*See also* DDR SDRAM.)

DDR3 SDRAM Type of SDRAM that transfers data at twice the rate of DDR2 SDRAM.

DDR4 SDRAM Type of SDRAM that offers higher density and lower voltages than DDR3, and can handle faster data transfer rates. Maximum theoretical capacity of DDR4 DIMMs is up to 512 GB.

DE (desktop environment) Name for the various user interfaces found in Linux distributions.

debug To detect, trace, and eliminate errors in computer programs.

decibels Unit of measurement typically associated with sound. The higher the number of decibels, the louder the sound.

dedicated server Machine that is not used for any client functions, only server functions.

default gateway In a TCP/IP network, the nearest router to a particular host. This router's IP address is part of the necessary TCP/IP configuration for communicating with multiple networks using IP.

definition file List of virus signatures that an antivirus program can recognize.

defragmentation (defrag) Procedure in which all the files on a hard disk drive are rewritten on disk so that all parts of each file reside in contiguous clusters. The result is an improvement in disk speed during retrieval operations.

degauss Procedure used to break up the electromagnetic fields that can build up on the cathode ray tube of a monitor; involves running a current through a wire loop. Most monitors feature a manual degaussing tool.

del (erase) Command in the command-line interface used to delete/erase files.

desktop User's primary interface to the Windows operating system.

desktop replacement Portable computer that offers the same performance as a full-fledged desktop computer; these systems are normally very heavy to carry and often cost much more than the desktop systems they replace.

device driver Program used by the operating system to control communications between the computer and peripherals.

Device Manager Utility that enables techs to examine and configure all the hardware and drivers in a Windows PC.

DFS (distributed file system) A storage environment where shared files are accessed from storage devices within multiple servers, clients, and peer hosts.

DHCP (Dynamic Host Configuration Protocol) Protocol that enables client hosts to request and receive TCP/IP settings automatically from an appropriately configured server.

differential backup Similar to an incremental backup. Backs up the files that have been changed since the last backup. This type of backup does not change the state of the archive bit.

digital camera Camera that simulates film technology electronically.

digital certificate Form in which a public key is sent from a Web server to a Web browser so that the browser can decrypt the data sent by the server.

Digital Living Network Alliance (DLNA) devices Devices that connect to a home network, discover each other, and share media. In theory, DLNA devices should work with minimal setup or fuss, even if sourced from different manufacturers.

digital zoom Software tool to enhance the optical zoom capabilities of a digital camera.

digitally signed driver A driver designed specifically to work with Windows that has been tested and certified by Microsoft to work stably with Windows.

digitizer The touchscreen overlay technology that converts finger and stylus contact into input data for the device to use.

DIMM (dual inline memory module) 32- or 64-bit type of DRAM packaging with the distinction that each side of each tab inserted into the system performs a separate function. DIMMs come in a variety of sizes, with 184-, 240-, and 288-pin being the most common on desktop computers.

DIN (Deutsches Institut für Normung) Round connector shell with pins or holes that was standardized by the German national standards body. Largely obsolete, DIN and mini-DIN connectors have been used by keyboards, mice, video systems, and other peripherals attached to computers.

dipole antennas Standard straight-wire antennas that provide the most omnidirectional function.

dir Command used in the command-line interface to display the entire contents of the current working directory.

directory Another name for a folder.

directory service Centralized index that each PC accesses to locate resources in the domain.

DirectX Set of APIs enabling programs to control multimedia, such as sound, video, and graphics. Used in Windows Vista and Windows 7 to draw the Aero desktop.

Disk Cleanup Utility built into Windows that can help users clean up their hard drives by removing temporary Internet files, deleting unused program files, and more.

disk cloning Taking a PC and making a duplicate of the hard drive, including all data, software, and configuration files, and transferring it to another PC. (*See* image deployment.)

disk duplexing Type of disk mirroring using two separate controllers rather than one; faster than traditional mirroring.

disk initialization A process that places special information on every hard drive installed in a Windows system.

Disk Management Snap-in available with the Microsoft Management Console that enables techs to configure the various disks installed in a system; available in the Computer Management Administrative Tool.

disk mirroring Process by which data is written simultaneously to two or more disk drives. Read and write speed is decreased, but redundancy in case of catastrophe is increased.

disk quota Application allowing network administrators to limit hard drive space usage.

disk striping Process by which data is spread among multiple (at least two) drives. Increases speed for both reads and writes of data. Considered RAID level 0 because it does not provide fault tolerance.

disk striping with parity Method for providing fault tolerance by writing data across multiple drives and then including an additional drive, called a parity drive, that stores information to rebuild the data contained on the other drives. Requires at least three physical disks: two for the data and a third for the parity drive. This provides data redundancy at RAID levels 5, 10, and 0+1 with different options.

disk thrashing Hard drive that is constantly being accessed due to lack of available system memory. When system memory runs low, a Windows system will utilize hard disk space as "virtual" memory, thus causing an unusual amount of hard drive access.

diskpart A fully functioning command-line partitioning tool.

display adapter Handles all the communication between the CPU and the monitor. Also known as a video card.

Display applet Tool in Windows XP and Windows 7 used to adjust display settings, including resolution, refresh rate, driver information, and color depth. (*See* Personalization applet for the comparable tool in Windows Vista.)

DisplayPort Digital video connector used by Apple Mac desktop models and some PCs, notably from Dell. Designed by VESA as a royalty-free connector to replace VGA and DVI.

distended capacitors Failed capacitors on a motherboard, which tend to bulge out at the top. This was especially a problem during the mid-2000s, when capacitor manufacturers released huge batches of bad capacitors.

distribution (distro) A specific variant of Linux.

DLP (data loss prevention) System or set of rules designed to stop leakage of sensitive information. Usually applied to Internet appliances to monitor outgoing network traffic.

DLP (digital light processing) Display technology that reflects and directs light onto a display surface using micromechanically operated mirrors.

DLT (digital linear tape) High-speed, magnetic tape storage technology used to archive and retrieve data from faster, online media such as hard disks.

DMA (direct memory access) modes Technique that some PC hardware devices use to transfer data to and from the memory without using the CPU.

DMA controller Resides between the RAM and the devices and handles DMA requests.

DMZ (demilitarized zone) A lightly protected or unprotected subnet network positioned between an outer firewall and an organization's highly protected internal network. DMZs are used mainly to host public address servers (such as Web servers).

DNS (domain name service) TCP/IP name resolution system that translates a host name into an IP address.

DNS domain Specific branch of the DNS name space. First-level DNS domains include .com, .gov, and .edu.

dock A bar at the bottom of the Mac OS X desktop where application icons can be placed for easy access.

docking station Device that provides a portable computer extra features such as a DVD drive or PC Card, in addition to legacy and modern ports. Similar to a port replicator. Also, a charging station for mobile devices.

document findings, actions, and outcomes Recording each troubleshooting job: what the problem was, how it was fixed, and other helpful information. (Step 6 of 6 in the CompTIA troubleshooting theory.)

Documents folder Windows folder for storing user-created files.

Dolby Digital Technology for sound reductions and channeling methods used for digital audio.

domain Groupings of users, computers, or networks. In Microsoft networking, a domain is a group of computers and users that share a common account database and a common security policy. On the Internet, a domain is a group of computers that share a common element in their hierarchical name. Other types of domains exist—e.g., broadcast domain, etc.

domain-based network Network that eliminates the need for logging on to multiple servers by using domain controllers to hold the security database for all systems.

DoS (denial of service) An attack on a computer resource that prevents it from performing its normal operations, usually by overwhelming it with large numbers of requests in an effort to monopolize its resources.

DOS (Disk Operating System) First popular operating system available for PCs. A text-based, single-tasking operating system that was not completely replaced until the introduction of Windows 95.

dot-matrix printer Printer that creates each character from an array of dots. Pins striking a ribbon against the paper, one pin for each dot position, form the dots. May be a serial printer (printing one character at a time) or a line printer.

double-sided RAM RAM stick with RAM chips soldered to both sides of the stick. May only be used with motherboards designed to accept double-sided RAM. Very common.

dpi (dots per inch) Measure of printer resolution that counts the dots the device can produce per linear (horizontal) inch.

DPMS (display power-management signaling) Specification that can reduce monitor power consumption by 75 percent by reducing/eliminating video signals during idle periods.

DRAM (dynamic random access memory or dynamic RAM) Memory used to store data in most personal computers. DRAM stores each bit in a "cell" composed of a transistor and a capacitor. Because the capacitor in a DRAM cell can only hold a charge for a few milliseconds, DRAM must be continually refreshed, or rewritten, to retain its data.

drive letter A letter designating a specific drive or partition.

DriveLock CMOS program enabling you to control the ATA security mode feature set. Also known as *drive lock*.

driver signing Digital signature for drivers used by Windows to protect against potentially bad drivers.

DS3D (DirectSound3D) Introduced with DirectX 3.0, a command set used to create positional audio, or sounds that appear to come from in front, in back, or to the side of a user. Merged with DirectSound into DirectAudio in DirectX 8. (*See also* DirectX.)

DSL (digital subscriber line) High-speed Internet connection technology that uses a regular telephone line for connectivity. DSL comes in several varieties, including asynchronous (ADSL) and synchronous (SDSL), and many speeds. Typical home-user DSL connections are ADSL with faster download speeds than upload speeds.

D-subminiature *See* DB connectors.

DTS (Digital Theatre Systems) Technology for sound reductions and channeling methods, similar to Dolby Digital.

dual boot Refers to a computer with two operating systems installed, enabling users to choose which operating system to load on boot. Can also refer to kicking a device a second time just in case the first time didn't work.

dual-channel architecture Using two sticks of RAM (either RDRAM or DDR) to increase throughput.

dual-channel memory Form of DDR, DDR2, and DDR3 memory access used by many motherboards that requires two identical sticks of DDR, DDR2, or DDR3 RAM.

dual-core CPUs that have two execution units on the same physical chip but share caches and RAM.

dual-scan passive matrix Manufacturing technique for increasing display updates by refreshing two lines at a time.

dual-voltage Type of power supply that works with either 110- or 220-volt outlets.

dumpster diving To go through someone's trash in search of information.

DUN (Dial-up Networking) Software used by Windows to govern the connection between the modem and the ISP.

duplexing Similar to mirroring in that data is written to and read from two physical drives, for fault tolerance. Separate controllers are used for each drive, both for additional fault tolerance and for additional speed. Considered RAID level 1. Also called *disk duplexing* or *drive duplexing*.

DVD (digital versatile disc) Optical disc format that provides for 4–17 GB of video or data storage.

DVD-ROM DVD equivalent of the standard CD-ROM.

DVD-RW/DVD+RW Incompatible rewritable DVD media formats.

DVD-Video DVD format used exclusively to store digital video; capable of storing over two hours of high-quality video on a single DVD.

DVI (Digital Visual Interface) Special video connector designed for digital-to-digital connections; most commonly seen on PC video cards and LCD monitors. Some versions also support analog signals with a special adapter.

dxdiag (DirectX Diagnostics Tool) Diagnostic tool for getting information about and testing a computer's DirectX version.

dye-sublimation printer Printer that uses a roll of heat-sensitive plastic film embedded with dyes, which are vaporized and then solidified onto specially coated paper to create a high-quality image.

dynamic disks Special feature of Windows that enables users to span a single volume across two or more drives. Dynamic disks do not have partitions; they have volumes. Dynamic disks can be striped, mirrored, and striped or mirrored with parity.

ECC (error correction code) Special software, embedded on hard drives, that constantly scans the drives for bad sectors.

ECC RAM/DRAM (error correction code DRAM) RAM that uses special chips to detect and fix memory errors. Commonly used in high-end servers where data integrity is crucial.

effective permissions User's combined permissions granted by multiple groups.

EFI (Extensible Firmware Interface) Firmware created by Intel and HP that replaced traditional 16-bit BIOS and added several new enhancements.

EFS (encrypting file system) Storage organization and management service, such as NTFS, that has the capability of applying a cipher process to the stored data.

EIA/TIA *See* TIA/EIA.

EIDE (Enhanced IDE) Marketing concept of hard drive–maker Western Digital, encompassing four improvements for IDE drives, including drives larger than 528 MB, four devices, increase in drive throughput, and non–hard drive devices. (*See* ATAPI, PIO mode.)

electric potential The voltage differential between any two objects, one of which is frequently ground or earth, resulting in a degree of attraction for the electrons to move from one of the objects to the other. A large difference between a person and a doorknob, for example, can lead to a shocking experience when the two touch. (*See* electrostatic discharge (ESD).)

electromagnetic interference (EMI) Electrical interference from one device to another, resulting in poor performance of the device being interfered with. Examples: Static on your TV while running a blow dryer, or placing two monitors too close together and getting a "shaky" screen.

electrostatic discharge (ESD) Uncontrolled rush of electrons from one object to another. A real menace to PCs, as it can cause permanent damage to semiconductors.

eliciting answers Communication strategy designed to help techs understand a user's problems better. Works by listening to a user's description of a problem and then asking cogent questions.

e-mail (electronic mail) Messages, usually text, sent from one person to another via computer. Can also be sent automatically to a group of addresses (mailing list).

emergency repair disk (ERD) Saves critical boot files and partition information and is the main tool for fixing boot problems in older versions of Windows. Newer versions of Windows call this a system repair disc (Windows Vista/7) or recovery drive (Windows 8/8.1 and 10).

eMMC (embedded MMC) A form of embedded flash memory widely seen in mobile devices.

emulator Software or hardware that converts the commands to and from the host machine into an entirely different platform.

encryption Making data unreadable by those who do not possess a key or password.

equipment rack A metal structure used in equipment rooms to secure network hardware devices and patch panels. Most racks are 19 inches wide. Devices designed to fit in such a rack use a height measurement called *units*, or simply *U*.

erase lamp Component inside laser printers that uses light to make the coating of the photosensitive drum conductive.

e-reader Mobile electronic device used for reading e-books.

Error-checking Windows graphical tool that scans and fixes hard drive problems. Often referred to by the name of the executable, chkdsk, or Check Disk. The Mac OS X equivalent is the Disk Utility, and Linux offers a command-line tool called fsck.

eSATA Serial ATA-based connector for external hard drives and optical drives.

escalate Process used when person assigned to repair a problem is not able to get the job done, such as sending the problem to someone with more expertise.

establish a plan of action and implement the solution After establishing and testing a theory about a particular problem, techs solve the problem. (Step 4 of 6 in the CompTIA troubleshooting theory.)

establish a theory of probable cause After identifying a problem, techs question the obvious to determine what might be the source of the problem. (Step 2 of 6 in the CompTIA troubleshooting theory.)

Ethernet Name coined by Xerox for the first standard of network cabling and protocols. Based on a bus topology.

Ethic of Reciprocity Golden Rule: Do unto others as you would have them do unto you.

EULA (End User License Agreement) Agreement that accompanies a piece of software, to which the user must agree before using the software. Outlines the terms of use for the software and also lists any actions on the part of the user that violate the agreement.

event auditing Feature of Event Viewer's Security section that creates an entry in the Security Log when certain events happen, such as a user logging on.

Event Viewer Utility made available in Windows as an MMC snap-in that enables users to monitor various system events, including network bandwidth usage and CPU utilization.

expand Command-line utility included with Windows that is used to access files within CAB files.

expansion bus Set of wires going to the CPU, governed by the expansion bus crystal, directly connected to expansion slots of varying types (PCI, AGP, PCIe, etc.).

expansion bus crystal Controls the speed of the expansion bus.

expansion slots Connectors on a motherboard that enable users to add optional components to a system. (*See also* AGP, PCI, and PCIe.)

ExpressCard The high-performance serial version of the PC Card that replaced PC Card slots on laptop PCs over the past decade. ExpressCard comes in two widths: 34 mm and 54 mm, called *ExpressCard/34* and *ExpressCard/54*.

extended partition Type of nonbootable hard disk partition. May only have one extended partition per disk. Purpose is to divide a large disk into smaller partitions, each with a separate drive letter.

Extensible Authentication Protocol (EAP) Authentication wrapper that EAP-compliant applications can use to accept one of many types of authentication. While EAP is a general-purpose authentication wrapper, its only substantial use is in wireless networks.

extension Two, three, four, five, or more letters that follow a filename and identify the type of file. Common file extensions are .zip, .exe, .doc, .java, and .xhtml.

external data bus (EDB) Primary data highway of all computers. Everything in your computer is tied either directly or indirectly to the external data bus. (*See also* frontside bus *and* backside bus.)

face lock Technology that enables use of facial features to unlock a mobile device or personal computer.

Fast User Switching Account option that is useful when multiple users share a system; allows users to switch without logging off.

FAT (file allocation table) Hidden table that records how files on a hard disk are stored in distinct clusters; the only way DOS knows where to access files. Address of first cluster of a file is stored in the directory file. FAT entry for the first cluster is the address of the second cluster used to store that file. In the entry for the second cluster for that file is the address for the third cluster, and so on until the final cluster, which gets a special end-of-file code. There are two FATs, mirror images of each other, in case one is destroyed or damaged. Also refers to the 16-bit file allocation table when used by Windows 2000 and later NT-based operating systems.

FAT16 File allocation table that uses 16 bits to address and index clusters. Used as the primary hard drive format on DOS and early Windows 95 machines; currently used with smaller-capacity (2 GB or less) flash media devices.

FAT32 File allocation table that uses 32 bits to address and index clusters. Commonly used with USB flash-media drives and versions of Windows prior to XP.

FAT64 (exFAT) A Microsoft-proprietary file system that breaks the 4-GB file-size barrier, supporting files up to 16 exabytes (EB) and a theoretical partition limit of 64 zettabytes (ZB). Envisioned for use with flash media devices with a capacity exceeding 2 TB.

FCS (Frame Check Sequence) Portion of an Ethernet frame used for error checking, most commonly with the CRC algorithm.

fdisk Disk-partitioning utility used in DOS and Windows 9*x* systems.

fiber-optic cable High-speed cable for transmitting data, made of high-purity glass sealed within an opaque tube. Much faster than conventional copper wire such as coaxial cable.

file Collection of any form of data that is stored beyond the time of execution of a single job. A file may contain program instructions or data, which may be numerical, textual, or graphical information.

file allocation unit Another term for cluster. (*See also* cluster.)

file association Windows term for the proper program to open a particular file; for example, the file association for opening or .mp3 files might be Winamp.

File Explorer A tool in Windows 8/8.1/10 that enables users to browse files and folders.

file format How information is encoded in a file. Two primary types are binary (pictures) and ASCII (text), but within those are many formats, such as BMP and GIF for pictures. Commonly represented by a suffix at the end of the filename; for example, .txt for a text file or .exe for an executable.

file server Computer designated to store software, courseware, administrative tools, and other data on a LAN or WAN. It "serves" this information to other computers via the network when users enter their personal access codes.

file system Scheme that directs how an OS stores and retrieves data on and off a drive; FAT32 and NTFS are both file systems. Used interchangeably with the term "data structure." (*See also* data structure.)

filename Name assigned to a file when the file is first written on a disk. Every file on a disk within the same folder must have a unique name. Filenames can contain any character (including spaces), except the following: \ / : * ? " < > |

Finder Mac OS X's file and folder browser.

fingerprint lock Type of biometric device that enables a user to unlock a mobile device using a fingerprint.

firewall Device that restricts traffic between a local network and the Internet.

FireWire (IEEE 1394) Interconnection standard to send wide-band signals over a serialized, physically thin connector system. Serial bus developed by Apple and Texas Instruments; enables connection of 63 devices at speeds up to 800 Mbps.

firmware Embedded programs or code stored on a ROM chip. Generally OS-independent, thus allowing devices to operate in a wide variety of circumstances without direct OS support. The system BIOS is firmware.

firmware upgrade Process by which the BIOS of a motherboard can be updated to reflect patched bugs and added features. Performed, usually, through CMOS, though some motherboard manufacturers provide a Windows program for performing a firmware upgrade.

fitness monitor Devices that encourage physical fitness by counting steps using accelerometers, registering heart rate through sensors, using GPS to track exercise, and offering vibration tools to remind the user to get moving. Fitness trackers fit into one of two type: fobs that clip to the body and more sophisticated fitness bands or watches.

Flash ROM ROM technology that can be electrically reprogrammed while still in the PC. Overwhelmingly the most common storage medium of BIOS in computers today, as it can be upgraded without a need to open the computer on most systems.

flatbed scanner Most popular form of consumer scanner; runs a bright light along the length of the tray to capture an image.

FlexATX Motherboard form factor. Motherboards built in accordance with the FlexATX form factor are very small, much smaller than microATX motherboards.

Flip 3D In the Aero desktop environment, a three-dimensional replacement for ALT-TAB. Accessed by pressing the WINDOWS KEY-TAB key combination.

floppy disk Removable storage media that can hold between 720 KB and 1.44 MB of data.

floppy drive System hardware that uses removable 3.5-inch disks as storage media.

flux reversal Point at which a read/write head detects a change in magnetic polarity.

FM synthesis Producing sound by electronic emulation of various instruments to more or less produce music and other sound effects.

form factor Standard for the physical organization of motherboard components and motherboard size. Most common form factors are ATX, microATX, and Mini-ITX.

format Command in the command-line interface used to format a storage device.

formatting Magnetically mapping a disk to provide a structure for storing data; can be done to any type of disk, including a floppy disk, hard disk, or other type of removable disk.

FPU (floating point unit) Formal term for math coprocessor (also called a numeric processor) circuitry inside a CPU. A math coprocessor calculates by using a floating point numerical system (which allows for decimals). Before the Intel 80486, FPUs were separate chips from the CPU.

fragmentation Occurs when files and directories get jumbled on a fixed disk and are no longer contiguous. Can significantly slow down hard drive access times and can be repaired by using the defrag utility included with each version of Windows. (*See also* defragmentation.)

frame A data unit transferred across a network. Frames consist of several parts, such as the sending and receiving MAC addresses, the data being sent, and the frame check sequence.

freeware Software that is distributed for free, with no license fee.

frequency Measure of a sound's tone, either high or low.

frontside bus Wires that connect the CPU to the main system RAM. Generally running at speeds of 66–133 MHz. Distinct from the expansion bus and the backside bus, though it shares wires with the former.

front-view projector Shoots the image out the front and counts on you to put a screen in front at the proper distance.

FRU (field replaceable unit) Any part of a PC that is considered to be replaceable "in the field," i.e., a customer location. There is no official list of FRUs—it is usually a matter of policy by the repair center.

FTP (File Transfer Protocol) Rules that enable two computers to talk to one another during a file transfer. Protocol used when you transfer a file from one computer to another across the Internet. FTP uses port numbers 20 and 21.

full-duplex Any device that can send and receive data simultaneously.

Full-Speed USB USB standard that runs at 12 Mbps. Also known as USB 1.1.

fully qualified domain name (FQDN) A complete, bottom-to-top label of a DNS host going from the specific host to the top-level domain that holds it and all of the intervening domain layers, each layer being separated by a dot. FQDNs are entered into browser bars and other utilities in formats like *mail.totalseminars.com*.

Function (fn) key Special key on many laptops that enables some keys to perform a third duty.

fuser assembly Mechanism in laser printers that uses two rollers to fuse toner to paper during the print process.

future-proofing Configuring a PC so that it will run programs (especially games) released in the coming years.

Gadgets Small tools, such as clocks or calendars, in Windows Vista and 7 that are placed on the Sidebar.

gain Ratio of increase of radio frequency output provided by an antenna, measured in decibels (dB).

gamepad An input device specifically designed for playing computer games. These usually consist of one or more thumbsticks, a directional pad, multiple face buttons, and two or more triggers.

GDI (graphical device interface) Component of Windows that utilizes the CPU rather than the printer to process a print job as a bitmapped image of each page.

general protection fault (GPF) Error code usually seen when separate active programs conflict on resources or data.

geometry Numbers representing three values: heads, cylinders, and sectors per track; defines where a hard drive stores data.

geotracking Feature in cellular phones that enables the cell phone companies and government agencies to use the ID or MAC address to pinpoint where a phone is at any given time.

giga Prefix for the quantity 1,073,741,824 (2^{30}) or for 1 billion. One gigabyte would be 1,073,741,824 bytes, except with hard drive labeling, where it means 1 billion bytes. One gigahertz is 1 billion hertz.

glasses Wearable computing device that enables a user to perform some computing functions via a pair of glasses.

Global Positioning System (GPS) Technology that enables a mobile device to determine where you are on a map.

globally unique identifier (GUID) partition table (GPT) Partitioning scheme that enables you to create more than four primary partitions without needing to use dynamic disks.

gpresult Windows command for listing group policies applied to a user.

GPU (graphics processing unit) Specialized processor that helps the CPU by taking over all of the 3-D rendering duties.

gpupdate Windows command for making immediate group policy changes in an individual system.

grayscale depth Number that defines how many shades of gray the scanner can save per dot.

grayware Program that intrudes into a user's computer experience without damaging any systems or data.

grep Linux command to search through text files or command outputs to find specific information or to filter out unneeded information.

group Collection of user accounts that share the same access capabilities.

Group Policy Means of easily controlling the settings of multiple network clients with policies such as setting minimum password length or preventing Registry edits.

GSM (Global System for Mobile Communications) Wireless data standard for mobile devices.

guest account Very limited built-in account type for Windows; a member of the Guest group.

GUI (graphical user interface) Interface that enables user to interact with computer graphically, by using a mouse or other pointing device to manipulate icons that represent programs or documents, instead of using only text as in early interfaces. Pronounced "gooey."

gyroscope Device that can detect the position of the tablet or phone in 3-D space.

HAL (hardware abstraction layer) Part of the Windows OS that separates system-specific device drivers from the rest of the operating system.

handshaking Procedure performed by modems, terminals, and computers to verify that communication has been correctly established.

hang Occurs when a computer or program stops responding to keyboard commands or other input; a computer or program in such a state is said to be 'hung.'

hang time Number of seconds a too-often-hung computer is airborne after you have thrown it out a second-story window.

hard drive Data-recording system using solid disks of magnetic material turning at high speeds to store and retrieve programs and data in a computer. Abbreviated HDD for *hard disk drive*.

hardware Physical computer equipment such as electrical, electronic, magnetic, and mechanical devices. Anything in the computer world that you can hold in your hand. A hard drive is hardware; Microsoft Word is not.

hardware protocol Defines many aspects of a network, from the packet type to the cabling and connectors used.

HBA (host bus adapter) Connects SATA devices to the expansion bus. Also known as the SATA controller.

HD (Hi-Definition) Multimedia transmission standard that defines high-resolution images and 5.1, 6.1, and 7.1 sound.

HDA (High Definition Audio) Intel-designed standard to support features such as true surround sound with many discrete speakers. Often referred to by its code name, Azalia.

HDD (hard disk drive) Data-recording system using solid disks of magnetic material turning at high speeds to store and retrieve programs and data in a computer.

HDMI (High Definition Multimedia Interface) Single multimedia connection that includes both high-definition video and audio. One of the best connections for outputting to television. Also contains copy protection features.

head actuator Mechanism for moving the arms inside a hard drive on which the read/write heads are mounted.

headphones Audio output device that sits on top of or in a user's ears.

heads Short for read/write heads used by hard drives to store data.

heat dope *See* thermal compound.

hex (hexadecimal) Base-16 numbering system using ten digits (0 through 9) and six letters (A through F). In the computer world, shorthand way to write binary numbers by substituting one hex digit for a four-digit binary number (e.g., hex 9 = binary 1001).

hibernation Power management setting in which all data from RAM is written to the hard drive before the system goes into Sleep mode. Upon waking up, all information is retrieved from the hard drive and returned to RAM.

hidden attribute File attribute that, when used, does not allow the dir command to show a file.

hierarchical directory tree Method by which Windows organizes files into a series of folders, called directories, under the root directory. (*See also* root directory.)

high gloss Laptop screen finish that offers sharper contrast, richer colors, and wider viewing angles than a matte finish, but is also much more reflective.

high-level formatting Format that sets up a file system on a drive.

high-voltage anode Component in a CRT monitor that has very high voltages of electricity flowing through it.

Hi-Speed USB USB standard that runs at 480 Mbps. Also referred to as USB 2.0.

home screen The default “desktop” of a mobile device.

home server PC A computer built to store files on a small office/home office (SOHO) network.

HomeGroup A Windows 7 feature that connects a group of computers using a common password—no special user names required. Each computer can be a member of only one homegroup at a time. Homegroups enable simple sharing of documents and printers between computers.

honesty Telling the truth—a very important thing for a tech to do.

horizontal cabling Cabling that connects the equipment room to the work areas.

host On a TCP/IP network, single device that has an IP address—any device (usually a computer) that can be the source or destination of a data packet. In the mainframe world, computer that is made available for use by multiple people simultaneously. Also, in virtualization, a computer running one or more virtual operating systems.

hostname Windows command for displaying the name of a computer.

hotspot Feature that enables a mobile device connected to a mobile data network to be used as a wireless access point (WAP) for other devices. Often these are stand-alone devices, though many cellular phones and data-connected tablets can be set up to act as hotspots.

hot-swappable Any hardware that may be attached to or removed from a PC without interrupting the PC’s normal processing.

HRR (horizontal refresh rate) Amount of time it takes for a monitor to draw one horizontal line of pixels on a display.

HTML (Hypertext Markup Language) ASCII-based, script-like language for creating hypertext documents such as those on the World Wide Web.

HTPC A home theater PC designed to attach to a TV or projector for movie and TV viewing.

HTTP (Hypertext Transfer Protocol) Extremely fast protocol used for network file transfers in the WWW environment. Uses port 80.

HTTPS (HTTP over Secure Sockets Layer) Secure form of HTTP used commonly for Internet business transactions or any time when a secure connection is required. Uses port 443. (*See also* HTTP.)

hub Electronic device that sits at the center of a star topology network, providing a common point for the connection of network devices. Hubs repeat all information out to all ports and have been replaced by switches, although the term "hub" is still commonly used.

hybrid A network topology that combines features from multiple other topologies, such as the star-bus topology.

hyperthreading CPU feature that enables a single pipeline to run more than one thread at once.

hypervisor Software that enables a single computer to run multiple operating systems simultaneously.

IaaS (Infrastructure as a Service) Cloud-hosted provider of virtualized servers and networks.

I/O (input/output) General term for reading and writing data to a computer. "Input" includes data entered from a keyboard, identified by a pointing device (such as a mouse), or loaded from a disk. "Output" includes writing information to a disk, viewing it on a monitor, or printing it to a printer.

I/O addressing Using the address bus to talk to system devices.

I/O advanced programmable interrupt controller (IOAPIC) Typically located in the Southbridge, acts as the traffic cop for interrupt requests to the CPU.

I/O base address First value in an I/O address range.

ICH (I/O Controller Hub) Official name for Southbridge chip found in Intel's chipsets.

icon Small image or graphic, most commonly found on a system's desktop, that launches a program when selected.

iCloud Apple cloud-based storage. iCloud enables a user to back up all iPhone or iPad data, and makes that data accessible from anywhere. This includes any media purchased through iTunes and calendars, contacts, reminders, and so forth.

ICS (Internet Connection Sharing) Windows feature that enables a single network connection to be shared among several machines.

IDE (integrated drive electronics) PC specification for small- to medium-sized hard drives in which the controlling electronics for the drive are part of the drive itself, speeding up transfer rates and leaving only a simple adapter (or "paddle"). IDE only supported two drives per system of no more than 504 MB each, and has been completely

supplanted by Enhanced IDE. EIDE supports four drives of over 8 GB each and more than doubles the transfer rate. The more common name for PATA drives. Also known as *intelligent drive electronics*. (*See* PATA.)

identify the problem To question the user and find out what has been changed recently or is no longer working properly. Step 1 of 6 in the CompTIA troubleshooting theory.

IEC-320 Connects the cable supplying AC power from a wall outlet into the power supply.

IEEE (Institute of Electronic and Electrical Engineers) Leading standards-setting group in the United States.

IEEE 1284 IEEE standard governing parallel communication.

IEEE 1394 IEEE standard governing FireWire communication. (*See also* FireWire.)

IEEE 1394a FireWire standard that runs at 400 Mbps.

IEEE 1394b FireWire standard that runs at 800 Mbps.

IEEE 802.11 Wireless Ethernet standard more commonly known as Wi-Fi.

ifconfig Linux command for finding out a computer's IP address information.

image deployment Operating system installation that uses a complete image of a hard drive as an installation media. Helpful when installing an operating system on a large number of identical PCs.

image file Bit-by-bit image of data to be burned on CD or DVD—from one file to an entire disc—stored as a single file on a hard drive. Particularly handy when copying from CD to CD or DVD to DVD.

IMAP4 (Internet Message Access Protocol version 4) An alternative to POP3 that retrieves e-mail from an e-mail server, like POP3; IMAP uses TCP port 143.

IMC (integrated memory controller) Memory controller circuitry built into the CPU that enables faster control over things like the large L3 cache shared among multiple cores.

IMEI (International Mobile Equipment Identity) A 15-digit number used to uniquely identify a mobile device, typically a smartphone or other device that connects to a cellular network.

impact printer Uses pins and inked ribbons to print text or images on a piece of paper.

impedance Amount of resistance to an electrical signal on a wire. Relative measure of the amount of data a cable can handle.

IMSI (International Mobile Subscriber Identity) A unique number that represents the actual user associated with a particular SIM card. The IMSI is usually available from the carrier, to ensure that stolen phones are not misused. The IMSI number can be used to unlock a phone as well.

incident report Record of the details of an accident, including what happened and where it happened.

incremental backup Backs up all files that have their archive bits turned on, meaning that they have been changed since the last backup. Turns the archive bits off after the files have been backed up.

Information Technology (IT) Field of computers, their operation, and their maintenance.

infrastructure mode Wireless networking mode that uses one or more WAPs to connect the wireless network nodes to a wired network segment.

inheritance NTFS feature that passes on the same permissions in any subfolders /files resident in the original folder.

ink cartridge Small container of ink for inkjet printers.

inkjet printer Uses liquid ink, sprayed through a series of tiny jets, to print text or images on a piece of paper.

installation disc Typically a CD-ROM or DVD that holds all the necessary device drivers.

instruction set All of the machine-language commands that a particular CPU is designed to understand.

integrity Always doing the right thing.

interface Means by which a user interacts with a piece of software.

Interrupt 13 (INT13) extensions Improved type of BIOS that accepts EIDE drives up to 137 GB.

interrupt/interruption Suspension of a process, such as the execution of a computer program, caused by an event external to the computer and performed in such a way that the process can be resumed. Events of this kind include sensors monitoring laboratory equipment or a user pressing an interrupt key.

inverter Device used to convert DC current into AC. Commonly used with CCFLs in laptops and flatbed scanners.

iOS The operating system of Apple mobile devices.

IP address Numeric address of a computer connected to the Internet. An IPv4 address is made up of four octets of 8-bit binary numbers translated into their shorthand

numeric values. An IPv6 address is 128 bits long. The IP address can be broken down into a network ID and a host ID. Also called *Internet address.*

ipconfig Command-line utility for Windows servers and workstations that displays the current TCP/IP configuration of the machine. Similar to ifconfig.

IPS (in-plane switching) Display technology that replaces the older twisted nematic (TN) panels for more accurate colors and a wider viewing angle.

IPsec (Internet Protocol security) Microsoft's encryption method of choice for networks consisting of multiple networks linked by a private connection, providing transparent encryption between the server and the client.

IPv4 (Internet Protocol version 4) Internet standard protocol that provides a common layer over dissimilar networks; used to move packets among host computers and through gateways if necessary. Part of the TCP/IP protocol suite. Uses the dotted-decimal format—*x.x.x.x*. Each *x* represents an 8-bit binary number, or 0-255. Here's an example: 192.168.4.1.

IPv6 (Internet Protocol version 6) Protocol in which addresses consist of eight sets of four hexadecimal numbers, each number being a value between 0000 and FFFF, using a colon to separate the numbers. Here's an example: FEDC:BA98:7654:3210:0800:200C:00CF:1234.

IrDA (Infrared Data Association) protocol Protocol that enables communication through infrared devices, with speeds of up to 4 Mbps.

IRQ (interrupt request) Signal from a hardware device, such as a modem or a mouse, indicating that it needs the CPU's attention. In PCs, IRQs are sent along specific IRQ channels associated with a particular device. IRQ conflicts were a common problem in the past when adding expansion boards, but the plug-and-play specification has removed this headache in most cases.

ISA (Industry Standard Architecture) Design found in the original IBM PC for the slots that allowed additional hardware to be connected to the computer's motherboard. An 8-bit, 8.33-MHz expansion bus was designed by IBM for its AT computer and released to the public domain. An improved 16-bit bus was also released to the public domain. Replaced by PCI in the mid-1990s.

ISDN (integrated services digital network) CCITT (Comité Consultatif Internationale de Télégraphie et Téléphonie) standard that defines a digital method for communications to replace the current analog telephone system. ISDN is superior to POTS telephone lines because it supports a transfer rate of up to 128 Kbps for sending information from computer to computer. It also allows data and voice to share a common phone line. DSL reduced demand for ISDN substantially. (*See also* POTS.)

ISO-9660 CD format to support PC file systems on CD media. Supplanted by the Joliet format and then the UDF format.

ISO file Complete copy (or image) of a storage media device, typically used for optical discs. ISO image files typically have a file extension of .iso.

ISP (Internet service provider) Company that provides access to the Internet, usually for money.

ITX A family of motherboard form factors. Mini-ITX is the largest and the most popular of the ITX form factors but is still quite small.

iwconfig Linux command for viewing and changing wireless settings.

jack (physical connection) Part of a connector into which a plug is inserted. Also referred to as a port.

Joliet Extension of the ISO 9660 format. Most popular CD format to support PC file systems on CD media. Joliet has been supplanted by UDF.

joule Unit of energy describing (in this book) how much energy a surge suppressor can handle before it fails.

joystick Peripheral often used while playing computer games; originally intended as a multipurpose input device.

Jump List A Windows 7 menu that shows context-sensitive information about whatever is on the taskbar.

jumper Pair of small pins that can be shorted with a shunt to configure many aspects of PCs. Often used in configurations that are rarely changed, such as master/slave settings on IDE drives.

Kerberos Authentication encryption developed by MIT to enable multiple brands of servers to authenticate multiple brands of clients.

kernel Core portion of program that resides in memory and performs the most essential operating system tasks.

keyboard Input device. Three common types of keyboards exist: those that use a mini-DIN (PS/2) connection, those that use a USB connection, and those that use wireless technology.

Keychain Mac OS X password management and storage service that saves passwords for computer and non-computer environments. Also, the *iCloud Keychain* adds synchronization among any OS X and iOS devices connected to the Internet for a user account.

Knowledge Base Large collection of documents and FAQs that is maintained by Microsoft. Found on Microsoft's Web site, the Knowledge Base is an excellent place to search for assistance on most operating system problems.

KVM (keyboard, video, mouse) switch Hardware device that enables multiple computers to be viewed and controlled by a single mouse, keyboard, and screen.

LAN (local area network) Group of computers connected via cabling, radio, or infrared that use this connectivity to share resources such as printers and mass storage.

laptop Traditional clamshell portable computing device with built-in LCD monitor, keyboard, and trackpad.

laser Single-wavelength, in-phase light source that is sometimes strapped to the head of sharks by bad guys. Note to henchmen: Lasers should never be used with sea bass, no matter how ill-tempered they might be.

laser printer Electro-photographic printer in which a laser is used as the light source.

Last Known Good Configuration Option on the Advanced Startup Options menu that enables your system to revert to a previous configuration to troubleshoot and repair any major system problems.

latency Amount of delay before a device may respond to a request; most commonly used in reference to RAM.

LBA (logical block addressing) Translation (algorithm) of IDE drives promoted by Western Digital as a standardized method for breaking the 504-MB limit in IDE drives. Subsequently universally adopted by the PC industry and standard on all EIDE drives.

LCD (liquid crystal display) Type of display commonly used on portable computers. LCDs have also replaced CRTs as the display of choice for desktop computer users. LCDs use liquid crystals and electricity to produce images on the screen.

LED (light-emitting diode) Solid-state device that vibrates at luminous frequencies when current is applied.

LED monitor LCD monitor that uses LEDs instead of CCFL tubes for backlighting, creating much higher contrast ratios and image quality.

Level 1 (L1) cache First RAM cache accessed by the CPU, which stores only the absolute most-accessed programming and data used by currently running threads. Always the smallest and fastest cache on the CPU.

Level 2 (L2) cache Second RAM cache accessed by the CPU. Much larger and often slower than the L1 cache, and accessed only if the requested program/data is not in the L1 cache.

Level 3 (L3) cache Third RAM cache accessed by the CPU. Much larger and slower than the L1 and L2 caches, and accessed only if the requested program/data is not in the L2 cache.

Li-Ion (Lithium-Ion) Battery commonly used in portable computing devices. Li-Ion batteries don't suffer from the memory effects of Nickel-Cadmium (Ni-Cd) batteries and provide much more power for a greater length of time.

Library Feature in Windows 7 and later that aggregates folders from multiple locations and places them in a single, easy-to-find spot in Windows Explorer or File Explorer. Default libraries in Windows include Documents, Music, Pictures, and Videos.

Lightning An eight-pin connector, proprietary to Apple, that can be inserted without regard to orientation. Used to connect mobile devices to a power or data source.

Lightweight Directory Access Protocol (LDAP) Protocol used by many operating systems and applications to access directories.

line of sight An unobstructed view between two devices. Required for IR communications.

link light An LED on NICs, hubs, and switches that lights up to show good connection between the devices.

Linux Open-source UNIX-clone operating system.

liquid cooling A method of cooling a PC that works by running some liquid—usually water—through a metal block that sits on top of the CPU, absorbing heat. The liquid gets heated by the block, runs out of the block and into something that cools the liquid, and is then pumped through the block again.

Live DVD The Windows installation media, which loads the Windows Preinstallation Environment (WinPE) directly from disc into memory and doesn't access or modify a hard drive or solid-state drive.

Local Security Policy Windows tool used to set local security policies on an individual system.

local user account List of user names and their associated passwords with access to a system, contained in an encrypted database.

Local Users and Groups Tool enabling creation and changing of group memberships and accounts for users.

location data Information provided by a mobile device's GPS; used for mapping functions as well as for location-aware services, such as finding nearby restaurants or receiving coupons for nearby shops.

log files Files created in Windows to track the progress of certain processes.

logical drives Sections of an extended partition on a hard drive that are formatted and (usually) assigned a drive letter, each of which is presented to the user as if it were a separate drive.

logon screen First screen of the Windows interface, used to log on to the computer system.

LoJack Security feature included in some BIOS/UEFI that enables a user to track the location of a stolen PC, install a key logger, or remotely shut down the stolen computer.

loopback plug Device used during loopback tests to check the female connector on a NIC.

Low-Speed USB USB standard that runs at 1.5 Mbps. Also called USB 1.1.

LPT port Commonly referred to as a printer port; usually associated with a local parallel port.

LPX First slimline form factor; replaced by NLX form factor.

ls Linux equivalent of the dir command, which displays the contents of a directory.

lumens Unit of measure for amount of brightness on a projector or other light source.

Mac (Also **Macintosh.**) Common name for Apple Computers' flagship operating system; runs on Intel-based hardware. CompTIA refers to the operating system as *Mac OS X*. Apple calls the current operating system *OS X*, dropping the Mac altogether.

MAC (media access control) address Unique 48-bit address assigned to each network card. IEEE assigns blocks of possible addresses to various NIC manufacturers to help ensure that the address is always unique. The Data Link layer of the OSI model uses MAC addresses to locate machines.

MAC address filtering Method of limiting wireless network access based on the physical, hard-wired address of the wireless NIC of a computing device.

machine language Binary instruction code that is understood by the CPU.

maintenance kits Set of commonly replaced printer components provided by many manufacturers.

MAM (mobile application management) Software enabling a company's IT department to manage mobile apps on employees' mobile devices.

mass storage Hard drives, optical discs, removable media drives, etc.

matte Laptop screen finish that offers a good balance between richness of colors and reflections, but washes out in bright light.

MBR (master boot record) Tiny bit of code that takes control of the boot process from the system BIOS.

MCC (memory controller chip) Chip that handles memory requests from the CPU. Although once a special chip, it has been integrated into the chipset or CPU on modern computers.

MCH (Memory Controller Hub) Intel-coined name for what is now commonly called the Northbridge.

md (mkdir) Command in the command-line interface used to create directories.

MDM (mobile device management) A formalized structure that enables an organization to account for all the different types of devices used to process, store, transmit, and receive organizational data.

mega- Prefix that stands for the binary quantity 1,048,576 (2^{20}) or the decimal quantity of 1,000,000. One megabyte is 1,048,576 bytes. One megahertz, however, is a million hertz. Sometimes shortened to *Meg*, as in "a 286 has an address space of 16 Megs."

megapixel Term used typically in reference to digital cameras and their ability to capture data.

memory Device or medium for temporary storage of programs and data during program execution. Synonymous with storage, although it most frequently refers to the internal storage of a computer that can be directly addressed by operating instructions. A computer's temporary storage capacity is measured in kilobytes (KB), megabytes (MB), or gigabytes (GB) of RAM (random-access memory). Long-term data storage on hard drives and solid-state drives is also measured in megabytes, gigabytes, and terabytes.

memory addressing Taking memory address from system RAM and using it to address non-system RAM or ROM so the CPU can access it.

Memory Stick Sony's flash memory card format; rarely seen outside of Sony devices.

mesh topology Network topology where each computer has a dedicated line to every other computer, most often used in wireless networks.

Metro UI The original name for the Windows 8 user interface. Due to legal concerns, it was rebranded the "Modern UI."

MFT (master file table) Enhanced file allocation table used by NTFS. (*See also* FAT.)

Micro Secure Digital (MicroSD) The smallest form factor of the SD flash memory standard. Often used in mobile devices.

micro USB USB connector commonly found on Android phones.

microATX (µATX) Variation of the ATX form factor, which uses the ATX power supply. MicroATX motherboards are generally smaller than their ATX counterparts but retain all the same functionality.

microBTX Variation of the BTX form factor. MicroBTX motherboards are generally smaller than their BTX counterparts but retain all the same functionality.

microdrive Tiny hard drives using the CompactFlash form factor. (*See also* CompactFlash (CF).)

microphone An input device for recording audio.

microprocessor "Brain" of a computer. Primary computer chip that determines relative speed and capabilities of the computer. Also called CPU.

Microsoft Certified IT Professional (MCITP) An advanced IT certification specifically covering Microsoft products.

MIDI (musical instrument digital interface) Interface between a computer and a device for simulating musical instruments. Rather than sending large sound samples, a computer can simply send "instructions" to the instrument describing pitch, tone, and duration of a sound. MIDI files are therefore very efficient. Because a MIDI file is made up of a set of instructions rather than a copy of the sound, modifying each component of the file is easy. Additionally, it is possible to program many channels, or "voices," of music to be played simultaneously, creating symphonic sound.

MIDI-enabled device External device that enables you to input digital sound information in the MIDI format; for example, a MIDI keyboard (the piano kind).

migration Moving users from one operating system or hard drive to another.

MIMO (multiple in/multiple out) Feature of 802.11n devices that enables the simultaneous connection of up to four antennas, greatly increasing throughput. 802.11ac also uses MU-MIMO, which gives a WAP the capability to broadcast to multiple users simultaneously.

mini-audio connector Very popular, 1/8-inch-diameter connector used to transmit two audio signals; perfect for stereo sound.

mini connector One type of power connector from a PC power supply unit. Supplies 5 and 12 volts to peripherals. Also known as a floppy connector.

mini-DIN Small connection most commonly used for keyboards and mice. Many modern systems implement USB in place of mini-DIN connections. Also called *PS/2*.

Mini-ITX The largest and the most popular of the three ITX form factors. At a miniscule 6.7 by 6.7 inches, Mini-ITX competes with microATX and proprietary small form factor (SFF) motherboards.

Mini-PCI Specialized form of PCI designed for use in laptops.

Mini-PCIe Specialized form of PCIe designed for use in laptops.

mini power connector Connector used to provide power to floppy disk drives.

Mini Secure Digital (MiniSD) The medium-sized form factor of the SD flash memory standard.

mini USB Smaller USB connector often found on digital cameras.

mirror set A type of mirrored volume created with RAID 1. (*See also* mirroring.)

mirrored volume Volume that is mirrored on another volume. (*See also* mirroring.)

mirroring Reading and writing data at the same time to two drives for fault tolerance purposes. Considered RAID level 1. Also called *drive mirroring*.

Mission Control A feature of Mac OS X that enables switching between open applications, windows, and more.

mkdir *See* md.

MMC (Microsoft Management Console) Means of managing a system, introduced by Microsoft with Windows 2000. The MMC enables an administrator to customize management tools by picking and choosing from a list of snap-ins. Available snap-ins include Device Manager, Users and Groups, and Computer Management.

MMX (multimedia extensions) Specific CPU instructions that enable a CPU to handle many multimedia functions, such as digital signal processing. Introduced with the Pentium CPU, these instructions are used on all ×86 CPUs.

mode Any single combination of resolution and color depth set for a system.

modem (modulator/demodulator) Device that converts a digital bit stream into an analog signal (modulation) and converts incoming analog signals back into digital signals (demodulation). An analog communications channel is typically a telephone line, and analog signals are typically sounds.

module Small circuit board that DRAM chips are attached to. Also known as a "stick."

Molex connector Computer power connector used by optical drives, hard drives, and case fans. Keyed to prevent it from being inserted into a power port improperly.

monaural Describes recording tracks from one source (microphone) as opposed to stereo, which uses two sources.

monitor Screen that displays data from a PC. Can use either a cathode ray tube (CRT) or a liquid crystal display (LCD) to display images.

motherboard Flat piece of circuit board that resides inside your computer case and has a number of connectors on it. Every device in a PC connects directly or indirectly to the motherboard, including CPU, RAM, hard drives, optical drives, keyboard, mouse, and video cards.

motherboard book Valuable resource when installing a new motherboard. Normally lists all the specifications about a motherboard, including the type of memory and type of CPU usable with the motherboard.

mount point Drive that functions like a folder mounted into another drive.

mouse Input device that enables users to manipulate a cursor on the screen to select items.

move Command in the command-line interface used to move a file from one location to another.

MP3 Short for MPEG Audio Layer 3, a type of compression used specifically for turning high-quality digital audio files into much smaller, yet similar-sounding, files.

MPA (Microsoft Product Activation) Anti-piracy measure introduced by Microsoft with the release of Windows XP. MPA prevents unauthorized use of Microsoft software by requiring the user to activate the software with special Microsoft activation servers.

MPEG-2 Moving Pictures Experts Group standard of video and audio compression offering resolutions up to 1280 × 720 at 60 frames per second.

MPEG-4 Moving Pictures Experts Group standard of video and audio compression offering improved compression over MPEG-2.

MS-CHAP Microsoft's variation of the Challenge Handshake Authentication Protocol that uses a slightly more advanced encryption protocol. Windows Vista uses MS-CHAP v2 (version 2), and does not support MS-CHAP v1 (version 1).

msconfig (System Configuration utility) Executable file that runs the Windows System Configuration utility, which enables users to configure a system's boot files and critical system files. Often used for the name of the utility, as in "just run msconfig."

MSDS (material safety data sheet) Standardized form that provides detailed information about potential environmental hazards and proper disposal methods associated with various computing components.

msinfo32 Provides information about hardware resources, components, and the software environment. Also known as System Information.

multiboot installation OS installation in which multiple operating systems are installed on a single machine.

multi rail A power supply configuration where the current is split into multiple pathways, each with a maximum capacity and its own Over Current Protection circuitry. CompTIA calls two-rail versions of this technology "dual rail."

multicore processing Using two or more execution cores on one CPU die to divide up work independently of the OS.

multifactor authentication Authentication schema requiring more than one unique authentication method. For example, a password and a fingerprint.

multimedia extensions (MMX) Originally an Intel CPU enhancement designed for graphics-intensive applications (such as games). It was never embraced but eventually led to improvements in how CPUs handle graphics.

multimeter Device used to measure voltage, amperage, and resistance.

multiple Desktops A GUI feature that enables a computer to have more than one Desktop, each with its own icons and background. Mac OS X supports multiple Desktops with Spaces. Most Linux distros use multiple Desktops, often called workspaces. Microsoft introduced the feature with Windows 10.

multisession drive Recordable CD drive capable of burning multiple sessions onto a single recordable disc. A multisession drive also can close a CD-R so that no further tracks can be written to it.

multitasking Process of running multiple programs or tasks on the same computer at the same time.

multi-touch Input method on many smartphones and tablets that enables you to use multiple fingers to do all sorts of fun things, such as using two fingers to scroll or swipe to another screen or desktop.

music CD-R CD using a special format for home recorders. Music CD-R makers pay a small royalty to avoid illegal music duplication.

mv The move command in Linux and Mac OS X.

My Computer An applet that enables users to access a complete listing of all fixed and removable drives contained within a system and to view/manage configuration properties of the computer. Also, an aspect of Windows Explorer.

Nano-ITX A 4.7 inch by 4.7 inch variation of the ITX form factor.

NAT (Network Address Translation) A means of translating a system's IP address into another IP address before sending it out to a larger network. NAT manifests itself by a NAT program that runs on a system or a router. A network using NAT provides the systems on the network with private IP addresses. The system running the NAT software has two interfaces: one connected to the network and the other connected to the larger network.

The NAT program takes packets from the client systems bound for the larger network and translates their internal private IP addresses to its own public IP address, enabling many systems to share a single IP address.

native resolution Resolution on an LCD monitor that matches the physical pixels on the screen.

navigation pane Windows 7's name for the Folders list in Windows Explorer.

net Command in Windows that enables users to view a network without knowing the names of the other computers on that network.

NetBIOS (Network Basic Input/Output System) Protocol that operates at the Session layer of the OSI seven-layer model. This protocol creates and manages connections based on the names of the computers involved.

NetBIOS Extended User Interface (NetBEUI) The default networking protocol for early versions of Windows.

netbook Small, low-power laptop used primarily for Web browsing.

network Collection of two or more computers interconnected by telephone lines, coaxial cables, satellite links, radio, and/or some other communication technique. Group of computers that are connected and that communicate with one another for a common purpose.

Network Interface in Windows Vista and Windows 7 for Windows Explorer; displays networked computers and other devices, such as network printers.

network attached storage (NAS) A device that attaches to a network for the sole purpose of storing and sharing files.

network connection A method for connecting two or more computers together. (*See also* network.)

network ID Logical number that identifies the network on which a device or machine exists. This number exists in TCP/IP and other network protocol suites.

network printer Printer that connects directly to a network.

network protocol Software that takes the incoming data received by the network card, keeps it organized, sends it to the application that needs it, and then takes outgoing data from the application and hands it to the NIC to be sent out over the network.

network technology A practical application of a topology and other critical standards to provide a method to get data from one computer to another on a network. It defines many aspects of a network, from the topology, to the frame type, to the cabling and connectors used.

NFC (near field communication) Mobile technology that enables short-range wireless communication between mobile devices. Now used for mobile payment technology such as Apple Pay and Google Wallet.

NIC (network interface card or controller) Expansion card or motherboard interface that enables a PC to connect to a network via a network cable. A *wireless NIC* enables connection via radio waves rather than a physical cable.

Ni-Cd (Nickel-Cadmium) Battery used in the first portable PCs. Heavy and inefficient, these batteries also suffered from a memory effect that could drastically shorten the overall life of the battery. (*See also* Ni-MH, Li-Ion.)

Ni-MH (Nickel-Metal Hydride) Battery used in early portable PCs. Ni-MH batteries had fewer issues with the memory effect than Ni-Cd batteries. Ni-MH batteries in computing devices have been replaced by Lithium-Ion batteries. (*See also* Ni-Cd, Li-Ion.)

nit Value used to measure the brightness of an LCD display. A typical LCD display has a brightness of between 100 and 400 nits.

NLQ (near-letter quality) Designation for dot-matrix printers that use 24-pin printheads.

NLX Second form factor for slimline systems. Replaced the earlier LPX form factor. (NLX apparently stands for nothing; it's just a cool grouping of letters.)

NMI (non-maskable interrupt) Interrupt code sent to the processor that cannot be ignored. Typically manifested as a BSoD.

NNTP (Network News Transfer Protocol) Protocol run by news servers that enable newsgroups.

non-system disk or disk error Error that occurs during the boot process. Common causes for this error are leaving a nonbootable floppy disk, CD, USB stick, or other media in the system while the computer is booting.

nonvolatile memory Storage device that retains data even if power is removed; typically refers to a ROM or flash ROM chip, but also could be applied to hard drives, optical media, and other storage devices.

normal backup Full backup of every selected file on a system. Turns off the archive bit after the backup.

Northbridge Chip that connects a CPU to memory, the PCI bus, Level 2 cache, and high-speed graphics. Communicates with the CPU through the frontside bus. Newer CPUs feature an integrated Northbridge.

notebook *See* laptop.

notification area Contains icons representing background processes, the system clock, and volume control. Located by default at the right edge of the Windows taskbar. Many users call this area the system tray.

nslookup Command-line program in Windows used to determine exactly what information the DNS server is providing about a specific host name.

ntdetect.com One of the critical Windows NT/2000/XP startup files.

NTFS (New Technology File System) Robust and secure file system introduced by Microsoft with Windows NT. NTFS provides an amazing array of configuration options for user access and security. Users can be granted access to data on a file-by-file basis. NTFS enables object-level security, long filename support, compression, and encryption.

NTFS permissions Restrictions that determine the amount of access given to a particular user on a system using NTFS.

ntldr (NT Loader) Windows NT/2000/XP boot file. Launched by the MBR or MFT, ntldr looks at the boot.ini configuration file for any installed operating systems.

NVIDIA Corporation One of the foremost manufacturers of graphics cards and chipsets.

NVMe (Non-Volatile Memory Express) SSD technology that supports a communication connection between the operating system and the SSD directly through a PCIe bus lane, reducing latency and taking full advantage of the speeds of high-end SSDs. NVMe SSDs come in a couple of formats, such as an add-on expansion card and a 2.5-inch drive, like the SATA drives for portables. NVMe drives are a lot more expensive currently than other SSDs, but offer much higher speeds.

NX bit Technology that enables the CPU to protect certain sections of memory. This feature, coupled with implementation by the operating system, stops malicious attacks from getting to essential operating system files. Microsoft calls the feature Data Execution Prevention (DEP).

object System component that is given a set of characteristics and can be managed by the operating system as a single entity.

object access auditing Feature of Event Viewer's Security section that creates an entry in the Security Log when certain objects are accessed, such as a file or folder.

ODBC Data Source Administrator Programming tool for configuring the Open Database Connectivity (ODBC) coding standard. Data Source Administrator enables you to create and manage entries called Data Source Names (DSNs) that point OBDC to a database. DSNs are used by ODBC-aware applications to query ODBC to find their databases.

offline files Windows 7/8/8.1/10 feature that enables storing a local, duplicate copy of files and folders on a hard drive. When the laptop connects to a network, Windows automatically syncs those offline files with the files and folders on a file server or other PC.

ohm(s) Electronic measurement of a cable's impedance.

open source Software environment that is not controlled by a central creator or distributer.

OLED (organic light-emitting diode) Display technology where an organic compound provides the light for the screen, thus eliminating the need for a backlight or inverter.

OpenGL One of two popular APIs used today for video cards. Originally written for UNIX systems but now ported to Windows and Apple systems. (*See also* DirectX.)

optical disc/media Types of data discs (such as DVDs, CDs, BDs, etc.) that are read by a laser.

optical drive Drive used to read/write to optical discs, such as CDs or DVDs.

optical mouse Pointing device that uses light rather than electronic sensors to determine movement and direction the mouse is being moved.

optical resolution Resolution a scanner can achieve mechanically. Most scanners use software to enhance this ability.

optical zoom Mechanical ability of most cameras to "zoom" in as opposed to the digital ability.

option ROM Alternative way of telling the system how to talk to a piece of hardware. Option ROM stores BIOS for the card in a chip on the card itself.

OS (operating system) Series of programs and code that creates an interface so users can interact with a system's hardware; for example, Windows, Mac OS X, and Linux.

OS X Current operating system on Apple Macintosh computers. Based on a UNIX core, early versions of OS X ran on Motorola-based hardware; current versions run on Intel-based hardware. The X is pronounced "ten" rather than "ex."

OSI seven-layer model Architecture model based on the OSI protocol suite that defines and standardizes the flow of data between computers. The seven layers are:

> **Layer 1, Physical layer** Defines hardware connections and turns binary into physical pulses (electrical or light). Repeaters and hubs operate at the Physical layer.
>
> **Layer 2, Data Link layer** Identifies devices on the Physical layer. MAC addresses are part of the Data Link layer. Bridges operate at the Data Link layer.
>
> **Layer 3, Network layer** Moves packets between computers on different networks. Routers operate at the Network layer. IP and IPX operate at the Network layer.
>
> **Layer 4, Transport layer** Breaks data down into manageable chunks. TCP, UDP, SPX, and NetBEUI operate at the Transport layer.
>
> **Layer 5, Session layer** Manages connections between machines. NetBIOS and Sockets operate at the Session layer.
>
> **Layer 6, Presentation layer** Can also manage data encryption; hides the differences between various types of computer systems.
>
> **Layer 7, Application layer** Provides tools for programs to use to access the network (and the lower layers). HTTP, FTP, SMTP, and POP3 are all examples of protocols that operate at the Application layer.

overclocking To run a CPU or video processor faster than its rated speed.

P1 power connector Provides power to ATX motherboards; 20-pin with original ATX motherboards, 24-pin on current units.

P4 power connector Provides additional 12-volt power for the CPU to motherboards that support Pentium 4 and later processors.

P8 and P9 connectors Provide power to old, AT-style motherboards.

PaaS (Platform as a Service) Cloud-based virtual server(s). These virtualized platforms give programmers tools needed to deploy, administer, and maintain a Web application.

packet Basic component of communication over a network. Group of bits of fixed maximum size and well-defined format that is switched and transmitted as a single entity through a network. Contains source and destination address, data, and control information.

page fault Minor memory-addressing error.

page file Portion of the hard drive set aside by Windows to act like RAM. Also known as *virtual memory* or *swap file*.

PAN (personal area network) Small wireless network created with Bluetooth technology and intended to link computers and other peripheral devices.

parallel execution When a multicore CPU processes more than one thread.

parallel port Connection for the synchronous, high-speed flow of data along parallel lines to a device, usually a printer.

Parental Controls Tool to enable monitoring and limiting of user activities; designed for parents to control the content their children can access.

parity Method of error detection where a small group of bits being transferred is compared to a single parity bit set to make the total bits odd or even. Receiving device reads the parity bit and determines if the data is valid, based on the oddness or evenness of the parity bit.

parity RAM Earliest form of error-detecting RAM; stored an extra bit (called the parity bit) to verify the data.

partition Section of the storage area of a hard disk. Created during initial preparation of the hard disk, before the disk is formatted.

partition boot table Sector of a partition that stores information important to its partition, such as the location of the OS boot files. Responsible for loading the OS on a partition.

partition table Table located in the boot sector of a hard drive that lists every partition on the disk that contains a valid operating system.

partitioning Electronically subdividing a physical hard drive into groups called partitions (or volumes).

passcode lock Mobile device security feature that requires you to type in a series of letters, numbers, or motion patterns to unlock the mobile device each time you press the power button.

passive matrix Technology for producing colors in LCD monitors by varying voltages across wire matrices to produce red, green, or blue dots.

passwd Linux command for changing a user's password.

password Key used to verify a user's identity on a secure computer or network.

Password Authentication Protocol (PAP) Oldest and most basic form of authentication. Also the least safe, because it sends all passwords in clear text.

password reset disk External storage media such as a floppy disk or USB flash drive with which users can recover a lost password without losing access to any encrypted, or password-protected, data. The password reset disk must be created proactively; if a user loses a password and did not already make a reset disk, it will be of no help to create one after the loss.

PATA (parallel ATA) Implementation that integrates the controller on the disk drive itself. (*See also* ATA, IDE, SATA.)

patch Small piece of software released by a software manufacturer to correct a flaw or problem with a particular piece of software.

patch cables Short (2 to 5 feet) UTP cables that connect patch panels to a switch or router.

patch panel A panel containing a row of female connectors (ports) that terminate the horizontal cabling in the equipment room. Patch panels facilitate cabling organization and provide protection to horizontal cabling.

path Route the operating system must follow to find an executable program stored in a subfolder.

PC Card Credit card–sized adapter card that adds functionality in older laptops and other computer devices. PC Cards come in 16-bit and CardBus parallel format and ExpressCard serial format. (*See also* PCMCIA.)

PC tech Someone with computer skills who works on computers.

PCI (Peripheral Component Interconnect) Design architecture for the expansion bus on the computer motherboard that enables system components to be added to the computer. Local bus standard, meaning that devices added to a computer through this port will use the processor at the motherboard's full speed (up to 33 MHz) rather than at the slower 8-MHz speed of the regular bus. Moves data 32 or 64 bits at a time rather than the 8 or 16 bits the older ISA buses supported.

PCIe (PCI Express) Serialized successor to PCI and AGP that uses the concept of individual data paths called lanes. May use any number of lanes, although a single lane (×1) and 16 lanes (×16) are the most common on motherboards.

PCIe 6/8-pin power connector Connector on some power supplies for powering a dedicated graphics card.

PCI-X (PCI Extended) Enhanced version of PCI, 64 bits wide. Typically seen in servers and high-end systems.

PCL (printer control language) Printer control language created by Hewlett-Packard and used on a broad cross section of printers.

PCM (pulse code modulation) Sound format developed in the 1960s to carry telephone calls over the first digital lines.

PCMCIA (Personal Computer Memory Card International Association) Consortium of computer manufacturers who devised the PC Card standard for credit card–sized adapter cards that add functionality in older notebook computers and other computer devices. (*See also* PC Card.)

Pearson VUE Company that administers the CompTIA A+ exams.

peer-to-peer network Network in which each machine can act as both a client and a server.

pen-based computing Input method used by many PDAs that combines handwriting recognition with modified mouse functions, usually in the form of a pen-like stylus.

Pentium Name given to the fifth and later generations of Intel microprocessors; original had a 32-bit address bus, 64-bit external data bus, and dual pipelining. Also used for subsequent generations of Intel processors—the Pentium Pro, Pentium II, Pentium III, and Pentium 4. Currently used as a budget label for Intel CPUs.

Performance Tab in Task Manager that tracks PC performance.

Performance Information and Tools Applet that provides a relative feel for how your computer stacks up against other systems using the Windows Experience Index.

Performance Logs and Alerts Snap-in enabling the creation of a written record of most everything that happens on the system.

Performance Monitor Windows tool for observing a computer's performance.

Performance Options Tool enabling users to configure CPU, RAM, and virtual memory settings.

peripheral Any device that connects to the system unit.

permission propagation Term to describe what happens to permissions on an object when you move or copy it.

persistence Phosphors used in CRT screens continuing to glow after being struck by electrons, long enough for the human eye to register the glowing effect. Glowing too long makes the images smeary, and too little makes them flicker.

personal safety Keeping yourself away from harm.

Personalization applet Windows Vista applet with which users can change display settings such as resolution, refresh rate, color depth, and desktop features. The Windows 7 version focuses on managing themes, desktop icons, mouse pointers, and account pictures. (For other options, *see* Display.)

PGA (pin grid array) Arrangement of a large number of pins extending from the bottom of the CPU package. There are many variations on PGA.

phablet Portmanteau of "phone" and "tablet." Colloquial term for a large phone. (And yes, I had to look up "portmanteau" as well. Love my editors!)

Phillips-head screwdriver Most important part of a PC tech's toolkit.

phishing The act of trying to get people to give their usernames, passwords, or other security information by pretending to be someone else electronically.

Phoenix Technologies Major producer of BIOS software for motherboards.

phosphor Electro-fluorescent material that coats the inside face of a cathode ray tube (CRT). After being hit with an electron, it glows for a fraction of a second.

photosensitive drum Aluminum cylinder coated with particles of photosensitive compounds. Used in a laser printer and often contained within the toner cartridge.

Pico-ITX A 3.8- by 2.8-inch version of the ITX form factor.

pin 1 Designator used to ensure proper alignment of floppy drive and hard drive connectors.

pinch Multi-touch gesture that enables you to make an image bigger or smaller.

pinned application Windows method of attaching programs to the taskbar. A pinned application gets a permanent icon displayed on the taskbar.

ping (packet Internet groper) Slang term for a small network message (ICMP ECHO) sent by a computer to check for the presence and aliveness of another. Used to verify the presence of another system. Also, the command used at a prompt to ping a computer.

pinwheel of death Mac OS X indicator that is the equivalent of a Windows unresponsive application; in this case, a spinning rainbow wheel.

PIO (programmed I/O) mode Series of speed standards created by the Small Form Factor Committee for the use of PIO by hard drives. Modes range from PIO mode 0 to PIO mode 4.

pipeline Processing methodology where multiple calculations take place simultaneously by being broken into a series of steps. Often used in CPUs and video processors.

pixel (picture element) In computer graphics, smallest element of a display space that can be independently assigned color or intensity.

PKI (public key infrastructure) Authentication schema where public keys are exchanged between all parties using digital certificates, enabling secure communication over public networks.

Play Store Storefront where Android users can purchase and download apps and digital media.

plug Hardware connection with some sort of projection that connects to a port.

plug and play (PnP) Combination of smart PCs, smart devices, and smart operating systems that automatically configure all necessary system resources and ports when you install a new peripheral device.

polygons Multisided shapes used in 3-D rendering of objects. In computers, video cards draw large numbers of triangles and connect them to form polygons.

polymorph virus Virus that attempts to change its signature to prevent detection by antivirus programs, usually by continually scrambling a bit of useless code.

POP3 (Post Office Protocol 3) One of the two protocols that receive e-mail from SMTP servers. POP3 uses TCP port 110. While historically most e-mail clients used this protocol, the IMAP4 e-mail protocol is now more common.

pop-up Irritating browser window that appears automatically when you visit a Web site.

port (networking) In networking, the number used to identify the requested service (such as SMTP or FTP) when connecting to a TCP/IP host. Examples: 80 (HTTP), 443, (HTTPS), 21 (FTP), 23 (Telnet), 25 (SMTP), 110 (POP3), 143 (IMAP), and 3389 (RDP).

port (physical connection) Part of a connector into which a plug is inserted. Physical ports are also referred to as jacks.

port forwarding Preventing the passage of any IP packets through any ports other than the ones prescribed by the system administrator.

port replicator Device that plugs into a USB port or other specialized port and offers common PC ports, such as serial, parallel, USB, network, and PS/2. Plugging a laptop into a port replicator can instantly connect the computer to nonportable components such as a printer, scanner, monitor, or full-sized keyboard. Port replicators are typically used at home or in the office with the nonportable equipment already connected.

port triggering Router function that enables a computer to open an incoming connection to one computer automatically based on a specific outgoing connection.

positional audio Range of commands for a sound card to place a sound anywhere in 3-D space.

POST (power-on self test) Basic diagnostic routine completed by a system at the beginning of the boot process to make sure a display adapter and the system's memory

are installed; it then searches for an operating system. If it finds one, it hands over control of the machine to the OS.

POST card Device installed into a motherboard expansion slot that assists in troubleshooting boot problems by providing a two-digit code indicating the stop of the boot process where the problem is occurring.

PostScript Language defined by Adobe Systems, Inc., for describing how to create an image on a page. The description is independent of the resolution of the device that will actually create the image. It includes a technology for defining the shape of a font and creating a raster image at many different resolutions and sizes.

power conditioning Ensuring and adjusting incoming AC wall power to as close to standard as possible. Most UPS devices provide power conditioning.

power good wire Used to wake up the CPU after the power supply has tested for proper voltage.

Power over Ethernet (PoE) Technology that provides power and data transmission through a single network cable.

power options Windows feature that enables better control over power use by customizing a balanced, power saver, or high-performance power plan.

power supply fan Small fan located in a system power supply that draws warm air from inside the power supply and exhausts it to the outside.

power supply unit Provides the electrical power for a PC. Converts standard AC power into various voltages of DC electricity in a PC.

Power Users group After Administrator/Administrators, the second most powerful account and group type in Windows. Power users have differing capabilities in different versions of Windows.

PowerShell *See* Windows PowerShell.

ppm (pages per minute) Speed of a printer.

PPP (Point-to-Point Protocol) Enables a computer to connect to the Internet through a dial-in connection and enjoy most of the benefits of a direct connection.

preboot execution environment (PXE) Technology that enables a PC to boot without any local storage by retrieving an OS from a server over a network.

primary corona Wire that is located near the photosensitive drum in a laser printer and is charged with extremely high voltage to form an electric field, enabling voltage to pass to the photosensitive drum, thus charging the photosensitive particles on the surface of the drum. Also called the *primary charge roller*.

primary partition Partition on a Windows hard drive that can store a bootable operating system.

print resolution Quality of a print image.

print spooler Area of memory that queues up print jobs that the printer will handle sequentially.

printed circuit board (PCB) Copper etched onto a nonconductive material and then coated with some sort of epoxy for strength.

printer Output device that can print text or illustrations on paper. Microsoft uses the term to refer to the software that controls the physical print device.

printhead Case that holds the printwires in a dot-matrix printer.

printwires Grid of tiny pins in a dot-matrix printer that strike an inked printer ribbon to produce images on paper.

PRL (Preferred Roaming List) A list that is occasionally and automatically updated to a phone's firmware by the carrier so that the phone will be configured with a particular carrier's networks and frequencies, in a priority order, that it should search for when it can't locate its home carrier network.

Problem Reports and Solutions Control Panel applet in Windows Vista that lists all Windows Error Reporting issues (plus a few easy-to-check items like firewall and anti-malware status).

Processes Tab in Task Manager that lists all running processes on a system. Frequently a handy tool for ending buggy or unresponsive processes.

processing The second step of the computing process, where the CPU completes the tasks that the user's input has given it.

product key Code used during installation to verify legitimacy of the software.

profile A list of settings that a calibration device creates when calibrating monitors and printers.

program/programming Series of binary electronic commands sent to a CPU to get work done.

Programs and Features Windows Control Panel applet; enables uninstalling or changing program options and altering Windows features.

projector Device for projecting video images from PCs or other video sources, usually for audience presentations. Available in front- and rearview displays.

prompt A character or message provided by an operating system or program to indicate that it is ready to accept input.

proprietary Technology unique to a particular vendor.

proprietary crash screen A screen, differing between operating systems, that indicates an NMI.

protective cover A case or sleeve that protects a mobile device from physical damage.

protocol Agreement that governs the procedures used to exchange information between cooperating entities. Usually includes how much information is to be sent, how often it is to be sent, how to recover from transmission errors, and who is to receive the information.

proxy server Device that fetches Internet resources for a client without exposing that client directly to the Internet. Usually accepts requests for HTTP, FTP, POP3, and SMTP resources. Often caches, or stores, a copy of the requested resource for later use. Common security feature in the corporate world.

ps Linux command for listing all processes running on the computer.

Public folder Folder that all users can access and share with all other users on the system or network.

punchdown tool A specialized tool for connecting UTP wires to a punchdown block.

pwd Linux command that displays the user's current path.

quad-channel architecture Feature similar to dual-channel RAM, but requiring four sticks instead of two.

Quality of Service (QoS) Policies that control how much bandwidth a protocol, PC, user, VLAN, or IP address may use.

queue Area where objects wait their turn to be processed. Example: the print queue, where print jobs wait until it is their turn to be printed.

Quick Launch toolbar Enables a user to launch commonly used programs with a single click in Windows.

QVGA Video display mode of 320 × 240.

RAID (redundant array of independent [or inexpensive] disks) Method for creating a fault-tolerant storage system. RAID uses multiple hard drives in various configurations to offer differing levels of speed/data redundancy.

RAID 0 Uses byte-level striping and provides no fault tolerance.

RAID 1 Uses mirroring or duplexing for increased data redundancy.

RAID 5 Uses block-level and parity data striping. Requires three or more drives.

RAID 6 Disk striping with extra parity. Like RAID 5, but with more parity data. Requires five or more drives, but you can lose up to two drives at once and your data is still protected.

RAID 0+1 A RAID 0 configuration created by combining two RAID 1s. Provides both speed and redundancy, but requires at least four disks.

RAID 10 The opposite of RAID 0+1, two mirrored RAID 0 configurations. Also provides both speed and redundancy, and also requires four disks.

rails Separate DC voltage paths within an ATX power supply.

RAM (random access memory) Memory that can be accessed at random—that is, memory which you can write to or read from without touching the preceding address. This term is often used to mean a computer's main memory.

RAMDAC (random access memory digital-to-analog converter) Circuitry used on video cards that support analog monitors to convert the digital video data to analog.

Raspberry Pi Latest generation of ultra-small, ARM-based computer motherboards with support for many operating systems and peripherals.

raster image Pattern of dots representing what the final product should look like.

raster line Horizontal pattern of lines that forms an image on the monitor screen.

rd (rmdir) Command in the command-line interface used to remove directories.

read-only attribute File attribute that does not allow a file to be altered or modified. Helpful when protecting system files that should not be edited.

ReadyBoost Windows feature enabling the use of flash media as dedicated virtual memory.

rearview projector Projector that shoots an image onto a screen from the rear. Rearview projectors are usually self-enclosed and very popular for TVs, but are virtually unheard of in the PC world.

reciprocity *See* Ethic of Reciprocity.

Recovery Console Command-line interface boot mode for Windows that is used to repair a Windows XP system suffering from massive OS corruption or other problems.

Recycle Bin Location to which files are moved when they are deleted from a modern Windows system. To permanently remove files from a system, they must be emptied from the Recycle Bin.

Refresh your PC Windows RE option in Windows 8 and later that rebuilds the OS, but preserves all user files and settings and any applications purchased from the Windows Store. Note well: Refresh deletes every other application on a system.

regedit.exe Program used to edit the Windows Registry.

region code Encoding that restricts you from playing DVD or Blu-ray Disc movies on a player that doesn't share the same region code.

register Storage area inside the CPU used by the onboard logic to perform calculations. CPUs have many registers to perform different functions.

registered RAM *See* buffered/registered DRAM.

registration Usually optional process that identifies the legal owner/user of the product to the supplier.

Registry Complex binary file used to store configuration data about a particular Windows system. To edit the Registry, users can use the applets found in the Control Panel or regedit.exe or regedt32.exe.

regsvr32 In contrast with regedit.exe, the regsvr32 command can modify the Registry in only one way, adding (or *registering*) dynamic link library (DLL) files as command components in the Registry.

Reliability and Performance Monitor Windows Vista's extended Performance applet.

remediation Repairing damage caused by a virus.

remnant Potentially recoverable data on a hard drive that remains despite formatting or deleting.

Remote Assistance Feature of Windows that enables users to give anyone control of his or her desktop over the Internet.

Remote Desktop Windows tool used to enable a local system to graphically access the desktop of a remote system.

Remote Desktop Protocol Protocol used for Microsoft's Remote Desktop tool. Uses port 3389.

remote network installation A common method of OS installation where the source files are placed in a shared directory on a network server. Then, whenever a tech needs to install a new OS, he or she can boot the computer, connect to the source location on the network, and start the installation from there.

removable media Any storage on a computer that can be easily removed. For example, optical discs, flash drives, or memory cards.

ren (rename) Command in the command-line interface used to rename files and folders.

Reset your PC Windows RE option in Windows 8 and later that nukes the system—deleting all apps, programs, user files, and user settings—and presents a fresh installation of Windows. Use Reset as the last resort when troubleshooting a PC. And back up data first, if possible.

resistance Difficulty in making electricity flow through a material, measured in ohms.

resistive touchscreen Type of touchscreen that responds to the pressure applied to the screen.

resistor Any material or device that impedes the flow of electrons. Electronic resistors measure their resistance (impedance) in ohms. (*See* ohm(s).)

resolution Measurement for monitors and printers expressed in horizontal and vertical dots or pixels. Higher resolutions provide sharper details and thus display better-looking images.

resources Data and services of a PC.

respect How all techs should treat their customers.

response rate Time it takes for all of the sub-pixels on the panel to go from pure black to pure white and back again.

restore point System snapshot created by the System Restore utility that is used to restore a malfunctioning system. (*See also* System Restore.)

RET (resolution enhancement technology) Technology that uses small dots to smooth out jagged edges that are typical of printers without RET, producing a higher-quality print job.

RFI (radio frequency interference) Another form of electrical interference caused by radio wave–emitting devices, such as cell phones, wireless network cards, and microwave ovens.

RG-6 Coaxial cabling used for cable television. It has a 75-ohm impedance and uses an F-type connector.

RG-58 Coaxial cabling used for 10Base2 networks.

ring Network topology where the computers form a circle and all data flows in one direction only.

RIP (raster image processor) Component in a printer that translates the raster image into commands for the printer.

riser card Special adapter card, usually inserted into a special slot on a motherboard, that changes the orientation of expansion cards relative to the motherboard. Riser cards are used extensively in slimline computers to keep total depth and height of the system to a minimum. Sometimes called a daughterboard.

RJ (registered jack) connector UTP cable connector, used for both telephone and network connections. RJ-11 is a connector for four-wire UTP; usually found in telephone connections. RJ-45 is a connector for eight-wire UTP; usually found in network connections.

RJ-11 *See* RJ (registered jack) connector.

RJ-45 *See* RJ (registered jack) connector.

rm Linux command for deleting files.

rmdir *See* rd (rmdir).

robocopy Powerful command-line utility for copying files and directories, even over a network.

ROM (read-only memory) Generic term for nonvolatile memory that can be read from but not written to. This means that code and data stored in ROM cannot be corrupted by accidental erasure. Additionally, ROM retains its data when power is removed, which makes it the perfect medium for storing BIOS data or information such as scientific constants.

root directory Directory that contains all other directories.

root keys Five main categories in the Windows Registry:
HKEY_CLASSES_ROOT
HKEY_CURRENT_USER
HKEY_USERS
HKEY_LOCAL_MACHINE
HKEY_CURRENT_CONFIG

router Device connecting separate networks; forwards a packet from one network to another based on the network address for the protocol being used. For example, an IP router looks only at the IP network number. Routers operate at Layer 3 (Network) of the OSI seven-layer model.

RS-232 Standard port recommended by the Electronics Industry Association (EIA) for serial devices.

run A single piece of installed horizontal cabling.

Run dialog box Command box in which users can enter the name of a particular program to run; an alternative to locating the icon in older versions of Windows. *Run* opens a program, folder, document or Web site. Supplanted in Windows Vista and later with the Search box.

S.M.A.R.T. (Self-Monitoring, Analysis, and Reporting Technology) Monitoring system built into hard drives.

S/PDIF (Sony/Philips Digital Interface Format) Digital audio connector found on many sound cards. Users can connect their computers directly to a 5.1/7.1 speaker system or receiver. S/PDIF comes in both a coaxial and an optical version.

SaaS (Software as a Service) Cloud-based service to store, distribute, and update programs and applications. The SaaS model provides access to necessary applications wherever you have an Internet connection, often without having to carry data with you or regularly update software. At the enterprise level, the subscription model of many SaaS providers makes it easier to budget and keep hundreds or thousands of computers up to date.

Safe mode Important diagnostic boot mode for Windows that runs only very basic drivers and turns off virtual memory.

safety goggles Protective glasses that keep stuff out of your eyes.

sampling Capturing sound waves in electronic format.

SATA (serial ATA) Serialized version of the ATA standard that offers many advantages over PATA (parallel ATA) technology, including thinner cabling, keyed connectors, and lower power requirements.

SATA bridge Adapter that allows PATA devices to be connected to a SATA controller.

SATA Express (SATAe) The newest version of SATA that ties capable drives directly into the PCI Express bus on motherboards. Each lane of PCIe 3.0 is capable of handling up to 8 Gbps data throughput. A SATAe drive grabbing two lanes, therefore, could move a whopping 16 Gbps through the bus.

SATA power connector 15-pin, L-shaped connector used by SATA devices that support the hot-swappable feature.

satellites Two or more standard stereo speakers to be combined with a subwoofer for a speaker system (i.e., 2.1, 5.1, 7.1, etc.).

Scalable Link Interface (SLI) Technology for connecting two or more NVIDIA GPUs together in a system.

scan code Unique code corresponding to each key on the keyboard, sent from the keyboard controller to the CPU.

SCSI (small computer system interface) Powerful and flexible peripheral interface popularized on the Macintosh and used to connect hard drives, optical drives, tape drives, scanners, and other devices to PCs of all kinds. Normal SCSI enables up to seven devices to be connected through a single bus connection, whereas Wide SCSI can handle 15 devices attached to a single controller.

SCSI chain Series of SCSI devices working together through a host adapter.

SCSI ID Unique identifier used by SCSI devices. No two SCSI devices may have the same SCSI ID.

SD (Secure Digital) Very popular format for flash media cards; also supports I/O devices.

SDK (software development kit) Software that used to create custom applications or add features to existing applications on your mobile device.

SDRAM (synchronous DRAM) DRAM that is synchronous, or tied to the system clock. This type of RAM is used in all modern systems.

sector Segment of one of the concentric tracks encoded on the disk during a low-level format. A sector holds 512 bytes of data.

sector translation Translation of logical geometry into physical geometry by the onboard circuitry of a hard drive.

sectors per track (sectors/track) Combined with the number of cylinders and heads, defines the disk geometry.

secure boot UEFI feature that secures the boot process by requiring properly signed software. This includes boot software and software that supports specific, essential components.

segment The connection between a computer and a switch.

self-grounding A less-than-ideal method for ridding yourself of static electricity by touching a metal object such as a computer case. Alternately, sending yourself to your own room as a form of punishment.

serial port Common connector on older PC. Connects input devices (such as a mouse) or communications devices (such as a modem). Also referred to as a COM port.

server Computer that shares its resources, such as printers and files, with other computers on a network. Example: network file system server that shares its disk space with a workstation that does not have a disk drive of its own.

service A program that runs in the background of a PC but displays no icons anywhere. You can view a list of services in the Windows Task Manager. Also, a program stored in a ROM chip.

service pack Collection of software patches released at one time by a software manufacturer.

Services Tab in Windows Task Manager that lists all running services on a system.

set-top box A device that adds "Smart TV" features, such as Internet streaming and show recording, to normal TVs.

Settings app Windows 10 tool that combines a huge number of otherwise disparate utilities, apps, and tools traditionally spread out all over your computer into one fairly unified, handy Windows app.

setupapi.log Log file that tracks the installation of all hardware on a system.

setuplog.txt Log file that tracks the complete installation process, logging the success or failure of file copying, Registry updates, and reboots.

sfc (System File Checker) Command-prompt program (sfc.exe) that scans, detects, and restores Windows system files, folders, and paths.

shadow mask CRT screen that allows only the proper electron gun to light the proper phosphors.

share-level security Security system in which each resource has a password assigned to it; access to the resource is based on knowing the password.

Shared Documents Windows premade folder that is accessible by all user accounts on the computer.

shared memory Means of reducing the amount of memory needed on a video card by borrowing from the regular system RAM, which reduces costs but also decreases performance.

shareware Program protected by copyright; holder allows (encourages!) you to make and distribute copies under the condition that those who adopt the software after preview pay a fee to the holder of the copyright. Derivative works are not allowed, although you may make an archival copy.

shunt Tiny connector of metal enclosed in plastic that creates an electrical connection between two posts of a jumper.

shutdown Windows and Linux command for shutting down the computer.

SID (security identifier) Unique identifier for every PC that most techs change when cloning.

sidebanding Second data bus for video cards; enables the video card to send more commands to the Northbridge while receiving other commands at the same time.

Sidebar *See* Windows Sidebar.

signal-to-noise ratio Measure that describes the relative quality of an input port.

signature Code pattern of a known virus; used by antivirus software to detect viruses.

SIMM (single in-line memory module) DRAM packaging distinguished by having a number of small tabs that install into a special connector. Each side of each tab is the same signal. SIMMs come in two common sizes: 30-pin and 72-pin.

simple file sharing Allows users to share locally or across the network but gives no control over what others do with shared files.

simple volume Volume created when setting up dynamic disks. Acts like a primary partition on a dynamic disk.

single rail Power supply configuration where all power is supplied along a single pathway.

single-sided RAM Has chips on only one side as opposed to double-sided RAM.

single source *See* closed source.

sleep timers A feature that enables you to put the computer into Standby after a set period of time, or to turn off the monitor or hard drive after a time, thus creating your own custom power scheme.

slimline Motherboard form factor used to create PCs that were very thin. NLX and LPX were two examples of this form factor.

slot covers Metal plates that cover up unused expansion slots on the back of a PC. Useful in maintaining proper airflow through a computer case.

smart battery Portable PC battery that tells the computer when it needs to be charged, conditioned, or replaced.

smart camera A digital camera incorporating the interface and computational features of a mobile device.

smart card Hardware authentication involving a credit card–sized card with circuitry that can be used to identify the bearer of that card.

SmartMedia Format for flash media cards; no longer used with new devices.

smartphone A cell phone enhanced to do things formerly reserved for fully grown computers, such as Web browsing, document viewing, and media consumption.

smart TV A television with network capabilities—both hardware and software—for use with streaming Internet video and audio.

smart watch A watch incorporating features of and communicating with a mobile device.

S/MIME (Secure/Multipurpose Internet Mail Extensions) Technology used to configure digital signature settings for e-mail, and contacts from a corporate address book, depending on how the corporate e-mail server is set up.

SMM (System Management Mode) Special CPU mode that enables the CPU to reduce power consumption by selectively shutting down peripherals.

SMTP (Simple Mail Transport Protocol) Main protocol used to send electronic mail on the Internet. Uses port 25.

snap-ins Small utilities that can be used with the Microsoft Management Console.

snapshot Virtualization feature that enables you to save an extra copy of the virtual machine as it is exactly at the moment the snapshot is taken.

SNMP (Simple Network Management Protocol) A set of standards for communication with devices connected to a TCP/IP network. Examples of these devices include routers, hubs, and switches. Uses port 161.

social engineering Using or manipulating people inside the networking environment to gain access to that network from the outside.

socket services Device drivers that support the PC Card socket, enabling the system to detect when a PC Card has been inserted or removed, and providing the necessary I/O to the device.

SO-DIMM (small-outline DIMM) Memory used in portable PCs because of its small size.

soft power Characteristic of ATX motherboards, which can use software to turn the PC on and off. The physical manifestation of soft power is the power switch. Instead of the thick power cord used in AT systems, an ATX power switch is little more than a pair of small wires leading to the motherboard.

software Single group of programs designed to do a particular job; always stored on mass storage devices.

solid core A cable that uses a single solid (not hollow or stranded) wire to transmit signals.

solid ink printers Printer that uses solid sticks of nontoxic "ink" that produce vibrant color documents with much less waste than color laser printers.

sound card Expansion card that can produce audible tones when connected to a set of speakers.

Southbridge Part of a motherboard chipset; handles all the inputs and outputs to the many devices in the PC.

Spaces Mac OS X feature enabling multiple desktops.

spam Unsolicited e-mails from both legitimate businesses and scammers that account for a huge percentage of traffic on the Internet.

spanned volume Volume that uses space on multiple dynamic disks.

SPD (serial presence detect) Information stored on a RAM chip that describes the speed, capacity, and other aspects of the RAM chip.

speaker Device that outputs sound by using magnetically driven diaphragm.

Spotify (spotify.com) Internet streaming music site.

sprite Bitmapped graphic, such as a BMP file, used by early 3-D games to create the 3-D world.

spyware Software that runs in the background of a user's PC, sending information about browsing habits back to the company that installed it onto the system.

SRAM (static RAM) RAM that uses a flip-flop circuit rather than the typical transistor/capacitor of DRAM to hold a bit of information. SRAM does not need to be refreshed and is faster than regular DRAM. Used primarily for cache.

SSD (solid-state drive) Data storage device that uses flash memory to store data.

SSH (Secure Shell) Terminal emulation program similar to Telnet, except that the entire connection is encrypted. Uses port 22.

SSID (service set identifier) Parameter used to define a wireless network; otherwise known as the network name.

SSL (Secure Sockets Layer) Security protocol used by a browser to connect to secure Web sites.

standard user account User account in Windows that has limited access to a system. Accounts of this type cannot alter system files, cannot install new programs, and cannot edit some settings by using the Control Panel without supplying an administrator password.

standoffs Small mechanical separators that screw into a computer case. A motherboard is then placed on top of the standoffs, and small screws are used to secure it to the standoffs.

star bus A hybrid network topology where the computers all connect to a central bus—a switch—but otherwise take the form of a star topology.

star topology Network topology where the computers on the network connect to a central wiring point, usually called a hub.

Start button Button on the Windows taskbar that enables access to the Start menu.

Start menu Menu that can be accessed by clicking the Start button on the Windows taskbar. Enables you to see all programs loaded on the system and to start them.

Start screen Windows 10 version of the Start menu, which functions as a combination of the traditional Start menu and the Windows 8/8.1 Modern UI.

Startup Repair A one-stop, do-it-all troubleshooting option that performs a number of boot repairs automatically.

static charge eliminator Device used to remove a static charge.

static IP address Manually set IP address that will not change.

stealth virus Virus that uses various methods to hide from antivirus software.

stepper motor One of two methods used to move actuator arms in a hard drive. (*See also* voice coil motor.)

stereo Describes recording tracks from two sources (microphones) as opposed to monaural, which uses one source.

stick Generic name for a single physical SIMM or DIMM.

Storage Spaces In Windows 8 and later, a software RAID solution that enables users to group multiple drives into a single storage pool.

STP (shielded twisted pair) Cabling for networks, composed of pairs of wires twisted around each other at specific intervals. Twists serve to reduce interference (also called crosstalk)—the more twists, the less interference. Cable has metallic shielding to protect the wires from external interference.

stranded core A cable that uses a bundle of tiny wire filaments to transmit signals. Stranded core is not quite as good a conductor as solid core, but it will stand up to substantial handling without breaking.

stream loading Process a program uses to constantly download updated information.

streaming media Broadcast of data that is played on your computer and immediately discarded.

stripe set Two or more drives in a group that are used for a striped volume.

striped volume RAID 0 volumes. Data is spread across two drives for increased speed.

strong password Password containing at least eight characters, including letters, numbers, and non-alphanumeric symbols.

structured cabling TIA/EIA standards that define methods of organizing the cables in a network for ease of repair and replacement.

stylus Pen-like input device used for pen-based computing.

su Older Linux command for gaining root access.

subnet mask Value used in TCP/IP settings to divide the IP address of a host into its component parts: network ID and host ID.

sub-pixels Tiny liquid crystal molecules arranged in rows and columns between polarizing filters used in LCDs.

subfolder A folder located inside another folder.

subwoofer Powerful speaker capable of producing extremely low-frequency sounds.

sudo Linux command for gaining root access.

Super I/O chip Chip specially designed to control low-speed, legacy devices such as the keyboard, mouse, and serial and parallel ports.

SuperSpeed USB A fast form of USB, with speeds up to 5 Gbps. Also called USB 3.0.

SuperSpeed+ USB Updated form of SuperSpeed USB providing speeds up to 10 Gbps. Also called USB 3.1.

surge suppressor Inexpensive device that protects your computer from voltage spikes.

SVGA (super video graphics array) Video display mode of 800 × 600.

swap file *See* page file.

swipe Gesture for mobile devices where you hold your finger on the screen and slide it across the screen, either right to left or top to bottom, depending on the type of application.

swipe lock Mobile device feature that uses a swipe gesture to unlock the mobile device.

switch Device that filters and forwards traffic based on some criteria. A bridge and a router are both examples of switches. In the command-line interface, a switch is a function that modifies the behavior of a command.

SXGA Video display mode of 1280 × 1024.

SXGA+ Video display mode of 1400 × 1050.

sync The process of keeping files on mobile devices up to date with the versions on desktop computers or over the Internet.

synchronize *See* sync.

syntax The proper way to write a command-line command so that it functions and does what it's supposed to do.

Sysprep (System Preparation Tool) Windows tool that makes cloning of systems easier by making it possible to undo portions of the installation.

system BIOS Primary set of BIOS stored on an EPROM or flash ROM chip on the motherboard. Defines the BIOS for all the assumed hardware on the motherboard, such as keyboard controller, floppy drive, basic video, and RAM.

system bus speed Speed at which the CPU and the rest of the PC operates; set by the system crystal.

system crystal Crystal that provides the speed signals for the CPU and the rest of the system.

system disk Any storage device with a bootable operating system.

system fan Any fan controlled by the motherboard but not directly attached to the CPU.

System File Checker *See* sfc.

System Monitor Utility that can evaluate and monitor system resources, such as CPU usage and memory usage.

System Preferences Mac OS X tool containing many administrative functions.

System Protection Feature in Windows that enables you to restore any previous version of a file or folder.

system resources In classic terms, the I/O addresses, IRQs, DMA channels, and memory addresses. Also refers to other computer essentials such as hard drive space, system RAM, and processor speed.

System Restore Utility in Windows that enables you to return your PC to a recent working configuration when something goes wrong. System Restore enables you to select a restore point and then returns the computer's system settings to the way they were at that restore point—all without affecting your personal files or e-mail.

system ROM ROM chip that stores the system BIOS.

system setup utility *See* CMOS setup program.

System Tools Menu containing tools such as System Information and Disk Defragmenter, accessed by selecting Start | Programs or All Programs | Accessories | System Tools.

system tray Contains icons representing background processes and the system clock. Located by default at the right edge of the Windows taskbar. Accurately called the notification area.

system unit Main component of the PC, in which the CPU, RAM, optical drive, and hard drive reside. All other devices—the keyboard, mouse, and monitor—connect to the system unit.

T568A Wiring standard for Ethernet cable.

T568B Wiring standard for Ethernet cable.

tablet A mobile device consisting of a large touchscreen, enabling the user to browse the Web, view media, and even play games.

Tablet PC Small portable computer distinguished by the use of a touchscreen with stylus and handwriting recognition as the primary modes of input.

tailgating Form of infiltration and social engineering that involves following someone else through a door as if you belong in the building.

Take Ownership Special permission allowing users to seize control of a file or folder and potentially prevent others from accessing the file/folder.

tap Touchscreen gesture where you press a spot on the screen to start an app or interact with a running app.

Task Manager Shows all running programs, including hidden ones, and is accessed by pressing CTRL-SHIFT-ESC. You can use the Task Manager to shut down an unresponsive application that refuses to close normally.

Task Scheduler Windows utility enabling users to set tasks to run automatically at certain times.

taskbar Contains the Start button, the notification area, the Quick Launch toolbar, and buttons for running applications. Located by default at the bottom of the desktop.

tasklist A command-line version of the Task Manager.

TCP/IP (Transmission Control Protocol/Internet Protocol) Communication protocols developed by the U.S. Department of Defense to enable dissimilar computers to share information over a network.

tech toolkit Tools a PC tech should never be without, including a Phillips-head screwdriver, a pair of tweezers, a flat-head screwdriver, a hemostat, a Torx wrench, a parts retriever, and a nut driver or two.

telecommunications room Area where all the cabling from individual computers in a network converges.

telephone scams Social engineering attack in which the attacker makes a phone call to someone in an organization to gain information.

Telnet Terminal emulation program for TCP/IP networks that allows one machine to control another as if the user were sitting in front of it. Uses port 23.

tera- Prefix that usually stands for the binary number 1,099,511,627,776 (2^{40}). When used for mass storage, it's often shorthand for 1 trillion bytes.

terminal Dumb device connected to a mainframe or computer network that acts as a point for entry or retrieval of information.

Terminal A command-line interface tool available in Mac OS X and various Linux distros.

terminal emulation Software that enables a computer to communicate with another computer or network as if the computer were a specific type of hardware terminal.

termination Using terminating resistors to prevent packet reflection on a network cable.

terminator Resistor that is plugged into the end of a bus cable to absorb the excess electrical signal, preventing it from bouncing back when it reaches the end of the wire. Terminators are used with coaxial cable and on the ends of SCSI chains. RG-58 coaxial cable requires resistors with a 50-ohm impedance. Also, a humanoid robot from the future designed by Skynet to destroy all human life. He'll be back.

test the theory Attempt to resolve the issue by either confirming the theory and learning what needs to be done to fix the problem, or by not confirming the theory and forming a new one or escalating. (Step 3 of 6 in the CompTIA troubleshooting theory.)

tethering The act of using a cellular-network-connected mobile device as a mobile hotspot.

texture Small picture that is tiled over and over again on walls, floors, and other surfaces to create the 3-D world.

TFT (thin film transistor) Type of LCD screen. (*See also* active matrix.)

theory of probable cause One possible reason why something is not working; a guess.

thermal compound Paste-like material with very high heat-transfer properties. Applied between the CPU and the cooling device, it ensures the best possible dispersal of heat from the CPU. Also called heat dope or thermal paste.

thermal printer Printer that uses heated printheads to create high-quality images on special or plain paper.

thick client CompTIA's name for a standard desktop computer. Runs desktop applications and meets recommended requirements for selected OS.

thin client A system designed to handle only very basic applications with an absolute minimum amount of hardware required by the operating system. Meets minimum requirements for selected OS.

thread Smallest logical division of a single program.

throttling Power reduction/thermal control capability allowing CPUs to slow down during low activity or high heat build-up situations. Intel's version is known as SpeedStep, AMD's as PowerNow!.

throw Size of the image a projector displays at a certain distance from the screen. Alternately, what you do with a computer that you just can't seem to get working.

Thunderbolt An open standards connector interface that is primarily used to connect peripherals to devices, including mobile devices, if they have a corresponding port.

TIA/EIA (Telecommunications Industry Association/Electronic Industries Alliance) Trade organization that provides standards for network cabling and other electronics.

tiers Levels of Internet providers, ranging from the Tier 1 backbones to Tier 3 regional networks.

Tiles The building blocks of Windows 8's Modern UI, as potentially "smart" app shortcuts, capable of displaying dynamic and changing information without even opening the app.

timbre Qualities that differentiate the same note played on different instruments.

Time Machine Mac OS X full backup tool that enables you to recover some or all files in the event of a crash; it also enables you to restore deleted files and recover previous versions of files.

TKIP (Temporal Key Integrity Protocol) Deprecated encryption standard that provided a new encryption key for every sent packet.

TN (twisted nematic) Older technology for LCD monitors. TN monitors produce a decent display for a modest price, but they have limited viewing angles and can't accurately reproduce all the color information sent by the video card.

tone generator *See* toner.

tone probe *See* toner.

toner A fine powder made up of plastic particles bonded to iron particles, used to create the text and images on a laser printer. Also, generic term for two devices used together—a tone generator and a tone locator (probe)—to trace cables by sending an electrical signal along a wire at a particular frequency. The tone locator then emits a sound when it distinguishes that frequency.

toner cartridge Object used to store the toner in a laser printer. (*See also* laser printer, toner.)

topology The way computers connect to each other in a network.

touch interface The primary user interface on modern mobile devices where keys are replaced with tactile interaction.

touchpad Flat, touch-sensitive pad that serves as a pointing device for most laptops.

touchscreen Monitor with a type of sensing device across its face that detects the location and duration of contact, usually by a finger or stylus.

tracert Windows command-line utility used to follow the path a packet takes between two hosts. Called traceroute in Mac OS X and Linux.

traces Small electrical connections embedded in a circuit board.

track Area on a hard drive platter where data is stored. A group of tracks with the same diameter is called a cylinder.

trackball Pointing device distinguished by a ball that is rolled with the fingers.

TrackPoint IBM's pencil eraser–sized joystick used in place of a mouse on laptops.

transfer corona Thin wire, usually protected by other thin wires, that applies a positive charge to the paper during the laser printing process, drawing the negatively charged toner particles off of the drum and onto the paper. Newer printers accomplish the same feat using a *transfer roller* that draws the toner onto the paper.

transfer rate Rate of data transferred between two devices, especially over the expansion bus.

transistor-transistor logic (TTL) A type of digital circuit found in early digital monitors.

transparency Effect in the Aero desktop environment (Windows Vista/7) that makes the edges of windows transparent.

triad Group of three phosphors—red, green, blue—in a CRT.

triple-channel architecture A chipset feature similar to dual-channel RAM, but requiring three matched sticks instead of two.

Trojan horse Program that does something other than what the user who runs the program thinks it will do. Used to disguise malicious code.

troubleshooting theory Steps a technician uses to solve a problem. CompTIA A+ defines six steps: identify the problem; establish a theory of probable cause; test the theory to determine cause; establish a plan of action to resolve the problem and implement a solution; verify full system functionality and if applicable implement preventive measures; and document findings, actions, and outcomes.

Trusted Platform Module (TPM) A hardware platform for the acceleration of cryptographic functions and the secure storage of associated information.

tunneling Creating an encrypted link between two programs on two separate computers.

TV tuner Typically an add-on device that allows users to watch television on a computer.

TWAIN (technology without an interesting name) Programming interface that enables a graphics application, such as a desktop publishing program, to activate a scanner, frame grabber, or other image-capturing device.

U (Units) The unique height measurement used with equipment racks; 1 U equals 1.75 inches.

UAC (User Account Control) Windows feature that enables standard accounts to do common tasks and provides a permissions dialog box when standard and administrator accounts do certain things that could potentially harm the computer (such as attempt to install a program).

UART (universal asynchronous receiver/transmitter) Device that turns parallel data into serial data and vice versa. The cornerstone of serial ports and modems.

UDF (universal data format) Replaced the ISO-9660 formats, enabling any operating system and optical drive to read UDF formatted disks.

UEFI (Unified Extensible Firmware Interface) Consortium of companies that established the UEFI standard that replaced the original EFI standard.

Ultra DMA Hard drive technology that enables drives to use direct memory addressing. Ultra DMA mode 3 drives—called ATA/33—have data transfer speeds up to 33 MBps. Mode 4 and 5 drives—called ATA/66 and ATA/100, respectively—transfer data at up to 66 MBps for mode 4 and 100 MBps for mode 5. Mode 6 pushed the transfer rate to 133 MBps. Modes 4, 5, and 6 require an 80-wire cable and a compatible controller to achieve these data transfer rates.

Ultrabook Thin, powerful laptop powered by Intel processors and built according to the Intel design specification. Competes directly with the Apple Mac Air.

unattended installation A type of OS installation where special scripts perform all the OS setup duties without human intervention.

unauthorized access Anytime a person accesses resources in an unauthorized way. This access may or may not be malicious.

unbuffered RAM RAM without a buffer chip; in other words, normal, consumer-grade RAM.

UNC (Universal Naming Convention) Describes any shared resource in a network using the convention *<server name>**<name of shared resource>*.

Unicode 16-bit code that covers every character of the most common languages, plus several thousand symbols.

unsigned driver Driver that has not gone through the Windows Certification Program to ensure compatibility. The Windows Certification Program was formerly known as the Windows Hardware Quality Labs and the Microsoft Windows Logo Program.

UPC (Universal Product Code) Bar code used to track inventory.

update Individual fixes for Windows that come out fairly often, on the order of once a week or so.

Upgrade Advisor Examines your hardware and installed software (in the case of an upgrade) and provides a list of devices and software that are known to have issues with it. The Upgrade Advisor is available for download at www.microsoft.com for Windows Vista and Windows 7. Windows 8/8.1 offers the Upgrade Assistant for similar purpose. The Get Windows 10 app generates a compatibility report that functions similarly.

upgrade installation Installation of Windows on top of an earlier installed version, thus inheriting all previous hardware and software settings.

UPS (uninterruptible power supply) Device that supplies continuous clean power to a computer system the whole time the computer is on. Protects against power outages and sags.

URL (uniform resource locator) An address that defines the location of a resource on the Internet. URLs are used most often in conjunction with HTML and the World Wide Web.

USB (universal serial bus) General-purpose serial interconnect for keyboards, printers, joysticks, and many other devices. Enables hot-swapping of devices.

USB host controller Integrated circuit that is usually built into the chipset and controls every USB device that connects to it.

USB hub Device that extends a single USB connection to two or more USB ports, almost always directly from one of the USB ports connected to the root hub.

USB root hub Part of the host controller that makes the physical connection to the USB ports.

USB thumb drive Flash memory device that uses the standard USB connection.

USB Type-C (connector) Reversible USB type cable that supports USB Super-Speed+ USB 3.1 with a top speed of 10 Gbps.

user account Container that identifies a user to an application, operating system, or network, including name, password, user name, groups to which the user belongs, and other information based on the user and the OS being used. Usually defines the rights and roles a user plays on a system.

User Accounts applet Applet in Control Panel that enables you to make changes to current accounts (local or global), and gives you access to the Settings charm (or app in Windows 10) when you opt to add a new account.

user interface Visual representation of the computer on the monitor that makes sense to the people using the computer, through which the user can interact with the computer. This can be a graphical user interface (GUI) like Windows 7 or a command-line interface like the Windows PowerShell or the Recovery Console.

user profiles Settings that correspond to a specific user account and may follow users regardless of the computers where they log on. These settings enable the user to have customized environment and security settings.

User's Files Windows default location for content specific to each user account on a computer. It is divided into several folders such as Documents, Pictures, Music, and Video.

Users group List of local users not allowed, among other things, to edit the Registry or access critical system files. They can create groups, but can only manage the groups they create.

USMT (User State Migration Tool) Advanced application for file and settings transfer of multiple users.

Utilities Mac OS X folder that contains tools for performing services on a Mac beyond what's included in System Preferences, including Activity Monitor and Terminal.

UTP (unshielded twisted pair) Popular type of cabling for telephone and networks, composed of pairs of wires twisted around each other at specific intervals. The twists serve to reduce interference (also called crosstalk). The more twists, the less interference. Unlike its cousin, STP, UTP cable has no metallic shielding to protect the wires from external interference. 1000BaseT uses UTP, as do many other networking technologies. UTP is available in a variety of grades, called categories, as follows:

> **CAT 1 UTP** Regular analog phone lines—not used for data communications.
>
> **CAT 2 UTP** Supports speeds up to 4 Mbps.
>
> **CAT 3 UTP** Supports speeds up to 16 Mbps.
>
> **CAT 4 UTP** Supports speeds up to 20 Mbps.
>
> **CAT 5 UTP** Supports speeds up to 100 Mbps.
>
> **CAT 5e UTP** Supports speeds up to 1000 Mbps.
>
> **CAT 6 UTP** Supports speeds up to 10 Gbps.
>
> **CAT 6a UTP** Supports speeds up to 10 Gbps.
>
> **CAT 7 UTP** Supports 10-Gbps networks at 100-meter segments; shielding for individual wire pairs reduces crosstalk and noise problems. CAT 7 is not a TIA /EIA standard.

V standards Standards established by CCITT for modem manufacturers to follow (voluntarily) to ensure compatible speeds, compression, and error correction.

vendor specific Stores that only sell products from one manufacturer, like the Apple store.

verify full system functionality Making sure that a problem has been resolved and will not return. (Step 5 of 6 in the CompTIA troubleshooting theory.)

vertices Used in the second generation of 3-D rendering; have a defined X, Y, and Z position in a 3-D world.

VESA (Video Electronics Standards Association) Consortium of computer manufacturers that standardizes improvements to common IBM PC components. VESA is responsible for the Super VGA video standard and the VLB bus architecture.

VGA (video graphics array) Standard for the video graphics adapter that was built into IBM's PS/2 computer. It supports 16 colors in a 640 × 480 pixel video display.

vi Linux and Mac OS X command-line tool for editing text files.

video capture Computer jargon for the recording of video information, such as TV shows or movies.

video card Expansion card that works with the CPU to produce the images displayed on your computer's display.

video display *See* monitor.

virtual assistant Voice-activated technology that responds to user requests for information. Virtual assistants can be used to search the Internet, make reminders, do calculations, and launch apps.

virtual machine (VM) A complete environment for a guest operating system to function as though that operating system were installed on its own computer.

virtual machine manager (VMM) *See* hypervisor.

virtual memory *See* page file.

virus Program that can make a copy of itself without your necessarily being aware of it. Some viruses can destroy or damage files. The best protection is to back up files regularly.

virus definition or data file Files that enable the virus protection software to recognize the viruses on your system and clean them. These files should be updated often. They are also called signature files, depending on the virus protection software in use.

virus shield Passive monitoring of a computer's activity, checking for viruses only when certain events occur.

VIS (viewable image size) Measurement of the viewable image that is displayed by a CRT rather than a measurement of the CRT itself.

VMM (virtual machine manager) *See* hypervisor.

voice coil motor One of two methods used to move actuator arms in a hard drive. (*See also* stepper motor.)

VoIP (Voice over Internet Protocol) Collection of protocols that makes voice calls over a data network possible.

volatile Memory that must have constant electricity to retain data. Alternatively, any programmer six hours before deadline after a nonstop, 48-hour coding session, running on nothing but caffeine and sugar.

volts (V) Measurement of the pressure of the electrons passing through a wire, or voltage.

volume Physical unit of a storage medium, such as tape reel or disk pack, that is capable of having data recorded on it and subsequently read. Also, a contiguous collection of cylinders or blocks on a disk that are treated as a separate unit.

volume boot sector First sector of the first cylinder of each partition; stores information important to its partition, such as the location of the operating system boot files.

voucher Means of getting a discount on the CompTIA A+ exams.

VPN (Virtual Private Network) Encrypted connection over the Internet between a computer or remote network and a private network.

VRM (voltage regulator module) Small card supplied with some CPUs to ensure that the CPU gets correct voltage. This type of card, which must be used with a motherboard specially designed to accept it, is not commonly seen today.

VRR (vertical refresh rate) The amount of time it takes for a CRT to draw a complete screen. This value is measured in hertz, or cycles per second. Most modern CRTs have a VRR of 60 Hz or better.

wait state Occurs when the CPU has to wait for RAM to provide code. Also known as pipeline stall.

WAP (wireless access point) Device that centrally connects wireless network nodes.

wattage (watts or W) Measurement of the amps and volts needed for a particular device to function.

wave table synthesis Technique that supplanted FM synthesis, wherein recordings of actual instruments or other sounds are embedded in the sound card as WAV files. When a particular note from a particular instrument or voice is requested, the sound processor grabs the appropriate prerecorded WAV file from its memory and adjusts it to match the specific sound and timing requested.

Web browser Program designed to retrieve, interpret, and display Web pages.

Web server A computer that stores and shares the files that make up Web sites.

webcam PC camera most commonly used for Internet video.

Welcome screen Logon screen for Windows. Enables users to select their particular user account by clicking on their user picture.

WEP (Wired Equivalent Privacy) Wireless security protocol that uses a standard 40-bit encryption to scramble data packets. Does not provide complete end-to-end encryption and is vulnerable to attack.

Wi-Fi Common name for the IEEE 802.11 wireless Ethernet standard.

Wi-Fi calling Mobile device feature that enables users to make voice calls over a Wi-Fi network, rather than a cellular network.

Wi-Fi Protected Setup (WPS) A standard included on many WAPs and clients to make secure connections easier to configure.

wide area network (WAN) A widespread group of computers connected using long-distance technologies.

wildcard Character used during a search to represent search criteria. For instance, searching for ***.docx** will return a list of all files with a .docx extension, regardless of the filename. The * is the wildcard in that search.

Windows 7 Version of Windows; comes in many different editions for home and office use, but does not have a Server edition.

Windows 7 Compatibility Center Microsoft Web page that lists the hardware and software that work with Windows 7.

Windows 8 Version of Windows noted for the Metro interface. Used for desktop and portable PCs and for mobile devices.

Windows Easy Transfer Windows method of transferring files and settings to a new PC.

Windows Explorer Windows utility that enables you to manipulate files and folders stored on the drives in your computer. Rebranded as File Explorer in Windows 8, 8.1, and 10.

Windows Hardware Certification Program Microsoft's rigorous testing program for hardware manufacturers, which hardware devices must pass before their drivers can be digitally signed.

Windows logo key Key on a keyboard bearing the Windows logo that traditionally brings up the Start menu, but is also used in some keyboard shortcuts.

Windows Memory Diagnostic Tool found in Windows 7 and later that can automatically scan a computer's RAM when encountering a problem.

Windows PowerShell Command-line tool included with Windows. Offers a number of powerful scripting tools for automating changes both on local machines and over networks.

Windows Preinstallation Environment (WinPE) The installation program for Windows.

Windows Recovery Environment (WinRE) A special set of tools in the Windows setup that enables you to access troubleshooting and repair features.

Windows Sidebar User interface feature in Windows Vista that enables users to place various gadgets, such as clocks, calendars, and other utilities, on the right side of their desktop.

Windows Update Microsoft application used to keep Windows operating systems up to date with the latest patches or enhancements. (*See* Automatic Updates.)

Windows Vista Version of Windows; comes in many different editions for home and office use, but does not have a Server edition.

Windows XP Version of Windows that replaced both the entire Windows 9*x* line and Windows 2000; does not have a Server version. No longer supported by Microsoft.

Windows XP Mode A Windows XP virtual machine that ships with Professional, Enterprise, and Ultimate editions of Windows 7 to enable users to run programs that don't work on Windows 7.

Wired (wired.com) Hip Internet news site.

work area In a basic structured cabling network, often simply an office or cubicle that potentially contains a PC attached to the network.

workgroup A simple, decentralized network that Windows PCs are configured to use by default.

worm Very special form of virus. Unlike other viruses, a worm does not infect other files on the computer. Instead, it replicates by making copies of itself on other systems on a network by taking advantage of security weaknesses in networking protocols.

WPA (Wi-Fi Protected Access) Wireless security protocol that uses encryption key integrity-checking/TKIP and EAP and is designed to improve on WEP's weaknesses. Supplanted by WPA 2.

WPA 2 (Wi-Fi Protected Access 2) Wireless security protocol, also known as IEEE 802.11i. Uses the Advanced Encryption Standard (AES) and replaces WPA.

WQUXGA Video display mode of 2560 × 1600.

wrapper *See* container file.

WSXGA Video display mode of 1440 × 900.

WSXGA+ Video display mode of 1680 × 1050.

WUXGA Video display mode of 1920 × 1200.

WVGA Video display mode of 800 × 480.

WWW (World Wide Web) System of Internet servers that supports documents formatted in HTML and related protocols. Can be accessed by applications that use HTTP and HTTPS, such as Web browsers.

www.comptia.org CompTIA's Web site.

WXGA Video display mode of 1280 × 800.

x64 Describes 64-bit operating systems and software.

x86 Describes 32-bit operating systems and software.

xcopy Command in the command-line interface used to copy multiple directories at once, which the copy command could not do.

xD (Extreme Digital) picture card Very small flash media card format.

Xeon Line of Intel CPUs designed for servers.

XGA (extended graphics array) Video display mode of 1024 × 768.

XPS (XML Paper Specification) print path Printing subsystem in Windows. Has enhanced color management and good print layout fidelity.

XT bus *See* PC bus.

ZIF (zero insertion force) socket Socket for CPUs that enables insertion of a chip without the need to apply pressure. Intel promoted this socket with its overdrive upgrades. The chip drops effortlessly into the socket's holes, and a small lever locks it in.

INDEX

Symbols

Numbers

A

B

C

D

E

F

G

H

I

M

N

O

P

Q

R

S

T

U

V

W

X

Z

LICENSE AGREEMENT

THIS PRODUCT (THE "PRODUCT") CONTAINS PROPRIETARY SOFTWARE, DATA AND INFORMATION (INCLUDING DOCUMENTATION) OWNED BY McGRAW-HILL EDUCATION AND ITS LICENSORS. YOUR RIGHT TO USE THE PRODUCT IS GOVERNED BY THE TERMS AND CONDITIONS OF THIS AGREEMENT.

LICENSE: Throughout this License Agreement, "you" shall mean either the individual or the entity whose agent opens this package. You are granted a non-exclusive and non-transferable license to use the Product subject to the following terms:
(i) If you have licensed a single user version of the Product, the Product may only be used on a single computer (i.e., a single CPU). If you licensed and paid the fee applicable to a local area network or wide area network version of the Product, you are subject to the terms of the following subparagraph (ii).
(ii) If you have licensed a local area network version, you may use the Product on unlimited workstations located in one single building selected by you that is served by such local area network. If you have licensed a wide area network version, you may use the Product on unlimited workstations located in multiple buildings on the same site selected by you that is served by such wide area network; provided, however, that any building will not be considered located in the same site if it is more than five (5) miles away from any building included in such site. In addition, you may only use a local area or wide area network version of the Product on one single server. If you wish to use the Product on more than one server, you must obtain written authorization from McGraw-Hill Education and pay additional fees.
(iii) You may make one copy of the Product for back-up purposes only and you must maintain an accurate record as to the location of the back-up at all times.

COPYRIGHT; RESTRICTIONS ON USE AND TRANSFER: All rights (including copyright) in and to the Product are owned by McGraw-Hill Education and its licensors. You are the owner of the enclosed disc on which the Product is recorded. You may not use, copy, decompile, disassemble, reverse engineer, modify, reproduce, create derivative works, transmit, distribute, sublicense, store in a database or retrieval system of any kind, rent or transfer the Product, or any portion thereof, in any form or by any means (including electronically or otherwise) except as expressly provided for in this License Agreement. You must reproduce the copyright notices, trademark notices, legends and logos of McGraw-Hill Education and its licensors that appear on the Product on the back-up copy of the Product which you are permitted to make hereunder. All rights in the Product not expressly granted herein are reserved by McGraw-Hill Education and its licensors.

TERM: This License Agreement is effective until terminated. It will terminate if you fail to comply with any term or condition of this License Agreement. Upon termination, you are obligated to return to McGraw-Hill Education the Product together with all copies thereof and to purge all copies of the Product included in any and all servers and computer facilities.

DISCLAIMER OF WARRANTY: THE PRODUCT AND THE BACK-UP COPY ARE LICENSED "AS IS." McGRAW-HILL EDUCATION, ITS LICENSORS AND THE AUTHORS MAKE NO WARRANTIES, EXPRESS OR IMPLIED, AS TO THE RESULTS TO BE OBTAINED BY ANY PERSON OR ENTITY FROM USE OF THE PRODUCT, ANY INFORMATION OR DATA INCLUDED THEREIN AND/OR ANY TECHNICAL SUPPORT SERVICES PROVIDED HEREUNDER, IF ANY ("TECHNICAL SUPPORT SERVICES"). McGRAW-HILL EDUCATION, ITS LICENSORS AND THE AUTHORS MAKE NO EXPRESS OR IMPLIED WARRANTIES OF MERCHANTABILITY OR FITNESS FOR A PARTICULAR PURPOSE OR USE WITH RESPECT TO THE PRODUCT. McGRAW-HILL EDUCATION, ITS LICENSORS, AND THE AUTHORS MAKE NO GUARANTEE THAT YOU WILL PASS ANY CERTIFICATION EXAM WHATSOEVER BY USING THIS PRODUCT. NEITHER McGRAW-HILL EDUCATION, ANY OF ITS LICENSORS NOR THE AUTHORS WARRANT THAT THE FUNCTIONS CONTAINED IN THE PRODUCT WILL MEET YOUR REQUIREMENTS OR THAT THE OPERATION OF THE PRODUCT WILL BE UNINTERRUPTED OR ERROR FREE. YOU ASSUME THE ENTIRE RISK WITH RESPECT TO THE QUALITY AND PERFORMANCE OF THE PRODUCT.

LIMITED WARRANTY FOR DISC: To the original licensee only, McGraw-Hill Education warrants that the enclosed disc on which the Product is recorded is free from defects in materials and workmanship under normal use and service for a period of ninety (90) days from the date of purchase. In the event of a defect in the disc covered by the foregoing warranty, McGraw-Hill Education will replace the disc.

LIMITATION OF LIABILITY: NEITHER McGRAW-HILL EDUCATION, ITS LICENSORS NOR THE AUTHORS SHALL BE LIABLE FOR ANY INDIRECT, SPECIAL OR CONSEQUENTIAL DAMAGES, SUCH AS BUT NOT LIMITED TO, LOSS OF ANTICIPATED PROFITS OR BENEFITS, RESULTING FROM THE USE OR INABILITY TO USE THE PRODUCT EVEN IF ANY OF THEM HAS BEEN ADVISED OF THE POSSIBILITY OF SUCH DAMAGES. THIS LIMITATION OF LIABILITY SHALL APPLY TO ANY CLAIM OR CAUSE WHATSOEVER WHETHER SUCH CLAIM OR CAUSE ARISES IN CONTRACT, TORT, OR OTHERWISE. Some states do not allow the exclusion or limitation of indirect, special or consequential damages, so the above limitation may not apply to you.

U.S. GOVERNMENT RESTRICTED RIGHTS: Any software included in the Product is provided with restricted rights subject to subparagraphs (c), (1) and (2) of the Commercial Computer Software-Restricted Rights clause at 48 C.F.R. 52.227-19. The terms of this Agreement applicable to the use of the data in the Product are those under which the data are generally made available to the general public by McGraw-Hill Education. Except as provided herein, no reproduction, use, or disclosure rights are granted with respect to the data included in the Product and no right to modify or create derivative works from any such data is hereby granted.

GENERAL: This License Agreement constitutes the entire agreement between the parties relating to the Product. The terms of any Purchase Order shall have no effect on the terms of this License Agreement. Failure of McGraw-Hill Education to insist at any time on strict compliance with this License Agreement shall not constitute a waiver of any rights under this License Agreement. This License Agreement shall be construed and governed in accordance with the laws of the State of New York. If any provision of this License Agreement is held to be contrary to law, that provision will be enforced to the maximum extent permissible and the remaining provisions will remain in full force and effect.